EDITORIAL BOARD

SAUL LEVMORE
DIRECTING EDITOR
William B. Graham Distinguished Service Professor of Law and
Former Dean of the Law School
University of Chicago

DANIEL A. FARBER
Sho Sato Professor of Law
University of California at Berkeley

HEATHER K. GERKEN
Dean and the Sol & Lillian Goldman Professor of Law
Yale University

SAMUEL ISSACHAROFF
Bonnie and Richard Reiss Professor of Constitutional Law
New York University

HAROLD HONGJU KOH
Sterling Professor of International Law and
Former Dean of the Law School
Yale University

THOMAS W. MERRILL
Charles Evans Hughes Professor of Law
Columbia University

ROBERT L. RABIN
A. Calder Mackay Professor of Law
Stanford University

HILLARY A. SALE
Agnes Williams Sesquicentennial Professor of Law,
Associate Dean for Strategy, and Professor of Management
Georgetown University

UNIVERSITY CASEBOOK SERIES®

SECURITIES REGULATION

CASES AND MATERIALS

FOURTEENTH EDITION

JOHN C. COFFEE, JR.
Adolf A. Berle Professor of Law
Columbia University School of Law

HILLARY A. SALE
Agnes Williams Sesquicentennial Professor of Law,
Associate Dean for Strategy, and Professor of Management
Georgetown University

CHARLES K. WHITEHEAD
Myron C. Taylor Alumni Professor of Business Law
Cornell University Law School

The publisher is not engaged in rendering legal or other professional advice, and this publication is not a substitute for the advice of an attorney. If you require legal or other expert advice, you should seek the services of a competent attorney or other professional.

University Casebook Series is a trademark registered in the U.S. Patent and Trademark Office.

© 1963, 1968, 1972, 1977, 1982, 1987, 1992, 1998, 2003 FOUNDATION PRESS
© 2007, 2009, 2012 THOMSON REUTERS/FOUNDATION PRESS
© 2015 LEG, Inc. d/b/a West Academic
© 2021 LEG, Inc. d/b/a West Academic
    444 Cedar Street, Suite 700
    St. Paul, MN 55101
    1-877-888-1330

Printed in the United States of America

ISBN: 978-1-64708-775-3

PREFACE TO THE FOURTEENTH EDITION

By John C. Coffee, Jr.*

Since the last edition in 2015, a good deal of legal water has gone over the dam: Initial Coin Offerings have become a recurring battleground between the SEC and aggressive entrepreneurs; the Commission has adopted Regulation Best Interest to subject brokers to a heightened standard (but one well short of a fiduciary duty); the Supreme Court has continued to debate the elements of Rule 10b–5 (and in at least one important decision has expanded its scope—*Lorenzo v. SEC*, 139 S.Ct. 1094 (2019)). A still surfacing trend may be the deepening skepticism of some Supreme Court Justices towards the Administrative State, and this has resulted in two recent battles for the SEC—*Kokesh v. SEC*, 137 S.Ct. 1635 (2017), and *Liu v. SEC*, 140 S.Ct. 1936 (2020)—which it has split. More such decisions may come as the SEC increasingly relies on administrative proceedings as its preferred means of enforcement.

With this edition, we welcome Professor Charles Whitehead of Cornell University Law School (and former research assistant to Professor Coffee) to our team. His energy and enthusiasm has shown itself in this edition as we have undertaken to condense and streamline this book. To be sure, this casebook continues to be longer than most of its competitors, but this is in large measure the product of our desire to give the instructor a broad choice of what to teach. One size does not fit all; a securities class at a rural school in a smaller state may appropriately have a different focus from that of a corresponding class at an urban law school in a major city. We do not expect (nor do we recommend) that users will cover every chapter in this book. Some may want to cover Tender Offers and the Williams Act; others may prefer to leave that for a different course on Mergers and Acquisitions and instead cover our chapter on Broker-Dealers. Still, others may wish to cover insider trading and criminal enforcement of the securities laws. We emphasize: It is your choice!

Finally, we wish to thank Roy Cohen, Amy Burr Hutchings, Serdar Inci, Maya Ben Meir, Olivia Brown, Hollie Chenault, Claire Creighton, Samantha Glazer, Jing Xu, Kyle Beck, Brandon Hanley, Elise Kletz,

---

* Professor Coffee is the Adolf A. Berle Professor of Law at Columbia University Law School and Director of its Center on Corporate Governance.

Prachee Sawant, and Junda Yu, our research assistants, for their considerable help and patience with us.

> JOHN C. COFFEE, JR.
>> Adolf A. Berle Professor of Law
>> Columbia University Law School
>
> HILLARY A. SALE
>> Agnes Williams Sesquicentennial Professor of Law,
>> Associate Dean for Strategy, and Professor of Management
>> Georgetown University
>
> CHARLES K. WHITEHEAD
>> Myron C. Taylor Alumni Professor of Business Law
>> Cornell University Law School

November, 2020

SUMMARY OF CONTENTS

PREFACE TO THE FOURTEENTH EDITION III
TABLE OF CASES XXIII
TABLE OF AUTHORITIES XLI

PART I. THE CAPITAL MARKETS: AN OVERVIEW

Chapter 1. The Institutional and Regulatory Framework 3
1. The Goals of Securities Regulation 3
2. An Overview of the Financial Markets 11
3. Forces Reshaping the Securities Markets 32
4. The Regulatory Framework 50
5. The Regulatory Process 58
6. Blue Sky Regulation 64

PART II. REGULATION OF THE DISTRIBUTION OF SECURITIES

SUBDIVISION A. THE UNDERWRITING PROCESS UNDER THE SECURITIES ACT OF 1933

Chapter 2. The Basic Structure and Prohibitions of the Securities Act 93
1. The Statutory Framework 93
2. The Pre-Filing Period ("Gun Jumping") 96
3. The Waiting Period 115
4. The Post-Effective Period 133
5. The JOBS Act and the FAST Act: Rationale and Impact 141
6. New Developments 147

Chapter 3. The Registration Process 153
1. The SEC's Integrated Disclosure System 153
2. Shelf Registration 161
3. Preparation of the Registration Statement 174
4. Qualitative Disclosure 190
5. New Approaches to Disclosure 206
6. Disclosure Policy and the Debate over the Efficient Market 225
7. Post-Filing Review and Restrictions 258
8. Regulation of Underwriters and the Distribution Process 262
9. Penny Stocks and Blank Check Offerings 270

SUBDIVISION B. COVERAGE OF THE REGULATION

Chapter 4. Definitions of "Security" and "Exempted Securities" 273
1. What Is a "Security"? 273
2. Exempted Securities: Sections 3(a)(2) Through 3(a)(8) 366

Chapter 5. The Private Offering Exemptions: Sections 4(a)(2) and 4(a)(5) 373

Chapter 6. Limited and Other Offering Exemptions 401
1. Regulation D: The Private Placement Safe Harbor 405
2. Regulation A Offerings 436
3. Intrastate Offerings: Section 3(a)(11), Rule 147, and Rule 147A 444
4. Other Exemptions: Rule 701 and Regulation CE 469
5. Exempted Exchanges and Reorganizations: Sections 3(a)(9) and 3(a)(10) and the Bankruptcy Code 475
6. Crowdfunding 501
7. Integration of Exemptions 507

SUBDIVISION C. THE OBLIGATION TO REGISTER RESALES OF SECURITIES BY PERSONS OTHER THAN THE ISSUER

Chapter 7. Offerings by Underwriters, Affiliates, and Dealers 523
1. The Concept of "Underwriter" 523
2. Going Public by the Back Door 537
3. The Section "4(1½)" Exemption 546
4. Statutory Restrictions on Distributions of Securities by Controlling Persons or Affiliates 557
5. Restrictions on Resales of Control Shares and Restricted Securities Under Rule 144 584
6. Rule 144A and the Private Resale Market 600
7. Section 4(a)(7) 608
8. Regulation S: An Exemption for Offerings Outside the United States 610

PART III. REGULATION OF TRADING IN SECURITIES

Chapter 8. Regulation of the Securities Markets 653
1. Introduction: Change in the Markets 653
2. The National Market System: Whose Interests Deserve Priority? 671
3. What Is an Exchange?: A Brief Survey from the 1934 Act to Regulation ATS 683
4. Primary Jurisdiction and the Struggle for Competitive Rates 697
5. The Over-the-Counter Market 709
6. Market Data 716
7. Technology and Infrastructure 720
8. Self Regulation in the Securities Industry 722

Chapter 9. Regulation of Broker-Dealers 727
1. Regulation Aimed at Fraud and Manipulation 741
2. Regulation Aimed at Protection from High Risk and Insolvency 758
3. Regulation Aimed at Establishing the Duties of Brokers to Their Customers 766

Chapter 10. Tender Offers, Management Buyouts, and Takeover Contests 791
1. An Overview of the Williams Act 797
2. Definitional Issues: Group, Tender Offer, and Bidder 817
3. Reforming the Tender Offer Process 867
4. Defensive Tactics: The Target Strikes Back 873
5. State Anti-Takeover Legislation 880
6. New Developments: The Changed Legal Landscape 902

PART IV. SECURITIES ENFORCEMENT AND CLASS ACTIONS

Chapter 11. Civil Liability Under the Securities Act of 1933 919
1. Section 11 of the 1933 Act 919
2. Section 12 of the 1933 Act 995
3. Section 17(a) of the 1933 Act 1028

Chapter 12. Rules 10b–5 and 14a–9: Fraud in Connection with a Purchase or Sale of a Security or the Solicitation of Proxies 1031
1. Introduction 1031
2. Rule 10b–5: Fraud in Connection with a Purchase or Sale of a Security 1037
3. Rule 14a–9: Proxy Fraud 1176
4. Section 18 1185

Chapter 13. Insider Trading 1187
1. "Insider" Trading 1191
2. Regulation FD 1244
3. SEC Rule 14e–3 and Tender Offers 1247
4. Section 16(b) Liability for Short Swing Profits 1255
5. Damages for Insider Trading 1280

Chapter 14. SEC Enforcement Actions 1289
1. Procedures 1290
2. Remedies 1297
3. SEC Enforcement and Professionals 1345

Chapter 15. Criminal Enforcement of the Federal Securities Laws 1441
1. Procedural Issues 1442
2. Criminal Prosecutions Under the Federal Securities Laws 1452
3. Stock Parking and "Regulatory" Violations 1457
4. Criminal Prosecutions Under Title 18 1471

Chapter 16. International Enforcement 1473
1. The Jurisdiction of U.S. Courts over Claims by Private Plaintiffs 1474

2. Government Extraterritorial Enforcement of the Securities Laws 1498

INDEX 1507

TABLE OF CONTENTS

PREFACE TO THE FOURTEENTH EDITION III
TABLE OF CASES XXIII
TABLE OF AUTHORITIES XLI

PART I. THE CAPITAL MARKETS: AN OVERVIEW

Chapter 1. The Institutional and Regulatory Framework 3
1. The Goals of Securities Regulation 3
2. An Overview of the Financial Markets 11
   A. The Structure of the Financial Markets: An Overview of the Non-Equity Markets 13
   B. The Equity Market 22
      (1) The Venture Capital Market 23
      (2) The Public Equity Market: Redefining the Role of Exchanges 24
3. Forces Reshaping the Securities Markets 32
   A. The Rise of Institutional Investors 33
   B. Globalization: Causes and Consequences 38
   C. Restructuring the Financial Services Industry: Deregulation and Reconsideration 41
   D. The Problem of Systemic Risk 42
   E. The Role of Gatekeepers 45
   F. Decline in IPOs 48
4. The Regulatory Framework 50
5. The Regulatory Process 58
6. Blue Sky Regulation 64

PART II. REGULATION OF THE DISTRIBUTION OF SECURITIES

SUBDIVISION A. THE UNDERWRITING PROCESS UNDER THE SECURITIES ACT OF 1933

Chapter 2. The Basic Structure and Prohibitions of the Securities Act 93
1. The Statutory Framework 93
   Introductory Note 93
2. The Pre-Filing Period ("Gun Jumping") 96
   A. Preliminary Negotiations Between Issuer and Underwriter 96
   B. The Traditional Dividing Line Between Pre-Filing Sales Publicity and Timely Disclosures of Corporate Information 100
      Securities Act Release No. 5180 103
   C. Downsizing the Quiet Period: The SEC's Revised Rules 105
   D. Broker-Dealer Activities During Registration 108
   E. The Problem of Biased Research 110
      Problem 2-1 112
      Problem 2-2 112

		Problem 2-3	113
		Problem 2-4	113
		Problem 2-5	113
		Problem 2-6	113
		Problem 2-7	113
		Problem 2-8	114
		Problem 2-9	114
		Problem 2-10	114
		Problem 2-11	114
		Problem 2-12	114
		Problem 2-13	115
		Problem 2-14	115
		Problem 2-15	115
	3.	The Waiting Period	115
		A. The Traditional Offering Documents	116
		B. The Free Writing Prospectus	122
		C. Road Shows and Electronic Communication	125
		D. Delivery During the Waiting Period	129
		Securities Act Release No. 4968	129
		Problem 2-16	130
		Problem 2-17	131
		Problem 2-18	131
		Problem 2-19	131
		Problem 2-20	131
		Problem 2-21	131
		Problem 2-22	131
		Problem 2-23	131
		Problem 2-24	132
		Problem 2-25	132
		Problem 2-26	132
		Problem 2-27	132
		Problem 2-28	132
		Problem 2-29	132
		Problem 2-30	133
		Problem 2-31	133
	4.	The Post-Effective Period	133
		A. The Procedure Surrounding Effectiveness: Rules 430A and 430B	133
		B. Prospectus Requirements in the Post-Effective Period	134
		Problem 2-32	140
		Problem 2-33	140
		Problem 2-34	140
		Problem 2-35	140
		Problem 2-36	140
	5.	The JOBS Act and the FAST Act: Rationale and Impact	141
		Problem 2-37	147
		Problem 2-38	147
		Problem 2-39	147
		Problem 2-40	147

6.	New Developments	147

Chapter 3. The Registration Process 153
1. The SEC's Integrated Disclosure System 153
   Securities Act Release No. 6383 157
2. Shelf Registration 161
   A. The Debate over Rule 415 161
   B. The Impact of Rule 415 164
      (1) Underwriting Fees 164
      (2) Equity Offerings 165
      (3) The Due Diligence Debate 166
      (4) The SEC's Compromise on Due Diligence: Rule 176 167
      (5) Automatic Shelf Registration 169
3. Preparation of the Registration Statement 174
   Introductory Note 174
   SEC Registration of Public Offerings Under the Securities Act of 1933 177
   Problem 3-1 189
   Problem 3-2 190
4. Qualitative Disclosure 190
   In the Matter of Franchard Corporation 190
5. New Approaches to Disclosure 206
   A. Soft Information: From Forbidden to Required 206
   Securities Act Release No. 6711 208
   Securities Act Release No. 6835 210
   Problem 3-3 216
   Problem 3-4 216
   Securities Act Release No. 7497 217
6. Disclosure Policy and the Debate over the Efficient Market 225
   A. What Makes the Market Efficient?: The Role of Underwriters 229
   The Mechanisms of Market Efficiency 230
   B. New Critiques of the Efficient Market Hypothesis 233
   C. How Do Investors Really Make Decisions: The Behavioral Economic Perspective 246
   D. Policy Implications 248
      (1) The Case for the Mandatory Disclosure System 248
      Market Failure and the Economic Case for a Mandatory Disclosure System 250
7. Post-Filing Review and Restrictions 258
   A. Post-Filing Processing 258
8. Regulation of Underwriters and the Distribution Process 262
   A. FINRA Review of Underwriter's Compensation 262
   B. Hot Issues: Oversubscription, Free Riding, and the Problem of Asymmetric Information 263
   Problem 3-5 266
   C. The SEC's Trading Rules 266
   D. Stabilization 268
   Problem 3-6 269

		E. Short Selling Around Public Offerings 269
9.		Penny Stocks and Blank Check Offerings 270
		Problem 3-7 272

SUBDIVISION B.   COVERAGE OF THE REGULATION

Chapter 4. Definitions of "Security" and "Exempted Securities" 273

1. What Is a "Security"? 273
   - A. "Investment Contract" 273
     - Securities & Exchange Commission v. W. J. Howey Co. 275
     - Securities and Exchange Commission v. Life Partners, Inc. 280
     - Securities and Exchange Commission v. Koscot Interplanetary, Inc. 289
     - Securities and Exchange Commission v. Edwards 296
     - Problem 4-1 301
   - B. The "Economic Realities" Test: Downsizing the Definition of Security 301
     - United Housing Foundation, Inc. v. Forman 301
     - International Brotherhood of Teamsters, Chauffeurs, Warehousemen and Helpers of America v. Daniel 307
     - (1) Condominiums and Real Estate Developments 312
       - Securities Act Release No. 5347 312
       - Problem 4-2 315
       - Problem 4-3 316
     - (2) Partnerships, Limited Partnerships, and Limited Liability Companies 316
       - a. Control in the Limited Partnership 316
         - Steinhardt Group Inc. v. Citicorp 316
       - b. The Special Case of Limited Liability Companies 322
       - c. Partnerships 324
       - d. Limited Partnerships 325
         - Problem 4-4 326
   - C. "Stock": The Return of Formalism 326
     - Landreth Timber Company v. Landreth 326
   - D. "Note" 332
     - Reves v. Ernst & Young 332
   - E. Special Debt Obligations 343
     - Problem 4-5 349
   - F. "Tokens" and Other Digital Assets 356
     - Securities Act Release No. 81207 356
     - Re: Pocketful of Quarters, Inc. 362
2. Exempted Securities: Sections 3(a)(2) Through 3(a)(8) 366
   - A. Section 3(a)(2) 366
   - B. Section 3(a)(3) 370
   - C. Sections 3(a)(4) to 3(a)(8) 371

Chapter 5. The Private Offering Exemptions: Sections 4(a)(2) and 4(a)(5) 373
Introductory Note 373
Securities and Exchange Commission v. Ralston Purina Co. 380
Doran v. Petroleum Management Corp. 386
Problem 5-1 399
Problem 5-2 399

Chapter 6. Limited and Other Offering Exemptions 401
1. Regulation D: The Private Placement Safe Harbor 405
   Securities Act Release No. 6389 405
   Securities Act Release No. 6455 416
   A. "General Solicitation or General Advertising" Under Regulation D 424
   B. Developments Under Regulation D 431
2. Regulation A Offerings 436
3. Intrastate Offerings: Section 3(a)(11), Rule 147, and Rule 147A 444
   A. Section 3(a)(11) 446
   Securities Act Release No. 4434 446
   Securities and Exchange Commission v. McDonald Investment Co. 451
   B. Rules 147 and 147A 457
   Securities Act Release No. 5450 457
   C. Developments Under Rule 147 and Rule 147A 467
4. Other Exemptions: Rule 701 and Regulation CE 469
   A. Rule 701 469
   B. Regulation CE 473
5. Exempted Exchanges and Reorganizations: Sections 3(a)(9) and 3(a)(10) and the Bankruptcy Code 475
   A. Section 2(a)(3) and the Theory of "Sale" 475
   B. Section 3(a)(9) 480
   Securities Act Release No. 646 484
   Securities Act Release No. 2029 486
   Notes on the Status of Section 3(a)(9) Exchanges 488
   C. Section 3(a)(10) 490
   Securities Act Release No. 312 493
   Notes on Reorganizations and Other Exchanges Under Section 3(a)(10) 494
   D. Bankruptcy Code 497
6. Crowdfunding 501
7. Integration of Exemptions 507
   Problem 6-1 514
   Problem 6-2 515
   Problem 6-3 515
   Problem 6-4 515
   Problem 6-5 515
   Problem 6-6 516
   Problem 6-7 516
   Problem 6-8 517

Problem 6-9 517
Problem 6-10 518
Problem 6-11 518
Problem 6-12 518
Problem 6-13 519
Problem 6-14 519
Problem 6-15 520
Problem 6-16 520
Problem 6-17 520
Problem 6-18 520
Problem 6-19 520
Problem 6-20 521
Problem 6-21 521

SUBDIVISION C.   THE OBLIGATION TO REGISTER RESALES OF SECURITIES BY PERSONS OTHER THAN THE ISSUER

Chapter 7. Offerings by Underwriters, Affiliates, and Dealers 523
1. The Concept of "Underwriter" 523
    A. Statutory and Presumptive Underwriters 523
        Securities and Exchange Commission v. Chinese Consolidated Benevolent Association, Inc. 527
        Notes on the *Chinese Consolidated Benevolent Association* Case 530
        Securities and Exchange Commission v. Guild Films Co. 531
        Notes on the *Guild Films* Case 535
        Problem 7-1 536
        Problem 7-2 537
        Problem 7-3 537
2. Going Public by the Back Door 537
    Securities and Exchange Commission v. Datronics Engineers, Inc. 537
    A. Spin-Offs, Reverse Mergers, and the Shell Game 541
3. The Section "4(1½)" Exemption 546
    The Section "4(1½)" Phenomenon: Private Resales of "Restricted" Securities 547
    Notes on the Section 4(1½) Exemption 555
4. Statutory Restrictions on Distributions of Securities by Controlling Persons or Affiliates 557
    In the Matter of Ira Haupt & Co. 557
    Who's "In Control"?—S.E.C. 564
    A. Transactions by Dealers and Brokers 569
        (1) The Dealer's Exemption 570
        (2) The Brokers' Exemption 571
            United States v. Wolfson 573
            Notes on Distribution of Securities by Controlling Persons or Affiliates 576
    B. From Ira Haupt to Rule 144 577
        (1) Sales by Controlling Persons 577

	(2)	"Investment Intent" and Resales of Securities Purchased in "Private Offerings"	579
	(3)	The Doctrine of "Change of Circumstances"	580
	(4)	The Fungibility Concept	581
		Problem 7-4	582
		Problem 7-5	583
		Problem 7-6	583
		Problem 7-7	583

5. Restrictions on Resales of Control Shares and Restricted Securities Under Rule 144 584
   A. Availability of Rule 144 586
   B. Current Public Information 586
   C. Holding Period 587
   D. Limitation on Amount of Securities Sold 590
   E. Manner of Sale 592
   F. Issuers with No or Only Nominal Operations 593
   G. Exclusivity and Operation of Rule 144 593
   H. Possible Modification 593
      Notes on Rule 145 594
      Problem 7-8 596
      Problem 7-9 597
      Problem 7-10 597
      Problem 7-11 598
      Problem 7-12 598
      Problem 7-13 598
      Problem 7-14 598
      Problem 7-15 598
      Problem 7-16 599
      Problem 7-17 599
      Problem 7-18 599
      Problem 7-19 600
      Problem 7-20 600

6. Rule 144A and the Private Resale Market 600
   Resale of Restricted Securities 602
   Notes on Rule 144A and the Private Resale Market 605
   Problem 7-21 607
   Problem 7-22 607
   Problem 7-23 608

7. Section 4(a)(7) 608

8. Regulation S: An Exemption for Offerings Outside the United States 610
   Offshore Offers and Sales 612
   Offshore Offers and Sales 629
   Notes on Regulation S 630
   Problem 7-24 636
   Problem 7-25 636
   Problem 7-26 637
   Problem 7-27 637

PART III. REGULATION OF TRADING IN SECURITIES

Chapter 8. Regulation of the Securities Markets 653
1. Introduction: Change in the Markets 653
   A. The Impact of Regulation on Market Structure 657
   B. Critiques of Contemporary Markets 667
2. The National Market System: Whose Interests Deserve Priority? 671
   Securities Exchange Act Release No. 51808 672
3. What Is an Exchange?: A Brief Survey from the 1934 Act to
   Regulation ATS 683
   Board of Trade of the City of Chicago v. Securities and Exchange
       Commission 686
   A. The Varieties of Alternative Trading Systems 690
      Securities Exchange Act Release No. 38672 691
   B. The SEC's Concerns 693
4. Primary Jurisdiction and the Struggle for Competitive Rates 697
   Gordon v. New York Stock Exchange 697
   Credit Suisse Secs. (USA) LLC v. Billing 700
5. The Over-the-Counter Market 709
   Lehl v. Securities and Exchange Commission 710
6. Market Data 716
7. Technology and Infrastructure 720
8. Self Regulation in the Securities Industry 722

Chapter 9. Regulation of Broker-Dealers 727
Introduction 727
Problem 9-1 741
Problem 9-2 741
1. Regulation Aimed at Fraud and Manipulation 741
   Problem 9-3 758
2. Regulation Aimed at Protection from High Risk and Insolvency 758
3. Regulation Aimed at Establishing the Duties of Brokers to Their
   Customers 766
   A. Regulation Best Interest 767
   B. The Duty of Best Execution 772
      Problem 9-4 773
   C. The Duty to Protect Limit Orders 773
      Problem 9-5 774
      Problem 9-6 775
      Problem 9-7 775
   D. Churning 775
      Nesbit v. McNeil 775
   E. The Penny Stock Reform Act of 1990 785
   F. The Financial Services Middle Market: Prospects for the
      Future 788

**Chapter 10. Tender Offers, Management Buyouts, and Takeover
   Contests 791**
Introduction 791

1. An Overview of the Williams Act 797
   A. The Section 13(d) Trip Wire 797
   B. Disclosure Under the Williams Act...799
   C. Substantive Rules 803
      Epstein v. MCA, Inc. 808
   D. Litigation Issues...816
2. Definitional Issues: Group, Tender Offer, and Bidder 817
   A. "Group" Therapy 817
      GAF Corp. v. Milstein..817
      Securities and Exchange Commission v. First City Financial
         Corp., Ltd. 831
   B. The Definition of "Tender Offer" 837
      Securities and Exchange Commission v. Carter Hawley Hale
         Stores, Inc. 837
      Hanson Trust PLC v. SCM Corporation...845
      Problem 10-1..858
      Problem 10-2..858
      Problem 10-3..858
   C. Who's the Bidder?...858
      MAI Basic Four, Inc. v. Prime Computer, Inc....................................859
3. Reforming the Tender Offer Process 867
   Securities Act Release No. 7760..867
4. Defensive Tactics: The Target Strikes Back 873
   A. The Williams Act's Application to the Target 873
   B. Federal Securities Law Implications of Defensive Tactics...............875
5. State Anti-Takeover Legislation 880
   A. The Case Law 881
      CTS Corporation v. Dynamics Corporation of America...................881
      Amanda Acquisition Corp. v. Universal Foods Corp. 891
   B. State Anti-Takeover Legislation After CTS: Constituency and
      Disgorgement Statutes 900
6. New Developments: The Changed Legal Landscape............................902
   A. The Friendly Tender Offer 902
   B. The Impact of Hedge Fund Activism 903
   C. Cross-Border Tender Offers 903
   D. Debt Tender Offers...906
   E. "Mini-Tenders" 907

PART IV. SECURITIES ENFORCEMENT
AND CLASS ACTIONS

The Role of Disclosure and Materiality in Securities Litigation and
   Enforcement 909
Statutory and Class Action Provisions Unique to Securities Litigation....910

Chapter 11. Civil Liability Under the Securities Act of 1933 919
1. Section 11 of the 1933 Act 919
   A. Introductory Note..919

	B.	Defendants and the Due Diligence Defense	922
		Escott v. BarChris Construction Corp.	922
		In re WorldCom, Inc. Securities Litigation	943
		Notes on Defendants and the "Due Diligence" Defense Under § 11	962
		Problem 11-1	970
	C.	Causation and Damages	971
		Akerman v. Oryx Communications, Inc.	971
		Note on Damages: Section 11 Limits Amount Recoverable	975
	D.	Section 11 Plaintiffs	976
		Hertzberg v. Dignity Partners, Inc.	976
		Notes on § 11 Plaintiffs: Who May Recover?	980
	E.	What Counts as a Misstatement Under Section 11?	982
		Omnicare, Inc. v. Laborers District Council Construction Industry Pension Fund	982
		Notes on Misstatements Under § 11	992
	F.	Statute of Limitations	993
	G.	Concurrent Jurisdiction	994
2.	Section 12 of the 1933 Act		995
	A.	Section 12(a)(1)	995
		Pinter v. Dahl	996
		Note on § 12(a)(1): Who Is a Seller?	1003
		Problem 11-2	1005
	B.	Section 12(a)(2)	1005
		Gustafson v. Alloyd Company, Incorporated	1006
		Notes on § 12 Post Gustafson: Reasonable Care Defense and Other Issues	1022
		Problem 11-3	1027
3.	Section 17(a) of the 1933 Act		1028

Chapter 12. Rules 10b–5 and 14a–9: Fraud in Connection with a Purchase or Sale of a Security or the Solicitation of Proxies 1031

1. Introduction 1031
   Notes on Cause of Action Under Rule 10b–5 1032
2. Rule 10b–5: Fraud in Connection with a Purchase or Sale of a Security 1037
   A. The Requirement That There Be Fraud 1037
      (1) Misstatements and Omissions 1037
           Santa Fe Industries, Inc. v. Green 1037
           Notes on Rule 10b–5 as a Remedy for Mismanagement 1043
      (2) The Duty to Update and the Duty to Correct 1047
           In re Time Warner Inc. Securities Litigation 1048
           In re Burlington Coat Factory Securities Litigation 1054
           Notes on the Duty to Update and the Duty to Correct 1058
           Problem 12-1 1060

	B.	Materiality	1061
		(1) Generally	1061
		Basic Incorporated v. Levinson	1061
		Matrixx Initiatives, Inc. v. Siracusano	1068
		Notes on Materiality	1079
		Problem 12-2	1080
		(2) Forward Looking Statements	1081
		In re Worlds of Wonder Securities Litigation	1083
		Note on Forward Looking Statements: The Private Securities Litigation Reform Act	1091
		Harris v. Ivax Corp.	1093
		(3) Reasons, Opinions, and Beliefs	1097
		Virginia Bankshares, Inc. v. Sandberg	1097
		Notes on Reasons, Opinions, and Beliefs	1101
		Problem 12-3	1102
	C.	The "in Connection with" Requirement	1103
		Semerenko v. Cendant Corp.	1103
		SEC v. Zandford	1107
		Note on the "in Connection with" Requirement	1111
	D.	Culpability	1112
		Ernst & Ernst v. Hochfelder	1112
		Notes on the Required Culpability of the Defendant	1120
		Problem 12-4	1122
	E.	Reliance and Causation	1123
		(1) Reliance and the Fraud-on-the-Market Presumption	1123
		Basic Incorporated v. Levinson	1123
		Halliburton Co. v. Erica P. John Fund, Inc.	1128
		Notes on the Fraud on the Market Theory	1140
		(2) Reasonable Reliance	1143
		Semerenko v. Cendant Corp.	1143
		Notes on Reasonable Reliance and Causation	1151
		(3) Loss Causation	1152
		Dura Pharmaceuticals, Inc. v. Michael Broudo	1152
		Erica P. John Fund, Inc. v. Halliburton Co.	1157
		Notes on Loss Causation	1162
		Problem 12-5	1165
	F.	Standing	1165
		Blue Chip Stamps v. Manor Drug Stores	1165
		Notes on Standing: The Purchaser Seller Requirement Under Rule 10b–5	1172
3.	Rule 14a–9: Proxy Fraud		1176
	A.	Implied Cause of Action	1177
	B.	Materiality	1177
		Notes on Materiality: What Facts Are Material?	1178
	C.	Culpability	1182
		Notes on Culpability Under Rule 14a–9	1184
	D.	Causation	1184
4.	Section 18		1185

Chapter 13. Insider Trading 1187
1. "Insider" Trading 1191
   A. Classical Insider Trading 1191
      Chiarella v. United States 1191
   B. Temporary Insiders, Tippers, and Tippees 1196
      Dirks v. SEC 1196
      Tippers and Tippees 1205
   C. The Misappropriation Theory 1207
      United States v. O'Hagan 1207
      Who Has a Duty to Disclose and SEC Regulations 1215
   D. The Second Circuit's Gift Theory 1220
      United States v. Martoma 1220
   E. The STOCK Act 1233
      Problem 13-1 1234
   F. 18 U.S.C. § 1348 1235
      United States v. Blaszczak 1236
2. Regulation FD 1244
3. SEC Rule 14e–3 and Tender Offers 1247
   United States v. O'Hagan 1248
   Rule 14e–3 Issues 1252
   Problem 13-2 1255
4. Section 16(b) Liability for Short Swing Profits 1255
   A. Introduction 1255
   B. Purchases and Sales 1257
      Kern County Land Co. v. Occidental Petroleum Corp. 1257
      "Purchase" and "Sale" 1264
      "Any Period of Less than Six Months" 1268
      "Profit Realized" 1268
   C. Officers and Directors 1269
      Feder v. Martin Marietta Corp. 1269
      Officer or Director 1274
   D. Beneficial Ownership 1275
      Ten Percent Holder 1276
      Problem 13-3 1278
   E. Rule 16b–3 and Employee Benefit Plans 1278
      The Sarbanes-Oxley Act 1279
5. Damages for Insider Trading 1280
   Elkind v. Liggett & Myers, Inc. 1280
   Statutory Developments 1286

Chapter 14. SEC Enforcement Actions 1289
1. Procedures 1290
   Note on Procedures: Formal Investigations 1291
   A. Special Issues: Proper Purpose 1293
   B. Right to Counsel 1293
   C. Confidentiality 1294
   D. Wells Submissions 1294
   E. Rules of Practice 1295
   F. Expanded Authority in Administrative Proceedings 1296

2.	Remedies..1297		
	A.	Injunctions and Ancillary Relief 1298	
		SEC v. Unifund SAL 1298	
	B.	Disgorgement and Ancillary Relief 1305	
		Liu v. SEC..1305	
		Notes on Disgorgement Remedy 1316	
		Notes on Injunctions and Receiverships.........................1317	
		Securities and Exchange Commission v. Bank of America Corporation...1319	
		Problem 14-1..1326	
	C.	Ex Parte Sanctions...1326	
	D.	New Statutory Remedies 1327	
		(1) Civil Fines...1327	
		(2) Cease and Desist Orders..1329	
		Valicenti Advisory Services, Inc. v. SEC 1330	
		WHX Corporation v. Securities and Exchange Commission..1334	
		(3) Corporate Bar Orders 1340	
		SEC v. Patel..1341	
		Note on the Corporate Bar Order: Sarbanes-Oxley 1344	
		(4) Collateral Bar Orders...1345	
3.	SEC Enforcement and Professionals 1345		
	A.	Securities Attorneys and Accountants.........................1345	
		(1) Introduction to Rule 102(e)....................................1345	
		(2) Rule 102(e) and Attorneys 1347	
		Carter & Johnson 1347	
		Notes on Rule 102(e): Over Time.......................................1366	
		SEC v. Fehn 1375	
		Problem 14-2..1382	
		(3) Accountants' Independence 1382	
			a. SEC Actions 1382
			b. The Sarbanes-Oxley Act....................................1386
	B.	Corporate Registrants, Officers, and Directors..........................1388	
		SEC v. World-Wide Coin Investments, Ltd. 1389	
		Notes on Sarbanes-Oxley and Dodd-Frank 1400	
	C.	Broker-Dealers 1404	
		In the Matter of John H. Gutfreund, et al. 1405	
		Notes on Broker-Dealers: Disciplinary Proceedings...................1417	
		Problem 14-3..1418	
		Notes on Broker-Dealers: SRO Regulation 1419	
	D.	Investment Advisers 1421	
		(1) Definition of "Investment Adviser" 1422	
		Lowe v. SEC..1422	
		Notes on Who Is an Investment Adviser 1427	
		Notes on Investment Advisers: The Dodd-Frank Act 1429	
		Problem 14-4..1431	
		(2) Scalping..1432	
		SEC v. Capital Gains Research Bureau, Inc. 1432	
		Problem 14-5 1439	

Chapter 15. Criminal Enforcement of the Federal Securities Laws 1441
1. Procedural Issues 1442
   SEC v. Dresser Industries, Inc. 1444
   A. Parallel Proceedings 1451
2. Criminal Prosecutions Under the Federal Securities Laws 1452
   United States v. Dixon 1453
   A. Knowing Versus Willful 1455
   B. Reliance on the Advice of Counsel 1457
3. Stock Parking and "Regulatory" Violations 1457
   United States v. Mulheren 1459
   Problem 15-1 1471
4. Criminal Prosecutions Under Title 18 1471

Chapter 16. International Enforcement 1473
1. The Jurisdiction of U.S. Courts over Claims by Private Plaintiffs 1474
   Morrison v. National Australia Bank, Ltd. 1475
   Notes on *Morrison* 1491
2. Government Extraterritorial Enforcement of the Securities Laws 1498
   A. Section 929P(b) of Dodd-Frank Act 1499
   B. Criminal Enforcement of the Securities Laws 1502
      Problem 16-1 1503
   C. The Challenges to Governmental Enforcement Efforts 1503

INDEX 1507

TABLE OF CASES

The principal cases are in bold type.

7547 Corp. v. Parker & Parsley Dev. Partners, L.P., 1175
A.T. Brod & Co. v. Perlow, 1176
Aaron v. S.E.C., 750, 1028, 1068, 1203
Abbey v. Control Data Corp., 200
Abell v. Potomac Ins. Co., 1003
Abrams v. Oppenheimer Gov't Sec., Inc., 1111
Absolute Activist Value Master Fund Ltd. v. Ficeto, 1492
Ackerberg v. Johnson, 397, 555
Ackerman v. Schwartz, 1003, 1004
Adair v. Bristol Tech. Sys., Inc., 982
Adler v. Klawans, 1277
Advanced Battery Technologies, Inc., In re, 1121
Advanta Corp. Sec. Litig., In re, 1106, 1121
AES Corp. Sec. Litig., In re, 203
Affiliated Ute Citizens v. United States, 1041, 1115, 1124, 1151
Ahern v. Gaussoin, 968
Akerman v. Oryx Communications, Inc., 971
Alaska Interstate Co. v. McMillian, 800
Aldrich v. McCulloch Properties, Inc., 307
Alexander Reid & Co., Inc., In re, 758
Alfus v. Pyramid Technology Corp., 1050
Allergan, Inc. v. Valeant Pharms. Int'l, Inc., 796
Alley v. Miramon, 1175
Allied Leisure Indus., Inc., 491
Allis-Chalmers Mfg. Co. v. Gulf & Western Industries, 1263
Alstead, Dempsey & Co., Inc., In the Matter of, 716, 1182
Amalgamated Clothing & Textile Workers v. J.P. Stevens & Co., 203
Amanda Acquisition Corp. v. Universal Foods Corp., 891
Ambler v. Whipple, 1310
American Bankers Ass'n v. S.E.C., 689
American Brewing Company, 478
American Equity Investment Life Ins. Co. v. S.E.C., 60
American Express Co. v. Italian Colors Restaurant, 765
American Standard, Inc. v. Crane Co., 1267
Ames Dep't Stores Inc. Stock Litig., In re, 1112
Amgen Inc. v. Connecticut Ret. Plans & Trust Funds, 916, 1129
Anderson v. Abbott Laboratories, 205
Andrews v. Prudential Securities, 1419, 1420
Angelastro v. Prudential-Bache Sec., Inc., 1105
AnnTaylor Stores Securities Litigation, In re, 1050
Apple Computer Sec. Litig., In re, 228, 1052, 1179
Arceneaux v. Merrill, Lynch, Pierce, Fenner & Smith, 781, 782
Argentinian Recovery Company LLC v. Multicanal S.A., 483, 491
Armstrong v. Exceptional Child Center, Inc., 1312
Arrow Distrib. Corp. v. Baumgartner, 1257, 1275
Arthur Andersen & Co. v. S.E.C., 53
Arthur Andersen LLP v. United States, 1470
Arthur James Huff, In the Matter of, 1415
Arthur Young & Co. v. Reves, 333, 336, 1059
Ashanti Goldfields Company Limited, 491
Ashcroft v. Iqbal, 990
Associated Randall Bank v. Griffin, Kubik, Stephens & Thompson, Inc., 1027
Astronics Corp. v. Protective Closures Co., 851
Bachynsky, United States v., 197
Backman v. Polaroid Corp., 1055
Badalamenti, United States v., 1463
Bair v. Krug, 1035
Ballan v. Upjohn Co., 203
Ballan v. Wilfred American Educational Corp., 197
Ballay v. Legg Mason Wood Walker, Inc., 1007, 1009
Banca Cremi, S.A. v. Alex Brown & Sons, Inc., 771
Banco Espanol de Credito v. Security Pacific National Bank, 14
Bank & Trust Co. of Old York Road v. Hankin, 1180
Baravati v. Josephthal, Lyon & Ross, Inc., 1420
Barbara v. New York Stock Exchange, 724
Barker v. Henderson, Franklin, Starnes & Holt, 1371
Barnes v. Osofsky, 981

Basic Inc. v. Levinson, 186, 200, 212, 214, 225, 257, 916, **1061**, **1123**, 1178
Basis Yield Alpha Fund v. Goldman Sachs Group, Inc., 1496
Bateman Eichler, Hill Richards, Inc. v. Berner, 1046
Bath Industries, Inc. v. Blot, 817, 821
Batterton v. Francis, 1250
Baurer v. Planning Group, Inc., 336
Baxter v. Palmigiano, 1447, 1452
Beaumont v. American Can Co., 74, 807
Beecher v. Able, 972, 973
Belknap v. Schild, 1310
Bell Atlantic Corp. v. Twombly, 1077, 1163
Berger v. Bishop Inv. Corp., 1033
Bersch v. Drexel Firestone, Inc., 95, 1487
Bershad v. McDonough, 1264
Bertoglio v. Texas Intern. Co., 197
Bilzerian, United States v., 836
Birnbaum v. Newport Steel Corp., 1166
Blaszczak, United States v., 1471
Blau v. Lamb, 1260, 1270
Blau v. Lehman, 1168, 1270
Blau v. Mission Corp., 1176
Blau v. Oppenheim, 1270
Blitz, United States v., 1469
Bloom, United States v., 1443
Blue Chip Stamp Co., United States v., 1166
Blue Chip Stamps v. Manor Drug Stores, 308, 328, 816, 1010, 1017, 1026, 1042, **1165**, 1283, 1472, 1487
BNS, Inc. v. Koppers Co., 892
Board of Governors v. Dimension Fin. Corp., 689
Board of Trade of the City of Chicago v. S.E.C., 684, **686**
Bolger v. Laventhol, Krekstein, Horwath & Horwath, 1175
Booth v. Varian Associates, 1263
Bosse v. Crowell Collier and Macmillan, 1174
Boston Sci. Corp Sec. Litig., In re, 197
Boyce Motor Lines, Inc. v. United States, 1215
Boyer, United States v., 1456
Bradford v. Moench, 347
Brascan Ltd. v. Edper Equities Ltd., 842, 844, 845, 851
Brennan v. Midwestern United Life Ins. Co., 1120
Brewster, United States v., 1234
Brophy v. Redivo, 778, 784
Brown-Forman Distillers Corp. v. New York State Liquor Authority, 887

Browning Debenture Holders' Committee v. DASA Corp., 479
Browning-Ferris Indus., Inc. Shareholder Derivative Litig., In re, 201
Brucker v. Thyssen-Bornemisza Europe N.V., 495
Bryan v. Brock & Blevins Co., 1042
Bryan, United States v., 1208
Bryant v. Avado Brands, Inc., 1122
BT Alex. Brown Inc., In re, 758
BT Securities Corp., In the Matter of, 771
Bua, In re, 1372
Bufalino, United States v., 1463, 1468
Burdell v. Denig, 1309
Burlington Coat Factory Securities Litigation, In re, **1054**, 1145, 1146, 1149
Busch v. Carpenter, 454, 456
Business Roundtable v. S.E.C., 60, 63, 724, 876
Butler v. Phlo Corp., 398
Buttrey v. Merrill Lynch, Pierce, Fenner & Smith, Inc., 1036
Byrnes v. Faulkner, Dawkins & Sullivan, 536, 573
C.R.A. Realty Corp. v. Fremont Gen. Corp., 1264
Cabell v. Markham, 821, 822
Cady v. Murphy, 1000, 1003
Cady, Roberts & Co., Matter of, 1191, 1197
Caiola v. Citibank, N.A., 354
California Pub. Emps.' Ret. Sys. v. ANZ Sec., Inc., 994
Callaghan v. Myers, 1311
Canadian Conquest Expl. Inc., 491
Capital General Corp., In re, 478
Capri v. Murphy, 1004
Carl M. Loeb, Rhoades & Co. and Dominick & Dominick, In the Matter of, 100
Carolina Wholesale Florists, Inc., 482
Carpenter v. United States, 1210, 1239, 1471
Carpenter, United States v., 1174
Carter & Johnson, In re, **1347**, 1380
Carter Hawley Hale Stores, Inc. v. The Limited, Inc., 838
Carter-Wallace, Inc., Securities Litigation, In re, 1072
Cascade Fund, LLLP v. Absolute Capital Mgmt. Holdings Ltd., 1492
Cashman v. Coopers & Lybrand, 968
Castellano v. Young & Rubicam, Inc., 1059
Caterpillar Inc., SEC Exch.Act Rel. No. 30532, In the Matter of, 213, 215

TABLE OF CASES xxv

Cendant Corp. Sec. Litig., In re, 1173
Central Bank of Denver, N.A. v. First Interstate Bank of Denver, N.A., 1017, 1371, 1375
CFTC v. British Am. Commodity Options Corp., 835
Chapman v. Dunn, 452, 456
Charles Hughes & Co. v. S.E.C., 712, 716
Checkosky v. S.E.C., 1346, 1367
Chemetron Corp. v. Business Funds, Inc., 1033
Chemical Bank v. Arthur Andersen & Co., 335, 478, 1104
Chemical Fund, Inc. v. Xerox Corp., 1277
Chestman, United States v., 736, 1240
Chevron, U.S.A., Inc. v. NRDC, 689, 1250
Chiarella v. United States, 1191, 1197, 1209, 1225
Chiarella, United States v., 1456
Chris-Craft Industries, Inc. v. Bangor Punta Corp., 101
Chromalloy American Corp. v. Sun Chemical Corp., 829, 837, 851, 1255
Church of the Holy Trinity v. United States, 304
CitiSource, Inc. Sec. Litig., In re, 1035
City Capital Assocs. Ltd. Partnership v. Interco, Inc., 862, 892
Clarence Z. Wurts, In the Matter of, 1418
Clark v. Kidder, Peabody & Co., 785
Cleary v. Perfectune, Inc., 1120
Clews v. Jamieson, 1310
Coates v. S.E.C., 1028, 1215
Cochran v. Channing Corp., 1172
Coffee v. Permian Corp., 1175
Cohen, United States v., 1469
Colan v. Mesa Petroleum Co., 1264
Colello v. S.E.C., 1504
Collins Sec. Corp. v. S.E.C., 1296
Colonial Realty Corp. v. Bache & Co., 727, 1035
Colonial Realty Corp. v. MacWilliams, 1268
Columbia General Inv. Corp. v. S.E.C., 261, 979
Columbia Securities Litigation, In re, 1050
Commerce Reporting Co. v. Puretec, Inc., 1176
Commonwealth Edison Co. v. Montana, 887
Comshare Inc. Sec. Litig., In re, 1122
Comverse Technology, Inc. Sec. Litig., In re, 199
Conley v. Gibson, 1156
Connecticut Nat. Bank v. Fluor Corp., 817
Consolidated Gold Fields PLC v. Minorco, S.A., 904
Continental Mktg. Corp. v. S.E.C., 287
Convergent Technologies Securities Litigation, In re, 228
Conway v. Icahn & Co., 737
Cook v. Avien, Inc., 1120
Cooke v. Teleprompter Corp., 202
Cooley v. Board of Wardens, 887, 888
Cooper v. Pickett, 1060
Cooperman v. Individual, Inc., 1181
Coopersmith v. Lehman Broth., Inc., 914
Copley Pharmaceutical, Inc. Securities Litigation, In re, 203
Copperweld Corp. v. Imetal, 800
Corenco Corp. v. Schiavone & Sons, Inc., 800
Cornwell v. Credit Suisse Group, 1492
Corr, United States v., 1469
Cort v. Ash, 1041, 1042
Cortec Indus., Inc. v. Sum Holding L.P., 1004
Coscia, United States v., 670
Costello v. Oppenheimer & Co., 782
Costello, Russotto & Co., In the Matter of the Application of, 712
Countrywide Fin. Corp. Derivative Litig., In re, 201
County Produce, Inc. v. United States Dep't of Agric., 1333
Cowin v. Bresler, 1172
Cowles v. Dow Keith Oil & Gas, Inc., 396
Craftmatic Sec. Litig. v. Kraftsow, 1003
Craighead v. E.F. Hutton & Co., Inc., 1028
Crane Co. v. American Standard, Inc., 877
Crane Co. v. Harsco Corp., 843
Crane Co. v. Westinghouse Air Brake Co., 755, 756, 877
Credit Suisse Secs. (USA) LLC v. Billing, 85, 86, **700**
Crosby, United States v., 1457
Crowley v. Montgomery Ward & Co., 287
CRTF Corp. v. Federated Dept. Stores, Inc., 804
CSX Corp. v. Children's Inv. Fund Management (UK) LLP, 829, 830
CTS Corp. v. Dynamics Corp. of America, 881, 891
Curran v. Merrill Lynch, Pierce, Fenner & Smith, Inc., 294
Cyan, Inc. v. Beaver Cty. Emples. Ret. Fund, 912, 995

Cytryn v. Cook, 1050
D.L. Cromwell Invs., Inc. v. NASD Regulation, Inc., 724
Daily v. Morgan, 331
Dan River, Inc. v. Icahn, 802, 837
Dan River, Inc. v. Unitex Ltd., 829, 1255
Danis v. USN Communications, Inc., 968
Dasho v. Susquehanna Corp., 1172
Data Probe Acquisition Corp. v. Datatab, Inc., 874
Davis v. Merrill Lynch, Pierce, Fenner & Smith, Inc., 783, 784
Davy v. S.E.C., 1346
de Kwiatkowski v. Bear Stearns & Co., 736, 738
Dean Witter Managed Futures Ltd. Partnership Litigation, In re, 736
Dean Witter Reynolds, Inc., In re, 1417
DeKwiatkowski v. Bear Stearns & Co., 650
Delafield & Delafield, In re, 1467
Dennis v. General Imaging, Inc., 1024
Department of Revenue of Ky. v. Davis, 367
Desaigoudar v. Meyercord, 201
DeSantis, United States v., 1456
Desiderio v. NASD, Inc., 1036
DeVita v. Sills, 1447
Diamond Foods, Inc. Derivative Litig., In re, 199
DiBona, United States v., 1294
Dickerson v. United States, 1128
Dickerson, United States v., 822
Digital Island Sec. Litig., In re, 813
Digital Realty Trust, Inc. v. Somers, 1291
Dirks v. S.E.C., 1052, 1127, **1196**, 1236, 1442
Dixon v. United States, 1119
Dixon, United States v., **1453**
Dolphin & Bradbury, Inc. v. S.E.C., 1121
Dopp v. Franklin National Bank, 1174
Doran v. Petroleum Management Corp., **386**
Drachman v. Harvey, 1040
Dubach v. Weitzel, 347
Dudley v. Southeastern Factor and Fin. Corp., 1175
Duker & Duker, In the Matter of, 712
Dunhill Securities Corp. v. Microthermal Applications, Inc., 74, 97
Dunn, United States v., 1109
Dura Pharmaceuticals, Inc. v. Broudo, **1152**, 1163
Durning v. Citibank, N.A., 1035

DVI, Inc. Secs. Litig., In re, 1159
D-Z Investment Co. v. Holloway, 856
E.F. Hutton and Company, Inc., In re, 774
E.ON AG v. Acciona, S.A., 906
Eastland v. United States Servicemen's Fund, 1234
Eaton Vance Distrib., Inc. v. Ulrich, 1420
eBay Inc. Shareholder Litigation, In re, 753
Echo Bay Resources Inc., 481
Edgar v. MITE Corp., 840, 882, 883, 888, 891, 902
Edward J. Mawod & Co. v. S.E.C., 1469
EEOC v. Arabian American Oil Co., 1477, 1488
Electronic Specialty Co. v. International Controls Corp., 802, 1060, 1281
Elizabeth v. Pavement Co., 1310, 1314
Elkind v. Liggett & Myers, Inc., 836, 1060, **1280**
Ellerin v. Massachusetts Mut. Life Ins. Co., 1277
Ellis v. Carter, 1033
Endo v. Albertine, 967
Endo v. Arthur Andersen & Co., S.C., 968
Energy Ventures, Inc. v. Appalachian Co., 845, 851
Epstein v. MCA, Inc., 808, 1255
Erica P. John Fund, Inc. v. Halliburton Co., 915, 916, **1157**
Ernst & Ernst v. Hochfelder, 874, 998, 1003, 1010, 1021, 1026, 1034, 1112, 1192
Escott v. BarChris Construction Corp., 922, 1117
Ettinger v. Merrill Lynch, Pierce, Fenner & Smith, Inc., 716
Europe & Overseas Commodity Traders v. Banque Paribas, 631
Exchange Nat'l Bank of Chicago v. Touche Ross & Co., 335
Exxon Corp. v. Governor of Maryland, 887, 889
Facebook, Inc., In re, 215
Falcone, United States v., 1227
Falls v. Fickling, 1174
Feder v. Frost, 1276
Feder v. Martin Marietta Corp., **1269**
Feiner v. SS & C Tech., Inc., 982
Feins v. American Stock Exch., Inc., 1036
Feit v. Leasco Data Processing Equipment Corp., 951, 964, 1117
Fencorp Co. v. Ohio Kentucky Oil Corp., 425

Ferraiolo v. Newman, 1270
Field v. Trump, 810, 813, 816, 1255
Fields v. Biomatrix, Inc., 913
Fields, United States v., 1450
Financial Planning Association v. S.E.C., 60, 766, 789
Findwhat Investor Group v. Findwhat.com, 1163, 1164
Finkel v. Stratton Corp., 93, 1028
Finkielstain v. Seidel, 1035
Finnerty v. Stiefel Laboratories, Inc., 1080
First Jersey Sec., Inc. v. Bergen, 62
First National Bank of Boston v. Bellotti, 888
First Pennsylvania Mortgage Trust, 482
First Trust & Savings Bank of Zanesville, Ohio v. Fidelity-Philadelphia Trust Co., 1024
First Union Discount Brokerage Services, Inc. v. Milos, 764
Fischman v. Raytheon, 1112, 1168
Fitzsimmons v. Barton, 95
Flamm v. Eberstadt, 1064, 1065, 1067
Florida Commercial Banks v. Culverhouse, 802, 816, 836, 1255
Florida Lime & Avocado Growers, Inc. v. Paul, 883
Florida State Bd. of Admin. v. Brick, 914
Flynn v. Bass Bros. Enterprises, Inc., 801
Follansbee v. Davis, Skaggs & Co., Inc., 778, 782
Foremost-McKesson, Inc. v. Provident Securities Co., 1276
Forkin v. Rooney, Pace, Inc., 784
Franchard Corporation, In the Matter of, 190
Frankel v. Slotkin, 1175
Franklin Savings Bank of New York v. Levy, 1024
Franklin v. Gwinnett County Public Schools, 1177
Fraser v. Fiduciary Trust Co. Int'l, 1173
Free Enterprise Fund v. Public Company Accounting Oversight Board, 63, 647
Freeman v. Venner, 1155
Friedman v. Salomon/Smith Barney, Inc., 85
Frigitemp Corp. v. Financial Dynamics Fund, Inc., 1193
FTC v. Bunte Brothers, Inc., 1114
FTC v. H.N. Singer, Inc., 1303
GAF Corp. v. Heyman, 197
GAF Corp. v. Milstein, 817
Gaines v. Haughton, 199, 1180

Gallagher v. Abbott Laboratories, 1059
Gannon v. Continental Ins. Co., 1147
Gansman, United States v., 1231
Gap Sec. Litig., In re, 1180
Garcia v. San Antonio Metro Transit Authority, 366
Gary Plastic Packaging Corp. v. Merrill Lynch, 288
Gearhart Industries, Inc. v. Smith Intern., Inc., 836, 1254
Geiger v. S.E.C., 573
Gelles v. TDA Indus., Inc., 1176
Geman v. S.E.C., 737
General Aircraft Corp. v. Lampert, 1255
General Electric Co. v. EPA, 1337
General Motors Class E Stock Buyout Sec. Litig., In re, 1081
Genzyme Corp. Sec. Litig., In re, 1121
George C. Kern, Jr., In the Matter of, 802
Georgiou, United States v., 1495
Gerber v. Computer Associates International, Inc., 813, 814
Gerstle v. Gamble-Skogmo, Inc., 1118
Gilbert, United States v., 1466, 1467
Gilead Scis. Sec. Litig., In re, 1163
Gilligan, Will & Co. v. S.E.C., 533, 549, 555, 580
Glennon v. Dean Witter Reynolds, Inc., 1420
Glosser v. Cellcor Inc., 967
Goldberg v. Meridor, 1043
Goldberger v. Baker, 1180
Golden v. Garafalo, 330, 332
Goldman v. Belden, 1060
Gollust v. Mendell, 1267
Goodwin v. Elkins & Co., 324
Gordon v. FDIC, 1448
Gordon v. New York Stock Exchange, 657, 697
Gould v. American-Hawaiian Steamship Co., 1182, 1184
Gould v. Ruefenacht, 331
Gould v. Tricon, Inc., 1024
Gould v. Winstar Comm., Inc., 1186
Graham v. S.E.C., 1417
Grand Casinos, Inc. Sec. Litig., In re, 915
Grandon v. Merrill Lynch & Co., 740
Gratz v. Claughton, 1268, 1269
Great Lakes Chemical Corporation v. Monsanto Company, 322, 332
Great Western United Corp. v. Kidwell, 884
Greater Iowa Corp. v. McLendon, 1168
Greebel v. FTP Software, Inc., 913, 914, 1121

Green v. Occidental Petroleum Corp., 1282
Greenberg, In re, 714
Greenfield v. Heublein, Inc., 1056
Gregory v. Helvering, 484
Grenader v. Spitz, 307
Griggs v. Pace Am. Group, Inc., 1176
Grin v. Shine, 1240
Grossman v. Novell, Inc., 1149
Grossman v. Waste Management, Inc., 202, 205
Grow Chemical Corp. v. Uran, 817
Gryl ex rel. Shire Pharm. Grp. PLC v. Shire Pharm. Grp. PLC, 60
Guenther v. Cooper Life Sciences, Inc., 981
Gulf Oil/Cities Service Tender Offer Litigation, In re, 1051
Gustafson v. Alloyd Co., Inc., 978, 981, **1006**
Gwozdzinsky v. Zell/Chilmark Fund, L.P., 1265
H.K. Porter Co., Inc. v. Nicholson File Co., 1253
H.P. Hood & Sons, Inc. v. Du Mond, 887
Haddy, United States v., 1469
Hall v. Geiger-Jones Co., 64
Halliburton Co. v. Erica P. John Fund, Inc., 225, 917, **1128**
Hallwood Realty Partners, L.P. v. Gotham Partners, LP, 827, 828
Halsey, Stuart & Co., Inc., In the Matter of, 755
Handler v. S.E.C., 1318
Handley Inv. Co. v. S.E.C., 712
Hanly v. Securities and Exchange Commission, 1024
Hanson Trust PLC v. SCM Corporation, 845
Haralson v. E. F. Hutton Group, Inc., 920
Harden v. Raffensperger, Hughes & Co., Inc., 535, 981
Harelson v. Miller Fin. Corp., 1003
Harris v. Ivax Corp., 207, **1093**
Harris v. Union Elec. Co., 1172
Hart v. Pulte Homes of Michigan, 294
Hatfield, United States v., 199
Hayes v. Gross, 1147
Head v. Head, 478
Hecht v. Harris, Upham & Co., 778, 782, 783
Heckmann v. Ahmanson, 879
Hedden v. Marinelli, 397
Heit v. Weitzen, 1186, 1281
Helstoski, United States v., 1234
Hemispherx Biopharma, Inc. v. Johannesburg Consolidated Investments, 826
Henderson v. Hayden, Stone Inc., 385

Henry, United States v., 1448
Heras, United States v., 1228
Herman & MacLean v. Huddleston, 968, 1032
Hertzberg v. Dignity Partners, Inc., **976**
Heublein, Inc. v. General Cinema Corp., 1267
Heungkuk Life Insurance Co. v. The Goldman Sachs Group, Inc., 1496
Hill York Corp. v. American Int'l Franchises, Inc., 389, 390, 995
Hines v. Davidowitz, 883
Hocking v. Dubois, 324
Hoffman v. Estabrook & Co., Inc., 1120
Holloway v. Peat, Marwick, Mitchell & Co., 335, 347
Hooper v. Mountain States Sec. Corp., 1172
Hoover Co. v. Fuqua Industries, 843
Horne Brothers, Inc. v. Laird, 1447
Hoskins, United States v., 1471
Houlihan v. Anderson-Stokes, Inc., 1175
Howing Co. v. Nationwide Corp., 1181, 1185
Humana, Inc. v. American Medicorp, Inc., 874
Hurley v. Federal Deposit Ins. Corp., 1141
Hyde Park Partners, L.P. v. Connolly, 898
ICICI Bank Limited, 491
IIT v. Vencap, Ltd., 1487
IIT, Int'l Inv. Trust v. Cornfeld, 1487
Ikon Office Solutions, Inc., In re, 1121
Independent Order of Foresters v. Donald, Lufkin & Jenrette, 736
Indiana Nat'l Corp. v. Rich, 1255
Indiana Public Retirement Systems v. SAIC, Inc., 202, 214
Initial Public Offering Antitrust Litigation, In re, 702
Initial Public Offering Securities Litigation, In re, 703
International Brotherhood of Teamsters, Chauffeurs, Warehousemen and Helpers of America v. Daniel, 307, 328, 330, 339, 1173
International Controls Corp. v. Vesco, 543, 1176
Investment Co. Institute v. Camp, 43
Ira Haupt & Co., In the Matter of, **557**
Isaacson, United States v., 1495, 1502
Isquith v. Caremark Int'l, Inc., 543, 1175

J. Bennett Grocock, Esq., In the Matter of, 1372
J.I. Case Co. v. Borak, 1167, 1177
Jablon v. Dean Witter & Co., 1036
Jackson v. Oppenheim, 1024
Jackson v. Virginia, 1463
Jackvony v. RIHT Fin. Corp., 1046, 1047
Jaffee & Co. v. S.E.C., 749, 750
James E. Ryan, In re, 716
James v. Gerber Products Co., 1174
Jammies Int'l, Inc. v. Nowinski, 1268
Janus Capital Group, Inc. v. First Derivative Traders, 1122, 1134
Jarecki v. G.D. Searle & Co., 1012
Jay Lapine, Esq., In the Matter of, 1372
Jeanes v. Henderson, 1175
Jennings v. Carson, 1310
Jiau, United States v., 1221
John H. Gutfreund, et al., In the Matter of, 1405
John Nuveen & Co., Inc. v. Sanders, 1026
John R. Sand & Gravel Co. v. United States, 1133
Johnston v. Bumba, 398, 425
Jones v. Alfred H. Mayer Co., 821
Jones v. S.E.C., 261, 724
Joseph I. Emas, In the Matter of, 1372
Joseph M. Salvani and MainstreetIPO.com, Inc., In the Matter of, 734
JWP, In re, 1022
Kagan v. Edison Bros. Stores, Inc., 1176
Kahn v. Securities and Exchange Commission, 757
Kahn v. Virginia Retirement System, 811, 813
Kaiser, United States v., 1456
Kalmanovitz v. G. Heileman Brewing Co., Inc., 874, 1254
Kamerman v. Steinberg, 816, 837, 879
Kansas v. Nebraska, 1309
Kaplan v. Rose, 1141
Kardon v. National Gypsum Co., 1032, 1126, 1196
Kas v. Financial Gen. Bankshares, Inc., 1180, 1181
Kassel v. Consolidated Freightways Corp., 888
Katt v. Titan Acquisitions Ltd., 814
Katyle v. Penn Nat'l Gaming, Inc., 1163
Katz v. Amos Treat & Co., 1002
KCD Financial Inc., In re, 425
Keating, Muething & Klekamp, In the Matter of, 1346

Keith v. Black Diamond Advisors, Inc., 323
Kendrick, United States v., 478
Kennecott Copper Corp. v. Curtiss-Wright Corp., 844, 851, 1178
Kennedy v. Josephthal & Co., Inc., 1151
Kerbs v. Fall River Industries, Inc., 1370
Kern County Land Co. v. Occidental Petroleum Corp., 1117, **1257**
Ketchum v. Green, 1104
Kevin D. Kunz, In the Matter of, 509
Keystone Mfg. Co. v. Adams, 1310
King v. Livent, Inc., 914
Kirk Tang Yuk, United States v., 1237
Kirsch Co. v. Bliss & Laughlin Indus., Inc., 837
Kirshner v. United States, 1174
Kitchens v. U.S. Shelter, 966
Klein v. Computer Devices, Inc., 981
Kline v. First W. Gov't Sec., Inc., 1085, 1150
K-N Energy, Inc. v. Gulf Interstate Co., 828
Koppel v. 4987 Corp., 1177
Koppers Co. v. American Express Co., 859, 861
Kordel, United States v., 1447, 1449, 1452
KPMG Peat Marwick, LLP, In re, 1338
KPMG, LLP v. S.E.C., 1337
Kramer v. Time Warner Inc., 813, 1181
Krome v. Merrill Lynch & Co., 716
Kronfeld v. Trans World Airlines, Inc., 1053, 1178
Kubik v. Goldfield, 571
Kushner v. Beverly Enters., Inc., 1121
Kwitek, United States v., 1463
L & B Hospital Ventures, Inc. v. Healthcare International, Inc., 325
Landreth Timber Co. v. Landreth, 326, 334, 1017
LaSalle National Bank, United States v., 1449, 1451
Lasker v. New York State Elec. & Gas Corp., 1102
Laven v. Flanagan, 964
Lawler v. Gilliam, 1003
Leasco Data Processing Equip. Corp. v. Maxwell, 1489
Lee Nat'l Corp. v. Segur, 1274
Lehl v. S.E.C., 710
Lehman Bros. Mortgage-Backed Sec. Litig., In re, 963
Lehman Bros. Sec. and ERISA Litig., In re, 963

Table of Cases

Leib v. Merrill Lynch, Pierce, Fenner & Smith, Inc., 737
Lentell v. Merrill Lynch & Co., 1163
Leonard, United States v., 323
Lerro v. Quaker Oats Co., 812, 813, 815
Levine v. NL Industries, Inc., 205, 206
Levy v. Marshall Capital Management, Inc., 1265
Lewis v. BT Investment Managers, Inc., 887
Lewis v. Fresne, 395
Lewis v. McGraw, 817, 1248
Lewis v. Mellon Bank, 1275
Lewis v. Varnes, 1275
Liberty Nat. Ins. Holding Co. v. Charter Co., 816, 836, 1255
Liberty Property Trust v. Republic Property Corporation, 321
Lilley v. Charren, 981
Lilley, United States v., 1456
List v. Fashion Park, Inc., 1196
Litton Indus., Inc. v. Lehman Bros. Kuhn Loeb Inc., 1151
Liu v. S.E.C., 1305, 1316
Lively v. Hirschfeld, 384, 396
Livingston v. Woodworth, 1310
Lone Star Ladies Inv. Club v. Schlotzsky's Inc., 1004
Longman v. Food Lion, Inc., 1101, 1179
Lorenzo v. S.E.C., 1122
Lormand v. United States Unwired, Inc., 1163
Los Angeles Trust Deed & Mortgage Exchange v. S.E.C., 293, 1318
Lovell v. City of Griffin, 1424, 1425
Lowe v. Nat'l Ass'n of Secs. Dealers, Inc., 725
Lowe v. S.E.C., 102, **1422**
LTV Corp. v. Grumman Corp., 843, 845, 851
LTV Securities Litigation, In re, 1124, 1127
Lucia v. S.E.C., 1295
Ludlow Corp. v. Tyco Laboratories, 842, 845, 851
Lyne v. Arthur Andersen & Co., 971
M. L. Lee & Co. v. American Cardboard & Packaging Corp., 97
Macfadden Holdings, Inc. v. JB Acquisition Corp., 885, 1178
Mader v. Armel, 1175
Madrid v. Gomez, 977
Magma Power Co. v. Dow Chem. Co., 1265
Mahaffy, United States v., 1240, 1472
Mahler, United States v., 1469
MAI Basic Four, Inc. v. Prime Computer, Inc., 859

Maldonado v. Dominguez, 1022, 1028
Maldonado v. Flynn, 201
Malone v. Microdyne Corp., 1088
Mandel, United States v., 1457
Manela v. Garantia Banking Ltd., 781
Manhattan General Equipment Co. v. Commissioner, 1119
Mankani, United States v., 1468
Mansbach v. Prescott, Ball & Turben, 784
Marine Bank v. Weaver, 279, 325, 328, 329, 332, 334, 1108
Mark v. FSC Securities Corp., 395, 427
Markewich v. Adikes, 1180
Marquette Cement Mfg. Co. v. Andreas, 1263, 1271
Marshall v. Vicksburg, 1306
Marshel v. AFW Fabric Corp., 1040
Mary S. Krech Trust v. Lakes Apartments, 395
Maryland Securities Co., In re, 714
Masel v. Villareal, 1121
Matek v. Murat, 324
Matrixx Initiatives, Inc. v. Siracusano, 909, **1068**, 1129
Matsushita Electric Industrial Co. v. Epstein, 812
Matthews, United States v., 1180
May & Co., Inc., In the Matter of Application of, 263
Mayer v. Chesapeake Insurance Co., 1276
Mayer v. Oil Field Systems Corp., 1175
McClure v. First Nat. Bank of Lubbock, Texas, 335
McDaniel v. Compania Minera Mar de Cortes, 555
McFarland v. Memorex Corp., 536
McMahon v. O'Keefe, 339
MDCM Holdings, Inc. v. Credit Suisse First Boston, 748
Mead Corp., United States v., 1108
Medhekar v. United States Dist. Ct., 915
Menasche, United States v., 1012
Menkes v. Stolt-Nielsen S.A., 201, 202
Mercer v. Jaffe, Snider, Raitt & Heuer, P.C., 1035
Merrill Lynch, Pierce, Fenner & Smith, Inc. v. Bobker, 806
Merrill Lynch, Pierce, Fenner & Smith, Inc. v. Livingston, 1275
Merrill Lynch, Pierce, Fenner & Smith, Inc. v. NASD, 62
Metro Serv. Inc. v. Wiggins, 914
meVC Draper Fisher Industries Juvetson Fund I, Inc. v. Millenium Partners, L.P., 828

TABLE OF CASES

Meyer v. Dans un Jardin, S.A., 295
Meyer v. Jinkosolar Holdings Co., Ltd., 1080
Mihara v. Dean Witter & Co., Inc., 777, 778, 779, 782
Miller v. Central Chinchilla Group, Inc., 287
Miller v. San Sebastian Gold Mines, Inc., 1172
Mills v. Electric Auto-Lite Co., 834, 1124
Milman v. Box Hill Sys. Corp., 982
Milnarik v. M-S Commodities, Inc., 294, 295
Minnesota v. Clover Leaf Creamery Co., 887
Minuse, United States v., 1466
Mishkin v. Peat, Marwick, Mitchell & Co., 14
Mississippi Valley Generating Co., United States v., 1437, 1438
Missouri Portland Cement Co. v. Cargill, Inc., 1178
Missud v. S.E.C., 59
Mitchell v. Robert DeMario Jewelry, Inc., 834
Mitchell v. Texas Gulf Sulphur Co., 1282
MITE Corp. v. Dixon, 884, 891
Molecular Technology Corp. v. Valentine, 1380
Monroe v. Hughes, 968, 1087
Moody's Corp. Sec. Litig., In re, 1142
Moore v. Kayport Package Express, Inc., 1003, 1004
Morales v. Reading & Bates Offshore Drilling Co., 1268
Mordaunt v. Incomco, 293
Morgan, United States v., 87
Morrison v. National Australia Bank, Ltd., 635, **1475**, 1499
Morton Salt Co., United States v., 1292
Mosher v. Kane, 1175, 1176
Mosser v. Darrow, 1200, 1438
Motz, United States v., 1472
Mowry v. Whitney, 1310
Mulheren, United States v., 1459, 1469
Murphy v. Cady, 1024
Musick, Peeler & Garrett v. Employers Ins. of Wausau, 1130
Mutual Shares Corp. v. Genesco, Inc., 1172
Myer v. Ward, 425
Myers v. Finkle, 1151
Naftalin, United States v., 999, 1010, 1013, 1029, 1034
NASD, In re, 714
NASDAQ Market-Makers Antitrust Litig., In re, 706
Nathenson v. Zonagen Inc., 1121

National Assn. of Manufacturers v. S.E.C., 61
National Assn. of Securities Dealers, In the Matter of, 87
National Assn. of Securities Dealers, Inc., United States v., 700
National Home Products, Inc. v. Gray, 1184
National Medical Enterprises, Inc. v. Small, 1275
National Tax Credit Partners, L.P. v. Havlik, 325
Natural Resources Defense Council v. S.E.C., 202, 205
Near v. Minnesota ex rel. Olson, 1425
Nelson v. Stahl, 323
Nesbit v. McNeil, 775
Netcoalition v. S.E.C., 718, 719
New Am. High Income Fund Sec. Litig., In re, 1180
New Jersey Carpenters Vacation Fund et al. v. Royal Bank of Scotland Group, PLC, et al., 963
New York v. United States, 366
New York, New Haven & Hartford Railroad Co., United States v., 479
Newcome v. Esrey, 93
Newharbor Partners v. F.D. Rich Co., 74, 97
Newman, United States v., 1220, 1223, 1235, 1240
Newmont Mining Corp. v. Pickens, 801
Newton v. Merrill, Lynch, Pierce, Fenner & Smith, Inc., 737, 772, 773
Nicholas Codispoti, In re, 714
Noa v. Key Futures, Inc., 285
Nolfi v. Ohio Kentucky Oil Corp., 425
Norex Petroleum Ltd. v. Blavatnik, 1496
Norlin Corporation v. Rooney, Pace Inc., 880
Norris & Hirshberg, Inc., In the Matter of, 781
Norris v. Wirtz, 1174
North Star Intern. v. Arizona Corporation Commission, 94
Northern Trust Co. v. Essaness Theatres Corp., 1196
Northland Capital Corp. v. Silver, 1176
Novak v. Kasaks, 1122
Number Nine Visual Tech. Corp. Sec. Litig., In re, 982
NVIDIA Securities Litigation, In re, 214
Nye v. Blyth Eastman Dillon & Co., 784
O'Connor & Assoc. v. Dean Witter Reynolds, Inc., 1252

Table of Cases

O'Connor v. R.F. Lafferty & Co., Inc., 770, 782, 1036
O'Hagan, United States v., 1110, 1189, **1207**, **1220**, 1225, **1236**, **1248**, 1480
O'Sullivan v. Trident Microsystems, Inc., 980
Ockerman v. May Zima & Co., 1141
Ohralik v. Ohio State Bar Assn., 1424
Old Dominion Copper Mining & Smelting Co. v. Lewisohn, 94
Omnicare, Inc. v. Laborers District Council Construction Industry Pension Fund, 982
One-O-One Enter., Inc. v. Caruso, 1046, 1047
Ontario Tchrs. Pension Plan Bd. v. Teva Pharmaceutical Indus. Ltd., 197
Ottmann v. Hanger Orthopedic Grp., Inc., 1121
Ozark Air Lines, Inc. v. Cox, 817, 822
Pacific Dunlop Holdings Inc. v. Allen & Co. Inc., 1007, 1009, 1011
Pacific Realty Trust v. APC Investments, Inc., 866
Packet Co. v. Sickles, 1310
Panter v. Marshall Field & Co., 844, 1254
Pappas v. Moss, 1040
Paramount Communications, Inc. v. Time Inc., 1049
Park & Tilford v. Schulte, 1265
Parkcentral Global Hub Ltd. v. Porsche Automobile Holdings SE, 1494
Parker Drilling Management Services, Ltd. v. Newton, 1314
Parklane Hosiery Co. v. Shore, 1297, 1317
Pasley v. Freeman, 1155
Pasquantino v. United States, 1485
Patsos v. First Albany Corp., 737
Patterson v. McLean Credit Union, 1133
Pavlidis v. New England Patriots Football Club, Inc., 1068
Peil v. Speiser, 1123, 1146
Pelletier v. Stuart-James Co., Inc., 1176
Peltz, United States v., 1454
Penhallow v. Doane's Administrators, 1310
Perl v. Smith Barney Inc., 736
Peter J. Kisch, In re, 716
Petersen v. Federated Dev. Co., 1174
Peterson v. Greenville, 1438
Peterson, United States v., 1457
Petrella v. Metro-GoldwynMayer, Inc., 1309

Petrobras Securities Litig., In re, 917, 1140, 1497, 1498
Pfeffer v. Cressaty, 1028
Pharo v. Smith, 1001
Philadelphia Nat. Bank, United States v., 700
Philadelphia v. New Jersey, 887
Philadelphia, City of v. Fleming Companies, 197, 1121
Phillips Petroleum Securities Litigation, In re, 837, 879
Pike v. Bruce Church, Inc., 898
Pin v. Texaco, Inc., 879
Pindus v. Fleming Co., Inc., 914
Pinter v. Dahl, **996**, 1003
Pinto-Thomaz, United States v., 1241
Piper v. Chris-Craft Industries, Inc., 840, 850, 874, 884, 896, 1040, 1041, 1253
Piper, Jaffray & Hopwood Inc. v. Ladin, 727
Plaine v. McCabe, 817, 874
Plumbers' Union Local No. 12 Pension Fund v. Swiss Reinsurance Company, 1501
Polaroid Corp. v. Disney, 804, 806, 807, 816, 1255
Polinsky v. MCA, Inc., 841
Polk v. Good, 879
Pontiac Policemen's and Firemen's Retirement System, City of v. UBS AG, 1493, 1495
Porter v. Warner Holding Co., 834, 1308
Portsmouth Square Inc. v. Shareholders Protective Committee, 802, 827
Powell, United States v., 1292
PR Diamonds, Inc. v. Chandler, 1121
Procter & Gamble Co. v. Bankers Trust Co., 354
Prudent Real Estate Trust v. Johncamp Realty, Inc., 865
Prudential Ins. Co. of America Sales Practices Litig., In re, 706
Prudential Sec. Inc., In the Matter of, 1417
Prudential Sec., Inc. v. Dalton, 1420
Pryor v. United States Steel Corp., 806, 816
Public Employees' Retirement System of Mississippi v. Merrill Lynch & Co. Inc., 963
Quail Cruises v. Agencia de Viagens, 1493
Quest Capital Strategies, Inc., In the Matter of, 1418
Rachal, United States v., 531
Radol v. Thomas, 801
Rathborne v. Rathborne, 543, 1176
Rattner v. Lehman, 1270, 1272
Ravens v. Iftikar, 914

Ray v. Atlantic Richfield Co., 883
Ray v. Karris, 1175
Raymond Motor Transportation, Inc. v. Rice, 887
Red Bank Oil Co., In the Matter of, 260
Reddy v. Commodity Futures Trading Comm'n, 1332
Redwine, United States v., 1463
Reese v. Malone, 1121
Regan, United States v., 1457, 1468
Reiter v. Cooper, 705
Rekant v. Desser, 1040
Reliance Electric Co. v. Emerson Electric Co., 1277
Reprosystem, B.V. v. SCM Corp., 1176
Resale of Restricted Securities, In the Matter of, 602
Retail Wholesale & Dep't Store Union Local 338 Ret. Fund v. Hewlett-Packard Co., 1080
Revak v. SEC Realty Corp., 294
Reves v. Ernst & Young, 298, 300, **332**, 1012, 1018
Revlon, Inc., In the Matter of, 874
Rex R. Rogers, In the Matter of, 1372
Rice v. Branigar Organization, Inc., 307
Richard R. Perkins, In the Matter of the Application of, 713
Richman v. Goldman Sachs Group, Inc., 201
Ridgely v. Keene, 1436
Riedel, United States v., 479
Riggs Nat'l Bank v. Allbritton, 866
Rissman v. Rissman, 1046
Rivanna Trawlers Unlimited v. Thompson Trawlers, Inc., 324
Rizek v. S.E.C., 781
Robert B. Orkin, In the Matter of the Application of, 712
Robinson v. Glynn, 323
Robinson v. TCI/US West Communications Inc., 1479
Rodriguez de Quijas v. Shearson/American Express, Inc., 765
Roeder v. Alpha Industries, Inc., 200, 201, 1180
Romag Fasteners, Inc. v. Fossil Group, Inc., 1309
Romano v. Merrill Lynch, Pierce, Fenner & Smith, 737
Rondeau v. Mosinee Paper Corp., 1248, 1298
Roosevelt v. E.I. Du Pont de Nemours & Co., 1177
Root v. Railway Co., 1308
Rosenberg v. XM Ventures, 826
Rosengarten v. ITT Corp., 200
Ross v. A. H. Robins Co., Inc., 1033, 1058, 1183, 1186
Ross v. Bank South, 1141
Royal Alliance Assoc., Inc., In the Matter of, 1418
Royal Am. Managers, Inc. v. IRC Holding Corp., 1003, 1004
Royal Bank of Scot. Group PLC Sec. Litig., In re, 1492, 1496
RP Acquisition Corp. v. Staley Continental, Inc., 892
Rubber Co. v. Goodyear, 1310
Rubin v. United States, 478, 999, 1175
Rubinson, United States v., 542
Ruckle v. Roto Am. Corp., 1172
Russell Motor Car Co. v. United States, 1018
Russello v. United States, 978
Russo, United States v., 1112
Ryder Int'l Corp. v. First Am. Nat'l Bank, 1003
S.E.C. v. Adler, 1217
S.E.C. v. Allison, 530
S.E.C. v. Alternative Energy Holdings, Inc., 398
S.E.C. v. American International Savings & Loan Association, 371
S.E.C. v. Amster & Co., 828
S.E.C. v. Arthur Young & Co., 968, 1292
S.E.C. v. Arvida Corp., 102
S.E.C. v. Associated Gas & Electric Co., 479
S.E.C. v. Bank of America Corporation, 1319
S.E.C. v. Bankosky, 1345
S.E.C. v. Banner Fund International, 294
S.E.C. v. Berlacher, 582
S.E.C. v. Bilzerian, 1318
S.E.C. v. Blatt, 835
S.E.C. v. Blavin, 834
S.E.C. v. Brigadoon Scotch Distrib. Co., 1292
S.E.C. v. Brown, 197, 1315
S.E.C. v. C.M. Joiner Leasing Corporation, 274, 309, 328, 329, 337
S.E.C. v. Capital Gains Research Bureau, Inc., 650, 825, 1041, **1432**, 1438
S.E.C. v. Carter Hawley Hale Stores, Inc., 810, **837**, 839, 851, 853
S.E.C. v. Caterinicchia, 1298
S.E.C. v. Cavanagh, 514, 530, 546
S.E.C. v. Certain Unknown Purchasers, 1504
S.E.C. v. Children's Hospital, 371
S.E.C. v. Chinese Consol. Benev. Ass'n, 527, 534
S.E.C. v. Clark, 1314
S.E.C. v. Cochran, 1059

Table of Cases

S.E.C. v. Coffey, 1431
S.E.C. v. Commonwealth Chemical Securities, Inc., 1303, 1469
S.E.C. v. Continental Commodities Corp., 293, 295
S.E.C. v. Continental Tobacco Co., 384, 389
S.E.C. v. Contorinis, 1314
S.E.C. v. Credit First Fund, LP, 427
S.E.C. v. Csapo, 1294
S.E.C. v. Culpepper, 534
S.E.C. v. Current Fin. Servs., 395
S.E.C. v. Datronics Engineers, Inc., 531, **537**
S.E.C. v. Dorozhko, 1243
S.E.C. v. Dresser Industries, Inc., 95, **1444**
S.E.C. v. Drucker, 1452
S.E.C. v. Drysdale Sec. Corp., 1112
S.E.C. v. Edwards, 296
S.E.C. v. Electronics Warehouse, Inc., 200
S.E.C. v. Empire Dev. Grp., LLC, 398
S.E.C. v. E-Smart Tech., 202
S.E.C. v. ETS Payphones, Inc., 297, 300
S.E.C. v. Eurobond Exch., Ltd., 1504
S.E.C. v. Fehn, 1375
S.E.C. v. First City Financial Corp., Ltd., **831**
S.E.C. v. First Jersey Secs., Inc., 1431
S.E.C. v. First Pac. Bancorp, 1341
S.E.C. v. Florafax Int'l, Inc., Litig. Rel. 10, 1318
S.E.C. v. Franklin Atlas Corp., 566
S.E.C. v. Geon Industries, Inc., 1067, 1068
S.E.C. v. Georgia-Pacific Corp., 878
S.E.C. v. Goldfield Deep Mines Co. of Nevada, 197
S.E.C. v. Goldman Sachs, 85, 1496, 1500
S.E.C. v. Guild Films Co., 531
S.E.C. v. Harwyn Industries Corp., 539, 542
S.E.C. v. Haswell, 1372
S.E.C. v. Higashi, 1294
S.E.C. v. Holschuh, 375, 995
S.E.C. v. Hughes Capital Corp., 1315
S.E.C. v. Hui Feng, 734
S.E.C. v. International Loan Network, Inc., 287
S.E.C. v. International Swiss Invs. Corp., 95
S.E.C. v. J.T. Wallenbrock & Assocs., 345, 1308
S.E.C. v. J.W. Barclay & Co., Inc., 1431
S.E.C. v. Jerry T. O'Brien, Inc., 1292
S.E.C. v. Joiner Corp., 277
S.E.C. v. Jones, 1301
S.E.C. v. Jos. Schlitz Brewing Co., 202
S.E.C. v. Kalvex Inc., 202
S.E.C. v. Kenton Capital, Ltd., 394, 398
S.E.C. v. Kimmes, 1469
S.E.C. v. Kokesh, 1316
S.E.C. v. Koscot Interplanetary, Inc., 289
S.E.C. v. Lauer, 294
S.E.C. v. Lehman Bros., 1120
S.E.C. v. Levine, 1303
S.E.C. v. Life Partners Holdings, Inc., 288
S.E.C. v. Life Partners, Inc., 280, 397
S.E.C. v. Longfin Corp., 1173
S.E.C. v. Lybrand, 546
S.E.C. v. Lyon, 582, 743
S.E.C. v. Management Dynamics, Inc., 1301
S.E.C. v. Mangan, 582
S.E.C. v. Manor Nursing Centers, Inc., 70, 835, 1298, 1304, 1318
S.E.C. v. Materia, 835, 1251, 1318
S.E.C. v. Mayhew, 1253
S.E.C. v. McDonald Investment Co., 451
S.E.C. v. Medic-Home Enter., Inc., 1318
S.E.C. v. Meek, 1293
S.E.C. v. Merchant Capital, LLC, 197, 325
S.E.C. v. Morgan Stanley & Co., 85
S.E.C. v. Murphy, 325, 374
S.E.C. v. Mut. Benefits Corp., 288
S.E.C. v. National Securities, Inc., 1034, 1174
S.E.C. v. National Student Marketing Corp., 1370, 1371
S.E.C. v. North Am. Research & Dev. Corp., 536, 571
S.E.C. v. Obus, 1225
S.E.C. v. Pace, 197, 199
S.E.C. v. Patel, 1341
S.E.C. v. Payne, 287
S.E.C. v. Posner, 1341
S.E.C. v. Professional Assocs., 325
S.E.C. v. Ralston Purina Co., 380, 555, 852, 1010, 1020
S.E.C. v. Resch-Cassin & Co., Inc., 755, 756, 1469
S.E.C. v. Ridenour, 725, 733
S.E.C. v. Savoy Indus., Inc., 1178
S.E.C. v. Scoville, 1502
S.E.C. v. SG Ltd., 296
S.E.C. v. Sierra Brokerage Servs, 545
S.E.C. v. Sloan, 1003, 1195, 1326
S.E.C. v. Spectrum, Ltd., 1372
S.E.C. v. Starmont, 102
S.E.C. v. Sunbeam Gold Mines Co., 381

S.E.C. v. Switzer, 1206
S.E.C. v. Techni-Culture, Inc., 1318
S.E.C. v. Telecom Marketing, Inc., 325
S.E.C. v. Texas Gulf Sulphur Co., 834, 836, 1028, 1067, 1187, 1193, 1306
S.E.C. v. Tome, 834, 835
S.E.C. v. Torr, 1301
S.E.C. v. Tourre, 1501
S.E.C. v. Traffic Monsoon, LLC, 1502
S.E.C. v. Tuchinsky, 468, 1004
S.E.C. v. Unifund SAL, 95, **1298**
S.E.C. v. Unique Fin. Concepts, Inc., 293
S.E.C. v. United Benefit Life Insurance Co., 371
S.E.C. v. Variable Annuity Life Ins. Co., 371
S.E.C. v. W. J. Howey Co., **275**, 290, 291, 298, 308, 313, 316, 319, 327, 329, 334, 335
S.E.C. v. Warde, 1226, 1253
S.E.C. v. Wencke, 1318
S.E.C. v. Wheeling-Pittsburgh Steel Corp., 1293
S.E.C. v. Whitman, 1294
S.E.C. v. Whittemore, 1314
S.E.C. v. Willis, 1216
S.E.C. v. World-Wide Coin Investments, Ltd., **1389**
S.E.C. v. Yun, 1207
S.E.C. v. Zandford, 784, 1059, **1107**
Salameh, United States v., 1228
Salcer v. Merrill Lynch, Pierce, Fenner and Smith, 319
Salesforce.com Securities Litigation, In re, 215
Salman v. United States, 1224, 1240
Salomon Analyst Metromedia Litigation, In re, 1159
Samuel B. Franklin & Co. v. S.E.C., 712
San Leandro Emergency Med. Group Profit Sharing Plan v. Philip Morris Co., Inc., 1059, 1101
Sanders v. Gardner, 265
Sanders v. John Nuveen & Co., 1024, 1025
Sanders v. Thrall Car Mfg. Co., 816, 837
SanDisk Corp., 491
Sanofi-Aventis Securities Litigation, In re, 1059
Santa Fe Industries, Inc. v. Green, 740, 785, **1037**, 1194
Sargent v. Genesco, Inc., 1174, 1175
SCA Hygiene Products Aktiebolag v. First Quality Baby Products, LLC, 1309
Schaffer v. CC Inv., LDC, 1265
Schaffer v. Timberland Co., 1142

Schiff, United States v., 1059
Schleicher v. Wendt, 1132, 1159
Schlick v. Penn-Dixie Cement Corp., 1040
Schneider v. Traweek, 969
Schoenbaum v. Firstbrook, 1040, 1172, 1474, 1476, 1477
Schreiber v. Burlington Northern, Inc., 874, 879, 1248
Schueneman v. Arena Pharmaceuticals, Inc., 1080
Schwartz v. Celestial Seasonings, Inc., 982
Scop, United States v., 1466
Screws v. United States, 1454
Seaboard World Airlines, Inc. v. Tiger Int'l, Inc., 802, 1178
Seaman Furniture Co., Inc., 482, 483
Searls v. Glasser, 1121
Sec. Act Rel. No. 97, 508
Sec. Act Rel. No. 131, 572
Sec. Act Rel. No. 285, 377
Sec. Act Rel. No. 305, 512
Sec. Act Rel. No. 312, **493**, 495
Sec. Act Rel. No. 646, **484**
Sec. Act Rel. No. 929, 477
Sec. Act Rel. No. 1459, 488
Sec. Act Rel. No. 1862, 525
Sec. Act Rel. No. 2029, **486**, 509
Sec. Act Rel. No. 3210, 475
Sec. Act Rel. No. 3224, 119
Sec. Act Rel. No. 3421, 572
Sec. Act Rel. No. 3844, 96
Sec. Act Rel. No. 4150, 264, 750
Sec. Act Rel. No. 4329, 259
Sec. Act Rel. No. 4412, 371
Sec. Act Rel. No. 4434, **446**, 453, 459, 460, 509
Sec. Act Rel. No. 4552, 509, 510
Sec. Act Rel. No. 4553, 59
Sec. Act Rel. No. 4968, **129**
Sec. Act Rel. No. 4982, 542
Sec. Act Rel. No. 5101, 129
Sec. Act Rel. No. 5103, 368
Sec. Act Rel. No. 5180, **103**, 104, 105, **356**
Sec. Act Rel. No. 5223, 584, 593
Sec. Act Rel. No. 5306, 584, 586
Sec. Act Rel. No. 5347, **312**
Sec. Act Rel. No. 5362, 1350
Sec. Act Rel. No. 5450, **457**, 468
Sec. Act Rel. No. 5550, 1383
Sec. Act Rel. No. 5699, 1048
Sec. Act Rel. No. 5758, 198
Sec. Act Rel. No. 5932, 594
Sec. Act Rel. No. 6084, 207, 220, 221, 1048
Sec. Act Rel. No. 6099, 584, 586, 587, 589
Sec. Act Rel. No. 6188, 312
Sec. Act Rel. No. 6231, 155
Sec. Act Rel. No. 6246, 370

xxxvi TABLE OF CASES

Sec. Act Rel. No. 6335, 167
Sec. Act Rel. No. 6363, 370
Sec. Act Rel. No. 6383, 157, 225, 969
Sec. Act Rel. No. 6389, 405
Sec. Act Rel. No. 6455, 416
Sec. Act Rel. No. 6499, 163
Sec. Act Rel. No. 6645, 372
Sec. Act Rel. No. 6661, 370
Sec. Act Rel. No. 6683, 426
Sec. Act Rel. No. 6711, 208, 1082
Sec. Act Rel. No. 6789, 745
Sec. Act Rel. No. 6835, 210
Sec. Act Rel. No. 6863, 612
Sec. Act Rel. No. 6864, 605
Sec. Act Rel. No. 6891, 271
Sec. Act Rel. No. 6897, 904
Sec. Act Rel. No. 6949, 442
Sec. Act Rel. No. 7168, 136
Sec. Act Rel. No. 7190, 629
Sec. Act Rel. No. 7233, 426
Sec. Act Rel. No. 7285, 427, 473, 474
Sec. Act Rel. No. 7314, 427
Sec. Act Rel. No. 7375, 745
Sec. Act Rel. No. 7390, 584
Sec. Act Rel. No. 7392, 629
Sec. Act Rel. No. 7497, 217
Sec. Act Rel. No. 7505, 631
Sec. Act Rel. No. 7593, 1369
Sec. Act Rel. No. 7644, 434, 435
Sec. Act Rel. No. 7759, 904
Sec. Act Rel. No. 7760, 867, 904
Sec. Act Rel. No. 7881, 92
Sec. Act Rel. No. 7943, 261, 512
Sec. Act Rel. No. 8098, 644
Sec. Act Rel. No. 8182, 223
Sec. Act Rel. No. 8350, 213
Sec. Act Rel. No. 8591, 105, 117, 122, 137, 170, 1023
Sec. Act Rel. No. 8812, 159
Sec. Act Rel. No. 8828, 427, 431
Sec. Act Rel. No. 8869, 584, 594
Sec. Act Rel. No. 8876, 159
Sec. Act Rel. No. 8891, 433
Sec. Act Rel. No. 9177, 431
Sec. Act Rel. No. 9415, 427, 433, 502
Sec. Act Rel. No. 9693, 643, 644
Sec. Act Rel. No. 9741, 443
Sec. Act Rel. No. 9877, 204
Sec. Act Rel. No. 10238, 445, 446
Sec. Act Rel. No. 10580, 110
Sec. Act Rel. No. 10699, 108
Sec. Act Rel. No. 10750, 213
Sec. Act Rel. No. 10763, 431, 432, 459, 461, 471, 474, 503, 506, 507, 508, 510, 514
Sec. Act Rel. No. 10786, 870
Sec. Exch. Act Rel. No. 2446, 748
Sec. Exch. Act Rel. No. 5276, 206
Sec. Exch. Act Rel. No. 7279, 759
Sec. Exch. Act Rel. No. 8995, 1048
Sec. Exch. Act Rel. No. 9310, 544
Sec. Exch. Act Rel. No. 13346, 1402

Sec. Exch. Act Rel. No. 13679, 725
Sec. Exch. Act Rel. No. 13787, 800
Sec. Exch. Act Rel. No. 14415, 680
Sec. Exch. Act Rel. No. 16045, 1363
Sec. Exch. Act Rel. No. 16112, 840
Sec. Exch. Act Rel. No. 16385, 844, 854, 857
Sec. Exch. Act Rel. No. 16410, 679
Sec. Exch. Act Rel. No. 16679, 708
Sec. Exch. Act Rel. No. 16888, 682
Sec. Exch. Act Rel. No. 17120, 1252
Sec. Exch. Act Rel. No. 17371, 87
Sec. Exch. Act Rel. No. 17831, 1372
Sec. Exch. Act Rel. No. 18482, 679
Sec. Exch. Act Rel. No. 19858, 662
Sec. Exch. Act Rel. No. 21439, 688
Sec. Exch. Act Rel. No. 21470, 787
Sec. Exch. Act Rel. No. 21962, 424
Sec. Exch. Act Rel. No. 22171, 798, 804, 805, 875, 876, 878, 880
Sec. Exch. Act Rel. No. 23170, 708
Sec. Exch. Act Rel. No. 23611, 749
Sec. Exch. Act Rel. No. 24633, 679
Sec. Exch. Act Rel. No. 24976, 857
Sec. Exch. Act Rel. No. 25893, 1367
Sec. Exch. Act Rel. No. 26100, 16
Sec. Exch. Act Rel. No. 26250, 761
Sec. Exch. Act Rel. No. 26708, 684
Sec. Exch. Act Rel. No. 26985, 16, 367
Sec. Exch. Act Rel. No. 27249, 760
Sec. Exch. Act Rel. No. 27445, 720
Sec. Exch. Act Rel. No. 27611, 685
Sec. Exch. Act Rel. No. 28869, 1265, 1266
Sec. Exch. Act Rel. No. 28899, 690
Sec. Exch. Act Rel. No. 29185, 720
Sec. Exch. Act Rel. No. 34961, 367
Sec. Exch. Act Rel. No. 35121, 876
Sec. Exch. Act Rel. No. 35124, 694
Sec. Exch. Act Rel. No. 35751, 774
Sec. Exch. Act Rel. No. 36724, 732, 1417
Sec. Exch. Act Rel. No. 36973, 771
Sec. Exch. Act Rel. No. 37260, 1279
Sec. Exch. Act Rel. No. 37542, 659
Sec. Exch. Act Rel. No. 37619A, 640
Sec. Exch. Act Rel. No. 38067, 749
Sec. Exch. Act Rel. No. 38672, 30, 691
Sec. Exch. Act Rel. No. 39670, 545
Sec. Exch. Act Rel. No. 39892, 1420
Sec. Exch. Act Rel. No. 40760, 696
Sec. Exch. Act Rel. No. 42208, 717, 718
Sec. Exch. Act Rel. No. 42450, 657, 682
Sec. Exch. Act Rel. No. 42758, 680
Sec. Exch. Act Rel. No. 42994, 1384
Sec. Exch. Act Rel. No. 43069, 908
Sec. Exch. Act Rel. No. 43154, 1244, 1247
Sec. Exch. Act Rel. No. 43602, 1384

Sec. Exch. Act Rel. No. 43862, 1385
Sec. Exch. Act Rel. No. 44568, 664
Sec. Exch. Act Rel. No. 45471, 644
Sec. Exch. Act Rel. No. 45742, 644
Sec. Exch. Act Rel. No. 45908, 89, 90
Sec. Exch. Act Rel. No. 46079, 221, 262
Sec. Exch. Act Rel. No. 46084, 644
Sec. Exch. Act Rel. No. 47226, 223
Sec. Exch. Act Rel. No. 49884, 224
Sec. Exch. Act Rel. No. 50103, 742, 744
Sec. Exch. Act Rel. No. 50699, 723
Sec. Exch. Act Rel. No. 50896, 85
Sec. Exch. Act Rel. No. 51217, 723
Sec. Exch. Act Rel. No. 51808, 24, 662, **672**
Sec. Exch. Act Rel. No. 53128, 28
Sec. Exch. Act Rel. No. 54684, 815
Sec. Exch. Act Rel. No. 56145, 641
Sec. Exch. Act Rel. No. 56152, 224
Sec. Exch. Act Rel. No. 56887, 472, 473
Sec. Exch. Act Rel. No. 58421, 753
Sec. Exch. Act Rel. No. 58592, 743
Sec. Exch. Act Rel. No. 58597, 805, 905
Sec. Exch. Act Rel. No. 58773, 744
Sec. Exch. Act Rel. No. 58774, 744
Sec. Exch. Act Rel. No. 58775, 744
Sec. Exch. Act Rel. No. 58785, 744
Sec. Exch. Act Rel. No. 58845, 662
Sec. Exch. Act Rel. No. 60448, 1292
Sec. Exch. Act Rel. No. 60997, 669
Sec. Exch. Act Rel. No. 61595, 744
Sec. Exch. Act Rel. No. 63010, 83, 85, 265, 754
Sec. Exch. Act Rel. No. 65708, 546
Sec. Exch. Act Rel. No. 65709, 546
Sec. Exch. Act Rel. No. 65710, 546
Sec. Exch. Act Rel. No. 69077, 720, 721
Sec. Exch. Act Rel. No. 73639, 720
Sec. Exch. Act Rel. No. 76639, 720, 721
Sec. Exch. Act Rel. No. 80295, 136
Sec. Exch. Act Rel. No. 86031, 728
Sec. Exch. Act Rel. No. 88216, 719
Sec. Exch. Act Rel. No. 641040, 1404
Securities Industry Ass'n v. Board of Governors of Federal Reserve System, 335
Seibert v. Sperry Rand Corp., 1179
Seinfeld v. Hospital Corp. of America, 1265
Selas Corp. of Am. v. Voogd, 1275
Semerenko v. Cendant Corp., **1103**, **1143**
Seymour v. McCormick, 1310
SG Cowen Sec. Corp. v. U.S. Dist. Ct. for N.D. of Cal., 915

S-G Securities, Inc. v. Fuqua Investment Co., 839
Shad v. Dean Witter Reynolds, Inc., 777
Shapiro v. Merrill Lynch, Pierce, Fenner & Smith, Inc., 1173, 1281
Shapiro v. UJB Fin. Corp., 981
Shaw v. Digital Equip. Corp., 1004
Shawnee Chiles Syndicate, 161
Shearson Lehman Bros., Inc., In re, 1417
Shearson Lehman Hutton, Inc. v. Wagoner, 736
Shearson/American Express, Inc. v. McMahon, 765
Sheldon v. S.E.C., 1346
Shell v. Hensley, 1040
Sherwood, United States v., 579
Shivangi v. Dean Witter Reynolds, Inc., 737
Shores v. Sklar, 1141
Siemers v. Wells Fargo & Co., 199
Silver v. McCamey, 1448
Silver v. New York Stock Exchange, 698, 700
Silverman v. Landa, 1263
Simon, United States v., 968
Simplystocks.com, 477
Simpson v. Southeastern Inv. Trust, 1178
Sisak v. Wings and Wheels Express, Inc., 817, 822
Skilling v. United States, 1442
Slagell v. Bontrager, 571
Sloane Overseas Fund, Ltd. v. Sapiens Int'l Corp., N.V., 1022
Smallwood v. Pearl Brewing Co., 841
Smith v. American Nat'l Bank & Trust Co., 1004
Smith v. Gross, 287
Smith, United States v., 1217, 1431
Smolowe v. Delendo Corp., 1270
Societe Generale Sec. Litig., In re, 1495
Software Toolworks Inc., In re, 967
Sorrell v. IMS Health, 102
Southern Development Co. v. Silva, 1155
Southern Pacific Co. v. Arizona, 888
Sparta Surgical Corp. v. National Ass'n of Sec. Dealers, 724
Speed v. Transamerica Corp., 1196
Spicer v. Chicago Bd. of Options Exch., Inc., 1036
Spies v. United States, 1454
Stack v. Lobo, 215
Stackhouse v. Toyota, 1495
Stadia Oil & Uranium Co. v. Wheelis, 572
Standard Sanitary Manufacturing Co. v. United States, 1447
Starr, United States v., 1468

State Teachers Retirement Bd. v. Fluor Corp., 1060
Staten Securities Corp., In re, 714
Stauffer v. Standard Brands, Inc., 1042
Steadman v. S.E.C., 1296
Stein, United States v., 1467
Steinhardt Group Inc. v. Citicorp, 316
Stella v. Graham-Paige Motors Corp., 1268
Steven Altman, Esq., In the Matter of, 1372
Stevens v. Liberty Packing Corp., 299
Stitch Fix, Inc. Securities Litigation, In re, 913
Stoneridge Investment Partners, LLC v. Scientific-Atlanta, Inc., 1073, 1130, 1159, 1371, 1488
Stoyas v. Toshiba Corporation, 1494, 1495
Stransky v. Cummins Engine Co., Inc., 1055, 1059
Stratte-Mcclure v. Morgan Stanley, 214
Stringer, United States v., 95
Stromfeld v. Great Atlantic & Pac. Tea Co., Inc., 851
Sundstrand Corp. v. Sun Chemical Corp., 1120
Super Stores, Inc. v. Reiner, 1267
Superintendent of Ins. of N.Y. v. Bankers Life & Casualty Co., 1040, 1042, 1109, 1173, 1483
Susquehanna Corp. v. Pan American Sulphur Co., 802
Swanson v. American Consumer Indus. Inc., 1175
Szur, United States v., 738
Tafflin v. Levitt, 347
Takeda v. Turbodyne Tech., Inc., 913
Taylor, United States v., 1455
Tcherepnin v. Knight, 304, 306, 330, 334, 1115
Teachers' Retirement System of Louisiana v. Hunter, 1163
Teamsters Local 282 Pension Trust Fund v. Angelos, 1149
Teicher v. S.E.C., 1345
Telxon Corp., Sec. Litig., In re, 914
Tenneco Securities Litigation, In re, 199
Texaco, Inc. v. Borda, 1448
Texas Int'l Airlines v. National Airlines, Inc., 1267
Thill Securities Corp., In re, 713
Third Point LLC. v. Ruprecht, 796
Thompson Ross Securities Co., In the Matter of, 501
Thrifty Shoppers Scrip Co. v. United States, 1166
Tilghman v. Proctor, 1308

Time Warner Inc. Securities Litigation, In re, 1048, 1060
Tomaszewski v. Trevena, Inc., 913
Topping v. Deloitte Touche Tohmatsu CPA, 914
Torres, United States v., 1228
Touche Ross & Co. v. Redington, 759, 1002, 1177, 1195
Touche Ross & Co. v. S.E.C., 1346
Transamerica Mortgage Advisors, Inc. v. Lewis, 1421
Treadway Companies, Inc. v. Care Corp., 816
Tricontinental Industries, Ltd. v. PricewaterhouseCoopers, 1163
Trustees of Dartmouth College v. Woodward, 888
TSC Industries, Inc. v. Northway, Inc., 864, 910, 987, 1052, 1136, 1178
Tull v. United States, 1309
U.S. S.E.C. v. Citigroup Global Markets Inc., 1324, 1325
UBS Sec. Litig., In re, 1495
Underhill v. Royal, 336
Unisys Sav. Plan Litig., In re, 36
United Housing Foundation, Inc. v. Forman, 281, 299, **301**, 308, 320, 327, 328, 330, 334
United Paperworkers Int'l Union v. International Paper Co., 1177, 1179
United States Steel Corp., In re, 206
Unity Gold Corp., In the Matter of, 488, 509
Universal Heritage Investments Corporation, In the Matter of, 1414
University Hill Foundation v. Goldman, Sachs & Co., 14
Unocal Corp. v. Mesa Petroleum Co., 807, 873
Unocal Corp. v. Pickens, 1335
URS Corp., 483
Uselton v. Commercial Lovelace Motor Freight, Inc., 312
Valence Tech. Sec. Litig., In re, 1023
Valicenti Advisory Services, Inc. v. S.E.C., 1330
Van Dyke v. Coburn Enters., Inc., 397
Vanderkam & Sanders, 477
Varghese v. China Chenghuo Pharmaceutical Holdings, Inc., 913
VeriFone Securities Litigation, In re, 215
Versyss Inc. v. Coopers and Lybrand, 979
Vilar, United States v., 1502
Villeneuve v. Advanced Business Concepts Corp., 293, 294
Vine v. Beneficial Finance Co., Inc., 1175

Virginia Bankshares, Inc. v. Sandberg, 986, 1085, **1097**, 1185
Virginia State Bd. of Pharmacy v. Virginia Citizens Consumer Council, Inc., 102
Vivendi Universal, S.A., In re, 1496
Vivendi, In re, 917, 1140
Voss & Co., Inc., In re, 714
W.R. Grace & Co., Securities Exchange Act Rel. No. 39, In the Matter of, 200
Wachovia Bank & Trust Co. v. National Student Marketing Corp., 1186
Wachovia Corp., 492
Waggoner v. Barclays PLC, 917, 1140, 1142
Walker v. Action Industries, Inc., 206, 1177
Walk-In Medical Centers, Inc. v. Breuer Capital Corp., 73
Wals v. Fox Hills Development Corporation, 294
Wamser v. J.E. Liss, Inc., 1005
Warner Communications Securities Litigation, In re, 1051
Warren v. Bokum Resources Corp., 807
Washburn v. Madison Square Garden Corp., 1253
Washington Public Power Supply System Securities Litigation, In re, 16
Weinberger v. Jackson, 964, 966
Weiner, United States v., 1456
Weissman v. NASD, Inc., 724
Wellman v. Dickinson, 827, 839
Wells Fargo Mortgage-Backed Certificates Litig., In re, 963
Wenderhold v. Cylink Corp., 914
Werner v. Werner, 1180
Wernes, United States v., 479
West v. Multibanco Comermex, S.A., 347
West Virginia v. Morgan Stanley & Co., 772
Western Air Lines, Inc. v. Sobieski, 479
Western Auto Supply Co. v. Gamble-Skogmo, Inc., 1257
Western Fed. Corp. v. Erickson, 397
Wharf (Holdings) Ltd. v. United Int'l Holdings, Inc., 1110
White, People v., 299
Whiting v. Dow Chem. Co., 1257
WHX Corporation v. Securities and Exchange Commission, 1334
Wielgos v. Commonwealth Edison Co., 207, 228
Wiley, United States v., 1468
Williams Secs. Litig.—WCG Subclass, In re, 1164
Wilson v. Comtech Telecommunications Corp., 1174
Wilson v. Great Am. Indus., Inc., 1181, 1184
Wilson v. Saintine Exploration & Drilling Corp., 1004
Winkler v. S.E.C., 1333
Winkler v. Wigley, 1060
WLR Foods, Inc. v. Tyson Foods, Inc., 891
Wolf Corp. v. S.E.C., 261
Wolf v. Banamex, 347, 348
Wolfson, United States v., 573, 1457
Wonsover v. S.E.C., 573
Wooden-Ware Co. v. United States, 1310
Woodward v. Metro Bank of Dallas, 1360
WorldCom, Inc. Securities Litigation, In re, 169, **943**, 950, 965, 967
Worlds of Wonder Securities Litigation, In re, 1083
Wright v. National Warranty Co., L.P., 396, 1005
Wunsch Auction Systems, Inc., 690
Yeaman, United States v., 197
Yoder v. Orthomolecular Nutrition Institute, Inc., 1173
Yoshikawa v. S.E.C., 1458
Zacharias v. S.E.C., 582
Zell v. InterCapital Income Securities, Inc., 35, 197
Ziemba v. Cascade Int'l, Inc., 1121
Zink v. Merrill Lynch Pierce Fenner & Smith, 93
Z-Seven Fund, Inc. v. Motorcar Parts & Accessories, 914
Zuckerman v. Franz, 842

Sec. Act § 17(a)(3) 750, 1028, 1029
Sec. Act § 17A 1121, 1500
Sec. Act § 18 ... 66, 401, 403, 404, 435, 436, 440, 470, 492, 609
Sec. Act § 18(a) 66
Sec. Act § 18(b) 403, 435
Sec. Act § 18(b)(3) 441
Sec. Act § 18(b)(4)(C) 503
Sec. Act § 18(b)(4)(D) 404
Sec. Act § 18(b)(4)(F) 403, 435
Sec. Act § 18(b)(4)(G) 609
Sec. Act § 19 .... 93, 875
Sec. Act § 19(b) 94, 1448
Sec. Act § 19(c) 876
Sec. Act § 19(d) 435
Sec. Act § 20 .... 93, 94, 415, 1117, 1289, 1327
Sec. Act § 20(a) 94, 1448
Sec. Act § 20(b) 380, 451, 537, 1298, 1378, 1448, 1450
Sec. Act § 20(e) 1340, 1344
Sec. Act § 22 .... 93, 95, 1498
Sec. Act § 22(a) 95
Sec. Act § 24 .... 93, 95, 1441, 1452
Sec. Act § 27 95
Sec. Act § 27(a)(3) 913
Sec. Act § 27(c)(1)(A) 1092
Sec. Act § 27A 126, 207, 1031, 1091
Sec. Act § 27A(b)(2)(D) 126
Sec. Act § 27A(c) 1092
Sec. Act § 27A(c)(1)(B) 1092
Sec. Act § 27A(c)(4) 1092
Sec. Act § 27A(f) 1092
Sec. Act § 27A(g)–(h) 1092
Sec. Act § 27A(i) 1092
Sec. Act § 27A(i)(E)–(F) 1092
Sec. Act § 28 .... 457, 460, 468, 630, 651
Sec. Act § 112(a)(1) 995
Sec. Act § 117(a) 981
Sec. Exch. Act § 2 4
Sec. Exch. Act § 3(a)(1) 653, 683, 685, 686, 688
Sec. Exch. Act § 3(a)(3) 340, 342, 343, 344, 345
Sec. Exch. Act § 3(a)(4) 725, 727, 733, 735
Sec. Exch. Act § 3(a)(5) 67, 725, 727, 733, 735
Sec. Exch. Act § 3(a)(9) 746, 907, 1035
Sec. Exch. Act § 3(a)(10) 273, 308, 333, 339, 342, 345, 359, 363, 746
Sec. Exch. Act § 3(a)(11) 472, 746
Sec. Exch. Act § 3(a)(14) 308, 478, 542
Sec. Exch. Act § 3(a)(22) 718
Sec. Exch. Act § 3(a)(22)(A) 717
Sec. Exch. Act § 3(a)(38) 592, 687
Sec. Exch. Act § 3(a)(51) 271, 727
Sec. Exch. Act § 3(a)(55) 355
Sec. Exch. Act § 3(a)(55)(B) 355

Sec. Exch. Act § 3(a)(55)(C) 355
Sec. Exch. Act § 3(a)(68) 355
Sec. Exch. Act § 3(f) 60
Sec. Exch. Act § 3(h) 502
Sec. Exch. Act § 3A 273, 354
Sec. Exch. Act § 5 .... 361, 639, 640, 653, 691
Sec. Exch. Act § 6 ...... 27, 28, 361, 603, 639, 640, 653, 722, 1035
Sec. Exch. Act § 6(a)(4) 699
Sec. Exch. Act § 6(b) 57, 689
Sec. Exch. Act § 6(b)(3) 689
Sec. Exch. Act § 6(b)(4) 689
Sec. Exch. Act § 6(e) 657, 697
Sec. Exch. Act § 7 .... 54, 640, 759, 762, 764
Sec. Exch. Act § 7(f) 763
Sec. Exch. Act § 8 .... 54, 640
Sec. Exch. Act § 8(a) 764
Sec. Exch. Act § 9 .... 640, 727, 755, 1032, 1033, 1040, 1116, 1117, 1169
Sec. Exch. Act § 9(a)(1) 1033, 1116
Sec. Exch. Act § 9(a)(2) 755, 756, 877, 1033, 1116
Sec. Exch. Act § 9(a)(4) 1117
Sec. Exch. Act § 9(a)(6) 268, 748, 1033
Sec. Exch. Act § 9(c) 1032
Sec. Exch. Act § 9(e) 1033, 1117
Sec. Exch. Act § 10 .... 727, 1028, 1031, 1032, 1116, 1183, 1187
Sec. Exch. Act § 10(a) 640, 742, 1116
Sec. Exch. Act § 10(b) 466, 537, 540, 635, 745, 748, 755, 756, 757, 920, 1019, 1022, 1032, 1034, 1037, 1039, 1040, 1041, 1042, 1043, 1061, 1062, 1063, 1068, 1069, 1073, 1076, 1078, 1080, 1092, 1093, 1103, 1104, 1105, 1106, 1107, 1108, 1109, 1110, 1111, 1112, 1113, 1114, 1115, 1116, 1117, 1118, 1119, 1120, 1124, 1126, 1128, 1129, 1130, 1131, 1145, 1146, 1158, 1159, 1167, 1168, 1169, 1173, 1183, 1189, 1191, 1192, 1193, 1194, 1195, 1197, 1198, 1199, 1207, 1208, 1209, 1210, 1211, 1212, 1213, 1214, 1215, 1225, 1233, 1236, 1244, 1248, 1249, 1250, 1298, 1299, 1300, 1347, 1358, 1359, 1362, 1367, 1375, 1376, 1378, 1379, 1380, 1382, 1456, 1473, 1474, 1475, 1476, 1477, 1478, 1479, 1480, 1481, 1482, 1483, 1484, 1486, 1487, 1488, 1489, 1490, 1491, 1492, 1493, 1494, 1495, 1497, 1499, 1501, 1502, 1503
Sec. Exch. Act § 10A 1289, 1386
Sec. Exch. Act § 10A(a) 1383
Sec. Exch. Act § 10A(b)(1) 1383
Sec. Exch. Act § 10A(b)(2) 1383
Sec. Exch. Act § 10A(b)(3) 1383
Sec. Exch. Act § 10A(i) 1387

Sec. Exch. Act § 10A(m) 1402
Sec. Exch. Act § 10C..................49, 56
Sec. Exch. Act § 11 653
Sec. Exch. Act § 11(b)....................709
Sec. Exch. Act § 11A.....646, 653, 658, 671, 716
Sec. Exch. Act § 11A(a)(1) 720, 721
Sec. Exch. Act § 11A(a)(1)(C) 658
Sec. Exch. Act § 11A(a)(1)(C)(v)....658
Sec. Exch. Act § 11A(a)(1)(D)........658
Sec. Exch. Act § 11A(a)(2) 720, 722
Sec. Exch. Act § 12 ....258, 259, 567, 644, 1235, 1373, 1388
Sec. Exch. Act § 12(a)....................153
Sec. Exch. Act § 12(b)...........100, 147, 153, 642, 643, 644, 650
Sec. Exch. Act § 12(g) 100, 153, 362, 363, 439, 441, 458, 472, 473, 600, 642, 643, 644, 650, 786
Sec. Exch. Act § 12(g)(1)........503, 643
Sec. Exch. Act § 12(g)(1)(A)...........642
Sec. Exch. Act § 12(g)(1)(B)...........642
Sec. Exch. Act § 12(g)(1)(G)...........642
Sec. Exch. Act § 12(g)(5)................643
Sec. Exch. Act § 12(g)(6)........502, 503
Sec. Exch. Act § 12(j)......................437
Sec. Exch. Act § 12(k).......1289, 1326, 1327
Sec. Exch. Act § 12(k)(2)................743
Sec. Exch. Act § 13 ....100, 118, 130, 258, 437, 458, 473, 586, 644, 786, 1373
Sec. Exch. Act § 13(a)...........215, 646, 1347, 1358, 1359, 1400
Sec. Exch. Act § 13(b)(2).....259, 1289, 1388, 1389, 1396, 1399
Sec. Exch. Act § 13(b)(2)(A)........1396, 1397, 1400
Sec. Exch. Act § 13(b)(2)(B)........1397, 1398, 1400
Sec. Exch. Act § 13(b)(4)–(7) 1388
Sec. Exch. Act § 13(d).....35, 259, 650, 791, 797, 798, 799, 817, 818, 831, 834, 835, 836, 837, 895, 901, 1178, 1187, 1254
Sec. Exch. Act § 13(d)(1)................818
Sec. Exch. Act § 13(d)(3).........796, 799
Sec. Exch. Act § 13(e) 35, 259, 650, 791, 797, 839, 876, 877, 895
Sec. Exch. Act § 13(g) 799
Sec. Exch. Act § 13(j).....................222
Sec. Exch. Act § 13(k).................1403
Sec. Exch. Act § 13(*l*)............222, 645
Sec. Exch. Act § 14 ....118, 259, 331, 1037, 1183, 1373
Sec. Exch. Act § 14(a).....56, 644, 822, 920, 1118, 1176, 1178, 1183, 1184
Sec. Exch. Act § 14(d).....35, 259, 650, 791, 838, 840, 920, 1178, 1187
Sec. Exch. Act § 14(d)–(f) 797, 895
Sec. Exch. Act § 14(d)(1)................799

Sec. Exch. Act § 14(d)(4)............ 1337, 1374
Sec. Exch. Act § 14(d)(5)........803, 805
Sec. Exch. Act § 14(d)(6)........803, 805
Sec. Exch. Act § 14(d)(7)........807, 812
Sec. Exch. Act § 14(e) 35, 259, 650, 756, 791, 817, 920, 1178, 1184, 1187, 1207, 1208, 1248, 1249, 1250, 1252, 1253, 1254
Sec. Exch. Act § 14(f).............650, 791
Sec. Exch. Act § 14(i) 49, 56, 204
Sec. Exch. Act § 14(j) 204
Sec. Exch. Act § 14A 49, 56, 204
Sec. Exch. Act § 14A(e)(2)............143
Sec. Exch. Act § 14A(e)(2)(B).........143
Sec. Exch. Act § 15............54, 56, 419, 640, 650, 733, 740, 765
Sec. Exch. Act § 15(a) 725, 731, 733, 735
Sec. Exch. Act § 15(a)(1)........502, 735
Sec. Exch. Act § 15(b) 557, 1289, 1405
Sec. Exch. Act § 15(b)(1).......725, 727, 732
Sec. Exch. Act § 15(b)(4).......727, 732, 759, 1317, 1328, 1404, 1417
Sec. Exch. Act § 15(b)(4)(A)–(H)....732
Sec. Exch. Act § 15(b)(4)(E)......... 732, 1410, 1413, 1415, 1416, 1417
Sec. Exch. Act § 15(b)(6).......727, 732, 1328, 1345, 1404, 1410, 1415, 1416, 1417
Sec. Exch. Act § 15(b)(7).......725, 727, 732, 760
Sec. Exch. Act § 15(b)(8)................641
Sec. Exch. Act § 15(b)(8)–(9)............62
Sec. Exch. Act § 15(c)......54, 653, 727, 733
Sec. Exch. Act § 15(c)(1) 755, 756, 757
Sec. Exch. Act § 15(c)(1)(D)...........733
Sec. Exch. Act § 15(c)(3) 733
Sec. Exch. Act § 15(c)(4) 1373, 1374
Sec. Exch. Act § 15(d) 100, 118, 130, 258, 259, 437, 439, 473, 586, 643, 644, 646, 786, 1235, 1373, 1375, 1376, 1377, 1378, 1380, 1382, 1388, 1400
Sec. Exch. Act § 15(f)...................1287
Sec. Exch. Act § 15(g) 727
Sec. Exch. Act § 15(h) 727
Sec. Exch. Act § 15(h)(1)..................66
Sec. Exch. Act § 15(i) 735
Sec. Exch. Act § 15(i)(3)................735
Sec. Exch. Act § 15(k) 727, 740
Sec. Exch. Act § 15(*l*)....................727
Sec. Exch. Act § 15(*o*) 56
Sec. Exch. Act § 15A...........29, 61, 62, 640, 641, 653, 709, 722, 1035
Sec. Exch. Act § 15A(b)(6) 62, 87
Sec. Exch. Act § 15A(b)(8) 63, 724

Sec. Exch. Act § 15A(f) 16
Sec. Exch. Act § 15A(g)(2) 1317
Sec. Exch. Act § 15A(*l*)(2) 557
Sec. Exch. Act § 15B 641, 722, 735, 1328
Sec. Exch. Act § 15C 16, 650, 722, 735, 1328
Sec. Exch. Act § 15E 57
Sec. Exch. Act § 15E(m) 57
Sec. Exch. Act § 15G 19
Sec. Exch. Act § 16 .... 331, 567, 644, 645, 1187, 1255, 1256, 1265
Sec. Exch. Act § 16(a) 259, 645, 1256, 1278, 1328
Sec. Exch. Act § 16(b) 34, 259, 901, 1167, 1168, 1191, 1256, 1257, 1258, 1259, 1260, 1261, 1262, 1263, 1265, 1266, 1267, 1268, 1269, 1270, 1271, 1274, 1275, 1276, 1277, 1278
Sec. Exch. Act § 16(c) 259
Sec. Exch. Act § 17 759
Sec. Exch. Act § 17(a) 757, 759, 1112
Sec. Exch. Act § 17A 64, 641, 653, 1328
Sec. Exch. Act § 17A(b) 686
Sec. Exch. Act § 17A(b)(3) 64
Sec. Exch. Act § 17A(c) 439
Sec. Exch. Act § 18 .... 1031, 1033, 1037, 1115, 1117, 1118, 1169, 1183, 1185, 1186
Sec. Exch. Act § 18(a) 1118, 1124, 1131
Sec. Exch. Act § 18(c) 1118
Sec. Exch. Act § 19 .... 653, 722
Sec. Exch. Act § 19(b) 641, 698, 699, 724
Sec. Exch. Act § 19(b)(1) 148
Sec. Exch. Act § 19(b)(9) 698, 699
Sec. Exch. Act § 19(c) 62, 63, 641, 724
Sec. Exch. Act § 20 .... 455, 1117, 1372
Sec. Exch. Act § 20(a) 317, 455, 1103, 1145, 1431, 1493
Sec. Exch. Act § 20(e) 56
Sec. Exch. Act § 20A 1173, 1187, 1286
Sec. Exch. Act § 20A(a) 1214
Sec. Exch. Act § 20A(b)(2) 1286
Sec. Exch. Act § 21 .... 1289, 1327
Sec. Exch. Act § 21(a) 659, 1405, 1448
Sec. Exch. Act § 21(b) 1448
Sec. Exch. Act § 21(c) 1292
Sec. Exch. Act § 21(d) 1301, 1378, 1442, 1443, 1448, 1450
Sec. Exch. Act § 21(d)(1) 1298, 1340
Sec. Exch. Act § 21(d)(2) 1344
Sec. Exch. Act § 21(e) 537, 1378
Sec. Exch. Act § 21A 200, 1187, 1233

Sec. Exch. Act § 21A(a)(2) 1286, 1287
Sec. Exch. Act § 21A(a)(3) 1287
Sec. Exch. Act § 21A(b) 1287
Sec. Exch. Act § 21A(g) 1233, 1234
Sec. Exch. Act § 21A(h) 1233
Sec. Exch. Act § 21A(h)(2) 1233
Sec. Exch. Act § 21B(a) 56
Sec. Exch. Act § 21C 215, 759, 1329
Sec. Exch. Act § 21C(c)(3) 1317
Sec. Exch. Act § 21C(f) 1345
Sec. Exch. Act § 21D 651
Sec. Exch. Act § 21D(a)(3) 913
Sec. Exch. Act § 21D(a)(3)(A) 914
Sec. Exch. Act § 21D(b)(2) 57
Sec. Exch. Act § 21D(b)(3)(B) 915
Sec. Exch. Act § 21E 126, 207, 651, 1031, 1091, 1121, 1122
Sec. Exch. Act § 21E(b)(2)(D) 126
Sec. Exch. Act § 21E(c) 1092
Sec. Exch. Act § 21E(c)(1)(A) 1092
Sec. Exch. Act § 21E(c)(1)(B) 1092
Sec. Exch. Act § 21E(c)(4) 1092
Sec. Exch. Act § 21E(f) 1092
Sec. Exch. Act § 21E(g)–(h) 1092
Sec. Exch. Act § 21E(i) 1092
Sec. Exch. Act § 21E(i)(1) 1092
Sec. Exch. Act § 21E(i)(E)–(F) 1092
Sec. Exch. Act § 21F 56, 1289, 1290
Sec. Exch. Act § 24 1503
Sec. Exch. Act § 25(a)(4) 1295
Sec. Exch. Act § 27 ...... 95, 1035, 1177, 1473, 1498, 1499
Sec. Exch. Act § 28(a) 895, 1168
Sec. Exch. Act § 28(e) 653, 697, 706, 707, 708, 709
Sec. Exch. Act § 29 323
Sec. Exch. Act § 29(b) 727, 1168
Sec. Exch. Act § 30A 54
Sec. Exch. Act § 32 1452
Sec. Exch. Act § 32(a) 1441, 1452, 1453, 1454, 1455, 1456, 1457
Sec. Exch. Act § 36 .... 651, 690

UNIVERSITY CASEBOOK SERIES®
SECURITIES REGULATION

CASES AND MATERIALS

FOURTEENTH EDITION

PART I

THE CAPITAL MARKETS: AN OVERVIEW

CHAPTER 1

THE INSTITUTIONAL AND REGULATORY FRAMEWORK

The federal securities laws regulate some, but not all, financial markets. Chiefly, they focus on those markets that allocate capital, moving it from savers through financial intermediaries (such as underwriters, dealers, and other financial firms) to users (that is, those who have productive uses for capital and are willing to pay a competitive return on the capital they use). Highly diverse in structure and operation, the capital markets link very different suppliers of capital principally with corporate (or other business) users; in some markets, retail investors are common, while in others they are excluded mainly in favor of sophisticated institutional investors. Although this process of intermediation between savers and users of capital is a primary focus of this casebook, the capital markets perform other functions as well. For example, the derivatives markets permit their users to hedge risks (such as the risks of interest rate or currency fluctuations or commodity price changes), but also to speculate.

Given these differences, it does not follow that all markets should be regulated in the same way. In some, private ordering may be feasible and the need for governmental oversight may be minimal. Although no simple generalization can explain the historical contingencies that cause the federal securities laws to apply only to certain markets, U.S. securities regulation—in particular, the Securities Act of 1933 ("Securities Act" or "1933 Act") and the Securities Exchange Act of 1934 ("Exchange Act" or "1934 Act"), which are a principal focus of this casebook—clearly varies in intensity depending on the extent to which individual investors participate in the particular market.

This chapter seeks to provide an abbreviated roadmap of, first, why there is a need to regulate the capital markets; second, the principal markets to which the federal securities laws apply; third, how these markets typically work and the forces changing them; and, fourth, the interwoven web of regulatory institutions—federal, state, and "self-regulatory"—that collectively regulate the capital markets, usually in cooperation, but sometimes in conflict.

1. THE GOALS OF SECURITIES REGULATION

The initial question is, why regulate? The fact that a market is very large does not alone imply that a federal agency should be created to oversee it. Many markets are adequately controlled simply by the common law of fraud and, even in the financial world, some enormous markets function with very little governmental regulation (for example, the currency market and the market for government securities). A distinctive feature of U.S. securities regulation is that it goes beyond simply proscribing fraud to requiring affirmative disclosure in connection with the issuance of securities. It also establishes a detailed and mandatory system of continuing, periodic disclosure with which "public" companies must comply. This continuing disclosure system focuses on the "secondary" market in which investors buy and sell securities, in contrast to the "primary" market in which issuers sell securities to investors.

Why should the securities markets be regulated in this pervasive fashion? Although this is a topic of controversy among academics (with some believing the current level of regulation is excessive), the justifications for such a mandatory disclosure system generally rely on some combination of the following:

1. *Consumer Protection.* The securities markets have long been thought to be effected with a special public interest. The first federal securities laws were passed during the early years of the Great Depression, following the stock market collapse in October 1929. Congress believed investors were systematically misled and overreached during the go-go decade of the 1920s.[1] They also found the 1929 stock market collapse to be a principal cause of the Great Depression, which was prolonged by a lack of investor confidence in the capital markets. Solvent corporations with good prospects could not raise capital.[2] These twin concerns—that investors were vulnerable in a manipulated marketplace *and* that others suffered when investors disinvested—explain why Congress declared in § 2 of the 1934 Act that "transactions in securities as commonly conducted upon securities exchanges and over-the-counter markets are effected with a national public interest which makes it necessary to provide for regulation and control of such transactions." The political judgment seemed obvious at the time: When Wall Street sneezed (as it massively did in October 1929), the rest of America could become seriously ill. As a result, Congress established the Securities and Exchange Commission ("Commission" or "SEC") in 1934 as an independent federal regulatory agency and gave it strong enforcement powers to serve as the "policeman of Wall Street."

---

[1] The House Report accompanying the Securities Act examined the decade after World War I and concluded:

> Fully half or $25,000,000 worth of securities floated during this period have been proved to be worthless. These cold figures spell tragedy in the lives of thousands of individuals who invested their life savings, accumulated after years of effort, in these worthless securities.

H.R.Rep. No. 85, 73d Cong., 1st Sess. 2 (1933).

[2] In recent years, historians have tended to assign greater causal weight to other events, such as the Hawley-Smoot Tariff Act of 1930 and a resulting trade war, in what caused the Great Depression. See Jackson, The World Trading System: Law and Policy of International Relations (1992) at 31. Under this view, the 1929 stock market crash may have precipitated an economic decline but other developments exacerbated and extended it.

Since 1929, there have been other sudden stock market declines (most notably, the 2008 financial crisis, discussed shortly). Indeed, the financial meltdown in 2008, which uniquely originated in the debt market, once again highlighted the close relationship between the capital markets and national economic health.

During the market boom of the 1920s, aggressive marketing (particularly by banks) convinced a large number of retail investors, estimated at between 15 and 20 million, to invest in the stock market. After the 1929 crash, disappointed and suspicious investors fled the market. As late as 1952, a New York Stock Exchange ("NYSE") study found that the number of stockholders in the United States was only an estimated 6,490,000 people—a fraction of the pre-crash level.[3] Aggressive salesmanship by the NYSE turned this around in the 1950s, convincing individuals to re-enter the marketplace. Still, the real point here is that investor confidence is a key, but subjective, variable. When it declines, the equity market can shrink—quickly and substantially. As a result, one of the most important goals of securities regulation, shared by all major market participants, is to preserve and maintain investor confidence.

From this perspective, the case for a paternalistic approach to securities regulation, focused on maintaining investor confidence, may be even greater today than during the Great Depression when the federal securities laws were first passed. At that time, only a relatively small percentage of the American public invested in securities (and even less in equity securities). Today, over one-half of American households' financial assets are invested in stocks, either directly or through mutual funds.[4] The majority of the American middle class has invested its retirement savings, directly or indirectly, in the stock market (and no longer only in bank savings accounts) and, thus, is more exposed than in 1929 to the possibility of a severe stock market decline. In light of this substantial investment in equity securities, it is not surprising that the 2008 financial crisis and market crash had severe consequences for the real economy.[5]

---

[3] See Traflet, A Nation of Small Shareholders: Marketing Wall Street after World War II (2013). This number came to only 4.2% of the U.S. population, whereas over 100 million Americans then had life insurance policies. The NYSE's campaign (known as the "Own Your Share of American Business" campaign) was highly successful, and by 1965, the number of shareholders had again risen to 20 million.

[4] See Kolchin, SIFMA Insights: Q: Who Owns Stock in America A: Individual Investors 14 (Oct. 2019), which states that American households invest 38.2% of their assets in equities directly and 18.5% in equities through mutual funds.

[5] For discussions of the impact of stock ownership on the U.S. economy, see Hu, Investor Beliefs and Government Neutrality, 78 Tex. L. Rev. 777, 794 (2000); see also Coates, The Privatization of the Securities Laws: Private vs. Political Choice of Securities Regulation, 41 Va. J. Int'l L. 531, 571 (2001). For detailed data on the growth in stock ownership, see Kennickell et al., Recent Changes in U.S. Family Finances: Results from the 1998 Survey of Consumer Finances, 86 Fed. Reserve Bull. 1, 15 (table 6) (2000) (showing growth in stock ownership by households); Tracy et al., Are Stocks Overtaking Real Estate in Household Portfolios? Fed. Reserve Bank N.Y., Current Issues Econ. & Fin., Apr. 1999, at 1–2 (table 1) (showing assets of U.S. households).

Nonetheless, the approach generally adopted by the federal securities laws is far from paternalistic. Instead, believing in investor self-determination, the federal securities laws permit high-risk products to be sold, even to retail investors, so long as full disclosure is made. This is critical: A primary goal of the federal securities laws is promoting full and accurate disclosure by issuers who wish to access the capital markets, sometimes affirmatively (by requiring certain types of information to be disclosed), sometimes through penalties (for material misstatements or omissions), and sometimes both.

2. *Systemic Risk and Financial Stability.* The 2008 financial crisis showed that financial institutions are closely interconnected—the failure of one can imply the failure of many. Although the SEC does not have jurisdiction over most financial institutions, it did have authority over the "shadow banks"—the large investment banks that were required to register with it as broker-dealers (this category included Lehman Brothers, which went bankrupt, and Bear Stearns and Merrill Lynch, which were acquired by commercial banks). The SEC was charged with ensuring their capital adequacy and monitoring their risk management practices. Studying the 2008 financial crisis, the Financial Crisis Inquiry Commission (created by Congress to investigate the crisis) concluded that the SEC (and other regulatory agencies) failed to meet their responsibilities in this regard.[6] As a result, the Dodd-Frank Wall Street Reform and Consumer Protection Act of 2010 ("Dodd-Frank Act"), discussed later in this chapter, attempted to strengthen regulatory oversight. Still, the proper structure for U.S. financial regulation continues to be debated, which is also discussed further below.

3. *Standardizing Disclosure.* Many markets sell fungible products (wheat, oil, diamonds, and so forth) whose grades and characteristics can be specified without great difficulty. Additionally, most transactions in these markets occur among professionals who expect to do business again and again and, therefore, value their reputation for honesty and fair dealing. Even in markets where transactions are not as easily standardized, self-help remedies, including personal inspection, are often available (for example, one can kick the tires at an automobile showroom or squeeze tomatoes in the supermarket). Such self-help is less feasible in the case of securities. Not only is it impossible for the typical buyer to examine the issuer, but the value of the security depends significantly on the issuer's likely future earnings. Thus, investors want reliable information about the issuer's financial condition (including likely future earnings), its competitive position, the status of its products, its contingent liabilities, the competence of its management—and a host of other matters. And the investor needs this information to be presented in a relatively standardized fashion to facilitate comparisons among issuers and securities. Absent such disclosures, it is questionable

---

[6] See The Financial Crisis Inquiry Commission, The Financial Crisis Inquiry Report xviii (2010).

whether most investors would be willing to invest funds in risky enterprises—but they certainly would reduce the price they are willing to pay in proportion to their uncertainty about a firm's value. Possibly for this reason, the level of disclosure required under the securities laws has historically exceeded the level of disclosure normally required by the laws of contract or fraud.[7] In short, for the securities markets to function efficiently, much more disclosure is required than in most other markets. For reasons discussed later in this casebook, this optimal level of disclosure may require governmental action and subsidization, principally because of the "public goods"-like character of securities information. Public goods often tend to be underprovided, and so mandatory regulation may be necessary.

4. *Inadequate Incentives to Disclose.* Conceivably, individual securities markets could solve the informational needs of investors without direct governmental intervention by adopting minimum listing standards for securities traded on them. In fact, the NYSE imposed such requirements on its listed companies for several decades before passage of the federal securities laws (although there is some debate about whether they enforced those requirements consistently before becoming subject to SEC oversight in the 1930s). Still, managers may resist disclosing adverse information about their firm for a variety of self-interested reasons, even if it is in the firm's long-term interest to maintain its credibility with investors by disclosing such information. Not only do managers fear being fired (or, at least, suffering a loss of pay), they may fear that disclosure of some forms of information will injure their firm by alerting competitors to important developments. Hence, one rationale for a mandatory disclosure system is that the private costs of disclosure can exceed its social costs, thus leading to lesser disclosure under a private ordering system, in which each firm chooses its own level of disclosure, than under a mandatory system. In short, a socially optimal level of disclosure may only be achievable through mandatory requirements.[8]

5. *Allocative Efficiency.* For many economists, the critical function of the federal securities laws is ensuring the accuracy of securities prices. By "accuracy," in the case of stocks, economists mean prices that conform to the fundamental value of the companies whose shares are traded.[9] In their view, the primary task of securities regulation is to encourage the price-correcting work of informed traders who use SEC-mandated disclosures to buy underpriced stocks and sell overpriced ones until their

---

[7] See Kronman, Mistake Disclosure, Information, and the Law of Contracts, 7 J. Legal Stud. 1 (1978) (noting absence of broad disclosure rules under the general law of contracts).

[8] For this argument, see Fox, Retaining Mandatory Securities Disclosure: Why Issuer Choice is Not Investor Empowerment, 85 Va. L. Rev. 1335 (1999).

[9] See Kahan, Securities Laws and the Social Costs of "Inaccurate" Stock Prices, 41 Duke L.J. 977 (1992); see also Gordon & Kornhauser, Efficient Markets, Costly Information, and Securities Research, 60 N.Y.U.L.Rev. 761 (1985); Gilson & Kraakman, The Mechanisms of Market Efficiency, 70 Va.L.Rev. 549 (1984).

prices conform to the shares' "fundamental" values.[10] This goal is considered even more important than the goal of investor protection, because the capital markets allocate a scarce resource—namely, capital—among competing users. By determining each issuer's cost of capital, the securities markets in theory serve as the nerve center for a capitalist economy, encouraging the flow of capital to businesses with superior prospects and penalizing less-efficient firms by requiring them to pay more for capital. In this view, the capital markets, and in particular the stock market, promote efficiency and economic growth and thereby benefit the public-at-large, not simply investors. The more one takes this view, the more one can justify a disclosure system having higher costs than most issuers would voluntarily incur to satisfy investors because, from this perspective, there is a public or social benefit that exceeds the private benefits of disclosure.

In recent years, this view has been much debated. Some believe that, while the goal of enhancing accuracy is valid, it must be balanced against the issuer's own interests in confidentiality.[11] Their primary fear is that excessively high disclosure standards will result in disclosures the firm's competitors can exploit. To illustrate, while disclosure of future business plans or new products should enhance the accuracy of securities prices, it may also allow competitors to mimic those plans; over time, this could reduce an issuer's incentive to invest in research and development. From this perspective, "accuracy enhancement is only one of a number of conflicting objectives which must be considered. . . ."[12]

Controversy also exists over whether the federal securities laws have improved market efficiency. Some argue that, by arming investors with private causes of action for fraud with the prospect of significant liability, the federal securities laws "reduce the amount of information that is provided by issuers."[13] This view rests on the premise that market forces alone would elicit a near-optimal level of disclosure. It overlaps with a lengthy debate about whether, historically, the introduction of the federal securities laws actually increased the amount of disclosure made available to investors.[14] Proponents of mandatory disclosure respond

---

[10] See Goshen & Parchomovsky, The Essential Role of Securities Regulation, 55 Duke L.J. 712, 715 (2006) (arguing that the essential role of "securities regulation is . . . to facilitate and protect the work of inform[ed] traders."). Although this view may seem in conflict with efficient market theory, it assumes the stock market is informationally efficient in responding quickly to new information, but not necessarily fundamentally efficient in reflecting fundamental value.

[11] See Kitch, The Theory and Practice of Securities Disclosure, 61 Brooklyn L.Rev. 763 (1995).

[12] Id. at 773.

[13] Id. at 770.

[14] Compare Benston, Required Disclosure and the Stock Market: An Evaluation of the Securities Exchange Act of 1934, 63 Am.Econ.Rev. 132 (Pt. 1) (1973) (concluding that mandatory disclosure system did not produce observable benefits to investors) with Friend & Westerfield, Required Disclosure and the Stock Market: Comment, 65 Am.Econ.Rev. 467 (1973) (disagreeing). For an historical assessment of disclosure before and after passage of the federal securities laws, see Seligman, The Historical Need for a Mandatory Corporate Disclosure System, 9 J.Corp.L. 1 (1983) (collecting evidence of disclosure failures prior to enactment of the

that recent empirical evidence shows that mandatory disclosure improves market efficiency.[15]

6. *Corporate Governance and "Agency Costs."* Corporate governance, in large part, is aimed at reducing "agency costs."[16] In that light, a crucial role of disclosure is assisting shareholders to gain greater control over their corporate managers. This is an alternative efficiency justification for mandatory disclosure under the federal securities laws, and some commentators see it as a more persuasive justification.[17] Under this interpretation, the principal purpose of mandatory disclosure is to address agency cost problems that may arise between stock promoters and investors, and between corporate managers and shareholders, by reducing the shareholders' cost of monitoring those agents (in particular, by mandating disclosure of the self-interested use of corporate assets by promoters and managers). Proponents argue, however, that this rationale justifies a considerably different disclosure system than today's "allocative efficiency" model.[18]

7. *Economic Growth, Innovation, and Access to Capital.* Not all industrial societies organize their economies around stock markets; indeed, active securities markets may be more the exception than the rule. Germany and Japan represent industrial systems that are more bank-centered than securities market-centered (although each has an active securities market). Yet, there is some evidence that countries with an active stock market experience more rapid economic growth.[19] Even apart from the question of relative growth rates, a significant qualitative difference is evident in the structure and performance of bank-centered versus market-centered economies: Bank-centered systems tend to be centralized, with greater industrial consolidation and fewer new market entrants. By contrast, economies organized around securities markets

---

federal securities laws); see also Seligman, The Transformation of Wall Street: A History of the Securities and Exchange Commission and Modern Corporate Finance, at 564–65 (1982).

[15] One important study found that, in the early 1980s, the SEC's introduction of the required "Management's Discussion and Analysis of Financial Condition and Results of Operations," which mandated the disclosure of certain forward-looking information, improved the accuracy of share pricing in the U.S. equity market. See Fox et al., Law, Share Price Accuracy and Economic Performance: The New Evidence, 102 Mich. L. Rev. 331 (2003).

[16] Agency costs are those costs that result from, or are incurred to control, an agent's behavior in a principal-agent relationship. See Jensen & Meckling, Theory of the Firm: Managerial Behavior, Agency Costs and Ownership Structure, 3 J.Fin.Econ. 305 (1976).

[17] See Mahoney, Mandatory Disclosure as a Solution to Agency Problems, 62 U.Chi.L.Rev. 1047 (1995).

[18] See id. at 1048.

[19] For the argument that economies organized around securities markets are more able to channel capital to emerging firms and spur economic growth in transitional countries, see Brown, Of Brokers, Banks and the Case for Regulatory Intervention in Russian Securities Markets, 32 Stan. J.Int'l L.Rev. 185 (1996). The recent experience of several Asian countries (most notably Korea, Taiwan, and Singapore) is often cited for this proposition. Correspondingly, those countries (including some in Eastern Europe) that have experienced difficulties in the transition to capitalism have often had extremely under-regulated securities markets, which in some cases have virtually collapsed due to fraud and investor distrust. See Coffee, Privatization and Corporate Governance: The Lessons from Securities Market Failure, 25 J. Corp. L. 1 (1999).

tend to favor new entrants, in particular start-ups that can convince investors of the value of their latest technological innovations. Thus, it may not be a coincidence that Silicon Valley developed in the United States, not in Germany or Japan. In bank-centered systems, there may be pressure for an entrepreneur with a new business to merge or otherwise affiliate with a larger corporate group as a precondition to bank financing. From this perspective, it is at least plausible that a legal system that facilitates an active equity market may also promote a more decentralized economy and a rapid pace of technological innovation.

8. *Reducing the Cost of Capital and the Tradeoffs.* Securities regulation may benefit issuers as well as investors. That is, if investors expect they are receiving full disclosure, and material failures will trigger enforcement actions, they are more likely to pay a higher price for a "safer" investment, meaning that the issuer benefits from a lower cost of capital. Issuers that already listed their stock in their home markets have found that their shares benefit from a positive price jump when they cross-list those shares on to a U.S. stock exchange. This may imply that investors believe they are receiving better disclosure or that stronger enforcement will deter the issuer from making a false statement.[20]

There is, however, a tradeoff here. In a global economy, issuers and investors can increasingly choose the market in which they wish to participate. If regulatory costs are higher in one market than another, issuers will predictably prefer the lower-cost market—unless that market has a higher cost of capital.

The result is a tradeoff between regulatory costs and benefits, and a balance must be struck. Today, unlike in the less-globalized past, "over-regulation" is more likely to cause issuers to flee a market and dissuade foreign issuers from cross-listing in a more expensive market, but "under-regulation" can produce a higher cost of capital, which can weaken or dampen the real economy and potentially increase unemployment. The optimal point where marginal costs and marginal benefits just balance is always elusive and debatable.

This problem of balance became more acute in the wake of the Sarbanes-Oxley Act of 2002 ("Sarbanes-Oxley Act") and the Dodd-Frank Act. Some of their provisions—most notably Section 404 of the Sarbanes-Oxley Act, which requires an annual audit of internal controls—significantly raised costs, particularly for smaller issuers, and caused some foreign issuers to leave, or not enter, the U.S. securities markets. In 2000, for example, nine out of every ten dollars raised by foreign companies through new stock offerings were raised in the United States. Then, possibly in response to the Sarbanes-Oxley Act's heightened requirements and the modernization of securities markets outside the United States, this pattern was reversed, with nine out of ten dollars

---

[20] For a fuller consideration of this theme, see Coffee, Law and the Market: The Impact of Enforcement, 156 U. Penn. L. Rev. 229 (2007).

raised by foreign companies through new listings in 2005 principally being in Europe.[21] More recently, some of the world's largest IPOs (including by Alibaba Group Holdings Limited, a China-based issuer, in 2014) returned to the United States. Nevertheless, as of 2019, even though the United States remains a top IPO market, only three out of ten dollars raised globally are through U.S. IPOs.[22]

The sense that over-regulation could cause the U.S. capital markets to lose global market share and experience slower growth has motivated some critics to demand a more rigorous (and quantified) cost-benefit review of proposed regulations before the regulators adopt them. This debate and the reaction of the D.C. Circuit Court of Appeals (which has invalidated a number of SEC rules on this ground) is considered later in this chapter.

The mixed evidence about where IPO issuers choose to list should be kept in perspective. The U.S. capital markets remain the world's largest, accounting for over 54% of global equity market capitalization and 48% of the world's corporate debt securities.[23] Arguably, the first responsibility of regulators is to maintain investor confidence in their own market, not to attract foreign listings. But regulatory costs do impose a constraint and, in a fully globalized world in which few barriers exist to the movement of capital, domestic as well as foreign issuers might flee a market in which the regulatory costs are too high. In turn, this possibility invites "regulatory arbitrage"—the deliberate relaxing of regulatory standards by one jurisdiction to attract listings and trading from another jurisdiction. Such a strategy may be competitive in the short-term, but—like the 2008 financial crisis, which many attribute to rapid and excessive deregulation—it may also result in an eventual stock market crash.

2. AN OVERVIEW OF THE FINANCIAL MARKETS

The securities markets are a subset of the broader financial markets that operate in the United States and globally. The federal securities laws apply unevenly to these markets, sometimes requiring the issuer of a security to enter the SEC's mandatory disclosure system, sometimes penalizing fraud, and sometimes not applying at all. This contrast is emphasized at the outset for several reasons:

---

[21] Id. at p. 6. Firms that do raise capital in the United States tend to do so in more lightly regulated private placements (typically pursuant to § 4(a)(2) of, and Rule 144A under, the 1933 Act) instead of registered public offerings.

[22] Ernst & Young, Global IPO Trends: Q4 2019 6, 9 (Dec. 2019).

[23] See Dimson et al., Summary Edition Credit Suisse Global Investment Returns Yearbook 2020 20 (Feb. 2020); Credit to Non-Financial Sector, Table F4.2: Total credit to non-financial corporations (core debt), BIS, https://stats.bis.org/statx/srs/table/f4.2; Mehta & Subramanian, Assessing Global Debt: Chapter 1 How Debt Has Evolved Since the Global Financial Crisis 13 (Davos Edition 2019); Vazza et al., U.S. Corporate Debt Market: The State Of Play In 2019, S&P Global (May 2019), https://www.spglobal.com/en/research-insights/articles/u-s-corporate-debt-market-the-state-of-play-in-2019.

First, financial markets are increasingly in direct competition. Issuers can seek capital in non-securities markets (for example, from direct loans by commercial banks), or they can issue bonds or notes in the U.S. securities markets, or they can seek financing in foreign capital markets. Which markets they choose to enter at any given time will depend on a variety of factors, including each market's relative cost of capital, the time needed to raise capital, and the degree of regulatory supervision and legal liability to which issuers may become subject.

Second, the line between the securities markets and other financial markets is sometimes unclear and has shifted in recent years. To some extent, this is the inevitable result of cross-market competition, as each market seeks to offer products that compete with its rivals. Hence, the futures market trades futures contracts on securities, and the securities markets trade options on securities—which can compete with each other economically. Competition also causes markets to copy each other's distribution techniques.[24]

Not surprisingly, regulatory conflict has sometimes arisen over the status of new financial instruments known as "derivatives"—including "swaps," options on other financial instruments, and futures (particularly futures based on stock market indices). These instruments are discussed in more detail later in this chapter, but the relevant point here is that the line between the securities markets and other financial markets can and has moved.

But why is this line important? Once a financial product is deemed to be a security, three legal conclusions typically follow: First, the SEC's mandatory disclosure system becomes applicable to the sale and trading of the instrument (unless the security falls within one of several exemptions from the federal securities laws); second, stiff federal antifraud rules apply that are considerably more favorable to the plaintiff than common law fraud; and third, the financial intermediaries that handle transactions in the financial product become subject to close, substantive regulation by the SEC. Several chapters in this casebook explain the significance of each of these consequences.

This opening section will attempt to provide an overview that places the securities markets in context by (A) providing a thumbnail sketch of the other principal capital markets; (B) profiling the economic actors—increasingly comprised of institutional investors—who dominate trading in the capital markets; and (C) surveying changes in market structure that have recently occurred. This chapter does not attempt to explain the

---

[24] For example, when a commercial bank makes a large loan to a corporate borrower, it often sells participations in all, or virtually all, the loan to other financial institutions (often mutual funds, small regional banks, and pension funds). This process of selling loan participations has elements in common with the traditional underwriting syndication by which underwriters buy and resell debt securities. The line between the loan participation market and the bond market at some point begins to blur.

law of securities regulation (that will come later), but instead focuses on the role of, and relationships among, markets and market participants.

A. THE STRUCTURE OF THE FINANCIAL MARKETS: AN OVERVIEW OF THE NON-EQUITY MARKETS

Financial markets match lenders and other investors with businesses seeking financing, enabling those with surplus funds to earn a favorable return while permitting those unable to finance their operations with internally-generated funds to obtain capital. At the same time, they permit investors to reduce their risk exposures through various strategies, such as portfolio diversification and hedging. They also provide "liquidity"—an important characteristic that essentially means that investors can buy or sell securities at any time without that transaction appreciably moving the market price.

The term "capital markets" generally refers to markets that deal in longer-term financial instruments (principally common and preferred stock, bonds, and so forth), while the term "money market" describes markets in which shorter-term debt instruments (typically with a maturity under one year) are issued and traded. Commercial banks tend to make loans (which typically are not securities) of intermediate duration (in the one- to five-year range), whereas corporate bonds often have maturities of ten years or longer. The following table of underwriting activity since 2005 shows both the diversity of securities that are underwritten by investment banks and the dominance of debt over equity issuances.

U.S. UNDERWRITING ACTIVITY[25] (in $billions)

YEAR	DEBT							EQUITY			TOTAL EQUITY AND DEBT
	Municipal	Treasury	Mortgage-Related	Corporate Debt	Federal Agency Securities	Asset-Backed	TOTAL DEBT	Preferred Stock	Common Stock	TOTAL EQUITY	
2005	407.1	746.1	2764.7	750.8	635.0	473.7	5777.5	20.8	165.3	186.2	5963.7
2006	387.9	788.5	2691.1	1058.3	691.8	658.2	6275.9	40.9	153.3	194.2	6470.1
2007	429.2	752.2	2434.6	1139.0	831.2	795.9	6382.1	62.9	164.0	226.9	6609.0
2008	389.3	1029.4	1394.0	712.7	924.8	215.2	4665.5	54.7	201.6	256.4	4921.8
2009	409.6	2197.2	2172.1	941.7	1244.4	177.9	7142.9	7.0	257.9	264.9	7407.8
2010	433.3	2319.8	2012.6	1053.3	1362.1	125.9	7307.0	6.2	213.0	219.2	7526.2
2011	295.1	2103.3	1724.8	1022.9	1025.3	151.0	6322.4	5.5	179.4	184.9	6507.3
2012	382.7	2304.6	2195.1	1368.9	925.5	259.0	7435.8	34.6	230.0	264.6	7700.4
2013	335.4	2140.0	2120.2	1376.6	652.9	304.1	6929.2	30.2	255.0	285.1	7214.4
2014	339.1	2215.2	1439.6	1435.4	558.7	393.4	6381.4	38.5	265.4	304.0	6685.4
2015	405.1	2122.4	1800.7	1490.7	645.5	333.4	6797.8	32.1	216.7	248.8	7046.6
2016	451.9	2169.4	2044.2	1519.1	927.9	325.4	7438.0	24.8	177.8	202.6	7640.5
2017	449.0	2224.3	1934.7	1642.2	731.3	550.3	7531.9	26.1	194.4	220.4	7752.3
2018	346.1	2684.7	1905.8	1333.1	653.6	516.9	7440.2	17.2	204.5	221.6	7661.8
2019	425.9	2935.5	2109.9	1415.3	989.4	310.2	8186.1	34.0	194.1	228.0	8414.1

---

[25] This chart is based on tables provided by the Securities Industry and Financial Markets Association's ("SIFMA") Capital Markets Fact Book 2019 and SIFMA Statistics, https://www.sifma.org/resources/archive/research/statistics/ (last visited June 11, 2020).

As the preceding table shows, debt underwritings dominate equity underwritings by a wide margin. Although we tend to think of debt offerings as consisting principally of corporate bonds, securitizations, including "Asset-Backed Debt" and "Mortgage-Related Debt" (the main category implicated in the 2008 financial crisis), significantly exceed the size of corporate debt issuances. Securitizations declined during and after the 2008 financial crisis, while corporate debt has continued to grow, although securitizations continue to significantly exceed corporate bonds.

The table does not even consider two additional markets discussed below—the Money Market and the Derivatives Market—each of which is also larger than the equity underwriting market.

1. *Money Market.* The money market consists of a group of short-term credit market instruments, including negotiable certificates of deposit (CDs), bankers' acceptances, treasury bills, and commercial paper. This market exists because the receivables paid to businesses, governments, and other economic units seldom coincide with their expenditures. Companies that have short-term surpluses typically hold them in interest-bearing money market instruments, which have low risk. Conversely, companies that have seasonal cash shortages or that need to finance accounts receivable also typically turn to the money market for short-term credit.[26] The instruments traded in this market usually have a maturity of from one day to one year, are characterized by a high degree of safety, and are commonly issued in units of $1 million or more. Some instruments in this market are considered securities for purposes of the federal securities laws, but others are not.[27]

Corporations typically raise funds in the money market by issuing short-term unsecured promissory notes, called "commercial paper." Although commercial paper notes are usually a security subject to the federal securities laws,[28] they are exempt from the 1933 Act's registration requirements so long as their maturity does not exceed nine months (exclusive of days of grace), they have an "investment grade" rating, and they arise out of, or their proceeds are used for, a "current transaction."[29] Investors usually do not have an opportunity to study financial statements about an issuer and instead rely on ratings issued by credit rating agencies. Those companies (the three major credit rating agencies are Moody's, Standard & Poor's, and Fitch) typically charge the issuer for rating its creditworthiness, which will effectively determine the

---

[26] For the standard reference source on the money market, see Stigum, The Money Market (3rd ed. 1990); see also Cook & Rowe, Instruments of the Money Market (6th ed. 1986).

[27] See, e.g., Mishkin v. Peat, Marwick, Mitchell & Co., 744 F.Supp. 531 (S.D.N.Y.1990) (bankers' acceptances and participations therein held not to be securities); Banco Espanol de Credito v. Security Pacific National Bank, 763 F.Supp. 36 (S.D.N.Y.1991) (very short-term loan notes held not to be securities).

[28] See University Hill Foundation v. Goldman, Sachs & Co., 422 F.Supp. 879 (S.D.N.Y.1976) (describing legal status and marketing procedures in the commercial paper market).

[29] See § 3(a)(3) of the 1933 Act.

interest rate payable on the commercial paper (or deny access to the market if no rating can be made). Securities are considered to be "investment grade" if they have a low risk of default, as determined by the credit rating agencies based on a relative scale. Commercial paper is attractive for creditworthy corporate borrowers, who typically will pay a lower interest rate on commercial paper than on commercial bank loans. The rate on commercial paper is usually a few "basis points" over the rate on CDs,[30] historically causing the market for commercial paper to grow exponentially,[31] even though it contracted following the 2008 financial crisis.[32]

2. *Government Securities Market.* Most national government treasuries conduct public auctions at which they sell their notes and bonds. The market for U.S. "government securities"[33] (including securities issued by the U.S. Treasury to finance the national debt and securities issued by government-sponsored enterprises, such as the Federal National Mortgage Association) is the world's largest securities market.

Significant differences exist between the government securities market and the major stock markets. First, the government securities market is highly concentrated and has only a limited number of significant actors (and little public participation). Trading treasury securities (or "treasuries," as they are known) occurs over-the-counter principally among financial institutions. Second, transactions in government securities can occur at different prices at the same time, because there is no centralized mechanism (such as a stock exchange floor or a computer network linking all traders) through which all buyers and sellers can meet and exchange bids and offers. Third, the principal market makers—the primary dealers—often possess valuable, nonpublic information about supply and demand imbalances. For example, if a primary dealer knows its customers intend to buy 80% of the securities being offered in an auction, then it also knows it has a greater chance of profiting if it buys more than 20% for its own account. Finally, the government securities market lacks what market experts call "transparency"—namely broad access to real-time pricing information and information about the size of investors' holdings. Proposals for

---

[30] A "basis point" is one-hundredth of one percent. Debt securities tend to be quoted in terms of the number of basis points by which they differ from some agreed benchmark (such as the "federal funds" rate on U.S. Treasury securities).

[31] See Perlow, Money Market Funds—Preserving Systemic Benefits, Minimizing Systemic Risks, 8 Berkeley Bus. L.J. 74 (2011); Frankel, Securitization: Structured Financing, Financial Asset Pools, and Asset-Backed Securities 7 (1991). See also Cochran et al., Money Market Fund Reform: SEC Rulemaking in the FSOC Era, 2015 Colum. Bus. L. Rev. 861, 871–72 (2015).

[32] See Federal Reserve Bank of St. Louis, Commercial Paper Outstanding, Federal Reserve Economic Data, https://fred.stlouisfed.org/series/COMPOUT (last visited June 17, 2020).

[33] The term "government securities" is defined in § 3(a)(42) of the 1934 Act. "Government securities" are exempt from most provisions of the federal securities laws, other than some antifraud rules.

reform have focused on developing more transparent electronic trading and reporting systems.

One last point deserves particular emphasis: Although the SEC has antifraud jurisdiction over any sale of government securities, its usual ability to regulate the practices of dealers is expressly limited by statute.[34] The Government Securities Act of 1986, which established a regulatory framework for this market, entrusted all rulemaking authority to the Treasury Secretary, with the SEC and banking regulators responsible only for enforcement.[35]

3. *Municipal Securities Market.* Municipal bond underwritings also dwarf equity offerings. The size of this market has grown substantially in recent years. In 2019, the total amount of municipal bond underwritings was $425.9 billion.[36]

For many years, conditions in the municipal securities market paralleled those in the government securities market, with one critical difference—the creditworthiness of local governmental units was often uncertain to doubtful. Although some SEC antifraud rules apply to municipal securities,[37] the Commission lacks the authority to require the registration of municipal securities or to regulate the conduct of their issuers. Observers reported that the quality of disclosure in this market and the reliability of financial information about municipal issuers was highly suspect. In response, in 1975, Congress passed a series of amendments to the 1934 Act that established the Municipal Securities Rulemaking Board ("MSRB"), which is subject to SEC oversight.

To improve municipal securities disclosure, the SEC focused its rulemaking on underwriters and those who market municipal securities. Initially, in 1989, the SEC adopted Rule 15c2–12, which, subject to certain exceptions, generally requires underwriters in municipal offerings of over $1 million to review the issuer's disclosure documents and distribute them to investors.[38] Although this obligation was imposed on underwriters, not issuers, it indirectly requires issuers to prepare a disclosure document. The SEC also emphasized that underwriters must have a reasonable basis for recommending the municipal securities being

---

[34] See § 15A(f) of the 1934 Act (providing that the Financial Industry Regulatory Authority ("FINRA"), the principal self-regulatory organization for broker-dealers, is not permitted to make rules concerning transactions by brokers or dealers in municipal securities).

[35] The Government Securities Act of 1986 added § 15C to the 1934 Act, which gave the Treasury Secretary jurisdiction over such matters as the financial responsibility, recordkeeping, custody, and use of customers' securities by government securities dealers. See Loss & Seligman, Securities Regulation (3d ed. 1990) at 3097–101.

[36] See SIFMA Statistics, https://www.sifma.org/resources/archive/research/statistics/ (last visited June 11, 2020).

[37] Rule 10b–5 under the 1934 Act applies to all securities, including municipal securities. See In re Washington Public Power Supply System Securities Litigation, 623 F.Supp. 1466 (W.D.Wash.1985), aff'd, 823 F.2d 1349 (9th Cir. 1987).

[38] See Exchange Act Release No. 26100 (Sept. 22, 1988); Exchange Act Release No. 26985 (June 28, 1989).

underwritten. These developments illustrate a familiar pattern in securities regulation: Through its enforcement and antifraud powers, the SEC can accomplish by the back door what it cannot achieve by the front door—namely, in this case, the gradual creation of a mandatory disclosure system within a particular market. The SEC took a similar back-door approach regarding periodic disclosures, prohibiting brokers and dealers from dealing in or recommending municipal securities unless the issuer provides annual financial information.

4. *Corporate Debt Market.* Although seldom attracting the same publicity (or controversy) that attends the equity market, the corporate debt market dwarfs the equity market in size, as the table at the beginning of this section shows. On average, the ratio of aggregate corporate debt offerings to aggregate equity offerings is five to one or even more. The bond market thus represents a much greater source of capital than the equity market.

Basically, the same SEC rules and disclosure obligations apply to firms that publicly issue debt securities as to those that publicly issue equity securities. In general, borrowers access the corporate debt market to raise medium- and long-term debt, whereas commercial paper usually has maturities of nine months or less. As with commercial paper, corporate debt offerings tend to be priced and sold based on credit ratings issued by the credit rating agencies.

Roughly half of all debt securities are issued to institutional investors in "private placement" transactions that are exempt from the SEC's registration requirements, whereas a much smaller percentage of equity securities, by dollar amount, are privately placed or otherwise issued in exempt transactions. For debt, private placements are disproportionately made by issuers that cannot obtain investment grade ratings (and whose securities are thus seen as "unsuitable" for certain institutional investors). The desire to avoid the cost and delay of SEC registration also motivates issuers to use the private placement exemption.

The secondary market for bonds is also quite different from the markets for equity securities. Although the daily trading volume of bonds is more than double that of common stock, the principal stock exchanges no longer list and trade bonds.[39] Instead, bonds are primarily screen-traded in a private and less-regulated market among dealers.[40] Dealers are linked through computer screens and telephone networks. Beginning in 2002, all broker-dealers were required to report trade prices,

---

[39] Although dominant in the 19th century, bond trading on the NYSE has long been minimal and, more recently, ceased altogether. In 1990, it was only 0.2% of all bond trading. See Colloton, Bondholder Communications—The Missing Link in High Yield Debt (1990) at 18. Today, bond trading has simply moved off the major exchanges.

[40] Although the market is informal and unregulated in structure, the brokers who participate in this market are subject to regulation by FINRA, which for example regulates the size of commissions. In general, however, there is far less transparency in the reporting of prices and commissions in this market than in the equity market.

quantities, and other information for certain debt instruments through the Trade Reporting and Compliance Engine (TRACE) system. The resulting transparency had a neutral or positive effect on bond liquidity and, since investors had more information, it also resulted in a greater ability to negotiate terms with dealers and lower trading costs.[41]

5. *Securitizations.* Asset-backed and mortgage-backed securities are primary examples of a financing technique known as "securitization." As the prior "U.S. Underwriting Activity" table shows, since 2005, the total value of "Asset-Backed Debt" and "Mortgage-Related Debt" has significantly exceeded Corporate Debt.

In a typical securitization, financial assets—such as mortgages, consumer loans, or accounts receivable—are transferred by their owners (typically the entities making the loans, also known as "originators") to a special purpose entity ("SPE") that issues bonds or notes whose proceeds typically are used to pay for the assets that were transferred to the SPE. Subsequent payments (for example, of interest and principal) made to the SPE on the financial assets it now holds are then used by the SPE to pay the holders of its bonds or notes.

Why are the financial assets transferred to an SPE (instead of the originators issuing their own debt securities against the same assets)? One key advantage of securitization is that it achieves "bankruptcy remoteness" for the securitized assets—meaning, if the originator later becomes insolvent, the claims of its creditors will not interrupt the flow of payments to investors who bought bonds or notes issued by the SPE. In other words, by transferring assets to the SPE in a way that ensures their "remoteness," the SPE's investors are protected from claims by the originators' creditors. For these investors, the only credit risk is the value of the pool of financial assets held by the SPE. As a result, the SPE's credit rating can be higher than the originator's (and, thus, the SPE can pay investors a lower interest rate).[42]

Also, the SPE's bonds or notes may be issued in different tranches, with the first tranche being denominated "senior debt" (with payments on that tranche made ahead of all other bonds or notes), a second tranche being subordinated to the first tranche, and so on. In light of the lower risk of the senior tranche, it can more easily obtain a "AAA" credit rating from the credit rating agencies and thus become an attractive investment for pension funds and other institutional investors that are interested only in safe, high-quality debt.

Securitizations began with residential mortgages in the 1970s and eventually spread to most other forms of financial assets (including, of

---

[41] See Bessembinder & Maxwell, Transparency and the Corporate Bond Market, 22 J. Econ. Persp. 217, 225–27 (2008); Edwards et al., Corporate Bond Market Transaction Costs and Transparency, 62 J. Fin. 1421, 1422–23 (2007); Goldstein et al., Transparency and Liquidity: A Controlled Experiment on Corporate Bonds, 20 Rev. Fin. Stud. 235, 237–38 (2007).

[42] See Schwarcz, The Alchemy of Asset Securitization, 1 Stan. J. L. Bus. & Fin. 132 (1994).

possible relevance to you, student loans). Unlike corporate bonds, there are no audited financial statements on which investors can rely to value the SPE's securities. For that matter, the SPE has no real operations, and the value of the SPE's financial assets often is not entirely transparent. Thus, securitized debt is typically marketed to investors based mainly on the rating assigned to the offering (or tranche) by the credit rating agencies.

Although not the only cause, the technology behind securitization clearly failed during the lead-up to the 2008 financial crisis. Why? The supply of mortgage funds increased dramatically after 2000 as a result of growth in asset-backed securitizations.[43] The next step was a collapse in mortgage lending standards—mortgage loan originators did not bear the risk of borrower default (since they quickly securitized their loans), and so they had less incentive to screen borrowers for creditworthiness. Investment banks also had little reason to resist the drop in lending standards; they knew they could successfully securitize those assets and sell the SPE's securities so long as they convinced a credit rating agency to give their offering an investment grade rating. (In fact, Title IX of the Dodd-Frank Act now requires securitizers to retain an economic interest in a material portion of the credit risk for any asset they sell or transfer to third parties.[44] This risk retention—or "skin-in-the-game"— requirement was intended to minimize the moral hazard problems that arose around investment banks.) Eventually, the housing bubble burst, and in its wake some famous investment banks (most notably, Lehman Brothers) became insolvent. Others (such as Merrill Lynch and Bear Stearns) were forced into mergers as those firms neared the brink of insolvency.

6. *Derivatives Market.* "Derivatives" are contracts or instruments that derive their value from the value of other instruments, commodities, or other assets "underlying" the derivative. Derivatives include forward contracts, futures, options, and swaps, but only futures and options trade on organized exchanges (or boards of trade). Historically, exchanges that traded derivatives originated in market centers where agricultural commodities were traded for future delivery. For example, a buyer might agree to pay a fixed price for a specified quantity of wheat that the seller agrees to deliver in the future. This allows the seller (perhaps a farmer) to lock in a favorable price in advance and also permits the buyer (perhaps a cereal-maker) to protect its cost of supply from volatile market changes.

In contrast to the debt or equity market, the market for derivatives typically does not provide capital to issuers. Instead, derivatives often involve side agreements on interest rates, currency rates, stock index levels, commodities prices, or similar market indices. Firms enter into

---

[43] See Mian & Sufi, The Consequences of Mortgage Credit Expansion: Evidence from the 2007 Mortgage Default Crisis (http://ssrn.com/abstract=1072304) (Dec. 2008).

[44] See § 941 of the Dodd-Frank Act (adding § 15G to the 1934 Act).

these agreements not to raise money, but to manage the risk of adverse market changes, such as changes in interest or currency rates or changes in other values or prices. Transactions in this market inherently are zero-sum; that is, one side's gain equals the other side's loss, depending on changes in the covered rates, values, or prices over the term of the transaction. Nevertheless, if both sides in a derivative are using it to help manage their risk exposures, then notwithstanding who ends up gaining or losing, both will benefit from the greater certainty provided by the arrangement.

Certain types of derivatives are described in more detail later in this casebook. In the meantime, we summarize some of the types of derivatives that grew almost exponentially over the last thirty years:

    a. *Traded Options.* An option gives the buyer, in return for paying a premium, the right (but not the obligation) to buy or sell shares of stock (or other financial assets) in the future at a fixed price (known as the "strike price") that is agreed upon today. Options traded on specialized options exchanges are not issued by the firms whose securities underlie those options.

For options to trade freely, their terms must be standardized. To do this, the securities options exchanges created the Options Clearing Corporation ("OCC"). The OCC is the issuer of all options, interposed between buyers and sellers so that there is no direct contractual relationship between them. This mitigates the risk of a counterparty defaulting.

In 1973, the Chicago Board Options Exchange ("CBOE") inaugurated a secondary market in options. Currently, the CBOE and the International Securities Exchange dominate trading in stock options. In addition to stock options, investors can also acquire options on a stock index. The best-known and most heavily traded stock index option on the CBOE is on the Standard & Poor's (S&P) 100, which is based on the value of 100 stocks that comprise the index.

    b. *Futures.* A futures contract is a contract to buy or sell a quantity of a financial asset or commodity at a fixed price on a future date. Futures on agricultural products and other commodities have existed for centuries. The U.S. market expanded its scope in the 1970s to trade contracts on financial assets (such as currencies and bonds). Then, in the 1980s, they began to trade futures on stock market indices. The most popular stock index future is the Standard & Poor's 500 index, a contract to buy or sell the value of the S&P 500 index multiplied by $250, which trades on the Chicago Mercantile Exchange ("CME"). The CME also created "e-mini futures" to permit smaller investments by a broader range of investors. The S&P 500 e-minis are one-fifth of the value of the larger contract ($50 rather than $250). The "e" in e-mini stands for electronic, since these futures trade electronically and, arguably, are more liquid than traditional futures.

Unlike options, stock index futures create an obligation (not a right) to deliver or receive the cash equivalent of a portfolio of stocks. A stock index option exposes its holder to the possible loss of the premium she paid to buy the option. Stock index futures, by contrast, obligate the holder to buy or sell the economic equivalent of the shares comprising the underlying stock index and, therefore, exposes the holder to substantially higher risk. Consequently, individual investors tend to trade options (where the risks and returns are less), while institutional investors tend to trade futures. Another critical difference between stock options and futures involves their regulation: Stock options are regulated by the SEC, while futures (including futures on stock indices) are regulated by the Commodity Futures Trading Commission ("CFTC").[45]

c. *Swaps*. This widely-used instrument requires a transactional explanation. Suppose you are a U.S. corporation that borrowed $100 million under a ten-year loan at a floating interest rate. In this case, you are exposed to a significant risk—the risk that, over the life of the loan, interest rates will rise and increase the amount you must pay on the loan. You can, however, fix your liability by agreeing to a "swap" transaction with a large financial institution (known as your swap "counterparty"). Under the terms of the swap, you agree to pay interest at a fixed rate (say, a small fraction above the current floating rate) to the counterparty, and the counterparty agrees to pay you interest at the floating rate (whatever it may be, from time to time, which amount you can use to pay what is owed on the floating-rate loan). Thus, if interest rates rise, you receive a net payment from the counterparty; if they fall, you make a net payment to the counterparty. But, basically, you pass the risk of rate fluctuations to the swap counterparty for a fee.[46] Other significant types of swaps include currency swaps, equity swaps, and credit default swaps.

Swaps do not trade on exchanges, but rather are entered into through the over-the-counter markets, typically between large banks and insurance companies, on the one hand, and their customers, on the other. This market is largely opaque because trading is conducted on a party-to-party, bilateral basis, without being reported to any exchange. This opacity may help explain why no exchange arose to handle these trades, even though using an exchange could reduce risk for all parties.

Since trading in swaps is conducted with a counterparty, rather than through a central market, each participant potentially faces credit risk as well as market risk; that is, it faces the market risk of changes in the index or other asset underlying the swap, and it may also face the credit

---

[45] The Commodities Exchange Act gives the CFTC exclusive jurisdiction over commodity futures contracts. See generally Johnson & Hazen, Commodities Regulation (2d ed. 1989); Markham, The History of Commodities Futures Trading and its Regulation (1987); GAO, Securities and Futures: How the Markets Developed and How They Are Regulated (1986).

[46] For an overview of swaps and their economic and regulatory context, see Hu, Swaps, The Modern Process of Financial Innovation and the Vulnerability of a Regulatory Paradigm, 138 U.Pa.L.Rev. 333 (1989). Although relatively new, the size of the swaps market dwarfs many other financial markets.

risk of its counterparty's ability to perform. Although it can partially protect itself by using collateral, the failure of a major swaps dealer can destabilize the financial markets. The Dodd-Frank Act mandates the use of clearinghouses, much like the OCC (which, among other things, will interpose a central counterparty between buyers and sellers), to minimize the risk of a counterparty defaulting.[47]

The appearance of swaps, single stock futures, and other hybrid instruments has blurred the line between securities and commodities. In the early 1980s, the SEC and CFTC negotiated a compromise that defined their respective jurisdictions. Although Congress adopted that compromise, ambiguous hybrid instruments continued (and continue) to be developed, sparking ongoing debate over these definitional (and jurisdictional) issues. Over time, partly to give greater legal certainty to transactions that totaled well over several trillion dollars (in notional amount), and partly reflecting the deregulatory mood at the time, Congress passed the Commodity Futures Modernization Act of 2000, which removed over-the-counter derivatives from the jurisdiction of both the SEC and the CFTC. This broad deregulation is now regarded as a contributing cause of the 2008 financial crisis because it left no agency with supervisory authority over the swaps market, which grew exponentially while remaining largely opaque. Filling this gap was an important part of the Dodd-Frank Act, discussed further later in this chapter.

B. THE EQUITY MARKET

Although smaller than the debt market, the equity market has a unique impact on the economy, both because stock prices influence and direct capital allocation, and because the equity market directly impacts corporate governance (partly due to managers today tending to be paid with stock options and other forms of equity-related compensation). As a company's stock price rises or falls, boards of directors and shareholders respond, as do activists and hostile bidders. Market efficiency is principally maintained by sophisticated analysts and traders, who continuously seek new information based on which to buy or sell stocks, thereby adjusting stock prices to reflect this new information. This competition is sufficiently rigorous that it is largely impossible for non-professionals to outperform the market by trading on the public disclosure of new information.

At the outset, it is useful to distinguish the primary market (sales of securities by issuers to investors) from the secondary market (trading transactions between investors). The secondary market dwarfs the primary market. For example, the value of equities traded in public

---

[47] For a concise history of clearinghouses in the United States, see Bernanke, Chairman, Fed. Res., Clearinghouses, Financial Stability, and Financial Reform, Speech at the 2011 Financial Markets Conference (Apr. 4, 2011), https://www.federalreserve.gov/newsevents/speech/bernanke20110404a.htm.

secondary markets may exceed the value of the common stock sold by issuers during the same year by more than 300-to-1.[48]

Of course, a secondary market arises only after the stock is issued in the primary market. Interestingly, the reverse is also often true: The promise of a secondary market is needed to facilitate primary issuances to public investors. As a practical matter, before an issuer can sell shares to the public, it will usually need to assure prospective investors of a secondary market to provide them with liquidity. If no such secondary market exists, the issuer may find it easier to make a private placement to a small, select group of sophisticated investors. Several exemptions in the 1933 Act permit such sales to be made without the same disclosure obligations of a public offering, but generally they also require the shares to be sold only to sophisticated investors and not resold for a defined period to public investors.

(1) THE VENTURE CAPITAL MARKET

Generally, start-up companies that have not yet marketed a product or earned significant revenues do not attempt to enter the public equity market with an IPO. This is less due to legal restrictions and more due to how difficult it is to value such early-stage businesses. Instead, in the United States, these kinds of companies can receive start-up capital through private placements to "angel" or "seed" investors or, at a later stage, to venture capital ("VC") investors. Some investors may be particularly sophisticated in certain high-tech industries, but all are (or should be) prepared to accept the higher risks of investing in start-ups. Also, unlike the more passive investors in public offerings, VC investors typically buy large blocks of stock and may negotiate for control rights (such as representation on the start-up's board and/or the right to veto certain transactions). VC investors normally do not acquire majority control, and they tend to invest in the company directly rather than buy shares issued to the founders. Their goal is to profit alongside the entrepreneurs in an IPO (or some other liquidity event), not to acquire the firm at this unproven stage from its founders.

The U.S. VC industry originated after World War II and was initially led by firms organized by the Rockefeller and Whitney families. The industry blossomed, however, with the emergence of Silicon Valley and the explosive growth of high technology after 1980. Over time, large corporations (such as Intel and Oracle) made substantial, but non-controlling, investments in many start-up firms, and these "strategic investors" became significant sources of venture capital.

The 1990s saw dynamic growth in early-stage investment, fueled mainly by the appearance of funds—often unregulated limited partnerships known as "venture capital funds"—that invested across a portfolio of businesses. A VC firm might raise capital by selling interests

---

[48] See SIFMA, Capital Markets Fact Book 2019 7, 24.

in a limited partnership that would invest in businesses the VC firm would later locate. The equity capital in such funds grew from around $5 billion in 1990 to over $136.5 billion in 2019, and the number of such firms grew over the same period from 100 to over 1,000.[49]

VC funds are typically formed for a limited period (up to ten years), with the limited partners having the right to withdraw their capital at the end of that period. Limited partners, however, prefer to profit on their investments quickly, either through an IPO or a strategic sale of the start-up, and so the fund's life may be shorter (between five and seven years). VC capital tends to be recycled into new VC funds, except that less successful VC firms are likely to fold as limited partners decide to reinvest with a more successful fund manager.[50]

(2) THE PUBLIC EQUITY MARKET: REDEFINING THE ROLE OF EXCHANGES

The U.S. market for equity securities has changed dramatically since the early 2000s due to changes both in trading technology and in legal reforms that have mandated greater competition among trading centers. The most important of these legal changes was the adoption of Regulation NMS in 2005.[51] Regulation NMS forbids a trading center from executing a transaction if a superior price is available on another trading center, thereby compelling price competition.[52]

This sudden appearance of intense competition contrasts with a long period in which trading volume was concentrated on just two exchanges: the NYSE and the Nasdaq Stock Market (also known as "Nasdaq" or "NASDAQ"). In 1900, over 100 stock exchanges operated in the United States. As information technology improved in the late 19th century (the most notable innovations being the stock ticker and the telephone), that number began to decline, and markets closed or consolidated since informational cost barriers no longer sheltered them from competition. As of 2020, the majority of U.S. equity trading continues to occur on the NYSE and Nasdaq, with some exchanges in specialized niches,[53] but as

---

[49] See National Venture Capital Association, Latest NVCA Yearbook Highlights Record Levels Reached by the U.S. Venture Ecosystem in 2018, https://nvca.org/pressreleases/latest-nvca-yearbook-highlights-record-levels-reached-u-s-venture-ecosystem-2018/ (last visited June 3, 2020); Hodges, US Venture Capital Investment Surpasses $130 Billion in 2019 for Second Consecutive Year, PRNewsWire (Jan. 14, 2020), https://www.prnewswire.com/news-releases/us-venture-capital-investment-surpasses-130-billion-in-2019-for-second-consecutive-year-300986237.html.

[50] See Gilson & Black, Does Venture Capital Require an Active Stock Market?, 12 J. Applied Corp. Fin. 35 (1999).

[51] See Exchange Act Release No. 51808 (June 9, 2005).

[52] A transaction at an inferior price is known as a "trade-through." Rule 611(a) of Regulation NMS requires that "[a] trading center shall establish, maintain, and enforce written policies and procedures that are reasonably designed to prevent trade-throughs on that trading center of protected quotations in NMS stocks. . . ."

[53] For example, the American Stock Exchange ("Amex"), once much larger than Nasdaq, lost out in this competition and was acquired by the NYSE in 2008. Renamed the NYSE MKT

described below, the nature of trading has changed significantly. The NYSE and Nasdaq have been eclipsed by newer automated trading platforms, permitted under Regulation ATS, that compete vigorously for trading volume. The result is greater liquidity in the market, but also trading that may be rigged in favor of institutions with more sophisticated trading technology.

Historically, the two dominant exchanges differed in several respects. The NYSE tended to list larger companies, while Nasdaq had the loyalty of many high-tech companies that preferred an electronic exchange. The NYSE was an example of an "auction" market, which meant that all orders to buy and sell from customers were routed to a single "specialist" in that stock, who in theory matched incoming buy and sell orders as an auctioneer. By law, the specialist was only a buyer or seller itself as a last resort (but it was obligated to buy or sell if no other buyer or seller was available). By contrast, Nasdaq was a "dealer" market, where multiple dealers competed for customers' buy and sell orders by offering superior price quotations. This structure encouraged competition, but it also meant that every transaction was between a customer and a dealer (without public "buy" orders crossing with public "sell" orders, as they often do in auction markets). Thus, the customer had to bear the cost of an intermediary, whose prices necessarily included a profit margin.

Whatever the merits of these two approaches, they have been overshadowed by more important developments, of which two stand out: First, although the NYSE and Nasdaq typically did not trade the same stocks, that has now changed entirely. Today, some 13 registered exchanges and 33 alternative trading systems ("ATSs") trade the same stocks and compete fiercely to attract trading, most notably by paying rebates to liquidity providers, as discussed below. Together, these venues (plus clearinghouses, depositories, and quote distributors) comprise the National Market System ("NMS"), the national system used by broker-dealers to fulfill trade orders for equity securities in the United States.

Second, the old trading systems (auction markets vs. dealer markets) have given way to computerized trading in which liquidity is provided by "high-frequency traders" who post limit orders to buy and sell stocks using computerized algorithms. These high-frequency traders are motivated, in part, by compensation when orders posted to buy or sell a stock are accepted by a counterparty. In these transactions, the high-frequency trader is referred to as the "maker" (because, in theory, it "makes" liquidity), and the party who accepts the order is known as the "taker" (who "took" the offered liquidity). The taker pays a fee per trade, which is mostly passed on to the liquidity provider (in this case, the high-frequency trader). This approach—known as the "maker/taker" system—

LLC in 2012, today it primarily trades "small cap" stocks. NYSE Amex Options, another fragment of the old Amex, now specializes in options trading and also is owned by the NYSE.

has largely replaced previous systems that relied on specialists or competing market makers.

Driving this change were SEC reforms that introduced ATSs and precluded a market from executing a transaction if a superior price was available elsewhere, as well as a shift from manual trading to automated trading that can occur in a millisecond (or less). As a result, the market structure for equity trading today is characterized by a dispersion of trading volume among exchanges and ATSs that offer a range of services to attract different types of market participants with different needs. The following table breaks down the allocation of trading among market centers in 2018:

Trading Centers and Estimated % of Share Volume in NMS Stocks (2018)[54]

NASDAQ	18.23%
NYSE & NYSE American	15.89%
NYSE ARCA	10.71%
NASDAQ BX & PSX	4.80%
IEX	3.08%
CHX	0.62%
NYSE American	0.37%
Off-Exchange Trading	46.30%

These changes eclipsed the once-dominant position of the NYSE. As late as January 2005, the NYSE executed approximately 79% of the consolidated share volume in NYSE-listed stocks (with the remaining volume split between Electronic Communications Networks ("ECNs," discussed below), Nasdaq, and regional exchanges). But by October 2009, the NYSE's percentage of NYSE-listed stocks had fallen to only 25%. At the same time, the volume of trading has soared—from 2.9 million daily trades in NYSE-listed stocks in 2005 to over a billion daily trades on NYSE in 2020.[55] And as the table indicates, there has also been a significant rise in off-exchange trading through ATSs, internal trading within broker-dealers (referred to as "internalization," described below), and other trading platforms. The result is a very different trading market than what existed as recently as a decade ago.

These changes have sparked considerable controversy because the new professional liquidity provider has certain advantages over both retail and institutional investors. Not only are proprietary trading firms

---

[54] See SIFMA Insights: US Equity Market Structure Primer 16–17 (July 2018). NMS stocks are those included within the SEC's consolidated quotation system.

[55] See Markets Diary, WSJ Markets (last visited June 10, 2020), https://www.wsj.com/market-data/stocks/marketsdiary.

offered payments for providing liquidity, but they also have a timing advantage that allows them to access the market more quickly than others. Specifically, they are permitted (for a fee) to place their computer servers very close to the trading center's servers so that their orders are received first. They also rent special computer lines from the trading centers so that they receive earlier news of orders reaching the center and transactions executed at the center. These practices—"colocation" (the placement of a high-frequency trader's server next to the trading center's server) and private feeds (that enable traders to learn of incoming orders ahead of others)—make possible a trading strategy known as "latency arbitrage." To illustrate, assume that orders reach different trading centers a fraction of a second apart and that high-frequency traders know from experience that, when a large order (to buy or sell) reaches one center, it is likely that other orders, within a fraction of a second, will reach other centers (probably because a large trader wants to spread its buying or selling across multiple venues to minimize their price impact). Using its timing advantages—based on colocation and private feeds—the high-frequency trader can send orders to other trading centers that will arrive just ahead of these other orders. Thus, it might decide to buy ahead of expected buy orders or raise the "asked" price it previously posted to sell shares. In this way, institutional investors will be surprised that available "asked" prices will vanish before they can accept them. In effect, even the buyer who placed the initial order will be "front run" by the high-frequency trader before it can buy on multiple trading centers.[56]

Whether such practices are fair or desirable certainly can be debated, but by providing liquidity to the market, one impact of the new maker/taker system appears to have been to reduce price "spreads" (essentially, the difference between the highest price a buyer is willing to pay for a share and the lowest price a seller is willing to accept for it). We will return to these issues later in the casebook, but for now, this chapter will introduce the principal players in our contemporary market structure.

a. *Registered Exchanges*

Traditionally, exchange trading accounted for most of the share volume in listed stocks. Today, that number has fallen with ATSs (including entities known as "dark pools") accounting for most of the balance, but with the allocation between exchanges and ATSs shifting regularly.[57] Exchanges must register with the SEC under § 6 of the 1934 Act and are subject to several regulatory requirements (such as supervising the brokers operating on them and needing to file proposed rule changes with the SEC) that ATSs can avoid. As of early 2020, there

---

[56] For a more detailed description of the practices and issues, see Lewis, Flash Boys: A Wall Street Revolt (2014).

[57] See SIFMA Insights: US Equity Market Structure Primer 17 (July 2018).

were 13 registered stock exchanges (several with a common parent) and some 33 ATSs (with this number changing often).[58]

1. *New York Stock Exchange.* The NYSE has a physical location with an actual trading floor. While once standard, this is becoming rarer, since most exchanges now trade electronically and do not use a trading floor. Even on the NYSE, the vast majority of trading today is automated and occurs within a second (often much less) of the order reaching the NYSE.

From its inception in 1792 until 2005, the NYSE was organized as a not-for-profit organization. Voting power was held by its seat holders (brokers who purchased "seats" or rights to trade on the exchange). In 2005, the NYSE "demutualized" as part of a merger with Archipelago Holdings, Inc., a former ATS. Now public, due to the merger, the NYSE's market value began to decline commensurate with its loss of market share to other exchanges. Struggling to find a new role for itself, it merged in 2007 with Euronext, the largest European exchange, which gave the NYSE control of a large derivatives exchange run by Euronext. Ultimately, this derivatives exchange proved to be its more valuable asset. In late 2012, the NYSE agreed to a merger for $8.2 billion with Intercontinental Exchange ("ICE"), a major derivatives exchange, which became the NYSE's parent company.

Today, the NYSE remains the principal exchange for stock trading but operates on a slightly reduced scale. The advent of ATSs and new exchanges has intensified the competition for market share with other trading platforms.

2. *Nasdaq.* Nasdaq (initially an acronym for "National Association of Securities Dealers Automated Quotations") is a computerized electronic dealer market. Over-the-counter dealer markets long predated Nasdaq, which only began operations in 1971. Nasdaq upgraded the technology underlying dealer markets from telephone contacts to an electronic screen on which all dealers' quotations were listed. Trading became computerized so that orders could be entered and securities purchased simply by hitting a computer button. For many years, Nasdaq's status was anomalous; it was not technically a national securities exchange (the SEC must approve exchanges under § 6 of the 1934 Act), but simply an electronic market owned by a "registered securities association" (the National Association of Securities Dealers ("NASD")). This anomaly ended in 2006 when the SEC approved Nasdaq's application to become a national securities exchange. It is now the "Nasdaq Stock Market LLC."[59]

Nasdaq later sought to expand into Europe through hostile bids to acquire the London Stock Exchange in 2006–2007 that ultimately failed.

---

[58] Id. at 18.

[59] See Exchange Act Release No. 53128 (Jan. 13, 2006). Nasdaq applied to become an exchange in 2001, but then spent five years negotiating details with the SEC, illustrating how complex the details were in converting a dealer market into an exchange.

It did, however, purchase a series of exchanges in the Nordic, Baltic, and Caucasus regions of Europe, which currently operate as Nasdaq Nordic.

The NASD was a self-regulatory organization that Congress created in 1938 under the Maloney Act, which added § 15A to the 1934 Act as a reform measure following several stock exchange scandals. Section 15A provided for a "registered securities association" that would be created to supervise broker-dealers. The NASD was founded the next year, in 1939, and it long remained the only such association. In 2007, the NASD merged with the regulatory arm of the NYSE to form the Financial Industry Regulatory Authority ("FINRA"). This consolidation simplified life for many broker-dealers who were NYSE members and, therefore, were required to comply with the often-different rules of both bodies. Today, every broker-dealer with public customers must belong to FINRA. Although the NASD had owned Nasdaq, it sold its ownership, recognizing that conflicts could arise between its dual roles as regulator and market-owner. Today, Nasdaq is owned by public and institutional shareholders.

3. *OTC Markets Group.* If a company is not a reporting company (or otherwise cannot qualify for the OTC Bulletin Board), it can still trade in an unregulated over-the-counter market, originally known as the "pink sheets" (published since 1904). This market relies on daily quotations for thinly-traded over-the-counter ("OTC") stocks.[60] The quotations are not firm "bid" or "asked" prices, because there is no assurance anyone will buy or sell at these prices. Historically, the quotations were published on long pink sheets, and the name "pink sheets" stuck, even though the quotations are now electronically disseminated. Only a few OTC companies file periodic reports with the SEC, and some border on insolvency.

In 2007, OTC Markets Group reorganized the pink sheets (and other OTC trading) into three separate marketplaces—OTCQX ("Best Market"), OTCQB ("Venture Stage Marketplace"), and OTC Pink ("Open Marketplace")—primarily based on the quality of a company's disclosures. The criteria range from OTCQX, which has financial, reporting, and other criteria, to OTC Pink, where there are no financial or reporting criteria.

More recently, problems have arisen with companies wishing to access the U.S. public market without filing a registration statement with the SEC. Those companies have looked to "reverse merge" with publicly-traded micro-cap companies as a way to become publicly-traded in the United States. The ongoing problem of going public "through the backdoor" is discussed later in this casebook.

---

[60] For an overview, see Molitor, Will More Sunlight Fade the Pink Sheets? Increasing Public Information About Non-Reporting Issuers With Quoted Securities, 39 Ind. L. Rev. 309 (2006).

b. *Electronic Communications Networks and Alternative Trading Systems*

ECNs are essentially matching systems on which buyers and sellers post trading interest; thus, they economize on the costs of trading by avoiding the intervention of a dealer (who usually charges a fee). The defining characteristic of an ECN is that its best-priced buy and sell orders are automatically included in the NMS consolidated quotation system, displayed on most brokers' trading screens, so that the orders improve the highest bid and the lowest asked price in the NMS (known, in the market's jargon, as the "NBBO" for "national best bid and offer"). Thus, by posting a superior bid or asked price on an ECN, a customer can ensure its offer to buy or sell will be filled before other transactions can be executed.

ECNs are regulated as ATSs. Under Regulation ATS, they must be registered as broker-dealers with the SEC and must join FINRA. This level of regulatory supervision is still less than that applicable to exchanges, although in 2005, both Instinet and Archipelago, the most successful of the ECNs, merged with Nasdaq and the NYSE, respectively, and Direct Edge, the largest of the ECNs, converted into a registered exchange in 2010.

A considerable range of ATSs appeared in the 1990s. Some were bulletin board systems on which institutions (often anonymously) indicated an interest in trading a stock at a specific price. Another institution could contact the first (by telephone or computer) and negotiate a price for a transaction between them. Other ATSs were crossing systems that executed at the midpoint of the bid/ask spread on another exchange. Still others used proprietary algorithms to match buy and sell orders, or they ran daily auctions to match buyers and sellers.

The growth of ATSs was deliberately spurred by the SEC's Order Handling Rules, which were introduced in 1996 in response to a scandal—the apparent manipulation of bid/ask spreads on Nasdaq by dealers who sought to maintain a minimum quarter-point spread. Faced with dealers who colluded to keep price spreads artificially wide, the SEC designed new rules to allow investors to post prices inside the dealers' spreads against which other investors could then trade on Nasdaq. These new rules succeeded in attracting new entrants into the market-making business. By 1997, the SEC estimated that some twenty ATSs accounted for 20% of the orders in Nasdaq-traded stocks and 4% in NYSE-listed stocks.[61] More recently, ECNs are estimated to handle approximately 40% of the trading volume on Nasdaq, but only 7% on the NYSE.[62] Nevertheless, the popularity of ECNs waned with the growth of high-

---

[61] See Exchange Act Release No. 38672 (June 4, 1997).

[62] See Anderson & Dyl, Trading Volume: NASDAQ and the NYSE, 63 Fin. Analysts J. 79, 80 (2007); Lobel, Nasdaq vs NYSE: Top 7 Differences Traders Should Know, DailyFX (Dec. 10, 2018), https://www.dailyfx.com/nas-100/NASDAQ-vs-NYSE.html (last visited June 17, 2020).

speed automated trading and the advent of Regulation NMS, which precludes trade-throughs (transactions at an inferior price to the NBBO) in NMS securities. As a result, some institutional customers—who may be willing to pay a price outside the NBBO for the flexibility of buying a large block of stock all at once—may no longer be able to use ECNs (as they did before) to execute such transactions.[63]

c. *Dark Pools*

Despite their mysterious name, dark pools are simply ATSs that are subject to Regulation ATS (and, thus, like any other ATS, must register with the SEC as a broker-dealer and become a member of FINRA). Most are operated by large multi-service banks and broker-dealers.

Dark pools are different from ECNs in that they do not provide their best-priced orders for inclusion in the NMS consolidated quotation system. Indeed, they are different from other markets because they do not disclose orders placed on them, but only completed trades.

Dark pools originally were used by institutions that traded large amounts of stock and feared their orders, if posted, would move the public market price adversely against them. They used dark pools to execute large trades with anonymity. For example, if a pension fund planned to sell several million shares of a particular stock, it might anticipate that the initial 100,000 shares it sold on the NYSE or Nasdaq would drive the price of that security down, and its interest in selling more shares would leak to the market. Thus, dark pools offered relative anonymity, but arguably at the price of reducing market transparency.

More recently, with the advent of the maker/taker system (under which high-frequency traders provide liquidity), dark pools have competed effectively with exchanges by offering both high rebates to liquidity providers and prices that are slightly inside the spreads posted by the exchanges. Dark pools may also charge lower fees than exchanges (in part because they are subject to less regulation). The number of dark pools changes each year, but as of 2020, there were more than thirty dark pools in the United States.[64]

d. *Broker-Dealer Internalization*

Another (and much used) way that securities are traded off an exchange is through broker-dealer internalization. Suppose a large broker-dealer has different customers who send it "market orders," some to buy and some to sell the same stock. Rather than taking these orders to an exchange or ATS (and paying the exchange or ATS a fee), the broker-dealer can do one of two things: It might act as an agent and cross

---

[63] Subject to some exceptions, Regulation NMS precludes transactions at inferior prices until all superior prices have been executed. Sometimes, a party seeking a large quantity of stock may be willing to pay a higher price if it can be assured of acquiring the larger block. Today, Regulation NMS may bar it from doing so unless it buys all intervening shares.

[64] See Osipovich, 'Dark Pools' Draw More Trading Amid Low Volatility, Wall St. J. (May 3, 2020).

the two orders at the midpoint of the bid/ask spread, thus benefiting both sides. Alternatively, it might serve as a dealer and buy from the seller and sell to the buyer at the then-prevailing NBBO price, leaving both sides no worse off and giving the broker-dealer a profit. In either scenario, broker-dealer internalization involves little danger to the customer because the broker-dealer is required to match the best price in the market.

The SEC has found that over 200 broker-dealers regularly internalize trades,[65] and internalization is estimated to account for 17.5% of the share volume in NMS stocks.[66] The amount would likely be higher but for one further complication: Recall that exchanges and other trading platforms pay brokers to send order flow to them for execution.[67] The availability of those payments means it may be more profitable for brokers to sell their order flow rather than to internalize execution. The upshot is that broker-dealer internalization may benefit (and likely will not hurt) customers, but it does represent one more means by which transactions are diverted from the principal markets and, thus, can contribute to market fragmentation.

e. *OTC Trading by Dealers*

A recent SEC study of trading in NMS stocks found that dealers trade nearly 25% of share volume without involving an exchange or ATS (either a dark pool or an ECN).[68] This is dealer-to-dealer trading that occurs over-the-counter. Some trading appears to represent efforts by broker-dealers to acquire a requested block of shares for a customer through multiple small trades. No special issue surrounds this activity, but it should remind us that by no means does trading occur exclusively through exchanges or ATSs.

3. FORCES RESHAPING THE SECURITIES MARKETS

While the preceding section described the principal actors in the contemporary capital markets, one also needs to understand the important changes that have reshaped the investor community and other dynamic forces at work since the federal securities laws were passed in the 1930s. The forces described in this section have already begun to compel regulators to redefine their roles: (1) the rise of institutional investors and the consequent "institutionalization" of the market; (2) the globalization of the securities markets (with the accompanying prospect that both capital and businesses may flee what they perceive to be an excessively restrictive legal regime); (3) the impact of technology and the internet; (4) the convergence of the banking and securities industries into

---

[65] See Concept Release on Equity Market Structure, Exchange Act Release No. 61358 (Jan. 14, 2010).
[66] 97 CCH SEC Docket 1337, 2122 (July 2010).
[67] See Note, The Perils of Payments for Order Flow, 107 Harv. L. Rev. 1675 (1994).
[68] See SIFMA Insights: US Equity Market Structure Primer 6 (July 2018).

a unified financial services industry; and (5) the gradual decline in IPOs over the past two decades.

A. THE RISE OF INSTITUTIONAL INVESTORS

The last half-century witnessed a quiet revolution in terms of the ownership of equity securities. From a time when ownership and control were clearly separated, and stock ownership was broadly dispersed, the pendulum has swung back towards a reconcentration of stock ownership.

In 1950, institutional investors owned approximately 6.1% of the total equity in U.S. public corporations. By 2018, that number had grown to 62.4%.[69] Mutual funds now hold 22.6% of all U.S. equities, and pension funds hold over 11.5%.[70] Even this focus on aggregate levels may understate the significance of institutional ownership for at least two reasons. First, among major public corporations (where institutions tend to concentrate their holdings), the ownership level is much higher. Looking at the ten largest U.S. corporations, the level of institutional ownership increased to 82% by 2017.[71] Overall, individual shareholders hold only 37.6% of all U.S. stocks, with most of the balance being held by institutions.[72] Second, institutional investors dominate the secondary market, accounting for about 70% of trading volume.[73] Thus, ownership has become highly concentrated, and collective action by institutions has become more feasible.

On this basis, institutional investors might seem to be in a position to dominate American corporate management, dictating financial and business strategies to them. But clearly, institutional investors do not behave as if they hold such power (although they have become increasingly active over the last few decades). Some commentators have argued that a leading reason institutions do not play a greater role in corporate governance is that they have been overregulated by the federal securities laws (and by state law) in a way that deliberately denies them the ability to hold a controlling block of stock in any public corporation.[74] From this perspective, the same populist tradition in American politics that underlay the passage of the federal securities laws also feared the

---

[69] See Kolchin, SIFMA Insights: Q: Who Owns Stock in America A: Individual Investors 14 (Oct. 2019).

[70] Id.

[71] McGrath, 80% of Equity Market Cap Held by Institutions, Pensions&Investments (Apr. 2017), https://www.pionline.com/article/20170425/INTERACTIVE/170429926/80-of-equity-market-cap-held-by-institutions. See also Fichtner et al., Hidden Power of the Big Three? Passive Index Funds, Re-concentration of Corporate Ownership, and New Financial Risk, 19 Business and Politics 298, 313 (2017).

[72] See Kolchin, SIFMA Insights: Q: Who Owns Stock in America A: Individual Investors 14 (Oct. 2019).

[73] See FINRA Staff, Institutional Investors: Get Smart About the "Smart Money", FINRA (Dec. 2015), https://www.finra.org/investors/insights/institutional-investors-get-smart-about-smart-money.

[74] The leading work expressing this view is Roe, Strong Managers, Weak Owners: The Political Roots of American Corporate Finance (1994). See also Morley, Too Big to Be Activist, 92 S.Cal.L.Rev. 1407 (Sept. 2019).

concentration of financial power (and, in particular, the dominance of New York and other East Coast financial interests). Responding to these pressures, Congress (and state legislatures) separated investment from commercial banking and otherwise sought to fragment the principal American financial institutions (banks, insurance companies, mutual funds and, more recently, pension funds) or at least deny them the ability to actively control corporate managements.

Others doubt that American law has forced investors into passivity by pointing to other factors that may have had a more significant influence. They cite factors such as a preference for liquidity (which is often inconsistent with holding a control block of stock) or the lack of any perceived payoff to institutional money managers from involvement in corporate governance.[75] Institutional investment preferences may also be inconsistent with a high degree of activism. In general, many institutional investors follow an investment strategy known as "indexing" under which they cease to pick individual stocks, but invest in the market as a whole (or at least hold a representative index, such as the S&P 500).[76] But such indexing invites passivity, mainly because there is less incentive to closely monitor an individual company in a portfolio if the investor's focus is on tracking the 500 stocks that comprise the S&P 500 index as a whole.[77]

Still, both sides in this debate agree that some SEC rules—most notably, the rules governing proxy solicitation, the regulation of takeover contests, and the rules under § 16(b) of the 1934 Act—can make communications among institutional investors legally risky and have sometimes chilled institutional activism.[78] Once, the proxy rules seemed to inhibit the formation of groups of institutional investors who might act to monitor corporate managements.[79] Group formation requires communication, and this process is slowed and made more costly if inter-institutional communications are deemed to be proxy solicitations (requiring the filing with the SEC of a proxy statement)[80] or require

---

[75] See Coffee, Liquidity Versus Control: The Institutional Investors As Corporate Monitor, 91 Colum.L.Rev. 1277 (1991); Rock, The Logic and (Uncertain) Significance of Institutional Shareholder Activism, 79 Geo.L.J. 445 (1991). Both of these authors stress that collective action problems may make institutional investors "rationally apathetic."

[76] As an investment strategy, indexing largely reflects acceptance by these institutions of the "efficient capital market hypothesis," which implies that the search for undervalued stocks in a liquid public market is futile.

[77] Some institutional investors hold several thousands of stocks in their portfolios. Also, institutional investors are increasingly investing in derivatives tied to stock indices, thus further weakening their focus on individual companies. See Coffee, Liquidity Versus Control: The Institutional Investors As Corporate Monitor, 91 Colum.L.Rev. 1277, 1340–42 (1991).

[78] See Coffee, The SEC and the Institutional Investor: A Half-Time Report, 15 Cardozo L.Rev. 837 (1994) (surveying impact of Williams Act rules and other obstacles).

[79] See Black, Shareholder Passivity Reexamined, 89 Mich.L.Rev. 520 (1990); see also Conard, Beyond Managerialism: Investor Capitalism?, 22 U.Mich.J.L.Ref. 117 (1988); Grundfest, The Subordination of American Capital, 27 J.Fin.Econ. 89 (1991).

[80] Rule 14a–1(*l*) under the 1934 Act defines a "solicitation" as a "communication to security holders under circumstances reasonably calculated to result in the procurement,

disclosure under the Williams Act once the "group" collectively owns more than 5% of the issuer's stock.[81] The SEC acknowledged the danger of over-regulation and amended its proxy rules to facilitate inter-shareholder communications when the shareholder is disinterested (as set out in the rule) and does not seek to obtain proxy authority.[82] Other rules continue to pose obstacles, however, and the debate over whether the SEC chills institutional activism continues.

Although it is common to speak of "institutions" as a uniform class, they can be quite different in their structures and behaviors, and they are regulated very differently. The major classes of institutional investor are: (1) mutual funds; (2) pension funds; (3) hedge funds; (4) bank trust departments; and (5) insurance companies. The federal securities laws do not directly regulate the last two, which have been mostly invisible as actors in corporate governance. The first three merit individual attention. Although public pension funds became increasingly active in the 1990s, mutual funds remained relatively passive, largely content to follow the traditional "Wall Street Rule" of selling shares when they disapproved of a firm's management but seldom openly challenging those managers. Hedge funds, by contrast, have been aggressive participants in corporate governance. In law and economic terms, the choice here has been between relying on "exit" (the ability to sell) versus "voice" (the ability to vote and pressure management in proxy and activist campaigns). What explains the difference in behavior? Here, it is useful to survey the major classes of institutional investor and understand their legal status.

 a. Mutual Funds. A mutual fund—or, in legal terminology, an "investment company"—is a "pool of assets consisting of securities belonging to the shareholders of the fund."[83] Such funds can be "closed-end" (which means their shares are traded among investors) or "open-end" (which means their securities are redeemable daily). Typically organized as a corporation in the United States, the mutual fund usually has no or *de minimus* employees, and instead contracts for advisory services with an investment adviser who may manage many, or even a whole family of, other mutual funds. The adviser makes the mutual fund's investment decisions. In the United States, public mutual funds are required to register with the SEC under the Investment Company

---

withholding or revocation of a proxy." A solicitation requires the filing with the SEC, and furnishing to each person solicited, of a detailed proxy statement unless otherwise exempted.

[81] The Williams Act added several sections to the 1934 Act (chiefly, §§ 13(d) and (e) and §§ 14(d) and (e)). These sections regulate tender offers and the process of acquiring control of a public corporation. Rule 13d–1 under the 1934 Act requires the filing with the SEC of a disclosure document, known as a Schedule 13D, once a "group" (as set forth in Rule 13d–5) beneficially owns more than 5% of any class of an equity security (other than non-voting securities) of a public company.

[82] See Rule 14a–2(b)(1) under the 1934 Act. Note also, in accordance with Rule 14a–2(b)(2), that the proxy statement requirements do not apply if the solicitation is made, otherwise than on behalf of the issuer, to ten or fewer persons.

[83] See Zell v. InterCapital Income Sec., Inc., 675 F.2d 1041, 1046 (9th Cir. 1982).

Act of 1940 ("Investment Company Act" or "1940 Act"), and their investment advisers must register under the Investment Advisers Act of 1940 ("Advisers Act"). The funds' sale of shares must also be registered under the 1933 Act.

Mutual funds have surpassed pension funds as the largest segment of financial intermediaries in the U.S. capital markets and hold 22.6% of corporate equities as of 2018.[84] Yet, mutual funds are subject to special rules regarding their ability to invest in equity securities. An investment company must choose whether it is a "diversified" or "nondiversified" mutual fund, with the vast majority choosing the former. If a mutual fund is "diversified," it must invest its assets in specified ways—with 75% of its assets being in cash, similarly liquid assets, or other securities, and with limits on the amount the fund can invest in the securities of any one issuer. As a practical matter, these limits severely discourage a mutual fund from investing more than 5% of its assets in a single stock or owning more than 10% of an issuer's outstanding stock.

Congress similarly sought to discourage mutual funds from utilizing undue leverage. Toward that end, it prohibited mutual funds from making purchases of securities on margin, selling securities short, or investing more than a small percentage of their assets in other investment companies.[85] These limitations significantly affect how mutual funds invest—they buy long (and not short), avoid leverage, and do not take significant equity positions in any one security. Additionally, as diversified investors, they are less likely to become involved in the corporate governance of a portfolio company because they are unlikely to significantly benefit if they own only a small percentage of its stock.

b. Pension Funds. Pension funds are closely regulated by federal law, chiefly the Employee Retirement Income Security Act of 1974 ("ERISA"). ERISA broadly preempts state fiduciary duty obligations, and in the case of defined benefit plans, it requires a fund to be reasonably diversified.[86] Again, as with diversified mutual funds, this is likely to chill the willingness of a pension fund to hold a large number of shares in any single issuer, and broad diversification invites passivity.

Nonetheless, in recent decades, pension funds have increased their investments in equity securities, from 26% of their assets in 1980 to 47.3% in 2019.[87] Public pension funds, in particular, have organized a series of well-known shareholder rebellions, supporting proxy fights and serving as lead plaintiffs in class action litigation. Why this difference? In some instances, due to the size of a pension fund's holdings and the

---

[84] See Kolchin, SIFMA Insights: Q: Who Owns Stock in America A: Individual Investors 14 (Oct. 2019).

[85] See §§ 12(a) and (d) of the 1940 Act.

[86] See 29 U.S.C. § 1104(a)(1) (defining prudent man standard). See also In re Unisys Sav. Plan Litig., 74 F.3d 420, 438 (3d Cir. 1996).

[87] See Gillers, Public Pension Plans Continue to Shift Into U.S. Stocks, Wall St. J. (Nov. 5, 2019); Clowes, The Money Flood: How Pension Funds Revolutionized Investing at 5–6 (2000).

publicity around its proposals, it may be seen as a low-cost means to focus pressure on management and build shareholder support for a takeover of the company. In the case of public pension funds, some argue that political pressures drive activist proposals that benefit the funds' managers, some of whom are elected officials, but may have little effect on (or even harm) the funds' investment performance.

c. *Hedge Funds.* A hedge fund, like a mutual fund, is an investment vehicle that holds a pool of securities (and perhaps other assets). The major difference is that hedge funds are largely unregulated. In general, so long as a hedge fund privately sells to less than 100 investors[88] or privately sells only to investors who each own not less than $5 million in investments,[89] the hedge fund escapes the obligation to register as an investment company under the 1940 Act.

For some time, the SEC sought to require hedge fund managers to register as investment advisers under the Advisers Act. Many advisers were exempt from registration as "private advisers" with only a few clients (the hedge fund, not its investors, being counted as one client). Although many advisers voluntarily registered, many did not. The Dodd-Frank Act resolved this standoff in 2010 by requiring large hedge fund managers to register with the SEC, subject to several exemptions.[90]

As institutional investors, hedge funds are unique. They can (and often do) sell short, use margin, and invest heavily in the securities of a single issuer. Since they are exempt from the 1940 Act and ERISA, they are not bound by diversification requirements, and typically they hold an undiversified portfolio.

Being exempt from the 1940 Act also permits hedge funds to pay very high performance fees to their investment managers, which would otherwise be barred. Many hedge fund managers charge their investors a standard "2% and 20%" fee—comprised of an annual fee of 2% of assets under management, plus 20% of any realized profits.

All in all, hedge funds tend to be aggressive investors since (1) they are not required to be diversified, (2) their managers benefit by receiving 20% of any realized profits, and (3) their investors expect short-term gains for the high fees they are charged. Some hedge funds specialize as "activist" investors, proactively seeking to reorganize or split-up companies they perceive to be overly diversified or underperforming. They may buy large stakes in a company, use margin and, in particular, sell short. Often, they do so in implicit (but undisclosed) groups that seek

---

[88] See § 3(c)(1) of the 1940 Act.

[89] See § 3(c)(7) of the 1940 Act. The term "qualified purchaser," which is used in this section, is defined in § 2(a)(51) of the 1940 Act.

[90] Sections 403 and 404 of the Dodd-Frank Act impose registration, record-keeping, and examination requirements on hedge fund managers, but § 410 subjects hedge fund managers with less than $100 million in assets under management to state, rather than federal, supervision. Venture capital fund advisers remain exempt from registration under § 407, and § 408 similarly exempts private fund managers with less than $150 million in assets under management in the United States.

to oust a company's managers or force a takeover. In the view of their critics, hedge funds have destabilized corporate governance, but their activism is very much a product of their unregulated status and their undiversified nature.

    d. Summary. As institutional investment has grown, institutions have not only become more active in corporate governance, they have begun to recognize that their interests may not align with those of retail investors. For example, the adoption of Regulation NMS, which prohibits trade-throughs, provided one of the first instances in which institutions lined up in opposition to retail investors, because institutions wanted the ability to buy shares in volume at prices outside the NBBO. More generally, institutions favor expansion of the private placement exemption and a greater ability to resell privately-placed securities into the public market. Major investment banks have also created special trading platforms for institutions to trade privately-placed securities from which individuals are largely excluded. (Certain rules discussed later—chiefly, Rule 144A—also distinguish between large institutions and other investors.) In a 2007 speech, the SEC's then-General Counsel characterized this process as "deretailization" and suggested it would intensify.[91] As it does, tensions between retail and institutional investors, which have never previously been significant, may grow and become more open.

B. GLOBALIZATION: CAUSES AND CONSEQUENCES

    Forty years ago, it would have been meaningless to talk about a worldwide securities market or global trading. Back then, local securities markets were protected by barriers to cross-border capital flow, currency differences, and the sheer improbability that new technologies could create functional equivalents of securities exchanges that were beyond the reach of any single regulator. Local securities exchanges were usually considered to be quasi-public entities and were protected by paternalistic governments from competitive pressure. All this changed during the 1990s.

    Change came from two different directions at the same time. First, institutional investors, particularly in the United States, recognized the need to diversify their portfolios to escape country-specific risk. They were attracted by the high rates of return in some emerging markets and the prospect that one national economy could decline while others surged; international portfolio diversification offered protection against this risk. As a result, institutional investors began investing significant portions of their portfolios in offshore investments. Second, with the fall of the Soviet Union, newly-emerging governments began to privatize national industries whose shares were transferred to the public. The scale of these programs dwarfed the local equity markets and required at

---

[91] See Cartwright, The Future of Securities Regulation (Oct. 24, 2007).

least a portion of the offering to be sold in the United States. These offerings started a broader migration of foreign companies seeking to list their securities in the U.S. market, in particular on the NYSE. As of early 2001, over 970 non-U.S. firms were listed on the NYSE, Nasdaq, or the American Stock Exchange.[92] Those numbers fell significantly between 2001 and 2010, but then slowly picked up; as of April 2020, there were 507 non-U.S. issuers listed on the NYSE alone.[93]

Why did these issuers migrate to the United States to cross-list on U.S. exchanges? Why did they later exit? The reasons vary. The entry of foreign issuers into the U.S. market may have represented a form of "bonding." That is, by subjecting themselves to public and private enforcement (by the SEC and class action plaintiffs), and by agreeing to reconcile their financial statements to U.S. generally accepted accounting principles (U.S. GAAP), foreign issuers credibly committed to making fuller and fairer disclosure—and thereby reduced their overall cost of capital.[94] European companies cross-listed their shares in the United States as one means to convert their stock into an attractive currency for stock-for-stock acquisitions of U.S. companies. In the case of emerging markets, particularly those in Latin America, trading in the shares also migrated to the United States in the wake of a cross-listing; often a substantial amount of trading in major Mexican and Brazilian stocks occurs on the NYSE, with the consequence that there is less liquidity in the local markets.

But, shortly after 2000, this migration of foreign issuers began to stall. In some measure, this resulted from passage of the Sarbanes-Oxley Act in 2002 and, more recently, the adoption of the Dodd-Frank Act in 2010, which raised regulatory costs for many issuers. Also, in some measure, this resulted from the burst of the high-tech bubble in 2000 (after which the U.S. IPO market dried up).

Beginning in 2002, foreign issuers began to find the costs of a U.S. listing dauntingly expensive, particularly the internal audit required by § 404 of the Sarbanes-Oxley Act.[95] IPOs by foreign issuers in the United States now appeared to be done elsewhere.[96] Yet, stricter regulation was not the only reason for the reversal. New U.S. regulation—most notably,

---

[92] See Gruson, Global Shares of German Corporations and their Dual Listings on the Frankfurt and New York Stock Exchanges, 22 U. Pa. J. Int'l Econ. L. 185 (2001).

[93] Current List of All Non-U.S. Issuers, NYSE, https://www.nyse.com/publicdocs/nyse/data/CurListofallStocks.pdf (last visited June 12, 2020).

[94] See Coffee, The Future As History: The Prospects for Global Convergence in Corporate Governance and Its Implications, 93 Nw. U. L. Rev. 641 (1999).

[95] See 15 U.S.C. § 7262 ("Management Assessment of Internal Controls"). Section 404, itself, does not require an audit, but only that the auditor "attest to, and report on" management's evaluation of the company's internal controls. However, in Auditing Standard No. 2, the Public Company Accounting Oversight Board determined that this attestation required an annual "audit" of internal controls. That proved to be unduly expensive for many smaller companies, as the SEC acknowledged in 2006.

[96] See Testimony of Donald Evans, Former Secretary of Commerce, Subcommittee on Capital Markets, Insurance and GSEs of the House Financial Services Committee, Apr. 6, 2006 (23 out of 25 largest IPOs in 2005 done outside the United States).

Regulation S and Rule 144A under the 1933 Act—eased the requirements for foreign issuers to sell securities to U.S. institutional investors without SEC registration. This new ability to more easily access U.S. institutional investors also lowered the relative benefit of tapping the U.S. public capital markets.

As a result, U.S. regulation of its own market is now subject to a new constraint—namely, costly regulation may encourage foreign markets to seek to attract foreign, conceivably even U.S., issuers if the SEC "over-regulates."[97] This issue has intensified as a result of the NYSE's merger with Euronext and Nasdaq's purchase of exchanges comprising Nasdaq Nordic. Such cross-border deals give both entities foreign trading platforms that may be mostly beyond the SEC's jurisdiction—perhaps a desirable outcome to the extent it creates "regulatory competition" that prunes inefficient or out-of-date regulation.[98]

Meanwhile, securities regulators around the world have sought to resist regulatory competition, instead focusing on how to harmonize their disclosure requirements to accommodate a global market. The International Organization of Securities Commissions, of which the SEC is a member, has led this effort and essentially reached international consensus on disclosure standards. Before full harmonization is possible, however, a similar agreement must be reached on accounting standards. Here, the SEC and the International Accounting Standards Committee appear to be resolving their differences, but at a slow pace.[99]

Globalization probably caused the SEC to relax (or "modernize") some standards. Rule 144A, adopted in 1991, permits foreign issuers and U.S. companies (in the case of equity, where the shares are not, when issued, of the same class as securities listed on a U.S. securities exchange) to privately sell securities to very large or sophisticated U.S. institutions, who can then trade the securities freely among themselves. This exemption from the SEC's registration requirements was motivated, in part, by a concern that U.S. institutions would go abroad to trade foreign-issued securities, thus leaving U.S. investment banks out of the transaction and potentially weakening the United States as a source of capital.

Will globalization produce a regulatory "race to the bottom" as issuers cross-list on exchanges with the least regulation? Or will it produce a "race to the top" where greater regulation assists in lowering

---

[97] This is not to concede that the potential loss of foreign issuer listings should cause the SEC to soften its regulatory stance. Arguably, the first goal of a securities regulator is to maintain investor confidence in its home market and thereby reduce the cost of capital. Maximizing foreign listings may only be a secondary consideration—but it is a consideration and thus a constraint.

[98] See Romano, Empowering Investors: A Market Approach to Securities Regulation, 107 Yale L. J. 2359 (1998); Choi & Guzman, Portable Reciprocity: Rethinking the International Reach of Securities Regulation, 71 S. Cal. L. Rev. 903 (1998).

[99] See White, A U.S. Imperative: High-Quality, Globally Accepted Accounting Standards (Jan. 5, 2017), https://www.sec.gov/news/statement/white-2016-01-05.html.

an issuer's cost of capital? The evidence is mixed, although there is some evidence that shows firms to be migrating to exchanges with the highest listing and disclosure standards to reduce their cost of capital and achieve other goals.[100]

No longer willing to accept SEC leadership on all policy issues (particularly following the 2008 financial crisis), regulators in the major securities markets have increasingly called for a common policy known as "mutual recognition."[101] Essentially, this policy mandates that the supervision of a financial institution should be left mainly to its home jurisdiction regulator, without other regulators seeking to impose additional rules or requirements. The rise of the internet was one of the first forces to push regulators toward such a policy because statements posted on a website can be seen worldwide and yet no such statement can feasibly comply with the often-conflicting rules of all jurisdictions. The SEC has shown some willingness to move in this direction, but how far it will or should move remains uncertain.[102]

C. Restructuring the Financial Services Industry: Deregulation and Reconsideration

For decades, banks, securities firms, and insurance companies were legislatively separated—legally unable to own or engage in the core activities of the others. Two principal statutes enforced this separation: the Glass-Steagall Act (a common name for certain provisions of the Banking Act of 1933), which denied banks the ability to underwrite securities, and the Bank Holding Act of 1956, which effectively separated banks from insurance companies. Although the Board of Governors of the Federal Reserve System ("Federal Reserve Board") gradually relaxed many of the prohibitions after 1980, full convergence among banks, securities firms, and insurance companies was not possible without legislative action. On at least ten different occasions, Congress considered legislation that would have removed or modified these restrictions. Yet, for a variety of reasons, each attempt failed—until the passage of the Financial Services Modernization Act of 1999 (also known as the "Gramm-Leach-Bliley Act" or "GLB") in late 1999. Congress reconsidered the wisdom of some of these steps after the 2008 financial crisis, and while not a retreat, the Dodd-Frank Act again imposes limits on risk-taking by systemically significant financial institutions.

---

[100] See Jackson & Pan, Regulatory Competition in International Securities Markets: Evidence from Europe in 1999—Part I, 56 Bus. Law. 653 (2001).

[101] In its recent Blueprint for reorganizing U.S. financial regulation, the Treasury Department defined "mutual recognition" as a policy "whereby financial intermediaries registered or supervised in a foreign jurisdiction are permitted access to U.S. markets without registering in the United States." See Treasury Department, Blueprint for a Modernized Financial Regulatory Structure 109 (2008). The Blueprint noted that the CFTC has followed this policy since the 1980s, but the SEC was only "considering" it.

[102] For an optimistic vision of the degree to which the SEC might defer to other regulators, see Tafara & Peterson, A Blueprint for Cross-Border Access to U.S. Investors: A New International Framework, 48 Harv. Int'l L. J. 31 (2007).

a. *Downsizing the Glass-Steagall Act.* Despite earlier failures, the passage of GLB reflected a sense that market developments already had outflanked many of the Glass-Steagall Act's restrictions, which seemed antiquated, and a newly-dominant view that financial convergence was desirable. The Glass-Steagall Act was a product of the Great Depression and the then-prevailing belief that involving banks in securities transactions had contributed to the severity of the 1929 stock market crash and the ensuing massive bank insolvencies. Although revisionist historians have increasingly challenged these assumptions, GLB incorporated several safeguards and procedures that showed continuing Congressional concern about banks straying too far from their traditional activities.

Essentially, GLB did the following: It repealed the restrictions on banks affiliating with companies that are "principally engaged" in securities underwriting; it authorized a new entity—a "financial holding company"—to engage in a list of financial activities, including insurance and securities underwriting; and it permitted financial holding companies to engage in "merchant banking," which meant they could hold equity stakes (including controlling positions) in non-financial firms.

GLB also preserved the existing system of "functional regulation" by mandating that most securities activities by a broker-dealer be overseen by the SEC; most insurance activities, by state insurance commissions; and most banking activities, by the Comptroller of the Currency, the Federal Reserve Board, or state banking agencies. As the Treasury Department concluded in its 2008 Blueprint,[103] the net result was a fragmented system of financial regulation with a different regulator for each category of institution. In retrospect, GLB may have failed in not allocating to any regulator the authority to supervise the broker-dealers' holding companies. This failure enabled the holding companies to significantly increase their leverage (their debt to equity ratios) after 2005, which appears to have contributed to the insolvency of several investment banks during the 2008 financial crisis.[104]

D. THE PROBLEM OF SYSTEMIC RISK

No sooner had the Glass-Steagall Act been repealed than the Enron scandal broke, resulting in enactment of the Sarbanes-Oxley Act. The subprime mortgage crisis followed, leading in 2010 to passage of the Dodd-Frank Act. These developments caused many to reconsider the wisdom of Glass-Steagall's repeal. Critics argued that the repeal enabled

---

[103] See The Department of Treasury, Blueprint for a Modernized Financial Regulatory Structure (2008).

[104] This is the conclusion that SEC Chairman Christopher Cox expressed to a Senate Committee in September 2008. See Testimony of Chairman Christopher Cox before the Committee on Banking, Housing and Urban Affairs, United States Senate, Sept. 23, 2008, at p. 4.

large financial institutions, acting as both investment and commercial banks, to structure and finance off-balance sheet transactions that were fraudulent or, at the least, denied full disclosure to public investors. They further claimed these questionable transactions were the product of conflicts of interest the Glass-Steagall Act would have precluded.[105] Others answered that the financial institutions that failed in 2008 belonged to the "shadow banking" sector that, in the first place, had been carved away from traditional banks by the Glass-Steagall Act. Thus, the argument went, the Glass-Steagall Act was just as likely to have been a cause of the financial crisis. The Dodd-Frank Act, in any event, did not reinstate the Glass-Steagall Act, but in several important respects, it did follow the Glass-Steagall Act's philosophy by restricting bank holding companies from engaging in activities deemed to be excessively risky.

In this light, it is useful to ask: What were the policies underlying the Glass-Steagall Act? Justice Stewart reviewed the legislative history of the Act in Investment Co. Institute v. Camp.[106] Congress foresaw three categories of hazards that might arise through the mixing of commercial and investment banking. First, the involvement of commercial banks in investment banking and securities activities might lead to the making of unsound loans and investments. Such loans might be made to companies of dubious credit, in whose stock the securities affiliate had invested, to bail out these firms or at least make their stock appear more attractive. Loans might also be made to customers to facilitate the purchase of securities, thereby encouraging speculation. Second, there was thought to be a danger of loss of public confidence in the commercial bank because of its association with an entity engaged in the high-risk activity of investment banking. In *Camp*, the Court noted that "pressures are created because the bank and the affiliate are closely associated in the public mind, and should the affiliate fare badly, public confidence in the bank might be impaired." Finally, the conflict between the promotional interests of the investment banker and the "obligation of the commercial banker to render disinterested investment advice" might lead to the bank's violation of its fiduciary responsibilities. Justice Stewart pointed out: "Congress had before it evidence that security affiliates might be driven to unload excessive holdings through the trust department of the sponsor bank."[107] Such fear of "unloading" shaky securities on customers (for example, by dumping stocks underwritten by the securities affiliate into accounts managed by the bank's trust department) particularly

---

[105] See Fanto, Subtle Hazards Revisited: The Corruption of a Financial Holding Company by a Corporate Client's Inner Circle, 70 Brook. L. Rev. 7, 8 (2004) (discussing how the entry of commercial banks into investment banking creates conflicts of interests that could lead to catastrophic failure).

[106] 401 U.S. 617, 629–34 (1971).

[107] Id. at 633 (citing Hearings Before a Subcomm. of the Senate Comm. on Banking and Currency, 71st Cong., 3d Sess., on the Operation of National and Federal Reserve banking systems, pursuant to S. Res. 71, at 237).

motivated Congress, which believed it saw evidence of such self-dealing by large banks during the 1920s.[108]

Whatever the basis for the Glass-Steagall Act's separation of commercial from investment banking, the 2008 financial crisis provided new evidence that large financial institutions could behave irresponsibly, and Congress acted on that perception by enacting the Dodd-Frank Act. As The Financial Crisis Inquiry Report, prepared by the Financial Crisis Inquiry Commission, found:

> We conclude a combination of excessive borrowing, risky investments, and lack of transparency put the system on a collision course with crisis.[109]

It added:

> In the years leading up to the crisis, too many financial institutions, as well as too many households, borrowed to the hilt, leaving them vulnerable to financial distress or ruin if the value of their investments declined even modestly. For example, as of 2007, the five major investment banks—Bear Stearns, Goldman Sachs, Lehman Brothers, Merrill Lynch, and Morgan Stanley—were operating with extraordinarily thin capital. By one measure, their leverage ratios were as high as 40 to 1, meaning for every $40 in assets there was only $1 in capital to cover losses. Less than a 3% drop in asset values could wipe out the firm. To make matters worse, much of their borrowing was short-term in the overnight market—meaning the borrowing had to be renewed each and every day.[110]

Because the five major investment banks were, at the time, regulated by the SEC, the conclusion is an overt critique of the SEC's performance as a monitor during the period leading up to the crisis.[111]

Responding to the concern that excessive leverage and a decline in financial discipline caused the 2008 crisis, the Dodd-Frank Act seeks to restrict the risk levels of large financial institutions. Among other things, it enacted a provision known as the "Volcker Rule," which restricted large financial institutions from engaging in proprietary trading or sponsoring

---

[108] Academics have been more skeptical about the purposes of the Glass-Steagall Act. Some believe it was intended to redirect the banking industry back to its traditional role as a supplier of commercial credit, while others argue it was purely the product of a clash of interest groups. Compare Langevoort, Statutory Obsolescence and the Judicial Process: The Revisionist Role of the Courts in Federal Banking Regulation, 85 Mich.L.Rev. 672, 716–17 (1987), with Macey, Special Interest Groups Legislation and the Judicial Function: The Dilemma of Glass-Steagall, 33 Emory L.J. 1, 4 (1984).

[109] See The Financial Crisis Inquiry Commission, The Financial Crisis Inquiry Report xix (2010).

[110] Id.

[111] Elsewhere, two of the authors of this casebook have attributed the SEC's poor performance to rapid deregulation and excessive confidence in self-regulation. See Coffee & Sale, Redesigning the SEC: Does the Treasury Have a Better Idea?, 95 Va. L. Rev. 707 (2009).

hedge funds.¹¹² The Volcker Rule was later amended, and many of its provisions were pulled back, but essentially it reflected a strategy—much like that underlying the Glass-Steagall Act—to confine commercial banks to less-risky activities.

The Dodd-Frank Act also rested on some fundamental assumptions about what caused financial institutions to race to higher leverage. First, it attributed much of the motivation to an excessively short-term system of executive compensation. Thus, The Financial Crisis Inquiry Report found:

> Compensation systems—designed in an environment of cheap money, intense competition, and light regulation—too often rewarded the quick deal. Often those systems encouraged the big bet—when the payoff on the upside could be huge and the downside limited.¹¹³

Second, the Dodd-Frank Act was premised on the view that the credit market perceived large financial institutions to be "too big to fail" and thus loaned funds to them at reduced rates in the belief that an implicit government guarantee protected them. As a result, large financial institutions could borrow more cheaply than their actual risk levels justified, and they did so excessively.

In response, the Dodd-Frank Act sought to dispel the market's faith in implicit government guarantees by restricting the powers of the Federal Reserve Board and the Federal Deposit Insurance Corporation to advance funds to troubled financial institutions (instead requiring that they be liquidated). The net result was less discretion on the part of the federal government to act as a lender of last resort—limiting the implicit government guarantee, but increasing the risk of panic if a major financial institution begins to totter on the brink of insolvency.¹¹⁴

E. THE ROLE OF GATEKEEPERS

The capital markets have long employed "gatekeepers"—independent professionals who pledge their "reputational capital" to protect the interests of dispersed investors who cannot easily take collective action themselves.¹¹⁵ Two key elements underlie the concept of a gatekeeper. First, a gatekeeper often has significant reputational capital, acquired over many years of performing similar services for numerous clients, which it pledges to assure the accuracy of the

---

[112] The Volcker Rule (named after Paul Volcker, the former chairman of the Federal Reserve Board, who suggested the rule) was codified in § 619 of the Dodd-Frank Act.

[113] See The Financial Crisis Inquiry Commission, The Financial Crisis Inquiry Report xix (2010).

[114] For a more complete discussion of this problem under the Dodd-Frank Act, see Coffee, Systemic Risk After Dodd-Frank: Contingent Capital and the Need for Regulatory Strategies Beyond Oversight, 111 Colum. L. Rev. 795 (2011).

[115] See Coffee, Gatekeepers: The Professions and Corporate Governance 2 (2006).

statements it makes or verifies.[116] Second, the gatekeeper receives a far smaller benefit for its role in verifying information than does the principal in the transaction the gatekeeper facilitates, and in some cases, the gatekeeper may be exposed to substantial legal liability for failing to fulfill its responsibilities adequately.[117]

To illustrate, suppose the founders of an early-stage company plan to undertake an IPO. They can expect a substantial increase in the value of their shareholdings, perhaps in the hundreds of millions of dollars, if the IPO is successful. Consequently, they have powerful incentives to present their company in the most favorable light possible—and even to misrepresent material facts in the company's registration statement filed with the SEC. By contrast, the firm's auditors expect a much smaller payoff (their audit fees and other fees as part of the IPO process) and have considerable reputational capital at risk. Moreover, the auditors face legal liability for any material misstatement or omission in the company's audited financial statements. Thus, gatekeepers are easier to deter—they are much more likely than the founders to cast an objective (and, perhaps, critical) eye on the company's disclosures as part of the offering process.

Consequently, the more the law makes the involvement of a gatekeeper mandatory, the more it enhances deterrence by a necessary actor whose compliance with the law it can more effectively influence. In addition to auditors, examples of gatekeepers include the credit rating agency that assigns a rating that reflects the issuer's or its securities' relative creditworthiness; the investment bank that provides a "fairness opinion" about the terms of an acquisition; and the law firm that issues a letter to the underwriters stating that nothing has come to its attention to cause it to believe there is a material misstatement or omission in the issuer's registration statement. The underwriters in a public offering are also gatekeepers in the sense that their reputations are implicitly pledged in support of the issuer and its securities. In each case, the market recognizes that the gatekeeper has a lower incentive to deceive than its client (even if it is the client who pays the gatekeeper's fees) and thus regards the gatekeeper's evaluation as more credible.

Nevertheless, during the late 1990s, gatekeeping seemingly failed in the wake of a series of financial scandals, all involving accounting irregularities. And leading up to the 2008 financial crisis, the gatekeepers again seemed to be asleep at their posts, permitting billions of dollars of securities to be issued that received an investment grade rating from the credit rating agencies based on pools of shaky subprime mortgages and related instruments.

What caused these scandals? Notwithstanding the theory of gatekeeping, the reality is that gatekeepers may change how they assess

---

[116] See id.
[117] See id. at 4–5.

relative harm and benefit. For example, the perceived risk of loss of reputational capital may decline, or the inducements offered to gatekeepers to breach their duties may increase, resulting in a greater willingness to take legal risk. Circumstances may also arise that cause the value of reputational capital to decline.[118] In addition, principal-agent problems can arise within gatekeeper firms, with the result that agents can rationally decide to risk the firm's reputational capital to a degree the firm as a whole would not.[119] Consequently, gatekeepers may sometimes acquiesce in managerial fraud, even though the apparent losses seem to dwarf the gains to be made from the individual client.

These reasons partly explain what occurred during the late 1990s and early 2000s. Take the case of Arthur Andersen, one of the largest public accounting firms in the 1990s, which got caught up in a series of accounting scandals that caused its fall in 2002. In theory, Arthur Andersen should not have acquiesced in any accounting irregularity because it had thousands of clients, each of whom paid fees that were modest in proportion to the firm's current and future revenues, but all of whom were attracted by Arthur Andersen's considerable reputational capital. Nevertheless, the 1990s were a period when accounting restatements were on the rise (one indication of widespread irregularities), several statutes were passed and cases decided that lowered potential legal liability, accounting firm revenues (from cross-selling services to audit clients) were significantly growing, and in a rising stock market, gatekeepers became less relevant and the value of their reputational capital declined.[120] These weaknesses, and the resulting gatekeeper failures, prompted the introduction of greater regulatory oversight through the Sarbanes-Oxley Act (described later in this chapter).

Similar factors influenced how credit rating agencies functioned during the period up to the 2008 financial crisis. No doubt, the credit rating agencies were not the only ones precipitating the crisis. However, for many large investors, an investment grade rating was a prerequisite to investing in subprime mortgage-backed securities, giving the rating agencies a significant lever over securitization activities at the root of the financial crisis. The broad perception was that rating agencies failed to conduct adequate due diligence on the securities they rated and recklessly provided ratings that failed to reflect the real risks of the securities that were sold. Like Arthur Andersen, the rating agencies should not have acquiesced to the inflated ratings. However, the securitization sponsors paid substantial fees to the rating agencies, the two principal rating agencies (Standard & Poor's and Moody's) competed for the same business (and so had an incentive to provide more favorable

---

[118] See id. at 67–69.
[119] See id. at 64–67.
[120] See Coffee, Gatekeeper Failure and Reform: The Challenge of Fashioning Relevant Reforms, 84 B.U.L.Rev. 301, 318–30 (2004).

ratings), and in some cases, rating agency employees aspired to join the investment banks that sponsored the securitizations they were asked to rate.[121] Like Arthur Andersen, the result was a weakened gatekeeping function that prompted legislative change in the Dodd-Frank Act (also discussed later in this chapter).

Gatekeepers continue to play significant roles in the capital markets. Yet, the problems that arose during the late 1990s and early 2000s illustrate the social cost of gatekeeper failure. Relying on reputational capital alone may not be sufficient. The question, going forward, is to what degree new statutes and regulations should begin to shape the gatekeeping function. Enhancing authority, and perhaps increasing liability, may be one approach—but attempts to fine tune the calculus around gatekeepers will continue to be at the forefront of capital markets regulation.

F. DECLINE IN IPOs

The U.S. IPO market has been steadily declining since the early 2000s. As noted before, part of this trend may reflect the increased burden placed on public companies by the Sarbanes-Oxley Act and the Dodd-Frank Act, and part may reflect the benefits of Regulation S and Rule 144A (and the declining value of accessing the U.S. public capital markets). In 2017, $1.5 trillion was raised through public offerings ($51.6 billion through IPOs) compared to over $3 trillion raised through private placements, more than 95% of which was under Regulation D (which includes a private placement exemption from SEC registration) and Rule 144A.[122]

Public offerings have always been expensive, but the Sarbanes-Oxley Act raised those costs considerably. For companies looking to go public, the Sarbanes-Oxley Act's requirements translate into a need for additional personnel, outside consultants, improvements in internal compliance systems, and heightened reporting—all of which raise the cost of going and remaining public. The Act also increased the potential for civil and criminal liability for directors and officers of the issuer. Its requirements were particularly burdensome for smaller firms that had limited resources to begin with. Perhaps, as a result, smaller IPOs declined sharply in 2002, the year in which the Sarbanes-Oxley Act was enacted.

More recently, the Dodd-Frank Act also increased the cost of being a public company in the United States. For example, Title IX of the Act authorized the SEC to adopt rules giving shareholders an advisory vote

---

[121] See Black, Whitehead & Coupland, The Nonprime Mortgage Crisis and Positive Feedback Lending, 3 J. L. Fin. & Acctg. 1 (2018).

[122] See Bauguess et al., Capital Raising in the U.S.: An Analysis of the Market for Unregistered Securities Offerings, 2009–2017 8 (Aug. 2018).

on executive compensation and golden parachutes.[123] Independence standards were also created for members of a public company's compensation committee,[124] and special disclosures were required about the relationship between executive compensation and the company's financial performance.[125]

The possible higher cost of an IPO is not the only explanation for a decline in IPOs. As explained later, economists have argued that start-ups typically receive a much higher price in the acquisition market than in the IPO market. Why? They find that larger, established companies will pay much more for a start-up firm than IPO investors due to synergies with their existing businesses. For example, strategic buyers can market a start-up's products globally, while the start-up cannot afford to leap to a global scale on its own. Symptomatically, many smaller IPOs have been unprofitable, and underwriters have become leary.

At the same time, Regulation D and Rule 144A have become increasingly popular alternatives to public offerings. First, Rule 144A allows issuers to access a majority of the IPO market without the delay or expense of SEC registration and with greater flexibility regarding what to disclose to prospective investors. "Qualified institutional buyers" (comprised mostly of large, sophisticated institutions, known as "QIBs"), who purchase in Rule 144A offerings, constitute 80% of the IPO market. Second, the rise of new trading platforms has enhanced the liquidity of secondary trading in securities sold pursuant to Regulation D and Rule 144A. Brokerage firms specialize in matching buyers and sellers of stock in privately-held companies, most notably, the Nasdaq Private Market that set a new annual record of $4.8 billion in transaction value in 2019.[126] In addition, the PORTAL ("Private Offering, Resale and Trading Through Automated Linkages") Alliance trades only securities that qualify under Rule 144A, adding a higher level of liquidity to the private placement process. Increasing liquidity reduced the discount that companies previously suffered when selling securities through a private placement.

The result has been a blurring of the line between public and private offerings. As selling securities in the private markets has become less costly, the calculus that favored going public thirty years ago has shifted. Greater costs in going and remaining public, along with the relative ease of a private placement, have increasingly pushed firms away from the

---

[123] See § 951 of the Dodd-Frank Act (adding § 14A to the 1934 Act). See Securities Act Release No. 9178 (Jan. 2011). A golden parachute is an agreement by a company to accelerate the vesting of an executive's benefits (such as stock options) and pay certain other benefits (such as a severance bonus) in the event of a change of control where the executive is terminated or demoted without cause.

[124] See § 952 of the Dodd-Frank Act (adding § 10C to the 1934 Act). See Securities Act Release No. 9330 (June 2012).

[125] See § 953(a) of the Dodd-Frank Act (amending § 14(i) of the 1934 Act).

[126] See Briganti, Nasdaq Private Market Sets New Annual Transaction Record in 2019, Nasdaq (Feb. 2020), http://ir.nasdaq.com/news-releases/news-release-details/nasdaq-private-market-sets-new-annual-transaction-record-2019 (last visited June 17, 2020).

IPO market. The trend is likely to continue as the SEC considers additional ways to ease restrictions in the private markets.

4. THE REGULATORY FRAMEWORK

a. Introduction. Financial regulation in the United States has long been organized along functional lines with a different regulator for each class of financial institution. In addition, the U.S.'s federalist structure enables many financial institutions to elect whether to be regulated at the state or federal level. This combination of a functional approach and federalism has resulted in a fragmented regulatory structure. For example, before the 2008 financial crisis, five agencies at the federal level shared regulatory and examination authority over banks and similar depository institutions: the Office of the Controller of the Currency; the Federal Reserve Board; the Federal Deposit Insurance Corporation ("FDIC"); the Office of Thrift Supervision ("OTS"); and the National Credit Union Administration. The Dodd-Frank Act eliminated only one of these agencies (the OTS), and it failed to combine the SEC and the CFTC (as the Treasury Department proposed in 2008). As investment banks failed or were acquired by commercial banks in the wake of 2008, the financial industry moved toward greater consolidation under the banks' regulators. Nevertheless, the Dodd-Frank Act left the fragmented regulatory structure largely intact.

This pattern of fragmented regulation is much less common outside the United States. Some (but not all) countries have a unified financial regulator, which has authority over the banking, insurance, securities, and investment advisory industries, as well as pension funds. Other countries (Australia and the Netherlands being leading examples) follow a "twin peaks" model that has one agency to monitor the safety and soundness of financial institutions and another to supervise their business conduct and assure investor protection. This bifurcated structure reflects the concern that a completely unified agency may give undue attention to protecting financial solvency at the expense of investor protection.[127]

Authority to oversee and regulate the securities markets is even more fragmented than in the banking industry. Partly for historical reasons, and partly because of the U.S.'s federal structure, authority over the securities industry is shared among three levels of regulators: the SEC, a federal administrative agency established by the 1934 Act; self-regulatory organizations ("SROs"), including the stock exchanges but of

---

[127] For example, a liberal litigation remedy permitting injured investors to sue underwriters and broker-dealers may work at odds with the goal of ensuring the financial soundness of the institutions that would be defendants in this litigation. Note that, for similar reasons, Title X of the Dodd-Frank Act established the Consumer Financial Protection Bureau, whose purpose is "to implement and, where applicable, enforce Federal consumer financial law consistently for the purpose of ensuring that all consumers have access to markets for consumer financial products and services and that markets for consumer financial products and services are fair, transparent, and competitive."

which the most important is FINRA, to which virtually all broker-dealers are required by law to belong; and state securities commissioners or other state officials who enforce state securities statutes popularly known as "blue sky laws." Even this description is incomplete because the United States also distinguishes between "securities" and "futures" and assigns the regulation of the latter to the CFTC, which is an independent federal administrative agency modeled along the same lines as the SEC. No other country makes this distinction between securities and futures. Compounding these line-drawing problems, the Dodd-Frank Act now divides swaps between these same two agencies, giving "security-based swaps" to the SEC and other swaps to the CFTC.

Dividing regulation along functional lines has been in place for decades, but it has been increasingly criticized for producing a slow and balkanized regulatory system that detracts from the competitiveness of the U.S. capital markets. In 2008, the Treasury Department proposed to consolidate most of the financial regulators, opting for a "twin peaks" model that separated prudential supervision from business conduct regulation and investor protection.[128] But the Treasury's "blueprint" for reform did not convince Congress (and, in any event, was presented on the eve of the 2008 financial crisis).

b. *Securities and Exchange Commission.* The SEC is an independent non-partisan agency created by the 1934 Act that is charged with administering and enforcing the federal securities laws. Above all, the SEC's primary responsibilities are to ensure the securities markets are fair and honest and provide investors with adequate disclosure. Organizationally, the Commission is comprised of five members: a Chairman and four Commissioners. Commission members are appointed by the President, with the advice and consent of the Senate, for five-year terms. The President designates the Chairman. Terms are staggered; one expires on June 5th of every year. Not more than three members may be of the same political party. Although the President appoints SEC Commissioners, the President may not remove a Commissioner, except for good cause.

Most importantly, the SEC is the tough cop of Wall Street. Historically, the SEC has acquired a reputation for zeal, integrity, and imagination that distinguishes it from many other federal agencies. Yet, over some recent periods (in particular, the 1990s), the SEC has been chronically underfunded as the size of the market and the SEC's enforcement obligations have expanded, while its staff has remained relatively constant.

c. *Commodity Futures Trading Commission.* Created by the Commodity Futures Trading Commission Act of 1972, the CFTC was

---

[128] For a more complete discussion of the "single peak" versus "twin peaks" models, see Coffee & Sale, Redesigning the SEC: Does the Treasury Have a Better Idea?, 95 Va. L. Rev. 707 (2009); see also Treasury Department, Blueprint for a Modernized Financial Regulatory Structure (2008).

patterned closely after the SEC as an independent federal commission with five commissioners appointed by the President, with the advice and consent of the Senate, and serving similar five-year staggered terms. The Act also authorized self-regulatory associations resembling FINRA and the significant delegation of authority to the SROs.

At the time of its creation, there was little overlap between the CFTC and the SEC, as futures trading related primarily to agricultural products. Thus, the CFTC was overseen by the Agriculture Committees of the House and Senate. Then, in 1975, the CFTC approved its first futures trading on financial assets. Trading in these contracts proved immensely popular, because they enabled companies to hedge interest rate risk.

This expansion in futures trading beyond agricultural products and other commodities produced friction with the SEC. Potentially, anything traded as a future could be traded as an option (which is a security), and vice versa. In 1981, the SEC and the CFTC negotiated an agreement that allocated jurisdiction between them and precluded (at least for the next twenty years) trading in single-stock futures and narrow-based stock indexes (because the SEC feared such products could be used to engage in insider trading that would be beyond the scope of the federal securities laws).[129]

    d.   Organization of the SEC. Internally, the SEC is organized into five principal divisions and several important advisory offices:

The Division of Corporation Finance has overall responsibility for assessing whether the 1933 Act's disclosure requirements are met by issuers who file a registration statement with the SEC. Much of its work involves reviewing (i) registration statements for public offerings, (ii) quarterly, annual, and other reports by public companies, (iii) proxy statements, and (iv) tender offer documents and related filings in mergers and acquisitions. It also has primary responsibility for rendering administrative interpretations of the 1933 Act and its rules and regulations.

The Division of Trading and Markets oversees the secondary trading markets, including the registration and performance of stock exchanges, ATSs, ECNs, broker-dealers, and other participants in these markets (such as transfer agents and clearing organizations).

The Division of Investment Management has special responsibility for mutual funds and investment advisers (and, more recently, public utilities). It reviews their financial responsibility, sales practices, advertising, and compliance with SEC rules.

---

[129] The prohibition on single-stock futures and narrow-based stock indexes was repealed by The Commodity Futures Modernization Act of 2000, which established a system of "coordinated regulation" between the SEC and CFTC to prohibit insider trading through the medium of futures or swaps.

The Division of Enforcement is charged with investigating possible violations of the federal securities laws and, when authorized by the Commission, undertaking enforcement actions, either by way of administrative proceedings or by seeking injunctions and civil penalties in federal court. Although it may cooperate with the Department of Justice and various U.S. Attorney's Offices, the SEC itself does not have the authority to commence criminal prosecutions.

Finally, the Division of Economic and Risk Analysis is the SEC's newest division, handling cost/benefit analyses for the Commission as part of its policy-making, rule-making, enforcement, and examination functions. As described below, recent court decisions have mandated such analyses and found the SEC's early attempts to be wanting.

Apart from these five main divisions, the SEC is comprised of several other offices. For example, the Office of the General Counsel provides legal advice and represents the Commission in appellate litigation. Often, it plays a significant role in the formulation of new policies within the Commission. The Office of International Affairs focuses on advancing international regulatory and enforcement cooperation, including the adoption of regulatory standards worldwide. And the Office of the Chief Accountant is responsible for accounting policies and most other matters relating to the form and content of financial information filed with the SEC. Through Regulation S–X and its Accounting Series Releases and Financial Reporting Releases, this office establishes the financial reporting requirements applicable to the federal securities laws.[130]

The SEC administers six statutes that comprise the federal securities laws: the Securities Act of 1933, the Securities Exchange Act of 1934, the Public Utility Holding Company Act of 1935 ("Public Utility Holding Company Act" or "PUHCA"), the Trust Indenture Act of 1939 ("Trust Indenture Act" or "TIA"), the Investment Company Act of 1940, and the Investment Advisers Act of 1940. Other statutes—most notably the Sarbanes-Oxley Act, the Dodd-Frank Act, and the Jumpstart Our Business Startups Act ("JOBS Act")—were enacted mainly in response to recent scandals, the 2008 financial crisis, and related developments, and most (but not all) of their provisions amended and expanded the scope and orientation of the 1934 Act.

The principal statutes covered in this casebook are the 1933 Act and the 1934 Act (although we touch on the other four statutes in our brief summaries below).

---

[130] Although the SEC has authority under the 1934 Act to promulgate its own accounting standards, it has long deferred to U.S. generally accepted accounting principles (U.S. GAAP) which today are set by the Financial Accounting Standards Board. U.S. "generally accepted auditing standards" (U.S. GAAS), in turn, are set by the American Institute of Certified Public Accountants. This practice of deference to the accounting profession was formally acknowledged in Accounting Series Release No. 150 (1973). See also Arthur Andersen & Co. v. SEC, [1978 Transfer Binder] Fed.Sec.L.Rep. (CCH) ¶ 96,374 (N.D.Ill. 1978) (deference to industry found not to represent unlawful delegation to a private body).

e. *1933 Act*. This casebook focuses principally on the 1933 Act. Essentially, absent an exemption, the Act prohibits the offer of a security unless a registration statement covering that security has been filed with the SEC, and it prohibits the sale of a security unless an SEC-filed registration statement covering that security is in effect. It also requires the delivery of a prospectus to a purchaser and to other persons to whom a written offer is made (although, as will be seen, this requirement has mostly been relaxed). Very favorable litigation remedies are given to purchasers of securities if the registration statement contains a material misstatement or omission (see § 11 of the 1933 Act) or if other material misstatements or omissions, including oral ones, are made by a seller (see § 12(a)(2) of the 1933 Act).

f. *1934 Act*. The 1934 Act covers far broader terrain than the 1933 Act. Public companies must enter the SEC's continuous disclosure system and file annual, quarterly, and other reports with the SEC. Pursuant to the 1934 Act, they must also distribute proxy statements before soliciting shareholder proxies or votes. Under § 15 of the 1934 Act, virtually all broker-dealers must register with the SEC, which has very broad rulemaking powers to define and proscribe the practices of broker-dealers it considers to be a "manipulative, deceptive, or other fraudulent device or contrivance" (see § 15(c)). In addition, the 1934 Act gives the SEC the authority to oversee the stock exchanges, ATSs, ECNs, as well as FINRA (the principal SRO for broker-dealers). Also, §§ 7 and 8 of the 1934 Act regulate the credit available to purchase securities—known as "margin"—by authorizing the Federal Reserve Board to establish limits on the amount of credit that can be extended in connection with a securities purchase.

The 1934 Act has been amended frequently; indeed, it has become the Christmas tree on which Congress regularly hangs new amendments. Notable examples include the Williams Act, passed in 1968, which amended how tender offers and other control acquisitions are regulated. Another amendment established the Securities Investor Protection Corporation, an analog to the FDIC, as one means to limit investor losses if their brokerage firm becomes insolvent. Additionally, in 1977, § 30A was added to the 1934 Act by the Foreign Corrupt Practices Act, which prohibits bribery, both foreign and domestic, and requires public firms to maintain internal accounting controls.

g. *Sarbanes-Oxley Act*. The Sarbanes-Oxley Act was passed in 2002, in the wake of the Enron, WorldCom, and other corporate scandals that highlighted accounting and financial reporting irregularities by major public corporations. In response, the 1934 Act was amended in a far-reaching effort to improve financial reporting by public companies, impose tighter oversight over the accounting profession, and regulate some areas of corporate governance that had been previously left to the states.

To do this, the Sarbanes-Oxley Act, among other things: created a self-regulatory body (the Public Company Accounting Oversight Board, also known as "PCAOB") to regulate the accounting profession, restricted consulting and other services an audit firm can provide the companies it audits to minimize conflicts of interest, and sought to increase auditor independence; directed the PCAOB to adopt auditing, quality control, ethics, independence, and other standards relating to the preparation of audit reports; and required the PCAOB to conduct compliance inspections of registered audit firms, and authorized the PCAOB to impose sanctions and levy fines.

The Sarbanes-Oxley Act also included some corporate governance provisions, including requiring a public company to have independent directors and an independent audit committee; imposing on a public company's lawyers a duty to disclose fraud or other misconduct to the company's officers or, if they failed to act "appropriately," to its audit committee, independent directors, or board as a whole; and requiring CEOs and CFOs of reporting companies to provide a prescribed certification of their company's financial statements, with enhanced criminal sanctions for certifications that are knowingly false.

In addition, the Act instructed the SEC to promulgate rules governing the independence and objectivity of securities analysts and protecting analysts from retaliation by their firms because of negative research or ratings.[131]

h. *Dodd-Frank Act.* Passed in 2010, the Dodd-Frank Act contains a potpourri of provisions, but its principal focus is on consumer protection (including the creation of the Consumer Financial Protection Bureau) and reducing the systemic risk of large financial institutions, while also averting the future public bailout of these institutions. Those of the Act's provisions that mostly relate to the capital markets are summarized below.

To reduce systemic risk, Title I of the Dodd-Frank Act created the Financial Stability Oversight Council ("FSOC") to monitor and regulate potential threats to the financial system, especially those posed by major financial firms (including non-bank institutions, such as broker-dealers) that are "too big to fail." The chairs of the SEC and the CFTC are members of the FSOC, which is chaired by the Secretary of the Treasury.

Title II established a procedure to liquidate systemically significant financial institutions. If the Treasury Secretary (after consulting with the President and other regulators) determines that liquidation of the institution is needed to mitigate the risk of serious adverse effect on U.S. financial stability, the Secretary may appoint the FDIC as receiver to liquidate the financial institution in a manner that mitigates that risk.

---

[131] Among other things, the SEC enacted Regulation AC, requiring broker-dealers to include in research reports a certification by the research analyst that the views expressed in the report accurately reflect the analyst's personal views and to disclose any compensation the analyst may have received.

Effectively, the FDIC already had this power concerning commercial banks, but the Dodd-Frank Act extended it to nonbank financial institutions, with the difference that (unlike commercial banks) no pre-funded reserve is required to be created.

To enhance consumer protection, Title IX of the Dodd-Frank Act authorized the SEC to promulgate rules that impose a common fiduciary duty on broker-dealers and investment advisers;[132] restrict pre-dispute mandatory arbitration (which was required by most agreements between broker-dealers and retail customers);[133] and adopt rules to protect whistleblowers and enhance their incentives to report securities violations.[134] In addition, the Act strengthened SEC enforcement authority by, among other things: lowering the intent standard in SEC actions against aiders and abetters of securities law violations from "knowingly" to "recklessly";[135] and authorizing broad use by the SEC of administrative proceedings before administrative law judges.[136]

Title IX also included certain corporate governance features. It authorized the SEC to adopt rules giving shareholders an advisory vote on executive compensation and golden parachutes (known as "say on pay" and "say on parachute" votes, respectively).[137] Independence standards were created for members of a public company's compensation committee,[138] and special disclosures were required about the relationship between executive compensation and the company's financial performance.[139] The SEC was also authorized to adopt rules permitting shareholders to nominate candidates for an issuer's board of directors and have such candidates listed on the issuer's own proxy materials (which would economize the costs of conducting a proxy fight and possibly give greater credibility to insurgent candidates).[140] In addition, under Title IX, brokers who are not the beneficial owners of

---

[132] See § 913 of the Dodd-Frank Act (amending § 15 of the 1934 Act). Most recently, the SEC enacted Regulation Best Interest (BI), which requires broker-dealers to act in the "best interest" of their retail customers.

[133] See § 921 of the Dodd-Frank Act (adding § 15(o) to the 1934 Act).

[134] See § 922 of the Dodd-Frank Act (adding § 21F to the 1934 Act).

[135] See §§ 929M, 929N, and 929O of the Dodd-Frank Act (amending § 15 of the 1933 Act, § 209 of the Advisers Act, and § 20(e) of the 1934 Act).

[136] See § 929P of the Dodd-Frank Act (amending § 8A of the 1933 Act, § 21B(a) of the 1934 Act, § 9(d)(1) of the Investment Company Act, and § 203(i)(1) of the Advisers Act).

[137] See § 951 of the Dodd-Frank Act (adding § 14A to the 1934 Act). See Securities Act Release No. 9178 (Jan. 2011).

[138] See § 952 of the Dodd-Frank Act (adding § 10C to the 1934 Act). See Securities Act Release No. 9330 (June 2012).

[139] See § 953(b) of the Dodd-Frank Act (directing the SEC to amend Regulation S–K under the 1933 Act to require each company to disclose a CEO pay ratio). See also § 953(a) of the Dodd-Frank Act (amending § 14(i) of the 1934 Act). The SEC proposed a pay versus performance rule in 2015, but it has not been adopted. See SEC, Dodd-Frank Implementation: Section 953, https://www.sec.gov/spotlight/dodd-frank-section.shtml#953) (last visited June 17, 2020).

[140] See § 971 of the Dodd-Frank Act (amending § 14(a) of the 1934 Act). See also Rule 14a–8 under the 1934 Act.

securities are prohibited from voting them on behalf of their beneficial owners without express instruction.[141]

Title IX also expanded the SEC's powers over nationally recognized statistical rating organizations ("NRSROs"), including the three major credit rating agencies (Moody's, Standard & Poor's, and Fitch). A new Office of Credit Ratings was authorized to examine NRSROs at least annually and to promulgate rules requiring NRSROs, among other things, to set up internal controls over the process for determining credit ratings; develop universal ratings across asset classes and types of issuers; adopt new professional standards requiring ratings analysts to pass qualifying exams and satisfy continuing education requirements; and observe certain conflict of interest standards that separate those who market a firm's services from those who rate the securities.[142] The Act also adopted a new liability provision under which private investors can sue credit rating agencies for a knowing or reckless failure to conduct a reasonable investigation.[143] This was a response to the broad perception that credit rating agencies had failed to perform adequate due diligence on the securities they rated leading up to the 2008 financial crisis.

In addition, Section 939G of the Dodd-Frank Act sought to impose liability on an NRSRO under § 11 of the 1933 Act for material misstatements or omissions related to its credit rating of asset-backed securities (including securitizations).[144] The NRSROs balked at this greater liability and refused to issue new ratings, causing the asset-backed securities market to freeze.[145] Amid the ensuing panic, the SEC agreed to "temporarily" freeze enforcement,[146] although the freeze is now in its ninth year.

Title VII assigned jurisdiction over "swaps" to the CFTC and jurisdiction over "security-based swaps" to the SEC. However, what constitutes a "swap" and a "security-based swap" is not always clear, requiring both Commissions to agree on a regulatory framework to implement Title VII that is described later in this casebook.

i. Public Utility Holding Company Act. Although no longer an important statute, since the SEC has mostly deregulated the field, PUHCA requires public utility holding companies (as defined) to secure approval from the Commission before issuing securities or otherwise changing their financial structures.

---

[141] See § 957 of the Dodd-Frank Act (amending § 6(b) of the 1934 Act).

[142] See §§ 931 to 939H of the Dodd-Frank Act (amending § 15E of the 1934 Act).

[143] See § 933 of the Dodd-Frank Act (amending §§ 15E(m) and 21D(b)(2) of the 1934 Act).

[144] See § 939G of Dodd-Frank Act (repealing Rule 436(g); Rule 436(g) exempts credit rating agencies from expert liability for their credit rating appearing in registration statements related to asset-backed securities).

[145] See Brody & Hanawalt, Dodd-Frank: Rating Agencies And The ABS Market, Law360 (Jan. 14, 2011), https://www.law360.com/articles/219571/dodd-frank-rating-agencies-and-the-abs-market.

[146] Id.

j. Trust Indenture Act. The TIA has a narrow but important focus. It applies to public offerings of debt securities in excess of $1 million and essentially specifies the form of indenture which must be used, including many of the indenture's substantive terms. The trust indenture is the contract that establishes the duties of the trustee who monitors and enforces the contractual rights of the bondholders. Among other things, the TIA basically attempts to prohibit the selection of a trustee with a disabling conflict of interest and establishes standards of conduct and responsibility for the trustee.

k. Investment Company Act. Investment companies—which term includes both "open-end" and "closed-end" mutual funds and money market funds—hold and manage a portfolio of securities for investment. Increasingly, middle-class Americans buy shares in mutual funds rather than attempting to pick stocks directly themselves. The 1940 Act specifies substantive corporate governance standards for the operation of such investment companies, including maintaining an independent board, providing for an annual review of the management contract between the investment company and its investment adviser, subjecting certain transactions between the investment company and its officers and directors to SEC approval, and regulating the investment company's capital structure.

l. Advisers Act. An investment adviser is in the business of providing investment advice to others for compensation. The Advisers Act requires such persons to register with the SEC (subject to some important exemptions), prohibits fraudulent and deceptive practices, regulates aspects of their compensation, and specifies some related requirements intended to ensure fair dealing. In essence, it does for investment advisers, on a lesser scale, what the 1934 Act does for broker-dealers.

5. THE REGULATORY PROCESS

Understanding the statutory framework only takes us part way towards understanding how the federal securities laws are interpreted, applied, and enforced. As an independent regulatory agency, the SEC must function and exercise its powers according to statutory and judicially-prescribed procedures and rules. In addition, the SEC oversees self-regulatory organizations that also enforce the securities laws.

a. Administrative Procedure Act. The SEC is subject to the Administrative Procedure Act ("APA"). The APA establishes the standards for judicial review of SEC administrative decisions and specifies procedures to be followed when the SEC is engaged in rulemaking. Typically, the SEC will give advance notice of rule proposals and will afford interested parties an opportunity to comment. It often acts at open meetings, and the discussions among Commissioners or with their staff at these meetings can be candid, sharp, and often revealing.

The SEC, however, does not act only through formal rulemaking. For example, it has never defined by rule what constitutes "insider trading," and it has resisted efforts aimed at legislative codification of this critical concept. Instead, it has made law on a case-by-case basis by pursuing an enforcement strategy. This "I-know-it-when-I-see-it" approach has been criticized on the grounds that it places a bureaucracy's interest in maximizing its discretionary power ahead of the industry's interest in bright-line standards and fair notice.[147]

The SEC staff has also developed a unique system of lawmaking by responding to inquiries from the bar about how it interprets (or will enforce) various provisions of the federal securities laws. If the staff agrees with an interpretation proposed by an attorney regarding a specific set of facts, it will state in its response that it will not recommend any enforcement action to the Commission if the attorney's client proceeds along the lines set out in the letter.[148] These "no-action" letters are made publicly available by the Commission and afford an important source of guidance for the bar. However, no-action letters are not binding on the Commission, which from time to time does overrule the staff, usually prospectively, and takes a position inconsistent with the staff's interpretation to date. No-action letters also are not binding on private parties, who may still challenge an interpretation the SEC's staff accepted. The staff may also change their views prospectively and cease to follow a position taken in an earlier no-action letter. In any case, controversy usually follows because practitioners understandably believe that no-action letters are intended to provide guidance that they cannot safely ignore. No matter how often the Commission repeats the mantra that no-action letters "only purport to represent the views of the officials who give them" or "set forth staff positions only" that "are not rulings of the Commission or its staff on questions of law or fact," the Commission's own contrary actions, not to speak of the contrary actions of the Commission's staff, belie that message to the practicing securities bar.[149] Nevertheless, on several occasions, controversy has arisen about the legal status of no-action letters. Repeatedly, courts have held that they are not judicially reviewable,[150] and are entitled to only limited

---

[147] The Commission was sharply criticized by one former Commissioner precisely on these grounds. See Karmel, Government by Prosecution (1981).

[148] See Securities Act Release No. 4553 (Nov. 6, 1962).

[149] For another critique of the uncertainty created by the SEC's refusal to treat no-action letters as a more formal source of law, see Loss, Summary Remarks, 30 Bus.Law. 163, 164–65 (1975). A more recent criticism is that there are a growing number of areas of law (such as the availability of exemptions from registration) where the staff refuses to issue no-action letters. See Nagy, Judicial Reliance on Regulatory Interpretations in SEC No-Action Letters: Current Problems and a Proposed Framework, 83 Cornell L. Rev. 921 (1998).

[150] See, e.g., Missud v. SEC, No. C-12-0161-DMR, 2012 WL 1225858 (N.D. Cal. Apr. 11, 2012) (holding that Exchange Act Rule 14a–8 "no-action" letters do not qualify as judicially reviewable SEC actions because they are written by SEC staff).

deference, since they amount to neither agency adjudication nor rule-making.[151]

Practitioners frequently accuse the SEC of avoiding "bright-line" rules in favor of vague or subjective tests that maximize agency discretion. Professor Homer Kripke once argued that, in part because the SEC is dominated by attorneys, it has developed a regulatory "theology" that is part law and part lore but cannot be confidently understood by non-specialists.[152] Its impact, he suggested, again was to maximize the agency's discretion to do what it wants under the circumstances.

    b.   *Cost-Benefit Analysis.* Over the last decade, financial regulators, and most notably the SEC, have been subjected to a new requirement—namely, that their rules must be grounded on an adequate cost-benefit analysis. This requirement has been imposed based less on the federal securities laws[153] and more on judicial interpretations of broad, policy-oriented language in several federal statutes, including the APA.[154] All of these decisions have been by the D.C. Circuit Court of Appeals, and the upshot has been an angry confrontation between those who feel the court has simply imposed its dislike of regulatory activism on the SEC and those who believe that greater use of cost-benefit analyses is essential to intelligent regulation. The fact that most of the cases have been initiated by a business trade or lobbying group seeking to invalidate new regulation has added fuel to this fire.

Proponents of cost-benefit analyses argue that existing law requires the SEC and CFTC to conduct a cost-benefit analysis before adopting regulations; they further insist that only a quantified analysis, which monetizes the costs and benefits of new regulation, will suffice.[155] By contrast, critics argue that expert judgment is essential to, and an inevitable component of, sound regulation and, to be effective, regulators

---

[151] See, e.g., Gryl ex rel. Shire Pharm. Grp. PLC v. Shire Pharm. Grp. PLC, 298 F.3d 136, 145 (2d Cir. 2002) (stating that "SEC no-action letters constitute neither agency rule-making nor adjudication and thus are entitled to no deference beyond whatever persuasive value they might have").

[152] See Kripke, The SEC and Corporate Disclosure: Regulation In Search of a Purpose (1979).

[153] Section 2(b) of the 1933 Act does require the SEC, when engaged in rulemaking, to consider not only "whether an action is necessary or appropriate in the public interest," but also "whether the action will promote efficiency, competition, and capital formation." See also § 3(f) of the 1934 Act (identical language). Neither provision, on its face, seems to mandate a quantified cost-benefit analysis.

[154] The first of these cases was Chamber of Commerce v. SEC, 412 F. 3d 133, 144 (D.C. Cir. 2005) (SEC requirement regarding board composition of mutual funds was invalid because SEC failed "adequately to consider the costs imposed upon funds"). The most notable of these decisions was Business Roundtable v. SEC, 647 F. 3d 1144 (D.C. Cir. 2014) (striking down the SEC's "proxy access" rule, which was authorized but not mandated by the Dodd-Frank Act). See also Goldstein v. SEC, 451 F. 3d 875 (D.C. Cir. 2006); Financial Planning Association v. SEC, 482 F. 3d 481 (D.C. Cir. 2007); American Equity Investment Life Ins. Co. v. SEC, 613 F. 3d 166 (D.C. Cir. 2010).

[155] See Committee on Capital Markets Regulation, A Balanced Approach to Cost-Benefit Reform (2013). See also Peirce, Economic Analysis by Federal Financial Regulators, 9 J.L. Econ & Pol'y 569 (2013).

must consider factors that cannot be quantified.[156] In their view, the judicial imposition of a "quantified" format for cost-benefit analyses paralyzes regulation.

This debate continues. Overall, the introduction of cost-benefit analyses has slowed SEC rulemaking. Changing direction slightly in 2014, the D.C. Circuit distinguished rules mandated by Congress (such as under the Dodd-Frank Act) from those proposed under the SEC's general rulemaking authority, and found that more discretion should be accorded the SEC in the former case.[157] This battle, however, is not over.

c. *Self-Regulatory Organizations.* The 1934 Act prescribes a concurrent and cooperative structure of regulation among the SEC and several specialized SROs. Justice William O. Douglas, an early SEC Chairman, described the strategy underlying this approach as that of giving the frontline enforcement responsibilities to the SROs, while the SEC "would keep the shotgun, so to speak, behind the door, well-oiled, cleaned and ready for use."[158]

Several different justifications underlie this approach. First, the SROs may receive a considerable degree of cooperation from the industry because they are populated with industry personnel. Second, because SROs finance their activities essentially by taxing the industry with dues, they increase the effective total enforcement budget for industry surveillance and monitoring. The SEC could not count on Congress to allocate equivalent funds to it if the SROs did not exist. Finally, this two-tier structure was probably an historical inevitability, because some of the SROs predated the SEC (the NYSE, for example, dates back to 1792). Although the 1934 Act granted the SEC significant authority over the stock exchanges, this two-tier structure of regulation represented an essential political accommodation.

The self-regulatory body with principal authority over broker-dealers was created in 1938 with the Maloney Act's addition of § 15A to the 1934 Act. Section 15A authorizes the registration of an association of brokers and dealers as a "national securities association." Only one such association has ever been established, formerly called the National Association of Securities Dealers. In 2007, the NASD merged with the regulatory arm of the NYSE to form FINRA.

SROs have broad disciplinary authority, subject to SEC review. The rules of the association must meet certain governance and law compliance objectives, including that they are "designed to prevent fraudulent and manipulative acts and practices, to promote *just and equitable principles of trade*, . . . to remove impediments to and perfect the mechanism of a free and open market and a national market system,

---

[156] For an incisive and trenchant critique, see Coates, Cost-Benefit Analysis of Financial Regulation: Case Studies and Implications (Working Paper 2014) (available at http://ssrn.com/abstract=2375396) (Jan. 2014).

[157] See National Association of Manufacturers v. SEC, 748 F. 3d 359 (D.C. Cir. 2014).

[158] See Douglas, Democracy and Finance 82 (1940).

and, in general, to protect investors and the public interest" (emphasis added).[159] The concept of "just and equitable principles of trade" was deliberately elastic. The idea behind self-regulation is that professionals in the marketplace "know it when they see it" and can recognize and discipline misconduct even when greater specificity would be required of a governmental agency. Thus, FINRA's Rules of Fair Practice (which provide the basis for most FINRA disciplinary actions) open with the requirement that members must "observe high standards of commercial honor and just and equitable principles of trade." This wording presumably is too vague a standard for criminal enforcement, but it can be enforced by FINRA, much like the rules of a private club. This ability to punish conduct that falls short of fraud, but is still socially undesirable, may be a distinctive advantage of self-regulation.

Under §§ 15(b)(8)–(9) of the 1934 Act, a broker-dealer may not effect a securities transaction unless it is a member of a registered securities association (today, FINRA) or unless it limits its activities to a single stock exchange of which it is a member. This effectively ensures that every broker-dealer dealing with public customers must join FINRA and comply with its rules; as a practical matter, suspension or expulsion by FINRA means disbarment from the industry.

SRO discipline can take a variety of forms: fines, censure, suspension from supervisory positions, or suspension from the industry (either permanently or temporarily). Both firms and individual employees are subject to discipline. In addition, FINRA can enforce not only its own rules but also the federal securities laws (statutes and regulations). Typically, FINRA's disciplinary process begins at the district level, where committees comprised of industry members hold hearings, reach decisions, and impose sanctions. Appeals can be taken to an internal appellate body (and further appeals to FINRA's board of directors and the SEC).[160] A possible downside of SRO enforcement is that constitutional protections (such as the privilege against self-incrimination) do not apply to private SRO bodies, while they do apply to proceedings brought by the DOJ and SEC.[161]

Procedural issues surround this self-regulatory structure, which delegates enormous discretion to an essentially private body. A policy question also surrounds the desirability of allowing competitors to discipline their business rivals. Still, courts have largely accepted SRO discipline against claims of procedural irregularity.[162] In part, they have relied on the requirement in § 15A of the 1934 Act that the SEC

---

[159] See § 15A(b)(6) of the 1934 Act.

[160] Under § 19(e) of the 1934 Act, the SEC can modify or overturn a FINRA-imposed sanction, but not increase it.

[161] See Birdthistle & Henderson, Becoming a Fifth Branch, 99 Cornell L. Rev. 1 (2013).

[162] See First Jersey Sec., Inc. v. Bergen, 605 F.2d 690 (3d Cir. 1979); Merrill Lynch, Pierce, Fenner & Smith v. NASD, 616 F.2d 1363 (5th Cir. 1980).

determine that an SRO's disciplinary rules "provide a fair procedure" for the disciplining of members and their associates.[163]

The SEC retains broad authority over the SROs (including the stock exchanges). Section 19(c) of the 1934 Act authorizes the SEC to "abrogate, add to, and delete from ... the rules of a self-regulatory organization ... as the Commission deems necessary or appropriate to insure the fair administration of the self-regulatory organization ... or otherwise in furtherance of the purposes of this title." Broad as this authority to amend an SRO's rules is, it is not unlimited. In the late 1980s, the SEC ordered the NYSE to adopt rules that denied listed companies the ability to issue supervoting stock that deviated from the traditional norm of "one share, one vote." (Such stock was often issued as part of a takeover defense.) The D.C. Circuit, however, invalidated those rules, finding that the SEC's authority under § 19(c) was essentially limited to rules that sought to create a national market system, not rules that regulated basic corporate governance.[164]

Other SROs exist, in addition to FINRA and the stock exchanges. A recent example is the Public Company Accounting Oversight Board, which was created by the Sarbanes-Oxley Act. PCAOB is a private body, established as a non-profit corporation, but subject to SEC oversight in much the same manner as FINRA. The PCAOB's five members are appointed by the SEC (after consultation with the Chairman of the Federal Reserve Board and the Treasury Secretary) for five-year terms.[165] Two (but only two) of PCAOB's five members must be certified public accountants.[166] These restrictions are intended to prevent the "capture" of PCAOB by the accounting profession.

Resolving a constitutional challenge to the PCAOB, the Supreme Court in 2009 largely upheld the PCAOB's structure (under which the SEC appoints PCAOB's board members), but found that the SEC could remove board members at any time (despite contrary statutory language) because greater protection from removal was contrary to vesting by Article II of the Constitution of executive power in the President. The net result was to affirm the SEC's ability to appoint PCAOB's members, but also to confer on the SEC a new non-statutory power of removal.[167]

Still another important SRO is the Municipal Securities Rulemaking Board, which regulates disclosure in the municipal securities market and

---

[163] See § 15A(b)(8) of the 1934 Act.

[164] See Business Roundtable v. SEC, 905 F.2d 406 (D.C.Cir. 1990). Ultimately, through a process of negotiation orchestrated by SEC Chairman Arthur Levitt, the three major exchanges were induced to adopt the same voting rule on a voluntary basis without any SEC direction or order to do so.

[165] See § 101(e)(5)(A) of the Sarbanes-Oxley Act.

[166] See § 101(e)(2) of the Sarbanes-Oxley Act. The chairperson, however, may not have been a practicing accountant for at least five years prior to her appointment to the PCAOB.

[167] See Free Enterprise Fund v. The Public Company Accounting Oversight Board, 561 U.S. 477 (2010).

municipal securities underwriters. Registered clearing agencies constitute another type of SRO.[168]

In the final analysis, the place and role of self-regulation will likely remain a hotly debated issue. Critics fear that self-regulation allows the industry to capture the regulatory process and even to focus its discipline on rivals and new entrants. Conversely, proponents argue that the industry invariably understands its own problems better than distant bureaucrats in a government agency. The debate will continue.

6. BLUE SKY REGULATION

Every American state has a statute regulating the offering of securities. Typically, these statutes—known as "blue sky laws"—effect a comprehensive system of regulation, requiring either registration of the securities with a state agency or the satisfaction of an applicable exemption. The statutes also impose registration and supervision requirements on securities professionals (such as broker-dealers and investment advisers) and create civil and criminal liabilities that broadly parallel the liabilities under the federal securities laws.

The term "blue sky" requires a special word of explanation. The first comprehensive state statute that regulated offerings and broker-dealers was adopted by Kansas in 1911 in reaction to fraudulent promoters who were believed to be luring gullible citizens into "speculative schemes which have no more basis than so many feet of 'blue sky'."[169] In general, the perception underlying these early statutes was that questionable East Coast promoters were swindling the honest local citizens by syndicating insubstantial offerings of "blue sky." Some more recent commentators have offered the more skeptical view that the enactment of the blue sky laws was an attempt by state banking regulators to expand "their regulatory turf" and advance "the financial interests of the banks under their supervision."[170] Clearly, the blue sky laws were part of the broad Progressive-era attempt to bring suspicious forms of business activity under closer governmental supervision, and financial syndications to the public were at this time viewed as highly suspect (possibly due to a general populist distrust of Eastern financial interests).

Later, with the passage of the federal securities laws, corporate issuers and securities professionals had to comply with dual and overlapping systems of regulation. Even more bothersome to corporate issuers were the different regulatory styles underlying these two legal regimes. As originally enacted, blue sky laws attempted to regulate the substantive fairness of the transaction and banned securities issuances within a state where the local blue sky administrator deemed them to be

---

[168] Section 17A of the 1934 Act requires the registration of clearing agencies; standards for the rules of such an agency are specified in § 17A(b)(3).

[169] See Hall v. Geiger-Jones Co., 242 U.S. 539, 550 (1917) (upholding Ohio "Blue Sky Law" and discussing statutory purposes).

[170] See Macey & Miller, Origin of the Blue Sky Laws, 70 Tex.L.Rev. 347, 351 (1991).

excessively risky, unfair, or overly generous to the promoters. Often, these statutes authorized the state blue sky administrator to preclude any offering in the state that the administrator found not to be "fair, just and equitable;" others authorized a ban if the terms of the offering were deemed to be "grossly unfair." Of course, some subjectivity surrounds these judgments. In any event, this form of "merit regulation" (which continues in a minority of the states today) contrasted sharply with the disclosure philosophy of the federal securities laws, which expects investors to protect their own interests once full disclosure is made.

Another criticism of merit regulation was that investors bore its costs. As an ABA Committee observed, when a securities offering is banned from one jurisdiction, the practical effect may be only that investors in that jurisdiction buy the stock in the secondary market (which is not covered by the blue sky laws) at the higher post-offering price.[171] From that perspective, merit regulation may paternalistically deny investors the opportunity to make high-risk, high-return investments and cost them the chance to buy at the often-lower offering price. In response to these criticisms, many states dropped merit regulation and moved to a full disclosure philosophy during the 1980s and early 1990s.[172] In addition, the National Conference of Commissioners on Uniform State Laws ("NCCUSL") adopted a Revised Uniform Securities Act ("RUSA") in 1985, which did not reject merit regulation, but limited the blue sky administrators' authority over more seasoned issuers.[173]

The adoption of RUSA by the NCCUSL in 1985 touched off a political battle. The North American Securities Administrators Association ("NASAA"), an organization of U.S., Canadian, and Mexican blue sky administrators, opposed the adoption of RUSA, seeing it as excessively deregulatory and overly restrictive of their ability to deal with novel abuses. In light of NASAA's opposition, RUSA has been adopted by only a few states, and the dominant statutory model remains the Uniform Securities Act, which was promulgated by the NCCUSL in 1956. The majority of states have "adapted" the Uniform Securities Act, adding or deleting their own pet provisions, although a few states have adopted RUSA. Notably, New York and California (the two most important states for securities offerings) have long had their own distinctive statutes based on neither model. California has been a strong "merit regulation" jurisdiction (along with Texas and Massachusetts), while New York basically administers an antifraud statute (but does apply merit

---

[171] See Report on State Merit Regulation of Securities Offerings, 41 Bus.Law. 785 (1986).

[172] For a discussion of these legislative battles and their mixed outcomes, see Sargent, The Challenge to Merit Regulation—Part I, 12 Sec.Reg.L.J. 276 (1984), and Sargent, Blue Sky Law—The Challenge to Merit Regulation—Part II, 12 Sec.Reg.L.J. 367 (1985).

[173] RUSA adopted a narrow exclusion from merit review for seasoned companies and placed certain restrictions on a blue sky administrator's ability to require the escrow of "cheap" stock held by promoters. See Hensley, The Development of a Revised Uniform Securities Act, 40 Bus.Law 721 (1985); Sargent, Some Thoughts on the Revised Uniform Securities Act, 14 Sec.Reg.L.J. 62 (1986).

regulation to a narrow spectrum of real estate and theatrical syndications). Not only do state blue sky statutes differ significantly (with some jurisdictions exempting the vast majority of offerings), but enforcement practices also vary at least as much. Due to budgetary constraints and the shifting philosophies of individual blue sky administrators, a state may move from an aggressive to a passive posture (and back again) over the course of a decade. The principal force for uniformity has been the NASAA, which seeks to coordinate the actions of its members when common interests exist.

In 1996, in the National Securities Markets Improvement Act ("NSMIA"), Congress amended § 18 of the 1933 Act to preempt state blue sky laws—*partially*. Under amended § 18(a), securities listed (or to be listed upon completion of an offering) on the NYSE, the Amex, or Nasdaq's National Market System are exempt from state registration procedures (but not their antifraud rules). In addition, the SEC is authorized to exempt securities listed on a regional stock exchange or sold to "qualified purchasers" (a term referring to sophisticated purchasers that the SEC is authorized to define by rule). Securities of registered investment companies (such as mutual funds) are also expressly exempted from state regulation. Finally, securities issued in certain transactions exempt from the federal registration requirements are also protected from state regulation (other than minimal notice filing requirements), and the JOBS Act extended this exemption. The upshot is that state blue sky registration requirements (but not a state's antifraud enforcement or investigatory authority) are confined to relatively small offerings (and then only if not sold to sophisticated or otherwise "qualified" investors).

The NSMIA also cut back on state broker-dealer registration requirements by adding § 15(h)(1) to the 1934 Act. This provision effectively preempts most substantive state regulation of broker-dealers. In effect, the state can enforce and monitor the SEC's requirements, but no more.

Finally, Title III of the NSMIA divided regulation of investment advisers between state and federal regulators, assigning to state regulation those advisers having assets under management of $25 million or less. The Dodd-Frank Act increased that minimum to $100 million,[174] with the result that many smaller investment advisers are supervised only at the state level.

---

[174] See § 410 of the Dodd-Frank Act (amending § 203A of the Advisers Act).

PART II

REGULATION OF THE DISTRIBUTION OF SECURITIES

SUBDIVISION A. THE UNDERWRITING PROCESS UNDER THE SECURITIES ACT OF 1933

An Overview

Perhaps the first point to be made about the role of underwriters is that use of an underwriter is not legally required, but tends to be a marketing necessity. Companies can "self-underwrite" and market their own securities to the public.[1] But they rarely do. Instead, corporate issuers go to investment banking firms to help them market their securities to investors for several reasons. Most obvious is the fact that investment banking firms have large inventories of clients who wish to purchase securities, whereas a young, start-up firm will typically have few such contacts. Often, investors purchase a portfolio of offerings from the same underwriter, relying on it to generate attractive returns for them across this portfolio, in effect conceding that the individual investor cannot tell a good deal from a bad one. In addition, the underwriter plays a special role as a "reputational intermediary" or "gatekeeper," who in effect pledges its reputational capital in order to assure investors that the issuer is reliable and honest. Such implicit assurances by the underwriter are credible for at least two reasons:

First, the underwriter has little to gain from fraud, because it receives a relatively modest underwriting fee (typically around 7% of the proceeds of an initial public offering) in comparison to the gains to the issuer and its management. Typically, the underwriter does not share in any equity appreciation (even if the stock price rises during the offering, each underwriter must sell its entire allotment at the original offering price).

---

[1] Such transactions do occur. However, if a corporate issuer markets its securities itself to investors, it will also have to register as a broker-dealer under the Securities Exchange Act of 1934 and possibly under various state laws because it will have come within the definition of a "dealer" in Section 3(a)(5) of the Securities Exchange Act of 1934. Nonetheless, with the development of the Internet, the prospect of such direct offerings, made by an issuer without an underwriter, is becoming feasible, including through "direct listings" on exchanges, as discussed later in this foreword.

Second, underwriters face high liability for even negligent errors. In addition, because major underwriters want to protect reputations that they developed over decades of working for many clients, they should logically not be willing to risk reputational damage for a single client in a transaction that will make only a modest contribution to the underwriter's annual revenues. The Securities Act of 1933 reinforces this natural tendency by basically holding the underwriter liable to purchasers in the offering for any material misstatement made by the issuer, *unless* the underwriter can affirmatively establish a "due diligence" defense which requires it to have conducted a reasonable investigation into the statements made in the issuer's registration statement. The policy rationale for placing this affirmative obligation on the underwriter to prove in effect its non-negligence is that it converts the underwriter into a vigilant gatekeeper who will therefore protect the public investor. Nonetheless, despite the existence of both these legal and market incentives that encourage the underwriter to monitor its client, the issuer, securities fraud does regularly occur, and sometimes underwriters appear to treat their legal exposure as simply a cost of business, which they can insure.

A second basic point about underwriting is that few brokerage firms engage in this activity. It is a specialization, and a capital intensive one. Historically, many of the most famous underwriting houses (e.g., Goldman Sachs or Lazard Freres) did not engage in retail brokerage operations, preferring to specialize in financing offerings that were chiefly sold to investor clients of other brokerage firms. Since the early 1980s, however, there has been a trend towards vertical integration, as traditional "financial" underwriters have merged with retail brokerage firms (for example, Morgan Stanley & Co. and Dean Witter merged during the 1990's). Smaller retail firms still are deterred from underwriting activities by the significant capital requirements needed to engage in this business;[2] however, they may still participate in underwritten offerings in a secondary role as marketers, but not as underwriters, as later discussed. Given the different specializations of different investment banking firms (some primarily financial institutions with little marketing presence and some primarily retail brokerage firms without the financial capacity to underwrite), the managing underwriter performs a delicate balancing act in many offerings by combining the financial strength of some firms with the marketing ability of others so that shares "underwritten" by the former are actually sold to clients of the latter.

A. *Varieties of Offerings.* A number of different techniques for selling securities by an issuer to unaffiliated investors can be used, some involving underwriters and some not. Each deserves a brief discussion.

---

[2] The SEC imposes "net capital" rules on all brokers, but these rules are particularly demanding in the capital that they require of firms that underwrite securities. See Rule 15c3–1 ("Net Capital Requirements for Brokers and Dealers") under the Securities Exchange Act.

Direct Offerings. Securities may be sold, without the use of an underwriter or marketing syndicate, in a direct offering by the issuer. Direct offerings by an issuer to the general market are very rare, but four other types of direct offerings are occasionally used: (a) a direct offering limited to existing shareholders, usually in the form of a "rights offering"; (b) an offer for sale by tender (or "Dutch auction"); (c) an "all or none" offering; or (d) a direct private placement.

(a) Rights Offerings. An issuer with a substantial shareholder base may seek to sell stock to its existing shareholders. The usual procedure is to make a "rights offering." In a rights offering, existing shareholders are offered warrants or rights to subscribe to securities of the issuer, usually at some small discount off the market price. Rights are allocated in proportion to the size of existing holdings of the issuer's securities. Those shareholders not wishing to buy can sell their warrants to others; thus, all shareholders gain something: either a discounted price or the profit on the sale of the warrant. Often, underwriters will be asked to make a "standby" commitment to buy the remaining shares that the shareholders do not buy at a slightly lower price. The basic advantage to the issuer from this approach is that the discount offered to existing shareholders may be less than the standard underwriter's discount.

(b) Dutch Auction. The "offer for sale by tender" (or "Dutch auction") is used by issuers more frequently in the United Kingdom than in the United States, but has attracted some attention in the U.S. in the wake of Google's use of such a procedure for its IPO in 2004.[3] Its advantage is that it maximizes the returns to the issuer, especially those companies doing their initial public offering. Investors bid for the stock at prices above a minimum price set by the company, but they do not pay the price that they offer. Rather, they pay the lower clearing price at which all shares can be sold. For example, if the issuer is selling 3 million shares and some shareholders offer to buy one million shares at $10 and other shareholders offer to buy one million shares at $9 and still other shareholders offer to buy two million shares at $8, all shareholders will pay $8 per share, which is the market clearing price. But because the offer is now over-subscribed, the shareholders offering to buy $8 will be prorated by 50%. In practice, the Dutch auction typically does utilize the investment advice of an experienced underwriter, who also typically gives some form of contingent underwriting commitment in case the public does not subscribe sufficiently to sell the entire offering. Institutional investors have, however, resisted the use of the Dutch Auction, precisely because it results in a higher, market-clearing price and thereby deprives them of the benefits (as the initial purchasers) of the typical first day run-up in an IPO. Despite Google's success with this approach in 2004, auctions involving the public sale of equity securities

---

[3] For a review of the issues in such auctions, see C. Hurt, What Google Can't Tell Us About Internet Auctions (And What It Can), 37 U. Tol. L. Rev. 403 (2006).

have been rare, probably because of the fear that institutional investors will boycott such offerings.

Although Dutch auctions are still uncommon in the United States, the United States Treasury Department now uses the Dutch auction technique to market federal government securities. Regulated issuers, such as public utilities, are required by law in some instances to use competitive, public bids among underwriters to sell their debt offerings. Also, some large issuers, such as Exxon Corporation, have used the Dutch auction to sell various forms of debt securities, with or without the use of underwriters.[4] The Dutch auction is intended to maximize the issuer's returns, eliminate or reduce underwriting commissions, and lower interest rates on new issues.

(c) *"All or None" Offerings.* In some situations where a minimum amount of funds are needed for a special purpose, securities may be offered by the issuer on an "all or none" basis. Thus, unless a designated number of shares are sold and paid for in full within a specified period, the offering will be terminated and all funds returned, with interest, to the subscribers. The subscribers' funds are placed "in escrow" with a designated depositary and do not become available for disposition until the terms of the offering are met. Some state securities administrators may require the use of an "all or none" offering under certain circumstances.[5]

(d) *Private Placements.* The last form of direct offering is a private placement. A private placement allows an issuer to sell securities (without registration with the SEC) to a limited number of institutional and other sophisticated investors. The most important factors leading an issuer to prefer a private placement of its securities, either by the issuer directly or with the assistance of an investment bank, are necessity, secrecy, speed, cost and lesser exposure to liability. Although investment banks often assist the issuer in a private placement, they act as the issuer's agent and do not buy the securities from the issuer to resell them to investors.

A private placement is far quicker than an initial public offering. The most important factor reducing the time required for a private placement is that a registration statement need not be filed with, and approved by, the SEC. In a private placement, the issuer or underwriter contacts a limited number of sophisticated purchasers to whom much of the detail required in a registration statement or statutory prospectus is unimportant. Although institutional and other sophisticated purchasers will want material investment information, it is made available to them

---

[4] Wall St.J., Oct. 29, 1976, p. 28, ed. 5; N.Y. Times, Nov. 17, 1976, at 84, col. 2. For the mechanics of Dutch auctions, see Exxon Corporation (Avail. April 7, 1977), Fed.Sec.L.Rep. (CCH) ¶ 81,198; Note, Auctioning New Issues of Corporate Securities, 71 Va.L.Rev. 1381 (1985).

[5] See SEC v. Manor Nursing Centers, Inc., 458 F.2d 1082 (2d Cir. 1972); SEC Securities Exchange Act Rules 10b–9, 15c2–4; Robbins, All-or-None Offerings, 19 Rev. of Sec. & Commodities Reg. 59 (1986); Robbins, All-or-None Offerings: An Update, 19 Rev. of Sec. & Commodities Reg. 181 (1986).

in the form of a fairly brief private placement memorandum, which is less difficult or time consuming to prepare and carries less potential liability. In addition, any written information can be supplemented by direct meetings between company officials and the prospective buyers. In dealing with sophisticated investors, the issuer (or its investment banker) can explain a highly speculative financing, or a highly technical offering, to a class of investors more likely to understand its terms than retail investors, and also more likely to commit the funds necessary to consummate a high-risk financing.

A private offering is also far less costly than a public offering. Several factors increase the costs of a public offering, including legal fees, accounting costs, registration expenses, underwriters' fees and printing bills. In a private placement, it may be possible to avoid a fresh audit, and legal expenses will be substantially less. The issuer may also be able to conduct the offering, itself, without a financial intermediary, such as an underwriter or broker-dealer. If an offering circular is required, there will be no prospectus to print. Finally, the transaction may be exempt from "blue sky" registration and regulatory requirements at the state level.

Although securities sold in private placements that are exempt from the registration requirements of the 1933 Act may not be resold into the public market without at least a six months holding period (which is necessary to satisfy an important SEC rule, known as Rule 144), institutional investors may often be able to resell such "restricted" securities to each other pursuant to another SEC Rule (Rule 144A), which is analyzed later in Chapter 9 (and thus private placement purchasers do enjoy some liquidity to this degree). Another major difference between the two forms of offerings is that the issuer and its placement agent are only liable for fraudulent statements or omissions, while in a public offering, the Securities Act of 1933 essentially imposes stricter liability upon them based on a negligence standard.

Direct Listings. A newly popular technique for offering shares to the public is the "direct listing." Essentially, it permits shares already sold to investors through private placements and other exemptions from registration to be listed on the New York Stock Exchange or Nasdaq. The issuer raises no capital by this means but does gain liquidity for its investors through an exchange listing. Procedurally, the issuer files (1) a registration statement covering shares already sold to institutional investors and other sophisticated investors in private placements; (2) a registration statement under the Securities Exchange Act of 1934; and (3) a listing application with the stock exchange. Once the stock is listed on an exchange, investors (including the issuer's own officers and employees) can now immediately sell and convert their shares into cash (with the result that increased liquidity will typically cause the shares to trade at a higher price). Once listed, the shares move from a few concentrated shareholders who bought in the earlier private placements to dispersed public shareholders. Also, the issuer gains the ability to sell additional shares to the market much more quickly and easily now that the issuer has become a public company (and entered the SEC's continuous reporting system by registering under the Securities Exchange Act of 1934). Direct listings cost considerably less than an initial public offering, because the issuer need not compensate an underwriter for marketing and selling its stock (although it must use a financial advisor, as discussed later in Chapter 2).

Who uses a "direct listing"? The first modern direct listing was done by Spotify, the music and streaming company, in 2018, and its example shows the type of issuer most likely to benefit from this transaction.[6] Spotify had raised equity capital in a series of private placements, several for over $1 billion. It was currently valued at an estimated $20 billion, and did not wish to raise capital, but its investors had little liquidity in the absence of a market listing. Also, a direct listing gave Spotify the ability to acquire other companies in mergers and acquisitions, using its own shares as the currency for these transactions. Finally, as examined in more detail in Chapter 2, a direct listing was much cheaper than an initial public offering, as it did not have to employ or pay an underwriter. Still, the absence of an underwriter may increase the possibility that others can exploit or manipulate the issuer's stock price, as discussed in Chapter 2.[7]

Underwriting. The term "underwriter" was borrowed from the field of insurance. It was originally used to describe those individuals or firms that insured the issuer against any loss in connection with an offering of securities if the public investors failed to subscribe fully to the issue. This arrangement is known as a "strict underwriting." The term "underwriting," however, has long since lost this meaning, and strict underwriting is rarely used today. The term "underwriter" now signifies a firm that specializes in the marketing of securities sold either by an issuer in a primary offering or by selling shareholders in secondary offerings. Section 2(a)(11) of the Securities Act of 1933 broadly defines an "underwriter" to mean any person who has purchased from the issuer (or controlling persons) (1) with a view to, or (2) offers or sells for an issuer in connection with, the distribution of any security, or (3) participates in any such undertaking.

Underwriters may be used in all forms of public offerings of securities, including all-or-none offerings, as well as in private placements; they render financial advice with respect to the method of financing, the type of security to be offered, the market to be reached, the manner of offering and serve as managers of the offering.

Types of Underwritings. The most common types of underwritings are three: (a) a firm commitment underwriting; (b) a "subscription"

---

[6] See Brent Horton, Spotify's Direct Listing: Is it a Recipe for Gatekeeper Failure?, 72 S.M.U. L. Rev. 177 (2019).
[7] Id.

offering (usually with a "standby" commitment from the underwriters); and (c) a "best-efforts" underwriting. In a firm commitment underwriting, the underwriter (or syndicate) agrees to purchase all or specific amounts of the offering for cash, possibly subject to certain "market-outs."[8] In a subscription offering, the issuer offers a new issue of its securities to its existing shareholders (usually at a discount to the current market price). The underwriters agree to "stand by" and purchase any shares not purchased by existing shareholders, at the expiration of a specified period. In a "best efforts" underwriting, the underwriter neither purchases the securities from the issuer nor resells them to the investing public; the underwriter agrees only to act as an agent of the issuer in marketing the issue to investors. Typically, the investment bank is paid only to the extent that it successfully sells the shares.

In smaller issues, the investment banker may market the issue solely by the use of its own organization; in larger issues, a syndicate of other dealers of securities is organized to facilitate the distribution. In these cases, the so-called managing underwriter receives a special commission for managing the offering, and the other members of the syndicate receive a concession off the public offering price as compensation for assuming part of the underwriting risk and for services. As indicated, in most cases the underwriting syndicate makes a firm commitment to the issuing company to take and pay for the securities directly and assume the same risk as any wholesaler and retailer in merchandising a product. In the case of "rights offerings" to existing shareholders, the underwriting group may merely agree to act as agent in reselling the securities, but nevertheless "underwrite" the issue by agreeing to take up and pay for any securities not subscribed for by the public. It was long customary to add a selling group of smaller broker-dealers who purchased a portion of the offering at a concession off the offering price, but assumed no part of the underwriting risk; their use has declined in recent years, but is still common. Finally, the investment banking firm may merely agree to use its best efforts to sell the securities for the issuer, without making a firm commitment.

In actual practice, the members of the underwriting syndicate usually purchase the securities outright and resell them to the public. In such purchase transactions, each underwriter commits itself only for a specified portion of the offering, rather than assuming a joint liability, in part because under Section 11 of the Securities Act of 1933, an

---

[8] In general, "market-out" clauses in firm commitment underwriting agreements are triggered only upon the occurrence of "a material, adverse event affecting the issuer that materially impairs the investment quality of the offered securities." Such a clause has generally been strictly read to refer only to an unforeseeable and extraordinary decline in the securities markets. See Walk-In Medical Centers, Inc. v. Breuer Capital Corp., 818 F.2d 260, 264 (2d Cir. 1987). See also SEC No-Action Letter, First Boston Corporation (Available Sept. 2, 1985), Fed.Sec.L.Rep. (CCH) ¶ 78,152.

underwriter's overall civil liability is limited to the total public offering price of the securities underwritten by it.

In a firm commitment underwriting, the issuer will discuss its proposed offering with several investment banking firms, from which it selects one or two to be the lead underwriter or underwriters. When the parties reach an understanding as to the type, nature and form of offering, this is usually reduced to writing, in a "letter of intent," which is usually expressly made not binding on either party.[9] The underwriter and issuer will arrive at a predicted public offering price for SEC filing fee purposes (this expected price may be moved up or down during the marketing process in response to demand and market conditions). After the registration statement becomes effective, the issuer and the lead underwriter will negotiate the final terms as to price and related matters. The final terms will be chiefly based upon the reaction to the marketing efforts of the underwriting syndicate in receiving indications of buyer interest. The underwriters will seek to, and often succeed in, obtaining such non-binding indications of interest from investors in amounts that may be a multiple of the actual shares to be sold (this process is called "book building"). When these indications of interest are a multiple of the shares to be sold, the underwriters know they have a "hot," oversubscribed offering, whose price will predictably rise in the secondary market. Still, underwriters do not directly profit from this appreciation, as they are required to sell all the shares they purchase at the initial offering price (even if the stock price is rising simultaneously in the secondary market).

At an early stage of the underwriting process, the lead underwriter will prepare a syndicate list and discuss it with the issuer. The issuer may be asked whether there are other security dealers who have shown an interest in the issuer and should be brought into the syndicate. News of the impending underwriting may have become a matter of general knowledge, and other underwriters may contact either the lead underwriter or the issuer and request that they be made members of the syndicate. In a registered offering, during the period between the filing of the registration statement and its effectiveness (the so-called waiting period), the preliminary prospectus will be widely distributed throughout the financial community, and, based on it, other underwriters will be solicited to become members of the syndicate. At the same time as the signing of the underwriting agreement (which typically occurs soon after the SEC declares the registration statement effective), the members of the syndicate will also enter into an "agreement among underwriters." This agreement will designate the underwriter or underwriters who will

---

[9] Several decisions have held that such a letter is not enforceable and creates no duty to negotiate further. See Dunhill Securities Corporation v. Microthermal Applications, Inc., 308 F.Supp. 195 (S.D.N.Y.1969); Beaumont v. American Can Co., 621 F.Supp. 484, 493 (S.D.N.Y.1985), aff'd, 797 F.2d 79 (2d Cir. 1986). Where, however, there is no language expressly making the letter of intent nonbinding, courts have divided over its enforceability. See Newharbor Partners v. F.D. Rich Co., 961 F.2d 294 (1st Cir. 1992) (collecting cases).

manage the offering and fix the various terms and agreements among the members of the syndicate. The underwriting agreement is executed by the issuer and the lead underwriter, acting as agent for the other underwriters in the syndicate, who thereby also become parties to the underwriting agreement.

During the waiting period, the underwriters may undertake a series of "roadshows" by which they and some members of the issuer's senior management travel around the country to meet with securities analysts, institutional investors, and possibly a few very wealthy individual investors, in order to market the offering. The general public, including even very experienced investors, are traditionally excluded from these meetings. Predictably, future earnings and other sensitive matters will often be discussed, and the roadshow system often amounted to a form of legally permissible selective disclosure in order to "hype" the offering.[10] Although the SEC has not sought to halt "roadshows," the participation of securities analysts working for the underwriters in these roadshows was banned (under the terms of the Global Settlement, which is discussed below), and the SEC also now requires as a practical matter that the issuer make available an electronic version of the "roadshow" to investors who request it.[11] More recently, as discussed later in this Chapter, the JOBS Act has largely lifted this bar and permitted analysts to appear at roadshows in the case of "emerging growth companies."

When the underwriting agreement is signed (usually shortly after the registration statement is declared effective), the underwriters are committed for the entire issue, subject to possible "market out" clauses in the underwriting agreement dealing with certain adverse contingencies, and it is only at this point that the issuer is relieved of risk and assured of receiving the proceeds when the offering is completed.

If investor interest is so disappointing during the marketing process as to indicate that the proposed amount of the issue cannot all be sold, the underwriters will advise either that the size of the offering be cut back or that the contemplated price be reduced or that the offering be deferred until market conditions improve. If, however, the issuer and underwriters agree on the price and related terms, the issuer will have a firm commitment from the group to purchase its securities. Conversely, if the offering is oversubscribed (that is, if the "indications of interest" received by each underwriter add up to an aggregate number that is, say, four or five times the number of shares to be sold), the underwriters will understand that the demand well exceeds the supply (at the estimated

---

[10] Regulation FD, which generally prohibits selective disclosure, contains an express exception for selective disclosures made "in connection with a securities offering." See Rule 100(b)(2)(iii), 17 C.F.R. § 243.100(b)(2)(iii). In recognizing this exception, the SEC appears to have been apprehensive that it would otherwise discourage roadshows. *Query*: Did it strike the right balance?

[11] The roadshow will sometimes today be deemed a "free writing prospectus," in which event it may be necessary to either file it or make it generally available. See Rule 433(d)(8), 17 C.F.R. § 230.433(d)(8). This topic is considered more fully in Chapter 2.

price range), and the stock is likely to rise in the secondary market. The underwriters may be reluctant to share this positive information with the issuer, because it may cause the issuer to hold out for a higher price in its negotiations with the underwriter. Partly as a result, initial public offerings are often "underpriced"; that is, the offering is sold at a price well below the secondary market price it reaches within hours after the offering begins. A Blue Ribbon Committee appointed by both the NYSE and NASD has recommended that, as a partial cure for underpricing, a committee of independent directors of the issuer should meet with the underwriters and learn in detail the status of their marketing efforts.[12] Query: Should it amount to insider trading if the underwriters fail to disclose material information known to them about market conditions (i.e., a high level of oversubscription) to the issuer at the time of their purchase of the issuer's stock?

A registered public offering is more complicated and time consuming than a private placement. It can typically take two to four months (and often longer) to arrange the financing, allow for the underwriters to make their due diligence investigation, and to prepare the registration statement. Depending upon the complexity of the company, and the workload of the SEC staff, it may take from a month to three months for the registration statement to be cleared by the SEC and become effective. By contrast, a private placement might be completed in as little as a week or two. A major factor in this time differential is the nature of the disclosure documents required.

Syndication. The managing underwriter will have completed the formation of the underwriting syndicate sometime after the registration statement is filed with the Securities and Exchange Commission. During the waiting period members of the syndicate will have tested the market by distributing the preliminary prospectus among securities dealers, and received non-binding indications of interest from prospective purchasers. On the basis of this accumulation of buyer interest, the allocation of the amount of securities to be purchased by each member of the syndicate will be made, thereby separating members of the syndicate into groups based upon the size of their purchase commitments.

In the formation of the underwriting syndicate for a large offering, the lead underwriter will usually organize a syndicate designed to give the widest possible distribution to the issue. In a large equity issue, the syndicate will comprise several groups of underwriters based upon the size of an underwriter's commitment. The first level will consist of "bulge-bracket underwriters"—a relatively small group of large investment banking firms, who bring substantial capital and prestige to the offering, in addition to their most important asset, that of distributing

---

[12] See NYSE/NASD IPO Advisory Committee, Report and Recommendations (May 2003) (available at http://www.finra.org/sites/default/files/Industry/p010373.pdf).

capability.[13] A second-tier or "mezzanine" group will normally consist of a combination of New York Stock Exchange member firms having branch offices outside of New York (called "wire houses" because, at least historically, the main office was connected with branch offices and correspondent brokers by private, leased telephone wires), and leading regional investment banking firms around the nation. Depending upon the size of the issue, the syndicate may also include other firms located throughout the United States and, in many cases, in financial centers throughout the world. Anywhere from ten to a hundred firms could be members of the underwriting group in any given issue. A combination of large institutionally-oriented firms, large wire houses, and locally based retailers has proven to be the most effective combination for achieving a good nationwide distribution and a reasonably satisfactory pricing of the offering from the standpoint both of the issuer and the underwriter.

After the registration statement is filed, the syndicate manager as well as the syndicate members will test the market for the offering, as their brokers call potential buyers to solicit "indications of interest"—i.e., non-binding requests for shares to be reserved for them; the preliminary prospectus will also be widely circulated to attract interest in the offering. If the offer is in demand, other broker-dealers may seek to become members of the syndicate or become members of the "selling group." Those firms that are not included in the syndicate can be invited to become members of the "selling group," and thus will not be excluded from participating in the offering. Members of the selling group serve as retailers of the securities. Only broker-dealers that are members of the Financial Industry Regulatory Authority ("FINRA"), the self-regulatory body of the brokerage industry, are eligible to become members of the underwriting syndicate or the selling group or to receive a concession off of the offering price.

Members of the syndicate may themselves deal directly with the public, or they may sell a portion of their shares to members of the "selling group." In actual practice, however, the "syndicate manager" or the lead underwriter will notify each underwriter of the amount of stock which it is to retain for sale. For example, a firm which has committed itself to take 10,000 shares may be told by the syndicate manager that it will be allocated only 5,000 shares of its 10,000 share allotment for sale to its own clients. The remainder of the securities go into the syndicate account, the "pot," which is under the direct control of the syndicate

---

[13] Much diplomacy surrounds the listing of the underwriters on the cover page of the prospectus or on the "tombstone ad." Some of the biggest underwriting firms (e.g., Goldman Sachs & Co., Merrill Lynch Capital Markets, and Morgan Stanley & Co.) have created a special or "bulge" bracket for themselves. In debt offerings, and less frequently in equity offerings, the "bulge" bracket is followed by a "mezzanine" bracket, a sub-major bracket and a bracket for the regional firms. Some major bracket firms have refused to accept a lesser status and will not participate without "star" billing. Nevertheless, institutional investors have become such a dominant factor in the new issue market that many new issues may be distributed by the "bulge" bracket underwriters, by forming a small syndicate, or even by a single underwriter. Just Like Film Stars, Wall Streeters Battle to Get Top Billing, Wall St. J., Jan. 15, 1986, p. 1, col. 4.

manager. These securities are used to satisfy the demand from (i) large institutional investors (which the syndicate manager handles in order to avoid duplication and/or competition among participating underwriters), and (ii) those firms which are members of the selling group, as distinguished from the underwriting group. Members of the selling group are liable solely for the amount of stock they have agreed to purchase. Securities dealers outside of the underwriting syndicate who have received indications of interest from their clients with respect to the offering will contact the syndicate manager asking to become a member of the selling group and obtain an allotment of stock. A selling group member gets compensated in the form of a selling concession, which typically amounts to 50–60% of the gross spread between the public offering price and the net amount received by the issuer.

This "gross spread" is the difference between the price to the issuer and the public offering price. It represents the compensation which is distributed among the managing underwriter, members of the underwriting syndicate and the members of the selling group—the "underwriting discounts and commissions" shown on the cover page of the prospectus or offering circular. The issuer sells the securities to the underwriting syndicate at a discount from the public offering price. In an initial public offering, this discount has long been in the range of 6¾% to 7%; indeed, there was so little variation that the Antitrust Division commenced an investigation into these pricing arrangements in the late 1990's, but later dropped it without taking action. The discount is considerably less for seasoned equity offerings by already public corporations and even less for debt offerings. Simply to illustrate the allocation of this discount within the underwriting group, let us assume that the issue is to be sold to the public for $10, with $9 going to the issuer. On this basis, the compensation might be sliced up as follows. First, the lead underwriter will receive a management fee of 20 cents per share for finding and packaging the issue, and to compensate it for managing the offering and "running the books." The next slice would be a fee of about 30 cents per share which is called the "gross underwriting fee." This fee both provides compensation to the underwriting group for their expenses, such as roadshows, "tombstone" advertising and stabilizing expenses, and represents compensation for the use of capital and for assuming the risk of the underwriting. The remaining 50 cents of the spread goes to the underwriting firm or the selling group member that actually sells the stock at retail for its marketing work.

Pricing. In the context of an initial public offering (or "IPO"), the pricing of the issue is the most sensitive matter to be negotiated between the underwriters and the issuer. As discussed below, there is considerable evidence that underwriters "underprice" a new issue so that the investors who purchase in the initial offering will receive an immediate return over the first day or two of trading. This run-up in price is intended to compensate the IPO investors for the riskiness of new offerings, but it tends to create a very volatile new issue aftermarket (because if the offering does not appreciate quickly, many investors who are expecting an immediate return will dump their shares, creating price pressure). In these price negotiations, both sides will come armed with data about other recent public offerings of similar companies and about the price/earnings ratios of comparable companies in the industry. The issuer will point to the fact that some of its rivals in the industry are trading at, say, 30:1 price/earnings multiples, and the underwriters will reply that the issuer's examples are all "seasoned" companies, while the untested character of the issuer's projected earnings stream requires application of a discount. The outcome of these negotiations is indeterminate, but relatively few deals fall apart at the last moment over price (unless market conditions suddenly turn sour).

In the case of a seasoned issuer, the price of the offering will have to be closely related to the existing market price. But this market price will in turn be affected by the decision to issue equity. The announcement of a public offering has a seemingly paradoxical impact on the market price for the issuer's stock: it goes down! A considerable body of research shows that the securities market responds negatively to an announcement of a common stock offering by a seasoned issuer.[14] There are two explanations for this phenomenon: First, corporate managers who have non-public access to material information about the firm's future cash flows may be more likely to issue equity securities when they perceive the firm to be overvalued by the market than when they perceive it to be undervalued.[15] In contrast, when they believe the firm is undervalued, they will prefer to issue debt securities. Aware of this incentive, investors may reduce the firm's value upon the announcement of a common stock issue, viewing the announcement as a signal of overvaluation. Second, an alternative explanation is that the demand for an issuer's stock is not perfectly elastic and thus any increase in supply will result in a new supply and demand equilibrium. Early research suggested that new issuances or the sale of large blocks created very little price pressure on common stock (unless the market viewed the sale or issuance as a signal of reduced earnings),[16] but more recent research has challenged this conclusion, suggesting that management must therefore incorporate an expectation of some share discount into its corporate financing decisions.[17]

---

[14] See Asquith and Mullins, Equity Issues and Offering Dilution, 15 J.Fin.Econ. 61 (1986); Barclay and Litzenberger, Announcement Effects of New Equity Issues and the Use of Intraday Price Data, 21 J.Fin.Econ. 71 (1988); Mikkelson and Partch, Valuation Effects of Security Offerings and the Issuance Process, 15 J.Fin.Econ. 31 (1986).

[15] For this explanation, see Myers and Majluf, Corporate Financing and Investment Decisions When Firms Have Information That Investors Do Not Have, 13 J.Fin.Econ. 187 (1984).

[16] See Scholes, The Market for Securities: Substitution Versus Price Pressure and the Effects of Information on Share Prices, 45 J.Bus. 179 (1972).

[17] See Loderer, Cooney and Van Drunen, The Price Elasticity of Demand for Common Stock, 46 J.Fin. 621 (1991); Asquith and Mullins, supra note 11; Masulis and Korwar, Seasoned Equity Offerings: An Empirical Investigation, 15 J.Fin.Econ. 91 (1986).

This perceived market penalty for equity offerings by seasoned issuers may contribute to an explanation of another puzzling phenomenon: seasoned corporations make very little use of equity public offerings to obtain capital. Instead, they rely heavily on retained earnings and debt.[18] For example, only $85 billion in stock was sold to the public in new issuances between 1980 and 1984, compared to the over $5.2 trillion in outstanding stock that was traded on registered exchanges between 1978 and 1985.[19]

B. *The New Issues Market.* The new issues market is at once extremely important, extremely volatile, and extremely "thin." The number of initial public offerings varies dramatically from year to year, following a seeming boom-or-bust cycle. Although experts disagree about how many IPOs occur each year (because they use different criteria to define IPOs), the following chart, prepared by Statista, is representative and shows the total number of IPOs from 1999 to 2019:[20]

Number of IPOs from 1999 to 2019

Year	Number
1999	486
2000	406
2001	84
2002	70
2003	71
2004	226
2005	206
2006	199
2007	213
2008	31
2009	63
2010	154
2011	125
2012	128
2013	222
2014	275
2015	170

---

[18] See Stout, The Unimportance of Being Efficient: An Economic Analysis of Stock Market Pricing and Securities Regulation, 87 Mich.L.Rev. 613, 645 and n. 179 (1988); see also Smith, Investment Banking and The Capital Acquisition Process, 15 J.Fin.Econ. 3 (1986).

[19] See Smith, supra note 18; Comment, Equity Financing for Public Corporations: Reasons and Methods to Encourage It, 138 U.Pa.L.Rev. 1411, 1419 n. 32 (1990).

[20] This table was prepared by Statistica, a statistical analytics firm, owned by Dell Software. Other studies show the same basic pattern.

2016	105
2017	160
2018	192
2019	159

This volatile pattern of an alternating "boom and bust" cycle in IPOs has been with us for some time.[21] IPOs increased to record numbers in 1999 and 2000, and then the bubble burst. The collapse of Enron and WorldCom in 2001 and 2002 further eroded investor confidence and produced stricter regulation in the form of the Sarbanes-Oxley Act of 2002. In 2008, an even greater financial crisis hit, and IPO activity basically halted over this period—a record drought. The Global IPO market similarly crashed with only 745 offerings worldwide over the first 11 months of 2008, in contrast to 1,790 for the same period in 2007.[22] The IPO market recovered modestly in 2009 and 2010, but did not truly rebound until 2013 and 2014. Still, despite some recovery, the number of IPOs in 2019 (159) was less than half the number in 1999 (486). What can explain this disparity? Some believe that stricter regulation (both the Sarbanes-Oxley Act and the Dodd-Frank Act) chilled IPOs. Possibly, there could be some truth to this hypothesis, but it does not explain the resurgence in IPO numbers immediately after the adoption of these statutes.

Thus, the more popular theory among financial economists is that the vast difference between the 1999 and the 2019 IPO numbers means that a deeper force is at work: namely, globalization. Globalization, they argue, has made it more profitable for a smaller firm to sell itself to a larger, global firm, which can speed a new product through development and sell it to a global market, than to do an IPO (and remain relatively small). The core of this hypothesis is that the merger marketplace will outbid the IPO marketplace because it can uniquely realize economies of scope.[23] As a result, larger firms may do an IPO, but smaller IPOs will decline in number (because these smaller firms can command a higher price in the merger marketplace). This seems to have happened, as IPOs of under $100 million have become increasingly uncommon and generally unprofitable to their investors.

Viewed from a different perspective, the long-run economic evidence on initial public offerings can only be described as puzzling. Numerous studies have found that IPOs tend to be underpriced over the short-run; for example, measured from the initial offering price to the market price at the end of the first day of trading, IPOs in the 1980's yielded an

---

[21] For data for earlier years, see Lowenstein, Shareholder Voting Rights: A Response to SEC Rule 19c–4 and to Professor Gilson, 89 Colum.L.Rev. 979, 994 (1989).

[22] See Stephen Taub, Global IPO Activity Plunges to 13-year Low, CFO.com (Dec. 9, 2008).

[23] See Xiaohui Gao, Jay R. Ritter, and Zhangyan Zhu, Where Have All the IPOs Gone?, 48 Journal of Financial and Quantitative Analysis 1663 (2013).

average initial return of 16.4%.[24] However this phenomenon of underpricing has been highly cyclical, with very high initial returns being reported across the new issue market for some years and then flat returns for other periods.[25] Over the years, financial economists have tried to explain this data in a variety of ways: (1) underpricing could represent an insurance premium for the higher legal liability underwriters face in IPOs; (2) it may reflect monopsony power held by investment banking firms vis-a-vis small issuers; or (3) it may be the result of investors' inability to judge IPOs on an individual basis so that they decide to invest on a portfolio basis at an average price, leading to the underpricing of higher quality offerings.[26]

None of these explanations, however, could explain the extraordinary underpricing that occurred in the late 1990's during the Nasdaq "high tech" boom. During this era, IPOs frequently rose 400%, 500%, and on occasion even higher, simply on their first day of trading. Recent studies have found that the average first day return was 44% for IPOs between 1997 and 1999 and that in 1999 (near the peak of the bubble) the average first day return (i.e., the difference between the first day closing price and the initial offering price at which IPO allocations were sold to favored investors) was 71.7%.[27] The extreme case was the IPO offering of VA Linux Systems, Inc. in December 1999, which was offered at $30 per share and closed the following day at $239.23.[28] Query: Should such an offering really be considered "successful"? If a stock is sold at an initial offering price of $10 per share and yet the very first trade in the secondary market is at $20 and the first day's closing price is $30 (as happened not infrequently in 1999 and 2000), this extraordinary underpricing should seemingly offend the issuer—on the ground that the underwriter had knowingly underpriced it and caused the issuer to receive only one third of the value that the market quickly

---

[24] See Ibbotson, Sindelar and Ritter, Initial Public Offerings, 1 J. App. Corp. Fin. 37 (1988) (sample of 8,668 IPOs going public in 1960–87); Tinic, Anatomy of Initial Public Offerings of Common Stock, 43 J.Fin. 789 (1988); Miller and Reilly, An Examination of Mispricing, Returns and Uncertainty for Initial Public Offerings, 16 Financial Management 33 (1987).

[25] Ibbotson and Jaffe, "Hot Issue" Markets, 30 J.Fin. 1027 (1975); Jay Ritter, The "Hot Issue" Market of 1980, 57 J.Bus. 215 (1984).

[26] For a survey of these theories and the related evidence, see Loderer, Sheehan and Kadlec, The Pricing of Equity Offerings, 29 J.Fin.Econ. 35 (1991). No similar pattern of underpricing is associated with seasoned offerings. In explaining this puzzling pattern of underpricing, a number of economists ascribe it to the impact of the liability provisions of the Securities Act of 1933. Under Section 11 of the Securities Act of 1933, the underwriter can only be held liable for the difference between the initial offering price and the lower price on the date of any lawsuit's filing. Hence, underpricing the initial offering price reduces the potential damages to the underwriter. For a critical review of this theory, see J. Alexander, The Lawsuit Avoidance Theory of Why Initial Public Offerings are Underpriced, 41 UCLA L. Rev. 17 (1993). One problem with this explanation is that underpricing is a worldwide phenomenon, while U.S. litigation remedies are unique to the U.S.

[27] See Norton Garfinkle, Burton Malkiel and Costin Bontas, Effect of Underpricing and Lock-Up Provisions in IPOs, 28 J. of Portfolio Management 50, 52 (2002). For the 71% figure for 1999, see Jay Ritter and Ivo Welch, A Review of IPO Activity, Pricing and Allocations, 57 J. Fin. 1795 (2002).

[28] See "VA Linux Soars a Record 698%," Wall Street Journal, December 10, 1999 at C1.

placed on this stock. The underwriter would presumably know that the stock was underpriced because it (and usually it alone) knows the ratio between the "indications of interest" it has received from potential purchasers and the number of shares to be sold (for example, if this ratio were as high as ten to one, as it sometimes was, the underwriter would know that it had a very hot offering). Yet, few such complaints were heard from issuers during this period. Instead, an intense competition developed among investors for allocation of stock in IPOs, as everyone anticipated that such an allocation amounted to "free money" because the IPO stock would predictably rise sharply in the secondary market.

What explains the puzzling phenomenon? There are many theories and a voluminous academic literature. Most observers acknowledge that two additional factors greatly influence IPO pricing: First, investment banking firms have close and multiple relationships with institutional investors. Conferring underpriced stock (or, in effect, free money) on institutions that buy in IPOs (most typically, mutual funds) may be a way of obtaining an institution's brokerage business or other advisory business from it. Institutions are estimated to purchase over 70% of the shares in "hot" IPO offerings,[29] and it is widely believed that underwriters allocate stock in "hot" (or oversubscribed) offerings to those institutions that have given them the most business. Underwriters employ informal formulas that relate brokerage commissions received to IPO allocations. The underwriters' loyalty to its institutional clients also explains why they vigorously oppose procedures, such as the Dutch auction, which allocate IPO stock to the highest bidder. Auctions imply that the IPO stock is less likely to be underpriced, and they thereby deny institutions the price discount that may cause them to be loyal to their underwriters and use their higher-priced brokerage services. Underpricing also benefits the underwriters in other ways, such as enabling them to confer allocations of "hot" IPO stock on prospective future clients, hopefully in return for future business—a practice known as "spinning" and now partially prohibited.[30] Arguably, underpricing is a glue that holds together the multi-service brokerage firm, encouraging institutions to use all its services in return for "hot" IPO allocations.

Still, even if favoritism for institutional investors understandably exists, it does not explain the issuer's passivity in tolerating IPO

---

[29] See K. Hanley and W. Wilhelm Jr., Evidence on the Strategic Allocation of Initial Public Offerings, 37 J. Fin. Econ. 239, 240 (1995).

[30] For studies of this practice, see S. Griffith, Spinning and Underpricing, 69 Brooklyn L. Rev. 583 (2004); L. Townsend, Can Wall Street's "Global Resolution" Prevent Spinning?: A Critical Evaluation of Current Alternatives, 34 Seton Hall L. Rev. 1121 (2004). Today, "spinning" or any allocation of shares in return for expected future investment banking business (i.e., a "quid pro quo" allocation) could violate FINRA Rule 5131(b). See Securities Exchange Act Release No. 63010 (September 29, 2010). The "anti-spinning" rule applies, however, only if the recipient executive's corporation has received investment banking services from the broker-dealer within the past 12 months or expects to be retained within the next 3 months for such services. The narrowness of this prohibition may suggest that the practice persists just outside the rule's boundaries.

underpricing.³¹ Here, the second factor comes into play. Insiders in most IPOs—i.e., officers, directors, and venture capitalists—own most of the existing stock in the firm. The underwriters usually require them to enter into "lock-up" agreements, which contractually bar these insiders from selling their shares in the secondary market until the expiration of a specified period after the effectiveness of the registration statement (usually, six months). This is done to assure investors that the insiders will not "bail out" and sell immediately after the offering. Underwriters insist on this because otherwise it would be difficult to market the stock to investors, but lock-up agreements have two consequences. First, they cause the insiders to focus less on the price of the stock at the time of the offering (which is when the underpricing occurs) and more on its likely price on the expiration of their lock-up (at which point they will typically sell a substantial portion of their shares to diversify their wealth). One explanation for why underpricing was tolerated by issuers is that the insiders whose stock is subject to "lock-ups" believe that a sharp first day price spike creates favorable publicity and attention for their company and maximizes the possibility that the stock price will remain high at the point when they become able to sell.³² Possibly too, the underwriters quietly agreed to encourage their "star" securities analysts to recommend the stock in a published report issued just before the lock-up expiration date is reached (this practice was called a "booster shot" in the parlance, but it is now restricted by FINRA rules). In the past, such services might have convinced the firm's controlling shareholders to accept considerable underpricing in return for coverage and publicity that maximized the stock price at this later lock-up expiration point, which was more important to them.

A second possible explanation is that lock-ups by their very nature create an imbalance in supply and demand that results in sharp price spikes on the offering day. For example, assume that 10 million shares are to be sold by the company, but 40 million shares are already held by the firm's founding shareholders, and the latter shares will be locked up for six months. Thus, only 10 million shares are in the public float in the secondary market. Arguably as a result, there is a supply and demand imbalance that produces a price spike until the lock-up expires. Supporting this interpretation is the fact that the typical IPO issuer's stock price usually does decline (and significantly) just before the lock-up expires.³³ (Of course, this could also be explained by the market anticipating that the stock is about to come under heavy selling pressure, both from insiders and from short-sellers, who tend to exploit this known

---

³¹ For an attempt to explain the issuer's passivity, see T. Lougheran & Jay Ritter, Why Don't Issuers Get Upset About Leaving Money on the Table in IPOs?, 15 Rev. Fin. Stud. 413 (2002) (finding that on average the IPO issuer leaves $9.1 million on the table because of underpricing).

³² For this explanation of underpricing, see A. Rajesh, L. Krigman, K. Womack, Strategic IPO Underpricing, Information Momentum, and Lockup Expiration Selling, 66 J. Fin. Econ. 105 (2002).

³³ See Garfinkle, Malkiel, and Bontas, supra note 27, at 54–56.

tendency). This supply and demand imbalance was further aggravated by the practice of many underwriters in imposing "anti-flipping" rules on their retail customers (but seldom on their institutional customers, who have more leverage). These rules warned the retail customer that if it sold (or "flipped") its IPO allocation during the period immediately after the offering (for example, the first month), it would receive no further IPO allocations (or at least not for a defined period).[34] In 2004, both the NASD and the NYSE proposed rules that would prohibit "flipping" restrictions by broker-dealers participating in IPOs, but neither FINRA (the successor to both self-regulatory bodies) nor the SEC acted quickly on these rules.[35] Only in 2010 was this "anti-flipping" rule finally adopted, with some exceptions.[36]

Still a third explanation is that the apparent underpricing may, at least sometimes, be a product of market manipulation. Because initial allocations of IPO stock are valuable, several class action lawsuits charged that underwriters required institutions who wanted allocations in "hot" offerings to agree, as a condition of their receipt, to buy additional stock in the secondary market at progressively higher prices on the first day of trading. This practice—known as "laddering"—creates an artificial demand for the stock and so results in a distorted price which is not the true product of the "real" supply and demand for the stock. It is also illegal, and the SEC settled "laddering" charges against several major underwriters in 2005 requiring each of them to pay a fine of $40 million.[37] An even larger antitrust class action alleging that IPO prices were manipulated by arrangements between underwriters and institutions was brought, but was rejected by the Supreme Court in an important decision on the relationship of the antitrust laws to the federal security laws. Essentially, the Court recognized an implied immunity from the

---

[34] Restrictions on "flipping" by retail purchasers imposed by multiple underwriters have been attacked on antitrust grounds as a restraint of trade. However, in a recent decision, "anti-flipping" restrictions have been upheld on the ground that such restrictions were consistent with the SEC's regulatory scheme and so had implied immunity from the antitrust laws. See Friedman v. Salomon/Smith Barney, Inc., 313 F.3d 796 (2d Cir. 2002). Subsequently, the Supreme Court held in Credit Suisse Sec. (USA) LLC v. Billing, 551 U.S. 264 (2007), that the federal securities laws implicitly precluded the application of the antitrust laws to conduct in connection with IPOs so long as the SEC had authority to regulate such conduct because the antitrust laws conflicted with the regulatory approach taken by the securities laws.

[35] Proposed NASD Rule 2712 and proposed NYSE Rule 470 would have prohibited a broker-dealer from attempting to recoup any portion of the underwriting commission paid to a broker or its employees if the shares were flipped by its customers. See Securities Exchange Act Release No. 50896 (December 28, 2004). In the past, such penalties were the primary mechanism used by the lead underwriter to enforce its policies against flipping. It led all participating brokers to monitor their clients' trading for fear of losing their underwriting profits.

[36] See Securities Exchange Act Release No. 63010 (September 29, 2010) (adopting renamed FINRA Rule 5131). The revised rule allows the managing underwriter to adopt such a penalty rule for the entire syndicate; thus, it bars the selective use of flipping penalties against smaller investors.

[37] See SEC v. Morgan Stanley & Co., Civil Action No. 1:05 CV 00166 (D.D.C. 2005); SEC v. Goldman Sachs & Co., Civil Action No. 05CV853 (S.D.N.Y. 2005).

antitrust laws for conduct that was within the regulatory jurisdiction of the SEC, even if it also violated the securities laws.[38]

There are also benign explanations for underpricing. These include: (1) the underwriter is a more experienced negotiator than the relatively inexperienced IPO issuer;[39] (2) informed investors may know more about the issuer's value than the issuer, itself;[40] (3) wise issuers interested in the long-run deliberately underprice in order to signal their quality and thereby win investor loyalty for the future;[41] and (4) underpricing is a form of compensation paid to the underwriters for future coverage by securities analysts.[42]

While the debate over the cause of underpricing will continue, one loser is obvious: the evidence is clear that those who buy IPO stocks in the secondary market during the interval between the end of the first trading day and the expiration of the lock-up period systematically lose.[43]

One related puzzle with IPO pricing merits special attention. IPOs tend to systematically underperform the market in the first year after the offering. Indeed, some studies show that, over a three year period following the IPO, issuing firms appear to underperform the market significantly, doing far worse than a sample of similar firms over the same period.[44] While there is substantial variation from year to year and across industries in this rate of underperformance, companies that went public in high volume years appear to fare the worst, so that, despite the initial underpricing, no gains in excess of the market average remain after three years. This data seems to support three generalizations: (1) the IPO market may not approach the informational efficiency of the deeper secondary markets (i.e., the exchanges); (2) investors are cyclically over optimistic about the earnings potential of emerging high growth companies; and (3) some investors who buy in the IPO secondary market are systematically prejudiced by current practices.

C. *The Fixed Price Offering and Resale Price Maintenance.* The typical underwriting agreement requires all the underwriters and selling group members to adhere to the public offering price as stated in the prospectus. Such a fixed price offering eliminates the prospect of competition among the underwriting group (particularly for the same

---

[38] See Credit Suisse Sec. (USA) LLC v. Billing, 551 U.S. 264 (2007).

[39] See A. Ljungquist, "IPO Underpricing" in HANDBOOKS IN FINANCE: EMPIRICAL CORPORATE FINANCE (2004). The problem with this argument is that venture capital firms are hardly inexperienced; yet, underpricing is particularly pronounced in deals in which they participate.

[40] See K. Rock, Why New Issues Are Underpriced, 15 J. Fin. Econ. 187 (1986).

[41] See R. G. Ibbotson, Price Performance of Common Stock New Issues, 2 J. Fin. Econ. 235 (1975); I. Welch, Seasoned Offerings, Imitation Costs and the Underpricing of Initial Public Offerings, 44 J. Fin. Econ. 421 (1989).

[42] M.T. Cliff and D.J. Denis, Do IPO Firms Purchase Analyst Coverage with Underpricing? (Working Paper) (available at http://www.ssrn.com/abstract_id=378201) (2003).

[43] See Garfinkle, Malkiel, and Bontas, supra note 27, at 56.

[44] Jay R. Ritter, The Long-Run Performance of Initial Public Offerings, 46 J.Fin. 3 (1991); see also Garfinkle, Malkiel, and Bontas, supra note 27.

institutional customers), but it essentially amounts to a price-fixing agreement. Early on, both the SEC and the courts held that such agreements did not violate the antitrust laws, although they could violate certain provisions of the securities laws.[45]

A practical problem arises under the Securities Act of 1933 because the offering price must be stated in the Prospectus (on the front cover), and any sales by underwriters below that price make the Prospectus false and misleading (unless it is amended or supplemented) and subject all of the underwriters to liability under Section 11 of the Act. Therefore, it is arguably impossible to carry out a fixed-price distribution without some sort of agreement, formal or informal, among all of the underwriters that they will adhere to the stated public offering price. Clearly, Congress did not think that fixed-price distributions were illegal when it enacted that statute.

Although sometimes evaded, the fixed offering price system remains politically popular with small investors, who do not like the idea of large institutions receiving a discount that they did not also get. As a result, in 1980, the SEC reversed its prior position and permitted the NASD to adopt rules enforcing resale price maintenance and thereby enforce fixed-price offerings. It reasoned that because the underwriting discount and selling group concessions were separately negotiated with respect to each new public issue, the NASD was not attempting to impose discounts and commissions in violation of § 15A(b)(6) of the 1934 Act.[46] Rather, the SEC said it was simply enforcing the voluntary agreement of the underwriters and selling group members to adhere to the offering price, until the managing underwriter released the group from those restrictions.

D. *The Role of the Securities Analyst.* A last player in the public offering process who needs to be introduced at this stage is the securities analyst. Analysts work both for brokerage firms (the so-called "sell side") and institutional investors and money managers (the so-called "buy side"). The research done by analysts on the buy side is usually kept confidential as proprietary information, but "sell side" research, including ratings and recommendations, is widely disseminated in order to encourage brokerage transactions by investors (as brokerage firms chiefly earn their revenues from brokerage commissions). Not surprisingly, buy recommendations usually outnumber sell

---

[45] One early SEC decision, In the Matter of National Association of Securities Dealers, 19 S.E.C. 424 (1945), found that an agreement to make an offering at a fixed price did not violate the Sherman Antitrust Act, but did violate what is now § 15A(b)(6) of the 1934 Act, which then forbade the rules of the NASD "to fix minimum profits, to impose any schedule of prices, or to impose any schedule or fix minimum rates of commission, allowances, discounts or other charges." See also United States v. Morgan, 118 F.Supp. 621, 699 (S.D.N.Y.1953) (resale price maintenance did not violate Sherman Act).

[46] See Securities Exchange Act Rel. No. 17371 (Dec. 31, 1980). Section 15A(b) of the 1934 Act is discussed supra at note 1. See generally, Price Maintenance in the Distribution of Securities, 56 Yale L.J. 333 (1947); Jennings, Self-Regulation in the Securities Industry: The Role of the Securities and Exchange Commission, 29 Law & Contemp. Probs. 663 (1964); Pickard & Djinis, NASD Disciplinary Proceedings: Practice and Procedure, 37 Bus.Law. 1213 (1982).

recommendations (in part because "buy" recommendations address all investors, while "sell" recommendations address only the much smaller population of investors who already own the stock or who are willing to sell it "short").

Securities analysts are chartered by a professional organization (The CFA Institute), which administers a continuing education program and conducts a rigorous examination for analysts who wish to become "chartered financial analysts" (or "CFAs"). As with other professional associations, The CFA Institute has adopted certain "best practice" standards consistent with the industry's view that the securities analyst is a professional, much like an attorney or an auditor. This view of the analyst as an objective professional conflicts, however, with the analyst's involvement in sales and marketing activities. During the 1990's, analysts became major participants in the IPO marketing process. At least in part, this was attributable to the fact that some analysts during this period acquired a celebrity status (often being featured on T.V. shows and quoted in newspaper stories), and investment bankers recognized that analyst support could sell a particular initial public offering. With this recognition came a sudden competition to hire "star" analysts, and well-recognized analysts increasingly migrated from small, boutique brokerage firms that specialized in research to large, integrated brokerage firms that specialized in underwriting (with this migration "star" analysts' salaries soared from relatively modest levels to the multi-million dollar range). Once hired by investment banking firms, analysts were regularly assigned to the "roadshows" at which prospective IPOs were sold to institutional investors.

But as the competition for analysts became more heated, conflicts of interest began to surface. Allegedly, some investment banking firms competed for IPOs by promising (implicitly or even explicitly) that their "star" analysts in the IPO firm's industry would issue a "strong buy" recommendation on the stock shortly after secondary trading began. At this point, an obvious conflict arises between the analyst's professional role as a neutral umpire, evaluating securities for investors, and the analyst's role as a salesman for the investment banking division of the analyst's firm.

After the collapse of the Nasdaq "high tech" market in 2000, pointed questions were raised in the media about the reasons for the persistence of many analysts in maintaining "buy" recommendations on stocks that fell 80% or more during this crash. Similarly, seventeen out of the eighteen analysts who followed Enron maintained buy recommendations on its stock up until shortly before its bankruptcy filing in 2001 (with the lone dissenting analyst working for a brokerage firm that did not have an investment banking department).

Discontent with the seeming conflicts surrounding analysts led to Congressional hearings in 2001, to rule-making by the NASD and the NYSE that was initiated in 2001, and, most importantly, to a civil action brought by the New York State Attorney General in 2002 against Merrill, Lynch & Co. The last action, brought by then New York Attorney General Eliot Spitzer, had particularly explosive consequences because the Attorney General filed a public affidavit which quoted excerpts from emails sent by Merrill Lynch securities analysts to their colleagues contemporaneously with buy recommendations issued by the firm, which emails seemingly trashed the stocks so recommended, describing the stocks in some cases as "pieces of junk" (and worse). The affidavit further quoted some analysts warning their superiors that several of the stocks recommended would cost small investors their retirement savings and implying that the buy recommendations were based only on the investment banking fees that they would generate for the firm. Over the following weeks, the market capitalization of Merrill Lynch sank by 20%, seemingly in response to this controversy. Meanwhile, the New York Attorney General announced an intent to achieve structural reforms that would separate securities research from investment banking (much as the Glass-Steagall Act had once separated commercial and investment banking), and the securities industry in turn objected to a single state's Attorney General attempting to restructure the securities industry in ways never suggested nor favored by the SEC.

Eventually, in 2002, not only Merrill Lynch, but also the other ten largest underwriters reached a settlement, popularly known as the "Global Research Settlement," with the SEC, the NYSE, the NASD, the New York Attorney General, and the various state securities commissioners, which required all of them to "separate completely the evaluation and determination of compensation for U.S.-based equity research analysts from . . . [the] investment banking business."[47] This settlement left underwriters still able to provide (and thus necessarily subsidize) securities research (if they chose to do so), but made certain that the underwriting division of the firm could not determine or influence analyst compensation decisions. Further, all communications between analysts and investment banking personnel were closely regulated. The premise here was that such prophylactic rules would leave securities analysts free to pursue their own individual desires to develop personal reputations for accurate and objective research, unconstrained by the threat of reduced compensation for negative research.

Contemporaneously with the Global Research Settlement, the SEC approved new rules, promulgated by both the NASD and the NYSE (and now enforced by FINRA), that similarly restricted investment banking influence and control over securities analysts.[48] These rules (NASD Rule 2711 and NYSE Rule 473) addressed analyst conflicts of interest in

---

[47] See Agreement Between the Attorney General of the State of New York and Merrill Lynch, Pierce, Fenner & Smith, Inc., dated May 21, 2002, at Paragraph 7.

[48] See Securities Exchange Act Release No. 34–45908 (May 16, 2002). Both these rules have been incorporated into the FINRA rulebook, but the NYSE rule applies only to broker-dealers who are members of the NYSE.

connection with the preparation and publication of research reports on equity securities and imposed the following restrictions:

1. No research analysts may be supervised or controlled by a firm's investment banking department;

2. Investment banking personnel may not discuss pending research reports with research analysts prior to their distribution (with certain limited exceptions);

3. Promises of favorable research in return for investment banking business are forbidden as is compensation to analysts tied to specific investment banking transactions;

4. Restrictions are placed on an analyst's personal trading, including in particular a prohibition on purchases by an analyst of an issuer's securities prior to an IPO;

5. Disclosures are mandated both about the brokerage firm's economic relationships with an issuer and about the percentage breakdown of its securities recommendations (i.e., the relative percentages of buy, sell and hold recommendations); and

6. No analyst research report may be disseminated by an underwriter in an IPO during a defined period following the effectiveness of the registration statement (this "blackout period" is intended to eliminate any conflict of interest that might tempt the underwriter to promote the IPO stock during this critical period).

In 2005, these rules were further amended to prohibit a research analyst from participating in a roadshow or otherwise communicating with a current or prospective customer in the presence of investment banking department personnel.[49] In 2014, however, FINRA agreed to relax these rules marginally in light of the JOBS Act.[50]

The securities industry was not happy with these reforms or the Global Research Settlement, and it found its opportunity to counterattack in the JOBS Act, which passed Congress in 2012. The JOBS Act sought to deregulate in order to facilitate IPOs and to ease the access of smaller issuers to the capital markets. Section 2(a)(3) of the Securities Act was amended to add the following sentence at its end:

---

[49] See Securities Act Release No. 34–51593 (April 21, 2005).

[50] In 2014, FINRA updated NASD Rule 2711 marginally and renamed it FINRA Rule 2241. The revised rule continues to (i) prohibit prepublication review, clearance or approval of research reports by investment banking personnel; (ii) restrict input by investment banking personnel into research coverage decisions; (iii) limit involvement in research department budget and compensation decisions to senior firm management (who are not involved in investment banking); and (iv) establish informational barriers to insulate research personnel from investment banking pressure. Other provisions were, however, relaxed. Possibly, the most notable change was the reduction in the post-IPO "quiet period" in which analysts could not publish research on the issuer to ten days. See Sec. Exch. Act Release No. 34–73622 (November 18, 2014). Rule 2241 specifically exempts offerings of "emerging growth companies" from its prohibition of analyst attendance or participation in roadshows.

"The publication or distribution by a broker or dealer of a research report about an emerging growth company that is the subject of a proposed public offering of the common equity securities of such emerging growth company pursuant to a registration statement that the issuer proposes to file, or has filed, or that is effective shall be deemed for purposes of paragraph (10) of this subsection and section 5(c) not to constitute an offer for sale or offer to sell a security, even if the broker or dealer is participating or will participate in the registered offering of the securities of the issuer."

The next and final sentence of Section 2(a)(3) then added a very broad definition of "research report" to cover both electronic and oral communications and recommendations. As a result, at least in the case of "emerging growth companies" (which term is broadly defined in Section 2(a)(19) of the Securities Act and will easily cover most IPO issuers), the securities analyst would appear to be free to make recommendations at roadshows or even in the "quiet period" before a registration statement is filed. Thus, the existing FINRA rules prohibiting analyst appearances at roadshows probably cannot be enforced with regard to emerging growth companies (although they can be applied to more seasoned issuers). However, FINRA has enforced its rules against using analysts to solicit underwriting business, imposing fines of $43.5 million against ten underwriting firms in 2014.[51] The SEC also takes the position that the JOBS Act provision does not suspend the obligations under the Global Research Settlement for those underwriters who joined in that settlement.

At present, the long-term impact of the JOBS Act and the foregoing rules remains uncertain. On the one hand, "sell side" securities research seems likely to remain dependent upon an economic subsidy from investment banking, because the "buy side" remains unwilling to pay for such research. On the other hand, "sell side" analysts do have their own incentives to develop personal reputations for accurate and useful research, which they are now freer to pursue. How these opposing forces will play out remains an open question. There is also evidence, that the market increasingly discounts the recommendations of "sell side" analysts who are connected with an underwriter of the issuer,[52] preferring to rely on independent analyst firms, who are unconnected to underwriters, or on "buy side" analysts. More problematic is the fact that in response to these new rules underwriting firms have reduced their employment of "sell side" analysts, and the number of companies that are

---

[51] See Gretchen Morgenson, "At Big Banks, a Lesson Not Learned," N.Y. Times, December 14, 2014. The fines were imposed in 2014 for analyst participation in marketing efforts in the Toys "R" Us offering in 2010, which was before the 2012 passage of the JOBS Act (and it is also not clear whether Toys "R" Us would have qualified as an a "emerging growth company").

[52] See Roni Michaely and Kent Womack, Conflict of Interest and the Credibility of Underwriter Analyst Recommendations, 12 Review of Financial Studies 653 (1999).

covered by securities analysts has probably declined, particularly at the lower end of the Nasdaq market.

The objectivity and independence of the securities analyst has also been significantly enhanced by another important SEC reform, which aimed at a different problem. Regulation FD, adopted in 2000,[53] now prohibits selective disclosure by corporate managements of material information to analysts, institutional investors, and shareholders likely to trade based on such information. Although aimed at selective disclosure, a variety of insider trading that had not been clearly prohibited by law, Regulation FD has reduced the ability of corporate managers to retaliate against, or threaten, analysts who published negative research about their companies. Prior to Regulation FD, the analyst could easily be cut off from the flow of sensitive information about the company and so had to be careful not to offend management with critical research or ratings. After Regulation FD, some forms of retaliation against the analyst remain possible, but the analyst cannot be wholly excluded from access to the flow of information because the company must release it to the market generally. For the future, management's ability to discipline the analyst has been marginally constrained by Regulation FD, but only time can tell whether analysts will become more independent and critical as a result.

E. *Future Directions.* Those who believe underpricing is a significant problem tend to prefer the Dutch auction as the efficient, market-based solution. Where Dutch auctions have been used (such as in Israel), there is evidence that underpricing is less prevalent.[54] But this system too has its critics, who believe that it produces a "winner's curse" and a likelihood that offerings will be overpriced (with the long-term result that investors might avoid IPO offerings). Although both institutional investors and underwriters resist Dutch auctions (many boycotting offerings in which such offerings are used), both Google and Morningstar have conducted highly successful IPOs using this technique. Nonetheless, as the world's capital markets converge, the evidence is that the American "bookbuilding" approach to underwritings is becoming more dominant and that the use of auctions in other countries is becoming less common.[55]

---

[53] See Securities Act Release No. 33–7881 (August 15, 2000). For the debate over the rule compare Merritt B. Fox, Regulation FD and Foreign Issuers: Globalization's Strains and Opportunities, 41 Va. J. Int'l L. 653 (2001) with William K.S. Wang, Selective Disclosure by Issuers, Its Legality and Ex Ante Harm: Some Observations In Response to Professor Fox, 42 Va. J. Int'l L. 869 (2002).

[54] See S. Kandel, O. Sarig, & A. Whol, The Demand for Stocks: An Analysis of IPO Auctions, 12 Rev. of Fin. Stud. 227 (No. 2 1999) (finding lower underpricing under Israeli auction system).

[55] See F. Degeorge, F. Derrien & K. Womack, Quid Pro Quo in IPOs: Why Book-Building is Dominating Auctions (SSRN Working Paper No. 582963 (December 2003)); F. Derrien & K. Womack, Auctions vs. Bookbuilding and the Control of Underpricing in Hot IPO Markets, 16 Rev. of Financial Stud. No. 1, 31 (2004).

CHAPTER 2

THE BASIC STRUCTURE AND PROHIBITIONS OF THE SECURITIES ACT

1. THE STATUTORY FRAMEWORK

Statutes

Securities Act, §§ 2, 3, 4, 5, 6, 7, 8, 9, 10 (and Schedule A), 11, 12, 13, 17, 19, 20, 22, 24.

Introductory Note

The Securities Act of 1933 has two basic objectives: (1) to provide investors with material financial and other information concerning new issues of securities offered for sale to the public; and (2) to prohibit fraudulent sales of securities. Its scope, however, is limited, for jurisdiction is always tied to some use of the mails or of interstate facilities to accomplish a forbidden transaction; however, the use of the "jurisdictional means" can almost always be found. Even the making of an interstate phone call or the sending of an email can support federal jurisdiction. We commence our study of the 1933 Act with a guided tour through the various sections of the statute.

The basic prohibitions are found in two groups of provisions: First, § 5 prescribes the rules compelling full disclosure (and § 12(a)(1) gives investors a right to rescind if § 5 is violated). Second, §§ 11, 17, and 12(a)(2) prohibit fraud or misrepresentation in interstate sales of securities. Sections 17, 11, and 12(a)(2) overlap to some extent, but violations of § 17 can trigger criminal sanctions, while the latter provisions exclusively authorize private civil actions. Section 17 also provides a basis for enforcement by the SEC through disciplinary proceedings or by way of an injunction. Although the Supreme Court has never decided whether a private right of action will be implied under § 17(a), lower courts have for some time refused to find any private cause of action created by that section.[1]

A key provision is § 5, which is the hinge on which most of the rest of the 1933 Act turns. Its overall purpose is to require that new issues of securities offered by the use of the mails or other instrumentalities of interstate commerce shall be registered with the Commission, and that a prospectus (filed as a part of the registration statement) shall be furnished to the purchaser prior to the sale or, in some cases, at the time of the delivery of the security after sale. Section 5 can only be understood, however, by

---

[1] Reversing an earlier trend, the Courts of Appeals have uniformly concluded that there is no private cause of action under § 17(a). See Zink v. Merrill Lynch Pierce Fenner & Smith, 13 F.3d 330 (10th Cir. 1993); Finkel v. The Stratton Corporation, 962 F.2d 169 (2d Cir. 1992); Newcome v. Esrey, 862 F.2d 1099, 1107 (4th Cir. 1988) (en banc).

taking § 2 into account, for that section defines a number of the technical terms used in § 5. Section 3 exempts from the operation of the 1933 Act (except for the antifraud provisions of §§ 17 and 12(a)(2)) a laundry list of different types of securities and transactions and thus further limits § 5. In addition, § 4 specifically provides that § 5 shall not apply to certain specified transactions (most notably, private placements) and thus further restricts the reach of § 5. Finally, although § 5 seemingly applies to "any person," we learn in § 4(a)(1) that the section does not apply to transactions by anyone unless the person is "an issuer, underwriter, or dealer"—something quite different. Again, these terms are words of art that are defined in § 2 and have meanings far broader than a lay person might expect.

The "registration statement" referred to in § 5 is defined in § 2(a)(8). Sections 6 through 8 set forth the procedures for registering securities, from the filing of the registration statement with the SEC until it becomes effective. Section 5 also regulates the use of the "prospectus." That term is defined in § 2(a)(10), and again the reach of this term is far broader than the ordinary person would expect and can reach any communication that offers securities or seeks to "condition the market" for them. The information required to be set forth in the registration statement is specified in § 7 (and, other than for a foreign government, or political subdivision, in Schedule A), and § 10 prescribes the contents of a prospectus.

Other sections of the 1933 Act are concerned with enforcement procedures. Sections 11 and 12 give private remedies to buyers of securities. The scope of those remedies is examined later in Chapter 13. Private remedies are rounded out by § 13, which fixes a short statute of limitations for §§ 11 and 12 actions; by § 14, which invalidates any contractual provision that attempts a waiver of remedies; and by § 15, which imposes joint and several liability upon persons in a control relationship with any person liable under §§ 11 or 12.[2]

To complete the overall picture, reference needs to be made to a number of miscellaneous sections. Section 18 partially preempts state "blue sky" laws that regulate the issuance and sale of securities to the extent the securities are listed on an exchange or meet certain other standards.[3] Section 19(a) gives the SEC rule-making powers, including the power to define accounting, technical, and trade terms used in the 1933 Act. It also contains an important good faith defense that immunizes from liability persons who rely on a rule or regulation of the Commission in good faith, even though it is later determined to be invalid.

The government may compel compliance with the 1933 Act in various ways. Sections 19(b) and 20(a) give the SEC investigative powers. Section 20

---

[2] This term, for example, would include the promoters in the case of Old Dominion Copper Mining & Smelting Co. v. Lewisohn, 210 U.S. 206 (1908), even though the securities were sold by the corporation, rather than the promoters. Although this case preceded the 1933 Act, it shows how the concept of control has long been construed.

[3] This topic and the impact of the National Securities Markets Improvements Act of 1996 was discussed earlier in Chapter 1. To the extent it is not preempted, a state may require merit review of out-of-state offerings of securities to be made within the state, even though the offering has met the disclosure requirements of the 1933 Act. See, e.g., North Star Intern. v. Arizona Corporation Commission, 720 F.2d 578 (9th Cir. 1983).

also authorizes the SEC to seek the judicial remedies of injunction and mandamus. This long-standing remedial power has been expanded in two important steps. First, the Securities Enforcement Remedies Act of 1990 authorizes the federal courts to issue cease-and-desist orders for violation of the securities laws, order the payment of penalties in addition to disgorgement, and prohibit persons from serving as officers and directors of public companies. Second, the Dodd-Frank Act expanded § 8A of the 1933 Act so that the SEC has the option of relying on administrative proceedings before administrative law judges. However, the power to institute criminal proceedings is exclusively vested in the Attorney General. Criminal penalties are specified in § 24.[4]

Court procedures are prescribed in §§ 9 and 22. Under § 9, a person aggrieved by an order of the Commission may have it reviewed in the United States Courts of Appeals. Jurisdiction over "offenses and violations" is vested in the United States district courts by virtue of § 22(a), although the state and territorial courts have concurrent jurisdiction with respect to civil actions under the 1933 Act. In suits in the federal courts, venue may be laid in the district where the defendant is found, is an inhabitant, or transacts business or where the offer or sale of the security occurred. Process runs throughout the world,[5] and the court may order security for costs under § 11(e).

With this preview of the overall structure of the 1933 Act, § 5 should be examined more closely. The section states the ground rules for making offers and sales of securities during three distinct periods of time: (1) the pre-filing period (the so-called "quiet period"); (2) the period between the filing of the

---

[4] The SEC is authorized to conduct investigations that may result in the "[i]nstitution of administrative proceedings looking to the imposition of remedial sanctions, initiation of injunctive proceedings in the courts, and, in the case of willful violation, reference of the matter to the Department of Justice for criminal prosecution." 17 C.F.R. § 202.5(b). The process is described in McLucas et al., An Overview of Various Procedural Considerations Associated With the Securities and Exchange Commission's Investigative Process, 45 Bus.Law. 625 (1990).

Congress and the courts have noted the "close working relationship" between the two agencies in their investigative capacities. See United States v. Stringer, 521 F.3d 1189 (9th Cir. 2008); SEC v. Dresser Industries, Inc., 628 F.2d 1368, 1386 (D.C.Cir. 1980) (*en banc*), cert. denied, 449 U.S. 993 (1980). The scope of the SEC's enforcement powers is described later in Chapter 19.

[5] Under § 22(a), process may be served "wherever the defendant may be found." Similar language appears in § 27 of the 1934 Act. In Fitzsimmons v. Barton, 589 F.2d 330 (7th Cir. 1979), nationwide service under § 27 and Fed.R.Civ.P. 4(e) withstood a constitutional attack on the basis of the Due Process Clause of the Fourteenth Amendment. In Bersch v. Drexel Firestone, Inc., 389 F.Supp. 446 (S.D.N.Y.1974), rev'd in part on other grounds, 519 F.2d 974 (2d Cir. 1975), cert. denied, 423 U.S. 1018 (1975), service of process on a British corporation by mailing a copy of the summons and complaint pursuant to F.R.C.P. Rule 4(i)(1)(D), return receipt requested, to its office outside the United States was held sufficient even though the envelope containing the summons and complaint was returned to the sender marked "delivery refused." The court held that defendant was "found" at its head office, despite its effort to avoid service of process merely by returning the papers. In SEC v. Unifund SAL, 910 F.2d 1028 (2d Cir. 1990), the district court ordered service of process to be made by sending all relevant papers to the defendant in care of the defendant's New York broker with instructions to forward the papers by overnight carrier to the defendant in Beirut. Service was held proper under § 27 of the 1934 Act and Fed.R.Civ.P. 4(e) and 4(i). See also SEC v. International Swiss Invs. Corp., 895 F.2d 1272 (9th Cir. 1990).

registration statement and the effective date (the so-called "waiting period"); and (3) the post-effective period.

Section 5(a) requires an "effective" registration statement as a precondition to the sale of a security; § 5(b) states the prospectus delivery requirements; and § 5(c) governs activities in the pre-filing period. Sections 5(b) and (c) were significantly relaxed by exemptive rules adopted by the SEC in 2005. Still, these exemptive rules have important preconditions and, therefore, they do not always apply. Hence, one must understand both the complex structure of § 5 and the SEC's more permissive rules. The only way to do this is to review § 5 in its entirety.

2. THE PRE-FILING PERIOD ("GUN JUMPING")

Statutes

Securities Act, §§ 2(a)(3), 2(a)(4), 2(a)(10), 2(a)(11), 2(a)(12), 4(a)(1), 5(c), 12(a)(1).

Rules and Regulations

Rules 135, 135a, 135c, 137, 138, 139, 163, 163A, 163B, 168, 169.[6]

A. PRELIMINARY NEGOTIATIONS BETWEEN ISSUER AND UNDERWRITER

Section 5(c) makes it unlawful for *any person* to make use of interstate facilities or the mails to offer to sell or to offer to buy any security before a registration statement with respect to the security has been filed with the SEC. Section 2(a)(3) defines the terms "sell" and "offer to sell" very broadly to embrace every attempt or offer to dispose of a security, for value. Even oral interstate telephone offers are proscribed, as it is immaterial whether the offer is made by means of a prospectus (as defined in § 2(a)(10)) or otherwise. Nor need there be a formal offer— any oral statement that seeks to "condition the market" or arouse interest in the issuer or its securities can be deemed an offer that violates § 5(c).[7] Indeed, unless § 5(c) were further qualified, it would literally prohibit normal trading transactions in outstanding securities, either on the stock exchanges or in the over-the-counter market, if the mails or interstate facilities were used. Limiting language precluding this overreach is found in § 4(a)(1), which excludes from § 5 transactions "by any person other than an issuer, underwriter, or dealer."

As a practical matter, § 5 does not become operational until an issuer has begun the process of preparing for an offering of its securities. At this

---

[6] Some explanation should be made as to the SEC's system of rule numbering. Since about 1940, the rules have been published in the Code of Federal Regulations, Title 17, Chapter II. The general rules and regulations under each act administered by the SEC appear as the following parts of Chapter II: Securities Act of 1933, part 230; Securities Exchange Act of 1934, part 240; Public Utility Holding Company Act of 1935, part 250; Trust Indenture Act of 1939, part 260; Investment Company Act of 1940, part 270; and Investment Advisers Act of 1940, part 275.

[7] See Securities Act Release No. 3844 (1957).

point, it is said to be "in registration" and must, in most cases, observe strict limits on what it can say about itself or the prospective offering. No bright line test establishes when an issuer is "in registration," but that point is clearly reached once any agreement relating to the offering (even if non-binding) is signed with any prospective underwriter.

Section 4(a)(1) is significant in two respects. On the one hand, the ordinary investor who is not engaged in the securities business, but who buys and sells securities for her own account, is free of any restrictions, so long as she does not engage in a transaction which would result in the person becoming an issuer, underwriter, or dealer.[8] (See §§ 2(a)(4), 2(a)(11), 2(a)(12)). On the other hand, standing alone, § 5(c) and § 4(a)(1) would prohibit an issuer, or a controlling person, proposing to offer securities from using the mails or interstate facilities to contact a managing or lead underwriter with a view to a public issue, and would preclude an underwriter from similarly approaching the issuer or controlling person, until a registration statement had been filed with the SEC. Clearly, however, negotiations at this level must take place in the pre-filing period if the transaction is to get off the ground. Therefore, § 2(a)(3) excludes from the definition of the terms "sale," "sell," "offer to sell," "offer for sale," "offer," and "offer to buy" as used in § 5(c), "preliminary negotiations or agreements" between an issuer or any affiliate and any underwriter who will be in privity of contract with the issuer or any affiliate.

a. The Initial Steps in the Pre-Filing Period. If an issuer and underwriter reach a tentative understanding that the underwriter will manage the issue, their mutual intention will sometimes be embodied in a "memorandum of understanding" or "letter of intent." This memorandum or letter will likely set forth the approximate amount of the issue, call for preparation of a registration statement and the formation of an underwriting group of which this underwriter will serve as manager, and determine how the various expenses of the offering will be allocated. This memorandum or letter may also indicate a proposed maximum and minimum offering price and a maximum percentage for underwriting discounts and dealer allowances, all subject, however, to market conditions. Finally, the memorandum or letter will state that it is not intended to be a binding commitment of either party, except as to any agreement regarding the assumption of expenses should the underwriting not materialize.[9]

---

[8] 1 Loss & Seligman, Securities Regulation 433 (3d ed. 1989). But see Morgan, Offers to Buy Under the Securities Act of 1933, 1982 Ariz.St.L.J. 809 (1982).

[9] Where a letter of intent stated that no liability was intended to be created, a prospective underwriter was denied recovery, in quantum meruit, for services performed and expenses incurred in implementing the letter. See Dunhill Securities Corp. v. Microthermal Applications, Inc., 308 F.Supp. 195 (S.D.N.Y. 1969); Newharbor Partners v. F.D. Rich Co., 961 F.2d 294 (1st Cir. 1992) (collecting cases). More ambiguity exists when there is no language expressly making the letter non-binding. See M. L. Lee & Co. v. American Cardboard & Packaging Corp., 424 F.2d 532 (3d Cir. 1970); 1 Securities Law Techniques § 18.04, app. 18C (A. Sommer ed. 1985) (sample letter of intent).

A great deal of activity occurs in the pre-filing period. A team must be organized to prepare the registration statement. The players will normally include the chief executive officer and the chief financial officer of the issuer, the lead underwriter and any co-manager, counsel for the issuer and for the underwriter, and the issuer's accountants. Potentially dozens of people may be involved in preparing the registration statement, and the average waiting period may last anywhere from thirty to more than sixty days, depending both on the SEC's case load at the time and how contentious the negotiations are between the issuer and the SEC's staff. Of course, the registrant chooses the filing date, but in practice, the SEC determines the effective date of the registration statement. It is important that no offer, not even an oral offer nor any attempt to solicit an offer to buy the security, occur during the pre-filing period, unless it is exempted by a special rule. Any such non-exempted public disclosure or announcement that tends to arouse interest in the offering may be deemed to be "gun jumping."[10]

Gun jumping is a serious matter, because any violation of § 5 can trigger a right to rescind under § 12(a)(1). In addition, the SEC may order a delay in the offering, and delay may be fatal (if market conditions change). Accordingly, during the waiting period counsel for the issuer must review all press releases or other communications emanating from the issuer to determine whether an offer to sell a security may be entailed. Certain large issuers, known as "Well-Known Seasoned Issuers" (or "WKSIs"), are exempted from the quiet period's prohibitions, but any written offer made by them must bear a mandated legend and be filed with the SEC. (See Rule 163). Thus, even in these cases, issuer's counsel must monitor the client's statements closely.

Unless a single underwriter is willing to take the full commitment (which is unusual), it will spread the risk by inducing other underwriters to join in an underwriting group in which each member will purchase a part of the offering directly from the issuer. The agreement among underwriters is the basic document that appoints the managing underwriter as the representative of the other underwriters to conclude negotiations with the issuer and defines their relationships with the manager and with each other. Typical matters covered by the agreement among underwriters are the number of shares to be purchased by each underwriter, the public offering price, the underwriting spread and the price to the issuer, and the discounts or concessions to be allowed to members of the selling group. The agreement also usually vests in the manager broad discretion (i) to engage in "stabilizing" activities in the immediate aftermarket (which is a technique by which underwriters set

---

[10] Prior to Google's initial public offering in 2004, its founders gave an interview to Playboy magazine. Although the interview was well before the offering process began, it was published well into the offering and was deemed by the SEC to fall within the meaning of "offer." Google was forced to disclose in its registration statement that it faced potential liability under § 5 for this interview. See Hurt, What Google Can't Tell Us About Internet Auctions (And What It Can), 37 U. Tol. L. Rev. 403, 422 (2006).

a floor under the stock's price to "protect" the offering from short-sellers and investor panic), (ii) to reserve from each underwriter's participation a certain number of shares to be offered to institutional investors and to selling group members, and (iii) otherwise to allocate the shares so as to balance supply with demand.

The "preliminary negotiations" exception from the terms "sell," "offer to sell," and the other definitions in § 2(a)(3) extends not only to the preliminary negotiations between the issuer and underwriters, but also to negotiation of the terms of the final underwriting agreement as well. Furthermore, the 1954 amendments made clear that the exception extends to negotiations and agreements between an affiliate of the issuer (which term includes any controlling person) and any underwriter. In addition, the language was enlarged to encompass negotiations and agreements among underwriters who are to be in privity of contract with an issuer or affiliate. As the Report of the Senate Committee put it: "The sole purpose of this [language] is to make clear that the usual agreement among underwriters as well as the agreement between the underwriters and the issuer (or controlling person, as the case may be) may be made before the registration statement has been filed."[11] Although the issuer can enter into an agreement with the prospective underwriters, neither it nor they may contact "selling group" members or other potential buyers, because selling group members will buy from the underwriters and, thus, will not be in privity with the issuer.

Apart from these activities between the issuer (or an affiliate) and the underwriters, § 5(c) forbids any further selling effort downstream before the registration statement has been filed. This would include sales activity by use of the mails or interstate facilities directed at dealers or any other prospective customers. A similar ban is placed upon dealers making offers to buy from the underwriters in the pre-filing period. However, as soon as a public offering is in the wind, the issuer may be inclined to shape its public relations program so as to release corporate information designed to awaken the interest of investors in the issuer and its securities. Once negotiations with the lead underwriter have commenced, news of the forthcoming offering travels fast in the financial world, and issuers, underwriters, and dealers are not easily kept under leash, despite these restraints on pre-filing selling activity.

When may the dissemination of information be regarded as a part of the normal flow of corporate information to security holders and the public, unrelated to selling effort, and when is it of a character calculated to arouse and stimulate investor and dealer interest and thus set in motion the processes of distribution? The following material sets forth the SEC's position on the problem of gun jumping.

---

[11] S.Rep.No. 1036, 83 Cong., 2d Sess. 11 (1954).

B. THE TRADITIONAL DIVIDING LINE BETWEEN PRE-FILING SALES PUBLICITY AND TIMELY DISCLOSURES OF CORPORATE INFORMATION

Section 5(c) of the 1933 Act prohibits offers to sell a security prior to the filing of a registration statement. At the same time, issuers subject to the reporting requirements of § 13 or § 15(d) of the 1934 Act and other publicly-held companies are under a duty to make prompt disclosure under the anti-fraud provisions of the securities laws or the timely disclosure policies of self-regulatory organizations.[12] Difficult questions of fact often arise as to whether an issuer is engaged in disseminating pre-filing sales publicity or is merely complying with its obligations of timely disclosure.

The traditional attitude of the SEC is well illustrated by In the Matter of Carl M. Loeb, Rhoades & Co. and Dominick & Dominick, 38 S.E.C. 843 (1959). There, Davis, the owner of extensive real estate holdings, formed Arvida Corporation, transferred his real estate to the corporation, and sought additional capital through an offering of stock to the public. When the financing proposals reached final form, a press release, issued on the letterhead of Loeb, Rhoades, a registered broker-dealer, was distributed to the New York press and to the principal wire services. The release stated that Arvida would have assets of over $100 million, representing Mr. Davis' investment, and some $25 to $30 million of additional capital would be raised through an offering of stock to the public. The release further stated that a public offering was scheduled to be made within 60 days through a nationwide investment banking group headed by Loeb, Rhoades and Dominick & Dominick, and Davis would transfer to Arvida over 100,000 acres "in the area of the Gold Coast" in Florida. The release identified the principal officers of Arvida and stated that the corporation proposed to undertake a "comprehensive program of orderly development" under which some land would be developed immediately into residential communities and other portions would be held for investment and future development. The release attracted such buying interest from security dealers that over 100 firms contacted the proposed underwriters for inclusion in the underwriting syndicate. Because of this pre-filing publicity, the SEC was able to obtain a

---

[12] A company that is subject to § 13 or § 15(d) of the 1934 Act is commonly referred to as a "reporting" company. In general, excluding certain types of issuers (e.g., banks, bank holding companies, and savings and loan holding companies), these companies comprise: (a) issuers with a class of securities listed or traded on a national securities exchange, e.g., the Nasdaq Global Market or the New York Stock Exchange (§ 12(b) of the 1934 Act); (b) issuers having total assets exceeding $10 million and a class of equity securities held of record by either (i) 2,000 or more persons or (ii) 500 or more persons who are not accredited investors (§ 12(g) of the 1934 Act); and (c) issuers with an effective 1933 Act registration statement (§ 15(d) of the 1934 Act). By registering securities under § 12(b) or § 12(g) of the 1934 Act, a company becomes subject to the periodic reporting requirements of § 13 of the 1934 Act. Note that few companies today have more than 1,000 shareholders of record because most shareholders today hold their stock in the "street name" of their broker or bank to facilitate easier trading.

permanent injunction for violations of § 5(c) by the proposed underwriters.[13]

Arvida subsequently filed a registration statement with respect to the proposed offering. The final prospectus disclosed that the properties were heavily mortgaged and a substantial part of the proceeds from the financing might be required to meet mortgage indebtedness and would be unavailable to develop the property. The Commission thereupon instituted proceedings against Loeb, Rhoades and Dominick & Dominick, seeking to suspend or expel them from membership in the National Association of Securities Dealers ("NASD," today merged into the Financial Industry Regulatory Association ("FINRA")). Although the Commission found willful violations of § 5(c) of the 1933 Act, it ultimately decided that, because of other mitigating factors, the drastic action of revocation, suspension, or expulsion of the underwriters from membership in the NASD was unnecessary.

A decade later, a more difficult case was presented in Chris-Craft Industries, Inc. v. Bangor Punta Corp., 426 F.2d 569 (2d Cir. 1970), which grew out of a bitter takeover battle for the control of Piper Aircraft Corporation between Chris-Craft Industries and Bangor Punta Corporation. Chris-Craft had made a cash tender offer for Piper stock. The Piper family thereupon negotiated a competing exchange offer of a package of securities from Bangor Punta Corporation under which all Piper shareholders would be entitled to exchange each share of Piper stock held by them for Bangor Punta securities and cash "having a value in the written opinion of The First Boston Corporation, of $80 or more."

Because the Bangor Punta exchange offer entailed a public offering of securities to the Piper Aircraft shareholders, Bangor Punta prepared to file a registration statement under the 1933 Act covering the proposed exchange offer. Upon the conclusion of the agreement between them, Bangor Punta and Piper management simultaneously issued a press release stating that Bangor Punta had "agreed to file a registration statement with the SEC covering the proposed exchange offer for any or all of the remaining outstanding shares of Piper Aircraft for a package of Bangor Punta securities to be valued in the judgment of The First Boston Corporation at not less than $80 per Piper share."

Chris-Craft sought a preliminary injunction to restrain Bangor Punta from making the exchange offer, claiming that the press release violated § 5(c) of the 1933 Act and Rule 135 promulgated thereunder. The contention was that Rule 135 exempts certain disclosures of pre-filing publicity from the definition of an "offer to sell" prohibited by § 5(c); that the categories of information privileged under the Rule are exclusive and do not permit a disclosure of the value of the securities to be offered; and that the announcement that the package of securities to be offered by

---

[13] SEC v. Arvida Corp., 169 F.Supp. 211 (S.D.N.Y. 1958).

Bangor Punta would have a value of $80 overstepped the exemption and made the press release an offer to sell.

Reversing the district court's conclusion that the press release did not violate § 5(c), the Second Circuit stated:

> When it is announced that securities will be sold at some date in the future and, in addition, an attractive description of these securities and of the issuer is furnished, it seems clear that such an announcement provides much the same kind of information as that contained in a prospectus. See SEC v. Arvida Corp., 169 F.Supp. 211 (S.D.N.Y.1958). Doubtless the line drawn between an announcement containing sufficient information to constitute an offer and one which does not must be to some extent arbitrary. A checklist of features that may be included in an announcement which does not also constitute an offer to sell serves to guide the financial community and the courts far better than any judicially formulated 'rule of reason' as to what is or is not an offer. Rule 135 provides just such a checklist, and if the Rule is not construed as setting forth an exclusive list, then much of its value as a guide is lost.

Some believe that the Commission's strong prophylactic rule against gun jumping may eventually encounter a First Amendment obstacle.[14] That has not yet happened, but remains an issue that could surface again in the future.

---

[14] For over 80 years it has been generally thought that the First Amendment of the United States Constitution was inapplicable to the 1933 Act restrictions on advertising in the offer and sale of securities. Thus, in SEC v. Starmont, 31 F.Supp. 264, 268 (E.D.Wash. 1939), the use of a publication, "Mining Truth," to sell securities was enjoined despite the claim of interference with "the rights of free press." Recently, however, doubts have been voiced as to whether the restrictions on the general advertising of securities are excluded from the First Amendment protections for commercial speech. See Virginia State Bd. of Pharmacy v. Virginia Citizens Consumer Council, Inc., 425 U.S. 748 (1976); Lowe v. SEC, 472 U.S. 181 (1985), rev'g, 725 F.2d 892 (2d Cir. 1984), rev'g, 556 F.Supp. 1359 (E.D.N.Y. 1983). In particular, the Supreme Court's 2011 decision in Sorrell v. IMS Health, 564 U.S. 552 (2011), hints that the Court may be narrowing its former commercial speech doctrine, but its impact remains difficult to assess.

Numerous articles have discussed whether the restrictions on advertising under the 1933 Act registration process, the regulation of advisers under the Investment Advisers Act of 1940, the regulation of proxy communications, and the anti-fraud and insider trading prohibitions under the 1934 Act unreasonably infringe First Amendment freedoms. See, e.g., Estreicher, Securities Regulation and the First Amendment, 24 Geo.L.Rev. 223 (1990); Neuborne, The First Amendment and Government Regulation of the Capital Markets, 55 Brooklyn L.Rev. 65 (1989); Winter, A First Amendment Overview, 55 Brooklyn L.Rev. 71, 74 (1989). If the Supreme Court were to adopt a more expansive view of First Amendment freedoms in this area, a significant part of the federal system of securities regulation might be disrupted or even dismantled.

Securities Act Release No. 5180
Securities and Exchange Commission.
August 16, 1971.

GUIDELINES FOR THE RELEASE OF INFORMATION BY ISSUERS WHOSE SECURITIES ARE IN REGISTRATION

The Commission today took note of situations when issuers whose securities are "in registration"[15] may have refused to answer legitimate inquiries from stockholders, financial analysts, the press or other persons concerning the company or some aspect of its business. The Commission hereby emphasizes that there is no basis in the securities acts or in any policy of the Commission which would justify the practice of non-disclosure of *factual* information by a publicly held company on the grounds that it has securities in registration under the Securities Act of 1933 ("Act"). Neither a company in registration nor its representatives should instigate publicity for the purpose of facilitating the sale of securities in a proposed offering. * * *

* * * It has been asserted that the increasing obligations and incentives of corporations to make timely disclosures concerning their affairs creates a possible conflict with statutory restrictions on publication of information concerning a company which has securities in registration. As the Commission has stated in previously issued releases, this conflict may be more apparent than real. Disclosure of factual information in response to inquiries or resulting from a duty to make prompt disclosure under the antifraud provisions of the securities acts or the timely disclosure policies of self-regulatory organizations, at a time when a registered offering of securities is contemplated or in process, can and should be effected in a manner which will not unduly influence the proposed offering.

* * *

Guidelines

The Commission strongly suggests that all issuers establish internal procedures designed to avoid problems relating to the release of corporate information when in registration. As stated above, issuers and their representatives should not initiate publicity when in registration, but should nevertheless respond to legitimate inquiries for factual information about the company's financial condition and business operations. * * *

It has been suggested that the Commission promulgate an all inclusive list of permissible and prohibited activities in this area. This is not feasible for the reason that determinations are based upon the particular facts of each case. However, the Commission as a matter of

---

[15] "In registration" is used herein to refer to the entire process of registration, at least from the time an issuer reaches an understanding with the broker-dealer which is to act as managing underwriter prior to the filing of a registration statement and the period of 40 to 90 days during which dealers must deliver a prospectus.

policy encourages the flow of factual information to shareholders and the investing public. Issuers in this regard should:

1. Continue to advertise products and services.

2. Continue to send out customary quarterly, annual and other periodic reports to stockholders.

3. Continue to publish proxy statements and send out dividend notices.

4. Continue to make announcements to the press with respect to factual business and financial developments; i.e., receipt of a contract, the settlement of a strike, the opening of a plant, or similar events of interest to the community in which the business operates.

5. Answer unsolicited telephone inquiries from stockholders, financial analysts, the press and others concerning factual information.

6. Observe an 'open door' policy in responding to unsolicited inquiries concerning factual matters from securities analysts, financial analysts, security holders, and participants in the communications field who have a legitimate interest in the corporation's affairs.

7. Continue to hold stockholder meetings as scheduled and to answer shareholders' inquiries at stockholder meetings relating to factual matters.[16]

In order to curtail problems in this area, issuers in this regard should avoid:

1. Issuance of forecasts, projections, or predictions relating but not limited to revenues, income, or earnings per share.[17]

2. Publishing opinions concerning values.

In the event a company publicly releases material information concerning new corporate developments during the period that a registration statement is pending, the registration statement should be amended at or prior to the time the information is released. If this is not done and such information is publicly released through inadvertence, the pending registration statement should be promptly amended to reflect such information.

The determination of whether an item of information or publicity could be deemed to constitute an offer—a step in the selling effort—in violation of section 5 must be made by the issuer in the light of all the facts and circumstances surrounding each case. The Commission recognizes that questions may arise from time to time with respect to the release of information by companies in registration and, while the

---

[16] Today, the position taken in Securities Act Release No. 5180 has been expanded. New SEC Rules 168 and 169 provide broad authority for the release of factual information, so long as no reference is made to the proposed offering.

[17] But, under Rule 168, forward-looking information may today be released by reporting companies during the quiet period, and under Rule 163, large seasoned issuers ("WKSIs") are largely exempt from the quiet period's prohibition on market conditioning.

statutory obligation always rests with the company and can never be shifted to the staff, the staff will be available for consultation concerning such questions. It is not the function of the staff to draft corporate press releases. If a company, however, desires to consult with the staff as to the application of the statutory requirements to a particular case, the staff will continue to be available, and in this regard the pertinent facts should be set forth in written form and submitted in sufficient time to allow due consideration.

* * *

C. DOWNSIZING THE QUIET PERIOD: THE SEC'S REVISED RULES

Although the goal of § 5(c) was to make the prospectus the exclusive source of information about the issuer and the offering, two problems quickly arose with a rule that is this prophylactic. First, public companies have existing shareholders who want ongoing disclosure of information and who are entitled to current reports under the 1934 Act. Thus, an inevitable tension existed between protecting new investors from market conditioning and providing current information to existing shareholders (who, in the case of a seasoned issuer, are likely to vastly outnumber the new investors in the public offering). Securities Act Release No. 5180 sought to accommodate both goals and strike a compromise, but increasingly existing shareholders became accustomed to receiving corporate projections as to future earnings and developments (which Release 5180 did not authorize). Second, companies legitimately need to communicate with customers, suppliers, and the public for reasons wholly unrelated to soliciting them as investors. Later, with the growth of electronic communications and the internet in the 1990s, the concept of a quiet period became increasingly difficult to enforce or sustain. Information, including information about an approaching offering, was everywhere. Not only securities analysts and investors, but also the media became fascinated with the IPO market, and in the 1990s, cable channels (such as CNN and CNBC) gave IPOs major attention. In 2001, the American Bar Association suggested to the SEC that, at least in the case of seasoned issuers, the goals of the quiet period had become infeasible, in part because a multitude of securities analysts would predictably follow and comment on pending and expected future developments. It recommended that, even in the case of IPOs, the quiet period be cut back to a period of 30 days prior to the filing of the registration statement.

In 2005, the SEC took this advice to heart and, in its offering reforms, significantly cut back on the quiet period. Specifically, Securities Act Release No. 8591 (July 19, 2005) downsized the quiet period by adopting the following rules:

(1) RULE 163A. This Rule applies to all issuers (with some limited exceptions) and exempts communication made "by or on behalf of an issuer" more than 30 days prior to the filing of the registration statement from the prohibition of § 5(c), at least if the communication "does not reference a securities offering that is or will be the subject of a registration statement." In effect, so long as the future public offering is not discussed or referenced, a bright-line 30-day rule now assures issuers that statements before that date cannot violate § 5(c). However, Rule 163A applies only to statements made by the issuer and its agents; thus, it would not exempt communications released by a prospective "offering participant"—for example, an underwriter or dealer.

(2) RULE 163. This Rule permits "Well-Known Seasoned Issuers" or "WKSIs" (a term that is discussed in detail later, but which is defined by Rule 405 to include the largest, most seasoned issuers) to engage in unrestricted oral and written selling activity before a registration statement is filed; in effect, such issuers are exempted from § 5(c). Again, however, conditions are attached to this exemption. Under Rule 163(b)(1), a mandatory legend must be included in any "written communication that is an offer" advising the offeree to obtain and read the prospectus and informing the offeree of the SEC's web site address where the prospectus can be downloaded. Under Rule 163(b)(2), every written communication made in reliance on this Rule must be filed with the SEC "promptly upon the filing of the registration statement." Also, the exemption again applies only to the issuer and not to "offering participants" (such as underwriters or dealers). Finally, any written offer made in reliance on Rule 163 will be deemed a "free writing prospectus" and a prospectus under § 2(a)(10) (see Rule 163(a)(1)), and thus can give rise to civil liability if it is materially inaccurate.

(3) RULE 168. Applicable only to reporting issuers and certain seasoned foreign private issuers (and, thus, not to most IPOs), this Rule exempts "the regular release or dissemination by or on behalf of an issuer . . . of communications containing factual business information or forward-looking information." The definitions in this Rule make clear that information such as projections of future revenues, income, or earnings per share, "[s]tatements about the issuer management's plans and objectives for future operations" and "[s]tatements about the issuer's future economic performance" are permitted (see Rule 168(b)). As with Rule 163A, no reference may be made to the approaching public offering and information about the offering may not be "released or disseminated as part of the offering activities in the registered offering" (see Rule 168(c)). Nor may "offering participants" (i.e., underwriters and selling group members) rely on this Rule. Finally, the Rule is available only where the issuer "has previously released or disseminated information of the type described in this rule in the ordinary course of its business" and the "timing, manner, and form in which the information is released or disseminated is consistent in material respects with similar past releases

or disseminations" (see Rule 168(d)). In short, Rule 168 permits forecasts, but only of a type previously made by the issuer.

(4) RULE 169. This Rule provides a more limited safe harbor for non-reporting issuers, which again authorizes "the regular release or dissemination by or on behalf of an issuer of communications containing factual business information." Again, the information must have been previously released and the "timing, manner, and form" of the release must be consistent in material respects with past practice. A key difference between Rules 169 and 168 is that Rule 169 does not cover "forward-looking information." Hence, forecasts are not permitted for an IPO issuer that is not a reporting company. Also, the audience to whom the information is released must consist of "persons, such as customers and suppliers, other than in their capacities as investors or potential investors in the issuer's securities," and the information must be released "by the issuer's employees or agents who historically have provided such information" (see Rule 169(d)(3)). In other words, press releases disseminated by an investor relations department would not qualify for this exemption.

(5) RULE 135. None of the rules adopted or amended by the SEC in its 2005 offering reforms permits an issuer (other than a WKSI) to announce a forthcoming offering of securities. Indeed, references to such a future offering are expressly excluded from Rule 163A. The one rule that does permit such an announcement is Rule 135, which was left unchanged by Release 8591. Rule 135 authorizes an issuer to disclose an intention to make a public offering, the amount and type of security, and the manner and purpose of the offering (but not the anticipated offering price). In addition, Rule 135 expressly forbids the issuer to identify the underwriters. Why? The intent is to constrain any downstream marketing efforts at this pre-filing stage, which might arise if potential investors could learn the identity of the underwriters and contact them. In *Chris-Craft Industries, Inc.* (described earlier in this chapter), the Second Circuit held that Rule 135 is the exclusive means by which a pre-filing announcement of an offering may be made. Today, a WKSI can disclose an offering and make statements that go beyond the safe harbor of Rule 135.

The relaxation of the 1933 Act's prophylactic rules did not stop with the 2005 reforms. The next major change came with the passage of the JOBS Act in 2012. This Act's new rules are discussed later in this chapter, but of particular importance was its authorization of "test-the-waters" communications. Specifically, it added § 5(d) to the 1933 Act, which permits certain smaller issuers (known as "emerging growth companies" or "EGCs") to engage in oral or written communications with certain institutional investors, either before or after the registration statement is filed.[18] Thus, for EGCs, § 5(d) overrides both § 5(c) and

---

[18] See the last two sentences of § 2(a)(3) of the 1933 Act. The term "emerging growth company" is now defined in § 2(a)(19) of the 1933 Act.

§ 5(b)(1) of the 1933 Act. Its purpose is to enable EGCs to discuss the feasibility of the offering with institutional investors: What proposed terms troubled them? What terms did they want? What price range is feasible?

Although the JOBS Act applied only to EGCs, the idea of "test-the-waters" communications became popular, and in late 2019, the SEC generalized this approach by adopting Rule 163B.[19] This Rule enables any issuer (not just EGCs), or persons authorized to act for the issuer (including underwriters), to engage in oral and written communications with investors who are either "qualified institutional buyers" (which term is defined in Rule 144A) or other institutional investors who qualify as "accredited investors" (as defined in Rule 501). This means that the underwriters can ignore the gun-jumping and, as discussed below, the "free writing" rules of the 1933 Act in dealing with virtually all institutional investors (but those rules remain in full force with respect to individual investors).

Rule 163B(b)(2) provides that any oral or written communication by the issuer, or any person authorized to act on its behalf, "will be deemed an 'offer' as defined in Section 2(a)(3) of the [Securities] Act." Thus, such communications will be subject to Rule 10b–5 and possibly § 12(a)(2) (but they do not need to be filed with the SEC).

D. BROKER-DEALER ACTIVITIES DURING REGISTRATION

The foregoing exemptions apply to the issuer and its agents, not broker-dealers, including both those who plan to join the offering and those that do not. Broker-dealers are, of course, subject to § 5 because they are by definition not exempted by § 4(a)(1) of the 1933 Act. Any written communication (or radio or T.V. advertisement) that offers a security will likely constitute a prospectus under § 2(a)(10), thus potentially creating liability for the broker-dealer under § 12(a)(1) of the 1933 Act.

Although the SEC traditionally sought to chill marketing efforts by broker-dealers that used any alternative to the registration statement (because it feared overly-optimistic research reports would inflate the stock during the waiting period), it became increasingly hard to justify barring the dissemination of research reports that are prepared by securities analysts, who usually are employed by broker-dealers but whose research often constitutes the most useful information for investors about a given offering. Broker-dealers typically employ securities analysts who research and evaluate companies, and their work clearly assists the efficient pricing of securities. The cost of a prophylactic rule that precluded the distribution of such research by all broker-dealers

---

[19] Rule 163B was proposed by the SEC in Securities Act Release No. 10607 (Feb. 19, 2019) and adopted in Securities Act Release No. 10699 (Sept. 25, 2019).

and their analysts began to seem like an excessive means of protecting investors from the perceived dangers of misleading promotional advice.

As a result, the SEC compromised. The three rules described next permit some distribution of research, opinions, and recommendations, including, to a limited extent, by broker-dealers participating in a distribution:

(1) RULE 137. If a broker-dealer is not participating in the offering and does not intend to participate, this Rule permits the broker to distribute research reports covering the securities of an issuer that is either about to file or has filed a registration statement. This Rule is not available if the broker-dealer received any direct or indirect compensation from the issuer, any other participant in the offering, or "[a]ny other person interested in the securities that are or will be the subject of the registration statement" (see Rule 137(b)). Although Rule 137 was long limited to "reporting" companies, the SEC liberalized the rule as part of its offering reforms in 2005 to apply to all issuers, including IPO (previously non-reporting) firms. Thus, a non-participating broker-dealer is free to describe its own views of the offering, unless it has been compensated for its views.

(2) RULE 138. An issuer that is proposing to issue common stock may also have outstanding a class of non-convertible debt or preferred stock. If broker-dealers who wish to participate in this offering are required to cease publishing research or recommendations concerning the issuer's non-convertible debt securities or preferred stock, this suspension of research might confuse investors and would, in any event, needlessly restrict potentially valuable research. As a result, Rule 138 allows a broker-dealer participating in the common stock offering to continue publishing research about non-convertible debt or preferred stock of the same issuer. Correspondingly, if the issuer is about to issue non-convertible debt or preferred stock, the broker-dealer may publish information, opinions, and recommendations about the issuer's common stock. Rule 138, however, is applicable only to reporting companies (and certain sizable foreign private companies). If the issuer is a non-reporting company, a broker-dealer not participating in the offering can still rely on Rule 137 to publish research reports and recommendations.

(3) RULE 139 AND RULE 139b. If an issuer meets the registrant requirements to use a Form S-3 (or, for foreign private issuers, Form F-3), has a market capitalization sufficient to satisfy the eligibility requirements of Form S-3 or Form F-3, and has satisfied its annual and quarterly reporting obligations under the 1934 Act for the past 12 months (or, alternatively, meets certain other standards in the case of a foreign issuer), a broker-dealer may publish "issuer-specific" research, opinions, and recommendations on such issuer, even though the broker-dealer is participating, or intends to participate, in the offering of the same class of the issuer's securities. The premise here is that such an issuer is

trading in a deep and efficient market and, therefore, is less susceptible to mispricing caused by overly "friendly" research.

Even if an issuer does not qualify for Form S-3 or Form F-3, Rule 139 provides alternatively that, if the issuer is a reporting company (or meets certain corresponding standards in the case of a foreign issuer), the broker-dealer who is participating, or intends to participate, in the offering may publish an "industry report" that covers the issuer; provided, that the "research report includes similar information with respect to a substantial number of issuers in the issuer's industry or sub-industry, or contains a comprehensive list of securities currently recommended by the broker or dealer" (see Rule 139(a)(2)(iii)). In this case, the report must give "no materially greater space or prominence in the publication" regarding the issuer than that given to other securities or issuers, and the broker-dealer must also publish or distribute its research reports "in the regular course of its business . . . [while] including similar information about the issuer or its securities in similar reports" and have previously covered the issuer in other reports (see Rule 139(a)(2)(v)). One reason for this Rule is that if a major broker-dealer—say, Merrill Lynch—had long recommended a particular stock and then dropped all reference to it from its list of recommended stocks (because it was about to participate in an offering of that issuer's securities), retail investors might be confused or interpret this suspension of coverage as an adverse signal.

In 2017, Congress mandated in the Fair Access to Investment Research Act that the SEC extend this same safe harbor to investment funds (e.g., mutual funds, exchange-traded funds, registered closed-end funds, and certain business development companies), and in 2018, the SEC adopted Rule 139b in response.[20] As with Rule 139, new Rule 139b authorizes both "issuer-specific reports" and "industry reports" and allows broker-dealers participating in the offering to use the exemption. In the case of issuer-specific reports, the Rule requires that the investment fund have been a reporting company for at least 12 months, have filed its periodic reports in a timely manner during the prior 12 months, and have an aggregate market value sufficient to qualify for Form S-3 (i.e., at least $75 million). The Rule 139b requirements for industry reports parallel those under Rule 139.

E. THE PROBLEM OF BIASED RESEARCH

Although the SEC liberalized the ability of broker-dealers to publish research during the offering, the principal self-regulatory organizations (then, the New York Stock Exchange ("NYSE") and the NASD, and today FINRA, the body into which they merged) restrict the dissemination of such research to reduce the pressure on analysts to inflate their recommendations. In so doing, they are responding to the widely-shared

---

[20] See Securities Act Release No. 10580 (Nov. 30, 2018). For an overview of this Rule, see Regulatory Developments 2018, 74 Bus. Law. 839 (Summer 2019).

perception that securities analysts may be compelled by the investment banking divisions of their broker-dealer firms, which typically subsidized their research departments, to be virtual cheerleaders and give "buy" recommendations to their firm's underwriting (and prospective) clients. This deep bias towards optimism in the case of IPOs was highlighted by New York Attorney General Eliot Spitzer in his 2002 investigation of research practices. Following a global settlement with all the major underwriting firms in 2002 (the "Global Settlement"), the NASD and the NYSE adopted rules that attempt to reduce this pressure. Chiefly, those rules restrict the influence of the investment banking division by limiting the ability of investment banking personnel to communicate with analysts and barring them from any role in determining security analyst compensation. Nevertheless, these rules also affect the offering process by restricting the publication of research at certain sensitive moments. For example, FINRA Rule 2241 precludes a broker-dealer who participated in an IPO from distributing a research report about an issuer client during a "quiet period" that extends until 10 days after the offering.[21] In addition, FINRA adopted new Rule 2242 with respect to debt offerings, although it contains no quiet period.

In addition, as later discussed in more detail, the JOBS Act permits a research analyst to distribute "research reports" (which include written and oral advice and recommendations) about "emerging growth companies" at virtually any time. This implies that Rules 137–139 may not apply to emerging growth companies (or at least to the activities of analysts working for underwriters in such offerings).

To further reduce the influence that underwriters had over analyst research, FINRA's rules preclude the participation by securities analysts in road shows that market the issuer's securities. Analysts also are barred from participating in "pitches" or other sales meetings at which underwriters solicit the business of a prospective corporate client. Although the JOBS Act permits an analyst to report her research at any time in the case of emerging growth companies, it does not necessarily follow from this that the analyst can participate in marketing efforts designed to win its employer the position of lead or managing underwriter.[22] Any attempt to promise favorable research for future business or other consideration violates FINRA's rules.

At the end of the day, someone must subsidize research analysts, who typically do not generate profits directly. During the 1990s, underwriting profits became the primary source of such subsidization. In

---

[21] In 2015, the SEC approved a new FINRA rule, Rule 2241 ("Research Analysts and Research Reports"), that shortened the former 25-day "quiet period" to 10 days for an IPO and only three days in the case of a follow-on equity offering. Offerings of "emerging growth companies" were carved out from this period in deference to the JOBS Act.

[22] In a "frequently asked questions" (or "FAQ") release issued in August 2012, the SEC took the position that the JOBS Act does not preempt FINRA's rules (including Rule 2241) and does not permit the parties to the Global Settlement to ignore their obligations under it. Arguably, this position could be challenged, but it has not been to date. See http://www.sec.gov/divisions/marketreg/tmjobsact-researchanalystsfaq.htm.

addition, the issuer remains largely free to retaliate by cutting off an analyst that criticizes it from further participation in conference calls or conferences. Even Regulation FD, adopted in 2000, which precludes selective disclosure, does not effectively prevent the issuer from retaliating against a skeptical analyst. As a result, the independence of securities analysts in large brokerage firms remains challenged.

Problems

New Corp., a privately-held company principally financed by six venture capital firms, needs to raise $250 million in an IPO to bring its new cell phone to market. Assume that New Corp.'s revenues in its last fiscal year were $1.4 billion. This new product significantly advances the state of the art, because it can make phone calls, receive and send emails, pick up T.V. and radio signals from a dedicated satellite with over 200 channels, including cable, and download a library of over 10,000 movies and music albums. It also has a computer chip that enables it to search the web, solve mathematical problems, and translate languages. Nevertheless, its feasibility will not be demonstrated until it can be mass-produced. Assume that New Corp. is not a reporting company and has not yet filed a registration statement.

PROBLEM 2-1

On January 10, New Corp.'s chief executive, Max Headroom, calls Thomas Whiteshoe, the head of corporate finance for Bache, Halsey and Co., a major underwriter, in New York from his office in Silicon Valley, California, and asks Whiteshoe if his firm would be willing to lead an underwriting group in an IPO for New Corp. that would raise at least $50 million in equity. Whiteshoe says his firm knows about New Corp. and would be very interested in serving as lead underwriter. "I can fly out there tomorrow with my team, and we could work out a letter of intent by the end of the week." "Let's do it," replies Headroom. By the end of the week, they have entered into a letter agreement that provides that Bache, Halsey will use its best efforts to effect a ten million share offering at a price consistent with other IPOs in the same industry. The agreement further provides that it creates no enforceable obligation, except that New Corp. will pay Bache, Halsey's reasonable expenses incurred in the offering. No registration statement has been filed. Any problems under § 5? Suppose, instead, this letter agreement did require Bache, Halsey to underwrite at least a minimum number of shares at a minimum price?

PROBLEM 2-2

Assume in the alternative that Ponderosa Partners, a venture capital firm owning 8% of New Corp., participates in these negotiations. It attends because it has a contractual right set forth in the private placement agreement by which it acquired its New Corp. shares to include these shares in the first registration statement filed by New Corp. After much negotiation, Ponderosa and Bache, Halsey agree that Bache, Halsey will seek to include half of Ponderosa's shares (i.e., 4%) in the offering. Any problems now under § 5?

PROBLEM 2-3

Also attending these meetings is Kleiner, Gilson Partners, another well-known West Coast venture capital firm, which owns 10% of New Corp., but has no contractual registration rights. It attends, in part, because it wishes to "monitor" the negotiations and make certain that Ponderosa does not receive any advantage over it, and, in part, because it serves as an investment advisor for several related hedge funds that may wish to buy in the offering. Any problem?

PROBLEM 2-4

Immediately following the letter of intent's execution, Whiteshoe calls senior executives at two other underwriters and invites them to join his firm as co-managing underwriters in the New Corp. offering. When they agree, a letter agreement among the three underwriters is executed. Permissible or not at this stage?

PROBLEM 2-5

Whiteshoe next emails some 50 other underwriting firms around the country, inviting them to join the prospective underwriting group. Permissible?

PROBLEM 2-6

Three of the smaller broker-dealers emailed by Whiteshoe respond that they are not in a position to underwrite (because of net capital problems). Still, they would each be willing to buy between 2,000 and 5,000 shares from Bache, Halsey in the offering if they can be given the usual selling discount. Is there any problem with their offer? What if Bache, Halsey agrees to their request, acknowledging they will be sold the shares at the initial offering price minus the standard retail selling discount?

PROBLEM 2-7

Following the letter of intent's execution, Bob Sales, New Corp.'s Vice President for Public Relations, purchases a full-page ad in Fortune Magazine, which has the headline, "Big Things Are Coming!" The advertisement describes the technological capability of New Corp.'s cell phone, which will not roll off the assembly line for at least another six months. Assume that New Corp. is negotiating with wholesalers who will carry its brand and hopes by this ad to attract their attention. Assume, in the alternative, that (a) New Corp. published a similar advertisement six months ago describing its new product or (b) it has never before paid for such an advertisement.

PROBLEM 2-8

Assume the same facts as in Problem 7, except that the Fortune ad now forecasts that New Corp. will have its new cell phone available for distribution by July 30, a date six months away. Although its ability to do so is uncertain, you may assume that this is a good faith estimate. Any problem now under § 5? What if, instead, New Corp. was a reporting company?

PROBLEM 2-9

The day after New Corp. enters into its letter of intent, it issues a press release indicating it intends to make an IPO of its common stock for approximately $50 million by the end of the year, with Bache, Halsey managing the offering for the underwriters. No copy of this press release is filed with the SEC. The press release is picked up by the Wall Street Journal, which announces the same facts the next day. Any problems? Query: Was anything left out of this notice that should have been stated?

PROBLEM 2-10

A month after issuing the foregoing press release, New Corp. publishes a second advertisement, this time in Forbes, again indicating that it will soon be producing a new, revolutionary cell phone with break-through capabilities, which product is now closer to production because of its previously announced IPO with several major underwriters. Is this announcement permissible? Would it be permissible if New Corp. were a reporting company?

PROBLEM 2-11

Assume that no one reacts or responds to the advertisement outlined in Problem 2-10 above. Forty days later, New Corp. files its registration statement on Form S-1. The SEC now advises New Corp. that its prior ad in Forbes violated § 5(c) of the Securities Act. In the alternative, assume that investors who purchased New Corp.'s stock in the subsequent IPO later seek rescission under § 12(a)(1) of the Securities Act because of the alleged § 5(c) violation. What defense can New Corp. raise to both claims? Would it make a difference if the former advertisement just proclaimed: "Major Break Through! New Corp Announces that its Revolutionary New Cell Phone will Soon be Available" (and then described its product in more detail, without discussing the contemplated IPO)?

PROBLEM 2-12

One week after New Corp.'s press release announcing its contemplated offering, IPO Securities, Inc., a broker-dealer that specializes in high-tech companies and IPOs, sends out a research report strongly recommending to investors that they buy shares in New Corp.'s offering. IPO Securities does not plan to participate in the underwriting group conducting the offering. Assume further that (a) it sells its research reports as independent research to a group of subscribers, including several members of the New Corp.

underwriting group, for $6,000 per month from each subscriber, and (b) New Corp. recently hired IPO Securities to develop a "shareholder relations plan" for New Corp. once it becomes publicly held.

PROBLEM 2-13

Following the IPO Securities research report, New Corp. receives phone calls and emails from a number of other securities analysts, each asking questions or requesting an interview. To handle these requests without undue waste of time or effort, New Corp. invites a group of ten of these analysts to its headquarters for a tour of its facilities, an inspection of its new product, and a joint interview with its CEO, Max Headroom. Any problems here?

PROBLEM 2-14

A broker-dealer that will participate in the offering publishes a comprehensive list of recommended securities and includes New Corp. among its "strong buys" (along with 50 other firms, with New Corp. receiving no special attention or prominence). The broker-dealer has long published such reports in the regular course of its business, but this is the first time it has listed New Corp. Would it make any difference if New Corp. were a reporting company?

PROBLEM 2-15

New Corp. publishes a "tombstone ad" in the Wall Street Journal, carrying only the information traditionally permitted in such an ad, and indicates that the securities may not be sold, nor may offers to buy be accepted, until a registration statement covering the securities has become effective. Can it do this?

3. THE WAITING PERIOD

Statutes

Securities Act, §§ 2(a)(10)(b), 5(a), 5(b), 10(a), 10(b).

Rules and Regulations

Rules 134, 135, 135a, 139, 164, 175, 418, 424, 430, 430A, 430B, 431, 433, 460, 461.

The moment the registration statement is filed with the SEC, § 5(c) by its terms drops out of the picture. This means that oral offers can now be made. Sales, of course, are still barred by § 5(a), and the underwriters also cannot accept customers' oral offers to buy. However, the underwriters can "build their book," collecting non-binding indications of interest from customers, which they hope to convert into sales once the registration statement is declared effective. This is critical to the underwriters because it allows them to "test the market" and lower (or raise) the security's price if the offering is undersold (or oversold). Absent such pre-effectiveness "book building," underwriters would face higher risk, and the underwriting discount might be correspondingly greater to compensate them for this higher risk.

But the underwriters' ability to market the offering during the waiting period is constrained by § 5(b)(1), which bars the underwriters and selling group members from distributing any prospectus relating to the security, "unless such prospectus meets the requirements of section 10." Given the broad definition of prospectus in § 2(a)(10), this prohibition essentially precludes any written communication that offers the security—unless the communication is specifically permitted by an SEC rule. This provision once gave a monopoly to the preliminary prospectus that is contained within the registration statement that the issuer has filed. Under Rule 430, the preliminary prospectus is defined to meet the requirements of § 10, and thus it can be distributed to investors before the registration statement is declared effective. But other forms of written communication were long prohibited by § 5(b)(1), thus giving the preliminary prospectus its de facto monopoly status. The statute's intent here was to prevent the issuer from using slick, promotional materials that would not contain the same substantive disclosures as the preliminary prospectus and might attempt to "hype" the offering by making statements the SEC would not allow in the registration statement. Such written materials were known as "free writing," because any such written material that fell outside a specific SEC rule permitting its use during the waiting period was banned. In short, what was not specifically permitted was prohibited.

This highly restrictive approach to marketing the offering ended in 2005, when the SEC adopted Rules 164 and 433, which now permit the issuer and the underwriters to use "free writing," but only on certain terms and conditions. As a result, today some written communications are deemed not to constitute a prospectus; others are deemed to constitute a "free writing prospectus," which is permitted but is subject to civil liability under § 12(a)(2) for materially false or misleading information; and finally, some communications can still violate § 5(b)(1) because they do not qualify as either a "free writing prospectus" or an exempted communication.

A. THE TRADITIONAL OFFERING DOCUMENTS

Although "free writing prospectuses" are now permitted, practices involving their use have not yet standardized. At least for the present, the principal offering documents remain the following:

1. *The Preliminary or "Red-Herring" Prospectus.* Originally, the Securities Act did not contemplate that the offering would be marketed prior to the effectiveness of the registration statement. However, the underwriting industry needed to pre-sell the offering to test the market and reduce its risk; thus, it lobbied the Commission to tolerate some marketing during the waiting period, so long as the only document used

was the prospectus filed with the Commission. The SEC rationalized this result by taking the position that the prospectus on file with the Commission (which included the mandatory "red herring" legend stating that it was not to be deemed an offer) did not constitute an offer to sell. Debatable as the distinction was that the SEC drew between "solicitation" (which was forbidden) and "dissemination of information" (which the "red herring" prospectus was viewed by the SEC as permissibly doing), the red herring prospectus was a practical accommodation by means of which material information then on file with the SEC could be distributed to potential investors in a document that enabled marketing to begin before effectiveness.[23]

In 1954, amendments to the 1933 Act legitimized this theory, and the "red herring" prospectus (now renamed the "preliminary prospectus") was expressly permitted, along with other communications the Commission chose by rule to exclude from § 2(a)(10). The practical effect was that underwriters could start their sales campaign as soon as the registration statement was filed and did not need to engage in the pretense that they were simply providing information to investors in the form of the "red herring" prospectus. Although offers to sell by the use of the mails or interstate facilities were no longer prohibited during the waiting period, they were closely regulated.

Here, it is important to understand clearly the relationship between § 5(b)(1) and § 10(b). Under § 5(b)(1), a prospectus that meets the requirements of § 10 may be used to make offers to sell during the waiting period. During this period, the statutory prospectus referred to in § 10(a) is not yet available, because much information—the price, the underwriters' discount, and the names of the underwriters—is not yet known. But § 10(b) authorizes the Commission to issue rules allowing the use, for § 5(b)(1) purposes, of a prospectus that summarizes or omits some of the information required by § 10(a) to be in the "statutory" (or "final") prospectus.

Rule 430 does just that, providing that a form of prospectus filed as a part of the registration statement shall be deemed to meet the requirements of § 10(b) for the purpose of § 5(b)(1) prior to the effective date of the registration statement, if it contains substantially the information required to meet the requirements of § 10(a). This document is often referred to as a § 10(b) prospectus to distinguish it from a § 10(a) prospectus. The red-herring tradition is carried forward in Regulation S–K, Item 501(b)(10), which requires any preliminary prospectus used before the effective date of the registration statement to contain the caption "Subject to Completion" and a specifically prescribed legend that disclaims any intention to make an offer to sell or solicit an offer to buy

---

[23] See Securities Act Release No. 8591 (Jul. 19, 2005). The name originated from the red ink legend disclaiming any intent to solicit offers to buy or make an offer to sell that appeared on each page of the "red herring" prospectus. See Lobell, Revision of the Securities Act, 48 Colum.L.Rev. 324 (1948); Dean, Twenty-Five Years of Federal Regulation by the Securities and Exchange Commission, 59 Colum.L.Rev. 697, 714–15 (1959).

the securities proposed to be offered. This is, of course, disingenuous. The underwriters are offering the stock for sale, although they cannot yet consummate the transaction.

2. *The Summary Prospectus.* Under Rule 431, a summary prospectus (or a preliminary summary prospectus) may be prepared and filed as a part of the registration statement. This type of prospectus, however, is available only if the registration statement form used to register the securities provides for its use. The conditions for use are prescribed by Rule 431 and by the authorizing form. In general, a summary prospectus may be used by domestic issuers that (1) have their principal business operations in the United States; (2) are reporting companies; and (3) have filed in a timely manner all reports under §§ 13, 14, or 15(d) of the 1934 Act for the twelve months preceding the offering and have also filed (not necessarily in a timely manner) all such reports for the three years prior to the filing of the registration statement. There are other criteria, including the absence of defaults in dividend or sinking fund obligations on preferred stock or debt obligations.

The summary prospectus (as well as the preliminary summary prospectus) is authorized pursuant to § 10(b) of the 1933 Act. That subsection provides that a § 10(b) prospectus filed as a part of the registration statement shall not be deemed to be a part of the registration statement for purposes of § 11, which imposes civil liability on issuers, underwriters, and others for material misstatements or omissions in registration statements. The summary prospectus is to be used for informational purposes only and, like the preliminary prospectus, does not qualify as a final prospectus meeting the requirements of § 10(a) of the 1933 Act.

3. *The "Tombstone Ad."* The Securities Act also envisaged one other way for reaching potential customers—the "tombstone ad," which derives its quaint name from the starkness of its contents. Even before 1954, § 2(a)(10)(b) excluded from the general definition of "prospectus" any communication in respect of a security "if it states from whom a written prospectus meeting the requirements of § 10 may be obtained and, in addition, does no more than identify the security, state the price thereof, [and] state by whom orders will be executed." The use of a tombstone ad was not permitted until after the registration statement had become effective. In 1954, however, § 2(a)(10) was amended to permit the use of an "identifying statement" during the waiting period as well, but still not in the pre-filing period. Although § 2(a)(10)(b) states that a statutory tombstone ad is not a "prospectus," it is silent as to whether it constitutes an "offer." Accordingly, § 5(c) effectively prohibits its use in the pre-filing period.

4. *The Identifying Statement.* Section 2(a)(10)(b) was also amended to permit the Commission to issue rules authorizing an expanded "tombstone ad" or "identifying statement" containing such additional information as it deems appropriate. The Commission responded by

issuing Rule 134, which permits the use of an enlarged statement so long as the conditions of the Rule are met.

Rule 134 enumerates 22 categories of information that may be included in the identifying statement. In addition to such matters as name of the issuer, title of the security, the contact information of the sender of the communication, and the identity of the underwriters—all of which are permitted by a tombstone ad—Rule 134 permits the communication to include a brief indication of the general type of business and certain specific information relating to senior securities (e.g., certain debt securities and preferred stock), if they are being offered.

In theory, the "tombstone ad" and "identifying statement" are not intended to serve as selling documents but serve "purely as a screening device to ascertain what persons [are] . . . sufficiently interested to warrant delivery to them of the statutory prospectus."[24] Certain mandatory provisions are designed to accomplish this objective. If the registration statement has not become effective, the identifying statement (1) must contain a red-herring-like legend stating that the securities may not be sold nor offers to buy be accepted prior to the effectiveness of the registration statement, and (2) must set forth the name and address of a person or persons from whom a § 10 prospectus may be obtained.

An identifying statement may be used during the waiting period to test the market for the securities and attain wider dissemination of the preliminary prospectus. To show how little has changed over the years, set forth below is an example of an identifying statement for a proposed offering of common shares of Owens-Illinois Inc., which appeared in various metropolitan newspapers in 1976 during the waiting period. After testing the market, the proposed offering was reduced from 2 million to 1.4 million shares. The tombstone ad that was used in the post-effective period is also set forth to show the changes that occurred in the composition of the underwriting syndicate. Tombstone ads and identifying statements do not look substantially different today.

---

[24] Securities Act Release No. 3224 (June 6, 1947), Memorandum of the Statutory Revision Committee addressed to the Commission, p. 2.

IDENTIFYING STATEMENT USED IN THE WAITING PERIOD

A registration statement relating to these securities has been filed with the Securities and Exchange Commission but has not yet become effective. These securities may not be sold nor may offers to buy be accepted prior to the time the registration statement becomes effective. This advertisement shall not constitute an offer to sell or the solicitation of an offer to buy nor shall there be any sale of these securities in any State in which such offer, solicitation or sale would be unlawful prior to registration or qualification under the securities laws of any such State.

Proposed New Issue   February 22, 1976

2,000,000
Common Shares
OWENS-ILLINOIS, INC.
($3.125 par value)

Owens-Illinois is one of the world's leading and most diversified manufacturers of packaging products. It is the world's largest manufacturer of glass containers. In addition to glass containers its products include semi-rigid plastic containers, metal and plastic closures for such containers, corrugated and solid fiber shipping containers and containerboard for such containers, metal cans, composite cans, paper and plastic bag and film products, disposable paper and plastic cups, tubs, lids and plates, and plywood. In addition, an important part of Owens-Illinois' business consists of specialized glass products, such as glass television bulbs (for color and black-and-white picture tubes), scientific and laboratory glassware, and glass tumblers and stemware for household and institutional use.

Lazard Frères & Co.   **Goldman, Sachs & Co.**

Bache Halsey Stuart Inc.   The First Boston Corporation   Blyth Eastman Dillon & Co.
Incorporated

Dillon, Read & Co. Inc.   Drexel Burnham & Co.   Hornblower & Weeks-Hemphill, Noyes
Incorporated   *Incorporated*

E. F. Hutton & Company Inc.   Kidder, Peabody & Co.   Kuhn, Loeb & Co.   Lehman Brothers
Incorporated   *Incorporated*

Loeb, Rhoades & Co.   Merrill Lynch, Pierce, Fenner & Smith   Paine, Webber, Jackson & Curtis
Incorporated   *Incorporated*

Reynolds Securities Inc.   Salomon Brothers   Smith Barney, Harris Upham & Co.
Incorporated

Wertheim & Co., Inc.   White, Weld & Co.   Dean Witter & Co.
Incorporated   *Incorporated*

Mitchell, Hutchins Inc.   Shearson Hayden Stone Inc.

ABD Securities Corporation   Basle Securities Corporation   Alex. Brown & Sons

F. Eberstadt & Co., Inc.   EuroPartners Securities Corporation   Robert Fleming
Incorporated

Kleinwort, Benson   Moseley, Hallgarten & Estabrook Inc.   New Court Securities Corporation
Incorporated

Oppenheimer & Co., Inc.   Piper, Jaffray & Hopwood
Incorporated

R. W. Pressprich & Co.   Shields Model Roland Securities   SoGen-Swiss International Corporation
Incorporated   *Incorporated*

Thomson & McKinnon Auchincloss Kohlmeyer Inc.   Spencer Trask & Co.
Incorporated

Tucker, Anthony & R. L. Day, Inc.   UBS-DB Corporation   Warburg Paribas Becker Inc.

Weeden & Co.   William D. Witter, Inc.   Wood, Struthers & Winthrop Inc.
Incorporated

Shuman, Agnew & Co., Inc.   Sutro & Co.   Birr, Wilson & Co., Inc.
Incorporated

Robertson, Colman, Siebel & Weisel   Stone & Youngberg

- -

Please send me a free copy of the Preliminary Prospectus of Owens-Illinois, Inc.

Name_____

Street_____ City_____ State_____ Zip____

Telephone_____
        (business)   (residence)

A copy of the Preliminary Prospectus may be obtained by mailing or delivering this coupon to any of the above firms or to Lazard Frères & Co., One Rockefeller Plaza, New York, N.Y. 10020 or Goldman, Sachs & Co., 55 Broad Street, New York, N.Y. 10004.

TOMBSTONE AD USED IN THE POST-EFFECTIVE PERIOD

This announcement is neither an offer to sell nor a solicitation of an offer to buy any of these securities. The offer is made only by the Prospectus.

NEW ISSUE

1,400,000 Common Shares

OWENS-ILLINOIS, INC.

($3.125 par value)

Price $57.50 Per Share

Copies of the Prospectus may be obtained only from such of the underwriters, including the undersigned, as may lawfully offer these securities in this State.

Lazard Frères & Co.	Goldman, Sachs & Co.

Bache Halsey Stuart Inc.	The First Boston Corporation	Blyth Eastman Dillon & Co. Incorporated
Dillon, Read & Co. Inc.	Drexel Burnham & Co. Incorporated	Hornblower & Weeks-Hemphill, Noyes Incorporated
E. F. Hutton & Company Inc.	Kidder, Peabody & Co. Incorporated	Kuhn, Loeb & Co. Lehman Brothers Incorporated
Loeb, Rhoades & Co.	Merrill Lynch, Pierce, Fenner & Smith Incorporated	Paine, Webber, Jackson & Curtis Incorporated
Reynolds Securities Inc.	Salomon Brothers	Smith Barney, Harris Upham & Co. Incorporated
Wertheim & Co., Inc.	White, Weld & Co. Incorporated	Dean Witter & Co. Incorporated
Mitchell, Hutchins Inc.		Shearson Hayden Stone Inc.
ABD Securities Corporation	Basle Securities Corporation	Alex. Brown & Sons
F. Eberstadt & Co., Inc.	EuroPartners Securities Corporation	Robert Fleming Incorporated
Kleinwort, Benson Incorporated	Moseley, Hallgarten & Estabrook Inc.	New Court Securities Corporation
Oppenheimer & Co., Inc.	Piper, Jaffray & Hopwood Incorporated	Prescott, Ball & Turben
R. W. Pressprich & Co. Incorporated	Shields Model Roland Securities Incorporated	SoGen-Swiss International Corporation
Thomson & McKinnon Auchincloss Kohlmeyer Inc.		Spencer Trask & Co. Incorporated
Tucker, Anthony & R. L. Day, Inc.	UBS-DB Corporation	Weeden & Co. Incorporated
William D. Witter, Inc.		Wood, Struthers & Winthrop Inc.
Bateman Eichler, Hill Richards Incorporated	Crowell, Weedon & Co.	Shuman, Agnew & Co., Inc.
Sutro & Co. Birr, Wilson & Co., Inc. Incorporated	Boettcher & Company	Bosworth, Sullivan & Company Incorporated
Foster & Marshall Inc.	Robertson, Colman, Siebel & Weisel	Stern, Frank, Meyer & Fox Incorporated
Stone & Youngberg		Jefferies & Company, Inc.

March 4, 1976

5. *The Broker's Card.* Rule 134(d) permits the broker (or anyone else) to send a written communication soliciting "from the recipient . . . an offer to buy the security or request the recipient to indicate whether he or she might be interested in the security." Such a letter must be accompanied or preceded by a prospectus that "meets the requirements

of section 10 of the Act," which essentially means a preliminary prospectus, and such prospectus must set forth the "price range where required by rule." Finally, the broker's letter must contain a mandatory legend indicating that the offer to buy may not be accepted, nor even partial payment made, until the registration statement has become effective. Typically, such a letter is sent by the broker to the client to provide the latter with a card by which the client can ask to have shares in the offering reserved for it on a non-binding basis. Such a letter, however, may not recommend or evaluate the security for the client without exceeding the authority granted by Rule 134(d).

In summary, therefore, prior to the 2005 revisions, the SEC permitted issuers, underwriters, and dealers to use the following methods to reach prospective purchasers during the waiting period: (1) oral offers to sell, whether face-to-face or by instrumentalities of interstate commerce (e.g., the telephone); (2) publication of a tombstone advertisement pursuant to § 2(a)(10)(b) or an identifying statement pursuant to Rule 134; (3) a preliminary prospectus that meets the conditions of Rule 430 or 430A (described below); (4) a preliminary summary prospectus that complies with Rule 431 and the applicable registration statement form; and (5) a broker's card under Rule 134(d). In addition, some very specialized exemptions permitted investment companies to engage in generic advertising (without referring to the name of the particular mutual fund) and to distribute a highly technical "Statement of Additional Information." See Rules 134b and 135a under the 1933 Act.

Many of these permissible communications, while still on the books, became dated as the result of a fundamental about-face by the SEC on the subject of free writing. The new approach, which expanded how prospective investors can be solicited, is described next.

B. THE FREE WRITING PROSPECTUS

In 2005, the Commission reversed its prior prohibition on "free writing" during the waiting period. Securities Act Release No. 8591 adopted Rules 164 and 433, which permit free writing during the waiting period if certain conditions are satisfied. Conceptually, Rule 405 defines (with some special exceptions) a written communication that constitutes an offer to sell or a solicitation to buy a security to be a "free writing prospectus," and Rule 433 deems a "free writing prospectus" that satisfies its conditions to be a § 10(b) prospectus, which can be used without violating § 5(b)(1) of the 1933 Act. In effect, most of what was previously forbidden by § 5(b)(1) has now become lawful—if the SEC's relatively modest conditions are satisfied.

Specifically, Rule 405 now defines a "free writing prospectus" as "any written communication as defined in this section that constitutes an offer to sell or a solicitation of an offer to buy the securities relating to a registered offering that is used after the registration statement in respect of the offering is filed . . . ," except for certain excluded communications. Although not initially apparent on the face of this definition, electronic communications, including emails, faxes, CD-ROMs, internet web sites, and even voicemail messages, today fall within the terms "graphic communication" and, by extension, "written communication" under Rule 405 and, accordingly, may constitute a free writing prospectus. Nevertheless, these written communications are possible during the waiting period if they satisfy Rules 164 and 433 under the 1933 Act.

The largest, most seasoned issuers—i.e., those that fall under Rule 405's definition of a "Well-Known Seasoned Issuer"—are permitted to use a free writing prospectus at any time; other issuers and their underwriters can use a free writing prospectus only after a registration statement is filed (thereby preserving some semblance of a quiet period for them).

The SEC's conditions for use of the free writing prospectus depend, among other things, on the size and status of the issuer and whether consideration has been paid for the dissemination of the free writing prospectus by the issuer or offering participant. Non-reporting issuers and unseasoned issuers (i.e., those reporting issuers not eligible to use Form S-3 or Form F-3 to register a primary offering) must both file a registration statement and precede or accompany the free writing prospectus with a copy of the preliminary prospectus (which, for this purpose, must normally set forth the security's expected price range) if they either prepare the free writing prospectus or pay any consideration for its dissemination (for example, if they pay for a newspaper advertisement). But they can satisfy this "precede or accompany" requirement by hyperlinking an electronic free writing prospectus to the most recent prospectus. In contrast, for seasoned issuers (i.e., reporting companies eligible to use Form S-3 or Form F-3 to register a primary offering), there is no need to precede or accompany the free writing prospectus with a preliminary prospectus. However, such an issuer must notify the recipient through a required legend about the filing of the registration statement and advise the recipient of the SEC's web site where it can access and download the prospectus. Finally, the Well-Known Seasoned Issuer can distribute a free writing prospectus even prior to filing the registration statement (because, under Rule 163, it is not subject to any quiet period restrictions).

Any free writing prospectus must include a legend specifying (i) the toll-free number established by the issuer and/or the underwriters at which the investor can request a copy of the prospectus, and (ii) the SEC's web site address at which the prospectus can also be obtained. The legend also may provide an email address at which the prospectus can be requested or web site at which they can be accessed (see Rule 433(c)(2)(ii)).

A free writing prospectus may include information not included in the registration statement, but it may not conflict with the information in the registration statement, including the periodic reports incorporated by reference therein (see Rule 433(c)(1)).

The issuer must file with the SEC any free writing prospectus that it prepares or any information in a free writing prospectus that an offering participant prepares based on information the issuer or its agents provided. Underwriters and other offering participants must also file any free writing prospectus that they use if they distribute it "in a manner reasonably designed to lead to its broad unrestricted dissemination" (Rule 433(d)(1)(ii)). Thus, an underwriter could circulate a memorandum to a limited group of institutional investors and not be obligated to file it with the Commission. A free writing prospectus that merely restates or stylistically revises a prior free writing prospectus also need not be filed with the SEC if it "does not contain substantive changes from or additions to a free writing prospectus previously filed with the Commission" (Rule 433(d)(3)). Issuers and offering participants are required to retain for three years any free writing prospectus that they use but have not filed with the SEC (see Rule 433(g)).

Rule 433(f) addresses the sensitive area of press and media interviews involving the issuer (including T.V. and radio appearances). It defines an interview or media appearance that "offers" the security to constitute a "written communication" and, hence, a free writing prospectus. It then distinguishes those "written communications" the issuer or an offering participant pays for or prepares from those they do not so prepare or pay for. In the latter case (which presumably is more common), the issuer or offering participant must file the "written communication" (which term includes a radio or T.V. transcript) with the SEC within four business days after the issuer or other offering participant "becomes aware of the publication, radio or television broadcast, or other dissemination . . ." (see Rule 433(f)(1)(ii)). Also, in the case of a non-reporting company, if the issuer or offering participant prepares or pays for the dissemination of the "written communication," Rule 433(b)(2)(i) requires that a § 10 prospectus accompany or precede the free writing prospectus—a condition that seems infeasible in the case of a T.V. appearance. In the case of web sites, the issuer can satisfy this "precede or accompany" requirement by hyperlinking the interview to the preliminary prospectus.

Predictably, a number of things can go wrong now that the free writing prospectus has been liberally authorized. Suppose an issuer fails to file a free writing prospectus by the time of its first use, as required by Rule 433(d). Does this mean that § 5 has been violated, which might permit rescission under § 12(b)(1)? Rule 164(b) provides a defense for "an immaterial or unintentional failure to file or delay in filing a free writing prospectus" if "[a] good faith and reasonable effort was made to comply" and "[t]he free writing prospectus is filed as soon as practicable after discovery of the failure to file." A similar good faith and reasonable effort defense is provided if the issuer fails to include the mandatory legend required by Rule 433 on the free writing prospectus (see Rule 164(c)). Obviously, these defenses are fact sensitive. What happens if the issuer or an offering participant fails to comply with a condition in Rule 433 and cannot meet Rule 164's "good faith and reasonable effort" defense? In such a case, the "written communication" would appear to be impermissible free writing that violates § 5(b)(1), unless it could be found to be exempt under some other rule (for example, Rule 134). This danger may dissuade many from making full use of the free writing prospectus.

C. ROAD SHOWS AND ELECTRONIC COMMUNICATION

1. *The Rise of the Road Show.* During the waiting period, the managing underwriters "build their book" (that is, they approach prospective investors to obtain non-binding commitments) and test the market for the offering. A key means for doing so is by staging "road shows" in which meetings are held with institutional investors in leading financial centers (both at home and abroad). This provides an opportunity to publicize the offering and to determine the price at which it can be sold. Originally, the road show developed as a means by which participating underwriters in the offering could demonstrate their "due diligence" to satisfy the statutory standard of a "reasonable investigation" under § 11(b) of the 1933 Act. In theory, participating underwriters did so by interviewing senior management in a series of conferences held in various cities across the country. Over time, this "due diligence" function gave way to a marketing function, as securities analysts for institutional buyers came to use the occasion to interview senior management (and seek projections—explicit or implicit—of future earnings and performance). As a result, issues arose as to the written materials that could be used at this stage. Typically, the issuer's executives would make a presentation that used charts, slides, or other visual aids, but no written materials (other than the preliminary prospectus) would be distributed; also, the press and public investors typically were excluded.

For years, the SEC found ways to rationalize that these communications did not amount to a "prospectus" or "free writing." Initially, it reasoned that these displays were merely oral offers (which are permitted during the waiting period). When the road show inevitably began to be broadcast on the internet, the SEC decided that such broadcasts were sufficiently dissimilar to radio or T.V. broadcasts (which are deemed to be prospectuses and, hence, would violate § 5(b)(1)), because of their narrower audience.[25] Also, issuers learned to limit access to their electronic road shows to pre-screened individuals (typically, institutional investors and very wealthy individuals), who were given a password that gave them access via an underwriter's website to the electronic road show. Because these password restrictions assured the SEC that little potential existed for retail investors to be defrauded, the

---

[25] See Exploration Inc., SEC No-Action letter (Oct. 9, 1986).

SEC issued a series of no-action letters accepting electronic road shows.[26] Still, the growing use of electronic road shows gave rise to other problems.

Inherently, road shows create a danger of selective disclosure. The issuer's executives could expect to be asked probing questions as to future results or projections at road shows—meaning that material information was often divulged at road shows that retail investors never learned. For this reason, the issuer's attorneys often advised its executives not to answer some questions, or they prepared a script of proposed answers. Nonetheless, projections were often released or acknowledged to be accurate at road shows, even though they were never contained in the registration statement. Of course, if the issuer's executives answered questions involving a securities analyst's future projections, they ran a risk of "adopting" the analyst's projections (and could conceivably face civil liability as if they had themselves made the projections). As a result, issuer's counsel sought to safeguard such projections by preparing and filing a "meaningful cautionary statement" with the SEC to obtain the protection of a special safe harbor for "forward looking information" that was enacted as part of the Private Securities Litigation Reform Act of 1995.[27]

Potentially, statements made at a road show could also constitute material, non-public information that the broader market did not possess. To protect issuers and others, a special (but debatable) exemption in Regulation FD exempts any oral communication made "in connection with the registered securities offering after filing of the registration statement for the offering under the Securities Act."[28] Thus, the issuer is not required to publicly disclose oral communications at a road show (although, as described below, an issuer must make available some form of the written communications revealed at a road show). Still, even though a road show's oral communications are exempt from Regulation FD, they could result in an insider trading violation if the various requirements for insider trading liability (such as a requisite fiduciary breach) can be established.

2. *The SEC's New Approach.* Having long sought to deny that road shows were marketing efforts that could amount to a prospectus, the SEC reversed course in 2005 as part of its offering reforms. Today, Rule 405 defines the term "graphic communication" to include "all forms of electronic media," including internet web sites, emails, faxes, videotapes, and "substantially similar messages widely distributed (rather than individually distributed) on telephone answering or voice mail systems,

---

[26] See Private Financial Network, SEC No-Action letter (Mar. 12, 1997); Charles Schwab & Co, Inc. SEC No-Action letter (Nov. 15, 1999, and Feb. 9, 2000).

[27] See § 27A of the 1933 Act and § 21E of the 1934 Act. It should be emphasized that this safe harbor applies only to reporting companies that file periodic reports under the 1934 Act and not to an initial public offering. See § 27A(b)(2)(D) of the 1933 Act and § 21E(b)(2)(D) of the 1934 Act.

[28] See Rule 100(b)(2)(iii)(F) of Regulation FD under the 1934 Act.

computers, computer networks and other forms of computer data compilation." The term "written communication" is then defined by Rule 405 to include "graphic communication." Thus, any graphic communication that constitutes an offer to sell or a solicitation of an offer to buy becomes a "free writing prospectus" under Rule 405's definition of that term.

Note that the term "graphic communication" (and, therefore, the term "written communication") includes an important exception: It does not include "a communication that, at the time of the communication, originates live, in real-time to a live audience and does not originate in recorded form or otherwise as a graphic communication, although it is transmitted through graphic means." (A radio or television broadcast, however, remains a "written communication" regardless of the means of transmission of the broadcast.) In other words, a road show that is communicated via the internet will not be considered a "graphic communication," even though it is transmitted using "graphic means," if it is a live, real-time broadcast to a live audience. A recording of that road show, however, is considered to be a "graphic communication."

As a result, if a road show presents only oral statements (or if it uses slides displayed on a screen that are shown simultaneously[29]), no written communication has been used, and § 5(b)(1) has not been violated. Nonetheless, if a recording of this same program is transmitted "graphically" (e.g., via the internet) or by television to remote sites, or if its main points are emailed by the issuer or underwriter to others, these communications fall within "graphic communications" under Rule 405. In addition, Rule 433(d)(8)(i) specifically defines "[a] road show for an offering that is a written communication" to be a free writing prospectus. Rule 433(d)(8)(i) then softens this blow by excluding most road shows from the obligation to file the free writing prospectus with the SEC. Still, Rule 433(d)(8)(ii) does require the road show to be filed with the SEC in the case of an offering of equity or convertible equity securities by a non-reporting issuer (i.e., the typical IPO), unless "at least one version of a *bona fide* electronic road show [is made] available without restriction by means of graphic communication to any person. . . ." A *"bona fide* electronic road show," in turn, is defined in Rule 433(h)(5) to include "if more than one road show that is a written communication is being used, . . . discussion of the same general areas of information regarding the issuer, [its] management, and the securities being offered as such other issuer road show or shows for the same offering that are written communications."

What does this language mean? Essentially, the issuer can prepare multiple versions of its road show, some containing projections and data that it does not want to share with retail investors for fear of liability.

---

[29] This special case of slides used to accompany an oral presentation at a road show is covered by a note to Rule 433(d)(8), which exempts such "simultaneous communication" from the scope of "graphic communications" and thus, by extension, "written communications".

The issuer must make one bona fide electronic road show available, and thus the two versions must largely parallel and probably not contradict each other. Nevertheless, the fact that the issuer can withhold some information from retail investors that it gives to sophisticated investors implies that selective disclosure remains alive and well in the offering process. Indeed, in the case of an offering by a seasoned issuer, Rule 433(d)(8)(i) does not require that any version of the road show be filed or made available to investors. Absent a mandatory requirement, issuers and underwriters appear to resist releasing projections to retail investors for fear of a securities class action if the projections are not met.

3. *Hyperlinks*. As corporations came to make use of web sites to reach customers and promote a general image, issues surfaced as to when statements on a web site by a corporation "in registration" violate § 5. During the waiting period, a written statement that arguably "conditions the market" for the offering could make such a statement a prospectus whose distribution likely violates § 5(b)(1). Even though the issuer's preliminary prospectus might also be on the web site, retail investors might read only the more streamlined, less legalistic materials and ignore the prospectus. For a time, the SEC handled these questions on a case-by-case basis, looking principally to the proximity between the alleged free writing on the web site and the preliminary prospectus. The closer the proximity and the more the statements approached market conditioning, the greater the likelihood that the SEC would find a § 5 violation. The SEC's approach—which depended on a doctrine sometimes called "envelope theory," because it analogized a web site to the mailing of statements in the same envelope with a preliminary prospectus—was often murky and gave little clear guidance as to when statements on a web site would be deemed impermissible free writing.

Today, Rule 433(e) provides a bright line test. Basically, it defines most material on an issuer's web site or a third party's web site that is hyperlinked by the issuer to be a free writing prospectus, which normally must be filed by the issuer with the SEC under Rule 433(d). An exception, however, is created for "historical issuer information that is identified as such and located in a separate section of the issuer's Web site containing historical issuer information, that has not been incorporated by reference into or otherwise included in a prospectus of the issuer for the offering . . . ." (see Rule 433(e)(2)). This exception for historical information seems a continuation of the old "envelope theory" under which information not in proximity to the prospectus (and not clearly sales oriented) was not viewed as free writing. Note again that if information on the issuer's web site does not fall within this special historical information exception and is not filed with the SEC, it would constitute impermissible free writing in violation of § 5(b)(1), unless the issuer cures the violation pursuant to its good faith and reasonable effort defense under Rule 164.

D. DELIVERY DURING THE WAITING PERIOD

A basic problem with the Securities Act is that delivery of the prospectus comes only with the delivery of the securities themselves (see § 5(b)(2)) or with a confirmation of sale (which is defined by § 2(a)(10) to be a prospectus precisely to force this confirmation to be accompanied or preceded by a § 10(a) statutory prospectus). Either way, the information thus delivered comes after the investment decision has been made. Delivered in this way, the prospectus may prove to be little more than a memento of the transaction, rather than informative disclosure. To remedy this problem, in 1969, the SEC adopted Rule 15c2–8 under the 1934 Act.[30]

In the case of a seasoned issuer that is a reporting company, Rule 15c2–8 simply requires the broker or dealer to respond to written requests for the preliminary prospectus. Thus, those who want the preliminary prospectus have a right to it. But in the case of an issuer that is not yet filing periodic reports under the 1934 Act (i.e., chiefly IPO issuers), Rule 15c2–8(b) requires the broker or dealer to "deliver a copy of the preliminary prospectus to any person who is expected to receive a confirmation of sale at least 48 hours prior to the sending of such confirmation." This mandatory delivery requirement for new issues closed a hole in the 1933 Act because otherwise the key disclosure document was only required to be delivered by underwriters or dealers with the confirmation of sale—well after the investment decision had been made. In effect, the 48-hour rule gives customers a "cooling off" period to reconsider before the customer can be called, after the registration statement goes effective, and asked to enter into a binding purchase commitment.

To further enforce this policy, the SEC conditions acceleration of the effectiveness of a registration statement in this IPO setting on the managing underwriter's written certification that it has satisfied the SEC's 48-hour rule:

Securities Act Release No. 4968
Securities and Exchange Commission.
April 24, 1969.

PRIOR DELIVERY OF PRELIMINARY PROSPECTUS

* * *

The Commission has declared its policy in Rule 460 that it will not accelerate the effective date of a registration statement unless the preliminary prospectus contained in the registration statement is distributed to underwriters and dealers who it is reasonably anticipated will be invited to participate in the distribution of the security to be offered or sold. The purpose of this requirement is to afford all persons

---

[30] See Securities Act Release No. 5101 (Nov. 19, 1970).

effecting the distribution a means of being informed with respect to the offering so that they can advise their customers of the investment merits of the security. Particularly in the case of a first offering by a nonreporting company, salesmen should obtain and read the current preliminary or final prospectus before offering the security to their clients.

The Commission also announced, in the exercise of its responsibilities in accelerating the effective date of a registration statement under Section 8(a) of the Securities Act of 1933, and particularly the statutory requirement that it have due regard to the adequacy of the information respecting the issuer theretofore available to the public, that it will consider whether the persons making an offering of securities of an issuer which is not subject to the reporting requirements of Section 13 or 15(d) of the Securities Exchange Act of 1934, have taken reasonable steps to furnish preliminary prospectuses to those persons who may reasonably be expected to be purchasers of the securities. The Commission will ordinarily be satisfied by a written statement from the managing underwriter to the effect that it has been informed by participating underwriters and dealers that copies of the preliminary prospectus complying with Rule 433(a) [the predecessor of Rule 430] have been or are being distributed to all persons to whom it is then expected to mail confirmations of sale not less than 48 hours prior to the time it is expected to mail such confirmations. Such distribution should be by air mail if the confirmations will be sent by air mail, or a longer period to compensate for the difference in the method of mailing the prospectus should be provided. Of course, if the form of preliminary prospectus so distributed was inadequate or inaccurate in material respects, acceleration will be deferred until the Commission has received satisfactory assurances that appropriate correcting material (including a memorandum of changes) has been so distributed.

* * *

Problems

Assume that New Corp. (which was earlier described in Problems 2-1–2-15) has now filed a registration statement covering an offering of 10,000,000 shares. It is still not a reporting company; nor has it previously sold securities to the public, but it earned revenues in its last fiscal year of $1.4 billion.

PROBLEM 2-16

Smithers, a registered representative in the Boston office of Bache, Halsey & Co., calls Mrs. Emily Thomas, a retired 75-year-old lady, and tells her this will likely be a hot offering that could run up in price on the first day. Being a greedy old lady, Mrs. Thomas says the offering sounds interesting. Smithers mails her a copy of the preliminary prospectus. What liability might Smithers face, either under § 5 or otherwise?

Problem 2-17

Smithers encloses in the envelope with the preliminary prospectus that he mails to Mrs. Thomas a small broker's card that invites her to request that a specified number of shares be reserved for her in the offering. Across the top of this card, he writes: "This could be a very interesting offer. I think 500 shares would be a good investment for you." If, as in-house counsel to Bache, Halsey, you learn of this a week later, what steps do you advise your client to take?

Problem 2-18

Armitage & Co., a broker-dealer that intends to join the New Corp. underwriting syndicate, publishes a monthly comprehensive list of securities that it is recommending to clients, and it now adds New Corp. to that list. Any problem? Would your answer change if New Corp. were a reporting company? Assume, in the alternative, that Armitage will not be a member of the New Corp. syndicate.

Problem 2-19

A Bache, Halsey registered representative mails a letter to several customers, offering New Corp. common stock, but he does not enclose a preliminary prospectus because he knows they have already received a New Corp. preliminary prospectus from other dealers at his firm. Any problems?

Problem 2-20

Mrs. Thomas calls back Smithers and says: "Yes, I want to buy 500 shares, and I am mailing you a check for 500 shares at the offering price." What must Smithers do?

Problem 2-21

Smithers also calls a small brokerage firm in Little Rock, Arkansas, and offers to reserve 1,000 shares for its customers once the registration statement becomes effective? Okay?

Problem 2-22

Smithers mails copies of the preliminary prospectus to all members of the Deepdale Golf Club (some 1,500), of which club he is also a member. Moreover, he calls 150 of them over the two days following his letter's receipt. Is this permissible?

Problem 2-23

Other members of the New Corp. syndicate send their own sales brochures, each slightly different, to their customers describing the New Corp. offering in very favorable terms. Can this be done? Under what conditions?

PROBLEM 2-24

Assume next that New Corp. has a long-standing company website, and it hyperlinks that website to the research report prepared by Armitage & Co., which is not planning to join the underwriting syndicate. What is the significance of this hyperlink?

PROBLEM 2-25

In the alternative to the preceding question, New Corp. does not hyperlink to any outside source, but it does include a separate section on its website, captioned "New Corp. Historical Financial Information," which sets forth financial information about New Corp. that is not incorporated by reference into its registration statement and that is not referred to in any offering document. Must New Corp. file this information with the SEC as a free writing prospectus?

PROBLEM 2-26

Bache, Halsey schedules road shows in four cities at which New Corp. management will speak to securities analysts and institutional investors. It also prepares an electronic version of this road show and makes it generally available to investors on both Bache, Halsey's website and New Corp.'s website. This electronic version is posted as of the date of the first actual road show, but it differs in that no projections as to next year's earnings or revenues are made. Must Bache, Halsey or New Corp. file the road show with the SEC as a free writing prospectus?

PROBLEM 2-27

New Corp.'s CEO, Jane Purcell, decides to appear on CNBC's new program, "IPO Week," to discuss her company. No payment is made by anyone to CNBC, or any affiliate thereof, with respect to this appearance. What must New Corp. do as a result of this appearance?

PROBLEM 2-28

Assume that Jane Purcell unintentionally misstates a fact about New Corp. in her T.V. interview on CNBC. What should counsel do?

PROBLEM 2-29

Instead of appearing on a T.V. show, Jane grants an interview with the host of the CNBC show and a Wall Street Journal reporter. Based on this interview, they each report favorably about New Corp. Must New Corp. distribute a preliminary prospectus to those reading or seeing these stories? Must it file the stories themselves with the SEC, or can it give the SEC only the materials and information provided to the media?

PROBLEM 2-30

Bache, Halsey modifies the free writing prospectus it was distributing to prospective investors (and which it had previously filed with the SEC) to bring the document more in line with the SEC's "plain English" policy. There are changes on virtually every page, and the document is made three pages shorter, but all the changes are non-substantive. Must this new document be filed with the SEC?

PROBLEM 2-31

New Corp. is very happy with a favorable story about it that unexpectedly appears in Fortune magazine. New Corp. did not supply information for this story. New Corp. emails this story to all participating underwriters and selling group members and also posts it on its website. Some of the underwriters also post it on their own websites. You are counsel to New Corp., and you learn of this days later. What should you do?

4. THE POST-EFFECTIVE PERIOD

Statutes and Regulations

Securities Act, §§ 2(a)(3), 2(a)(10), 4, 5, 10.

Securities Act Rules 153, 153a, 172, 173, 174, 424, 427, 430A, 430B, 430C, 431, 463; Regulation S–K, Items 501 and 502, particularly Item 502(e).

Exchange Act Rule 15c2–8.

Uniform Commercial Code § 8–319.

A. THE PROCEDURE SURROUNDING EFFECTIVENESS: RULES 430A AND 430B

For many years, the normal practice among underwriters and issuers was to "price" the offering (set a price, but not contractually bind the issuers, underwriters, or purchasers) the evening before the SEC was expected to declare the registration statement effective and then to file a pre-effective "pricing amendment" the next morning that would contain all price-related information. Once the SEC declared this amended registration statement effective (after the dawn filing of the pricing amendment), the issuer and underwriters could contractually agree to issue and buy the securities, and sales to investors could be consummated. This procedure protected the underwriters from last minute adverse market movements, but required a somewhat frenzied ritual of printing the pricing amendment and flying copies of it to Washington, D.C., for a morning filing when the SEC opened for business.

As a part of a general deregulatory program in the 1990s, the SEC adopted Rule 430A, which permits a registration statement to be declared effective without inclusion of price-related information (e.g., the public offering price, the underwriting discount, the use of proceeds, the identity of the underwriting syndicate, and other price-dependent factors, such as conversion rates and call dates). Under Rule 430A, this information could be disclosed to the SEC in a revised form of prospectus filed pursuant to Rule 424(b) not later than the second business day following the date of determination of the offering pricing or the date of its first use, whichever was earlier. If such a delayed filing was not made on a timely basis (typically, by the fifteenth business day after the effectiveness of the registration statement (see Rule 430A(a)(3)), however, a formal post-effective amendment would need to be filed (which is a step the issuer and underwriters wish to avoid, because it restarts the running of the statute of limitations and creates a new date on which the accuracy of the registration statement is tested for purposes of liability under § 11 of the 1933 Act). Although the idea of a prospectus that lacks the price of the security and other essential marketing terms may seem anomalous, the net impact of Rule 430A is to permit the registration statement to be declared effective prior to the final pricing negotiations between the issuer and the underwriters (or between both and the institutional investors who are often the principal buyers). For the issuer, this means that it will not necessarily be engaged in simultaneous negotiations with both the SEC and the underwriters.

Rule 430A does contain one meaningful limitation. Although it is possible to cut back the size of the offering if marketing problems are encountered, the reductions in price and volume may not represent more than a 20% reduction in the maximum aggregate offering price (as stated in the registration statement when declared effective). Any greater cutback or a decrease in volume or change in price range that materially changes the registration statement disclosure instead requires a post-effective amendment.

A post-effective prospectus that omits the Rule 430A pricing information may be used after effectiveness and prior to pricing. See Rule 430A(c). A preliminary prospectus that meets these conditions may continue to be used in this interval between effectiveness and pricing. Although this document will not itself satisfy the prospectus delivery obligations under § 5(b), that problem has been resolved by other means, as next discussed.

B. Prospectus Requirements in the Post-Effective Period

Section 5(b)(2) mandates delivery of a § 10(a) final prospectus at or before delivery of a security for sale or after sale. Also, Rule 10b–10 under the 1934 Act mandates the broker-dealer to provide each customer a confirmation of sale containing specified information. Since this document "confirms the sale," it is a prospectus under the definition in § 2(a)(10) but it does not qualify as a § 10 prospectus. (Note that the definition of "free writing prospectus" does not include sales confirmations.) Thus, in light of § 5(b)(1), a broker-dealer obligated to deliver a Rule 10b–10 confirmation must find a way to remove it from the definition of "prospectus." Traditionally, the standard way to do so was to precede or accompany the confirmation with a § 10(a) final prospectus (see § 2(a)(10)(a) of the 1933 Act).

In addition, § 5(a)(2) restricts movement and delivery of the security by providing that it is unlawful to use the mails or interstate facilities to transport a security for the purpose of sale or for delivery after sale, unless a registration statement is in effect as to such security. The result is to prohibit such deliveries in both the pre-filing period and during the waiting period. Although oral interstate offers to sell may be made during the waiting period, so long as no actual sale is made, § 5(a)(2) forestalls the possibility of using interstate facilities or the mails to transport a security either for the purpose of sale or for delivery after sale in the pre-effective period. Furthermore, even in the case of face-to-face transactions or intrastate sales made without the use of the mails or interstate facilities, § 5(a)(2) forbids use of these media to deliver the security following a sale.

From a policy perspective, the problem with these delivery rules is that they achieved nothing of importance. While they forced the prospectus to accompany the security and the confirmation of sale, this information came after the investment decision had been made. As one commentator put it: "the buyer in these transactions gets his prospectus more as a memento than as a vehicle of information."[31] This anomaly—that the statutory prospectus was delivered after the investment decision—was heightened by adoption of earlier-noted Rule 430A, which allows the omission of most price-related information from the statutory prospectus. But as Rule 430A(c) makes clear, price-related information needs to be communicated to investors in some document to satisfy § 5(b)(2).

Just how is this delivery to be effected? For decades, the pricing amendment would incorporate all material information into the final prospectus, and this document would be printed on the eve of effectiveness and so could be mailed out with the confirmation of sale shortly after the moment of effectiveness. However, Rule 430A eliminated the need to prepare such a last minute and costly document (to the industry's great relief). More importantly, an unrelated development arose that aggravated the timing problem. In 1995, the SEC (in conjunction with the Federal Reserve Board) shortened the settlement time for a securities transaction (typically involving the delivery of securities against payment) from five business days to (in most cases) the third business day following the trade date (or, in the industry's parlance, "T+3"). Since 2017, this period has been further shortened to the second business day following the trade date (or

---

[31] Lobell, Revision of the Securities Act, 48 Colum.L.Rev. 313, 323 (1948).

"T+2").³² The industry wanted these changes (as they meant that underwriters and other sellers of securities would get paid more quickly), but this compression of the settlement cycle complicated the problem of mailing out a statutory prospectus (with the confirmation of sale) in this telescoped time period. In light of the 1995 change, the securities industry convinced the SEC to adopt what became known as its T+3 Prospectus Delivery Rules.³³ Specifically, Rule 434 (now repealed) was promulgated to allow the information traditionally required to be included in the final prospectus to be delivered instead to investors in piecemeal fashion in multiple documents.

Nevertheless, Rule 434 was a complicated stopgap solution that still left the industry mailing multiple documents to investors, probably after their investment decisions had been made. In 2005, the SEC cut through the Gordian knot of the delivery requirements under § 5 by adopting the position that "access equals delivery." Under Rule 172, the issuer is now exempted both from any requirement under § 5(b)(1) to send a § 10(a) prospectus that accompanies or precedes a confirmation of sale and from any requirement under § 5(b)(2) to similarly send a § 10(a) prospectus with or prior to delivery of the securities. To be sure, there still must be a final prospectus, and the same procedure under which pricing information is added after effectiveness under Rules 430A, 430B, and 430C remains intact. But there is no longer any obligation to make physical delivery of the final prospectus. Instead, new Rule 173 requires underwriters and dealers to deliver within two business days after the sale either (1) a copy of the final prospectus or (2) "a notice to the effect that the sale was made pursuant to a registration statement..." (or pursuant to certain other limited circumstances). Predictably, underwriters will elect the latter, simpler option. For dealers (but not underwriters), even this notice is waived by Rule 174 in the case of reporting companies. Thus, Rule 173 requires such a notice mainly for underwriters and dealers in IPOs. Also, compliance with Rule 173 is not a condition to reliance on Rule 172 (see Rule 173(c)).

Rule 172 does not cover the entire waterfront. It does not apply to business combinations, investment companies, and certain business development companies (see Rule 172(d)). It is also inapplicable if the Commission has brought a pending proceeding under §§ 8(d) or 8(e) of the Act. In these cases, the underwriter must still make delivery.

Interestingly, Rule 15c2–8 was not changed. Thus, its rule requiring delivery of a preliminary prospectus 48 hours before the sending of a confirmation of sale remains intact. This is one context where access is not equated with delivery.

  a. Free Writing in the Post-Effective Period. One further nuance remains to the prohibitions of § 5(b)(1). Recall that § 2(a)(10) defines a

---

  ³² See Rule 15c6–1 under the 1934 Act. For the latest revision, see Exchange Act Release No. 80295 (May 30, 2017).

  ³³ See Securities Act Release No. 7168 (May 11, 1995).

"prospectus" to include any written communication that "offers any security for sale or confirms the sale of any security." But clause (a) to § 2(a)(10) then excludes from this definition any communication sent or given after the effective date (other than a § 10(b) prospectus) if it is proved that prior to or at the same time a written prospectus meeting the requirements of § 10(a) was sent or given to the person to whom the communication was directed. Thus, § 2(a)(10) permits selling literature to be sent to a prospective buyer *after the effective date*, so long as this communication has been preceded or is accompanied by a final § 10(a) prospectus. However, what happens when the issuer "delivers" the prospectus by means of Rule 172? Here, the SEC's possibly surprising answer is that, although Rule 172 satisfies the issuer's obligations for purposes of mailing a confirmation of sale and delivering the shares, it does not amount to sending or giving the final prospectus for purposes of § 2(a)(10)(a).[34] At first glance, this seems odd, but the result is clearly policy driven. The SEC wants sales literature to constitute a free writing prospectus. If the filing of the final prospectus for purposes of Rule 172 also meant that sales literature sent after the final prospectus was filed should be deemed to fall within § 2(a)(10)(a), then the sales literature would be exempted by that clause, it would not constitute a "free writing prospectus," and thus, it would not need to be filed with the SEC under Rule 433(d). Equally important, the sales literature would not give rise to liability under § 12(a)(2) for any material misstatements or omissions. To avoid this result, the Commission decided to be highly formalistic and deem the final prospectus, although delivered for purposes of § 5(b)(2), not to have been "sent or given" for purposes of § 2(a)(10)(a).

 b. The Duration of the Delivery Obligation. Suppose the underwriters quickly sell off their allotted shares in the first day of the offering to retail investors. Does this end their responsibility to deliver a final prospectus? The literal answer under § 5 is no—but this answer is today largely irrelevant. The answer is negative because, even though retail investors can resell their shares without any concern for § 5 because of the exemption afforded by § 4(a)(1), issuers, underwriters, and broker-dealers must still pay heed to the requirements of § 5 and the specific exemptions applicable to each of them under § 4.

 Section 5's prospectus delivery obligations apply to "any person," including dealers not participating in the offering. What was the original reason for requiring even those dealers to deliver a prospectus? One goal of the Securities Act was to enhance transparency by widely circulating the prospectus in the aftermarket; thus, § 5 required even dealers not participating in the offering to deliver a prospectus for a defined period to inform secondary market participants. Because these non-participating dealers were not exempted by § 4(a)(1), they had to rely on

---

[34] Securities Act Release No. 8591 (Jul. 19, 2005) states (at footnote 561): "A final prospectus only filed as provided in Rule 172 will not be considered to be sent or given prior to or with a written offer within the meaning of clause (a) of Securities Act Section 2(a)(10)."

§ 4(a)(3), which requires delivery of the final prospectus for a variety of periods depending upon the issuer's status. Today, these requirements are overshadowed by Rule 172, which finds any delivery requirement (including a dealer's) to be satisfied by electronic access.

Nonetheless, these rules can still be important in special contexts. Under § 4(a)(3), underwriters are required to deliver a final prospectus so long as they have unsold allotments (see § 4(a)(3)(C)). Thus, in a very slow offering, an underwriter is still required to make delivery, for example, six months later, if it continues to sell securities from its unsold allotment. Under the terms of § 4(a)(3)(B), dealers (including an underwriter no longer acting as an underwriter and not selling securities from an unsold allotment) are required to make delivery for a 40-day period after the later of the effective date of the registration statement or the commencement of the offering. A 1964 amendment, which added the final sentence to § 4(a)(3), extended this 40-day period to 90 days in the case of an issuer that had not previously sold securities under an effective registration statement (i.e., an IPO).

These requirements imposed a substantial logistical burden on dealers, and they lobbied for relief. The 1964 amendments gave the Commission the power, by rule or order, to prescribe a shorter period than the 40- or 90-day periods in § 4(a)(3) for the delivery of prospectuses. Under this authority, the SEC issued Rule 174, which provides that dealers (again, including an underwriter no longer acting as an underwriter) need not deliver a prospectus to the purchaser if the issuer was a reporting company prior to the filing of the registration statement. (Moreover, the obligation of a dealer to deliver a prospectus is entirely dispensed with if the registration statement is on Form F-6 (for registration of American Depositary Receipts issued against securities of foreign issuers to be deposited with an American depositary).) Where a registration statement relates to offerings to be made from time to time (which is known as "shelf registration," and is considered in the next chapter), the prospectus delivery requirements are dispensed with upon expiration of the initial prospectus delivery period specified in § 4(a)(3) following the first bona fide offering of the securities.

Today, the prospectus delivery obligations of dealers and underwriters have been greatly simplified by Rule 172, which treats access as equivalent to delivery. But there remain circumstances in which § 4(a)(3), and also Rule 174 and Rule 153 (described below), are relevant. For example, imagine after an offering conducted abroad by a foreign issuer (and presumably in full compliance with Regulation S), a U.S. broker-dealer acquires some shares in the secondary market and brings them back to the United States and sells them in the U.S. Regulation S exempts certain foreign offerings from the reach of § 5, but it does not exempt resales in the United States. Thus, the broker-dealer reselling into the United States would need to comply with § 4(a)(3) or be exempted by Rule 174 if the foreign issuer were a reporting company.

Rule 174 also remains relevant because, for transactions where it is applicable, it excuses compliance (in the case of reporting companies) with new Rule 173's notice requirement (see Rule 173(a)). Similarly, Rule 153 sets forth a simplified means for brokers and dealers to comply with § 5(b)(2)'s prospectus delivery requirement in transactions with other brokers or dealers effected on a national securities exchange (among other venues). In addition, compliance with Rule 153 excuses providing the notice of registration required by Rule 173 (see Rule 173(f)(1)).

c. Online Offerings. With the broad acceptance of email communications in the late 1990s, some brokers sought to redesign the interaction between underwriters and retail clients, so that it was no longer necessary to reach investors by telephone after a registration statement was declared effective to secure oral agreement to purchase the securities. Logistically, it was difficult to telephone hundreds (and possibly thousands) of retail customers within a limited period and secure their final post-effective agreement to accept shares earlier reserved for them out of an underwriter's allocation. Particularly as the size of IPOs grew during the late 1990s, this need to secure post-effective agreement proved to be a practical obstacle for the online brokerage industry, most of whose customers were retail investors.

In response, one online broker, Wit Capital Corporation, secured the SEC's consent in 1999 to a significant revision in the procedures by which shares are sold to investors in a public offering. Under the no-action letter that Wit Capital received, it was permitted to solicit revocable offers to buy from investors during the waiting period, which it could accept after the effective date of the registration statement. Thus, instead of the customer accepting the underwriter's offer to sell after the effective date, the underwriter confirmed by email or fax to the customer its acceptance of the customer's offer to buy. Formal as this distinction may sound, its practical significance was that it eliminated any need to contact the customer on the morning of effectiveness. The SEC, however, subjected the use of this procedure to several important conditions.[35] First, customers who made a conditional offer to buy before the effective date could withdraw the offer at any time before Wit Capital accepted it. Second, Wit Capital would need to obtain a reconfirmation email from each customer after the time of pricing and within two business days of the expected date of effectiveness; such a reconfirmation would also remain valid for only five business days (thus ensuring, in the event the effective date was significantly delayed, that the customer's consent would need to be secured again). In effect, this procedure precluded long-term advance offers to buy from the customer, and required Wit Capital to contact the customer and obtain the customer's agreement just prior to effectiveness (and after pricing).

---

[35] See Wit Capital Corporation, 1999 SEC No-Act. LEXIS 620 (Jul. 14, 1999).

Problems

New Corp.'s registration statement is declared effective on September 1. New Corp. will become a reporting company and will be listed on Nasdaq.

PROBLEM 2-32

Bache, Halsey has prepared a glossy brochure that it mails to its customers the day after effectiveness. Can Bache, Halsey treat this material as being exempted by § 2(a)(10)(a)? Or what must it do?

PROBLEM 2-33

Bache, Halsey sends a preliminary prospectus 48 hours in advance to each customer to whom it expects to send a confirmation of sale in compliance with Rule 15c2–8. Then, it emails to its customers (including even those who have not consented to electronic delivery) confirmations of sale containing the information specified in Rule 10b–10. Nothing else is done, except that Bache, Halsey delivers shares to those shareholders requesting to hold them in their own name. Any problem?

PROBLEM 2-34

Goldman, Lynch is a dealer that has not participated in the offering. Two weeks after the effectiveness of the New Corp. registration statement, it recommends to a long-standing client that it purchase several thousand shares of New Corp. The customer agrees to do so. On making the purchase and delivering the shares to its customer, must Goldman, Lynch deliver a copy of the final prospectus? Must it do anything else?

PROBLEM 2-35

Blythe & Co., a small broker-dealer that did not participate in the New Corp. offering, is asked by a customer to purchase 200 shares of New Corp. common stock in the secondary market in the week following New Corp.'s effectiveness. It does so, but neither includes a final prospectus, nor provides the notice specified in Rule 173. Any problem here?

PROBLEM 2-36

New Corp. decides to merge with Big Co. On the merger's approval, New Corp.'s shareholders are to receive two shares of Big Co. for each share they hold in New Corp. A registration statement on Form S-4 covering this transaction is declared effective on September 1. Must copies of the final prospectus be delivered to these shareholders?

5. THE JOBS ACT AND THE FAST ACT: RATIONALE AND IMPACT

The Jumpstart Our Business Startups Act ("JOBS Act"),[36] passed by Congress in 2012, was primarily an attempt to improve access to the public capital markets for smaller companies. Its premise was that smaller companies were deterred or precluded from going public by regulatory burdens, particularly those imposed by the Sarbanes-Oxley Act and the Dodd-Frank Act. As discussed below, that premise is highly debatable because much evidence suggests that smaller IPOs are simply not viable for other reasons. Nonetheless, many of the changes made by the JOBS Act are important.

Title I of the JOBS Act created what it termed an "on ramp" for a special class of smaller companies known as "emerging growth companies." Under § 2(a)(19) of the 1933 Act, an "emerging growth company" is defined to mean an issuer that has total annual gross revenues of less than $1 billion.[37] However, this status as an emerging growth company is lost upon the earliest of the following events to occur:

A. the last day of the fiscal year of the issuer during which it had total annual gross revenues of $1 billion or more;

B. the last day of the fiscal year following the fifth anniversary of its IPO;

C. the date on which the issuer has issued more than $1 billion in non-convertible debt over the prior three years; or

D. the date on which the issuer is deemed to be a "large accelerated filer" (which, under Rule 12b–2 under the 1934 Act, requires the issuer to have a public float of $700 million or more).[38]

Thus, on the date of its IPO, the typical issuer can normally expect a five-year period (i.e., the "on ramp") during which it will be exempt from many of the requirements otherwise applicable to a reporting company.

What are the specific benefits that an emerging growth company gains under the JOBS Act? The principal benefits include:

1. *Confidential Review of the Registration Statement.* An emerging growth company may confidentially submit its draft registration statement to the SEC for non-public review.[39] This may protect the issuer from embarrassment if the SEC challenges its accounting or has other adverse comments that require significant revision. However, the confidential submission (and all amendments to it) must be made publicly

---

[36] Pub L. No. 112–106, 126 Stat. 306 (2012) (codified in various sections of 15 U.S.C.).
[37] The $1 billion threshold is subject to inflation indexing every five years.
[38] See § 2(a)(19) of the 1933 Act.
[39] See § 6(e)(1) of the 1933 Act.

available no later than 15 days before the commencement of a road show. Thus, the privacy obtained is short-lived, but the provision does permit the issuer to revise its disclosures quietly if the SEC objects and thereby avoid a higher profile public dispute. It also permits an emerging growth company to assess the nature and extent of disclosures it must make in a registration statement before formally deciding to file with the SEC.

In 2017, in an effort to encourage more IPO filings, the SEC extended its policy on confidential review and now permits all IPO filings to be made confidentially, even in the case of very large issuers that do not qualify as emerging growth companies.[40]

2. *Test-the-Waters Communications.* Under § 5(d) of the 1933 Act, an emerging growth company, or any person authorized to act on its behalf, may engage in oral or written communications with potential investors that are "qualified institutional buyers" or institutional "accredited investors." This standard includes most institutional investors.[41] The goal of this provision is to enable the issuer to test the feasibility of the offering before undertaking the costs of preparing and filing a registration statement with the SEC. As a result, the gun-jumping rules of § 5(c) are cut back for an emerging growth company, which in theory could line up investors willing to buy all its stock before even filing a registration statement. As noted earlier, recently adopted Rule 163B extends this same approach to all issuers (and those authorized to act for them) in their dealings with most institutional investors. This fundamentally changes how underwriters (and other agents of the issuers) can approach and deal with institutional versus individual investors.

3. *Required Disclosures.* An emerging growth company must include only two years of audited financial statements in its registration statement (in contrast to the three years required for other issuers).[42] An emerging growth company may also limit its disclosures in the section on Management's Discussion and Analysis of Financial Condition and Results of

---

[40] See Note, Going Public Secretly: The SEC's Unavailing Effort to Increase Initial Public Offerings through Confidential Review, 2019 Colum. Bus. L.Rev. 305. Opinions vary as to whether this policy is having any effect on the number of IPOs.

[41] These terms are defined in Rule 144A and Rule 501 under Regulation D. Effectively, if an institutional investor not formed for the specific purpose of acquiring the offered securities has at least $5 million in total assets, it will qualify as an "accredited investor," and no such financial requirement applies to banks, brokers and dealers, or insurance companies (see Rules 501(a)(1) and (a)(7)).

[42] See § 7(a)(2)(A) of the 1933 Act.

Operations in its registration statement so as to only cover the same two-year period.

4. *Accounting Standards.* An emerging growth company may delay the adoption of accounting standards that have different effective dates for public and private companies until those standards apply to private companies.[43] The SEC will request an emerging growth company to disclose in the Risk Factors section of its registration statement that this could cause its financial statements not to be comparable with those of other issuers. To date, this provision has not been triggered by any new accounting standards.

5. *Corporate Governance Rules.* Under Title I of the JOBS Act, an emerging growth company will not be subject to a variety of corporate governance provisions that apply to other public companies, including "Say-on-Pay," "Say-on-Frequency" and "Say-on-Golden Parachute" votes (which votes were required by the Dodd-Frank Act).[44] Once an issuer ceases to be an emerging growth company, those votes will be required.[45] Certain disclosures about the relationship between executive compensation and the firm's financial performance and about the CEO's compensation relative to that of the median employee (which were required by the Dodd-Frank Act) are also waived in the case of an emerging growth company.[46]

Today, there is no requirement for the mandatory rotation of audit firms. However, if such a rule were adopted in the future, emerging growth companies would be exempted. Other new auditing standards adopted by the PCAOB will not apply to an emerging growth company, unless the SEC specifically determines that such a requirement is necessary or appropriate for the protection of investors.[47]

Finally, an emerging growth company is exempted from the requirement that the auditor must attest to the adequacy of (and audit) the issuer's internal controls.[48] This did significantly reduce the audit fees to which an emerging growth company would otherwise have been subject.

---

[43] See § 7(a)(2)(B) of the 1933 Act.

[44] See § 14A(e)(2) of the 1934 Act.

[45] The timing of these votes at a former emerging growth company is governed by § 14A(e)(2)(B) of the 1934 Act. If the emerging growth company held such a status for less than two years, the votes must be held by the end of the third year following its IPO; otherwise, the vote must be within one year of the loss of that status.

[46] These requirements were imposed by § 953(b)(1) of the Dodd-Frank Act.

[47] See JOBS Act § 104 (amending Sarbanes-Oxley Act § 103(a)(3)).

[48] Management of an emerging growth company must still establish, maintain and annually assess their company's internal controls over financial reporting, but the auditor's report on those controls (which requires an expensive audit) was waived. See JOBS Act § 103 (amending Sarbanes-Oxley Act § 404(b)).

6. *Research Reports.* Under revised § 2(a)(3) of the 1933 Act, securities analysts, including those working for the underwriters, may circulate "research reports" (which term is broadly defined to include both oral and electronic communications) about an emerging growth company to investors, both before and after the registration statement is filed.[49] Thus, analysts can effectively tout a stock that their employer is underwriting. The JOBS Act does not invalidate FINRA rules that restrict other analyst activities,[50] and in 2014, FINRA imposed sanctions on ten underwriters who used their analysts to try to convince an issuer to hire them for its IPO.[51] Still, FINRA does not attempt to bar analysts from discussing their research at a road show in the case of an emerging growth company.[52]

In overview, few of these benefits seem financially significant (although confidential review is widely used and the exemption from § 404(b)'s requirements for an audit of internal controls did clearly reduce auditing expenses). Revealingly, emerging growth companies are not fully exploiting these opportunities where doing so might incur the market's displeasure. Thus, many emerging growth companies are including three years of financial results, despite the JOBS Act's permission to use only two years, because their underwriters have advised them that the market wants more information. The active use of analyst research reports to market the offering (either before or after the filing of the registration statement) has not yet developed, and "test the waters" solicitations have largely been limited to meetings introducing the issuer's management to institutional investors. The one provision in the JOBS Act that has been widely adopted is confidential review. Most eligible issuers are using it, but most institutional investors will review the issuer's confidential submission to the SEC before they attend the road show.

In 1997, there were 168 IPOs that listed on exchanges with an initial market capitalization of less than $75 million, but in 2012, there were

---

[49] The term "research report" is defined in § 2(a)(3) of the 1933 Act.

[50] Sections 105(c) and (d) of the JOBS Act do preclude both the SEC and FINRA from adopting or maintaining rules that bar a broker-dealer from publishing a research report, but these provisions do not prohibit FINRA from restricting analyst participation in sales meetings with a potential underwriting client. The SEC takes the position that these FINRA rules are not preempted.

[51] In 2014, FINRA fined ten underwriting firms a total of $43.5 million for violating FINRA rules that forbid underwriters to use their analysts to solicit investment banking business by promising favorable research. The underwriting firms were competing in 2010 for the role of underwriter in a planned IPO by Toys "R" Us (which offering never transpired). See Morgenson, At Big Banks, a Lesson Not Learned, N.Y. Times (Dec. 12, 2014), at B-1.

[52] As noted earlier, in 2015, the SEC approved a new FINRA rule, Rule 2241 ("Research Analysts and Research Reports"), that shortened the former 25-day "quiet period" to 10 days for an IPO and only three days in the case of a follow-on equity offering.

only seven such IPOs.[53] To date, the JOBS Act does not seem to be reversing this trend. What then is causing "the death of the small IPO"? Proponents of the JOBS Act believed the leading causes were increased regulatory costs following the passage of the Sarbanes-Oxley Act (and, in particular, increased auditing costs caused by § 404(b) of the Sarbanes-Oxley Act, which was interpreted to require an annual audit of internal controls) and reduced analyst coverage of smaller companies (which was allegedly caused by Regulation FD and the Global Settlement (described earlier), which restricted analysts' ability to hype IPO stocks). But scholarship has found only weak to mixed evidence that increased regulatory costs disproportionately burdened smaller companies.[54] The claim that restrictions on analysts changed the "market ecosystem" in a way that prejudices smaller companies has also drawn scholarly skepticism, as analyst coverage empirically has not declined significantly.[55]

What then has happened? One view is that globalization has disadvantaged smaller firms, which need to grow quickly to survive. Under this view, increased regulatory costs and changes within financial intermediaries (including how they support analysts) have had little impact. Still, broader structural changes in the economy may necessitate that firms grow so as to be able to operate on a global scale, and this forces smaller firms to "eat or be eaten."[56] In effect, the merger market may offer these firms a larger premium than does the IPO market.

This debate will continue, but one empirical fact is clear: Smaller firms that do undertake an IPO and list on an exchange do not remain there for long. One recent study found that, from 1996 to 2012, only 55% of small IPOs remained listed on an exchange for five years (while 61.3% and 67.1% of middle and large capitalization firms remained listed).[57] To date, the most counter-intuitive finding about the impact of the JOBS Act is that it may have actually increased the costs of going public. One study of 312 EGC IPOs between April 2012 and April 2015 finds no reduction in the direct costs of issuance, accounting, legal, or underwriting fees for emerging growth companies, but a significant increase in "underpricing," which is an indirect cost of issuance.[58] Although this study found no increase in IPO volume as a result of the

---

[53] See Davidoff Solomon & Rose, The Disappearing Small IPO and the Lifecycle of the Small Firm (Jul. 2014) at 1, http://ssrn.com/abstract=2400488.

[54] See Coates & Srianivasan, SOX after Ten Years: A Multidisciplinary Review, 28 Acct'g Horizons 627 (2014).

[55] See Gao, Ritter & Zhu, Where Have All the IPOs Gone?, 48 J. Fin. & Quant. Anal. 1663 (2013).

[56] Gao, Ritter & Zhu are the leading proponents of this "economies of scope" theory. But see also Bova et al., The Sarbanes-Oxley Act and the Exit Strategies of Private Firms, 31 Contemp. Acct'g Res. 818 (2014) (smaller firms are more likely to be acquired than do an IPO).

[57] See Davidoff Solomon & Rose, The Disappearing Small IPO and the Lifecycle of the Small Firm (Jul. 2014), http://ssrn.com/abstract=2400488.

[58] See Chaplinsky, Hanley & Moon, The JOBS Act and the Costs of Going Public, 55 J. Acct'g Res. 795 (2017).

JOBS Act, another study, in 2014, concluded that the JOBS Act led to an additional 21 IPOs annually or a 25% increase over pre-JOBS Act levels.[59] This debate will likely continue. None of this proves that scaled disclosure is a poor policy choice for smaller firms, but it does suggest that reforms do not always achieve their intended objective.

    a. What Does It Cost? One recent study of IPOs after the JOBS Act found that IPO expenses (excluding the underwriting discount) came to $4.2 million on average, with emerging growth companies spending $3.7 million and other issuers spending $5.9 million.[60] Because the latter issuers are larger and probably undertake more sizable offerings, this finding does not demonstrate that the JOBS Act reduced costs for emerging growth companies, but it may suggest that smaller IPOs (i.e., under $75 million) may be too expensive to be feasible.

    b. How Long Does It Take? The same study found that the timeline for non-emerging growth companies was shorter than for emerging growth companies, with the period from the first SEC filing to IPO pricing being 116 days compared to 128 days for emerging growth companies that filed confidentially and 249 days for emerging growth companies that did not file confidentially.[61] No obvious reason for this disparity is apparent.

    c. The FAST Act: The Latest Step in Deregulation. The Fixing America's Surface Transportation Act ("FAST Act") became law in 2015. Only a small portion of that statute dealt with the federal securities laws, but it basically extended or broadened some of the existing JOBS Act provisions. The JOBS Act had permitted an emerging growth company to confidentially file its registration statement with the SEC, but then precluded such a company from conducting a road show until 25 days after the public filing of its registration statement. The FAST Act shortened this 25-day delay to a 15 days and also provided that, if an emerging growth company filed confidentially but then ceased to be an emerging growth company, it would still be treated as an emerging growth company until the earlier of the date on which it consummated its IPO or one year after it ceased to be an emerging growth company.[62] Small stuff, but clearly Congress wanted to reinforce the JOBS Act.

Problems

Assume now that New Corp.'s gross revenues were $250 million in the fiscal year prior to its IPO. It is also not a reporting company.

---

[59] See Dambra, Field & Gustafson, The JOBS Act and IPO Volume: Evidence that Disclosure Costs Affect the IPO Decision, 116 J. Fin. Econ. 121 (2015). The authors report that biotechnology and pharmaceutical firms particularly benefitted from the JOBS Act because those firms, in their view, had higher disclosure costs.

[60] See Proskauer Rose LLP., 2014 IPO Study (2014) at 2 (study of 100 IPOs that were priced in 2013, the first year after the JOBS Act).

[61] Id. at 11. On average, emerging growth companies that filed confidentially made their first public filing 50 days after their first confidential submission.

[62] See § 6(e) of the 1933 Act.

PROBLEM 2-37

Prior to New Corp. filing its registration statement, Thomas Smith, an analyst with Bache, Halsey & Co., the lead underwriter for the proposed offering, sends a five-page letter to 25 pension and mutual funds (and also posts this letter on a blog that he runs for Bache, Halsey), analyzing New Corp.'s recent financial performance and describing it as "stellar" and "off-the-charts." Can this be done?

PROBLEM 2-38

New Corp. posts Smith's letter on its own web site. Any problem?

PROBLEM 2-39

Again prior to New Corp.'s filing of its registration statement, New Corp.'s CEO, Max Headroom, invites investment officers from six major insurance companies, three large hedge funds, and two sizable mutual funds to the company's headquarters for what he describes as a "preliminary road show." Can this be done?

PROBLEM 2-40

New Corp. files its registration statement on March 1, seeking confidential review by the SEC. On April 5, the SEC responds with a letter of comments, and New Corp. files its first pre-effective amendment to its registration statement on April 12. All these documents are made publicly available on April 21, and New Corp. schedules its first formal road show in New York City for May 2nd. Any problem?

6. NEW DEVELOPMENTS

The key development in recent years has been the growth of large privately-held companies—sometimes called "unicorns"—that have raised billions of dollars in capital in successive rounds of private placements. These companies still lack liquidity, with the result that their investors cannot easily find buyers (and their sales may depress the market price for their stock). In response, these companies have departed from the traditional IPO game plan, as discussed below:

a. *Direct Listings.* If a privately-held company has already secured the capital it needs for the immediate future, it makes little sense for it to make an initial public offering and raise superfluous capital, paying high fees to an underwriter. Instead, its real need is to effect a listing on a stock exchange so that its shareholders can trade their shares (and there is no need to pay an underwriter to do this). The New York Stock Exchange was happy to oblige this desire to list without issuing new shares (as it profits from the secondary trading of companies listed on it). In principle, to list on an exchange, a company would only need to register under the 1934 Act (as § 12(b) of that Act specifically requires 1934 Act registration before a company may list on an exchange) and then file a listing application with the exchange. In 2017, the NYSE sought to amend its rules to encourage direct listings, but because amendment of a stock exchange's rules requires SEC approval, the NYSE needed the SEC to approve its new direct listing rule.[63] The SEC surprised the NYSE by insisting that an issuer must also register its shares under the 1933 Act, even though no new shares were to be issued.[64] This ensured greater transparency, but it also raised the possibility that the issuer might have potential liability under the 1933 Act (whose § 11 essentially provides strict liability for material misstatements or omissions made by an issuer in a registration statement).

Spotify did the first registered direct listing on the New York Stock Exchange in 2017.[65] Essentially, Spotify achieved three objectives: (1) by listing on the NYSE, it obtained liquidity for its investors (including its employees and officers who held its stock), and its stock price rose significantly after its listing; (2) given its $20 billion valuation, Spotify could easily qualify for "automatic shelf registration" (which is discussed in the next chapter) and thus could quickly issue shares to effect mergers and acquisitions; and (3) Spotify avoided having to pay an expensive fee to an underwriter (although it was required to hire a financial advisor at a lower fee). Under the NYSE's new direct listing rule, Spotify was required to provide a valuation from a financial advisor or expert certifying it had a market value of at least $250 million (but this was no problem for Spotify, which then had an estimated market value of around $20 billion). The $250 million requirement suggests that the SEC may not be ready to see this new direct listing procedure used by smaller companies, which might directly access the public markets without using an underwriter.

Although the NYSE's direct listing procedure did not contemplate the sale of any shares, the obvious question that arose in the wake of Spotify's listing was whether a private company could now list its outstanding shares and also sell new shares at the same time (without employing an underwriter). In 2019, the NYSE responded to this desire and proposed to amend its direct listing rule to permit issuers to both list outstanding shares and issue new shares simultaneously. However, the SEC refused to approve this revised rule (without publicly explaining its reasons).[66]

---

[63] See § 19(b)(1) of, and Rule 19b–4 under, the 1934 Act.

[64] See Exchange Act Release No. 82627 (Feb. 2, 2018). For the new rule, see NYSE Listed Company Manual § 102.01B.

[65] For an overview, see Horton, Spotify's Direct Listing: Is It A Recipe for Gatekeeper Failure?, 72 S.M.U. L. Rev. 177 (2019). Subsequent to the Spotify offering, other companies have also conducted successful direct listings, with their stock price then rising. In 2019, Slack Technologies, Inc. was the most notable example.

[66] In November 2019, the NYSE filed a rule proposal to permit issuers to both list outstanding shares and sell additional shares without using an underwriter. In December 2019, the SEC rejected this proposed rule change. See Mondaq Business Briefing (Feb. 4, 2020). However, the SEC later approved a resubmission with changes.

Why was the SEC skeptical? Although the SEC has not explained, one plausible reason may be that the prospect of stock manipulation goes up in "underwriter-less" offerings. Normally, the underwriter "stabilizes" the stock price during an offering (meaning it will buy the stock, if necessary, so that the price does not fall below the offering price).[67] In the absence of an underwriter, the risk increases that short sellers or others could seek to manipulate the stock's price, either up or down. Nonetheless, when the NYSE submitted a revised proposal in 2020 under which an issuer could do a direct listing and sell its shares in a primary offering (without using an underwriter), the SEC approved it, but later stayed its decision when a group of institutional investors objected. Although the cost advantages of such a procedure are attractive to privately-held companies (especially the "unicorns"), a troubling question is whether "underwriter-less" offerings of stock will place investors at greater risk. Also, direct listings may permit issuers to escape Section 11 liability on the shares sold in direct listings because "tracing" such shares is difficult to impossible.[68]

b. *The Cost Advantages.* Although the costs of an IPO vary, PriceWaterhouseCoopers has estimated that the costs for an IPO of around $300 million (which is a medium-sized IPO) will come to over $44 million, consisting of:[69]

Item	Amount
SEC Registration Fee	$200,000
Listing Fee	$250,000
Printing Costs	$600,000
Auditors Fees	$1,700,000
Legal Fees and Expenses	$3,100,000
Transfer Agent and Registrar Fees	N/A
Underwriter's Fee	$37,000,000
Miscellaneous Fees and Expenses	$1,600,000
Total:	$44,350,000

Obviously, the major expense is the underwriter's fee, which is estimated to be 84% of the total IPO fees.

So what did Spotify pay to its financial advisors? According to its prospectus, Spotify paid $35 million for a direct listing of securities

---

[67] Stabilization is regulated by Rule 104 of Regulation M under the 1934 Act.

[68] The "tracing" requirement, which is unique to Section 11, is discussed later in Chapter 11, which analyzes Section 11.

[69] PWC Deals, Considering An IPO? An Insight Into the Costs Post-Jobs Act (2015), at 10.

valued at over $20 billion[70]—far below the 7 to 7.5% underwriter's commission that has been standard. Other recent IPOs by large unicorns have involved underwriting fees of $85 to $176 million.[71] Of course, the financial advisor in a direct listing takes no risk and sells no shares, and thus it should charge far less. Nonetheless, the cost savings from a direct listing have greatly interested private companies that are considering how best to enter the public markets.

c. The IPO Ratchet. Traditionally, the principal investors in private placements by prospective IPO issuers were venture capital and private equity firms. More recently, mutual funds have begun to invest in late round private placements by likely candidates for an IPO, hoping to steal a march on other mutual funds that wait to invest until the IPO takes place. Mutual funds, as investors in private placements, appear to have very different interests than venture capital funds. While the latter are primarily interested in board representation and voting rights, mutual funds have shown more interest in protection against a decline in the value of their investments.[72] Mutual funds appear to seek two types of provisions: (1) redemption rights that allow them to exit (possibly if the IPO is delayed) and (2) a pricing "ratchet" that entitles them to receive additional shares if the IPO prices below the value at which they bought shares in their private placement. These provisions impose risks on the shareholders who buy in the IPO. For example, if the last private placement was at $20 per share and the IPO prices at $16 per share, the issuer might have to issue additional shares to the mutual fund investors who negotiated such a "ratchet" clause in the private placement. In the WeWork attempted IPO in 2019 (which ultimately collapsed), some analysts computed the value of the additional shares that would have had to be paid to SoftBank, the principal investor in WeWork, as potentially exceeding $500 million.[73] But no disclosure of this risk was made in the WeWork prospectus.

d. The Increased Use of Non-GAAP Financial Metrics. Financial results must be disclosed pursuant to Regulation S–X under the 1933 Act, but issuers may also explain their results in other ways. For example, one of the most popular alternatives is to stress EBITDA (earnings before interest, taxes, depreciation and amortization), which is designed to give investors a measure of cash flow. The issuer's ability to

---

[70] See Horton, *Spotify's Direct Listing: Is It A Recipe for Gatekeeper Failure?*, 72 S.M.U. L. Rev. 177, 200 (2019).

[71] Id. at 199–200 (estimating that Spotify would have paid "around $130 million" to a traditional underwriter).

[72] See Chemenko, Lerner & Zeng, *Mutual Funds as Venture Capitalists?: Evidence from Unicorns* (2019), https://ssrn.com/abstract=2897254; Gornall & Strebulav, *Squaring Venture Capital Valuations with Reality* (2019), https://ssrn.com/abstract=2955455.

[73] See Renaissance Capital, *WeWork's anti-dilution provisions could grant $400 million to Softbank and others* (Sept. 12, 2019); Rooney, *WeWork investors like Softbank have an obscure protection worth millions in a devalued IPO* (Sept. 24, 2019), at https://www.cnbc.com/2019/09/24/softbank-has-a-multi-million-dollar-protection-in-weworks-ipo.html.

use these metrics is governed by Regulation G,[74] which requires the issuer to accompany the non-GAAP financial metric with "[a] presentation of the most directly comparable financial measure calculated and presented in accordance with Generally Accepted Accounting Principles (GAAP)" and a "reconciliation" of the differences between the two measures.

In recent years, the use of non-GAAP financial metrics has soared, with the percentage of S&P 500 firms that used at least one such metric rising from 59% in 1996 to 97% in 2018.[75] More dubiously, some firms are relying on many such metrics as part of their disclosures, including some very exotic ones. An extreme case involved WeWork, an office space leasing firm, which in 2019 employed a metric it called "community adjusted EBITDA," which allowed the firm to exclude marketing costs. The impact of this metric was to flip WeWork from a $1.9 billion loss for 2018 to a $467 million profit.[76] Convinced that this could be misleading to investors, the SEC demanded that WeWork exclude this measure from the prospectus for its IPO. WeWork refused, and an elaborate negotiation began, which ended when the offering was canceled (largely because of investor dismay over self-dealing and persistent losses, as well as the unusual financial presentation). WeWork's use of a specially designed metric to downplay its losses may have been extreme, but it was not unique. Uber, for example, used a metric called "core platform adjusted net revenue" to help it explain its losses. Even more recently, some issuers are attempting to introduce a new metric—EBITDAC (with the "C" standing for Covid-19). Under this metric, the issuer would add back to its earnings the estimated costs (or possibly even the lost revenues) caused it by the Covid-19 pandemic. Of course it is uncertain that these numbers can be reliably estimated. SEC observers believe the SEC's staff will give enhanced scrutiny to the use of such metrics.

---

[74] See Rule 100 of Regulation G under the 1933 Act.
[75] See Eaglesham & Brown, WeWork Was Wrestling with SEC over Key Financial Metric Just Before It Scrapped IPO, Wall Street Journal Online (Nov. 10, 2019) (citing study by Audit Analytics, a research firm).
[76] Id.

CHAPTER 3

THE REGISTRATION PROCESS

Statutes

Securities Act, §§ 6(a), 10(a).

Exchange Act, §§ 12(a), 12(b), 12(g), Rule 12g–1.

Rules and Regulations

Rules 176, 406, 411, 415, 421.

Regulation S–K Items 103, 301, 302, 303.

1. THE SEC'S INTEGRATED DISCLOSURE SYSTEM

a. Introduction. The preceding chapter principally examined the statutory provisions of the Securities Act of 1933 as they are likely to apply to an initial public offering ("IPO"). In an IPO, the issuer is not yet subject to the ongoing reporting obligations of the Securities Exchange Act of 1934. Not so in the case of a seasoned company, which is likely to be subject to both the 1933 and 1934 Acts. That is, if, at the end of its fiscal year, the issuer has $10 million in total assets and a specified number of shareholders of record, in general it is required to register under § 12(g) of the 1934 Act (using Form 10, which an issuer can also use to register a class of securities for trading on a U.S. exchange) and enter the SEC's periodic disclosure system—which, among other obligations, requires it to file annual reports on Form 10-K and, for the first three quarters of each year, quarterly reports on Form 10-Q.[1]

Given this continuing disclosure obligation, it appears unnecessary and excessive to require such a "reporting" issuer—one that is already making continuing disclosures—to delay its public offering and follow the same registration procedures (often taking four or more months) as a first-time IPO issuer, particularly when public investors are already trading its outstanding securities in the secondary market. With perfect hindsight, one can say that the disclosures provided under the two statutes should have been integrated to streamline the process and spare the seasoned issuer from having to start from scratch each time it filed a registration statement with the SEC. Through integration, the seasoned "reporting" issuer could utilize the periodic disclosures it makes under the 1934 Act and supplement them with information about the offering's terms and any material changes in its prior disclosures.

---

[1] See Rule 12g–1 under the 1934 Act. In 2012, § 501 of the Jumpstart Our Business Startups ("JOBS") Act raised the requisite number of shareholders of record from 500 to 2,000. However, companies that list on an exchange (including Nasdaq) are independently required by § 12(b) of the 1934 Act to become "reporting companies."

Self-evident as this insight might seem today, it was first pointed out in a famous law review article by Milton Cohen,[2] who observed that the SEC's disclosure system would have been quite different "if the 1933 and 1934 Acts . . . had been enacted in the opposite order."[3] In that event, the first statute would have created "a statutory scheme of continuous disclosures covering issuers of actively traded securities,"[4] and with this scheme in place, the logical question for the draftsperson of the second statute would have been what additional disclosures were needed when the company came to make a public offering of its securities. Presumably, given the existence of a continuous disclosure system, the additional disclosures necessary to register the issuer's securities for sale could have been simplified, and overlapping, duplicative, and inconsistent disclosures might have been eliminated. Most of all, the seasoned issuer would have quicker access to the capital market and would not need to undertake the slow process of SEC review and comment that surrounded the typical registration statement.

The SEC came slowly to accept this idea of integrating the disclosures required under the 1933 and 1934 Acts. Over its first four decades, the SEC administered the two statutes independently and, as a result, separate and distinct disclosure systems evolved under each. This dual system spawned sometimes inconsistent interpretations, and each disclosure document—registration statement, periodic report, and proxy statement—had its own requirements, definitions, and instructions, with little standardization. In particular, the financial statements used in 1933 Act documents could differ from those used in 1934 Act documents.

The first step toward integration occurred in 1977 when the SEC adopted Regulation S–K, which prescribed a single standard set of instructions for filing forms under the 1933 and 1934 Acts. Thus, today, when the same type of information is mandated in various forms under either Act, a single set of instructions applies.

More drastic surgery was performed in January 1980 when the SEC adopted sweeping revisions to Form 10-K (the annual report filed by a public company), Rule 14a–3 under the 1934 Act (which prescribes the annual report to shareholders under the proxy rules), Regulation S–X (which governs the requirements for financial statements under the 1933 and 1934 Acts), and Regulation S–K (which prescribes instructions for filings under the 1933 and 1934 Acts). The effect of these amendments was, at last, to promulgate uniform financial disclosure requirements for virtually all documents required to be filed under the 1933 or 1934 Act. In particular, the SEC mandated that the audited financial statements included in annual reports to shareholders under the 1934 Act must comply with the requirements of Regulation S–X. Simultaneously, Regulation S–X was amended to eliminate most of the differences with

---

[2] Cohen, "Truth in Securities" Revisited, 79 Harv. L. Rev. 1340 (1966).
[3] Id. at 1341.
[4] Id.

the requirements of U.S. generally accepted accounting principles. Today, the requirements for financial disclosures appear in Regulation S–X, and the requirements for non-financial disclosures appear in Regulation S–K. Yet, in the relatively recent past, securities regulation was a hodgepodge of inconsistent and uncoordinated standards.

Besides establishing a common disclosure standard, the SEC also developed the concept of a "basic information package" that disclosure documents under the 1933 and 1934 Acts should contain:

> The Commission's review of the purpose and utility of the Form 10-K led it to believe that there is a basic information package which most, if not all, investors expect to be furnished. Further, it has become apparent that this basic information package, which in the context of Form 10-K developed to support the current information requirements of an active trading market, is virtually identical to the similar information package independently developed in connection with the registration and sale of newly issued shares under the Securities Act. The essential content of these Form 10-K and registration statement information packages includes audited financial statements, a summary of selected financial data appropriate for trend analysis, and a meaningful description of the registrant's business and financial condition.[5]

This "basic information package" was defined to include audited financial statements for the issuer's two most recent fiscal years (both balance sheets as of the end of the two years, and income statements and statements of changes in financial position for each of those two years), plus selected financial information from the last five years to indicate trends in sales, income, liabilities, and dividends, and information about the issuer's stock price.[6] In addition, the SEC required the "basic information package" to include a Management's Discussion and Analysis of Financial Condition and Results of Operations ("MD&A"). The MD&A presents the issuer through management's own eyes and highlight trends that are likely to affect the issuer's liquidity or profitability in the future.[7] In effect, the issuer must make forecasts about material "trends and uncertainties" that may affect it. (The MD&A requirement is discussed in more detail later in this chapter.)

Today, this basic information package appears in the issuer's annual report to shareholders, which must precede or accompany the issuer's

---

[5] Securities Act Release No. 6231 (Sept. 2, 1980).

[6] In addition to Regulation S–X under the 1933 Act, the financial components of this "basic information package" are specified in Items 301 and 302 of Regulation S–K under the 1933 Act. Item 301 requires selected financial data for five years, and Item 302 requires data relating to net sales, gross profit, income (or loss), and earnings per share for each full quarter for the two most recent fiscal years and any subsequent interim period for which financial statements are required by Regulation S–X.

[7] The required MD&A disclosures are set forth in Item 303 of Regulation S–K under the 1933 Act.

proxy statement, its annual report on Form 10-K, and its registration statement. When the SEC developed the concept of the basic information package, it also drew a distinction between "registrant-specific" information and "transaction-specific" information. The Form 10-K a reporting company files under the 1934 Act basically provides registrant-specific information, including the basic information package and more detailed information about the issuer's business, properties, officers and directors, and recent developments. The 1933 Act registration statement also includes this basic information package but otherwise concentrates on "transaction-specific" information about the proposed offering. For example, how are the proceeds of the offering to be used? What dilution, if any, will the offering cause to existing shareholders? What are the specific terms of the new security being issued (e.g., default conditions, covenants, convertibility, sinking fund, and so forth)? Such information arises at the time of a public offering and, thus, could not have been previously disclosed in a Form 10-K.

Marking the significant next step in the evolution of integrated disclosure, in 1981, the SEC classified issuers by their level of seasoning and permitted incorporation by reference of 1934 Act reports into a 1933 Act registration statement, at least in the case of the most seasoned class of issuers. Essentially, the SEC divided issuers into two categories.[8] The first category of issuer consisted of unseasoned companies that had not previously filed 1934 Act reports. Thus, logically, the registration statement for such a company should include all information—both company-specific information and transaction-specific information—in one document, the Form S-1 registration statement.[9]

The second, more seasoned category of issuer was authorized to use Form S-3, which contained a basic information package providing transaction-specific information but omitting most company-specific information. The issuer was permitted to incorporate by reference such information from the issuer's Form 10-K and other 1934 Act filings, without attempting to restate or summarize it, and provide any material updates in the registration statement itself. Incorporation by reference

---

[8] In 2005, as described below, the SEC further revised this classification system into four categories (Well-Known Seasoned Issuers, Seasoned Issuers, Unseasoned Issuers, and Non-Reporting Issuers). In addition, some specially disfavored companies are deemed "ineligible" issuers, such as companies with a recent enforcement history.

[9] Note that, in parallel with Forms S-1 and S-3, the SEC has forms designated for foreign private issuers on Form F-1 and F-3. Our focus in this chapter is on the forms used by U.S. registrants. Forms S-2 and F-2 have been discontinued and are no longer used.

Today, public issuers that do not meet the requirements to use Form S-3 can provide investors with transaction-specific information in a Form S-1 registration statement and company-specific information in listed 1934 Act reports that are specifically incorporated by reference (with material updates in the registration statement itself). See Items 11A and 12 of Form S-1 under the 1933 Act. This is a somewhat exceptional practice—it is often efficient simply to present both company- and transaction-specific information directly in the Form S-1 registration statement—but when it is done, the prospectus and incorporated reports may all be bundled together in one, somewhat cumbersome, disclosure document. With the advent of the internet, the incorporated documents may be made available on the issuer's website, although as a practical matter the issuer may still choose to bundle them with the prospectus.

meant that the special liability rules of the 1933 Act (specifically, §§ 11 and 12(a)(2)) applied to the incorporated information, without the information being expressly set out in the registration statement. For the SEC to permit such company-specific information to be omitted from the registration statement implied that the SEC had substantially accepted the central concept of the "efficient capital market hypothesis" ("ECMH")—namely, that publicly disclosed information (here, the information in the 1934 Act reports) had already been evaluated by the market and incorporated into the security's price.

The Commission summarized its new tripartite categorization of issuers in Securities Act Release No. 6383, which also stressed the important difference between "registrant-specific" and "transaction-specific" information:

Securities Act Release No. 6383
Securities and Exchange Commission.
March 3, 1982.

ADOPTION OF INTEGRATED DISCLOSURE SYSTEM

* * *

Generally, it is the registrant-oriented portion of the information relating to a public offering, as opposed to the transaction-specific information, which sometimes may be satisfied otherwise than through full prospectus presentation. Much of this registrant-oriented information is the same as that which is required to be presented in annual reports to the Commission on Form 10-K and in annual reports to security holders, as well as in quarterly and current reports on Forms 10-Q and 8-K, respectively. Information about the offering, however, will not have been reported on in any other disclosure document or otherwise have been publicly disseminated and thus will be required to be presented in the prospectus in all cases.

The registration statement for the first category is Form S-1. It requires complete disclosure to be set forth in the prospectus and permits no incorporation by reference. Form S-1 is to be used by registrants in the Exchange Act reporting system for less than three years [now 12 months or if the registrant has not filed "in a timely manner" all 1934 Act reports required to be filed during the preceding 12 months, except certain filings on Form 8-K—Eds.] and also may be used by any registrants who choose to do so or for whom no other form is available.

* * *

Form S-3, in reliance on the efficient market theory, allows maximum use of incorporation by reference of Exchange Act reports and requires the least disclosure to be presented in the prospectus and delivered to investors. Generally, the Form S-3 prospectus will present the same transaction-specific information as will be presented in a Form

S-1 ... prospectus. Information concerning the registrant will be incorporated by reference from Exchange Act reports. The prospectus will not be required to present any information concerning the registrant unless there has been a material change in the registrant's affairs which has not been reported in an Exchange Act filing or the Exchange Act reports incorporated by reference do not reflect certain restated financial statements or other financial information.

* * *

---

1. *Integrated Disclosure: Was Efficient Market Theory the Rationale or a Makeweight?* Although Securities Act Release No. 6383 states its "reliance on the efficient market theory," skeptics have doubted it explains the SEC's motivation for integrating the 1933 Act's and 1934 Act's disclosure systems.[10] They suggest the costs of maintaining two distinct systems of disclosure simply outweighed the benefits.

At the time, the Form S-3 could be used for any debt security that was rated "investment grade" by a nationally recognized statistical rating organization (i.e., a credit rating agency), representing a sensible cost/benefit judgment in light of the lower risk of such securities. Use of the Form S-3 is no longer tied to a credit rating, which now relies on different objective criteria relating to the issuer's access to the public debt markets—such as whether the issuer has issued $1 billion in registered non-convertible securities, other than common equity, for cash, over the prior three years or has outstanding $750 million of such non-convertible securities.

Since its adoption in 1982, the SEC has liberalized the eligibility requirements to use Form S-3. The current eligibility rules typically require the aggregate market value for the issuer's voting stock held by non-affiliates (i.e., its "public float") to be $75 million or more for a primary offering of stock for cash. This reduction by half from the original $150 million threshold seems to reflect a political accommodation and not any belated SEC recognition that the boundaries of the efficient market had suddenly expanded.

Even the $75 million requirement was relaxed in 2007 when the SEC permitted issuers that have been "reporting" companies for at least one year and have a class of stock listed on a national securities exchange to use Form S-3 to effect smaller primary offerings. Specifically, use of the Form S-3 is now possible without regard to the issuer's size or earnings, so long as (i) the issuer meets the Registrant Requirements in General Instruction I(A) and is not a shell company, (ii) the offering is a primary offering for cash, and (iii) the aggregate market value of the securities sold during the prior 12 months does not exceed one-third of the

---

[10] See Langevoort, Theories, Assumptions and Securities Regulation: Market Efficiency Revisited, 140 U.Pa.L.Rev. 851 (1992).

aggregate market value of the issuer's common stock held by non-affiliates (i.e., its public float).[11] With this change, the Form S-3 is now generally available, at least for smaller offerings, to virtually all seasoned companies.

While the SEC's judgment underlying the Form S-3 seems sound—namely, that investors in primary and secondary markets need the same information to transact in securities—one critical difference between these two markets should be underscored: The issuer has a far greater incentive to deceive when it is selling stock (and will receive the proceeds) in a primary offering than when the only trading is between investors in the secondary market. For this reason, § 11 of the 1933 Act places virtually "strict liability" on the issuer for material misstatements or omissions in the issuer's registration statement. It also imposes liability without proof of fault on third parties (i.e., underwriters, experts, directors, and auditors) to give them a strong incentive to test the adequacy of the issuer's disclosures. As will be seen later in this chapter, much of the current debate surrounding 1933 Act disclosure has centered on the continued ability of these third parties to play this "gatekeeping" role as verifiers of the issuer's disclosures within the very time-constrained limits of shelf registration (which, as described below, relies on Form S-3).

2. *Smaller Reporting Companies.* The next significant relaxation of the 1933 Act's requirements came in 1992 when the SEC introduced streamlined registration procedures for "small business issuers." Originally, such an issuer was defined as a U.S. or Canadian issuer with revenues of less than $25 million during its last fiscal year and with an aggregate market value for its voting stock held by non-affiliates of less than $25 million. Such small companies rarely trade in an efficient market, but this relaxation reflected the political need for the SEC to simplify capital-raising for small businesses (who argued they were disproportionately affected by the costs of registration, and therefore, did not have access to the public capital market). Inevitably, inflation resulted in progressively fewer companies qualifying for inclusion within this category, and pressure built for its further liberalization.

In 2007, the SEC expanded this category of smaller issuer, renaming them "smaller reporting companies," dropping the $25 million in revenues test, and permitting issuers with a public float of less than $75 million to qualify for its scaled-down disclosure standard.[12] The SEC

---

[11] See Securities Act Release No. 8812 (June 26, 2007) (proposing revised eligibility conditions). The SEC adopted this proposal in December 2007. The instructions specifying these new eligibility conditions for smaller issuers are set forth in General Instruction I(B)(6) of Form S-3. The $75 million aggregate market value requirement continues to be set forth in General Instruction I(B)(1) of Form S-3, but does not need to be satisfied by issuers qualifying instead under Instruction I(B)(6).

[12] See Securities Act Release No. 8876 (Dec. 19, 2007). As discussed earlier, a reporting issuer with less than a $75 million public float can still use Form S-3 for smaller offerings where the aggregate market value of the securities sold during the prior 12 months does not exceed one-third of the aggregate market value of the issuer's public float.

amended the definition again in 2018 to require (determined on an annual basis) (i) a public float of less than $250 million or (ii) less than $100 million in annual revenues and (a) no public float or (b) a public float of less than $700 million.[13] Today, qualifying companies are permitted to follow simplified versions of Regulation S–K and Regulation S–X in preparing a Form S-1 or Form S-3 registration statement and Form 10-K annual report.[14]

3. *Management's Discussion and Analysis.* When the SEC adopted its integrated disclosure system, it recognized the need to upgrade disclosure under the 1934 Act, which often was cursory and mechanical. To achieve more meaningful 1934 Act disclosure, the Commission designed a new disclosure requirement—the Management's Discussion and Analysis of Financial Condition and Results of Operations ("MD&A")—for 1934 Act periodic reports. In other words, there was a tradeoff—the Commission sought to upgrade the reporting requirements under the 1934 Act (in particular, by focusing on the quality of disclosure regarding the issuer's financial condition and earnings) at the same time it integrated the 1933 Act's and 1934 Act's two disclosure systems to permit public issuers to incorporate their 1934 Act filings by reference to satisfy the bulk of their 1933 Act disclosure requirements.

Item 303 of Regulation S–K sets forth the required MD&A disclosures and calls for a narrative discussion, written from management's perspective, of the company's current financial position and future prospects. Essentially, the registrant must disclose and assess any known trends, demands, commitments, events, or uncertainties that it considers "reasonably likely" to have a material impact on its financial condition or earnings. In a series of releases during the 1980s, the SEC tightened these requirements and increased the quantification of future possibilities a registrant must undertake. The philosophy and requirements of the MD&A are discussed later in this chapter.

4. *EDGAR.* The Electronic Data Gathering, Analysis, and Retrieval ("EDGAR") System was another major step—moving the SEC from a paper-based technology to the world of electronic communications and a searchable database. Although first introduced for 1934 Act filings, today EDGAR requires domestic registrants to file both their periodic reports under the 1934 Act and their registration statements under the 1933 Act by electronic transmissions to the SEC. One advantage of EDGAR is that information is often available on the SEC's website

---

[13] See Rule 405 under the 1933 Act. The definition of "smaller reporting company" includes separate thresholds that must be satisfied by an issuer that exceeds one of the basic thresholds, and so no longer qualifies as a smaller reporting company, but later expects to re-qualify.

[14] See SEC, Changeover to the SEC's New Smaller Reporting Company System by Small Business Issuers and Non-Accelerated Filer Companies A Small Entity Compliance Guide (Jan. 25, 2008), https://www.sec.gov/info/smallbus/secg/smrepcosysguid.pdf (last visited June 12, 2020).

almost immediately after its filing with the SEC.[15] Among other benefits, EDGAR permits investors to easily access the 1934 Act reports that are incorporated by reference into an issuer's 1933 Act registration statement and prospectus.

2. SHELF REGISTRATION

A. THE DEBATE OVER RULE 415

Although the reaction of the bar and the investment banking community to the introduction of integrated disclosure was favorable and even laudatory, a far more critical reception greeted the next major SEC initiative: shelf registration. Traditionally, securities were registered for a specific, discrete offering, whose terms were negotiated with a group of underwriters and whose co-managers had reached at least a preliminary and non-binding agreement with the issuer before the registration statement was filed with the SEC.

This view that registration was for a one-time, specific offering was thought to be required by the last sentence of § 6(a) of the 1933 Act, which provides that "[a] registration statement shall be deemed effective only as to the securities specified therein as proposed to be offered." Precisely what this sentence means has always been something of a mystery, as the 1933 Act's legislative history gives little indication of Congress's purpose.[16] From early on, however, the SEC read this section to prevent an issuer from registering stock for sale at some undefined later point when the information in the registration statement might become "stale."[17]

In fact, the 1933 Act makes clear that a § 10(a) final prospectus cannot be used longer than the 9- and 16-month period specified in § 10(a)(3) of the 1933 Act. Pursuant to § 10(a)(3), when a prospectus (contained in a registration statement) is used more than nine months after the registration statement's effective date, the information contained in the prospectus cannot be of a date more than 16 months prior to such use. So, hypothetically, if a registration statement was declared effective on February 1, 2019, and the prospectus was used after November 1, 2019 (more than nine months after February 1, 2019), the prospectus could continue under § 10(a) so long as the information in it (i.e., the audited financial statements) is not of a date more than 16 months prior to the time the prospectus is used. Thus, the problem of stale information was always recognized and addressed by the Securities Act, suggesting that § 6(a)'s last sentence served no clear purpose.

---

[15] The SEC's website is at http://www.sec.gov.
[16] See Hodes, Shelf Registration: The Dilemma of the Securities and Exchange Commission, 49 Va. L. Rev. 1106, 1108–10 (1963).
[17] See Shawnee Chiles Syndicate, 10 S.E.C. 109, 113 (1941) ("The policy behind the last sentence of Section 6(a) is to assure investors that the registration statement and prospectus on which they rely, so far as is reasonably possible, provide current information.").

Still, in principle, it is easy to imagine a world in which the issuer registered securities for a future offering whose timing and purpose were not yet known at the time the issuer filed its registration statement. This would maximize the issuer's flexibility and allow it to respond quickly to new market conditions and opportunities. Once the methodology of integrated disclosure was perfected, such a delayed or continuous offering became increasingly feasible because the registration statement and final prospectus would no longer necessarily go stale. The issuer's subsequently-filed 1934 Act periodic reports would be automatically incorporated by reference, thus keeping the registration statement and final prospectus current or, in the vernacular, "evergreen."

The term used to describe such a registration of securities for delayed future sale at some indeterminate date (or continuous sale over a prolonged period) was "shelf registration"—because the issuer in effect registered the securities and put them "on the shelf" to later be "taken down" (i.e., later sold under the registration statement) from the shelf in a future offering. Despite § 6(a) of the 1933 Act, the Commission had always accepted "shelf registration" for limited purposes, such as the registration of warrants or convertible securities, where the time of actual sale could not be known at the time of filing. Such registration statements were kept "evergreen" by an annual, post-effective amendment that included the financial information from the issuer's current annual report on Form 10-K. The SEC accepted these "traditional shelf registration" statements based on an administrative compromise under which the registrant filed an "undertaking" in its initial registration statement that committed it to file a post-effective amendment to the registration statement to reflect in the prospectus any material changes in information. This allowed the SEC's staff to review the revised prospectus before its use and postponed the commencement of the statute of limitations period prescribed in § 13 of the Securities Act with respect to § 11 actions.

To implement its integrated disclosure system, the SEC originally divided registrants into three categories: (1) companies widely followed by professional research analysts; (2) companies subject to the 1934 Act's periodic reporting requirements for at least three years but not widely followed by research analysts; and (3) companies subject to the 1934 Act's reporting requirements for less than three years. The first category was permitted to use a short-form registration statement (Form S-3) that relies on incorporation by reference of 1934 Act reports (see Rules 411 and 412 under the 1933 Act) and permits minimal disclosure in the prospectus. The second category was permitted to use Form S-2 (which, as noted below, has since been abolished) that combined incorporation by reference of 1934 Act reports with supplemental information. The third category, consisting of unseasoned issuers, was required to use Form S-1 that requires full disclosure of both company-specific and transaction-specific information (specific incorporation by reference of listed 1934 Act reports, but not subsequently-filed 1934 Act reports, is permitted today[18]). More recently, the SEC reduced this tripartite division into a dual one, abolishing Form S-2 in 2005, and allowing companies to use Form S-3 if they (i) are "reporting" companies for at least 12 months, (ii) have filed "in a timely manner" all reports required to be filed during the preceding 12 months, and (iii) otherwise satisfy both the Registrant Requirements and Transaction Requirements of Form S-3.[19] Issuers that do not meet the requirements of Form S-3, and for whose securities no other form is authorized or prescribed, use the Form S-1.[20]

Companies eligible to use Form S-3 are also permitted to employ shelf registration in "at the market" offerings (typically where a publicly-traded company gradually sells newly-issued shares into the secondary market through a designated broker-dealer at prevailing market prices), based on the SEC's premise that these firms trade in an efficient market in which a company's prior disclosures are immediately reflected in its share price. To accomplish this objective, the SEC greatly expanded the scope of Rule 415 under the 1933 Act. As revised, Rule 415's new goal was to enable issuers to time periodic public offerings of their securities to take advantage of favorable "market windows." Still, Rule 415 had many critics, particularly within the investment banking community, who asserted it caused more harm than good.

It may seem curious that a deregulatory rule, such as Rule 415, was vehemently resisted by the investment banking community. Investment bankers justified their opposition by claiming the Rule's expedited procedures gave them too little time to engage in due diligence (which § 11 of the 1933 Act requires if underwriters are to satisfy their affirmative defense under § 11(b)). Thus, they argued, they might be exposed to liability from which they could not successfully defend themselves. One SEC Commissioner dissented from the adoption of Rule 415 on this basis.[21] In response, the SEC argued that due diligence might be done in advance of any specific offering by engaging in continuous due diligence, such as by appointing an outside law firm to review and discuss with management the issuer's Form 10-K and other 1934 Act filings.

An alternative explanation for why investment bankers opposed Rule 415 looks to its predictable impact on competition. If a shelf registration statement could be filed and declared effective by the SEC a year or more in advance of a contemplated offering, then when the issuer later decides that market conditions are favorable to make an offering, it could seek competitive bids from underwriters as to their underwriting discount. Indeed, it was even conceivable the issuer could dispense with underwriters altogether and directly sell its securities to a small group

---

[18] See Item 12 of Form S-1 under the 1933 Act.
[19] See Instructions I.A. and I.B. of Form S-3 under the 1933 Act.
[20] See Instruction I. of Form S-1 under the 1933 Act.
[21] See Securities Act Release No. 6499 (Dec. 17, 1983) (dissent of Commissioner Barbara Thomas).

of institutional investors. As discussed below, investment bankers did win some concessions in the final version of Rule 415, including a requirement (now deleted) that an underwriter must be used in any shelf offering. In effect, the industry successfully lobbied for a rule that at the time secured their position as underwriters.

B. The Impact of Rule 415

(1) Underwriting Fees

Although much controversy surrounded the adoption of shelf registration, one impact of Rule 415 today is fairly certain: It introduced a heightened degree of competition into the market for underwriting services.

This was particularly evident in the differential between the average underwriting discount on non-shelf offerings and shelf offerings. The SEC's Advisory Committee on the Capital Formation and Regulatory Process reported that, from 1993 to 1995, the median underwriting commission for a public offering of common stock was 7.0% on Form S-1, 6.0% on Form S-2 (which form, you will recall, is no longer used today), 5.0% on non-shelf offerings on Form S-3, and only 4.6% for shelf offerings on Form S-3.[22] The reason for this differential most likely lies, in part, in the practical leverage that shelf registration affords corporate officers in seeking competitive bids—calling up rival underwriters and asking for a bid for a "take-down" offering later that same week.

By contrast, the classic Form S-1 involves an extended process of collaboration between the underwriters and the issuer in preparing the registration statement before the critical pricing moment was reached. To a considerable degree, the traditional delay surrounding a public offering locked the issuer into its choice of underwriters and reduced its leverage in pricing negotiations. At the outset of this extended period, it was too early to expect the underwriters to commit to a price for the still-distant offering. But, toward the end of the process, calling off the offering (due to a pricing dispute) would likely result in greater harm to the issuer than the underwriting group. After all, the issuer had invested time and money, which would not be recouped if the offering were canceled; it might desperately need the funds; and it might suffer a severe reputational loss, particularly if the market suspected the offering was canceled because the underwriters discovered an undisclosed problem.

Since underwriting discounts were likely to be reduced by Rule 415, a political compromise was needed to enable the SEC to adopt the Rule. Accordingly, as originally adopted, Rule 415 still protected underwriters by requiring the issuer to use an underwriter in an "at the market" equity

---

[22] See SEC Report of the Advisory Committee on the Capital Formation and Regulatory Process, App. A, at table 4 (1996); see also Kidwell, Marr & Thompson, Shelf Registration: Competition and Market Efficiency, 30 J.L. & Econ. 181 (1987).

offering (no longer required today). In part, this responded to investment bankers' fears that large corporations would simply bypass underwriters and directly market offerings to institutional investors, for example, by soliciting a small group of mutual funds to buy all the shares in an equity offering. As revised (but also no longer required today), Rule 415 also limited shelf offerings of voting stock to 10% of the issuer's total outstanding voting stock, thereby requiring the issuer to use a more traditional form of underwriting for very large offerings.

Why should the SEC protect the industry in this fashion if issuers believed they did not need the services of underwriters? Why not permit costly financial intermediaries (such as underwriters) to wither away if they are no longer needed? One possible response is that an underwriter is a natural "gatekeeper"—that is, it is the best-positioned party to test the accuracy of the issuer's registration statement. In the absence of underwriters, sophisticated institutional buyers might quickly resell "untested" securities purchased in a shelf-registered offering to less-sophisticated public investors. In any event, in its 2005 offering reforms, after over 20 years of experience with the Rule, the SEC deleted from Rule 415 the requirement that the issuer use an underwriter and the 10% limitation on the issuance of voting stock.

(2) EQUITY OFFERINGS

Initially, Rule 415 was little used for equity offerings (although it was immediately exploited for debt offerings).[23] The most likely explanation relates to the typical decline in an issuer's stock price upon announcement of an equity offering, perhaps due to the market's sense that managers may decide to issue new stock when they believe the stock price has peaked. After all, if the managers believe, based on nonpublic information, that the stock price will soon rise further, they would logically delay making an offering. Whether for that reason, or due to the possibility that a large supply of new stock creates an imbalance between supply and demand that depresses market price, adverse market reaction to news of an impending equity offering by a public issuer is well-established.[24] This same negative reaction occurred when an equity shelf registration statement was filed with the SEC (referred to as "filing a shelf"), and sometimes it was severe.[25] As a result, managers were reluctant to file an equity shelf and incur an immediate stock price penalty for a still-distant offering. From their perspective, the transaction cost savings were more than offset by the market penalty.

---

[23] See Denis, Shelf Registration and the Market for Seasoned Equity Offerings, 64 J.Bus. 189 (1991).

[24] See Barclay & Litzenberger, Announcement Effects of New Equity Issuers and the Use of Intraday Price Data, 21 J.Fin.Econ. 71 (1988).

[25] For one study finding no significant differences in market reaction to announcements of the filing of shelf registration statements versus traditional equity offerings, see Moore, Peterson & Peterson, Shelf Registrations and Shareholder Wealth: A Comparison of Shelf and Traditional Equity Offerings, 41 J.Fin. 451 (1986).

In response to this problem, the SEC amended shelf registration procedures in 1993 to eliminate the need to specify the number of shares that were being registered for potential future sale. Under this new "universal registration statement," the issuer must identify only the classes of securities being registered (debt, equity, warrants, and so forth) and the aggregate expected proceeds from all sales. Since most shelf registration statements are for debt securities, and the listing of additional equity classes does not mean that common stock will actually be sold, this process apparently reduced the penalty for registering equity securities (in effect, by masking the intended equity sales). But, while favorable to issuers, did this action benefit investors (the SEC's traditional constituency)? In any event, the use of shelf registration statements for equity offerings picked up markedly after 1993.[26]

(3) THE DUE DILIGENCE DEBATE

Academics have vigorously debated the impact of Rule 415 on the underwriters' ability to perform due diligence. Professor Barbara Banoff concluded that Rule 415 "clearly benefits issuers, investors and the economy as a whole."[27] Professor Merritt Fox, taking a broader view of the economic role the securities markets play in the national economy, questioned Professor Banoff's conclusions. He argued that the market "monitors and structures the allocation of scarce resources in the economy." Concerned about the decline in due diligence, he concluded: "The improvement in the quality of information about an issuer that results from underwriter due diligence enhances efficient allocation of resources of the economy. Short-form and shelf registration—the heart of the integrated disclosure program—can be expected to reduce the amount of due diligence underwriters perform, and therefore reduce the benefits to the economy that flow from that activity." Accordingly, he concluded, "the benefits of the traditional level of underwriter due diligence are worth their accompanying costs."[28]

This debate is likely to continue. Yet, today it is clear underwriters do not apply the same level of due diligence under shelf registration as they do in IPOs, even though they face potentially serious litigation damages.

---

[26] Between January 1994 and December 1995, a review of all registration statements covering common stock showed that issuers filed 486 such shelf registration statements on Form S-3 covering common stock as opposed to 416 such non-shelf registration statements on Form S-3, 310 such registration statements on Form S-1, and 79 such registration statements on Form S-2 (which form is no longer used today) or S-11. See Report of Advisory Committee on the Capital Formation and Regulatory Processes, App. A table 2. (SEC 1996). In short, the "universal shelf" succeeded in extending shelf registration to equity securities.

[27] Banoff, Regulatory Subsidies, Efficient Markets, and Shelf Registration: An Analysis of Rule 415, 70 Va.L.Rev. 135 (1984).

[28] Fox, Shelf Registration, Integrated Disclosure, and Underwriter Due Diligence: An Economic Analysis, 70 Va.L.Rev. 1005 (1984).

(4) THE SEC'S COMPROMISE ON DUE DILIGENCE: RULE 176

At the time the SEC adopted shelf registration, many underwriters objected that their inability to conduct due diligence under the time constraints it created unfairly exposed them to liability under § 11 of the 1933 Act. To alleviate these concerns, the Commission adopted Rule 176, which was "intended to make explicit what circumstances may bear upon the determination of what constitutes a reasonable investigation and reasonable ground for belief as these terms are used in Section 11(b) of the Securities Act."[29]

Analyzing the role of due diligence in an integrated disclosure system, the Commission emphasized the continuing need for close monitoring of the issuer by underwriters:[30]

> [T]he Securities Act imposes a high standard of conduct on specific persons, including underwriters and directors, associated with a registered public offering of securities. . . .
>
> The principal goal of integration is to simplify disclosure and reduce unnecessary repetition and redelivery of information which has already been provided, not to alter the roles of participants in the securities distribution process as originally contemplated by the Securities Act. The integrated disclosure system, past and proposed, is thus not designed to modify the responsibility of underwriters and others to make a reasonable investigation. Information presented in the registration statement, whether or not incorporated by reference, must be true and complete in all material respects and verified where appropriate. Likewise, nothing in the Commission's integrated disclosure system precludes conducting adequate due diligence. This point can be demonstrated by addressing the two principal concerns which have been raised.
>
> First, . . . commentators have expressed concern about the short time involved in document preparation. There also may be a substantial reduction in the time taken for pre-effective review at the Commission. As to the latter point, however, commentators . . . themselves noted that due diligence generally is performed prior to filing with the Commission, rendering the time in registration largely irrelevant. As to the former point, there is nothing which compels an underwriter to proceed prematurely with an offering. Although, as discussed below, he may wish to arrange his due diligence procedures over time for the purpose of avoiding last minute delays in an offering environment characterized by rapid market changes, in the

---

[29] Securities Act Release No. 6335 (Aug. 6, 1981), Fed.Sec.L.Rep. (CCH) No. 926, Special Rep., 2d Extra Ed. (Aug. 13, 1981), at 65.
[30] Id. at 88–91.

final analysis the underwriter is never compelled to proceed with an offering until he has accomplished his due diligence.

The second major concern relates to the fact that documents, prepared by others, often at a much earlier date, are incorporated by reference into the registration statement. Again, it must be emphasized that due diligence requires a reasonable investigation of all the information presented therein and any information incorporated by reference. If such material contains a material misstatement, or omits a material fact, then, in order to avoid liability, a subsequent document must be filed to correct the earlier one, or the information must be restated correctly in the registration statement. Nothing in the integrated disclosure system precludes such action.

The Commission specifically rejects the suggestion that the underwriter needs only to read the incorporated materials and discuss them with representatives of the registrant and named experts. Because the registrant would be the sole source of virtually all information, this approach would not, in and of itself, include the element of verification required by the case law and contemplated by the statute.

Thus, verification in appropriate circumstances is still required, and if a material misstatement or omission has been made, correction by amendment or restatement must be made. For example, a major supply contract on which the registrant is substantially dependent should be reviewed to avoid the possibility of inaccurate references to it in the prospectus. On the other hand, if the alleged misstatement in issue turns on an ambiguity or nuance in the drafted language of an incorporated document making it a close question as to whether a violation even has been committed, then the fact that a particular defendant did not participate in preparing the incorporated document, when combined with judgmental difficulties and practical concerns in making changes in prepared documents, would seem to be an appropriate factor in deciding whether "reasonable belief" in the accuracy of statements existed and thus in deciding whether to attach liability to a particular defendant's conduct.

In sum, the Commission strongly affirms the need for due diligence and its attendant vigilance and verification. . . .

Nonetheless, little has happened despite the SEC's encouragement to develop new due diligence procedures to preserve the underwriter's traditional role in verifying information. Most public companies do not conduct year-round due diligence or appoint counsel for later-to-be-determined underwriters. Since, under shelf registration, the issuer gained the leverage to choose among underwriters—in terms of both price and the underwriters' ability to meet the issuer's schedule—few underwriters dared to object to expedited schedules that precluded meaningful due diligence. Although both underwriters and directors relied on Rule 176, hoping that courts would tolerate reduced due diligence efforts in view of the new integrated disclosure system, this also did not happen. The leading decision found that the SEC, in adopting Rule 176, had not intended to relax the due diligence obligations of underwriters or directors.[31] As discussed later in this casebook, the *WorldCom* court found that Rule 176 did not significantly reduce or modify the duties of underwriters or directors, and it also limited the degree to which both could rely on accountants as experts under § 11 of the Securities Act. The result has been a dilemma that has still not resolved itself. Put simply, the old statutory norms requiring underwriters, directors, and accountants to conduct a "reasonable investigation" still appear to apply in court when an offering turns sour. These requirements, however, are no longer observed in practice because, under the pressure of expedited time schedules, underwriters appear unable to perform any meaningful due diligence, instead choosing to accept the business risk of § 11 liability.

(5) AUTOMATIC SHELF REGISTRATION

In 2005, the SEC again simplified the capital-raising process, this time for "well-known seasoned issuers" ("WKSIs"), by creating a system of "automatic shelf registration" that effectively guaranteed WKSIs immediate access to the securities markets, uninterrupted by any period of SEC review. Essentially, these qualifying issuers are permitted to register unspecified amounts of different types of securities on registration statements (on Form S-3 or, for foreign private issuers, Form F-3) that become effective immediately upon filing with the SEC. SEC review of the registration statement before its effectiveness is simply eliminated for this class of large, seasoned issuers. The registration statement remains effective for three years (subject to the issuer updating its financial information, most likely by incorporating subsequently-filed 1934 Act reports). As a result, qualifying issuers now have maximum flexibility to sell unlimited amounts of securities whenever they deem market conditions to be propitious. The new system also contemplates that much of the information formerly included in initial, or "base," prospectuses can now be omitted at the time the registration statement becomes effective (for example, whether the offering is a primary offering or a secondary offering). This information will be added later when it becomes known to the issuer, and the issuer then files a revised prospectus at or shortly after the time of sale.

  a. Well-Known Seasoned Issuer. As described earlier, in its 2005 offering reforms, the SEC recognized a new category of issuer—the "well-known seasoned issuer"—that is eligible to use "automatic shelf registration" and thereby enjoy immediate and unlimited market access.

---

[31] See In re WorldCom, Inc. Sec. Litigation, 346 F.Supp.2d 628 (S.D.N.Y. 2004).

Generally, to qualify as a WKSI, a U.S. private company must meet the Registrant Requirements of Instruction I.A. of Form S-3 (among other things, meaning it must be current and timely (other than with respect to a limited class of Form 8-K reports) in its 1934 Act reporting for the past 12 months) and it cannot be an "ineligible issuer" (as defined in Rule 405 under the 1933 Act). In addition, it must have a worldwide market capitalization for its common stock (both voting and non-voting shares) of at least $700 million (excluding shares held by affiliates). Alternatively, the issuer must have issued $1 billion in non-convertible securities, other than common stock (e.g., debt securities or non-convertible preferred stock), in the last three years in registered primary offerings for cash, but only in the case of offerings of such non-convertible securities, unless it also has an aggregate market value for its common stock (voting and non-voting shares) of at least $75 million held by non-affiliates.[32] The SEC adopted the WKSI standard after finding that, in 2004, such issuers represented 30% of listed issuers—but 95% of U.S. equity market capitalization and 96% of the total debt raised in registered offerings.[33] Also, the SEC found that, between 1997 and 2004, issuers meeting the WKSI standard were followed, on average, by 12 sell-side securities analysts, suggesting that their securities traded in an efficient market.

Not only do WKSIs enjoy the benefits of automatic shelf registration, but under Rule 163, with some exceptions, they are exempt from the prohibitions in § 5(c) and the "quiet period," provided they (i) include a mandated legend (set forth in Rule 163(b)(1)(i)) in every written communication that is made in reliance on this Rule and (ii) with some exceptions, file such communications with the SEC (in accordance with Rule 163(b)(2)). Underwriters and other offering participants are not protected by Rule 163, and so under that rule they must continue to respect the quiet period's constraints on market conditioning.[34]

  b. Other Classes of Issuers. In Securities Act Release No. 8591, the SEC classified all issuers into four categories: (1) WKSIs; (2) Seasoned Issuers (firms that are not WKSIs but can avail themselves of Form S-3); (3) Unseasoned Issuers (reporting companies that do not meet the eligibility requirements of Form S-3); and (4) Non-reporting Issuers (issuers not yet required to file periodic reports under the 1934 Act).[35]

---

[32] See Rule 405 under the 1933 Act and Instruction I.(D)(1)(a) of Form S-3.

[33] See Securities Act Release No. 8591 *29 (Jul. 19, 2005).

[34] Note, however, that Rule 163B under the 1933 Act permits any issuer, or any person authorized to act on its behalf, to engage in oral or written communications with potential investors that are, or are reasonably believed to be, "qualified institutional buyers" or institutional "accredited investors," either prior to or following the filing of a registration statement, to determine whether such investors might have an interest in a contemplated registered securities offering. The rule is non-exclusive and an issuer may rely on other Securities Act communications rules or exemptions when determining how, when, and what to communicate about a contemplated securities offering.

[35] Securities Act Release No. 8591 also uses the term "ineligible issuers," which refers to certain disfavored issuers, including "blank check companies" (issuers with no identified business plan or assets), shell companies, "penny stock issuers" (issuers with unlisted securities

The third and fourth categories of issuers must use Form S-1, which traditionally did not incorporate by reference information from 1934 Act periodic reports. Thus, Form S-1 issuers had to set out in full both company-specific and transaction-specific information.

Today, following the 2005 offering reforms, an Unseasoned Issuer that is ineligible to use Form S-3 can opt into the integrated disclosure system using Form S-1, once it has filed at least one Form 10-K, if it (1) is current in its 1934 Act filings and (2) makes the information incorporated by reference readily available on a website. However, the Form requires the issuer to specifically incorporate listed 1934 Act filings by reference, without the ability to incorporate subsequently-filed 1934 Act reports. (Material updates from the incorporated 1934 Act reports are typically included in the registration statement.) This means that incorporation by reference does not help a Form S-1 registration statement stay evergreen.[36]

By contrast, a Form S-3 eligible issuer (categories one and two above) will use a prospectus that is mostly confined to transaction-specific information and incorporates by reference company-specific information from its 1934 Act reports. Form S-3 registration statements permit the issuer to specifically incorporate listed 1934 Act reports by reference *and also* incorporate subsequently-filed 1934 Act reports *prospectively*. Material updates from the incorporated 1934 Act reports are typically included in the registration statement (including, when securities are taken down from a shelf, the prospectus used at the time of takedown). As noted before, this permits the Form S-3 registration statement to remain evergreen.[37]

c. *Post-Effective Procedure.* WKSIs can automatically register unlimited amounts of different securities (common stock, bonds, warrants, convertible securities, and so forth) for three years and then determine during those three years not only what securities to sell but who will sell them (i.e., the issuer or, for example, a selling shareholder). This goes well beyond the practice under Rule 430A, which permits the exclusion of price-related information at the time the registration statement is declared effective. For WKSIs, the registration statement need not include more than a general description of the type of security that will be sold until the post-effective decision is made to sell securities. In general, Rule 409 under the 1933 Act permits a registrant to omit from the registration statement information that is either unknown or not "reasonably available" to the registrant. More specifically, under Securities Act Release No. 8591, the "base prospectus" included in an

---

trading at prices under $5 per share), issuers delinquent in their 1934 Act filing obligations, and issuers that have been the subject of enforcement proceedings within the past three years. These "ineligible issuers" cannot use shelf registration or enjoy the other benefits of the recent offering reforms.

[36] See Instruction VII. and Items 11A and 12 of Form S-1 under the 1933 Act.
[37] See Item 12 of Form S-3 under the 1933 Act.

automatic shelf registration statement may also omit information relating to: (1) whether the offering is primary or secondary; (2) the description of the securities to be offered; (3) the names of any selling security holders; and (4) the plan of distribution and participating underwriters. Thus, the base prospectus in the initial registration statement need only identify, in general terms, the names and classes of securities to be registered and need not specify the allocation of securities among those classes. (A WKSI can subsequently add new classes to its registration statement by post-effective amendment, if it chooses.) Omitted information will be added later by means of (1) a post-effective amendment to the registration statement, (2) a prospectus supplement (or an entirely new prospectus), or (3) incorporation by reference from the issuer's 1934 Act reports.

What legal liability attaches to a prospectus that is filed, or material that is incorporated by reference, after the original effective date of the registration statement? Section 11 liability, at the time securities are taken down from a shelf, is addressed by Rule 430B.[38] Basically, if the conditions to using Rule 430B are satisfied,[39] the Rule provides that information in a subsequently-filed prospectus or document incorporated (or deemed incorporated) by reference "shall be deemed to be part of and included in the registration statement on the earlier of the date such subsequent form of prospectus is first used or the date and time of the first contract of sale of securities in the offering to which such subsequent form of prospectus relates"[40]—in other words, at the time securities are taken down from the shelf. This has important liability consequences because § 11 works off of what is in the registration statement at the time of effectiveness.

Since § 11 liability is tied to effectiveness, when is the registration statement deemed to be effective with respect to the *new* information filed or incorporated by reference after the registration statement's original effective date? Here, Rule 430B(f) draws an important distinction between the issuer and underwriters, on the one hand, and the issuer's directors, certain signatories, and experts, on the other. The date on which a form of prospectus is deemed to be part of and included in the registration statement—in other words, at the time of takedown—shall be deemed, for purposes of § 11 liability, to be a new effective date for the issuer and any underwriter, but not for the issuer's directors, officers, or experts. The new effective date will apply to information in the registration statement, any prospectus relating to the offering, and

---

[38] Rule 430C under the 1933 Act also addresses information contained in a form of prospectus filed with the SEC after the original effective date, but only if Rules 430A, Rule 430B, and Rule 430D are not applicable. In general, shelf registration will be accomplished using Rule 430B.

[39] See Rule 430B(b) under the 1933 Act.

[40] See Rule 430B(f)(1) under the 1933 Act. The SEC separately advised that the date of first use is not the date a prospectus is given to a purchaser, but rather refers to the date the prospectus is available to the managing underwriter, syndicate member, or any prospective purchaser.

any materials incorporated by reference therein (that have not been modified or superseded).[41] In other words, when there is a shelf takedown, only the issuer and underwriters at the time will be liable under § 11 for the information included or incorporated by reference into the registration statement (including in the related prospectus).

The new effective date for the issuer's directors, certain signatories, and any experts is determined differently. For a director,[42] a new effective date will arise upon the filing of a prospectus (pursuant to § 10(a)(3)) to include information so that the prospectus is not "stale"[43] or to reflect any facts or events arising after the effective date of the registration statement which represents a "fundamental change" in the information in the registration statement.[44]

The same applies to any person who signs a report or document incorporated by reference into the registration statement—the new effective date is determined, with respect to that signatory, only if the report or document is filed so that the prospectus is not "stale" or to reflect a "fundamental change."[45] Any person signing any report or document incorporated by reference in the prospectus, other than a document filed to update the prospectus pursuant to § 10(a)(3) or to reflect a fundamental change, is deemed not to be a person who signed the registration statement as a result.

The effective date remains unchanged for auditors whose consent was originally required[46] to be named as experts in an existing registration statement concerning their report on the issuer's audited financial statements or any other report or opinion—in other words, it remains the original effective date. The effective date, however, changes at the time when a prospectus (or any 1934 Act report incorporated by reference into the prospectus) or post-effective amendment to the registration statement contains new audited financial statements or another report or opinion as to which the auditor is an expert and for which a new consent is required to be filed with the SEC.[47] For any other expert, the filing of a new prospectus also does not trigger a new effective date and does not require the filing of a new consent, unless the prospectus (including any 1934 Act reports incorporated by reference therein) includes a new report or opinion where the expert's consent is required.[48]

No statement made in a prospectus or incorporated document will, as to a purchaser of securities with a contract of sale prior to the new

---

[41] See Rules 430B(f)(2) and (4) under the 1933 Act.
[42] See Rule 430B(f)(4) under the 1933 Act.
[43] See § 10(a)(3) of the 1933 Act.
[44] See Item 512(a)(1)(ii) of Regulation S–K under the 1933 Act.
[45] See Rule 430B(f)(4) under the 1933 Act.
[46] See § 7(a) of the 1933 Act.
[47] See Rule 430B(f)(5) under the 1933 Act.
[48] See Rules 430B(f)(3) and (f)(5) under the 1933 Act.

effective date, modify or supersede any statement made in the registration statement or prospectus (including the incorporated documents) prior to such effective date.[49] Likewise, any statement in a document incorporated by reference into a registration statement will be deemed to be modified or superseded by a later statement in the prospectus that is part of the registration statement or a subsequently-filed incorporated document to the extent such later statement modifies or replaces the prior statement.[50] To illustrate, if the registration statement originally is effective on March 1, there is a takedown of securities on April 1, and the issuer files its annual report on Form 10-K with the SEC on April 2 (which is incorporated by reference into the prospectus forming part of the registration statement), only those purchasing on and after April 2 may assert a claim under § 11 for any misstatement or omission in the annual report at the time of takedown. If another takedown occurs on May 1, and the related prospectus includes statements that modify the information in the Form 10-K annual report filed on April 2, then those statements will be deemed to modify or replace the statements in the earlier-filed annual report.

Liability under § 12(a)(2) of the 1933 Act, unlike § 11, is based on the information included or incorporated by reference into the prospectus at the time of sale, not at the time the registration statement became effective. Here, Rule 159 makes clear that, for purposes of § 12(a)(2), in determining whether a prospectus or oral statement includes any material misstatement or omission, any information conveyed to the purchaser after the time of sale (including a contract of sale) will not be taken into account. Presumably, since the statute of frauds does not extend to oral contracts for securities,[51] the sale will occur at the time a customer orally agrees with her broker to purchase the securities relating to the prospectus or oral statement.

3. PREPARATION OF THE REGISTRATION STATEMENT

Statutes and Regulations

Securities Act, §§ 6, 7.

Regulation C, Regulation S–K.

Forms S-1, S-3.

Introductory Note

The preparation of a 1933 Act registration statement, especially that of an issuer going public, is a demanding and intricate undertaking, which can

---

[49] See Rule 430B(g) under the 1933 Act.

[50] See Rule 412(a) under the 1933 Act.

[51] See, e.g., Uniform Commercial Code § 8–113, "Statute of Frauds Inapplicable," which states: "A contract or modification of a contract for the sale or purchase of a security is enforceable whether or not there is a writing signed or record authenticated by a party against whom enforcement is sought, even if the contract or modification is not capable of performance within one year of its making."

challenge the imagination and ingenuity of the securities lawyer. A great deal of expertise must be acquired in practice, preferably by working with competent and experienced securities lawyers.

Regulation S–K contains the standard instructions applicable to the non-financial portion of the registration statements filed under the 1933 Act and registration statements, periodic reports, and proxy statements filed under the 1934 Act; it was issued as part of the Commission's integrated disclosure program.

Under the 1933 Act, the applicable legal rules probably are best understood by first studying the statute and Regulation C, then moving to Form S-1, and thereafter analyzing a well-drafted prospectus in light of the statute, rules, and form. It is also helpful to prepare a cross-reference sheet (sometimes referred to as a "form check") showing the location in the registration statement (including the prospectus contained therein, as well as Part II of the registration statement) of the information that must be included in response to the various items of Form S-1. There are also a few useful books devoted to "going public," and the mechanics of preparing a 1933 Act registration statement, written from the lawyer's point of view.[52]

Although the process of going public is costly and time-consuming, it is also alluring. In a period of rising stock prices and business expansion, the managers of private companies may be dazzled by the supposed advantages of going public, with the opportunity to cash-in on the increased net worth of the company. Once into a recession, however, those perceived advantages may begin to fade. Thus, businesspeople who take their companies public in a rising "bull market" may suddenly wish to have it both ways by "going private" after stock prices plunge during a later "bear market."

The motivations for "going public" include:

1. To raise funds for such corporate purposes as increasing working capital, expanding plants and equipment, investing in research and development, retiring existing debt, or diversification of operations;

2. To enable early-stage shareholders to sell or hold a liquid security (which can also be used as collateral for loans);

3. To gain prestige, become better known, and obtain a wider market for the company's products or services, particularly if the company is engaged in distributing goods or services to the consumer public;

4. To gain a currency (i.e., stock) with which the issuer may acquire other businesses without expending cash, borrowing, or increasing leverage;

5. To enable the adoption of stock options and other employee benefit plans as a means of attracting and retaining personnel; and

6. To improve the company's net worth, thereby enabling the company to raise funds on more favorable terms.

The disadvantages, which are often overlooked during periods of business expansion, include:

---

[52] See, e.g., Jacobs, Manual of Corporate Forms for Securities Practice (Aug. 2019).

1. The relatively high cost of an IPO as a means of raising capital (particularly if the offering size is small);

2. The full disclosure obligations of reporting companies regarding salaries, transactions with management, conflicts-of-interest, and information as to sales, profits, and competitive positions, all of which become available to shareholders and competitors; the consequence may be to convey valuable business intelligence to one's rivals;

3. The loss of flexibility in management arising from practical, if not legal, limitations on salaries and fringe benefits, self-dealing transactions, and the necessity of acting only after approval of outside directors or shareholders;

4. Increased costs of administration, and legal, accounting, and other fees, associated with operating as a company subject to the reporting requirements of the 1934 Act;

5. Possible loss of control over dividend policy, since the market may expect a constant payout;

6. The business decisions of a public company may be affected by short-term considerations arising from management's preoccupation with day-to-day stock market prices, or quarterly financial results, rather than a consideration of long-term benefits;

7. If a sufficiently large proportion of the company's shares are sold to the public, the company may become a candidate for a takeover bid, with a loss of control by the insiders;

8. The threat of liability in class actions if the company's stock price drops (with the issuer facing virtually strict liability under § 11 of the 1933 Act if the registration statement contained a material misstatement or omission when it became effective); and

9. Finally, the supposed advantages of an active public market for the company's shares may not develop, so that the shares sell at a discount below the price anticipated on the basis of earnings and book value.

---

1. *What Does It Cost?* A study of over 100 IPOs in 2019 found that IPO expenses (excluding the underwriting discount) came to $5.64 million on average.[53] Both the underwriting discount and the other expenses should be less for a seasoned issuer (which tends to have a less elaborate series of roadshows).

On a percentage basis, an industry survey found that in 2018 the total costs of an IPO (i.e., the underwriting discount plus direct out-of-pocket costs) came to 11.77% of the offering size for initial offerings registered on Form S-1.[54] Since some costs are relatively fixed, the smaller the offering size, the higher the percentage that goes to legal, accounting, and administrative costs. As a result, smaller IPOs may be

---

[53] See Proskauer Rose LLP, 2019 IPO study at 57.
[54] Id. at 40.

an inefficient way to raise capital; IPO offerings under $75 million are relatively less common.

Perhaps even more important are the imputed costs of executive time. One estimate is that during registration, the chief financial officer will spend 75% of her time on the offering, and the chief executive officer, 40%.[55]

Excerpt from: William W. Barker

SEC Registration of Public Offerings Under the Securities Act of 1933
52 Bus.Law. 65 (1996)[a]

INTRODUCTION

The staff of the Division of Corporation Finance (Division) at the Securities and Exchange Commission (Commission) knows public offerings. More than 8800 registration statements were filed with the Commission during fiscal year 1995 under the Securities Act of 1933 (Securities Act), registering more than $823 billion of securities. Of these 8800 registration statements, 1520 statements were selected for full review by the staff, including all of the 1000 initial public offerings that were filed. This was in addition to the staff's examination of other securities filings.

	Total	Billion $	Full Review	Billion $	IPOs	Billion $
1995	8832	$823	1520	$265	1000	$123
1994	8651	$815	1730	$226	1382	$117
1993	7815	$868	1670	$261	989	$113*

* * *

The time that an issuer spends "in registration" varies.[3] Over the past few years, a first-time issuer could expect to spend seventy days in registration, on average, with some first-time issuers spending as little

---

[55] See Loeb & Whalen, IPOs in the 1990s: Company Counsel's Role, PLI Advanced Securities Law Workshop 300, at 313 (1995).

[a] Reprinted with permission of the author. Mr. Barker was Senior Counsel to the Division of Corporation Finance at the SEC.

[*] There were 1,045 public offerings in 2019, see FINRA, Key Statistics for 2019, https://www.finra.org/media-center/statistics, and the total dollar amount raised from public offerings in 2019 was $1.2 trillion, see SEC, Facilitating Capital Formation and Expanding Investment Opportunities by Improving Access to Capital in Private Markets, 85 Fed. Reg. 17956, 17957 (Mar. 31, 2020).

[3] "In registration" means the total number of days between the date that a registration statement is first filed with the Commission and the date it is declared effective.

as forty-five days, or as many as ninety days or more, in registration.[4] At the upper end of this range, the time spent in registration must seem interminable, prompting issuers to wonder what could be done to speed the process along. Even at the lower end of the range, it is always desirable for the registration process to run more smoothly.

The comment process is predictable, which should work to an issuer's advantage. Most disclosure and other problems are recurring and can be avoided, resulting in a shorter and smoother registration process for any issuer. The primary constant in the review process is the time allotted for the staff to review filings and provide comments, which runs about thirty days from the date a registration statement is filed initially with the Commission to the date of the first round of comments, and five calendar days for each amendment. There are fewer variables in the review process than issuers may imagine.

The purposes of this Article are: (i) to illustrate that the length of time an issuer spends in registration depends on factors largely within an issuer's control, (ii) to describe the most common pitfalls to be avoided, and (iii) to explain what can be done by issuers to speed along the registration process. Registration statements that are declared effective within the more expeditious time range are drafted by counsel who understand the staff's role in the registration process, avoid likely comments, and work with the staff to resolve problems quickly.

THE DIVISION OF CORPORATION FINANCE

GENERAL

The Division is staffed with lawyers, financial analysts, and accountants who provide a broad range of services in connection with the examination of public offerings filed under the Securities Act, proxy solicitations and reports filed under the Securities Exchange Act of 1934 (Exchange Act), and filings made under the Trust Indenture Act of 1939. Most Division lawyers have two or three years of previous law firm experience, and many also hold an M.B.A. or LL.M. degree. All Division financial analysts hold M.B.A. degrees. All Division accountants are certified public accountants, each person having a minimum of three years of prior public accounting experience, usually with a "Big Six" accounting firm or the equivalent....

---

[4] Of the 70 days referred to in the text, 37 days are attributed to the staff; that is, 30 days for the initial review of the registration statement and seven days for amendments. The remaining 33 days are attributed to the time taken by the issuer to respond to staff comments. In comparison, the total elapsed time in registration for repeat issuers is about 77 days, with the additional seven days attributed to the issuer. Registration statements not resolved within this time frame are generally those with significant problems or are complex filings that simply require more response time.

CHAIN OF COMMAND

[There are seven industry Division offices that examine registration statements and other filings.]* . . . Issuers are assigned to a particular examining office on the basis of the standard industrial code (SIC) activity which generates the most significant portion of the issuer's revenues. * * *

TEAM APPROACH

Registration statements are examined by a team consisting of a staff attorney or financial analyst (commonly called "examiners") and a staff accountant. The examination team changes from registration statement to registration statement. The examiner's work is reviewed by the Assistant Director or a senior staff member, usually a lawyer. The accountant's work is reviewed by an Assistant Chief Accountant.

After receiving the registration statement, the examiner will make any necessary referrals, including referrals to support offices or other divisions within the Commission, state regulators, or other federal agencies. Such referrals may lead to further or more accurate disclosure. Except for international offerings, initial public offerings usually do not require support offices of the Division to become involved in the review of a registration statement.

The staff examines the registration statement carefully. Examiners first review the registration statement for major structural defects, sometimes called "show stoppers," which would prevent the transaction from going forward until resolved. Examiners then scrutinize the prospectus and Part II information, including exhibits, for compliance with other applicable federal securities laws. . . .

The preliminary results of the staff review of an initial filing and amendments are described in written internal memoranda, or "examination reports." The examination reports are the Commission's nonpublic written records of the analyses, thoughts, and impressions of the respective members of the examination team, whether or not expressed in the comment letter to the issuer that follows. Pursuant to * * * the rules of the Freedom of Information Act (FOIA),[23] staff examination reports are not required to be produced in response to a FOIA request by an outside party.

The accounting and nonaccounting portion of the examination and review of registration statements proceed separately. The accounting portion of the staff review passes from the staff accountant to an Assistant Chief Accountant. The nonaccounting portion of the staff

---

* The seven industry offices are: Energy & Transportation; Life Sciences; Real Estate & Construction; Finance; Manufacturing; Technology; and Trade & Services. See SEC, Disclosure Program Realignment Announcement (Sept. 27, 2019)—Eds.

[23] See 17 C.F.R. § 200.80(b)(4) (1996); see also 5 U.S.C. § 552(a)–(d) (1994). An overview of the subject is found in Robert G. Belair, SEC FOIA Practice, REV. OF SEC. & COMM. REG., Jan. 24, 1990, at 11.

review passes from the examiner to a senior staff member. Throughout the examination process, however, the examiners and accountants exchange ideas and work together to develop comments. This is particularly true of accounting or financial issues that need to be drawn out in the text of the prospectus. Both portions of the staff review come together in the hands of the examiner shortly before comments are communicated to the issuer. Comments will not be communicated to an issuer until both portions have been reviewed by supervisory staff. Sending accounting and nonaccounting comments out to issuers as they become available invariably causes more problems and delays than are avoided.

The examiner is the "point person" responsible for monitoring the involvement of other examining offices and divisions, the status of the accounting staff review, coordinating and compiling the comment letter, and communicating staff views to the issuer. The legal and accounting staff remain autonomous in most matters because neither group has authority to direct the activities or pace of the other.

THE SELECTIVE REVIEW PROCESS

Rule 202.3 of the Commission's Rules of Practice and Investigation provides that registration statements, proxy statements, periodic reports, trust indenture filings, and similar documents filed with the Commission are routed to the Division. The Division initially passes upon the adequacy of disclosure and recommends initial action to be taken. The Division does not have the resources necessary to examine all registration statements and other documents filed with the Commission each year. As a result, the selective review process was implemented in 1980.

Registration statements are "screened" in the appropriate examining office, according to predetermined criteria, to select which of four levels of review is appropriate: (i) deferred review, (ii) monitor, (iii) no review, or (iv) full review.[26] While the Division's detailed screening procedures are nonpublic, as most practitioners probably are aware from personal experience, the selective review process is financially oriented and very practical. Registration statements filed by first-time issuers will be assigned a full and thorough review.[27] Subsequently, issuers are selected for review on an "as needed" basis.[28] In the selective review system, it is important nothing be left to chance so that no filing that

---

[26] See Expediting Registration Statements Filed Under the Securities Act of 1933, Securities Act Release No. 4934, [1967–1969 Transfer Binder] Fed.Sec.L.Rep. (CCH) ¶ 77,677, at 83,345 (Nov. 21, 1968); Division of Corporation Finance's Procedures to Curtail Time in Registration Under the Securities Act, Securities Act Release No. 5231, [1971–1972 Transfer Binder] Fed.Sec.L.Rep. (CCH) ¶ 78,509, at 81,103 (Feb. 3, 1972).

[27] See Richard H. Rowe, SEC Review Practices: A Primer, INSIGHTS, Jan. 1990, at 22.

[28] Issuers also may receive a full review based upon the nature of the transaction (e.g., exchange offers and merger proxies filed on Form S-4), special industry concerns, outstanding comments on reports filed under the Exchange Act, or simply because it has been two or three years since the issuer's last full review.

should be reviewed "slips by" unnoticed. Consequently, it is to an issuer's advantage to communicate with the staff regarding any prefiling, filing, or disclosure issues, or other questions an issuer may have.

Filings that are deficient materially or incomplete when filed may receive a deferred review. Common examples of materially deficient filings are registration statements filed with financial statements that are stale or registration statements filed with incomplete financial or other information. Materially deficient filings are summarily rejected from the review process by the staff issuance of a "bed-bug letter" outlining the material deficiencies which prevent further review. Bed-bugged filings will not proceed any further in the review process and the thirty-day review period will not begin again until an amendment is filed that does not contain comparable deficiencies. The staff usually is unwilling to expedite the thirty-day review period when an amendment correcting the deficiencies is filed, for to do so would delay unfairly more conscientious filers. For the same reason, the staff will not consider reviewing portions of the registration statement that are not deficient while the deficient portions are being corrected. The issuer may lose the number of days between the date the deficient filing was made and the date upon which the issuer was notified that the filing was bed-bugged.

Repeat issuers often receive a "no review" when there is little or no practical purpose served by subjecting an issuer, or the staff, to another full review. The most common example of no reviews are offerings filed by issuers who very recently had another registration statement fully reviewed, are current and timely in their reporting obligations under the Exchange Act, have not had financial difficulties, and do not raise any enforcement issues. There are no published criteria describing the type of financial difficulties that will trigger review, but, "like pornography, a lawyer should know what financial difficulties are when he or she sees them."

There also are less rigorous types of reviews. Specific aspects of a registration statement may be targeted by the staff for review or monitoring. An issuer that may otherwise qualify for a "no review" may be monitored for aspects of the offering that are of special interest to the staff or that are different from the last fully reviewed registration statement filed. Issues that commonly result in monitoring include outstanding comments on Exchange Act reports, unusual securities or plans of distribution, and enforcement interest in the issuer. Similarly, reports filed under the Exchange Act may be selected for "financial statement only" review by the accounting staff, which targets the issuer's financial statements and the Management's Discussion and Analysis (MD&A) section of the report. Often, the purpose of monitoring a filing is to examine only one or two issues of interest to the staff and to ensure that those issues are in compliance with the federal securities laws. Where an offering is monitored, as opposed to being reviewed fully, comments tend to be fewer and more focused, and available in less than thirty days. Depending on the issues, it may be possible for the staff to review proposed changes in draft form rather than by amendment.

PREFILING CONSIDERATIONS

The hard work is completed before the registration statement is filed with the Commission. Avoiding disclosure and other registration problems begins early by addressing any transactional, disclosure, or accounting obstacles an issuer may have, considering the documents to be filed, and planning in order to avoid delays.

PRELIMINARY ISSUES

* * *

An issuer should conduct as much industry research as possible. Many staff comments, particularly those made with respect to the Business and MD&A sections, will be drawn from recent newspapers, magazines, trade publications, electronic data bases, and industry, market, or investment reports. These sources provide valuable insight into sales, trends, competition, and other facets of the issuer's business. The staff catches most "gun jumping" issues as a result of research through comprehensive news and industry data bases.[47]

"MODEL" PROSPECTUSES

The best advice to an issuer is to shop carefully. One of the problems with selecting a model is that only approximately fifteen to twenty percent of all registration statements filed with the Commission are reviewed fully in the selective review process. Consequently, many of the remaining registration statements not reviewed fully contain errors, making them poor models. There also are subjective elements in the review process to consider. A good model will reflect the types of comments likely to be raised in connection with the issuer's registration statement. At a minimum, registration statements used as models should be those that were given a full review by the staff, have the same SIC as the issuer, and were reviewed in the same Assistant Director group that will review the issuer's registration statement. If necessary, select a second model covering the accounting presentation. Select models that are straightforward, balanced, and fairly representative of good disclosure practices throughout the issuer's industry.

* * *

PRESENTATION OF THE REGISTRATION STATEMENT

Present the disclosure in a clear, concise, and understandable fashion as required by Rule 421. Write short, simple sentences in plain English. Grammar and writing software are available to aid in this task. Gratuitous or repetitive information should be deleted because it

---

[47] Potentially offending news articles or other material that may condition the market prior to the effective date of the registration statement should be drawn to the staff's attention rather than waiting to see whether the staff will notice. . . .

obscures material information and makes the prospectus more difficult to read. Superior registration statements contain almost no repetition.

The prospectus should be informative. Try to anticipate the types of questions a reader might raise concerning how the issuer makes money, the market for the issuer's products, marketing and distribution, and which products and product lines generate material revenues. Questions not answered easily within the four corners of the prospectus by a casual reading probably will result in comments. * * *

PREFILING AND OTHER CONFERENCES

The Commission has an established policy of making its staff available to issuers in advance of filing a registration statement, a service that is probably under-utilized.[56] Face-to-face meetings are rare because of the time involved. Although meetings usually are unnecessary, the staff will take the time to meet with anyone who requests a meeting. Informal conference calls are much more common and can be arranged with the staff reviewing the registration statement. A conference call can be used to discuss unusual problems that the issuer must overcome to accomplish registration or simply to discuss a novel or unique accounting or legal issue likely to become the subject of comment. In addition, because the staff reviews so many registration statements, issues unfamiliar in counsel's experience may be fairly common to the staff. The staff enjoys participating in conference calls with other professionals, particularly when it believes that its time has been well-spent.

In preparing for conference calls, it is helpful to study the treatment of the same or similar issues in other offerings, particularly accounting issues, which tend to be more concrete than others.[57] While not required, the issuer should address any concerns to be covered in the conference call in an advance letter to the staff. The letter should outline the facts and issues to be discussed, the treatment of the issues in similar filings, and the issuer's rationale and proposed solutions. It is helpful to

---

[56] See Guides for Preparation and Filing of Registration Statements, Securities Act Release No. 4936, [1967–1969 Transfer Binder] Fed.Sec.L.Rep. (CCH) ¶ 77,636, at 83,370 (Dec. 9, 1968); see also Commission's Rules of Practice and Investigation, Pre-filing Assistance and Interpretative Advice, 17 C.F.R. § 202.2 (1996). Rule 202.2 directs the staff to provide assistance to prospective issuers and the general public. This assistance may concern the availability of an exemption, the application of a statute or rule, preparation of registration statements, and the scope of the items contained in the forms. No-action letters are examples of interpretive advice. Novel or unique plans of distribution are sometimes submitted to the Division's Office of Chief Counsel and/or the Assistant Director for pre-review to ensure legal compliance. One example of pre-review occurred when a firm commitment underwriting of common stock was proposed to take place concurrently with a self-underwritten offering to customers through coupons attached to products. See Boston Beer Co. (SEC File No. 33–96162) (Rule 424(b)(4) prospectus, filed Nov. 22, 1995) (consumer offering) (on file with The Business Lawyer, University of Maryland School of Law); Boston Beer Co. (SEC File No. 33–96164) (Rule 424(c) prospectus, filed Nov. 29, 1995) (firm commitment) (on file with The Business Lawyer, University of Maryland School of Law).

[57] Disclosure in prior registration statements may be more or less authoritative depending upon: (i) whether a particular model was given a full review, (ii) whether the issue in question was raised by the staff, (iii) if any factual differences impacted materiality, (iv) the staff's level of experience, and (v) if the disclosure in question represents the views of the Division at the Chief Counsel or Chief Accountant level or higher.

memorialize the results of the meeting in a letter back to the staff after the conference call.

THE STAFF'S ROLE IN THE REGISTRATION PROCESS
* * *

ROLE OF THE STAFF IN EXAMINING FILINGS

The Commission does not have the authority to approve or disapprove offerings for lack of merit. The only standard that must be met in the registration of securities is adequate and accurate disclosure of the material facts concerning the issuer's business, finances, securities, proposed offering, and risks. * * *

THE STAFF'S COMMENT LETTER

Much of the exchange between staff and issuers previously occurred informally over the telephone and without documentation. Now these exchanges more appropriately take place through detailed written correspondence intended to document the comment process. Rule 202.3 of the Commission's Rules of Practice and Investigation establishes the basis for the review process and, indirectly, the basis for the current comment process. For example, if the registration statement appears to afford inadequate disclosure through omission of material information or noncompliance with generally accepted accounting principles, the usual practice is to bring the deficiencies to the attention of the issuer through a letter. * * *

Today's comment letter is more extensive than the original "deficiency letter" sent out by the staff in the early days of the registration process to stave off stop order proceedings. Though sent out over the signature of an Assistant Director or senior staff member, a comment letter is a collection of questions and perceived deficiencies raised by staff attorneys, accountants, and analysts. These individuals possess differing levels of experience, are located in different examining offices or divisions, and are positioned at various levels of staff or management.

The comment letter fulfills two purposes. It documents staff concerns regarding the adequacy and accuracy of the information contained in the registration statement and reflects the staff's consideration of different facets of the offering, such as legal compliance of underwriting arrangements and the plan of distribution. As a result of comments, the staff receives issuer revisions or, where there is disagreement, information supporting and documenting the issuer's belief that it has a reasonable basis for its actions.

Comment letters are surrounded by a unique internal protocol that results from the type of integrated examination registration statements receive. Because comment letters are an integrated effort among the legal, financial, and accounting disciplines, a cursory reading of a comment letter may indicate that four or more staff members contributed comments to the letter. Additional comments may be contributed by staff members in support offices or other divisions depending upon the issues involved in the offering. To avoid altering the substance of the various staff members' concerns, and to assure comments are given to issuers in a timely manner, comments provided to the examiner by these persons are included in the comment letter without any editorial changes.

In reviewing the registration statement to ensure the adequacy and accuracy of the disclosure, the staff issues two types of comments: (i) comments requesting supplemental information as provided in Rule 418; and (ii) comments requesting revision to the registration statement, including requests for clarification as provided in Rule 421. The disclosure in the registration statement is the responsibility of the issuer and the issuer's representatives. Over the years, the staff's shorthand instruction—"advise or revise"—has conveyed the notion that comments may be addressed either in the issuer's response letter or by revision to the registration statement, so long as the staff's underlying concern regarding the adequacy or accuracy of the proposed disclosure is resolved. * * *

THE ISSUER'S RESPONSE LETTER

The issuer's response letter sets the tone for the remainder of the review process. Well-written response letters will result in a smoother and more efficient review process because the staff will work first on amendments that can be completed quickly. Avoiding a few simple mistakes can increase the success rate of responses to staff comments and will result in fewer rounds of comments.

Choose battles carefully. Giving the staff all information and revisions requested in the comment letter is the fastest route to "going effective." . . .

It usually is unproductive to dispute whether a comment should have been included in the comment letter; one should instead focus on the response. A well-reasoned response often can persuade the staff quickly not to pursue a comment that will not lead to meaningful disclosure. . . . Because comments can be waived only by supervisory staff, which may require additional time, focusing upon the adequacy and accuracy of the existing disclosure in the response letter usually is the most expedient approach to resolving comments.[176]

---

[176] A 10% test often is employed as a general rule of thumb to gauge materiality, particularly with respect to financial matters. This is not intended, however, to be a bright-line test. As explained in Comment of Proposed Guides, Securities Act Release No. 5622, [1975–1976 Transfer Binder] Fed.Sec.L.Rep. (CCH) ¶ 80,305, at 85,690 (Oct. 1, 1975), the determination of materiality depends on particular facts and is not subject to objective rules. In some cases, such as bank holding companies and insurance companies, where the figures may be large, the staff has not accepted the argument that a certain figure is not material because it is less than a certain percentage of, for example, a loan portfolio or total assets. Some dollar amounts simply may be too large not to be considered qualitatively material. There also may be other more relevant reference points to be taken into consideration. The test for materiality, as enunciated by the Supreme Court, is whether a reasonable investor would consider the particular fact

Issuers frequently fail to provide the staff with data and other information necessary for the staff to determine whether the issue has complied with the comments. Each response should briefly indicate *how* the issuer has complied with the comment. Responses also should state the page numbers where disclosure in response to each comment is located. The language used in the comment will often indicate the disclosure the staff is seeking or the approach suggested by the staff. Making the staff search the amended registration statement for disclosure in response to each of the staff comments slows the process.

When a comment is not complied with, the most common shortcoming in response letters is the failure to provide sufficient factual information for the staff to either agree or disagree with the issuer's position. Thus, the comment will be reissued. To avoid this, detail the factual basis for disagreement in the response letter and focus the analysis on the *reasons* the disclosure is believed to be adequate. * * *

A question frequently arises whether staff comments should be addressed by letter, in a draft, or by amendment. The staff prefers revisions be provided by pre-effective amendment, which is available immediately to the public, rather than in a response letter or in draft form, which is not available publicly. To a lesser extent, the staff would also like to avoid issuers treating the staff's informal review of draft changes as an opportunity to take a "free bite at the apple." Requests for the staff to review draft responses therefore are more likely to be accepted in response to later rounds of comments when there are only a few issues left outstanding. Comments impacting Part II of the registration statement, including the undertakings required by Item 512 of Regulation S–K, disclosure of recent sales of unregistered securities that is required by Item 701 of Regulation S–K, and exhibits required by Item 601 of Regulation S–K must be made by pre-effective amendment.

Most issuers receive at least two rounds of comment and will file at least two amendments, assuming that no additional "voluntary" amendments are filed. Where the last changes agreed to by the issuer are minor, changes may be made in the final prospectus filed under Rule 424(b) after the effective date at the discretion of the Assistant Director.[182] Issuers should be aware this is the exception, not the rule, and the practice varies throughout the Division.

---

important in making an investment decision. See Basic Inc. v. Levinson, 485 U.S. 224, 238–40 (1988). * * *

[182] Whether a change may be made by pre-effective amendment or in the 424(b) final prospectus often depends on how significant the change is and the impact of the change upon the issuer's liability. The liability provisions of Section 11 of the Securities Act apply to a "registration statement," composed of the prospectus and the Part II information. See 15 U.S.C. § 77k (1994). The liability provisions of section 12 of the Securities Act apply only to the "prospectus" portion of the registration statement. Id. § 77*l*. Because section 11 liability does not attach to changes filed in a final Rule 424(b) prospectus, the staff prefers that all revisions be made to the registration statement on a pre-effective basis. See 17 C.F.R. § 230.424(b) (1996).

"GOING EFFECTIVE"

The process of submitting acceleration requests and going effective is much more troublesome and misunderstood than it should be. Section 8(a) provides that a registration statement will become effective, automatically, twenty days after filing with the Commission, or on such earlier date as the Commission may determine. The twenty-day statutory delay in the effective date of the registration statement prescribed by section 8(a) may be delayed indefinitely by affixing the delaying amendment proscribed by Rule 473(a).

The procedure for requesting acceleration is straightforward and has been made easier by changes to the rules. Requests for the acceleration of the effective date must be submitted under Rule 461 at least forty-eight hours before the desired effective date. The acceleration request may be made by letter, facsimile, or orally.

The staff will make every effort to meet reasonable requests and work with issuers to resolve any outstanding concerns. Issuers should appreciate, however, that concerns which persist until this point in the review process are likely to be important. Before the registration statement can be declared effective, all staff comments must be resolved. The issuer should also plan on filing a pre-effective amendment containing any material agreed upon changes that have not been previously filed. This is made easier by EDGAR. Any necessary clearances from the [the Financial Industry Regulatory Authority, also known as FINRA] should also be provided to the staff before requesting acceleration. Additionally, the Assistant Director needs approximately two days at the end of the staff review to work the filing into his or her schedule, and to work out any remaining disclosure issues in order to ensure the disclosure is complete and accurate.

The [two business day] period provided in Rule 461 normally is sufficient to accomplish all of these tasks, provided the acceleration request is not submitted prematurely. This sometimes occurs when an acceleration request is submitted with an amendment that will draw additional comments. Acceleration requests submitted prematurely may be met with a telephone call requesting a written withdrawal of the request. Removing the delaying amendment as provided in Rule 473(b) and causing the registration statement to become effective under section 8(a) of the Securities Act is not practical for most issuers.[188]

One of the staff's objectives is to facilitate efficient and timely access to the capital markets. The staff does not exercise the kind of broad discretion to delay issuers sometimes described by commentators and, at the Division level, does not have authority to deny acceleration. Having due regard for the adequacy of information available to the public

---

[188] [See 17 C.F.R. § 230.461] The delaying amendment must not only be removed, but it must also be replaced by language required by Rule 473(b) announcing: "This registration statement shall hereafter become effective in accordance with the provisions of section 8(a) of the Securities Act of 1933." Id. § 230.473(b).

regarding the issuer, and the ease with which information regarding the issuer, its capital structure, and securities can be understood, Rule 461(b) states, "it is the general policy of the Commission * * * to permit acceleration of the effective date of the registration statement as soon as possible after the filing of appropriate amendments, if any." The staff is mindful that a refusal to accelerate the effective date of a registration statement would pass the matter to the Commission and require the type of substantial support for a stop order that is set out in Rule 461(b)(1) through (b)(7), which would principally require that the prospectus is not reasonably concise and understandable, is incomplete or misleading in a material respect, that the Commission is making an investigation of the issuer or underwriters, or that there is market manipulation involved. Whether or not a stop order could be supported, a misstep at this point can derail an offering. * * *

THE INFORMAL APPEAL PROCESS

There is opportunity for frustration in the comment process. Honest disagreements about the application of statutes, regulations, or accounting principles are common. The staff comments, passing as they do from hand to hand, are not always models of clarity or direction. It may not always be clear what change in the filing or what additional information is being requested by the staff. The basis for a comment may not be clear. Additional information or disclosure called for by a comment may seem burdensome. Positions on legal and accounting issues change and the rationale for positions are not always publicized. Interpretation of Division policy may differ somewhat between various Assistant Director groups. * * *

It is important that issuers have confidence in the registration process and believe they are being treated fairly, particularly when the staff's objectives are not perfectly aligned with the issuer or counsel's objectives. Issuers are entitled and encouraged to seek any necessary clarification or explanation of the staff's actions, including whether a position taken by the staff represents the views of the Division, is particular to that examining office, or is the view of the examiner or accountant. It is for exactly this reason that the telephone numbers of the Division's supervisory staff are included at the end of each comment letter.

Most concerns can be resolved over the telephone. * * *

When a problem or question cannot be resolved between the examiner or staff accountant and the issuer, or the issuer believes it is not receiving prompt attention, is being treated unfairly, requires an explanation, or has some other concern, the issuer has several means by which to obtain satisfaction. It is perfectly acceptable for the issuer to request the matter be raised with supervisory staff immediately above the examiner and accountant. The examiner or accountant will arrange a conference call. The issuer also may contact the supervisory staff, including the Assistant Director, directly by telephone. The supervisory staff are often able to provide a more satisfying explanation than the examiner or staff accountant has provided, or may modify or waive a comment if that is the appropriate solution. Some issuers simply find it comforting to hear the same answer at a higher level.

The line of informal appeal to be followed depends upon the nature of the problem. Legal and financial problems that cannot be resolved between the issuer and the Assistant Director may be appealed to the Chief Counsel, one of the Associate Directors, the Deputy Director, or Director of the Division. Accounting problems that cannot be resolved between the issuer and the Assistant Chief Accountant may be appealed to the Deputy Chief Accountant or Chief Accountant. Informal appeal is used to determine whether or not there is a general agreement with the position that is being taken by the staff, or simply where the issuer continues to believe the staff position is in error. The process need not take long because telephone calls usually are sufficient to provide for a complete exchange of views.

CONCLUSION

* * *

The duration of the registration process seems to depend more upon the issuer and counsel, rather than upon the staff. Experience indicates that avoiding recurring disclosure problems at the drafting stage of the registration statement, before it is filed with the Commission, will result in a much shorter and smoother registration for any issuer. Issuers who file registration statements that are declared effective at the short end of the range are always those issuers who begin with the end in mind—by ensuring that their registration statements contain the disclosure that the staff will look for and by avoiding disclosure pitfalls that will trigger comments. These registration statements are those that always provide an investor with all the information suggested by the regulations, in addition to other information necessary to evaluate intelligently the business of the issuer, market for its products, revenues, and risks. * * *

Problems

PROBLEM 3-1

XYZ Industries completed its IPO on March 15, 2012. It was also effective on its Form 10 under the 1934 Act, where it registered its common stock for trading on Nasdaq. As a result, XYZ became subject to the periodic reporting requirements of the 1934 Act. The offering sold 10 million shares (or 50% of XYZ's outstanding common stock) at $5 per share for $50 million to unaffiliated investors; its founders held the other 50% of XYZ's common stock. Since then, XYZ has filed all 1934 Act reports in a timely manner. Another 5 million shares were sold in early 2013 for $6 per share to public investors. It is now December 2013, XYZ's current stock price is $4 per share, and XYZ would like to do another public offering of 10 million shares (or approximately $40 million) and has found an underwriter to assist it. They would like to use "shelf registration." What restrictions do they face at this point and in the near future? Alternatively, what if XYZ, which made a substantial profit last year, were to offer non-convertible debt securities?

PROBLEM 3-2

Alternatively, it is now late 2013, and XYZ Industries has prospered. Currently, the market value of its common stock is slightly more than $1.5 billion, and the public holds 60% of its shares. It would like to register up to $600 million in common stock for sale from time to time. It wants to get to the market as soon as possible because it believes market conditions are favorable. What additional options are now available to it? Would it matter if it was currently delinquent by 20 days in filing its Form 10-K? What if, instead, it was delinquent in filing a Form 8-K?

4. QUALITATIVE DISCLOSURE

Statutes and Regulations

Securities Act, §§ 7, 8, and 8A.

Regulation C, Rules 400–418, 421, 425, 461, 481.

In the Matter of Franchard Corporation
Securities and Exchange Commission, 1964.
42 S.E.C. 163.

■ CARY, CHAIRMAN: These are consolidated proceedings pursuant to Sections 8(c) and 8(d) of the Securities Act of 1933 ("Securities Act") to determine whether a stop order should issue suspending the effectiveness of three registration statements filed by Franchard Corporation, formerly Glickman Corporation ("registrant"), and whether certain post-effective amendments filed by the registrant should be declared effective. * * *

I. FACTS

A. Background

Louis J. Glickman ("Glickman") has for many years been a large-scale real estate developer, operator and investor. From 1954 to 1960 he acquired control of real estate in this country and in Canada by means of "syndication" arrangements. * * * Glickman conducted some of these syndication activities and certain other phases of his real estate business through a number of wholly owned corporations, the most important of which was Glickman Corporation of Nevada, now known as Venada Corporation ("Venada").

In May of 1960, Glickman caused registrant to be formed in order to group under one entity most of the publicly owned corporations and limited partnerships under his control. Registrant was to operate on a so-called "cash flow" basis, i.e., the amount available for distribution to its stockholders was to be gauged by the excess of cash receipts over cash disbursements, without reference to such non-cash deductions from gross receipts as depreciation and leasehold amortization. Registrant's stock was divided into two classes, Class A common and Class B common, with the B stockholders given the right to elect ²/₃ of registrant's directors until 1971, when all outstanding B shares become A shares. Glickman established control of registrant by acquiring 450,000 of its 660,000 authorized B shares for $1 per share. He exercised a dominant role in the management of registrant's affairs as president at the time of its formation and later as its first chairman of the board.

The first of the three registration statements here involved ("1960 filing") became effective on October 12, 1960. * * *

The second of the three registration statements ("first 1961 filing") became effective on October 2, 1961 * * *. All of the A shares offered to the public for cash under the 1960 filing and the first 1961 filing were sold as were the A shares offered under the second 1961 filing, and the exchange offer in the 1960 filing was accepted by most of the offerees.

B. *Glickman's Withdrawals and Pledges*

Registrant's 1960 prospectus stated that Glickman had from time to time advanced substantial sums to the partnerships and corporations that were about to become subsidiaries of the registrant. It also said that he had advanced $211,000 to the registrant for the purpose of defraying its organization and registration costs and that this advance would be repaid without interest out of the proceeds of the public offering. On October 14, 1960—two days after the effective date of registrant's 1960 filing—Glickman began secretly to transfer funds from the registrant to Venada, his wholly owned corporation. Within two months the aggregate amount of these transfers amounted to $296,329. By October 2, 1961, the effective date of registrant's first 1961 filing, Glickman had made 45 withdrawals which amounted in the aggregate to $2,372,511. Neither the 1961 prospectuses nor any of the effective amendments to the 1960 filing referred to these transactions.

All of registrant's prospectuses stated that Glickman owned most of its B as well as a substantial block of its A stock. On the effective date of the 1960 filing Glickman's shares were unencumbered. In the following month, however, he began to pledge his shares to finance his personal real estate ventures. By August 31, 1961, all of Glickman's B and much of his A stock had been pledged to banks, finance companies, and private individuals. On the effective dates of the two 1961 filings the loans secured by these pledges aggregated about $4,250,000. The effective interest rates on these loans ran as high as 24% annually. Glickman retained the right to vote the pledged shares in the absence of a default on the loans. The two 1961 filings made no mention of Glickman's pledges or the loans they secured.

C. *Action of the Board of Directors*

In May 1962 the accountants who had audited the financial statements in registrant's 1960 and 1961 filings informed its directors that Glickman had from time to time diverted funds from the registrant's treasury to Venada. The directors then met with Glickman, who assured them that the withdrawals had been without wrongful intent and would not recur. Glickman agreed to repay all of the then known unauthorized withdrawals with the interest at the rate of 6%. Registrant's directors soon discovered that Glickman had made other withdrawals, and they retained former United States District Court Judge Simon H. Rifkind to determine Glickman's liability to registrant. Glickman agreed to be bound by Judge Rifkind's determination and was continued in office.

In a report submitted on August 20, 1962, Judge Rifkind found that Glickman had on many occasions withdrawn substantial sums from registrant; that Bernard Mann, who was registrant's as well as Venada's treasurer but not a member of registrant's board of directors, was the only one of registrant's officers who had known of the withdrawals and had collaborated with Glickman in effecting them; that registrant's inadequate administrative procedures had to some extent facilitated Glickman's wrongdoing; and that all of the withdrawals had been made good with 6% interest. Judge Rifkind also found that 6% was an inadequate interest rate because Glickman and Venada had been borrowing at appreciably higher interest rates from commercial finance companies and others. Accordingly, he concluded that registrant was entitled to additional interest from Glickman and from Venada in the amount of $145,279. Registrant has not thus far been able to collect any part of this sum.[10]

On November 30, 1962, registrant's directors learned that Glickman had continued to make unauthorized withdrawals after he had promised to desist from so doing and after the issuance of the Rifkind report, that Glickman and his wife had pledged all of their shares of the registrant's stock, and that Glickman and Venada were in financial straits. Glickman and Mann thereupon resigned from all of their posts with the registrant, and Glickman sold all his B stock and some of his Class A stock to a small group of investors. Monthly cash distributions to A stockholders, which registrant had made every month since its inception, were discontinued in January 1963, and registrant changed its name from Glickman Corporation to Franchard Corporation.

II. ALLEGED DEFICIENCIES—ACTIVITIES OF MANAGEMENT

A. *Glickman's Withdrawals of Registrant's Funds and Pledges of His Shares*

Of cardinal importance in any business is the quality of its management. Disclosures relevant to an evaluation of management are particularly pertinent where, as in this case, securities are sold largely

---

[10] In February 1963 Glickman and Venada filed petitions in the United States District Court . . . seeking arrangements with their creditors pursuant to Chapter XI of the Bankruptcy Act. . . .

on the personal reputation of a company's controlling person. The disclosures in these respects were materially deficient. The 1960 prospectus failed to reveal that Glickman intended to use substantial amounts of registrant's funds for the benefit of Venada, and the 1961 prospectuses made no reference to Glickman's continual diversion of substantial sums from the registrant. Glickman's pledges were not discussed in either the effective amendments to the 1960 filings or in the two 1961 filings.

In our view, these disclosures were highly material to an evaluation of the competence and reliability of registrant's management—in large measure, Glickman. In many respects, the development of disclosure standards adequate for informed appraisal of management's ability and integrity is a difficult task. How do you tell a "good" business manager from a "bad" one in a piece of paper? Managerial talent consists of personal attributes, essentially subjective in nature, that frequently defy meaningful analysis through the impersonal medium of a prospectus. Direct statements of opinion as to management's ability, which are not susceptible to objective verification, may well create an unwarranted appearance of reliability if placed in a prospectus. The integrity of management—its willingness to place its duty to public shareholders over personal interest—is an equally elusive factor for the application of disclosure standards.*

Evaluation of the quality of management—to whatever extent it is possible—is an essential ingredient of informed investment decision. * * * Appraisals of competency begin with information concerning management's past business experience, which is elicited by requirements that a prospectus state the offices and positions held with the issuer by each executive officer within the last five years. With respect to established companies, management's past performance, as shown by comprehensive financial and other disclosures concerning the issuer's operations, furnish a guide to its future business performance. To permit judgments whether the corporation's affairs are likely to be conducted in the interest of public shareholders, the registration requirements elicit information as to the interests of insiders which may conflict with their duty of loyalty to the corporation. Disclosures are also required with respect to the remuneration and other benefits paid or proposed to be paid to management as well as material transactions between the corporation and its officers, directors, holders of more than 10 percent [now 5%—Eds.] of its stock, and their associates.

Glickman's withdrawals were material transactions between registrant and its management, and the registration forms on which registrant's filings were made called for their disclosure. Registrant's argument that the withdrawals were not material because Glickman's

---

* Is it realistic to expect that there can or will be meaningful disclosure regarding the quality of management in the prospectus? Nonetheless, the SEC's forms focus on this issue. See Form S–1, Item 11(k), and Item 401 of Regulation S–K under the 1933 Act.—Eds.

undisclosed indebtedness to registrant never exceeded 1.5% of the gross book value of registrant's assets not only minimizes the substantial amounts of the withdrawals in relation to the stockholders' equity and the company's cash flow, but ignores the significance to prospective investors of information concerning Glickman's managerial ability and personal integrity. * * *

A description of Glickman's activities was important on several grounds. First, publication of the facts pertaining to Glickman's withdrawals of substantial funds and of his pledges of his control stock would have clearly indicated his strained financial position and his urgent need for cash in his personal real estate ventures. * * *

Second, disclosure of Glickman's continual diversion of registrant's funds to the use of Venada, his wholly owned corporation, was also germane to an evaluation of the integrity of his management. This quality is always a material factor. * * *

Third, Glickman's need for cash * * * gave him a powerful and direct motive to cause registrant to pursue policies which would permit high distribution rates and maintain a high price for registrant's A shares. * * * Investors were entitled to be apprised of these facts and such potential conflicts of interest.

Finally, the possibility of a change of control was also important to prospective investors. As we have noted, registrant's public offerings were largely predicated on Glickman's reputation as a successful real estate investor and operator. Disclosure of Glickman's secured loans, the relatively high interest rates that they bore, the secondary sources from which many of the loans were obtained, and the conditions under which lenders could declare defaults would have alerted investors to the possibility of a change in the control and management of registrant * * *.

* * *

With respect to disclosure of pledged shares, registrant is not aided by pointing out that our registration forms under the Securities Act and the reports required under the Securities Exchange Act do not call for disclosure of encumbrances on a controlling stockholder's shares, and that proposals to require such disclosures in reports filed with us under the Securities Exchange Act have not been adopted. The fact that such disclosures are not required of all issuers and their controlling persons in all cases does not negate their materiality in specific cases. The registration forms promulgated by us are guides intended to assist registrants in discharging their statutory duty of full disclosure. They are not and cannot possibly be exhaustive enumerations of each and every item material to investors in the particular circumstances relevant to a specific offering. The kaleidoscopic variety of economic life precludes any attempt at such an enumeration. The preparation of a registration statement is not satisfied, as registrant's position suggests, by a mechanical process of responding narrowly to the specific items of the applicable registration form. On the contrary, Rule 408 under the Securities Act makes clear to prospective registrants that: "In addition to the information expressly required to be included in a registration statement, there shall be added such further material information, if any, as may be necessary to make the required statements in the light of the circumstances under which they were made, not misleading."

B. Activities of Registrant's Directors

Another issue raised in these proceedings concerns the disclosure to be required in a prospectus regarding the adequacy of performance of managerial functions by registrant's board of directors. The Division urges that the prospectuses, by identifying the members of the board of directors, impliedly represented that they would provide oversight and direction to registrant's officers. * * *

It was obvious * * * that Glickman would exercise the dominant role in managing registrant's operations and the prospectuses contained no affirmative representations concerning the participation of the directors in registrant's affairs. Moreover, the board met regularly and received information as to registrant's affairs from Glickman and in connection with the preparation of registrant's registration statements, post-effective amendments, and periodic reports filed with us. It is clear we are not presented with a picture of total abdication of directorial responsibilities. Thus, the question posed by the Division must be whether the prospectuses were deficient in not disclosing that the directors, in overseeing the operations of the company, failed to exercise the degree of diligence which the Division believes was required of them under the circumstances in the context of the day-to-day operations of the company. We find no deficiencies in this area.

This is an issue raising fundamental considerations as to the functions of the disclosure requirements of the Securities Act. The civil liability provisions of Section 11 do establish for directors a standard of due diligence in the preparation of a registration statement—a federal rule of directors' responsibility with respect to the completeness and accuracy of the document used in the public distribution of securities. The Act does not purport, however, to define federal standards of directors' responsibility in the ordinary operations of business enterprises and nowhere empowers us to formulate administratively such regulatory standards. The diligence required of registrant's directors in overseeing its affairs is to be evaluated in the light of the standards established by state statutory and common law.

In our view, the application of these standards on a routine basis in the processing of registration statements would be basically incompatible with the philosophy and administration of the disclosure requirements of the Securities Act. Outright fraud or reckless indifference by directors might be readily identifiable and universally condemned. But activity short of that, which may give rise to legal restraints and liabilities, invokes significant uncertainty. * * * To generally require information in

Securities Act prospectuses as to whether directors have performed their duties in accordance with the standards of responsibility required of them under state law would stretch disclosure beyond the limitations contemplated by the statutory scheme and necessitated by considerations of administrative practicality. * * * [T]he disclosures sought here by the staff would require evaluation of the entire conduct of a board of directors in the context of the whole business operations of a company in the light of diverse and uncertain standards. In our view, this is a function which the disclosure requirements of the Securities Act cannot effectively discharge. It would either result in self-serving generalities of little value to investors or grave uncertainties both on the part of those who must enforce and those who must comply with that Act.

* * *

V. CONCLUSIONS

The deficiencies we have found in registrant's effective filings are serious. * * * Omissions of so material a character would normally require the issuance of a stop order.

Here, however, several factors taken together lead us to conclude that the distribution of copies of this opinion to all of registrant's past and present stockholders, as registrant has proposed, will give adequate public notice of the deficiencies in registrant's effective filings, and that neither the public interest nor the protection of investors requires the issuance of a stop order. Among those factors are Glickman's departure, the transfer of his controlling B shares to a management which has made a substantial financial commitment in registrant's securities, and registrant's voluntary disclosures to our staff prior to the initiation of these proceedings. Registrant also filed post-effective amendments to its 1960 filings which, though admittedly inadequate, represented a bona fide effort to remedy the deficiencies in its effective filings. In addition, * * * unusually extensive publicity was given to the true facts affecting registrant's affairs and to the resulting deficiencies in its effective filings.

Any new post-effective amendment should conform to the views expressed in this opinion. After the Division has reviewed such amendment, it will communicate its views with respect to it to the registrant, and thereafter the matter will be submitted to us for appropriate action.

* * *

---

a. Integrity Disclosures. The Commission's concern in *Franchard*, that investors be provided with qualitative information enabling them to appraise the character, integrity, and ability of the issuer's management, has today been codified in a series of provisions in Subpart 400 of Regulation S–K under the 1933 Act that focus on managerial experience, compensation, stock ownership, and conflicts of interest.

Item 401(f) of Regulation S–K requires registrants to disclose "certain legal proceedings" that "occurred during the past ten years and that are material to an evaluation of the ability or integrity of any director, person nominated to become a director or executive officer of the registrant." Listed under this heading are proceedings that include: (1) bankruptcy or reorganization petitions; (2) criminal convictions or a "pending criminal proceeding" (excluding traffic violations and "other minor offenses"); (3) any order, judgment, or decree enjoining or otherwise limiting the individual from engaging in the futures, commodities, or securities business, or "[e]ngaging in any type of business practice;" and (4) any order, judgment, or decree enjoining or otherwise limiting the individual from "[e]ngaging in any activity . . . in connection with any violation of Federal or State securities laws or Federal commodities laws."

Regulation S–K focuses only on events that occurred within the past ten years and does not require disclosure of pending civil litigation. Nonetheless, courts have sometimes found pending civil litigation[56] and securities law adjudications before the mandated disclosure period to have been material on specific facts.[57] The SEC has maintained, regarding a prior five-year rule, that it was only a "guide to disclosure" and "events occurring outside this period may be material and should be

---

[56] In Zell v. InterCapital Income Securities, Inc., 675 F.2d 1041 (9th Cir. 1982), the failure to disclose pending securities litigation against the investment adviser of a mutual fund was found to be material where the proxy statement related to the management contract between the adviser and the fund. See also SEC v. Merchant Capital, 483 F.3d 747, 771–72 (11th Cir. 2007) (holding that the issuer's failure to disclose the existence of a contemporaneous cease and desist order that prohibited it from selling identical unregistered securities in California was misleading); SEC v. Pace, 173 F.Supp.2d 30 (D.D.C. 2001) (embezzlement of any amount of money from corporation by officer would be material). However, in the City of Philadelphia v. Fleming Companies, 264 F.3d 1245, 1256–57 (10th Cir. 2001), the failure to disclose pending litigation was not found to be material. Similarly, in GAF Corp. v. Heyman, 724 F.2d 727 (2d Cir. 1983), the Second Circuit did not find allegations of fraud brought against a contestant in a proxy fight by his own sister to be material where the case resulted in only a settlement, not an adjudication. See also Ontario Tchrs. Pension Plan Bd. v. Teva Pharmaceutical Indus. Ltd., 432 F.Supp.3d 131, 167 (D.Conn.) (quoting Ciresi v. Citicorp, 782 F.Supp. 819, 823 (S.D.N.Y. 1991) ("the law does not impose a duty to disclose uncharged, unadjudicated wrongdoing or mismanagement")); In re Bos. Sci. Corp Sec. Litig., 490 F.Supp.2d 142, 159 (D.Mass. 2007) (quoting Ballan v. Wilfred American Educational Corp., 720 F.Supp. 241, 248–49 (E.D.N.Y. 1989) ("The SEC's proxy disclosures do not require a company's management to confess guilt to uncharged crimes or to accuse itself of antisocial or illegal policies.")).

[57] See United States v. Bachynsky, 415 F.App'x 167, 171–72 (11th Cir. 2014) (holding that issuer's failure to disclose its controlling shareholder's prior convictions was misleading even though the convictions occurred before the mandated disclosure period); SEC v. Brown, 740 F.Supp.2d 148, 159 (D.D.C. 2010) (holding that the issuer's failure to disclose CEO's prior conviction for conspiracy to commit securities fraud was misleading notwithstanding that the CEO's conviction was before the mandated disclosure period); Bertoglio v. Texas Intern. Co., 488 F.Supp. 630 (D.Del. 1980) (the failure to disclose in a proxy statement a 15-year-old adjudication of securities law violations was material where there was also pending civil litigation alleging securities law violations). An even more expansive holding is United States v. Yeaman, 194 F.3d 442 (3d Cir. 1999) (Company A must disclose that Company B was subject to an SEC order where one of Company A's officers and directors was a controlling shareholder of Company B). But see SEC v. Goldfield Deep Mines Co. of Nevada, 758 F.2d 459 (9th Cir. 1985) (failure to disclose 17-year-old conviction for embezzlement was not material, even though defendant had also violated state securities laws just over five years ago).

disclosed."[58] Accordingly, the provisions in Subpart 400 of Regulation S–K are not necessarily exclusive. In *Franchard,* for example, the Commission focused at length on the possibility that Glickman's strained financial position would affect his management style and give him "a powerful and direct motive to cause registrant to pursue policies" that favored current dividends over future growth.

Query: An affirmative requirement to disclose criminal convictions and other "bad acts" risks an adverse reaction from investors. The response, in some cases, may simply be to remove the director or officer who implicates the troubling disclosure. From that perspective, to what extent are these requirements crafted to inform investors of management's integrity, and to what extent are they likely to go further to shape the composition of the issuer's board and officers?

In *Franchard,* the SEC also noted the increased possibility of a sudden change in control if Glickman were forced to sell his interest. Item 403 requires disclosure of management's beneficial securities ownership, including any "arrangements, known to the registrant, including any pledge by any person of securities of the registrant . . ., the operation of which may at a subsequent date result in a change of control of the registrant."[59] This drafting seems to reflect the Commission's concerns in *Franchard.*

Perhaps the most important provision in Subpart 400 of Regulation S–K is Item 404, which covers conflict of interest transactions. Item 404(a), for example, requires disclosure of any transaction exceeding $120,000 where the registrant was or is to be a "participant," and where any executive officer, director, director nominee, or beneficial owner of more than 5% of the registrant's voting securities, or immediate family member of any of the foregoing, "had or will have a direct or indirect material interest." For these purposes, a "transaction" is broadly defined to include any financial transaction, arrangement, or relationship or any series of similar transactions, arrangements, or relationships, including indebtedness and guarantees of indebtedness.[60] Item 404(b) then requires the registrant to disclose its policies and procedures for the review, approval, or ratification of any transaction required to be reported under Item 404(a). Item 404(b) also requires the registrant to disclose any transaction described under Item 404(a) that was not required under its policies and procedures to be reviewed, approved, or ratified, or where such policies and procedures were not followed. (Again, *query*: Is it likely an issuer would be concerned about investor reaction if it disclosed it had no policies or procedures for some or all of the Item

---

[58] Securities Act Release No. 5758 (Nov. 2, 1976); see also SEC v. Brown, 740 F.Supp.2d 148, 159 (D.D.C. 2010) (SEC maintaining that the time limitation in Regulation S–K is "irrelevant because the sole test for determining whether information must be disclosed is whether it is material, i.e., whether there is a substantial likelihood that a reasonable investor would consider it important").

[59] See Item 403(c) of Regulation S–K under the 1933 Act.

[60] See Instruction 2. to Item 404(a) of Regulation S–K under the 1933 Act.

404(a) transactions or, even worse, that it violated those policies and procedures? Is this another example of how mandatory disclosure requirements can affect corporate governance?)

 b. Case Law. Given the breadth of the disclosure obligation, it is necessary to examine with particular care those cases in which the courts have found immaterial (or have otherwise excused) the failure to disclose unlawful acts or other conduct seemingly bearing on management's integrity. A leading case is Gaines v. Haughton,[61] in which plaintiffs alleged that Lockheed's failure to disclose extensive payments to foreign governments and officials in its proxy statement constituted a material omission. Upholding summary judgment for the defendants, the Ninth Circuit offered the following standard for when unlawful or questionable conduct was material to shareholders:

> We draw a sharp distinction * * * between allegations of director misconduct involving a breach of trust or self-dealing—the nondisclosure of which is presumptively material—and allegations of simple breach of fiduciary duty/waste of corporate management—the nondisclosure of which is never material for § 14(a) purposes * * *. The distinction between "mere" bribes and bribes coupled with kickbacks to the directors makes a great deal of sense, indeed it is fundamental to a meaningful concept of materiality under § 14(a) and the preservation of state corporate law.[62]

Where directors received a personal benefit from an unlawful transaction, courts have generally found its nondisclosure to constitute a material omission.[63] Where, however, the illegality is on behalf of the company and does not involve a personal benefit to the officer, courts have employed a variety of theories to shield the individual defendants from liability. Sometimes, as in *Gaines,* they have found the omission to be immaterial; at other times, they have found a lack of scienter. Still, on other occasions, they have relied on a doctrine known as "transaction causation" to justify dismissal—namely, because the alleged loss from the unlawful payment preceded the proxy statement or other disclosure

---

 [61] 645 F.2d 761 (9th Cir. 1981); see also In re AGNC Inv. Corp., 2018 WL 3239476, at *5 (D. Md. July 3, 2018) ("[U]nlike acts of mere corporate mismanagement, which may not need to be disclosed in a proxy statement relating to a Board election, self-dealing, dishonesty, and deceit benefiting the directors are 'presumptively material' facts."); In re Diamond Foods, Inc. Derivative Litig., 2012 WL 1945814, at *7 (N.D. Cal. May 29, 2012) (stating "their claim is not one of mismanagement but rather one of self-dealing, which is presumptively material").

 [62] 645 F.2d at 776–78. See also In re Tenneco Securities Litigation, 449 F.Supp. 528 (S.D.Tex. 1978).

 [63] See, e.g., United States. v. Hatfield, 724 F.Supp.2d 321, 328 (E.D.N.Y 2010) (finding that a jury could conclude that undisclosed information regarding an executive's use of corporate funds for excessive personal spending is material); In re Comverse Technology, Inc. Sec. Litig., 543 F.Supp.2d 134, 138, 151 (E.D.N.Y 2008) (holding that company's failure to disclose executive's option-backdating scheme was a material omission); Siemers v. Wells Fargo & Co., 2007 WL 1140660 at *8 (N.D.Cal. 2007) ("[A]ny intentional misappropriation . . . would have been material to investors."). For a recent holding that embezzlement of even a modest amount by an officer from his corporation was material, see SEC v. Pace, 173 F.Supp.2d 30 (D.D.C. 2001).

document, the omission to disclose it did not cause the loss.[64] It is also important to remember that, even if an omitted fact is clearly material, it does not follow that there is an immediate duty to disclose it. Thus, a number of courts have relied on Basic Inc. v. Levinson[65] to find that, even though an illegal bribe was material, there was no affirmative duty of disclosure.[66] However, if other statements by the issuer seem to imply the absence of illegality, this can give rise to a "half truth" that is actionable and requires disclosure of the omitted information.

Much depends on who is suing. Although private plaintiffs face numerous obstacles, the SEC may often be given greater judicial deference.[67] Also, the defendant may prefer to settle (and not litigate) with the SEC for a variety of reasons not applicable to a private litigant. Finally, the SEC may use other remedies not available to a private plaintiff. In one important corporate governance dispute, the SEC decided a board permitted excessive retirement benefits to be paid to its retiring CEO and failed to disclose a related-party transaction between the company and the CEO's son. The company consented to a cease-and-desist order not to commit further violations of the federal securities laws (without admitting or denying the Commission's charges). However, not content simply to settle with the defendant company, the Commission issued a public report, pursuant to § 21A of the 1934 Act, that criticized the company's outside directors and asserted they failed to discharge their affirmative responsibilities to make adequate disclosure.[68] "Punishment by publicity" may be the last option for the SEC in dealing with issues that combine self-dealing with poor corporate governance.

c. Unadjudicated Charges. Suppose an individual knows that law enforcement authorities are investigating her for criminal law violations, but she maintains her innocence. In such circumstances, must the individual disclose in a proxy statement or registration statement that an investigation is ongoing—where she has not been charged with a crime? Read literally, Item 401(f) of Regulation S–K only requires disclosure of convictions within the past ten years or being "named subject of a pending criminal proceeding (excluding traffic violations and other minor offenses)." Could a CEO who knew of a criminal investigation, and who expected to be indicted next week, go effective with a registration statement today without disclosing this fact?

---

[64] See Abbey v. Control Data Corp., 603 F.2d 724, 732 (8th Cir. 1979); Rosengarten v. ITT Corp., 466 F.Supp. 817, 827–28 (S.D.N.Y. 1979).

[65] 485 U.S. 224 (1988). *Basic* held that silence was generally not actionable, absent a duty to disclose. While such a duty might arise at the time a proxy statement is circulated, there would be no such duty to disclose or update on a daily basis.

[66] See Roeder v. Alpha Industries, Inc., 814 F.2d 22 (1st Cir. 1987).

[67] See SEC v. Electronics Warehouse, Inc., 689 F.Supp. 53 (D.Conn. 1988), aff'd, 891 F.2d 459 (2d Cir. 1989) (pending criminal action against corporate president must be disclosed, despite his good faith belief in his innocence).

[68] See In the Matter of W.R. Grace & Co., Exchange Act Release No. 39,157 (Sept. 30, 1997).

Technically, no charge is pending, and no adjudication has occurred—but is it still material enough that it must be disclosed?[69]

   d. *Private Litigation.* Most cases brought by private plaintiffs have rejected attempts to use the failure to make integrity disclosures about management's conduct or character as a basis for private damages. In the proxy context, a few cases have granted injunctive relief and ordered a new proxy solicitation before a shareholders' meeting could be held. Sometimes, as in *Gaines* (discussed earlier), the successful defense has been based on causation theories; at other times, the court found there was no duty to disclose at the particular time under *Basic* because the company was neither trading nor soliciting proxies.[70] And, since the passage of the Private Securities Litigation Reform Act of 1995 ("PSLRA") (which requires a plaintiff to "state with particularity facts giving rise to a strong inference" of fraud), courts have recurrently ruled that a mere fiduciary breach does not indicate scienter, because it could be based only on negligence. Even in cases based on the proxy rules (where Rule 14a–9 under the 1934 Act does not require scienter to be alleged), some circuits have held that, for the allegations to be actionable, they must "sound in fraud" (which a fiduciary breach, standing alone, does not necessarily do).[71] Still, some cases in the wake of the 2008 subprime mortgage debacle have found this heightened scienter standard satisfied when the plaintiff alleged, not only a fiduciary breach, but also violations of internal underwriting standards on making subprime loans as a means to enhance executive compensation.[72]

   e. *Law Violations Not Involving Senior Management.* Item 401 of Regulation S–K applies by its terms only when a director, senior

---

[69] Courts have reached different conclusions on whether the non-disclosure of criminal investigations is material information. Cases that have found such information to be material have tended to involve executive self-dealing or a substantial financial risk to the company. Compare Richman v. Goldman Sachs Group, Inc., 868 F.Supp.2d 261, 274 (S.D.N.Y. 2011) (finding that Goldman Sachs was not obligated to disclose certain employees were being investigated by the SEC for wrongdoing), and Browning-Ferris Indus., Inc. Shareholder Derivative Litig., 830 F.Supp. 361, 369–70 (S.D. Tex. 1993) (holding that Item 401(f) did not require the company to disclose that a corporate manager was under DOJ investigation for collusion), *with* Roeder v. Alpha Indus., Inc. 814 F.2d 22, 26 (concluding that allegations of corporate bribery could be material because the allegations jeopardized the company's ability to secure government contracts), and Maldonado v. Flynn, 597 F.2d 789, 796–97 (2d Cir. 1979) (holding that, although allegations of corporate mismanagement may be immaterial, allegations involving executive self-dealing are material); Menkes v. Stolt-Nielsen S.A., 2005 WL 3050970, at *6 (D.Conn. Nov. 10 2005) ("[M]anagement may be compelled to disclose uncharged illegal conduct when there is insider trading . . . or when disclosure is necessary to prevent another statement from misleading the public."). See also SEC Staff Accounting Bulletin No. 99, 64 Fed. Reg. 45,150, 45,151 (Aug. 19, 1999) (concealment of an unlawful transaction is a consideration that may render a misstatement as material).

[70] See, e.g., Roeder v. Alpha Indus., Inc., 814 F.2d 22 (1st Cir. 1987); Menkes v. Stolt-Nielsen S.A., 2005 WL 3050970, at *7 (D.Conn. Nov. 10, 2005) ("[O]bligation to disclose uncharged illegal conduct does not arise from the materiality of [the] information alone."). For a general discussion of the law, see Ferrara, Starr & Steinberg, Disclosure of Information Bearing on Management Integrity and Competence, 76 Nw.L.Rev. 555 (1981).

[71] See, e.g., Desaigoudar v. Meyercord, 223 F.3d 1020, 1022–23 (9th Cir. 2000).

[72] See In re Countrywide Fin. Corp. Derivative Litig., 554 F.Supp.2d 1044 (C.D. Cal. 2008).

manager, or 5% beneficial owner, or an immediate family member, was involved in a violation of law or a pending legal proceeding. Assume, instead, that lower-echelon officials were involved in under-the-table payments to bribe potential customers, and the amounts involved were not large enough by themselves to be material to the company. While the involvement of directors, managers, and large shareholders may be *per se* material (at least in a civil proceeding),[73] other theories must be relied upon when they are not implicated. The SEC has advanced at least two theories with some success in its enforcement litigation: (1) unlawful practices are material when they constitute the company's basic method of competition; and (2) illegality is material when it exposes the company to economically material sanctions (either in the form of fines or other financial penalties, or disqualifications from doing business in a jurisdiction or line of business, upon conviction).[74] In effect, these decisions rely on a more quantitative theory of materiality, rather than a qualitative focus on managerial integrity (as in *Franchard*), because the behavior threatens the company's financial position or casts its basic business model in a materially different light.

 f. Antisocial Conduct Not Involving Violations of Law. Although most private cases have declined to find material forms of misbehavior that did not involve actual violations of law or conflicts of interest, there have been noteworthy exceptions to this generalization. The most visible case is one where the magnitude of the company's potential liabilities is itself material. Thus, in Grossman v. Waste Management, Inc.,[75] the court held it to be a material omission to fail to disclose the registrant's potential liabilities for the required cleanup of toxic waste under environmental laws. Such a standard is consistent with *Basic*'s traditional probability/magnitude tradeoff for determining materiality. Courts, however, have seldom gone beyond this point.

 In Natural Resources Defense Council v. SEC,[76] the D.C. Circuit refused to expand the definition of materiality to include the special interests of the "ethical investor." Similarly, allegations that all directors

---

[73] See SEC v. Black, 2008 WL 4394891, at *12 (N.D. Ill. Sept. 24, 2008); SEC v. Kalvex Inc., 425 F.Supp. 310, 315 (S.D.N.Y. 1975); Cooke v. Teleprompter Corp., 334 F.Supp. 467 (S.D.N.Y. 1971). But see SEC v. E-Smart Tech. (D.D.C. 2015), 82 F.Supp.3d 97, 116 (finding that reasonable minds could disagree on whether information regarding the CEO's reimbursements for personal expenses is material).

[74] See Ind. Pub. Retirement Sys. v. SAIC, Inc., 818 F.3d 85, 97 (concluding that information about rogue employee's illegal kickback system and the potential, resulting city fines was material information under Regulation S–K); SEC v. Jos. Schlitz Brewing Co., 452 F.Supp. 824 (E.D.Wis. 1978) (where licenses to sell beer at risk because of unlawful payments to tavern owners, such practices were material although amounts paid were immaterial). But see Menkes v. Stolt-Nielsen S.A., 2005 WL 3050970, at *9 (Nov. 10 2005) (holding that Regulation S–K does not mandate the disclosure of criminal misconduct by employees).

[75] 589 F.Supp. 395 (N.D. Ill. 1984).

[76] 606 F.2d 1031, 1051 (D.C.Cir. 1979). See also Chairman Clayton, Statement on Proposed Amendments to Modernize and Enhance Financial Disclosures; Other Ongoing Disclosure Modernization Efforts; Impact of the Coronavirus; Environmental and Climate-Related Disclosure, SEC (Jan. 30, 2020) (discussing the threshold issues of mandating environmental and climate-related disclosures).

were willfully involved in a campaign to engage in anti-union activities in violation of the federal labor laws were found not to be material, where no allegation of self-dealing or personal benefit was made.[77] Note, however, that statements that the company is not involved in such conduct or that the company's activities were in compliance with law may constitute material affirmative misrepresentations.[78] In addition, even if environmental liabilities are not yet material, or do not involve misconduct by senior managers, there remains the distinct possibility that such liabilities constitute a future trend, uncertainty, or commitment that may become material in the future and so may need to be disclosed in the MD&A section of the registration statement or periodic report (which we discuss further below).

    g.   *Executive Compensation.* Item 402 of Regulation S–K requires detailed disclosure of compensation (including stock awards, stock options, and pension benefits) for the registrant's principal executive officer ("PEO"), principal financial officer ("PFO"), three of the most highly-compensated executive officers other than the PEO or PFO (whose adjusted total compensation is $100,000 or more), and up to two of the most highly-compensated non-executive officers. That disclosure includes a "Compensation Discussion and Analysis" ("CD&A"), which is intended to explain all material elements of compensation of the named executive officers, including the objectives of the compensation programs, what the program is designed to reward, each element of compensation, how the registrant determines the amount to pay for each element, and whether (and, if so, how) the registrant has considered the most recent shareholder "say-on-pay" advisory vote (pursuant to § 14A of the 1934 Act and Rule 14a–20 thereunder) in determining executive compensation. The CD&A "should focus on the material principles underlying the registrant's executive compensation policies and decisions and the most important factors relevant to analysis of those policies and decisions."[79]

    The 2008 financial crisis was viewed, to some degree, as a failure of corporate governance. Consequently, the Dodd-Frank Act contains several provisions that relate to governance and compensation. Section 953(b) of the Dodd-Frank Act directed the SEC to amend Item 402 of Regulation S–K (which it did by adding Item 402(u)) to require each company, with limited exceptions, to disclose: the median of the annual total compensation of all its employees, excluding its PEO; the annual total compensation of its PEO; and the ratio of these two amounts. Section 951 of the Dodd-Frank Act directed the SEC to adopt rules giving shareholders an advisory vote on executive compensation (known as the

---

    [77]   See Amalgamated Clothing & Textile Workers v. J.P. Stevens & Co., 475 F.Supp. 328 (S.D.N.Y. 1979), vacated as moot per curiam, 638 F.2d 7 (2d Cir. 1980).

    [78]   See In re Copley Pharmaceutical, Inc. Securities Litigation, [1995 Transfer Binder] Fed.Sec.L.Rep. (CCH) Para. 98,695 (D.Mass. 1995); In re AES Corp. Sec. Litig., 825 F.Supp. 578 (S.D.N.Y. 1993); Ballan v. Upjohn Co., 814 F.Supp. 1375 (W.D.Mich. 1992).

    [79]   See Instruction 3. to Item 402(b) of Regulation S–K under the 1933 Act.

"say-on-pay" vote).[80] Item 402(u)'s new ratio is designed to provide a company-specific metric that shareholders might find useful as part of say-on-pay voting, although, in light of how recently it has been adopted, the impact of say-on-pay voting on CEO compensation is still inconclusive. In dissent, two Commissioners noted the substantial costs of the new Item, estimated by the SEC as $1.3 billion in initial compliance costs and $526 million in ongoing annual costs, and queried whether there was a clear statement of purpose or benefits in the Dodd-Frank Act or the SEC's adopting release.[81]

Section 953(a) of the Dodd-Frank Act added new § 14(i) to the 1934 Act, which directs the SEC to adopt a rule requiring each issuer to disclose in any proxy or consent solicitation for an annual meeting of shareholders the relationship between executive compensation and the issuer's financial performance. The SEC proposed a "pay-versus-performance" disclosure rule in 2015, pursuant to which a public company would be required to provide a clear description of the relationship between executive compensation paid to senior executives and the company's cumulative total shareholder return ("TSR"). Each issuer would also disclose the relationship between the company's TSR and that of a peer group chosen by the company over each of the five most recently completed fiscal years. The proposed rule has not been passed (and is unlikely to be adopted in the near-term), even though some companies have started making voluntary disclosures.

Finally, § 955 of the Dodd-Frank Act added § 14(j) of the 1934 Act, which directed the SEC to adopt a rule requiring disclosure in any proxy or consent solicitation for an annual meeting of shareholders whether any director or employee is permitted to hedge or offset any decrease in the market value of any equity securities granted to them as compensation or otherwise held by them. The SEC's new rule, appearing in Item 407(i) of Regulation S–K, directs the issuer to disclose any practices or policies on hedging activities concerning equity securities of the issuer or any affiliate of the issuer.[82] The issuer must also disclose categories of hedging transactions that are permitted or, if it has no policies or procedures regarding hedging, the fact of their absence.[83]

h. The Special Case of Environmental Liabilities. Environmental liabilities receive special attention in Item 103 of Regulation S–K. On its face, Item 103 simply requires disclosure of "any material pending legal proceedings, other than ordinary routine litigation incidental to the business." The instructions to this Item then explain that no information needs to be disclosed regarding litigation involving a claim for damages

---

[80] See § 951 of the Dodd-Frank Act (adding § 14A to the 1934 Act). See Securities Act Release No. 9178 (Jan. 25, 2011).
[81] Securities Act Release No. 9877 (Aug. 5, 2015).
[82] See Instruction 1. to Item 407(i) of Regulation S–K under the 1933 Act.
[83] See Item 407(i)(4) of Regulation S–K under the 1933 Act.

that is 10% or less of the registrant's current assets.[84] However, a special instruction says that administrative and judicial proceedings arising under federal, state, or local laws "regulating the discharge of materials into the environment or primar[il]y for the purpose of protecting the environment shall not be deemed 'ordinary routine litigation incidental to the business'" and shall be disclosed when, among other circumstances, a governmental authority is a party to the proceeding unless the registrant "reasonably believes that such proceeding will result in ... monetary sanctions ... of less than $300,000" or, at the election of the registrant, such other threshold that the registrant determines is reasonably designed to result in disclosure of a proceeding that is material to the business or financial condition and does not exceed the lesser of $1 million or one percent of the current assets of the registrant and its subsidiaries on a consolidated basis.[85] In effect, the Commission has given environmental liabilities a preferred status under its disclosure rules, although it has resisted other attempts to use the federal securities laws as a lever to promote social goals unrelated to investor interests.

In Natural Resources Defense Council, Inc. v. SEC,[86] the D.C. Circuit upheld the Commission's determination that the focus of its disclosure policy should remain on economically significant information and rejected the claim that a special priority should be given to environmental concerns under the National Environmental Policy Act. Still, despite the SEC's victory, plaintiffs have sometimes been successful in convincing courts that the issuer's failure to disclose uncharged violations of the environmental laws was material under circumstances where a failure to disclose other liabilities might have been upheld.[87] In a decision dealing with environmental liabilities, Levine v. NL Industries, Inc., the Second Circuit specifically focused on Item 101(c)(xii) of Regulation S–K, which provides in part that:

> Appropriate disclosure also shall be made as to the material effects that compliance with Federal, State and local provisions ... regulating the discharge of materials into the environment ... may have upon the capital expenditures, earnings and competitive position of the registrant and its subsidiaries.

Construing this provision in a case where the registrant had carelessly operated a uranium processing plant, the Second Circuit gave a

---

[84] See Instruction 2. to Item 103 of Regulation S–K under the 1933 Act.

[85] See Item 103(c)(3)(iii) of Regulation S–K under the 1933 Act.

[86] 606 F.2d 1031 (D.C.Cir. 1979).

[87] Compare Grossman v. Waste Management, Inc., 589 F.Supp. 395, 407–08 (N.D.Ill. 1984) (omissions of disclosures of environmental liabilities were actionable), and Levine v. NL Industries, Inc., 717 F.Supp. 252 (S.D.N.Y. 1989), aff'd, 926 F.2d 199 (2d Cir. 1991) (failure to disclose potential environmental liability for serious penalties in Form 10-K not material where Items 101 and 103 of Regulation S–K do not require disclosure of contingent liabilities not yet asserted by any party). Outside the environmental context, no similar rule seems to require disclosure of violations of other federal regulatory statutes or rules. See Anderson v. Abbott Laboratories, 140 F.Supp.2d 894 (N.D.Ill. 2001) (distinguishing *Grossman*).

considerably broader interpretation to the disclosure obligation than had the district court:

> The district court's opinion might be read as interpreting this section to require disclosure only of the cost of complying with environmental regulations, but not the cost of failing to comply with them.... Such an inference would be incorrect. Disclosure of potential costs for violations of environmental laws, if material, is ordinarily required.[88]

Thus, while the district court in *Levine* ruled that unasserted claims did not need to be disclosed in the registrant's annual report on Form 10-K, the Second Circuit's decision seems to suggest that an estimate of future liabilities must be made by an issuer that has (in the SEC's words) "a policy or approach toward compliance with environmental regulations which is reasonably likely to result in substantial fines, penalties, or other significant effects on the corporation."[89] In effect, although Item 103 ("Legal Proceedings") does not require disclosure of unasserted claims, Item 101 ("Description of Business") may require such disclosure where those claims are likely to be asserted based on a management "policy or approach toward compliance with environmental regulations." *Query:* Can environmental liabilities be distinguished from other regulatory schemes that provide for substantial penalties? Should a managerial policy of "flouting the law" now require disclosure without any claim having been asserted? Or is the Second Circuit especially sensitive to environmental concerns?

5. NEW APPROACHES TO DISCLOSURE

A. SOFT INFORMATION: FROM FORBIDDEN TO REQUIRED

Historically, the SEC took a "just the facts, ma'am" approach to disclosure and discouraged the inclusion of forward-looking information or projections. Indeed, in 1956, the SEC listed "predictions as to specific future market values, earnings, or dividends" as types of information that, because of their potential to mislead, should generally not be included in proxy statements.[90] There was a latent paternalism in this policy, which many commentators began to criticize during the 1970s on the grounds that it denied the market precisely the types of information the market considered most valuable. Some suggested that the SEC was overly preoccupied with making disclosures fully comprehensible to a hypothetical layman who did not, in fact, read disclosure documents and

---

[88] Levine v. NL Industries, Inc., 926 F.2d 199, 203 (2d Cir. 1991). Ultimately, the Second Circuit affirmed summary judgment for defendants because they were indemnified by the U.S. Department of Energy and thus faced no economic exposure to loss.

[89] Id. (quoting In re United States Steel Corp., Exchange Act Release No. 16,233 (Sept. 27, 1979)).

[90] See Walker v. Action Industries, Inc., 802 F.2d 703, 707 (4th Cir. 1986) (discussing Exchange Act Release No. 5276). This footnote to Rule 14a–9 under the 1934 Act, precluding the use of such projections, was eliminated in 1976.

who had, in any event, little impact on price determination;[91] others saw the SEC's policy as defensive, protecting it from potentially embarrassing charges it failed to detect fraud in filings made with it. Many commentators suggested that the SEC's hostility towards projections and other soft information rendered disclosure documents sterile—both unreadable and unread.[92] In response to these critics, the SEC organized a study of corporate disclosure during the mid-1970s, which recommended a significant change in policy, including a greater receptivity to projections and estimates.[93] Gradually and over time, the SEC came to accept the legitimacy of "soft information" (i.e., information about an issuer that inherently involves some subjective analysis or extrapolation, such as projections or estimates). An important milestone was reached in 1979 when the SEC adopted Rule 175 under the 1933 Act and Rule 3b–6 under the 1934 Act to encourage the use of such information in SEC filings.[94] Both Rules created safe harbors for certain defined types of "forward-looking statements" by specifying that a statement "shall be deemed not to be a fraudulent statement . . . unless it is shown that such statement was made or reaffirmed without a reasonable basis or was disclosed other than in good faith."[95] Later, in 1995, a far broader and almost ironclad safe harbor for forward-looking information was added to both the 1933 Act and the 1934 Act by the Private Securities Litigation Reform Act; these safe harbors essentially immunize a "forward-looking" statement if it is accompanied by a "meaningful cautionary statement."[96]

Issuers remain hesitant about including projections in prospectuses and registration statements, largely out of anxiety over the low bar to finding liability under § 11 of the 1933 Act for a material misstatement or omission. In fact, however, judicial decisions have been extremely protective to date.[97]

---

[91] The most influential critic in this debate was Professor Homer Kripke. See Kripke, The Myth of the Informed Layman, 28 Bus.Law. 631 (1973); Kripke, The SEC, the Accountants, Some Myths and Some Realities, 45 N.Y.U.L.Rev. 1151 (1970); Kripke, A Search for a Meaningful Securities Disclosure Policy, 31 Bus.Law. 293 (1975).

[92] Mann, Prospectuses: Unreadable or Just Unread?—A Proposal to Reexamine Policy Against Permitting Projections, 40 Geo.Wash. L.Rev. 222 (1971); Schneider, Nits, Grits and Soft Information in SEC Filings, 121 U.Pa.L.Rev. 254 (1972).

[93] See Report of the Advisory Committee on Corporate Disclosure to the Securities and Exchange Commission. For an excellent overview of this debate and the gradual transition in SEC philosophy, see Kripke, The SEC and Corporate Disclosure: Regulation in Search of a Purpose (1979).

[94] See Securities Act Release No. 6084 (June 25, 1979).

[95] See Rule 175(a) under the 1933 Act and Rule 3b–6(a) under the 1934 Act. The term "forward-looking statement" is defined in Rule 175(c) and Rule 3b–6(c).

[96] The PSLRA added Section 27A to the 1933 Act and Section 21E to the 1934 Act. The application of these safe harbors is discussed later in this casebook.

[97] See Wielgos v. Commonwealth Edison Co., 892 F.2d 509 (7th Cir. 1989) (dealing with Rule 175), and Harris v. Ivax Corp., 182 F.3d 799 (11th Cir. 1999) (addressing statutory safe harbors).

a. When Are Projections Mandatory: MD&A

During the late 1980s, the SEC's most important initiative to enhance disclosure standards was strengthening the Management's Discussion and Analysis of Financial Condition and Results of Operations ("MD&A"). Two important SEC releases related to this expansion are excerpted below:

Securities Act Release No. 6711
Securities and Exchange Commission.
April 24, 1987.

CONCEPT RELEASE ON MANAGEMENT'S DISCUSSION AND ANALYSIS OF FINANCIAL CONDITION AND OPERATIONS

* * *

II. The Purpose of MD&A and Current Requirements

The Commission has long recognized the need for a narrative explanation of the financial statements, because a numerical presentation and brief accompanying footnotes alone may be insufficient for an investor to judge the quality of earnings and the likelihood that past performance is indicative of future performance. MD&A is intended to give the investor an opportunity to look at the company through the eyes of management by providing both a short and long-term analysis of the business of the company. The Item [303 of Regulation S–K] asks management to discuss the dynamics of the business and to analyze the financials. . . .

A wide range of corporate events and changes may warrant MD&A disclosure. The examples provided by the Commission in 1974 are still useful illustrations:

* * *

1. Material changes in product mix or in the relative profitability of lines of business;

2. Material changes in advertising, research, development, product introduction or other discretionary costs;

3. The acquisition or disposition of a material asset other than in the ordinary course of business;

4. Material and unusual charges or gains, including credits or charges associated with discontinuation of operations;

5. Material changes in assumptions underlying deferred costs and the plan for amortization of such costs;

6. Material changes in assumed investment return and in actuarial assumptions used to calculate contributions to pension funds; and

7. The closing of a material facility or material interruption of business or completion of a material contract.

Perhaps the most misunderstood aspect of MD&A is its relationship to statements of a prospective nature. MD&A requires disclosure of "known trends or any known demands, commitments, events or uncertainties that will result in or that are reasonably likely to result in the registrant's liquidity increasing or decreasing in any material way."[14] Additionally, the Item calls for a description of any known material trends in the registrant's capital resources and any expected changes in the mix or cost of such resources. Elsewhere, the Item requires disclosure of known trends or uncertainties that are reasonably expected to have a material impact on net sales, revenues, or income from continuing operations. The Instructions add that MD&A "shall focus specifically on material events and uncertainties known to management that would cause reported financial information not to be necessarily indicative of future operating results or of future financial condition."

Conversely, Instruction 7 of Item 303(a) states that registrants are encouraged, but not required, to supply "forward-looking" information. The Instruction was not intended to detract from the requirements noted above but instead to make clear that "forward-looking information" (as that term is used in the Instruction) should be distinguished from presently known data that is reasonably expected to have a material impact on future results.

> Both required disclosure regarding the future impact of presently known trends, events or uncertainties and optional forward-looking information may involve some prediction or projection. The distinction between the two rests with the nature of the prediction required. Required disclosure is based on currently known trends, events, and uncertainties that are reasonably expected to have material effects, such as: a reduction in the registrant's product prices; erosion in the registrant's market share; changes in insurance coverage; or likely non-renewal of a material contract. In contrast, optional forward-looking disclosure involves anticipating a future trend or event or anticipating a less predictable impact of a known event, trend, or uncertainty.*

* * *

---

[14] 17 CFR 229.303(a)(1).

* Instruction 7. of Item 303(a) has since been modified; currently, it states that "[a]ny forward-looking information supplied is expressly covered by the safe harbor rule for projections." However, the distinction between disclosure based on "currently known trends, events, and uncertainties" and disclosure that "involves anticipating a future trend or event or anticipating a less predictable impact of a known event, trend, or uncertainty" is still useful.—Eds.

Securities Act Release No. 6835
Securities and Exchange Commission.
May 18, 1989.

INTERPRETIVE RELEASE: MANAGEMENT'S DISCUSSION AND ANALYSIS OF FINANCIAL CONDITION AND RESULTS OF OPERATIONS

* * *

The Commission has determined that interpretive guidance is needed regarding the following matters: prospective information required in MD&A * * *.

B. Prospective Information

Several specific provisions in Item 303 require disclosure of forward-looking information.

* * *

A disclosure duty exists where a trend, demand, commitment, event or uncertainty is both presently known to management and reasonably likely to have material effects on the registrant's financial condition or results of operations. Registrants preparing their MD&A disclosure should determine and carefully review what trends, demands, commitments, events or uncertainties are known to management. In the following example, the registrant discloses the reasonably likely material effects on operating results of a known trend in the form of an expected further decline in unit sales of mature products:

> While market conditions in general remained relatively unchanged in 1987, unit volumes declined 10% as the Company's older products, representing 40% of overall revenues, continue to approach the end of their life cycle. Unit volumes of the older products are expected to continue to decrease at an accelerated pace in the future and materially adversely affect revenues and operating profits.

In preparing the MD&A disclosure, registrants should focus on each of the specific categories of known data. For example, Item 303(a)(2)(i) requires a description of the registrant's material "commitments" for capital expenditures as of the end of the latest fiscal period. However, even where no legal commitments, contractual or otherwise, have been made, disclosure is required if material planned capital expenditures result from a known demand, as where the expenditures are necessary to a continuation of the registrant's current growth trend. Similarly, if the same registrant determines not to incur such expenditures, a known uncertainty would exist regarding continuation of the current growth trend. If the adverse effect on the registrant from discontinuation of the growth trend is reasonably likely to be material, disclosure is required. Disclosure of planned material expenditures is also required, for example, when such expenditures are necessary to support a new, publicly announced product or line of business.

In the following example, the registrant discusses planned capital expenditures, and related financing sources, necessary to maintain sales growth:

> The Company plans to open 20 to 25 new stores in fiscal 1988. As a result, the Company expects the trend of higher sales in fiscal 1988 to continue at approximately the same rate as in recent years. Management estimates that approximately $50 to $60 million will be required to finance the company's cost of opening such stores. In addition, the Company's expansion program will require increases in inventory of about $1 million per store, which are anticipated to be financed principally by trade credit. Funds required to finance the Company's store expansion program are expected to come primarily from new credit facilities with the remainder provided by funds generated from operations and increased lease financings. The Company recently entered into a new borrowing agreement with its primary bank, which provides for additional borrowings of up to $50 million for future expansion. The Company intends to seek additional credit facilities during fiscal 1988.
>
> * * *

Events that have already occurred or are anticipated often give rise to known uncertainties. For example, a registrant may know that a material government contract is about to expire. The registrant may be uncertain as to whether the contract will be renewed, but nevertheless would be able to assess facts relating to whether it will be renewed. More particularly, the registrant may know that a competitor has found a way to provide the same service or product at a price less than that charged by the registrant, or may have been advised by the government that the contract may not be renewed. The registrant also would have factual information relevant to the financial impact of non-renewal upon the registrant. In situations such as these, a registrant would have identified a known uncertainty reasonably likely to have material future effects on its financial condition or results of operations, and disclosure would be required.

In the following example, the registrant discloses the reasonably likely material effect of a known uncertainty regarding implementation of recently adopted legislation:

> The Company had no firm cash commitments as of December 31, 1987 for capital expenditures. However, in 1987, legislation was enacted which may require that certain vehicles used in the Company's business be equipped with specified safety equipment by the end of 1991. Pursuant to this legislation, regulations have been proposed which, if promulgated, would

require the expenditure by the company of approximately $30 million over a three-year period.

Where a trend, demand, commitment, event or uncertainty is known, management must make two assessments:

(1) Is the known trend, demand, commitment, event or uncertainty likely to come to fruition? If management determines that is not reasonably likely to occur, no disclosure is required.

(2) If management cannot make that determination, it must evaluate objectively the consequences of the known trend, demand, commitment, event or uncertainty, on the assumption that it will come to fruition. Disclosure is then required unless management determines that a material effect on the registrant's financial condition or results of operations is not reasonably likely to occur.[15]

Each final determination resulting from the assessments made by management must be objectively reasonable, viewed as of the time the determination is made * * *

---

1. *Significance.* In January 2020, the SEC proposed various amendments to Item 303. Among them was a proposal to codify certain of the Instructions in Item 303(a):

> We are also proposing to codify Commission guidance that states that a registrant should provide a narrative explanation of its financial statements that enables investors to see a registrant "through the eyes of management" into the description of MD&A objectives. We believe that emphasizing the purpose of MD&A at the outset of the Item will provide clarity and focus to registrants as they consider what information to discuss and analyze. Our intent is to facilitate a thoughtful discussion and analysis, and encourage management to disclose factors specific to the registrant's business, which management is in the best position to know, and underscore materiality as the overarching principle of MD&A. Our proposal is intended to serve as a reminder to registrants as they prepare their MD&A that the general purpose of the disclosure is to provide both a historical and prospective analysis of the registrant's financial condition and results of operations, with particular emphasis on the registrant's prospects for the future. This principles-based approach is also well-suited to elicit

---

[15] MD&A mandates disclosure of specified forward-looking information, and specifies its own standard for disclosure—i.e., reasonably likely to have a material effect. This specific standard governs the circumstances in which Item 303 requires disclosure. The probability/magnitude test for materiality approved by the Supreme Court in Basic, Inc. v. Levinson, 485 U.S. 224 (1988), is inapposite to Item 303 disclosure.

disclosure about complex and often rapidly evolving areas, without the need to continuously amend the text of the rule to impose bright-line or prescriptive requirements.[98]

MD&A disclosure is required in registration statements, the annual report on Form 10-K, and quarterly reports on Form 10-Q. Thus, the process of estimating the impact of trends, demands, commitments, events, and uncertainties that may have a material effect on an issuer's financial condition or results of operations is a constant and continuing one for publicly-held companies. Moreover, when MD&A disclosure is required, the SEC has said the disclosures must be "quantified to the extent reasonably practicable."[99] The Instructions to Item 303 state that "[t]he [MD&A] shall focus specifically on material events and uncertainties known to management that would cause reported financial information not to be necessarily indicative of future operating results or of future financial condition. This would include descriptions *and amounts* of (A) matters that would have an impact on future operations and have not had an impact in the past, and (B) matters that have had an impact on reported operations and are not expected to have an impact upon future operations" (emphasis added).[100]

2. *SEC Expansion of the MD&A's Role.* Responding to Enron and the wave of accounting irregularity cases in the late 1990s and early 2000s, in 2001, the Commission reminded registrants that, under existing MD&A requirements, a registrant should address the material implications of uncertainties associated with the methods, assumptions, and estimates underlying the registrant's critical accounting measurements. The SEC also encouraged companies to explain the effects of their critical accounting policies and the judgments made in applying them. In 2002, the Commission proposed rules requiring a discussion of accounting estimates a company made in applying its accounting policies and the initial adoption of an accounting policy that had a material impact on its financial presentation. Those rules were never adopted, although the SEC advised registrants that MD&A disclosure should consider accounting estimates or assumptions (i) where the nature of the estimates or assumptions was material due to the levels of subjectivity and judgment needed to account for highly uncertain matters or the susceptibility of such matters to change and (ii) where the impact of the estimates and assumptions on financial condition or operating performance was material.[101]

In January 2020, the SEC proposed new rules to explicitly require disclosure of critical accounting estimates, with the goal of "providing greater insight on the uncertainties involved in creating and applying an accounting policy and how significant accounting policies of registrants

---

[98] Securities Act Release No. 10750 (Jan. 30, 2020).
[99] See In the Matter of Caterpillar Inc., Exchange Act Release No. 30532 (Mar. 31, 1992).
[100] Instruction 3. to Item 303(a) of Regulation S–K under the 1933 Act.
[101] See Securities Act Release No. 8350 (Dec. 19, 2003).

faced with similar facts and circumstances may differ."[102] A "critical accounting estimate" involves a significant level of estimation uncertainty and has had or is reasonably likely to have a material impact on the registrant's financial condition or results of operations. For each estimate, registrants would be required to disclose, to the extent material, why the estimate is subject to uncertainty, how much each estimate has changed during the reporting period, and the sensitivity of the reported amounts to the material methods, assumptions, and estimates underlying the estimate's calculation. Further, companies will be required to update this information and disclose any material changes in estimates and their impact in their quarterly reports on Form 10-Q. Although this proposed change is far from revolutionary, it illustrates the lasting impact of corporate scandals on disclosure policy and suggests that a continuing accordion-like expansion of the MD&A is predictable.

3. *Principles-Based Approach to Disclosure.* In August 2020, the SEC amended Items 101, 103, and 105 of Regulation S-K relating to a registrant's description of its business, legal proceedings, and risk factors. The SEC adopting release explained that the amendments were intended to improve disclosures for investors and ease compliance burdens for companies by, among other things, adopting a principles-based approach to disclosure.[103] The amendments are part of a continued, incremental move by the SEC away from prescriptive disclosure requirements towards a more principles-based, registrant-specific approach to disclosure. In practice, this means a move towards a regime that requires each registrant to tailor disclosure to its unique circumstances, requiring that it (and its advisors) use judgment to evaluate the registrant's circumstances and disclose factors that are most specific to the registrant's business, with the goal of a more focused and thoughtful discussion and analysis.

4. *Private Litigation.* Because the MD&A uses its own unique test of materiality that departs from the probability/magnitude formula of Basic v. Levinson,[104] some courts have found that material departures from the requirements of Item 303 are not enough to support a private antifraud action.[105] That is, even if management is aware of known

---

[102] Securities Act Release No. 10750 (Jan. 30, 2020).

[103] The amendments also require new descriptions, where material to an understanding of the business, of (i) a company's "human capital resources" and (ii) "any human capital measures or objectives that the registrant focuses on in managing the business (such as, depending on the nature of the registrant's business and workforce, measures or objectives that address the development, attraction and retention of personnel)." Disclosures may relate to workforce diversity and compensation, health and safety, training and skills, and turnover rates. Each company will need to consider its industry and particular circumstances in determining what its human capital resources are and how to describe resources that are material to an understanding of its business.

[104] 485 U.S. 224 (1988).

[105] Compare Indiana Public Retirement Systems v. SAIC, Inc., 818 F.3d 85 (2d Cir. 2016), and Stratte-Mcclure v. Morgan Stanley, 776 F.3d 94 (2d Cir. 2015), where the Second Circuit found that a public company that omits disclosure required by Item 303 violates a duty to disclose under Rule 10b–5, *with* In re NVIDIA Securities Litigation, 768 F.3d 1046, 1054 (9th

adverse trends or uncertainties and fails to disclose them, this omission is not actionable under Rule 10b–5—unless, at a minimum, the trend or uncertainty would have been material under the *Basic* standard. More broadly, some courts have said that the failure to disclose a forecast of future events is not actionable under the federal securities laws. More modestly, others have simply held that the failure to reveal inconsistent internal forecasts is insufficient to demonstrate scienter.[106]

5. *SEC Enforcement.* Nonetheless, the SEC can enforce its MD&A requirement, particularly by administrative enforcement proceedings. In In the Matter of Caterpillar Inc.,[107] the SEC brought an administrative proceeding against Caterpillar under § 21C of the 1934 Act for failing to comply with § 13(a) of the 1934 Act, and Rules 13a–1 and 13a–13 thereunder, based on the following facts: In its Form 10-K for 1989, Caterpillar failed to disclose that 23% of its net profits were attributable to its Brazilian subsidiary ("CBSA"). This contribution by CBSA to Caterpillar's overall earnings was hidden by Caterpillar's consolidated accounting system; also, several non-operating items of income (involving mainly currency translations and tax loss carryforwards) substantially increased CBSA's earnings for 1989. At the same time, hyperinflation in Brazil was leading to dramatic political changes that made CBSA's future ability to contribute to Caterpillar's 1990 earnings highly uncertain. By June 1990, a new Brazilian austerity program indicated to Caterpillar's management that CBSA would suffer substantial losses. After this was publicly announced, Caterpillar's stock dropped by 9%. The Commission found that Caterpillar had failed to comply with Item 303 by failing to disclose the nature and extent of CBSA's contribution to Caterpillar's earnings and by failing to indicate the known uncertainty surrounding CBSA's ability to continue to make its past contribution (which uncertainty had been clearly recognized by Caterpillar's management).

While securities analysts have largely welcomed the SEC's new insistence on disclosure (and quantification) of known trends and uncertainties, some academic commentators are skeptical. Professor Edmund Kitch has argued that these heightened standards deprive the issuer of proprietary information and permit its business rivals to gain significant competitive advantages over it:

> It is impossible for a management to prepare a "good" MD&A disclosure—that is, a disclosure that truly achieves the objectives of the required disclosure—without revealing a good deal about what it thinks about its businesses, the markets in

---

Cir. 2014), and In re VeriFone Securities Litigation, 11 F.3d 865, 870 (9th Cir. 1993), where the Ninth Circuit found that Item 303 does not create a duty to disclose for purposes of Rule 10b–5.

[106] See, e.g., In re Facebook, Inc., 986 F.Supp.2d 487, 507–08 (S.D.N.Y. 2013); In re Salesforce.com Securities Litigation, 2005 WL 6327481 at 7–9 (N.D. Cal. 2005).

[107] See Exchange Act Release No. 30532 (Mar. 31, 1992).

which its businesses operate, and how those markets will evolve.[108]

How great was the competitive advantage that competitors could have gained if Caterpillar complied with Item 303? Still, Professor Kitch's broader point is worthy of attention: A public disclosure system, particularly one that requires projections as to future profitability, informs not only investors but also competitors. Nevertheless, even if public disclosure may harm competitiveness, diversified investors—who are more likely to own a portfolio of stocks that includes shares of the registrant and its competitors—could benefit from the disclosure. Does this counterbalance the potentially negative impact of MD&A disclosure on competition?

Problems

PROBLEM 3-3

Fifteen years ago, Ajax Corp. sold its chemical division to Achilles Industries, and the latter gave Ajax a broad release from any liability to Achilles for environmental problems or future clean-up costs. The chemical division's principal site, however, has proven to be a toxic minefield and was subsequently made into a Superfund site. Possibly as a negotiating tactic in its battles with the environmental authorities, Achilles has disclosed it may be forced to file for bankruptcy due to the costs associated with cleaning up this site. Ajax doubts that Achilles will file for bankruptcy, but it is aware that, if Achilles does, it could be named as a "potentially responsible party" and forced to share in the clean-up costs. If it were forced to contribute, Ajax's share could be between $25 and $60 million (and the latter number would be material to Ajax), but it cannot really estimate these costs because it is not able to visit the site. Ajax is also unable to make any objective prediction as to whether Achilles will file for bankruptcy or whether the environmental authorities will sue Ajax in such an event. Ajax must soon file its annual report on Form 10-K. Must it disclose anything about its contingent liability for the Superfund site, even if it believes the possibility that Achilles will file for bankruptcy to be only around 40%?

PROBLEM 3-4

Morgan Financial Services, Inc. has a shareholder-approved qualified stock option plan that authorizes its Compensation Committee to grant options to management to purchase up to 30 million of shares over a defined period. The plan requires that all options be granted at the market price of the stock on the date of grant by the Compensation Committee. On July 1, 2002, the Committee granted an option to its CEO, Dudley Doright, to purchase 1 million shares at the then-market price of $30 per share. However, one week before, on June 24, 2002, Morgan's stock price had fallen to $27 per share (its lowest for the year). In granting the stock option, the

---

[108] Kitch, The Theory and Practice of Securities Disclosure, 61 Brook.L.Rev. 763, 859 (1995).

Committee never discussed what the current price was, and did not date the corporate minutes, leaving this task to Morgan's Assistant Secretary. The Assistant Secretary, however, backdated the option to June 24th (and, hence, to $27 per share). Five years later, in 2007, these details were uncovered as part of an overall review of stock option practices shortly before Doright's stock option expired. As it turns out, Morgan's stock price fell in 2003 to $25 per share (before Doright's stock option vested and became exercisable), and the stock price never again reached $27. Doright's counsel argued that the whole matter is immaterial because there was "not a dollar's loss or dilution to any shareholder." But, while no longer CEO, Doright remained as Chairman of the Board. Was the option-backdating material? What if Doright had retired from all corporate offices in 2006?

b. *Note on "Plain English Disclosure"*

In 1998, the SEC revised Rules 421, 461, and 481 of Regulation C to require registrants to employ "plain English" in writing certain sections of the registration statement and prospectus. These new rules followed a several-year pilot project that convinced the SEC that simpler, more readable prospectuses were feasible. Technically, only the cover pages, summary, and risk factors sections are covered by the "plain English" rule (Rule 421(d)), but the new communications philosophy is now strongly encouraged by the SEC's staff. In determining the date on which a registration statement will become effective, the SEC may refuse to accelerate the effective date "[w]here there has not been a bona fide effort to make the prospectus reasonably concise, readable, and in compliance with the plain English requirements . . . in order to facilitate an understanding of the information in the prospectus."[109] Although retail investors have applauded the "plain English" rule, it may sometimes make it difficult for the issuer to describe highly complex matters to sophisticated investors. Disclosure policy necessarily involves tradeoffs and can generate a reasonable dispute over whose interests deserve priority.

In the adopting release, the Commission, itself, was plain and concise about the changes it expected:

Securities Act Release No. 7497
Securities and Exchange Commission.
January 28, 1998.

Plain English Disclosure

* * *

Full and fair disclosure is one of the cornerstones of investor protection under the federal securities laws. If a prospectus fails to communicate information clearly, investors do not receive that basic

---

[109] See Rule 461(b)(1) under the 1933 Act.

protection. Yet, prospectuses today often use complex, legalistic language that is foreign to all but financial or legal experts. The proliferation of complex transactions and securities magnifies this problem. A major challenge facing the securities industry and its regulators is assuring that financial and business information reaches investors in a form they can read and understand.

In response to this challenge, we undertake today a sweeping revision of how issuers must disclose information to investors. This new package of rules will change the face of every prospectus used in registered public offerings of securities. Prospectuses will be simpler, clearer, more useful, and we hope, more widely read.

First, the new rules require issuers to write and design the cover page, summary, and risk factors section of their prospectuses in plain English. Specifically, in these sections, issuers will have to use: short sentences; definite, concrete, everyday language; active voice; tabular presentation of complex information; no legal or business jargon; and no multiple negatives. Issuers will also have to design these sections to make them inviting to the reader. In response to comments, the new rules will not require issuers to limit the length of the summary, limit the number of risk factors, or prioritize risk factors.

Second, we are giving guidance to issuers on how to comply with the current rule that requires the entire prospectus to be clear, concise, and understandable. Our goal is to purge the entire document of legalese and repetition that blur important information investors need to know.

* * *

III. *Rules on How to Prepare Prospectuses*

A. Plain English Rule—Rule 421(d)

Rule 421(d), the plain English rule, requires you to prepare the front portion of the prospectus in plain English. You must use plain English principles in the organization, language, and design of the front and back cover pages, the summary, and the risk factors section. Also, when drafting the language in these front parts of the prospectus, you must comply substantially with six basic principles:

- Short sentences;
- Definite, concrete, everyday language;
- Active voice;
- Tabular presentation or bullet lists for complex material, whenever possible;
- No legal jargon or highly technical business terms; and
- No multiple negatives.

A number of comment letters noted that our rule dictates how to write the front of the prospectus. They are correct. We have seen marked improvement in the clarity of disclosure when pilot participants have used these widely recognized, basic principles of clear writing. We believe the benefits to investors support mandating the use of these writing principles for the front of the prospectus.

In addition, you must design the cover page, summary, and risk factors section to make them easy to read. You must format the text and design the document to highlight important information for investors. The rule permits you to use pictures, charts, graphics, and other design features to make the prospectus easier to understand.

B. Clear, Concise, and Understandable Prospectuses—Rule 421(b)

Rule 421(b) currently requires that the entire prospectus be clear, concise, and understandable. This requirement is in addition to the plain English rule we are adopting, which applies only to the front of the prospectus.

We are adopting, as proposed, amendments to Rule 421(b). These amendments provide guidance on how to prepare a prospectus that is clear, concise, and understandable. The amendments set out four general writing techniques that you must follow and list four conventions to avoid when drafting the prospectus. As several comment letters noted, these amendments codify our earlier interpretive advice.

Amended Rule 421(b) requires you to use the following techniques when writing the entire prospectus:

- Present information in clear, concise sections, paragraphs, and sentences. Whenever possible, use short explanatory sentences and bullet lists;
- Use descriptive headings and subheadings;
- Avoid frequent reliance on glossaries or defined terms as the primary means of explaining information in the prospectus. Define terms in a glossary or other section of the document only if the meaning is unclear from the context. Use a glossary only if it facilitates understanding of the disclosure; and
- Avoid legal and highly technical business terminology.

The new note to Rule 421(b) provides guidance on how to comply with the rule's general requirements. The note lists the following drafting conventions to avoid because they make your document harder to read:

- Legalistic or overly complex presentations that make the substance of the disclosure difficult to understand;
- Vague boilerplate explanations that are readily subject to differing interpretations;
- Complex information copied directly from legal documents without any clear and concise explanation of the provision(s); and

- Repetitive disclosure that increases the size of the document, but does not enhance the quality of the information.

C. Comments on Proposed Amendments to Rule 421(b) and Rule 421(d)

Several comment letters stated that we should permit public companies to use legal and technical business terminology. The letters noted, for example, that high technology companies must use technical terms to distinguish their products or services from others in the industry. We recognize that certain business terms may be necessary to describe your operations properly. But, you should avoid using excessive technical jargon that only your competitors or an industry specialist can understand.

You should write the disclosure in your prospectus for investors. When you use many highly technical terms, the investor must learn your dictionary of terms to understand your disclosure. If technical terms are unavoidable, you should make every effort to explain their meaning the first time you use them.

* * *

---

c. *The Sarbanes-Oxley Act and Post-Enron Disclosure*

The bankruptcy of Enron in late 2001 proved a catalyst for change, both for the markets and the SEC. In particular, as the SEC recognized, Enron's collapse demonstrated significant shortcomings in the SEC's existing disclosure system, mainly as it related to the ability of issuers to (1) hide off-balance sheet liabilities that significantly reduced the issuer's liquidity and capital resources; (2) engage in trading activities involving non-exchange-traded derivatives, where the issuer could inflate its earnings depending upon the "fair value" it assigned to those contracts; and (3) conceal relationships and transactions with related parties. Since the Financial Accounting Standards Board, not the SEC, determines "generally accepted accounting principles" ("GAAP"), the SEC could not respond to Enron by tightening GAAP itself. Instead, the Commission turned to the MD&A to better disclose the impact of off-balance-sheet and derivatives transactions.[110] In addition, the Commission decided that its disclosure system had become "antiquated" and needed to be strengthened by a more immediate obligation to disclose material information on a "real-time" basis.

To do so, the Commission proposed an overhaul of Form 8-K, which called for accelerated disclosure of a significantly larger number of

---

[110] See Securities Act Release No. 8056 (Jan. 25, 2002). It should be emphasized here that the Commission did not require the disclosure of material information as soon as it became known, but rather mandated new and earlier reporting dates for certain specified material events.

transactions, in many cases within two business days after the transaction.[111] Responding to the delayed disclosures in Enron, the Commission proposed that issuers would be required to disclose on new Form 8-K, on an expedited basis, directors' and executive officers' transactions in company equity securities, transactions outside the ordinary course of the issuer's business, and changes in critical accounting policies.[112] Similarly, the due dates for Form 10-K and Form 10-Q would be accelerated, depending on the market capitalization of the issuer, to 60 days after the end of the fiscal year (in the case of Form 10-K) and 30 days after the end of the first three quarters (in the case of Form 10-Q). Lastly, the Commission required a company's chief executive officer and chief financial officer to certify, to the best of their knowledge, that the information contained in each annual and quarterly report is true in all important respects and contains all information about the company of which they are aware that they believe important to a reasonable investor.[113]

Congress, however, did not wait for the SEC to adopt its own proposed rules. Instead, it legislated them in substance, in some cases going considerably further than the SEC had proposed. Specifically, the Sarbanes-Oxley Act of 2002 did the following to require increased disclosures in response to specific abuses that came to light after the Enron scandal:

1. *Executive Certifications.* Section 302 of the Sarbanes-Oxley Act directed the SEC to adopt rules requiring the chief executive officer and the chief financial officer to certify they have reviewed each annual and quarterly report and concluded, "based on the officer's knowledge," that the report does not contain a material misstatement or omission and "the financial statements, and other financial information included in the report, fairly present in all material respects the financial condition and results of operations of the issuer as of, and for, the periods presented in the report."[114] In addition, these officers must certify the adequacy of the issuer's internal financial controls.[115] Adding suspenders to § 302's belt, § 906 of the Sarbanes-Oxley Act amended the federal criminal code to require additional certification by the same two executive officers regarding periodic reports containing financial statements and made it a felony to make knowingly false statements in that certification.[116]

2. *"Real-Time" Issuer Disclosures.* Section 409 of the Sarbanes-Oxley Act mandates that reporting companies "shall disclose to the public

---

[111] Securities Act Release No. 8089 (Apr. 23, 2002).

[112] See SEC Press Release No. 2002–22 (Feb. 13, 2002) and Securities Act Release No. 8089 (Apr. 23, 2002).

[113] Exchange Act Release No. 46079 (June 14, 2002).

[114] See §§ 302(a)(2) and (a)(3) of the Sarbanes-Oxley Act.

[115] See §§ 302(a)(4) and (a)(5) of the Sarbanes-Oxley Act.

[116] See 18 U.S.C. § 1350. This section specifies a fine of up to $1 million and a criminal sentence of up to ten years to knowingly provide a false certification and elevates the penalty to a $5 million fine and a 20-year sentence for a "willfully" false certification.

on a rapid and current basis such additional information concerning material changes in the financial condition or operations of the issuer, in plain English, which may include trend and qualitative information and graphic presentations, as the Commission determines . . . is necessary or useful for the protection of investors and in the public interest."[117] In response, the SEC amended Form 8-K not to require the issuance of earnings releases or similar announcements, but if made (typically on a quarterly and annual basis), to require such releases and announcements to be filed on Form 8-K. Public disclosure of financial information for a completed fiscal period in a presentation that is made orally, telephonically, by webcast, by broadcast, or by similar means is not required to be filed if (1) the presentation occurs within 48 hours of a related release or announcement that is filed on Form 8-K; (2) the presentation is broadly accessible to the public; and (3) the information in the webcast is posted on the company's website.[118]

The SEC amended Form 8-K again the following year, among other things, to add or expand items in the Form and shorten the Form 8-K filing deadline for most items to four business days after the occurrence of an event requiring disclosure on Form 8-K.[119] Among the new items, Items 2.03 and 2.04 responded to some of the accounting problems that precipitated the Enron collapse. Item 2.03 requires disclosure of a direct financial obligation that is material to the company. More importantly, if the company becomes directly or contingently liable for a material obligation arising out of an off-balance-sheet arrangement, the company is also required to disclose that arrangement. Item 2.04 requires the company to file a Form 8-K if a triggering event causes an increase or acceleration of a direct financial obligation that is material to the company. Likewise, a Form 8-K must be filed if a triggering event causes an off-balance-sheet arrangement to increase or accelerate, or causes a company's contingent obligation under an off-balance-sheet arrangement to become a direct financial obligation, and the consequences are material to the company.

The SEC limited some specific disclosure requirements that were proposed—but, even if a specific item was not affirmatively required, the SEC reminded registrants of the catch-all need to ensure that disclosures that are made are accurate: "We once again . . . remind companies that any disclosure made in a report on Form 8-K must include all other material information, if any, that is necessary to make the required disclosure, in the light of the circumstances under which it is made, not misleading."[120]

3. *Off-Balance Sheet Items and Pro Forma Figures.* Section 401 of the Sarbanes-Oxley Act added a new § 13(j) to the 1934 Act requiring the

---

[117] This provision is codified as § 13(*l*) of the 1934 Act.
[118] See Item 2.02 of Form 8-K under the 1934 Act.
[119] See Securities Act Release No. 8400 (Aug. 2004).
[120] Id.

SEC to adopt rules requiring that Form 10-Ks and Form 10-Qs "disclose all material off-balance sheet transactions, arrangements, obligations (including contingent obligations), and other relationships of the issuer with unconsolidated entities or other persons, that may have a material current or future effect on financial condition, changes in financial condition, results of operations, liquidity, capital expenditures, capital resources, or significant components of revenues or expenses." In response, the SEC introduced new requirements to disclose off-balance sheet arrangements and amended its MD&A requirements to explicitly require each registrant to explain these off-balance sheet arrangements in a separately captioned subsection.[121]

A related problem is that issuers may publish data that are not directly related to their audited financial disclosures or, in a market boom, that emphasize growing revenues while ignoring a corresponding rise in costs. The result can be projections based on "adjusted," "normalized," or "underlying" earnings—typically profits after the company determines that certain expenses are unusual or one-off items and so eliminates them in presenting, for example, "adjusted" earnings to investors. Critics describe such one-sided measures (of which the best known is "EBITDA"—earnings before interest, taxes, depreciation, and amortization) as "earnings before the bad stuff," and, standing alone, they argue, these projected earnings may mislead investors.

To address this problem, the Sarbanes-Oxley Act required the SEC to adopt rules requiring that pro forma financial information in SEC reports or press releases be presented so as to (1) not contain a material misstatement or omission, or otherwise be materially misleading, and (2) reconcile such pro forma information "with the financial condition and results of operations of the company under generally accepted accounting principles."[122] In response, the SEC promulgated Regulation G and Item 10(e) of Regulation S–K under the 1933 Act. They require that, when a non-GAAP financial measure is used, the issuer must include a presentation of the most directly comparable GAAP financial measure and a reconciliation of the two figures.[123]

This continues to be an area of interest for the SEC. In 1996, approximately 60% of Standard & Poor's 500 companies (a portfolio of 500 large companies listed on U.S. stock exchanges) reported at least one non-GAAP earnings-per-share figure; more recently, that amount has increased to 97%.[124] Consequently, the SEC continues to caution companies to carefully consider the usefulness of non-GAAP measures to investors, as well as their accuracy and completeness. When commenting on filed registration statements, the SEC staff's most common concern

---

[121] See Securities Act Release No. 8182 (Jan. 28, 2003).
[122] See § 401(b) of the Sarbanes-Oxley Act.
[123] See Exchange Act Release No. 47226 (Jan. 23, 2003).
[124] See McKeon, Audit Analytics, Long-Term Trends in Non-GAAP Disclosures: A Three-Year Overview (Oct. 10, 2018).

around non-GAAP metrics has been that the registrant presented them with undue prominence.[125] Several recent SEC enforcement actions have also focused on prominence, as well as on whether the non-GAAP disclosures were materially misleading.

4. *Internal Control Report.* Section 404(a) of the Sarbanes-Oxley Act mandates the SEC to develop a new "internal control report," which must be included in each Form 10-K and must assess the effectiveness of management's internal controls over financial reporting. Then, under § 404(b), the company's outside auditor must "attest to, and report on," this assessment.

Although not anticipated at the time the Sarbanes-Oxley Act was passed, § 404 proved to be the most costly and controversial provision of the Act, because the Public Company Accounting Oversight Board (which, subject to SEC oversight, establishes auditing and related professional practice standards for registered public accounting firms in preparing and issuing audit reports) interpreted § 404(b) to require a full-scale audit of a reporting issuer's internal controls before the auditor could make its attestation. Under its Auditing Standard No. 2,[126] the auditor was required to test and evaluate both the design and the operating effectiveness of a company's internal controls before it could be satisfied with management's assessment, which proved to be expensive. Smaller companies and foreign issuers particularly protested the application of § 404 to them and largely escaped coverage.

The dilemma is that internal controls tend to be weakest in small-cap companies, but the cost of full compliance may be prohibitive for them. Thus, while the Dodd-Frank Act subsequently tightened other financial controls, it effectively exempted issuers with a market capitalization of $75 million or less from the obligation of having their auditors attest to their managements' evaluation of their internal controls.[127] Even this step did not end the downsizing of § 404. To spur job creation, the Jumpstart Our Business Startups ("JOBS") Act, passed in 2012, exempts "emerging growth companies" from § 404(b).[128] Thus, § 404(a) requires management to review its internal controls in the case of an emerging growth company, but there is no obligation of the auditor to audit the internal controls of such a company.

---

[125] See Hallas & Usvyatsky, Audit Analytics, Trends in SEC Non-GAAP Comment Letters 2016–2018 (Oct. 16, 2018).

[126] See Exchange Act Release No. 49884 (June 23, 2004). This auditing standard was significantly relaxed in 2007 with the adoption of Auditing Standard No. 5. See Exchange Act Release No. 56152 (Jul. 27, 2007). Nonetheless, an evaluation by the auditor of the company's internal controls was still required.

[127] See § 989G of the Dodd-Frank Act (adding a new § 404(c) to the Sarbanes-Oxley Act, exempting issuers with less than $75 million in market capitalization from the attestation requirement).

[128] See § 103 of the JOBS Act (amending § 404(b) of the Sarbanes-Oxley Act). The term "emerging growth company" is defined in § 2(a)(19) of the 1933 Act. In a nutshell, it is a company with total annual gross revenues of less than $1 billion, but loses this designation upon the occurrence of events listed in § 2(a)(19).

5. *SEC Review of Public Companies.* Section 408 of the Sarbanes-Oxley Act requires the SEC to review disclosures made by reporting companies "on a regular and systematic basis," at least once every three years. This appears to have been a response to published reports that the financially-pressed SEC had not been able to review Enron's filings for several years.

As the accounting rules applicable to public companies have become more complex, the JOBS Act's provisions, initially directing the SEC staff to permit confidential review of a proposed registration statement by an emerging growth company before it was filed,[129] has been extended by the SEC to all IPOs and secondary offerings of publicly-traded stocks in the first year after an IPO. By submitting on a confidential basis, the issuer can learn the SEC's position and revise its disclosures—or simply choose not to go forward with a public offering (perhaps due to concerns over the types of information that would be disclosed to competitors, as described earlier)—before its registration statement is released to the public.

6. *Code of Ethics.* Section 406 of the Sarbanes-Oxley Act requires a reporting company to disclose "whether or not, and if not, the reason therefor, such issuer has adopted a code of ethics for senior financial officers." Any change or waiver of this code must be disclosed on Form 8-K by filing such Form, dissemination by the internet, or other electronic means.

6. DISCLOSURE POLICY AND THE DEBATE OVER THE EFFICIENT MARKET

At times, both the SEC[130] and the Supreme Court[131] have characterized the market for publicly-traded securities as "efficient." In so doing, they are alluding to a fundamental concept known as the Efficient Capital Market Hypothesis ("ECMH"). The central and least disputed claim of the ECMH is that available information about securities traded in the principal securities markets is impounded into stock prices with sufficient speed that even sophisticated investors cannot systematically profit by trading on newly-available information. Thus, the most common definition of an efficient market is that prices in

---

[129] See § 6(e) of the 1933 Act.

[130] In adopting its integrated disclosure system, the Commission acknowledged that its deregulatory policy was premised on the assumption that "investors are protected by the market's analysis of information about certain companies which is widely available . . . and that such analysis is reflected in the price of the securities offered." Securities Act Release No. 6235 (1980). See also Securities Act Release No. 6383 (1982). For an analysis of the differences between the standard ECMH and the SEC's more qualified acceptance of it, see Pickholz & Horahan, The SEC's Version of the Efficient Market Theory and Its Impact on Securities Law Liabilities, 39 Wash. & Lee L.Rev. 943 (1982).

[131] See Halliburton Co. v. Erica P. John Fund, Inc., 573 U.S. 258, 268 (2014) (affirming the presumption that market prices reflect all publicly-available information, including material misrepresentations); see also Basic Inc. v. Levinson, 485 U.S. 224 (1988).

such a market "fully reflect" all "available" information.[132] But what do "fully reflect" and "available" mean? A clearer definition is that a market is efficient with respect to specific information "if prices act *as if* everyone knows the information."[133] That is, the security's price is the same as the price that would exist if everyone had complete information, even though it is demonstrable that all do not have the same information.

Not even the strongest proponent of the ECMH argues that the market's judgment will always (or even usually) prove correct in the long run. Too much uncertainty is inherent in economic life for this assertion to be true. Rather, the central claim of the ECMH is that consensus valuation of an efficient market will be the best-possible, least-biased measure of value at any given time. The ECMH developed historically from the empirical observation that traders cannot exploit "available information" to develop profitable trading or arbitrage strategies. Still, we know that some traders—i.e., those using "inside" information—do profit, and thus, some forms of non-public information can be successfully exploited. Accordingly, one must carefully specify what one means by "available information."

In a much-cited article, Professor Eugene Fama distinguished three different versions or ways of interpreting the ECMH: "weak," "semi-strong," and "strong."[134] The "weak" form of the theory claims only that the history of securities prices provides no useful information to the investor; that is, knowing that a stock has risen three points in the last hour or day will not tell the investor whether the next price movement will be positive or negative. The "semi-strong" theory makes the same assessment about publicly-released information (such as the information contained in SEC filings). Finally, the "strong" form of the theory hypothesizes that even non-public information is reflected in share price. As Fama demonstrated, some empirical studies support each of these interpretations, but the weight of the evidence underlying the "semi-strong" version has accumulated to the point that there is no serious challenge today to its claim that the market absorbs and reflects new information with great speed.

But, if so, so what? The policy implications of the ECMH to securities regulation and disclosure policy are more controversial than the theory. One implication of the ECMH is that stock prices will move unpredictably—or, in the jargon, will follow a "random walk." This implication follows because, if stock prices incorporate all available

---

[132] See Gilson & Kraakman, The Mechanisms of Market Efficiency, 70 Va.L.Rev. 549, 554 (1984).

[133] See Beaver, Market Efficiency, 56 Acct.Rev. 23, 35 (1981). For an even more precise definition—that the market is efficient with respect to a specific information set if revealing that information to all traders would not alter stock prices or the composition of stock portfolios—see Latham, Informational Efficiency and Information Subsets, 41 J.Fin. 39, 40 (1986).

[134] Fama, Efficient Capital Markets: A Review of the Theory and Empirical Work, 25 J.Fin. 383 (1970).

information, they will move only when truly new (i.e., unforeseen) information becomes available. This tendency for stock prices to move unpredictably was observed early in the 1900s,[135] and the formal theory of market efficiency is essentially an attempt to explain such random movements.

The next implication is far more debatable. Many read the ECMH to imply that, in an efficient market, "every security's price equals its investment value at all times."[136] This claim that there can be no divergence between the corporation's "intrinsic" or "investment value" and its market price, because securities prices incorporate all available information, is premised on additional assumptions that are not always carefully specified. These additional assumptions include: (1) all investors are equally rational; (2) all investors have relatively costless access to the available information; and (3) arbitrage opportunities will be exploited until any evident disparity between "investment value" and market price is eliminated.[137] Others challenge these assumptions on the grounds that the market is "speculatively efficient" (in the sense that its movements cannot be predicted) but not "allocatively efficient" (in the sense that there is no divergence between "investment" and "market" value).[138] In principle, when all the preconditions of the formal model are satisfied, there should be an identity between asset and securities values,[139] but few believe the theoretical conditions for such an identity actually exist.

Researchers have found evidence that conflicts (or co-exists in considerable tension) with the idea that the market is "fundamentally efficient" (i.e., that securities prices represent the intrinsic value of the company). One such body of evidence appears to find excessive volatility in the stock markets.[140] Markets seem to overreact to new information, and securities prices adjust only gradually to such announcements, swinging back and forth before reaching a new equilibrium level.[141] Also, many of the securities traded on Nasdaq may simply trade outside the range of the efficient market, because many of these securities are not widely followed by securities analysts.[142] Thus, momentum trading—in

---

[135] See Bachlier, Theory of Speculation (1900), reprinted in P. Cootner, The Random Character of Stock Prices 17 (1964). For a general history of the efficient markets literature, see LeRoy, Efficient Capital Markets and Martingales, 27 J.Econ.Lit. 1583 (1989).

[136] See Alexander & Sharpe, Fundamentals of Investments 67 (1985).

[137] Id.

[138] See Gordon & Kornhauser, Efficient Markets, Costly Information, and Securities Research, 60 N.Y.U.L.Rev. 761 (1985); see also Wang, Some Arguments That the Stock Market Is Not Efficient, 19 U.C. Davis L.Rev. 341 (1986).

[139] See Gilson & Kraakman, The Mechanisms of Market Efficiency, 70 Va.L.Rev. 549, 558 (1984).

[140] See Campbell and Shiller, The Dividend Price Ratio and Expectations of Future Dividends and Discount Factors, 1 Rev. Fin. Stud. 192 (1988).

[141] See Bernard & Thomas, Post-Earnings Announcement Drifts: Delayed Price Response or Risk Premium?, 27 J. Acct. Res. 1 (1989).

[142] See Hong et al., Bad News Travels Slowly: Size, Analyst Coverage and the Profitability of Momentum Strategies, 55 J. Fin. 265 (2000).

other words, trading based on recent prices as an indicator of future prices—may be possible in such a market, at least for a while.

Beyond these empirical objections, a powerful theoretical case can be made that the preconditions for market efficiency cannot fully exist. Financial economists use the term "efficiency paradox" to refer to a fundamental conflict between the need of securities analysts and other market professionals for an acceptable return on their investment in acquiring and verifying securities information, and the impossibility of such a return if the securities market is perfectly efficient. Inevitably, information collection is costly, and such activities will be reduced or suspended if a positive return is not obtainable; at that point, the market becomes less efficient. As a result, Professors Sanford Grossman and Joseph Stiglitz, both noted economists, have argued that a perfectly efficient market is impossible.[143] Rather, the market may experience oscillating cycles of near-perfect efficiency, followed by relative inefficiency, as traders suspend the costly pursuit of new information when returns from such activity fade, but then later resume their search for new information once the market becomes less efficient. Ultimately, they argue, some "equilibrium level of disequilibrium" will be attained—meaning that the market will absorb information quickly, but not so quickly as to deny professionals a "normal" profit.

Courts, however, have sometimes bordered on reading the ECMH to imply that stocks will always trade at their investment value. The leading example is Wielgos v. Commonwealth Edison Co.,[144] in which an investor brought a class action on behalf of the purchasers of the stock of Commonwealth Edison issued under a shelf registration statement on Form S-3. The plaintiff alleged that projections made by the issuer as to when certain nuclear generators would be operational and approved by the Nuclear Regulatory Commission were materially misleading. Writing for the Seventh Circuit, Judge Easterbrook acknowledged that the projections were based on plainly unrealistic assumptions, but still affirmed the grant of summary judgment for the defendants because, he concluded, market professionals must have known the projections were wrong. The opinion opens with an observation that suggests the market can seldom be fooled:

> The Securities and Exchange Commission believes that markets correctly value the securities of well-followed firms, so that new sales may rely on information that has been digested and expressed in the security's price.[145]

---

[143] See Grossman & Stiglitz, On the Impossibility of Informationally Efficient Markets, 70 Am.Econ.Rev. 393 (1980).

[144] 892 F.2d 509 (7th Cir. 1989). For a similar view that an efficient market will see-through misleading projections, see Cooke v. Manufactured Homes, Inc., 998 F.2d 1256, 1262–63 (4th Cir. 1993); In re Apple Computer Securities Litigation, 886 F.2d 1109, 1116 (9th Cir. 1989); In re Convergent Technologies Securities Litigation, 721 F.Supp. 1133 (N.D.Cal. 1988), aff'd, 948 F.2d 507 (9th Cir. 1991).

[145] 892 F.2d at 510.

It is doubtful that the Commission believes this (it probably accepts only the more modest conclusion that the costs of requiring additional disclosure by publicly-held firms, already subject to the 1934 Act's continuous disclosure system, outweighs the benefits). More importantly, economic theory does not necessarily make this strong of a claim. Fischer Black, a prominent financial economist, has argued that a reasonable definition of an efficient market is "one in which price is within a factor of 2 of value, i.e., the price is more than half of value and less than twice value."[146] If this test defines "efficiency," then misleading predictions and statements about events or matters, where it is difficult or costly for the market to verify the provided information, may also be impounded into stock prices. In short, the market may quickly reflect misinformation as well as accurate information. As a result, it is important to focus in more detail in this section on:

(1) The forces or mechanisms that make the market efficient—and how the law can facilitate or retard them;

(2) The critiques of market efficiency—are there other explanations that can explain the same phenomena of seemingly random price movements?; and

(3) Does the theory really dictate policy consequences? Are there realistic policy options that truly hinge on its validity?

A. WHAT MAKES THE MARKET EFFICIENT?: THE ROLE OF UNDERWRITERS

While economists have concentrated on measuring the market's efficiency in responding to new information, legal scholars have focused more on understanding the forces that enhance or inhibit market efficiency. In one well-known article, Professors Ronald Gilson and Reinier Kraakman argue that the level of market efficiency is essentially determined by two factors: (1) the relative cost of acquiring, processing, and verifying different types of information, and (2) the initial distribution of the information among traders in the market. Thus, they claim, some types of information that are more costly to acquire or difficult to verify may not be impounded by the market into price as quickly as, for example, the financial information in SEC filings, which not only comes partially verified by the issuer's public accountants, but is also distributed widely to the entire market. Moreover, cost determines the distribution of a specific type of information among traders. The lower the cost of acquiring it, the wider its distribution in the market, and, ultimately, the more effective the market will be at impounding it into price. Based on this starting point, they then examine how the market attempts to economize on the costs of information acquisition and

---

[146] Black, Noise, 41 J.Fin. 529, 533 (1986).

verification. In particular, they propose a different way of understanding the role of the investment banker.

Excerpt from: Ronald J. Gilson and Reinier H. Kraakman

The Mechanisms of Market Efficiency
70 Virginia Law Review 549, 612–21 (1984).

* * *

The core of our analysis, then, is that the cost of information critically determines market efficiency because it dictates not only the amount of information attending a particular security but also the distribution of that information among traders, which in turn determines the operative capital market mechanism. This focus on information costs also identifies the invisible hand that moves the market toward greater informational efficiency. Information market incentives lead to economizing on information costs and thus to the availability of more effective capital market mechanisms. The result is an integrated understanding of the mechanisms of market efficiency that we believe provides both theoretical insights and new opportunities for employing the market efficiency concept to inform regulatory policy.

In this section we apply our synthesis of the operation of the capital and information markets to * * * explain the investment banker's role in increasing the efficiency of the market's response. * * *

A. *The Role of the Investment Banker*

* * *

Investment bankers are typically seen as having two principal functions in the distribution of securities. First, investment bankers serve as distributors for the issuer, providing the sales force and facilities necessary to sell the securities to the public. Second, they provide a form of risk sharing or insurance, at least in connection with "firm commitment underwriting," that relieves the issuer of some of the risks inherent in the offering of a security. But even taken together, these two functions do not entirely explain the modern underwriter's role. While distribution is obviously an important function, a sizable percentage of the total underwriting compensation goes to participants who do not actually engage in selling the security. Nor does risk sharing account for the remainder of the modern underwriting function, since the underwriter need bear little risk even in a firm commitment underwriting. In a typical firm commitment underwriting, the price that the underwriter pays to the issuer is not set, and the underwriter is not committed to purchase the securities, until approximately twenty-four hours before the registration statement is declared effective and the public sale of the securities commences. The issuer thus bears virtually all risk of changed market conditions prior to the commencement of sale.

Moreover, the practice of soliciting "indications of interest"—non-binding statements of intent to buy the securities—from prospective purchasers during the period between the filing of the registration statement and the commencement of sales further reduces the risk that the securities will be priced too high.

The only risk that then remains for the underwriter to "share" is that of a change in market conditions during the short period, typically no more than a week, required by the underwriter to complete the sale. But even here the underwriter need bear little risk; the futures and options markets permit it to hedge the risk of market changes during the offering period. For example, if the underwriter fears that interest rates may rise while it is trying to sell a fixed rate bond, it can eliminate all risk by selling treasury bills for future delivery. Similar hedging of overall market conditions is possible in equity offerings through the use of futures markets in various stock composites.

If distribution and risk sharing do not adequately account for the investment banker's function, some additional factor must be at work. Our analysis suggests that investment bankers play a third role, that of an information and reputational intermediary, which is particularly important in the context of new issues and other innovations.

Recall the problem facing an innovative issuer. Buyers find it too expensive to determine for themselves whether the issuer's new form of security warrants a higher price; and even if the issuer could educate them individually, the verification problem remains. Buyers still must be convinced of the accuracy of the information the issuer provides. A reputable investment banker may be able to solve both problems. Processing costs are obviously lower for a single investment banker than for a disparate group of individual buyers. This fact reflects the savings that accrue both from collectivization and from the potential for scale and scope economies in information processing.

From our perspective, however, the investment banker's role in reducing verification costs is even more critical. The difficulty confronting the issuer and prospective buyers is that determining the quality of the issuer's information is expensive ex ante, but not ex post. Before the sale, prospective buyers must incur verification costs to assess the issuer's good faith; after the sale, the issuer's behavior will reveal the quality of the information at virtually no cost. In this setting, a common technique for economizing on information costs is for sellers to make capital investments in brand name or reputation as a means of signaling the quality of the information. By making the investment in reputation, the seller signals its belief that when the purchaser learns the truth ex post, the quality of the information provided by the seller ex ante will be proved high. If the original information proves to be of low quality, the value of the seller's investment in reputation will diminish. Thus, the seller's investment in reputation demonstrates that it is not in his interest to misrepresent the accuracy of its information; and the buyer can rely upon that signal in lieu of engaging in costly verification itself.

The disadvantage of this economizing technique, however, is that in many cases it may not be available to an information seller. First, the seller may lack the capital to invest in a reputation. Second, it may lack the time to build a reputation prior to the contemplated sale. Third, even if the seller is willing to invest the necessary time and resources, prospective buyers may still harbor doubts about its good faith—an investment in reputation cannot wholly eliminate the incentive to behave opportunistically. Suppose, for example, that an issuer contemplates going to the capital market only once, and thereafter intends to finance its growth internally. In that case, an investment in reputation may be not a bond but bait, willingly lost in order to catch a more valuable fish. The gains from opportunism may well exceed the costs of lost reputation. Finally, each of these three difficulties—of money, time, and lingering suspicion—are particularly acute when an issuer makes its first offering.

It is in this setting that the critical role of the investment banker as a reputational intermediary becomes clear. In essence, the investment banker rents the issuer its reputation. The investment banker represents to the market (to whom *it,* and not the issuer, sells the security) that it has evaluated the issuer's product and good faith and that it is prepared to stake its reputation on the value of the innovation. Moreover, because the investment banker, unlike the issuer, is certain to be a "repeat player" in the capital markets, there are no final period problems to dampen the signal of value.

The investment banker's role as an informational and reputational intermediary can dramatically affect the efficiency of the market's response to an innovative security. As the cost of information about the security is reduced, information is more widely distributed and, therefore, more effectively reflected in market price. Of course, the market never becomes *completely* efficient with respect to the innovative security. Information costs are always greater than zero: information concerning the innovation will not be perfectly processed, and the investment banker's signal, itself costly, will not be perfectly credible. The market price of the innovative security will therefore still be lower than it would be if information costs were zero. Nonetheless, the investment banker helps make the market *more* efficient than it otherwise would be. And from our perspective, a more complete picture of the role of this critical actor in the capital markets demonstrates the value of understanding the relationship between information costs and market efficiency.

* * *

B. NEW CRITIQUES OF THE EFFICIENT MARKET HYPOTHESIS

Excerpt from: Andrei Shleifer and Lawrence H. Summers

The Noise Trader Approach to Finance
4 Journal of Economic Perspectives 19–33 (1990).

If the efficient markets hypothesis was a publicly traded security, its price would be enormously volatile. Following Samuelson's (1965) proof that stock prices should follow a random walk if rational competitive investors require a fixed rate of return and Fama's (1965) demonstration that stock prices are indeed close to a random walk, stock in the efficient markets hypothesis rallied. Michael Jensen was able to write in 1978 that "the efficient markets hypothesis is the best established fact in all of social sciences."

Such strong statements portend reversals, the efficient markets hypothesis itself notwithstanding. Stock in the efficient markets hypothesis lost ground rapidly following the publication of Shiller's (1981) and Leroy and Porter's (1981) volatility tests, both of which found stock market volatility to be far greater than could be justified by changes in dividends.[a] The stock snapped back following the papers of Kleidon (1986) and Marsh and Merton (1986)[b] which challenged the statistical validity of volatility tests. A choppy period then ensued, where conflicting econometric studies induced few of the changes in opinion that are necessary to move prices. But the stock in the efficient markets hypothesis—at least as it has traditionally been formulated—crashed along with the rest of the market on October 19, 1987. Its recovery has been less dramatic than that of the rest of the market.

This paper reviews an alternative to the efficient markets approach that we and others have recently pursued. Our approach rests on two assumptions. First, some investors are not fully rational and their demand for risky assets is affected by their beliefs or sentiments that are not fully justified by fundamental news. Second, arbitrage—defined as trading by fully rational investors not subject to such sentiment—is risky and therefore limited. The two assumptions together imply that changes in investor sentiment are not fully countered by arbitrageurs and so affect security returns. We argue that this approach to financial markets is in many ways superior to the efficient markets paradigm.

Our case for the noise trader approach is threefold. First, theoretical models with limited arbitrage are both tractable and more plausible than

---

[a] Shiller, Do Stock Prices Move Too Much to be Justified by Subsequent Changes in Dividends?, 71 American Economic Review 421 (1981); Leroy & Porter, Stock Price Volatility: Tests Based on Implied Variance Bounds, 49 Econometrica 97 (1981)—Eds.

[b] Kleidon, 94 Journal of Political Economy 953 (1986); Marsh & Merton, 76 American Economic Review 483 (1986)—Eds.

models with perfect arbitrage. The efficient markets hypothesis obtains only as an extreme case of perfect riskless arbitrage that is unlikely to apply in practice. Second, the investor sentiment/limited arbitrage approach yields a more accurate description of financial markets than the efficient markets paradigm. The approach not only explains the available anomalies, but also readily explains broad features of financial markets such as trading volume and actual investment strategies. Third, and most importantly, this approach yields new and testable implications about asset prices, some of which have been proved to be consistent with the data. It is absolutely *not true* that introducing a degree of irrationality of *some* investors into models of financial markets "eliminates all discipline and can explain anything."

The Limits of Arbitrage

We think of the market as consisting of two types of investors: "arbitrageurs"—also called "smart money" and "rational speculators"—and other investors. Arbitrageurs are defined as investors who form fully rational expectations about security returns. In contrast, the opinions and trading patterns of other investors—also known as "noise traders" and "liquidity traders"—may be subject to systematic biases. In practice, the line between arbitrageurs and other investors may be blurred, but for our argument it helps to draw a sharp distinction between them, since the arbitrageurs do the work of bringing prices toward fundamentals.

Arbitrageurs play a central role in standard finance. They trade to ensure that if a security has a perfect substitute—a portfolio of other securities that yields the same returns—then the price of the security equals the price of that substitute portfolio. If the price of the security falls below that of the substitute portfolio, arbitrageurs sell the portfolio and buy the security until the prices are equalized, and vice versa if the price of a security rises above that of the substitute portfolio. When the substitute is indeed perfect, this arbitrage is riskless. As a result, arbitrageurs have perfectly elastic demand for the security at the price of its substitute portfolio. Arbitrage thus assures that relative prices of securities must be in line for there to be no riskless arbitrage opportunities. Such riskless arbitrage is very effective for derivative securities, such as futures and options, but also for individual stocks and bonds where reasonably close substitutes are usually available.

Although riskless arbitrage ensures that relative prices are in line, it does not help to pin down price levels of, say, stocks or bonds as a whole. These classes of securities do not have close substitute portfolios, and therefore if for some reason they are mispriced, there is no riskless hedge for the arbitrageur. For example, an arbitrageur who thinks that stocks are underpriced cannot buy stocks and sell the substitute portfolio, since such a portfolio does not exist. The arbitrageur can instead simply buy stocks in hopes of an above-normal return, but this arbitrage is no longer riskless. If the arbitrageur is risk-averse, his demand for underpriced stocks will be limited. With a finite number of arbitrageurs, their combined demand curve is no longer perfectly elastic.

Two types of risk limit arbitrage. The first is fundamental risk. Suppose that stocks are selling above the expected value of future dividends and an arbitrageur is selling them short. The arbitrageur then bears the risk that the realization of dividends—or of the news about dividends—is better than expected, in which case he loses on his trade. Selling "overvalued" stocks is risky because there is always a chance that the market will do very well. Fear of such a loss limits the arbitrageur's original position, and keeps his short-selling from driving prices all the way down to fundamentals.

The second source of risk that limits arbitrage comes from unpredictability of the future resale price. Suppose again that stocks are overpriced and an arbitrageur is selling them short. As long as the arbitrageur is thinking of liquidating his position in the future, he must bear the risk that at that time stocks will be *even more* overpriced than they are today. If future mispricing is more extreme than when the arbitrage trade is put on, the arbitrageur suffers a loss on his position. Again, fear of this loss limits the size of the arbitrageur's initial position, and so keeps him from driving the price all the way down to fundamentals.

Clearly, this resale price risk depends on the arbitrageur having a finite horizon. If the arbitrageur's horizon is infinite, he simply sells the stock short and pays dividends on it in all the future periods, recognizing that the present value of those is lower than his proceeds from the short sale. But there are several reasons that it makes sense to assume that arbitrageurs have short horizons. Most importantly, arbitrageurs have to borrow cash or securities to implement their trades, and as a result must pay the lenders *per period* fees. These fees cumulate over the period that the position remains open, and can add up to large amounts for long term arbitrage. The structure of transaction costs thus induces a strong bias toward short horizons. In addition, the performance of most money managers is evaluated at least once a year and usually once every few months, also limiting the horizon of arbitrage. As a result of these problems, resources dedicated to long-term arbitrage against fundamental mispricing are very scarce.

Japanese equities in the 1980s illustrate the limits of arbitrage. During this period, Japanese equities have sold at the price earnings multiples of between 20 and 60, and have continued to climb. Expected growth rates of dividends and risk premia required to justify such multiples seem unrealistic. Nonetheless, an investor who believes that Japanese equities are overvalued and wants to sell them short, must confront two types of risk. First, what if Japan actually does perform so well that these prices are justified? Second, how much more out of line can prices get, and for how long, before Japanese equities return to more realistic prices? Any investor who sold Japanese stocks short in 1985, when the price earnings multiple was 30, would have lost his shirt as the multiples rose to 60 in 1986.

These arguments that risk makes arbitrage ineffective actually understate the limits of arbitrage. After all, they presume that the arbitrageur knows the fundamental value of the security. In fact, the arbitrageur might not exactly know what this value is, or be able to detect price changes that reflect deviations from fundamentals. In this case, arbitrage is even riskier than before. Summers * * * shows that a time series of share prices which deviate from fundamentals in a highly persistent way looks a lot like a random walk.[c] Arbitrageurs would have as hard a time as econometricians in detecting such a deviation, even if it were large. An arbitrageur is then handicapped by the difficulty of identifying the mispricing as well as by the risk of betting against it. Are economists certain that Japanese stocks are overpriced at a price earnings ratio of 50?

Substantial evidence shows that, contrary to the efficient markets hypothesis, arbitrage does not completely counter responses of prices to fluctuations in uninformed demand. Of course, identifying such fluctuations in demand is tricky, since price changes may reflect new market information which changes the equilibrium price at which arbitrageurs trade. Several recent studies do, however, avoid this objection by looking at responses of prices to changes in demand that do not plausibly reflect any new fundamental information because they have institutional or tax motives.

For example, Harris and Gurel and Shleifer examine stock price reactions to inclusions of new stocks into the Standard & Poor 500 stock index.[d] Being added to the S & P 500 is not a plausible example of new information about the stock, since stocks are picked for their representativeness and not for performance potential. However, a stock added to the S & P 500 is subsequently acquired in large quantities by the so-called "index funds," whose holdings just represent the index. Both Harris and Gurel and Shleifer find that announcements of inclusions into the index are accompanied by share price increases of 2 to 3 percent. Moreover, the magnitude of these increases over time has risen, paralleling the growth of assets in index funds. Clearly, the arbitrage trade in which rational speculators sell the new stock and buy back close substitutes is not working here. And simply selling short the newly included stock on the theory that it is now overpriced must be too risky.

---

[c] Summers, Does the Stock Market Rationally Reflect Fundamental Values?, 41 Journal of Finance 591 (1986)—Eds.

[d] Harris & Gurel, Price and Volume Effects Associated with Changes in the S & P 500: New Evidence for the Existence of Price Pressure, 41 Journal of Finance 851 (1986); Shleifer, Do Demand Curves for Stocks Slope Down?, 41 Journal of Finance 579 (1986)—Eds.

Further evidence on price pressure when no news is transmitted comes from Ritter's[e] work on the January effect. The January effect is the name for the fact that small stocks have outperformed market indices by a significant percentage each January over the last 50 or so years. Ritter finds that small stocks are typically sold by individual investors in December—often to realize capital losses—and then bought back in January. These share shifts explain the January effect as long as arbitrage by institutions and market insiders is ineffective, since aggressive arbitrage should eliminate the price effects of temporary trading patterns by individual investors. Either risk or borrowing constraints keep arbitrageurs from eliminating the price consequences of year-end trading.

Less direct evidence also shows that news is not the only force driving asset prices, suggesting that arbitrage is not successful in eliminating the effects of uninformed trading on prices. For example, French and Roll[f] look at a period when the U.S. stock market was closed on Wednesdays and find that the market is less volatile on these days than on Wednesdays when it is open. By focusing on Wednesdays, they control for the intensity of release of public information. This result may reflect incorporation of private information into prices during open hours, but it may also reflect the failure of arbitrage to accommodate intraday demand shifts. Roll[g] demonstrates that most idiosyncratic price moves in individual stocks cannot be accounted for by public news. He finds that individual stocks exhibit significant price movements unrelated to the market on days when there are no public news about these stocks. A similar and more dramatic result is obtained for the aggregate stock market by Cutler, Poterba, and Summers,[h] who find that the days of the largest aggregate market movements are not the days of most important fundamental news and vice versa. The common conclusion of these studies is that news alone does not move stock prices; uninformed changes in demand move them too.

Investor Sentiment

Some shifts in investor demand for securities are completely rational. Such changes could reflect, for example, reactions to public announcements that affect future growth rate of dividends, risk, or risk aversion. Rational demand changes can also reflect adjustment to news conveyed through the trading process itself. Finally, rational demand changes can reflect tax trading or trading done for institutional reasons of the types discussed above.

---

[e]   Ritter, The Buying and Selling Behavior of Individual Investors at the Turn of the Year, 43 Journal of Finance 701 (1988)—Eds.

[f]   French & Roll, Stock Return Variances: The Arrival of Information and the Reaction of Traders, 17 Journal of Financial Economics 5 (1986)—Eds.

[g]   Roll, R-squared, 43 Journal of Finance 541 (1988)—Eds.

[h]   Cutler, Poterba & Summers, What Moves Stock Prices?, 15 Journal of Portfolio Management 4 (1989)—Eds.

But not all demand changes appear to be so rational; some seem to be a response to changes in expectations or sentiment that are not fully justified by information. Such changes can be a response to pseudo-signals that investors believe convey information about future returns but that would not convey such information in a fully rational model. An example of such pseudo-signals is advice of brokers or financial gurus. We use the term "noise traders" to describe such investors * * *. Changes in demand can also reflect investors' use of inflexible trading strategies or of "popular models" that Shiller describes in this journal. One such strategy is trend chasing. Although these changes in demand are unwarranted by fundamentals, they can be related to fundamentals, as in the case of overreaction to news.

These demand shifts will only matter if they are correlated across noise traders. If all investors trade randomly, their trades cancel out and there are no aggregate shifts in demand. Undoubtedly, some trading in the market brings together noise traders with different models who cancel each other out. However, many trading strategies based on pseudo-signals, noise, and popular models are correlated, leading to aggregate demand shifts. The reason for this is that judgment biases afflicting investors in processing information tend to be the same. Subjects in psychological experiments tend to make the same mistake; they do not make random mistakes.

Many of these persistent mistakes are relevant for financial markets. For example, experimental subjects tend to be overconfident,[i] which makes them take on more risk. Experimental subjects also tend to extrapolate past time series, which can lead them to chase trends. Finally, in making inferences experimental subjects put too little weight on base rates and too much weight on new information,[j] which might lead them to overreact to news.

The experimental evidence on judgment biases is corroborated by survey and other evidence on how investors behave. For example, extrapolation is a key feature of the popular models discovered by the surveys Shiller describes in this journal.[k] He finds that home buyers as well as investors in the crash of 1987 seem to extrapolate past price trends. Similar results have been found by Frankel and Froot (1986)[l] in their analysis of exchange rate forecasts during the mid-1980s: over the short horizon, professional forecasters expect a price trend to continue even when they expect a long run reversion to fundamentals.

---

[i] Kahneman, Slovic & Tversky, Judgment Under Uncertainty: Heuristics and Biases (1982)—Eds.

[j] Tversky & Kahneman, Evidential Impact of Base Rates, in Kahneman, Slovic & Tversky, Judgment Under Uncertainty: Heuristics and Biases (1982)—Eds.

[k] Shiller, Speculative Prices and Popular Models, 4 Journal of Economic Perspectives 55 (1990)—Eds.

[l] Frankel & Froot, Understanding the US Dollar in the Eighties: The Expectations of Chartists and Fundamentalists, Economic Record (Special Issue) (1986)—Eds.

* * *

Learning and imitation may not adversely affect noise traders either. When noise traders earn high average returns, many other investors might imitate them, ignoring the fact that they took more risk and just got lucky. Such imitation brings more money to follow noise trader strategies. Noise traders themselves might become even more cocky, attributing their investment success to skill rather than luck. As noise traders who do well become more aggressive, their effect on demand increases.

The case against the importance of noise traders also ignores the fact that new investors enter the market all the time, and old investors who have lost money come back. These investors are subject to the same judgment biases as the current survivors in the market, and so add to the effect of judgment biases on demand.

These arguments suggest that the case for long run unimportance of noise traders is at best premature. In other words, shifts in the demand for stocks that do not depend on news or fundamental factors are likely to affect prices even in the long run.

Explaining the Puzzles

When arbitrage is limited, and investor demand for securities responds to noise and to predictions of popular models, security prices move in response to these changes in demand as well as to changes in fundamentals. Arbitrageurs counter the shifts in demand prompted by changes in investor sentiment, but do not eliminate the effects of such shifts on the price completely.

In this market, prices vary more than is warranted by changes in fundamentals, since they respond to shifts in investor sentiment as well as to news. Stock returns are predictably mean-reverting, meaning that high stock returns lead to lower expected stock returns. This prediction has in fact been documented for the United States as well as the foreign stock prices by Fama and French (1988)[m] and Poterba and Summers (1988).[n]

The effects of demand shifts on prices are larger when most investors follow the finance textbooks and passively hold the market portfolio. In this case, a switch in the sentiment of some investors is not countered by a change of position of all the market participants, but only of a few arbitrageurs. The smaller the risk bearing capacity of arbitrageurs, the bigger the effect of a sentiment shift on the price. A simple example highlights this point. Suppose that all investors are sure that the market is efficient and hold the market portfolio. Now suppose that one investor

---

[m] Fama & French, Permanent and Temporary Components of Stock Market Prices, 96 Journal of Political Economy 246 (1988)—Eds.

[n] Poterba & Summers, Mean Reversion in Stock Prices: Evidence and Implications, 22 Journal of Financial Economics 27 (1988)—Eds.

decides to hold additional shares of a particular security. Its price is driven to infinity.

This approach fits very neatly with the conventional nonacademic view of financial markets. On that view, the key to investment success is not just predicting future fundamentals, but also predicting the movement of other active investors. Market professionals spend considerable resources tracking price trends, volume, short interest, odd lot volume, investor sentiment indexes and numerous other gauges of demand for equities. Tracking these possible indicators of demand makes no sense if prices responded only to fundamental news and not to investor demand. They make perfect sense, in contrast, in a world where investor sentiment moves prices and so predicting changes in this sentiment pays. The prevalence of investment strategies based on indicators of demand in financial markets suggests the recognition by arbitrageurs of the role of demand.

Not only do arbitrageurs spend time and money to predict noise trader moves, they also make active attempts to take advantage of these moves. When noise traders are optimistic about particular securities, it pays arbitrageurs to create more of them. These securities might be mutual funds, new share issues, penny oil stocks, or junk bonds: anything that is overpriced at the moment. * * *

When they bet against noise traders, arbitrageurs begin to look like noise traders themselves. They pick stocks instead of diversifying, because that is what betting against noise traders requires. They time the market to take advantage of noise trader mood swings. If these swings are temporary, arbitrageurs who cannot predict noise trader moves simply follow contrarian strategies. It becomes hard to tell the noise traders from the arbitrageurs.

But saying that a market affected by investor sentiment looks realistic is hardly a rigorous test. To pursue this line of thought, we must derive and test implications that are not obvious and perhaps that are new. We consider first the implications of unpredictability or randomness of changes in investor sentiment. Second, we look at implications of strategies followed by investors who buy when prices rise and sell when prices fall, possibly because their expectations are simple extrapolations.

Implications of Unpredictability of Investor Sentiment

Even without taking a position on how investor sentiment moves, we can learn something from the observation that it moves in part unpredictably. Even if arbitrageurs know that noise traders are pessimistic today and hence will on average become less pessimistic in the future, they cannot be sure when this will happen. There is always a chance that noise traders become even more pessimistic first. This unpredictability contributes to resale price risk, since the resale price of an asset depends on the state of noise trader sentiment. If investor sentiment affects a broad range of assets in the same way, this risk from its unpredictability becomes systematic. Systematic risk has a price in equilibrium. Consequently, assets subject to whims of investor sentiment should yield higher average returns than similar assets not subject to such whims. Put differently, assets subject to unpredictable swings in investor sentiment must be underpriced in the market relative to their fundamental values.

* * * [Commentators cite two forms of evidence to support this argument:] First, stocks are probably subject to larger fluctuations of investor sentiment than bonds. In this case, equilibrium returns on stocks must be higher than warranted by their fundamentals—the latter being given by dividends and by covariation of dividends with consumption. In particular, the difference between average returns on stocks and on bonds—the risk premium—must be higher than is warranted by fundamentals. Such excess returns on stocks are in fact observed in the U.S. economy.

* * *

The second application we examined involves the pricing of closed-end mutual funds. These funds, like open-end funds, hold portfolios of other securities, but unlike open-end funds, have a fixed number of shares outstanding. As a result, an investor who wants to liquidate his holdings of a closed-end fund must sell his shares to other investors; he cannot just redeem his shares as with an open-end fund. Closed-end funds present one of the most interesting puzzles in finance, because their fundamental value—the value of the assets in their portfolios—is observed, and tends to be systematically higher than the price at which these funds trade. The pervasiveness of discounts on closed-end funds is a problem for the efficient markets hypothesis: in the one case where value is observed, it is not equal to the price.

De Long, Shleifer, Summers and Waldmann[o] argue that investor sentiment about closed-end funds changes, and that this sentiment also affects other securities. When investors are bullish about closed-end funds, they drive up their prices relative to fundamental values, and discounts narrow or turn into premiums. When investors in contrast are bearish about closed-end funds, they drive down their prices and discounts widen. Any investor holding a closed-end fund bears two kinds of risk. The first is the risk from holding the fund's portfolio. The second is the resale price risk: at the time the investor needs to sell the fund the discount might widen. If investor sentiment about closed-end funds affects many other securities as well, bearing the resale price risk should be rewarded. That is, closed-end funds should on average sell at a discount. Put differently, the reason there are discounts *on average* is that discounts fluctuate, and investors require an extra return for bearing the risk of fluctuating discounts.

---

[o] De Long et al., Noise Trader Risk in Financial Markets, 98 Journal of Political Economy 703 (1990)—Eds.

This theory explains why arbitrage does not effectively eliminate discounts on closed-end funds. An arbitrageur who buys a discounted fund and sells short its portfolio runs the risk that at the time he liquidates his position the discount widens and so his arbitrage results in a loss. An arbitrageur with an infinite horizon need not worry about this risk. But if the arbitrageur faces some probability of needing to liquidate his position in finite time, the risk from unpredictability of investor sentiment at the time he liquidates prevents him from aggressive betting that would eliminate discounts.

* * *

Implications of Positive Feedback Trading

One of the strongest investor tendencies documented in both experimental and survey evidence is the tendency to extrapolate or to chase the trend. Trend chasers buy stocks after they rise and sell stocks after they fall: they follow positive feedback strategies. Other strategies that depend on extrapolative expectations are "stop loss" orders, which prescribe selling after a certain level of losses, regardless of future prospects, and portfolio insurance, which involves buying more stocks (to raise exposure to risk) when prices rise and selling stocks (to cut exposure to risk) when prices fall.

When some investors follow positive feedback strategies—buy when prices rise and sell when prices fall—it need no longer be optimal for arbitrageurs to counter shifts in the demand of these investors. Instead, it may pay arbitrageurs to jump on the bandwagon themselves. Arbitrageurs then optimally buy the stocks that positive feedback investors get interested in when their prices rise. When price increases feed the buying of other investors, arbitrageurs sell out near the top and take their profits. The effect of arbitrage is to stimulate the interest of other investors and so to contribute to the movement of prices away from fundamentals. Although eventually arbitrageurs sell out and help prices return to fundamentals, in the short run they feed the bubble rather than help it to dissolve. * * *

The presence of positive feedback traders in financial markets also makes it easier to interpret historical episodes, such as the sharp market increase and the crash of 1987. According to standard finance, the market crash of October 1987 reflected either a large increase in risk premiums because the economy became a lot riskier, or a large decrease in expected future growth rate of dividends. These theories have the obvious problem that they do not explain what news prompted a 22 percent devaluation of the American corporate sector on October 19. Another problem is that there is no evidence that risk increased tremendously—volatility indeed jumped up but came back rapidly as it usually does—or that expected dividend growth has been revised sharply down. An examination of OECD long-term forecasts shows no downward revision in forecasts of long run growth rates after the crash, even though the crash itself could have adversely affected expectations. Perhaps most strikingly, Seyhun

(1989)ᵖ finds that corporate insiders bought stocks in record numbers during and after the crash, and moreover bought more of the stocks that later had a greater rebound. Insiders did not share the view that growth of dividends will slow or that risk will increase and *they were right!* Fully rational theories have a clear problem with the crash.

The crash is much easier to understand in a market with significant positive feedback trading. Positive feedback trading can rationalize the dramatic price increase during 1987, as more and more investors chase the trend. Positive feedback trading, exacerbated by possible front-running by investment banks, can also explain the depth of the crash once it has started. One still needs a theory of what broke the market on October 19, but the bad news during the previous week might have initiated the process, albeit with some lag. A full theory of the crash remains to be developed: prospects for such a theory look a lot brighter, however, if it incorporates positive feedback trading.

Conclusion

This paper has described an alternative to the efficient markets paradigm that stresses the roles of investor sentiment and limited arbitrage in determining asset prices. We have shown that the assumption of limited arbitrage is more general and plausible as a description of markets for risky assets than the assumption of perfect arbitrage which market efficiency relies on. With limited arbitrage, movements in investor sentiment are an important determinant of prices. We have also shown that this approach yields a large number of implications about the behavior of both investors and speculative prices which are consistent with the evidence. Perhaps most importantly, we have shown that this approach yields some new testable implications about security returns. Some of these implications, such as the ones on closed-end funds, have been tested and confirmed. It is thus not the case that the investor sentiment approach deprives finance of the discipline to which it is accustomed.

Assuming that our approach has some explanatory power and therefore intellectual merit, what are its implications for welfare and for policy? There are two normative issues relevant to the evaluation of noise trading. First, should something be done to prevent noise traders from suffering from their errors? Second, do noise traders impose a cost on the rest of market participants and, if so, how can this cost be reduced? Although answers to these questions ultimately turn on open empirical problems, both theory and empirical work permit some tentative remarks.

Investors who trade on noise or on popular models are worse off than they would be if their expectations were rational (if welfare is computed with respect to the correct distribution of returns). They need not lose

---

ᵖ Seyhun, Fads or Fundamentals: Some Lessons from Insiders' Response to the Crash of 1987 (1989).

money on average, as the simplest logic might suggest. But even if they earn higher average returns, it is because they bear more risk than they think. And even if they get rich over time, it is only because they underestimate the risk and get lucky. If investors had perfect foresight and rationality, they would know that noise trading always hurts them.

Whether the government should do anything to save noise traders from themselves depends on the social welfare function. People are allowed to participate in state lotteries, to lose fortunes in casinos, or to bet on the racetrack even though benevolent observers know that they are being taken to the cleaners. The case for making it costly for investors to bet on the stock market to protect them from their own utility losses is in principle identical to the case for prohibiting casinos, horse races, and state lotteries.

Noise trading, however, can also affect the welfare of the rest of the community. One effect is to benefit arbitrageurs who take advantage of noise traders. These benefits accrue both to those who bet against noise traders and those who feed their demand by providing financial services. Interestingly, the combined receipts of the NYSE member firms amounted to a sixth of the total U.S. corporate income in 1987. Of course, some of these benefits to arbitrageurs are also a social *opportunity* cost as valuable human and other resources are allocated to separating noise traders from their money.

But noise trading also has a private cost, as it makes returns on assets more risky, and so can reduce physical investment. The overall impact of noise trading on the rest of the market participants and society can be negative. Some have also argued that noise trading in foreign exchange markets distorts the flow of goods between countries and leads to inefficient choice of production. Others have argued that noise trading forces managers to focus on the short term, and to bias the choice of investments against long-term projects. The policy reaction to noise trading can be dangerous as well; for example, sharp contractions of money supply by the Federal Reserve have often been justified as responses to excessive speculation. In this case, the consequences of such policies are more costly than the speculation itself.

Awareness of these costs of noise trading raises the question of what (if anything) should be done about it. Some businessmen and economists have proposed short term capital gains taxes as a way to cripple noise trading, while others * * * have advocated transaction taxes to the same end. It is not our goal in this paper to evaluate these proposals. We note, however, that one benefit of the research on markets where investor sentiment matters is to allow a more systematic evaluation of these proposals.

---

1. *Behavioral Theories.* The foregoing noise trading critique by Professors Shleifer and Summers stays essentially within the domain of

financial economics and asserts that markets can remain inefficient because it is too costly and risky for arbitrageurs to correct them. This theme of the limits on arbitrage (which, in turn, are partly attributable to traditional limitations imposed on short selling) has been picked up by several other economists.[147] Still, some critics go further and suggest there are systematic psychological and cognitive biases at work that distort markets from time to time. One leading behavioral finance theorist, Professor Robert Shiller, argues that contagions can dominate valuation because investors are heavily influenced by each other, not just by market fundamentals.[148] Moreover, with improvements in information technology, the vulnerability of the market to fads, rumors, and misinformation increases (for example, misinformed investors on online "chat rooms" can convince each other through repetition of wildly inaccurate information).

This view of the market dates back at least to a famous metaphor coined by John Maynard Keynes in the 1930s. Like Professor Shiller, he believed the market reflected investors strategically attempting to assess what other investors were likely to do (e.g., how they would react to a new announcement or world development). Keynes suggested that this process was not unlike the "beautiful baby" contests then popular in the London newspapers, in which contestants competed to be selected as the most beautiful child from a number of pictures, with the winner being determined by which baby received the most votes. Hence, he concluded, the best strategy was not to choose the child's inherent characteristics (i.e., market fundamentals), but rather to predict which child the other entrants would consider most beautiful (i.e., guess what the noise traders would do).[149]

Recent research can be read to support this view of the market because it seems to show that investors routinely overreact or underreact to corporate announcements—a persistent phenomenon that some attribute to the psychological tendency of investors to be overconfident about the accuracy of the information they possess.[150] Investor overreaction can be partially attributed to institutional forces (such as a high ratio of buy to sell recommendations across the market) or to innate investor psychology. Whatever the explanation, a growing body of opinion believes that finance theory must be supplemented by reference to social and psychological theories and forces to understand market behavior adequately.

---

[147] See, e.g., Hong & Stein, Disagreement and the Stock Market, 21 J. Econ. Persp. 109 (2007); Baker & Wurglar, Investor Sentiment in the Stock Market, 21 J. Econ. Persp. 129 (2007).

[148] See Shiller, Market Volatility 379–400 (1989).

[149] See Keynes, The General Theory of Employment, Interest and Money 156 (1936).

[150] See Barber & Odean, Trading Is Hazardous to Your Wealth: The Common Stock Investment Performance of Individual Investors, 55 J. Fin. 773 (2000); Daniel, Hirschleifer & Subrahmanyam, Investor Psychology and Security Markets Under-and-Overreacting, 53 J. Fin. 1839 (1998).

2. *Noise Theory.* The new popularity of noise trading as an explanation for market inefficiency may owe a good deal to the euphemistic character of this phrase. Essentially, noise theory posits that factors unrelated to fundamental news or rational expectations about market values can cause stock prices to deviate from their consensus values for non-trivial periods if all traders possess the same information. Some have suggested that financial economists have been able to accept this phrase—but not the nearly equivalent idea that "irrational" forces could move the market.[151]

C. How Do Investors Really Make Decisions: The Behavioral Economic Perspective

Traditional economic models view the investor as an entirely rational decision-maker, without biases or emotions, and with an unlimited cerebral capacity to process complex information. Psychologists view the individual very differently and, over the last quarter-century, a new discipline—behavioral economics—has emerged that seeks to apply the insights of psychology to actual economic decision-making.[152] The starting point for this approach is the recognition that humans have limited information-processing abilities and, as a result, remain inattentive to much available information. Given these difficulties, individuals take shortcuts; they simplify decision-making by adopting rules of thumb, or "heuristics," to reach decisions without processing all available information. This results in the introduction of predictable biases into investors' decisions.

Behavioral economics has identified several recurring heuristics that systematically result in cognitive errors by individual investors. These errors are likely to be individually costly to investors, but it is less clear if they have a market-wide impact on securities prices. The most well-known of these heuristics are the following:

(1) OVERCONFIDENCE.

The psychology literature has documented over and over again that most individuals are overconfident; that is, concerning investment decisions, they tend to believe they are more knowledgeable or skillful than they actually are.[153] For example, investors who are initially successful in trading online become increasingly aggressive in their

---

[151] See Leroy, Efficient Capital Market Theory and Martingales, 27 J. Econ. Lit. 1583, 1612 (1989) (asserting that the phrase "noise trading" has "sanitize[d] irrationality" and rendered it "palatable" to many financial economists).

[152] This approach to the study of decision-making under uncertainty begins with the work of Amos Tversky and Daniel Kahneman (for which the latter won the Nobel Prize in Economics after the death of the former). See Tversky & Kahneman, Judgment Under Uncertainty: Heuristics and Biases, 185 Science 1124 (1974); Kahneman & Tversky, Prospect Theory: An Analysis of Decision Under Risk, 47 Econometrica 263 (1979).

[153] See Barber & Odean, The Courage of Misguided Convictions, Financial Analysts Journal (Special Issue on Behavioral Finance) (1999).

trading, ignoring that the transaction costs of such trading exceed their gains.[154] Males seem to be more afflicted than females by this bias.[155]

(2) DIVERSIFICATION BIAS.

Faced with uncertainty, individuals tend to choose a little bit of everything.[156] This may sound sensible, but it often results in poor asset allocation decisions. One well-known study asked employees to allocate their retirement savings among five funds, of which four were fixed-income and one equity. Another group of employees was then given a choice among five other funds, four equity and one debt. The first group allocated 43% to equity, while the second group 68%. The inference here is that the menu of options significantly affected the choices made by these otherwise-similar employees.[157]

(3) LOSS AVERSION.

Investors seem willing to accept more risk to avoid a loss than to realize a gain. Whether at the race track or in playing the stock market, individuals take greater gambles when they are attempting to recover a loss or restore the status quo than when they are confronting the same risk for the first time.[158] Such behavior, of course, can be financially disastrous, but it can also be manipulated. For example, if a salesperson or broker gives a client the sense that she is behind some benchmark, the client may become more aggressive.

(4) STATUS QUO BIAS.

What an investor currently owns may seem preferable simply by virtue of its possession.[159]

(5) REPRESENTATIVENESS BIAS.

Individuals tend to judge long-term probabilities based on recent experience.[160] Thus, investors may assume, if the stock market has increased dramatically over the last two or three years, that it will continue to do so and at the same pace. The result can be a bubble if all or most investors exhibit the same bias. The basic cognitive error here is

---

[154] See Barber & Odean, Trading is Hazardous to Your Wealth: The Common Stock Investment Performance of Individual Investors, 55 J. Fin. 773 (2000) (finding that, over a five-year period, the most active traders at a discount brokerage firm averaged a 11.4% return while, over the same period, the market return for a non-trading investor was 17.9%).

[155] See Barber & Odean, Boys Will Be Boys: Gender, Overconfidence and Common Stock Investment, 116 Q. J. Econ. 261 (2001) (male traders exhibit greater overconfidence in their trading patterns).

[156] See Read & Loewenstein, Diversification Bias: Explaining the Discrepancy in Variety Seeking Between Combined and Separated Choices, 1 J. of Experimental Psychol.: Applied 34 (1995).

[157] See Benartzi & Thaler, Naive Diversification Strategies in Defined Contribution Savings Plans, 91 Am. Econ. Rev. 79 (2001).

[158] See Odean, Are Investors Reluctant to Realize Their Losses?, 53 J. Fin. 1775 (1998).

[159] See Kahneman, Knetsch & Thaler, Anomalies: The Endowment Effect, Loss Aversion and Status Quo Bias, 5 J. Econ. Persp. 193 (1991).

[160] See Tversky & Kahneman, Availability: A Heuristic for Judging Frequency and Bias, 5 Cognitive Psych. 207 (1973); Tversky & Kahneman, Judgment Under Uncertainty: Heuristics and Biases, 185 Science 1124 (1974).

attempting to judge an entire population or long-term probability based on a limited data sample.

(6) FAMILIARITY BIAS.

Closely related to the bias towards recency and the status quo is a tendency to place a higher value on what is known and familiar.[161] This may partly explain why investors prefer home country securities over foreign ones.

Emotions also play a role in investment decision-making. Factors as irrelevant as the weather seem to influence decisions.[162] Both positive and negative emotions can lead investors to ignore, or at least be less sensitive to, risk distributions. The happier the investor, the more likely the investor is to pursue opportunities with low probabilities of success.[163] Of course, the financial services industry understands marketing and can exploit these tendencies.

All told, the evidence produced by behavioral theorists has probably convinced most (but not all) researchers that stock price movements cannot be explained exclusively by neo-classical finance theory. A social-psychological dimension is needed for a full understanding of stock price behavior.[164]

D. POLICY IMPLICATIONS

(1) THE CASE FOR THE MANDATORY DISCLOSURE SYSTEM

How should policymakers respond to the growing evidence that investors are systematically less than rational? On the one hand, there is a danger of excessive paternalism, but, on the other, there may be some need to recognize that mandatory disclosure is not the optimal regulatory answer in all cases. If investors under-diversify, or if they make systematically suboptimal asset allocation decisions, one policy response might be greater investment in investor education; specifically, the SEC might sponsor education programs designed to offset the influence of media and the industry, which tend to glamorize and oversell the prospect of easy wealth through securities trading.[165] Still, the chronic

---

[161] See Heath & Tversky, Preferences and Beliefs: Ambiguity and Choice Under Uncertainty, 4 J. Risk & Uncertainty 5 (1991).

[162] See Hirshleifer & Shumway, Good Day Sunshine: Stock Returns and the Weather, 58 J. Fin. 1009 (2003).

[163] See MacGregor et al., Imagery, Affect and Financial Judgment, 1 J. Psychol. & Fin. Mkts. 104 (2000).

[164] For an incisive review, see Cunningham, From Random Walks to Chaotic Crashes: The Linear Genealogy of the Efficient Capital Market Hypothesis, 62 Geo. Wash. L. Rev. 546 (1994).

[165] For an evaluation of such a policy, see Hu, Faith and Magic: Investor Beliefs and Government Neutrality, 78 Tex. L. Rev. 777 (2000). An alternative perspective is that the SEC is as equally subject as investors to behavioral biases (as well as political biases). For this view, see Choi & Pritchard, Behavioral Economics and the SEC, 56 Stan. L. Rev. 1 (2003).

problem with this answer is that those most needing investor education are also the least likely to participate in it.

Of course, it is not only investors that are subject to behavioral biases. Regulators may be subject to the same biases.[166] Market failures may be more than matched by governmental failures. Major reform programs have the potential to be dominated by special interests.

Even if there is an element of irrationality in investor behavior, this does not mean we should abandon the goal of an efficient market. Thus, an alternative perspective sees the SEC's mandatory disclosure system as the best answer to this problem. From that perspective, the SEC's system of mandatory disclosure essentially operates as a means of economizing on information costs.[167] By collectivizing the acquisition of securities information, the securities laws reduce potentially duplicative and socially wasteful investments by private parties. Even more importantly, by collecting and disseminating information through the SEC, the federal securities laws essentially subsidize a public good that would otherwise be undersupplied. The classic example of a public good is a lighthouse. It cannot be privately financed because there is no feasible way to tax the passing ships that benefit from it. Similarly, the SEC benefits investors in a manner that could not be achieved through private ordering because many free riders would escape paying.

Thus, even if the securities markets are inefficient, it does not follow that society should give up on the pursuit of greater efficiency (to protect investors, to promote allocative efficiency, and to reduce the cost of capital). Indeed, any strategy that successfully reduces the cost of capital would produce real macroeconomic benefits for the entire society, not just investors. From this perspective, the SEC's mandatory disclosure system may represent the lowest cost means of correcting the private market's failure to provide adequate securities research and verification. This explanation emphasizes the "public goods" nature of securities research, which in turn implies that research will be underprovided because its value cannot be fully captured by those who produce it. This view, in turn, helps us understand why securities analysts and other professionals may find it difficult to earn adequate compensation for their efforts.

---

[166] See Choi & Pritchard, Behavioral Economics and the SEC, 56 Stan. L. Rev. 1 (2003).

[167] See Coffee, Market Failure and the Economic Case for a Mandatory Disclosure System, 70 Va.L.Rev. 717 (1984).

Excerpt from: John C. Coffee, Jr.

Market Failure and the Economic Case for a Mandatory Disclosure System
70 Virginia Law Review 717, 725–33 (1984).

* * *

I. A PUBLIC GOODS PERSPECTIVE

Easy as it is today to criticize the original premise of the federal securities laws—i.e., that mandatory disclosure would enable the small investor to identify and invest in higher quality and lower risk securities—such criticism does not take us very far because its target has shifted. The securities markets have evolved significantly since the 1930's, and one of the most important developments is the appearance of the professional securities analyst.[19] Little known in 1934 and common today, the analyst seems likely to become the critical mechanism of market efficiency because on-line computerization of SEC-filed data makes access to such information both immediate and relatively costless to the analyst.*

The work of the securities analyst can be subdivided into two basic functions. First, the analyst searches for information obtainable from non-issuer sources bearing on the value of a corporate security. Often, this information is critical because the issuer's performance may be substantially dependent on exogenous factors—e.g., interest rates, the behavior of competitors, governmental actions, consumer attitudes, and demographic trends—about which the issuer has no special knowledge or the analyst has superior access. Second, the analyst verifies, tests, and compares the issuer's disclosures, both to prevent deliberate fraud and to remove the unconscious bias that usually affects all forms of information transfer.

Although individual investors could also perform these search and verification functions, the professional securities analyst typically can do so at a lower cost because there appear to be significant economies of scale and specialization associated with these tasks. As a result, most accounts explaining the stock market's efficiency assign a substantial

---

[19] The SEC's Advisory Committee on Corporate Disclosure found that there were some 14,646 professional securities analysts employed by financial institutions, brokerage firms, and consulting services as of 1977. * * * Presumably, this profession has survived because it performs a useful service. Typically, the chief source of firm-specific data used by the analyst appears to come from personal conversations with managers. Id. at 66–68. That managers do divulge information in this fashion to analysts provides some support for the theory of voluntary disclosure discussed below. * * *

* The number of securities analysts has dropped in recent years, partly due to greater U.S. regulation under the Sarbanes-Oxley Act and other regulation in Europe. For instance, the number of analysts working at the world's 12 largest investment banks fell from more than 6,500 at the end of 2012 to less than 5,000 during the first half of 2019. Nevertheless, the role and importance of securities analysts remains, perhaps even more so in light of the new regulation around research and analysts.—Eds.

responsibility to the competition among analysts for securities information.

In principle, the information volume developed by securities analysts is determined by the usual market forces and should result in the usual equilibrium: analysts should invest in verifying and obtaining material information about corporate securities until the marginal cost of this information to them equals their marginal return. Ordinarily, this private equilibrium should also result in allocative efficiency: social resources would be devoted to information verification until the social costs rose to meet the social benefits. There is a basic flaw, however, in this simple neoclassical analysis, and it involves a recurring problem that arises whenever a public good is produced.

A. Market Failure as a Cause of Insufficient Securities Research

Public goods are a well-known economic concept. What has not been adequately recognized, however, is the degree to which information about corporate securities from non-issuer sources resembles (albeit imperfectly) a public good. The key characteristic of a public good is the non-excludability of users who have not paid for it; people benefit whether or not they contribute to the costs of acquiring the good, in part because consumption of the good by one user does not diminish its availability to others.... The net result is that public goods tend to be underprovided.

Securities information displays this key characteristic of non-excludability. It seldom can be confined to a single user because many people have a motive to leak it. When the corporate insider tips a friend of a material impending development, the information does not stop with the tippee, but tends to be passed on. In fact, it is generally in the tippee's interest, once he has traded, to inform others to create excitement and induce a market upswing. Otherwise, the tippee achieves only the dubious victory of owning an undervalued security, and as the Wall Street Traders' credo says: "A bargain that remains a bargain is no bargain." Subsequent users thus gain a largely gratuitous benefit from material information leaked to them, although the value of the benefit quickly diminishes because of the market's rapid adjustment.

As applied to the securities analyst, the public goods-like character of securities research implies that the analyst cannot obtain the full economic value of his discovery, and this in turn means that he will engage in less search or verification behavior than investors collectively desire. The public goods character of securities research is illustrated by the well-known commercial: "When E.F. Hutton talks, people listen." Indeed, people do listen, but the eavesdroppers do not pay for what they receive; they are, in the parlance, "free riders." Typically, securities research is reduced to an analyst's report that is circulated among prominent institutional investors in return for expected future commissions or other investment banking business. Contracting for research in this fashion is presumably more efficient than each institutional investor employing its own analysts (which also happens) because of the economies of scale and specialization. Once securities research is initially disseminated in this fashion (or any similar fashion), however, free riding is predictable: news leaks out almost immediately because the confidentiality of a circulated report cannot be protected for long and because institutional investors have an incentive (after they trade) to make the analyst's report a self-fulfilling prophecy by encouraging others to trade. Either way, those in the tippee chain do not compensate the analyst. As a result, securities research is likely to be undercompensated. This undercompensation implies that there is underinvestment in securities research in terms of the aggregate wealth it creates or preserves. Thus, we are back to the classic public goods problem: so long as the free riders do not have to pay, the commodity will be underprovided.

A related problem with securities research involves the difficulties inherent in contracting for it. Normally, compensation for such research is on an ex post basis because the investor cannot know its value in advance. * * * The only objective test of the advice's value is the ultimate occurrence of the predicted market reaction. Although the buyer of valuable information should be willing to compensate the provider (at least to the extent that the buyer wishes to obtain such information from him in the future), the ex post and unilateral character of the payment results in less compensation being paid than if the negotiation were on a bilateral basis.

This problem is further complicated because payment typically is not made in cash. Rather, the user directs some of its brokerage business to the firm whose analyst supplied the information. In effect, the institutional investor pays above market price for brokerage services to obtain valuable research; the investor purchases advice with nothing more than the promise of future brokerage commissions at a premium rate. This premium is evidenced by the recent appearance of discount brokers, who offer only clearing services and provide no investment advice. The cost of such brokerage is estimated to be fifty percent below that of full service brokerage firms. Thus, the customer has his choice of financial services—a simple clearing service or a clearing service plus advice.

This curious institutional structure has two important implications, which the neoclassical critics of mandatory disclosure have simply ignored. First, there is clearly an incentive for the buyer to cheat on the implicit deal; he can use the investment advice provided by the full service firm and then steer the majority of his brokerage business to the discount firm. Second, the persistence of full service firms and the very survival of the securities analyst as a profession in the face of this price competition suggest that consumers do want securities advice and research, both on the individual client and institutional investor levels.

Otherwise, brokerage firms would fire their analysts to cut costs. Moreover, one cannot dismiss this evident demand for securities research as an irrational preference because the consumers include the most sophisticated of institutional investors.

These contractual problems, in combination with the public goods nature of securities research, help explain how a mandatory disclosure system benefits investors. Put simply, if market forces are inadequate to produce the socially optimal supply of research, then a regulatory response may be justified. Although securities advisers are regulated only in the most minimal way by the federal securities laws, they are in effect heavily subsidized by these statutes. Thus, the contemporary impact of the '34 Act may lie less in providing usable information to the ultimate investor than it does in reducing costs for the securities analyst. Indeed, the detailed periodic reports that "reporting" companies file under the '34 Act are chiefly useful only to the professional analyst and not the individual trader. It is therefore no surprise that the professional investment community has long supported the continuous disclosure system of the '34 Act: to them the system implies cost savings.

What do these cost savings imply for the structure and efficiency of the securities market? To the extent that mandated disclosure reduces the market professional's marginal cost of acquiring and verifying information, it increases the aggregate amount of securities research and verification provided. That is, because the analyst as a rational entrepreneur will increase his output until his marginal cost equals his marginal return, it follows axiomatically that the collectivization of securities information will produce more information. Over time, excess returns to securities analysts will induce new competitors to enter the market, which will increase the competitiveness of the industry. Casual empiricism suggests that both these predictions can be observed in the post-1934 experience of the securities industry. Certainly, the volume of securities research is much higher today than in 1934, and the very title "securities analyst" would not have been understood back then.

The unresolved question is why these cost savings were not clearly reflected in stock price increases or any other observable impact immediately following the '34 Act's passage? Although the one existing study of the market's reaction to the '34 Act's adoption may have been too methodologically flawed to capture any changes that occurred, another possible answer is that all the gains were captured by informed traders and other market professionals in the form of cost reductions. Arguably, these traders received the same approximate volume of information both before and after 1934, but simply obtained this data at a lower price after the '34 Act. Yet this answer seems incomplete; it ignores that the securities analyst—or his predecessor in that era— should produce more information if he has a lower marginal cost.

This argument that lower costs for the securities analyst should result in more information production takes us only so far. As Professors

Easterbrook and Fischel correctly observe, it is theoretically possible that too much information is already produced, particularly because not all, or even most, investors need to be well informed for the market to be efficient. Yet they stop at this point, which seems to be the threshold where close analysis should begin.

According to the SEC Advisory Committee on disclosure, only about 1,000 of the 10,000 odd "reporting" companies registered under the '34 Act are regularly followed by securities analysts. In the absence of analyst monitoring and in the presence of erratic trading, there is considerable reason to doubt that the market for the other 9,000 firms is "efficient," even in some cases in the "weak" sense of that term. Although other mechanisms exist by which to achieve efficiency, their efficacy is unproven and highly debatable. The desirability of expending social resources to improve the efficiency of the trading in these smaller issues can also be reasonably disputed. What seems to be beyond argument, however, is the consequence of increasing the securities analysts' marginal costs for obtaining or verifying information. If we repealed the '34 Act, and thereby increased analysts' marginal costs, the number of companies regularly followed by analysts would likely decline below this 1,000 figure. In short, cost reductions for analysts imply broader coverage of firms, and cost increases imply the converse. This conclusion, in turn, leads to the bottom line: the more firms that are closely followed by analysts, the greater assurance both that capital markets will be allocatively efficient and that the game will be fair with respect to such companies.

* * *

In 1934, institutional investors represented only a small fraction of equity securities trading; the dominant figure was still the professional trader, who relied more on rumors, tips, and personal contacts than on hard data. Only with the later appearance (probably in the 1960's) of the institutional investor—and in particular, a nationwide population of institutional investors—did the institutional structure arise that could support the modern securities analyst. In this light, the '34 Act becomes the logical, if premature, answer to a problem that had yet to emerge: how to increase the volume of securities research, which then was not even in demand. In 1934, any gains that the Act created may well have been fully captured by a small coterie of professional traders, but with the subsequent expansion of the industry, the cost savings that the '34 Act engendered helped to create the securities analyst as a distinct profession. That this result was serendipitous does not make it any less desirable.

B. Social Waste and the Problem of Excess Research

This hypothesis that a mandatory disclosure system reduces the costs incurred by market professionals has another important corollary: aggregate social wealth is arguably increased because the partial collectivization of securities information that the '34 Act mandates in effect economizes on the total amounts expended in pursuing trading gains. From a social welfare perspective, trading gains do not create additional wealth; one party's gain comes at the other party's loss, whereas the process of researching and verifying securities information consumes real resources. Although securities research sometimes creates social wealth (both by perfecting the allocative efficiency of the capital markets and by facilitating the entrepreneur's ability to raise capital for wealth-creating projects), the '34 Act chiefly addresses the secondary trading market. Here, one can view the participants as engaged in pursuing trading gains that do not affect aggregate shareholder wealth. Their expenditures in pursuit of such gains therefore represent social waste, as Professor Hirschleifer long ago pointed out in a classic article. In this light, a major significance of a mandatory disclosure system is that it can reduce these costs. Rival firms do not need to incur expenses to produce essentially duplicative data banks when a central securities data bank is in effect created at the SEC. Thus, rather than the '34 Act producing too much information (as Professors Easterbrook and Fischel suggest), it probably reduces wasteful duplication by establishing a central information repository.

This claim that wasteful duplication is eliminated by a mandatory disclosure system may sound inconsistent with the earlier assertion that inadequate securities research occurs because of the public goods-like character of securities information. Yet there is no contradiction. Financial professionals may simultaneously expend both too little and too much resources on verifying and obtaining information. The first problem arises because too few companies are followed or are researched inadequately; the second, because investigations by one analyst are duplicated by another. Still, the existence of a central information repository in the form of the SEC is at least a partial answer to both problems.

C. Allocative Efficiency: The Public Interest in Adequate Securities Research

Which of the last two problems discussed—too much research or too little—is more serious? This question is important because the design of an optimal disclosure system depends in large part on how one answers it. Two very different perspectives are possible on the securities market. If we see it as simply a "fair game" in which securities prices are "unbiased" (that is, prices are as likely to move in the buyer's favor as the seller's), there is little cause for regulatory intervention (except possibly to prevent insider trading). Moreover, because in this light the securities market is essentially a "zero-sum game"—that is, one side's gain in every transaction is the other side's loss—society has no reason to encourage the parties to invest their resources in this nonproductive attempt to obtain wealth at the other's expense. So viewed, a mandatory disclosure system would be justifiable principally as a means of minimizing the wasted resources devoted to the pursuit of trading gains.

Conversely, if we view the securities market as the principal allocative mechanism for investment capital, the behavior of securities prices is important not so much because of their distributive consequences on investors but more because of their effect on allocative efficiency. In this light, it is important not only that the game be fair, but that it be accurate—that is, that capital be correctly priced. Depending on a firm's share price, its cost for obtaining capital will be either too high or low as compared to the cost that would prevail in a perfectly efficient market. In either case, society's mechanism for allocating scarce investment capital among competing users becomes distorted, even though the game remains equally fair to buyers and sellers. From this perspective, the critical empirical question shifts from whether the federal securities laws improved the mean return to investors to whether they reduced the variance associated with these returns. That is, if the federal securities laws reduced the dispersion associated with the returns on new issues, it can reasonably be inferred that they made the market for new issues more allocatively efficient. Professor Stigler appears to acknowledge this point: "Price dispersion," he writes, "is a manifestation—and, indeed, it is a measure—of ignorance in the market."[47] The greater this variance associated with securities returns, the greater the uncertainty and heterogeneity of investor expectations, and the less the likelihood that our capital allocation mechanism is working efficiently. Yet the stock market may still appear efficient to the extent that prices move randomly and mandatory public disclosures appear not to cause price adjustments.

Once the focus is shifted to the degree of dispersion associated with securities prices in the presence or absence of a mandatory disclosure system, the empirical issue is narrowed. Every scholar who has investigated the impact of the federal securities laws—including Stigler, Bentson, Jarrell, and Friend—appears to agree that price dispersion declined after the passage of the Securities Act of 1933. The most logical conclusion to draw from this evidence is that allocative efficiency was enhanced and that investors thereby benefited. The key point then is that the social benefit of the federal securities laws may exceed their benefit to investors. The beneficiaries of increased allocative efficiency include virtually all members of society, not just investors. In this light, it is myopic to view the '34 Act as simply a subsidy for investors or to denigrate its benefits as merely trading gains.

This focus on allocative efficiency should also frame future research efforts. Rather than debate endlessly the effect that the federal securities laws had a half century ago, it is time to turn to issues of greater contemporary significance. For example, has the recent trend toward deregulation in connection with the administration of the '34 Act been associated with any increase in price dispersions or market volatility? To ask this question is not to answer it. Testable hypotheses, however, can

---

[47] Stigler, The Economics of Information, 69 J.Pol.Econ. 213, 214 (1961).

be framed: for example, one could inquire whether price dispersion has increased following the adoption of the integrated disclosure system in 1982 and the expanded use of shelf registration statements. If not, the cost reductions to corporate issuers associated with these regulatory reforms would seem justified. Clearly, however, this question cannot be safely answered by looking only at the market's immediate reaction to these developments or only at the change, if any, in mean returns to investors. Once we recognize that there is a social interest associated with an allocatively efficient capital market, then it is an overly narrow form of social cost accounting to calculate only the costs to issuers and benefits to investors.

---

1. *Market Efficiency and the Fraud-on-the-Market Doctrine.* The growing evidence that the efficiency of the market is less "robust" and more contestable than originally envisioned has special implications for securities litigation. In 1988, the Supreme Court accepted the Fraud-on-the-Market Doctrine, which assumes that investors rely on market price to reflect all available material information about a stock.[168] This greatly encouraged securities litigation by simplifying class certification. Increasingly, however, it became clear that not all investors do rely on market price.[169] Many buy stocks believing the market price undervalues the stock; other investors are indexed and do not care if a stock is undervalued or overvalued because, in their view, the shares will average out.

Based on this and similar arguments, corporate defendants asked the Court to reconsider the Fraud-on-the-Market Doctrine, which it did in Halliburton Co. v. Erica P. John Fund, Inc.[170] Yet, despite the claims of defendants that modern economic theory had "undermined" the doctrine, the Court's majority held it remained valid and no "special justification" existed for overturning it as a long-settled precedent. Still, the Court viewed the doctrine's presumption of investor reliance on publicly available information more as a sound generalization than a scientific fact—a generalization, it said, that rested "on the fairly modest premise that 'market professionals generally considered most publicly announced material statements about companies, thereby affecting stock market prices.'"[171] As for the "academic debate" over the doctrine, the Court further noted that critics of market efficiency "have not refuted the modest premise underlying the presumption of reliance. Even the foremost critic of the efficient-markets hypothesis acknowledges that public information generally affects stock prices."[172] In light of the new

---

[168] Basic, Inc. v. Levinson, 485 U.S. 224 (1988).
[169] On this theme, see Lev & de Villiers, Stock Price Crashes and 10b–5 Damages: A Legal, Economic and Policy Analysis, 47 Stan. L. Rev. 7 (1999).
[170] 573 U.S. 258 (2014).
[171] Id at 272.
[172] Id.

evidence, however, the Court did slightly "tweak" the doctrine by allowing defendants to contest at class certification whether the alleged misstatement or omission had "price impact" (i.e., did it affect the actual market price of the stock?).

7. POST-FILING REVIEW AND RESTRICTIONS

Statutes

    Securities Act, § 8.

    Exchange Act, §§ 12, 13, 15(d), Rule 15c2–8.

Rules and Regulations

    Rules 460, 461, 463, 473, 477.

A. POST-FILING PROCESSING

Under § 8 of the Securities Act, a registration statement becomes effective on "the twentieth day after the filing thereof,"[173] unless it is the subject of a refusal order[174] or stop order[175] by the Commission, or the Commission determines to make it effective on an earlier date (i.e., if effectiveness is "accelerated").[176]

This statutory scheme originally contemplated, in the usual case, that the registration statement would be filed; it would be reviewed by the Commission and information about the issue would be disseminated during the 20-day "waiting period"; the registration statement would become effective at the end of 20 days; and the offering would commence. For several reasons, however, it has not worked out this way.

a. Delaying Amendments. During the early history of the Commission, it was possible for offerings with no unusual problems to become effective within the basic 20-day period or even earlier. By an amendment to the statute in 1940, the SEC was given power, not only to consent to the filing of all amendments "as of" the original filing, but also to shorten this basic period. During this early era, many registration statements were made effective 15 to 18 days after the original filing.

If there were deficiencies in the registration statement that had not been corrected by amendment, and the 20-day period was about to expire, the Commission would generally suggest to the issuer that it file a "delaying amendment" to prevent the registration statement "from becoming effective in deficient form," unless the Commission thought the deficiencies were so serious as to warrant a stop-order proceeding. Since any amendment, no matter how trivial, starts a new 20-day period, such a delaying amendment can consist merely of changing one word on the

---

[173] See § 8(a) of the 1933 Act.
[174] See § 8(b) of the 1933 Act.
[175] See § 8(d) of the 1933 Act.
[176] See § 8(a) of the 1933 Act.

front cover of the registration statement. For example, the approximate date of the proposed public offering is required to be stated on the cover page, and it was generally expressed in some language such as: "As soon as practicable after the effective date of the Registration Statement." Back then, a delaying amendment might consist, for example, of simply changing the word "practicable" to "possible." A second delaying amendment, if one was required, could consist of changing the word "possible" back to "practicable."

The sort of procedure described above has become obsolete. Since the late 1950s, instead of receiving the SEC's letter of comment within about ten days after filing, there has been a delay of one to three months (or more) before the letter is forthcoming. This delay is attributable to a tremendous increase in the number of filings, combined with the failure of Congress to provide adequate staffing to the Commission to handle the workload. Consequently, the possibility of becoming effective during the basic 20-day period originally set by Congress has become practically nonexistent.

To eliminate the need for the issuer to file meaningless amendments, the SEC adopted Rule 473 that, in effect, permits a permanent delaying amendment to be filed along with the original registration statement.[177] Few issuers have been willing to confront the Commission by omitting this amendment.

    b. *Entry Into the Exchange Act.* As part of the IPO process, company counsel must educate the directors and officers of the newly public company regarding their ongoing responsibilities as a public company under the federal securities laws, particularly the 1934 Act.

As a result of going public, an issuer becomes subject to the periodic reporting requirements of § 13 by virtue of § 15(d) of the Exchange Act. In all probability, the company must also comply with the registration provisions of § 12 of the Exchange Act (a registration requirement under the 1934 Act to admit the registrant's securities for trading on a U.S. securities exchange, in addition to the registration requirement under the 1933 Act). A registrant under the 1934 Act must comply with numerous provisions: the proxy rules (§ 14); recapture of short-swing profits (§ 16(b)); the beneficial ownership reporting requirements (§ 16(a)); restrictions on short sales (§ 16(c)); the tender offer and reporting provisions of the Williams Act (§§ 14(d) and (e) and §§ 13(d) and (e)); the Foreign Corrupt Practices Act (§ 13(b)(2)); and the obligation to furnish annual reports to shareholders (§ 14 and Rules 14a–6 and 14c–3). Today, the Sarbanes-Oxley Act has added more duties to these traditional obligations, as discussed earlier, of which § 404's obligation to assess internal controls is likely to be the most costly, and § 302's requirement that the CEO and CFO certify their company's financial results may be the most feared.

---

[177] Securities Act Release No. 4329 (Feb. 21, 1961).

c. *Use of Proceeds.* Under Rule 463, an issuer filing its first registration statement under the 1933 Act must report on its use of proceeds in the first periodic report it subsequently files under the 1934 Act. This reporting obligation, which applies only to first-time registrants, continues until the later of the time at which the proceeds of the offering are fully applied or the offering is terminated. Essentially, Rule 463 is an antifraud protection, which allows the SEC to monitor whether proceeds have been applied in accordance with what is disclosed in the prospectus.

d. *Acceleration.* The decision whether to grant a request for acceleration is made by the Director of the Division of Corporation Finance, to whom the Commission has delegated this power. Requests for acceleration must be made in writing by the registrant, the managing underwriters of the offering, and the selling security holders, if any, in compliance with the conditions specified in Rule 461. The conditions governing the granting of acceleration are set forth in Rules 460 and 461.

To qualify for acceleration, Rule 460 states that the underwriters and participating dealers must have sufficient numbers of the preliminary prospectus to secure their adequate distribution a reasonable time in advance of the anticipated effective date of the registration statement. Today, with electronic delivery, this condition no longer poses any substantial obstacle. Rule 15c2–8 under the 1934 Act also requires that all brokers or dealers participating in the distribution take reasonable steps to furnish preliminary prospectuses to those who make a written request for copies and, in the case of an IPO, requires that preliminary prospectuses be sent at least 48 hours in advance of the mailing of the confirmation of sale. Rule 461 specifies the process by which acceleration is requested and the information that must be furnished to the SEC's Division of Corporation Finance.

e. *Refusal and Stop Orders.* The Commission generally does not use its powers to refuse a registration statement under § 8(b) because such an order requires it to act within ten days after the filing of the registration statement. At least in recent years, such quick action has not been possible. Furthermore, in the case of a refusal order, the deficiencies must be apparent "on the face" of the registration statement. This requirement may raise difficulties if the proceedings show there are deficiencies but there is an argument over whether they are "apparent." Under Red Bank Oil Co., 20 S.E.C. 863 (1945), a stop order is equally available whenever a refusal order might be issued, and it is not subject to either of these limitations. Thus, a stop order proceeding normally is instituted by the Commission. Instances in which the Commission has found it necessary to institute stop order proceedings have been relatively few in comparison to the large number of registration statements that have been filed.[178]

f. Withdrawal of Registration Statement. A controversy long surrounded the asserted right of a registrant to voluntarily withdraw a registration statement prior to effectiveness, despite the opposition of the SEC based on public interest considerations. A prior version of Rule 477 provided that a registration statement, or any amendment or exhibit thereto, could be withdrawn upon application of the registrant only if the Commission found such withdrawal consistent with the public interest and the protection of investors and, therefore, consented to the withdrawal. This rule seemingly reversed the result in Jones v. SEC,[179] in which the Supreme Court, in a sharply divided decision, sustained the right of a registrant to withdraw its registration statement prior to the effective date, despite objections by the SEC. Since the registrant had not commenced business, and there were no securities outstanding in the hands of the public, the Court saw no public interest issue involved in that case.

The validity of Rule 477 was sustained in a series of cases, typically because the registrant's securities were already outstanding in the hands of the public at the time of the proposed withdrawal of the registration statement.[180] Why did the SEC care if the registrant wished to call off an offering? The SEC's concern, in part, seemed to be that it would remain possible for the registrant to resort to Regulation A or another exemption following its withdrawal and capitalize on its prior sales efforts, thereby defeating the investor's right to public disclosure from a registration statement.

Nonetheless, in 2001, the SEC revised Rule 477 so that an issuer's application to withdraw a pre-effective registration statement becomes effective upon filing unless the Commission objects within 15 days after such filing.[181] This revision still permits the SEC to halt what it suspects is an attempt to substitute a fraudulent exempt offering for a public offering, but it also enables the issuer to control timing in most cases. This change is important for issuers because it reduces the prospect that a later offering will be "integrated" with the prior public offering (and thereby forfeit its exempt status). This problem of "integrating" offerings is considered later in this casebook.

---

[178] But see McLucas, Stop Order Proceedings Under the Securities Act of 1933: A Current Assessment, 40 Bus. Law. 515 (1985) (indicating an increasing use of this device).

[179] 298 U.S. 1 (1936).

[180] See Columbia General Investment Corp. v. SEC, 265 F.2d 559 (5th Cir. 1959); Wolf Corp. v. SEC, 115 U.S.App.D.C. 75, 317 F.2d 139 (1963).

[181] Securities Act Release No. 7943 (Jan. 26, 2001).

8. REGULATION OF UNDERWRITERS AND THE DISTRIBUTION PROCESS

Statutes and Regulations

Securities Act, § 8.

Regulation M, Rules 460, 461.

To this point, the chapter has focused primarily on the issuer. But underwriters are also closely regulated during the distribution process by the SEC and FINRA, as well as by state blue sky commissioners to the extent their jurisdiction is not preempted.

A. FINRA REVIEW OF UNDERWRITER'S COMPENSATION

For decades, the National Association of Securities Dealers ("NASD") and, today, its successor, the Financial Industry Regulatory Authority ("FINRA"), have reviewed and restricted the amount of compensation underwriters may receive in connection with a public offering. This review is premised, in part, on FINRA Conduct Rule 2010, which requires FINRA members to comply with "high standards of commercial honor and just and equitable principles of trade."[182] Based on these principles, FINRA Conduct Rule 2710 elaborately specifies the information that FINRA will consider in reviewing underwriter compensation.[183] FINRA reads this Rule as entitling it to reject any offering where "unfair or unreasonable compensation" will be paid to any of its members. But what is unfair or unreasonable about compensation the issuer and the underwriter negotiate between themselves? As a practical matter, abuses have chiefly arisen in cases involving unseasoned companies that find it difficult to enter the public market and are willing to pay high compensation to any underwriter willing to handle their securities. In such cases, some underwriting firms seek additional compensation in the form of "cheap stock" (i.e., stock purchased below the market or offering price) or warrants to purchase stock in the future. The fear may be that an overcompensated underwriter (particularly in a best efforts offering) will overreach its customers to obtain excessive compensation. By contrast, it becomes understandable that certain high-quality offerings, such as shelf-registered offerings on Form S-3 and certain debt offerings, are exempt from FINRA review.

Procedurally, the managing underwriter files the underwriting documents and the prospectus with FINRA, where a Committee on Corporate Financing (whose membership is secret) reviews it. Although few clear guidelines exist governing what constitutes "unreasonable" compensation in FINRA's eyes, an underwriter may not: (1) purchase

---

[182] See FINRA Rule 2010.
[183] See Exchange Act Release No. 42619 (Apr. 4, 2000).

securities of the issuer at a price significantly below the offering price within a 12-month period before the offering; (2) receive warrants to purchase issuer securities in excess of 10% of the securities to be offered or warrants having an exercise price below the offering price or a maturity in excess of five years; (3) obtain an over-allotment option exceeding 15% of the offering; or (4) sell warrants or stock received from the issuer as compensation until one year after the offering is completed.

The guidelines on overall compensation are vaguer and vary based on the size of the offering and the risks incurred by the underwriters.

> In determining the maximum amount of compensation that is considered fair and reasonable, [FINRA] considers the size of the offering and the amount of risk assumed by the underwriter, which is determined by whether the offering is being underwritten on a firm commitment or best efforts basis and whether the offering is an initial or secondary offering. The maximum guideline amount generally will vary directly with the amount of risk assumed by the underwriter and inversely with the dollar amount of offering proceeds. Firm commitment offerings are permitted higher levels of compensation than best efforts offerings due to the risk involved in an underwriter purchasing the securities for resale versus simply utilizing its best efforts to place the securities for the issuer. In addition, a firm commitment initial public offering (IPO) is generally permitted higher compensation than a firm commitment secondary offering because the underwriter is dealing with an unseasoned issuer and is likely to incur higher costs in introducing the issuer to prospective underwriters and investors. The higher percentage levels of compensation permitted in smaller offerings recognizes that certain fixed costs are involved in any distribution, regardless of size.[184]

Violations of FINRA's rules on compensation can result in disciplinary sanctions.[185]

B. Hot Issues: Oversubscription, Free Riding, and the Problem of Asymmetric Information

During the waiting period, the underwriters will often learn that demand for the offering far outstrips supply (a "hot issue"). At the contemplated offering price, they may learn they can sell not just 5 million shares (as originally planned), but 8 million. This information indicates that the secondary market price should rise because, as the allocation to those who wish to purchase in the offering is cut back, the unsatisfied demand will cause the secondary market price to jump at the

---

[184] FINRA, Notice To Members 92–53, Underwriting Compensation Received by Members in Public Corporate Equity Offerings.
[185] See, e.g., In the Matter of Application of May & Co., Inc., 44 S.E.C. 412 (Sept. 8, 1970).

outset of the offering. Of course, the underwriters could raise the offering price until supply and demand balance. This would make it more difficult, however, for underwriters to market the stock and would deny their investor clients the expected first-day appreciation.

A potential alternative is for the underwriters (or some of them) to exploit their knowledge that an issue is "hot" by subscribing themselves for a significant portion of their own allotment—in effect, jumping in front of their clients based on non-public information that the offering is oversubscribed. This further reduction in supply available to public investors will aggravate the supply/demand imbalance, making it even more likely the secondary market price will immediately rise. Conversely, an underwriter may sell portions of a "hot" offering to its partners, officers, employees, or friendly parties with whom it engages in reciprocal business transactions.

Both the SEC and FINRA have long objected to such practices. In the SEC's view, the statement in the registration statement that the securities will be offered to the public at the public offering price amounts to a representation that would become materially false if most shares were withheld for underwriters, insiders, or their affiliates.[186] Thus, the issuer needs to make a bona fide offering to the public to avoid making a material misrepresentation.

FINRA views the underwriter as a conduit through which securities in an underwritten offering should freely pass from the issuer to the public. Under its fair practice rules, FINRA insists that the underwriter cannot "free ride"—it cannot siphon off securities intended for the public to itself, its affiliates, or others in a position to direct future business to the underwriter, based on its knowledge that the offering is oversubscribed.[187] Likewise, the underwriter cannot sell such securities to directors, officers, employees, and associated persons of the underwriter, as well as other broker-dealers, and with limited exceptions, to immediate family members of those persons who are restricted from buying.

FINRA also does not permit the underwriter to raise the primary offering price if, during the distribution, the secondary market price rises above that price. In effect, this built-in profit must go to the subscribing investors.

There is no private cause of action available to plaintiffs for violation of the FINRA rules. However, arbitration panels have awarded punitive and substantial compensatory damages where stock in a hot IPO has

---

[186] See Securities Act Release No. 4150 (Oct. 23, 1959).

[187] See Free-Riding and Withholding, NASD Interpretations of the Board of Governors, NASD Manual (IM–2110–1); see also FINRA Conduct Rule 2110.

been allocated to affiliates of the underwriter in violation of these rules.[188]

When an offering is oversubscribed, powerful institutional buyers (e.g., mutual funds and pension funds) may insist that their desired allocation not be cut back (but instead that smaller investors bear the brunt of the rationing). These institutions may threaten not to participate in future offerings by the lead underwriter for a defined period (referred to as the "penalty box") if they do not receive their full allocation. Although the SEC may prefer that some stock be distributed to public investors, SEC rules do not significantly restrict the underwriters' discretion in allocating stock in an oversubscribed offering. Predictably, this means that those with the least leverage get cut back the most.

Two limitations are imposed on the underwriters' discretion (in addition to the "free-riding" prohibition, described above). First, shares in an IPO may not be allocated in return for payment of above-normal or "excessive" brokerage commissions. During the IPO boom of the late 1990s, it was alleged that hedge funds, which were particularly interested in "hot" IPO shares, offered to pay inflated brokerage commissions to the underwriter on other transactions as one means to obtain them. Arguably, such payments represented a bribe or kickback. In 2002, the SEC and the NASD (before the creation of FINRA) settled charges against Credit Suisse First Boston Corporation, a major underwriter, relating to its IPO allocation practices for total fines, plus disgorgement, of $100 million.[189] The SEC claimed these excessive commissions were calculated to pay the underwriter between one-third and two-thirds of the customers' trading gains on the IPO shares.

Slowly following up on these enforcement actions, in 2010, FINRA adopted Rule 5131(a), which prohibits a broker-dealer (or associated person) from allocating shares in a new issue for "compensation that is excessive in relation to the services provided by the member."[190] Although phrased in very general terms, the Rule does empower FINRA to discipline an underwriter or selling group member that sells its allocation to the highest bidder or in return for inflated charges for other services.

The second limitation on the underwriters' discretion involves "spinning"—the deliberate allocation by an underwriter of hot issue shares in the offering of one issuer to the officers and directors of another issuer in return for past or to obtain future business.[191] To curb this abuse, FINRA Rule 5131(b) prohibits a broker-dealer from allocating

---

[188] See Sanders v. Gardner, 7 F.Supp.2d 151 (E.D.N.Y. 1998) (upholding arbitration panel award of punitive damages for violation of "free-riding" rule).

[189] See SEC Litigation Release No. 17327 (Jan. 22, 2002), 2002 SEC LEXIS 147.

[190] See FINRA Rule 5131(a) (adopted in Exchange Act Release No. 63010 (Oct. 5, 2010)).

[191] See NASD Sends Members Warning Concerning Allocation of Hot IPOs, (BNA) Sec. Reg. & L. Rep., Vol. 29, no. 47, at 1667 (1998).

shares in a new issue to the account of an executive officer or director of a company: (i) that is an investment banking client of the broker-dealer; (ii) that paid compensation to the broker-dealer for investment banking services within the past 12 months; (iii) that expects to retain the broker-dealer for investment banking services within the next three months; or (iv) on the express or implied condition that such executive officer or director, on behalf of the company, will retain the underwriter for the performance of future investment banking services.[192] The Rule, however, is subject to several exceptions, and its narrowness suggests that "spinning" may still occur just outside the Rule's boundaries.

Rule 5131 also attempts to deal with the chronic underpricing of IPOs by requiring underwriters to provide more detailed information, in the form of periodic reports to a pricing committee of the IPO issuer's board, about the indications of interest received from investors and the allocation of shares to institutional investors.[193] The premise is that, if the board realizes the degree to which the offering is hot (and institutions are demanding allocations in it), they may seek to price their offering more aggressively.

Problem

PROBLEM 3-5

The allocation of stock in hot IPOs has long been a controversial issue. Inevitably, large or repeat customers appear to receive preference over retail customers in the allocation of shares in hot IPOs. Suppose, then, that FINRA proposes, under pressure from Congress, an allocation rule under which underwriters must do one of the following:

(a) allocate IPO shares on a "first-come, first-served" basis to the persons who first request an allocation (probably subject to some ceiling—say 10,000 shares—on this right of priority); or

(b) prorate the shares the underwriter is to receive among all its customers who request allocations (thus, if the underwriter intends to buy 1 million shares and receives indications of interest from its customers for 2 million shares, every customer would receive at least 50% of its requested allocation).

Would such rules be preferable to the current system (in fact, variations on these rules are in effect in some other countries)? What would be their likely impact?

C. THE SEC'S TRADING RULES

When the issuer has had prior offerings, and its stock is traded in the secondary market, the offering price in a primary offering will typically be its trading price in the secondary market. This price could be inflated, however, if the underwriters were to undertake significant

---

[192] See Exchange Act Release No. 63010 (Oct. 5, 2010) (adopting Rule 5131).
[193] See FINRA Rule 5131(d) (adopted in Securities Act Release No. 63010) (Oct. 5, 2010).

purchases of the issuer's stock in the period immediately prior to the offering. Even in the case of an IPO, the offering's success would be greatly assisted if the issuer or underwriters (or agents of either) were to buy stock in the secondary market after the primary offering commenced to cause the secondary market price to rise above the fixed price in the offering. Purchases in both contexts are inherently suspicious because the buyer's intent may be to manipulate the price of the stock to assure the success of the offering. For this reason, the SEC has long restricted the ability of issuers and underwriters to buy what they are selling during a distribution. For many years, this restriction was embodied in Rule 10b–6 under the 1934 Act, but in 1997, the SEC codified a series of trading rules in Regulation M under the 1934 Act.

Rule 101 of Regulation M focuses on (i) underwriters, (ii) brokers or dealers who have agreed to participate or who are participating in a distribution of securities, and (iii) "affiliated purchasers," which term includes those acting in concert with the above persons or who control any participant in the distribution.[194] Such persons are prohibited from making purchases or bids during a "distribution" until they have completed their participation in the distribution.

Rule 101's prohibition applies during a "restricted period," which depends on the trading volume associated with the security. When a security has an average daily trading volume ("ADTV") of $100,000 or more, and its issuer has a public float of $25 million or more,[195] Rule 100 specifies that the restricted period begins one business day prior to the determination of the offering price (or such later time when the person becomes a distribution participant). Otherwise, the restricted period begins on the later of five business days prior to the determination of the offering price or the date on which the person becomes a distribution participant. Rule 101 grants an exemption from these restrictions for certain "excepted securities," including securities having an ADTV of at least $1 million and a public float of at least $150 million. In these "excepted" cases, although Regulation M does not bar a broker-dealer from purchasing or bidding for the security during the distribution, it is still potentially open to the Commission or a private party seeking to prove manipulative intent in violation of Rule 10b–5.

Rule 102 applies similar prohibitions to the issuer, selling shareholders, and their affiliates, while Rule 103 provides an exception for "passive" market-making on Nasdaq. This permits an underwriter to make a secondary market in the stock so long as it does not bid for or purchase the stock at a price that exceeds the highest independent bid.

It is important to understand that Regulation M applies broadly to any "distribution," a term defined by Rule 100 to cover "an offering of securities, whether or not subject to regulation under the Securities Act,

---

[194] See Rule 101 of Regulation M under the 1934 Act.
[195] "Float" refers to the value of the stock held by public investors (i.e., not by insiders or "affiliates").

that is distinguished from ordinary trading transactions by the magnitude of the offering and the presence of special selling efforts and selling methods." Conceivably, an attempt by a large but non-controlling shareholder to liquidate its substantial stake (say, 15%) could amount to a "distribution" and thus make Regulation M applicable, even though registration of the securities is not required.

D. STABILIZATION

The underwriters' great fear during a distribution is that the secondary market price will fall below the fixed offering price. This could be the result of (1) exogenous changes in the outside world (i.e., some surprise announcement or unexpected news); (2) a loss of confidence in the offering by short-term oriented investors ("flippers") who hoped for immediate stock appreciation in the first hours of the offering and were disappointed; or (3) the activities of short-sellers (who want the aftermarket price to fall once they have made substantial short sales). To guard against the latter two possibilities, the underwriting group typically attempts to place a floor under the secondary market price during the period of the distribution by placing a standing offer to buy all stock offered in the market at below the offering price. This is called "stabilizing" the stock (i.e., the fixing of a security market's price through purchases or bids at the offering price to preclude or retard any decline in price below the offering price during the distribution). Stabilization was long permitted within certain defined boundaries by a special rule (Rule 10b–7), which was later codified in Regulation M as Rule 104.

Section 9(a)(6) of the 1934 Act prohibits "pegging, fixing, or stabilizing the price" of a security in contravention of the SEC's rules. Rule 104 is both an exception to Rule 101 (which broadly forbids purchases and bids during a distribution) and a safe harbor that protects the underwriter from any claim it has "manipulated" the stock's price. Thus, by complying with Rule 104, the underwriter avoids liability under § 9(a)(6) and Rule 10b–5. Under Rule 104, underwriters can bid for the stock so long as they do not exceed the lower of the offering price or "last independent transaction price for the security in the principal market."[196] Thus, if the offering price is $100 and the secondary market price rises to $102, the underwriters may not stabilize (i.e., peg the price) at that level. Stabilizing is also forbidden in an "at-the-market offering."[197]

Stabilizing activities can be suspended at any time and will typically be halted once the distribution is completed (i.e., once all allotments have been sold by the underwriters). In effect, this means that the floor placed under the stock's price can suddenly be removed, and the stock's price, which had seemed stable, can suddenly nosedive. For this reason,

---

[196] See Rule 104(f)(2) under the 1934 Act.

[197] See Rule 104(e) under the 1934 Act. "At-the-market" offerings have no fixed-offering price; securities are sold to investors at the then-current secondary market price.

sophisticated investors may be cautious of the offering if the price does not immediately rise in the aftermarket, because a stable aftermarket price is often illusory (since it may be artificially and temporarily maintained by the underwriters).

Problem

PROBLEM 3-6

Stabilization is a means of protecting the issuer against a raid by short-sellers, who hope to create and profit from panic. But stabilization may mislead the retail investor who may think that a "flat" offering (i.e., one with no initial run-up in price) shows a stable market and a relative equilibrium between supply and demand for the stock. In fact, the "flat" price may be the consequence of underwriters placing a temporary floor under the offering price; when that temporary floor is removed, the stock will likely decline. Would it be simpler just to preclude short-selling for some period (say, ten days) after the IPO offering begins? Or would this reform aggravate the problem by producing a more volatile, less reliable market? Alternatively, in light of the strong tendency toward underpricing in IPOs, are stabilizing purchases justifiable on this ground? What would happen if the current rule did not exist? How would underwriters likely respond if they could not stabilize?

E. SHORT SELLING AROUND PUBLIC OFFERINGS

Public offerings have proven to be an inviting target for short-sellers. Sometimes acting in concert, they sell the stock in large quantities on or before the offering date to drive the price down and cover their short sales at a lower price. Although stabilizing purchases by the underwriters may offset these short sales, the underwriters will usually cease "stabilizing" the market once they have sold their allotments. The price may decline immediately afterward as the market maker responds to the imbalance of sales and purchases.

What makes a public offering a special target for short selling? One possible answer is that short sellers can uniquely protect themselves from the normal risk that the stock price may rise in the aftermarket, which would force them to cover at a loss. They can do so by subscribing for shares in the offering at the offering price. Of course, this is another example of "free-riding" because they may intend to purchase the offered shares only if the aftermarket price rises. (If it falls, they are likely to default on their purchase and, instead, buy shares in the secondary market at a price below the offering price.) As a result, short sellers can view primary offerings as presenting them with a "can't lose" opportunity.

In response, underwriters lobbied the SEC for protection, and in the 1990s, the Commission adopted Rule 10b–22, which has now been codified as Rule 105 in Regulation M. Rule 105 does not forbid short selling in connection with a public offering, but rather prohibits any person from covering a short sale with "offered securities [purchased] from an underwriter or broker or dealer participating in the offering" if the short sale occurred within a prescribed period that usually begins five business days before the pricing of the offered security and ends with the pricing of the security. This Rule does not apply to shelf registrations (where the market is believed to be too deep for short selling to have much effect) or best efforts underwritings (where there tends not to be a fixed offering price). Although Rule 105 chills short selling on the eve of a public offering, it has proven difficult to enforce because of difficulty in detecting violations. Some public offerings remain plagued by short-selling campaigns, but it is uncertain whether Rule 105 is being violated.

9. PENNY STOCKS AND BLANK CHECK OFFERINGS

Although the federal securities laws are based on a disclosure philosophy that assumes that informed investors can protect themselves, and thus do not authorize the SEC to engage in the same "merit review" that some state securities regulators conduct,[198] Congress passed a clear exception in 1990 to deal with what are termed "blank check" offerings. In the Securities Enforcement Remedies and Penny Stock Reform Act of 1990,[199] Congress found that "blank check" registration had "been used extensively for abusive and fraudulent practices in the penny stock market."[200] As the name implies, "blank check" offerings involve newly-formed companies without a preexisting history or assets; the investor, in effect, is asked to trust the promoter (i.e., to write it a blank check) to use the offering proceeds to acquire virtually any kind of assets the promoter considers attractive. Indeed, because the promoter often has no specific business plans, there is relatively little to disclose (other than the promoter's prior history and the obvious risks in such an offering). Not infrequently, the secondary market in such stocks was manipulated by the promoter to give the impression of a rising stock price, even though the proceeds of the offering were not re-invested or were actually diverted into the promoter's own pockets.

In response, the 1990 legislation directed the SEC to prescribe specific rules applicable to "blank check" offerings. Under § 7(b) of the 1933 Act, the Commission may require such issuers to (1) provide additional disclosures, both before and after the registration statement is declared effective; (2) place limitations on the use of proceeds obtained

---

[198] "Merit review" today has largely disappeared, mainly because federal law preempts state "blue sky" registration in the case of stocks listed on a national securities exchange or sold in certain exempt offerings. See § 18 of the 1933 Act.

[199] Penny Stock Market Fraud: Hearing on H.R. 4497 Before the Subcomm. on Telecomm. and Fin. of the Comm. on Energy and Commerce, 101st Cong. 31 (1989). See also Pub. L. No. 101–429, 104 Stat. 931, Tit. V. (1990). This legislation also amended the 1934 Act for the purpose of "curbing the pervasive fraud and manipulation in the penny stock market." House Comm. on Energy and Commerce, Penny Stock Reform Act of 1990, H.R. Rep. No. 101–617, at 7 (1990).

[200] Id. at 22.

in such an offering and on the distribution of the securities sold; and (3) provide a right of rescission to shareholders.

Section 7(b) applies only to registration statements filed by issuers that are "blank check companies," which term is defined in § 7(b)(3) to mean "any development stage company that is issuing a penny stock . . . and that . . . (A) has no specific business plan or purpose; or (B) has indicated that its business plan is to merge with an unidentified company or companies." The term "penny stock" is defined in § 3(a)(51) of the 1934 Act to include any equity security other than a security registered on a national securities exchange or authorized for quotation on Nasdaq that meets criteria set by the SEC. To prevent evasion, subsection (B) of § 3(a)(51) also grants the Commission the authority to designate as a penny stock any security that is registered on an exchange or quoted on Nasdaq, if trading in the security also occurs outside the exchanges or in the non-Nasdaq over-the-counter market. The SEC's rule defining "penny stock" is Rule 3a51–1 under the 1934 Act.

Notably, § 7(b) is intended to cover "blank check" offerings and does not extend to "blind pool" offerings. A "blind pool" offering may raise funds to acquire still-unidentified assets (for example, real estate investments in a specific market), but so long as there is a "specific business plan" (i.e., to operate motels or suburban garden apartments according to some operating criteria), the issuer is exempt from the "blank check" designation under § 7(b)(3)(A).

What is most distinctive about § 7(b) is the substantive authority it confers on the SEC to regulate the use of proceeds and to provide investors with a continuing right of rescission (on terms specified by the SEC). This authority closely resembles the merit authority exercised by state blue sky commissioners. The SEC has sometimes used this authority aggressively. In particular, the SEC adopted Rule 419 to govern 1933 Act registration statements relating to an offering by a blank check company.[201] The Commission summarized the rule, in part, this way:[202]

> [P]roposed new Securities Act Rule 419 would require funds received and securities issued in an offering of penny stock by a blank check company to be placed in an escrow or trust account . . . until specified conditions have been met. These conditions would include the filing of a post-effective amendment upon the consummation of an acquisition if the business or assets being

---

[201] Securities Act Release No. 6891 (Apr. 17, 1991) [1990–1991 Transfer Binder] Fed.Sec.L.Rep. (CCH) ¶ 84,728. One should distinguish blank check companies, formed under Rule 419, from the recent wave of special purpose acquisition companies ("SPACs") that raised more than $40 billion in 2020. SPACs, like blank check companies, pool funds to finance a merger or acquisition within a set timeframe with a company or companies that usually have not yet been identified. SPACs, however, typically are not regulated under Rule 419 because they do not issue penny stocks, although in practice many of the Rule 419 requirements may be mirrored in a SPAC offering.

[202] Id. at 81,503.

acquired met specified criteria. Purchasers would have the opportunity to have their deposited funds (less certain withdrawals) returned upon receipt of the prospectus describing the acquisition. If these conditions had not been met within 18 months, the funds would be required to be returned to the purchaser.

In addition, the 1934 Act's Penny Stock Rules (Rules 15g–1 through 15g–9 and Schedule 15G) provide for a risk disclosure document, require monthly customer account statements concerning penny stocks held for customers, and mandate special continuing disclosures as to compensation, market quotations, and whether the broker-dealer is acting as the sole market maker for the security. Clearly, these rules use disclosure less to inform investors than to chill this type of offering.

Problem

PROBLEM 3-7

As part of the Securities Enforcement Remedies and Penny Stock Reform Act of 1990, Congress authorized the SEC to pass new rules designed to reduce fraud in the buying and selling of "penny stocks" by regulating the use of proceeds and giving investors a right of rescission. These rules made it more costly for underwriters, brokers, and anyone else (including agents, finders, and consultants, among others) participating in the sale and distribution of penny stocks (defined as stocks with a price of less than $5). The goal was to raise the quality of all equity offerings, including those in the penny stock category and the non-penny stock category. Do you think the statute was successful? How might you design an empirical study to test the efficacy of this statute?

SUBDIVISION B. COVERAGE OF THE REGULATION

CHAPTER 4

DEFINITIONS OF "SECURITY" AND "EXEMPTED SECURITIES"

1. WHAT IS A "SECURITY"?

Statutes

Securities Act, §§ 2(a)(1), 2A, 3(a)–(c).

Exchange Act, §§ 3(a)(10) and 3A.

A. "INVESTMENT CONTRACT"

DEFINITION OF A "SECURITY": A STUDY
IN STATUTORY INTERPRETATION

The federal securities laws apply to an instrument or contract only if it qualifies as a "security." The scope of that definition, therefore, is jurisdictional—affecting the breadth of the federal securities laws, as well as limiting the reach of certain other laws. For example, the authority of the Consumer Financial Protection Bureau ("CFPB") is circumscribed, in part, by the authority of the SEC—so what qualifies as a "security" affects both the SEC's reach as well as the CFPB's limits.

But how broad is that term? Little doubt exists that a share of stock is a security (except, as we will see, in some cases), and few would expect that an ownership interest in Florida orange trees would amount to a security (but it does, as we will see, in some cases). In construing what constitutes a security, the federal securities laws look less to the instrument than to the underlying business relationship.

The key terms in the federal securities laws have meanings quite different from their dictionary definitions. Securities Act § 2(a)(1) and Exchange Act § 3(a)(10) each define a "security" in both specific and general terms. Thus, there is no single test for determining what constitutes a security. The purpose of the two-part test was "to include within the definition the many types of instruments that in our commercial world fall within the ordinary concept of a security."[1]

The list of specific instruments includes any "note," "stock," "bond," and "debenture," and, in a recent addition, any "security-based swap." Then there follows a laundry-list of more general catch-all phrases, such as any "evidence of indebtedness," any "certificate of interest or

---

[1] H.R.Rep. No. 85, 73 Cong., 1st Sess. 11 (1933).

participation in any profit-sharing agreement," any "investment contract," and any "instrument commonly known as a 'security.'" This broad reach creates some inevitable uncertainty, but it also prevents transaction planners from sidestepping the federal securities laws by simply calling an instrument by a name that is not listed in the statutory definition.

This statutory flexibility works both ways. Both the specific and the general definitions in the Securities Act and the Exchange Act are said to apply "unless the context otherwise requires." Thus, although an instrument seemingly falls into any of the statutory definitions of security, it nevertheless may not be held to be a security under the federal securities laws if the context otherwise requires. For many years, this language has been used to exclude many types of debt obligations from the coverage of the federal securities laws, despite their inclusion in the foregoing lists, where these obligations arose in traditional banking or mercantile contexts.

In Securities and Exchange Commission v. C.M. Joiner Leasing Corporation,[2] the Supreme Court initially considered the application of the statute to the sale of interests in oil and gas leases, coupled with the promise by the seller to drill test wells located to discover the oil-producing possibilities of the surrounding land. Justice Jackson noted that the definition was similar to those found in many state "blue sky" laws and considered what rules of statutory construction might serve to ascertain the legislative intent. In rejecting the argument that the Act should be strictly construed, he stated:[3]

> In the Securities Act the term "security" was defined to include by name or description many documents in which there is common trading for speculation or investment. Some, such as notes, bonds, and stocks, are pretty much standardized and the name alone carries well-settled meaning. Others are of more variable character and were necessarily designated by more descriptive terms, such as "transferable share," "investment contract," and "in general any interest or instrument commonly known as a security." We cannot read out of the statute these general descriptive designations merely because more specific ones have been used to reach some kinds of documents. Instruments may be included within any of these definitions, as a matter of law, if on their face they answer to the name or description. However, the reach of the Act does not stop with the obvious and commonplace. Novel, uncommon, or irregular devices, whatever they appear to be, are also reached if it be proved as [a] matter of fact that they were widely offered or dealt in under terms or courses of dealing which established their

---

[2] 320 U.S. 344 (1943).
[3] Id. 350–51.

character in commerce as "investment contracts," or as "any interest or instrument commonly known as a 'security.'"

In applying the two tests for a security under § 2(a)(1), Justice Jackson first applied the specific instruments test to determine whether the oil leasehold interests were included in the specifically designated instruments. Obviously, the list of specific instruments did not include divided interests in oil and gas. He, therefore, proceeded to the second test by considering terms of a more variable character, specifically "investment contract." Noting that the leasehold interests were sold on the condition that the purchasers would share in any appreciation in value of their lease interests if oil were discovered on adjacent land, Justice Jackson concluded that these leaseholds constituted "investment contracts" and, therefore, were "securities."

Joiner Leasing did not attempt to specify precise criteria, but in retrospect it is clear that all the investors were mutually dependent on the promoter's promise to conduct test drilling. This factor of interdependency loomed even larger in the next case considered by the Supreme Court on the meaning of "security."

Securities & Exchange Commission v. W. J. Howey Co.

Supreme Court of the United States, 1946.
328 U.S. 293, 66 S.Ct. 1100, 90 L.Ed. 1244.

■ MR. JUSTICE MURPHY delivered the opinion of the Court.

This case involves the application of § 2(a)(1) of the Securities Act of 1933 to an offering of units of a citrus grove development coupled with a contract for cultivating, marketing and remitting the net proceeds to the investor.

The Securities and Exchange Commission instituted this action to restrain the respondents from using the mails and instrumentalities of interstate commerce in the offer and sale of unregistered and non-exempt securities in violation of § 5(a) of the Act. The District Court denied the injunction, * * * and the Fifth Circuit Court of Appeals affirmed the judgment * * *. We granted certiorari * * *.

* * * The respondents, W. J. Howey Company and Howey-in-the-Hills Service, Inc., are Florida corporations under direct common control and management. The Howey Company owns large tracts of citrus acreage in Lake County, Florida. During the past several years it has planted about 500 acres annually, keeping half of the groves itself and offering the other half to the public "to help us finance additional development." Howey-in-the-Hills Service, Inc., is a service company engaged in cultivating and developing many of these groves, including the harvesting and marketing of the crops.

Each prospective customer is offered both a land sales contract and a service contract, after having been told that it is not feasible to invest in a grove unless service arrangements are made. While the purchaser is free to make arrangements with other service companies, the superiority of Howey-in-the-Hills Service, Inc., is stressed. Indeed, 85% of the acreage sold during the 3-year period ending May 31, 1943, was covered by service contracts with Howey-in-the-Hills Service, Inc.

The land sales contract with the Howey Company provides for a uniform purchase price per acre or fraction thereof, varying in amount only in accordance with the number of years the particular plot has been planted with citrus trees. Upon full payment of the purchase price the land is conveyed to the purchaser by warranty deed. Purchases are usually made in narrow strips of land arranged so that an acre consists of a row of 48 trees. During the period between February 1, 1941, and May 31, 1943, 31 of the 42 persons making purchases bought less than 5 acres each. The average holding of these 31 persons was 1.33 acres and sales of as little as 0.65, 0.7 and 0.73 of an acre were made. These tracts are not separately fenced and the sole indication of several ownership is found in small land marks intelligible only through a plat book record.

The service contract, generally of a 10-year duration without option of cancellation, gives Howey-in-the-Hills Service, Inc., a leasehold interest and "full and complete" possession of the acreage. For a specified fee plus the cost of labor and materials, the company is given full discretion and authority over the cultivation of the groves and the harvest and marketing of the crops. The company is well established in the citrus business and maintains a large force of skilled personnel and a great deal of equipment, including 75 tractors, sprayer wagons, fertilizer trucks and the like. Without the consent of the company, the land owner or purchaser has no right of entry to market the crop; thus there is ordinarily no right to specific fruit. The company is accountable only for an allocation of the net profits based upon a check made at the time of picking. All the produce is pooled by the respondent companies, which do business under their own names.

The purchasers for the most part are non-residents of Florida. They are predominantly business and professional people who lack the knowledge, skill and equipment necessary for the care and cultivation of citrus trees. They are attracted by the expectation of substantial profits. * * * Many of these purchasers are patrons of a resort hotel owned and operated by the Howey Company in a scenic section adjacent to the groves. The hotel's advertising mentions the fine groves in the vicinity and the attention of the patrons is drawn to the groves as they are being escorted about the surrounding countryside. They are told that the groves are for sale; if they indicate an interest in the matter they are then given a sales talk.

It is admitted that the mails and instrumentalities of interstate commerce are used in the sale of the land and service contracts and that no registration statement or letter of notification has ever been filed with the Commission in accordance with the Securities Act of 1933 and the rules and regulations thereunder.

Section 2(a)(1) of the Act defines the term "security" to include the commonly known documents traded for speculation or investment. This definition also includes "securities" of a more variable character, designated by such descriptive terms as "certificate of interest or participation in any profit-sharing agreement," "investment contract" and "in general, any interest or instrument commonly known as a 'security.'" The legal issue in this case turns upon a determination of whether, under the circumstances, the land sales contract, the warranty deed and the service contract together constitute an "investment contract" within the meaning of § 2(a)(1) * * *.

The term "investment contract" is undefined by the Securities Act or by relevant legislative reports. But the term was common in many state "blue sky" laws in existence prior to the adoption of the federal statute and, although the term was also undefined by the state laws, it had been broadly construed by state courts so as to afford the investing public a full measure of protection. Form was disregarded for substance and emphasis was placed upon economic reality. An investment contract thus came to mean a contract or scheme for "the placing of capital or laying out of money in a way intended to secure income or profit from its employment." State v. Gopher Tire & Rubber Co., 146 Minn. 52, 56, 177 N.W. 937, 938. This definition was uniformly applied by state courts to a variety of situations where individuals were led to invest money in a common enterprise with the expectation that they would earn a profit solely through the efforts of the promoter or of some one other than themselves.

By including an investment contract within the scope of § 2(a)(1) of the Securities Act, Congress was using a term the meaning of which had been crystallized by this prior judicial interpretation. It is therefore reasonable to attach that meaning to the term as used by Congress, especially since such a definition is consistent with the statutory aims. In other words, an investment contract for purposes of the Securities Act means a contract, transaction or scheme whereby a person invests his money in a common enterprise and is led to expect profits solely from the efforts of the promoter or a third party, it being immaterial whether the shares in the enterprise are evidenced by formal certificates or by nominal interests in the physical assets employed in the enterprise. Such a definition necessarily underlies this Court's decision in S.E.C. v. Joiner Corp., 320 U.S. 344, and has been enunciated and applied many times by lower federal courts. It permits the fulfillment of the statutory purpose of compelling full and fair disclosure relative to the issuance of "the many types of instruments that in our commercial world fall within the ordinary concept of a security." H.Rep. No. 85, 73d Cong., 1st Sess., p. 11. It embodies a flexible rather than a static principle, one that is capable of adaptation to meet the countless and variable schemes devised by those who seek the use of the money of others on the promise of profits.

The transactions in this case clearly involve investment contracts as so defined. The respondent companies are offering something more than fee simple interests in land, something different from a farm or orchard coupled with management services. They are offering an opportunity to contribute money and to share in the profits of a large citrus fruit enterprise managed and partly owned by respondents. They are offering this opportunity to persons who reside in distant localities and who lack the equipment and experience requisite to the cultivation, harvesting and marketing of the citrus products. Such persons have no desire to occupy the land or to develop it themselves; they are attracted solely by the prospects of a return on their investment. Indeed, individual development of the plots of land that are offered and sold would seldom be economically feasible due to their small size. Such tracts gain utility as citrus groves only when cultivated and developed as component parts of a larger area. A common enterprise managed by respondents or third parties with adequate personnel and equipment is therefore essential if the investors are to achieve their paramount aim of a return on their investments. Their respective shares in this enterprise are evidenced by land sales contracts and warranty deeds, which serve as a convenient method of determining the investors' allocable shares of the profits. The resulting transfer of rights in land is purely incidental.

Thus all the elements of a profit-seeking business venture are present here. The investors provide the capital and share in the earnings and profits; the promoters manage, control and operate the enterprise. It follows that the arrangements whereby the investors' interests are made manifest involve investment contracts, regardless of the legal terminology in which such contracts are clothed. The investment contracts in this instance take the form of land sales contracts, warranty deeds and service contracts which respondents offer to prospective investors. And respondents' failure to abide by the statutory and administrative rules in making such offerings, even though the failure result from a bona fide mistake as to the law, cannot be sanctioned under the Act.

This conclusion is unaffected by the fact that some purchasers choose not to accept the full offer of an investment contract by declining to enter into a service contract with the respondents. The Securities Act prohibits the offer as well as the sale of unregistered, non-exempt securities. Hence it is enough that the respondents merely offer the essential ingredients of an investment contract.

* * *

Reversed.

"Unique" Investments. Both in *Howey* and *Joiner Leasing*, the term "investment contract" was applied to arrangements (small interests in a citrus grove coupled with a service contract in *Howey*; oil lease assignments in *Joiner Leasing*) that were not susceptible to trading on exchanges or in other securities markets. More recently, however, the Court has retreated from applying the term "investment contract" to at least some forms of "unique" business arrangements that could not be traded in the securities markets. In Marine Bank v. Weaver, 455 U.S. 551 (1982), which is discussed further below, the plaintiffs pledged a bank certificate of deposit to secure a bank loan to a company and, in return, received a share of the company's net profits along with the right to use a pasture and barn owned by the company. They also received the right to veto future loans to the company, thereby giving them at least some right to participate in control of the enterprise. Did this amount to an investment contract?

The Court said "no," distinguishing prior cases:

> The usual instruments found to constitute securities in prior cases involved offers to a number of potential investors, not a private transaction in this case. In *Howey*, for example, 42 persons purchased interests in a citrus grove during a 4 month period.... The instruments involved in *C.M. Joiner Leasing* and *Howey* had equivalent values to most persons and could have been traded publicly.
>
> Here, in contrast, ... the unique agreement they negotiated was not designed to be traded publicly. Id. at 559–560.

Although the Court may have exaggerated how easy it would have been to publicly trade interests in a small citrus grove, *Marine Bank* probably does mean that a privately-negotiated transaction, offered only to a single investor or a very small number of investors, and involving rights not easily valued (such as the right to use a barn and pasture), will not be deemed to involve the offer or sale of securities.

Does this make sense, and should the *Weaver* decision be generalized to mean that all privately-negotiated, "unique" transactions that cannot be publicly traded should not be deemed securities? Some have argued that, in such one-on-one transactions, there are no economies of scale that justify placing the disclosure costs on the issuer. See Carney, Defining a Security: The Addition of a Market-Oriented Contextual Approach to Investment Contract Analysis, 33 Emory L. J. 311 (1984). Arguably, this creates too strong an incentive to custom-design financial contracts to avoid the federal securities laws. Thus, others reply that § 4(a)(2) of the 1933 Act (the issuer's private placement exemption) better addresses this problem, because it greatly reduces the costs of disclosure to the issuer, while still holding the issuer liable for fraud under Rule 10b–5 under the 1934 Act.

Securities and Exchange Commission v. Life Partners, Inc.

United States Court of Appeals for the District of Columbia Circuit, 1996.
87 F.3d 536.

■ Before WALD, GINSBURG and HENDERSON.

■ GINSBURG, CIRCUIT JUDGE: A viatical settlement is an investment contract pursuant to which an investor acquires an interest in the life insurance policy of a terminally ill person—typically an AIDS victim—at a discount of 20 to 40 percent, depending upon the insured's life expectancy. When the insured dies, the investor receives the benefit of the insurance. The investor's profit is the difference between the discounted purchase price paid to the insured and the death benefit collected from the insurer, less transaction costs, premiums paid, and other administrative expenses.

Life Partners, Inc., "LPI," ... arranges these transactions and performs certain post-transaction administrative services. The SEC contends that the fractional interests marketed by LPI are securities, and that LPI violated the [federal securities laws] by selling them without first complying with the registration and other requirements of those Acts. The district court agreed and preliminarily enjoined LPI from making further sales.

* * *

We agree with the district court that viatical settlements are not exempt from the securities laws because they are insurance contracts. Contrary to the district court, however, we conclude that LPI's contracts are not securities subject to the federal securities laws because the profits from their purchase do not derive predominantly from the efforts of a party or parties other than the investors. . . .

I. BACKGROUND

* * *

Although some promoters of viatical settlements do register them as securities under the federal securities laws, LPI observes that registration under the federal securities laws means higher costs for investors and correspondingly lower prices for terminally ill policy holders, and objects that any significant administrative delay . . . might be fatal in this time sensitive context.

* * *

. . . LPI sells fractional interests in insurance policies to retail investors, who may pay as little as $650 and buy as little as 3% of the benefits of a policy. In order to reach its customers, LPI uses some 500 commissioned "licensees," mostly independent financial planners. For its efforts, LPI's net compensation is roughly 10% of the purchase price after payment or referral and other fees. . . .

[The structure of LPI's transactions have] gone through three iterations during the course of this litigation. In each, LPI performed or performs a number of pre-purchase functions: Specifically, even before assembling the investors, LPI evaluates the insured's medical condition, reviews his insurance policy, negotiates the purchase price, and prepares the legal documents. The difference among the three versions is that LPI performs ever fewer (and ultimately no) post-purchase functions.

[In the original Version, LPI or an agent, were the record owners of the insurance policies. An independent escrow agent performed most of the post-purchase administrative functions, holding the policy, disbursing all funds, and filing the death claim. Under Version II, the investors were the owners of record and thus were in privity with the insurance company. Although investors were told that they did not need to use the escrow agent's post-purchase services, these services were offered to them on an optional basis, which most took. Under Version III, LPI ceased to provide any post-purchase services to purchasers either directly or through any agent. All such services became the sole responsibility of the investor; however, an escrow agent was still available to provide services as the agent of the investor.]

II. ANALYSIS

[The Court first rejected LPI's argument that the viatical settlements were insurance contracts exempted under Section 3(a)(8) of the Securities Act, relying on the SEC's argument that the seller of a viatical settlement was actually "giving up the protection of an insurance policy," not acquiring protection against future risks.] . . . We turn next to the question whether the contracts are properly characterized as securities. . . . That determination is controlled by the Supreme Court's decision in *Howey* which . . . holds that an investment contract is a security subject to the Act if investors purchase with (1) an expectation of profits arising from (2) a common enterprise that (3) depend upon the efforts of others. . . .

1. Expectation of Profits

. . . LPI maintains that under United Housing Foundation, Inc. v. Forman, 421 U.S. 837 (1975), profits must be derived from "either capital appreciation resulting from the development of the initial investment or a participation in earnings resulting from the use of the investors' funds," neither of which obtains with respect to viatical contracts. . . .

The Court's general principle we think, is only that the expected profits must, in conformity with ordinary usage, be in the form of a financial return on the investment, not in the form of consumption. This principle distinguishes between buying a note secured by a car and buying the car itself.

The asset acquired by an LPI investor is a claim on future death benefits. The buyer is obviously purchasing not for consumption—unmatured claims cannot be currently consumed—but rather for the prospect of a return on his investment. As we read the *Forman* gloss on *Howey,* that is enough to satisfy the requirement that the investment be made in the expectation of profits.

2. Common Enterprise

The second element of the *Howey* test for a security is that there be a "common enterprise." So-called horizontal commonality—defined by the pooling of investment funds, shared profits, and shared losses—is ordinarily sufficient to satisfy the common enterprise requirement.... Here, LPI brings together multiple investors and aggregates their funds to purchase the death benefits of an insurance policy. If the insured dies in a relatively short time, then the investors realize profits; if the insured lives a relatively long time, then the investors may lose money or at best fail to realize the return they had envisioned; i.e., they experience a loss of the return they could otherwise have realized in some alternative investment of equivalent risk. Any profits or losses from an LPI contract accrue to all of the investors in that contract; i.e., it is not possible for one investor to realize a gain or loss without each other investor gaining or losing proportionately, based upon the amount that he invested. In that sense, the outcomes are shared among the investors; the sum that each receives is a predetermined portion of the aggregate death benefit.

LPI claims, however, that there is no pooling and therefore no shared profits or losses because each investor acquires his own interest in the policy.... It seems to us that the pooling issue reduces to the question whether there is a threshold percentage of a policy that must be sold before an investor can be assured that his purchase of a smaller percentage interest will be consummated. If not, then each investor's acquisition is independent of all the other investors' acquisitions and LPI is correct in asserting that there is no pooling. On the other hand, if LPI must have investors ready to buy some minimum percentage of the policy before the transaction will occur, then the investment is contingent upon a pooling of capital.

When we raised this point at oral argument, the SEC contended that inter-dependency among investors was not necessary to a determination that their funds are pooled; the test, according to the Commission, is whether the funds are "commingled." In this context, however, commingling in itself is but an administrative detail; it is the interdependency of the investors that transforms the transaction substantively into a pooled investment.... Many of the post-purchase administrative functions (e.g., monitoring the insured's health, collecting the death benefit) involve costs that are seemingly invariant to the number of investors or the percentage of a policy that has been sold. Neither LPI nor the investors would be anxious to spread these costs over contracts representing much less than the full value of a policy.

Therefore, we think that pooling is in practice an essential ingredient of the LPI program; that is, any individual investor would find that the profitability if not the completion of his or her purchase depends upon completion of the larger deal. Because LPI's viatical settlements entail this implicit form of pooling, and because any profits or losses accrue to all investors (in proportion to the amount invested), we conclude that all three elements of horizontal commonality—pooling, profit sharing, and loss sharing—attend the purchase of a fractional interest through LPI. . . .

    3.   Profits Derived Predominantly from the Efforts of Others

The final requirement of the *Howey* test for an investment to be deemed a security is that the profits expected by the investor be derived from the efforts of others. In this connection, the SEC suggests that investors in LPI's viatical settlements are essentially passive; their profits, the Commission argues, depend predominantly upon the efforts of LPI, which provides pre-purchase expertise in identifying existing policyholders and, together with Sterling, provides post-purchase management of the investment. Meanwhile, LPI argues that its pre-purchase functions are wholly irrelevant and that the post-purchase functions, by whomever performed, should not count because they are only ministerial. On this view, once the transaction closes, the investors do not look to the efforts of others for their profits because the only variable affecting profits is the timing of the insured's death, which is outside of LPI's and Sterling's control. By its terms *Howey* requires that profits be generated "solely" from the efforts of others. Although the lower courts have given the Supreme Court's definition of a security broader sweep by requiring that profits be generated only "predominantly" from the efforts of others, . . . they have never suggested that purely ministerial or clerical functions are by themselves sufficient; indeed, quite the opposite is true. . . . Because post-purchase entrepreneurial activities are the "efforts of others" most obviously relevant to the question whether a promoter is selling a "security," we turn first to the distinction between those post-purchase functions that are entrepreneurial and those that are ministerial; thereafter, we consider the relevance of pre-purchase entrepreneurial services.

Ministerial versus entrepreneurial functions, post purchase. In Version I of its program, LPI and not the investor could appear as the owner of record of the insurance policy. LPI's ownership gave it the ability, post-purchase, to change the party designated as the beneficiary of the policy, indeed to substitute itself as beneficiary. That ability tied the fortunes of the investors more closely to those of LPI in the sense that it made the investors dependent upon LPI's continuing to deal honestly with them, at least to the extent of not wrongfully dropping them as beneficiaries. This does not, however, establish an association between the profits of the investors and the "efforts" of LPI. Nothing that LPI could do by virtue of its record ownership had any effect whatsoever upon the near exclusive determinant of the investors' rate of return, namely how long the insured survives. . . . The promoter's "efforts" not to engage in criminal or tortious behavior, or not to breach its contract are not the sort of entrepreneurial exertions that the *Howey* Court had in mind when it referred to profits arising from "the efforts of others."

In Version II LPI no longer appeared as the record owner of a policy, but LPI and Sterling continued to offer the following post-purchase services: holding the policy, monitoring the insured's health, paying premiums, converting a group policy into an individual policy where required, filing the death claim, collecting and distributing the death benefit (if requested), and assisting an investor who might wish to resell his interest. LPI characterizes these functions as clerical and routine in nature, not managerial or entrepreneurial, and therefore unimportant to the source of investor expectations. The district court seemed to agree with LPI about the character if not the significance of most post-purchase services, for it described them as "often ministerial in nature."

The Commission disputes the district court's characterization of post-purchase services as ministerial, but attempt to portray only one service in particular as entrepreneurial: we refer to the secondary market that LPI purportedly makes. By establishing a resale market, according to the SEC, LPI links the profitability of the investments it sells to the success of its own efforts. We find this argument unconvincing for several reasons. First, there is no evidence in the record before us that investors actually seek to liquidate their investments prior to the receipt of death benefits. Second, there is no evidence that LPI's potential assistance adds value to the investment contract, an investor could, for all that appears, get the same help with resale (if any is needed) through any one of the many firms that sell viatical settlements. Third, LPI is quite specific in warning its clients that

> viatical transactions are not liquid assets. There is no established market for the resale of such policies. They should be purchased only by persons who are willing and able to hold the policy until it matures . . .

LPI's promise of help in arranging for the resale of a policy is not an adequate basis upon which to conclude that the fortunes of the investors are tied to the efforts of the company, much less that their profits derive "predominantly" from those efforts.

In Version III LPI provides no post-purchase services. All such services are the sole responsibility of the investors, who may purchase them from Sterling or not, as they choose. The district court minimized the significance of this choice, stating that "it is neither realistic nor feasible for multiple investors, who are strangers to each other, to perform post-purchase tasks without relying on the knowledge and expertise of a third party . . ." . . . As we have seen, none of Sterling's post-purchase services can meaningfully affect the profitability of the investment. It is therefore of no moment whether Sterling performs those services usually or always, or whether it does so as the agent of LPI or as the agent of the investor.

In sum, the SEC has not identified any significant non-ministerial service that LPI or Sterling performs for investors once they have purchased their fractional interests in a viatical settlement. Nor do we find that any of the ministerial functions have a material impact upon the profits of the investors. Therefore, we turn to the question whether LPI's prepurchase services count as "the efforts of others" under the *Howey* test.

Entrepreneurial functions, pre-purchase. LPI's assertion that its prepurchase efforts are irrelevant receives strong, albeit implicit, support from the Ninth Circuit decision in Noa v. Key Futures, Inc., 638 F.2d 77 (1980) (per curiam). In that case, which involved investments in silver bars, the court observed that the promoter made pre-purchase efforts to identify the investment and to locate prospective investors; offered to store the silver bars at no charge for a year after purchase and to repurchase them at the published spot price at any time without charging a brokerage fee. The court concluded, however, that these services were only minimally related to the profitability of the investment: "Once the purchase . . . was made, the profits to the investor depended upon the fluctuations of the silver market, not the managerial efforts of [the promoter]." Id. at 79–80. . . .

In [these cases], the courts of appeals regarded the promoter's pre-purchase efforts as insignificant to the question whether the investments—in silver bars and parcels of land, respectively—were securities. The different outcomes trace wholly to the promoters' commitment to perform meaningful post-purchase functions in [one case but not the other].

Even if [LPI's investor played a significant prepurchase role in setting their own purchase criteria], the district court appropriately characterized LPI's pre-purchase efforts as "undeniably essential to the overall success of the investment." The investors rely heavily, if not exclusively, upon LPI to locate insureds and to evaluate them and their policies, as well as to negotiate an attractive purchase price.

The SEC urges us to go even further than did the district court, however, in appraising the significance of LPI's pre-purchase activities insofar as they count toward "the efforts of others." The Commission reminds us that the Supreme Court did not draw a bright line distinction in *Howey* between pre- and post-purchase efforts, and notes that LPI may continue to perform some functions, such as preparing the preliminary agreement and evaluating the insured's policy and medical file, right up to the closing of the transaction. . . .

Absent compelling legal support for the Commission's theory—and the Commission actually furnishes no support at all—we cannot agree that the time of sale is an artificial dividing line. It is a legal construct but a significant one. If the investor's profits depend thereafter predominantly upon the promoter's efforts, then the investor may benefit from the disclosure and other requirements of the federal securities laws.

But if the value of the promoter's efforts has already been impounded into the promoter's fees or into the purchase price of the investment, and if neither the promoter nor anyone else is expected to make further efforts that will affect the outcome of the investment, then the need for federal securities regulation is greatly diminished. . . .

While we doubt that pre-purchase services should ever count for much, for present purposes we need only agree with the district court that pre-purchase services cannot by themselves suffice to make the profits of an investment arise predominantly from the efforts of others, and that ministerial functions should receive a good deal less weight than entrepreneurial activities. . . .

In this case it is the length of the insured's life that is of overwhelming importance to the value of the viatical settlements marketed by LPI. As a result, the SEC is unable to show that the promoter's efforts have a predominant influence upon investors' profits; and because all three elements of the *Howey* test must be satisfied before an investment is characterized as a security, we must conclude that the viatical settlements marketed by LPI are not securities. . . .

■ WALD, CIRCUIT JUDGE, dissenting.

. . . I part company with the majority . . . because I believe that the third requirement of the *Howey* test, that (3) the expected profits be generated solely from the efforts of other, is also met here . . . I would distinguish between investments that satisfy the *Howey* third prong and those which do not by focusing on the kind and degree of dependence between the investors' profits and the promoter's activities. I believe that the third prong of the *Howey* test can be met by prepurchase managerial activities of a promoter when it is the success of these activities, either entirely or predominantly, that determines whether profits are eventually realized. . . .

When profits depend on the intervention of market forces, there will be public information available to an investor by which the investor could assess the likelihood of the investment's success. Thus, for example, a purchaser of silver bars has access to information on the trends in silver prices, an investor in paintings can get a sense, at least generally, of how the market for artwork is faring, and a purchaser of an undeveloped lot has access to information on growth trends in the area. . . .

Where profits depend on the success of the promoter's activities, however, there is less access to protective information and the type of information that is needed is more specific to the promoter. . . . This need for information holds true in regard to investors prior to purchase as much as to investors who have committed their funds—indeed, more so, if they are to avoid over-risky investments. . . .

I believe that the majority's position, precluding any pre-purchase managerial activities of a promoter from ever satisfying the third prong of the *Howey* test, is unwarranted and will serve to undercut the necessary flexibility of our securities laws ... Therefore, I respectfully dissent.

---

1. *Managerial Efforts: When and by Whom.* The *Howey* test is now read by all courts to require the showing of three elements: (1) an expectation of profits arising from (2) a common enterprise that (3) depends predominantly for its success on the efforts of others. Even though the *Howey* decision appears to say that an investment contract can be found only if profits are to be derived "solely" from the managerial efforts of the promoter or third parties, subsequent courts have re-interpreted "solely" to mean "predominantly," recognizing that promoters could otherwise circumvent the federal securities laws by simply assigning investors some nominal role in the enterprise.[4]

Most of the interpretive issues under the *Howey* test have involved either the meaning of commonality or the nature of the managerial or entrepreneurial efforts that the promoter can provide without giving rise to a security. A number of colorful cases have involved animal breeding programs in which the promoter sells the breeding stock to investors and promises to repurchase the offspring they raise.[5] Sometimes, in these cases, substantial efforts are required of the investors simply to obtain any offspring. For example, in Miller v. Central Chinchilla Group, Inc.,[6] the investors had to expend considerable efforts to raise chinchillas (which have a high mortality rate) to be able to resell them to the promoters at the agreed, above-market price. The Eighth Circuit focused on the promoters' representation that only minimal care was required. Finding that the investment could only yield a profit if the promoters could continue their pyramid scheme by finding new investors to buy the offspring raised by prior investors, the Eighth Circuit concluded that the promoters played the critical role and hence the breeding program amounted to an investment contract.

Subtract the feature of a pyramid scheme, and most franchise/franchisee relationships will not be found to constitute investment contracts under *Howey* because the efforts required of the franchisee/investor are too significant.[7] Where, however, the franchisee is used not simply as a sales agent, but as a source of capital for the production of the product (as the next case illustrates), some courts find

---

[4] See SEC v. International Loan Network, Inc., 968 F.2d 1304, 1308 (D.C.Cir. 1992) (profits must be "expected to accrue, if not solely, at least predominantly from the efforts of others").

[5] See Smith v. Gross, 604 F.2d 639 (9th Cir. 1979) (earthworms); Continental Mktg. Corp. v. SEC, 387 F.2d 466 (10th Cir. 1967) (beavers); SEC v. Payne, 35 F.Supp. 873 (S.D.N.Y.1940) (a pre-*Howey* case involving silver foxes).

[6] 494 F.2d 414 (8th Cir. 1974).

[7] See Crowley v. Montgomery Ward & Co., 570 F.2d 875 (10th Cir. 1975).

that the uncertain line between a legitimate franchise and an unregistered investment contract has been crossed.[8]

Life Partners drew a new distinction between pre- and post-purchase services. A number of commentators have doubted the wisdom of drawing this distinction.[9] The SEC has also resisted the majority's decision, although it succeeded in a later case largely by showing that the defendant's post-purchase activities were more substantial than in *Life Partners*. In Securities and Exchange Commission v. Larry W. Tyler & Advanced Fin. Servs., Inc.,[10] the SEC prevailed by emphasizing the secondary market the defendant created to provide liquidity for the fractional viatical shares it sold.[11] But for this fact, the court noted it would be inclined to follow *Life Partners*. Other cases, however, have rejected the D.C. Circuit's approach.[12] In particular, in SEC v. Mut. Benefits Corp.,[13] the Eleventh Circuit rejected the distinction between pre-purchase managerial activities and post-purchase efforts, essentially agreeing with Judge Wald's dissent in *Life Partners*. Investors in viatical contracts, it said, relied on the promoter's pre-purchase services. For an overview, see Levin, Killing Life Partners: Why Viatical Settlements Are "Securities" in Light of SEC v. Mutual Benefits Corp. and Other Recent Cases that Explicitly Reject SEC v. Life Partners, 6 J. Bus. & Sec. L. 71 (2005/2006).

If accepted by other courts, *Life Partners*' distinction between pre- and post-purchase services could have great significance for securitization transactions, such as collateralized debt obligations (or "CDOs"). Typically, the promoter in such asset-backed financings assembles a pool of financial assets (for example, mortgages, credit card receivables, or auto loans) and sells interests in them to investors. Although the instruments in such transactions are typically considered securities, in some cases, the promoter's services are largely or entirely pre-purchase and consist of selecting and screening the assets.

---

[8] See SEC v. Aqua-Sonic Products Corp., 687 F.2d 577 (2d Cir. 1982) (franchise agreement was an investment contract where circumstances made it clear that franchisee was neither able nor expected to sell firm's product to customers). However, those courts that require "horizontal commonality" (as next discussed) will probably still not find the franchisor/franchisee relationship to amount to an "investment contract."

[9] See Albert, The Future of Death Futures: Why Viatical Settlements Must Be Classified As Securities, 19 Pace L. Rev. 345 (1999); Lann, Viatical Settlements: An Explanation of the Process, An Analysis of State Regulations, and An Examination of Viatical Settlements As Securities, 46 Drake L. Rev. 923 (1998).

[10] 2002 WL 257645 (N.D.Tex. 2002).

[11] The district court relied heavily on Gary Plastic Packaging Corp. v. Merrill Lynch, 756 F.2d 230 (2d Cir. 1985), in which the Second Circuit found that the heavily advertised provision of such a secondary market by the seller could convert certificates of deposit, which ordinarily are not securities, into an investment package that constitutes a security.

[12] For a recent example, see SEC v. Life Partners Holdings, Inc., 2013 U.S. Dist. LEXIS 184376 (W. D. Tex. Dec. 3, 2013).

[13] 408 F.3d 737 (11th Cir. 2005).

Securities and Exchange Commission v. Koscot Interplanetary, Inc.
United States Court of Appeals, Fifth Circuit, 1974.
497 F.2d 473.

■ Before: RIVES, GEWIN and RONEY, CIRCUIT JUDGES.

■ GEWIN, CIRCUIT JUDGE: This appeal emanates from a district court order denying an injunction sought by the Securities & Exchange Commission (SEC) against Koscot Interplanetary, Inc., (Koscot) for allegedly violating the federal securities laws. Specifically, the SEC maintained that the pyramid promotion enterprise operated by Koscot was within the ambit of the term security, as employed by the Securities Act of 1933 and the Securities Exchange Act of 1934, that as such it had to be registered with the SEC pursuant to the '33 Act, and that the manner in which Koscot purveyed its enterprise to potential investors contravened the anti-fraud provisions of the '34 Act. In a comprehensive opinion, * * *, the district court denied the injunction holding that the Koscot Scheme did not involve the sale of a security. Because of our disagreement with the district court's reasoning, we reverse.

I

A. *The Koscot Scheme*

The procedure followed by Koscot in the promotion of its enterprise can be synoptically chronicled. A subsidiary of Glenn W. Turner Enterprises, Koscot thrives by enticing prospective investors to participate in its enterprise, holding out as a lure the expectation of galactic profits. All too often, the beguiled investors are disappointed by paltry returns.

The vehicle for the lure is a multi-level network of independent distributors, purportedly engaged in the business of selling a line of cosmetics. At the lowest level is a "beauty advisor" whose income is derived solely from retail sales of Koscot products made available at a discount, customarily of 45%. Those desirous of ascending the ladder of the Koscot enterprise may also participate on a second level, that of supervisor or retail manager. For an investment of $1,000, a supervisor receives cosmetics at a greater discount from retail price, typically 55%, to be sold either directly to the public or to be held for wholesale distribution to the beauty advisors. In addition, a supervisor who introduces a prospect to the Koscot program with whom a sale is ultimately consummated receives $600 of the $1,000 paid to Koscot. The loftiest position in the multi-level scheme is that of distributor. An investment of $5,000 with Koscot entitles a distributor to purchase cosmetics at an even greater discount, typically 65%, for distribution to supervisors and retailers. Moreover, fruitful sponsorship of either a supervisor or distributor brings $600 or $3,000 respectively to the sponsor.

The SEC does not contend that the distribution of cosmetics is amenable to regulation under the federal securities laws. Rather, it maintains that the marketing of cosmetics and the recruitment aspects of Koscot's enterprise are separable and that only the latter are within the definition of a security. * * *

The modus operandi of Koscot and its investors is as follows. Investors solicit prospects to attend Opportunity Meetings at which the latter are introduced to the Koscot scheme. Significantly, the investor is admonished not to mention the details of the business before bringing the prospect to the meeting, a technique euphemistically denominated the "curiosity approach." * * *

Thus, in the initial stage, an investor's sole task is to attract individuals to the meeting.

Once a prospect's attendance at a meeting is secured, Koscot employees, frequently in conjunction with investors, undertake to apprise prospects of the "virtues" of enlisting in the Koscot plan. The meeting is conducted in conformity with scripts prepared by Koscot. * * * The principal design of the meetings is to foster an illusion of affluence. Investors and Koscot employees are instructed to drive to meetings in expensive cars, preferably Cadillacs, to dress expensively, and to flaunt large amounts of money. It is intended that prospects will be galvanized into signing a contract by these ostentations displayed in the evangelical atmosphere of the meetings. * * *

The final stage in the promotional scheme is the consummation of the sale. If a prospect capitulates at * * * an Opportunity Meeting * * *, an investor will not be required to expend any additional effort. Less fortuitous investors whose prospects are not as quickly enticed to invest do have to devote additional effort to consummate a sale, the amount of which is contingent upon the degree of reluctance of the prospect.

* * *

The district court rebuffed the SEC's effort to subject Koscot's promotional scheme to the federal securities laws. * * *

Of * * * immediate concern is the reasoning employed by the district court in rejecting the SEC's contention that Koscot sold "investment contracts," for it is our disagreement with this conclusion that prompts us to reverse. The district court correctly cited * * * language from SEC v. W. J. Howey Co., * * * as the standard controlling its disposition of the case.

* * *

This test subsumes within it three elements: first, that there is an investment of money; second, that the scheme in which an investment is made functions as a common enterprise; and third, that under the scheme, profits are derived solely from the efforts of individuals other than the investors. * * *. The district court pretermitted a consideration of the first two elements in finding that the third component of the test was not satisfied because Koscot investors expended effort in soliciting recruits to meetings, in participating in the conduct of meetings, and in attempting to consummate the sale of distributorships and subdistributorships. * * *

II

Thus, we are called upon to address that which the court below did not consider—whether the Koscot scheme satisfies the first two elements of the *Howey* test—and that which the district court did consider—whether the scheme satisfies the third component of the test. The latter inquiry entails, in the first instance, a determination of whether the "solely from the efforts of others" standard is to be literally or functionally applied. We address these issues seriatim.

A. *The First Two Elements*

Since it cannot be disputed that purchasers of supervisorships and distributorships made an investment of money, * * * our initial concern is whether the Koscot scheme functions as a common enterprise. As defined by the Ninth Circuit, "[a] common enterprise is one in which the fortunes of the investor are interwoven with and dependent upon the efforts and success of those seeking the investment or of third parties." SEC v. Glenn W. Turner Enterprises, Inc., supra at 482 n. 7. The critical factor is not the similitude or coincidence of investor input, but rather the uniformity of impact of the promoter's efforts.

[T]his definition comports with the standard applied by the Supreme Court * * * in *Howey*, supra. * * *

Similarly, here, the fact that an investor's return is independent of that of other investors in the scheme is not decisive. Rather, the requisite commonality is evidenced by the fact that the fortunes of all investors are inextricably tied to the efficacy of the Koscot meetings and guidelines on recruiting prospects and consummating a sale. * * *

B. *The Third Element—Solely from the Efforts of Others*

As was noted earlier, the critical issue in this case is whether a literal or functional approach to the "solely from the efforts of others" test should be adopted, i.e., whether the exertion of some effort by an investor is inimical to the holding that a promotional scheme falls within the definition of an investment contract. We measure the viability of the SEC's advocacy of a functional approach by its compatibility with the remedial purposes of the federal securities acts, the language employed and the derivation of the test utilized in *Howey*, and the decisions in this circuit and other federal courts.

1. The Legal Standard

* * *

A literal application of the *Howey* test would frustrate the remedial purposes of the Act. As the Ninth Circuit noted in SEC v. Turner

Enterprises, Inc., supra at 482, "[i]t would be easy to evade [the *Howey* test] by adding a requirement that the buyer contribute a modicum of effort." The admitted salutary purposes of the Acts can only be safeguarded by a functional approach to the *Howey* test.

Moreover, a close reading of the language employed in *Howey* and the authority upon which the Court relied suggests that, contrary to the view of the district court, we need not feel compelled to follow the "solely from the efforts of others" test literally. Nowhere in the opinion does the Supreme Court characterize the nature of the "efforts" that would render a promotional scheme beyond the pale of the definition of an investment contract. Clearly the facts presented no issue of how to assess a scheme in which an investor performed mere perfunctory tasks. Indeed, * * * the Court observed that "the promoters *manage, control* and *operate* the enterprise." 328 U.S. at 300 (emphasis added).

* * *

In view of * * * our analysis of the import of the language in and the derivation of the *Howey* test, we hold that the proper standard in determining whether a scheme constitutes an investment contract is that explicated by the Ninth Circuit in SEC v. Glenn W. Turner Enterprises, Inc., supra. In that case, the court announced that the critical inquiry is "whether the efforts made by those other than the investor are the undeniably significant ones, those essential managerial efforts which affect the failure or success of the enterprise." Id. at 482.

* * *

2. Application of the Test to the Instant Facts

Having concluded that the district court misperceived the controlling standard, it becomes incumbent upon us to determine whether Koscot's scheme falls with[in] the standard adopted.

Our task is greatly simplified by the Ninth Circuit's decision in SEC v. Glenn W. Turner Enterprises, Inc., supra. The promotional scheme confronting the Ninth Circuit is largely paralleled by that exposed before this court. * * *

As in the Koscot scheme, the initial task of a purchaser of a Dare plan was to lure prospects to meetings, denominated Adventure Meetings. These were characterized by the same overzealous and emotionally charged atmosphere at which the illusion of affluence fostered in Opportunity Meetings was created and relied upon in securing sales. The Adventure Meetings were run according to script but, as the Ninth Circuit noted, "The Dare People, not the purchaser— 'salesmen', run the meetings and do the selling." 474 F.2d at 479. * * *

The recruitment role played by investors in Koscot coincides with that played by investors in Dare to be Great. That investors in the latter did not participate in Adventure Meetings while they do in the Koscot scheme is insignificant. Since Koscot's Opportunity Meetings are run according to preordained script, the deviation from which would occasion disapprobation or perhaps exclusion from the meetings, the role of investors at these meetings can be characterized as little more than a perfunctory one. Nor does the fact that Koscot investors may have devoted more time than did Dare investors to closing sales transmute the essential congruity between the two schemes. The act of consummating a sale is essentially a ministerial not managerial one, * * * one which does not alter the fact that the critical determinant of the success of the Koscot Enterprise lies with the luring effect of the opportunity meetings. As was noted earlier, investors are cautioned to employ the "curiosity approach" in attracting prospects. Once attendance is secured, the sales format devised by Koscot is thrust upon the prospect. An investor's sole contribution in following the script is a nominal one. Without the scenario created by the Opportunity Meetings and Go-Tours, an investor would invariably be powerless to realize any return on his investment.

III

We confine our holding to those schemes in which promoters retain immediate control over the essential managerial conduct of an enterprise and where the investor's realization of profits is inextricably tied to the success of the promotional scheme. Thus, we acknowledge that a conventional franchise arrangement, wherein the promoter exercises merely remote control over an enterprise and the investor operates largely unfettered by promoter mandates presents a different question than the one posed herein. But the Koscot scheme does not qualify as a conventional franchising arrangement.

* * *

Accordingly, this cause is reversed and remanded for further proceedings consistent with this opinion.

---

1. *"Vertical" Versus "Horizontal" Commonality.* In finding a common enterprise, the *Koscot* court focused on the vertical commonality between investors and promoters. Under this approach, a common enterprise may be found when the activities of the promoter are the dominant factor in the investment's success—even though there is no pooling of funds or interests by multiple investors.[14] Even among courts that accept vertical commonality, most insist upon some interdependence or mutuality of interest between the promoter's financial success and that of its investors.[15] This latter view—known as "strict vertical

---

[14] The Fifth and the Eleventh Circuits are probably the strongest proponents of the "vertical commonality" test. See, e.g., SEC v. ETS Payphones, Inc., 408 F.3d 727 (11th Cir. 2005); SEC v. Unique Fin. Concepts, Inc., 196 F.3d 1195 (11th Cir. 1999); SEC v. Continental Commodities Corp., 497 F.2d 516 (5th Cir. 1974); Villeneuve v. Advanced Business Concepts Corp., 698 F.2d 1121, 1124 (11th Cir. 1983), aff'd en banc 730 F.2d 1403 (11th Cir. 1984).

[15] See Mordaunt v. Incomco, 686 F.2d 815 (9th Cir. 1982). The First, Ninth, and Eleventh Circuits have taken this position. See, e.g., Los Angeles Trust Deed & Mortgage Exchange v.

commonality" as opposed to "broad vertical commonality"—"requires that the fortunes of investors be tied to the fortune of the promoter" (as opposed to the investors' fortunes being "linked only to the *efforts* of the promoter"[16]). As a practical matter, this means the promoter must share in the profits and not simply receive a flat fee.

Other Circuits, however, appear to insist upon horizontal commonality—in short, that there must be a pooling of investor funds.[17] Usually, there will also be a pro rata distribution of profits among the investors. A leading case is Wals v. Fox Hills Development Corporation,[18] in which the plaintiff bought a one-week time-sharing interest in a golf course condominium and simultaneously entered into an annually renewable agreement with the developer under which the developer would rent the unit during that week on behalf of the plaintiff (with the rental proceeds being split on a 70/30 basis between the plaintiff and the developer). Rejecting the argument that this agreement created a common enterprise between the developer of the condominium and the owner of this one-week interest, Judge Posner wrote for the Seventh Circuit:

> The [1933] Act is a disclosure statute. It requires promoters and issuers to make uniform disclosure to all investors, and this requirement makes sense only if the investors are obtaining the same thing, namely an undivided share in the same pool of assets and profits. This is not what the plaintiffs in this case received * * *. Their investment was in a specific time slice of a specific apartment, the physical and temporal characteristics of which (including price) differed from those of other apartments.[19]

Nonetheless, a year later, in SEC v. Lauer,[20] Judge Posner authored another opinion for the Seventh Circuit in which he found that an investment in a specially-designed package of high-yield securities was, itself, a security, even though the investment package was sold by the broker only to a single investor. Although defendants predictably argued, based on *Wals,* that no "horizontal commonality" was present, Judge Posner answered their arguments as follows:

SEC, 285 F.2d 162 (9th Cir. 1962); Villaneuve v. Advanced Business Concepts Corp., 698 F. 2d 1121 (11th Cir. 1983).

[16] See Revak v. SEC Realty Corp., 18 F.3d 81, 88 (2d Cir. 1994). In *Revak*, the Second Circuit did not decide if strict vertical commonality was sufficient, but it rejected broad vertical commonality as insufficient.

[17] This approach is clearly favored by the Third, Sixth, and Seventh Circuits and probably originated with the Seventh Circuit's decision in Milnarik v. M-S Commodities, Inc., 561 F.2d 274 (7th Cir. 1972). See also Curran v. Merrill Lynch, Pierce, Fenner & Smith, Inc., 622 F.2d 216 (6th Circ. 1980); SEC v. Banner Fund International, 211 F.3d 602 (D.C.Cir. 2000); Hart v. Pulte Homes of Michigan, 735 F.2d 1001, 1004 (6th Cir. 1984); Salcer v. Merrill, Lynch, Pierce, Fenner & Smith, Inc., 682 F.2d 459, 460 (3d Cir. 1982).

[18] 24 F.3d 1016 (7th Cir. 1994).

[19] Id. at 1019.

[20] 52 F.3d 667 (7th Cir. 1995).

[I]t is the character of the investment vehicle, not the presence of multiple investors, that determines whether there is an investment contract. Otherwise, a defrauder who was content to defraud a single investor * * * would have immunity from the federal securities laws. That would not make any sense, and is not contemplated by any of the cases that require horizontal commonality.[21]

Thus, an intention to involve multiple investors can sometimes result in horizontal commonality, even though no other investors participate; in effect, it may be enough that there was an intent to pool.

Some commentators argue that the requirement of horizontal commonality is formalistic and lacks any relationship to the policy goals of the 1933 Act.[22] Nonetheless, there is at least one context in which most courts seem inclined to require it: discretionary trading accounts managed by securities and commodities brokers. Suppose, for example, a broker contracts with a customer to receive a specified percentage of the gains from his discretionary trading in the account for the customer. If horizontal commonality is required, this relationship cannot give rise to a common enterprise or a security (because there is no pooling of investor funds).[23] Note that, even if vertical commonality is deemed sufficient, the "strict vertical commonality" approach will find a common enterprise only if the broker is compensated out of the profits from its trading for the customer.[24] Conversely, if the broker does not share the financial risks of the discretionary trading account (for example, if it is compensated on a commission basis), then only the "broad vertical commonality" approach would result in the relationship amounting to a common enterprise.[25]

Some commentators argue that both the horizontal and vertical approaches to commonality are overinclusive.[26] Why, they argue, should it make a difference whether a single investor or two brothers open a discretionary commodities trading account with a commodities broker? In the latter case, horizontal commonality seems present, but unimportant. Correspondingly, when an investor and a broker share the profits from a discretionary trading account, their interests are aligned. Although this pattern satisfies the vertical commonality approach, it is unclear why a federal remedy is needed where the conflicts of interest

---

[21] Id. at 670.

[22] See Gordon, Common Enterprise and Multiple Investors, 3 Colum.Bus.L.Rev. 635, 660–62 (1988).

[23] See Milnarik v. M-S Commodities, Inc., 457 F.2d 274 (7th Cir. 1972), cert. denied, 409 U.S. 887 (1972); see also Bines and Thel, Investment Management Arrangements and the Federal Securities Laws, 58 Ohio St. L.J. 459 (1997); Prendergast, Discretionary Trading Accounts—Revisited, 16 Rev.Sec.Reg. 854 (1983).

[24] See Meyer v. Dans un Jardin, S.A., 816 F.2d 533 (10th Cir. 1987).

[25] See SEC v. Continental Commodities Corp., 497 F.2d 516 (5th Cir. 1974).

[26] See Karjala, Federalism, Full Disclosure, and the National Markets in the Interpretation of Federal Securities Law, 80 Nw.U.L.Rev. 1473, 1508 (1986).

are minimal, but not where the broker is paid by a single investor on a pure commission basis (which relationship creates an incentive to churn the account and, hence, a greater conflict of interest, but fails the "strict vertical commonality" standard). Also, if the discretionary account is trading commodities subject to the jurisdiction of the Commodity Futures Trading Commission, is it wise to overlay SEC jurisdiction on top of the CFTC's simply because the broker has discretionary authority? Does this create an unwise potential for regulatory turf battles?

2. *Commonality and the Internet.* In SEC v. SG Ltd.,[27] the First Circuit reversed the district court and held that the "virtual shares" generated by an internet game were securities. The defendant operated a website under the name of "StockGeneration," where visitors could buy "virtual shares" of "virtual companies" on a "virtual stock exchange." One such company was known as the "privileged company," and the website indicated that its shares would constantly rise by ten percent each month (that is, the computer—not any market—was programmed to result in this appreciation). Participants had to invest real money to buy shares, and if participants referred new players to the site, they would receive a percentage of the new player's payments. Finding this to be a game or lottery, not a common enterprise, the district court dismissed the SEC's complaint, which alleged a *Howey*-style investment contract. The First Circuit, however, agreed with the SEC and, in particular, found the requisite "horizontal commonality" to be present because the defendant pooled the investors' funds in a single account that was used to pay the appreciation on the "privileged company." In addition, the SEC alleged that the only way the defendant could pay a guaranteed increased price on such shares was through the new infusion of money through a "Ponzi" or pyramid-type scheme. Similarly, the SEC argued that the payments made to contestants for referring new players also came from this pooled fund, as the defendant had no other source of funds. Finally, because the contestants themselves could do nothing to increase the value of the stocks in the game, the third prong ("predominantly dependent upon the efforts of others") of *Howey* was found to be satisfied.

Query: What if the defendant designed the game so that existing contestants only received payments from the new contestants they referred to the website? Would this be more like *Koscot*? Would Circuits that required horizontal commonality dismiss the SEC's complaint?

Securities and Exchange Commission v. Edwards
Supreme Court of the United States, 2004.
540 U.S. 389, 124 S.Ct. 892, 157 L.Ed.2d 813.

■ JUSTICE O'CONNOR delivered the opinion of the Court.

"Opportunity doesn't always knock . . . sometimes it rings." App. 113 (ETS Payphones promotional brochure). And sometimes it hangs up. So

---

[27] 265 F.3d 42 (1st Cir. 2001).

it did for the 10,000 people who invested a total of $300 million in the payphone sale-and-leaseback arrangements touted by respondent under that slogan. The Securities and Exchange Commission (SEC) argues that the arrangements were investment contracts, and thus were subject to regulation under the federal securities laws. In this case, we must decide whether a moneymaking scheme is excluded from the term "investment contract" simply because the scheme offered a contractual entitlement to a fixed, rather than a variable, return.

I

Respondent Charles Edwards was the chairman, chief executive officer, and sole shareholder of ETS Payphones, Inc. (ETS). ETS, acting partly through a subsidiary also controlled by respondent, sold payphones to the public via independent distributors. The payphones were offered packaged with a site lease, a 5-year leaseback and management agreement, and a buyback agreement. All but a tiny fraction of purchasers chose this package, although other management options were offered. The purchase price for the payphone packages was approximately $7,000. Under the leaseback and management agreement, purchasers received $82 per month, a 14% annual return. Purchasers were not involved in the day-to-day operation of the payphones they owned. ETS selected the site for the phone, installed the equipment, arranged for connection and long-distance service, collected coin revenues, and maintained and repaired the phones. Under the buyback agreement, ETS promised to refund the full purchase price of the package at the end of the lease or within 180 days of a purchaser's request.

In its marketing materials and on its website, ETS trumpeted the "incomparable pay phone" as "an exciting business opportunity," in which recent deregulation had "open[ed] the door for profits for individual pay phone owners and operators." According to ETS, "[v]ery few business opportunities can offer the potential for ongoing revenue generation that is available in today's pay telephone industry." App. 114–115 (ETS brochure); id., at 227 (ETS website); see id., at 13 (Complaint PP 37–38).

The payphones did not generate enough revenue for ETS to make the payments required by the leaseback agreements, so the company depended on funds from new investors to meet its obligations. In September 2000, ETS filed for bankruptcy protection. The SEC brought this civil enforcement action the same month. It alleged that respondent and ETS had violated the registration requirements of §§ 5(a) and (c) of the Securities Act of 1933, 15 U.S.C. §§ 77e(a), (c), the antifraud provisions of both § 17(a) of the Securities Act of 1933, 15 U.S.C. § 77q(a) and § 10(b) of the Securities Exchange Act of 1934, as amended, 15 U.S.C. § 78j(b), and Rule 10b–5 thereunder, 17 CFR § 240.10b–5 (2003). The District Court concluded that the payphone sale-and-leaseback arrangement was an investment contract within the meaning of, and therefore was subject to, the federal securities laws. SEC v. ETS Payphones, Inc., 123 F.Supp.2d 1349 (ND Ga. 2000). The Court of

Appeals reversed. 300 F.3d 1281 (CA11 2002) (per curiam). It held that respondent's scheme was not an investment contract, on two grounds. First, it read this Court's opinions to require that an investment contract offer either capital appreciation or a participation in the earnings of the enterprise, and thus to exclude schemes, such as respondent's, offering a fixed rate of return. Id., at 1284–1285. Second, it held that our opinions' requirement that the return on the investment be "derived solely from the efforts of others" was not satisfied when the purchasers had a contractual entitlement to the return. Id., at 1285. We conclude that it erred on both grounds.

II

"Congress' purpose in enacting the securities laws was to regulate *investments*, in whatever form they are made and by whatever name they are called." Reves v. Ernst & Young, 494 U.S. 56, 61, (1990). To that end, it enacted a broad definition of "security," sufficient "to encompass virtually any instrument that might be sold as an investment." Ibid. Section 2(a)(1) of the 1933 Act, 15 U.S.C. § 77b(a)(1), and § 3(a)(10) of the 1934 Act, 15 U.S.C. § 78c(a)(10), in slightly different formulations which we have treated as essentially identical in meaning, Reves, supra, 494 U.S. 56 at 61, n. 1, 108 L.Ed.2d 47, 110 S.Ct. 945, define "security" to include "any note, stock, treasury stock, security future, bond, debenture, . . . investment contract, . . . [or any] instrument commonly known as a 'security'." "Investment contract" is not itself defined.

The test for whether a particular scheme is an investment contract was established in our decision in SEC v. W. J. Howey Co., 328 U.S. 293 (1946). We look to "whether the scheme involves an investment of money in a common enterprise with profits to come solely from the efforts of others." 328 U.S. 293 at 301. This definition "embodies a flexible rather than a static principle, one that is capable of adaptation to meet the countless and variable schemes devised by those who seek the use of the money of others on the promise of profits." Id., 328 U.S. 293 at 299.

In reaching that result, we first observed that when Congress included "investment contract" in the definition of security, it "was using a term the meaning of which had been crystallized" by the state courts' interpretation of their " 'blue sky' " laws. Id., 328 U.S. 293 at 298. (Those laws were the precursors to federal securities regulation and were so named, it seems, because they were "aimed at promoters who 'would sell building lots in the blue sky in fee simple.' " 1 Loss & Seligman, Securities Regulation 36, 31–43 (3d ed. 1998) (quoting Mulvey, Blue Sky Law, 36 Can. L. Times 37 (1916)).) The state courts had defined an investment contract as "a contract or scheme for 'the placing of capital or laying out of money in a way intended to secure income or profit from its employment,' " and had "uniformly applied" that definition to "a variety of situations where individuals were led to invest money in a common enterprise with the expectation that they would earn a profit solely through the efforts of the promoter or [a third party]." Howey, supra, 328

U.S. 293 at 298, (quoting State v. Gopher Tire & Rubber Co., 146 Minn. 52, 56, 177 N. W. 937, 938 (1920)). Thus, when we held that "profits" must "come solely from the efforts of others," we were speaking of the profits that investors seek on their investment, not the profits of the scheme in which they invest. We used "profits" in the sense of income or return, to include, for example, dividends, other periodic payments, or the increased value of the investment.

There is no reason to distinguish between promises of fixed returns and promises of variable returns for purposes of the test, so understood. In both cases, the investing public is attracted by representations of investment income, as purchasers were in this case by ETS' invitation to "'watch the profits add up.'" App. 13 (Complaint P 38). Moreover, investments pitched as low-risk (such as those offering a "guaranteed" fixed return) are particularly attractive to individuals more vulnerable to investment fraud, including older and less sophisticated investors. See S. Rep. No. 102–261, Vol. 2, App., p. 326 (1992) (Staff Summary of Federal Trade Commission Activities Affecting Older Consumers). Under the reading respondent advances, unscrupulous marketers of investments could evade the securities laws by picking a rate of return to promise. We will not read into the securities laws a limitation not compelled by the language that would so undermine the laws' purposes.

Respondent protests that including investment schemes promising a fixed return among investment contracts conflicts with our precedent. We disagree. No distinction between fixed and variable returns was drawn in the blue sky law cases that the *Howey* Court used, in formulating the test, as its evidence of Congress' understanding of the term. Howey, supra, 328 U.S. 293 at 298, and n 4. Indeed, two of those cases involved an investment contract in which a fixed return was promised. People v. White, 124 Cal. App. 548, 550–551, 12 P.2d 1078, 1079 (1932) (agreement between defendant and investors stated that investor would give defendant $5,000, and would receive $7,500 from defendant one year later); Stevens v. Liberty Packing Corp., 111 N. J. Eq. 61, 62–63, 161 A. 193, 193–194 (1932) ("ironclad contract" offered by defendant to investors entitled investors to $56 per year for 10 years on initial investment of $175, ostensibly in sale-and-leaseback of breeding rabbits).

None of our post-*Howey* decisions is to the contrary. In United Housing Foundation, Inc. v. Forman, 421 U.S. 837 (1975), we considered whether "shares" in a nonprofit housing cooperative were investment contracts under the securities laws. We identified the "touchstone" of an investment contract as "the presence of an investment in a common venture premised on a reasonable expectation of profits to be derived from the entrepreneurial or managerial efforts of others," and then laid out two examples of investor interests that we had previously found to be "profits." Id., 421 U.S. 837 at 852. Those were "capital appreciation resulting from the development of the initial investment" and "participation in earnings resulting from the use of investors' funds." Ibid. We contrasted those examples, in which "the investor is 'attracted solely by the prospects of a return'" on the investment, with housing cooperative shares, regarding which the purchaser "is motivated by a desire to use or consume the item purchased." Id., at 852–853 (quoting Howey, supra, at 300.) Thus, *Forman* supports the commonsense understanding of "profits" in the *Howey* test as simply "financial returns on . . . investments." 421 U.S. 837 at 853.

* * *

We hold that an investment scheme promising a fixed rate of return can be an "investment contract" and thus a "security" subject to the federal securities laws. The judgment of the United States Court of Appeals for the Eleventh Circuit is reversed, and the case is remanded for further proceedings consistent with this opinion.

It is so ordered.

---

1. *Fixed Returns*. Prior to *Edwards*, some had imagined that the *Howey* test did not apply to fixed returns, as such returns resemble debt obligations—"notes"—which are governed by the standard set forth in Reves v. Ernst & Young, 494 U.S. 56 (1990) (set out later in this chapter). The line between *Howey* and *Reves* remains uncertain after *Edwards*. Economically, the sale and leaseback arrangement in *Edwards* was substantially the same as a secured loan, which is often evidenced by a note. Thus, while there was no note in *Edwards*, the same economic outcome could have been accomplished in a transaction that uses a note, which raises a question: What would have been the outcome in *Edwards* if the sale-leaseback transaction used a note? Should that relatively minor change in structure—arguably more form than substance—dictate whether *Reves* or *Howey* is applicable?

2. *Commonality*. Curiously, the Court in *Edwards* never addressed the issue of whether horizontal commonality was necessary (which seems not to have been present on the facts of *Edwards*).

3. *Outcome on Remand*. The Eleventh Circuit on remand concluded that the sale and leaseback arrangements in *Edwards* were investment contracts and emphasized the investors' reliance on the promoters' managerial efforts; in particular, the promoters were responsible for maintenance of the phones and the decision where to locate them. See SEC v. ETS Payphones, Inc., 408 F.3d 727 (11th Cir. 2005). The Eleventh Circuit has long followed the vertical commonality test, and, thus, the outcome could have been different in other Circuits.

Problem

PROBLEM 4-1

Yoga Studios, Inc., a very California corporation, wants to create a nationwide chain and establish itself as the best-known school and studio for yoga exercises and meditation. The company has begun nationally advertising its trademark, the "Yoga Bear"—a patient, meditating, vegetarian bear. But the capital requirements of building a nationwide chain from a local chain in Northern California are simply too high, so it chooses to go the franchise route. For $100,000, it will sell a franchisee its name and train its staff in its approach to yoga; the franchisee also receives the exclusive franchise within a defined geography. Under the franchise agreement, the franchisor retains control over the services that may be provided and products that may be sold, and the franchisor will supply the franchisees with a broad variety of meditative and holistic health products. All employees who deal with the public must be "certified" under the franchisor's training course, but the franchisee can hire and fire its employees, offer additional products that do not compete with any of Yoga Studios' products, sponsor additional services, and set prices. Initially, the venture is a success and 80 franchises are sold. But then a scandal erupts when it is discovered that Yoga Studios' special brand of ginseng contains a minute quantity of marijuana ("to facilitate the meditative experience"). Customers flee, and the franchisees sue in a class action, alleging they have been unlawfully sold a security without registration. What is your analysis of the legal issues?

B. THE "ECONOMIC REALITIES" TEST: DOWNSIZING THE DEFINITION OF SECURITY

United Housing Foundation, Inc. v. Forman
Supreme Court of the United States, 1975.
421 U.S. 837, 95 S.Ct. 2051, 44 L.Ed.2d 621.

■ MR. JUSTICE POWELL delivered the opinion of the Court.

The issue in these cases is whether shares of stock entitling a purchaser to lease an apartment in Co-op City, a state subsidized and supervised nonprofit housing cooperative, are "securities" within the purview of the Securities Act of 1933 and the Securities Exchange Act of 1934.

I

Co-op City is a massive housing cooperative in New York City. Built between 1965 and 1971, it presently houses approximately 50,000 people on a 200-acre site containing 35 high-rise buildings and 236 town houses. The project was organized, financed, and constructed under the New York State Private Housing Finance Law, commonly known as the Mitchell-Lama Act, enacted to ameliorate a perceived crisis in the availability of decent low-income urban housing. In order to encourage private developers to build low-cost cooperative housing, New York provides them with large long-term, low-interest mortgage loans and substantial tax exemptions. Receipt of such benefits is conditioned on a willingness to have the State review virtually every step in the development of the cooperative. See N.Y.Priv.Hous.Fin.Law §§ 11–37, as amended (1962 and Supp.1974–1975). The developer also must agree to operate the facility "on a nonprofit basis," § 11–a(2a), and he may lease apartments only to people whose incomes fall below a certain level and who have been approved by the State.

The United Housing Foundation (UHF), a nonprofit membership corporation established for the purpose of "aiding and encouraging" the creation of "adequate, safe and sanitary housing accommodations for wage earners and other persons of low or moderate income," * * * was responsible for initiating and sponsoring the development of Co-op City. Acting under the Mitchell-Lama Act, UHF organized the Riverbay Corporation (Riverbay) to own and operate the land and buildings constituting Co-op City. Riverbay, a nonprofit cooperative housing corporation, issued the stock that is the subject of this litigation. UHF also contracted with Community Services, Inc. (CSI), its wholly owned subsidiary, to serve as the general contractor and sales agent for the project. As required by the Mitchell-Lama Act, these decisions were approved by the State Housing Commissioner.

To acquire an apartment in Co-op City an eligible prospective purchaser must buy 18 shares of stock in Riverbay for each room desired. The cost per share is $25, making the total cost $450 per room, or $1,800 for a four-room apartment. The sole purpose of acquiring these shares is to enable the purchaser to occupy an apartment in Co-op City; in effect, their purchase is a recoverable deposit on an apartment. The shares are explicitly tied to the apartment: they cannot be transferred to a nontenant; nor can they be pledged or encumbered; and they descend, along with the apartment, only to a surviving spouse. No voting rights attach to the shares as such: participation in the affairs of the cooperative appertains to the apartment, with the residents of each apartment being entitled to one vote irrespective of the number of shares owned.

Any tenant who wants to terminate his occupancy, or who is forced to move out, must offer his stock to Riverbay at its initial selling price of $25 per share. In the extremely unlikely event that Riverbay declines to repurchase the stock, the tenant cannot sell it for more than the initial purchase price plus a fraction of the portion of the mortgage that he has paid off, and then only to a prospective tenant satisfying the statutory income eligibility requirements.

* * *

In May 1965, subsequent to the completion of the initial planning, Riverbay circulated an Information Bulletin seeking to attract tenants for what would someday be apartments in Co-op City. After describing the nature and advantages of cooperative housing generally and of Co-op City in particular, the Bulletin informed prospective tenants that the total estimated cost of the project, based largely on an anticipated construction contract with CSI, was $283,695,550. Only a fraction of this sum, $32,795,550, was to be raised by the sale of shares to tenants. The remaining $250,900,000 was to be financed by a 40-year low-interest mortgage loan from the New York Private Housing Finance Agency. After construction of the project the mortgage payments and current operating expenses would be met by monthly rental charges paid by the tenants. While these rental charges were to vary, depending on the size, nature, and location of an apartment, the 1965 Bulletin estimated that the "average" monthly cost would be $23.02 per room, or $92.08 for a four-room apartment.

Several times during the construction of Co-op City, Riverbay, with the approval of the State Housing Commissioner, revised its contract with CSI to allow for increased construction costs. In addition, Riverbay incurred other expenses that had not been reflected in the 1965 Bulletin. To meet these increased expenditures, Riverbay, with the Commissioner's approval, repeatedly secured increased mortgage loans from the State Housing Agency. Ultimately the construction loan was $125 million more than the figure estimated in the 1965 Bulletin. As a result, while the initial purchasing price remained at $450 per room, the average monthly rental charges increased periodically, reaching a figure of $39.68 per room as of July 1974.

These increases in the rental charges precipitated the present lawsuit. Respondents, 57 residents of Co-op City, sued in federal court on behalf of all 15,372 apartment owners, and derivatively on behalf of Riverbay, seeking upwards of $30 million in damages, forced rental reductions, and other "appropriate" relief. Named as defendants (petitioners herein) were UHF, CSI, Riverbay, several individual directors of these organizations, the State of New York, and the State Private Housing Finance Agency. The heart of respondents' claim was that the 1965 Co-op City Information Bulletin falsely represented that CSI would bear all subsequent cost increases due to factors such as inflation. Respondents further alleged that they were misled in their purchases of shares since the Information Bulletin failed to disclose several critical facts. On these bases, respondents asserted two claims under the fraud provisions of the federal Securities Act of 1933, as amended, § 17(a) * * * and the Securities Exchange Act of 1934, as amended, § 10(b), * * * and * * * Rule 10b–5. * * *

Petitioners, while denying the substance of these allegations, moved to dismiss the complaint on the ground that federal jurisdiction was lacking. They maintained that shares of stock in Riverbay were not "securities" within the definitional sections of the federal Securities Acts. * * *

The District Court granted the motion to dismiss. * * *

The Court of Appeals for the Second Circuit reversed * * *.

In view of the importance of the issues presented we granted certiorari. * * * As we conclude that the disputed transactions are not purchases of securities within the contemplation of the federal statutes, we reverse.

* * *

II

* * *

A

We reject at the outset any suggestion that the present transaction, evidenced by the sale of shares called "stock," must be considered a security transaction simply because the statutory definition of a security includes the words "any * * * stock." Rather we adhere to the basic principle that has guided all of the Court's decisions in this area:

> [I]n searching for the meaning and scope of the word "security" in the Act[s], form should be disregarded for substance and the emphasis should be on economic reality. Tcherepnin v. Knight, 389 U.S. 332, 336 (1967).

See also *Howey,* supra, at 298.

The primary purpose of the Acts of 1933 and 1934 was to eliminate serious abuses in a largely unregulated securities market. The focus of the Acts is on the capital market of the enterprise system: the sale of securities to raise capital for profit-making purposes, the exchanges on which securities are traded, and the need for regulation to prevent fraud and to protect the interest of investors. Because securities transactions are economic in character Congress intended the application of these statutes to turn on the economic realities underlying a transaction, and not on the name appended thereto. Thus, in construing these Acts against the background of their purpose, we are guided by a traditional canon of statutory construction:

> [A] thing may be within the letter of the statute and yet not within the statute, because not within its spirit, nor within the intention of its makers. Church of the Holy Trinity v. United States, 143 U.S. 457, 459 (1892).

* * *

In holding that the name given to an instrument is not dispositive, we do not suggest that the name is wholly irrelevant to the decision whether it is a security. There may be occasions when the use of a traditional name such as "stocks" or "bonds" will lead a purchaser justifiably to assume that the federal securities laws apply. This would clearly be the case when the underlying transaction embodies some of the significant characteristics typically associated with the named instrument.

In the present case respondents do not contend, nor could they, that they were misled by use of the word "stock" into believing that the federal securities laws governed their purchase. Common sense suggests that people who intend to acquire only a residential apartment in a state-subsidized cooperative, for their personal use, are not likely to believe that in reality they are purchasing investment securities simply because the transaction is evidenced by something called a share of stock. These shares have none of the characteristics "that in our commercial world fall within the ordinary concept of a security." H.R.Rep. No. 85, supra, at 11. Despite their name, they lack what the Court in *Tcherepnin* deemed the most common feature of stock: the right to receive "dividends contingent upon an apportionment of profits." 389 U.S., at 339. Nor do they possess the other characteristics traditionally associated with stock: they are not negotiable; they cannot be pledged or hypothecated; they confer no voting rights in proportion to the number of shares owned; and they cannot appreciate in value. In short, the inducement to purchase was solely to acquire subsidized low-cost living space; it was not to invest for profit.

B

The Court of Appeals, as an alternative ground for its decision, concluded that a share in Riverbay was also an "investment contract" as defined by the Securities Acts. Respondents further argue that in any event what they agreed to purchase is "commonly known as a 'security' " within the meaning of these laws. In considering these claims we again must examine the substance—the economic realities of the transaction—rather than the names that may have been employed by the parties. We perceive no distinction, for present purposes, between an "investment contract" and an "instrument commonly known as a 'security.' " In either case, the basic test for distinguishing the transaction from other commercial dealings is

> whether the scheme involves an investment of money in a common enterprise with profits to come solely from the efforts of others. *Howey,* 328 U.S., at 301.[16]

This test, in shorthand form, embodies the essential attributes that run through all of the Court's decisions defining a security. The touchstone is the presence of an investment in a common venture premised on a reasonable expectation of profits to be derived from the entrepreneurial or managerial efforts of others. By profits, the Court has meant either capital appreciation resulting from the development of the initial investment, as in *Joiner,* supra (sale of oil leases conditioned on promoters' agreement to drill exploratory well), or a participation in

---

[16] This test speaks in terms of "profits to come *solely* from the efforts of others." (Emphasis supplied.) Although the issue is not presented in this case, we note that the Court of Appeals for the Ninth Circuit has held that "the word 'solely' should not be read as a strict or literal limitation on the definition of an investment contract, but rather must be construed realistically, so as to include within the definition those schemes which involve in substance, if not form, securities." SEC v. Glenn W. Turner Enterprises, 474 F.2d 476, 482, cert. denied, 414 U.S. 821 (1973). We express no view, however, as to the holding of this case.

earnings resulting from the use of investors' funds, as in Tcherepnin v. Knight, supra (dividends on the investment based on savings and loan association's profits). In such cases the investor is "attracted solely by the prospects of a return" on his investment. *Howey,* supra, at 300. By contrast, when a purchaser is motivated by a desire to use or consume the item purchased—"to occupy the land or to develop it themselves," as the *Howey* Court put it, ibid.—the securities laws do not apply. See also *Joiner,* supra.

In the present case there can be no doubt that investors were attracted solely by the prospect of acquiring a place to live, and not by financial returns on their investments. The Information Bulletin distributed to prospective residents emphasized the fundamental nature and purpose of the undertaking * * *.

Nowhere does the Bulletin seek to attract investors by the prospect of profits resulting from the efforts of the promoters or third parties. On the contrary, the Bulletin repeatedly emphasizes the "non-profit" nature of the endeavor. It explains that if rental charges exceed expenses the difference will be returned as a rebate, not invested for profit. It also informs purchasers that they will be unable to resell their apartments at a profit since the apartment must first be offered back to Riverbay "at the price * * * paid for it." Id., at 163a. In short, neither of the kinds of profits traditionally associated with securities was offered to respondents.

* * *

There is no doubt that purchasers in this housing cooperative sought to obtain a decent home at an attractive price. But that type of economic interest characterizes every form of commercial dealing. What distinguishes a security transaction—and what is absent here—is an investment where one parts with his money in the hope of receiving profits from the efforts of others, and not where he purchases a commodity for personal consumption or living quarters for personal use.

* * *

Since respondents' claims are not cognizable in federal court, the District Court properly dismissed their complaint. The judgment below is therefore

Reversed.

* * *

---

1. *Investment Versus Consumption: The Gray Intermediate Zone.* Although *Forman* can easily be read as a statement that the federal securities laws do not apply to consumption decisions, even if instruments resembling securities are purchased, many cases can arise in which there are mixed elements of investment and consumption. The Co-op City development in *Forman* was a subsidized, non-profit

cooperative as to which both the Supreme Court and the Second Circuit agreed there was no "possible profit on a resale"—but should the outcome be different if there was some potential for profit? What result, for example, in the case of a non-subsidized, private cooperative or condominium that permits its shareholders to sell their stock for a profit to new tenants? See Grenader v. Spitz, 537 F.2d 612 (2d Cir. 1976) (where profit motive is "purely incidental" to purchase of residential housing, shares in cooperative did not constitute securities). The prevailing rule today is that the factfinder should look to the purchaser's "primary motive." Was it investment or consumption? See Rice v. Branigar Organization, Inc., 922 F.2d 788 (11th Cir. 1991). Determining the primary motive, however, may require a trial and, thus, introduces considerable uncertainty into the law. Suppose a real estate developer markets subdivided lots in a real estate development. Could these interests be securities based on the developer's efforts to market the development as a whole (even though most buyers would buy for consumption and would develop their lots themselves)? See Aldrich v. McCulloch Properties, Inc., 627 F.3d 1036 (10th Cir. 1980) (whether lots in a development constituted securities could not be determined simply from the pleadings). For a fuller discussion of cooperatives, see Goforth, Application of the Federal Securities Laws to Equity Interests in Traditional and Value-Added Agricultural Cooperatives, 6 Drake J. Agric. L. 31 (2001).

2. *Investment Versus Entertainment.* In SEC v. SG Ltd. (discussed earlier), the defendants claimed they were only marketing an internet investment game in which persons could buy "virtual shares" as entertainment and not as a security. Defendants convinced the district court but lost on appeal. One of the issues in that case was the existence of horizontal commonality. But, even if that is present, isn't it possible that an internet game, viewed in terms of its economic reality, could be more like entertainment than an investment contract? For example, what if each share cost only 5 cents and no one could invest more than $50? Seemingly, the amount at stake should be a relevant consideration in whether the federal securities laws apply.

International Brotherhood of Teamsters, Chauffeurs, Warehousemen and Helpers of America v. Daniel

Supreme Court of the United States, 1979.
439 U.S. 551, 99 S.Ct. 790, 58 L.Ed.2d 808.

■ MR. JUSTICE POWELL delivered the opinion of the Court.

This case presents the question whether a noncontributory, compulsory pension plan constitutes a "security" within the meaning of the Securities Act of 1933 and the Securities Exchange Act of 1934 (Securities Acts).

I

In 1954 multiemployer collective bargaining between Local 705 of the International Brotherhood of Teamsters, Chauffeurs, Warehousemen, and Helpers of America and Chicago trucking firms produced a pension plan for employees represented by the Local. The plan was compulsory and noncontributory. Employees had no choice as to participation in the plan, and did not have the option of demanding that the employer's contribution be paid directly to them as a substitute for pension eligibility. The employees paid nothing to the plan themselves.

* * *

The petitioners moved to dismiss the first two counts of the complaint on the ground that respondent had no cause of action under the Securities Acts. The District Court denied the motion. * * * It held that respondent's interest in the Pension Fund constituted a security within the meaning of § 2(a)(1) of the Securities Act and § 3(a)(10) of the Securities Exchange Act because the plan created an "investment contract" as that term had been interpreted in SEC v. W.J. Howey Co. * * *. It also determined that there had been a "sale" of this interest to respondent within the meaning of § 2(3) of the Securities Act and § 3(a)(14) of the Securities Exchange Act. It believed respondent voluntarily gave value for his interest in the plan, because he had voted on collective-bargaining agreements that chose employer contributions to the Fund instead of other wages or benefits.

[T]he Court of Appeals for the Seventh Circuit affirmed. * * * We granted certiorari and now reverse.

II

"The starting point in every case involving construction of a statute is the language itself." Blue Chip Stamps v. Manor Drug Stores, 421 U.S. 723, 756 (1975) (Powell, J., concurring); * * *. In spite of the substantial use of employee pension plans at the time they were enacted, neither § 2(a)(1) of the Securities Act nor § 3(a)(10) of the Securities Exchange Act, which define the term "security" in considerable detail and with numerous examples, refers to pension plans of any type. Acknowledging this omission in the statutes, respondent contends that an employee's interest in a pension plan is an "investment contract," an instrument which is included in the statutory definitions of a security.

To determine whether a particular financial relationship constitutes an investment contract, "[t]he test is whether the scheme involves an investment of money in a common enterprise with profits to come solely from the efforts of others." Howey, supra, * * *. This test is to be applied in light of "the substance—the economic realities of the transaction—rather than the names that may have been employed by the parties." United Housing Foundation, Inc. v. Forman, 421 U.S. 837, 851–852 (1975). * * * Looking separately at each element of the Howey test, it is apparent that an employee's participation in a noncontributory, compulsory pension plan such as the Teamsters' does not comport with the commonly held understanding of an investment contract.

A. Investment of Money

An employee who participates in a noncontributory, compulsory pension plan by definition makes no payment into the pension fund. He only accepts employment, one of the conditions of which is eligibility for a possible benefit on retirement. Respondent contends, however, that he has "invested" in the Pension Fund by permitting part of his compensation from his employer to take the form of a deferred pension benefit. By allowing his employer to pay money into the Fund, and by contributing his labor to his employer in return for these payments, Respondent asserts he has made the kind of investment which the Securities Acts were intended to regulate.

In order to determine whether respondent invested in the Fund by accepting and remaining in covered employment, it is necessary to look at the entire transaction through which he obtained a chance to receive pension benefits. In every decision of this Court recognizing the presence of a "security" under the Securities Acts, the person found to have been an investor chose to give up a specific consideration in return for a separable financial interest with the characteristics of a security. See * * * *Howey*, supra (money paid for purchase, maintenance, and harvesting of orange grove); SEC v. C.M. Joiner Leasing Corp., 320 U.S. 344 (1943) (money paid for land and oil exploration). * * * In every case the purchaser gave up some tangible and definable consideration in return for an interest that had substantially the characteristics of a security.

In a pension plan such as this one, by contrast, the purported investment is a relatively insignificant part of an employee's total and indivisible compensation package. No portion of an employee's compensation other than the potential pension benefits has any of the characteristics of a security, yet these noninvestment interests cannot be segregated from the possible pension benefits. Only in the most abstract sense may it be said that an employee "exchanges" some portion of his labor in return for these possible benefits.[12] He surrenders his labor as a whole, and in return receives a compensation package that is substantially devoid of aspects resembling a security. His decision to accept and retain covered employment may have only an attenuated relationship, if any, to perceived investment possibilities of a future pension. Looking at the economic realities, it seems clear that an employee is selling his labor primarily to obtain a livelihood, not making an investment. * * *

---

[12] This is not to say that a person's "investment," in order to meet the definition of an investment contract, must take the form of cash only rather than of goods and services. See *Forman*, supra, 421 U.S., at 852 n. 16.

B. Expectation of Profits From a Common Enterprise

As we observed in *Forman,* the "touchstone" of the *Howey* test "is the presence of an investment in a common venture premised on a reasonable expectation of profits to be derived from the entrepreneurial or managerial efforts of others." 421 U.S., at 852. The Court of Appeals believed that Daniel's expectation of profit derived from the Fund's successful management and investment of its assets. To the extent pension benefits exceeded employer contributions and depended on earnings from the assets, it was thought they contained a profit element. The Fund's trustees provided the managerial efforts which produced this profit element.

As in other parts of its analysis, the court below found an expectation of profit in the pension plan only by focusing on one of its less important aspects to the exclusion of its more significant elements. It is true that the Fund, like other holders of large assets, depends to some extent on earnings from its assets. In the case of a pension fund, however, a far larger portion of its income comes from employer contributions, a source in no way dependent on the efforts of the Fund's managers. The Local 705 Fund, for example, earned a total of $31 million through investment of its assets between February 1955, and January 1977. During this same period employer contributions totaled $153 million. Not only does the greater share of a pension plan's income ordinarily come from new contributions, but unlike most entrepreneurs who manage other people's money, a plan usually can count on increased employer contributions, over which the plan itself has no control, to cover shortfalls in earnings.

The importance of asset earnings in relation to the other benefits received from employment is diminished further by the fact that where a plan has substantial preconditions to vesting, the principal barrier to an individual employee's realization of pension benefits is not the financial health of the Fund. Rather, it is his own ability to meet the Fund's eligibility requirements. Thus, even if it were proper to describe the benefits as a "profit" returned on some hypothetical investment by the employee, this profit would depend primarily on the employee's efforts to meet the vesting requirements, rather than the Fund's investment success. When viewed in light of the total compensation package an employee must receive in order to be eligible for pension benefits, it becomes clear that the possibility of participating in a plan's asset earnings "is far too speculative and insubstantial to bring the entire transaction within the Securities Acts," *Forman,* supra, at 856.

III

The court below believed that its construction of the term "security" was compelled not only by the perceived resemblance of a pension plan to an investment contract, but also by various actions of Congress and the SEC with regard to the Securities Acts. In reaching this conclusion, the court gave great weight to the SEC's explanation of these events, an explanation which for the most part the SEC repeats here. Our own review of the record leads us to believe that this reliance on the SEC's interpretation of these legislative and administrative actions was not justified. * * *

As we have demonstrated above, the type of pension plan at issue in this case bears no resemblance to the kind of financial interests the Securities Acts were designed to regulate. Further, the SEC's present position is flatly contradicted by its past actions. Until the instant litigation arose, the public record reveals no evidence that the SEC had ever considered the Securities Acts to be applicable to noncontributory pension plans. In 1941, the SEC first articulated the position that voluntary, contributory plans had investment characteristics that rendered them "securities" under the Acts. At the same time, however, the SEC recognized that noncontributory plans were not covered by the Securities Acts because such plans did not involve a "sale" within the meaning of the statutes. . . .

* * *

IV

If any further evidence were needed to demonstrate that pension plans of the type involved are not subject to the Securities Acts, the enactment of ERISA in 1974 would put the matter to rest. Unlike the Securities Acts, ERISA deals expressly and in detail with pension plans. ERISA requires pension plans to disclose specified information to employees in a specified manner, . . . in contrast to the indefinite and uncertain disclosure obligations imposed by the antifraud provisions of the Securities Acts. . . . Further, ERISA regulates the substantive terms of pension plans, setting standards for plan funding and limits on the eligibility requirements an employee must meet. For example, with respect to the underlying issue in this case—whether respondent served long enough to receive a pension—§ 203(a) of ERISA now sets the minimum level of benefits an employee must receive after accruing specified years of service, and § 203(b) governs continuous service requirements. Thus if respondent had retired after § 1053 took effect, the Fund would have been required to pay him at least a partial pension. The Securities Acts, on the other hand, do not purport to set the substantive terms of financial transactions.

The existence of this comprehensive legislation governing the use and terms of employee pension plans severely undercuts all arguments for extending the Securities Acts to noncontributory, compulsory pension plans. Congress believed that it was filling a regulatory void when it enacted ERISA, a belief which the SEC actively encouraged. Not only is the extension of the Securities Acts by the court below unsupported by the language and history of those Acts, but in light of ERISA it serves no general purpose. * * * Whatever benefits employees might derive from the effect of the Securities Acts are now provided in more definite form through ERISA.

V

We hold that the Securities Acts do not apply to a noncontributory, compulsory pension plan. Because the first two counts of respondent's complaint do not provide grounds for relief in federal court, the District Court should have granted the motion to dismiss them. The judgment below is therefore

Reversed.

* * *

---

1. *Aftermath.* Following *Daniel,* in which the SEC unsuccessfully argued, as an amicus curiae, that the federal securities laws applied to noncontributory pension plans, the SEC issued Securities Act Release No. 6188 (Feb. 1, 1980), which announced that it would thereafter deem only those pension plans that were both voluntary and contributory to constitute securities. See also Uselton v. Commercial Lovelace Motor Freight, Inc., 940 F.2d 564 (10th Cir. 1991) (reading *Daniel* as limited to compulsory, noncontributory plans). Is this the critical distinction in the Supreme Court's analysis in *Daniel*? Or is it the existence of ERISA, an alternative regulatory regime, which also applies to voluntary, contributory plans?

(1) CONDOMINIUMS AND REAL ESTATE DEVELOPMENTS

Securities Act Release No. 5347
Securities and Exchange Commission.
January 4, 1973.

GUIDELINES AS TO THE APPLICABILITY OF THE FEDERAL SECURITIES LAWS TO OFFERS AND SALES OF CONDOMINIUMS OR UNITS IN A REAL ESTATE DEVELOPMENT

The Securities and Exchange Commission today called attention to the applicability of the federal securities laws to the offer and sale of condominium units, or other units in a real estate development, coupled with an offer or agreement to perform or arrange certain rental or other services for the purchaser. The Commission noted that such offerings may involve the offering of a security in the form of an investment contract or a participation in a profit sharing arrangement within the meaning of the Securities Act of 1933 and the Securities Exchange Act of 1934. Where this is the case any offering of any such securities must comply with the registration and prospectus delivery requirements of the Securities Act, unless an exemption therefrom is available, and must comply with the anti-fraud provisions of the Securities Act and the Securities Exchange Act and the regulations thereunder. In addition, persons engaged in the business of buying or selling investment contracts or participations in profit sharing agreements of this type as agents for others, or as principal for their own account, may be brokers or dealers within the meaning of the Securities Exchange Act, and therefore may be required to be registered as such with the Commission under the provisions of Section 15 of that Act. * * *

The offer of real estate as such, without any collateral arrangements with the seller or others, does not involve the offer of a security. When the real estate is offered in conjunction with certain services, a security, in the form of an investment contract, may be present. The Supreme Court in Securities and Exchange Commission v. W. J. Howey Co., 328 U.S. 293 (1946) set forth what has become a generally accepted definition of an investment contract * * *.

The *Howey* case involved the sale and operation of orange groves. The reasoning, however, is applicable to condominiums.

* * *

The existence of various kinds of collateral arrangements may cause an offering of condominium units to involve an offering of investment contracts or interests in a profit sharing agreement. The presence of such arrangements indicates that the offeror is offering an opportunity through which the purchaser may earn a return on his investment through the managerial efforts of the promoters or a third party in their operation of the enterprise.

For example, some public offerings of condominium units involve rental pool arrangements. Typically, the rental pool is a device whereby the promoter or a third party undertakes to rent the unit on behalf of the actual owner during that period of time when the unit is not in use by the owner. The rents received and the expenses attributable to rental of all the units in the project are combined and the individual owner receives a ratable share of the rental proceeds regardless of whether his individual unit was actually rented. The offer of the unit together with the offer of an opportunity to participate in such a rental pool involves the offer of investment contracts which must be registered unless an exemption is available.

Also, the condominium units may be offered with a contract or agreement that places restrictions, such as required use of an exclusive rental agent or limitations on the period of time the owner may occupy the unit, on the purchaser's occupancy or rental of the property purchased. Such restrictions suggest that the purchaser is in fact investing in a business enterprise, the return from which will be substantially dependent on the success of the managerial efforts of other persons. In such cases, registration of the resulting investment contract would be required.

In any situation where collateral arrangements are coupled with the offering of condominiums, whether or not specifically of the types discussed above, the manner of offering and economic inducements held out to the prospective purchaser play an important role in determining whether the offerings involve securities. In other words, condominiums, coupled with a rental arrangement, will be deemed to be securities if they are offered and sold through advertising, sales literature, promotional schemes or oral representations which emphasize the economic benefits to the purchaser to be derived from the managerial efforts of the promoter, or a third party designated or arranged for by the promoter, in renting the units.

In summary, the offering of condominium units in conjunction with any one of the following will cause the offering to be viewed as an offering of securities in the form of investment contracts:

1. The condominiums, with any rental arrangement or other similar service, are offered and sold with emphasis on the economic benefits to the purchaser to be derived from the managerial efforts of the promoter, or a third party designated or arranged for by the promoter, from rental of the units,

2. The offering of participation in a rental pool arrangement; and

3. The offering of a rental or similar arrangement whereby the purchaser must hold his unit available for rental for any part of the year, must use an exclusive rental agent or is otherwise materially restricted in his occupancy or rental of his unit.

In all of the above situations, investor protection requires the application of the federal securities laws.

If the condominiums are not offered and sold with emphasis on the economic benefits to the purchaser to be derived from the managerial efforts of others, and assuming that no plan to avoid the registration requirements of the Securities Act is involved, an owner of a condominium unit may, after purchasing his unit, enter into a non-pooled rental arrangement with an agent not designated or required to be used as a condition to the purchase, whether or not such agent is affiliated with the offeror, without causing a sale of a security to be involved in the sale of the unit. Further a continuing affiliation between the developers or promoters of a project and the project by reason of maintenance arrangements does not make the unit a security.

* * *

* * * Whether an offering of securities is involved necessarily depends on the facts and circumstances of each particular case. The staff of the Commission will be available to respond to written inquiries on such matters.

* * *

Re-Assessment. Confident as the SEC's words are in the foregoing release, they were written in 1973, well before the Circuits split over the question of "vertical" versus "horizontal" commonality. In those Circuits that accept "strict vertical commonality," more would need to be shown than the importance of the promoter's managerial efforts; some sharing of the profits would be necessary. In those Circuits that agree with Judge Posner's analysis in Wals v. Fox Hills Development Corporation (discussed earlier), what facts would the SEC need to show before a purchaser of a condominium unit in a ski lodge could be said to have purchased a security?

Problems

PROBLEM 4-2

(a) Samantha Jones, a young associate with the law firm of Dewey, Cheatem & Howe, is making a substantial income and wants to invest in a ski country condominium. Her problem is she can rarely take weekends off and will probably only use the condo three or four weekends each year. For this reason, she is particularly attracted by the brochures her real estate agent gave her for Ski Lodge Condos ("Ski Lodge"), a development being constructed by a major resort company. Ski Lodge stresses the strong economic return and tax shelter advantages associated with acquiring a unit in its development. It also encourages condo owners to place their unit on the market with Ski Lodge for a weekend rental to tourists if the owner notifies management that she will not be occupying the unit that weekend. Tourists pay between $500 and $700 to rent the unit for a weekend, and, over the year, rental income of $15,000 or more is possible. For Samantha, this economic return makes the purchase price ($250,000) acceptable. Assume next that the rental income received with respect to a unit that is rented out for the weekend is allocated according to one of the following three formulas:

(1) all rental income is allocated pro rata among all owners who notify management their unit is available for rent that weekend, regardless of whether the unit is actually rented (management suggests this technique prevents them from "playing favorites" and directing rentals to preferred clients);

(2) rental income is allocated only to the unit that was occupied and in the amount paid by the tenant, minus a $150 service charge that management deducts and keeps; or

(3) rental income, again, is allocated on a unit-by-unit basis that reflects the actual occupancy of the unit, but it is shared on a 2/3:1/3 basis, with management keeping one-third of the rental income for its services in advertising the unit to the ski vacation market and soliciting rentals.

Under which of these options, if any, does the arrangement between Samantha and Ski Lodge amount to a security?

(b) Assume Samantha buys a unit in Ski Lodge and makes substantial improvements to it, for example, by installing a hot tub, a mini-bar, a sound system, and a luxurious king-size bed. The total cost of these improvements is $25,000, and, as a result, the unit now rents for more than any other unit in the Ski Lodge development (i.e., $850 per weekend). Does this additional factor change your analysis? Under all, or only some, of the three rental allocation formulas discussed in part (a) above?

PROBLEM 4-3

Chateau Napa is a financially-strained California winery that makes excellent cabernet. Typically, it ages its wine in oak casks for three years after harvesting. This is costly, and so to solve its cash flow problems, it offers investors the opportunity to buy cases of the latest vintage of its cabernet that has just been placed in casks (and, thus, is three years from sale) at a price equal to one-half the price of a case in its current vintage. Wine lovers, however, must purchase a minimum of three cases for a price of $1,000. To secure its promised future delivery, Chateau Napa gives a mortgage covering ten acres of its vineyard to a trustee appointed to represent all the "future delivery" wine purchasers. Chateau Napa gives its purchaser of the minimum three cases "a future delivery receipt," and a secondary market quickly springs up on the internet (without Chateau Napa encouraging it in any way) in these certificates, with prices fluctuating as forecasts are made about whether this year's wine harvest will be a vintage year. All told, Chateau Napa raises some $1.5 million by this technique. But does this amount to an investment contract?

(2) PARTNERSHIPS, LIMITED PARTNERSHIPS, AND LIMITED LIABILITY COMPANIES

a. *Control in the Limited Partnership*

Steinhardt Group Inc. v. Citicorp

United States Court of Appeals, Third Circuit, 1997.
126 F.3d 144.

■ Before: BECKER and MANSMANN, CIRCUIT JUDGES, and HOEVOLER, DISTRICT JUDGE.

■ MANSMANN, CIRCUIT JUDGE.

In this appeal, we are asked to decide whether a highly structured securitization transaction negotiated between Citicorp and an investor in a limited partnership constitutes an "investment contract" as that term is defined by the Supreme Court in SEC v. W.J. Howey Co. Examining the economic reality of the transaction as a whole, we conclude that the limited partner retained pervasive control over its investment in the limited partnership such that it cannot be deemed a passive investor under *Howey* and its progeny. Accordingly, we find the securitization transaction here does not constitute an investment contract. We will, therefore, affirm the judgment of the district court.

I.

* * *

A.

The controversy here arises out of alleged violations of Sections 10(b) and 20(a) of the Securities Exchange Act of 1934, and Rule 10b–5 involving the "securitization" of a pool of delinquent residential mortgage loans ("Mortgage Loans") and real estate owned by Citicorp as a result of foreclosed loans ("REO") The plaintiffs are The Steinhardt Group Inc. ("Steinhardt" Group) and C.B. Mtge., L.P. ("C.B.Mtge."). . . .

The fraudulent conduct alleged in the amended complaint arises out of a severe financial crisis faced by Citicorp during the early 1990's. With bad loans and illiquid assets threatening the very existence of the nation's then-largest banking institution, Citicorp was looking for a way to extricate itself from its financial problems. The securitization transaction was thus conceived by Citicorp to remove the nonperforming assets from its financial books and replace them with cash.

In essence, the securitization required Citicorp to create an investment vehicle—a limited partnership ultimately named Bristol Oaks, L.P.—that would issue both debt securities, in the form of nonrecourse bonds, and equity securities, in the form of partnership interests, to investors. Bristol would acquire title to the nonperforming Mortgage Loans and REO properties and would retain Ontra, Inc. to manage and liquidate the assets. Then Bristol would obtain bridge financing from Citibank and CNAI; shortly thereafter, CSI would securitize and underwrite a public offering of bonds and other debt securities to pay off the bridge financing. All of the investors' money was to be paid to Bristol and become the capital of that investment vehicle. The return on these investments was to come from the same pool of assets.

During late 1993 and the first half of 1994, representatives of CSI made a series of written and oral presentations to the Steinhardt Group in which they described returns of 18% or more annually by investing in Bristol. Throughout these presentations and in other meetings and telephone discussions, Citicorp explained how it had created the proprietary "Citicorp Non-Performing Loan Model" (the "Pricing Model"), based on its own past experience, intimate knowledge of the assets at issue, and the valuation of such assets. Citicorp represented the Pricing Model to be an accurate means of pricing the Mortgage Loans and REO properties in the portfolio and of providing the Steinhardt Group with the promised 18% or greater returns. In particular, Citicorp represented to the Steinhardt Group that no institution in America had more experience in single-family residential mortgages, or more knowledge about the process of collecting on defaulted mortgage loans. Moreover, Citicorp touted not only its longstanding reputation in the banking industry, but also how the assumptions in the Pricing Model were firmly grounded upon Citicorp's own unparalleled experience and expertise.

A series of factual assumptions lies at the core of the Pricing Model. First, Citicorp assumed that the most accurate "proxy" for the values of the REO and the properties mortgaged for the Mortgage Loans would be Broker's Price Opinions ("BPOs"). These BPOs would be obtained from independent real estate brokers reflecting collateral value as well as the proceeds that would be obtained within six months if the properties were listed for sale. In addition, these BPOs were to provide "as is" values indicating what the properties were worth in light of their overall exterior and interior physical condition. Finally, an integral component of Citicorp's valuation methodology was obtaining BPOs for all of the assets, rather than just a sampling, thereby resulting in a more accurate valuation of the portfolio and significantly reducing the investment risk.

Under the Pricing Model, Citicorp represented the BPOs would be used to calculate a current Loan-to-Value ("LTV") ratio for each of the properties. The LTV ratio was used to project the probability of possible outcomes with respect to each of the Mortgage Loans, as well as the ultimate cash proceeds that would flow from each of the possible resolutions. The Pricing Model further assumed that each of the existing and to-be-foreclosed REO properties could be sold for 98% of the BPO, which Citicorp represented to be conservative and designed to assure realization of its promised 18% return on the portfolio. . . .

According to the amended complaint, Citicorp knew at the time it made these representations that several of the assumptions underlying the Pricing Model were false. Steinhardt claims that Citicorp obtained inflated valuations by promising the brokers they would later be hired to list the properties for sale if the BPOs were satisfactory to Citicorp. The inflated valuations, in turn, caused the assets to be overpriced, which resulted in the overstatement of future cash flow. Steinhardt further contends that [Citicorp] failed to follow its own internal controls for insuring unbiased appraisals, that it employed brokers not on Citicorp's approved list, and that it required brokers to provide large numbers of valuations within grossly inadequate periods of time, which further undermined their accuracy. Although Citicorp was allegedly warned repeatedly by one of its own officers that the assets were overpriced, these warnings were never revealed to Steinhardt. Rather, Steinhardt contends these warnings were actively concealed in order to induce it to invest in Bristol.

* * *

According to the amended complaint, Steinhardt first learned of Citicorp's allegedly fraudulent scheme in 1995 through conversations with a former officer of CMI, which ultimately led to an investigation and the discovery of the alleged fraud. On December 1, 1995, Bristol and BHT (collectively the "Partnerships"), sent Citibank and CNAI a repurchase notice for more than 2,300 assets; however, Citibank and CNAI refused to honor their obligations to repurchase these assets. . . .

II.

The outcome of this dispute hinges upon whether, under the circumstances, the securitization transaction constitutes an investment contract within the meaning of section 2(1) of the Securities Act of 1933. In order to invoke the protections of the federal securities laws, an investor must show, as a threshold matter, that the instrument in question is a security. Section 2(1) of the Act sets forth the definition of the term "security." Included in this definition are several catch-all categories which were designed to cover other securities interests not specifically enumerated in the statute. . . . One such category is the "investment contract."

The term investment contract has not been defined by Congress, nor does the legislative history to the 1933 and 1934 Acts illuminate what Congress intended by the term investment contract. The interpretation of this term has thus been left to the judiciary. In 1946, the Supreme Court took up the task of defining the parameters of an investment contract in the seminal case of SEC v. W.J. Howey. The Court stated:

> an investment contract for purposes of the Securities Act means a contract, transaction or scheme whereby a person invests his money in a common enterprise and is led to expect profits solely from the efforts of the promoter or a third party. . . .

* * *

Clearly Steinhardt has alleged sufficient facts to meet the first prong of *Howey*. The Steinhardt Group, through its affiliate, C.B. Mtge., has invested $42 million dollars in Bristol with the expectation of receiving a return on its investment of approximately 18%. Thus, the facts alleged show that Steinhardt has undertaken some degree of economic risk. . . .

Regarding the second prong, commonality, we have previously applied a horizontal commonality approach in determining whether a particular investment constitutes a security. See, Salcer v. Merrill Lynch, Pierce, Fenner and Smith, 682 F.2d 459, 460 (3d Cir. 1982). . . . In the case before us, Steinhardt maintains that the district court erred in concluding that horizontal commonality was not adequately pleaded. In the alternative, Steinhardt argues that vertical commonality exists here and urges us to find that vertical commonality can satisfy the *Howey* common enterprise prong. On the other hand, the Citicorp Defendants agree with the district court's finding as to the common enterprise element but disagree with the court's ruling insofar as it found that the third element of the Howey test was adequately pleaded—the "solely from the efforts of others" element. The Citicorp Defendants entreat us to find that Steinhardt negotiated such pervasive control over its investment in Bristol Oaks that it cannot meet the third element of *Howey*. . . .

The third prong of the Supreme Court's test in *Howey* test requires that the purchaser be attracted to the investment by the prospect of a profit on the investment rather than a desire to use or consume the item purchased. United Housing Foundation, Inc. v. Forman, 421 U.S. 837, 853–54, 95 S.Ct. 2051, 2060–61, 44 L.Ed.2d 621 (1975) (court concluded that sale of shares in a housing cooperative did not give rise to a securities transaction where none of the promotional materials emphasized profit and there was a low probability the shares would actually produce a profit). In analyzing this element, the courts have also looked at whether the investor has meaningfully participated in the management of the partnership in which it has invested such that it has more than minimal control over the investment's performance.

* * *

To resolve the issue of whether Steinhardt's involvement in the Bristol Oaks Limited Partnership was limited to that of a passive investor, we must look at the transaction as a whole, considering the arrangements the parties made for the operation of the investment vehicle in order to determine who exercised control in generating profits for the vehicle. The Limited Partnership Agreement ("LPA"), which establishes the relative powers of the partners in running the enterprise, therefore governs our inquiry.

Section 3.1(f) of the LPA, as amended, requires that "the Managing Partner shall not have the right to take any of the following actions ('Material Actions') without the consent of . . . a Majority of the Partners (or pursuant to an approved Business Plan). . . ." The "Material Actions", set forth in section 3.1(f) of the LPA, include most tasks that are crucial to turning the mortgages and REO into profit, which is the basic purpose of Bristol Oaks, e.g., entering into any written or verbal material agreement or transaction with any borrower outside of the Loan Documents; giving any material consent required to be obtained by any borrower under the Loan Documents; modifying or amending any of the Loan Documents; exercising any rights under the Loan Documents; selling, exchanging, securitizing, conveying, or otherwise voluntarily disposing of, or placing any encumbrance on, the Properties. Under the LPA, a "Majority of the Partners" is defined as "those Partners holding greater than fifty percent (50%) of the Percentage Interests . . .", meaning that Steinhardt alone constitutes a "Majority of the Partners."

Steinhardt approved the interim business plan and although Citicorp drafted that plan, Steinhardt retains the power to amend that plan as it wishes in one of two ways: (1) in its capacity as "Majority of the Partners," Steinhardt can propose and approve a new business plan; and (2) if the general partner proposes a new business plan, Steinhardt retains veto power, which it can exercise merely by declining to approve the proposed change within fifteen business days. Thus, we agree with the Citicorp Defendants that "Steinhardt's consent is required for the taking of any 'Material Action,' whether through its control over the business plan, or through its veto power over 'Material Actions' that fall outside the parameters of the business plan."

The LPA further provides that where a Majority of the Partners proposes a Material Action, the general partner "shall use best efforts to implement such Material Action at the Partnership's expense on the terms proposed by such Majority of the Partners," i.e., Steinhardt. If the general partner refuses to act with such best efforts in pursuit of Steinhardt's proposals, Steinhardt can remove and replace the general partner without notice.

As the above provisions demonstrate, the LPA gives Steinhardt pervasive control over the management of the Partnership. Indeed, these quite significant powers are far afield of the typical limited partnership agreement whereby a limited partner leaves the control of the business to the general partners. We find the agreement altogether consistent with the arrangement before us: Steinhardt, a sophisticated investor, made a $42 million capital contribution in Bristol Oaks, thereby becoming a 98.79% partner through a highly negotiated transaction.

* * *

Thus, accepting, as we must, the facts as alleged in the amended complaint, we do not find Steinhardt is entitled to relief under *Howey* and its progeny.

III.

We find that the rights and powers assigned to Steinhardt under the LPA were not nominal, but rather, were significant and, thus, directly affected the profits it received from the Partnership. Accordingly, we hold Steinhardt's investment in the Bristol Oaks Limited Partnership does not constitute an investment contract.

Because we find that Steinhardt was not a passive investor, we need not consider whether the securitization here constituted a common enterprise. We will, therefore, affirm the judgment of the district court.

---

1. *How Much Control Is Too Much?* Two real estate developers formed a real estate development trust and together constituted two out of the three initial trustees. Later, the trust's board was expanded to six trustees (including the same original two). Did their status as founding trustees give them sufficient control under *Steinhardt* so that their interests would not constitute securities when they later sued for securities fraud? The D.C. Circuit held that if the two founders entered into a transaction with the defendant expecting that control would shift to a broader board, with the founders becoming minority members of the board prior to the closing of the transaction, then the two founders could sue for securities fraud and were not barred by the *Steinhardt* decision. See Liberty Property Trust v. Republic Property Corporation, 577 F.3d 335 (D.C. Cir. 2009).

b. *The Special Case of Limited Liability Companies*

Courts have disagreed over whether interests in limited liability companies ("LLCs") constitute securities, but most agree that the answer depends on the facts. In Great Lakes Chemical Corporation v. Monsanto Company, 96 F.Supp.2d 376, 391–92 (D. Del. 2000), the district court rejected the idea that there could even be a presumption that interests in LLCs were securities, noting:

> In comparison with limited partnerships, the Delaware Limited Liability Company Act permits a member in an LLC to be an active participant in management and still to retain limited liability. 6 Del. C. §§ 18–303. Thus, there is no statutory basis, as with limited partnerships, to presume that LLC members are passive investors entitled to protection under the federal securities laws.
>
> The Delaware Limited Liability Company Act grants parties substantial flexibility in determining the character of an LLC. Accordingly, the terms of the operating agreement of each LLC will determine whether its membership interests constitute securities. The presumptions that courts have articulated with respect to general partnerships and limited partnerships do not apply to LLCs. Rather, to determine whether a member's profits are to come solely from the efforts of others, it is necessary to consider the structure of the particular LLC at issue, as provided in its operating agreement.
>
> In the present case, the Members of [the LLC] had no authority to directly manage [the LLC's] business and affairs. Section 5.1(a) of the LLC Agreement states:
>
>> Except as otherwise expressly set forth in this Agreement, the Members shall not have any authority, right or power to bind the Company, or to manage or control, or to participate in the management or control of, the business and affairs of the Company in any manner whatsoever. Such management shall in every respect be the full and complete responsibility of the Board alone as provided in this Agreement.
>
> The Members, however, had the power to remove any Manager with or without cause, and to dissolve the company. [The plaintiff] exercised this authority on October 5, 1999, when it filed a Certificate of Cancellation with the State of Delaware, dissolving [the LLC] as a separate entity. . . .
>
> The powers held by [the plaintiff] were comparable to those of *Steinhardt*, in that [plaintiff] had the authority to remove [the LLC's] managers without cause. Because [the plaintiff] was the sole owner of [the LLC], its power to remove managers was not diluted by the presence of other ownership interests. See

Williamson, 645 F.2d at 423 (noting that a partner in a general partnership might be deemed to be a passive investor if there were a sufficient number of other partners to dilute the partner's voting rights). [Plaintiff's] authority to remove managers gave it the power to directly affect the profits it received from [the LLC]. Thus, the court finds that [Plaintiff's] profits from NSC did not come solely from the efforts of others. See Howey, 328 U.S. at 299.

While the district court in *Great Lakes* looked to the operative agreement to determine who had control, the Second Circuit has stressed that, in applying the *Howey* test to LLCs, "courts can (and should) look beneath the formal terms of a relationship to the reality of the parties' positions to evaluate whether the 'reasonable expectation was one of significant investor control.'" See United States v. Leonard, 529 F.3d 83, 90 (2d Cir. 2008) (citation omitted). After such an inquiry (and in a criminal case), the Second Circuit concluded:

> In sum, upon consideration of the totality of the circumstances, we conclude that the jury could have determined that, notwithstanding the organization documents drafted to suggest active participation by members, the defendants sought and expected passive investors for [the two LLCs], and therefore the interests they marketed constituted securities . . .

Id. at 91. Both courts (the district court in *Great Lakes* and the Second Circuit in *Leonard*) might have agreed with the other on the facts of the two cases. But the Second Circuit, as with the Fifth Circuit in the Williamson v. Tucker case, discussed below, insisted on examining how the interests were marketed and who acquired them before determining their status as securities.

The courts remain split on whether LLCs should be characterized as securities, but most decisions take the view that the specific facts of the business relationship need to be examined in terms of the *Howey* criteria.[28] That is, the answer is not the same for all LLCs.

Commentators have suggested that private ordering should be permitted to resolve this issue and that the LLC's members should be able to opt out of the securities laws, such as through an express provision in the LLC agreement declaring their investments not to be securities. See McGinty, The Limited Liability Company: Opportunity for Selective Securities Law Deregulation, 64 U. Cin. L. Rev. 369 (1996). But opting out raises special issues. For example, should § 29 of the 1934 Act (which forbids waivers of the federal securities laws) bar such opting out?

---

[28] See Robinson v. Glynn, 349 F. 3d 166, 173 (4th Cir. 2003) (finding interests not to be securities). For decisions finding LLCs to be securities under the *Howey* test, see, e.g., Nelson v. Stahl, 173 F.Supp.2d 153 (S.D.N.Y.2001); Keith v. Black Diamond Advisors, Inc., 48 F.Supp.2d 326, 354 (S.D.N.Y.1999). For overviews, see Garrison & Knoepfle, Limited Liability Company Interests As Securities: A Proposed Framework for Analysis, 33 Am. Bus. L.J. 577 (1996); Sargent, Are Limited Liability Company Interests Securities?, 19 Pepp. L. Rev. 1069 (1992).

For such a view, see Welle, Freedom of Contract and the Securities Laws: Opting Out of Securities Regulation by Private Agreement, 56 Wash. & Lee L. Rev. 519 (1999). Finally, Professor Ribstein has argued for the view that the securities laws should inherently not apply to general partnerships and LLCs, but should presumptively apply to corporations and limited partnerships, on the grounds that this would give investors a "bright line" choice through their selection of the organizational form. See Ribstein, Form and Substance in the Definition of a "Security": The Case of Limited Liability Companies, 51 Wash. & Lee L. Rev. 807 (1994).

c. *Partnerships*

General partnerships have rarely been found to be securities, even when most partners in the partnership remain passive.[29] Still, in Williamson v. Tucker, 645 F.2d 404 (5th Cir. 1981),[30] the Fifth Circuit offered the following much-cited formula for determining when a general partnership interest could constitute a security:

> A general partnership or joint venture interest can be designated a security if the investor can establish, for example, that (1) an agreement among the parties leaves so little power in the hands of the partner or venturer that the arrangement in fact distributes power as would a limited partnership; or (2) the partner or venturer is so inexperienced and unknowledgeable in business affairs that he is incapable of intelligently exercising his partnership or venture powers; or (3) the partner or venturer is so dependent on some unique entrepreneurial or managerial ability of the promoter or manager that he cannot replace the manager of the enterprise or otherwise exercise meaningful partnership or venture powers.[31]

Although *Williamson* indicates that the mere form of the organization (general partnership vs. limited partnership) is not necessarily dispositive, most subsequent cases have indicated that a general partner who seeks to characterize his partnership interest as a security faces a high barrier. Few such plaintiffs have been successful.[32] Indeed, one scholar, surveying all the cases, found that plaintiffs overwhelmingly lose when they attempt to assert that a general partnership interest is a security (winning in only 25% of the cases), but win by a higher

---

[29] See Rivanna Trawlers Unlimited v. Thompson Trawlers, Inc., 840 F.2d 236 (4th Cir. 1988); Matek v. Murat, 862 F.2d 720 (9th Cir. 1988); Goodwin v. Elkins & Co., 730 F.2d 99 (3d Cir. 1984).

[30] *Williamson's* criteria appear to have been accepted by the Ninth Circuit in an en banc decision. See Hocking v. Dubois, 885 F.2d 1449 (9th Cir. 1989), cert. denied, 494 U.S. 1078 (1990).

[31] Id. at 424.

[32] See, e.g., Rivanna Trawlers Unlimited v. Thompson Trawlers, Inc., 840 F.2d 236 (4th Cir. 1988). For a review of the cases supporting this generalization, see Karjala, Federalism, Full Disclosure, and the National Markets in the Interpretation of Federal Securities Law, 80 Nw. L. Rev. 1473, 1511 (1986).

percentage when they seek to characterize a limited partnership interest as a security (succeeding in 80% of the cases).[33]

d. Limited Partnerships

As just noted, most decisions do find limited partnership interests to constitute securities.[34] Thus, *Steinhardt* represents an exceptional case. Still, according to Judge Easterbrook, writing for the Seventh Circuit, the test for whether a limited partnership interest falls outside the definition of "security" is whether the interest "carrie[s] more control than normal investment units."[35] The degree of control is critical, he found, under the Supreme Court's decision in Marine Bank v. Weaver (discussed earlier and again below).[36]

In SEC v. Merchant Capital, LLC, 483 F.3d 747 (11th Cir. 2007).[37] an SEC enforcement action, the Commission sued promoters who sold partnership interests in 28 limited liability partnerships to some 485 persons for over $26 million. Virtually all the partners, however, had significant assets, and more than 75% had a net worth exceeding $500,000. Under each partnership agreement, the partners had the right to elect the Managing General Partner who would run the partnership. All potential partners were informed they were expected to participate in the operation of their partnership, but "their actual duties would be limited to checking a box on ballots that would be periodically sent to them." The SEC argued that the *Williamson* presumption against a partnership interest being deemed an "investment contract" should not govern because each partner had limited liability and, hence, less incentive to participate in control. The 11th Circuit, however, concluded that the real test was a partner's expectation of an ability to participate in control. Finding that any one of the three tests specified in *Williamson* would make the partnership interest an investment contract, the court determined that all three tests were easily satisfied. In its view, there was simply no "realistic alternative" to the promoter serving as managing general partner and, thus, it had "permanent control" over each partnership, resulting in an investment contract.

---

[33] See Gabaldson, A Sense of a Security: An Empirical Study, 25 J. Corp. L. 307, 335 (2000).

[34] See, e.g., SEC v. Murphy, 626 F.2d 633 (9th Cir. 1980); L & B Hospital Ventures, Inc. v. Healthcare International, Inc., 894 F.2d 150 (5th Cir.), cert. denied, 498 U.S. 815 (1990).

[35] See National Tax Credit Partners, L.P. v. Havlik, 20 F.3d 705, 709 (7th Cir. 1994).

[36] 455 U.S. 551 (1982).

[37] In general, the SEC has been far more successful than private plaintiffs in establishing that partnership interests are securities. See SEC v. Professional Assocs., 731 F.2d 349, 357 (6th Cir. 1984) (noting that at least some investors were "entirely passive"); SEC v. Telecom Marketing, Inc., 888 F.Supp. 1160, 1166 (N.D.Ga. 1995) ("investors were targeted for their ignorance of law, accounting, and the . . . industry").

Problem

PROBLEM 4-4

Morgan Bank wishes to transfer some risky loans (at a large discount) to a sophisticated purchaser. The purchaser—Hedged Risk Associates ("HRA"), a large hedge fund—is only willing to purchase these risky assets if Morgan will manage them and assume some of the risk. They strike a deal in which: the loans will be transferred to a limited partnership, LHIW Partners; Morgan will be the General Partner (and will receive 10% of the profits and losses); and HRA will be the sole limited partner (with 90% of the profits and losses). Morgan will service the loans and sue any borrowers who default. On that basis, HRA will contribute 90% of the previously agreed purchase price for the loans (which price is 65% of the loans' face value). Under the terms of the LHIW limited partnership, Morgan must agree to liquidate the partnership, sell the assets, foreclose on the assets, or take any other financial measure with respect to these assets as 51% in interest of the limited partners instruct it (and HRA is the only limited partner). Six months later, HRA concludes that Morgan defrauded it by failing to disclose how close the loans were to defaulting (and how many were actually in default). It brings suit under Rule 10b–5 under the 1934 Act. What result on Morgan's motion to dismiss? Would it make a difference if HRA took a 45% limited partnership interest, and another hedge fund, Pequot Partners—managed by the same investment adviser—took the other 45% limited partnership interest, with Morgan still holding the residual 10% interest?

C. "STOCK": THE RETURN OF FORMALISM

Landreth Timber Company v. Landreth
Supreme Court of the United States, 1985.
471 U.S. 681, 105 S.Ct. 2297, 85 L.Ed.2d 692.

■ JUSTICE POWELL delivered the opinion of the Court.

This case presents the question whether the sale of all of the stock of a company is a securities transaction subject to the antifraud provisions of the federal securities laws (the Acts).

I

Respondents Ivan K. Landreth and his sons owned all of the outstanding stock of a lumber business they operated in Tonasket, Washington. The Landreth family offered their stock for sale through both Washington and out-of-state brokers. Before a purchaser was found, the company's sawmill was heavily damaged by fire. Despite the fire, the brokers continued to offer the stock for sale. Potential purchasers were advised of the damage, but were told that the mill would be completely rebuilt and modernized.

Samuel Dennis, a Massachusetts tax attorney, received a letter offering the stock for sale. On the basis of the letter's representations concerning the rebuilding plans, the predicted productivity of the mill, existing contracts, and expected profits, Dennis became interested in acquiring the stock. He talked to John Bolten, a former client who had retired to Florida, about joining him in investigating the offer. After having an audit and an inspection of the mill conducted, a stock purchase agreement was negotiated, with Dennis the purchaser of all of the common stock in the lumber company. Ivan Landreth agreed to stay on as a consultant for some time to help with the daily operations of the mill. Pursuant to the terms of the stock purchase agreement, Dennis assigned the stock he purchased to B & D Co., a corporation formed for the sole purpose of acquiring the lumber company stock. B & D then merged with the lumber company, forming petitioner Landreth Timber Co. Dennis and Bolten then acquired all of petitioner's Class A stock, representing 85% of the equity, and six other investors together owned the Class B stock, representing the remaining 15% of the equity.

After the acquisition was completed, the mill did not live up to the purchasers' expectations. Rebuilding costs exceeded earlier estimates, and new components turned out to be incompatible with existing equipment. Eventually, petitioner sold the mill at a loss and went into receivership. Petitioner then filed this suit seeking rescission of the sale of stock and $2,500,000 in damages, alleging that respondents had widely offered and then sold their stock without registering it as required by the Securities Act of 1933 (the 1933 Act). Petitioner also alleged that respondents had negligently or intentionally made misrepresentations and had failed to state material facts as to the worth and prospects of the lumber company, all in violation of the Securities Exchange Act of 1934 (the 1934 Act).

Respondents moved for summary judgment on the ground that the transaction was not covered by the Acts because under the so-called "sale of business" doctrine, petitioner had not purchased a "security" within the meaning of those Acts. The District Court granted respondents' motion and dismissed the complaint for want of federal jurisdiction. It acknowledged that the federal statutes include "stock" as one of the instruments constituting a "security," and that the stock at issue possessed all of the characteristics of conventional stock. Nonetheless, it joined what it termed the "growing majority" of courts that had held that the federal securities laws do not apply to the sale of 100% of the stock of a closely held corporation. * * * Relying on United Housing Foundation, Inc. v. Forman, 421 U.S. 837 (1975), and SEC v. W.J. Howey Co., 328 U.S. 293 (1946), the District Court ruled that the stock could not be considered a "security" unless the purchaser had entered into the transaction with the anticipation of earning profits derived from the efforts of others. Finding that managerial control of the business had passed into the hands of the purchasers, and thus that the transaction was a commercial venture rather than a typical investment, the District Court dismissed the complaint.

The United States Court of Appeals for the Ninth Circuit affirmed the District Court's application of the sale of business doctrine. [W]e granted certiorari. We now reverse.

II

It is axiomatic that "[t]he starting point in every case involving construction of a statute is the language itself." Blue Chip Stamps v. Manor Drug Stores, 421 U.S. 723, 756 (1975) (POWELL, J., concurring); accord, Teamsters v. Daniel, 439 U.S. 551, 558 (1979). Section 2(a)(1) of the 1933 Act . . . defines a "security". . . .

* * *

As we have observed in the past, this definition is quite broad, Marine Bank v. Weaver, 455 U.S. 551, 556 (1982), and includes both instruments whose names alone carry well-settled meaning, as well as instruments of "more variable character [that] were necessarily designated by more descriptive terms," such as "investment contract" and "instrument commonly known as a 'security.'" SEC v. C.M. Joiner Leasing Corp., 320 U.S. 344, 351 (1943). The face of the definition shows that "stock" is considered to be a "security" within the meaning of the Acts. As we observed in United Housing Foundation, Inc. v. Forman, 421 U.S. 837 (1975), most instruments bearing such a traditional title are likely to be covered by the definition.

As we also recognized in *Forman,* the fact that instruments bear the label "stock" is not of itself sufficient to invoke the coverage of the Acts. Rather, we concluded that we must also determine whether those instruments possess "some of the significant characteristics typically associated with" stock, recognizing that when an instrument is both called "stock" and bears stock's usual characteristics, "a purchaser justifiably [may] assume that the federal securities laws apply,". . . . We identified those characteristics usually associated with common stock as (i) the right to receive dividends contingent upon an apportionment of profits; (ii) negotiability; (iii) the ability to be pledged or hypothecated; (iv) the conferring of voting rights in proportion to the number of shares owned; and (v) the capacity to appreciate in value.

Under the facts of *Forman,* we concluded that the instruments at issue there were not "securities" within the meaning of the Acts. That case involved the sale of shares of stock entitling the purchaser to lease an apartment in a housing cooperative. The stock bore none of the characteristics listed above that are usually associated with traditional stock. Moreover, we concluded that under the circumstances, there was no likelihood that the purchasers had been misled by use of the word "stock" into thinking that the federal securities laws governed their purchases. The purchasers had intended to acquire low-cost subsidized living space for their personal use; no one was likely to have believed that he was purchasing investment securities. Ibid.

In contrast, it is undisputed that the stock involved here possesses all of the characteristics we identified in *Forman* as traditionally associated with common stock. Indeed, the District Court so found. Moreover, unlike in *Forman*, the context of the transaction involved here—the sale of stock in a corporation—is typical of the kind of context to which the Acts normally apply. It is thus much more likely here than in *Forman* that an investor would believe he was covered by the federal securities laws. Under the circumstances of this case, the plain meaning of the statutory definition mandates that the stock be treated as "securities" subject to the coverage of the Acts.

Reading the securities laws to apply to the sale of stock at issue here comports with Congress' remedial purpose in enacting the legislation to protect investors by "compelling full and fair disclosure relative to the issuance of 'the many types of instruments that in our commercial world fall within the ordinary concept of a security.'" SEC v. W.J. Howey Co., 328 U.S., at 299 (quoting H.R.Rep. No. 85, 73d Cong., 1st Sess., 11 (1933)). Although we recognize that Congress did not intend to provide a comprehensive federal remedy for all fraud, Marine Bank v. Weaver, 455 U.S. 551, 556 (1982), we think it would improperly narrow Congress' broad definition of "security" to hold that the traditional stock at issue here falls outside the Acts' coverage.

III

Under other circumstances, we might consider the statutory analysis outlined above to be a sufficient answer compelling judgment for petitioner. Respondents urge, however, that language in our previous opinions, including *Forman*, requires that we look beyond the label "stock" and the characteristics of the instruments involved to determine whether application of the Acts is mandated by the economic substance of the transaction. Moreover, the Court of Appeals rejected the view that the plain meaning of the definition would be sufficient to hold this stock covered, because it saw "no principled way," 731 F.2d, at 1353, to justify treating notes, bonds, and other of the definitional categories differently. We address these concerns in turn.

A

It is fair to say that our cases have not been entirely clear on the proper method of analysis for determining when an instrument is a "security." This Court has decided a number of cases in which it looked to the economic substance of the transaction, rather than just to its form, to determine whether the Acts applied. In SEC v. C.M. Joiner Leasing Corp., for example, the Court considered whether the 1933 Act applied to the sale of leasehold interests in land near a proposed oil well drilling. In holding that the leasehold interests were "securities," the Court noted that "the reach of the Act does not stop with the obvious and commonplace." 320 U.S., at 351. Rather, it ruled that unusual devices such as the leaseholds would also be covered "if it be proved as matter of fact that they were widely offered or dealt in under terms or courses of dealing which established their character in commerce as 'investment contracts,' or as any interest or instrument commonly known as a 'security.' " Ibid.

* * *

Respondents contend that *Forman* and the cases on which it was based require us to reject the view that the shares of stock at issue here may be considered "securities" because of their name and characteristics. Instead, they argue that our cases require us in every instance to look to the economic substance of the transaction to determine whether the *Howey* test has been met. According to respondents, it is clear that petitioner sought not to earn profits from the efforts of others, but to buy a company that it could manage and control. Petitioner was not a passive investor of the kind Congress intended the Acts to protect, but an active entrepreneur, who sought to "use or consume" the business purchased just as the purchasers in *Forman* sought to use the apartments they acquired after purchasing shares of stock. Thus, respondents urge that the Acts do not apply.

We disagree with respondents' interpretation of our cases. First, it is important to understand the contexts within which these cases were decided. All of the cases on which respondents rely involved unusual instruments not easily characterized as "securities." Thus, if the Acts were to apply in those cases at all, it would have to have been because the economic reality underlying the transactions indicated that the instruments were actually of a type that falls within the usual concept of a security. In the case at bar, in contrast, the instrument involved is traditional stock, plainly within the statutory definition. There is no need here, as there was in the prior cases, to look beyond the characteristics of the instrument to determine whether the Acts apply.

* * *

Second, we would note that the *Howey* economic reality test was designed to determine whether a particular instrument is an "investment contract," not whether it fits within *any* of the examples listed in the statutory definition of "security." Our cases are consistent with this view. Teamsters v. Daniel, 439 U.S., at 558 (appropriate to turn to the *Howey* test to "determine whether a particular financial relationship constitutes an investment contract"); United Housing Foundation, Inc. v. Forman, 421 U.S. 837 (1975); see supra, at 689. Moreover, applying the *Howey* test to traditional stock and all other types of instruments listed in the statutory definition would make the Acts' enumeration of many types of instruments superfluous. Golden v. Garafalo, 678 F.2d 1139, 1144 (C.A.2 1982). See Tcherepnin v. Knight, 389 U.S. 332, 343 (1967).

Finally, we cannot agree with respondents that the Acts were intended to cover only "passive investors" and not privately negotiated transactions involving the transfer of control to "entrepreneurs." The 1934 Act contains several provisions specifically governing tender offers, disclosure of transactions by corporate officers and principal stockholders, and the recovery of short-swing profits gained by such persons. See, e.g., 1934 Act, §§ 14, 16. Eliminating from the definition of "security" instruments involved in transactions where control passed to the purchaser would contravene the purposes of these provisions. Accord, Daily v. Morgan, 701 F.2d 496, 503 (C.A.5 1983). Furthermore, although § 4(2) of the 1933 Act exempts transactions not involving any public offering from the Act's registration provisions, there is no comparable exemption from the antifraud provisions. Thus, the structure and language of the Acts refute respondents' position.

* * *

IV

We also perceive strong policy reasons for not employing the sale of business doctrine under the circumstances of this case. By respondents' own admission, application of the doctrine depends in each case on whether control has passed to the purchaser. It may be argued that on the facts of this case, the doctrine is easily applied, since the transfer of 100% of a corporation's stock normally transfers control. We think even that assertion is open to some question, however, as Dennis and Bolten had no intention of running the sawmill themselves. Ivan Landreth apparently stayed on to manage the daily affairs of the business. Some commentators who support the sale of business doctrine believe that a purchaser who has the ability to exert control but chooses not to do so may deserve the Acts' protection if he is simply a passive investor not engaged in the daily management of the business. Easley, Recent Developments in the Sale-of-Business Doctrine: Toward a Transactional Context-Based Analysis for Federal Securities Jurisdiction, 39 Bus.Law. 929, 971–972 (1984); Seldin, When Stock is Not a Security: The "Sale of Business" Doctrine Under the Federal Securities Laws, 37 Bus.Law. 637, 679 (1982). In this case, the District Court was required to undertake extensive fact-finding, and even requested supplemental facts and memoranda on the issue of control, before it was able to decide the case.
* * *

More importantly, however, if applied to this case, the sale of business doctrine would also have to be applied to cases in which less than 100% of a company's stock was sold.[38] This inevitably would lead to difficult questions of line-drawing. The Acts' coverage would in every case depend not only on the percentage of stock transferred, but also on such factors as the number of purchasers and what provisions for voting and veto rights were agreed upon by the parties. As we explain more fully in Gould v. Ruefenacht, post, at 701, decided today as a companion to this case, coverage by the Acts would in most cases be unknown and unknowable to the parties at the time the stock was sold. These

---

[38] In Gould v. Ruefenacht, 471 U.S. 701 (1985), which was decided the same day as *Landreth Timber*, the Court held that the sale of 50 percent of the stock of a business corporation entailed the sale of a security—Eds. Note.

uncertainties attending the applicability of the Acts would hardly be in the best interests of either party to a transaction. Cf. Marine Bank v. Weaver, 455 U.S., at 559 n. 9 (rejecting the argument that the certificate of deposit at issue there was transformed, chameleon-like, into a "security" once it was pledged). Respondents argue that adopting petitioner's approach will increase the workload of the federal courts by converting state and common-law fraud claims into federal claims. We find more daunting, however, the prospect that parties to a transaction may never know whether they are covered by the Acts until they engage in extended discovery and litigation over a concept as often elusive as the passage of control. Accord, Golden v. Garafalo, 678 F.2d 1145–1146.

V

In sum, we conclude that the stock at issue here is a "security" within the definition of the Acts, and that the sale of business doctrine does not apply. The judgment of the United States Court of Appeals for the Ninth Circuit is therefore

Reversed.[39]

■ JUSTICE STEVENS, dissenting. [The opinion is omitted.]

The Contrast with Other Entities. Under *Landreth*, stock is always a security (at least, unless it is purchased for consumption under *Forman*). But, if one buys 100% of the interest in an LLC (as was the case in *Great Lakes Chemical Corporation v. Monsanto Company*), then under *Howey*, there is no "investment contract" because the purchaser is not substantially dependent on the efforts of another (as it is buying a business that it will run). Similarly, a limited partnership interest is presumptively a security unless the investor purchases a majority interest that is accompanied by control rights (which acquisition will likely trigger the *Steinhardt* doctrine). Is this difference in treatment sensible? If not, in which direction should it change?

D. "NOTE"

Reves v. Ernst & Young
Supreme Court of the United States, 1990.
494 U.S. 56, 110 S.Ct. 945, 108 L.Ed.2d 47.

■ JUSTICE MARSHALL delivered the opinion of the Court.

This case presents the question whether certain demand notes issued by the Farmer's Cooperative of Arkansas and Oklahoma Co-Op

---

[39] For further analysis, see Hazen, Taking Stock of Stock and the Sale of Closely Held Corporations: When is Stock Not a Security?, 61 N.C.L.Rev. 393 (1983); Rosin, Functional Exclusions from the Definition of a Security (pts. 1–2), 28 So.Tex.L.Rev. 333, 375 (1986–1987).

are "securities" within the meaning of § 3(a)(10) of the Securities Exchange Act of 1934. We conclude that they are.

I

The Co-Op is an agricultural cooperative that, at the time relevant here, had approximately 23,000 members. In order to raise money to support its general business operations, the Co-Op sold promissory notes payable on demand by the holder. Although the notes were uncollateralized and uninsured, they paid a variable rate of interest that was adjusted monthly to keep it higher than the rate paid by local financial institutions. The Co-Op offered the notes to both members and nonmembers, marketing the scheme as an "Investment Program." Advertisements for the notes, which appeared in each Co-Op newsletter, read in part: "YOUR CO-OP has more than $11,000,000 in assets to stand behind your investments. The Investment is not Federal *[sic]* insured but it is . . . Safe . . . Secure . . . and available when you need it." App. 5 (ellipses in original). Despite these assurances, the Co-Op filed for bankruptcy in 1984. At the time of the filing, over 1,600 people held notes worth a total of $10 million.

After the Co-Op filed for bankruptcy, petitioners, a class of holders of the notes, filed suit against Arthur Young & Co., the firm that had audited the Co-Op's financial statements (and the predecessor to respondent Ernst & Young). Petitioners alleged, *inter alia,* that Arthur Young had intentionally failed to follow generally accepted accounting principles in its audit, specifically with respect to the valuation of one of the Co-Op's major assets, a gasohol plant. Petitioners claimed that Arthur Young violated these principles in an effort to inflate the assets and net worth of the Co-Op. Petitioners maintained that, had Arthur Young properly treated the plant in its audits, they would not have purchased demand notes because the Co-Op's insolvency would have been apparent. On the basis of these allegations, petitioners claimed that Arthur Young had violated the antifraud provisions of the 1934 Act as well as Arkansas' securities laws.

Petitioners prevailed at trial on both their federal and state claims, receiving a $6.1 million judgment. Arthur Young appealed, claiming that the demand notes were not "securities" under either the 1934 Act or Arkansas law, and that the statutes' antifraud provisions therefore did not apply. A panel of the Eighth Circuit, agreeing with Arthur Young on both the state and federal issues, reversed. Arthur Young & Co. v. Reves, 856 F.2d 52 (1988). We granted certiorari to address the federal issue . . . and now reverse the judgment of the Court of Appeals.

II

A

This case requires us to decide whether the note issued by the Co-Op is a "security" within the meaning of the 1934 Act. Section 3(a)(10) of that Act is our starting point.

* * *

The fundamental purpose undergirding the Securities Acts is "to eliminate serious abuses in a largely unregulated securities market." United Housing Foundation, Inc. v. Forman, 421 U.S. 837, 849 (1975). In defining the scope of the market that it wished to regulate, Congress painted with a broad brush. It recognized the virtually limitless scope of human ingenuity, especially in the creation of "countless and variable schemes devised by those who seek the use of the money of others on the promise of profits," SEC v. W.J. Howey Co., 328 U.S. 293, 299 (1946), and determined that the best way to achieve its goal of protecting investors was "to define 'the term "security" in sufficiently broad and general terms so as to include within that definition the many types of instruments that in our commercial world fall within the ordinary concept of a security.'" *Forman,* supra, at 847–848 (quoting H.R.Rep. No. 85, 73d Cong., 1st Sess., 11 (1933)). Congress therefore did not attempt precisely to cabin the scope of the Securities Acts. Rather, it enacted a definition of "security" sufficiently broad to encompass virtually any instrument that might be sold as an investment.

Congress did not, however, "intend to provide a broad federal remedy for all fraud." Marine Bank v. Weaver, 455 U.S. 551, 556 (1982). Accordingly, "[t]he task has fallen to the Securities and Exchange Commission (SEC), the body charged with administering the Securities Acts, and ultimately to the federal courts to decide which of the myriad financial transactions in our society come within the coverage of these statutes." *Forman,* supra, at 848. In discharging our duty, we are not bound by legal formalisms, but instead take account of the economics of the transaction under investigation. See, e.g., Tcherepnin v. Knight, 389 U.S. 332, 336 (1967) (in interpreting the term "security," "form should be disregarded for substance and the emphasis should be on economic reality"). Congress' purpose in enacting the securities laws was to regulate *investments,* in whatever form they are made and by whatever name they are called.

A commitment to an examination of the economic realities of a transaction does not necessarily entail a case-by-case analysis of every instrument, however. Some instruments are obviously within the class Congress intended to regulate because they are by their nature investments. In Landreth Timber Co. v. Landreth, 471 U.S. 681 (1985), we held that an instrument bearing the name "stock" that, among other things, is negotiable, offers the possibility of capital appreciation, and carries the right to dividends contingent on the profits of a business enterprise is plainly within the class of instruments Congress intended the securities laws to cover. *Landreth Timber* does not signify a lack of concern with economic reality; rather, it signals a recognition that stock is, as a practical matter, always an investment if it has the economic characteristics traditionally associated with stock. Even if sparse exceptions to this generalization can be found, the public perception of common stock as the paradigm of a security suggests that stock, in whatever context it is sold, should be treated as within the ambit of the Acts. Id., at 687, 693.

We made clear in *Landreth Timber* that stock was a special case, explicitly limiting our holding to that sort of instrument. Id., at 694. Although we refused finally to rule out a similar *per se* rule for notes, we intimated that such a rule would be unjustified. Unlike "stock," we said, " 'note' may now be viewed as a relatively broad term that encompasses instruments with widely varying characteristics, depending on whether issued in a consumer context, as commercial paper, or in some other investment context." Ibid. (citing Securities Industry Assn. v. Board of Governors, FRS, 468 U.S. 137, 149–153 (1984)). While common stock is the quintessence of a security, *Landreth Timber,* supra, at 693, and investors therefore justifiably assume that a sale of stock is covered by the Securities Acts, the same simply cannot be said of notes, which are used in a variety of settings, not all of which involve investments. Thus, the phrase "any note" should not be interpreted to mean literally "any note," but must be understood against the backdrop of what Congress was attempting to accomplish in enacting the Securities Acts.

Because the *Landreth Timber* formula cannot sensibly be applied to notes, some other principle must be developed to define the term "note." A majority of the Courts of Appeals that have considered the issue have adopted, in varying forms, "investment versus commercial" approaches that distinguish, on the basis of all of the circumstances surrounding the transactions, notes issued in an investment context (which are "securities") from notes issued in a commercial or consumer context (which are not). See, e.g., McClure v. First Nat. Bank of Lubbock, Texas, 497 F.2d 490, 492–494 (C.A.5 1974); Holloway v. Peat, Marwick, Mitchell & Co., 879 F.2d 772, 778–779 (C.A.10 1989), cert. pending sub nom. Peat, Marwick Main & Co., No. 89–532.

The Second Circuit's "family resemblance" approach begins with a presumption that *any* note with a term of more than nine months is a "security." See, e.g., Exchange Nat'l Bank of Chicago v. Touche Ross & Co., 544 F.2d 1126, 1137 (C.A.2 1976). Recognizing that not all notes are securities, however, the Second Circuit has also devised a list of notes that it has decided are obviously not securities. Accordingly, the "family resemblance" test permits an issuer to rebut the presumption that a note is a security if it can show that the note in question "bear[s] a strong family resemblance" to an item on the judicially crafted list of exceptions, id., at 1137–1138, or convinces the court to add a new instrument to the list. See, e.g., Chemical Bank v. Arthur Andersen & Co., 726 F.2d 930, 939 (C.A.2 1984).

In contrast, the Eighth and District of Columbia Circuits apply the test we created in SEC v. W.J. Howey Co., 328 U.S. 293 (1946), to determine whether an instrument is an "investment contract" to the determination whether an instrument is a "note." Under this test, a note is a security only if it evidences "(1) an investment; (2) in a common enterprise; (3) with a reasonable expectation of profits; (4) to be derived from the entrepreneurial or managerial efforts of others." Arthur Young & Co. v. Reves, 856 F.2d, at 54. Accord Baurer v. Planning Group, Inc., 215 U.S.App.D.C. 384, 391–393, 669 F.2d 770, 777–779 (1981). See also Underhill v. Royal, 769 F.2d 1426, 1431 (C.A.9 1985) (setting forth what it terms a "risk capital" approach that is virtually identical to the *Howey* test).

We reject the approaches of those courts that have applied the *Howey* test to notes; *Howey* provides a mechanism for determining whether an instrument is an "investment contract." The demand notes here may well not be "investment contracts," but that does not mean they are not "notes." To hold that a "note" is not a "security" unless it meets a test designed for an entirely different variety of instrument "would make the Acts' enumeration of many types of instruments superfluous," Landreth Timber, 471 U.S., at 692, and would be inconsistent with Congress' intent to regulate the entire body of instruments sold as investments, see supra, at 3–5.

The other two contenders—the "family resemblance" and "investment versus commercial" tests—are really two ways of formulating the same general approach. Because we think the "family resemblance" test provides a more promising framework for analysis, however, we adopt it. The test begins with the language of the statute; because the Securities Acts define "security" to include "any note," we begin with a presumption that every note is a security.[3] We nonetheless recognize that this presumption cannot be irrebuttable. As we have said, supra, at 949, Congress was concerned with regulating the investment market, not with creating a general federal cause of action for fraud. In an attempt to give more content to that dividing line, the Second Circuit has identified a list of instruments commonly denominated "notes" that nonetheless fall without the "security" category. See Exchange Nat. Bank, supra, at 1138 (types of notes that are not "securities" include "the note delivered in consumer financing, the note secured by a mortgage on a home, the short-term note secured by a lien on a small business or some of its assets, the note evidencing a 'character' loan to a bank customer, short-term notes secured by an assignment of accounts receivable, or a note which simply formalizes an open-account debt incurred in the ordinary course of business (particularly if, as in the case of the customer of a broker, it is collateralized)"); Chemical Bank, supra, at 939 (adding

---

[3] The Second Circuit's version of the family resemblance test provided that only notes *with a term of more than nine months* are presumed to be "securities." See supra, at 6. No presumption of any kind attached to notes of less than nine months duration. The Second Circuit's refusal to extend the presumption to *all* notes was apparently founded on its interpretation of the statutory exception for notes with a maturity of nine months or less. Because we do not reach the question of how to interpret that exception, see infra, at 13, we likewise express no view on how that exception might affect the presumption that a note is a "security."

to list "notes evidencing loans by commercial banks for current operations").

We agree that the items identified by the Second Circuit are not properly viewed as "securities." More guidance, though, is needed. It is impossible to make any meaningful inquiry into whether an instrument bears a "resemblance" to one of the instruments identified by the Second Circuit without specifying what it is about *those* instruments that makes *them* non-"securities." Moreover, as the Second Circuit itself has noted, its list is "not graven in stone," ibid., and is therefore capable of expansion. Thus, some standards must be developed for determining when an item should be added to the list.

An examination of the list itself makes clear what those standards should be. In creating its list, the Second Circuit was applying the same factors that this Court has held apply in deciding whether a transaction involves a "security." First, we examine the transaction to assess the motivations that would prompt a reasonable seller and buyer to enter into it. If the seller's purpose is to raise money for the general use of a business enterprise or to finance substantial investments and the buyer is interested primarily in the profit the note is expected to generate, the instrument is likely to be a "security." If the note is exchanged to facilitate the purchase and sale of a minor asset or consumer good, to correct for the seller's cash-flow difficulties, or to advance some other commercial or consumer purpose, on the other hand, the note is less sensibly described as a "security." See, e.g., Forman, 421 U.S., at 851 (share of "stock" carrying a right to subsidized housing not a security because "the inducement to purchase was solely to acquire subsidized low-cost living space; it was not to invest for profit"). Second, we examine the "plan of distribution" of the instrument, SEC v. C.M. Joiner Leasing Corp., 320 U.S. 344, 353 (1943), to determine whether it is an instrument in which there is "common trading for speculation or investment," id., at 351. Third, we examine the reasonable expectations of the investing public: The Court will consider instruments to be "securities" on the basis of such public expectations, even where an economic analysis of the circumstances of the particular transaction might suggest that the instruments are not "securities" as used in that transaction. Compare Landreth Timber, 471 U.S., at 687, 693 (relying on public expectations in holding that common stock is always a security) with id., at 697–700 (Stevens, J., dissenting) (arguing that sale of business to single informed purchaser through stock is not within the purview of the Acts under the economic reality test). See also *Forman,* supra, at 851. Finally, we examine whether some factor such as the existence of another regulatory scheme significantly reduces the risk of the instrument, thereby rendering application of the Securities Acts unnecessary. See, e.g., Marine Bank, 455 U.S., at 557–559, and n. 7.

We conclude, then, that in determining whether an instrument denominated a "note" is a "security," courts are to apply the version of the "family resemblance" test that we have articulated here: a note is presumed to be a "security," and that presumption may be rebutted only by a showing that the note bears a strong resemblance (in terms of the four factors we have identified) to one of the enumerated categories of instrument. If an instrument is not sufficiently similar to an item on the list, the decision whether another category should be added is to be made by examining the same factors.

B

Applying the family resemblance approach to this case, we have little difficulty in concluding that the notes at issue here are "securities." Ernst & Young admits that "a demand note does not closely resemble any of the Second Circuit's family resemblance examples." Brief for Respondent 43. Nor does an examination of the four factors we have identified as being relevant to our inquiry suggest that the demand notes here are not "securities" despite their lack of similarity to any of the enumerated categories. The Co-Op sold the notes in an effort to raise capital for its general business operations, and purchasers bought them in order to earn a profit in the form of interest.[4] Indeed, one of the primary inducements offered purchasers was an interest rate constantly revised to keep it slightly above the rate paid by local banks and savings and loans. From both sides, then, the transaction is most naturally conceived as an investment in a business enterprise rather than as a purely commercial or consumer transaction.

As to the plan of distribution, the Co-Op offered the notes over an extended period to its 23,000 members, as well as to nonmembers, and more than 1,600 people held notes when the Co-Op filed for bankruptcy. To be sure, the notes were not traded on an exchange. They were, however, offered and sold to a broad segment of the public, and that is all we have held to be necessary to establish the requisite "common trading" in an instrument. See, e.g., *Landreth Timber,* supra (stock of closely held corporation not traded on any exchange held to be a "security"); Tcherepnin, 389 U.S., at 337 (nonnegotiable but transferable "withdrawable capital shares" in savings and loan association held to be a "security"); Howey, 328 U.S., at 295 (units of citrus grove and maintenance contract "securities" although not traded on exchange).

The third factor—the public's reasonable perceptions—also supports a finding that the notes in this case are "securities". We have consistently identified the fundamental essence of a "security" to be its character as

---

[4] We emphasize that by "profit" in the context of notes, we mean "a valuable return on an investment," which undoubtedly includes interest. We have, of course, defined "profit" more restrictively in applying the *Howey* test to what are claimed to be "investment contracts." See, e.g., Forman, 421 U.S., at 852 ("[P]rofit" under the *Howey* test means either "capital appreciation" or "a participation in earnings"). To apply this restrictive definition to the determination whether an instrument is a "note" would be to suggest that notes paying a rate of interest not keyed to the earning of the enterprise are not "notes" within the meaning of the Securities Acts. Because the *Howey* test is irrelevant to the issue before us today, see supra, at 7, we decline to extend its definition of "profit" beyond the realm in which that definition applies.

an "investment." See supra, at 949, 951. The advertisements for the notes here characterized them as "investments," see supra, at 948, and there were no countervailing factors that would have led a reasonable person to question this characterization. In these circumstances, it would be reasonable for a prospective purchaser to take the Co-Op at its word.

Finally, we find no risk-reducing factor to suggest that these instruments are not in fact securities. The notes are uncollateralized and uninsured. Moreover, unlike the certificates of deposit in *Marine Bank*, supra, at 557–558, which were insured by the Federal Deposit Insurance Corporation and subject to substantial regulation under the federal banking laws, and unlike the pension plan in Teamsters v. Daniel, 439 U.S. 551, 569–570 (1979), which was comprehensively regulated under the Employee Retirement Income Security Act of 1974, 88 Stat. 829, 29 U.S.C. § 1001 *et seq.*, the notes here would escape federal regulation entirely if the Acts were held not to apply.

The court below found that "[t]he demand nature of the notes is very uncharacteristic of a security," 856 F.2d, at 54, on the theory that the virtually instant liquidity associated with demand notes is inconsistent with the risk ordinarily associated with "securities." This argument is unpersuasive. Common stock traded on a national exchange is the paradigm of a security, and it is as readily convertible into cash as is a demand note. The same is true of publicly traded corporate bonds, debentures, and any number of other instruments that are plainly within the purview of the Acts. The demand feature of a note does permit a holder to eliminate risk quickly by making a demand, but just as with publicly traded stock, the liquidity of the instrument does not eliminate risk all together. Indeed, publicly traded stock is even more readily liquid than are demand notes, in that a demand only eliminates risk when and if payment is made, whereas the sale of a share of stock through a national exchange and the receipt of the proceeds usually occur simultaneously.

We therefore hold that the notes at issue here are within the term "note" in § 3(a)(10).

III

Relying on the exception in the statute for "any note . . . which has a maturity at the time of issuance of not exceeding nine months," [Section 3(a)(10)], respondent contends that the notes here are not "securities," even if they would otherwise qualify. Respondent cites Arkansas cases standing for the proposition that, in the context of the state statute of limitations, "[a] note payable on demand is due immediately." See, e.g., McMahon v. O'Keefe, 213 Ark. 105, 106, 209 S.W.2d 449, 450 (1948) (statute of limitations is triggered by the date of issuance rather than by date of first demand). Respondent concludes from this rule that the "maturity" of a demand note within the meaning of § 3(a)(10) is immediate, which is, of course, less than nine months. Respondent therefore contends that the notes fall within the plain words of the exclusion and are thus not "securities."

Petitioners counter that the "plain words" of the exclusion should not govern. Petitioners cite the legislative history of a similar provision of the 1933 Act, [§ 3(a)(3)], for the proposition that the purpose of the exclusion is to except from the coverage of the Acts only commercial paper—short-term, high quality instruments issued to fund current operations and sold only to highly sophisticated investors. See S.Rep. No. 47, 73d Cong., 1st Sess., 948, 950 (1933); H.R.Rep. No. 85, 73d Cong., 1st Sess., 15 (1933). Petitioner also emphasizes that this Court has repeatedly held (see supra, at 3–6) that the plain words of the definition of a "security" are not dispositive, and that we consider the economic reality of the transaction to determine whether Congress intended the Securities Acts to apply. Petitioner therefore argues, with some force, that reading the exception for short-term notes to exclude from the Acts' coverage investment notes of less than nine months duration would be inconsistent with Congress' evident desire to permit the SEC and the courts flexibility to ensure that the Acts are not manipulated to investors' detriment. If petitioners are correct that the exclusion is intended to cover only commercial paper, these notes, which were sold in a large scale offering to unsophisticated members of the public, plainly should not fall within the exclusion.

We need not decide, however, whether petitioners' interpretation of the exception is correct, for we conclude that even if we give literal effect to the exception, the notes do not fall within its terms.

Respondent's contention that the demand notes fall within the "plain words" of the statute rests entirely upon the premise that Arkansas' statute of limitations for suits to collect demand notes is determinative of the "maturity" of the notes, as that term is used in the *federal* Securities Acts. The "maturity" of the notes, however, is a question of federal law. To regard States' statutes of limitations law as controlling the scope of the Securities Acts would be to hold that a particular instrument is a "security" under the 1934 Act in some States, but that the same instrument is not a "security" in others. Compare *McMahon,* supra, at 106 (statute runs from date of note) with 42 Pa.Cons.Stat. § 5525(7) (1988) (statute runs "from the later of either demand or any payment of principal of or interest on the instrument"). We are unpersuaded that Congress intended the Securities Acts to apply differently to the same transactions depending on the accident of which State's law happens to apply.

The Chief Justice's argument in partial dissent is but a more artful statement of respondent's contention, and it suffers from the same defect. The Chief Justice begins by defining "maturity" to mean the time when a note becomes due. Post, at 957 (quoting Black's Law Dictionary 1170 (3d ed. 1933)). Because a demand note is "immediately 'due' such that an action could be brought at any time without any other demand than the suit," post, at 957, the Chief Justice concludes that a demand note is due immediately for purposes of the federal securities laws. Even if the Chief Justice is correct that the "maturity" of a note corresponds to the time at which it "becomes due," the authority he cites for the proposition that, as a matter of federal law, a demand note "becomes due" immediately (as opposed to when demand is made or expected to be made) is no more dispositive than is Arkansas case law. The Chief Justice's primary source of authority is a treatise regarding the *state* law of negotiable instruments, particularly the Uniform Negotiable Instruments Law. See M. Bigelow, The Law of Bills, Notes, and Checks v–vii (W. Lile rev. 1928). The quotation upon which the Chief Justice relies is concerned with articulating the general *state* law rule regarding when suit may be filed. The only other authority the Chief Justice cites makes plain that state-law rules governing when a demand note becomes due are significant only in that they control the date on which statutes of limitation begin to run and whether demand must precede suit. See 8 C.J. Bills and Notes § 602, p. 406 (1916). Indeed, the treatise suggests that States were no more unanimous on those questions in 1933 than they are now. Ibid. In short, the dissent adds nothing to respondent's argument other than additional authority for what "maturity" means in certain state-law contexts. The dissent provides no argument for its implicit, but essential, premise that state rules concerning the proper method of collecting a debt control the resolution of the federal question before us.

Neither the law of Arkansas nor that of any other State provides an answer to the federal question, and as a matter of federal law, the words of the statute are far from "plain" with regard to whether demand notes fall within the exclusion. If it is plausible to regard a demand note as having an immediate maturity because demand *could* be made immediately, it is also plausible to regard the maturity of a demand note as being in excess of nine months because demand *could* be made many years or decades into the future. Given this ambiguity, the exclusion must be interpreted in accordance with its purpose. As we have said, we will assume for argument's sake that petitioners are incorrect in their view that the exclusion is intended to exempt only commercial paper. Respondent presents no competing view to explain why Congress would have enacted respondent's version of the exclusion, however, and the only theory that we can imagine that would support respondent's interpretation is that Congress intended to create a bright-line rule exempting from the 1934 Act's coverage *all* notes of less than nine months' duration, because short-term notes are, as a general rule, sufficiently safe that the Securities Acts need not apply. As we have said, however, demand notes do not necessarily have short terms. In light of Congress' broader purpose in the Acts of ensuring that investments of all descriptions be regulated to prevent fraud and abuse, we interpret the exception not to cover the demand notes at issue here. Although the result might be different if the design of the transaction suggested that both parties contemplated that demand would be made within the statutory period, that is not the case before us.

IV

For the foregoing reasons, we conclude that the demand notes at issue here fall under the "note" category of instruments that are "securities" under the 1933 and 1934 Acts. We also conclude that, even under respondent's preferred approach to § 3(a)(10)'s exclusion for short-term notes, these demand notes do not fall within the exclusion. Accordingly, we reverse the judgment of the Court of Appeals and remand the case for further proceedings consistent with this opinion.

So ordered.

■ CHIEF JUSTICE REHNQUIST, with whom JUSTICE WHITE, JUSTICE O'CONNOR, and JUSTICE SCALIA join, concurring in part and dissenting in part.

I join Part II of the Court's opinion, but dissent from part III and the statements of the Court's judgment in parts I and IV. In Part III, the court holds that these notes were not covered by the statutory exemption for "any note ... which has a maturity at the time of issuance of not exceeding nine months.". . . .

* * *

In construing any terms whose meanings are less than plain, we depend on the common understanding of those terms at the time of the statute's creation. * * *

* * *

To be sure, demand instruments were considered to have "the peculiar quality of having two maturity dates—one for the purpose of holding to his obligation the party primarily liable (e.g. maker), and the other for enforcing the contracts of parties secondarily liable (e.g. drawer and indorsers)." M. Bigelow, supra, § 350, 266. But only the rule of immediate maturity respecting makers of demand notes has any bearing on our examination of the exemption; the language in the Act makes clear that it is the "maturity at time of issuance" with which we are concerned. [§ 3(a)(10)] Accordingly, in the absence of some compelling indication to the contrary, the maturity date exemption must encompass demand notes because they possess "maturity at the time of issuance of not exceeding nine months."

Petitioners and the lower court decisions cited by Justice Stevens rely, virtually exclusively, on the legislative history of § 3(a)(3) of the *1933* Act for the proposition that the terms "any note" in the exemption in § 3(a)(10) of the 1934 Act encompass only notes having the character of short-term "commercial paper" exchanged among sophisticated traders. I am not altogether convinced that the legislative history of § 3(a)(3) supports that interpretation even with respect to the terms "any note" in the exemption in § 3(a)(3), and to bodily transpose that legislative history to another statute has little to commend it as a method of statutory construction.

The legislative history of the 1934 Act—under which this case arises—contains nothing which would support a restrictive reading of the exemption in question. Nor does the legislative history of § 3(a)(3) of the 1933 Act support the asserted limited construction of the exemption in § 3(a)(10) of the 1934 Act. Though the two most pertinent sources of congressional commentary on § 3(a)(3)—H.R.Rep. No. 85, 73d Cong., 1st Sess. 15 (1933) and S.Rep. No. 47, 73d Cong., 1st Sess. 3–4 (1933)—do suggest an intent to limit § 3(a)(3)'s exemption to short-term commercial paper, the references in those reports to commercial paper simply did not survive in the language of the enactment. Indeed, the Senate report stated "[n]otes, drafts, bills of exchange, and bankers' acceptances *which are commercial paper* and arise out of current *commercial, agricultural, or industrial* transactions, *and which are not intended to be marketed to the public,* are exempted. . . ." S.Rep. No. 47, supra (emphasis added). Yet the provision enacted in § 3(a)(3) of the 1933 Act exempts "*[a]ny* note, draft, bill of exchange, or banker's acceptance which arises out of a current transaction or the proceeds of which have been or are to be used for current transaction, and which has a maturity at the time of issuance of not exceeding nine months, . . ." [Section 3(a)(3)] (emphasis added).

Such broadening of the language in the enacted version of § 3(a)(3), relative to the prototype from which it sprang, cannot easily be dismissed in interpreting § 3(a)(3). *A fortiori,* the legislative history's restrictive meaning cannot be imputed to the facially broader language in a different provision of another act. Although I do not doubt that both the 1933 and 1934 Act exemptions encompass short-term commercial paper, the expansive language in the statutory provisions is strong evidence that, in the end, Congress meant for commercial paper merely to be a subset of a larger class of exempted short-term instruments.

* * *

E. Special Debt Obligations

In *Reves* and earlier in *Landreth Timber*, the Supreme Court recognized that conventional "stock" is different from other categories of instruments. Traditional stock is the "quintessence" of a security. In contrast, an instrument bearing the label "note" encompasses instruments with widely varying characteristics depending on whether the instrument was issued in an investment context, and therefore is a security, or was issued in a commercial or consumer context, and thus constitutes a non-security.[40]

---

[40] 494 U.S. at 62. On the legislative history concerning the extent to which "notes" and other debt instruments should be deemed to be "securities," see Rosin, Historical Perspectives on the Definition of a Security, 28 S.Tex.L.Rev. (pt. 2) 575 (1987).

At the same time, the Court rejected the use of the *Howey* test in the case of "notes," indicating that the application of *Howey* should be confined to determining whether an instrument is an "investment contract" and perhaps to other instruments of a more variable character. As the Court put it:[41] "To hold that a 'note' is not a 'security' unless it meets a test designed for an entirely different variety of instrument would make the Act's enumeration of many types of instruments superfluous. . . . (quoting *Landreth Timber*) and would be inconsistent with Congress' intent to regulate the entire body of instruments sold as investments. . . ."

The Court adopted a variation of the "family resemblance" test formulated by Judge Friendly as a framework for analysis, rather than the investment/commercial test previously used by some Circuits. Because the statute defines a security to include "any note," there is a presumption that every note is a security. The Court then adopted the list of securities identified by Judge Friendly as constituting non-securities: (1) a note delivered in consumer financing; (2) a note secured by a home mortgage; (3) a short-term note secured by a lien on a small business or some of its assets; (4) a note evidencing a "character" loan to a bank customer; (5) short-term notes secured by an assignment of accounts receivable; (6) a note formalizing an open-account debt incurred in the ordinary course of business; and (7) notes evidencing loans by commercial banks for current operations.

The Court then suggested some standards to apply when separating "note" instruments which were securities from those which were non-securities: (1) what motivations normally would prompt a reasonable buyer and seller to enter into such a transaction; (2) what was the issuer's "plan of distribution" in offering the instrument; (3) what were the reasonable expectations of the investing public; and (4) were there risk-reducing features of the instrument, including another regulatory regime, thereby rendering application of the federal securities laws unnecessary.

Commercial Paper. Although these guidelines may be helpful in borderline situations, they do not account for the vast changes in commercial banking practices since 1933. For example, when Congress was considering § 3(a)(3) of the 1933 Act, which exempts short-term notes issued to evidence a loan for current operations, the Senate Report described the difference between commercial banking and investment banking this way:[42]

---

[41] 494 U.S. at 64.

[42] Sen.Banking & Currency Comm., Stock Exchange Practices, S.Rep. No. 1455, 73d Cong., 2d Sess. 155 (1934), reprinted in 3 Legislative History of the Securities Act of 1933 and Securities Exchange Act of 1934, at Item 21 (Ellenberger & Mahar eds. 1973). The quotation is also reprinted and discussed in Rosin, Historical Perspectives on the Definition of a Security, 28 S.Tex.L.Rev. 57, at 587 (1987). This is the second part of a two-part article. For part I, see Rosin, Functional Exclusions From the Definition of a Security, 28 S.Tex.L.Rev. 331 (1986).

The primary function of commercial banking is to furnish short-term credits for financing production and distribution of consumable goods. By their nature, such loans should be self-liquidating. A sharp line of demarcation should exist between the function of the commercial banker and the investment banker. Long-term capital financing . . . is the proper field of the investment banker, since such loans are not self-liquidating within the prescribed limits of short-term commercial banking operations.

The sharp line of demarcation between commercial banking and investment banking, previously imposed by the Glass-Steagall Act, has long since been abandoned, both by the courts and Congress. But where, then, should the line be drawn between commercial paper, which historically arose from commercial banking relationships, and other instruments that were historically underwritten by investment banks?

In *Reves,* the Court left open the question of whether commercial paper and certificates of deposit with a stated maturity of less than nine months are within the short-term "note" exclusion of the Exchange Act. The Court found it unnecessary to resolve this question because demand notes may not necessarily mature in less than nine months. But this issue still overhangs the law in this area. Although the 1933 Act has an exemption from registration for commercial paper (§ 3(a)(3)), the 1934 Act excludes short-term notes from its definition of a security (see the exclusion at the end of § 3(a)(10) of the 1934 Act). The SEC has long taken the position that this language in § 3(a)(10) applies only to investment-grade commercial paper, but after *Reves,* this became an open question.[43]

Of course, many transactions in which a "note" is issued may be exempt from the 1933 Act's registration requirements, but if a "security" transaction occurs, the antifraud provisions of the 1933 and 1934 Acts will still apply. Commercial banks engage in many creative lending activities that go far beyond traditional commercial banking practices. In these situations, when will the "note" be regarded as being used in a commercial rather than investment context?

Certificates of Deposit. In Marine Bank v. Weaver, 455 U.S. 551 (1982), discussed in *Landreth Timber* and *Reves,* the Court held that a certificate of deposit issued by a bank regulated by the federal government and insured by the Federal Deposit Insurance Corporation was not a "security" under the federal securities laws. Sam and Alice Weaver had purchased a $50,000 certificate of deposit from Marine Bank. The instrument had a six-year maturity and was insured by the Federal Deposit Insurance Corporation. The Weavers subsequently pledged the

---

These articles trace the origins and legislative history of the definition of a "security" under the 1933 and 1934 Acts.

[43] For a decision supporting the SEC's position that the exemption in § 3(a)(10) applies only to high quality commercial paper, see SEC v. J. T. Wallenbrock & Associates, 313 F.3d 532 (9th Cir. 2002).

certificate to the Bank to guarantee a $65,000 loan made by the Bank to Columbus Packing Company as part of a business transaction between the Weavers and Columbus. At the time, Columbus owed the Bank $33,000 for prior loans and was substantially overdrawn on its checking account. The Weavers claimed that Bank officers told them Columbus would use the $65,000 loan as working capital in its business but instead the Bank applied the loan to pay Columbus' overdue obligations to it as well as debts owed to third persons. Columbus became bankrupt four months later.

The Weavers brought a Rule 10b–5 action for fraud, asserting that had they known of Columbus' precarious financial condition and the Bank's plans, they would not have guaranteed the loan. The Court, relying on the *Daniel* case (included earlier in this chapter), held that a government-insured certificate of deposit was unique, differed from other long-term obligations, and was not a "security." The reason: "This certificate of deposit was issued by a federally regulated bank which is subject to the comprehensive set of regulations governing the banking industry.... The ... purchaser of a certificate of deposit is virtually guaranteed payment in full, whereas the holder of an ordinary long-term debt obligation assumes the risk of the borrower's insolvency. The definition of security in the 1934 Act provides that an instrument which seems to fall within the broad sweep of the Act is not considered a security if the context otherwise requires. It is unnecessary to subject issuers of bank certificates of deposit to liability under the antifraud provisions of the federal securities laws since the holders of bank certificates of deposit are abundantly protected under the federal banking laws. We therefore hold that the certificate of deposit purchased by the Weavers is not a security."[44]

The "comparable protection" rationale applied in *Daniel* and *Marine Bank* has come under some criticism.[45] First, the idea that it is impossible to lose your money if you put it in a bank (or in a pension plan regulated under ERISA) has proven, in retrospect, to be demonstrably false. Second, federal deposit insurance only protects against bank insolvency, not bank fraud against customers. Indeed, Chief Justice Burger admitted that not all certificates of deposit are non-securities. In footnote 11, he had this to say: "It does not follow that a certificate of deposit ... invariably falls outside the definition of a security as defined by the federal statutes. Each transaction must be analyzed and evaluated on the basis of the content of the instruments in question, the purposes

---

[44] 455 U.S. at 557–59.

[45] See, e.g., Arnold, "When is a Car a Bicycle?" and Other Riddles: The Definition of a Security Under the Federal Securities Laws, 33 Cleve.St.L.Rev. 448, 474 (1984–85) ("The *Weaver* decision immediately preceded the collapse of Penn Square Bank. In that failure and several failures since then, it appears as if uninsured depositors stand to lose a significant portion of their principal."); Steinberg & Kaulbach, The Supreme Court and the Definition of "Security": The "Context" Clause, "Investment Contract" Analysis, and Their Ramifications, 40 Vand.L.Rev. 489, 492 (1987) ("not only is *Weaver* riddled with ambiguity, the decision is simplistic, and its understanding of securities law is weak").

intended to be served, and the factual setting as a whole."[46] Third, federal bank regulation may be intended more to protect the solvency and stability of banks than the interests of investors.[47]

Risk Reduction: How Far Does This Rationale Extend? Although *Marine Bank* and *Daniel* looked only to federal regulatory systems, several Circuits have applied the comparable regulation rationale to cover issuers regulated by state law and foreign issuers subject only to foreign regulation.[48] *Reves* did not address whether federal courts may consider state (or foreign) regulation of a note when considering whether a note is a security. When applying the fourth factor on risk reduction, however, the Court emphasized that the instruments considered in *Marine Bank* and *Daniel* were subject to comprehensive regulation under federal law and that the notes in *Reves* "would escape federal regulation entirely if the [federal securities laws] were held not to apply."[49]

Curiously enough, the question of whether state banking regulation would preempt the federal securities laws was then pending before the Court in Holloway v. Peat, Marwick, Mitchell & Co.[50] Rather than deciding *Holloway*, the Court remanded the case for further consideration in light of *Reves*. On remand, the *Holloway* court adhered to its decision that passbook savings certificates and thrift certificates issued by a state bank and a trust company were securities within the meaning of the federal securities laws.

The Court of Appeals in *Holloway* noted that the *Reves* Court emphasized the role of federal regulation in *Marine Bank* and *Daniel*. Moreover, the court pointed out that *Reves* rejected the resort to state law to determine when a demand note matures in favor of federal law. Accordingly, the court reaffirmed its holding "that under the supremacy clause, U.S. Const., art. VI, cl. 2, our focus must be on *federal* regulation; state regulatory schemes cannot displace the [Securities] Acts."[51] Yet,

---

[46] See Jones, Footnote 11 of Marine Bank v. Weaver: Will Unconventional Certificates of Deposit Be Held Securities, 24 Hous.L.Rev. 492 (1987); Quinn, After Reves v. Ernst & Young, When Are Certificates of Deposit "Notes" Subject to Rule 10b–5 of the Securities Exchange Act?, 46 Bus.Law. 173, 179 (1990).

[47] See Kornegay, Bank Loans As Securities: A Legal and Financial Economic Analysis of the Treatment of Marketable Bank Assets Under the Securities Acts, 40 UCLA L. Rev. 799 (1993).

[48] See, e.g., Dubach v. Weitzel, 135 F.3d 590 (8th Cir. 1998); Wolf v. Banamex, 739 F.2d 1458 (9th Cir. 1984), cert. denied, 469 U.S. 1108 (1985); West v. Multibanco Comermex, S.A., 807 F.2d 820 (9th Cir. 1987), cert. denied, 482 U.S. 906 (1987); Tafflin v. Levitt, 865 F.2d 595 (4th Cir. 1989), aff'd as to unrelated issue, 493 U.S. 455 (1990). Contra Holloway v. Peat, Marwick, Mitchell & Co., 879 F.2d 772 (10th Cir. 1989), aff'd after remand, 900 F.2d 1485 (10th Cir. 1990), cert. denied sub nom. KPMG Peat, Marwick v. Holloway, 498 U.S. 958 (1990) (savings certificates and passbook accounts issued by financial institutions regulated by the state were securities).

[49] 494 U.S. at 69.

[50] 879 F.2d 772 (10th Cir. 1989), aff'd after remand, 900 F.2d 1485 (10th Cir. 1990), cert. denied sub nom. KPMG Peat, Marwick v. Holloway, 498 U.S. 958 (1990).

[51] 900 F.2d 1485, 1488. One post-*Holloway* decision in the 10th Circuit even found thrift certificates and passbook savings accounts at a state-regulated bank to amount to "securities." See Bradford v. Moench, 809 F.Supp. 1473, 1483 (D. Utah 1992). This result seems unlikely to be followed by other Circuits.

other Circuits have held the opposite, finding that state and even foreign regulation is sufficient.[52]

The significance of this issue comes into clearer focus when one realizes that whether certificates of deposit are "notes," thus making them securities under the Exchange Act, "has particular importance today in light of the increasing number of failed lending institutions and widespread allegations that many of these lenders committed fraud. Although depositors with federally insured lenders will be able to recover their deposits, many certificates of deposit are not adequately insured or are uninsured. Because Exchange Act Rule 10b–5 probably provides the most attractive remedy for depositors who can allege fraud, litigation over its applicability to certificates of deposit is likely to increase."[53] There is also no private right of action under the federal banking laws.[54]

Most courts have focused only on regulation as a risk-reducing factor, but at least one considered the existence of collateral. In Bass v. Janney Montgomery Scott Inc., 210 F.3d 577 (6th Cir. 2000), the Sixth Circuit found that notes should not be deemed securities where they were secured by assets of the borrower and stock in a subsidiary of the borrower. How far can this approach be pushed? The defendant in Stoiber v. S.E.C., 161 F.3d 745 (D.C.Cir. 1998), argued that contractual provisions in a loan agreement sufficiently reduced risk to affect the note/security determination. The D.C. Circuit refused to buy this argument, finding that contractual provisions, which were in essence early acceleration clauses, "are significantly less valuable than collateral or insurance and not by our thinking an adequate substitute for the protection of the federal securities laws."[55]

Overlap with "Investment Contract" and the Howey Test. Many ambiguous instruments can be analyzed under either the *Reves* test or the *Howey* test. For example, viatical settlements may be assessed under both standards.[56] What happens, however, if the instrument is deemed to be a security under one test but not the other? Presumably, the definition of "security" in § 2(a)(1) is disjunctive, but *Reves* can be read to mean there are instruments Congress did not want classified as securities. To the extent courts have given primary weight to the *Reves* test, and considered *Howey* only secondarily, they have seemed inclined to classify ambiguous instruments as non-securities. For example, in Great Rivers Cooperative of Southeastern Iowa v. Farmland Industries, Inc., 198 F.3d 685 (8th Cir. 1999), "capital credits" issued by an agricultural cooperative to its members were found not to constitute

---

[52] See Wolf v. Banamex, 739 F.2d 1458 (9th Cir. 1984), cert. denied, 469 U.S. 1108 (1985).

[53] After Reves v. Ernst & Young, When Are Certificates of Deposit "Notes" Subject to Rule 10b–5 of the Securities Exchange Act, 46 Bus.Law. 173 (1990).

[54] Id.

[55] 161 F.3d at 751–52.

[56] In SEC v. Tyler, 2002 U.S. Dist. LEXIS 2952, 2002 WL 257645 (N.D. Tex., Feb. 22, 2002), the district court found the viatical settlements at issue to constitute securities under both tests.

securities, even though the credits (1) were transferable (but only with the consent of the defendant's board); (2) represented retained equity in the firm that was issued by the defendant in an attempt to raise capital; (3) were purchased by the members in return for shares in the cooperative that they surrendered; (4) entitled their members to receive distributions of the defendant's earnings; and (5) were dependent for their economic value on the managerial efforts of the defendant's officers.[57] Essentially, a majority of the holders of the credits received them as a result of converting their common stock into capital credits. Yet, in the Eighth Circuit's opinion, overshadowing these factors was that the holders had entered into a commercial relationship with the cooperative and viewed the credits as "patronage refunds or equity interests reflecting a membership or former membership in that cooperative...."[58] Still, in *Edwards* (included earlier in this casebook), the Court considered an ambiguous sale/leaseback arrangement in which the investor received a fixed return exclusively in terms of the *Howey* test. Could this imply that *Reves* will be limited to cases in which there is an instrument, a "note," that evidences indebtedness? No clear trend is evident yet.

Problem

PROBLEM 4-5

(a) Suppose a business corporation finds itself in financial difficulties. It owes its suppliers for goods sold on an open-account basis. To avoid bankruptcy, the company issues term notes to 45 of its trade creditors evidencing the debts. Is this a commercial or investment transaction?

(b) In Gary Plastic Packaging Corp. v. Merrill Lynch, Pierce, Fenner & Smith, Inc., 756 F.2d 230 (2d Cir. 1985), the defendant broker-dealer offered federally insured $100,000 certificates of deposit ("CDs") of savings banks to the public and agreed to maintain a secondary market in the CDs. In addition, Merrill Lynch offered a variety of other services, which included screening banks to determine which offered the most competitive yields, monitoring the creditworthiness of the banks, and negotiating for the best terms with these banks. The plaintiff alleged: (1) the defendant failed to disclose that the interest rates on their CDs were lower than the interest rates paid by the banks on direct sales of CDs; and (2) the defendants pocketed the difference between the rates as an undisclosed commission. Were the CDs sold through the Merrill Lynch program securities? The Second Circuit said yes, but would the D.C. Circuit majority in *Life Partners* (included earlier in this casebook) agree? Or would they classify these services as "pre-purchase" services? Should this distinction matter when applying the *Reves* criteria rather than the *Howey* criteria?

(c) Along with nine other sophisticated investors, Mr. Brooke Trout, a highly sophisticated investor, is approached by a broker-dealer,

---

[57] 198 F.3d at 796-98.
[58] Id. at 700.

Montgomery, Inc., who solicits them to provide bridge loans in the amount of $100,000 each (or $1 million in total) to Technifuture Inc., a start-up company expected to conduct an IPO in approximately 12 to 18 months once it has brought its new digital email phone into production. The loans will bear interest at 13%, and each will be independently secured by real estate owned by Technifuture or its controlling shareholders. Trout hopes to supply Technifuture with computer software through a firm he controls. When Technifuture goes into bankruptcy, Trout sues Montgomery for misleading statements that it allegedly made. Montgomery moves to dismiss the lawsuit on the basis that the notes are not securities. What result?

Loan Participations. Increasingly, commercial banks syndicate the loans they make to corporate borrowers to institutional investors (in particular, foreign banks, insurance companies, and mutual funds). The commercial bank may charge for its services in originating the loan by retaining the spread between the actual interest rate on the loan (say, 10.25%) and the lower rate at which the institution investors agree to purchase their participations (say, 10.10%). So long as the latter rate exceeds the money market rate on comparable instruments of a similar risk level, the institutional purchasers may not object to this retention by the bank. But what is the legal status of these loan participations?

In Banco Espanol de Credito v. Security Pacific National Bank, 973 F.2d 51 (2d Cir. 1992), Security Pacific made short-term loans, ranging in duration from overnight to one year (with most being for less than one month), to Integrated Resources, a large financial services conglomerate, to finance the latter's current business operations. Security Pacific sold participation interests in its Integrated Resources loan portfolio to some 11 financial institutions, each of which agreed to buy without recourse against Security Pacific and to conduct its own credit analysis of the borrower. These institutions previously purchased other "loan notes" from Security Pacific, which specialized in this form of syndication, and had signed a Master Participation Agreement with Security Pacific, covering the terms on which Security Pacific would offer participations in short-term loans made to many of its corporate borrowers. When Integrated Resources defaulted and went into bankruptcy in 1989, several loan participants sued Security Pacific, asserting that the instruments were securities and they had been sold to the investors while Security Pacific was in possession of material, non-public information about Integrated Resource's declining financial condition.

Applying the four *Reves* factors, a divided Second Circuit panel affirmed the district court's dismissal of the complaint on the ground that Security Pacific's "loan notes" were not securities:

> In addressing the first *Reves* factor, the district court found that Security Pacific was motivated by a desire to increase lines of credit to Integrated while diversifying Security Pacific's risk, that Integrated was motivated by a need for short-term credit

at competitive rates to finance its current operations, and that the purchasers of the loan participations sought a short-term return on excess cash. Based on these findings, the district court concluded that "the overall motivation of the parties was the promotion of commercial purposes" rather than an investment in a business enterprise.

Weighing the second *Reves* factor—the plan of distribution of the instrument—the district court observed that only institutional and corporate entities were solicited and that detailed individualized presentations were made by Security Pacific's sales personnel. The district court therefore concluded that the plan of distribution was "a limited solicitation to sophisticated financial or commercial institutions and not to the general public." We agree.

The plan of distribution specifically prohibited resales of the loan participation without the express written permission of Security Pacific. This limitation worked to prevent the loan participation from being sold to the general public, thus limiting eligible buyers to those with the capacity to acquire information about the debtor. . . .

With regard to the third factor—the reasonable perception of the instrument by the investing public—the district court considered the expectations of the sophisticated purchasers who signed MPA's [Master Participation Agreements] and determined that these institutions were given ample notice that the instruments were participations in loans and not investments in a business enterprise.

Finally, the district court noted that the Office of the Comptroller of the Currency has issued specific policy guidelines addressing the sale of loan participation. Thus, the fourth factor—the existence of another regulatory scheme—indicated that application of the securities laws was unnecessary.

Thus, under the *Reves* family resemblance analysis, as properly applied by the district court, we hold that the loan participations in the instant case are analogous to the enumerated category of loans issued by banks for commercial purposes and therefore do not satisfy the statutory definition of "notes" which are "securities". . . .[59]

Seeing Security Pacific's loan participation program in an entirely different light, Judge Oakes dissented, concluding that the majority decision "makes bad banking law and bad securities law, and stands on its head the law of this Circuit and of the Supreme Court in *Reves*. . . .":

---

[59] 973 F.2d at 55–56.

> ... [T]he loan note program engaged in by Security Pacific, while bearing a superficial resemblance to traditional loan participations, differs from those traditional participations in several important respects, including (1) who the participants are; (2) what the purposes of the purchasers or participants are; and (3) what the promotional basis used in marketing the loan notes is. The participants, rather than being commercial lenders who engage in traditional loan participations, were instead in many cases non-financial entities not acting as commercial lenders but making an investment, and even though there were some banks that purchased the so-called loan notes, they generally did so not through their lending departments but through their investment and trading departments ... The promotional literature put out by Security Pacific advertised the so-called loan notes as competitive with commercial paper, a well-recognized security under the Security Act. ...
>
> Beyond that, ... these loan notes differ from traditional loan participations in the scope of information available to the purchasers. In the traditional loan participation, participants generally engage in one-to-one negotiation with the lead lender, and at times with the borrower, and can inspect all information, public and non-public, that is relevant, and consequently are able to do their own credit analysis. Here, Security Pacific did not provide the participants with non-public information it had, provided only publicly-available documents or ratings, and the purchasers were not in a position to approach the hundred or more possible borrowers in the program and conduct their own examinations. ...[60]

Accordingly, Judge Oakes concluded that the loan participants did not have the opportunity to verify information that "normal" loan participants had in those forms of bank syndication that were traditionally beyond the scope of the federal securities laws.

When certiorari was applied for, the Supreme Court requested the views of the Solicitor General. Although the Solicitor General characterized the Second Circuit's decision as "flawed," it advised against granting certiorari (possibly because the federal banking agencies were concerned that a contrary ruling would expose banks to significantly heightened liabilities). In any event, the Supreme Court declined to grant certiorari.

Although the result in *Banco Espanol* is debatable, the controversy was inevitable. With increased competition in the financial services industry, a convergence of banking and brokerage firms has resulted, and traditional distinctions between how banks and brokerage firms behave

---

[60] Id. at 56–57. For another criticism of the majority's reasoning, see Roberts & Quinn, Leveling the Playing Field: The Need for Investor Protection for Bank Sales of Loan Participations, 63 Fordham L. Rev. 2115 (1995).

no longer provide very useful guideposts for the future. Indeed, had the Second Circuit found the short-term loans that Security Pacific was syndicating (which typically were between ten days and one month in duration) to be securities, would it have been feasible for Security Pacific to market them? Although Security Pacific could have made a private placement of such notes, the preparation of a private placement memorandum for each such offering (particularly those where the loan would be outstanding for less than ten days) seems disproportionate.

The Second Circuit later returned to the topic of loan participations in Pollack v. Laidlaw Holdings, Inc., 27 F.3d 808 (2d Cir. 1994).[61] This time, the instruments were uncollateralized participations in mortgages, which had been sold in many cases by brokers and investment advisers to unsophisticated investors. The Second Circuit reversed the district court, which found the instruments not to be securities based in part on *Banco Espanol,* and distinguished *Banco Espanol* on the grounds that it did not apply to "broad-based, unrestricted sales to the general investing public."[62]

Swaps. Derivatives are financial instruments whose value derives from that of another asset or measure (such as a stock, a stock index, interest rates, currency values, commodity values, and so forth) to which they are pegged. One particularly important form of derivative is the swap. A swap is a contract between two parties (usually called "counterparties") under which they agree to periodically exchange a series of cash flows over time. Why? Usually, the goal is to protect one side (or both sides) from, for instance, interest rate or currency fluctuations.[63] For example, the simplest swap agreement is a fixed-for-floating interest rate swap.[64] Under this form of agreement, one counterparty agrees to make fixed-rate payments to the other, while the second party agrees to make payments whose amounts "float" with prevailing interest rates (or some other index or rate to which the counterparties agree). The payments are calculated and made periodically, such as every six months over the life of the swap agreement. If prevailing interest rates rise above the fixed rate, the second party (who pays the floating rate) will incur a net loss on the contract at that time; if prevailing rates fall below the fixed rate, it will receive a net gain. Typically, the motivation for the party paying the fixed rate is to protect itself, as an issuer, against an interest rate rise on its own outstanding floating debt, because the payments it receives under the swap contract will, to that extent, offset any increase it incurs on its

---

[61] For a similar result, also emphasizing that those solicited were individuals, not institutions, see Stoiber v. SEC, 161 F.3d 745 (D.C.Cir. 1998).

[62] 27 F.3d at 814.

[63] In the following example, both counterparties transfer risk to each other. However, in instances when one counterparty transfers risk to another, it may pay the other counterparty a fee for assuming that risk.

[64] For a fuller discussion of swaps, see Romano, A Thumbnail Sketch of Derivative Securities and Their Regulation, 55 Md.L.Rev. 1 (1996).

own interest rate expense. Correspondingly, the party making the floating rate payments may fear a decline in interest rates (because, for example, it may hold a portfolio of floating rate securities), and so, under the swap contract, it protects itself against the danger that floating rates will fall below the fixed rate. Regardless of which party "wins" or "loses" under the swap, both counterparties benefit from the greater certainty that the agreement provides—namely, in this example, greater control over their exposures to interest rates.

Typically, swaps are not traded on exchanges but are customized contracts written for a specific corporate debtor or financial institution by a swaps dealer (usually, a commercial bank, investment bank, insurance company, or an affiliate). Also, in most swaps, the two sides do not make the two reciprocal streams of payments; rather, the party obligated to make the payment simply pays the other party the differential (the "net amount") between the two payments to be made on each payment date.

Do such swap contracts amount to "securities" under the *Reves* criteria? For a time, considerable uncertainty surrounded this issue, and the SEC asserted in some enforcement actions that certain swaps, in substance, amounted to options and thus constituted securities.[65] In response to both a recommendation by a President's Working Group and enormous lobbying pressure from the banking industry, Congress adopted the Commodity Futures Modernization Act of 2000 ("CFMA"), which contained amendments to both the 1933 and 1934 Acts that exempted both "security-based swap agreements" and "non-security-based swap agreements" from the definition of "security."[66] Effectively, these two terms covered the waterfront and exempted all swap agreements from registration (although "security-based swap agreements" remained subject to the SEC's antifraud and anti-manipulation authority).

This deregulation of swaps was revisited and largely reversed by the Dodd-Frank Act, which restored "security-based swaps" to the SEC's jurisdiction, while giving the CFTC regulatory authority over other swaps. This division of authority makes the definition of "security-based swap" critical. If a financial instrument qualifies as a "security-based swap," not only does it become subject to the 1933 and 1934 Acts, but the person dealing in those instruments may be classified as a "security-based swap dealer" or "major security-based swap participant," subject

---

[65] However, in Procter & Gamble Co. v. Bankers Trust Co., 925 F.Supp. 1270 (S.D.Ohio 1996), the district court found that interest rate swaps were not securities under the *Reves* test. It emphasized that the defendant bank's motive was "to generate a fee and commission, while P & G's expressed motive was, in substantial part, to reduce its funding costs." It also emphasized that the swaps would not be distributed to the market in the manner of securities and hence failed to meet *Reves*'s second prong. But see Caiola v. Citibank, N.A., 295 F.3d 312 (2d Cir. 2002) (finding cash-settled "synthetic" options on a specific stock to be securities, but also finding equity swaps not to be securities).

[66] The CFMA added § 2A to the 1933 Act and § 3A to the 1934 Act. These sections have been modified by the Dodd-Frank Act.

to SEC jurisdiction. (Further complicating matters, note that there is a definitional and regulatory difference between "security-based swaps" and "security-based swap agreements.")

New § 3(a)(68) of the 1934 Act defines "security-based swap" as "any agreement, contract, or transaction" that qualifies as a "swap" under the Commodity Exchange Act, and "is based on—

(I) an index that is a narrow-based security index, including any interest therein or on the value thereof;

(II) a single security or loan, including any interest therein or on the value thereof; or

(III) the occurrence, nonoccurrence, or extent of the occurrence of an event relating to a single issuer of a security or the issuers of securities in a narrow-based security index, provided that such event directly affects the financial statements, or financial condition, or financial obligations of the issuer."

This language was deliberately crafted to reach credit default swaps on corporate bonds or corporate loans (even though such loans would not normally be securities). Credit default swaps are typically triggered by a "credit event," which subparagraph III above references. Under the above definition, an equity swap based on the S&P 500 index would not be a "security-based swap" (because the S&P 500 index is broad-based), but an equity swap based on a small index of stocks might be.

Many interpretive issues arise under these definitions. For example, what is a "narrow-based security index"? Section 3(a)(55) of the 1934 Act provides a definition,[67] but the multiplicity of securities indexes now in use do not all fall clearly on one side or the other of its lines.

In response to these and other interpretive problems, the SEC and the CFTC created new rules that partly reflect a jurisdictional compromise between the two regulators.[68] The rules (and interpretive guidance) further define and provide guidance on the terms "swap," "security-based swap," "mixed swap," and "security-based swap agreement" in accordance with the Dodd-Frank Act. The scope of the terms determines which transactions, and parties to a transaction, are subject to SEC or CFTC regulation and enforcement.

---

[67] Sections 3(a)(55)(B) and (C) focus on the concentration level of the securities index and deem it a "narrow-based security index" if it meets any of four criteria: (1) the index has nine or fewer components; (2) a component security comprises more than 30% of the index's weighting; (3) the five highest weighted securities in the aggregate compose more than 60% of the index's weighting; or (4) the lowest weighted securities comprising, in the aggregate, 25% of the index's weighting have an average daily trading volume of less than $50 million (subject to some exceptions).

[68] "Further Definition of 'Swap,' 'Security-Based Swap,' and 'Security-Based Swap Agreement'; Mixed Swaps; Security-Based Swap Agreement Recordkeeping," CFTC and SEC Joint Final Rule; Interpretations; Request for Comment on an Interpretation, 77 Fed. Reg. 48208 (Aug. 30, 2012).

The SEC and the CFTC declined to address all of the definitional issues raised by the Dodd-Frank Act, instead focusing on the most commonly-transacted products, including foreign exchange and currency derivatives, commodity and security forwards, total return swaps, and credit default swaps. Among other things, the rules exclude certain consumer and commercial transactions from the product definitions, include a safe harbor for certain insurance products, and set out a process for parties to request a public determination by the Commissions of the definitional status of a particular product.

The Commissions declined to provide a bright-line definition of "security-based swap agreement," but did provide several examples as guidance. Some swaps, classified as "mixed swaps," are simultaneously treated as security-based swaps and swaps, subject to joint SEC-CFTC oversight. The Commissions interpret what constitutes a "mixed swap" narrowly, but the term generally refers to derivatives with multiple underlying references—at least one of which is characteristic of a security-based swap and another that is characteristic of a swap, such as a derivative tied to both an oil corporation's stock and the price of oil.

F. "Tokens" and Other Digital Assets

Despite nearing its 80th anniversary, *Howey* remains a vibrant part of the federal securities laws. Most recently, the *Howey* analysis has been applied to determine whether "tokens" and other digital assets—namely, media of exchange in binary format ("computer code") that use cryptography to secure transactions and verify the transfer of assets—are securities subject to the federal securities laws. The Securities Act release below and the following SEC Division of Corporation Finance no-action letter for Pocketful of Quarters, Inc. highlight the durability of *Howey* as novel instruments continue to arise.

Securities Act Release No. 81207
Securities and Exchange Commission.
July 25, 2017.

REPORT OF INVESTIGATION

PURSUANT TO SECTION 21(a) OF THE SECURITIES EXCHANGE ACT OF 1934: THE DAO

I. Introduction and Summary

The United States Securities and Exchange Commission's ("Commission") Division of Enforcement ("Division") has investigated whether The DAO, an unincorporated organization; Slock.it UG ("Slock.it"), a German corporation; Slock.it's co-founders; and intermediaries may have violated the federal securities laws. The Commission has determined not to pursue an enforcement action in this matter based on the conduct and activities known to the Commission at this time. . . .

The DAO is one example of a Decentralized Autonomous Organization, which is a term used to describe a "virtual" organization embodied in computer code and executed on a distributed ledger or blockchain. The DAO was created by Slock.it and Slock.it's co-founders, with the objective of operating as a for-profit entity that would create and hold a corpus of assets through the sale of DAO Tokens to investors, which assets would then be used to fund "projects." The holders of DAO Tokens stood to share in the anticipated earnings from these projects as a return on their investment in DAO Tokens. In addition, DAO Token holders could monetize their investments in DAO Tokens by re-selling DAO Tokens on. . .web-based platforms ("Platforms") that supported secondary trading in the DAO Tokens.

* * *

The investigation raised questions regarding the application of the U.S. federal securities laws to the offer and sale of DAO Tokens, including the threshold question whether DAO Tokens are securities. . . .

* * *

II. Facts

A. Background

From April 30, 2016 through May 28, 2016, The DAO offered and sold approximately 1.15 billion DAO Tokens in exchange for a total of approximately 12 million Ether ("ETH"). . . used on the Ethereum Blockchain.[6] As of the time the offering closed, the total ETH raised by The DAO was valued in U.S. Dollars ("USD") at approximately $150 million.

* * *

B. The DAO

"The DAO" is the "first generation" implementation of the White Paper concept of a DAO Entity, and it began as an effort to create a "crowdfunding contract" to raise "funds to grow company in the crypto space." . . . The DAO was to be "decentralized" in that it would allow for voting by investors holding DAO Tokens. All funds raised were to be held at an Ethereum Blockchain "address" associated with The DAO and DAO Token holders were to vote on contract proposals, including proposals to The DAO to fund projects and distribute The DAO's anticipated earnings from the projects it funded. The DAO was intended to be "autonomous" in that project proposals were in the form of smart contracts that exist on the Ethereum Blockchain and the votes were administered by the code of The DAO.

---

[6] Ethereum, developed by the Ethereum Foundation, a Swiss nonprofit organization, is a decentralized platform that runs smart contracts on a blockchain known as the Ethereum Blockchain.

* * *

["The DAO Website", run by Slock.it's co-founders, described how the DAO operated and included a link for purchase of DAO Tokens]. Slock.it's co-founders also promoted The DAO by soliciting media attention and by posting almost daily updates on The DAO's status on The DAO and Slock.it websites and numerous online forums relating to blockchain technology. [In these posts, the co-founders offered information on purchasing DAO Tokens, submitting proposals, and voting]. Slock.it also created an online forum on The DAO Website, as well as administered "The DAO Slack" channel, an online messaging platform in which over 5,000 invited "team members" could discuss and exchange ideas about The DAO in real time.

1. DAO Tokens

In exchange for ETH, The DAO created DAO Tokens (proportional to the amount of ETH paid) that were then assigned to the Ethereum Blockchain address of the person or entity remitting the ETH. A DAO Token granted the DAO Token holder certain voting and ownership rights. According to promotional materials, The DAO would earn profits by funding projects that would provide DAO Token holders a return on investment.

* * *

... All of the ETH raised in the offering as well as any future profits earned by The DAO were to be pooled and held in The DAO's Ethereum Blockchain address. The token price fluctuated... depending on when the tokens were purchased during the Offering Period.

* * *

DAO Token holders were not restricted from re-selling DAO Tokens acquired in the offering, and DAO Token holders could sell their DAO Tokens in a variety of ways in the secondary market...

In addition to secondary market trading on the Platforms, after the Offering Period, DAO Tokens were to be freely transferable on the Ethereum Blockchain.

* * *

2. Participants in The DAO

... DAO Token holders expected Contractors to submit proposals for projects that could provide DAO Token holders returns on their investments.

* * *

ETH raised by The DAO was to be distributed to a Contractor to fund a proposal only on a majority vote of DAO Token holders. DAO Token holders were to cast votes, which would be weighted by the number of tokens they controlled, for or against the funding of a specific proposal....

Before any proposal was put to a vote by DAO Token holders, it was required to be reviewed by one or more of The DAO's "Curators." . . . Curators of a DAO Entity had "considerable power" . . . [and] performed crucial security functions and maintained ultimate control over which proposals could be submitted to, voted on, and funded by The DAO.

III. Discussion

The Commission is aware that virtual organizations and associated individuals and entities increasingly are using distributed ledger technology to offer and sell instruments such as DAO Tokens to raise capital. These offers and sales have been referred to, among other things, as "Initial Coin Offerings" or "Token Sales." . . .

* * *

A. DAO Tokens Are Securities

1. Foundational Principles of the Securities Laws Apply to Virtual Organizations or Capital Raising Entities Making Use of Distributed Ledger Technology

Under Section 2(a)(1) of the Securities Act and Section 3(a)(10) of the Exchange Act, a security includes "an investment contract." *See* 15 U.S.C. §§ 77b–77c. An investment contract is an investment of money in a common enterprise with a reasonable expectation of profits to be derived from the entrepreneurial or managerial efforts of others. . . . This definition embodies a *"flexible rather than a static principle,* one that is capable of adaptation to meet the countless and variable schemes devised by those who seek the use of the money of others on the promise of profits." *Howey,* 328 U.S. at 299 (emphasis added). The test "permits the fulfillment of the statutory purpose of compelling full and fair disclosure relative to the issuance of 'the many types of instruments that in our commercial world fall within the ordinary concept of a security.'" *Id.* In analyzing whether something is a security, "form should be disregarded for substance," *Tcherepnin v. Knight,* 389 U.S. 332, 336 (1967), "and the emphasis should be on economic realities underlying a transaction, and not on the name appended thereto." *United Housing Found.,* 421 U.S. at 849.

2. Investors in The DAO Invested Money

* * *

Investors in The DAO used ETH to make their investments, and DAO Tokens were received in exchange for ETH. Such investment is the type of contribution of value that can create an investment contract under *Howey.* . . .

3. With a Reasonable Expectation of Profits

Investors who purchased DAO Tokens were investing in a common enterprise and reasonably expected to earn profits through that enterprise when they sent ETH to The DAO's Ethereum Blockchain address in exchange for DAO Tokens. [DAO was a for-profit entity, its objective was to fund projects with the expectation of a return on investments, and the investments (ETH) were pooled to fund those projects]. . . . Depending on the terms of each particular contract, DAO Token holders stood to share in potential profits from the contracts. Thus, a reasonable investor would have been motivated, at least in part, by the prospect of profits on their investment of ETH in The DAO.

4. Derived from the Managerial Efforts of Others

a. The Efforts of Slock.it, Slock.it's Co-Founders, and The DAO's Curators Were Essential to the Enterprise

. . . The DAO's investors relied on the managerial and entrepreneurial efforts of Slock.it and its co-founders, and The DAO's Curators, to manage The DAO and put forth project proposals that could generate profits for The DAO's investors.

Investors' expectations were primed by the marketing of The DAO and active engagement between Slock.it and its co-founders with The DAO and DAO Token holders. To market The DAO and DAO Tokens, Slock.it created The DAO Website on which it published the White Paper. . . [and] also created and maintained other online forums that it used to provide information to DAO Token holders about how to vote and perform other tasks related to their investment. Slock.it appears to have closely monitored these forums. . . Through their conduct and marketing materials, Slock.it and its co-founders led investors to believe that they could be relied on to provide the significant managerial efforts required to make The DAO a success.

Investors in The DAO reasonably expected Slock.it and its co-founders, and The DAO's Curators, to provide significant managerial efforts after The DAO's launch. The expertise of The DAO's creators and Curators was critical [for operational support, risk management, and decisions on proposals]. . . .the Curators exercised significant control over the order and frequency of proposals, and. . . DAO Token holders' votes were limited to proposals whitelisted by the Curators. . .

b. DAO Token Holders' Voting Rights Were Limited

Although DAO Token holders were afforded voting rights, these voting rights were limited. [DAO Token holders primarily relied on Slock.it's, the co-founders', and the Curators' managerial efforts]. . . .

The voting rights afforded DAO Token holders did not provide them with meaningful control over the enterprise, because (1) DAO Token holders' ability to vote for contracts was a largely perfunctory one; and (2) DAO Token holders were widely dispersed and limited in their ability to communicate with one another.

* * *

[Due to the limitations listed above] DAO Token holders [were not able to] to exercise meaningful control over the enterprise through the voting process, rendering the voting rights of DAO Token holders akin to those of a corporate shareholder. . . .

. . . [Slock.it's, its co-founders', and the Curators'] efforts, not those of DAO Token holders, were the "undeniably significant" ones, essential to the overall success and profitability of any investment into The DAO. . . .

B. Issuers Must Register Offers and Sales of Securities Unless a Valid Exemption Applies

The definition of "issuer" is broadly defined to include "every person who issues or proposes to issue any security" and "person" includes "any unincorporated organization." 15 U.S.C. § 77b(a)(4). . . .

The DAO, an unincorporated organization, was an issuer of securities, and information about The DAO was "crucial" to the DAO Token holders' investment decision. . . . The DAO was "responsible for the success or failure of the enterprise," and accordingly was the entity about which the investors needed information material to their investment decision. . . .

During the Offering Period, The DAO offered and sold DAO Tokens in exchange for ETH through The DAO Website, which was publicly-accessible, including to individuals in the United States. . . . [b]ecause DAO Tokens were securities, The DAO was required to register the offer and sale of DAO Tokens, unless a valid exemption from such registration applied.

* * *

C. A System that Meets the Definition of an Exchange Must Register as a National Securities Exchange or Operate Pursuant to an Exemption from Such Registration

Section 5 of the Exchange Act makes it unlawful for any broker, dealer, or exchange, directly or indirectly, to effect any transaction in a security, or to report any such transaction, in interstate commerce, unless the exchange is registered as a national securities exchange under Section 6 of the Exchange Act, or is exempted from such registration. *See* 15 U.S.C. § 78e.

* * *

IV. Conclusion and References for Additional Guidance

Whether or not a particular transaction involves the offer and sale of a security—regardless of the terminology used—will depend on the facts and circumstances, including the economic realities of the transaction. Those who offer and sell securities in the United States must comply with the federal securities laws, including the requirement to register with the Commission or to qualify for an exemption from the registration requirements of the federal securities laws. . . . These requirements apply to those who offer and sell securities in the United States, regardless whether the issuing entity is a traditional company or a decentralized autonomous organization, regardless whether those securities are purchased using U.S. dollars or virtual currencies, and regardless whether they are distributed in certificated form or through distributed ledger technology.

* * *

Re: Pocketful of Quarters, Inc.
Response of the Division of Corporation Finance

July 25, 2019

Re: Pocketful of Quarters, Inc. Incoming letter dated July 25, 2019

Based on the facts presented, the Division will not recommend enforcement action to the Commission if, in reliance on your opinion as counsel that the Quarters are not securities, PoQ offers and sells the Quarters without registration under Section 5 of the Securities Act and does not register Quarters as a class of equity securities under Section 12(g) of the Exchange Act. Capitalized terms have the same meanings as defined in your letter.

In reaching this position, we particularly note that:

- PoQ will not use any funds from Quarters sales to build the Quarters Platform, which has been fully developed and will be fully functional and operational immediately upon its launch and before any of the Quarters are sold;
- the Quarters will be immediately usable for their intended purpose (gaming) at the time they are sold;
- PoQ will implement technological and contractual provisions governing the Quarters and the Quarters Platform that restrict the transfer of Quarters to PoQ or to wallets on the Quarters Platform;
- gamers will only be able to transfer Quarters from their Quarters Hot Wallets for gameplay to addresses of Developers with Approved Accounts or to PoQ in connection with participation in e-sports tournaments;
- only Developers and Influencers with Approved Accounts will be capable of exchanging Quarters for ETH at pre-determined exchange rates by transferring their Quarters to the Quarters Smart Contract;
- to create an Approved Account, Developers and Influencers will be subject to KYC / AML checks at account initiation as well as on an ongoing basis;
- Quarters will be made continuously available to gamers in unlimited quantities at a fixed price;

- there will be a correlation between the purchase price of Quarters and the market price of accessing and interacting with Participating Games; and
- PoQ will market and sell Quarters to gamers solely for consumptive use as a means of accessing and interacting with Participating Games.

This position is based on the representations made to the Division in your letter. Any different facts or conditions might require the Division to reach a different conclusion. Further, this response expresses the Division's position on enforcement action only and does not express any legal conclusion on the question presented or on the applicability of any other laws, including the Bank Secrecy Act and anti-money laundering and related frameworks.

Sincerely,

Jonathan A. Ingram
Chief Legal Advisor, FinHub
Division of Corporation Finance

July 25, 2019

VIA ELECTRONIC SUBMISSION

Securities Act of 1933 Sections 2(a)(1) and 5 Securities Exchange Act of 1934 Sections 3(a)(10) and 12(g)

Office of Chief Counsel Division of Corporation Finance Securities and Exchange Commission 100 F Street, N.E. Washington, D.C. 20549

Re: Pocketful of Quarters, Inc.

Dear Sir or Madam:

Pocketful of Quarters, Inc. ("PoQ" and together with its affiliates and subsidiaries, the "Company"), a privately-held Delaware corporation with its principal place of business in the State of Connecticut, was founded to address one of the biggest frustrations facing players of on line video games today: the inability to use gaming credits, coins or other units of value purchased in, or earned playing, one online video game in other online games. PoQ proposes to offer Quarters (as defined below) for sale to those persons playing or seeking to play online video games ("gamers") without registration under the Securities Act of 1933, as amended (the "Securities Act"), and the Securities Exchange Act of 1934, as amended (the "Exchange Act," and, together with the Securities Act, the "Securities Acts").

I. Factual Background

a. The problem of in-game currency fragmentation

* * *

Gamers' inability to efficiently use their in-game currencies stems from the fact that current in-game currencies are not compatible across different games...[t]hese siloed video game economies result in large unspent balances of in-game currencies that represent significant lost value for gamers and leave game developers with frustrated customers.

b. The Quarters Platform

To prevent the loss of value resulting from in-game currency fragmentation, improve player experience, and enhance gameplay behavior, PoQ has financed and developed a new platform for gamers that leverages the benefits of blockchain[2] technology (the "Quarters Platform")... to significantly improve the user experience for gamers by creating a universal gaming token. The Quarters Platform includes two smart contracts,[3] the "Quarters Smart Contract" and the "Q2 Smart Contract," as well as two independent blockchain-based cryptographically protected tokens:[4] the "Quarters," which are the subject of this letter, and the "Q2 Tokens," which are securities.

* * *

i. A common in-game currency

Unlike any other in-game currency that exists to date, Quarters will interact across any Participating Game to provide gamers with a "wallet for all of your games." To use the Quarters Platform, gamers will go to www.pocketfulofquarters.com (the "PoQ Website") and register on line to create a "hot wallet"[8] that allows them to store their Quarters (a "Quarters Hot Wallet"). Gamers will then be able to purchase Quarters using U.S. Dollars on the PoQ Website or through distribution channels such as the Apple App Store or the Google Play Store... Alternatively,

---

[2] A "blockchain" is a distributed ledger maintained and updated (through a consensus mechanism) by a number of network participants, as compared to a traditional database that is stored in a central, permissioned, server.

[3] "Smart contracts" are pre-programmed coded functions that allow for self-execution at specified times and/or based on reference to the occurrence or non-occurrence of an action or event (including data external to the network provided by third-party sources, known as "oracles"), generally through the use of a distributed computing platform such as the Ethereum Blockchain.

[4] "Cryptographic tokens" are instances of computer code maintained on a blockchain-based ledger that are encrypted (secured) using cryptography, with each token typically representing a specific value or amount on the relevant ledger.

[8] A digital asset "wallet" is software that interfaces with one or more blockchain(s) and stores public and private keys allowing wallet holders to monitor their digital asset balances and digitally sign transaction instructions to send and receive digital assets. A "hot wallet" is one that is connected to the Internet.

gamers may purchase Quarters by sending ETH[10] directly to the Quarters Smart Contract.

Once the Quarters Platform has launched, gamers will be able to immediately use the Quarters stored in their Quarters Hot Wallet. . . By design, Quarters will have no value outside of their use in Participating Games.

* * *

ii. Why blockchain?

The Quarters Platform relies on blockchain technology to provide transparency and security. The ability for all parties—gamers, Developers and Influencers—to view and audit all transactions is critical to gain the trust needed for large-scale adoption of a new gaming token accepted for use in multiple otherwise unrelated games. The Quarters Smart Contract and the Q2 Smart Contract developed for the Quarters Platform ensure that Developers, Influencers, and Q2 Token investors are all paid in a secure and transparent fashion.

* * *

c. Quarters

i. Use of proceeds; manner of sale

. . . the sale of Quarters is not an effort to raise seed or other capital or to otherwise attract "investors" seeking to profit from their purchase of Quarters or from the growth of an "ecosystem." Instead, funds received from the sales of Quarters will be held in the Quarters Smart Contract in ETH and used to remunerate Developers, Influencers and Q2 Token holders as further described herein.

The Company will market and sell Quarters to gamers solely for consumptive use as a means of accessing and interacting with the range of Participating Games. The marketing material and the sales documentation for Quarters will explicitly disclose that Quarters are for use in Participating Games only, should not be viewed or acquired as an investment, and that gamers should not expect to derive any economic profits from any Quarters they purchase. . . . The Company, its agents and employees . . . will not otherwise refer to an investment opportunity or potential profits in connection with the sale of Quarters.

ii. Key characteristics of Quarters

Two key characteristics of the Quarters are their unlimited supply and fixed price. Quarters will be made continuously available to gamers in unlimited quantities. . . [and] Quarters will be offered for sale at a fixed price for either retail or wholesale purchases. Given the complementary characteristics of unlimited supply and a fixed sales price, price appreciation of Quarters will be highly unlikely, if not

---

[10] ETH means any amount {including any fractional amount equal to or greater than one Wei) of the digital token commonly known as "Ether" exchanged on the Ethereum Blockchain.

practically impossible. It will also not be possible for Quarters to trade in any secondary markets... because the terms of the Approved Account Agreement will prohibit Approved Accounts from transferring Quarters other than to the Quarters Smart Contract or, in the case of Developers, to gamers in connection with Gamer Rewards.

* * *

iii. How gamers use Quarters

...[G]amers will be able to use Quarters for one thing only: engaging with Participating Games by transferring Quarters to an Approved Account either to enter e-sports tournaments or make purchases during gameplay. In other words, the sole benefit to gamers of purchasing Quarters will be the ability to use them in Participating Games. The Company will prohibit gamers from transferring their Quarters to other gamers or trading them in any secondary markets by restricting the functionality of gamers' Quarters Hot Wallets...

* * *

2. EXEMPTED SECURITIES: SECTIONS 3(a)(2) THROUGH 3(a)(8)

Sections 3 and 4 of the Securities Act provide certain specific exemptions from the broad registration and prospectus requirements of § 5. It is important, however, to understand that the antifraud provisions of both the 1933 Act (other than § 11) and 1934 Act remain generally applicable, with some notable exceptions.

Although, at first glance, § 3 seems to exempt securities, while § 4 exempts transactions, a closer reading reveals that many of § 3's exemptions are, in fact, for transactions. Section 3(a)(1), repealed in 1987, was a transition section. It exempted from the registration requirements of the Securities Act securities that were offered to the public prior to or shortly after adoption of the Act. After fifty-plus years, § 3(a)(1) was finally recognized to be obsolete. The 1987 amendment reserved paragraph (1) for future use and retained the numbering of the remaining subsections.[69]

A. SECTION 3(a)(2)

Originally, § 3(a)(2) was at least partially premised on the assumption that serious constitutional issues would arise if federal legislation subjected the issuance of state and municipal securities to federal regulation. That is less likely today, although the Supreme Court's devotion to federalism has been inconsistent.[70]

---

[69] S.Rep. No. 100–105, 100th Cong., 1st Sess. 15–16 (1987).

[70] Compare Garcia v. San Antonio Metro Transit Authority, 469 U.S. 528 (1985) (rejecting a constitutional attack on the application of federal minimum wage laws to a state transit authority) with New York v. United States, 505 U.S. 144 (1992) (striking down federal

In any event, § 3(a)(2) exempts much more than the securities of federal, state, and municipal bodies and other public authorities. Its scope has been expanded by a series of amendments that also cover, among others: (1) certain types of industrial development bonds, the interest on which is excludable from gross income under § 103(a)(1) of the Internal Revenue Code; (2) interests and participations in the traditional forms of common trust funds maintained by banks as investment vehicles in which the bank holds the assets in a bona fide fiduciary capacity; (3) interests and participations in collective trust funds maintained by banks for funding certain stock bonus, pension or profit-sharing plans which meet the requirements for qualification under § 401(a) of the Internal Revenue Code; and (4) any interest or participation in a "separate account" maintained by an insurance company for funding certain stock bonus, pension or profit-sharing plans which meet the requirements for qualification under IRC § 401(a) and certain annuity plans under IRC § 404(a)(2).

Why are so many different types of securities squeezed within § 3(a)(2) (and not another provision in § 3)? Consider the reach of § 12(a)(2), which relates to material misstatements and omissions in prospectuses. Securities subject to § 3(a)(2) or § 3(a)(14) are expressly carved out from liability under § 12(a)(2), and since they are exempt from registration, sales of those securities are also not subject to disclosure-related liability under § 11. Given a choice, § 3(a)(2) offers an attractive means to limit liability under the antifraud provisions of the Securities Act.

a. Municipal Securities. The municipal securities market was discussed earlier in Chapter 1, along with the SEC's efforts to improve disclosure in it by regulating the brokers and dealers active in this market through Rule 15c2–12. Effectively, Rule 15c2–12 requires a disclosure document (known as the "official statement") for municipal securities offerings above a minimal floor (over $1,000,000), even though an exemption from § 5 of the 1933 Act is available under § 3(a)(2). Adopted in 1989 and amended in 1994,[71] Rule 15c2–12 was a response to the default on bonds issued by the Washington Public Power System (WPPS) and the near-default on New York City's bonds in the mid-to-late 1970s. Both episodes, and the later default by Orange County, California, in the late 1980s, disrupted the municipal securities market and gave rise to calls for reform and increased regulation.

---

liability provisions imposed on states that failed to handle hazardous waste as mandated by federal law). See also Dept. of Revenue of Ky. v. Davis, 553 U.S. 328 (2008) (discussing history of tax exemption for municipal bonds).

[71] See Exchange Act Release No. 26,985 (June 28, 1989) and Exchange Act Release No. 34,961 (Nov. 10, 1994). To the extent applicable, Rule 15c2–12 requires participating underwriters in a municipal securities offering to obtain and review a copy of the issuer's official statement and provide it to requesting customers, thus on a modest level establishing a basic disclosure requirement.

Another amendment extended § 3(a)(2) to exempt certain industrial development bonds ("IDBs").[72] IDBs are a form of revenue bond used by a municipality or other governmental subdivision to attract industry, provide housing, or for other commercial purposes. Typically, the municipality issues revenue bonds to finance the construction of an industrial facility for a private corporation. The corporation rents the facility on a long-term basis for an amount that covers principal and interest on the bonds. The bonds are secured solely by a pledge of the revenues and a mortgage on the facilities, so that payment of the bonds is dependent on the credit of the private corporation rather than the municipal issuer. Thus, IDBs actually are "private activity" bonds that are funded by an industrial or commercial enterprise and conceptually are "indistinguishable from other corporate debt securities" that are subject to the registration requirements of the 1933 Act.[73] They have been widely used by retail chain stores and other private entrepreneurs because they provide tax advantages for the bondholder, a lower-cost of funding for the industrial enterprise (as compared to competitors), and an exemption from the disclosure obligations of the 1933 Act. The Tax Equity and Fiscal Responsibility Act of 1982 (TEFRA) placed restrictions on the type of facilities financed with small issue IDBs and otherwise curtailed their use,[74] and the Tax Reform Act of 1986 further curbed the abuses of this tax bonanza for certain private sector beneficiaries.

b. Securities Issued or Guaranteed by a Bank. The application of § 3(a)(2) to banks is more complicated than it appears from a first reading of this section. Of course, § 3(a)(2) exempts stock or bonds issued by a bank, but it does not apply to securities issued by a bank holding company.[75] The § 3(a)(2) exemption is available, however, for financial institutions (known as "industrial loan companies") that function as the economic equivalent of a commercial bank (by taking deposits and

---

[72] See Securities Act Release No. 5103 (Nov. 6, 1970) with respect to the exemption of IDBs under § 3(a)(2) where the proceeds were to be used to provide a narrow range of specified facilities. The exemption applied only to issues that did not exceed $5 million, which was later increased to $10 million. Rule 131 under the 1933 Act and Rule 3b–5 under the 1934 Act deny the exemption to governmental obligations that are funded by payments received from an industrial or commercial enterprise for the use of such facilities. In that case, the obligations are deemed to be a separate "security" issued by the private entity and the exemption is not available. However, these rules do not apply to revenue bonds or other evidences of indebtedness issued by a governmental entity to finance a revenue-producing public project to be operated by that entity.

[73] The SEC sponsored the Industrial Development Bond Act of 1978, which would have subjected these bonds to the registration requirements of the 1933 Act. S. 3323, 95th Cong., 2d Sess. (1978). The bill died for lack of support. For the history of IDBs and a discussion of abuses arising from their use, see Hellige, Industrial Development Bonds: The Disclosure Dilemma, 6 J. Corp. L. 291 (1981).

[74] See McGee, The Impact of TEFRA and the 1984 Act on Small Issue Industrial Development Bonds, 33 Emory L.J. 779 (1984); Leifer & Plump, Uses of Industrial Development Bonds, 42 N.Y.U.Ann.Inst. on Fed.Tax. 7–1 (1984).

[75] See Bankers Trust Co., SEC No-Action Letter, [1971–72 Transfer Binder] Fed.Sec.L.Rep. (CCH) ¶ 78,474 (Sept. 22, 1971).

making loans) but are not actually regulated as a bank under state law.[76] These financial institutions typically have Federal Deposit Insurance Corporation (FDIC) insurance and are subject to regulation that is similar to bank regulation under state law.

The significance of § 3(a)(2) has been enhanced by the surge of structured financings and asset-backed securitizations. Sometimes, in these transactions, a bank guarantees that a pool of assets (usually mortgages or accounts receivable) will be sufficient to pay the principal and interest on debt securities issued by a nominal debtor set up to acquire and hold the pool of assets. Almost any form of an income-producing instrument with standardized terms can be pooled, thereby permitting the firm that holds these instruments to free up capital for other uses. For example, if the sales financing subsidiary of General Motors or Ford sells its accounts receivable (auto loans) to such a nominal debtor, which pays for them by issuing bonds in the public market, the addition of a major bank's guarantee that the pooled auto loans will be sufficient to pay principal and interest on the bonds will satisfy the bonds' purchasers as well as the requirements of § 3(a)(2), thereby eliminating the need for SEC registration.[77]

The success of commercial banks in providing this service led to a clamor from their principal rivals, insurance companies, that the § 3(a)(2) exemption should be expanded to cover securities guaranteed by them as well. Predictably, banks sought to keep their competitors out of this business. The SEC also resisted pressure to expand § 3(a)(2) to cover insurers, fearing, in part, that the adequacy of state insurance regulation was questionable. Instead, the SEC suggested that § 3(a)(2) be repealed as an overbroad exemption and be replaced by a grant of authority to the SEC to exempt those securities or transactions where registration was not necessary.[78] Neither the banking nor insurance industries liked this idea, and Congress has never acted on it.

Does a foreign bank that has established a branch in the United States qualify for the § 3(a)(2) exemption? The SEC has taken the position that a U.S. branch or agency of a foreign bank is entitled to rely on the exemption if "the nature and extent of Federal and/or State regulation and supervision of that particular branch or agency is substantially equivalent to that applicable to Federal or State chartered domestic banks doing business in the same jurisdiction."[79] The U.S. branches of foreign banks are also permitted to use the § 3(a)(2) exemption, subject to a special, non-discriminatory condition that the

---

[76] See Morris Plan Co. of California, SEC No-Action Letter, 1990 SEC No-Act. LEXIS 797 (May 7, 1990).

[77] See Report by the United States Securities and Exchange Commission on the Financial Guarantee Market: The Use of the Exemption in Section 3(a)(2) of the Securities Act of 1933 by Banks and the Use of Insurance Policies to Guarantee Debt Securities (Aug. 28, 1987).

[78] Id. at 95.

[79] See Securities Act Release No. 6661 (Sept. 23, 1986).

foreign branches of U.S. banks in the foreign bank's home jurisdiction receive parity of treatment.[80]

c. *Keoghs and IRAs.* Keogh plans are tax-deferred retirement plans established by self-employed individuals for the benefit of themselves and their employees. The plans enable these taxpayers to obtain some of the tax advantages previously available only to employees under corporate plans. The House Committee Report explained that § 3(a)(2) "does not exempt interests or participations issued by either bank collective trust funds or insurance company separate accounts in connection with 'H.R. 10 plans,' because of their fairly complex nature as an equity investment and because of the likelihood that they could be sold to self-employed persons, unsophisticated in the securities field."[81]

The Employee Retirement Security Act of 1974 (ERISA) established IRAs (Individual Retirement Accounts), which permit employees who are not covered under a corporate or Keogh plan to obtain tax benefits comparable to those provided under such plans. Additionally, the Revenue Act of 1978 created "Simplified Employee Pensions," which provide for simplified reports to the IRS and to employees. Congress did not extend the § 3(a)(2) exemption to these plans, and they have the same status as IRAs under the securities laws.[82]

In 1981, the Commission adopted Rule 180, which exempts from registration Keogh tax-qualified retirement plans established by a single employer or by interrelated partnerships. However, the exemption is confined to law firms, accounting firms, investment banking firms, and investment advisory or pension consulting firms, or firms that have secured independent expert investment advice in connection with their plans.[83]

B. SECTION 3(a)(3)

This section sets forth the "commercial paper" exemption and has two clear requirements: (1) the maturity of the instrument must not exceed nine months; and (2) the debt must arise out of a current transaction. Thus, if the issuer sought to finance the construction or acquisition of an industrial plant by issuing commercial paper (with the expectation that it would continually roll over these notes on maturity), it seems unlikely that the "current transaction" requirement would be satisfied.[84] The SEC also reads this exemption to apply only to "prime-quality, negotiable commercial paper of a type not ordinarily purchased

---

[80] See Securities Act Release No. 6661 (Sept. 29, 1986). Nondiscriminatory treatment of foreign banks was required by the 1978 International Banking Act.

[81] H.R.Rep. No. 91–1382, 91st Cong., 2d Sess. 44 (1970).

[82] Securities Act Release No. 6246 (Oct. 9, 1980).

[83] Securities Act Release 6363 (Nov. 24, 1981). See Rule 180(a)(3)(i) and (ii).

[84] In addition, if an instrument contains an automatic rollover provision providing for reinvestment in new securities on maturity (unless the investor opts out), the Commission has indicated that the exemption will likely not be available. See Securities Act Release No. 4412 (Sept. 20, 1961).

by the general public." See Securities Act Release No. 4412 (Sept. 20, 1961). However, the *Reves* decision (included earlier in this casebook) shows the Court to be divided as to whether the statutory language actually codifies this additional condition.

C. SECTIONS 3(a)(4) TO 3(a)(8)

Under the § 3(a)(4) exemption, the securities must be issued by an entity that is organized and operated *exclusively* for charitable purposes. In SEC v. Children's Hospital, 214 F.Supp. 883 (D.Ariz. 1963), the court enjoined the issuing institution from using the exemption where ten percent of the net proceeds were to be paid to the promoters as compensation for their services in planning and supervising the construction of the facility.[85] Similarly, the exemption granted to securities of savings and loan associations by § 3(a)(5) was denied to a Maryland association where the vast majority of the shares were sold to the public, not to provide loans for members but to use the proceeds to acquire slow-moving, dubious assets from the control group or their associates. Thus, although operating in the guise of a savings and loan association, the company failed to meet the test that substantially all of its business must be confined to making loans to members.[86]

The § 3(a)(8) exemption was long the subject of a controversy over the status of so-called "variable annuities." Section 3(a)(8) exempts "insurance" and "annuity" contracts when "subject to the supervision of the insurance commissioner . . . of any State or Territory of the United States or the District of Columbia." This clearly covers the fixed annuities that insurance companies have traditionally issued, under which the annuitant is offered a specified and definite amount beginning at a certain time in the future.

In contrast, the variable annuity was invented to provide a hedge against inflation. Under these contracts, a greater portion of the premiums collected are invested in common stocks, and the periodic benefits payable to the annuitant depend on the success of the insurance company's investment policy. In a sense, the annuitant's interest in the portfolio of securities is much like that of an investor in a mutual fund. Because the variable annuity "places all the investment risks on the annuitant, none on the company" and "the concept of 'insurance' involves some investment risk-taking on the part of the company," the Supreme Court held that it was not an "annuity" for purposes of the § 3(a)(8) exemption.[87]

---

[85] The California Corporations Code § 25100(J) codifies this principle by denying its analogous charitable exemption "if any promoter thereof expects or intends to make a profit directly or indirectly from any business or activity associated with the organization or operation of such nonprofit organization or from remuneration received from such nonprofit organization."

[86] SEC v. American International Savings & Loan Association, 199 F.Supp. 341 (D.Md. 1961).

[87] SEC v. Variable Annuity Life Ins. Co., 359 U.S. 65 (1959). And see SEC v. United Benefit Life Insurance Co., 387 U.S. 202 (1967), holding that a "flexible fund annuity" contract

The Supreme Court's decision did not end the battle. In response, the insurance industry created a modified type of annuity that provides certain guarantees of principal and interest, regardless of investment results. The SEC has now accepted this instrument, generally known as a "guaranteed investment contract," as entitled to an exemption from registration under § 3(a)(8) if it is issued and marketed under certain conditions.

These conditions are specified in Rules 151 and 151A, which establish "safe harbors" under the § 3(a)(8) exemption. To qualify, the annuity contract must: (1) be issued by a corporation (the insurer) that is subject to the supervision of a state insurance commissioner, a bank commissioner, or an agency or officer performing like functions; (2) provide certain guarantees or assurances that amounts payable by the issuer under the contract will, in fact, be paid; and (3) not be marketed primarily as an investment. The rule thus covers single premium deferred annuities.[88]

Apart from §§ 3(a)(2) to 3(a)(8), the securities falling in the other paragraphs of § 3(a) possess no inherent characteristics that should make them the subjects of a permanent exemption from SEC registration. They are, in reality, transaction exemptions and will be discussed later in this casebook. In addition, § 3(b) gives the SEC statutory authority to exempt certain securities transactions if their registration is not necessary for the public interest. The maximum amount of any such issue may not exceed $5,000,000 (§ 3(b)(1)) or $50,000,000 (§ 3(b)(2)). Section 3(c) grants the Commission an exemptive authority with respect to securities issued by a small business investment company under the Small Business Investment Act of 1958. Consideration of § 3(b) will be taken up later in this casebook.

---

did not come within the § 3(a)(8) insurance exemption of the 1933 Act. On "Insurance Products," see 2 Loss & Seligman, Securities Regulation 1000–20 (3d ed. 1989).

[88] See Securities Act Release No. 6645 (May 29, 1986).

CHAPTER 5

THE PRIVATE OFFERING EXEMPTIONS: SECTIONS 4(a)(2) AND 4(a)(5)

Statutes and Regulations

Securities Act, §§ 2(a)(2), 2(a)(4), 2(a)(15), 4(a)(1), 4(a)(2), 4(a)(5).

Introductory Note

Public offerings are expensive, time-consuming, require governmental approval, and carry heightened liability. For all these reasons, issuers would like to avoid registration, particularly in the case of smaller offerings where the costs of registration may be prohibitive. But, for many years, the SEC and the courts resisted the efforts of issuers to rely on exemptions from registration. Then, beginning in the 1970s, the attitude of the SEC—and later, the courts—slowly began to shift. This chapter will focus primarily on the case law, leaving the contours of the SEC's exemptive rules for later.

Initially, it is essential to clarify some terms. We have been using the words "issuer" and "underwriter" without paying very much attention to what they mean in terms of the Securities Act. Although § 5 broadly prohibits the use of the channels of interstate commerce or the mails to sell a security unless a registration statement is in effect, § 4(a)(1) specifically exempts "transactions by any person other than an issuer, underwriter, or dealer." These terms, therefore, serve to separate those persons who are subject to the § 5 registration and prospectus requirements from those who may ignore them. In this chapter, we explore the concept of "issuer" and the transaction exemptions that are applicable to issuers in connection with the offer and sale of securities. Later, we will consider the meaning of the terms "underwriter" and "dealer" and their obligation to comply with the registration and prospectus requirements of the 1933 Act.

To minimize confusion, we note at the outset that the "private placement" exemption was long denominated as § 4(2), but the Dodd-Frank Act added a new § 4(b), thus requiring the exemption to become § 4(a)(2). However, the court decisions, SEC releases, and other excerpts in this casebook may still refer to it as § 4(2).

1. *Who Is an "Issuer"?* An "issuer" is defined in § 2(a)(4) of the 1933 Act. In many cases there is not much difficulty in identifying the issuer of a security, although it need not be a corporation. Indeed, the issuer may be almost any juridical "person," since that term is defined in § 2(a)(2) to include

an individual, a partnership, a trust or other unincorporated association, and a foreign or domestic government or its political subdivisions.[1]

The scope of who can be an "issuer" is broad in other respects as well. The term includes persons who propose to issue a security, even if no securities are actually issued. The act of issuing a security arises from the creation of a right in some other person in the form of an investment contract, whether or not evidenced by a written instrument, such as a share of stock. Thus, when a promoter proposes to take a preincorporation subscription for shares in a corporation that is not yet formed, he intends to issue a security in the form of a "preorganization certificate or subscription" (included within § 2(a)(1)'s definition of "security"). Obviously, the corporation cannot be the issuer since it is not yet in existence. The contract thus is made with the promoter, who has become an issuer (although this might be a surprise to him).

If no exemption from registration is available, an added burden arises in having to register preincorporation subscriptions, because the underlying security will also be subject to registration. In actual practice, therefore, the promoter will usually dispense with the use of preorganization certificates of subscription. Instead, the corporation will be formed and the securities proposed to be issued will be registered without going through the extra motions. When this procedure is not followed, however, any preorganization selling activity, except preliminary negotiations or agreements between the issuer and an underwriter (as contemplated by § 2(a)(3)), is forbidden, unless an exemption from registration is available.

In SEC v. Murphy, 626 F.2d 633 (9th Cir. 1980), the court engaged in a search to determine the "issuer" in connection with a complex promotion entailing the sale of limited partnership interests. Murphy was a founder, director, and officer of Intertie, a corporation engaged in financing, construction, and management of cable television systems. Intertie promoted limited partnerships to which it sold newly-packaged cable TV systems. Intertie would purchase an existing television system on credit. It would then sell the system to a newly-organized partnership and lease back the system from the partnership. ISC, a brokerage firm, unaffiliated with Intertie or Murphy, sold the limited partnership interests. An ISC representative was usually the general partner of the limited partnership, but neither Murphy nor Intertie were partners. Murphy was the architect of this promotion by which Intertie received approximately $7.5 million from 400 investors in 30 partnerships. He participated actively in the offerings. In an SEC injunction proceeding alleging violation of the registration and antifraud provisions of the Securities Acts, the court held Murphy to be an issuer of the securities: "[W]hen a person organizes or sponsors the organization of limited partnerships and is primarily responsible for the success or failure of the venture for which the partnership is formed, he will

---

[1] The 1934 Act has similar, but not identical, definitions of "issuer" and "person." See §§ 3(a)(8) (issuer) and 3(a)(9) (person).

be considered an issuer for purposes of determining the availability of the private offering exemption."[2]

There are a number of anomalous types of securities where the "issuer" is not readily identifiable. These include certificates of deposit; voting trust certificates; certificates of interest in unincorporated associations; investment trusts and business trusts; equipment trust certificates; and fractional undivided interests in oil, gas, and other mineral rights. As to these securities, § 2(a)(4) describes in some detail the persons who shall be treated as issuer for purposes of the 1933 Act. Thus, in the case of oil, gas, and mineral rights generally, the issuer is any owner of such right (whether whole or fractional) who splits up his right into fractions for the purpose of making a public offering of those interests. Designation of the issuer has a bearing on who must sign the registration statement as well as determining possible liability under § 11 of the 1933 Act (which effectively makes issuers strictly liable for material misstatements or omissions).

2. *The Private Offering Exemptions.* A number of transaction exemptions are available to enable an issuer to avoid the registration requirements of the 1933 Act. Issuers who avail themselves of these exemptions remain subject to certain of the antifraud provisions of the 1933 and 1934 Acts, including Rule 10b–5. Indeed, the disclosure obligations under these civil remedies help fill the void left by the absence of the protection afforded by registration.

One set of these exemptions is available where the transaction by the issuer does not involve any public offering of securities. Two of the private offering exemptions are statutory: § 4(a)(2) and § 4(a)(5). Section 4(a)(2), which is commonly referred to as the "private placement" exemption, excludes from registration "transactions by an issuer not involving any public offering." Such an exemption is absolutely essential for there to be a workable system of federal securities regulation. It would be unreasonable, when any business is formed and capital is obtained from anyone outside of the entrepreneurial group, for federal registration to be required unless some other exemption were available, such as Regulation A or the intrastate offering exemption (discussed later in this casebook). As noted below, § 4(a)(5) is rarely used today, and so this chapter's principal focus is on § 4(a)(2) and the evolution of judicial interpretations of this provision.

At one end of the private placement spectrum is the case in which business people about to start a new business or expand a small, closely-held business, need additional capital. Frequently, the most immediate sources of "angel" or "seed" capital for such start-up companies are members of the family, or friends, or business, professional, or social acquaintances. So long as offerings were confined to a limited number of these persons, who presumably knew the principals and were willing to make an investment in the projected enterprise, it was generally assumed that the nonpublic offering exemption was available. The purchase, however, must be for

---

[2] 626 F.2d at 644. Accord SEC v. Holschuh, 694 F.2d 130 (7th Cir. 1982). The court noted that § 4(a)(1) is a transaction exemption and one who participates or is a "substantial factor" in unlawful sales satisfies the test for primary liability in an enforcement action for injunctive relief.

"investment" and not with a view to resale. The result was the saving of enormous costs entailed by registration, such as legal and accounting fees, underwriting expenses, printing costs, and the like.

At the other end of the spectrum, well-established public companies may prefer to make a private placement of investment-grade securities with insurance companies, pension funds, foundations, and other institutional investors. The motive may be cost savings or time, a fear that a public offering will depress the market price of outstanding shares, or a desire to restrict the communication of sensitive, material information to a limited audience. Underwriters and some banks have specialized in making these private placements, and again, it was generally assumed that the private offering exemption was available because of the sophistication of the offerees of the securities. The number of participants was not thought to be significant.

In between these types of financing, there developed a grey area as to which it was difficult for lawyers to give opinions with any confidence. Moreover, beginning in the 1950s, start-up, growth companies were organized in which more remote sources of capital were tapped, such as wealthy individuals, venture capital firms, small business investment companies, and institutional investors, including mutual funds. Sometimes a group of investors would provide the seed capital for the first round of financing with a view toward further participation in later rounds of financing as the business expanded.

During the 1980s, spurred both by academic criticism and congressional pressure, the SEC used its exemptive powers to expansively broaden the opportunities for an issuer to offer and sell substantial amounts of securities without registration under the 1933 Act. Indeed, it is now possible for a start-up company to save time and money, undergo less regulation, and raise as much or more investment capital through one or more private placements than by resorting to registered public offerings. Yet, that was not always the case. The present regime is the result of an evolutionary process extending over a number of years. Initially, the § 4(a)(2) exemption embodied a very vague and imprecise concept: a nonpublic offering. What defined such an offering was not self-evident, and the resulting uncertainty likely impeded capital formation. With the adoption of Regulation D in 1982 (discussed in the next chapter), new "bright-line" standards facilitated substantial offerings of securities without 1933 Act registration, because they eliminated most legal uncertainty. Partly in consequence, the venture capital industry burgeoned in the 1980s.

In addition to Regulation D, Rule 701 permits offers and sales of securities to employees, consultants, and business advisers under various forms of stock incentive and compensatory benefit plans without 1933 Act registration. (Rule 701 is also discussed in the next chapter.) This chapter will trace the transformation of the early, largely amorphous concepts of a nonpublic offering into the present specific conditions which now allow offers and sales of securities without having to incur enormous registration expenditures or to accept the legal uncertainty that formerly surrounded use of the private placement exemption. In overview, it should be understood that this is a context in which increased legal clarity contributed greatly to the growth of a distinctive industry: the venture capital business, which in turn fueled the growth of Silicon Valley.

The Statutory Standard. Section 4(a)(2) exempts "transactions by an issuer not involving any public offering" from the registration requirements of the 1933 Act. The exemption is self-determining, with the burden of proof being placed on the issuer and others relying upon the exemption. However, the statute and legislative history throw very little light on its scope. The House Committee Report contained the cryptic statement that these transactions were exempted "so as to permit an issuer to make a specific or an isolated sale of its securities to a particular person, but if a sale . . . should be made generally to the public that transaction would come within the purview of the Act." The Committee further emphasized that the bill "carefully exempts from its application transactions where there is no practical need for its application or where the public benefits are too remote."[3]

Administrative Interpretations. In the early years of the administration of the 1933 Act, the SEC and various commentators suggested a number of criteria for determining what constituted a nonpublic offering.

(1) *Number of Offerees.* At the lower end of the spectrum, the SEC's General Counsel early on expressed the view that an offering to not more than approximately 25 persons is not an offering to a substantial number of persons and presumably does not involve a public offering.[4] In practice, however, offers and sales were sometimes made of large blocks of investment quality securities to institutional investors. In some cases, the number approached 100, but the Commission did not raise any question regarding the availability of the private offering exemption if all were institutional investors, such as insurance companies and pension trusts. As to these persons, numbers seemed less important. The policy of treating institutional investors differently for both issuer transactions and resales in the secondary market was formally legitimized in 1990 by the adoption of Rule 144A, which regulates certain private resales of securities by institutions (and is discussed later in this casebook).

(2) *Availability of Information.* The availability of information to the offerees is a key factor in establishing the exemption. Some argue it is essentially the only factor that should be considered. They stress that this appears "to be the proper approach, since disclosure is in fact all that the registration process provides by way of investor protection (apart from the antifraud provisions)."[5]

(3) *Access to Information.* The access test may be met in two ways: (1) by actually furnishing such information directly to the offeree; or (2) by the offeree having access to such information as an employee, by virtue of a family relationship, or through economic bargaining power. See SEC v. Ralston Purina Co., which appears below.

---

[3] H.R. No. 85, 73d Cong., 1st Sess. 16 (1933).
[4] General Counsel's Opinion, Securities Act Release No. 285 (Jan. 24, 1935).
[5] Schneider, Section 4(2) in 12th Ann. Inst. on Sec. Reg. 295, 296 (PLI 1981).

(4) *Nature of the Offerees.* The Commission and courts have always taken into account the financial sophistication of the offeree. At some point, the offeree's ability to bear the economic risk of the investment was also a factor (and it may still influence some judicial decisions), but the SEC later rejected such a test as an improperly paternalistic standard that distinguished among investors based on their wealth rather than their sophistication.

(5) *Relationship to the Issuer and Each Other.* If the offerees had a special relationship to the issuer (for example, if they were major customers, family members of the CEO, or partners at its law firm or investment banking firm), this gave them special knowledge of the issuer and distinguished them from the public generally.[6]

(6) *Manner of Offering.* The concept of a private offering precludes general advertising or general solicitation through which offers are made. As originally viewed by the SEC, private offerings were negotiated between the participants on a face-to-face basis.

(7) *Limitation on Resales.* The purchase must be for investment, not with a view to resale. This factor is partly based on the notion that, if there are resales, the numbers limitation could be exceeded. It was also based on § 4(a)(1) which exempts from the provisions of § 5 "transactions by any person *other than* an issuer, underwriter, or dealer." Because § 2(a)(11) defines an underwriter as "any person who has purchased from an issuer *with a view to* . . . the distribution of any security," an investor who buys securities with the intent of making a resale is likely to be involved in a "distribution," which essentially is a public offering not exempt under § 4(a)(2).

In actual practice, however, application of the § 4(a)(2) exemption proved to be extremely difficult, so that it became a source of uncertainty and controversy among lawyers in the securities bar. In 1974, the Commission sought to provide "more objective standards" under the private offering exemption by adopting former Rule 146. The Rule provided that transactions by an issuer shall not be deemed to involve any public offering, within the meaning of § 4(a)(2), if they were part of an offering that met all of the conditions of the Rule.

The adoption of former Rule 146 did not stem the tide of criticism of the stringent criteria imposed by § 4(a)(2) as interpreted by the courts. (See particularly Doran v. Petroleum Management Corp., set out below.) Although Rule 146 was described by the Commission as a "safe harbor" from the pitfalls of § 4(a)(2), it imposed even more stringent and subjective standards upon issuers and their representatives regarding the qualifications of an offeree with respect to her knowledge and experience in financial matters and ability to evaluate and bear the risks of a prospective investment.

In 1980, the Commission responded to this criticism by issuing Rule 242 (which was later replaced by Regulation D). Although Rule 242 was

---

[6] This factor was stressed in the General Counsel's Opinion, Securities Act Release No. 285 (Jan. 24, 1935).

promulgated pursuant to the Commission's authority under § 3(b), the small issue exemption, it was essentially a private offering exemption in that it prohibited public solicitation and general advertising, and it limited offers and sales only to specified types of persons and to a maximum number of offerees and purchasers. The Rule introduced the concept of an "accredited investor," defined to include various types of institutional and other investors, corresponding to the list later enumerated in § 2(a)(15) of the 1933 Act.

These rules were originally quite restrictive and limited the total dollar amount that could be sold under them to accredited investors to $2 million in any six-month period. With the election of President Ronald Reagan in 1980, Congress's mood became more deregulatory as it grew concerned that American business, and particularly small business, had experienced difficulty in raising investment capital and decided that part of the problem arose from difficulties in complying with the stringent criteria imposed by § 4(a)(2) and former Rule 146. Congress, therefore, took action to aid small business by enacting the Small Business Incentive Act of 1980.[7] A new section, § 4(6), later renumbered by the Dodd-Frank Act as § 4(a)(5), was added to the 1933 Act that provides an additional statutory exemption for offers and sales by an issuer to "accredited investors" if the offer and sale does not exceed the dollar limit allowed under § 3(b)(1) (currently $5 million), and if there is no advertising or public solicitation entailed in the offer. Section 4(a)(5) thus adopted the "accredited investor" concept used in former Rule 242 and that term was defined in § 2(a)(15). In addition, § 2(a)(15) granted the Commission authority to enlarge the definition to include additional purchasers as accredited investors based upon "such factors as financial sophistication, net worth, knowledge and experience in financial matters, or amount of assets under management." Thus, the list of accredited investors was expanded by the SEC in Rule 215. And, since there is no limit on offers or sales to accredited investors under § 4(a)(5), numbers of offerees or investors (so long as they are accredited) became irrelevant.

Regulation D replaced Rule 146 and dropped many of its restrictions. Rule 501(a) of Regulation D essentially tracks §§ 4(a)(5) and 2(a)(15), but there are significant differences that should be recognized. For example, unlike § 4(a)(5), Rule 506(c) of Regulation D permits general solicitation; and while general solicitation is restricted under Rule 506(b), unlike § 4(a)(5), sales can be made up to 35 *non*-accredited investors. Not only is Rule 506 unlimited in the aggregate amount that can be offered, Regulation D has clearer, bright-line standards on how to satisfy the exemption, including with respect to aggregation, integration, and solicitation. Section 4(a)(5) does not seem to affirmatively require a disclosure document to be provided to offerees or investors. Rule 502(b) requires such a disclosure document, but only in the case of sales to non-accredited investors (and thus, again, supplies a broader exemption with clearer guidelines than § 4(a)(5)). In light of the foregoing, reliance on § 4(a)(5) has largely been overtaken by Regulation D. The key premise underlying Regulation D was that wealthy investors (at least those defined as "accredited investors") did not need the mandatory

---

[7] Pub. Law 96–477, § 602.

disclosure that SEC registration provided. However, an unrecognized byproduct of the quantitative definition given to the term "accredited investor" was that inflation over time would stretch that definition to cover a large percentage of investors, which helps explain why Regulation D has become so popular.

Section 4(a)(2), Rule 506, and § 4(a)(5) are interrelated, although they contain differing conditions for their use. Persons who acquire securities from issuers in a transaction complying with any of these exemptions receive securities that are unregistered; they are thus deemed to be "restricted securities" and can only be reoffered or resold if registered or pursuant to an exemption from the registration requirements of the Securities Act.

Statutes and Regulations

Securities Act, §§ 2(a)(15), 4(a)(2), 4(a)(5).

Securities and Exchange Commission v. Ralston Purina Co.

Supreme Court of the United States, 1953.
346 U.S. 119, 73 S.Ct. 981, 97 L.Ed. 1494.

■ MR. JUSTICE CLARK delivered the opinion of the Court.

Section 4(1)[8] of the Securities Act of 1933 exempts "transactions by an issuer not involving any public offering" from the registration requirements of § 5. We must decide whether Ralston Purina's offerings of treasury stock to its "key employees" are within this exemption. On a complaint brought by the Commission under § 20(b) of the Act seeking to enjoin respondent's unregistered offerings, the District Court held the exemption applicable and dismissed the suit. The Court of Appeals affirmed. The question has arisen many times since the Act was passed; an apparent need to define the scope of the private offering exemption prompted certiorari.

* * *

Ralston Purina manufactures and distributes various feed and cereal products. Its processing and distribution facilities are scattered throughout the United States and Canada, staffed by some 7,000 employees. At least since 1911 the company has had a policy of encouraging stock ownership among its employees; more particularly, since 1942 it has made authorized but unissued common shares available to some of them. Between 1947 and 1951 * * * Ralston Purina sold nearly $2,000,000 of stock to employees without registration and in so doing made use of the mails.

In each of these years, a corporate resolution authorized the sale of common stock "to employees * * * who shall, without any solicitation by the Company or its officers or employees, inquire of any of them as to how

---

[8] In 1964, the second clause of former paragraph (1) was redesignated as § 4(2). Act of Aug. 20, 1964, § 12, 78 Stat. 580. As noted previously, today it is designated as § 4(a)(2)—Eds.

to purchase common stock of Ralston Purina Company." A memorandum sent to branch and store managers after the resolution was adopted, advised that "The only employees to whom this stock will be available will be those who take the initiative and are interested in buying stock at present market prices." Among those responding to these offers were employees with the duties of artist, bakeshop foreman, chow loading foreman, clerical assistant, copywriter, electrician, stock clerk, mill office clerk, order credit trainee, production trainee, stenographer, and veterinarian. The buyers lived in over fifty widely separated communities scattered from Garland, Texas to Nashua, New Hampshire and Visalia, California. The lowest salary bracket of those purchasing was $2,700 in 1949, $2,435 in 1950 and $3,107 in 1951. The record shows that in 1947, 243 employees bought stock, 20 in 1948, 414 in 1949, 411 in 1950, and the 1951 offer, interrupted by this litigation, produced 165 applications to purchase. No records were kept of those to whom the offers were made; the estimated number in 1951 was 500.

The company bottoms its exemption claim on the classification of all offerees as "key employees" in its organization. Its position on trial was that "A key employee * * * is not confined to an organization chart. It would include an individual who is eligible for promotion, an individual who especially influences others or who advises others, a person whom the employees look to in some special way, an individual, of course, who carries some special responsibility, who is sympathetic to management and who is ambitious and who the management feels is likely to be promoted to a greater responsibility." That an offering to all of its employees would be public is conceded.

The Securities Act nowhere defines the scope of § 4(1)'s private offering exemption. Nor is the legislative history of much help in staking out its boundaries. The problem was first dealt with in § 4(1) of the House Bill, H.R. 5480, 73d Cong., 1st Sess., which exempted "transactions by an issuer not with or through an underwriter; * * *." The bill, as reported by the House Committee, added "and not involving any public offering." H.R.Rep. No. 85, 73d Cong., 1st Sess. 1. This was thought to be one of those transactions "where there is no practical need for * * * [the bill's] application or where the public benefits are too remote." Id., at 5. The exemption as thus delimited became law. It assumed its present shape with the deletion of "not with or through an underwriter" by § 203(a) of the Securities Exchange Act of 1934, * * * a change regarded as the elimination of superfluous language. H.R.Rep. No. 1838, 73d Cong., 2d Sess. 41.

Decisions under comparable exemptions in the English Companies Acts and state "blue sky" laws, the statutory antecedents of federal securities legislation have made one thing clear—to be public, an offer need not be open to the whole world. In Securities and Exchange Comm. v. Sunbeam Gold Mines Co., 9 Cir. 1938, 95 F.2d 699, 701, this point was made in dealing with an offering to the stockholders of two corporations about to be merged. Judge Denman observed that:

> In its broadest meaning the term "public" distinguishes the populace at large from groups of individual members of the public segregated because of some common interest or characteristic. Yet such a distinction is inadequate for practical purposes; manifestly, an offering of securities to all red-headed men, to all residents of Chicago or San Francisco, to all existing stockholders of the General Motors Corporation or the American Telephone & Telegraph Company, is no less "public" in every realistic sense of the word, than an unrestricted offering to the world at large. Such an offering, though not open to everyone who may choose to apply, is none the less "public" in character, for the means used to select the particular individuals to whom the offering is to be made bear no sensible relation to the purposes for which the selection is made. * * * To determine the distinction between "public" and "private" in any particular context, it is essential to examine the circumstances under which the distinction is sought to be established and to consider the purposes sought to be achieved by such distinction.

The courts below purported to apply this test. * * *

Exemption from the registration requirements of the Securities Act is the question. The design of the statute is to protect investors by promoting full disclosure of information thought necessary to informed investment decisions. The natural way to interpret the private offering exemption is in light of the statutory purpose. Since exempt transactions are those as to which "there is no practical need for [the bill's] application," the applicability of § 4(1) should turn on whether the particular class of persons affected need the protection of the Act. An offering to those who are shown to be able to fend for themselves is a transaction "not involving any public offering."

The Commission would have us go one step further and hold that "an offering to a substantial number of the public" is not exempt under § 4(1). We are advised that "whatever the special circumstances, the Commission has consistently interpreted the exemption as being inapplicable when a large number of offerees is involved." But the statute would seem to apply to a "public offering" whether to few or many. It may well be that offerings to a substantial number of persons would rarely be exempt. Indeed nothing prevents the Commission, in enforcing the statute, from using some kind of numerical test in deciding when to investigate particular exemption claims. But there is no warrant for superimposing a quantity limit on private offerings as a matter of statutory interpretation.

The exemption, as we construe it, does not deprive corporate employees, as a class, of the safeguards of the Act. We agree that some employee offerings may come within § 4(1), e.g., one made to executive personnel who because of their position have access to the same kind of information that the act would make available in the form of a registration statement. Absent such a showing of special circumstances, employees are just as much members of the investing "public" as any of their neighbors in the community. Although we do not rely on it, the rejection in 1934 of an amendment which would have specifically exempted employee stock offerings supports this conclusion. The House Managers, commenting on the Conference Report said that "the participants in employees' stock-investment plans may be in as great need of the protection afforded by availability of information concerning the issuer for which they work as are most other members of the public." H.R.Rep. No. 1838, 73d Cong., 2d Sess. 41.

Keeping in mind the broadly remedial purposes of federal securities legislation, imposition of the burden of proof on an issuer who would plead the exemption seems to us fair and reasonable. * * * Agreeing, the court below thought the burden met primarily because of the respondent's purpose in singling out its key employees for stock offerings. But once it is seen that the exemption question turns on the knowledge of the offerees, the issuer's motives, laudable though they may be, fade into irrelevance. The focus of inquiry should be on the need of the offerees for the protections afforded by registration. The employees here were not shown to have access to the kind of information which registration would disclose. The obvious opportunities for pressure and imposition make it advisable that they be entitled to compliance with § 5.

Reversed.

■ THE CHIEF JUSTICE and MR. JUSTICE BURTON dissent.

---

1. *Ralston Purina's Criteria. Ralston Purina* essentially formulated a dual standard: (1) investors had to be able "to fend for themselves," which presumably required some level of economic sophistication; and (2) investors had to receive "access to the kind of information which registration would disclose." Left open was whether this access requirement required the actual preparation of a registration statement-like document or whether the offered availability of the information would be sufficient. The SEC, however, did not win a total victory in *Ralston Purina*. It had long relied on numerical criteria involving the number of offerees, and the Court expressed skepticism about this standard. Instead, the Court appears to have decided that the public interest would be adequately protected by assigning to the issuer the burden of proof with respect to the availability of the exemption. In light of these statements, the SEC backed off of numerical criteria, but strictly interpreted the issuer's need to satisfy the burden of proof with respect to each offeree.

In interpreting *Ralston Purina*'s standards, the early response of the federal courts was to place a high burden on those seeking to use the exemption. Generally, they required a high standard of sophistication. Thus, in Lively v. Hirschfeld,[9] the defendants sought to establish a private placement on the basis that the offeree "had such information and capabilities that the registration statements and disclosures were not needed by them or would not add anything to what they had available." One of the plaintiffs was an airline pilot possessing "considerable business experience" who had purchased stocks from time to time. He was given information as to the number of outstanding shares, the stock structure, and the names of the officers. He sought no further information, and none was withheld.

In applying the *Ralston Purina* standard, the Tenth Circuit said: "The 'need' requirement is strict. The Supreme Court in its description of a possible 'private' group in *Ralston Purina* includes only persons of exceptional business experience, and [in] 'a position where they have regular access to all the information and records which would show the potential for the corporation.'" The court concluded that the offerees did not possess "unusual business experience and skill" nor "the degree of access to the type of data as would meet the standard."[10] It was this kind of language that aroused foreboding among securities lawyers.

In the same year, the Fifth Circuit decided Hill York Corp. v. American International Franchises, Inc.[11] Thirteen people had paid $5,000 each for stock in a fast-food franchising corporation. All of the purchasers were sophisticated businessmen and attorneys who planned to do business with the issuer, not the average person on the street. The record, however, contained no evidence of the total number of offerees. The plaintiffs brought an action to rescind the transaction and, in a jury trial, were awarded rescission of the stock sale and damages on the basis of violations of §§ 5 and 12(a)(2) of the 1933 Act. In affirming the judgment, the court approved the trial court's jury charge "that every offeree had to have information equivalent to that which a registration statement would disclose." The court also rejected the contention that a high degree of business or legal sophistication on the part of the offerees would be enough to establish the exemption. Even if the offerees were lawyers and businessmen, if they did not possess the information required to be contained in a registration statement, "they could not bring their sophisticated knowledge of business affairs to bear in deciding whether or not to invest. . . ."[12]

Hill York was followed in the Fifth Circuit by a bombshell decision, SEC v. Continental Tobacco Co., 463 F.2d 137 (5th Cir. 1972). In *Continental Tobacco*, a written prospectus, including unaudited financial statements prepared by a certified public accountant, was used in the offering. Moreover, the offerees who purchased signed "investment

---

[9] 440 F.2d 631, 632 (10th Cir. 1971).
[10] Id. at 633.
[11] 448 F.2d 680 (5th Cir. 1971).
[12] Id. at 690.

letters" acknowledging receipt of the prospectus, which was designed to give them all the information a registration statement would have afforded. Nevertheless, the court held that, even if the prospectus sent to the purchasers contained all the information that registration would have disclosed, "that fact alone would not justify the exemption." The court emphasized that the purchasers did not have the opportunity to inspect the corporation's records or verify the statements made in the prospectus, and that at least some of the purchasers had never met any officers of the company prior to acquiring the stock, thereby denying them "access." Even more frightening to the securities bar was the SEC's argument in its brief to the Fifth Circuit that those relying on the exemption had to show that each offeree had a relationship to the issuer that made such person the equivalent of an insider. Although the Fifth Circuit did not adopt this proposed standard, the SEC's assertion of it created great uncertainty. At a minimum, in *Hill York* and *Continental Tobacco*, the courts seemed to be formulating a standard under which the exemption was lost unless: (1) the offer was made to a limited number of offerees; (2) all of whom must be sophisticated purchasers having some relation to each other and to the issuer; (3) with access to all the information a registration statement would disclose; and (4) with an actual opportunity to inspect the company's records or otherwise verify for themselves the statements made to them as inducements for the purchase.

On the same day *Continental Tobacco* was decided, in Henderson v. Hayden, Stone Inc.,[13] the Fifth Circuit allowed a wealthy investor who had invested $180,000 in a speculative start-up company to rescind the transaction and get his money back, even though he was aware at the time of the transaction that the stock was not registered. The plaintiff managed his own investment portfolio of several million dollars, had some six brokerage accounts, read the leading financial publications, and, admittedly, could only be described as a sophisticated investor. Although the evidence showed that sales had actually been made only to seven other individuals, the Fifth Circuit reversed the district court because defendants failed to establish how many other *offers* may have been made by those engaged in the selling effort. In light of the burden of proof on the defendant, it was apparently to be presumed that a solicitation involving unqualified offerees had been made unless the defendant could prove otherwise. In response, securities counsel began to keep written logs of private placement brochures to ensure that no offer could be made until the offeree had been prescreened.

On the basis of these decisions, some commentators contended that the private offering exemption had been destroyed for all practical purposes.[14] Although the defendants in these cases failed to meet the

---

[13] 461 F.2d 1069 (5th Cir. 1972).

[14] See Kripke, Wrap-up, in Revolution in Securities Regulation, 29 Bus.Law. 185, 187 (Mar. 1974); Kripke, SEC Rule 146: A "Major Blunder," N.Y.L.J., Jul. 5, 1974; Goldberg, Private

burden of proof placed upon persons claiming entitlement to the exemption, there had been no showing of fraud or abuse; clearly, the costs and risks associated with use of the private placement exemption were rising—with arguably no one benefiting from this increased rigor. Two years later, the Commission adopted Rule 146 to provide "more objective standards" for determining when sales by an issuer would be deemed to be a transaction not involving a public offering within the meaning of § 4(a)(2).

Slowly, the tide began to turn. In Woolf v. S. D. Cohn & Co.[15] and Doran v. Petroleum Management Corp. (set out below), the Fifth Circuit sought to explain, and perhaps to limit, *Continental Tobacco*. As you read *Doran*, which follows, what are your answers to the following questions: (1) How, if at all, does *Doran* limit *Continental Tobacco*? (2) What factors are relevant in determining whether an offering qualifies for the § 4(a)(2) exemption? (3) When does an offeree have access? How is the existence of access to be determined? What is the relationship between access and offeree sophistication? (4) In *Doran*, the issuer was not a 1934 Act reporting company. Would access to information exist whenever the issuer is a 1934 Act reporting company? Should these 1934 Act reports be deemed inherently accessible to offerees?

Doran v. Petroleum Management Corp.

United States Court of Appeals, Fifth Circuit, 1977.
545 F.2d 893.

■ Before GOLDBERG, DYER and SIMPSON, CIRCUIT JUDGES.

■ GOLDBERG, CIRCUIT JUDGE:

In this case a sophisticated investor who purchased a limited partnership interest in an oil drilling venture seeks to rescind. The question raised is whether the sale was part of a private offering exempted by § 4(2) of the Securities Act of 1933, from the registration requirements of that Act. * * *[1]

I. Facts

Prior to July 1970, Petroleum Management Corporation (PMC) organized a California limited partnership for the purpose of drilling and operating four wells in Wyoming. The limited partnership agreement provided for both "participants," whose capital contributions were to be used first to pay all intangible expenses incurred by the partnership, and

---

Placements and Restricted Securities § 2.16[a] (rev. ed. 1975); Marsh, Who Killed the Private Offering Exemption?, A Legal Whodunit, 71 Nw.U.L.Rev. 470 (1977).

[15] 515 F.2d 591 (5th Cir. 1975), reh. denied 521 F.2d 225, on remand 546 F.2d 1252 (5th Cir. 1977), cert. denied 434 U.S. 831 (1977).

[1] . . . The SEC's adoption of Rule 146 . . . which establishes a sufficient set of conditions for coming within the exemption, does not bear directly on the case at bar. The transaction at issue began in 1970, and the plaintiff filed suit in 1972. Rule 146 was not adopted until 1974. It applies to offers commencing on or after June 10, 1974.

"special participants," whose capital contributions were to be applied first to pay tangible drilling expenses.

PMC and Inter-Tech Resources, Inc., were initially the only "special participants" in the limited partnership. They were joined by four "participants." As found by the district court, PMC contacted only four other persons with respect to possible participation in the partnership. All but the plaintiff declined.

During the late summer of 1970, plaintiff William H. Doran, Jr., received a telephone call from a California securities broker previously known to him. The broker, Phillip Kendrick, advised Doran of the opportunity to become a "special participant" in the partnership. PMC then sent Doran the drilling logs and technical maps of the proposed drilling area. PMC informed Doran that two of the proposed four wells had already been completed. Doran agreed to become a "special participant" in the Wyoming drilling program. In consideration for his partnership share, Doran agreed to contribute $125,000 toward the partnership. Doran was to discharge this obligation by paying PMC $25,000 down and in addition assuming responsibility for the payment of a $113,643 note owed by PMC to Mid-Continent Supply Co. Doran's share in the production payments from the wells was to be used to make the installment payments on the Mid-Continent note.

Pursuant to this arrangement, on September 16, 1970, Doran executed a promissory note, already signed by the President and Vice President of PMC in their individual capacities, for $113,643 payable to Mid-Continent. On October 5, 1970, Doran mailed PMC a check for $25,000. He thereby became a "special participant" in the Wyoming drilling program.

* * *

Following the cessation of production payments between November 1971 and August 1972 and the decreased yields thereafter, the Mid-Continent note upon which Doran was primarily liable went into default. Mid-Continent subsequently obtained a state court judgment against Doran, PMC, and the two signatory officers of PMC for $50,815.50 plus interest and attorney's fees.

On October 16, 1972, Doran filed this suit in federal district court seeking damages for breach of contract, rescission of the contract based on violations of the Securities Acts of 1933 and 1934, and a judgment declaring the defendants liable for payment of the state judgment obtained by Mid-Continent.

The court below found that the offer and sale of the "special participant" interest was a private offering because Doran was a sophisticated investor who did not need the protection of the Securities Acts. . . . Doran filed this appeal.

II. The Private Offering Exemption

No registration statement was filed with any federal or state regulatory body in connection with the defendants' offering of securities. Along with two other factors that we may take as established—that the defendants sold or offered to sell these securities, and that the defendants used interstate transportation or communication in connection with the sale or offer of sale—the plaintiff thus states a prima facie case for a violation of the federal securities laws. . . .

The defendants do not contest the existence of the elements of plaintiff's prima facie case but raise an affirmative defense that the relevant transactions came within the exemption from registration found in § 4(2). Specifically, they contend that the offering of securities was not a public offering. The defendants, who of course bear the burden of proving this affirmative defense, must therefore show that the offering was private. . . .

This court has in the past identified four factors relevant to whether an offering qualifies for the exemption. The consideration of these factors, along with the policies embodied in the 1933 Act, structure the inquiry. . . . The relevant factors include the number of offerees and their relationship to each other and the issuer, the number of units offered, the size of the offering, and the manner of the offering. Consideration of these factors need not exhaust the inquiry, nor is one factor's weighing heavily in favor of the private status of the offering sufficient to ensure the availability of the exemption. Rather, these factors serve as guideposts to the court in attempting to determine whether subjecting the offering to registration requirements would further the purposes of the 1933 Act.

* * *

In the case at bar, the defendants may have demonstrated the presence of the latter three factors. A small number of units offered, relatively modest financial stakes, and an offering characterized by personal contact between the issuer and offerees free of public advertising or intermediaries such as investment bankers or securities exchanges—these aspects of the instant transaction aid the defendants' search for a § 4(2) exemption.

Nevertheless, with respect to the first, most critical, and conceptually most problematic factor, the record does not permit us to agree that the defendants have proved that they are entitled to the limited sanctuary afforded by § 4(2). We must examine more closely the importance of demonstrating both the number of offerees and their relationship to the issuer in order to see why the defendants have not yet gained the § 4(2) exemption.

A. *The Number of Offerees*

Establishing the number of persons involved in an offering is important both in order to ascertain the magnitude of the offering and in order to determine the characteristics and knowledge of the persons thus identified.

The number of offerees, not the number of purchasers, is the relevant figure in considering the number of persons involved in an offering. Hill York Corp. v. American International Franchises, Inc. . . . [448 F.2d 680, 691 (5th Cir. 1971)]. A private placement claimant's failure to adduce any evidence regarding the number of offerees will be fatal to the claim. SEC v. Continental Tobacco Co. . . . [463 F.2d 137, 161 (5th Cir. 1972)]. The number of offerees is not itself a decisive factor in determining the availability of the private offering exemption. Just as an offering to few may be public, so an offering to many may be private. . . . Nevertheless, "the more offerees, the more likelihood that the offering is public." Hill York Corp. v. American International Franchises, Inc., supra, 448 F.2d at 688. In the case at bar, the record indicates that eight investors were offered limited partnership shares in the drilling program—a total that would be entirely consistent with a finding that the offering was private.

The defendants attempt to limit the number of offerees even further, however. They argue that Doran was the sole offeree because all others contacted by PMC were offered "participant" rather than "special participant" interests. The district court, which did not issue a finding of fact or conclusion of law with respect to this argument, appears to have assumed that there were eight offerees.

The argument is, in any event, unsupported by the record. . . . We must therefore reject the argument that Doran was the sole offeree.

In considering the number of offerees solely as indicative of the magnitude or scope of an offering, the difference between one and eight offerees is relatively unimportant. Rejecting the argument that Doran was the sole offeree is significant, however, because it means that in considering the need of the offerees for the protection that registration would have afforded we must look beyond Doran's interests to those of all his fellow offerees. Even the offeree-plaintiff's 20–20 vision with respect to the facts underlying the security would not save the exemption if any one of his fellow offerees was blind.

B. *The Offerees' Relationship to the Issuer*

Since SEC v. Ralston, supra, courts have sought to determine the need of offerees for the protections afforded by registration by focusing on the relationship between offerees and issuer and more particularly on the information available to the offerees by virtue of that relationship. * * * Once the offerees have been identified, it is possible to investigate their relationship to the issuer.

The district court concluded that the offer of a "special participant" interest to Doran was a private offering because Doran was a sophisticated investor who did not need the protections afforded by registration. It is important, in light of our rejection of the argument that Doran was the sole offeree, that the district court also found that all four "participants" and all three declining offerees were sophisticated investors with regard to oil ventures.

The need of the offerees for the protection afforded by registration is, to be sure, a question of fact dependent upon the circumstances of each case.... Nevertheless, the trial court's conclusion with respect to the availability of the private offering exemption may be set aside if induced by an erroneous view of the law....

1. *The role of investment sophistication*

The lower court's finding that Doran was a sophisticated investor is amply supported by the record, as is the sophistication of the other offerees. Doran holds a petroleum engineering degree from Texas A & M University. His net worth is in excess of $1,000,000. His holdings of approximately twenty-six oil and gas properties are valued at $850,000.

Nevertheless, evidence of a high degree of business or legal sophistication on the part of all offerees does not suffice to bring the offering within the private placement exemption. We clearly established that proposition in Hill York Corp. v. American International Franchises, Inc., supra, 448 F.2d at 690. We reasoned that "if the plaintiffs did not possess the information requisite for a registration statement, they could not bring their sophisticated knowledge of business affairs to bear in deciding whether or not to invest...." Sophistication is not a substitute for access to the information that registration would disclose.... As we said in *Hill York*, although the evidence of the offerees' expertise "is certainly favorable to the defendants, the level of sophistication will not carry the point. In this context, the relationship between the promoters and the purchasers and the 'access to the kind of information which registration would disclose' become highly relevant factors." 448 F.2d at 690.

In short, there must be sufficient basis of accurate information upon which the sophisticated investor may exercise his skills. Just as a scientist cannot be without his specimens, so the shrewdest investor's acuity will be blunted without specifications about the issuer. For an investor to be invested with exemptive status he must have the required data for judgment.

2. *The requirement of available information*

* * *

The requirement that all offerees have available the information registration would provide has been firmly established by this court as a necessary condition of gaining the private offering exemption. * * *

More specifically, we shall require on remand that the defendants demonstrate that all offerees, whatever their expertise, had available the information a registration statement would have afforded a prospective investor in a public offering. Such a showing is not independently sufficient to establish that the offering qualified for the private placement exemption, but it is necessary to gain the exemption and is to be weighed along with the sophistication and number of the offerees, the number of units offered, and the size and manner of the offering. * * * Because in this case these latter factors weigh heavily in favor of the private offering exemption, satisfaction of the necessary condition regarding the availability of relevant information to the offerees would compel the conclusion that this offering fell within the exemption.

* * *

C. On Remand: The Issuer-Offeree Relationship

In determining on remand the extent of the information available to the offerees, the district court must keep in mind that the "availability" of information means either disclosure of or effective access to the relevant information. The relationship between issuer and offeree is most critical when the issuer relies on the latter route.

To begin with, if the defendants could prove that all offerees were actually furnished the information a registration statement would have provided, whether the offerees occupied a position of access pre-existing such disclosure would not be dispositive of the status of the offering. If disclosure were proved and if, as here, the remaining factors such as the manner of the offering and the investment sophistication of the offerees weigh heavily in favor of the private status of the offering, the absence of a privileged relationship between offeree and issuer would not preclude a finding that the offering was private. . . .

Alternatively it might be shown that the offeree had access to the files and record of the company that contained the relevant information. Such access might be afforded merely by the position of the offeree or by the issuer's promise to open appropriate files and records to the offeree as well as to answer inquiries regarding material information. In either case, the relationship between offeree and issuer now becomes critical, for it must be shown that the offeree could realistically have been expected to take advantage of his access to ascertain the relevant information.[12] Similarly the investment sophistication of the offeree assumes added importance, for it is important that he could have been expected to ask the right questions and seek out the relevant information.

* * *

1. Disclosure or access: a disjunctive requirement

That our cases sometimes fail clearly to differentiate between "access" and "disclosure" as alternative means of coming within the private offering exemption is, perhaps, not surprising. Although the *Ralston Purina* decision focused on whether the offerees had "access" to

---

[12] For example, the offeree's ability to compel the issuer to make good his promise may depend on the offeree's bargaining power or on his family or employment relationship to the issuer.

the required information, . . . the holding that "the exemption question turns on the knowledge of the offerees," could be construed to include possession as well as access. Such an interpretation would require disclosure as a necessary condition of obtaining a private offering notwithstanding the offerees' access to the information that registration would have provided.

Both the Second and the Fourth Circuits, however, have interpreted *Ralston Purina* as embodying a disjunctive requirement. . . .

The cases in this circuit are not inconsistent with this view. . . .

* * *

Although Rule 146 cannot directly control the case at bar, we think its disjunctive requirement that the private offering claimant may show either "access" or "disclosure" expresses a sound view that this court has in fact implicitly accepted. . . .

2. *The role of insider status*

Once the alternative means of coming within the private placement exemption are clearly separated, we can appreciate the proper role to be accorded the requirement that the offerees occupy a privileged or "insider" status relative to the issuer. That is to say, when the issuer relies on "access" absent actual disclosure, he must show that the offerees occupied a privileged position relative to the issuer that afforded them an opportunity for effective access to the information registration would otherwise provide.[18] When the issuer relies on actual disclosure to come within the exemption, he need not demonstrate that the offerees held such a privileged position. Although mere disclosure is not a sufficient condition for establishing the availability of the private offering exemption, and a court will weigh other factors such as the manner of the offering and the investment sophistication of the offerees, the "insider" status of the offerees is not a necessary condition of obtaining the exemption.

Because the line between access and disclosure has sometimes been obscured, some have interpreted this court's decision in *Continental* [described *supra* in this chapter] as limiting the § 4(2) exemption to insider transactions.[19] As we pointed out in our recent decision in *Woolf*, however, such fears are unfounded. 515 F.2d at 610.

---

[18] That all offerees are in certain respects "insiders" does not ensure that the issuer will gain the private placement exemption. An insider may be an insider with respect to fiscal matters of the company, but an outsider with respect to a particular issue of securities. He may know much about the financial structure of the company but his position may nonetheless not allow him access to a few vital facts pertaining to the transaction at issue. If Doran had effective access to all information that registration would provide, he would be a transactional insider. That is all we require regarding the availability of information. If, on the other hand, his inside knowledge was incomplete or his access ineffective, he would be a transactional outsider despite the fact that we might consider him an "insider" for other purposes.

[19] For example, one commentator has written that "if Continental Tobacco represents the current state of the law regarding private placement exemption in non-Rule 146 transactions (highly doubtful), its availability is limited to insider transaction." 2 S. Goldberg,

The language from *Continental* that gave rise to those fears consists in the court's findings that "Continental did not affirmatively prove that all offerees of its securities had received both written and oral information concerning Continental, that all offerees of its securities had access to any additional information which they might have required or requested, and that all offerees of its securities had personal contacts with the officers of Continental." 463 F.2d at 160. It is possible to read this as a list of the necessary conditions for coming within the § 4(2) exemption, and therefore to infer that a private placement claimant must show the "insider" status of the offerees. Properly viewed in context, however, these statements were not clearly intended to establish necessary conditions, but only to point to the manifold weaknesses of the defendant's claim which, taken together, precluded private offering status.

In *Continental,* the court admittedly agreed with the SEC's position that even if the prospectus that Continental had sent to purchasers contained all the information registration would disclose, that fact alone would not justify the exemption. 463 F.2d at 160. That is doubtless true, since even if all the purchasers of Continental's securities had received full disclosure, the defendant would not have established that all offerees had received full disclosure. Because Continental had failed to sustain its burden of demonstrating the number of offerees, moreover, even the fact that all known offerees might have received disclosure would still have been insufficient to ensure the availability of the exemption. But the court's language in *Continental* should not be read as requiring in addition to full disclosure to all offerees a demonstration of the offerees' insider status.

Rather, the court's language regarding Continental's failure to show that all offerees had access to the requisite information and that all offerees had personal contacts with Continental's officers may be read as foreclosing the possible alternative route to the § 4(2) exemption. Because the prospectus did not contain all the information registration would provide and because it was not established that all offerees received the prospectus, it was clear that Continental could not rely upon actual disclosure. The additional language in *Continental,* though admittedly subject to other interpretations, may be read as making clear that there was in that case no privileged relationship between the offerees and the issuer that might have compensated for the defendant's palpable failure to disclose.

Although the disjunctive nature of the requirement is, to be sure, not made explicit in *Continental,* it is important that the pertinent conclusion of fact held clearly erroneous in that case was that "the offerees . . . were

---

Private Placements and Restricted Securities § 2.16[e] (1975). See also Schwartz, The Private Offering Exemption—Recent Developments, 37 Ohio St.L.J. 1, 19 (1976), and cases cited therein; Rediker, The Fifth Circuit Cracks Down on Not-So-Private Offerings, 25 Ala.L.Rev. 289, 311–17 (1973).

furnished and/or provided access to the same type of information that would have been provided in a registration statement...." 463 F.2d at 159. In order to hold this conclusion clearly erroneous, it was thus necessary to show that the defendant had failed to prove either disclosure or access.

In any event, absent a clear and unambiguous indication to the contrary, we do not read *Continental* as requiring insider status. We think that any such requirement would inhibit the ability of business to raise capital without the expense and delay of registration under circumstances in which the offerees did not need the protection of registration....

Rule 146 offers some rays of sunlight into the limbos and uncertain depths of § 4(2). The cases cast at best a faint beacon toward the horizon of decision. While we appreciate full well that the test we have fashioned remains too fluid to enable the would-be private offering issuer to feel entirely secure, we are confident that, at long last, the safe harbor of Rule 146 will provide that security and that few private placement claimants will stray far from that harbor....

* * *

IV. Conclusion

An examination of the record and the district court's opinion in this case leaves unanswered the central question in all cases that turn on the availability of the § 4(2) exemption. Did the offerees know or have a realistic opportunity to learn facts essential to an investment judgment? We remand so that the trial court can answer that question.

* * *

---

1. *Sophistication and Information.* Doran is clear that sophisticated investors still need information. But that need can be satisfied in one of two ways: (1) by furnishing the relevant information or (2) by providing effective access to that information. If the access route were chosen, then the relationship between the offeree and the issuer "becomes critical" (in *Doran*'s phrase), as it "must be shown that the offeree could realistically have been expected to take advantage of his access to ascertain the relevant information." Still, *Doran* clearly backs away from any requirement that offerees must be insiders or have a relationship among themselves (as the SEC argued in *Continental Tobacco*).

2. *Subsequent Cases.* In Securities and Exchange Commission v. Kenton Capital, Ltd.,[16] defendant was a Cayman Islands corporation that, through a sales agent in the United States, sought to raise capital to finance a "trading program" in securities and other instruments.

---

[16] 69 F.Supp.2d 1 (D.D.C.1998).

Apparently on his own initiative, the sales agent projected returns of 3750% per week for 40 weeks, which the defendant later conceded were not achievable. Over 40 investors agreed to invest some $1,700,000 in the defendant's trading program—at which point the SEC learned of the scheme and brought an injunctive action in federal court. The SEC conceded that the number of offerees was limited and that no general solicitation had occurred, but it challenged both the investors' sophistication and their access to relevant information. The court found as follows:

> Defendants support their allegation that their offerees were sophisticated by evidence that they screened their offerees. Wallace [the defendant's President] testified that he developed a checklist of information that was required of all investors, which was included in the material that Kenton sent to investors. Closer examination of this list, however, reveals that the information requested therein consisted of a photocopy of the investor's passport, a copy of the investor's driver's license or social security card, and a bank reference showing the investor to be in good standing with a bank. This information is wholly irrelevant to the sophistication of the offerees. The Court is equally unimpressed by Wallace's contention that Kenton's minimum investment requirement provided any safeguard of investor sophistication.[17]

The court added that, even if sophistication were established, it would still not be a substitute for access to the information that registration would disclose, citing *Doran*.

Although a minimum investment requirement did not work in *Kenton Capital*, cases upholding the private placement exemption have often looked to the size of the investment made by the plaintiff, particularly as a proportion of the total offering or of all outstanding shares.[18]

3. *Pre-Screening Procedures.* Although the screening procedures employed in *Kenton Capital*, supra, were deemed insufficient, more elaborate procedures, typically involving a substantial "investor questionnaire," are frequently used today by broker-dealers to determine whether an offeree is qualified, and courts have given these some weight.[19] But questionnaires do not automatically satisfy the sophistication standard. In Mark v. FSC Securities Corp.,[20] a brokerage firm formed a limited partnership to invest in the Arabian horse industry. In an action by investors to rescind their purchases of limited

---

[17] Id. at 11. Accord SEC v. Current Fin. Servs., 100 F.Supp.2d 1 (D.D.C.2000).

[18] See, e.g., Lewis v. Fresne, 252 F.3d 352, 358 (5th Cir. 2001) (purchase of 29% of outstanding shares is consistent with private character of offering).

[19] See, e.g., Mary S. Krech Trust v. Lakes Apartments, 642 F.2d 98 (5th Cir. 1981) (approving use of "formidable" due diligence investigation).

[20] 870 F.2d 331 (6th Cir. 1989).

partnership interests, the general partner of the partnership testified as to the investor suitability and wealth standards his brokerage firm used to identify investors and also testified that the investors had represented in their subscription agreements that they were sophisticated and had received sufficient information to make an informed investment decision. Nonetheless, the Sixth Circuit found this evidence insufficient because it only indicated the standard operating procedures that the brokerage firm used and did not satisfy the issuer's burden of demonstrating it had a reasonable basis for concluding that the actual investors in this offering were sophisticated. Apparently, the issuer's burden of proof required it to present evidence as to each investor. Conversely, in Wright v. National Warranty Co.,[21] the Sixth Circuit refused to permit husband and wife investors to disavow statements and representations made to the issuer in which they represented they had sufficient business experience to invest in the proposed private placement. But how far should this principle of estoppel be carried? Should it be sufficient that the investor makes a conclusory representation that it is a qualified offeree with substantial business and investing experience? In general, courts continue to place the burden of proof on the defendants.

4. *The Meaning of Sophistication.* How sophisticated must an offeree be in order for the private placement exemption to be available? Does the answer depend to some degree on the character of the disclosures made or the degree of access the offeree receives to information about the issuer?

Obviously, "sophistication" is not an either/or issue, and degrees of sophistication exist. An experienced, successful businessperson may have had considerable success, founded her own company, negotiated many complex transactions, and yet be uninformed with regard to a technical area of finance (such as derivatives). Thus, an ABA position paper on the scope of the § 4(a)(2) exemption concluded:

> The relevant inquiry should be whether the investor can understand and evaluate the nature of the risk based upon the information supplied to him. The relevant inquiry should not be whether the investor is *au courant* in all of the latest nuances and techniques of corporate finance.[22]

Nonetheless, courts have sometimes seemingly required a higher standard. In Lively v. Hirschfeld,[23] the Tenth Circuit indicated that only

---

[21] 953 F.2d 256 (6th Cir. 1992). In *Wright*, the plaintiffs were the company's incoming chief financial officer and his wife (who purchased at the time he was hired). Although both had access to all corporate information, they sought to assert that the CFO's wife was insufficiently experienced. It is not surprising that the court was unsympathetic to this claim on these facts, and thus the decision may not apply broadly.

[22] See Section 4(2) and Statutory Law: A Position Paper of the Federal Regulation of Securities Committee, Section of Corporation, Banking and Business Law of the American Bar Association, 31 Bus.Law. 485 (1975).

[23] 440 F.2d 631 (10th Cir. 1971). But see Cowles v. Dow Keith Oil & Gas, Inc., 752 F.2d 508 (10th Cir. 1985).

"persons of exceptional business experience" would satisfy the standard for an offeree under § 4(a)(2). *Doran* instead seemed to focus more on the quality of the disclosure provided by the issuer. The Eighth Circuit has gone further than other circuits and seemingly subordinated sophistication to the access-to-information requirement, emphasizing the economic bargaining power of the offerees.[24] Another Eighth Circuit decision assumed that a buyer of restricted securities was sophisticated because his net income exceeded $200,000, his net worth was over $1 million, and his trading account had a balance of approximately $500,000.[25] But do net income and net worth necessarily equate to sophistication?

Special problems exist when an issuer seeks to obtain summary judgment on the availability of the § 4(a)(2) exemption. In Hedden v. Marinelli,[26] one investor held a bachelor's degree in economics from Stanford and a law degree from U.C. Hastings and was the founding director of a bank; the other investor was a former CEO of the company whose stock he was purchasing. Still, the court refused to grant summary judgment on the issue of sophistication.

One commentator has found that courts examine the issue of sophistication in a variety of different contexts under the federal securities laws and, across this continuum, tend to place primary emphasis on the professional status and investment experience of the investor, including exposure to and prior consultation with investment professionals.[27] This would make sense, but the case law under § 4(a)(2) continues to show courts looking to talismanic factors, such as personal wealth or apparent bargaining power.

Courts have also continued to place the burden on the issuer of identifying and establishing the requisite qualifications of all offerees where the claimed exemption is based on § 4(a)(2).[28] As will be seen, this contrasts sharply with the standards under Regulation D.

5. *Access and Furnishing*. The strictness of the § 4(a)(2) exemption is evident in other respects. An individual who was the issuer's founder and a former director and officer was still found to lack access to

---

[24] See Van Dyke v. Coburn Enters., Inc., 873 F.2d 1094, 1098 (8th Cir. 1989) (conditions of § 4(a)(2) were satisfied where offerees "had the economic bargaining power to demand any information necessary to make an informed investment decision").

[25] See Ackerberg v. Johnson, 892 F.2d 1328 (8th Cir. 1989).

[26] 796 F.Supp. 432 (N.D.Cal. 1992).

[27] See Fletcher, Sophisticated Investors Under the Federal Securities Laws, 1988 Duke L.J. 1081.

[28] See, e.g., SEC v. Life Partners, Inc., 912 F.Supp. 4 (D.D.C.1996) (defendants "have the burden of identifying all offerees, and because [they] cannot provide this information, defendants' offerings do not qualify for exemption under Section 4(2)"), rev'd on other grounds, 87 F.3d 536 (D.C.Cir. 1996); see also Western Fed. Corp. v. Erickson, 739 F.2d 1439 (9th Cir. 1984) (failure to identify all offerees, even where a numbering system was used on the offering brochures, caused loss of exemption).

information after the time of his resignation.[29] Another decision found the § 4(a)(2) exemption to be unavailable where the investor did not receive the "same" information as a registration statement would disclose.[30] These decisions under § 4(a)(2) stand in stark contrast to what the outcomes would have been under Regulation D if these same individuals qualified under its liberal standard for "accredited investor."

6. *The ABA's Position.* The SEC's principal safe harbor, Regulation D, for private placements relaxes a number of the conditions discussed above for § 4(a)(2). In 2010, the ABA's Committee on Federal Regulation of Securities (whose members included a number of former SEC officials) published a report urging courts to apply basically the same standards as they would to an offering under Regulation D (even if the offering did not comply with Regulation D).[31] In particular, this would imply that only the qualifications of purchasers (and not offerees) could be considered, that the number of offerees would be generally irrelevant, and that information would not need to be furnished to most prospective investors in the case of a reporting company. To date, however, the courts do not appear to be heeding this advice and the number of offerees (and their sophistication) remains relevant in private offerings not conducted under Regulation D.[32]

7. *A Concluding Thought: Rules Versus Standards.* In this chapter, we have seen courts develop somewhat vague and uncertain standards under the broad language of § 4(a)(2). In the next chapter, we will see the SEC promulgate several bright-line rules (most notably, Regulation D) that reduced the uncertainty for issuers. This may remind you of the classic choice between "rules" and "standards." Rules are specific ("Drive at no more than 60 m.p.h."), while standards ("Drive at a reasonable speed.") are looser. Each has its advantages and disadvantages. Standards provide the regulatory agency with greater flexibility and ensure that no case just outside the line of a rule escapes the reach of regulation, but complying with those standards, and anticipating their reach, may be needlessly difficult. Rules minimize uncertainty and are easier to enforce (when they apply) but permit

---

[29] See Butler v. Phlo Corp., 2001 U.S. Dist. LEXIS 10809, Fed. Sec. L. Rep. (CCH) Para. 91,499 (S.D.N.Y. 2001).

[30] See SEC v. Empire Dev. Grp., LLC, 2008 U.S. Dist. LEXIS 43509 (S.D.N.Y. 2008). Some courts have looked to Schedule A of the 1933 Act to determine what information should be disclosed in a qualifying private placement.

[31] See Committee on Federal Regulation of Securities, Law of Private Placements (Non-Public Offerings) Not Entitled to Benefits of Safe Harbors—A Report, 66 The Business Lawyer 85 (Nov. 2010).

[32] For decisions focusing on the number of offerees, see, e.g., SEC v. Alternative Energy Holdings, Inc., 2014 U.S. Dist. LEXIS 66401 (D. Idaho 2014); SEC v. Empire. Dev. Group, LLC, 2008 U.S. Dist. LEXIS 43509 (S.D.N.Y. 2008). Still, at least one court has found that only the status of purchasers (and not offerees) should control. See Johnston v. Bumba, 764 F.Supp. 1263, 1273 (N.D. Ill. 1991), aff'd on other grounds, 983 F.2d 1072 (7th Cir. 1992). That remains a minority position. See SEC v. Kenton Capital, Ltd., 69 F.Supp.2d 1, 11–12 (D.D.C. 1998) (refusing to read Regulation D's standards into private placements not done pursuant to that rule).

capable lawyers to comply with the black letter of the rules while skirting their intended scope. Consider this choice further after you have finished the next chapter.

Problems

PROBLEM 5-1

BioTech, Inc., a young start-up that is not yet a reporting company, needs to raise $10,000,000 to complete the testing of a potential drug, which, if successful, promises to have broad applications and be a major innovation in cancer treatment. But there is no reliable way to estimate whether it will prove successful. The most that can be said is that (i) the drug looked promising in trials on mice and (ii) it has at least a 10% chance of providing significant benefits for humans. If successful, the drug could make BioTech worth $1 billion or more to the major pharmaceutical companies that would wish to acquire it for its new drug.

At present, BioTech has very limited funds and could not afford the cost, time, or delay incident to a public offering. Nor do underwriters want to touch it, given the high risk it faces. BioTech, however, is a potentially interesting investment for some institutional investors and some high-wealth "angel" investors who like to invest in high-risk start-ups.

BioTech's CEO, Dickie Nerd, knows he needs a capital infusion within weeks to stay in business. Without the assistance of counsel or an investment banker, he approaches over 100 institutions and high-wealth investors, asking them if they would be interested in private equity investments in the bio-tech area, but making no attempt to comply with any exemptive rules (because he is simply unaware of their existence).

Assume Mr. Nerd finds some 20 persons or entities that may be willing to provide such financing. He probably approached some persons who would not qualify as accredited investors, and none of those he found who are interested in investing (all of whom would qualify as accredited investors) has any prior relationship with BioTech. Mr. Nerd does not believe there is time (or money) available to prepare a disclosure document equivalent to a registration statement. But he is quite willing to answer questions, take the investors on a tour of the company, and give them free rein to inspect whatever they like and talk to whomever they please inside the company. You are brought in at the last minute to serve as counsel for the company. Can you structure this offering (without significantly changing the foregoing facts) to be an exempt private placement? Both Mr. Nerd and the investors want you to deliver such an opinion as a condition of the closing.

PROBLEM 5-2

(a) The Tucson Cowboys Inc., a triple-A minor league baseball team with a relatively good earnings history, wants to raise $8 million to build a new stadium. They are prepared to sell a 25% interest to each of two former superstars who recently retired—Barry Bondie and Manuel Romirez. Both players have ample resources to pay $4 million each, but neither graduated from college nor has any experience with financial statements. The Tucson Cowboys have not prepared any disclosure document remotely resembling a prospectus; also, because their controlling shareholder does not like to deal with lawyers, they do not know about, and have made no attempt to comply with, any SEC exemptive rule. But they have hired a registered representative from a local brokerage firm to represent both of the proposed investors and evaluate the transaction for them. They will give the representative complete access to their books and will answer any questions he has. They expect to pay the representative $25,000 for his services (and this payment will be disclosed to both investors). Will this work? What else would you recommend without fundamentally changing the transaction?

(b) In the alternative, suppose the net worth of each player is under $1 million and they are being asked to invest $200,000 each. Their motivation to invest is partly to obtain jobs as bench coaches with the team hopefully to begin working their way back to the major leagues as coaches. What result now?

CHAPTER 6

LIMITED AND OTHER OFFERING EXEMPTIONS

Statutes and Regulations

Securities Act, §§ 2(a)(3), 3(a)(7), 3(a)(9)–(11), 3(b), 4(a)(2), 4(a)(6), 4A, 5, 18.

Regulations A, CE, D, and Crowdfunding.

Rules 145, 147, 147A, 149, 150, 152, 155, 701, 1001.

Bankruptcy Code, §§ 364, 1125, 1145.

As described in the previous chapter, judicial interpretation of a vague, statutory exemption (§ 4(a)(2)) led to uncertainty that impeded capital-raising. In response, the SEC promulgated several rule-based limited offering exemptions, which set forth more precise safe harbors and avoided the soft-edged concepts that had developed under judicial interpretations of § 4(a)(2). In addition, several other exemptions from § 5—both statutory and SEC rule-based, as well as in the Bankruptcy Code—may be relied upon by small, start-up businesses and some larger, more-seasoned issuers that wish to avoid the costs, delays, or liabilities of SEC registration.

The exemptions this chapter covers are:

(1) Regulation D, which codifies the § 4(a)(2) private placement exemption and also relies on the § 3(b) small issue exemption;

(2) Regulation A, which provides a form of "mini-registration;"

(3) § 3(a)(11) and Rules 147 and 147A, which provide exemptions for intrastate offerings;

(4) Rule 701, which exempts offers and sales of securities by non-reporting issuers under a compensatory employee benefit plan;

(5) Regulation CE, which applies to limited offerings in California (but, perhaps in the future, could be generalized to other states);

(6) the § 3(a)(9) exemption for the exchange of securities by an issuer with its existing security holders, the § 3(a)(10) exemption for securities issued as part of a judicially- or administratively-approved exchange, and certain exemptions under the Bankruptcy Code; and

(7) the "crowdfunding" exemption (§ 4(a)(6)), which was added by the Jumpstart Our Business Startups ("JOBS") Act in 2012.

Historically, Regulation A was the most popular exemption, but it has been eclipsed by Regulation D due to its lower cost and the absence of a statutory ceiling on amounts that can be raised under Rule 506.

Adopted by the SEC in 1982, Regulation D relies for its authority on § 3(b) and § 4(a)(2). It was designed to coordinate a series of prior limited offering exemptions, to streamline the requirements applicable to private offers and sales of securities, and to provide a more reliable safe harbor for issuers if all the conditions of Regulation D are met.

Today, Regulation D is the most commonly used method of capital-raising in the United States. The SEC reports the following usage of various types of offerings from 2014 to 2017:[1]

Number of Offerings by Type of Offering and Year

Year	Regulation D	Public Equity	Public Debt	Rule 144A[2]	Other Private[3]
2014	33,429	1,176	1,576	1,813	674
2015	34,877	985	1,565	1,761	287
2016	35,793	821	1,636	1,500	450
2017	37,785	976	1,846	2,099	1,217

To illustrate Regulation D's dominance, in 2017, only 78 Regulation A offerings were completed,[4] compared to 37,785 Regulation D offerings.[5] Financial companies, such as hedge funds, private equity funds, and other private investment funds, comprised the bulk of the Regulation D offerings.[6] Between 2009 and 2017, non-financial firms, especially small businesses, made about 100,700 offerings.[7] Of those, about 78% of Regulation D offerings were for amounts less than $20 million,[8] and only

---

[1] Bauguess et al., Capital Raising in the U.S.: An Analysis of the Market for Unregistered Securities Offerings, 2009–2017, SEC Division of Economic Risk and Analysis 9 (Aug. 2018). The number of investors in Regulation D offerings is limited compared to the number in public offerings. Only 398,000 investors participated in Regulation D offerings in 2017 (91% of whom were "accredited investors"). This limited number is likely due to the restrictive definition of the term "accredited investor" and concerns by issuers and broker-dealers if they sell to non-accredited investors for reasons discussed later in this chapter.

[2] Rule 144A is a resale exemption from § 5 that is discussed later in this casebook.

[3] Includes offerings conducted under Regulations A, S, and Crowdfunding and § 4(a)(2). Regulation S covers offers and sales of securities outside the United States; it is discussed later in this casebook.

[4] Id. at 45. These are Regulation A offerings that were completed; the number does not include offerings that were qualified under Regulation A but not completed.

[5] In 2019, in dollar amounts, the SEC estimated that $1,558 billion was raised under Regulation D and $1 billion was raised under Regulation A. See Securities Act Release No. 10763, at 9 (Mar. 4, 2020). This indicates that individual Regulation A offerings tend to be larger in size than Regulation D offerings—which is certainly consistent with the raising of the Regulation A ceiling.

[6] In 2017, pooled investment funds raised $1,671 billion, while non-financial issuers raised only $105 billion. Id. at 5.

[7] Id.

[8] Id. at 45 (based on Table 16, showing 29,389 offerings under Regulation D below $20 million, compared to 37,785 total offerings under Regulation D). The cut-off is $20 million, because in March 2015, the SEC adopted new rules under Regulation A that divided the Regulation into two tiers: Tier 1, for securities offerings up to $20 million; and Tier 2, for

15% were offerings of more than $50 million.[9] The median amount sold in Regulation D offerings was less than $2 million,[10] indicating that Regulation D was preferred even when Regulation A was available.

Regulation D offerings also raise significant amounts of capital. From 2014 to 2017, issuers raised an average of about $1.4 trillion per year under Regulation D. In 2017, the private markets (including sales under Regulation D and Rule 144A) raised more than $3 trillion in capital, compared with $1.5 trillion raised in registered offerings in the public markets.[11] Since filings are not required for most private offerings, the private offering amount likely underestimates the total amount of capital raised in unregistered placements. As described later in this chapter, the popularity of Regulation D has soared since amendments introduced in the JOBS Act permitted issuers to conduct general solicitations (e.g., using radio, TV, the internet, or even billboards) so long as sales are made only to accredited investors.

Several other factors also explain the popularity of Regulation D:

First, the issuer escapes SEC oversight (because it need not file a disclosure document with the SEC).

Second, the issuer need not prepare an elaborate disclosure document (at least if it sells exclusively to "accredited investors," as defined in Rule 501(a) under the 1933 Act); this reduces cost and enables a faster offering process.

Third, the issuer escapes state securities registration requirements. State requirements are preempted for "covered securities" under § 18(b) of the 1933 Act. Section 18(b)(4)(F) includes as a "covered security" any security exempted under "Commission rules or regulations issued under section 4(a)(2)." Since Rule 506 of Regulation D relies on § 4(a)(2) of the 1933 Act, § 18 preempts state registration requirements for securities offered and sold under that Rule. Section 18(b)(4)(F), however, permits a state to require a "notice filing" to the extent such a requirement was in effect on September 1, 1996.

For most small businesses, the principal alternative to Regulation D is Regulation A (Rules 251 to 263 under the 1933 Act), which was significantly expanded by the JOBS Act in 2012 to permit an issuer to sell securities under Tier 1, for offerings of up to $20 million in a 12-month period, and under Tier 2, for offerings of up to $50 million in a 12-

---

offerings up to $50 million. Regulation A is discussed later in this chapter. See Rule 251 of Regulation A under the 1933 Act.

[9] Bauguess et al., Capital Raising in the U.S.: An Analysis of the Market for Unregistered Securities Offerings, 2009–2017, SEC Division of Economic Risk and Analysis 45 (Aug. 2018) (based on Table 16, showing 32,265 offerings under Regulation D below $50 million, compared to 37,785 total offerings under Regulation D).

[10] Id. at 16–17.

[11] Id. at 7. The balance in favor of private offerings appears to have continued. The SEC reported in March 2020 that, in 2019, registered offerings accounted for $1.2 trillion (30.8%) of capital raised, while private markets accounted for $2.7 trillion (69.2%). See Securities Act Release No. 10763, at 8 (Mar. 4, 2020).

month period. The prior ceiling was $5 million. Both Regulation A and Regulation D are exemptions from registration under § 5 of the 1933 Act and, therefore, do not subject the issuer or its directors or officers, or the broker-dealers selling its securities, to liabilities arising under § 11 of the 1933 Act.

As described below, there are certain requirements applicable to both Tier 1 and Tier 2 offerings, including company eligibility requirements, the filing of a Form 1-A "offering statement" for review by the SEC staff before the statement is "qualified," and the disqualification of "bad actors." (Regulation D also has a "bad actor" disqualification.)

Additional requirements apply to Tier 2 offerings, partly reflecting the ability of Tier 2 offerings to be listed on a national securities exchange. They include limits on the amount a non-accredited investor may invest in an unlisted Tier 2 offering, requirements for audited financial statements, and the filing of ongoing reports. Like Regulation D, issuers in Tier 2 offerings are not required under § 18 of the 1933 Act to register or qualify their offerings with state securities regulators.[12]

Securities sold under Regulation D are "restricted securities," as defined in Rule 144(a)(3) (which is discussed later in this casebook), that cannot immediately be resold in the public markets. In contrast to Regulation D, compliance with Regulation A results in the issuance of "unrestricted" securities that may be freely resold by the purchaser. In fact, as noted before, Tier 2 securities can be traded on a national securities exchange. Also, unlike Regulation D, a Tier 2 offering can be conducted as a public offering, without limitation on the eligibility of any purchaser if the securities are listed on a national securities exchange.

Nevertheless, unlike Regulation A, Rule 506 of Regulation D has no ceiling on the amount of securities that can be offered or sold in reliance on it. Offerings under Regulation D also are not subject to the formal disclosure requirements of Regulation A. These appear to be quite important for issuers.[13]

Regulation A is discussed later in this chapter. The next section discusses Regulation D and includes excerpts from key SEC releases relating to that Regulation.

---

[12] See § 18(b)(4)(D) of the 1933 Act.

[13] Prior to May 2018, Regulation A issuers—unlike Rule 506 issuers—could not be publicly reporting companies. Regulation A was amended to permit its use by publicly reporting companies, which may make it more accessible to some issuers that previously relied on Regulation D.

1. REGULATION D: THE PRIVATE PLACEMENT SAFE HARBOR

Statutes and Regulation

Securities Act, §§ 3(b), 4(a)(2).

Regulation D.

Securities Act Release No. 6389
Securities and Exchange Commission.
March 8, 1982.

REGULATION D—REVISION OF CERTAIN EXEMPTIONS
FROM REGISTRATION UNDER THE SECURITIES ACT
OF 1933 FOR TRANSACTIONS INVOLVING
LIMITED OFFERS AND SALES

The Commission announces the adoption of a new regulation governing certain offers and sales of securities without registration under the Securities Act of 1933 and a uniform notice of sales form to be used for all offerings under the regulation. The regulation replaces three exemptions and four forms, all of which are being rescinded. The new regulation is designed to simplify and clarify existing exemptions, to expand their availability, and to achieve uniformity between federal and state exemptions in order to facilitate capital formation consistent with the protection of investors. [The bracketed language in this Release and certain footnotes reflect updates or other changes made by the Editors.]

* * *

II. Discussion

A. *Overview*

Regulation D is a series of six rules, designated Rules [500]–506 [with Rule 505 in reserve], that establishes three exemptions from the registration requirements of the Securities Act.... The regulation is designed to simplify existing rules and regulations, to eliminate any unnecessary restrictions that those rules and regulations place on issuers, particularly small businesses, and to achieve uniformity between state and federal exemptions in order to facilitate capital formation consistent with the protection of investors.

Rules 501–503 set forth definitions, terms, and conditions that apply generally throughout the regulation. The exemptions of Regulation D are contained in Rules 504–506. Rules 504 and 505 [Rule 505 was subsequently rescinded by the SEC.] ... provide exemptions from registration under Section 3(b) of the Securities Act. Rule 506 succeeds Rule 146 and relates to transactions that are deemed to be exempt from registration under Section 4(2) of the Securities Act.

Rule 504 generally expands Rule 240 by increasing the amount of securities sold in a 12 month period from $100,000 to [currently

$5,000,000],[14] eliminating the ceiling on the number of investors, and removing the prohibition on payment of commissions or similar remuneration. Rule 504 also removes restrictions on the manner of offering and on resale if an offering is conducted exclusively in states where it is registered and where a disclosure document is delivered under the applicable state law. . . . Rule 504 does not prescribe specific disclosure requirements. Rule 504 is an effort by the Commission to set aside a clear and workable exemption for small offerings by small issuers to be regulated by state "Blue Sky" requirements and to be subject to federal anti-fraud provisions and civil liability provisions such as Section 12(2). Therefore, the exemption is not available to issuers that are subject to the reporting obligations of the Securities Exchange Act of 1934 . . . or are investment companies as defined under the Investment Company Act of 1940. . . .

Rule 506 takes the place of Rule 146. As under its predecessor, Rule 506 is available to all issuers for offerings sold to not more than 35 purchasers. Accredited investors, however, do not count towards that limit. Rule 506 requires an issuer to make a subjective determination that each purchaser meets certain sophistication standards, a provision that narrows a similar requirement as to all offerees under Rule 146. The new exemption retains the concept of the purchaser representative so that unsophisticated purchasers may participate in the offering if a purchaser representative is present.[15]

* * *

III. Synopsis

The following section-by-section discussion of the provisions of Regulation D, the significant commentary on the proposals, and the revisions made to the proposed regulation are included to assist in understanding the regulation as adopted. Attention is directed to the text of Regulation D for a more complete understanding. Attention is also directed to the chart following the synopsis which compares the provisions of Regulation D exemptions to those of predecessor exemptions.

A. *Preliminary Notes*

[Rule 500 of] Regulation D contains [seven paragraphs]. [Rule 500(a)] . . . reminds issuers that Regulation D offerings, although exempt from Section 5 of the Securities Act, are not exempt from antifraud or civil liability provisions of the federal securities laws. The note also reminds issuers conducting Regulation D offerings of their obligation to furnish whatever material information may be needed to make the required disclosure not misleading.

---

[14] The SEC recently proposed increasing Rule 504's ceiling to $10 million. See Securities Act Release No. 10763 (Mar. 4, 2020).

[15] This paragraph describes what is now Rule 506(b) of Regulation D under the 1933 Act. Rule 506(c), which was subsequently adopted by the SEC, is described below.

[Rule 500(b)] underscores an issuer's obligation to comply with applicable state law and highlights certain areas of anticipated differences between Regulation D at the federal and state levels. . . .

[Rule 500(c)] makes clear that reliance on any particular exemption in Regulation D does not act as an [exclusive] election. An issuer may always claim the availability of any other applicable exemption. Several commentators believed this note should address specifically the availability of an exemption under Section 4(2) of the Securities Act. The Commission has reworded the note by including language that appeared in proposed Rule 506(a) and clarified the specific availability of Section 4(2).

[Rule 500(d)] specifies that Regulation D is available only to the issuer of the securities and not to its affiliates or others for resales of the issuer's securities. The [Rule] further provides that Regulation D exemptions are only transactional. . . .

[Rule 500(g) was added in 1990 when Regulation S was adopted. Securities offered and sold outside the United States in conformity with Regulation S may be conducted at the same time as offers and sales in the United States in accordance with Regulation D without causing the two transactions to be integrated. The provisions of Rule 500(g) do not apply if the issuer elects to rely solely on Regulation D, rather than Regulation S, for offers and sales made to persons outside the United States.]

B. *Rule 501—Definitions and Terms Used in Regulation D*

Rule 501 sets forth, alphabetically, definitions that apply to the entire regulation.

* * *

1. *Accredited investor.* . . .

The following subsections review the eight categories of accredited investor in Rule 501(a).

a. Rule 501(a)(1)—Institutional Investors. Rule 501(a)(1) repeats the listing of institutional investors included in Section 2(15)(i) of the Securities Act [although the category in Rule 501(a)(1) is broader than under § 2(15)(i)]. One such investor is an employee benefit plan within the meaning of Title I of the Employee Retirement Income Security Act of 1974 ("ERISA"), the investment decisions for which are made by a bank, insurance company, or registered investment adviser. The Commission recognizes, and several commentators noted, that many plans have internalized the function of the plan fiduciary and thus could not qualify under the proposed category. For this reason the Commission believes it is appropriate to extend accredited investor status to any ERISA plan with total assets in excess of $5,000,000.

b. Rule 501(a)(2)—Private Business Development Companies. This category applies to private business development companies as defined in Section 202(a)(22) of the Investment Advisers Act of 1940. . . .

c. Rule 501(a)(3)— . . . [T]he Commission has determined that this category can be expanded to all organizations that are described as exempt organizations in Section 501(c)(3) of the Internal Revenue Code. Additionally, the Commission has lowered the asset level to $5 million. [Note that Rule 501(a)(3) is not limited to tax-exempt organizations. It also covers any corporation, business trust, or partnership "not formed for the specific purpose of acquiring the securities offered" with total assets exceeding $5 million. "Total assets" refers to a firm's assets without subtracting liabilities.]

d. Rule 501(a)(4)—Directors, Executive Officers and General Partners. Rule 501(a)(4) provides that certain insiders of the issuer are accredited investors. As proposed, the category pertained only to directors and executive officers. A number of comment letters recommended that the provision be modified to cover general partners of limited partnerships. The category thus has been revised to include general partners of issuers, as well as directors, executive officers and general partners of those general partners.

* * *

f. Rule 501(a)[(5)]—$1,000,000 Net Worth Test. This category extends accredited investor status to any natural person whose net worth at the time of purchase [exceeds] $1,000,000. Net worth may be either the individual worth of the investor or the joint net worth of the investor and the investor's spouse [or spousal equivalent]. . . .[16] [In 2011, to conform the accredited investor definition to the requirements of § 413(a) of the Dodd-Frank Wall Street Reform and Consumer Protection Act ("Dodd-Frank Act"), the SEC amended the net worth test, when determining accredited investor status, to (i) exclude as an asset the value of an individual's primary residence, (ii) exclude as a liability indebtedness secured by that primary residence (e.g., a mortgage) up to the estimated market value of the primary residence, and (iii) include as a liability indebtedness secured by that primary residence in excess of the estimated market value of the primary residence.[17]]

---

[16] As discussed later in this chapter, the Dodd-Frank Wall Street Reform and Consumer Protection Act of 2010 ("Dodd-Frank Act") authorizes the SEC (subject to some timing limitations) to index the $1 million net worth test and to adjust the $200,000 income test under Rule 501(a)(6) to account for inflation. The SEC normally can modify its own rules without special legislation, but the Dodd-Frank Act precluded any modification of these thresholds before 2014. That time period having now expired, today the SEC could increase these thresholds to reflect the impact of inflation, but it would likely encounter strong resistance from the financial industry. For reference, if these thresholds were adjusted for inflation, the net worth threshold would exceed $2.5 million and the income threshold would exceed $500,000 for individuals and $740,000 for an investor and the investor's spouse or spousal equivalent.

[17] See Rule 501(a)(5)(i) under the 1933 Act.

g. Rule 501(a)[(6)]—$200,000 Income Test. A natural person who has an income in excess of $200,000 in each of the last two years [or joint income with that person's spouse or spousal equivalent in excess of $300,000 in each of those years] and who reasonably expects [to reach the same income level] in the current year is an accredited investor.

* * *

[h.] [Rule 501(a)(7)—Trusts With Total Assets Exceeding $5,000,000. Any trust with total assets in excess of $5,000,000, not formed for the specific purpose of acquiring the securities offered, whose purchase is directed by a "sophisticated person" as described in Rule 506(b)(2)(ii), is an accredited investor. A "sophisticated person" is defined in Rule 506(b)(2)(ii) as a person who "has such knowledge and experience in financial and business matters that he is capable of evaluating the merits and risks of the prospective investment."]

[i.] Rule 501(a)(8)—Entities Made up of Certain Accredited Investors. The proposed definition of accredited investor did not take into account an entity owned entirely by accredited investors. Rule 501(a)(8) of the final regulation extends accredited investor status to entities in which all the equity owners are accredited investors.... [Rules 501(a)(9)–(13) include natural persons with certain professional certifications and designations, such as a Series 7, 65, or 82 license (for persons in the securities industry), or other credentials issued by an accredited educational institution; with respect to investments in a private fund, a person who is a "knowledgeable employee" of the fund; any entity with investments over $5 million that was not formed for the specific purpose of investing in the securities offered; and "family offices" with at least $5 million in assets under management and their "family clients."]

* * *

C. *Rule 502—General Conditions to be Met*

Rule 502 sets forth general conditions that relate to all offerings under Rules 504 [and] 506. These cover guidelines for determining whether separate offers and sales constitute part of the same offering under principles of integration, requirements as to specific disclosure requirements in Regulation D offerings, and limitations on the manner of conducting the offering and on the resale of securities acquired in the offering.

* * *

1. *Integration.* Rule 502(a) provides that all sales that are part of the same Regulation D offering must be integrated. The rule provides a safe harbor for all offers and sales that take place at least six months before the start of or six months after the termination of the Regulation D offering, so long as there are no offers and sales excluding those [under]

employee benefit plans, of . . . securities [of the same or a similar class] within either of these six-month periods.[18]

* * *

[Recall that Rule 500(g) states that offers and sales of securities within the United States that are made in compliance with Regulation D will not be integrated with coincident offers and sales made in accordance with Regulation S.]

2. *Information Requirements.* Rule 502(b) provides when and what type of disclosure must be furnished in Regulation D offerings. If an issuer sells securities under Rule 504 or only to accredited investors, then Regulation D does not mandate any specific disclosure. If securities are sold under Rule . . . 506 to any investors that are not accredited, then Rule 502(b)(1) requires delivery of the information specified in Rule 502(b)(2) to all purchasers [a reasonable time prior to sale]. The type of information to be furnished varies depending on the size of the offering and the nature of the issuer.

* * *

The specific disclosure requirements are as follows:

[For non-reporting companies, the obligation to provide information under Rule 502(b) is subject to an ambiguous clause in Rule 502(b)(2)(i), which mandates the required disclosures "to the extent material to an

---

[18] The SEC recently proposed amendments to the integration rules. See Securities Act Release No. 10763 (Mar. 4, 2020). The proposals would establish new Rule 152, which would replace current Rules 152 and 155. New Rule 152 provides a general framework and four safe harbors, replacing the various safe harbors currently set forth in various 1933 Act exemptions.

1. Proposed General Principle of Integration—For offerings not covered by a safe harbor, offers and sales are not integrated if, based on the particular facts and circumstances, the issuer can establish that each offering complies with the registration requirements of the 1933 Act or an exemption from registration is available for the particular offering. The proposed facts and circumstances analysis of integration replaces the traditional five-factor test.
2. Proposed Safe Harbor 1—Any offering made more than 30 calendar days before the commencement of any other offering, or more than 30 calendar days after the termination or completion of any other offering, will not be integrated; provided that, for an exempt offering for which general solicitation is not permitted, the purchasers either were not solicited through the use of general solicitation or established a substantive relationship with the issuer prior to the commencement of the offering for which general solicitation is not permitted.
3. Proposed Safe Harbor 2—Offers and sales made in compliance with Rule 701 or Regulation S will not be integrated with other offerings.
4. Proposed Safe Harbor 3—A 1933 Act-registered offering will not be integrated if made subsequent to:
   • a terminated or completed offering for which general solicitation is not permitted;
   • a terminated or completed offering for which general solicitation is permitted and made only to qualified institutional buyers and institutional accredited investors; or
   • an offering for which general solicitation is permitted that terminated or completed more than 30 calendar days prior to the commencement of the registered offering.
5. Proposed Safe Harbor 4—Offers and sales made in reliance on an exemption for which general solicitation is permitted would not be integrated if made subsequent to any prior terminated or completed offering.

understanding of the issuer, its business, and the securities being offered." *Query*: When is such information *not* material?

For non-reporting companies, the obligation to disclose non-financial information principally depends on whether the issuer is eligible to use Regulation A. If the issuer is eligible to use Regulation A, it must provide the same information required in a Regulation A offering circular. If the issuer is not eligible to use Regulation A, it must provide the same information required in a prospectus used in a registered public offering.

For non-reporting companies, the financial information that must be disclosed varies significantly with the size of the offering, with different requirements becoming applicable depending on whether the offering is below $2,000,000, between $2,000,000 and $7,500,000, or above $7,500,000. Even for the offerings below $2,000,000, the issuer must, at a minimum, provide an audited balance sheet, dated within 120 days of the start of the offering; more extensive audited financial statements are required for larger categories of offerings.[19]

As described below, if the issuer is a reporting company, Rule 502(b)(2)(ii), in most instances, requires that it furnish purchasers with filings the issuer already made under the 1934 Act's continuous disclosure system. Hence, for reporting issuers, Regulation D is satisfied simply by using disclosures they already filed with the SEC.]

* * *

a. Non-reporting companies. Disclosure requirements for companies that are not subject to the reporting obligations of the Exchange Act are set forth in Rule 502(b)(2)(i). These requirements are keyed to the size of the offering. . . .

b. Reporting companies. Companies that are subject to Exchange Act reporting obligations must furnish the same kind of disclosure regardless of the size of the offering. These issuers, however, have an option as to the form that this disclosure may take. Under Rule 502(b)(2)(ii)(A), a reporting company may provide its most recent annual report to shareholders, assuming it is in accordance with Rule 14a–3 or 14c–3 under the Exchange Act, the definitive proxy statement filed in connection with that annual report, and, if requested in writing, the most recent Form 10-K. Alternatively, those issuers may elect under Rule 502(b)(2)(ii)(B) to provide the information contained in the most recent of its Form 10-K or a Form S-1 registration statement under the Securities Act or a Form 10 registration statement under the Exchange Act. Although the requirement under subparagraph (B) refers to specific forms, it does not mandate delivery of the actual reference documents.

---

[19] In an effort to harmonize disclosure under Regulation A and Regulation D, the SEC has proposed, in Regulation D offerings up to $20 million, to require issuers to comply with the disclosure standards that apply to a Regulation A Tier 1 offering, and in Regulation D offerings greater than $20 million, to require issuers to provide audited financial statements and comply with the requirements of Regulation S–X, similar to Regulation A Tier 2 offerings. See Securities Act Release No. 10763 (Mar. 4, 2020).

An issuer, for instance, may choose to prepare and deliver a separate document that contains the necessary information.

Regardless of the issuer's choice of disclosure in subparagraph (A) or (B), Rule 502(b)(2)(ii)(C) requires the basic information to be supplemented by information contained in certain Exchange Act reports filed after the distribution or filing of the report or registration statement in question. Further, the issuer must provide certain information regarding the offering and any material changes in the issuer's affairs that are not disclosed in the basic documents.

* * *

c. *Other information requirements.* The balance of Rule 502(b)(2) provides for the treatment of exhibits [in Rule 502(b)(2)(iii)], the right of purchasers that are not accredited to receive information which was furnished to accredited investors [in Rule 502(b)(2)(iv)], . . . the right of all purchasers to ask questions of the issuer concerning the offering [in Rule 502(b)(2)(v)], and a specific obligation by the issuer to disclose all material differences in terms or arrangements as between security holders in a business combination or exchange offer [in Rule 502(b)(2)(vi)]. . . .

3. *Manner of Offering.* Rule 502(c) prohibits the use of general solicitation or general advertising[20] in connection with Regulation D offerings, except in certain cases under Rule 504.[21] . . .

4. *Limitations on Resale.* Securities acquired in a Regulation D offering, with the exception of certain offerings under Rule 504, have the status of securities acquired in a transaction under Section 4(2) of the Securities Act. As further provided in Rule 502(d), the issuer shall exercise reasonable care to assure that purchasers of securities are not underwriters, which reasonable care will include certain inquiry as to investment purpose, [written] disclosure of resale limitations [to each purchaser prior to sale that the securities have not been registered and, therefore, cannot be resold unless they are registered or an exemption from registration is available,] and placement of a legend on the certificate[s] . . . .

---

[20] As discussed later in this chapter, the ban on general solicitation has been lifted if sales are made exclusively to persons the issuer reasonably believes to be accredited investors and the other requirements of Rule 506(c) are satisfied.

[21] Notwithstanding the prohibition on general solicitation or general advertising, an issuer that is a reporting U.S. company (and certain foreign issuers) may publish a limited notice pursuant to Rule 135c under the 1933 Act that it proposes to make, is making, or has made an unregistered offering of securities, so long as the notice is not used to condition the U.S. market for the securities being offered. In addition, pursuant to Rule 135e under the 1933 Act, a foreign private issuer, a foreign governmental issuer, a selling security holder of either of them, or their representatives, will not be deemed to have offered a security for sale by virtue of providing any journalist with access to (i) its press conferences held outside the United States, (ii) meetings with the issuer's or selling security holder's representatives outside the United States, or (iii) written press-related materials released outside the United States, in each case at or in which an offering of securities is discussed, so long as the requirements of Rule 135e are satisfied.

D. *Rule 503—Filings of Notice of Sales*

The Commission is adopting a uniform notice of sales form for use in offerings under both Regulation D and Section [4(a)(5)] of the Securities Act. . . . As with the predecessor forms, issuers will furnish information on Form D mainly by checking appropriate boxes. The form requires an indication of the exemptions being claimed.

Rule 503 sets forth the filing requirements for Form D. The notice is due 15 days after the first sale of securities in an offering under Regulation D. . . .

* * *

E. *Rule 504—Exemption for Offers and Sales Not Exceeding [$5,000,000]*[22]

Rule 504, which replaces Rule 240, provides an exemption under Section 3(b) of the Securities Act for certain offers and sales not exceeding an aggregate offering price of [$5,000,000]. . . . Proceeds from securities sold within the preceding 12 months in all transactions exempt under [Rule 504] or in violation of Section 5(a) of the Securities Act must be included in computing the aggregate offering price under Rule 504. The exemption is not available to investment companies or issuers subject to Exchange Act reporting obligations [or certain development stage companies that either have no specific business plan or purpose or have indicated that their business plan is to engage in a merger or acquisition with an unidentified company or companies, or other entity or person]. Commissions or similar transaction related remuneration may be paid.

As under Rule 240, the exemption under Rule 504 does not mandate specific disclosure requirements. However, the issuer remains subject to the antifraud and civil liability provisions of the federal securities laws and must also comply with state requirements.

Offers and sales under Rule 504 must be made in accordance with all the . . . terms and conditions in [Rule 501 and Rule 502(a) (regarding integration), (c) (regarding manner of offering), and (d) (regarding resale limitations)]. However, if the entire offering is made exclusively in states that require registration and the delivery of a disclosure document, and if the offering is in compliance with those requirements, then the general limitations on the manner of offering [Rule 502(c)] and on resale [Rule 502(d)] will not apply. [Note that Rule 504(b) also permits the issuer to escape the general solicitation prohibition of Rule 502(c) and the limitations on resale of Rule 502(d) if the offering is made (i) in one or more states that do not provide for the registration of securities or the public filing or delivery of a disclosure document before sale, if the securities have been registered in a state that does provide for such registration, public filing, and delivery, and offers and sales are made in accordance with such provisions, and the disclosure document is

---

[22] The SEC recently proposed increasing Rule 504's ceiling to $10 million. See Securities Act Release No. 10763 (Mar. 4, 2020).

delivered before sale to all purchasers (including those in states that have no such procedure); or (ii) exclusively according to a state law exemption that permits general solicitation and general advertising so long as sales are made only to accredited investors.]

* * *31

G. *Rule 506—Exemption for Offers and Sales Without Regard to Dollar Amount*

Rule 506 relates to transactions that are deemed to be exempt under Section 4(2) of the Securities Act. It modifies and replaces Rule 146. Like its predecessor, Rule [506(b)] exempts offers and sales to no more than 35 purchasers. Whereas Rule 146 excludes certain purchasers from the count, Rule [506(b)] excludes accredited investors in computing the number of purchasers. More significantly, Rule 506 modifies the offeree qualification principles of Rule 146 in two ways. First, [Rule 506(b)(2)(ii)] requires that only purchasers meet the sophistication standard [and that standard may be met alone or with a "purchaser representative" (see Rule 501(i) (requirements for a "purchaser representative"))]. Second, the rule eliminates the economic risk test. Commentators endorsed both modifications.

[Rule 506 was subsequently amended to include Rule 506(c), which permits general solicitation or general advertising, but (among other requirements) requires the issuer to "take reasonable steps to verify" that the purchasers are accredited investors. Rule 506(c) is discussed in more detail later in this chapter.]

H. *Rule 507—Disqualification Relating to Exemptions Under Rules 504 . . . and 506*

Rule 507, adopted in 1989, disqualifies issuers from using Regulation D, if the issuer, any predecessor or affiliate has been found by a court to have violated the Form D filing requirements specified in Rule 503. [Rule 507(b), however, states that the disqualification will not apply

---

31   . . . [T]he Commission is aware that in computing the aggregate offering price issuers frequently misunderstand the interaction of the concepts of aggregation and integration as applicable under Rule [504(b)(2)] . . . . Aggregation is the principle by which an issuer determines the dollar worth of exempt sales available directly under Section 3(b) of the Securities Act. Integration is a principle under which an issuer determines overall characteristics of its offering. The following examples illustrate the application of these concepts. An issuer that has conducted an offering under Rule [504] in [December] 1982 must aggregate the proceeds from that offering with the proceeds of a Rule [504] offering conducted in [May] 1982. If the May offering had been under Rule 506, however, it would not need to be aggregated with the December offering. In either case, the [May and December offerings] should be exempt from principles of integration by virtue of the safe harbor provision in Rule 502(a). If a Rule 506 offering had been conducted in July 1982, the integration safe harbor would not be available as to a subsequent Rule [504] offering in December. Although the proceeds from the July 506 offering would not be added to the December [504] aggregate offering price under aggregation principles, they would have to be included if the two offerings could be integrated. Assuming the two offerings were integrated, then the issuer would have to evaluate all characteristics of the combined transactions, e.g., number of investors, aggregate offering price, etc., when determining the availability of an exemption.

if the SEC determines, upon a showing of good cause, that it is not necessary under the circumstances that the exemption be denied.]

I. *Rule 508—Insignificant Deviations From a Requirement of Regulation D*

Rule 508, adopted in 1989, provides that isolated failures to comply with Regulation D will not necessarily cause the loss of an exemption. Although Form D is still required to be filed, it is no longer a condition to an exemption under Regulation D. Rule 508 responds to the criticism that the limited offering rules are too complex and impose intolerable risks for inadvertent violations.

[More specifically, Rule 508 provides that a person failing to comply with a term, condition, or requirement of Rule 504 or 506 will not lose the exemption if the person shows:

(1) The failure to comply did not pertain to a term, condition, or requirement "directly intended to protect the individual or entity to whom securities were offered or sold;"

(2) The failure to comply was "insignificant with respect to the offering as a whole," except that failing to comply with Rule 502(c) (no general solicitation or general advertising), Rule 504(b)(2) (the aggregate offering price cap), and Rule 506(b)(2)(i) (the 35 purchasers cap) is deemed to be significant to the offering as a whole; and

(3) A good faith and reasonable attempt was made to comply with Rule 504 or 506.

Even if a person retains its exemption, in reliance on Rule 508, the SEC may bring an action under § 20 of the 1933 Act for failing to strictly comply with Rule 504 or 506.]

* * *

---

1. *Relative Use.* Rule 506 consistently dominates Rule 504 in offerings that rely on Regulation D. The SEC reports that between 2009 and 2017, 97.2% of all offerings under Regulation D and 99.9% of all funds raised under Regulation D were pursuant to Rule 506.[23]

---

[23] Bauguess et al., Capital Raising in the U.S.: An Analysis of the Market for Unregistered Securities Offerings, 2009–2017, SEC Division of Economic Risk and Analysis 13–14 (Aug. 2018). More recently, the SEC reported that, for Regulation D offerings in 2019, $1,558 billion (99.99%) was raised under Rule 506, while only $0.23 billion was raised under Rule 504. See Securities Act Release No. 10763, at 9 (Mar. 4, 2020).

Securities Act Release No. 6455
Securities and Exchange Commission.
March 3, 1983.

Interpretive Release on Regulation D

* * *

[The bracketed language in this Release reflects updates or other changes made by the Editors.]

1. General

The definition of "accredited investor" includes any person who comes within or "who the issuer reasonably believes" comes within one of the enumerated categories "at the time of the sale of the securities to that person." What constitutes "reasonable" belief will depend on the facts of each particular case. For this reason, the staff generally will not be in a position to express views or otherwise endorse any one method for ascertaining whether an investor is accredited.

(1) *Question:* A director of a corporate issuer purchases securities offered under Rule [506]. Two weeks after the purchase, and prior to completion of the offering, the director resigns due to a sudden illness. Is the former director an accredited investor?

Answer: Yes. The preliminary language to Rule 501(a) provides that an investor is accredited if he falls into one of the enumerated categories "at the time of the sale of securities to that person." One such category includes directors of the issuer. See Rule 501(a)(4). The investor in this case had that status at the time of the sale to him.

2. Certain Institutional Investors—Rules 501(a)(1)–(3)

(2) *Question:* A national bank purchases $100,000 of securities from a Regulation D issuer and distributes the securities equally among ten trust accounts for which it acts as trustee. Is the bank an accredited investor?

Answer: Yes. Rule 501(a)(1) accredits a bank acting in a fiduciary capacity.

(3) *Question:* An ERISA employee benefit plan will purchase $200,000 of the securities being offered. The plan has less than $5,000,000 in total assets and its investment decisions are made by a plan trustee who is not a bank, insurance company, or registered investment adviser. Does the plan qualify as an accredited investor?

Answer: Not under Rule 501(a)(1). Rule 501(a)(1) accredits an ERISA plan that has a plan fiduciary which is a bank, [savings and loan association,] insurance company, or registered investment adviser or that has total assets in excess of $5,000,000. [Nor can the plan qualify as an accredited investor under Rule 501(a)(5) or (6). They apply only to natural persons, not juristic persons.] * * *

(5) *Question:* A not-for-profit, tax exempt hospital with total assets of $3,000,000 is purchasing $100,000 of securities in a Regulation D offering. The hospital controls a subsidiary with total assets of $3,000,000. Under generally accepted accounting principles, the hospital may combine its financial statements with that of its subsidiary. Is the hospital accredited?

Answer: Yes, under Rule 501(a)(3). Where the financial statements of the subsidiary may be combined with those of the investor, the assets of the subsidiary may be added to those of the investor in computing total assets for purposes of Rule 501(a)(3).

3. Insiders—Rule 501(a)(4)

(6) *Question:* The executive officer of a parent of the corporate general partner of the issuer is investing in the Regulation D offering. Is that individual an accredited investor?

Answer: Rule 501(a)(4) accredits only the directors and executive officers of the general partner itself. Unless the executive officer of the parent can be deemed an executive officer of the subsidiary, that individual is not an accredited investor.

* * *

5. Natural Persons—Rules 501(a)(5)–(6)

Rules 501(a)(5) and (6) apply only to natural persons. Paragraph (5) accredits any natural person with a net worth at the time of purchase in excess of $1,000,000. . . . [T]he rule permits the use of joint net worth of [a] couple [which may be calculated by reference to the investor and her spouse or spousal equivalent]. Paragraph (6) accredits any natural person whose income has exceeded $200,000 [or joint income with the person's spouse or spousal equivalent has exceeded $300,000] in each of the two most recent years and is reasonably expected to [reach the same income level in the current year.]

(20) *Question:* A corporation with a net worth of $2,000,000 purchases securities in a Regulation D offering. Is the corporation an accredited investor under Rule 501(a)(5)?

Answer: No. Rule 501(a)(5) is limited to "natural" persons.

(21) *Question:* In calculating net worth for purposes of Rule 501(a)(5), may the investor include the estimated fair market value of his principal residence as an asset?

[*Answer:* Pursuant to § 413(a) of the Dodd-Frank Act, the SEC amended the net worth test, when determining accredited investor status, to (i) exclude as an asset the value of an individual's primary residence, (ii) exclude as a liability indebtedness secured by that primary residence (e.g., a mortgage) up to the estimated market value of the primary residence, and (iii) include as a liability indebtedness secured by that primary residence in excess of the estimated market value of the primary residence. See Rule 501(a)(5)(i).]

(22) *Question:* May a purchaser take into account income of a spouse [or spousal equivalent] in determining possible accreditation under Rule 501(a)(6)?

[*Answer:* Yes. An individual who had net income in excess of $200,000 in each of the most recent years or joint income with that person's spouse or spousal equivalent in excess of $300,000 in each of those years, and has a reasonable expectation of reaching the same income level in the current year, qualifies as an accredited investor.]

(23) *Question:* May a purchaser include unrealized capital appreciation in calculating income for purposes of Rule 501(a)(6)?

Answer: Generally, no.

6. Entities Owned By Accredited Investors—Rule 501(a)(8)

Any entity in which all equity owners are accredited investors under any of the qualifying categories is accredited under Rule 501(a)(8).

(24) *Question:* All but one of the shareholders of a corporation are accredited investors by virtue of net worth or income. The unaccredited shareholder is a director who bought one share of stock in order to comply with a requirement that all directors be shareholders of the corporation. Is the corporation an accredited investor under Rule 501(a)(8)?

Answer: No. Rule 501(a)(8) requires "all of the equity owners" to be accredited investors. The director is an equity owner and is not accredited. Note that the director cannot be accredited under Rule 501(a)(4). That provision extends accreditation to a director of the issuer, not of the investor.

(25) *Question:* Who are the equity owners of a limited partnership?

Answer: The limited partners.

* * *

(30) *Question:* May a trust be accredited under Rule 501(a)(8) if all of its beneficiaries are accredited investors?

Answer: Generally, no. Rule 501(a)(8) accredits any entity if all of its "equity owners" are accredited investors. The staff does not interpret this provision to apply to the beneficiaries of a conventional trust. The result may be different, however, in the case of certain non-conventional trusts where, as a result of powers retained by the grantors, a trust as a legal entity would be deemed not to exist. Thus, where the grantors of a revocable trust are accredited investors under Rule 501(a)(5) (i.e., net worth exceeds $1,000,000) and the trust may be amended or revoked at any time by the grantors, the trust is accredited because the grantors will be deemed the equity owners of the trust's assets. Similarly, where the purchase of Regulation D securities is made by an Individual Retirement Account and the participant is an accredited investor, the account would be accredited under Rule 501(a)(8).

* * *

C. Executive Officer—Rule 501(f)

The definition of executive officer in Rule 501(f) is the same as that in Rule 405 of Regulation C.

(37) *Question:* The executive officer of the parent of the Regulation D issuer performs a policy making function for its subsidiary. May that individual be deemed an "executive officer" of the subsidiary?

Answer: Yes.

D. Purchaser Representative—Rule [501(i)]

A purchaser representative is any person who satisfies, or who the issuer reasonably believes satisfies, four conditions enumerated in Rule [501(i)]. Beyond the obligations imposed by that rule, any person acting as a purchaser representative must consider whether or not he is required to register as a broker-dealer under section 15 of the Securities Exchange Act of 1934 or as an investment adviser under section 203 of the Investment Advisers Act of 1940.

(38) *Question:* May the officer of a corporate general partner of the issuer qualify as a purchaser representative under Rule [501(i)]?

Answer: Rule [501(i)] provides that "an affiliate, director, officer or other employee of the issuer" may not be a purchaser representative unless the purchaser has one of three enumerated relationships with the representative. The staff is of the view that an officer or director of a corporate general partner comes within the scope of "affiliate, director, officer or other employee of the issuer."

(39) *Question:* May the issuer in a Regulation D offering pay the fees of the purchaser representative?

Answer: Yes. Nothing in Regulation D prohibits the payment by the issuer of the purchaser representative's fees. Rule [501(i)(4)], however, requires disclosure of this fact.

* * *

III. *Operational Conditions*

A. Integration—Rule 502(a)

* * *

(53) *Question:* An issuer conducts offering (A) under Rule 504 of Regulation D that concludes in January. Seven months later the issuer commences offering (B) under Rule 506. During that seven month period the issuer's only offers or sales of securities are under an employee benefit plan (C). Must the issuer integrate (A) and (B)?

Answer: No. Rule 502(a) specifically provides that (A) and (B) will not be integrated. [Regarding the employee benefit plan, see also Rule 701(f).]

B. Calculation of the Number of Purchasers—Rule 501(e)

Rule 501(e) governs the calculation of the number of purchasers in offerings that rely . . . on [Rule 506(b)]. [Rule 506(b)] limit[s] the number of non-accredited investors to 35. Rule 501(e) has [three] parts. The first excludes certain purchasers from the calculation. The second establishes basic principles for counting of corporations, partnerships, or other entities. [The third concerns non-contributory employee benefit plans within the meaning of Title I of ERISA. Such plans are to be counted as one purchaser where the trustee makes all investment decisions for the plan.]

(54) *Question:* One purchaser in a [Rule 506(b)] offering is an accredited investor. Another is a first cousin of that investor sharing the same principal residence. Each purchaser is making his own investment decision. How must the issuer count these purchasers for purposes of meeting the 35 purchaser limitation?

Answer: The issuer is not required to count either investor. The accredited investor may be excluded under Rule 501(e)(1)(iv), and the first cousin may then be excluded under Rule 501(e)(1)(i).

(55) *Question:* An accredited investor in a Rule [506(b)] offering will have the securities she acquires placed in her name and that of her spouse. The spouse will not make an investment decision with respect to the acquisition. How many purchasers will be involved?

Answer: The accredited investor may be excluded from the count under Rule 501(e)(1)(iv) and the spouse may be excluded under Rule 501(e)(1)(i). The issuer may also take the position, however, that the spouse should not be deemed a purchaser at all because he did not make any investment decision, and because the placement of the securities in joint name may simply be a tax or estate planning technique.

(56) *Question:* An offering is conducted in the United States under Rule [506(b)]. At the same time certain sales are made overseas. Must the foreign investors be included in calculating the number of purchasers?

Answer: Offers and sales of securities to foreign persons made outside the United States in such a way that the securities come to rest abroad generally do not need to be registered under the Act. This basis for non-registration is separate from Regulation D and offers and sales relying on this interpretation are not required to be integrated with a coincident domestic offering. Thus, assuming the sales in this question rely on this interpretation, foreign investors would not be counted. [See also Regulation S and Rule 500(g) of Regulation D.]

(57) *Question:* An investor in a Rule 506 offering is a general partnership that was not organized for the specific purpose of acquiring the securities offered. The partnership has ten partners, five of whom do not qualify as accredited investors. The partnership will make an investment of $100,000. How is the partnership counted and must the issuer make any findings as to the sophistication of the individual partners?

Answer: Rule 501(e)(2) provides that the partnership shall be counted as one purchaser. The issuer is not obligated to consider the sophistication of each individual partner.

* * *

(59) *Question:* An investor in a Rule 506 offering is an investment partnership that is not accredited under Rule 501(a)(8). Although the partnership was organized two years earlier and has made investments in a number of offerings, not all the partners have participated in each investment. With each proposed investment by the partnership, individual partners have received a copy of the disclosure document and have made a decision whether or not to participate. How do the provisions of Regulation D apply to the partnership as an investor?

Answer: The partnership may not be treated as a single purchaser. Rule 501(e)(2) provides that if the partnership is organized for the specific purpose of acquiring the securities offered, then each beneficial owner of equity interests should be counted as a separate purchaser. Because the individual partners elect whether or not to participate in each investment, the partnership is deemed to be reorganized for the specific purpose of acquiring the securities in each investment. Thus, the issuer must look through the partnership to the partners participating in the investment. The issuer must satisfy the conditions of Rule 506 as to each partner.

C. Manner of Offering—Rule 502(c)

* * *

In analyzing what constitutes a general solicitation, the staff considered a solicitation by the general partner of a limited partnership to limited partners in other active programs sponsored by the same general partner. In determining that this did not constitute a general solicitation the Division underscored the existence and substance of the pre-existing business relationship between the general partner and those being solicited. The general partner represented that it believed each of the solicitees had such knowledge and experience in financial and business matters that he or she was capable of evaluating the merits and risks of the prospective investment. . . .

(60) *Question:* If a solicitation were limited to accredited investors, would it be deemed in compliance with Rule 502(c)?

Answer: The mere fact that a solicitation is directed only to accredited investors will not mean that the solicitation is in compliance with Rule 502(c). Rule 502(c) relates to the nature of the offering not the nature of the offerees.

D. Limitations on Resale—Rule 502(d)

Rule 502(d) makes it clear that Regulation D securities have limitations on transferability and requires that the issuer take certain precautions to restrict the transferability of the securities.

(61) *Question:* An investor in a Regulation D offering wishes to resell his securities within [six months] after the offering. The issuer has agreed to

register the securities for resale. Will the proposed resale under the registration statement violate Rule 502(d)?

Answer: No. The function of Rule 502(d) is to restrict the unregistered resale of securities. Where the resale will be registered, however, such restrictions are unnecessary.

IV. *Exemptions*

A. Rule 504

Rule 504 is an exemption under section 3(b) of the Securities Act available to non-reporting and non-investment companies [and issuers that are not a development stage company that either has no specific business plan or purpose or has indicated that its business plan is to engage in a merger or acquisition with an unidentified company or companies, or other entity or person] for offerings not in excess of [$5,000,000].

* * *

(63) *Question:* An issuer proposes to make an offering under Rule 504 in two states. The offering will be registered in one state and the issuer will deliver a disclosure document pursuant to the state's requirements. The offering will be made pursuant to an exemption from registration in the second state. Must the offering satisfy the limitations on the manner of offering and on resale in paragraphs (c) and (d) of Rule 502?

Answer: An offering under Rule 504 is exempted from the manner of sale and resale limitations ... if it is registered in *each* state in which it is conducted and ... if a disclosure document is required by state law. [Note, however, Rule 504(b) also permits the issuer to escape the general solicitation prohibition of Rule 502(c) and the limitations on resale of Rule 502(d) if the offering is made (i) in one or more states that do not provide for the registration of securities or the public filing or delivery of a disclosure document before sale, if the securities have been registered in a state that does provide for such registration, public filing, and delivery, and offers and sales are made in accordance with such provisions, and the disclosure document is delivered before sale to all purchasers (including those in states that have no such procedure); or (ii) exclusively according to a state law exemption that permits general solicitation and general advertising so long as sales are made only to accredited investors.]

(64) *Question:* The state in which the offering will take place provides for "qualification" of any offer or sale of securities. The state statute also provides that the securities commissioner may condition qualification of an offering on the delivery of a disclosure document prior to sale. Would the issuer be making its offering in a state that "provides for [the] registration of the securities, and require[s] the [public filing and] delivery [to investors] of a [substantive] disclosure document before sale" if its offering were qualified in this state on the condition that it deliver a disclosure document before sale to each investor?

Answer: Yes.

(65) *Question:* If an issuer is registering securities at the state level, are there any specific requirements as to resales outside of that state if the issuer is attempting to come within the provision in Rule 504 that waives the limitations on the manner of offering and on resale in Rules 502(c) and (d)?

Answer: No. The issuer, however, must intend to use Rule 504 to make bona fide sales in that state and not to evade the policy of Rule 504 by using sales in one state as a conduit for sales into another state. *See* [Rule 500(f).]

* * *

C. Questions Relating to [Rule 504]

... [Rule 504(b)(2)] require[s] that the offering not exceed a specified aggregate offering price. The allowed aggregate offering price, however, is reduced by the aggregate offering price for all securities sold within the last twelve months in reliance on [Rule 504] or in violation of section 5(a) of the Securities Act.

(67) *Question:* An issuer preparing to conduct an offering of equity securities under [Rule 504] raised $2,000,000 from the sale of debt instruments under [Rule 504] eight months earlier. How much may the issuer raise in the proposed equity offering?

Answer: $3,000,000. A specific condition to the availability of [Rule 504] for the proposed offering is that its aggregate offering price not exceed $5,000,000 less the [aggregate offering price] for *all* securities sold under [Rule 504] [or in violation of § 5(a) of the 1933 Act] within the last 12 months.

(68) *Question:* An issuer is planning a [Rule 504] offering. Ten months earlier the issuer conducted a Rule 506 offering. Must the issuer consider the previous Rule 506 offering when calculating the allowable aggregate offering price for the proposed [Rule 504] offering?

Answer: No. The Commission issued Rule 506 under section 4(2), and [Rule 504(b)(2)] requires that the aggregate offering price be reduced by previous sales under [Rule 504] [or in violation of § 5(a) of the 1933 Act].

(69) *Question:* Seven months before a proposed Rule 504 offering the issuer conducted a rescission offer under Rule 504. The rescission offer was for securities that were sold in violation of section 5 more than 12 months before the proposed Rule 504 offering. Must the aggregate offering price for the proposed Rule 504 offering be reduced either by the amount of the rescission offer or the earlier offering in violation of section 5?

Answer: No. The offering in violation of section 5 took place more than 12 months earlier and thus is not required to be included when satisfying the limitation in [Rule 504(b)(2)]. The staff is of the view that the rescission offer relates back to the earlier offering and therefore should not be included as an adjustment to the aggregate offering price for the proposed Rule 504 offering.

(70) *Question:* [Rule 504] contain[s] examples as to the calculation of the allowed aggregate offering price for a particular offering. Do these examples contemplate integration of the offerings described?

Answer: No. The examples have been provided to demonstrate the operation of the limitation on the aggregate offering price in the absence of any integration questions.

* * *

A. "General Solicitation or General Advertising" Under Regulation D

Rule 502(c) limits the manner in which securities may be offered or sold pursuant to Regulation D. First, in most cases, general solicitation or general advertising will be fatal to the § 4(a)(2) exemption. This is also true in the case of Rule 506(b) under Regulation D. Second, in accordance with § 4(b) of the 1933 Act, as amended by the JOBS Act, general solicitation or general advertising subject to Rule 506(c) under Regulation D is permissible if the issuer takes "reasonable steps to verify" that the purchasers are accredited investors.

The net effect is to force practitioners to focus (in different contexts) on two issues: (1) When does a communication result in general solicitation or general advertising (sometimes jointly referred to as "general solicitation")?; and (2) If a general solicitation is used, what "reasonable steps" must an issuer or its agent take to verify that all purchasers are accredited investors?

    a. General Solicitation or General Advertising. Clearly, a T.V., radio, or newspaper advertisement is a general solicitation or general advertising. But what about emails sent to all the members of a country club to which the promoter belongs? Or to all fellow owners in the promoter's co-op? In such closer cases, the SEC's staff has long stressed the need for a pre-existing relationship between the issuer (or broker acting on its behalf) and the offeree for the communication not to amount to a general solicitation. When the solicitation has been broader, and with only a general economic or professional status used to filter out the general public, the SEC has tended to find a general solicitation. For example, in In the Matter of Kenman Corp.,[24] a broker-dealer solicited investors for a limited partnership offering, in part by using (1) a list of officers at 50 Fortune 500 companies, (2) a list of physicians in California, (3) a list of persons who had previously invested $10,000 or more in real estate offerings syndicated by other broker-dealers, (4) a list of managerial employees at Hughes Aircraft Company, and (5) a list of company presidents of firms based in Morris County, New Jersey. On

---

[24] See Exchange Act Release No. 21962 (Apr. 19, 1985).

this basis, where neither the issuer nor the broker had a prior relationship with the potential investors, and little, if anything, connected the persons on these lists, the SEC concluded a general solicitation had occurred.[25]

Courts have had little difficulty finding the mass mailing of a "confidential memorandum" to 2,500 persons to constitute a general solicitation.[26] Grayer issues emerge when a communication describing an offering is sent to a smaller and more targeted audience. Given that the SEC's staff attempts to distinguish "limited" from "general" communications in terms of whether the issuer or its agent had some preexisting relationship with the recipient of the communication, the obvious next question is: What counts as a pre-existing relationship? The SEC's staff takes the position that the relationship should enable the issuer or its agent "to be aware of the financial circumstances or sophistication of the persons with whom the relationship exists. . . ."[27]

Read literally, Rule 502(c) prohibits general solicitation and general advertising by the issuer or any person acting on its behalf. But what if a third party publishes a newsletter that discusses all forthcoming private placements? One SEC no-action letter addressed such a case and could not conclude a general solicitation had not occurred, although a critical factor may have been that the issuers prepared the materials used in the newsletter and paid for their publication.[28] A different result was reached in the case of matching services, where both investors and

---

[25] It is not uncommon for startup incubators, universities, and others involved in early-stage businesses to hold "demo days" that permit startups to profile themselves to prospective investors. Are demo days (or invitations to demo days) a "general solicitation"? To clarify this, the SEC has proposed new Rule 148, which would provide that certain demo day communications will not be deemed to be a general solicitation or general advertising. For these purposes, a "demo day" means a seminar or meeting by a college, university, or other institution of higher education, a local government, a nonprofit organization, or an "angel investor group," incubator, or accelerator. The sponsor is not permitted to make investment recommendations or provide investment advice to attendees of the event; engage in any investment negotiations between the issuer and investors attending the event; charge attendees of the event any fees, other than reasonable administrative fees; receive any compensation for making introductions between attendees and issuers, or for investment negotiations between the parties; or receive any compensation with respect to the event that would require it to register as a broker-dealer or investment adviser. Advertising for the event cannot reference any specific offering of securities by an issuer, and information conveyed at the event regarding the offering of securities by the issuer must be limited. See Securities Act Release No. 10763 (Mar. 4, 2020).

[26] See Johnston v. Bumba, 764 F.Supp. 1263 (N.D.Ill.1991). See also Myer v. Ward, 2017 WL 6733726 (comparing the facts to *Johnston*); Nolfi v. Ohio Kentucky Oil Corp., No. 5:06CV260, 2008 WL 2048014 at *7 (N.D. Ohio May 12, 2008), aff'd sub nom. Fencorp Co. v. Ohio Kentucky Oil Corp., 675 F.3d 933 (6th Cir. 2012) (describing scenarios that may or may not constitute a general solicitation); In re KCD Financial Inc., SEC Opinion 34–80340, Mar. 29, 2017 (when determining if there is a solicitation, the dispositive issue is whether all offerees, and not just all purchasers, had a pre-existing substantive relationship with the issuer or its agent).

[27] See Mineral Lands Research & Marketing Corp., SEC No-Action Letter (Dec. 4, 1985). In this no-action request, an issuer proposed to offer securities to 600 persons who were clients of an insurance broker who was also an officer of the issuer. Since these facts alone were an insufficient basis to judge whether the required pre-existing relationship existed, the SEC staff concluded it could not grant the requested no-action relief.

[28] See J.D. Manning, Inc. SEC No-Action Letter (Feb. 27, 1986).

entrepreneurs paid to learn of transactions or investors who met their stated criteria. In a 1994 no-action letter, the SEC's staff found that a general solicitation had not occurred where a nonprofit corporation maintained a computerized database that sought to match investors with investment opportunities.[29] This system, however, did not inform the issuers of the names of potential investors, but only notified investors of the forthcoming offerings that seemed of interest to them. Also, all investors were required to represent that they were accredited investors or otherwise experienced in financial matters.[30]

Logically, it was but a small leap from such a computerized databank to the internet. Initially, however, the SEC seemed skeptical about using the internet to reach investors. In an important 1995 release, it said:

> The placing of [offering] materials on the Internet would not be consistent with the prohibitions against general solicitation in Rule 502(c) of Regulation D.[31]

More recently, and after some prodding, the SEC's staff has become more internet-friendly. The critical step has been the development of a password-protected procedure to qualify the potential offeree as an accredited investor before an offer is made.[32] Typically, a broker-dealer or other agent of the issuer places an investor questionnaire on its internet home page. Investors who complete this questionnaire are evaluated to determine if they qualify as an accredited investor. If they do, they are given a password to review any current and future private placement offering materials on the site. In effect, this new methodology permits a solicitation of accredited investors who volunteer to be solicited.

Some commentators argued that the SEC's continued insistence on determining whether a general solicitation has occurred is inconsistent with Regulation D's primary emphasis on the sophistication of the actual purchasers.[33] To a degree, the SEC listened. In 1987, it requested comment on whether it should narrow the scope of its prohibition on general solicitation,[34] and in 1992, it amended Regulation D to remove

---

[29] See Texas Capital Network, Inc., SEC No-Action Letter (Feb. 23, 1994); see also The Colorado Capital Alliance, Inc., SEC No-Action Letter, 1995 SEC No-Act. LEXIS 503 (May 4, 1995); Michigan Growth Capital Symposium, SEC No-Action Letter, 1995 SEC No-Act. LEXIS 499 (May 4, 1995) (University of Michigan annual symposium to match investors and entrepreneurs did not amount to a general solicitation).

[30] The no-action letter noted, however, that even if an investor participated in the network, it "would not relieve a participating entrepreneur from, nor be a substitute for, the required independent evaluation of an investor's accreditation or sophistication." Texas Capital Network, Inc., SEC No-Action Letter (Feb. 23, 1994).

[31] See Securities Act Release No. 7233, at example 20 (Oct. 13, 1995).

[32] See IPONET SEC No-Action Letter, 1996 SEC No-Act. LEXIS 642 (Jul. 26, 1996); see also Lamp Technologies, Inc., SEC No-Action Letter, 1997 SEC No-Act. LEXIS 638 (May 29, 1997).

[33] See Sargent, The New Regulation D: Deregulation, Federalism, and the Dynamics of Regulatory Reform, 68 Wash. U. L. Q. 225 (1990); Daugherty, Rethinking the Ban on General Solicitation, 38 Emory L.J. 67 (1989).

[34] See Securities Act Release No. 6683 (Jan. 16, 1987).

Rule 502(c)'s prohibition on general solicitation in the case of Rule 504 offerings. In 1994, it adopted new Rule 135c, which is discussed below. Then, in 1995, the SEC indicated it was considering removing or scaling back Rule 502(c) and requested comments on the proposal.[35] Instead, it adopted Regulation CE (Rule 1001), which applies only to California offerings (and is discussed later in this chapter). Next, in 2007, the Commission proposed, but never adopted, a new category—"large accredited investors," basically comprised of institutional investors—to whom limited advertising would be permitted.[36]

This to-ing and fro-ing came to an end with Title II of the JOBS Act, which directed the SEC to do what it had long considered, but never quite been willing to do—namely, eliminate the ban on general solicitation and advertising for certain offerings. In 2013, the SEC implemented this provision with a bifurcated approach, either requiring an issuer to avoid a general solicitation (Rule 506(b)) or to take reasonable steps to verify that purchasers in an offering involving a general solicitation or general advertising are accredited investors (Rule 506(c)).[37] In offerings outside Rule 506(c), a general solicitation or general advertising remains fatal to any private placement exemption.

b. *"Reasonable Steps to Verify."* It is important to note that the definition of "accredited investor" includes "any person . . . who the issuer *reasonably believes* comes within any of the [enumerated] categories" (emphasis added). Rule 501(a) relaxed the standards applicable to assessing a purchaser's qualifications, compared to what was judicially required of offerees under § 4(a)(2). In other words, an investor may not actually fall within one of Rule 501(a)'s categories of accredited investor, but in light of the "reasonable belief" standard in determining whether a purchaser is an accredited investor, that purchaser may still qualify as an accredited investor for purposes of the Regulation D exemption. This reflects, in part, the possibility that a person could provide false or misleading information or documentation to an issuer.

Rule 501(a) does not specify what an issuer must do to establish its "reasonable belief," reflecting the need for flexibility in assessing whether a purchaser is accredited—but keeping in mind that the burden of showing compliance with Regulation D remains with the issuer. What does "reasonable belief" require? In Mark v. FSC Securities Corp.,[38] the

---

[35] See Securities Act Release No. 7285 (May 1, 1994) (Commission determined to defer "action on the general solicitation question"); Securities Act Release No. 7314 (Jul. 25, 1994) (Commission requested comments on whether the general solicitation prohibitions should be scaled back).

[36] See Securities Act Release No. 8828 (Aug. 3, 2007).

[37] See Securities Act Release No. 9415 (Jul. 10, 2013).

[38] 870 F.2d 331 (6th Cir. 1989); see also SEC v. Loomis, 969 F.Supp.2d 1226 (E.D. Cal. 2013) (holding that the issuer violated Rule 506 when its offering memorandum to potential investors mentioned securities were only available to accredited investors, but never affirmatively investigated whether purchasers were actually accredited investors); SEC v. Credit First Fund, LP, 2006 WL 4729240, at *13 (C.D. Cal. Feb. 13, 2006) (holding that a blank

defendant broker-dealer circulated a subscription letter to investors in which they were asked to represent they had "sufficient knowledge and experience in business affairs to enable [them] to evaluate the risks of the investment" and provided them with an offeree questionnaire to set forth their investment background. Although the Sixth Circuit acknowledged that a review of each executed subscription agreement could have provided the issuer with a "reasonable belief" sufficient to satisfy Rule 506, it found that only a general awareness of these procedures and the investors' representations was insufficient. In short, evidence as to "the circumstances under which those sales were intended to have been made" was not enough.[39] Having shown nothing more, the issuer failed its burden of proving the exemption's availability.

Rule 506(c) steps beyond Rule 501(a)'s "reasonable belief" standard, requiring the issuer to "take reasonable steps to verify" that a purchaser is accredited. This "reasonable steps" approach incorporates a "principles-based" method for verification of accredited investor status as well as a non-exclusive list of verification methods. The additional requirement, in part, reflected concerns that, by not prohibiting a general solicitation or general advertising, the offering could become available to unaccredited investors or result in fraud.

The principles-based method of verification requires an objective determination by the issuer (or those acting on its behalf) as to whether the steps taken are "reasonable" in the context of the particular facts and circumstances of each purchaser and transaction. Rule 506(c) also includes a non-exclusive list of verification methods that issuers may but are not required to use when seeking to satisfy the verification requirement but only with respect to natural person purchasers.

With the principles-based approach, the SEC wished to provide flexibility in the verification process but also acknowledged the need for some additional guidance:[40]

> ... [W]e are adopting as a condition of new Rule 506(c) the requirement that issuers take "reasonable steps to verify" that purchasers of the offered securities are accredited investors. This requirement is separate from and independent of the requirement that sales be limited to accredited investors, and must be satisfied even if all purchasers happen to be accredited investors. We are also including in Rule 506(c) a nonexclusive list of methods that issuers may use to satisfy the verification requirement. As discussed above, a number of commenters urged the Commission to provide greater certainty for issuers that the verification requirement has been satisfied by providing a non-exclusive list of methods for verifying the

---

copy questionnaire did not support defendant's alleged reasonable belief of investors' sophistication).

[39] 870 F.2d at 337.
[40] Id.

accredited investor status of purchasers in Rule 506(c) offerings. Upon further consideration, we have concluded that a general requirement that issuers take "reasonable steps to verify" that the purchasers are accredited investors, combined with a non-exclusive list of verification methods that are deemed to meet this requirement, would maintain the flexibility of the verification standard while providing additional clarity and certainty that this requirement has been satisfied if one of the specified methods is used. We have specified methods for verifying the accredited investor status of natural persons because we believe that the potential for uncertainty and the risk of participation by non-accredited investors is highest in offerings involving natural persons as purchasers.

* * *

Under Rule 506(c), issuers are required to take reasonable steps to verify the accredited investor status of purchasers. . . .[W]hether the steps taken are "reasonable" will be an objective determination by the issuer (or those acting on its behalf), in the context of the particular facts and circumstances of each purchaser and transaction. Among the factors that issuers should consider under this facts and circumstances analysis are:

- the nature of the purchaser and the type of accredited investor that the purchaser claims to be;
- the amount and type of information that the issuer has about the purchaser; and
- the nature of the offering, such as the manner in which the purchaser was solicited to participate in the offering, and the terms of the offering, such as a minimum investment amount.

. . . [T]hese factors are interconnected and are intended to help guide an issuer in assessing the reasonable likelihood that a purchaser is an accredited investor—which would, in turn, affect the types of steps that would be reasonable to take to verify a purchaser's accredited investor status. After consideration of the facts and circumstances of the purchaser and of the transaction, the more likely it appears that a purchaser qualifies as an accredited investor, the fewer steps the issuer would have to take to verify accredited investor status, and vice versa. For example, if the terms of the offering require a high minimum investment amount and a purchaser is able to meet those terms, then the likelihood of that purchaser satisfying the definition of accredited investor may be sufficiently high such that, absent any facts that indicate that the purchaser is not an accredited investor, it may be reasonable for the issuer to take fewer steps to verify or, in certain cases, no additional steps to verify accredited investor status other than to confirm that the purchaser's cash investment is not being financed by a third party.

* * *

The SEC faced pressure from rival sides as to what would constitute "reasonable steps to verify" a purchaser's status. Consumer groups lobbied the SEC to require actual verification of the investor's status and mandate special disclosures in such offerings (for fear that wealthy, but unsophisticated, investors would be overreached). The financial services industry argued that investors should be able to continue to self-certify that they are accredited investors (with issuers being able to rely on such self-certifications). Predictably, the SEC compromised. Rule 506(c) was drafted so as not to mandate any specific procedure that issuers were required to follow, although reasonable efforts to verify the purchaser's status would still be necessary.

In addition, as noted in the foregoing excerpt, Rule 506(c)(2)(ii) provides a safe harbor for verifying whether a natural person is an accredited investor. Specifically, the issuer can rely (unless it has contrary knowledge) on any of the following four non-exclusive and non-mandatory methods:

(a) a review of Internal Revenue Service forms (including Form W-2) for the two most recent years (to determine if Rule 501(a)(6)'s annual income test is satisfied) plus receipt of "a written representation from the purchaser that he or she has a reasonable expectation of reaching the income level necessary to qualify as an accredited investor during the current year;"

(b) a review of, among other documents, bank or brokerage statements, tax assessments, appraisals by independent third parties, or credit reports (to determine if the investor qualifies as an accredited investor based on Rule 501(a)(5)'s net worth test);

(c) written confirmation by a broker-dealer, investment adviser, licensed attorney, or certified public accountant that "such person or entity has taken reasonable steps to verify that the purchaser is an accredited investor within the prior three months and has determined that such person is an accredited investor;" or

(d) certification from an investor who previously purchased in an offering by the same issuer under Rule 506(b), prior to the effective date of Rule 506(c), and continues to hold such securities, that she qualifies as an accredited investor at the time of sale in the new offering.

Although the SEC has provided guidance on how it will interpret its guidelines,[41] it has also made clear it will not provide specific rulings or issue no-action letters in individual cases.[42]

B. DEVELOPMENTS UNDER REGULATION D

1. *Rule 144.* Securities issued under Regulation D are "restricted securities," as defined in Rule 144(a)(3). Traditionally, under Rule 144, such securities had to be held (with certain limited resales permitted) for at least one year before they could be resold into the public market, subject to the other conditions of Rule 144 being satisfied. As discussed later in this casebook, the current holding period for securities of publicly reporting companies is six months and for non-reporting companies is 12 months. The greater liquidity (and reduced discount) that resulted from shortening the holding period to six months significantly increased the attractiveness of Regulation D and private placements in general.

2. *Adjusting the Definition of "Accredited Investor" for Inflation.* For some time, the SEC has recognized that the $1,000,000 net worth test and the $200,000 and $300,000 income test for defining "accredited investor" have been trivialized by the impact of inflation since Regulation D's adoption in 1982. In 2007, the SEC proposed that these tests be adjusted for inflation and that a new category of individual accredited investor who holds $750,000 in investments be recognized.[43] The financial industry resisted these proposed higher tests, fearing they would restrict the availability of the private placement exemption.

Congress addressed this issue in the Dodd-Frank Act but changed the law only modestly. To address an investor who is "house rich, but cash poor" (for example, a retiree with an expensive home), § 413 of the Act instructed the SEC to exclude the value of a natural person's primary residence from the $1 million net worth test, and authorized the SEC, after a thorough review, to make adjustments to the definition of "accredited investor," but it also directed the SEC not to otherwise modify the $1 million net worth test during the four years following enactment of the Dodd-Frank Act. The change to the net worth test appears in Rule 501(a)(5).[44]

---

[41] See http://www.sec.gov/divisions/corpfin/guidance/securitiesactrules-interps.htm.

[42] The SEC is considering changes to Rule 506(c)'s verification requirement, noting that it may be creating uncertainty for issuers and inadvertently encouraging issuers (and those acting on their behalf) to rely only on the non-exclusive list of verification procedures. Accordingly, the SEC reaffirmed and updated its prior guidance on the principles-based method for verification and, in particular, what may be considered "reasonable steps" to verify an investor's accredited investor status. It also proposed adding a new item to the non-exclusive list of procedures that would allow an issuer to establish that an investor, for which the issuer previously took reasonable steps to verify as an accredited investor, remains an accredited investor as of the time of a subsequent sale if the investor provides a written representation to that effect and the issuer is not aware of information to the contrary. See Securities Act Release No. 10763 (Mar. 4, 2020).

[43] Securities Act Release No. 8828 (Aug. 3, 2007).

[44] See Securities Act Release No. 9177 (Jan. 25, 2011).

The SEC was also instructed to make further periodic reviews of the definition of "accredited investor" "not earlier than 4 years after the date of enactment and not less frequently than once every 4 years thereafter." As a result, the SEC could change the $1 million net worth test and the $200,000/$300,000 income test, although to date, it has shown little inclination to adjust either standard.

3. *"Bad Actor" Disqualification.* Regulation D is unavailable in connection with a sale of securities if any of the following has engaged in certain specified conduct that violates the law (including, but not limited to, the federal securities laws):[45]

(i) an issuer, including any predecessor or affiliated issuer,

(ii) a director, executive officer, or other officer participating in the offering,

(iii) a general partner or managing member of the issuer,

(iv) a beneficial holder of 20% or more of the issuer's outstanding voting equity securities,

(v) any promoter connected with the issuer at the time of sale,

(vi) any investment manager of a pooled investment fund issuer, or any person paid for soliciting purchasers, including any general partner or managing member of an investment manager or solicitor, and

(vii) any director, executive officer, or other officer participating in the offering of any general partner or managing member specified in paragraph (vi).

The prohibition covers persons subject to an SEC or other order imposing restrictions on, and any person or entity convicted of any felony or misdemeanor with respect to, the purchase or sale of a security. It also covers any person subject to certain other SEC orders, as well as final orders by the Commodity Futures Trading Commission, any state securities commission, or any state banking or insurance commission that bars such person from associating with a regulated entity. The SEC, however, retains the ability to waive a disqualification under Rule 506(d)(2) (and it has done so, sometimes by a closely divided vote in the case of some major banks). Consequently, not only can the issuer be denied the availability of Regulation D if any of its directors or officers falls under a "bad actor" disqualification, but Regulation D can also be lost if any broker-dealer, or any officer or director of a broker-dealer, that is soliciting investors on its behalf is deemed to be a "bad actor."

Rule 262 of Regulation A had long prohibited the use of Regulation A (absent an SEC exemption) with respect to certain "bad actors." Section 926 of the Dodd-Frank Act required the SEC to adopt rules disqualifying

---

[45] The SEC is considering additional changes to the "bad actor" disqualification in Regulation D, as well as in Regulation A and Regulation Crowdfunding, including changes that will further conform the Regulation D, Regulation A, and Regulation Crowdfunding disqualifications. See Securities Act Release No. 10763 (Mar. 4, 2020).

felons and other "bad actors" from relying on Rule 506, and the SEC complied by adding new Rule 506(d) (which went beyond Rule 262 at the time, although Rule 262 and Rule 506(d) are now largely consistent).

The "bad actor" disqualification was adopted at the same time the SEC adopted Rule 506(c). Reflecting concerns that the ability to undertake a general solicitation or general advertising under Rule 506(c) could increase the risk of fraud, the SEC noted that part of its motivation in crafting a bad actor disqualification was to "preserv[e] the integrity of the Rule 506(c) market and minimiz[e] the incidence of fraud.... We are adopting today the bad actor disqualification for Rule 506 offerings mandated by the Dodd-Frank Act, which may address some of those concerns."[46] The Dodd-Frank Act did not address Rule 504, but the SEC extended the same disqualifying provisions in Rule 504(b)(3).

4. *Rule 503*. Initially, Regulation D's availability was conditioned on the filing of a Form D within 15 days after the first sale of securities under Regulation D. In 1989, the SEC adopted Rule 507 and changed the language of Rule 503. The net effect is that Regulation D's availability is now denied by Rule 507 for failing to file a Form D only if there has been an injunction enjoining the issuer (or a predecessor or affiliate) for failing to comply with Rule 503. Even then, the issuer can seek relief from the Commission "upon a showing of good cause" that the exemption should not be denied.

In February 2008, Securities Act Release No. 8891 mandated that Form D be filed electronically. This response was an indirect rebuff to commentators who had requested that the Form D filing requirement be eliminated entirely. At the same time, the SEC amended Form D to require additional disclosures about brokerage rates practices and compensation. Also, a minor amendment was made to Rule 502(c)(2) to create a safe harbor for the Form D filing (which, after being electronically filed, is publicly accessible on the Commission's website) from the prohibition against general solicitation and general advertising. Modest as these changes were, they implied that the Commission was not ready to consider more significant revisions that had been proposed.

Nevertheless, the SEC periodically revisits Rule 503's notice requirement. Most recently, in 2013, the SEC proposed additional disclosures on Form D for Rule 506(c) offerings.[47] Under the proposal, Rule 507 would also be amended to disqualify issuers and affiliates who failed to comply with the new Form D requirements, thereby making the filing of a Form D truly mandatory. The SEC did not act on these (and other related) proposals.

5. *Rule 508*. Rule 508 responded to the securities bar's repeated request for an "innocent and immaterial" defense to asserted violations of Regulation D. Those favoring the defense argued that Regulation D's

---

[46] Securities Act Release No. 9415 (Jul. 10, 2013).
[47] See Securities Act Release No. 9416 (Jul. 10, 2013).

complexity made "innocent" mistakes likely. The SEC's staff had long resisted this defense before it was adopted in 1989. Although Rule 508 expresses a new and forgiving SEC approach to minor transgressions, Rule 508 has clear boundaries. In particular, the conditions in Regulation D relating to general solicitation and general advertising (Rule 502(c)), Rule 504's dollar ceiling (Rule 504(b)(2)), and Rule 506(b)'s numerical purchaser limit (Rule 506(b)(2)(i)) are expressly placed beyond the scope of this defense. As a result, such errors or misjudgments can seemingly never be deemed immaterial. Should this imply that the other conditions are less important?

6. *Fraud and Rule 504.* Rule 504 has long been thought to invite fraud because it permits (1) issuers to sell freely tradeable securities, (2) to an unlimited number of purchasers, (3) through a general solicitation of investors. Hence, small, non-reporting "penny stock" issuers could market their offerings to the world under Rule 504 (currently, up to a 12-month $5 million aggregate ceiling) and not experience the same liquidity discount that investors would impose on "restricted securities" sold under Rule 506 (which securities cannot be freely resold, typically until the 6-month or one year holding period under Rule 144 has expired[48]).

After a series of fraudulent transactions in the late 1990s involving "microcap companies," the SEC amended Rule 504 by conditioning its availability for public offerings on the existence of state regulation over the offering.[49] Rule 504(b) now permits the issuer to escape the general solicitation prohibition of Rule 502(c) and the limitations on resale of Rule 502(d) only if the offering is made (i) exclusively in one or more states that provide for the registration of the securities under state law and require the public filing and delivery of a "substantive disclosure document" (i.e., a prospectus); (ii) in one or more states that do not provide for the registration of securities or the public filing or delivery of a disclosure document before sale, if the securities have been registered in a state that does provide for such registration, public filing, and delivery, and offers and sales are made in accordance with such provisions, and the disclosure document is delivered before sale to all purchasers (including those in states that have no such procedure); or (iii) exclusively according to a state law exemption that permits general solicitation and general advertising so long as sales are made only to accredited investors.

The Commission opted not to follow an earlier proposal to make Rule 504 securities "restricted securities" and, thus, not freely tradeable. It justified its compromise as "an effective way to combat the abuses we have described and at the same time preserve the ability of legitimate small businesses to raise capital."[50] If the Commission had restricted

---

[48] The resale exemption provided by Rule 144 under the 1933 Act is discussed later in this casebook.

[49] See Securities Act Release No. 7644 (Feb. 25, 1999).

[50] Id.

resales under Rule 504, it (and many smaller companies) feared that firms relying on Rule 504 would only be able to raise capital at a significant discount below what could be obtained if the securities were freely tradeable. Today, if an issuer does not register its securities in a qualifying state,[51] it can still use Rule 504, but under Rule 504(b), it may not make a general solicitation or general advertising and must advise purchasers they are buying "restricted securities."

7. *Rule 135c.* Rule 502(c) provides "that publication by an issuer of a notice in accordance with Rule 135c ... shall not be deemed to constitute general solicitation or general advertising for purposes of this rule." Rule 135c permits a reporting company (and certain foreign issuers) to publicly announce that it proposes to make, is making, or has made an unregistered offering. Its rationale is that public companies must inform their shareholders of important activities, and a total ban on disclosing any unregistered offerings would deny them material information. Although the Rule has no relevance to small, non-public issuers, public companies that make an unregistered offering may disclose it in a manner similar to what they can disclose under Rule 135 when proposing to make a registered public offering.

8. *Blue Sky Exemptions and the ULOE.* As noted earlier, one advantage of a Rule 506 offering is that the securities are "covered securities" under § 18(b) of the 1933 Act and, thus, are exempt from state registration and qualification requirements.

Section 18(b)(4)(F) includes as a "covered security" any security exempt from § 5 under "Commission rules or regulations issued under section 4(a)(2)." Since Rule 506 (unlike Rule 504) relies on § 4(a)(2) of the 1933 Act, § 18 preempts state registration and qualification requirements for securities sold under that Rule. Section 18(b)(4)(F), however, permits a state to require a "notice filing" to the extent such a requirement was in effect on September 1, 1996.

If a security is not exempt by § 18, the SEC and the North American Securities Administrators Association, Inc. ("NASAA")[52] have established special procedures to coordinate state and federal standards. Specifically, the NASAA has adopted a Uniform Limited Offering Exemption ("ULOE") for enactment at the state level. The ULOE was expressly contemplated by § 19(d) of the 1933 Act, which Congress passed in 1980.[53] The ULOE exempts any offering from state registration if it complies with Rule 505 (which the SEC has since rescinded) or Rule

---

[51] The vast majority of states require registration of Rule 504 offerings, although New York and the District of Columbia do not. See Securities Act Release No. 7644 at n. 12 (Feb. 25, 1999).

[52] The NASAA is a voluntary organization that represents state and provincial securities regulators in the United States (including its territories and districts), Canada, and Mexico.

[53] Section 19(d) of the 1933 Act authorizes the SEC to "cooperate" with the NASAA to achieve "greater uniformity in Federal-State securities matters." The ULOE was an outgrowth of that cooperation. Nonetheless, in 1996, Congress decided to largely preempt state registration requirements by adding § 18 to the 1933 Act.

506, so long as certain additional conditions are met. Virtually every state has adopted some form of non-public limited offering exemption, thereby eliminating duplicative regulation of small issues at the state level.[54]

The ULOE also has certain limitations not contained in Regulation D (for example, it restricts the commissions that can be paid to brokers or sales agents). More importantly, it includes a suitability standard for sales to non-accredited investors, which requires that the investment be "suitable for the purchaser upon the basis of the facts, if any, disclosed by the purchaser as to the purchaser's other security holdings, financial situation and needs." The ULOE then adds that, if the investment does not exceed 10% of the investor's net worth, it is presumed to be suitable. Since the NASAA is a voluntary association, it cannot impose the ULOE on its members, and individual states have modified its requirements, including the suitability standard. Thus, state procedures under the ULOE are far from uniform.[55]

Finally, offerings under Rule 504 are neither "covered securities" under § 18 of the 1933 Act nor do they qualify under the ULOE. Many states, however, have adopted a Small Corporate Offering Registration (known as "SCOR") form, which allows for a simple check-the-box, question-and-answer format for registration. It is not an exemption from state registration but provides a simplified procedure for registering an offering.

2. REGULATION A OFFERINGS

Statutes and Regulations

    Securities Act, § 3(b).

    Regulation A and Forms.

Regulation A (Rules 251 to 263 under the 1933 Act) arises under § 3(b) of the 1933 Act, the "small offering" exemption. Acting under the authority of § 3(b), the SEC has issued regulations that include Regulation A (as well as Rule 504 under Regulation D).

The SEC is authorized under § 3(b)(1) to exempt from § 5 offers and sales of securities (in addition to the other classes exempted by § 3) if it finds that 1933 Act protection "is not necessary in the public interest and for the protection of investors by reason of the small amount involved or the limited character of the public offering." The aggregate amount of securities offered under § 3(b)(1) may not exceed $5 million. Partly to counteract inflation, the JOBS Act amended § 3(b) to add new § 3(b)(2).

---

[54] See Berkeley & Parisi, 1 Securities Law Techniques § 2.06 (2020); Rapp, Blue Sky Regulation of Regulation D Offerings and Private Placements, SU032 ALI-ABA 275 (2013).

[55] See generally Cohn & Yadley, Capital Offense: The SEC's Continuing Failure to Address Small Business Financing Concerns, 4 N.Y.U. J. L. & Bus. 10 (2007).

The new offering ceiling under § 3(b)(2) is $50 million during any 12-month period.[56]

The securities that may be offered under Regulation A are limited to equity securities, debt securities, and debt securities convertible or exchangeable into equity interests, including any guarantees of such securities.[57] For these types of securities, Regulation A provides a "mini-registration" process for U.S. and Canadian companies.[58] It is not available to, among others, "blank check" development companies, investment companies, issuers subject to an SEC order pursuant to § 12(j) of the 1934 Act within the preceding five years, issuers that have not filed with the SEC the ongoing reports required by Regulation A (described below) within the preceding two years, and issuers who are subject to a "bad actor" disqualification.[59] Regulation A's "bad actor" persons and triggering events are substantially the same as those in Regulation D and Regulation Crowdfunding (discussed later in this chapter).[60]

Regulation A has two offering "tiers" that vary based on size and requirements. Aggregate sales in a Tier 1 offering may not exceed $20 million during any 12-month period. A Tier 2 offering may not exceed $50 million during any 12-month period.[61] In addition, secondary sales by affiliates of the issuer can be made up to a maximum of $6 million (of a total of $20 million) for Tier 1 offerings, and up to a maximum of $15 million (of a total of $50 million) for Tier 2 offerings.[62] Secondary sales, in general, cannot exceed 30% of the aggregate offering price in the

---

[56] Section 401 of the JOBS Act amended § 3(b) of the 1933 Act and instructed the SEC in new § 3(b)(2) to "add a class of securities to the securities exempted pursuant to this section" with a ceiling during any 12-month period of $50 million.

[57] See Rule 261(c) under the 1933 Act.

[58] In May 2018, § 508 of the Economic Growth, Regulatory Relief, and Consumer Protection Act directed the SEC to amend Regulation A to permit its use by a publicly reporting company. The SEC amended Regulation A by deleting the prior restriction on use by a company subject to continuous reporting under the 1934 Act. See Economic Growth, Regulatory Relief, and Consumer Protection Act, Pub. L. No. 115–174, § 508, 132 Stat. 1296 (2018).

[59] See Rules 251(b) and 262 under the 1933 Act. The SEC has proposed amending Regulation A to provide that an issuer that is subject to the continuous reporting requirements of § 13 or § 15(d) of the 1934 Act will not be eligible to use Regulation A if the issuer does not file all the required 1934 Act reports during the two years prior to filing a Regulation A offering statement. Under the proposal, if an issuer is delayed in filing a 1934 Act report, it must become current in its reports over the last two years to become eligible to use Regulation A again. See Securities Act Release No. 10763 (Mar. 4, 2020).

[60] Recall that the "bad actor" disqualifications extend beyond the issuer to include its directors, executive officers, and other officers participating in the offering, beneficial holders of 20% or more of the issuer's outstanding voting equity securities, any promoter connected with the issuer at the time of sale, and any person paid for soliciting purchasers. The SEC is considering changes to the "bad actor" disqualification in Regulation D, Regulation A, and Regulation Crowdfunding, including changes that will further conform the Regulation D, Regulation A, and Regulation Crowdfunding disqualifications. See Securities Act Release No. 10763 (Mar. 4, 2020).

[61] Section 401 of the JOBS Act requires the SEC to review the § 3(b)(2) offering limitation every two years. Recently, the SEC proposed raising the maximum Tier 2 offering amount to $75 million and the maximum offering amount for secondary sales to $22.5 million. See Securities Act Release No. 10763 (Mar. 4, 2020).

[62] See Rule 251(a) under the 1933 Act.

issuer's first Regulation A offering or in any subsequent Regulation A offering qualified within one year of the first Regulation A offering.[63]

The basic Regulation A offering process is initiated when a company files an offering statement on Form 1-A with the SEC. The SEC staff can comment on the Form 1-A and require revisions before the offering statement is "qualified" (analogous to being "effective" for a registration statement). Regulation A also provides for delayed or continuous offerings, analogous to a registered shelf, for issuers that are subject to Regulation A's continuous filing requirements (described below).[64] Regulation A issuers may "test the waters," orally or in writing, at any time before the filing or qualification of an offering statement, "to determine whether there is any interest in a contemplated securities offering" (discussed further below).[65]

The offering statement on Form 1-A is not a registration statement for purposes of § 11 of the 1933 Act, although its format resembles a registration statement. The offering statement in a Tier 1 offering need not contain audited financial statements (unless the issuer has audited financial statements); the offering statement in a Tier 2 offering must contain audited financial statements.[66] Just as the registration statement contains a prospectus, the offering statement contains a component known as the "offering circular."[67] Although the offering statement is not subject to § 11, the offering circular and other disclosures made in Regulation A offerings are subject to liability under § 12(a)(2) of the 1933 Act (which essentially is a negligence-based standard).

After filing the offering statement, and before it is qualified, oral offers may be made and written offers may also be made through a preliminary offering circular (in addition to continued "testing the waters").[68] A preliminary offering circular must be provided by issuers not subject to Regulation A's continuing reporting requirements at least 48 hours before sale to any person who indicated an interest in the Regulation A offering.[69]

After SEC review, the Form 1-A offering statement is declared "qualified" by a "notice of qualification." Only after the offering statement has been qualified may the securities be sold.[70] Information relating to offering price, underwriters, amount of proceeds, and other related

---

[63] Id.

[64] See Rule 251(d)(3) under the 1933 Act. See also Rule 253(g) (regarding offering circular supplements).

[65] See Rule 255 under the 1933 Act.

[66] See Part F/S of Form 1-A under the 1933 Act.

[67] See Rule 253 under the 1933 Act.

[68] See Rule 251(d)(1) under the 1933 Act. A preliminary offering circular must contain a "red herring" legend on its cover page. See Rule 254(a) under the 1933 Act.

[69] See Rule 251(d)(2) under the 1933 Act.

[70] Id.

information may be omitted from a qualified offering circular, so long as that information is subsequently filed with the SEC.[71]

Final offering circulars must be delivered by each underwriter or dealer to purchasers within 25 days (if the security is listed on a national securities exchange) or 90 days after qualification of the offering statement. Delivery may be satisfied by a notice that the sale was made pursuant to a qualified offering statement, together with a link to the final offering circular.[72]

The issuer in a Regulation A offering is not required to become a 1934 Act reporting company solely as a result of qualifying an offering statement (unlike an issuer in a registered public offering who must become a reporting company under § 15(d) of the 1934 Act). Regulation A, however, has its own periodic reporting requirements for Tier 2 issuers.[73] Under Regulation A, Tier 2 issuers must file annual, semi-annual, and current reports (but not quarterly reports). The annual reports must include audited financial statements.[74] This is a major difference from Regulation D offerings, where no such ongoing obligation arises.

Securities issued in a Tier 2 offering are not included in determining whether an issuer is subject to § 12(g) of the 1934 Act and, thus, must satisfy the 1934 Act's reporting requirements, so long as the issuer is current in its Regulation A periodic reporting obligations, has hired a transfer agent registered with the SEC under § 17A(c) of the 1934 Act, and has a public float of less than $75 million or, in the absence of a public float, annual revenues of less than $50 million. (Recall that, in general, § 12(g) registration is required if the company has total assets of more than $10 million and a class of equity security held of record by 2,000 persons or 500 persons who are not accredited investors.) An issuer that exceeds the $75 million or $50 million threshold, and as a result, would exceed the § 12(g) thresholds, is granted a two-year transition period (so long as the issuer remains current in its Regulation A periodic reports) before it must include the Regulation A securities in determining whether it must register a class of securities, and satisfy the 1934 Act's reporting requirements, pursuant to § 12(g).[75]

There are two principal advantages of Regulation A over Regulation D. First, securities issued under Regulation A are not "restricted securities" (unlike securities sold under Rule 506) and, thus, they can be freely resold. In fact, shares sold in a Tier 2 offering can list and trade on

---

[71] See Rules 253(b) and (c) under the 1933 Act.

[72] See Rule 251(d)(2). This is consistent with the "access equals delivery" model, where sales are made on the basis of offers conducted during the pre-qualification period and the final offering circular is filed and available on the SEC's website.

[73] A Tier 2 issuer's duty to file reports under Regulation A is deemed to have been met if the issuer becomes a reporting company under § 13 or § 15(d) of the 1934 Act and files the required 1934 Act reports. See Rule 257(b)(6) under the 1933 Act.

[74] See Rule 257(b) under the 1933 Act.

[75] See Rule 12g5–1 under the 1934 Act.

a national securities exchange. Second, Tier 1 offerings may be made to an unlimited number of purchasers, with no cap on the number or minimum qualification of the investors, and Tier 2 offerings that are listed on a national securities exchange also have no limitations[76] (whereas Rule 506(b) imposes a ceiling of 35 sophisticated non-accredited investors to whom sales can be made, and Rule 506(c) requires that all purchasers be accredited investors).

Despite these attractions, Regulation A largely fell into disuse after 2000. There were only three qualified Regulation A offerings in 2010 (compared to over 30,000 Regulation D offerings). The JOBS Act tried to jumpstart Regulation A by raising the ceiling from $5 million up to $50 million.[77] Popularly known as "Regulation A+," it was hoped that the new ceiling would provide a realistic alternative to a Rule 506 offering.

Regulation A could be an attractive means to conduct a smaller IPO, perhaps through the internet, with subsequent trading on a national securities exchange.[78] Alternatively, under Regulation A, a non-reporting issuer can offer and sell securities to public retail investors (which it cannot do under Regulation D), subject to limitations on the amount a non-accredited investor may invest in a Tier 2 offering.[79]

To ease potential issuer concerns around filing a publicly-available offering statement with the SEC, Rule 252(d) permits non-public review by the SEC staff of a draft offering statement prior to public filing if the issuer has never before sold securities under Regulation A or an effective registration statement. Presumably, questions can be resolved before an issuer finds itself obligated to disclose sensitive or competitive information publicly. Moreover, the SEC staff's review of Regulation A offering statements tends to be quicker and less formal than registration statements, and filing fees tend to be less. In addition, as noted earlier, a qualified offering statement is not subject to liability under § 11 of the 1933 Act because an offering statement is not a registration statement. Finally, Rule 256 defines all purchasers in Tier 2 (but not Tier 1) offerings as "qualified purchasers" and, thus, in accordance with § 18 of the 1933

---

[76] If a Tier 2 offering is not listed on a national securities exchange at the time of qualification, sales can only be made to accredited investors or to non-accredited purchasers where the aggregate purchase price is not more than 10% of the greater of such purchaser's annual income or net worth (for natural persons) or revenue or net assets (for a non-natural person). See Rule 251(d)(2)(C) under the 1933 Act.

[77] Although Regulation A offerings climbed, that effort met with only limited success. In 2017, only 78 Regulation A offerings were completed, compared to 37,785 Regulation D offerings. See Bauguess et al., Capital Raising in the U.S.: An Analysis of the Market for Unregistered Securities Offerings, 2009–2017, SEC Division of Economic Risk and Analysis 9, 45 (Aug. 2018).

[78] See Gregg, Regulation A Initial Public Offerings on the Internet: A New Opportunity for Small Businesses, 1 J. Small & Emerging Bus. L 417 (1997).

[79] See Rule 251(d)(2)(C) under the 1933 Act.

Act, preempts state registration and qualification requirements for all Tier 2 offerings.[80]

Issuers, thus, face a tradeoff. Offerings under both Regulation A (Tier 2) and Regulation D are exempt from state registration and qualification requirements. Regulation A offerings can be publicly sold (without restriction on general solicitation or general advertising) to anyone (in the case of Tier 2 securities, if they are listed on a national securities exchange, otherwise only to accredited investors or purchasers subject to a cap on how much they can invest). Securities sold under Regulation A are not "restricted securities," but they require the use of an SEC-reviewed offering statement and potential liability under § 12(a)(2) of the 1933 Act. Tier 2 offerings, unlike under Regulation D, must also include audited financial statements, and they subject the issuer to a continuous reporting obligation (but shareholders who bought in a Tier 2 offering, where the requirements of Rule 12g5–1 under the 1934 Act have been met, will not be counted toward the number of recordholders required to become a reporting company pursuant to § 12(g) of the 1934 Act).

By contrast, Rule 506 offerings can be made publicly only if sales are limited to accredited investors. Sales under Rule 506 may be made to up to 35 non-accredited purchasers, but only if the issuer refrains from general solicitation or general advertising. Regulation D offerings require less disclosure than under Regulation A (if the securities are sold only to accredited investors), and there is no prior SEC review of the disclosure materials. Finally, the disclosures are subject only to Rule 10b–5 (which requires proof of scienter and special pleading standards).

Regulation A contains a "testing the waters" procedure that permits issuers to gauge investor interest before proceeding forward.[81] Under Rule 255, prior to the filing of any offering statement, an issuer may "test the waters" orally or in writing, including through television, radio, the

---

[80] See Rule 256 under the 1933 Act. See also § 18(b)(3) of the 1933 Act (treating securities offered or sold to a qualified purchaser as "covered securities" not subject to state registration or qualification requirements).

[81] The SEC is proposing a new exemption that will permit an issuer to solicit indications of interest in any exempt offering, either orally or in writing, using generic solicitation of interest materials, prior to determining the exemption under which the offering may be conducted. This new exemption, which is substantially based on Rule 255, is proposed to be set forth in new Rule 241. The proposed Rule includes several conditions intended to ensure appropriate investor protections, including requiring materials used under the exemption to bear a specified legend or disclaimer. Depending on the method of dissemination, offers under Rule 241 may be considered a general solicitation. If soliciting generic indications of interest under the proposed Rule is done in a manner that constitutes general solicitation, and the issuer ultimately decides to conduct an unregistered offering under an exemption that does not permit general solicitation, the issuer must analyze whether the generally solicited offer and the subsequent private offering could be integrated, thereby making the exemption unavailable. (In some circumstances, the issuer may be able to rely on one of the new integration safe harbors, also being proposed at the same time as new Rule 241, if it waits 30 days following termination of the generic solicitation of interest before commencing the private offering.) The antifraud provisions of the federal securities laws will apply to the generic solicitations. As proposed, Rule 241 does not provide for the preemption of state securities law registration and qualification requirements. See Securities Act Release No. 10763 (Mar. 4, 2020).

internet, or other means, "to determine whether there is any interest in a contemplated securities offering."[82] The rationale for this procedure is that the preparation of a disclosure document (such as the offering statement) is costly, and incurring those costs may be inadvisable without knowing if there is investor interest.[83] Any written communication under Rule 255(c) "may include a means by which a person may indicate to the issuer that such person is interested in a potential offering," including contact details such as the potential investor's name, address, telephone number, and email address.[84] Money cannot be solicited or accepted, nor is a commitment (binding or otherwise) permitted, until the offering statement has been qualified.[85] Rule 255(a) provides that testing-the-waters communications "are deemed to be an offer of a security for sale for purposes of the antifraud provisions of the federal securities laws." Thus, misstatements or omissions may result in liability under § 12(a)(2) of the 1933 Act or Rule 10b–5 under the 1934 Act.

Although the testing-the-waters rationale is understandable, it is open to some criticism. For example, once an investor reads the testing-the-waters disclosure document and becomes interested, is this investor as likely to read the offering statement? Or, will the latter document simply become a memento of the transaction, drafted in abstruse lawyer-like detail to disclose all risks because it is no longer the principal marketing document?

Regulation A also has a special integration rule. Rule 251(c) precludes the integration of a Regulation A offering with (1) *any* prior offers or sales of securities and (2) later offers or sales that are registered (subject to Rule 255(e), described below), made in compliance with Rule 701 or pursuant to an employee benefit plan, exempt under Regulation S (discussed later in this casebook, but generally covering offers and sales outside the United States) or § 4(a)(6) of the 1933 Act (relating to crowdfunding, discussed later in this chapter), or made more than six months after completion of the Regulation A offering.[86] Thus, an offering pursuant to Regulation D that ended one month before the Regulation A offering commenced will not be integrated with the Regulation A offering. Commentators have suggested that the language of Rule 251(c) provides

---

[82] See Rule 255(a) under the 1933 Act. Any solicitation materials used after publicly filing the offering statement must be preceded or accompanied by a preliminary offering circular or contain a notice informing potential investors where and how the most current preliminary offering circular can be obtained. See Rule 255(b) under the 1933 Act.

[83] See Securities Act Release No. 6949 (Jul. 30, 1992).

[84] This process is analogous to the broker's card exemption in Rule 134(d) under the 1933 Act for registered offerings.

[85] See Rule 255(a) under the 1933 Act.

[86] As noted before, the SEC recently proposed amendments to the integration rules. See Securities Act Release No. 10763 (Mar. 4, 2020). The proposals would establish new Rule 152, which would replace current Rules 152 and 155. New Rule 152 provides a general framework and four safe harbors, replacing the various safe harbors currently set forth in various 1933 Act exemptions.

"two-sided" protection from integration, assuring the issuer both that the Regulation A exemption will not be lost *and* that the exemption for the prior or subsequent offering will also be secure.[87] In addition, the SEC has indicated that concurrent exempt offerings, that take place alongside Regulation A offerings, may be made without integration so long as each offering complies with the requirements of the relevant exemption:

> [A]n offering made in reliance on Regulation A should not be integrated with another exempt offering made by the issuer, provided that each offering complies with the requirements of the exemption that is being relied upon for the particular offering. For example, an issuer conducting a concurrent exempt offering for which general solicitation is not permitted will need to be satisfied that purchasers in that offering were not solicited by means of the offering made in reliance on Regulation A, including without limitation any "testing the waters" communications. Alternatively, an issuer conducting a concurrent exempt offering for which general solicitation is permitted, for example, under Rule 506(c), could not include in any such general solicitation an advertisement of the terms of a Regulation A offering, unless that advertisement also included the necessary legends for, and otherwise complied with, Regulation A.[88]

Although Rule 251(c) clearly provides greater protection than Rule 502(a) for a prior offering, its other principal difference is less obvious: Under Rule 502(a), an offering "made more than six months before the start of a Regulation D offering or . . . made more than six months after completion of a Regulation D offering" will not be integrated "so long as during those six-month periods there are no offers or sales of securities by or for the issuer that are of the same or a similar class as those offered or sold under Regulation D." In other words, the six-month periods must be "clean"—meaning that no offers or sales of the same or a similar class of securities may occur during that period to get the benefit of Rule 502(a)'s safe harbor. Rule 251(c) does not require a "clean" six months. Recall that prior offers and sales of securities are not integrated. Subsequent offers and sales, made more than six months after completion of the Regulation A offering, also are not integrated, even if they are a "dirty" six months (that is, offers or sales of securities occurred during that interval).

After testing the waters, and finding there is substantial investor demand, an issuer may choose to abandon its Regulation A offering in favor of a registered public offering. Pursuant to Rule 255(e), the abandoned offering will not be integrated with the subsequent registered offering if only qualified institutional buyers (as defined in Rule 144A

---

[87] Bradford, Regulation A and the Integration Doctrine: The New Safe Harbor, 55 Ohio St. L.J. 255 (1994).

[88] See Securities Act Release No. 9741 (Mar. 25, 2015).

under the 1933 Act, which is discussed later in this casebook) and institutional accredited investors were solicited. If others were solicited, the abandoned Regulation A offering will still not be subject to integration if the issuer and its agents wait at least 30 days between the last solicitation of interest under Regulation A and the filing of the registration statement with the SEC.[89]

Finally, like Rule 508 of Regulation D, Rule 260 provides that isolated, insignificant failures to comply with Regulation A will not necessarily cause a loss of the exemption. Among other things, the failures to comply must be "insignificant with respect to the offering as a whole, provided that any failure to comply with Rule 251(a) [amounts that can be sold under Regulation A], [Rule 251(b)] [issuer qualifications], and [Rule 251(d)(1)] [when offers can be made] and [Rule 251(d)(3)] [continuous or delayed offerings] are deemed to be significant to the offering as a whole." Those failures do not get the benefit of the Rule 260 safe harbor.[90]

3. INTRASTATE OFFERINGS: SECTION 3(a)(11), RULE 147, AND RULE 147A

Statutes and Regulations

Securities Act, § 3(a)(11).

Rules 147 and 147A.

Section 4 of the 1933 Act provides a list of transaction-based exemptions, while § 3 lists securities that are, themselves, exempt (e.g., most government securities (§ 3(a)(2)) and commercial paper (§ 3(a)(3)). Section 3, however, is deceptive because it also includes exemptions that are transaction-based. The clearest example is § 3(a)(11)'s exemption for offerings limited to a single state or territory. Section 3(b), which is the basis for Rule 504 and Regulation A, is another example.

This section discusses § 3(a)(11) and the Rule 147 safe harbor for the § 3(a)(11) exemption. It also discusses the new intrastate offering exemption in Rule 147A. Although Rules 147 and 147A parallel each other in many ways, Rule 147A falls outside the scope of § 3(a)(11) in two significant respects: It permits issuers to make offers accessible to out-of-state residents, although all sales must be made only to residents of the issuer's state or territory to ensure the intrastate nature of the exemption, and it permits issuers to be incorporated out-of-state so long

---

[89] Note, too, that new Rule 163B under the 1933 Act permits any issuer, or any person authorized to act on its behalf, to engage in oral or written communications with potential investors that are, or are reasonably believed to be, "qualified institutional buyers" or institutional "accredited investors," either prior to or following the filing of a registration statement, to determine whether such investors might have an interest in a contemplated registered securities offering. The rule is non-exclusive, and if offers in an offering were made only to "qualified institutional buyers" or institutional "accredited investors," the issuer may also rely on Rule 163B in proceeding with the registered public offering.

[90] Rule 260(a)(2) under the 1933 Act.

as they can demonstrate the in-state nature of their business. Neither provision is permitted under the express language of § 3(a)(11), but the SEC believed both changes were required by current market practices. Since both changes are outside the statutory limitations of § 3(a)(11), Rule 147A was adopted by the SEC pursuant to its general exemptive authority under § 28 of the 1933 Act.[91] Rule 147 remains consistent with § 3(a)(11)'s requirements.

Regarding offers to out-of-state residents, the SEC was concerned that "offers made over the Internet that can be viewed by a significant number of out-of-state residents are not consistent with Section 3(a)(11) and Rule 147, even if such offers include prominent disclosure stating that sales will be made only to residents of the same state or territory as the issuer."[92] Thus, consistent with the intrastate nature of the exemption, Rule 147A "permit[s] issuers to engage in general solicitation and general advertising of their offerings, using any form of mass media, including unrestricted, publicly-available Internet websites, so long as sales of securities so offered are made only to residents of the state or territory in which the issuer is resident."[93] Rule 147 and Rule 147A require issuers to include prominent disclosure in all offering materials stating that sales will be made only to residents of the same state or territory as the issuer. The SEC noted, however, that "[n]othing in this disclosure requirement . . . will prevent state authorities from imposing additional disclosure requirements or other requirements on offers or sales made to persons within their states."[94]

With respect to incorporation, the SEC stated, "We continue to believe that using a principal place of business requirement in lieu of an in-state formation requirement to establish the issuer's residency is more consistent with modern business practices in which issuers are permitted to incorporate or organize in states other than the state or territory of their principal place of business, for example, to take advantage of well-established bodies of corporate or partnership law."[95] Put differently, founders are more likely to organize in jurisdictions where business entity laws are consistent with modern business practices or provide greater flexibility. As the SEC noted, "[C]ompanies may have strong incentives to select perceived favorable regimes, such as that of Delaware."[96] Thus, so long as there are geographical ties to the location of investment and employment, which Rule 147A retains, states will continue to benefit from intrastate capital-raising without issuers losing

---

[91] Section 28 grants the SEC the authority to "exempt any person, security, or transaction, or any class or classes of persons, securities, or transactions" from the 1933 Act "to the extent that such exemption is necessary or appropriate in the public interest, and is consistent with the protection of investors."

[92] Securities Act Release No. 10238 (Oct. 26, 2016).

[93] Id.

[94] Id.

[95] Id.

[96] Id.

the ability to benefit from being organized in more favorable jurisdictions.

Why retain Rule 147 that, on its face, is less flexible than Rule 147A? Here, the SEC reflected on § 3(a)(11)'s and Rule 147's reliance on state blue sky laws to regulate intrastate offerings. State laws had been drafted with § 3(a)(11) and Rule 147 expressly in mind, so repealing Rule 147 would require changes in state regulation as well. Accordingly, the SEC decided to adopt new Rule 147A, while "also retaining amended Rule 147 as a safe harbor under Section 3(a)(11) to preserve the continued availability of existing state exemptive provisions that are specifically conditioned upon issuer reliance on Section 3(a)(11) and Rule 147."[97] For the time being, § 3(a)(11) and Rule 147 may continue to be the safe harbors on which many issuers rely, at least until state laws are amended to reflect new Rule 147A.

A. SECTION 3(a)(11)

Securities Act Release No. 4434
Securities and Exchange Commission.
December 6, 1961.

SECTION 3(a)(11) EXEMPTION FOR LOCAL OFFERINGS

The meaning and application of the exemption from registration provided by Section 3(a)(11) . . . have been the subject of court opinions, releases of the Securities and Exchange Commission . . . and opinions and interpretations expressed by the staff of the Commission in response to specific inquiries. This release is published to provide in convenient and up-to-date form a restatement of the principles underlying Section 3(a)(11) as so expressed over the years and to facilitate an understanding of the meaning and application of the exemption.[98]

General Nature of Exemption

Section 3(a)(11), as amended in 1954, exempts from the registration and prospectus requirements of the Act:

Any security which is a part of an issue offered and sold only to persons resident within a single State or Territory, where the issuer of such security is a person resident and doing business within, or, if a corporation, incorporated by and doing business within, such State or Territory.

The legislative history of the Securities Act clearly shows that this exemption was designed to apply only to local financing that may practically be consummated in its entirety within the State or Territory

---

[97] Securities Act Release No. 10238 (Oct. 26, 2016).

[98] Since publication of the 1937 release, the Investment Company Act of 1940 ("1940 Act") was enacted, and under § 24(d) of the 1940 Act, the § 3(a)(11) exemption is not available for an investment company registered or required to be registered under the 1940 Act.

in which the issuer is both incorporated and doing business. As appears from the legislative history, by amendment to the Act in 1934, this exemption was removed from Section 5(c) and inserted in Section 3, relating to "Exempted Securities", in order to relieve dealers of an unintended restriction on trading activity. This amendment was not intended to detract from its essential character as a transaction exemption.[99]

"Issue" Concept

A basic condition of the exemption is that the *entire issue* of securities be offered and sold exclusively to residents of the state in question. Consequently, an offer to a non-resident which is considered a part of the intrastate issue will render the exemption unavailable to the entire offering.

Whether an offering is "a part of an issue", that is, whether it is an integrated part of an offering previously made or proposed to be made, is a question of fact and depends essentially upon whether the offerings are a related part of a plan or program.... Thus, the exemption should not be relied upon in combination with another exemption for the different parts of a single issue where a part is offered or sold to non-residents.

The determination of what constitutes an "issue" is not governed by state law.... Any one or more of the following factors may be determinative of the question of integration: (1) are the offerings part of a single plan of financing; (2) do the offerings involve issuance of the same class of security; (3) are the offerings made at or about the same time; (4) is the same type of consideration to be received, and (5) are the offerings made for the same general purpose.[100]

Moreover, since the exemption is designed to cover only those security distributions, which, as a whole, are essentially local in character, it is clear that the phrase "sold only to persons resident" as used in Section 3(a)(11) cannot refer merely to the initial sales by the issuing corporation to its underwriters, or even the subsequent resales by the underwriters to distributing dealers. To give effect to the fundamental purpose of the exemption, it is necessary that the entire issue of securities shall be offered and sold to, and come to rest only in the hands of residents within the state. If any part of the issue is offered or sold to a non-resident, the exemption is unavailable not only for the

---

[99] See Report of the Securities and Exchange Commission to the Committee on Interstate and Foreign Commerce, dated Aug. 7, 1941, on Proposals for Amendments to the Securities Act of 1933 and the Securities Exchange Act of 1934, at p. 24, where, in referring to §§ 3(a)(1), 3(a)(9), 3(a)(10), 3(a)(11), and 3(b) of the 1933 Act, it was said: "Since these are in reality transaction exemptions, the Commission proposes and representatives of the securities' industry agree that they should be re-designated as transaction exemptions and transferred to Section 4...."

[100] As noted before, the SEC recently proposed amendments to the integration rules. See Securities Act Release No. 10763 (Mar. 4, 2020). The proposals would establish new Rule 152, which would replace current Rules 152 and 155. New Rule 152 provides a general framework and four safe harbors, replacing the various safe harbors currently set forth in various 1933 Act exemptions.

securities so sold, but for all securities forming a part of the issue, including those sold to residents. . . . It is incumbent upon the issuer, underwriter, dealers and other persons connected with the offering to make sure that it does not become an interstate distribution through resales. It is understood to be customary for such persons to obtain assurances that purchases are not made with a view to resale to non-residents.

Doing Business Within the State

In view of the local character of the Section 3(a)(11) exemption, the requirement that the issuer be doing business in the state can only be satisfied by the performance of substantial operational activities in the state of incorporation. The doing business requirement is not met by functions in the particular state such as bookkeeping, stock record and similar activities or by offering securities in the state. Thus, the exemption would be unavailable to an offering by a company made in the state of its incorporation of undivided fractional oil and gas interests located in other states even though the company conducted other business in the state of its incorporation. While the person creating the fractional interests is technically the "issuer" as defined in Section 2(4) of the Act, the purchaser of such security obtains no interest in the issuer's separate business within the state. Similarly, an intrastate exemption would not be available to a "local" mortgage company offering interests in out-of-state mortgages which are sold under circumstances to constitute them investment contracts. Also, the same position has been taken of a sale of an interest, by a real estate syndicate organized in one state to the residents of that state, in property acquired under a sale and leaseback arrangement with another corporation organized and engaged in business in another state.

If the proceeds of the offering are to be used primarily for the purpose of a new business conducted outside of the state of incorporation and unrelated to some incidental business locally conducted, the exemption should not be relied upon. . . . So also, a Section 3(a)(11) exemption should not be relied upon for each of a series of corporations organized in different states where there is in fact and purpose a single business enterprise or financial venture whether or not it is planned to merge or consolidate the various corporations at a later date. . . .

Residence Within the State

Section 3(a)(11) requires that the entire issue be confined to a single state in which the issuer, the offerees and the purchasers are residents. Mere presence in the state is not sufficient to constitute residence as in the case of military personnel at a military post. . . . The mere obtaining of formal representations of residence and agreements not to resell to non-residents or agreements that sales are void if the purchaser is a non-resident should not be relied upon without more as establishing the availability of the exemption.

An offering may be so large that its success as a local offering appears doubtful from the outset. Also, reliance should not be placed on the exemption for an issue which includes warrants for the purchase of another security unless there can be assurance that the warrants will be exercised only by residents. With respect to convertible securities, a Section 3(a)(9) exemption may be available for the conversion.

A secondary offering by a controlling person in the issuer's state of incorporation may be made in reliance on a Section 3(a)(11) exemption provided the exemption would be available to the issuer for a primary offering in that state. It is not essential that the controlling person be a resident of the issuer's state of incorporation.

Resales

From these general principles it follows that if during the course of distribution any underwriter, any distributing dealer (whether or not a member of the formal selling or distributing group), or any dealer or other person purchasing securities from a distributing dealer for resale were to offer or sell such securities to a non-resident, the exemption would be defeated. In other words, Section 3(a)(11) contemplates that the exemption is applicable only if the entire issue is distributed pursuant to the statutory conditions. Consequently, any offers or sales to a non-resident in connection with the distribution of the issue would destroy the exemption as to all securities which are a part of that issue, including those sold to residents regardless of whether such sales are made directly to non-residents or indirectly through residents who as part of the distribution thereafter sell to non-residents. It would furthermore be immaterial that sales to non-residents are made without use of the mails or instruments of interstate commerce. Any such sales of part of the issue to non-residents, however few, would not be in compliance with the conditions of Section 3(a)(11), and would render the exemption unavailable for the entire offering including the sales to residents.

This is not to suggest, however, that securities which have actually come to rest in the hands of resident investors, such as persons purchasing without a view to further distribution or resale to non-residents, may not in due course be resold by such persons, whether directly or through dealers or brokers, to non-residents without in any way affecting the exemption. The relevance of any such resales consists only of the evidentiary light which they might cast upon the factual question whether the securities had in fact come to rest in the hands of resident investors. If the securities are resold but a short time after their acquisition to a non-resident this fact, although not conclusive, might support an inference that the original offering had not come to rest in the state, and that the resale therefore constituted a part of the process of primary distribution; a stronger inference would arise if the purchaser involved were a security dealer. It may be noted that the non-residence of the underwriter or dealer is not pertinent so long as the ultimate distribution is solely to residents of the state.

Use of the Mails and Facilities of Interstate Commerce

The intrastate exemption is not dependent upon non-use of the mails or instruments of interstate commerce in the distribution. Securities issued in a transaction properly exempt under this provision may be offered and sold without registration through the mails or by use of any instruments of transportation or communication in interstate commerce, may be made the subject of general newspaper advertisement (provided the advertisement is appropriately limited to indicate that offers to purchase are solicited only from, and sales will be made only to residents of the particular state involved), and may even be delivered by means of transportation and communication used in interstate commerce, to the purchasers. Similarly, securities issued in a transaction exempt under Section 3(a)(11) may be offered without compliance with the formal prospectus requirements applicable to registered securities. Exemption under Section 3(a)(11), if in fact available, removes the distribution from the operation of the registration and prospectus requirements of Section 5 of the Act. It should be emphasized, however, that the civil liability and anti-fraud provisions of Sections 12(2) and 17 of the Act nevertheless apply and may give rise to civil liabilities and to other sanctions applicable to violations of the statute.

Conclusion

In conclusion, the fact should be stressed that Section 3(a)(11) is designed to apply only to distributions genuinely local in character. From a practical point of view, the provisions of that section can exempt only issues which in reality represent local financing by local industries, carried out through local investment. Any distribution not of this type raises a serious question as to the availability of Section 3(a)(11). Consequently, any dealer proposing to participate in the distribution of an issue claimed to be exempt under Section 3(a)(11) should examine the character of the transaction and the proposed or actual manner of its execution by all persons concerned with it with the greatest care to satisfy himself that the distribution will not, or did not, exceed the limitations of the exemption. Otherwise the dealer, even though his own sales may be carefully confined to resident purchasers, may subject himself to serious risk of civil liability under Section 12(1) of the Act for selling without prior registration a security not in fact entitled to exemption from registration. In Release No. 4386, we noted that the quick commencement of trading and prompt resale of portions of the issue to non-residents raises a serious question whether the entire issue has, in fact, come to rest in the hands of investors resident in the state of the initial offering.

The Securities Act is a remedial statute, and the terms of an exemption must be strictly construed against one seeking to rely on it. . . . The courts have held that he has the burden of proving its availability. . . .

Securities and Exchange Commission v. McDonald Investment Co.

United States District Court, D. Minn., 1972.
343 F.Supp. 343.

MEMORANDUM OPINION

■ NEVILLE, DISTRICT JUDGE: The question presented to the court is whether the sale exclusively to Minnesota residents of securities, consisting of unsecured installment promissory notes of the defendant, a Minnesota corporation, whose only business office is situated in Minnesota, is exempt from the filing of a registration statement under § 3(a)(11) of the 1933 Securities Act, when the proceeds from the sale of such notes are to be used principally, if not entirely, to make loans to land developers outside of Minnesota. Though this is a close question, the court holds that such registration is required and the defendants have not satisfied their burden of proving the availability of an exemption under the Act; this despite the fact that the securities have heretofore been duly registered with the Securities Commissioner of the State of Minnesota for whom this court has proper respect.

Plaintiff, the Securities and Exchange Commission, instituted this lawsuit pursuant to § 20(b) of the 1933 Securities Act. The defendants are McDonald Investment Company, a Minnesota corporation, and H. J. McDonald, the company's president, treasurer, and owner of all the company's outstanding common stock. Plaintiff requests that the defendants be permanently enjoined from offering for sale and selling securities without having complied with the registration requirements of Section 5 of the Act.

Plaintiff and defendants have stipulated to the following pertinent facts: The defendant company was organized and incorporated in the State of Minnesota on November 6, 1968. The principal and only business office from which the defendants conduct their operations is located in Rush City, Minnesota, and all books, correspondence, and other records of the company are kept there.

Prior to October 19, 1971, the defendants registered an offering for $4,000,000 of its own installment notes with the Securities Division of the State of Minnesota pursuant to Minnesota law. The prospectus offering these installment notes became effective on October 19, 1971 by a written order of the Minnesota Commissioner of Securities making the registration and prospectus effective following examination and review by the Securities Division. Sales of the installment notes, according to the amended prospectus of January 18, 1972, are to be made to Minnesota residents only. Prior to the institution of this action, the defendants were enjoined from their past practices of selling, without Securities and Exchange Commission registration, notes secured by lien land contracts and first mortgages on unimproved land located at various places in the United States, principally Arizona. The defendant company is said to have sold $12,000,000 of such to some 2,000 investors. The present plan contemplates that those purchasing defendant company's securities henceforth will have only the general unsecured debt obligation of the company, though the proceeds from the installment notes will be lent to land developers with security taken from them in the form of mortgages or other liens running to the defendant corporation. The individual installment note purchasers will not, however, have any direct ownership or participation in the mortgages or other lien security, nor in the businesses of the borrowers.

No registration statement as to the installment notes described in McDonald Investment Company's amended prospectus is in effect with the United States Securities and Exchange Commission, nor has a registration statement been filed with the Commission. Furthermore, the defendants will make use of the means and instruments of transportation and communication in interstate commerce and of the mails to sell and offer to sell the installment notes though only to residents of Minnesota.

* * *

The plaintiff predicates its claim for a permanent injunction on the ground that the defendants will be engaged in a business where the income producing operations are located outside the state in which the securities are to be offered and sold and therefore not available for the 3(a)(11) exemption. Securities and Exchange Commission v. Truckee Showboat, 157 F.Supp. 824 (S.D.Cal.1957); Chapman v. Dunn, 414 F.2d 153 (6th Cir. 1969). While neither of these cases is precisely in point on their facts, the rationale of both is clear and apposite to the case at bar.

In *Truckee* the exemption was not allowed because the proceeds of the offering were to be used primarily for the purpose of a new unrelated business in another state, i.e., a California corporation acquiring and refurbishing a hotel in Las Vegas, Nevada. Likewise, in *Dunn* the 3(a)(11) exemption was unavailable to an offering by a company in one state, Michigan, of undivided fractional oil and gas interests located in another state, Ohio. The *Dunn* court specifically stated:

> ... [I]n order to qualify for the exemption of § 3(a)(11), the issuer must offer and sell his securities only to persons resident within a single State and the issuer must be a resident of that same State. *In addition to this, the issuer must conduct a predominant amount of his business within this same State.* This business which the issuer must conduct within the same State refers to the income producing operations of the business in which the issuer is selling the securities. . . . [Emphasis added]

This language would seem to fit the instant case where the income producing operations of the defendant, after completion of the offering, are to consist entirely of earning interest on its loans and receivables invested outside the state of Minnesota. While the defendant will not participate in any of the land developer's operations, nor will it own or control any of the operations, the fact is that the strength of the installment notes depends perhaps not legally, but practically, to a large degree on the success or failure of land developments located outside Minnesota, such land not being subject to the jurisdiction of the Minnesota court. The investor obtains no direct interest in any business activity outside of Minnesota, but legally holds only an interest as a creditor of a Minnesota corporation, which of course would be a prior claim on the defendant's assets over the shareholder's equity, now stated to be approximately a quarter of a million dollars.

This case does not evidence the deliberate attempt to evade the Act as in the example posed by plaintiff of a national organization or syndicate which incorporates in several or many states, opens an office in each and sells securities only to residents of the particular state, intending nevertheless to use all the proceeds whenever realized in a venture beyond the boundaries of all, or at best all but one of the states. See Securities & Exchange Commission v. Los Angeles Trust Deed & Mortgage Exchange, 186 F.Supp. 830, 871 (S.D.Cal.1960), aff'd 285 F.2d 162 (9th Cir. 1960). Defendant corporation on the contrary has been in business in Minnesota for some period of time, is not a "Johnny come lately" and is not part of any syndicate or similar enterprise; yet to relieve it of the federal registration requirements where none or very little of the money realized is to be invested in Minnesota, would seem to violate the spirit if not the letter of the Act.

Persuasive language is found in the Securities and Exchange Commission Release No. 4434, December 6, 1961, relating to exemptions for local offerings:

> [The court quotes a portion of Securities Act Release No. 4434, included immediately above, under the heading, "Doing Business Within the State."]

Exemptions under the Act are strictly construed, with the burden of proof on the one seeking to establish the same. . . .

Defendant notes that agreements with land developers will by their terms be construed under Minnesota law; that the income producing activities will be the earning of interest which occurs in Minnesota; that the Minnesota registration provides at close proximity all the information and protection that any investor might desire; that whether or not registered with the Securities and Exchange Commission, a securities purchaser has the protection of [§ 12(a)(2) of the 1933 Act] which attaches liability to the issuer whether or not registration of the securities are exempted for fraudulent or untrue statements in a prospectus or made by oral communications; that plaintiff blurs the distinction between sale of securities across state lines and the operation of an intrastate business; and that if injunction issues in this case it could issue in any case where a local corporation owns an investment out of the particular state in which it has its principal offices and does business such as accounts receivable from its customers out of state. While these arguments are worthy and perhaps somewhat more applicable to the facts of this case than to the facts of *Truckee* and *Chapman*, supra, on balance and in carrying out the spirit and intent of the Securities Act of 1933, plaintiff's request for a permanent injunction should be granted.

---

1. *Recurring Issues Under § 3(a)(11)*. The open-ended language of § 3(a)(11) rendered its exemption fraught with peril. For example, what happened if:

   (1) the issuer conducted 75% of its business in its state of incorporation, but 25% in two others;

   (2) the issuer conducted nearly all of its business in its state of incorporation, but the proceeds of the offering would be chiefly used to expand its retail stores in another;

   (3) it conducted all its business in its state of incorporation, but it was a "hot" stock and 50% of the initial purchasers resold the stock over-the-counter within the first year to out-of-state residents (many within days after the offering); or

   (4) a single offer was made to an out-of-state resident (and this offeree did not buy)?

These issues eventually resulted in the SEC adopting the Rule 147 and, later, the Rule 147A safe harbors. Still, not all intrastate offerings are conducted pursuant to a safe harbor, and thus, these issues remain.

2. *Leading Cases*. Busch v. Carpenter[101] arose out of an offer and sale of shares in the amount of $500,000 by Sonic Petroleum, Inc., a Utah corporation ("Sonic"), solely to residents of Utah in reliance on the § 3(a)(11) exemption. Following the offering, Sonic did not engage in any business activity but did maintain its corporate office, books, and records in Utah.

Seven months after the intrastate offering, Carpenter, the President of Sonic, was contacted by Mason, an Illinois oil and gas promoter, about a merger of Sonic with Mason's operations in Illinois. As a result of these negotiations, Sonic issued a controlling block of stock to Mason and acquired an Illinois drilling corporation that was privately owned by Mason and his family. Upon becoming president of the new company, renamed Mason Oil, Mason withdrew $350,000 of the net proceeds of $435,000 that remained from the intrastate offering and transferred it to Illinois.

After joining forces, Mason and Carpenter set up Norbil Investments, a brokerage account in Utah, so that Mason and his friends could buy shares of Sonic. Plaintiffs were residents of California who bought shares in the open market through Norbil within seven months after the initial offering. They brought a § 12(a)(1) action against the

---

[101] 827 F.2d 653 (10th Cir. 1987).

officers and directors of Sonic at the time of the intrastate offering, including Carpenter, its then-president, to recover the purchase price of their shares.

Plaintiffs claimed that the exemption was lost for two distinct reasons: (1) the securities had not "come to rest" in the hands of the Utah residents who resold their stock within seven months of the offering since the initial purchasers had not bought with investment intent; and (2) the issuer did not meet the "doing business within" condition of § 3(a)(11). Liability was sought to be imposed upon defendants as controlling persons under § 15 of the 1933 Act.[102] The district court rejected these contentions and granted summary judgment to the defendants. On appeal to the Tenth Circuit, the SEC appeared as amicus on behalf of the plaintiffs. The Court of Appeals rejected the plaintiffs' and the SEC's first (or "coming to rest") theory, but accepted their second (or "doing business within") theory and remanded.

With respect to the "coming to rest" requirement, the Court of Appeals opined:

> We reject Amicus' argument. The intrastate offering exemption requires that the issue be "offered and sold only to persons resident within a single state." . . . In our view, a seller seeking summary judgment makes a prima facie showing that the offering was consummated within a state by showing that the stock was sold only to residents of that state. We disagree with Amicus that, in order to be entitled to summary judgment, the issuer should be required to disprove all the possible circumstances that might establish the stock has not come to rest. It seems more logical to us to impose on the other party the burden of producing some contrary evidence on this issue when the seller claiming the exemption has satisfied the facial requirement of the statute. In the face of defendants' undisputed showing that all of the original buyers were Utah residents, plaintiffs were therefore required to produce evidence that the stock had not come to rest but had been sold to people who intended to resell it out of state.
>
> . . . [T]he interstate purchases by Mason and others of freely traded shares several months after the completion of the intrastate offering do not, without more, impugn the investment intent of the original buyers or otherwise imply an effort to

---

[102] In general, for § 15 of the 1933 Act and § 20 of the 1934 Act, the mere existence of control is not alone a basis for liability. Section 15 of the 1933 Act provides that persons in a control relationship with persons liable under § 11 or § 12 of the 1933 Act will be jointly and severally liable, "unless the controlling person had no knowledge of or a reasonable ground to believe in the existence of the facts by reason of which the liability of the controlled person is alleged to exist." Section 20(a) of the 1934 Act has a different formulation. It provides for the joint and several liability of a controlling person "unless the controlling person acted in good faith and did not directly or indirectly induce the act or acts constituting the violation or cause of action."

evade the federal securities laws. Norbil served as a conduit for over-the-counter purchases made by Olsen & Company [a brokerage firm] on behalf of Mason and various acquaintances. Although Carpenter did collect from buyers, pay Olsen, and transfer the stock certificates to their new owners, there is simply no indication that those who sold through Norbil had not originally purchased their stock for investment purposes.

With respect to the "doing business within" requirement, the Court added:

> Although neither the statute nor its legislative history defines the doing business requirement, courts have uniformly held that it refers to activity that actually generates revenue within an issuer's home state.... [The court then discussed Chapman v. Dunn, 414 F.2d 153 (6th Cir. 1969); SEC v. Truckee Showboat, Inc., 157 F.Supp. 824 (S.D.Cal.1957); and SEC v. McDonald Investment Co., described and excerpted earlier.]
>
> These cases make clear that an issuer cannot claim the exemption simply by opening an office in a particular state. Conducting substantially all income-producing operations elsewhere defeats the exemption.... Doing business under the 1933 Act means more than maintaining an office, books, and records in one state....
>
> Viewing the evidence and drawing reasonable inferences most favorably to plaintiffs, a fact issue exists regarding whether Sonic's plans for the use of proceeds are distinguishable from the issuer's plans in *Truckee*.... Here the corporation never did more than maintain its office, books, and records in Utah. This was not sufficient to make a prima facie showing of compliance with the intrastate offering exemption. While its prospectus stated that no more than twenty percent of all proceeds would be used outside of Utah, Sonic nonetheless transferred essentially all of its assets to Mason in Illinois. The record contains no evidence, moreover, of any prior efforts whatever at locating investment opportunities within Utah. These considerations support a reasonable inference that Sonic may have intended all along to invest its assets outside the state....
>
> * * *
>
> ... Accordingly, we conclude that a genuine issue of material fact exists precluding summary judgment in favor of all defendants.[103]

---

[103] Busch v. Carpenter, 827 F.2d 653, 658–59 (10th Cir. 1987). *Busch* is consistent with the leading case on "doing business within" the state, Chapman v. Dunn, 414 F.2d 153 (6th Cir. 1969). There, the Michigan issuer sold fractional undivided interests in oil and gas leases in another jurisdiction (Ohio). The Sixth Circuit ruled that the issuer "must conduct a predominant amount of its business within this same State" to qualify under § 3(a)(11). Id. at 158–159.

B. RULES 147 AND 147A

Much as the SEC promulgated Regulation D to cure uncertainties for issuers under § 4(a)(2), so did it promulgate Rule 147 to give clearer guidance to issuers as to what is necessary to comply with § 3(a)(11), which was at least as uncertain in its scope. Rule 147A was adopted to reflect changes in the capital markets that conflict with § 3(a)(11)'s statutory limitations, while still retaining the intrastate nature of the offering.

Securities Act Release No. 5450
Securities and Exchange Commission.
January 7, 1974.

NOTICE OF ADOPTION OF RULE 147 UNDER THE SECURITIES ACT OF 1933

* * *

The Securities and Exchange Commission today adopted Rule 147 which defines certain terms in, and clarifies certain conditions of, Section 3(a)(11) of the Securities Act of 1933 ("the Act"). Section 3(a)(11) (the "intrastate offering exemption") exempts from the registration requirements of Section 5 of the Act, securities that are part of an issue offered and sold only to persons resident within a single state or territory, if the issuer is a person resident and doing business within that state or territory. . . . [The bracketed language in this Release reflects updates or other changes made by the Editors. Since much of Rule 147 is paralleled by Rule 147A, some of the bracketed language reflects sections that apply to both Rules.]

In developing the definitions in, and conditions of, Rule 147 the Commission has considered the legislative history and judicial interpretations of Section 3(a)(11) as well as its own administrative interpretations. The Commission believes that adoption of the rule, which codifies certain of these interpretations, is in the public interest, since it will be consistent with the protection of investors and provide, to the extent feasible, more certainty in determining when the exemption provided by that Section of the Act is available. [Recall that, unlike Rule 147, Rule 147A was adopted by the SEC pursuant to its general exemptive authority under § 28 of the 1933 Act.] Moreover, the Commission believes that local businesses seeking financing solely from local sources should have objective standards to facilitate compliance with Section 3(a)(11) and the registration provisions of the Act, and that the rule will enable such businesses to determine with more certainty whether they may use the exemption in offering their securities. The rule also will give more assurance that the intrastate offering exemption is used only for the purpose that Congress intended, i.e., local financing of companies primarily intrastate in character. Neither Section 3(a)(11) nor Rule 147 [nor Rule 147A] provides an exemption from the civil liability provisions of Section 12(2) of the Act, the anti-fraud provisions of the Act or of the Securities Exchange Act of 1934 ("Exchange Act"), the registration and periodic reporting provisions of Sections 12(g) and 13 of the Exchange Act, or any applicable state laws.

Rule 147 is another step in the Commission's continuing efforts to provide protection to investors and, where consistent with that objective, to add certainty, to the extent feasible, to the determination of when the registration provisions of the Act apply. . . .

Background and Purpose

Congress, in enacting the federal securities laws, created a continuous disclosure system designed to protect investors and to assure the maintenance of fair and honest securities markets. The Commission, in administering and implementing these laws, has sought to coordinate and integrate the disclosure system with the exemptive provisions provided by the laws. Rule 147 is a further effort in this direction.

Section 3(a)(11) was intended to allow issuers with localized operations to sell securities as part of a plan of local financing. Congress apparently believed that a company whose operations are restricted to one area should be able to raise money from investors in the immediate vicinity without having to register the securities with a federal agency. In theory, the investors would be protected both by their proximity to the issuer and by state regulation. Rule 147 reflects this Congressional intent and is limited in its application to transactions where state regulation will be most effective. The Commission has consistently taken the position that the exemption applies only to local financing provided by local investors for local companies.[2] To satisfy the exemption, the entire issue must be offered and sold [in the case of Rule 147A, just sold] exclusively to residents of the state in which the issuer is resident and doing business. An offer or sale [in the case of Rule 147A, just sale] of part of the issue to a single non-resident will destroy the exemption for the entire issue.

Certain basic questions have arisen in connection with interpreting Section 3(a)(11). They are:

1. what transactions does the Section cover;
2. what is "part of an issue" for purposes of the Section;
3. when is a person "resident within" a state or territory for purposes of the Section; and
4. what does "doing business within" mean in the context of the Section?

The courts and the Commission have addressed themselves to these questions in the context of different fact situations, and some general guidelines have been developed. Certain guidelines were set forth by the

---

[2] See, e.g., Securities Act Release No. 4434 (Dec. 6, 1961).

Commission in Securities Act Release No. 4434 and, in part, are reflected in Rule 147. However, in certain respects, as pointed out below, the rule differs from past interpretations.

* * *

The "Part of an Issue" Concept

The determination of what constitutes "part of an issue" for purposes of the exemption, i.e. what should be "integrated", has traditionally been dependent on the facts involved in each case. The Commission noted in Securities Act Release 4434 that "any one or more of the following factors may be determinative of the question of integration:

"1. are the offerings part of a single plan of financing;

"2. do the offerings involve issuance of the same class of security;

"3. are the offerings made at or about the same time;

"4. is the same type of consideration to be received; and

"5. are the offerings made for the same general purpose."

In this connection, the Commission generally has deemed intrastate offerings to be "integrated" with those registered or private offerings of the same class of securities made by the issuer at or about the same time.[104]

... As adopted, [Rules 147 and 147A] provide[ ] in Subparagraph [(g)] that, for purposes of the rule only, certain offers and sales of securities, discussed below, will be deemed not to be [integrated], but the rule does not otherwise define [what offers and sales are included in an "offering".] Accordingly, as to offers and sales not within [(g)], issuers who want to rely on [Rule 147 or Rule 147A] will have to determine whether their offers and sales are part of an issue by applying the five factors cited above.

The "Person Resident Within" Concept

The object of the Section 3(a)(11) exemption, i.e., to restrict the offering to persons within the same locality as the issuer who are, by reason of their proximity, likely to be familiar with the issuer and protected by the state law governing the issuer, is best served by interpreting the residence requirement narrowly. In addition, the determination of whether all parts of the issue have been sold only to residents can be made only after the securities have "come to rest" within the state or territory. Rule 147 retains these concepts but provides more

---

[104] As noted before, the SEC recently proposed amendments to the integration rules. See Securities Act Release No. 10763 (Mar. 4, 2020). The proposals would establish new Rule 152, which would replace current Rules 152 and 155. New Rule 152 provides a general framework and four safe harbors, replacing the various safe harbors currently set forth in various 1933 Act exemptions. Under its Proposed General Principle of Integration, an issuer will determine whether offers and sales are to be integrated based on the particular facts and circumstances. The proposed facts and circumstances analysis of integration replaces the traditional five-factor test set forth here.

objective standards for determining when a person is considered a resident within a state for purposes of the rule and when securities have come to rest within a state. [Recall that the offering restriction requirements do not appear in Rule 147A. This is discussed in more detail below.]

The "Doing Business Within" Requirement

Because the primary purpose of the intrastate exemption was to allow an essentially local business to raise money within the state where the investors would be likely to be familiar with the business and with the management, the doing business requirement has traditionally been viewed strictly. . . .

Rule 147 reinforces these requirements by providing specific percentage amounts of business that must be conducted within the state, and of proceeds from the offering that must be spent in connection with such business. [The specific requirements in Rules 147(c)(2) and 147A(c)(2), by which an issuer can demonstrate it is "doing business within" a state or territory, is satisfied if *any one* of the requirements is met.] In addition, [Rules 147(c)(1) and 147A(c)(1)] require[ ] that the principal [place of business] of the issuer be within the state. [As Rule 147(c)(1) and Rule 147A(c)(1) provide, the "principal place of business" is where "the officers, partners or managers of the issuer primarily direct control and coordinate the activities of the issuer." Rule 147(c)(1) also requires the issuer to be incorporated or organized in the state; that requirement is not in Rule 147A.]

Synopsis of Rule 147 [and Rule 147A]

. . . [Rule 147(a) states] that the rule does not raise any presumption that the Section 3(a)(11) exemption would not be available for transactions which do not satisfy all of the provisions of the rule. . . . [Since Rule 147A was issued pursuant to § 28, and not under § 3(a)(11), Rule 147A(a) simply states that it is an exemption from § 5 of the 1933 Act. It is not available to investment companies registered or required to be registered under the Investment Company Act of 1940.]

As initially proposed, the rule was intended not to be available for secondary transactions. . . . [Accordingly, Rules 147(b) and 147A(b) state that the exemption relates to "[a]n issuer, or any person acting on behalf of the issuer." In addition, Rule 147A(a) states that it applies to "[o]ffers and sales by or on behalf of an issuer."] [I]n accordance with long standing administrative interpretations of Section 3(a)(11), the intrastate offering exemption may be available for secondary offers and sales by controlling persons of the issuer, if the exemption would have been available to the issuer.[6] [Recall that Rule 147, not Rule 147A, is issued under § 3(a)(11).]

---

[6] Securities Act Release No. 4434 (December 6, 1961).

2. [Manner of Offers and Sales—Rules 147(b) and 147A(b)]

[Rule 147(b)] provides that offers . . . and sales of securities that meet all the conditions of the rule will be deemed to come within the exemption provided by Section 3(a)(11). Those conditions are: (1) the issuer must be resident [including incorporated or organized] and doing business within the state or territory in which the securities are offered and sold (Rule 147(c)); (2) the *offerees* and purchasers must be resident within such state or territory (Rule 147(d)); (3) resales for a period of [six] months [from the date of the sale by the issuer of a security] must be limited as provided (Rule 147(e) and (f)). In addition, the revised rule provides that certain offers and sales of securities by or for the issuers will [not be integrated with certain other offers and sales] (Rule 147(g)).

[Rule 147A(b) provides that offers and sales of securities that meet all the conditions of the rule may be made "using any form of general solicitation and general advertising." Those conditions are: (1) the issuer must be resident (but *not* required to be incorporated or organized) and doing business within the state or territory in which the securities are sold (Rule 147A(c)); (2) the purchasers (*not* offerees) must be resident within such state or territory (Rule 147A(d)); and (3) resales for a period of six months from the date of the sale by the issuer of a security must be limited as provided (Rule 147A(e) and (f)). Rule 147A also provides that certain offers and sales of securities by or for the issuers will not be integrated with certain other offers and sales (Rule 147A(g)).]

3. ["Integration With Other Offerings"—Rules 147(g) and 147A(g)][105]

[Rule 147's integration safe harbor has been revised since the Rule was first adopted. Similar to Regulation A, Rules 147(g) and 147A(g) preclude integration with (1) *any* prior offers or sales of securities and (2) later offers or sales that are registered (subject to Rule 147(h) and Rule 147A(h), described below), made in compliance with Regulation A, Rule 701, Regulation S (discussed later in this casebook, but generally covering offers and sales outside the United States), or § 4(a)(6) of the 1933 Act (relating to crowdfunding, discussed later in this chapter), made pursuant to an employee benefit plan, or made more than six months after completion of the offering. Thus, an offering pursuant to Regulation D that ended one month before the Rule 147 or 147A offering commenced will not be integrated with the Rule 147 or 147A offering. Also, like Regulation A, Rules 147(g) and 147A(g) do not require a "clean" six months. Recall that prior offers and sales of securities are not integrated. Subsequent offers and sales, made more than six months after completion of the Rule 147 or Rule 147A offering, also are not integrated,

---

[105] As noted before, the SEC recently proposed amendments to the integration rules. See Securities Act Release No. 10763 (Mar. 4, 2020). The proposals would establish new Rule 152, which would replace current Rules 152 and 155. New Rule 152 provides a general framework and four safe harbors, replacing the various safe harbors currently set forth in various 1933 Act exemptions.

even if they are a "dirty" six months (that is, offers or sales of securities occurred during that interval).

After making offers under Rule 147 or Rule 147A, and finding there is substantial investor demand, an issuer may choose to abandon its exempt offering in favor of a registered public offering. Pursuant to Rule 147(h) and Rule 147A(h), the abandoned offering will not be integrated with the subsequent registered offering if only qualified institutional buyers (as defined in Rule 144A under the 1933 Act, which is discussed later in this casebook) and institutional accredited investors were solicited. If others were solicited, the abandoned offering will still not be subject to integration if the issuer waits at least 30 days between the last offer made in reliance on Rule 147 or Rule 147A, as the case may be, and the filing of the registration statement with the SEC.[106]

Finally, an issuer that previously conducted an intrastate offering pursuant to Rule 147 or Rule 147A may not conduct another intrastate offering pursuant to either Rule 147 or Rule 147A, i.e., reliance on both Rules is precluded, in a different state or territory for six months from the last sale in such offering.[107]]

4. Nature of the Issuer—Rule 147(c) [and Rule 147A(c)]—"Person Resident Within"—Rule 147(c)(1) [and Rule 147A(c)(1)]

[Rule 147(c)(1)] defines the situations in which issuers would be deemed to be "resident within" a state or territory. [For Rule 147(c), a] corporation, limited partnership or business trust [or other form of business organization] must be incorporated or organized pursuant to the laws of such state or territory [, and it must have its "principal place of business" in such state or territory. An issuer shall be deemed to have its principal place of business "in a state or territory in which the officers, partners or managers of the issuer primarily direct, control and coordinate the activities of the issuer."] . . . A general partnership or other form of business entity that is not formed under a specific state or territorial law must have its principal [place of business] within the state or territory. The rule also provides that an individual who is deemed an issuer, e.g., a promoter issuing preincorporation certificates, will be deemed a resident if his principal residence is in the state or territory. . .

[Rule 147A(c) provides that an issuer is resident in a state or territory in which it has its principal place of business. The term "principal place of business" has the same definition as in Rule 147(c).]

---

[106] Note, too, that new Rule 163B under the 1933 Act permits any issuer, or any person authorized to act on its behalf, to engage in oral or written communications with potential investors that are, or are reasonably believed to be, "qualified institutional buyers" or institutional "accredited investors," either prior to or following the filing of a registration statement, to determine whether such investors might have an interest in a contemplated registered securities offering. The rule is non-exclusive, and if offers were made only to "qualified institutional buyers" or institutional "accredited investors," the issuer may also rely on Rule 163B in proceeding with the registered public offering.

[107] See Instruction to paragraph (c)(1) in Rule 147 under the 1933 Act and Instruction to paragraph (c) in Rule 147A under the 1933 Act.

5. Nature of the Issuer—Rule 147(c) [and Rule 147A(c)]—Doing Business Within—Rule 147(c)(2) [and Rule 147A(c)(2)]

[Rule 147(c)(2) and Rule 147A(c)(2)] provide[ ] that the issuer will be deemed to be "doing business within" a state or territory . . . if [at least one of the following requirements is satisfied]:

(1) at least 80 percent of its gross revenues and those of its subsidiaries on a consolidated basis (a) for its most recent fiscal year (if the first offer of any part of the issue is made during the first six months of the issuer's current fiscal year) or (b) for the subsequent six-month period, or for the twelve months ended with that period (if the first offer of any part of the issue is made during the last six months of the issuer's current fiscal year) were derived from the operation of a business or [of real] property located in or [from the] rendering of services within the state or territory; [or]

(2) at least 80 percent of the issuer's assets and those of its subsidiaries on a consolidated basis at the end of the most recent . . . semi-annual [fiscal] period prior to the first offer of any part of the issue are located within such state or territory; [or]

(3) at least 80 percent of the net proceeds to the issuer from the sales made pursuant to the rule are intended to be and are used in connection with the operation of a business or [of real] property, [the purchase of real property located in,] or the rendering of services within such state or territory; [or]

(4) [a majority of the issuer's employees are based in the state or territory].

* * *

The provisions of paragraph (c) are intended to assure that the issuer is primarily a local business. . . . The following examples demonstrate the manner in which these standards would be interpreted:

Example 1. X corporation is incorporated in State A and has its only warehouse, only manufacturing plant and only office in that state. X's only business is selling products throughout the United States and Canada through mail order catalogs. X annually mails catalogs and order forms from its office to residents of most states and several provinces of Canada. All orders are filled at and products shipped from X's warehouse to customers throughout the United States and Canada. All the products shipped are manufactured by X at its plant in State A. These activities are X's sole source of revenues.

Question. Is X deriving more than 80 percent of its gross revenues from the "operation of a business or . . . rendering of services" within State A?

Interpretive Response. Yes, this aspect of the "doing business within" standard is satisfied.

Example 2. Assume the same facts as Example 1, except that X has no manufacturing plant and purchases the products it sells from corporations located in other states.

Question. Is X deriving more than 80 percent of its gross revenues from the "operation of a business or . . . rendering of services" within State A?

Interpretive Response. Yes, this aspect of the "doing business within" standard is satisfied.

Example 3. Y Corporation is incorporated in State B and has its only office in that state. Y's only business is selling undeveloped land located in State C and State D by means of brochures mailed from its office throughout the United States.

Question. Is Y deriving more than 80 percent of its gross revenues from the "operation of a business or of property or rendering of services" within State B?

Interpretive Response. There are not sufficient facts to respond. If Y owns an interest in the developed land, it might not satisfy the "80 percent of assets" standard [or] the "80 percent of gross revenues" standard. Moreover, [it is unclear whether Y intends to] use more than 20 percent of the proceeds of any offerings made pursuant to the rule in connection with the acquisition of the undeveloped land.

Example 4. Z company is a firm of engineering consultants organized under the laws of State E with its only office in that state. During any year, Z will provide consulting services for projects in other states. 75 percent of Z's work in terms of man hours will be performed at Z's offices where it employs some 50 professional and clerical personnel. Z has no employees located outside of State E. However, professional personnel visit project sites and clients' offices in other states. Approximately 50 percent of Z's revenue is derived from clients located in states other than State E.

Question. Is Z deriving more than 80 percent of its gross revenues from "rendering services" within State E?

Interpretive Response. Yes, this aspect of the "doing business within" standard is satisfied.

Example 5. The facts are the same as in Example 4. In addition, at the end of Z's most recent fiscal quarter 25 percent of its assets are represented by accounts receivable from clients in other states.

Question. Does Z satisfy the "assets" standard?

Interpretive Response. Yes, Z satisfies the "assets" standard. For purposes of the rule, accounts receivable arising from a business conducted in the state would generally be considered to be located at the principal office of the issuer.

6. Offerees and Purchasers: Persons Resident—Rule 147(d) [and Purchasers: Persons Resident—Rule 147A(d)]

[Rule 147(d)] provides that offers and sales may be made only to persons resident within the state or territory [or to persons who the issuer reasonably believes, at the time of the offer and sale, are residents of the state or territory in which the issuer is resident]. An individual offeree or purchaser of any part of an issue would be deemed to be a person resident within the state or territory if such person has his principal residence in the state or territory. Temporary residence, such as that of many persons in the military service, would not satisfy the provisions of paragraph (d). In addition, if a person purchases securities on behalf of other persons, the residence of those persons must satisfy paragraph (d). If the offeree or purchaser is a business organization its residence will be deemed the state or territory in which it has its principal [place of business, as defined earlier], unless it is an entity organized for the specific purpose of acquiring securities in the offering, in which case it will be deemed to be a resident of a state only if all of the beneficial owners of interests in such entity are residents of the state. [Likewise, a trust that is not deemed under the law of its creation to be a separate legal entity is deemed to be a resident of each state or territory in which its trustee or trustees are resident.[108]]

[A written representation from purchasers of in-state residency status will not, without more, be sufficient to establish a reasonable belief that such purchasers are in-state residents.[109]]

* * *

[Rule 147A(d) parallels Rule 147(d), except that it extends only to sales. Rule 147A does not restrict offers to persons outside the issuer's state or territory.]

7. Limitations on Resales—Rule 147(e) [and Rule 147A(e)]

Paragraph (e) of [Rule 147 and Rule 147A] provides that . . . for a period of [six] months from the date of the . . . sale by the issuer of [a security], resales of [such security] by any person shall be made only to persons resident within the [issuer's] state or territory. . . .

Persons who acquire securities from issuers in transactions complying with the rule would acquire unregistered securities that could only be reoffered and resold pursuant to an exemption from the registration provisions of the Act.

. . . The Commission has determined that it is in the public interest to adopt a specific time period, . . . which provides the necessary protections to investors against interstate trading markets springing up before the securities have come to rest within the state. . . .

---

[108] See Instruction to paragraph (d)(1) of Rule 147 and Rule 147A under the 1933 Act.
[109] See Instruction to paragraph (d) of Rule 147 and Rule 147A under the 1933 Act.

A note to the rule indicates that where convertible securities are sold pursuant to the rule, resales of either the convertible security, or if it is converted, of the underlying security, could be made during the period specified in paragraph (e) only to residents of the state. However, the conversion itself, if pursuant to Section 3(a)(9) of the Act, would not begin a new period. In the case of warrants and options, sales upon exercise, if done in reliance on the rule, would begin a new period.

8. Precautions Against Interstate ... Sales—Rule 147(f) [and Rule 147A(f)]

Paragraph (f) of [Rule 147 and Rule 147A] requires issuers to take steps to preserve the exemption provided by the rule, since any resale of any part of the issue before it comes to rest within the state to persons resident in another state or territory will, under the Act, be in violation of Section 5. The required steps are: (i) placing a legend on the certificate or other document evidencing the security stating that the securities have not been registered under the Act and setting forth the limitations on resale contained in paragraph (e); (ii) issuing stop transfer instructions to the issuer's transfer agent, if any, with respect to the securities, or, if the issuer transfers its own securities, making a notation in the appropriate records of the issuer; and (iii) obtaining a written representation from each purchaser as to his residence. Where persons other than the issuer are reselling securities of the issuer during the time period specified in paragraph (e) of the rule, the issuer would, if the securities are presented for transfer, be required to take steps (i) and (ii). In addition, the rule requires that the issuer disclose in writing the limitations on resale imposed by paragraph (e) . . . .

Operation of Rule 147 [and Rule 147A]

* * *

[Rule 147 and Rule 147A are nonexclusive rules.] ... The Commission ... emphasizes that the exemption[s] provided by Section 3(a)(11) [and Rule 147 and Rule 147A are not exemptions] from the civil liability provisions of Section 12(2) or the anti-fraud provisions of Section 17 of the Act or of Section 10(b) of the Securities Exchange Act of 1934. The Commission further emphasizes that Rule 147 [and Rule 147A are] available only for transactions by issuers and [are] not available for secondary offerings.

In view of the objectives and policies underlying the Act, the rule would not be available to any person with respect to any offering which, although in technical compliance with the provisions of the rule, is part of a plan or scheme by such person to make interstate offers or sales of securities. In such cases, registration would be required. In addition, any plan or scheme that involves a series of offerings by affiliated organizations in various states, even if in technical compliance with the rule, may be outside the parameters of the rule and of Section 3(a)(11)[, as the case may be,] if what is being financed is in effect a single business enterprise.

* * *

C. DEVELOPMENTS UNDER RULE 147 AND RULE 147A

1. *State Regulation and NSMIA*. In 1996, Congress enacted the National Securities Market Improvement Act of 1996 ("NSMIA") to reduce the costs incident to a "dual system of regulation" that required many issuers to register securities both at the federal and state levels. Although NSMIA eliminated state blue sky review of registered offerings and Rule 506 private placements, and Regulation A Tier 2 offerings (by SEC rule) and § 4(a)(7) offerings (by statute) are also not subject to state review, by most accounts NSMIA had "virtually no effect on an issuer making instate offerings."[110] Some academics have criticized state regulators for persisting in maintaining state-specific compliance regulations that increase compliance costs: "[S]tates had the power to neutralize any of the federal rules that improve access to capital by small (or large) issuers. By enacting or letting stand more restrictive state rules, state regulators were able to exercise hegemony over the SEC, thus effectively neutralizing the new balance struck at the federal level between capital formation and investor protection."[111]

Would this be a fair criticism if applied to state rules applicable to § 3(a)(11), Rule 147, or Rule 147A offerings? Section 18 of the 1933 Act, which preempts state blue sky registration and qualification of most offerings, does not apply to § 3(a)(11), Rule 147, or Rule 147A. The premise is that federal regulation of these offerings is unnecessary since the offering or sales will take place in only one jurisdiction that will regulate the offering. Hence, the danger of multiple states imposing inconsistent and/or overlapping standards seems minimal.

A further premise of § 3(a)(11) and Rule 147 is that state regulation is adequate to protect investors in legitimately "local" offerings. Rule 147A is based on a similar premise. But is this true?

Under § 3(a)(11), Rule 147, and Rule 147A, there is neither a requirement of investor sophistication nor a disclosure requirement. Similarly, no limitation is placed on the number of purchasers or the aggregate offering size. Moreover, Rule 147A has no limitation on general solicitation or general advertising. In these regards, § 3(a)(11), Rule 147, and Rule 147A are far more open-ended than exemptions based on § 3(b) or § 4(a)(2).[112] The result is a substantially greater reliance on oversight

---

[110] See Dorsch, National Securities Market Improvement Act: How Improved is the Securities Market?, 36 Duq. L. Rev. 365, 377 (1998).

[111] See Campbell, The Impact of NSMIA on Small Issuers, 53 Bus. Law. 575, 580 (1998).

[112] Possibly due to the *de minimis* constraints imposed by Rule 147 (and now Rule 147A), the SEC has never adopted the "innocent and immaterial" defense included in Regulation A (Rule 260) and Regulation D (Rule 508). That defense permits the issuer to show it substantially complied with the exemption's terms even if there was an insubstantial departure.

by state regulators—with the practical difficulty of registering or qualifying a securities offering in all likelihood varying from state to state.

Still, an issuer that is resident in a state where registration is unduly difficult is not without a remedy, particularly if it is prepared to sell to only accredited investors, which limits the issuer's disclosure obligations. It may simply choose to rely on Rule 506 of Regulation D (which preempts state review).

2. *"Doing Business Within."* In a series of no-action letters, the SEC's staff has vacillated in the strictness of its approach to the "doing business within" requirement under § 3(a)(11) and Rule 147. These letters predate the SEC's adoption of Rule 147A.

Sometimes, the staff has been quite strict. For example, in a 1991 no-action letter request,[113] an issuer sought clarification under Rule 147(c)(2) where it proposed to acquire and service the loan portfolios of several insolvent out-of-state financial institutions from the Federal Deposit Insurance Corporation and another receiver. The purchased loan portfolios would have been serviced exclusively from offices within the state, but the original lenders had made most of the loans to out-of-state entities. The SEC declined to issue the requested ruling, noting "that more than 20% of the net proceeds to be received from the proposed offering may be used in connection with services to be performed outside of the state. . . ." Sensible result? One commentator has described the result as "hopelessly confused."[114] Yet, in an earlier no-action letter under § 3(a)(11), the staff permitted a limited partnership to invest most of its assets in other limited partnerships that would operate outside the state.[115] Does this elevate form over substance?

3. *Secondary Transactions.* Both Securities Act Release No. 5450 (which adopted Rule 147) and Securities Act Release No. 4434 (which contains the fullest SEC statement on § 3(a)(11)) indicate that the intrastate offering exemption may be available for secondary offers and sales by controlling persons of the issuer if the exemption would have been available to the issuer itself. Nonetheless, some decisions have disagreed. In SEC v. Tuchinsky,[116] the court said that "the exemption created by this section is limited to the original issue of the securities and does not exempt secondary distribution" (citing Vol. III Loss & Seligman, Securities Regulation 1142–44 and nn. 5–6 (3d. ed. 1989)). Even if an exemption were not available in the past, should the SEC use its exemptive power under § 28 of the 1933 Act (the same basis for the creation of Rule 147A) to create such an exemption?

---

[113] See First Commerce of America, Inc., 1991 SEC No-Act. LEXIS 1121 (Sept. 30, 1991); [1991–1992 Transfer Binder] Fed.Sec.L.Rep. (CCH) ¶ 76,029.

[114] See Haft, Analysis of Key SEC No-Action Letters (1995–1996 ed.).

[115] See The Professional Consultants, Inc., SEC No-Action Letter (Dec. 19, 1980).

[116] See [1992 Transfer Binder] Fed.Sec.L.Rep. (CCH) ¶ 96,917 (S.D.Fla. June 29, 1992), 1992 WL 226302, at *11–12.

4. OTHER EXEMPTIONS: RULE 701 AND REGULATION CE

Statutes and Regulations

Securities Act, § 3(b).

Rules 701, 1001.

A. RULE 701

Venture capital and start-up companies often attract and hold key employees by offering them incentive compensation, including in the form of stock option, profit-sharing, and stock purchase plans. Beginning in the 1980s, privately-held companies began using stock options to compensate a far broader range of employees than before, including middle- and even lower-level staff. The goal was to enable employees to share in any appreciation in the firm's value and, thus, better align their self-interest with the interest of the company.

For public companies, it was relatively simple to register a continuing offer of securities to employees—for example, covering stock options and warrants, and later covering stock issued upon exercise of the options or warrants—by filing and keeping current a Form S-8 registration statement. Form S-8 is the SEC form used for the shelf registration of securities issued under an employee benefit plan.

For non-reporting companies, which most likely were pre-IPO, the problem was more difficult. *Ralston Purina* (excerpted and discussed earlier in this casebook) required the issuer to register the stock (and options and warrants) it offered its employees, unless an exemption was available. The costs of registration—including, among others, the legal and accounting fees, the new public disclosures the company must make, the ongoing reporting obligations, and the corporate governance responsibilities of being a public company—were often disproportionately high for a small, non-reporting company to consider incurring.

Rule 701 was a response to this problem, tailored to meet the needs of non-reporting issuers. Adopted in 1988, it provides a non-exclusive exemption under § 3(b) for offers and sales of securities by non-reporting issuers to directors, officers, and employees, among others, where such offers and sales are pursuant to a written compensatory benefit plan or a written compensation (employment) contract established by the issuer and certain of its affiliates.[117]

The premise of Rule 701 is that compensatory benefit plans are not an attempt to raise capital by the issuer, but rather to use stock, stock options, and related compensation to bind the employees to the firm. Thus, Preliminary Note 5 to the Rule states:

---

[117] See Rules 701(b) and (c) under the 1933 Act.

This rule is not available for plans or schemes to circumvent this [compensatory] purpose, such as to raise capital.... In ... [such] cases, registration under the [1933] Act is required unless another exemption is available.

Perhaps reflecting the incentive nature of securities sold under Rule 701, Rule 701 securities are "restricted securities," as defined in Rule 144 (discussed later in this casebook),[118] subject to restriction on resale, and they are not exempt from blue sky regulation under § 18 of the 1933 Act. That makes it more difficult to transfer securities received under Rule 701 and, as restricted securities issued by a non-reporting company, those who expect to resell their securities under Rule 144 may be required to hold them for at least one year[119] (or longer, if transfers are contractually or otherwise restricted by the securities' terms).

Partly to enforce the restriction on capital-raising, Rule 701 limits the amount of securities that can be sold during any consecutive 12-month period. The total amount may not exceed the greatest of $1,000,000 or amounts determined under two different formulae. In general, the first formula limits this amount to 15% of the issuer's total assets, while the second restricts the amount to no more than 15% of the issuer's outstanding securities of the same class. Each limit is measured as of the issuer's most recent balance sheet date (if no older than its last fiscal year-end).[120]

Note the special rules regarding options. For example, Rule 701(d)(3)(i) provides that "[o]ptions must be valued based on the exercise price of the option," and Rule 701(d)(3)(ii) states that "the aggregate sales price is determined when an option grant is made (without regard to when the option becomes exercisable)." Rule 701(d)(1) also instructs that "sales of securities underlying options must be counted as sales on the date of the option grant." Likewise, Rule 701(d)(3)(iii) states that, in calculating outstanding securities (for purposes of the 15% cap described in the preceding paragraph), securities underlying all currently exercisable or convertible securities, including options, other than those issued under Rule 701, should be treated as outstanding. Regarding disclosure, Rule 701(e)(6) states that the delivery of any required materials must be made "a reasonable period of time" before the exercise date.

---

[118] See Rule 701(g) under the 1933 Act.

[119] See Rule 144(d)(1)(ii) under the 1933 Act. Rule 144 is discussed later in this casebook.

[120] Non-cash consideration is "valued by reference to *bona fide* sales of that consideration made within a reasonable time or, in the absence of such sales, on the fair value as determined by an accepted standard." Rule 701(d)(3)(i) under the 1933 Act. With respect to options, "[o]ptions must be valued based on the exercise price of the option," Rule 701(d)(3)(i) under the 1933 Act, and "sales of securities underlying options must be counted as sales on the date of the option grant," Rule 701(d)(1) under the 1933 Act.

All Rule 701 offerings are deemed to be part of a single discrete offering that is not subject to integration with any other offers or sales.[121] Similarly, in light of Rule 701's compensatory nature, aggregation is limited to only sales under Rule 701 within the prior 12 months (and does "not affect 'aggregate offering prices' in other exemptions, and amounts of securities sold in reliance on other exemptions do not affect the amount that may be sold in reliance on" Rule 701).[122]

Rule 701 generally does not require affirmative disclosures about the issuer (other than the issuer providing plan participants with a copy of the compensatory benefit plan or contract relating to the compensation). Rule 701(e), however, requires affirmative disclosure if the issuer sells more than $10 million in securities during any consecutive 12-month period. In that case, the issuer must provide, among other things, the same financial statements as are used in a Regulation A offering statement, dated no earlier than 180 days before the issuance of securities under Rule 701,[123] as well as "[i]nformation about the risks associated with investment in the securities sold pursuant to the compensatory benefit plan or compensation contract."[124] Rule 701's exemption does not extend to antifraud liability, which could still arise under Rule 10b–5 under the 1934 Act.

Google ran afoul of Rule 701's disclosure requirements during the two years prior to its 2004 IPO when it issued over $80 million in stock options to its employees without providing the financial statements required by Rule 701(e). In response, the SEC brought and settled an administrative cease-and-desist order against Google and its general counsel.[125]

Rule 701 can be used to offer securities, not only to directors, officers, and employees, but also to consultants and advisers who "provide *bona fide* services" to the issuer or certain affiliates that "are not in connection with the offer or sale of securities in a capital-raising transaction, and do not directly or indirectly promote or maintain a market for the issuer's securities."[126] The exemption recognizes that individuals who perform valuable services for start-up companies often are not employees (in part, because the start-up cannot afford to hire many employees). Still, the ability to issue unregistered securities to "consultants and advisers" could open the door to evasion, and some could potentially be little more

---

[121] See Rule 701(f) under the 1933 Act. As noted before, the SEC recently proposed amendments to the integration rules. See Securities Act Release No. 10763 (Mar. 4, 2020). The proposals would establish new Rule 152, which would replace current Rules 152 and 155. New Rule 152 provides a general framework and four safe harbors, replacing the various safe harbors currently set forth in various 1933 Act exemptions.

[122] Rule 701(d)(3)(iv) under the 1933 Act.

[123] See Rule 701(e)(4) under the 1933 Act.

[124] See Rule 701(e)(3) under the 1933 Act.

[125] See SEC Press Release 2005–06 (Jan. 15, 2005).

[126] See Rule 701(c)(1). See also Herff Jones, Inc., SEC No-Action Letter, 1990 SEC No-Act. LEXIS 1026 (Nov. 13, 1990) (stock plan that covered sales representatives who were not employees complied with Rule 701).

than disguised underwriters. Hence, the exclusion of services in connection with "a capital-raising transaction" attempts to strike a balance that recognizes the legitimacy of consultants and advisors, but rules some services off-limits—on its face, excluding, for example, underwriters and the lawyers who work on an offering. An issuer might still attempt to stretch Rule 701 to designate potential investors as nominal "consultants and advisers." In such a case, the SEC presumably could turn to Preliminary Note 5 (quoted previously).

When stock is sold to a consultant or adviser, the value of services performed by the adviser must be counted against the aggregate offering price ceilings under Rule 701(d)(2). However, the value of services performed by an employee in the regular course of her employment is not so counted.[127]

Rule 701 did not solve all problems. Indeed, the very popularity of Rule 701 resulted in additional complications with compensatory stock options. At the time, Exchange Act § 12(g) required an issuer with 500 or more holders of record of a class of equity security (which includes stock options[128]) and total assets in excess of $10 million to register that class under the Exchange Act and begin periodic reporting. If a private company had 500 or more optionholders of record (and more than $10 million in total assets), it would have been required to register under the Exchange Act and begin periodic reporting, even though it had not yet conducted an IPO. Increasingly, private non-reporting companies began to approach the point at which they had 500 optionholders of record, even though their common stock was held of record by less than the 500-person threshold. This problem was addressed by the JOBS Act in 2012, which moved the number of recordholders from 500 to 2,000.

Prior to 2012, however, the SEC still needed to address the impending recordholder concerns. Accordingly, in Exchange Act Release No. 56887 (Dec. 3, 2007), the SEC adopted two exemptions to spare private companies from costly Exchange Act registration and reporting. Those exemptions remain in place, even following the JOBS Act amendment.

First, the SEC amended Rule 12h–1 under the 1934 Act to exempt private companies that do not already have a class of security registered under § 12(g), and that otherwise meets Rule 12h–1's requirements, from becoming obligated to register under § 12(g) with respect to the issuance of stock options "held only by those persons described in Rule 701(c) . . .

---

[127] This distinction, which is not obvious on the face of the Rule, was made in Securities Act Release No. 6768 (Apr. 20, 1988). Note, however, that "[t]he value of services exchanged for securities issued must be measured by reference to the value of the securities issued." Rule 701(d)(3) under the 1933 Act. Compare Rule 501(c), which (like Rule 701(d)(3)) addresses the value of non-cash consideration received for securities but, unlike Rule 701, does not specifically address the value of services. Perhaps this specific focus on services reflects Rule 701's compensatory nature.

[128] See § 3(a)(11) of the 1934 Act.

or their permitted transferees."[129] The Rule 12h–1 exemption requires, among other things, that the stock options be restricted so as to permit their transfer only to family members or an executor or guardian of the optionholder.[130]

Second, the SEC amended Rule 12h–1 to provide a further exemption for issuers that were already reporting companies to spare them from registering an additional class of compensatory stock options.[131] Here, the Commission's rationale was that, because such an issuer was already filing periodic reports under § 13 or § 15(d) of the 1934 Act, the existing reports "will provide the appropriate information to optionholders."[132] As a result of both amendments to Rule 12h–1, compensatory stock options are now largely exempt from § 12(g)'s 1934 Act registration requirement.

B. REGULATION CE

In 1996, the SEC adopted a new form of exemption in Rule 1001.[133] Essentially, it combines features of both the intrastate exemption (§ 3(a)(11)) and the small issue exemption (§ 3(b)).

Rule 1001 provides an exemption that tracks a California state law exemption set forth in § 25102(n) of the California Corporations Code ("CCC"). CCC § 25102(n) permits, among others, certain California corporations and foreign business entities (in the case of foreign business entities, corporations with more than one-half of their outstanding voting securities owned by persons having addresses in California and that satisfy specified property, payroll, and sales factor tests, but excluding corporations listed on a national securities exchange or wholly-owned subsidiaries of an otherwise exempt corporation[134]) to sell their securities to "qualified purchasers" (or persons the issuer reasonably believes, after reasonable inquiry, to be "qualified purchasers") who meet criteria similar to, but more liberal than, those set forth in the definition of "accredited investor" in Rule 501(a) under the 1933 Act. For example, the CCC definition of "qualified purchaser" includes (i) any person purchasing $150,000 or more of securities in the offering (provided the purchaser, or the issuer reasonably believes the purchaser, herself or with her professional advisor, has the capacity to protect her own interests in the transaction, or the investment (including mandatory assessments) does not exceed 10% of the purchaser's net worth or joint net worth with her spouse) (a "CCC excluded purchaser"), and (ii) with respect to certain voting common stock or preferred stock, and so long as the investment does not exceed 10% of the purchaser's net worth, (a) a

---

[129] Rule 12h–1(f)(1)(iii) under the 1934 Act.
[130] See Rule 12h–1(f)(1)(iv) under the 1934 Act.
[131] See Rule 12h–1(g) under the 1934 Act.
[132] See Exchange Act Release No. 56887 (Dec. 3, 2007) at *46.
[133] See Securities Act Release No. 7285 (May 1, 1996).
[134] See Cal. Corp. Code § 2115, referenced in Cal. Corp. Code § 25102(n)(1).

natural person who, individually or jointly with her spouse, has a net worth of $250,000 if her gross income exceeds $100,000 (and she reasonably expects her gross income to exceed $100,000 during the current tax year), or (b) a natural person who, individually or jointly with her spouse, has a net worth of $500,000.[135]

The sum of all cash and other consideration to be received in a Rule 1001 offering cannot exceed $5 million, minus the offering price of all other securities sold in the same offering, whether pursuant to Rule 1001 or another exemption.[136] Rule 1001 offerings are not aggregated with other offerings; rather, the $5 million ceiling applies on an offering-by-offering basis. Standard integration concepts, however, do apply, meaning that a Rule 1001 offering can be integrated with other offerings so that exemptions can be forfeited by some or all of them.[137]

The CCC exemption, on which Rule 1001 relies, permits a general announcement of the proposed offering, including to non-qualified investors, limited to specified information as one way to "test the waters" for the offering.[138] In addition, although not a condition to relying on CCC § 25102(n), each natural person who purchases securities (including organizations specifically formed by natural persons to acquire the securities) must receive, at least five business days before purchasing, a written offering disclosure statement that meets the requirements of Regulation D as well as any other information required by California regulation. The disclosure obligation does not extend to all purchasers, including, for example, a CCC excluded purchaser.[139] No telephone solicitation is permitted until the issuer has determined the prospective purchaser is a qualified purchaser.[140] In addition, Rule 1001(c) provides that securities issued under Regulation CE are "restricted securities" subject to the resale limitations.[141]

Most importantly, in Securities Act Release No. 7285, which adopted Rule 1001, the Commission indicated its willingness "to provide the same exemption for each state that enacts a transactional exemption incorporating the same standards used by California." The SEC's goal was to facilitate capital-raising by small businesses by providing a coordinated federal-state exemption without losing investor protection. On that basis, the Commission captioned Rule 1001 "Regulation CE" for "Coordinated Exemptions" in anticipation of other states enacting

---

[135] See Cal. Corp. Code § 25102(n)(2).

[136] See Rule 1001(b) under the 1933 Act.

[137] See Securities Act Release No. 7285 at n. 31 (May 1, 1996). As noted before, the SEC recently proposed amendments to the integration rules. See Securities Act Release No. 10763 (Mar. 4, 2020). Under its Proposed General Principle of Integration, an issuer will determine whether offers and sales are to be integrated based on the particular facts and circumstances. The proposed facts and circumstances analysis of integration replaces the traditional five-factor test.

[138] See Cal. Corp. Code § 25102(n)(5).

[139] See Cal. Corp. Code § 25102(n)(4).

[140] See Cal. Corp. Code § 25102(n)(6).

[141] See Rule 1001(c) under the 1933 Act.

similar statutes. The New York State Bar Association's Securities Committee, however, voiced concern that this approach could create a "confusing patchwork of similar, but not identical approaches" that undercuts the uniformity of the federal securities laws.[142]

5. EXEMPTED EXCHANGES AND REORGANIZATIONS: SECTIONS 3(a)(9) AND 3(a)(10) AND THE BANKRUPTCY CODE

Statutes and Regulations

Securities Act, §§ 2(a)(3), 3(a)(7), 3(a)(9), 3(a)(10).

Rules 149, 150.

Bankruptcy Code, §§ 364, 1125, 1145.

A. SECTION 2(a)(3) AND THE THEORY OF "SALE"

Statutes and Regulations

Securities Act, § 2(a)(3).

Under § 5 of the 1933 Act, absent an exemption, it is unlawful to "sell" a security unless a registration statement is in effect. Section 2(a)(3) defines "sale" to include "every contract of sale or disposition of a security . . . , for value." In most instances, it is clear when a sale of a security has occurred. In some cases, however, whether an issuance of securities is a "sale," as used in the 1933 Act, may be less clear.

a. Warrants, Options, and Conversion Rights. In a typical rights offering (or "rights issue"), shareholders are issued subscription warrants without consideration. The warrants provide the shareholders the right (but not the obligation) to purchase new shares, in proportion to their existing holdings, at a discount to the market price. In general, since there is no § 2(a)(3) "sale" of the warrants—they are issued without consideration to existing shareholders—§ 5 is never triggered. The warrants themselves need not be registered. A warrant (or other convertible security), however, if immediately exercisable, constitutes an offer to sell the underlying security.[143]

---

[142] See "N.Y. Lawyers Voice Concerns Over California Registration Exemptions," Sec.Reg. & L.Rep. (BNA) (Sept. 15, 1995). For a sharp criticism of Regulation CE as an unwise delegation of federal power to state authorities, see Bradford, The SEC's New Regulation CE Exemption: Federal-State Coordination Run Rampant, 52 U.Miami L.Rev. 429 (1998).

[143] See Securities Act Release No. 3210 (Apr. 9, 1947). This conclusion is consistent with how § 2(a)(3) treats conversion and subscription rights that are not exercisable until a future date. Section 2(a)(3) provides, in relevant part:

The issue or transfer of a right or privilege, when originally issued or transferred with a security, giving the holder of such security the right to convert such security into another security of the same issuer or of another person, or giving a right to subscribe to another security of the same issuer or of another person, which right cannot be exercised until some future date, shall not be deemed to be an offer or sale of such other security; but the issue or transfer of such other security upon the exercise of such right of conversion or subscription shall be deemed a sale of such other security.

In the case of convertible securities or warrants that are registered with the SEC, where such securities are convertible or exercisable within one year, the SEC's view is that the underlying securities should also be registered at that time.[144] If not convertible or exercisable within one year, the issuer may choose not to register the underlying securities (consistent with the analysis in the next paragraph). Absent an exemption, however, the underlying securities must be registered no later than the date such securities become convertible or exercisable by their terms.[145] Likewise, when securities are convertible only at the option of the issuer, then absent an exemption, the underlying securities must be registered when the convertible securities are registered, since the investor's entire investment decision will have occurred at the time she purchases the convertible securities.[146]

Section 2(a)(3) also addresses rights to convert a security into another security and rights to subscribe to another security (together, "conversion rights") that are *not* immediately exercisable. In that case, the issue or transfer of a conversion right "which right cannot be exercised until some future date, shall not be deemed to be an offer or sale of such other security; but the issue or transfer of such other security upon the exercise of such right . . . shall be deemed a sale of such other security." According to the House Report:[147]

> This makes it unnecessary to register such a security prior to the time that it is to be offered to the public, although the conversion right or the right to subscribe must be registered. When the actual securities to which these rights appertain are offered to the public, the bill requires registration as of that time. This permits the holder of any such right of conversion or warrant to subscribe to judge whether upon all the facts it is advisable for him to exercise his rights.

A question that often arises is whether, at the time the underlying security is "sold" (i.e., issued upon exercise of a conversion right), the sale of that security is exempt from § 5 or requires an effective registration statement. In general, absent an exemption, new securities issued upon exercise of the conversion right must be registered with the SEC. In some instances, however, § 3(a)(9) (which is discussed below) may provide an exemption for sale of the underlying security.

Thus, it follows that a security that is immediately convertible into another security entails an offer of the security into which it may be converted.

[144] See SEC Division of Corporation Finance, Compliance and Disclosure Interpretations, Question 103.3 (Sept. 22, 2016).

[145] See id.

[146] The SEC's view is that the security holder, by purchasing a convertible security that is convertible only at the option of the issuer, is effectively deciding to accept the underlying security. See SEC Division of Corporation Finance, Compliance and Disclosure Interpretations, Question 103.4 (Sept. 22, 2016).

[147] H.R.Rep. No. 85, 73d Cong., 1st Sess. 11 (1933).

b. *Stock Dividends.* An issuer may choose to issue stock as a dividend rather than cash (or something else of value). Conventional stock dividends "are exempt without express provision as they do not constitute a sale, not being given for value."[148] Although waiver of a right could constitute "value" under § 2(a)(3), the SEC General Counsel has opined that, when a company declares a dividend that is payable, at the shareholder's election, in cash or securities, "neither the declaration of the dividend, nor the distribution of securities to stockholders who elect to take the dividend in that form, would . . . constitute a sale within the meaning of the Securities Act, and no registration of the securities so distributed would be required by that Act." If, however, the board were to be so ill-advised as to declare a cash dividend, and then permit its shareholders to receive stock in exchange for waiving rights to a cash payment, the General Counsel opined that a "sale of securities" might be entailed. This conclusion was based on the prevailing view that shareholders entitled to receive a dividend become the company's creditors. Those shareholders cannot be divested of their rights by board action. Instead, under this arrangement, the shareholders would be "paying" for the stock by waiving their rights to a cash dividend, resulting in a sale.[149]

c. *"Free Stock."* In the late 1990s, to increase subscribers, some internet companies devised a series of "stock giveaway" or "free stock" programs under which people who registered on (or simply visited) a company's website would receive company stock. This arrangement made sense to the issuers, who could charge more to advertisers if they had a larger subscriber base (which became even more important to an issuer approaching an IPO). The companies argued that no sale was made to these share recipients, who paid nothing and made no commitment to the issuer. In a series of no-action letters, the SEC staff rejected those positions, finding that issuing securities in return for a person registering on, or simply visiting, an issuer's website would be a "sale" under § 2(a)(3).[150] Indeed, even if the recipient only sent a self-addressed envelope to the issuer, the SEC staff took the position that such a "registration" conferred "value" on the issuer and, therefore, fell within § 2(a)(3).[151]

In the website cases, the stock recipient did something that involved a concrete, tangible act—such as registering on a website. Assume, instead, a company's 100% shareholder gives away stock to several hundred people (while still retaining a controlling interest) to help create a market for that stock. In one such case, the SEC still found that § 5 had been violated, because the "value" requirement under § 2(a)(3) hinges

---

[148] H.R.Rep. No. 152, 73d Cong., 1st Sess. 25 (1933).

[149] See Securities Act Release No. 929 (1936). See also SEC Division of Corporation Finance, Compliance and Disclosure Interpretations, Question 103.1 (Sept. 22, 2016).

[150] See Simplystocks.com, 1999 WL 51836 (SEC No-Action Letter), 1999 SEC No-Act. LEXIS 131 (Feb. 4, 1999); Vanderkam & Sanders, 1999 SEC No-Act. LEXIS 96 (Jan. 27, 1999).

[151] See Jones and Rutten, 1999 SEC No-Act. LEXIS 555 (June 8, 1999).

"not only on whether the recipient of the security gives something of value . . . but also on whether value is received from any other source."[152] In this case, the controlling shareholder received the benefit of a public market, even if the minority shareholders paid nothing.

Query: Suppose a beer manufacturer offers one share of stock for each purchase of one case of beer. The company can demonstrate there has been no change in the price at which it sells beer. That price is set by state law and has remained constant for some time. Has a "sale" occurred? Note, in this regard, § 2(a)(3) reads in part that "[a]ny security given or delivered with, or as a bonus on account of, any purchase of securities *or any other thing*, shall be conclusively presumed to constitute a part of the subject of such purchase and to have been offered and sold for value" (emphasis added).[153]

d. *Pledge of Securities.* Prior to Rubin v. United States,[154] the Courts of Appeals were divided about whether a pledge of securities as collateral for a loan involved a "sale or disposition of a security or interest in a security, for value" within the meaning of § 2(a)(3) and, therefore, a "sale" for purposes of § 17(a) of the 1933 Act. Section 17(a) is an antifraud statute the SEC may use, for example, if there has been a material misstatement or omission in the offer or sale of securities. Some Circuits relied on the clause "unless the context otherwise requires" at the beginning of § 2 to conclude the transaction fell outside the definition of "sale." In economic reality, they reasoned, it merely consisted of transferring the possession of securities from a borrower to a creditor to secure a loan. No sale or other disposition would occur until foreclosure following a default on the loan.

In *Rubin*, the Supreme Court settled the matter, affirming a criminal conviction for fraud under § 17(a) of the 1933 Act by a defendant who pledged worthless stock to a bank as collateral for a commercial loan. The Court found the terms of the 1933 Act to be "unambiguous" in determining that a pledge involved a "disposition of . . . [an] interest in a security, for value." Justice Blackmun concurred but concluded that a pledge of stock as collateral simply constituted a "disposition" within the meaning of § 2(a)(3), also noting the parallel provision of § 3(a)(14) of the 1934 Act (which omits the words "for value"). Accordingly, the pledge of securities may also be subject to the antifraud provisions of Rule 10b–5 under the 1934 Act.[155]

---

[152] See In re Capital General Corp., [1993 Transfer Binder] Fed. Sec. L. Rep. [CCH] ¶ 85,223 (1993) at 84,425. See also the *Datronics* opinion, which is discussed later in this casebook.

[153] For the SEC's position, see American Brewing Company, 1999 WL 38280 (SEC. No-Action Letter) (Jan. 27, 1999).

[154] 449 U.S. 424 (1981).

[155] See Head v. Head, 759 F.2d 1172 (4th Cir. 1985); Chemical Bank v. Arthur Andersen & Co., 726 F.2d 930 (2d Cir. 1984); United States v. Kendrick, 692 F.2d 1262 (9th Cir. 1982), cert. denied 461 U.S. 914 (1983).

e. *Exchanges and Amendments of Articles or Indentures.* Although the § 2(a)(3) definition of "sale" does not expressly include "exchange," courts have had no difficulty finding an exchange of securities to be a sale. As one court put it: "[O]ne may sell a security and be paid therefor in cash, or in another security, or in any other object of value such as a house. . . ."[156] Congress obviously took this view in enacting §§ 3(a)(9) and 3(a)(10), discussed next, which exempt certain types of exchanges of securities from the registration requirements of the 1933 Act.

The matter seems quite clear when the security holder voluntarily surrenders a certificate evidencing a security and, in return, receives an entirely different certificate. But sometimes, rather than a change in certificates, an issuer may make substantial changes to the terms of the security represented by a single certificate. In SEC v. Associated Gas & Electric Co.,[157] for example, extending the maturity date of a bond (evidenced by stamping the outstanding certificates with a legend) was held to be a new issue and sale of a security under the Public Utility Holding Company Act of 1935. Modification of the original obligation by negotiation between bondholders and the issuer was deemed to be equivalent to exchanging a new security for an old one. On that basis, a material change in the rights of other outstanding securities—by way of a charter amendment or otherwise—even if authorized by law, may involve the issue and sale of a new security.[158]

There is some inconsistency in the case law in this area. In Browning Debenture Holders' Committee v. DASA Corp.,[159] the issuer needed its bondholders to waive protective covenants in the bond indenture so that it could sell certain assets. To obtain their consent, the issuer proposed a sweetener—a favorable change in the bondholders' conversion rights, which the bondholders were asked to vote to approve. Dissident bondholders sued, arguing that the substantial change in conversion rights amounted to an offer to sell a new security. The court disagreed, noting that the original bond indenture authorized amendments based on a two-thirds vote. Despite this decision, the SEC continues to insist that any material amendment to a security's economic or voting rights amounts to the sale of a new security.[160]

---

[156] United States v. Riedel, 126 F.2d 81, 83 (7th Cir. 1942); see also United States v. Wernes, 157 F.2d 797 (7th Cir. 1946).

[157] 99 F.2d 795 (2d Cir. 1938).

[158] United States v. New York, New Haven & Hartford Railroad Co., 276 F.2d 525 (2d Cir. 1960), cert. denied 362 U.S. 961 (1960); Western Air Lines, Inc. v. Sobieski, 191 Cal.App.2d 399, 12 Cal.Rptr. 719 (1961); McGuigan & Aiken, Amendment of Securities, 9 Rev. of Sec.Reg. 935 (1976).

[159] [1974–1975 Transfer Binder] Fed. Sec. L. Rep. (CCH) Para. 95,071 (S.D.N.Y. 1975).

[160] The SEC, however, does not find a minor change, such as an alteration in par value or an increase in authorized stock, to be the sale of a new security. See INDRESCO, Inc., SEC No-Action Letter, [1996 Transfer Binder] Fed. Sec. L. Rep. (CCH) Para. 77,123 (Oct. 31, 1995).

B. SECTION 3(a)(9)

Statutes and Regulations

Securities Act, § 3(a)(9).

Rules 149, 150.

Section 3(a)(9) is a transactional exemption tucked away amidst other § 3 exemptions that mostly apply to classes of securities (specifically, §§ 3(a)(1)—3(a)(8) of the 1933 Act). It permits a company to issue new securities exclusively in exchange for existing securities, without SEC registration, so long as no one is paid for soliciting the exchange. Section 3(a)(9)'s existence can be traced to the economic exigencies of the early Depression when many businesses were forced to exchange equity securities (or a package of equity and debt securities) for outstanding senior securities on which they could no longer pay interest or principal at maturity.[161]

Today, § 3(a)(9) is more commonly used by issuers that are not in financial peril, although its popularity still spikes upward during times of crisis, like the COVID-19 pandemic. The most common transaction remains an offer by an issuer to swap a new security for an outstanding senior security (often one whose principal is approaching maturity). However, an exchange transaction can also be used to take a company private in a leveraged buyout (with the company's shareholders receiving debt securities plus cash for their common stock) or to issue special "superweighted" voting stock as a defensive measure against a hostile takeover. Although most § 3(a)(9) exchanges are voluntary, an involuntary exchange can be compelled under many state laws if there is a shareholder-approved amendment of the certificate of incorporation (or if state law otherwise permits a mandatory exchange). In such cases, a proxy solicitation will be used if the company is a reporting company, but the exemption under the 1933 Act is likely to come from § 3(a)(9).

In general, the four main requirements of § 3(a)(9) are as follows:

1. *Same issuer.* The issuer of the outstanding securities being surrendered must be the same as the issuer of the new securities being offered in exchange.

2. *Offer only to existing security holders.* The exchange must be offered exclusively to the issuer's existing security holders.

3. *No additional consideration from security holders.* With limited exception,[162] existing security holders should only be required to deliver the outstanding securities being exchanged, with no other payment being necessary.

---

[161] See H.R.Rep. No. 152, 73rd Cong., 1st Sess. 25 (1933).

[162] See Rule 150 under the 1933 Act. The waiver of accrued but unpaid dividends would not make the § 3(a)(9) exemption unavailable. See SEC Division of Corporation Finance, Compliance and Disclosure Interpretations, Question 125.04 (Sept. 22, 2016).

4. *No remuneration for the solicitation.* The issuer must not pay any commission or other remuneration for the solicitation of the exchange.

Section 3(a)(9)'s "same issuer" requirement means that the new securities being issued and the outstanding securities being surrendered must originate from a single issuer. This concept seems straightforward, but a number of factors can complicate matters. For example, in one case, the SEC staff granted no-action relief under § 3(a)(9) when a finance subsidiary exchanged debt securities, guaranteed by its parent, for securities of the parent. The no-action request emphasized the economic reality of the transaction, noting the subsidiary was established to finance the parent's activities and, therefore, had minimal assets and liabilities of its own.[163] Nevertheless, in general, the SEC staff takes the view that a parent and subsidiary are different issuers. Section 3(a)(9) is unavailable when a subsidiary has outstanding debentures that are guaranteed by the parent and proposes to exchange them for new debentures that do not have the guarantee.[164]

Another concern with issuer identity arises when, through a merger, acquisition, or other transaction, an issuer unconditionally assumes the securities of another issuer. The SEC staff believes the § 3(a)(9) exemption is available so long as the obligations relating to the target company's debt securities have been fully and unconditionally assumed by the issuer of the new securities. "Once the issuer has fully and unconditionally assumed the obligations on the debt securities of the other issuer, the transaction becomes the exchange of that obligation for the new security of the issuer with its existing security holders."[165]

Securities Act Release No. 2029 indicates that the term "exclusively" in § 3(a)(9) is read by the SEC to have two consequences: First, the § 3(a)(9) offering must be made exclusively to an existing class of security holders; that is, shares of the same class (or a similar class) may not be contemporaneously offered to other investors for other consideration. Second, the issuer must offer the exchange exclusively for a class of outstanding securities. Security holders should not be asked to contribute cash or other consideration.

Regarding the first consequence, if the exchange occurs when there is a contemporaneous offering to other prospective investors, the issuer must take care to keep the two offerings separate to avoid their being "integrated" into a single transaction. The topic of integration has been

---

[163] See SEC No-Action Letter, Echo Bay Resources Inc., 1998 SEC No-Act. LEXIS 591 (May 18, 1998).

[164] See SEC Division of Corporation Finance, Compliance and Disclosure Interpretations, Question 125.05 (Sept. 22, 2016). The SEC staff considers the guarantee and the debentures to be separate securities. Thus, exchanging the parent guarantee for the subsidiary's unguaranteed debentures does not involve an exchange by the same issuer, even if exchange of the debentures themselves may be exempt from registration.

[165] See SEC Division of Corporation Finance, Compliance and Disclosure Interpretations Question 125.02 (Sept. 22, 2016).

raised already and is addressed further later in this chapter. If integrated, however, the entire transaction must satisfy the requirements of a single exemption. Whether the two offerings will be integrated depends on the circumstances. But if an issuer, for example, purports to do a § 4(a)(2) private placement for cash, and at the same time does a § 3(a)(9) exchange offer of the same securities, the two offerings may be integrated into a single transaction. In that case, the § 3(a)(9) exemption will be lost (since some investors paid cash in the now-integrated single transaction). The issuer may be able to fit both offerings under § 4(a)(2) or seek to rely on another exemption from § 5, if available.[166]

Regarding the second consequence, there is no barrier to the *issuer* offering cash plus a new class of securities in exchange for an outstanding class of securities.[167] Rule 150 under the 1933 Act expressly permits "payments made by the issuer, directly or indirectly, to its security holders in connection with an exchange of securities for outstanding securities, when such payments are part of the terms of the offer of exchange." Rather, § 3(a)(9) prohibits the existing security holder from being asked to make a further cash or property investment. Even this barrier has been relaxed slightly. Rule 149 permits the issuer to request a security holder to pay cash to the extent "necessary to effect an equitable adjustment" in the dividends or interest for the exchanged security "as between such security holder and other security holders" in the exchange.

Suppose an issuer has accrued dividends of $30 per share on its outstanding preferred stock, and offers to exchange three shares of common stock for one share of preferred stock (resulting in loss of the $30 in accrued dividends). Does this exchange, which requires the preferred stockholder to surrender a future payment, meet the "exclusively" test? The SEC interprets § 3(a)(9) to only bar the investor from investing new consideration, and thus it has not objected to such an exchange under § 3(a)(9). Indeed, the SEC has even permitted an exchange under § 3(a)(9) where shareholders were required to release claims underlying a securities fraud lawsuit as a condition of the exchange.[168]

---

[166] As noted earlier, the SEC recently proposed amendments to the integration rules. See Securities Act Release No. 10763 (Mar. 4, 2020). The proposals would establish new Rule 152, which would replace current Rules 152 and 155. New Rule 152 provides a general framework and four safe harbors, replacing the various safe harbors currently set forth in various 1933 Act exemptions. Under its Proposed General Principle of Integration, an issuer will determine whether offers and sales are to be integrated based on the particular facts and circumstances. The proposed facts and circumstances analysis of integration replaces the traditional five-factor test.

[167] The SEC Staff has provided no-action relief even when the consideration is paid by an affiliate of the issuer. See Carolina Wholesale Florists, Inc., SEC No-Action Letter, 1976 WL 12584 (Sept. 27, 1976).

[168] See First Pennsylvania Mortgage Trust, SEC No-Action Letter, 1997 WL 13863 (Feb. 4, 1977); see also SEC Division of Corporation Finance, Compliance and Disclosure Interpretations, Question 125.04 (Sept. 22, 2016); Seaman Furniture Co., Inc., 1989 SEC No-Act. LEXIS 1014 (Oct. 10, 1989).

One practical barrier to using § 3(a)(9) is that the issuer cannot hire an underwriter or other agent to solicit security holders. Section 3(a)(9) prohibits payment of any "commission or other remuneration . . . directly or indirectly for soliciting such exchange." This limitation can create practical difficulties for issuers that believe they need an active dealer/manager to solicit the exchanges. Although the issuer can use its own employees, that may not be practical; nor may sophisticated investors place much weight on their analyses. If employees are used, they should not be paid a special bonus or other type of remuneration for their solicitation activities (i.e., they should be paid their regular salary), and they should attend to their regular duties, with solicitation being only an additional assignment.[169]

The SEC's staff, however, has relaxed the prohibition in various no-action letters.[170] In one important no-action letter, a financially troubled issuer won permission to use an investment bank (that was also the company's financial adviser) to meet with a committee of institutional investors to discuss the issuer's proposed restructuring through an exchange offer. The investment bank's services included: performing financial analyses; assisting the issuer in formulating a restructuring proposal; advising the issuer on the terms of the new securities to be issued in the restructuring; participating in meetings between the issuer's representatives and legal and financial advisors of the committee; and speaking by telephone with representatives of the legal and financial advisors of the committee. To obtain the no-action relief, the issuer represented that the investment bank would only play an informational role. It would not express to the committee's advisors their views on the fairness of the proposed restructuring or the value of the new securities to be issued or make any recommendation regarding the restructuring or proposed exchange.[171] Although § 3(a)(9) does not specify the types of fees that third parties can receive, the SEC's staff has indicated in no-action letters that an adviser may receive a fixed fee for its services, not contingent upon the success of the exchange, plus reasonable expenses related to the exchange. A fixed fee eliminates one factor that might support the inference that the adviser had an incentive to engage in an impermissible solicitation. *Query*: Investment banks typically have a "liability management," "restructuring," or "workout" team that specializes in debt restructurings. They assist an issuer in creating a restructuring plan and managing the exchange, perhaps also

---

[169] See URS Corp., SEC No-Action Letter, 1975 WL 11259 (May 8, 1975).

[170] The SEC staff has issued no-action letters that permit a financial advisor to undertake certain activities, including pre-launch discussions with sophisticated security holders, so long as the financial advisor is not paid a success fee. For examples of the types of activities of a third party, such as a financial advisor, that are consistent with § 3(a)(9), see Seaman Furniture Co., Inc., 1989 SEC No-Act. LEXIS 1014 (Oct. 10, 1989).

[171] See id. In a different matter, a court found an underwriter's activities in soliciting noteholders to approve an informal reorganization to be sufficiently connected to a later exchange solicitation to bar reliance on § 3(a)(9). See Argentinian Recovery Company LLC v. Multicanal S.A., 331 B.R. 537, Fed. Sec. L. Rep. (CCH) Para. 93,584 (S.D.N.Y. 2005).

meeting with various large security holders. In these meetings, can the line between "providing information" and "making recommendations" be effectively monitored? More generally, should the SEC liberalize § 3(a)(9) when that exemption requires no disclosure statement and contains no restrictions on the nature of investors to whom the offer can be made?[172]

Securities Act Release No. 646
Securities and Exchange Commission.
February 3, 1936.

[In 1936, the SEC General Counsel issued two interpretive letters relating to § 3(a)(9) of the 1933 Act. The first letter concerned a proposed exchange of bonds with three noteholders. In responding to the query, the General Counsel had this to say:]

* * *

I believe Section 3(a)(9) is applicable only to exchanges which are bona fide, in the sense that they are not effected merely as a step in a plan to evade the registration requirements of the Act. For example, Corporation A, as part of such a plan, might issue a large block of its securities to Corporation B, and might then issue new securities to Corporation B in exchange for the first-issued securities, with the understanding that such new securities are to be offered to the public by Corporation B. In my opinion, the mere fact that the exchange in such case might comply with the literal conditions of Section 3(a)(9) would not avail to defeat the necessity for registration of the securities issued in such exchange. Cf. Gregory v. Helvering, 293 U.S. 465.

In determining whether a particular exchange had been effected merely as a step in a plan to evade the registration requirements of the Act, I believe that a court would take into account various factors such as the length of time during which the securities received by the issuer were outstanding prior to their surrender in exchange, the number of holders of the securities originally outstanding, the marketability of such securities, and also the question whether the exchange is one which was dictated by financial considerations of the issuer and not primarily in order to enable one or a few security holders to distribute their holdings to the public. * * *

The second opinion of the General Counsel was in reply to an inquiry whether securities previously received by a controlling stockholder in a bona fide exchange exempt under § 3(a)(9) should be registered before being offered to the public through an underwriter. The relevant portion of the opinion follows:

---

[172] For the view that § 3(a)(9) represents an overbroad exemption in its present form, see Hicks, Recapitalizations Under Section 3(a)(9) of the Securities Act of 1933, 61 Va.L.Rev. 1057 (1995).

In order to make clear my position on this question, I must briefly review the legislative histories of the present Section 3(a)(9) and of Section 2(11) of the Securities Act of 1933.

The last sentence of Section 2(11) . . . by defining an underwriter to include a person purchasing from one in a control relation with the issuer, makes the exemption afforded by Section 4(1) inapplicable to transactions by such a person and thus necessitates registration before distribution to the public of securities acquired from a person in a control relation. The report of the House Committee, which considered the identical language in the bill then before the Committee (H.R. 5480), leaves no doubt as to the reason for this requirement . . . .

* * *

Section 2(11) thus gives expression to the clear intent of Congress to subject to the registration requirements of the Act any redistribution of securities purchased from persons in a control relation with the issuer.[a]

Turning to the present Section 3(a)(9), I call your attention to the fact that, although this Section in terms excepts *securities* issued in certain transactions of exchange, its predecessor, Section 4(3) exempted only such *transactions* of exchange. Consequently, before the 1934 amendments, distribution by a controlling person through an underwriter of stock previously issued in a transaction exempt under former Section 4(3), was subject to the registration requirements. The reasons for the relevant amendment therefore become important.

The question early arose whether dealers' transactions in securities exchanged in a Section 4(3) transaction were exempt from the registration requirements of the Securities Act. Section 4(1) specifically excepts from the dealers' exemption

> "transactions within one year after the first date upon which a security was bona fide offered to the public";

but in order to effectuate the evident purpose of the Act, the Federal Trade Commission took the position that dealers' transactions in securities originally issued in a transaction exempt under Section 4(3) were exempt, even though such dealers' transactions were effected within a year of the first offering of such securities.

> "[T]he purpose of the amendment changing Section 4(3) to Sections 3(a)(9) and 3(a)(10) was to incorporate in the Act this opinion of the Commission. [This] appears from the . . . report of the Conference Committee which considered these amendments."

---

[a] See H.R. 85, 73d Cong., 1st Sess., pp. 13–14.

* * *

This language clearly evidences that the Congressional intent was merely to offer a more adequate statutory basis for the Commission's previous interpretation, and not to alter the fundamental requirement of Section 2(11).

Moreover, the fact that the securities in question fall within Section 3(a) does not necessarily preclude consideration of the necessity of their registration before certain transactions therein can be effected. Sections 3(a)(2) to 3(a)(8) inclusive describe classes of securities which are of such an intrinsic nature that it is evident that Congress felt that, regardless of the character of the transaction in which they have been or are to be issued or publicly offered, their registration was not necessary for the protection of investors. . . . In the language of House Report No. 85, quoted supra, a large public offering of such securities possesses all the dangers attendant upon a new offering by their issuer.

* * *

In view of the Congressional purpose in enacting the last sentence of Section 2(11), the legislative history of the present Section 3(a)(9), and the lack of any rational basis for the continuance of the exemption provided by Section 3(a)(9) to a later offering of securities by an underwriter, it is my opinion that securities received in a Section 3(a)(9) exchange should be registered before their public distribution through an underwriter by a person in control of their issuer.

Securities Act Release No. 2029
Securities and Exchange Commission.
August 8, 1939.

[Letter of SEC General Counsel Relating to §§ 3(a)(9) and 4(1) (the predecessor to current § 4(a)(2)).]

* * *

You have requested an opinion as to the applicability of Section 3(a)(9) and the second clause of Section 4(1) of the Securities Act of 1933 in the following circumstances:

The subject company has an "open end" mortgage upon its properties, the only issue of bonds now outstanding thereunder being denoted as Series A bonds. It is proposed to create two new series of bonds under the mortgage, to be called Series B and Series C bonds respectively, for the purpose of refunding the outstanding bonds. The Series B and Series C bonds will differ substantially from each other in respect of maturity date, interest rate, redemption prices and default provisions.

The Series B bonds will be offered in exchange to the holders of the outstanding Series A bonds on the basis of an equal principal amount of Series B bonds for those of Series A, with interest adjustment. No commission or other remuneration will be paid or given, directly or indirectly, for soliciting such exchange.

The necessary funds to redeem any unexchanged Series A bonds will be raised by the sale for cash of Series C bonds. The Series C bonds will be offered and sold to not more than twelve insurance companies, which will agree to purchase for investment and without a view to distribution.

If the proposed exchange offer and the proposed cash offer were isolated transactions, it would be clear that no registration under the Securities Act would be required. The Series B bonds would be exempted as securities "exchanged by the issuer with its existing security holders exclusively where no commission or other remuneration is paid or given directly or indirectly for soliciting such exchange;" and the offering and sale of the Series C bonds would be exempted by the second clause of Section 4(1), as "transactions by an issuer not involving any public offering." The interdependence of the two offerings, however, requires a more comprehensive analysis of the Act.

Section 3(a)(9) contains no language expressly limiting the exemption to securities forming part of an issue the whole of which is sold as specified in the exempting provision. At first reading, therefore, Section 3(a)(9) appears to confer exemption upon any security exchanged with the issuer's existing security holders, even though other securities of the same class, as a part of the same plan of financing, are sold to other than existing security holders, or to existing security holders otherwise than by way of exchange. Such a construction, however, gives insufficient weight to the use of the word "exclusively," as employed both in Section 3(a)(9) and in its predecessor, former Section 4(3). In neither section is the grammatical function of the word entirely clear; but in order to avoid an interpretation which would reject the word as pure surplusage, it is necessary to adopt the view that the exemption is available only to securities constituting part of an issue which, as a whole, is exchanged in conformity with the requirements of the section.

This conclusion appears to be supported by the legislative history of Section 3(a)(9) .... [T]he changes in the proposed Section 3(a)(9) made in conference were "intended only to clarify its meaning" (H.R. (Conf.) Rep. No. 1838, 73rd Cong., 2nd Sess., p. 40).

Interpretation of the so-called "private offering" exemption provided by the second clause of Section 4(1) presents similar considerations. You will note that the clause in question does not exempt every transaction which is not itself a public offering, but only transactions "not involving any public offering." Accordingly, I am of the opinion that the exemption is not available to securities privately offered if any other securities comprised within the same issue are made the subject of a public offering.

It appears, therefore, that both with respect to Section 3(a)(9) and with respect to Section 4(1) the necessity of registering the Series B and Series C bonds depends upon whether they should be deemed separate issues or merely parts of a single issue. I believe it unnecessary at this time to enter into any extended discussion of what constitutes an "issue" for the purposes of the Act. The opinion of the Commission in In the Matter of Unity Gold Corporation (Securities Act Release No. 1776) discusses this question as it arises under Section 3(b) of the Act. The point is also touched upon, at least inferentially, in the discussion of Section 3(a)(11) contained in Securities Act Release No. 1459. Whatever may be the precise limits of the concept of "issue" when all securities involved are of the same class, I do not believe that securities of different classes can fairly be deemed parts of a single "issue." Since on the facts submitted the Series B and Series C bonds appear to be securities of different classes, they constitute separate "issues," and may be offered and sold in the manner above described without being registered under the Securities Act.[a]

In expressing this opinion I do not mean to imply that any difference in the incidents of two blocks of securities, however trivial, renders the blocks separate classes and consequently separate "issues" for the purposes of the Act. In this case, however, the differences between the Series B and Series C bonds are, I believe, sufficiently substantial to warrant treating them as separate classes even though they will be issued under the same mortgage indenture.

* * *

NOTES ON THE STATUS OF SECTION 3(a)(9) EXCHANGES

1. *Convertible Securities.* Section 3(a)(9) applies to the conversion of convertible stock (such as preferred stock that is convertible into common stock). The interrelationship of §§ 3(a)(9) and 2(a)(3) merits special attention. If the convertible security is immediately convertible, then absent an exemption from § 5, both the convertible securities and the underlying securities must be registered with the SEC.

The question arises, what if the conversion feature is not immediate? As noted earlier in this chapter, § 2(a)(3) provides that "[t]he issue or transfer of a right or privilege, when originally issued or transferred with a security, giving the holder of such security the right to convert such security into another security of the same issuer" is not an offer or sale of the underlying security if the right cannot be exercised until some future date. Thus, in 2018, if a company issues convertible preferred stock that cannot be converted into common stock until 2020, there is no obligation to register the common stock on the date the convertible stock

---

[a] In 1939, the integration doctrine was at an early stage in its development. This opinion discusses its application in the context of §§ 4(a)(2) and 3(a)(9). See the section on "Integration of Exemptions" later in this chapter.—Eds.

is issued. Section 2(a)(3) provides that the subsequent conversion will be a sale, but if § 3(a)(9) is available, there is no need for registration with the SEC. There still remains the question of whether an offer is being made that violates § 5(c) once the right to convert becomes exercisable, even if the later conversion (the deemed sale) will be exempt under § 3(a)(9). Here, the SEC's position has wavered over the years, but currently it agrees that § 3(a)(9) exempts the continuing offer of the common stock once the conversion feature becomes exercisable, as well as the actual conversion.[173]

In the foregoing exchanges, each offeree is free to accept or reject the offer as an individual matter. This element of individual consent differentiates voluntary exchanges from corporate reorganizations and recapitalizations involving a "cram-down," in which non-consenting security holders are bound by the vote of a majority, subject to any right of appraisal. Nevertheless, in some instances, these reorganizations or recapitalizations—if subject to judicial or administrative approval—may rely on § 3(a)(10), which is discussed in the next section.

2. *Resales.* Section 3(a)(9) exempts only the exchange transaction, not a subsequent resale by the investor who makes the exchange. "Generally, the Commission appears to consider the Section 3(a)(9) exchange a neutral event. The new securities received by the Holder in the exchange are subject to the same resale limitations as the old securities that the Holder surrendered in the Section 3(a)(9) transaction. Accordingly, a Holder in possession of freely tradeable securities prior to the Section 3(a)(9) exchange will possess freely tradeable securities after the exchange. Conversely, if the Holder's old securities were restricted, the Holder's new Section 3(a)(9) Securities also will be deemed restricted."[174] Thus, for most investors, the exemption that will permit them to immediately resell the new securities is § 4(a)(1). That is, if the securities surrendered are not "restricted securities" (as defined in Rule 144, which is discussed later in this casebook), the securities received in the exchange will also not be "restricted" and can be resold immediately.

A controlling person, however, may remain a controlling person, and should it seek to resell the exchanged security, the resale may involve an underwriter under the last sentence of § 2(a)(11). Hence, a controlling person typically must comply with the "trickle" provisions of Rule 144 or make a private resale, options that are discussed later in this casebook.

A non-controlling shareholder may also need to rely on an exemption (other than § 4(a)(1)) if the securities it surrendered in the exchange were issued under an exemption, such as § 3(a)(11), or Rule 147 or Rule 147A, or § 4(a)(2). Recall that securities issued in reliance on § 4(a)(2) are "restricted securities." An exchange of restricted securities under

---

[173] See Loss, Fundamentals of Securities Regulation at 280–281 (2d ed. 1988).

[174] Campbell, Resales of Securities Under the Securities Act of 1933, 52 Wash. & Lee L.Rev. 1333, 1357 (1995).

§ 3(a)(9) does not free them for immediate resale.[175] Instead, the holder must wait until the applicable holding period under Rule 144 is satisfied (but, in calculating the hold period, it may tack on the length of time it held the exchanged securities to the holding period for the new securities) or resell the securities in reliance on Rule 144A or the so-called "§ 4(1½)" exemption, if available.

C. SECTION 3(a)(10)

Statute

Securities Act, § 3(a)(10).

Section 3(a)(10) provides an exemption from § 5 for offers and sales of securities in court- or governmentally-approved exchange transactions. Although the history is sparse, § 3(a)(10) apparently was designed to exempt judicially or administratively approved reorganizations or recapitalizations on the theory that, if the plans were approved as to "fairness," after a hearing at which all affected security holders could appear, there would be no need for additional regulation. The "fairness" hearing before a court or administrative agency was assumed to be "a substitute for the protection afforded to the investor by the information which would otherwise be made available through registration."[176]

The premise of § 3(a)(10) is that fairness hearings will protect the affected security holders. This is debatable, with the quality of scrutiny varying across state and federal agencies and tribunals that are authorized to approve a transaction's fairness. Even if the review is thorough, the hearing may do little to inform the secondary market of the issuer or the securities being issued. As a result, § 3(a)(10) can permit a distribution of unregistered securities to the public market, arguably with less-than-adequate disclosure.

In general, to rely on § 3(a)(10), the following conditions must be satisfied (bracketed language in the following excerpt reflects updates or clarifications by the Editors):[177]

- The securities must be issued in exchange for securities, claims, or property interests; they cannot be offered for cash. [Note that § 3(a)(10) only covers the original issuance of options, warrants, and other convertible securities, not

---

[175] See SEC Division of Corporation Finance, Compliance and Disclosure Interpretations, Question 125.08 (Sept. 22, 2016). For a fuller discussion, see Campbell, Resales of Securities Under the Securities Act of 1933, 52 Wash. & Lee L.Rev. 1333, 1356–59 (1995).

[176] Securities Act Release No. 312 (Mar. 15, 1933). For the most recent expression of the SEC's views on this hearing requirement, see SEC Division of Corporation Finance, Division of Corporation Finance, Staff Legal Bulletin No. 3A (CF) (June 18, 2008); SEC No-Action, Interpretive and Exemptive Letters, 3(a)(10)-Exemption for Exchanges After a Fairness Hearing (last visited Jul. 9, 2020), http://www.sec.gov/divisions/corpfin/cf-noaction.shtml#3a10.

[177] SEC Division of Corporation Finance, Division of Corporation Finance, Staff Legal Bulletin No. 3A (CF) (June 18, 2008).

- their later exercise or conversion.[178] § 3(a)(9) or another exemption may be available then.]

- A court or authorized governmental entity must approve the fairness of the terms and conditions of the exchange. [It is the SEC staff's view that the term "any court" may include a foreign court.[179] In Staff Legal Bulletin No. 3 (Oct. 20, 1999), the SEC's Division of Corporation Finance indicated it will permit the § 3(a)(10) exemption to apply to approvals by foreign courts, provided the reviewing court (i) approves the fairness of the terms and conditions of the exchange, (ii) holds a hearing open to all affected persons to whom securities will be issued, and (iii) provides adequate notice of the hearing to all such persons.[180] In Argentinian Recovery Company LLC v. Multicanal S.A.,[181] this position was upheld, subject to the proviso that the foreign court has jurisdiction to hold a hearing on the fairness of the terms. *Query*: Is there any obvious limit on this procedure? To date, the SEC has only extended § 3(a)(10) to settlements approved by courts that follow traditional common law principles. Suppose a local court in an emerging market approves the issuance of shares after providing proper notice and holding a hearing, but it is not in a common law jurisdiction? Is it too ethnocentric to restrict § 3(a)(10) to the traditional common law process?]

- For governmental entities, the federal or state authorizing statute must expressly require the entity to affirmatively conclude that the exchange is fair to the security holders participating in the exchange.[182]

At the federal level, facilitating legislation sufficient to permit the use of § 3(a)(10) exists under the Public Utility Holding Company Act[183] and the Investment Company Act of 1940.[184]

---

[178] See Canadian Conquest Expl. Inc., SEC No-Action Letter, 1989 WL 245804 (Apr. 6, 1989); Allied Leisure Indus., Inc., SEC No-Action Letter, 1979 WL 14401 (Oct. 4, 1979).

[179] See, e.g., SanDisk Corp., SEC No-Action Letter, 2006 WL 2805149 (Sept. 21, 2006); Anglogold Ltd., SEC No-Action Letter, 2004 WL 111629 (Jan. 15, 2004).

[180] The Division has granted no-action letters on this basis for judicially approved amalgamations under English, Australian, Singaporean, and Indian procedures. See, e.g., ICICI Bank Limited, 2001 WL 161753 (SEC No-Action Letter, Dec. 13, 2001). In Ashanti Goldfields Company Limited, 2002 WL 1359408 (SEC No-Action Letter, June 19, 2002), the SEC staff gave its no-action approval to a "Scheme of Arrangement" approved by the Grand Court of the Cayman Islands.

[181] 331 B.R. 537, Fed. Sec. L. Rep. (CCH) Para. 93,584 (S.D.N.Y. Sept. 28, 2005).

[182] See SEC Division of Corporation Finance, Division of Corporation Finance, Staff Legal Bulletin No. 3A (CF) (June 18, 2008).

[183] 15 U.S.C. §§ 79, 79k(e).

[184] 15 U.S.C. §§ 80a–17(b), 17(d).

[At the state level, several states have adopted regulations that govern fairness hearings. Currently, California, Oregon, Washington, Utah, Idaho, Michigan, North Carolina, and Montana have held fairness hearings subject to § 3(a)(10).[185] In a number of other jurisdictions, states have comparable legislation relating to regulated industries, such as insurance, public utilities, and banking. Thus, a Florida banking authority's approval of a bank acquisition fell within § 3(a)(10) when the state agency was expressly authorized to pass upon (and did pass upon) the fairness of the merger.[186] Note, also, securities that rely on § 3(a)(10) are removed from the definition of "covered securities" in § 18 of the 1933 Act and, accordingly, are subject to the registration or qualification provisions of the state securities laws. An issuer may rely upon a fairness hearing conducted under state securities law to perfect its reliance on § 3(a)(10). Since § 3(a)(10) securities are carved out from § 18, they are not exempt from the registration or qualification provisions of any state securities law.]

- The reviewing court or authorized governmental entity must:
  o find, before approving the transaction, that the terms and conditions of the exchange are fair to those to whom securities will be issued; and
  o be advised before the hearing that the issuer will rely on the Section 3(a)(10) exemption based on the court's or authorized governmental entity's approval of the transaction.
- The court or authorized governmental entity must hold a hearing before approving the fairness of the terms and conditions of the transaction.
- A governmental entity must be expressly authorized by law to hold the hearing, although it is not necessary that the law require the hearing.
- The fairness hearing must be open to everyone to whom securities would be issued in the proposed exchange.
- Adequate notice must be given to all those persons. [The SEC staff has noted that the antifraud requirements of the federal securities laws govern disclosures to persons in connection with fairness hearings.[187]]

---

[185] See Hunton & Williams, Client Alert 2 (Mar. 2017).

[186] See Wachovia Corp., SEC No-Action Letter, 1998 WL 60783 (Feb. 10, 1998).

[187] See SEC Division of Corporation Finance, Division of Corporation Finance, Staff Legal Bulletin No. 3A (CF) (June 18, 2008).

- There cannot be any improper impediments to the appearance by those persons at the hearing.

Securities Act Release No. 312
Securities and Exchange Commission.
March 15, 1935.

[The following is an excerpt from an interpretive letter of the SEC General Counsel with respect to exchange transactions under Section 3(a)(10).]

* * *

I shall take up in order the three questions you have raised as to the interpretation of [Section 3(a)(10)].

1. Is adequate notice to all persons to whom it is proposed to issue securities of the hearing on the fairness of their issuance necessary for an exemption under Section 3(a)(10)?

Although the wording of Section 3(a)(10) does not demand such notice, in my opinion this requirement is to be implied from the necessity for a "hearing . . . at which all persons to whom it is proposed to issue securities . . . shall have the right to appear." To give substance to this express requirement, some adequate form of notice seems necessary. The usual practice of giving notice to persons who will receive securities in reorganizations, mergers and consolidations supports this view. Of course, the question of what mode of notice is adequate cannot be answered in the abstract but may vary with the facts and circumstances in each case.

2. Is a grant of "express authorization of law" to a state governmental authority to approve the fairness of the terms and conditions of the issuance and exchange of securities necessary for an exemption under Section 3(a)(10), or is express authorization merely to approve the terms and conditions sufficient?

The punctuation and grammatical construction of the last clause of Section 3(a)(10) indicate that the words "expressly authorized . . . by law" were not intended to modify "[any] court[,] or [by any] official[ ] or agenc[y] of the United States". In my opinion a State governmental authority (with the possible exception of a banking or insurance commission) must possess express authority of law to approve the *fairness* of the terms and conditions of the issuance and exchange of the securities in question. This interpretation seems necessary to give meaning to the express requirement of a hearing upon the fairness of such terms and conditions, which must subsume authority in the supervisory body to pass upon the fairness from the standpoint of the investor, as well as the issuer and consumer, and to disapprove terms and conditions because unfair either to those who are to receive the securities or to other security holders of the issuer, or to the public. This requirement seems the more essential in that the whole justification for the exemption afforded by Section 3(a)(10) is that the examination and approval by the body in question of the fairness of the issue in question is a substitute for the protection afforded to the investor by the information which would otherwise be made available to him through registration. The requisite express authorization of law to approve the fairness of such terms and conditions, however, probably need not necessarily be in haec verba but, to give effect to the words "express" and "by law", must be granted clearly and explicitly.

3. Does a hearing by an authority expressly authorized by law to hold such a hearing satisfy the requirement of a hearing in Section 3(a)(10), if the state law does not require a hearing?

I believe that, as a corollary to the view expressed in my answer to the second question, supra, and in order that a hearing have legal sanction, the approving authority must be expressly authorized by law to hold the hearing; but in my opinion it is unnecessary that the hearing be mandatory under applicable state law. Therefore, if state law expressly authorizes the approving authority to hold a hearing on the fairness of the terms and conditions of the issuance and exchange of securities, and such a hearing is in fact held, this requirement of Section 3(a)(10) is satisfied. * * *

NOTES ON REORGANIZATIONS AND OTHER EXCHANGES UNDER SECTION 3(a)(10)

1. *Advantages to the Issuer.* From the issuer's perspective, § 3(a)(10) has some distinct advantages over a § 3(a)(9) exchange (either to settle litigation or to restructure a financially strained company). First, unlike § 3(a)(9) (and its "exclusively" limitation), a § 3(a)(10) exchange can occur at the same time as an offering for cash. Second, § 3(a)(10) is not subject to the § 3(a)(9) requirement that the issuer of the outstanding securities and the securities surrendered must be the same. Thus, it is easier to effect a reorganization involving multiple companies under § 3(a)(10). Third, there is no limitation on commissions or other remuneration paid to solicitors (as there is under the final clause of § 3(a)(9)); this enables the issuer to use broker-dealers to solicit security holders.

Note, however, that § 3(a)(10) has some doctrinal issues. For example, when the court or agency mails out a hearing notice to affected security holders, no exemption clearly protects this communication (since the court or agency has not yet determined "fairness").[188] Also, an agency

---

[188] Clearly, this notice does not fall within Rule 135 under the 1933 Act since there is no registration statement. Practitioners believe that, so long as the notice strictly conforms to judicial or agency rules, the SEC will raise no objection. See Mann, The Section 3(a)(10) Exemption: Recent Interpretations, 22 UCLA L.Rev. 1247 (1975). Likewise, the SEC's Division of Corporation Finance staff has said, "A practical issue arises because many statutes governing

that lacks statutory authority to approve the exchange's fairness may not qualify under § 3(a)(10), even if the agency is authorized to consider the effect of the proposed transaction on consumers or the public interest.

2. *Reorganization of Financially-Distressed Entities.* Securities issued under a plan of reorganization are subject to the supervision of the bankruptcy court. Unlike § 3(a)(10), solicitation of approval of a plan of reorganization must be accompanied by a disclosure statement approved by the bankruptcy court as being adequate.[189] The court is authorized to hold a hearing on the plan, and confirmation is conditioned on finding that the plan "does not discriminate unfairly, and is fair and equitable, with respect to each class of claims or interests that is impaired under, and has not accepted, the plan."[190] The Bankruptcy Code, therefore, represents a departure from the § 3(a)(10) model. Certain of the issues around securities issued pursuant to the Bankruptcy Code are discussed next in this chapter.

3. *Settlement of Litigation.* SEC no-action letters reveal the use of § 3(a)(10) in connection with securities issued in negotiated litigation settlements subject to court supervision. Unlike state governmental agencies, U.S. courts do not need an express grant of authority to approve the fairness of the terms of a securities exchange.[191]

Professor Barbara A. Ash, after reviewing approximately 60 publicly-available no-action letters, concluded that the SEC "staff has consistently taken a no-action position based on counsel's opinion as to the availability of section 3(a)(10) irrespective of whether the issuer was one of the defendants or a corporation, a substantial number of whose securities happened to be held by one or more of the defendants."[192] As to the usefulness of § 3(a)(10) in settlements, Professor Ash found:[193]

> Since § 3(a)(10) may be relied on in connection with the settlement of litigation of almost any nature, it is of widespread utility. As noted above, the amount of litigation under the

---

fairness hearings require security holders to vote before the hearing, at a time when the issuer cannot be certain that it will be able to rely on the Section 3(a)(10) exemption. In these situations, the Division has not objected to a vote before the fairness hearing, even though this means an investment decision is made before the fairness hearing. The Division takes this view because the timing is required by the governing statute and, under that statute, the transaction is not effected unless the court or authorized governmental entity approves it. In the Division's view, the issuer should submit to the court or authorized governmental entity the disclosure materials offering the securities before it mails them to the offerees." SEC Division of Corporation Finance, Division of Corporation Finance, Staff Legal Bulletin No. 3A (CF) (June 18, 2008).

[189] See 11 U.S.C. § 1125.
[190] Id. at §§ 1128 (hearing), 1129 (confirmation).
[191] Securities Act Release No. 312 (Mar. 15, 1935), at p. 490.
[192] Ash, Reorganizations and Other Exchanges Under Section 3(a)(10) of the Securities Act of 1933, 75 Nw.U.L.Rev. 1, 38 (1980). For an example of the use of § 3(a)(10) in settling litigation, see Brucker v. Thyssen-Bornemisza Europe N.V., 424 F.Supp. 679, 690–91 (S.D.N.Y.1976).
[193] Ash, Reorganizations and Other Exchanges Under Section 3(a)(10) of the Securities Act of 1933, 75 Nw.U.L.Rev. 1, 38–39 (1980).

federal securities laws has become rather substantial and often lends itself to a settlement agreement involving the issuance of securities. In more than a majority of the approximately sixty no-action letters referred to above, the underlying litigation was pursuant to the Federal securities laws, frequently the antifraud provisions of the Act or the Exchange Act or the federal proxy rules, and in one case interestingly enough section 3(a)(10) itself. In addition, the no-action letters indicate that section 3(a)(10) is quite often useful to the settlement of litigation arising from various provisions of the state corporation codes and to court-supervised liquidations, distributions for the benefit of creditors, and various other insolvency-related issuances of securities not pursuant to the Federal Bankruptcy Act. . . . [T]here appears to be no limitation, even in the Commission's view, on the availability of the Exchange Exemption because of the nature of the litigation proposed to be settled.

4. *Resales.* Section 3(a)(10) covers sales by the issuer and not resales of securities received in a § 3(a)(10) transaction. Public offers and resales of § 3(a)(10) securities typically by affiliates of the target issued as part of a reclassification, merger or consolidation, or transfer-of-assets reorganization (each as described in Rule 145(a) under the 1933 Act) that are subject to shareholder vote are addressed as follows (emphases added):[194]

> [I]t is the Division's view that securities received in a Rule 145(a) transaction *not involving a shell company* that was exempt under Section 3(a)(10) may generally be resold without regard to Rule 144 if the sellers are not affiliates of the issuer of the Section 3(a)(10) securities and have not been affiliates within 90 days of the date of the Section 3(a)(10)-exempt transaction, as such securities would not constitute "restricted securities" within the meaning of Rule 144(a)(3) under the Securities Act. In the event that the securities are held by affiliates of the issuer, those holders may be able to resell the securities in accordance with the provisions of Rule [144(b)(2)].
>
> When a Rule 145(a) transaction is exempt from Securities Act registration under Section 3(a)(10) and *any party to that transaction is a shell company*, other than a business combination related shell company, then the Rule 145(c) and (d) resale limitations apply to any party to that transaction (other than the issuer of the Section 3(a)(10) securities) and to any person who is an affiliate of such party at the time such transaction is submitted for vote or consent. In those situations, holders who are deemed to be underwriters under Rule 145(c)

---

[194] SEC Division of Corporation Finance, Division of Corporation Finance, Staff Legal Bulletin No. 3A (CF) (June 18, 2008).

may resell their securities without registration in the manner permitted by Rule 145(d).

Rules 144 and 145 are discussed later in this casebook—but, as indicated in the preceding excerpt, whether a shell company is involved in a Rule 145(a) transaction is likely to change its regulatory treatment, largely due to abuses that historically occurred when shell companies were involved in Rule 145(a) transactions.

Note that Rule 145(c) is focused on public offers or resales of securities received in a Rule 145(a) transaction. It does not extend to private resales, which presumably can rely on another exemption (e.g., § 4(1½), Rule 144, or Rule 144A) from registration.

Rule 145 is also focused on public resales by the parties to a Rule 145(a) transaction, other than the issuer, and affiliates of such parties. Public resales by *non*-affiliates generally may rely on the § 4(a)(1) exemption.

Finally, in some instances, the SEC may treat a non-affiliate security holder, who receives a substantial block of stock as part of a Rule 145(a) transaction, as an underwriter, even though it is not an affiliate. In that case, the SEC may require any resales to meet the same requirements under Rule 145(d) (as noted above) to exempt its resales. Resales that otherwise are not exempted, of course, can also be covered by an effective registration statement.[195]

D. BANKRUPTCY CODE

Statutes

Bankruptcy Code, §§ 364, 1125, 1145.

Securities Act, § 3(a)(7).

a. *Bankruptcy Code §§ 1125 and 1145.* The Bankruptcy Reform Act of 1978[196] made significant changes in the application of the federal securities laws to the issuance of securities during a bankruptcy reorganization and the resale of such securities. The result has been some conflict because the Bankruptcy Reform Act fundamentally sought to reduce costs, including through scaled-down disclosure. Section 1145 of the Bankruptcy Code provides a limited exemption from § 5's registration requirements for the offer and sale of securities pursuant to a plan of reorganization under Chapter 11 of the Bankruptcy Code.[197] This exemption reflects Congress's decision to move away from

---

[195] See generally Campbell, Resales of Securities Under the Securities Act of 1933, 52 Wash. & Lee L.Rev. 1333 (1995).

[196] The bankruptcy laws were generally revised by the 1978 Act and enacted as Title 11, Bankruptcy, of the United States Code by Pub.L. 96–598, Nov. 6, 1978, 92 Stat. 2549.

[197] Note that § 3(a)(7) of the 1933 Act also exempts the issuance of trustee or receiver certificates with court approval. In addition, § 364(f) of the Bankruptcy Code exempts the issuance of certain unsecured debt securities from § 5 of the 1933 Act. Both are discussed below in this section.

predecessor Chapter X, in which the SEC played a substantial role in bankruptcy reorganizations. As a result, § 1145 provides that the registration requirements of § 5 of the 1933 Act (as well as state blue sky laws) do not apply to the offer or sale under a plan of reorganization of securities of a debtor, an affiliate of the debtor, or a successor to the debtor issued principally in exchange for the debtor's existing debts and securities to anyone other than an "underwriter" (although the Bankruptcy Code defines this critical term more narrowly than the 1933 Act[198]). Securities sold in a § 1145 transaction are deemed to have been issued in a public offering. As a result, non-affiliate creditors who receive these securities can resell them without restriction.

Section 1145 has two principal benefits. First, it permits debtors in bankruptcy to avoid the expensive and time-consuming process of preparing and filing a registration statement with the SEC. Instead, the debtor's limited assets can be put to better use, for example, in repaying its creditors. A distribution under § 1145 also does not trigger the continuing reporting obligations of the 1934 Act, including complying with the costly audit and certification requirements of the Sarbanes-Oxley Act.

The second benefit arises from a § 1145 distribution being deemed a "public offering." Congress concluded that creditors who receive securities for claims under a plan of reorganization would look to resell them quickly. As a result, securities issued to parties other than "underwriters" (as defined in § 1145) are deemed to be "public" and not "restricted" (as defined in Rule 144 under the 1933 Act). That means, for non-affiliates of the issuer, those securities can be immediately resold into the public market pursuant to § 4(a)(1) of the 1933 Act. This enhances liquidity and, in turn, the effectiveness of the reorganization process. If the holder is an affiliate, the securities are likely to be resold pursuant to Rule 144, which includes volume limitations, as well as requirements regarding the public availability of information about the reorganized debtor, but without being required to comply with Rule 144(d)'s holding period requirement.[199] If the creditor is deemed to be an

---

[198] The definition of "underwriter" for this purpose is set forth in § 1145(b)(1) of the Bankruptcy Code. Portions of it parallel the definition in § 2(a)(11) of the 1933 Act, although § 1145(b)(1) excludes from underwriter status any person who sells securities only in "ordinary trading transactions."

[199] Rule 144 is discussed later in this casebook. The problem of resales of securities issued under § 1145 is complicated by the drafting of §§ 1145(a)(1) and 1145(b)(3). Section 1145(a) exempts from § 5 of the 1933 Act the issuance of exchange securities by the debtor, except with respect to an "underwriter" as defined under § 1145(b). Section 1145(b)(1)(D)'s definition of "underwriter" includes an issuer, as used in § 2(a)(11) of the 1933 Act. The purpose of subsection (D) was to exclude an issuer or controlling person from the exemption granted in § 1145(b)(3). There is nothing in the legislative history, however, that indicates other exemptions might not be available, including the exemption in Rule 144 for sales by controlling persons. Otherwise, § 1145 would permanently preclude the availability of the § 4(a)(1) exemption and prohibit any resales by affiliates without SEC registration. Under Rule 144, affiliates of issuers that are subject to 1934 Act reporting requirements, and who hold control shares, may resell such securities by complying with Rule 144, other than the holding period requirement of Rule 144(d). In the Calstar, Inc. no-action letter, the SEC staff recognized the ambiguity in § 1145 and

underwriter, it may not resell the securities without finding an exemption from, or complying with, the registration and prospectus delivery requirements of the 1933 Act.[200]

These two benefits, however, raise a concern. An integral feature of a corporate reorganization is the restructuring of the debtor's capital and debt. That process necessarily involves the exchange of new debt or equity securities for outstanding claims or interests. In principle, some exchanges could be handled under § 3(a)(9), at least in cases where the claimants in bankruptcy hold a security, but registration would still be required when claimants are owed money or hold property claims. Since existing security holders wish to quickly resell securities they receive in an exchange, without an exemption, a substantial portion of the funds needed to revitalize the business would be absorbed by the 1933 Act's registration expenses. Balanced against this concern over cost was a concern over disclosure. If a plan of reorganization entails the issuance of securities in exchange for outstanding claims or interests, some disclosure obligations should be imposed upon the debtor-issuer of the new securities. This problem was resolved by § 1125 of the Bankruptcy Code, which supplants the disclosure obligations otherwise applicable under the 1933 Act with a regime run under the supervision of the bankruptcy court. Congress concluded that aspects of the reorganization process, such as the use of a disclosure statement, serve the basic objectives of the 1933 Act and, therefore, make its protections less necessary. The balance that was struck favored preserving debtor resources over spending them on the 1933 Act registration process.

Consider, however, the difference in disclosure standards between a prospectus and a bankruptcy disclosure statement. A prospectus is prepared based on regulations that affirmatively mandate specific, itemized disclosure to provide potential investors with information to make informed investment decisions. By contrast, under § 1125, the adequacy of disclosure is determined not only based on the investors' informational needs, but also on the debtor's ability to make the desired disclosures. Section 1125 carefully avoids using the securities laws' fundamental concept of "materiality." Instead, pursuant to § 1125, a disclosure statement must provide "adequate information," meaning information that, "as far as is reasonably practicable in light of the nature and history of the debtor and the condition of the debtor's books and records," would enable "a hypothetical investor . . . to make an informed

---

allowed affiliates to resell reorganization securities issued under §§ 1145(a)(1) and (2) in compliance with Rule 144, other than the Rule 144(d) holding period. See Calstar, Inc. [1985–86 Transfer Binder] Fed.Sec.L.Rep. (CCH) ¶ 78,137 at 76,619 (Sept. 26, 1985).

[200] In addition, § 1145(a)(4) provides an exemption for resales of securities received in a transaction under § 1145(a)(1) or (2) through a stockbroker, provided certain conditions are met. The sale must occur before the expiration of 40 days after the first date on which the security was bona fide offered to the public by the issuer or by or through an underwriter; and the issuer must furnish a disclosure statement approved under § 1125, as well as supplementary information, if the court so orders. The exemption is patterned on § 4(a)(3)(A) of the 1933 Act.

judgment about the plan"—in other words, "to provide the information that a reasonable, typical investor needs to make an informed decision about voting for or against the plan of reorganization." In determining whether the disclosure statement provides "adequate information," the court may consider "the cost of providing additional information." Ultimately, whether the disclosure is adequate will depend on what the bankruptcy court decides is appropriate, factoring in "the condition of the debtor's books and records" and the cost of additional disclosure.

In substance, §§ 1125 and 1145 override the federal securities laws' focus on investors and replaces that standard with a balancing test that factors in the debtor's capacity to make disclosures. Moreover, § 1125 includes a broad safe harbor that exempts a person who participates, in good faith, "in the offer, issuance, sale, or purchase of a security, offered or sold under the plan" from liability "on account of such solicitation or participation, for violation of any applicable law, rule, or regulation governing . . . the offer, issuance, sale, or purchase of securities," including the antifraud provisions of the federal securities laws. Even if the disclosure document is materially misleading, defendants who solicit sales or approvals on the basis of such disclosures in good faith apparently enjoy the protections of the § 1125 safe harbor.

Although lawyers who prepare disclosure statements are often guided by the standards in the federal securities laws, the principal focus is on obtaining approval of the reorganization plan—the level of disclosure in a registration statement is not required. The result is less public disclosure than what one would expect in a registered public offering—in particular for buyers and sellers in the secondary market, who may never actually see the disclosure statement. As a practical matter, this may not be a significant concern if trading is among sophisticated investors, familiar with the risks of securities issued as part of a reorganization. To that extent, the full disclosure requirements of the 1933 Act may not be necessary.

b. Section 3(a)(7) of the 1933 Act; § 364 of the Bankruptcy Code. Section 364(a) of the Bankruptcy Code permits a trustee who is authorized to operate the business of a debtor to issue securities in the ordinary course of business, unless the court orders otherwise. Subsections (b) and (c) permit the trustee to issue securities not in the ordinary course of business, with approval of the court. Section 364(f) exempts offers and sales of securities under § 364(a) from the registration requirements of § 5 of the 1933 Act, the Trust Indenture Act of 1939 (which, among other things, regulates the formal written agreement (an "indenture") for certain public bond issuances), and state securities laws, except as to a person that is an underwriter as defined in § 1145(b). Although § 364(f) is a necessary exemption from registration for securities issued in the ordinary course of business under § 364(a), it seems redundant as applied to court-authorized securities that are also exempt from § 5 registration under § 3(a)(7) of the 1933 Act. With respect to certificates of indebtedness issued by a receiver or a trustee or debtor in possession, with the approval of the court, § 3(a)(7) continues to apply and provide an express exemption from the § 5 registration and prospectus provisions.

The conventional view has been that § 3(a)(7) of the 1933 Act is a security rather than a transactional exemption.[201] Curiously enough, the legislative history indicates that the House Committee on the Judiciary understood § 364, § 3(a)(7), and § 3(a)(10) to be transactional exemptions, not perpetual exemptions that "run with" the security.[202] Moreover, the "underwriter" limitation in § 364(f) supports the argument that § 364(f) is a transactional exemption. Nevertheless, the accepted view is that § 3(a)(7), unlike § 3(a)(10), is a security exemption permitting resales without restriction.

6. CROWDFUNDING

Statutes and Regulations

    Securities Act, §§ 4(a)(6), 4A.

    Regulation Crowdfunding.

The concept of "crowdfunding" derives from the efforts (and considerable success) of internet sites, such as Kickstarter and Facebook. Generally, those sites sought contributions or sold products, creating informal mechanisms for connecting entrepreneurs seeking to raise modest amounts of money with prospective donors or customers. Most sites did not offer or sell securities, or if they did, they risked violating § 5's registration requirements.

Probably the most controversial provision of the JOBS Act was Title III ("Crowdfunding"), which added § 4(a)(6) to the 1933 Act to exempt from § 5 the crowdfunded sale of securities in an aggregate annual amount of not more than $1.07 million[203] and with a dollar amount of sales to any single investor being severely limited. The rationale was that small offerings should be encouraged, with less formality, when investors risk only small amounts. That is, if the offering is under $1.07 million, and no retail investor can invest more than 5% or 10% of her income or net worth, it was appropriate to permit entrepreneurs to avoid the costs

---

[201] Thompson Ross Securities Co., 6 S.E.C. 1111, 1118 (1940); 7 Hicks, Exempted Transactions Under the Securities Act of 1933 § 1.01 [3] (1991 rev.); 2 Collier, Bankruptcy & 364.07 (15th ed. 1980); Orlanski, Resale of Securities, 53 Am. Bankr.L.J. 327, 348 (1979). Contra, Mitchell, Securities Regulation in Bankruptcy Reorganizations, 54 Am.Bankr. L.J. 99, 108, 137 (1980).

[202] H.R.Rep. No. 95–595, 95th Cong., 1st Sess. 236–38 (1977).

[203] Under § 4A(h) of the 1933 Act, the SEC is required to adjust the dollar amounts in § 4(a)(6) "not less frequently than once every 5 years, by notice published in the Federal Register, to reflect any change in the Consumer Price Index for All Urban Consumers published by the Bureau of Labor Statistics." The maximum offering limit of $1.07 million is $1.0 million adjusted to reflect changes in the Consumer Price Index. See also Rule 100 of Regulation CF under the 1933 Act.

of SEC registration, even though they could be selling securities to unsophisticated buyers.

Offers and sales under § 4(a)(6) can be effected online, with the market functioning over the internet, although each transaction must be conducted through a broker or "funding portal" that is registered with the SEC (in the case of funding portals, not required to meet the standards (including capital adequacy) applicable to broker-dealers).[204] Title III also added § 4A of the 1933 Act, which requires, among other things, that issuers and funding portals provide certain information to investors and potential investors and provide notices and other information to the SEC.[205] The SEC, in turn, issued new rules to implement §§ 4(a)(6) and 4A in Regulation Crowdfunding ("Regulation CF").

a. Issuer Eligibility. The $1.07 million annual ceiling makes crowdfunding appealing to early-stage start-up entrepreneurs, perhaps who have little more than an idea or concept. (Regulation D and Regulation A offerings are typically preferred by issuers seeking higher amounts of capital.) The crowdfunding exemption is available to domestic issuers other than reporting companies, investment companies, or companies with no specific business plan or whose business plan is to engage in a merger or acquisition with an unidentified company or companies.[206] Regulation CF, like Regulation D and Regulation A, provides that the crowdfunding exemption is also subject to "bad actor" disqualifications that bar reliance on the exemption.[207] In addition, an issuer that sold securities under § 4(a)(6), but failed to provide to the SEC and its investors the annual reports required by Regulation CF during the two years immediately preceding a later offering, is barred from relying on Regulation CF until it is no longer delinquent.[208]

b. Investor Limits. Regulation CF does not restrict investors based on sophistication, but it does limit each investor's maximum annual investment when all or a portion of it is made through an offering that relies on the crowdfunding exemption. In the case of an investor with an

---

[204] See § 4(a)(6)(C) of, and Rules 100(a)(3), 400 and 401 of Regulation CF under, the 1933 Act. FINRA also oversees funding portals. They must first meet the eligibility requirements to become a FINRA member, and then comply with FINRA's Funding Portal Rules. Among other things, FINRA examines the funding portals and requires them to issue periodic reports. See FINRA Rules 100, 110, 200, 300, 800, 900, and 1200 (eff. Jan. 29, 2016).

[205] Title III also added § 3(h) of the 1934 Act, which requires the SEC to adopt rules to exempt a "funding portal" from registering as a broker-dealer under § 15(a)(1) of the 1934 Act; mandates the SEC to establish "bad actor" disqualification provisions under which an issuer is unable to rely on § 4(a)(6) if the issuer or an intermediary is subject to a disqualifying event; and adds § 12(g)(6) of the 1934 Act, which requires the SEC to adopt rules to exempt securities acquired under § 4(a)(6) from the 1934 Act's registration and reporting requirements.

[206] See § 4A(f) of, and Rule 100(b) of Regulation CF under, the 1933 Act.

[207] See Rules 100(b)(4) and 503 of Regulation CF under the 1933 Act. The SEC is considering changes to the "bad actor" disqualification in Regulation D, Regulation A, and Regulation CF, including changes that will further conform the Regulation D, Regulation A, and Regulation CF disqualifications. See Securities Act Release No. 10763 (Mar. 4, 2020).

[208] See Rule 100(b)(5) of Regulation CF under the 1933 Act.

annual income or net worth of less than $107,000, the maximum investment across all issuers raising capital under § 4(a)(6) during any 12-month period is the greater of $2,200 or 5% of the lesser of the investor's annual income or net worth. If the investor has an annual income and net worth equal to or greater than $107,000, the ceiling on her purchase during any 12-month period is 10% of the lesser of her annual income or net worth, subject to a maximum amount of $107,000.[209]

Purchasers of securities sold under § 4(a)(6) are required to hold them for at least one year, unless they resell to the issuer, an accredited investor, or a family member or trust, among others, or unless the resale is registered with the SEC.[210]

    c. *State Regulation.* Securities sold in a crowdfunding are "covered securities" under § 18(b)(4)(C) of the 1933 Act, which preempts state registration and qualification requirements. The states' antifraud authority (and some notice filings) are retained. State regulation of funding portals is also largely preempted.

    d. *Disclosure Requirements.* Crowdfunding purchasers are excluded from the 2,000 recordholder threshold under § 12(g)(1) of the 1934 Act, which means that sales to them will not cause a start-up business to become a 1934 Act reporting company.[211] Rather, Regulation CF sets out its own disclosure requirements for issuers and creates a regulatory framework for funding portals.

For issuers, Regulation CF requires that they file certain disclosures with the SEC on Form C[212] and provide these disclosures to investors and the funding portals facilitating the offering.[213] The disclosures are intended to help minimize the risk of fraud, in light of the high failure rate of start-ups and small businesses, the relative lack of sophistication of many purchasers, and the unique level of anonymity that the internet provides issuers.[214]

Regulation CF includes a laundry list of issuer disclosure requirements. They include, among others, disclosures relating to the

---

[209] See § 4(a)(6)(B) of, and Rule 100(a)(2) of Regulation CF under, the 1933 Act. The SEC is considering changes to Regulation CF that would no longer apply any investment limits for accredited investors and permit non-accredited investors to determine their investment limit based on the *greater* (not lesser, as under the current Regulation) of their annual income or net worth. In addition, the SEC is proposing an exemption, in new Rule 206, to permit issuers to test-the-waters, orally or in writing, with all potential investors prior to filing a Form C with the SEC. Certain legends and other conditions will be required. See Securities Act Release No. 10763 (Mar. 4, 2020).

[210] See § 4A(e) of, and Rule 501 of Regulation CF under, the 1933 Act.

[211] See § 12(g)(6) of, and Rule 12g–6 under, the 1934 Act.

[212] See Rules 201 and 203 of Regulation CF under the 1933 Act. Material amendments to the Form C are filed on Form C/A, and periodic updates on the offering are filed on Form C-U. Annual filings are made on Form C-AR, which must be filed within 120 days of the end of the issuer's fiscal year. The SEC's goal is to have these filings posted by the portal on its website.

[213] See Rule 201 of Regulation CF under the 1933 Act.

[214] Crowdfunding, 80 Fed. Reg. 71,387, 71,488–91 (Nov. 16, 2015).

issuer's directors and officers, beneficial owners of 20% or more of the issuer's voting equity securities, business (including anticipated business plans), "material factors that make an investment in the issuer speculative or risky," use of proceeds, capital structure (including indebtedness), and certain related-party transactions. Regulation CF also requires the issuer to discuss its financial condition, including, to the extent material, liquidity, capital resources, and historical results of operations.[215] Additionally, Regulation CF requires the issuer to provide financial statements, whose level of detail and verification (from certification by the issuer's principal executive officer up to audited financial statements) varies depending on the amount of capital raised under § 4(a)(6) within the preceding 12 months.[216] Finally, Regulation CF requires issuers to file annual reports with the SEC (including financial statements and a description of the issuer's financial condition) and post them on the issuer's website.[217]

Issuers are restricted from advertising the terms of a crowdfunded offering, except for limited notices that direct investors to the applicable funding portal.[218] Issuers and their agents can communicate with investors and potential investors about the terms of an offering[219] through communications channels that each portal is required to maintain,[220] so long as the issuer and its agents identify themselves in those communications. The issuer, or someone acting on its behalf, can compensate a person for promoting the offering through the portal communication channels so long as each communication clearly discloses the receipt of that compensation.[221]

e. *Use of Intermediaries to Reduce Fraud Risk.* Regulation CF relies on intermediaries, such as brokers and funding portals, to reduce the risk of fraud—in effect, treating them as "gatekeepers" through whom crowdfunding issuers must pass to access the public markets.[222] To that end, a funding portal is prohibited from offering investment advice or recommendations; soliciting purchases, sales, or offers to buy securities offered or displayed on its platform; compensating anyone for any such solicitation or based on the sale of securities through its platform; or holding, managing, possessing, or otherwise handling investors' funds or securities.[223]

The portal, however, may (among other things) apply objective criteria to highlight offerings on its platform; provide search functions or

---

[215] See Rule 201(s) of Regulation CF under the 1933 Act.
[216] See Rule 201(t) of Regulation CF under the 1933 Act.
[217] See Rule 202 of Regulation CF under the 1933 Act.
[218] See Rules 204(a) and (b) of Regulation CF under the 1933 Act.
[219] See Rule 204(c) of Regulation CF under the 1933 Act.
[220] See Rule 303(c) of Regulation CF under the 1933 Act.
[221] See Rule 205 of Regulation CF under the 1933 Act.
[222] See § 4(a)(6)(C) of, and Rule 100(a)(3) of Regulation CF under, the 1933 Act.
[223] See Rule 402(a) of Regulation CF under the 1933 Act.

other tools that investors can use to search, sort, or categorize offerings; and compensate a third party for referring a person to the portal, so long as the third party does not provide the portal with any "personally identifiable information of any potential investor" and the compensation (other than if paid to a broker-dealer) is not tied to the purchase or sale of a security through the portal's platform.[224] The permissibility of posting news, such as market news and news about a particular issuer or industry, on a portal platform is a facts and circumstances determination, and portals must be sensitive to ensure they are not violating the prohibition on giving investment advice and recommendations. Finally, each portal must keep records of all investors who purchase or attempt to purchase securities on its platform, all issuers who offer, sell, or attempt to offer or sell securities in its platform, and all communications that occur on or through the platform.[225]

In addition, under Regulation CF, intermediaries must deny access to issuers if they have a reasonable basis for believing that the issuer or the offering presents the potential for fraud "or otherwise raises concerns about investor protection."[226] The intermediary "must deny access if it reasonably believes that it is unable to adequately or effectively assess the risk of fraud of the issuer or its potential offering."[227] In addition, the intermediary must have a reasonable basis for believing that an admitted issuer complies with the Regulation's disclosure requirements (which may include reliance on issuer representations unless the intermediary has reason to question their reliability).[228] Finally, an intermediary must deny access to an issuer that is subject to a "bad actor" disqualification. To satisfy this requirement, the intermediary must, at a minimum, conduct a background and securities enforcement regulatory history check on each issuer and its directors, officers, and 20% beneficial owners of the issuer's voting equity securities.[229]

The intermediary must make the information provided by the issuer available to investors through its platform.[230] An intermediary must also provide investors with educational materials that, among other things, explains "the risks associated with each type of security [offered through the intermediary] . . . , [and t]he need for the investor to consider whether investing in a [crowdfunded security] is appropriate for that investor."[231] Additionally, § 4A(a)(4) requires each intermediary to ask investors questions that demonstrate their understanding of the investment risks.

---

[224] See Rule 402(b) of Regulation CF under the 1933 Act.
[225] See Rule 404 of Regulation CF under the 1933 Act.
[226] See Rule 301(c)(2) of Regulation CF under the 1933 Act.
[227] See id.
[228] See Rule 301(a) of Regulation CF under the 1933 Act.
[229] See Rule 301(c)(1) of Regulation CF under the 1933 Act.
[230] See Rule 303(a) of Regulation CF under the 1933 Act.
[231] See Rule 302(b) of Regulation CF under the 1933 Act.

f. Liability for Material Misstatements or Omissions. The JOBS Act created a new liability provision, § 4A(c), which generally parallels § 12(a)(2) of the 1933 Act with respect to material misstatements or omissions in any written or oral communication in the offer or sale of a crowdfunded security. Section 4A(c), however, extends liability not just to the issuer but also to its directors and principal officers. In addition, "any person who offers or sells the security in such offering" may be liable for such material misstatement or omission. The SEC declined to exempt funding portals or other intermediaries from this provision. Instead, liability under § 4A(c) turns on the facts and circumstances of the particular matter. The SEC believes there are appropriate steps an intermediary may take in exercising "reasonable care." These steps include establishing policies and procedures that are reasonably designed to achieve compliance with Regulation CF and conducting a review of the issuer's offering documents to evaluate whether they contain materially false or misleading information.

g. More Smoke than Fire? When the JOBS Act was enacted in 2012, many believed that crowdfunding would be a "game-changer," easing the burden on small businesses seeking to raise relatively small amounts of capital.[232] Yet, five years following the adoption of Regulation CF, crowdfunding has largely fallen flat. What happened?

Some attribute the failure to § 4(a)(6)'s low ceiling of $1.07 million.[233] Others attribute it to the extensive disclosure and other requirements of Regulation CF. Both may be correct. Combining the two has resulted in disproportionately high costs for an offering exemption with a low ceiling. In 2019, the SEC estimated that the transactional costs in a crowdfunded offering ranged between 14.69% and 22.92% of offering proceeds. Those figures do not include the annual costs of ongoing disclosures, which the SEC estimates fall between $4,000 and $32,700.[234] They also do not include the costs to intermediaries of complying with the screening, notification, recordkeeping, and other requirements of Regulation CF. Those costs can be particularly substantial for portals that otherwise are barred from pursuing sources of revenue that broker-dealers typically have, such as investment advice, making recommendations, and soliciting purchases and sales of securities. Finally, as noted before, § 4A(c) imposes negligence-based liability on issuers (including directors and officers) and intermediaries for material misstatements or omissions.

The result has likely been a mismatch between the benefits of raising capital through crowdfunding and the compliance and related

---

[232] See, e.g., Kalil & Rand, The Promise of Crowdfunding and American Innovation, The White House President Barack Obama (June 8, 2016).

[233] As a result, the SEC has proposed raising the crowdfunding ceiling to $5 million. See Securities Act Release No. 10763 (Mar. 4, 2020).

[234] Thomas, Making Equity Crowdfunding Work for the Unaccredited Crowd, 4 Harv. Bus. L. Rev. Online 62, 65–66 (2014), http://www.hblr.org/?p=3773; Crowdfunding, 78 Fed. Reg. 66,428, 66,521 & n.918 (proposed Nov. 5, 2013).

costs imposed by Regulation CF, especially in light of alternatives such as Regulation D and Regulation A. Like any good start-up, this may require the SEC to "pivot" if it decides to support further crowdfunding initiatives. Recent SEC proposals—to increase the crowdfunding ceiling to $5 million, among others—suggest they are interested in doing so.[235]

7. INTEGRATION OF EXEMPTIONS

Regulations

Rules 152, 155.

The 1933 Act contains several discrete transactional exemptions from the registration and prospectus delivery requirements of § 5 that are available to issuers. Among these are the private offering exemptions (§ 4(a)(2), § 4(a)(5), and Rule 506 of Regulation D); the limited offering exemptions (Rules 504 and 701 and Regulation A); the intrastate exemption (§ 3(a)(11) and Rule 147, and most recently, Rule 147A); and the §§ 3(a)(9) and 3(a)(10) exemptions for certain exchanges and reorganizations.

As these sections are construed, for an exemption to be available, each transaction must satisfy all the conditions of a single exemption. Moreover, where there are a series of offerings, every proposed unregistered (or registered) offering may be linked with a prior or subsequent offering. If such linkage occurs, two or more ostensibly discrete offerings may be deemed to comprise a single transaction.

The doctrine of integration entails the process of combining multiple offerings into a single transaction. The effect may be to destroy one or more exemptions that each offering, when looked at separately, purported to rely on without integration.

For example, assume A, B, and C form X Corp. in State Y and issue shares to themselves at $10 per share in reliance on the § 4(a)(2) private placement exemption. A is a resident of State Z; B and C are residents of State Y. So far, there is no problem. Immediately after, X Corp. makes a public offering of shares at the same price in reliance on the § 3(a)(11) intrastate exemption, with offers and sales being restricted to residents of State Y. Each individual offering satisfies the exemption it purportedly relies on. If, however, the two offerings are integrated into a single transaction, the § 4(a)(2) exemption is nullified (since, as integrated, the transaction includes a public offering in State Y) and the § 3(a)(11) exemption is unavailable (since, as integrated, the transaction includes out-of-state sales). Absent another exemption, such as Rule 506(c) under

---

[235] Currently, there is no restriction on the type of security that may be offered and sold in reliance on Regulation CF. The SEC has proposed a change that would limit eligible securities to equity securities, debt securities, and securities convertible or exchangeable to equity interests, including any guarantees of such securities. See Securities Act Release No. 10763 (Mar. 4, 2020).

the 1933 Act (if sales are made only to accredited investors), the integrated offerings will violate § 5 of the 1933 Act.

Alternatively, two years later, suppose X Corp. makes another intrastate offering of common stock in compliance with § 3(a)(11), followed by a later 1933 Act registered offering of common stock in which sales are made to residents outside State Y. If these two offerings are integrated, the § 3(a)(11) exemption is nullified, although the registered offering may remain unaffected. In this case, the concept would result in only "one-way" integration.

The underlying policy behind the integration doctrine is that issuers should not be permitted to avoid registration by splitting what is essentially a single financing into two or more ostensibly separate and distinct offerings, each of which, if regarded discretely, would qualify under one of the exemptions. We have already encountered the integration doctrine in several contexts. It may be helpful at this point to bring the threads together.[236]

a. Genesis of the Doctrine. The integration doctrine first emerged in connection with § 3(a)(11), which makes the intrastate exemption hinge upon the *entire issue* being offered and sold only to residents of the state in question.[237] Although the SEC stated that whether an offering

---

[236] As noted earlier, the SEC recently proposed amendments to the integration rules. See Securities Act Release No. 10763 (Mar. 4, 2020). The proposals would establish new Rule 152, which would replace current Rules 152 and 155. New Rule 152 provides a general framework and four safe harbors, replacing the various safe harbors currently set forth in various 1933 Act exemptions.

1. Proposed General Principle of Integration—For offerings not covered by a safe harbor, offers and sales are not integrated if, based on the particular facts and circumstances, the issuer can establish that each offering complies with the registration requirements of the 1933 Act or an exemption from registration is available for the particular offering. The proposed facts and circumstances analysis of integration replaces the traditional five-factor test.
2. Proposed Safe Harbor 1—Any offering made more than 30 calendar days before the commencement of any other offering, or more than 30 calendar days after the termination or completion of any other offering, will not be integrated; provided that, for an exempt offering for which general solicitation is not permitted, the purchasers either were not solicited through the use of general solicitation or established a substantive relationship with the issuer prior to the commencement of the offering for which general solicitation is not permitted.
3. Proposed Safe Harbor 2—Offers and sales made in compliance with Rule 701 or Regulation S will not be integrated with other offerings.
4. Proposed Safe Harbor 3—A 1933 Act-registered offering will not be integrated if made subsequent to:
    1. a terminated or completed offering for which general solicitation is not permitted;
    2. a terminated or completed offering for which general solicitation is permitted and made only to qualified institutional buyers and institutional accredited investors; or
    3. an offering for which general solicitation is permitted that terminated or completed more than 30 calendar days prior to the commencement of the registered offering.
5. Proposed Safe Harbor 4—Offers and sales made in reliance on an exemption for which general solicitation is permitted would not be integrated if made subsequent to any prior terminated or completed offering.

[237] Securities Act Release No. 97 (Dec. 28, 1933), 11 Fed.Reg. 10,949 (1946).

will be regarded as a part of a larger offering and, thus, integrated is a question of fact, it added:[238]

> Any one or more of the following factors may be determinative of the question of integration: (1) are the offerings part of a single plan of financing; (2) do the offerings involve issuance of the same class of security; (3) are the offerings made at or about the same time; (4) is the same type of consideration to be received, and (5) are the offerings made for the same general purpose.

According to this formulation, it is possible that the presence of a single factor may cause two offerings to be parts of a single issue.[239] The same five-part formulation appears in the note to Rule 502(a).

The "issue" concept is also read into the § 4(a)(2) private offering exemption, since that exemption, with some exceptions, is available only to "transactions by an issuer *not involving any* public offering" (emphasis added). In Securities Act Release No. 4552, the SEC again stated, with respect to the § 4(a)(2) exemption, that the determination of whether offerings should be integrated "depends on the particular facts or circumstances," but that the five factors set forth above "should be considered." Nothing was said regarding what weight to give the various factors or whether a single factor might be determinative.

Section 3(a)(9) has also imported the "issue" concept. Recall that this is accomplished by reading the word "exclusively" in § 3(a)(9) as modifying both "exchanged" and "security holders." Accordingly, an exchange of securities with existing security holders cannot be combined with a § 4(a)(2) private offering of the same class of securities to institutional investors.[240] Indeed, if the exchange with existing security holders is itself a public offering, and the two offerings are integrated, the private offering exemption will also be lost. If, however, the offerings

---

[238] Securities Act Release No. 4434 (Dec. 6, 1961). See also In re Unity Gold Corp., 3 S.E.C. 618 (1938) (considering whether offerings constituted separate issues).

[239] One example where the SEC found different offerings to have the same general purpose and to be part of a single plan of financing is In the Matter of Kevin D. Kunz, Exchange Act Release No. 452901 (Jan. 16, 2002), aff'd 2003 U.S. App. LEXIS 6011 (10th Cir. 2003). There, an issuer was ordered by the State of Nevada to make rescission offers to investors in prior offerings. It simultaneously offered these investors rescission or the ability to invest in its own notes or in mortgages that it held issued by third parties. The issuer prepared six private placement memoranda that offered the rescission or reinvestment opportunity, and in total, it sold to 138 non-accredited investors. The SEC concluded that these offerings should be integrated (thus exceeding the maximum limit on the number of non-accredited purchasers). Even though different classes of securities may have been involved, the SEC found that the offerings were at the same time and for the same general purpose, involved the same plan of financing, and investors paid the same consideration (i.e., release of their legal claims relating to the prior offerings). Clearly then, the failure of a single criterion in this five-factor test does not prevent integration.

[240] See Securities Act Release No. 2029 (Aug. 8, 1939). This Release, which expresses the views of the SEC General Counsel, pre-dates the five-factor test described earlier. Presumably, consideration of those factors would also be relevant today in determining whether the two offerings constitute a single "issue" of securities.

entail different "issues" of securities (including substantively different terms), the exemption may not be lost.[241]

The "issue" concept also arises under § 3(b), which authorizes the SEC by rule or regulation to add any class of securities to those exempted in § 3. Section 3(b)(1) specifies that no such issue shall be exempted "where the aggregate amount at which such issue is offered to the public exceeds $5,000,000." Section 3(b)(2) provides that the aggregate amount of all securities offered and sold during a 12-month period "in reliance on the exemption added in accordance with this paragraph shall not exceed $50,000,000." In both instances, the question arises whether integrating two offerings into a single transaction will cause it to exceed the limits of § 3(b).

Recall, however, that many exemptions contain integration safe harbors. Rule 502(a) provides a six-month safe harbor so that securities sold under Regulation D will be immunized from integration. However, offers or sales by the issuer of the same or similar class of securities as that offered under Regulation D during the "window period" causes a loss of the safe-harbor (in effect, requiring a "clean" six months). Absent a safe harbor, to determine whether two or more offerings should be integrated, one should apply the five-factor test set forth above.[242]

The Rule 502(a) safe harbor requires a "clean" six months. Other exemptions, such as Regulation A (Rule 251(c)), Rule 147(g), and Rule 147A(g), still provide a safe harbor from integration with offers or sales after six months, even if during the window-period there were offers or sales of the same or similar class of securities, permitting a "dirty" six months. They also make clear that prior offers and sales will not be integrated. This difference in the safe harbor provisions raises the possibility that a Rule 506 transaction, followed six months and one day later by a Rule 147 transaction, may result in forward integration so as to destroy the Rule 506 exemption (if the six months are "dirty"), although the Rule 147 transaction would remain intact. In that respect, one should note that the safe-harbor provisions of Rule 502(a), Rule 147(g) and Rule 147A(g) provide a shield for their respective offerings, but none of those provisions provides a safe-harbor for the other exempt offering. To the contrary, recall that commentators have suggested that the language of Rule 251(c) provides "two-sided" protection from integration (e.g., an offering pursuant to Regulation D that ended one month before the Regulation A offering commenced will not be integrated with the Regulation A offering), assuring the issuer both that the

---

[241] See Securities Act Release No. 4552 (Nov. 6, 1962).

[242] As noted before, the SEC recently proposed amendments to the integration rules. See Securities Act Release No. 10763 (Mar. 4, 2020). The proposals would establish new Rule 152, which would replace current Rules 152 and 155. New Rule 152 provides a general framework and four safe harbors, replacing the various safe harbors currently set forth in various 1933 Act exemptions. Under its Proposed General Principle of Integration, an issuer will determine whether offers and sales are to be integrated based on the particular facts and circumstances. The proposed facts and circumstances analysis of integration replaces the traditional five-factor test set forth here.

Regulation A exemption will not be lost *and* that the exemption for the prior or subsequent offering will also be secure.[243]

If an issuer were to make a Rule 506 offering separated by more than a "clean" six months from a § 3(a)(9), § 3(a)(11), or § 4(a)(2) offering, the latter offering—not having the benefit of a safe harbor—could lose its exemption if the conditions for integration under the five-factor test are applicable. The integration, however, would only be "one way." Relying on the Rule 502(a) safe harbor, the Rule 506 offering would not be affected. Knowing this risk, and considering the five factors, securities counsel may advise its client to arrange its transactions so that they constitute different plans of financing and achieve different general purposes using different classes of securities, whenever feasible.

Finally, recall the clean "two-sided" integration safe harbor in Rule 701(f). Offerings exempt under Rule 701 (pursuant to compensatory benefit plans or contracts) "are deemed to be a part of a single, discrete offering and are not subject to integration with any other offers or sales"—shielding both the Rule 701 offering and the other offering from integration.

b. *Rule 152*. In an effort to protect issuers from technical traps that could deny them access to the public capital market, the SEC adopted Rule 152, which states: "The phrase 'transactions by an issuer not involving any public offering' in section 4(a)(2) . . . shall be deemed to apply to transactions not involving any public offering at the time of said transactions although subsequently thereto the issuer decides to make a public offering and/or files a registration statement."

Absent Rule 152, an issuer that made a private placement and found it needed more capital to achieve its objective could be denied access to the public capital market for a time because the subsequent public offering could be integrated with the earlier private placement. Arguably, there is little reason to restrict the issuer. (*Query*: Does it serve a public purpose to place hurdles in the way of an issuer that wishes to register securities, with the attendant greater disclosure that accompanies a registration statement?)

Still, despite Rule 152's efficient purpose, some ambiguities exist. First, the antecedent of "thereto" is not self-evident. Must the decision to make a public offering and/or file a registration statement be subsequent to the abandonment or completion of the § 4(a)(2) offering? Second, does the issuer escape integration simply because it later files a registration statement? The ambiguous "and/or" in Rule 152 literally applies to "any public offering," whether registered or unregistered.

Originally, the purpose of Rule 152 was to allow "those who have contemplated or begun to undertake a private offering to register securities without incurring any risk of liability as a consequence of

---

[243] Bradford, Regulation A and the Integration Doctrine: The New Safe Harbor, 55 Ohio St. L.J. 255 (1994).

having first contemplated or begun to undertake a private offering."[244] Thus, if a private offering failed, it could be converted into a public offering.[245] If, however, a private offering and/or a registered offering are planned at the same time, the rule literally appears to offer no protection. In reality, most "high-tech" start-up firms probably contemplate an eventual IPO from the day they are formed.

Despite ambiguities in Rule 152, the SEC staff issued several no-action letters that, in effect, accepted the idea of an initial "seed round venture financing" of a start-up company, notwithstanding the issuer's "contemplation" of an eventual registered public offering at the time of the placement.[246] Those rulings permitted planning for the second-phase public offering to commence while the first private offering was still in progress. But what if work on the public offering began before all the privately placed securities in the initial private offering were sold to investors? In a much-discussed 1990 no-action letter to Black Box, Inc.,[247] the SEC staff concluded that the critical date was the filing of the registration statement for the second offering. So long as the purchasers in the first offering were unconditionally bound by this date, even though the closing had not yet occurred, the second offering would meet the "subsequently thereto" requirement in Rule 152. However, if there was any renegotiation of the private offering after the filing date for the public offering, Rule 152 could not be satisfied, and the two offerings would presumably be integrated.

    c.   *Rule 155.* Eventually, the SEC recognized the need for a clearer safe harbor than Rule 152, and they adopted Rule 155 in 2001.[248] Rule 155 is two-sided; it applies to both (a) a public offering following the abandonment of a prior private offering, and (b) a private offering

---

[244] Securities Act Release No. 305 (Mar. 2, 1935), quoted in Deaktor, Integration of Securities Offerings, 31 U.Fla.L.Rev. 465, 497 n.206 (1979).

[245] Note, too, that new Rule 163B under the 1933 Act permits any issuer, or any person authorized to act on its behalf, to engage in oral or written communications with potential investors that are, or are reasonably believed to be, "qualified institutional buyers" or institutional "accredited investors," either prior to or following the filing of a registration statement, to determine whether such investors might have an interest in a contemplated registered securities offering. The rule is non-exclusive, and if offers in the private offering were made only to "qualified institutional buyers" or institutional "accredited investors," the issuer may rely on Rule 163B in proceeding with the registered public offering.

[246] See Verticom, Inc., 1986 SEC No-Act. LEXIS 1751 (Feb. 12, 1986); BBI Assocs., 1986 SEC No-Act. LEXIS 3036 (Dec. 29, 1986). The scenario of multiround high-tech start-up financing is more fully described in the request for a no-action letter in *Verticom*.

What is the difference between "contemplating" and "planning" an IPO? At some stage of the financing, the documents may contain extensive provisions granting piggy-back and demand registration rights to the venture investors. One would hope these arrangements are still only contemplative.

[247] See Black Box, Inc., 1990 SEC No-Act. LEXIS 926 (June 26, 1990). A later no-action letter helped further lay out the details of this position. See Squadron, Ellenoff, Pleasant & Lehrer, 1992 S.E.C. No-Act. LEXIS 363 (Feb. 28, 1992). See also Glover, The Offerings that Precede An Initial Public Offering—How to Preserve Exemptions And Avoid Integration, 24 Sec.Reg.L.J. 3 (1996).

[248] See Securities Act Release No. 7943 (Feb. 5, 2001).

following the abandonment of a prior public offering.[249] The preconditions to Rule 155's application require a clean break between the private and public offerings. They are also intended to assure that investors understand the differences between their legal protections in the two types of offerings.

Unlike Rule 152, Rule 155 does not require the future public offering not to have been contemplated or foreseen at the time of the private placement. When the public offering follows the abandoned private offering, Rule 155(b) requires that (i) all offering activity in the private offering has terminated and (ii) the issuer files its registration statement at least 30 calendar days after the termination of all offering activity in the private offering unless securities in the private offering were offered only to persons who were (or were reasonably believed to be) accredited or sophisticated investors.[250] In the reverse case, where the private offering follows the abandonment of the public offering, Rule 155(c) again conditions the safe harbor on a thirty-day period elapsing after the withdrawal of the registration statement. To expedite this process, Rule 477 was amended to permit an issuer to withdraw its registration statement prior to its effectiveness (disclosing in its application that it may undertake a subsequent private offering in reliance on Rule 155(c)), unless the SEC objects within 15 calendar days after the issuer applies for withdrawal.

Still, Rule 155 is limited in some important respects. First, Rule 155(a) defines a private offering as an offering that is exempt from registration under §§ 4(a)(2) or 4(a)(5) or Rule 506 of Regulation D. Hence, Rule 155 does not apply to Rule 504 offerings; nor would it have any application to a § 3(a)(11), Rule 147, or Rule 147A intrastate offering, a § 3(a)(10) reorganization, or a § 3(a)(9) exchange offering. Even more basic is the fact that Rule 155 only applies when the initial offering (private or public) was abandoned and no securities were sold pursuant to it.

Finally, it should be underscored that Rule 155 is only a safe harbor. Transactions that do not quite come within its four corners might still be exempt under traditional integration criteria. Or, in some cases, the issuer may be able to fall back onto Rule 152.

---

[249] Why is the latter safe harbor necessary when there were no sales in the abandoned public offering? Since a public offering inherently involves a general solicitation, §§ 4(a)(2) and 4(a)(5) and Rule 506(b) cannot be satisfied if they are integrated with even an abandoned prior public offering.

[250] Recall, as well, new Rule 163B under the 1933 Act, which permits any issuer, or any person authorized to act on its behalf, to engage in oral or written communications with potential investors that are, or are reasonably believed to be, "qualified institutional buyers" or institutional "accredited investors," either prior to or following the filing of a registration statement, to determine whether such investors might have an interest in a contemplated registered securities offering. The rule is non-exclusive, and if offers in the abandoned private offering were made only to "qualified institutional buyers" or institutional "accredited investors," the issuer may rely on Rule 163B in proceeding with the registered public offering.

d. *Foreign Offerings.* The SEC has taken the position that the registration provisions of § 5 of the 1933 Act "are primarily intended to protect American investors." Accordingly, sales of securities that "come to rest" abroad generally will not be integrated with contemporaneous sales in the United States, provided that precautions are taken to ensure securities that come to rest abroad will not flow back into the hands of U.S. investors. These principles are formalized in Regulation S, which, among other things, governs offshore offerings by domestic issuers, as well as in Rule 500(g) of Regulation D.[251]

e. *Uncertainty.* Even if Rules 152 and 155 answer some problems, the integration doctrine remains open-ended and inherently ambiguous. Despite innumerable no-action letters and a few decisions,[252] the five-factor test is poorly defined, in part because its factors seem to overlap, and in part because its application to any specific set of facts is debatable. Academic commentators have criticized its broad scope,[253] and an ABA task force suggested it "seriously needs rethinking."[254] Only the bright-line six-month tests of Regulation D, Regulation A, and Rules 147 and 147A, the flat prohibition against integrating with prior offerings in Regulation A and Rules 147 and 147A, and the two-way safe harbor of Rule 701 give any workable certainty to the practitioner. Some would simply discard the doctrine as outmoded.[255] Going forward, as changes facilitate access to the public markets (especially for large issuers), and as the ceiling on exempt offerings has (and continues to be) raised, the question is whether issuers will need to continue to raise capital through multiple exempt offerings. To the extent these become less necessary, additional industry pressure for reform may subside.[256]

Problems

PROBLEM 6-1

BioTech, Inc. ("BioTech") again faces a capital-raising crisis: It must raise $10 million quickly, or it will not be able to continue operations, even

---

[251] Regulation S is discussed later in this casebook.

[252] See, in particular, SEC v. Cavanagh, 1 F.Supp.2d 337, 364 (S.D.N.Y.), aff'd 155 F.3d 129 (2d Cir. 1998) (focusing on how offerings were viewed by those structuring them and the investing public).

[253] See Bradford, Transaction Exemptions in the Securities Act of 1933: An Economic Analysis, 45 Emory L. J. 591 (1996).

[254] See Committee on Federal Regulation of Securities, Integration of Securities Offerings: Report of the Task Force on Integration, 41 Bus. Law 595 (1986).

[255] See Campbell, The Overwhelming Case for Elimination of the Integration Doctrine Under the Securities Act of 1933, 89 Ky. L.J. 289 (2001–02).

[256] As noted earlier, the SEC recently proposed amendments to the integration rules. See Securities Act Release No. 10763 (Mar. 4, 2020). The proposals would establish new Rule 152, which would replace current Rules 152 and 155. New Rule 152 provides a general framework and four safe harbors, replacing the various safe harbors currently set forth in various 1933 Act exemptions. Under its Proposed General Principle of Integration, an issuer will determine whether offers and sales are to be integrated based on the particular facts and circumstances. The proposed facts and circumstances analysis of integration replaces the traditional five-factor test.

though it has a "miracle drug" that may end up being just that. Its CEO, Dickie Nerd, approaches and makes offers to nearly 100 potential investors. Eventually, he finds 20 accredited investors who will invest the capital. As BioTech's attorney, you must decide: Can this offering be considered exempt from registration under § 4(a)(2) (now pursuant to Rule 506 of Regulation D)? What information or access must BioTech provide?

PROBLEM 6-2

Same problem and same facts, except that now Nerd has found 30 accredited investors, as well as three sophisticated persons who do not qualify as accredited investors. Again, there is the same need to act quickly and at low cost. What advice do you give as BioTech's securities counsel?

PROBLEM 6-3

Suppose, despite the use of some reasonable efforts to comply with Rule 506, BioTech sells to one individual, a non-accredited investor, who lacks the requisite sophistication to be "capable of evaluating the merits and risks of the prospective investment." Can the other investors rescind if BioTech's stock price later declines?

PROBLEM 6-4

Buzz's Steakhouse, Inc. ("Buzz") is a local chain of "steak and ale" restaurants doing business in New York, New Jersey, and Pennsylvania. It has a loyal clientele, some of whom are eager to invest in this family-owned business. Between January 1 and February 28, 2007, Buzz sells 1,000,000 shares of its common stock at $4.50 per share to some 30 investors, most of who are loyal customers, but none of who are accredited or sophisticated investors. In September, it contacts some institutional investors and sells another 2,000,000 shares, this time at $8 per share to ten of them. Assume there were no offers made between March 1, 2007, and September 10, 2007. Has Buzz complied with Regulation D?

PROBLEM 6-5

Amalgamated Widget, Inc. ("AWI") is a well-known reporting company with a market capitalization of just over $10 billion. It runs the largest chain of sporting goods stores and one of the largest pizzeria companies in the United States. Thus, everyone knows it and is familiar with its commercials extolling its sneakers and pizzas (which smell remarkably alike). Since AWI is already so widely recognized, it decides to do a sizeable private placement of stock in February 2016 for nearly $2 billion (or 20% of its market capitalization) under Rule 506(c), including through general solicitation and general advertising. It knows that some non-accredited investors will attempt to buy because it is offering its shares for $1 below market price on the date of the offering. Thousands of investors apply, and as general counsel to AWI, you must deal with the following cases:

(a) several investors have provided photocopies of their executed Form 1099 tax returns for 2014, which show each to have made more than $200,000 in that year; some also provide returns for 2012 and/or 2013. You are worried that these photocopies might be fraudulent and not reflect their actual incomes for those years;

(b) some investors provide a brokerage statement showing that they hold more than $1 million of securities in such account;

(c) Jones, a resident of New Jersey, provides a letter from Smith, who is an experienced and respected tax attorney practicing with a major law firm in New York City. The letter states Smith's view that, after a reasonable investigation by him of Jones's status, Jones is an accredited investor;

(d) despite a bank statement for one investor (Klein) showing him to have $1.5 million in total assets, you are aware that your brokerage firm just liquidated Klein's account for failure to meet the firm's margin call for $700,000.

Is the information sufficient in each case? Or is more needed? Explain.

PROBLEM 6-6

Returning to Buzz, assume, in the alternative, that Buzz wishes to offer only 120,000 of its shares at $8 per share to some 15 or 20 loyal customers. It does not want to prepare a formal prospectus or similar offering document, and it realizes its prospective investors are ordinary people who do not have any special investment experience. Buzz's friendly broker, Hot Shot Securities, believes it can find investors for Buzz by inviting them to "investment seminars" it sponsors by advertising in northern New Jersey and Westchester newspapers. As securities counsel, what is your advice?

PROBLEM 6-7

(a) New Co., incorporated in 2006 in Delaware, has 2,000,000 shares of common stock currently outstanding, held by some 45 shareholders. New Co. is not a reporting company. Its balance sheet currently shows negative equity, and it has no prospect of profits this year. Most of its shareholders (approximately 25) are also its officers and/or employees. Those shareholders are computer engineers and web design specialists who hope to help New Co. launch the latest advance in micro-communications—a hand-held communications device that can translate oral speech into emails (and vice versa) and send them around the globe instantaneously. If it is successful, there will be extraordinary profits; if not, none. Given that the company represents an "all-or-nothing" gamble, New Co.'s board adopts an employee stock option plan under which it reserves 500,000 shares of New Co.'s common stock. So far, New Co. has granted options relating to 100,000 shares pursuant to this plan during the first four months of this year (without registering the stock or preparing or distributing any disclosure document to its employees). Is this permissible? If so, how many stock options may it grant under its stock option plan during the remainder of this year?

(b) Roughly contemporaneously with granting options for 200,000 shares, New Co. sells 200,000 shares in a private placement to ten institutional investors. Any problems?

(c) Shyster and Dimwitty, a law firm, handled the incorporation of New Co. and assisted in drafting its employee stock option plan. It is willing to take an option under the stock option plan (which, by its terms, extends to consultants and advisers) instead of a cash payment of its fees. Is this permissible?

PROBLEM 6-8

(a) In addition to selling 4,000,000 shares of its stock to ten institutions (all of whom easily qualify as accredited investors) at $2 per share, Start-up Corp., a newly formed corporation, plans to sell 1,000,000 shares of the same class of stock at the same price to several corporate officers, including Ms. Judy Jones, the Corporate Secretary, Vice President, and Deputy General Counsel. Ms. Jones earns approximately $175,000 per year and has a net worth (with her spouse or spousal equivalent) of approximately $500,000. It is imperative to Start-up Corp. that it avoids the cost and delay of preparing a full-scale disclosure document. In this light, can Start-up Corp. sell to Ms. Jones?

(b) In addition, Start-up Corp. has contemporaneously received an offer from Venture LLP, a recently organized Massachusetts limited partnership with ten limited partners, to buy 1,000,000 shares at the same $2 price per share. Of Venture's ten limited partners, eight are highly experienced in private equity investments, and each has a net worth of well over $1 million. The remaining two limited partners, university professors in economics who teach finance courses, each possess a net worth of below $1 million. They were given their limited partnership stakes in return for advisory services—past and prospective—that they have performed or will perform for the partnership. Can Start-up Corp. accept this offer? What must it do if it accepts this offer?

PROBLEM 6-9

To create incentives for key employees, New Corp., upon its organization in January 2006, adopted an employee stock option plan under which it reserved 500,000 shares of common stock. From February 15 through December 2006, New Corp. granted options to purchase a total of 400,000 shares of common stock to 72 employees under the plan (such options were granted every other month by the Board of Directors). The options were granted at prices ranging from $.10 to $.50 per share. Each option had a term of five years and was exercisable each year for 20% of the shares covered by that option, subject to the continued employment of the optionee. Each employee received a summary of the stock option plan, but no further information regarding New Corp.'s business or prospects. The company intends to continue to grant options under the plan. Currently, New Corp.

has 600,000 shares of its common stock outstanding. Can this offering qualify for an exemption from registration?

PROBLEM 6-10

If the preceding offering does qualify for an exemption, is that exemption lost when New Corp. sells 2,000,000 shares of its common stock on January 15, 2007, to 15 accredited investors and six sophisticated individuals in an otherwise qualified private placement? Will the two offerings be integrated?

PROBLEM 6-11

Start-Up Corp., a Delaware corporation and non-reporting company, is a high-tech venture capital-financed company that is approaching an eventual IPO. As of December 31, 2011, it had total assets of $100 million and 50 million shares of common stock outstanding (mostly held by institutional investors). In 2012, it hired several high-level executives to staff itself for its upcoming IPO. All previous stock options were issued at a $1 per share exercise price. In 2012, Start-Up Corp. issued options to purchase 6 million shares to several new executives, including a new chief operating officer, a new chief financial officer, and a new treasurer, giving them the same disclosures it gave to prior option holders (basically, a copy of its stock option plan and their employment agreement, but no financial disclosures). Most of these executives exercised their options in 2012. These executives were highly sophisticated (although not necessarily wealthy), but Start-Up Corp. was also making other private placements at the same time to various institutional investors. Do you see any problem? If this transaction were still pending, what practical advice would you give Start-Up Corp.'s general counsel?

PROBLEM 6-12

Jersey Co. ("Jersey") is a privately-held New Jersey corporation with its principal place of business in the Meadowlands of New Jersey. The company derives virtually all of its revenues from amusement parks it operates in New Jersey. It owns no assets outside of New Jersey, and it plans to use the proceeds of a $7 million offering of its convertible debentures to finance the expansion of its Wilderness Adventure Park in the southern New Jersey pinelands. Fifty percent of its common stock is owned by four members of the Soprano family, well-known New Jersey entrepreneurs. On June 30, 2003, Jersey sells $3 million of these debentures to the New Jersey State Pension Fund and $2 million to Jersey Investments ("Investments"), a newly-organized limited partnership with ten limited partners (and a corporate general partner that is a New Jersey corporation). Investments is organized under the New Jersey limited partnership statute and has its office in Newark, New Jersey. Eight of the ten limited partners reside in New Jersey, with the other two residing in New York. On September 30, 2003, the last $2 million of the debentures are sold to the pension funds of two New Jersey-based unions.

(a) Do you see any problems with this offering to this point?

(b) On November 1, 2003, Tony Soprano, an officer and large shareholder of Jersey, sells 50,000 shares (or 8% of Jersey's outstanding common stock) to five local businessmen, all residents of New Jersey, for $1.5 million. No disclosure document is prepared or delivered, and three of the businessmen do not qualify as accredited investors. Are there any problems?

(c) On April 2, 2004, over nine months after it acquired its debentures, the New Jersey State Pension Fund sells half of its Jersey debentures to the New York State Pension Fund in a private sale that they negotiate. Any problem?

(d) On December 5, 2003, Jersey files a registration statement on Form S-1 covering the sale of $20 million in convertible debentures. It is declared effective on February 5, 2004. Assume, in the alternative, that the same $20 million is sold on the same date pursuant to a Regulation A offering. Any issues?

(e) On October 15, 2003, Jersey, at the direction of its controlling shareholders, loans $3.5 million to two New York corporations, Gambino Operations, Inc. and Bonnano Properties Co., both privately-held firms. The transactions close in New Jersey and are documented with notes obligating each borrower to pay interest at the compounded annual rate of 12½%. "It was just too good an offer to refuse," explains Tony Soprano, a Jersey director. Any problem?

(f) In the alternative to (e) above, Jersey decides to use $7 million from the proceeds of its $20 million debenture offering to repay a high-interest bank loan it earlier secured from First National Bank of Philadelphia. Is the issue now any different than in (e)?

PROBLEM 6-13

"Wild Bill" Hickock, a Texas oil promoter, forms a Texas master limited partnership in which he offers limited partnership interests exclusively to Texas residents. The limited partnership's principal place of business is in San Antonio, where it maintains its bank accounts and business records. The partnership principally invests in limited partnership interests in other limited partnerships, which are also organized under Texas limited partnership law, but which then invest in oil and gas ventures located outside of Texas. Assume that these limited partnerships also have their principal place of business in Texas. Can this two-tier structure qualify under Rule 147(c) (or Rule 147A(c))?

PROBLEM 6-14

Two New York lawyers have started an internet website that helps New Yorkers find lawyers in New York. Its revenues come from lawyer advertising on the website. To expand, the two promoters want to sell common stock in their new company to New York attorneys, so they place a marketing document on their website that offers the stock to all New York attorneys (and only to them). What advice would you give them?

PROBLEM 6-15

Webco, Inc., a Delaware corporation ("Webco"), announces it will donate ten shares of its common stock, traded at $5 per share on Nasdaq, to the International AIDS Foundation, a respected and independent foundation, for each person who sends it an email with a return address on or before December 1, 2003. Webco's counsel requests "as a formality" a no-action letter from the SEC's staff that such a donation will not violate § 5 of the 1933 Act. As the SEC attorney responding to this no-action request, what is your response?

PROBLEM 6-16

XYZ Inc., a reporting company ("XYZ"), faces a liquidity crisis. It cannot pay the soon-to-be-due principal on the bonds of its wholly-owned subsidiary, Subsidiary Co., which mature at the end of this year. Hence, it offers the following exchange: 3 shares of XYZ's stock, currently trading at $30 per share, for each $100 in principal of the debt represented by the bonds. The bonds are held by approximately 400 holders, most of whom are institutions, as well as by several individuals. XYZ hopes to be able to pay the debt in full of those who do not accept its offer. What are the exemptions from registration available for this offering?

PROBLEM 6-17

Assume the same facts as in Problem 6-16, except that the debt is now owed by XYZ (not its subsidiary) and elaborate negotiations are conducted between a committee representing the institutional investors and XYZ, which is represented in these negotiations by its investment adviser, Goldman, Merrill (which later charges a $4 million fee for its services). Ultimately, they reach a revised deal under which the bondholders will be given two shares of XYZ stock plus $34 in cash for each $100 in principal amount of debt exchanged by them. Does any aspect of this transaction raise securities law problems? Evaluate.

PROBLEM 6-18

The foregoing exchange was made on April 1, 2008. XYZ pays $275 million in cash and, as a result, finds itself facing a cash flow problem. XYZ, therefore, sells 1 million shares of its preferred stock, which carries a 10% annual cumulative dividend, to a group of 20 large institutional investors on September 1, 2008. Do you see any problem here?

PROBLEM 6-19

ABC Industries ("ABC") sold $50,000,000 of its 7% bonds in a private placement on June 1, 2006. Now, in early April 2007, ABC offers bondholders a chance to exchange those bonds for its common stock at a favorable ratio. The transaction will comply with § 3(a)(9). Joe Retail, an accredited investor, purchased $100,000 of ABC's bonds (at the time, he was an Executive Vice President of ABC, but he retired on December 30, 2006), and he exchanged all his bonds for ABC common stock. A week later, on April 5, 2007, he decided to sell the common stock. Can he sell? When and under what conditions?

PROBLEM 6-20

Two local bus companies in New Jersey announced a stock-for-stock merger. Assume that under New Jersey law, the New Jersey Transportation Commission must approve any such merger and, under its governing statute, it must consider the impact of the merger on "consumer safety, efficient operations, the public's need for low-cost public transportation, and the public interest generally." Assume the Commission holds an elaborate, ten-day public hearing, after notifying everyone, including shareholders of both companies, and hears detailed testimony from dissident minority shareholders of one company that the merger is unfair to them. Nonetheless, the Commission expressly finds the merger to be fair to all concerned, including the minority shareholders. Does this approval qualify for purposes of § 3(a)(10)?

PROBLEM 6-21

Software Co. is a reporting company listed on Nasdaq. It files a registration statement on Form S-3 for an offering of 10 million shares of common stock on June 1, 2007, but then market conditions deteriorate. Its underwriters tell it that the offering is currently infeasible. They suggest, however, that they can place 2 to 3 million shares with a small group of pension funds in a private "PIPE" transaction at a price of $1.50 per share. What, if any, are the legal obstacles to such an offering?

SUBDIVISION C. THE OBLIGATION TO REGISTER RESALES OF SECURITIES BY PERSONS OTHER THAN THE ISSUER

CHAPTER 7

OFFERINGS BY UNDERWRITERS, AFFILIATES, AND DEALERS

Statutes and Regulations

Securities Act, §§ 2(a)(2), 2(a)(11), 4(a)(1), 4(a)(7).

Rules 141, 142, 144, 145, 405.

Regulation S, and Form 144.

1. THE CONCEPT OF "UNDERWRITER"

A. STATUTORY AND PRESUMPTIVE UNDERWRITERS

a. Statutory Underwriters. Section 5 prohibits the use of interstate facilities or the mails to sell a security unless a registration statement is in effect as to that security. However, § 4(a)(1) specifically exempts transactions "by any person other than an issuer, underwriter, or dealer." Thus, only issuers, underwriters, and dealers are subject to the registration and prospectus-delivery requirements of the 1933 Act. We have already explored the meaning of the term "issuer" as used in the Securities Act. We now consider the complicated concept of "underwriter." Once again, we will see that key terms are defined not by their conventional meaning but by reference to the purposes of the Securities Act.

The definition of "underwriter" is found in § 2(a)(11). The term means "any person who": [1] "has purchased from an issuer [or controlling person] with a view to, or [2] offers or sells for an issuer [or a controlling person] in connection with, the distribution of any security, or [3] participates or has a direct or indirect participation in any such undertaking, or [4] participates or has a participation in the direct or indirect underwriting of any such undertaking."

The addition above of the bracketed language ("or controlling person") takes account of the last sentence of § 2(a)(11), which defines the term "issuer" as used therein to include, in addition to an issuer, any person in a control relationship with the issuer. Thus, one who buys from an affiliate of an issuer can become an "underwriter" under § 2(a)(11).

The House Committee Report described the meaning of the term "underwriter" this way:[1]

> The term [underwriter] is defined broadly enough to include not only the ordinary underwriter, who for a commission promises to see that an issue is disposed of at a certain price, but also includes as an underwriter the person who purchases an issue outright with the idea of then selling that issue to the public. The definition of underwriter is also broad enough to include two other groups of persons who perform functions, similar in character, in the distribution of a large issue. The first of these groups may be designated as the underwriters of the underwriter, a group who, for a commission, agree to take over pro rata the underwriting risk assumed by the first underwriter. The second group may be termed participants in the underwriting or outright purchase, who may or may not be formal parties to the underwriting contract, but who are given a certain share or interest therein.
>
> The term "underwriter," however, is interpreted to exclude the dealer who receives only the usual distributor's or seller's commission. This limitation, however, has been so phrased as to prevent any genuine underwriter passing under the mark of a distributor or dealer. The last sentence of this definition, defining "issuer" to include not only the issuer but also affiliates or subsidiaries of the issuer and persons controlling the issuer, has two functions. The first function is to require the disclosure of any underwriting commission which, instead of being paid directly to the underwriter by the issuer, may be paid in an indirect fashion by a subsidiary or affiliate of the issuer to the underwriter. Its second function is to bring within the provisions of the bill redistribution whether of outstanding issues or issues sold subsequently to the enactment of the bill. All the outstanding stock of a particular corporation may be owned by one individual or a select group of individuals. At some future date they may wish to dispose of their holdings and to make an offer of this stock to the public. Such a public offering may possess all the dangers attendant upon a new offering of securities. Wherever such a redistribution reaches significant proportions, the distributor would be in the position of controlling the issuer and thus able to furnish the information demanded by the bill. This being so, the distributor is treated as equivalent to the original issuer and, if he seeks to dispose of the issue through a public offering, he becomes subject to the

---

[1] Report of Committee on Interstate and Foreign Commerce, H.R.Rep.No.85, 73d Cong., 1st Sess., 13–14 (1933).

act. The concept of control herein involved is not a narrow one, depending upon a mathematical formula of 51 percent of voting power, but is broadly defined to permit the provisions of the act to become effective wherever the fact of control actually exists.

The somewhat uncertain question of who is an underwriter is addressed, in the first instance, by two SEC rules. First, Rule 141 makes clear that the dealer's "commission" referred to in § 2(a)(11) is the usual "spread" between the underwriter's offering price to dealers and the public offering price, provided the profit margin is usual and customary for the type and size of the offering. The rule applies whether the dealer buys outright and resells the security or whether it is acting merely as a broker. Note that there is a second implication to Rule 141: if you are not an "underwriter" under this rule, then you cannot engage in preliminary negotiations or agreements with the issuer prior to the filing of the registration statement because § 2(a)(3) exempts only "underwriters" (and only those who are, or are to be, in privity of contract with the issuer).

Second, Rule 142 permits persons who are not affiliated with the issuer or underwriter to commit with the underwriter to purchase all or a part of any unsold portion of the offering after the lapse of a specified period following the commencement of the offering, if the securities are acquired for investment and not with a view to distribution. According to the SEC's General Counsel, this rule was adopted "in recognition of the value of secondary capital in facilitating the flow of investment funds into industry, and of the fact that the owners of such secondary capital cannot practicably perform the duty of thorough investigation and analysis imposed by the Act of the underwriter proper."[2] The rule thus makes clear "that a person who does no more than agree with an underwriter to take over some or all of the undistributed portion of the issue, and who purchases for investment any securities which his commitment thus obliges him to take up, does not thereby subject himself to liability as an underwriter of the securities of the issue actually distributed to the public."[3] As a practical matter, the rule opens the way for institutional investors, such as insurers, investment companies, and pension funds, to make an advance commitment to purchase stock on a "standby" basis at a discount to the initial offering price if the public does not purchase all the offering—without incurring the liabilities of an underwriter. However, Rule 142 requires that (i) the securities must be purchased "for investment and not with a view to distribution," and (ii) the agreement not be directly with the issuer. Thus, under Rule 142, these institutional investors cannot distribute the securities, nor can they have a control relationship with the issuer or any principal underwriter.

    b. *Presumptive Underwriters.* Sometimes, often during periods of a strong new issues market, a wealthy individual or institutional investor

---

[2] Opinion of General Counsel, SEC Securities Act Release No. 1862 (Dec. 13, 1938).
[3] Id.

may purchase a large block of a registered offering, presumably for investment, and after that resell the securities to the public without the use of a statutory prospectus. To cope with this situation, the SEC and its staff developed the "presumptive underwriter" doctrine. As first formulated, the doctrine established an administrative rule-of-thumb that any person who purchased ten percent or more of a registered offering was presumed to be an underwriter within the meaning of § 2(a)(11) of the 1933 Act. The rule was first enunciated and applied in business combination transactions under Rule 145 (discussed earlier in this casebook). Although never officially adopted by formal action of the Commission, the doctrine, nevertheless, is applied in practice by the SEC staff. A definition of the doctrine, consistent with Commission practice, has been formulated in these terms:

> A person may be deemed to be an underwriter, within the meaning of § [2(a)(11)] of the Securities Act, if such person purchases or acquires a significant percentage of the securities offered pursuant to a registered distribution, except that such purchaser is not deemed to be an underwriter if he resells such securities in limited quantities.[4]

The SEC staff applies the presumptive underwriter doctrine in individual cases to prevent unrestricted resales, by purchasers of large blocks of registered offerings, free of the disclosure requirements generally applicable to registered offerings. Under the doctrine, such purchases followed by a resale creates a presumption that the seller is a statutory underwriter unless the burden is rebutted by showing a change of circumstance or other justifiable cause. The Commission's practice is gleaned from SEC staff no-action letters responding to interpretive requests. In practice, the Commission generally advises that such resales will not violate the Securities Act if such resales do not exceed the quantity limitations of Rule 144 or Rule 145, considered later in this chapter.[5]

The doctrine, however, should not be applied woodenly where a person or entity is not engaging or otherwise participating in a distribution. Thus, the SEC's staff gave a no-action letter that an insurance company would not be considered an underwriter in connection with recurrent purchases of large amounts of registered securities for investment so long as the securities were acquired from the issuer or an underwriter in the ordinary course of the insurer's business, and no arrangement existed between the insurer and others to participate in the distribution of the securities. Insurance companies and pension funds must make investments that are sufficiently liquid to meet

---

[4] Ahrenholz & Van Valkenberg, The Presumptive Underwriter Doctrine: Statutory Underwriter Status for Investors Purchasing a Specified Portion of a Registered Offering, 1973 Utah L. Rev. 773, 775–76 (1973).

[5] For an analysis and critique of the presumptive underwriter doctrine as an instrument in securities law enforcement, see 2 Loss & Seligman, Securities Regulation 1114–15 (3d ed. 1989); Nathan, Presumptive Underwriters, 8 Rev. Sec. Reg. 881 (1975).

foreseeable obligations as well as unforeseen demands. This need for portfolio liquidity requires such institutional investors to be certain that, when purchasing securities, they will be able to resell the securities if the need arises without being tagged as a "presumptive underwriter."[6]

Securities and Exchange Commission v. Chinese Consolidated Benevolent Association, Inc.

United States Circuit Court of Appeals, Second Circuit, 1941.
120 F.2d 738.

■ AUGUSTUS N. HAND, CIRCUIT JUDGE. The Securities and Exchange Commission seeks to enjoin the defendant from the use of any instruments of interstate commerce or of the mails in disposing, or attempting to dispose, of Chinese Government bonds for which no registration statement has ever been made.

The defendant is a New York corporation organized for benevolent purposes having a membership of 25,000 Chinese. On September 1, 1937, the Republic of China authorized the issuance of $500,000,000 in 4% Liberty Bonds, and on May 1, 1938 authorized a further issue of $50,000,000 in 5% bonds. In October 1937, the defendant set up a committee which has had no official or contractual relation with the Chinese government for the purpose of:

(a) Uniting the Chinese in aiding the Chinese people and government in their difficulties.

(b) Soliciting and receiving funds from members of Chinese communities in New York, New Jersey and Connecticut, as well as from the general public in those states, for transmission to China for general relief.

All the members of the committee were Chinese and resided in New York City. Through mass meetings, advertising in newspapers distributed through the mails, and personal appeals, the committee urged the members of Chinese communities in New York, New Jersey and Connecticut to purchase the Chinese government bonds referred to and offered to accept funds from prospective purchasers for delivery to the Bank of China in New York as agent for the purchasers. At the request of individual purchasers and for their convenience the committee received some $600,000 to be used for acquiring the bonds, and delivered the moneys to the New York agency of the Bank of China, together with written applications by the respective purchasers for the bonds which they desired to buy. The New York agency transmitted the funds to its branch in Hong Kong with instructions to make the purchases for the account of the various customers. The Hong Kong bank returned the bonds by mail to the New York branch which in turn forwarded them by

---

[6] American Council of Life Insurance (avail. June 10, 1983), Fed.Sec.L.Rep. (CCH) [1983–84 Transfer Binder] ¶ 77,526.

mail to the purchasers at their mailing addresses, which, in some cases, were in care of the defendant at its headquarters in New York. Neither the committee, nor any of its members, has ever made a charge for their activities or received any compensation from any source. The Bank of China has acted as an agent in the transactions and has not solicited the purchase of bonds or the business involved in transmitting the funds for that purpose.

No registration statement under the Securities Act has ever been made covering any of the Chinese bonds advertised for sale. Nevertheless the defendant has been a medium through which over $600,000 has been collected from would-be purchasers and through which bonds in that amount have been sold to residents of New York, New Jersey and Connecticut.

Motions for judgment were made by both parties upon pleadings setting forth the foregoing facts. As a result the court below entered a decree denying complainant's motion, granting defendant's motion and dismissing the complaint. The Commission has taken an appeal from the decree, which, in our opinion, ought to be reversed.

It should be observed at the outset that the Commission is not engaged in preventing the solicitation of contributions to the Chinese government, or its citizens. Its effort is only to prevent the sale of Chinese securities through the mails without registry. * * *

Section 5 of the Act provides as follows. [The court quotes §§ 5(a)(1) and (2) imposing the registration and prospectus requirements in connection with sales of securities by the use of interstate facilities or the mails.]

Section 4 provides the following exemptions from the requirements of Section 5 supra:

> Sec. 4. The provisions of section 5 shall not apply to any of the following transactions:
>
> (1) Transactions by any person other than an issuer, underwriter, or dealer; * * *.

Under Section 2(11) an "underwriter" is defined as: "any person who has purchased from an issuer with a view to, or sells for an issuer in connection with, the distribution of any security, or participates or has a direct or indirect participation in any such undertaking; * * *".

We think that the defendant has violated Section 5(a) of the Securities Act when read in connection with Section 2(3) because it engaged in selling unregistered securities issued by the Chinese government when it solicited offers to buy the securities "for value". The solicitation of offers to buy the unregistered bonds, either with or without compensation, brought defendant's activities literally within the prohibition of the statute. Whether the Chinese government as issuer authorized the solicitation, or merely availed itself of gratuitous and even unknown acts on the part of the defendant whereby written offers to buy, and the funds collected for payment, were transmitted to the Chinese banks does not affect the meaning of the statutory provisions which are quite explicit. In either case the solicitation was equally for the benefit of the Chinese government and broadly speaking was for the issuer in connection with the distribution of the bonds.

* * *

Under Section 4(1) the defendant is not exempt from registration requirements if it is "an underwriter". The court below reasons that it is not to be regarded as an underwriter since it does not sell or solicit offers to buy "for an issuer in connection with, the distribution" of securities. In other words, it seems to have been held that only solicitation authorized by the issuer in connection with the distribution of the Chinese bonds would satisfy the definition of underwriter contained in Section 2(11) and that defendant's activities were never for the Chinese government but only for the purchasers of the bonds. Though the defendant solicited the orders, obtained the cash from the purchasers and caused both to be forwarded so as to procure the bonds, it is nevertheless contended that its acts could not have been for the Chinese government because it had no contractual arrangement or even understanding with the latter. But the aim of the Securities Act is to have information available for investors. This objective will be defeated if buying orders can be solicited which result in uninformed and improvident purchases. It can make no difference as regards the policy of the act whether an issuer has solicited orders through an agent, or has merely taken advantage of the services of a person interested for patriotic reasons in securing offers to buy. The aim of the issuer is to promote the distribution of the securities, and of the Securities Act is to protect the public by requiring that it be furnished with adequate information upon which to make investments. Accordingly the words "[sell] for an issuer in connection with the distribution of any security" ought to be read as covering continual solicitations, such as the defendant was engaged in, which normally would result in a distribution of issues of unregistered securities within the United States. Here a series of events were set in motion by the solicitation of offers to buy which culminated in a distribution that was initiated by the defendant. We hold that the defendant acted as an underwriter.

There is a further reason for holding that Section 5(a)(1) forbids the defendant's activities in soliciting offers to buy the Chinese bonds. Section 4(1) was intended to exempt only trading transactions between individual investors with relation to securities already issued and not to exempt distributions by issuers. The words of the exemption in Section 4(1) are: "Transactions by any person other than an issuer, underwriter, or dealer; * * * ". The issuer in this case was the Republic of China. The complete transaction included not only solicitation by the defendant of offers to buy, but the offers themselves, the transmission of the offers and the purchase money through the banks to the Chinese government, the acceptance by that government of the offers and the delivery of the bonds to the purchaser or the defendant as his agent. Even if the defendant is not itself "an issuer, underwriter, or dealer" it was participating in a transaction with an issuer, to wit, the Chinese Government. The argument on behalf of the defendant incorrectly assumes that Section 4(1) applies to the component parts of the entire transaction we have mentioned and thus exempts defendant unless it is an underwriter for the Chinese Republic. Section 5(a)(1), however, broadly prohibits sales of securities irrespective of the character of the person making them. The exemption is limited to "transactions" by persons other than "issuers, underwriters or dealers". It does not in terms or by fair implication protect those who are engaged in steps necessary to the distribution of security issues. To give Section 4(1) the construction urged by the defendant would afford a ready method of thwarting the policy of the law and evading its provisions.

It is argued that an injunction ought not to be granted because the interests of a foreign state are involved. But the provisions for registration statements apply to issues of securities by a foreign government. (See Section 2(a)(2) and Section 7.) Section 6(a), moreover, permits a registration relating to securities issued by a foreign government to be signed by the underwriter, which we have held the defendant to be.

* * *

The decree is reversed with directions to the District Court to deny the defendant's motion to dismiss and to issue the injunction as prayed for in the bill of complaint. * * *

NOTES ON THE *CHINESE CONSOLIDATED BENEVOLENT ASSOCIATION* CASE

1. *Promoters.* Based on the *Chinese Consolidated Benevolent Association* case, it is fairly easy to see how those who promote the sale of unregistered securities can be classified as underwriters. If a person arranges for research reports or other promotional efforts designed to stimulate market interest or trading to occur, that person may fall within the definition of an "underwriter" as one who "participates . . . in any such undertaking."[7] But, as seen next, this same broad statutory language can also ensnare creditors and institutional investors.

2. *Underwriter or Issuer?* Persons who actively promote the sale of unregistered securities invite SEC enforcement actions. Sometimes, they are sued as underwriters on the theory that they have "participated" in a distribution.[8] Other times, the SEC will sue officers, directors or control

---

[7] See SEC v. Allison, [1982 Transfer Binder] Fed. Sec. L. Rep. (CCH) ¶ 98,774 (N.D. Cal. 1982) (quoting § 2(a)(11) of the 1933 Act).

[8] See SEC v. Cavanagh, 1 F.Supp.2d 337 (S.D.N.Y.), aff'd 155 F.3d 129 (2d Cir. 1998).

persons as issuers under § 2(a)(4).[9] Despite the liberality with which courts have, to date, accepted the idea that promoters and controlling persons could be deemed issuers, the statutory structure of the 1933 Act suggests that they are more logically reached under § 2(a)(11), which expressly contemplates that those who buy from a controlling person with an intent to distribute are underwriters.[10]

Securities and Exchange Commission v. Guild Films Co.
United States Court of Appeals, Second Circuit, 1960.
279 F.2d 485.

■ MOORE, CIRCUIT JUDGE. This is an appeal * * * from an order by the district court * * * granting a preliminary injunction to restrain the sale of 50,000 shares of Guild Films Company, Inc. common stock by two of the appellants, the Santa Monica Bank and The Southwest Bank of Inglewood. Pending a final determination of this action, the preliminary injunction was issued "unless and until" a registration statement should be filed under the Securities Act of 1933.

Section 5 of the Act makes it unlawful for anyone, by any interstate communication or use of the mails, to sell or deliver any security unless a registration statement is in effect. Section 4 provides, however, that "the provisions of section 5 * * * shall not apply to * * * (1) Transactions by any person other than an issuer, underwriter, or dealer." The banks claim that they come within this exemption to the registration requirements. The district court rejected this claim, holding that the banks were "underwriters" within the meaning of the Act. While the issue involved can be simply stated, a rather complete discussion of the facts is necessary.

The Original Loans by the Banks and the Security Therefor

On September 17, 1958, the Santa Monica Bank and The Southwest Bank of Inglewood jointly agreed to loan Hal Roach, Jr., $120,000 represented by two notes. * * *

The loans were * * * secured * * * by 30,000 shares of [F.L. Jacobs Co.] stock. Roach had used a large part of the proceeds of the loans to purchase a substantial number of the 30,000 Jacobs shares put up as collateral.

The Jacobs Stock and the Renewal Notes

Roach was an officer, director, and the controlling shareholder of F. L. Jacobs Co. * * * This company controlled the Scranton Corp. which owned Hal Roach Studios, which in turn owned both W-R Corp. and Rabco T.V. Production, Inc.

---

[9] See United States v. Rachal, 473 F.2d 1338 (5th Cir. 1973).

[10] See SEC v. Datronics Engineers, Inc., 490 F.2d 250 (4th Cir. 1973), which appears later in this chapter.

W-R Corp. and Guild Films, Inc. had made an agreement on January 23, 1959, under which W-R Corp. was to obtain 400,000 shares of Guild Films common stock (the registration of 50,000 shares of this stock is here in dispute) and a number of promissory notes in exchange for certain film properties. The stock was not registered with the S.E.C., but Guild Films agreed to use its best efforts to obtain registration. However, seeking to come within an exemption provided in section 4 of the Securities Act, the parties provided the following in their agreement:

> Stock Taken for Investment: W-R warrants, represents and agrees that all of the said 400,000 shares of Guild's common stock being contemporaneously issued hereunder, whether registered in the name of W-R or in accordance with the instructions of W-R, are being acquired for investment only and not for the purpose or with the intention of distributing or reselling the same to others. Guild is relying on said warranty and representation in the issuance of said stock.

On February 5, 1959, for reasons discussed below, Roach directed that 100,000 shares of the Guild Films stock be issued in the name of W-R Corp. and 100,000 shares (represented by two 50,000 share certificates) in the name of Rabco. Meacham, the treasurer of Guild Films, directed that the transfer agent stamp this restriction on the stock certificates:

> The shares represented by this certificate have not been registered under the Securities Act of 1933. The shares have been acquired for investment and may not be sold, transferred, pledged or hypothecated in the absence of an effective registration statement for the shares under the Securities Act of 1933 or an opinion of counsel to the company that registration is not required under said Act.

The remaining 200,000 shares were not issued as the promised film properties were never transferred.

Although the Guild Films stock was issued "for investment only," the district court found that Roach "unquestionably" purchased it in order to have it resold. * * * These findings are uncontested.

* * *

[In December, 1958, the lending banks learned that the Jacobs stock had been suspended from trading on the New York Stock Exchange. The Santa Monica Bank asked Roach to liquidate the loan because the Jacobs stock, which was then being traded over-the-counter, had dropped to $5 a share and was not deemed by the bank to be acceptable collateral. Roach asked the banks for more time to deposit acceptable collateral and make a cash payment on the note. As negotiations continued the banks agreed to defer action until February 10, 1959.]

* * *

On that date Roach wired The Southwest Bank that he had sent 50,000 shares of Guild Films stock to the Santa Monica Bank. By a divided vote the Loan Committee of The Southwest Bank decided to renew the note, making it payable "On 'Demand' if 'No Demand' then all due March 18, 1959." On February 12th, one of the 50,000 share Guild Films certificates in the name of Rabco T.V. Productions was received by the Santa Monica Bank. The restrictive legend quoted above was stamped on the face of the certificate. * * *

* * *

On February 12th, the Santa Monica Bank and The Southwest Bank learned that the Jacobs stock had been suspended from all trading by the S.E.C. The Santa Monica Bank immediately telegraphed Roach demanding payment by February 16th, and stating that otherwise the stock would be sold to liquidate the loan. Roach failed to pay and the banks attempted to sell the securities through brokers on the American Stock Exchange.

The Guild Films transfer agent refused to transfer the stock to the banks because of the stamped restriction. The Santa Monica Bank then wired Guild Films that unless the stock was released or exchanged for unrestricted securities, the matter would be taken to the American Stock Exchange and the S.E.C. "for their assistance and release." Guild Films refused to act; it also refused an offer to exchange the 50,000 shares for 25,000 shares of unrestricted stock; and no application for registration was made to the S.E.C.

In August, 1959, the Santa Monica Bank brought an action against Guild Films in the New York Supreme Court to compel the transfer of the stock. On September 18, 1959, that court ordered the transfer of the stock to the bank. The court based its order on a referee's report which found that the stock was exempt from the Securities Act of 1933. The Santa Monica Bank thereupon ordered 9,500 shares of the Guild Films stock sold. The S.E.C. learned of the sale and notified the bank and Guild Films that the stock could not be sold without registration. The bank then sought a Commission ruling that the stock was exempt. Despite an adverse opinion by the Commission, the bank sold an additional 10,500 shares on September 24, 1959. At that point, the Commission filed this suit to restrain the delivery of these shares and the sale of the remainder of the stock. The district court granted a preliminary injunction against delivery and further sale.

The Securities Act of 1933 was primarily intended to "protect investors by requiring registration with the Commission of certain information concerning securities offered for sale." Gilligan, Will & Co. v. S.E.C., 2 Cir., 1959, 267 F.2d 461, 463. An exemption from the provisions of § 5 of the Act was provided by § 4(1) for "transactions by any person other than an issuer, underwriter or dealer" because it was felt that no protection was necessary in these situations. * * * The primary question involved in this case is: were appellants issuers, underwriters or dealers within this exemption?

An "underwriter" is defined in § 2(11) as "any person who has purchased from an issuer with a view to, or sells for an issuer in connection with, the distribution of any security, * * * or participates or has a participation in the direct or indirect underwriting of any such undertaking * * *." The burden of proof is on the one seeking an exemption. * * *

The banks cannot be exempted on the ground that they did not "purchase" within the meaning of § 2(11). The term, although not defined in the Act, should be interpreted in a manner complementary to "sale" which is defined in § 2(3) as including "every * * * disposition of * * * a security or interest in a security, for value * * *." In fact, a proposed provision of the Act which expressly exempted sales "by or for the account of a pledge holder or mortgagee selling or offering for sale or delivery in the ordinary course of business and not for the purpose of avoiding the provisions of the Act, to liquidate a bona fide debt, a security pledged in good faith as collateral for such debt," was not accepted by Congress.

* * *

Nor is it a defense that the banks did not deal directly with Guild Films. This court has recently stated that "the underlying policy of the Act, that of protecting the investing public through the disclosure of adequate information, would be seriously impaired if we held that a dealer must have conventional or contractual privity with the issuer in order to be an 'underwriter'." S.E.C. v. Culpepper, 2 Cir., 1959, 270 F.2d 241, 246, following S.E.C. v. Chinese Consol. Benev. Ass'n, 2 Cir., 1941, 120 F.2d 738 * * *. It was held in these two cases that § 4(1) "does not in terms or by fair implication protect those who are engaged in steps necessary to the distribution of a security issue. To give Section 4(1) the construction urged by the defendant would afford a ready method of thwarting the policy of the law and evading its provisions." S.E.C. v. Chinese Consol. Benev. Ass'n, supra * * *.

The banks have contended that they were "bona fide pledgees" and therefore "entitled upon default to sell the stock free of restrictions." They assume that "good faith" in accepting the stock is a sufficient defense. See Loss, Securities Regulation, 346 (1951). But the statute does not impose such a "good faith" criterion. The exemption in § 4(1) was intended to permit private sales of unregistered securities to investors who are likely to have, or who are likely to obtain, such information as is ordinarily disclosed in registration statements. * * * The "good faith" of the banks is irrelevant to this purpose. It would be of little solace to purchasers of worthless stock to learn that the sellers had acted "in good faith." Regardless of good faith, the banks engaged in steps necessary to this public sale, and cannot be exempted.

Without imputing to the banks any participation in a preconceived scheme to use the pledge of these securities as a device for unlawful distribution, it may be noted that when the 50,000 shares of Guild Films stock were received on February 12, 1959, the banks knew that they had been given unregistered stock and that the issuer had specifically forbidden that the stock "be sold, transferred, pledged or hypothecated in the absence of an effective registration statement for the shares under the Securities Act of 1933 or an opinion of counsel to the company that registration is not required under said Act." Furthermore, from Roach's prior unfulfilled promises, the banks should have known that immediate sale was almost inevitable if they were to recoup their loans from the security received. On February 11, 1959, the day before the stock was received, the S.E.C. suspended trading in the Jacobs stock. And on the very day that the stock was received, appellants wired Roach that they would call the loan unless payment were made. For months the banks had threatened action but declined to act; circumstances finally required action. The banks cannot now claim that this possibility was unforeseeable. The district court properly enjoined the threatened violation.

Affirmed.

NOTES ON THE *GUILD FILMS* CASE

1. *How Little Does It Take?* Section 2(a)(11) states that anyone who "participates or has a direct or indirect participation in any such undertaking" is a statutory underwriter. This "participation" standard is obviously intended to be broad. But how broad? In Harden v. Raffensperger, Hughes & Co., Inc.,[11] the issuer was itself a broker-dealer that wished to underwrite an offering by its subsidiary. Under NASD rules, such "self underwriting" required that it employ a "qualified independent underwriter" to review the pricing of the offering (in light of the issuer's conflict of interest) and to perform due diligence with regard to the registration statement. The defendant, Raffensperger, Hughes & Co., Inc., was hired to perform these limited functions, but it did not offer or sell the securities. Nonetheless, it was found liable under § 11. The Seventh Circuit reached this conclusion on two grounds. First, it said that the words "participates" or "takes part" in an underwriting were "broad enough to encompass all persons who engage in steps necessary to the distribution of securities."[12] *Query:* Would this standard make even the printer of the prospectus liable? Second, and more importantly, it noted that the NASD had determined that "qualified independent underwriters are subject to section 11 liability."[13] *Query:* Would "independent" underwriters have sufficient incentive to perform due

---

[11] 65 F.3d 1392 (7th Cir. 1995).
[12] Id. at 1400.
[13] Id. at 1401.

diligence (to the degree that the 1933 Act intended) if they were insulated from liability under § 11?

In Byrnes v. Faulkner, Dawkins & Sullivan,[14] the owners of unregistered shares exercised a "piggyback" right to include shares they owned in a registration statement filed by the company. But they did not actively promote the offering in any way. The registration statement indicated they might be deemed to be statutory underwriters. When the registration statement became effective, they sold their shares through a broker but failed to include a statutory prospectus with the confirmation of sale. Their purchasers argued that the sale violated § 5. Because the sellers "arranged to have their stock included in . . . [the issuer's] registration statements and were identified as putative underwriters," the court concluded that they "therefore became participants in the . . . distribution and accordingly became underwriters."[15] Sound result?

This is not the only possible standard. Other cases have read the word "participates" in § 2(a)(11) to focus on whether the defendant has furnished assistance that facilitated the issuer's distribution.[16] *Byrnes* does seem to expose venture capitalists and institutional investors to liability when they exercise contractual rights to include unregistered stock acquired earlier in a private placement in an initial public offering. In contrast, other courts have ruled that such investors should not be deemed underwriters, at least where they neither contribute professional services nor share in the economic risks of the offering.[17]

Problems

PROBLEM 7-1

Your old college roommate and the best man at your wedding has launched a small start-up company in Silicon Valley. He convinces you to invest $200,000, and, because you are "best lawyer he knows" (he was always good at flattery), to write the first draft of the registration statement for a small offering where his firm is chiefly buying the stock of a rival firm in an exchange offer. But they are also looking for additional financing, and he convinces you to give him the email addresses of 100 or so of your law firm's better-heeled clients. He solicits them to invest, and about 20 do. He uses your name as a reference with several, and a few call you to ask your opinion (which is favorable if "you are willing to accept some risk"). Are you an underwriter?

---

[14] 550 F.2d 1303 (2d Cir. 1977).
[15] Id. at 1312.
[16] See, e.g., SEC v. North Am. Research & Dev. Corp., 424 F.2d 63 (2d Cir. 1970).
[17] See McFarland v. Memorex Corp., 493 F.Supp. 631, 644–46 (N.D.Cal.1980), modified on other grounds, 581 F.Supp. 878 (N.D.Cal.1984); see also, O'Hare, Institutional Investors, Registration Rights, and the Specter of Liability Under Section 11 of the Securities Act of 1933, 1996 Wisc.L.Rev. 217.

CHAPTER 7   OFFERINGS BY UNDERWRITERS, AFFILIATES, AND DEALERS   537

PROBLEM 7-2

Your law firm has a unique practice of representing IPO clients on a "stock only" basis. That is, rather than charging the $1 million to $1.5 million fee charged by comparable firms, your firm will take stock (valued at the initial offering price) in lieu of cash. The offering was initially priced at $25 per share, but because the price rose on the first day to $60, your firm has made a bundle and would like to realize its profit as soon as it can. Although your firm's stock was fully registered, it agreed to a lock-up under which the firm would not sell any shares until six months after the offering. Is the firm now an underwriter as one who "participates" in a distribution? What if, during the period between one month after the offering and the end of the lock-up agreement, your firm occasionally buys the issuer's stock in the secondary market (because the lead underwriter, who also is buying, advises you that otherwise the stock price will slip)?

PROBLEM 7-3

Dana runs a blog where she comments on the economy, markets, and, on occasion, particular stocks. When one of her favorite companies went public, Dana wrote a series of blog posts extolling the virtues of the company, the quality of its products, and its commitment to doing good for the world. She even included a link on her website where her readers could access the company's regulatory filings and, when the company eventually offered its stock for sale, a link that connected her readers to the company's prospectus. Dana received no compensation or consideration of any kind for her actions. Has Dana violated § 5?

2. GOING PUBLIC BY THE BACK DOOR

Securities and Exchange Commission v. Datronics Engineers, Inc.

United States Court of Appeals, Fourth Circuit, 1973.
490 F.2d 250, cert. denied 416 U.S. 937.

■ Before BRYAN, SENIOR CIRCUIT JUDGE, and FIELD and WIDENER, CIRCUIT JUDGES.

■ ALBERT A. BRYAN, SENIOR CIRCUIT JUDGE: The Securities and Exchange Commission in enforcement of the Securities Act of 1933, § 20(b), and the Securities Exchange Act of 1934, § 21(e), sought a preliminary injunction to restrain Datronics Engineers, Inc., its officers and agents, as well as related corporations, from continuing in alleged violation of the registration and antifraud provisions of the Acts. The breaches are said to have been committed in the sale of unregistered securities, § 5 of the 1933 Act, and by the employment of false representations in their sale, § 10(b) of the 1934 Act, and Rule 10b–5 of the Commission.

Summary judgment went for the defendants, and the Commission appeals. We reverse.

Specifically, the complaint charged transgressions of the statutes by Datronics, assisted by the individual defendants, in declaring, and effectuating through the use of the mails, "spin-offs" to and among its stockholders of the unregistered shares of stock owned by Datronics in other corporations. With exceptions to be noted, and since the decision on appeal rests on a motion for summary judgment, there is no substantial dispute on the facts. Datronics was engaged in the construction of communications towers. Its capital stock was held by 1000 shareholders and was actively traded on the market. All of the spin-offs occurred within a period of 13 months * * * and the spun-off stock was that of nine corporations, three of which were wholly owned subsidiaries of Datronics and six were independent corporations.

The pattern of the spin-offs in each instance was this: Without any business purpose of its own, Datronics would enter into an agreement with the principals of a private company. The agreement provided for the organization by Datronics of a new corporation, or the utilization of one of Datronics' subsidiaries, and the merger of the private company into the new or subsidiary corporation. It stipulated that the principals of the private company would receive the majority interest in the merger-corporation. The remainder of the stock of the corporation would be delivered to, or retained by, Datronics for a nominal sum per share. Part of it would be applied to the payment of the services of Datronics in the organization and administration of the proposed spin-off, and to Datronics' counsel for legal services in the transaction. Datronics was bound by each of the nine agreements to distribute among its shareholders the rest of the stock.

Before such distribution, however, Datronics reserved for itself approximately one-third of the shares. Admittedly, none of the newly acquired stock was ever registered; its distribution and the dissemination of the false representations were accomplished by use of the mails.

I. Primarily, in our judgment each of these spin-offs violated § 5 of the Securities Act in that Datronics caused to be carried through the mails an unregistered security "for the purpose of sale or for delivery after sale". Datronics was actually an issuer, or at least a coissuer, and not exempted from § 5 by § 4(1) of the Act, as "any person other than an issuer".

Datronics and the other appellees contend, and the District Court concluded, that this type of transaction was not a sale. The argument is that it was no more than a dividend parceled out to stockholders from its portfolio of investments. A noteworthy difference here, however, is that each distribution was an obligation. Their contention also loses sight of the definition of "sale" contained in § 2 of the 1933 Act. As pertinent here that definition is as follows:

When used in this subchapter, unless the context otherwise requires—

* * *

(3) The term "sale" or "sell" shall include every contract of sale or *disposition* of a security or interest in a security, *for value.* The term "offer to sell", "offer for sale", or "offer" shall include every attempt or offer to dispose of, or solicitation of an offer to buy, a security or interest in a security, *for value.* * * * (Accent added.)

As the term "sale" includes a "disposition of a security", the dissemination of a new stock among Datronics' stockholders was a sale. However, the appellees urged, and the District Court held, that this disposition was not a statutory sale because it was not "for value", as demanded by the definition. Here, again, we find error. Cf. Securities and Exchange Commission v. Harwyn Industries Corp., 326 F.Supp. 943, 954 (S.D.N.Y.1971). Value accrued to Datronics in several ways. First, a market for the stock was created by its transfer to so many new assignees—at least 1000, some of whom were stockbroker-dealers, residing in various States. Sales by them followed at once—the District Judge noting that "[i]n each instance dealing promptly began in the spun-off shares". This result redounded to the benefit not only of Datronics but, as well, to its officers and agents who had received some of the spun-off stock as compensation for legal or other services to the spin-off corporations. Likewise, the stock retained by Datronics was thereby given an added increment of value. The record discloses that in fact the stock, both that disseminated and that kept by Datronics, did appreciate substantially after the distributions.

This spurious creation of a market whether intentional or incidental constituted a breach of the securities statutes. Each of the issuers by this wide spread of its stock became a publicly held corporation. In this process and in subsequent sales the investing public was not afforded the protection intended by the statutes. Further, the market and the public character of the spun-off stock were fired and fanned by the issuance of shareholder letters announcing future spin-offs, and by information statements sent out to the shareholders.

Moreover, we think that Datronics was an underwriter within the meaning of the 1933 Act. Hence its transactions were covered by the prohibitions, and were not within the exemptions, of the Act. §§ 3(a)(1) and 4(1) of the 1933 Act. By definition, the term underwriter "means any person who has purchased from an issuer with a view to, or offers or sells for an issuer in connection with, the distribution of any security, or participates or has a direct or indirect participation in any such undertaking. * * *" § 2(11) of the 1933 Act. Clearly, in these transactions the merger-corporation was an issuer; Datronics was a purchaser as well as a co-issuer; and the purchase was made with a view to the distribution of the stock, as commanded by Datronics' preacquisition agreements. By this underwriter distribution Datronics violated § 5 of the 1933 Act—sale of unregistered securities.

II. The Commission charged a violation by Datronics and its officers of § 10(b) of the 1934 Act and of Rule 10b–5. The breach occurred through untrue factual statements incident to the spin-offs. The District Court quite justifiably found that "in certain instances misleading statements were made by" Datronics and the individual defendants. This finding was reiterated by the District Court in discussing the announcements which were made to Datronics' stockholders with each spin-off.

A common explanation of the distribution to its stockholders was that it was "impractical" for Datronics itself to run the merger-corporations. Of course, as the minority stockholder, Datronics could not do so. The District Court termed the explanation false and a "pure subterfuge".

Since, however, the District Court was of the opinion that the distribution of the stock among Datronics' shareholders was not a sale, it held that the "misleading statements" were not outlawed by § 10(b) or by Commission Rule 10b–5. These provisions condemn such misrepresentations only when they are used "in connection with the purchase or sale of any security". Inasmuch as we believe there was a sale in each spin-off, we cannot agree with the District Court's determination. * * *

This was one of the trial court's reasons for not granting an injunction. Other grounds were that there was no indication that in the future the defendants might violate the statutes in suit; that the officers and agents who formulated and executed the spin-offs were no longer connected with Datronics; and that the present officers and agents assured the District Court that no more spin-offs of this kind would be indulged in. Moreover, the Court felt that by its interpretative releases the Commission had led Datronics and its codefendants to believe that spin-offs were not proscribed by these statutes. The Court was also persuaded by the failure of the Commission to act more vigilantly. While the issuance of an injunction is discretionary, it seems to us that overall, notwithstanding these considerations, the facts in this case warranted the grant of an injunction. * * *

Finally, a summary of the activities of Datronics is conclusively convincing that they violated the statutes in question, and should now be restrained to prevent recurrences. To begin with, it is noteworthy that they were not isolated or minimal transgressions. There were, to repeat, nine sales and distributions of unregistered stocks in little more than a year. They were huge in volume, ranging from 75,000 to 900,000 shares. The distribution was not confined to a small number of recipients; nor was it incidental to Datronics' corporate functions. Concededly, none of the several distributions had a business purpose. In short, the spin-offs seemingly constituted the major operation of Datronics at the time.

We cannot read the releases or letters of the Commission or its abstention from earlier suits as evincing express or implied approval of the repeated and large-scale violations as are here. The releases do not approve or condone a campaign, such as Datronics engaged in, to develop means and opportunities to promote spin-offs. Indeed, one of Datronics' agents was a "finder" of opportunities for spin-offs.

The dismissal order of the District Court will be vacated, and the cause remanded for the entry of a judgment sustaining the appellant's motion for the preliminary injunction sought in its complaint.

▪ WIDENER, CIRCUIT JUDGE (concurring):

I concur in the issuance of the temporary injunction * * *.

I note that the opinion of the court may not be broadly enough read to cast doubt upon the legitimate business acquisition of one company by another, or the legitimate business merger of two companies, although a market for securities spun off as a consequence of the transfer may be thereby created; for, as the opinion of the court recites, the market created by Datronics' spin-offs was spurious, doubtless meaning illegitimate, however actual it might have been, and Datronics caused the consummation of the transactions complained of without any business purpose of its own.

In my own opinion, the root of this case is the pre-existing agreement between Datronics and the various companies whose stocks it spun off with no apparent purpose other than the incidental benefits of creation of a public market for the stock. If the transactions were with a view to creating a public market for the stock which the various companies could not otherwise do absent compliance with the statute, then I think Datronics may be held to be an underwriter. The value requirement of a sale, for the issuer did receive value, I think, may be satisfied by the exchange of stock of the various companies with Datronics or by the exchange of stock of the various companies for services of Datronics. See also 58 Va.L.Rev. 1451.[18]

* * *

A. SPIN-OFFS, REVERSE MERGERS, AND THE SHELL GAME

a. Restricting Back Door Entry to the Market. The *Datronics* case may seem like slightly strained reasoning in support of the correct policy result. The policy problem is that the trading of securities of inactive or shell corporations can easily be manipulated, and spin-offs were regularly used to effect "pump and dump" schemes. In the 1960s, a

---

[18] On motions to reconsider, the defendants represented to the court that no more spin-offs would be undertaken. On that basis, the court rescinded that part of the opinion which required the trial court to award a preliminary injunction, and remanded for a determination by the district court, consistent with the remainder of the opinion, of whether an injunction should or should not be issued restraining Datronics in respect of those transactions the court found to be impermissible. Datronics' request for a rehearing en banc was denied—Eds.

technique first came into use by which a private company could achieve the status of a public company without a 1933 Act registration, in effect going public through the back door. A variety of patterns were used, but the overall objective remained the same. The most popular of these devices was that employed in the *Datronics* case—a privately-held company wishing to "go public" would issue additional stock to a second publicly-held company (usually a shell corporation with few assets, other than its stockholder list), which would then distribute most of the stock to its public shareholders as a dividend, keeping a portion as its "fee" for acting as the conduit in this operation. It would then repeat the operation again and again for different companies desiring a public market for their stocks without any of the disclosures required by the 1933 Act or 1934 Act.

In SEC v. Harwyn Industries Corp.,[19] the SEC sought to plug this potential loophole in the 1933 Act by seeking to enjoin various forms of spin-offs of a subsidiary's shares to the parent's stockholders without registration, thereby converting the subsidiary into a public firm whose unregistered shares would then be traded in the market. The court held that the *Harwyn* spin-offs "violated the spirit and purpose of the registration requirements of § 5 of the 1933 Act." Nevertheless, the court concluded that defendant's interpretation of §§ 2(a)(3) and 5 was "neither frivolous nor wholly unreasonable" and was made in good faith and on the advice of counsel. The court was moved by the somewhat ambivalent attitude of the SEC, both before and after the SEC's Interpretative Release No. 4982.[20] That Release emphasized that the appropriate test for when a spin-off required registration was whether it had a proper business purpose. Upon assurance by counsel for defendants in *Harwyn* that their clients would no longer engage in distributions of the type in question without registration (because the SEC had now set forth its views), the court denied the SEC's motion for a preliminary injunction.

The *Datronics* case delivered the coup de grace to the more blatant forms of the spin-off and shell game, while still permitting conventional spin-offs. Indeed, in United States v. Rubinson,[21] defendants who persisted in engaging in spin-offs, followed by the resale of worthless securities to the unsuspecting public, were convicted for violating the registration and antifraud provisions of the federal securities laws. In addition, the SEC recognized that the definition of "sale" in § 3(a)(14) of the 1934 Act does not have the same "for value" requirement as the definition in § 2(a)(3) of the 1933 Act, and, thus, it did need to engage in

---

[19] 326 F.Supp. 943 (S.D.N.Y.1971).
[20] Securities Act Release No. 4982 (July 2, 1969).
[21] 543 F.2d 951 (2d Cir. 1976), cert. denied 429 U.S. 850 (1976).

the same elaborate (and possibly strained) analysis of the benefits to the issuer as was necessary in *Datronics*.[22]

In any event, the SEC's thinking about spin-offs changed over subsequent years. De-emphasizing its earlier focus in Release 4982 on the existence of a "proper business purpose," the Commission shifted to an emphasis on whether adequate disclosures had been made at the time of the spin-off. Later decisions also held that spin-offs that receive adequate disclosure are not sales or purchases of securities.[23] After issuing a multitude of no-action letters on the line between spin-offs that require registration and those that do not, the staff of the Division of Corporation Finance codified them in Staff Legal Bulletin No. 4 in 1997.[24] In that bulletin, the staff took the position that a spin-off will not be required to be registered if each of the following five conditions are satisfied:

1. *No consideration.* The parent corporation's shareholders must provide no consideration for the spun-off shares (otherwise, obviously there is a sale).

2. *Pro-rata distribution of shares.* The spin-off must be pro-rata to the parent corporation's shareholders with no surrender of rights or value required by those who receive the spun-off shares.

3. *Adequate information.* The parent corporation must provide adequate information to both its shareholders and the market. If the subsidiary to be spun off is not a reporting company, the parent must (1) provide an information statement by the date of the spin-off that describes the transaction and complies with Regulation 14A or 14C under the 1934 Act and (2) cause the subsidiary to promptly register as a reporting company under the 1934 Act. Where the subsidiary is a reporting company, it must have been subject to the 1934 Act's reporting requirements for at least 90 days, be current in its 1934 Act reports, and provide certain specific disclosures about the transaction.

4. *Valid business purpose.* Where there is a valid business purpose for the transaction, the SEC staff's view is that the spin-off transaction is less likely to amount to a sale. What constitutes an invalid purpose? The bulletin gave several examples, such as creating a public market for a development stage subsidiary that had no specific business plan or objective (other than seeking a merger). The common premise underlying

---

[22] Thus, in International Controls Corp. v. Vesco, 490 F.2d 1334 (2d Cir.), cert. denied, 417 U.S. 932 (1974), a much simpler analysis was used to find that a spin-off amounted to a sale of securities.

[23] See Isquith v. Caremark International, Inc., 136 F.3d 531 (7th Cir. 1998); Rathborne v. Rathborne, 683 F.2d 914, 919–20 (5th Cir. 1982) (sale still results if transactions produce "fundamental change in the nature" of the investment). *Rathborne* emphasized, however, that if the shareholder received the same proportionate interest in the parent and the spun-off subsidiary, a "fundamental change" would be unlikely to result. *Query*: Would this standard produce a different result in *Datronics*?

[24] See 1997 SEC No-Act. LEXIS 869 (Sept. 16, 1997).

these examples was that an attempt to market a company through the back door without adequate information is an invalid purpose.

5. *Restricted securities.* Where a parent corporation spins off "restricted securities," the parent corporation may be deemed an underwriter of those securities for at least two years. If, however, the parent has held the subsidiary's stock for at least two years prior to the spin-off, the parent will not be deemed an underwriter. (This interpretation apparently applies only to stock acquired by the parent and not to the stock of subsidiaries it created itself.)

b. *Rule 15c2–11.* In addition, the SEC's staff advised that affiliates of the parent that acquire shares in a spin-off may be required to hold such shares as restricted securities and sell them only pursuant to Rule 144 or some other exemption.

In an entirely different and earlier approach to end the spin-off game, the SEC sought to regulate the broker-dealers who trade such securities. In 1971, the Commission adopted Rule 15c2–11 under the 1934 Act for the purpose of preventing a broker or dealer from initiating or resuming quotations with respect to a security in the absence of adequate information concerning the security and the issuer.[25] In adopting the rule, the SEC emphasized that the rule was particularly applicable in connection with the distribution of securities of "shell" corporations by means of a "spin-off" device. The Commission noted, however, that the potential for fraud and manipulation also existed whenever a broker or dealer submitted quotations concerning any infrequently traded security in the absence of adequate information. Rule 15c2–11 illustrates the SEC's use of the antifraud provisions of the 1934 Act to buttress the disclosure provisions of the 1933 Act.

Nonetheless, the efficacy of Rule 15c2–11 is open to debate. Although it creates a clear disincentive for the broker-dealer who has no information about a non-reporting issuer from beginning to trade that stock, this disincentive is undercut in several ways. Subsection (f)(3) of the Rule includes a "piggyback" exception that allows a broker-dealer to rely on the quotations of another broker-dealer that initially complied with the information review requirement so long as the conditions of that subsection are met. Once the conditions are met, a broker-dealer can "piggyback" on either its own or other broker-dealers' previously published quotations. These exceptions may well overwhelm the rule.

Although the Securities Enforcement Remedies and Penny Stock Reform Act of 1990 (the "Penny Stock Act") gave the SEC additional authority to deal with fraud and abuse in penny stocks, the definition of a "penny stock" is somewhat arbitrarily limited, in most cases, to stocks priced at less than five dollars.[26] Promoters quickly learned that they

---

[25] Exchange Act Release No. 9310 (Sept. 13, 1971).

[26] See Rule 3a51–1. To escape the definition of a "penny stock," not only must the stock be priced at $5 or more per share, but the issuer must also meet certain fairly modest financial criteria (e.g., net tangible assets in excess of $2 million or certain other levels).

could escape the more onerous provisions of the Penny Stock Act if they priced the security at $5 or more per share.

Thus, the 1990s witnessed a major resurgence of trading in low-priced, illiquid stocks that traded in non-transparent markets. The balance traded in over-the-counter markets, including the NASDAQ bulletin board. Most of the issuers at the lower end of this market were unlikely to be reporting companies. Hence, the problem of back door listings resurfaced as a major problem, largely because new technological innovations made the Internet and OTC electronic bulletin boards an effective substitute for a stock exchange listing. Faced with endemic problems in its bulletin board market, the NASD responded in 1997 by purging most non-reporting companies from that market (with the result that those firms could trade only in the over-the-counter "pink sheets").[27] Although concerned about the loss of liquidity, the SEC supported this proposal, and, in 1998, it proposed amendments to tighten Rule 15c2–11 to deal with "microcap" fraud by requiring all brokers to possess and review more current information about an issuer when they publish price quotations for the issuer's securities.[28] The effect of these amendments might have been to chill the willingness of brokers to publish quotations for non-reporting issuers; possibly for this reason and possibly because of lobbying pressure, the Commission waited until late 2019 to repropose the same amendments.[29]

c. *Continuing Use of the Backdoor.* The dimensions of the "microcap" market continue to grow. As of June 2020, there were 10,974 securities trading in the OTC Market, including 9,585 securities in the pink sheets.[30]

Although the spin-off was the preferred technique at the time of *Datronics*, the more popular technique today has become the use of a reverse merger to acquire a listing. Under this technique, a non-public company merges with a shell corporation, paying a modest premium over the market price for the shell company's stock (which is usually a penny stock). This may set the stage for a follow-up "pump and dump" scheme. More recently, a number of Chinese-incorporated companies have used the reverse merger technique to obtain listings (without registration), partly as a means of accessing the U.S. capital markets.

The SEC has sometimes challenged reverse mergers when special facts are present. See SEC v. Sierra Brokerage Servs, 608 F.Supp.2d 923 (S.D. Ohio 2009) ("gifts" of shell company stock amounted to unregistered "sales" in violation of § 5 and appeared to be preludes to a "pump and

---

[27] See Knight, "NASD Tries to Reduce the Risk of OTC Trading," Wash. Post (Dec. 15, 1997).

[28] See Exchange Act Release No. 39670 (Feb. 17, 1998).

[29] See Publication or Submission of Quotations Without Specified Information, SEC Release No. 34–87115 [File No. S7-14-19] (Sept. 25, 2019).

[30] See OTC Markets: Stock Screener, https://www.otcmarkets.com/research/stock-screener (last visited June 6, 2020).

dump" scheme). Despite these occasional challenges by the SEC,[31] the number of such "back door" entries into the public market appears to continue. Sometimes, the shell corporation purports to comply with Rule 15c2–11 to qualify for over-the-counter trading, but the company is "sold" to the acquiring company's management largely for its existing status as a publicly-traded company. In extreme cases, the owners of the shell corporation may sell part of the shell company's stock to the purchasers of the operating business in "matched" trades that are publicly reported to create the illusion of a rising market price.[32] Such examples help explain why, when the SEC amended Rule 145 under the 1933 Act in 2007 to generally delete the former "presumptive underwriter" provisions in Rules 145(c) and (d), it still retained that doctrine in cases of mergers involving "shell companies" (which term is defined in Rule 405 under the 1933 Act).

As public concern grew over reverse mergers to obtain listings (most of which have recently been by companies based in China), the major stock exchanges tightened their listing standards in 2011, most notably by requiring the company to maintain a specified minimum share price for a sustained period prior to making a listing application.[33] Commentators have suggested additional standards before a foreign issuer should be able to obtain a listing on a U.S. exchange through a reverse merger, including an independent forensic report on the issuer, the execution of a consent to service of process in the U.S. by foreign controlling persons, and a longer seasoning period.[34] But, to date, the SEC has been unwilling to adopt or encourage such tougher measures.

3. THE SECTION "4(1½)" EXEMPTION

The exemptions to § 5 surveyed so far do not cover every instance in which the need for SEC registration is absent. Let's suppose that Acme, Inc. raises $10 million in a private placement to sophisticated persons under § 4(a)(2). In this offering, John D. Rockefeller V buys $1 million, and two months later, he is asked by his friend, J.P. Morgan VI, if he would sell him $500,000 because the latter did not hear of the placement in time to buy. Rockefeller would be happy to sell to Morgan (who both are wealthy and sophisticated). But can he? Rockefeller has not held nearly long enough to satisfy Rule 144 and might be deemed an underwriter under § 4(a)(1) because of the "view to distribution" test in

---

[31] See SEC v. Lybrand, 200 F.Supp.2d 384 (S.D.N.Y.2002) (finding violations of both § 5 and Rule 10b–5 where promoters made repetitive sales of shell corporations); SEC v. Cavanagh, 1 F.Supp.2d 337 (S.D.N.Y.1998).

[32] Such conduct will violate the antifraud rules as well as § 5. "Matched trades" are pre-arranged buys and sells that have not been exposed to the market and, hence, often represent inflated or otherwise fictitious prices.

[33] See, e.g., Exchange Act Release No. 65710 (Nov. 8, 2011) (AMEX); Exchange Act Release No. 65709 (Nov. 15, 2011) (NYSE); Exchange Act Release No. 65708 (Nov. 15, 2011) (Nasdaq).

[34] See Exchange Act Release No. 65710 (Nov. 8, 2011), 76 FR 70790 at p. 12 (noting proposed reforms that were not adopted).

§ 2(a)(11)'s definition of underwriter. Also, § 4(a)(2), on its face, is of little help because it only exempts "transactions by an issuer," and no issuer would be involved in this sale from Rockefeller to Morgan. But is there any conceivable need for the securities laws to block this innocuous transaction (when Morgan could have easily bought directly from Acme)?

The implication of this example is that an exemption falling midway between §§ 4(a)(1) and 4(a)(2) would be desirable. Over time, with little statutory basis, courts and the SEC have come to recognize such an exemption for "private resales."

Excerpt from: Carl W. Schneider

The Section "4(1½)" Phenomenon: Private Resales of "Restricted" Securities*
34 Business Lawyer 1961–1978 (1979).[a]

INTRODUCTION

The purpose of this Report is to consider the available methods by which a person may resell privately securities initially issued in a private placement ("restricted securities") without registration under the Securities Act of 1933. This variety of sale has become popularly known as "section 4(1½)" transactions, primarily because the SEC, in no-action letters and other pronouncements, frequently has required that such resales meet at least some of the established criteria for exemptions under both section 4(1) and section 4(2).[3] In this Report the term "Holder" is used to refer to a person who holds restricted securities and the term "Purchaser" to refer to a person who purchases restricted securities from a Holder.

* * *

OVERVIEW OF THE 4(1½) PHENOMENON

* * *

Our initial inquiry in analyzing the scope of permissible sales of Restricted Securities is to determine what subsection within section 4 is applicable. Sections 4(3), 4(4) and 4(5) may be ruled out summarily. Because section 4(2) exempts only "transactions *by an issuer*" and a sale by a Holder is not a sale "by an issuer", a literal reading of this section makes it inapplicable as the basis for an exemption. Of necessity, one

---

[*] A Report to the Committee on Federal Regulation of Securities from the Study Group on Section "4(1½)" of the Subcommittee on 1933 Act * * *.

[a] Copyright 1979 by the American Bar Association. All rights reserved. Reproduced with the permission of the American Bar Association and its Section of Corporation, Banking and Business Law.

[3] In this Report, the phrases "4(1½) transaction" or "4(1½) Sale" are used generically to describe resales of restricted securities otherwise than through holders in public markets.

then must turn to section 4(1), which exempts "transactions by any person other than an issuer, underwriter, or dealer." Recognizing that the Holder, by hypothesis, is not an "issuer" (as defined in section 2(4)) and assuming that he is not a "dealer", the critical inquiry is whether he or his Purchaser may be deemed an "underwriter", as defined in section 2(11) of the 1933 Act. To avoid "underwriter" status, the Holder (i) must not have purchased the shares from the issuer "with a view to" their "distribution" and (ii) must not offer or sell the shares "for an issuer in connection with, the distribution".

The term "distribution," although central to the "underwriter" analysis, is not defined in the 1933 Act, and it is at this point that section 4(2) concepts are typically introduced and the "underwriter" analysis becomes confusing. Because a "distribution", in the context of section 4(1), is generally considered to be functionally equivalent to a "public offering" as used in section 4(2), it seems reasonable in defining "distribution" to borrow by analogy from judicial and administrative interpretations of the term "public offering". Moreover, in considering a resale of Restricted Securities soon after the Holder has acquired them from the issuer, the application of section 4(2) standards to the resale may be necessary to assure that the issuer's original section 4(2) exemption is not vitiated by the resale.

Separate from the line of decisions and SEC staff positions that apply section 4(2) standards in determining whether a "distribution" is involved is the theory that section 4(2) may independently provide an exemption for sales by a Holder.

Against this general background of inconsistent application of various criteria and the lack of any clear agreement on even the applicable theory of exemption, we turn first to an analysis of the legislative history of section 4.

Legislative History

The legislative history of the 1933 Act sheds little light on any of the questions posed above. * * *

* * * James Landis, a principal draftsman of H.R. 5480, commented upon the general scope of the 1933 Act as follows:

> "Public offerings" as distinguished from "private offerings" proved to be the answer [to the question what scope the 1933 Act was to have]. The sale of an issue of securities to insurance companies or to a limited group of experienced investors was certainly not a matter of concern to the federal government. That bureaucracy, untrained in these matters as it was, could hardly equal these investors for sophistication, provided only it was their own money that they were spending. And so the conception of an exemption for all sales, other than by an issuer, underwriter, or dealer came into being, replacing the concept of

"isolated transactions" theretofore traditional to blue sky legislation.[14]

The precise process by which the desire to exempt a sale by an issuer to a small group of sophisticated investors as described by Landis led to an exemption for sales by a person other than an "issuer, underwriter, or dealer" is unclear. The first part of the quoted language seems more appropriately directed to validating the private offering exemption of section 4(2) than the exemption of section 4(1). * * *

* * *

There is some support for the theory that section 4(1) was designed to cover resales in much the same fashion as section 4(2) was aimed at delineating the scope of the exemption for sales by an issuer. One House Report on this legislation reflects a primary intention to distinguish between regular trading and distributions (whether made by the issuer, affiliates or nonaffiliates).[19]

* * *

The Report also indicates that the regulation of sales of control securities was intended to be effected by shaping the definition of "underwriter" in section 2(11) and incorporating that term in the section 4(1) exemption:

* * *

From this [Report] one may draw some support for the notions that section 4(2) is properly addressed solely to issuers and that section 4(1) above should govern all resales, including sales of both Restricted Securities and securities held by controlling persons. * * *

JUDICIAL INTERPRETATIONS

Judicial efforts to identify the statutory provision to be applied to sales of restricted securities and to define the parameters of the appropriate exemption have been far more successful than legislative endeavors and generally support the view that section 4(1) is the provision to be applied.

The earliest such cases were United States v. Sherwood[22] and Gilligan, Will & Co. v. SEC.[23] In *Sherwood*, criminal contempt proceedings were brought against Sherwood, the holder of 8 percent of a company's stock, for violating an injunction prohibiting sales of the company's stock absent registration or the availability of an exemption. The stock in question had been acquired by Sherwood from one Doyle, who had received the stock from the issuer. The court found that

---

[14] Landis, The Legislative History of the Securities Act of 1933, 28 Geo.Wash.L.Rev. 29, 37 (1959).

[19] House of Representatives Report No. 85, at 5 (May 4, 1933) (hereinafter cited as "H.Rep. 85").

[22] 175 F.Supp. 480 (S.D.N.Y.1959) (discussed [infra at page 579]).

[23] 267 F.2d 461 (2d Cir. 1959) (discussed [infra at page 580]).

Sherwood was not a control person, had not acquired the stock with a view to distribution, and therefore was not an "underwriter". The fact that Sherwood had held the shares two years persuaded the court of Sherwood's investment intent. Sherwood's sales of the stock were found to be exempt under section 4(1).

In *Gilligan, Will* two registered dealers had participated in the placement of $3,000,000 of convertible debentures of Crowell-Collier Publishing Co. Gilligan, a partner of Gilligan, Will & Co., purchased $100,000 of the debentures for his own account and made representations that he purchased for investment. Notwithstanding these representations, Gilligan quickly sold $45,000 of the debentures to one Louis Alter, and Gilligan also made offers to two other potential purchasers, selling $5,000 of debentures to one of them. Ten months after these sales, Gilligan, Will & Co., Gilligan and Alter converted their debentures into common stock and sold the stock at a profit on the American Stock Exchange.

Gilligan and Alter later subscribed to an additional $200,000 of debentures which they similarly converted to common stock. Gilligan, Will & Co. also was active in selling $200,000 of the debentures to a mutual fund, and as a result of this transaction, other parties received warrants to purchase Crowell-Collier stock.

In a subsequent SEC enforcement action, Gilligan, Will attempted to have its own acts viewed in isolation, claiming that they were not "underwriters" because the transactions effected by them, viewed alone, did not constitute a "public offering." Similar transactions had been effected by another dealer contemporaneously with Gilligan, Will's transactions. Taken together, however, the total number of offerees was quite small. In addition to Gilligan and Alter, only two other offerees were involved. The defendants stipulated that none of the four offerees had access to the kind of information made available by registration. The court found that, even though the number of offerees was small, the offering could not be viewed as a "private" one, under the criteria established for the section 4(2) exemption, in the *Ralston Purina* case. Accordingly, Gilligan, Will was held to be an "underwriter", having purchased with a view to public distribution.

Although the result in *Gilligan, Will* is not surprising, the court's analysis of the defendants' claims of exemption is instructive. The court focused on the section 4(1) exemption, and determined that the initial inquiry was whether a "distribution" was involved. In determining the existence of a "distribution" the court noted that the term was equivalent to "public offering"[24] and turned to the *Ralston Purina* decision for instruction on that point. Finding that the Ralston "access" requirement had not been met, the court held that a "distribution" had occurred.

---

[24] Id. at 466 (citing H.R. Rep.No. 1838, 73d Cong., 2d Sess. (1934) at 41).

The court also recognized that a person could rely on the section 4(1) exemption even if a "distribution" had occurred, provided that person's acquisition of the shares had not been with a "view" to the subsequent distribution. In this part of its analysis, the court (i) rejected the particular "change of circumstances" asserted by the defendants (without rejecting the concept) and (ii) held that a ten-month holding period was not sufficient to establish that the defendants had not acquired the stock with a "view" to distribution.[26]

* * *

A clearer analysis of the statutory exemptions is present in Value Line Income Fund, Inc. v. Marcus.[34] This case involved an attempted rescission of an agreement between a mutual fund and Marcus, the principal shareholder and president of a machinery company, in which the mutual fund agreed to purchase one-half of Marcus' shares in the company. The transaction was completed as planned, but when the stock declined drastically in price within a year, Value Line sought to rescind the agreement on the ground that Marcus had made fraudulent representations and the shares had not been registered.

The two major defendants in *Value Line* were Marcus, the "Holder", and Van Alstyne, Noel & Co. ("Vanco"), the party through whom Marcus sold his shares to Value Line. Vanco was unaware of any misrepresentations made by Marcus, and more importantly, the court found that Vanco was neither an issuer, underwriter, or dealer, and therefore the transaction was considered exempt under section 4(1). Marcus, as a control person, was an "issuer" for purposes of determining whether Vanco was an "underwriter."[35] The only offerings of Marcus' stock made by Vanco were to mutual funds, which were recognized as highly sophisticated investors with sufficient "access" for private offering purposes. The court found there was no "distribution" or "view to distribution" by Vanco, with the result that Vanco was not an "underwriter" under section 2(11) and was entitled to rely upon the section 4(1) exemption. On the same analysis, the section 4(1) exemption was found to be available to Marcus.

Like * * * *Gilligan, Will,* * * * *Value Line* recognizes that private resales may be made in reliance on section 4(1). Moreover, *Value Line* is particularly significant in its recognition that such resales may be made immediately after the shares are acquired, provided the ultimate purchasers are persons to whom the issuer could have made a valid direct sale under section 4(2).

* * *

---

[26] 267 F.2d at 466–68.

[34] [1964–1966 Transfer Binder] Fed.Sec.L.Rep. (CCH) ¶ 91,523, 94,953 (S.D.N.Y.1965).

[35] Id. at ¶ 94,969.

In summary, our review of the cases dealing with the section 4(1½) phenomenon indicates the following:

1. The appropriate exemptive provision is section 4(1) and not 4(2).
2. No particular holding period is required.
3. The Purchasers' sophistication and access to information appear to have been viewed as essential in * * * the * * * decisions.
4. The number of purchasers, viewed alone, is not dispositive of the availability of an exemption.
5. Restrictions on resales by a Purchaser generally have not been required.
6. No decision has articulated an affirmative duty on a Holder to provide registration-type information to a Purchaser.

SEC INTERPRETATIONS

a. *The Staff No-Action Letters*

General

The SEC Staff has never enunciated the statutory basis on which it has permitted private resales of Restricted Securities, and the staff letters are relatively few in number and show little consistency. On a number of occasions, the staff has implied that the section 4(2) exemption would be applicable. Yet in one letter the Staff expressly repudiated the notion that the section 4(2) exemption is available to any party other than the issuer and suggested that section 4(1) might be the appropriate theory on which to base private resales. Similarly, the most recent step in the evolution of paragraph (e)(3)(G) of rule 144 further supports the section 4(1) basis for section 4(1½) sales by indicating that private resales can be made in reliance upon the section 4(1) exemption if the sale is one "not involving any public offering." * * *

* * *

Qualification of Purchasers

The staff letters are mixed with respect to the necessity that the purchaser be a sophisticated investor. Most staff letters make no reference to this requirement. A few, however, grant no-action requests upon the express condition that the purchaser be somewhat sophisticated. * * * In two letters the staff went even further, requiring the purchaser to be able "to afford the risk of the highly speculative investment."

Access to or Furnishing of Information

The staff has grappled somewhat unsuccessfully with the question whether the Purchaser must have access to registration-type information or be supplied such information by the Holder. In one letter the staff required that "prospective purchasers * * * be limited to persons who have access to the same information about [the issuer's] stock that a registration statement would provide." In others, the staff has required that the seller advise all offerees where information regarding the issuer might be obtained, and in one letter the staff merely required the seller to disclose all information regarding the issuer that was known to the seller.

Restrictions on Purchaser's Resales

The staff letters tend uniformly to provide that Purchasers of restricted securities are deemed to have received restricted shares and may not resell them *publicly* without compliance with the registration provisions of the Act. In a few letters the staff also has required that restrictive legends and stop-transfer orders be placed upon the shares. In a number of other letters, however, the staff has denied that it has any power to require the placement or removal of restrictive legends.

GENERAL GUIDELINES: THEORY AND PRACTICE

a. *Basis of Exemption*

Initially, we conclude that the only proper statutory basis for section 4(1½) sales is section 4(1). We consider that the limiting phrase "by an issuer" in section 4(2) poses an insurmountable barrier to reliance on that exemption as an affirmative basis for the exemption of section 4(1½) sales. As discussed below, however, we consider it appropriate to apply certain section 4(2) criteria to limit the manner in which some varieties of section 4(1½) transactions may otherwise be effected.

b. *Sales of Restricted Securities*

Where a nonaffiliate proposes to sell Restricted Securities, the critical inquiries in determining his status as an "underwriter" are whether his acquisition was made "with a view to * * * distribution" and whether his sale is to be made "for an issuer in connection with" a "distribution". Because these phrases appear in the disjunctive in section 2(11), strict statutory analysis indicates that if either question is answered in the affirmative, the Holder would not be entitled to rely upon section 4(1). As discussed below, however, even a purchase made subjectively "with a view to * * * distribution" may under certain conditions be made under section 4(1). Each of these phrases in section 2(11) focuses, first, on the status of the shares in the hands of the Holder (specifically, have they "come to rest") and second, whether his sales constitute a "distribution".

Under the traditional (pre-rule 144) approach, the prevailing view of securities law practitioners was that once restricted securities had "come to rest" (in the sense that the resales would not be a further step in the issuer's distributive process), there should be no restriction on the manner of resale. Analytically, such resales by definition would not vitiate the issuer's 4(2) exemption and would be sufficiently removed from the original placement that (i) the Holder's resale would not be deemed "for" the issuer and (ii) the Holder's original purchase would not be deemed to have been made with the proscribed "view". We think that this traditional approach has continuing validity and that the section 4(1) exemption should be available if the Holder can demonstrate (i) that he did not acquire the restricted securities from the issuer or an affiliate "with a view to" distribution *and* (ii) that the resale is not being made "for an issuer" (or in the case of the resale of restricted securities acquired from an affiliate, for the affiliate). The best objective evidence on these questions will be the length of time the Holder has owned the securities. If he has established a sufficiently long holding period, this alone should demonstrate conclusively that (i) his original acquisition was not "with a view" to distribution and (ii) that the resale is not being made "for the issuer". With respect to each of these standards, the mere length of the holding period should be sufficient. In this regard, we suggest that a Holder who subjectively intended when he acquired the Restricted Securities, to "distribute" them, may nevertheless thereafter resell them in reliance on section 4(1) if his actual retention of them has been consistent with the opposite intent.

In the case of restricted securities that have not "come to rest", the Holder may nevertheless sell them if the sale does not constitute a "distribution" (unless, as discussed below, the sale may be considered part of the original placement). In determining whether a "distribution" will result from the Holder's sale, we consider the better view to be that only the manner of sale and the number of purchasers are relevant. In short, only the quantitative aspects of the term "distribution" should be considered. We find no basis in the language or legislative history of the 1933 Act to impose the requirements that the Purchaser be sophisticated or have access to registration-type information. Accordingly, a Holder should be able to dispose of restricted securities provided there are few purchasers and the securities are not offered by means of mass communications. Nor, analytically, should there be any particular limit on the amount that may be sold. Obviously, some reasonable limitations must be observed on these points but there are no hard and fast rules. Similarly, the use of a broker to locate a few purchasers should not be ruled out, provided reasonable restrictions are placed on the breadth of the broker's solicitation efforts. Thus, even if the restricted securities have not "come to rest" at the time of resale, if under this second step of the "underwriter" analysis, one determines that no "distribution" will result, section 4(1) will be available.

If the restricted securities have been acquired from the issuer under circumstances in which it cannot be concluded that the shares have come to rest after their sale in the section 4(2) transaction, it is appropriate for section 4(2) requirements of offeree sophistication and access to be applied to the Holder resales. But this is appropriate only for the purpose of assuring that the issuer's original section 4(2) exemption for its sale to the Holder is not lost.

c. *Status of Securities in the Purchaser's Hands*

As a theoretical matter, a Purchaser of restricted securities can resell immediately so long as he adheres to the standards discussed above for the Holder's sale (*i.e.*, "privately") and his resales (and all others occurring around the same time) do not result in a "distribution" or otherwise vitiate the issuer's original section 4(2) exemption. The Purchaser thus is essentially in the same position as the Holder and should be able to make resales in the same fashion described herein for Holders.

* * *

NOTES ON THE SECTION 4(1½) EXEMPTION

1. *Purchaser Sophistication.* The foregoing, somewhat expansive interpretation of the § 4(1½) exemption focuses primarily on whether the distribution has "come to rest"—a mode of analysis that gives little weight to the sophistication of the buyer but instead focuses on quantitative criteria about the number of purchasers and the manner of sale. Yet, continuing uncertainty surrounds the legitimacy of this approach. If the scope of the § 4(1½) exemption is to be determined, at least in part, by reference to the criteria applicable to an issuer's private placement under § 4(a)(2), buyer sophistication may be at the heart of the inquiry. In Gilligan, Will & Co. v. SEC,[35] the Second Circuit seemed to say precisely this: that the term "distribution" in § 2(a)(11) is to be read in light of the criteria applicable to an issuer exemption under § 4(a)(2). Still, to date, most courts have been able to duck the issue of whether full compliance is necessary with the standards announced in SEC v. Ralston Purina Co.[36] to satisfy the § 4(1½) exemption. In Value Line Fund, Inc. v. Marcus,[37] discussed in the preceding excerpt, all five offerees were obviously sophisticated mutual funds. Similarly, in Ackerberg v. Johnson,[38] the plaintiff had a net worth over $1,000,000, had read a 99-page private placement memorandum prepared by the broker for the seller, and was found by the court to be a "sophisticated investor." Thus, the Eighth Circuit had no difficulty upholding the availability of the § 4(1½) exemption, both on the grounds that the seller had held the privately-placed securities for at least four years prior to the sale (which implied that the distribution had come to rest), and that the purchaser could fend for himself (thus satisfying *Ralston Purina*). Conversely, in SEC v. Manus,[39] the defendant, who was a controlling person, held the

---

[35] 267 F.2d 461 (2d Cir. 1959).
[36] 346 U.S. 119 (1953).
[37] [1964–1965 Transfer Binder] Fed.Sec.L.Rep. (CCH) ¶ 91,523 (S.D.N.Y. 1965).
[38] 892 F.2d 1328 (8th Cir. 1989).
[39] [1981–1982 Transfer Binder] Fed.Sec.L.Rep. (CCH) ¶ 98,307 (S.D.N.Y.1981). See also McDaniel v. Compania Minera Mar de Cortes, 528 F.Supp. 152 (D.Ariz.1981).

stock for four years and then sold to relatively unsophisticated buyers (a junior high school teacher and several other individuals who had not invested before). Not surprisingly, that defendant lost.

In contrast, Rule 144 ignores the sophistication of the buyer and basically permits resale to anyone if the securities have been held for the requisite holding period and, if resold by an affiliate, are resold in small quantities (i.e., normally 1% or less) that are unlikely to impact the market. The policy issue then is this: Should the § 4(1½) exemption be interpreted more in keeping with Rule 144's quantitative criteria or, instead, according to *Ralston Purina*?

2. *Other Criteria.* A consensus exists that a general solicitation will destroy the availability of the § 4(1½) exemption. Still, some no-action letters permitted the holders of large blocks to publicly advertise their availability, at least when the entire block was to be sold to one purchaser.[40] Sellers sometimes prepare a private placement memorandum when seeking to rely on the § 4(1½) exemption (although this could equally be based on a controlling person's fear of antifraud liability under Rule 10b–5). In contrast, no information furnishing obligation exists under Regulation D in the case of "accredited investors." Should the § 4(1½) exemption require more information than Regulation D? Should changes to the general solicitation restrictions in Rule 506 offerings be paralleled here to allow at least accredited investors to make private sales with general solicitation to other accredited investors?

3. *The Future of the § 4(1½) Exemption.* In the wake of the 1997 reduction in holding period to six months under Rule 144, and the development of an active resale market under Rule 144A, it might have been expected that the § 4(1½) exemption would no longer matter much. Its availability seemed most important in the case of affiliates of the issuer who wanted to sell large blocks of stock. The common stock of public domestic issuers generally will not qualify for Rule 144A (because, as discussed below, Rule 144A is not available for the common stock of companies whose shares are listed). For non-affiliates, Rule 144, today, probably provides a much simpler and less uncertain means to transfer restricted securities.

Still, the importance of this exemption has recently surfaced in a new context. Since 2000 and the collapse of the Internet bubble, the time it takes for a new company, even a very promising one, to move from the venture capital stage to an IPO has grown longer. Employees of the company may be forced to exercise stock options at this pre-IPO stage or else see them expire. This delay creates an enhanced desire for liquidity on the part of insiders; that is, shareholders in privately-held or venture capital companies may need to sell stock prior to the IPO.

---

[40] See Schneider, Section 4(1½)—Private Resales of Restricted or Control Securities, 49 Ohio St.L.J. 501, 507 (1988).

New institutions have arisen to service their needs: most notably, brokerage firms that specialize in matching buyers and sellers of stock in privately-held companies. The best-known of these firms includes SecondMarket (which facilitated Facebook's pre-IPO trading), SharesPost, and EquityZen.[41] Nasdaq acquired SecondMarket in 2015 (to be integrated into the Nasdaq Private Market), signaling Nasdaq's belief that more companies are staying private for longer periods.[42] Likewise, in 2019, the Nasdaq Private Market set a new annual record of $4.8 billion in transaction value.[43]

Such sales could be made pursuant to the § 4(1½) exemption (at least if the buyer was a sophisticated investor) or pursuant to Rule 144 (if the seller held the stock for a year or more and was not an affiliate). The rules applicable to such transactions remain only partially resolved (although the SEC has insisted that firms running such a matching service register as broker-dealers under the 1934 Act). The existence of markets for stock of privately held companies may prove to be a double-edged sword. On the one hand, they give new companies access to capital (and perhaps lower the cost of capital to them), thereby encouraging economic growth. On the other hand, these firms often have greater risk, higher informational asymmetries, and are associated with more fraud. Such markets for "emerging companies" have a history of collapsing after a series of scandals. This does not imply that they are undesirable, but regulatory oversight may be important for their survival.

4. STATUTORY RESTRICTIONS ON DISTRIBUTIONS OF SECURITIES BY CONTROLLING PERSONS OR AFFILIATES

In the Matter of Ira Haupt & Co.
Securities and Exchange Commission, 1946.
23 S.E.C. 589.

FINDINGS AND OPINION OF THE COMMISSION

This proceeding was instituted under Sections 15(b) and 15A(*l*)(2) of the Securities Exchange Act of 1934 to determine whether Ira Haupt & Co. ("Respondent") willfully violated Section 5(a) of the Securities Act of 1933 and, if so, whether the revocation of its registration as a broker-dealer and its expulsion or suspension from membership in the National Association of Securities Dealers, Inc. ("NASD"), a registered securities association, would be in the public interest.

---

[41] See Coren, Startup Employees Now Have a Good Way to Sell Their Shares Before an IPO, Quartz (Oct. 2017).

[42] See Stynes & Hope, Nasdaq Acquires SecondMarket, Buys Out SharesPost's Stake in Joint Venture, Wall St. J. (Oct. 2015).

[43] See Briganti, Nasdaq Private Market Sets New Annual Transaction Record in 2019, GlobalNewsWire (Feb. 2020).

The alleged violation of Section 5(a) is based on respondent's sale, for the accounts of David A. Schulte, a controlled corporation of Schulte's, and the David A. Schulte Trust (sometimes hereinafter referred to collectively as the "Schulte interests"), of approximately 93,000 shares of the common stock of Park & Tilford, Inc., during the period November 1, 1943, to June 1, 1944. It is conceded that the Schulte interests were in control of Park & Tilford during this period, that the sales were effected by use of the mails and instrumentalities of interstate commerce, and that the stock was not covered by a registration statement under the Securities Act.

After appropriate notice a hearing was held before a trial examiner. At the hearing a stipulation of facts was submitted in lieu of testimony. A trial examiner's report was waived, briefs and reply briefs were filed, and we heard argument.

* * *

[David A. Schulte was the president and director of Park & Tilford, Inc. The company had 243,731 shares of common stock outstanding, of which the Schulte interests owned 225,482 shares or 92 per cent, and the public 18,249 shares or 8 per cent. Schulte had been a long time customer of respondent brokerage firm. In December 1943, during the period of wartime shortages, Schulte announced that Park & Tilford was issuing a dividend in whiskey to its shareholders at cost. Ira Haupt, the senior partner of respondent, testified that Schulte called him, explained that, with the announcement of the liquor plan, it was likely that the market would become "terribly active" and placed a standing order to sell from one to three hundred shares at every quarter or half point so as "to create an orderly market." As anticipated, the trading became extremely active and in a rising market Haupt was able to dispose of some 90,000 shares at prices ranging from 58 to 96. The market was further stimulated when Park & Tilford offered to sell stockholders up to six cases of whiskey for each share of stock. At this point the wartime Office of Price Administration stepped in and limited resale prices of both the purchase rights and the whiskey, and the stock fell to 30. All told, during a six months period, respondent disposed of some 93,000 shares of stock for the Schulte interests, by use of the facilities of the New York Stock Exchange, the public's holdings thereby increasing to 115,344 shares or 46 per cent.]

* * *

It is conceded that respondent's transactions in Park & Tilford stock for the account of the Schulte interests constitute a violation of Section 5(a) unless an exemption was applicable to such transactions. Respondent contends that * * * the following [exemption] was applicable:
* * *

Section 4(2)a which exempts

> Brokers' transactions, executed upon customers' orders on any exchange or in the open or counter market, but not the solicitation of such orders.

The applicability of the foregoing [exemption] involves the following subissues:

(1) Was Respondent an "underwriter" as that term is defined in Section 2(11)?

* * *

(3) Is the brokerage exemption of Section 4(2) [the predecessor of § 4(4)] available to an underwriter who effects a distribution of an issue for the account of a controlling stockholder through the mechanism of a stock exchange?

If the violation of Section 5(a) is established, there are the further questions whether the violation was "willful" and, if so, whether it is in the public interest to revoke respondent's registration, or to expel or suspend it from the NASD.

1. *Was Respondent an "Underwriter"?*

Section 2(11) defines an "underwriter" as

> any person who * * * sells for an issuer in connection with, the distribution of any security * * * As used in this paragraph the term "issuer" shall include * * * any person * * * controlling * * * the issuer * * *

The purpose of the last sentence of this definition is to require registration in connection with secondary distributions through underwriters by controlling stockholders. This purpose clearly appears in the House Report on the Bill which states that it was intended:

> to bring within the provisions of the bill redistribution whether of outstanding issues or issues sold subsequently to the enactment of the bill. All the outstanding stock of a particular corporation may be owned by one individual or a select group of individuals. At some future date they may wish to dispose of their holdings and to make an offer of this stock to the public. Such a public offering may possess all the dangers attendant upon a new offering of securities. Wherever such a redistribution reaches significant proportions, the distributor would be in the position of controlling the issuer and thus able to furnish the information demanded by the bill. This being so, the distributor is treated as equivalent to the original issuer and, if he seeks to dispose of the issue through a public offering, he becomes subject to the act.

---

a   The Securities Acts Amendments of 1964, 78 Stat. 565, recast § 4 so that former § 4(2) is now § 4(a)(4)—Eds.

It is conceded that the Schulte interests controlled Park & Tilford and the respondent was, therefore, "selling for" a person in control of the issuer. However, respondent denies that these sales were effected "in connection with the distribution of any security." It asserts that at no time did it intend, nor was it aware that Schulte intended, a distribution of a large block of stock. It emphasizes that, in connection with the sales by which Schulte disposed of approximately 52,000 shares over a period of 6 months, each order was entered by Schulte to maintain an orderly market and was limited to 200 to 300 shares at a specific price; that the authority to sell 73,000 shares for the Trust was dependent upon a market price of at least 80; that the total amount which would be sold was never fixed or ascertained, and that consequently it did not intend to sell in connection with a distribution.

"Distribution" is not defined in the Act. It has been held, however, to comprise "the entire process by which in the course of a public offering the block of securities is dispersed and ultimately comes to rest in the hands of the investing public." In this case, the stipulated facts show that Schulte, owning in excess of 50,000 shares, had formulated a plan to sell his stock over the exchange in 200 share blocks "at 59 and every quarter up" and that the trust, holding 165,000 shares, specifically authorized the sale over the exchange of 73,000 shares "at $80 per share or better." A total of 93,000 shares was in fact sold by respondent for the account of the Schulte interests pursuant to these authorizations. We think these facts clearly fall within the above quoted definition and constitute a "distribution." We find no validity in the argument that a predetermination of the precise number of shares which are to be publicly dispersed is an essential element of a distribution. Nor do we think that a "distribution" loses its character as such merely because the extent of the offering may depend on certain conditions such as the market price. Indeed, in the usual case of an offering at a price, there is never any certainty that all or any specified part of the issue will be sold. And where part of an issue is outstanding, the extent of a new offering is almost always directly related to variations in the market price. Such offerings are not any less a "distribution" merely because their precise extent cannot be predetermined.

Nor can we accept respondent's claim that it was not aware of the distribution intended by the Schulte interests. * * *

* * *

We conclude from the foregoing facts that respondent was selling for the Schulte interests, controlling stockholders of Park & Tilford, in connection with the distribution of their holdings in the stock and was, therefore, an "underwriter" within the meaning of the Act.

* * *

3. Is the Brokerage Exemption of Section 4(2) Available to an Underwriter Who Effects a Distribution of an Issue for the Account of a Controlling Stockholder Through the Mechanism of a Stock Exchange?

Respondent's final argument on this phase of the case is that, notwithstanding the inapplicability of * * * [Section] 4(1) and even though respondent may be found to be an underwriter, its transactions fall within Section 4(2) which exempts "brokers' transactions, executed upon customers' orders on any exchange * * * but not the solicitation of such orders." * * *

* * *

It is clear from Section 4(1), read in conjunction with Section 2(11), that public distributions by controlling persons, through underwriters, are intended generally to be subject to the registration and prospectus requirements of the Act. Section 4(1) exempts transactions "by any person other than an issuer, underwriter, or dealer," "transactions by an issuer not involving a public offering" and "transactions by a dealer" other than those "within one year after the first date upon which the security was bona fide offered to the public * * * by or through an underwriter * * *" This shows a specific intention to subject to the registration and prospectus requirements public offerings by issuers or by or through "underwriters." And, as we have seen, Section 2(11) defines "underwriter" to include any person who sells for the issuer or a person controlling the issuer in connection with the distribution of a security.

These sections, by their terms, provide that whenever anyone controlling an issuer makes a public distribution of his holdings in the controlled corporation by selling through another person acting for him in connection with the distribution, the sales by which the distribution is accomplished are transactions by an underwriter which are subject to the registration requirements. Applied to such transactions by which substantial quantities of securities are disposed of to the public, the registration requirement is consistent with and calculated to further the general purpose of the Act to provide investors with pertinent information as a means of self-protection. The legislative history of the Act strongly sustains this conclusion.

We find nothing in the language or legislative history of Section 4(2) to compel the exemption of this type of secondary distribution and the consequent overriding of the general objectives and policy of the Act. On the contrary, there are affirmative indications that Section 4(2) was meant to preserve the distinction between the "trading" and "distribution" of securities which separates the exempt and non-exempt transactions under Section 4(1). This conclusion becomes apparent on examination of the legislative comments on Sections 4(1) and 4(2).

* * *

*** [I]n discussing the limited exemption for dealers in the third clause of Section 4(1),[b] the House Report again emphasized the distinction between "trading" and "distribution":

> *** Recognizing that a dealer is often concerned not only with the *distribution* of securities but also with *trading* in securities, the dealer is exempted as to *trading* when such *trading* occurs a year after the public offering of the securities. Since before that year the dealer might easily evade the provisions of the act by a claim that the securities he was offering for sale were not acquired by him in the process of *distribution* but were acquired after such process had ended, transactions during that year are not exempted. The period of a year is arbitrarily taken because, generally speaking, the average public offering has been distributed within a year and the imposition of requirements upon the dealer so far as that year is concerned is not burdensome. (Emphasis added.)

From the foregoing, it is apparent that transactions by an issuer or underwriter and transactions by a dealer during the period of *distribution* (which period for purposes of administrative practicality is arbitrarily set at one year) must be preceded by registration and the use of a prospectus. It is likewise apparent that Congress intended that, during this period, persons other than an issuer, underwriter, or dealer should be able to *trade* in the security without use of a prospectus. Since such persons would carry on their trading largely through the use of brokers (who are included in the general definition of dealers), such trading through brokers without the use of a prospectus could be permitted during the first year after the initial offering only if there were a special exemption for dealers acting as brokers. *** That this was the specific purpose of Section 4(2) is clearly seen from the comment on this provision by the House Committee which considered the legislation:

> Paragraph (2) exempts the ordinary brokerage transaction. *Individuals may thus dispose of their securities according to the method which is now customary without any restrictions imposed either upon the individual or the broker. This exemption also assures an open market for securities at all times, even though a stop order against further distribution of such securities may have been entered.* Purchasers, provided they are not dealers, may thus in the event that a stop order has been entered, cut their losses immediately, if there are losses, by disposing of the securities. *On the other hand, the entry of a stop order prevents any further distribution of the security.* (Emphasis added.)

---

[b] Originally, the dealers' exemption appeared in § 4(1). In 1954, the exemption was moved to § 4(a)(3) and the one-year period was reduced to 40 days.

To summarize: Section 4(2) permits individuals to sell their securities through a broker in an ordinary brokerage transaction, during the period of distribution or while a stop order is in effect, without regard to the registration and prospectus requirements of Section 5. But the process of distribution itself, however carried out, is subject to Section 5.

* * *

We conclude that Section 4(2) cannot exempt transactions by an underwriter executed over the Exchange in connection with a distribution for a controlling stockholder. * * *

WILLFULNESS

* * * We find that Respondent knew that it was effecting a distribution for a controlling person and that no registration statement was in effect for the securities being distributed. Since Respondent was fully aware of what it was doing, its violation was willful within the meaning of the Act.

PUBLIC INTEREST

Even though Respondent willfully violated the Securities Act, its registration as a broker-dealer may not be revoked, and it may not be suspended or expelled from the NASD, unless such action is found to be in the public interest.

* * *

[W]e cannot overlook the fact that respondent, in the course of a public distribution of securities, engaged in a willful violation of the Securities Act—a violation which, the evidence indicates, would have been regarded as such even under previous interpretations of Section 4(2)—and, by its failure to insist on registration and the attendant disclosure of information, made it possible for the distribution to be effected to an uninformed public which suffered heavy losses. Accordingly, we find it appropriate in the public interest and for the protection of investors to suspend Respondent from membership in the NASD for a period of 20 days.

An appropriate order will issue.

Excerpt from: A. A. Sommer, Jr.

Who's "In Control"?—S.E.C.
21 Business Lawyer 559, 559–583 (1966).*

A basic concept running through all of the statutes administered by the Securities and Exchange Commission is that of "control". * * * Some of the statutes administered by the Securities and Exchange Commission contain definitions of "control"; the Securities Act of 1933 and the Securities Exchange Act of 1934, however, the two statutes of most significance for most businesses, and the statutes which are discussed in this paper, do not include such definitions. The absence of a definition, however, has not prevented the Commission by rule, ruling and releases from limning the outlines of a definition and it has not mitigated the vital importance of determining the meaning of "control".

* * *

Who Is A Controlling Person?

* * * [T]he situation of a "controlling person" may be perilous—and expensive. When so much attaches to the identification of a person within that category it would be most desirable if the identification could be done with certainty and precision, as, for instance, can often be done under the Internal Revenue Code. Alas, such is rarely the case with key concepts in the structure of federal securities law, and this is particularly true in the case of the concept of "control". Like so many key notions the imprecise limits of the term have been limned through the painstaking process of rule, interpretation, judicial decision and ad hoc determinations in "no action letters". Out of these there has come no mathematical standard, no slide rule computation, no certain rule which can infallibly guide counsel and client in making this most important determination—a determination which can be costly if wrongly made. Often, of course, the answer is easily arrived at; for instance, concluding that a holder of 90% of the voting power of a corporation whose stock is unencumbered and who personally runs the affairs of the corporation is a controlling person demands no subtlety. Often, however, the problem is more complex. In those situations it has become axiomatic that in deciding who is a "controlling person" the entire situation within the corporation at the time of determination, together with some of the history of the corporation, must be considered; single factors—shareholdings, offices held, titles, conduct—are rarely determinative, at least not in the close cases (clearly that ninety percent shareholder will rarely, if ever, enjoy the luxury of being found not to be in control even if every other conceivable pointer in the direction of control is lacking).

---

* Reprinted with the permission of the author and the American Bar Association and its Section of Corporations, Banking, and Business Law. Copyright 1966 by the American Bar Association.

The Securities Act itself is of little help in determining who is a controlling person. * * * The Commission through Rule 405 under the Securities Act has sought to clarify the meaning of the concept of "control":

> The term "control" (including the terms "controlling," "controlled by" and "under common control with") means the possession, direct or indirect, of the power to direct or cause the direction of the management and policies of a person, whether through the ownership of voting securities, by contract, or otherwise.

This definition introduces some new notions in addition to those intimated by Section 15 of the Securities Act: control is a "power" (Section 15 speaks of one who "controls," which implies exercise of the power), it may be possessed directly or indirectly, it may exist by reason of ownership of voting securities, contract or "otherwise," and the power is the power to direct or "cause the direction of management and policies" of another person (almost always a corporation). With Section 15 of the Securities Act and Rule 405 as starters, we must look principally to reported determinations, Commission and court, supplemented by logical analysis of the concept, for further delineation of this elusive notion. The administrative and judicial determinations arise in a variety of contexts; in some cases the issue is whether a person is a controlling person, thus establishing a purchaser of his stock for distribution as an underwriter; in others the question is whether a person was a "parent" of a registrant under the 1933 or 1934 Act and hence should have been identified as such in filings with the Commission; and in some few instances the question has been the derivative liability of an alleged controlling person under Section 15 of the Securities Act or Section 20 of the Securities Exchange Act.

Some basic notions should preliminarily be recognized. The *power* to control, even if unexercised, may constitute a person a controlling person. In the Walston and Co.[16] case the principal creditor of the registrant, who was the principal source of its business, had options to acquire the interests of others in the company, and received 90% of profits, had nevertheless not actively participated in the direction of the business; the Commission nonetheless held that it had the *power* to control if it so wished and hence was a controlling person of Walston and should have been so disclosed.

Correlatively, those who exercise control by the sufferance of those with the power to control may also be controlling persons. In North Country Uranium and Minerals Ltd.,[17] the holder of only a nominal amount of stock was held to be a controlling person of the defendant company because he actively managed the enterprise, which he had been

---

[16] 7 S.E.C. 937 (1940).
[17] 37 S.E.C. 608 (1957).

instrumental in organizing, without interference from the clearly dominant shareholder who would apparently be also considered a controlling person because of his *power* to control. Similarly, in SEC v. Franklin Atlas Corp.,[18] the president and person who actually ran the corporation was not a shareholder, but because of the actuality of his control—even though subject to termination at the whim of those who controlled the stock—he was held to be a controlling person.

Thus either *the power to control* or *the actual exercise of control*, even though by sufferance of another who possesses the ultimate power to control, is sufficient to make a person a controlling person. This duality is in a sense reducible to the single notion of power to control: the person who actually controls with the acquiescence of the one having the ultimate power is realistically exercising, one might say by terminable default, the power of the other person.

Chairman Cohen of the Commission once suggested a very practical criterion for determining the person or group in control: what individual or group has the power to cause a registration statement under the Securities Act to be signed? At least one court has also used this standard for determining the identity of controlling persons. Registration statements can only be filed by an issuer and must be signed by the registrant, a majority of the board of directors, the chief executive officer, the chief financial officer, and the chief accounting officer. Obviously the statement can only be signed by the registrant under authority from the board of directors. So it would appear that control is in the hands of whoever or whatever group can cause a majority of the board to authorize the registrant's signature on the statement. At first blush it would appear this criterion offered a simple escape from their problems for purported controlling persons: simply arrange for the board to be presented with a proposal that a registration statement be signed and filed for the shares of the ostensible controlling person and have the board refuse to permit the registrant to sign and file the statement—presto, the purported controlling person has flunked the test: he could not produce a majority vote to sign the statement and he may therefore sell without the expense and bother of a registration statement. Needless to say, any board refusal other than a simon-pure bona fide refusal could be of no avail. Furthermore, for a refusal to be of any significance, the person proposing that the corporation file a registration statement with respect to his shares must agree to indemnify the registrant for its expenses in connection with the registration; otherwise, the board might well refuse—and probably should refuse—to authorize signing and filing on the legitimate ground that the corporation could not properly incur expenses for the benefit of a shareholder.

---

[18] 154 F.Supp. 395 (S.D.N.Y.1957).

With these propositions as starters, it is possible to discern some further guides in Commission and court cases and logical analysis of the concept of control.

* * *

* * * The initial source of power of necessity must be ownership of voting securities, not only because of the specific mention of this in Rule 405, but because under modern corporation law the power of management is *ultimately*—in theory and law, if not in practice—in the hands of the holders of voting securities. * * *

* * *

How little stock may a person own or have the power to vote and still be considered a controlling person? This depends upon many circumstances. Principal among these are the distribution of the other shares and the other relationships the shareholder has with the corporation and with other shareholders. Initially, record or beneficial ownership of (or right to vote) 10% or more of the voting stock of a corporation has become something of a benchmark and when this is encountered a red warning flag should run up. Schedule A to the Securities Act of 1933, the proxy statement rules, and many of the registration forms promulgated by the Commission require disclosure of all persons who own of record or beneficially more than 10% of any class of stock of the issuer, and the reporting and penalty provisions of Section 16 of the Securities Exchange Act (the so-called "insider trading" provisions) apply to the beneficial owners of more than 10% of a class of equity security registered pursuant to Section 12 of that Act. While there is nothing in the statutes or the regulations or rulings by the Commission which says such a holder is *ipso facto* a controlling person, generally such degree of ownership should create caution and might be regarded as creating a rebuttable presumption of control, especially if such holdings are combined with executive office, membership on the board, or wide dispersion of the remainder of the stock.

That such a percentage of ownership or right to vote is not *conclusive* evidence of control, however, is almost self-evident. In a situation in which one person owned 89% of the voting stock and the other 11% was owned by an antagonist, it is evident the owner of the 11% is not a controlling person (barring the improbable situation where unanimous shareholder action is required): he could not cause the company to file a registration statement and he could not elect a majority of the board; in fact, unless the size of the board and cumulative voting combine to afford him board representation, he is powerless save for the rights which belong to any shareholder regardless of holdings, e.g. right to inspect books, to bring a derivative suit, to secure the fair value of his shares in certain circumstances. On the other hand, ownership of less than 10% of the voting power of a corporation does not automatically spell non-control. Apart from the circumstance that a holder of less than 10% may be a member of a group which controls, a person with less than 10% may alone be a controlling person; generally to be such his ownership would have to be combined with dominant executive office and fairly wide dispersion of the remainder of the voting power. It has been suggested that ownership of as little as 5% of a corporation's stock by an officer or director may give rise to a presumption that such a person is a member of a control group.

* * *

When—and why—a person who owns or has the right to vote a minority of the outstanding stock of a corporation may be considered in control is not easily answered. The holder of twenty or twenty-five percent of stock of a widely and publicly held company could be defeated in a proxy contest; if he asserts control based upon his acquisition of a substantial interest the majority of the board and the officers might defy him and deny him any board representation until the next shareholders' meeting, or accord him only representation proportionate to his holdings. Victor Muscat and his associates suffered this fate in 1962 when they purchased 29 percent of the shares of B.S.F. Co. Upon demanding control of the Board of Directors, they were rebuffed. * * * One thus rebuffed could hardly be called a controlling person. Thus in many instances more than a substantial minority stockholding, even in a corporation with widely held stock, is the prerequisite to the establishment of control; such a holding may really constitute control only when it has actually resulted in the yielding of control by those who have previously possessed it. Thus, while unencumbered ownership of more than fifty percent of the outstanding voting power of a corporation will usually constitute control even though unexercised simply because the power to control is there, ownership of substantially less than 50% of the stock may be indicative of control only if the power inherent in the voting power has in some fashion been manifested through the exercise of control, usually through the election of a favorably inclined majority of the board of directors.

* * *

THE CONTROLLING GROUP

There are innumerable instances in which a single person does not appear to have actual operating control or the power to control. Then the problem is to identify the *group* which is in control and those who constitute the group. The search for the group commences when the search for the individual in control or having the power to control fails. Is there always a controlling person or a controlling group in every corporation? I would suggest that there is: someone runs the show or some group runs the show, some person has the power to run the show or some group has that power. As a beginning, it may be safely suggested that simply being a member of the board of directors, or an officer of the company, does not automatically constitute one a member of the controlling group. At least as far as the directors are concerned, this is self-evident: if the corporation is subject to cumulative voting requirements some, and perhaps one short of a majority, of the directors

may be quite hostile to management and to the majority of the board; it would obviously be wrong to call them members of the controlling group. It is less obvious that principal executive officers are not *ipso facto* members of the controlling group, since they serve at the will of the board and hence it may be fairly implied they would be compliant with the will of whoever controls the board; however, even then a situation is conceivable where an officer with an employment contract may be out of step with the controlling group, but perhaps the fact of his contract alone may be sufficient to cause him to be considered a controlling person if his prerogatives are broad enough. In some instances it may be pertinent to distinguish "inside" directors (i.e. directors who are officers and involved in the active management of the corporation) from "outside" directors (i.e. those *not* a part of active management); obviously "inside" directors would be more likely to be found to be in control, but this would stem from roles and positions over and above that of being a director. In general, however, unless a person or identifiable group clearly is in control by reason of possession *and* use of voting power, all directors and policy-making officers are presumptively members of the controlling group and only compelling evidence to the contrary should remove them from the group. Generally there must be some homogeneity among individuals if they are to be regarded as members of the controlling group, some significant business characteristic or relationship or course of conduct that affords an element of unity. It is clear from the legislative history of the Securities Act, judicial decisions and releases of the Commission that some "cement", other than mere association on a board, or the circumstance that adding up the holdings of a number of people yields an actual or working majority of the voting power of the corporation, is necessary to constitute individuals a controlling group.
* * *

* * *

The question of control is subtle and difficult in many instances. Often, to be sure, the focus of control is simply determined. Just as often, and perhaps oftener particularly in corporations in which there is substantial public participation in ownership, the answer is clouded. Ultimately the test is briefly stated: taking into account history, family, business affiliations, shareholdings, position and all the other circumstances, what person or what group calls the day-to-day shots? The shots in major matters? What person or what group could, if it wished, call those shots? When these are identified the controlling persons and the controlling group are identified. * * *

* * *

A. TRANSACTIONS BY DEALERS AND BROKERS

The registration and prospectus requirements of § 5 are always applicable to issuers and underwriters who, by definition, are engaged in the process of distribution of a block of securities to the public. This is not so for dealers despite § 4(a)(1).

(1) THE DEALER'S EXEMPTION

Section 4(a)(3) exempts transactions by a dealer (including an underwriter who is no longer acting as such with respect to the security involved in such transaction) with three exceptions. These exceptions, in effect, fix periods during which dealers are subject to the registration and prospectus delivery requirements of § 5. The purpose of this limited exemption was to force dealers to deliver the prospectus during the period following effectiveness in order to inform the market of the issuer and its securities. With the Internet, this purpose has become dated, and hence, SEC rules have granted broad exemptions that largely eclipse § 4(a)(3). That is, Rules 172 and 174 dispense with the prospectus delivery requirement for dealers in most registered offerings. Still, § 4(a)(3) remains relevant in some special contexts and, therefore, cannot be ignored.

Since an amendment in 1954, the statutory language of § 4(a)(3) has required delivery of the prospectus by dealers during three time periods:

> (A) transactions taking place prior to the expiration of forty days after the first date upon which the security was bona fide offered to the public by the issuer or by or through an underwriter,
>
> (B) transactions in a security, as to which a registration statement has been filed, taking place prior to the expiration of forty days after the effective date of such registration statement or prior to the expiration of forty days after the first date upon which the security was bona fide offered to the public by the issuer or by or through an underwriter after such effective date, whichever is later (excluding in the computation of such forty days any time during which a stop order issued under section 8 is in effect as to the security), or such shorter period as the Commission may specify by rules and regulations or order, and
>
> (C) transactions as to securities constituting the whole or a part of an unsold allotment to or subscription by such dealer as a participant in the distribution of such securities by the issuer or by or through an underwriter.

As (B) states, the SEC may specify shorter time periods by rules and regulations or order, and thus dealers remain protected by Rules 172 and 174, but only to the extent they apply.

The term "dealer" is defined in § 2(a)(12) to mean "any person who engages either for all or part of his time, directly or indirectly, as agent, broker, or principal, in the business of offering, buying, selling, or otherwise dealing or trading in securities issued by another person." This definition includes a broker as well as a principal trading for her own account. According to the House Report, the goal of this definition was "to subject brokers to the same advertising restrictions that are imposed upon dealers, so as to prevent the broker from being used as a cloak for the sale of securities."[44] At the same time, under § 2(a)(11), a dealer is excluded from the definition of "underwriter," even if she purchases securities from an underwriter at a price below the public offering price and resells the securities to the public, so long as the "commission" or "spread" is not in excess of the usual and customary distributor's or seller's commission.

In its original form, the Securities Act imposed a period of one year during which dealers not participating in the distribution of a new issue were required to deliver prospectuses in connection with trading transactions. In 1954, this period was reduced to 40 days. In supporting the change, the SEC had this to say: "The 1-year provision has long been recognized as unrealistic, since dealers trading in a security publicly offered within 1 year find themselves unable to obtain prospectuses. This fact has rendered compliance by dealers and enforcement by the Commission difficult."[45]

Because Rules 172 and 174 eliminate any prospectus delivery requirement in most registered offerings, the continuing significance of § 4(a)(3) lies in its application to an exempt offering made to the public. For example, in a Regulation S offering (which is discussed later in this chapter), the dealer will remain under an obligation to deliver a prospectus for the period up to 40 days "after the first date upon which the security was bona fide offered to the public by the issuer or by or through an underwriter." This is a hidden reef onto which even experienced dealers can crash. How does one calculate the 40 days under § 4(a)(3)? In Kubik v. Goldfield,[46] the court held that a bona fide offer to the public dated from the time when another dealer entered quotations in the National Daily Quotations Service "pink sheets," even though there was no relationship or collaboration between the dealers.[47]

(2) THE BROKERS' EXEMPTION

This brokers' exemption, now contained in § 4(a)(4), is discussed at length in the *Haupt* case. Its purpose is to permit the ordinary investor to sell her securities without being subject to the prospectus delivery requirements of § 5. Of course, the customer's part of the transaction is exempt under § 4(a)(1), but such sales will almost always be made through a broker, and since brokers are included within the definition of

---

[44] H.R.Rep. No. 85, 73d Cong., 1st Sess. 14 (1933).

[45] Hearings on S. 2846 Before a Subcommittee of the Senate Committee on Banking and Currency, 83d Cong., 2d Sess. 6 (1954).

[46] 479 F.2d 472 (3d Cir. 1973). Cf. Slagell v. Bontrager, 616 F.Supp. 634 (W.D.Pa.1985) (interpreting § 13 of the 1933 Act and holding that the limitation period began when the purchaser was first offered the security).

[47] Cf. SEC v. North American Research & Development Corp., 280 F.Supp. 106 (S.D.N.Y.1968), aff'd in part, 424 F.2d 63 (2d Cir. 1970).

dealer in § 2(a)(12), the dealer's exemption may not be available to the broker. For example, a stop order issued after a registration statement has been declared effective, by suspending its effectiveness, closes the mails and channels of interstate commerce to further sales of the security by issuers and underwriters and by dealers selling for their own account. It was to keep the securities markets open to the investing public that § 4 exempted "brokers' transactions executed upon customers' orders on any exchange or in the over-the-counter market but not the solicitation of such orders."

With the adoption of Rules 172 and 174, the brokers' exemption has come to have its greatest significance in cases where the client seeks to sell unregistered securities. Here, the *Haupt* case illustrates the chief problem for the broker. The narrow purpose of the exemption was explained by the Federal Trade Commission, which administered the 1933 Act for about a year before the SEC was established: "The exemption . . . applies only to the broker's part of a [brokerage] transaction. It does not extend to the customer. Whether the customer is excused from complying with the registration requirements of Section 5 depends upon his own status or upon the character of the particular transaction . . . [Thus,] an issuer selling through a broker on the stock exchange would be subject to Section 5 of this Act."[48] This statement, although accurate as far as it goes, can be misunderstood, because the *Haupt* case teaches that a broker who sells for a controlling person in *connection with the distribution* of a security becomes an underwriter and thereby loses his broker's exemption. Of course, the brokers' exemption is never available to issuers.[49]

Section 4(a)(4) is far from clear as to the meaning of the phrase "solicitation of such orders." In a brokerage transaction, the broker might solicit the seller's order or the buyer's order. Rule 154, as adopted by the SEC in 1951, provided that the "term solicitation of such orders . . . shall be deemed to include the solicitation of an order to buy a security, but shall not be deemed to include the solicitation of an order to sell a security." By way of further amplification, the Commission said:[50]

> [I]f the broker solicits the purchaser to buy the security, Section 4(2) [now § 4(a)(4)] does not provide an exemption *either for the solicitation itself or for the resulting transaction.* On the other

---

[48] FTC Securities Act Release No. 131 (March 13, 1934).

[49] Stadia Oil & Uranium Co. v. Wheelis, 251 F.2d 269 (10th Cir. 1957). But Rule 144, considered later, also was thought to provide protection to the controlling shareholder if all of the applicable conditions of the rule were met. "Although the Rule was expressly directed at § 4(4), it was obviously contemplated that the seller's part of the transaction would be considered to be exempt under § 4(1) whenever the broker's part came within the Rule." 3 Loss & Seligman, Securities Regulation 1476 n. 642 (3d Ed. Rev. 1999); When Corporations Go Public 30–31 (Israels and Duff eds. 1962); S.E.C. Problems of Controlling Stockholders and in Underwritings 44 (Israels ed. 1962). However, the *Wolfson* case, which appears later in this chapter, rejects this view if the controlling person deceives his broker.

[50] Securities Act Release No. 3421 (Aug. 2, 1951). On the brokers' exemption, see 3 Loss & Seligman, Securities Regulation 1467–77 (3d Ed. Rev. 1999).

hand, if the broker does not solicit the purchaser to buy, the mere fact that he may solicit the seller to sell will not destroy any exemption otherwise available to him under Section 4(2); this construction is based on the fact that the statute is designed primarily for the protection of buyers rather than for the protection of sellers. [Emphasis supplied.]

It should also be noted that the prospectus delivery requirements are not restricted to transactions between brokers and public customers; they have also been held to be applicable to transactions between two broker-dealers.[51]

The SEC continues to read the § 4(a)(4) exemption narrowly. It insists that a broker relying on § 4(a)(4) must make a careful inquiry into the status of the securities being offered for sale when the customer is selling a substantial quantity. Even in cases with facts far less dramatic than those in the *Haupt* case, the SEC has disciplined brokers who failed to conduct an adequate investigation into whether the securities being sold were restricted.[52] As will be seen, Rule 144 today provides practical relief for the broker by providing a specific safe harbor.

When should a broker recognize that a distribution is in progress and, hence, it cannot rely on § 4(a)(4) under *Haupt*? In Geiger v. SEC,[53] the D.C. Circuit found that the unregistered sale of 0.5 percent of the outstanding shares by controlling shareholders and officers of a shell corporation violated § 5 because it amounted to a distribution. Although 0.5% was a low figure, the critical factor to the D.C. Circuit was that the stock was moving from controlling insiders to members of the general public who needed the protection of the 1933 Act.

United States v. Wolfson
United States Court of Appeals, Second Circuit, 1968.
405 F.2d 779, certiorari denied 394 U.S. 946 (1969).

■ Before MOORE, WOODBURY and SMITH, CIRCUIT JUDGES.

■ WOODBURY, SENIOR CIRCUIT JUDGE:

It was stipulated at the trial that at all relevant times there were 2,510,000 shares of Continental Enterprises, Inc., issued and outstanding. The evidence is clear, indeed is not disputed, that of these the appellant Louis E. Wolfson himself with members of his immediate family and his right hand man and first lieutenant, the appellant Elkin B. Gerbert, owned 1,149,775 or in excess of 40%. The balance of the stock was in the hands of approximately 5,000 outside shareholders. The government's undisputed evidence at the trial was that between August

---

[51] Byrnes v. Faulkner, Dawkins & Sullivan, 550 F.2d 1303, 1310 (2d Cir. 1977).
[52] Wonsover v. SEC, 205 F.3d 408 (D.C. Cir. 2000) (broker disciplined where it failed to investigate further even though the seventeen individuals selling same security through it all shared one address).
[53] 363 F.3d 481 (D.C. Cir. 2004).

1, 1960, and January 31, 1962, Wolfson himself sold 404,150 shares of Continental through six brokerage houses, that Gerbert sold 53,000 shares through three brokerage houses and that members of the Wolfson family, including Wolfson's wife, two brothers, a sister, the Wolfson Family Foundation and four trusts for Wolfson's children sold 176,675 shares through six brokerage houses.

Gerbert was a director of Continental. Wolfson was not, nor was he an officer, but there was ample evidence that nevertheless as the largest individual shareholder he was Continental's guiding spirit in that the officers of the corporation were subject to his direction and control and that no corporate policy decisions were made without his knowledge and consent. Indeed Wolfson admitted as much on the stand. No registration statement was in effect as to Continental; its stock was traded over-the-counter.

The appellants do not dispute the foregoing basic facts. They took the position at the trial that they had no idea during the period of the alleged conspiracy, stipulated to be from January 1, 1960, to January 31, 1962, that there was any provision of law requiring registration of a security before its distribution by a controlling person to the public. On the stand in their defense they took the position that they operated at a level of corporate finance far above such "details" as the securities laws; as to whether a particular stock must be registered. They asserted and their counsel argued to the jury that they were much too busy with large affairs to concern themselves with such minor matters and attributed the fault of failure to register to subordinates in the Wolfson organization and to failure of the brokers to give notice of the need. Obviously in finding the appellants guilty the jury rejected this defense, if indeed, it is any defense at all.

The appellants assert numerous claims of error. We shall dispose of the claims more or less in the order of their importance.

Section 5 of the Act in pertinent part provides: "(a) Unless a registration statement is in effect as to a security, it shall be unlawful for any person, directly or indirectly—

"(1) to make use of any means or instruments of transportation or communication in interstate commerce or of the mails to sell or offer to buy such security through the use or medium of any prospectus or otherwise; * * *."

However, § 4 of the Act exempts certain transactions from the provisions of § 5 including:

"(1) Transactions by any person other than an issuer, underwriter, or dealer."

The appellants argue that they come within this exemption for they are not issuers, underwriters or dealers. At first blush there would appear to be some merit in this argument. The immediate difficulty with it, however, is that § 4(1) by its terms exempts only "transactions," not classes of persons * * * and ignores § 2(11) of the Act which defines an "underwriter" to mean any person who has purchased from an issuer with a view to the distribution of any security, or participates directly or indirectly in such undertaking unless that person's participation is limited to the usual and customary seller's commission, and then goes on to provide:

> "As used in this paragraph the term 'issuer' shall include, in addition to an issuer, any person directly or indirectly *controlling* or controlled by *the issuer*, or any person under direct or indirect common control with the 'issuer.' " (Italics supplied.)

In short, the brokers provided outlets for the stock of issuers and thus were underwriters. * * * Wherefore the stock was sold in "transactions by underwriters" which are not within the exemption of § 4(1), supra.

But the appellants contend that the brokers in this case cannot be classified as underwriters because their part in the sales transactions came within § 4(4) which exempts "brokers' transactions executed upon customers' orders on any exchange or in the over-the-counter market but not the solicitation of such orders." The answer to this contention is that § 4(4) was designed only to exempt the brokers' part in security transactions. * * * Control persons must find their own exemptions.

There is nothing inherently unreasonable for a broker to claim the exemption of § 4(4), supra, when he is unaware that his customer's part in the transaction is not exempt. Indeed, this is indicated by the definition of "brokers' transaction" in * * * Rule 154 [which is discussed [infra at page 577] and was the predecessor of Rule 144] which provides:

> "(a) The term 'brokers' transaction" in Section 4(4) of the act shall be deemed to include transactions by a broker acting as agent for the account of any person controlling, controlled by, or under common control with, the issuer of the securities which are the subject of the transaction where:

> "(4) The broker is *not aware* of circumstances indicating * * * that the transactions are part of a distribution of securities on behalf of his principal."

And there can be no doubt that appellants' sale of over 633,000 shares (25% of the outstanding shares of Continental and more than 55% of their own holdings), was a distribution rather than an ordinary brokerage transaction. See Rule 154(6) which defines "distribution" for the purpose of paragraph (a) generally as "substantial" in relation to the number of shares outstanding and specifically as a sale of 1% of the stock within six months preceding the sale if the shares are traded on a stock exchange.

Certainly if the appellants' sales, which clearly amounted to a distribution under the above definitions had been made through a broker or brokers with knowledge of the circumstances, the brokers would not be entitled to the exemption. It will hardly do for the appellants to say that because they kept the true facts from the brokers they can take advantage of the exemption the brokers gained thereby.

* * *

In conclusion it will suffice to say that full consideration of the voluminous record in this rather technical case discloses no reversible error.

Affirmed.

NOTES ON DISTRIBUTION OF SECURITIES BY CONTROLLING PERSONS OR AFFILIATES

1. *Defining Control.* Rule 405 under the 1933 Act provides a functional but sweeping definition of control, which it defines as "the possession, direct or indirect, of the power to direct or cause the direction of the management and policies of a person, whether through the ownership of voting securities, by contract, or otherwise." This definition does not require the actual exercise of power, and hence a passive owner, such as the proverbial widow or playboy heir who has never participated in management, can be said to possess control. Still, commentators have suggested that the legislative history supports a narrower definition, under which a controlling person could compel the filing of a registration statement.[54] The premise here is that Congress intended to force controlling persons to register their shares because they alone hold sufficient power to force the corporation to register the stock for them.

2. *Shelf Registration.* Traditionally, registering the stock of a controlling shareholder for resale would have been expensive and perhaps burdensome for the corporation if it placed them "in registration" with the SEC at a sensitive time. To mitigate this problem, the SEC has long permitted the use of Form S-8 to register not only stock options and other securities offered to employees under employee benefit plans, but also the resale of those securities upon the exercise of an option (or other purchase) by the employee. In addition, Rule 415(a)(1) permits shelf registration (that is, a continuous or delayed offering of the securities) by "persons other than the registrant" and of "[s]ecurities which are to be issued upon the exercise of outstanding options, warrants or rights." Thus, at a relatively low cost, the issuer could include a controlling person's stock within its shelf registration statement, thereby allowing the control person to sell from time to time, and the Form S-8 could cover all stock purchased by any person pursuant to stock options or other rights. But the decision to cover these securities had to be made in advance, and it increased the registration fee charged by the SEC.

Today, the process has been greatly simplified. As part of the 2005 offering reforms, new Rule 430B authorizes a simplified shelf registration statement for issuers that qualify to use Form S-3, under

---

[54] See Campbell, Defining Control in Secondary Distributions, 18 B. C. L. Rev. 37 (1976).

which the identity of the selling shareholders need not be disclosed in advance. Instead, this information can be added later by means of a prospectus supplement, an amendment to the registration statement, or a 1934 Act filing that is incorporated by reference into the registration statement. This permits a disclose-as-you-go approach to sales by control shareholders without the need for advance registration (and, in the case of the Well-Known Seasoned Issuer, this registration statement becomes effective upon filing).[55]

B. FROM IRA HAUPT TO RULE 144

(1) SALES BY CONTROLLING PERSONS

Before the *Haupt* case, there was great uncertainty as to the rules governing sales of securities by controlling persons. That case entailed a massive distribution of equity securities through the facilities of the stock exchange by control persons relying upon the exemption provided in § 4(a)(4) for brokers' transactions. The *Haupt* case also cast doubt as to the quantity of shares that a controlling person might sell in brokerage transactions without thereby engaging in a "distribution" of securities. Although the sale of a few hundred shares by a controlling person over the stock exchange might not amount to a distribution of securities, it was impossible to determine when additional sales (possibly by other persons belonging to the same control group) would be regarded as sufficient to destroy the exemption; also, it was not clear what holding period would suffice to establish that the purchase was made with an investment intent, and not with a view to a distribution, at the time of the purchase.

In 1954, the securities industry lobbied for an amendment to the 1933 Act to "[r]estore the 'broker's exemption' . . . so as to give relief from the popular interpretation" of the *Haupt* opinion.[56] The Commission recommended instead that the matter be handled by a rule, and Congress acquiesced, the Senate Committee expressing the hope that the SEC "will give favorable consideration to a rule that will deal effectively with the problem."[57] The upshot was that, in 1954, the Commission revised Rule 154, the predecessor of Rule 144, to clarify and limit the scope of the broker's exemption embodied in § 4(a)(4) with respect to secondary sales by controlling persons (or others belonging to the same control group) in reliance on the exemption.

Rule 154 defined the term "brokers' transactions" in § 4(a)(4) of the Act to include transactions by a broker acting as an agent for a control

---

[55] This approach of disclosing sales by controlling shareholders in 1934 Act reports (rather than in the registration statement) was first proposed in the 1996 report of an SEC Advisory Committee. See Report of the Task Force on Disclosure Simplification 51 (Mar. 5, 1996), https://www.sec.gov/news/studies/smpl.htm.

[56] Hearings on S. 2846 before a Subcommittee of the Senate Committee on Banking and Currency, 83d Cong., 2d Sess. 4 (1954).

[57] S.Rep. No. 1036, 83d Cong., 2d Sess. 7 (1954).

person, provided: (1) the buy order was not solicited from purchasers; (2) the broker performed no more than the usual brokerage functions; and (3) the broker was not aware of circumstances indicating that the transaction was a part of the distribution or that the broker's principal was an underwriter. The number of securities that could be sold within a specified period was prescribed by defining "distribution" in the negative; no "distribution" would be entailed if a transaction or series of transactions did not involve an amount of sales "substantial in relation to the number of shares of the security outstanding and the aggregate volume of trading in such security." More specifically, the rules defined the term "distribution" to not include a sale or series of sales of securities, which, together with all other sales of the same person within the preceding six months, in the case of a security traded over-the-counter, did not exceed 1% of the outstanding shares, and in the case of stock exchange transactions, did not exceed the lesser of 1% of the outstanding shares of the class or the largest reported volume of trading on securities exchanges during any one week within the four calendar weeks preceding the receipt of the sell order. Under these "leakage" provisions, controlling persons were permitted to make limited sales of control shares under conditions that would not disrupt the trading market for the securities and where only normal brokerage functions were performed. However, the rule provided no avenue for the sale of securities that the control person would otherwise be unable to sell without registration, such as investment securities acquired under the private offering exemption. Resales of such securities would constitute the controlling person an underwriter, irrespective of Rule 154.

Rule 154, like § 4(a)(4), exempted only the broker's part of the transaction; it did not protect the controlling person who might have violated the Act. And, through a curious method of drafting, the Securities Act does not subject controlling persons to the registration and prospectus requirements of § 5 in specific terms. A controlling person is not an issuer as that term is used in § 4(a)(1), but such a person is defined as an issuer under § 2(a)(11) solely for the purpose of determining who is an "underwriter." Accordingly, it could be argued that the broker who sold for the controlling person with knowledge that it was participating in a distribution would be subject to criminal penalties, whereas no specific substantive provision of the 1933 Act by its terms imposes liability upon the controlling person. Alternatively, if the broker, after a reasonable investigation, reasonably believed it was not participating in a distribution by a controlling person so that it would be exempt from liability by virtue of Rule 154, would the controlling person still be exempt from liability by virtue of the lacunae in the regulatory scheme? The *Wolfson* case, set out earlier in this chapter, gave a negative answer to this question. Because Rule 154 and § 4(a)(4) are transaction exemptions, the exemption is not available to anyone participating in the forbidden transaction.

(2) "INVESTMENT INTENT" AND RESALES OF SECURITIES PURCHASED IN "PRIVATE OFFERINGS"

For many years, a thorny problem persisted regarding the circumstances under which the holder of securities (whether or not a controlling person) could make resales of securities purchased in a private placement. Persons purchasing securities in a nonpublic offering, pursuant to the § 4(a)(2) exemption, must purchase for investment and not with a view to distribution of the securities; otherwise, they will be deemed to be an "underwriter" as defined in § 2(a)(11).

To prove investment intent, the practice developed of having the purchaser sign an "investment letter" asserting that she was taking the securities for investment and not with a view to their later distribution. Clearly, such an investment covenant was worthless if the purchaser disproved the assertion by turning around and reselling the securities shortly after their purchase. The SEC took the position that the investor's original intent was best evidenced by the investor's subsequent actions. If you sold within a year or two, then the SEC would read this conduct to demonstrate the falsity of your original claim of investment intent. This, in turn, presented the question of how long the purchaser had to hold the securities to establish an "investment intent." Was she ever to be relieved of this hurdle against the resale of the securities?

This was the question clearly presented in United States v. Sherwood.[58] Sherwood owned eight percent of the shares in a Canadian corporation that he acquired in a private purchase from one Doyle, a control person of the issuer. A criminal contempt proceeding was brought against Sherwood for violating an injunction prohibiting sales of these securities in violation of the registration provisions of the 1933 Act or the availability of an exemption from registration. The court ruled that Sherwood was not a control person, had not purchased the shares with a view to distribution, and, therefore, was not an underwriter. The evidence established that Sherwood had held the securities for two years prior to any resale. The court concluded that the evidence was sufficient to establish an intention to purchase for investment and not with a view to distribution.

The "two-year rule" declared in *Sherwood* to be sufficient to establish a presumption of investment intent was relied on by some securities lawyers in counseling clients, but other more cautious (or conscientious) lawyers recommended a waiting period of three to five years before making resales.[59] And, in the pre-Rule 144 period, on occasion the SEC's

---

[58] 175 F.Supp. 480 (S.D.N.Y.1959).

[59] For the history of this period and the origin of the "Cohen two-year rule," named after Commissioner Manuel F. Cohen, later Chairman of the Commission, see 3 Loss & Seligman, Securities Regulation 1478–504 (3rd Ed. Rev. 1999).

staff would issue no-action letters advising investors it would accept a resale after five years.[60]

(3) THE DOCTRINE OF "CHANGE OF CIRCUMSTANCES"

If the length of holding the securities did not itself furnish sufficient evidence of an original "investment intent," the investor had one possible defense remaining: the investor could claim it had an investment intent at the time of purchase, but changed that intent later because of some fundamental and unforeseen change of circumstances. Although the SEC's staff recognized, in principle, that a resale could be motivated by a "change of circumstances" between the original purchase and the subsequent resale, it frequently disagreed with the investor as to whether the change of circumstances was foreseeable. For example, an investor who purchased securities in a private placement may suffer a heart attack and seek to sell the stock after only a ten-month holding period based on this asserted change of circumstances (in particular, the need to engage in estate planning). The SEC's staff, however, might respond that given the investor's age or overall health, the need for estate planning was foreseeable.

In Gilligan, Will & Co. v. SEC,[61] an enforcement proceeding was brought by the SEC against the Gilligan firm, a registered broker-dealer, and its partners, asserting that the defendants had engaged as underwriters in a distribution of securities without registration in violation of § 5 of the 1933 Act. The securities were part of a private placement of Crowell-Collier Publishing Company convertible debentures sold to four specific purchasers, including Gilligan. Although these purchasers represented they purchased the debentures for investment, they converted the securities and resold the stock received on conversion on the stock exchange at a profit. The defendants argued that § 4(a)(2), applicable to issuer transactions, was not applicable in this case; that whether there was a distribution should be judged solely by their acts and intentions; and that their purchases and resales were

---

[60] The Commission's staff often received requests for no-action letters from counsel, on behalf of a client, setting forth facts concerning a proposed sale of securities with an opinion of counsel to the effect that registration under the Securities Act was not required on the basis of a claimed exemption and a request that the staff advise whether they concurred in the opinion. During the period prior to Rule 144's adoption, the staff might or might not give such a no-action letter in reply to these requests. If it did so, an authorized member of the staff would sign the letter, which in substance states that, on the basis of the facts set forth in the letter, no action will be recommended to the Commission if the proposed sales are made in the manner described without registration under the 1933 Act in reliance on counsel's opinion that registration is not required. Common subjects for no-action letters in the pre-Rule 144 period were requests concerning the availability of the private offering exemption or the existence (or non-existence) of "control." Requests for no-action letters, particularly based on alleged changes of circumstances, became a substantial burden for the SEC's staff, and this burden may have been a major factor in the Commission's decision to adopt a bright line rule in the form of Rule 144. Today, in light of Rule 144, the SEC's staff no longer responds to no-action requests seeking rulings on changes of circumstances.

[61] 267 F.2d 461 (2d Cir. 1959).

exempt under § 4(a)(1) because their resales did not amount to a "public offering" and hence they were not underwriters.

On appeal, the Second Circuit, relying on the *Ralston Purina* test under § 4(a)(2), held that the resales by the defendants did amount to a "public offering" and a "distribution" because the purchasers were not in a position to "fend for themselves." Hence, deciding the same standards applied in both contexts, the court held the defendants to be underwriters and their transactions not to be exempt under § 4(a)(1).

The defendants also contended that the conversion and sales of stock occurred more than ten months after purchasing the debentures, thereby establishing a presumption of investment intent. Moreover, they asserted, the failure of Crowell-Collier to continue to operate profitably resulted in a change of circumstances that would lead a prudent investor to sell. The court rejected this argument, concluding that an intention to retain the securities only if Crowell-Collier operated at a profit was "equivalent to a 'purchase . . . with a view to . . . distribution' within the statutory definition of underwriters in § 2(11)." The upshot of *Gilligan, Will* was uncertainty as to when the "change of circumstances" doctrine could be relied upon.

(4) THE FUNGIBILITY CONCEPT

Now largely abandoned, the fungibility doctrine formerly treated shares of the same class held by an investor to be subject to the most restrictive conditions applicable to any shares of that same (or even a similar) class. The doctrine was developed to protect the integrity of the holding period concept.

Suppose A buys 10,000 shares of stock in the trading market. One month later, A buys an additional 10,000 shares of the same stock in a private placement pursuant to the § 4(a)(2) exemption. May A now sell 5,000 shares of the unrestricted stock, which was previously purchased publicly, without sacrificing the § 4(a)(2) exemption? Under the fungibility concept, as applied by the Commission's staff, A could not; A's entire 20,000 shares were now locked-up and could not be resold until the expiration of the holding period for the shares purchased in the § 4(a)(2) private placement.

If, however, the transactions were reversed, and A made a purchase of shares in a private placement followed by a purchase of the same shares in the trading markets, it was less certain whether the doctrine of fungibility applied to restrict the sale of the after-acquired securities. Moreover, uncertainty existed when there was a series of purchases of shares from an issuer pursuant to the § 4(a)(2) exemption. Even though the holding period may have expired for an earlier purchase, it was by no means certain whether those shares were locked-in as a result of the subsequent purchases or whether resales of those securities could be made without destroying the § 4(a)(2) exemption.

The "Wheat Report" focused on these problems and concluded that the doctrines governing the resale of securities purchased pursuant to the § 4(a)(2) exemption were "of uncertain application, created serious administrative burdens and produce[d] results incompatible with the policy objectives of the [1933] Act."[62] The Commission thereupon rescinded Rule 154 and adopted Rule 144 to solve these problems as they related to controlling and non-controlling persons.

The new rule built upon Rule 154 and regulates resales of securities held by controlling persons pursuant to the § 4(a)(4) brokerage exemption. Unlike Rule 154, however, Rule 144 also applies to resales of investment securities held by controlling persons. In addition, Rule 144 also regulates resales by non-controlling persons of securities acquired in a private placement by permitting limited resales of those securities in brokerage transactions after they have been held at risk for a period that was initially two years but later was shortened by the Commission to six months if the issuer was a "reporting" company that made timely filings, and one year otherwise. In adopting Rule 144, the SEC indicated it was abandoning the fungibility doctrine. Limitations on privately-placed securities would apply just to those securities and not to shares purchased in the open market. Still, from time to time, the SEC's staff seeks to revive this virtually-extinct doctrine, which appears to survive in a twilight state as a doctrine of last resort.[63]

Problems

PROBLEM 7-4

Investor A purchases common stock in a private placement by a major airline on May 30, 2019. Shortly thereafter, a terrorist-induced air crash shocks the markets and collapses the price of airline stocks. Investor A sells the shares on July 1, 2019, claiming that the terrorist disaster was totally unforeseen and represented an historically fundamental change of circumstances. Assume that, as an attorney in the SEC's Enforcement Division, you were asked to advise the Commission and its staff whether this is a legitimate claim that should be accepted.

---

[62] SEC, "Disclosure to Investors"—Report and Recommendations to the Securities and Exchange Commission From the Disclosure Policy Study, "The Wheat Report," 160–77 (1969).

[63] The SEC has unsuccessfully attempted to raise this doctrine in connection with PIPE (Private Investments in Public Equity) transactions. When a publicly-held firm announces it has made a large private placement of its stock, its market price usually declines. Hence, the private placement investors, who typically buy at a discount to the market price, often hedge their investments by selling short in order to lock-in the spread. The SEC's staff has argued that the borrowed shares sold short are "fungible" with the privately-placed stock the investor holds and so their disposition amounts to an unregistered sale of restricted stock. To date, the SEC has not prevailed on this theory in most cases based on these or similar facts seeking to find violations of the 1933 Act. See SEC v. Berlacher, No. 07 Civ. 3800, 2010 WL 3566790 (E.D. Pa. Jan. 23, 2008); SEC v. Lyon, 529 F.Supp.2d 444 (S.D.N.Y. 2008); SEC v. Mangan, 598 F.Supp.2d 731 (W.D.N.C. 2008). But see Zacharias v. SEC, 569 F.3d 458, 464–68 (D.C. Cir. 2009) (per curiam), which adopted a more expansive reading of the 1933 Act.

Problem 7-5

Ebarka Eban, a 7' 3" center who plays in the European Basketball League, is the first draft choice in the first round of this year's NBA draft. He signs with the New York Knicks on August 30, 2015—a team which, as usual, finished last—for $50 million over five years plus one million shares in the Knicks, which are sold to him on that date in a valid private placement at $1.50 per share (the trading price on Nasdaq was then $8 per share and the 1 million shares represent 5% of the Knicks's outstanding shares). A week later, Eban pledges his shares in the Knicks to the Bank of New York as partial collateral for a $60 million loan, which he promptly uses to buy a controlling stake in a franchise in the European Basketball League. On February 8, 2015, Eban announces he will play that season for his European team, and thereby (i) breaches his contract with the Knicks and (ii) defaults on his loan with the Bank of New York. The Bank of New York wants to sell the shares it received in the Eban pledge on Nasdaq, which is where the Knicks are traded. Can it?

Problem 7-6

In Problem 7-5, assume now that Eban buys 1 million Knicks shares from the Knicks at $1.50 per share after becoming their first draft choice (when the market price was $8 per share). Two months later, he is injured in a motorcycle accident, and uncertainty exists about his ability to play next year. Because Eban's employment contract required him not to ride motorcycles (and only Rolls Royces), an employment negotiation follows, at the end of which Eban is traded to the Nets for a second round draft choice in next year's draft, gives back half his cash bonus, and sells his 1 million Knicks shares back to Mr. J. Dolan, the Knicks's controlling shareholder, for $2.25 per share (when the market price was $5 per share). The sale of the Knicks shares occurs six months and two days after Eban's acquisition of the shares. Any securities law problems here?

Problem 7-7

The Rutgers family has always controlled Rutgers Industries, a reporting company traded on Nasdaq, since their grandfather, Raritan Rutgers, founded it in 1925. But today, they own only 28% of the stock among them. Nevertheless, on the nine-person Rutgers board, they hold five seats. When the oldest Rutgers director—Brunswick Rutgers—dies suddenly, the family decides to replace him with their family lawyer, Somerset Trenton. Because Trenton owns no Rutgers shares, they have the company sell him 2 million shares (or 2% of the outstanding shares) at a price of $3 per share on October 1, 2016, in a private placement. Rutgers is behind in its filing of 1934 Act reports, and, as a result, Rule 144 is not available to its usual extent. Rutgers's average weekly trading volume ranges between 250,000 and 500,000 shares per week. Nonetheless, on his retirement from his law firm on October 30, 2017, Trenton (who remains a director of Rutgers) sells 1.5 million Rutgers shares on Nasdaq on November 5, 2017, in an unsolicited broker's transaction. Can he do this? What if he resigned from his position on the Rutgers board on the same day he resigned from his law firm?

5. RESTRICTIONS ON RESALES OF CONTROL SHARES AND RESTRICTED SECURITIES UNDER RULE 144[64]

Rule 144 creates a safe harbor for the sale of securities under the exemption set forth in § 4(a)(1) of the 1933 Act. In effect since 1972,[65] it has spawned a vast body of interpretations, chiefly in SEC no-action letters. In 2007, the SEC significantly amended Rule 144 to reduce the holding period it mandated to six months in the case of reporting companies, with a one-year holding period otherwise, and to simplify many of its requirements. These changes likely made private placements more attractive to many issuers, in part by reducing the illiquidity discount normally applicable to privately-placed securities. Overall, Rule 144 has eliminated much of the previous uncertainty concerning public sales by control persons ("affiliates") and holders of privately-placed securities (or, in the language of Rule 144, "restricted securities"[66]). Rule 144 has been revised several times, and thus students must take care when reading a discussion about it that they are reading a description of the current rule.[67]

Rule 144 applies to two quite different contexts: (i) the sale of "control" securities by an affiliate; and (ii) the sale of "restricted securities" sold in a private placement or other exempt offering. Basically, Rule 144 exempts either sale from any claim that the seller was an underwriter (and, thus, not exempt under § 4(a)(1) of the 1933 Act) if the following basic conditions are met:

---

[64] The material in this section derives in large part from an article written by James Fogelson, a deceased partner of the law firm of Wachtell, Lipton, Rosen & Katz. See Fogelson, Rule 144: A Summary Review, 29 Bus. Law. 1183–203 (1974). This article was updated for prior editions of this book by Jesse M. Brill, Publisher/Editor of The Corporate Counsel, and Robert A. Barron, Esq., Sr. Vice President, Salomon Smith Barney Inc. (Retired). The casebook authors wish to acknowledge their appreciation of the efforts of Messrs. Brill and Barrow in updating Mr. Fogelson's much respected article.

[65] The original adopting release was Securities Act Release No. 5223 (Jan. 11, 1972).

[66] The term "restricted securities" is defined in Rule 144(a)(3) to cover certain securities received in transactions that are exempt from registration, specifically: (i) securities acquired directly or indirectly from the issuer, or from an affiliate of the issuer, in a transaction or chain of transactions not involving any public offering; (ii) securities acquired directly or indirectly from the issuer that are subject to the resale limitations of Rule 502(d) under Regulation D or Rule 701(c); (iii) securities acquired in a transaction or chain of transactions meeting the requirements of Rule 144A; (iv) securities acquired from the issuer in a transaction subject to the conditions of Regulation CE; (v) equity securities of domestic issuers acquired in a transaction or chain of transactions subject to the conditions of Rules 901 or 903 under Regulation S; (vi) certain securities acquired in a transaction under Rule 801; (vii) certain securities acquired in a transaction under Rule 802; and (viii) securities acquired from the issuer in a transaction subject to the exemption under § 4(a)(5) of the 1933 Act.

[67] Rule 144 has been significantly revised or reinterpreted in a series of SEC releases. See, e.g., Securities Act Release No. 5306 (Sept. 26, 1972); Securities Act Release No. 6099 (Aug. 2, 1979); Securities Act Release No. 6862 (April 23, 1990); Securities Act Release No. 7390 (Feb. 20, 1997); and Securities Act Release No. 8869 (Dec. 7, 2007).

(1) Adequate current public information is available with respect to the issuer (unless the securities have been held by a non-affiliate for at least one year, in which case this requirement is no longer applicable to such a non-affiliate).

(2) If the securities are restricted securities, a holding period of at least six months (in the case of a reporting company) or at least one year (in the case of a nonreporting company) must be satisfied.[68] However, where a six-month holding period is applicable and has expired, the current information requirement noted above will still apply and may preclude sales by a non-affiliate for another six months if current information is not available.

(3) In the case of affiliates, the amount of equity securities sold in each three-month period may not exceed the greater of (i) 1% of the outstanding securities of that class or (ii) the average weekly trading volume (as defined) over a four-week trading period prior to the date of the notice referred to in (5) below. In the case of debt securities, this maximum level is raised to ten percent of the tranche (or class) over each three-month period. As a result of the 2007 amendment, non-affiliates are not subject to this volume restriction and may freely resell their securities after satisfying the requisite holding period, subject only to the current information requirement of Rule 144(c) discussed earlier.

(4) In the case of affiliates, the sales are made in ordinary brokerage transactions, transactions directly with a market maker, or riskless principal transactions.

(5) In the case of affiliates, except for smaller sales (i.e., sales in any period of three months below the lesser of 5,000 shares or $50,000), the seller files a notice of sale on Form 144 with the SEC and, in the case of listed securities, the principal exchange, concurrently with either placing the order to sell with a broker or executing the sale directly with a market maker.[69]

The premise of Rule 144 is that sales that meet these requirements—in particular, the holding period and volume restrictions of Rules 144(d) and (e), respectively—amount to only a "trickle" and not to the full scale "distribution" that is required under the definition of "underwriter" in § 2(a)(11) of the Securities Act. If the sale cannot be said to have been made by an underwriter, then the exemption afforded by § 4(a)(1) of the Securities Act is available.

---

[68] When an affiliate sells unrestricted securities, the sale is subject to the Rule, but there is no holding period requirement under such circumstances.

[69] See Rule 144(h) under the 1933 Act.

A. AVAILABILITY OF RULE 144

Rule 144 may be utilized notwithstanding the fact that the holder of restricted securities (1) has contractual registration rights, or (2) the shares are covered by an effective registration statement.[70]

Once, under its now-abandoned "fungibility doctrine," the SEC insisted that private sales be aggregated with any public sales or sales under any other statutory exemption when determining the total volume of sales that could be made without amounting to a distribution. But this doctrine was largely dropped when the SEC adopted Rule 144 in 1972. As a result, today, concurrent sales under Rule 144 or pursuant to an effective registration statement or pursuant to some other exemption (such as Regulation A) are permitted.

The SEC has also permitted utilization of Rule 144 by security holders whose shares were purchased in purported private placements that did not comply with the private offering exemption and, therefore, were sold illegally. Similarly, the illegal issuance of stock (which would entitle the holder to rescind its purchase) will not toll the holding period.[71] Although the issuer has violated the law, the SEC does not wish to penalize the purchaser if the purchaser can meet the Rule's requirements.

B. CURRENT PUBLIC INFORMATION

The current public information requirement in Rule 144(c) is met if the issuer is subject to the reporting requirements of §§ 13 or 15(d) of the 1934 Act and has filed all required reports under these sections during the 12 months preceding such sale (or for such shorter period that the issuer was required to file such reports), other than Form 8-K reports. Alternatively, if the issuer is not subject to the reporting requirements of the 1934 Act, Rule 144(c)(2) permits such an issuer to make publicly available the information specified in paragraphs (b)(5)(i)(A) to (N), inclusive, and paragraph (b)(5)(i)(P) of Rule 15c2–11 under the 1934 Act, and thereby satisfy Rule 144(c). Rule 15c2–11 specifies the information that must be made publicly available before a broker-dealer may make a market in an over-the-counter security, and Rule 144(c)(2) simply declares that if such information is publicly available, a Rule 144 seller may also rely upon it. This provision does not, however, apply to a reporting company. Thus, Rule 144 sales may not be made in the case of a reporting issuer that is delinquent in its periodic filings based upon the issuer making publicly available the information specified in Rule 15c2–11.

---

[70] See Securities Act Release No. 5306 (Sept. 26, 1972), at 153–54; Securities Act Release No. 6099 (Aug. 2, 1979), at question 84; Electro-Nucleonics, Inc. (letter available July 20, 1972), [1972–1973 Transfer Binder] Fed. Sec. L. Rep. (CCH) ¶ 78,891.

[71] Hadron, Inc. (letter avail. July 31, 1981), [1981–82 Transfer Binder] Fed. Sec. L. Rep. (CCH) ¶ 77,041.

When an issuer registers securities under the 1934 Act for the first time, the 90-day waiting period in Rule 144(c)(1) commences on the effective date of the 1934 Act registration statement. Effectively, this amounts to a mandatory 90-day lock-up period for unregistered sales by senior executives, because as "control persons" they need to rely on Rule 144, whether the stock is "restricted" or not.

The 1934 Act's periodic reporting forms require issuers to state whether they have been subject to the reporting requirements for the past 90 days and have met the reporting requirements for the past 12 months (or such shorter period to which the issuer has been subject). Unless she knows or has reason to believe that the issuer has not complied with the reporting requirements, the Rule 144 seller is entitled to rely on the issuer's statement in the latest of such reports or on a written statement from the issuer that the reports have been filed. An issuer that has received an extension of time to file a 1934 Act report has not filed all required reports for Rule 144 purposes but will be deemed to be current when the filing is made.

Compliance with the publicly-available information provision is a factual question to be decided on a case-by-case basis. The SEC has taken the position that information about a nonreporting company is publicly available for Rule 144 purposes if the company distributes reports containing the 15c2–11 information to its shareholders, brokers, market makers, and any other interested persons, and if information about the company is published in a recognized financial reporting service.[72] It is insufficient if the company simply furnishes the 15c2–11 information to the broker through which the Rule 144 sale is to be made.[73]

For non-affiliates, the only Rule 144 requirement that such a seller must observe (other than the holding period requirement of Rule 144(d)) is Rule 144(c)(1)'s current information requirement. For non-affiliates, the need to satisfy this requirement continues for one year after the later of the date on which the securities were acquired from the issuer or from an affiliate of the issuer. In effect, this may add six months to a non-affiliate seller's holding period (if the issuer is a reporting company). Conversely, if the issuer is not a reporting company, then the non-affiliate purchaser must hold for one year in any event, but need not be further concerned about Rule 144(c).

C. Holding Period

A major policy predicate of Rule 144 is that the acquirer of restricted securities must assume the full economic risk of a holding period. This holding period is six months in the case of a reporting company and one year in the case of a non-reporting company. In all cases, restricted securities must have been fully paid for and held for the requisite holding

---

[72] Securities Act Release No. 6099 (Aug. 2, 1979), at Question 20.
[73] Id. at Illustration to Question 20.

period before they can be sold under Rule 144. But what is the reason for this requirement? The justification for this holding period and the need for economic risk-bearing is that it distinguishes the Rule 144 seller from a securities dealer or underwriter who might be serving as a mere conduit for the flow of securities from the issuer to the general public. An underwriter would generally not be willing to bear the economic risk of the securities for such a period simply to earn an underwriter's profit.

If securities are purchased from the issuer with a note or other obligation, they are not considered fully paid unless: (1) the note or obligation is with full recourse, (2) the note or obligation is paid in full before the sale, and (3) there is adequate collateral, other than the purchased securities, the fair market value of which is, throughout the holding period, equal to the unpaid portion of the purchase price. The holding period is tolled for any periods during which the fair market value of the collateral falls below the unpaid portion of the purchase price. Excess collateral may be withdrawn without affecting the holding period.

Shares of stock issuable upon exercise of options at a stated price are not fully paid until the option has been exercised and the exercise price has been fully paid. Note, however, that if the securities were acquired from the issuer solely upon cashless exercise of an option or warrant issued by the issuer, the newly-acquired securities would be deemed to have been acquired at the same time as the option or warrant. This tacking provision only applies if the holder purchased the option or warrant, creating an economic risk to the holder, and it does not apply in the case of employee stock options.

If restricted securities are purchased on an installment basis, the holding period commences on a staggered basis. The holding period is tolled only for those securities which do not meet the full-recourse or collateralization requirements.

The SEC's staff takes the position that where money is borrowed from a third-party, non-affiliate lender (e.g., a bank) to purchase restricted securities; the loan is not directly or indirectly guaranteed by the issuer; and the restricted securities are pledged as the only collateral for a normal full-recourse loan, then the restricted securities are considered fully paid and the holding period is deemed to have commenced upon purchase of the restricted securities.

Fungibility does not apply to Rule 144 situations. The acquisition of restricted securities will not restart the holding period on previously acquired restricted securities. Likewise, fungibility does not apply in non-Rule 144 situations. The acquisition of restricted securities does not taint unrestricted securities previously acquired.[74] The holder merely must be able to trace the securities to their purchase dates.

---

[74] See Borden & Fleischman, The Continuing Development of Rule 144: Significant SEC Staff Interpretations, Eighth Annual Institute on Securities Regulation 91, 126–27 (1977).

A private sale of restricted or control securities pursuant to the "Section 4(1½) exemption" will start a new holding period if the seller is an affiliate of the issuer. Otherwise, the holding period can be satisfied by the purchaser tacking the holding period of the prior non-affiliate seller to her own holding period. However, the holding period of the prior holder cannot be tacked to the holding of the subsequent holder if the prior holder was an affiliate of the issuer. Only if the prior holder was a non-affiliate of the issuer is tacking permitted. Partners who receive restricted securities as distributions by their partnership may also tack their holding periods to that of the partnership.[75]

Tacking is also permitted for stock dividends and stock splits, recapitalizations (including recapitalizations resulting in changes in par values), reincorporations that do not result in changes in the business or management, conversions of convertible securities (provided the security is convertible into securities of the same issuer), warrants (provided that the only consideration surrendered upon exercise of the warrant consists of other securities of the same issuer), and securities acquired as contingent payments in business combinations. In each of these situations, for Rule 144 purposes, the subsequently-acquired securities are deemed to have been acquired at the time the related restricted securities were acquired.

Stock dividends on restricted securities are restricted securities for Rule 144 purposes; however, the holding period for securities acquired as a dividend is deemed to have commenced as of the date the securities on which the dividend was paid were acquired.

Tacking is permitted for bona fide pledgees, donees of gifts, and trusts. Restricted securities are deemed to have been acquired when they were acquired by the pledgor, donor, or settlor. The SEC has taken the position that multiple donees or beneficiaries need not aggregate horizontally, provided they do not otherwise act in concert.

Where an estate is an affiliate, tacking is permitted, and the volume restriction applies. Moreover, where a beneficiary who is an affiliate receives restricted securities from the estate, tacking is permitted of both the decedent and the estate holding periods. If the affiliated beneficiary is a trustee or executor under the instrument as well, the trust or estate is deemed to be an affiliate and, thus, the amount limitations apply. Where the estate is not an affiliate or the securities are sold by a beneficiary who is not an affiliate, no holding period is required, and the amount limitations and the manner of sale requirement do not apply even if one or more beneficiaries (other than the trustee, as discussed immediately above) are affiliates, but the current information requirement of Rule 144(c) does continue to apply. However, where the trustee or executor is an affiliate (even though the securities are

---

[75] It should be noted that tacking is permitted only if the distribution does not require the distributee to furnish additional consideration as, for example, when her partnership interest is being redeemed. Securities Act Release No. 6099 (Aug. 2, 1979), at Question 34 n.11.

unrestricted securities in the hands of the non-affiliated trust or estate), the trustee or executor must aggregate her personal sales with those of the trust or estate. Conversely, the non-affiliated trust or estate need not aggregate its sales with those of the trustee or executor for purposes of the volume restriction. The special provisions for an estate apply only to restricted securities acquired by the estate from the decedent, not to restricted securities acquired otherwise, such as by exchange of securities owned by the decedent, to which Rule 144 applies fully.

D. LIMITATION ON AMOUNT OF SECURITIES SOLD

In the case of affiliates, the ceiling on the amount of equity securities which may be sold pursuant to the Rule in any three-month period is the greater of 1% of the outstanding securities of the class being sold, or the average weekly volume of that class on all exchanges or reported through the consolidated transaction reporting system for the four calendar weeks prior to the filing of the notice of sale. Sales pursuant to registered offerings and pursuant to Regulation A, Regulation S, and § 4 of the 1933 Act are not aggregated with Rule 144 sales in determining the amount permitted to be sold under the Rule.

There is no prohibition on sales in successive three-month periods, but carry-forward and accumulation are not permitted.

Both restricted and unrestricted securities are aggregated in determining the amount limitation for sales by affiliates.

The 2007 amendments made two important changes in the volume restrictions in Rule 144(e): First and most importantly, they eliminated the volume restriction for any person who is not an affiliate of the issuer at the time of sale and has not been an affiliate of the issuer during the preceding three months. Thus, if the CEO of a reporting company resigned or was terminated, she would, presumably, be free to sell unrestricted securities after three months. This former CEO would also be able to sell her restricted securities after three months if (1) the holding period in Rule 144(d) has been met and (2) Rule 144(c)'s current information requirement is satisfied.

Second, the 2007 amendments relaxed the volume restrictions on the sale of debt securities (which rules today apply only to affiliates and persons who have been affiliates within the prior three months). In the case of debt securities, the amount of debt securities sold for the account of such an affiliate of the issuer may not exceed ten percent of the principal amount of the tranche attributable to the securities sold. This ten percent limitation includes both sales of restricted and unrestricted debt securities held by the issuer. All such sales from the same tranche (or class) made within any three-month period must be aggregated. For this purpose, it should be noted that non-participatory preferred stock (i.e., preferred stock which receives a fixed dividend and does not share in residual earnings) is considered a debt security, and the ten percent ceiling is computed in terms of the number of shares in the class. To illustrate, if in March 2012, a reporting company sold $100 million in 10% Senior Notes (either in a public offering or a private placement), an affiliate who had held for the requisite holding period could sell, in any three-month period, up to $10 million (and would have to aggregate all sales of restricted and unrestricted Senior Notes from the same March 2012 offering that the affiliate sold over this three-month period).

Sales by affiliates and other persons acting in concert are also aggregated. The mere fact that several affiliates sell at the same time will not, in and of itself, be considered acting in concert, but it does give rise to a situation that must be considered carefully. Where investors who include one or more affiliates have agreed not to sell more than a specified percentage of their securities during a specified period, the SEC's staff has taken the position that this constitutes an agreement to act in concert. The treatment, for aggregation purposes, of several funds or other accounts under the same investment management is not covered specifically in the Rule, but the SEC's staff has indicated that, in the case of two trusts managed by the same bank, it would treat each trust as a separate person, notwithstanding common trustees, so long as the trusts are not administered in a manner that results in them acting in concert.

"Person" is defined in Rule 144 to include relatives of the seller who share a permanent home with the seller, trusts and estates in which the seller and such relatives collectively own a 10% or greater beneficial interest or which any of them serves as trustee or executor, and corporations or other entities in which the seller, such relatives, and such trusts and estates, together, have a 10% equity interest or own 10% of a class of equity securities. Thus, in determining the amount that an affiliate may sell, sales by all those deemed to be the same "person" as the affiliate are aggregated for the purpose of Rule 144. But aggregation is not required by a non-affiliated trust or estate that wishes to dispose of unrestricted securities—even though the trustee, executor, or beneficiary is an affiliate. The trustee or executor who is an affiliate, however, would be required to aggregate her personal sales with those of the trust or estate under such circumstances. An institutional investor or other person who owns 10% or more of any class of equity securities of a company is considered one person with such company for the purpose of Rule 144, and, therefore, the institutional investor would need to inquire of all companies in which it holds a 10% interest to determine if any of them had or planned transactions in a restricted security which the institution wishes to sell under Rule 144. Directors of charitable foundations are not deemed to act in a capacity similar to that of a trustee or executor for the purpose of Rule 144; thus, aggregation is not required. In the pledge, gift, and trust contexts, the pledgee, donee, or beneficiary must aggregate its sales with those of the pledgor, donor, or settler, respectively. Such aggregation terminates six months (or one year in the case of a non-reporting issuer) after the original transfer to the pledgee, donee, or trust. In the case of an estate, there is no limitation on the amount it can sell if the estate (or beneficiary of the estate who is selling) is not, itself, an affiliate of the issuer.

Section (e)(3)(i) of the Rule is a rather confusingly-drafted provision which provides that where both convertible securities, and the underlying securities into which they are convertible, are being sold, the amount of the underlying securities for which the convertible securities being sold may be converted is aggregated with other sales of the underlying securities in determining the aggregate amount of both securities allowed to be sold. Thus, the amount limitations of paragraph (e) cannot be circumvented by selling an amount of the underlying securities in compliance with those limits, while at the same time selling an amount of the convertible securities that would meet the amount limitations for the convertible securities if they were looked at separately, but that would have resulted in an excessive sale of the underlying securities if the convertible securities had first been converted and the sale of both blocks of securities had taken place.

E. Manner of Sale

Sales of equity securities by affiliates under the Rule can be made in brokers' transactions within the meaning of § 4(a)(4) of the 1933 Act, transactions directly with "a market maker" as defined in the 1934 Act, or riskless principal transactions as defined in the Rule. The seller of equity securities that is an affiliate cannot solicit or arrange for the solicitation of buy orders or make any payment in connection with the sale other than usual commissions to the broker who executes the order. No limitation is placed on the manner of sale in the case of non-affiliates or in the case of resale of debt securities held by an affiliate.

A "market maker" is defined in § 3(a)(38) of the 1934 Act as either (1) a specialist who is permitted to act as a dealer, (2) a dealer who acts as a block positioner, or (3) a dealer who holds itself out as willing to buy and sell a particular security for its own account on a regular or continuous basis.

A market maker is precluded from specifically soliciting buy orders for securities the market maker wishes to buy in a Rule 144 transaction. However, a solicitation will not be implied from the fact that the market maker continues to engage in normal market making activities. The only requirement is that the market maker not engage in a special campaign to solicit buyers for the shares it proposes to purchase pursuant to Rule 144. However, once the market maker consummates a purchase of securities in a Rule 144 transaction, the securities are freed of their restrictive character. The market maker may then solicit buy orders for such shares.

Brokers' transactions are defined as those in which the broker (1) does no more than execute a sell order as agent for the usual commission and (2) does not solicit buy orders in anticipation of or in connection with the transaction. The broker may inquire of other brokers who have indicated an interest within the preceding 60 days. Such inquiry may also be made of clients, institutional and non-institutional, who are bona fide and unsolicited and indicated an interest, within the preceding ten days. Brokers should maintain written records of such indications to substantiate their bona fide nature.

Brokers can continue to make a two-way market in an equity security for which they have a Rule 144 sale order from an affiliate if, prior to receipt of the order, they were making such market, and published bid and asked quotes for the security on each of at least 12 out of the preceding 30 calendar days with no more than four business days in succession without such two-way quotations.

F. Issuers with No or Only Nominal Operations

Rule 144(i) makes Rule 144 unavailable for issuers with only nominal assets or assets consisting of cash and cash equivalents and only nominal assets. This change, added in 2007, was intended to restrict the practical ability of such a shell company to use this Rule.

G. Exclusivity and Operation of Rule 144

The preliminary note to Rule 144 states that the Rule is not exclusive. This means that an affiliate or non-affiliate may also sell pursuant to (1) a registration statement, (2) an exempt transaction, (3) Regulation S, or (4) Regulation A.

Rule 144 is not available where there is technical compliance, but the Rule 144 sales are part of a plan to effect a distribution.[76] Rule 144 does not exempt sales from the antifraud, civil liability, or short-swing profits provisions of the securities laws. The SEC position is that the Rule is to be strictly construed, and persons selling under the Rule have the burden of proving its availability.

H. Possible Modification

In 2014, legislation was introduced in the House of Representatives that would direct the SEC to shorten the holding period under Rule 144 to three months, but the House never acted on the proposed bill. At this point, if the holding period were shortened further, the line between public and private transactions would become very thin indeed, and issuers might increasingly prefer to issue stock to accredited investors in Rule 506 offerings using a general solicitation rather than registering the same stock.

---

[76] Securities Act Release No. 5223 (Jan. 11, 1972), at 81,061. The SEC's staff, however, has indicated that Rule 144 provides a safe harbor for sales of restricted securities even where sales pursuant to the Rule would seriously impact the trading market for the issuing company's shares. See WCS Int'l. (letter avail. Jan. 12, 1979).

NOTES ON RULE 145

Rule 145 provides that exchanges of securities in connection with certain covered transactions—involving reclassifications, mergers or consolidations, and transfer-of-assets reorganizations (each as described in Rule 145(a))—that are subject to a shareholder vote constitute sales of those securities.[77] As the preliminary note to Rule 145 states: "The thrust of the rule is that an *offer, offer to sell, offer for sale,* or *sale* occurs when there is submitted to security holders a plan or agreement pursuant to which such holders are required to elect, on the basis of what is in substance a new investment decision, whether to accept a new or different security in exchange for their existing security." Unless an exemption from § 5 is available, Rule 145(a) requires the registration of these sales.[78]

Note that Rule 145 defines Rule 145(a) transactions as involving sales of securities, but with respect to those sales, it does not itself provide an exemption from the registration requirements of the 1933 Act. Consequently, absent an exemption from § 5 of the 1933 Act (e.g., §§ 3(a)(9)–(11), § 4(a)(2), Rule 147, Rule 147A, Regulation A, or Regulation D), issuers must register the Rule 145 securities with the SEC. If restricted securities are issued as part of a Rule 145(a) transaction, resales will be subject to the same rules that otherwise govern resales of those securities.

A prior version of Rule 145(c) deemed persons who were parties[79] to a Rule 145(a) transaction, other than the issuer, and affiliates of such parties to be engaged in a distribution and, therefore, to be underwriters in connection with any offer or sale of Rule 145(a) securities received within a defined period of time. Doing so foreclosed reliance on the § 4(a)(1) exemption for the resale of those securities. In 2007, in Securities Act Release No. 8869, the SEC eliminated the "presumptive underwriter" provision in most cases.[80] Today, the presumption only applies to public offers or sales by a party to a Rule 145(a) transaction, other than the issuer, and affiliates of such party if the transaction involves a shell company (other than one used solely to complete the transaction). The SEC retained the provision for shell companies "based on our experience with transactions involving shell companies that have resulted in abusive sales of securities."[81] In other words, the Rule 145(c)

---

[77] For a discussion of complexities around defining what transaction are included under Rule 145, see Kim, A Study on Rule 145 of the Securities Act of 1933: How to Provide Clarity and Predictability in Rule 145 Transactions, 40 Akron L. Rev. 131 (2007); Campbell, Rule 145: Mergers, Acquisitions and Recapitalizations Under the Securities Act of 1933, 56 Fordham L. Rev. 277 (1987).

[78] See Securities Act Release No. 5932 (May 15, 1978).

[79] Rule 145(e)(2) defines a "party" as "the corporations, business entities, or other persons, other than the issuer, whose assets or capital structure are affected by the transactions specified in" Rule 145(a).

[80] See Securities Act Release No. 8869 (Dec. 6, 2007).

[81] Id.

"presumptive underwriter" doctrine remains applicable to public offers or resales, typically by affiliates of the target (in an acquisition or transfer of assets) or reclassified company, of securities received in a Rule 145(a) transaction when a company with only "nominal" assets or operations (i.e., a shell company) is a party to the transaction.

Under Rule 145(c), the presumptive underwriter doctrine extends only to public offers or sales of securities received in a Rule 145(a) transaction. It does not extend to private resales, which may rely on another exemption (e.g., § 4(1½), Rule 144, or Rule 144A) from registration. Rule 145 is also focused on public resales by parties to a Rule 145(a) transaction, other than the issuer, and affiliates of such parties. Accordingly, public resales by non-affiliates generally are not considered to be distributions and, therefore, the reselling security holders are not "underwriters" and can continue to rely on the § 4(a)(1) exemption. Note that, in some instances, the SEC may treat a non-affiliate security holder, who receives a substantial block of stock as part of a Rule 145(a) transaction, as an underwriter, even though it is not an affiliate (and, therefore, falls outside the presumptive underwriter definition in Rule 145(c)). In that case, the SEC may require any resale to meet the same requirements under Rule 145(d) (described below) as a presumptive underwriter must do to be exempt from § 5's registration requirements.[82]

Notwithstanding Rule 145(c)'s presumptive underwriter doctrine, under Rule 145(d), a presumptive underwriter is not deemed to be engaged in a distribution and, therefore, not to be an underwriter of securities acquired in a Rule 145(a) transaction that was registered under the 1933 Act, if:

- the issuer is not (or has ceased to be) a shell company, the issuer is a reporting company and has filed the requisite 1934 Act reports for the preceding 12 months (other than reports on Form 8-K), and the issuer has filed current information with the SEC reflecting its status as no longer being a shell company; and

- one of the following three conditions is met:
    o the securities are sold in accordance with Rule 144's current public information, volume limitation, manner of sale, and brokers' transactions requirements, and at least 90 days have elapsed since the date the securities were acquired from the issuer in the Rule 145(a) transaction;

---

[82] See Kim, A Study on Rule 145 of the Securities Act of 1933: How to Provide Clarity and Predictability in Rule 145 Transactions, 40 Akron L. Rev. 131, 160 (2007); Campbell, Resales of Securities Under the Securities Act of 1933, 52 Wash. & Lee L.Rev. 1333, 1370–72 (1995).

○ the seller is not, and has not been for at least three months, an affiliate of the issuer, at least six months have elapsed since the date the securities were acquired from the issuer in the Rule 145(a) transaction, and current information regarding the issuer is publicly available; or

○ the seller is not, and has not been for at least three months, an affiliate of the issuer, and at least one year has elapsed since the date the securities were acquired from the issuer in the Rule 145(a) transaction.

Note that, under Rule 145, affiliates of a party (other than the issuer) to a Rule 145(a) transaction that hold stock acquired pursuant to § 3(a)(9), § 3(a)(10) or Regulation A may also resell under Rule 145(d). Although paragraph (d) on its face is limited to resales of "registered securities," the SEC takes the position that Rule 145(d) is still available for resales of exempted securities.[83]

Rule 145(d), however, is subject to some practical limitations regardless of whether the resales are of "registered securities" or not. If the issuer (the acquiring company) is a reporting company under the 1934 Act and its securities are traded in an organized market, Rule 145(d) provides a workable framework for short-term resales (after 90 days) within the amount limitations of Rule 144 (see Rule 145(d)(2)(i)). The ability to execute sales through brokers' transactions, which is one of Rule 145(d)(2)(i)'s requirements, is more likely if the securities are traded in an organized (and liquid) market. If, however, the issuer is not a reporting company, it may be difficult to meet Rule 145(d)'s "current information" requirements, resulting in a one-year holding period (see Rule 145(d)(2)(iii)). This limitation, however, is analogous to what would be required if resales were conducted under Rule 144.

Problems

PROBLEM 7-8

Medium Tech, Inc. is a Nasdaq-listed "reporting" company that designs software and web sites for large corporate clients. Becky Gill was hired by Medium Tech two years ago, at which point she purchased 10,000 shares from Medium Tech in a private sale (the purchase price was $120,000, and she paid $20,000 in cash and gave a full recourse promissory note for $100,000, which was secured by a pledge of securities having a market value

---

[83] See Kim, A Study on Rule 145 of the Securities Act of 1933: How to Provide Clarity and Predictability in Rule 145 Transactions, 40 Akron L. Rev. 131, 164–66 (2007); Campbell, Rule 145: Mergers, Acquisitions and Recapitalizations Under the Securities Act of 1933, 56 Fordham L. Rev. 277, 327 (1987); see also, e.g., SEC Division of Corporation Finance, Staff Legal Bulletin No. 3A (CF) (June 18, 2008) (noting that § 3(a)(10) securities received in a Rule 145(a) transaction not involving a shell company "may generally be resold without regard to Rule 144 if the sellers are not affiliates of the issuer;" but where a party is a shell company, the Rule 145(d) resale limitations will apply).

of $80,000). Becky paid off this note in full three months ago. Becky's title is Director of Web Design for Medium Tech, which is an important creative position, but does not make her an executive officer (she does not perform a policymaking function). Becky now owns 25,000 shares in Medium Tech, having also purchased 5,000 shares in the open market on Nasdaq last week and 10,000 shares on the exercise of a stock option three months ago. Becky was awarded the stock option under the company's employee stock option plan, which is a "qualified" plan. She is not quite clear on whether shares received under the stock option plan are registered. You are counsel to Merrill, Shearson, the brokerage firm, which she has asked to help her sell all of the stock she can without registration (she wants to buy a ski chalet in Colorado). Medium Tech has 1,400,000 shares outstanding, and its average weekly trading volume over the last four weeks has been 10,000, 13,000, 16,000, and 14,000 shares, respectively. Advise Becky as to what she can and cannot now sell.

PROBLEM 7-9

Same facts as in the preceding problem, except that now (1) Becky Gill has been promoted to Executive Vice President and made a director of Medium Tech (and, therefore, may be considered an affiliate of Medium Tech), (ii) Becky financed her purchase two years ago of 10,000 Medium Tech shares with a full-recourse bank loan (not a loan from Medium Tech), and the bank received no collateral other than a pledge of the Medium Tech shares, and (iii) Becky gave 2,000 of the 5,000 shares she recently purchased in the market to her 19-year-old son, Ronald, as a birthday present. Ronald sold those shares last week to buy a "really hot" car. Now, how many shares can Becky sell immediately?

PROBLEM 7-10

(a) Donald Duck is the Vice Chairman of Disney Enterprises, Inc., the movie studio. On January 10, 2016, he makes a gift of 1 million shares to each of his three nephews, Huey, Dewey, and Louie (none of whom live with Donald). The 3 million shares have been held by Donald Duck for over ten years. Disney has 100 million shares of its common stock outstanding, and its average weekly trading volume is 600,000 shares. On June 30, 2016, Huey, Dewey, and Louie each independently decides to sell 500,000 shares. Any problem?

(b) Same facts as before, but Huey, Dewey, and Louie agree that sales of 500,000 shares by each of them would depress the market. Thus, they agree that Huey will sell in Week One, Dewey in Week Two, and Louie in Week Three. Assume further that Louie has become an affiliate of Disney. Any problem now?

(c) Same facts as before, except that Huey, Dewey, and Louie—all very eligible bachelors—share a swinging East Side townhouse.

PROBLEM 7-11

Widget Corp., a reporting company listed on Nasdaq, has recently done a series of exempt transactions. On March 1, 2016, it sold 50,000 shares (or just under 1% of its outstanding common stock) to Bill Jones, a Widget Vice President (who is not a controlling person or affiliate), pursuant to his employment contract, which was entered into several months ago when Widget was not yet a reporting company. Widget relies on Rule 701 for its exemption. On April 15, 2016, it sold 3 million shares in an intrastate offering under § 3(a)(11), including 30,000 shares to Mike Smith, a retail investor. It is now November 1, 2016, and both shareholders would like to sell and want an opinion from you, their counsel, that they are free to use Rule 144. Can you give it to each of them? What can you advise each?

PROBLEM 7-12

Assume next that Widget Corporation made a $20 million private placement of its stock in February 2016 under Rule 506, selling to some 60 investors, some accredited and some not. Several of the non-accredited investors would probably not qualify as sophisticated. One of these is Homer Pyle, an ex-Marine Corps veteran and now a member of Congress. Pyle bought 60,000 shares at $5 per share and would like to sell them at their current price ($14 per share). It is now December 2016, and the average weekly trading volume for Widget is 30,000 shares. Can he rely on Rule 144?

PROBLEM 7-13

Bill Smith is a director of Widget and its largest shareholder, with 24% of its common stock. He wants to cause Mike Jones, Chief Operating Officer of Intel, to join Widget as its new CEO. He is prepared to sell Jones 1% of Widget's stock at a price $2 below the current market price from his own personal holdings. Assume Widget has made all requisite filings with the SEC. Can Smith use Rule 144 to cover this transaction?

PROBLEM 7-14

Tardy Corp. just listed on Nasdaq 90 days ago, but already it has become six months late in filing its Form 10-Q. Joe Jones, a Tardy salesman (but not an officer or affiliate), owns 10,000 shares of Tardy common stock that he purchased six months ago in the open market. Sally Smith, a small but sophisticated investor, bought 10,000 shares of Tardy in a Tardy private placement 15 months ago. Prudence Jones, another sophisticated investor, bought 10,000 shares of Tardy two years ago in another private placement. Assume the average weekly trading volume for Tardy is 50,000 shares. Which of these investors, if any, can sell today under Rule 144?

PROBLEM 7-15

On September 1, 2016, Delta Corp., a privately-held, non-reporting company, sells 1 million shares of its common stock to Tom Prince, its incoming chief executive officer, at $10 per share. Prince gives his demand note bearing interest at 10% per annum in return for the shares and also pledges the stock to Delta as collateral for this loan. In early 2014, Delta Corp. does an initial public offering and lists on Nasdaq. Delta Corp. now has 80 million shares outstanding and an average weekly trading volume of 200,000 shares, and its stock price has risen to $25 per share. On September 15, 2017, Prince secures another loan from City Bank for $10,000,000 and uses that loan to pay down the Delta loan. He pledges half of his Delta stock (or 500,000 shares) to secure the City Bank loan. On September 30, 2017, he sells 150,000 of his shares to Mellon Investors, a hedge fund, at $22 per share in a private sale (i.e., $3 below the then-market price). On March 30, 2018, Prince wishes to sell 200,000 additional Delta shares on Nasdaq. Do you see any problems with either of these sales?

Problem 7-16

Donald Duck is a senior officer, director, and 10% shareholder of Disney, Inc., a publicly-held company. He sells one million shares (equal to 0.9% of Disney's outstanding common stock) on January 15, 2017, and then dies of a heart attack on January 20, 2017 (after becoming upset about a commercial that employed the Aflac duck, which he considered "stereotypical"). His only beneficiaries are Huey, Dewey, and Louie, who now live separately; each would like to sell the 500,000 shares on February 20, 2017, that each expects to receive from Donald's estate. Can they each make their contemplated sales under Rule 144? What if the executor of Donald's estate was also a director and vice-chairman of Disney, owning 8% himself? Can he sell any of Donald's Disney stock?

Problem 7-17

XYZ Industries, Inc., owns 51% of the stock of Internet Ventures, Inc., a reporting company that is listed on Nasdaq. XYZ Industries, in turn, is controlled by the Rockyfella family, with John D. Rockyfella, the family's patriarch, owning 8% and his wife, Mabel, owning 5% of XYZ Industries. On January 15, 2017, XYZ Industries sells 900,000 shares of Internet Ventures pursuant to Rule 144, and on February 1, it sells another 500,000 shares to a hedge fund in a private sale that did not involve any public offering. John D. Rockyfella has become disenchanted with Internet Ventures, but he only owns 2% of its stock. On February 15, he asks your law firm if he can sell those shares in the public market. The partner in charge of the Rockyfella account asks you to research this question and advise him of how much stock John D. Rockyfella may immediately sell and under what conditions. Assume that Internet Ventures has 100 million shares outstanding, and its average weekly trading volume is 250,000 shares.

Problem 7-18

Assume the same facts as in the preceding problem, except that XYZ Industries, Inc. and the AIGG Insurance Company (which are not affiliated) also hold 9% Debentures, due in 2030, issued by Internet Ventures pursuant to a registered public offering of its debt in 2015. Each firm holds $20 million of these debentures ($100 million of these debentures were issued originally in 2015). Internet Ventures has no other debt securities outstanding. Both want to sell these debentures immediately (and they have no material, nonpublic information about Internet Ventures). To what extent can each do so?

PROBLEM 7-19

Passive Corp.'s assets consist almost exclusively of cash and cash equivalents, and it has only nominal operations (it sold most of its assets for cash in 2014, and it simply re-invests its cash in bank certificates of deposit and rolls these over when they mature). It is, however, a reporting company, which has made all of its filings under the 1934 Act on a timely basis. Robert Promoter, Passive's chief executive, owns 5% of its common stock and wants to sell a block amounting to 1% of Passive's common stock into the public market pursuant to Rule 144 during every three-month period until he has sold all his shares. May he rely on Rule 144 for these contemplated sales?

PROBLEM 7-20

Los Pollos Hermanos ("LPH") has been a 1934 Act reporting company since going public three years ago and is current in its filings. LPH sold an additional $3 million of common stock through a Rule 506 offering seven months after the IPO. Werner Heisenberg is an accredited investor who bought 10,000 shares in the Regulation D offering. Three months after buying these shares, Heisenberg pledged the shares as collateral for a loan he obtained from the Bank of Albuquerque. Heisenberg has become insolvent and ceased to make loan payments, and the Bank seized the collateral and wishes to sell immediately to pay down the loan. As counsel to the Bank, you have been asked if the Bank can freely sell the shares. What questions do you have for Bank personnel before you determine your answer?

6. RULE 144A AND THE PRIVATE RESALE MARKET

Adopted in 1990 (18 years after Rule 144), Rule 144A did a number of things at once: (1) it greatly increased liquidity within the market for privately-placed securities, permitting an active institutional market to develop for the trading of such securities; (2) it increased the capital that issuers could raise in unregistered transactions by reducing the illiquidity discount because now institutions could resell the unregistered securities prior to the expiration of Rule 144's holding period; and, most importantly, (3) it enabled foreign issuers to access U.S. institutional investors without having to formally enter the U.S. public markets by listing on an exchange or registering under § 12(g) of the 1934 Act. This last impact of Rule 144A was the product of its interplay with Regulation S, which will be discussed later in this chapter. Together, they facilitated the development of an international market in unregistered securities. The size of the Rule 144A market dwarfs those of other exempt and unregistered offerings. In 2017, Rule 144A offerings amounted to approximately 37% of total capital raised in unregistered securities placements in the United States (a category that also includes private placements and intrastate offerings) and constituted 24% of total capital raised in all underwritten transactions.[84]

Much of this growth has been fueled by foreign private issuers looking to access the U.S. capital markets without needing to register under the 1933 and 1934 Acts.[85] In combination with Regulation S, Rule 144A allows these issuers to make an integrated worldwide simultaneous offering, registering their securities and selling them to the public in some jurisdictions, but accessing only large institutional investors in the United States. Even when a global offering is not attempted, foreign issuers could make modest changes in their offering to comply with Rule 144A and sell a portion of the offering to U.S. "qualified institutional buyers." In effect, a portion of foreign offerings would be reserved for U.S. institutional investors and sold to them in compliance with Regulation S and Rule 144A.[86] Because Rule 144A(e) expressly precludes integration, eligible issuers can conduct such a worldwide offering without fear that their public offers and sales outside the United States will block their ability to rely on Rule 144A. In overview, the popularity of Rule 144A with foreign issuers as an alternative to U.S. registration may testify to their fear of the SEC (or of the potential for class action litigation in the United States if the offerings were made to the public).

In this light, it may seem surprising that Rule 144A has one major limitation: it cannot be utilized by issuers for securities of a class that is already listed on a U.S. securities exchange (or Nasdaq) or that is closely similar. This is the "fungibility" exception to Rule 144A (specifically, Rule 144A(d)(3)). Why is it that a small foreign issuer or a domestic, non-reporting company can use Rule 144A when IBM, Microsoft, and General Electric cannot? Certainly, the latter's securities are safer investments, and their issuers might well want to use the Rule. The answer to this puzzle is that extending Rule 144A to listed securities was resisted because it would likely create a two-tier market, in which the listed stock would trade at one price on the NYSE or Nasdaq and at a slightly lower price in the Rule 144A market. Not surprisingly, the exchanges objected to this possibility. As a result of their pressure, Rule 144A was drafted so that it can only be used for the shares of unlisted domestic and foreign issuers.[87]

---

[84] See Bauguess et al., Capital Raising in the U.S.: An Analysis of the Market for Unregistered Securities Offerings, 2009–2017 7–8 (Aug. 2018).

[85] See Swan et al., Investing in Foreign Securities Offerings and Avoiding Rule 144A Pitfalls: Tips for the International Investment Manager, 16 The Investment Lawyer 1–2 (2009).

[86] See Jackson & Pan, Regulatory Competition in International Securities Markets: Evidence from Europe in 1999—Part I, 56 Bus. Law. 653, 667–71 (2007).

[87] The "fungibility exclusion" can sometimes be outflanked (but at a cost that may prohibitive). A listed company can design a security that is of a different class than its listed security and sell that by means of Rule 144A. Rule 144A(d)(3) specifies economic tests to determine if the two classes are substantially identical. Although issuers do design non-fungible, hybrid securities, common stock simply cannot be sold by a company whose common

Finally, it should be understood that although Rule 144A created a giant international market, it is technically only an exemption for the resale of securities. The issuer itself will typically issue the securities in foreign transactions under Regulation S or domestically through a private placement under § 4(a)(2). Rule 144A covers the resale of those unregistered securities to very large institutional investors that the Rule defines as "qualified institutional buyers" (or "QIBs"). But it does permit a rapid re-entry into the U.S. institutional market, at least in the case of foreign issuers.

Resale of Restricted Securities
Securities Act Release No. 6862.
April 23, 1990.

A. GENERAL

* * *

Rule 144A sets forth a non-exclusive safe harbor from the registration requirements of Section 5 of the Securities Act for the resale of restricted securities to specified institutions by persons other than the issuer of such securities. The transactions covered by the safe harbor are private transactions that, on the basis of a few objective standards, can be defined as outside the purview of Section 5, without the necessity of undertaking the more usual analysis under Sections 4(1) and 4(3) of the Securities Act. Each transaction will be assessed under the Rule individually. The exemption for an offer and sale complying with the Rule will be unaffected by . . . transactions by other sellers. The Commission wishes to emphasize that Rule 144A is not intended to preclude reliance on traditional facts-and-circumstances analysis to prove the availability of an exemption outside the safe harbor it provides.

* * *

In the case of securities originally offered and sold under Regulation D of the Securities Act, a person that purchases securities from an issuer and immediately offers and sells such securities in accordance with the Rule is not an "underwriter" within the meaning of Rule 502(d) of Regulation D. Issuers making a Regulation D offering, who generally must exercise reasonable care to assure that purchasers are not underwriters, therefore would not be required to preclude resales under Rule 144A. Similarly, the fact that purchasers of securities from the issuer may purchase such securities with a view to reselling such securities pursuant to the Rule will not affect the availability to such issuer of an exemption under Section 4(2) of the Securities Act from the registration requirements of the Securities Act.

---

stock is listed on a U.S. exchange. Also, creating alternative, non-fungible classes of securities may clutter up the issuer's balance sheet and confuse investors; generally, issuers are reluctant to create new classes of stock simply to secure an exemption.

B. ELIGIBLE SECURITIES

Rule 144A would not extend to the offer or sale of securities that, when issued, were of the same class as securities listed on a national securities exchange registered under Section 6 of the Exchange Act or quoted in an automated inter-dealer quotation system. Accordingly, privately-placed securities that, at the time of their issuance, were fungible with securities trading on a U.S. exchange or quoted in NASDAQ would not be eligible for resale under the Rule.

Where American Depositary Shares ("ADSs") are listed on a U.S. exchange or quoted in NASDAQ, the deposited securities underlying the ADSs also would be considered publicly traded, and thus securities of the same class as the deposited securities could not be sold in reliance on the Rule . . . . Under the Rule, a convertible security is to be treated as both the convertible and the underlying security unless, at issuance, it is subject to an effective conversion premium of at least 10 percent.

C. ELIGIBLE PURCHASERS

1. *Types of Institutions Covered*

As discussed above, except for registered broker-dealers, to be a "qualified institutional buyer" an institution must in the aggregate own and invest on a discretionary basis at least $100 million in securities of issuers that are not affiliated with the institution.

a. *Banks and Savings and Loan Associations*

Banks, as defined in Section 3(a)(2) of the Securities Act, and savings and loan associations as referenced in Section 3(a)(5)(A) of the Act, must, in addition to owning and investing on a discretionary basis at least $100 million in securities, have an audited net worth of at least $25 million, as demonstrated in their latest published annual financial statements . . . . As federally-insured depository institutions, domestic banks and savings and loans are able to purchase securities with funds representing deposits of their customers. These deposits are backed by federal insurance funds administered by the Federal Deposit Insurance Corporation ("FDIC"). In light of this government support, these financial institutions are able to purchase securities without placing themselves at risk to the same extent as other types of institutions. In this respect, banks and savings and loans effectively are able to purchase securities using public funds. Therefore, the amount of securities owned by a bank or savings and loan institutions may not, on its own, be a sufficient measure of such institution's size and investment sophistication . . . . A combined securities ownership and net worth test [was therefore adopted] . . . .

b. *Registered Broker-Dealers*

* * *

Commenters stated that the definition of qualified institutional buyer, as reproposed, would exclude a number of registered broker dealers from acting as intermediaries in the Rule 144A resale market. They also stated that if the $100 million test was retained for registered broker-dealers in all situations, significant segments of the registered broker-dealer community, whose participation was important to the efficient functioning of the market, would be excluded from participation in the market as principals.

In response to these comments, the Rule as adopted provides that a broker-dealer registered under the Exchange Act which in the aggregate owns and invests on a discretionary basis at least $10 million in securities of issuers that are not affiliated with the broker-dealer is a qualified institutional buyer. Additionally, the Rule provides that registered broker-dealers acting as riskless principals for identified qualified institutional buyers would themselves be deemed to be qualified institutional buyers . . . .

D. INFORMATION REQUIREMENT

* * *

As adopted, availability of the Rule is conditioned upon the holder and a prospective purchaser designated by the holder having the right to obtain from the issuer, upon the holder's request to the issuer, certain basic financial information, and upon such prospective purchaser having received such information at or prior to the time of sale, upon such purchaser's request to the holder or the issuer. This information is required only where the issuer does not file periodic reports under the Exchange Act, and does not furnish home country information to the Commission pursuant to Rule 12g3–2(b). Additionally, the Rule has been revised to exempt from the information requirement securities issued by a foreign government . . . . The holder must be able to obtain, upon request, and the prospective purchaser must be able to obtain and must receive if it so requests, the following information (which shall be reasonably current in relation to the date of resale under Rule 144A): a very brief statement of the nature of the issuer's business and of its products and services offered, comparable to that information required by subparagraphs [(H) and (I) of Exchange Act Rule 15c2–11(b)(5)]; and its most recent balance sheet and profit and loss and retained earnings statements, and similar financial statements for such part of the two preceding fiscal years as it has been in operation. The financial information required is the same as that required by [subparagraphs (L) and (M) of Rule 15c2–11(b)(5)]. The financial statements should be audited to the extent audited financial statements are reasonably available.

The Commission does not believe that the limited information requirement should impose a significant burden on those issuers subject to the requirement. Many foreign issuers that will be subject to the requirement, which were the focus of the commenters' concern, will have securities traded in established offshore markets, and already will have made the required information publicly available in such markets. Even for domestic issuers, the required information presents only a portion of that which would be necessary before a U.S. broker or dealer could submit for publication a quotation for the securities of such an issuer in a quotation medium in the United States .... Financial statements meeting the timing requirements of the issuer's home country or principal trading markets would be considered sufficiently current for purposes of the information requirement of the Rule ....

The Rule does not specify the means by which the right to obtain information would arise. The obligation could be, inter alia, imposed in the terms of the security, by contract, by corporate law, by regulatory law, or by rules of applicable self-regulatory organizations.

E. OTHER REQUIREMENTS

Although the Rule imposes no resale restrictions, a seller or any persons acting on its behalf must take reasonable steps to ensure that the buyer is aware that the seller may rely on the exemption from the Securities Act's registration requirements afforded by Rule 144A.

* * *

NOTES ON RULE 144A AND THE PRIVATE RESALE MARKET

1. *General Solicitation.* Originally, Rule 144A made a condition of the Rule's availability that the securities be offered and sold only to QIBs. The JOBS Act superseded that requirement, permitting a general solicitation to be used in connection with a Rule 144A offering as well as in connection with a Rule 506(c) offering. Sales under Rule 144A, however, can only be made to persons reasonably believed to be QIBs.

2. *PORTAL.* Contemporaneously with the adoption of Rule 144A in 1990, the SEC approved the creation by the NASD (later managed by NASDAQ) of an electronic market to trade Rule 144A securities.[88] Known as PORTAL (for the "Private Offering, Resale and Trading through Automated Linkages" system), this market traded only securities that qualify under Rule 144A and only permitted investors who qualify as QIBS to trade. Prior approval by PORTAL of the investor as a QIB was necessary before it could trade, and this requirement was further enforced by a clearance and settlement system which The Depository Trust Company ("DTC") administered to prevent the leakage of Rule 144A securities into public markets. PORTAL got off to a shaky start,[89] failing to develop as a primary trading facility as initially planned; debt

---

[88] See Securities Act Release No. 6864 (April 30, 1990).

[89] In its first two years, PORTAL attracted only 75 subscribers out of an estimated universe of over 3,300 QIBs. See Bostwick, The SEC Response to Internationalization and Institutionalization: Rule 144A Merit Regulation of Investors, 27 Law & Policy In International Business 423, n.75 (1996).

and equity securities continued to be privately traded among QIBs outside of PORTAL. In 2006, NASDAQ requested the SEC for approval to re-establish a trading system for equity securities only, and, in 2007, NASDAQ ceased operating the PORTAL market in favor of joining the PORTAL Alliance, which it created with certain other financial institutions for privately-placed equity securities. From 2009, DTC no longer required Rule 144A debt or equity securities to be PORTAL-designated for clearance and settlement.

Notwithstanding these growing pains, PORTAL added a unique level of liquidity to the private placement process. It made Rule 144A attractive to foreign issuers, who could have done offshore offerings but were instead attracted by the prospects of a liquid secondary market (which did not exist in their home country).[90] Many went on to become "reporting companies" and graduate to a listing on Nasdaq or the NYSE.

3. *Documentation and Form.* Although envisioned as a form of private placement, Rule 144A offerings have come to look more like public offerings. Typically, they involve a disclosure document that more or less parallels the prospectus contained in a Form S-1 registration statement, with similar financial statements, risk factors, and, often, a Management's Discussion and Analysis of Financial Condition and Results of Operations (MD&A). Unlike a typical private placement, where the investment banker functions only as an agent of the issuer, in a Rule 144A offering, the major investment banks will purchase the securities from the issuer as the "initial purchasers" and then resell to the QIB purchasers, thus functionally paralleling the role of underwriters.

4. *Information Requirement.* Some controversy has surrounded Rule 144A's information requirement in subsection (d)(4) of the Rule. Under Regulation D, no information must normally be provided to an accredited investor, nor must information be provided under the statutory exemption in § 4(a)(6). On average, these investors are less sophisticated and have less bargaining power than QIBs. If information need not be provided to such investors in the primary offering, why should it be required at the time of the secondary market transaction? Perhaps, the answer was that the SEC's attention in Rule 144A was focused on foreign issuers who would conduct their primary offerings abroad (under the protective auspices of Regulation S), and the SEC wanted to ensure that securities of such issuers could not reach the U.S. secondary markets (such as PORTAL) without some commitment by the issuer to provide continuing information.

5. *Fungibility Exclusion.* The public policy of denying Rule 144A to listed securities seems debatable. While extending Rule 144A to listed securities would permit large institutional investors to buy the listed

---

[90] See Sjostrom, The Birth of Rule 144A Equity Offerings, 56 UCLA L. Rev. 409, 411–12 (2008).

security in an off-exchange transaction at a cheaper price (but subject to less liquidity) than a retail investor could, that is what happens in most markets: namely, the large volume purchaser gets a discount. For the near future, however, the 2005 offering reforms that gave Well-Known Seasoned Issuers immediate access to the market probably mean there will be little interest on the part of these issuers in lobbying for liberalization of Rule 144A. Logically, they should prefer selling to the entire market, rather than to only a segment of it at a discount.

6. *Rules 138 and 139.* In 2005, the SEC amended Rules 138 and 139 to clarify that research reports issued in compliance with either of those rules would not be considered an offer or a general solicitation in connection with a Rule 144A offering. At the time, Rule 144A made a condition of the Rule's availability that the securities be offered and sold only to QIBs, raising the concern that research reports distributed to institutional investors who were not QIBs could cause Rule 144A's availability to be lost. With the JOBS Act amendment to Rule 144A, so that it no longer restricts offers to only QIBs, this concern has largely fallen by the wayside, although the amendments to Rules 138 and 139 remain.

Problems

PROBLEM 7-21

United States Industries, a reporting company whose common stock is listed on the New York Stock Exchange makes a private placement of $100 million in face amount of 7% Convertible Debentures through Goldman Brothers, its placement agent. The debentures were purchased at their face value without any discount. The purchasers are 20 or so large institutional investors, most of whom would satisfy the definition of "qualified institutional buyer" in Rule 144A(a)(1)(i). Both these institutions and United States Industries would like to admit the debentures to the PORTAL system. Each $1,000 debenture is convertible into 20 shares of United States Industries, which, on the date the offering closed, was trading at $40 per share. Do these securities qualify for Rule 144A?

PROBLEM 7-22

(a) Widget Corp., a non-reporting issuer, sells $50 million of its Convertible Debentures to two distributors—Citybank and J.P. Morganbank—who, in turn, resell to 20 QIBs. A general solicitation is used. Citybank and J.P. Morganbank indicated on their websites, both preceding and following their purchase from Widget, that they would be offering the Widget debentures to QIBs. One of these QIBs—Lafayette Securities—resells four months later to five wealthy investors, none of whom are QIBs (although all are accredited investors). What exposure does Lafayette have? And what exposure do Widget, Citybank, and the QIB purchasers (other than Lafayette) face because of Lafayette's sale?

(b) Assume now that one of Lafayette's purchasers was not a QIB and received no information or disclosure document from Lafayette, Widget, Citybank, or anyone else. What results now for all the parties?

PROBLEM 7-23

Quick Chips, a non-reporting company in Silicon Valley that produces microchips, is evaluating two capital-raising alternatives. First, it could sell 5 million shares of its common stock in a private placement through a local broker-dealer, with the purchasers being largely accredited investors (and a few QIBs). Second, it could do a Rule 144A transaction, using a large commercial bank as its "distributor." The small brokerage firm (which lacks the contacts with QIBs to do a Rule 144A offering) argues that it can sell to a wider audience of persons (i.e., to non-QIB accredited investors, sophisticated persons, and even unsophisticated persons with a qualified purchaser representative), and it will charge a comparable fee. As securities counsel to Quick Chips, you are asked to explain what the advantages of a Rule 144A offering—both legal and economic—might be.

7. SECTION 4(a)(7)

Congress passed the Fixing America's Surface Transportation ("FAST") Act in 2015.[91] Included in the FAST Act was an amendment to the 1933 Act—new §§ 4(a)(7) and 4(d)—that created a new exemption from § 5 for private resales of securities. This new exemption may ease the ability of some securities holders to privately resell securities acquired in unregistered offerings.

Specifically, § 4(a)(7) creates a non-exclusive exemption from § 5 for the private resale of restricted securities to "accredited investors."[92] The class of securities to be sold must have been authorized and outstanding for a period of 90 days[93] and cannot be part of an unsold allotment.[94] In addition, the issuer must be "engaged in business;" it cannot be in the organizational stage or in bankruptcy or receivership; and it cannot otherwise fail to satisfy the business requirement under § 4(d)(6). For non-reporting issuers, § 4(a)(7) also requires a variety of specified information that is "reasonably current" to be provided to prospective buyers, including the issuer's most recent balance sheet, statement of profit and loss, and similar financial statements, prepared in accordance with generally accepted accounting principles ("GAAP"), for such part of the two preceding fiscal years as the issuer has been in operation.[95] In that case, § 4(a)(7) is unlikely to be available to a seller unless the documentation for the original sale permits resales pursuant to § 4(a)(7)

---

[91] Fixing America's Surface Transportation Act, Pub. L. No. 114–94, 129 Stat. 1312 (2015).
[92] See § 4(d)(1) of the 1933 Act. The term "accredited investors" is defined in Rule 501(a) of Regulation D under the 1933 Act.
[93] See § 4(d)(8) of the 1933 Act.
[94] See § 4(d)(7) of the 1933 Act.
[95] See § 4(d)(3) of the 1933 Act.

or the issuer consents to, and assists in the seller's compliance with, § 4(a)(7).

Securities acquired under § 4(a)(7) are deemed to have been acquired in a transaction not involving a public offering or distribution (for purposes of the underwriter definition in § 2(a)(11) of the 1933 Act).[96] The seller (who cannot be the issuer or an issuer subsidiary[97] or a "bad actor"[98]) cannot engage in a general solicitation with respect to offers to buy or sell the securities.[99] Securities sold under § 4(a)(7) remain "restricted" and cannot be resold in the absence of another exemption.[100] Such securities are also "covered securities" under § 18 of the 1933 Act, which preempts state securities law registration and qualification requirements, although certain notice requirements may still apply.[101]

Since § 4(a)(7) is a non-exclusive safe harbor, sellers can also rely on other exemptions that permit the resale of restricted securities, such as § 4(1½), Rule 144, and Rule 144A. Unlike these other exemptions, § 4(a)(7) includes issuer disqualifications and restricts resales by "bad actors."

There may, however, still be advantages to relying on § 4(a)(7). Section 4(a)(7) is analogous to § 4(1½). Yet, for many, the black letter guidance in § 4(a)(7) provides greater certainty than § 4(1½). That same certainty also means the requirements of § 4(a)(7) may be more restrictive. Non-reporting issuers must provide specific financial disclosure, prepared in accordance with GAAP, although the information need not be audited or reviewed.[102]

Unlike Rule 144, § 4(a)(7) does not have a holding period requirement. Additionally, § 4(a)(7) may be more viable for affiliates looking to resell securities since it does not have volume restrictions for affiliate resales. Nevertheless, securities resold pursuant to § 4(a)(7) remain restricted, and purchasers cannot freely resell them as they may with securities purchased in a Rule 144 transaction.

Section 4(a)(7) permits resales to a wider universe of investors than Rule 144A. Resales can be made to "accredited investors" rather than to Rule 144A's narrower class of "qualified institutional buyers." In addition, resales under § 4(a)(7) are not subject to the fungibility limitation of Rule 144A.

---

[96] See § 4(e)(1) of the 1933 Act.
[97] See § 4(d)(4) of the 1933 Act.
[98] See § 4(d)(5) of the 1933 Act. The criteria to be a "bad actor" are set forth in Rule 506(d) of Regulation D under the 1933 Act and in § 3(a)(39) of the 1934 Act.
[99] See § 4(d)(2) of the 1933 Act. This prohibition against general solicitation is consistent with § 4(a)(2) and Rule 506(b) in Regulation D under the 1933 Act.
[100] See § 4(e)(1) of the 1933 Act.
[101] See § 18(b)(4)(G) of the 1933 Act.
[102] See Greene et al., U.S. Regulation of the International Securities and Derivatives Markets § 7.01 470 (11th and 12th Editions 2014–2017).

8. REGULATION S: AN EXEMPTION FOR OFFERINGS OUTSIDE THE UNITED STATES

For the issuer seeking to avoid the costs, delay, and potential liability associated with the registration of securities, an obvious tactic is to issue the securities abroad. The problem with this technique is that the 1933 Act does not, on its face, exempt extraterritorial offerings from its reach. To the contrary, § 5 of the 1933 Act applies to any offering or sale in "interstate commerce," and § 2(a)(7) defines "interstate commerce" to include "trade or commerce in securities or any transportation or communication relating thereto ... between any foreign country and any State, Territory, or the District of Columbia." Section 5's worldwide reach results in considerable overbreadth that potentially subjects to the registration requirements of § 5 both U.S. issuers who sought to sell securities abroad (for example, by making phone calls from the United States) and foreign issuers whose securities entered the United States through resales.

Such a literal interpretation of § 5's scope would produce dismay from foreign issuers and U.S. issuers with foreign operations, and might result in confrontations with regulators in other countries. Not surprisingly, the SEC has never attempted to extend § 5 to its fullest conceivable reach. The problems inherent in extraterritorial offerings first became apparent in the 1960s with the development of the Eurobond market. Essentially, due to persistent U.S. balance-of-payments deficits (caused, in large part, by the Cold War and the stationing of U.S. troops in Europe), European financial institutions held large reserves of dollar deposits that they were prepared to lend at lower interest rates than domestic U.S. financial institutions. To tap this attractive financial market, U.S. issuers wanted to make bond offerings in Europe. But they could foresee that some of the issued securities would re-enter the United States—with the possible result that the SEC would consider these issuers to have made a public offering in violation of § 5. To enable U.S. issuers to access this market, the SEC issued Release No. 4708 in 1964, which stated that the U.S. securities laws were "primarily intended to protect American investors" and concluded that debt securities could be sold by U.S. issuers without need for registration under the 1933 Act if "the offering is made under circumstances reasonably designed to preclude distribution or redistribution of the securities within, or to nationals of, the United States."

Over the next 25 years, the SEC interpreted and re-interpreted Release 4708 in a voluminous series of no-action letters that still left some continuing uncertainties. Cautious counsel developed an elaborate set of contractual provisions to satisfy this Release. Typically, these procedures required (1) a "lock-up" of the securities and their release to buyers in definitive form at a delayed point (usually 90 days after the closing) that was sufficiently after the completion of the distribution to ensure the offering had ended and the securities had come to rest; and

(2) an express agreement by the underwriters that they would not sell to U.S. nationals or residents. The obvious difficulty with this approach was that it denied U.S. institutional investors the ability to participate in foreign offerings. As U.S. institutional investors increasingly desired to diversify their portfolios on an international basis, pressure developed to reconsider Release 4708.

Regulation S, which was adopted in 1990, essentially reflects a shift from a "national" approach focused on protecting U.S. nationals (wherever located) to a "territorial" approach (which permits U.S. and foreign issuers to sell unregistered securities in foreign markets, even to U.S. nationals). Structurally, Regulation S consists of a general statement (in Rule 901) and two specific safe harbors (in Rules 903 and 904). Rule 903 provides a safe harbor for participants in a distribution (referred to as "distributors"), including issuers, underwriters, and selling group members. In turn, Rule 904 sets forth a safe harbor for resales by others, including investors who acquire securities in a U.S. private placement or in a transaction exempt from registration under Rule 144A.

Rule 903 focuses on the relative likelihood that securities of the issuer will enter U.S. markets. As a result, it subdivides issuers into three categories: (1) foreign issuers without "substantial U.S. market interest" (or "SUSMI") for their securities (see Rule 903(b)(1)); (2) foreign or U.S. issuers that are "reporting" companies under the 1934 Act and foreign issuers of debt securities (see Rule 903(b)(2)); and (3) all other issuers (see Rule 903(b)(3)).

In the case of a foreign issuer that falls into the first category because it lacks SUSMI, Rule 903's safe harbor is available as long as the securities are offered and sold in an "offshore transaction," and no "directed selling efforts" are made in the United States. The buyer in such a case may be a U.S. national, and the entire transaction can be planned and preparatory activities undertaken in the United States, because the transaction will be deemed an "offshore transaction" under Rule 902(h) so long as the buyer is outside the United States at the time the "buy offer is originated" or the transaction is executed on the "physical trading floor" of a foreign securities exchange.

In the case of the second category ("reporting" companies and foreign issuers of debt securities), there are additional requirements: a 40-day "restricted period" is required during which offers or sales may not be made to U.S. persons; "offering restrictions" must be implemented; and a notice requirement becomes applicable.

In the case of the third category (all other issuers),[103] more elaborate procedural requirements are specified, including certification and lock-

---

[103] Although described broadly as "all other issuers," this third category is likely to be very small and will chiefly consist of U.S. issuers selling equity that are not reporting companies and a few foreign issuers that have a "substantial U.S. market interest."

up requirements for debt securities and a one-year restricted period, coupled with a stop-transfer restriction, for equity securities. These restrictions parallel the former standards under Release 4708. In addition, Rule 905 treats the equity securities of U.S. issuers acquired pursuant to Regulation S to be "restricted securities" as defined in Rule 144.

The rationale for this tripartite classification is explained below in the adopting release.

Offshore Offers and Sales
Securities Act Release No. 6863.
April 24, 1990.

* * * Regulation S as adopted includes two safe harbors. One safe harbor applies to offers and sales by issuers, securities professionals involved in the distribution process pursuant to contract, their respective affiliates, and persons acting on behalf of any of the foregoing (the "issuer safe harbor"), and the other applies to resales by persons other than the issuer, securities professionals involved in the distribution process pursuant to contract, their respective affiliates (except certain officers and directors), and persons acting on behalf of any of the foregoing (the "resale safe harbor"). An offer, sale or resale of securities that satisfies all conditions of the applicable safe harbor is deemed to be outside the United States within the meaning of the General Statement and thus not subject to the registration requirements of Section 5.

Two general conditions apply to the safe harbors. First, any offer or sale of securities must be made in an "offshore transaction," which requires that no offers be made to persons in the United States and that either: (i) the buyer is (or the seller reasonably believes that the buyer is) offshore at the time of the origination of the buy order, or (ii) for purposes of the issuer safe harbor, the sale is made in, on or through a physical trading floor of an established foreign securities exchange, or (iii) for purposes of the resale safe harbor, the sale is made in, on or through the facilities of a designated offshore securities market, and the transaction is not pre-arranged with a buyer in the United States. Second, in no event could "directed selling efforts" be made in the United States in connection with an offer or sale of securities made under a safe harbor. "Directed selling efforts" are activities undertaken for the purpose of, or that could reasonably be expected to result in, conditioning of the market in the United States for the securities being offered. Exceptions to the general conditions are made with respect to offers and sales to specified institutions not deemed U.S. persons, notwithstanding their presence in the United States.

The issuer safe harbor distinguishes three categories of securities offerings, based upon factors such as the nationality and reporting status of the issuer and the degree of U.S. market interest in the issuer's securities. The first category of offerings has been expanded from the Proposals and includes: securities offered in "overseas directed offerings," securities of foreign issuers in which there is no substantial U.S. market interest, securities backed by the full faith and credit of a foreign government, and securities issued pursuant to certain employee benefit plans. The term "overseas directed offerings" includes an offering of a foreign issuer's securities directed to any one foreign country, whether or not the issuer's home country, if such offering is conducted in accordance with local laws, offering practices and documentation. It also includes certain offerings of a domestic issuer's non-convertible debt securities, specified preferred stock and asset-backed securities denominated in the currency of a foreign country, which are directed to a single foreign country, and conducted in accordance with local laws, offering practices and documentation. The second category has been revised to include offerings of securities of U.S. reporting issuers and offerings of debt securities, asset-backed securities and specified preferred stock of foreign issuers with a substantial U.S. market interest. * * *

The issuer safe harbor requires implementation of procedural safeguards, which differ for each of the three categories, to ensure that the securities offered come to rest offshore. Offerings under the first category may be made offshore under the issuer safe harbor without any restrictions beyond the general conditions. Offerings made in reliance on the other two categories are subject to additional safeguards, such as restrictions on offer and sale to or for the account or benefit of U.S. persons.

The resale safe harbor has been expanded from the Proposals to allow reliance thereon by certain officers and directors of the issuer or distributors. In such a transaction, no remuneration other than customary broker's commissions may be paid. Otherwise, the resale safe harbor is adopted substantially as reproposed. Under the resale safe harbor, dealers and others receiving selling concessions, fees or other remuneration in connection with the offering (such as sub-underwriters) must comply with requirements designed to reinforce the applicable restriction on directed selling efforts in the United States and the offshore transaction requirement. * * *

The safe harbors are not exclusive and are not intended to create a presumption that any transaction failing to meet their terms is subject to Section 5. Reliance on one of the safe harbors does not affect the availability of any exemption from the Securities Act registration requirements upon which a person may be able to rely.

Regulation S relates solely to the applicability of the registration requirements of Section 5 of the Securities Act. The Regulation does not limit in any way the scope or applicability of the antifraud or other provisions of the federal securities laws or provisions of state law relating to the offer and sale of securities.

* * *

At or around the time of adoption of this Regulation, the Department of the Treasury is adopting regulations establishing new procedures applicable to foreign-targeted offerings of bearer debt obligations. Persons contemplating issuance of such obligations in reliance on this Regulation are advised to direct their attention also to the Treasury regulations. . . .

II. BACKGROUND AND INTRODUCTION

The registration requirements of the Securities Act literally apply to any offer or sale of a security involving interstate commerce or use of the mails, unless an exemption is available. The term "interstate commerce" includes "trade or commerce in securities or any transaction or communication relating thereto . . . between any foreign country and any State, Territory or the District of Columbia. . . ." The Commission, however, historically has recognized that registration of offerings with only incidental jurisdictional contacts should not be required. In Release 4708, the Commission stated that it would not take any enforcement action for failure to register securities of U.S. corporations distributed abroad solely to foreign nationals, even though the means of interstate commerce were used, if the distribution was effected in a manner that would result in the securities coming to rest abroad.

* * *

The development of active international trading markets and the significant increase in offshore offerings of securities, as well as the significant participation by U.S. investors in foreign markets, present numerous questions under the U.S. securities laws. For companies raising capital abroad, a principal issue under the federal securities laws is the reach across national boundaries of the registration requirements under Section 5 of the Securities Act.

The Regulation adopted today is based on a territorial approach to Section 5 of the Securities Act. The registration of securities is intended to protect the U.S. capital markets and investors purchasing in the U.S. market, whether U.S. or foreign nationals. Principles of comity and the reasonable expectations of participants in the global markets justify reliance on laws applicable in jurisdictions outside the United States to define requirements for transactions effected offshore. The territorial approach recognizes the primacy of the laws in which a market is located. As investors choose their markets, they choose the laws and regulations applicable in such markets.

* * *

Regulation S relates solely to the applicability of the registration requirements of Section 5 of the Securities Act, and does not limit the scope or extraterritorial application of the antifraud or other provisions of the federal securities laws or provisions of state law relating to the offer and sale of securities. The antifraud provisions have been broadly applied by the courts to protect U.S. investors and investors in U.S.

markets where either significant conduct occurs within the United States (the "conduct" test) or the conduct occurs outside the United States but has a significant effect within the United States or on the interests of U.S. investors (the "effects" test). It is generally accepted that different considerations apply to the extraterritorial application of the antifraud provisions than to the registration provisions of the Securities Act. While it may not be necessary for securities sold in a transaction that occurs outside the United States, but touching this country through conduct or effects, to be registered under United States securities laws, such conduct or effects have been held to provide a basis for jurisdiction under the antifraud provisions of the United States securities laws.

III. DISCUSSION OF REGULATIONS

A. General Statement

Rule 901(a) is a general statement of the applicability of the registration provisions of the Securities Act. The General Statement provides that any offer, offer to sell, sale, or offer to buy that occurs within the United States is subject to Section 5 of the Securities Act, while any such offer or sale that occurs outside the United States is not subject to Section 5. The determination as to whether a transaction is outside the United States will be based on the facts and circumstances of each case. If it can be demonstrated that an offer or sale of securities occurs "outside the United States," the registration provisions of the Securities Act will not apply, regardless of whether the conditions of the safe harbor are met. For a transaction to qualify under the General Statement, both the sale and the offer pursuant to which it was made must be outside the United States. * * *

B. Safe Harbors

Rules 903 and 904 set forth non-exclusive safe harbors for extraterritorial offers, sales and resales of securities. The safe harbors include conditions to protect against indirect, unregistered, non-exempt offerings into the U.S. capital markets.

An offer or sale by an issuer, a distributor, an affiliate of either, or any person acting on behalf of any of the foregoing, that meets the applicable conditions of the issuer safe harbor (Rule 903) is outside the United States for the purposes of Rule 901. For purposes of the Regulation, the term "distributor" includes all underwriters, dealers, and other persons who are participating in a distribution of securities pursuant to contractual arrangements, such as sub-underwriters, but does not include persons participating pursuant to contract only in ancillary positions, such as fiscal agents or persons hired to perform clearing services.

Distributors and their affiliates are not prevented by the Regulation from engaging in secondary transactions in securities of the same class being distributed, provided the securities are not borrowed or replaced with shares from the offering. Once the distribution has ended and any applicable restricted period specified in Rule 903 has expired, distributors that have sold their allotments will no longer have distributor status and therefore will be able to use Rule 904's resale safe harbor. So long as a distributor still holds some portion of its allotment, it will continue to be unable to rely on Rule 904 with respect to the offer and sale of the unsold allotment.

The resale safe harbor is available for offers and sales by all persons except an issuer, a distributor, an affiliate of either (other than specified officers and directors), and any person acting on behalf of any of the foregoing. An offer or sale that meets the applicable conditions of Rule 904 is outside the United States for the purposes of Rule 901. Unlike the reproposal, resales of securities by officers and directors who may be affiliates of the issuer or distributor, and thus would have been ineligible to use the resale safe harbor, may be made in reliance upon that safe harbor provided specified conditions are met. Of course, the resale safe harbor is not available for such officers and directors if they are being used as conduits to sell securities for persons ineligible to rely upon the resale safe harbor.

1. General Conditions

Two general conditions apply to all offers, sales and resales made in reliance on the safe harbors. First, such an offer or sale must be made in an "offshore transaction." Second, no "directed selling efforts" may be made in the United States in connection with an offer or sale of securities in reliance on such safe harbors.

a. Requirement of Offshore Transaction

An "offshore transaction" is a transaction in which no offer is made to a person in the United States and either of two additional sets of requirements is met. The first alternative requires at the time the buy order is originated, that the buyer be outside the United States (or the seller and any person acting on its behalf reasonably believe that the buyer is outside the United States). The second alternative covers certain transactions executed in, on or through the facilities of a designated offshore securities market (unless the seller or a person acting on its behalf knows that the transaction was prearranged with a buyer in the United States) and certain transactions executed in, on or through the physical trading floor of an established foreign securities exchange located outside the United States.

The first alternative focuses on the location of the buyer for two reasons. First, the location of the buyer overseas clearly and objectively provides evidence of the offshore nature of the transaction. The requirement that the buyer itself, rather than its agent, be outside the United States reduces evidentiary difficulties and problems in administering the Regulation, both for regulators and private parties attempting to ensure compliance with the conditions of the safe harbor. Second, the buyer's location outside the United States supports the expectation that the buyer is or should be aware that the transaction is not subject to registration under the Securities Act.

When the buyer is a corporation or partnership, if an authorized employee places the buy order while abroad, the requirement that the buyer be outside the United States will be satisfied. When the buyer is an investment company, if an authorized person employed by either such company or its investment adviser places the buy order outside the United States, the requirement that the buyer be outside the United States will be satisfied.

The second alternative definition of "offshore transaction" provides that certain transactions executed in, on or through certain offshore securities markets are offshore transactions, without regard to the location of the person originating the buy order. In order to be considered a sale of securities in, on or through the facilities of an offshore securities market, the sale must be effected outside the United States under the auspices and supervision of such a securities market, by or through a member of such market or any other person authorized to effect such sales thereon. Such execution of a transaction in a foreign marketplace provides objective evidence of the foreign locus of the transaction. Moreover, buyers in such markets may be presumed to rely on the regulatory protections afforded by local law and not U.S. registration requirements. * * *

b. *Directed Selling Efforts*

A person making an offer or sale otherwise in accordance with the conditions of the issuer safe harbor will be unable to rely on the provisions of the safe harbor if any directed selling efforts are being made in the United States by an issuer, a distributor, any of their respective affiliates, or any person acting on behalf of any of the foregoing. With respect to resales under Rule 904, a directed selling effort by the seller, any of its affiliates, or any person acting on behalf of either, will preclude reliance on the resale safe harbor by that seller; directed selling efforts by any other person will not affect the seller's ability to rely on the resale safe harbor.

Under the issuer safe harbor, directed selling efforts in the United States may not be made during the period the issuer, the distributors, their respective affiliates or persons acting on behalf of any of the foregoing, are offering and selling the securities and, for offerings under the second and third safe harbor categories, during the restricted period as well.

"Directed selling efforts" are those activities that could reasonably be expected, or are intended, to condition the market with respect to the securities being offered in reliance upon the Regulation. This provision precludes, *inter alia,* marketing efforts in the United States designed to induce the purchase of the securities purportedly being distributed abroad. Activities such as mailing printed material to U.S. investors, conducting promotional seminars in the United States, or placing advertisements with radio or television stations broadcasting into the United States or in publications with a general circulation in the United States, which discuss the offering or are otherwise intended to condition, or could reasonably be expected to condition, the market for the securities purportedly being offered abroad, constitute directed selling efforts in the United States.

Publications with a general circulation in the United States, as defined in the Regulation, include all publications printed primarily for distribution in the United States, and all publications that, on average during the preceding 12 months, have had a circulation in the United States of 15,000 copies or more per issue.

The definition of directed selling efforts specifically excludes several forms of advertisements. First, an advertisement will not be deemed a directed selling effort under the Regulation if publication of the advertisement is required by foreign or U.S. law or the rules or regulations of a U.S. or foreign regulatory or self-regulatory authority, such as a stock exchange, provided that the advertisement contains no more information than legally required and includes a statement to the effect that the securities have not been registered under the Securities Act and may not be offered or sold in the United States (or to a U.S. person, if the advertisement relates to an offering under the second or third issuer safe harbor categories) absent registration or an applicable exemption from the registration requirements. * * *

Distribution or publication in the United States of information, opinions or recommendations concerning the issuer or any class of its securities could constitute directed selling efforts, depending upon the facts and circumstances. Directed selling efforts will not be deemed to exist, however, if the information, opinion or recommendation of a distributor or its affiliate with respect to a reporting issuer: (i) is contained in a publication that is distributed with reasonable regularity in its normal course of business, and includes similar information, opinions or recommendations in that issue with respect to a substantial number of companies in the issuer's industry or sub-industry, or contains a comprehensive list of securities recommended by such entity; (ii) is given no materially greater space or prominence in such publication than that given to securities of other issuers; and (iii) with respect to an opinion or recommendation, is no more favorable to the issuer than the opinion or recommendation published by the entity in its last issue addressing the issuer or its securities. When the issuer is not a reporting issuer, the effect on the market of publication or distribution of information, opinions or recommendations about the issuer or its securities can be expected to be more significant due to the possible absence of other publicly available information about the issuer. Distributors and their affiliates should exercise even greater caution in publication or distribution of information, opinions or recommendations concerning non-reporting issuers or their securities.

An isolated, limited contact with the United States generally will not constitute directed selling efforts that result in a loss of the safe harbor for the entire offering. The Regulation likewise is not intended to inhibit routine activities conducted in the United States for purposes other than inducing the purchase or sale of the securities being distributed abroad, such as routine advertising and corporate communications. The dissemination of routine information of the character and content normally published by a company, and unrelated to a securities selling effort, generally would not be directed selling efforts under the Regulation. For example, press releases regarding the financial results of the issuer or the occurrence of material events with respect to the issuer generally will not be deemed to be "directed selling efforts."

* * *

Legitimate selling activities carried out in the United States in connection with an offering of securities registered under the Securities Act or exempt from registration pursuant to the provisions of Section 3 or 4 of the Securities Act will not constitute directed selling efforts with respect to offers and sales made under Regulation S.

* * *

2. *Issuer Safe Harbor*

The issuer safe harbor is available for issuers, distributors, their respective affiliates, and persons acting on behalf of any of the foregoing. The issuer safe harbor distinguishes among three classes of securities, with varying procedural safeguards imposed to have the securities offered come to rest offshore. The criteria used to divide securities into three groups, such as nationality and reporting status of the issuer and the degree of U.S. market interest in the issuer's securities, were chosen because they reflect the likelihood of flowback into the United States and the degree of information available to U.S. investors regarding such securities.

* * *

a. *Category 1: Foreign Issuers With No Substantial U.S. Market Interest; Overseas Directed Offerings; Securities Backed by the Full Faith and Credit of a Foreign Government; Employee Benefit Plans*

The first issuer safe harbor category is available for offers and sales of securities of foreign issuers with no "substantial U.S. market interest" for their securities, securities offered and sold in "overseas directed offerings," securities backed by the full faith and credit of a foreign government, and securities offered and sold pursuant to certain employee benefit plans. Securities issued by foreign entities that do not have a substantial U.S. interest in their securities may be expected to flow back or remain in their major or home market, and are not likely to flow into the United States following an offshore offering. Flowback concerns also are limited where securities of a foreign issuer, even with a substantial U.S. market, are offered and sold in an offering directed at residents of a single foreign jurisdiction and conducted in accordance with local laws, and customary local practices and documentation. Flowback concerns are reduced where a U.S. issuer's non-convertible debt securities, asset-backed securities and non-participating preferred stock denominated in a currency other than U.S. dollars are offered and sold in an offering directed at residents of a single foreign jurisdiction, and the offering is conducted in accordance with local laws, and customary local practices and documentation. Securities offered and sold pursuant to employee benefit plans established and administered under foreign law are less likely to flow back into the United States where steps are taken to preclude sales to U.S. residents (other than employees on temporary assignment in the United States) and other conditions specified in the Regulation are met.

Offers and sales of securities included in this category may be made in reliance on the safe harbor without any limitations or restrictions other than the general conditions that the transaction be offshore and that no directed selling efforts be made in the United States. Offers and sales of securities to U.S. investors who are overseas at such time will not preclude reliance on the safe harbor for securities in this category. Of course, trading of a substantial amount of such securities in the United States shortly after they had been offered offshore may indicate a plan or scheme to evade the registration provisions; where a transaction is part of such a plan or scheme, Regulation S is not available.

(1) "Substantial U.S. Market Interest"

* * *

A "substantial U.S. market interest" in a class of a foreign issuer's equity securities is defined to exist where at the commencement of the offering (a) the securities exchanges and inter-dealer quotation systems in the United States in the aggregate constitute the single largest market for such securities in the shorter of the issuer's prior fiscal year or the period since the issuer's incorporation or (b) 20 percent or more of the trading in the class of securities took place in, on or through the facilities of securities exchanges and inter-dealer quotation systems in the United States and less than 55 percent of such trading took place in, on or through the facilities of securities markets of a single foreign country in the shorter of the issuer's prior fiscal year or the period since the issuer's incorporation.

Commenters on the Reproposing Release expressed concern that defining substantial U.S. market interest by use of percentage and numerical tests would present difficulties because records of trading in an issuer's equity securities may be inaccessible or incomplete. In response to those concerns, the Regulation as adopted permits an issuer to rely upon its reasonable belief as to the existence of a substantial U.S.

market interest. Where a foreign or domestic market does not record all trading in a security, only the trading that is recorded (to the extent such information is available to the issuer), is otherwise known to the issuer, or can be reasonably measured or approximated need be considered. Where a substantial market for the issuer's equity securities does not record trading volume, the issuer may reasonably believe there is not a substantial U.S. market interest in that class of securities where less than 20 percent of the class is held of record by persons for whom a U.S. address appears on the records of the issuer, its transfer agent, voting trustee, depositary or person performing similar functions.

A "substantial U.S. market interest" in an issuer's debt securities is dependent upon the aggregation of three types of securities. In addition to traditional debt securities, outstanding non-convertible capital stock, the holders of which are entitled to a preference in payment of dividends and in distribution of assets on liquidation, dissolution or winding up of the issuer, but are not entitled to participate in residual earnings or assets of the issuer (referred to hereinafter as "non-participating preferred stock"), is now included in the measurement of U.S. market interest in debt. * * *

With respect to debt securities, substantial U.S. market interest is measured at the commencement of the offering and is defined as: (A) the issuer's debt securities, its non-participating preferred stock and its asset-backed securities, in the aggregate, being held of record by 300 or more U.S. persons; (B) $1 billion or more of the principal amount outstanding of its debt securities, the greater of liquidation preference or par value of its non-participating preferred stock, and the principal amount or principal balance of its asset-backed securities, in the aggregate, being held of record by U.S. persons; and (C) 20 percent or more of the principal amount outstanding of its debt securities, the greater of liquidation preference or par value of its non-participating preferred stock, and the principal amount or principal balance of its asset-backed securities, in the aggregate, being held of record by U.S. persons.

Substantial U.S. market interest in warrants is measured by the level of market interest in the securities to be purchased upon exercise of the warrants. Substantial U.S. market interest in non-participating preferred stock and asset-backed securities is measured by use of the debt securities test in the definition.

Foreign issuers with no "substantial U.S. market interest" are eligible to rely on the first category of the issuer safe harbor, whether or not they are reporting under the Exchange Act, have securities listed on a U.S. exchange or quoted on NASDAQ, or sponsor an American depositary receipt ("ADR") facility.

* * *

(2) "Overseas Directed Offerings"

* * * "Overseas directed offering" [in Rule 903(b)(ii)] includes two classes of securities offerings. The first class involves offerings of securities of foreign issuers directed to residents of a single country other than the United States made in accordance with local laws, and customary practices and documentation of that country. The second class involves offerings of nonconvertible debt securities, asset-backed securities and non-participating preferred stock of domestic issuers directed to residents of a single foreign country in accordance with local laws, and customary practices and documentation of that country, provided that the principal and interest of the securities are denominated in a currency other than U.S. dollars and the securities are neither convertible into U.S. dollar-denominated securities nor linked to U.S. dollars in a manner that has the effect of converting the securities into U.S. dollar-denominated securities. Related currency or interest rate swap transactions that are commercial in nature will not cause securities denominated in a currency other than the U.S. dollar to be treated as if they were denominated in U.S. dollars.

Of particular importance in the concept of "overseas directed offering" is the requirement that such offerings be "directed" at a single country. Where the foreign issuer, a distributor, any of their respective affiliates, or a person acting on behalf of any of the foregoing, knows or is reckless in not knowing that a substantial portion of the offering will be sold or resold outside that country, the offering will not qualify as an overseas directed offering.

* * *

b. *Category 2: Reporting Issuers; Non-Reporting Foreign Issuers' Debt Securities; Non-Reporting Foreign Issuers' Non-Participating Preferred Stock and Asset-Backed Securities*

Securities of all domestic issuers that file reports under the Exchange Act are subject, under the second safe harbor category, both to the general conditions that an offer or sale be an offshore transaction and that no directed selling efforts may be made in the United States, and to specified selling restrictions. Securities of foreign reporting issuers with substantial U.S. market interest are subject to the same restrictions. The selling restrictions applicable to the second category are designed to protect against an indirect unregistered public offering in the United States during the period the market is most likely to be affected by selling efforts offshore. In the event flowback of reporting issuers' securities does occur after the restricted period, the information relating to such securities publicly available under the Exchange Act generally should be sufficient to ensure investor protection.

The second category also applies to offerings of debt securities of any non-reporting foreign issuer. The inclusion of those offerings in this category reflects the view that offering restrictions applicable to the category provide adequate protection against an indirect U.S. distribution because of the generally institutional nature of the debt market and the trading characteristics of debt securities. Moreover, because debt securities are usually issued in separate classes or series, debt securities can be tracked more easily to detect use of offshore transactions to evade the registration obligation for distributions into the United States.

Reflecting public comment, certain equity securities of non-reporting foreign issuers have been moved to this category from the more restrictive third issuer safe harbor category because of the similarity of the market for these securities to the debt market. Non-participating preferred stock and asset-backed securities of non-reporting foreign issuers are now included in the second category.

Two types of selling restrictions exist for securities in the second category—"transactional restrictions" and "offering restrictions."

(1) Transactional Restrictions

Transactional restrictions require that the securities sold under the safe harbor prior to the expiration of a 40-day restricted period not be offered or sold to or for the benefit or account of a U.S. person. Persons relying on the second issuer safe harbor category are required to ensure (by whatever means they choose) that any non-distributor to whom they sell securities is a non-U.S. person and is not purchasing for the account or benefit of a U.S. person. Transactional restrictions also require a distributor selling securities to certain securities professionals to send a confirmation or notice to such purchasers advising that the purchaser is subject to the same restrictions on offers and sales that apply to a distributor.

(a) U.S. Person

Rule 902(*o*) contains a definition of the term "U.S. person." Unlike no-action letters pursuant to Release 4708, U.S. residency rather than U.S. citizenship is the principal factor in the test of a natural person's status as a U.S. person under Regulation S. Thus, for example, a French citizen resident in the United States is a U.S. person.

Trusts and estates generally are U.S. persons for purposes of the Regulation if any trustee, executor or administrator is a U.S. person. In response to commenters' concerns with respect to the competitive effects on U.S. professional fiduciaries, the definition of U.S. person has been revised so that an estate with a U.S. professional fiduciary acting as executor or administrator is not deemed a U.S. person if: an executor or administrator who is not a U.S. person has sole or shared investment discretion with respect to the estate assets, and the estate is governed by foreign law. An exclusion from the definition of U.S. person is provided for a trust with a U.S. professional fiduciary acting as trustee, provided a trustee who is not a U.S. person has sole or shared investment discretion with respect to the trust assets, and no beneficiary (and no settlor if the trust is revocable) is a U.S. person.

With respect to forms of business organization, such as corporations and partnerships, the definition codifies and elaborates on positions set forth in no-action letters. With regard to such entities, the place of incorporation or organization generally controls. The status of subsidiaries and affiliated companies, which generally have separate legal identities, is determined according to the place of incorporation or organization. An entity organized under foreign law by a U.S. person principally for the purpose of investing in unregistered securities is a U.S. person unless organized and owned by accredited investors (as defined in Regulation D) who are not natural persons, estates or trusts.

A branch or agency of a foreign entity is treated as a U.S. person if it is located in the United States. Branches and agencies of U.S. banks and insurance companies located outside the United States are not treated as U.S. persons, if they: (i) operate for valid business reasons; (ii) are engaged in the banking or insurance business; and (iii) are subject to substantive local banking or insurance regulation.

With respect to fiduciary accounts (other than trusts and estates), the definition generally treats the person with the investment discretion as the buyer; therefore the status of that person governs. Thus, where a U.S. person has discretion to make investment decisions for the account of a non-U.S. person, the account is treated as a U.S. person. Conversely, where a non-U.S. person makes investment decisions for the account of a U.S. person, that account is not treated as a U.S. person. Several exceptions from that general principle, however, are established in the definition.

* * *

(b) Measurement of the Restricted Period

The 40-day restricted period begins to run on the later of the date of the closing of the offering or the date the first offer of the securities to persons other than distributors is made.

(2) Offering Restrictions

"Offering restrictions" are procedures that must be adopted with regard to the entire offering by the issuer, distributors, their respective affiliates, and all persons acting on behalf of any of the foregoing, in order for a transaction to be in compliance with the second or third categories of the issuer safe harbor. Failure to implement the offering restrictions precludes the availability of the issuer safe harbor for all parties. In effect, offering restrictions are procedures set up by such persons to ensure compliance with the transactional restrictions, particularly the restrictions on offer or sale of the securities to or for the account or benefit of U.S. persons. When the issuer, a distributor, an affiliate of either, or a person acting on behalf of any of the foregoing, is the seller of securities, that person is in a position to ensure, and should ensure, that procedures designed to discourage flowback are used with respect to the entire offering.

* * *

The offering restrictions require distributors, who by definition are participating in the distribution pursuant to a contractual arrangement, to contract that all their offers and sales of the securities will be made in accordance with the safe harbor (or pursuant to registration under the Securities Act or an exemption therefrom).

The issuer, distributors, their respective affiliates, and persons acting on behalf of any of the foregoing, must ensure that certain materials disclose that the securities have not been registered and may not be offered or sold in the United States or to a U.S. person (other than a distributor), unless registered or an exemption from registration is available. Disclosure of the restrictions must appear in any prospectus, offering circular or other document (other than a press release) used in connection with the distribution prior to the expiration of the restricted period. All advertisements relating to the securities are subject to that requirement. The disclosure may appear in summary form on prospectus cover pages and in advertisements.

c. *Category 3: Non-Reporting U.S. Issuers; Equity Offerings by Non-Reporting Foreign Issuers With Substantial U.S. Market Interest*

All securities not covered by the prior two categories fall into this residual category, which is subject to procedures intended to protect against an unregistered U.S. distribution where there is little (if any) information available to the marketplace about the issuer and its securities and there is a significant likelihood of flowback. This category includes securities of non-reporting U.S. issuers and equity securities of non-reporting foreign issuers with substantial U.S. market interest in their equity securities.

As in the case of securities of reporting issuers, offerings of securities in this category are subject to the two general conditions and to offering and transactional restrictions. Offering restrictions that must be adopted for offerings of these securities are the same as for offerings of securities of reporting issuers. In contrast to offerings in the second category, more restrictive transactional restrictions to prevent flowback are applicable.

In essence, the restrictive procedures are similar to those that evolved under the no-action letters involving Release 4708. * * * These distinguish between debt and equity securities, recognizing that debt securities are generally sold in institutional markets and that the likelihood of flowback is less than in the case of common equity. The category includes a restricted period of one year for equity securities and forty days for debt securities. Two types of a non-reporting U.S. issuers' securities, which would include non-convertible, nonparticipating preferred stock and asset-backed securities, will be subject to the same restrictions as debt securities in the third category, including a 40-day restricted period rather than a one-year restricted period. Offerings of securities of a non-reporting foreign issuer of those two types have been added to the second issuer safe harbor category.

* * * Prior to the expiration of the one-year restricted period, the securities may not be sold to U.S. persons or for the account or benefit of U.S. persons (other than distributors). Purchasers of the securities (other than distributors) are required to certify that they are not U.S. persons and are not acquiring the securities for the account or benefit of a U.S. person other than persons who purchased securities in transactions exempt from the registration requirements of the Securities Act. Such purchasers are also required to agree only to sell the securities in accordance with the registration provisions of the Securities Act or an exemption therefrom, or in accordance with the provisions of the Regulation.

With respect to equity securities of domestic issuers, the safe harbor requires that a legend be placed on the shares stating that transfer is prohibited other than in accordance with the Regulation. The safe harbor further requires that any issuer, by contract or a provision in its bylaws, articles, charter or comparable document, refuse to register any transfer of equity securities not made in accordance with the provisions of the Regulation. Where bearer securities are being sold, or foreign law prevents an issuer from refusing to register securities transfers, use of reasonable procedures, such as a legend, will suffice to satisfy the requirement designed to prevent transfer of equity securities other than in accordance with the Regulation.

Purchasers of debt securities offered under the third issuer safe harbor category (other than distributors) are subject to different restrictions than equity purchasers under this category. Prior to the expiration of the forty day restricted period, the securities may not be sold to U.S. persons or for the account or benefit of U.S. persons (other than distributors). The debt securities must be represented by temporary global securities not exchangeable for definitive securities until expiration of the restricted period. Upon expiration, persons exchanging their temporary global security for the definitive security are required to certify beneficial ownership by: a non-U.S. person or a U.S. person who purchased securities in a transaction that did not require registration under the Securities Act.

Distributors selling equity or debt securities prior to the expiration of the restricted period are required to send a confirmation or other notice to purchasers who are distributors, dealers or persons receiving remuneration in connection with the sale. The notice must state that the purchaser is subject to the same restrictions on offers and sales as the distributor. Non-distributors are not required to send such a confirmation or notice.

3. *Resale Safe Harbor*

* * *

Persons other than: (1) dealers and persons receiving a selling concession, fee or other remuneration in respect of the securities offered or sold, which may include sub-underwriters (all referred to herein as "securities professionals"), and (2) affiliated officers and directors eligible to rely upon the resale safe harbor, may resell any securities in reliance on this safe harbor, with no restrictions other than the general conditions that the offer and sale be made in an offshore transaction (including offers and sales in a designated offshore securities market not prearranged with a buyer in the United States) and without directed selling efforts within the United States.

Resales by securities professionals also are subject to the offshore transaction requirement and the prohibition on directed selling efforts (and the conditions applying to affiliated officers and directors, as applicable). In addition, if the securities being resold are not in the first issuer safe harbor category and the resale is made prior to the expiration of any applicable restricted period, neither the securities professional nor any person acting on its behalf may knowingly offer or sell to a U.S. person. Further, if the selling securities professional or a person acting on its behalf knows the purchaser of the securities is a securities professional, the seller is required to send a confirmation or other notice of the applicable restrictions to the purchaser.

The resale safe harbor is available for the resale offshore of any securities, whether or not acquired in an offshore transaction under Regulation S. Resales pursuant to Rule 904 of securities originally placed privately will not affect the validity of the private placement exemption relied upon by the issuer.

4. *Safe Harbor Protections*

If an issuer, distributor, any of their respective affiliates (other than officers and directors relying on the resale safe harbor), or any person acting on behalf of any of the foregoing: (1) fails to comply with the offering restrictions; or (2) engages in a directed selling effort in the United States, the Rule 903 safe harbor is unavailable to any person in connection with the offering of securities. If the issuer, a distributor, any of such respective affiliates, or any person acting on behalf of any of the foregoing, fails to comply with any other requirement of the issuer safe harbor, the safe harbor is not available for any offer or sale in reliance thereon made by the person failing to comply, its affiliates or persons acting on their behalf. The availability of Rule 903 for other persons' offers and sales of securities is unaffected.

Under the reproposal, the failure to comply with the conditions, other than the offering restrictions and the restrictions on directed selling efforts in the United States, would have precluded reliance upon the safe harbor only for non-complying offers and sales. Under Rule 903 as adopted, reliance upon the safe harbor for all offers and sales made by a non-complying person and its affiliates is precluded as an appropriate incentive to comply fully with the conditions of the safe harbor.

The availability of the Rule 904 resale safe harbor generally is unaffected by the actions of the issuer, distributor, their respective affiliates (other than certain officers and directors relying upon Rule 904), or persons acting on behalf of any of the foregoing. An offer or sale of securities made in compliance with the provisions of Rule 904 is within the safe harbor, notwithstanding non-complying offers or resales by other unaffiliated persons not acting on behalf of the seller.

As Preliminary Note 2 states, the Regulation is not available to any transaction or series of transactions that, although in technical compliance with the rules, is part of a plan or scheme to evade the registration provisions of the Securities Act. Thus, for example, a participant in a distribution, regardless of whether it literally takes all steps required for reliance upon the protection of the Regulation, does not have the protection of the Regulation if it knows or is reckless in not knowing that a person to whom it sells securities in reliance upon the Regulation will not comply with the requirements. Clearly, if an underwriter were told by a dealer to whom it intended to sell securities in reliance upon Rule 903 that the dealer had a customer in New York waiting for the securities, that underwriter would not be able to rely upon the protection of the Rule in connection with its sale to that dealer, even if the underwriter complied with all the Regulation's requirements. The same would be true if the underwriter knew or was reckless in not knowing that the dealer to whom it intended to sell had consistently sold to U.S. residents in violation of resale restrictions in other offerings made pursuant to the safe harbor provisions of the Regulation. If, on the other hand, an underwriter sold to a dealer and the dealer sold to a customer in the United States, and the underwriter did not know and was not reckless in failing to know that the non-conforming sale would occur, the underwriter would not lose the protection of the safe harbor.

C. *Interaction with Other Securities Act Provisions*

1. *Contemporaneous U.S. and Offshore Offerings*

Offshore transactions made in compliance with Regulation S will not be integrated with registered domestic offerings or domestic offerings that satisfy the requirements for an exemption from registration under the Securities Act, even if undertaken contemporaneously. Resales of securities offered and sold in offshore transactions pursuant to Rule 144A are consistent with Rule 904. Of course, the securities sold pursuant to Rule 144A would be restricted securities.

* * *

Offshore Offers and Sales
Securities Act Release No. 7392.
February 20, 1997.

* * *

Since the adoption of Regulation S in 1990, the Commission has become aware of uses of Regulation S that the rule not only did not contemplate, but in fact expressly prohibited. Some issuers, affiliates and others involved in the distribution process are using Regulation S as a guise for distributing securities into the U.S. markets without the protections of registration under Section 5 of the Securities Act. In June 1995, the Commission issued an interpretive release that listed certain problematic practices under Regulation S and requested comment on whether the Regulation should be amended to limit its vulnerability to abuse.[8]

As a result of the continuation of certain of these abusive practices and in response to the comment letters received on the Interpretive Release, the Commission is proposing to stop these abusive practices by amending Regulation S for placements of equity securities by domestic companies. In addition, although abusive practices involving the equity securities of foreign issuers are not as evident as with domestic issuers, there is equal potential for abuse where the principal trading market for those securities is in the United States. Therefore, the Commission also is proposing to amend the safe harbor procedures for placements of equity securities of foreign issuers where the principal market for those securities is in the United States. In general, the "principal market" would be in the United States if more than half of the trading in that security takes place in the United States.

These Regulation S proposals would:

- classify these equity securities placed offshore under Regulation S as "restricted securities" within the meaning of Rule 144;
- align the Regulation S restricted period for these equity securities with the Rule 144 holding periods by lengthening from 40 days (currently applicable to reporting issuers) or one year (currently applicable to non-reporting issuers) to two years the period during which persons relying on the Regulation S safe harbor may not sell these equity securities to U.S. persons (unless pursuant to registration or an exemption);
- impose certification, legending and other requirements now only applicable to sales of equity securities by non-reporting issuers;

---

[8] Securities Act Release No. 7190 (June 27, 1995) (the "Interpretive Release").

- require purchasers of these securities to agree not to engage in hedging transactions with regard to such securities unless such transactions are in compliance with the Securities Act;
- prohibit the use of promissory notes as payment for these securities;
- make clear that offshore resales under Rule 901 or 904 of equity securities of these issuers that are "restricted securities," as defined in Rule 144, will not affect the restricted status of those securities.

The combination of these proposed amendments should prevent the sale of equity securities offshore under Regulation S in transactions that effectively result in unregistered distributions of the securities into the U.S. markets

* * *

NOTES ON REGULATION S

1. *Structure of Regulation S.* Although it adopts a broad "territorial" approach to § 5's registration requirement, Regulation S essentially does so by the narrow definitional tactic of defining the terms "offer," "offer to sell," "sell," and "offer to buy." This definitional approach was taken because, at the time Regulation S was adopted, the 1933 Act did not authorize the SEC to adopt broader exemptions based on policy considerations. Today, § 28 of the 1933 Act would seemingly authorize exemptions on such a basis.

2. *Abuse of Regulation S.* As originally adopted, Regulation S represented an immediate liberalization over prior Release 4708, which required a 90-day "seasoning" period. Under Regulation S, foreign issuers without SUSMI had no "restricted" or seasoning period, and reporting issuers only had a 40-day period. Release 7392 noted that one consequence of this liberalization was that financial intermediaries were arbitraging the spread between the lower sale price of the security in the foreign market and its price in the U.S. trading market. Arbitrageurs would buy stocks at a substantial discount in the foreign Regulation S offerings and dump them in the U.S. market 40 days later. Typically, the intermediaries also hedged their holdings over this "seasoning" period by short selling the same security (if it was traded in a U.S. market) at or before the time they bought it in the foreign market. Alternatively, they could purchase their investment with promissory notes (possibly even on a non-recourse basis) so that they were not obligated to pay for the securities before they were resold. Or, they would use even more sophisticated hedging strategies involving options futures, equity swaps, or other derivatives. To combat this, in 1995, the SEC suggested in Release 7190 that purchasers who sold securities short into the United States at or about the same time they bought the same type of securities

under Regulation S were, in effect, reselling the securities in the United States that they had purchased abroad under Regulation S. *Query:* Did this assertion involve an exhumation of the long-dead fungibility doctrine the SEC had seemingly abandoned with the adoption of Rule 144?

3. *1998 Reforms.* Following up quickly on its 1997 criticisms of the misuse of Regulation S, in 1998, the Commission amended Rule 903 to increase the period (now described as the "distribution compliance period") from 40 days to one year, during which an offer or sale of equity securities of a U.S. issuer (or certain foreign issuers) could not be made to a U.S. person (other than a distributor).[104] In 2007, in line with the amendment of Rule 144 that shortened its holding period to six months (in the case of a reporting company), the distribution compliance period was similarly shortened to six months in the case of a reporting company (but remains one year for a non-reporting company). See Rule 903(b)(3). Effectively, this added delay ended the incentive to use Regulation S as an alternative to a Regulation D private placement. In addition, to achieve full equivalence, equity securities of U.S. issuers that are acquired from the issuer, a distributor, or an affiliate of either were made "restricted securities" so that they could only be sold in compliance with Rule 144 (or pursuant to some other exemption—for example, Rule 144A). See Rule 905.

The 1998 reforms also required purchasers (other than distributors) of equity securities of U.S. issuers to certify they are not U.S. persons and are not acquiring the securities for the benefit of U.S. persons. In addition, all U.S. issuers of equity securities in Regulation S transactions must (i) place into effect a stop transfer instruction to prevent resales not in accordance with Regulation S, and (ii) include a restrictive legend on the share certificates forbidding resales in violation of the 1933 Act. Previously, such restrictions were required of only non-reporting U.S. issuers.

U.S. issuers are also now obligated to report Regulation S sales of equity securities on a quarterly basis on Form 10-Q (thereby also alerting the SEC's staff).

4. *Rule 901.* Rule 901 states very generally that "the terms 'offer,' 'offer to sell,' 'sell,' 'sale,' and 'offer to buy' shall be deemed . . . not to include offers and sales that occur outside the United States." It had been thought that this broad statement would have little impact, with the real work of Regulation S being performed by the much more complicated Rule 903 and the two resale rules, Rules 904 and 905. However, in *Europe & Overseas Commodity Traders v. Banque Paribas*,[105] the Second Circuit upheld the dismissal of a complaint based on Rule 901 that alleged a securities transaction occurred within the United States, even though it was unable to conclude that there were no "directed selling

---

[104] See Securities Act Release No. 7505 (Feb. 17, 1998).
[105] 147 F.3d 118 (2d Cir. 1998).

efforts" in the United States or that the offer was made in an "offshore transaction"—the two critical prerequisites for the application of Rule 903. Essentially, a French investment bank was syndicating the securities of a foreign issuer to foreign institutional investors, and, in connection therewith, called a foreign agent of a foreign institution who was then working in Florida. This agent faxed back his purchase order from Florida. Finding these contacts with the United States to be *de minimis*, the Second Circuit upheld dismissal based on Rule 901, even though it acknowledged that the plaintiffs had adequately pled that "directed selling efforts" had reached into the United States. Hence, Rule 901 may work for defendants, even when the safe harbor of Rule 903 is unavailable.

5. *TEFRA D.* A long-standing federal tax policy disfavors the use of bearer bonds because experience has convinced the IRS that many holders of bearer bonds will fail to report interest earned on them. Thus, § 163(f) of the Internal Revenue Code disallows the issuer an interest deduction on such bonds, and § 4701 also imposes an excise tax on the issuer. Because bearer bonds are standard in European markets, however, a compromise was necessary between competing IRS and SEC policies. Shortly after the adoption of Regulation S, the Treasury Department adopted new regulations, known as "TEFRA D," that partially shield the issuer from these penalties if, during the 40-day restricted period, the bearer bonds are only sold abroad under "arrangements reasonably designed to ensure that such obligation will be sold . . . only to a person who is not a United States person." See Treas.Reg. § 1.163–5(c)(1)(i). The impact of TEFRA D is, generally, to preclude underwriters or selling group members from selling debt securities in bearer form to U.S. investors.

6. *Business Implications.* As discussed below, a principal significance of Regulation S may lie in its interface with Rule 144A. Together with Rule 144A, Regulation S permits U.S. investment banks to participate as underwriters in an unregistered offshore offering that normally would be closed to U.S. investors. Although the distributor may not directly sell "Category 2" or "Category 3" securities to a U.S. person for a specified period, a U.S. person can buy securities of U.S. issuers from those who buy from the distributor (either pursuant to Rule 904, Rule 144A, or another exemption) and bring them back to the U.S. market (subject to Rule 905). In effect, Regulation S provides a safe harbor for sales of securities outside the United States, and Rule 144A provides a safe harbor for resales of those securities to QIBs in the United States. Furthermore, the Regulation S resale safe harbor (Rule 904) can provide a critical exit from the Rule 144A market to offshore markets, where liquidity for some securities might be substantially greater than in the United States.

Among the other practical implications of Regulation S are the following:

(1) It shortens the restrictions on continuous offerings. Many issuers in the Eurobond market make continuous offerings of their debt securities and were subject to resale restrictions because these individual offerings could be integrated. Regulation S provides that each identifiable tranche of securities will be subject to a separate seasoning requirement, thus ending the likelihood of integration.

(2) Under Regulation S, underwriters can offer and sell unseasoned securities in some circumstances to (i) discretionary accounts of U.S. investors where the account is managed or co-managed by a fiduciary located outside the United States and (ii) U.S. fiduciaries who have discretionary authority over the accounts of foreign investors.

(3) Under the resale safe harbor of Rule 904, securities privately placed in the United States or sold under Rule 144A can immediately be resold abroad, including on foreign securities exchanges.

7. *Relationship with Rule 144A.* Regulation S's interrelationship with Rule 144A is complex, and the topic is best divided into two subparts:

a. Resales Outside the United States. Under Rule 904, securities sold abroad can be immediately resold abroad so long as (1) the "offshore transaction" requirement is satisfied; (2) there are no directed selling efforts in the United States; and (3) the party making the resale is not a dealer, officer, director, or affiliate of the issuer, or a person receiving a selling concession or other fee or remuneration. If the seller falls into this third category, then it is treated much as if it were a distributor, and Rule 904(b)(1) requires that the seller must not know its buyer is a U.S. person and, if the buyer is a dealer or person receiving a selling concession, the seller must send the buyer a confirmation setting out the applicable transfer restrictions. For resales by an officer or director of the issuer who is an affiliate of the issuer solely on that basis, Rule 904(b)(2) requires that no selling concession, fee, or other remuneration (other than a standard brokerage commission) be paid in connection with the resale.

With these modest exceptions, the party buying stock from the distributor in an offering by a foreign issuer may resell freely, including to a U.S. person who is outside the United States (or who is reasonably believed to be so by the seller). Securities issued by foreign issuers are generally deemed unrestricted and may be resold anywhere by their purchasers, including into the United States.[106] Only the distributor,

---

[106] If the foreign issuer's securities trade in the United States and it has SUSMI, it will generally fall into Category 2 of Rule 903, and a 40-day "distribution compliance period" becomes applicable. See Rule 903(b)(2)(iii). If, however, the foreign issuer's equity securities trade in the United States and it has SUSMI, but is not a "reporting company," it falls under Rule 903(b)(3) and the distribution compliance period becomes one year. Note, however, that in connection

dealer, or person receiving a selling concession, fee, or other remuneration from the distributor is subject to any "seasoning" requirement.

Suppose a foreign issuer makes an international offering, simultaneously selling securities in Europe, the United States, and Japan. Assume further that the U.S. tranche of this offering is a private placement. The securities privately placed by the foreign issuer in the United States may be resold immediately outside the United States, including on a foreign exchange. This ability to resell restricted securities outside the United States greatly enhances the liquidity of foreign securities and gives investors in the U.S. private placement essentially the same liquidity as investors in the public offering in Europe of those same securities.

b. *Resales in the United States*. When a foreign issuer sells securities abroad, those securities will be subject to several possible limitations on their U.S. resale. First, a dealer will be subject to a limitation up to 40 days following the date of the offering by virtue of § 4(a)(3)(A) of the Securities Act; indeed, an underwriter or dealer that is holding an "unsold allotment" is restricted indefinitely by § 4(a)(3)(C). Second, a "distribution compliance period" may apply, which will be 40 days if the foreign issuer has SUSMI and is a reporting company, but one year if the foreign issuer has SUSMI and is not a reporting company. After expiration of the applicable distribution compliance period, securities sold in a Regulation S offering, other than the equity securities of U.S. issuers (which are covered by Rule 905), are generally unrestricted, unless they are part of an unsold allotment, in which case the bar on U.S. sales by dealers under § 4(a)(3)(C) of the Securities Act applies.

But even in the special case when the one year distribution compliance period is applicable, Rule 903(b)(3)(iii) still permits even the equity securities of a U.S. issuer to be sold by a purchaser from the distributor to a U.S. person pursuant to either Rule 904 or Rule 144A. Section 4(a)(3)(A) may restrict broker-dealers seeking to resell securities issued under Regulation S in the United States for up to 40 days following the offering, but it is not a barrier to sales by others.[107] Pursuant to Rule 905, however, the equity securities of a U.S. issuer

---

with resales, the "distribution compliance period" only applies to a distributor, a dealer, or a person receiving a selling concession, fee, or other remuneration, not to, for example, a retail purchaser. Moreover, as later discussed, Rule 144A provides an exemption to even these special requirements.

[107] Resales under Rule 144A, as well as Rule 904, may also be possible so long as the requirements of Rule 144A are satisfied. If the securities are listed on a U.S. exchange or Nasdaq, for example, the fungibility exception of Rule 144A will normally make that Rule inapplicable.

become "restricted securities," and they do not become unrestricted following the expiration of the distribution compliance period.[108]

In the case of foreign securities and debt securities, neither of which is within Rule 905, it may be possible to "wash" them by sales outside the United States in a Rule 904 transaction followed by their resale in the U.S. public markets, even during the distribution compliance period. This is because the investor holding the securities following the Rule 904 resale is not subject to the distribution compliance period, unless the investor is a dealer or a person who has received a selling concession, fee, or other remuneration.[109] This possibility of a "washing" transaction has concerned the SEC, and in a clearly pre-arranged case, the SEC might assert that Preliminary Note 2 to Regulation S applies and overrides the Rule's exemption.[110] But, such evasion is not possible if the equity securities were issued by a U.S. issuer because Rule 905 will apply. Finally, even if securities not covered by Rule 905 can be "washed" in a Rule 904 transaction, dealers will remain subject to the 40-day restriction of § 4(a)(3)(A) before they can sell into the public U.S. markets.

8. *Impact of Morrison v. National Australia Bank, Ltd.* In 2010, the Supreme held in Morrison v. National Australia Bank (which appears later in this casebook)[111] that § 10(b) of the 1934 Act did not apply to purchases and sales of securities made outside the United States, even if the fraud originated in the United States. The impact of *Morrison* on Regulation S and § 5 of the 1933 Act is uncertain. Regulation S purports to preclude sales of certain securities to U.S. persons outside the United States during "distribution compliance periods," even though there have been no "directed selling efforts" in the United States and the transaction is an "offshore transaction." Arguably, this is beyond the regulatory reach of the 1933 Act, which may be similarly read to apply only to domestic transactions. Conversely, the language of § 5 differs from that of § 10(b) of the 1934 Act. While the latter requires a purchase or sale, the former focuses, at least in part, on whether offers have been made prior to the filing of a registration statement. Such offers, if they emanate from within the United States or are made to persons within the United States, could support jurisdiction, even if the sale occurs abroad. Arguably, to the extent that *Morrison* relied on the language of § 10(b), which it read to require a purchase or sale within the United States, § 5 may only require that an offer be made from within the United States. Even this interpretation, however, would not permit Regulation S to

---

[108] This means that the volume restrictions of Rule 144(e) and the brokerage transaction requirement of Rules 144(f) and (g) may apply even after the expiration of Rule 144(d)'s holding period. Of course, these provisions apply only to transactions by affiliates.

[109] See Rule 904(b).

[110] Preliminary Note 2 to Regulation S states that transactions that are in "technical compliance with these rules" will not be exempt if they are "part of a plan or scheme to evade the registration provisions of the [Securities] Act."

[111] 56 U.S. 247 (2010).

reach so broadly as to preclude offers or sales to U.S. persons abroad. In addition, *Morrison* articulated a strong presumption against the extraterritorial application of U.S. law, and this may also lead courts to read Regulation S narrowly. In short, the literal language of Regulation S may be followed to obtain its safe harbor, but it is unclear whether its distribution compliance periods can truly govern after *Morrison*.

Subsequent to *Morrison*, Congress passed legislation, as part of the Dodd-Frank Act, intended to restore the SEC's extraterritorial jurisdiction (discussed later in this casebook), but its application to the special context of § 5 and Regulation S remains unresolved. Because Regulation S is a safe harbor rule, no direct challenge to it is likely, but the SEC may still be reluctant to enforce it aggressively.

Problems

PROBLEM 7-24

Belgian Industries is a Belgium incorporated company, listed on the Euronext Stock Exchange, with over 70% of its shareholders being Belgians. It is not a U.S. reporting company, but it does occasionally trade on the Nasdaq Bulletin Board, with such trading never accounting for more than 10% of the overall trading in its stock. On December 20, 2017, it makes an offering of 10,000,000 shares of its common stock in Europe pursuant to Rule 903. You may assume that (i) offering restrictions were implemented, (ii) no "directed selling efforts" were made by anyone in the United States, (iii) all offers and sales were made in "offshore transactions," and (iv) the securities carry a legend to the effect that transfers are prohibited, except in accordance with the provisions of Regulation S or pursuant to an exemption from registration under the 1933 Act. After the offering, 100 million shares of Belgian Industries' common stock are outstanding (and the average weekly trading volume is roughly 50,000 shares per week). Jacques Café, a wealthy Belgian investor, bought 800,000 shares of Belgian's stock in the December offering. He, thereafter, sold 400,000 shares on January 15, 2018, to a U.S. broker-dealer, XYZ Securities, Inc., in a transaction negotiated in Europe. Between January 20 and January 23, 2018, XYZ Securities sold 250,000 Belgian Industries shares over the Nasdaq Bulletin Board to ten different buyers (presumably none of whom are QIBs). Are these sales in compliance with the requirements of the 1933 Act? Explain specifically why or why not, discussing the relevant rules and/or exemptions.

PROBLEM 7-25

Small Co., a Delaware corporation that is not a reporting company, makes an offering of common stock in Europe on January 15, 2017, selling some 5 million shares through a combination of U.S. and European distributors. Offering restrictions are implemented; no directed selling efforts are made in the United States; the legend and stop transfer order mandated by Rule 903(b)(3)(iii) are properly complied with; and all offers and sales by the distributors are made in offshore transactions. The Gallic Fund, a French mutual fund and a QIB, buys 250,000 shares on January 15, and on February 1, it sells its shares to CalPERS, the California pension fund, pursuant to Rule 144A. Is this permissible? Can CalPERS resell, and to whom and when?

PROBLEM 7-26

Assume now that Small Co. in Problem 7-20 is a reporting company listed on the New York Stock Exchange. On January 30, 2017, it makes a Regulation S offering of its common stock in Europe through two American investment banks—Merrill, Sachs and Goldman, Lynch—acting as distributors. They sell 100,000 shares of Small Co.'s common stock to:

(a) the London office of the Hartford Insurance Co., which sells insurance in the U.K. subject to U.K. regulation;

(b) the Quantitative Fund, one of the U.S.'s largest hedge funds, in what purports to be a Rule 144A transaction; and

(c) a discretionary account managed by a large U.S. broker-dealer for Count Bernadotte, the billionaire Swedish industrialist.

Which of these sales is permissible under Regulation S?

PROBLEM 7-27

Small Co. has 100 million shares of its common stock outstanding after the above Regulation S offering, and its average weekly trading volume is 500,000 shares. The Little Fund, a small U.S. mutual fund that does not qualify as a QIB, purchased 2 million shares of Small Co. on January 31, 2017, from the Gallic Fund, a French mutual fund that acquired the shares in the original Regulation S offering by Small Co., but Little Fund quickly sours on its investment. On March 15, it sells 500,000 shares, on April 1, it sells 300,000 shares, and on April 30, it sells 400,000 shares—all on the New York Stock Exchange. Any problem here? What can it do?

PART III

REGULATION OF TRADING IN SECURITIES

THE SECURITIES EXCHANGE ACT OF 1934: AN OVERVIEW

The Securities Act of 1933 is a more or less coherent and unified statute directed almost entirely at two fundamental objectives: full disclosure in connection with the distribution of securities and the prevention of fraud in the sale of securities. The Securities Exchange Act of 1934 (the "1934 Act"), on the other hand, is something of a hodge-podge of different provisions, many of which are largely unrelated to each other. Over time, whenever there has been a crisis or a new challenge, Congress's typical response has been to amend the 1934 Act to deal with the new issue or problem. The two most recent examples are: (1) the 2001–2002 corporate governance and accounting scandals, which began with the Enron bankruptcy and resulted in the Sarbanes-Oxley Act of 2002; and (2) the 2008 financial meltdown, which ultimately produced the Dodd-Frank Act of 2010. Both these statutes have different focal points (Sarbanes-Oxley focused largely on accounting controls, while Dodd-Frank was more concerned with protecting the solvency of major financial institutions), but both led to significant revisions to the Securities Exchange Act.

Unlike the 1933 Act, the 1934 Act's primary focus is not on the issuance of securities, but on the secondary markets in which securities trade and on the provision of adequate and continuing disclosure to those trading in these markets. In order to ensure full and fair disclosure in these markets, the 1934 Act took a number of interrelated steps:

1. *The SEC.* The 1934 Act created the Securities and Exchange Commission to replace the less specialized Federal Trade Commission (which had originally been given jurisdiction over the Securities Act of 1933). Possibly, the intent of some was to substitute a more industry-friendly regulator, but the history of the SEC during the 1930's shows this hope to have been ill-founded.

2. *The Stock Exchanges.* The 1934 Act adopted a comprehensive system of federal regulation over the stock exchanges, including the specialists and broker-dealers who worked on them. Section 5 of the 1934 Act subjected all exchanges to an SEC registration requirement, and § 6 dictated that their rules, regulations, system of governance, and operating procedures meet certain public interest standards. These

provisions of the 1934 Act posed a potential barrier to the evolution of new electronic trading systems (in particular, entities known as "ECNs" and "Dark Pools") that functionally compete with traditional exchanges but that would have substantial difficulty in complying with many of the standards and conditions specified in § 6. The evolution of these new institutions was facilitated and shaped by a series of SEC rules, beginning with the SEC's Order Handling Rules in 1996,[1] continuing with Regulation ATS in 1998, and finally culminating in Regulation NMS in 2005 (which are all discussed in Chapter 10). These rules encouraged and enabled new entrants to compete with traditional market makers, changed the handling of order flow to introduce greater competition, but also required these new entities to register with the SEC as broker-dealers (although not as exchanges).

    3. *Speculation and Short Selling.* Because there was substantial concern in the 1930's about excessive speculation in the securities markets, §§ 7 and 8 established a system of margin regulation that placed controls over the amount of credit that could be extended to finance the purchase of securities. Similarly, § 9 authorized the SEC to prohibit manipulation and to restrict options trading, and § 10(a) gave the SEC power to regulate and restrict short-selling. Both options trading and short-selling were regarded in that Depression era as risky speculative practices that required close regulation in order not to destabilize the markets.[2] More recently, the Commission has both shown greater tolerance for short selling by adopting Regulation SHO, which exempts some heavily traded stocks from special rules that limited when short sales can be made to a rising stock market. Still, after the 2008 financial crisis, the SEC's attitude towards short selling seemingly changed, and it prohibited an abusive practice known as "naked short selling" in 2009. This topic is addressed in Chapter 11.

    4. *Self-Regulatory Organizations.* Another major focus of the 1934 Act involved granting the SEC jurisdiction over broker-dealers. Section 15 ("Registration and Regulation of Brokers and Dealers") of the 1934 Act was the first step in this direction, and it continues to serve as the SEC's authority for broad rules regulating broker-dealer conduct, operations, and financial condition (many of which are prophylactic rules that require no showing of fraud—such as the "net capital" rule). In 1938, a further and, to some extent, duplicative step was taken with the passage of the Maloney Act, which added § 15A to the 1934 Act. This provision established a system of self-regulation for broker-dealers paralleling that earlier created for the exchanges under §§ 5 and 6. Formally, § 15A provided for the registration of an association of broker-

---

[1] See Securities Exchange Act Release No. 37619A (September 6, 1996).

[2] This concern about excessive speculation in the securities markets may no longer rank high on the SEC's agenda, but it continues to be stressed by some commentators. See Stout, Are Stock Markets Costly Casinos? Disagreements, Market Failure, and Securities Regulation, 81 Va. L. Rev. 611 (1995). For a rejoinder, see Mahoney, Is There a Cure for "Excessive" Trading?, 81 Va. L. Rev. 713 (1995).

dealers that would act as a self-regulatory body. Only one such organization—the National Association of Securities Dealers ("NASD")—has ever been created under § 15A. In 2007, the NASD merged with the regulatory arm of the New York Stock Exchange to form the Financial Industry Regulatory Authority ("FINRA").[3] This merger had been sought by the larger broker-dealer firms, which were typically members of both bodies and believed that this subjected them to duplicative and sometimes conflicting regulatory standards. FINRA is currently governed by a Board of Governors of twenty-three members, with eleven governors being "public" members having no affiliation with the industry. Today (although not originally), all brokers and dealers who deal with the public must become members of FINRA, because § 15(b)(8) of the 1934 Act makes it "unlawful for any registered broker or dealer to effect any transaction in * * * any security * * * unless such broker or dealer is a member of a securities association registered pursuant to Section 15A of this title * * *."[4]

FINRA is not the only self-regulatory organization. The exchanges also enforce rules and administer disciplinary sanction. In 1975, two other SROs were created, one to monitor registered clearing agencies,[5] and the other—the Municipal Securities Rulemaking Board ("MSRB")—to establish rules regulating the conduct of municipal securities brokers and dealers with respect to transactions in such securities.[6] The net result is that all broker-dealers are as a practical matter subject to the active and overlapping oversight of at least two (and often three) monitors (the SEC's and at least one SRO), any one (or all) of which can take disciplinary action for violations of their rules. In 1975, Congress enhanced the authority of the SEC over its SROs by amending § 19(b) and (c) of the 1934 Act so that (i) any rule change proposed by an SRO must today be approved by the SEC in order to become effective, and (ii) the SEC may in its discretion "abrogate, add to, and delete from" the SRO's rules "as the Commission deems necessary or appropriate to insure the fair administration of the self-regulatory organization * * * [or] otherwise in furtherance of the purposes of this title * * * " Despite this enhanced power, the SROs are far from pawns of the SEC, and the relationship between the SEC and the exchanges (and, in the past, between the SEC and the NASD) have at times been adversarial.[7] This topic of self regulation is addressed in more detail in Chapters 10 and 11.

---

[3] This merger and the amendment of the bylaws and constitution of the former NASD had to be approved (and was approved) by the SEC. See Exchange Act Release No. 56,145, 72 Fed. Reg. 42,169, at 42,170 (July 26, 2007).

[4] There are some modest exceptions to this requirement, including one for a broker or dealer who effects transactions exclusively on a securities exchange of which it is a member.

[5] See § 17A of the 1934 Act. Clearing agencies handle the clearance and settlement of securities transactions and the safeguarding of investors' funds and securities in their custody.

[6] See § 15B of the 1934 Act. All municipal securities dealers, including banks, must register with the SEC. The MSRB is composed of fifteen members appointed by the SEC.

[7] In 1996, the SEC brought a disciplinary action against the NASD, which chiefly charged the NASD with inadequate supervision over dealers in the Nasdaq market who

The newest SRO is the Public Company Accounting Oversight Board, which was created by Congress in 2002 in the wake of a series of accounting scandals to supervise the standard setting process for auditing standards and to assume the disciplinary and investigative functions formerly handled by the accounting profession internally.

5. *The Continuous Disclosure System.* A principal focus of the 1934 Act was the creation of a continuous disclosure system for publicly held companies. Several different provisions of the 1934 Act combine to produce this continuous disclosure system. Section 12 requires the registration of "listed" or "reporting" companies. Section 13 requires such reporting companies to file certain periodic reports to keep current the information supplied in the initial registration statement. Section 14 and Regulation 14A thereunder, regulate the solicitation of proxies by registered corporations. Section 16 provides for the recapture of certain "short-swing" profits made in connection with short-term trading (i.e., less than six months) in the securities of their companies by officers, directors and 10% stockholders of registered corporations.

Prior to 1964, these various regulations applied only to corporations with securities listed on a national securities exchange. The Securities Acts Amendments of 1964 extended their application to certain publicly-held corporations whose securities were traded in the over-the-counter markets. For several decades, a company was required to register a class of equity securities with the SEC if, as of the last day of its fiscal year, that class was held of record by 500 or more holders *and* the issuer has more than $10 million in total assets.[8] Then, in 2012, intending to reduce regulatory costs for smaller companies, Congress passed the JOBS Act, which amended § 12(g) to require registration only when an issuer with $10 million in total assets also has a class of equity securities held of record by either (i) 2,000 persons, or (ii) 500 persons who are not "accredited investors" (as such term is defined in SEC rules).[9] As a practical matter, a company that wishes to list on an exchange will be required to register under § 12(b) of the 1934 Act, but those that do not so list will generally find that the 2,000 record ownership test gives them great latitude and will seldom, if ever, require 1934 Act registration. Still,

---

regularly "backed away" from filling orders placed by certain disfavored customers. This proceeding was related to more general allegations of collusive price-fixing by Nasdaq market makers that produced several large antitrust settlements. For the SEC's findings, see Report Pursuant to Section 21(a) of the Securities Exchange Act of 1934 Regarding the NASD and the NASDAQ Market [1996 Transfer Binder], Fed. Sec. L. Rep. (CCH), Para. 85,824 (Aug. 8, 1996).

[8] Total assets refers to the asset side of the balance sheet without any reduction for liabilities. Thus, a firm with $20 million in assets and $22 million in liabilities may be insolvent, but it is nonetheless covered and required to register if it has the requisite number of shareholders. See Rule 12g5–2.

[9] Section 501 of the JOBS Act added § 12(g)(1)(A) and (B) to the 1934 Act. In the case of an issuer that is a bank or a bank holding company, the alternative "accredited investor" test is not applicable, and only record ownership by 2,000 persons or more requires a bank or bank holding company to register. See § 12(g)(1)(B). The term "accredited investor" is defined in Rule 501 under the 1933 Act and was discussed earlier in Chapter 6. Insurance companies are also exempted from 1934 Act registration by § 12(g)(1)(G).

such unlisted issuers will need to maintain adequate records to demonstrate that they have less than 500 record shareholders who are not accredited investors, and, as a result, some issuers may adopt bylaws to preclude share transfers to non-accredited investors.[10]

Many believe that the use of a record ownership requirement for setting the threshold under § 12(g)(1) has arguably become dated at a time when most shareholders own shares beneficially, holding them in "street name" with their broker-dealer or bank (which facilitates a quick sale and easier market access). As a result, the new record ownership rule in § 12(g) potentially allows companies with thousands of beneficial shareholders and substantial assets to escape the SEC's continuous disclosure system. As a practical matter, however, companies with such a dispersed ownership almost invariably are listed on an exchange and so must register under § 12(b). The JOBS Act did not change the reporting obligations of listed companies. Principally, it has simplified life for companies that hope to conduct an IPO in the future, but were approaching the old 500 shareholder of record limit because of their use of stock options.[11]

Foreign private issuers are also permitted to avoid becoming reporting companies (to the extent they are not listed on an exchange) if they comply with the provisions of Rule 12g3–2, which requires them to provide the same information to the SEC as they file with their home country or home stock exchange or otherwise distribute (or are required to distribute) to their security holders. This exemptive rule encouraged some foreign issuers to trade only in the over-the-counter markets, not Nasdaq or the NYSE, to avoid 1934 Act registration. For the future, because unlisted foreign companies will be sheltered by the 2,000 shareholder of record test in § 12(g), they thus may not need to rely on Rule 12g3–2 to trade in over-the-counter markets.

Issuers may subsequently delist as "reporting" companies pursuant to Rule 12g–4 if the issuer's largest class of registered equity securities (i) is held of record by less than 300 persons, or (ii) is held by less than 500 persons and its total assets have not exceeded $10,000,000 on the last day of the issuer's three most recent fiscal years. In addition, foreign issuers may delist under Rule 12g–4(a)(2) if they have less than 300 persons resident in the United States who hold their equity securities of record.

Even if an issuer is not required to register by § 12(g), § 15(d) of the 1934 Act still requires most public companies to comply with the 1934

---

[10] See Securities Act Release No. 33–9693 (December 18, 2014). This Release also provided a non-exclusive safe harbor by which issuers can satisfy the less than 500 accredited investor test.

[11] Section 502 of the JOBS Act amended Section 12(g)(5) of the 1934 Act to exclude from the definition of "held of record" shares received by persons pursuant to an "employee compensation plan" in transactions exempt from registration. Thus, the combination of this provision and the 2,000 shareholder of record test ensures that few companies will be required to become "reporting" companies prior to their IPO.

Act's reporting requirements. It provides that an issuer that files a registration statement that becomes effective under the 1933 Act must thereafter comply with the periodic reporting requirements of § 13 of the 1934 Act—even if it does not have 2,000 shareholders of record. Thus, once a company does an initial public offering, it will be required to become a "reporting" company under the 1934 Act, regardless of whether it has the requisite number of shareholders of record. Foreign issuers (whether covered by § 12(g) or § 15(d)) do not, however, become subject to the 1934 Act's proxy rules or its "short-swing" trading provisions in § 16.[12] Finally, banks, bank holding companies, and savings and loan holding companies are able to terminate their registration under § 12(g) and suspend reporting under § 15(d) if the issuer's largest class of equity securities is held of record by less than 1,200 persons.[13]

Except in the case of certain highly regulated issuers (e.g., banks, insurance companies, savings and loan holding companies, and investment companies) who are exempted from § 12's reporting requirements, the basic effect of § 12 and § 15(d) is to subject those companies trading in public secondary markets to a continuing disclosure requirement. Such issuers are required to file an initial registration form (either on Form 8-A or Form 10) and thereafter to file annual and quarterly reports on Forms 10-K and 10-Q, respectively. Until the passage of the Sarbanes-Oxley Act in 2002, the 1934 Act's continuous disclosure system contemplated annual and quarterly filings, supplemented by only occasional "current reports" on Form 8-K. In response to Enron and related scandals in which highly material information reached the market only belatedly, the Commission in 2002 implemented a series of changes intended to shift this continuous disclosure system to a more current, "real time" basis. These changes both accelerated the filing deadlines for annual and quarterly reports and, more importantly, required many more events to be disclosed on Form 8-K, which must typically be filed within four business days (and sometimes only two business days) after the event.[14] The premise underlying these proposals is that additional and more timely disclosure by companies of significant events will diminish the opportunities for deception and earnings manipulation. Some of the changes were clearly driven by the accounting scandals of that era (Enron, WorldCom, and others) in which the impact of fundamental and questionable accounting policies has been hidden from investors.[15] Their impact (especially the

---

[12] See Rule 3a12–3 (exempting "foreign private issuer," as defined in Rule 3b–4, from proxy rules and § 16). Thus, the foreign issuer now has to comply with the annual and periodic reporting pursuant to § 13, but not the proxy rules, of § 14(a).

[13] See Securities Act Release No. 33–9693, supra note 10. This revision was legislatively mandated for banks and bank holding companies by Section 601 of the JOBS Act, and the Commission decided to treat savings and loan companies similarly.

[14] See Securities Exchange Act Release No. 46084 (June 25, 2002); Securities Exchange Act Release No. 45742 (April 12, 2002); Securities Exchange Act Release No. 45471 (April 23, 2002).

[15] Hence in 2002 the Commission adopted rules requiring enhanced disclosure of "critical accounting policies." See Securities Act Release No. 8098 (May 10, 2002). These disclosures are

four business day filing deadline) is to increase significantly the responsibilities of counsel—both in-house and outside counsel—to monitor, detect and report a broad series of events on a rapid and continuing basis.

Form 8-K normally requires disclosure within four business days after the occurrence of the event (and in a few cases within two business days).[16] The scope of what must be reported on Form 8-K has also been broadened so that, for example, any "material definitive agreement not made in the ordinary course of business" or any "direct financial obligation that is material to the registrant" must be promptly disclosed.[17] Taken together, these proposals show the Commission intent on recasting its system of continuous disclosure, shifting from periodic reports to constant "real time" reports. The Sarbanes-Oxley Act, enacted in the wake of the Enron, WorldCom, and related scandals, codified this SEC initiative, requiring reporting companies to disclose "on a rapid and current basis such additional information concerning material changes in the financial condition or operations of the issuer, in plain English, which may include trend or qualitative information . . ., as the Commission determines . . . is necessary or useful for the protection of investors and in the public interest."[18] In particular, the foregoing "plain English" requirement may necessitate changes in the style of financial reporting, especially in the footnotes to financial statements.

In addition, the Sarbanes-Oxley Act amended § 16(a) of the Securities Exchange Act to require that any change in the ownership of equity securities of an officer, director, or 10% beneficial owner of a reporting company be reported to the SEC on a Form 4 "before the end of the second business day on which the subject transaction has been executed." This two business day rule has already had considerable significance because it effectively precludes the backdating of stock options (a practice that was not widely known at the time of Sarbanes-Oxley's enactment).[19] Those wishing to backdate options had to file late under § 16 and thereby signal to the SEC the possibility of an irregularity.

6. *Criminal Enforcement of the Continuous Disclosure System.* In response to a series of scandals involving financial irregularity, Congress

---

required in the "Management Discussion and Analysis" section of both a registration statement and annual and quarterly reports.

[16] See Form 8-K, General Instruction B.

[17] See Items 1.01 and 2.03 of Form 8-K.

[18] Section 409 ("Real Time Issuer Disclosures") of the Sarbanes-Oxley Act added a new Section 13(*l*) to the 1934 Act containing this language.

[19] One study estimates that 23% of options granted prior to August 29, 2003 to top executives pursuant to at-the-market stock option plans were "backdated or otherwise manipulated," but only 10% of the options granted after that date were similarly tainted. August 29, 2003 was the date that the two business day filing period under § 16(a) took effect. See Randall A. Heron and Erik Lie, "What Faction of Stock Option Grants to Top Executives Have Been Backdated or Manipulated?" (Working Paper July 14, 2006). The implication then is that greater transparency does reduce the incidence of fraud.

required in 2002 that the chief executive and chief financial officer of every reporting company certify under oath with respect to periodic reports containing financial statements that are filed pursuant to Section 13(a) or 15(d) of the 1934 Act that "the information contained in the periodic report fairly presents, in all material respects, the financial condition and results of operations of the issuer." Although criminal penalties already existed for knowingly filing false information with the Commission, this new provision—18 U.S.C. § 1350—deliberately adds to the formality of the process and requires the senior officers to accept personal responsibility. However, liability attaches only to knowing or willful violations, and hence corporate officials can continue to defend on the grounds that they were deceived by subordinates. The developing practice seems to be that the certifying senior officials will demand parallel certifications from line officials beneath them with responsibility for divisional financial statements. Note that the mandated certification makes no reference to "generally accepted accounting principles" (or "GAAP"), thus suggesting that financial statements prepared in accordance with GAAP could still be found not to "fairly present" the issuer's financial condition or results of operations.

7. *The National Market System.* In 1975, in the most comprehensive revision of the 1934 Act to that point, the Securities Acts Amendments of 1975 sought to integrate and encourage competition among the various market systems that were then rapidly evolving. Some of the impetus for this legislation was technological, as new trading systems (Nasdaq and alternative trading systems) had only recently appeared; also, institutional investors were just arriving on the scene as a major force and were clamoring for changes. More fundamental, however, was Congress's desire to encourage competition by ending the long prevailing system under which brokerage commissions were set by the regulatory fiat of the exchanges and not by market forces. To most, minimum brokerage commissions, imposed by the exchanges, looked suspiciously like price fixing in the guise of regulation. Section 6(e) of the 1934 Act effectively ended fixed commissions as of May 1, 1975, and under competition, brokerage rates declined radically almost overnight. In addition, § 11A of the 1934 Act, adopted as part of these 1975 amendments, specified criteria by which the SEC was instructed to oversee the national market system. Fundamentally, § 11A endorses a philosophy of multiple competing (but linked) markets in preference to a single centralized marketplace (which might have otherwise evolved from the starting point of the New York Stock Exchange).

In the late 1990's, following disclosures that Nasdaq dealers had failed to compete, but rather had seemingly developed collusive customs and procedures that maintained artificially wide spreads in the secondary market for Nasdaq-traded securities, the Commission adopted new "Order Handling Rules" under § 11A in an attempt to encourage competition. As discussed in Chapter 10, these rules had the impact of encouraging the appearance and growth of alternative trading systems (including "dark pools") that now account for a significant fraction of the trading in equity securities. Although the appearance of these new alternative trading systems has given rise to a host of new issues, these changes have also been accompanied by a major reduction in the spreads quoted in secondary markets (and hence to the cost of trading). The SEC's efforts to implement its vision of a national market system in a world now populated by these alternative trading systems culminated in 2005 with its adoption of Regulation NMS, which is reviewed next in Chapter 8. Simply put, the impact of Regulation NMS has been transformational. Also, it has again proven the Law of Unintended Consequences. Largely because of Regulation NMS, the NYSE has shrunk from a near monopolist to a relatively inconsequential (and low profit) player in the securities marketplace.

8. *Accounting Reform.* The Sarbanes-Oxley Act significantly restructured the regulation of the accounting profession. First, Title I of this Act creates the Public Company Accounting Oversight Board (the "PCAOB") under the aegis of the SEC to oversee the audit of public companies.[20] Accounting firms that audit publicly held companies are required to register with it, and the board is authorized to establish auditing, quality control, ethics, independence and related standards that will be binding on such firms. The lead audit partner for every client must be rotated every five years in an effort to preclude "clubby" relationships between the client and auditor, but the Sarbanes-Oxley Act stopped short of requiring mandatory rotation of the audit firm (although a further study of this possible reform was required). The PCAOB is given investigative and disciplinary powers over both accounting firms and their associated persons that are roughly comparable to those given FINRA over the brokerage industry. In particular, the PCAOB is instructed to conduct a continuing program of inspections to assess the degree of compliance by each registered public accounting firm with the rules of the PCAOB and the SEC. This is intended as a substitute for the accounting profession's long-standing system of "peer review," under which selected audits of each accounting firm were periodically reviewed by a comparable firm for compliance with professional standards. The Sarbanes-Oxley Act also prohibits public accounting firms from providing nine specified types of consulting services to audit clients in the belief

---

[20] Because the Sarbanes-Oxley Act gave the power to appoint the PCAOB's five board members only to the SEC and made the PCAOB's board members removable for cause only by the SEC (and not by the President), this unique status gave rise to constitutional challenge. Those seeking to invalidate the PCAOB claimed that this structure infringed the President's appointment power under the Constitution and also the separation of powers. In Free Enterprise Fund v. Public Company Accounting Oversight Board, 130 S.Ct. 3138 (2010), the Supreme Court largely upheld this structure, but did find it impermissible for Congress to have placed "dual for-cause" limitations on the President's power of removal (i.e., the President could only remove the SEC's Commissioners "for cause" and they in turn can only remove PCAOB board members for cause). Although the Court invalidated this provision on separation of powers grounds, the net effect was only to enable the SEC to remove PCAOB members without cause. In other respects, the validity of SEC appointment of PCAOB members was affirmed.

that the pursuit of such revenues compromises the firm's independence.[21] It further requires that the audit committee of a public corporation's board of directors be "directly responsible for the appointment, compensation, and oversight" of the auditor (including the resolution of any disagreements between management and the auditor regarding financial reporting). The auditor must report directly to the audit committee, and the Sarbanes-Oxley Act mandates that the audit committee approve any other services that the audit firm is to provide to the corporation. In short, the Sarbanes-Oxley Act seems to vest sole responsibility for the choice, compensation, dismissal, and oversight of the audit firm in the audit committee, to the exclusion of the management and possibly the full board and the shareholders. To this extent, the Sarbanes-Oxley Act overrode any contrary state corporation law.

Although the PCAOB has been generally regarded as a success, the Trump Administration proposed in early 2020 that its functions be merged back into the SEC and the independent agency abolished, allegedly as a cost-saving measure.[22]

9. *Attorneys and Other Professionals.* The Sarbanes-Oxley Act was potentially as sweeping in its treatment of lawyers. The Sarbanes-Oxley Act requires the SEC to promulgate rules governing the professional responsibilities of attorneys practicing before it. In particular, Section 307 of the Act mandates the SEC to adopt rules that require an attorney to "report evidence of a material violation of securities laws or breach of fiduciary duty or similar violation by the company or any agent" to the corporation's chief legal officer or chief executive officer. If those persons do not take appropriate action, the rules similarly require that the evidence be reported to the audit committee or some similar committee of independent directors. This provision, added late in the statute's passage by a floor amendment, appears to have been a response to a rejection of similar rules proposed by an ABA Task Force by the American Bar Association's House of Delegates in 2001.

The Sarbanes-Oxley Act also required the promulgation of SEC rules restricting analyst conflicts of interest and protecting analysts from internal retaliation because of negative research reports or ratings. Independently, the SEC adopted Regulation AC ("analyst certification")

---

[21] The prohibited services include: (i) bookkeeping services related to accounting records or financial statements of the client; (ii) financial information systems design and implementation; (iii) appraisal or valuation services, including fairness opinions; (iv) actuarial services; (v) internal audit outsourcing services; (vi) management or human resources services; (vii) broker-dealer or investment banking services; (viii) legal or expert services related to the audit; (ix) any other service that the Board deems impermissible. Most of these categories of consulting activities had earlier been prohibited to auditors by SEC rules, adopted two years earlier after a long and contentious battle between the SEC and the accounting industry. Notably still not covered is the provision of tax advice, which audit firms have long provided to their audit clients.

[22] For a critique of this proposal by a former SEC Chairman, see Arthur Levitt, "Without An Independent Watchdog, Who Will Audit the Auditors?," The Wall Street Journal, February 20, 2020 at A-17.

in 2002, to require analysts to certify that the views they express are their own and not the product of pressure from investment banking personnel or clients.[23]

10. *The Credit Ratings Agencies.* In 2006, Congress enacted the Credit Rating Agency Reform Act of 2006 (the "CRARA") to accomplish two basic purposes: (1) to encourage new competitors to enter the credit rating market, which had long been dominated by three firms (Moody's, Standard & Poor's, and Fitch), and (2) to authorize the SEC to exercise greater oversight over the credit rating agencies, whose failure to anticipate the bankruptcies of Enron and WorldCom (until just days before their respective filings) had elicited considerable criticism and a sense that the agencies were compromised by the fact that their revenues came from the corporations that they rated. CRARA added new Section 15G to the Securities Exchange Act, which establishes procedures for credit rating agencies that wish to be treated as "Nationally Recognized Statistical Rating Organizations" (or "NRSROs") to register with the SEC. Both because of SEC rules and the rules of other regulators relating to pension funds and commercial banks, many institutional investors can only purchase debt securities if they are rated "investment grade" by an NRSRO. The procedure created by Section 15G was intended to encourage new entrants to become NRSROs, and it limited SEC discretion in the belief that the SEC, perhaps fearing a "race to the bottom," had long resisted recognizing new NRSROs.

CRARA also requires a credit rating agency registering with the SEC to disclose its general methods and procedures in its application and to establish written policies "to address and manage any conflicts of interest that may arise from such business." The SEC is also given authority "to prohibit, or require the management and disclosure of, any conflicts of interest relating to the issuance of credit ratings" by NRSROs.[24] CRARA, however, denies the SEC any authority to regulate the "substance of credit ratings or the procedures or methodologies by which any ... [NRSRO] determines credit ratings."[25]

Passed in 2006, a year before the subprime mortgage crisis surfaced in 2007, CRARA was less a response to the apparent inflation of debt ratings associated with collateralized debt obligations (or "CDOs") than to the oligopolistic power of the Big Three ratings agencies. Ratings inflation was, however, a focus of the Dodd-Frank Act, passed in 2010 in the wake of the 2008 financial meltdown, which statute greatly enhanced the SEC's supervisory powers over the ratings agencies. These provisions were discussed earlier in Chapter One, but they still leave the SEC

---

[23] Regulation AC requires analysts to certify the truthfulness of their views in research reports and public appearances and to disclose whether they have received any compensation related to the specific recommendation provided in those reports or appearances. See SEC News Digest Issue 2002–144 (July 26, 2002).

[24] See Section 15G(h)(2), 15 U.S.C. § 78o–7(h)(2).

[25] See Section 15G(c)(2), 15 U.S.C. § 78o–7(c)(2).

without power to review the substantive methodologies used by the ratings agencies.

11. *The Williams Act.* In 1968, the Williams Act (named after its sponsor, Senator Harrison A. Williams) was enacted to add Subsections (d) and (e) to Section 13 and Subsections (d), (e) and (f) to Section 14 of the 1934 Act. These provisions regulate tender offers and certain other corporate control transactions by requiring the offeror to prepare and file a disclosure document prior to making a tender offer and to disclose acquisitions above the 5% level of any class of the equity security of any "reporting" company registered under §§ 12(b) or (g). Most (but not all of its provisions) are limited to tender offers for, or acquisitions of, equity securities of "reporting" companies. Recurrent litigation has surrounded the definition of "tender offer," which the Act does not define, and the scope of the "best price" rule which requires the bidder to pay the same price to any holder that it pays to some holders. Chapter 10 reviews the Williams Act's requirements in detail.

12. *Brokers and Investment Advisers.* Although the Dodd-Frank Act was not primarily aimed at broker-dealers or investment advisers, it did attempt to address a long-standing tension between them. As a result of a Supreme Court decision,[26] investment advisers owe a fiduciary duty to their clients. But the obligations of brokers to their clients are largely determined by state law (and the states are fundamentally split, with many states holding that brokers only owe a fiduciary duty to their clients when the broker holds discretionary trading authority).[27] The Dodd-Frank Act instructed the SEC to study this area and find a common standard for brokers and investment advisers.[28] After some study and much lobbying, the SEC finally crafted a compromise in 2019, adopting a package of rulemakings and interpretations intended to enhance the quality and transparency of retail investors' relationship with their brokers and investment advisers. At the center of this new regulatory approach is Regulation Best Interest,[29] which establishes new standards of conduct for brokers and investment advisers. This topic is covered in Chapter 9, but a political controversy continues as to whether these changes are truly substantive or largely cosmetic.

13. *Other Provisions.* Even prior to the 2002 Act, the 1934 Act was the subject of significant revisions in 1986, 1995, and 1996. The Government Securities Act of 1986 eliminated the exemption for government securities brokers and dealers, which chiefly applied to commercial banks. A new § 15C of the Exchange Act provides for their registration and regulation. Registered securities brokers and dealers under § 15 and municipal securities dealers under § 15B that also act as

---

[26] See SEC v. Capital Gains Research Bureau, Inc., 375 U.S. 180 (1963).

[27] This topic is covered in Chapter 11, but for a representative case, see DeKwiatkowski v. Bear Stearns & Co., 306 F.3d 1293 (2d Cir. 2002).

[28] See Section 913 of the Dodd-Frank Act of 2010.

[29] 17 C.F.R. § 240.15*l*–1 (2019).

government securities brokers and dealers must notify their appropriate regulatory government agencies that they are a government securities broker or dealer. The Federal Reserve Board, the Secretary of the Treasury and the SEC now share regulatory authority over government securities brokers and dealers. In 1995, Congress passed the Private Securities Litigation Reform Act of 1995, chiefly to curb perceived abuses in the securities class action field. This Act added § 21D ("Private Securities Litigation") and § 21E ("Application of Safe Harbor for Forward-Looking Statements"), whose impacts are reviewed in later chapters.

14. *Blue Sky Laws and SEC's Exemptive Authority.* Finally, as described earlier in Chapter 1, the balance of power between state and federal regulators was significantly altered by the National Securities Markets Improvements Act of 1996, which curtailed the authority of state regulators, both with regard to the registration of public offerings, brokers and investment advisers. That Act also added § 28 to the 1933 Act and § 36 to the 1934 Act, which each granted the SEC broad exemptive authority, permitting it to override express provisions of these statutes to the extent the SEC finds such an "exemption is necessary or appropriate in the public interest, and is consistent with the protection of investors." As a result, today the SEC has broad authority to deregulate and potentially could supercede, or grant exemptions regarding, virtually any provision in the 1933 or 1934 Acts.

CHAPTER 8

REGULATION OF THE SECURITIES MARKETS

Statutes and Regulations

Exchange Act, §§ 3(a)1, 5, 6, 11, 11A, 15(c), 15A, 17A, 19, and 28(e).

Regulation ATS.

Regulation NMS.

1. INTRODUCTION: CHANGE IN THE MARKETS

Once upon a time, the world of securities markets was settled and stable. Around the globe, exchanges had de facto monopolies, protected by national boundaries from international competition, and thus were able to enjoy the quiet life. In most cases, they were run as not-for-profit, club-like enterprises in the interests of their various constituencies—i.e., brokers, specialists, and listed firms. Today, two of the dominant forces reshaping the modern world—globalization and technological change—are also reshaping the securities markets. Globalization has created international competition among markets, and both the NYSE and Nasdaq have actively competed not only to solicit foreign firms to list, but also to acquire a foreign exchange or exchanges. Virtually all exchanges have privatized and are today run not as private clubs, but as profit-maximizing businesses. Foreign listings on the NYSE peaked at around 17% in 2002, but since then have declined as the Sarbanes-Oxley Act (and other factors) raised at least the perceived costs of a U.S. listing to foreign firms.

Technology has had a similarly destabilizing impact, giving rise to new electronic trading markets: most notably, electronic communications networks (or "ECNs") and "dark pools", which are each described in more detail below. From only a 9% market share of Nasdaq trading in 1996, ECNs grew to account for 40% of Nasdaq trading by 2003, but since have declined just as significantly in volume, in part yielding to an even newer variety of alternative trading system, known as "dark pools."[1] Increasingly, rival trading centers—exchanges and alternative trading systems—compete in terms of speed of execution and the incentives they offer to traders to post limit orders on them.

But the greatest factor inducing change in the markets has been regulation. If one turns the clock back only twenty years, trading in

---

[1] See Daniel Gray, The Essential Role of Regulation In Promoting Equity Market Competition, 1 Brook. J. Corp. Fin. & Com. L. 395, 403 (2007).

equity securities could be fairly described with the following generalizations:

1. Trading in an issuer's stock largely occurred on only one trading venue (typically, the NYSE or Nasdaq), as exchanges competed for the listing of stocks, but not for trading in the same stock.

2. The customer's order went to an intermediary (either the specialist on the NYSE or the market maker on Nasdaq) who executed the order. Although the specialist at the NYSE might auction the customer's order off to traders on the NYSE's trading floor (and could only, itself, trade with the customer if no one else on the floor was willing to trade), trades would generally occur within the bid/asked spread set by the specialist. This process was manual and slow.

3. Both the NYSE and Nasdaq held a near monopoly in the trading of the stocks they listed. Other trading venues were unable to attract significant volume (in part because markets with greater volume could offer superior prices).

4. Exchanges were owned by the brokers who held "seats" on them, and Nasdaq was owned by the National Association of Securities Dealers (which was the regulatory association to which virtually all brokers belonged). Arguably, this "clubby" arrangement may have restricted the incentive of exchanges and Nasdaq to compete or innovate (as their owners may have been primarily interested in maintaining a profitable brokerage business).

Today, this has all changed. Specialists have disappeared, and traditional market makers have receded into the background and play no more than a modest, marginal role. The dominance of both the NYSE and Nasdaq has ended. New exchanges have appeared and have attracted trading volume, based on more rapid technology and the controversial practice of paying for order flow. At present, there are twenty-three registered stock exchanges, but this number is somewhat misleading as many of these exchanges are owned by three principal owners.[2] No one of these exchanges accounts for more than 25% of the trading in the market (the NYSE has 25% and Nasdaq has 20%). Most stocks (although they typically list on only one exchange) trade on many of these markets.

---

[2] Those principal owners are: the NYSE, Nasdaq, and Cboe Global Markets Inc. ("Cboe"), which stands for "Chicago Board Options Exchange" and which owns four exchanges. Nasdaq acquired several of the principal regional exchanges, including the Boston and Philadelphia Stock Exchanges; the NYSE acquired the American Stock Exchange, and the Cboe (which operates the largest U.S. options exchange) acquired both the Chicago Stock Exchange and BATS Global Markets; BATS had been a new and ambitious stock exchange operator that ran four U.S. stock exchanges (and others outside the U.S.) until it encountered operating problems and sold out in 2017. As later discussed, new stock exchanges continue to register with the SEC, including in 2020.

So, where then does the rest of the trading occur? Nearly 40 dark pools share a constantly fluctuating volume that is currently around 15% of total market volume.[3] The remaining trading (around 20 to 25%) is largely internalized trading (that is, a broker will trade its own customers' buy and sell orders against each other at the NBBO (the National Best Bid and Offered prices that are constantly posted under SEC rules). Or (and most commonly), it will sell its order flow to another broker or dark pool that will similarly execute these trades at the NBBO.[4]

This raises an even more basic question: if the specialist and the market maker have largely disappeared, who trades with the retail customer or the institutional investor who wishes to buy or sell stock? The short answer is that a new and largely unregulated market participant—the high-frequency trader (or "HFT")—now appears on the buy or sell side of about 50% of all trades.[5] They have largely replaced the specialist and the market maker, and they trade based on algorithms that they program into their computers to respond to new information so that their quotes are adjusted on a second by second basis. But to understand their role, one first has to understand that each trading venue (exchange or alternative trading system) participates in a national electronic limit order book where a computer matches incoming marketable orders from retail and institutional traders with standing limit orders posted earlier by other traders (mainly, the HFTs). In this environment, the HFTs are the principal suppliers of liquidity (or the "makers" of liquidity in industry parlance), while the retail and institutional customers are the "takers" of liquidity. Roughly three-quarters of all trades are executed in such open limit order books, with most of the remaining trading involving "internalization" (i.e., a broker matching the buy and sell orders of its own retail customers at the prevailing NBBO price without taking the orders to any exchange).

But, what motivates the HFT trader to post limit orders (both in good times and bad). Here, the initial answer is that the exchanges offer them compensation for doing so. Customers of the exchange (both retail and institutional) pay a modest fee to the exchange for trading there. The exchange in turn pays most of this fee to the HFT trader who posts a limit order—but only when that limit order to buy or sell posted by the HFT trader is accepted by the customer. In these transactions, the HFT trader is referred to as the "maker" (because it in theory provided the liquidity) and the customer who traded against this limit order is known as the "taker" (because it took the offered liquidity). This approach—known as the "maker/taker" system—has largely replaced the older

---

[3] See Rhodi Preece, Dark Pools, Internalization and Equity Market Quality, CFA Institute Codes, Standards, and Position Papers 12–15 (2012).

[4] Id.

[5] Who are these HFT traders? Two of the largest and best known are Citadel Securities LLC and Virtu Financial Inc. Both are relatively young firms, founded in 2001 and 2008 respectively, that have grown to great size and profitability by finding a new way to make markets.

systems of a specialist serving as an auctioneer or of competing market makers.

It is not simply the expected rebate from the exchange (paid by the "taker" in its fee to the exchange) that motivates the HFT trader to offer liquidity. It also believes that it has better information about the direction of the market than other traders. In particular, HFTs receive a timing advantage that allow them to access the market more quickly than other traders. Specifically, they are permitted (for a fee to the exchange) to place their computer servers very close to the exchange's servers so that their orders are received first by the exchange. They also rent special computer lines from the exchanges and other trading venues so that they receive earlier news of orders reaching the exchange and transactions executed at the exchange. These practices—"colocation" (the placement of a high frequency trader's server next to the exchange's server) and private feeds (which enable these traders to learn of incoming orders ahead of all others)—make possible a trading strategy known as "latency arbitrage." This practice is further described later in this Chapter, but, to illustrate, assume that orders reach different exchanges a fraction of a second apart and that high frequency traders know from experience that when a large order (to buy or sell) reaches one exchange, it is likely that other orders within a fraction of a second will reach other exchanges (probably because an institutional trader wants to spread its buying or selling across multiple exchanges to minimize its price impact). Using its timing advantages based on colocation and special feeds, the high frequency trader can send out orders to the other exchanges that will arrive ahead of these other orders. Thus, it might decide to buy ahead of expected buy orders or to raise its own "asked" price that it previously posted. In this way, institutional investors will be surprised that available "asked" prices that they see on their trading screen vanish before they can intersect with them. In effect, even the buyer who placed the initial order may be "front run" by the high frequency trader before it can buy on multiple exchanges. This accounts for the vanishing quotations and seemingly illusory prices that are at the center of Michael Lewis's "Flash Boys" critique of current market structure.[6]

Whether such practices are fair or desirable certainly can be debated, but one impact of the new "maker/taker" system for providing liquidity is that price spreads have further narrowed.

Indeed, this tendency for new developments to reduce trading costs has been a consistent phenomenon. For example, when electronic communication networks (or ECNs) first appeared in the 1990s, the effective spreads on Nasdaq stocks quickly declined by approximately

---

[6] Much controversy was stoked by the publication of Michael Lewis's FLASH BOYS: A Wall Street Revolt (2014), which alleged that the stock market was being "manipulated" by high frequency traders based on their superior access to information and executions. At bottom, the phenomenon involved here is latency arbitrage.

30%.[7] Perhaps it should not surprise that the entry of new competitors improved both prices and the quality of services. But what enabled these new competitors to enter the market for equity trading services and succeed so quickly? Historically, new competitors had faced steep barriers to entry into this market. One of the oldest axioms about securities markets is that "liquidity attracts liquidity." That is, as a market gains increased trading volume in a stock, liquidity improves, thereby enabling the market to offer superior prices at lower costs. Economists call this a "network effect,"[8] because each new user of the market increases the value of the market to both existing and prospective users. Because the dominant market will continue to attract liquidity, competition between markets is difficult to maintain. Thus, the two major stock exchanges—the NYSE and Nasdaq—long competed only for listings, but did not compete over the trading in individual stocks.

Multiple factors explain the rapid changes in equity market structure (including increased competition and technology), but probably the leading factor was regulatory change. Three episodes stand out, and are next discussed:

A. THE IMPACT OF REGULATION ON MARKET STRUCTURE

1. *The 1975 Amendments.* The driving force behind the 1975 amendments to the Securities Exchange Act was the Congressional desire to end the system of fixed brokerage commission rates set by the New York Stock Exchange for transactions on it. Although this system had been in effect since the founding of the New York Stock Exchange in 1792, the dealers who held seats on the NYSE effectively held the power to set a mandatory commission rate and thereby preclude price competition. The Supreme Court had found such a system to be lawful because the SEC had "primary jurisdiction" over the securities markets and had long tolerated this system.[9] Yet, even if "lawful" price fixing was tolerable to the Court, it was not to Congress, and the 1975 amendments added § 6(e) to the Securities Exchange Act which prohibited any system of fixed commissions, effective as of May 1, 1976 (a date known to the brokerage industry as "May Day").[10]

Although the industry had predicted that such a tough reform would cause many brokerage firms to fail because they could not survive in a fully competitive environment, exactly the opposite happened. As brokerage rates fell, trading by investors went up, resulting in an increase in aggregate commission revenues. In effect, regulation and

---

[7] See Securities Exchange Act Release No. 42,450 (Feb. 23, 2000), 65 Fed. Reg. 10,577 at 10,584.

[8] See Larry Harris, TRADING AND EXCHANGES: Market Microstructure for Practitioners, 526, 535–36 (2003).

[9] See Gordon v. New York Stock Exchange, 422 U.S. 659 (1975), which is set forth infra at p. 697.

[10] See Section 6(e) of the Securities Exchange Act of 1934, 15 U.S.C. § 78f.

increased competition saved the industry from the costly mistake of fixed (and inflated) commissions.

Less noticed at the time, but at least equally important, was the adoption of Section 11A ("National Market System for Securities") as an amendment to the Securities Exchange Act. It both specified criteria that the SEC was to follow in shaping a "National Market System" and expressed a preference for the "linking of all markets for qualified securities through communication and data processing facilities" over the growth of a single market to absorb all trading (which would have been the NYSE).[11] The criteria specified by Congress deserve special attention. Section 11A(a)(1)(C) provides:

"It is in the public interest and appropriate for the protection of investors and the maintenance of fair and orderly markets to assure—

(i) economically efficient execution of securities transactions;

(ii) fair competition among brokers and dealers, among exchange markets, and between exchange markets and markets other than exchange markets;

(iii) the availability to brokers, dealers, and investors of information with respect to quotations for and transactions in securities;

(iv) the practicability of brokers executing investors' orders in the best market; and

(v) an opportunity, consistent with the provisions of clauses (i) and (ii) of this subparagraph, for investors' orders to be executed without the participation of a dealer."[12]

Although the goals of Section 11A seemed laudable, there were sharp tensions among them. Subparagraph 11A(a)(1)(C)(v) called for fostering an "opportunity" for transactions that did not involve a dealer. This was possible on the NYSE where the specialist could match buyers and sellers and on new private markets (most notably Instinet) where institutional investors could directly communicate with each other, but not on Nasdaq (where all orders were entered on the Nasdaq screen by dealers).

Progress towards a "national market system" was slow prior to 2000. Nasdaq, which had only been formed in 1971, grew rapidly, but mainly by acquiring new listings (especially in high-tech industries, which preferred an "electronic" market to the still largely manual NYSE). Regional exchanges—such as Boston, Philadelphia, and Chicago—were unable to attract sufficient liquidity to offer superior prices and thus they specialized either in smaller, local companies or in options (which the NYSE did not trade).

---

[11] See Section 11A(a)(1)(D) of the Securities Exchange Act of 1934, 15 U.S.C. § 78k–1.

[12] See Section 11A(a)(1)(C) of the Securities Exchange Act of 1934, 15 U.S.C. § 78k–1.

2. *The Nasdaq Collusion Scandal and the SEC's Response.* A major scandal that cast a shadow over Nasdaq broke in 1994 when evidence surfaced that Nasdaq dealers were collusively maintaining artificially wide bid/asked spreads on Nasdaq stocks. Specifically, two finance professors published an academic study that concluded that Nasdaq market-makers were purposefully avoiding odd-eighth quotes (that is they would only quote prices in quarter point intervals) in order to widen the spread.[13] In effect, by declining to trade on the odd eighths of a point, dealers were collectively conspiring to maintain the spread at a minimum of a quarter of a point. Tape recordings subpoenaed by the SEC and the Department of Justice suggested that such a pricing convention had developed, and the broker dealers who violated it were subjected to threats and intimidation. All told, the practice resembled a massive price-fixing conspiracy to maintain artificially wide bid/asked spreads on Nasdaq. Although this issue was never resolved in court, the major market makers settled a private class action by paying a then record $1.1 billion settlement in 1997. In 1996, the SEC censured the NASD[14] and forced a formal reorganization under which the latter's regulatory functions were placed in a separate subsidiary, NASD Regulation, Inc., in order to maintain their independence.

This episode also faced the SEC with a dilemma: if thousands of brokers had failed to compete for an extended period, how could it restore competition among brokers that did not want to compete? It needed to develop a new source of competition, and to this end, it invented the "Electronic Communications Network" (or "ECN"). Recognizing that institutional and public customers could potentially compete with dealers, and thereby narrow spreads, the SEC developed an ingenious order handling procedure for introducing greater competition into the Nasdaq market. Assume for the moment that 20 dealers trade a Nasdaq stock, each quoting a bid and asked price. Assume next that the highest "bid" price is $20 and the lowest "asked" price is $20.25. If this spread of 25 cents between the highest bid and the lowest asked price (which is known in the market's jargon as the "NBBO" for "national best bid and offer") is still artificially wide (as it seems here, where the spread is 25 cents), how can it be feasibly narrowed? Under the SEC's Order Handling Rules, customers were enabled to place a "limit order" to buy or sell a stock at a price between the bid/asked spread.[15]

---

[13] See William Christie & Paul Schultz, Why Do NASDAQ Market Makers Avoid Odd-Eighth Quotes 49 J. Fin. 1813 (1994) A voluminous literature followed provided alternative interpretations and theories.

[14] See Report Pursuant to Section 21(a) of the Securities Exchange Act of 1934 Regarding the NASD and the Nasdaq Market, See Exch. Act Rel. No. 37542 (August 8, 1996). Section 21(a) authorizes the Commission to publish reports of its investigations. This report found that the NASD had failed adequately "to comply with certain NASD rules and, without reasonable justification or excuse, to enforce compliance with the Exchange Act and the rules and regulations thereunder." Id. at *1 to *2.

[15] A "limit order" is an order to buy or sell a stock at a specific price. Alternatively, a customer can enter a "market order": namely, orders to buy or sell at the best available price in the market. Adopted in 1996, Rule 604 ("Display of Customer Limit Orders") of Regulation NMS

Customers could not place limit orders on the Nasdaq screen on their own; they had to use an ECN to do this (in part because retail customers might default). Effectively, the SEC's Order Handling Rules recognized the ECN and gave the customer the ability to use the ECN to post a price inside the dealer's spread. The customer does this by entering what is known as a "limit order" at any price and in any quantity that the customer wishes on the ECN.[16] Other customers can search through these posted limit orders and decide to accept (in whole or in part) any such order. For example, suppose that for a particular stock the highest bid price on Nasdaq was $10 per share and the lowest asked price was a $10.10 per share (i.e., a spread of 10 cents, which was once common, but today would be unusually wide).[17] A customer not satisfied with buying or selling at these prices could instead post a limit order to buy (or sell) a specified quantity of shares at $10.05 on an ECN, and the ECN would match this order with any counterparty willing to sell (or buy) at this price, or at a better price. Thus, if Sarah posted a limit order to buy at $10.05, a seller entering a market order would be matched with her order. Or, if Bill had earlier entered a limit order to sell at $10.04, these two transactions would be matched, and both would do better than if they had traded at the dealers' best posted prices on Nasdaq. In short, ECNs offered customers a means of improving on the dealer's price to their mutual benefit.

But there is one downside to using an ECN: prices could change and the customer's posted offer might never be hit. That is, suppose Sarah again posts a limit offer to buy at $10.05 per share and there are no corresponding offers to sell at this price or a lower price in the system.

---

now requires market makers on Nasdaq and exchange specialists, as well, to display customer limit orders that improve the inside spread (but it does not require a market maker to accept a limit order). Most major market makers will accept limit orders, and limit orders now outnumber market orders.

[16] Traditionally, most orders, both in auction markets and dealer markets, were "market orders"—i.e., orders to buy or sell at the best available price in the market. "Limit orders" are instead orders for a specified quantity and at a specific price that may be away from the current market price. Once, limit orders were primarily used as a form of insurance (the customer might go away from the market—for example, on vacation—and want to protect itself from any market decline). Sometimes, the customer was shopping for a better price. Today, however, limit orders are primarily the means by which HFT traders provide liquidity to the market.

[17] It may be useful here to add a word on market terminology. Suppose the limit order book for a hypothetical stock (Widget Corporation) looks as follows:

Bids		Offers	
Price	Shares	Price	Shares
10.00	500	10.10	600
9.58	600	10.11	600
9.56	500	10.12	400
9.54	400	10.15	400

In market terminology, this market would be described in shorthand as "10.00 to 10.10, 500 by 600," meaning that the best bid was 10.00 (with a total 500 shares available at that price) and the best offer was 10.10 (with a total of 600 shares available at that price). This description leaves out much information that would greatly interest the institutional investor (for example, how much more stock is available at slightly higher or lower prices—i.e., information about the "depth" of the market).

Possibly, a new trader might later search this ECN and find Sarah's superior price and trade with her. But it is also possible that the "asked" price of the stock might rise to $10.20 based on new information that reaches the market, in which case Sarah's offer will not be executed. That is her choice and her risk: either to post a limit order on an ECN or to send a "market order" to her broker who will search Nasdaq for the then best available price.

The rapid growth of the ECNs was directly attributable to this SEC policy change: the adoption of the Order Handling Rules.[18] Prior to these rules, the trading in Nasdaq stocks was divided principally between two markets: (i) the public dealer market (or Nasdaq), and (ii) a private agency market operated by the original forerunner of the ECNs, Instinet, on which institutions could trade with each other. The public traded on Nasdaq, and its prices reflected only market maker quotations. Institutions tended to trade on Instinet (which also operated on an "after hours" basis when Nasdaq was closed), and Instinet frequently offered better prices and narrower spreads, but these prices were only available to Instinet subscribers who traded with each other without the intervention of a dealer. In response, the Order Handling Rules required Nasdaq market makers to include in their quotes (or send to others that would do so) customer limit orders that improved on their own published quotes. Thus, in our earlier example in which Sarah placed an order to buy at $10.05 that was midway between the best bid price of $10.00 and the best asked price of $10.20, the ECN would enter her bid on the Nasdaq screen and thereby change the inside spread to $10.05 (bid) and $10.10 (asked). Essentially, this rule change allowed customers to place their limit orders on the Nasdaq screen where other customers could accept them, thereby allowing public orders to interact with public orders, as they had regularly done on the NYSE. In hindsight, these reforms were highly successful (although they were controversial at the time) and introduced greater price competition, as a host of new ECNs were quickly formed to exploit this new technique.

The implication of this example is that competition in the securities markets does not arise automatically, but tends to be the product of regulatory actions that foster it. The SEC had long sought to promote competition in the trading markets through a variety of tools. These included: (1) insisting upon price transparency, (2) assuring non-discriminatory access to markets; and (3) imposing a duty of best execution upon brokers. Price transparency permits a non-dominant market to compete by enabling it to assure its customers that its prices are as good as those obtainable elsewhere. Non-discriminatory access precludes the dominant market from forbidding its traders to trade elsewhere. The duty of best execution requires brokers to search for the best market to which to take their customers' orders.

---

[18] See "Order Execution Obligations," Securities Exchange Act Release No. 37,619A, 61 Fed. Reg. 48,290 (Sept. 12, 1996).

The next step towards an integrated, national stock market was Nasdaq's introduction in 2002 of an electronic trading system, called SuperMontage.[19] Effectively, this system converted Nasdaq into an electronic limit order book. Under it, dealers posted their own limit orders, with which customer limit orders competed. The former privileged position of dealers as the only source of quotations on Nasdaq was abandoned. The NYSE had earlier adopted an automated small order execution system, which was gradually expanded. The specialist continued to supply some of the liquidity on the NYSE until 2008, when the NYSE largely eliminated specialists.[20] They survive in a limited fashion (but are today known as "designated market makers") with their primary role being running the opening and closing auctions each trading day. Thus, as of no later than 2008, both the NYSE and Nasdaq had become essentially electronic limit order markets.

3. *Regulation NMS*. Although the Order Handling Rules and later changes at the NYSE increased competition, they still did not bring the NYSE and Nasdaq into actual price competition. The SEC's next (and more controversial) step was taken in 2005, when the SEC adopted Regulation NMS, which includes a "trade-through" rule that generally prevents a market from executing trades at prices inferior to automated quotes that are displayed in other markets.[21] Effectively, this required the automated routing of orders to the market displaying the best quotation. Once this was done, the NYSE, Nasdaq, regional exchanges, and alternative trading systems were all trading in one consolidated limit order book. The unforeseen consequences of this rule are examined later in this chapter.

Increased competitive pressure had one further impact on the world of exchanges: the old "clubby" world of exchanges organized as not-for-profit entities gave way to a more entrepreneurial environment in which exchanges have been privatized (or "demutualized" in the industry's preferred term) so that they are now owned by shareholders. In Europe, the major exchanges were privatized in the 1990s. Proponents of privatization argued that shareholder control would simplify the internal decision-making process within exchanges, making exchanges more focused on profit maximization and more effective competitors. In the absence of privatized ownership, a variety of constituencies might

---

[19] See Securities Exchange Act Release No. 34–19,858 (June 9, 1983). See also David Lipton, Governance of our Securities Markets and the Failure to Allocate Regulatory Responsibility, 34 Cath. U. L. Rev. 397 (1985); Mark Biondi, Market Making in the Electronic Age, 32 Loy. U. Chi. L. J. 815, 869 (2001).

[20] See Sec. Exch. Act Release No. 58,845 (October 24, 2008) (discussing the NYSE's transition from "specialists" to "designated market makers").

[21] See Exchange Act Release No. 51,808 (June 9, 2005) (adopting Regulation NMS). Rule 611 ("Order Protection Rule") is the "trade-through" rule adopted by Regulation NMS. See 17 C.F.R. § 242.611. It requires "trading centers" to "establish, maintain and enforce written policies and procedures that are reasonably designed to prevent trade-throughs on that trading center . . ." A "trade-through" arises when a security is traded on one trading venue at a price inferior to an available price on another exchange or trading venue.

contend for influence, and each might hold veto powers over the exchange's decisions, thereby producing paralysis. But, as seat holders turned into shareholders and exchanges became for-profit entities, concerns next arose about the self-regulatory responsibilities of exchanges. Regulation is not a profit center, and a for-profit corporation may have limited interest in serving as a regulator, or may be conflicted in the case of firms that are its clients. Thus, in the demutualization process, the SEC has sought to insulate and assure adequate funding for the self-regulatory arm of exchanges (most notably, by creating FINRA— the product of the merger in 2007 of the NASD and the NYSE's regulatory arm).[22]

As privatization converted exchanges into profit-maximizing entrepreneurial entities, one of the first moves of both the NYSE and Nasdaq was to buy the ECNs that had competed most aggressively with them. Nasdaq acquired Instinet and Brut, both successful ECNs. The NYSE went public in 2005 by means of a merger with Archipelago Holdings Inc. ("ARCA"), which had been an ECN until it effectively acquired the Pacific Coast Stock Exchange in 2000. The NYSE operates ARCA as an independent market; thus, it functions more like an ECN than a traditional exchange. Next, in 2007, the new parent corporation created by this merger, the NYSE Group, Inc., acquired Euronext N.V., which operated stock exchanges in Paris, Brussels, Amsterdam, and Lisbon (and also a futures exchange in London). Finally, in 2013, the Intercontinental Exchange ("ICE"), a primarily derivatives exchange founded in 2000, acquired the NYSE, ending the independent existence of an exchange that traced its roots to 1792.

The internal structure of markets has also changed, with significant convergence occurring. Although it has long been conventional to distinguish dealer or "quote-driven markets" from auction or "order-driven markets," both have moved in recent years to a hybrid model. As discussed above, customer limit orders now can be posted on the Nasdaq screen. Conversely, the vast majority of trades on the NYSE, an auction market, are now executed on an automated basis without any specialist matching buy and sell orders. The originally sharp differences between "order driven" and "quote driven" markets began to blur in the late 1990's when the SEC adopted its "Order Handling Rules" that permit persons other than dealers to transact with public customers in the Nasdaq market. Correspondingly, when Regulation NMS was adopted in 2005, the SEC required the NYSE to offer automated, electronic execution for

---

[22] For succinct reviews of these developments, see Roberta Karmel, Turning Seats Into Shares: Causes and Implications of Demutualizations of Stock and Futures Exchanges, 53 Hastings L. J. 367 (2002); Andreas Fleckner, Stock Exchanges at the Crossroads, 74 Fordham L. Rev. 2541 (2006); Norman S. Poser, The Stock Exchange of the United States and Europe: Automation, Globalization and Consolidation, 22 U. Pa. J. Int'l Eco. L. 497 (2001); Reena Aggarwal, Demutualization and Corporate Governance of Stock Exchanges, 15 J. App. Corp. Fin. 105 (2002).

most transactions, which its institutional customers (who wanted faster executions) had long desired.

Another dramatic change from these developments has been the significant narrowing in the size of the average spreads in the equity markets. Once, an eighth of a point (that is, 12.5 cents) was the minimum increment in which securities were quoted, and spreads of a quarter to a half point were normal, even in the case of widely traded stocks. Since April 9, 2001, all U.S. equity markets by law have been quoting stocks in decimals. Today, spreads are often as narrow as one cent and have tended to average approximately 1.9 cents in the more actively traded stocks.[23] This dramatic reduction in spreads, which constitute the principal component in investors' trading costs, has been the direct result of successful SEC policy initiatives, most importantly its Order Handling Rules, which are discussed below.

The evolution of trading mechanisms in the securities markets continued. A variation on the ECN model—known as "dark pools"—has become increasingly popular over the last decade. Originally, they allowed institutions to trade with each other on a basis that was intended to protect their anonymity (because large institutions feared that by exposing trading interest they would be front run or otherwise move the market in a manner adverse to them). Dark pools (and there are now over forty of them, mostly operated by large broker-dealers) are alternative trading systems that differ from ECNs in that their best-priced quotations are not included within the consolidated quotation data disseminated to the market, but remain hidden from public customers. In short, they disclose their trades, but not their quotes. The anonymity they offer to the institutional trader is probably their primary attraction to traders. Yet, the significant undisplayed trading interest on such trading systems poses a basic policy tradeoff: dark pools may offer superior prices, but they also exclude the public (and others) and may arguably produce reduced transparency. As a result, the SEC has proposed changes, discussed later in this chapter, that may require increased transparency on their part.

Once exchanges and alternative trading systems were locked into a truly centralized market (as Regulation NMS effectively did), the largest market no longer had a natural superiority. Instead, the tactical question became: how could rival markets attract those traders most willing to improve the NBBO spread and thereby automatically win transactions under Regulation NMS, which prohibited "trade-throughs"—i.e., transactions on one market inferior to quoted prices on another market. In short order, some trading venues began to experiment with rebates, which were paid by the market center to those traders willing to post

---

[23] See Securities Exchange Act Release No. 44568 (July 18, 2001) at *1 n. 3 (citing Nasdaq Decimalization Impact Study at 2, 15–16).

limit orders on them.[24] Relatively quickly, these practices evolved into what is now known as the "maker/taker system"—under which trading venues (i.e., exchanges and dark pools) pay the provider of liquidity (the "maker") a fee each time a limit order that it posts on that market is accepted by a "taker" of liquidity (basically a trader who places a market order that is matched in the trading venue's limit order book with that limit order).[25] These rebates to the "maker" are paid by the exchange or alternative trading center out of "access" fees charged by the market to the "taker" of liquidity. Thus, in reality, the "taker" pays the market center, which pays most of that fee to the "maker." The "access fee" that can be charged to the "taker" is restricted by Regulation NMS,[26] and this ceiling in effect limits what can be paid to both the "maker" and the market center (as no market would rationally pay the "maker" more than it receives from the "taker"). Thus, the SEC's rules under Regulation NMS effectively amount to rate regulation (not unlike that of a public utility commission), which limits the total compensation payable in the maker/taker system.

The new competition among market centers has also forced exchanges, dealers, and ECNs to reconsider their business models. Clearly, they operate secondary trading markets, but they also generate and sell information (price quotations and transaction reports) both to vendors who disseminate such information to the market and the HFTs (who pay for "co-location" and private data feeds that enable them to receive information ahead of the rest of the market). This production of price and trade information accounts for a significant proportion of the revenues of exchanges and dark pools, and the entitlement to such information is increasingly producing conflicts, litigation and political jockeying for position among market participants. In particular, because HFTs pay substantial amounts for "co-location" services and private data feeds that represent a significant proportion of the revenues of these trading venues, HFTs may acquire disproportionate influence at exchanges and other trading venues. These problems are further assessed later in this chapter.

4. *A Summary.* What was the bottom line impact of Regulation NMS? Most believe that it did cause the relative decline of the NYSE, as once all exchanges were linked in a consolidated limit order book, its size and greater liquidity no longer mattered. Most (but not all) also believe that Regulation NMS encouraged the appearance of high frequency

---

[24] See Stanislav Dolgopolov, The Maker-Taker Pricing Model And Its Impact on The Securities Market Structure: A Can of Worms for Securities Fraud?, 8 Va. L. & Bus. Rev. 231 (2014).

[25] Technically, the trading venue pays for each non-marketable limit order that it receives and that is executed upon. Id. No payment would be made for a limit order that was at the inside spread (because it is equivalent to a market order). Some markets (but very few) have an alternative "taker/maker system" under which the taker is paid a fee, while the maker posting a limit order pays the access fee. Id.

[26] See Rule 610(c) of Regulation NMS, 17 C.F.R. § 242. 610(c) (capping "access fees" at $0.003 per share for stocks trading at $1.00 per share or more).

traders. Once one exchange began to pay rebates to such traders, other exchanges had little choice but to comply.

Even more fundamentally, Regulation NMS required all traders to buy or sell at the best offered price, and thereby ignore other possible considerations, such as the quickest executions or the greatest reliability of the offered price being available. Arguably, investors had previously weighed all these variables, before Regulation NMS ruled that price must be the dominant consideration.

More generally, stock exchanges (including both the NYSE and Nasdaq) no longer appear to be playing any significant role in corporate governance. This may be partly attributable to Regulation NMS, but even more so to privatization. Once exchanges became owned by value-maximizing shareholders, they lost interest in enforcing corporate governance standards (which paid little in the way of return to shareholders).

Finally, in the wake of Regulation NMS, there has been a significant increase in the number of U.S. exchanges. Still, a skeptic might respond that some of these exchanges have been short-lived and none have yet been able to attract significant listings. This may reflect the earlier-noted "network effect" that benefits established exchanges, such as the NYSE and Nasdaq, because listings seem to attract listings. Possibly, the best example here is the short life cycle of BATS Global Markets, which began as an ECN in 2005, became a registered exchange in 2008, negotiated mergers, and soon accounted for 10–12% of equity trading volume. Yet, it was not able to attract listings, and when it encountered operational problems, it sold out to the Cboe in 2017.

Other new exchanges have aimed at attracting a narrower audience. Two examples show this:

 1. The Investors Exchange ("IEX"), which was the focus of Michael Lewis's FLASH BOYS, sought to distinguish itself by adopting a "low latency" policy that slowed trading time to discourage HFT traders and thus protect institutional investors. Although it accounts for 3% of U.S. equity trading, IEX has only been able to attract a single listing (which later returned to Nasdaq).

 2. The Long-Term Exchange, which received SEC approval to register as an exchange in 2019, seeks to attract new IPO issuers by allowing them to use "tenured voting" under which shareholders gain additional votes the longer they hold their shares. Its hope is that this incentive will attract new high-tech companies, as it may protect them from takeovers and hedge fund activism. To date, this exchange has not attracted listings, but it only began to operate in August, 2020.

The only current threat to the domination of the NYSE and Nasdaq is a brand new exchange, approved by the SEC in 2020, known as the

Members Exchange ("MEMX"), which was organized by major brokers, HFT traders, and institutional investors (including Fidelity, Morgan Stanley and Citadel Securities). Its goal is to greatly reduce trading cost to those who trade on it (and who organized it). Only one prediction can be made with confidence here: competition has increased and more new entrants are possible.

B. CRITIQUES OF CONTEMPORARY MARKETS

In 2014, Michael Lewis, a best-selling author with a special interest in Wall Street, published FLASH BOYS: A Wall Street Revolt, which essentially pronounced the equity markets to be "rigged" in favor of HFTs, dark pools, and other insiders. His accusations hit a nerve with the public and have resulted in a series of investigations and hearings. But is the market "rigged"? Here, it is necessary to consider both sides of this story after first identifying the critical new players and practices.

1. *Favoritism Toward High Frequency Trading?* Some new exchanges have reduced their response times to less than 1 millisecond, and soon trading is likely to occur in nanoseconds. Although all exchanges are required to report their quotations and transactions to centralized consolidators, who make it publicly available, exchanges can also sell this data to private subscribers, who as a practical matter can obtain this data and respond to it a fraction of a second faster than if they relied upon the centralized display. Further, these exchanges may offer "co-location services" that allow HFTs to place their computer servers physically next to the exchange's matching engine—again giving the HFTs the ability to act on new market information a millisecond faster than other traders. Predictably, such time advantages translate into profit, and this helps to explain the rapid growth of certain new exchanges (such as BATS and Direct Edge), which specialized in serving such traders. None of this could have happened, however, without Rule 611's prohibition of trade-throughs.

As an example showing the importance and value of time advantages, traders were willing to pay up to $6,000 per month for two-second early access to the University of Michigan Consumer Survey, which was released by Thomson Reuters. Although two seconds may not sound like much of an advantage, one academic paper estimates that the full advantage of the information was impounded into stock prices in as little as 15 milliseconds (and no more than 200 milliseconds) after Thomson Reuters released the information to paying subscribers.[27] For reference, an eye blink takes 300 milliseconds.

2. *"Latency Arbitrage."* Probably the practice that has been most controversial and that FLASH BOYS most criticized is politely called "latency arbitrage" (or, less politely, "electronic front running"). Assume

---

[27] See Grace Xing Hu, Jun Pan, Jiang Wang, "Early Peek Advantage?," 126 J. Fin. Econ. 399 (2017).

that an HFT has purchased "co-location" at the major exchanges and dark pools and also has private data feeds from each. This enables it to learn about transaction occurring on each exchange or dark pool and also to learn about orders reaching the exchanges, sooner in each case than other traders. It can now cancel outstanding orders and submit new orders in less than a millisecond. Suppose next that a large institutional investor wishes to sell a large block of stock (say, one million shares), and it prudently breaks up this order into smaller orders and sends them to every exchange in order to avoid any concentrated impact on any one exchange. Inevitably, this institutional trader's order will reach one exchange first. There, it will be detected by the HFT's co-location facility, which is equipped with algorithms that enable it to recognize that such an order is statistically associated with other similar orders reaching other exchanges. The HFT's computer recognizes that this pattern implies a likely price decline in the stock. On this assumption that other sell orders are on route to other exchanges, the HFT's computer can automatically exploit this knowledge by both (i) sending sell orders to other exchanges that arrive before the institutional trader's original sell orders, and (ii) cancelling any buy orders it had in the stock and substituting only a lower buy order in anticipation of a likely price decline. All this can occur in as a little as a millisecond. Thus, its sell orders will be executed first before the price decline in the stock, and it can lower its bid price to buy at a lower price after the decline, thereby making an arbitrage profit.

Note, however, that this is not classic "frontrunning" because the HFT owes no duty to the institutional trader. Still, it is profiting from its earlier knowledge and ability to trade almost instantaneously. Many see this as unfair, but defenders point out that because the HFT can profit in this fashion it will continue to post limit orders that narrow the bid/asked spread. From their perspective, narrow bid/asked spreads require that we in effect subsidize HFTs in this fashion, enabling them to realize trading profits so that they will compete to post limit orders with narrow spreads. But at what point is the subsidy too high? Also, although some HFTs seem primarily interested in the rebates they receive from trading venues for providing liquidity, others seem more interested in trading profits based on their ability to trade in as little as a millisecond.

3. *"Dark Pools."* As discussed above, significant markets with real liquidity now exist that are not included in the consolidated quotation data for NMS stocks that is disseminated to the public. The justification for permitting a "dark pool" not to disclose quotations on it is that this enables large institutional traders to protect their anonymity and avoid front-running. That is, they can attempt to withhold from the market their desire to sell a million shares in Widget Corp and simply submit limit orders at the midpoint of the bid/asked spread to several dark pools, knowing that their undisclosed, but marketable, limit orders will interact

with any new market orders that come to the dark pool. Thus, they can sell without their large order triggering a market reaction

This may be a legitimate desire, but the Commission has become concerned that such undisplayed or "non-public" trading interest could result in reduced transparency, market fragmentation, and potentially a two-tiered market system. In response, it proposed to redefine the terms "bid" or "offer" so as to include "indications of interest" (or "IOIs"), which are messages, functionally resembling quotations, that dark pools privately send to certain market participants, indicating immediately exercisable trading interest on them.[28] As a practical matter, the recipient of an IOI knows that if the dark pool is indicating that it has actionable trading interest available on it in a specific NMS stock, then the price has to be at least equal to the NBBO (because trade-throughs are forbidden by Rule 611 of Regulation NMS, both on exchanges and alternative trading systems). The Commission's proposal would have forced IOIs to be displayed on the consolidated quotation system (although it would exempt IOIs for very large orders in a NMS stock).[29] This proposal, however, has not been adopted.

In addition, the SEC proposed in this same release to revise the order display requirements in Regulation ATS. Currently, an ATS must only display its best-priced orders when its average daily trading volume in the particular security exceeds 5%. Although Release 60997 proposed to lower that threshold to 0.25% of average daily trading volume,[30] this proposal has also not been adopted. FINRA has, however, proposed its own rules to require more disclosures by ATSs.[31]

Conversely, there is the alternative possibility that institutional investors have been victimized by dark pools. Unlike other markets, dark pools can and do exclude those traders they do not want to deal with, and some have traditionally excluded HFTs on the ground that their rapid trading amounted to front running that injured the dark pools' institutional clients. Institutional traders often want to avoid trading venues populated by HFTs. But it is expensive for trading venues to exclude HFTs that are willing to pay large amounts for co-location services. In a much publicized suit in 2014, the New York Attorney General brought an action against Barclays alleging that it had misrepresented the extent to which its dark pool was free of HFT

---

[28] See Securities Exchange Act Release No. 60997 ("Regulation of Non-Public Trading Interest") (November 13, 2009).

[29] To accomplish this goal, Release 60997 proposed to redefine the terms "bid" and "offer" in Rule 600(b)(8) of Regulation NMS to include most IOIs; thus, under Rule 602 of Regulation NMS and Rule 301(b)(3) of Regulation ATS, these IOIs would have to enter the consolidated quotation system.

[30] This proposal would have amended Rule 301(b)(3)(i)(B) of Regulation ATS.

[31] FINRA is considering whether to amend FINRA Rules 4552, 6150, 6170, 6480 and 6720 to require ATSs to report to FINRA at least weekly their volume information and number of trades.

trading.³² On disclosure of these allegations, many institutions ceased to use Barclay's dark pool. In short, many market participants have grievances and doubt that the current system fully protects their interests.

4. *"Pinging" and "Spoofing."* Market participants have adverse interests. Although institutional investors want to hide their undisplayed buying or selling interest (and so use dark pools to do so), other participants (most obviously HFTs) want to discover this undisplayed liquidity. One technique they use to discover that hidden liquidity is known as "pinging." An HFT may send a very small (say 100 share) order to a dark pool at the midpoint of the spread for a stock to discover if there is undisplayed liquidity there. If its order is immediately accepted, this active trader now knows that there is hidden liquidity there and may automatically adjust its algorithmic trading. Of course the dark pool could refuse to accept such a small order (but its loyalty may be at least as much to the HFTs as to its institutional traders).

HFTs are also vulnerable to predatory behavior. Because their trading is automatically triggered by market events to which their algorithms respond, aggressive traders sometimes attempt to cause these programs to respond by submitting orders that are almost immediately cancelled (but not before they trigger the HFTs algorithms). This practice is known as "spoofing," which is defined by the Commodity Exchange Act to mean making a bid or offer "with the intent to cancel the bid or offer before execution."³³ The Dodd-Frank Act amended the Commodity Exchange Act to criminalize "spoofing" in the commodities markets,³⁴ and in 2016, a commodities trader was convicted under this statute for such conduct.³⁵ Conceivably, similar prosecutions could be brought under Rule 10b–5. Should Rule 10b–5 be extended this far?

5. *Exotic Orders.* Order types are instructions traders use to tell an exchange how a buy or sell order should be executed (immediately or only under certain contingencies). Critics believe that HFTs sometimes use esoteric order types to gain advantages over other traders. The most controversial order types—known as "Hide and Slide" and "Hide Not Slide"—were developed by Direct Edge, a dark pool that converted itself into an exchange, and it permits those who use it (primarily HFTs) to ensure that their orders will be filled ahead of earlier entered orders.³⁶

---

³² See People ex rel. Schneiderman v. Barclays, 47 Misc. 3d 862 (2015). This suit was brought pursuant to the New York Blue Sky statute, known as the "Martin Act." For a review of this pending litigation, see David Beehler and Thomas Berndt, "Lawsuits Reveal Risks Lurking Below Surface of Dark Pools," Law360 (September 4, 2014).

³³ See 7 U.S.C. § 6c(a)(5)(C) (Commodity Exch. Act § 4c(a)(5)(C)).

³⁴ Id.

³⁵ See United States v. Coscia, 177 F.Supp.3d 1087 (N. D. Ill. 2016). For an overview, see "DOJ's 1st Anti-Spoofing Prosecution Reflects 2 Trends," Law360, October 23, 2014. Prior to this defendant's indictment, the CFTC had first settled with him (a prominent commodities trader) under a settlement that required him to pay $3.7 million in penalties. Id.

³⁶ See Scott Patterson, "How One Whistleblower Turned the Tables on High Frequency Traders," Wall Street Journal Blog, August 6, 2014 (describing whistleblower complaints filed

Although any trader could in theory use a "sliding" order (or other variants), most are unaware of their existence, which the exchange may communicate only to favored clients. In 2014, the SEC reached a settlement involving a substantial penalty with BATS over its use of exotic order types that gave favored clients faster execution than other clients.[37]

2. THE NATIONAL MARKET SYSTEM: WHOSE INTERESTS DESERVE PRIORITY?

Statutes and Regulations

    Exchange Act, § 11A.

    Regulation ATS.

    Regulation NMS.

The 1975 Securities Acts Amendments, which ended fixed brokerage commissions, contemplated much greater changes than simply the abolition of fixed commissions. They envisioned a national market system that would ensure investors competitive markets and "best execution" of their trades and otherwise satisfy the aspirational goals set forth in Section 11A of the Securities Exchange Act.

In theory, the competition among markets would prevent specialists on the then primary exchanges (NYSE or AMEX) from charging monopolistic prices for trading in listed securities. Bid and asked spreads in listed securities would tighten in the face of competitive pressure. In practice, however, active price competition did not develop between market centers (at least to the extent the Commission had hoped). Until recently, only a lesser form of competition developed between market centers: namely, competition for stock listings (particularly among high technology stocks that became the subject of continuing battles between Nasdaq and the NYSE).

What explains the initially limited progress toward price competition? At best, the 1975 Securities Act Amendments had an incomplete vision of what a national market should look like. Many believe that the five goals listed above in § 11A are in considerable tension. For example, the narrowest spread and the maximum degree of liquidity are inversely related. Market makers will not expend large amounts of capital to handle a large order when the spreads (which represent their profit from trading) are razor thin. Instead, they will break a large order up into smaller units, thereby providing less liquidity and also delaying the execution of the customer's order. At this point,

---

by Haim Bodek, a former high speed trader, which resulted in SEC sanctions against Direct Edge.

    [37] See Scott Patterson, "BATS Faces Big Trading Fine—Potential SEC Settlement Over Treatment of Investors May Be for Record Amount," The Wall Street Journal, December 5, 2014 at C-1.

different consumers of the market's services can have different definitions of what the optimal market system should look like. For example, institutional customers typically prefer high liquidity to the narrowest possible price spread, while retail customers (who trade in small volumes) logically have the reverse preference.

One answer to these differing preferences might be different markets for different investors, letting each use the market of its choice. But this solution would raise the SEC's deepest fear: market fragmentation—namely, the concern that as new market centers sprang up, securities could come to trade at different prices in different markets at the same time. Also, fragmented markets might imply an overall loss in market efficiency.

For the SEC, the greatest challenge in the design of the national market system has been the tension between its desire to foster competition and its fear of market fragmentation. This issue came to a head as the NYSE and Nasdaq began to trade the same securities, based on different trading systems and rules. In general, Nasdaq is a more automated market and can execute orders quicker. But the NYSE's auction system permits public orders to trade with each other without the intervention of a dealer and at prices that often are between the bid/asked spread. A particularly controversial difference between the two markets was their treatment of "trade-throughs" (i.e., trades at prices inferior to the inside bid and asked spread (or "NBBO" for "National Best Bid and Offer")). For a considerable time, a fierce lobbying battle saw institutional and retail investors on opposite sides. Could one exchange trade a security at a price inferior to the best available price on another exchange? Prior to Regulation NMS, this was common and was justified as necessary to encourage faster executions and greater liquidity. The Commission's final position, adopted in 2005, is explained below:

Securities Exchange Act Release No. 51808
Securities and Exchange Commission.
June 9, 2005.

REGULATION NMS

* * *

B. NMS Principles and Objectives

1. Competition Among Markets and Competition Among Orders

The NMS is premised on promoting fair competition among individual markets, while at the same time assuring that all of these markets are linked together, through facilities and rules, in a unified system that promotes interaction among the orders of buyers and sellers in a particular NMS stock. The NMS thereby incorporates two distinct types of competition—competition among individual markets and competition among individual orders—that together contribute to efficient markets. Vigorous competition among markets promotes more efficient and innovative trading services, while integrated competition among orders promotes more efficient pricing of individual stocks for all types of orders, large and small. Together, they produce markets that offer the greatest benefits for investors and listed companies.

Accordingly, the Commission's primary challenge in facilitating the establishment of an NMS has been to maintain an appropriate balance between these two vital forms of competition. It particularly has sought to avoid the extremes of: (1) isolated markets that trade an NMS stock without regard to trading in other markets and thereby fragment the competition among buyers and sellers in that stock; and (2) a totally centralized system that loses the benefits of vigorous competition and innovation among individual markets. Achieving this objective and striking the proper balance clearly can be a difficult task. Since Congress mandated the establishment of an NMS in 1975, the Commission frequently has resisted suggestions that it adopt an approach focusing on a single form of competition that, while perhaps easier to administer, would forfeit the distinct, but equally vital, benefits associated with both competition among markets and competition among orders.

. . .

The difficulty, however, is that competition among multiple markets trading the same stocks can detract from the most vigorous competition among orders in an individual stock, thereby impeding efficient price discovery for orders of all sizes. The importance of competition among orders has long been recognized. Indeed, when Congress mandated the establishment of an NMS, it well stated this basic principle: "Investors must be assured that they are participants in a system which maximizes the opportunities for the most willing seller to meet the most willing buyer." To the extent that competition among orders is lessened, the quality of price discovery for all sizes of orders can be compromised. Impaired price discovery could cause market prices to deviate from fundamental values, reduce market depth and liquidity, and create excessive short-term volatility that is harmful to long-term investors and listed companies. More broadly, when market prices do not reflect fundamental values, resources will be misallocated within the economy and economic efficiency—as well as market efficiency—will be impaired.

2. Serving the Interests of Long-Term Investors and Listed Companies

In its extended review of market structure issues and in assessing how best to achieve an appropriate balance between competition among markets and competition among orders, the Commission has been guided by a firm belief that one of the most important goals of the equity markets is to minimize the transaction costs of long-term investors and thereby to reduce the cost of capital for listed companies. These functions are inherently related because the cost of capital of listed companies is influenced by the transaction costs of those who are willing to accept the risk of holding corporate equity for an extended period.

. . .

The objective of minimizing short-term price volatility offers an important example where the interests of long-term investors can diverge from those of short-term traders. Deep and liquid markets that minimize volatility are of most benefit to long-term investors. Such markets help reduce transaction costs by furthering the ability of investors to establish and unwind positions in a stock at prices that are as close to previously prevailing prices as possible. Indeed, the 1975 Senate Report on the NMS emphasized that one of the "paramount" objectives for the NMS is "the maintenance of stable and orderly markets with maximum capacity for absorbing trading imbalances without undue price movements."

Excessively volatile markets, in contrast, can generate many opportunities for traders to earn short-term profits from rapid price swings. Short-term traders, in particular, typically possess the systems capabilities and expertise necessary to enter and exit the market rapidly to exploit such price swings. Moreover, short-term traders have great flexibility in terms of their choice of stocks, choice of initially establishing a long or short position, and time of entering and exiting the market. Long-term investors (both institutional and retail), in contrast, typically have an opinion on the long-term prospects for a company. They therefore want to buy or sell a particular stock at a particular time. These investors thus are inherently less able to exploit short-term price swings and, indeed, their buying or selling interest often can initiate short-term price movements. Efficient markets with maximum liquidity and depth minimize such price movements and thereby afford long-term investors an opportunity to achieve their trading objectives with the lowest possible transaction costs.

The Commission recognizes that it is important to avoid false dichotomies between the interests of short-term traders and long-term investors, and that many difficult line-drawing issues potentially can arise in precisely defining the difference between the two terms. For present purposes, however, these issues can be handled by simply noting that it makes little sense to refer to someone as "investing" in a company for a few seconds, minutes, or hours.

Short-term traders and market intermediaries unquestionably provide needed liquidity to the equity markets and are essential to the welfare of investors. Consequently, much, if not most, of the time the interests of long-term investors and short-term traders in market quality issues such as speed and operational efficiency will coincide. Indeed, implementation of Regulation NMS likely will lead to a significant expansion of automated trading in exchange-listed stocks that both benefits all investors and opens up greater potential for electronic trading in such stocks than currently exists. But when the interests of long-term investors and short-term traders conflict in this context, the

Commission believes that its clear responsibility is to uphold the interests of long-term investors.

. . .

In assessing the current state of the NMS and formulating its rule proposals, the Commission has focused on the interests of these millions of Americans who depend on the performance of their equity investments for such vital needs as retirement security and their children's college education. Their investment returns are reduced by transaction costs of all types, including the explicit costs of commissions and mutual fund fees. But the largely hidden costs associated with the prices at which trades are executed often can dwarf the explicit costs of trading. For example, the implicit transaction costs associated with the price impact of trades and liquidity search costs of mutual funds and other institutional investors is estimated at more than $30 billion per year. Such hidden costs eat away at the long-term returns of millions of individual mutual fund shareholders and pension plan participants. One of the primary objectives of the NMS is to help reduce such costs by improving market liquidity and depth. The best way to promote market depth and liquidity is to encourage vigorous competition among orders. As a result, the Commission cannot merely focus on one type of competition—competition among markets to provide trading services—at the expense of competition among orders. The interests of U.S. long-term investors and listed companies require that the NMS continue to promote both types of competition.

---

1. *What Did Regulation NMS Actually Do?* In 2005, after years of debate, the SEC adopted its new governing rule for the national market system, but only by a closely divided 3–2 vote. Why the controversy? The political answer is that different interest groups wanted different things—all of which are inherently desirable. Regulation NMS's most controversial provision is its "trade-through rule" (Rule 611), which requires trading centers to establish, maintain and enforce written policies and procedures reasonably designed to prevent the execution of trades in NMS securities at prices inferior to "protected quotations" displayed by other trading centers.

On the practical level, this implied that Nasdaq had to seek to prevent trades on it that were inferior to the NBBO.[38] Why did this rule

---

[38] Rule 611 requires policies and procedures reasonably designed to prevent the execution of trades at prices inferior prices to "protected quotations" from other trading centers. A "protected quotation" is defined by Rule 600 to mean a quotation in a NMS stock that "is displayed by an automated trading system" and "that is the best bid or best offer" of a national securities exchange or Nasdaq. Thus, if the bid/asked spread on Nasdaq for a particular stock were initially $12 bid and $12.15 asked and then an ECN placed a limit order to buy at $12.05, this bid, even if for a small amount, would become the best publicly displaced bid, and the NBBO would become $12.05 and $12.15 as a result. The $12.05 bid would receive a mandatory priority, and Nasdaq could not permit (without at least potentially violating Rule 611) a trade for 5,000 shares to be executed at $12.00, while the $12.05 bid remained outstanding (even if it were only

impact Nasdaq more severely? Historically, the NYSE and the regional exchanges that belonged to the Intermarket Trading System had long been subject to such a "trade-through" rule, but Nasdaq was not. Thus, trades on Nasdaq in stocks listed elsewhere could occur at inferior prices to the quotations on other markets. Brokers who traded at such prices still had to justify how trading at an inferior price satisfied their duty of "best execution" to their client. But frequently the argument would be that their client wanted more volume than the NYSE specialist would supply at the superior price. Or, the client wanted an instantaneous transaction (before prices changed in a volatile market), and it could trade more quickly (and in higher volume) on Nasdaq's automated market than on the slower NYSE. Ultimately, the SEC's adoption of a rule prohibiting trade-throughs was intended to encourage and reward the display of public limit orders, but it favored the NYSE over Nasdaq. However, as discussed below, the SEC insisted as its price for extending the trade-through rule to Nasdaq that the NYSE become a faster, more automated exchange.

Rule 611 also threatened the ECNs because they could less easily match orders at prices inferior to the best price (or NBBO) in the national market system, even if some of their customers wanted precisely that. Revealingly, both Archipelago and Instinet decided to merge with the NYSE and Nasdaq, respectively, as it became evident that the SEC would adopt Regulation NMS.

Other provisions in Regulation NMS were nearly as controversial, although they affected a smaller population. Regulation NMS's "Access Rule" (Rule 610) requires fair and non-discriminatory access to quotations, and, towards this end, places a limit on access fees to "harmonize" the pricing of quotations across different markets. Protecting the best displayed prices against trade-throughs would be meaningless if broker-dealers and trading centers could not access those prices fairly and efficiently. Thus, Rule 610 prohibits a trading center from imposing unfairly discriminatory terms that inhibit access by any person. Rule 610 also limits the fees that any trading center can charge for access to its quotations to no more than $0.003 per share. This ceiling seemingly resolved a long-standing dispute about whether other brokers had to pay an "access fee" to ECNs when the latter displayed the "best" price in a stock. But this policy placed the SEC in the position of a rate-setting agency, much like a public utility commission.

Regulation NMS also adopted a "Sub-Penny Rule" (Rule 612), which prohibits market participants from accepting, ranking, or displaying orders, quotations, or indications of interest in a pricing increment smaller than a penny. Effectively, this prevents institutional investors and dealers from stepping ahead of limit orders posted by retail customers by offering a one tenth of a cent price improvement. Once

---

for 200 shares). Viewed in this light, Rule 611 encourages customers—both small and large—to place limit orders into the national market system and thereby narrow the bid/asked spread.

again, this is a case where the proponents of market efficiency and free competition would argue that excessive deference was being paid by the SEC to concerns about fairness.

Finally, the Commission revised its "Market Data Rules" (Rules 601–603) governing the consolidating, distribution and displaying of market information. The sale of market information to vendors (for example, Reuters and Bloomberg) had become a principal profit center for exchanges and other trading centers and necessarily involved infighting over the allocation of these profits.

Of all these rules, clearly the most controversial was the "trade-through" rule, which effectively requires that orders to buy or sell securities be routed to the market with the "best" price (that is, the lowest price in the case of an order to buy). Why should this be controversial? For some institutional investors, trading on the NYSE was sometimes unattractive even at the "best" price, because executions were slow and large orders often had to be broken up into smaller units. Worse, the institution's identity might be inferred by other traders during this slow trading process (thus causing the market to move adversely to them before they had completed their planned large purchases or sales). By trading electronically on a dark pool, an ECN, or Nasdaq, they could trade faster and in larger volume and with greater anonymity, even if to do so they had to sacrifice some small discount off the best price.

2. *In Whose Interests?* The interests of institutional investors and retail investors may necessarily be in conflict with regard to the National Market System's priorities. Large mutual funds prefer high liquidity (i.e., the ability to buy and sell in large volume without affecting the market price) to the narrowest spread, while retail investors (who trade in smaller quantities) prefer a narrow spread and protection against trade-throughs. Critics of the "trade-through" rule accused the SEC of paternalistically deciding that "best price" was more important than speed or anonymity, when sophisticated investors believed otherwise. But retail investors may be unable to monitor whether their brokers are truly complying with their duty of best execution. Release 51808 justifies its position by focusing on the interests of "long-term investors."

On the simplest level, this issue can be visualized in terms of whether the government should make such a choice for investors. Proponents of a free market would argue that if, for example, the ordinary consumer, seeking to buy a small amount of groceries, goes to a delicatessen, rather than a supermarket, because the consumer can make some minimal purchases quickly without waiting in a checkout line, government regulation should not prevent the consumer from doing so, even if the customer thereby pays more and saves only a little time. In reply, the SEC might respond that the difference between this example about the market for groceries and the market for securities is that a broker is an agent whom the small investor cannot easily monitor. In particular, brokers have conflicts of interest that may compromise their loyalty to their clients' interest, as some market makers paid brokers a small rebate for directing their order flow to their market. Hence, a trade-through rule may be a means to prevent such incentives from distorting the flow of orders to the superior market. From a policy perspective, much depends on whether a competitive market for broker services adequately restrains the potential for broker misconduct. If it does, the case for a trade-through rule may weaken.

Another asserted problem with any "trade-through" rule is that it may chill the incentive to innovate. Why should a smaller market center attempt to innovate with new technology that allows its customers to obtain some benefit (speed, anonymity, greater trading volume, etc.) if all trades must be routed to the market that has concentrated only on offering the best price? From this perspective, the real issue is whether public policy should seek to promote competition for individual orders based on best price or competition among trading platforms based on a variety of criteria.

These arguments were not ignored by the SEC, which did condition its trade-through rule on quotations being immediately and automatically accessible. Because the trade-through rule only protects quotations that can be automatically executed on an immediate basis, this condition forced the NYSE to move toward significantly greater use of electronic trading and away from its traditional trading floor dominated by the specialist (whose manual execution of trades was inevitably slower).

From the SEC staff's perspective, this compromise of a universal trade-through rule with the precondition that a trading center offer immediate electronic trading for it to be applicable avoided the danger of market fragmentation (i.e., the risk that the national market could divide into multiple pools that traded the same security at different prices), while also protecting institutional customers from the danger that slow markets would expose them to adverse price changes.

3. *The Evolution of the NMS.* Although progress toward a national market system was slow in the first decades after the 1975 Securities Act Amendments, some important reforms were implemented. Over this period, the SEC principally sought to enhance price transparency (so that investors could know immediately which market center was offering the superior price) and to eliminate restrictions that prevented brokers from taking customer orders to a market offering superior prices.

The most important SEC steps were its Order Handling Rules and Regulation NMS. These have already been discussed, but the SEC also implemented the goal of a truly "national market system" in other important ways that are next discussed:

a. Transaction and Quotation Information. The 1975 Securities Act Amendments caused an informational revolution. Market transparency and meaningful price competition require that investors be able to see the quotations being offered and the transactions actually being executed across markets on a close to real time basis. As a practical matter, a precondition is that transaction and quotation information from different markets be consolidated into a single stream of data that is available to all market participants and investors.[39] In 1979, the SEC took the first major step to this end by approving a real-time quotation and transaction reporting system for exchange-listed securities that collected information on quotations and transactions, from the primary and regional exchanges and the over-the-counter market, then consolidated this information, and disseminated it to the public.[40] Together, consolidated quotations and the consolidated tape (administered by a consortium of the exchanges known as the Consolidated Tape Association ("CTA")) made possible the Intermarket Trading System ("ITS"), so that an investor could compare prices on competing markets. The accessibility of the ITS to the ordinary investor remained a problem, but because trade-throughs on the ITS were forbidden, a price improvement on any exchange benefited all investors. Later, a similar system for collecting, consolidating and reporting quotations and transactions on Nasdaq was similarly established.[41]

During the early 1980s, the Commission extended last-sale transaction reporting to a broad number of over-the-counter stocks (such securities being known today as the National Market System).[42] In addition, the Commission imposed an obligation on market makers and specialists in exchange-listed or National Market System ("NMS") securities to report immediately all changes in their bid and asked quotations and to execute at their quoted prices subject to Commission guidelines.[43] These changes brought a wave of sunlight to the over-the-counter market, which had historically been characterized by illusory price quotations and uncertainty as to the then prevailing price. As a result, the transition to a National Market System was achieved on the *informational* level: market participants had easy access to current and reliable information about most securities in which there was active trading. Yet, as noted at the end of this Chapter, the system created to collect and transmit this information—chiefly, the CTA and the

---

[39] Today, this obligation is governed by Rules 601–603 of Regulation NMS. See 17 C.F.R. § 292.601–603.

[40] Originally, Rule 11Ac1–1 required the exchanges to establish the Consolidated Quotation Plan. See Securities Exchange Act Release No. 16,410 (Dec. 7, 1979). Today, this rule has been moved to Regulation NMS, and the dissemination of transaction reports is governed by Rule 601 and the dissemination of quotations by Rule 602.

[41] The Nasdaq equivalent to the Consolidated Quotation Plan is known as the Nasdaq-UTP Plan.

[42] See Rules 601 and 602 of Regulation NMS. In 1987, the Commission largely ceded to the stock exchanges and the NASD the responsibility for determining the standards for eligibility for inclusion in the NMS. See Securities Exchange Act Release No. 24633 (June 23, 1987).

[43] See Rule 602 of Regulation NMS. This obligation to report bid and asked prices gave rise to the "consolidated quotation system." See Securities Exchange Act Release No. 18482 (1982).

Consolidated Quotation System ("CQS")—was a governmentally created monopoly, which some believe resulted in excessive costs and discriminated against new entrants. Hence, one of the newer issues in securities regulation, discussed below, is how to determine these charges and allocate the revenues.

    b. *"Off-Board" Trading Restrictions.* Since early in its existence, the NYSE prohibited members from trading NYSE-listed securities away from the NYSE. Although such a prohibition, which was long embodied in NYSE Rule 390, obviously restricted competition, the SEC moved slowly to repeal it, gradually chipping away at it (although it had clear authority under the 1975 Securities Acts Amendments to order its immediate repeal). The SEC's principal concern was that market fragmentation might result if broker-dealers could "internalize" order flow (that is, trade themselves with their own customers in off-exchange transactions at the then prevailing spread) if Rule 390 were eliminated. After a series of SEC partial steps that cut back on Rule 390, the NYSE itself sought and received SEC approval for the repeal of Rule 390.[44] The restriction had ultimately become an embarrassment for the NYSE that it could not easily defend.

    c. *Firm Quotations.* Prior to 1978, the quotes disseminated on Nasdaq did not specify size (or the number of shares to which the quote applied). Market makers also did not always honor their quotes and might refuse to trade at the specified price in any volume. Also, some market makers might simply suspend operations for the day if market conditions soured or they feared excessive volatility. In 1978, the SEC adopted the "Firm Quote Rule," (today, Rule 602), to deal with problems.[45] The rule requires broker-dealers who maintain quotes for a security to promptly disseminate these quotations and to honor them by executing transactions at the quoted prices and sizes. In 1996, the SEC extended this rule to apply to Nasdaq market makers who issued quotations on exchange-listed securities, at least if the market maker is responsible for more than one percent of the volume in the security.[46] As a result, a significant number of NASD enforcement and arbitration disputes came to focus on "backing away" complaints in which the assertion is made that a market maker had failed to honor its quotation.

    d. *The Rise and Fall of the ECNs.* Although some ECNs predated the Order Handling Rules, their explosive growth in the late 1990's seems primarily attributable to those rules. Not only could public customers seek matching transactions on an ECN, but now they were assured that, if their limit order was or became superior to other orders on the ECN, it would be displayed on the Nasdaq screen; thus, all brokers would be required to execute against their limit order if it became part of the inside spread (the NBBO). This was important because the inherent

---

44   See Securities Exchange Act Release No. 42,758 (May 5, 2000).

45   See Securities Exchange Act Release No. 14415 (Jan. 26, 1978).

46   See Securities Exchange Act Release No. 37619A (Sept. 6, 1996) at *42.

problem with matching systems (which most ECNs are) is that a user can encounter only limited liquidity within them and thus can be left behind if the broader market moves adversely. The Order Handling Rules addressed this problem by integrating orders within the ECN with those in the broader market.[47] In effect, they gave customers the opportunity to obtain an execution inside the bid/asked spread established by Nasdaq's dealers, because their limit order, if inside that spread, would automatically revise the bid/asked spread. New Rule 611 further enforces this right by requiring the market center to police against trade throughs at inferior prices.

A second major advantage of ECNs was their lower execution costs. Because customer orders can interact with each other without the intervention of a market-maker, retail customers flocked to ECNs to avoid paying a spread. Although ECNS charge their subscribers access fees, these fees were no more than $.015 per share as of late 2001[48] and may be even lower if the subscriber qualifies for a volume discount.

A final advantage of ECNs was that market-makers could use them to trade anonymously. If a market-maker wishes to display a quotation on an ECN that is different than its publicly offered spread, it may do so under the Order Handling Rules (so long as the superior price is accessible to the public generally). Thus, if a market-maker on Nasdaq was offering an aggressively high "offer" price (the price at which it will sell) but wishes to reduce its inventory of that stock for liquidity reasons, it could offer a lower offer price on an ECN. If that lower offer price were the best offer price on that ECN, it would be displayed on the Nasdaq screen—but under the ECN's name, not the market maker's name. This ability to trade on an anonymous basis is important to market-makers who want to signal their belief above future price directions in stocks, but cannot afford to hold a large inventory of the stock.

Rapid as the rise of ECNs was, their decline was equally quick. First, they were leapfrogged by the "dark pools," which offered greater anonymity to their users and were also exempt, as alternative trading systems, from any public display obligation (at least until the dark pool's average daily trading volume in any NMS security exceeded 5%). The ECNs' original advantage was their ability to allow users to obtain prices inside the Nasdaq market makers' spreads. But with Regulation NMS in 2005, intermarket competition eroded those inflated spreads. Equally important, ECNs found that if they converted to exchanges, they could obtain a larger share of the revenue for market data.

---

[47] A technical qualification is necessary here. Regulation ATS requires that the orders of any subscriber, including a retail customer, must be displayed on Nasdaq if they represent the ECN's best bid or offer price—but only if the ECN is large enough to account for a minimum percentage of trading in the specific security (5%). Hence, many smaller ECNs do not need to display their orders on the consolidated display.

[48] See Borrelli, Market Making in the Electronic Age, 32 Loy. U. Chi. L. J. 815, 859 (2001).

e. *Decimalization.* Although the Order Handling Rules reduced the price spreads in the equity markets, their impact was in turn overshadowed by decimalization. Since the founding of the NYSE, U.S. securities markets had quoted securities in minimum increments of eighths of a dollar. This tradition dated back to the days when Spanish doubloons, which could be broken physically into "pieces of eight," were the principal currency of exchange, but it was increasingly anachronistic in an era when computerization had reduced trading costs and the volume of trading had increased exponentially. To many, the convention of quoting in terms of minimum increments of one eighths represented the last lawful price-fixing agreement.

Believing that this convention produced excessive profits for traders, Congressional leaders of both parties introduced in March 1997 the "Common Cents Stock Pricing Act of 1997," which would have required the quotation of equity securities in decimals within one year. Although the bill was opposed by each of the NYSE, the Amex, and the NASD, each yielded to Congressional pressure and voted within months to begin trading stocks in decimals, rather than fractions.

f. *"Internalization."* The repeal of off-board restrictions (chiefly NYSE Rule 390, discussed earlier) has made it possible for a broker-dealer when it receives an order from a client to "internalize" the order, either trading with the client, itself, as a principal or effecting an "in-home cross" by crossing another client's shares as the counterparty, without in either case exposing the transaction to the market. The Commission has concerns about the "internalization" of order flow, a practice that, it notes, leads to "the withholding of retail orders from other market centers for the purpose of executing them 'in house' as principal, without exposing those orders to buying and selling interest in those other market centers. . . ."[49] What are the SEC's fears if this transaction must occur at the NBBO (i.e., the best price then available in the market)? Essentially, it has two concerns: (1) the dealer may not search for price improvement by exposing the order to others, but will prefer to trade at the existing price because it is the counterparty; and (2) the withdrawal of a large volume of trading from the principal market results in market fragmentation and the possibility that price determination in the principal market will be less accurate.

Although it is clear that the SEC is not prepared to ban internalization, possible compromises include requiring the dealer who internalizes order flow to grant comparable price improvement.[50]

---

[49] See Securities Exchange Act Release No. 16888 (June 11, 1980).

[50] This was the NYSE's proposal at the time it repealed Rule 390. See Securities Exchange Act Release No. 42450 (Feb. 23, 2000) at *5.

3. WHAT IS AN EXCHANGE?: A BRIEF SURVEY FROM THE 1934 ACT TO REGULATION ATS

Another word on which a great deal hinges in securities law—like the words "offer," "underwriter," "prospectus," or "security"—is the word "exchange." The SEC has special powers over exchanges, as opposed to brokers who are acting in a manner similar to an exchange. Exchanges must be open to all members, must engage in costly self-regulation activities, and must secure SEC approval for changes in their rules. Thus, a dark pool wishing to exclude HFTs or other unwelcome traders might not be able to do so if it operated as an exchange. Indeed, in the *Board of Trade v. SEC* case set forth below, the Seventh Circuit noted that the special options trading market there at issue could not have survived if it were required to register as an exchange.

The term "exchange" is broadly defined by § 3(a)(1) of the 1934 Act to mean

> any organization, association, or group of persons, * * * which constitutes, maintains, or provides a market place or facilities for bringing together purchasers and sellers of securities or for otherwise performing with respect to securities the functions commonly performed by a stock exchange as that term is generally understood, and includes the market place and the market facilities maintained by such exchange.

For many years, this definition posed no problem for securities regulators because the concept of an exchange was in fact "generally understood" (as § 3(a)(1) assumed). However, the combination of the technological capacity afforded by the computer plus the growth in institutional trading eventually resulted in the appearance of proprietary trading systems.[51] The initial such alternative trading system, Instinet, which began operations in 1969, essentially functioned as a clearinghouse in which large institutions interested in trading large quantities of securities could trade directly with each other.[52] Instinet operates without any specialist or market maker and does not itself quote a bid/asked spread in the manner of a dealer; rather, its subscribers furnish all quotes and orders to it. Subscribers could either execute transactions automatically based on the then price of a security on its

---

[51] Originally, these trading systems were sometimes called the "fourth market" to distinguish them from (1) the exchanges, (2) the over-the-counter dealer market, and (3) the "third market," which consists of market makers trading exchange-listed securities on Nasdaq in competition with the exchange's specialist. For a fuller description, see 6 L. Loss & J. Seligman, Securities Regulation, at 2577, 2662–2663 (3d ed. 1990). Prior to the mid-1990's, these systems primarily serviced institutional investors seeking to trade sizable blocks. Some eleven different proprietary trading systems had received no-action letters from the SEC's staff as of April 1989, indicating that the staff would not object to their commencing trading operations without registering as an exchange. Id. at 2659.

[52] Instinet provides last sale and quotation information on exchange-listed and over-the-counter securities, but also permits its subscribers (chiefly, bank trust departments, mutual and pension funds, and other institutional investors) to execute transactions through its computer facility.

primary exchange (i.e., the NYSE or the American Stock Exchange) or simply advertise their purchasing and selling interest and then engage in direct negotiations with each other. In other trading systems, large institutions could trade whole portfolios of exchange-listed securities with each other.[53] For the most part, institutions did not use these trading systems on a large scale as a cheaper substitute for the market, but rather employed them to trade either after the primary market had closed or when they wished to pursue trading strategies without attracting the market's attention.[54]

On the policy level, the SEC seems to have accepted the appearance of proprietary trading systems as a natural evolutionary development. While it required that those operating a trading system register as a broker-dealer, it distinguished these systems from exchanges on the following grounds:

> The Commission believes that the proprietary trading systems that have developed to date are distinguishable in function from exchange markets. These proprietary systems offer to participants the capacity to execute automatically transactions based on derivative pricing.... These systems have not, however, evolved into interdealer quotation or transaction mechanisms in which participants enter two-sided quotations on a regular or continuous basis, thus ensuring a liquid marketplace.[55]

Eventually, existing exchanges challenged the willingness of the Commission's staff to grant no-action letters to proprietary trading systems. In Board of Trade of the City of Chicago v. Securities and Exchange Commission,[56] the Seventh Circuit found the particular proprietary trading system there at issue to be

> "neither fish nor fowl, neither an exchange after the pattern of the Board of Trade and the New York Stock Exchange nor an over-the-counter market after the fashion of the NASDAQ. Developments in automation and communication are bound to produce more of these hard-to-classify entities. Section 3(a)(1) is

---

[53] While it existed, the POSIT (Portfolio System for Institutional Trading) system allowed the trading of equity portfolios by customers such as mutual funds. The system permitted its subscribers to post an indication of interest to be matched on a confidential basis against other orders in the system. POSIT specialized in facilitating program trading for indexed investors. Some estimate that its transactions in combination with those on Instinet accounted for up to 50% of the volume in program trading. See Stern, "A Dwindling Monopoly," Forbes, May 13, 1991, at 64. Other systems specialized in debt or government securities.

[54] Because large institutional traders can pursue portfolio trading strategies on Instinet or similar systems without attracting the market's attention, they favored this "fourth market" (which essentially consisted of institutions trading with institutions) because it enabled them to avoid signaling their trading intentions to the broader market as a whole.

[55] See Securities Exchange Act Release No. 26708 (Apr. 11, 1989), 43 S.E.C. Dock. 979, 984.

[56] 883 F.2d 525 (7th Cir. 1989).

a product of the '30s, [the proprietary trading system] a product of the 80's."[57]

The Seventh Circuit remanded the case to the SEC for a formal determination of whether the particular proprietary trading system was an "exchange."

On remand, the SEC stuck to its guns and insisted that the Delta trading system (which three firms had collectively developed to trade options on federal government securities) did not amount to an exchange. In part, the SEC clearly based its determination on its fear that a strict interpretation of § 3(a)(1) would result in a "straitjacket" on the evolution of new forms of trading systems. It concluded:

> In summary, employing an expansive interpretation of Section 3(a)(1) results in potential conflicts with other central regulatory definitions under the Act as well as adverse effects on innovation and competition. Rather, each system must be analyzed in light of the statutory objectives and the particular facts and circumstances of that system. In conducting such an analysis, the central focus of the Commission's inquiry should be whether the system is designed, whether through trading rules, operational procedures or business incentives, to centralize trading and provide buy and sell quotations on a regular or continuous basis so that purchasers and sellers have a reasonable expectation that they can regularly execute their orders at those price quotations. The means employed may be varied, ranging from a physical floor or trading system (where orders can be centralized and executed) to other means of intermediation (such as a formal market making system or systemic procedures such as a consolidated order book or regular single price auction).[58]

The Commission also relied on the "absence of complete * * * standardization" in the terms of the options quoted by Delta and the fact that the lack of "regulatory requirements to ensure two-sided quotations make the development of regular or continuous trading unlikely." Although the Commission noted that an embryonic trading system might well grow into a "continuous or regular auction market," it concluded that the Delta trading system was still at too early and formative a stage to make that prediction.

In overview, the principal criteria stressed by Release 27611 for defining an exchange were centralized trading, continuous two-sided quotations, the expectation of liquidity, and the standardization of terms. However, as a practical matter, the Commission's decision not to deem the Delta system an exchange chiefly served to protect those emerging

---

[57] Id. at 535. Writing for the Seventh Circuit panel, Judge Easterbrook added: "We could not find a single case under § 3(a)(1) discussing which attributes (if any) are necessary, and which are sufficient, for sorting a trading apparatus into the 'exchange bin.' " Id.

[58] See Securities Exchange Act Release No. 27611 (January 12, 1990).

trading systems that did not provide continuous trading (but which were either passive systems which adopted prices derived from another system or systems that functioned as electronic bulletin boards through which potential trading partners could negotiate price and others terms). In general, the Commission resisted the mandatory classification of new trading systems as exchanges, preferring to allow them to opt for the less restrictive alternative of broker-dealer registration.

Meanwhile, with the stage thus set, the case went back to the Seventh Circuit the next year:

Board of Trade of the City of Chicago v. Securities and Exchange Commission

United States Court of Appeals, Seventh Circuit, 1991.
923 F.2d 1270.

■ POSNER, CIRCUIT JUDGE. This case is before us for the second time * * * The question we must answer this time is whether a system for trading options on federal government securities that has been put together by RMJ, a broker; Delta, a clearing agency; and SPNTCO, a bank (the last playing an essentially custodial role unnecessary to discuss further) is an "exchange" within the meaning of section 3(a)(1) of the Securities Exchange Act of 1934, in which event it must register with the Securities Exchange Commission. The Commission, faced as it was merely with an application by Delta to register as a clearing agency under section 17A(b) of the Act, thought it unnecessary to decide whether the Delta system—as we shall call the trading system put together by the three firms—is an exchange. We disagreed in our first opinion. We held that the Commission could not, as it had done, approve Delta's application without deciding whether the system whose trades it intended to clear could lawfully operate without registering as an exchange. We therefore remanded the case to the Commission for a determination of the system's status. The Commission held that it was not an exchange, and therefore adhered to its decision to register Delta as a clearing house. The Board of Trade and the Chicago Mercantile Exchange again petition for review. They are concerned about competition from the Delta system. We held in our first opinion that this concern gives them standing to challenge the Commission's decision to allow Delta to become a registered clearing house.

An ingenious device for facilitating the purchase and sale of securities, the Delta system works roughly as follows. * * * The system specifies the form of option contract that shall be the security traded. Some of the terms of the contract are fixed, such as the maximum term of the option and the day of the month on which it expires. Others are left open to be negotiated by the parties, such as the premium, the exercise price, and the month of expiration. The traders, who consist not only of securities dealers but also of banks, pension funds, and other institutional investors, communicate their buy or sell offers to RMJ, which enters the offers in the system's computer. Delta, the clearing agency, monitors the computer and when it sees a matching buy and sell offer it notifies the traders that they have a deal (but doesn't tell them with whom) and it takes the necessary steps to effectuate the completed transaction. The interposition of Delta between the traders protects the anonymity of each from the other as well as guaranteeing to each that the other will honor the terms of the option traded.

The fixing of some standardized terms so that one trader is not offering to buy apples and the other offering to sell oranges; the guarantees of anonymity and performance; the pooling of buy and sell offers in a single (electronic) place—these essential features of the Delta system are methods for creating a market that will bring together enough buy and sell offers to enable transacting at prices that will approximate the true market values of the things traded. Does this make the Delta system an exchange, that is, "any organization, association, or group of persons * * * which constitutes, maintains, or provides a market place or facilities for bringing together purchasers and sellers of securities or for otherwise performing with respect to securities the functions commonly performed by a stock exchange as that term is generally understood"? There is no doubt that the Delta system creates an electronic marketplace for securities traders, and the petitioners say that no more is required to establish that the system must register as an exchange. The Commission's reply emphasizes the words "generally understood." The Delta system is not—not quite, anyway—what is generally understood by the term "stock exchange." It lacks a trading floor. It lacks specialists, who enhance the liquidity of an exchange by using their own capital to trade against the market when the trading is light, in order to buffer price swings due to the fewness of offers rather than to changes in underlying market values. Not all conventional exchanges have specialists, but those that do not have brokers who trade for their own account as well as for their customers' accounts, and the additional trading enhances the market's liquidity. It is fitting that such brokers are called "market makers." Securities Exchange Act of 1934, § 3(a)(38). RMJ does not trade for its own account in the Delta system.

The petitioners reply that the words "generally understood" apply only to functions other than the central one of "provid[ing] a market place or facilities for bringing together purchasers and sellers of securities." In other words, they want us to put a comma after "sellers of securities." This done, they argue as follows: the statute defines exchange as any entity that provides a facility for bringing together purchasers and sellers of securities, whether or not in providing that facility it is performing an exchange function as the term exchange is generally understood; the Delta system provides a facility for bringing together purchasers and sellers of securities; therefore Delta is an exchange.

Unless the petitioners can be permitted to add their own punctuation to the statute, we do not think that their reading is any more persuasive, even at the literal level, than the Commission's reading, which places the provision of a market place or of other facilities for bringing securities traders together among those functions performed by a stock exchange as the term is generally understood, and thus subjects "provid[ing] a market place or facilities" to the qualifying force of "generally understood." Moreover, if the petitioners are to be consistent in advancing a "literal" reading of the statute, they should read "bring together" literally too. But even an admitted exchange does not literally "bring together" purchasers and sellers of securities, except when the floor brokers are trading for their own account. It does not bring them into physical propinquity. And a broker's waiting room, which does bring purchasers and sellers of securities into physical propinquity, is not an exchange. We therefore question whether the petitioners have a coherent approach to the interpretation of the statute.

The consequence of their interpretation must also give us pause. The Delta system cannot register as an exchange, because the statute requires that an exchange be controlled by its participants, who must in turn be registered brokers or individuals associated with such brokers. Securities and Exchange Act of 1934, §§ 6(b)(3), (c)(1); Securities Exchange Act Release No. 21439, 49 Fed.Reg. 44577, 44578 (Oct. 31, 1984). So all the financial institutions that trade through the Delta system would have to register as brokers, and RMJ, Delta, and the bank would have to turn over the ownership and control of the system to the institutions. The system would be *kaput*. One must question an interpretation of the definitional provision that would automatically prevent competition for the exchanges from an entity that the exchanges are unable to show poses a threat to the safety of investors by virtue of not being forced to register and assume the prescribed exchange format. As the Commission stresses, each of the three firms that constitute the Delta system is comprehensively regulated; no regulatory gaps are created by declining to place the system itself in the exchange pigeonhole; the only thing that such classification would do would be to destroy the system.

What is true is that the Delta system differs only in degree and detail from an exchange. Its trading floor is a computer's memory. Its structure is designed to encourage liquidity, though not to the same extent as the structure of an exchange is. Section 3(a)(1) is broadly worded. No doubt (considering the time when and circumstances in which it was enacted) this was to give the Securities and Exchange Commission maximum control over the securities industry. So the Commission could have interpreted the section to embrace the Delta system. But we do not think it was compelled to do so. The statute is not crystal clear; on the contrary, even when read literally, which is to say without regard to context and consequence, it does not support the petitioners' argument without repunctuation of the statute and without overlooking the impossibility of a consistently literal reading. An administrative agency has discretion to interpret a statute that is not crystal clear. Chevron v. Natural Resources Defense Council, 467 U.S. 837, 844–45, 104 S.Ct. 2778, 2782–83, 81 L.Ed.2d 694 (1984). The Securities and Exchange Commission can determine better than we generalist judges whether the protection of investor and other interests within the range of the statute is advanced, or retarded, by placing the Delta system in a classification that will destroy a promising competitive innovation in the trading of securities. Of course, if the statute were unambiguous, the Commission would have to bow. Board of Governors v. Dimension Financial Corp., 474 U.S. 361, 106 S.Ct. 681, 88 L.Ed.2d 691 (1986); American Bankers Ass'n v. SEC, 804 F.2d 739, 744 (D.C.Cir. 1986). It has not been given the power of statutory revision. But in this case there is enough play in the statutory joints that its decision must be affirmed.

■ FLAUM, CIRCUIT JUDGE, dissenting.

No doubt there is some ambiguity in the statutory definition of "exchange." The ambiguity lies in the broad formula Congress adopted: "as that term is generally understood." On one point, however, the statute is not ambiguous. An organization that "constitutes, maintains, or provides a market place or facilities for bringing together purchasers and sellers of securities" is an exchange. The statute makes it unnecessary to speculate whether bringing together buyers and sellers is one of the "generally understood" functions of an exchange; it makes *that* function a determinative characteristic, sufficient unto itself to confer exchange status. Entities that *"otherwise"* perform the functions of a stock exchange—whatever those may be—may also constitute exchanges, but the statute leaves no doubt that bringing together buyers and sellers is the principal function of an exchange. Since—as the majority acknowledges—we cannot ignore an unequivocal statutory mandate, I respectfully dissent from the court's decision to defer to an SEC interpretation that does.

* * *

1. *Square Pegs and Round Holes.* The immediate problem for an alternative trading system, if it were deemed to be an exchange, is that the 1934 Act mandates a governance structure for exchanges based on a conception of them as not-for-profit organizations run for the benefit of participating dealers. Proprietary systems are, of course, run for their own benefit (or that of their owners). Section 6(b) of the 1934 Act contemplates that an exchange will be essentially a membership organization, administered on a not-for-profit basis. Thus § 6(b)(3) requires "fair representation" of its members in the selection of the directors, and § 6(b)(4) contemplates that the rules of the exchange will provide for "the equitable allocation" of costs among members and other

users of its facilities. Neither of these sections contemplate a privately owned "exchange," such as the Delta System (or the contemporary NYSE). Also, "dark pools," which are today organized as alternative trading systems, may want to exclude HFT traders (in order to attract institutional traders), which exclusion would not be possible on an exchange.

In 1934, Congress was obviously looking to the existing structure of exchanges as more-or-less private clubs organized for trading purposes and did not contemplate that anyone could "own" the technological equivalent of a trading floor. This was, of course, an anomaly that the SEC could today correct through exemptive rulemaking under § 36 ("General Exemptive Authority") of the 1934 Act. But § 36 did not exist at the time of the Delta System case, and any exemptive rulemaking proceeding would then have been both lengthy and subject to legal challenge.

A. THE VARIETIES OF ALTERNATIVE TRADING SYSTEMS

New trading systems continue to be developed, and any taxonomy of them is likely to become dated quickly. Still, some basic distinctions should be understood:

1. *Matching Systems.* These allow participants to display firm, priced orders to other participants and to execute automatically against other orders in the system. The Instinet Corporation ("Instinet"), was the leading and first example of this type.

2. *Crossing Systems.* These allow participants to enter unpriced orders, which are then executed with matching interest on the other side at a single price, usually derived from the primary public market for each crossed security. The attraction of these systems is that they allow institutional investors to split the bid/asked spread. That is, if two pension funds see a spread of $18 bid and $18½ asked, they would each prefer to execute a transaction between them at $18¼ than to accept an inferior price from dealers. The leading example of such a "passive" system was POSIT (Portfolio System for Institutional Trading). ECNs and "dark pools", however, came to occupy this same market niche, and POSIT closed.

3. *Single-Price Auction Systems.* These systems allow participants to enter priced orders, which a computer then compares to determine the single price at which the largest volume of orders can be executed. All orders are then matched and executed at that price. The best known example of this type of system was the Arizona Stock Exchange.[59] For example, if the "auction price" that best equalizes supply and demand is 42⅜, then all orders to buy at 42½ and higher would be filled at 42⅜, and

---

[59] Securities Exchange Act Release No. 28,899 (Feb. 28, 1991); see also Wunsch Auction Systems, Inc., 1991 WL 178593 (S.E.C.) (Feb. 28, 1991).

all orders to sell at 42¼ or less would be filled at 42⅜.[60] A special attraction of this system is the ability of each customer to see at all times (on its own computer terminal) the bids and offers made by all other users.

4. *The Arizona Aftermath.* Interestingly, the Arizona Stock Exchange, which was a single-price auction system, did not ask the Commission to rule that it was not an exchange. Instead, it asked for and received an exemption under the last clause of § 5 of the 1934 Act based on the "limited volume of transactions effected on such exchange." To the extent that such systems were successful, it follows that they would begin to execute far more than a "limited volume of transactions." Thus, as new trading systems grew, the problem of identifying the defining criteria of an "exchange" was becoming more central and had to be faced by the Commission.

Securities Exchange Act Release No. 38672
Securities and Exchange Commission.
May 23, 1997.

REGULATION OF EXCHANGES

Stock markets play a critical role in the economic life of the United States. The phenomenal growth of the U.S. markets over the past 60 years is a direct result of investor confidence in those markets. Technological trends over the past two decades have also contributed greatly to this success. In particular, technology has provided a vastly greater number of investment and execution choices, increased market efficiency, and reduced trading costs. These developments have enhanced the ability of U.S. exchanges to implement efficient market linkages and advanced the goals of the national market system ("NMS").

At the same time, however, technological changes have posed significant challenges for the existing regulatory framework, which is ill-equipped to respond to innovations in U.S. and cross-border trading. Specifically, two key developments highlight the need for a more forward-looking, flexible regulatory framework: (1) the exponential growth of trading systems that present comparable alternatives to traditional exchange trading; and (2) the development of automated mechanisms that facilitate access to foreign markets from the United States.

---

[60] Buy orders set below 42⅜ and sell orders set above 42⅜ will go unfilled, and orders exactly at 42⅜ will be filled on a first come, first served basis. For a fuller explanation, see Stern, "A Dwindling Monopoly," Forbes, May 13, 1991, at 65.

The Commission estimates that alternative trading systems[1] currently handle almost 20 percent of the orders[2] in over-the-counter ("OTC") stocks and almost 4 percent of orders in securities listed on the New York Stock Exchange ("NYSE"). The explosive growth of alternative trading systems over the past several years has significant implications for public secondary market regulation. Even though many of these systems provide essentially the same services as traditional markets, most alternative trading systems are regulated as broker-dealers. As a result, they have been subject to regulations designed primarily to address traditional brokerage, rather than market, activities. For example, these systems are typically subject to oversight by self-regulatory organizations ("SROs") that themselves operate exchanges or quotation systems, which raises inherent competitive concerns.

At the same time, alternative trading systems are not fully integrated into the national market system. As a result, activity on alternative trading systems is not fully disclosed to, or accessible by, public investors. The trading activity on these systems may not be adequately surveilled for market manipulation and fraud. Moreover, these trading systems have no obligation to provide investors a fair opportunity to participate in their systems or to treat their participants fairly, nor do they have an obligation to ensure that they have sufficient capacity to handle trading demand. These concerns together with the increasingly important role of alternative trading systems, call into question the fairness of current regulatory requirements, the effectiveness of existing NMS mechanisms, and the quality of public secondary markets.

* * *

B. ALTERNATIVES FOR REVISING DOMESTIC MARKET REGULATION

The questions raised by technological developments in the U.S. markets could be addressed in a variety of ways. . . .

First, the Commission could continue to regulate alternative trading systems as broker-dealers and develop rules applicable to these systems, and their supervising SROs, that would more actively integrate these systems into NMS mechanisms. The Commission could, for example, require alternative trading systems to provide additional audit trail information to SROs, to assist SROs in their surveillance functions, and to adopt standard procedures for ensuring adequate system capacity and

---

[1] Trading systems not registered as exchanges have been referred to in previous Commission releases as "proprietary trading systems," "broker-dealer trading systems," and "electronic communications networks." The latter two terms are defined in Rule 17a–23 and 11Ac1–1 under the Securities Exchanges Act of 1934 ("Exchange Act"), 17 CFR 240.17a–23 and 240.11Ac1–1, respectively. The term "alternative trading systems" will be used throughout this release to refer generally to automated systems that centralize, display, match, cross, or otherwise execute trading interest, but that are not currently registered with the Commission as national securities exchanges or operated by a registered securities association.

[2] For purposes of this release, the term "order" generally means any firm trading interest, including both limit orders and market maker quotations.

the integrity of their system operations. The Commission could then require SROs to integrate trading on alternative trading systems into their ongoing, real-time surveillance for market manipulation and fraud, and to develop surveillance and examination procedures specifically targeted to alternative trading systems they supervise. In addition, the Commission could require alternative trading systems to make all orders in their systems available to their supervising SROs, and require such SROs to incorporate those orders into the public quotation system. The Commission could also require that alternative trading systems provide the public with access to these orders on a substantially equivalent basis as provided to system participants.

Alternatively, the Commission could integrate alternative trading systems into the national market system as securities exchanges, by adopting a tiered approach to exchange regulation. The first tier, under this type of approach, could consist of the majority of alternative trading systems, those that have limited volume or do not establish trading prices, which could be exempt from traditional exchange requirements. For example, exempt exchanges could be required to file an application and system description with the Commission, report trade, maintain an audit trail, develop systems capacity and other operational standards, and cooperate with SROs that inspect their regulated participants. Most alternative trading systems currently regulated as broker-dealers would be exempt exchanges.

The second tier of exchanges under this approach could consist of alternative trading systems that resemble traditional exchanges because of their significant volume of trading and active price discovery. These systems could be regulated as national securities exchanges. The Commission could then use its exemptive authority to eliminate barriers that would make it difficult for these non-traditional markets to register as exchanges, by exempting such systems from any exchange registration requirements that are not appropriate or necessary in light of their business structure or other characteristics. For example, the Commission could exempt alternative trading systems that register as exchanges from requirements that exchanges have a traditional membership structure, and from requirements that limit exchange participation to registered broker-dealers. The Commission could also use its exemptive authority to reduce or eliminate those exchange requirements that are incompatible with the operation of for-profit, non-membership alternative trading systems.

* * *

B. THE SEC'S CONCERNS

The SEC had historically displayed an attitude of benign neglect toward alternative trading systems; this was a product both of their low volume and the fear that close regulation would retard their evolution as competitive alternatives to the traditional markets.[61] By the time of the foregoing Concept Release in 1997, the growth of alternative trading systems (then amounting to 20% of Nasdaq volume, but later exceeding 40% once "dark pools" matured) had convinced the SEC that such systems could no longer be treated as infants to be sheltered in a protective legal nursery. Rather, hard issues about their operation and regulation had to be faced. Among these issues, the following stood out:

1. *Market Access.* Small investors may not have access to the principal alternative trading systems (such as Instinet), which primarily serve institutional investors and other large traders. Thus, if there are superior prices available on such systems, small investors may not benefit from them. On the other hand, the access issue was not easy to resolve because alternative trading systems may not be willing to guarantee execution if one of the trading parties defaults. This risk of default is greatest in the case of the individual investor, and is eliminated in the national securities markets by the market's own guarantee that the trade will be executed at the agreed price. An alternative trading system may not be willing to assume this cost and may therefore wish to exclude smaller traders in order to minimize counterparty trading risk (i.e., the risk that the other party to a trade will default).

2. *Market Transparency.* As the foregoing Concept Release noted, the SEC's 1996 investigation of Nasdaq trading found that the majority of the bids and offers displayed by Instinet and SelectNet (then, the two most significant alternative trading systems for Nasdaq securities) were better than those posted publicly on Nasdaq. The SEC believed this lack of transparency was harmful to investors in several ways. Because Nasdaq dealers could trade with each other through non-public trading systems, they had reduced economic incentive to reduce their price spreads and compete based on price. The resulting wider public spreads, of course, increased the transaction costs for public investors and indirectly the cost of capital to corporate issuers. In response to these findings, the Commission introduced new order handling rules in 1996, which required a market maker or specialist to make publicly available any superior prices that it privately offers through certain types of alternative trading systems (known as electronic communications networks or "ECNs"). These order handling rules permit an ECN to satisfy this obligation on behalf of market makers using its system by submitting its best market maker bid/ask quotation to the exchange or Nasdaq for inclusion into the public quotation displays (the so-called "ECN Display Alternative"). Although these reforms served to integrate orders submitted by broker-dealers to private trading systems into the broader public quotation system, they were subject to a significant limitation: institutional orders placed with alternative trading systems

---

[61] In 1994, the SEC did adopt Rule 17a–23, which is a recordkeeping and reporting rule for broker-dealers that operate alternative trading systems. The rule requires a broker-dealer to report quarterly the trading volume on such system and to provide a description of the trading system. See Securities Exchange Act Release No. 35124 (Dec. 20, 1994).

It needs to be underscored that Regulation ATS does not integrate all orders into the national market system. Rather, its fair access rules create an exclusion for systems that match customers' orders without displaying them or that execute orders pursuant to an automated quotation system.[69]

4. PRIMARY JURISDICTION AND THE STRUGGLE FOR COMPETITIVE RATES

Statutes

Exchange Act, §§ 6(e) and 28(e).

Gordon v. New York Stock Exchange
United States Supreme Court, 1975.
422 U.S. 659, 95 S.Ct. 2598, 45 L.Ed.2d 463.

■ MR. JUSTICE BLACKMUN delivered the opinion of the Court.

This case presents the problem of reconciliation of the antitrust laws with a federal regulatory scheme in the particular context of the practice of the securities exchanges and their members of using fixed rates of commission. The United States District Court for the Southern District of New York and the United States Court of Appeals for the Second Circuit concluded that fixed commission rates were immunized from antitrust attack because of the Securities and Exchange Commission's authority to approve or disapprove exchange commission rates and its exercise of that power.

I

In early 1971 petitioner Richard A. Gordon, individually and on behalf of an asserted class of small investors, filed this suit against the New York Stock Exchange, Inc. (NYSE), the American Stock Exchange, Inc. (Amex), and two member firms of the exchanges. The complaint challenged a variety of exchange rules and practices and, in particular, claimed that the system of fixed commission rates, utilized by the exchanges at that time for transactions less than $500,000, violated §§ 1 and 2 of the Sherman Act, 15 U.S.C. §§ 1 and 2. Other challenges in the complaint focused on (1) the volume discount on trades over 1,000 shares, and the presence of negotiated rather than fixed rates for transactions in excess of $500,000; (2) the rules limiting the number of exchange memberships; and (3) the rules denying discounted commission rates to nonmembers using exchange facilities.

---

maximum limit on fees, and does not expressly provide that they must be paid by non-subscribers to the ECN. Nonetheless, brokers are today paying access fees to ECNs.

[69] For example, some alternative trading systems matched orders received overnight at the market's opening price, or they matched unpriced orders at the midpoint of the bid and offer spread. Such systems are not subject to the fair access rules. See Rule 301(b)(5)(iii).

Respondents moved for summary judgment on the ground that the challenged actions were subject to the overriding supervision of the Securities and Exchange Commission (SEC) under § 19(b) of the Securities Exchange Act of 1934, and, therefore, were not subject to the strictures of the antitrust laws. The District Court granted respondents' motion as to all claims * * *. Dismissing the exchange membership limitation and the Robinson-Patman Act contentions as without merit, the court focused on the relationship between the fixed commission rates and the Sherman Act mandates. It utilized the framework for analysis of antitrust immunity in the regulated securities area that was established a decade ago in Silver v. New York Stock Exchange, 373 U.S. 341 (1963). Since § 19(b)(9) of the Exchange Act authorized the SEC to supervise the Exchanges "in respect of such matters as * * * the fixing of reasonable rates of commission," the court held applicable the antitrust immunity reserved in *Silver* for those cases where "review of exchange self-regulation [is] provided through a vehicle other than the antitrust laws." 373 U.S., at 360. It further noted that the practice of fixed commission rates had continued without substantial challenge after the enactment of the 1934 Act, and that the SEC had been engaged in detailed study of the rate structure for a decade, culminating in the requirement for abolition of fixed rates as of May 1, 1975.

On appeal, the Second Circuit affirmed. . . .

* * *

IV

This Court has considered the issue of implied repeal of the antitrust laws in the context of a variety of regulatory schemes and procedures. Certain axioms of construction are now clearly established. Repeal of the antitrust laws by implication is not favored and not casually to be allowed. Only where there is a "plain repugnancy between the antitrust and regulatory provisions" will repeal be implied. * * *

The starting point for our consideration of the particular issue presented by this case, viz., whether the antitrust laws are impliedly repealed or replaced as a result of the statutory provisions and administrative and congressional experience concerning fixed commission rates, of course, is our decision in *Silver*. There the Court considered the relationship between the antitrust laws and the Securities Exchange Act, and did so specifically with respect to the action of an exchange in ordering its members to remove private direct telephone connections with the offices of a nonmember. Such action, absent any immunity derived from the regulatory laws, would be a *per se* violation of § 1 of the Sherman Act. 373 U.S., at 347. Concluding that the proper approach to the problem was to reconcile the operation of the antitrust laws with a regulatory scheme, the Court established a "guiding principle" for the achievement of this reconciliation. Under this principle, "[r]epeal is to be regarded as implied only if necessary to make the

Securities Exchange Act work, and even then only to the minimum extent necessary." Id., at 357.

In *Silver*, the Court concluded that there was no implied repeal of the antitrust laws in that factual context because the Exchange Act did not provide for SEC jurisdiction or review of particular applications of rules enacted by the exchanges. It noted:

> "Although the Act gives to the Securities and Exchange Commission the power to request exchanges to make changes in their rules, § 19(b), and impliedly, therefore, to disapprove any rules adopted by an exchange, see also § 6(a)(4), it does not give the Commission jurisdiction to review particular instances of enforcement of exchange rules." Ibid.

* * *

It is patent that the case presently at bar is, indeed, that "different case" to which the Court in *Silver* referred. In contrast to the circumstances of *Silver*, § 19(b) gave the SEC direct regulatory power over exchange rules and practices with respect to "the fixing of reasonable rates of commission." Not only was the SEC authorized to disapprove rules and practices concerning commission rates, but the agency also was permitted to require alteration or supplementation of the rules and practices when "necessary or appropriate for the protection of investors or to insure fair dealings in securities traded in upon such exchange." Since 1934 all rate changes have been brought to the attention of the SEC, and it has taken an active role in review of proposed rate changes during the last 15 years. Thus, rather than presenting a case of SEC impotence to affect application of exchange rules in particular circumstances, this case involves explicit statutory authorization for SEC review of all exchange rules and practices dealing with rates of commission and resultant SEC continuing activity.

* * *

In sum, the statutory provision authorizing regulation, § 19(b)(9), the long regulatory practice, and the continued congressional approval illustrated by the new legislation, point to one, and only one, conclusion. The Securities Exchange Act was intended by the Congress to leave the supervision of the fixing of reasonable rates of commission to the SEC. Interposition of the antitrust laws, which would bar fixed commission rates as *per se* violations of the Sherman Act, in the face of positive SEC action, would preclude and prevent the operation of the Exchange Act as intended by Congress and as effectuated through SEC regulatory activity. Implied repeal of the antitrust laws is, in fact, necessary to make the Exchange Act work as it was intended; failure to imply repeal would render nugatory the legislative provision for regulatory agency supervision of exchange commission rates.

Affirmed.

■ [JUSTICES DOUGLAS and STEWART each wrote concurring opinions.]

Credit Suisse Secs. (USA) LLC v. Billing
United States Supreme Court, 2007.
551 U.S. 264, 127 S.Ct. 2383, 168 L.Ed.2d 145.

■ JUSTICE BREYER delivered the opinion of the Court.

A group of buyers of newly issued securities have filed an antitrust lawsuit against underwriting firms that market and distribute those issues. The buyers claim that the underwriters unlawfully agreed with one another that they would not sell shares of a popular new issue to a buyer unless that buyer committed (1) to buy additional shares of that security later at escalating prices (a practice called "laddering"), (2) to pay unusually high commissions on subsequent security purchases from the underwriters, or (3) to purchase from the underwriters other less desirable securities (a practice called "tying"). The question before us is whether there is a " 'plain repugnancy' " between these antitrust claims and the federal securities law. See Gordon v. New York Stock Exchange, Inc., 422 U.S. 659, 682 (1975) (quoting United States v. Philadelphia Nat. Bank, 374 U.S. 321, 350–351 (1963)). We conclude that there is. Consequently we must interpret the securities laws as implicitly precluding the application of the antitrust laws to the conduct alleged in this case. See 422 U.S., at 682, 689, 691; see also United States v. National Assn. of Securities Dealers, Inc., 422 U.S. 694 (1975) (NASD); Silver v. New York Stock Exchange, 373 U.S. 341 (1963).

I

A

The underwriting practices at issue take place during the course of an initial public offering (IPO) of shares in a company. An IPO presents an opportunity to raise capital for a new enterprise by selling shares to the investing public. A group of underwriters will typically form a syndicate to help market the shares. The syndicate will investigate and estimate likely market demand for the shares at various prices. It will then recommend to the firm a price and the number of shares it believes the firm should offer. Ultimately, the syndicate will promise to buy from the firm all the newly issued shares on a specified date at a fixed, agreed-upon price, which price the syndicate will then charge investors when it resells the shares. When the syndicate buys the shares from the issuing firm, however, the firm gives the syndicate a price discount, which amounts to the syndicate's commission. See generally L. Loss & J. Seligman, Fundamentals of Securities Regulation 66–72 (4th ed. 2001).

At the heart of the syndicate's IPO marketing activity lie its efforts to determine suitable initial share prices and quantities. At first, the syndicate makes a preliminary estimate that it submits in a registration statement to the Securities and Exchange Commission (SEC). It then conducts a "road show" during which syndicate underwriters and representatives of the offering firm meet potential investors and engage in a process that the industry calls "book building." During this time, the underwriters and firm representatives present information to investors about the company and the stock. And they attempt to gauge the strength of the investors' interest in purchasing the stock. For this purpose, underwriters might well ask the investors how their interest would vary depending upon price and the number of shares that are offered. They will learn, among other things, which investors might buy shares, in what quantities, at what prices, and for how long each is likely to hold purchased shares before selling them to others.

On the basis of this kind of information, the members of the underwriting syndicate work out final arrangements with the issuing firm, fixing the price per share and specifying the number of shares for which the underwriters will be jointly responsible. As we have said, after buying the shares at a discounted price, the syndicate resells the shares to investors at the fixed price, in effect earning its commission in the process.

B

In January 2002, respondents, a group of 60 investors, filed two antitrust class-action lawsuits against the petitioners, 10 leading investment banks. They sought relief under § 1 of the Sherman Act, ch. 647, 26 Stat. 209, as amended, 15 U.S.C. § 1; 2(c) of the Clayton Act, 38 Stat. 730, as amended by the Robinson-Patman Act, 49 Stat. 1527, 15 U.S.C. § 13(c); and state antitrust laws. App. 1, 14. The investors stated that between March 1997 and December 2000 the banks had acted as underwriters, forming syndicates that helped execute the IPOs of several hundred technology-related companies. *Id.*, at 22. Respondents' antitrust complaints allege that the underwriters "abused the ... practice of combining into underwriting syndicates" by agreeing among themselves to impose harmful conditions upon potential investors—conditions that the investors apparently were willing to accept in order to obtain an allocation of new shares that were in high demand. *Id.*, at 12.

These conditions, according to respondents, consist of a requirement that the investors pay "additional anticompetitive charges" over and above the agreed-upon IPO share price plus underwriting commission. In particular, these additional charges took the form of (1) investor promises "to place bids ... in the aftermarket at prices above the IPO price" (*i.e.*, "laddering" agreements); (2) investor "commitments to purchase other, less attractive securities" (*i.e.*, "tying" arrangements); and (3) investor payment of "non-competitively determined" (*i.e.*, excessive) "commissions," including the "purchas[e] of an issuer's shares in follow-up or 'secondary' public offerings (for which the underwriters would earn underwriting discounts)." *Id.*, at 12–13. The complaint added that the underwriters' agreement to engage in some or all of these practices artificially inflated the share prices of the securities in question. *Id.*, at 32.

The underwriters moved to dismiss the investors' complaints on the ground that federal securities law impliedly precludes application of antitrust laws to the conduct in question. (The antitrust laws at issue include the commercial bribery provisions of the Robinson-Patman Act.) The District Court agreed with petitioners and dismissed the complaints against them. See In re Initial Public Offering Antitrust Litigation, 287 F.Supp.2d 497, 524–525 (SDNY 2003) (IPO Antitrust). The Court of Appeals for the Second Circuit reversed, however, and reinstated the complaints. 426 F.3d 130, 170, 172 (2005). We granted the underwriters' petition for certiorari. And we now reverse the judgment of the Court of Appeals.

* * *

II

* * *

B

These principles, applied to the complaints before us, considerably narrow our legal task. For the parties cannot reasonably dispute the existence here of several of the conditions that this Court previously regarded as crucial to finding that the securities law impliedly precludes the application of the antitrust laws.

First, the activities in question here—the underwriters' efforts jointly to promote and to sell newly issued securities—is central to the proper functioning of well-regulated capital markets. The IPO process supports new firms that seek to raise capital; it helps to spread ownership of those firms broadly among investors; it directs capital flows in ways that better correspond to the public's demand for goods and services. Moreover, financial experts, including the securities regulators, consider the general kind of joint underwriting activity at issue in this case, including road shows and book-building efforts essential to the successful marketing of an IPO. See Memorandum *Amicus Curiae* of SEC in *IPO Antitrust,* Case No. 01 CIV 2014 (WHP) (SDNY), pp. 15, 39–40, App. D to Pet. for Cert. 124a, 138a, 155a–157a (hereinafter Brief for SEC). Thus, the antitrust complaints before us concern practices that lie at the very heart of the securities marketing enterprise.

Second, the law grants the SEC authority to supervise all of the activities here in question. Indeed, the SEC possesses considerable power to forbid, permit, encourage, discourage, tolerate, limit, and otherwise regulate virtually every aspect of the practices in which underwriters engage. See, *e.g.,* 15 U.S.C. §§ 77b(a)(3), 77j, 77z–2 (granting SEC power to regulate the process of book-building, solicitations of "indications of interest," and communications between underwriting participants and their customers, including those that occur during road shows); § 78*o*(c)(2)(D) (granting SEC power to define and prevent through rules and regulations acts and practices that are fraudulent, deceptive, or manipulative); § 78i(a)(6) (similar); § 78j(b) (similar). Private individuals who suffer harm as a result of a violation of pertinent statutes and regulations may also recover damages. See §§ 78bb, 78u–4, 77k.

Third, the SEC has continuously exercised its legal authority to regulate conduct of the general kind now at issue. It has defined in detail, for example, what underwriters may and may not do and say during their road shows. Compare, *e.g.*, Guidance Regarding Prohibited Conduct In Connection with IPO Allocations, 70 Fed. Reg. 19672 (2005), with Regulation M, 17 CFR §§ 242.100–242.105 (2006). It has brought actions against underwriters who have violated these SEC regulations. See Brief for SEC 13–14, App. D to Pet. for Cert. 136a–138a. And private litigants, too, have brought securities actions complaining of conduct virtually identical to the conduct at issue here; and they have obtained damages. See, *e.g.*, In re Initial Pub. Offering Securities Litigation, 241 F.Supp.2d 281 (SDNY 2003).

The preceding considerations show that the first condition (legal regulatory authority), the second condition (exercise of that authority), and the fourth condition (heartland securities activity) that were present in *Gordon* and *NASD* are satisfied in this case as well. Unlike *Silver*, there is here no question of the existence of appropriate regulatory authority, nor is there doubt as to whether the regulators have exercised that authority. Rather, the question before us concerns the third condition: Is there a conflict that rises to the level of incompatibility? Is an antitrust suit such as this likely to prove practically incompatible with the SEC's administration of the Nation's securities laws?

III

* * *

B

We accept the premises of respondents' argument—that the SEC has full regulatory authority over these practices, that it has actively exercised that authority, but that the SEC has *disapproved* (and, for argument's sake, we assume that it will continue to disapprove) the conduct that the antitrust complaints attack. Nonetheless, we cannot accept respondents' conclusion. Rather, several considerations taken together lead us to find that, even on these prorespondent assumptions, securities law and antitrust law are clearly incompatible.

First, to permit antitrust actions such as the present one *still* threatens serious securities-related harm. For one thing, an unusually serious legal line-drawing problem remains unabated. In the present context only a fine, complex, detailed line separates activity that the SEC permits or encourages (for which respondents must concede antitrust immunity) from activity that the SEC must (and inevitably will) forbid (and which, on respondents' theory, should be open to antitrust attack).

For example, in respect to "laddering" the SEC forbids an underwriter to "solicit customers prior to the completion of the distribution regarding whether and at what price and in what quantity they intend to place immediate aftermarket orders for IPO stock," 70 Fed. Reg. 19675–19676 (emphasis deleted); 17 CFR §§ 242.100–242.105. But at the same time the SEC permits, indeed encourages, underwriters (as part of the "bookbuilding" process) to "inquir[e] as to a customer's desired future position in the longer term (for example, three to six months), and the price or prices at which the customer might accumulate that position without reference to immediate aftermarket activity." 70 Fed. Reg. 19676.

It will often be difficult for someone who is not familiar with accepted syndicate practices to determine with confidence whether an underwriter has insisted that an investor buy more shares in the immediate aftermarket (forbidden), or has simply allocated more shares to an investor willing to purchase additional shares of that issue in the long run (permitted). And who but a securities expert could say whether the present SEC rules set forth a virtually permanent line, unlikely to change in ways that would permit the sorts of "laddering-like" conduct that it now seems to forbid? Cf. Gordon, supra, at 690–691.

Similarly, in respect to "tying" and other efforts to obtain an increased commission from future sales, the SEC has sought to prohibit an underwriter "from demanding . . . an offer from [its] customers of any payment or other consideration [such as the purchase of a different security] in addition to the security's stated consideration." 69 Fed. Reg. 75785 (2004). But the SEC would permit a firm to "allocat[e] IPO shares to a customer because the customer has separately retained the firm for other services, when the customer has not paid excessive compensation in relation to those services." *Ibid.*, n. 108. The National Association of Securities Dealers (NASD), over which the SEC exercises supervisory authority, has also proposed a rule that would prohibit a member underwriter from "offering or threatening to withhold" IPO shares "as consideration or inducement for the receipt of compensation that is excessive in relation to the services provided." *Id.*, at 77810. The NASD would allow, however, a customer legitimately to compete for IPO shares by increasing the level and quantity of compensation it pays to the underwriter. See *Ibid.* (describing NASD Proposed Rule 2712(a)).

Under these standards, to distinguish what is forbidden from what is allowed requires an understanding of just when, in relation to services provided, a commission is "excessive," indeed, so "excessive" that it will remain *permanently* forbidden, see Gordon, 422 U.S., at 690–691. And who but the SEC itself could do so with confidence?

* * *

Now consider these factors together—the fine securities-related lines separating the permissible from the impermissible; the need for securities-related expertise (particularly to determine whether an SEC rule is likely permanent); the overlapping evidence from which reasonable but contradictory inferences may be drawn; and the risk of inconsistent court results. Together these factors mean there is no practical way to confine antitrust suits so that they challenge only activity of the kind the investors seek to target, activity that is presently unlawful and will likely remain unlawful under the securities law. Rather, these factors suggest that antitrust courts are likely to make unusually serious mistakes in this respect. And the threat of antitrust mistakes, *i.e.*, results that stray outside the narrow bounds that plaintiffs seek to set, means that underwriters must act in ways that will avoid not simply conduct that the securities law forbids (and will likely continue to forbid), but also a wide range of joint conduct that the securities law permits or encourages (but which they fear could lead to an antitrust lawsuit and the risk of treble damages). And therein lies the problem.

This kind of problem exists to some degree in respect to other antitrust lawsuits. But here the factors we have mentioned make mistakes unusually likely (a matter relevant to Congress' determination of which institution should regulate a particular set of market activities). And the role that joint conduct plays in respect to the marketing of IPOs, along with the important role IPOs themselves play in relation to the effective functioning of capital markets, means that the securities-related costs of mistakes is unusually high.

* * *

In sum, an antitrust action in this context is accompanied by a substantial risk of injury to the securities markets and by a diminished need for antitrust enforcement to address anticompetitive conduct. Together these considerations indicate a serious conflict between, on the one hand, application of the antitrust laws and, on the other, proper enforcement of the securities law.

* * *

The upshot is that all four elements present in *Gordon* are present here: (1) an area of conduct squarely within the heartland of securities regulations; (2) clear and adequate SEC authority to regulate; (3) active and ongoing agency regulation; and (4) a serious conflict between the antitrust and regulatory regimes. We therefore conclude that the securities laws are "clearly incompatible" with the application of the antitrust laws in this context.

The Second Circuit's contrary judgment is

Reversed.

---

1. *Primary Jurisdiction.* The primary jurisdiction doctrine, relied upon in *Gordon* and greatly extended in *Credit Suisse*, is "specifically applicable to claims properly cognizable in court that contain some issue within the special competence of an administrative agency."[70] When properly invoked, this doctrine permits the court to make "a 'referral' to the agency, staying further proceedings so as to give the parties reasonable opportunity to seek an administrative ruling." Until recently,

---

[70] See Reiter v. Cooper, 507 U.S. 258, 268 (1993).

attempts to invoke this doctrine in areas involving the SEC's special competence had met with little success.[71] *Credit Suisse* gives, however, vastly enhanced significance to the primary jurisdiction doctrine because it found an implied antitrust immunity with respect to a practice that the SEC actively opposed (rather than silently tolerated).

2. *"Soft Dollars" and § 28(e)*. Fixed commissions had given rise to an evasionary tactic known as "give-ups," under which institutional customers with economic leverage would demand that their broker share its fixed commission with another broker who provided the institutional client with some free service (such as securities research or computer services). In this way, they negotiated a hidden discount that partially (and, ultimately, largely) undercut the fixed commission system. As a result, numerous "research boutique" brokerage firms grew up, supported by the "give-up" system with its hidden discounts. Although the competitive need to utilize give-ups as a way of outflanking fixed commissions ended in 1975, the practice survived. First, money managers secured legislative protection for paying above-market brokerage commissions. Fearing that in the absence of legislative authorization they would be forced to use the lowest priced broker or otherwise would be liable to their clients for breach of fiduciary duty, institutional money managers successfully lobbied Congress for the addition of § 28(e) to the 1934 Act. Essentially, § 28(e) creates a "safe harbor" that allows money managers to pay above-market commission rates in return for special services that the broker either provides or arranges for. These special services—known in the trade as "soft dollars"—chiefly consist of research and advisory services or computer facilities made available to the money manager. Obviously, there is a potential for a substantial conflict of interest, because such services may not necessarily benefit the clients that the money manager serves as a fiduciary. Suppose, for example, that the special research is presented to the money manager's leading employees at a seminar held at a ski lodge in Vail, Colorado during the January season. Is this research or employee compensation—or both?

By its terms, § 28(e) applies to protect the money manager from being found to have breached its fiduciary responsibilities because it paid an above-market commission only when it "determined in good faith that such amount of commission was reasonable in relation to the value of the brokerage and research services provided by such member broker or dealer, viewed in terms of either that particular transaction or [its] * * * overall responsibilities with respect to the accounts for which [it] * * * exercises investment discretion." As a result, the degree to which § 28(e) covers "give-ups" remains uncertain, even two decades years after its adoption.[72] Clearly, it was intended to preempt common law principles or

---

[71] See In re NASDAQ Market-Makers Antitrust Litig., 169 F.R.D. 493 (S.D.N.Y.1996); In re Prudential Ins. Co. of America Sales Practices Litig., 962 F.Supp. 450 (D.N.J.1997).

[72] For overviews, see Blanc, "Soft Dollars," 18 Rev. Sec. & Comm. Reg. 51 (1985); Myers, Directed Brokerage and "Soft Dollars" Under ERISA: New Concerns for Plan Fiduciaries, 42

any other state or federal law interpretations that would expose fiduciaries to liability solely because they failed to obtain the lowest brokerage commission available. But it does not absolve fiduciaries from all liability. The House Report accompanying the legislation made the following distinction:

> [A] challenge to fiduciary conduct must be premised on the basis that a fiduciary has failed to use reasonable business judgment in selecting his broker and valuing the services rendered. It is, of course, expected that money managers paying brokers an amount which is based upon the quality and reliability of the broker's services including the availability and value of research, would stand ready and be required to demonstrate that such expenditures were bona fide.[73]

For the SEC, the major question in interpreting the scope of § 28(e) has been that of allocating between true "research" costs and other costs. In a 1986 release, it drew the following distinction:

> [T]he controlling principle to be used to determine whether something qualifies as research is whether it provides lawful and appropriate assistance to the money manager in the performance of his investment decision-making responsibilities. In making this determination, the fact that a product or service is readily and customarily available and offered to the general public on a commercial basis does not dictate that the product or service is not research * * *.
>
> In many cases, a product or service termed "research" may serve other functions that are not related to the making of investment decisions. For example, management information systems may integrate such diverse functions as trading, execution, accounting, recordkeeping and other administrative matters, such as measuring the performance of accounts. Where a product obtained with soft dollars has a mixed use, a money manager faces a conflict of interest in obtaining that product by causing his clients to pay more than competitive brokerage commission rates. Therefore, the Commission believes that where a product has a mixed use, a money manager should make a reasonable allocation of the cost of the product according to its use. The percentage of the service or specific component that provides assistance to a money manager in the investment decision-making process may be paid for in commission dollars, while those services that provide administrative or non-

---

Bus. Law. 553 (Feb.1987); Herzel, Paying Up On Stock Brokerage Commissions Under Section 28(e) of the Securities Exchange Act, 31 Bus. Law. 1479 (1976).

[73] H.R.Rep. No. 94–123, 94th Cong., 1st Sess. 95 (1975); see also 6 Loss and Seligman, supra note 67, at 2886–87.

research assistance are outside the section 28(e) safe harbor and must be paid for by the money manager using his own funds.[74]

In this same Release, the Commission restated its prior position that a money manager could pay "soft dollars" to a broker for research produced by third parties. Research may even be delivered directly by the third party to the money manager (and not routed through the broker for redelivery to the money manager) so long as the broker/money manager contract specifies that the "research" is to be "provided by" the broker. As practices have evolved, the Commission will not object to a money manager paying "reasonable" soft dollar commissions to a broker for "third party" research so long as the manager does not commit itself to performing a minimum number of transactions in return for the research. However, the manager may, with the beneficiaries' consent, obligate itself to pay directly for the cost of research if a minimum number of transactions does not occur.[75] At this point, however, there seems to be little to distinguish "third party" research paid for with "soft dollars" from the old-fashioned customer directed "give-up."

After much hesitation, the SEC returned in 2006 to the topic of "soft dollars" and again sought to restrict the use of "soft dollars." A 1998 SEC staff study and much commentary had suggested that the shareholders of mutual funds were in fact compensating their investment advisers through soft dollars for conference fees, office rent, computer hardware, office administration and other amenities that money managers should cover out of their own budgets. Activists wanted the SEC to rein in "soft dollars." Market practices had also changed, at least in some sectors of the market. For example, Fidelity Investments, the giant mutual fund adviser, sought to increase transparency by separating the fees it paid for stock research and trading, paying each separately.[76] Other brokers have developed "commission-sharing arrangements" under which money managers go to one broker for trading and another for research, building up credits with the former who then contracts for research with the latter.[77] The premise to this approach is that the first broker would not overpay the latter, and that the true cost of trading is thereby revealed.

Against this backdrop, the Commission unanimously voted in July 2006 to issue a new interpretive release to provide "guidance" on money managers' use of client commissions to pay for research and related services. The release sets forth somewhat clearer eligibility criteria; specifically, money managers may use commissions only to pay for eligible research services, including traditional research reports and market data, but not mass-marketed publications, computer hardware,

---

[74] Securities Exchange Act Release No. 23,170 (1986).

[75] See 6 Loss and Seligman, supra note 51, at 2892–93; see also Securities Exchange Act Rel. No. 16,679 (1980).

[76] See A. Dale, Wall Street Makes "Soft Dollar Pitch," The Wall Street Journal, July 11, 2006 at C-3.

[77] Id.

or other items that benefit only the money manager. Once eligibility criteria are satisfied, the money manager must also make appropriate use of the research or services provided and must make a good faith determination that the commissions paid were reasonable in light of the value of the services received. For "mixed-use" items, the release again requires an allocation. In overview, the Commission appears caught in the crossfire between mutual fund investors who are suspicious of "soft dollars" and a brokerage industry that has come to rely upon them and is unable to make more than modest interpretive changes. But competitive forces may be widening the cracks in the foundation underlying the soft dollar system.

One last point must be understood about § 28(e): by its own terms, it can never be violated. It is simply a "safe harbor," and when transactions fall outside that safe harbor, it is still necessary to look to the statutory or common law defining the relevant fiduciary obligation.

5. THE OVER-THE-COUNTER MARKET

Statutes and Regulations

Exchange Act, §§ 11(b) and 15A.

Regulation ATS.

Exchange Act Rules 10b–10, 11b–1, 11Aa3–1, 11Ac1–1.

Not all securities trade on exchanges. Over the long history of U.S. securities markets, the majority of stocks traded instead on over-the-counter markets. In these markets, there was no specialist or electronic market that automatically executed an order at an offered price. Transactions instead were negotiated by buyer and seller. Although Nasdaq was originally an over-the-counter market, it offered firm bid and offered prices that a customer could accept electronically. Once Congress adopted the National Market System, a "Firm Quote Rule" became mandatory, which required the dealer to provide firm quotes for Nasdaq-listed securities that the customer could accept electronically,[78] and Nasdaq's own rules require that last sale reports must be reported by dealers within 90 seconds of execution. With such data, investors could easily ascertain the best bid and asked prices and could rely on these prices more or less as confidently as they could on the quotations on an exchange. However, other over-the-counter securities issued by companies that did not meet the issuer qualification standards for the NMS were not subject to these rules. In such cases, last sale prices are not necessarily reported, and current information may be lacking on the bid/asked prices available from all dealers. In such an environment, a customer wishing to purchase or sell such a security becomes both

---

[78] See Rule 602(b) of Regulation NMS.

dependent on the dealer to learn what the best current price is and more vulnerable to exploitation.

Today, the over-the-counter market (basically, those stocks beneath the level of Nasdaq's Bulletin Boards) remains outside the National Market System and may have only limited transparency. Up to 10,000 stocks may be listed in this market (the number varies constantly), and most are "penny stocks," implying both that they are not "reporting companies" and that they trade for less than $5 per share. Prices in this market are volatile, and are sometimes manipulated, often through "pump and dump" schemes in which co-conspirators release false positive information, bid the stock up in transactions among themselves, and then "dump" their holdings at inflated prices onto unsuspecting investors.

Organizationally, the contemporary over-the-counter market is run by the OTC Markets Group, which is the successor to the former "Pink Sheets", which was a listing service that for nearly a century published pricing information (but not firm quotes) on literally pink sheets. Although it is based in New York City, it is an electronic market with no fixed trading floor,[79] and its prices must be negotiated between buyer and seller, with the result that prices may vary from transaction to transaction; nor are brokers in this market required to report transactions promptly.

Brokers trading on any market are subject to a duty of best execution (as further discussed in Chapter 11). But in addition, the NASD (and now FINRA) have promulgated additional rules to limit the possible overreaching of customers by brokers in this non-transparent market, as next discussed:

Lehl v. Securities and Exchange Commission
United States Court of Appeals, Tenth Circuit, 1996.
90 F.3d 1483.

■ Before ANDERSON, MCWILLIAMS, and ENGEL, CIRCUIT JUDGES.

■ ANDERSON, CIRCUIT JUDGE.

Daniel R. Lehl petitions for review of a final order by the Securities and Exchange Commission ("SEC") sustaining disciplinary action taken against him by a registered securities association, the National Association of Securities Dealers, Inc. ("NASD"). Based on our review of the record, we affirm the SEC's order.

In 1990, Lehl was a securities salesman associated with First Choice Securities in Denver. First Choice was a registered member of the NASD and Lehl was a registered representative. Between July 17 and August 3, 1990, Lehl sold 285,000 shares of stock in Champions Sports, Inc., to

---

[79] The OTC Markets Group has three levels of markets: OTCQX, OTCQB, and Pink Sheets, with the last listing the most speculative of stocks.

retail customers in eleven separate transactions. Lehl charged his customers 6.5 cents per share, the "execution price" established by his firm. The Denver branch of First Choice obtained the stock from the firm at a "strike price" of 5 cents per share. Each of these prices was posted daily on a board in the front of the Denver office. The difference between the strike price and the execution price constituted the firm's "gross commission" on each transaction, from which Lehl's individual commissions were paid. Lehl knew these facts. He did not know, however, and never inquired into, the price per share the firm had paid for its Champions stock, which was in fact 3.125 cents in nine of the transactions and 3.5 cents in the other two.

In 1991, the NASD commenced disciplinary proceedings against First Choice and various individuals associated with the firm, including Lehl, for their actions in marketing Champions stock. The NASD District Business Conduct Committee found Lehl had violated the NASD Rules of Fair Practice by charging unfair and excessive prices without proper disclosure to his customers. The Committee censured Lehl and ordered him to requalify by examination as a registered representative. On appeal, the NASD National Business Conduct Committee affirmed and added a $5000 fine, plus costs. On de novo review, the SEC affirmed in pertinent part and sustained the NASD's sanctions. Lehl seeks review of the SEC's adverse decision.

* * *

The SEC found Lehl violated Sections 1 and 4 of the NASD Rules of Fair Practice, Article III. Section 1 reads: "A member, in the conduct of his business, shall observe high standards of commercial honor and just and equitable principles of trade." Section 4 reads:

> In "over-the-counter" transactions, whether in "listed" or "unlisted" securities, if a member . . . sells for his own account to his customer, he shall . . . sell at a price which is fair, taking into consideration all relevant circumstances, including market conditions with respect to such security at the time of the transaction, the expense involved, and the fact that he is entitled to a profit. . . .

See also NASD Rules of Fair Practice, art. I, § 5 ("Persons associated with a member shall have the same duties and obligations as a member under these Rules of Fair Practice."), reprinted in Resp't Br., Statutory Addendum at 2A.

In his petition, Lehl advances five reasons why he should not be held accountable for selling Champions stock at unfair markups: (1) the SEC's findings of misconduct varied from the misconduct charged against him; (2) the NASD never properly adopted its markup policy; (3) SEC enforcement of the NASD markup policy is an improper regulation of securities prices; (4) the SEC improperly calculated the markups; and (5) the record contains insufficient evidence to support the SEC's finding that Lehl was personally culpable. We will address each of these contentions in turn.

* * *

2. *The NASD Markup Policy.* Lehl next argues that the SEC never formally approved the NASD markup policy, as required for any changes in registered association rules. See 15 U.S.C. § 78s(b)(1). The NASD policy, which interprets Sections 1 and 4 as they relate to markups, prohibits registered representatives from entering into "any transaction with a customer in any security at any price not reasonably related to the current market price of the security." NASD Mark-Up Policy, Interpretation of the Board of Governors, *reprinted* in Resp't Br., Statutory Addendum at 4A. . . .

Lehl nevertheless focuses his argument specifically on a guideline within that interpretation, the so-called "5% policy."[4] He argues that the SEC employed the 5% policy as a substantive rule in this case, sanctioning him for selling Champions stock at prices exceeding 5% of the market price—even though the NASD never formally adopted the policy as a rule. We disagree with the premise of this argument. "[T]here is no hard and fast '5 percent rule' as complained of by petitioner. The Commission did not discipline him merely because his commissions were in excess of 5 per cent." Samuel B. Franklin & Co. v. SEC, 290 F.2d 719, 725 (9th Cir.), *cert. denied*, 368 U.S. 889, 82 S.Ct. 142, 7 L.Ed.2d 88 (1961). Rather it found, without reference to the 5% policy, that markups of 86% and 100% over market price were unfair. A substantial body of established case law supports this determination, independent of the 5% policy. E.g., Duker & Duker, Exchange Act Release No. 2350, 6 S.E.C. 386, 1939 WL 1332, at *3 (Dec. 19, 1939) ("Judged by any standards," markup of 44% was "plainly excessive and unreasonable.") (pre-5% policy); Charles Hughes & Co. v. SEC, 139 F.2d 434, 435 (2d Cir. 1943) (prices marked up 40% were "very substantially over those prevailing in the . . . market"), *cert. denied*, 321 U.S. 786, 64 S.Ct. 781, 88 L.Ed. 1077 (1944); Samuel B. Franklin & Co., 290 F.2d at 725 (markups greater than 20% were clearly excessive and not reasonably related to market prices); Costello, Russotto & Co., Exchange Act Release No. 7729, 42 S.E.C. 798, 1965 WL 6611, at *3 (Oct. 22, 1965) ("We have repeatedly held that markups of more than 10 percent are unfair even in the sale of low priced securities. . . ."); cf. Robert B. Orkin, Exchange Act Release No. 32,035,

---

[4] To guide its members in determining when a price is "reasonably related to the current market price," the NASD surveyed industry pricing practices, concluding that the vast majority of transactions occurred at markups of 5% or less. It then issued guidelines setting 5% as a benchmark of reasonableness, to be considered with other relevant factors. The NASD cautioned, however, that the 5% policy "is a guide—not a rule"; that a "mark-up pattern of 5% or even less may be considered unfair or unreasonable"; and that "[i]n the case of certain low-priced securities, such as those selling below $10.00, a somewhat higher percentage may sometimes be justified." See Handley Inv. Co. v. SEC, 354 F.2d 64, 65 (10th Cir. 1965); Samuel B. Franklin & Co. v. SEC, 290 F.2d 719, 725 (9th Cir.), cert. denied, 368 U.S. 889, 82 S.Ct. 142, 7 L.Ed.2d 88 (1961); NASD Mark-Up Policy, reprinted in Resp't Br., Statutory Addendum at 4A.

53 S.E.C. Docket 1963, 1993 WL 89023, at *4 n. 30 (Mar. 23, 1993) (markups ranging from 16% to 100% make challenge to 5% policy "largely academic"), aff'd, 31 F.3d 1056 (11th Cir. 1994). Lehl's attack on the 5% policy in this case fails.

3. *NASD Regulatory Authority.* Lehl next argues that the SEC's enforcement of the "NASD markup rules" is an improper regulation of securities prices. See 15 U.S.C. § 78o–3(b)(6) (rules of registered securities association may not fix rates of commissions). We disagree. As the SEC has observed in rejecting a similar contention, "[t]he NASD does not set prices, but merely requires that whatever prices its members set be fair to retail customers. As Congress has noted, this policy serves "to protect investors against "gouging" and promotes just and equitable principles of trade." Richard R. Perkins, Exchange Act Release No. 32,188, 53 S.E.C. Docket 2442, 1993 WL 128738, at *3 (Apr. 21, 1993) (quoting S.Rep. No. 75, 94th Cong., 1st Sess. 28, *reprinted in* 1975 U.S.C.C.A.N. 179, 206) (citation corrected) (and noting further that the SEC has "rejected similar arguments before"); see also R. Vol. 3 at 2261 n.22 (same). In this case, the SEC did not sanction Lehl for selling securities above a certain price or for receiving commissions in excess of a fixed rate, but rather for selling securities to his customers at prices that were blatantly unfair. Lehl's attack on the NASD's regulatory authority fails.

* * *

For the foregoing reasons, we AFFIRM the order of the SEC.

---

1. *Note on Mark-Up Policy.* Since 1943, the NASD (and later FINRA) have enforced an interpretation of its Rules of Fair Practice that deems it inconsistent with "just and equitable" principles of trade for a member to enter into any transaction with a customer at a price not reasonably related to the current market price of the security.[80] In 1943, the NASD surveyed its members and determined that 47% of transactions by its members were made at mark-ups of 3% or less and 71% of the transactions were affected at mark-ups of 5% or less. Based on this evidence, the NASD adopted a 5% guideline to determine when mark-ups became excessive.[81]

A guideline is by no means a prophylactic rule, and the NASD (and now FINRA) have identified a variety of factors that need to be considered in determining the fairness of a mark-up in an individual case. These include:

---

[80] See Interpretation of the Board of Governors, NASD Mark-Up Policy, CCH NASD Manual, Rule 2154 at 2054–61.

[81] See In re Thill Securities Corp., 42 S.E.C. 89, 91 n. 4 (1964).

a. *The type of security involved.* Generally, mark-ups on equity securities may be larger than mark-ups on debt securities.[82]

b. *The availability of the security.* When the market in a stock is inactive, the dealer will usually spend more time and effort obtaining the security, thus justifying a higher mark-up. When there is an active market, and less effort is needed to obtain the stock, the same mark-up is not justified.[83]

c. *The price of the security.* Although there is no direct correlation, the percentage of mark-up or rate of commission generally increases as the price of the security decreases. Handling costs tend to be the same for both high and low priced securities, and thus justify a commission that is higher on a percentage basis in the case of the low priced securities. However, where the size of the transaction is large, even though the security's price is low, higher mark-ups may not be justified.[84]

d. *The amount of money involved in the transaction.* A transaction that involves a small amount of money may warrant a higher percentage of mark-up to cover handling costs.[85]

e. *Disclosure to the customer.* Any disclosure made to the customer before the transaction about the mark-up will be considered, but is not alone a justification for a commission otherwise "unfair or excessive in light of all the other relevant circumstances."[86]

f. *The pattern of mark-ups.* The NASD will look beyond the individual transaction to the overall pattern of the member's mark-ups to determine if they are generally excessive.

g. *The nature of the member's business.* A dealer that provides other services, such as research, advice or financial planning, may be justified in charging a higher mark-up.

The NASD's mark-up policy applies not only to stock traded over-the-counter, but also to the rarer case in which the broker contacts existing shareholders of a small company to acquire stock for its client. In general, both the NASD and FINRA have vigorously enforced this mark-up policy and brought a number of disciplinary proceedings for charging excessive mark-ups.[87] At the same time, the NASD also revised

---

[82] See In re Staten Securities Corp., 47 S.E.C. 766, 768 (1982).
[83] See In re NASD, 17 S.E.C. 459, 466–67 (1944).
[84] See In re Maryland Securities Co., 40 S.E.C. 443, 446 (1960).
[85] See In re Greenberg, 40 S.E.C. 133, 136 (1960).
[86] CCH NASD Manual, Rule 2154 (now FINRA Rule 2154).
[87] For representative cases, see, e.g., In re Nicholas Codispoti, Securities Exchange Act Release No. 24946 (Sept. 29, 1987); In re Voss & Co., Inc., Securities Exchange Act Release No. 21301 (Sept. 10, 1984).

its policy to require more detailed procedures to establish what the prevailing price was. In the case of securities not traded over Nasdaq, determining the prevailing price (to which the mark-up is then added) is often the principal issue in the case. In 1988, the SEC approved an amendment to the NASD Rules of Fair Practice requiring the member to mark customer order tickets for each transaction in a non-Nasdaq stock to indicate the dealers contacted and the price quotations received in order to determine the prevailing price.[88] Also in 1988, the NASD issued an interpretation restating its "5% Policy" that set forth the following rules for determining the "prevailing market price."

    a.   When there is a competitive market for the securities, the prices paid by other dealers to the market maker under review are to be considered the most accurate reflection of the prevailing market price.

    b.   Market makers who engage in principal transactions with their retail clients are normally entitled to the "inside" spread, and the best available price (i.e., the "inside" asked price) would be used to calculate the mark-up. Where the dealer does not make a market in the security, it may use its contemporaneous cost as the primary basis from which to compute a mark-up.

    c.   Where there is no independent market or where the market maker dominates the market, the contemporaneous prices paid by the market maker for the stock are the best available evidence of the prevailing market price, and such cost should be used as the basis for the mark-up.

    d.   A dominant market maker may not use its own quoted spread as the basis for a mark-up (as it would be entitled to if there was a competitive market in the stock), but should use its cost.[89]

FINRA has vacillated in its policy on markups. In 2011, it proposed to abandon the 5% ceiling, fearing that some brokers were treating it as an authority to charge high markups of up to 5%. But, in 2013, it reversed itself and restored the 5% rule, apparently concluding that a more indefinite rule would be hard to enforce. In any event, markups today appear to be closer to 2% than 5%, and FINRA has made clear to its members that markups below 5% can be found to be excessive in certain cases.

Independently, the SEC has also enforced its own mark-up policy under the antifraud provisions of the federal securities laws. In 1943, the Second Circuit accepted the SEC's position that the duty of fair dealing

---

    [88]   See NASD Notice to Members 88–83 (discussed in Mathews & Citera, "Markups" in PLI, Trading Practices, the Portfolio Execution Process), and Soft-Dollar Arrangements (L. Pickard, ed., 1989) at 195.

    [89]   See Mathews & Citera, supra note 88, at 196.

included an implied representation that the price a dealer charges bears a "reasonable relationship" to the prevailing market price.[90] Absent disclosure, the dealer thus violates Rule 10b–5 if its price is "substantially different" from the prevailing market price.[91] When the mark-up exceeds ten percent of the "prevailing market price," the SEC has repeatedly held in administrative proceedings that such a mark-up is fraudulent per se.[92]

Rule 10b–10 partially implements the SEC's policy on mark-ups by specifying what must be disclosed on the confirmation of sale sent to the customer. In some circumstances, it requires specific disclosure of the mark-up.[93] Generally, Rule 10b–10 requires disclosure of the net price to the customer, but does not require disclosure of mark-ups. Compliance with Rule 10b–10 does not, however, create a safe harbor that absolves the dealer from liability for excessive mark-ups.[94]

6. MARKET DATA

Statutes and Regulations

Exchange Act, § 11A.

Exchange Act Rules 11Aa3–1.

Rules 603 and 610 of Regulation NMS.

One of the greatest successes surrounding the introduction of the NMS system was the market infrastructure that the SEC essentially imposed to give all investors immediate access to the same "core" information about NMS-listed securities. But this early success appears to have faded more recently, possibly because of the desire of exchanges to maximize their revenues from the sale of market data. Under the NMS structure (as detailed in Rule 603), information about quotations and transactions is sent by each exchange or market venue to one of two "securities information processors" (or "SIPs"), who aggregate this information from each exchange and market center and funnel it to commercial publishers (basically, Bloomberg, Dow Jones, and Reuters) who distribute it to their subscribers (mainly, broker-dealers) electronically. The two SIPs are not in competition with each other,[95] and their costs are borne by brokers (or passed on by them to their customers).

---

[90] Charles Hughes & Co. v. SEC, 139 F.2d 434 (2d Cir. 1943).

[91] See, e.g., Ettinger v. Merrill Lynch, Pierce, Fenner & Smith, Inc., 835 F.2d 1031 (3d Cir. 1987); In re James E. Ryan, 47 S.E.C. 759 (1982).

[92] See Alstead, Dempsey & Co., Securities Exchange Act Release No. 20825 (April 5, 1984); In re Peter J. Kisch, Securities Exchange Act Release No. 19005 (Aug. 24, 1982).

[93] See Rule 10b–10(a)(2)(ii)(A)–(B). For equity securities in the National Market System, the rule requires disclosures based on which an intelligent customer can calculate the mark-up.

[94] Ettinger v. Merrill Lynch, Pierce, Fenner & Smith, 835 F.2d 1031 (3d Cir. 1987); Krome v. Merrill Lynch & Co., 637 F.Supp. 910, 915–16 (S.D.N.Y.1986).

[95] The two current "securities information processors" each have an exclusive relationship with one group of exchanges. The CTA/CQ SIP, which is largely owned by the NYSE's parent, basically handles securities listed on the NYSE, while the UTP SIP largely

For a long time, this system worked relatively well, and enabled brokers to quickly discover the "best bid and best offer" (or "NBBO") for any NMS security, so that brokers could easily fulfill the duty of best execution that they owed their customers by trading for them at the inside spread price that the SIPs provided. But, as trading became much more rapid after the adoption of Regulation NMS in 2005, traders found that they could profit from algorithmic trading and particularly from gaining even a millisecond advantage in trading time (or "low latency" in the vocabulary of traders). One means to achieve low latency was "co-location"—that is, paying exchanges to allow the trader to place its computer's server next to the exchange's server (and then programming the computer to trade instantly based on installed algorithms). Another technique was for the exchange to sell private feeds of its market data to HFT traders. By this latter means, sophisticated traders could acquire information before it became fully available through the SIP and the commercial publishers to whom the SIP supplied market information. Also, exchanges learned and responded to the desire of HFT traders to gain more information than was transmitted to the SIP—for example, information about the "depth of the market" and how much stock was available at prices inferior to the NBBO.

Here, it is critical to understand that securities exchanges basically generate revenue from three sources: (1) listing fees charged to listed companies; (2) fees and expenses charged to member firms for trading on them; and (3) market data fees, which are paid for transaction, quotation and other information. Increasingly, this third source has become more important, and a decade ago, it was a primary reason that some ECNs converted to exchanges (to gain a greater share of these fees).

The discount brokers have long claimed that the exchanges' fees were excessive and exceeded the reasonable costs of gathering the information. The conflict is at bottom between the owners of the property right and its users, because the market data fees typically are borne by the broker-dealer. That is, while the exchange sells its data to a vendor (for example, Bloomberg), the vendor charges a fee to its subscribers, who are mostly broker-dealers, and the latter typically cannot fully pass on these costs to their customers. In 1998, when this controversy first came to a boil, the exchanges received $414 million in market data fees, while Schwab paid in that year a total of $20 million for access to NYSE data alone.[96]

Brokers and exchanges have strongly divergent and antagonistic positions here.[97] Many discount brokers want market data fees to be closely tied to the costs actually incurred in generating this data.

---

handles Nasdaq-listed securities. The term "securities information processor" is defined in Section 3(a)(22)(A) of the 1934 Act.

[96] See David Ignatius, "Putting a Meter on the Flow of Information," Washington Post, June 30, 1999, at A-31.

[97] For an overview of the issues, see Securities Exchange Act Release No. 42208 (Dec. 9, 1999).

Inevitably, this would involve the SEC in rate regulation, much like a public utility commission, and the SEC's competence at such a task is open to doubt. Conversely, the exchanges would prefer that each exchange be able to sell its own data to vendors. Yet, brokers fear that the major exchanges still have a sufficiently dominant position that they would be able to overcharge.

The SEC has long sought a compromise. As long ago as 2000, it appointed an advisory committee to develop recommendations, which was chaired by then Dean Joel Seligman of Washington University Law School. This Advisory Committee on Market Information reported in 2001 and recommended that the institutional structure for the collection of market data be revised to provide for multiple consolidators of market data.[98] Today, each exchange must report "core data" (i.e., the price and size of its most recent trade and its current best bid and offer) to one of two SIPs for consolidation,[99] and each disseminates the consolidated information to broker-dealers and data vendors.[100] The SEC must approve the fees charged for core data,[101] and a broker-dealer is required to purchase consolidated core data and make it available to investors.[102]

Although the distribution of "core data" is closely regulated and the SEC has long required these fees to be related to costs,[103] the greater problem is that the SIPs have not kept pace with the private market. Having a regulatory monopoly, the SIP rationally has little incentive to innovate or invest in new technology (while the exchanges and other market centers that compete do—at least, if they can charge for it). In 2006, NYSE Arca (which was the former Archipelago ECN) proposed to charge for its "depth-of-book" data (which it had formerly provided at no cost); this data showed all outstanding limit orders to sell or buy stocks at prices away from the best prices (i.e., the inside spread) on the exchange and was a measure of the liquidity on the exchange. NYSE Arca was required to file (and did file) a proposed rule change with the SEC and show that its proposed charge for the distribution of non-core market data was "fair and reasonable" and "not unreasonably discriminatory."[104]

---

[98] See Report of the Advisory Committee on Market Information (Sept. 14, 2001); see also Schroeder, "Market Data Report Backs Multiple Consolidators," Securities Industry News, October 1, 2001.

[99] This obligation is imposed by Rules 601 and 602 of Regulation NMS. See 17 C.F.R. §§ 242.601, 242.602.

[100] See Rule 603 ("Distribution, Consolidation and Display of Information with Respect to Quotations for and Transactions in NMS Stocks). 17 C.F.R. § 242.603.

[101] See Rule 608(b) ("Filing and Amendment of National Market System Plans"). See 17 C.F.R. § 242.608.

[102] See Rule 603(c) ("Distribution, Consolidation, and Display of Information with Respect to Quotations for and Transactions in NMS Stocks"). See 17 C.F.R. § 242.603(c).

[103] Because of the mandatory requirement that brokers purchase core data and the arguably oligopolistic position of the exchanges, the SEC has insisted that core data fees "should bear some relationship to cost." See Netcoalition v. S.E.C., 615 F.3d 525, 529 n. 2 (citing Securities Exchange Act Release No. 42208 (Dec. 17, 1999)).

[104] Although non-core data is not required by the SEC to be included in the consolidated data stream or displayed by brokers to investors, an exchange is an "exclusive processor" of securities information under Section 3(a)(22) of the Securities Exchange Act and must distribute

The SEC approved NYSE Arca's proposed rule change, even though its proposed charge for this data was not cost based. Instead, the SEC found that NYSE Arca's "market-based" charges were acceptable because NYSE Arca was subject to significant competitive based forces in setting the prices for its product. A coalition of broker-dealers and internet companies promptly sued in the D.C. Circuit to overturn the SEC's rulings. In *NetCoalition v. Securities and Exchange Commission*,[105] the D.C. Circuit agreed with the plaintiffs and invalidated the SEC's order, finding that the SEC had failed to show that NYSE Arca was adequately subject to competitive forces. Although the D.C. Circuit recognized that order flow competition was a powerful force, it would not accept that it adequately constrained market prices for an informational product that was used by only a limited number of sophisticated investors. In short, it did not believe that an excessive price would cause NYSE Arca to lose sufficient order flow to discipline its pricing decisions.

Facing the recognition that the NMS's system for disclosure of market data had fallen behind the private markets, the SEC, after a series of hearings and reports, finally proposed action in early 2020. In Securities Exchange Act Release No. 34–88216 ("Market Data Infrastructure"), it announced two basic policy changes:

(1) it would require more mandatory disclosure (particularly about the "depth of the market") that exchanges and other market centers would have to disclose contemporaneously; and

(2) it responded to the slowness of the existing SIP system by proposing a system of multiple competing SIPs, along with rules that would permit market centers and others to "self aggregate."[106]

A new Rule 614 was also proposed to be added to Regulation NMS to change the governance structure for the regulation of market data and to minimize potential conflicts of interest. These proposals are still at an intermediate stage and will attract controversy. If adopted in their current version, they will mean that there will no longer be a single NBBO, but different SIPs and self-aggregators will specify different NBBOs. These changes are unlikely to replace the centrality of HFTs as the principal suppliers of liquidity to the equity markets, but they may usher in other still unanticipated changes (just as did Regulation NMS in 2005).

---

information on terms that are "fair and reasonable" and "not unreasonably discriminatory." See Rule 603(a)(1)–(2), 17 C.F.R. § 242.603(a).

[105] 615 F.3d 525 (D.C. Cir. 2010).

[106] See Securities Exchange Act Rel. No. 34–88216 ("Market Data Infrastructure") (February 14, 2020).

7. TECHNOLOGY AND INFRASTRUCTURE

Statutes and Regulations

Exchange Act, § 11A(a)(1) and (2).

Regulation Systems Compliance and Integrity ("Regulation SCI").

The U.S. securities markets have simultaneously enhanced the speed, capacity, and sophistication of trading systems and experienced increased operational problems with automated systems, including large scale failures, delays, losses of liquidity, and intrusions. Given the interconnected nature of the U.S. securities markets, even seemingly minor problems at a single entity can have system-wide effects causing widespread damage. For over two decades, SEC oversight of the technology underlying the U.S. securities markets was conducted pursuant to a voluntary compliance program based on a general set of principles.[107] But high-profile operational failures at exchanges caused the Commission to abandon that voluntary policy in 2014 and supersede it with Regulation Systems Compliance and Integrity (better known as "Regulation SCI").[108] In short, the technological infrastructure underlying the securities markets became a regulatory priority because automation increases the costs and risks associated with technological glitches, bugs and failures.

Regulation SCI principally applies to self-regulatory organizations (which includes the exchanges), high volume alternative trading systems, securities information plan processors (or "SIPs"), and clearing agencies and requires these entities to establish written policies and procedures reasonably designed to ensure that their systems have levels of capacity, integrity, resiliency, and security adequate to maintain their operational capability. In addition, these entities are required to participate in regular testing of the operation of their business continuity and disaster recovery plan and to take corrective action with respect to certain events (including systems disruptions, compliance issues, and system intrusions) and to notify the SEC of such events. Regulated entities were also required to conduct a review of their systems by qualified personnel at least annually and submit quarterly reports regarding material changes in their systems.

The adoption of Regulation SCI marked a shift from a voluntary to a mandatory policy and followed a series of well publicized failures.[109] These included:

---

[107] See Sec. Exch. Act Release No. 27445 (November 16, 1989) and Sec. Exch. Act Release No. 29185 (May 9, 1991). These two releases, each titled "Automated Systems of Self Regulatory Organizations," established the Commission's "Automation Review Policy."

[108] See Sec. Exch. Act Release No. 73639 (November 19, 2014).

[109] Some of these events are discussed in Sec. Exch. Act Release No. 69077 (March 8, 2013) at 20–23. More recent events are discussed in Sec. Exch. Act Release No. 73639, supra note 108.

(1) The May 10, 2010 "Flash Crash". On that date, the prices of many U.S-based equity products (stocks, options, and derivatives) experienced extraordinary rapid declines and recoveries. The SEC's staff found over 20,000 trades on that date in at least 300 securities that were executed at prices more than 60% away from their values just moments before.[110] The staff concluded that "the interaction between automated execution programs and algorithmic trading strategies can quickly erode liquidity and result in disorderly markets . . .";[111]

(2) The initial public offerings of BATS Global Markets, Inc. and Facebook, Inc., in 2012, were disrupted by "software bugs" that delayed or shut down these offerings;

(3) Computer hackers penetrated Nasdaq's computer network in 2011;

(4) Both Nasdaq and the Chicago Board Option Exchanges experienced major, multi-hour delays in the opening of trading in 2013; and

(5) Securities information processors were unable recurrently to process quotes from exchanges because of technical failures.[112]

In response, Regulation SCI does the following:

1. Rule 1001(a) requires regulated entities to develop comprehensive written policies and procedures to achieve capacity, integrity, resiliency, availability and security.

2. Rule 1001(b) mandates similar policies to achieve systems compliance.

3. Rule 1002 requires corrective actions, Commission notification, and dissemination of reports in the wake of certain defined events.

4. Rule 1003 requires notification of the Commission of system changes and periodic review.

5. Rules 1005–1007 mandate record-keeping, electronic filing on new Form SCI, and access to the systems of an "SCI entity."

SEC jurisdiction for Regulation SCI is predicated on § 11A(a)(1) of the 1934 Act, which finds both that "[t]he securities markets are an important national asset which must be preserved and strengthened" and that "[i]t is in the public interest . . . to assure . . . economically efficient execution of securities transactions." The 1934 Act then directs

---

[110] See Securities Exch. Act Release No. 69077, supra note 109, at pp. 20–21.
[111] Id at 21.
[112] See Sec. Exch. Act. Release No. 73639, supra note 109, at 11 to 15.

the Commission in § 11A(a)(2) "to carry out the objectives set forth in paragraph (1) of this subsection."

Today, "SCI events"—meaning system disruptions, system compliance problems and system intrusions (by hackers or others)—are recognized as requiring prompt disclosure and corrective efforts, lest the victim become itself the target of SEC enforcement. Recent reviews of Regulation SCI have generally praised the SEC's efforts in designing and enforcing this regulation.[113]

8. SELF REGULATION IN THE SECURITIES INDUSTRY

Statutes and Regulations

Exchange Act, §§ 6, 15A, 15B, 15C, 19.

Because the NYSE and other exchanges existed for well over a century before the SEC was created, a system of self-regulation was already in place at the time the federal securities laws were enacted, which they largely adopted. In effect, SEC regulation was overlaid on top of exchange regulation, rather than substituted for it. Still, because the Congress was dissatisfied with the performance of the exchanges during the late 1920's, when it believed that "pools" and other conspiracies manipulated securities prices, the 1934 Act required the registration of all securities exchanges with the SEC and gave the Commission strong enforcement powers over them.[114] Later in 1938, Congress passed the Maloney Act, which authorized the creation of a similar self-regulatory body to regulate broker-dealers (many of whom were not NYSE members).[115] Although Section 15A authorized the formation of multiple such self-regulatory associations, only one—the National Association of Securities Dealers ("NASD"), founded in 1939—was ever formed.[116] Following the NASD's merger in 2007 with the regulatory arm of the NYSE to form the Financial Industry Regulatory Authority ("FINRA"), FINRA is today the self-regulatory body responsible for the oversight of all broker-dealers dealing with the public (although each stock exchange continues to oversee certain trading and listing issues).

The merits of self-regulation have long been debated, but at least in theory, two important advantages can be posited for such a two-tiered structure of regulation, with the SEC and "self-regulatory organizations" (or "SROs") sharing overlapping authority. First, SROs have the ability

---

[113] See Alexander Osipovich, "Fixes Spark by 'Flash Crash' Worked Well in Recent Turmoil," The Wall Street Journal at B-1, May 6, 2020; Kristin Johnson, Regulating Innovation: High Frequency Trading in Dark Pools, 42 J. Corporation Law 833 (2017); Note, The Need for Speed: Regulating Approaches to High Frequency Trading in the U.S. and the European Union, 50 Vanderbilt J. Transnational Law 1359 (2017).

[114] See Section 6 of the Securities Exchange Act of 1934.

[115] See Section 15A of the Securities Exchange Act of 1934.

[116] It was actually a successor to an earlier body, the Code Committee, created in 1933 as part of the National Recovery Act, which Act was later held unconstitutional by the Supreme Court.

to tax the relevant industry to fund their monitoring and enforcement costs. This is in contrast to the SEC, which depends on a sometimes parsimonious Congress for its annual appropriation; thus this two-tier structure implies some level of assured financing. "Taxing the industry" is simple to achieve because the ability to practice in the industry or profession can be conditioned on registration and payment of membership fees. Second, while the SEC is primarily an anti-fraud enforcement agency, SROs can be authorized to employ a lower threshold of regulatory attention and discipline negligence or unprofessional conduct that falls short of fraud. Both FINRA and its predecessor, the NASD, have long promulgated and enforced Rules of Fair Practice, which obligate its members to "observe high standards of commercial honor and just and equitable principles of trade"[117]—in short, the rules that honest merchants would naturally observe. In practice, these rules authorize enforcement and sanctions in cases that anti-fraud rules would often have difficulty reaching. In addition, because the rules of private bodies (as both the NYSE and FINRA remain in the eyes of courts) do not give rise to implied causes of action, SRO regulations authorize only public enforcement and not private enforcement, which may arguably make it possible for SRO rules to establish more aspirational standards.

A. *Governance.* Historically, both the NYSE and the NASD were non-profit organizations owned by their members. In 2005, the NYSE merged with Archipelago Holdings Inc., and in the process the NYSE was transformed from a not-for-profit corporation, in which the voting power was held by its seat holders, to a public corporation, NYSE Group, Inc., which is owned by more or less the same cross-section of shareholders that own other U.S. public corporations. Almost simultaneously, Nasdaq merged with Instinet, one of the largest and the oldest ECN, in a transaction that also gave it a broad public ownership. In response, the SEC indicated that it expected publicly held SROs, such as the exchanges, to conform to the same governance standards as publicly held companies under Sarbanes Oxley.[118] In early 2005, the NYSE conformed to this policy, adopting an "Independence Policy" for its Board of Directors that essentially paralleled its standards for listed companies.[119] Pursuant to a settlement with the SEC, FINRA revised its board so that today it has a majority of outside "public" directors. Specifically, it has a board of twenty-four members, thirteen of which are "public" members having no affiliation with the industry; ten of which are representatives of the industry (broken down among various constituencies of the broker-dealer industry (e.g., small broker-dealers, medium-sized broker-dealers, large broker-dealers, and certain

---

[117] NASD Rules of Fair Practice, Article III (1992) (now set forth in FINRA Rule 2010).
[118] See Securities Exchange Act Release No. 50699 (Nov. 18, 2004) ("Fair Administration and Governance of Self-Regulatory Organizations").
[119] See Securities Exchange Act Release No. 51217 (Feb. 16, 2005).

specialized dealers)); the final and twenty-fourth member is FINRA's CEO.

B. *Rule-Making*. Rules of all self-regulatory organizations must be approved by the SEC.[120] In addition, under Section 19(c) of the 1934 Act, the SEC "may abrogate, add to, and delete from . . . the rules of self-regulatory organization." This seemingly broad power to impose rules on SROs is, however, subject to judicial limitations. The SEC cannot use this power to impose its preferred rules of corporate governance on listed companies, but must show that the purposes of any such SEC amendment are to advance the goals of the National Market System.[121]

C. *Enforcement*. SROs have an obligation to enforce compliance with both their own rules and the federal securities laws. Correspondingly, the SEC can enforce SRO rules, and it can bring its own overlapping charges without regard to considerations of double jeopardy or res judicata.[122] Procedurally, § 15A(b)(8) of the 1934 Act requires that the rules of the NASD must "provide a fair procedure." But FINRA and the NYSE, in disciplining their members are regarded as private actors and hence are not subject to the Fifth Amendment's privilege against self-incrimination. This means that they can suspend and/or expel any member or associated person who refuses to testify before it or who pleads the Fifth Amendment before it—at least so long as the SRO acts independently of government influence and not as an agent of the state.[123] With the merger of the NASD and the NYSE's regulatory arm into FINRA, the premise that FINRA is an entirely private body may receive increasing judicial skepticism.

D. *Immunity*. Courts have long given SROs near absolute immunity with regard to their statutorily-delegated regulatory or disciplinary functions.[124] With the privatization of the NYSE and Nasdaq, however, courts have begun to consider the limits on this immunity. In Weissman v. NASD, Inc.,[125] the Eleventh Circuit has held that this immunity stops at the point at which the SRO begins to pursue its own private commercial interests that are independent of its quasi-governmental role. There, plaintiff sued the NASD because of advertisements it had published that allegedly touted the virtues of WorldCom, a NASD-listed company. Plaintiff asserted that he had relied to his detriment on these ads. Finding such advertisements to be

---

[120] See Section 19(b) of the Securities Exchange Act of 1934.

[121] See Business Roundtable v. SEC, 905 F.2d 406 (D.C.Cir. 1990) (invalidating SEC-imposed "one share, one vote" rule as a listing condition for NYSE and Nasdaq traded companies because it exceeded SEC's authority under Section 19(c)).

[122] See Jones v. SEC, 115 F.3d 1173 (4th Cir. 1997).

[123] See D.L. Cromwell Invs., Inc. v. NASD Regulation, Inc., 279 F.3d 155 (2d Cir. 2002).

[124] See Barbara v. New York Stock Exchange, 99 F.3d 49, 59 (2d Cir. 1996); Sparta Surgical Corp. v. National Ass'n of Sec. Dealers, 159 F.3d 1209, 1215 (9th Cir. 1998).

[125] 500 F.3d 1293 (11th Cir. 2007). For a review of the implications of this case, see Springer, Weissman v. NASD: Piercing the Veil of Absolute Immunity of an SRO under the Securities Exchange Act of 1934, 33 Del. J. Corp. L. 451 (2008).

intended to promote the Nasdaq market, the Eleventh Circuit found them to be outside the scope of the absolute immunity that the NASD enjoyed for its quasi-governmental activities. With its absolute immunity thus curbed, the NASD may find itself the target of more litigation in the future. Still, so long as the NASD is exercising a supervisory responsibility, its immunity remains near absolute.[126]

E. *SEC Jurisdiction.* Section 15(a) of the 1934 Act prohibits any person from acting as a broker or a dealer in securities unless registered with the SEC or otherwise exempted from registration. Both the terms "broker" and "dealer" are broadly defined in §§ 3(a)(4) and (5), respectively, of the 1934 Act. A broker is defined as a person "engaged in the business of effecting transactions in securities for the accounts of others," while a dealer is a person who engages "in the business of buying and selling securities for his own account." Note the emphasis in both definitions on the phrase "in the business;" it is intended to distinguish professionals who act for others or make markets as a profession from very active personal investors.[127]

Under § 15(b)(1) of the 1934 Act, the SEC has authority to deny (or to revoke) a broker-dealer registration—after "notice of the grounds . . . and opportunity for hearing." Also, under § 15(b)(7), the SEC is empowered to set "standards of operational capability," both for the broker-dealer and "all natural persons associated with such broker or dealer." These standards may specify such minimum "standards of training, experience, competence and such other qualifications as the Commission finds necessary or appropriate in the public interest or for the protection of investors." Accordingly, in conjunction with FINRA, the Commission can (and has) established a testing program for entry into the broker-dealer industry that is the functional equivalent of the Bar exam for lawyers.[128]

F. *The Pros and Cons of Self Regulation.* The usual argument against self regulation emphasizes the dangers of regulatory capture: the process will be dominated by the industry and will primarily serve to insulate it from new entrants and increased competition. Another claim is that it adds "a layer of arguably redundant regulation" on the existing system of SEC regulation, which raises costs in return for little added benefit.[129] Proponents of self-regulation typically reply that industry rule-making is (or at least can be) more flexible and detailed, more sensitive to market nuances, and more able to deal with ethical and moral issues that a governmental agency cannot as legitimately regulate.

---

[126] See Lowe v. Nat'l Ass'n of Secs. Dealers, Inc., 548 F. 3d 110 (D.C. Cir. 2008).

[127] See SEC v. Ridenour, 913 F.2d 515 (8th Cir. 1990); see also Lipton, A Primer on Broker-Dealer Registration, 36 Cath. U. L. Rev. 899 (1987).

[128] See Securities Exchange Act Release No. 13679 (June 27, 1977).

[129] For a skeptical assessment of self-regulation from an industry participant, see Miller, Self-Regulation of the Securities Markets: A Critical Examination; 42 Wash. & Lee L. Rev. 853 (1985); see also Smythe, Government Supervised Self-Regulation in the Securities Industry and the Antitrust Laws: Some Suggestions for an Accommodation, 62 N. C. L. Rev. 475 (1984).

Also, self-regulation invites the participation of the regulated, thereby increasing the prospect of law compliance. To some degree, a measure of self-regulation seems inevitable; the SEC could not feasibly regulate floor activities on the stock exchanges, where decisions must be made, or disputes resolved between market participants, within hours (or even minutes) of the moment at which they arise. This debate over the degree of reliance that should be placed on self-regulation will predictably continue. The terms of the debate have, however, been significantly changed by the now nearly universal privatization of exchanges.

CHAPTER 9

REGULATION OF BROKER-DEALERS

Statutes and Regulations

Exchange Act, §§ 3(a)(4), 3(a)(5), 3(a)(51), 9, 10, 15(b)(1), 15(b)(4), 15(b)(6), 15(b)(7), 15(c), 15(g), 15(h), 15(k), 15(*l*), 29(b).

Rules 10b–3, 10b–5, 10b–10, 10b–16, 15c1–1 through 15c1–9.

Regulation Best Interest (Rule 15*l*–1).

Introduction

As with other financial service industries, the broker-dealer industry is closely regulated. The SEC, multiple SROs, and state "blue sky" authorities share oversight responsibilities, as described below. In addition, broker-dealers may be liable to their customers, either in court or in arbitration proceedings, for asserted breaches of fiduciary duties owed to the customer or for breach of SRO rules.[1]

1. *Why Regulate?* As with securities regulation generally, it is important to question the need for the special (and detailed) regulation of broker-dealers. After all, most intermediaries in other parts of the economy do not need to pass an examination, obtain a license, and subject themselves to thousands of pages of rules in order to connect consenting adults in legal transactions. So why are broker-dealers one of the most heavily regulated professions in our economy?

One answer is that conflicts of industry are pervasive (and perhaps uniquely so) in this industry. Brokers may be compensated both by the issuers of securities for marketing their stock and by the buyers (their brokerage clients). Even when they serve only their own client, brokers have an incentive to encourage rapid trading of the account (and sometimes "churning" the account, as later discussed) to maximize their commissions. More generally, although federal securities law insists on continuing disclosure by issuers, investors do not necessarily read or consider these disclosures and may instead rely on the recommendations of their brokers.

---

[1] The vast majority of decisions do not recognize an implied cause of action for breach of a stock exchange or FINRA rule. See Colonial Realty Corp. v. Bache & Co., 358 F.2d 178 (2d Cir. 1966). Some courts do, however, view the violation of such a rule as evidence of negligence. See Piper, Jaffray & Hopwood Inc. v. Ladin, 399 F.Supp. 292, 298 (S.D.Iowa 1975). In any event, even if there is no private cause of action that may be asserted in court, arbitration panels often take a broader view of their responsibilities and award damages based on equitable principles, as discussed later in this introduction.

Of course, the federal securities laws have long prohibited fraud by brokers; their clients may sue them under Rule 10b–5, and the SEC has a variety of enforcement tools discussed later in this chapter. But what if the broker's advice falls short of fraud, but is still negligently given or otherwise potentially affected by a conflict of interest? This is an area where federal securities has just been significantly revised. From the outset and until 2019, the broker's duty to its client (absent fraud) was determined by state law and the standards of self-regulatory organizations (the NASD and then FINRA). Such self regulation is common to many professions (for example, bar associations and the states prescribe professional standards for attorneys). State law with respect to brokers varied: in most states, a broker was not considered a fiduciary to its client (absent special factors, such as discretionary trading authority being given by the client to the broker), while in other states (most notably, California), the broker was deemed a fiduciary to its clients.

In fairness, a reasonable case can be made that self-regulation should work. High-quality market professionals, be they underwriters or brokers, should be expected to support regulation, insofar as it provides a credible signal that they are not cheating their clients. This is the fundamental premise of self-regulation: namely, that the industry has a strong incentive to police itself in order to maintain its reputation.

Nonetheless, in the Dodd-Frank Act, Congress directed the SEC to determine if a uniform minimum standard could be drafted, in large part, because there was a sharp difference in the legal exposure faced by brokers and investment advisers (as the latter are considered to be fiduciaries to their clients).[2] After much study and even more political controversy, the SEC acted in 2019, adopting a new regulation—Regulation Best Interest—which requires that the broker "when making a recommendation of any securities transaction or investment strategy involving securities. . .to a retail customer. . .shall act in the best interest of the retail customer at the time the recommendation is made. . ."[3] This new rule was expressly "designed to improve investor protection by enhancing the quality of broker-dealer recommendations to retail customers and reducing the potential harm to retail customers that may be caused by conflicts of interest,"[4] but what was probably most important is what it did not do: it did not make the broker a fiduciary to its client. This compromise was controversial and further revision of the rule (in a different administration) is possible (but will be a political "hot potato").

To understand Regulation Best Interest (or "Regulation B.I." in shorthand), it is necessary to locate it against a background that includes (1) a history of self-regulation, (2) a long-standing, but never fully

---

[2] See Section 913 of the Dodd-Frank Act (requiring study and report).
[3] See 17 CFR § 240.15*l*–1(a). See Exchange Act Release No. 34–86031 (June 5, 2019).
[4] See Release No. 34–86031 at 16.

rationalized, distinction between the obligations owed to clients of broker-dealers versus those owed to clients by investment advisors, (3) a series of studies by the SEC and the RAND Institute showing investor confusion over this difference,[5] (4) a Department of Labor Fiduciary Rule that imposed a fiduciary duty, but was judicially vacated,[6] and (5) the efforts of several states and many commentators to impose a higher standard. As will be seen, one of the most important questions relating to this new rule is whether it will result in the preemption of state law that does impose a fiduciary duty on brokers.[7]

While issuers and brokers both have incentives to regulate themselves, issuers are not repeat players (they make few and widely separated public offerings), whereas brokers are repeat players, thus giving brokers stronger incentives to institute self regulation.

2. *The Origin of Self-Regulation.* In 1792, the New York state legislature made contracts for the sale of stock owned by others unenforceable in New York courts.[8] Accordingly, the only way that the growing stock brokerage industry in New York could continue to expand and flourish was to create its own shadow legal system that could, through private rules, enforce such bargains. This early form of private enforcement built primarily on efforts at cartelization by brokers. The form of private regulation we know today arrived in much its current form in 1817, when a group of nearly 30 brokers formed the New York Stock and Exchange Board. The Board grew and changed as the market for securities increased over the next few decades. The average daily trading volume increased more than fifty fold during this period, as the number of securities listed grew from about 25 to over 100. In response, the Board increased the formality of its membership processes and the rules by which it conducted its business. By 1860, the Board "dominated securities trading in New York," in part because its reputation allowed it to determine the prices at which other trades would happen most effectively. The Board created this reputation in part through its creation of a "miniature legal system" that included rules governing trading and disputes among brokers. For transactions happening off the exchanges, initially on the curb in front (the "curb" market) and then in what became the "over-the-counter" market, another self regulatory body, known

---

[5] See Staff of the U.S. Securities and Exchange Commission, Study on Investment Advisers and Broker-Dealers. As Required by Section 913 of the Dodd-Frank Wall Street Reform and Consumer Protection Act (2011); Angela A. Hung et al, Investor and Industry Perspectives on Investment Advisers and Broker-Dealers, RAND Institute for Civil Justice (2008).

[6] The Department of Labor's rule applied only to pension and other funds subject to ERISA. See 82 Fed. Reg. 16902 (April 7, 2017).

[7] The SEC's adopting release takes no position on preemption; nonetheless, as discussed later in this chapter, there is a substantial chance that state law standards differing from Regulation Best Interest will be preempted.

[8] See NY Laws, 40th Sess., c. 275, §§ 11, 20 (April 15, 1817) (continuing in force a statute passed in 1792). For a discussion of these laws, see Stuart Banner, ANGLO-AMERICAN SECURITIES REGULATION: Cultural and Political Roots, 1690–1860, 171–75 (1998) (also noting that this statute was repealed in 1858).

eventually as the National Association of Securities Dealers ("NASD") arose to serve similar regulatory function as the NYSE.

After the securities laws were passed in the wake of the 1929 crash, the NYSE and other SROs were given a significant role to continue their regulatory mission during the New Deal in conjunction with administrative agencies. According to the leading history of the SEC, the SROs "retain[ed] the initial responsibility for preventing fraud or unfairness, both because [they] could act swiftly and more subtly than a government bound by due process standards and could avoid the 'bureaucratic blight' of too intrusive a government police force."[9] As noted above, the regulatory arm of the NYSE and the NASD were combined into FINRA in 2007. Today, FINRA, a private corporation, is the primary cop on the beat for broker-dealers.

3. *FINRA's Power*. The power of self regulation is the ability to do what the government cannot do, given the limits of the Constitution and the fear some have of government action. The ability to police conduct that the government could not easily get at, because of constitutional and political constraints, was a primary reason self-regulation was enshrined in the New Deal securities regulatory scheme. The Maloney Act amendments to the securities laws were passed in 1938 after a major scandal: the former CEO of the New York Stock Exchange was sent to prison for defrauding his clients. Under this Act, the Commission was given power to form a new self-regulatory organization: the NASD, which later became FINRA. Speaking to the Hartford Bond Club, SEC Chairman, and later Supreme Court Justice, William O. Douglas described the virtues of self-regulation this way:

> By and large, government can operate satisfactorily only by proscription. That leaves untouched large areas of conduct and activity; some of it susceptible of government regulation but in fact too minute for satisfactory control; some of it lying beyond the periphery of the law in the realm of ethics and morality. Into these large areas of self-government, and self-government alone, can effectively reach.[10]

FINRA Rule 2010 is a good example of this power. This rule states: "A member . . . shall observe high standards of commercial honor and just and equitable principles of trade." Indefinite as this is, it allows FINRA to discipline its members and to levy penalties against brokers who engage in socially undesirable conduct but that would be too difficult or costly to prove violates other, more specific rules. A general, ethical rule like this is especially important both because it can fill gaps and because it can serve as a protective safeguard backing up more specific rules. In other words, the vagueness of Rule 2010 is its power, in that it lowers monitoring and enforcement costs, as well as provides a safety net to

---

[9] Joel Seligman, The Transformation of Wall Street, at 158.
[10] Id at 186.

catch bad brokers who would escape punishment in a more legalistic environment. A vague, ethical rule like 2010 may be peculiarly within the power of a SRO to use. To tolerate the use of such a powerful and ill-defined rule, members must have faith that the discretion it grants to those sitting in judgment will be exercised wisely. If members are behind a veil of ignorance, that is, they do not know whether they will be judged or sitting in judgment, then they will be more likely to agree to be bound by such a rule than if they know the discretion will be exercised by non-industry members, such as government agents.

4. *FINRA's Disciplinary Process.* If a broker allegedly violates a FINRA rule, FINRA conducts an investigation, and, if warranted, brings an enforcement action before a FINRA hearing officer. Any decision of the hearing officer can be appealed to the National Adjudicatory Council ("NAC"), a quasi-judicial, appellate body comprised of an equal number of industry insiders (seven) and outsiders (seven). Appeals from the NAC (pronounced "knack"), are to the FINRA board of directors, followed by the SEC, then the circuit courts, and even the Supreme Court. Despite this appellate oversight, most of FINRA's disciplinary actions do not get substantial government review. This is especially notable because relevant constitutional limits, e.g., the Fourth and Fifth Amendments, do not apply to FINRA, as it has not yet been declared a state actor.

5. *The Cartelization Problem.* Although self regulation is a potentially powerful regulatory tool, it is also a way for the industry to protect itself from external competition or regulation that might be social welfare enhancing. It is not a coincidence that one of the first acts of the NYSE was to fix brokerage commissions, a practice that persisted for the next hundred and fifty years.[11] Self regulation also failed on many occasions. A special study conducted under William Cary, President Kennedy's chair of the SEC, found that industry self-regulation consistently had been self-interested and self-protective, often failing to produce standards of conduct superior to those that existed before the enactment of the securities laws. As a consequence, over the next several decades, various amendments to the securities laws were passed to tighten SEC control over the regulatory policies of the SROs. These included authorizing the SEC to approve SRO rules, giving it the power to initiate SRO rules, and requiring that brokers satisfy various SEC standards.[12]

6. *SEC Authority over Broker-Dealers.* Section 15(a) of the 1934 Act prohibits any person from acting as a broker or a dealer unless

---

[11] The SEC ended fixed commissions for large transactions (>$500,000) in 1972; fixed commissions for retail transactions ended in 1975.

[12] For a full discussion of the growing "governmentalization" of SROs, see William A. Birdthistle and M. Todd Henderson, "Becoming a Fifth Branch," 99 Cornell Law Review 1 (2013). For example, pursuant to a settlement with the SEC following a price-fixing scandal involving industry-wide collusion in securities pricing, FINRA is now required to have a majority of public members and only a minority of industry members. Clearly it looks a lot less like a private club today.

registered with the SEC or expressly exempted. But registration is not automatic. Section 15(b)(1) of the 1934 Act authorizes the SEC to deny registration for certain specified reasons, and § 15(b)(4) empowers it to "censure, place limitations on the activities, functions, or operations of, suspend for a period not exceeding twelve months, or revoke the registration of any broker or dealer if it finds . . . [that such action] . . . is in the public interest and that such broker or dealer" has engaged in certain specified forms of misconduct (including, in both cases, making false statements in any application or report required to be filed with the SEC).[13]

In short, broker-dealers can be thrown out of the industry, or otherwise disciplined to a less drastic extent, if at any time they run seriously afoul of the SEC. Similarly, under § 15(b)(6), the SEC has equivalent authority over any person "associated" with a broker-dealer, meaning that the Commission can enter a lifetime disbarment order barring an individual from any employment or other association with a broker-dealer.

The SEC has used Section 15(b)(4)(E) to require more rigorous compliance procedures. In a well-known case involving Prudential Securities, the Commission found that Prudential had failed to adequately supervise the sale of approximately $8 billion in limited partnership interests in some 700 offerings between 1980 and 1990, which offerings involved material misrepresentations about "potential yields, safety and purported liquidity of the investments."[14]

Section 15(b)(7) also gives the Commission important additional authority by prohibiting any broker or dealer from effecting any transaction in, or inducing the purchase or sale of any security, "unless such broker or dealer meets such standards of operational capability and such broker or dealer and all natural persons associated with [such broker or dealer] and meets such standards of training, experience, competence, and such other qualifications as the Commission finds necessary or appropriate in the public interest or for the protection of investors." Effectively, this provision authorizes the Commission to

---

[13] Section 15(b)(4) describes in subsections 15(b)(4)(A) through (H) the various forms of misconduct that can trigger Commission disciplinary action. The subsection that has received the greatest SEC attention in recent years is Section 15(b)(4)(E), which covers not only willful aiding and abetting, but also the willful failure "reasonably to supervise with a view to preventing violations of the provisions of such statutes, rules and regulations," any employee subject to its supervision. However, section 15(b)(4)(E) further provides that "no person shall be deemed to have failed reasonably to supervise any other person" if it has established procedures and a system for applying such procedures, which would reasonably be expected to prevent and detect. . .any such violation by such other person." In short, adequate compliance procedures seemingly supply a defense that immunizes the broker from liability for its employee's violation.

[14] Prudential Sec. Inc., 51 SEC 726, 737 (1993). SEC Litig. Rel. 13, 840, 55 SEC Dock. 709 (October 21, 1993). The SEC took similar action against PaineWebber for its sale of $3 billion in limited partnership interests. See Securities Exchange Act Rel. No. 36,724 (January 17, 1996). Probably, the most publicized failure to supervise case involved Kidder Peabody & Co. in 1994 for with respect to an employee (Jett) who reported enormous false, profits. As a result, Kidder Peabody's parent, General Electric shut down the century old brokerage firm.

establish tests and training standards to regulate entry into the profession. Finally, § 15(c) contains several broad antifraud provisions specifically directed at broker-dealers that authorize the Commission to adopt rules and regulations to define "such acts and practices as are manipulative, deceptive or otherwise fraudulent."[15]

Beyond these antifraud rules, the 1934 Act also focuses on regulating the financial soundness of broker-dealers. Thus, § 15(c)(3) empowers the Commission to prescribe rules and regulations "to provide safeguards with respect to the financial responsibility and related practices of brokers and dealers, including . . . the acceptance of custody and use of customers' securities and the carrying and use of customers' deposits or credit balances." Here, the concern is with the solvency of a broker-dealer as a financial institution (much like a bank or a savings and loan association) that holds "other people's money." Pursuant to this authority, the SEC has adopted elaborate and detailed rules regulating the capital structure of broker-dealers.[16]

The broad scope of SEC authority over broker-dealers is further enhanced by an expansive definition of the terms "broker" and "dealer", and the limited scope of the exemptions from § 15's registration requirement. Section 3(a)(4) of the 1934 Act defines "broker" as "any person engaged in the business of effecting transactions in securities for the account of others," and § 3(a)(5) defines "dealer" as "any person engaged in the business of buying and selling securities for [such person's] own account." The phrase "in the business" in both definitions is intended to distinguish the professional market maker from simply an "active investor" who trades frequently. Sometimes, however, the line can be close between these two. In SEC v. Ridenour,[17] a bond account executive at a broker-dealer was found, himself, to be a broker-dealer subject to § 15(a)'s registration requirement, where he actively traded bonds for his own account with a regular clientele of institutional clients. The court found that the defendant's "level of activity . . . made him more than an active investor,"[18] but perhaps the key factor was his attempt to develop his own clientele of trading clients who relied on his services. In general, the more open, public, and regular the behavior, the more an individual appears to be "in the business" and hence a broker.

Grayer issues surface, however, when the person or entity wishing to avoid the "broker" characterization is offering what it claims is only technical assistance or a communication mechanism. In its no-action letters, the SEC's staff has permitted a firm to create a web site that provided information and disclosure documents concerning both registered and exempt offerings without registering as a broker.[19] But

---

[15] See § 15(c)(1)(D) of the 1934 Act.
[16] See Rules 15c3–1 to 15c3–3.
[17] 913 F.2d 515 (8th Cir. 1990).
[18] Id. at 517.
[19] Internet Capital Corp., No-Action Letter (avail. Dec. 24, 1997).

when another proposed a web-based communications system that would enable municipal bond issuers to conduct an auction for their bonds, the staff found this conduct to cross the line. "A person effects transactions in securities," it wrote in denying the no-action letter request, "if he or she participates in such transactions at 'key points in the chain of distribution.' "[20] Assisting the issuer to structure the transaction or find potential purchasers constituted, it said, such impermissible "participation."

Employees of an issuer could in theory also be deemed a "broker" because of their work, for example, in a shareholder relations department, seeking to induce purchase of the firm's shares. Here, however, the SEC has provided a protective safe harbor in the form of Rule 3a4–1, which indicates that participation in certain specified activities (which do not involve oral solicitations of public investors) does not require registration as a broker.

More surprising and illustrative of the extraordinarily broad reach of the term "broker" in the SEC's view has been the SEC's use of its "broker" concept against attorneys who provide some form of investment advice to their clients. Immigration attorneys had learned to use a special program that allows foreign nationals to obtain permanent residence in the U.S. if they make a requisite investment (usually $500,000) in a real estate project in a poverty-stricken neighborhood. This "Immigrant Investment Program" (or "EB-5" as it is generally known) requires the persons representing a foreign client to find an eligible program. Casinos and luxury resort hotels (including those in Las Vegas) have exploited this program, often paying attorneys to choose their projects. In SEC v. Hui Feng, the Commission successfully sued a New York attorney (who was a native born Chinese) who represented Chinese clients seeking visas.[21] His clients bought limited partnership interests in ventures that he recommended (and the attorney had clear conflicts of interest as he received payments from the sponsors of these projects). The Commission successfully argued that the attorney was a "broker" because he recommended specific projects in return for a fee. The practical message here for attorneys is that they have to find a registered broker to work with them.[22]

---

[20] MuniAuction Inc., [2000 Transfer Binder] [CCH] Fed. Sec. L. Rep. Para. 77,830 (March 13, 2000). For a similar case involving a firm that offered to auction "hot" IPOs for issuers, see In the Matter of Joseph M. Salvani and MainstreetIPO.com, Inc., Securities Exchange Act Release No. 44590 (July 26, 2001).

[21] 935 F.3d 721 (9th Cir. 2019)

[22] Arguably, the defendant attorney in this case was serving more as an investment adviser to his clients (who were in no position to find an eligible investment on their own), and the Investment Advisers Act exempts attorneys from its definition of Investment Advisers. See Section 202(a)(11) of the Investment Advisers Act of 1940, 15 U.S.C. § 80b–2(a)(11). Although nothing excuses the obvious conflict of interest in this case, attorneys—whether acting as executors or tax advisers—have historically provided some investment advice to clients.

Relatively few exemptions exist from § 15(a). The most important exemptions are for (1) banks,[23] (2) firms that deal exclusively in exempt securities,[24] (3) persons who do business "exclusively intrastate" and who do "not make use of any facility of a national securities exchange,"[25] and (4) foreign brokers who have only "indirect" contacts with U.S. investors.[26] The SEC also permits issuers to maintain electronic bulletin boards on which their shareholders may trade their stock without the issuer being required to register as a broker-dealer.[27]

The registration issue looms large for many types of investment funds. The regulatory costs of registering and subjecting oneself to the ongoing reporting and regulatory requirements of FINRA and the SEC are high, especially for smaller funds or firms, because they cannot spread the regulatory costs across a larger asset base. (Arguably regulation can have an anti-competitive impact because if larger firms successfully lobby for higher regulatory costs, they can achieve an advantage over smaller entrants.) Private equity funds, for example, are often engaged in providing services that resemble investment-banking services, such as "solicitation, negotiation, or execution of [securities] transactions." If a private equity fund manager charges success-based fees when the fund sells a portfolio company, it may meet this standard, and therefore be a broker-dealer under § 15. It is for this reason that many large private equity funds, like Apollo Global Management, Blackstone, and KKR, are registered as brokers. Many smaller private equity funds are not, but the SEC's attitude towards them is uncertain.

7. *State Authority*. The Uniform Securities Act requires the annual registration of broker-dealers doing business in the jurisdiction and provides for broad disciplinary powers in the state agency. However, the National Securities Markets Improvements Act of 1996 added § 15(i) to the 1934 Act, which imposes substantial limitations on the authority of state blue sky regulators over broker-dealers. Basically, § 15(i) restricts state blue sky regulation of broker-dealers by precluding capital, operational, or record-keeping rules that are in addition to those established by the SEC. It also permits associated persons of a broker-dealer not registered in the particular jurisdiction to engage in certain limited transactions in that jurisdiction on behalf of a broker-dealer that is so registered.[28] Although this restriction limits state oversight, no

---

[23] See §§ 3(a)(4), 3(a)(5).

[24] Section 15(a)(1) specifically exempts transactions in "an exempted security, or commercial paper, bankers' acceptances, or commercial bills." Many of these dealers will, however, be subject to § 15B ("Municipal Securities") or § 15C ("Government Securities Brokers and Dealers") of the 1934 Act.

[25] See § 15(a)(1).

[26] See Rule 15a–6 (exempting certain limited activities, such as execution of unsolicited transactions and the provision of research to institutional investors).

[27] See Portland Brewing Co., No-Action Letter (available Dec. 14, 1999).

[28] See § 15(i)(3).

restriction was placed by the Act on state anti-fraud rules relating to broker-dealers or on state enforcement powers.

8. *Common Law Duties.* Notwithstanding somewhat limited oversight powers for state regulators, the common law still applies to customer-broker relations. A broker is an agent to the customer and thus owes the duties established by the law of agency. Whether the broker is also a "fiduciary," who arguably owes a duty to warn the customer of risks or to disclose adverse information about the issuer that is in the broker's possession, depends on state law. Here, the prevailing rule is that where the account is "non-discretionary," meaning that the customer makes the investment decisions and the stock broker merely receives and executes the customer's orders, the relationship does not give rise to general fiduciary duties, such as a duty to warn the customer about the specific risks involved.[29] In Independent Order of Foresters v. Donald, Lufkin & Jenrette,[30] the Second Circuit announced this rule, which relied on New York law,[31] in a case involving a seemingly sophisticated institutional investor who complained that its investment banker had not warned it about the dangers inherent in certain derivative securities.[32] The logic of these cases is essentially that the fiduciary relationship requires that there be two critical elements that are not present in the case of a simple non-discretionary brokerage account: (1) reliance by the customer on the broker, and (2) domination and control by the broker.[33] Thus, the majority state rule deems the broker normally to owe a fiduciary duty that is bounded by the scope of the relationship with the client and that requires the broker only to perform diligently the instructions given to it by the client. In contrast, in the case of a discretionary account, where the broker does exercise trading authority, a fuller fiduciary relationship would arise, and the broker would be under a duty for example, to investigate the securities and possibly to warn the customer as to adverse information or risks known to the broker.

This summary is, however, deceptively simple, in several respects. First, even in the case of a non-discretionary account, some duties are owed. For example, at a minimum, the broker has a duty to execute requested trades promptly and seek their best execution.[34] The failure to consider alternative markets offering superior prices could thus be a

---

[29] See Independent Order of Foresters v. Donald, Lufkin & Jenrette, 157 F.3d 933, 940 (2d Cir. 1998); see also de Kwiatkowski v. Bear, Stearns & Co., 306 F.3d 1293 (2d Cir. 2002).

[30] Id.

[31] See In re Dean Witter Managed Futures Ltd. Partnership Litigation, 282 A.D.2d 271, 724 N.Y.S.2d 149 (2001); Perl v. Smith Barney Inc., 230 A.D.2d 664, 646 N.Y.S.2d 678, 680 (1996).

[32] However, the Second Circuit declined to dismiss and reinstated claims that the defendant broker-dealer had caused an employee of the plaintiff institutional investor to breach his fiduciary duties to the plaintiff by authorizing the purchase of the risky securities in return for kickbacks.

[33] See United States v. Chestman, 947 F.2d 551, 568–69 (2d Cir. 1991) (en banc) (defining when a fiduciary relationship arises for purposes of insider trading law).

[34] See Shearson Lehman Hutton, Inc. v. Wagoner, 944 F.2d 114, 120 (2d Cir. 1991).

breach of duty, even if the fiduciary duty is limited simply to the execution of the transaction.[35] Further, if the terms of the account require the customer's specific authorization, it violates the broker's duty to execute unauthorized trades.[36]

Second, the broker can assume a greater duty, possibly by the representations it makes to its customer about its special competence or capacity.[37] More importantly, some decisions find that, even in the case of the non-discretionary account, the broker has "the duty to recommend a stock only after studying it sufficiently to become informed as to its nature, price and financial prognosis."[38] Third, the existence of a fiduciary relationship is a question of state law, and some states have a more liberal attitude than does New York. In Patsos v. First Albany Corp.,[39] the Massachusetts Supreme Court found that a fiduciary relationship existed where the broker-dealer's registered representative had assured his customer-plaintiffs that if they followed his investment advice, they could make "a great deal of money."[40] Following his advice, they bought $8 million of the stock of a single small bank, approximately one-half of which was purchased on a margin account. Later, the broker induced his clients to use even greater margin, thereby increasing their leverage and potential exposure. Although the Massachusetts Supreme Court agreed that a simple brokerage relationship is not fiduciary in character, it found that special facts could show that a sufficient "degree of discretion" had been entrusted to the broker to create a full fiduciary relationship.[41] A customer's "lack of investment acumen" could also be an important factor, it said, in determining whether a full fiduciary relationship existed.[42] Other decisions have taken a similarly liberal stance.[43] Still others waffle on this issue by finding that the scope of the fiduciary relationship is a factual question for the jury to resolve.

Finally, once the broker makes a recommendation to the client, everything changes, and it becomes possible for the client to contest whether the broker had a reasonable basis for its recommendation and whether it adequately disclosed the risks known to it to the customer.[44]

---

[35] See Newton v. Merrill, Lynch, Pierce, Fenner & Smith, Inc., 135 F.3d 266 (3d Cir. 1998) (en banc).

[36] See Conway v. Icahn & Co., 16 F.3d 504, 510 (2d Cir. 1994).

[37] Geman v. SEC, 334 F.3d 1183 (10th Cir. 2003).

[38] See Leib v. Merrill Lynch, Pierce, Fenner & Smith, Inc., 461 F.Supp. 951, 953 (E.D.Mich.1978).

[39] 433 Mass. 323, 741 N.E.2d 841 (2001).

[40] Id. at 844.

[41] Id. at 849–50.

[42] Id. at 850–51.

[43] See Romano v. Merrill Lynch, Pierce, Fenner & Smith, 834 F.2d 523, 530 (5th Cir. 1987).

[44] See Leib v. Merrill Lynch, Pierce, Fenner & Smith, 461 F.Supp. 951, 953 (E.D. Mich. 1978) (broker must "disclose any personal interest the broker may have in a particular recommended security"). But see Shivangi v. Dean Witter Reynolds, Inc., 825 F.2d 885 (5th Cir. 1987).

An illustrative, if controversial, recent decision on the scope of the fiduciary relationship is de Kwiatkowski v. Bear Stearns.[45] There, in a case involving an extremely experienced and wealthy private investor (to whom the jury awarded a recovery of $111.5 million plus interest based on the broker's negligence), the district court ruled that the broker owed even this sophisticated, nondiscretionary account customer a duty to investigate issuers whose securities were under consideration, to refrain from self-dealing, and to report any conflicting or personal interest that the broker may have had in the transaction. As a result, it upheld the jury's apparent finding that the defendant's failure to provide its customer with certain information that it possessed breached the broker's duty of reasonable care. The basis for this unusual result seems to have been the court's finding that, over the course of dealing with this very large account, the defendant undertook in fact the role of investment adviser and was relied upon by the plaintiff to provide him with the information that the defendant omitted to provide. On appeal, the Second Circuit reversed, finding that, although the broker owes a duty of reasonable care to the client, this duty "begins and ends with each transaction" and does not comprehend any ongoing or open-ended duty to warn the client or monitor the client's account.[46] The broker cannot be held liable for a failure to warn a nondiscretionary client, it said, in the absence of clear evidence that it had contractually agreed to undertake a substantial advisory role. Even though the broker may volunteer advice, this does not create an ongoing duty to continue to do so.

Criminal law also defines and enforces the fiduciary duties owed by brokers to their customers, and criminal liability has not depended on whether a full fiduciary relationship exists between the broker and the customer. Where exorbitant commissions were not disclosed, it has been held sufficient, in order to uphold a conviction for breaching the duty of "honest services" under 18 U.S.C. § 1346 (one of the federal mail and wire fraud statutes), that simply a relationship of trust and confidence existed between the broker and the customer. In United States v. Szur,[47] the Second Circuit recently upheld criminal convictions of brokers who agreed to market the controlling stake of a majority holder in a small corporation to their retail customers in return for commissions that were agreed in advance to be fifty percent of any proceeds received from these sales. Although defendants protested that they owed no fiduciary duty (and the Second Circuit agreed), it still found a relationship of trust and confidence to accompany any broker-customer relationship, with the result that the failure to disclose excessive commissions was a material omission that amounted to fraud.

9. *Suitability.* Under leading case law (e.g., *de Kwiatkowski*), brokers are not subject to a traditional fiduciary duty standard. But

---

[45] 126 F.Supp.2d 672 (S.D.N.Y.2000).
[46] de Kwiatkowski v. Bear Stearns & Co., 306 F.3d 1293 (2d Cir. 2002).
[47] 289 F.3d 200 (2d Cir. 2002).

FINRA does require brokers to put clients' interests above their own. FINRA imposes obligations on brokers to understand their clients' interests, and put them in investments that match these interests. FINRA Rule 2111 imposes an affirmative obligation on broker-dealers to advise customers that certain securities are excessively risky (or "unsuitable" in the industry parlance) for their economic position or needs.[48] This doctrine—known as the "suitability doctrine"—rests on the premise that brokers have an obligation to know their customer and make only recommendations that are "suitable" to their customer's needs and financial position.[49] As will be seen, this suitability doctrine has been largely superseded by Regulation Best Interest to the extent that this new rule applies, but some investors (such as institutional investors) are not covered by Regulation Best Interest, and so must still rely on "suitability" principles.

Although it is unlikely that investors can sue their brokers in private civil actions based on FINRA's "suitability" rules or the SEC's Regulation Best Interest, commentators report that arbitration panels do regularly enforce these norms by requiring broker-dealers to share in the losses experienced by customers who are advised to buy "unsuitable" or other securities that are not in their best interest.[50] Indeed, the Arbitrator's Manual that governs these proceedings advises arbitrators that they are to do equity and may go "beyond the written law."[51] Also, arbitrators may award punitive damages (which the federal securities laws preclude) on state law theories.

10. *The Impact of Dodd-Frank.* Section 913(g) ("Authority to Establish A Fiduciary Duty for Brokers And Dealers") of the Dodd-Frank Act amended both the Securities Exchange Act (with respect to brokers and dealers) and the Investment Advisers Act (with respect to investment advisers), seeking to harmonize the standards of conduct and obligations applicable to both. Specifically, it sought to reconcile the applicable standards by stating:

> "The Commission may promulgate rules to provide that the standard of conduct for all brokers, dealers, and investment advisers, when providing personalized investment advice about securities to retail customers (and such other customers as the Commission may by rule provide), shall be to act in the best interest of the customer without regard to the financial or other

---

[48] See FINRA Manual, Duties and Conflicts, Rule 2111 ("Suitability") (2008).

[49] This was long set forth in the FINRA Manual at Rule 2310 ("Recommendations for Customers"), which required FINRA members to have "reasonable grounds for believing that the recommendation is suitable for such customer upon the basis of the facts, if any, disclosed by such customer as to his other holdings and as to his financial situation and needs." This has now been moved to FINRA Rule 2111.

[50] See Lewis Lowenfels and Alan Bromberg, Beyond Precedent: Arbitral Extensions of Securities Law, 57 Bus. Law. 999 (2002).

[51] Id. at 1001 (citing Secs. Industry Conference on Arbitration, THE ARBITRATOR'S MANUAL 2 (2001)).

interest of the broker, dealer, or investment adviser providing the advice."[52]

Although § 913(g) is captioned "Authority to Establish A Fiduciary Duty for Brokers and Dealers," it is doubtful that this language, requiring only that the broker or dealer act in the "best interests" of the customer, actually created a traditional fiduciary obligation. Indeed, § 913(g)(1) adds a new § 15(k) ("Standard of Conduct") to the Securities Exchange Act (§ 15 is the principal provision of that Act regulating brokers and dealers), and the last sentence of this new provision states:

> "Nothing in this Section shall require a broker or dealer or registered representative to have a continuing duty of care or loyalty to the customer after providing personalized investment advice about securities."

This seems to mean that, if the broker or dealer later changes (or even reverses) its views and recommendation, it has no obligation to warn the customer to whom it previously recommended the same security.

Further compounding the confusion about the scope of a broker-dealer's obligations to the customer is an SEC doctrine, known as "shingle theory," whose continued survival is at best uncertain. Under this theory, a person's act of going into the brokerage business (i.e., "hanging out his shingle" as a professional) amounts to an implied representation that he or she will deal fairly with customers.[53] This implied representation theory once allowed the SEC to view unfair conduct as also a fraudulent misrepresentation. Still, in the wake of Santa Fe Industries, Inc. v. Green[54] and the Supreme Court's insistence in this and other cases on the need for an actual misrepresentation or omission, rather than simply a breach of fiduciary duty, before Rule 10b–5 becomes applicable, it is doubtful that federal courts will give this doctrine much substantive weight in federal court litigation.[55]

When the SEC issued its § 913 report in January 2011; it recommended adopting a uniform fiduciary duty on brokers and investment advisors. The report relied on customer confusion about the duties of brokers and investment advisors as a main justification for its proposal.

---

[52] Section 913(g)(2) adds this language by adopting a new Section 211(g) to the Investment Advisers Act of 1940. This section also defines the term "retail customer."

[53] The theory originates with Charles Hughes & Co. v. SEC, 139 F.2d 434 (2d Cir. 1943). That case involved a dealer who charged higher than normal mark-ups on securities. As discussed later in this Chapter, excessive mark-ups are regularly challenged by FINRA on a variety of theories (not simply involving a breach of fiduciary duty) and occasionally by the SEC under Rule 10b–5.

[54] 430 U.S. 462 (1977).

[55] See Robert Karmel, Is Shingle Theory Dead?, 52 Wash. & Lee L. Rev. 1271 (1995). Some cases do, however, still refer to it. See Grandon v. Merrill Lynch & Co., 147 F.3d 184 (2d Cir. 1998). Administrative law judges in SEC proceedings may also rely on the doctrine.

Problems

PROBLEM 9-1

Ed X. Cutor worked for many years in the trust and estate side of a major bank, helping to settle major estates. Based on that experience, he forms his own firm—Ed X. Cutor Services, Inc.—and advertises on his firm's web site (and other web sites) its willingness to locate buyers for illiquid controlling blocks held by estates. He also contacts dealers that make markets in firms in which a CEO or large shareholder has recently died to offer his services. His services include helping the buyer to value the block and make the best offer. Is Ed or his firm a broker who must register under § 15(a)?

PROBLEM 9-2

MainStreetIPO.com has created a website on which IPO issuers are invited to auction their shares under a Dutch auction methodology. The issuer will still register its stock with the SEC and all settlements will be handled by a registered broker-dealer, but MainStreetIPO will handle the auction and its software will determine the clearing price. Based on its advertising, several thousand customers have registered with it. Is MainStreetIPO a broker-dealer? Any advice on how to redesign its relationship with the issuer to avoid registration?

1. REGULATION AIMED AT FRAUD AND MANIPULATION

A. *Regulation of Short Sales.* One of the most controversial securities law topics for the last several centuries has been whether to regulate short sales and, if so, how to do it.[56] While Wall Street is often vilified as earning profits from mere money lending, as opposed to actually "making" things, special scorn is reserved by many for short sellers who profit from bad news and economic decline, of firms or the economy as a whole. It is one thing to reap unearned profits in good times, it is quite another to do the same on the backs of suffering investors. (Of course, neither of these descriptions is entirely accurate, but that is the conventional wisdom of many Main Street critics.) Before we can understand short selling and its regulation, we have to first know what it is.

What is selling short? A Senate investigation of stock market practices in 1934 described short selling this way: "Short selling is a device whereby the speculator sells stock which he does not own, anticipating that the price will decline and that he will thereby be enabled to 'cover,' or make delivery of the stock sold by purchasing it at the lesser price. If the decline materializes, the short seller realizes as a profit the differential between the sales price and the lower purchase or

---

[56] For a brief history, see L. Loss and J. Seligman, Fundamentals of Securities Regulation 699–703 (3d ed. 1995).

covering price."[57] Daniel Drew, a nineteenth century stock market manipulator, characterized the consequences of a failure to "cover" a short-sale in his oft quoted jingle: "He that sells what isn't his'n, Must buy it back or go to prison."[58]

Following the stock market crash of 1929, it was a common (if unproven) view that professional speculators had regularly conducted "bear raids" through short sales, thereby deriving enormous profits while accelerating the stock market decline and postponing recovery.[59] Today, however, it is also recognized that short selling has legitimate justifications, including to hedge risk, to provide liquidity, and to correct the seeming optimistic bias of a market overly influenced by sell side analysts.

When the 1934 Act was before Congress, it was recognized that previous attempts in other countries to outlaw short sales had ended in failure and that most such laws were later repealed. Thus, rather than adopting an inflexible statute, § 10(a) simply delegates to the SEC the authority to regulate short sales of any security registered on a national securities exchange. The section is applicable whether the short sale is effected on an exchange or in the over-the-counter market, and it applies to all persons, not just broker-dealers. Still, the Commission's rules on short selling have long focused on the broker-dealer who effects such a sale for its customer.

Implementing § 10(a), the SEC has long sought to strike a balance that recognized both that (a) concentrated short selling in a declining market can be a tool to destabilize and manipulate the market, and (b) "short selling provides the market with two important benefits: market liquidity and pricing efficiency."[60] For many years, the heart of the SEC's policy was its "tick test," which restricted short selling in a declining market. Former Rule 10a–1 prohibited any person from effecting a short sale of any exchange-traded security at a price (1) below the last reported

---

[57] Stock Exchange Practices, Report of Com. on Banking & Currency, S.Rep. No. 1455, 73d Cong., 2d Sess. (1934) 50.

[58] See B. White, The Book of Daniel Drew 180 (1910). John Steele Gordon in his history of early Wall Street also attributes this quotation to Daniel Drew, without the citation of any source except "Wall Street tradition." Gordon, The Scarlet Woman of Wall Street 73 (1988). We have followed these authors in crediting him with its authorship, although it seems unlikely that "Uncle Daniel" (also known as the "Great Bear" because of his bear raids) in fact originated this bon mot since he was the most notorious short-seller in the entire history of Wall Street. See Gordon, passim. Mr. Gordon at another point quotes Commodore Vanderbilt as saying in response to a reporter's badgering him for a statement regarding a "corner" he had engineered in a particular stock and the squeeze he was putting on the short-sellers: "Don't you never buy anything you don't want, nor sell anything you hain't got." Id. at p. 85. Possibly this vernacular response was later transformed by some unknown literary artist into the traditional, more elegant, couplet quoted above.

[59] See L. Loss and J. Seligman, supra note 56, at 699–700.

[60] See Securities Exchange Act Release No. 50103 (July 28, 2004), 69 FR at 48009. Economic critics have long objected to restrictions on short selling on the ground that it reduces the incentives of market professionals to seek out and act on negative information and thereby interferes with market efficiency. See Macey, Mitchell & Netter, Restrictions on Short Sales: An Analysis of the Uptick Rule and Its Role in View of the October 1987 Stock Market Crash, 74 Cornell L. Rev. 799 (1989).

price at which such security was sold, or (2) at the same price, unless that price was above the next preceding price at which a sale of such security was reported. In stock market jargon, short sales on a minus-tick or a zero-minus tick were prohibited.

In 2007, the SEC rescinded the "tick test," believing that the introduction of decimalization had largely eroded its impact. With decimalization, even a one penny price increase (after a steady fall in the price) would permit a seller to make a substantial short sale. A determined short seller could either wait for a small price rise to execute a major short sale or, possibly, contrive to cause such a modest price increase in order to make a larger short sale. Also, options dealers were not subject to the tick test, and thus it did not preclude persons from buying put options, with the options dealer then hedging its position in the options market by selling short in the equity market.

The SEC's decision to abandon the tick test, and thus liberalize short selling, was based in part on a multi-year randomized trial conducted by the SEC. The Commission liberalized short selling for a random set of the Russell 3000, and collected data on the impact of the change. This randomized trial was the first in the SEC's history, but appears to have proven an effective regulatory tool.

In 2008 when a number of financial institutions came under sustained short selling pressure, sometimes under circumstances in which false rumors appear to have been spread for manipulative purposes, the SEC reconsidered its approval of short selling. Rather than restore the tick test, however, the SEC took a variety of other actions in 2008 to constrain concentrated short selling. For a brief period in October 2008, at the height of the financial turmoil, the SEC (following earlier action taken by the U.K.'s securities regulator) banned all short selling of the stocks of financial institutions pursuant to § 12(k)(2) of the Securities Exchange Act, which authorizes the SEC to take "emergency action" for a ten business day period.[61] More or less simultaneously, the SEC also sought to restrict "naked" short selling. The term "naked" short selling refers to short sales that are made without the seller having earlier borrowed the securities to make delivery on the settlement date.[62] Under Rule 203(b) of Regulation SHO (which governs short selling), a broker may not accept a short sale order in an equity security from a customer unless the broker or dealer has either itself borrowed the stock or has: "reasonable grounds to believe that the security can be borrowed so that it can be delivered on the date delivery is due."[63] The broker could,

---

[61] See Securities Exchange Act Release No. 58592 (Sept. 18, 2008) (temporarily prohibiting short selling of stocks of specified financial institutions). Under § 12(k)(2) of the 1934 Act, the SEC can adopt an emergency rule for ten business days, which rule can be extended up to a maximum duration of 30 calendar days.

[62] See SEC v. Lyon, 529 F.Supp.2d 444, 448 n. 1 (S.D.N.Y. 2008). The seller's motivation for not borrowing may be to save the interest charges that it must pay to the lender. Or, it may simply be unable to find securities to borrow.

[63] See Rule 203(b)(1)(ii), 17 CFR § 242.203(b)(1)(ii).

however, rely on the customer's representation to it that the customer had located shares to borrow. Alternatively, the broker could rely on "Easy to Borrow" lists, but the Adopting Release for Regulation SHO stressed that the information used to generate such a list "must be less than 24 hours old."[64] The Commission's firmness on this point was based on the recognition that "naked" short sales frequently disrupt the market when the short seller fails to deliver on the delivery date (e.g., the second business day after the date of the transaction—or "T+2"). Over recent years, "naked" short selling appears to have increased, as shown by corresponding increases in "failures to deliver."

In 2008, the SEC tightened the rules on "naked" short selling in three respects that all related to broker-dealers:

First, it amended Regulation SHO to require the broker to deliver securities on the settlement date, including by purchasing or borrowing securities so as to close out the "fail to deliver" position by the opening of trading on the next business day following the date of the failure to deliver.[65]

Second, it adopted a new antifraud rule—Rule 10b–21—covering deception about the short seller's intention or ability to deliver securities by the settlement date.[66] This rule was specifically designed to cover instances in which the customer misrepresented to the broker that it had "located" securities to enable it to deliver by the settlement date.

Third, the SEC eliminated an exemption for option market-makers from Regulation SHO.[67] Under that exemption, option market makers had not been required to "locate" securities to borrow in order to sell short and had more time to close out failure to deliver positions.

The combined effect of these rules appears to reduce, but not eliminate, naked short selling and the incidence of failures to deliver. Nonetheless, the SEC remains under continuing pressure from the business community to restore some form of the former tick test. In response, in 2010, the SEC adopted amendments to Regulation SHO, which establish a short-sale related circuit breaker test.[68] Under these amendments, securities markets must adopt and enforce restrictions precluding short sales in a security if the security's price drops 10% or more from its closing price on the prior day.

A final restriction on short selling is contained in Rule 105 of Regulation M, which rule seeks to prevent manipulative short selling of securities in anticipation of a public offering. Originally, the rule was

---

[64] Securities Exchange Act Release No. 50103, 69 Fed. Reg. 48008 at 48014.
[65] See Securities Exchange Act Release No. 58773 (Oct. 14, 2008).
[66] See Securities Exchange Act Release No. 58774 (Oct. 14, 2008).
[67] See Securities Exchange Act Release No. 58775 (Oct. 14, 2008). The Commission also adopted rules requiring large institutional investment managers to report their short sales to the SEC (but not to the public) on new Form SH. See Securities Exchange Act Release No. 58785 (Oct. 15, 2008).
[68] See Securities Exchange Act Release No. 61595 (February 26, 2010).

adopted by the SEC under § 10(b), at the request of the NASD, based on concerns by issuers that short selling prior to a public offering "can and does have the effect of driving down the price of the securities to be distributed."[69] In this context, the short selling may result in either a lowering of the public offering price or the cancellation of the proposed offering. Today, the content of this rule has been moved to Rule 105 of Regulation M, which became effective in 1997 as part of a general codification of the Commission's rules on trading practices during a distribution.[70] The scope of Rule 105 has also been marginally narrowed. It now applies only to short sales during the five business days prior to the pricing of the offering. As to these covered short sales, Rule 105 makes it unlawful to cover short sales of equity securities of the same class as securities offered for cash pursuant to a 1933 Act registration statement, or a notification on Form 1-A under Regulation A, with any securities purchased from an underwriter or broker or dealer participating in the offering. Rule 105 only applies to firm commitment underwritings; it does not apply to shelf-offerings under Rule 415.

Under Rule 105(d), the Commission can grant exemptions from this prohibition on covering short sales out of the securities in the offering, and typically it will do so based on special terms and conditions. It must be emphasized that Rule 105 does not prohibit short sales in connection with a distribution; such "bear raids" by those who believe the offering price is unrealistically high (particularly in the aftermarket of an IPO) do continue to occur. Rather, Rule 105 precludes the short seller using securities it has reserved in the offering to cover its sales, because this makes the transaction essentially riskless to the short seller. If the offering price goes up, it will break even; if it goes down, it would typically decline its allocation and profit on the short sale.

B. *Manipulation During a Distribution: Regulation M.* An issuer (and the underwriters assisting it) in a distribution have an obvious incentive to attempt to raise the issuer's stock price just prior to the time of the offering. By buying the stock (even in fairly modest amounts) in the period immediately preceding the offering, they may be able to inflate the issuer's stock price in order to obtain a higher price in the offering (or simply give the false impression that there is widespread demand for the stock). Of course, this is the essence of manipulation: that is, purchases intended to artificially peg the security's price, and not based on any investment decision as to the security's inherent value.

Relying on its authority under § 10(b) of the 1934 Act to proscribe "manipulative or deceptive devices or contrivances," the SEC since 1955 has prohibited the issuer and other participants in a distribution from bidding for or purchasing securities that were the subject of a current or contemplated distribution. For many years, these prohibitions were

---

[69] See Securities Act Release No. 6789 (Aug. 25, 1988) [1988–1989 Transfer Binder] Fed.Sec.L.Rep. (CCH) ¶ 84,315, at 89,384.

[70] See Securities Act Release No. 7375 (December 20, 1996).

contained in Rules 10b–6, 10b–7 and 10b–8. These rules were extremely technical and were subject to numerous exceptions that sometimes seemed to overwhelm the principal prohibitions.

Accordingly, in 1997, in a deregulatory effort long sought by the industry, the SEC reorganized these trading rules, collecting them under a new Regulation M, simplifying their prohibitions and narrowing their scope. Rule 101 now applies to underwriters (including prospective underwriters) and any broker, dealer "or other person who has agreed to participate or is participating in the distribution" (all such persons being defined by Rule 100 as "distribution participants"). Rule 102 reaches the issuer or any other person (such as a selling shareholder) on whose behalf the distribution is being conducted. "Distribution" is for this purpose broadly defined by Rule 100 to mean:

> an offering of securities, whether or not subject to registration under the Securities Act, that is distinguished from ordinary trading transactions by the magnitude of the offering and the presence of special selling efforts and selling methods.

Thus, Regulation M could easily apply to an exempt intrastate offering under § 3(a)(11), or to a § 3(a)(9) or § 3(a)(10) offering. Regulation M's prohibition against buying what you are selling applies only for a relatively brief "restricted period", which varies depending upon the average daily trading volume ("ADTV") in the stock and the nature of the transaction. For issuers with an average daily trading volume of $100,000 or more and that also have a "public float value" (i.e., the value of stock held by public shareholders and not affiliates) of $25 million or more, the restricted period is briefer and only begins on the later of one business day prior to the pricing of the offering or such time as the broker-dealer or other person becomes a distribution participant; the restricted period continues until such person completes its participation in the distribution. For issuers that do not satisfy this high trading volume standard, the "restricted period" begins on the later of five business days prior to the pricing of the stock or such later point at which the person becomes a distribution participant, and it continues similarly until the person completes its participation in the distribution. (These time periods are shorter than the prior time periods of two or nine business days, depending upon trading volume, under former Rule 10b–6). In the case of mergers, acquisitions and exchange offers, the restricted period is typically longer and begins on the day that proxy solicitations or other offering materials are first disseminated to security holders and continues until the completion of the distribution.

Regulation M is subject to a number of important exceptions. Under Rule 101(c)(1), "actively-traded securities" are exempted on the apparent premise that such securities cannot be feasibly manipulated. For this exemption to become applicable, the securities must have an ADTV of $1 million and be issued by a company with a public float of at least $150 million. As of 1995, it was estimated that some 1,900 companies would qualify for this exemption. Although dealers and underwriters are thus no longer subject to trading restrictions on actively traded securities, issuers and selling shareholders remain subject to such restrictions during a distribution, even if the security is "actively traded." The apparent rationale is that broker-dealers have legitimate reasons for wanting to buy stock during a distribution, but issuers have less justification. Also, it needs to be understood that Regulation M is not a safe harbor. If intent to manipulate can be shown, a dealer, underwriter or any other person would presumably violate Rule 10b–5, even if it had complied with the applicable rules under Regulation M.

Regulation M also accords special significance to the existence of "information barriers" (sometimes called "Chinese Walls"). Under Rule 100, the term "affiliated purchaser" is defined so as to exclude affiliates of underwriters, selling shareholders, or issuers so long as the underwriter or issuer maintains and enforces written "information barriers" and obtains an annual independent assessment of the operation of such barrier.

Rules 101 and 102 apply not only to the security being distributed, but also to any "reference security." This term is defined by Rule 100 to mean "a security into which a security that is the subject of a distribution ('subject security') may be converted, exchanged or exercised or which, under the terms of the subject security being distributed, may in whole or in significant part determine the value of [such] security." On this basis, if common stock were being distributed, trading in a convertible debt security convertible into that common stock would not be affected by Regulation M, but if the same convertible debt were being distributed, trading in the underlying common stock would be restricted. Trading in options and other derivative securities are thus also outside the scope of Rules 101 and 102 (whereas they were formerly covered by Rule 10b–6).

C. *"Laddering."* Suppose in an oversubscribed or "hot" offering the underwriter tells a prospective customer that it can receive an allocation of 5,000 shares but only if it agrees to purchase another 5,000 shares (or perhaps 10,000 or even more shares) in the aftermarket on the first day of the offering. Sometimes, the arrangement allegedly calls for the customer to make its required aftermarket purchases only after the market price in the secondary market reaches a specified level (hence the term "laddering," as the secondary market purchases are pre-arranged on a "ladder" of ascending prices).[71] The impact of any such "tie-in" arrangement is to create an artificial demand for the shares, which should increase the first day price spike seen in many "hot" offerings.

Still, it is important to ask: Who is the victim? Importantly, it is not the customer who agrees to this "tie-in." This customer willingly agreed to buy additional shares at a possibly inflated price in order to obtain an

---

[71] See Peter Beshar, "The New Wave of Securities Litigation—The Laddering Cases" in How to Prepare an Initial Public Offering 2001, 343 (PLI Corporate Law and Practice Course Handbook Series No. BO-01BW, 2001).

initial allocation that this customer probably regards as "free money." The real victim is the third-party customer who buys in the aftermarket, not knowing that the price of the security has been artificially inflated. In Staff Legal Bulletin No. 10, the SEC's Division of Market Regulation announced its view in 2000 that any "tie-in" arrangement that requires the customer to buy additional shares in the aftermarket as a condition of receiving an allocation in the offering violated Rules 101 and 102 of Regulation M.[72] Staff Legal Bulletin No. 10 also warned that the anti-manipulation provisions of § 17(a) of the 1933 Act and § 10(b) of the 1934 Act would also be violated by such conduct.

After the collapse of the Internet IPO bubble in the early 2000s, a number of class actions alleging manipulative "laddering" were brought, and ultimately settled, in the Southern District of New York. Some also alleged that the underwriter reached an agreement whereby the purchaser who received the allocation in a "hot" IPO was required to split its profits with the underwriter (thereby possibly defrauding the issuer as well as the secondary market issuer, because such a profit-sharing agreement gives the underwriter a strong incentive to underprice the stock).[73] With the collapse of the IPO bubble in 2000, these practices faded, but could return in the future.

D. *Stabilization.* In principle, § 9(a)(6) of the 1934 Act prohibits transactions for the purpose of "pegging, fixing, or stabilizing" the price of a security, but only when they are "in contravention of such rules and regulations as the Commission may prescribe as necessary or appropriate in the public interest or for the protection of investors." In 1940 in its Statement of Policy on the Pegging Fixing and Stabilizing of Security Prices,[74] the majority of the Commission, interpreted this ambiguous provision as a mandate to the Commission to *regulate* rather than *prohibit* stabilizing transactions by an underwriting syndicate to facilitate a distribution of securities.

Thus, the SEC recognizes one major exception to the prohibitions in Regulation M on the issuer or the underwriters buying what they are selling for certain purchases conducted by underwriters during a distribution in order to "stabilize" the security's price (or, more accurately, to prevent or retard the decline of the security's price below the offering price). Such purchasing could also in theory be deemed "manipulative" (because it seeks to "peg" the price of the distributed security), but a long history of SEC interpretations has largely carved them out of the SEC's trading rules in order to facilitate distributions.

The present rules developed as a result of this approach consist of a general prohibition in Rules 101 and 102 against any "distribution participant" bidding for or purchasing the security being distributed or

---

[72] See 2000 SEC No-Act LEXIS 820 (August 25, 2000). See Rule 101(a).

[73] See MDCM Holdings, Inc. v. Credit Suisse First Boston, 216 F.Supp.2d 251 (S.D.N.Y. 2002) (declining to dismiss complaint containing such allegations).

[74] Securities Exchange Act Release No. 2446 (March 18, 1940).

any security of the same class, with exceptions for, among other things, any stabilizing transactions carried out in conformity with Rule 104.

New Rule 104, which replaced old Rule 10b–7 at the time that Regulation M was codified, has a broader scope than its predecessor. Under Rule 104(a), all stabilizing activities are covered in connection with any securities "offering" (a term which the adopting release indicates is deliberately broader than the conventional term "distribution"); because Rule 104 is an exemptive rule, this broader scope authorizes the underwriters to continue buying the stock for a longer period.[75] Otherwise, Rule 104 largely continues the prior practices with regard to stabilizing, which (1) require any person entering the stabilizing bid to grant priority to independent bids (see Rule 104(c)), (2) permit only one stabilizing bid to be made at a time in any market (see Rule 104(d)), and (3) require disclosure to the market of the stabilizing bid (Rule 104(h)). However, Rule 104 does give the underwriters greater freedom and discretion in stabilizing because it enables the underwriter to initiate and change its stabilizing bid based upon the current independent price in the market, provided that their bid does not exceed the offering price.[76] Also, in recognition of the global nature of securities markets and the increasing prevalence of international offerings, Rule 104 permits stabilizing bids to be made with reference to independent prices in the principal market for the security. Thus, if the principal market were in London and the offering were being conducted in both the U.S. and the U.K., a U.S. underwriter would enter a stabilizing bid at the highest independent U.K. market price, even if this were above the U.S. price, so long as it did not exceed the offering price.

E. *Shelf Registration and Trading Practices.* Over the long history of Rule 10b–6, which was the precursor to Regulation M, the fact pattern that caused the greatest difficulty was the shelf registration by selling shareholders of a substantial quantity of stock for a continuous offering. Suppose one shareholder buys during a period when it is not selling, but other shareholders in the same group are selling—could this be a reciprocal agreement? In *Jaffee & Company*,[77] thirty-four selling shareholders had registered shares and were buying and selling. The SEC took the position that each holder had to coordinate its individual purchases with the sales of the other thirty-three shareholders so as to assure that purchases and sales did not overlap within any restricted period. In 1986, the SEC relaxed this relatively strict position, requiring the selling shareholder thereafter to observe the requisite restricted period only with respect to its own sales transactions.[78]

---

[75] See Exchange Act Release No. 38067 ("Anti-manipulation Rules Concerning Securities Offerings") (December 20, 1996).

[76] See Rule 104(f)(2) and (4).

[77] See 44 SEC 285 (1970), affirmed in part and vacated in part, Jaffee & Co. v. SEC, 446 F.2d 387 (2d Cir. 1971).

[78] See Securities Exchange Act Release No. 23,611 (September 11, 1986).

F. *Scienter*. Originally, courts did not require the SEC to prove that a defendant intentionally violated the SEC's trading practices rules, but only that the challenged practice could "distort the . . . market."[79] But this pro-enforcement attitude may not survive Ernst & Ernst v. Hochfelder[80], which today requires all plaintiffs, including the SEC, to demonstrate scienter in order to make out a violation of Rule 10b–5.[81] The Commission, however, has continued to maintain that it can adopt prophylactic rules to regulate the distribution process. This issue may be litigated again in the wake of the adoption of Regulation M, but Regulation M is also phrased as an anti-manipulation rule.

Importantly, § 17(a)(2) and (3) of the 1933 Act do not require scienter to be proved, thus making this section an attractive theory of liability for the SEC to assert (although private parties may not sue under § 17).

G. *"Hot Issues," "Free Riding" and "Withholding": SEC and NASD Interpretations*. Attempts to support the price of a security occur in weak or declining markets, where "sticky" offerings (or extended ones) are common. In contrast, the reverse pattern is typical in the "bull markets" that often typify the IPO marketplace. In this world, the issuer and its underwriters do not necessarily want to sell to the "mere" public, but may wish to reserve shares for the affiliates of underwriters, for other underwriters who are not participating in the offering (or their personnel), and for insiders at favored clients—all in the expectation of reciprocity. The SEC and the NASD have fought this pattern for decades. In one of its first releases on this topic, "Preliminary Report on Practices in Distributions of 'Hot Issues',"[82] the SEC addressed the allocation of hot issues in 1959:

> The practices in question involve a combination of some or all of the following elements:
>
> 1. In addition to allotments of the offered securities to his own customers and to selling group dealers, if any, the underwriter may allot a portion of the offering at the public offering price to trading firms active in the over-the-counter market. These firms are expected to commence making a market in such securities at or immediately after the start of the public offering. Some of these firms sell their allotments at prices substantially in excess of the public offering price stated in the prospectus, and in some cases bid for and purchase the security while they are distributing their allotments. The

---

[79] See Jaffee & Co. v. SEC, 446 F.2d 387, 391 (2d Cir. 1971).

[80] 425 U.S. 185 (1976); see also Aaron v. SEC, 446 U.S. 680 (1980) (*Hochfelder's* standard applies to SEC as well as to private plaintiffs).

[81] Aaron v. SEC, supra note 80, distinguished Rule 10b–5 from Sections 17(a)(2) and (3) and found that the SEC did not have to plead scienter under these two subsections of § 17(a).

[82] See "Preliminary Report on Practices in Distribution of Hot Issues," Securities Act Release No. 4150 (Oct. 23, 1959).

inquiry also discloses that such distributions may be made by these firms without any use of a prospectus.

. . .

2. Underwriters and selling group dealers may allot a substantial portion of the securities acquired by them to partners, officers, employees or relatives of such persons ('insiders'), to other broker-dealers with whom they may have reciprocal arrangements or to 'insiders' of such other broker-dealers. Such allotments are made notwithstanding the fact that customers of such firms are unable to obtain a part of the original distribution and therefore could only purchase the securities in the market at the higher price.

Following this SEC Release in 1959, the NASD issued an Interpretation with respect to "Free-Riding and Withholding." That Interpretation, as amended, concluded:[83]

FREE-RIDING AND WITHHOLDING
Introduction

"(1) This Interpretation is based upon the premise that members have an obligation to make a bona fide public distribution at the public offering price of securities of a public offering which trade at a premium in the secondary market whenever such secondary market begins (a 'hot issue') regardless of whether such securities are acquired by the member as an underwriter, as a selling group member, or from a member participating in the distribution as an underwriter or a selling group member, or otherwise. The failure to make a bona fide public distribution when there is a demand for an issue can be a factor in artificially raising the price. Thus, the failure to do so, especially when the member may have information relating to the demand for the securities or other factors not generally known to the public, is inconsistent with high standards of commercial honor and just and equitable principles of trade and leads to an impairment of public confidence in the fairness of the investment banking and securities business. Such conduct is, therefore, in violation of Article III, Section 1 of the Association's Rules of Fair Practice [today Rule 2110—eds.] and this Interpretation thereof which establishes guidelines in respect to such activity.

* * *

Interpretation

"Except as provided herein, it shall be inconsistent with high standards of commercial honor and just and equitable principles of trade and a violation of Article III, Section 1 of the Association's Rules of Fair Practice for a member, or a person associated with a member, to fail to make a bona fide public distribution at the public offering price of

---

[83] For the current and nearly identical text of this rule, see FINRA Manual, Rule 5130, discussed below, which was largely derived from this interpretation and from NASD Rule 2790.

securities of a public offering which trade at a premium in the secondary market whenever such secondary market begins regardless of whether such securities are acquired by the member as an underwriter, a selling group member or from a member participating in the distribution as an underwriter or selling group member, or otherwise. Therefore, it shall be a violation of Article III, Section 1 for a member, or a person associated with a member, to:

1. Continue to hold any of the securities so acquired in any of the member's accounts;

2. Sell any of the securities to any officer, director, general partner, employee or agent of the member or of any other broker/dealer, or to a person associated with the member or with any other broker/dealer, or to a member of the immediate family of any such person;

3. Sell any of the securities to a person who is a finder in respect to the public offering or to any person acting in a fiduciary capacity to the managing underwriter, including, among others, attorneys, accountants and financial consultants, or to a member of the immediate family of any such person;

4. Sell any securities to any senior officer of a bank, savings and loan institution, insurance company, registered investment company, registered investment advisory firm or any other institutional type account, domestic or foreign, or to any person in the securities department of, or to any employee or any other person who may influence or whose activities directly or indirectly involve or are related to the function of buying or selling securities for any bank, savings and loan institution, insurance company, registered investment company, registered investment advisory firm, or other institutional type account, domestic or foreign, or to a member of the immediate family of any such person; . . .

6. Sell any of the securities, at or above the public offering price, to any other broker/dealer; provided, however, a member may sell all or part of the securities acquired as described above to another member broker/dealer upon receipt from the latter of written assurances that such purchase would be made in order to fill orders for bona fide public customers, other than those enumerated in paragraphs (1), (2), (3), (4) or (5) above, at the public offering price as an accommodation to them and without compensation for such. . . .

H. *Spinning.* A principal target of SEC and FINRA enforcement has been the underwriter who allocates some of its stock in a "hot" offering to its own officers or directors or to personnel at another underwriter (even if the latter is not participating in the offering).

Regulators obviously fear that reciprocal understandings would develop under which "hot" allocations would be exchanged. But can the underwriter give an allocation in a "hot" offering to a prospective client (or, more likely, the CEO of such a prospective client)? Now, the underwriter's goal is to use allocations in hot offerings to win future business, and this practice is known as "spinning." Although "spinning" is inconsistent with the idea in the foregoing release that NASD members "have an obligation to make a bona fide public distribution at the public offering price," spinning did not violate any of the actual prohibitions in the foregoing release or in NASD Conduct Rule 2110. Thus, underwriters had a strong incentive to allocate IPO stock to venture capital firms (or their insiders) in the hope that such firms would steer their next IPO to the underwriter. In a well-known Delaware corporate law case dealing with this same practice, underwriters allocated shares in the IPOs of other companies to directors of eBay as a form of rebate on the fees eBay paid to its underwriters. The court found these payments to be illegal, on the ground that the rebates belonged to the firm, and could not be taken by the directors except in accord with corporate law rules about disclosure and ratification.[84]

Slowly and arguably incompletely, FINRA has restricted spinning. In the wake of a wave of lawsuits in 2000 to 2001 challenging IPO practices, the NASD sought to reform the IPO allocation process. In mid-2002, it announced proposed rules that would expressly curb both "spinning" and "laddering." Today, FINRA Rule 5130, originally adopted by the NASD in 2003 and re-adopted by FINRA in 2008, governs the allocation of stock in IPOs to securities industry personnel and precludes the allocation of stock in IPOs to such personnel or to "reward persons who are in a position to direct future business to NASD members."[85] This new rule amends and replaces the NASD's former "Free-Riding and Withholding Interpretation" earlier quoted. Under Rule 5130, a FINRA member may not sell shares in a "new issue" to a "restricted person" or to any account in which a restricted person has a significant beneficial interest. The term "restricted person" includes most broker-dealer personnel, portfolio managers of bank, insurance and mutual fund companies, or managers of other institutional accounts. The basic goal is to preclude quid pro quo allocations of IPO shares to persons in a position to direct future business to the underwriter in reciprocation for the IPO allocation.

Going further, the NASD proposed a rule in 2003 to restrict the practice of "spinning" (i.e., the allocation of shares to officers or directors of prospective investment banking clients). The proposed rule would have expressly prohibited both spinning and "quid pro quo allocations" (offering IPO shares for the receipt of "compensation that is excessive in

---

[84] In re eBay Inc. Shareholder Litigation, 2004 WL 253521 (Del. Ch. 2004).
[85] See Securities Exchange Act Release No. 58421 (August 25, 2008) (re-adopting old NASD Rule 2790 as FINRA Rule 5130 with minor changes).

relation to the services provided by the NASD member"). This latter reference to excessive compensation was a reaction to reports that some underwriters had "sold" IPO allocations to hedge funds in return for very high brokerage commissions, which commissions were determined after the fact and effectively amounted to as much as 25% of the first day's runup in the IPO stock's price. The proposed rule sat quietly from 2003 to 2010, when it was finally adopted.[86] However, the rule, as adopted, has been relaxed. As adopted, FINRA Rule 5131(b) now prohibits the allocation of new issue shares to the account of an executive officer or director of a company: (1) if the company is currently an investment banking services client of the broker-dealer or the broker-dealer has received compensation for investment banking services within the past 12 months, (2) if the broker-dealer expects to provide, or expects to be retained by the company for such services, within the next 3 months, or (3) if there is an "express or implied condition that such executive officer or director, on behalf of the company will retain" the broker-dealer for future investment banking services. The narrowness of this drafting (and the short 3 months limit) suggests that spinning may yet persist in a somewhat more veiled format.

Rule 5131 is a complex rule with limitations,[87] but it is backstopped by Rule 2110, which can always be deployed to police conduct that FINRA deems unethical or unprofessional. The threat of this vague rule undoubtedly deters some conduct on the margin, as compliance professionals within broker-dealers cannot readily predict when it will be used.

As part of its 2010 reforms, FINRA also revised FINRA Rule 5131(a) to prohibit any broker-dealer from offering, or threatening to withhold, shares in a new issue "as consideration or inducement for the receipt of compensation that is excessive in relation to the services provided by the" broker-dealer. This was a response to practices under which some institutional clients (most typically, hedge funds) paid very high brokerage commissions for the receipt of "hot" IPO allocations. Still, if this is unethical, is it also wrong or unethical to direct IPO allocations to institutional clients that have paid the broker-dealer larger aggregate annual brokerage commissions (even if they may pay a much smaller commission per share)? It is generally believed that underwriters allocate IPO shares on the latter basis (and thereby prefer mutual funds,

---

[86] See Securities Exchange Act Release No. 63010 (Sept. 29, 2010).

[87] In 2014, FINRA amended Rule 5131 to ease compliance for certain funds-of-funds, which are investment funds that invest in other investment funds. The regulatory complexity for these funds in complying with Rule 5131 was significant, because each investor in each fund must be identified to ensure they are not in violation of the rule. The amendment allows private funds to certify compliance with the rule even though the fund does not look through investors to its underlying beneficial owners to determine whether such beneficial owners are public company officers or are covered by Rule 5131. For the exception to apply, the fund must: (1) be managed by an investment adviser; (2) have assets under management of more than $50 million; (3) own less than 25% of the account; (4) not have any investor with an interest of more than 25%; and (5) not be formed for the purpose of investing in the account.

which pay very large aggregate annual commissions but very low per share commissions). When shares are allocated to institutions instead of to retail customers, the underwriter's motivation is probably to obtain or hold future brokerage business. This practice will likely persist, as it is deeply embedded in the structure of multi-service investment banking firms. Should there instead be a broader "equal opportunity" rule that gives all customers an equal entitlement to IPO allocations? Is this feasible? Or, should the underwriter's preference for the large institution that may want a significant piece of the offering be considered justified because the institution is in reality a wholesale purchaser, who in most markets receives a priority over retail customers?

I. *Manipulation: The General Issues.* Section 9 of the Securities Exchange Act of 1934 is designed to prohibit manipulation of the securities markets. It has been termed by the SEC the "very heart of the act."[88] Section 9 applies only to listed securities, but the prohibitions in that section have been held to be incorporated into §§ 10(b) and 15(c)(1), which prohibit "manipulative" devices with respect to over-the-counter securities also.[89] In addition to various specific provisions aimed at the more notorious practices of the "pools" of the 1920's, such as wash sales, matched orders, and tipster sheets, § 9(a)(2) contains a general prohibition against effecting "a series of transactions * * * creating actual or apparent active trading in * * * or raising or depressing the price of" a security *"for the purpose of inducing the purchase or sale of such security by others."* The first part of the requirement of this section would be met by almost any conceivable market activity, other than a single purchase or sale. *Any* series of transactions would almost inevitably create actual or apparent trading or raise or depress the price of the security dealt in. The crucial question is the *purpose* for which the transactions are affected: unlawful activities are those done for the purpose of inducing the purchase or sale of such security by others. However, as the Commission stated in the *Halsey, Stuart*[90] case: "There is not here (as indeed there rarely is) any subjective evidence of such a purpose. If found, it must, as in most cases, be inferred from the circumstances of the case."

In Crane Company v. Westinghouse Air Brake Company[91] the Second Circuit had no difficulty in determining that the purchases by American Standard of the Westinghouse Air Brake stock were made for the purpose of manipulating the market in that stock and defeating the Crane tender offer. Although it was true that that was a particularly aggravated case (because the purchases on the floor of the exchange were accompanied by off-board sales at a loss), the Court nonetheless stated that: "When a person who has a 'substantial, direct pecuniary interest in

---

[88] See 3 Loss, Securities Regulation 1549 (2d ed. 1961).
[89] Securities and Exchange Commission v. Resch-Cassin & Co., Inc., 362 F.Supp. 964 (S.D.N.Y.1973).
[90] In the Matter of Halsey, Stuart & Co., Inc., 30 S.E.C. 106, 123–24 (1949).
[91] 419 F.2d 787 (2d Cir. 1969).

the success of a proposed offering takes active steps to effect a rise in the market' in the security, we think that a finding of manipulative purpose is prima facie established."[92]

In Securities and Exchange Commission v. Resch-Cassin & Co., Inc.[93] a brokerage firm, which was the principal market maker in a security following a public offering, ran the price up in thirty-four minutes on one day from $11 to $16 and in another 20 day period from $13 to $17.5; but in less than two months after the issue came out at $10, the price was down to $4. The court said:

> Of course, once it is established that a price rise occurred, it becomes necessary to show that defendants caused it. There are various factors which characterize attempts by manipulators to raise the price of an over-the-counter security: (a) price leadership by the manipulator; (b) dominion and control of the market for the security; (c) reduction in the floating supply of the security; and (d) the collapse of the market for the security when the manipulator ceases his activity. As already discussed herein, the tactic of inserting successively higher bids in the pink sheets has the effect of giving an appearance of activity. However, it also has the effect of causing a price rise. Similarly, the use of actual purchases and sales at successively higher prices not only has the effect of giving an appearance of activity, it raises the price of the over-the-counter security. * * *
>
> It is true, of course, that § 9(a)(2) of the Exchange Act requires that any manipulation be for the purpose of inducing the purchase or sale of such security by others'. Although defendants claim they were engaged in normal trading', it seems clear that their transactions in Africa stock were designed to induce others to purchase the security. Here they were engaged in the distribution of the stock and obviously had the purpose of inducing the purchase of the security by others. They had an obvious incentive to artificially influence the market price of the security in order to facilitate its distribution or increase its profitability. Here the defendants used the manipulated after-market to sell the Africa stock to the public.[94]

J. *The General Fraud Sections as Applied to Broker-Dealers.* Section 17(a) of the Securities Act of 1933, § 10(b) (as implemented by Rule 10b–5) of the Securities Exchange Act, and § 15(c)(1) of the Securities Exchange Act all prohibit manipulative, deceptive and

---

[92] 419 F.2d at 795.

[93] 362 F.Supp. 964 (S.D.N.Y.1973).

[94] 362 F.Supp. at 976–77. See also L. Lowenfels, Sections 9(a)(1) and 9(a)(2) of the Securities Exchange Act of 1934: An Analysis of Two Important Anti-Manipulation Provisions Under the Federal Securities Laws, 85 Nw. U. L.Rev. 698, at 702–705 (1991); Poser, Stock Market Manipulation and Corporate Control Transactions, 40 U. Miami L. Rev. 671 (1986) (discussing § 14(e) of the 1934 Act prohibiting manipulative activity in connection with tender offers).

fraudulent actions in the securities markets. Section 17(a) outlaws: (1) any device, scheme, or artifice to defraud; (2) any untrue statement of a material fact or any omission to state a material fact necessary to make the statements made not misleading; and (3) any transaction, practice, or course of business which operates or would operate as a fraud or deceit. Section 10(b) itself refers only to "any manipulative or deceptive device or contrivance," but Rule 10b–5 has copied the language of the three subdivisions of § 17(a). Section 15(c)(1) refers to "any manipulative, deceptive, *or other fraudulent* device or contrivance." But again Rule 15c1–2 has incorporated into this section the substance of the three subdivisions of § 17(a).

The major differences between these three sections and the rules implementing them are that § 17(a) applies only to *sales,* whereas §§ 10(b) and 15(c)(1) apply to both purchases and sales, and that § 15(c)(1) applies only to a "broker or dealer," whereas §§ 17(a) and 10(b) apply to "any person." There are other minor variations in language, which are not too significant. In connection with a revocation proceeding against a broker-dealer involving allegedly fraudulent sales of securities, the Commission uniformly cites all three sections (and their related rules).

K. *"Shingle Theory."* "Shingle theory" was developed by the Commission as a basis for a liberalized finding of statutory fraud under these sections in cases where no intentional misstatement or omission on the part of the broker-dealer could be established. In brief, the theory is that when a broker-dealer goes into business (hangs out his "shingle") he impliedly represents that he will deal fairly and competently with his customers and that he will have an adequate basis for any statements or recommendations which he makes concerning securities. But how far does this representation extend? In Kahn v. Securities and Exchange Commission, Judge Clark, in a concurring opinion, stated that under this theory the broker-dealer "implicitly warrants the soundness of statements of stock value."[95] Today this statement unquestionably goes much too far, as scienter must, of course, be proven in any action based on Rule 10b–5.

Shingle theory was set forth for the first time in a 1944 case, Charles Hughes & Co. v. SEC.[96] The charge in that case, as in most of the early cases involving shingle theory, was that the broker-dealer sold securities to his customers at prices greatly in excess of their market value and without disclosure of the market value, thus making false his implied representation that he would deal with them fairly and at prices reasonably related to market value. Today, the survival of "shingle theory" is open to serious question,[97] but it still remains possible that if

---

[95] 297 F.2d 112 (2d Cir. 1961).
[96] Charles Hughes & Co. v. SEC, 139 F.2d 434 (2d Cir. 1943), cert. denied, 321 U.S. 786 (1944).
[97] See Roberta Karmel, Is the Shingle Theory Dead?, 52 Wash. & Lee L. Rev. 1271 (1995).

a broker-dealer makes optimistic statements to its customers about a security without any factual basis, the SEC will view this as violating a broker's implied representation that he will have a reasonably adequate basis for any such statements.[98]

Problem

PROBLEM 9-3

Barbary Hedges LLP is a billion dollar (or medium-sized) hedge fund, and its portfolio is roughly one half the size of the larger mutual fund families. As a result, its aggregate brokerage commissions with any underwriter are also less than those of most large mutual funds. Thus, when Barbary seeks an allocation in "hot" IPOs from Merrill, Chase, the underwriter, it usually gets a much smaller allocation than it wants. To solve this problem, it begins on its own to pay those broker-dealers who are also underwriters a commission that is more than double the standard commission for an institution (i.e., it now pays roughly 1% of the transaction's size). You are counsel at Merrill Chase. If your firm did not request this excess commission and if it assigns IPO allocations more or less in proportion to aggregate brokerage commissions received from its clients, can it accept this additional compensation? Or, can it accept the commissions but then not increase its IPO allocation to Barbary?

2. REGULATION AIMED AT PROTECTION FROM HIGH RISK AND INSOLVENCY

As in the case of other financial institutions, federal regulatory policy toward broker-dealers seeks to ensure their financial soundness.[99] The regulatory objective is not only protection of the customers of the individual firm, but, in light of the interdependence of firms, protection of the system from a domino-like cascade of failing firms. As discussed below, this is achieved through direct regulation, financial controls, segregation of customer funds, and a governmentally administered insurance system. Some rules also indirectly reduce the overall financial risk to the system. For example, the SEC requires that every contract for the purchase or sale of a security (with some exceptions for exempted and governmental securities and commercial paper) settle not later than the second business day after the contract was executed.[100] By requiring a short settlement cycle (now known as "t+2"), the Commission reduced the overall risk to the system from longer-term extensions of credit.

Beyond seeking to reduce aggregate risk, federal policy, since the inception of the 1934 Act, has paternalistically sought to discourage the individual investor from pursuing heavily leveraged investment

---

[98] See In re BT Alex. Brown Inc., Securities Exchange Act Release No. 42145 (Nov. 17, 1999); In re Alexander Reid & Co., Inc., Securities Exchange Act Release No. 6727 (1962).

[99] For an overview of federal policy toward financial institutions, see Clark, The Soundness of Financial Intermediaries, 86 Yale L.J. 1 (1976).

[100] See Rule 15c6–1 ("settlement cycle"), 17 C.F.R. § 240.15c6–1.

strategies in securities. Toward this end, § 7 of the 1934 Act subjects broker-dealers and other lenders and borrowers to margin controls that are intended to prevent "excessive" use of credit for the purpose of purchasing or carrying securities. Because, under the margin rules, a customer can only borrow 50% of the purchase price of a security from his or her broker, these rules may have the effect of diverting investments to things other than securities. For instance, during the height of the 2008 housing bubble, individuals could borrow (from a bank) 100% of the value of a $1 million home, but could borrow (from a stock broker) only 50% of the value of a $1 million stock investment. The greater leverage available in the home investment case may have made it a much more attractive investment, and may have contributed to the bubble in housing prices.

A. *Broker-Dealer Record-Keeping.* Section 17(a) of the 1934 Act requires broker-dealers to keep extensive records. Under Rule 17a–5, every broker-dealer who clears transactions or carries customer accounts must file both monthly and quarterly reports (known as FOCUS reports) with FINRA and the SEC on its financial condition. The same rule also requires the broker-dealer to send periodically to its customers specified information about its financial position.[101] A broker-dealer that overstates its income or assets is subject to SEC discipline and sanctions, because necessarily the FOCUS reports it files with the Commission will be overstated.[102] Thus, Rule 17a–5 provides a jurisdictional hook for cases involving a variety of forms of misconduct that wrongfully transfer customer funds to the broker-dealer.

Other rules under § 17 require broker-dealers to keep specified records and to preserve these records for specified periods.[103] These include: blotters containing daily itemized records of all purchases and sales of securities, ledgers of the firm's income and expense and capital accounts, ledger accounts as to each customer account, and a memorandum of each brokerage order.[104] These records are subject to periodic inspections by government regulators (state and federal), and the net result is not unlike the standard examination procedures that a bank or a savings and loan association undergoes.

Section 17(a) does not give a defrauded creditor any private right of action (either against the broker-dealer or its auditors).[105] Rather, the Supreme Court viewed it as a tool to aid regulators, not as a grant of rights to investors.

---

[101] See Rule 17a–5(c).

[102] See Securities Exchange Act Litig. Release No. 14865 ("In the Matter of Gruntal & Co. Inc.") (April 9, 1996) (broker-dealer subjected to cease and desist order under § 21C of the 1934 Act and other sanctions under § 15(b)(4) of the 1934 Act for overstating earnings on its FOCUS report by diverting customer funds to broker-dealer's own account).

[103] See Rule 17a–4 (six year preservation required).

[104] See Rule 17a–3.

[105] See Touche Ross & Co. v. Redington, 442 U.S. 560, 569 (1979).

B. *The Net Capital Rules.* Based on authority granted it by § 15(b)(7) of the 1934 Act, the SEC directly regulates the capital of broker-dealers, requiring high liquidity in order to protect customers and creditors of broker-dealers from financial exposure in the event of broker insolvency. The key rule—Rule 15c3–1—"requires registered broker-dealers to maintain sufficient liquid assets to enable firms that fall below the minimum net capital requirements to liquidate in an orderly fashion without the need for a formal proceeding."[106] Setting a liquidation threshold equal to the aggregate of customer accounts promotes orderly self-liquidations of financially distressed broker-dealers and reduces the costs incurred in bankruptcy proceedings. Still, the cost of such a policy is considerable: necessarily some broker-dealers are forced into liquidation that are not insolvent and that would not become insolvent (but that have crossed the early warning thresholds imposed by Rule 15c3–1). Also, the rule heavily impacts broker-dealer behavior: they cannot easily hold investments in securities, because the rule writes down such investments to a fraction of their market value. In the industry, this is referred to as "taking a haircut," and it induces broker-dealers to maintain high cash reserves. The rule also restricts entry into the broker-dealer industry by imposing high minimum capital requirements. Here, as above, we see the tension between regulation and cartelization risk.

Nonetheless, the Commission justifies Rule 15c3–1 (which has been in force since 1965) on three grounds:

> First, firms handling customer funds and securities should have sufficient capital so that they are not dependent upon customer assets to make up the principal working capital of the firm. Second, firms should have adequate capital, resources, and equipment so that the securities markets function smoothly and efficiently and market participants have the resulting confidence to carry out business responsibly. Finally, if the liability of a broker-dealer to its customers from violations of state and federal law is to be a deterrent to improper conduct, a firm should be required to maintain a reasonable financial stake in its business.[107]

Rule 15c3–1 uses a dual measuring standard for a broker-dealer's capital requirements. Two types of financial ratio computations are specified: (1) an "aggregate indebtedness standard" which generally prohibits the broker or dealer from permitting its aggregate indebtedness to exceed 1500 percent of its net capital, and (2) an "alternative standard," which requires that a broker not permit its net capital to be less than the greater of $250,000 or two percent of aggregate debit items as computed under the rule.[108] A broker-dealer who carries customer

---

[106] See Securities Exchange Act Release No. 27,249 (Sept. 15, 1989).
[107] Id.
[108] See Rule 15c3–1(a)(1)(i) and (ii).

accounts must also maintain net capital of not less than $250,000.[109] This requirement often induces smaller brokers to use larger clearing brokers to hold and service their customers' accounts. This undoubtedly reduces customer risk, but it also concentrates economic activity in larger brokers, and inhibits competition for these services.

Another aspect of the net capital rule is the requirement that broker-dealers maintain fully paid customer securities in a "segregated" account with the brokerage firm or a bank.[110] Often, this is arranged between the brokerage firm and the Depositary Trust Company ("DTC").[111] These rules also restrict the "hypothecation" of customer securities: that is, their use by the broker-dealer as collateral for its own borrowings or short sales.

C. *Securities Investor Protection Corporation.* The SIPC was established in 1970, and registered broker-dealers are required to become members. SIPC was created in the wake of the "back-office crisis" of 1967–70. The crisis was caused by lax back office documentation of trades. Over the period 1964 to 1968, average daily volume on the NYSE grew by 265 percent. Reflecting "an industrywide loss of control of record-keeping procedures," the number of complaints against brokers rose from about 4000 in 1968 to over 12,000 just one year later.[112] According to the leading history of Wall Street, this period saw "the most serious failure of securities self-regulation in the [SEC]'s history."[113] The government's own study of the problem concluded that, during the late 1960s, the "industry concentrated its resources on sales, and paid insufficient attention to properly handling and processing the business brought in by its sales efforts."[114] SIPC was designed to prevent customer losses from badly managed brokerages, as opposed to badly performing investments, and to prevent a run on solvent brokers in the event of a spike in customer complaints across the industry.

Essentially, the SIPC insures the accounts of customers with brokerage firms in much the same manner as the Federal Deposit Insurance Corporation ("FDIC") does for the banking industry.[115] As with the FDIC, there are ceilings on this insurance (securities in customer accounts are covered by the SIPC up to $500,000 in the event of a broker-dealer's insolvency). Another advantage of this insurance system is that

---

[109] See Rule 15c3–1(a)(2)(i).

[110] See Rule 15c3–3(c); see also Rule 8c–1.

[111] See Securities Exchange Act Release No. 26,250 (November 3, 1988) (detailing procedures for "memo segregation" by DTC).

[112] Joel Seligman, The Transformation of Wall Street at 451.

[113] Id at 450.

[114] SEC, Study of Unsafe and Unsound Practices of Brokers and Dealers: Report and Recommendations of the Securities and Exchange Commission, H.R. Doc. No. 92–231 (1971) at p. 95.

[115] See 15 U.S.C. § 78aaa (authorizing SIPC). The broker membership requirement is codified at 15 U.S.C. § 78ccc(a)(2)(A). For a review of the SIPC's performance, see Bloomenthal & Salcito, Customer Protection from Brokerage Failures: The Securities Investor Protection Corporation and the SEC, 54 U. Colo. L. Rev. 161 (1983).

it spares the customer the delay involved in bankruptcy and insolvency reorganizations. The downside of this insurance system, like all others, is what economists call "moral hazard." Knowing that brokerage accounts are insured against broker insolvency, investors will take less care on the margin in choosing a broker. This may mean average broker quality, along some dimensions, will be lower in a world with the SIPC than without.

Importantly, however, SIPC does not cover losses from bad decisions. This significantly reduces the value of the safety net. According to the Wall Street Journal, nearly 80% of the arbitration awards from 2012 were not paid because the defendant brokers did not have the money to cover the claims or insurance to cover the conduct.[116] Neither FINRA nor the SEC require insurance that would fill this gap.

D. *Credit Regulation. The Margin Requirements.* Section 7 of the 1934 Act subjects broker-dealers, most other lenders, and borrowers to margin controls that are intended to prevent "excessive" use of credit for the purpose of purchasing or carrying securities. Congress's intent was to chill speculation in securities trading (which from the vantage point of 1934 seemed a major cause of the 1929 stock market crash).

Section 7(a) requires the Federal Reserve Board ("FRB") to prescribe regulations with respect to the amount of credit that may be initially extended and subsequently maintained on any security, other than an exempt security. Although the FRB has the authority to promulgate the regulations and to fix from time to time the minimum margin level (currently 50%), the SEC and the SROs are charged with the responsibility of enforcing the margin rules with respect to broker-dealers. The current regulation governing lending on securities by broker-dealers is designated Regulation T. There is a similar, but by no means identical, regulation governing loans by banks secured directly or indirectly by margin stock "for the purpose * * * of buying or carrying margin stock,"[117] which is designated Regulation U, and relatively new regulations governing lending by persons other than broker-dealers and banks, who engage in the business of making loans for the purpose of

---

[116] "Is Your Adviser Insured?," WALL ST. J., Dec. 27, 2014.

[117] For a discussion of the differences between the regulation of lending on securities by broker-dealers, on the one hand, and by banks, on the other, prior to 1968, see Report of Special Study of the Securities Markets, H.Doc.No.95, 88th Cong., 1st Sess., Pt. 4 at 15–25 (1963).

The primary difference prior to that time was that broker-dealers could not lend at all on over-the-counter securities, whereas lending by banks on such securities was completely unregulated. By Act of July 29, 1968, 82 Stat. 452, Section 7 of the Securities Exchange Act was amended to give the FRB the authority to regulate credit on OTC securities and to eliminate the prohibition against broker-dealers lending on such securities. While the current Regulation T permits lending by broker-dealers on any securities, the required margin is 100% with respect to over-the-counter securities which are neither exempted securities nor on the list of "OTC Margin Stocks" issued by the FRB. On the other hand, a bank may lend on any such securities without regard to the margin requirement, and may assign a loan value to such collateral of any amount (not exceeding 100% of current market).

buying or carrying margin securities (Regulation G)[118] and governing borrowing by persons in the United States from either domestic or foreign lenders (Regulation X).[119]

Basically, Regulation T provides for two types of accounts that may be maintained for a customer by a broker-dealer: a "margin account" and a "cash account" (i.e., an account which is not subject to the margin requirements).

In a margin account, the loan value of the account must be maintained at the current required level, i.e., under the currently required 50% "margin" the debit balance of an account cannot be permitted to exceed 50% of the current market value of the securities held as collateral in the account in connection with any additional purchase of securities.[120]

Although the FRB has authority to require maintenance levels of margin as well as initial levels, it has never done so; therefore, Regulation T never requires "margin calls" if no new securities are purchased.[121] This is a matter regulated entirely by the rules of the stock exchanges and the contract between the customer and the broker-dealer.[122] For example, Rule 431 of the New York Stock Exchange requires (with some exceptions) that an account maintain a margin level of not less than twenty-five percent with respect to the securities "long" in the account. Thus, if an investor purchased securities using fifty percent margin from the broker-dealer, and the value of the securities so purchased falls, the broker must make a "margin call" (i.e., a demand for additional cash or collateral) once this "maintenance" margin level is reached. Or, the broker will be required to liquidate the securities in the account to pay off the customer's indebtedness to it. Such "margin calls" often occur in rapidly falling markets and were thought by Congress to accelerate the market's decline.

Brokers often specify "house maintenance margin" limits in their brokerage agreements with customers, which are stricter than the levels

---

[118] 12 C.F.R. Part 207 (§ 207.0 et seq.) effective March 11, 1968. This regulation in general conforms to Regulation U applicable to banks.

[119] 12 C.F.R. Part 224 (§ 224.1 et seq.). This regulation was authorized by Act of October 26, 1970, P.L. 91–508, 84 Stat. 1124, adding subsection (f) to Section 7 of the Securities Exchange Act. While primarily intended to stop the practice of United States persons borrowing from foreign lenders in order to evade the margin requirements, the statute and Regulation X originally applied to any borrowing, whether domestic or foreign, and thus for the first time made the borrower as well as the lender guilty of an offense when there is a violation of the margin rules. In 1984, Regulation X was revised to apply to a domestic borrowing *only* if "the borrower willfully causes the credit to be extended in contravention of Regulations G, T, or U." Basically, Regulation X simply says that the borrower is prohibited from borrowing if the lender is prohibited from lending by these regulations.

[120] 12 C.F.R. §§ 220.4, 220.12.

[121] The withdrawal of cash or securities from a margin account is not permitted, however, even though no new securities are being purchased, if thereafter the adjusted debit balance of the account would exceed the maximum loan value of the securities remaining, with certain exceptions. 12 C.F.R. § 220.4(e).

[122] Report of Special Study of the Securities Markets, H.Doc.No.95, 88th Cong., 1st Sess. Pt. 4, pp. 5–6 (1963); 12 C.F.R. § 220.3(c).

specified by the stock exchanges. These agreements may entitle the broker-dealer to make a margin call with virtually no notice or grace period or simply to liquidate the customer's securities if the house maintenance margin level is exceeded.[123] In contrast, federal law, which applies only to the initial margin requirement on a purchase, gives the customer four business days to satisfy any margin call.[124]

In addition to the FRB margin rules, in 1970, the SEC adopted Rule 10b–16. It requires a broker-dealer extending credit to a customer in a margin transaction to disclose the credit terms to the customer. Following the "Truth in Lending" paradigm, the rule provides, among other things, that at the opening of the account, the customer shall be furnished a written statement of the conditions under which the interest charge will be imposed, the method of computing the interest, and the conditions under which additional collateral can be required.

The National Securities Market Improvements Act of 1996 effected some significant deregulation in the scope of the margin rules and the FRB's authority. First, it repealed former § 8(a) and amended § 7 of the 1934 Act, which together had authorized the FRB to regulate the sources of credit for broker-dealers, and substituted a weaker requirement under which the FRB could regulate loans to broker dealers only if it found that such rules were necessary or appropriate in the public interest or for the protection of investors. The FRB has expressly declined to make any such finding.[125] Hence, broker-dealers are not restricted today in their own pursuit of credit by the margin-setting authority of the FRB.

Also, in 1996, the FRB amended its own Regulation T to relax substantially the former restrictions on the "arranging for" credit by broker-dealers. Today, a broker-dealer may effectively arrange for credit that it, itself, could not advance.[126] That is, the broker-dealer may arrange for credit that does not otherwise violate the lending provisions of the FRB's margin regulations (such as from an unregulated or foreign lender), but it may not arrange for credit from a lender that would itself violate Regulations G, T or U. Part of the rationale for this significant change was the increasingly global character of the market in which

---

[123] Such agreements are enforceable, even when no notice is given. See First Union Discount Brokerage Services, Inc. v. Milos, 997 F.2d 835 (11th Cir. 1993).

[124] 12 C.F.R. § 220.4(c)(3). This provision of Regulation T, adopted in 1998, works off on an SEC rule, Rule 15c6–1. Section 220.4(c)(3) of Regulation T requires that a margin call be satisfied "within one payment period after the margin deficiency was created." Section 220.2 then defines "payment period" to mean "the number of business days in the standard settlement cycle in the United States, as defined in paragraph (a) of SEC Rule 15c6–1 . . . plus two business days." Rule 15c6–1 requires all contracts for the purchase or sale of securities to settle within two business days—i.e., "t+2" (subject to several exceptions). Hence, Section 220.2 defines "payment period" to mean four business days.

[125] See Federal Reserve System, "Securities Credit Transactions; Borrowings by Brokers and Dealers," 61 F.R. 60166 (November 26, 1996).

[126] See Federal Reserve System, "Securities Credit Transactions; Review of Regulation T," 61 F.R. 20386 (May 6, 1996). Section 7 of the 1934 Act forbids a broker-dealer from "arranging" credit on terms forbidden by the FRB, but it does not restrict the FRB's ability to permit broker-dealers to arrange credit on terms they cannot themselves advance.

broker-dealers operated and the prospect that U.S. broker-dealers would be at a competitive disadvantage to foreign broker-dealers who could arrange for credit without restriction.

E. *Arbitration.* Almost all contracts between customers and brokers (known as brokerage agreements) include a provision requiring all disputes arising under the contract to be decided by a FINRA arbitration panel. The Supreme Court has upheld mandatory arbitration provisions under the 1934 Act in Shearson/American Express Inc. v. McMahon in 1987, and under the 1933 Act in Rodriguez de Quijas v. Shearson/American Express Inc. in 1989.[127] Accordingly, FINRA operates one of the largest arbitration forums in the world. Historically, arbitration panels (of three) included both industry and non-industry representatives, but in 2011 FINRA made a pilot program of all public arbitrators permanent, so that today customers have the option of a panel of all non-industry members. According to FINRA, "giving investors the ability to have an all-public panel will increase public confidence in the fairness of our dispute resolution process."[128] No appeals are available within the arbitration process, but there are some bases for review under state and federal law.[129]

Although arbitration is well established for most disputes, in 2011, broker Charles Schwab tried to extend its scope. It sent amendments to its brokerage contract to its nearly 7 million customers requiring them to agree to waive their rights to participate in class action lawsuits arising under the brokerage agreement. FINRA brought an enforcement action against Schwab alleging that the waiver violated FINRA rules. The FINRA Board ultimately found the Schwab agreement violated the rules and that the Federal Arbitration Act did not preempt the FINRA rules limiting arbitration in this context.[130] The argument under the rules is complex and subsidiary to the question of whether the FAA limited FINRA's authority to write rules that restrict the accessibility of arbitration. The Supreme Court has taken an expansive view of the preemptive power of the FAA, declaring that nothing short of a clear congressional override of the FAA can limit the availability of arbitration.[131] Arguably, there is such an override today: Section 921(a) of the Dodd-Frank Act specifically amends section 15 of the '34 Act to give the SEC authority to restrict the scope of brokerage arbitration agreements. Seemingly, this statute would be redundant if the SEC (and thus FINRA) already had this power prior to the Dodd-Frank Act, when the rules in question in *Schwab* were promulgated. In any event, the issue has not proceeded further, either to the SEC or the courts.

---

[127] 482 U.S. 220 (1987); 490 U.S. 477 (1989).
[128] http://www.finra.org/Newsroom/NewsReleases/2011/P122877.
[129] Federal Arbitration Act, 9 U.S.C. § 10.
[130] https://www.finra.org/media-center/news-releases/2014/board-decision-finds-Charles-Schwab-Co-violated-finra-rules.
[131] See, e.g., American Express Co. v. Italian Colors Restaurant, 570 U.S. 228 (2013).

3. REGULATION AIMED AT ESTABLISHING THE DUTIES OF BROKERS TO THEIR CUSTOMERS

Historically, the federal securities laws did not address whether or when brokers were fiduciaries to their clients. This issue was left to state law (and the states were divided). Unless the federal antifraud rules were violated by false or reckless statements by a broker, the federal securities laws also did not address the broker's obligations with respect to recommendations about securities that the broker made to the client. This gap was instead filled by the "suitability obligation" that the NASD (and later FINRA) enforced, which barred the broker from making an unsuitable recommendation to the client based on what the broker knew about the client's needs and expectations from information the client had provided. This obligation, which is discussed later in this chapter, was derived from the historic "know your customer" rule that the New York Stock Exchange had developed in the 19th Century (largely to protect itself from the impact of a client's collapse).[132] What then changed that the SEC adopted Regulation Best Interest in 2019, thereby imposing a uniform federal rule with respect to recommendation by brokers to retail clients about securities? The answer begins with the fact that investment advisers do owe their clients a fiduciary duty, and in the inevitable competition between these two closely related professions, investment advisers marketed themselves as the preferable choice for clients because they had to meet fiduciary standards. Further, although brokers are exempt (if certain conditions are satisfied) from the Investment Advisers Act, investment advisers had successfully litigated and overturned an SEC rule that had attempted to expand and simplify that exemption.[133] Customers were confused about the differences in the obligations owed by the two professions.

Against this backdrop, Congress added Section 913 to the Dodd-Frank Act in 2010, which required the SEC to conduct a study to evaluate the effectiveness of the current standards regulating broker-dealers and investment advisers and posed the question of whether there were regulatory gaps in the standards for the protection of retail customers that needed to be addressed.

In 2011, the Commission published the requested study, and it recommended that a uniform fiduciary standard of conduct should be imposed when either brokers or investment advisers provided investment advice and recommendations to retail customers.[134] The

---

[132] The NYSE's original fear was that a client's failure could cause a broker's failure, and the collapse of a substantial broker could set off a parade of falling dominoes that could imperil the exchange. Ironically then, the Know Your Customer rule was originally intended to protect the exchange more than the customer.

[133] See Fin. Planning Association v. Securities Exchange Commission, 482 F.3d 481 (D.C. Cir. 2007).

[134] See Staff of the U.S. Securities and Exchange Commission, Study on Investment Advisers and Broker-Dealers Required by Section 913 of Dodd-Frank Wall Street Reform and

proposed standard would have required broker-dealers to act in the best interest of their retail customers and was to be no less rigorous than the fiduciary standard applied to investment advisers, except that broker-dealers would not have any continuing duty of care or loyalty after providing their investment advice or recommendation.

This proposal began a political and lobbying battle which delayed the Commission until 2019, but the rule that ultimately emerged was quite similar to what the staff had proposed in 2011—except that Regulation Best Interest took even greater care to indicate that it was not imposing a fiduciary duty.

A. REGULATION BEST INTEREST

1. *What Does It Say?* A remarkably succinct rule, Regulation Best Interest has two basic provisions: First, Rule 15*l*–1(a)(1) opens with a one sentence general obligation that the broker (and any natural person who is an associated person) must "act in the best interest of the retail customer at the time the recommendation is made." Then, Rule 15*l*–I(a)(2) specifies that this general obligation shall be deemed to have been satisfied if the broker (or associated person) satisfies four component obligations. These four component obligations are:

(a) A Disclosure Obligation. This requires written "full and fair disclosure" to the retail customer of all material facts relating to the scope and terms of the relationship, including

(a) "the material fees and costs that apply to the... customer's transactions, holdings, and accounts,"

(b) the type and scope of services provided, including "any material limitations on the securities or investment strategies involving securities that may be recommended," and

(c) "all material facts relating to conflicts of interest that are associated with the recommendation."

(b) A Care Obligation. The broker (or any associated person) must exercise reasonable diligence, care and skill to (i) understand the risks, rewards, and costs associated with the recommendation, (ii) have a reasonable basis to believe that the recommendation is in the best interest of a particular retail customer based on that customer's investment profile, and (iii) does not place the financial or other interest of the broker, dealer or associated persons ahead of the interest of the retail customer.

(c) Conflict of Interest Obligation. The broker or dealer must establish, maintain and enforce written policies designed

---

Consumer Protection Act (2011), available at www.sec.gov/news/studies/2011/913studyfinal/pdf.

to (i) identify and disclose all conflicts of interest associated with its recommendation, (ii) identify and mitigate any conflict that creates an incentive for an associated person to place the interest of the broker or dealer or the natural person ahead of the interest of the retail customer; and (iii) identify, disclose, and prevent any material limitations placed on the securities or investment strategy recommended to the retail customer from causing the broker, dealer or associated person from placing its interests ahead of the retail customer.

(d) Compliance Obligation. The broker or dealer must establish, maintain, and enforce written policies and procedures reasonably designed to achieve compliance with Regulation Best Interest.

In short, if the broker or dealer (or the associated person) satisfies these four components, it has satisfied the general obligation to act in the best interest of the retail customer.

2. *What Does Regulation Best Interest Not Say?* The regulation clearly does not:

(a) create a fiduciary duty;

(b) authorize a private cause of action;

(c) apply to institutional investors; or

(d) require the broker or dealer (or associated person) to place the client's interests ahead of its own (rather, a tie is valid).

3. *Likely Impacts of Regulation Best Interest.* First, even if Regulation Best Interest does not give rise to a private cause of action and will thus not allow an investor to sue in federal court, it is likely to affect the outcome in arbitration proceedings and favor the plaintiff investor.

Second, Regulation Best Interest is clear that it applies to all individual investors, even if they are wealthy and sophisticated.

Third, a possible adverse impact of Regulation Best Interest is that it may entail high record-keeping and transaction costs that will force smaller broker-dealers into mergers with, or sales to, larger rivals. Here only time will tell.

4. *Preemption.* As earlier noted, state law differs on whether a broker is a fiduciary to the client. Regulation Best Interest specifies a single standard which seems below that which might be required of a fiduciary. For example, Regulation Best Interest applies only at the time of the recommendation and does not require the broker to warn the client later that the securities have become too risky to continue to be suitable for the client because of a change in circumstances. A fiduciary (including an investment adviser) may well be required to give such a warning. Suppose a state that views the broker as a fiduciary would require the

broker to give such a warning. Is this higher standard now preempted by Regulation Best Interest? In other words, is Regulation Best Interest only a minimum standard (so that states can require more), or is it a mandatory uniform standard that precludes any additional requirement? The SEC could have specified an answer in its adopting release (for example, it could have said that it did not mean to bar higher standards), but it said nothing, ducking the issue (with the result that the case for preemption is enhanced).

This issue of preemption never arose in the past with regard to the "suitability rules" of the NASD (and now FINRA) because both these bodies were regarded as private organizations with no authority to override state law. But the SEC, as a public body, can.

5. *Gray Areas.* The SEC has made clear that recommendations of investment strategies (e.g., "municipal bonds make sense for you") or account types ("you should try an advisory account with an annual fee") are also covered by Regulation Best Interest. This is new, and will involve questions about conflict of interest disclosures. Also "hold" recommendations as well as "buy" or "sell" recommendations are covered (even though these will not be covered by Rule 10b–5).

The SEC made clear that it is not requiring the broker to recommend the lowest cost option to the client (where the brokerage firm's own products compete with others), but when the broker recommends its own firm's products that cost more than competitors' products, this context is particularly sensitive from both a disclosure and a conflict of interest perspective.

Regulation Best Interest also requires the broker-dealer to "mitigate" conflict of interests, particularly where recommendations "create an incentive for any natural person who is an associated person of a broker dealer to place the interest of the broker or dealer, or such natural person, ahead of the interest of the retail person" (see Rule 15c–1(a)(2)(iii)(B)). This will raise difficult questions about incentive compensation paid to associated persons at brokerage firms. Going even further, Rule 15*l*–1(a)(2)(iii)(D) requires the broker-dealer to "eliminate any sales contests, sales quotas, bonuses, and non-cash compensation that are based on the sales of specific securities or specific types of securities with a limited period of time." No more all-expense trips to the Caribbean for the winner!

Finally, the SEC has indicated that if a broker exercises investment discretion, it may be required also to register as an investment adviser.[135]

---

[135] Brokers are exempt from the Investment Advisers Act of 1940 so long as their activities are "solely incidental" to brokerage services. The SEC has indicated, however, that the exercise of investment discretion over a client's account is generally not "solely incidental." See Investment Advisers Act Release No. 5249 (June 5, 2019). Still, the SEC also stated in this release that some "limited exercise of discretionary authority" would be permissible for a broker. Id at 14–17. This will involve very fine distinctions.

6. *Litigation.* Although Regulation Best Interest does not create any private cause of action, it is predictable that an aggressive plaintiff's attorney may plead that the broker failed to disclose a material omission: namely, that the recommended security was not in his client's best interest. This will be difficult because the complaint must plead facts with particularity giving rise to a strong inference of fraud, but the same attempt was made in the past with regard to allegedly "unsuitable" securities (but it rarely worked).[136]

7. *Form CRS.* At the time it adopted Regulation Best Interest, the SEC also adopted Form CRS and related rules which require both the broker and the investment adviser to provide a brief relationship summary to their retail clients.[137] This summary must follow a prescribed order and use standardized headings (to maximize comparability). The SEC explained that Form CRS was intended to "reduce retail investor confusion in the marketplace for brokerage and investment advisory services and to assist retail investors with the process of deciding whether to engage...a particular firm or financial professional..."[138] Form CRS is intended to be short and will focus on services provided, fees and costs, conflicts of interest and disciplinary history. If material facts change, the form must be updated.

8. *Suitability Obligations.* Although Regulation Best Interest did not repeal FINRA's suitability rules,[139] it made them largely irrelevant. In response, FINRA (which actually opposed the adoption of Regulation Best Interest as superfluous) has announced that it will defer to Regulation Best Interest in any case where it applies. However, there are cases in which it does not apply. For example, Regulation Best Interest applies only to recommendations made to retail customers, while FINRA's rules apply more broadly to recommendations made to institutions as well. Also FINRA rules apply to pension funds and others, not reached by Regulation Best Interest. Nonetheless, the SEC's rules largely today overshadow FINRA's and will be enforced by both the SEC and FINRA.

9. *Institutional Investors.* Institutional investors clearly do not fall within Regulation Best Interest, but as a result they can fall back on

---

[136] See e.g., O'Connor v. R.F. Lafferty & Co., Inc., 965 F.2d 893 (10th Cir. 1992) (considering but rejecting a Rule 10b–5 claim that securities recommended were unsuitable).

[137] This requirement is set forth in new rules under both the Securities Exchange Act (Rule 17a–14) and under the Advisers Act (Rule 204–5). See Advisers Act Release No. 5247 (June 5, 2019).

[138] Advisers Act Release No. 5247 (June 5, 2019) at p.5.

[139] FINRA has multiple rules addressing suitability, but the key rule has long been Rule 2111, which requires a FINRA member in making a recommendation with respect to a security to "have a reasonable basis to believe that a recommended transaction or investor strategy... is suitable for the customer, based on the information obtained through the reasonable diligence of the [member] or associated person..." FINRA's rules also include Rule 2090 which requires the member to "know its customer" (which was copied from the old NYSE Rule).

FINRA's suitability rules, which do cover institutional investors.[140] In a 1996 interpretation, the NASD (now FINRA) indicated its view that the obligation to make only suitable recommendations applies to institutional customers as well—unless the broker determines that the customer is capable of making an "independent assessment of the opportunities and risks presented by a potential investment, market factors and other investment considerations."[141] This inquiry by the broker requires that it determine both that (1) these factors will be evaluated, and (2) that the persons making the decision have the experience, capacity, and access to information to conduct such a suitability analysis. Recent experience with investments in derivatives by certain institutional investors (most notably in the cases of Orange County and Procter and Gamble[142]) suggests that even the most experienced institutions may lack capacity in some areas. Still, it is difficult to reconcile paternalistic protection for institutional investors with the overall structure of securities regulation as a primarily disclosure-based regime.

Courts have tended to take a generally narrow view of the duty owed by brokers to sophisticated investors, especially entities. Banca Cremi, S.A. v. Alex Brown & Sons, Inc. is a representative case.[143] In *Banca Cremi*, a sophisticated international bank sued a major investment banking firm under Rule 10b–5, after it lost some $21 million investing in high risk derivatives, allegedly based on the investment bank's advice and recommendation. Finding the plaintiff bank to be sophisticated and experienced, to have access to all relevant information from multiple sources, and to be aware of the risks associated with the general class of derivative instruments, the Fourth Circuit affirmed the district court's grant of summary judgment for the defendant on the primary ground that the plaintiff had behaved recklessly and could not satisfy its own duty to exercise due diligence. It was important to this result that the two parties had dealt with each other as principal to principal, with the result that a common law fiduciary duty never arose.

In this light, consider the different case of a small college in the boondocks or a regional school board with some investment funds. Is it similar to or different from an individual investor? Should it be owed a fiduciary duty by an investment bank that convinces it to buy a risky form of derivatives? In practice, arbitration panels appear less willing to apply the essentially paternalistic suitability doctrine to justify

---

[140] For a strong defense of this position, see Norman Poser, Liability of Broker-Dealers for Unsuitable Recommendations to Institutional Investors, 2001 B.Y.U. L. Rev. 1493 (2001).

[141] See Securities Exchange Act Release No. 36,973 (March 14, 1996).

[142] An enforcement action was brought by the SEC against the old Bankers Trust for its allegedly reckless behavior in such trading. See In the Matter of BT Securities Corp., [1994–1995 Transfer Binder] Fed.Sec.L.Rep. (CCH) Para. 85,477 (December 22, 1994).

[143] 132 F.3d 1017 (4th Cir. 1997).

recoveries for even small institutions like these. Sometimes, however, the institutional client may find it more attractive to sue in state court.[144]

B. THE DUTY OF BEST EXECUTION

The duty of best execution once required brokers to search multiple markets to obtain the best price for their customers. That was necessary because, prior to Regulation NMS's prohibition of trade-throughs, multiple markets might simultaneously trade the same security at different prices. Although there is no SEC rule requiring best execution, FINRA Rule 5310 ("Best Execution and Interpositioning") requires a broker-dealer (and persons associated with it) in any transaction for a customer, to:

> use reasonable diligence to ascertain the best dealer market for the subject security and to buy or sell in such market so that the resultant price to the customer is as favorable as possible under prevailing market conditions.

In determining whether the "reasonable diligence" test has been satisfied, Rule 5310 considers four factors:

> (A) the character of the market for the security (e.g., price volatility, relative liquidity, and pressure on available communications); (B) the size and type of transaction; (C) the number of markets checked; (D) accessibility of the quotation; and (E) the terms and conditions of the order which result in the transaction, as communicated to the member. . . .[145]

Once, this almost ineffable standard raised some stark litigation issues. In Newton v. Merrill Lynch Pierce Fenner & Smith,[146] the issue was whether the leading brokers in the industry had collectively violated their duty of best execution by trading at the NBBO ("national best bid and offer") on Nasdaq and ignoring potentially superior quotes on ECNs. Although this sounds like self-serving conduct, a plausible rebuttal can be made that this is not necessarily the case. Orders on the ECNs (at superior prices) were often for small quantities that might not remain firm when the broker sought to access them and seek more shares. Thus, the brokers *might* have a customer-serving reason for routing the trade in a way that *seemed* to be at an inferior price. Nonetheless, the Third Circuit found that a systematic failure to seek out superior prices in an alternative market system could be found by a jury to be a deceptive practice. Although it remanded the case for further findings about the viability of this alternative, it denied class certification on other grounds, and the case was not tried.

---

[144] See West Virginia v. Morgan Stanley & Co., 459 S.E.2d 906 (W. Va. 1995) (holding broker liable where state law barring speculative investments by state investment fund was violated).

[145] See FINRA Rule 5310.

[146] 135 F.3d 266 (3d Cir. 1998) (en banc).

Today, in light of both the SEC's Order Handling Rules that make an ECN's best price part of the NMS system and Regulation NMS that prohibits trade-throughs, the implementation of the duty of best execution seems much simpler than in the past.[147] But, if a stock is traded over-the-counter and not quoted on Nasdaq, issues can frequently arise, because the lowest price quoted may not be "firm" or current or may be for a much smaller quantity than a seemingly less attractive quote (but covering a larger order size). Issues can also arise, even with regard to Nasdaq-listed stocks, as to when a broker is subject to the duty of best execution. For example, suppose one broker refers its customer's order for execution to another broker-dealer. Is the latter executing broker also subject to the duty of best execution?[148]

In theory, Rule 10b–5 can be used to enforce the duty of best execution (if its elements, including the requirement of scienter, are satisfied),[149] but the duty's contours will more likely be adjudicated in arbitration proceedings brought by customers against their broker-dealer.

Problem

PROBLEM 9-4

Dean Reynolds & Co., a registered broker-dealer, pays its registered representatives higher compensation for principal trades of Nasdaq stocks in which it is the principal market maker than for other sales. Joe B. Sales, a registered representative with Dean Reynolds, calls Mr. and Mrs. Smith to recommend that they purchase stock in Keldon Oil Co., knowing that he would receive a higher commission, because Dean Reynolds makes the market in that stock. When Dean Reynolds sells stock to a customer as a dealer, it charges them the inside asked spread (i.e., the NBBO asked price) plus a mark-up. Dean Reynolds's mark-up is always less than its standard brokerage commission. Should it and Joe B. Sales be liable (either in court or in an arbitration proceeding) when Keldon Oil's stock price falls and the Smiths commence an action?

C. THE DUTY TO PROTECT LIMIT ORDERS

Assume that a customer gives a broker dealer a limit order to sell 5,000 shares of XYZ Corp. at $17.5 at a time when the inside quotation (the "NBBO") is $17 bid and $17.125 asked. Later, the NBBO widens to

---

[147] Some issues may still arise when stock is traded on Nasdaq and on ECN or over-the-counter sites that are not integrated into Nasdaq, because of the uncertain trade-off between the customer's desire for speed of execution and the customer's desire for price improvement, which two goals tend to be inversely related. See Jonathan Macey and Maureen O'Hara, The Law and Economics of Best Execution, 6 J. of Fin. Intermediation 188 (1997).

[148] In July, 2002, the NASD sent a notice to members indicating its view that the duty did normally apply to the executing broker under these circumstances, at least if the order ultimately came from a customer of the routing broker. See NASD Notice to Members 02–40 (July, 2002).

[149] See Newton v. Merrill, Lynch, 135 F.3d 266 (3d Cir. 1998) (failure to disclose that broker has not traded at best available price can violate Rule 10b–5).

$17 bid and $17.5 asked. At this point, the broker-dealer sells 5,000 of its own shares at $17.5. It never executes its customer's limit order because the market price of XYZ thereafter declines, and it defends its own trading on the grounds that the bid price (the price at which it would buy) never rose to $17.5.

In an important 1988 case, the SEC found that a broker-dealer who traded in this fashion had "traded ahead" of its customer's limit order in breach of its fiduciary duty to the customer for whom it held the limit order.[150] The majority of a divided SEC found that the broker's selling its own stock from its inventory at $17.5, when it could have instead executed its customer's limit order, gave an unlawful priority to the broker's own interests over that of the customer to whom it owed a fiduciary duty (the minority replied that the existence of a fiduciary duty depended on state law and could not be assumed in this fashion). Although this decision was controversial at the time, it has since been codified in FINRA Rule 5320, which requires a market-maker not to trade ahead of a customer's limit order at a price equal to or better than the limit order price.[151] However, broker-dealers have no obligation to accept limit orders (although most do) and may charge a higher commission for doing so.

Although this problem can still arise today, the SEC's Order Handling Rules have reduced its frequency by causing an inside-the-quote limit order to automatically improve the NBBO, at least if it is publicly displayed; hence, such an order today would have an automatic priority.

Problems

PROBLEM 9-5

Friendly Brokerage Co., a registered broker-dealer, makes a market in the stock of Widget Corp., a Nasdaq-listed company. Currently, the NBBO (or inside spread) is $17 bid and $17 1/8 asked. Joe D. Trader gives them a limit order to sell for 5,000 shares at $17¼. Later, the NBBO widens to $17 and $17¼. But at this point Friendly, itself, sells 4,000 shares for its own account. Shortly thereafter, Widget's stock price falls back below $16 per share. When Joe complains, Friendly explains that the bid price never moved up to $17¼ (or even close). Nonetheless, Joe D. thinks that Friendly stepped in front of his sell order and so brings an arbitration proceeding under NASD rules against Friendly Brokerage for his lost profit at $17¼. What result?

---

[150] See In re E.F. Hutton and Company, Inc., Securities Exchange Act Release No. 25887 (July 6, 1988). This case is widely known as the "Manning" decision, after the name of the plaintiff, William Manning.

[151] See Securities Exchange Act Release No. 35751 ("Limit Order Protection on Nasdaq") (May 22, 1995). FINRA Rule 5320.

PROBLEM 9-6

Mrs. Jones, an elderly widow living on a pension, has much of her late husband's estate invested in the stock market (on his deathbed advice to her). Her broker is Merrill, Schwab & Co., which has information in its files showing Mrs. Jones to be a person of relatively modest means. Teddy Fastpitch is the new broker assigned by Merrill, Schwab to handle Mrs. Jones's account. Assume in the alternative that:

(a) He recommends that she buy 1,000 shares of Volatile Co., a Nasdaq traded software company, known for its price fluctuations, in order "to put a little life in her account;" or

(b) Mrs. Jones, who is just a little bit greedy, asks his recommendation about Volatile Co. because her bridge partner, Mrs. Smith, made $2,500 last month, investing in it. Fastpitch tells her to "go ahead; it may make sense to liven up your portfolio;" or

(c) He makes no recommendations, but just executes her order for Volatile without comment, even though he knows it is very risky.

Either way, Mrs. Jones buys 2,000 shares at $10 and the stock promptly falls to $2. She brings an arbitration proceeding based on NASD arbitration rules, alleging that Fastpitch breached the "suitability rule," and she uses her nephew, Irving Brilliant, as her attorney. What result?

PROBLEM 9-7

Bank Brazil, a Brazilian bank with almost $5 billion in assets, bought some $40 million in collateralized mortgage obligations ("CMOs") from Kuhn, Lehman & Co., an investment banking firm with a specialization in this area. Bank Brazil bought a particularly risky form of CMO (known as an "inverse floater," whose interest rate is inverse to the market's rate). When interest rates rose generally in 2007, Bank Brazil lost over half the value of its investment. It claimed that it relied on Kuhn, Lehman & Co's predictions about the direction of interest rates. Bank Brazil has, however, its own internal staff of economic experts and securities experts. The evidence will show that Kuhn, Lehman was well aware that the trend in interest rates was very adverse to Bank Brazil (and expected that trend to continue), but it gave no warning to Bank Brazil. What result in its suit against Kuhn, Lehman under Rule 10b–5 based on suitability claims?

D. CHURNING

Nesbit v. McNeil
United States Court of Appeals, Ninth Circuit, 1990.
896 F.2d 380.

■ Before WRIGHT, TANG and FERNANDEZ, CIRCUIT JUDGES.

■ FERNANDEZ, CIRCUIT JUDGE:

Virginia H. Nesbit and the W. Wallace Nesbit Trust ("plaintiffs") brought this action against Steve McNeil and Black & Company, Inc.

("defendants") and alleged that the defendants had churned the plaintiffs' investment accounts. Among other things, plaintiffs sought to recover for violations of . . . the Securities and Exchange Act of 1934 § 10(b) and Rule 10b–5, and under the State of Oregon securities laws [Or.Rev.Stat. § 59.135 (1987)]. The district court directed a verdict against the plaintiffs on the Oregon securities law claim, and submitted the federal securities claim to the jury. The jury brought in a verdict against defendants, and awarded damages in the amount of the excess commissions generated by the churning of the plaintiffs' accounts. The district court denied a motion for judgment notwithstanding the verdict, and entered judgment accordingly.

Defendants now appeal and claim that the district court erred because it did not permit the offset of trading gains against the excess commissions, because the evidence of churning was insufficient to support the verdict, and because the plaintiffs' claims were barred by the statute of limitations in whole or in part. Defendants also claim that they should not have been required to disgorge the full amount of excess commissions, but only their net gain on those commissions.

* * *

We affirm the district court on each of these issues.

BACKGROUND FACTS

Virginia H. Nesbit was a retired school teacher and the widow of W. Wallace Nesbit, a businessman. Upon his death, Mr. Nesbit left a portfolio of securities that were rather conservative although not necessarily highly successful. Those, as well as other assets, were divided between Mrs. Nesbit and the W. Wallace Nesbit Trust ("the Trust"). Mrs. Nesbit was the trustee of the Trust. From then until 1974, the investments remained conservative and did not do very well. By 1974, there had been a significant loss of value. Mrs. Nesbit then opened accounts for herself and the Trust at Black & Company, Inc. They were opened through Steve McNeil, who was the son of a friend of Mrs. Nesbit. The equity in Mrs. Nesbit's account was then $167,463, and the equity in the Trust's account was $44,177. Mrs. Nesbit, who was not knowledgeable in these matters, told the defendants that her investment objectives for herself and the Trust were stability, income and growth. Defendants claim that she told them she wanted to recoup the losses that had been suffered previously.

Defendants then embarked on a course of conduct that extended over a period of eleven and one half years. By the time the accounts were closed out in October of 1985, the equity in Mrs. Nesbit's account was $301,711, and the equity in the Trust's account was $92,844. There can be little dispute that this was a substantial increase in value. However, the activities of defendants during those eleven and one half years are called into question in this case.

Plaintiffs have pointed out that defendants first liquidated some of the securities in plaintiffs' portfolio. Mr. McNeil then embarked on a course of trading that involved 150 issues, one thousand trades, and an overall transaction value of $4,400,000. While the plaintiffs' account values did grow by $182,915 during the period in question, the defendants' commissions came to $250,000. Moreover, the investments chosen by defendants were not the kind of investments that one would purchase if one sought a stable, income-producing portfolio. Rather, they were often speculative in nature and were not income-producing. By the time the accounts terminated, many of the investments had accrued losses.

By 1984, Mrs. Nesbit became concerned about the level of activity in the accounts. She kept in closer contact with Mr. McNeil, and the level of trading decreased, but did not end entirely. She became even more concerned in 1985. At that time she discovered losses in the portfolio when calls were made upon her by lenders to whom she had pledged certain of the securities. Her concerns increased when the handling of the accounts was questioned by Ronald Linn, an analyst at Titan Capital, and were not particularly allayed when visits with Mr. McNeil brought forth an apology and an expression of embarrassment at the list of losing stocks. All of this ultimately led to the closing of the accounts in October of 1985. Over one year later, plaintiffs filed this action.

* * *

DISCUSSION

Although the principal question before us is whether plaintiffs can recover damages for churning when they have had an increase in portfolio values that exceeds the amount of commissions they were charged, the defendants have also claimed that there was insufficient evidence to support the verdict, and that the action is barred by the statute of limitations. If defendants were to prevail on either of the latter issues, there would be no need to consider the damage issue. Therefore, we will address them first.

A. *Sufficiency of the Evidence.*

The detection and proof of churning is not a simple matter. Churning can only be identified when one considers the whole history of an account, and even then expert testimony is virtually essential. Shad v. Dean Witter Reynolds, Inc., 799 F.2d 525, 530 (9th Cir. 1986). As we explained in Mihara v. Dean Witter & Co., Inc., 619 F.2d 814, 820–21 (9th Cir. 1980):

> When a securities broker engages in excessive trading in disregard of his customer's investment objectives for the purpose of generating commission business, the customer may hold the broker liable for churning in violation of Rule 10b–5. * * * In order to establish a claim of churning, a plaintiff must show (1) that the trading in his account was excessive in light of

his investment objectives; (2) that the broker in question exercised control over the trading in the account; and (3) that the broker acted with the intent to defraud or with the wilful and reckless disregard for the interests of his client. [citations omitted]

Plaintiffs presented substantial evidence on each of these elements, as our statement of background facts has shown. This case involves a relatively unsophisticated investor, who relied upon a person in whom she had confidence—the son of a family friend—to handle her portfolio in a safe and income-generating manner. There can be little doubt that Mr. McNeil did exercise a great deal of de facto control over that account, and the mere fact that he told his client what was being done does not change that situation. This case is quite unlike Brophy v. Redivo, 725 F.2d 1218 (9th Cir. 1984), where the only real claim was that certain transactions had been executed without plaintiff's permission and even against her directions. Here the gravamen of the complaint is that the defendants used their position to overtrade in the account and to do so in a way that they knew did not meet the client's true investment desires and objectives. See Follansbee v. Davis, Skaggs & Co., Inc., 681 F.2d 673, 676 (9th Cir. 1982); Mihara v. Dean Witter & Co., 619 F.2d at 821; Hecht v. Harris, Upham & Co., 430 F.2d 1202, 1209 (9th Cir. 1970). In other words, there was a good deal of evidence about the relationship between the parties and Mr. McNeil's control over the account. That is underscored by Mr. McNeil's embarrassment when he was confronted with the condition of certain securities toward the end of the period. His apology showed that he had something to be embarrassed about; he was not simply executing orders at the direction of Mrs. Nesbit. In addition, the testimony of plaintiffs' expert showed that one could infer the necessary degree of scienter arising out of the handling of this account, and demonstrated that there was excessive trading.

Defendants contend that there was insufficient evidence of excessive trading in the account. Relying on this circuit's comments that expert testimony is virtually essential, see Shad, 799 F.2d at 530, defendants argue that Nesbit's expert did not present objective statistical evidence of excessive trading. In particular, they complain that the expert did not testify about a turnover ratio for the account as a whole or for an annualized period[3] and that the commission ratio[4] indicated there was no churning.

Although courts often rely on the turnover ratio and commission ratio to indicate excessive trading, no single factor or test identifies excessive trading. See 2 A. Bromberg & L. Lowenfels, Securities Fraud

---

[3] The turnover ratio is the ratio of the total cost of the purchases made for the account during a given period of time to the amount invested. 2 A. Bromberg & L. Lowenfels, Securities Fraud and Commodities Fraud § 5.7(322) (1988).

[4] The commission ratio is "the ratio of the broker's commissions generated by the account to the size of the customer's investment in that account." 2 A. Bromberg & L. Lowenfels, Securities Fraud and Commodities Fraud § 5.7(322) (1988).

and Commodities Fraud § 5.7(310) & (322) (1988). Certainly these ratios can make the presence of excessive trading fairly obvious. Id. However, that does not mean that lower ratios will preclude a finding of excessive trading.

Here, Mr. Olson testified that in his expert opinion the 1,000 trades, the high amount of commission compared to the value of the account, the volume of trading, and the presence of losing stock that had been held for some time all pointed toward an improper handling of this account, considering the investment objectives of the client. While defendants have presented evidence and arguments to the contrary, we are in no position to say that the jury improperly found against them on this record. We will not second guess the jury's determination of the facts, where, as here, the evidence is in conflict and there is substantial evidence to support the jury's decision.

* * *

C. *The Measurement of Damages.*

As we have already noted, defendants obtained commissions of $250,000 from the plaintiffs. The jury found that $134,000 of that constituted excess commissions. At the same time, the value of plaintiffs' accounts increased in the sum of $182,915. Defendants claimed below, and continue to claim, that the plaintiffs' portfolio gain should be offset against the plaintiffs' commission loss, as a result of which plaintiffs can recover no damages whatever. The district court disagreed, and gave the following instruction to the jury: "If you find that the plaintiffs have proven their claims for churning, excessive trading, plaintiffs may recover as damages any commissions they paid as a result of the churning in excess of commissions that would have been reasonable on transactions during the pertinent time period." The district court did not go on to instruct the jury that it could then offset the trading gains against those commission losses. We agree with the district court.

We begin with the rather straightforward principle announced in Mihara v. Dean Witter & Co., Inc., 619 F.2d at 826, where we said that, "While damage for churning are limited to commissions and interest, plaintiff's claim as to the suitability of the securities purchased would also encompass trading losses." As the Fifth Circuit Court of Appeals explained in Miley v. Oppenheimer & Co., Inc., 637 F.2d at 326, there are two separate and distinct possible harms when an account has been churned, and those are:

> First, and perhaps foremost, the investor is harmed by having had to pay the excessive commissions to the broker. * * * Second, the investor is harmed by the decline in the value of his portfolio * * * as a result of the broker's having intentionally and deceptively concluded transactions, aimed at generating fees, which were unsuitable for the investor. The intentional and deceptive mismanagement of a client's account, resulting in a

decline in the value of that portfolio, constitutes a compensable violation of both the federal securities laws and the broker's common law fiduciary duty, regardless of the amount of the commissions paid to the broker.

In the case at hand, the plaintiffs only suffered one of those harms, but there is no reason to find that they should be denied a recovery because their portfolio increased in value, either because of or in spite of the activities of the defendants.

* * *

As a final attack on damages, the defendants rely on a portion of the Supreme Court's decision in Randall v. Loftsgaarden, id., for the proposition that the plaintiff must lean upon the concept of unjust enrichment in order to recover. Reasoning from that proposition, defendants ask that the brokers' expenses be deducted from the commissions and that plaintiffs recover, at most, the difference. It is true that *Randall* addresses the question of unjust enrichment at 478 U.S. 661–64, 106 S.Ct. 3152–53, but it does not mandate the theory suggested by defendants. The core of the defendants' position must be that if a broker defrauds a client of a commission, the broker ought to be able to deduct the expenses he incurred in perpetrating the fraud and then return the rest to the client. We believe that the very statement of the proposition refutes it, and not a shard of judicial precedent supports it. *Randall,* on the other hand, merely offers the possibility that even if a plaintiff has not lost as much as a defendant has gained, the plaintiff should recover that gain from the defendant. To apply that to a situation where defendant has not netted as much as he has taken from the plaintiff would stand *Randall* on its head. It takes no hierophant to discover that.

Therefore, we must reject defendants' assault on the damage award in this case.

[Plaintiffs' claim under the Oregon Securities Law was rejected.]

CONCLUSION

We have been presented with the rather unusual case of plaintiffs whose portfolios increased while under the guidance and control of the defendants, and who still chose to bring an action to recover commissions that they had paid to those same defendants.

The jury before which this case was tried could have decided that defendants were perfectly honest brokers, who were being victimized by rather greedy clients. The jury did not do so. Instead, it found that plaintiffs were indeed wronged by the defendants' churning of the accounts. That determination was supported by substantial evidence. As we have noted, the jury's determination that the statute of limitations had not run in this case was also properly supported.

As a result, the defendants were properly required to disgorge the inappropriate portion of their commissions, even if the portfolio itself increased in value, since, as we have shown, issues regarding the performance of the portfolio are separate from issues related to excess commissions. Just as there can be gains or losses when trading is appropriate, there can be gains or losses when it is inappropriate. The propriety of the trading determines the right to a commission. The same evidence may also influence the right to recover for losses, but that does not mean that gains should undermine the plaintiffs' right to recover improper commissions. The wrongs are separate, and the result of each should be analyzed separately.

* * *

AFFIRMED.

---

1. *Churning Litigation.* Rule 15c1–7 prohibits what is generally known as "churning," i.e., excessive trading by a broker for an account in which he or she holds discretionary powers, for the purpose of collecting commissions. In In the Matter of Norris & Hirshberg, Inc., the Commission stated that, although the Rule itself specifically applies only to cases where the broker or dealer has been "vested" with discretionary powers, either orally or in writing, "the handling of a customer's account may become fraudulent whenever the broker or dealer is in a position to determine the volume and frequency of transactions by reason of the customer's willingness to follow the suggestions of the broker or dealer and he abuses the customer's confidence by overtrading."[152]

Judicial decisions have placed even greater emphasis on the existence of "control" on the part of the broker over the account. Where the client retains control, but blindly follows the broker's recommendation to trade aggressively, courts have tended to favor the defendant broker. In Arceneaux v. Merrill, Lynch, Pierce, Fenner & Smith, the Eleventh Circuit required the plaintiff to "prove three elements in order to establish a cause of action for churning: (1) the trading in his account was excessive in light of the customer's investment objectives; (2) the broker in question exercised control over the trading in the account; and (3) the broker acted with the intent to defraud or with willful and reckless disregard for the investor's interest."[153] But what shows control? Even if the client retains investment discretion, the fact

---

[152] 21 S.E.C. 865 (1946), aff'd, 177 F.2d 228 (D.C.Cir. 1949). For a general overview of the development of this doctrine, see Note, Churning by Securities Dealers, 80 Harv. L. Rev. 869 (1967).

[153] 767 F.2d 1498, 1501 (11th Cir. 1985); for a more recent statement of this formula, see Rizek v. SEC, 215 F.3d 157, 162 (1st Cir. 2000). Other decisions stress that the heart of a churning case is the use of the broker's authority over an account to generate excessive commissions, while at the same time leading the customer to believe that the broker is attempting to fulfill the customer's objectives. See Manela v. Garantia Banking Ltd., 5 F.Supp.2d 165 (S.D.N.Y.1998). This verbal formula seemingly gives a greater role to evidence of deception.

that the client automatically follows the broker's recommendations may constitute sufficient evidence to sustain a jury verdict (as the *Arceneaux* case ultimately held).[154]

Other cases have in contrast focused on the intelligence and experience of the client and framed the test in terms of whether the customer "has sufficient intelligence and understanding to evaluate the broker's recommendations and reject one when he thinks it unsuitable."[155] One commentator has suggested that the test should focus on whether the broker has invited the customer's trust and then breached that trust.[156] Finally, "churning" and unsuitability cases tend to overlap. Thus, even when there is insufficient control by the broker over the account to establish a churning case, it might still be argued that the broker made unsuitable recommendations in order to maximize its commissions.[157]

The *Nesbit* case is thus typical. Mrs. Nesbit was not knowledgeable in investment matters. She told her broker that the investment objectives for herself and the trust were stability, income, and growth. Although her broker was vested with discretionary powers, Mrs. Nesbit regularly received written confirmations of each transaction over a period of eleven years without raising any objections either to a failure to meet her investment objectives or as to the excessive commissions. Only then did she become concerned about the level of activity in the accounts.

2. *Excessive Trading.* Courts typically look to the "turnover ratio" in determining if trading is excessive. That ratio compares the total cost of purchases made for an account (typically over a one year period) to the total amount invested in the account. Some decisions have suggested that a turnover ratio in excess of six reflects excessive trading.[158] Of course, trading can only be excessive in terms of the customer's investment objectives, and the aggressive customer may want "excessive" trading. Courts also sometimes look to the commissions earned on the account, either as a percentage of the individual broker's income or the branch office's commission revenues.[159] Trading patterns are also relevant: "in and out" day trading in which securities are bought and sold on the same day is particularly suspicious. From an economic perspective, there is a view that the best standard for comparison would be to match the account with a mutual fund having a similar risk preference and determine if the

---

[154] See also Mihara v. Dean Witter & Co., 619 F.2d 814 (9th Cir. 1980).

[155] See Follansbee v. Davis, Skaggs & Co., 681 F.2d 673, 677 (9th Cir. 1982).

[156] See O'Hara, The Elusive Concept of Control in Churning Claims under Federal Securities and Commodities Law, 75 Geo. L.J. 1875 (1987).

[157] O'Connor v. R.F. Lafferty & Co., 965 F.2d 893 (10th Cir. 1992), represents such a case in which these overlapping allegations were raised.

[158] For representative cases, see e.g., Arceneaux v. Merrill Lynch, Pierce, Fenner & Smith, 767 F.2d 1498 (11th Cir. 1985); Mihara v. Dean Witter & Co., 619 F.2d 814, 821 (9th Cir. 1980); Costello v. Oppenheimer & Co., 711 F.2d 1361, 1369 (7th Cir. 1983).

[159] See Hecht v. Harris, Upham & Co., 283 F.Supp. 417 (N.D.Cal.1968), aff'd in part, 430 F.2d 1202 (9th Cir. 1970).

account traded significantly more frequently than the fund over the same period.[160]

3. *Damages.* What damages should the victim receive: the excessive commissions or the decline in portfolio value? In Hecht v. Harris, Upham & Co., the Ninth Circuit allowed only the former and denied any decline in market value.[161] This result was partly based on a specific factual issue involving waiver and estoppel issue in that case. Although the plaintiff customer had regularly received confirmations and was thus deemed by the Ninth Circuit to have been estopped to deny knowledge of the transactions in her account, the Ninth Circuit still permitted her to claim lack of knowledge that her account was excessively traded. But as a result, it limited the damages to the excessive commissions.

Later cases have generally rejected the result reached in *Hecht* with respect to portfolio damages.[162] As the *Nesbit* court makes clear, the investor may recover *both* the excessive commission charged by the broker and the decline in value of the investor's portfolio resulting from the "churning" of the account. Furthermore, if the portfolio increases in value, the gain will not be offset against the excessive commissions charged by the broker to reduce the damages.

Davis v. Merrill Lynch, Pierce, Fenner & Smith, Inc.,[163] was an egregious churning case brought on behalf of an eighty-seven year old widow. The account had a value of about $144,000 at the beginning and a value of $197,000 at the end of the trading period, so that the account realized a cumulative net profit of $53,000 during the period it was churned. If the account had not been churned, however, the portfolio would have had a further increase in value of about $56,000. The Eighth Circuit, following *Nesbit,* upheld an award of $44,000 in damages for excessive trading despite the increase in the value of the portfolio. Adding a new twist, however, the court upheld an additional award of $56,000 for the loss in portfolio value arising from churning, plus punitive damages of $2,000,000. The Court stated:

> Churning is a species of fraud prohibited by Section 10(b) and Rule 10b–5 regardless of whether the account's profits or its principal is misappropriated. Under the law of this circuit, if an account earned $50,000 but would have earned $100,000 if it was not churned, the customer has sustained actual damages in

---

[160] See Winslow and Anderson, A Model for Determining the Excessive Trading Element in Churning Claims, 68 N.C. L. Rev. 327 (1990).

[161] 430 F.2d 1202 (9th Cir. 1970).

[162] Rolf v. Blyth, Eastman Dillon & Co., 570 F.2d 38 (2d Cir. 1978), cert. denied, 439 U.S. 1039 (1978); Miley v. Oppenheimer & Co., 637 F.2d 318 (5th Cir. 1981); Davis v. Merrill Lynch, Pierce, Fenner & Smith, Inc., 906 F.2d 1206 (8th Cir. 1990); Hatrock v. Edward D. Jones & Co., 750 F.2d 767 (9th Cir. 1984).

[163] 906 F.2d 1206 (8th Cir. 1990). The Nesbit and Davis cases are discussed in Booth, New Churning Cases Add Twist to Claims for Portfolio Damages, Nat'l L.J., June 24, 1991, at 34.

the amount of $50,000 plus excess commissions paid. * * * Because Mrs. Davis paid over $40,000 in commissions and would have earned over $50,000 more than she did had her account not been churned, it is nonsensical to argue that she did not suffer actual damages as a result of the churning.[164]

In some situations, an award of portfolio damages may require the comparison of profit or loss in the portfolio during the trading period with the performance of a comparable well-recognized index such as the Dow Jones Industrials or the Standard and Poor's Index, or a specialized index or a combination of indexes.[165] Thus in Miley v. Oppenheimer & Co., both the market and the value of the portfolio had declined.[166] The court held that compensatory damages for portfolio losses should be measured by the decline in the value of the portfolio in excess of the average decline in the stock market during the time in which the broker handled the account. Moreover, in the absence of either a specialized portfolio or the availability of a more accurate measure, the actual portfolio loss should be reduced by the average percentage decline in value of the Dow Jones Industrials or the Standard and Poor's Index during the relevant period. This method was said to prevent the award of windfall profits arising from the ordinary hazards of the stock market.[167]

4. *Unauthorized Transactions, Churning, and the "in Connection with" Requirement.* Suppose a broker trades securities in a nondiscretionary account without the customer's permission. Of course, this is actionable, but does it violate Rule 10b–5? Some courts have said that the broker's failure to disclose the transaction to the client is a material omission of the fact that it is not dealing fairly with the customer,[168] but others have found that it is no more than a contractual breach.[169] These more conservative courts had expressed doubt that there was a sufficient connection between the trade and any implied misrepresentation to satisfy the "in connection with" standard under Rule 10b–5.

The Supreme Court's decision in SEC v. Zandford may resolve this issue in favor of plaintiffs.[170] In *Zandford*, a broker misused a discretionary brokerage account set up by an elderly father to provide for his severely mentally handicapped daughter. The broker misappropriated the funds. The broker defended against the SEC's suit

---

[164] 906 F.2d at 1218–19.

[165] On the economic aspects, see J. Lorie, P. Dodd & M. Kimpton, The Stock Market: Theories and Evidence Ch. 3 (2d ed. 1985).

[166] 637 F.2d 318 (5th Cir. 1981).

[167] Miley v. Oppenheimer & Co., Inc., 637 F.2d 318, 327 (5th Cir. 1981).

[168] See Mansbach v. Prescott, Ball & Turben, 598 F.2d 1017, 1026–27 (6th Cir. 1979); see also Nye v. Blyth Eastman Dillon & Co., 588 F.2d 1189 (8th Cir. 1978).

[169] See, e.g., Brophy v. Redivo, 725 F.2d 1218, 1220 (9th Cir. 1984); Forkin v. Rooney, Pace, Inc., 804 F.2d 1047, 1049–50 (8th Cir. 1986) (unauthorized rescission of trade not actionable deception).

[170] 535 U.S. 813 (2002).

for restitution by arguing that his conduct amounted only to embezzlement and not securities fraud. This defense won in the Fourth Circuit, but lost in the Supreme Court, which relaxed the "in connection with" requirement, finding it sufficient "that the scheme to defraud and the sale of securities coincide."[171] Apparently, today as in the past, when the Court discovers a true villain, legal rules can be bent.

In any event, the "in connection with" requirement is less of a problem in churning cases, because the court can view the churning trades as themselves fraudulent or deceptive acts which violate Rule 10b–5 without the need for any material misrepresentation or omission.[172] Still, it remains debatable whether such conduct more resembles the type of fiduciary breach that must be established under state law standards under Sante Fe Industries, Inc. v. Green.[173]

E. THE PENNY STOCK REFORM ACT OF 1990

The Securities Enforcement and Penny Stock Reform Act of 1990 has been called "the most significant attack on securities fraud and white collar crime in many years."[174] The first four titles of the Act deal with civil enforcement remedies. Title V is the Penny Stock Reform Act; it mandates and authorizes the SEC to provide greater protection to investors in those low priced securities known as "penny stocks."

---

1. *Revised SEC Rules.* Pursuant to the Penny Stock Reform Act of 1990, the SEC has adopted Rules 15g–1 through 15g–9. Rule 3a51–1 also defines penny stocks as basically stocks trading below $5 per share (but with numerous qualifications). Although some of these rules are traditional disclosure rules, requiring generic disclosure of risks inherent to the Penny Stock Market (Rule 15g–2) or disclosures about broker compensation (Rules 15g–4 and 15g–5), Rule 15g–9 imposes a direct affirmative suitability obligation on the broker or dealer that must be satisfied prior to the transaction being effected. In addition, Rule 15g–9 also requires delivery of a document (Schedule 15G) that seeks to discourage the investor from entering the transaction. Finally, Rule 15g–9 effectively chills high pressure "cold call" telephone selling tactics by requiring that the investor's account first be approved by the broker, that the broker then deliver certain elaborately mandated written disclosures, and finally that the customer give written instructions before a penny

---

[171] Id. at 822.

[172] See Clark v. Kidder, Peabody & Co., 636 F.Supp. 195, 198 (S.D.N.Y.1986).

[173] 430 U.S. 462 (1977). On these themes, see Langevoort, Fraud and Deception by Securities Professionals, 61 Tex. L. Rev. 1247, 1279–83 (1983).

[174] Legislative statement of Rep. Edward Markey, 136 Cong. Rec. H8532 (daily ed. Oct. 1, 1990).

stock transaction can be effected. This is the use of disclosure less to provide sunlight than to disrupt certain abusive marketing practices.[175]

2. *Rule 15c2–11.* Many "penny stocks" are not reporting companies under § 12(g) of the 1934 Act. In such cases Rule 15c2–11 basically prohibits the broker-dealer from quoting an over-the-counter security that is not quoted on NASDAQ unless it has on hand specified information about the security and the issuer.

The information to be accumulated depends on the classification of the issuer. In the case of 1933 Act and 1934 Act reporting companies, the broker-dealer must have on hand the most recent 1933 Act prospectus, the annual, quarterly and current reports filed pursuant to sections 13 or 15(d) of the 1934 Act, and a copy of the Offering Circular used in any Regulation A offering. Similar documented financial and other available information must be obtained with respect to insurance companies exempt from reporting requirements under § 12(g) of the 1934 Act, foreign private issuers, and American Depository Receipts (ADRs) that represent deposited shares of such foreign issuers. In addition, the broker-dealer is required to have on hand any other material information (including adverse information) that comes to its attention or possession before the submission of a quotation with respect to such securities.

Having collected and retained this information, the broker-dealer is prohibited from quoting any such over-the-counter security unless it first determines that, based on such documents and information, it has "a reasonable basis under the circumstances for believing that the * * * information is accurate in all material respects, and that the sources of [such] information are reliable." (Rule 15c2–11(a)).

But this is not all. There are sixteen other items of current information with respect to issuers and their securities that must be collected and preserved by the broker-dealer. The broker-dealer must also make these reasonably available upon request to any person expressing an interest in a proposed transaction in any such security. These items list information about the issuer, its securities, the nature of its business, the products or services offered, its facilities, its most recent balance sheet and income statement, and similar financial information for the two preceding fiscal years.

If a broker-dealer makes such information available to others upon request, it:

> shall not constitute a representation by the broker or dealer that such information is accurate, but shall constitute a representation * * * that the information is reasonably current in relation to the day the quotation is submitted, that the broker or dealer has a reasonable basis under the circumstances for

---

[175] For a fuller description of practices in this market, see Goldstein, Ramshaw and Ackerson, An Investment Masquerade: A Descriptive Overview of Penny Stock Fraud and the Federal Securities Laws, 47 Bus.Law. 773 (1992).

believing the information is accurate in all material respects, and that the information was obtained from sources which the broker or dealer has a reasonable basis for believing are reliable.[176]

While this does not make the broker-dealer a guarantor of the accuracy of the information, and at least literally does not impose upon the broker any duty of investigation or "due diligence" beyond going to what the broker reasonably believes are reliable sources, the possible exposure to civil liability of a broker-dealer quoting a non-registered security is obvious. The Rule was adopted in large part to prohibit broker-dealers from establishing arbitrary quotations for infrequently traded over-the-counter securities.[177]

The effectiveness of Rule 15c2–11 is, however, subject to some potentially crippling limitations on its application. Under subparagraph (f)(3), a "piggyback" exception exempts securities that have been quoted in an interdealer quotation system (such as the OTC Bulletin Board) where they have been quoted on "at least 12 days within the previous 30 calendar days, with no more than 4 business days in succession without a quotation." Effectively, this means that once one dealer quotes the stock (presumably based on compliance with the Rule), others can piggyback on its efforts and need not have current information in their possession. In addition, under Rule 15c2–11(f)(3)(iii), even the original dealer is freed from this obligation to have current information once the stock has been quoted for this requisite period. This is known as "self piggybacking", and it implies that no dealer may actually possess at any given time the information described in Rule 15c2–11(b).

As a result of this curious state of affairs, the NASD estimated as of 1997 that nearly half of the companies traded on its Bulletin Board (which then had no listing or eligibility standards) were not reporting companies.[178] To resolve this unhappy state of affairs, the NASD took a drastic step in 1999 and required issuers on its OTC Bulletin Board to become "reporting" companies registered under § 12(g)(1) of the Securities Act (with some special exemptions for banks and other regulated companies) or face delisting.[179] As a consequence, over 3,000 companies were required to delist, most of whom fled to the Pink Sheets,

---

[176] See Rule 15c2–11(a)5.

[177] Exchange Act Release No. 21470 (Nov. 8, 1984), 31 SEC Dock. 797, 798 (1984).

[178] See Knight, NASD Tries to Reduce the Risk of OTC Trading, Washington Post, December 15, 1997, at p. F23.

[179] Some 5,601 companies were then quoted on the OTCBB, and pursuant to this new standard, some 3,187 companies were found to be ineligible. (Some 205 of these issuers deemed ineligible were subsequently able to qualify). Correspondingly, between 1999 and 2000, the number of securities quoted on the Pink Sheets surged from about 1,000 to 4,000. See M. Molitor, Will More Sunlight Fade the Pink Sheets? Increasing Public Information About Non-Reporting Issuers With Quoted Securities, 39 Ind. L. Rev. 309 (2006).

which is a virtually unregulated market.[180] Thus, the problem remained and only its location changed.[181]

Ultimately, on the policy level, Rule 15c2–11 seems likely to function mainly as a deterrent to dissuade brokers from trading penny stocks, unless and until the SEC creates some centralized and electronic repository, accessible to both brokers and customers, for Rule 15c2–11 information. Only then will it realistically provide information to investors.

F. THE FINANCIAL SERVICES MIDDLE MARKET: PROSPECTS FOR THE FUTURE

An array of professionals—brokers, investment advisers, banks, insurance agents, and financial planners—provide financial advice to middle class Americans, much of it focused on assisting them to meet retirement income objectives. These professionals are regulated very differently, and occasionally turf wars break out between them.

1. *The Continuing Broker/Investment Adviser Turf War.* Brokers have long been exempted from the Investment Advisers Act, but only to the extent that they performed traditional brokerage functions for which they were compensated on a commission basis. Yet, middle-income Americans typically do not trade securities frequently, but rather pursue a diversified buy-and-hold policy. Thus, the brokerage industry has long sought to move from commission-based compensation to fee-based compensation under which they would charge retail customers an annual fee based on the assets in their account. The advantage, of course, is that this is recurring revenue. To justify this charge, brokerage firms argue that they are providing financial planning services. The problem that this justification created, however, was that the Investment Advisers Act of 1940 only exempted brokers from its application when, in the language of its Section 202(a)(11), the broker's services were "solely incidental to the conduct of his business as a broker and receives no special compensation therefor." A broker who provided advice and charged a fee to the account for this advice did not seem to meet this definition, particularly if the account had few or no transactions. Thus, the brokerage industry prevailed upon the SEC to adopt a special exemptive rule, based upon what is now § 202(2)(11)(G), which exempts from the Investment Advisers Act "such other persons not within the intent of this paragraph, as the Commission may designate by rules and regulations or order." The D.C. Circuit struck down the Commission's proposed rule in Financial Planning Association v. Securities and Exchange

---

[180] The Over-The-Counter Market has also recently begun to impose minimum disclosure standards, but continues to have no quantitative or qualitative standards for listing. See Molitor, supra note 179.

[181] There were, however, clear beneficiaries of the NASD's policy. The remaining companies on the OTCBB escaped the taint that had previously enveloped them, and the Bulletin Board is now considered a more reputable market.

Commission,[182] finding that the provision was unambiguous and hence not subject to SEC modification.

The aftermath of *Financial Planning Association* has not been that brokerage firms have abandoned their attempt to charge their clients an annual fee based on assets under management, but that brokers providing advice to such fee-based accounts would also have to register as investment advisers. Of course, this implies that they would become fiduciaries to their clients. Possibly, this suggests that legal liability is secondary to market pressure in terms of what motivates brokerage firm managers.

2. *"Rogue Brokers"*. One problem still hovers over the brokerage industry despite long efforts to resolve it: "rogue brokers" who move from firm to firm, despite a troubling disciplinary record. One survey by the Government Accountability Office ("GAO") found that of the 470,000 brokers then active, some 10,000 had at least one formal disciplinary action taken against them, and 816 had three or more such actions.[183] These brokers may be terminated by their brokerage firm, but still move to other firms (possibly because they had a good earnings history or possibly because their original employer fears defamation liability if it discloses fully its experience with this broker[184]).

Section 918(b) of the Dodd-Frank Act directed the SEC to conduct a study of ways to improve the access of retail investors to information about both brokers and investment advisers and to identify additional information that should be made available. In response, the SEC published a study in 2011 recommending a more unified public disclosure database covering both brokers and investment advisers,[185] and subsequently, at the SEC's urging, information about investment advisers has been added to FINRA's BrokerCheck website, which is an easily accessible on-line tool that enables investors to check broker's records. Critics, however, still object that "rogue brokers" are often able to expunge their records and thus escape true transparency.[186]

---

[182] 482 F.3d 481 (D.C. Cir. 2007).

[183] See GAO, Actions Needed to Better Protect Investors against Unscrupulous Brokers, at 3 (1994); see also Joint Regulatory Sales Practices Sweep Report, 1995–1996 Fed. Sec. L. Rep. (CCH) ¶ 85,742 (1994).

[184] To address this problem, the Uniform Securities Act now provides that the forms filed by brokerage firms dealing with employee terminations are legally privileged and cannot be used as evidence to support a defamation or similar action.

[185] See Study on Investment Advisers and Broker-Dealers (January 21, 2011), available at www.sec.gov/news/studies/2011/913studyfinal/pdf.

[186] See Seth E. Lipner, The Expungement of Customer Complaint CRD Information Following the Settlement of a FINRA Arbitration, 19 Fordham J. Corp. & Fin. L. 57 (2013); Note, What You Do Not Know Can Hurt You: How the FINRA Expungement Process is Endangering Future Investors Through a Lack of Information, 42 Hofstra L. Rev. 1227 (2014).

CHAPTER 10

TENDER OFFERS, MANAGEMENT BUYOUTS, AND TAKEOVER CONTESTS

Statutes
  Exchange Act, §§ 13(d) and (e), 14(d), (e) and (f).
Rules and Regulations
  Rules 10b–18, 13e–1 to 13e–4.
  Regulations 13A, 13D–G, 14D, 14E.
  Schedule 13D, Schedule TO.

Introduction

Probably no area of corporate and securities law has produced equivalent controversy, resulted in more legislation, or yielded as many academic theories, as has the topic of hostile takeovers. The one common denominator in takeovers has been constant change. As tactics changed, the tide of the battle regularly ebbed and flowed. More recently, the number of hostile takeovers has declined, but hedge fund activists have appeared on the scene to perform much of the same role as the hostile bidder did in the past.

Thus, it is useful to start with a brief historical review. Prior to the Williams Act's passage in 1968, bidders could make very short tender offers, lasting only several days. At least in theory, shareholders of the target could be coerced by such offers, because if they spurned the bidder's premium and the offer succeeded, they might be left holding a minority interest in an illiquid stock controlled by the bidder. Fear of the unknown bidder and its potential plans for their corporation might also stampede shareholders into tendering because widely dispersed public shareholders could not easily unite to take collective action in response to a hostile bid, even if they perceived it to be inadequate. In response, Congress passed the Williams Act in 1968 to fill a perceived gap in the disclosure received by target shareholders and to authorize the SEC to adopt rules regulating certain substantive aspects of tender offers.

Although the passage of the Williams Act initially slowed the growth of the takeover movement, bidders quickly discovered techniques by which to regain the advantage. During the 1970s and early 1980s, the bidder would typically employ a three-stage attack: (1) quietly buying up to 5% of the class (at which point § 13(d) of the Williams Act required it to file within ten days thereafter a disclosure document known as a

Schedule 13D), (2) launching a hostile tender offer for control, and (3) merging out shortly thereafter any remaining minority interest that had failed to tender. As an additional tactic to pressure shareholders, bidders might also structure their offer as a "two-tier" partial bid in which they offered an above-market tender offer premium for 50% of the stock, but announced a plan to merge out the remaining minority shareholders at a lower price once they obtained control (thus, the tender offer was said to be "front-loaded").

In response to these coercive tactics, target managements resorted to rough-and-tumble defensive tactics of their own:

(1) a target might seek a friendly acquisition partner (a "white knight") or an institutional investor (a "white squire") who would acquire a blocking position so that the bidder could not safely acquire a controlling position or effect a squeeze-out merger;

(2) it might grant a "lock-up" to some third party, either of its stock or of certain "crown jewel" assets, (usually, this would involve giving the third party an option to buy assets or stock at a below-market price, possibly in return for its agreement to make a counter-offer at a higher price);

(3) it might repurchase its own shares in order to drive their price above the tender offer; or

(4) most likely, it would adopt (or utilize a previously adopted) "poison pill" shareholder rights plan (typically, this involves a distribution of options or warrants that, in order to dilute the bidder's holdings in the target, entitles all target shareholders, other than the bidder, to purchase the target's stock at an extremely attractive below-market price under specified circumstances, such as the bidder crossing a specified threshold—say 15%—of the target's stock).

Almost invariably, the bidder went to court to enjoin any of these defensive measures ("scorched earth" tactics in its view) as a breach of target management's fiduciary duties to its shareholders. More recently, the target's defense would also rely on whatever anti-takeover statute its jurisdiction of incorporation had adopted; these statutes might require a statutorily defined "fair price" or a supermajority vote, disenfranchise the bidder's shares, grant special compensation to employees, authorize the target to recapture gains from certain large shareholders, or simply preclude a follow-up merger for a designated "moratorium" period.

These takeover contests spawned epic legal battles, but, for the most part, the legal issues involved were those of state corporate law and the common law of fiduciary duties. This Chapter will leave these state law issues to your course in Corporations and instead focus on takeovers from a federal securities law perspective. From that perspective, it is far from clear that target shareholders need much protection from bidders, for two reasons. First, the indisputable fact about takeovers is that the target shareholders profit significantly from them.[1] Although greater ambiguity surrounds the impact of takeovers on bidder shareholders,[2] on bondholders,[3] and on employees,[4] the measurable losses suffered by these other constituencies, even when aggregated, clearly do not begin to approach the stock price gains to target shareholders. Second, target shareholders have an effective armory of self-help weapons against "unfair" hostile bids, which target managements are more than ready to employ.

From this starting point that shareholders are "net gainers" from takeovers, it sensibly can be asked: why should takeovers be subject to special federal regulation (other than the general antifraud rules that apply to all securities transactions)? Arguably, federal regulation may only give self-interested target managements another weapon with which to ward off lucrative bids that their own shareholders desire. From this perspective, if the intended beneficiaries of the Williams Act (i.e. shareholders) need little protection, the statute might sensibly be given a minimalist interpretation in order to prevent it from interfering with the market's healthy functioning. The force of this argument was underscored by an unmistakable shift in the tide of battle favoring the target following the adoption of the Williams Act. As a result of a variety of factors—especially potent defensive tactics (most notably, the poison pill), state anti-takeover statutes, and the decline in junk bond financing—fewer hostile takeovers were for a time launched.

Tactics then changed. Bidders announced a combined tender offer and proxy fight, seeking to oust the incumbent board at the target in a proxy contest and then elect their own nominees who could then redeem the "poison pill" so that the tender offer could proceed unimpeded. For a time, this approach faced the problem that many companies had "staggered" boards so that the bidder would have to win two elections before it could succeed (which was longer than most bidders could wait). More recently, activist shareholders have induced most public companies to abandon staggered boards so that only a few companies still have this defense. As a result, the balance of advantage may have swung back to the bidder (except when the target can find a third party bidder to offer an even higher premium).

---

[1] For a summary of the statistical evidence from "event studies" of takeover stocks, see Jarrell, Brickley and Netter, The Market for Corporate Control: The Empirical Evidence Since 1980, 2 Journal of Economic Perspectives 49 (1988) (on average, 30% abnormal gain on announcement of tender offer).

[2] Different studies show bidder shareholders experiencing small gains, no gains, or small losses on the announcement of a takeover. Some commentators believe that the market's reaction understates the expected loss to the bidder's shareholders from overpayment because the market already anticipated the loss. See Black, Bidder Overpayment in Takeovers, 41 Stan.L.Rev. 597 (1989).

[3] See Asquith & Wizman, Event Risk, Covenants and Bondholder Returns in Leveraged Buyouts, 27 J.Fin.Econ. 195 (1990).

[4] Coffee, Shareholders Versus Managers: The Strain in The Corporate Web, 85 Mich.L.Rev. 1 (1986).

The balance of advantage in the takeover wars may shift again from time to time, but it is important to focus on the justifications for regulation. The standard answer to the claim that takeovers are overregulated involves the special problem of coercion: dispersed shareholders are incapable of collective action in a takeover, and various offensive tactics, such as the two-tier partial bid,[5] may coerce them into selling at prices well below that at which a single owner of all the target stock would be willing to sell.[6] So viewed, the Williams Act's disclosure and timing provisions may make sense primarily as a means by which to reduce coercion and facilitate an auction market in which bidders compete on an equal footing to acquire control so that shareholders will receive higher takeover premiums. From this perspective, the Williams Act should serve mainly to ensure a level playing field on which the contestants do battle.

An alternative justification for regulation is that the time delays mandated by the Williams Act encourage auctions to develop by providing time for third party bidders to enter the battle and make higher bids. The evidence suggests that the actual impact of the Williams Act has been to increase takeover premiums[7], but, as a consequence, it may reduce the number of bids made. The unresolved question is whether shareholders on average are better off if takeover premia are higher, but fewer bids are made. Even the desirability of a competitive auction market for takeovers has been the subject of much academic debate.[8]

---

[5] In a "two-tier" bid, the acquirer offers a high price for that percentage of the shares necessary to give it majority control (which, for example, may be only 35% if it already owns 15%) and then indicates that it plans to merge out the remaining shareholders at a lower price. Even if it offers the same price for the "back end," this amount may only be received much later, possibly in the form of debt securities that will trade below their face value, and without interest to cover the intervening period. As a result, this approach increases the pressure to tender into the front-end.

[6] The shareholders' problem can be explained as a variant of the standard "prisoner's dilemma." If shareholders believe the offer is inadequate, they could in theory hold out, but in a world where the second-step merger may be at a lower price (or may be a delayed payment of the same price, given the time value of money), a shareholder who holds out will be in a worse-off position if other shareholders tender and the offer is successful. Then the holdouts will become minority shareholders in a thinly traded or untraded firm. The "front-loaded" tender offer exacerbates this problem by offering a special advantage to those who defect from any implicit agreement not to tender. In short, in a setting where shareholders would be best off not tendering, it is likely that shareholders who cannot organize will be forced to tender. See Carney, Shareholder Coordination Costs, Shark Repellents and Takeout Mergers: The Case Against Fiduciary Duties, 1983 A.B.F.Res.J. 341.

[7] Studies have found that in the wake of the Williams Act's passage, the average premium over the pre-offer price in a cash tender offer rose from 32% to nearly 53%. See Jarrell and Bradley, The Economic Effects of Federal and State Regulation of Cash Tender Offers, 23 J.L. & Econ. 371 (1980).

[8] Those who favor auctions believe that they direct the target's assets to the most efficient user (i.e., the firm that will realize the greatest synergy from the combination). See Gilson, Seeking Competitive Bids Versus Pure Passivity in Tender Offer Defense, 35 Stan.L.Rev. 51 (1982). Those who oppose auctions believe that, unless the first bidder's search costs are rewarded, bidders will be deterred from making takeover bids, and the number of bids will decline. See Easterbrook & Fischel, Auctions and Sunk Costs in Tender Offers, 35 Stan.L.Rev. 1 (1982). Proponents of auctions doubt that search costs play a large role in takeovers. Another critique of auctions is that, absent unique synergies, auctions waste social

Thus, while it can be debated whether the Williams Act has made shareholders as a class better off, it almost certainly has protected smaller shareholders from coercive tactics that might have forced them to tender at lower prices.

The legislative history of the Williams Act reveals a Congressional desire to preserve a fair balance in takeover contests so that managerial defensive tactics could only be used up to the point where they were likely to increase value for target shareholders. Indeed, the chief draftsman of the Williams Act (Senator Harrison Williams of New Jersey) observed that "extreme care" had been taken in writing the legislation to avoid "tipping the scales either in favor of management or in favor of the person making the takeover bid."[9] Still, any notion that the Williams Act places substantive limitations on the defensive tactics available to management (other than those that directly contravene the Act's few regulatory provisions) was forcefully rejected by the Supreme Court in Schreiber v. Burlington Northern, Inc.[10] As a result, the Williams Act necessarily constrains bidders much more than target managements.

Is this desirable? Another way to frame this issue is to ask: to what degree should the law treat target management as the negotiating agent of the target shareholders? Some commentators believe that because target shareholders cannot negotiate for themselves, their management should be given substantial discretion to do so on their behalf.[11] Others believe that target management has too substantial a conflict of interest to be accorded much discretion. If so, the Williams Act may provide a superior means by which to promote auctions and raise premiums. Even if it were not Congress's intent to promote auctions when it passed the Williams Act, the evidence seems to show that the chief effect of the Act has been to enable target shareholders to capture the vast majority of the gains from takeovers, with bidders receiving only statistically insignificant gains on average.

Until recently, the takeover drama was essentially between two actors: bidder and target (with possibly a third actor, the "white knight" bidder waiting in the wings). Then, probably around 2005, the environment changed, and a new actor appeared: the "activist" hedge fund. These funds often assemble a coalition of other activist investors to pursue a specific agenda: e.g., forcing a sale of the subject company, replacing senior management, inducing the target to spin off substantial assets or buy back shares, etc. All these strategies hint at a possible takeover battle and raise the expected takeover premium. These activists

---

resources. See Schwartz, The Fairness of Tender Offer Prices in Utilitarian Theory, 17 J. Legal Stud. 165 (1988).

[9] 113 Cong.Rec. 24664; see also U.S.Code Cong. & Admin.News 1968, at 2813; H.R.Rep. No. 1711, 90th Cong., 2d Sess., 4 (1968).

[10] 472 U.S. 1 (1985).

[11] See, e.g., Leebron, Games Corporations Play: A Theory of Tender Offers, 61 N.Y.U.L.Rev. 153 (1986); Haddock, Macey & McChesney, Property Rights in Assets and Resistance to Tender Offers, 73 Va.L.Rev. 701 (1987).

can assemble a coalition of other activist institutions holding as much as 20% or more of the issuer's stock without any of them making a Williams Act filing, at least so long as (1) no individual fund acquires more than 5% prior to the announcement of their campaign, and (2) each participant maintains its own freedom to act in its own interests so they have no agreement to act in concert and hence are not a "group" under § 13(d)(3) of the 1934 Act. Typically, the public announcement of this campaign (usually disclosed by means of a Schedule 13D filing when the lead fund does cross the 5% threshold) produces a significant market reaction (around 7% to 8%, net of other market movements) that benefits all the participants in this coalition.[12] A recent Delaware Chancery Court decision described this strategy as the formation of a "wolf pack,"[13] and the popularity of this tactic owes much to the recent liberalization of the SEC's rules regarding both proxy and Williams Act solicitations.[14]

The continuing evolution of takeover tactics was illustrated in 2014 when the best-known of these activist funds, Pershing Square Capital Management ("Pershing"), teamed up with a strategic bidder for an over $62 billion takeover bid for Allergan, Inc., a prominent pharmaceutical company.[15] Although Pershing did make a capital contribution to the bidder and agreed to share its gains with the bidder, it did not tender for the target's shares or accept any liability for the acquisition costs. This procedure raised the question of whether the strategic bidder had in effect simply tipped Pershing in return for its contribution of capital—in violation of SEC Rule 14e–3 under the Williams Act. The district court hearing the case declined to enjoin the tender offer, but did find "serious questions" about whether Rule 14e–3 had been violated and whether Pershing should be viewed as an exempt co-bidder in the tender offer.[16] The bottom line is that considerable uncertainty now exists about when and how activist funds and strategic bidders can affiliate in order to make a tender offer. Further developments in the efforts of bidders and hedge funds to strike partnerships for purposes of a takeover bid seem likely, and newer and even more novel patterns may yet emerge

This chapter examines the current regulatory balance that has been struck between underregulation and overregulation, recognizing that the only constant about takeovers has been constant and often sudden change.

---

[12] See Alon Brav, Wei Jiang, Frank Partnoy, and Randall Thomas, Hedge Fund Activism, Corporate Governance and Firm Performance, 63 J. Fin. 1729 (2008)

[13] See Third Point LLC. v. Ruprecht, 2014 Del. Ch. LEXIS 64 (May 2, 2014).

[14] See Thomas Briggs, Corporate Governance and the New Hedge Fund Activism: An Empirical Analysis, 32 J. Corp. L 681 (Summer 2007); John C. Coffee, Jr. and Darius Palia, The Wolf at the Door: The Impact of Hedge Fund Activism on Corporate Governance, 41 J. Corp. L. 545 (2016).

[15] Allergan, Inc. v. Valeant Pharms. Int'l, Inc., 2014 U.S. Dist. LEXIS 156227 (C.D. Cal. Nov. 4, 2014).

[16] Id at * 24 and * 39.

1. AN OVERVIEW OF THE WILLIAMS ACT

Enacted in 1968 and amended in 1970, the Williams Act was a product of both a Congressional sense that "something had to be done" about corporate takeovers and a Congressional irresolution about what precisely should be done. Although the original force behind the introduction of the Williams Act was probably the desire of target managements to obtain protection from takeover bids made by brash, young entrepreneurs who were the beneficiaries of the 1960s "bull market" (which enabled firms with high price/earnings ratios to exchange their securities for the lower valued securities of target firms), the draft legislation was substantially modified during the Congressional hearings on the advice of the SEC. Because of the concerns of a number of academic critics that a "strong" statute would entrench incumbent (and perhaps inefficient) management, the legislative history to the Williams Act displays a strong desire to "avoid tipping the balance of regulation in favor of management or in favor of the person making the takeover bid."[17] As a result, the Williams Act is avowedly neutral, but seeks to assist shareholder decision-making through a potpourri of disclosure provisions, antifraud rules, substantive regulations governing the conduct of tender offers, and a substantial grant of rulemaking authority to the SEC.

Organizationally, the Williams Act added Section 13(d) and (e) and Section 14(d)–(f) to the 1934 Act. Its principal provisions are briefly summarized below.

A. THE SECTION 13(d) TRIP WIRE

Essentially, § 13(d) mandates that a person or "group" who becomes the beneficial owner of more than 5 percent of a class of an equity security of a publicly held company must file a disclosure document (either a Schedule 13D or shorter document, known as a Schedule 13G, depending on the circumstances). In most cases, the person or group will be required to use a Schedule 13D, which must be filed within ten days after the purchase or act that crosses the 5 percent threshold. However, certain institutional investors who acquire "such securities in the ordinary course of [their] business and not with a purpose nor with the effect of changing or influencing the control of the issuer" may instead use a short-form statement, known as Schedule 13G, which need not be filed until within 45 days after the end of the calendar year (and only then if the investor or group continues to own 5% at year end).[18] Copies of either Schedule must also be transmitted to the relevant stock exchanges and the target company.

---

[17] S.Rep. No. 550, 90th Cong., 1st Session 3 (1967); see also Rondeau v. Mosinee Paper Corp., 422 U.S. 49, 58–59 (1975) (reviewing legislative history).

[18] See Rule 13d–1(b)(1)(i).

The instructions to Schedule 13D require the reporting person or group to disclose information approximating that which would have to be disclosed in a contested proxy fight: the identity and background of the party or group making the filing, the source of funding, the number of shares owned by them, any contracts or arrangements with respect to the shares and, most importantly, the purpose of the transaction (including whether it is to acquire control). If any "material" changes occur in any of the information so disclosed in Schedule 13D, Rule 13d–2 requires that the information be "promptly" updated. As a practical matter, the SEC usually interprets "promptly" in this context to mean within two business days.[19] Rule 13d–2 further indicates that an acquisition or disposition of 1% or more of the class will be deemed "material," and lesser acquisitions or dispositions may also be material depending on their facts. In consequence, once a potential acquirer crosses the 5% threshold of a publicly held company subject to § 14(d), it must anticipate that it is entering a fishbowl of public disclosure in which its every action and possible motive will be subject to close scrutiny not only by the target, but also by market professionals (the arbitrageurs or "arbs") who invest or speculate in takeover stocks.

In efforts to outflank § 13(d), bidders have utilized a variety of techniques, including options, nominees, and other, more informal agreements, but they have usually been thwarted by Rule 13d–3 under the Securities Exchange Act, which attributes beneficial ownership to any person (and hence requires a Schedule 13D filing by such person) if that person holds either voting power or investment power (i.e., the right to dispose of the shares). Thus, any understanding under which shares would be voted or sold at the direction of any person gives that person beneficial ownership of the shares and necessitates a Schedule 13D if the person's total ownership (i.e., legal and beneficial) exceeds five percent of the class. The scope of Rule 13d–3's concept of "grouphood" has spawned much litigation, which is analyzed later in this Chapter.

Two basic policy questions surround § 13(d): First, do shareholders really benefit from the "distant early warning" system that § 13(d) establishes? Critics of the Williams Act argue that its true beneficiary is target management, which gains time to put takeover defenses in place or to find a white knight. Specifically, they argue that § 13(d) increases both the cost and risk of takeovers, and by lowering the bidder's expected return it may decrease the likelihood of a takeover bid being made in the first instance.[20] Conversely, defenders of the Williams Act reply that, but for § 13(d), most of the gains from a takeover would be captured by the bidder, which could assemble a controlling position (without actually

---

[19] In Securities Exchange Act Release No. 34–22171 (June 26, 1985), the Commission declined to specify a precise rule for determining whether an amendment was "prompt," but indicated that in the case of Schedule 13D "promptness" must be "judged * * * by the market's sensitivity to a particular change of fact triggering the obligation to amend * * *."

[20] For a forceful statement of this perspective, see Macey & Netter, Regulation 13D and the Regulatory Process, 65 Wash.U.L.Q. 131 (1987).

making a tender offer) by quietly effecting steady "creeping control" purchases in the open market that do not alert market professionals or potential other bidders. Thus, § 13(d) arguably achieves a "fairer" allocation of the gains between the bidder and the target's shareholders. However, there is also some evidence that the competitive character of the takeover market erodes away all gains for the bidder once it loses the benefit of secrecy.[21]

A second area of concern about the regulations underlying § 13(d) is their impact on institutional investors. Are they impeded from joining together to take collective action to resist corporate management? Suppose a half dozen institutions, each of whom owns 1%–2% of the common stock of a corporation subject to the Williams Act, wish to oppose a proposal by the corporation's management to adopt a "shark repellent" charter amendment or to award themselves lucrative "golden parachute" contracts. Collectively, these institutions (typically mutual funds and public pension funds) have no desire to lead a takeover or to oust management, but in the aggregate they may own well over 5% of a class. Must they file a Schedule 13D as a "group"? Under Rule 13d–5, when "two or more persons agree to act together for the purpose of acquiring, holding, *voting,* or disposing of equity securities of an issuer, the group formed thereby shall be deemed to have acquired beneficial ownership, for purposes of Sections 13(d) and 13(g) of the Act, as of the date of such agreement, of all equity securities of that issuer beneficially owned by any such persons" (emphasis added).[22] Some commentators have suggested that § 13(d) contributes to the overregulation of institutional investors and deters them from greater involvement in corporate governance.[23] Alternatively, others report a pattern under which one investor (often an activist hedge fund) tips other institutional investors that it is about to cross the 5% threshold and will disclose in its Schedule 13D that it will ask management to spin off assets, sell the company, or declare a large special dividend. It knows that this disclosure will usually raise the market price of the company's stock (at least for a period) and that it and its allies can profit from purchases made before such an announcement. Under current law, this does not amount to insider trading; nor, absent an agreement to act in concert, do these entities amount to a group. Hence, there are those who believe current law underregulates as well as those who believe it overregulates.

B. DISCLOSURE UNDER THE WILLIAMS ACT

Above all, the Williams Act is a disclosure statute, and § 14(d)(1) implements this purpose by requiring the bidder to prepare and file a

---

[21] See Black, Bidder Overpayment in Takeovers, 41 Stan.L.Rev. 597 (1989).

[22] Interestingly, § 13(d)(3) does not refer to "voting," but only to a group formed "for the purpose of acquiring, holding, or disposing." Do the SEC's rules overregulate here?

[23] See Gilson & Kraakman, Reinventing the Outside Director: An Agenda for Institutional Investors, 43 Stan.L.Rev. 863 (1991); Black, Shareholder Passivity Reexamined, 89 Mich.L.Rev. 520 (1990).

disclosure statement with the SEC. Today, the document filed with the SEC is the Schedule TO, and it will include all prior communications sent by the bidder to security holders. The actual tender offer itself will be set forth in a separate document, incorporated within the Schedule TO, which will typically have earlier been summarized in a newspaper advertisement and mailed or sent to security holders who request it. Increasingly, it is a lengthy document, because most bidders believe it necessary to include their own financial statements in these documents. Although the case law provides few clear guidelines, it has indicated that such financial information may be material to a target shareholder in determining whether to tender (in part because the shareholder might decide that it was more attractive to remain as a minority shareholder under a new, more efficient management).[24] In 1977, the SEC amended Regulation 14D to state that financial information had to be included when it was "material."[25] This tautological advice hardly resolved the ambiguities, but the Release did point to several nonexclusive factors that the bidder should evaluate.[26]

Why should the bidder be required to make detailed disclosures about its own financial condition? Arguably, given the usual premium over the prior market price in a takeover, the investment decision for the target shareholder is as simple as deciding whether to exchange a $5 bill for a $10 bill. One answer to this claim may be that a tender offer can be only a partial bid, thus ensuring that most shareholders will continue to own some shares in the target after the tender offer is consummated. Another is that some shareholders may believe (or wish to determine whether) the offer is inadequate. Or perhaps, they believe that they will gain more from becoming minority investors in the target company under the bidder's new, presumably more efficient management. These theories are subject to powerful rejoinders: an efficient market should imply that it is desirable to accept a premium over the market, and target shareholders seldom have the opportunity to remain as minority shareholders under the new management, because the bidder usually merges out the non-tendering shareholders through a squeeze-out merger within a year or two after the tender offer. Still, courts have

---

[24] See Corenco Corp. v. Schiavone & Sons, Inc., 362 F.Supp. 939 (S.D.N.Y.1973), aff'd, 488 F.2d 207 (2d Cir. 1973); Alaska Interstate Co. v. McMillian, 402 F.Supp. 532 (D.Del.1975); Copperweld Corp. v. Imetal, 403 F.Supp. 579 (W.D.Pa.1975).

[25] Securities Exchange Act Release No. 13787 (July 21, 1977).

[26] These included, without limitation: "(1) the terms of the tender offer, particularly those terms concerning the amount of securities being sought, such as any or all, a fixed minimum with a right to accept additional shares tendered, all or none, and a fixed percentage of the outstanding; (2) whether the purpose of the offer is for control of the subject company; (3) the plans or proposals of the bidder described in Item 5 of the Schedule; and (4) the ability of the bidder to pay for the securities sought in the tender offer and/or to repay any loans made to the bidder * * *." Id. For an intriguing case applying these criteria, see Prudent Real Estate Trust v. Johncamp Realty, Inc., 599 F.2d 1140, 1147 (2d Cir. 1979) (noting differences between an "any and all" offer and a partial bid). Johncamp Realty reasoned that target shareholders might have a reason to be interested in the bidder's poor financial condition even in an "any and all" bid for fear that "control of the company might otherwise pass into irresponsible hands." Query: Would not disclosure of this information increase the pressure?

reasoned that if all the shareholders were fully informed and knew the bidder's estimates of the value of the target's assets, they might reject the offer.

On this basis, some courts have held that "tender offer materials must disclose soft information, such as * * * asset appraisals based upon predictions regarding economic and corporate events," but they have limited this obligation to disclose projections and appraisals to circumstances where "the predictions underlying the appraisal are substantially certain to hold."[27] For bidders, this can be a substantial disclosure burden, particularly when their source of information may be speculative or out of date. Moreover, how far does this obligation to disclose the bidder's estimate of the target's potential value go? For example, could a court require a bidder to disclose its reservation or "walk away" price at which it would abandon its efforts to acquire control? This seems unlikely, but if this disclosure is not material, why should the law require disclosure of the projections and asset appraisals based upon which this bottom line price has been determined? Perhaps, the answer is that such disclosure will encourage new bidders to enter the fray, but is it appropriate to compel disclosure of proprietary information when the bidder owes no fiduciary duty to the target shareholders?

Another much debated disclosure issue arises when a bidder commences a tender offer without first obtaining firm financing for the funds necessary to pay for the shares. Although it is obviously necessary for the bidder to disclose its source and amounts of funds,[28] suppose the bidder discloses only that it has received a letter from its investment banker that the banker is "highly confident" that it can secure the financing before the time of acceptance.[29] In addition, suppose the tender offer is made conditional on the bidder's obtaining adequate financing by the end of the tender offer period. Courts have accepted such conditional offers on the theory that the Williams Act, as primarily a disclosure statute, only requires the bidder to disclose the information it knows and does not impose substantive restrictions, except those expressly set forth in the statute or the SEC's rules thereunder. On the other hand, an attempt by the bidder to withdraw its offer because it did not consider the financing terms available to it to be attractive might not fare as well, even if the bidder disclosed clearly that it was reserving the right to do so "in its sole discretion."[30]

---

[27] Radol v. Thomas, 772 F.2d 244, 252–53 (6th Cir. 1985); see also Flynn v. Bass Bros. Enterprises, Inc., 744 F.2d 978 (3d Cir. 1984).

[28] Disclosure of this information is required by Item 7 of Schedule TO.

[29] See Newmont Mining Corp. v. Pickens, 831 F.2d 1448 (9th Cir. 1987), (permitting offer to proceed based on Drexel Burnham's "highly confident" letter). Query: What is the investment banker's liability if it proves to have been "overconfident" and cannot finance the offer?

[30] Both the SEC and standard contract law tend to view "sole discretion" clauses as actually imposing an objective standard of reasonableness. The SEC's staff has informed bidders that any attempt to use a subjective "sole discretion" standard may be viewed as a material amendment of the offer, requiring its extension.

Although some early takeover bids were enjoined on disclosure grounds, most federal courts have since heeded Judge Henry Friendly's admonition that courts should not "impose an unrealistic requirement of laboratory conditions that might make the * * * [Williams Act] a potent tool for incumbent management to protect its own interests against the desires and welfare of the stockholders."[31] As a result, courts today will rarely grant the target corporation more than a temporary injunction, halting the tender offer pending corrective disclosure, and almost never require the bidder to divest itself of shares already acquired (or to cease to vote them).[32]

Procedurally, the bidder has a choice as to how to disclose under the Williams Act. Under Rule 14d–4, it may choose either "long-form publication" or "summary publication." The former involves publication in a newspaper or newspapers of general circulation of the bidder's offer, which publication must set forth the full terms of its offer. The alternative of summary publication permits the publication of a "summary advertisement of the tender offer" plus a mailing of the full terms to each security holder who requests the full terms in response to the summary advertisement. This second approach is generally the more practical and less costly option. Under Rule 14d–6, summary publication can be quite concise and basically resembles a "tombstone" ad.

The target corporation is also subject to a disclosure obligation under the Williams Act. Rule 14d–9 provides that any person who solicits or makes a recommendation to shareholders in respect of a tender offer must file a Schedule 14D-9, which must basically disclose any conflicts of interest and also requires the target to disclose any recent or pending negotiations and transactions relating to the takeover bid in which the target company is engaged.[33] The obligation to file a Schedule 14D-9 cannot be avoided by the target management, because under Rule 14e–2, the target is required, no later than 10 business days from the date the tender offer is first published or sent, to give its security holders a statement disclosing its position on the offer (i.e., whether it recommends acceptance, rejection, or is unable to take a position). This statement must "also include the reasons for the position * * *." Because this

---

[31] See Electronic Specialty Co. v. International Controls Corp., 409 F.2d 937, 948 (2d Cir. 1969). See also, Susquehanna Corp. v. Pan American Sulphur Co., 423 F.2d 1075 (5th Cir. 1970); Seaboard World Airlines, Inc. v. Tiger International, Inc., 600 F.2d 355 (2d Cir. 1979).

[32] For decisions limiting the relief to corrective disclosure or refusing to grant damages (even to shareholders) for misstatements under § 13(d) or § 14(d), see Rondeau v. Mosinee Paper Corp., 422 U.S. 49 (1975); Dan River, Inc. v. Icahn, 701 F.2d 278 (4th Cir. 1983) (reversing "sterilization" order); Florida Commercial Banks v. Culverhouse, 772 F.2d 1513 (11th Cir. 1985) (appropriate remedy is corrective disclosure); Portsmouth Square Inc. v. Shareholders Protective Committee, 770 F.2d 866 (9th Cir. 1985).

[33] So long as an "agreement in principle" has not been reached, the target need not disclose the parties or terms if it believes this would "jeopardize" the negotiations. See Instructions to Item 7 to Schedule 14D-9. The failure of Allied Stores Corp., a target corporation, to disclose such defensive negotiations resulted in an important case, discussed infra, on an attorney's responsibilities under the federal securities laws. See In the Matter of George C. Kern, Jr., Securities Act Release No. 29356 (June 21, 1991).

mandatory Rule 14e–2 statement requires a recommendation, it in turn triggers the obligation to file a Schedule 14D-9.[34]

Finally, Rule 14e–8 prohibits market announcements of tender offers without both a bona fide intent and reasonable belief by the party making the announcement in its ability to complete the bid. This rule is intended less to regulate the bidder than to prevent market manipulation by those who would buy before the announcement and sell on the market's reaction to the news. Although Rule 10b–5 would also reach a false statement, Rule 14e–8 reaches a negligent or incurably optimistic bidder who lacks a "reasonable" belief in its ability to complete the bid.

C. SUBSTANTIVE RULES

The Williams Act sets forth a rudimentary framework within which takeover contests must be conducted. For example, Section 14(d)(5) states that shareholders may withdraw their tendered shares either within the first seven days of the offer or after sixty days from its commencement. Similarly, Section 14(d)(6) requires bidders to prorate shares received during the first ten days of the offer if the offer is oversubscribed; for example, if the bidder tenders for 50% and all shares are tendered, then each tendering shareholder will have 50% of its shares accepted and 50% of its shares returned. Clearly, the purpose of these provisions is to reduce the pressure to tender on the shareholder. Absent a proration rule, bidders might announce a "first-come, first-served" policy on acceptance so that in a partial bid those who tendered after the first few days would likely have all their shares returned.

Although both §§ 14(d)(5) and 14(d)(6) of the Williams Act state "bright line" standards, their significance has been largely eclipsed by subsequent SEC rules that extend both the length of the tender offer and the period during which proration and withdrawal rights continue. Today, Rule 14e–1 requires a 20 business day duration for a tender offer, and Rule 14d–8 continues proration rights for the life of the tender offer. This raises an obvious question about the SEC's authority. If the Williams Act specifies a seven day withdrawal period and a ten day proration period, what authority does the SEC have to adopt rules requiring a longer duration or longer withdrawal or proration periods? The SEC's answer is that § 14(e) of the Williams Act authorizes the Commission to adopt rules "reasonably designed to prevent such acts and practices as are fraudulent, deceptive, or manipulative." Thus, although a seven day tender offer may not be inherently fraudulent, a rule requiring a 20-day period is still "reasonably designed" to prevent fraud and deception. The scope of the SEC's power in this area remains debatable and has never reached the Supreme Court. However, in

---

[34] Rule 14d–9(f) states this explicitly.

Schreiber v. Burlington Northern, Inc.,[35] the Supreme Court held that § 14(e) does not prohibit manipulation unless there has been some element of deception through a material misrepresentation or omission. If so, where is the requisite deception in an openly disclosed seven-day tender offer?

Before examining the SEC's rules in more detail, one other important consequence should be noted that follows from the SEC's decision to utilize § 14(e) as a basis for rulemaking. While § 14(d) applies only to equity securities registered pursuant to 12 of the 1934 Act (and some miscellaneous exempt issuers), § 14(e) applies more broadly to all tender offers. Thus, tender offers for debt securities or for the equity securities of a privately held company are subject to the rules promulgated under § 14(e), but not those under § 14(d).

1. *Timing and Duration Rules.* Rule 14e–1(a) mandates that a tender offer be held open for at least 20 business days from the date the offer is first published, sent, or given to security holders. In addition, Rule 14e–1(b) requires that a tender offer be held open for an additional ten business days in the event of an "increase or decrease in the percentage of the class of securities being sought or the consideration offered" (and also in the event of a change in the dealer's soliciting fee). Obviously, both rules are intended to reduce the pressure on shareholders to tender, and they also have the effect (whether or not intended) of giving the target additional time to find a "white knight" or to make its own counter-proposal.

Interpretive issues can arise under Rule 14e–1 as to whether clause (a) or clause (b) applies to a given transaction. For example, suppose a bidder announces a change from a 100% bid (usually referred to as an "any and all" tender offer) to a partial two-tier bid (which, it announces, will be followed by a squeeze-out merger at a lower cash price). Is this an amendment under Rule 14e–1(b) requiring only a ten business day extension, or a new offer requiring a twenty business day minimum period under Rule 14e–1(a)?[36]

In addition to these rules, the Commission has followed a policy of requiring that a minimum period of time remain in the offering period following any material change in the information received by investors.[37] Where the new information is disseminated by a press release that reaches the market generally, the Commission will typically deem five business days to be an adequate remaining period during which investors

---

[35] 472 U.S. 1 (1985). But see Polaroid Corp. v. Disney, 862 F.2d 987 (3d Cir. 1988) (upholding SEC's authority to promulgate Rule 14d–10, known as the "All Holders Rule," even though it was only tangentially related to ensuring complete disclosure).

[36] See CRTF Corp. v. Federated Dept. Stores, Inc., 683 F.Supp. 422 (S.D.N.Y.1988) (finding ten day extension sufficient). Query: Would the result be the same if the offered consideration changed from cash to debentures? The SEC's staff has suggested that the 20 day period would be necessary in this case.

[37] See Securities Exchange Act Release No. 34–23421 (July 11, 1986) and Securities Exchange Release No. 34–24296 (April 3, 1987).

can evaluate the new information; otherwise, if the information is only mailed to shareholders, it may require ten business days. In one representative case, the SEC found that the waiver by the bidder of a minimum share condition in its offer was such a material change in information to require a five business day extension after dissemination of the information, even though the bidder did not increase or decrease the shares it sought so as to come within Rule 14e–1(b).[38]

An important timing rule governs the commencement of a tender offer: Under Rule 14d–2(a), a tender offer commences "on the date when the bidder has first published, sent or given the means to tender to security holders." Under prior rules, a pre-commencement announcement of an intent to commence a tender offer could actually start the statutory period running, but the SEC ultimately decided that this created too much of a trap for the unwary and now allows pre-commencement communications so long as the communication does not include a means for tendering the shares and such communication is eventually filed under cover of the Schedule TO.[39]

2. *Withdrawal and Proration.* Although § 14(d)(5) provides that shares tendered in a tender offer may be withdrawn during the first seven days of the offer, Rule 14d–7 overshadows this statutory provision by extending withdrawal rights for the life of the offer.[40] However, Rule 14d–11 permits bidders to extend the offer for a "subsequent offering period" without withdrawal rights in order to acquire the remaining shares after a successful offer. Little, if any, pressure is placed on shareholders by this provision.

Similarly, § 14(d)(6) requires the bidder to prorate shares received during the first ten days if the offer is oversubscribed, but Rule 14d–8 extends the proration period throughout the life of the offer. One justification for these rules, which obviously rest on an uncertain jurisdictional foundation, is that without them the purpose of the twenty business day rule (Rule 14e–1(a)) would be frustrated, because in a partial bid if bidders could limit proration rights to the first ten days of the offer, then target shareholders would be under substantial pressure to tender within that time period (particularly if the bidder announced

---

[38] See Securities Exchange Act Release No. 34–24296 (April 13, 1987).

[39] See Rule 14d–2(b).

[40] Rule 14d–7 does permit a bidder to curtail withdrawal rights during a "subsequent offering period," which it is permitted to add onto its tender offer in order to receive additional shares. See Rule 14d–7(a)(2). For example, if a bidder obtains a majority of the shares in its tender offer, it may wish to add such an additional period to encourage shareholders who initially resisted its offer to now tender into this subsequent offering period at the same price. This both helps those shareholders who initially resisted and who may now wish to tender (rather than hold stock in a controlled and possibly illiquid company), and it allows the bidder to cross the threshold specified under state law (typically, 80%) at which it can do a short-form merger without a shareholder vote. The subsequent offering period is governed by Rule 14d–11. Formerly, the "subsequent offering period" had to last between three and twenty business days, but in 2008 the SEC deleted the 20 day maximum length, thereby leaving the maximum length to the bidder's discretion. See Securities Exchange Act Release No. 58597 (Sept. 19, 2008).

that it intended to follow up its partial bid with a squeeze-out merger at a lower price). To date, courts have upheld the validity of these rules.[41]

To protect the flanks of Rule 14d–8, Rule 14e–4 prohibits "short tendering"—that is, tendering more securities into a partial bid than the shareholder owns. For example, if the bid were for 50%, the shareholder who owns 1% may face the risk that half of this stock may be returned (and may decline in value once the bidder becomes the company's controlling shareholder). Thus, to avoid this risk of proration, many sophisticated shareholders would tender much more than they owned. But if as a result more shares are tendered into the proration pool, other shareholders will suffer greater proration. To prevent unfairness to those who were honest, Rule 14e–4 prohibits (1) short tendering, (2) tendering coupled with the immediate sale into the market or the purchase of a call option ("hedged tendering"), and (3) tendering the same security to multiple bidders ("multiple tendering").[42] Rule 14e–4 bars short tendering not only by the owner of securities; but also by a broker tendering for its customer.

3. *Anti-Discrimination Rules.* Section 14(d)(7) sets forth the Williams Act's "best price" rule: each security holder is entitled to the best price paid to any other security holder pursuant to the tender offer. Thus, a shareholder who tenders into the initial offer at, for example, $23.50 per share must receive the higher price if the bidder subsequently increases its offer to $25. But what happens if the bidder accepts all shares at $23.50 and then, after the apparent conclusion of the tender offer, pays $25 per share to the largest shareholder who had held out and not tendered? A variant on this fact pattern arose in Field v. Trump,[43] where the bidder "withdrew" its offer at $22.50 per share, purchased at $25 per share the shares of a shareholder group that owned 18.4% of the target's stock and also held two seats on the target's board, and then reinstated its tender offer at a price of $23.50 per share. The Second Circuit found that the original tender offer at $22.50 and the later tender offer at $23.50 could be "integrated" into a continuous offer, because otherwise "successive tender offers interrupted by withdrawals * * * [could render] the 'best-price rule' * * * meaningless." Therefore, the bidder was required to purchase plaintiff's shares at the higher price. Still, the question remains: at what point should a bidder's post-tender

---

[41] See Pryor v. United States Steel Corp., 794 F.2d 52 (2d Cir. 1986) (proration rule valid and shareholders have private right of action to enforce it); Field v. Trump, 850 F.2d 938 (2d Cir. 1988); Polaroid Corp. v. Disney, 862 F.2d 987 (3d Cir. 1988) ("All Holders Rule" upheld).

[42] For a decision applying these rules, see Merrill Lynch, Pierce, Fenner & Smith v. Bobker, 808 F.2d 930 (2d Cir. 1986). For a more general perspective, see Dennis, This Little Piggy Went to Market: The Regulation of Risk Arbitrage After Boesky, 52 Alb. L. Rev. 841 (1989). Although prohibiting short tendering was not controversial, the prohibition on hedged tendering was. Why should a shareholder be forbidden to sell a call option on stock that the shareholder has tendered (but still owns and could withdraw)?

[43] 850 F.2d 938 (2d Cir. 1988).

purchase of target securities of the same class be sufficiently distant to escape integration?[44]

Two SEC rules protect the flanks of § 14(d)(7)'s "best price" rule. Rule 14d–10 (the "All Holders Rule") requires that a tender offer be open to all holders of the class. Thus, a bidder cannot limit its tender offer to a limited group (for example, institutional shareholders or target management). Of course, if the group is small enough and private purchases are individually negotiated, such a limited purchasing program will probably not amount to a "tender offer." Interestingly, Rule 14d–10 appears to have been adopted not in response to any abusive tactic by bidders, but to trump a defensive tactic by targets. In response to a hostile bid from Mesa Petroleum (which was controlled by Boone Pickens), Unocal Corp. made a discriminatory self-tender offer for its own shares at a price well above Mesa's offer, which self-tender was open to all shareholders, except Mesa Petroleum. This tactic was upheld by the Delaware Supreme Court,[45] but, although losing the battle, the SEC later won the war by adopting Rules 14d–10 and 13e–4(f)(8).[46] In their wake, a discriminatory self-tender by a target is today unlawful, as federal securities law has effectively preempted a tactic that was permissible under state corporate law.

Rule 14e–5 also enforces this same norm of equal treatment of target shareholders. Subject to some limited exceptions, Rule 14e–5 prohibits a bidder (or its affiliates or agents) from purchasing (or making arrangements to purchase) equity securities that are the subject of the tender offer otherwise than pursuant to the tender offer during the pendency of the offer. Once the offer commences, no private purchase can be arranged or consummated by the bidder with any shareholder.[47]

Issues have arisen about the William Act's "best price" and antidiscrimination rules in a variety of settings. For example, a bidder may make a tender offer, call it off, purchase shares in the open market at a price below the tender price, and then reinstate its tender offer. Can those who sold in the open market at a price below the tender offer price claim that these various steps should be integrated and that therefore

---

[44] Should a court look to the six month safe harbor in Rule 502(a) of Regulation D with respect to the integration of successive sales of unregistered securities? Is this too long given the pace of takeovers? Or, does the obviously egalitarian purpose underlying § 14(d)(7) justify requiring such a time frame before the parties can safely pay insiders more than other shareholders?

[45] See Unocal Corp. v. Mesa Petroleum Co., 493 A.2d 946 (Del.1985).

[46] Rule 13e–4 applies to issuer self-tenders, whereas Rule 14d–10 applies to tender offers by third parties. In Polaroid Corp. v. Disney, 862 F.2d 987 (3d Cir. 1988), the SEC's authority to adopt Rule 14d–10 was upheld, but the Third Circuit found that the target corporation lacked standing to raise a violation of the rule on behalf of its shareholders.

[47] Rule 14e–5 is a successor to a long-standing former rule, Rule 10b–13. A complicated question, which has never been fully resolved, involves who has standing to sue under that rule (besides the SEC). Compare Beaumont v. American Can Co., 797 F.2d 79 (2d Cir. 1986) (non-tendering shareholder may not sue) and Warren v. Bokum Resources Corp., 433 F.Supp. 1360 (D.N.M.1977) (tendering shareholders have cause of action). Rule 14e–5 does not bar purchases outside the tender offer during the subsequent offering period. See Rule 14e–5(a).

they should get the higher tender offer price?[48] Even trickier problems arise when a target officer or a controlling shareholder receives some additional or different consideration that the other shareholders do not receive. What if this consideration was paid by the bidder in the form of an employment contract ostensibly intended to secure the officer's continued employment after the bidder took control of the target? Here, as the next case shows, the critical language in Rule 14d–10 that must be construed is its requirement that "the consideration paid to any security holder for securities tendered in the tender offer is the highest consideration paid to any other security holder for securities tendered in the tender offer."

Epstein v. MCA, Inc.
United States Court of Appeals, Ninth Circuit, 1995.
50 F.3d 644.

■ Before: NORRIS, WIGGINS and O'SCANNLAIN, CIRCUIT JUDGES.

■ NORRIS, CIRCUIT JUDGE:

In 1990, Matsushita Electrical Co., Ltd, ("Matsushita") acquired MCA, Inc. ("MCA") for $6.1 billion. The acquisition was accomplished through a tender offer of $71 per share of MCA common stock.

Lew Wasserman, MCA's chairman and chief executive officer at the time, owned 4,953,927 shares of MCA common stock worth $351,728,817 at the tender price of $71 per share. His cost basis was 3 cents per share. Rather than tender his shares at the tender offer price, Wasserman entered into a separate agreement with Matsushita, known as the "Capital Contribution and Loan Agreement," pursuant to which Wasserman exchanged his shares for preferred stock in a wholly-owned Matsushita subsidiary called "MEA Holdings." Matsushita agreed to fund MEA Holdings by contributing 106% of the tender price multiplied by the number of MCA shares Wasserman exchanged. The MEA Holdings preferred stock Wasserman received pays a dividend of 8.75% annually, is secured by letters of credit, and is redeemable upon the death of Wasserman or his wife, but in no event earlier than five years from the date of the exchange. Wasserman was 77 at the time. It is not disputed that the transaction was designed to be a tax-free exchange of Wasserman's MCA stock under Internal Revenue Code § 351(a) * * *. [Plaintiffs sued claiming that this transaction violated Rule 14d–10, the all holders/best-price rule. The Ninth Circuit first held that a private cause of action could be maintained for a violation of this rule and then turned to the facts of the Wasserman transaction.]

---

[48] For the answer that they can indeed integrate these transactions, see Field v. Trump, 850 F.2d 938 (2d Cir. 1988).

II. THE WASSERMAN TRANSACTION

Captioned the "Equal treatment of securities holders," Rule 14d–10 prohibits a bidder from making a tender offer that is not open to all shareholders or that is made to shareholders at varying prices. The gist of plaintiffs' claims is that Matsushita violated the antidiscrimination requirements of the Rule by paying Wasserman and Sheinberg [MCA's President—eds.] premiums pursuant to the tender offer.

Negotiations between Matsushita and MCA began in August 1990, when a representative of Matsushita telephoned MCA's financial advisor to express interest in acquiring MCA. During the course of the talks, Matsushita stressed that it wanted Wasserman and Sheinberg to commit their shares to Matsushita in advance of the friendly takeover and to remain in MCA's employment for five years. On the morning of November 26, 1990, Matsushita and Wasserman entered into the Capital Contribution and Loan Agreement, pursuant to which Wasserman agreed to exchange his MCA shares for preferred stock in a subsidiary Matsushita would create called "MEA Holdings."

Performance of the Capital Contribution and Loan Agreement was conditioned on the tender offer in several respects. First, neither Matsushita nor Wasserman was obligated to perform the Agreement if any of the conditions of the tender offer were not satisfied. *See* Capital Contribution and Loan Agreement § 7(c). If, for example, Matsushita did not acquire 50% of MCA's common stock as a result of the tender offer, the Wasserman deal would be off. Second, the timing of performance was tied to the tender offer. The Wasserman exchange was scheduled to take place "immediately following the time at which shares of MCA Common Stock are accepted for payment pursuant to and in accordance with the terms of the offer * * *." Id. § 2(a). Third, the amount of cash Matsushita was required to contribute in order to fund MEA Holdings was dependent upon the tender price, with Matsushita agreeing to contribute to MEA Holdings 106% of the "highest price paid * * * for any shares of MCA Common Stock, pursuant to the [tender] offer." Id. at § 1(c). Finally, the redemption value of Wasserman's preferred stock was set as the tender price. Id. Thus if Matsushita increased the tender price at the last minute in response to a competitive bid for MCA, Matsushita would have been required to increase both its funding of MEA Holdings and the amount paid upon the redemption of the Wasserman preferred stock.

Moments after signing the Capital Contribution and Loan agreement, Matsushita and MCA announced the $71 per share tender offer. Shareholders were given from the time of the announcement until 12:01 A.M. on December 29, 1990 to tender their shares. The owners of 91% of MCA's common stock did so, and at 12:05 A.M., Matsushita accepted all tendered shares for payment. At 1:25 A.M., Matsushita exchanged Wasserman's shares for MEA Holdings preferred stock pursuant to the Capital Contribution and Loan Agreement. MCA was merged into Matsushita as a wholly owned subsidiary on January 3, 1991.

Whether the Wasserman transaction violated Rule 14d–10 depends upon whether Wasserman received greater consideration than other MCA shareholders "during such tender offer," Rule 14d–10(a)(2), or whether he received a type of consideration not offered to other MCA shareholders "in a tender offer." Rule 14d–10(c).

Matsushita argues that the Wasserman transaction falls outside the Rule's ambit because it closed *after* the tender offer period expired. The tender offer period, Matsushita contends, ended when it accepted the tendered MCA shares for payment—at 12:05 A.M. on December 29, 1990, one hour and 20 minutes before Wasserman's shares were exchanged. In Matsushita's view, liability under Rule 14d–10 boils down to a pure question of timing: the Rule is simply a "mechanical provision" concerned with "payments to shareholders of a target corporation only *during a specifically-defined tender offer period.*" Brief of Matsushita at 23 (emphasis in original). Outside that period, Matsushita insists, "Rule 14d–10 is without effect" because the Rule "is engaged (or not engaged) depending upon *when payment is made.*" Id. at 23, 35 (emphasis in original).

Although Matsushita argues that Rule 14d–10 is designed to operate only during a "specifically-defined tender offer period," neither the phrase "tender offer period" nor a specific time frame is to be found in the Rule's text. To be sure, section (a)(2) of the Rule prohibits paying one security holder more than another "during such tender offer." But the term "tender offer," as used in the federal securities laws, has never been interpreted to denote a rigid period of time. On the contrary, in order to prevent bidders from circumventing the Williams Act's requirements, Congress, the SEC, and the courts have steadfastly refused to give the term a fixed definition. Instead, we have held that "[t]o serve the purposes of the Williams Act, there is a need for flexibility in fashioning a definition of a tender offer." SEC v. Carter Hawley Hale Stores, Inc., 760 F.2d 945 (9th Cir. 1985) * * *.

An inquiry more in keeping with the language and purposes of Rule 14d–10 focuses not on when Wasserman was paid, but on whether the Wasserman transaction was an integral part of Matsushita's tender offer. If it was, Matsushita violated Rule 14d–10 because it paid him, pursuant to the tender offer, different, and perhaps more valuable consideration than it offered to other shareholders.

Matsushita contends that the Wasserman transaction cannot be deemed a part of the tender offer because it was merely a private exchange of stock, structured to take place after the tender offer finished. But Matsushita's assumption that the Wasserman transaction was private, rather than a part of the tender offer, begs the question. In Field v. Trump, 850 F.2d at 944, the Second Circuit held that "[w]hether [an] acquisition of shares in a corporation is part of the tender offer for purposes of the Act cannot be determined by rubber-stamping the label used by the acquiror." To hold otherwise, the court stated, would render "virtually all of the provisions of the Williams Act, including its filing and disclosure requirements," subject to evasion "simply by an offeror's announcement that offers to purchase * * * stock were private purchases." Id. Thus, the court observed that because the Williams Act and its implementing regulations do not define the term "tender offer," "[c]ourts faced with the question of whether purchases of a corporation's shares are privately negotiated or are part of a tender offer have applied a functional test that scrutinizes such purchases in the context of various salient characteristics of tender offers and the purposes of the Williams Act." Id. at 943–44. *See also* SEC Release No. 34–22198, 1985 WL 61507, 1985 SEC LEXIS 1175, at *7 (July 1, 1985) ("[T]he fact that * * * different consideration is offered to different holders of the same class of securities, does not mean that a tender offer has not been made under the Williams Act. Rather, if such a transaction is found to be a tender offer, then the tender offer would not have been made in compliance with the all-holders requirement").

Because the terms of the Wasserman Capital Contribution and Loan Agreement were in several material respects conditioned on the terms of the public tender offer, we can only conclude that the Wasserman transaction was an integral part of the offer and subject to Rule 14d–10's requirements. Two facts compel this conclusion: first, the redemption value of Wasserman's preferred stock incorporated the tender offer price by reference, and second, the Capital Contribution and Loan Agreement was conditioned on the tender offer's success. If the tender offer failed, Wasserman would have remained the owner of his MCA stock. This is precisely the arrangement Matsushita made with its shareholders through its public tender offer: if an insufficient number of shares were tendered, each shareholder too would have retained ownership of her MCA stock. The deal Matsushita made with Wasserman thus differed from the tender offer in only one material respect—the type (and possibly the value) of consideration provided. Rule 14d–10(c)(1) forbids just such a transaction.

To be sure, the fact that a private purchase of stock and a public tender offer are both part of a single plan of acquisition does not, by itself, render the purchase a part of a tender offer for purposes of Rule 14d–10. Rule 14d–10 does not prohibit transactions entered into or effected before, or after, a tender offer—provided that all material terms of the transaction stand independent of the tender offer. Thus a bidder who purchases shares from a particular shareholder before a tender offer begins does not violate Rule 14d–10. See, e.g., Kahn v. Virginia Retirement System, 13 F.3d 110 (4th Cir. 1993) (bidder's *unconditional* private purchase of target's shares two days before tender offer was formally announced did not violate section 14(d)(7) and rule 14d–10), *cert. denied,* 114 S.Ct. 1834, 128 L.Ed.2d 462 (1994).

If, in advance of the tender offer, Wasserman had become unconditionally obligated to exchange his MCA shares, the transaction would not have violated Rule 14d–10, even if Matsushita believed that acquiring Wasserman's shares was a first step in acquiring MCA. In such a case, both Wasserman and Matsushita would have assumed the burdens of their agreement despite the risk that an anticipated tender offer should fail, or command a different price. But such a course was not followed. Matsushita sought to acquire MCA *without* purchasing the holdings of individual shareholders block by block and accordingly subjecting itself to the risk that it would end up with a huge investment in MCA stock, but without control. The tender offer device is designed to avoid this risk, but only if holders of the same security are offered precisely the same consideration * * *.

Accordingly, we reverse the summary judgment in favor of Matsushita * * *, reverse the district court's order denying plaintiff's motion for partial summary judgment that the Wasserman transaction did violate Rule 14d–10, and remand for further proceedings on the question whether the consideration Wasserman received in exchange for his MCA stock had a greater value than what plaintiffs received and, if so, how much greater * * *.

---

1. *MCA Distinguished.* The *MCA* case was reversed by the Supreme Court on unrelated grounds (a prior class action in Delaware Chancery Court was found to preclude it[49]). Even though the Supreme Court did not reach the issues of scope and standing under Rule 14d–10, other appellate courts have disagreed with the approach of the Ninth Circuit in its *MCA* decision and suggested a much narrower, more formalistic reading of Rule 14d–10. The leading such decision is Lerro v. Quaker Oats Co.[50] In it, the Quaker Oats Company ("Quaker") offered $14 in cash for all the shares of Snapple Beverage Corporation (for a total of $1.7 billion). At least thirty-five percent of Snapple was owned by a single investor (Thomas H. Lee), and Quaker entered into a separate Distributor Agreement with a company controlled by him, which granted this company the exclusive right to distribute in certain Midwestern states certain Snapple and Gatorade products. Focusing on the expected profits under this agreement, plaintiffs contended that the agreement provided Mr. Lee with extra compensation in violation of Rule 14d–10 and § 14(d)(7) of the 1934 Act. Hence, a similar amount had to be paid, plaintiffs asserted, to every other security holder who tendered shares pursuant to the tender offer.

The district court dismissed this claim on the ground that because the distributorship agreement had been signed prior to the commencement of the tender offer, it fell outside Rule 14d–10, which

---

[49] See Matsushita Electric Industrial Co. v. Epstein, 516 U.S. 367 (1996).
[50] 84 F.3d 239 (7th Cir. 1996).

applies only to "consideration paid to any other security holder during such tender offer."[51] The Seventh Circuit agreed, but did not limit its holding to this factual setting alone. Plaintiffs also contended that the tender offer and the merger were a single integrated transaction, and hence because the Distributor Agreement was conditioned on the merger's approval, it should be seen, they argued, as having been negotiated and closed as part of that integrated transaction. Such a rule, the Seventh Circuit responded, would "imperil countless ordinary transactions, * * * [including] simple employment agreements under which the surviving entity promises to employ managers for stated terms or give severance pay."[52] However, the Seventh Circuit opinion conceded that if an investor, such as Mr. Lee, were paid $14 during the tender offer along with other shareholders, but an additional $6 one month later, this "boot" could be treated as having been paid during the tender offer.[53]

Although the Lerro v. Quaker Oats decision thus acknowledges that a "boot" transaction (which it did not define) would fall within the proscription of Rule 14d–10, its basic approach is to fashion a bright-line test that gives practitioners certainty. Under it, the key question is: did the shareholder sell shares in the period between the public announcement of the tender offer and its expiration or withdrawal? This approach may be criticized as underinclusive. For example, suppose a bidder pays the same amount to all shareholders, but also pays the target CEO $5 million in cash for signing a noncompete agreement. These are the facts of Gerber v. Computer Associates International, Inc.,[54] but there the district court refused to dismiss the complaint, and the Second Circuit affirmed,[55] with the latter partially ducking the issue by noting that because the agreement followed the press release announcing the tender offer, a tender offer had actually begun. Although the Second Circuit in Field v. Trump and the Ninth Circuit in *MCA* have formulated an "integral part" test, the Seventh Circuit (and a number of district courts) prefer the bright-line test of *Lerro*. The Third Circuit has fashioned an apparent compromise standard that rejects *Lerro*'s bright-line formalism but requires the plaintiff to plead scienter and allege facts with particularity that demonstrate the motive for the side payment.[56] Before concluding that the Seventh Circuit's "bright line" standard is underinclusive, however, one needs to consider the problems that lurk in

---

[51] See Lerro v. Quaker Oats Co., 897 F.Supp. 1131 (N.D.Ill.1995). Other courts have reached a similar result. See, e.g., Kramer v. Time Warner Inc., 937 F.2d 767, 778–79 (2d Cir. 1991); Kahn v. Virginia Retirement System, 783 F.Supp. 266, 269–70 (E.D.Va.1992), aff'd on other grounds, 13 F.3d 110 (4th Cir. 1993). For the view that *Lerro* states the better approach, see Janon A. Gonzalez, Sunglasses: The Secret to Making Tender Offers Fashionable, 1 NYU J. of Law & Business 335 (2005).

[52] 84 F.3d 239, 244.

[53] Id. at 245.

[54] 2000 U.S. Dist. LEXIS 21727 (E.D.N.Y. Nov. 7, 2000).

[55] 303 F.3d 126 (2d Cir. 2002).

[56] In re Digital Island Sec. Litig., 357 F.3d 322 (3d Cir. 2004).

the more expansive, "integral part" tests of the Second and Ninth Circuits, as next examined.

2. *Overinclusion and Employment Agreements.* The "integral part" test swept very broadly if the bidder sought to negotiate to retain target employees or to cause them to enter into noncompete agreements. Even when these employees owned too few shares to be capable of meaningful resistance to the tender offer, plaintiffs have still been successful in asserting violations of Rule 14d–10, at least to the extent of defeating motions to dismiss. For example, in Pererz v. Chiron Corp.,[57] the bidder granted "put" options at the tender offer price to non-tendering, option-holding employees, thereby insulating them from any future decline in the target's stock price. Under *MCA*, this was, however, viewed as an "integral part" of the tender offer, and hence the action could not be dismissed. In Gerber v. Computer Associates Int'l, Inc.,[58] a payment made to the target's chief executive officer for signing a noncompete agreement was found by a jury to constitute additional compensation for his shares. While Gerber involved a chief executive officer whose 25% ownership seemingly controlled the company, the share ownership held by the officers in Katt v. Titan Acquisitions[59] was under 2%, and yet the district court still rejected a motion to dismiss a complaint that alleged that the acquirer's willingness to honor the target executives' employment agreements violated Rule 14d–10, even though the employment agreements had been adopted or amended by the target, itself, months before the tender offer when the target decided to put itself up for sale.[60]

The stakes in these cases were often enormous because of the "best price" rule. Given the damages inherent in Rule 14d–10, one commentator has recently observed that:

> A claim that a 0.1% holder of a twenty billion dollar company received an extra five million dollars in compensation would carry damages of five billion dollars.[61]

As a result, some acquirers began to favor a statutory merger over a tender offer, even though a merger took longer and was more expensive to the parties, because it could not trigger Rule 14d–10.

Eventually, in 2006, the SEC adopted an amendment to Rule 14d–10's best price rule so as to restrict its application in cases involving

---

[57] 1996 U.S. Dist. LEXIS 22503 (N.D.Cal. May 8, 1996).

[58] 303 F.3d 126 (2d Cir. 2002). A key, but unstated, distinction between those cases that have imposed liability and those that have not appears to be the percentage of ownership held by the defendants. Obviously, persons holding only a 1% block cannot determine the success of the tender offer, while those with a control block can and so may be able to command a premium.

[59] 133 F.Supp.2d 632 (M.D.Tenn.2000).

[60] Ultimately, this case was dismissed on summary judgment. See Katt v. Titan Acquisitions Ltd., 244 F.Supp.2d 841 (M.D. Tenn. 2003).

[61] See Note, Employment Agreements and Tender Offers: Reforming the Problematic Treatment of Severance Plans Under Rule 14d–10, 102 Colum. L. Rev. 774, 808 (2002); see also Gonzalez, supra note 51.

employment compensation.[62] Under it, Rule 14d–10(a)(2) was amended to clarify that the best price rule applies only with respect to the consideration offered and paid for securities tendered in the tender offer. In addition, the amendments add a new provision to Rule 14d–10(c) creating an exemption from the third-party best price rule for payments made or to be made, or benefits granted or to be granted, pursuant to employment compensation, severance or other employment benefits arrangements that are entered into by the bidder or the target company with current or future employees and directors of the target company.[63] Finally, for purposes of this new subsection (d), a payment or other arrangement is deemed to be permissible employment compensation or other qualifying employee benefits (and thus exempt from Rule 14d–10), if it was approved by the compensation committee (or another committee of independent directors) of either the acquirer's or the target's board of directors. The premise here appears to be that independent directors would not approve a bribe to the target company's officers. Rule 14d–10 litigation appears to have been reduced by this new rule, but still remains possible in the case of controlling shareholders or where the compensation is not approved by independent directors.

3. *When Does the Offer Commence?* Although there is some tension between the *Quaker Oats* and *MCA* decisions, their combined effect is to place great weight on Rule 14d–2(a), which defines when a tender offer commences. Because the Distributor Agreement and the Merger Agreement in *Quaker Oats* were signed on November 1, 1994 and the tender offer was announced on November 4th, defendants believed that they were in the clear. Plaintiffs contended that because the terms of the offer had already been communicated to Mr. Lee as of the time that he caused the Distributor Agreement to be signed, the offer had been commenced as of that earlier moment under the then applicable provision of Rule 14d–2(a)(5), which looked to the time "the tender offer is first published or sent or given to security holders by the bidder by any means not otherwise referred to in paragraphs (a)(1) through (a)(4) of this rule." The Seventh Circuit rejected this expansive theory, saying that under Rule 14d–2(a)(5), one looked to the "definitive announcement, not negotiations looking toward an offer."[64] This result seems clearly correct, but the Rule has since been revised to drop this clause, possibly in an effort to avoid the interpretation rejected in this case. Still, the risks and damages that could flow from the inadvertent or premature announcement of a tender offer remain real.

---

[62] See Securities Exchange Act Release No. 54684 (Nov. 1, 2006). A corresponding change was also made for Rule 13e–4(f)(8)(ii) for issuer self-tender offers.

[63] No analogous safe harbor was created under the issuer best-price rule for self-tender offers.

[64] 84 F.3d 239, 245.

D. LITIGATION ISSUES

Litigation in takeover battles has gained a somewhat disreputable reputation, because the litigants often are seeking not a judicial victory, but one or more of several ulterior purposes: to harass their adversary, to gain a discovery "window" into their opponent's planning, or, at best, to require corrective disclosure that will delay the consummation of the offer.[65] In general, courts have recognized this tendency and tend to resist allowing courtroom battles to decide the outcome of a fundamentally economic contest.[66]

Possibly as a result of a skeptical view of takeover litigation, courts have sometimes imposed significant obstacles on the private plaintiff seeking to enforce the Williams Act. First, as a matter of standing, the Supreme Court made clear in *Chris-Craft* that a bidder does not have a private right of action to sue for damages because it is not among those for whose "especial benefit" the statute was enacted.[67] Still, almost all courts have held that target shareholders have standing to assert violations and seek damages under §§ 14(d)(6) and 14(d)(7) of the Williams Act[68] and have similar standing to seek injunctive relief under § 13(d).[69] But they have resisted shareholder standing to seek damages or divestment under § 13(d).[70] Several decisions have also permitted the target company to sue on behalf of its shareholders, but only to seek equitable relief or corrective disclosure, not divestment.[71]

In the case of § 14(e), it is clear that the statute intentionally abolished the purchaser/seller requirement of Blue Chip Stamps v. Manor Drug Stores.[72] However, courts have disagreed on whether the

---

[65] For a candid statement of these ulterior purposes by a leading takeover practitioner, see Wachtell, Special Tender Offer Litigation Tactics, 32 Bus.Law. 1433 (1977).

[66] Although injunctions requiring corrective disclosure are granted, these will seldom resolve the battle. Injunctions that enjoin the offer or "sterilize" the shares (i.e., preclude the bidder from voting them) are strongly disfavored. See Rondeau v. Mosinee Papers Corp., 422 U.S. 49 (1975).

[67] Piper v. Chris-Craft Industries, Inc., 430 U.S. 1, 35 (1977).

[68] Polaroid Corp. v. Disney, 862 F.2d 987, 996–97 (3d Cir. 1988); Field v. Trump, 850 F.2d 938, 946 (2d Cir. 1988); Pryor v. United States Steel Corp., 794 F.2d 52, 57–58 (2d Cir. 1986).

[69] In Treadway Companies, Inc. v. Care Corp., 638 F.2d 357, 380 (2d Cir. 1980), the Second Circuit held that "an injunction will issue for a violation of § 13(d) only on a showing of irreparable harm to the interests which the section seeks to protect." See also CSX Corporation v. The Children's Investment Fund Management (UK) LLP, 654 F.3d 276 (2d Cir. 2011) (declining to issue injunction against the voting of shares even if a § 13(d) violation was shown).

[70] See Kamerman v. Steinberg, 891 F.2d 424 (2d Cir. 1989); Sanders v. Thrall Car Mfg. Co., 582 F.Supp. 945 (S.D.N.Y.1983), aff'd, 730 F.2d 910 (2d Cir. 1984). Shareholders who purchased at a relevant time period may, however, have a suit under Rule 10b–5 against a bidder who files a materially false Schedule 13D or Schedule 14D-1.

[71] Compare Florida Commercial Banks v. Culverhouse, 772 F.2d 1513 (11th Cir. 1985) (permitting suit for equitable relief) and Liberty Nat. Ins. Holding Co. v. Charter Co., 734 F.2d 545 (11th Cir. 1984) (rejecting injunctive suit seeking divestment).

[72] 421 U.S. 723 (1975).

plaintiff must still have relied on a misrepresentation or omission.[73] The more recent tendency is to permit a shareholder to recover based on a showing of causal injury, and not to require individual reliance; thus, proof that sufficient other shareholders were misled to approve the transaction suffices to show causation.[74] Another unique causation issue in the tender offer context arises when the bidder withdraws, or fails to commence, a tender offer because of allegedly false statements or deceptive conduct by the target or a rival bidder. Can shareholders sue the party whose misstatement caused the bidder to withdraw, claiming to have relied on its misstatement, even though they never had the chance to have their shares accepted? In Panter v. Marshall Field & Co.,[75] the Seventh Circuit found that a withdrawal by the bidder precludes reliance by the individual shareholder. Sound result?

Must the plaintiff prove scienter to establish a prima facie case under § 14(e)? On its face, § 14(e) so closely resembles § 17 of the 1933 Act as to suggest that scienter need not be proven with respect to alleged material misrepresentations or omissions. Nonetheless, some cases have read § 14(e) in pari materia with Rule 10b–5 and required scienter in damage actions.[76]

2. DEFINITIONAL ISSUES: GROUP, TENDER OFFER, AND BIDDER

A. "GROUP" THERAPY

GAF Corp. v. Milstein
United States Court of Appeals, Second Circuit, 1971.
453 F.2d 709.

■ Before KAUFMAN and MANSFIELD, CIRCUIT JUDGES, and LEVET, DISTRICT JUDGE.

■ KAUFMAN, CIRCUIT JUDGE. This appeal involves the interpretation of section 13(d) of the Securities Exchange Act, hitherto a largely unnoticed provision[2] added in 1968 by the Williams Act. We write, therefore, on a

---

[73] Compare Lewis v. McGraw, 619 F.2d 192, 195 (2d Cir. 1980) with Plaine v. McCabe, 797 F.2d 713 (9th Cir. 1986).

[74] See Plaine v. McCabe, supra note 73.

[75] 646 F.2d 271 (7th Cir. 1981). Prior to Panter, the Second Circuit held in Lewis v. McGraw, 619 F.2d 192 (2d Cir. 1980) that fraud by the target company would not support an action under § 14(e) where its effect was to cause the bid never to have been made. Panter extends this holding to the case of an announced, but withdrawn, offer.

[76] See Connecticut Nat. Bank v. Fluor Corp., 808 F.2d 957 (2d Cir. 1987); see also Lowenstein, Section 14(e) of the Williams Act and Rule 10b–5 Comparisons, 71 Geo.L.J. 1311 (1983).

[2] We are aware of only four other cases which considered the section. Bath Industries, Inc. v. Blot, 305 F.Supp. 526 (E.D.Wis.1969), aff'd, 427 F.2d 97 (7th Cir. 1970); Ozark Air Lines, Inc. v. Cox, 326 F.Supp. 1113 (E.D.Mo.1971); Sisak v. Wings and Wheels Express, Inc., CCH Fed.Sec.L.Rep. ¶ 92,991 (S.D.N.Y. Sept. 9, 1970); Grow Chemical Corp. v. Uran, 316 F.Supp.

relatively *tabula rasa,* despite the burgeoning field of securities law. Essentially, section 13(d) requires any person, after acquiring more than 10% (now 5%[4]) of a class of registered equity security, to send to the issuer and the exchanges on which the security is traded and file with the Commission the statement required by the Act. Although the section has not attracted as much comment as section 14(d), also added by the Williams Act and requiring disclosure by persons engaging in tender offers, the section has potential for marked impact on holders, sellers and purchasers of securities.

GAF Corporation filed its complaint in the United States District Court for the Southern District of New York alleging that Morris Milstein, his two sons, Seymour and Paul, and his daughter, Gloria Milstein Flanzer, violated section 13(d) of the Securities Exchange Act first by failing to file the required statements and then by filing false ones. The complaint also alleged violation of section 10(b) based on the same false statements and, in addition, market manipulation of GAF stock. The Milsteins moved for dismissal under Rule 12(b)(6), F.R.Civ.P., on the ground that the complaint failed to state a claim on which relief could be granted or, in the alternative, for summary judgment under Rule 56. Judge Pollack aptly framed the issues involved:

> The ultimate issue presented by the defendants' motion to dismiss the first count is whether, organizing a group of stockholders owning more than 10% of a class of equity securities with a view to seeking control is, without more, a reportable event under Section 13(d) of the Exchange Act; and as to the second count, whether in the absence of a connected purchase or sale of securities, the target corporation claiming violation of Section 10 and Rule 10b(5), has standing to seek an injunction against a control contestant for falsity in a Schedule 13D filing.

324 F.Supp. 1062, 1064–1065 (S.D.N.Y.1971). Judge Pollack granted the Milsteins' motion to dismiss under Rule 12(b)(6), and GAF has appealed. We disagree with Judge Pollack's determination that GAF failed to state a claim under section 13(d) and Rule 13d–1 promulgated thereunder, and thus reverse his order in this respect, but we affirm the dismissal of the second claim of the complaint on the ground that GAF, as an issuer, has no standing under section 10(b).

Before considering the merits of the issues involved on appeal, a statement of the facts as presented in the complaint and the briefs is in order. We note also that in this posture of the proceeding we must accept as true all well pleaded allegations in the complaint.

---

891 (S.D.N.Y.1970). See generally Comment, Section 13(d) and Disclosure of Corporate Equity Ownership, 119 U.Pa.L.Rev. 853 (1971).

[4] As of December 22, 1970, section 13(d)(1) was amended to require filing after the acquisition of 5%. Act of December 22, 1970, Pub.L. No. 91–567, § 1, 84 Stat. 1497, amending Securities Exchange Act § 13(d)(1), 15 U.S.C. § 78m(d)(1).

The four Milsteins received 324,166 shares of GAF convertible preferred stock, approximately 10.25% of the preferred shares outstanding, when The Ruberoid Company, in which they had substantial holdings, was merged into GAF in May, 1967. They have not acquired any additional preferred shares since the merger.

The complaint informs us that at some time after July 29, 1968, the effective date of the Williams Act, the Milsteins "formed a conspiracy among themselves and other persons to act as a syndicate or group for the purpose of acquiring, holding, or disposing of securities of GAF with the ultimate aim of seizing control of GAF for their own personal and private purposes." It is necessary for our purposes to examine only a few of the nine overt acts GAF alleged were taken in furtherance of this conspiracy.

The complaint alleged that initially the Milsteins sought senior management and board positions for Seymour Milstein with GAF. When this sinecure was not forthcoming, the Milsteins allegedly caused Circle Floor Co., Inc., a company in their control, to reduce its otherwise substantial purchases from GAF. It also charged that the Milsteins thereafter undertook a concerted effort to disparage its management and depress the price of GAF common and preferred stock in order to facilitate the acquisition of additional shares. On May 27, 1970, the Milsteins filed a derivative action in the district court, charging the directors, *inter alia,* with waste and spoliation of corporation assets. A companion action was filed in the New York courts. GAF further alleged that these actions were filed only to disparage management, to depress the price of GAF stock and to use discovery devices to gain valuable information for their takeover conspiracy.

In the meantime, the complaint tells us, Paul and Seymour Milstein purchased respectively 62,000 and 64,000 shares of GAF common stock. When GAF contended that the Milsteins were in violation of section 13(d) because they had not filed a Schedule 13D as required by Rule 13d–1, the Milsteins, although disclaiming any legal obligation under section 13(d), filed such a schedule on September 24, 1970. In their 13D statement (appended to the complaint), the Milsteins disclosed their preferred and common holdings and stated they "at some future time [might] determine to attempt to acquire control of GAF. * * * " They also stated that they had "no present intention as to whether or not any additional securities of GAF [might] be acquired by them in the future. * * * " Indeed, within the next two months, commencing with October 2, Paul and Seymour each purchased an additional 41,650 shares of common. The Milsteins thereafter filed a Restated and Amended Schedule 13D on November 10 to reflect these new purchases.

Then, on January 27, 1971, the Milsteins filed a third Schedule 13D, disclosing their intention to wage a proxy contest at the 1971 annual meeting. Although the statement again disclaimed any present intention to acquire additional shares, Paul purchased 28,300 shares of common stock during February, 1971. These last purchases, which brought the Milsteins' total common holdings to 237,600 shares having a value in excess of $2 million and constituting 1.7% of the common shares outstanding, were reflected in a February 23 amendment to the January 27 Schedule 13D.

The last essential datum for our purposes is the proxy contest. On May 10, 1971, it was announced that GAF management had prevailed at the April 16 meeting by a margin of some 2 to 1.

GAF's complaint in this action filed on December 16, 1970, requested that the Milsteins be preliminarily and permanently enjoined from (1) acquiring or attempting to acquire additional GAF stock; (2) soliciting any proxy from a GAF shareholder to vote GAF stock; (3) voting any shares of GAF stock held or acquired during the conspiracy; and (4) otherwise acting in furtherance of the conspiracy. It asks for this relief "until the effects of the conspiracy have been fully dissipated and the unlawful acts committed pursuant to the conspiracy fully corrected. * * *"

I.

At the time the conspiracy allegedly was formed, section 13(d)(1) in relevant part provided:

> Any person who, after acquiring directly or indirectly the beneficial ownership of any equity security of a class which is registered pursuant to section 12 of this title * * *, is directly or indirectly the beneficial owner of more than 10 per centum of such class shall, within ten days after such acquisition, send to the issuer of the security at its principal executive office, by registered or certified mail, send to each exchange where the security is traded, and file with the Commission, a statement. * * *

This section, however, exempts from its filing requirements any acquisition which, "together with all other acquisitions by the same person of securities of the same class during the preceding twelve months, does not exceed 2 per centum of that class." Section 13(d)(6)(B). Section 13(d)(3), which is crucial to GAF's claim, further provides that "[w]hen two or more persons act as a partnership, limited partnership, syndicate, or other group for the purpose of acquiring, holding, or disposing of securities of an issue, such syndicate or group shall be deemed a 'person' for the purposes of [section 13(d)]." On the assumption that the facts alleged in the complaint are true, we cannot conclude other than that the four Milsteins constituted a "group" and thus, as a "person," were subject to the provisions of section 13(d). We also are aware of the charge that the Milsteins agreed after July 29, 1968, to hold their GAF preferred shares for the common purpose of acquiring control of GAF. Furthermore, the individuals collectively or as a "group" held more than 10% of the outstanding preferred shares—a registered class of securities.

Since the section requires a "person" to file only if he acquires more than 2% of the class of stock in a 12-month period after July 29, 1968,[12] the principal question presented to us is whether the complaint alleges as a matter of law that the Milstein *group* "acquired" the 324,166 shares of preferred stock owned by its members after that date. We conclude that it does and thus that it states a claim under section 13(d).

The statute refers to "acquiring directly or indirectly the beneficial ownership of securities." Thus, at the outset, we are not confronted with the relatively simple concept of legal title, but rather with the amorphous and occasionally obfuscated concepts of indirect and beneficial ownership which pervade the securities acts.

The Act nowhere explicitly defines the concept of "acquisition" as used in section 13(d). Although we are aware of Learned Hand's warning "not to make a fortress out of the dictionary," Cabell v. Markham, 148 F.2d 737, 739 (2d Cir.), aff'd, 326 U.S. 404 (1945), some light, although dim, is shed by Webster's Third International Dictionary. It tells us that "to acquire" means "to come into possession [or] control." If the allegations in the complaint are true, then the group, which must be treated as an entity separate and distinct from its members, could have gained "beneficial control" of the voting rights of the preferred stock[13] only after its formation, which we must assume occurred after the effective date of the Williams Act. Manifestly, according to the complaint, the group when formed acquired a beneficial interest in the individual holdings of its members. We find ourselves in agreement with the statement of the Court of Appeals for the Seventh Circuit in Bath Industries, Inc. v. Blot, 427 F.2d 97, 112 (7th Cir. 1970), that in the context of the Williams Act, where the principal concern is focused on the battle for corporate control, "voting control of stock is the only relevant element of beneficial ownership." Thus, we hardly can agree with Judge Pollack that the language of the statute compels the conclusion that individual members must acquire shares before the group can be required to file.

We are well aware of the first catechism of statutory construction which teaches that we should begin the process of interpretation with "the language of the statute itself," see Jones v. Alfred H. Mayer Co., 392 U.S. 409, 420 (1968); that, however, is *toto caelo* from saying that the process must end there or that we are required to blind ourselves to other relevant aids to construction, particularly when dealing with a statute as complex as the one before us. The wisdom of Learned Hand guides us again: "it is one of the surest indexes of a mature and developed jurisprudence * * * to remember that statutes always have some purpose

---

[12] The Milsteins concede that their group would have been required to file if the individual members had acquired additional preferred shares after the effective date of the Williams Act and within a 12-month period which amounted to more than 2% of the outstanding shares.

[13] The convertible preferred stock votes share-for-share with the common stock. Each share of preferred is convertible into 1.25 shares of common stock.

or object to accomplish, whose sympathetic and imaginative discovery is the surest guide to their meaning." Cabell v. Markham, supra, 148 F.2d at 739. See also United States v. Dickerson, 310 U.S. 554, 562 (1940). We are, therefore, totally puzzled by the experienced trial judge's conclusion that "the legislative reports should not be resorted to here since the specific statutory language is clear. * * *" 324 F.Supp. at 1067. Indeed, the statute before us is anything but a model of clarity[14] and the ritualistic approach to statutory interpretation which the district judge suggests would close off the only light available to illumine the statute.

The legislative history, as well as the purpose behind section 13(d), bear out our interpretation. Any residual doubt over its soundness is obviated by the following clear statement appearing in both the House and Senate reports accompanying the Williams Act:

> [Section 13(d)(3)] would prevent a group of persons who seek to pool their voting or other interests in the securities of any issuer from evading the provisions of the statute because no one individual owns more than 10 per cent of the securities. *The group would be deemed to have become the beneficial owner, directly or indirectly, of more than 10 percent of a class of securities at the time they agreed to act in concert. Consequently, the group would be required to file the information called for in section 13(d)(1) within 10 days after they agree to act together, whether or not any member of the group had acquired any securities at that time.* S.Rep. No. 550, 90th Cong., 1st Sess. 8 (1967); H.R.Rep. No. 1711, 90th Cong., 2d Sess. 8–9 (1968), U.S.Code Cong. & Admin.News p. 2818 (Emphasis added).

Indeed, Professor Loss, one of the foremost scholars of securities law, reached the same interpretation in his treatise, citing this passage. 6 L. Loss, Securities Regulation 3664 (Supp.1969).

The Senate and House reports and the Act as finally enacted, contrary to appellees' contention,[15] are entirely consistent in our view. This conclusion is buttressed by a consideration of the purpose of the Act. The 1960's on Wall Street may best be remembered for the pyrotechnics of corporate takeovers and the phenomenon of conglomeration. Although individuals seeking control through a proxy contest were required to comply with section 14(a) of the Securities Exchange Act and the proxy rules promulgated by the SEC, and those making stock tender offers were required to comply with the applicable provisions of the Securities Act,

---

[14] The meaning of "acquiring" hardly could be considered plain when two district court judges recently failed to agree on whether an inheritance of stock was an "acquisition." Compare Sisak v. Wings and Wheels Express, Inc., CCH Fed.Sec.L.Rep. ¶ 92,991 (S.D.N.Y.1970), with Ozark Air Lines, Inc. v. Cox, 326 F.Supp. 1113 (E.D.Mo.1971).

[15] Appellees in their brief "concede" that the 1968 committee reports are "against" them. Professor Loss, co-counsel for the Milsteins both in this and the lower court, informed us at the argument that the view set forth in his treatise was "a mistake" and that this passage is "diametrically opposed to the text of the statute" and the purpose and intent of the Williams Act.

before the enactment of the Williams Act there were no provisions regulating cash tender offers or other techniques of securing corporate control. According to the committee reports:

> The [Williams Act] would correct the current gap in our securities laws by amending the Securities Exchange Act of 1934 to provide for full disclosure in connection with cash tender offers and other techniques for accumulating large blocks of equity securities of publicly held companies. S.Rep. No. 550 at 4; H.R.Rep. No. 1711 at 4, U.S.Code Cong. & Admin.News p. 2814.

Specifically, we were told, "the purpose of section 13(d) is to require disclosure of information by persons who have acquired a substantial interest, or increased their interest in the equity securities of a company by a substantial amount, within a relatively short period of time." S.Rep. No. 550 at 7; H.R.Rep. No. 1711 at 8, U.S.Code Cong. & Admin.News p. 2818. Otherwise, investors cannot assess the potential for changes in corporate control and adequately evaluate the company's worth. See generally Comment, Section 13(d) and Disclosure of Corporate Equity Ownership, 119 U.Pa.L.Rev. 853, 854–55, 858, 865–66 (1971).

That the purpose of section 13(d) is to alert the marketplace to every large, rapid aggregation or accumulation of securities, regardless of [the] technique employed, which might represent a potential shift in corporate control is amply reflected in the enacted provisions. Section 13(d)(1)(C) requires the person filing to disclose any intention to acquire control. If he has such an intention, he must disclose any plans for liquidating the issuer, selling its assets, merging it with another company or changing substantially its business or corporate structure. It is of some interest, moreover, that section 13(d)(6)(D) empowers the Commission to exempt from the filing requirements "any acquisition * * * as not entered into for the purpose of, and not having the effect of, changing or influencing the control of the issuer *or otherwise* as not comprehended within the purpose of [section 13(d)]." (Emphasis added.)

The alleged conspiracy on the part of the Milsteins is one clearly intended to be encompassed within the reach of section 13(d). We have before us four shareholders who together own 10.25% of an outstanding class of securities and allegedly agreed to pool their holdings to effect a takeover of GAF. This certainly posed as great a threat to the stability of the corporate structure as the individual shareholder who buys 10.25% of the equity security in one transaction. A shift in the *loci* of corporate power and influence is hardly dependent on an actual transfer of legal title to shares, and the statute and history are clear on this.

In light of the statutory purpose as we view it, we find ourselves in disagreement with the interpretation of *Bath Industries,* supra, that the group owning more than 10%, despite its agreement to seize control, in addition, must agree to acquire more shares before the filing requirement of section 13(d) is triggered. The history and language of section 13(d) make it clear that the statute was primarily concerned with disclosure of *potential changes* in control resulting from new aggregations of stockholdings and was not intended to be restricted to only individual stockholders who made future purchases and whose actions were, therefore, more apparent.[18] See Comment, Section 13(d) and Disclosure of Corporate Equity Ownership, 119 U.Pa.L.Rev. 853, 869–72 (1971). It hardly can be questioned that a group holding sufficient shares can effect a takeover without purchasing a single additional share of stock.

Two "policy" considerations have been advanced against our interpretation. First, the district judge warned that "[t]he inherent difficulty of ascertaining when a group was formed is akin to an attempt to grasp quicksilver." 324 F.Supp. at 1068. This supposed difficulty, however, would not be dissipated even under his view—that individual members must acquire more than 2% after July 29, 1968, before the group can be compelled to file. The court still would be required to determine whether the individuals indeed constituted a "group." But, we hardly envision this as an insuperable obstacle to stating a claim in a complaint. GAF, in order to succeed on the merits, will have to carry its burden of proof by a fair preponderance of the evidence. It will have to produce evidence establishing that the conspiracy came into being after July 29, 1968, with the purpose of seizing control. If GAF should succeed on the merits, any difficulty in pinpointing the precise date, as distinguished from an approximate time, when the conspiracy was formed and the group became subject to section 13(d) can be one of the elements considered by the district judge in fashioning appropriate equitable relief.

The Milsteins also caution us against throwing our hook into the water and catching too many fish—namely, hundreds of families and other management groups which control companies with registered securities and whose members collectively own more than 5% of a class of the company's stock. Although this problem is not part of the narrow issue we must decide, we cannot close our eyes to the implications of our decision. Upon examination, however, the argument while superficially appealing proves to be totally without substance. Management groups *per se* are not customarily formed for the purpose of "acquiring, holding, or disposing of securities of [the] issuer" and would not be required to file unless the members conspired to pool their securities interests for one of the stated purposes.[20]

---

[18] Section 13(d)(3) refers to groups formed "for the purpose of acquiring, holding, *or* disposing of securities." Bath Industries would read out "holding" and "disposing."

[20] The more difficult question, and a question we need not decide on this appeal, is whether management groups which expressly agree to pool their interests to fight a potential takeover are subject to section 13(d). Nor do we intimate any view on whether an insurgent group which has filed under section 13(d) and subsequently is successful in its takeover bid remains subject to the section. In any event, as we have already indicated, the Commission can forestall any untoward effects under the exemptive power conferred upon it by section 13(d)(6)(D).

II

It is not sufficient that we merely conclude that the allegations of the complaint state a violation of section 13(d). We also must determine whether GAF has standing to assert those violations. Here, unlike in our prior discussion we write with the aid of substantial precedent.

* * *

III

The more difficult question is whether GAF has standing under section 13(d) to seek an injunction against allegedly false and misleading filings. The Milsteins in their brief argue that "the short answer" is that false filing does not violate the section that requires the filing—i.e., section 13(d)—but rather the penal provision on false filings, section 32(a), or one of the antifraud provisions, for example, section 10(b). This response, deceptively pleasing in its simple, compartmental approach to the Securities Exchange Act, immediately brings to mind the Supreme Court's instruction that the securities acts should not be construed technically and restrictively, but "flexibly to effectuate [their] remedial purposes." S.E.C. v. Capital Gains Research Bureau, Inc., 375 U.S. 180, 195 (1963). With this teaching in mind, we conclude that the obligation to file *truthful* statements is implicit in the obligation to file with the issuer, and *a fortiori*, the issuer has standing under section 13(d) to seek relief in the event of a false filing.

The Williams Act was entitled "An Act Providing for full disclosure of corporate equity ownership of securities under the Securities Exchange Act of 1934." In particular, section 13(d) was intended to alert investors to potential changes in corporate control so that they could properly evaluate the company in which they had invested or were investing. Disclosure which is false or misleading subverts this purpose. In some instances, a false filing may be more detrimental to the informed operation of the securities markets than no filing at all. We also find support for our conclusion in section 13(d)(2) which places a continuing obligation on the person filing to amend his statements "[i]f any material change occurs in the facts set forth." Indeed, it is an argument not without force to urge that false statements immediately place those required to file in violation of Rule 13d–2 which requires "prompt" amendment.[23]

* * *

---

[23] GAF informs us that the Milsteins' first Schedule 13D, dated September 24, 1970, was false because it disclaimed any present intention to acquire additional stock, whereas Paul and Seymour Milstein purchased 83,800 shares of GAF common stock within the next two months. The Milsteins, however, did not amend their Schedule 13D until after these purchases were completed. Thus, even assuming that the statement filed on September 24 accurately and truthfully reflected their intentions, clearly those intentions changed when the Milsteins decided to make the additional purchases and before those purchases were actually completed.

IV

In reversing that part of Judge Pollack's order which dismissed Claim I of GAF's complaint on the ground that it failed to state a claim on which relief could be granted, we emphasize that we are not yet called upon to determine whether the Milsteins have in fact violated section 13(d), or, if they have, what relief would be appropriate. That part of Judge Pollack's order dismissing Claim II of the complaint under section 10(b) is affirmed. Costs to the appellant.

---

1. *Who Can Form a Group?* Suppose a beneficial holder of 7% of the common stock of a target company (which is a "reporting" company) enters into discussions with several hedge funds and private equity firms that have no beneficial ownership of the target's stock, but the talks clearly contemplate a takeover of the target by these firms collectively. Has a "group" been formed for purposes of Section 13(d)(3)? The answer of the case law may seem surprising: No! Although neither the text of Section 13(d)(1) or Section 13(d)(3) expressly requires beneficial ownership, the decisions have held that each member of a Section 13(d)(3) group must be a beneficial owner of the target's securities. See Hemispherx Biopharma, Inc. v. Johannesburg Consolidated Investments, 553 F.3d 1351 (11th Cir. 2008); Rosenberg v. XM Ventures, 274 F.3d 137 (3d Cir. 2001). The rationale for this position is "each member of the group must have something to pool."[77] That is, the purpose of Section 13(d)(3) is to prevent a de facto control group from being secretly formed without triggering § 13(d) reporting because each member owned less than 5%. But, if an entity has no beneficial ownership, it cannot contribute to the formation of such a group or otherwise outflank Section 13(d)(3)'s goal. Also, if persons who were not beneficial owners could form a Section 13(d)(3) group (because, for example, one additional group member held more than 5%), the scope of Section 13(d)(3) could become extremely broad as a result of Rule 13d–5's inclusion of "voting" as among the purposes that trigger a group's formation (as next discussed). For example, suppose a 7% beneficial owner discussed how to vote on a disputed proxy issue with several investment bankers and institutional investors (or even its own lawyers) who were all not beneficial owners. Unless the definition of "group" is limited to beneficial owners, such an aggregation could arguably be deemed a Section 13(d)(3) group. Note, however, that the definition of beneficial ownership under Rule 13d–3 is broad and includes the direct or indirect possession of voting or investment power over securities. Thus, if a shareholder and a non-shareholder reached an agreement under which they shared voting or dispositive power over a specific block of shares, both would be deemed to be the beneficial owners of those shares by Rule 13d–3(a). Finally, even though a non-beneficial owner

---

[77] See Rosenberg v. XM Ventures, 274 F.3d 137, 146 (3d Cir. 2001).

cannot join a Section 13(d)(3) group, agreements or understandings that it reaches with a more than 5% beneficial owner may require the latter to amend its Schedule 13D to make fuller disclosure (if, for example, the latter's investment purpose changed to a control-seeking purpose).

2. *What Makes a Group?* Today, Rule 13d–5 goes beyond the statutory language in § 13(d)(3) quoted in *GAF* to state that a "group" arises "[w]hen two or more persons agree to act together for the purpose of acquiring, holding, *voting*, or disposing of equity securities" (emphasis added). No reference to "voting" appears in § 13(d)(3), which speaks only of "acquiring, holding or disposing." Should voting together be treated the same as acquiring or holding together? Does this chill, for example, the willingness of mutual and pension funds to join together to vote against a management proxy proposal that they consider ill-advised? Of course, the impact of Rule 13d–5 depends on the sanctions available for its violation. In that light, see SEC v. First City Financial Corp., Ltd., infra, p. 831.

Showing that a collection of entities have acquired more than 5% of a class of the securities of a target company and have a common purpose is not by itself sufficient to demonstrate the formation of a Section 13(d)(3) group. Rather, as the Second Circuit has ruled:

> "[W]hether a group exists under section 13(d)(3) turns on whether there is sufficient direct or circumstantial evidence to support the inference of a *formal or informal understanding between [members] for the purpose of acquiring, holding, or disposing of the securities.*"[78]

Close questions can arise under this standard. In Wellman v. Dickinson,[79] the Second Circuit focused on the word "disposing" in § 13(d)(3) and held that five target company shareholders became a "group" when they reached an understanding under which they agreed to sell their stock if a third party could be found to make a takeover proposal for their company. Their unsuccessful defense was that there had been no understanding or agreement on any specific set of terms or any specific takeover proposal, but only a collective willingness to "go with the deal." Is the desire to find a lucrative bidder the same as a purpose to dispose?

Conversely, in Portsmouth Square Inc. v. Shareholders Protective Committee,[80] a committee of shareholders, who solicited funds from other shareholders by requesting an assignment of their dividends in order to fund litigation to challenge the conduct of insiders who had just effected a change in control of the corporation, were found not to be a "group" under § 13(d). Although their "grouphood" was clear in terms of their

---

[78] See CSX Corporation v. The Children's Investment Fund Management (UK) LLP, 654 F.3d 276, 283 (2d Cir. 2011); see also Hallwood Realty Partners, L.P. v. Gotham Partners, LP, 286 F.3d 613, 617 (2d Cir. 2008).

[79] 682 F.2d 355 (2d Cir. 1982).

[80] 770 F.2d 866, 874 (9th Cir. 1985).

level of organization, they lacked the requisite purpose of "acquiring, holding, voting or disposing" in common, as their goal was instead to sue in common. The court stated that their agreement to act together "invoked neither voting power nor investment power" (referring to the twin tests under Rule 13d–3(a)).

In the contemporary environment, the most important issue about "grouphood" involves the recurring pattern of the "activist" hedge fund that tips other funds that it will soon cross the 5% threshold and file a Schedule 13D announcing some campaign to change the target corporation. Assuming that the other hedge funds buy on this information and that they collectively hold more than 5%, are they a group? Assume further, however, that no one has agreed—explicitly or implicitly—to act in concert with the initial "activist" fund, although they may later vote in favor of proxy resolutions proposed by the initial "activist." On similar facts, a number of decisions have found that there is no group.[81] But variations on this fact pattern may change the results.

3. *Investment Purpose.* Suppose a "group" says that it is holding securities "for investment purposes," but it is in fact considering and evaluating a range of options. Item 4 to Schedule 13D requires the reporting person to state the "purpose of the acquisition of securities" and then lists a variety of specific transactions (sales, changes in dividend policy, or changes in board composition, etc.) that must be disclosed if the reporting person has "plans or proposals * * * which relate to" them. In K-N Energy, Inc. v. Gulf Interstate Co.,[82] the court held the claim that a group was holding "for investment purposes" to be materially false when the evidence indicated that it was in fact seeking to influence corporate affairs. Arguably, this doctrine may provide management with a weapon by which to threaten and silence dissident or activist shareholders who seek to persuade management to change corporate policy. In practice, however, courts typically require only corrective disclosure and rarely, if ever, grant injunctive relief for disclosure violations in takeover battles.

Even the SEC has lost in this context. In SEC v. Amster & Co.,[83] the district court did grant summary judgment against the SEC where it had brought an injunctive action against arbitrageurs who took a position in Graphic Scanning Corp. and characterized their investment in their Schedule 13D as being "for the purpose of making an investment in the Company and not with the present intention of acquiring control. * * *" The SEC charged that defendants later abandoned their investment intent, but failed to amend Item 4 of their Schedule 13D promptly to reflect their new intent to acquire control. Rejecting the SEC's claim that "§ 13(d) requires disclosure whenever 'the securities purchaser has a

---

[81] See, e.g., Hallwood Realty Partners, L.P. v. Gotham Partners, 286 F. 3d 613 (2d Cir. 2002); meVC Draper Fisher Industries Juvetson Fund I, Inc. v. Millenium Partners, L.P., 260 F.Supp.2d 616, 631–633 (S.D.N.Y. 2003).

[82] 607 F.Supp. 756 (D.Colo.1983).

[83] 762 F.Supp. 604 (S.D.N.Y.1991).

perceptible desire to influence substantially the issuer's operations' " the court concluded that such a "desire" does rise to level of a "control" purpose that must be disclosed by an amendment to the Schedule 13D. A mere "desire" to influence operations was insufficient, the court said, adding: "If the hot air balloon of desire is separated from the ballast of control purpose or intent, it is free to soar wherever an advocate's winds may blow. * * * [T]he reporting of desires not yet transformed into purpose or intent could mislead investors in manners contrary to the statute's purpose. To change the metaphor, the SEC argues for a 13(d) "Streetcar Named Desire." I do not think that streetcar runs." Although the *Amster* decision may (or may not) signal a shift in the winds of judicial opinion, earlier decisions do seem to have required disclosure of a control purpose whenever the reporting person took any significant step to influence the issuer (or began to prepare to launch a proxy fight or tender offer). See Chromalloy American Corp. v. Sun Chemical Corp., 611 F.2d 240, 246–47 (8th Cir. 1979); Dan River, Inc. v. Unitex Ltd., 624 F.2d 1216, 1226 n. 9 (4th Cir. 1980). Should the SEC's proposed "perceptible desire to influence substantially the issuer's operations" be the test of "grouphood"? Recent decisions strongly suggest otherwise. See CSX Corporation v. The Children's Investment Fund Management (UK) LLP, 654 F.3d 276, 283 (2d Cir. 2011). Note that Item 4 to Schedule 13D also requires reporting persons to disclose any plans or proposals which "relate to or would result in" a change of control, apparently regardless of whether the reporting person has a control purpose.

4. *Can Swaps Confer Beneficial Ownership?* Two hedge funds (TCI and 3G) sought to change the management policies of CSX, a large railroad company. To this end, they purchased CSX shares and entered into cash-settled, total-return equity swaps referencing CSX stock with various banks as counterparties. Total return swaps are contracts in which the parties agree to exchange sums equivalent to the income streams on specified assets. The "long side" of such a swap contract will be paid the returns (dividends plus stock appreciation) on a specified number of shares of a designated company, and the "short side" receives an interest rate on the principal amount that would be needed to buy that number of shares. As a result, the financial return to the long party is roughly equivalent to having borrowed from the short party to buy the specified number of shares, and such a swap enables the long side to increase its investment in a stock without buying the shares. Although the banks on the "short side" need not buy shares in the referenced stock, they are highly likely to do so in order to hedge their risk if the referenced shares appreciate (they may also be willing to vote those shares as the long party would prefer). The two hedge funds took care that no one bank held more than 5% of CSX's stock. Based on their position as owners of CSX shares and holders of a larger quantity of total return equity swaps on CSX stock, the two hedge funds undertook a proxy fight in 2008 to elect a minority slate of directors to CSX's board of directors. CSX promptly sued, alleging that the two funds had formed a Section 13(d)(3)

group based on their beneficial ownership of the CSX shares held by the banks as a hedge against the CSX-referenced equity swaps. The District Court rejected the claim that either hedge fund was the beneficial owner of the bank-owned CSX shares based on Rule 13d–3(a) (which looks to whether a person has beneficial ownership of shares based on voting or investment power over them), but it did find that one hedge fund (TCI) was the beneficial owner of these shares under Rule 13d–3(b). That latter rule states:

> "Any person who, directly or indirectly, creates or uses a trust, proxy, power of attorney, pooling arrangement or any other contract, arrangement, or device with the purpose or effect of divesting such person of beneficial ownership of a security or preventing the vesting of such beneficial ownership as part of a plan or scheme to evade the reporting requirements of section 13(d) or (g) of the Act shall be deemed for purposes of such sections to be the beneficial owner of such security."

Because TCI had sought to avoid disclosure of the swaps, the District Court treated TCI as the beneficial owner of the CSX shares held by the banks on the short side of its swaps. However, the District Court declined to "sterilize" the shares (i.e., prevent them from being voted), but did enjoin the defendants from future violations of Section 13(d).[84]

On appeal to the Second Circuit, the panel indicated that they did not accept the District Court's finding that TCI held beneficial ownership over the CSX shares held by the banks and vacated the injunction, but remanded for further findings as to whether the shares owned outright by the two hedge funds gave rise to a Section 13(d)(3) group.[85] The SEC indicated throughout the litigation that it did not believe that beneficial ownership can be predicated upon equity swaps.

Nonetheless, on the policy level, the issue remains open, and critics of takeovers want legislative reform if the SEC will not reconsider its position. Bidders can today easily leverage their investment through equity swaps and seemingly escape a disclosure obligation under Section 13(d) (at least so long as the collective outright stock ownership of the group members remains below 5%). Should they be able to do so? *Query*: Could CSX have alleged that the hedge funds and the banks collectively formed a group? (It actually alleged only that the two hedge funds were a group). If the swaps had not been cash settled, and the short side had been obligated to deliver the CSX shares to TCI on the termination of the swap, would this create beneficial ownership in TCI?

---

[84] CSX Corp. v. Children's Investment Fund Management (UK) LLP, 562 F.Supp.2d 511 (S.D.N.Y. 2008).

[85] CSX Corp. v. Children's Investment Fund Management (UK) LLP, 654 F.3d 276 (2d Cir. 2011).

Securities and Exchange Commission v. First City Financial Corp., Ltd.
United States Court of Appeals, District of Columbia Circuit, 1989.
890 F.2d 1215.

■ Before EDWARDS, GINSBURG and SILBERMAN, CIRCUIT JUDGES.

■ SILBERMAN, CIRCUIT JUDGE.

Section 13(d) of the Securities Exchange Act of 1934, 15 U.S.C. § 78m(d), requires any person who has directly or indirectly obtained the beneficial ownership of more than 5 percent of any registered equity security to disclose within 10 days certain information to the issuer, the exchanges on which the security trades, and to the Securities and Exchange Commission ("SEC"). The SEC charged appellants, First City Financial Corporation, Ltd. ("First City") and Marc Belzberg, with deliberately evading section 13(d) and its accompanying regulations in their attempted hostile takeover of Ashland Oil Company ("Ashland") by filing the required disclosure statement after the 10 day period. The district court concluded that appellants had violated the statute; it then enjoined them from further violations of section 13(d) and ordered them to disgorge all profits derived from the violation. See SEC v. First City Financial Corp., et al. 688 F.Supp. 705 (D.D.C.1988). * * *

I.

The SEC's case is based on its contention that on March 4, 1986 Marc Belzberg, a vice-president of First City, telephoned Alan ("Ace") Greenberg, the Chief Executive Officer of Bear Stearns, a large Wall Street brokerage firm, and asked Greenberg to buy substantial shares of Ashland for First City's account. Appellants claim that Greenberg "misunderstood" Belzberg: the latter intended only to recommend that Bear Stearns buy Ashland for its own account.

* * *

[O]n March 4, Marc Belzberg telephoned Greenberg and engaged him in a short conversation that would be the centerpiece of this litigation. At his deposition, Greenberg described the conversation in the following manner:

> [Marc Belzberg] called me and said something to the effect that—something like, "It wouldn't be a bad idea if you bought Ashland Oil here," or something like that. And I took that to mean that we were going to do another put and call arrangement that we had done in the past. * * * I was absolutely under the impression I was buying at their risk and I was going to do a put and call.[4]

---

[4] Large investors sometimes purchase stock through "put and call agreements." Under these agreements, a broker such as Bear Stearns would purchase the stock subject to the agreement and place it in its own account. The agreement entitles the investor to "call" or purchase the shares from the broker for an agreed upon period at an agreed upon price, the cost

While Greenberg interpreted Marc Belzberg's call as an order to purchase Ashland stock on behalf of First City, Marc Belzberg later claimed that he intended only to recommend that Greenberg buy stock for himself, that is, for Bear Stearns, and that Greenberg apparently misunderstood Belzberg. Immediately after the phone call, Greenberg purchased 20,500 Ashland shares. If purchased for First City, those shares would have pushed First City's Ashland holdings above 5 percent and triggered the beginning of the 10 day filing period of section 13(d). In that event, First City would have been obliged to file a Schedule 13D disclosure statement on March 14 with the SEC.

Between March 4 and 14, Greenberg purchased an additional 330,700 shares of Ashland stock for First City costing more than $14 million. Greenberg called Marc Belzberg periodically during those ten days to discuss various securities, including Ashland. In these conversations, Greenberg reported to Marc Belzberg the increasing number of Ashland shares Greenberg had accumulated. According to Greenberg, Belzberg replied to these reports by saying, " 'Fine, keep going,' or something to that effect." Greenberg also characterized Belzberg's response as "grunt[ing]" approvingly. Belzberg did not squarely deny that testimony; he testified that he, Belzberg, said "uh-huh, I think it's cheap." Over the March 15–16 weekend, Marc Belzberg met with his father and uncles in Los Angeles to discuss Ashland. On Sunday, March 16, Samuel Belzberg decided that First City should continue to buy Ashland stock. Marc Belzberg then advised his father that Greenberg had accumulated a block of Ashland shares that "First City could acquire quickly." Samuel Belzberg later testified that he had no prior knowledge of the Greenberg purchases.

Returning to New York the next morning, March 17, Marc Belzberg called Greenberg and arranged a written put and call agreement for the 330,700 shares Bear Stearns had accumulated. During that conversation, Marc Belzberg did not mention a price to Greenberg. Several days later, Marc Belzberg received the written agreement with a "strike price," or the price Bear Stearns was charging First City, of $43.96 per share. This price was well below the then market price of $45.37; thus, the total March 17 put and call price was almost $500,000 below market. Marc Belzberg apparently expressed no surprise that Bear Stearns was charging almost half a million dollars less than market value. He later testified that he believed that Bear Stearns was acting as a "Santa Claus" and that Greenberg was giving him "a bit of a break" to gain more business from First City in the future.

When Blumenstein, the officer responsible for ensuring First City's compliance with the federal securities laws, noticed the strike price, he

---

to the broker plus interest and a small commission. At the same time, the broker has the right to "put" or sell the shares to the investor at the same price. As a result, the investor rather than the broker bears all of the market risks in buying the stock. The put and call agreements were developed apparently in response to the pre-merger notification requirements of the Hart-Scott-Rodino Act.

immediately met with Marc Belzberg. Blumenstein recognized that the computation of the price reflected only the cost to Bear Stearns of acquiring the stock over the two week period before the written agreement (plus interest and commission), thus creating an inference that First City was the beneficial owner of the securities before March 17. After Blumenstein outlined the problem to Belzberg, the two men called Greenberg on a speakerphone. Belzberg later testified, "I informed Mr. Greenberg [during that conversation] that the letter [the written agreement] was incorrect, that I didn't care what the price of the stock was that he bought for himself, I didn't care what day he made the trades for himself, that I was buying stock from him as of today." Belzberg then testified that Greenberg said, "[Y]ou're right, the letter's wrong, I didn't read it before it went out, throw it out and I will send you a corrected copy." Greenberg, however, testified that Belzberg referred only to an error in the calculation of interest and not to the date on which First City acquired the stock. At the end of the conversation, Belzberg suggested he pay $44.00 per share, 4 cents per share higher than the original strike price but still $1.36, or a total of nearly $450,000, below the market price. At trial, Belzberg admitted to picking the $44 figure "out of the air" and that he "did not want the price [he] was paying to relate to [Greenberg's] cost." Between March 17 and 25, on Marc Belzberg's instructions, Greenberg bought another 890,100 Ashland shares on behalf of First City using several put and call agreements.

After these purchases, Samuel Belzberg sent a letter to Ashland's management, informing them of First City's holdings in their stock and proposing a friendly takeover of the company. Ashland rejected the offer, and on the morning of March 25 the company issued a press release disclosing that First City held between 8 and 9 percent of Ashland's stock. Almost immediately, the price of Ashland stock rose 10 percent to $52.25. The next day, on March 26, First City filed the Schedule 13D disclosure statement required by section 13(d). The statement indicated that First City had accumulated 9 percent of Ashland stock and intended to launch a tender offer for the remaining shares at $60 per share. The market price of Ashland stock then rose to $55, peaking at $55.75 per share the next day. * * *

The district court found that Marc Belzberg and First City entered into an informal put and call agreement on March 4 and then deliberately violated the 10 day filing requirement of section 13(d). The district court, in an extensive opinion, relied primarily on First City's acknowledged ultimate purpose to take over Ashland, Greenberg's understanding of his March 4 telephone conversation with Marc Belzberg, the subsequent conversations between Belzberg and Greenberg, and the suspicious price of the March 17 written agreement. The court discounted Marc Belzberg's "misunderstanding" explanation as "self-serving, inconsistent with his later actions and [not] squar[ing] with the objective evidence." 688 F.Supp. at 712. Belzberg, to put it bluntly, was not credited. The court also refused to consider Greenberg's later testimony that there might have been an "honest misunderstanding" since Greenberg reached that conclusion based only on Belzberg's suggestions and statements. See id. at 720.

The district court permanently enjoined appellants from future violations of section 13(d) because they violated the statute deliberately, showed no "remorse," and were engaged in a business which presented opportunities to violate the statute in the future. See id. at 725–26. The court also ordered appellants to disgorge approximately $2.7 million, representing their profits on the 890,000 shares of Ashland stock acquired between March 14 and 25. The court reasoned that appellants were able to purchase these shares at an artificially low price due to their failure to make the section 13(d) disclosure on March 14. See id. at 726–28. Appellants appeal the district court's finding of violation as unsupported by the evidence and a product of judicial bias. They further contend that the district court abused its discretion in ordering the injunction and disgorgement remedies.

* * *

IV.

The district court directed disgorgement of profits, and appellants' challenge to this aspect of the order presents an issue of first impression—whether federal courts have the authority to employ that remedy with respect to section 13(d) violations and whether it is appropriate in this sort of case. Appellants also claim that the amount ordered disgorged is excessive. We reject both arguments and affirm the district court's order on these issues as well.

Appellants, by claiming that Congress did not explicitly authorize a monetary remedy for section 13(d) violations, misapprehend the source of the court's authority. Disgorgement is an equitable remedy designed to deprive a wrongdoer of his unjust enrichment and to deter others from violating the securities laws. See SEC v. Tome, 833 F.2d 1086, 1096 (2d Cir. 1987), cert. denied, 486 U.S. 1014, 108 S.Ct. 1751, 100 L.Ed.2d 213 (1988); SEC v. Blavin, 760 F.2d 706, 713 (6th Cir. 1985); SEC v. Texas Gulf Sulphur Co., 446 F.2d 1301, 1307 (2d Cir.), cert. denied, 404 U.S. 1005, 92 S.Ct. 561, 30 L.Ed.2d 558 (1971). "Unless otherwise provided by statute, all the inherent equitable powers of the District Court are available for the proper and complete exercise of that jurisdiction." Porter v. Warner Holding Co., 328 U.S. 395, 398, 66 S.Ct. 1086, 1089, 90 L.Ed. 1332 (1946); see also Mitchell v. Robert DeMario Jewelry, Inc., 361 U.S. 288, 291–92, 80 S.Ct. 332, 334–35, 4 L.Ed.2d 323 (1960). We see no indication in the language or the legislative history of the 1934 Act that even implies a restriction on the equitable remedies of the district courts. See Mills v. Electric Auto-Lite Co., 396 U.S. 375, 391, 90 S.Ct. 616, 625, 24 L.Ed.2d 593 (1970). Disgorgement, then, is available simply because the relevant provisions of the Securities Exchange Act of 1934, sections

21(d) and (e), 15 U.S.C. §§ 78u(d) and (e), vest jurisdiction in the federal courts.

Indeed, appellants concede that disgorgement is rather routinely ordered for insider trading violations despite a similar lack of specific authorizations for that remedy under the securities law. See, e.g., SEC v. Tome, 833 F.2d at 1096; SEC v. Materia, 745 F.2d 197, 201 (2d Cir. 1984); see generally L. Loss, Fundamentals of Securities Regulation 1004–11 (1988). But they seek to distinguish section 13(d) violations as a "technical" transgression of reporting rules that really do not cause injury. In contrast, they argue, insider trading under modern theory is tantamount to theft; an actual injury is inflicted on the individual or institution entitled to confidentiality. Section 13(d), however, is the pivot of the entire Williams Act regulation of tender offers. To be sure, some may doubt the usefulness of that statute generally or the section 13(d) requirement specifically, but it is hardly up to the judiciary to second-guess the wisdom of Congress' approach to regulating takeovers. Suffice it for us to note that section 13(d) is a crucial requirement in the congressional scheme, and a violator, it is legislatively assumed, improperly benefits by purchasing stocks at an artificially low price because of a breach of the duty Congress imposed to disclose his investment position. The disclosure of that position—a holding in excess of 5 percent of another company's stock—suggests to the rest of the market a likely takeover and therefore may increase the price of the stock. Appellants circumvented that scheme, and the theory of the statute, by which we are bound, is that the circumventions caused injury to other market participants who sold stock without knowledge of First City's holdings. We therefore see no relevant distinction between disgorgement of inside trading profits and disgorgement of post-section 13(d) violation profits.

* * *

Since disgorgement primarily serves to prevent unjust enrichment, the court may exercise its equitable power only over property causally related to the wrongdoing. The remedy may well be a key to the SEC's efforts to deter others from violating the securities laws, but disgorgement may not be used punitively. See SEC v. Blatt, 583 F.2d 1325, 1335 (5th Cir. 1978); SEC v. Manor Nursing Centers, Inc., 458 F.2d 1082, 1104 (2d Cir. 1972). Therefore, the SEC generally must distinguish between legally and illegally obtained profits. See CFTC v. British Am. Commodity Options Corp., 788 F.2d 92, 93 (2d Cir.), cert. denied, 479 U.S. 853, 107 S.Ct. 186, 93 L.Ed.2d 120 (1986)....

If exact information were obtainable at negligible cost, we would not hesitate to impose upon the government a strict burden to produce that data to measure the precise amount of the ill-gotten gains. Unfortunately, we encounter imprecision and imperfect information. Despite sophisticated econometric modelling, predicting stock market responses to alternative variables is, as the district court found, at best speculative. Rules for calculating disgorgement must recognize that separating legal from illegal profits exactly may at times be a near-impossible task. See, e.g., Elkind v. Liggett & Myers, Inc., 635 F.2d 156, 171 (2d Cir. 1980).

Accordingly, disgorgement need only be a reasonable approximation of profits causally connected to the violation. In the insider trading context, courts typically require the violator to return all profits made on the illegal trades, see, e.g., SEC v. Texas Gulf Sulphur Co., 446 F.2d 1301, 1307 (2d Cir.). . . .

Although the SEC bears the ultimate burden of persuasion that its disgorgement figure reasonably approximates the amount of unjust enrichment, we believe the government's showing of appellants' actual profits on the tainted transactions at least presumptively satisfied that burden. Appellants, to whom the burden of going forward shifted, were then obliged clearly to demonstrate that the disgorgement figure was not a reasonable approximation. . . .

* * *

Placing the burden on the defendants of rebutting the SEC's showing of actual profits, we recognize, may result, as it has in the insider trader context, in actual profits becoming the typical disgorgement measure. But the line between restitution and penalty is unfortunately blurred, and the risk of uncertainty should fall on the wrongdoer whose illegal conduct created that uncertainty. * * *

New Teeth for § 13(d). With the decision in *First City Financial Corp.*, the SEC acquired a powerful new weapon to combat stock parking. Note also that use of the "put and call" agreements discussed in footnote 4 of the court's opinion have in other cases been criminally prosecuted.[86] *Query:* would disgorgement be equally appropriate if the defendants had filed a timely Schedule 13D but instead of disclosing a control purpose had simply claimed an "investment" purpose? Does the market really believe such claims about purpose when the parties are well-known takeover raiders? Should they justify the very heavy financial penalties imposed in *First City Financial*?

Private Remedies. Although the SEC can now sue for disgorgement (and indeed may seek it in an administrative proceeding under new Section 21B(e) of the 1934 Act), private plaintiffs have fewer remedies available to them. Most federal courts have recognized an implied right of action in the target to seek equitable relief for violations of § 13(d).[87] However, the Supreme Court's decision in *Rondeau v. Mosinee Paper*

---

[86] See United States v. Bilzerian, 926 F.2d 1285 (2d Cir. 1991).

[87] See Florida Commercial Banks v. Culverhouse, 772 F.2d 1513 (11th Cir. 1985); Gearhart Industries, Inc. v. Smith Intern., Inc., 741 F.2d 707 (5th Cir. 1984). However, in Liberty Nat. Ins. Holding Co. v. Charter Co., 734 F.2d 545 (11th Cir. 1984), the Eleventh Circuit found that there was no implied right in the target to seek divestment.

Corp.,[88] which overruled an injunction "sterilizing" the shares held by a defendant who failed to file a Schedule 13D (apparently out of simple ignorance), has been read by most lower federal courts as a virtual bar to the use of divestment or sterilization as remedies in § 13(d) cases.[89] Typically, courts will grant only a temporary injunction pending corrective disclosure.[90]

When shareholders (rather than the target company) sue, standing is again recognized, but courts have not read § 13(d) as authorizing an award of damages.[91] On the other hand, shareholders may have a valid claim under Rule 10b–5 if they purchased shares during an interval in which a materially inaccurate Schedule 13D filed by a defendant was misinforming the market.[92]

B. THE DEFINITION OF "TENDER OFFER"

Securities and Exchange Commission v. Carter Hawley Hale Stores, Inc.
United States Court of Appeals, Ninth Circuit, 1985.
760 F.2d 945.

■ Before: GOODWIN, SNEED, and SKOPIL, CIRCUIT JUDGES.

■ SKOPIL, CIRCUIT JUDGE.

The issue in this case arises out of an attempt by The Limited ("Limited"), an Ohio corporation, to take over Carter Hawley Hale Stores, Inc. ("CHH"), a publicly-held Los Angeles corporation. The SEC commenced the present action for injunctive relief to restrain CHH from repurchasing its own stock in an attempt to defeat the Limited takeover attempt without complying with the tender offer regulations. The district court concluded CHH's repurchase program was not a tender offer. The SEC appeals from the district court's denial of its motion for a preliminary injunction. We affirm.

FACTS AND PROCEEDINGS BELOW

On April 4, 1984 Limited commenced a cash tender offer for 20.3 million shares of CHH common stock, representing approximately 55% of the total shares outstanding, at $30 per share. Prior to the announced offer, CHH stock was trading at approximately $23.78 per share (pre-tender offer price). Limited disclosed that if its offer succeeded, it would

---

[88] 422 U.S. 49 (1975).

[89] See Dan River, Inc. v. Icahn, 701 F.2d 278 (4th Cir. 1983).

[90] A few decisions have granted a short "cooling-off" period for the revised disclosures to reach and be digested by the market. See Kirsch Co. v. Bliss & Laughlin Indus., Inc., 495 F.Supp. 488 (W.D.Mich.1980) (30 day cooling off period). But see, Chromalloy American Corp. v. Sun Chemical Corp., 611 F.2d 240 (8th Cir. 1979).

[91] See Kamerman v. Steinberg, 891 F.2d 424 (2d Cir. 1989); Sanders v. Thrall Car Mfg. Co., 582 F.Supp. 945 (S.D.N.Y.1983), aff'd, 730 F.2d 910 (2d Cir. 1984).

[92] In re Phillips Petroleum Securities Litigation, 881 F.2d 1236 (3d Cir. 1989).

exchange the remaining CHH shares for a fixed amount of Limited shares in a second-step merger.

In compliance with section 14(d) of the Securities Exchange Act of 1934 ("Exchange Act"), Limited filed a Schedule 14D-1 disclosing all pertinent information about its offer. The schedule stated that (1) the offer would remain open for 20-days, (2) the tendered shares could be withdrawn until April 19, 1984, and (3) in the event the offer was oversubscribed, shares would be subject to purchase on a pro rata basis.

While CHH initially took no public position on the offer, it filed an action to enjoin Limited's attempted takeover. Carter Hawley Hale Stores, Inc. v. The Limited, Inc., 587 F.Supp. 246 (C.D.Cal.1984). CHH's motion for an injunction was denied. Id. From April 4, 1984 until April 16, 1984 CHH's incumbent management discussed a response to Limited's offer. During that time 14 million shares, about 40% of CHH's common stock, were traded. The price of CHH stock increased to approximately $29.25 per share. CHH shares became concentrated in the hands of risk arbitrageurs.

On April 16, 1984 CHH responded to Limited's offer. CHH issued a press release announcing its opposition to the offer because it was "inadequate and not in the best interests of CHH or its shareholders." CHH also publicly announced an agreement with General Cinema Corporation ("General Cinema"). CHH sold one million shares of convertible preferred stock to General Cinema for $300 million. The preferred shares possessed a vote equivalent to 22% of voting shares outstanding. General Cinema's shares were to be voted pursuant to CHH's Board of Directors recommendations. General Cinema was also granted an option to purchase Walden Book Company, Inc. a profitable CHH subsidiary, for approximately $285 million. Finally, CHH announced a plan to repurchase up to 15 million shares of its own common stock for an amount not to exceed $500 million. If all 15 million shares were purchased, General Cinema's shares would represent 33% of CHH's outstanding voting shares.

CHH's public announcement stated the actions taken were "to defeat the attempt by Limited to gain voting control of the company and to afford shareholders who wished to sell shares at this time an opportunity to do so." CHH's actions were revealed by press release, a letter from CHH's Chairman to shareholders, and by documents filed with the Securities and Exchange Commission ("SEC")—a Schedule 14D-9 and Rule 13e-1 transaction statement. These disclosures were reported by wire services, national financial newspapers, and newspapers of general circulation. Limited sought a temporary restraining order against CHH's repurchase of its shares. The application was denied. Limited withdrew its motion for a preliminary injunction.

CHH began to repurchase its shares on April 16, 1984. In a one-hour period CHH purchased approximately 244,000 shares at an average price of $25.25 per share. On April 17, 1984 CHH purchased approximately 6.5

million shares in a two-hour trading period at an average price of $25.88 per share. By April 22, 1984 CHH had purchased a total of 15 million shares. It then announced an increase in the number of shares authorized for purchase to 18.5 million.

On April 24, 1984, the same day Limited was permitted to close its offer and start purchasing, CHH terminated its repurchase program having purchased approximately 17.5 million shares, over 50% of the common shares outstanding. On April 25, 1984 Limited revised its offer increasing the offering price to $35.00 per share and eliminating the second-step merger. The market price for CHH then reached a high of $32.00 per share. On May 21, 1984 Limited withdrew its offer. The market price of CHH promptly fell to $20.62 per share, a price below the pre-tender offer price.

On May 2, 1984, two and one-half weeks after the repurchase program was announced and one week after its apparent completion,[1] the SEC filed this action for injunctive relief. The SEC alleged that CHH's repurchase program constituted a tender offer conducted in violation of section 13(e) of the Exchange Act, and Rule 13e–4. On May 5, 1984 a temporary restraining order was granted. CHH was temporarily enjoined from further stock repurchases. The district court denied the SEC's motion for a preliminary injunction, finding the SEC failed to carry its burden of establishing "the reasonable likelihood of future violations * * * [or] * * * a 'fair chance of success on the merits' * * *." SEC v. Carter Hawley Hale Stores, Inc., 587 F.Supp. 1248, 1257 (C.D.Cal.1984) (citations omitted). The court found CHH's repurchase program was not a tender offer because the eight-factor test proposed by the SEC and adopted in Wellman v. Dickinson, 475 F.Supp. 783 (S.D.N.Y.1979), aff'd on other grounds, 682 F.2d 355 (2d Cir. 1982), cert. denied, 460 U.S. 1069 (1983), had not been satisfied. SEC v. Carter Hawley Hale Stores, Inc., 587 F.Supp. at 1255. The court also refused to adopt, at the urging of the SEC, the alternative test of what constitutes a tender offer as enunciated in S-G Securities, Inc. v. Fuqua Investment Co., 466 F.Supp. 1114 (D.Mass.1978). 587 F.Supp. at 1256–57. On May 9, 1984 the SEC filed an emergency application for an injunction pending appeal to this court. That application was denied.

DISCUSSION

* * *

The SEC urges two principal arguments on appeal: (1) the district court erred in concluding that CHH's repurchase program was not a tender offer under the eight-factor *Wellman* test, and (2) the district court erred in declining to apply the definition of a tender offer enunciated in *S-G Securities,* 466 F.Supp. at 1126–27. Resolution of these issues on

---

[1] In addition to seeking to enjoin further stock purchases, the SEC sought preliminary injunctive relief requiring CHH to issue 17.9 million shares of its common stock to trustees who, pending a trial on the merits, would be required to vote such shares in the same proportion as the votes of unaffiliated shareholders. This matter therefore is not moot.

appeal presents the difficult task of determining whether CHH's repurchase of shares during a third-party tender offer itself constituted a tender offer.

1. *The Williams Act.*

   A. *Congressional Purposes*

   The Williams Act amendments to the Exchange Act were enacted in response to the growing use of tender offers to achieve corporate control. Edgar v. MITE Corp., 457 U.S. 624, 632 (1982) (citing Piper v. Chris-Craft Industries, 430 U.S. 1, 22 (1977)). Prior to the passage of the Act, shareholders of target companies were often forced to act hastily on offers without the benefit of full disclosure. See H.R.Rep. No. 1711, 90th Cong., 2d Sess. (1968), reprinted in 1968 U.S.Code, Cong. & Admin.News 2811 ("House Report 1711").[2] The Williams Act was intended to ensure that investors responding to tender offers received full and fair disclosure, analogous to that received in proxy contests. The Act was also designed to provide shareholders an opportunity to examine all relevant facts in an effort to reach a decision without being subject to unwarranted pressure. House Report 1711.

   This policy is reflected in section 14(d), which governs third-party tender offers, and which prohibits a tender offer unless shareholders are provided with certain procedural and substantive protections including: full disclosure; time in which to make an investment decision; withdrawal rights; and pro rata purchase of shares accepted in the event the offer is oversubscribed.

   * * *

   B. *Issuer Repurchases Under Section 13(e)*

   Issuer repurchases and tender offers are governed in relevant part by section 13(e) of the Williams Act and Rules 13e–1 and 13e–4 promulgated thereunder.

   The SEC argues that the district court erred in concluding that issuer repurchases, which had the intent and effect of defeating a third-party tender offer, are authorized by the tender offer rules and regulations. The legislative history of these provisions is unclear. Congress apparently was aware of an intent by the SEC to regulate issuer tender offers to the same extent as third-party offers. Senate Hearings 214–16, 248; Exchange Act Release No. 16,112 [1979] Fed.Sec.L.Rptr. (CCH) ¶ 82,182 at 82,205 (Aug. 16, 1979) (proposed amendments to tender offer rules). At the same time, Congress recognized issuers might engage in "substantial repurchase programs

---

[2] For additional discussion of the concerns giving rise to the Williams Act amendments, see Full Disclosure of Corporate Equity Ownership and in Corporate Takeover Bids: Hearing on S. 510 Before the Subcommittee on Securities of the Senate Committee on Banking and Currency, 90th Cong., 1st Sess. (1967) ("Senate Hearings"); Takeover Bids: Hearing on H.R. 14475, and S. 510 Before the Subcommittee on Commerce and Finance of the House Committee on Interstate and Foreign Commerce, 90th Cong., 2d Sess. (1968) ("House Hearings").

* * * inevitably affect[ing] market performance and price levels." House Hearings at 14–15; see also House Report 1711 at 2814–15. Such repurchase programs might be undertaken for any number of legitimate purposes, including with the intent "to preserve or strengthen * * * control by counteracting tender offer or other takeover attempts. * * * " House Report 1711 at 2814; House Hearings at 15. Congress neither explicitly banned nor authorized such a practice. Congress did grant the SEC authority to adopt appropriate regulations to carry out congressional intent with respect to issuer repurchases. The legislative history of section 13(e) is not helpful in resolving the issues.

There is also little guidance in the SEC Rules promulgated in response to the legislative grant of authority. Rule 13e–1 prohibits an issuer from repurchasing its own stock during a third-party tender offer unless it discloses certain minimal information. The language of Rule 13e–1 is prohibitory rather than permissive. It nonetheless evidences a recognition that not all issuer repurchases during a third-party tender offer are tender offers. Id. In contrast, Rule 13e–4 recognizes that issuers, like third parties, may engage in repurchase activity amounting to a tender offer and subject to the same procedural and substantive safeguards as a third-party tender offer. The regulations do not specify when a repurchase by an issuer amounts to a tender offer governed by Rule 13e–4 rather than 13e–1.[3]

We decline to adopt either the broadest construction of Rule 13e–4, to define issuer tender offers as virtually all substantial repurchases during a third-party tender offer, or the broadest construction of Rule 13e–1, to create an exception from the tender offer requirements for issuer repurchases made during a third-party tender offer. Like the district court, we resolve the question of whether CHH's repurchase program was a tender offer by considering the eight-factor test established in *Wellman,* 587 F.Supp. at 1256–57.[4]

To serve the purposes of the Williams Act, there is a need for flexibility in fashioning a definition of a tender offer. See Smallwood v. Pearl Brewing Co., 489 F.2d 579 (5th Cir.), cert. denied 419 U.S. 873 (1974). The *Wellman* factors seem particularly well suited in determining when an issuer repurchase program during a third-party tender offer will

---

[3] The procedural and substantive requirements that must be complied with under Rule 13e–4 differ from those under Rule 13e–1. An issuer engaged in a repurchase under Rule 13e–1 is required to file a brief statement with the SEC setting forth the amount of shares purchased; the purpose for which the purchase is made; and the source and amount of funds used in making the repurchase. CHH complied with the requirements of Rule 13e–1.

An issuer engaged in a tender offer under Rule 13e–4 must comply with more burdensome regulations. All the substantive and procedural protections for shareholders come into play under Rule 13e–4 including: full disclosure; time in which to make investment decisions; withdrawal rights; and requirements for pro rata purchase of shares. CHH did not comply with Rule 13e–4.

[4] We have followed the *Wellman* test in another context, see Polinsky v. MCA, Inc., 680 F.2d 1286, 1290–91 (9th Cir. 1982) (open market purchases made in anticipation of a tender offer met none of the *Wellman* indicia), but have not addressed the question of the applicability of the *Wellman* factors to issuer repurchase programs during third-party tender offers.

itself constitute a tender offer. *Wellman* focuses, *inter alia,* on the manner in which the offer is conducted and whether the offer has the overall effect of pressuring shareholders into selling their stock. *Wellman,* 475 F.Supp. at 823–24. Application of the *Wellman* factors to the unique facts and circumstances surrounding issuer repurchases should serve to effect congressional concern for the needs of the shareholder, the need to avoid giving either the target or the offeror any advantage, and the need to maintain a free and open market for securities.

2. *Application of the Wellman Factors.*

Under the *Wellman* test, the existence of a tender offer is determined by examining the following factors:

> (1) Active and widespread solicitation of public shareholders for the shares of an issuer; (2) solicitation made for a substantial percentage of the issuer's stock; (3) offer to purchase made at a premium over the prevailing market price; (4) terms of the offer are firm rather than negotiable; (5) offer contingent on the tender of a fixed number of shares, often subject to a fixed maximum number to be purchased; (6) offer open only for a limited period of time; (7) offeree subjected to pressure to sell his stock; [and (8)] public announcements of a purchasing program concerning the target company precede or accompany rapid accumulation of a large amount of target company's securities.

475 F.Supp. at 823–24.

Not all factors need be present to find a tender offer; rather, they provide some guidance as to the traditional indicia of a tender offer. Id. at 824; see also Zuckerman v. Franz, 573 F.Supp. 351, 358 (S.D.Fla.1983).

The district court concluded CHH's repurchase program was not a tender offer under *Wellman* because only "two of the eight indicia" were present. 587 F.Supp. at 1255. The SEC claims the district court erred in applying *Wellman* because it gave insufficient weight to the pressure exerted on shareholders; it ignored the existence of a competitive tender offer; and it failed to consider that CHH's offer at the market price was in essence a premium because the price had already risen above pre-tender offer levels.

A. *Active and Widespread Solicitation*

The evidence was uncontroverted that there was "no direct solicitation of shareholders." 587 F.Supp. 1253. No active and widespread solicitation occurred. See Brascan Ltd. v. Edper Equities Ltd., 477 F.Supp. 773, 789 (S.D.N.Y.1979) (no tender offer where defendant "scrupulously avoided any solicitation upon the advice of his lawyers"). Nor did the publicity surrounding CHH's repurchase program result in a solicitation. 587 F.Supp. 1253–54. The only public announcements by CHH were those mandated by SEC or Exchange rules. See Ludlow Corp.

v. Tyco Laboratories, 529 F.Supp. 62, 68–69 (D.Mass.1981) (schedule 13d filed by purchaser could not be characterized as forbidden publicity); Crane Co. v. Harsco Corp., 511 F.Supp. 294, 303 (D.Dela.1981) (Rule 13e–1 transaction statement and required press releases do not constitute a solicitation); but cf. S-G Securities, Inc., 466 F.Supp. at 1119–21 (tender offer present where numerous press releases publicized terms of offer).

B. *Solicitation for a Substantial Percentage of Issuer's Shares*

Because there was no active and widespread solicitation, the district court found the repurchase could not have involved a solicitation for a substantial percentage of CHH's shares. 587 F.Supp. 1253–54. It is unclear whether the proper focus of this factor is the solicitation or the percentage of stock solicited. The district court probably erred in concluding that, absent a solicitation under the first *Wellman* factor, the second factor cannot be satisfied, see Hoover Co. v. Fuqua Industries, [1979–80] Fed.Sec.L.Rptr. (CCH) ¶ 97,107 at 96,148 n. 4 (N.D.Ohio 1979) (second *Wellman* factor did not incorporate the type of solicitation described in factor one), but we need not decide that here. The solicitation and percentage of stock elements of the second factor often will be addressed adequately in an evaluation of the first *Wellman* factor, which is concerned with solicitation, and the eighth *Wellman* factor, which focuses on the amount of securities accumulated. In this case CHH did not engage in a solicitation under the first *Wellman* factor but did accumulate a large percentage of stock as defined under the eighth *Wellman* factor. An evaluation of the second *Wellman* factor does not alter the probability of finding a tender offer.

C. *Premium Over Prevailing Market Price*

The SEC contends the open market purchases made by CHH at market prices were in fact made at a premium not over market price but over the pre-tender offer price. At the time of CHH's repurchases, the market price for CHH's shares (ranging from $24.00 to $26.00 per share) had risen above the pre-tender offer price (approximately $22.00 per share). Given ordinary market dynamics, the price of a target company's stock will rise following an announced tender offer. Under the SEC's definition of a premium as a price greater than the pre-tender offer price, a premium will always exist when a target company makes open market purchases in response to a tender offer even though the increase in market price is attributable to the action of the third-party offeror and not the target company. See LTV Corp. v. Grumman Corp., 526 F.Supp. 106, 109 & n. 7 (E.D.N.Y.1981) (an increase in price due to increased demand during a tender offer does not represent a premium). The SEC definition not only eliminates consideration of this *Wellman* factor in the context of issuer repurchases during a tender offer, but also underestimates congressional concern for preserving the free and open market. The district court did not err in concluding a premium is determined not by reference to pre-tender offer price, but rather by reference to market price. This is the definition previously urged by the

SEC, Exchange Act Release No. 16,385 [1979–80] Fed.Sec.L.Rptr. (CCH) ¶ 82,374 at 82,605 (Nov. 29, 1979) (footnotes omitted) (proposed amendments to tender offer rules) (premium defined as price "in excess of * * * the current market price * * *"), and is the definition we now apply. See LTV Corp., 526 F.Supp. at 109 & n. 7.

D. *Terms of Offer Not Firm*

There is no dispute that CHH engaged in a number of transactions or purchases at many different market prices. 587 F.Supp. at 1254.

E. *Offer Not Contingent on Tender of Fixed Minimum Number of Shares*

Similarly, while CHH indicated it would purchase up to 15 million shares, CHH's purchases were not contingent on the tender of a fixed minimum number of shares. 587 F.Supp. at 1254.

F. *Not Open for Only a Limited Time*

CHH's offer to repurchase was not open for only a limited period of time but rather was open "during the pendency of the tender offer of The Limited." 587 F.Supp. at 1255. The SEC argues that the offer was in fact open for only a limited time, because CHH would only repurchase stock until 15 million shares were acquired. The fact that 15 million shares were acquired in a short period of time does not translate into an issuer-imposed time limitation. The time within which the repurchases were made was a product of ordinary market forces, not the terms of CHH's repurchase program.

G–H. *Shareholder Pressure and Public Announcements Accompanying a Large Accumulation of Stock*

With regard to the seventh *Wellman* factor, following a public announcement, CHH repurchased over the period of seven trading days more than 50% of its outstanding shares. 587 F.Supp. at 1255. The eighth *Wellman* factor was met.

The district court found that while many shareholders may have felt pressured or compelled to sell their shares, CHH itself did not exert on shareholders the kind of pressure the Williams Act proscribes. Id.

While there certainly was shareholder pressure in this case, it was largely the pressure of the marketplace and not the type of untoward pressure the tender offer regulations were designed to prohibit. See Panter v. Marshall Field & Co., 646 F.2d 271, 286 (7th Cir.) (where no deadline and no premium, shareholders "were simply not subjected to the proscribed pressures the Williams Act was designed to alleviate"), cert. denied, 454 U.S. 1092 (1981); Brascan Ltd. v. Edper Equities, 477 F.Supp. at 789–92 (without high premium and threat that the offer will disappear, large purchases in short time do not represent the kind of pressure the Williams Act was designed to prevent); Kennecott Copper Corp. v. Curtiss-Wright Corp., 449 F.Supp. 951, 961 (S.D.N.Y.), aff'd in relevant part, rev'd in part, 584 F.2d 1195, 1207 (2d Cir. 1978) (where no deadline and no premium, no pressure, other than normal pressure of the marketplace, exerted on shareholders).

CHH's purchases were made in the open market, at market and not premium prices, without fixed terms and were not contingent upon the tender of a fixed minimum number of shares. CHH's repurchase program had none of the traditional indicia of a tender offer. See, e.g., Energy Ventures, Inc. v. Appalachian Co., 587 F.Supp. 734, 739 (D.Del.1984) (major acquisition program involving open market purchases not subject to tender offer regulation); Ludlow Corp. v. Tyco Laboratories, Inc., 529 F.Supp. at 68 (no tender offer where shareholders not pressured into making hasty ill-advised decision due to premium, fixed terms, or active solicitation); LTV Corp. v. Grumman, 526 F.Supp. at 109 (massive buying program, with attendant publicity, made with intent to defeat third-party tender offer, not itself a tender offer); Brascan Ltd. v. Edper Equities, 477 F.Supp. at 792 (the pressure the Williams Act attempts to eliminate is that caused by "a high premium with a threat that the offer will disappear within a certain time").

The shareholder pressure in this case did not result from any untoward action on the part of CHH. Rather, it resulted from market forces, the third-party offer, and the fear that at the expiration of the offer the price of CHH shares would decrease.

The district court did not abuse its discretion in concluding that under the *Wellman* eight factor test, CHH's repurchase program did not constitute a tender offer.

* * *

Affirmed.

Hanson Trust PLC v. SCM Corporation
United States Court of Appeals, Second Circuit, 1985.
774 F.2d 47.

■ Before MANSFIELD, PIERCE and PRATT, CIRCUIT JUDGES.

■ MANSFIELD, CIRCUIT JUDGE.

Hanson Trust PLC, HSCM Industries, Inc., and Hanson Holdings Netherlands B.V. (hereinafter sometimes referred to collectively as "Hanson") appeal from an order of the Southern District of New York, 617 F.Supp. 832 (1985), Shirley Wohl Kram, Judge, granting SCM Corporation's motion for a preliminary injunction restraining them, their officers, agents, employees and any persons acting in concert with them, from acquiring any shares of SCM and from exercising any voting rights with respect to 3.1 million SCM shares acquired by them on September 11, 1985. The injunction was granted on the ground that Hanson's September 11 acquisition of the SCM stock through five private and one open market purchases amounted to a "tender offer" for more than 5% of SCM's outstanding shares, which violated §§ 14(d)(1) and (6) of the

Williams Act and rules promulgated by the Securities and Exchange Commission (SEC) thereunder. See 17 C.F.R. §§ 240.14(e)(1) and 240.14d–7. We reverse.

The setting is the familiar one of a fast-moving bidding contest for control of a large public corporation: first, a cash tender offer of $60 per share by Hanson, an outsider, addressed to SCM stockholders; next, a counterproposal by an "insider" group consisting of certain SCM managers and their "White Knight," Merrill Lynch Capital Markets (Merrill), for a "leveraged buyout" at a higher price ($70 per share); then an increase by Hanson of its cash offer to $72 per share, followed by a revised SCM-Merrill leveraged buyout offer of $74 per share with a "crown jewel" irrevocable lock-up option to Merrill designed to discourage Hanson from seeking control by providing that if any other party (in this case Hanson) should acquire more than one-third of SCM's outstanding shares (66⅔% being needed under N.Y.Bus.L. § 903(a)(2) to effectuate a merger), Merrill would have the right to buy SCM's two most profitable businesses (consumer foods and pigments) at prices characterized by some as "bargain basement." The final act in this scenario was the decision of Hanson, having been deterred by the SCM-Merrill option (colloquially described in the market as a "poison pill"), to terminate its cash tender offer and then to make private purchases, amounting to 25% of SCM's outstanding shares, leading SCM to seek and obtain the preliminary injunction from which this appeal is taken. A more detailed history of relevant events follows.

SCM is a New York corporation with its principal place of business in New York City. Its shares, of which at all relevant times at least 9.9 million were outstanding and 2.3 million were subject to issuance upon conversion of other outstanding securities, are traded on the New York Stock Exchange (NYSE) and Pacific Stock Exchange. Hanson Trust PLC is an English company with its principal place of business in London. HSCM, a Delaware corporation, and Hanson Holdings Netherlands B.V., a Netherlands limited liability company, are indirect wholly-owned subsidiaries of Hanson Trust PLC.

On August 21, 1985, Hanson publicly announced its intention to make a cash tender offer of $60 per share for any and all outstanding SCM shares. Five days later it filed the tender offer documents required by § 14(d)(1) of the Williams Act and regulations issued thereunder. The offer provided that it would remain open until September 23, unless extended, that no shares would be accepted until September 10, and that

> Whether or not the Purchasers [Hanson] purchase Shares pursuant to the Offer, the Purchasers may thereafter determine, subject to the availability of Shares at favorable prices and the availability of financing, to purchase additional Shares in the open market, in privately negotiated transactions, through another tender offer or otherwise. Any such purchases of additional Shares might be on terms which are the same as,

or more or less favorable than, those of this Offer. The Purchasers also reserve the right to dispose of any or all Shares acquired by them. Offer to Purchase For Cash Any and All Outstanding Shares of Common Stock of SCM Corporation (Aug. 26, 1985) at 21.

On August 30, 1985, SCM, having recommended to SCM's stockholders that they not accept Hanson's tender offer, announced a preliminary agreement with Merrill under which a new entity, formed by SCM and Merrill, would acquire all SCM shares at $70 per share in a leveraged buyout sponsored by Merrill. Under the agreement, which was executed on September 3, the new entity would make a $70 per share cash tender offer for approximately 85% of SCM's shares. If more than two-thirds of SCM's shares were acquired under the offer the remaining SCM shares would be acquired in exchange for debentures in a new corporation to be formed as a result of the merger. On the same date, September 3, Hanson increased its tender offer from $60 to $72 cash per share. However, it expressly reserved the right to terminate its offer if SCM granted to anyone any option to purchase SCM assets on terms that Hanson believed to constitute a "lock-up" device. Supplement Dated September 5, 1985, to Offer to Purchase, at 4.

The next development in the escalating bidding contest for control of SCM occurred on September 10, 1985, when SCM entered into a new leveraged buyout agreement with its "White Knight," Merrill. The agreement provided for a two-step acquisition of SCM stock by Merrill at $74 per share. The first proposed step was to be the acquisition of approximately 82% of SCM's outstanding stock for cash. Following a merger (which required acquisition of at least 66⅔%), debentures would be issued for the remaining SCM shares. If any investor or group other than Merrill acquired more than one-third of SCM's outstanding shares, Merrill would have the option to buy SCM's two most profitable businesses, pigments and consumer foods, for $350 and $80 million respectively, prices which Hanson believed to be below their market value.

Hanson, faced with what it considered to be a "poison pill," concluded that even if it increased its cash tender offer to $74 per share it would end up with control of a substantially depleted and damaged company. Accordingly, it announced on the Dow Jones Broad Tape at 12:38 P.M. on September 11 that it was terminating its cash tender offer. A few minutes later, Hanson issued a press release, carried on the Broad Tape, to the effect that "all SCM shares tendered will be promptly returned to the tendering shareholders."

At some time in the late forenoon or early afternoon of September 11 Hanson decided to make cash purchases of a substantial percentage of SCM stock in the open market or through privately negotiated transactions. Under British law Hanson could not acquire more than 49% of SCM's shares in this fashion without obtaining certain clearances, but acquisition of such a large percentage was not necessary to stymie the SCM-Merrill merger proposal. If Hanson could acquire slightly less than one-third of SCM's outstanding shares it would be able to block the $74 per share SCM-Merrill offer of a leveraged buyout. This might induce the latter to work out an agreement with Hanson, something Hanson had unsuccessfully sought on several occasions since its first cash tender offer.

Within a period of two hours on the afternoon of September 11 Hanson made five privately-negotiated cash purchases of SCM stock and one open-market purchase, acquiring 3.1 million shares or 25% of SCM's outstanding stock. The price of SCM stock on the NYSE on September 11 ranged from a high of $73.50 per share to a low of $72.50 per share. Hanson's initial private purchase, 387,700 shares from Mutual Shares, was not solicited by Hanson but by a Mutual Shares official, Michael Price, who, in a conversation with Robert Pirie of Rothschild, Inc., Hanson's financial advisor, on the morning of September 11 (before Hanson had decided to make any private cash purchases), had stated that he was interested in selling Mutual's Shares' SCM stock to Hanson. Once Hanson's decision to buy privately had been made, Pirie took Price up on his offer. The parties negotiated a sale at $73.50 per share after Pirie refused Price's asking prices, first of $75 per share and, later, of $74.50 per share. This transaction, but not the identity of the parties, was automatically reported pursuant to NYSE rules on the NYSE ticker at 3:11 P.M. and reported on the Dow Jones Broad Tape at 3:29 P.M.

Pirie then telephoned Ivan Boesky, an arbitrageur who had a few weeks earlier disclosed in a Schedule 13D statement filed with the SEC that he owned approximately 12.7% of SCM's outstanding shares. Pirie negotiated a Hanson purchase of these shares at $73.50 per share after rejecting Boesky's initial demand of $74 per share. At the same time Rothschild purchased for Hanson's account 600,000 SCM shares in the open market at $73.50 per share. An attempt by Pirie next to negotiate the cash purchase of another large block of SCM stock (some 780,000 shares) from Slifka & Company fell through because of the latter's inability to make delivery of the shares on September 12.

Following the NYSE ticker and Broad Tape reports of the first two large anonymous transactions in SCM stock, some professional investors surmised that the buyer might be Hanson. Rothschild then received telephone calls from (1) Mr. Mulhearn of Jamie & Co. offering to sell between 200,000 and 350,000 shares at $73.50 per share, (2) David Gottesman, an arbitrageur at Oppenheimer & Co. offering 89,000 shares at $73.50, and (3) Boyd Jeffries of Jeffries & Co., offering approximately 700,000 to 800,000 shares at $74.00. Pirie purchased the three blocks for Hanson at $73.50 per share. The last of Hanson's cash purchases was completed by 4:35 P.M. on September 11, 1985.

In the early evening of September 11 SCM successfully applied to Judge Kram in the present lawsuit for a restraining order barring

Hanson from acquiring more SCM stock for 24 hours. On September 12 and 13 the TRO was extended by consent pending the district court's decision on SCM's application for a preliminary injunction. Judge Kram held an evidentiary hearing on September 12–13, at which various witnesses testified, including Sir Gordon White, Hanson's United States Chairman, two Rothschild representatives (Pirie and Gerald Goldsmith) and stock market risk-arbitrage professionals (Robert Freeman of Goldman, Sachs & Co., Kenneth Miller of Merrill Lynch, and Danial Burch of D.F. King & Co.). Sir Gordon White testified that on September 11, 1985, after learning of the $74 per share SCM-Merrill leveraged buyout tender offer with its "crown jewel" irrevocable "lock-up" option to Merrill, he instructed Pirie to terminate Hanson's $72 per share tender offer, and that only thereafter did he discuss the possibility of Hanson making market purchases of SCM stock. Pirie testified that the question of buying stock may have been discussed in the late forenoon of September 11 and that he had told White that he was having Hanson's New York counsel look into whether such cash purchases were legally permissible.

SCM argued before Judge Kram (and argues here) that Hanson's cash purchases immediately following its termination of its $72 per share tender offer amounted to a *de facto* continuation of Hanson's tender offer, designed to avoid the strictures of § 14(d) of the Williams Act, and that unless a preliminary injunction issued SCM and its shareholders would be irreparably injured because Hanson would acquire enough shares to defeat the SCM-Merrill offer. Judge Kram found that the relevant underlying facts (which we have outlined) were not in dispute * * * and concluded that "[w]ithout deciding what test should ultimately be applied to determine whether Hanson's conduct constitutes a 'tender offer' within the meaning of the Williams Act * * * SCM has demonstrated a likelihood of success on the merits of its contention that Hanson has engaged in a tender offer which violates Section 14(d) of the Williams Act." * * * The district court, characterizing Hanson's stock purchases as "a deliberate attempt to do an 'end run' around the requirements of the Williams Act," * * * made no finding on the question of whether Hanson had decided to make the purchases of SCM before or after it dropped its tender offer but concluded that even if the decision had been made after it terminated its offer preliminary injunctive relief should issue. From this decision Hanson appeals.

Discussion

A preliminary injunction will be overturned only when the district court abuses its discretion. * * *

Since, as the district court correctly noted, the material relevant facts in the present case are not in dispute, this appeal turns on whether the district court erred as a matter of law in holding that when Hanson terminated its offer and immediately thereafter made private purchases of a substantial share of the target company's outstanding stock, the purchases became a "tender offer" within the meaning of § 14(d) of the Williams Act. Absent any express definition of "tender offer" in the Act, the answer requires a brief review of the background and purposes of § 14(d).

* * *

The typical tender offer, as described in the Congressional debates, hearings and reports on the Williams Act, consisted of a general, publicized bid by an individual or group to buy shares of a publicly-owned company, the shares of which were traded on a national securities exchange, at a price substantially above the current market price. * * * The offer was usually accompanied by newspaper and other publicity, a time limit for tender of shares in response to it, and a provision fixing a quantity limit on the total number of shares of the target company that would be purchased.

Prior to the Williams Act a tender offeror had no obligation to disclose any information to shareholders when making a bid. The Report of the Senate Committee on Banking and Currency aptly described the situation: "by using a cash tender offer the person seeking control can operate in almost complete secrecy. At present, the law does not even require that he disclose his identity, the source of his funds, who his associates are, or what he intends to do if he gains control of the corporation."

* * *

The purpose of the Williams Act was, accordingly, to protect the shareholders from that dilemma by insuring "that public shareholders who are confronted by a cash tender offer for their stock will not be required to respond without adequate information." Piper v. Chris-Craft Industries, 430 U.S. 1, 35 (1977); Rondeau v. Mosinee Paper Corp., 422 U.S. 49, 58 (1975).

Congress took "extreme care," 113 Cong.Rec. 24664 (Senator Williams); id. at 854 (Senator Williams), however, when protecting shareholders, to avoid "tipping the balance of regulation either in favor of management or in favor of the person making the takeover bid." * * *

Congress finally settled upon a statute requiring a tender offer solicitor seeking beneficial ownership of more than 5% of the outstanding shares of any class of any equity security registered on a national securities exchange first to file with the SEC a statement containing certain information specified in § 13(d)(1) of the Act, as amplified by SEC rules and regulations. Congress' failure to define "tender offer" was deliberate. Aware of "the almost infinite variety in the terms of most tender offers" and concerned that a rigid definition would be evaded, Congress left to the court and the SEC the flexibility to define the term.
* * *

Although § 14(d)(1) clearly applies to "classic" tender offers of the type described above * * *, courts soon recognized that in the case of privately negotiated transactions or solicitations for private purchases of stock many of the conditions leading to the enactment of § 14(d) for the most part do not exist. The number and percentage of stockholders are usually far less than those involved in public offers. The solicitation involves less publicity than a public tender offer or none. The solicitees, who are frequently directors, officers or substantial stockholders of the target, are more apt to be sophisticated, inquiring or knowledgeable concerning the target's business, the solicitor's objectives, and the impact of the solicitation on the target's business prospects. In short, the solicitee in the private transaction is less likely to be pressured, confused, or ill-informed regarding the businesses and decisions at stake than solicitees who are the subjects of a public tender offer.

These differences between public and private securities transactions have led most courts to rule that private transactions or open market purchases do not qualify as a "tender offer" requiring the purchaser to meet the pre-filing strictures of § 14(d). Kennecott Copper Corp. v. Curtiss-Wright Corp., 449 F.Supp. 951, 961 (S.D.N.Y.), aff'd in relevant part, 584 F.2d 1195, 1206–07 (2d Cir. 1978); Stromfeld v. Great Atlantic & Pac. Tea Co., Inc., 496 F.Supp. 1084, 1088–89 (S.D.N.Y.), aff'd mem., 646 F.2d 563 (2d Cir. 1980); SEC v. Carter Hawley Hale Stores, Inc., 760 F.2d 945, 950–53 (9th Cir. 1985); Brascan Ltd. v. Edper Equities, Ltd., 477 F.Supp. 773, 791–92 (S.D.N.Y.1979); Astronics Corp. v. Protective Closures Co., 561 F.Supp. 329, 334 (W.D.N.Y.1983); LTV Corp. v. Grumman Corp., 526 F.Supp. 106, 109 (E.D.N.Y.1981); Energy Ventures, Inc. v. Appalachian Co., 587 F.Supp. 734, 739–41 (D.Del.1984); Ludlow v. Tyco Laboratories, Inc., 529 F.Supp. 62, 67 (D.Mass.1981); Chromalloy American Corp. v. Sun Chemical Corp., 474 F.Supp. 1341, 1346–47 (E.D.Mo.), aff'd, 611 F.2d 240 (8th Cir. 1979). The borderline between public solicitations and privately negotiated stock purchases is not bright and it is frequently difficult to determine whether transactions falling close to the line or in a type of "no man's land" are "tender offers" or private deals. This has led some to advocate a broader interpretation of the term "tender offer" than that followed by us in Kennecott Copper Corp. v. Curtiss-Wright Corp., supra, 584 F.2d at 1207, and to adopt the eight-factor "test" of what is a tender offer, which was recommended by the SEC and applied by the district court in Wellman v. Dickinson, 475 F.Supp. 783, 823–24 (S.D.N.Y.1979), aff'd on other grounds, 682 F.2d 355 (2d Cir. 1982), cert. denied, 460 U.S. 1069 (1983), and by the Ninth Circuit in SEC v. Carter Hawley Hale Stores, Inc., supra. The eight factors are:

(1) active and widespread solicitation of public shareholders for the shares of an issuer;

(2) solicitation made for a substantial percentage of the issuer's stock;

(3) offer to purchase made at a premium over the prevailing market price;

(4) terms of the offer are firm rather than negotiable;

(5) offer contingent on the tender of a fixed number of shares, often subject to a fixed maximum number to be purchased;

(6) offer open only for a limited period of time;

(7) offeree subjected to pressure to sell his stock;

* * *

[(8)] public announcements of a purchasing program concerning the target company precede or accompany rapid accumulation of large amounts of the target company's securities. (475 F.Supp. at 823–24).

Although many of the above-listed factors are relevant for purposes of determining whether a given solicitation amounts to a tender offer, the elevation of such a list to a mandatory "litmus test" appears to be both unwise and unnecessary. As even the advocates of the proposed test recognize, in any given case a solicitation may constitute a tender offer even though some of the eight factors are absent or, when many factors are present, the solicitation may nevertheless not amount to a tender offer because the missing factors outweigh those present. Id., at 824; *Carter,* supra, at 950.

We prefer to be guided by the principle followed by the Supreme Court in deciding what transactions fall within the private offering exemption provided by § 4(1) of the Securities Act of 1933, and by ourselves in *Kennecott Copper* in determining whether the Williams Act applies to private transactions. That principle is simply to look to the statutory purpose. In S.E.C. v. Ralston Purina Co., 346 U.S. 119 (1953), the Court stated, "the applicability of § 4(1) should turn on whether the particular class of persons affected need the protection of the Act. An offering to those who are shown to be able to fend for themselves is a transaction 'not involving any public offering.'" Id., at 125. Similarly, since the purpose of § 14(d) is to protect the ill-informed solicitee, the question of whether a solicitation constitutes a "tender offer" within the meaning of § 14(d) turns on whether, viewing the transaction in the light of the totality of circumstances, there appears to be a likelihood that unless the pre-acquisition filing strictures of that statute are followed there will be a substantial risk that solicitees will lack information needed to make a carefully considered appraisal of the proposal put before them.

Applying this standard, we are persuaded on the undisputed facts that Hanson's September 11 negotiation of five private purchases and one open market purchase of SCM shares, totalling 25% of SCM's outstanding stock, did not under the circumstances constitute a "tender offer" within the meaning of the Williams Act. Putting aside for the moment the events preceding the purchases, there can be little doubt that the privately negotiated purchases would not, standing alone, qualify as a tender offer, for the following reasons:

(1) In a market of 22,800 SCM shareholders the number of SCM sellers here involved, six in all, was miniscule compared with the numbers involved in public solicitations of the type against which the Act was directed.

(2) At least five of the sellers were highly sophisticated professionals, knowledgeable in the market place and well aware of the essential facts needed to exercise their professional skills and to appraise Hanson's offer, including its financial condition as well as that of SCM, the likelihood that the purchases might block the SCM-Merrill bid, and the risk that if Hanson acquired more than 33⅓% of SCM's stock the SCM-Merrill lockup of the "crown jewel" might be triggered. Indeed, by September 11 they had all had access to (1) Hanson's 27-page detailed disclosure of facts, filed on August 26, 1985, in accordance with § 14(d)(1) with respect to its $60 tender offer, (2) Hanson's 4-page amendment of that offer, dated September 5, 1985, increasing the price to $72 per share, and (3) press releases regarding the basic terms of the SCM-Merrill proposed leveraged buyout at $74 per share and of the SCM-Merrill asset option agreement under which SCM granted to Merrill the irrevocable right under certain conditions to buy SCM's consumer food business for $80 million and its pigment business for $350 million.

(3) The sellers were not "pressured" to sell their shares by any conduct that the Williams Act was designed to alleviate but by the forces of the market place. Indeed, in the case of Mutual Shares there was no initial solicitation by Hanson; the offer to sell was initiated by Mr. Price of Mutual Shares. Although each of the Hanson purchases was made for $73.50 per share, in most instances this price was the result of private negotiations after the sellers sought higher prices and in one case price protection, demands which were refused. The $73.50 price was not fixed in advance by Hanson. Moreover, the sellers remained free to accept the $74 per share tender offer made by the SCM-Merrill group.

(4) There was no active or widespread advance publicity or public solicitation, which is one of the earmarks of a conventional tender offer. Arbitrageurs might conclude from ticker tape reports of two large anonymous transactions that Hanson must be the buyer. However, liability for solicitation may not be predicated upon disclosures mandated by Stock Exchange Rules. See S.E.C. v. Carter Hawley Hale Stores, Inc., supra, 760 F.2d at 950.

(5) The price received by the six sellers, $73.50 per share, unlike that appearing in most tender offers, can scarcely be dignified with the label "premium." The stock market price on

September 11 ranged from $72.50 to $73.50 per share. Although risk arbitrageurs sitting on large holdings might reap sizeable profits from sales to Hanson at $73.50, depending on their own purchase costs, they stood to gain even more if the SCM-Merrill offer of $74 should succeed, as it apparently would if they tendered their shares to it. Indeed, the $73.50 price, being at most $1 over market or 1.4% higher than the market price, did not meet the SEC's proposed definition of a premium, which is $2.00 per share or 5% above market price, whichever is greater. SEC Exchange Act Release No. 16,385 (11/29/79) [1979–80] Fed.Sec.L.Rep. ¶ 82,374.

(6) Unlike most tender offers, the purchases were not made contingent upon Hanson's acquiring a fixed minimum number or percentage of SCM's outstanding shares. Once an agreement with each individual seller was reached, Hanson was obligated to buy, regardless what total percentage of stock it might acquire. Indeed, it does not appear that Hanson had fixed in its mind a firm limit on the amount of SCM shares it was willing to buy.

(7) Unlike most tender offers, there was no general time limit within which Hanson would make purchases of SCM stock. Concededly, cash transactions are normally immediate but, assuming an inability on the part of a seller and Hanson to agree at once on a price, nothing prevented a resumption of negotiations by each of the parties except the arbitrageurs' speculation that once Hanson acquired 33⅓% or an amount just short of that figure it would stop buying.

In short, the totality of circumstances that existed on September 11 did not evidence any likelihood that unless Hanson was required to comply with § 14(d)(1)'s pre-acquisition filing and waiting-period requirements there would be a substantial risk of ill-considered sales of SCM stock by ill-informed shareholders.

There remains the question whether Hanson's private purchases take on a different hue, requiring them to be treated as a *"de facto"* continuation of its earlier tender offer, when considered in the context of Hanson's earlier acknowledged tender offer, the competing offer of SCM-Merrill and Hanson's termination of its tender offer. After reviewing all of the undisputed facts we conclude that the district court erred in so holding.

In the first place, we find no record support for the contention by SCM that Hanson's September 11 termination of its outstanding tender offer was false, fraudulent or ineffective. Hanson's termination notice was clear, unequivocal and straight-forward. Directions were given, and presumably are being followed, to return all of the tendered shares to the SCM shareholders who tendered them. Hanson also filed with the SEC a statement pursuant to § 14(d)(1) of the Williams Act terminating its tender offer. As a result, at the time when Hanson made its September 11 private purchases of SCM stock it owned no SCM stock other than those shares revealed in its § 14(d) pre-acquisition report filed with the SEC on August 26, 1985.

The reason for Hanson's termination of its tender offer is not disputed: in view of SCM's grant of what Hanson conceived to be a "poison pill" lock-up option to Merrill, Hanson, if it acquired control of SCM, would have a company denuded as the result of its sale of its consumer food and pigment businesses to Merrill at what Hanson believed to be bargain prices. Thus, Hanson's termination of its tender offer was final; there was no tender offer to be "continued." Hanson was unlikely to "shoot itself in the foot" by triggering what it believed to be a "poison pill," and it could not acquire more than 49% of SCM's shares without violating the rules of the London Stock Exchange.

Nor does the record support SCM's contention that Hanson had decided, before terminating its tender offer, to engage in cash purchases. Judge Kram referred only to evidence that "Hanson had *considered* open market purchases before it announced that the tender offer was dropped" (emphasis added) but made no finding to that effect. Absent evidence or a finding that Hanson had decided to seek control of SCM through purchases of its stock, no duty of disclosure existed under the federal securities laws.

Second, Hanson had expressly reserved the right in its August 26, 1985, pre-acquisition tender offer filing papers, whether or not tendered shares were purchased, "*thereafter* * * * to purchase additional Shares in the open market, in privately negotiated transactions, through another tender offer or otherwise." (Emphasis added). * * * Thus, Hanson's privately negotiated purchases could hardly have taken the market by surprise. Indeed, professional arbitrageurs and market experts rapidly concluded that it was Hanson which was making the post-termination purchases.

Last, Hanson's prior disclosures of essential facts about itself and SCM in the pre-acquisition papers it filed on August 26, 1985, with the SEC pursuant to § 14(d)(1), are wholly inconsistent with the district court's characterization of Hanson's later private purchases as "a deliberate attempt to do an 'end run' around the requirements of the Williams Act." * * *

In the present case we conclude that since the district court erred in ruling as a matter of law that SCM had demonstrated a likelihood of success on the merits, based on the theory that Hanson's post-tender offer private purchases of SCM constituted a *de facto* tender offer, it was an abuse of discretion to issue a preliminary injunction. Indeed, we do not believe that Hanson's transactions raise serious questions going to the merits that would provide a fair ground for litigation. In view of this holding it becomes unnecessary to rule upon the district court's determination that the balance of hardships tip in favor of SCM and that absent preliminary relief it would suffer irreparable injury. However, our decision is not to be construed as an affirmance of the district court's resolution of these issues.

* * *

The order of the district court is reversed, the preliminary injunction against Hanson is vacated, and the case is remanded for further proceedings in accordance with this opinion. The mandate shall issue forthwith.

Unconventional Offers. Both *Hanson Trust* and *Carter Hawley Hale* deal with large-scale open market purchasing (or "street sweeps"). This is not the most common pattern. More often litigated have been privately negotiated purchases from a limited group of purchasers. In Hoover Co. v. Fuqua Industries, Inc.,[93] the court held that an offer made to over one hundred members of the family of the founder of the company amounted to a tender offer. Although earlier decisions had found offers to a limited group of sophisticated purchasers not to be a tender offer,[94] the *Hoover* court found that the family shareholders who were there solicited had little in common, had not worked for the company, and owned widely varying shareholdings. Thus, it found the solicitation of the family to be "the equivalent of a solicitation of all the public shareholders." *Query:* should an offer limited to fifty to one hundred of the senior officers of a target corporation be deemed a tender offer? Note that if the answer is yes, Rule 14d–10 requires that the offer be made to all shareholders.

In Wellman v. Dickinson,[95] the court found that a solicitation to sell stock in a target company made to thirty large institutional holders and nine individuals was a tender offer, applying the eight "factors" which are discussed in the *Carter Hawley Hale* case. The solicitation was carried out like a military operation with thirty different representatives of the brokerage firm, each sitting with a lawyer, telephoning the solicitees at 4 p.m. New York time after the close of the New York Stock Exchange and giving them only one hour to decide whether or not to accept the offer, which was at a substantial premium over market. By this operation, the offeror acquired approximately thirty-four percent of the outstanding stock of the target company. The solicitees had been alerted earlier to expect a phone call at 4 p.m. New York time, but were not given the exact price that was going to be offered until those phone calls were made after the close of the market. Judge Carter indicated that in his opinion all the "factors" were satisfied except one, the widespread publication of the offer to the general body of shareholders. It would not

---

[93] Fed.Sec.L.Rep. (CCH) Para. 97,107 (N.D.Ohio 1979). For a case involving a widespread telephone solicitation of shareholders, see Cattlemen's Investment Co. v. Fears, 343 F.Supp. 1248 (W.D.Okl.1972).

[94] See Kennecott Copper Corp. v. Curtiss-Wright Corp., 584 F.2d 1195, 1206 (2d Cir. 1978); D-Z Investment Co. v. Holloway, Fed.Sec.L.Rptr. (CCH) Para. 94,771 (S.D.N.Y.1974).

[95] 475 F.Supp. 783 (S.D.N.Y.1979), aff'd on other grounds, 682 F.2d 355 (2d Cir. 1982).

appear that the *Hanson Trust* case has overruled that decision, although the court did not approve the automatic use of these "factors."

Street Sweeps. In 1979, the SEC proposed, but never adopted, a definition of tender offer that would have included many street sweeps.[96] Under Proposed Rule 14d–1(b)(1), the term "tender offer" would have had four elements: (1) one or more offers to purchase, or solicitations of offers to sell, securities of a single class; (2) during any 45 day period; (3) directed to more than 10 persons; and (4) seeking the acquisition of more than 5% of the class. However, an exception was also proposed for open market purchases by a broker or its customer at the then current market price on a national securities exchange or in the over-the-counter market if three conditions were present: (1) the open market purchases were unsolicited; (2) the broker or dealer performed only the customary functions of a broker or dealer; and (3) the broker or dealer received no more than the customary commission or markup for executing the trade. Does this deal adequately with the "street sweep"? Note that the transaction in *Carter Hawley Hale* would probably not have been a tender offer under the proposed rule, as the purchases were at the then current market price and the other criteria of the open market exemption were also seemingly satisfied.

In 1987, the SEC again proposed, but never adopted, a special rule to deal with street sweeps.[97] Proposed Rule 14d–11 would provide that after the termination of a tender offer a bidder could not for 30 days increase its beneficial ownership in the target by 10 percent or more (except by means of another tender offer). Also, any other person (such as arbitrageurs) would be similarly precluded for ten days. The proposed rule seems to have been a direct response to the *Hanson Trust* case and the problem of the confused aftermarket following the termination of a tender offer.

Obviously, there was an egalitarian dimension to Proposed Rule 14d–11, because the chief beneficiaries of street sweeps are professional investors, who have easy access to the market within the short time frames during which street sweeps occur, while "little" investors typically miss out. An expansive definition of tender offer (without any exclusion for open market purchasing at the market price) might be defended on the ground that it promotes equality of treatment among stockholders. From such a policy perspective, one may well ask a broader question: should not the tender offer be the preferred and indeed mandatory technique for the hostile acquisition (as it is in effect in Great Britain)?

---

[96] Securities Exchange Act Release No. 16385 (Oct. 1, 1987).
[97] Securities Exchange Act Release No. 24976. For an overview, see Oesterle, The Rise and Fall of Street Sweep Takeovers, 1989 Duke L.J. 202. An equivalent to proposed Rule 14a–11 has, however, been adopted for issuer self-tenders. See Rule 13e–4(f)(6) (ten business day cooling off period).

Problems

PROBLEM 10-1

Bidder Co., a New York Stock Exchange-listed company, would like to acquire Target, Inc., which is a "reporting" company and the third largest firm in its principal industry. Because Bidder Co. expects resistance and primarily fears starting an auction, it quietly approaches some twenty institutions, who collectively own 33% of Target, and asks each of them at what price they would be prepared to sell their entire interest in Target. Target was trading in the range of $16 to $17 per share. Three institutions immediately agree to sell at prices between $19 and $20 per share. Five more sell at prices between $21 and $22 after extensive negotiations. Bidder has now acquired 8% and knows that it will soon have to file a Schedule 13-D, disclosing its more than 5% ownership. It now approaches again the remaining dozen institutions and tells them it is their "final chance" to sell and that they may otherwise do less well. Ten of these twelve sell at prices between $22 and $24, with eight also negotiating a "best price" protection that they will receive any higher price Bidder pays anyone else over the next six months for Target shares. As a result, all ten of these firms will receive $24 per share. Bidder now files its schedule 13D, and Target sues to enjoin and rescind these purchases as an illegal tender offer. What result in this litigation?

PROBLEM 10-2

Same facts as before, except that after buying not less than 25% of the stock, Bidder now approaches Bobbie Wasserman, Target's CEO, who also owns 1% of the Target stock, and offers him the same $24 price offered to the institutions. He accepts, and, one week later, now owning 25%, Bidder commences an offer for the remaining stock at $21 per share. Outraged shareholders sue Wasserman for his shares, and Bidder, claiming that Rule 14d–10 has been violated. What result?

PROBLEM 10-3

Same facts as before, but now Wasserman, when approached, agrees to support a tender offer at $23 per share for all shares and to tender his stock into it. Bidder also agrees at this meeting to an employment contract under which Wasserman will receive compensation of $8 million next year, which is more than three times his current level and the equivalent of a $1.50 increase in the tender offer to all shareholders. Again, shareholders sue, alleging a violation of Rule 14d–10 in that the employment contract is a de facto premium to Wasserman, which violates Rule 14d–10. What result now?

C. WHO'S THE BIDDER?

Of course, the party or parties making the contractual offer are included within the term "bidder". So also is a controlling parent of the actual bidder.⁹⁸ But what about an investment bank that arranges and contributes financing and otherwise plays a role that is "central to the offer"?⁹⁹ In this area, as the next case shows, courts have struggled to draw a clear line.

MAI Basic Four, Inc. v. Prime Computer, Inc.

United States Court of Appeals, First Circuit, 1989.
871 F.2d 212.

■ Before CAMPBELL, CHIEF JUDGE, COFFIN, SENIOR CIRCUIT JUDGE, and BOWNES, CIRCUIT JUDGE.

■ COFFIN, SENIOR CIRCUIT JUDGE.

This expedited appeal arises out of the efforts of a group of companies in the computer industry, MAI Basic Four, Choice Corporation, and Brooke Partners, L.P. (collectively Basic), to take over control of Prime Computer, Inc. (Prime). Although Basic filed the first complaint, attacking Massachusetts anti-takeover statutes in connection with its November 15, 1988, tender offer, the present issues flow from the district court's action on Prime's counterclaim. In this counterclaim Prime alleged, principally, that Basic had violated the Williams Act Amendments to the Securities Exchange Act (the Act), by failing to disclose in its Offer to Purchase sufficient information concerning the involvement, interests, and condition of its investment advisor, investor, and underwriter, Drexel Burnham Lambert, Inc. (Drexel). It contended that Drexel fell under the Act's disclosure requirements because it was in reality a "bidder." SEC Rule 14d–1(b)(1); Rule 14d–6; SEC Schedule 14D–1.

Prime sought a preliminary injunction against consummation of the tender offer, which was granted on December 9, 1988. The injunction has survived several subsequent proceedings in which supplemental disclosures made by Basic were considered. The inquiry on this appeal is whether the district court committed either an error of law or abuse of discretion in continuing to enjoin the consummation of the offer pending receipt of further information from Basic regarding Drexel.

THE TENDER OFFER

The elements of the tender offer are as follows. Basic is offering $20 a share in cash for all shares of Prime, a price that exceeds the pre-offer market price. As of the date of oral argument, March 2, 1989, approximately 61 percent of Prime stock had been tendered, 46 percent on a fully diluted basis.¹ The offer is conditioned upon there being

---

⁹⁸ The definition of "bidder" in SEC Rule 14d–1(g)(2) includes "any person who makes a tender offer or on whose behalf a tender offer is made."

⁹⁹ See Koppers Co. v. American Express Co., 689 F.Supp. 1371, 1388 (WD Pa. 1988) (finding investment bank was a bidder).

1 That is, after taking into account additional shares projected to be issued in connection with (or in response to) the tender offer.

tendered, prior to its expiration, 67 percent of the shares on a fully diluted basis. * * * The financing consists of $20 million in cash, supplied by Brooke Partners, L.P.; $650 million in bank financing; and $875 million in high yield, interest bearing, increasing rate notes (*i.e.*, "junk bonds"), placement to be arranged by Drexel. Upon consummation of the offer, Basic intends to merge itself and Prime and cash out any remaining Prime stockholders at $20 a share.

DREXEL'S INVOLVEMENT

Drexel's past, present, and contemplated roles in connection with the offer lie at the heart of this appeal. Since 1986 Drexel has been associated in arranging financing for Basic's principal stockholders, Bennett S. LeBow and William Weksel, in several other acquisitions (of Liggett Group, Inc. and of Western Union Corp.) in which Drexel has obtained both substantial fees and equity positions. In the spring of 1988, Drexel tried unsuccessfully to interest Prime in buying MAI Basic Four. Subsequently, Basic decided to be the acquirer. Drexel's undertaking, as financial advisor for this transaction, is to "include, but not be limited to * * * advising and assisting [Basic] in determining the possible alternative ways in which the Transaction might be structured, and advising and assisting [Basic] with respect to the completion of the Transaction."

Drexel has an equity interest in MAI Basic Four, Inc., which will be 5 percent on a diluted basis, with a right to purchase at half price another 9 percent. In addition to this 14 percent of direct interest, it possesses, through two intermediary partnership entities, a one-third equity interest in LeBow, Inc., and, through another entity, a 17 percent equity interest in Brooke Partners. LeBow, Inc., is the sole owner of L. Holdings, which is Brooke's sole general partner. As of the date of the offer, Drexel also, through a stockholders agreement, had the right to name one of the three directors of LeBow, Inc., with veto power over some corporate actions. During this litigation, the agreement was changed to remove Drexel's right to a board member, but Drexel continues to have the right to attend board meetings and is guaranteed first refusal in future underwriting and placement.

Drexel's role in placing $875 million in junk bonds will entitle it to $65 million in fees, if the placement is successful. At the moment, the record indicates that none of these notes have been sold. Even if the offer fails, Drexel will be entitled to 15 percent of any profit Basic realizes from selling Prime stock now held. There is some ambiguity with regard to a further role Drexel may have in relation to the notes. The offer to Purchase merely reflects Drexel's view that it is "highly confident" that it can place the $875 million of notes and its agreement "to use its best efforts to arrange the financing."

CONTENTIONS OF THE PARTIES

The positions taken by the parties could not be farther apart. Basic * * * challenges the court's finding that Drexel is a bidder. Finally it argues that even if Drexel could be considered a bidder, no additional disclosure is required by the Act. When asked why Basic could not readily furnish the kind of information concerning Drexel that was provided in *Interco,* counsel's response was that other questions would be asked and that "no amount of disclosure is ever going to be enough."

Prime, on the other hand, maintains that Drexel should, as a bidder, furnish all items of information required for compliance with Schedule 14D-1. In oral argument counsel stated, without citing any authority, that even if Drexel is not a bidder, it is still such a key participant that its financial condition was material information which must be more thoroughly disclosed under the Williams Act.

* * *

DISCUSSION

The facts in this case bear some similarity to those in Koppers Co. v. American Express Co., 689 F.Supp. 1371 (W.D.Pa.1988), where an investment bank was held to be a bidder for purposes of Rule 14d. In Koppers, two Shearson entities, Shearson Holdings and its subsidiary Shearson Lehman, and their indirect subsidiary, SL-Merger, Inc., were found collectively to have become aggressively involved in a takeover plan at an early stage; to have contributed $23.05 million for purchasing shares of the target; to own 46 percent of the Class B common stock in the target; to have committed themselves to a contribution of $570 million for notes or preferred stock; and to have earned large brokerage fees. The court accepted, as criteria for a bidder, "those who are central to the offer," 689 F.Supp. at 1388 (citation omitted), "playing a central participatory role," being "a motivating force," "one of the principal planners and players." Id. at 1390. It acknowledged the multiple roles of the Shearson entities—advisor, underwriter, equity partner, financier, broker-dealer—deeming these roles as far surpassing that of an investment banker. The court labelled Shearson "a major equity participant," "one of the entities on whose behalf the tender offer is made." Id.

In the case at bar, Drexel has equity interests in various affiliates associated with LeBow. It has a background of association with Basic and other LeBow interests. Like Shearson in Koppers, Drexel participated in the planning of the Prime tender offer very early, well before the offer. It had a director with veto power in LeBow, Inc., the sole owner of the general partner of Brooke Partners. Brooke in turn supplied the entire $20 million of equity for this highly leveraged deal, which funds Drexel was instrumental in raising through earlier tender offers. Drexel has relinquished this directorship, but only after commencement of the tender offer and without explication. Of course the projected equity position of Drexel is far less than Shearson's 46 percent interest in Koppers. Finally, Drexel will enjoy substantial fees, perhaps in excess of $65 million, for its heavy participation in the offer.

In a similar vein, the present case is at least somewhat distinguishable from City Capital Assocs. Ltd. Partnership v. Interco, Inc., 860 F.2d 60 (3d Cir. 1988). In *Interco,* the court of appeals pointed out that Drexel was not engaged by the acquirer until after the tender offer was made. The court distinguished *Koppers* on the basis that Drexel was to have no representation on the board of the surviving entity, id. at 63 n. 5., and emphasized that there was no indication that Drexel had any control over the offer or that it would have any other role than that of investor. Id. at 63. . . .

Given Drexel's early and pervasive role in the planning and execution of the present offer, its erstwhile board representation in the corporation controlling the sole equity participant in the bidder group, and record evidence sufficient to reasonably suggest an expectation, though not a contractual obligation, that Drexel would itself provide additional financing if it could not place the $875 in junk bonds elsewhere, we might accept the approach of the Third Circuit while distinguishing *Interco* on its facts. Such a decision on our part would be consistent with one of the formulations of the test in *Interco,* that if a stockholder in an acquirer "is in a position to have a significant impact on the future of that corporation, information about the stockholder may well be material to a decision of stockholders of the target whether to take the offer or hang on with the hope of a greater return." Id. at 65.

But we recognize that in the end the court in *Interco* concluded that financial statements are not required from an entity that will wind up as a minority stockholder. It reached this result based on the perceived need for a bright-line test in the takeover context, requiring a narrow construction of Rule 14d–1(b)(1), and a strict application of Schedule 14D-1, General Instruction G, Item 9, 17 C.F.R. § 240.14d–100, reading the latter to indicate that "bidder" under the SEC regulations means an entity formally making a tender offer and those who *control* it. Because the traditional indicia of control were lacking, ipso facto Drexel was deemed not to be a bidder. We think the more realistic prescription is that of *Interco's* dissenter, who wrote:

> [I]n the event of doubt on a particular disclosure question, courts should exercise liberality in order to carry out the remedial purposes of the [Williams Act]. Excess information may well be harmless, but inadequate disclosure could be disastrous to the shareholder.

860 F.2d at 68 (Weis, J., dissenting). The more flexible, fact-based approach advocated by Judge Weis is consistent with our reading of the Williams Act.

The purpose of the Williams Act was explained by an often quoted report of the House Interstate and Foreign Commerce Committee as follows:

> The persons seeking control * * * have information about themselves and about their plans which, if known to investors, might substantially change the assumptions on which the market price is based. This bill is designed to make the relevant facts known so that shareholders have a fair opportunity to make their decision.

H.R.Rep. No. 1711, 90th Cong., 2d Sess. 2, reprinted in 1968 U.S.Code Cong. & Admin.News 2811, 2813.

Section 14(d) of the Act governs the disclosures required of those initiating tender offers. Section 14(d)(1) bars an offer by

> any person, directly or indirectly * * * if, after consummation thereof, such person would, directly or indirectly, be the beneficial owner of more than 5 per centum of such class, unless * * * such person has filed with the Commission a statement containing such of the information specified in section 78m(d) of this title, and such additional information as the Commission may by rules and regulations prescribe as necessary or appropriate in the public interest or for the protection of investors.

15 U.S.C. § 78n(d)(1). The statute then defines "person":

> When two or more persons act as a partnership, limited partnership, syndicate, or other group for the purpose of acquiring, holding, or disposing of securities of an issuer, such syndicate or group shall be deemed a "person" for purposes of this subsection.

Williams Act § 14(d)(2), 15 U.S.C. § 78n(d)(2).

The SEC Rule, 14d–1(b)(1) * * * uses the word "bidder" in place of "person" in the statute. It defines a bidder as "any person who makes a tender offer or on whose behalf a tender offer is made." Id. The SEC, in a 1979 Release, stated that bidder was a "shorthand reference[ ] to [a] principal participant[ ] in a tender offer." Exchange Act Release No. 15,548 [1979 Transfer Binder] Fed.Sec.L.Rep. (CCH) ¶ 81,935, at 81,216 (Feb. 5, 1979). We read the "on whose behalf" language of Rule 14d–1(b)(1) to incorporate the "group" concept of sections 13(d) and 14(d) of the Williams Act. As pointed out by Judge Weis in *Interco,* the statute authorizes the SEC to require "additional information," but does not appear to grant the Commission discretion to narrow the definition of "person" explicitly defined in the Act.

Our interpretation of bidder under Rule 14d–1(b)(1) is consistent with the statute. Section 14(d) of the Act, as quoted supra, by explicit cross-reference incorporates the scope of the disclosure requirements of

§ 13(d), 15 U.S.C. § 78m(d). The definition of "person" in § 14(d)(2) is identical to the formulation found in § 13(d)(3). The legislative history of the latter section contradicts an exclusive focus on control, a factor provisionally raised in Schedule 14D-1, General Instruction G, Item 9, in determining who is a bidder under the regulation. * * *

We distill from these guides, which use the words "directly or indirectly," "on whose behalf," "principal participant[ ]," and "any contract, understanding, relationship, agreement or other arrangement" that there is no bright, hard-line test for bidder under the regulation. We empathize with the Third Circuit when it said in *Interco*, "[t]his is an area of law in which predictability is of crucial importance." 860 F.2d at 64. But we are skeptical. We suspect that any bright-line test, separating those who are subject to the Williams Act from those who are not, would merely invite the ingenuity of resourceful counsel to place their client formally on the desired side of the line, whatever the underlying reality may be.

In this case we cannot say that, as a matter of law, an active advisor-broker-financier-participant who owns less than a majority interest in the surviving entity is not a bidder where, as here, there has been a history of close association, equity sharing, board representation and involvement from the beginning of the present offer, and where there is the possibility of the advisor-broker being the indispensable key to the offer's success. Nor can we say that while a 46 percent stockholder qualifies as a bidder, a 14 percent direct stockholder with other indirect equity interests cannot qualify. At a minimum it is evident that Drexel has "act[ed] as a partnership, limited partnership, * * * or other group for the purpose of acquiring, holding, or disposing of securities of an issuer." 15 U.S.C. § 78n(d)(2). We are not convinced that the district court erred in determining that Prime demonstrated a likelihood of success on the merits, and therefore affirm the court's ruling that Drexel is a bidder.

This does not end our inquiry. We must determine whether the information still required by the court is "material."

> An omitted fact is material if there is a substantial likelihood that a reasonable shareholder would consider it important in deciding how to vote. * * * [This standard] does not require proof of a substantial likelihood that disclosure of the omitted fact would have caused the reasonable investor to change his vote. What the standard does contemplate is a showing of a substantial likelihood that, under all the circumstances, the omitted fact would have assumed actual significance in the deliberations of the reasonable shareholder.

TSC Indus., Inc. v. Northway, Inc., 426 U.S. 438, 449, 96 S.Ct. 2126, 2132, 48 L.Ed.2d 757 (1976). In pointing out that materiality under Item 9 depends on the facts and circumstance of a given case, the SEC has explained:

These may include, but are not limited to * * * (4) the ability of the bidder to pay for the securities sought in the tender offer and/or to repay any loans made by the bidder or its affiliates in connection with the tender offer or otherwise. It should be noted that the factors described above are not exclusive nor is it necessary that any or all such factors be present in order to trigger the materiality test.

Filing and Disclosure Relating to Tender Offers, Exchange Act Release No. 13,787, 42 Fed.Reg. at 38,346 (July 21, 1977).

It is not clear to us that the financial strength or vulnerability of Drexel, including the adverse impact of Drexel's plea bargain and other legal difficulties, is immaterial to Prime shareholders' deliberations. As opposed to the "highly confident" opinion of Drexel and the conclusory report that Drexel has over $2 billion of capital, and despite the argument that Drexel has recently financed far larger deals, the *Interco* submission indicated an equity of $1.4 billion as of June 24, 1988, *before* the $650 million plea bargain. As Judge Friendly put it:

In applying [the materiality] test to a cash tender offer, it is necessary to appreciate the problem faced by a stockholder of the target company in deciding whether to tender, to sell or to hold part or all of his securities. It is true that, in the case of an "any and all" offer such as that here at issue, a stockholder who has firmly decided to tender has no interest in the financial position of the offeror *other than its ability to pay* * * * since he will have severed all financial connections with the target.

Prudent Real Estate Trust v. Johncamp Realty, Inc., 599 F.2d 1140, 1147 (2d Cir. 1979) (emphasis added). Even assuming the professed ability to pay the offered price,

[T]he shareholder of the target company faces a hard problem in determining the most advantageous course of action, a problem whose difficulty is enhanced by his usual ignorance of the course other shareholders are adopting. If the bidder is in a flourishing financial condition, the stockholder might decide to hold his shares in the hope that, if the offer was only partially successful, the bidder might raise his bid after termination of the offer. * * * *Per contra,* a poor financial condition of the bidder might cause the shareholder to accept for fear that control of the company would pass into irresponsible hands.

Id. That shareholders might reasonably hold out for a higher offer is supported by the determination of the Delaware Chancery Court, rejecting Basic's challenge to the institution of takeover defenses by Prime directors, that the directors reasonably relied on independent investment bankers' valuation of Prime stock between $23 and $28 per share. In turn, whether Drexel be seen as weak or strong is a legitimate datum for Prime stockholders.

Nor can we discount the possible impact of Drexel's plea bargain and other legal difficulties as immaterial. This area of corporate cannibalism is not a neat and tidy one. We must rely to a large extent on the judgment of the trial judge who lives with the case. * * *

This leads us to the issue of remedy. We see no reason, even though we have upheld the district court's decision that Drexel is to be considered a bidder, to require a full Schedule 14D-1 disclosure in the exercise of the court's equitable power. We agree with the court in Pacific Realty Trust v. APC Investments, Inc., 685 F.2d 1083, 1086 (9th Cir. 1982), that a curative disclosure is sufficient. See also Riggs Nat'l Bank v. Allbritton, 516 F.Supp. 164, 182 (D.D.C.1981).

We affirm the order of the district court. We further direct that if Basic files with the SEC 1) current financial statements of Drexel, 2) identification of all Drexel-affiliated officers and directors, and 3) disclosure of recent trading in shares by Drexel, then the district court, upon determining that these disclosures appear accurate and reasonably equivalent to the information voluntarily disclosed in *Interco* (but brought up to date), shall vacate the injunction insofar as it is based on nondisclosure. * * *

Materiality Revisited. Why is financial information about a minority shareholder of the bidder material to the shareholders of the target? The First Circuit panel relied on Judge Friendly's statement in *Johncamp Realty, Inc.* that the poor financial condition of the bidder might cause shareholders to accept "for fear that control of the company would pass into irresponsible hands." But if such information will tend to stampede the shareholders into tendering, why should disclosure policy force the bidder to disclose it and thus increase the pressure on target shareholders? Suppose to the contrary that Drexel were in strong financial shape. Would it then be a realistic scenario for the target shareholders to fail to tender "in the hope that * * * the bidder might raise his bid after the termination of the offer?" Isn't it more likely that the bidder will simply use a squeeze-out merger to eliminate holdout shareholders at the same price or at an even lower price?

As a policy matter, an expansive definition of materiality can be defended on the ground that it fosters an auction market and drives up the premiums in takeovers. But the counter-argument is that if the bidder can be delayed interminably in disclosure litigation and forced to pay a higher premium, such a legal policy will reduce the incentive to make a takeover bid and hence eventually reduce the number of takeovers.[100] In light of this debate, what balance does the SEC strike in its instructions to Schedules 13D and 14D-1?

---

[100] Compare Rosenzweig, Target Litigation, 85 Mich.L.Rev. 110 (1986) (target litigation should be discouraged as contrary to shareholder interests) with Jarrell, The Wealth Effects of

3. REFORMING THE TENDER OFFER PROCESS

In late 1999, after much debate, the SEC revised takeover procedures significantly with its adoption of Regulation M–A, whose principal goal, as next described, was to achieve greater transactional parity between cash offers and equity offers. This required significant deregulation and relaxing of the normal rules surrounding the issuance of equity securities (which were analyzed in Chapter 2).

Securities Act Release No. 7760
Securities and Exchange Commission.
October 22, 1999.

* * *

Last fall, we proposed comprehensive changes to the various regulatory schemes applicable to issuer and third-party tender offers, mergers, going-private transactions and security holder communications. The proposed changes were prompted by an increase in the number of transactions where securities are offered as consideration; an increase in the number of hostile transactions involving proxy or consent solicitations; and significant technological advances that have resulted in more and faster communications with security holders and the markets. Because these trends have continued since we issued the Proposing Release and commenters, for the most part, viewed the proposals as favorable, we are adopting the proposals, with some modification.

As we noted in the Proposing Release, the existing regulatory framework imposes a number of restrictions on communications with security holders and the marketplace. In addition, the disparate regulatory treatment of cash and stock tender offers may unduly influence a bidder's choice of offering cash or securities in a takeover transaction. We also noted unnecessary differences in regulatory requirements between tender offers and other types of extraordinary transactions, such as mergers. Finally, we noted that the multiple regulatory schemes that can apply to a transaction may impose additional compliance costs without necessarily providing a sufficient marginal benefit to security holders. Our goals in proposing and adopting these changes are to promote communications with security holders and the markets, minimize selective disclosure, harmonize inconsistent disclosure requirements and alleviate unnecessary burdens associated with the compliance process, without a reduction in investor protection.

* * *

We believe these new rules and revisions should provide participants in the securities markets sufficient flexibility to accommodate changes in

---

Litigation by Targets: Do Interests Diverge in a Merger?, 28 J.L. & Econ. 151 (1985) (target litigation drives up takeover premiums).

deal structure and advances in technology that continue to occur in today's markets. Briefly, the new rules and amendments adopted today will:

* * *

- balance the treatment of stock and cash tender offers by permitting both issuer and third-party stock tender offers to commence as early as the filing of a registration statement;
- simplify and integrate the various disclosure requirements for tender offers, going-private transactions, and other extraordinary transactions in a new series of rules within Regulation S–K, called "Regulation M–A";

* * *

F. Disclosure Requirements for Tender Offers and Mergers

1. Schedules Combined and Disclosure Requirements Moved to Subpart 1000 of Regulation S–K ("Regulation M–A")

Currently, there are different disclosure schedules for issuer tender offers, third-party tender offers and going-private transactions. Since a given transaction may involve more than one of these regulatory schemes, a company may be required to file a separate disclosure document to satisfy each applicable disclosure regime. In addition, the disclosure requirements appearing in the rules and schedules can often lead to duplicative, and sometimes inconsistent, requirements. In light of the increased pressure to announce a business combination transaction soon after it is entered into and the attendant requirement to file mandated disclosure documents quickly, we proposed to integrate, simplify and update the disclosure requirements currently in the rules and schedules. Our basic approach was to combine all the disclosure requirements in one central location in a subpart of Regulation S–K, called Regulation M–A. The specific disclosure requirements in schedules were keyed to items under Regulation M–A in a manner consistent with the integrated disclosure system previously adopted for proxy and registration statements.

All commenters addressing the proposed changes in this area believed that it was time to update and simplify the disclosure requirements for business combination transactions. We are adopting Regulation M–A substantially as proposed. This series of disclosure items incorporates all the current disclosure requirements for issuer and third-party tender offers, tender offer recommendation statements and going-private transactions. The new regulation includes some disclosure items for cash merger proxy statements as well. We have made slight modifications, where necessary, to harmonize and clarify the requirements, as well as a few substantive changes that are discussed below in more detail. In some cases the disclosure requirements may appear different, but that is because we have made an effort to draft the items in Regulation M–A using clear, plain language. In the future, we expect to expand this new regulation to cover additional disclosure items as necessary.

We are combining current Schedules 13E-4 and 14D-1 (the schedules now used for issuer and third-party tender offers, respectively), into new Schedule TO, as proposed. In addition, we are changing the rules to allow one filing to satisfy both the tender offer and going-private disclosure requirements. As a result, the information required by Schedules 14D-1, 13E-4 and 13E-3 can be disclosed in one combined filing. We believe that these revisions will reduce the need to file two or more schedules for what is essentially the same transaction.

We have included an instruction in new Schedule TO, as proposed, listing the specific line items that must be complied with for different types of transactions. In addition, we have revised the current instruction requiring information that is incorporated by reference to be filed as an exhibit. As revised, filers can incorporate information included in documents previously filed electronically on EDGAR without refiling that information as an exhibit to the schedule. To the extent that the existing schedules permit filers to include negative answers in the schedule, but not in the disclosure document sent to security holders, filers will continue to have the ability to omit that information from documents sent to security holders.

At this time we are not extending the one filing satisfies all approach to encompass transactions involving the Securities Act and proxy rules as well as the tender offer and going-private rules. In the future, we may consider integrating the requirements further, to permit the satisfaction of the disclosure required under all four regulatory schemes with one filing.

We also are revising the rules that require filing persons to include a fair and adequate summary of the information required by the schedules in the disclosure document sent to security holders. Instead of specifying some items and excluding others, as the current rules do, the revised rules simply require that the document given to security holders summarize all items in the schedule (except for exhibits). As noted in the Proposing Release, this change is not intended to increase the amount of information that is given to security holders. Instead, it is intended to simplify the requirements. We expect filers to exercise their judgment in determining the specific information that must be included in the disclosure document sent to security holders to provide a fair and adequate summary. We are not, however, changing the current requirement that certain disclosure required in a going-private transaction be set forth in full in the disclosure document delivered to security holders.

The Goal of Transaction Parity. The basic thrust of Regulation M–A is to deregulate shareholder communications incident to most forms of business combinations and takeovers in order to ensure that acquirers offering equity securities do not operate at a substantial disadvantage to those offering cash. Prior to these rules, a prospective acquirer who proposed to exchange its securities for securities of the target (either in a friendly merger or a less frequent hostile exchange offer) operated at a substantial disadvantage to a bidder (either friendly or hostile) who offered cash. The acquirer who offered stock had to register its securities and could not commence its exchange offer until the SEC had reviewed the registration statement covering these securities and declared it effective. Even if the SEC expedited its review, this factor added an element of uncertainty. In contrast, a cash bidder could consummate a cash tender offer, which only has to remain open for 20 business days (or, typically, about a month), much more quickly. The upshot was an incentive for a bidder to use cash instead of stock because the longer the period before the offer could be consummated, the more vulnerable the bidder was to a "disruptive" higher bid by a hostile, third party.

Rule 162 seeks to reduce this incentive to prefer cash over stock by permitting an offeror to solicit tenders of securities in an exchange offer "before a registration statement is effective as to the security offered, so long as no securities are purchased until the registration statement is effective and the tender offer has expired in accordance with the tender offer rules." Of course, such an exchange bidder would have to distribute a preliminary prospectus to target shareholders, but in effect cash and exchange offers can now be commenced at the same point and consummated equivalently—at least so long as the SEC's staff quickly reviews and declares effective the exchange offer's registration statement within the 20 business day period mandated by the tender offer rules. To date, the SEC's staff has been able to meet this goal of processing registration statements in exchange offers within this period.[101]

Publicity and Gun-Jumping. Prior to the new rules, any announcement of an exchange offer by the bidder could be seen as a "gun-jumping" violation under Section 5(c) of the Securities Act, unless a registration statement covering the offered securities had already been filed. This meant that an issuer had to file its registration statement before it could safely announce an exchange offer; also, written materials might violate the prohibition on the use of "free writing" under Section 5(b) of the 1933 Act. These problems effectively chilled the exchange bidder and created another unintended legal advantage for the cash bidder. The new rules end (or at least reduce substantially) this disparity. Under Rule 165(a), an offeror of securities to be issued in a business

---

[101] To this same end of fostering transactional parity, the SEC adopted in 2020 new simplified accounting rules addressing what must be disclosed in a registration statement relating to a merger or exchange offer, which reduced the "pro forma" disclosures that have to be made on such occasions. See Securities Act Release No. 33-10786 ("Amendments to Financial Disclosures about Acquired or Disposed Businesses") (May 20, 2020).

combination may make an offer to sell, or may solicit an offer to buy, those securities beginning with the first public announcement of the transaction, so long as any written communication made in connection with, or relating to, the transaction is filed under Rule 425 and such "prospectus" contains a prescribed legend. Further, once the registration statement is filed relating to the proposed business combination, Rule 165(b) provides that any written communication made in connection with, or relating to, the transaction will not constitute a "Section 10" prospectus or other form of unlawful "free writing" (and thus need not comply with the disclosure requirements of Section 10 of the 1933 Act), so long as the written communication is filed under Rule 424 or Rule 425 with the SEC and contains a prescribed legend. Anti-fraud liability under Section 12(a)(2) of the 1933 Act will, however, attach to these communications.

Proxy Rule Reform. A similar exemptive rule was adopted under the proxy rules, so that the offeror could begin at once to solicit proxies prior to filing a proxy statement. Under Rule 14a–12, a proxy solicitation may now be made before shareholders are given a proxy statement if, basically, (1) all proxy soliciting material is given to the SEC, and (2) a definitive proxy statement is sent to shareholder at or before the time that they are given proxy or consent cards or forms.

Commencement of the Offer. Prior to the revised rules, a bidder who disclosed its intention to make a cash tender offer was required to formally commence (or withdraw) the offer within five business days. The point of this rule was to minimize market uncertainty and preclude deceptive stock manipulation tactics. This rule has now been repealed. Bidders and targets may now communicate freely with shareholders undeterred by the threat that a statement may inadvertently trigger a tender offer (or force an embarrassing withdrawal of one that was never truly commenced). The only restriction is that a letter of transmittal (or similar instructions on how to tender) may not be sent prior to commencement (this parallels the equivalent restriction under the proxy rules barring a proxy card being distributed ahead of the proxy statement).

To discourage attempts to manipulate the market by misleading announcements of intended tender offers, the SEC has adopted a new Rule 14e–8, which makes it fraudulent for a person to announce a plan to make a tender offer if the person does not have a bona fide intent to launch the offer within a reasonable time period or lacks a reasonable belief that it will have the means to purchase the securities for which it has tendered.

Because Rule 165's exemption from the 1933 Act's gun-jumping rules is conditioned on an obligation to file all written communications with the SEC after the first public announcement of the transaction, it is still possible that an issuer could blunder and violate the 1933 Act. The term "public announcement" is broadly defined in Rule 165(f)(3), and an issuer who casually indicated its intention to make a tender or exchange offer could thus violate the 1933 Act if it failed to file written communications released after this point.

Subsequent Offering Period. Under the revised rules, a bidder may (but need not) tender for shares during a "subsequent offering period" that would follow the date all conditions to its offer were satisfied and the bidder accepted the tendered shares. Shares would have to be purchased as they are tendered during this period, and corresponding tendering shareholders would not have withdrawal rights. The subsequent offer period could be as short as three business days and could be extended by the bidder up to a maximum period of 20 business days.

The purpose of this additional period seems to be to permit the bidder to tender for the remaining shares once it has clearly acquired control in the initial tender offer. This would either allow the bidder to clean up the transaction, acquiring all remaining shares without the typical back-end merger, or to raise its level of ownership to the percentage level under state law (typically, 90%) that enabled it to effect a short-form merger without a shareholder vote.

Rule 14e–5. Replacing old Rule 10b–13, new Rule 14e–5 similarly precludes (subject to a list of exceptions) any purchase by a bidder, its affiliates, or advisors of the securities subject to a tender offer (or securities convertible or exchangeable into the same) other than pursuant to the offer. The rule applies from the time the tender offer is announced until the offer expires. During any subsequent offering period, however, purchases outside the offer are permitted, so long as the form and amount of consideration are the same as that offered in the tender offer.

Disclosure Forms. Consolidating the forms and specific disclosure requirements for different types of business combinations, the SEC has adopted "Regulation M–A" as a new subpart of Regulation S–K. It now sets forth the disclosure requirements for issuer tender offers, third-party tender offers and going private transactions. Former Schedule 13E-4 (used in "going private" transactions) and Schedule 14D-1 (used in third party tender offers) have been merged into new Schedule TO. Schedule 13E-3 will still be used when a "going private" transaction is to be effected by a means other than a tender offer. Offers to purchase in cash tender offers and proxy statements in cash mergers are now required to include a "plain English" summary term sheet that highlights in bullet point fashion the principal terms of the transaction.

Impact. The SEC did not grant all the requests of the "M & A" bar for regulatory relief. Despite urging from the bar, the SEC did not provide that registration statements in the case of business combinations would become effective on filing (although it has promised rapid review), and it refused to extend the safe harbor for forward-looking information to tender and exchange offers. Still, the new rules appear to make it possible to effect an exchange offer as quickly as a cash tender offer. Given that there are also tax advantages to the use of equity securities as the currency for business combinations and that exchange offers do not require the bidder to negotiate with a bank or other financial institution over financing terms, exchange offers are becoming more popular and may come to rival the cash tender offers in frequency.

4. DEFENSIVE TACTICS: THE TARGET STRIKES BACK

A fundamental fact about the regulation of takeovers in the United States is that the bidder and target are chiefly regulated by different bodies of law: the bidder by federal law; and the target by state corporate law. The result is an asymmetry that many see as producing inconsistent and even contradictory bodies of law.[102] At a minimum, there has clearly been a tension between federal and state regulation, with the SEC at times seeking to preempt some state statutes and also to preclude defensive tactics that state courts have expressly upheld. (One example was the adoption of the "All Holders" Rule to preclude a discriminatory self-tender by the target corporation—a result expressly upheld in Unocal Corp. v. Mesa Petroleum Co.,[103] the leading Delaware decision on takeover defenses).

A. THE WILLIAMS ACT'S APPLICATION TO THE TARGET

The Williams Act applies to the target as well as to the bidder. Schedule 14D-9 must be filed by any person who makes a solicitation or recommendation to target shareholders, and this clearly covers the target company and its management, because Rule 14e-2 requires the target to notify its shareholders of its position with respect to the offer not later than 10 business days from the commencement of the tender offer. This mandatory recommendation in turn triggers the filing of a Schedule 14D-9, which in turn must be updated in the event of a material change. Thus, if midway through a tender offer the target enters into serious negotiations with a third party that wishes to buy a material portion of the target's assets, an amendment of the Schedule 14D-9 may be necessary in order to respond to Item 7 of that Schedule, which requires disclosure of "Certain Negotiations and Transactions by the Subject Company."[104] The instructions to Item 7 may, however, provide an escape clause for the target: disclosure is not required "if no agreement in principle has been reached" and disclosure would "in the opinion of the Board of Directors * * * jeopardize continuation of such negotiations."

---

[102] For such a critique, see Fiflis, Of Lollipops and Law—A Proposal for a National Policy Concerning Tender Offer Defenses, 19 U.C. Davis L.Rev. 303 (1986).

[103] 493 A.2d 946 (Del.1985).

[104] This was essentially the fact pattern in In the Matter of George C. Kern, Jr., SEC Administrative File No. 3–6869, [1988–1989 Transfer Binder] Fed. Sec. L. Rep. (CCH) Para. 84,342 (Nov. 14, 1988).

Even then, a statement that preliminary discussions or negotiations are under way (without naming the target) is required.[105]

Rule 14d–5 also applies to the target and is a corollary to a similar provision in the proxy rules. Under it, the target must choose whether to give the bidder a shareholder list or to mail its tender materials for it. (Predictably, it chooses the latter).

Any misstatement by the target can produce litigation brought by the bidder against the target under § 14(e) of the Williams Act. Under § 14(e), the target need not have purchased or sold securities to bring suit. Although the Supreme Court's decision in Piper v. Chris-Craft Indus., Inc.[106] implies that the bidder lacks standing to sue the target for damages (on the theory that only the target shareholders were the intended beneficiaries of the Williams Act), most courts do permit the bidder to seek injunctive relief for corrective disclosure.[107] Nontendering shareholders other than the bidder can sue the target under § 14(e) for monetary damages where they can allege that but for a fraudulent statement or omission they would have tendered.[108] Of course, the target is also subject to Rule 10b–5 liability to those shareholders who purchased or sold its stock during a period when the market was affected by any material misstatement made by it.

Potentially, § 14(e) could have severely constrained target management's ability to engage in self-interested defensive tactics. However, to employ § 14(e) in this way, courts would have had to read the term "manipulative" in § 14(e) to cover fully disclosed conduct that was in breach of the target management's fiduciary duties to its shareholders. Exactly such a construction was considered and decisively rejected by the Supreme Court in Schreiber v. Burlington Northern, Inc., 472 U.S. 1 (1985). Instead, the Court ruled:

> We hold that the term 'manipulative' as used in § 14(e) requires misrepresentation or nondisclosure. It connotes 'conduct designed to deceive or defraud investors by controlling or artificially affecting the price of securities.' Ernst & Ernst v. Hochfelder, 425 U.S. 185 at 199. Without misrepresentation or nondisclosure, § 14(e) has not been violated.

Subsequent decisions have assumed that a fully disclosed defensive tactic, however egregious, is thus immune from attack under § 14(e).[109]

---

[105] If the Schedule 14D-9 states that negotiations are not under way but that such discussions are possible, a prompt amendment is required when negotiations commence. See In the Matter of Revlon, Inc., Securities Exchange Act Rel. No. 34–23320 (June 16, 1986).

[106] 430 U.S. 1 (1977).

[107] See Humana, Inc. v. American Medicorp, Inc., 445 F.Supp. 613 (S.D.N.Y.1977).

[108] See Plaine v. McCabe, 797 F.2d 713 (9th Cir. 1986). Even when the bidder is a target shareholder, it may not seek monetary damages under § 14(e). See Kalmanovitz v. G. Heileman Brewing Co., 769 F.2d 152 (3d Cir. 1985).

[109] See Data Probe Acquisition Corp. v. Datatab, Inc., 722 F.2d 1 (2d Cir. 1983).

B. FEDERAL SECURITIES LAW IMPLICATIONS OF DEFENSIVE TACTICS

Some defensive tactics that are permissible under state law still touch upon and may be precluded by federal law:

1. *Supervoting Stock and the One-Share/One-Vote Controversy.* The takeover defensive tactic that probably most implicates the interests of the federal securities laws is the dual class recapitalization. Clearly, the one insurmountable deterrent to a hostile takeover is for the company's founders (or its management) to hold majority control of the company. There are two basic ways target management can gain such voting control: (1) it can buy the company (or most of it)—a process typically called a "leveraged buyout" and specifically regulated by § 13(e) of the Williams Act; or (2) it can effect a recapitalization (typically just prior to its IPO) under which one class of voting stock (held by it) gains much greater voting power relative to the other class (held by the public shareholder).

One major obstacle existed to the use of dual class recapitalizations. Since 1926, the New York Stock Exchange (NYSE) had required listed companies to afford shareholders equal voting rights on a per share basis. This policy—known as the "one-share, one-vote" rule—precluded the largest U.S. corporations from adopting dual class recapitalizations. Yet, because neither the American Stock Exchange (AMEX) or the National Association of Securities Dealers Automatic Quotation System (NASDAQ) had a similar policy against unequal voting rights, the NYSE was exposed to the competitive threat that issuers would delist from it and move to either of them. Faced with this threat, the NYSE proposed in 1986 to amend its rules to permit dual class recapitalizations, so long as any modification of existing shareholders' voting rights was approved by a majority of both the independent directors and the disinterested shareholders.[110]

Under § 19 of the 1934 Act, proposed changes in the rules of a national securities exchange are subject to SEC approval before they can become effective. During 1986 and the first half of 1987, the SEC sought to negotiate a compromise among the NYSE, AMEX and NASDAQ under which each would agree to some form of a "one-share, one-vote" policy. When these efforts proved unsuccessful, the SEC proposed a new Rule 19c–4, which would prohibit the listing of the securities of an issuer if, after May 15, 1987, the issuer "issues any class of security or takes any other corporate action that would have the effect of nullifying, restricting or disparately reducing the per share voting rights of holders of an outstanding class" of common stock.[111] Note that this Rule did not

---

[110] For the text of the NYSE's proposal, see 18 Sec.Reg. & L.Rep. (BNA), No. 37, at 1389–92 (Sept. 19, 1986).

[111] Securities Exchange Act Release No. 34–24623 ("Voting Rights Listing Standards—Proposed Disenfranchisement Rule") (June 22, 1987).

preclude the issuance of low voting or nonvoting stock, but only supervoting stock that could reduce the voting power of existing stockholders. Its premise was that investors dealing at arms' length with the corporation could decide to buy lower voting stock without the need for special SEC protection, but that existing shareholders were exposed to coercion and seduction through the use of "sweeteners" and related techniques.[112]

Rule 19c–4 was formally adopted in 1988,[113] and was quickly challenged in court by the Business Roundtable on the ground that the SEC had exceeded its jurisdiction under § 19(c) to impose rules on the exchanges. In Business Roundtable v. SEC,[114] the D.C. Circuit agreed with the Business Roundtable and invalidated the Rule. The D.C. Circuit's decision did not, however, affect the status of the various exchanges' own rules (each of the NYSE, the AMEX, and NASDAQ had in the interim adopted a rule to comply with Rule 19c–4). After much negotiation, assisted by some SEC prodding, the three principal markets worked out a common "one share, one vote" standard.[115] This revised standard forbids only the issuance of high-voting stock that reduces the voting power of existing shareholders, but not the issuance of low-voting stock (which does not dilute existing shareholders). Thus, "dual capitalization" voting structures continue to be used, with the low-voting stock typically issued at the time of the company's IPO. The stock exchanges' revised new standard also grandfathered those companies that had been listed with dual class voting structures under the prior rules, and even permits them to issue additional shares under those classes. But it did preclude them from creating new classes of supervoting stock in the future that would reduce the voting rights of common shareholders. In addition, foreign issuers were exempted from these voting rights standards in deference to their often very different systems of corporate governance.

2. *Issuer Repurchases.* Issuer repurchases are regulated by the federal securities laws in several respects: First, when any third party commences a tender offer for a publicly held target (i.e., one subject to § 13(e) of the 1934 Act), Rule 13e–1 states that the target may not purchase its own shares until it has disclosed certain factual information (including the amount to be purchased, the source of funds, and the markets it is entering). Essentially, the purpose of this rule is to prevent

---

[112] The SEC appears to have adopted an approach recommended by Professor Gilson in this regard. See Gilson, Evaluating Dual Class Common Stocks: The Relevance of Substitutes, 75 Va. L. Rev. 807 (1982).

[113] Securities Exchange Act Release No. 34–25891 (July 7, 1988).

[114] 905 F.2d 406 (D.C.Cir. 1990).

[115] See Securities Exchange Act Release No. 35121 (December 19, 1994) (approving joint shareholder voting rights policy of NYSE, AMEX, and NASDAQ). Essentially, this policy forbids listing on the NYSE or AMEX or inclusion in the Nasdaq system of "companies that disenfranchise shareholders of public common stock." See 1994 SEC LEXIS 4072 at *4.

manipulation and deception, as shareholders might otherwise attribute the market rise to the prospect of a rival third party bid.[116]

Second, if the purchasing program amounts to a tender offer, then Rule 13e–4 must be complied with. Although the target corporation is exempt from § 14(d) of the Williams Act by virtue of § 14(d)(8)(B), the SEC has adopted virtually equivalent rules under § 13(e). As a result, the same disclosure statement must be prepared, and Rule 13e–4(f)(8) parallels Rule 14d–10 by requiring that the offer be open to all holders. Hence, the target could not make a discriminatory offer that excluded the bidder from participating (as it did in *Unocal*). Also, in response to the *Hanson Trust* case, the SEC adopted a "cooling off" period that prevents the issuer or an affiliate from purchasing shares that were the subject of its offer until the expiration of at least ten business days after the termination of the offer.[117] The target is also partially exempt from SEC Rules that prohibit persons from buying outside their own tender offer.[118]

Suppose even before a takeover bid is made, a potential target corporation suspects that it is about to be put "in play," and it begins an open-market purchasing campaign for its own stock in order to boost its stock price. This program will not violate Rule 13e–1 because no tender offer has yet been announced. However, it can violate § 9(a)(2) of the 1934 Act or Rule 10b–5 as being "manipulative" in its intent, *unless* the purchasing program complies with Rule 10b–18. Rule 10b–18 is a "safe harbor" rule, and noncompliance with its restrictions does not create any presumption of unlawful conduct.[119] Essentially, the Rule establishes restrictions on the timing, price, volume and manner of purchase, which, if complied with by the issuer, protect it from the claim that it has manipulated the market for its stock. These restrictions basically require that:

(i) the issuer purchase through only one broker or dealer on a single day (in order to prevent any appearance of a broad market interest in the stock if multiple dealers were used);

(ii) the issuer's purchases do not constitute the opening transaction or come during the last half hour of trading;

(iii) the issuer may not purchase at a price above the market price (i.e., it may not cause the price to increase); and

---

[116] Undisclosed open-market purchasing of the target stock could violate not only Rule 13e–1, but in addition might be found "manipulative" and therefore in violation of both § 9(a)(2) of the 1934 Act and Rule 10b–5 if their purpose were to drive the target's stock price above the tender price. See Crane Co. v. Westinghouse Air Brake Co., 419 F.2d 787 (2d Cir. 1969). However, the Supreme Court's *Piper* decision may bar one bidder from suing another for damages in such a case. See Crane Co. v. American Standard, Inc., 603 F.2d 244 (2d Cir. 1979).

[117] See Rule 13e–4(f)(6). No similar "cooling off" period has been adopted for third party tender offers, although the SEC did propose such a general rule.

[118] See Rule 14e–5 ("Prohibiting Purchases Outside of a Tender Offer"). Rule 14e–5 replaced former Rule 10b–13, which for decades stated basically the same prohibition.

[119] See Rule 10b–18(d).

(iv) the volume of its purchases may not exceed 25% of the average daily trading volume (as determined over the four prior calendar weeks) in the case of a publicly traded security or, in the case of other securities, the volume over a several day period may not exceed 1/20 of 1% of the outstanding shares of the security (exclusive of shares held by affiliates).

These basic restrictions are subject to numerous exceptions and qualifications (for example, block trades and purchases pursuant to Rule 13e–1 are exempt). Still, Rule 10b–18 has an importance that transcends the takeover context because as a practical matter it establishes "bright line" limitations on issuer repurchases. Its adoption was motivated by the practices of acquisition-minded companies that used their shares as their preferred currency for acquisitions; supporting their stock price by buying their shares thus enabled them to use an inflated currency for their acquisitions. During the 1960s the SEC brought several injunctive actions against such practices,[120] and in 1970 it proposed Rule 13e–2.[121] This rule was never adopted, although it long supplied the governing criteria used by the SEC in manipulation cases. Rule 10b–18 was adopted in 1982 and generally followed the standards contained in Proposed Rule 13e–2.[122] Although Rule 13e–2 was proposed to be mandatory, so that any purchases above its limits were unlawful, Rule 10b–18 is only a safe harbor.

One final rule that an issuer must consider in repurchasing its own securities is Rule 102 of Regulation M, which precludes the issuer from buying stock that is the subject of a distribution. If, for example, the issuer has outstanding warrants or a class of convertible securities, it is technically engaged in a distribution of securities and thus must secure an exemption from Rule 102. The issuer can, however, apply for a specific exemption from the SEC.

3. *Greenmail.* The tactic known as "greenmail" consists of buying off the putative bidder by the target repurchasing its shares from the bidder, either at a premium over the market or at the market price in a market inflated by takeover rumors, and then requiring the bidder to sign a "standstill agreement" whereby the bidder agrees not to acquire additional shares in the target for a defined period (usually five to ten years). The problem with this defensive tactic is that it often simply attracts a second bidder who also wants the same largesse (this is referred to as "double dipping"). Once a takeover target is identified in the market's eye, it often cannot escape just by in effect bribing the first bidder on the scene to go away.

---

[120] See Securities and Exchange Commission v. Georgia-Pacific Corp., Fed.Sec.L.Rep. (CCH) Para. 91,680 (1966).

[121] See Sec. Exch. Act Rel. No. 34–8930 (July 13, 1970).

[122] See Sec. Exch. Act Rel. No. 34–19244 (Nov. 17, 1982). Rule 13e–2 limited issuer purchases to 15% of the daily trading volume, whereas Rule 10b–18 relaxes this test to 25%.

Legal challenges to greenmail are typically framed in terms of state law issues of the fiduciary responsibilities of target directors and officers. Only one decision appears to have enjoined greenmail payments,[123] and Delaware law has been especially tolerant of such payments.[124] Under federal law, the open and disclosed payment of greenmail would not amount to deception or manipulation.[125] Indeed, this result seems a necessary consequence of Schreiber v. Burlington Northern, Inc.,[126] which held that "manipulation" under 14(e) requires a showing of deception. Still, misstatements about either the putative bidder's intent or about the target's conduct might support an action under Rule 10b–5 if plaintiffs purchased during the period that such statement affected the market.[127]

On the policy level, an academic debate has long surrounded greenmail. Although the dominant view has been that such practices serve to entrench management, others argue that the putative bidder provides a service for other shareholders by identifying an undervalued target and stimulating an auction.[128] This argument is premised on the fact that the average stock price gains on the announcement of a Schedule 13D filing by the putative bidder usually exceed the average loss on the announcement of a greenmail repurchase. Still, at least one problem with this argument is that net gains remaining after the greenmail repurchase tend to gradually disappear unless there is a subsequent successful offer.[129] Another problem with the optimistic thesis that greenmail benefits shareholders by initiating a gradual auction is that much of it is invisible: bidders may contact target management and arrange a sale at a premium without crossing the 5% threshold in order to avoid publicity, litigation and subsequent bidder "double dipping."[130]

The prevalence of greenmail transactions has been chilled to a degree by I.R.C. § 5881, enacted in 1987, which imposes a 50% nondeductible excise tax on the profit realized from the receipt of greenmail (this results in an overall 84% effective rate of taxation on such profits). The definition of "greenmail" in this statute is, however,

---

[123] See Heckmann v. Ahmanson, 168 Cal.App.3d 119, 214 Cal.Rptr. 177 (1985).

[124] See Polk v. Good, 507 A.2d 531 (Del.1986) (transaction valid unless sole or primary purpose was to perpetuate management in control).

[125] Pin v. Texaco, Inc., 793 F.2d 1448 (5th Cir. 1986); see also Kamerman v. Steinberg, 891 F.2d 424 (2d Cir. 1989) (shareholder who did not purchase or sell may not sue derivatively to seek damages for greenmail absent proof that issuer was deceived).

[126] 472 U.S. 1 (1985).

[127] See In re Phillips Petroleum Securities Litigation, 881 F.2d 1236 (3d Cir. 1989).

[128] Compare Macey & McChesney, A Theoretical Analysis of Corporate Greenmail, 95 Yale L.J. 13 (1985) with Gordon & Kornhauser, Takeover Defense Tactics: A Comment on Two Models, 96 Yale L.J. 295 (1986).

[129] See Ang & Tucker, The Shareholder Wealth Effects of Corporate Greenmail, 11 J.Fin.Res. 265 (1988) (gains from first bidder's appearance vanish if greenmail is not followed by a subsequent, successful bid).

[130] For a discussion of other forms of disguised greenmail, see Gilson, Drafting an Effective Greenmail Prohibition, 88 Colum.L.Rev. 329 (1988).

seriously underinclusive, as it applies only to corporate payments to a stockholder (1) who has held the stock for less than 2 years, and (2) who has made or threatened to make a tender offer for the stock. Obviously, a sophisticated "greenmailer" will avoid making or threatening a tender offer or will at least keep its threat implicit.

4. *The NYSE's 20% Rule.* Even when the target corporation's issuance of shares to a white knight, ESOP or other ally does not constitute a fiduciary breach, it may violate a New York Stock Exchange Rule that requires shareholder approval of certain transactions, including any issuance of stock exceeding 20% of the corporation's common stock (either in a single transaction or in an integrated series of transactions).[131] In Norlin Corporation v. Rooney, Pace Inc.,[132] Norlin issued shares amounting to approximately 49% of its outstanding stock to a wholly-owned Panamanian subsidiary, in order to ward off a threatened hostile takeover. Norlin claimed that the law of Panama permitted its subsidiary to vote its shares in Norlin. While the Second Circuit rejected this argument, it rested its injunction invalidating the stock issuance on an alternative ground as well: the prospect of delisting from the New York Stock Exchange for violation of its listing standard threatened shareholders with irreparable injury and thus justified an injunction. In particular, both the District Court and the Second Circuit focused on the likely loss of liquidity to investors if the NYSE delisted Norlin.[133] *Query:* would delisting from the NYSE constitute a significant injury today if the corporation could list on another exchange or on NASDAQ (where some substantial corporations eligible for the NYSE prefer to list)? Note, however, that NASDAQ today has the same shareholder approval rule as the NYSE. Finally, if the target corporation is the subject of competitive bidding between two corporate bidders and it acts to prefer one by granting a stock lockup in excess of 20%, how can the threat of delisting injure its shareholders when it is about to disappear anyway?

5. STATE ANTI-TAKEOVER LEGISLATION

Although the Williams Act is avowedly neutral between bidder and target, the states have not been neutral, but have sided consistently with the target. Commentators disagree about the motivation for such legislation. Some see state anti-takeover statutes as simply the product of individual target companies overreaching a compliant state legislature

---

[131] Originally, the ceiling on stock issuances without shareholder approval was 18½%, but in 1989 the NYSE raised it to 20% and the NASD adopted a similar limit for NASDAQ-listed stocks. See Sec.Exch. Act Rel. No. 34–27035 (NYSE rule) (July 14, 1989) and Sec.Exch. Act Rel. No. 34–27489 (NASDAQ rule) (Nov. 30, 1989). See also NYSE Listed Company Manual at § 312.03.

[132] 744 F.2d 255 (2d Cir. 1984).

[133] Id. at 268.

(in which out-of-state shareholders have little voice or influence),[134] while others believe an anti-takeover political consensus has developed among a broad coalition of groups that is driven by the latent (and sometimes explicit) desire to protect non-shareholder constituencies from risk.[135] Clearly, whether as the result of ignorance or distaste for what they have seen, the public at large, as revealed by public opinion polls, is skeptical and suspicious of hostile takeovers.[136] This section will examine, first, the case law and, second, the newer forms of anti-takeover statutes.

A. THE CASE LAW

CTS Corporation v. Dynamics Corporation of America

Supreme Court of the United States, 1987.
481 U.S. 69, 107 S.Ct. 1637, 95 L.Ed.2d 67.

■ JUSTICE POWELL delivered the opinion of the Court.

This case presents the questions whether the Control Share Acquisitions Chapter of the Indiana Business Corporation Law, Ind.Code § 23–1–42–1 et seq. (Supp.1986), is preempted by the Williams Act or violates the Commerce Clause of the Federal Constitution, Art. I, § 8, cl. 3.

I

A

On March 4, 1986, the Governor of Indiana signed a revised Indiana Business Corporation Law. That law included the Control Share Acquisitions Chapter. Beginning on August 1, 1987, the Act will apply to any corporation incorporated in Indiana, unless the corporation amends its articles of incorporation or bylaws to opt out of the Act. Before that date, any Indiana corporation can opt into the Act by resolution of its board of directors. The Act applies only to "issuing public corporations." The term "corporation" includes only businesses incorporated in Indiana.
* * *

The Act focuses on the acquisition of "control shares" in an issuing public corporation. Under the Act, an entity acquires "control shares" whenever it acquires shares that, but for the operation of the Act, would bring its voting power in the corporation to or above any of three thresholds: 20%, 33⅓%, or 50%. An entity that acquires control shares does not necessarily acquire voting rights. Rather, it gains those rights only "to the extent granted by resolution approved by the shareholders of

---

[134] Romano, The Political Economy of Takeover Statutes, 73 Virginia L. Rev. 111 (1987) (describing enactment of takeover statutes).

[135] See, e.g., Johnson & Millon, Missing the Point About State Takeover Statutes, 87 Mich.L.Rev. 846 (1989).

[136] Romano, The Future of Hostile Takeovers: Legislation and Public Opinion, 57 Cinn.L.Rev. 457 (1988) (noting negative public perception of hostile takeovers).

the issuing public corporation." Section 9 requires a majority vote of all disinterested shareholders holding each class of stock for passage of such a resolution. The practical effect of this requirement is to condition acquisition of control of a corporation on approval of a majority of the pre-existing disinterested shareholders.

The shareholders decide whether to confer rights on the control shares at the next regularly scheduled meeting of the shareholders, or at a specially scheduled meeting. The acquiror can require management of the corporation to hold such a special meeting within 50 days if it files an "acquiring person statement,"[4] requests the meeting, and agrees to pay the expenses of the meeting. See § 23–1–42–7. If the shareholders do not vote to restore voting rights to the shares, the corporation may redeem the control shares from the acquiror at fair market value, but it is not required to do so. § 23–1–42–10(b). Similarly, if the acquiror does not file an acquiring person statement with the corporation, the corporation may, if its bylaws or articles of incorporation so provide, redeem the shares at any time after 60 days after the acquiror's last acquisition. § 23–1–42–10(a).

B

On March 10, 1986, appellee Dynamics Corporation of America (Dynamics) owned 9.6% of the common stock of appellant CTS Corporation, an Indiana corporation. On that day, six days after the Act went into effect, Dynamics announced a tender offer for another million shares in CTS; purchase of those shares would have brought Dynamics' ownership interest in CTS to 27.5%. Also on March 10, Dynamics filed suit in the United States District Court for the Northern District of Illinois, alleging that CTS had violated the federal securities laws in a number of respects no longer relevant to these proceedings. On March 27, the Board of Directors of CTS, an Indiana corporation, elected to be governed by the provisions of the Act, see § 23–1–17–3.

Four days later, on March 31, Dynamics moved for leave to amend its complaint to allege that the Act is pre-empted by the Williams Act and violates the Commerce Clause, Art. I, § 8, cl. 3. Dynamics sought a temporary restraining order, a preliminary injunction, and declaratory relief against CTS's use of the Act. On April 9, the District Court ruled that the Williams Act pre-empts the Indiana Act and granted Dynamics' motion for declaratory relief. * * * Relying on JUSTICE WHITE's plurality opinion in Edgar v. MITE Corp., 457 U.S. 624 (1982), the court concluded that the Act "wholly frustrates the purpose and objective of Congress in striking a balance between the investor, management, and the takeover bidder in takeover contests." * * * A week later, on April 17, the District Court issued an opinion accepting Dynamics' claim that the Act violates the Commerce Clause. This holding rested on the court's conclusion that

---

[4] An "acquiring person statement" is an information statement describing, inter alia, the identity of the acquiring person and the terms and extent of the proposed acquisition. See § 23–1–42–6.

"the substantial interference with interstate commerce created by the [Act] outweighs the articulated local benefits so as to create an impermissible indirect burden on interstate commerce." Id., at 406. The District Court certified its decisions on the Williams Act and Commerce Clause claims as final under Fed.Rule Civ.Proc. 54(b). Ibid.

* * *

II

The first question in this case is whether the Williams Act pre-empts the Indiana Act. As we have stated frequently, absent an explicit indication by Congress of an intent to pre-empt state law, a state statute is pre-empted only

> "where compliance with both federal and state regulations is a physical impossibility * * *," Florida Lime & Avocado Growers, Inc. v. Paul, 373 U.S. 132, 142–143 (1963), or where the state "law stands as an obstacle to the accomplishment and execution of the full purposes and objectives of Congress." Hines v. Davidowitz, 312 U.S. 52, 67 (1941) * * *. Ray v. Atlantic Richfield Co., 435 U.S. 151, 158 (1978).

Because it is entirely possible for entities to comply with both the Williams Act and the Indiana Act, the state statute can be pre-empted only if it frustrates the purposes of the federal law.

* * *

B

The Indiana Act differs in major respects from the Illinois statute that the Court considered in Edgar v. MITE Corp., 457 U.S. 624 (1982). After reviewing the legislative history of the Williams Act, Justice White, joined by Chief Justice Burger and Justice Blackmun (the plurality), concluded that the Williams Act struck a careful balance between the interests of offerors and target companies, and that any state statute that "upset" this balance was pre-empted. Id., at 632–634.

The plurality then identified three offending features of the Illinois statute. Justice White's opinion first noted that the Illinois statute provided for a 20-day precommencement period. During this time, management could disseminate its views on the upcoming offer to shareholders, but offerors could not publish their offers. The plurality found that this provision gave management "a powerful tool to combat tender offers." Id., at 635. This contrasted dramatically with the Williams Act: Congress had deleted express precommencement notice provisions from the Williams Act. According to the plurality, Congress had determined that the potentially adverse consequences of such a provision on shareholders should be avoided. Thus, the plurality concluded that the Illinois provision "frustrate[d] the objectives of the Williams Act." Ibid. The second criticized feature of the Illinois statute was a provision for a hearing on a tender offer that, because it set no deadline, allowed management " 'to stymie indefinitely a takeover,' " id., at 637 (quoting MITE Corp. v. Dixon, 633 F.2d 486, 494 (C.A.7 1980)). The plurality noted that " 'delay can seriously impede a tender offer,' " 457 U.S. at 637 (quoting Great Western United Corp. v. Kidwell, 577 F.2d 1256, 1277 (C.A.5 1978) (Wisdom, J.)), and that "Congress anticipated that investors and the takeover offeror would be free to go forward without unreasonable delay," 457 U.S., at 639. Accordingly, the plurality concluded that this provision conflicted with the Williams Act. The third troublesome feature of the Illinois statute was its requirement that the fairness of tender offers would be reviewed by the Illinois Secretary of State. Noting that "Congress intended for investors to be free to make their own decisions," the plurality concluded that " '[t]he state thus offers investor protection at the expense of investor autonomy—an approach quite in conflict with that adopted by Congress.' " Id., at 639–640 (quoting MITE Corp. v. Dixon, supra, at 494).

C

As the plurality opinion in *MITE* did not represent the views of a majority of the Court,[6] we are not bound by its reasoning. We need not question that reasoning, however, because we believe the Indiana Act passes muster even under the broad interpretation of the Williams Act articulated by Justice White in *MITE*. As is apparent from our summary of its reasoning, the overriding concern of the *MITE* plurality was that the Illinois statute considered in that case operated to favor management against offerors, to the detriment of shareholders. By contrast, the statute now before the Court protects the independent shareholder against the contending parties. Thus, the Act furthers a basic purpose of the Williams Act, " 'plac[ing] investors on an equal footing with the takeover bidder,' " Piper v. Chris-Craft Industries, 430 U.S., at 30 (quoting the Senate Report accompanying the Williams Act, S.Rep. No. 550, 90th Cong., 1st Sess., 4 (1967)).

The Indiana Act operates on the assumption, implicit in the Williams Act, that independent shareholders faced with tender offers often are at a disadvantage. By allowing such shareholders to vote as a group, the Act protects them from the coercive aspects of some tender offers. If, for example, shareholders believe that a successful tender offer will be followed by a purchase of nontendering shares at a depressed price, individual shareholders may tender their shares—even if they doubt the tender offer is in the corporation's best interest—to protect themselves from being forced to sell their shares at a depressed price. As the SEC explains: "The alternative of not accepting the tender offer is virtual assurance that, if the offer is successful, the shares will have to

---

[6] Justice White's opinion on the preemption issue, 457 U.S. at 630–640, was joined only by Chief Justice Burger and by Justice Blackmun. Two Justices disagreed with Justice White's conclusion. See id., at 646–647 (Powell, J., concurring in part); id., at 655 (Stevens, J. concurring in part and concurring in judgment). Four Justices did not address the question. See id., at 655 (O'Connor, J., concurring in part); id., at 664 (Marshall, J., with whom Brennan, J. joined, dissenting); id., at 667 (Rehnquist, J., dissenting).

be sold in the lower priced, second step." Two-Tier Tender Offer Pricing and Non-Tender Offer Purchase Programs, SEC Exchange Act Rel. No. 21079 (June 21, 1984), [1984 Transfer Binder] CCH Fed.Sec.L.Rep. ¶ 83,637, p. 86,916 (footnote omitted) (hereinafter SEC Release No. 21079). See Lowenstein, Pruning Deadwood in Hostile Takeovers: A Proposal for Legislation, 83 Colum.L.Rev. 249, 307–309 (1983). In such a situation under the Indiana Act, the shareholders as a group, acting in the corporation's best interest, could reject the offer, although individual shareholders might be inclined to accept it. The desire of the Indiana Legislature to protect shareholders of Indiana corporations from this type of coercive offer does not conflict with the Williams Act. Rather, it furthers the federal policy of investor protection.

In implementing its goal, the Indiana Act avoids the problems the plurality discussed in *MITE*. Unlike the *MITE* statute, the Indiana Act does not give either management or the offeror an advantage in communicating with the shareholders about the impending offer. The Act also does not impose an indefinite delay on tender offers. Nothing in the Act prohibits an offeror from consummating an offer on the 20th business day, the earliest day permitted under applicable federal regulations, see 17 CFR § 240.14e–1(a) (1986). Nor does the Act allow the state government to interpose its views of fairness between willing buyers and sellers of shares of the target company. Rather, the Act allows *shareholders* to evaluate the fairness of the offer collectively.

D

The Court of Appeals based its finding of pre-emption on its view that the practical effect of the Indiana Act is to delay consummation of tender offers until 50 days after the commencement of the offer. 794 F.2d, at 263. As did the Court of Appeals, Dynamics reasons that no rational offeror will purchase shares until it gains assurance that those shares will carry voting rights. Because it is possible that voting rights will not be conferred until a shareholder meeting 50 days after commencement of the offer, Dynamics concludes that the Act imposes a 50-day delay. This, it argues, conflicts with the shorter 20-business-day period established by the SEC as the minimum period for which a tender offer may be held open. 17 CFR § 240.14e–1 (1986). We find the alleged conflict illusory.

The Act does not impose an absolute 50-day delay on tender offers, nor does it preclude an offeror from purchasing shares as soon as federal law permits. If the offeror fears an adverse shareholder vote under the Act, it can make a conditional tender offer, offering to accept shares on the condition that the shares receive voting rights within a certain period of time. The Williams Act permits tender offers to be conditioned on the offeror's subsequently obtaining regulatory approval. E.g., Interpretive Release Relating to Tender Offer Rules, SEC Exchange Act Rel. No. 34–16623 (Mar. 5, 1980), 3 CCH Fed.Sec.L.Rep. ¶ 24,284I, p. 17,758, quoted in Macfadden Holdings, Inc. v. JB Acquisition Corp., 802 F.2d 62, 70

(C.A.2 1986). There is no reason to doubt that this type of conditional tender offer would be legitimate as well.

Even assuming that the Indiana Act imposes some additional delay, nothing in *MITE* suggested that *any* delay imposed by state regulation, however short, would create a conflict with the Williams Act. The plurality argued only that the offeror should "be free to go forward without *unreasonable* delay." 457 U.S., at 639 (emphasis added). In that case, the Court was confronted with the potential for indefinite delay and presented with no persuasive reason why some deadline could not be established. By contrast, the Indiana Act provides that full voting rights will be vested—if this eventually is to occur—within 50 days after commencement of the offer. This period is within the 60-day maximum period Congress established for reinstitution of withdrawal rights in 15 U.S.C. § 78n(d)(5). We cannot say that a delay within that congressionally determined period is unreasonable.

Finally, we note that the Williams Act would pre-empt a variety of state corporate laws of hitherto unquestioned validity if it were construed to pre-empt any state statute that may limit or delay the free exercise of power after a successful tender offer. State corporate laws commonly permit corporations to stagger the terms of their directors. See Model Business Corp. Act § 37 (1969 draft) in 3 Model Business Corp. Act Ann. (2d ed. 1971) (hereinafter MBCA); American Bar Foundation, Revised Model Business Corp. Act § 8.06 (1984 draft) (1985) (hereinafter RMBCA). By staggering the terms of directors, and thus having annual elections for only one class of directors each year, corporations may delay the time when a successful offeror gains control of the board of directors. Similarly, state corporation laws commonly provide for cumulative voting. See MBCA § 33, par. 4; RMBCA § 7.28. By enabling minority shareholders to assure themselves of representation in each class of directors, cumulative voting provisions can delay further the ability of offerors to gain untrammeled authority over the affairs of the target corporation. See Hochman & Folger, Deflecting Takeovers: Charter and By-Law Techniques, 34 Bus.Law. 537, 538–539 (1979).

In our view, the possibility that the Indiana Act will delay some tender offers is insufficient to require a conclusion that the Williams Act pre-empts the Act. The longstanding prevalence of state regulation in this area suggests that, if Congress had intended to pre-empt all state laws that delay the acquisition of voting control following a tender offer, it would have said so explicitly. The regulatory conditions that the Act places on tender offers are consistent with the text and the purposes of the Williams Act. Accordingly, we hold that the Williams Act does not pre-empt the Indiana Act.

III

As an alternative basis for its decision, the Court of Appeals held that the Act violates the Commerce Clause of the Federal Constitution. We now address this holding. On its face, the Commerce Clause is nothing more than a grant to Congress of the power "[t]o regulate Commerce * * * among the several States * * *," Art. I, § 8, cl. 3. But it has been settled for more than a century that the Clause prohibits States from taking certain actions respecting interstate commerce even absent congressional action. See, e.g., Cooley v. Board of Wardens, 12 How. 299 (1852). The Court's interpretation of "these great silences of the Constitution," H.P. Hood & Sons, Inc. v. Du Mond, 336 U.S. 525, 535 (1949), has not always been easy to follow. Rather, as the volume and complexity of commerce and regulation has grown in this country, the Court has articulated a variety of tests in an attempt to describe the difference between those regulations that the Commerce Clause permits and those regulations that it prohibits. See, e.g., Raymond Motor Transportation, Inc. v. Rice, 434 U.S. 429, 441, n. 15 (1978).

A

The principal objects of dormant Commerce Clause scrutiny are statutes that discriminate against interstate commerce. See, e.g., Lewis v. BT Investment Managers, Inc., 447 U.S. 27, 36–37 (1980); Philadelphia v. New Jersey, 437 U.S. 617, 624 (1978). See generally Regan, The Supreme Court and State Protectionism: Making Sense of the Dormant Commerce Clause, 84 Mich.L.Rev. 1091 (1986). The Indiana Act is not such a statute. It has the same effects on tender offers whether or not the offeror is a domiciliary or resident of Indiana. Thus, it "visits its effects equally upon both interstate and local business," Lewis v. BT Investment Managers, Inc., supra, at 36.

Dynamics nevertheless contends that the statute is discriminatory because it will apply most often to out-of-state entities. This argument rests on the contention that, as a practical matter, most hostile tender offers are launched by offerors outside Indiana. But this argument avails Dynamics little. "The fact that the burden of a state regulation falls on some interstate companies does not, by itself, establish a claim of discrimination against interstate commerce." Exxon Corp. v. Governor of Maryland, 437 U.S. 117, 126 (1978). See Minnesota v. Clover Leaf Creamery Co., 449 U.S. 456, 471–472 (1981) (rejecting a claim of discrimination because the challenged statute "regulate[d] evenhandedly * * * without regard to whether the [commerce came] from outside the State"); Commonwealth Edison Co. v. Montana, 453 U.S. 609, 619 (1981) (rejecting a claim of discrimination because the "tax burden [was] borne according to the amount * * * consumed and not according to any distinction between in-state and out-of-state consumers"). Because nothing in the Indiana Act imposes a greater burden on out-of-state offerors than it does on similarly situated Indiana offerors, we reject the contention that the Act discriminates against interstate commerce.

B

This Court's recent Commerce Clause cases also have invalidated statutes that may adversely affect interstate commerce by subjecting activities to inconsistent regulations. E.g., Brown-Forman Distillers

Corp. v. New York State Liquor Authority, 476 U.S. 573 (1986); Edgar v. MITE Corp., 457 U.S., at 642 (plurality opinion of White, J.); Kassel v. Consolidated Freightways Corp., 450 U.S. 662, 671 (1981) (plurality opinion of Powell, J.). See Southern Pacific Co. v. Arizona, 325 U.S. 761, 774 (1945) (noting the "confusion and difficulty" that would attend the "unsatisfied need for uniformity" in setting maximum limits on train lengths); Cooley v. Board of Wardens, supra, at 319 (stating that the Commerce Clause prohibits States from regulating subjects that "are in their nature national, or admit only of one uniform system, or plan of regulation"). The Indiana Act poses no such problem. So long as each State regulates voting rights only in the corporations it has created, each corporation will be subject to the law of only one State. No principle of corporation law and practice is more firmly established than a State's authority to regulate domestic corporations, including the authority to define the voting rights of shareholders. See Restatement (Second) of Conflict of Laws § 304 (1971) (concluding that the law of the incorporating State generally should "determine the right of a shareholder to participate in the administration of the affairs of the corporation"). Accordingly, we conclude that the Indiana Act does not create an impermissible risk of inconsistent regulation by different States.

C

The Court of Appeals did not find the Act unconstitutional for either of these threshold reasons. Rather, its decision rested on its view of the Act's potential to hinder tender offers. We think the Court of Appeals failed to appreciate the significance for Commerce Clause analysis of the fact that state regulation of corporate governance is regulation of entities whose very existence and attributes are a product of state law. As Chief Justice Marshall explained:

> A corporation is an artificial being, invisible, intangible, and existing only in contemplation of law. Being the mere creature of law, it possesses only those properties which the charter of its creation confers upon it, either expressly, or as incidental to its very existence. These are such as are supposed best calculated to effect the object for which it was created. Trustees of Dartmouth College v. Woodward, 4 Wheat. 518, 636 (1819).

See First National Bank of Boston v. Bellotti, 435 U.S. 765, 822–824 (1978) (Rehnquist, J., dissenting). Every State in this country has enacted laws regulating corporate governance. By prohibiting certain transactions, and regulating others, such laws necessarily affect certain aspects of interstate commerce. This necessarily is true with respect to corporations with shareholders in States other than the State of incorporation. Large corporations that are listed on national exchanges, or even regional exchanges, will have shareholders in many States and shares that are traded frequently. The markets that facilitate this national and international participation in ownership of corporations are essential for providing capital not only for new enterprises but also for established companies that need to expand their businesses. This beneficial free market system depends at its core upon the fact that a corporation—except in the rarest situations—is organized under, and governed by, the law of a single jurisdiction, traditionally the corporate law of the State of its incorporation.

* * *

D

Dynamics' argument that the Act is unconstitutional ultimately rests on its contention that the Act will limit the number of successful tender offers. There is little evidence that this will occur. But even if true, this result would not substantially affect our Commerce Clause analysis. We reiterate that this Act does not prohibit any entity—resident or nonresident—from offering to purchase, or from purchasing, shares in Indiana corporations, or from attempting thereby to gain control. It only provides regulatory procedures designed for the better protection of the corporations' shareholders. We have rejected the "notion that the Commerce Clause protects the particular structure or methods of operation in a * * * market." Exxon Corp. v. Governor of Maryland, 437 U.S., at 127. The very commodity that is traded in the securities market is one whose characteristics are defined by state law. Similarly, the very commodity that is traded in the "market for corporate control"—the corporation—is one that owes its existence and attributes to state law. Indiana need not define these commodities as other States do; it need only provide that residents and nonresidents have equal access to them. This Indiana has done. Accordingly, even if the Act should decrease the number of successful tender offers for Indiana corporations, this would not offend the Commerce Clause.

IV

On its face, the Indiana Control Share Acquisitions Chapter evenhandedly determines the voting rights of shares of Indiana corporations. The Act does not conflict with the provisions or purposes of the Williams Act. To the limited extent that the Act affects interstate commerce, this is justified by the State's interests in defining the attributes of shares in its corporations and in protecting shareholders. Congress has never questioned the need for state regulation of these matters. Nor do we think such regulation offends the Constitution. Accordingly, we reverse the judgment of the Court of Appeals.

It is so ordered.

---

1. *Was the Indiana Statute Truly Preclusive?* Some commentators believe that the Indiana "control share acquisition" statute at issue in *CTS* could not block a determined bidder and may actually assist it. Contrasting Indiana's statute with "fair price" and "redemption"

statutes, Professor Roberta Romano predicted that "shareholders may tender more frequently under a control share statute than a fair price provision."[137] Ordinarily, antitakeover defenses seek to prevent the shareholders from voting, but the Indiana statute actually entitled them to vote on the offer. Although the Indiana statute effectively also mandated a 50-day delay before the bidder can obtain a vote and pursue its offer, today a target board could probably secure approximately the same delay through the use of a poison pill. Thus, to believe that the bidder is really disadvantaged by the vote requirement, one must believe that the target shareholders who hold its shares prior to the commencement of a takeover would vote differently on its mandated referendum than would the shareholders who thereafter acquire those shares. Proponents of this statutory approach evidently believe that the "true" shareholders will vote down an offer that the "arbs" and "speculators" who acquire takeover stocks would approve. This is a questionable premise, as the "true" shareholders have arguably "voted with their feet" by tendering to the arbitrageurs.

2. *Delaware's Response.* Within days after the Supreme Court's decision in *CTS,* Delaware began to draft an antitakeover statute. After considering and rejecting an Indiana-style control share acquisition statute, the Corporate Law Section of the Delaware State Bar Association turned instead to New York State for a precedent and largely borrowed N.Y.Bus.Corp.L. § 912. This form of statute—known as a "moratorium" or "business combination" statute—imposes no obstacle to a tender offer, but delays any second-step merger for several years (5 years in New York; 3 years in Delaware). As adopted, Delaware Gen.Corp.Law § 203 (see Statutory Supplement) bars an acquirer of more than 15% of the voting stock of a Delaware corporation from effecting a "business combination" (as defined) between it and the target for three years. The practical impact of such an antitakeover statute is to bar the financing of "bust-up" takeovers. Because the bidder cannot get access to the target's assets for the moratorium period, it cannot issue junk bonds based largely on the target's liquidation value. Thus, a moratorium statute may not preclude a well-financed Whale Co. from a takeover of Minnow Inc., but it does largely deter Minnow from tendering for Whale.

3. *The Post-CTS Case Law.* The first decisions after *CTS* involved the new Delaware statute.[138] Each found that the Delaware statute left hostile bidders "a meaningful opportunity for success" while also concluding that a statute that wholly insulated targets from bidders would not pass constitutional muster under a Commerce Clause analysis, even after CTS. At least implicitly, these decisions seemed to continue to

---

[137] Romano, The Political Economy of Takeover Statutes, 73 Va.L.Rev. 111, 169 (1987).

[138] See BNS Inc. v. Koppers Co., Inc., 683 F.Supp. 458 (D.Del.1988); RP Acquisition Corp. v. Staley Continental, Inc., 686 F.Supp. 476 (D.Del.1988); City Capital Associates LP v. Interco, Inc., 696 F.Supp. 1551 (D.Del.1988).

use a balancing mode of analysis: that is, a state could pursue legitimate corporate governance objectives in a way that chilled takeovers, so long as it did not wholly preclude them. But, as the next case (which also involves a "moratorium" statute, but one stricter than Delaware's) illustrates, the tide turned quickly.[139]

Amanda Acquisition Corp. v. Universal Foods Corp.

United States Court of Appeals, Seventh Circuit, 1989.
877 F.2d 496.

■ Before BAUER, CHIEF JUDGE, EASTERBROOK, CIRCUIT JUDGE, and WILL, SENIOR DISTRICT JUDGE.

■ EASTERBROOK, CIRCUIT JUDGE.

States have enacted three generations of takeover statutes in the last 20 years. Illinois enacted a first-generation statute, which forbade acquisitions of any firm with substantial assets in Illinois unless a public official approved. We concluded that such a statute injures investors, is preempted by the Williams Act, and is unconstitutional under the dormant Commerce Clause. MITE Corp. v. Dixon, 633 F.2d 486 (7th Cir. 1980). The Supreme Court affirmed the judgment under the Commerce Clause, Edgar v. MITE Corp., 457 U.S. 624, 643–46 (1982). * * *

Indiana enacted a second-generation statute, applicable only to firms incorporated there and eliminating governmental veto power. Indiana's law provides that the acquiring firm's shares lose their voting power unless the target's directors approve the acquisition or the shareholders not affiliated with either bidder or management authorize restoration of votes. We concluded that this statute, too, is inimical to investors' interests, preempted by the Williams Act, and unconstitutional under the Commerce Clause. Dynamics Corp. of America v. CTS Corp., 794 F.2d 250 (7th Cir. 1986). This time the Supreme Court did not agree. It thought the Indiana statute consistent with both [the] Williams Act and Commerce Clause. CTS Corp. v. Dynamics Corp. of America, 481 U.S. 69, 107 S.Ct. 1637, 95 L.Ed.2d 67 (1987). Adopting Justice White's view of preemption for the sake of argument, id. at 81, 107 S.Ct. at 1645, the Court found no inconsistency between state and federal law because Indiana allowed the bidder to *acquire* the shares without hindrance. Such a law makes the shares less attractive, but it does not regulate the process of bidding. As for the Commerce Clause, the Court took Indiana's law to be regulation of internal corporate affairs, potentially beneficial because it would allow investors to avoid the "coercion" of two-tier bids and other tactics. * * *

Wisconsin has a third-generation takeover statute. Enacted after *CTS,* it postpones the kinds of transactions that often follow tender offers (and often are the reason for making the offers in the first place). Unless

---

[139] For another decision rejecting the "meaningful opportunity for success" standard, see WLR Foods, Inc. v. Tyson Foods, Inc., 65 F.3d 1172 (4th Cir. 1995).

the target's board agrees to the transaction in advance, the bidder must wait three years after buying the shares to merge with the target or acquire more than 5% of its assets. We must decide whether this is consistent with the Williams Act and Commerce Clause.

I

* * *

No firm incorporated in Wisconsin and having its headquarters, substantial operations, or 10% of its shares or shareholders there may "engage in a business combination with an interested stockholder . . . for 3 years after the interested stockholder's stock acquisition date unless the board of directors of the [Wisconsin] corporation has approved, before the interested stockholder's stock acquisition date, that business combination or the purchase of stock", Wis.Stat. § 180.726(2). An "interested stockholder" is one owning 10% of the voting stock, directly or through associates (anyone acting in concert with it), § 180.726(1)(j). A "business combination" is a merger with the bidder or any of its affiliates, sale of more than 5% of the assets to bidder or affiliate, liquidation of the target, or a transaction by which the target guarantees the bidder's or affiliates debts or passes tax benefits to the bidder or affiliate, § 180.726(1)(e). The law, in other words, provides for almost hermetic separation of bidder and target for three years after the bidder obtains 10% of the stock—unless the target's board consented before then. No matter how popular the offer, the ban applies: obtaining 85% (even 100%) of the stock held by non-management shareholders won't allow the bidder to engage in a business combination, as it would under Delaware law. See BNS, Inc. v. Koppers Co., 683 F.Supp. 458 (D.Del.1988); RP Acquisition Corp. v. Staley Continental, Inc., 686 F.Supp. 476 (D.Del.1988); City Capital Associates L.P. v. Interco, Inc., 696 F.Supp. 1551 (D.Del.), affirmed, 860 F.2d 60 (3d Cir. 1988). Wisconsin firms cannot opt out of the law, as may corporations subject to almost all other state takeover statutes. In Wisconsin it is management's approval in advance, or wait three years. Even when the time is up, the bidder needs the approval of a majority of the remaining investors, without any provision disqualifying shares still held by the managers who resisted the transaction, § 180.726(3)(b). The district court found that this statute "effectively eliminates hostile leveraged buyouts". As a practical matter, Wisconsin prohibits any offer contingent on a merger between bidder and target, a condition attached to about 90% of contemporary tender offers.

* * *

II

Courts try to avoid constitutional adjudication. There is no escape for us today, however. * * *

A

If our views of the wisdom of state law mattered, Wisconsin's takeover statute would not survive. Like our colleagues who decided *MITE* and *CTS*, we believe that antitakeover legislation injures shareholders.[5] Managers frequently realize gains for investors via voluntary combinations (mergers). If gains are to be had, but managers balk, tender offers are investors' way to go over managers' heads. If managers are not maximizing the firm's value—perhaps because they have missed the possibility of a synergistic combination, perhaps because they are clinging to divisions that could be better run in other hands, perhaps because they are just not the best persons for the job—a bidder that believes it can realize more of the firm's value will make investors a higher offer. Investors tender; the bidder gets control and changes things. Michael Bradley, Anand Desai & E. Han Kim, Synergistic Gains from Corporate Acquisitions and Their Division Between the Stockholders of Target and Acquiring Firms, 21 J.Fin.Econ. 3 (1988). The prospect of monitoring by would-be bidders, and an occasional bid at a premium, induces managers to run corporations more efficiently and replaces them if they will not.

Premium bids reflect the benefits for investors. The price of a firm's stock represents investors' consensus estimate of the value of the shares under current and anticipated conditions. Stock is worth the present value of anticipated future returns—dividends and other distributions. Tender offers succeed when bidders offer more. Only when the bid exceeds the value of the stock (however investors compute value) will it succeed. A statute that precludes investors from receiving or accepting a premium offer makes them worse off. It makes the economy worse off too, because the higher bid reflects the better use to which the bidder can put the target's assets. (If the bidder can't improve the use of the assets, it injures itself by paying a premium.)

Universal, making an argument common among supporters of antitakeover laws, contends that its investors do not appreciate the worth of its business plans, that its stock is trading for too little, and that if investors tender reflexively they injure themselves. If only they would wait, Universal submits, they would do better under current

---

[5] Because both the district court and the parties—like the Williams Act—examine tender offers from the perspective of equity investors, we employ the same approach. States could choose to protect "constituencies" other than stockholders. Creditors, managers, and workers invest human rather than financial capital. But the limitation of our inquiry to equity investors does not affect the analysis, because no evidence of which we are aware suggests that bidders confiscate workers' and other participants' investments to any greater degree than do incumbents—who may (and frequently do) close or move plants to follow the prospect of profit. Joseph A. Grundfest, a Commissioner of the SEC, showed in Job Loss and Takeovers, address to University of Toledo College of Law, Mar. 11, 1988, that acquisitions have no logical (or demonstrable) effect on employment. See also Brown & Medoff, The Impact of Firm Acquisitions on Labor, in Corporate Takeovers: Causes and Consequences 9 (A. Auerbach ed. 1988); Roberta Romano, The Future of Hostile Takeovers: Legislation and Public Opinion, 57 U.Cin.L.Rev. 457 (1988); C. Steven Bradford, Protecting Shareholders from Themselves? A Policy and Constitutional Review of a State Takeover Statute, 67 Neb.L.Rev. 459, 529–34 (1988).

management. A variant of the argument has it that although smart investors know that the stock is underpriced, many investors are passive and will tender; even the smart investors then must tender to avoid doing worse on the "back end" of the deal. State laws giving management the power to block an offer enable the managers to protect the investors from themselves.

Both versions of this price-is-wrong argument imply: (a) that the stock of firms defeating offers later appreciates in price, topping the bid, thus revealing the wisdom of waiting till the market wises up; and (b) that investors in firms for which no offer is outstanding gain when they adopt devices so that managers may fend off unwanted offers (or states adopt laws with the same consequence). Efforts to verify these implications have failed. The best available data show that if a firm fends off a bid, its profits decline, and its stock price (adjusted for inflation and market-wide changes) never tops the initial bid, even if it is later acquired by another firm. Stock of firms adopting poison pills falls in price, as does the stock of firms that adopt most kinds of anti-takeover amendments to their articles of incorporation. Studies of laws similar to Wisconsin's produce the same conclusion: share prices of firms incorporated in the state drop when the legislation is enacted.

Although a takeover-*proof* firm leaves investors at the mercy of incumbent managers (who may be mistaken about the wisdom of their business plan even when they act in the best of faith), a takeover-*resistant* firm may be able to assist its investors. An auction may run up the price, and delay may be essential to an auction. Auctions transfer money from bidders to targets, and diversified investors would not gain from them (their left pocket loses what the right pocket gains); diversified investors would lose from auctions if the lower returns to bidders discourage future bids. But from targets' perspectives, once a bid is on the table an auction may be the best strategy. The full effects of auctions are hard to unravel, sparking scholarly debate. Devices giving managers some ability to orchestrate investors' responses, in order to avoid panic tenders in response to front-end-loaded offers, also could be beneficial, as the Supreme Court emphasized in *CTS,* 481 U.S. at 92–93, 107 S.Ct. at 1651–52. ("Could be" is an important qualifier; even from a perspective limited to targets' shareholders given a bid on the table, it is important to know whether managers use this power to augment bids or to stifle them, and whether courts can tell the two apart.)

State anti-takeover laws do not serve these ends well, however. Investors who prefer to give managers the discretion to orchestrate responses to bids may do so through "fair-price" clauses in the articles of incorporation and other consensual devices. Other firms may choose different strategies. A law such as Wisconsin's does not add options to firms that would like to give more discretion to their managers; instead it destroys the possibility of divergent choices. Wisconsin's law applies even when the investors prefer to leave their managers under the gun, to allow the market full sway. Karpoff and Malatesta found that state anti-takeover laws have little or no effect on the price of shares if the firm already has poison pills (or related devices) in place, but strongly negative effects on price when firms have no such contractual devices. To put this differently, state laws have bite only when investors, given the choice, would deny managers the power to interfere with tender offers (maybe already *have* denied managers that power).

B

Skepticism about the wisdom of a state's law does not lead to the conclusion that the law is beyond the state's power, however. We have not been elected custodians of investors' wealth. States need not treat investors' welfare as their summum bonum. Perhaps they choose to protect managers' welfare instead, or believe that the current economic literature reaches an incorrect conclusion and that despite appearances takeovers injure investors in the long run. Unless a federal statute or the Constitution bars the way, Wisconsin's choice must be respected.

Amanda relies on the Williams Act of 1968, incorporated into §§ 13(d), (e) and 14(d)–(f) of the Securities Exchange Act of 1934. The Williams Act regulates the conduct of tender offers. Amanda believes that Congress created an entitlement for investors to receive the benefit of tender offers, and that because Wisconsin's law makes tender offers unattractive to many potential bidders, it is preempted. See *MITE*, 633 F.2d at 490–99, and Justice White's views, 457 U.S. at 630–40.

Preemption has not won easy acceptance among the Justices for several reasons. First there is § 28(a) of the '34 Act, 15 U.S.C. § 78bb(a), which provides that "[n]othing in this chapter shall affect the jurisdiction of the securities commission * * * of any State over any security or any person insofar as it does not conflict with the provisions of this chapter or the rules and regulations thereunder." Although some of the SEC's regulations (particularly the one defining the commencement of an offer) conflict with some state takeover laws, the SEC has not drafted regulations concerning mergers with controlling shareholders, and the Act itself does not address the subject. States have used the leeway afforded by § 28(a) to carry out "merit regulation" of securities—"blue sky" laws that allow securities commissioners to forbid sales altogether, in contrast with the federal regimen emphasizing disclosure. So § 28(a) allows states to stop some transactions federal law would permit, in pursuit of an approach at odds with a system emphasizing disclosure and investors' choice. Then there is the traditional reluctance of federal courts to infer preemption of "state law in areas traditionally regulated by the States." States have regulated corporate affairs, including mergers and sales of assets, since before the beginning of the nation.

Because Justice White's views of the Williams Act did not garner the support of a majority of the Court in *MITE*, we reexamined that subject in *CTS* and observed that the best argument for preemption is the

Williams Act's "neutrality" between bidder and management, a balance designed to leave investors free to choose. * * *

There is a big difference between what Congress *enacts* and what it *supposes* will ensue. Expectations about the consequences of a law are not themselves law. To say that Congress wanted to be neutral between bidder and target—a conclusion reached in many of the Court's opinions, e.g., Piper v. Chris-Craft Industries, Inc., 430 U.S. 1, 97 S.Ct. 926, 51 L.Ed.2d 124 (1977)—is not to say that it also forbade the states to favor one of these sides. Every law has a stopping point, likely one selected because of a belief that it would be unwise (for now, maybe forever) to do more. * * * Nothing in the Williams Act says that the federal compromise among bidders, targets' managers, and investors is the only permissible one. * * *

The Williams Act regulates the *process* of tender offers: timing, disclosure, proration if tenders exceed what the bidder is willing to buy, best-price rules. It slows things down, allowing investors to evaluate the offer and management's response. Best-price, proration, and short-tender rules ensure that investors who decide at the end of the offer get the same treatment as those who decide immediately, reducing pressure to leap before looking. After complying with the disclosure and delay requirements, the bidder is free to take the shares. *MITE* held invalid a state law that increased the delay and, by authorizing a regulator to nix the offer, created a distinct possibility that the bidder would be unable to buy the stock (and the holders to sell it) despite compliance with federal law. Illinois tried to regulate the process of tender offers, contradicting in some respects the federal rules. Indiana, by contrast, allowed the tender offer to take its course as the Williams Act specified but "sterilized" the acquired shares until the remaining investors restored their voting rights. Congress said nothing about the voting power of shares acquired in tender offers. Indiana's law reduced the benefits the bidder anticipated from the acquisition but left the process alone. So the Court, although accepting Justice White's views for the purpose of argument, held that Indiana's rules do not conflict with the federal norms.

CTS observed that laws affecting the voting power of acquired shares do not differ in principle from many other rules governing the internal affairs of corporations. Laws requiring staggered or classified boards of directors delay the transfer of control to the bidder; laws requiring supermajority vote for a merger may make a transaction less attractive or impossible. 481 U.S. at 85–86, 107 S.Ct. at 1647–48. Yet these are not preempted by the Williams Act, any more than state laws concerning the *effect* of investors' votes are preempted by the portions of the Exchange Act, 15 U.S.C. § 78n(a)–(c), regulating the process of soliciting proxies. Federal securities laws frequently regulate process while state corporate law regulates substance. Federal proxy rules demand that firms disclose many things, in order to promote informed voting. Yet states may permit or compel a supermajority rule (even a unanimity rule) rendering it all but impossible for a particular side to prevail in the voting. * * * Are the state laws therefore preempted? How about state laws that allow many firms to organize without traded shares? Universities, hospitals, and other charities have self-perpetuating boards and cannot be acquired by tender offer. Insurance companies may be organized as mutuals, without traded shares; retailers often organize as co-operatives, without traded stock; some decently large companies (large enough to be "reporting companies" under the '34 Act) issue stock subject to buy-sell agreements under which the investors cannot sell to strangers without offering stock to the firm at a formula price; Ford Motor Co. issued non-voting stock to outside investors while reserving voting stock for the family, thus preventing outsiders from gaining control (dual-class stock is becoming more common); firms issue and state law enforces poison pills. All of these devices make tender offers unattractive (even impossible) and greatly diminish the power of proxy fights, success in which often depends on buying votes by acquiring the equity to which the vote is attached. None of these devices could be thought preempted by the Williams Act or the proxy rules. If they are not preempted, neither is Wis.Stat. § 180.726.

Any bidder complying with federal law is free to acquire shares of Wisconsin firms on schedule. Delay in completing a second-stage merger may make the target less attractive, and thus depress the price offered or even lead to an absence of bids; it does not, however, alter any of the procedures governed by federal regulation. Indeed Wisconsin's law does not depend in any way on how the acquiring firm came by its stock: open-market purchases, private acquisitions of blocs, and acquisitions via tender offers are treated identically. Wisconsin's law is no different in effect from one saying that for the three years after a person acquires 10% of a firm's stock, a unanimous vote is required to merge. Corporate law once had a generally-applicable unanimity rule in major transactions, a rule discarded because giving every investor the power to block every reorganization stopped many desirable changes. (Many investors could use their "hold-up" power to try to engross a larger portion of the gains, creating a complex bargaining problem that often could not be solved.) Wisconsin's more restrained version of unanimity also may block beneficial transactions, but not by tinkering with any of the procedures established in federal law.

* * *

C

The Commerce Clause, Art. I, § 8 cl. 3 of the Constitution, grants Congress the power "[t]o regulate Commerce * * * among the several States". * * *

When state law discriminates against interstate commerce expressly—for example, when Wisconsin closes its border to butter from

Minnesota—the negative Commerce Clause steps in. The law before us is not of this type: it is neutral between inter-state and intra-state commerce. Amanda therefore presses on us the broader, all-weather, be-reasonable vision of the Constitution. Wisconsin has passed a law that unreasonably injures investors, most of whom live outside of Wisconsin, and therefore it *has* to be unconstitutional, as Amanda sees things. Although Pike v. Bruce Church, Inc., 397 U.S. 137, 90 S.Ct. 844, 25 L.Ed.2d 174 (1970), sometimes is understood to authorize such general-purpose balancing, a closer examination of the cases may support the conclusion that the Court has looked for discrimination rather than for baleful effects. * * * At all events, although *MITE* employed the balancing process described in *Pike* to deal with a statute that regulated all firms having "contacts" with the state, *CTS* did not even cite that case when dealing with a statute regulating only the affairs of a firm incorporated in the state, and Justice Scalia's concurring opinion questioned its application. * * * Although the scholars whose writings we cited in Part II.A conclude that laws such as Wisconsin's injure investors, Wisconsin is entitled to give a different answer to this empirical question—or to decide that investors' interests should be sacrificed to protect managers' interests or promote the stability of corporate arrangements.

Illinois's law, held invalid in *MITE,* regulated sales of stock elsewhere. Illinois tried to tell a Texas owner of stock in a Delaware corporation that he could not sell to a buyer in California. By contrast, Wisconsin's law, like the Indiana statute sustained by *CTS,* regulates the internal affairs of firms incorporated there. Investors may buy or sell stock as they please. Wisconsin's law differs in this respect not only from that of Illinois but also from that of Massachusetts, which forbade any transfer of shares for one year after the failure to disclose any material fact, a flaw that led the First Circuit to condemn it. Hyde Park Partners, L.P. v. Connolly, 839 F.2d 837, 847–48 (1st Cir. 1988).

Buyers of stock in Wisconsin firms may exercise full rights as investors, taking immediate control. No interstate transaction is regulated or forbidden. True, Wisconsin's law makes a potential buyer less willing to buy (or depresses the bid), but this is equally true of Indiana's rule. Many other rules of corporate law—supermajority voting requirements, staggered and classified boards, and so on—have similar or greater effects on some persons' willingness to purchase stock. * * * States could ban mergers outright, with even more powerful consequences. * * * Wisconsin did not allow mergers among firms chartered there until 1947. We doubt that it was violating the Commerce Clause all those years. * * * Every rule of corporate law affects investors who live outside the state of incorporation, yet this has never been thought sufficient to authorize a form of cost-benefit inquiry through the medium of the Commerce Clause.

* * *

The long run takes time to arrive, and it is tempting to suppose that courts could contribute to investors' welfare by eliminating laws that impose costs in the short run. * * * The price of such warfare, however, is a reduction in the power of competition among states. Courts seeking to impose "good" rules on the states diminish the differences among corporate codes and dampen competitive forces. Too, courts may fail in their quest. How do judges know which rules are best? Often only the slow forces of competition reveal that information. Early economic studies may mislead, or judges (not trained as social scientists) may misinterpret the available data or act precipitously. Our Constitution allows the states to act as laboratories; slow migration (or national law on the authority of the Commerce Clause) grinds the failures under. No such process weeds out judicial errors, or decisions that, although astute when rendered, have become anachronistic in light of changes in the economy. Judges must hesitate for these practical reasons—and not only because of limits on their constitutional competence—before trying to "perfect" corporate codes.

* * *

. . . The Commerce Clause does not demand that states leave bidders a "meaningful opportunity for success". . . A state with the power to forbid mergers has the power to defer them for three years. Investors can turn to firms incorporated in states committed to the dominance of market forces, or they can turn on legislators who enact unwise laws. The Constitution has room for many economic policies. "[A] law can be both economic folly and constitutional." *CTS,* 481 U.S. at 96–97, 107 S.Ct. at 1653–54 (Scalia, J., concurring). Wisconsin's law may well be folly; we are confident that it is constitutional.

Was the Decision Overwritten? Amanda Acquisition gives *CTS* a very broad interpretation: First, the negative impact of the Commerce Clause simply precludes discriminatory legislation and does not require "that states leave bidders 'a meaningful opportunity for success' " (as the earlier decisions involving the Delaware statute had required). Second, the preemption claim is dismissed because the Williams Act is said not to mandate a neutral balance between bidder and target, but only to regulate "the process of tender offers." Because "investors have no right to receive tender offers," *Amanda Acquisition* declares that state law may prevent a bidder from launching a takeover bid; provided that it not interfere with the process of the tender offer should a bidder proceed. *Query:* Is this a sensible interpretation of Congressional intent? Would Congress have wanted to insist on neutrality between bidder and target at the federal level, but then allow the Williams Act to be rendered an empty formality by state legislation?

More importantly, is such a view of preemption consistent with the Court's analysis in *CTS*? A plausible reading of the *CTS* decision is that it permits a state to protect shareholders from coercion so long as it does not unduly favor management. Arguably, the Indiana statute maximized shareholder power and so promoted the Williams Act's goals. In contrast, the Wisconsin statute presents a far clearer case of undue favoritism: the statute contains none of the escape clauses in the Delaware statute (such as the provision making the statute inapplicable if 85% in interest tender), employs a lower threshold (5% of the target's shares as opposed to Delaware's 15%), and has no opt-out provision.

B. STATE ANTI-TAKEOVER LEGISLATION AFTER CTS: CONSTITUENCY AND DISGORGEMENT STATUTES

At least nominally, state takeover legislation before *CTS* (and even the Delaware and Wisconsin statutes after it) sought to protect shareholders from the allegedly coercive character of hostile takeovers. More recently, however, the focus has shifted from protecting shareholders to protecting "stakeholders": employees, bondholders, local communities and other constituencies. Perhaps their protection was always a motivating force behind state antitakeover laws, but traditionally the negative impact of the Commerce Clause posed a formidable barrier to legislation restricting plant closings or worker terminations. After *CTS*, this barrier seemed less formidable, and legislatures became more explicit about their intended beneficiaries. Initially, these statutes authorized directors to consider the "long-term" interests of the corporation (in contrast, it seemed, to the "short-term" interests of shareholders).[140] Next, statutes began to permit the board to consider the interests of non-shareholder constituencies. At least 26 states have adopted some form of constituency legislation, although in most every case these statutes permit, but do not require, the board to consider the interests of non-shareholder constituencies.[141] Some, however, expressly authorize the board to subordinate shareholder interests to those of other constituencies.[142]

This statutory reformulation of the duties of directors raises numerous questions. In the case where the statute provides that the board may consider non-shareholder interests, but does not expressly authorize subordination of shareholder interests, should such legislation be read as changing the board's responsibilities or as simply codifying the common law (which clearly permitted some consideration of other interests if consistent with long-term shareholder welfare)? Consider the views on this topic of the American Bar Association's Committee on

---

[140] New York's statute, passed in 1988, authorized the board to consider whether a poison pill (or "shareholder rights plan") should be "imposed, enforced or waived in the best long-term and short-term interests of the corporation and its shareholders considering, without limitation, the prospects for potential growth, development, productivity and profitability of the corporation." See N.Y.Bus.Corp.Law § 505(a)(2)(ii).

[141] For a survey of these statutes, see Committee on Corporate Laws, Other Constituencies Statutes: Potential for Confusion, 45 Bus.Law. 2253 (1990).

[142] See 15 Pa. Cons. Stat. § 516 (1990).

Corporate Laws (which has declined to add a constituency provision to the ABA's Revised Model Business Corporations Act):

> The Committee has concluded that permitting—much less requiring—directors to consider [non-shareholder] interests without relating such consideration in an appropriate fashion to shareholder welfare (as the Delaware courts have done) would conflict with directors' responsibility to shareholders and could undermine the effectiveness of the system that has made the corporation an efficient device for the creation of jobs and wealth.
>
> The Committee believes that the better interpretation of these statutes, and one that avoids such consequences, is that they confirm what the common law has been: directors may take into account the interests of other constituencies but only as and to the extent that the directors are acting in the best interests, long as well as short term, of the shareholders and the corporation.[143]

The most controversial of the state antitakeover statues is probably the Pennsylvania "disgorgement" statute.[144] Section 2572 of this legislation announces that its purposes are to prevent greenmail, "promote a stable relationship among the various parties involved" in public corporations, and "ensure that speculators who put * * * corporations 'in play' do not misappropriate corporate values for themselves at the expense of the corporation and groups affected by corporate actions." Section 2575 then announces its unique enforcement strategy: investors who join a control group that acquires 20% of a Pennsylvania corporation's voting power are made liable to the corporation for profits on shares acquired within two years prior to the point at which the person or group became a "controlling person" if they are disposed of within 18 months after that point. In effect, Pennsylvania has enlarged the "short swing" liability provisions of § 16(b) of the 1934 Act, and effectively mandated a period of illiquidity of at least 18 months after the investor becomes a member of a control group. Moreover, the definition of "control" and "control group" is largely borrowed from § 13(d) of the 1934 Act and thus has sufficient breadth to reach institutional investors who might join together in a proxy contest or similar effort to oppose takeover defenses.

Many institutional investors perceived the Pennsylvania statute as an attempt at intimidation directed at them. They lobbied Pennsylvania chartered corporations to exercise their statutory right to opt out of the Pennsylvania statute. During a three month opt-out period that ended in July 1990, 67 out of approximately 300 public corporations subject to the Pennsylvania statute (including 11 of the 16 Fortune 500 companies

---

[143] Committee on Corporate Laws, supra note 141, at 2268–9.

[144] Sections 2571–2576 of Title 15 of the Pennsylvania Consolidated Statutes are included in the Statutory Supplement.

chartered in Pennsylvania) did exercise their right to opt out.[145] Does this send a message to other states considering such a statute? Or is it more relevant that well over 200 firms remained subject to the statute?

Is the Pennsylvania statute constitutional, even after *CTS* and *Amanda Acquisition*? Suppose your client is a public pension fund in Arizona that has no contacts with the state of Pennsylvania. It buys a 1% block in a Pennsylvania chartered corporation and allegedly cooperates with a group of other investors who organize a proxy contest to oust the incumbent management. The proxy fight is unsuccessful, but there is a general market rise across the securities markets anyway; it sells its stock 15 months later over the New York Stock Exchange, and the corporation sues to recapture the profits. Is this an out of state market transaction that Pennsylvania cannot regulate under Edgar v. MITE or is it an aspect of corporate governance that *CTS* would say Pennsylvania law can control?

6. NEW DEVELOPMENTS: THE CHANGED LEGAL LANDSCAPE

A. THE FRIENDLY TENDER OFFER

Once, friendly deals were done as mergers and hostile deals were launched as tender offers. That has changed. Today, a friendly deal may still be structured as a merger, but on its announcement, the acquirer will commence (as agreed with the target) a tender offer for 100% of the target's shares. Why? The main reason is the timing advantage that this gives the parties to the deal over a potential hostile bidder who seeks to challenge it. A merger involving public firms may take several months to consummate, as a special meeting of the target's shareholders must be held to approve the merger, a proxy statement must be prepared, proxies must be solicited, and time must be given to beneficial owners to respond. In contrast, a tender offer may be consummated after 20 business days.[146] Such a period may not give a potential rival bidder sufficient time to secure financing or even achieve agreement within its own board as to the deal and its pricing. Also, even if the hostile bidder is willing to top the first bidder's price, it will be forced to offer a significant premium over that price, or otherwise the risk is high that the target shareholders will tender to the first bidder because they know that if a majority of the shares are tendered to the first bidder, the hostile bidder will call off its tender offer. The inability of the target shareholders to determine how their fellow shareholders will decide makes them reluctant to take the risk that the first bid will obtain a majority of the shares, leaving those who wanted to tender to the second bid out in the cold and forced to wait

---

[145] See 22 Sec.Reg. & Law Rptr. 1177 (August 10, 1990).

[146] See Rule 14e–1(a) (specifying a minimum duration for a tender offer of not less than 20 business days).

for the later merger. Once again, shareholders can be coerced to favor even a lower bid (if it is the first to close).

B. THE IMPACT OF HEDGE FUND ACTIVISM

Another reason that hostile bids may have declined is that hedge fund activists have seemingly come to play the same (or at least a largely parallel) role to the hostile bidder. Suppose the stock price of a conglomerate firm has performed poorly, and market analysts attribute its poor performance to its unwieldly portfolio of unrelated companies (which offer no collective synergy). Historically, since the 1980's at least, this pattern might have attracted a hostile bidder who would attempt a "bust-up" takeover, which might even sell off enough of the target's subsidiaries to more than cover its acquisition cost.[147] Today, the economic actor most likely to respond to this pattern of negative synergy is the activist hedge fund. It can acquire a 5–7% stake in the target and then seek representation on its board. Its threat will be that, unless it is given several seats on the board, it will launch a proxy fight for control. These threats have generally caused the risk-averse managements of these targets to give the activist fund the requested board representation.[148] Once it has secured representation on the board, the activist fund will likely push for the sale of some divisions, stock buy-backs, and increased leverage. Ultimately this may produce the same end result as if a "bust-up" takeover had been successfully implemented, except that it costs far less to acquire a 5–7% stake than to pursue a tender offer for the entire target firm.

Issues surround such hedge fund engagements, in part because the other shareholders of the target are generally denied any voice or opportunity to decide on the election of the hedge fund's candidates to its board (because management either enlarges the board or uses vacant directorships to appoint the activist's nominees to those slots). Actual proxy fights occur, but are a small minority of these cases.[149]

C. CROSS-BORDER TENDER OFFERS

The increasingly international character of the world's securities markets can create a special problem for U.S. investors. The regulatory systems for handling takeovers differ markedly around the world and reflect very different philosophies. Thus, it may be impossible to comply with inconsistent statutes. Suppose U.S. investors hold a small percentage of the stock of an English or European company that is listed

---

[147] This assumes (as was often the case) that the value of the target as a whole was less than the value of its various subsidiaries—in short, it had "negative synergy" because the whole was worth less than the sum of its parts.

[148] See John C. Coffee, Jr., Robert J. Jackson, Jr., Joshua R. Mitts, and Robert E. Bishop, Activist Directors and Agency Costs: What Happens When An Activist Director Goes On The Board?, 104 Cornell L. Rev. 381 (2019).

[149] For a fuller discussion, see Coffee, Jackson, Mitts, and Bishop, supra note 148.

both on a U.S. exchange and on the London Exchange, which company becomes the subject of a tender offer. Faced with the complexity of the U.S. securities laws, a foreign bidder might well decide to exclude them from its offer rather than undertake the costs of compliance or face the prospect of litigation in the United States.[150] In addition, express regulatory conflicts can arise between the Williams Act and, for example, the City Code on Takeovers that regulates British takeovers. While the SEC had dealt with these problems on an administrative basis in several instances (usually by allowing bidders to make dual offers, one under British law and one to American security holders under the Williams Act), it proposed an exemption in 1991 under which the Williams Act's substantive rules would not apply when the percentage of U.S. shareholdings in the target were under ten percent.[151]

Eventually the SEC adopted a two-tier exemptive structure, which became effective in 2000.[152] Tender offers for the securities of foreign private issuers are now exempt from most of the substantive provisions of the Williams Act when U.S. investors hold ten percent or less of the class sought in the tender offer; this is known as a "Tier I" exemption. In addition, when the level of U.S. ownership is below 10%, Rules 801 and 802 under the Securities Act of 1993 provide corresponding exemptions from the registration requirements of § 5 for securities issued in rights offerings or business combinations.[153] When U.S. investors hold forty percent or less of the foreign private issuer's securities, a more limited exemption provides relief from certain provisions of the Williams Act (but not from securities registration requirements); this is known as a "Tier II" exemption.[154] Typically, the Tier II acquirer will make separate (but equal) offers to U.S. and foreign holders, which may have slightly different terms and procedures.

Rule 802, which exempts the foreign private issuer engaged in a business combination or exchange offer from any obligation to comply

---

[150] Although the SEC does not deny the ability of foreign bidders to exclude U.S. investors from a foreign tender offer, both it and American courts interpret that power carefully and may assert U.S. jurisdiction if any offering materials enter the United States. See Consolidated Gold Fields PLC v. Minorco, S.A., 871 F.2d 252 (2d Cir. 1989) (where offering materials given to British nominees and thus would predictably be passed on to the U.S. beneficial holders, U.S. jurisdiction existed and U.S. investors could not be excluded under the all-holders rule).

[151] See Securities Act Rel. No. 33–6897 (June 5, 1991).

[152] See Securities Act Release No. 7759 (October 22, 1999); see also Securities Act Release No. 7760 (October 22, 1999).

[153] If the issuer publishes or distributes an informational document in connection with the offering, Rule 802(a)(3) (in the case of an exchange offer or business combination) and Rule 801(a)(4) (in the case of a rights offering) require the issuer to furnish an English translation of that document to the SEC on Form CB by the first business day after its publication or dissemination.

[154] The scope of the Tier I exemption is set forth in Rule 14d–1(c), and the scope of the Tier II exemption is set forth in Rule 14d–1(d). In particular, Rule 14d–1(d)(2) allows the bidder not to extend the withdrawal rights otherwise required by § 14(d)(5) and to make parallel tender offers to U.S. holders and foreign holders (if the terms of the U.S. offer are "at least as favorable"). The bidder may also give notices of extensions in accordance with the "home jurisdiction law," rather than U.S. law.

with § 5 of the Securities Act when U.S. investors hold ten percent or less of the subject company's securities, contains one important substantive condition: U.S. investors must be permitted "to participate in the exchange offer or business combination on terms at least as favorable as those offered any other holder of the subject securities."[155] This was intended to discourage bidders from simply excluding U.S.-based shareholders from their tender offer. Query: although the intent here is to assure equal treatment, does this create the same problems as the "best price" provisions of Rule 14d–10 used to create? That is, what happens if one European shareholder receives a special bonus in the form of an ostensible employment contract or non-compete agreement?

While these rules provide exemptions from the Williams Act and the 1933 Act's registration requirements, the antifraud and anti-manipulation provisions of the federal securities laws continue to apply to cross-border transactions (at least if the purchase or sale transaction occurs in the U.S. or on a U.S. exchange).

The SEC's Tier I and Tier II exemptions have proven difficult to apply. In part, this is because bidders are often unable to estimate the level of U.S. beneficial ownership in a foreign company, but it is even more a result of the fact that U.S. institutions tend today collectively to own more than 10% in most substantial foreign corporations that are publicly held. In 2008, the SEC marginally liberalized its exemption for cross-border tender offers by (1) permitting U.S. beneficial ownership to be calculated as of any date not more than 60 days before or not more than 30 days after the public announcement of the transaction, (ii) providing an alternative test for determining eligibility for its exemptions based on a comparison of the average daily trading volume of the subject company's securities in the U.S. market with its worldwide average trading volume; and (iii) exempting subsequent bidders from the Williams Act's rules if the initial bidder was exempted (even if U.S. ownership levels subsequently rose).[156]

Nonetheless, some critics continue to believe that the cross-border rules either remain a trap for the unwary or "imperialistically" impose U.S. law on foreign markets. For example, suppose that a Spanish company engages in an aggressive buying program for the stock of another Spanish company (of which U.S. investors own more than 10%) in response to a German company's tender offer for the same company. Can U.S. shareholders obtain an injunction, either because the would-be Spanish acquirer made an unconventional tender offer for the company or because it failed to file a Schedule 13D after it crossed the 5% ownership level? On roughly these facts, a federal court did grant an injunction on the Schedule 13D claim, but refused to find that an unconventional tender offer had been made (where the Spanish bidder

---

[155] See Rule 802(a)(2).
[156] See Securities Exchange Act Release No. 58597 (Sept. 19, 2008).

purchased in a "street sweep" that involved U.S. investors on the Madrid stock exchange).[157]

D. DEBT TENDER OFFERS

Tender offers for debt securities are not subject to Section 14(d) (and thus Regulation 14D does not apply), but they are subject to Section 14(e) (and by extension Regulation 14E). Although Rule 14e–1 requires that any tender offer be open for a minimum period of 20 business days, the SEC's staff regularly gives exemptions through no-action letters with respect to this provision, typically permitting seven to ten-day tender offers. The SEC's justification is that debt tender offers are extremely sensitive to prevailing market interest rates, which fluctuate rapidly and cannot be easily predicted even 20 business days in advance.

Debt tender offers also characterized by other unusual formats, including:

1) "Waterfall" tender offers, which are made for a maximum amount of more than the debt outstanding under any one class of debt security, so that typically debt securities in more than one class will be retired, with an uncertain excess spilling over to less senior classes. Because most tender offer rules (including the proration and withdrawal rules) do not apply to tender offers regulated only by Section 14(e), such an offer might be made on a "first come, first served" basis or might not be open to all holders.

2) "Dutch Auction" tender offers, which ask each holder to specify the price at which it is willing to sell so that the bidder can begin with the cheapest prices offered, then move upward until it has purchased all the securities it is willing to buy.[158]

The bidder in most debt tender offers is typically the issuer of the bonds. Although it might have negotiated a redemption right entitling it to buy back its bonds if interest rates fell, it prefers to repurchase them in the market. To this end, debt tender offers are often made deliberately coercive. Probably the most serious issue associated with debt tender offers is the frequent use of "exit consents" under which those tendering in the offer also vote (as a condition of their tender's eligibility) to wave restrictive debt covenants. Thus, those who hold out and do not tender risk that they will wind up holding bonds that are without protective

---

[157] See E.ON AG v. Acciona, S.A., 468 F.Supp.2d 559 (S.D.N.Y. 2007) (denying motion to dismiss and finding subject matter jurisdiction to exist); E.ON AG v. Acciona, S.A., 2007 WL 316874 (S.D.N.Y. 2007) (granting injunction with regard to Schedule 13D violations, but declining, at least partially in deference to principles of international comity, to find that unconventional offers in Europe and U.S. amounted to a tender offer).

[158] For a fuller discussion of the procedures and techniques in debt tender offers, see Charles T. Haag and Zachary A. Keller, Honored in the Breach: Issues in the Regulation of Tender Offers for Debt Securities, 9 N.Y.U. J.L. & Bus. 199 (2012).

financial covenants. This is obviously coercive, but has been quietly accepted by the SEC in this context of debt tender offers.[159] Another criticism of the SEC's approach to these offers is its use of "no-action" letters, not to interpret ambiguities in the law, but to grant blanket exemptions for these tender offers (such as its frequent waiver of the 20 business day rule). Critics argue that this is an inappropriate use of the "no-action" letter procedure.[160]

Possibly as a deterrent to excesses in this area, the SEC's staff has sometimes taken the position that when financial covenants are stripped from bonds or other material changes are made, it is equivalent to the issuance of "new" securities for old securities. As a result, the "new," covenant-less bonds might have to be registered under the 1933 Act or an exemption from registration must be found. Still, what about the exemption under § 3(a)(9) of the 1933 Act for an exchange of securities?[161] Is it really relevant when the issuer has no interest typically in reselling the bonds?

Note finally that although "exit consent" solicitations can waive or amend many provisions in the indenture, the Trust Indenture Act prohibits (in the case of publicly held debt) the modification of the principal amount, the interest rate, or the maturity date. But, does this provision matter if everything else can be amended and the old bonds can be subordinated to other securities?

E. "MINI-TENDERS"

A tender offer that results in the bidder owning less than 5 percent of any class of the target's stock is exempt from Section 14(d)—but not from Section 14(e).[162] The SEC and others have reported that they have "observed an increase in tender offers that would result in the bidder holding not more than five percent of a company's securities."[163] The SEC was concerned that these offers were not accompanied by adequate disclosures, were structured as "first-come, first served" offers without proration or withdrawal rights in order to maximize the pressure on shareholders, and in some cases were even made below the stock market price of the target. One ploy reported by the SEC was for the bidder in such a "mini-tender" to tender at or just above the then market price but deny any withdrawal rights. Then, if the market price rose, the issuer could buy at a now below market price by denying shareholders the right

---

[159] Id.

[160] Id.

[161] For the view that new rules are not needed see Note, Debt Tender Offer Techniques and the Problem of Coercion, 91 Colum.L.Rev. 846 (1991). For a counter-view, see Coffee & Klein, Bondholder Coercion: The Problem of Constrained Choice in Debt Tender Offers and Recapitalizations, 58 U.Chi.L.Rev. 1207 (1991).

[162] In contrast, issuer self-tenders are governed by Rule 13e–4, which applies to all tender offers by an issuer for any class of its equity securities and in any amount, at least if the issuer has at least one class registered under the 1934 Act.

[163] See Securities Exchange Act Release No. 43069 (July 24, 2000).

to withdraw. In some other cases, issuers were found not to have made prompt payment in violation of Rule 14e–1(c). Similar problems were reported in connection with tender offers for limited partnership interests.

Although Securities Exchange Act Release No. 43069, which was issued by the SEC in mid-2000, did not adopt any new substantive rules, it warned bidders that certain of the foregoing practices could be found to be fraudulent or manipulative on their facts, specified "recommended" minimum disclosures for such mini-tender offers, and advised bidders in mini-tenders to use a pro-rata acceptance procedure to avoid excessive pressure on shareholders to tender. Some critics have doubted that the SEC has the authority to enforce these proposed standards.[164]

---

[164] See Miriam R. Albert, Because We Said So: The SEC's Overreaching Efforts to Regulate Mini-Tender Offers, 45 Ariz. L. Rev. 897 (2003).

PART IV

SECURITIES ENFORCEMENT AND CLASS ACTIONS

The earlier portions of this book covered in great detail the ex-ante regulation of offerings, both primary and secondary, public and private, as well as the people and entities involved in offerings. This half of the book focuses on the enforcement surrounding securities transactions. The provisions of the securities laws are enforced both by public officials (the Department of Justice for criminal enforcement and the Securities and Exchange Commission for civil enforcement) and through private litigation. The next few chapters of the book focus on private enforcement, while Chapters 14 and 15 cover public enforcement and Chapter 16 covers both private and public international enforcement.

THE ROLE OF DISCLOSURE AND MATERIALITY IN SECURITIES LITIGATION AND ENFORCEMENT

Liability under the securities laws and regulations deploys the same disclosure basics as the registration provisions. In general, disclosure is required where the law imposes a duty to do so. Absent a requirement to do so, companies do not have to disclose any, or all, information that might impact stock prices. This limitation is particularly true with respect to contingent and future events. That said, once an actor makes a public statement, she must not omit relevant information where that information would be necessary to make the public statement, in light of the circumstances in which it was made, not misleading.[1] As a result, once an actor makes a public statement, even one that was not required pursuant to a statute or regulation, it assumes a duty to disclose the information necessary to ensure that statement is not misleading. That duty extends to information not otherwise required to be disclosed: although to create liability, the statement and the alleged omission must be substantively linked, and the omission must actually make the disclosure misleading.[2]

Further, whether a particular disclosure or omission is required depends on whether it is material. Courts and the SEC have long refused

---
[1] See 17 C.F.R. 240.10b–5(b).
[2] See Matrixx Initiatives, Inc. v. Siracusano, 563 U.S. 27 (2011).

to define materiality as a particular number or percentage. Instead, the long-prevailing definition of materiality focuses on whether there is a substantial likelihood that a reasonable investor would find the information important in making a decision to buy or sell stock because it would significantly alter the "total mix" of information available.[3] As a result, when other information negating or neutralizing an alleged misstatement or omission is present in the market, courts have found a lack of materiality. The standard for materiality is an objective one, focused on a reasonable investor. Statements must be sufficiently concrete to be actionable. Further, there are several key doctrines that play into the definition of materiality. In broad strokes, the categories are: speculative or contingent information; vague or "puffing" statements; and forward-looking information. Materiality is covered in more detail in Chapter 12.

STATUTORY AND CLASS ACTION PROVISIONS UNIQUE TO SECURITIES LITIGATION

A. *Class Actions Generally.* Private securities litigation has received considerable attention from Congress, academics, business organizations, and investor groups. The Supreme Court has also played a significant role in the shaping of securities-related claims and opportunities to litigate them.

As in other areas, like civil rights and employment law, securities class actions provide an important vehicle for bringing claims against corporate actors and deterring securities wrongdoing. Of course, individuals can bring their own claims against a company or its officers and directors for a breach of the securities laws. Litigation is, however, expensive and, for individual investors, the likely recovery is sufficiently small that the cost of litigating outweighs the potential recovery. Particularly, given the limited resources of the SEC for public enforcement, class actions are arguably an important part of the enforcement regime.

Nevertheless, class actions are not without costs. Although there is considerable debate about, for example, how to measure the costs, whether the studies that purport to do so are accurate, or whether the number of claims far exceed any possible wrongdoing, those arguments are regularly balanced, both by the courts and Congress, with the sense that class actions provide a necessary tool in the enforcement arsenal.

Class counsel and their role in securities class actions have received the greatest attention. There are several arguments surrounding their role. First, the actual plaintiffs rarely play a role in these cases. Instead, the lawyers make the decisions and call the shots. Second, the economic interests of the lawyer may differ from those of the class. For example, the lawyers may be inclined to exit the litigation, through settlement, at

---

[3] TSC Industries, Inc. v. Northway, Inc., 426 U.S. 438 (1976).

an earlier stage, in order to pursue other claims or balance their investment in the litigation, rather than staying in for longer and increasing the potential recovery. Third, opponents of class actions argue that the recoveries for the plaintiffs are small, while fees to the lawyers are high. The lawyers, they argue, settle cases too cheaply.[4] Of course, fees are what make the cases attractive to lawyers, and to the extent we believe there is wrongdoing or that enforcement is valuable, fees are arguably a necessary tradeoff for ex post enforcement.

Another point of contention is the evaluation of investor "losses." It is simple to measure the total decline in a stock's price over a specified period, but the decline attributable to the defendant's misconduct (i.e., any material misstatement or omission) may be only a small fraction of the total decline that the stock experienced. A defendant is liable for only that portion of the plaintiff's economic losses that the plaintiff can show were proximately caused by the defendant's actionable misrepresentations or omissions. Thus, for example, a stock may fall fifty points in a single day following disclosure of previously undisclosed material information, but some of this decline may be attributable to external developments in the world, in the financial markets, or in the general industry. As a result, a methodology that compares the settlement size to the total investors' economic losses on their investment tends systematically to overstate the losses that were legally recoverable. The *Dura Pharmaceuticals* case, covered in Chapter 12, explores this issue in more detail.

There is one more puzzle worth considering. The amount of damages in securities class actions is typically proportional to the number of trades made during the class period. The more turnover there is, the more damages plaintiffs can claim. Of course, the fact that for every buyer there is a seller (and thus the net social losses are approximately zero) suggests the number of buyers and sellers should not matter to the damages. After all, zero times anything is zero. In addition, if the court determines damages in part by stock price drops, and if the market anticipates this, even trivial securities fraud cases could lead to enormous damages. Traders could effectively drive down the price in anticipation of recovering all their gains back in securities fraud damages. We know this does not happen, but there are no easy answers

---

[4] What causes (and what can correct) this "cheap" settlement tendency in class actions is a more debatable question. Academic commentary suggests that prevailing methods of calculating fee awards (whether on an hourly basis or a fixed percentage of the recovery) may lead counsel to settle for too little. See John C. Coffee, Understanding the Plaintiff's Attorney: The Implications of Economic Theory for Private Enforcement of Law, 86 Colum. L. Rev. 669, 717 (1986); Jonathan R. Macey & Geoffrey P. Miller, The Plaintiffs' Attorney's Role in Class Actions and Derivative Actions: Economic Analysis and Recommendations for Reform, 58 U. Chi. L. Rev. 1 (1991). See generally Cornerstone Research, Securities Class Settlements—2019 Review and Analysis (2019) (showing median settlements are typically less than 10% of "Simplified Tiered Damages," which is calculated by "simplifying assumptions to estimate per-share damages and trading behavior" because calculating "actual economic losses borne by shareholders . . . requires more in-depth economic analysis.")

as to why or to the question of why the stock price drop is our source of estimating the damages in these cases.

B. *Private Securities Litigation Reform Act of 1995.* Congress debated all of these issues, and more, when it passed the Private Securities Litigation Reform Act of 1995 (the "1995 Act" or "PSLRA"). There were a number of political and social developments, including the election of Republican majorities in both Houses of Congress for the first time in over forty years and an increasing disenchantment with securities class actions (and possibly with private enforcement of law in general) that contributed to the pressure for the PSLRA. The 1995 Act also responded to academic critiques of securities litigation.

The PSLRA has had several impacts on the world of securities litigation. One of the early effects was a perceived growth of class actions in state courts, where the standards for the claims were less defined. In 1998, however, Congress passed the Securities Litigation Uniform Standards Act (SLUSA) to preempt certain class actions that allege fraud under state law. In response to years of confusion over the effect of SLUSA, a unanimous Supreme Court in Cyan Inc., v. Beaver City. Emples. Ret. Fund,[5] held state-law suits are removable, but suits alleging only Securities Act violations are not. Thus, SLUSA did not deprive state courts of their concurrent jurisdiction over class actions brought under the Securities Act.

As Chapters 11 and 12 make clear, claims under the Securities Act and the Exchange Act can overlap and be brought simultaneously. The result is that the pleading of the claims and their proof also overlap. The PSLRA made many changes to both statutes and the way in which these claims are litigated. In general, as a result of the PSLRA, class actions proceed as follows: the plaintiffs' attorneys file a complaint, discovery is stayed, and the defendants file a motion to dismiss. One of the key issues at the motion to dismiss stage is the level of particularity required for the plaintiffs to withstand the motion to dismiss. The discovery stay and particularized pleading, at least with respect to fraud claims, are both required by the PSLRA.

As part of the focus on controlling the externalities created by class actions, the PSLRA also contained provisions establishing qualifications for lead plaintiffs and lead counsel, as well as requiring the plaintiffs' lawyers to file notice of the litigation. Cases that survive the motion to dismiss and have lead counsel and plaintiffs confirmed generally move forward to the class certification stage. At this stage, cases must meet the elements of Federal Rule of Civil Procedure 23 before, for example, moving to trial. In reality, of course, few of these cases try. Instead, cases that can survive all of the procedural hurdles generally move to settlement.

---

[5] Cyan, Inc. v. Beaver Cty. Emples. Ret. Fund, 138 S.Ct. 1061 (2018).

Lead Plaintiff and Counsel Provisions. As mentioned above, the PSLRA made revisions to the ways in which representative plaintiffs and plaintiffs' counsel are selected in federally filed securities class actions. The key provisions appear in § 27 of the Securities Act and Section 21D of the Exchange Act.

The first change is the development of the status of lead plaintiff. Class actions function with a representative plaintiff, but in response to the concern that securities class actions were being filed without review or serious input from those injured, § 27(a)(3) of the Securities Act and § 21D(a)(3) of the Exchange Act require the court to appoint a lead plaintiff. The process starts with a rebuttable presumption that the class member with the largest financial stake is the "most adequate plaintiff."[6] After notice to all members of the proposed class, which allows for others to contest the proposed lead plaintiff, the court makes the selection.[7] The PSLRA also limits to five the number of cases in which a lead plaintiff can serve during any three year period.

One of the questions that can arise is who can oppose the selection of the lead plaintiffs. Some courts have ruled that a defendant may not oppose a plaintiff's motion regarding satisfaction of the lead plaintiff provision, but may object to the adequacy of certification and notice when these are prerequisites to consideration of a motion for lead plaintiff.[8] Other courts have ruled that nothing in the 1995 Act precludes or limits the right of the defendants to challenge a motion to appoint lead plaintiff

---

[6] In some cases, multiple plaintiffs have proposed to combine their stakes in order to have the largest financial stake. Courts in some circuits have allowed aggregation. In Cendant Corp. Litig., Judge Becker correctly explained that the 1995 Act contemplates a "group" serving as lead plaintiff and noted that the SEC had urged "that groups with more than five members are too large to work effectively." 264 F.3d 201, 267 (3d Cir. 2001). See generally Jill E. Fisch, Aggregation, Auctions, and Other Developments in the Selection of Lead Counsel Under the PSLRA, 64 Law & Contemp. Probs. 53, 65–78 (Spr.-Sum. 2001). The PSLRA, however, does not define "group" and as such courts consider aggregation on a case by case basis. See, e.g., In re Stitch Fix, Inc. Securities Litigation, 393 F.Supp.3d (N.D. Cal. 2019) ("[T]he clear consensus in our district is that a group of investors who had no pre-existing relationship with one another, and whose relationship and group status were forged only by a lawyer, is not appropriate to be lead plaintiff based on their aggregated losses."); Tomaszewski v. Trevena, Inc., 383 F.Supp.3d 409 (E.D. Pa. 2019) (concluding that "a relationship based on informed communication among the members as to forming a group need only predate the motions for appointment as lead plaintiff" to satisfy the Third Circuit's "adequate pre-existing relationship" requirement).

[7] The PSLRA does not set forth criteria to calculate the "largest financial interest." The courts, however, have identified four factors to weigh in selecting a lead plaintiff: "(1) the total number of shares purchased during the class period; (2) the net shares purchased during the class period (in other words, the difference between the number of shares purchased and the number of shares sold during the class period)[;] (3) the net funds expended during the class period (in other words, the difference between the amount spent to purchase shares and the amount received for the sale of shares during the class period); and (4) the approximate losses suffered." Varghese v. China Chenghuo Pharmaceutical Holdings, Inc., 589 F.Supp.2d 388, 394–95 (S.D.N.Y. 2008). Of these four factors, "approximate loss" is the "most important element of the test." Id.

[8] See, e.g., Greebel v. FTP Software, Inc., 939 F.Supp. 57, 61 (D. Mass. 1996), aff'd, 194 F.3d 185 (1st Cir. 1999). In Takeda v. Turbodyne Tech., Inc., the court ruled that the defendants have no standing to oppose the appointment of a lead plaintiff, but addressed their concerns sua sponte. 67 F.Supp.2d 1129 (C.D. Cal. 1999). In Fields v. Biomatrix, Inc., the court held that even if defendants do not have standing, a court may sua sponte consider the issues raised by them. 198 F.R.D. 451 (D.N.J. 2000).

and class counsel,[9] while some have held that only class members "may seek to rebut the presumption."[10] The courts generally have not permitted interlocutory appeals to lead plaintiff appointments.[11]

Once selected, the lead plaintiff, in turn, selects and retains counsel. Although early on there were some skirmishes around who in fact had the power to retain counsel, the courts have generally held that barring some significant reason to take over the process, the decision belongs to the lead plaintiff. In fact, in one key case, In re Cendant Corp. Sec. Litig.,[12] the Third Circuit rejected the trial court's decision to select lead counsel by an auction, with potential counsel bidding for the job. As part of the bidding process, bidders submitted proposed fee and other arrangements. In the end, the trial court chose the same lawyers as the lead plaintiff. Nevertheless, when the case settled, the court approved arrangement resulted in a very large fee to the lawyers. The Third Circuit rejected the proposed and approved fee for the lawyers on the theory that the lead plaintiffs were not allowed to choose the counsel and, in the process, negotiate and approve the fee arrangement. That role, the Court held, was consistent with the statutory role of lead plaintiff, and, as a result, the fee resulting from the auction process was invalid.

Notice and Stay Provisions. The PSLRA also included additional procedural provisions. The notice and stay provisions are particularly noteworthy.

(a) *Notice Provisions.* Under § 21D(a)(3)(A), early notice to class members must be published in a widely circulated national business-oriented publication or wire service. A notice filed in the Business Wire satisfies the "widely circulated" requirement of § 21D(a)(3)(A). The provision was not designed to ensure notice to the entire class "but merely to those sophisticated and institutional investors that Congress deemed presumptively most adequate to serve as lead plaintiffs."[13] "[T]he description of the claims in the notice must be congruent with the claims as alleged in the pleadings."[14] Courts have enforced the requirement that a motion to serve as lead plaintiff must be filed within 60 days of the date on which the notice advising of the pendency of the action is published.[15]

---

[9] King v. Livent, Inc., 36 F.Supp.2d 187, 190 (S.D.N.Y. 1999).

[10] In re Cendant Corp. Litigation, 264 F.3d 201, 269 (3d. Cir. 2001).

[11] Pindus v. Fleming Co., Inc., 146 F.3d 1224, 1227 (10th Cir. 1998); Metro Serv. Inc. v. Wiggins, 158 F.3d 162 (2d Cir. 1998); Florida State Bd. of Admin. v. Brick, 210 F.3d 371 (6th Cir. 2000); Z-Seven Fund, Inc. v. Motorcar Parts & Accessories, 231 F.3d 1215 (9th Cir. 2000).

[12] 264 F.3d 201 (3d Cir. 2001).

[13] Greebel v. FTP Software, Inc., 939 F.Supp. 57, 62–64 (D. Mass. 1996), aff'd, 194 F.3d 185 (1st Cir. 1999).

[14] Wenderhold v. Cylink Corp., 188 F.R.D. 577, 579 (N.D. Cal. 1999) (citing Ravens v. Iftikar, 174 F.R.D. 651, 656–661 (N.D. Cal. 1997)).

[15] See, e.g., Topping v. Deloitte Touche Tohmatsu CPA, 95 F.Supp.3d 607, 619–20 (S.D.N.Y. 2015); In re Telxon Corp., Sec. Litig., 67 F.Supp.2d 803, 818 (N.D. Ohio 1999) ("The PSLRA is unequivocal and allows for no exceptions . . . The plain language of the statute precludes consideration of a financial loss asserted for the first time in a complaint, or any other pleading, for that matter, filed after the sixty (60) day window has closed.") But see, e.g., Coopersmith v. Lehman Broth., Inc., 344 F.Supp.2d 783, 790–93 (D. Mass. 2004) (concluding

(b) *Stay Provisions.* Section 21D(b)(3)(B) requires that all discovery and other proceedings be stayed during the pendency of any motion to dismiss "unless the court finds . . . that particularized discovery is necessary to preserve evidence or to prevent undue prejudice" to any party,[16] including discovery required by Rule 26 of the Federal Rules of Civil Procedure.[17] The discovery stay applies to both plaintiffs and defendants.

In SG Cowen Sec. Corp. v. U.S. Dist. Ct. for N.D. of Cal.,[18] the court held that the provision prohibits limited discovery to allow a plaintiff to uncover facts sufficient to satisfy the Act's pleading requirements. As the court earlier stated, "Congress clearly intended that complaints in these securities actions should stand or fall based on the actual knowledge of the plaintiffs rather than information produced by the defendants after the action has been filed."[19]

In an appropriate case the court will lift the automatic stay of discovery to the limited extent of permitting plaintiffs to preserve the status quo by serving on defendants and third parties subpoenas *duces tecum* for the purpose of preserving evidence.[20]

C. *The Evolving Law on Class Certifications.* In addition to pleading and other hurdles, class action complaints must also survive the class certification motion. In general, plaintiffs will file a motion to certify the class, invoking the provisions of Federal Rule of Civil Procedure 23. Defendants sometimes oppose these motions, depending, in part, on whether the parties have already agreed to settle the case.

Rule 23 requires the court to review several factors, some of which overlap with the merits of the underlying case. Typically, however, this debate occurs at a time when discovery is not yet complete, making merits-based determinations problematic. In recent years, the level of proof, or evidence, required at class certification has become a hotly contested issue in the courts. Several important cases are summarized below.

Erica P. Johnson Fund v. Halliburton ("Halliburton I"). In *Halliburton I,* the Supreme Court explored pleading and class certification in the context of a securities claim.[21] The Court held that a plaintiff relying on the fraud-on-the-market theory to establish reliance did not have to separately establish loss causation in order to obtain class

---

the 60-day limitation can be extended in certain circumstances as "[t]he PSLRA does not require speed over due consideration of appropriate candidates.")

[16] 15 U.S.C. § 78u–4(b)(3)(B).
[17] Medhekar v. U.S. Dist. Ct., 99 F.3d 325 (9th Cir. 1996).
[18] 189 F.3d 909 (9th Cir. 1999).
[19] Medhekar v. U.S. Dist. Ct., 99 F.3d at 328.
[20] 15 U.S.C. § 78u–4(b)(3)(C). See, e.g., Grand Casinos, Inc. Sec. Litig., 988 F.Supp. 1270 (D. Minn. 1997).
[21] Erica P. John Fund, Inc. v. Halliburton Co., 563 U.S. 804 (2011).

certification.[22] In his majority opinion, Chief Justice Roberts rejected the Fifth Circuit's requirement of proof of loss causation at the class certification stage, as "not justified" by prior case law.[23]

The fraud-on-the-market theory is covered in Chapter 12. In short, a key aspect of Rule 23 and the invocation of a class action is that the claims of the plaintiffs be sufficiently similar, with the focus being on whether individual aspects of claims predominate. Some claims of securities fraud require reliance. Most individual investors do not read all of the filings of a company. Instead, they buy in the open market, in theory relying on the market price as impacted by company statements and the analysts, brokers, and others who translate that information to the market. As a result, proof of reliance would either differ from one individual to the next or be indirect and based on market price. Either way, absent a mechanism making reliance on market price available for reliance, the plaintiffs would not be able to join as a class. The rebuttable presumption of fraud on the market, adopted by the Court in Basic v. Levinson,[24] created that mechanism.

Reliance has been referred to by the Court as transaction causation, and it differs from loss causation. This distinction was one of many the Court made in *Halliburton I*. In fact, in *Halliburton I*, Chief Justice Roberts stated that requiring proof of loss causation in order to invoke the rebuttable presumption of reliance under the fraud-on-the-market theory would:

> [C]ontravene[ ] *Basic's* fundamental premise—that an investor presumptively relies on a misrepresentation so long as it was reflected in the market price at the time of his transaction. The fact that a subsequent loss may have been caused by factors other than the revelation of a misrepresentation has nothing to do with whether an investor relied on the misrepresentation in the first place, either directly or presumptively through the fraud-on-the-market theory. Loss causation has no logical connection to the facts necessary to establish the efficient market predicate to the fraud-on-the-market theory.[25]

Amgen v. Connecticut Retirement Plans and Trust Funds. At issue in *Amgen* was the question of whether the plaintiffs should be required to prove materiality at the class certification stage, rather than at trial.[26] The Supreme Court rejected Amgen's argument, holding that Rule 23(b) requires only a showing that questions common to the class predominate, but not that they are a question common to all class members. The Court also held that materiality is subject to an objective standard. As a result, proof for one individual would be proof for all. Thus, if the plaintiffs were

---

[22] Id. at 2186.
[23] Id. at 2185.
[24] 485 U.S. 224 (1988).
[25] 563 U.S. 804, 813 (2011).
[26] Amgen Inc. v. Connecticut Ret. Plans & Trust Funds, 568 U.S. 455 (2013).

unable to prove materiality, the entire case would fail for all plaintiffs/class members, and not for just for some individuals. In reaching its holding, the Court emphasized that the role of Rule 23(b)(3) is to determine the best method of adjudication, not to adjudicate the case in its entirety.

Halliburton v. Erica P. Johnson Fund ("Halliburton II"). In *Halliburton II,* the Court revisited the fraud-on-the-market theory, upholding it, but opening the door for further class certification issues.[27] In doing so, the Court distinguished reliance from materiality. As a result, defendants can now attempt to rebut the fraud-on-the-market theory of reliance at the class certification stage. Note that had the *Amgen* defendants prevailed, the burden would have been on the plaintiffs to *prove* materiality at the certification stage, as opposed to at trial.

Waggoner v. Barclays PLC. Following *Halliburton II*, the Second Circuit clarified the fraud-on-the-market theory of reliance at the class certification stage. The court addressed *Basic*'s presumption of reliance in Waggoner v. Barclays PLC,[28] affirming a decision certifying a class based on the price maintenance theory[29] and clarifying that defendants seeking to rebut the *Basic* presumption at the class certification stage must do so by a preponderance of the evidence.[30]

---

[27] Halliburton Co. v. Erica P. John Fund, Inc., 573 U.S. 258 (2014).

[28] 875 F.3d 79 (2d. Cir. 2017).

[29] Price maintenance theory recognizes "that statements that merely maintain inflation already extant in a company's stock price, but do not add to that inflation, nonetheless affect a company's stock price." Waggoner v. Barclays PLC, 875 F.3d 79, 104 (quoting In re Vivendi, 838 F.3d 223, 256 (2d. Cir. 2016)).

[30] Id. The burden of proof standard was reaffirmed in In Ark. Teachers Ret. Sys. v. Goldman Sachs Grp., Inc., clarifying that defendants did not need to "conclusively prove a complete absence of price impact". 879 F.3d 474 (2d. Cir. 2018). While declining to adopt a particular test for market efficiency, the Second Circuit held it was proper for the district court to decline to "view direct and indirect evidence as distinct requirements, opting instead for a holistic analysis based on the totality of the evidence presented." In re Petrobras Securities Litig., 862 F.3d 250, 277 (2d Cir. 2017).

CHAPTER 11

CIVIL LIABILITY UNDER THE SECURITIES ACT OF 1933

Statutes and Regulations

Securities Act, §§ 11, 12, 15, 17.

Rules 156, 176, 436.

This chapter covers the causes of action arising under the Securities Act of 1933. Sections 11 and 12 are provisions of the Securities Act that provide for private liability for buyers.[1] Section 11 establishes liability for misstatements or omissions in registration statements and § 12 applies for rescission or damages related to the prospectus. Section 11 applies to issuers, underwriters, and experts. Section 12 applies to "dealers." The two provisions can, however, overlap.

Generally, §§ 11 and 12 do not require a heightened state of mind or, *scienter*. Thus, they are not "fraud" claims. Some courts, however, apply the "sounds-in-fraud" doctrine to these claims.

This chapter also covers § 17. Section 17 does not create an express private right of action. The Securities Exchange Commission and the Department of Justice deploy § 17 as an enforcement tool. Whether § 17(a) provides a private right of action remains an open question. If it does, it may be an increasingly popular avenue for plaintiffs to pursue securities class actions, since the Supreme Court (and some lower federal courts) have substantially lessened the attractiveness of § 10 and Rule 10b–5 for those purposes.

1. SECTION 11 OF THE 1933 ACT

A. INTRODUCTORY NOTE

At the core of § 11 of the Securities Act of 1933 is a relatively simple concept.[2] The issuer and a list of statutorily defined potential defendants (including the underwriter and outside experts such as the accountant) can be held liable if the registration statement, when it became effective, contained a material misrepresentation or omission. Ironically, § 11 did

---

[1] On § 11 law generally, see Jennifer O'Hare, Institutional Investors, Registration Rights, and the Specter of Liability under Section 11 of the Securities Act of 1933, 1996 Wis. L. Rev. 217; Barry D. Hunter, Liability of Issuer's Counsel in the Wake of Central Bank of Denver—To Whom Is the Lawyer's Due Diligence Due?, 86 Ky. L.J. 413 (1997–1998).

[2] On the history of the 1933 Act, see Joel Seligman, The Transformation of Wall Street: A History of the Securities and Exchange Commission and Modern Corporate Finance chs. 2, 3 (rev. ed. 1995); James M. Landis, The Legislative History of the Securities Act of 1933, 28 Geo. Wash. L. Rev. 29 (1959).

not produce a substantial recovery for 30 years. It is, however, now used more frequently. As a result, it is worth parsing the provision with care.

Any person who acquired a registered security, whether in the registration process or in the secondary market, may sue under § 11.[3] Under § 11(a) the plaintiff has to prove only that "any part of the registration statement, when such part became effective, contained an untrue statement of a material fact or omitted to state a material fact required to be stated therein or necessary to make the statements therein not misleading." In Chapter 12 we examine how a plaintiff proves material misrepresentations or omissions. Materiality, on the one hand, and misrepresentations or omissions, on the other hand, are separate concepts. Simply put, a material misstatement or omission is one that a reasonable investor would consider significant in making an investment decision, with a focus on the probability and/or the magnitude of an event. Proof of materiality and of misrepresentations or omissions are identical, or virtually so, under each of the antifraud remedies addressed in detail in this book (§§ 11 and 12 of the 1933 Act; §§ 10(b), 14(a), 14(d), and 14(e) of the 1934 Act). The lessons of Chapter 12 with respect to materiality and misrepresentations or omissions are equally applicable here.

Normally, the plaintiff need not prove reliance unless the plaintiff bought after the issuer had made generally available to its security holders an earnings statement covering a period of at least a year beginning after the effective date. Even then, "reliance may be established without proof of the reading of the registration statement by such person."[4]

The plaintiff need not prove causation either, but damages are reduced to the extent that the defendant proves that the damages did not result from its misconduct.[5]

Section 11(a) identifies potential defendants. These persons are: (1) the registrant (i.e., the issuing corporation, which is included as a "person who signed the registration statement," since all registration statements must be signed by the issuer even when they relate to a secondary offering); (2) all directors of the issuer (including all persons who are named as "about to become" directors); (3) all other persons who sign the registration statement (i.e., the principal executive officer, the principal financial officer, and the principal accounting officer of the issuer, who must sign even if they are also directors); (4) all underwriters of the offering; and (5) any "expert" who is named as having prepared or certified any part of the registration statement (this would always

---

[3] When shares are bought in the open or secondary market, they must be "traced" to the registered offering. See Hillary A. Sale, Disappearing Without a Trace: Sections 11 and 12(a)(2) of the 1933 Securities Act, 75 Wash. L. Rev. 429 (2000).

[4] § 11(a), last par.; cf. Haralson v. E. F. Hutton Group, Inc., 919 F.2d 1014, 1032 (5th Cir. 1990).

[5] § 11(e).

include the independent accountants who certify the financial statements and occasionally other persons who "expertise" particular statements in the registration statement, such as geologists who give opinions on mineral reserves or lawyers who give title opinions on real property or other legal matters). In addition, § 15 reaches anyone the plaintiff can show to be in control of any of these persons. Liability of control persons is analyzed in Chapter 12.

Under § 11 an issuer's liability is absolute with one exception: the issuer, like all defendants, can show that the plaintiff knew of the untruth or omission at the time the plaintiff acquired the security.[6] For other defendants, an elaborate series of reasonable care or due diligence defenses are available:

(A) A defendant might establish that before the effective date of that part of the registration statement, or upon becoming aware of its effectiveness, the defendant had taken appropriate steps to sever all described connections with the issuer, and had advised the issuer and the Commission in writing that he or she took such action and would not be responsible for that part of the statement, or the defendant gave reasonable public notice that part of the statement had become effective without his or her knowledge and the defendant subsequently severed all connections with the issuer and gave notice to the issuer and Commission.[7]

(B) A nonexpert defendant (often a director, officer, or underwriter), sued on a "nonexpertised" portion of a registration statement as well as an expert sued on an "expertised" portion must establish that "he had, after reasonable investigation, reasonable ground to believe and did believe, at the time such part of the registration statement became effective," that it was true and complete.[8] The standard of reasonableness is defined in § 11(c) to be "that required of a prudent man in the management of his own property."

(C) A nonexpert defendant sued on an "expertised" portion of the registration statement has a double negative defense: that "he had no reasonable ground to believe and did not believe, at the time such part of the registration statement became effective, that the statements therein were untrue or that there was an omission to state a material fact required to be stated therein or necessary to make the statements therein not misleading."[9]

---

[6] § 11(a).

[7] §§ 11(b)(1)–(2).

[8] §§ 11(b)(3)(A)–(B).

[9] § 11(b)(3)(C). In 1995, as part of the Private Securities Litigation Reform Act, the Commission was authorized by amended § 11(f) to limit by rule the liability of outside directors.

B. Defendants and the Due Diligence Defense

The following two cases explore the due diligence defense and make clear its potential power. In effect, the due diligence defense converts a strict liability cause of action into one that is negligence-like.

Escott v. BarChris Construction Corp.
United States District Court, S.D.N.Y., 1968.
283 F.Supp. 643.

■ McLean, District Judge.

This is an action by purchasers of 5-1/2 per cent convertible subordinated fifteen year debentures of BarChris Construction Corporation (BarChris). Plaintiffs purport to sue on their own behalf and "on behalf of all other and present and former holders" of the debentures.

* * *

The action is brought under Section 11 of the Securities Act of 1933. Plaintiffs allege that the registration statement with respect to these debentures filed with the Securities and Exchange Commission, which became effective on May 16, 1961, contained material false statements and material omissions.

Defendants fall into three categories: (1) the persons who signed the registration statement; (2) the underwriters, consisting of eight investment banking firms, led by Drexel & Co. (Drexel); and (3) BarChris's auditors, Peat, Marwick, Mitchell & Co. (Peat, Marwick).

The signers, in addition to BarChris itself, were the nine directors of BarChris, plus its controller, defendant Trilling, who was not a director. Of the nine directors, five were officers of BarChris, i.e., defendants Vitolo, president; Russo, executive vice president; Pugliese, vice president; Kircher, treasurer; and Birnbaum, secretary. Of the remaining four, defendant Grant was a member of the firm of Perkins, Daniels, McCormack & Collins, BarChris's attorneys. He became a director in October 1960. Defendant Coleman, a partner in Drexel, became a director on April 17, 1961, as did the other two, Auslander and Rose, who were not otherwise connected with BarChris.

* * *

In general, BarChris's method of operation was to enter into a contract with a customer, receive from him at that time a comparatively small down payment on the purchase price, and proceed to construct and equip the bowling alley. When the work was finished and the building delivered, the customer paid the balance of the contract price in notes, payable in installments over a period of years. BarChris discounted these notes with a factor and received part of their face amount in cash. The factor held back part as a reserve.

In 1960 BarChris began a practice which has been referred to throughout this case as the "alternative method of financing." In substance this was a sale and leaseback arrangement. It involved a distinction between the "interior" of a building and the building itself, i.e., the outer shell. In instances in which this method applied, BarChris would build and install what it referred to as the "interior package." Actually this amounted to constructing and installing the equipment in a building. When it was completed, it would sell the interior to a factor, James Talcott Inc. (Talcott), who would pay BarChris the full contract price therefor. The factor then proceeded to lease the interior either directly to BarChris's customer or back to a subsidiary of BarChris. In the latter case, the subsidiary in turn would lease it to the customer.

Under either financing method, BarChris was compelled to expend considerable sums in defraying the cost of construction before it received reimbursement.[4] As a consequence, BarChris was in constant need of cash to finance its operations, a need which grew more pressing as operations expanded.

In December 1959, BarChris sold 560,000 shares of common stock to the public at $3.00 per share. This issue was underwritten by Peter Morgan & Company, one of the present defendants.

By early 1961, BarChris needed additional working capital. The proceeds of the sale of the debentures involved in this action were to be devoted, in part at least, to fill that need.

The registration statement of the debentures, in preliminary form, was filed with the Securities and Exchange Commission on March 30, 1961. A first amendment was filed on May 11 and a second on May 16. The registration statement became effective on May 16. The closing of the financing took place on May 24. On that day BarChris received the net proceeds of the financing.

By that time BarChris was experiencing difficulties in collecting amounts due from some of its customers. Some of them were in arrears in payments due to factors on their discounted notes. As time went on those difficulties increased. Although BarChris continued to build alleys in 1961 and 1962, it became increasingly apparent that the industry was overbuilt. Operators of alleys, often inadequately financed, began to fail. Precisely when the tide turned is a matter of dispute, but at any rate, it was painfully apparent in 1962.

In May of that year BarChris made an abortive attempt to raise more money by the sale of common stock. It filed with the Securities and Exchange Commission a registration statement for the stock issue which it later withdrew. In October 1962 BarChris came to the end of the road. On October 29, 1962, it filed in this court a petition for an arrangement

---

[4] Under the sale and leaseback arrangement, Talcott paid part of the price to BarChris as the work progressed.

under Chapter XI of the Bankruptcy Act. BarChris defaulted in the payment of the interest due on November 1, 1962 on the debentures.

* * *

The registration statement in its final form contained a prospectus as well as other information. Plaintiffs' claims of falsities and omissions pertain solely to the prospectus, not to the additional data. The prospectus contained, among other things, a description of BarChris's business, a description of its real property, some material pertaining to certain of its subsidiaries, and remarks about various other aspects of its affairs. It also contained financial information. It included a consolidated balance sheet as of December 31, 1960, with elaborate explanatory notes. These figures had been audited by Peat, Marwick. It also contained unaudited figures as to net sales, gross profit and net earnings for the first quarter ended March 31, 1961, as compared with the similar quarter for 1960. In addition, it set forth figures as to the company's backlog of unfilled orders as of March 31, 1961, as compared with March 31, 1960, and figures as to BarChris's contingent liability, as of April 30, 1961, on customers' notes discounted and its contingent liability under the so-called alternative method of financing. Plaintiffs challenge the accuracy of a number of these figures. They also charge that the text of the prospectus, apart from the figures, was false in a number of respects, and that material information was omitted.

* * *

Summary

For convenience, the various falsities and omissions which I have discussed in the preceding pages are recapitulated here. They were as follows:

1.	*1960 Earnings*		
	(a) *Sales*		
		As per prospectus	$ 9,165,320
		Correct figure	8,511,420
		Overstatement	$ 653,900
	(b) *Net Operating Income*		
		As per prospectus	$ 1,742,801
		Correct figure	1,496,196
		Overstatement	$ 246,605
	(c) *Earnings per Share*		
		As per prospectus	$ .75
		Correct figure	.65
		Overstatement	$ .10

* * *

5.	Earnings Figures for Quarter ending March 31, 1961	
	(a) *Sales*	
	As per prospectus	$ 2,138,455
	Correct figure	1,618,645
	Overstatement	$ 519,810
	(b) *Gross Profit*	
	As per prospectus	$ 483,121
	Correct figure	252,366
	Overstatement	$ 230,755
6.	*Backlog as of March 31, 1961*	
	As per prospectus	$ 6,905,000
	Correct figure	2,415,000
	Overstatement	$ 4,490,000
7.	*Failure to Disclose Officers' Loans Outstanding and Unpaid on May 16, 1961*	$ 386,615
8.	*Failure to Disclose Use of Proceeds in Manner not Revealed in Prospectus*	
	Approximately	$ 1,160,000
9.	*Failure to Disclose Customers' Delinquencies in May 1961 and BarChris's Potential Liability with Respect Thereto*	
	Over	$ 1,350,000
10.	*Failure to Disclose the Fact that BarChris was Already Engaged, and was about to be More Heavily Engaged, in the Operation of Bowling Alleys*	

* * *

[The contingent liabilities as of December 31, 1960 arose from BarChris's selling practices. BarChris used two financing methods. Under the first method, the corporation accepted customers' installment notes with maturities up to seven years as part payment for products sold or services performed. The notes were generally discounted to financial institutions. BarChris began using an alternative financing method in 1960, comprised of one of two types of contracts. Under Type A alternative method contracts, BarChris sold the bowling alley to a factor, James Talcott Inc., and Talcott then leased the property directly to a

[BarChris customer. In Type A contracts, BarChris guaranteed the customer's performance in an amount equal to 25% of the customer's total obligation to Talcott under the lease. In Type B alternative method contracts, BarChris sold the bowling alley to Talcott, who leased back the property to a BarChris subsidiary, BarChris Leasing Corporation, which then leased the property to the customer. In Type B arrangements, BarChris was liable to the extent of 100% for the performance by its subsidiary of its obligations under the leases.]

[With respect to the contingent liabilities for 1960, the prospectus stated that under the second, alternative, method of financing, the Company was contingently liable in an amount equal to 25% of the customers' aggregate unexpired rental payments under both types of contracts. Although this was correct as to the Type A contracts, the contingent liabilities on Type B contracts were up to 100%, and therefore understated to the extent of 75% of unpaid balances under the leases.]

[The court found several BarChris transactions particularly troubling. The Capitol Lanes project, also named Heavenly Lanes, appeared on BarChris's prospectus as a completed contract in the amount of $330,000 in 1960. BarChris, however, had not found an outside buyer. BarChris had sold the lanes to Talcott purely as a financing mechanism, who then leased it back to a newly created BarChris subsidiary. BarChris overstated its 1960 earnings by $330,000 because of this contract.]

[BarChris signed a contract in 1960 for $150,000 to build an annex onto Howard Lanes. Rather than selling the building to Howard Lanes, BarChris retained title to the annex through a subsidiary and leased the annex to Howard. Despite retaining title to the annex BarChris included the contract in its 1960 sales. BarChris overstated its earnings from the Howard Lanes transaction by $150,000.]

[BarChris incorrectly listed $519,810.00 in its prospectus as sales from two transactions. The contracts were actually contingent liabilities. In the Bridge transaction, BarChris had a construction contract for $269,810 with Biel Land & Development Company. On March 24, 1961, however, BarChris acquired Biel—before the transaction closed. Another BarChris subsidiary, Parkway Lanes, Inc., was then to operate Bridge. BarChris included the full value of the contract in its prospectus as a 1961 Q1 sale, despite never receiving payment from Biel. BarChris also incorrectly included $250,000 as a 1961 Q1 sale when it made the contract with Yonkers Lanes, Inc., a BarChris subsidiary. By March 18, 1961, no buyer had emerged for the property built for Yonkers. BarChris, undeterred, incorrectly classified the $250,000 as a sale rather than a liability.]

[BarChris included six alley projects with T-Bowl, a portion of the 'backlog' contracts, as 'jobs in progress' on the March 18, 1961 meeting of the BarChris executive committee. No corporation named T-Bowl existed on March 18, and the corporation's formation was dependent on securing highly speculative financing. The only existence of the projects were six unexecuted, standard-form purchase contracts that BarChris's in-house counsel advised were legally unenforceable. Despite these infirmities, the six projects appeared as scheduled, unfilled orders in BarChris's financial information. Although T-Bowl eventually incorporated on May 2, 1961, no contracts or buyer existed in March 1961.]

Materiality

It is a prerequisite to liability under Section 11 of the Act that the fact which is falsely stated in a registration statement, or the fact that is omitted when it should have been stated to avoid misleading, be 'material.' The regulations of the Securities and Exchange Commission pertaining to the registration of securities define the word as follows:

"The term 'material', when used to qualify a requirement for the furnishing of information as to any subject, limits the information required to those matters as to which an average prudent investor ought reasonably to be informed before purchasing the security registered."

* * *

On all the evidence I find that these balance sheet errors were material within the meaning of Section 11.

* * *

The "Due Diligence" Defenses

Section 11(b) of the Act provides that:

"* * * no person, other than the issuer, shall be liable * * * who shall sustain the burden of proof—

* * *

(3) that (A) as regards any part of the registration statement not purporting to be made on the authority of an expert * * * he had, after reasonable investigation, reasonable ground to believe and did believe, at the time such part of the registration statement became effective, that the statements therein were true and that there was no omission to state a material fact required to be stated therein or necessary to make the statements therein not misleading; * * * and (C) as regards any part of the registration statement purporting to be made on the authority of an expert (other than himself) * * * he had no reasonable ground to believe and did not believe, at the time such part of the registration statement became effective, that the statements therein were untrue or that there was an omission to state a material fact required to be stated therein or necessary to make the statements therein not misleading * * *."

Section 11(C) defines "reasonable investigation" as follows:

"In determining, for the purpose of paragraph (3) of subsection (b) of this section, what constitutes reasonable investigation and reasonable ground for belief, the standard of reasonableness shall be that required of a prudent man in the management of his own property."

Every defendant, except BarChris itself, to whom, as the issuer, these defenses are not available, and except Peat, Marwick, whose position rests on a different statutory provision, has pleaded these affirmative defenses. Each claims that (1) as to the part of the registration statement purporting to be made on the authority of an expert (which, for convenience, I shall refer to as the "expertised portion"), he had no reasonable ground to believe and did not believe that there were any untrue statements or material omissions, and (2) as to the other parts of the registration statement, he made a reasonable investigation, as a result of which he had reasonable ground to believe and did believe that the registration statement was true and that no material fact was omitted. As to each defendant, the question is whether he has sustained the burden of proving these defenses. Surprising enough, there is little or no judicial authority on this question. No decisions directly in point under Section 11 have been found.

Before considering the evidence, a preliminary matter should be disposed of. The defendants do not agree among themselves as to who the "experts" were or as to the parts of the registration statement which were expertised. Some defendants say that Peat, Marwick was the expert, others say that BarChris's attorneys, Perkins, Daniels, McCormack & Collins, and the underwriters' attorneys, Drinker, Biddle & Reath, were also the experts. On the first view, only those portions of the registration statement purporting to be made on Peat, Marwick's authority were expertised portions. On the other view everything in the registration statement was within this category, because the two law firms were responsible for the entire document.

The first view is the correct one. To say that the entire registration statement is expertised because some lawyer prepared it would be an unreasonable construction of the statute. Neither the lawyer for the company nor the lawyer for the underwriters is an expert within the meaning of Section 11. The only expert, in the statutory sense, was Peat, Marwick, and the only parts of the registration statement which purported to be made upon the authority of an expert were the portions which purported to be made on Peat, Marwick's authority.

The parties also disagree as to what those portions were. Some defendants say that it was only the 1960 figures (and the figures for prior years, which are not in controversy here). Others say in substance that it was every figure in the prospectus. The plaintiffs take a somewhat intermediate view. They do not claim that Peat, Marwick expertised every figure, but they do maintain that Peat, Marwick is responsible for a portion of the text of the prospectus, i.e., that pertaining to "Methods of Operation," because a reference to it was made in footnote 9 to the balance sheet.

Here again, the more narrow view is the correct one. The registration statement contains a report of Peat, Marwick as independent public accountants dated February 23, 1961. This relates only to the consolidated balance sheet of BarChris and consolidated subsidiaries as of December 31, 1960, and the related statement of earnings and retained earnings for the five years then ended. This is all that Peat, Marwick purported to certify. It is perfectly clear that it did not purport to certify the 1961 figures, some of which are expressly stated in the prospectus to have been unaudited.

Moreover, plaintiffs' intermediate view is also incorrect. The cross reference in footnote 9 to the "Methods of Operation" passage in the prospectus was inserted merely for the convenience of the reader. It is not a fair construction to say that it thereby imported into the balance sheet everything in that portion of the text, much of which had nothing to do with the figures in the balance sheet.

I turn now to the question of whether defendants have proved their due diligence defenses. The position of each defendant will be separately considered.

* * *

Kircher

Kircher was treasurer of BarChris and its chief financial officer. He is a certified public accountant and an intelligent man. He was thoroughly familiar with BarChris's financial affairs. He knew the terms of BarChris's agreements with Talcott. He knew of the customers' delinquency problem. He participated actively with Russo in May 1961 in the successful effort to hold Talcott off until the financing proceeds came in. He knew how the financing proceeds were to be applied and he saw to it that they were so applied. He arranged the officers' loans and he knew all the facts concerning them.

Moreover, as a member of the executive committee, Kircher was kept informed as to those branches of the business of which he did not have direct charge. He knew about the operation of alleys, present and prospective. He knew that Capitol was included in 1960 sales and that Bridge and Yonkers were included in first quarter 1961 sales despite the fact that they were not sold. Kircher knew of the infirmities in customers' contracts included in the backlog figure. Indeed, at a later date, he specifically criticized Russo's handling of the T-Bowl situation. In brief, Kircher knew all the relevant facts.

Kircher worked on the preparation of the registration statement. He conferred with Grant [a BarChris director whose law firm was securities counsel to BarChris] and on occasion with Ballard [underwriters' counsel]. He supplied information to them about the company's business. He had the prospectus and understood it. He knew what it said and what it did not say.

Kircher's contention is that he had never before dealt with a registration statement, that he did not know what it should contain, and that he relied wholly on Grant, Ballard and Peat, Marwick to guide him. He claims that it was their fault, not his, if there was anything wrong with it. He says that all the facts were recorded in BarChris's books where these "experts" could have seen them if they had looked. He says that he truthfully answered all their questions. In effect, he says that if they did not know enough to ask the right questions and to give him the proper instructions, that is not his responsibility.

There is an issue of credibility here. In fact, Kircher was not frank in dealing with Grant and Ballard. He withheld information from them. But even if he had told them all the facts, this would not have constituted the due diligence contemplated by the statute. Knowing the facts, Kircher had reason to believe that the expertised portion of the prospectus, i.e., the 1960 figures, was in part incorrect. He could not shut his eyes to the facts and rely on Peat, Marwick for that portion.

As to the rest of the prospectus, knowing the facts, he did not have a reasonable ground to believe it to be true. On the contrary, he must have known that in part it was untrue. Under these circumstances, he was not entitled to sit back and place the blame on the lawyers for not advising him about it.

Kircher has not proved his due diligence defenses.

* * *

Birnbaum

Birnbaum was a young lawyer, admitted to the bar in 1957, who, after brief periods of employment by two different law firms and an equally brief period of practicing in his own firm, was employed by BarChris as house counsel and assistant secretary in October 1960. Unfortunately for him, he became secretary and a director of BarChris on April 17, 1961, after the first version of the registration statement had been filed with the Securities and Exchange Commission. He signed the later amendments, thereby becoming responsible for the accuracy of the prospectus in its final form.

Although the prospectus, in its description of "management," lists Birnbaum among the "executive officers" and devotes several sentences to a recital of his career, the fact seems to be that he was not an executive officer in any real sense. He did not participate in the management of the company. As house counsel, he attended to legal matters of a routine nature. Among other things, he incorporated subsidiaries, with which BarChris was plentifully supplied. Among the subsidiaries which he incorporated were Capitol Lanes, Inc. which operated Capitol, Yonkers Lanes, Inc. which eventually operated Yonkers, and Parkway Lanes, Inc. which eventually operated Bridge. He was thus aware of that aspect of the business.

Birnbaum examined contracts. In that connection he advised BarChris that the T-Bowl contracts were not legally enforceable. He was thus aware of that fact.

One of Birnbaum's more important duties, first as assistant secretary and later as full-fledged secretary, was to keep the corporate minutes of BarChris and its subsidiaries. This necessarily informed him to a considerable extent about the company's affairs. Birnbaum was not initially a member of the executive committee, however, and did not keep its minutes at the outset. According to the minutes, the first meeting which he attended, "upon invitation of the Committee," was on March 22, 1961. He became a member shortly thereafter and kept the minutes beginning with the meeting of April 24, 1961.

It seems probable that Birnbaum did not know of many of the inaccuracies in the prospectus. He must, however, have appreciated some of them. In any case, he made no investigation and relied on the others to get it right. Unlike Trilling, he was entitled to rely upon Peat, Marwick for the 1960 figures, for as far as appears, he had no personal knowledge of the company's books of account or financial transactions. But he was not entitled to rely upon Kircher, Grant and Ballard for the other portions of the prospectus. As a lawyer, he should have known his obligations under the statute. He should have known that he was required to make a reasonable investigation of the truth of all the statements in the unexpertised portion of the document which he signed. Having failed to make such an investigation, he did not have reasonable ground to believe that all these statements were true. Birnbaum has not established his due diligence defenses except as to the audited 1960 figures.

Auslander

Auslander was an "outside" director, i.e., one who was not an officer of BarChris. He was chairman of the board of Valley Stream National Bank in Valley Stream, Long Island. In February 1961 Vitolo asked him to become a director of BarChris. Vitolo gave him an enthusiastic account of BarChris's progress and prospects. As an inducement, Vitolo said that when BarChris received the proceeds of a forthcoming issue of securities, it would deposit $1,000,000 in Auslander's bank.

In February and early March 1961, before accepting Vitolo's invitation, Auslander made some investigation of BarChris. He obtained Dun & Bradstreet reports which contained sales and earnings figures for periods earlier than December 31, 1960. He caused inquiry to be made of certain of BarChris's banks and was advised that they regarded BarChris favorably. He was informed that inquiry of Talcott had also produced a favorable response.

On March 3, 1961, Auslander indicated his willingness to accept a place on the board. Shortly thereafter, on March 14, Kircher sent him a copy of BarChris's annual report for 1960. Auslander observed that

BarChris's auditors were Peat, Marwick. They were also the auditors for the Valley Stream National Bank. He thought well of them.

Auslander was elected a director on April 17, 1961. The registration statement in its original form had already been filed, of course without his signature. On May 10, 1961, he signed a signature page for the first amendment to the registration statement which was filed on May 11, 1961. This was a separate sheet without any document attached. Auslander did not know that it was a signature page for a registration statement. He vaguely understood that it was something "for the SEC."

Auslander attended a meeting of BarChris's directors on May 15, 1961. At that meeting he, along with the other directors, signed the signature sheet for the second amendment which constituted the registration statement in its final form. Again, this was only a separate sheet without any document attached. Auslander never saw a copy of the registration statement in its final form.

At the May 15 directors' meeting, however, Auslander did realize that what he was signing was a signature sheet to a registration statement. This was the first time that he had appreciated that fact. A copy of the registration statement in its earlier form as amended on May 11, 1961, was passed around at the meeting. Auslander glanced at it briefly. He did not read it thoroughly.

At the May 15 meeting, Russo and Vitolo stated that everything was in order and that the prospectus was correct. Auslander believed this statement.

In considering Auslander's due diligence defenses, a distinction is to be drawn between the expertised and non-expertised portions of the prospectus. As to the former, Auslander knew that Peat, Marwick had audited the 1960 figures. He believed them to be correct because he had confidence in Peat, Marwick. He had no reasonable ground to believe otherwise.

As to the non-expertised portions, however, Auslander is in a different position. He seems to have been under the impression that Peat, Marwick was responsible for all the figures. This impression was not correct, as he would have realized if he had read the prospectus carefully. Auslander made no investigation of the accuracy of the prospectus. He relied on the assurance of Vitolo and Russo, and upon the information he had received in answer to his inquiries back in February and early March. These inquiries were general ones, in the nature of a credit check. The information which he received in answer to them was also general, without specific reference to the statements in the prospectus, which was not prepared until some time thereafter.

It is true that Auslander became a director on the eve of the financing. He had little opportunity to familiarize himself with the company's affairs. The question is whether, under such circumstances,

Auslander did enough to establish his due diligence defense with respect to the non-expertised portions of the prospectus.

Although there is a dearth of authority under Section 11 on this point, an English case under the analogous Companies Act is of some value. In Adams v. Thrift [1915] 1 Ch. 557, aff'd [1915] 2 Ch. 21, it was held that a director who knew nothing about the prospectus and did not even read it, but who relied on the statement of the company's managing director that it was "all right," was liable for its untrue statements.

Section 11 imposes liability in the first instance upon a director, no matter how new he is. He is presumed to know his responsibility when he becomes a director. He can escape liability only by using that reasonable care to investigate the facts which a prudent man would employ in the management of his own property. In my opinion, a prudent man would not act in an important matter without any knowledge of the relevant facts, in sole reliance upon representations of persons who are comparative strangers and upon general information which does not purport to cover the particular case. To say that such minimal conduct measures up to the statutory standard would to all intents and purposes, absolve new directors from responsibility merely because they are new. This is not a sensible construction of Section 11, when one bears in mind its fundamental purpose of requiring full and truthful disclosure for the protection of investors.

I find and conclude that Auslander has not established his due diligence defense with respect to the misstatements and omissions in those portions of the prospectus other than the audited 1960 figures.

* * *

Grant

Grant became a director of BarChris in October 1960. His law firm was counsel to BarChris in matters pertaining to the registration of securities. Grant drafted the registration statement for the stock issue in 1959 and for the warrants in January 1961. He also drafted the registration statement for the debentures. In the preliminary division of work between him and Ballard, the underwriters' counsel, Grant took initial responsibility for preparing the registration statement, while Ballard devoted his efforts in the first instance to preparing the indenture.

Grant is sued as a director and as a signer of the registration statement. This is not an action against him for malpractice in his capacity as a lawyer. Nevertheless, in considering Grant's due diligence defenses, the unique position which he occupied cannot be disregarded. As the director most directly concerned with writing the registration statement and assuring its accuracy, more was required of him in the way of reasonable investigation than could fairly be expected of a director who had no connection with this work.

There is no valid basis for plaintiffs' accusation that Grant knew that the prospectus was false in some respects and incomplete and misleading in others. Having seen him testify at length, I am satisfied as to his integrity. I find that Grant honestly believed that the registration statement was true and that no material facts had been omitted from it.

In this belief he was mistaken, and the fact is that for all his work, he never discovered any of the errors or omissions which have been recounted at length in this opinion, with the single exception of Capitol Lanes. He knew that BarChris had not sold this alley and intended to operate it, but he appears to have been under the erroneous impression that Peat, Marwick had knowingly sanctioned its inclusion in sales because of the allegedly temporary nature of the operation.

Grant contends that a finding that he did not make a reasonable investigation would be equivalent to holding that a lawyer for an issuing company, in order to show due diligence, must make an independent audit of the figures supplied to him by his client. I do not consider this to be a realistic statement of the issue. There were errors and omissions here which could have been detected without an audit. The question is whether, despite his failure to detect them, Grant made a reasonable effort to that end.

Much of this registration statement is a scissors and paste-pot job. Grant lifted large portions from the earlier prospectuses, modifying them in some instances to the extent that he considered necessary. But BarChris's affairs had changed for the worse by May 1961. Statements that were accurate in January were no longer accurate in May. Grant never discovered this. He accepted the assurances of Kircher and Russo that any change which might have occurred had been for the better, rather than the contrary.

It is claimed that a lawyer is entitled to rely on the statements of his client and that to require him to verify their accuracy would set an unreasonably high standard. This is too broad a generalization. It is all a matter of degree. To require an audit would obviously be unreasonable. On the other hand, to require a check of matters easily verifiable is not unreasonable. Even honest clients can make mistakes. The statute imposes liability for untrue statements regardless of whether they are intentionally untrue. The way to prevent mistakes is to test oral information by examining the original written record.

There were things which Grant could readily have checked which he did not check. For example, he was unaware of the provisions of the agreements between BarChris and Talcott. He never read them. Thus, he did not know, although he readily could have ascertained, that BarChris's contingent liability on Type B leaseback arrangements was 100 per cent, not 25 per cent. He did not appreciate that if BarChris defaulted in repurchasing delinquent customers' notes upon Talcott's demand, Talcott could accelerate all the customer paper in its hands, which amounted to over $3,000,000.

As to the backlog figure, Grant appreciated that scheduled unfilled orders on the company's books meant firm commitments, but he never asked to see the contracts which, according to the prospectus, added up to $6,905,000. Thus, he did not know that this figure was overstated by some $4,490,000.

Grant was unaware of the fact that BarChris was about to operate Bridge and Yonkers. He did not read the minutes of those subsidiaries which would have revealed that fact to him. On the subject of minutes, Grant knew that minutes of certain meetings of the BarChris executive committee held in 1961 had not been written up. Kircher, who had acted as secretary at those meetings, had complete notes of them. Kircher told Grant that there was no point in writing up the minutes because the matters discussed at those meetings were purely routine. Grant did not insist that the minutes be written up, nor did he look at Kircher's notes. If he had, he would have learned that on February 27, 1961 there was an extended discussion in the executive committee meeting about customers' delinquencies, that on March 8, 1961 the committee had discussed the pros and cons of alley operation by BarChris, that on March 18, 1961 the committee was informed that BarChris was constructing or about to begin constructing twelve alleys for which it had no contracts, and that on May 13, 1961 Dreyfuss, one of the worst delinquents, had filed a petition in Chapter X.

Grant knew that there had been loans from officers to BarChris in the past because that subject had been mentioned in the 1959 and January 1961 prospectuses. In March Grant prepared a questionnaire to be answered by officers and directors for the purpose of obtaining information to be used in the prospectus. The questionnaire did not inquire expressly about the existence of officers' loans. At approximately the same time, Grant prepared another questionnaire in order to obtain information on proxy statements for the annual stockholders' meeting. This questionnaire asked each officer to state whether he was indebted to BarChris, but it did not ask whether BarChris was indebted to him.

* * *

As far as customers' delinquencies [are] concerned, although Grant discussed this with Kircher, he again accepted the assurances of Kircher and Russo that no serious problem existed. He did not examine the records as to delinquencies, although BarChris maintained such a record. Any inquiry on his part of Talcott or an examination of BarChris's correspondence with Talcott in April and May 1961 would have apprised him of the true facts. It would have led him to appreciate that the statement in this prospectus, carried over from earlier prospectuses, to the effect that since 1955 BarChris had been required to repurchase less than one-half of one per cent of discounted customers' notes could no longer properly be made without further explanation.

Grant was entitled to rely on Peat, Marwick for the 1960 figures. He had no reasonable ground to believe them to be inaccurate. But the matters which I have mentioned were not within the expertised portion of the prospectus. As to this, Grant was obliged to make a reasonable investigation. I am forced to find that he did not make one. After making all due allowances for the fact that BarChris's officers misled him, there are too many instances in which Grant failed to make an inquiry which he could easily have made which, if pursued, would have put him on his guard. In my opinion, this finding on the evidence in this case does not establish an unreasonably high standard in other cases for company counsel who are also directors. Each case must rest on its own facts. I conclude that Grant has not established his due diligence defenses except as to the audited 1960 figures.

The Underwriters and Coleman

The underwriters other than Drexel made no investigation of the accuracy of the prospectus. One of them, Peter Morgan, had underwritten the 1959 stock issue and had been a director of BarChris. He thus had some general familiarity with its affairs, but he knew no more than the other underwriters about the debenture prospectus. They all relied upon Drexel as the "lead" underwriter.

Drexel did make an investigation. The work was in charge of Coleman, a partner of the firm, assisted by Casperson, an associate. Drexel's attorneys acted as attorneys for the entire group of underwriters. Ballard did the work, assisted by Stanton.

On April 17, 1961 Coleman became a director of BarChris. He signed the first amendment to the registration statement filed on May 11 and the second amendment constituting the registration statement in its final form, filed on May 16. He thereby assumed a responsibility as a director and signer in addition to his responsibility as an underwriter.

* * *

[The court described various inquiries Coleman made before becoming a director.]

After Coleman was elected a director on April 17, 1961, he made no further independent investigation of the accuracy of the prospectus. He assumed that Ballard was taking care of this on his behalf as well as on behalf of the underwriters.

* * *

The formal opinion which Ballard's firm rendered to the underwriters at the closing on May 24, 1961 made clear * * * what he had done. The opinion stated (italics supplied):

In the course of the preparation of the Registration Statement and Prospectus by the Company, we have had numerous conferences with representatives of and counsel for the Company and with its auditors and we have raised many questions regarding the business of the Company. Satisfactory answers to such questions were in each case given us, and all other information and documents we requested have been supplied. We are of the opinion that the *data presented* to us are accurately reflected in the Registration Statement and Prospectus and that there has been omitted from the Registration Statement no material facts *included in such data*. Although *we have not otherwise verified* the completeness or accuracy of the information furnished to us, on the basis of the foregoing and with the exception of the financial statements and schedules (which this opinion does not pass upon), we have no reason to believe that the Registration Statement or Prospectus contains any untrue statement of any material fact or omits to state a material fact required to be stated therein or necessary in order to make the statements therein not misleading.

Coleman testified that Drexel had an understanding with its attorneys that "we expect them to inspect on our behalf the corporate records of the company including, but not limited to, the minutes of the corporation, the stockholders and the committees of the board authorized to act for the board." Ballard manifested his awareness of this understanding by sending Stanton to read the minutes and the major contracts. It is difficult to square this understanding with the formal opinion of Ballard's firm which expressly disclaimed any attempt to verify information supplied by the company and its counsel.

In any event, it is clear that no effectual attempt at verification was made. The question is whether due diligence required that it be made. Stated another way, is it sufficient to ask questions, to obtain answers which, if true, would be thought satisfactory, and to let it go at that, without seeking to ascertain from the records whether the answers in fact are true and complete?

I have already held that this procedure is not sufficient in Grant's case. Are underwriters in a different position, as far as due diligence is concerned?

The underwriters say that the prospectus is the company's prospectus, not theirs. Doubtless this is the way they customarily regard it. But the Securities Act makes no such distinction. The underwriters are just as responsible as the company if the prospectus is false. And prospective investors rely upon the reputation of the underwriters in deciding whether to purchase the securities.

* * *

The purpose of Section 11 is to protect investors. To that end the underwriters are made responsible for the truth of the prospectus. If they may escape that responsibility by taking at face value representations made to them by the company's management, then the inclusion of underwriters among those liable under Section 11 affords the investors no additional protection. To effectuate the statute's purpose, the phrase "reasonable investigation" must be construed to require more effort on the part of the underwriters than the mere accurate reporting in the prospectus of "data presented" to them by the company. It should make no difference that this data is elicited by questions addressed to the company officers by the underwriters, or that the underwriters at the time believe that the company's officers are truthful and reliable. In order to make the underwriters' participation in this enterprise of any value to the investors, the underwriters must make some reasonable attempt to verify the data submitted to them. They may not rely solely on the company's officers or on the company's counsel. A prudent man in the management of his own property would not rely on them.

It is impossible to lay down a rigid rule suitable for every case defining the extent to which such verification must go. It is a question of degree, a matter of judgment in each case. In the present case, the underwriters' counsel made almost no attempt to verify management's representations. I hold that that was insufficient.

On the evidence in this case, I find that the underwriters' counsel did not make a reasonable investigation of the truth of those portions of the prospectus which were not made on the authority of Peat, Marwick as an expert. Drexel is bound by their failure. It is not a matter of relying upon counsel for legal advice. Here the attorneys were dealing with matters of fact. Drexel delegated to them, as its agent, the business of examining the corporate minutes and contracts. It must bear the consequences of their failure to make an adequate examination.

The other underwriters, who did nothing and relied solely on Drexel and on the lawyers, are also bound by it. It follows that although Drexel and the other underwriters believed that those portions of the prospectus were true, they had no reasonable ground for that belief, within the meaning of the statute. Hence, they have not established their due diligence defense, except as to the 1960 audited figures.[26]

The same conclusions must apply to Coleman. Although he participated quite actively in the earlier stages of the preparation of the prospectus, and contributed questions and warnings of his own, in addition to the questions of counsel, the fact is that he stopped his participation toward the end of March 1961. He made no investigation after he became a director. When it came to verification, he relied upon his counsel to do it for him. Since counsel failed to do it, Coleman is bound by that failure. Consequently, in his case also, he has not established his due diligence defense except as to the audited 1960 figures.

---

[26] In view of this conclusion, it becomes unnecessary to decide whether the underwriters other than Drexel would have been protected if Drexel had established that as lead underwriter, it made a reasonable investigation.

Peat, Marwick

Section 11(b) provides:

"Notwithstanding the provisions of subsection (a) no person * * * shall be liable as provided therein who shall sustain the burden of proof—

* * *

"(3) that * * * (B) as regards any part of the registration statement purporting to be made upon his authority as an expert * * * (a) he had, after reasonable investigation, reasonable ground to believe and did believe, at the time such part of the registration statement became effective, that the statements therein were true and that there was no omission to state a material fact required to be stated therein or necessary to make the statements therein not misleading * * *."

This defines the due diligence defense for an expert. Peat, Marwick has pleaded it.

The part of the registration statement purporting to be made upon the authority of Peat, Marwick as an expert was, as we have seen, the 1960 figures. But because the statute requires the court to determine Peat, Marwick's belief, and the grounds thereof, "at the time such part of the registration statement became effective," for the purposes of this affirmative defense, the matter must be viewed as of May 16, 1961, and the question is whether at that time Peat, Marwick, after reasonable investigation, had reasonable ground to believe and did believe that the 1960 figures were true and that no material fact had been omitted from the registration statement which should have been included in order to make the 1960 figures not misleading. In deciding this issue, the court must consider not only what Peat, Marwick did in its 1960 audit, but also what it did in its subsequent "S-1 review." The proper scope of that review must also be determined.

* * *

The 1960 Audit

Peat, Marwick's work was in general charge of a member of the firm, Cummings, and more immediately in charge of Peat, Marwick's manager, Logan. Most of the actual work was performed by a senior accountant, Berardi, who had junior assistants, one of whom was Kennedy.

Berardi was then about thirty years old. He was not yet a C.P.A. He had had no previous experience with the bowling industry. This was his first job as a senior accountant. He could hardly have been given a more difficult assignment.

After obtaining a little background information on BarChris by talking to Logan and reviewing Peat, Marwick's work papers on its 1959 audit, Berardi examined the results of test checks of BarChris's accounting procedures which one of the junior accountants had made, and he prepared an "internal control questionnaire" and an "audit program." Thereafter, for a few days subsequent to December 30, 1960, he inspected BarChris's inventories and examined certain alley construction. Finally, on January 13, 1961, he began his auditing work which he carried on substantially continuously until it was completed on February 24, 1961. Toward the close of the work, Logan reviewed it and made various comments and suggestions to Berardi.

It is unnecessary to recount everything that Berardi did in the course of the audit. We are concerned only with the evidence relating to what Berardi did or did not do with respect to those items which I have found to have been incorrectly reported in the 1960 figures in the prospectus. More narrowly, we are directly concerned only with such of those items as I have found to be material.

Capitol Lanes

First and foremost is Berardi's failure to discover that Capitol Lanes had not been sold. This error affected both the sales figure and the liability side of the balance sheet. Fundamentally, the error stemmed from the fact that Berardi never realized that Heavenly Lanes and Capitol were two different names for the same alley. In the course of his audit, Berardi was shown BarChris's contract file. He examined the contracts in the file and made a list of them. The file must have included a contract with an outside purchaser for Heavenly Lanes, although no such contract was ever produced at the trial, for Berardi included Heavenly on his list. Apparently there was no contract in the file for a lane named Capitol because that name did not appear on Berardi's list.

Kircher also made a list of jobs. Heavenly was on his list. Capitol was not. Berardi compared the two lists and satisfied himself that he had the proper jobs to be taken into account. Berardi assumed that Heavenly was to be treated like any other completed job. He included it in all his computations.

The evidence is conflicting as to whether BarChris's officers expressly informed Berardi that Heavenly and Capitol were the same thing and that BarChris was operating Capitol and had not sold it. I find that they did not so inform him.

Berardi did become aware that there were references here and there in BarChris's records to something called Capitol Lanes. He also knew that there were indications that at some time BarChris might operate an alley of that name.

* * *

Berardi testified that he inquired of Russo about Capitol Lanes and that Russo told him that Capitol Lanes, Inc. was going to operate an alley some day but as yet it had no alley. Berardi testified that he understood that the alley had not been built and that he believed that the rental payments were on vacant land.

I am not satisfied with this testimony. If Berardi did hold this belief, he should not have held it. The entries as to insurance and as to "operation of alley" should have alerted him to the fact that an alley existed. He should have made further inquiry on the subject. It is apparent that Berardi did not understand this transaction.

In any case, he never identified this mysterious Capitol with the Heavenly Lanes which he had included in his sales and profit figures. The vital question is whether he failed to make a reasonable investigation which, if he had made it, would have revealed the truth.

Certain accounting records of BarChris, which Berardi testified he did not see, would have put him on inquiry. One was a job cost ledger card for job no. 6036, the job number which Berardi put on his own sheet for Heavenly Lanes. This card read "Capitol Theatre (Heavenly)." In addition, two accounts receivable cards each showed both names on the same card, Capitol and Heavenly. Berardi testified that he looked at the accounts receivable records but that he did not see these particular cards. He testified that he did not look on the job cost ledger cards because he took the costs from another record, the costs register.

The burden of proof on this issue is on Peat, Marwick. Although the question is a rather close one, I find that Peat, Marwick has not sustained that burden. Peat, Marwick has not proved that Berardi made a reasonable investigation as far as Capitol Lanes was concerned and that his ignorance of the true facts was justified.

Howard Lanes Annex

Berardi also failed to discover that this alley was not sold. Here the evidence is much scantier. Berardi saw a contract for this alley in the contract file. No one told him that it was to be leased rather than sold. There is no evidence to indicate that any record existed which would have put him on notice. I find that his investigation was reasonable as to this item.

* * *

The S-1 Review

The purpose of reviewing events subsequent to the date of a certified balance sheet (referred to as an S-1 review when made with reference to a registration statement) is to ascertain whether any material change has occurred in the company's financial position which should be disclosed in order to prevent the balance sheet figures from being misleading. The scope of such a review, under generally accepted auditing standards, is limited. It does not amount to a complete audit.

Peat, Marwick prepared a written program for such a review. I find that this program conformed to generally accepted auditing standards. * * *

Berardi made the S-1 review in May 1961. He devoted a little over two days to it, a total of 20-1/2 hours. He did not discover any of the errors or omissions pertaining to the state of affairs in 1961 which I have previously discussed at length, all of which were material. The question is whether, despite his failure to find out anything, his investigation was reasonable within the meaning of the statute.

* * *

In substance, what Berardi did is similar to what Grant and Ballard did. He asked questions, he got answers which he considered satisfactory, and he did nothing to verify them. For example, he obtained from Trilling a list of contracts. The list included Yonkers and Bridge. Since Berardi did not read the minutes of subsidiaries, he did not learn that Yonkers and Bridge were intercompany sales. The list also included Woonsocket and the six T-Bowl jobs, Moravia Road, Milford, Groton, North Attleboro, Odenton and Severna Park. Since Berardi did not look at any contract documents, and since he was unaware of the executive committee minutes of March 18, 1961 (at that time embodied only in Kircher's notes), he did not learn that BarChris had no contracts for these jobs. Trilling's list did not set forth contract prices for them, although it did for Yonkers, Bridge and certain others. This did not arouse Berardi's suspicion.

* * *

Apparently the only BarChris officer with whom Berardi communicated was Trilling. He could not recall making any inquiries of Russo, Vitolo or Pugliese. As to Kircher, Berardi's testimony was self-contradictory. At one point he said that he had inquired of Kircher and at another he said that he could not recall making any such inquiry.

There had been a material change for the worse in BarChris's financial position. That change was sufficiently serious so that the failure to disclose it made the 1960 figures misleading. Berardi did not discover it. As far as results were concerned, his S-1 review was useless.

Accountants should not be held to a standard higher than that recognized in their profession. I do not do so here. Berardi's review did not come up to that standard. He did not take some of the steps which Peat, Marwick's written program prescribed. He did not spend an adequate amount of time on a task of this magnitude. Most important of all, he was too easily satisfied with glib answers to his inquiries.

This is not to say that he should have made a complete audit. But there were enough danger signals in the materials which he did examine to require some further investigation on his part. Generally accepted accounting standards required such further investigation under these circumstances. It is not always sufficient merely to ask questions.

Here again, the burden of proof is on Peat, Marwick. I find that that burden has not been satisfied. I conclude that Peat, Marwick has not established its due diligence defense.

* * *

In re WorldCom, Inc. Securities Litigation
United States District Court, S.D.N.Y., 2004.
346 F.Supp.2d 628.

■ COTE, DISTRICT JUDGE:

This Opinion addresses issues related to an underwriter's due diligence obligations. Following the conclusion of fact discovery, several of the parties in this consolidated securities class action arising from the collapse of WorldCom, Inc. ("WorldCom") have filed for summary judgment.

* * *

It is undisputed that at least as of early 2001 WorldCom executives engaged in a secretive scheme to manipulate WorldCom's public filings concerning WorldCom's financial condition. Because those public filings were incorporated into the registration statements for the two bond offerings, the underwriters are liable for those false statements unless they can show that they were sufficiently diligent in their investigation of WorldCom in connection with the bond offerings.

* * *

Procedural History

WorldCom announced a massive restatement of its financials on June 25, 2002. It reported its intention to restate its financial statements for 2001 and the first quarter of 2002. According to that announcement, "[a]s a result of an internal audit of the company's capital expenditure accounting, it was determined that certain transfers from line cost expenses[1] to capital accounts during this period were not made in accordance with generally accepted accounting principles (GAAP)." The amount of transfers was then estimated to be over $3.8 billion. Without the improper transfers, the company estimated that it would have reported a net loss for 2001 and the first quarter of 2002. On July 21, it filed for bankruptcy. A restatement of WorldCom's financials was issued in 2004 in connection with WorldCom's emergence from bankruptcy. WorldCom restated its financial information for the years ending 2000 and 2001. The restatement included approximately $76 billion in adjustments, which reduced WorldCom's net equity from approximately $50 billion to approximately minus $20 billion.

* * *

WorldCom's Accounting Strategies

* * *

[WorldCom's auditor,] Andersen was unaware of the manipulation of line costs through this capitalization scheme.

---

[1] Line costs, which are transmission costs, are described below. They were the single largest operating expense incurred by WorldCom.

* * *

The improper capitalization of line costs continued through the first quarter of 2002. WorldCom's internal audit department had completed its last audit of WorldCom's capital expenditures in approximately January of 2002, and had not uncovered any evidence of fraud. In May of 2002, it began another audit of the company's capital expenditures. The fraudulent capitalization of line cases was uncovered as a result of a May 21 meeting between the company's internal auditors and the WorldCom director in charge of tracking capital expenditures. During that meeting the director used the term "prepaid capacity" to explain the difference between two sets of schedules that he was being shown. The auditors were unfamiliar with the term. After asking questions of several people about "prepaid capacity," Eugene Morse, a member of WorldCom's internal audit group, used a new software tool to investigate WorldCom's books and was able to uncover the transfer of line costs to capital accounts in a matter of hours.[15]

On June 17, David Myers, WorldCom's former controller, admitted to the internal audit team that there was "no support" for the prepaid capacity entries and that there was "no standard" supporting the entries. He explained that the "entries had been booked based on what they thought the margins should be." Myers told the team, "if we couldn't get the costs down that we might as well shut the doors of the business, that we can't continue." On June 20, during a meeting in which Sullivan [Scott Sullivan was CFO at WorldCom] was confronted with the fraud, Myers told internal audit that the capitalization of line costs had started in the first quarter of 2001. As of that time, the internal audit team thought that the capitalization of line costs had begun in the second quarter of 2001, and was no longer trying to find out how far back the entries went.

Andersen and the 1999 Form 10-K

Andersen had been the auditor for WorldCom or its predecessors for almost twenty years. It issued an unqualified or "clean" opinion for the WorldCom annual financial statements for 1997 through 2000. After the public disclosure of the accounting fraud, Andersen withdrew its support for the WorldCom 2001 Form 10-K, but it never withdrew its audit opinions for the 1999 or 2000 Form 10-Ks.

* * *

2000 Offering

On May 24, 2000, WorldCom conducted a public offering of debt securities by issuing approximately $5 billion worth of bonds ("2000 Offering"). It filed a registration statement dated April 12, 2000, and

---

[15] Morse testified that without that software tool and without access to the general ledger (which the internal audit department did not have), it would have taken him weeks of digging to uncover the fraud. In his opinion, someone with access to the general ledger or someone who asked those who made the questionable entries for the documentation to support the entries, could also have uncovered the fraud.

prospectus supplement dated May 19, 2000 (collectively "2000 Registration Statement") that incorporated by reference among other things the WorldCom Form 10-K for the year ending December 31, 1999, and its Form 10-Q for the quarter ended March 31, 2000. [Salomon Smith Barney] was the book runner and, with J.P. Morgan, was the co-lead manager.[19]

* * *

The 2000 Registration Statement included a section labeled "experts." It explained that the year-end WorldCom consolidated financial statements

> have been audited by Arthur Andersen LLP, independent public accountants, as indicated in their report with respect thereto, and are included in the MCI WorldCom's Annual Report on Form 10-K for the year ended December 31, 1999, and are incorporated herein by reference, in reliance upon the authority of such firm as experts in accounting and auditing in giving such reports.

* * *

The only written record of due diligence performed by the Underwriter Defendants for the 2000 Offering is a May 26 memorandum prepared by Cravath, Swaine & Moore ("Cravath"), counsel to the Underwriter Defendants. The memorandum reflects due diligence conducted from May 15 to 23.[23] It describes a May 17 telephone conversation in which Sullivan was asked questions about the Sprint merger, whether WorldCom had experienced problems integrating either SkyTel or MCI, and whether there were any other material issues.[24] In that conversation, Sullivan predicted overall growth for the year 2000 would be about 14%, represented that the proceeds for the 2000 Offering would be used to repay "commercial debt," reported that WorldCom was experiencing a very competitive environment but that there were no changes in that environment since 1999, and stated that there were no other material issues than the ones he described in the call. The memorandum then outlines the board minutes for WorldCom, lists its public filings, refers to its press releases, and discusses Sprint documents.

* * *

Andersen created an undated worksheet in connection with WorldCom's first quarter 2000 unaudited financial statement. The worksheet was an eleven-page Andersen form entitled "U.S. GAAS

---

[19] A book runner is responsible for pricing the offering and allocating shares to institutional and retail investors. A lead manager determines the amount of shares reserved for its own sales efforts and the amount of the offering for other members of the syndicate.

[23] The memorandum indicated that due diligence for WorldCom for the period prior to August 17, 1999 was contained in a document of that date.

[24] The memorandum does not identify who participated in the conversation with Sullivan.

Review of Interim Financial Statements of a Public Company," and was a vital step in preparing a "comfort letter" for a company and underwriters. The form reflects tasks to be performed, with boxes to indicate whether the task had been "done" or was "N/A." Most of the tasks had one of those two boxes checked, some had both boxes checked, and one task—reading the financial statements and disclosures in the client's draft Form 10-Q—was left blank. Brief comments were handwritten next to some of the tasks. The form paragraph that appears directly above the engagement partner's signature, states: "Based on the results of the review procedures, we are not aware of any material modifications that should be made to the interim financial statements for them to be in conformity with generally accepted accounting principles consistently applied."

A "comfort letter" for the first quarter 2000 unaudited financial statement is dated May 19, is eight pages long, and indicates that it is written at the request of WorldCom. In it, Andersen reaffirms its audits, including those incorporated in the 2000 Registration Statement. It warns that having not audited any financial statements for any period subsequent to December 31, 1999, it is unable to express any opinion on the unaudited consolidated balance sheet of WorldCom as of March 31, 2000, or the results of operations or cash flows as of any date subsequent to December 31, 1999. The letter indicates, however, that Andersen had performed the procedures specified by the American Institute of Certified Public Accountants for a review of interim financial information as described in SAS No. 71 on the unaudited condensed consolidated balance sheet as of March 31, 2000, and related statements, and had made certain inquiries of WorldCom officials who have responsibility for financial and accounting matters. Andersen represented that nothing had come to its attention as a result of that work that caused Andersen to believe that "[a]ny material modifications should be made to the unaudited condensed consolidated financial statements [for the first quarter of 2000], incorporated by reference in the Registration Statement, for them to be in conformity with generally accepted accounting principles" or that "[t]he unaudited condensed consolidated financial statements . . . do not comply as to form in all material respects with the applicable accounting requirements of the Act and the related published rules and regulations." The letter concludes that it is offered to "assist the underwriters in conducting and documenting their investigation" of the affairs of WorldCom in connection with the offering of securities covered by the 2000 Registration Statement. A two page May 23 Andersen letter reaffirmed the May 19 letter.

* * *

The Underwriter Defendants' Credit Assessment of WorldCom as of Early 2001

[After the Form S-3 shelf offering in 2000, and before the 2001 offering] [i]n February 2001, several of the Underwriter Defendants downgraded WorldCom's credit rating due to their assessment of WorldCom's deteriorating financial condition. Then, during the weeks that followed, several of the Underwriter Defendants made a commitment to WorldCom to help it restructure its massive credit facility. In doing so, there is evidence that at least some of the Underwriter Defendants internally expressed concern again about WorldCom's financial health. WorldCom had required the banks to participate in the restructuring of the credit facility if a bank wished to play a significant role in its next bond offering, the 2001 Offering. That offering turned out to be the largest public debt offering in American history. The Lead Plaintiff contends that the evidence of the Underwriter Defendants' concerns about WorldCom's financial condition in the months immediately preceding the 2001 Offering undercuts their contention that the due diligence that they performed in connection with the 2001 Offering was reasonable.

As noted, several of the Underwriter Defendants downgraded WorldCom as a credit risk in February 2001. At the same time, one of the major credit rating agencies publicly announced that it was downgrading long-term WorldCom debt.

* * *

Within weeks of these decisions to downgrade WorldCom's credit rating, the Underwriter Defendants had to consider whether to participate in WorldCom's restructuring of its credit facility, which was a line of credit extended to WorldCom by several of the banks, and whether to compete for investment banking positions in the bond offering that WorldCom hoped to undertake that Spring. WorldCom had a $10.25 billion credit facility with affiliates of some of the banks and it wanted to restructure that facility in a $8 to 10 billion transaction. WorldCom informed banks that they could only participate as an underwriter on the 2001 Offering if they agreed to participate in the restructuring. WorldCom also let banks know that the greater a bank's commitment to the credit facility, the greater the role it could have in the offering. With a commitment of at least $800 million to the new credit facility, a bank was promised a role as "joint book running manager" in the offering. Bank of America calculated that if it were successful in becoming a joint book running manager, it could earn 20 to 25% of an expected investment banking fee of $10 to 12.5 million.

There is evidence that several of the Underwriter Defendants decided to make a commitment to the restructuring of the credit facility and to attempt to win the right to underwrite the 2001 Offering, while at the same time reducing their own exposure to risk from holding WorldCom debt by engaging in hedging strategies, such as credit default swaps.[29] For example, as early as March 23, J.P. Morgan identified one

---

[29] A credit default swap enables a lender to hedge its exposure to a borrower. The lender enters into a swap contract and pays a premium for credit default protection to the swap seller.

of its three key objectives in connection with the restructuring of the credit facility and its participation in the 2001 Offering as: "to minimize exposure after $800MM initial commitment...." The memorandum recommended developing a strategy that would give up some participation in the 2001 Offering in return for reducing the bank's exposure under the credit facility down to $600 million. It concluded, "Lets [sic] make this a true team effort: first class execution for the client, attractive economics for JPM and the *minimum credit exposure*." (Emphasis supplied.) Within less than a month, J.P. Morgan wanted to reduce its exposure to $500 million. By May 22, through a carefully managed entry into the market, J.P. Morgan had entered a $150 million credit default swap, out of a goal of $200 million, to reduce its exposure in the event of a default by WorldCom. J.P. Morgan personnel structured its activities so that neither WorldCom nor any of J.P. Morgan's investment banking rivals would learn what it was doing. A May 16 e-mail captured the problem with these words: "if WCOM gets any sense that we're laying off exposure DURING the syndication process (and wouldn't SSB love to pass that along), it would not be good news. Understandably" this point is "Jennifer's greatest and principal concern." Jennifer Nason was the bank's due diligence team leader for the 2001 Offering.

* * *

2001 Offering

Through the 2001 Offering WorldCom issued $11.9 billion worth of notes. The May 9, 2001 registration statement and May 14, 2001 prospectus supplement (collectively, "2001 Registration Statement") for the 2001 Offering incorporated WorldCom's 2000 10-K and first quarter 2001 Form 8-K dated April 26, 2001.

J.P. Morgan and SSB served as co-book runners. Each of the Underwriter Defendants for the 2001 Offering have stated that they relied on the due diligence performed by SSB and J.P. Morgan. Cravath again represented the Underwriter Defendants.

A May 16, 2001 memorandum prepared by Cravath describes the due diligence conducted from April 19 through May 16, 2001 in connection with the 2001 Offering. On April 23, the Underwriter Defendants forwarded due diligence questions to WorldCom. The due diligence for the 2001 Offering included telephone calls with WorldCom on April 30 and May 9, and a May 9 telephone call with Andersen and WorldCom. The due diligence inquiry also included a review of WorldCom's board minutes, 1998 revolving credit agreement, SEC filings, and press releases from April 19 to May 16, 2001.

During the April 30 telephone call, two bankers from J.P. Morgan and SSB, and two attorneys from Cravath spoke with Sullivan. Sullivan

---

In the event of a failure to pay, the swap seller agrees to pay the lender the value of the loan. If there is no failure to pay, the lender has lost only the premium.

explained that WorldCom intended to use half of the proceeds from the 2001 Offering "to repay the balance of its outstanding commercial paper, to retire debt and to fund a portion of the Company's negative free cash flow." When asked whether WorldCom had significant reserves for bad receivables, Sullivan responded that WorldCom had a general $1.1 billion reserve. Sullivan indicated that WorldCom was comfortable with the current earnings per share, that there were no issues that could affect the company's credit rating, and that the company had nothing material to disclose that had not been discussed with the investment bankers. When asked about the competitive environment, Sullivan answered that

> the general economic slowdown has not had a material impact on the Company's business, however the telecommunication environment has affected the Company. In particular, he was surprised that receivables declined in the first quarter. Despite this, the Company is selling through the rough parts of the telecommunications slowdown and the number of new installations is still strong.

On May 9, Sullivan confirmed that there were no material changes since the April 30 telephone call.

On May 9, a banker from J.P. Morgan and two Cravath attorneys spoke by telephone with Sullivan and Stephanie Scott of WorldCom and with representatives of Andersen. Andersen indicated that it had not issued any management letters to WorldCom and that there were no accounting concerns. WorldCom and Andersen assured J.P. Morgan that there was nothing else material to discuss. In neither the April 30 due diligence telephone call nor the May 9 call did Sullivan disclose the $771 million capitalization of line costs.

On May 9 and 16, Andersen issued comfort letters for the WorldCom first quarter 2001 financial statement. The 2001 comfort letters stand in contrast to the 2000 comfort letter, which expressed that nothing had come to Andersen's attention to cause it to believe that "[a]ny material modifications should be made to the unaudited condensed consolidated financial statements described in 4(a)(1), incorporated by reference in the Registration Statement, for them to be in conformity with generally accepted accounting principles" or that "[t]he unaudited condensed consolidated financial statements . . . do not comply as to form in all material respects with the applicable accounting requirements of the Act and the related published rules and regulations." In 2001, by comparison, the letters indicated that nothing had come to Andersen's attention that caused it to believe that the financial statements "were not determined on a basis substantially consistent with that of the corresponding amounts in the audited consolidated balance sheets of WorldCom as of December 31, 2000 and 1999, and the consolidated statements of operations, shareholders' investment and cash flows for each of the three years in the period ended December 31, 2000. . . ." A J.P. Morgan banker and a Cravath attorney noticed the absence of the "negative GAAP assurance" in the 2001 comfort letter. An SSB banker noted that the issue was important to understand but advised against getting "too vocal" about it since "WorldCom's a bear to deal with on that subject."

Some of the investment bankers responsible for performing due diligence in connection with the 2001 Offering were aware of their own bank's credit concerns regarding WorldCom, and some were not. For instance, the lead investment banker for J.P. Morgan testified that she was unaware of her bank's memorandum downgrading WorldCom's risk rating. Two investment bankers at Deustche Bank testified that they were aware that their bank had downgraded WorldCom's credit rating. One testified that he believed that the downgrading was "too early"; the other testified that the downgrading was not inconsistent with the information that was in the public domain.

* * *

III. The Underwriter Defendants' Motion for Summary Judgment; The Financial Statements

The Underwriter Defendants move for summary judgment with respect to the financial statements that were incorporated into the Registration Statements. They assert that there is no dispute that they acted reasonably in relying on Andersen's audits and comfort letters. The Underwriter Defendants contend that they were entitled to rely on WorldCom's audited financial statements and had no duty to investigate their reliability so long as they had "no reasonable ground to believe" that such financial statements contained a false statement. They also assert that they were entitled to rely in the same way on Andersen's comfort letters for the unaudited quarterly financial statements incorporated into the Registration Statements.

* * *

A. *Role of the Underwriter*

An underwriter is commonly understood to be a "person who buys securities directly or indirectly from the issuer and resells them to the public, or performs some act (or acts) that facilitates the issuer's distribution." In re WorldCom, Inc. Sec. Litig., 308 F.Supp.2d 338, 343 (S.D.N.Y. 2004). As the SEC has observed, in enacting Section 11, "Congress recognized that underwriters occupied a unique position that enabled them to discover and compel disclosure of essential facts about the offering. Congress believed that subjecting underwriters to the liability provisions would provide the necessary incentive to ensure their careful investigation of the offering." The Regulation of Securities Offerings, SEC Release No. 7606A, 63 Fed. Reg. 67174, 67230. At the same time, Congress specifically rejected the notion of underwriters as insurers. H.R. Conf. Rep. No. 73–152, at 277 (1933); SEC Rel. 7606A, 63 Fed. Reg. at 67230. Rather, it imposed upon underwriters the obligation to "exercise diligence of a type commensurate with the confidence, both as to integrity and competence," placed in them by those purchasing securities. H.R. Conf. Rep. No. 73–152, at 277.

Underwriters must "exercise a high degree of care in investigation and independent verification of the company's representations." Feit v. Leasco Data Processing Equip. Corp., 332 F.Supp. 544, 582 (E.D.N.Y. 1971). Overall, "[n]o greater reliance in our self-regulatory system is placed on any single participant in the issuance of securities than upon the underwriter." Chris-Craft, 480 F.2d at 370. Underwriters function as "the first line of defense" with respect to material misrepresentations and omissions in registration statements. As a consequence, courts must be "particularly scrupulous in examining the[ir] conduct." Feit, 332 F.Supp. at 581.

B. *The "Due Diligence" Defenses*

* * *

Although the requirements of due diligence vary depending on whether the registration statement has been made in part or in whole on the authority of an expert, the standard for determining what constitutes a reasonable investigation and reasonable ground for belief is the same: "[T]he standard of reasonableness shall be that required of a prudent man in the management of his own property." 15 U.S.C. § 77k(c).

Courts have distinguished between these two standards by labeling them the due diligence defense and the reliance defense, referring in the latter case to the reliance permitted by the statute on an expert's statement.

* * *

C. *Accountants as Experts*

Although Section 11(b) furnishes different standards, depending on whether a statement is made on the authority of an expert, the statute does not define the term "expert." Section 11(a)(4) lists professions that give a person authority to make a statement, which on consent can be included in a registration statement. 15 U.S.C. § 77k(a)(4). The list of professions includes an accountant. Id. Thus, while Section 11(b) does not define the term expert or explain what sort of documents and/or work constitutes that "made on an expert's authority," it is settled that an accountant qualifies as an expert, and audited financial statements are considered expertised portions of a registration statement.

Not every auditor's opinion, however, qualifies as an expert's opinion for purposes of the Section 11 reliance defense. To distinguish among auditor's opinions, some background is in order. While financial statements are prepared by the management of a company, an accountant serving as the company's auditor may give an opinion as to whether the financial statements have been presented in conformity with GAAP. This opinion is given after the accountant has performed an audit of the company's books and records. Audits are generally completed once a year, in connection with a company's year-end financial statements. There are ten audit standards with which an auditor must comply in performing its annual audit. They are known as Generally Accepted Auditing Standards ("GAAS"). If an auditor signs a consent to have its opinion on financial statements incorporated into a company's public filings, the opinion may be shared with the public through incorporation.

Public companies are also required under the Exchange Act to file quarterly financial statements, which are referred to as interim financial statements. While not subject to an audit, interim financial statements included in Form 10-Q quarterly reports are reviewed by an independent public accountant using professional standards and procedures for conducting such reviews, as established by GAAS. The standards for the review of interim financial statements are set forth in Statement of Auditing Standards No. 71, Interim Financial Information ("SAS 71"). When a public company files a registration statement for a sale of securities, the auditor is customarily asked by underwriters to provide a comfort letter. The comfort letter will contain representations about the auditor's review of the interim financial statements. Guidance about the content of comfort letters is contained in the Statement on Auditing Standards No. 72, Letters for Underwriters and Certain Other Requesting Parties ("SAS 72"). There is frequently more than one comfort letter for a transaction: an initial comfort letter, and a second or "bringdown" comfort letter issued closer to the time of closing.

In order for an accountant's opinion to qualify as an expert opinion under Section 11(b)(3)(C), there are three prerequisites. First, it must be reported in the Registration Statement. Second, it must be an audit opinion. Finally, the accountant must consent to inclusion of the audit opinion in the registration statement.

In an effort to encourage auditor reviews of interim financial statements, the SEC acted in 1979 to assure auditors that their review of unaudited interim financial information would not subject them to liability under Section 11.

* * *

The objective of a review of interim financial information differs significantly from the objective of an examination of financial statements in accordance with generally accepted auditing standards. The objective of an audit is to provide a reasonable basis for expressing an opinion regarding the financial statements taken as a whole. A review of interim financial information does not provide a basis for the expression of such an opinion, because the review does not contemplate a study and evaluation of internal accounting control; tests of accounting records and of responses to inquiries by obtaining corroborating evidential matter through inspection, observation, or confirmation; and certain other procedures ordinarily performed during an audit. A review may bring to the accountant's attention significant matters affecting the interim financial information, but it does not provide assurance that the accountant will become aware of all significant matters that would be disclosed in an audit. (emphasis supplied)

* * *

In sum, underwriters can rely on an accountant's audit opinion incorporated into a registration statement in presenting a defense under Section 11(b)(3)(C). Underwriters may not rely on an accountant's comfort letters for interim financial statements in presenting such a defense. Comfort letters do not "expertise any portion of the registration statement that is otherwise non-expertised."

D. *Integrated Disclosure, Shelf Registration, and Rule 176*

* * *

Together, the mechanism of incorporation by reference and the expansion of shelf registration significantly reduced the time and expense necessary to prepare public offerings, thus enabling more "rapid access to today's capital markets." As the SEC recognized, these changes affected the time in which underwriters could perform their investigations of an issuer. Underwriters had weeks to perform due diligence for traditional registration statements. By contrast, under a short-form registration regime, "[p]reparation time is reduced sharply" thanks to the ability to incorporate by reference prior disclosures.

These two innovations triggered concern among underwriters. Members of the financial community worried about their ability "to undertake a reasonable investigation with respect to the adequacy of the information incorporated by reference from periodic reports filed under the Exchange Act into the short form registration statements utilized in an integrated disclosure system." Specifically, underwriters expressed concern that

> this reduction in preparation time, together with competitive pressures, will restrict the ability of responsible underwriters to conduct what would be deemed to be a reasonable investigation, pursuant to Section 11, of the contents of the registration statement.... [I]ssuers may be reluctant to wait for responsible underwriters to finish their inquiry, and may be receptive to offers from underwriters willing to do less.

Because an underwriter could select among competing underwriters when offering securities through a shelf registration, some questioned whether an underwriter could "afford to devote the time and expense necessary to conduct a due diligence review before knowing whether it will handle an offering and that there may not be sufficient time to do so once it is selected." Others doubted whether they would have the chance "to apply their independent scrutiny and judgment to documents prepared by registrants many months before an offering."

Because of concerns like those described here, the SEC introduced Rule 176 in 1981 "to make explicit what circumstances may bear upon the determination of what constitutes a reasonable investigation and reasonable ground for belief as these terms are used in Section 11(b)." Rather than give underwriters a "safe harbor from liability for statements made in incorporated Exchange Act reports," as some suggested should happen, the SEC turned to the American Law Institute's proposed Federal Securities Code for guidance. Rule 176, which largely mirrors Section 1704(g) of the Code, provides in relevant part:

> In determining whether or not the conduct of a person constitutes a reasonable investigation or a reasonable ground for belief meeting the standard set forth in section 11(c), relevant circumstances include, with respect to a person other than the issuer. [sic]
>
> (a) The type of issuer;
>
> (b) The type of security;
>
> (c) The type of person;
>
> . . .
>
> (f) Reasonable reliance on officers, employees, and others whose duties should have given them knowledge of the particular facts (in the light of the functions and responsibilities of the particular person with respect to the issuer and the filing);
>
> (g) When the person is an underwriter, the type of underwriting arrangement, the role of the particular person as an underwriter and the availability of information with respect to the registrant; and
>
> (h) Whether, with respect to a fact or document incorporated by reference, the particular person had any responsibility for the fact or document at the time of the filing from which it was incorporated.

Although "[n]o court has ever been called upon to interpret Rule 176," the SEC's own commentary on the rule makes clear that Rule 176 did not alter the fundamental nature of underwriters' due diligence obligations. At the time Rule 176 was finalized, the SEC took care to explain that integrated disclosure was intended to "simplify disclosure and reduce unnecessary repetition and redelivery of information," not to "modify the responsibility of underwriters and others to make a reasonable investigation." Instead, emphasizing that "nothing in the Commission's integrated disclosure system precludes conducting adequate due diligence," the SEC advised underwriters concerned about the time pressures created by integrated disclosure to "arrange [their] due diligence procedures over time for the purpose of avoiding last minute delays in an offering environment characterized by rapid market changes." It also reminded them that an underwriter is "never compelled to proceed with an offering *until he has accomplished his due diligence.*" (emphasis supplied). And the SEC warned underwriters that the verification "required by the case law and contemplated by the statute" would still be required in appropriate circumstances. As recently as December 1998, the SEC recalled that it "expressly rejected the consideration of competitive timing and pressures when evaluating the reasonableness of an underwriter's investigation."

The SEC's intent to maintain high standards for underwriter due diligence is confirmed by its many discussions of appropriate due diligence techniques in the integrated disclosure system. In proposing Rule 176, the SEC acknowledged that different investigatory methods would be needed "in view of the compressed preparation time and the volatile nature of the capital markets." Nonetheless, it emphasized that such techniques must be "*equally thorough.*" (emphasis supplied). Among the strategies recommended by the SEC were the development of a "reservoir of knowledge about the companies that may select the underwriter to distribute their securities registered on short form registration statements" through a "careful review of [periodic Exchange Act] filings on an ongoing basis," consultation of analysts' reports, and active participation in the issuer's investor relations program, especially analysts and brokers meetings.

At the time the SEC finalized the shelf registration rule two years later, it again recognized that "the techniques of conducting due diligence investigations of registrants qualified to use short form registration . . . would differ from due diligence investigations under other circumstances." Nonetheless, it stressed the use of "anticipatory and continuous due diligence programs" to augment underwriters' fulfillment of their due diligence obligations. Among other practices, the SEC approvingly noted the increased designation of one law firm to act as underwriters' counsel, which "facilitates continuous due diligence by ensuring on-going access to the registrant on the underwriters' behalf"; the holding of "Exchange Act report 'drafting sessions,'" which allow underwriters "to participate in the drafting and review of periodic disclosure documents before they are filed"; and "periodic due diligence sessions," such as meetings between prospective underwriters, their counsel, and management shortly after the release of quarterly earnings.

* * *

E. *Case Law: Reliance Defense*

Over thirty-five years ago, the Honorable Edward C. McLean of this District observed that "there is little or no judicial authority" on how a defendant can successfully establish his affirmative defenses under Section 11. This remains true today. Neither the Supreme Court nor the Second Circuit has explored this area of law in any significant way.

* * *

Nevertheless, underwriters' reliance on audited financial statements may not be blind. Rather, where "red flags" regarding the reliability of an audited financial statement emerge, mere reliance on an audit will not be sufficient to ward off liability.

* * *

[T]he phrase "red flags" can be used to describe two different concepts. First, red flags can be those facts which come to a defendant's attention that would place a reasonable party in defendant's position "on notice that the audited company was engaged in wrongdoing to the detriment of its investors." * * *

The phrase "red flags," or "storm warnings," may also describe facts or circumstances that "would suggest to an investor of ordinary intelligence the probability that she has been defrauded." The Second Circuit, for example, has found that a company's taking three substantial reserve charges over four years should have "alert[ed] any reasonable investor that something is seriously wrong." Where such red flags arise, a duty of inquiry arises and knowledge of the fraud is imputed to the investor with consequences as to whether or not a claim has been filed within the statute of limitations.

* * *

F. *Case Law: Due Diligence Defense*

Just as there is little judicial elaboration of the reliance defense, so too there is "little judicial gloss" on the due diligence defense afforded to underwriters for non-expertised portions of a registration statement.

* * *

G. *The Application of the Law to This Motion*

The Underwriter Defendants have moved for summary judgment on each of the alleged misstatements in the 2000 and 2001 Registration Statements. The Underwriter Defendants analyze each of the misstatements (as opposed to the omissions) that the Lead Plaintiff has alleged as quintessentially matters of accounting. Most of the misstatements are financial figures from WorldCom's Exchange Act reports that were incorporated by reference into the Registration Statements. Additional misstatements include management's comparison of financial figures from one period to the next, statements by WorldCom's management describing accounting policies and future expectations, and the use of proceeds. The Underwriter Defendants contend that they are entitled to summary judgment on their affirmative defenses of reliance and due diligence because they were entitled to rely on Andersen's audits and comfort letters. The analysis that follows distinguishes between the expertised and non-expertised statements which are the subject of this motion.

1. *Audited Financial Statements*

The Underwriter Defendants contend that they were entitled to rely on Andersen's unqualified "clean" audit opinions for WorldCom's 1999 and 2000 Form 10-Ks as expertised statements under Section 11(b)(3)(C). Their motion for summary judgment on their reliance defense is denied.

a. *2000 Registration Statement*

The Lead Plaintiff points to one issue that it contends gave the Underwriter Defendants a reasonable ground to question the reliability of WorldCom's 1999 Form 10-K. According to the computations presented by the Lead Plaintiff, WorldCom's reported E/R [expense to revenue] ratio was significantly lower than that of the equivalent numbers of its two closest competitors, Sprint and AT & T.[47] The Lead Plaintiff argues that, in the extremely competitive market in which WorldCom operated, that discrepancy triggered a duty to investigate such a crucial measurement of the company's health. The Lead Plaintiff has shown that there are issues of fact as to whether the Underwriter Defendants had reasonable grounds to believe that the 1999 Form 10-K was inaccurate in the lines related to the E/R ratio reflected in that filing.

The Underwriter Defendants argue that the difference in the E/R ratios was insufficient as a matter of law to put the Underwriter Defendants on notice of any accounting irregularity. In support of this, they point to the fact that this difference was publicly available information and no one else announced a belief that it suggested the existence of an accounting fraud at WorldCom.

The fact that the difference was publicly available information does not absolve the Underwriter Defendants of their duty to bring their expertise to bear on the issue. The Underwriter Defendants do not dispute that they were required to be familiar with the Exchange Act filings that were incorporated by reference into the Registration Statement. If a "prudent man in the management of his own property," upon reading the 1999 Form 10-K and being familiar with the other relevant information about the issuer's competitors would have questioned the accuracy of the figures, then those figures constituted a red flag and imposed a duty of investigation on the Underwriter Defendants. A jury would be entitled to find that this difference was of sufficient importance to have triggered a duty to investigate the reliability of the figures on which the ratio was based even though the figures had been audited.

The Underwriter Defendants contend that an audited figure can never constitute a red flag and impose a duty of investigation. This argument mischaracterizes the Lead Plaintiff's position. The Lead Plaintiff has pointed to facts extraneous to WorldCom's audited figures to argue that a reasonable person would have inquired further about the

---

[47] WorldCom's E/R ratio was 43%. The expert for the Lead Plaintiff calculates that AT & T's equivalent ratio was 46.8% and Sprint's was 53.2%.

discrepancy between the audited figures and the comparable information from competitors. As discussed above, the existence of red flags can create a duty to investigate even audited financial statements.

The Underwriter Defendants argue that the standard that should apply is whether they had "clear and direct notice" of an "accounting" problem. They argue that case law establishes that "ordinary business events" do not constitute red flags. They are wrong. There is no basis in law to find a requirement that a red flag arises only when there is "clear and direct" notice of an accounting issue. The standard under Section 11 is whether a defendant has proven that it had "no reasonable ground to believe and did not believe" that a registration statement contained material misstatements, a standard given meaning by what a "prudent man" would do in the management of his own property. Nor is the bar lowered because there is an expert's opinion on which an underwriter is entitled to rely. The "prudent man" standard applies to Section 11(b)(3)(C). Finally, what constitutes an ordinary business event and what constitutes a red flag is an issue of fact. These are exquisitely fact intensive inquiries that depend on the circumstances surrounding a particular issuer and the alleged misstatement. There is no category of information which can always be ignored by an underwriter on the ground that it constitutes an ordinary business event. What is ordinary in one context may be sufficiently unusual in another to create a duty of investigation by a "prudent man."

* * *

b. *2001 Registration Statement*

The Lead Plaintiff points to three issues that it contends imposed upon the Underwriter Defendants a duty to investigate the reliability of WorldCom's 2000 Form 10-K. They are the discrepancy between WorldCom's E/R ratio and that of its competitors; the deterioration in the MCI long-distance business, which the Lead Plaintiff alleges should have caused them to question the accuracy of WorldCom's reported assets;[50] and Ebbers' personal financial situation, which gave him both the motive and opportunity to inflate WorldCom's stock price through manipulation.

The Underwriter Defendants' general arguments about the nature of the reliance defense insofar as it concerns audited information have already been addressed. The arguments that are particular to the individual red flags identified by the Lead Plaintiff are addressed below. The Underwriter Defendants have shown that they are entitled to summary judgment on the issue of whether Ebbers' financial situation constituted a red flag that imposed upon them the duty of inquiry.

* * *

---

[50] When WorldCom acquired MCI for $47 billion, $29 billion of that purchase price was attributed to goodwill, which is treated as an intangible asset.

2. *Interim Financial Statements*

The Underwriter Defendants contend that, pursuant to Sections 11(b)(3)(A) and 12(a)(2), they were entitled to rely on Andersen's comfort letters for WorldCom's unaudited interim financial statements for the first quarter of 2000 and 2001 so long as the Lead Plaintiff is unable to show that the Underwriter Defendants were on notice of any accounting red flags. They argue that this statement of the due diligence defense is particularly appropriate because WorldCom was a seasoned issuer and the Registration Statements were part of the integrated disclosure system that allowed the Exchange Act periodic reports to be incorporated by reference. The Underwriter Defendants contend that "Form S-3 issuers" like WorldCom are only required to include transaction-related information in a Form S-3 prospectus and that the information contained in the Exchange Act filings which are incorporated by reference do not need to be repeated. They argue that in the context of integrated disclosure for shelf registrations, and as a result of SEC Rule 176, the focus is on an underwriter's continuous learning about an "industry" and reasonable reliance on other professionals, such as an issuer's auditor. As a consequence, they contend that there is no difference from the point of view of the underwriter between audited and unaudited financial statements so long as the underwriter receives an auditor's comfort letter. According to the Underwriter Defendants, so long as there are no red flags that bring the auditor's assessment into question, the receipt of a comfort letter "goes a long way to establish" due diligence with respect to all matters of accounting. They ask for a legal ruling that "an underwriter's investigation of accounting issues is reasonable when it rests on the independent auditor's SAS 71 review for interim financial statements," at least in the context of seasoned issuers engaged in a shelf registration. Finally, they argue that it is material that no amount of reasonable diligence could have uncovered the capitalization of line costs since the WorldCom management deliberately concealed it from Andersen and every other outsider and would never have given them any documents or information that would have revealed the fraud.

Andersen issued a May 19 comfort letter and May 23 bringdown comfort letter for the 2000 Offering. Andersen issued comfort letters on May 9 and 16 for the 2001 Offering. These comfort letters addressed the only interim financial statements that were incorporated by reference in the Registration Statements. In connection with the latter Offering, the Underwriter Defendants emphasize that J.P. Morgan and SSB had recently had occasion to work closely with WorldCom on other projects. The two firms had participated in the two tracking stock realignment of WorldCom announced in November 2000, and J.P. Morgan had acted as a lead manager and sole book-runner for WorldCom's $2 billion private placement in December 2000. They point to these activities as part of their continuous due diligence for WorldCom.

To prevail on their due diligence defense at trial, the Underwriter Defendants must show that they conducted a reasonable investigation and that after such an investigation that they had reasonable ground to believe that the statements in the Registration Statements, including the information in the unaudited interim financial statements, were true. In judging that investigation, a jury will have to consider the non-exclusive list of factors enumerated in Rule 176. Insofar as Rule 176 is concerned, there does not appear to be any dispute that WorldCom was a "well-established" issuer, that the notes at issue were investment-grade debt securities, that SSB and J.P. Morgan assigned experienced personnel to the due diligence teams, that they spoke to the issuer's CFO and in 2001 also spoke to Andersen, that the underwriting was a firm commitment underwriting, that the underwriting was through a shelf registration, that many analysts and credit reporting agencies followed and reported on WorldCom, that the issuer and not the Underwriter Defendants had responsibility for preparing the interim financial statements, and that Andersen and not the Underwriter Defendants had responsibility for reviewing the interim financial statements.

The Lead Plaintiff has shown that there are questions of fact, however, as to whether the Underwriter Defendants conducted a reasonable investigation in either 2000 or 2001. It points to what it contends is evidence of the limited number of conversations with the issuer or its auditor, the cursory nature of the inquiries, the failure to go behind any of the almost formulaic answers given to questions, and the failure to inquire into issues of particular prominence in the Underwriter Defendants' own internal evaluations of the financial condition of the issuer or in the financial press. It argues in particular with respect to 2001, that having internally downgraded WorldCom's credit rating and having taken steps to limit their exposure as WorldCom creditors, the Underwriter Defendants were well aware that WorldCom was in a deteriorating financial position in a troubled industry, and that a reasonable investigation would have entailed a more searching inquiry than that undertaken by the Underwriter Defendants. Given the enormity of these two bond offerings, and the general deterioration in WorldCom's financial situation, at least as of the time of the 2001 Offering, they argue that a particularly probing inquiry by a prudent underwriter was warranted. These issues of fact require a jury trial.

The Underwriter Defendants have framed their summary judgment motion in a way that is incompatible with their burden of proving their due diligence defense under Section 11. They seek to restrict the inquiry on their due diligence solely to the work undertaken with respect to the interim financial statements and therefore to restrict it to a determination of whether any red flags existed that would put them on notice of a duty to make an inquiry of the interim financial statements. This formulation converts the due diligence defense into the reliance defense and balkanizes the task of due diligence.

In order to succeed with a due diligence defense, the Underwriter Defendants will have to show that they conducted a reasonable investigation of the non-expertised portions of the Registration Statements and thereafter had reasonable ground to believe that the interim financial statements were true. In assessing the reasonableness of the investigation, their receipt of the comfort letters will be important evidence, but it is insufficient by itself to establish the defense.

It is important to note that even if no reasonable investigation would have uncovered a fraud, an underwriter will prevail on its defense if [it] can show it did conduct a reasonable investigation. Conversely, an underwriter must conduct a reasonable investigation to prevail on the due diligence defense, even if it appears that such an investigation would have proven futile in uncovering the fraud. Without a reasonable investigation, of course, it can never be known what would have been uncovered or what additional disclosures would have been demanded.

The Underwriter Defendants argue that if they are not entitled to rely on a comfort letter, the costs of capital formation in the United States will be substantially increased since underwriters will have to hire their own accounting firms to rehash the work of the issuer's auditor. Nothing in this Opinion should be read as imposing that obligation on underwriters or the underwriting process. The term "reasonable investigation" encompasses many modes of inquiry between obtaining comfort letters from an auditor and doing little more, on one hand, and having to re-audit a company's books on the other. Nonetheless, if aggressive or unusual accounting strategies regarding significant issues come to light in the course of a reasonable investigation, a prudent underwriter may choose to consult with accounting experts to confirm that the accounting treatment is appropriate and that additional disclosure is unnecessary.

Underwriters perform a different function from auditors. They have special access to information about an issuer at a critical time in the issuer's corporate life, at a time it is seeking to raise capital. The public relies on the underwriter to obtain and verify relevant information and then make sure that essential facts are disclosed.[53] Acting with the degree of diligence that applies to a prudent man when managing his own property, underwriters should ask those questions and seek those answers that are appropriate in the circumstances. They are not being asked to duplicate the work of auditors, but to conduct a reasonable investigation. If their initial investigation leads them to question the accuracy of financial reporting, then the existence of an audit or a comfort letter will not excuse the failure to follow through with a subsequent investigation of the matter. If red flags arise from a reasonable

---

[53] Reflecting on underwriters' role as the procurer and verifier of critical issuer-specific information, some academic commentators describe them as "reputational intermediaries" or "gatekeepers." See, e.g., John Coffee, Gatekeeper Failure and Reform: The Challenge of Fashioning Relevant Reforms, 84 B.U. L. Rev. 301, 302 n.1, 308 nn.13–14 (2004).

investigation, underwriters will have to make sufficient inquiry to satisfy themselves as to the accuracy of the financial statements, and if unsatisfied, they must demand disclosure, withdraw from the underwriting process, or bear the risk of liability.

An underwriter should, and the Underwriter Defendants here certainly did, have the "business and financial expertise to identify the weak points in an issuer's business and financial condition and to assess the adequacy of an issuer's disclosure in this regard." It is in part because underwriters have taken their responsibilities seriously in this regard that, from the perspective of over seventy years, the Securities Act has been an effective instrument of regulation. The question the jury will have to decide here is whether the Underwriter Defendants have fulfilled that obligation in the context of the two WorldCom Offerings.

The Underwriter Defendants contend that they will be able to show at trial that the continuous due diligence that they performed with respect to WorldCom amounted to a reasonable investigation for both Offerings. This Opinion does not address the likelihood of that showing because the Underwriter Defendants have not moved for summary judgment on that ground. For that reason, it is also unnecessary to address their arguments about the difficulty of meeting the traditional standard for due diligence in the context of integrated disclosure and shelf registrations. In any event, the Underwriter Defendants have not shown that the prudent man standard in Section 11 has been diluted by any regulatory changes. The processes through which and the timing in which due diligence is performed have changed, but the ultimate test of reasonable conduct in the specific circumstances of an offering remains unchanged.

* * *

For the reasons stated herein, the parties' motions for summary judgment are each granted in part and denied in part.

* * *

NOTES ON DEFENDANTS AND THE "DUE DILIGENCE" DEFENSE UNDER § 11

1. *Who Are § 11 Defendants?* Section 11 imposes civil liability for misstatements or omissions of material facts in a securities offering registration statement. Potential § 11 defendants include the issuer, underwriters, directors, accountants (or others who have prepared or certified reports or valuations in connection with the registration statement), and any other person who signed the registration statement.[10]

Plaintiffs tried to expand the class of § 11 defendants, arguing credit rating agencies should be liable as underwriters for misstatements or

---

[10] § 11(a).

omissions in securities offering documents. Thus far this theory of liability has proved unpersuasive.[11] Significantly, in In re Lehman Brothers,[12] the Second Circuit affirmed the district court's dismissal of three class action complaints seeking to hold rating agencies liable.

The plaintiffs in *Lehman Brothers* filed three class actions arising from the purchase of $155 billion worth of mortgage pass-through certificates between 2005 and 2007. In connection with the offering, the credit rating agencies provided models enabling the transaction to be structured such that the certificates achieved the desired rating. The plaintiffs claimed this rating was a necessary prerequisite to the certificates' distribution in the market, and the models the credit rating agencies provided were outdated and flawed. As a result, they argued, the ratings assigned to the certificates did not accurately represent their risk. The plaintiffs alleged the active involvement of the credit rating agencies qualified them as underwriters, and accordingly they should be liable under § 11 for misstatements and omissions in the offering documents.

The Second Circuit rejected the plaintiffs' argument and held credit rating agencies are not underwriters for the purpose of the securities laws. The court held the rating agencies' participation in "the mere structuring or creation of securities does not constitute participation in statutory underwriting."[13] Instead, the court explained, "[t]he plain language of the statute limits liability to persons who participate in the purchase, offer, or sale of securities for distribution," and because the credit rating agencies' efforts in creating and structuring certificates occurred during only the initial stages of securitization, they did not qualify as underwriters.[14]

The Second Circuit also found support in prior case law, the law in other circuits, and legislative history to support its view that to qualify as a statutory underwriter the participation in underwriting "must be in the statutorily enumerated distributional activities, not in non-distributional activities that may *facilitate* the eventual distribution by others."[15] The court reasoned that to hold otherwise could create the "implausible result of transforming every lawyer, accountant, and other professional whose work is theoretically 'necessary' to bringing a security to market into an 'underwriter' subject to strict liability under § 11, a dramatic outcome that Congress provided no sign of intending."[16]

---

[11] See e.g., In re Lehman Bros. Sec. and ERISA Litig., 681 F.Supp.2d 495 (S.D.N.Y. 2010); New Jersey Carpenters Vacation Fund et al. v. Royal Bank of Scotland Group, PLC et al., 720 F.Supp.2d 254 (S.D.N.Y. 2010); In re Wells Fargo Mortgage-Backed Certificates Litig., 712 F.Supp.2d 958 (N.D. Cal. 2010); Public Employees' Retirement System of Mississippi v. Merrill Lynch & Co. Inc., 714 F.Supp.2d 475 (S.D.N.Y. 2010).

[12] In re Lehman Bros. Mortgage-Backed Sec. Litig., 650 F.3d 167 (2d Cir. 2011).

[13] Id. at 184.

[14] Id.

[15] Id. at 178.

[16] Id. at 182.

2. *Outside Directors.* This phrase refers to directors who are not otherwise employed by the issuer and who normally have other full-time occupations. In *BarChris* the court held that although the outside director can delegate a duty of investigation, he or she is liable if the person to whom this duty was delegated does not perform it properly.

BarChris also held two outside directors (a lawyer and an investment banker) with relevant areas of expertise to a higher standard than that of a run-of-the-mill outside director. The court, however, rejected the contention that when the law firm prepared the registration statement, it "expertised" the entire prospectus. The court also concluded the investment banker was not liable individually as an underwriter but only in conjunction with his firm. But, the court did hold when the attorney or underwriter directors undertook the laboring oar in the preparation of the registration statement, they made themselves liable *as directors* when their performance fell short of what the court considered proper for an attorney or investment banker engaged in that task. Thus, the court apparently judged them by the standards applicable to their professions, rather than those that might apply to a director who had no expertise in the registration process and did not undertake to oversee compliance with the requirements.

Similarly in Feit v. Leasco Data Processing Equip. Corp.,[17] Judge Weinstein concluded that Hodes, a partner in a law firm representing the issuer, was so intimately involved in the preparation of the registration statement "that to treat him as anything but an insider would involve a gross distortion of the realities of [the issuer's] management."

Subsequent cases have been more kind to outside directors. In Laven v. Flanagan,[18] for example, the court found outside directors' reliance on representations of management was not unreasonable, particularly when confirmed by investigations conducted by Price Waterhouse and Merrill Lynch. The court noted:

> Their work was imperfect, to the regret of plaintiff and certainly, in light of its $57.3 million dollar loss, to Curtiss-Wright. But their activities were a far cry from the passive and total reliance on company management that defeated the due diligence defense in Escott v. BarChris. As such, we must deem it to have been a reasonable effort to seek verification of the truth of the registration statement.[19]

In Weinberger v. Jackson,[20] the court seemingly went further:

> Since Valentine was an outside director, he was not obliged to conduct an independent investigation into the accuracy of all the statements contained in the registration statement. He

---

[17] 332 F.Supp. 544, 576 (E.D.N.Y.1971).
[18] 695 F.Supp. 800 (D.N.J.1988).
[19] Id. at 812.
[20] 1990–1991 Fed. Sec. L. Rep. (CCH) ¶ 95,693 at 98,256 (N.D. Cal. 1990).

could rely upon the reasonable representations of management, if his own conduct and level of inquiry were reasonable under the circumstances. He was reasonably familiar with the company's business and operations. He regularly attended board meetings at which the board discussed every aspect of the company's business. And he reviewed the company's financial statements. He was familiar with the company's development of its new product lines. He was involved with various company decisions. He reviewed six drafts of the registration statement and saw nothing suspicious or inconsistent with the knowledge that he had acquired as a director. And he discussed certain aspects of the registration statement with management.

With respect to the alleged misrepresentations about shipment of the lines of products, he could not reasonably have noticed any ambiguity in the phrase "in quantity" in light of his understanding of the company's business and its practice of increasing production from the time a new model is first introduced. With respect to alleged misrepresentations regarding the availability of software, Valentine knew what the prospectus stated, that is, that software was provided by outside vendors, and that application software might not be available for new models when they are first introduced.

Plaintiffs argue that Valentine did not make specific inquiries of the company's management with respect to the representations contained in the prospectus. But he had no duty to do so as long as the prospectus statements were consistent with the knowledge of the company which he had reasonably acquired in his position as director. He was also given comfort by the fact that the prospectus and the information in it were reviewed by underwriters, counsel and accountants. This met the standards of due diligence and reasonable inquiry.

The *WorldCom* opinion does not address the status of the directors because they agreed to a settlement requiring the directors to pay $18 million, which represented 20% of each director's personal net worth (minus certain spousal and retirement assets). In addition, their insurers paid $36 million—for a total of $54 million.[21] The court initially rejected this settlement because the settling parties sought approval of a stipulation that the liability of the other non-director defendants would only be reduced by the total net worth of the directors. When the court rejected this provision as inconsistent with the proportionate liability provisions of the PSLRA, the plaintiffs backed out of the settlement and threatened to take the directors to trial. As a result, the personal exposure of directors under § 11 seemed very high (in part because liability insurance could not hope to cover the potential $17 billion in

---

[21] See In re WorldCom, Inc. Sec. Litig., 2005 WL 335201 (S.D.N.Y. 2005).

liability for WorldCom's bonds). In this light, the issue has arisen: do directors need their own counsel (rather than rely on corporate or underwriter's counsel) to establish and document their due diligence defense?

3. *Inside Directors and Officers.* The *BarChris* court held these defendants to a very high standard of diligence. The *Feit* court added:

> Inside directors with intimate knowledge of corporate affairs and of the particular transactions will be expected to make a more complete investigation and have more extensive knowledge of facts supporting or contradicting inclusions in the registration statements than outside directors.[22]

This demanding due diligence standard for inside or employee directors and officers has endured because of their familiarity with corporate operations and records.[23]

4. *Underwriters.* The *BarChris* court indicated that although perhaps not as high as that of the "inside" defendants, the standard of diligence for underwriters is also very high because the public looks to them for an independent, disinterested investigation of the business and for advice regarding the issue. Underwriters are the central gatekeepers of the capital markets.

The members of the underwriting syndicate other than the managing or so-called "lead" underwriter typically do not undertake an investigation of the issuer at all but rely entirely upon the managing underwriter to do an investigation for them. The syndicate members are entitled to rely upon this investigation if it in fact complies with the statutory requirements.[24] Conversely, it is fairly inferable from the *BarChris* opinion that if the performance falls short, the syndicate members are equally liable. Whether the underwriting syndicate might have some action against the managing underwriter for such a failure is debatable. The typical "agreement among underwriters" attempts to negate any fiduciary relationship between the managing underwriter and the other syndicate members. The theory is that reputation in a repeat-play game among underwriters provides the primary deterrent to shirking or cheating by the lead underwriter. Cases like Enron, however, raise questions as to whether the theory holds up in practice.

The lurking fear that members of the underwriting syndicate will not be permitted to rely upon the investigation by the managing underwriter has led to a ritual known as the "due diligence meeting." Shortly before the effective date of the registration statement, representatives of the underwriters gather in a room with officers of the

---

[22] 332 F.Supp. at 578.

[23] See Kitchens v. U.S. Shelter, 1988–1989 Fed. Sec. L. Rep. (CCH) ¶ 93,920 at 90,155 (D.S.C. 1988).

[24] See, e.g., Weinberger v. Jackson, 1990–1991 Fed. Sec. L. Rep. (CCH) ¶ 95,693 at 98,255 (N.D. Cal. 1990).

issuer, ostensibly to question the officers about the company's affairs as disclosed in the registration statement. In fact, the questions are more likely to be about matters not disclosed in the registration statement, but which may be useful in selling the issue, such as: "what is the projection for next quarter's earnings?" This meeting, largely a formality, is unlikely to save the other underwriters if the managing underwriter has failed in its duty of investigation.

In In re Software Toolworks Inc., [25] the court held an underwriter need not conduct due diligence into the "expertised" parts of a prospectus such as certified financial statements if the underwriter had no reasonable grounds to believe the expertised statements were misleading. The Ninth Circuit found a "red flag," a "backdated" agreement allegedly permitting Toolworks to recognize income in an earlier year. The court found the underwriter defendant was entitled to summary judgment, in part, because the underwriter confronted the accountant on this issue, insisted that the accountant reconfirm that the income recognition was proper, and contacted other accounting firms to verify the appropriateness of the Toolworks' accountant's revenue recognition methods.

The underwriter was *not* entitled to summary judgment, however, with regard to the period after a preliminary prospectus was filed until the effective date, when the underwriters did little more than rely on Toolworks' assurances that specified sales transactions were legitimate.[26]

The *In re WorldCom, Inc. Sec. Litig.*[27] court provided further guidance on the underwriters' due diligence, making clear that underwriters must perform reasonable investigations into non-expertised portions of the registration statement. In doing so, the court rejected the underwriters' argument that they need only perform due diligence on interim financials, and only on areas where red flags existed. The court also stressed the appropriate standard is that which applies to a prudent person managing her own property.

5. *"Experts" and Liability with Respect to "Expertised Portions" of the Registration Statement.* An expert is liable under § 11 with respect to only those portions of a registration statement expressly stated to be made on his or her authority as an expert. The *BarChris* court properly rejected contentions that the accountants were liable for all of the figures

---

[25] 50 F.3d at 623.

[26] Id. at 625–626. See also Endo v. Albertine, 863 F.Supp. 708, 731–733 (N.D.Ill.1994) (questions of fact whether an underwriter was entitled to due diligence defenses); Glosser v. Cellcor Inc., 1994–1995 Fed. Sec. L. Rep. (CCH) ¶ 98,424 at 90,914 (Del. Ch. 1994) (question of fact whether defendant could prove due diligence defense).

[27] 346 F.Supp.2d 628 (S.D.N.Y. 2004). See also International Rectifier Sec. Litig., 1997 Fed. Sec. L. Rep (CCH) ¶ 99,469 at 97,140 (C.D. Cal. 1997) (listing factors for reasonableness determination, including familiarity with issuer's finances, knowledge of issuer's industry, interviews with or inquiries of issuer's customers or other third parties, and verification from issuer and/or outside accountants on information in prospectus).

in the registration statement, even those that were uncertified, and that the lawyer was liable for the entire statement because he or she wrote it. An expert's investigation should conform to the standards generally considered appropriate in his or her profession. The *BarChris* court found the accountants neither met those standards, nor indeed even complied with their own written procedures for an S-1 review. In the *Simon* case,[28] however, the Second Circuit held compliance with the standards of the profession would not necessarily insulate an accountant even from criminal prosecution—if the court considered them too lax. Presumably, lax standards would not insulate him from liability under § 11 either.

Subsequently, in Monroe v. Hughes,[29] the Ninth Circuit added:

> We have held that an accountant's good faith compliance with Generally Accepted Accounting Principles and Generally Accepted Auditing Standards discharges the accountant's professional obligation to act with reasonable care. See SEC v. Arthur Young & Co., 590 F.2d 785, 788–789 (9th Cir. 1979). A corollary rule, however, is that compliance with GAAP and GAAS do not immunize an accountant who consciously chooses not to disclose on a registration statement a known material fact.[30]

In *Hughes* the court declined to hold an accountant liable when there was compliance with Generally Accepted Accounting Principles (GAAP), but there was no disclosure of deficiencies in internal accounting controls.[31]

Attorneys who assist in the preparation of the registration statement do not thereby become experts for purposes of § 11 liability.[32] An attorney who also acts as a director or officer, or who signs the registration statement or otherwise provides a legal opinion outside of

---

[28] United States v. Simon, 425 F.2d 796 (2d Cir. 1969).

[29] 31 F.3d 772 (9th Cir. 1994).

[30] Id. at 774.

[31] An accountant can be liable for notes to the financial statement to the extent that he or she prepare or certifies them. In Endo v. Arthur Andersen & Co., S.C., 163 F.3d 463 (7th Cir. 1999), the court declined to hold an accountant liable for the republication of a note made by a former auditor, holding that (1) the accountant did not purport to certify that footnote and (2) the former accountant could be held liable. Cf. Cashman v. Coopers & Lybrand, 877 F.Supp. 425, 434–435 (N.D.Ill.1995) (accountant can be liable for expertised materials in registration statement even if they were prepared by others); Danis v. USN Communications, Inc., 121 F.Supp.2d 1183 (N.D.Ill.2000) (auditor can be held liable under § 11 unless the auditor establishes a due diligence defense).

[32] Ahern v. Gaussoin, 611 F.Supp. 1465 (D. Or. 1985) (rejecting attorney liability where attorneys had extensive knowledge of the corporation in question business' affairs and a high degree of involvement in the note offering). See also Herman & MacLean v. Huddleston, 459 U.S. 375, 386 (1983) (stating, "certain individuals who are involved in preparing the registration generally cannot be reached by a section 11 action. These include . . . lawyers not acting as 'experts'. . ."); In re ZZZZ Best Sec. Litig., 1989 U.S. Dist. LEXIS 8083 (holding the opinion letter required by Regulation S–K does not subject the attorney to further § 11 liability).

routine registration preparation, however, may be subject to § 11 liability.[33]

In 1982, when the Commission permitted disclosure of ratings for debt and preferred stock by nationally recognized statistical rating organizations (NRSROs), it adopted Rule 436(g) to exclude such ratings from § 11(a)(4).[34] As discussed in Chapter 1, however, the SEC "temporarily" froze enforcement of this rule when the NRSROs threatened to stop issuing new ratings. The freeze continues today.

Earlier the Commission had adopted Rules 436(c)–(d). Rule 436(c) excludes an independent accountant's report on unaudited interim financial information (as defined in Rule 436(d)) from consideration as part of a registration statement "prepared or certified by an accountant or a report prepared or certified by an accountant within the meanings of sections 7 and 11 of the Act."

An incidental impact of § 11 with a unique effect for auditors is to continue the auditor's responsibility until the effective date rather than the date of the audit opinion. It is always possible that information available to the auditor at the opinion date might justify one audit opinion, and additional information available at or near the effective date might then *require* a different opinion.[35]

With respect to an "expertised portion" of the registration statement, the non-expert defendants have a relaxed burden. No investigation need be shown, and the defendant must prove only that he "had no reasonable ground to believe, and did not believe," that the statements were false. Thus, ignorance is sufficient with respect to these statements, unless the defendant had some reason to question them. The *BarChris* court absolved all of the defendants of liability for the errors in the certified financial statements, except the accountants who certified them and the insiders who knew or should have known that they were false. Of course, they were all held liable for misstatements in other portions of the same prospectus.

6. *Securities Offering Reform.* In light of the *WorldCom* decision and its treatment of Rule 176 as not constituting a safe harbor, do underwriters and/or directors need a new "safe harbor" defense? As discussed in Chapter 2, when the SEC reformed the securities offering provisions in 2005, it permitted the use of a free writing prospectus that includes information in addition to that contained in the prospectus that is part of the registration statement. This free writing prospectus does not become part of the registration statement—unless the issuer decides that it should be. As a result, the free writing prospectus material is not

---

[33] 283 F.Supp. 643 at 690. See also Schneider v. Traweek, 1990 WL 132716 (lawyer consented to the inclusion of his materially false and misleading tax opinion in the registration statement).

[34] Sec. Act Rel. 6383, 24 SEC Dock. 1262, 1282–1283 (1982).

[35] See R. James Gormley, Accountants' Professional Liability—A Ten Year Review, 29 Bus. Law. 1205, 1217 (1974).

subject to § 11. Note, however, that § 12(a)(2) and other antifraud liability under the securities laws apply to the free writing prospectus.

7. *How Much Diligence Is Due?*[36] For the issuer, the only defense available under § 11 is to prove that the plaintiff at the time of his acquisition of the security knew of the untruth or omission. This defense is also available to all defendants. That said, it is of little practical significance in a class action, because the defendants could not prove it as to more than a handful of the plaintiffs, if it could be proven for any. All defendants other than the issuer, however, have the defense that they had, "after reasonable investigation, reasonable grounds to believe and did believe" that the statements were true and complete. This defense is commonly referred to as the "due diligence defense." Under this requirement, mere passive ignorance is insufficient. There must be an affirmative belief based upon reasonable grounds and upon reasonable investigation. The 1933 Committee report states that this defense casts a burden of "competence as well as innocence" upon the persons involved in an issue of securities.[37]

Problem

PROBLEM 11-1

In March of year two, AmericasBank sold $480 million of subordinated debt on a Form S-3 registration statement. Form S-3 incorporates by reference the registrant's latest annual report on Form 10-K and subsequent periodic reports on Forms 10-Q and 8-K. Annual and periodic reports were prepared by AmericasBank management. The underwriting firm of Bixwell Golden was hired to be lead underwriter in the preparation of the Form S-3 in January of year one.

At the time, banks in the geographic region where AmericasBank was located were experiencing relatively high bankruptcy rates as a result of a spate of commercial loan failures. Bixwell Golden asked its law firm of Navis Jones & Ito to conduct due diligence. Partner Sarah Jones worked with three associates over a two-week period to distribute questionnaires to management; review prior SEC filings; review AmericasBank's material contracts; and review board minutes. All minutes were provided in a timely fashion except AmericasBank Executive Committee meeting minutes for year one which had not been typed up yet. Jones asked AmericasBank CEO Ralph Smith about the delay and was informed "there were no problems in the minutes, just an overworked staff."

Shortly after the March offering a federal depository institution regulator announced it had initiated a formal investigation of AmericasBank's recordkeeping citing concerns about whether there had

---

[36] See Clifton A. Lake, Comment, Escott v. Barchris: How Much Diligence is Due?, 17 Kan. L. Rev. 651 (1969), from which this heading is borrowed.

[37] H.R. Rep. No. 85, 73d Cong., 1st Sess. 9 (1933).

been an appropriate evaluation of the collateral for commercial loans in its home region.

AmericasBank's subordinated debt, which had been sold at $100 per bond, slumped to $86, and in May of year two a § 11 lawsuit was filed against: (1) the board of directors of AmericasBank; (2) the underwriter Bixwell Golden; and (3) Navis Jones & Ito.

During discovery, the missing Executive Committee meeting minutes for year one were typed up. They revealed ongoing discussions between the Executive Committee (which included three inside directors: Ralph Smith; CFO Paula Larsen; and executive vice president Harriet Zahn) and the federal depository institution regulator. The federal depository institution regulator had proposed a consent settlement, in February of year two which the Executive Committee rejected. Three long time outside directors, attorney Sarah Jones and business executives Peter Quirk and Hazel Choi, did not attend the Executive Committee meetings.

How should a court rule in a § 11 lawsuit with respect to each of the defendants?

C. CAUSATION AND DAMAGES

The plaintiff does not have the affirmative burden to prove either reliance or causation in a § 11 case,[38] but the defendant can advance causation as a defense to the plaintiff's damages claim under the proviso in § 11(e), which states:

> *Provided,* that if the defendant proves that any portion or all of such damages represents other than the depreciation in value of such security resulting from such part of the registration statement, with respect to which his liability is asserted, not being true or omitting to state a material fact required to be stated therein or necessary to make the statements therein not misleading, such portion of or all such damages shall not be recoverable.

Section 11(e) thus creates a type of "negative causation" or, more grandly, "comparative causation with a reverse twist."[39]

Akerman v. Oryx Communications, Inc.
United States Court of Appeals, Second Circuit, 1987.
810 F.2d 336.

■ Before: VAN GRAAFEILAND, MESKILL, and NEWMAN, CIRCUIT JUDGES.

■ MESKILL, CIRCUIT JUDGE:

* * *

---

[38] See, e.g., Lyne v. Arthur Andersen & Co., 772 F.Supp. 1064, 1067 (N.D.Ill.1991).

[39] 9 Louis Loss & Joel Seligman, Securities Regulation 4251 (3d ed. 1992).

This case arises out of a June 30, 1981, initial public offering of securities by Oryx, a company planning to enter the business of manufacturing and marketing abroad video cassettes and video discs of feature films for home entertainment. Oryx filed a registration statement and an accompanying prospectus dated June 30, 1981, with the Securities and Exchange Commission (SEC) for a firm commitment offering of 700,000 units. Each unit sold for $4.75 and consisted of one share of common stock and one warrant to purchase an additional share of stock for $5.75 at a later date.

The prospectus contained an erroneous *pro forma* unaudited financial statement relating to the eight month period ending March 31, 1981. It reported net sales of $931,301, net income of $211,815, and earnings of seven cents per share. Oryx, however, had incorrectly posted a substantial transaction by its subsidiary to March instead of April when Oryx actually received the subject sale's revenues. The prospectus, therefore, overstated earnings for the eight month period. Net sales in that period actually totaled $766,301, net income $94,529, and earnings per share three cents.

Oryx's price had declined to four dollars per unit by October 12, 1981, the day before Oryx revealed the prospectus misstatement to the SEC. The unit price had further declined to $3.25 by November 9, 1981, the day before Oryx disclosed the misstatement to the public. After public disclosure, the price of Oryx rose and reached $3.50 by November 25, 1981, the day this suit commenced.

Plaintiffs allege that the prospectus error rendered Oryx liable for the stock price decline pursuant to sections 11 and 12(2) of the Securities Act of 1933. In July 1982, Oryx moved for summary judgment on the grounds, *inter alia*, that the misstatement was not material for purposes of establishing liability under section 11 and that the misstatement had not actually caused the price decline for purposes of damages under section 11.

* * *

Plaintiffs in the Akermans' situation, if successful, would be entitled to recover the difference between the original purchase price and the value of the stock at the time of suit. 15 U.S.C. § 77k(e). A defendant may, under section 11(e), reduce his liability by proving that the depreciation in value resulted from factors other than the material misstatement in the registration statement. 15 U.S.C. § 77k(e). A defendant's burden in attempting to reduce his liability has been characterized as the burden of "negative causation." Beecher v. Able, 435 F.Supp. 397, 409 (S.D.N.Y.1975).

The district court determined that plaintiffs established a *prima facie* case under section 11(a) by demonstrating that the prospectus error was material "as a theoretical matter." Akerman, 609 F.Supp. at 366–68. The court, however, granted defendants' motion for summary judgment on damages under section 11(e), stating: "[Defendants] have carried their heavy burden of proving that the [Oryx stock price] decline was caused by factors other than the matters misstated in the registration statement." The precise issue on appeal, therefore, is whether defendants carried their burden of negative causation under section 11(e).

Defendants' heavy burden reflects Congress' desire to allocate the risk of uncertainty to the defendants in these cases. Defendants' burden, however, is not insurmountable; section 11(e) expressly creates an affirmative defense of disproving causation.

* * *

The misstatement resulted from an innocent bookkeeping error whereby Oryx misposted a sale by its subsidiary to March instead of April. Oryx received the sale's proceeds less than one month after the reported date. The prospectus, moreover, expressly stated that Oryx "expect[ed] that [the subsidiary's] sales will decline." Indeed, Morris Akerman conceded that he understood this disclaimer to warn that Oryx expected the subsidiary's business to decline.

Thus, although the misstatement may have been "theoretically material," Akerman, 609 F.Supp. at 366, when it is considered in the context of the prospectus' pessimistic forecast of the performance of Oryx's subsidiary, the misstatement was not likely to cause a stock price decline. Indeed, the public not only did not react adversely to disclosure of the misstatement, Oryx's price actually *rose* somewhat after public disclosure of the error.

The applicable section 11(e) formula for calculating damages is "the difference between the amount paid for the security (not exceeding the price at which the security was offered to the public) and . . . the value thereof as of the time such suit was brought." 15 U.S.C. § 77k(e). The relevant events and stock prices are:

Date	Event	Oryx Stock Price
June 30, 1981	Initial public offering	$4.75
October 15, 1981	Disclosure of error to SEC	$4.00
November 10, 1981	Disclosure of error to public	$3.25
November 25, 1981	Date of suit	$3.50

The price decline before disclosure may not be charged to defendants. See Beecher v. Able, 435 F.Supp. 397, 407 (S.D.N.Y.1975) (price decline before misstatement revealed not attributable to defendants under section 11(e)). At first blush, damages would appear to be zero because there was no depreciation in Oryx's value between the time of public disclosure and the time of suit.

The Akermans contended at trial, however, that the relevant disclosure date was the date of disclosure to the SEC and not to the public. Under plaintiffs' theory, damages would equal the price decline subsequent to October 15, 1981, which amounted to fifty cents per share. Plaintiffs attempted to support this theory by alleging that insiders privy to the SEC disclosure—Oryx's officers, attorneys and accountants, and underwriters and SEC officials—sold Oryx shares and thereby deflated its price before public disclosure. The district court attributed "at least possible theoretical validity" to this argument. After extensive discovery, however, plaintiffs produced absolutely no evidence of insider trading. Plaintiffs' submissions and oral argument before us do not press this theory.

The Akermans first attempted to explain the public's failure to react adversely to disclosure by opining that defendant-underwriter Moore & Schley used its position as market maker to prop up the market price. This theory apparently complemented the Akermans' other theory that insiders acted on knowledge of the disclosure to the SEC to deflate the price before public disclosure. The Akermans failed after extensive discovery to produce any evidence of insider trading and have not pressed the theory on appeal.

The district court invited statistical studies from both sides to clarify the causation issue. Defendants produced a statistical analysis of the stocks of the one hundred companies that went public contemporaneously with Oryx. The study tracked the stocks' performances for the period between June 30, 1981 (initial public offering date) and November 25, 1981 (date of suit). The study indicated that Oryx performed at the exact statistical median of these stocks and that several issues suffered equal or greater losses than did Oryx during this period. Defendants produced an additional study which indicated that Oryx stock "behaved over the entire period . . . consistent[ly] with its own inherent variation."

Plaintiffs offered the following rebuttal evidence. During the period between SEC disclosure and public disclosure, Oryx stock decreased nineteen percent while the over-the-counter (OTC) composite index rose five percent (the first study). During this period, therefore, the OTC composite index outperformed Oryx by twenty-four percentage points. Plaintiffs also produced a study indicating that for the time period between SEC disclosure and one week after public disclosure, eighty-two of the one hundred new issues analyzed in the defendants' study outperformed Oryx's stock.

Plaintiffs' first study compared Oryx's performance to the performance of the OTC index in order to rebut a comparison offered by defendants to prove that Oryx's price decline resulted not from the misstatement but rather from an overall market decline. As previously stated, defendants' comparison indicated that the OTC index generally declined for the period between Oryx's offering date and the date of suit.

The parties' conflicting comparisons, however, lack credibility because they fail to reflect any of the countless variables that might affect the stock price performance of a single company. Statistical analyses must control for relevant variables to permit reliable inferences.

The studies comparing Oryx's performance to the other one hundred companies that went public in May and June of 1981 are similarly flawed. The studies do not evaluate the performance of Oryx stock in relation to the stock of companies possessing any characteristic in common with Oryx, *e.g.*, product, technology, profitability, assets or countless other variables which influence stock prices, except the contemporaneous initial offering dates.

Perhaps more important, the Akermans' study of the one hundred new issues focuses on a time frame which controverts one of their own theories explaining the public's failure to react adversely to disclosure. The Akermans argue that the thin market in Oryx stock prevented immediate public reaction to disclosure of the prospectus error. Their study, however, measures Oryx's performance from SEC disclosure to *one week* after public disclosure. A thin market, according to the Akermans' own explanation, would not reflect the impact of bad news in such a short time period (one week). This internal inconsistency seriously undercuts the probative value of the Akermans' study.

Finally, we note that this time period drew its relevance from the Akermans' theory that insider trading deflated Oryx's price during this period. As previously stated, this theory has no support even after extensive discovery and is not pressed on appeal.

Granting the Akermans every reasonable, favorable inference, the battle of the studies is at best equivocal; the studies do not meaningfully point in one direction or the other.

* * *

Defendants met their burden, as set forth in section 11(e), by establishing that the misstatement was barely material and that the public failed to react adversely to its disclosure. With the case in this posture, the plaintiffs had to come forward with "specific facts showing that there is a genuine issue for trial." Despite extensive discovery, plaintiffs completely failed to produce any evidence, other than unreliable and sometimes inconsistent statistical studies and theories, suggesting that Oryx's price decline actually resulted from the misstatement.

* * *

NOTE ON DAMAGES: SECTION 11 LIMITS AMOUNT RECOVERABLE

Section 11(e) also caps each individual underwriter's liability at the total price of the securities underwritten by it. Section 11(g) adds a further cap on § 11 damages by providing: "[i]n no case shall the amount recoverable under this section exceed the price at which the security was offered to the public." This provision limits the plaintiff who purchased in the open market rather than in the course of a distribution. When the plaintiff disposes of the security in the open market before suit, the measure of damages is purchase price less resale price (with no mention of interest or of deducting income received on the security as in § 12). If the market *goes up pending suit*, and the plaintiff disposes of the security before judgment, the defendant gets the benefit of the increase over the value at the time of suit. If the market goes *down*, and the plaintiff disposes of the security pending suit, the plaintiff still gets only the difference between the purchase price and the value at the time of suit. Thus, it is to the plaintiff's advantage not to hold the security after filing suit if he or she wants to be sure of receiving damages.

D. SECTION 11 PLAINTIFFS

Hertzberg v. Dignity Partners, Inc.
United States Court of Appeals, Ninth Circuit, 1999.
191 F.3d 1076.

■ Before: THOMPSON and FLETCHER, CIRCUIT JUDGES, and LASNIK, DISTRICT JUDGE.

■ W. FLETCHER, CIRCUIT JUDGE:

This case arises out of alleged misstatements and omissions contained in Appellee Dignity Partners, Inc.'s ("Dignity's") registration statement filed with the Securities and Exchange Commission for an initial public offering of Dignity common stock. Dignity was in the business of buying the rights to life insurance proceeds from people with AIDS, paying a lump sum up front, and taking over the responsibility for paying the premiums. Shortly after the offering, the fact that AIDS patients were living longer than expected because of new AIDS treatments became public knowledge. As a result of the longer lives of the insured, Dignity posted huge losses, and the stock plummeted.

Plaintiffs/appellants Hertzberg, Derosa, and Feinman ("Hertzberg") are investors who purchased Dignity stock on the open market more than 25 days after the initial offering but before the news of the longer life expectancy or large losses became public knowledge. They brought a class action for several violations of the securities laws by Dignity, including violation of Section 11 of the Securities Act of 1933 ("Securities Act"), 15 U.S.C. § 77K ("Section 11"). Hertzberg claims that Dignity knew of the longer life expectancy but failed to disclose it in the registration statement. The district court dismissed the Section 11 causes of action on the ground that, because appellants had not bought their stock in the initial public offering, or within 25 days thereof, they did not have standing to bring the claim.

* * *

We reverse the district court's holding that the original named plaintiffs lacked standing under Section 11.

* * *

BACKGROUND

* * *

Dignity moved to dismiss Hertzberg's Section 11 claims because the named plaintiffs had not purchased their shares "in" the registered offering. The district court, ruling from the bench, held that because the named plaintiffs purchased their stock more than 25 days after the registration statement was filed, they did not have standing to bring an action under Section 11. It therefore dismissed their Section 11 claims.

* * *

DISCUSSION

We review the district court's interpretation of Section 11 *de novo*. In determining the meaning of a statute, we look first to its text. Section 11(a) provides that where a material fact is misstated or omitted from a registration statement accompanying a stock filing with the Securities and Exchange Commission, "any person acquiring such security" may bring an action for losses caused by the misstatement or omission. 15 U.S.C. § 77K(a). The district court read this phrase as if it had been written, "any person acquiring such security *on the first day of an initial public offering or in the twenty-five day period thereafter.*"[3] This reading adds a significant limitation not found in the original text.

The term "any person" is quite broad, and we give words their ordinary meaning. According to Webster's Third New Int'l Dictionary (3d ed. 1986), "any" means "one, no matter what one"; "ALL"; "one or more discriminately from all those of a kind." This broad meaning of "any" has been recognized by this circuit. Madrid v. Gomez, 150 F.3d 1030, 1036 (9th Cir. 1998) (the court must accept "the plain meaning of the word 'any.' In its conventional usage, 'any' means 'ALL-used to indicate a maximum or whole.' It certainly does not mean 'some.'") (citations omitted).

The limitation on "any person" is that he or she must have purchased "such security." Clearly, this limitation only means that the person must have purchased a security issued under that, rather than some other, registration statement. While it might present a problem of proof in a case in which stock was issued under more than one registration

---

[3] The district court ruled from the bench and did not issue a written decision, so we are not certain where it got the 25-day period. Such a 25-day period was most likely borrowed from the 25-day after-market period of 17 C.F.R. § 230.174. However, this section pertains to false statements in prospectuses (a Section 12 violation), not registration statements (a Section 11 violation). We note that defendant does not seriously argue in support of the 25-day period. Rather, it argues that *any* after-market purchase is excluded from the protection of Section 11, whether made one day or 26 days after the initial public offering.

statement, the only Dignity stock ever sold to the public was pursuant to the allegedly misleading registration statement at issue in this case. Thus, as long as Hertzberg is suing regarding this security, he is "any person purchasing such security," regardless of whether he bought in the initial offering, a week later, or a month after that.

Further, paragraph (e) of Section 11 uses "the amount paid for the security (not exceeding the price at which the security was offered to the public)" as the baseline for measuring damages. 15 U.S.C. § 77k(e); see also 15 U.S.C. § 77k(g). Such a provision would be unnecessary if only a person who bought in the actual offering could recover, since, by definition, such a person would have paid "the price at which the security was offered to the public." We will "avoid a reading which renders some words altogether redundant." Gustafson v. Alloyd Co., Inc., 513 U.S. 561, 574 (1995).

Finally, Dignity believes that its reading of Section 11 is supported by the Supreme Court's decision in *Gustafson*. We believe that Dignity is mistaken. In *Gustafson*, the Supreme Court interpreted Section 12 of the Securit[ies] Act, 15 U.S.C. § 77l, rather than Section 11, and limited its decision to determining what was a "prospectus" under Section 12. Dicta in *Gustafson* indicate that a suit under Section 12 may only be maintained by a person who purchased the stock in the offering under the prospectus, but the Court gave no indication that it intended this restriction to apply to Section 11.

Dignity relies on the Supreme Court's statements in *Gustafson* that Section 12 is a companion to Section 11 for its claim that Section 11 applies only to people who purchased their stock in the initial offering. However, while Section 11 and Section 12 are indeed parallel statutes, their wording is significantly different as to who can bring a suit. As already noted, Section 11 permits suit without restriction by "any person acquiring such security." Section 12, by contrast, permits suit against a seller of a security by prospectus only by "the person purchasing such security *from him*," thus specifying that a plaintiff must have purchased the security directly from the issuer of the prospectus. 15 U.S.C. § 77l(a)(2) (emphasis added).

Congress's decision to use "from him" in Section 12 but not in Section 11 must mean that Congress intended a different meaning in the two sections. See Russello v. United States, 464 U.S. 16, 23 (1983) ("[W]here Congress includes particular language in one section of a statute but omits it in another section of the same Act, it is generally presumed that Congress acts intentionally and purposefully in the disparate inclusion or exclusion.") (citations and internal quotation marks omitted). Further, there is nothing in the reasoning or underlying logic of *Gustafson* that indicates that we should read into Section 11 the express privity requirement of Section 12.

Other circuits that have addressed this issue agree with our reading of the text and have uniformly allowed for recovery by purchasers in the aftermarket. Versyss Inc. v. Coopers and Lybrand, 982 F.2d 653, 657 (1st Cir. 1992) (Section 11 "is remarkably stringent where it applies, readily imposing liability on ancillary parties to the registration statement (like accountants) for the benefit *even of purchasers after the original offering*") (emphasis added); Barnes, supra, 373 F.2d 269 (2d Cir. 1967); Columbia General Inv. Corp. v. SEC, 265 F.2d 559, 562 (5th Cir. 1959) ("Persons other than those who purchase the new stock under the Registration may be affected in point of fact and may, under certain circumstances, have remedies in point of law for misrepresentations in a Registration"). We are unaware of any circuit that in light of *Gustafson* has either reconsidered its view or has disagreed with the circuits that have previously decided the question. Two district courts, in addition to the district court in this case, have read *Gustafson* in the manner suggested by Dignity, but for the reasons given above, we believe they have misread both *Gustafson* and Section 11.

Where the meaning of a statute is clear from the text, we need look no further. However, we note that even if we were to find the wording of the statute ambiguous, the legislative history supports Hertzberg's reading of Section 11.

The House Report accompanying the version of the bill that ultimately became the Securities Act of 1933 provides:

> the civil remedies accorded by [Section 11] are given to all purchasers ... regardless of whether they bought their securities *at the time of the original offer or at some later date*, provided, of course, that the remedy is prosecuted within the period of limitations provided by section 13.

H.R. Rep. No. 73–85, at 22 (emphasis added). By expressly referring to purchasers who bought their securities at "some later date" other than "at time of the original offer," the Report makes it clear that purchasers in the aftermarket are intended to have a cause of action under the Section. Similarly, when Congress amended Section 11 in 1934 to add a requirement of proof of reliance on the registration statement if there had been an intervening earning statement, the House Report stated:

> The basis of this provision is that in all likelihood the purchase and price of the security purchased after publication of such an earning statement will be predicated upon that statement rather than upon the information disclosed upon registration.

H.R. Rep. 73–1838 at 41. By referring to purchases after publication of an earning statement, the Report makes clear that purchasers in the aftermarket are within the group of purchasers provided a cause of action by Section 11.

Dignity does not effectively counter this legislative history. Rather, it points to comments made regarding an alternate bill which was never enacted, S. 875. This circuit relies on official committee reports when considering legislative history, not stray comments by individuals or other materials unrelated to the statutory language or the committee reports. Dignity also cites pieces of the legislative history that show Congress meant Section 11 to deal with new offerings of securities. But that issue has never been in dispute. As discussed above, all the stock ever publicly issued by Dignity was sold in the single offering at issue in this case. The difficulties of tracing stock to a particular offering present in some cases are thus not present here.

* * *

Reversed and remanded.

NOTES ON § 11 PLAINTIFFS: WHO MAY RECOVER?

1. *Oral Presentations.* Section 11 liability is limited to material misrepresentations or omissions in the registration statement. Roadshow presentations, analysts' reports, and statements to investment publications do not establish a § 11 claim.[40]

2. *Other Documents.* Liability under § 11 is based on information provided at the time the registration statement becomes effective, including information in the Rule 430A final prospectus and any Rule 430B prospectus supplement. A preliminary prospectus under Rule 430 will not, however, give rise to § 11 liability if errors are corrected before the effective date. Nor will a tombstone ad under Rule 134, because it is not filed as part of the registration statement, or a summary prospectus prepared under Rule 431. Information contained in a registration statement or a prospectus that is part of a registration statement, filed after the time of sale of the securities, is included in the registration statement for the purposes of § 11 liability.

For shelf offerings, the liability for issuers and underwriters will be determined on the takedown date, but liability for signing officers, directors, and experts will be determined as of the effective date of the registration statement or the most recent annual report on Form 10-K or 20-F. See 17 C.F.R. § 230.430B(f). As a result, the issuer and underwriters may be subject to liability that other defendants may escape. This reform followed the *WorldCom* decision[41] and was likely motivated by the timing implications of shelf offerings. Outside directors, in particular, are not in a position to complete due diligence at the time of a shelf takedown.

3. *Purchasers.* It is clear under the express terms of § 11 of the 1933 Act that the plaintiff must be a purchaser of a security ("any person acquiring such security"). Section 11 expressly eliminates any privity requirement between the plaintiff and the issuer as a defendant. Section 11 does not require privity of contract between the plaintiff and collateral defendants, such as directors and officers. Any purchaser in the market

---

[40] O'Sullivan v. Trident Microsystems, Inc., 1993–1994 Fed. Sec. L. Rep. (CCH) ¶ 98,116.
[41] 346 F.Supp.2d 628 (S.D.N.Y. 2004).

at any time before the statute of limitations has run may sue for a violation of that Section.

4. *Tracing.* In the period before the United States Supreme Court decision in Gustafson v. Alloyd Co., the lower federal courts consistently had held that any investor who acquired a registered security, whether in the process of a securities distribution or in the open market, could sue under § 11.[42] The open market purchaser, however, had to trace his or her particular securities to securities sold in the registered offering.[43] This is an unavoidable result of a statutory scheme that registers *units*, not *classes*, of securities.[44]

In the pre-*Gustafson* period these and other lower federal court cases consistently held that the plain language of § 11 provided a lawsuit for "any person acquiring such security." As Judge Friendly reasoned in Barnes v. Osofsky,[45] the most natural reading of this statutory language is to provide a remedy to both those who were original purchasers and those who could trace the lineage of their shares to the newly offered ones. Either a limitation of § 11 liability solely to those in direct privity with the initial sellers or a broader concept of liability extending to *all* holders of the same class of stock "would be inconsistent with the overall statutory scheme."[46] Judge Friendly recognized that the House Report accompanying the Securities Act provided further support for this construction when it stated that § 11 provided a remedy to purchasers "regardless of whether they bought their securities at the time of the original offer or at some later date."[47]

The Gustafson v. Alloyd Co., Inc.[48] majority opinion does not address this issue. The case concerns which purchasers have standing to sue under § 12(2) (now § 12(a)(2)) of the Securities Act. Section 12(a)(2) limits liability to sellers who make misrepresentations or omissions "by means of a prospectus," thus, the Supreme Court held that liability was limited to registered offerings by issuers and their controlling shareholders. The Court did not address whether § 11 provided standing to shareholders who could trace their purchases to a registration statement. It did, however, recognize that another section of the 1933 Act, § 17(a), applied both to a fraudulent scheme in an initial offer or sale of securities *and* in the course of open market trading.[49] *Gustafson*, therefore supports the

---

[42] 513 U.S. 561 (1995).

[43] See, e.g., Barnes v. Osofsky, 373 F.2d 269 (2d Cir. 1967); Shapiro v. UJB Fin. Corp., 964 F.2d 272, 286 (3d Cir. 1992).

[44] See, e.g., Klein v. Computer Devices, Inc., 591 F.Supp. 270, 273 n. 7 (S.D.N.Y.1984); Guenther v. Cooper Life Sciences, Inc., 759 F.Supp. 1437, 1439 (N.D.Cal.1990) ("The burden of tracing shares to a particular public offering rests with plaintiffs"); Harden v. Raffensperger, Hughes & Co., Inc., 933 F.Supp. 763 (S.D.Ind.1996); Lilley v. Charren, 936 F.Supp. 708, 715 (N.D.Cal.1996).

[45] 373 F.2d 269 (2d Cir. 1967).

[46] Id. at 272.

[47] Id. at 273, citing H.R. Rep. No. 85, 73d Cong., 1st Sess. 5 (1933).

[48] 513 U.S. 561 (1995).

[49] Id. at 577.

inference that each section of the 1933 Act deserves a separate analysis. Most post-*Gustafson* cases have followed Hertzberg v. Dignity Partners and allowed tracing.[50]

E. WHAT COUNTS AS A MISSTATEMENT UNDER SECTION 11?

Section 11 covers misstatements in a registration statement, but what exactly is a "misstatement"? To be sure, a statement must be objectively false to be deemed a misstatement. But must the plaintiff prove the speaker of the misstatement knew that it was false when it was made? In 2013, the Sixth Circuit answered that question "no," since it viewed § 11 as more or less a strict liability provision. The case set up a circuit split with several other circuits, including the Second and Ninth, which held the opposite. In 2015, the Supreme Court resolved the split in the following case:

Omnicare, Inc. v. Laborers District Council Construction Industry Pension Fund

Supreme Court of the United States, 2015.
575 U.S. 175, 135 S.Ct. 1318, 191 L.Ed.2d 253 (2015).

■ JUSTICE KAGAN delivered the opinion of the Court.

Before a company may sell securities in interstate commerce, it must file a registration statement with the Securities and Exchange Commission (SEC). If that document either "contain[s] an untrue statement of a material fact" or "omit[s] to state a material fact . . . necessary to make the statements therein not misleading," a purchaser of the stock may sue for damages. . . . This case requires us to decide how each of those phrases applies to statements of opinion.

I

The Securities Act of 1933 . . . protects investors by ensuring that companies issuing securities (known as "issuers") make a "full and fair disclosure of information" relevant to a public offering. . . . The linchpin of the Act is its registration requirement. With limited exceptions not relevant here, an issuer may offer securities to the public only after filing a registration statement. . . . That statement must contain specified information about both the company itself and the security for sale. . . .

---

[50] See, e.g., Schwartz v. Celestial Seasonings, Inc., 178 F.R.D. 545, 555–556 (D.Colo.1998); Adair v. Bristol Tech. Sys., Inc., 179 F.R.D. 126, 132–133 (S.D.N.Y.1998); In re Number Nine Visual Tech. Corp. Sec. Litig., 51 F.Supp.2d 1, 25–26 (D.Mass.1999) (standing under § 11 for plaintiffs who purchased securities in aftermarket trading and can "trace" the purchase to a public offering); Feiner v. SS & C Tech., Inc., 47 F.Supp.2d 250, 251–252 (D.Conn.1999) (tracing permitted both under §§ 11 and 12(a)(2)); Milman v. Box Hill Sys. Corp., 192 F.R.D. 105 (S.D.N.Y.2000) (a class may be formed on the basis of secondary market purchasers who can trace their securities to a registered offering under § 11).

Beyond those required disclosures, the issuer may include additional representations of either fact or opinion.

Section 11 of the Act promotes compliance with these disclosure provisions by giving purchasers a right of action against an issuer or designated individuals (directors, partners, underwriters, and so forth) for material misstatements or omissions in registration statements. As relevant here, that section provides:

> "In case any part of the registration statement, when such part became effective, contained an untrue statement of a material fact or omitted to state a material fact required to be stated therein or necessary to make the statements therein not misleading, any person acquiring such security . . . [may] sue."
>
> . . . .

Section 11 thus creates two ways to hold issuers liable for the contents of a registration statement—one focusing on what the statement says and the other on what it leaves out. Either way, the buyer need not prove (as he must to establish certain other securities offenses) that the defendant acted with any intent to deceive or defraud. . . .

This case arises out of a registration statement that petitioner Omnicare filed in connection with a public offering of common stock. Omnicare is the nation's largest provider of pharmacy services for residents of nursing homes. Its registration statement contained (along with all mandated disclosures) analysis of the effects of various federal and state laws on its business model, including its acceptance of rebates from pharmaceutical manufacturers. . . . Of significance here, two sentences in the registration statement expressed Omnicare's view of its compliance with legal requirements:

- "We believe our contract arrangements with other healthcare providers, our pharmaceutical suppliers and our pharmacy practices are in compliance with applicable federal and state laws." . . .

- "We believe that our contracts with pharmaceutical manufacturers are legally and economically valid arrangements that bring value to the healthcare system and the patients that we serve." . . .

Accompanying those legal opinions were some caveats. On the same page as the first statement above, Omnicare mentioned several state-initiated "enforcement actions against pharmaceutical manufacturers" for offering payments to pharmacies that dispensed their products; it then cautioned that the laws relating to that practice might "be interpreted in the future in a manner inconsistent with our interpretation and application." . . . And adjacent to the second statement, Omnicare noted that the Federal Government had expressed "significant concerns" about some manufacturers' rebates to pharmacies and warned that business might suffer "if these price concessions were no longer provided." . . .

Respondents here, pension funds that purchased Omnicare stock in the public offering (hereinafter Funds), brought suit alleging that the company's two opinion statements about legal compliance give rise to liability under § 11. Citing lawsuits that the Federal Government later pressed against Omnicare, the Funds' complaint maintained that the company's receipt of payments from drug manufacturers violated anti-kickback laws.... Accordingly, the complaint asserted, Omnicare made "materially false" representations about legal compliance.... And so too, the complaint continued, the company "omitted to state [material] facts necessary" to make its representations not misleading. The Funds claimed that none of Omnicare's officers and directors "possessed reasonable grounds" for thinking that the opinions offered were truthful and complete.... Indeed, the complaint noted that one of Omnicare's attorneys had warned that a particular contract "carrie[d] a heightened risk" of liability under anti-kickback laws.... At the same time, the Funds made clear that in light of § 11's strict liability standard, they chose to "exclude and disclaim any allegation that could be construed as alleging fraud or intentional or reckless misconduct."...

The District Court granted Omnicare's motion to dismiss.... In the court's view, "statements regarding a company's belief as to its legal compliance are considered 'soft' information" and are actionable only if those who made them "knew [they] were untrue at the time."... The court concluded that the Funds' complaint failed to meet that standard because it nowhere claimed that "the company's officers knew they were violating the law."... The Court of Appeals for the Sixth Circuit reversed.... It acknowledged that the two statements highlighted in the Funds' complaint expressed Omnicare's "opinion" of legal compliance, rather than "hard facts."... But even so, the court held, the Funds had to allege only that the stated belief was "objectively false"; they did not need to contend that anyone at Omnicare "disbelieved [the opinion] at the time it was expressed."...

We granted certiorari, 571 U. S. 1236 (2014), to consider how § 11 pertains to statements of opinion. We do so in two steps, corresponding to the two parts of § 11 and the two theories in the Funds' complaint. We initially address the Funds' claim that Omnicare made "untrue statement[s] of ... material fact" in offering its views on legal compliance.... We then take up the Funds' argument that Omnicare "omitted to state a material fact ... necessary to make the statements [in its registration filing] not misleading."... Unlike both courts below, we see those allegations as presenting different issues. In resolving the first, we discuss when an opinion itself constitutes a factual misstatement. In analyzing the second, we address when an opinion may be rendered misleading by the omission of discrete factual representations. Because we find that the Court of Appeals applied the wrong standard, we vacate its decision.

II

The Sixth Circuit held, and the Funds now urge, that a statement of opinion that is ultimately found incorrect—even if believed at the time made—may count as an "untrue statement of a material fact." . . . As the Funds put the point, a statement of belief may make an implicit assertion about the belief's "subject matter": To say "we believe X is true" is often to indicate that "X is in fact true." . . . In just that way, the Funds conclude, an issuer's statement that "we believe we are following the law" conveys that "we in fact are following the law"—which is "materially false," no matter what the issuer thinks, if instead it is violating an anti-kickback statute. . . .

But that argument wrongly conflates facts and opinions. A fact is "a thing done or existing" or "[a]n actual happening." Webster's New International Dictionary 782 (1927). An opinion is "a belief[,] a view," or a "sentiment which the mind forms of persons or things." *Id.*, at 1509. Most important, a statement of fact ("the coffee is hot") expresses certainty about a thing, whereas a statement of opinion ("I think the coffee is hot") does not. See *ibid.* ("An opinion, in ordinary usage . . . does not imply . . . definiteness . . . or certainty"); 7 Oxford English Dictionary 151 (1933) (an opinion "rests[s] on grounds insufficient for complete demonstration"). Indeed, that difference between the two is so ingrained in our everyday ways of speaking and thinking as to make resort to old dictionaries seem a mite silly. And Congress effectively incorporated just that distinction in § 11's first part by exposing issuers to liability not for "untrue statement[s]" full stop (which would have included ones of opinion), but only for "untrue statement[s] of . . . *fact*." § 77k(a) (emphasis added).

Consider that statutory phrase's application to two hypothetical statements, couched in ways the Funds claim are equivalent. A company's CEO states: "The TVs we manufacture have the highest resolution available on the market." Or, alternatively, the CEO transforms that factual statement into one of opinion: "I *believe*" (or "I think") "the TVs we manufacture have the highest resolution available on the market." The first version would be an untrue statement of fact if a competitor had introduced a higher resolution TV a month before—even assuming the CEO had not yet learned of the new product. The CEO's assertion, after all, is not mere puffery, but a determinate, verifiable statement about her company's TVs; and the CEO, however innocently, got the facts wrong. But in the same set of circumstances, the second version would remain true. Just as she said, the CEO really did believe, when she made the statement, that her company's TVs had the sharpest picture around. And although a plaintiff could later prove that opinion erroneous, the words "I believe" themselves admitted that possibility, thus precluding liability for an untrue statement of fact. That remains the case if the CEO's opinion, as here, concerned legal compliance. If, for example, she said, "I believe our marketing practices are lawful," and actually did think that, she could not be liable for a false statement of fact—even if she afterward discovered a longtime violation of law. Once again, the statement would have been true, because all she expressed was a view, not a certainty, about legal compliance.

That still leaves some room for § 11's false-statement provision to apply to expressions of opinion. As even Omnicare acknowledges, every such statement explicitly affirms one fact: that the speaker actually holds the stated belief. . . . For that reason, the CEO's statement about product quality ("I believe our TVs have the highest resolution available on the market") would be an untrue statement of fact—namely, the fact of her own belief—if she knew that her company's TVs only placed second. And so too the statement about legal compliance ("I believe our marketing practices are lawful") would falsely describe her own state of mind if she thought her company was breaking the law. In such cases, § 11's first part would subject the issuer to liability (assuming the misrepresentation were material).

In addition, some sentences that begin with opinion words like "I believe" contain embedded statements of fact—as, once again, Omnicare recognizes. . . . Suppose the CEO in our running hypothetical said: "I believe our TVs have the highest resolution available because we use a patented technology to which our competitors do not have access." That statement may be read to affirm not only the speaker's state of mind, as described above, but also an underlying fact: that the company uses a patented technology. See *Virginia Bankshares, Inc.* v. *Sandberg*, 501 U.S. 1083, 1109 (1991) (SCALIA, J., concurring in part and concurring in judgment) (showing that a statement can sometimes be "most fairly read as affirming separately both the fact of the [speaker's] opinion and the accuracy of the facts" given to support or explain it (emphasis deleted)). Accordingly, liability under § 11's false-statement provision would follow (once again, assuming materiality) not only if the speaker did not hold the belief she professed but also if the supporting fact she supplied were untrue.

But the Funds cannot avail themselves of either of those ways of demonstrating liability. The two sentences to which the Funds object are pure statements of opinion: To simplify their content only a bit, Omnicare said in each that "we believe we are obeying the law." And the Funds do not contest that Omnicare's opinion was honestly held. Recall that their complaint explicitly "exclude[s] and disclaim[s]" any allegation sounding in fraud or deception. . . . What the Funds instead claim is that Omnicare's belief turned out to be wrong—that whatever the company thought, it was in fact violating anti-kickback laws. But that allegation alone will not give rise to liability under § 11's first clause because, as we have shown, a sincere statement of pure opinion is not an "untrue statement of material fact," regardless whether an investor can ultimately prove the belief wrong. That clause, limited as it is to factual statements, does not allow investors to second-guess inherently subjective and uncertain assessments. In other words, the provision is not, as the Court of Appeals and the Funds would have it, an invitation to Monday morning quarterback an issuer's opinions.

III

A

That conclusion, however, does not end this case because the Funds also rely on § 11's omissions provision, alleging that Omnicare "omitted to state facts necessary" to make its opinion on legal compliance "not misleading." ... As all parties accept, whether a statement is "misleading" depends on the perspective of a reasonable investor: The inquiry (like the one into materiality) is objective. Cf. *TSC Industries, Inc.* v. *Northway, Inc.*, 426 U.S. 438, 445 (1976) (noting that the securities laws care only about the "significance of an omitted or misrepresented fact to a reasonable investor"). We therefore must consider when, if ever, the omission of a fact can make a statement of opinion like Omnicare's, even if literally accurate, misleading to an ordinary investor.

Omnicare claims that is just not possible. On its view, no reasonable person, in any context, can understand a pure statement of opinion to convey anything more than the speaker's own mindset. ... As long as an opinion is sincerely held, Omnicare argues, it cannot mislead as to any matter, regardless what related facts the speaker has omitted. Such statements of belief (concludes Omnicare) are thus immune from liability under § 11's second part, just as they are under its first.

That claim has more than a kernel of truth. A reasonable person understands, and takes into account, the difference we have discussed above between a statement of fact and one of opinion. ... She recognizes the import of words like "I think" or "I believe," and grasps that they convey some lack of certainty as to the statement's content. See, *e.g.*, Restatement (Second) of Contracts § 168, Comment *a*, p. 456 (1979) (noting that a statement of opinion "implies that [the speaker] ... is not certain enough of what he says" to do without the qualifying language). And that may be especially so when the phrases appear in a registration statement, which the reasonable investor expects has been carefully wordsmithed to comply with the law. When reading such a document, the investor thus distinguishes between the sentences "we believe X is true" and "X is true." And because she does so, the omission of a fact that merely rebuts the latter statement fails to render the former misleading. In other words, a statement of opinion is not misleading just because external facts show the opinion to be incorrect. Reasonable investors do not understand such statements as guarantees, and § 11's omissions clause therefore does not treat them that way.

But Omnicare takes its point too far, because a reasonable investor may, depending on the circumstances, understand an opinion statement to convey facts about how the speaker has formed the opinion—or, otherwise put, about the speaker's basis for holding that view. And if the real facts are otherwise, but not provided, the opinion statement will mislead its audience. Consider an unadorned statement of opinion about legal compliance: "We believe our conduct is lawful." If the issuer makes that statement without having consulted a lawyer, it could be misleadingly incomplete. In the context of the securities market, an investor, though recognizing that legal opinions can prove wrong in the end, still likely expects such an assertion to rest on some meaningful legal inquiry—rather than, say, on mere intuition, however sincere. Similarly, if the issuer made the statement in the face of its lawyers' contrary advice, or with knowledge that the Federal Government was taking the opposite view, the investor again has cause to complain: He expects not just that the issuer believes the opinion (however irrationally), but that it fairly aligns with the information in the issuer's possession at the time. Thus, if a registration statement omits material facts about the issuer's inquiry into or knowledge concerning a statement of opinion, and if those facts conflict with what a reasonable investor would take from the statement itself, then § 11's omissions clause creates liability.

An opinion statement, however, is not necessarily misleading when an issuer knows, but fails to disclose, some fact cutting the other way. Reasonable investors understand that opinions sometimes rest on a weighing of competing facts; indeed, the presence of such facts is one reason why an issuer may frame a statement as an opinion, thus conveying uncertainty.... Suppose, for example, that in stating an opinion about legal compliance, the issuer did not disclose that a single junior attorney expressed doubts about a practice's legality, when six of his more senior colleagues gave a stamp of approval. That omission would not make the statement of opinion misleading, even if the minority position ultimately proved correct: A reasonable investor does not expect that *every* fact known to an issuer supports its opinion statement.

Moreover, whether an omission makes an expression of opinion misleading always depends on context. Registration statements as a class are formal documents, filed with the SEC as a legal prerequisite for selling securities to the public. Investors do not, and are right not to, expect opinions contained in those statements to reflect baseless, off-the-cuff judgments, of the kind that an individual might communicate in daily life. At the same time, an investor reads each statement within such a document, whether of fact or of opinion, in light of all its surrounding text, including hedges, disclaimers, and apparently conflicting information. And the investor takes into account the customs and practices of the relevant industry. So an omission that renders misleading a statement of opinion when viewed in a vacuum may not do so once that statement is considered, as is appropriate, in a broader frame. The reasonable investor understands a statement of opinion in its full context, and § 11 creates liability only for the omission of material facts that cannot be squared with such a fair reading.

These principles are not unique to § 11: They inhere, too, in much common law respecting the tort of misrepresentation. The Restatement of Torts, for example, recognizes that "[a] statement of opinion as to facts not disclosed and not otherwise known to the recipient may" in some circumstances reasonably "be interpreted by him as an implied statement" that the speaker "knows facts sufficient to justify him in forming" the opinion, or that he at least knows no facts "incompatible with [the] opinion." When that is so, the Restatement explains, liability may result from omission of facts—for example, the fact that the speaker failed to conduct any investigation—that rebut the recipient's predictable inference. . . . Similarly, the leading treatise in the area explains that "it has been recognized very often that the expression of an opinion may carry with it an implied assertion, not only that the speaker knows no facts which would preclude such an opinion, but that he does know facts which justify it." . . . That is especially (and traditionally) the case, the treatise continues, where—as in a registration statement—a speaker "holds himself out or is understood as having special knowledge of the matter which is not available to the plaintiff." . . .

And the purpose of § 11 supports this understanding of how the omissions clause maps onto opinion statements. Congress adopted § 11 to ensure that issuers "tell[ ] the whole truth" to investors. H. R. Rep. No. 85, 73d Cong., 1st Sess., 2 (1933) (quoting President Roosevelt's message to Congress). For that reason, literal accuracy is not enough: An issuer must as well desist from misleading investors by saying one thing and holding back another. Omnicare would nullify that statutory requirement for all sentences starting with the phrases "we believe" or "we think." But those magic words can preface nearly any conclusion, and the resulting statements, as we have shown, remain perfectly capable of misleading investors. . . . Thus, Omnicare's view would punch a hole in the statute for half-truths in the form of opinion statements. And the difficulty of showing that such statements are literally false—which requires proving an issuer did not believe them, . . .—would make that opening yet more consequential: Were Omnicare right, companies would have virtual *carte blanche* to assert opinions in registration statements free from worry about § 11. That outcome would ill-fit Congress's decision to establish a strict liability offense promoting "full and fair disclosure" of material information. . . .

Omnicare argues, in response, that applying § 11's omissions clause in the way we have described would have "adverse policy consequences." . . . According to Omnicare, any inquiry into the issuer's basis for holding an opinion is "hopelessly amorphous," threatening "unpredictable" and possibly "massive" liability. . . . And because that is so, Omnicare claims, many issuers will choose not to disclose opinions at all, thus "depriving [investors] of potentially helpful information." . . .

But first, that claim is, just as Omnicare labels it, one of "policy"; and Congress gets to make policy, not the courts. The decision Congress made, for the reasons we have indicated, was to extend § 11 liability to all statements rendered misleading by omission. In doing so, Congress no doubt made § 11 less cut-and-dry than a law prohibiting only false factual statements. Section 11's omissions clause, as applied to statements of both opinion and fact, necessarily brings the reasonable person into the analysis, and asks what she would naturally understand a statement to convey beyond its literal meaning. And for expressions of opinion, that means considering the foundation she would expect an issuer to have before making the statement.... All that, however, is a feature, not a bug, of the omissions provision.

Moreover, Omnicare way overstates both the looseness of the inquiry Congress has mandated and the breadth of liability that approach threatens. As we have explained, an investor cannot state a claim by alleging only that an opinion was wrong; the complaint must as well call into question the issuer's basis for offering the opinion.... And to do so, the investor cannot just say that the issuer failed to reveal its basis. Section 11's omissions clause, after all, is not a general disclosure requirement; it affords a cause of action only when an issuer's failure to include a material fact has rendered a published statement misleading. To press such a claim, an investor must allege that kind of omission—and not merely by means of conclusory assertions. See *Ashcroft* v. *Iqbal*, 556 U.S. 662, 678 (2009) ("Threadbare recitals of the elements of a cause of action, supported by mere conclusory statements, do not suffice"). To be specific: The investor must identify particular (and material) facts going to the basis for the issuer's opinion—facts about the inquiry the issuer did or did not conduct or the knowledge it did or did not have—whose omission makes the opinion statement at issue misleading to a reasonable person reading the statement fairly and in context.... That is no small task for an investor.

Nor does the inquiry such a complaint triggers ask anything unusual of courts. Numerous legal rules hinge on what a reasonable person would think or expect. In requiring courts to view statements of opinion from an ordinary investor's perspective, § 11's omissions clause demands nothing more complicated or unmanageable. Indeed, courts have for decades engaged in just that inquiry, with no apparent trouble, in applying the common law of misrepresentation....

Finally, we see no reason to think that liability for misleading opinions will chill disclosures useful to investors. Nothing indicates that § 11's application to misleading factual assertions in registration statements has caused such a problem. And likewise, common-law doctrines of opinion liability have not, so far as anyone knows, deterred merchants in ordinary commercial transactions from asserting helpful opinions about their products. That absence of fallout is unsurprising. Sellers (whether of stock or other items) have strong economic incentives to ... well, *sell* (*i.e.*, hawk or peddle). Those market-based forces push back against any inclination to underdisclose. And to avoid exposure for omissions under § 11, an issuer need only divulge an opinion's basis, or else make clear the real tentativeness of its belief. Such ways of conveying opinions so that they do not mislead will keep valuable information flowing. And that is the only kind of information investors need. To the extent our decision today chills *misleading* opinions, that is all to the good: In enacting § 11, Congress worked to ensure better, not just more, information.

B

Our analysis on this score counsels in favor of sending the case back to the lower courts for decision. Neither court below considered the Funds' omissions theory with the right standard in mind—or indeed, even recognized the distinct statutory questions that theory raises.... We therefore follow our ordinary practice of remanding for a determination of whether the Funds have stated a viable omissions claim (or, if not, whether they should have a chance to replead).

In doing so, however, we reemphasize a few crucial points pertinent to the inquiry on remand. Initially, as we have said, the Funds cannot proceed without identifying one or more facts left out of Omnicare's registration statement.... The Funds' recitation of the statutory language—that Omnicare "omitted to state facts necessary to make the statements made not misleading"—is not sufficient; neither is the Funds' conclusory allegation that Omnicare lacked "reasonable grounds for the belief" it stated respecting legal compliance.... At oral argument, however, the Funds highlighted another, more specific allegation in their complaint: that an attorney had warned Omnicare that a particular contract "carrie[d] a heightened risk" of legal exposure under anti-kickback laws.... On remand, the court must review the Funds' complaint to determine whether it adequately alleged that Omnicare had omitted that (purported) fact, or any other like it, from the registration statement. And if so, the court must determine whether the omitted fact would have been material to a reasonable investor—*i.e.,* whether "there is a substantial likelihood that a reasonable [investor] would consider it important." *TSC Industries*, 426 U.S., at 449.

Assuming the Funds clear those hurdles, the court must ask whether the alleged omission rendered Omnicare's legal compliance opinions misleading in the way described earlier—*i.e.,* because the excluded fact shows that Omnicare lacked the basis for making those statements that a reasonable investor would expect.... Insofar as the omitted fact at issue is the attorney's warning, that inquiry entails consideration of such matters as the attorney's status and expertise and other legal information available to Omnicare at the time.... Further, the analysis of whether Omnicare's opinion is misleading must address the statement's context.... That means the court must take account of whatever facts Omnicare *did* provide about legal compliance, as well as any other hedges, disclaimers, or qualifications it included in its registration statement. The court should consider, for example, the information Omnicare offered that States had initiated enforcement actions against drug manufacturers for giving rebates to pharmacies, that the Federal Government had expressed concerns about the practice, and that the relevant laws "could "be interpreted in the future in a manner" that would harm Omnicare's business. See App. 95–96, 136–137; *supra,* at 3.

* * *

With these instructions and for the reasons stated, we vacate the judgment below and remand the case for further proceedings.

It is so ordered.

NOTES ON MISSTATEMENTS UNDER § 11

1. *Who Won?* The Court seemingly took the middle road in *Omnicare,* giving defendants a reprieve from the Sixth Circuit's broad reading of § 11 (as a strict liability provision, even for opinions) but giving the plaintiffs a chance to make a claim that the registration statement omitted facts relevant to the defendant's statement of opinion. Both sides declared victory. The defense bar seized on Justice Kagan's statement that meeting the pleading requirement in these cases going forward would be "no small task for an investor," who must "identify particular . . . facts going to the basis for the issuer's opinion . . . whose omission makes the opinion statement at issue misleading to a reasonable person reading the statement fairly and in context." For the plaintiffs' bar, however, *Omnicare* makes it clear the cause of action is available in the Second and Ninth Circuits, which is where almost all of the securities fraud action is.

2. *New Grounds for Litigation?* While one might think the expressions of opinions are not crucial parts of the registration statement, and that issuers could safely jettison them, there are potentially many grounds for litigation. The word "believe" appears fairly commonly in S-1s (for example, it appeared nearly 100 times in the S-1 of Twitter), and opinions are commonly found in accounting data. Lawyers likely used these words believing they insulated assertions from liability. This is no longer clearly the case. Courts have also held that financial reserves, goodwill, and other gray-area accounting terms are opinions. Now, courts will have to decide whether the pleadings allege sufficient supporting facts to make any opinion claims not misleading in light of the views of a reasonable investor. As in other areas, in the securities context and more generally, where pleading standards like these have played out in the lower courts, there is likely to be much litigation ahead before the Court's standard works its way to a workable rule.

3. *Back Door Due Diligence Requirement?* In arguably the most interesting part of the opinion, the Court discusses the importance of due

diligence to any defense of an opinion statement that turns out to be false in fact. Justice Kagan writes:

> Registration statements as a class are formal documents, filed with the SEC as a legal prerequisite for selling securities to the public. Investors do not, and are right not to, expect opinions contained in those statements to reflect baseless, off-the-cuff judgments, of the kind that an individual might communicate in daily life. At the same time, an investor reads each statement within such a document, whether of fact or of opinion, in light of all its surrounding text, including hedges, disclaimers, and apparently conflicting information. And the investor takes into account the customs and practices of the relevant industry.

The *Escott* case above sets out the law on the diligence that is required for defendants to avail themselves of statutory defenses to § 11 claims. What do you think is added by the due diligence requirement the Court suggests is necessary for opinion statements? In a concurrence (joined by no other justice), Justice Scalia suggests the Court's objective test for determining whether sufficient due diligence was performed is inappropriate. He argues instead for a subjective test:

> When a client receives advice from his lawyer, it is surely implicit in that advice that the lawyer has conducted a reasonable investigation—reasonable, that is, *in the lawyer's estimation*. The client is relying on the expert lawyer's judgment for the amount of investigation necessary, no less than for the legal conclusion. To be sure, if the lawyer conducts an investigation that he does not believe is adequate, he would be liable for misrepresentation. And if he conducts an investigation that he believes is adequate but is *objectively unreasonable* (and reaches an incorrect result), he may be liable for malpractice. But on the latter premise he is not liable for misrepresentation; all that was implicit in his advice was that he had conducted an investigation *he* deemed adequate. To rely on an expert's opinion is to rely on the expert's evaluation of *how much time to spend* on the question at hand.

Which test do you think is more consistent with the statutory language? With the purpose of § 11? With the securities laws as a whole?

F. STATUTE OF LIMITATIONS

Section 13 of the Act presents two time limitations on the initiation of § 11 suits:

> No action shall be maintained to enforce any liability created under [§ 11] unless brought within one year after the discovery of the untrue statement or the omission, or after such discovery should have been made by the exercise of reasonable diligence . . . . In no event shall any such action be brought to enforce a

liability created under [§ 11] more than three years after the security was bona fide offered to the public.

The one-year limitation encourages "diligent prosecution of known claims," and the three-year statute of repose provides certainty to potential defendants.[51] In *ANZ Sec., Inc.*,[52] the Supreme Court refused to toll this three-year bar for an individual who opted out of a timely-filed class-action. Although the plaintiff would have been a member of the class, the Court held that adjudicating the individual complaint more than three years after the securities offering was contrary to Congress's intent—"to offer defendants full and final security after three years."[53]

G. CONCURRENT JURISDICTION

The '33 Act gave federal and state courts concurrent jurisdiction over '33 Act claims. Concerned with class-action abuses,[54] Congress passed the Private Securities Litigation Reform Act of 1995 (PSLRA), which increased the pleading standard for some class-action claims at the federal level. The PSLRA, however, resulted in unintended consequences: plaintiffs and their representatives began bringing claims in state courts.[55]

Congress then passed the Securities Litigation Uniform Standards Act of 1998 (SLUSA). SLUSA provides that defendants can remove "covered class actions" (suits seeking damages on behalf of more than 50 people)[56] to federal court where the class files in state court and asserts state-law securities claims.[57] The effect is to eliminate certain private securities class actions under state "Blue Sky" fraud statutes alleging in substance (i) a misrepresentation or omission of a material fact, or (ii) the use of manipulation, a deceptive device, or a contrivance in connection with the purchase or sale of a security.[58]

Until recently, state courts were split over whether SLUSA modified the '33 Act grant of concurrent jurisdiction to prohibit state courts from adjudicating class actions alleging *solely* claims under the Act. Section 77v(a) of SLUSA confirms state-court concurrent jurisdiction over '33 Act claims, "except as provided in section 77p of this title with respect to covered class actions. . .".[59] Section 77p provides that, "no case arising

---

[51] Cal. Pub. Emps.' Ret. Sys. v. ANZ Sec., Inc., 137 S.Ct. 2042, 2045 (2017).

[52] Id.

[53] Id. at 2052.

[54] For example, PSLRA required a class's lead plaintiff in a federal suit to file a sworn certificate to ensure the plaintiff had not purchased the relevant security "at the direction of plaintiff's counsel." § 77z–1(a)(2)(A)(ii).

[55] For a discussion of the backdrop to this legislation, see Richard W. Painter, Responding to a False Alarm: Federal Preemption of State Securities Fraud Causes of Action, 84 Cornell L. Rev. 1 (1998).

[56] 15 U.S.C. § 77p(f)(2).

[57] 15 U.S.C. § 77p(c).

[58] 15 U.S.C. § 78bb(f)(1).

[59] 15 U.S.C. § 77v(a).

under this Act and brought in any State court of competent jurisdiction shall be removed to any court of the United States."[60]

A unanimous Supreme Court resolved the dispute in *Cyan*,[61] holding (1) state courts have jurisdiction over actions alleging violations of only the Securities Act, and (2) defendants may not remove such actions to federal court. Defendants *may* remove to federal court covered class actions described in § 77p(b): "class action[s] based upon the statutory or common law of any State." Simply put, state-law suits are removable, but suits alleging only '33 Act claims are not. Thus, SLUSA did not deprive state courts of their concurrent jurisdiction over class actions brought under the '33 Act.

2. SECTION 12 OF THE 1933 ACT

A. SECTION 12(a)(1)

Section 12(a)(1), § 12(1) until 1995, provides that "[a]ny person who offers or sells a security in violation of Section 5 shall be liable to the person purchasing such security from him." Liability is near absolute. The plaintiff need only prove that:

(1) the defendant was a seller;

(2) the jurisdictional requirement of interstate commerce was satisfied;[62]

(3) the defendant failed to comply with the § 5 registration or prospectus requirement, typically by such means as an unregistered offer or sale or failure to timely deliver a prospectus or securities;[63]

(4) the action is not barred by the statute of limitations; and

(5) the plaintiff made adequate tender when seeking the remedy of rescission (rather than damages).[64]

The only practical defense available to the defendant under § 12(a)(1) is proving that the particular security or transaction was exempt from § 5. The defendant's culpability is irrelevant in a § 12(a)(1) action.[65]

---

[60] 15 U.S.C. § 77p.
[61] Cyan, Inc. v. Beaver Cty. Emples. Ret. Fund, 138 S.Ct. 1061 (2018).
[62] See 9 Louis Loss & Joel Seligman, Securities Regulation 4208–4211 (3d ed. 1992).
[63] Id. at 4194–4197.
[64] Section 12 requires "tender of such security" for rescission. See id. at 4241–4242.
[65] See, e.g., Hill York Corp. v. American Int'l Franchises, Inc., 448 F.2d 680, 694 n. 19 (5th Cir. 1971); SEC v. Holschuh, 694 F.2d 130, 137 n. 10 (7th Cir. 1982).

Pinter v. Dahl
Supreme Court of the United States, 1988.
486 U.S. 622, 108 S.Ct. 2063, 100 L.Ed.2d 658.

■ JUSTICE BLACKMUN delivered the opinion of the court.

The question[ ] presented by this case [is] * * * whether one must intend to confer a benefit on himself or on a third party in order to qualify as a "seller" within the meaning of § 12(1).

I

The controversy arises out of the sale prior to 1982 of unregistered securities (fractional undivided interests in oil and gas leases) by petitioner Billy J. "B.J." Pinter to respondents Maurice Dahl and Dahl's friends, family, and business associates. Pinter is an oil and gas producer in Texas and Oklahoma, and a registered securities dealer in Texas. Dahl is a California real estate broker and investor, who, at the time of his dealings with Pinter, was a veteran of two unsuccessful oil and gas ventures. In pursuit of further investment opportunities, Dahl employed an oil field expert to locate and acquire oil and gas leases. This expert introduced Dahl to Pinter. Dahl advanced $20,000 to Pinter to acquire leases, with the understanding that they would be held in the name of Pinter's Black Gold Oil Company and that Dahl would have a right of first refusal to drill certain wells on the leasehold properties. Pinter located leases in Oklahoma, and Dahl toured the properties, often without Pinter, in order to talk to others and "get a feel for the properties." Upon examining the geology, drilling logs, and production history assembled by Pinter, Dahl concluded, in the words of the District Court, that "there was no way to lose."

After investing approximately $310,000 in the properties, Dahl told the other respondents about the venture. Except for Dahl and respondent Grantham, none of the respondents spoke to or met Pinter or toured the properties. Because of Dahl's involvement in the venture, each of the other respondents decided to invest about $7,500.[2]

Dahl assisted his fellow investors in completing the subscription-agreement form prepared by Pinter. Each letter-contract signed by the purchaser stated that the participating interests were being sold without the benefit of registration under the Securities Act, in reliance on Securities and Exchange Commission (SEC or Commission) Rule 146, 17 CFR § 230.146 (1982). In fact, the oil and gas interests involved in this suit were never registered with the Commission. Respondents' investment checks were made payable to Black Gold Oil Company. Dahl received no commission from Pinter in connection with the other respondents' purchases.

---

[2] The venture included still others who were either interested in additional ventures organized by Pinter or were new investors who met Pinter through sources other than Dahl. Those investors are not parties to this litigation.

When the venture failed and their interests proved to be worthless, respondents brought suit against Pinter in the United States District Court for the Northern District of Texas, seeking rescission under § 12(1) of the Securities Act, 15 U.S.C. § 77*l*(1), for the unlawful sale of unregistered securities.

In a counterclaim, Pinter alleged that Dahl, by means of fraudulent misrepresentations and concealment of facts, induced Pinter to sell and deliver the securities. Pinter averred that Dahl falsely assured Pinter that he would provide other qualified, sophisticated, and knowledgeable investors with all the information necessary for evaluation of the investment. Dahl allegedly agreed to raise the funds for the venture from those investors, with the understanding that Pinter would simply be the "operator" of the wells. Pinter also asserted, on the basis of the same factual allegations, that Dahl's suit was barred by the equitable defenses of estoppel and *in pari delicto*.[6]

The District Court, after a bench trial, granted judgment for respondent-investors. The court concluded that Pinter had not proved that the oil and gas interests were entitled to the private-offering exemption from registration. Accordingly, the court ruled that, because the securities were unregistered, respondents were entitled to rescission pursuant to § 12(1).[7] The court also concluded that the evidence was insufficient to sustain Pinter's counterclaim against Dahl. The District Court made no mention of the equitable defenses asserted by Pinter, but it apparently rejected them.

* * *

The Court of Appeals * * * considered whether Dahl was himself a "seller" of the oil and gas interests within the meaning of § 12(1), for if he was, the court assumed, he could be held liable in contribution for the other plaintiffs' claims against Pinter.[9] Citing Fifth Circuit precedent,

---

[6] Pinter contended that all the respondents should be estopped from recovery because of Dahl's fraudulent conduct. He asserted his *in pari delicto* defense solely against Dahl.

[7] Having reached this conclusion, the District Court found it unnecessary to consider respondents' § 12(2) claim. The court rejected respondents' claim under § 10(b) and Rule 10b–5.

[9] Because none of the other plaintiffs sought recovery from Dahl, Dahl's liability on their claims is at issue only if contribution is available to Pinter.

The Court of Appeals addressed Pinter's contention that Dahl was liable as a § 12(1) seller and thus should be accountable to Pinter in contribution for the amounts awarded to the other plaintiffs. It is not entirely clear how this claim was raised below. Pinter's pleadings do not state an explicit cause of action for contribution against Dahl, although Pinter did move, albeit unsuccessfully, to realign Dahl as a third-party defendant, based on Pinter's assertion that Dahl was a "seller" of the unregistered securities to the remaining plaintiffs and had made the allegedly actionable misrepresentations to them in connection with the sales. Presumably, the Court of Appeals construed Pinter's affirmative defense for contributory fault and his incorporation of this defense into his counterclaims, as effectively seeking contribution.

Unlike § 11 of the Securities Act, see 15 U.S.C. § 77k(f), § 12 does not expressly provide for contribution. The Court of Appeals did not reach the question whether Pinter is entitled to contribution under § 12(1) because it found that Dahl was not a seller for purposes of § 12(1), and therefore would not be the proper subject of a contribution claim. The parties have not raised or addressed the contribution issue before this Court, and we express no view as to whether a right of contribution exists under § 12(1).

the court described a statutory seller as "(1) one who parts with title to securities in exchange for consideration or (2) one whose participation in the buy-sell transaction is a substantial factor in causing the transaction to take place." While acknowledging that Dahl's conduct was a "substantial factor" in causing the other plaintiffs to purchase securities from Pinter, the court declined to hold that Dahl was a "seller" for purposes of § 12(1). Instead, the court went on to refine its test to include a threshold requirement that one who acts as a "promoter" be "motivated by a desire to confer a direct or indirect benefit on someone other than the person he has advised to purchase." The court reasoned that "a rule imposing liability (without fault or knowledge) on friends and family members who give one another gratuitous advice on investment matters unreasonably interferes with well-established patterns of social discourse." Ibid. Accordingly, since the court found no evidence that Dahl sought or received any financial benefit in return for his advice, it declined to impose liability on Dahl for "mere gregariousness."

* * *

III

* * *

In determining whether Dahl may be deemed a "seller" for purposes of § 12(1), such that he may be held liable for the sale of unregistered securities to the other investor-respondents, we look first at the language of § 12(1). See Ernst & Ernst v. Hochfelder, 425 U.S. 185, 197 (1976). That statute provides, in pertinent part: "Any person who . . . offers or sells a security" in violation of the registration requirement of the Securities Act "shall be liable to the person purchasing such security from him." 15 U.S.C. § 77*l*. This provision defines the class of defendants who may be subject to liability as those who offer or sell unregistered securities. But the Securities Act nowhere delineates who may be regarded as a statutory seller, and the sparse legislative history sheds no light on the issue. The courts, on their part, have not defined the term uniformly.

At the very least, however, the language of § 12(1) contemplates a buyer-seller relationship not unlike traditional contractual privity. Thus, it is settled that § 12(1) imposes liability on the owner who passed title, or other interest in the security, to the buyer for value. Dahl, of course, was not a seller in this conventional sense, and therefore may be held liable only if § 12(1) liability extends to persons other than the person who passes title.[20]

---

[20] The "offers or sells" and the "purchasing such security from him" language that governs § 12(1) also governs § 12(2), which provides a securities purchaser with a similar rescissionary cause of action for misrepresentation. See 15 U.S.C. § 77*l*. Most courts and commentators have not defined the defendant class differently for purposes of the two provisions.

The question whether anyone beyond the transferor of title, or immediate vendor, may be deemed a seller for purposes of § 12 has been litigated in actions under both § 12(1) and § 12(2).

A

In common parlance, a person may offer or sell property without necessarily being the person who transfers title to, or other interest in, that property. We need not rely entirely on ordinary understanding of the statutory language, however, for the Securities Act defines the operative terms of § 12(1). Section 2(3) defines "sale" or "sell" to include "every contract of sale or disposition of a security or interest in a security, for value," and the terms "offer to sell," "offer for sale," or "offer" to include "every attempt or offer to dispose of, or solicitation of an offer to buy, a security or interest in a security, for value." 15 U.S.C. § 77b(3). Under these definitions, the range of persons potentially liable under § 12(1) is not limited to persons who pass title. The inclusion of the phrase "solicitation of an offer to buy" within the definition of "offer" brings an individual who engages in solicitation, an activity not inherently confined to the actual owner, within the scope of § 12. Indeed, the Court has made clear, in the context of interpreting § 17(a) of the Securities Act, 15 U.S.C. § 77q(a), that transactions other than traditional sales of securities are within the scope of § 2(3) and passage of title is not important. See United States v. Naftalin, 441 U.S. 768, 773 (1979). We there explained: "The statutory terms ['offer' and 'sell'], which Congress expressly intended to define broadly, . . . are expansive enough to encompass the entire selling process, including the seller/agent transaction." Ibid. See also Rubin v. United States, 449 U.S. 424, 430 (1981) ("It is not essential under the terms of the Act that full title pass to a transferee for the transaction to be an 'offer' or a 'sale' ").

Determining that the activity in question falls within the definition of "offer" or "sell" in § 2(3), however, is only half of the analysis. The second clause of § 12(1), which provides that only a defendant "from" whom the plaintiff "purchased" securities may be liable, narrows the field of potential sellers.[21] Several courts and commentators have stated that the purchase requirement necessarily restricts § 12 primary liability to the owner of the security. Thus, an offeror, as defined by § 2(3), may incur § 12 liability only if the offeror also "sells" the security to the plaintiff, in the sense of transferring title for value.

We do not read § 12(1) so restrictively. The purchase requirement clearly confines § 12 liability to those situations in which a sale has taken place. Thus, a prospective buyer has no recourse against a person who touts unregistered securities to him if he does not purchase the securities. The requirement, however, does not exclude solicitation from the category of activities that may render a person liable when a sale has taken place. A natural reading of the statutory language would include

---

Decisions under § 12(2) addressing the "seller" question are thus relevant to the issue presented to us in this case, and, to that extent, we discuss them here. Nevertheless, this case does not present, nor do we take a position on, the scope of a statutory seller for purposes of § 12(2).

[21] One important consequence of this provision is that § 12(1) imposes liability on only the buyer's immediate seller; remote purchasers are precluded from bringing actions against remote sellers. Thus, a buyer cannot recover against his seller's seller.

in the statutory seller status at least some persons who urged the buyer to purchase. For example, a securities vendor's agent who solicited the purchase would commonly be said, and would be thought by the buyer, to be among those "from" whom the buyer "purchased," even though the agent himself did not pass title. See Cady v. Murphy, 113 F.2d 988, 990 (CA1) (finding broker acting as agent of the owner liable as a statutory seller), cert. denied, 311 U.S. 705 (1940).

The Securities Act does not define the term "purchase." The soundest interpretation of the term, however, is as a correlative to both "sell" and "offer," at least to the extent that the latter entails active solicitation of an offer to buy. This interpretation is supported by the history of the phrase "offers or sells," as it is used in § 12(1). As enacted in 1933, § 12(1) imposed liability on "[a]ny person who . . . sells a security." 48 Stat. 84. The statutory definition of "sell" included "offer" and the activities now encompassed by that term, including solicitation. Id., at 74. The words "offer or" were added to § 12(1) by the 1954 amendments to the Securities Act, when the original definition of "sell" in § 2(3) was split into separate definitions of "sell" and "offer" in order to accommodate changes in § 5. 68 Stat. 683, 686. Since "sells" and "purchases" have obvious correlative meanings, Congress' express definition of "sells" in the original Securities Act to include solicitation suggests that the class of those from whom the buyer "purchases" extended to persons who solicit him. The 1954 amendment to § 12(1) was intended to preserve existing law, including the liability provisions of the Act. H.R. Rep. No. 1542, 83d Cong., 2d Sess., 26 (1954), U.S.Code Cong. & Admin.News 1954, p. 2973; S.Rep. No. 1036, 83d Cong., 2d Sess., 18 (1954); Loss, at 884. Hence, there is no reason to think Congress intended to narrow the meaning of "purchased from" when it amended the statute to include "solicitation" in the statutory definition of "offer" alone.

The applicability of § 12 liability to brokers and others who solicit securities purchases has been recognized frequently since the passage of the Securities Act. It long has been "quite clear," that when a broker acting as agent of one of the principals to the transaction successfully solicits a purchase, he is a person from whom the buyer purchases within the meaning of § 12 and is therefore liable as a statutory seller. Indeed, courts had found liability on this basis prior to the 1954 amendment of the statute. Had Congress intended liability to be restricted to those who pass title, it could have effectuated its intent by not adding the phrase "offers or" when it split the definition of "sell" in § 2(3).

An interpretation of statutory seller that includes brokers and others who solicit offers to purchase securities furthers the purposes of the Securities Act—to promote full and fair disclosure of information to the public in the sales of securities. In order to effectuate Congress' intent that § 12(1) civil liability be *in terrorem*, the risk of its invocation should be felt by solicitors of purchases. The solicitation of a buyer is perhaps the most critical stage of the selling transaction. It is the first stage of a traditional securities sale to involve the buyer, and it is directed at producing the sale. In addition, brokers and other solicitors are well positioned to control the flow of information to a potential purchaser, and, in fact, such persons are the participants in the selling transaction who most often disseminate material information to investors. Thus, solicitation is the stage at which an investor is most likely to be injured, that is, by being persuaded to purchase securities without full and fair information. Given Congress' overriding goal of preventing this injury, we may infer that Congress intended solicitation to fall under the mantle of § 12(1).

Although we conclude that Congress intended § 12(1) liability to extend to those who solicit securities purchases, we share the Court of Appeals' conclusion that Congress did not intend to impose rescission based on strict liability on a person who urges the purchase but whose motivation is solely to benefit the buyer. When a person who urges another to make a securities purchase acts merely to assist the buyer, not only is it uncommon to say that the buyer "purchased" from him, but it is also strained to describe the giving of gratuitous advice, even strongly or enthusiastically, as "soliciting." Section 2(3) defines an offer as a "solicitation of an offer to buy . . . for value." The person who gratuitously urges another to make a particular investment decision is not, in any meaningful sense, requesting value in exchange for his suggestion or seeking the value the titleholder will obtain in exchange for the ultimate sale. The language and purpose of § 12(1) suggest that liability extends only to the person who successfully solicits the purchase, motivated at least in part by a desire to serve his own financial interests or those of the securities owner. If he had such a motivation, it is fair to say that the buyer "purchased" the security from him and to align him with the owner in a rescission action.

B

Petitioner is not satisfied with extending § 12(1) primary liability to one who solicits securities sales for financial gain. Pinter assumes, without explication, that liability is not limited to the person who actually parts title with the securities, and urges us to validate, as the standard by which additional defendant-sellers are identified, that version of the "substantial factor" test utilized by the Fifth Circuit before the refinement espoused in this case. Under that approach, grounded in tort doctrine, a nontransferor § 12(1) seller is defined as one "whose participation in the buy-sell transaction is a substantial factor in causing the transaction to take place." Pharo v. Smith, 621 F.2d 656, 667 (C.A.5 1980). The Court of Appeals acknowledged that Dahl would be liable as a statutory seller under this test.

We do not agree that Congress contemplated imposing § 12(1) liability under the broad terms petitioners advocate. There is no support in the statutory language or legislative history for expansion of § 12(1) primary liability beyond persons who pass title and persons who "offer," including those who "solicit" offers. Indeed, § 12's failure to impose express liability for mere participation in unlawful sales transactions suggests that Congress did not intend that the section impose liability on participants' collateral to the offer or sale. When Congress wished to create such liability, it had little trouble doing so. Cf. Touche Ross & Co. v. Redington, 442 U.S. 560, 572 (1979).[26]

The deficiency of the substantial-factor test is that it divorces the analysis of seller status from any reference to the applicable statutory language and from any examination of § 12 in the context of the total statutory scheme. Those courts that have adopted the approach have not attempted to ground their analysis in the statutory language. Instead, they substitute the concept of substantial participation in the sales transaction, or proximate causation of the plaintiff's purchase, for the words "offers or sells" in § 12. The "purchase from" requirement of § 12 focuses on the defendant's relationship with the plaintiff-purchaser. The substantial-factor test, on the other hand, focuses on the defendant's degree of involvement in the securities transaction and its surrounding circumstances. Thus, although the substantial-factor test undoubtedly embraces persons who pass title and who solicit the purchase of unregistered securities as statutory sellers, the test also would extend § 12(1) liability to participants only remotely related to the relevant aspects of the sales transaction. Indeed, it might expose securities professionals, such as accountants and lawyers, whose involvement is only the performance of their professional services, to § 12(1) strict liability for rescission. The buyer does not, in any meaningful sense, "purchas[e] the security from" such a person.[27]

---

[26] Congress knew of the collateral participation concept and employed it in the Securities Act and throughout its unified program of securities regulation. Liabilities and obligations expressly grounded in participation are found elsewhere in the Act, see, e.g., 15 U.S.C. § 77b(11) (defining "underwriter," who is liable under § 5, as including direct and indirect participants), and in the later Roosevelt administration securities Acts. For example, § 9 of the 1934 Act, passed by the same Congress that enacted the Securities Act, creates a private right of action that expressly imposes liability on participants. 15 U.S.C. § 78i(e).

Section 11 of the Securities Act, 15 U.S.C. § 77k, lends strong support to the conclusion that Congress did not intend to extend § 12 primary liability to collateral participants in the unlawful securities sales transaction. That section provides an express cause of action for damages to a person acquiring securities pursuant to a registration statement that misstates or omits a material fact. Section 11(a) explicitly enumerates the various categories of persons involved in the registration process who are subject to suit under that section, including many who are participants in the activities leading up to the sale. There are no similar provisions in § 12, and therefore we may conclude that Congress did not intend such persons to be defendants in § 12 actions.

[27] For similar reasons, we reject the Commission's suggestion that persons who "participate in soliciting the purchase" may be liable as statutory sellers. The Commission relies on Katz v. Amos Treat & Co., 411 F.2d 1046 (C.A.2 1969), where the court held that an attorney who had been "a party to the solicitation" of the plaintiff-purchaser was liable under § 12(1) because he had placed the brokerage firm for which he worked in a position "to tackle [the purchaser] for the money" owed on an investment he had made. Although in Katz the attorney spoke directly to the plaintiff prior to the delivery of money in plaintiff's investment, the "party to a solicitation" concept could easily embrace those who merely assist in another's solicitation efforts. See Schneider, 51 Tenn. L. Rev., at 273 (suggesting that the Katz approach allows courts to interpret solicitation activities "rather broadly"). It is difficult to see more than a slight

* * *

The broad remedial goals of the Securities Act are insufficient justification for interpreting a specific provision " 'more broadly than its language and the statutory scheme reasonably permit.' " Touche Ross, 442 U.S., at 578, quoting SEC v. Sloan, 436 U.S. 103, 116 (1978). We must assume that Congress meant what it said.

The substantial-factor test reaches participants in sales transactions who do not even arguably fit within the definitions set out in § 2(3); it "would add a gloss to the operative language of [§ 12(1)] quite different from its commonly accepted meaning." Ernst & Ernst v. Hochfelder, 425 U.S., at 199. We conclude that Congress did not intend such a gross departure from the statutory language. Accordingly, we need not entertain Pinter's policy arguments. Being merely a "substantial factor" in causing the sale of unregistered securities is not sufficient in itself to render a defendant liable under § 12(1).

C

We are unable to determine whether Dahl may be held liable as a statutory seller under § 12(1). The District Court explicitly found that "Dahl solicited each of the other plaintiffs (save perhaps Grantham) in connection with the offer, purchase, and receipt of their oil and gas interests." We cannot conclude that this finding was clearly erroneous. It is not clear, however, that Dahl had the kind of interest in the sales that make him liable as a statutory seller.

* * *

IV

The judgment of the Court of Appeals is vacated, and the case is remanded for further proceedings consistent with this opinion.

It is so ordered.

NOTE ON § 12(a)(1): WHO IS A SELLER?

The lower courts have generally extended the Supreme Court's § 12(a)(1) analysis in *Pinter* to § 12(a)(2).[66] After *Pinter* the law is settled that brokers or other agents—persons who are not sellers in the sense of passing title—may be held liable under §§ 12(a)(1) or 12(a)(2).[67]

---

difference between this approach and the participation theory, which we have concluded does not comport with Congress' intent.

[66] See, e.g., Abell v. Potomac Ins. Co., 858 F.2d 1104, 1113–1115 (5th Cir. 1988); Moore v. Kayport Package Express, Inc., 885 F.2d 531, 535–537 (9th Cir. 1989); Royal Am. Managers, Inc. v. IRC Holding Corp., 885 F.2d 1011, 1016–1017 (2d Cir. 1989); Craftmatic Sec. Litig. v. Kraftsow, 890 F.2d 628, 635–636 (3d Cir. 1989); Ryder Int'l Corp. v. First Am. Nat'l Bank, 943 F.2d 1521, 1527–1529 (11th Cir. 1991); Ackerman v. Schwartz, 947 F.2d 841, 844–845 (7th Cir. 1991).

[67] Pinter v. Dahl, 486 U.S. 622, 642–643 (1988). This result was common before Pinter, based on the logic that a broker for a seller is a "person who sells." See Cady v. Murphy, 113 F.2d 988 (1st Cir. 1940); Lawler v. Gilliam, 569 F.2d 1283, 1287–1288 (4th Cir. 1978); Harelson v. Miller Fin. Corp., 854 F.2d 1141 (9th Cir. 1988).

It is not inevitable, however, that officers, directors, employees, or other nonbroker agents of the seller who actively participate in the sale will be liable based on status alone.[68] *Pinter* focused on solicitation of sales "motivated at least in part by a desire to serve his own financial interests or those of the securities owner." The Second Circuit, for example, followed *Pinter* in holding that two general partners in a coal mining venture were liable to the limited partners under § 12(a)(2) because they had prepared and circulated a prospectus to the plaintiffs. The "seller" status of a lawyer-promoter whose law firm drafted the prospectus and performed other legal work in connection with the venture did not preclude the general partners from being sellers because the lawyer's promotional efforts were "directly attributable" to the general partners.[69] In contrast, the courts have exonerated attorneys, accountants, and board members who did not own the relevant security, initiate or participate in sales negotiations, or otherwise appear to solicit sales.[70]

Subject to exceptions involving statutory controlling persons, it seems quite clear that § 12 contemplates an action by a buyer against only *his or her immediate seller*.[71] Issuers, however, are an exception to this rule. Although some courts had held that issuers are not sellers, and, therefore, not proper defendants in firm commitment underwritings,[72] the SEC recently promulgated regulations clarifying that in primary offerings, issuers are sellers for the purposes of § 12(a)(2).[73] In effect, unlike § 11, § 12 incorporates a privity requirement.[74]

---

[68] See Smith v. American Nat'l Bank & Trust Co., 982 F.2d 936, 941–942 (6th Cir. 1992); SEC v. Tuchinsky, 1992 Fed. Sec. L. Rep. (CCH) ¶ 96,917 at 93,803 (S.D.Fla.1992).

[69] Capri v. Murphy, 856 F.2d 473, 478 (2d Cir. 1988).

[70] See, e.g., Wilson v. Saintine Exploration & Drilling Corp., 872 F.2d 1124, 1126–1127 (2d Cir. 1989) (attorney); Moore v. Kayport Package Express, Inc., 885 F.2d 531, 537 (9th Cir. 1989) (attorney and accountant); Royal Am. Managers, Inc. v. IRC Holding Corp., 885 F.2d 1011, 1017 (2d Cir. 1989) (attorney and director); Ackerman v. Schwartz, 947 F.2d 841, 845 (7th Cir. 1991) (attorney).

[71] See, e.g., Cortec Indus., Inc. v. Sum Holding L.P., 949 F.2d 42 (2d Cir. 1991).

[72] See, e.g., Shaw v. Digital Equip. Corp., 82 F.3d 1194, 1215–1216 (1st Cir. 1996) (holding that in a firm commitment underwriting issuer does not pass title to the securities, and, therefore, the issuer and officers are not "sellers" under Section 12(a)(2), unless they actively solicit the plaintiffs' purchase to further their own financial motives). See also Lone Star Ladies Inv. Club v. Schlotzsky's Inc., 238 F.3d 363, 369–370 (5th Cir. 2001).

[73] See 17 C.F.R. § 230.159A. Rule 159A's coverage extends to communications including a preliminary prospectus or prospectus of the issuer filed pursuant to Rule 424 or 497; a free writing prospectus prepared by, on behalf of, or used or referred to by the issuer and, for open-end management investment companies, any profile relating to the offering pursuant to Rule 498; a portion of any other free writing prospectus (or for registered investment or business development company issuers any advertisement pursuant to Rule 482) relating to the offering containing material information about the issuer or its securities provided by or on behalf of the issuer; and any other communication that is an offer as the offering made by the issuer to such purchase. See 17 C.F.R. § 230.159A.

[74] See also William Fisher, Parsing Pinter Four Years Later: Defining a Statutory Seller under Section 12 of the Securities Act, 21 Sec. Reg. L.J. 46 (1993); Jack E. Karns, Edwin A. Doty & Steven S. Long, Accountant and Attorney Liability as "Sellers" of Securities under Section 12(2) of the Securities Act of 1933: Judicial Rejection of the Statutory, Collateral Participant Status Cause of Action, 74 Neb. L. Rev. 1 (1995).

Problem

PROBLEM 11-2

Howard Ripple, an attorney, wrote a tax opinion that was circulated to investors in a limited partnership known as Organized Equipment Leasing (OEL). Ripple's letter described specific tax credits and deductions that would be available to investors. Several "facts" that Ripple described in his letter were fictitious and the Internal Revenue Service subsequently disallowed each of the tax credits and deductions Ripple described.

Over 110 investors have now brought a § 12(a)(1) lawsuit against Ripple, among others. Will this suit succeed?

Would it make any difference if Ripple wrote personal notes to each investor bringing suit recommending that, "You should consider this investment seriously. It is a winner!"

Would it make any difference if Ripple's law firm was paid on a sliding scale basis depending on the dollar value of limited partnership units sold?

B. SECTION 12(a)(2)

Section 12(a)(2) imposes liability on any person who offers or sells a security by means of a prospectus or oral communication that includes a material misrepresentation or omission.[75] Section 12(a)(2) also has a jurisdictional requirement. The seller must use "any means of or instruments of transportation or communication in interstate commerce or of the mails." The Pinter v. Dahl definition of "seller" in the context of § 12(a)(1) applies equally to § 12(a)(2). As with the antifraud provisions generally, concepts such as materiality, misrepresentation, omission, and fact have a generic meaning. For § 12(a)(2), a plaintiff is not required to prove reliance, only that he or she did not know of the material misrepresentation or omission, normally a far easier matter.[76]

Defendants have two statutory defenses. Section 12(a)(2) itself creates a "reasonable care" defense for a defendant who can sustain the burden of proof "that he did not know, and in the exercise of reasonable care could not have known" of a material misrepresentation or omission. In 1995, Congress added a new subsection, 12(b), to allow the defendant to reduce the amount recoverable under § 12(a)(2) by proving that the material misrepresentation or omission did not cause the depreciation in value of the security. This "loss causation" or "negative causation" defense is similar, if not identical, to the § 11 causation defense.

Unlike the more frequently employed Rule 10b–5, § 12(a)(2) provides the plaintiff a mandatory right of rescission upon tender of the subject

---

[75] Including an exempt security other than a security exempted by § 3(a)(2) or (14)
[76] See, e.g., Wright v. National Warranty Co., L.P., 953 F.2d 256, 262 (6th Cir. 1992); Wamser v. J.E. Liss, Inc., 838 F.Supp. 393, 398 (E.D. Wis. 1993).

security. Alternatively, plaintiffs may seek rescissory damages if they have sold the security and cannot tender.

When the seller of a security is the issuer or an underwriter, a plaintiff may be able to bring a claim under §§ 11 and 12(a)(2). When the ultimate seller is a dealer, only § 12(a)(2) will be available.

As with the antifraud remedies, a plaintiff can sue the controlling person of a § 12(a) seller, as well as the seller. Until it was resolved in 1995, the most significant question under § 12(a)(2) was its scope: was it limited to registered securities offerings "by means of a prospectus" or did the definition of prospectus in what was then § 2(10) (now § 2(a)(10)) extend to secondary distributions?

Gustafson v. Alloyd Company, Incorporated
Supreme Court of the United States, 1995.
513 U.S. 561, 115 S.Ct. 1061, 131 L.Ed.2d 1.

■ JUSTICE KENNEDY delivered the opinion of the Court.

Under § 12(2) of the Securities Act of 1933 buyers have an express cause of action for rescission against sellers who make material misstatements or omissions "by means of a prospectus." The question presented is whether this right of rescission extends to a private, secondary transaction, on the theory that recitations in the purchase agreement are part of a "prospectus."

I

Petitioners Gustafson, McLean, and Butler (collectively Gustafson) were in 1989 the sole shareholders of Alloyd, Inc., a manufacturer of plastic packaging and automatic heat-sealing equipment. Alloyd was formed, and its stock was issued, in 1961. In 1989, Gustafson decided to sell Alloyd and engaged KPMG Peat Marwick to find a buyer. In response to information distributed by KPMG, Wind Point Partners II, L.P., agreed to buy substantially all of the issued and outstanding stock through Alloyd Holdings, Inc., a new corporation formed to effect the sale of Alloyd's stock. The shareholders of Alloyd Holdings were Wind Point and a number of individual investors.

In preparation for negotiating the contract with Gustafson, Wind Point undertook an extensive analysis of the company, relying in part on a formal business review prepared by KPMG. Alloyd's practice was to take inventory at year's end, so Wind Point and KPMG considered taking an earlier inventory to use in determining the purchase price. In the end they did not do so, relying instead on certain estimates and including provisions for adjustments after the transaction closed.

On December 20, 1989, Gustafson and Alloyd Holdings executed a contract of sale. Alloyd Holdings agreed to pay Gustafson and his coshareholders $18,709,000 for the sale of the stock plus a payment of $2,122,219, which reflected the estimated increase in Alloyd's net worth from the end of the previous year, the last period for which hard financial data were available. Article IV of the purchase agreement, entitled "Representations and Warranties of the Sellers," included assurances that the company's financial statements "present fairly ... the Company's financial condition" and that between the date of the latest balance sheet and the date the agreement was executed "there ha[d] been no material adverse change in ... [Alloyd's] financial condition." The contract also provided that if the year-end audit and financial statements revealed a variance between estimated and actual increased value, the disappointed party would receive an adjustment.

The year-end audit of Alloyd revealed that Alloyd's actual earnings for 1989 were lower than the estimates relied upon by the parties in negotiating the adjustment amount of $2,122,219. Under the contract, the buyers had a right to recover an adjustment amount of $815,000, from the sellers. Nevertheless, on February 11, 1991, the newly formed company (now called Alloyd, Co., the same as the original company) and Wind Point brought suit in the United States District Court for the Northern District of Illinois, seeking outright rescission of the contract under § 12(2) of the Securities Act of 1933. Alloyd (the new company) claimed that statements made by Gustafson and his coshareholders regarding the financial data of their company were inaccurate, rendering untrue the representations and warranties contained in the contract. The buyers further alleged that the contract of sale was a "prospectus," so that any misstatements contained in the agreement gave rise to liability under § 12(2) of the 1933 Act. Pursuant to the adjustment clause, the defendants remitted to the purchasers $815,000 plus interest, but the adjustment did not cause the purchasers to drop the lawsuit.

Relying on the decision of the Court of Appeals for the Third Circuit in Ballay v. Legg Mason Wood Walker, Inc., 925 F.2d 682 (1991), the District Court granted Gustafson's motion for summary judgment, holding "that section 12(2) claims can only arise out of the initial stock offerings." Although the sellers were the controlling shareholders of the original company, the District Court concluded that the private sale agreement "cannot be compared to an initial offering" because "the purchasers in this case had direct access to financial and other company documents, and had the opportunity to inspect the seller's property."

On review, the Court of Appeals for the Seventh Circuit vacated the District Court's judgment and remanded for further consideration in light of that court's intervening decision in Pacific Dunlop Holdings Inc. v. Allen & Co. Inc., 993 F.2d 578 (1993). In *Pacific Dunlop* the court reasoned that the inclusion of the term "communication" in the Act's definition of prospectus meant that the term prospectus was defined "very broadly" to include all written communications that offered the sale of a security. Rejecting the view of the Court of Appeals for the Third Circuit in *Ballay*, the Court of Appeals decided that § 12(2)'s right of action for rescission "applies to any communication which offers any security for sale ... including the stock purchase agreement in the present case." We granted certiorari to resolve this Circuit conflict, and we now reverse.

II

The rescission claim against Gustafson is based upon § 12(2) of the 1993 Act, 48 Stat. 84, as amended, 15 U.S.C. § 77*l*(2).

* * *

As this case reaches us, we must assume that the stock purchase agreement contained material misstatements of fact made by the sellers and that Gustafson would not sustain its burden of proving due care. On these assumptions, Alloyd would have a right to obtain rescission if those misstatements were made "by means of a prospectus or oral communication." The parties (and the courts of appeals) agree that the phrase "oral communication" is restricted to oral communications that relate to a prospectus. The determinative question, then, is whether the contract between Alloyd and Gustafson is a "prospectus" as the term is used in the 1933 Act.

Alloyd argues that "prospectus" is defined in a broad manner, broad enough to encompass the contract between the parties. This argument is echoed by the dissents. Gustafson, by contrast, maintains that prospectus in the 1933 Act means a communication soliciting the public to purchase securities from the issuer.

Three sections of the 1933 Act are critical in resolving the definitional question on which the case turns: § 2(10), which defines a prospectus; § 10, which sets forth the information that must be contained in a prospectus; and § 12, which imposes liability based on misstatements in a prospectus. In seeking to interpret the term "prospectus," we adopt the premise that the term should be construed, if possible, to give it a consistent meaning throughout the Act. That principle follows from our duty to construe statutes, not isolated provisions.

A

We begin with § 10.

* * *

Although § 10 does not define what a prospectus is, it does instruct us what a prospectus cannot be if the Act is to be interpreted as a symmetrical and coherent regulatory scheme, one in which the operative words have a consistent meaning throughout. There is no dispute that the contract in this case was not required to contain the information contained in a registration statement and that no statutory exemption was required to take the document out of § 10's coverage. Cf. 15 U.S.C. § 77c. It follows that the contract is not a prospectus under § 10. That does not mean that a document ceases to be a prospectus whenever it omits a required piece of information. It does mean that a document is not a prospectus within the meaning of that section if, absent an exemption, it need not comply with § 10's requirements in the first place.

An examination of § 10 reveals that, whatever else "prospectus" may mean, the term is confined to a document that, absent an overriding exemption, must include the "information contained in the registration statement." By and large, only public offerings by an issuer of a security, or by controlling shareholders of an issuer, require the preparation and filing of registration statements. See 15 U.S.C. §§ 77d, 77e, 77b(11). It follows, we conclude, that a prospectus under § 10 is confined to documents related to public offerings by an issuer or its controlling shareholders.

This much (the meaning of prospectus in § 10) seems not to be in dispute. Where the courts are in disagreement is with the implications of this proposition for the entirety of the Act, and for § 12 in particular. Compare Ballay v. Legg Mason Wood Walker, Inc., 925 F.2d, at 688–689 (suggesting that the term prospectus is used in a consistent manner in both §§ 10 and 12), with Pacific Dunlop Holdings Inc. v. Allen & Co., 993 F.2d, at 584 (rejecting that view). We conclude that the term "prospectus" must have the same meaning under §§ 10 and 12. In so holding, we do not, as the dissent by Justice Ginsburg suggests, make the mistake of treating § 10 as a definitional section. Instead, we find in § 10 guidance and instruction for giving the term a consistent meaning throughout the Act.

The 1933 Act, like every Act of Congress, should not be read as a series of unrelated and isolated provisions. Only last term we adhered to the "normal rule of statutory construction" that "identical words used in different parts of the same act are intended to have the same meaning." That principle applies here. If the contract before us is not a prospectus for purposes of § 10—as all must and do concede—it is not a prospectus for purposes of § 12 either.

The conclusion that prospectus has the same meaning, and refers to the same types of communications (public offers by an issuer or its controlling shareholders), in both §§ 10 and 12 is reinforced by an examination of the structure of the 1933 Act. Sections 4 and 5 of the Act together require a seller to file a registration statement and to issue a prospectus for certain defined types of sales (public offerings by an issuer, through an underwriter). See 15 U.S.C. §§ 77d, 77e. Sections 7 and 10 of the Act set forth the information required in the registration statement and the prospectus. See §§ 77g, 77j. Section 11 provides for liability on account of false registration statements; § 12(2) for liability based on misstatements in prospectuses. See 15 U.S.C. §§ 77k, 77*l*. Following the most natural and symmetrical reading, just as the liability imposed by § 11 flows from the requirements imposed by §§ 5 and 7 providing for the filing and content of registration statements, the liability imposed by § 12(2) cannot attach unless there is an obligation to distribute the prospectus in the first place (or unless there is an exemption).

Our interpretation is further confirmed by a reexamination of § 12 itself. The section contains an important guide to the correct resolution of the case. By its terms, § 12(2) exempts from its coverage prospectuses relating to the sales of government-issued securities. See 15 U.S.C. § 77*l* (excepting securities exempted by § 77c(a)(2)). If Congress intended § 12(2) to create liability for misstatements contained in any written communication relating to the sale of a security—including secondary market transactions—there is no ready explanation for exempting government-issued securities from the reach of the right to rescind granted by § 12(2). Why would Congress grant immunity to a private seller from liability in a rescission suit for no reason other than that the seller's misstatements happen to relate to securities issued by a governmental entity? No reason is apparent. The anomaly disappears, however, when the term "prospectus" relates only to documents that offer securities sold to the public by an issuer. The exemption for government-issued securities makes perfect sense on that view, for it then becomes a precise and appropriate means of giving immunity to governmental authorities.

The primary innovation of the 1933 Act was the creation of federal duties—for the most part, registration and disclosure obligations—in connection with public offerings. See, e.g., Ernst & Ernst v. Hochfelder, 425 U.S. 185, 195 (1976) (the 1933 Act "was designed to provide investors with full disclosure of material information concerning public offerings"); Blue Chip Stamps v. Manor Drug Stores, 421 U.S. 723, 752 (1975) ("The 1933 Act is a far narrower statute [than the Securities Exchange Act of 1934 (1934 Act)] chiefly concerned with disclosure and fraud in connection with offerings of securities—primarily, as here, initial distributions of newly issued stock from corporate issuers"); United States v. Naftalin, 441 U.S. 768, 777–778 (1979) ("[T]he 1933 Act was primarily concerned with the regulation of new offerings"); SEC v. Ralston Purina Co., 346 U.S. 119, 122, n. 5 (1953) (" '[T]he bill does not affect transactions beyond the need of public protection in order to prevent recurrences of demonstrated abuses' "), quoting H.R. Rep. No. 85, 73d Cong., 1st Sess., 7 (1933). We are reluctant to conclude that § 12(2) creates vast additional liabilities that are quite independent of the new substantive obligations the Act imposes. It is more reasonable to interpret the liability provisions of the 1933 Act as designed for the primary purpose of providing remedies for violations of the obligations it had created. Indeed, §§ 11 and 12(1)—the statutory neighbors of § 12(2)—afford remedies for violations of those obligations. See § 11, 15 U.S.C. § 77k (remedy for untrue statements in registration statements); § 12(1), 15 U.S.C. § 77*l*(1) (remedy for sales in violation of § 5, which prohibits the sale of unregistered securities). Under our interpretation of "prospectus," § 12(2) in similar manner is linked to the new duties created by the Act.

On the other hand, accepting Alloyd's argument that any written offer is a prospectus under § 12 would require us to hold that the word "prospectus" in § 12 refers to a broader set of communications than the same term in § 10. The Court of Appeals was candid in embracing that conclusion: "[T]he 1933 Act contemplates many definitions of a prospectus. Section 2(10) gives a single, broad definition; section 10(a) involves an isolated, distinct document—a prospectus within a prospectus; section 10(d) gives the Commission authority to classify many." Pacific Dunlop Holdings Inc. v. Allen & Co., 993 F.2d, at 584. The dissents take a similar tack. In the name of a plain meaning approach to statutory interpretation, the dissents discover in the Act two different species of prospectuses: formal (also called § 10) prospectuses, subject to both §§ 10 and 12, and informal prospectuses, subject only to § 12 but not to § 10. Nowhere in the statute, however, do the terms "formal prospectus" or "informal prospectus" appear. Instead, the Act uses one term—"prospectus"—throughout. In disagreement with the Court of Appeals and the dissenting opinions, we cannot accept the conclusion that this single operative word means one thing in one section of the Act and something quite different in another. The dissenting opinions' resort to terms not found in the Act belies the claim of fidelity to the text of the statute.

Alloyd, as well as Justice Thomas in his dissent, respond that if Congress had intended § 12(2) to govern only initial public offerings, it would have been simple for Congress to have referred to the § 4 exemptions in § 12(2). The argument gets the presumption backwards. Had Congress meant the term "prospectus" in § 12(2) to have a different meaning than the same term in § 10, that is when one would have expected Congress to have been explicit. Congressional silence cuts against, not in favor of, Alloyd's argument. The burden should be on the proponents of the view that the term "prospectus" means one thing in § 12 and another in § 10 to adduce strong textual support for that conclusion. And Alloyd adduces none.

B

Alloyd's contrary argument rests to a significant extent on § 2(10), or, to be more precise, on one word of that section. Section 2(10) provides that "[t]he term 'prospectus' means any prospectus, notice, circular, advertisement, letter, or communication, written or by radio or television, which offers any security for sale or confirms the sale of any security." 15 U.S.C. § 77b(10). Concentrating on the word "communication," Alloyd argues that any written communication that offers a security for sale is a "prospectus." Inserting its definition into § 12(2), Alloyd insists that a material misstatement in any communication offering a security for sale gives rise to an action for rescission, without proof of fraud by the seller or reliance by the purchaser. In Alloyd's view, § 2(10) gives the term "prospectus" a capacious definition that, although incompatible with § 10, nevertheless governs in § 12.

The flaw in Alloyd's argument, echoed in the dissenting opinions, is its reliance on one word of the definitional section in isolation. To be sure, § 2(10) defines a prospectus as, *inter alia*, a "communication, written or by radio or television, which offers any security for sale or confirms the sale of any security." 15 U.S.C. § 77b(10). The word "communication," however, on which Alloyd's entire argument rests, is but one word in a list, a word Alloyd reads altogether out of context.

The relevant phrase in the definitional part of the statute must be read in its entirety, a reading which yields the interpretation that the term prospectus refers to a document soliciting the public to acquire securities. We find that definition controlling. Alloyd's argument that the phrase "communication, written or by radio or television," transforms any written communication offering a security for sale into a prospectus cannot consist with at least two rather sensible rules of statutory construction. First, the Court will avoid a reading which renders some words altogether redundant. See United States v. Menasche, 348 U.S. 528, 538–39 (1955). If "communication" included every written communication, it would render "notice, circular, advertisement, [and] letter" redundant, since each of these are forms of written communication as well. Congress with ease could have drafted § 2(10) to read: "The term 'prospectus' means any communication, written or by radio or television, that offers a security for sale or confirms the sale of a security." Congress did not write the statute that way, however, and we decline to say it included the words "notice, circular, advertisement, [and] letter" for no purpose.

The constructional problem is resolved by the second principle Alloyd overlooks, which is that a word is known by the company it keeps (the doctrine of *noscitur a sociis*). This rule we rely upon to avoid ascribing to one word a meaning so broad that it is inconsistent with its accompanying words, thus giving "unintended breadth to the Acts of Congress." Jarecki v. G.D. Searle & Co., 367 U.S. 303, 307 (1961). The rule guided our earlier interpretation of the word "security" under the 1934 Act. The 1934 Act defines the term "security" to mean, *inter alia*, "any note." We concluded nevertheless that in context "the phrase 'any note' should not be interpreted to mean literally 'any note,' but must be understood against the background of what Congress was attempting to accomplish in enacting the Securities Acts." Reves v. Ernst & Young, 494 U.S. 56, 63 (1990). These considerations convince us that Alloyd's suggested interpretation is not the correct one.

There is a better reading. From the terms "prospectus, notice, circular, advertisement, or letter," it is apparent that the list refers to documents of wide dissemination. In a similar manner, the list includes communications "by radio or television," but not face-to-face or telephonic conversations. Inclusion of the term "communication" in that list suggests that it too refers to a public communication.

When the 1933 Act was drawn and adopted, the term "prospectus" was well understood to refer to a document soliciting the public to acquire securities from the issuer. See Black's Law Dictionary 959 (2d ed. 1910) (defining "prospectus" as a "document published by a company . . . or by persons acting as its agents or assignees, setting forth the nature and objects of an issue of shares . . . and inviting the public to subscribe to the issue"). In this respect, the word prospectus is a term of art, which accounts for Congressional confidence in employing what might otherwise be regarded as a partial circularity in the formal, statutory definition. See 15 U.S.C. § 77b(10) ("The term 'prospectus' means any prospectus. . . ."). The use of the term prospectus to refer to public solicitations explains as well Congress' decision in § 12(2) to grant buyers a right to rescind without proof of reliance. See H.R. Rep. No. 85, 73d Cong., 1st Sess., 10 (1933) ("The statements for which [liable persons] are responsible, although they may never actually have been seen by the prospective purchaser, because of their wide dissemination, determine the market price of the security. . . .").

The list of terms in § 2(10) prevents a seller of stock from avoiding liability by calling a soliciting document something other than a prospectus, but it does not compel the conclusion that Alloyd urges us to reach and that the dissenting opinions adopt. Instead, the term "written communication" must be read in context to refer to writings that, from a functional standpoint, are similar to the terms "notice, circular, [and] advertisement." The term includes communications held out to the public at large but that might have been thought to be outside the other words in the definitional section.

C

Our holding that the term "prospectus" relates to public offerings by issuers and their controlling shareholders draws support from our earlier decision interpreting the one provision of the Act that extends coverage beyond the regulation of public offerings, § 17(a) of the 1933 Act. See United States v. Naftalin, 441 U.S. 768 (1979). In *Naftalin*, though noting that "the 1933 Act was primarily concerned with the regulation of new offerings," the Court held that § 17(a) was "intended to cover any fraudulent scheme in an offer or sale of securities, whether in the course of an initial distribution or in the course of ordinary market trading." The Court justified this holding—which it termed "a major departure from th[e] limitation [of the 1933 Act to new offerings]"—by reference to both the statutory language and the unambiguous legislative history. The same considerations counsel in favor of our interpretation of § 12(2).

The Court noted in *Naftalin* that § 17(a) contained no language suggesting a limitation on the scope of liability under § 17(a). See id., at 778, ("the statutory language . . . makes no distinctions between the two kinds of transactions"). Most important for present purposes, § 17(a) does not contain the word "prospectus." In contrast, as we have noted, § 12(2) contains language, i.e., "by means of a prospectus or oral communication," that limits § 12(2) to public offerings. Just as the absence of limiting language in § 17(a) resulted in broad coverage, the presence of limiting language in § 12(2) requires a narrow construction.

Of equal importance, the legislative history relied upon in *Naftalin* showed that Congress decided upon a deliberate departure from the general scheme of the Act in this one instance, and "made abundantly clear" its intent that § 17(a) have broad coverage. See Naftalin, 441 U.S., at 778 (quoting legislative history stating that " 'fraud or deception in the sale of securities may be prosecuted regardless of whether . . . or not it is of the class of securities exempted under sections 11 or 12.' " S. Rep. No. 47, 73d Cong., 1st Sess., 4 (1933)). No comparable legislative history even hints that § 12(2) was intended to be a free standing provision effecting expansion of the coverage of the entire statute. The intent of Congress and the design of the statute require that § 12(2) liability be limited to public offerings.

D

It is understandable that Congress would provide buyers with a right to rescind, without proof of fraud or reliance, as to misstatements contained in a document prepared with care, following well established procedures relating to investigations with due diligence and in the context of a public offering by an issuer or its controlling shareholders. It is not plausible to infer that Congress created this extensive liability for every casual communication between buyer and seller in the secondary market. It is often difficult, if not altogether impractical, for those engaged in casual communications not to omit some fact that would, if included, qualify the accuracy of a statement. Under Alloyd's view any casual communication between buyer and seller in the aftermarket could give rise to an action for rescission, with no evidence of fraud on the part of the seller or reliance on the part of the buyer. In many instances buyers in practical effect would have an option to rescind, impairing the stability of past transactions where neither fraud nor detrimental reliance on misstatements or omissions occurred. We find no basis for interpreting the statute to reach so far.

III

The * * * [SEC], as *amicus*, and Justice Ginsburg in dissent, rely on what they call the legislative background of the Act to support Alloyd's construction. With a few minor exceptions, however, their reliance is upon statements by commentators and judges written after the Act was passed, not while it was under consideration. Material not available to the lawmakers is not considered, in the normal course, to be legislative history. After-the-fact statements by proponents of a broad interpretation are not a reliable indicator of what Congress intended when it passed the law, assuming extratextual sources are to any extent reliable for this purpose.

The SEC does quote one contemporaneous memorandum prepared by Dean Landis. The statement is quite consistent with our construction. Landis observed that, in contrast to the liabilities imposed by the Act " 'that flow from the fact of non-registration or registration,' " dealings may violate § 12(2) " 'even though they are not related to the *fact* of registration.' " This, of course, is true. The liability imposed by § 12(2) has nothing to do with the *fact* of registration, that is with the failure to file a registration statement that complies with §§ 7 and 11 of the Act. Instead, the liability imposed by § 12(2) turns on misstatements contained in the prospectus. And, one might point out, securities exempted by § 3 of the Act do not require registration, although they are covered by § 12. Landis' observation has nothing to do with the question presented here: whether a prospectus is a document soliciting the public to purchase securities from the issuer.

The SEC also relies on a number of writings, the most prominent a release by the [FTC], stating that § 12(2) applied to securities outstanding on the effective date of the 1933 Act. Again, this is an issue not in dispute. Although the Act as passed exempted securities from registration if sold by the issuer within 60 days of the passage of the Act, see 1933 Securities Act, § 3(a)(1), the limitation did not apply to § 12(2). See 15 U.S.C. § 77*l*. Instead, actions brought under § 12(2) are subject to the limitation of actions provision in § 13. See 15 U.S.C. § 77m (one year from the date of discovery). A buyer who discovered a material omission in a prospectus after the passage of the Act could sue for rescission under § 12(2) even though the prospectus had been issued before enactment of the statute. This tells us nothing one way or the other, however, about whether the term "prospectus" is limited to a document soliciting the public to purchase securities from the issuer.

In large measure the writings on which both the SEC and Justice Ginsburg rely address a question on which there is no disagreement, that is, "to what securities does § 12(2) apply?" We agree with the SEC that § 12(2) applies to every class of security (except one issued or backed by a governmental entity), whether exempted from registration or not, and whether outstanding at the time of the passage of the Act or not. The question before us is the coverage of § 12(2), and the writings offered by the SEC are of little value on this point.

If legislative history is to be considered, it is preferable to consult the documents prepared by Congress when deliberating. The legislative history of the Act concerning the precise question presented supports our interpretation with much clarity and force. Congress contemplated that § 12(2) would apply only to public offerings by an issuer (or a controlling shareholder). The House Report stated: "The bill affects only new offerings of securities. . . . It does not affect the ordinary redistribution of securities unless such redistribution takes on the characteristics of a new offering." H.R. Rep. No. 85, 73d Cong., 1st Sess., 5 (1933). The observation extended to § 12(2) as well. Part II, § 6 of the House Report is entitled "Civil Liabilities." It begins: "Sections 11 and 12 create and define the civil liabilities imposed by the act.... Fundamentally, these sections entitle the buyer of securities sold upon a registration statement ... to sue for recovery of his purchase price." It will be recalled that as to private transactions, such as the Alloyd purchase, there will never have been a registration statement. If § 12(2) liability were imposed here, it would cover transactions not within the contemplated reach of the statute.

* * *

Justice Ginsburg argues that the omission from the 1933 Act of the phrase "offering to the public" that appeared in the definition of "prospectus" in the British Companies Act of 1929 suggests that the drafters of the American bill intended to expand its coverage. We consider it more likely that the omission reflected instead the judgment that the words "offering to the public" were redundant in light of the understood meaning of "prospectus." Far from suggesting an intent to depart in a dramatic way from the balance struck in the British Companies Act, the legislative history suggests an intent to maintain it. In the context of justifying the "civil liabilities" provisions that hold "all those responsible for statements upon the face of which the public is solicited ... to standards like those imposed by law upon a fiduciary," the House Report stated: "The demands of this bill call for the assumption of no impossible burden, nor do they involve any leap into the dark. Similar requirements have for years attended the business of issuing securities in other industrialized nations." So, too, the Report provided: "The committee is fortified in these sections [that is, §§ 11 and 12] by similar safeguards in the English Companies Act of 1929. What is deemed necessary for sound financing in conservative England ought not to be unnecessary for the more feverish pace which American finance has developed." These passages confirm that the civil liability provisions of the 1933 Act, §§ 11 and 12, impose obligations on those engaged in "the business of issuing securities," in conformance, not in contradiction to, the British example.

* * *

In sum, the word "prospectus" is a term of art referring to a document that describes a public offering of securities by an issuer or controlling shareholder. The contract of sale, and its recitations, were not held out to the public and were not a prospectus as the term is used in the 1933 Act.

The judgment of the Court of Appeals is reversed, and the case is remanded for further proceedings consistent with this opinion.

It is so ordered.

■ JUSTICE THOMAS, with whom JUSTICE SCALIA, JUSTICE GINSBURG, and JUSTICE BREYER join, dissenting.

From the majority's opinion, one would not realize that § 12(2) was involved in this case until one had read more than half-way through. In contrast to the majority's approach of interpreting the statute, I believe the proper method is to begin with the provision actually involved in this case, § 12(2), and then turn to the 1933 Act's definitional section, § 2(10), before consulting the structure of the Act as a whole. Because the result of this textual analysis shows that § 12(2) applies to secondary or private sales of a security as well as to initial public offerings, I dissent.

I

A

As we have emphasized in our recent decisions, " '[t]he starting point in every case involving construction of a statute is the language itself.' " Landreth Timber Co. v. Landreth, 471 U.S. 681, 685 (1985) (quoting Blue Chip Stamps v. Manor Drug Stores, 421 U.S. 723, 756 (1975) (Powell, J., concurring)). See also Central Bank of Denver, N.A. v. First Interstate Bank of Denver, N.A., 511 U.S. 164, 171–175 (1994). Unfortunately, the majority has decided to interpret the word "prospectus" in § 12(2) by turning to sources outside the four corners of the statute, rather than by adopting the definition provided by Congress.

* * *

There is no reason to seek the meaning of "prospectus" outside of the 1933 Act, because Congress has supplied just such a definition in § 2(10). That definition is extraordinarily broad:

"When used in this subchapter, unless the context otherwise requires—

. . . .

"(10) The term 'prospectus' means any prospectus, notice, circular, advertisement, letter, or communication, written or by radio or television, which offers any security for sale or confirms the sale of any security." 15 U.S.C. § 77b(10).

For me, the breadth of these terms forecloses the majority's position that "prospectus" applies only in the context of initial distributions of securities. Indeed, § 2(10)'s inclusion of a prospectus as only one of the many different documents that qualify as a "prospectus" for statutory purposes indicates that Congress intended "prospectus" to be more than a mere "term of art." Likewise, Congress' extension of prospectus to include documents that merely confirm the sale of a security underscores Congress' intent to depart from the term's ordinary meaning. Section 2(10)'s definition obviously concerns different types of communications rather than different types of transactions. Congress left the job of exempting certain classes of transactions to §§ 3 and 4, not to § 2(10). We should use § 2(10) to define "prospectus" for the 1933 Act, rather than, as the majority does, use the 1933 Act to define "prospectus" for § 2(10).

The majority seeks to avoid this reading by attempting to create ambiguities in § 2(10). According to the majority, the maxim *noscitur a sociis* (a word is known by the company it keeps) indicates that the circulars, advertisements, letters, or other communications referred to by § 2(10) are limited by the first word in the list: "prospectus." Thus, we are told that these words define the forms a prospectus may take, but the covered communications still must be "prospectus-like" in the sense that they must relate to an initial public offering. *Noscitur a sociis*, however, does not require us to construe every term in a series narrowly because of the meaning given to just one of the terms. See Russell Motor Car Co. v. United States, 261 U.S. 514, 519 (1923); cf. Reves v. Ernst & Young, 494 U.S. 56, 64.

The majority uses the canon in an effort to *create* doubt, not to *reduce* it. The canon applies only in cases of ambiguity, which I do not find in § 2(10). "*Noscitur a sociis* is a well-established and useful rule of construction where words are of obscure or doubtful meaning; and then, but only then, its aid may be sought to remove the obscurity or doubt by reference to the associated words." Russell, supra, 261 U.S. at 520. There is obvious breadth in "notice, circular, advertisement, letter, or communication, written or by radio or television." To read one word in a long list as controlling the meaning of all the other words would defy common sense; doing so would prevent Congress from giving effect to expansive words in a list whenever they are combined with one word with a more restricted meaning. Section 2(10)'s very exhaustiveness suggests that "prospectus" is merely the first item in a long list of covered documents, rather than a brooding omnipresence whose meaning cabins that of all the following words. The majority also argues that a broad definition of prospectus makes much of § 2(10) redundant. See ante, at 1069. But the majority fails to see that "communication, written or by radio or television" is a catch all. It operates as a safety net that Congress used to sweep up anything it had forgotten to include in its definition.

* * *

B

* * *

The majority transforms § 10 into the tail that wags the 1933 Act dog. An analogy will illustrate the point. Suppose that the Act regulates cars, and that § 2(10) of the Act defines a "car" as any car, motorcycle, truck, or trailer. Section 10 of this hypothetical statute then declares that a car shall have seatbelts, and § 5 states that it is unlawful to sell cars without seatbelts. Section 12(2) of this Act then creates a cause of action for misrepresentations that occur during the sale of a car. It is reasonable to conclude that §§ 5 and 10 apply only to what we ordinarily refer to as "cars," because it would be absurd to require motorcycles and trailers to have seatbelts. But the majority's reasoning would lead to the further conclusion that § 12(2) does not cover sales of motorcycles, when it is clear that the Act includes such sales.

C

* * *

The majority argues that § 4's exemption suggests a contrary conclusion. According to the majority, if Congress had intended § 12(2) to apply to private, secondary transactions, it would have said so explicitly. This reasoning goes too far, for it would render § 4 superfluous. After all, if the majority applied its approach to § 5 (which prohibits the sale of a security without first registering the security or without first sending a prospectus), then it would conclude—even in the absence of § 4—that § 5 refers only to initial offerings. But this would have precluded any need to include § 4 at all.

The majority claims that under my reading, "there is no ready explanation for exempting" government securities from § 12(2). But Congress could have concluded that it was unnecessary to impose liability on the private or secondary sellers of a government security because information concerning government securities is already available either from the markets or from government entities. Or Congress could have chosen not to burden government securities with the costs that might accrue from additional liabilities on initial or secondary sales.

* * *

III

The majority's analysis of § 12(2) is motivated by its policy preferences. Underlying its reasoning is the assumption that Congress could never have intended to impose liability on sellers engaged in secondary transactions. Adopting a chiding tone, the majority states that "[w]e are reluctant to conclude that § 12(2) creates vast additional liabilities that are entirely independent of the new substantive obligations that the Act enumerates." Yet, this is exactly what Congress did in § 17(a) of the 1933 Act as well as in § 10(b) of the 1934 Act. Later, the majority says: "[I]t is not plausible to infer that Congress created this extensive liability for every casual communication between buyer and seller in the secondary market." It is not the usual practice of this Court to require Congress to explain why it has chosen to pursue a certain policy. Our job simply is to apply the policy, not to question it.

I share the majority's concern that extending § 12(2) to secondary and private transactions might result in an unwanted increase in securities litigation. But it is for Congress, and not for this Court, to determine the desired level of securities liability. As we said last Term in *Central Bank of Denver*, policy considerations " 'cannot override our interpretation of the text and structure of the Act, except to the extent that they may help to show that adherence to the text and structure would lead to a result "so bizarre" that Congress could not have intended it.' " 511 U.S., at 188 (1994). The majority is concerned that a contrary reading would have a drastic impact on the thousands of private and secondary transactions by imposing new liabilities and new transaction costs. But the majority forgets that we are only enforcing *Congress'* decision to impose such standards of conduct and remedies upon sellers. If the majority believes that § 12(2)'s requirements are too burdensome for the securities markets, it must rely upon the other branches of government to limit the 1933 Act.

* * *

For the foregoing reasons, I respectfully *dissent*.

■ JUSTICE GINSBURG, with whom JUSTICE BREYER joins, dissenting.

A seller's misrepresentation made "by means of a prospectus or oral communication" is actionable under § 12(2) of the Securities Act of 1933. To limit the scope of this civil liability provision, the Court maintains that a communication qualifies as a prospectus only if made during a public offering.[1] Communications during either secondary trading or a private placement are not "prospectuses," the Court declares, and thus are not covered by § 12(2).

As Justice Thomas persuasively demonstrates, the statute's language does not support the Court's reading. Section 12(2) contains no terms expressly confining the provision to public offerings, and the statutory definition of "prospectus"—"any prospectus, notice, circular, advertisement, letter, or communication, written or by radio or television, which offers any security for sale or confirms the sale of any security," § 2(10), 15 U.S.C. § 77b(10)—is capacious.

The Court presents impressive policy reasons for its construction, but drafting history and the longstanding scholarly and judicial understanding of § 12(2) caution against judicial resistance to the statute's defining text. I would leave any alteration to Congress.

* * *

II

Most provisions of the Securities Act govern only public offerings, and the legislative history pertaining to the Act as a whole shares this orientation. Section § 17(a) of the Act, 15 U.S.C. § 77q(a), however, is not limited to public offerings; that enforcement provision, this Court has recognized, also covers secondary trading. The drafting history is at least consistent with the conclusion that § 12(2), like § 17(a), is not limited to public offerings.

The drafters of the Securities Act modeled this federal legislation on the British Companies Act, 19 & 20 Geo. 5, ch. 23 (1929). See Landis, The Legislative History of the Securities Act of 1933, 28 Geo. Wash. L. Rev. 29, 34 (1959) (Landis and the other drafters "determined to take as the base of [their] work the English Companies Act"); see also SEC v. Ralston

---

[1] I understand the Court's definition of a public offering to encompass both transactions that must be registered under § 5, 15 U.S.C. § 77e, and transactions that would have been registered had the securities involved not qualified for exemption under § 3, 15 U.S.C. § 77c.

Purina Co., 346 U.S. 119, 123 (1953) (characterizing the Companies Act as a "statutory anteceden[t]" of federal securities laws). The Companies Act defined "prospectus" as "any prospectus, notice, circular, advertisement, or other invitation, *offering to the public* for subscription or purchase any shares or debentures of a company," 19 & 20 Geo. 5, ch. 23, § 380(1) (1929) (emphasis added). Though the drafters of the Securities Act borrowed the first four terms of this definition, they did not import from the British legislation the language limiting prospectuses to communications "offering [securities] to the public." This conspicuous omission suggests that the drafters intended the defined term "prospectus" to reach beyond communications used in public offerings.

* * *

Commentators writing shortly after passage of the Act understood § 12(2) to cover resales and private sales, as well as public offerings. Felix Frankfurter, organizer of the team that drafted the statute, firmly stated this view. See Frankfurter, The Federal Securities Act: II, 8 Fortune 53, 108 (1933) (Act "seeks to terminate the facilities of the mails and of interstate commerce for dishonest or unfair dealings in the sale of *all* private or foreign government securities, *new or old*") (emphasis added). William O. Douglas expressed the same understanding. See Douglas & Bates, The Federal Securities Act of 1933, 43 Yale L.J. 171, 183 (1933) (noting that, except for transactions involving securities exempt under § 3(a)(2), 15 U.S.C. § 77c(a)(2), no securities or transactions are exempt from § 12(2)).

* * *

In light of the text, drafting history, and longstanding scholarly and judicial understanding of § 12(2), I conclude that § 12(2) applies to a private resale of securities. If adjustment is in order, as the Court's opinion powerfully suggests it is,[8] Congress is equipped to undertake the alteration. Accordingly, I dissent from the Court's opinion and judgment.

---

[8] Section 12(2) did not become prominent in Securities Act litigation until this Court held in Ernst & Ernst v. Hochfelder, 425 U.S. 185 (1976), that an action for civil damages under § 10(b) of the Securities Exchange Act of 1934, 48 Stat. 891, 15 U.S.C. § 78j(b), and Securities and Exchange Commission Rule 10b–5, 17 CFR § 240.10b–5 (1975), requires proof of scienter. See Loss, The Assault on Securities Act Section 12(2), 105 Harv. L. Rev. 908, 910 (1992).

Though the Court of Appeals' reading of § 12(2) shows fidelity to the statute Congress passed, this Court's opinion makes noteworthy practical and policy points. As the Court observes, ante, at 1071, under the Court of Appeals' reading, § 12(2) would equip buyers with a rescission remedy for a negligent misstatement or omission even if the slip did not cause the buyer's disenchantment with the investment. And, in light of the "free writing" provision of § 2(10)(a), 15 U.S.C. § 77b(10)(a) (a communication will not be deemed a "prospectus" if its recipient was previously sent a prospectus meeting the requirements of § 10), the Court of Appeals' reading, ironically, would leave a seller more vulnerable in private transactions than in public ones.

NOTES ON § 12 POST GUSTAFSON: REASONABLE CARE DEFENSE AND OTHER ISSUES

1. *What Explains the Outcome in Gustafson?* The term "prospectus" is defined (by the statute and courts) in exceedingly broad terms—it covers any communication that offers a security for sale. As we've seen, "offer" is also defined very broadly to cover all communications that "condition the public mind." So what explains Justice Kennedy's statement in *Gustafson* that a prospectus is: "a term of art referring to a document that describes a public offering of securities by an issuer or controlling shareholder"? Do you think the Court's hostility to private, securities class actions colored its interpretation of "prospectus"? Should it?

2. *The Upside of Gustafson.* While *Gustafson* is a strained reading of the statutory language and the regulatory scheme, there is a potential upside in the clarity it brings to the various liability provisions. Section 11 covers misstatements in registration statements; § 12(a)(1) covers violations of the gun-jumping rules; and § 12(a)(2) covers misstatements in the selling of a public offering. Do you think this clarity justifies the Court's opinion in *Gustafson*?

3. *Section 10(b) and Alloyd's Claim.* After *Gustafson*, Alloyd no longer has a claim under § 12(a)(2). As we will see when we focus on the 1934 Act causes of action, companies like Alloyd have potential claims under § 10(b) of that Act, as well as state law contract claims.

4. *Section 12 After Gustafson. Gustafson* left a number of questions unresolved. Suppose, for example, a defendant violates § 5, fails to register a security and sells the security by means of a private placement offering circular. Will the plaintiff be deprived of § 12(a)(2) because the defendant violated the law and did not register? To date, the lower courts have reached equivocal results. "[P]rivate placement memoranda like those at issue are not 'prospectuses' for the purposes of a claim under [§ 12(a)(2)]."[77] The court stated in JWP Inc. Sec. Litig.: "If the * * * plaintiffs wish to contend that the * * * offerings should have been registered, * * * the appropriate basis for that claim would be [§ 12(a)(1)], which provides for rescission of sales of securities improperly accomplished without registration."[78] Compare Sloane Overseas Fund, Ltd. v. Sapiens Int'l Corp., N.V.[79]: "Regulation S offerings are not exempted pursuant to §§ 3, 4 of the 1933 Act, 15 U.S.C. § 12(2) * * * if it is a public offering."

Section 12(a)(2) states that its scope includes exempt *securities* other than those exempted by § 3(a)(2) or 3(a)(14). Will an offering of

---

[77] In re JWP, 928 F.Supp. 1239, 1259 (S.D.N.Y.1996).

[78] Ibid. Similarly in Maldonado v. Dominguez, 137 F.3d 1 (1st Cir. 1998), the court unequivocally held, citing Gustafson, "the Supreme Court conclusively decided that section 12(2) applies exclusively to 'initial public offerings.'" Id. at 8.

[79] 941 F.Supp. 1369, 1376 (S.D.N.Y.1996).

commercial paper be subject to § 12(a)(2) even though these offerings are not made employing a § 10 prospectus? Section 3 is labeled "Exempted Securities," but it is generally recognized that the intrastate exemption in § 3(a)(11) is for an exempted transaction, not an exempted security.[80] If a private placement under § 4(2) is not subject to § 12(a)(2), should an intrastate exempt transaction under § 3(a)(11) also be outside the scope of § 12(a)(2)?[81]

5. *Standing.* As discussed earlier in the chapter, attorneys have deployed *Gustafson* to cabin the standing of § 11 plaintiffs who purchase in the aftermarket. Similar issues occur under Section 12(a)(2). *Gustafson* states that liability attaches when prospectus distribution is required.[82] Thus, at least for some courts, unless prospectus delivery was required, plaintiffs cannot sue under § 12(a)(2).

6. *Rule 159.* Section 12(a)(2) liability attaches to a prospectus or other oral communication. The SEC promulgated interpretive Rule 159 to clarify that liability attaches to misstatements or omissions at the time of sale, and not, for example, to modifications made later. The date of the sale contract, of course, may occur prior to delivery of a final prospectus. Any changes in a final prospectus, then, are not included in the "prospectus" for purposes of § 12(a)(2) liability. Further, the same timing applies to determinations of whether the purchaser knew of the untruth or omission.[83]

7. *Free Writing Prospectus Liability.* The free writing prospectus is subject to liability under § 12(a)(2) but not under § 11 unless the issuer chooses to file it as part of the registration statement. In addition, the 2005 offering reforms attempt to limit liability for a free writing prospectus to the provider of the information in it and the user. For example, if an issuer provides information for a free writing prospectus, it and any offering participant that uses the free writing prospectus on the basis of issuer information, could be subject to § 12(a)(2) liability. The issuer and other offering participants may not, however, be subject to liability.[84] In addition, Rule 433(a) provides that a free writing prospectus is "deemed" public regardless of the distribution method, increasing the potential for § 12(a)(2) liability in the post-*Gustafson* world.

---

[80] See 3 Louis Loss & Joel Seligman, Securities Regulation 1142–1144 (3d ed. rev. 1999).

[81] For a variety of views on these and related questions, see Elliot J. Weiss, Securities Act Section 12(2) after Gustafson v. Alloyd Co.: What Questions Remain?, 50 Bus. Law. 1209 (1995); Therese H. Maynard, The Impact of Gustafson and Its Methodology, 24 Sec. Reg. L.J. 61 (1996); Edmund Kitch, Gustafson v. Alloyd Co.: An Opinion that Did Not Write, 1995 Sup. Ct. Rev. 99; Peter Letsou, The Scope of Section 12(2) of the Securities Act of 1933: A Legal and Economic Analysis, 45 Emory L.J. 95 (1996); Therese H. Maynard, A Requiem: Reflections on Gustafson, 57 Ohio St. L.J. 1327 (1996); Elliot J. Weiss, Some Further Thoughts on Gustafson v. Alloyd Co., 65 U. Cinn. L. Rev. 137 (1996).

[82] See, e.g., In re Valence Tech. Sec. Litig., 1996 WL 37788 (N.D. Cal.).

[83] See 17 C.F.R. § 230.159 and SEC Securities Offering Reform Release 33–8591 (July 19, 2005).

[84] Securities Act Release No. 33–8591 (2005).

8. *The Reasonable Care Defense.* Section 12(a)(2) provides a defense if a defendant sustains the burden of proof that "he did not know, and in the exercise of reasonable care could not have known," of the untruth or omission. This provision is read as saying that the defendant may escape liability if he proves that, "*if* he [or she] had exercised reasonable care, he [or she] would not have known." The Section thus imposes liability based on simple negligence and the defendant has the burden of establishing that he or she was free of negligence.

There is no defense under § 12(a)(2), as there is in § 11, based upon the "expertising" of certain statements. For example, if there is a misstatement in financial statements that were "expertised" by independent accountants, a director of the issuer could defend under § 11 on the ground that he or she simply accepted their figures and "had no reasonable ground to believe" that they were erroneous, as in the *BarChris* case. This defense is not available under § 12(a)(2). Instead, a director must show that "in the exercise of reasonable care [he or she] could not have known" of the error.[85] Does reasonable care in this situation require the director to investigate the figures of the independent accounts? There is relatively little case law addressing the meaning of reasonable care in § 12(a)(2) itself.[86] But one case, Franklin Savings Bank of New York v. Levy,[87] involving an action against Goldman, Sachs by a purchaser of Penn Central commercial paper, raises the issue:

> We have held that where a broker-dealer makes a representation as to the quality of the security he sells, he impliedly represents that he has an adequate basis in fact for the opinion he renders. Hanly v. Securities and Exchange Commission, 415 F.2d 589, 596–97 (2d Cir. 1969). We see no reason why that theory is not at least equally appropriate in cases involving § 12(2) of the 1933 Act.
>
> Here Goldman, Sachs became an exclusive source of the Penn Central notes in issue. It was a professional vendor admittedly recommending this paper for sale to an institution authorized by statute only to invest in prime paper. Such an undertaking implies that Goldman, Sachs has conducted an ongoing investigation of Penn Central's financial condition. If Goldman, Sachs failed to exercise reasonable professional care in

---

[85] See Gould v. Tricon, Inc., 272 F.Supp. 385 (S.D.N.Y.1967). See generally Comm. on Fed. Reg. of Sec., Report of Task Force on Sellers' Due Diligence and Similar Defenses under the Federal Securities Laws, 48 Bus. Law. 1185 (1993); Therese H. Maynard, The Affirmative Defense of Reasonable Care under Section 12(2) of the Securities Act of 1933, 69 Notre Dame L. Rev. 57 (1993).

[86] The earliest decision is Murphy v. Cady, 30 F.Supp. 466, 468–469 (D.Me.1939). See also First Trust & Savings Bank of Zanesville, Ohio v. Fidelity-Philadelphia Trust Co., 214 F.2d 320 (3d Cir. 1954); Jackson v. Oppenheim, 533 F.2d 826, 829 n. 7 (2d Cir. 1976); Sanders v. John Nuveen & Co., 524 F.2d 1064 (7th Cir. 1975); Dennis v. General Imaging, Inc., 918 F.2d 496, 505 (5th Cir. 1990).

[87] 551 F.2d 521 (2d Cir. 1977).

assembling and evaluating the financial data, particularly in view of the worsening condition of Penn Central, then its representation that the paper was credit worthy and high quality was untrue in fact and misleading no matter how honestly but mistakenly held. This view does not render Goldman, Sachs an insurer as appellants claim liable for some catastrophe beyond its control. Rather, it in fact makes the dealer responsible to Franklin if it is unable to shoulder the burden of establishing that it was not reasonable for it to have determined on March 16, 1970 that the quality of the paper it was purveying was less than that represented.[88]

9. *Due Diligence Defense and Reasonable Care Defense Compared.* In Sanders v. John Nuveen & Co., Inc.,[89] the Seventh Circuit found no difference in the reasonable investigation required by § 11 and the § 12(a)(2) defense of reasonable care. The court stated in part:

> It is not at all clear that Congress intended to impose a higher standard of care under § 12(2). The difference in language appeared in the House bill and was retained in the Act as agreed to by the Joint Conference Committee and as passed by both Houses. See H.R. 5480, 73d Cong., 1st Sess. §§ 11 & 12 (1933). The Conference Committee report, in its discussion of the standard of liability imposed for a misleading registration statement, describes the standard adopted not as one of "reasonable investigation," but one of "reasonable care." H.R. Rep. No. 152, 73d Cong., 1st Sess. 26 (1933) (Conference Report). More specifically, Congress does not appear to have intended that a different standard apply to underwriters. Thus, the House Report draws no distinction between an underwriter's burden in the case of misleading statements in a prospectus, for which it can be liable only under § 12(2) and its § 11 duty to conduct a "reasonable investigation." H.R. Rep. No. 85, 73d Cong., 1st Sess. 9 (1933). The difference in language can be explained not as an attempt to impose different duties of care under §§ 11 and 12, but by the fact that § 12(2) imposes the duty on all sellers of securities, while § 11 imposes liability only on specified groups of persons having such a close relationship with the registration statement that the 1933 Act, before it was amended the following year, treated them as fiduciaries. See Securities Act of 1933, ch. 38, § 11(c), 48 Stat. 74, 83 (1933); Securities Exchange Act of 1934, ch. 404, § 206(c), 48 Stat. 881, 907 (1934). Thus the general duty of reasonable care, the specific requirements of which are determined by the circumstances of the case, was to be applied in § 11 only to persons who had a stronger connection with a registration

---

[88] Id. at 527.
[89] 619 F.2d 1222 (7th Cir. 1980).

statement than a seller necessarily has to a prospectus, so a more stringent articulation of the standard was appropriate.

In the circumstances of this case, the reasonable care standard required the reasonable investigation described in *Sanders II*. Since what constitutes reasonable care under § 12(2) depends upon the circumstances, we, of course, do not intimate that the duty of a seller under § 12(2) is always the same as that of an underwriter in a registration offering under § 11.[90]

The Supreme Court denied *certiorari*, but Justice Powell, joined by Justice Rehnquist, dissented on the ground that the lower court failed to distinguish the standards of care applicable under § 11 and what is now § 12(a)(2) (then § 12(2)) in John Nuveen & Co., Inc. v. Sanders.[91] Justice Powell wrote in part:

> Section 11(a) of the 1933 Act imposes liability on certain persons for selling securities in a registered public offering pursuant to a materially false or misleading registration statement. A registered offering is the class of financial transactions for which Congress prescribed the most stringent regulation. The standard of care imposed on an underwriter is that it must have "had, after *reasonable investigation*, reasonable ground to believe and did believe" that the registration statement was accurate. Section 11(b)(3)(A) of the Act (emphasis added).
>
> Liability in this case was not imposed on petitioner under § 11, but under § 12(2). Under the latter section, it is necessary for sellers to show only that they "did not know, and in the exercise of *reasonable care* could not have known," that their statements were false or misleading. (Emphasis added).
>
> In providing standards of care under the 1933 Act, Congress thus used different language for different situations. "Reasonable *investigation*" is required for registered offerings under § 11, but nothing more than "mer[e] . . . 'reasonable *care*' " is required by § 12(2). (emphasis added) W.O. Douglas & G.E. Bates, The Federal Securities Act of 1933, 43 Yale L.J. 173, 208 (1933). The difference in language is significant, because in the securities acts Congress has used its words with precision. See, e.g., Ernst & Ernst v. Hochfelder, 425 U.S. 185, 198–201 (1976); Blue Chip Stamps v. Manor Drug Stores, 421 U.S. 723, 755, 756 (1975) (Powell J., concurring). "Investigation" commands a greater undertaking than "care." See W.O. Douglas & G.E. Bates, supra, at 208, n. 205.[92]

---

[90] Id. at 1228.
[91] 450 U.S. 1005 (1981).
[92] Id. at 1008–09.

As the *Software Toolworks*[93] court suggested, the law remains unsettled as to whether the § 11 reasonable investigation standard is identical, similar, or materially different from the § 12(a)(2) reasonable care standard.[94] Perhaps most significantly the court in *Software Toolworks* suggested that even if there are different standards under §§ 11 and 12(a)(2), the analysis of each on summary judgment may be identical.

Problem

PROBLEM 11-3

Opus Mortgages sells mortgage related investments. Among other things, it will provide individual mortgages to specific homeowners and sell portfolios of mortgages to investors.

To sell these investments, Opus has a sales force that makes "cold" (unsolicited) telephone calls in which the mortgage brokers read from a script. The script states in part that "each mortgage is individually secured" and explains in detail the system of matching individual investments to individual mortgages.

Opus has twice been the subject of investigations by the State Attorney General. Two years ago, the State Attorney General and Opus signed a consent order under which Opus agreed to have financial records audited. The consent order was negotiated for Opus by general counsel and vice president, Lawrence Haydn. In the next two years, Haydn on three occasions attempted to hire an accountant to audit the financial records of Opus. On each occasion the accountant was unable to give an unqualified opinion because, as the accountant put it, "the recordkeeping is a disaster area. I am unable to determine whether or not Opus is, in fact, matching mortgages." On several occasions Haydn reassured officials of the State Attorney General's office that he was making a good faith effort to comply with the consent order.

More recently, after the State Attorney General had received several complaints from individuals about Opus, a second investigation began. This investigation discovered, among other things: (1) that the same "script" and offering circular had been used without change; (2) that no audited financial records had ever been produced; (3) that the late chief executive officer of Opus, Koernke, had misappropriated (stolen) $7 million of Opus assets; and (4) because no matching system had ever fully been in place, Opus was forced to liquidate. The $7 million stolen by Koernke was not recovered.

Haydn subsequently has been sued for federal securities law violations by a class of investors. Can Haydn be held liable under § 12(a)(2) of the Securities Act of 1933? If so, is he entitled to a reasonable care defense?

---

[93] 50 F.3d 615, 621 (9th Cir. 1994).

[94] Cf. Associated Randall Bank v. Griffin, Kubik, Stephens & Thompson, Inc., 3 F.3d 208, 213 (7th Cir. 1993) (rejecting suggestion that there is no difference between the reasonable investigation standard in § 11 and reasonable care standard in § 12(a)(2)).

3. SECTION 17(a) OF THE 1933 ACT

Section 17(a) of the 1933 Act is identical to Rule 10b–5 (promulgated pursuant to section 10 of the 1934 Act) with respect to its substantive provisions. The Commission copied § 17(a) when it adopted Rule 10b–5. The coverage of the two provisions, however, is not identical. Section 17(a) applies only to an "offer or sale," while Rule 10b–5 applies to a "purchase or sale." Section 17(a) applies to an *offer to sell*, but Rule 10b–5 does not. Rule 10b–5 applies to a purchase of a security by the defendant, but § 17(a) does not. The coverage of § 17(a) is, however, almost identical to the coverage of the express civil liability provision in § 12(a)(2) of the 1933 Act. The sole exception is that § 17(a) covers all offers and sales exempt from registration by the provisions of § 3, but § 12(a)(2) does not cover transactions in two of the exempt securities, government and bank securities.

After a few early decisions upheld a private right of action under § 17(a),[95] more recent cases, with few exceptions,[96] have generally rejected the implication of a private cause of action under § 17(a).[97]

The courts have also addressed the question of the appropriate standard for culpability under § 17(a). Recall that § 11 has a negligence-like standard, and that § 12 has a strict liability standard. Rule 10b–5, which is covered in a separate chapter, has a higher recklessness standard.

In Aaron v. SEC,[98] the Supreme Court addressed two questions: whether the *scienter* requirement applied in an injunction action by the Commission as well as a private damage action; and whether that requirement existed under § 17(a) of the 1933 Act as well as under Rule 10b–5. The Court held, first, that the Commission must meet the same requirements regarding the fault of the defendant in an injunction action as a private plaintiff must in an action for damages or other relief, but that the *scienter* requirement does not exist under two of the three clauses of § 17(a). The Court said:

> The language of § 17(a) strongly suggests that Congress contemplated a scienter requirement under § 17(a)(1), but not under § 17(a)(2) or § 17(a)(3). The language of § 17(a)(1), which makes it unlawful "to employ any device, scheme, or artifice to defraud," plainly evinces an intent on the part of Congress to

---

[95] See, e.g., Pfeffer v. Cressaty, 223 F.Supp. 756 (S.D.N.Y. 1963); cf. Judge Friendly dictum in SEC v. Texas Gulf Sulphur Co., 401 F.2d 833, 867 (2d Cir. 1968); Coates v. SEC, 394 U.S. 976 (1969); "Once it had been established, however, that an aggrieved buyer has a private action under § 10(b) of the 1934 Act, there seemed little practical point in denying the existence of such an action under § 17—with the important proviso that fraud, as distinct from mere negligence, must be alleged."

[96] See Craighead v. E.F. Hutton & Co., Inc., 899 F.2d 485, 492–493 (6th Cir. 1990).

[97] Finkel v. Stratton Corp., 962 F.2d 169, 174–175 (2d Cir. 1992) (citing cases from seven other circuits); Maldonado v. Dominguez, 137 F.3d 1 (1st Cir. 1998).

[98] 446 U.S. 680 (1980).

proscribe only knowing or intentional misconduct. Even if it be assumed that the term "defraud" is ambiguous, given its varied meanings at law and in equity, the terms "device," "scheme," and "artifice" all connote knowing or intentional practices. Indeed, the term "device," which also appears in § 10(b), figured prominently in the Court's conclusion in *Hochfelder* that the plain meaning of § 10(b) embraces a scienter requirement.

By contrast, the language of § 17(a)(2), which prohibits any person from obtaining money or property "by means of any untrue statement of a material fact or any omission to state a material fact," is devoid of any suggestion whatsoever of a scienter requirement. As a well-known commentator has noted, "[there] is nothing on the face of Clause (2) itself which smacks of *scienter* or intent to defraud." 3 L. Loss, Securities Regulation 1442 (2d ed. 1961). In fact, this Court in *Hochfelder* pointed out that the similar language of Rule 10b–5(b) "could be read as proscribing . . . any type of material misstatement or omission . . . that has the effect of defrauding investors, whether the wrongdoing was intentional or not."

Finally, the language of § 17(a)(3), under which it is unlawful for any person "to engage in any transaction, practice, or course of business which *operates* or *would operate* as a fraud or deceit," (emphasis added) quite plainly focuses upon the *effect* of particular conduct on members of the investing public, rather than upon the culpability of the person responsible. This reading follows directly from *Capital Gains*, which attributed to a similarly worded provision in § 206(2) of the Investment Advisers Act of 1940 a meaning that does not require a "showing [of] deliberate dishonesty as a condition precedent to protecting investors." 375 U.S. at 200.

It is our view, in sum, that the language of § 17(a) requires scienter under § 17(a)(1), but not under § 17(a)(2) or § 17(a)(3). Although the parties have urged the Court to adopt a uniform culpability requirement for the three subparagraphs of § 17(a), the language of the section is simply not amenable to such an interpretation. This is not the first time that this Court has had occasion to emphasize the distinctions among the three subparagraphs of § 17(a). In United States v. Naftalin, 441 U.S. 768, 774, the Court noted that each subparagraph of § 17(a) "proscribes a distinct category of misconduct. Each succeeding prohibition is meant to cover additional kinds of illegalities— not to narrow the reach of the prior sections." (Footnote omitted) Indeed, since Congress drafted § 17(a) in such a manner as to compel the conclusion that scienter is required under one subparagraph but not under the other two, it would take a very clear expression in the legislative history of congressional intent to the contrary to justify the conclusion that the statute does not mean what it so plainly seems to say.[99]

---

[99] Id. at 695–97.

CHAPTER 12

RULES 10b–5 AND 14a–9: FRAUD IN CONNECTION WITH A PURCHASE OR SALE OF A SECURITY OR THE SOLICITATION OF PROXIES

Statutes and Regulations

Federal Rule of Civil Procedure 23.

Securities Act, § 27A.

Exchange Act, §§ 10, 18, 21E.

Rules 10b–5, 14a–9.

1. INTRODUCTION

Rule 10b–5 is the basic antifraud provision of the federal securities laws. The Rule reaches fraud "in connection with a purchase or sale of a security." Recall that §§ 11 and 12 of the Securities Act address fraud in securities distributions and is covered in Chapter 11. Rule 14a–9 is limited to fraud in a proxy solicitation and § 18 of the Securities Exchange Act imposes liability on any person who shall make or cause to be made any materially false or misleading statement in a filing required by the Securities Exchange Act.

As a practical matter Rule 10b–5 applies to three types of fraud: (1) misrepresentations or omissions in corporate statements (which can include proxy statements and offering documents); (2) trading while in possession of material nonpublic information, called "insider trading"; and (3) manipulation. The basic elements of a Rule 10b–5 violation overlap for each type of fraud. Although Rule 10b–5 is the primary mechanism for enforcing these antifraud goals today, this was not the original intent. For example, § 16(b), which disgorges profits from insiders' sales within a six-month window, was the initial prohibition against insider trading. But, as we will see below, a variety of factors make it the key antifraud provision today.

One of those present at the genesis of the Rule described its humble origins this way:

> I do not remember if we got there that morning or after lunch. We passed a piece of paper around to all the commissioners. All the commissioners read the rule and they tossed it on the table,

indicating approval. Nobody said anything except Sumner Pike. 'Well,' he said, 'we are against fraud, aren't we?' That is how it happened. Louis [Loss] is absolutely right that I never thought that twenty-odd years later it would be the biggest thing that had ever happened.[1]

Section 10(b) of the Securities Exchange Act was a residual provision that followed more specific prohibitions against market manipulation in §§ 9 and 10. As one of the drafters stated of the somewhat broader version initially denominated § 9(c) in the Securities Exchange Bill: "Subsection (c) says, 'Thou shalt not devise any other cunning devices.' "[2]

Rule 10b–5 is one long sentence:

It shall be unlawful for any person, directly or indirectly, by the use of any means or instrumentality of interstate commerce, or of the mails, or of any facility of any national securities exchange,

(1) to employ any device, scheme, or artifice to defraud,

(2) to make any untrue statement of a material fact or to omit to state a material fact necessary in order to make the statements made, in the light of the circumstances under which they were made, not misleading, or

(3) to engage in any act, practice, or course of business which operates or would operate as a fraud or deceit upon any person,

in connection with the purchase or sale of any security.

NOTES ON CAUSE OF ACTION UNDER RULE 10b–5

1. *Implied Cause of Action.* Note that Rule 10b–5 does not include an express private cause of action. In 1947, a federal district court implied one.[3] In 1971, the Supreme Court in Superintendent of Insurance of the State of New York v. Bankers Life and Casualty Co.[4] stated in a footnote: "It is now established that a private right of action is implied under § 10(b)," and the *Herman & MacLean*[5] decision resolved the question. In its 2008 decision in Stoneridge Investment Partners, LLC v. Scientific Atlanta, Inc.,[6] the Supreme Court further noted that the 1995 Private Securities Litigation Reform Act's provisions relating to the implied right of action ratified it.[7] Yet, as we'll see below, many of the Court's decisions can be justified only on the ground that they curtail a private cause of action that had grown out of control and resulted in too

---

[1] Conference on Codification of the Federal Securities Laws, 22 BUS. LAW. 793, 921–23 (1967).

[2] Stock Exchange Regulation, Hearings before House Comm. on Interstate & Foreign Commerce, 73d Cong., 2d Sess. 115 (1934) (testimony of Thomas Corcoran).

[3] Kardon v. National Gypsum Co., 73 F.Supp. 798 (E.D. Pa. 1947).

[4] 404 U.S. 6 n.9 (1971).

[5] Herman & MacLean v. Huddleston, 459 U.S. 375 (1983).

[6] 552 U.S. 148, 128 S.Ct. 761 (2008).

[7] Id. at 773.

much nuisance in litigation. Interestingly, in response to one of these decisions, *Central Bank of Denver,* Congress reinstated a public cause of action—in § 20(e)—that gave the SEC authority to pursue actions against those who aid and abet violations of the securities laws.

This back-and-forth among different Supreme Courts—one implying a private cause of action and others cutting back on it—obscures a fairly straightforward policy debate about the scope of private lawyers in enforcing the public interest in reducing securities fraud. Private lawyers bring resources, information, investigatory skills, and strong incentives to prosecute cases (since their pay depends on winning and is proportional to any judgment). On the other hand, private lawyers may be less public spirited and may bring cases that have primarily nuisance value.

2. *Purchases and Sales.* Section 10(b) by its terms applies to "any security registered [i.e., listed] on a national securities exchange or any security not so registered," and is all-inclusive. Originally the great majority of private civil suits instituted under the Rule concerned closely held corporations with securities not actively traded in any market. In recent years public corporations have been the primary target of these actions.

3. *Overlapping Causes of Action.* Another important Rule 10b–5 issue involved whether a plaintiff could sue under Rule 10b–5 if an express civil liability provision of the 1933 Act or the 1934 Act also applied. The unanimous decision in *Herman & MacLean* held that a Rule 10b–5 lawsuit can be concurrent with a § 11 claim. Rule 10b–5 lawsuits also run concurrent with lawsuits under § 12(a)(2) of the 1933 Act;[8] § 9 of the 1934 Act;[9] and § 18 of the 1934 Act.[10] The *Herman & MacLean* court stated:

> The Securities Act of 1933 and the Securities Exchange Act of 1934 "constitute interrelated components of the federal

---

[8] See Ellis v. Carter, 291 F.2d 270 (9th Cir. 1961) (upholding concurrent claims); Berger v. Bishop Inv. Corp., 695 F.2d 302, 308 (8th Cir. 1982) (upholding concurrent claims).

[9] In Chemetron Corp. v. Business Funds, Inc., 682 F.2d 1149 (5th Cir. 1982), the court initially held that an action could not be maintained under Rule 10b–5 where an action was available under § 9(e) of the 1934 Act, because § 9 only prohibited certain willful misconduct; therefore, the plaintiff was not assuming a greater burden of proof by suing under Rule 10b–5 and to recognize such a right of action would nullify the procedural restrictions applicable to an action under § 9. In fact, the court indicated that the plaintiff would have a *lesser* burden of proof under Rule 10b–5 because of the requirement that certain additional facts be proven under the express provisions of § 9(a)(1), (2) and (6). Judge Jerre Williams dissented from this decision.

The Supreme Court granted certiorari in this case and then vacated the judgment and remanded the case for "further consideration in the light of [the Supreme Court decision in] Herman & MacLean v. Huddleston." On remand, Judge Gee, who wrote the original majority opinion, adhered to his former opinion even "in the light of" the decision in the Herman & MacLean case, but Judge Reavley changed his vote and Judge Williams wrote the new majority opinion upholding the Rule 10b–5 action despite the alleged conflict with § 9. Chemetron Corporation v. Business Funds, Inc., 718 F.2d 725 (5th Cir. 1983). The Fifth Circuit then granted a hearing in the case en banc, but the lawsuit was settled before that en banc hearing.

[10] See Ross v. A.H. Robins Co., Inc., 607 F.2d 545 (2d Cir. 1979) (upholding concurrent remedies).

regulatory scheme governing transactions in securities." Ernst & Ernst v. Hochfelder, 425 U.S. 185, 206 (1976). The Acts created several express private rights of action, one of which is contained in § 11 of the 1933 Act. In addition to the private actions created explicitly by the 1933 and 1934 Acts, federal courts have implied private remedies under other provisions of the two laws. Most significantly for present purposes, a private right of action under § 10(b) of the 1934 Act and Rule 10b–5 has been consistently recognized for more than 35 years. The existence of this implied remedy is simply beyond peradventure.

The issue in this case is whether a party should be barred from invoking this established remedy for fraud because the allegedly fraudulent conduct would apparently also provide the basis for a damage action under § 11 of the 1933 Act. The resolution of this issue turns on the fact that the two provisions involve distinct causes of action and were intended to address different types of wrongdoing.

* * *

Since § 11 and § 10(b) address different types of wrongdoing, we see no reason to carve out an exception to § 10(b) for fraud occurring in a registration statement just because the same conduct may also be actionable under § 11. Exempting such conduct from liability under § 10(b) would conflict with the basic purpose of the 1933 Act: to provide greater protection to purchasers of registered securities. It would be anomalous indeed if the special protection afforded to purchasers in a registered offering by the 1933 Act were deemed to deprive such purchasers of the protections against manipulation and deception that § 10(b) makes available to all persons who deal in securities.

While some conduct actionable under § 11 may also be actionable under § 10(b), it is hardly a novel proposition that the Securities Exchange Act and the Securities Act "prohibit some of the same conduct." United States v. Naftalin, 441 U.S. 768, 778 (1979) (applying § 17(a) of the 1933 Act to conduct also prohibited by § 10(b) of the 1934 Act in an action by the SEC). " 'The fact that there may well be some overlap is neither unusual nor unfortunate.' " Ibid., quoting SEC v. National Securities, Inc., 393 U.S. 453, 468 (1969). In savings clauses included in the 1933 and 1934 Acts, Congress rejected the notion that the express remedies of the securities laws would preempt all other rights of action.

* * *

A cumulative construction of the securities laws also furthers their broad remedial purposes.[11]

4. *Persons.* The 1975 amendment to the 1934 Act's definition of "person" in § 3(a)(9) to include governments, appeared to resolve that Rule 10b–5 could be used in litigation against municipalities and other governments.[12] Section 3(a)(9), however, does not resolve whether the 11th Amendment may bar such lawsuits.[13]

5. *Violations of the Rules of the Stock Exchanges, FINRA, and Implied Causes of Action.* Under §§ 6 and 15A of the 1934 Act, the stock exchanges and FINRA must adopt rules that, among other things, "are designed to prevent fraudulent and manipulative acts and practices, to promote just and equitable principles of trade, * * * and, in general, to protect investors and the public interest." Section 19(g) requires the SROs to enforce their own rules against their members and persons associated with those members. Section 21(d) authorizes the Commission to bring an injunctive action to prevent a violation of the rules of the exchanges and FINRA, as well as the provisions of the statute and the Commission's own rules. Section 27 of the 1934 Act, confers exclusive jurisdiction on the federal courts of appeal to enforce any liability or duty created by the 1934 Act. Section 27 refers only to such liabilities or duties created "by this title [i.e., the act itself] or the rules and regulations thereunder," and makes no mention of rules of SROs as do the other sections mentioned above.

Under this statutory scheme, is there any basis for implying a cause of action for a violation of one of the rules of the self-regulatory organizations? Even if the statute and the rules of the SROs create a cause of action, would the federal courts have any jurisdiction to entertain it in view of the language in § 27?

In Colonial Realty Corp. v. Bache & Co.,[14] the court held that there was no cause of action for a violation of the requirement under the rules of the NYSE and the NASD (now FINRA) that their members observe "just and equitable principles of trade." Judge Friendly refused, however, to say that there might never be an implied cause of action for violating SRO rules. He stated:

---

[11] 459 U.S. 375, 380–81 (1983).

[12] See, e.g., CitiSource, Inc. Sec. Litig., 694 F.Supp. 1069 (S.D.N.Y. 1988).

[13] Cf. Finkielstain v. Seidel, 857 F.2d 893 (2d Cir. 1988) (holding that it would not dismiss an action against the Maryland Deposit Insurance Corporation as barred by the 11th Amendment); Durning v. Citibank, N.A., 950 F.2d 1419 (9th Cir. 1991) (11th Amendment did not bar an action against Wyoming Community Development Authority when offering circulars expressly disclaimed that state was liable for the bonds); Bair v. Krug, 853 F.2d 672 (9th Cir. 1988) (11th Amendment barred federal securities law claims against state officials with regulatory oversight of state chartered thrift company); Mercer v. Jaffe, Snider, Raitt & Heuer, P.C., 730 F.Supp. 74, 78 (W.D. Mich. 1990), aff'd without op., 933 F.2d 1008 (6th Cir. 1991) (11th Amendment barred securities claims against State of Michigan).

[14] 358 F.2d 178 (2d Cir. 1966), cert. denied, 385 U.S. 817 (1966).

What emerges is that whether the courts are to imply federal civil liability for violation of exchange or dealer association rules by a member cannot be determined on the simplistic all-or-nothing basis urged by the two parties; rather, the court must look to the nature of the particular rule and its place in the regulatory scheme, with the party urging the implication of a federal liability carrying a considerably heavier burden of persuasion than when the violation is of the statute or an SEC regulation. The case for implication would be strongest when the rule imposes an explicit duty unknown to the common law.[15]

Similarly, in Buttrey v. Merrill Lynch, Pierce, Fenner & Smith, Inc.[16] the Seventh Circuit upheld a cause of action against a broker-dealer for violating Rule 405 of the New York Stock Exchange—the so-called "know your customer" rule.

Subsequently the pendulum swung the other way. In 1980, the Ninth Circuit in Jablon v. Dean Witter & Co.[17] held that under the *Redington* and *Transamerica* cases there could be no implication of a private right of action for a violation of any of the rules of the SROs, and indicated that its opinion in the *Buttrey* case had been overruled by those decisions of the Supreme Court. Virtually every subsequent appellate decision has agreed that there is no implied cause of action under the federal securities laws for violation of an SRO rule.[18]

This Chapter also provides a brief overview of Rule 14a–9, which allows for litigation over fraudulent proxy materials.

Recall that shareholder voting occurs in two key circumstances: when management is conducting a proxy process for the election of the board of directors and when shareholders are soliciting proxies on their own, for example, to attempt to take over the company. Generally, in a large publicly held corporation, individual shareholders are viewed as passive and relatively small owners. They tend to go along with management on many issues and, if dissatisfied, to sell their shares and invest elsewhere. For someone who owns a small number of shares, the cost of being involved exceeds the gains. Thus, in economic terms, when these shareholders "fail" to participate, it is perceived to be rational. For

---

[15] Id. at 182.

[16] 410 F.2d 135 (7th Cir. 1969), cert. denied, 396 U.S. 838 (1969).

[17] 614 F.2d 677 (9th Cir. 1980).

[18] See, e.g., Spicer v. Chicago Bd. of Options Exch., Inc., 977 F.2d 255 (7th Cir. 1992) (§ 6(b) does not create private cause of action for investors who allege that marketmakers violated Chicago Board Options Exchange Rules); VeriFone Sec. Litig., 11 F.3d 865, 870 (9th Cir. 1993) ("It is well established that violation of an exchange rule will not support a private claim"); Feins v. American Stock Exch., Inc., 81 F.3d 1215 (2d Cir. 1996) (no private cause of action for monetary damages resulting from denial of application of membership in SRO); Desiderio v. NASD, Inc., 191 F.3d 198, 208 (2d Cir. 1999) (there is no private right of action available under the Securities Exchange Act to redress denials of membership in an exchange or to challenge an exchange's failure to follow its own rules). But see O'Connor v. R.F. Lafferty & Co., Inc., 965 F.2d 893, 897 (10th Cir. 1992) (holding that unsuitability doctrine premised on NYSE and NASD rules is recognized as a violation of Rule 10b–5 and analyzed as either an omission case or a fraudulent practices case).

smaller shareholders, exiting the firm may be a more efficient form of discipline than trying to exercise voice in how the firm is governed.[19] For larger or more well-informed shareholders, however, the benefits of exercising their voice may exceed the costs. For example, institutional investors and hedge-fund owners, who own shares in larger blocks and do not suffer from the same collective action problems as individual shareholders, have been shifting the dynamic and engaging in various contests with the board of directors.

Federal proxy regulation controls much of this process. As with other areas of the securities laws, proxy regulation is disclosure-based. Section 14 of the Securities Exchange Act provides the SEC with the authority to regulate the proxy process. The term "proxy" has several different meanings, including: the right to vote for another, the voter who has the right to vote for another, and the document that controls that relationship. Thus, when a corporation solicits proxies from its shareholders, it is collecting the voting cards to cast the actual ballots. In effect, it is a form of absentee voting, with, in most cases, the corporation controlling the information the shareholders receive. Given the importance of the voting rights at stake, the SEC has interpreted its mandate very broadly, designing detailed rules for the proxy process.

At the end of this Chapter, § 18 is discussed briefly. It is an infrequently used provision of the Securities Exchange Act.

2. Rule 10b–5: Fraud in Connection with a Purchase or Sale of a Security

A. The Requirement That There Be Fraud

(1) Misstatements and Omissions

Santa Fe Industries, Inc. v. Green

Supreme Court of the United States, 1977.
430 U.S. 462, 97 S.Ct. 1292, 51 L.Ed.2d 480.

■ Mr. Justice White delivered the opinion of the Court.

The issue in this case involves the reach and coverage of § 10(b) of the Securities Exchange Act of 1934 and Rule 10b–5 thereunder in the context of a Delaware short-form merger transaction used by the majority stockholder of a corporation to eliminate the minority interest.

I

In 1936, petitioner Santa Fe Industries, Inc. ("Santa Fe"), acquired control of 60% of the stock of Kirby Lumber Corporation ("Kirby"), a Delaware corporation. Through a series of purchases over the succeeding years, Santa Fe increased its control of Kirby's stock to 95%; the purchase

---

[19] Albert O. Hirschman, Exit, Voice, and Loyalty (1970).

prices during the period 1968–1973 ranged from $65 to $92.50 per share. In 1974, wishing to acquire 100% ownership of Kirby, Santa Fe availed itself of § 253 of the Delaware Corporation Law, known as the "short-form merger" statute. Section 253 permits a parent corporation owning at least 90% of the stock of a subsidiary to merge with that subsidiary, upon approval by the parent's board of directors, and to make payment in cash for the shares of the minority stockholders. The statute does not require the consent of, or advance notice to, the minority stockholders. However, notice of the merger must be given within 10 days after its effective date, and any stockholder who is dissatisfied with the terms of the merger may petition the Delaware Court of Chancery for a decree ordering the surviving corporation to pay him the fair value of his shares, as determined by a court-appointed appraiser subject to review by the court. Del. Gen. Corp. Law §§ 253, 262.

Santa Fe obtained independent appraisals of the physical assets of Kirby—land, timber, buildings, and machinery—and of Kirby's oil, gas, and mineral interests. These appraisals, together with other financial information, were submitted to Morgan Stanley & Company ("Morgan Stanley"), an investment banking firm retained to appraise the fair market value of Kirby stock. Kirby's physical assets were appraised at $320 million (amounting to $640 for each of the 500,000 shares); Kirby's stock was valued by Morgan Stanley at $125 per share. Under the terms of the merger, minority stockholders were offered $150 per share.

The provisions of the short-form merger statute were fully complied with. The minority stockholders of Kirby were notified the day after the merger became effective and were advised of their right to obtain an appraisal in Delaware court if dissatisfied with the offer of $150 per share. They also received an information statement containing, in addition to the relevant financial data about Kirby, the appraisals of the value of Kirby's assets and the Morgan Stanley appraisal concluding that the fair market value of the stock was $125 per share.

Respondents, minority stockholders of Kirby, objected to the terms of the merger, but did not pursue their appraisal remedy in the Delaware Court of Chancery. Instead, they brought this action in federal court on behalf of the corporation and other minority stockholders, seeking to set aside the merger or to recover what they claimed to be the fair value of their shares. The amended complaint asserted that, based on the fair market value of Kirby's physical assets as revealed by the appraisal included in the information statement sent to minority shareholders, Kirby's stock was worth at least $772 per share. The complaint alleged further that the merger took place without prior notice to minority stockholders; that the purpose of the merger was to appropriate the difference between the "conceded pro rata value of the physical assets" and the offer of $150 per share—to "freez[e] out the minority stockholders at a wholly inadequate price," and that Santa Fe, knowing the appraised value of the physical assets, obtained a "fraudulent appraisal" of the stock from Morgan Stanley and offered $25 above that appraisal "in order to lull the minority stockholders into erroneously believing that [Santa Fe was] generous." This course of conduct was alleged to be "a violation of Rule 10b–5 because defendants employed a 'device, scheme, or artifice to defraud' and engaged in an 'act, practice or course of business which operates or would operate as a fraud or deceit upon any person, in connection with the purchase or sale of any security.'" Morgan Stanley assertedly participated in the fraud as an accessory by submitting its appraisal of $125 per share although knowing the appraised value of the physical assets.

* * *

The language of § 10(b) gives no indication that Congress meant to prohibit any conduct not involving manipulation or deception. Nor have we been cited to any evidence in the legislative history that would support a departure from the language of the statute. "When a statute speaks so specifically in terms of manipulation and deception, . . . and when its history reflects no more expansive intent, we are quite unwilling to extend the scope of the statute. . . ." Thus the claim of fraud and fiduciary breach in this complaint states a cause of action under any part of Rule 10b–5 only if the conduct alleged can be fairly viewed as "manipulative or deceptive" within the meaning of the statute.

III

It is our judgment that the transaction, if carried out as alleged in the complaint, was neither deceptive nor manipulative and therefore did not violate either § 10(b) of the Act or Rule 10b–5.

As we have indicated, the case comes to us on the premise that the complaint failed to allege a material misrepresentation or material failure to disclose. The finding of the District Court, undisturbed by the Court of Appeals, was that there was no "omission" or "misstatement" in the information statement accompanying the notice of merger. On the basis of the information provided, minority shareholders could either accept the price offered or reject it and seek an appraisal in the Delaware Court of Chancery. Their choice was fairly presented, and they were furnished with all relevant information on which to base their decision.[14]

---

[14] In addition to their principal argument that the complaint alleges a fraud under clauses (a) and (c) of Rule 10b–5, respondents also argue that the complaint alleges nondisclosure and misrepresentation in violation of clause (b) of the Rule. Their major contention in this respect is that the majority stockholder's failure to give the minority advance notice of the merger was a material nondisclosure, even though the Delaware short-form merger statute does not require such notice. Brief for Respondents, at 27. But respondents do not indicate how they might have acted differently had they had prior notice of the merger. Indeed, they accept the conclusion of both courts below that under Delaware law they could not have enjoined the merger because an appraisal proceeding is their sole remedy in the Delaware courts for any alleged unfairness in the terms of the merger. Thus, the failure to give advance notice was not a material nondisclosure within the meaning of the statute or the Rule. Cf. TSC Industries, Inc. v. Northway, Inc., 426 U.S. 438 (1976).

We therefore find inapposite the cases relied upon by respondents and the court below, in which the breaches of fiduciary duty held violative of Rule 10b–5 included some element of deception.[15] Those cases forcefully reflect the principle that "[s]ection 10(b) must be read flexibly, not technically and restrictively" and that the statute provides a cause of action for any plaintiff who "suffer[s] an injury as a result of deceptive practices touching its sale [or purchase] of securities. . . ." Superintendent of Insurance v. Bankers Life & Casualty Co., 404 U.S. 6, 12–13 (1971). But the cases do not support the proposition, adopted by the Court of Appeals below and urged by respondents here, that a breach of fiduciary duty by majority stockholders, without any deception, misrepresentation, or nondisclosure, violates the statute and the Rule.

It is also readily apparent that the conduct alleged in the complaint was not "manipulative" within the meaning of the statute. "Manipulation" is "virtually a term of art when used in connection with securities markets." Ernst & Ernst, 425 U.S., at 199. The term refers generally to practices, such as wash sales, matched orders, or rigged prices, that are intended to mislead investors by artificially affecting market activity. See, e.g., § 9 of the 1934 Act (prohibiting specific manipulative practices); Ernst & Ernst, supra; Piper v. Chris-Craft Industries, Inc., 430 U.S., at 43 (Rule 10b–6, also promulgated under

---

[15] The decisions of this Court relied upon by respondents all involved deceptive conduct as part of the Rule 10b–5 violation alleged. Affiliated Ute Citizens v. United States, 406 U.S. 128 (1972) (misstatements of material fact used by bank employees in position of market maker to acquire stock at less than fair value); Superintendent of Insurance v. Bankers Life & Cas. Co., 404 U.S. 6, 9 (1971) ("seller [of bonds] was duped into believing that it, the seller, would receive the proceeds"). Cf. SEC v. Capital Gains Research Bureau, 375 U.S. 180 (1963) (injunction under Investment Advisers Act of 1940 to compel registered investment adviser to disclose to his clients his own financial interest in his recommendations).

We have been cited to a large number of cases in the Courts of Appeals, all of which involved an element of deception as part of the fiduciary misconduct held to violate Rule 10b–5. E.g., Schoenbaum v. Firstbrook, 405 F.2d 215, 220 (C.A.2 1968) (en banc), cert. denied, 395 U.S. 906 (1969) (majority stockholder and board of directors "were guilty of deceiving" the minority stockholders); Drachman v. Harvey, 453 F.2d 722, 733, 736, 737 (C.A.2 1971) (en banc) (Rule 10b–5 violation alleged on facts found "indistinguishable" from Superintendent of Insurance v. Bankers Life & Cas. Co.); Schlick v. Penn-Dixie Cement Corp., 507 F.2d 374 (C.A.2 1974), cert. denied, 421 U.S. 976 (1975) (scheme of market manipulation and merger on unfair terms, one aspect of which was misrepresentation); Pappas v. Moss, 393 F.2d 865, 869 (C.A.3 1968) ("if a 'deception' is required in the present context [of § 10(b) and Rule 10b–5], it is fairly found by viewing this fraud as though the 'independent' stockholders were standing in the place of the defrauded corporate entity," where the board of directors passed a resolution containing at least two material misrepresentations and authorizing the sale of corporate stock to the directors at a price below fair market value); Shell v. Hensley, 430 F.2d 819, 825 (C.A.5 1970) (derivative suit alleging that corporate officers used misleading proxy materials and other reports to deceive shareholders regarding a bogus employment contract intended to conceal improper payments to the corporation president and regarding purchases by the corporation of certain securities at excessive prices); Rekant v. Desser, 425 F.2d 872, 882 (C.A.5 1970) (as part of scheme to cause corporation to issue Treasury shares and a promissory note for grossly inadequate consideration, corporate officers deceived shareholders by making affirmative misrepresentations in the corporation's annual report and by failing to file any such report the next year). See Recent Cases, 89 Harv. L. Rev. 1917, 1926 (1976) (stating that no appellate decision before that of the Court of Appeals in this case and in Marshel v. AFW Fabric Corp., 533 F.2d 1277 (CA2), vacated and remanded for a determination of mootness, 429 U.S. 881 (1976), "had permitted a 10b–5 claim without some element of misrepresentation or nondisclosure") (footnote omitted).

§ 10(b), is "an antimanipulative provision designed to protect the orderliness of the securities market during distributions of stock" and "to prevent stimulative trading by an issuer in its own securities in order to create an unnatural and unwarranted appearance of market activity"); 2 A. Bromberg, Securities Law: Fraud § 7.3 (1975); 3 L. Loss, Securities Regulation 1541–70 (2d ed. 1961); 6 id., at 3755–3763 (2d ed. Supp.1969). Section 10(b)'s general prohibition of practices deemed by the SEC to be "manipulative"—in this technical sense of artificially affecting market activity in order to mislead investors—is fully consistent with the fundamental purpose of the 1934 Act "to substitute a philosophy of full disclosure for the philosophy of *caveat emptor*...." Affiliated Ute Citizens v. United States, 406 U.S. 128, 151 (1972), quoting SEC v. Capital Gains Research Bureau, 375 U.S. 180, 186 (1963). Indeed, nondisclosure is usually essential to the success of a manipulative scheme. No doubt Congress meant to prohibit the full range of ingenious devices that might be used to manipulate securities prices. But we do not think it would have chosen this "term of art" if it had meant to bring within the scope of § 10(b) instances of corporate mismanagement such as this, in which the essence of the complaint is that shareholders were treated unfairly by a fiduciary.

IV

The language of the statute is, we think, "sufficiently clear in its context" to be dispositive here, Ernst & Ernst, 425 U.S., at 201; but even if it were not, there are additional considerations that weigh heavily against permitting a cause of action under Rule 10b–5 for the breach of corporate fiduciary duty alleged in this complaint. Congress did not expressly provide a private cause of action for violations of § 10(b). Although we have recognized an implied cause of action under that section in some circumstances, we have also recognized that a private cause of action under the anti-fraud provisions of the Securities Exchange Act should not be implied where it is "unnecessary to ensure the fulfillment of Congress' purposes" in adopting the Act. Piper v. Chris-Craft Industries, 430 U.S. at 41. As we noted earlier, the Court repeatedly has described the "fundamental purpose" of the Act as implementing a "philosophy of full disclosure"; once full and fair disclosure has occurred, the fairness of the terms of the transaction is at most a tangential concern of the statute. As in Cort v. Ash, 422 U.S. 66, 78, 80 (1975), we are reluctant to recognize a cause of action here to serve what is "at best a subsidiary purpose" of the federal legislation.

A second factor in determining whether Congress intended to create a federal cause of action in these circumstances is "whether 'the cause of action [is] one traditionally relegated to state law....'" Piper v. Chris-Craft Industries, Inc., 430 U.S., at 949, quoting Cort v. Ash, 422 U.S., at 78. The Delaware Legislature has supplied minority shareholders with a cause of action in the Delaware Court of Chancery to recover the fair value of shares allegedly undervalued in a short-form merger. Of course, the existence of a particular state law remedy is not dispositive of the question whether Congress meant to provide a similar federal remedy, but as in *Piper* and *Cort*, we conclude that "it is entirely appropriate in this instance to relegate respondent and others in his situation to whatever remedy is created by state law."

The reasoning behind a holding that the complaint in this case alleged fraud under Rule 10b–5 could not be easily contained. It is difficult to imagine how a court could distinguish, for purposes of Rule 10b–5 fraud, between a majority stockholder's use of a short-form merger to eliminate the minority at an unfair price and the use of some other device, such as a long-form merger, tender offer, or liquidation, to achieve the same result; or indeed how a court could distinguish the alleged abuses in these going private transactions from other types of fiduciary self-dealing involving transactions in securities. The result would be to bring within the Rule a wide variety of corporate conduct traditionally left to state regulation. In addition to posing a "danger of vexatious litigation which could result from a widely expanded class of plaintiffs under Rule 10b–5," Blue Chip Stamps v. Manor Drug Stores, 421 U.S. 723, 740 (1975), this extension of the federal securities laws would overlap and quite possibly interfere with state corporate law. Federal courts applying a "federal fiduciary principle" under Rule 10b–5 could be expected to depart from state fiduciary standards at least to the extent necessary to ensure uniformity within the federal system.[16] Absent a clear indication of congressional intent, we are reluctant to federalize the substantial portion of the law of corporations that deals with transactions in securities, particularly where established state policies of corporate regulation would be overridden. As the Court stated in Cort v. Ash: "Corporations are creatures of state law, and investors commit their funds to corporate directors on the understanding that, except where federal law *expressly* requires certain responsibilities of directors with respect to stockholders, state law will govern the internal affairs of the corporation."

We thus adhere to the position that "Congress by § 10(b) did not seek to regulate transactions which constitute no more than internal corporate mismanagement." Superintendent of Insurance v. Bankers Life & Cas. Co., 404 U.S., at 12. There may well be a need for uniform federal fiduciary standards to govern mergers such as that challenged in

---

[16] For example, some States apparently require a "valid corporate purpose" for the elimination of the minority interest through a short-form merger, whereas other States do not. Compare Bryan v. Brock & Blevins Co., 490 F.2d 563 (C.A.5), cert. denied, 419 U.S. 844 (1974) (merger arranged by controlling stockholder for no business purpose except to eliminate 15% minority stockholder violated Georgia short-form merger statute) with Stauffer v. Standard Brands, Inc., 41 Del.Ch. 7 (Sup. Ct. 1962) (Delaware short-form merger statute allows majority stockholder to eliminate the minority interest without any corporate purpose and subject only to an appraisal remedy). Thus to the extent that Rule 10b–5 is interpreted to require a valid corporate purpose for elimination of minority shareholders as well as a fair price for their shares, it would impose a stricter standard of fiduciary duty than that required by the law of some States.

this complaint. But those standards should not be supplied by judicial extension of § 10(b) and Rule 10b–5 to "cover the corporate universe."

The judgment of the Court of Appeals is reversed, and the case is remanded for further proceedings consistent with this opinion.

* * *

NOTES ON RULE 10b–5 AS A REMEDY FOR MISMANAGEMENT

1. *State Law Fiduciary Breaches.* Santa Fe v. Green makes clear that claims based solely on state law fiduciary duty breaches are not actionable under Rule 10b–5 absent material misrepresentations or omissions. If the claim involves misleading disclosures or omissions about, for example, a state law remedy, Rule 10b–5 may, however, provide a remedy. Consider Goldberg v. Meridor, a Second Circuit case[20] that addressed a derivative action on behalf of UGO charging that its parent, Maritimecor, had caused it to issue shares to the parent for all of its assets and liabilities in an unfair transaction and on the basis of nondisclosure or misleading disclosure of material facts that were known to all the directors. Judge Friendly's majority opinion stated that[21]:

> [T]here is deception of the corporation (in effect, of its minority shareholders) when the corporation is influenced by its controlling shareholder to engage in a transaction adverse to the corporation's interests (in effect, the minority shareholders' interests) and *there is nondisclosure or misleading disclosures as to the material facts of the transaction* [italics supplied] * * *. [W]e do not read *Green* as ruling that no action lies under Rule 10b–5 when a controlling corporation causes a partly owned subsidiary to sell its securities to the parent in a fraudulent transaction and fails to make a disclosure or, as can be alleged here, makes a misleading disclosure. * * *

> Defendants contend that even if all this is true, the failure to make a public disclosure or even the making of a misleading disclosure would have no effect, since no action by stockholders to approve the UGO-Maritimecor transaction was required.

* * *

> When, as in a derivative action, the deception is alleged to have been practiced on the corporation, even though all the directors were parties to it, the test [of materiality] must be whether the facts that were not disclosed or were misleadingly disclosed to the shareholders "would have assumed actual significance in the deliberations" of reasonable and disinterested directors or

---

[20] 567 F.2d 209 (2d Cir. 1977), cert. denied, 434 U.S. 1069 (1978).
[21] Id. at 217–20.

created "a substantial likelihood" that such directors would have considered the "total mix" of information available to have been "significantly altered."

* * *

Beyond this Goldberg and other minority shareholders would not have been without remedy if the alleged facts had been disclosed.

* * *

The availability of injunctive relief if the defendants had not lulled the minority stockholders of UGO into security by a deceptive disclosure, as they allegedly did, is in sharp contrast to *Green*, where the disclosure following the merger transaction was full and fair, and, as to the pre-merger period, respondents accepted "the conclusion of both courts below that under Delaware law they could not have enjoined the merger because an appraisal proceeding is their sole remedy in the Delaware courts for any alleged unfairness in the terms of the merger," * * *.[22]

2. *Oral Misstatements.* Violations can occur with written or oral misstatements. But *Santa Fe* requires deception for Rule 10b–5 violations. In Wharf (Holdings) Limited v. United International Holdings, Inc.,[23] the Supreme Court held that the deception element can be satisfied when a promisor secretly intends not to honor a promise at the time of making the promise. The facts in *Wharf (Holdings)* were as follows:

[Eds. United International Holdings, Inc., a Colorado-based company, sued The Wharf (Holdings) Limited, a Hong Kong firm, arguing that Wharf had sold it an option to buy 10% of the stock of a new Hong Kong cable television system, and at the time of the sale Wharf secretly intended not to permit United to exercise the option. A jury found in United's favor.]

The relevant facts, viewed in the light most favorable to the verdict winner, United, are as follows. In 1991, the Hong Kong government announced that it would accept bids for the award of an exclusive license to operate a cable system in Hong Kong. Wharf decided to prepare a bid. Wharf's chairman, Peter Woo, instructed one of its managing directors, Stephen Ng, to find a business partner with cable system experience. Ng found United. And United sent several employees to Hong Kong to

---

[22] Cf. Virginia Bankshares, Inc. v. Sandberg, 501 U.S. 1083 (1991) (causation could not be established when there was no link between alleged misrepresentations to minority shareholder and any state remedy).

[23] 532 U.S. 588 (2001).

help prepare Wharf's application, negotiate contracts, design the system, and arrange financing.

United asked to be paid for its services with a right to invest in the cable system if Wharf should obtain the license. During August and September 1992, while United's employees were at work helping Wharf, Wharf and United negotiated about the details of that payment. Wharf prepared a draft letter of intent that contemplated giving United the right to become a co-investor, owning 10% of the system. But the parties did not sign the letter of intent. And in September, when Wharf submitted its bid, it told the Hong Kong authorities that Wharf would be the system's initial sole owner, although Wharf would also "consider" allowing United to become an investor.

In early October 1992, Ng met with a United representative, who told Ng that United would continue to help only if Wharf gave United an enforceable right to invest. Ng then orally granted United an option with the following terms: (1) United had the right to buy 10% of the future system's stock; (2) the price of exercising the option would be 10% of the system's capital requirements minus the value of United's previous services (including expenses); (3) United could exercise the option only if it showed that it could fund its 10% share of the capital required for at least the first 18 months; and (4) the option would expire if not exercised within six months of the date that Wharf received the license. The parties continued to negotiate about how to write documents that would embody these terms, but they never reduced the agreement to writing.

In May 1993, Hong Kong awarded the cable franchise to Wharf. United raised $66 million designed to help finance its 10% share. In July or August 1993, United told Wharf that it was ready to exercise its option. But Wharf refused to permit United to buy any of the system's stock. Contemporaneous internal Wharf documents suggested that Wharf had never intended to carry out its promise. For example, a few weeks before the key October 1992 meeting, Ng had prepared a memorandum stating that United wanted a right to invest that it could exercise if it was able to raise the necessary capital. A handwritten note by Wharf's Chairman Woo replied, "No, no, no, we don't accept that." In September 1993, after meeting with the Wharf board to discuss United's investment in the cable system, Ng wrote to another Wharf executive, "How do we get out?" In December 1993, after United had filed documents with the Securities Exchange Commission representing that United was negotiating the acquisition of a 10% interest in the cable system, an internal Wharf memo stated that "[O]ur next move should be to claim that our directors got quite *upset* over these representations. . . . Publicly, we *do not* acknowledge [United's] opportunity" to acquire the 10% interest. (emphasis in original). In the margin of a December 1993 letter from United discussing its expectation of investing in the cable system, Ng wrote, "Be careful, must deflect this! How?" Other Wharf documents referred to the need to "back ped[al]," and "stall."[24]

3. *Plaintiff's Due Diligence.* In face-to-face transactions, the defendant can also mount a defense if he or she can show that the plaintiff lacked due diligence and the plaintiff's scienter was the same as that applied to defendants. Due diligence, of course, suggests a negligence standard, but the *Ernst & Ernst* culpability standard requires intentional or reckless misconduct.[25]

4. *Nonreliance/Integration Clauses.* Cases have explored nonreliance clauses in stock purchase agreements that purport to preclude damages under the federal securities laws for oral statements prior to the date of the agreement.[26] In Rissman v. Rissman,[27] Judge Easterbrook concluded:

> [W]e now follow those cases by holding that a written anti-reliance clause precludes any claim of deceit by prior representations. The principle is functionally the same as a doctrine long accepted in this circuit: that a person who has received written disclosure of the truth may not claim to rely on contrary oral falsehoods. A non-reliance clause is not identical to a truthful disclosure, but it has a similar function: it ensures that both the transaction and any subsequent litigation proceed on the basis of the parties' writings, which are less subject to the vagaries of memory and the risks of fabrication.
>
> Memory plays tricks. Acting in the best of faith, people may "remember" things that never occurred but now serve their interests. Or they may remember events with a change of emphasis or nuance that makes a substantial difference to meaning. Express or implied qualifications may be lost in the folds of time. A statement such as "I won't sell at current prices" may be recalled years later as "I won't sell." Prudent people protect themselves against the limitations of memory (and the temptation to shade the truth) by limiting their dealings to those memorialized in writing, and promoting the primacy of

---

[24] Id. at 590–92.

[25] Cf. also Bateman Eichler, Hill Richards, Inc. v. Berner, 472 U.S. 299 (1985) (the defendant is also entitled to the in pari delicto defense but only when the plaintiff bears at least substantially equal responsibility for the violations for which he or she seeks redress). We will examine in pari delicto later.

[26] See, e.g., Jackvony v. RIHT Fin. Corp., 873 F.2d 411 (1st Cir. 1989); One-O-One Enter., Inc. v. Caruso, 848 F.2d 1283 (D.C. Cir. 1988).

[27] 213 F.3d 381 (7th Cir. 2000).

the written word is a principal function of the federal securities laws.

Failure to enforce agreements such as the one between Arnold and Randall could not make sellers of securities better off in the long run. Faced with an unavoidable risk of claims based on oral statements, persons transacting in securities would reduce the price they pay, setting aside the difference as a reserve for risk. If, as Arnold says, Randall was willing to pay $17 million and not a penny more, then a legal rule entitling Arnold to an extra $95 million if Tiger should be sold in the future would have scotched the deal (the option value of the deferred payment exceeds 1 cent), leaving Arnold with no cash and the full risk of the venture. Arnold can't have both $17 million with certainty and a continuing right to 1/3 of any premium Randall negotiates for the firm, while bearing no risk from the fickle toy business; that would make him better off than if he had held his shares throughout.

* * *

Arnold calls the no-reliance clauses "boilerplate," and they were; transactions lawyers have language of this sort stored up for reuse. But the fact that language has been used before does not make it less binding when used again. Phrases become boilerplate when many parties find that the language serves their ends. That's a reason to enforce the promises, not to disregard them. * * * Judges need not speculate about the reason a clause appears or is omitted, however; what matters when litigation breaks out is what the parties actually signed.[28]

(2) THE DUTY TO UPDATE AND THE DUTY TO CORRECT

As discussed above, the U.S. securities regulation regime does not require continuous disclosure of material facts by issuers. Rather issuers have to make only periodic disclosures, except in a relatively narrow group of circumstances. Nevertheless, there are special rules regarding stale information.

Clause (2) of Rule 10b–5 prohibits the "[omission] to state a material fact necessary in order to make the statement made, in the light of the circumstances under which they were made, not misleading." The Commission has stated that:

> depending on the circumstances, there is a duty to correct statements made in any filing . . . if the statements either have

---

[28] Id. at 384–85. Judge Rover concurred in this result but wrote separately to urge that in fact the two cases that the majority relies upon, Jackvony v. RIHT Fin. Corp., 873 F.2d 411 (1st Cir. 1989) and One-O-One Enter. v. Caruso, 848 F.2d 1283 (D.C. Cir. 1988), were conventional justifiable reliance cases and did not base their conclusions on written antireliance clauses but on a broader review of surrounding circumstances. Id. at 384–89.

become inaccurate by virtue of subsequent events, or are later discovered to have been false and misleading from the outset, and the issuer knows or should know that persons are continuing to rely on all or any material portion of the statements.[29]

Courts have addressed both duties to update projections and to correct issuer statements about historical facts, as well as duties to correct statements made by others that can be attributed to the issuer.

In re Time Warner Inc. Securities Litigation
United States Court of Appeals, Second Circuit, 1993.
9 F.3d 259.

■ Before NEWMAN, CHIEF JUDGE, WINTER and MINER, CIRCUIT JUDGES.

■ JON O. NEWMAN, CHIEF JUDGE:

This appeal from the dismissal of a securities fraud complaint requires us to consider the recurring issue of whether stock fraud claims are sufficiently pleaded to warrant at least discovery and perhaps trial. Three separate issues are presented: (1) whether a corporation has a duty to update somewhat optimistic predictions about achieving a business plan when it appears that the plan might not be realized, (2) whether a corporation has a duty to disclose a specific alternative to an announced business plan when that alternative is under active consideration, and (3) whether a corporation is responsible for statements in newspapers and security analyst reports that are attributed to unnamed corporate personnel.

* * *

Plaintiffs' complaint alleged that defendant Time Warner, Inc. and four of its officers had misled the investing public by statements and omissions made in the course of Time Warner's efforts to reduce its debt. The District Court dismissed the complaint with prejudice for failure to adequately plead material misrepresentations or omissions attributable to the defendants and for failure to adequately plead scienter. We hold that the complaint's allegations of scienter and certain of its allegations concerning omissions are adequate to survive a motion to dismiss, and we accordingly reverse the order of dismissal and remand.

Background

On June 7, 1989, Time, Inc. received a surprise tender offer for its stock from Paramount Communications. Paramount's initial offer was $175 per share, in cash, and was eventually increased to $200 per share.

---

[29] Sec. Act Rel. 6084, 17 SEC Dock. 1048, 1054 (1979); see also Sec. Ex. Act Rel. 8995 (1970) (a company that has complied with the reporting requirements "still has an obligation to make full and prompt announcement of facts regarding the company's financial condition"); Sec. Act Rel. 5699, 9 SEC Dock. 472, 474 (1976) ("this responsibility may extend to situations where management knows its previously disclosed assessments no longer have a reasonable basis").

See Paramount Communications, Inc. v. Time Inc., 571 A.2d 1140, 1147–49 (Del. 1989). Time's directors declined to submit this offer to the shareholders and continued discussions that had begun somewhat earlier concerning a merger with Warner Communications, Inc. Eventually, Time and Warner agreed that Time would acquire all of Warner's outstanding stock for $70 per share, even though this acquisition would cause Time to incur debt of over $10 billion. Time shareholders and Paramount were unsuccessful in their effort to enjoin the Warner acquisition, which was completed in July 1989.

Thus, in 1989, Time Warner, Inc., the entity resulting from the merger, found itself saddled with over $10 billion in debt, an outcome that drew criticism from many shareholders. The company embarked on a highly publicized campaign to find international "strategic partners" who would infuse billions of dollars of capital into the company and who would help the company realize its dream of becoming a dominant worldwide entertainment conglomerate. Ultimately, Time Warner formed only two strategic partnerships, each on a much smaller scale than had been hoped for. Faced with a multi-billion dollar balloon payment on the debt, the company was forced to seek an alternative method of raising capital—a new stock offering that substantially diluted the rights of the existing shareholders. The company first proposed a variable price offering on June 6, 1991. This proposal was rejected by the SEC, but the SEC approved a second proposal announced on July 12, 1991. Announcement of the two offering proposals caused a substantial decline in the price of Time Warner stock. From June 5 to June 12, the share price fell from $117 to $94. By July 12, the price had fallen to $89.75.

* * *

Discussion

* * *

I. Existence of an actionable misrepresentation or omission

A. Anonymous statements to reporters and analysts

We first consider whether the District Court properly concluded that Rule 9(b) required dismissal of allegations of fraudulent statements when the complaint failed to identify the speaker. The complaint contains excerpts from a variety of newspaper stories and security analyst reports. Some of these accounts contain anonymous quotes or paraphrases of statements from alleged Time Warner insiders. Others merely report upon Time Warner's activities. In both cases, plaintiffs allege that some as yet unknown agents of Time Warner made misleading statements (or omitted to disclose material information) in discussions with the reporter or analyst. These reports and stories, excerpted in the complaint at ¶¶ 42, 44–47, 49, 54, 58–62, 65, 69, 72, generally confirm that negotiations concerning strategic alliances are ongoing and add little to the statements for which Time Warner is concededly responsible. But some of the statements implied in the reports and stories would bolster plaintiffs' case considerably.

* * *

Rule 9(b) requires that "[i]n all averments of fraud or mistake, the circumstances constituting fraud or malice shall be stated with particularity." Judge Lasker understood Rule 9(b) to require, at a minimum, that the plaintiff identify the speaker of the allegedly fraudulent statements. We believe that he was correct. Plaintiffs rely on several district court decisions that they claim apply a less strict rule for statements attributed to corporate "spokespersons," see In re AnnTaylor Stores Securities Litigation, 807 F.Supp. 990, 1004 (S.D.N.Y.1992); Cytryn v. Cook, 1990 WL 128233 (N.D.Cal. July 2, 1990), and for statements by newspapers and analysts allegedly caused by corporate employees, see Alfus v. Pyramid Technology Corp., 764 F.Supp. 598, 603 (N.D.Cal.1991); In re Columbia Securities Litigation, 747 F.Supp. 237, 245 (S.D.N.Y.1990). These cases are distinguishable on their facts, in that they involve official press releases. None of these cases sanctions the pleading of fraud through completely unattributed statements, even when the plaintiff alleges on information and belief that the unattributed statement was made by an agent of the defendant.

Just as 10b–5 litigation, however resolved, risks adverse consequences, as we have noted, a strict application of Rule 9(b) in the context of unattributed statements also risks unfortunate effects. A scheming corporation could inflate its stock price through fraudulent statements whispered to reporters or analysts. If the reporters or analysts refused to reveal their sources and if no one inside the corporation leaked to the stockholders or to regulators the identity of the speakers, the corporation would have perpetuated a fraud that could not be remedied by a private civil action under the federal securities laws. For several reasons, however, we have some confidence that this is not a sufficiently likely scenario to justify a rule that would permit a suit alleging unattributed statements to survive a motion to dismiss.

As an initial matter, the function of financial reporters and security analysts is to determine the truth about the affairs of publicly traded companies. Few reporters or analysts would knowingly abet a fraud, and many will detect and reveal a corporation's efforts to use them as a channel for fraudulent statements. Additionally, investors tend to discount information in newspaper articles and analyst reports when the author is unable to cite specific, attributable information from the company. Thus, the opportunity to manipulate stock prices through the planting of false stories is somewhat limited. Finally, the effect of a less strict construction of Rule 9(b) would be only to allow discovery on the issue of the linkage between the corporation and the newspaper stories or analyst reports. Sometimes, of course, plaintiff's counsel would be able to use discovery to determine the identity of the speaker, and would find that this speaker was a person for whom the corporation was responsible.

But far more often, we suspect, this would not be the case. Either the corporation is not responsible for the statements, in which case it has been unnecessarily burdened either by the expense of discovery or by a settlement extracted under threat of such discovery, or it is responsible, and having exhibited sufficient devotion to a fraudulent scheme so as to prevent attribution of statements in advance of discovery, it will often attempt and sometimes succeed in stonewalling discovery.

* * *

B. Attributed statements and corporate press releases

We next focus on those statements as to which there is no issue of attribution. While plaintiffs claim that these statements were misleading, in that they exaggerated the likelihood that strategic alliances would be made, plaintiffs primarily fault these statements for what they did not disclose. The nondisclosure is of two types: failure to disclose problems in the strategic alliance negotiations, and failure to disclose the active consideration of an alternative method of raising capital.

* * *

1. Affirmative misrepresentations. We agree with the District Court that none of the statements constitutes an *affirmative* misrepresentation. Most of the statements reflect merely that talks are ongoing, and that Time Warner hopes that the talks will be successful. There is no suggestion that the factual assertions contained in any of these statements were false when the statements were made. As to the expressions of opinion and the projections contained in the statements, while not beyond the reach of the securities laws, the complaint contains no allegations to support the inference that the defendants either did not have these favorable opinions on future prospects when they made the statements or that the favorable opinions were without a basis in fact.

2. Nondisclosure of problems in the strategic alliance negotiations. The allegations of nondisclosure are more serious. Plaintiffs' first theory of nondisclosure is that the defendants' statements hyping strategic alliances gave rise to a duty to disclose problems in the alliance negotiations as those problems developed. We agree that a duty to update opinions and projections may arise if the original opinions or projections have become misleading as the result of intervening events. See In re Gulf Oil/Cities Service Tender Offer Litigation, 725 F.Supp. 712, 745–49 (S.D.N.Y.1989) (material misstatements or omissions adequately set forth alleging that defendants had expressed a strong interest in consummating a merger and had not disclosed a later "change of heart"); In re Warner Communications Securities Litigation, 618 F.Supp. 735, 752 (S.D.N.Y.1985) (approving settlement), aff'd, 798 F.2d 35 (2d Cir. 1986). But, in this case, the attributed public statements lack the sort of definite positive projections that might require later correction. The statements suggest only the hope of any company, embarking on talks with multiple partners, that the talks would go well. No identified defendant stated that he thought deals would be struck by a certain date, or even that it was likely that deals would be struck at all. Cf. In re Apple Computer Securities Litigation, 886 F.2d 1109, 1118–19 (9th Cir. 1989) (Chairman of the Board stated that new computer product would be "phenomenally successful the first year out of the chute," etc.), cert. denied, 496 U.S. 943 (1990). These statements did not become materially misleading when the talks did not proceed well.[4]

3. Nondisclosure of alternative methods of raising capital. Still more serious is the allegation of a failure to disclose the simultaneous consideration of the rights offering as an alternative method of raising capital. As an initial matter, of course, a reasonable investor would probably have wanted to know of consideration of the rights offering. Though both the rights offering and strategic alliances would have brought capital into the corporation, the two acts would have directly opposite effects on the price of Time Warner stock. A successful strategic alliance, simultaneously opening new markets and reducing debt, would have improved the corporation's expected profit stream, and should have served to drive up the share price. An offering of new shares, in contrast, would dilute the ownership rights of existing shareholders, likely decrease dividends, and drive down the price of the stock.

But a corporation is not required to disclose a fact merely because a reasonable investor would very much like to know that fact. Rather, an omission is actionable under the securities laws only when the corporation is subject to a duty to disclose the omitted facts. As Time Warner pointedly reminds us, we have not only emphasized the importance of ascertaining a duty to disclose when omissions are at issue but have also drawn a distinction between the concepts of a duty to disclose and materiality. It appears, however, that the distinction has meaning only in certain contexts. For example, where the issue is whether an individual's relationship to information imposed upon him a duty to disclose, the inquiry as to his duty is quite distinct from the inquiry as to the information's materiality. See Dirks v. SEC, 463 U.S. 646 (1983). On the other hand, where the disclosure duty arises from the combination of a prior statement and a subsequent event, which, if not disclosed, renders the prior statement false or misleading, the inquiries as to duty and materiality coalesce. The undisclosed information is material if there is "a substantial likelihood that the disclosure of the omitted fact would have been viewed by the reasonable investor as having significantly altered the 'total mix' of information available." TSC Industries, Inc. v. Northway, Inc., 426 U.S. 438, 449 (1976). If a reasonable investor would so regard the omitted fact, it is difficult to

---

[4] Although the statements are generally open-ended, there is one sense in which they have a solid core. The statements represent as fact that serious talks with multiple parties were ongoing. If this factual assertion ceased to be true, defendants would have had an obligation to update their earlier statements. But the complaint does not allege that the talks ever stopped or ceased to be "serious," just that they eventually went poorly.

imagine a circumstance where the prior statement would not be rendered misleading in the absence of the disclosure. As *Glazer* makes clear, one circumstance creating a duty to disclose arises when disclosure is necessary to make prior statements not misleading.

We have previously considered whether disclosure of one business plan required disclosure of considered alternatives in Kronfeld v. Trans World Airlines, Inc., 832 F.2d 726 (2d Cir. 1987), cert. denied, 485 U.S. 1007 (1988). In *Kronfeld*, the defendant, TWA's parent corporation, failed to disclose in the prospectus for a new issue of TWA stock that it was contemplating termination of its relationship with TWA. Because the prospectus discussed "in some detail the relationship between TWA" and the parent, we held that a fact question was presented as to whether it was materially misleading not to disclose the possibility of termination. In effect, the alternative, if disclosed, would have suggested to investors that the various guarantees extended from the parent to TWA might be meaningless. In the pending case, the District Court understood the obligation to disclose alternate business plans to be limited to the context of mutually exclusive alternatives. It is true that *Kronfeld* involved such alternatives—the TWA parent could not both maintain and terminate its relations with TWA—and that this case does not. Time Warner potentially could have raised all its needed capital from either strategic alliances or a rights offering, or it could have raised some part of the necessary capital using each approach.

We believe, however, that a disclosure duty limited to mutually exclusive alternatives is too narrow. A duty to disclose arises whenever secret information renders prior public statements materially misleading, not merely when that information completely negates the public statements. Time Warner's public statements could have been understood by reasonable investors to mean that the company hoped to solve the *entire* debt problem through strategic alliances. Having publicly hyped strategic alliances, Time Warner may have come under a duty to disclose facts that would place the statements concerning strategic alliances in a materially different light.

It is important to appreciate the limits of our disagreement with the District Court. We do not hold that whenever a corporation speaks, it must disclose every piece of information in its possession that could affect the price of its stock. Rather, we hold that when a corporation is pursuing a specific business goal and announces that goal as well as an intended approach for reaching it, it may come under an obligation to disclose other approaches to reaching the goal when those approaches are under active and serious consideration. Whether consideration of the alternate approach constitutes material information, and whether nondisclosure of the alternate approach renders the original disclosure misleading, remain questions for the trier of fact, and may be resolved by summary judgment when there is no disputed issue of material fact. We conclude here only that the allegations in this complaint of nondisclosure of the rights offering are sufficient to survive a motion to dismiss.

* * *

In re Burlington Coat Factory Securities Litigation
United States Court of Appeals, Third Circuit, 1997.
114 F.3d 1410.

■ Before: GREENBERG, ALITO, and ROTH, CIRCUIT JUDGES.

■ ALITO, CIRCUIT JUDGE:

Burlington Coat Factory Warehouse Corporation ("BCF"), a Delaware corporation based in New Jersey, announced its fourth quarter and full fiscal year results for 1994 on September 20, 1994. The results were below the investment community's expectations, and BCF's common stock fell sharply, losing approximately 30% in one day. Within a day of the initial announcement, the first investor suit was filed. In the next few days, the company made additional explanatory disclosures, and the stock price fell even further. More investor suits were filed. The action at hand is the product of the consolidation of these suits.

* * *

The district court dismissed the case both for failure to state claims on which relief could be granted and for failure to plead those claims with adequate particularity.

* * *

BCF is one of the leading retailers of coats in the United States. Its specialty is selling brand name clothes at discount prices. By mid-1993, BCF was operating a total of 185 stores in 39 states. The stores ranged in size from 16,000 to 133,000 square feet and featured outerwear (coats, jackets, and raincoats) and complete lines of clothing for men, women, and children.

* * *

On September 20, 1994, BCF reported its year-end revenues and earnings for fiscal 1994. These results were below the market's expectations, with the earnings per share for fiscal 1994 being $1.12 as compared to the $1.37 that analysts had been predicting. On September 20 itself, the price of BCF stock fell almost 30%, from $23.25 to $15.75 per share. Between September 20 and September 23 both BCF and outside analysts attempted to explain the reasons for the worse-than-expected results. By the close of the market on September 23, 1994, the price of BCF stock had fallen to $13.63.

* * *

Duties to Update and Correct

Plaintiffs * * * assert that BCF had a duty to correct the November 1, 1993, expression of comfort with the analysts' projections. In particular, plaintiffs point to the refusal of BCF's CEO, Monroe Milstein, in an interview given to Reuters—reported on March 22, 1994—to comment on analysts' earnings projections for both the third quarter of 1994 and the full year. Plaintiffs assert that on March 22, 1994, and at other unspecified points in time after November 1, 1993, defendants had had a duty to correct the November 1 earnings projection. Although plaintiffs characterize their claim as a "duty to correct" claim, they appear to be asserting both a duty to correct and a duty to update.

The Seventh Circuit explained in Stransky v. Cummins Engine Co., Inc., 51 F.3d 1329 (7th Cir. 1995), that the duty to correct is analytically different from the duty to update, although litigants, as appears to be the case here, often fail to distinguish between the two.

* * *

(a) Duty to Correct

The *Stransky* court articulated the duty to correct as applying:

> when a company makes a *historical statement* that, at the time made, the company believed to be true, but as revealed by *subsequently discovered* information actually was not. The company then must correct the prior statement within a reasonable time.

51 F.3d at 1331–32 (emphasis added); see also Backman v. Polaroid Corp., 910 F.2d 10, 16–17 (1st Cir. 1990) (in banc) ("Obviously, if a disclosure is in fact *misleading when made*, and the speaker thereafter learns of this, there is a duty to correct it.") (emphasis added). We have no quarrel with the *Stransky* articulation, except to note that we think the duty to correct can also apply to a certain narrow set of forward-looking statements. We will attempt to illustrate the kinds of circumstances we have in mind with an example.

Imagine the following situation. A public company in Manhattan makes a forecast that appears to it to be reasonable at the time made. Subsequently, the company discovers that it misread a vital piece of data that went into its forecast. Perhaps a fax sent by the company's factory manager in some remote location was blurry and was reasonably misread by management in Manhattan as representing sales for the past quarter as 100,000 units as opposed 10,000 units. Manhattan management then makes an erroneous forecast based on the information it has at the time. A few weeks later, management receives the correct sales figures by mail. So long as the correction in the sales figures was material to the forecast that was disclosed earlier, we think there would likely be a duty on the part of the company to disclose either the corrected figures or a corrected forecast. In other words, there is an implicit representation in any forecast (or statement of historical fact) that *errors* of the type we have identified will be corrected. This duty derives from the implicit factual representation that a public company makes whenever it makes a forecast, i.e., that the forecast was reasonable at the time made. What is crucial to recognize is that the error, albeit an honest one, was one that had to do with information *available at the time the forecast was made* and that the error in the information was subsequently discovered.

Plaintiffs phrase their claim as based on a "duty to correct." * * * [A]s to the "duty to correct" claim, plaintiffs have failed to allege how and what the specific error or set of errors might have been that went into the November 1, 1993, forecast. Nor have the plaintiffs identified the specific times at which those errors were discovered, so as to allow correction and trigger defendants' alleged duty. Therefore, the "duty to correct" claim (to the extent one is being made) fails Rule 9(b)'s pleading standards. In any event, we think plaintiffs' claim is better characterized as a "duty to update" claim.

(b) Duty to Update

The duty to update, in contrast to the duty to correct, concerns statements that, although reasonable at the time made, become misleading when viewed in the context of subsequent events. See Greenfield v. Heublein, Inc., 742 F.2d 751, 758 (3d Cir. 1984). In *Greenfield*, we explained that updating might be required if a prior disclosure "[had] become materially misleading in light of subsequent events." However, although we have generally recognized that a duty to update might exist under certain circumstances, we have not clarified when such circumstances might exist. Specifically, we have not addressed the question whether a duty to update might exist for ordinary, run-of-the-mill forecasts, such as the earnings projection in this case.

At issue here is the statement of BCF's CAO on November 1, 1993, that he was comfortable with analyst projections of $1.20 to $1.30 as a mid-range for earnings per share in fiscal 1994. Plaintiffs' argument appears to be that, as BCF obtained information in the period subsequent to November 1, 1993, that would have produced a material change in the earnings projection for fiscal 1994, there was an ongoing duty to disclose this information. In essence then, the claim is that the disclosure of a single specific forecast produced a continuous duty to update the public with either forecasts or hard information that would in any way change a reasonable investor's perception of the originally forecasted range. We decline to hold that the disclosure of a single, ordinary earnings forecast can produce such an expansive set of disclosure obligations.

For a plaintiff to allege that a duty to update a forward-looking statement arose on account of an earlier-made projection, the argument has to be that the projection contained an implicit factual representation that remained "alive" in the minds of investors as a continuing representation. Determining whether such a representation is implicit in an ordinary forecast is a function of what a reasonable investor expects as a result of the background regulatory structure. In particular, we note three features of the existing federal securities disclosure apparatus:

1. Except for specific periodic reporting requirements (primarily the requirements to file quarterly and annual reports), there is no general duty on the part of a company to provide the public with all material information. See Time Warner, 9 F.3d at 267 ("a corporation is not required to disclose a fact merely because a reasonable investor would very much like to know that fact"). Thus, possession of material nonpublic information alone does not create a duty to disclose it.

2. Equally well settled is the principle that an accurate report of past successes does not contain an implicit representation that the trend is going to continue, and hence does not, in and of itself, obligate the company to update the public as to the state of the quarter in progress.

3. Finally, the existing regulatory structure is aimed at encouraging companies to make and disclose internal forecasts by protecting them from liability for disclosing internal forecasts that, although reasonable when made, turn out to be wrong in hindsight. See Stransky, 51 F.3d at 1333. Companies are *not* obligated either to produce or disclose internal forecasts, and if they do, they are protected from liability, except to the extent that the forecasts were unreasonable when made. See Glassman, 90 F.3d at 631. The regulatory structure seeks to encourage companies to disclose forecasts by providing companies with some protection from liability. However, where it comes to affirmative disclosure requirements, the current regulatory scheme focuses on backward-looking "hard" information, not forecasts. See id. (citing Frank H. Easterbrook and Daniel R. Fischel, The Economic Structure of Corporate Law, 305–06 (1991)). Increasing the obligations associated with disclosing reasonably made internal forecasts is likely to deter companies from providing this information—a result contrary to the SEC's goal of encouraging the voluntary disclosure of company forecasts.

Based on features one and two, we do not think it can be said that an ordinary earnings projection contains an implicit representation on the part of the company that it will update the investing public with all material information that relates to that forecast. Under existing law, the market knows that companies have neither a specific obligation to disclose internal forecasts nor a general obligation to disclose all material information. We conclude that ordinary, run-of-the-mill forecasts contain no more than the implicit representation that the forecasts were made reasonably and in good faith. Just as the accurate disclosure of a line of past successes has been ruled not to contain the implication that the current period is going just as well, disclosure of a specific earnings forecast does not contain the implication that the forecast will continue to hold good even as circumstances change.

Finally, the federal securities laws, as they stand today, aim at encouraging companies to disclose their forecasts. A judicially created rule that triggers a duty of continuous disclosure of all material information every time a single specific earnings forecast is disclosed would likely result in a drastic reduction in the number of such projections made by companies. It is these specific earnings projections that are the most useful to investors in deciding whether to invest in a firm's securities. The only types of projections that would be exempt from the duty of continuous disclosure advocated by plaintiffs, and hence the only types of projections that would likely be disclosed under the rule proposed by plaintiffs, would be vague expressions of hope and optimism that are of little use to investors. Therefore, apart from the fact that plaintiffs' disclosure theory has no support in the existing regulatory structure, adopting it would severely undermine the goal of encouraging the maximal disclosure of information useful to investors. Cf. Hillson, 42 F.3d at 219 (increasing the level of liability for projections would produce a result contrary to the goals of full disclosure that underlie the federal securities laws). In sum, under the existing disclosure apparatus, the voluntary disclosure of an ordinary earnings forecast does not trigger any duty to update.

* * *

NOTES ON THE DUTY TO UPDATE AND THE DUTY TO CORRECT

1. *Duty to Correct.* As both *Time Warner* and *Burlington Coat* suggest, the courts have long recognized that a corporation owes a duty to correct a statement that it believed was true when made but subsequent events reveal was not, in fact, true when made. This duty to correct persists as long as the prior statements remain "alive." As the District Court in Ross v. A.H. Robins Co., Inc.[30] explained:

> Both Section 10(b) and Rule 10b–5 are silent as to the effect of time on the duty to correct, but logic compels the conclusion that time may render statements immaterial and end any duty to correct or revise them. In measuring the effect of time in a particular instance, the type of later information and the importance of earlier information contained in a prior statement must be considered. Thus, general financial information in a two-year-old annual report may be stale and immaterial. However, no general rule of time can be applied to all circumstances. Rather, a "particular duty to correct a specific prior statement exists as long as traders in the market could reasonably rely on the statement."

2. *Duty to Update. Burlington Coat* illustrates that the courts are divided about whether a corporation also has a duty to update a statement that was true when made but because of subsequent events

---

[30] 465 F.Supp. 904, 908 (S.D.N.Y. 1979), rev'd on other grounds, 607 F.2d 545 (2d Cir. 1979).

became untrue. Some recent cases have suggested that this duty is very narrow.[31] In fact, the Seventh Circuit has rejected the existence of a duty to update in such a situation asserting that Rule 10b–5 does not encompass such a duty because the duty to update comes after the original statement in question and Rule 10b–5 restricts liabilities to "circumstances under which they were made."[32]

    3. *Duty to Disclose.* As discussed in the cases above, an omission is actionable only when there is a duty to disclose. This duty might arise in circumstances where there is a pre-existing, fiduciary duty to disclose such as with broker-dealers or in close corporations.[33] There are also some cases that suggest a duty to disclose when circumstances give investors reason to rely upon an individual as a source of complete and accurate information.[34]

    4. *Third-Party Statements.* In limited circumstances, an issuer may also be responsible for correcting or updating third party statements when the issuer is the source of the inaccuracies or is responsible for their dissemination. Normally, however, the mere presence of rumors or

---

    [31] See, e.g., United States v. Schiff, 602 F.3d 152 (3d Cir. 2010), declining to hold a company liable for its failure to update information relating to sales volumes. In so holding, the court noted that "the duty has only been plausible in cases where the initial statement concerns fundamental changes in the nature of the company—such as a merger, liquidation, or takeover attempt—and when subsequent events produce an 'extreme' or 'radical change' in the continuing validity of that initial statement."

    In In re Sanofi-Aventis Securities Litigation, 774 F.Supp.2d 549 (S.D.N.Y. 2011), the court held that a company did not have a duty to update statements about the safety of its product when those statements concerned only currently available safety information and were not forward-looking.

    Cf. San Leandro Emergency Med. Group Profit Sharing Plan v. Philip Morris Co., Inc., 75 F.3d 801 (2d Cir. 1996), which declined to find a material omission when a cigarette manufacturer considered a marketing plan to lower cigarette prices and increase market share while publicly stating that the company was committed to increased prices to sustain profits. In this case, unlike *Time Warner*, there was uncertainty whether the company had in fact committed itself to a new marketing strategy and foreclosed all alternatives.

    But cf. Shaw v. Digital Equip. Corp., 82 F.3d 1194, 1205 (1st Cir. 1996), analyzing Item 11(a) of Form S-3:

> The primary purpose of the "material changes" disclosure requirement of Item 11(a), then, is to ensure that the prospectus provides investors with an update of the information required to be disclosed in the incorporated Exchange Act filings, including the information provided in those filings concerning "known trends and uncertainties" with respect to "net sales or revenues or income from continuing operations." 17 C.F.R. § 229.303(a)(3)(ii).

    [32] Stransky v. Cummings Engine Co., 51 F.3d 1329, 1333 (7th Cir. 1995); see also Gallagher v. Abbott Laboratories, 269 F.3d 806 (7th Cir. 2001) (adhering to *Stransky* and its progeny in again refusing to acknowledge a duty to update).

    [33] SEC v. Zandford, 535 U.S. 813 (2002) ("any distinction between omissions and misrepresentations is illusory in the context of a broker who has a fiduciary duty to her clients"); Castellano v. Young & Rubicam, Inc., 257 F.3d 171 (2d. Cir. 2001) ("closed corporations that purchase their own stock have a special obligation to disclose to sellers all material information"); see also SEC v. Cochran, 214 F.3d 1261 (10th Cir. 2000) (duty to disclose bid rigging may exist between municipal bond firm officer and government agency client).

    [34] See Arthur Young & Co. v. Reves, 937 F.2d 1310 (8th Cir. 1991) (duty to disclose imposed on agricultural cooperative's accounting firm who assisted in sale of demand notes to members). But see Jensen v. Kimble 1 F.3d 1073 (10th Cir. 1993) (no duty to disclose despite finding of relationship of trust and confidence because the promoter specifically refused to share information).

publicly circulating inaccuracies concerning the issuer does not require a response.[35] For example, in Elkind v. Liggett & Myers, Inc.,[36] the Second Circuit observed:

> We have no doubt that a company may so involve itself in the preparation of reports and projections by outsiders as to assume a duty to correct material errors in those projections. This may occur when officials of the company have, by their activity, made an implied representation that the information they have reviewed is true or at least in accordance with the company's views.[37]

But a company assumes no duty to disclose its own internal earnings forecasts or to warn analysts that it does not share their optimistic view if it merely reviewed analyst reports and made suggestions as to factual and descriptive matters while adhering to a policy not to comment on earnings forecasts.[38]

Problem

PROBLEM 12-1

In year one, Mondo Electronics secured a patent for a new type of "multi-thermal" battery (MTB). Its CEO, Mitch Mondo, announced in a December year one press conference that the MTB was a "breakthrough" for the battery-powered automobile. On the basis of "systematic 6-month tests," he announced that the MTB would allow the "typical United States or foreign made automobile to drive up to 50 hours without recharging at speeds of up to 90 miles per hour."

Mondo's CFO explained that when full production of 10,000 batteries was achieved at Mondo's plant late in year two, the cost per battery would be $250, which would permit retail sales of the battery at $500 per battery and approximately double Mondo's net income.

---

[35] See, e.g., Electronic Specialty Co. v. International Controls Corp., 409 F.2d 937, 949 (2d Cir. 1969), item in Wall Street Journal column "Heard on the Street" held not attributable to the issuer: "While a company may choose to correct a misstatement in the press not attributable to it, cf. SEC v. Texas Gulf Sulphur Co., 401 F.2d 833, 857–59, 866–69 (concurring opinion) (2d Cir. 1968), we find nothing in the securities legislation requiring it to do so." See also State Teachers Retirement Bd. v. Fluor Corp., 654 F.2d 843, 850 (2d Cir. 1981): "A company has no duty to correct or verify rumors in the marketplace unless these rumors can be attributed to the company."

[36] 635 F.2d 156 (2d Cir. 1980).

[37] Id. at 163; see also Goldman v. Belden, 754 F.2d 1059, 1069 (2d Cir. 1985); Cooper v. Pickett, 137 F.3d 616, 623–24 (9th Cir. 1997); Winkler v. Wigley, 242 F.3d 369 (2d Cir. 2000).

[38] Elkind v. Liggett & Myers, 635 F.2d 156, 163 (2d Cir. 1980). Cf. In re Time Warner Inc. Sec. Litig., 794 F.Supp. 1252, 1258–59 (S.D.N.Y. 1992), aff'd in part & rev'd in part, 9 F.3d 259 (2d Cir. 1993):

Only statements attributable to the defendants, or omissions by them, can support the claims against them. * * * [N]either the alleged statements by anonymous Time Warner sources which are quoted in the complaint nor analysts' and journalists' reports allegedly based on information gleaned from Time Warner sources may be attributed to the defendants.

By February of year two, Mondo's engineers had learned that:

(1) They had underestimated the weight of the typical sedan and minivan, with the consequence that the typical battery driven could achieve top speeds up to 60 miles per hour.

(2) Tests over 18 months disclosed that the MTB deteriorated over time and between 12 and 18 months the MTB needed to be recharged an average of once every 28 hours.

(3) More comprehensive engineering data revealed an average cost per battery of $260.

(4) The same engineering study revealed that full production at Mondo's plant could only produce 8,000 batteries per year.

Which, if any, of this data would Mondo be required to reveal under Rule 10b–5?

B. MATERIALITY

(1) GENERALLY

Basic Incorporated v. Levinson
Supreme Court of the United States, 1988.
485 U.S. 224, 108 S.Ct. 978, 99 L.Ed.2d 194.

■ BLACKMUN, J., delivered the opinion of the Court, in which BRENNAN, MARSHALL, and STEVENS, JJ., joined, and in Parts I, II, and III of which WHITE and O'CONNOR, JJ., joined. WHITE, J., filed an opinion concurring in part and dissenting in part, in which O'CONNOR, J., joined. REHNQUIST, C.J. and SCALIA and KENNEDY, JJ., took no part in the consideration or decision of the case.

■ JUSTICE BLACKMUN:

This case requires us to apply the materiality requirement of § 10(b) of the Securities Exchange Act of 1934 (1934 Act), and the Securities and Exchange Commission's Rule 10b–5, promulgated thereunder, in the context of preliminary corporate merger discussions.

* * *

I

Prior to December 20, 1978, Basic Incorporated was a publicly traded company primarily engaged in the business of manufacturing chemical refractories for the steel industry. As early as 1965 or 1966, Combustion Engineering, Inc., a company producing mostly alumina-based refractories, expressed some interest in acquiring Basic, but was deterred from pursuing this inclination seriously because of antitrust concerns it then entertained. In 1976, however, regulatory action opened the way to a renewal of Combustion's interest. The "Strategic Plan," dated October 25, 1976, for Combustion's Industrial Products Group included the objective: "Acquire Basic Inc. $30 million."

Beginning in September 1976, Combustion representatives had meetings and telephone conversations with Basic officers and directors, including petitioners here,[2] concerning the possibility of a merger.[3] During 1977 and 1978, Basic made three public statements denying that it was engaged in merger negotiations.[4] On December 18, 1978, Basic asked the New York Stock Exchange to suspend trading in its shares and issued a release stating that it had been "approached" by another company concerning a merger. On December 19, Basic's board endorsed Combustion's offer of $46 per share for its common stock, and on the following day publicly announced its approval of Combustion's tender offer for all outstanding shares.

Respondents are former Basic shareholders who sold their stock after Basic's first public statement of October 21, 1977, and before the suspension of trading in December 1978. Respondents brought a class action against Basic and its directors, asserting that the defendants issued three false or misleading public statements and thereby were in violation of § 10(b) of the 1934 Act and of Rule 10b–5. Respondents alleged that they were injured by selling Basic shares at artificially depressed prices in a market affected by petitioners' misleading statements and in reliance thereon.

The District Court adopted a presumption of reliance by members of the plaintiff class upon petitioners' public statements that enabled the court to conclude that common questions of fact or law predominated over particular questions pertaining to individual plaintiffs. See Fed. Rule Civ. Proc. 23(b)(3). The District Court therefore certified respondents' class. On the merits, however, the District Court granted summary judgment for the defendants. It held that, as a matter of law, any misstatements were immaterial: there were no negotiations ongoing at

---

[2] In addition to Basic itself, petitioners are individuals who had been members of its board of directors prior to 1979: Anthony M. Caito, Samuel Eels, Jr., John A. Gelbach, Harley C. Lee, Max Muller, H. Chapman Rose, Edmund G. Sylvester, and John C. Wilson, Jr. Another former director, Mathew J. Ludwig, was a party to the proceedings below but died on July 17, 1986, and is not a petitioner here.

[3] In light of our disposition of this case, any further characterization of these discussions must await application, on remand, of the materiality standard adopted today.

[4] On October 21, 1977, after heavy trading and a new high in Basic stock, the following news item appeared in the Cleveland Plain Dealer:

"[Basic] President Max Muller said the company knew no reason for the stock's activity and that no negotiations were under way with any company for a merger. He said Flintkote recently denied Wall Street rumors that it would make a tender offer of $25 a share for control of the Cleveland-based maker of refractories for the steel industry."

On September 25, 1978, in reply to an inquiry from the New York Stock Exchange, Basic issued a release concerning increased activity in its stock and stated that "management is unaware of any present or pending company development that would result in the abnormally heavy trading activity and price fluctuation in company shares that have been experienced in the past few days."

On November 6, 1978, Basic issued to its shareholders a "Nine Months Report 1978." This Report stated:

"With regard to the stock market activity in the Company's shares we remain unaware of any present or pending developments which would account for the high volume of trading and price fluctuations in recent months."

the time of the first statement, and although negotiations were taking place when the second and third statements were issued, those negotiations were not "destined, with reasonable certainty, to become a merger agreement in principle."

The United States Court of Appeals * * * reversed the District Court's summary judgment, and remanded the case. The court reasoned that while petitioners were under no general duty to disclose their discussions with Combustion, any statement the company voluntarily released could not be " 'so incomplete as to mislead.' " In the Court of Appeals' view, Basic's statements that no negotiations were taking place, and that it knew of no corporate developments to account for the heavy trading activity, were misleading. With respect to materiality, the court rejected the argument that preliminary merger discussions are immaterial as a matter of law, and held that "once a statement is made denying the existence of any discussions, even discussions that might not have been material in absence of the denial are material because they make the statement made untrue."

* * *

We granted certiorari, to resolve the split among the Courts of Appeals as to the standard of materiality applicable to preliminary merger discussions.

* * *

II

* * *

The Court previously has addressed various positive and common-law requirements for a violation of § 10(b) or of Rule 10b–5. The Court also explicitly has defined a standard of materiality under the securities laws, see TSC Industries, Inc. v. Northway, Inc., 426 U.S. 438 (1976), concluding in the proxy-solicitation context that "[a]n omitted fact is material if there is a substantial likelihood that a reasonable shareholder would consider it important in deciding how to vote." Acknowledging that certain information concerning corporate developments could well be of "dubious significance," the Court was careful not to set too low a standard of materiality; it was concerned that a minimal standard might bring an overabundance of information within its reach, and lead management "simply to bury the shareholders in an avalanche of trivial information— a result that is hardly conducive to informed decisionmaking." It further explained that to fulfill the materiality requirement "there must be a substantial likelihood that the disclosure of the omitted fact would have been viewed by the reasonable investor as having significantly altered the 'total mix' of information made available." We now expressly adopt the *TSC Industries* standard of materiality for the § 10(b) and Rule 10b–5 context.

III

The application of this materiality standard to preliminary merger discussions is not self-evident. Where the impact of the corporate development on the target's fortune is certain and clear, the *TSC Industries* materiality definition admits straightforward application. Where, on the other hand, the event is contingent or speculative in nature, it is difficult to ascertain whether the "reasonable investor" would have considered the omitted information significant at the time. Merger negotiations, because of the ever-present possibility that the contemplated transaction will not be effectuated, fall into the latter category.[9]

A

Petitioners urge upon us a Third Circuit test for resolving this difficulty. Under this approach, preliminary merger discussions do not become material until "agreement-in-principle" as to the price and structure of the transaction has been reached between the would-be merger partners. By definition, then, information concerning any negotiations not yet at the agreement-in-principle stage could be withheld or even misrepresented without a violation of Rule 10b–5.

Three rationales have been offered in support of the "agreement-in-principle" test. The first derives from the concern expressed in *TSC Industries* that an investor not be overwhelmed by excessively detailed and trivial information, and focuses on the substantial risk that preliminary merger discussions may collapse: because such discussions are inherently tentative, disclosure of their existence itself could mislead investors and foster false optimism. The other two justifications for the agreement-in-principle standard are based on management concerns: because the requirement of "agreement-in-principle" limits the scope of disclosure obligations, it helps preserve the confidentiality of merger discussions where earlier disclosure might prejudice the negotiations; and the test also provides a usable, bright-line rule for determining when disclosure must be made.

None of these policy-based rationales, however, purports to explain why drawing the line at agreement-in-principle reflects the significance of the information upon the investor's decision. The first rationale, and the only one connected to the concerns expressed in *TSC Industries*, stands soundly rejected, even by a Court of Appeals that otherwise has accepted the wisdom of the agreement-in-principle test. "It assumes that investors are nitwits, unable to appreciate—even when told—that mergers are risky propositions up until the closing." Flamm v. Eberstadt, 814 F.2d, at 1175. Disclosure, and not paternalistic withholding of accurate information, is the policy chosen and expressed by Congress. We have recognized time and again, a "fundamental purpose" of the various

---

[9] We do not address here any other kinds of contingent or speculative information, such as earnings forecasts or projections.

securities acts, "was to substitute a philosophy of full disclosure for the philosophy of *caveat emptor* and thus to achieve a high standard of business ethics in the securities industry." SEC v. Capital Gains Research Bureau, Inc., 375 U.S. 180, 186 (1963). The role of the materiality requirement is not to "attribute to investors a child-like simplicity, an inability to grasp the probabilistic significance of negotiations," Flamm v. Eberstadt, 814 F.2d, at 1175, but to filter out essentially useless information that a reasonable investor would not consider significant, even as part of a larger "mix" of factors to consider in making his investment decision. TSC Industries, Inc. v. Northway, Inc., 426 U.S., at 448–449.

The second rationale, the importance of secrecy during the early stages of merger discussions, also seems irrelevant to an assessment whether their existence is significant to the trading decision of a reasonable investor. To avoid a "bidding war" over its target, an acquiring firm often will insist that negotiations remain confidential, and at least one Court of Appeals has stated that "silence pending settlement of the price and structure of a deal is beneficial to most investors, most of the time." Flamm v. Eberstadt, 814 F.2d, at 1177.

We need not ascertain, however, whether secrecy necessarily maximizes shareholder wealth—although we note that the proposition is at least disputed as a matter of theory and empirical research—for this case does not concern the *timing* of a disclosure; it concerns only its accuracy and completeness. We face here the narrow question whether information concerning the existence and status of preliminary merger discussions is significant to the reasonable investor's trading decision. Arguments based on the premise that some disclosure would be "premature" in a sense are more properly considered under the rubric of an issuer's duty to disclose. The "secrecy" rationale is simply inapposite to the definition of materiality.

The final justification offered in support of the agreement-in-principle test seems to be directed solely at the comfort of corporate managers. A bright-line rule indeed is easier to follow than a standard that requires the exercise of judgment in the light of all the circumstances. But ease of application alone is not an excuse for ignoring the purposes of the securities acts and Congress' policy decisions. Any approach that designates a single fact or occurrence as always determinative of an inherently fact-specific finding such as materiality, must necessarily be overinclusive or underinclusive. In *TSC Industries* this Court explained: "The determination [of materiality] requires delicate assessments of the inferences a 'reasonable shareholder' would draw from a given set of facts and the significance of those inferences to him. . . ." After much study, the Advisory Committee on Corporate Disclosure cautioned the SEC against administratively confining materiality to a rigid formula.[14] Courts also would do well to heed this advice.

We therefore find no valid justification for artificially excluding from the definition of materiality information concerning merger discussions, which would otherwise be considered significant to the trading decision of a reasonable investor, merely because agreement-in-principle as to price and structure has not yet been reached by the parties or their representatives.

B

The Sixth Circuit explicitly rejected the agreement-in-principle test, as we do today, but in its place adopted a rule that, if taken literally, would be equally insensitive, in our view, to the distinction between materiality and the other elements of an action under Rule 10b–5:

> "When a company whose stock is publicly traded makes a statement, as Basic did, that 'no negotiations' are underway, and that the corporation knows of 'no reason for the stock's activity,' and that 'management is unaware of any present or pending corporate development that would result in the abnormally heavy trading activity,' information concerning ongoing acquisition discussions becomes material *by virtue of the statement denying their existence*. . . .
>
> ". . . In analyzing whether information regarding merger discussions is material such that it must be affirmatively disclosed to avoid a violation of Rule 10b–5, the discussions and their progress are the primary considerations. However, once a statement is made denying the existence of any discussions, even discussions that might not have been material in absence of the denial are material because they make the statement made untrue." 786 F.2d, at 748–749 (emphasis in original).

This approach, however, fails to recognize that, in order to prevail on a Rule 10b–5 claim, a plaintiff must show that the statements were *misleading* as to a *material* fact. It is not enough that a statement is false or incomplete, if the misrepresented fact is otherwise insignificant.

C

Even before this Court's decision in *TSC Industries*, the Second Circuit had explained the role of the materiality requirement of Rule 10b–5, with respect to contingent or speculative information or events, in

---

[14] "Although the Committee believes that ideally it would be desirable to have absolute certainty in the application of the materiality concept, it is its view that such a goal is illusory and unrealistic. The materiality concept is judgmental in nature and it is not possible to translate this into a numerical formula. The Committee's advice to the [SEC] is to avoid this quest for certainty and to continue consideration of materiality on a case-by-case basis as problems are identified."

Report of the Advisory Committee on Corporate Disclosure to the Securities and Exchange Commission 327 (House Committee on Interstate and Foreign Commerce, 95th Cong., 1st Sess.) (Comm.Print) (1977).

a manner that gave that term meaning that is independent of the other provisions of the Rule. Under such circumstances, materiality "will depend at any given time upon a balancing of both the indicated probability that the event will occur and the anticipated magnitude of the event in light of the totality of the company activity." SEC v. Texas Gulf Sulphur Co., 401 F.2d, at 849. Interestingly, neither the Third Circuit decision adopting the agreement-in-principle test nor petitioners here take issue with this general standard. Rather, they suggest that with respect to preliminary merger discussions, there are good reasons to draw a line at agreement on price and structure.

In a subsequent decision, the late Judge Friendly, writing for a Second Circuit panel, applied the *Texas Gulf Sulphur* probability/magnitude approach in the specific context of preliminary merger negotiations. After acknowledging that materiality is something to be determined on the basis of the particular facts of each case, he stated:

> "Since a merger in which it is bought out is the most important event that can occur in a small corporation's life, to wit, its death, we think that inside information, as regards a merger of this sort, can become material at an earlier stage than would be the case as regards lesser transactions—and this even though the mortality rate of mergers in such formative stages is doubtless high."

SEC v. Geon Industries, Inc., 531 F.2d 39, 47–48 (C.A.2 1976). We agree with that analysis.

Whether merger discussions in any particular case are material therefore depends on the facts. Generally, in order to assess the probability that the event will occur, a factfinder will need to look to indicia of interest in the transaction at the highest corporate levels. Without attempting to catalog all such possible factors, we note by way of example that board resolutions, instructions to investment bankers, and actual negotiations between principals or their intermediaries may serve as indicia of interest. To assess the magnitude of the transaction to the issuer of the securities allegedly manipulated, a factfinder will need to consider such facts as the size of the two corporate entities and of the potential premiums over market value. No particular event or factor short of closing the transaction need be either necessary or sufficient by itself to render merger discussions material.[17]

---

[17] To be actionable, of course, a statement must also be misleading. Silence, absent a duty to disclose, is not misleading under Rule 10b–5. "No comment" statements are generally the functional equivalent of silence. See In Re Carnation Co., supra. See also New York Stock Exchange Listed Company Manual § 202.01 (premature public announcement may properly be delayed for valid business purpose and where adequate security can be maintained); American Stock Exchange Company Guide §§ 401–405 (similar provisions).

It has been suggested that given current market practices, a "no comment" statement is tantamount to an admission that merger discussions are underway. See Flamm v. Eberstadt, 814 F.2d, at 1178. That may well hold true to the extent that issuers adopt a policy of truthfully denying merger rumors when no discussions are underway, and of issuing "no comment" statements when they are in the midst of negotiations. There are, of course, other statement

As we clarify today, materiality depends on the significance the reasonable investor would place on the withheld or misrepresented information.[18] The fact-specific inquiry we endorse here is consistent with the approach a number of courts have taken in assessing the materiality of merger negotiations. Because the standard of materiality we have adopted differs from that used by both courts below, we remand the case for reconsideration of the question whether a grant of summary judgment is appropriate on this record.[20]

* * *

In Matrixx Initiatives Inc. v. Siracusano, the Supreme Court returned (for the first time in over 20 years) to the linchpin issue of materiality and largely reaffirmed its decision in Basic, Inc. v. Levinson.

Matrixx Initiatives, Inc. v. Siracusano

Supreme Court of the United States, 2011.
563 U.S. 27, 131 S.Ct. 1309, 179 L.Ed.2d 398.

■ JUSTICE SOTOMAYOR delivered the opinion of the Court.

This case presents the question whether a plaintiff can state a claim for securities fraud under § 10(b) of the Securities Exchange Act of 1934, and Securities and Exchange Commission (SEC) Rule 10b–5, based on a

---

policies firms could adopt; we need not now advise issuers as to what kind of practice to follow, within the range permitted by law. Perhaps more importantly, we think that creating an exception to a regulatory scheme founded on a prodisclosure legislative philosophy, because complying with the regulation might be "bad for business," is a role for Congress, not this Court. See also id., at 1182 (opinion concurring in the judgment and concurring in part).

[18] We find no authority in the statute, the legislative history, or our previous decisions, for varying the standard of materiality depending on who brings the action or whether insiders are alleged to have profited. See, e.g., Pavlidis v. New England Patriots Football Club, Inc., 737 F.2d 1227, 1231 (C.A.1 1984) ("A fact does not become more material to the shareholder's decision because it is withheld by an insider, or because the insider might profit by withholding it"); cf. Aaron v. SEC, 446 U.S. 680, 691 (1980) ("[s]cienter is an element of a violation of § 10(b) and Rule 10b–5, regardless of the identity of the plaintiff or the nature of the relief sought").

We recognize that trading (and profit making) by insiders can serve as *an* indication of materiality. We are not prepared to agree, however, that "[i]n cases of the disclosure of inside information to a favored few, determination of materiality has a different aspect than when the issue is, for example, an inaccuracy in a publicly disseminated press release." SEC v. Geon Industries, Inc., 531 F.2d 39, 48 (C.A.2 1976). Devising two different standards of materiality, one for situations where insiders have traded in abrogation of their duty to disclose or abstain (or for that matter when any disclosure duty has been breached), and another covering affirmative misrepresentations by those under no duty to disclose (but under the ever-present duty not to mislead), would effectively collapse the materiality requirement into the analysis of defendant's disclosure duties.

[20] The Sixth Circuit rejected the District Court's narrow reading of Basic's "no developments" statement, which focused on whether petitioners knew of any reason for the activity in Basic stock, that is, whether petitioners were aware of leaks concerning ongoing discussions. See also Comment, Disclosure of Preliminary Merger Negotiations Under Rule 10b–5, 62 Wash. L. Rev. 81, 82–84 (1987) (noting prevalence of leaks and studies demonstrating that substantial trading activity immediately preceding merger announcements is the "rule, not the exception"). We accept the Court of Appeals' reading of the statement as the more natural one, emphasizing management's knowledge of *developments* (as opposed to leaks) that would explain unusual trading activity.

pharmaceutical company's failure to disclose reports of adverse events associated with a product if the reports do not disclose a statistically significant number of adverse events. Respondents, plaintiffs in a securities fraud class action, allege that petitioners, Matrixx Initiatives, Inc., and three of its executives (collectively Matrixx), failed to disclose reports of a possible link between its leading product, a cold remedy, and loss of smell, rendering statements made by Matrixx misleading. Matrixx contends that respondents' complaint does not adequately allege that Matrixx made a material representation or omission or that it acted with scienter because the complaint does not allege that Matrixx knew of a statistically significant number of adverse events requiring disclosure. We conclude that the materiality of adverse event reports cannot be reduced to a bright-line rule. Although in many cases reasonable investors would not consider reports of adverse events to be material information, respondents have alleged facts plausibly suggesting that reasonable investors would have viewed these particular reports as material. Respondents have also alleged facts "giving rise to a strong inference" that Matrixx "acted with the required state of mind." 15 U.S.C. A. § 78u–4(b)(2)(A). We therefore hold, in agreement with the Court of Appeals for the Ninth Circuit, that respondents have stated a claim under § 10(b) and Rule 10b–5.

I

A

Through a wholly owned subsidiary, Matrixx develops, manufactures, and markets over-the-counter pharmaceutical products. Its core brand of products is called Zicam. All of the products sold under the name Zicam are used to treat the common cold and associated symptoms. At the time of the events in question, one of Matrixx's products was Zicam Cold Remedy, which came in several forms including nasal spray and gel. The active ingredient in Zicam Cold Remedy was zinc gluconate. Respondents allege that Zicam Cold Remedy accounted for approximately 70 percent of Matrixx's sales.

Respondents initiated this securities fraud class action against Matrixx on behalf of individuals who purchased Matrixx securities between October 22, 2003, and February 6, 2004. The action principally arises out of statements that Matrixx made during the class period relating to revenues and product safety. Respondents claim that Matrixx's statements were misleading in light of reports that Matrixx had received, but did not disclose, about consumers who had lost their sense of smell (a condition called anosmia) after using Zicam Cold Remedy. Respondents' consolidated amended complaint alleges the following facts, which the courts below properly assumed to be true.

In 1999, Dr. Alan Hirsch, neurological director of the Smell & Taste Treatment and Research Foundation, Ltd., called Matrixx's customer service line after discovering a possible link between Zicam nasal gel and a loss of smell "in a cluster of his patients." Dr. Hirsch told a Matrixx employee that "previous studies had demonstrated that intranasal application of zinc could be problematic." He also told the employee about at least one of his patients who did not have a cold and who developed anosmia after using Zicam.

In September 2002, Timothy Clarot, Matrixx's vice president for research and development, called Miriam Linschoten, Ph.D., at the University of Colorado Health Sciences Center after receiving a complaint from a person Linschoten was treating who had lost her sense of smell after using Zicam. Clarot informed Linschoten that Matrixx had received similar complaints from other customers. Linschoten drew Clarot's attention to "previous studies linking zinc sulfate to loss of smell." Clarot gave her the impression that he had not heard of the studies. She asked Clarot whether Matrixx had done any studies of its own; he responded that it had not but that it had hired a consultant to review the product. Soon thereafter, Linschoten sent Clarot abstracts of the studies she had mentioned. Research from the 1930's and 1980's had confirmed "[z]inc's toxicity." Clarot called Linschoten to ask whether she would be willing to participate in animal studies that Matrixx was planning, but she declined because her focus was human research.

By September 2003, one of Linschoten's colleagues at the University of Colorado, Dr. Bruce Jafek, had observed 10 patients suffering from anosmia after Zicam use. Linschoten and Jafek planned to present their findings at a meeting of the American Rhinologic Society in a poster presentation entitled "Zicam tm Induced Anosmia." (internal quotation marks omitted). The American Rhinologic Society posted their abstract in advance of the meeting. The presentation described in detail a 55-year-old man with previously normal taste and smell who experienced severe burning in his nose, followed immediately by a loss of smell, after using Zicam. It also reported 10 other Zicam users with similar symptoms.

Matrixx learned of the doctors' planned presentation. Clarot sent a letter to Dr. Jafek warning him that he did not have permission to use Matrixx's name or the names of its products. Dr. Jafek deleted the references to Zicam in the poster before presenting it to the American Rhinologic Society.

The following month, two plaintiffs commenced a product liability lawsuit against Matrixx alleging that Zicam had damaged their sense of smell. By the end of the class period on February 6, 2004, nine plaintiffs had filed four lawsuits.

Respondents allege that Matrixx made a series of public statements that were misleading in light of the foregoing information. In October 2003, after they had learned of Dr. Jafek's study and after Dr. Jafek had presented his findings to the American Rhinologic Society, Matrixx stated that Zicam was " 'poised for growth in the upcoming cough and cold season' " and that the company had " 'very strong momentum.' " Matrixx further expressed its expectation that revenues would " 'be up in excess of 50% and that earnings, per share for the full year [would] be in the 25 to 30 cent range.'" In January 2004, Matrixx raised its revenue guidance, predicting an increase in revenues of 80 percent and earnings per share in the 33-to-38-cent range.

In its Form 10-Q filed with the SEC in November 2003, Zicam warned of the potential "'material adverse effect'" that could result from product liability claims, "'whether or not proven to be valid.'" It stated that product liability actions could materially affect Matrixx's "'product branding and goodwill,'" leading to reduced customer acceptance. It did not disclose, however, that two plaintiffs had already sued Matrixx for allegedly causing them to lose their sense of smell.

On January 30, 2004, Dow Jones Newswires reported that the Food and Drug Administration (FDA) was "'looking into complaints that an over-the-counter common-cold medicine manufactured by a unit of Matrixx Initiatives, Inc. (MTXX) may be causing some users to lose their sense of smell'" in light of at least three product liability lawsuits. Matrixx's stock fell from $13.55 to $11.97 per share after the report. In response, on February 2, Matrixx issued a press release that stated:

> "All Zicam products are manufactured and marketed according to FDA guidelines for homeopathic medicine. Our primary concern is the health and safety of our customers and the distribution of factual information about our products. Matrixx believes statements alleging that intranasal Zicam products caused anosmia (loss of smell) are completely unfounded and misleading.
>
> "In no clinical trial of intranasal zinc gluconate gel products has there been a single report of lost or diminished olfactory function (sense of smell). Rather, the safety and efficacy of zinc gluconate for the treatment of symptoms related to the common cold have been well established in two double-blind, placebo-controlled, randomized clinical trials. In fact, in neither study were there any reports of anosmia related to the use of this compound. The overall incidence of adverse events associated with zinc gluconate was extremely low, with no statistically significant difference between the adverse event rates for the treated and placebo subsets.
>
> "A multitude of environmental and biologic influences are known to affect the sense of smell. Chief among them is the common cold. As a result, the population most likely to use cold remedy products is already at increased risk of developing anosmia. Other common causes of olfactory dysfunction include age, nasal and sinus infections, head trauma, anatomical obstructions, and environmental irritants."

The day after Matrixx issued this press release, its stock price bounced back to $13.40 per share.

On February 6, 2004, the end of the class period, Good Morning America, a nationally broadcast morning news program, highlighted Dr. Jafek's findings. (The complaint does not allege that Matrixx learned of the news story before its broadcast.) The program reported that Dr. Jafek had discovered more than a dozen patients suffering from anosmia after using Zicam. It also noted that four lawsuits had been filed against Matrixx. The price of Matrixx stock plummeted to $9.94 per share that same day. Zicam again issued a press release largely repeating its February 2 statement.

On February 19, 2004, Matrixx filed a Form 8-K with the SEC stating that it had "'convened a two-day meeting of physicians and scientists to review current information on smell disorders'" in response to Dr. Jafek's presentation. According to the Form 8-K, "'In the opinion of the panel, there is insufficient scientific evidence at this time to determine if zinc gluconate, when used as recommended, affects a person's ability to smell.'" A few weeks later, a reporter quoted Matrixx as stating that it would begin conducting "'animal and human studies to further characterize these post-marketing complaints.'"

On the basis of these allegations, respondents claimed that Matrixx violated § 10(b) of the Securities Exchange Act and SEC Rule 10b–5 by making untrue statements of fact and failing to disclose material facts necessary to make the statements not misleading in an effort to maintain artificially high prices for Matrixx securities.

B

Matrixx moved to dismiss respondents' complaint, arguing that they had failed to plead the elements of a material misstatement or omission and scienter. The District Court granted the motion to dismiss. Relying on In re Carter-Wallace, Inc., Securities Litigation, 220 F.3d 36 (2d Cir. 2000), it held that respondents had not alleged a "statistically significant correlation between the use of Zicam and anosmia so as to make failure to public[ly] disclose complaints and the University of Colorado study a material omission." The District Court similarly agreed that respondents had not stated with particularity facts giving rise to a strong inference of scienter. See 15 U.S.C.A. § 78u–4(b)(2)(A) (Feb. 2011 Supp.). It noted that the complaint failed to allege that Matrixx disbelieved its statements about Zicam's safety or that any of the defendants profited or attempted to profit from Matrixx's public statements.

The Court of Appeals reversed. Noting that "'[t]he determination [of materiality] requires delicate assessments of the inferences a "reasonable shareholder" would draw from a given set of facts and the significance of those inferences to him,'" the Court of Appeals held that the District Court had erred in requiring an allegation of statistical significance to establish materiality. It concluded, to the contrary, that the complaint adequately alleged "information regarding the possible link between Zicam and anosmia" that would have been significant to a reasonable investor. Turning to scienter, the Court of Appeals concluded that "[w]ithholding reports of adverse effects of and lawsuits concerning the product responsible for the company's remarkable sales increase is 'an extreme departure from the standards of ordinary care,'" giving rise to a strong inference of scienter.

We granted certiorari, and we now *affirm*.

II

Section 10(b) of the Securities Exchange Act makes it unlawful for any person to "use or employ, in connection with the purchase or sale of any security . . . any manipulative or deceptive device or contrivance in contravention of such rules and regulations as the Commission may prescribe as necessary or appropriate in the public interest or for the protection of investors." 15 U.S.C. § 78j(b). SEC Rule 10b–5 implements this provision by making it unlawful to, among other things, "make any untrue statement of a material fact or to omit to state a material fact necessary in order to make the statements made, in the light of the circumstances under which they were made, not misleading." 17 CFR § 240.10b–5(b). We have implied a private cause of action from the text and purpose of § 10(b).

To prevail on their claim that Matrixx made material misrepresentations or omissions in violation of § 10(b) and Rule 10b–5, respondents must prove "(1) a material misrepresentation or omission by the defendant; (2) scienter; (3) a connection between the misrepresentation or omission and the purchase or sale of a security; (4) reliance upon the misrepresentation or omission; (5) economic loss; and (6) loss causation." Stoneridge Investment Partners, LLC v. Scientific-Atlanta, Inc., 552 U.S. 148, 157 (2008). Matrixx contends that respondents have failed to plead both the element of a material misrepresentation or omission and the element of scienter because they have not alleged that the reports received by Matrixx reflected statistically significant evidence that Zicam caused anosmia. We disagree.

A

We first consider Matrixx's argument that "adverse event reports that do not reveal a statistically significant increased risk of adverse events from product use are not material information."

1

To prevail on a § 10(b) claim, a plaintiff must show that the defendant made a statement that was "*misleading* as to a *material* fact." Basic, 485 U.S., at 238. In *Basic*, we held that this materiality requirement is satisfied when there is " 'a substantial likelihood that the disclosure of the omitted fact would have been viewed by the reasonable investor as having significantly altered the "total mix" of information made available.' " We were "careful not to set too low a standard of materiality," for fear that management would " 'bury the shareholders in an avalanche of trivial information.' "

Basic involved a claim that the defendant had made misleading statements denying that it was engaged in merger negotiations when it was, in fact, conducting preliminary negotiations. The defendant urged a bright-line rule that preliminary merger negotiations are material only once the parties to the negotiations reach an agreement in principle. We observed that "[a]ny approach that designates a single fact or occurrence as always determinative of an inherently fact-specific finding such as materiality, must necessarily be overinclusive or underinclusive." We thus rejected the defendant's proposed rule, explaining that it would "artificially exclud[e] from the definition of materiality information concerning merger discussions, which would otherwise be considered significant to the trading decision of a reasonable investor."

Like the defendant in *Basic*, Matrixx urges us to adopt a bright-line rule that reports of adverse events associated with a pharmaceutical company's products cannot be material absent a sufficient number of such reports to establish a statistically significant risk that the product is in fact causing the events. Absent statistical significance, Matrixx argues, adverse event reports provide only "anecdotal" evidence that "the user of a drug experienced an adverse event at some point during or following the use of that drug." Accordingly, it contends, reasonable investors would not consider such reports relevant unless they are statistically significant because only then do they "reflect a scientifically reliable basis for inferring a potential causal link between product use and the adverse event."

As in *Basic*, Matrixx's categorical rule would "artificially exclud[e]" information that "would otherwise be considered significant to the trading decision of a reasonable investor." Matrixx's argument rests on the premise that statistical significance is the only reliable indication of causation. This premise is flawed: As the SEC points out, "medical researchers . . . consider multiple factors in assessing causation." Statistically significant data are not always available. For example, when an adverse event is subtle or rare, "an inability to obtain a data set of appropriate quality or quantity may preclude a finding of statistical significance." Moreover, ethical considerations may prohibit researchers from conducting randomized clinical trials to confirm a suspected causal link for the purpose of obtaining statistically significant data.

A lack of statistically significant data does not mean that medical experts have no reliable basis for inferring a causal link between a drug and adverse events. As Matrixx itself concedes, medical experts rely on other evidence to establish an inference of causation. We note that courts frequently permit expert testimony on causation based on evidence other than statistical significance. We need not consider whether the expert testimony was properly admitted in those cases, and we do not attempt to define here what constitutes reliable evidence of causation. It suffices to note that, as these courts have recognized, "medical professionals and researchers do not limit the data they consider to the results of randomized clinical trials or to statistically significant evidence."

The FDA similarly does not limit the evidence it considers for purposes of assessing causation and taking regulatory action to statistically significant data. In assessing the safety risk posed by a product, the FDA considers factors such as "strength of the association," "temporal relationship of product use and the event," "consistency of findings across available data sources," "evidence of a dose-response for the effect," "biologic plausibility," "seriousness of the event relative to the disease being treated," "potential to mitigate the risk in the population," "feasibility of further study using observational or controlled clinical study designs," and "degree of benefit the product provides, including availability of other therapies." It "does not apply any single metric for determining when additional inquiry or action is necessary, and it certainly does not insist upon 'statistical significance.'"

Not only does the FDA rely on a wide range of evidence of causation, it sometimes acts on the basis of evidence that suggests, but does not prove, causation. For example, the FDA requires manufacturers of over-the-counter drugs to revise their labeling "to include a warning as soon as there is reasonable evidence of an association of a serious hazard with a drug; a causal relationship need not have been proved." 21 CFR § 201.80(e). More generally, the FDA may make regulatory decisions against drugs based on postmarketing evidence that gives rise to only a suspicion of causation. See FDA, The Clinical Impact of Adverse Event Reporting ("[A]chieving certain proof of causality through postmarketing surveillance is unusual. Attaining a prominent degree of suspicion is much more likely, and may be considered a sufficient basis for regulatory decisions" (footnote omitted)).

This case proves the point. In 2009, the FDA issued a warning letter to Matrixx stating that "[a] significant and growing body of evidence substantiates that the Zicam Cold Remedy intranasal products may pose a serious risk to consumers who use them." The letter cited as evidence 130 reports of anosmia the FDA had received, the fact that the FDA had received few reports of anosmia associated with other intranasal cold remedies, and "evidence in the published scientific literature that various salts of zinc can damage olfactory function in animals and humans." It did not cite statistically significant data.

Given that medical professionals and regulators act on the basis of evidence of causation that is not statistically significant, it stands to reason that in certain cases reasonable investors would as well. As Matrixx acknowledges, adverse event reports "appear in many forms, including direct complaints by users to manufacturers, reports by doctors about reported or observed patient reactions, more detailed case reports published by doctors in medical journals, or larger scale published clinical studies." As a result, assessing the materiality of adverse event reports is a "fact-specific" inquiry that requires consideration of the source, content, and context of the reports. This is not to say that statistical significance (or the lack thereof) is irrelevant—only that it is not dispositive of every case.

Application of *Basic*'s "total mix" standard does not mean that pharmaceutical manufacturers must disclose all reports of adverse events. Adverse event reports are daily events in the pharmaceutical industry; in 2009, the FDA entered nearly 500,000 such reports into its reporting system. The fact that a user of a drug has suffered an adverse event, standing alone, does not mean that the drug caused that event. The question remains whether a *reasonable* investor would have viewed the nondisclosed information " 'as having *significantly* altered the "total mix" of information made available.' " Basic, 485 U.S., at 232 (quoting TSC Industries, 426 U.S., at 449; emphasis added). For the reasons just stated, the mere existence of reports of adverse events—which says nothing in and of itself about whether the drug is causing the adverse events—will not satisfy this standard. Something more is needed, but that something more is not limited to statistical significance and can come from "the source, content, and context of the reports." This contextual inquiry may reveal in some cases that reasonable investors would have viewed reports of adverse events as material even though the reports did not provide statistically significant evidence of a causal link.

Moreover, it bears emphasis that § 10(b) and Rule 10b–5(b) do not create an affirmative duty to disclose any and all material information. Disclosure is required under these provisions only when necessary "to make . . . statements made, in the light of the circumstances under which they were made, not misleading. 17 CFR § 240.10b–5(b); see also Basic, 485 U.S., at 239, n. 17 ("Silence, absent a duty to disclose, is not misleading under Rule 10b–5"). Even with respect to information that a reasonable investor might consider material, companies can control what they have to disclose under these provisions by controlling what they say to the market.

2

Applying *Basic*'s "total mix" standard in this case, we conclude that respondents have adequately pleaded materiality. This is not a case about a handful of anecdotal reports, as Matrixx suggests. Assuming the complaint's allegations to be true, as we must, Matrixx received information that plausibly indicated a reliable causal link between Zicam and anosmia. That information included reports from three medical professionals and researchers about more than 10 patients who had lost their sense of smell after using Zicam. Clarot told Linschoten that Matrixx had received additional reports of anosmia. (In addition, during the class period, nine plaintiffs commenced four product liability lawsuits against Matrixx alleging a causal link between Zicam use and anosmia.) Further, Matrixx knew that Linschoten and Dr. Jafek had presented their findings about a causal link between Zicam and anosmia to a national medical conference devoted to treatment of diseases of the nose.

Their presentation described a patient who experienced severe burning in his nose, followed immediately by a loss of smell, after using Zicam—suggesting a temporal relationship between Zicam use and anosmia.

Critically, both Dr. Hirsch and Linschoten had also drawn Matrixx's attention to previous studies that had demonstrated a biological causal link between intranasal application of zinc and anosmia. Before his conversation with Linschoten, Clarot, Matrixx's vice president of research and development, was seemingly unaware of these studies, and the complaint suggests that, as of the class period, Matrixx had not conducted any research of its own relating to anosmia. See, e.g., App. 84a (referencing a press report, issued after the end of the class period, noting that Matrixx said it would begin conducting " 'animal and human studies to further characterize these post-marketing complaints' "). Accordingly, it can reasonably be inferred from the complaint that Matrixx had no basis for rejecting Dr. Jafek's findings out of hand.

We believe that these allegations suffice to "raise a reasonable expectation that discovery will reveal evidence" satisfying the materiality requirement, Bell Atlantic Corp. v. Twombly, 550 U.S. 544, 556 (2007), and to "allo[w] the court to draw the reasonable inference that the defendant is liable for the misconduct alleged," Iqbal, 556 U.S., at 678. The information provided to Matrixx by medical experts revealed a plausible causal relationship between Zicam Cold Remedy and anosmia. Consumers likely would have viewed the risk associated with Zicam (possible loss of smell) as substantially outweighing the benefit of using the product (alleviating cold symptoms), particularly in light of the existence of many alternative products on the market. Importantly, Zicam Cold Remedy allegedly accounted for 70 percent of Matrixx's sales. Viewing the allegations of the complaint as a whole, the complaint alleges facts suggesting a significant risk to the commercial viability of Matrixx's leading product.

It is substantially likely that a reasonable investor would have viewed this information " 'as having significantly altered the "total mix" of information made available.' " Basic, 485 U.S., at 232 (quoting TSC Industries, 426 U.S., at 449). Matrixx told the market that revenues were going to rise 50 and then 80 percent. Assuming the complaint's allegations to be true, however, Matrixx had information indicating a significant risk to its leading revenue-generating product. Matrixx also stated that reports indicating that Zicam caused anosmia were " 'completely unfounded and misleading' " and that " 'the safety and efficacy of zinc gluconate for the treatment of symptoms related to the common cold have been well established.' " Importantly, however, Matrixx had evidence of a biological link between Zicam's key ingredient and anosmia, and it had not conducted any studies of its own to disprove that link. In fact, as Matrixx later revealed, the scientific evidence at that time was " 'insufficient . . . to determine if zinc gluconate, when used as recommended, affects a person's ability to smell.' "

Assuming the facts to be true, these were material facts "necessary in order to make the statements made, in the light of the circumstances under which they were made, not misleading." 17 CFR § 240.10b–5(b). We therefore affirm the Court of Appeals' holding that respondents adequately pleaded the element of a material misrepresentation or omission.

B

Matrixx also argues that respondents failed to allege facts plausibly suggesting that it acted with the required level of scienter. "To establish liability under § 10(b) and Rule 10b–5, a private plaintiff must prove that the defendant acted with scienter, 'a mental state embracing intent to deceive, manipulate, or defraud.'" Tellabs, 551 U.S., at 319 (quoting Ernst & Ernst v. Hochfelder, 425 U.S. 185, 193–194, and n. 12 (1976)). We have not decided whether recklessness suffices to fulfill the scienter requirement. Because Matrixx does not challenge the Court of Appeals' holding that the scienter requirement may be satisfied by a showing of "deliberate recklessness," see 585 F.3d at 1180 (internal quotation marks omitted), we assume, without deciding, that the standard applied by the Court of Appeals is sufficient to establish scienter.

Under the PSLRA, a plaintiff must "state with particularity facts giving rise to a strong inference that the defendant acted with the required state of mind." 15 U.S.C. A. § 78u–4(b)(2)(A) (Feb. 2011 Supp.). This standard requires courts to take into account "plausible opposing inferences." Tellabs, 551 U.S., at 323. A complaint adequately pleads scienter under the PSLRA "only if a reasonable person would deem the inference of scienter cogent and at least as compelling as any opposing inference one could draw from the facts alleged." In making this determination, the court must review "all the allegations holistically." The absence of a motive allegation, though relevant, is not dispositive.

Matrixx argues, in summary fashion, that because respondents do not allege that it knew of statistically significant evidence of causation, there is no basis to consider the inference that it acted recklessly or knowingly to be at least as compelling as the alternative inferences. "Rather," it argues, "the most obvious inference is that petitioners did not disclose the [reports] simply because petitioners believed they were far too few * * * to indicate anything meaningful about adverse reactions to use of Zicam." Matrixx's proposed bright-line rule requiring an allegation of statistical significance to establish a strong inference of scienter is just as flawed as its approach to materiality.

The inference that Matrixx acted recklessly (or intentionally, for that matter) is at least as compelling, if not more compelling, than the inference that it simply thought the reports did not indicate anything meaningful about adverse reactions. According to the complaint, Matrixx was sufficiently concerned about the information it received that it informed Linschoten that it had hired a consultant to review the product, asked Linschoten to participate in animal studies, and convened a panel of physicians and scientists in response to Dr. Jafek's presentation. It successfully prevented Dr. Jafek from using Zicam's name in his presentation on the ground that he needed Matrixx's permission to do so. Most significantly, Matrixx issued a press release that suggested that studies had confirmed that Zicam does not cause anosmia when, in fact, it had not conducted any studies relating to anosmia and the scientific evidence at that time, according to the panel of scientists, was insufficient to determine whether Zicam did or did not cause anosmia.[15]

These allegations, "taken collectively," give rise to a "cogent and compelling" inference that Matrixx elected not to disclose the reports of adverse events not because it believed they were meaningless but because it understood their likely effect on the market. Tellabs, 551 U.S., at 323, 324. "[A] reasonable person" would deem the inference that Matrixx acted with deliberate recklessness (or even intent) "at least as compelling as any opposing inference one could draw from the facts alleged." We conclude, in agreement with the Court of Appeals, that respondents have adequately pleaded scienter. Whether respondents can ultimately prove their allegations and establish scienter is an altogether different question.

* * *

For the reasons stated, the judgment of the Court of Appeals for the Ninth Circuit is *Affirmed*.

NOTES ON MATERIALITY

1. *Class Certification.* The Supreme Court addressed proof of materiality in the context of class certification in Amgen Inc. v. Connecticut Retirement Plans & Trust Funds.[39] The Court held:

> Because the question of materiality is common to the class, and because a failure of proof on that issue would not result in questions "affecting only individual members" predominating, Fed. Rule Civ. Proc. 23(b)(3), Connecticut Retirement was not required to prove the materiality of Amgen's alleged misrepresentations and omissions at the class-certification stage. This is not a case in which the asserted problem—i.e., that the plaintiff class cannot prove materiality—"exhibits some fatal dissimilarity" among class members that would make use of the class-action device inefficient or unfair. Nagareda, Class Certification in the Age of Aggregate Proof, 84 N.Y.U.L. Rev. 97,

---

[15] One of Matrixx's *amici* argues that "the most cogent inference regarding Matrixx's state of mind is that it delayed releasing information regarding anosmia complaints in order to provide itself an opportunity to carefully review all evidence regarding any link between Zicam and anosmia." Brief for Washington Legal Foundation as Amicus Curiae 26. We do not doubt that this may be the most cogent inference in some cases. Here, however, the misleading nature of Matrixx's press release is sufficient to render the inference of scienter at least as compelling as the inference suggested by *amicus*.

[39] 568 U.S. 455 (2013).

107 (2009). Instead, what Amgen alleges is "a fatal similarity— [an alleged] failure of proof as to an element of the plaintiffs' cause of action." Ibid. Such a contention is properly addressed at trial or in a ruling on a summary-judgment motion. The allegation should not be resolved in deciding whether to certify a proposed class. Ibid.[40]

2. *Half-Truths*. As discussed above in Matrixx "[d]isclosure is required under [§ 10(b) and Rule 10b–5(b)] only when necessary "to make . . . statements made, in the light of the circumstances under which they were made, not misleading". If a company speaks but fails to speak completely, it might be liable for an omission that makes the statement misleading to a reasonable investor.[41] The half-truth doctrine does not prohibit silence, rather it prohibits misleading the public by not speaking completely. This inquiry is highly dependent on the circumstances.

Problem

PROBLEM 12-2

Humongous Mega Movies, Inc. (HMM, Inc.) earned over $100 million in net profits last year.

(1) Would it be material to a reasonable investor that:

(a) Its CEO, Herman Humongous, who last year earned $12.5 million in executive compensation, embezzled $10,000 from petty cash last year?

(b) Its Co-CEO, Marie Mega, has very high blood pressure and elevated cholesterol and has been ordered by her physician to take a one month vacation and try to relax? Last year Marie Mega was the executive producer of the most successful HMM film which alone was responsible for 50 percent of HMM's net profits.

Herman Humongous, Chief Executive Officer of HMM, Inc., had dinner last night with his business school classmate, Frieda Durkheim, Chief Executive Officer of Lawrence Co. Both HMM and Lawrence are listed on the New York Stock Exchange (NYSE).

---

[40] Id. at 470.

[41] See, e.g., Schueneman v. Arena Pharmaceuticals, Inc., 840 F.3d 698 (9th Cir. 2016) (fraudulent for a pharmaceutical company to tout confidence in FDA approval based on preclinical animal studies, without revealing the FDA expressed concern with the studies and the data was not favorable towards FDA approval); Meyer v. Jinkosolar Holdings Co., Ltd., 761 F.3d 245 (2d Cir. 2014) (fraudulent to detail pollution-preventing equipment and 24-hour environmental monitoring teams without disclosing such efforts do not comply with regulations regarding the company's use of dangerous chemicals when violation may pose significant financial risk); Finnerty v. Stiefel Laboratories, Inc., 756 F.3d 1310 (11th Cir. 2014) (fraudulent for company that touts 160-year family owned, privately held history with no plans to change that, to fail to disclose sale of the company under consideration). But see, e.g., Retail Wholesale & Dep't Store Union Local 338 Ret. Fund v. Hewlett-Packard Co., 845 F.3d 1268 (9th Cir. 2017) (not fraudulent to not disclose officer's ethical standards violation when publishing the corporation's ethical standards as statement did not "reasonably suggest that there would be no violations of the standards").

This morning average daily volume trebled on HMM, Inc. and its stock price was up 15 percent.

(2) If the appropriate NYSE representative telephones and asks if HMM, Inc. has any information about why the price and volume are up, can HMM's public relations officer state "absolutely none"?

(3) Suppose Durkheim had presented Humongous with a two-page proposed "merger of equals" and Humongous had turned it down. Could the public relations officer still state, "I know of absolutely nothing to allow for the stock price and volume increases"?

(4) Suppose Durkheim presented Humongous with a two-page proposed "merger of equals" and Humongous said, "I'll take it to my board for consideration next week." Could the public relations officer then state, "I know of nothing to account for the stock price and volume increases"?

(2) Forward Looking Statements

Basic v. Levinson was limited to premerger negotiations and did not generally address other forms of contingent or forward-looking statements or prospectuses,[42] but its holding that materiality "will depend at any given time upon a balancing of both the indicated probability that the event will occur and the anticipated magnitude of the event in light of the totality of the company activity" provides a general approach to forward-looking or soft information.[43]

The SEC was the most significant driving force for mandatory disclosure of forward-looking statements. Item 303(a) of Regulation S–K effectively requires management to disclose certain estimates and projections in its Management's Discussion and Analysis of Financial Condition and Results of Operations (the "MD&A"), a required item in both the Annual Report on Form 10-K and the Quarterly Report on Form 10-Q. Specifically, the MD&A must contain a description of "known trends * * * demands, commitments, events or uncertainties that will result in or that are reasonably likely to result in the registrant's liquidity increasing or decreasing in any material way."[44] Similar disclosure is required of "any known trends or uncertainties that have had or that the registrant reasonably expects will have a material favorable or unfavorable impact on net sales or income from continuing operations."[45]

The SEC has drawn the following distinction between required disclosures and voluntary forward-looking disclosures:

> Both required disclosure regarding the future impact of presently known trends, events or uncertainties and optional

---

[42] 485 U.S. at 232 n.9.

[43] The lower courts have applied the Basic-Texas Gulf Sulphur test to other contingent events. See, e.g., General Motors Class E Stock Buyout Sec. Litig., 694 F.Supp. 1119 (D. Del. 1988).

[44] Item 303(a)(1), Regulation S–K.

[45] Item 303(a)(3), Regulation S–K.

forward-looking information may involve some prediction or projection. The distinction between the two rests with the nature of the prediction required. Required disclosure is based on currently known trends, events and uncertainties that are reasonably expected to have material effects, such as a reduction in the registrant's product prices; erosion in the registrant's market share; changes in insurance coverage; or the likely non-renewal of a material contract. In contrast, optional forward-looking disclosure involves anticipating a future trend or event or anticipating a less predictable impact of a known event, trend or uncertainty.[46]

Is this distinction clear? Or, does it really imply that the registrant must make affirmative disclosure of all "trends" and "uncertainties" other than the most speculative? Conceptually, the SEC's position on the MD&A poses the question of whether the registrant is subject to an affirmative disclosure obligation, even though Basic, Inc. v. Levinson seemed to say that silence was not actionable in the absence of such a duty to speak.

When the Commission adopted its safe harbor rules for forward-looking statements in 1979, it waffled on the significance of the disclosure of risk factors and assumptions to accompany a forward-looking statement. The Commission generally requires the disclosure of risk factors in registration statements and prospectuses, but these requirements do not specifically address forward-looking statements. The Private Securities Litigation Reform Act of 1995 also addressed this issue, as the notes following the next case make clear.

Under the "bespeaks caution" doctrine, cautionary language, as part of the "total mix" of the information available, may render a forward-looking statement immaterial or make it unreasonable for an investor to rely upon the statement. Generalized cautionary language accompanying a prediction, however, is not always sufficient to gain the protection of the doctrine and courts have cautioned that "inclusion of general cautionary language regarding a prediction [does] not excuse the alleged failure to reveal known material, adverse facts."[47] The next case introduces the "bespeaks caution" doctrine applicable to forward-looking statements.

---

[46] Sec. Act Rel. 6711, 38 SEC Dock. 138, 140–141 (1987).
[47] Rubinstein v. Collins, 20 F.3d 160, 171 (5th Cir. 1994).

In re Worlds of Wonder Securities Litigation
United States Court of Appeals, Ninth Circuit, 1994.
35 F.3d 1407.

■ Before: FLETCHER, HALL, and WIGGINS, CIRCUIT JUDGES.

■ CYNTHIA HOLCOMB HALL, CIRCUIT JUDGE:

In this appeal, we consider the saga of Worlds of Wonder, Inc. ("WOW"), a toy company that sold $80 million of "junk bonds" to the investing public in June 1987. When WOW defaulted on its very first interest payment and filed for bankruptcy just six months later, rendering the securities worthless, a class of disappointed investors filed this securities-fraud action, naming as defendants WOW's officers, directors, auditors, underwriters, and major shareholders. The district court granted summary judgment in favor of all defendants and the investors appealed. After considering a myriad of issues, we affirm in part and reverse in part.

I.

In 1985, Donald Kingsborough formed WOW to manufacture and distribute "The World of Teddy Ruxpin," a product line featuring animated toy bears and accessories. Teddy Ruxpin was an immediate success, becoming a top seller for the 1985 Christmas season and generating net sales of $93 million in WOW's first fiscal year, which ended March 31, 1986. Shortly thereafter, WOW launched "Lazer Tag," a product line featuring infrared toy weapons. Lazer Tag became another instantaneous hit and, as Teddy Ruxpin continued to move briskly off the shelves, WOW posted two of the ten best-selling toys of the 1986 Christmas season. Ultimately, WOW recorded net sales of $327 million for fiscal 1987, which ended March 31, 1987.

Hoping to fund further expansion, WOW conducted a public offering of unsecured 9% convertible subordinated debentures on June 4, 1987 ("the Debenture Offering"), raising $80 million. (In common parlance, the debentures were "junk bonds" because they bore an above-market interest rate to compensate for the risk associated with their "below investment grade" rating). This additional infusion of capital, however, proved inadequate to sustain the corporation's uncontrolled growth and, almost immediately, WOW commenced a series of public disclosures that led to sharp declines in the market price of the debentures and, eventually, to a total financial collapse.

On July 27, 1987, the corporation reported losses of $10 million for the first quarter of fiscal 1988, ending June 30, 1987. Shortly thereafter, on August 7, 1987, WOW terminated fifteen percent of its domestic workforce (fifty-five employees) and announced reductions in capital expenditures. Two months later, the corporation disclosed that it had laid off another seventeen percent of its workforce (sixty employees) and engaged in further cost-cutting measures. On November 9, 1987, WOW reported net losses of $43 million for the second quarter of fiscal 1988, ending September 30, 1987, and announced price reductions on Teddy Ruxpin and Lazer Tag. Finally, after 1987 Christmas sales fell far below projections, WOW defaulted on the first interest payment of the debentures and, shortly thereafter, filed for bankruptcy on December 21, 1987, rendering the securities worthless.

* * *

II.

* * *

A.

In concluding that the "textual part" of the Debenture Prospectus was not false or misleading, the district court analyzed the plaintiffs' claims of misrepresentation under the rubric of the "bespeaks caution" doctrine:

> ... The doctrine holds that economic projections, estimates of future performance, and similar optimistic statements in a prospectus are not actionable when precise cautionary language elsewhere in the document adequately discloses the risks involved. It does not matter if the optimistic statements are later found to have been inaccurate or based on erroneous assumptions when made, provided that the risk disclosure was conspicuous, specific, and adequately disclosed the assumptions upon which the optimistic language was based. . . .
>
> In the context of a summary judgment motion, . . . [t]he doctrine holds that where a prospectus contains adequate cautionary language disclosing specific risks, no reasonable inference can be drawn that a statement regarding those risks was misleading.

The court also analyzed the plaintiffs' claims in the context of information about WOW known to the market at the time of the offering:

> ... [T]he major rating agencies classified [WOW's] debentures as "junk bonds." That this fact was widely disseminated throughout the market is reflected by the 9% interest rate for the debentures, which was substantially higher than the market rate for lower risk securities. Since WOW was widely considered in the marketplace to be a risky investment, Plaintiffs' allegations that statements in or omissions from the Debenture Prospectus were misleading deserve especially careful scrutiny. . . .

On appeal, the plaintiffs contend that the district court erred by adopting and applying the bespeaks caution doctrine and by granting summary judgment despite evidence indicating that the textual part of the Debenture Prospectus contained material misstatements and omissions. We consider these contentions in order.

1.

* * *

[T]he doctrine, when properly construed, merely represents the pragmatic application of two fundamental concepts in the law of securities fraud: materiality and reliance. The Fifth Circuit recently explained:

> The "bespeaks caution" doctrine ... reflects a relatively recent, ongoing, and somewhat uncertain evolution in securities law, an evolution driven by the increase in and the unique nature of fraud actions based on predictive statements. In essence, predictive statements are just what the name implies: predictions. As such, any optimistic projections contained in such statements are necessarily contingent. Thus, the "bespeaks caution" doctrine has developed to address situations in which optimistic projections are coupled with cautionary language—in particular, relevant specific facts or assumptions—affecting the reasonableness of reliance on and the materiality of those projections. To put it another way, the "bespeaks caution" doctrine reflects the unremarkable proposition that statements must be analyzed in context.

Rubinstein, 20 F.3d at 167 (footnotes omitted).

* * *

In this case, the district court applied the doctrine narrowly:

> ... [A]n overbroad application of the doctrine would encourage management to conceal deliberate misrepresentations beneath the mantle of broad cautionary language. To prevent this from occurring, the bespeaks caution doctrine applies only to precise cautionary language which directly addresses itself to future projections, estimates or forecasts in a prospectus. By contrast, blanket warnings that securities involve a high degree of risk [are] insufficient to ward against a federal securities fraud claim.

WOW, 814 F.Supp. at 858 (citations and quotations omitted); see Kline v. First W. Gov't Sec., Inc., 24 F.3d 480, 489 (3d Cir. 1994) ("application of the 'bespeaks caution' doctrine ... requires that the language bespeaking caution relate directly to that to which plaintiffs claim to have been misled"). As a result, notwithstanding the plaintiffs' shrill arguments to the contrary, the court's context-specific approach entirely comports with Virginia Bankshares, Inc. v. Sandberg, 501 U.S. 1083 (1991), in which the Supreme Court noted that "[w]hile a misleading statement will not always lose its deceptive edge simply by joinder with others that are true, the true statements may discredit the other one so obviously that the risk of real deception drops to nil. . . . [Therefore,] publishing accurate facts . . . can render a misleading proposition too unimportant to ground liability."

* * *

2.

Turning to the merits, the plaintiffs claim the textual disclosures in the Debenture Prospectus were false or misleading in four general areas: liquidity, internal controls, revenue recognition, and sales performance. We consider each in order.

a.

The plaintiffs first contend that the prospectus was false and misleading because it stated that WOW expected to have sufficient cash to operate through March 31, 1988. The prospectus made the following disclosures regarding liquidity:

Seasonality of Quarterly Results. . . . There can be no assurance that the Company can maintain sufficient flexibility with respect to its working capital needs, manufacturing capacity and supplies of raw materials, tools and components to be able to minimize the adverse effects of an unanticipated shortfall in seasonal demand. . . .

Capital Requirements. . . . To meet seasonal working capital requirements, the Company has borrowed, and expects to continue to borrow, substantial amounts . . . the Company anticipates that the proceeds of this offering, together with cash flow from operations, existing lines of credit and new bank credit facilities presently being negotiated, will provide sufficient funds to meet the Company's capital needs through March 31, 1988. However, if the Company is unable to obtain adequate capital from this offering and such new bank credit facilities on acceptable terms, its operations would be adversely affected. . . .

Liquidity and Capital Resources. Since its inception, the Company's internally generated cash flow has not been sufficient to finance accounts receivable, inventory and capital equipment needs, as well as support growth. . . .

To meet seasonal working capital requirements, management expects to continue to borrow substantial amounts under its bank line of credit and its import financing line, both of which it expects to replace or extend prior to expiration. Based on its current plan of operations, management anticipates that existing credit facilities and new bank facilities presently being negotiated, together with the proceeds of the offering of the Debentures and funds from operations, will be sufficient to meet the Company's short-term cash requirements through March 31, 1988.

After reviewing the document, the district court concluded that the prospectus "clearly bespoke caution on the serious risks WOW's liquidity crisis posed to investors. . . . Plaintiffs are not entitled to an inference that they were misled in the face of such disclosures." We agree.

* * *

Given the plaintiffs' lack of probative evidence and the Debenture Prospectus' specific references to WOW's continuing cash shortfall and borrowing requirements, the district court was correct to conclude that the prediction of liquidity was not materially misleading as a matter of law.

* * *

b.

The plaintiffs next argue that the following Debenture Prospectus description of WOW's internal controls was materially misleading:

Information Systems and Control Procedures. The Company's business has grown dramatically in the last year, and the Company's development of its management information system and other systems and control procedures has at times lagged behind this growth. While the Company continues to upgrade its systems, procedures and controls to meet the demand of its expansion, there can be no assurance that the Company can successfully implement these enhancements or that these enhancements will keep pace with the growth.

The plaintiffs contend that, in fact, WOW's internal controls at the time of the offering had "crippling deficiencies" and that "no reasonable investor reading the Prospectus would have concluded that there were any existing problems with controls." The district court disagreed: "Plaintiffs ignore the fact that the Prospectus included an express disclaimer that 'there can be no assurances' that WOW's existing internal controls would continue to be adequate given the rapid pace at which the company was growing. The Prospectus made no predictions to the contrary. Thus, the Prospectus adequately bespoke caution regarding this potential risk to WOW's investors. As a matter of law, Plaintiffs cannot have been misled." This conclusion is correct for several reasons. First, contrary to the plaintiffs' assertions, the Debenture Prospectus did not state or imply that WOW's internal control problems were "in the past" and not ongoing. Rather, the prospectus clearly warned that the company's attempt to improve internal controls could prove to be inadequate. Second, the plaintiffs presented no evidence that WOW's internal controls at the time of the offering were materially deficient. Indeed, the allegedly "devastating" management letter issued by Deloitte (two-and-a-half months after the Debenture Offering) concluded that, although "significant problems" existed, WOW's internal controls had no material weaknesses. And, third, WOW probably would not have needed to disclose even serious internal-control deficiencies. Cf. Monroe v. Hughes, 31 F.3d 772, 776 (9th Cir. 1994) (holding that an auditor need not disclose internal controls).

The Debenture Prospectus, which noted that WOW had struggled to maintain sufficient internal controls, clearly erred on the side of *over* disclosure and was therefore not misleading. We affirm the district court on this point.

c.

The plaintiffs next argue that the Debenture Prospectus was misleading because it failed to disclose that WOW engaged in various tactics to "pump up" revenue figures without completing actual sales. Specifically, the plaintiffs contend the prospectus misleadingly omitted WOW's observance of "price protection" (the right to reimbursement in the event of post-sale price reductions), "stock balancing" (the post-sale right to exchange non-defective products for different merchandise), and "guaranteed sales" (the unqualified right to return non-defective products).

The argument regarding price protection and stock balancing is without merit for several reasons. First, the plaintiffs introduced "no evidence that, at the time of the Debenture offering, WOW's management could have foreseen that WOW would have to reduce prices to [the extent it actually did so in late 1987]. Thus, the alleged practice of price protection did not pose a foreseeable risk to WOW's investors at the time of the Debenture offering, so WOW had no duty to disclose it." The speculative impact of future exchanges and price reductions was not material. See Hanon, 976 F.2d at 506 ("potential action to be taken sometime in the distant future is not an item appropriately made a part of a public disclosure because of its speculativeness"). And, second, the plaintiffs concede that price protection is a common practice in the toy industry. The undisputed evidence also indicates that stock balancing is commonplace in the industry. As a result, WOW had no duty to disclose its observance of those practices.

Although a slightly closer call, the plaintiffs' contention regarding guaranteed sales fares no better. We agree that a company that "substantially overstate[s] its revenues by reporting consignment transactions as sales . . . mak[es] false or misleading statements of material fact." Malone v. Microdyne Corp., 26 F.3d 471, 478 (4th Cir. 1994). And we acknowledge that the plaintiffs did present some evidence that WOW engaged in guaranteed sales prior to the Debenture Offering, particularly in the final quarter of fiscal 1987.

The evidence indicates, however, that Deloitte analyzed WOW's sales practices and concluded that, "[w]hile it is true that on a few occasions prior to the 1987 audit, WOW made the business decision to permit customers to return or exchange nondefective products, these returns were minimal in number, and did not have a material impact on WOW's financial statements taken as a whole." As the district court noted, "[j]ust because some of WOW's customers were allowed a refund does not mean that . . . WOW had a practice of offering guaranteed sales to all its customers. Giving an unsatisfied customer a refund is a normal business method of dealing with an unsatisfied customer. It is not a violation of securities laws for WOW to fail to disclose such an obvious practice to potential investors."

The plaintiffs' evidence of guaranteed sales is speculative, nebulous, and nowhere purports to quantify the degree to which WOW engaged in this "normal business" practice. As such, it does not rise to the level of a material omission.

* * *

d.

Finally, the plaintiffs argue that the following Debenture Prospectus disclosures misstated WOW's performance in the first quarter of fiscal 1988 and generally hid the fact that, at the time of the Debenture Offering, sales of and demand for WOW products had declined precipitously:

Seasonality of Quarterly Results. ... The Company anticipates that net sales for the quarter ending June 30, 1987 will be less than those for each of the prior three quarters, and the Company expects to report a loss for the quarter. ...

Net Sales. ... Because sales of toys are highly seasonal, the Company would generally expect net sales to be lower in the first half of the calendar year. The Company's net sales in the first quarter of fiscal 1987 were lower than net sales in each of the preceding two quarters. Similarly, the Company expects net sales for the first quarter of fiscal 1988 to be lower than sales for each of the prior three quarters. At the same time, the Company is continuing to expand its operations in anticipation of the Christmas selling season. As a result, the Company expects to report a net loss for the first quarter of fiscal 1988 proportionally greater than the net loss reported for the first quarter of fiscal 1987.

The plaintiffs contend the prospectus was misleading because it did not state that (1) WOW's performance in the first quarter (which ended a month after the Debenture Offering) would be "substantially" lower than the first quarter of the preceding year or (2) WOW's net quarterly loss would be "disproportionally greater" than that of the prior year. We reject this argument for several reasons.

First, as Smith Barney explains, "[t]he only reasonable reading [of the prospectus] is that, in light of the lower first quarter sales and the higher first quarter operating expenses the company was then expecting, WOW's net loss ... was expected to constitute a 'greater proportion' of net revenue than ... during the first quarter of 1987." The prospectus did not imply that WOW's first quarter 1988 losses would be proportional to its first quarter 1987 losses.

Second, the prospectus clearly warned that WOW expected lower net sales. WOW was under no duty to disclose the precise extent of the anticipated revenue drop. . . . The plaintiffs complain that the prospectus failed to disclose the extent to which first quarter sales lagged behind WOW's internal projections. The quarter, however, was not yet complete; had WOW actually disclosed its internal business plan, the plaintiffs probably would now be contending that no basis existed for such a prediction. Cf. Convergent Technologies, 948 F.2d at 516 ("It is just good general business practice to make . . . projections for internal corporate use. There is no evidence, however, that the estimates were made with such reasonable certainty even to *allow* them to be disclosed to the public.") (quotation omitted).

The plaintiffs also argue that the Debenture Prospectus violated section 11 by failing generally to reveal "WOW's crisis of sales and demand." The district court disagreed: "Plaintiffs submit no admissible evidence to show that WOW's sales had decreased so dramatically at the time of the Debenture offering that WOW's management could have known about, and thus would have had a duty to disclose, the impending collapse of Lazer Tag sales. Plaintiffs cannot use the benefit of 20–20 hindsight to turn management's business judgment into securities fraud." We agree.

The plaintiffs argue that WOW's sales, for Lazer Tag in particular, began a dramatic collapse in January 1987 and that, because revenues prior to the Debenture Offering fell below WOW's internal business plan, WOW was required to disclose that "fact" in the Debenture Prospectus. The prospectus, however, fully disclosed WOW's sales for each of the eight completed fiscal quarters of its existence (through March 31, 1987). This disclosure revealed a significant decline in both net sales and net income for the first three months of 1987. The plaintiffs' complaint that WOW should have disclosed the ramifications of that drop in sales (i.e., that the decline was due to more than "normal seasonality") is without merit. See Convergent Technologies, 948 F.2d at 513 ("The challenged statements do not imply any comparison between the rate of past and future growth. They simply report past performance and assert specific limited predictions for the future."); see generally Trump Casino, 7 F.3d at 375 ("The federal securities laws do not ordain that the issuer of a security compare itself in myriad ways to its competitors, whether favorably or unfavorably.").

* * *

Just four days prior to the Debenture Offering, WOW commenced a production schedule implementing the corporation's optimistic business plan, which projected $542 million in sales. As the Officers note, if demand actually had dried up, the "[p]laintiffs cannot explain why WOW's entire senior and middle management would have lied to themselves about the Company's business outlook." See Apple Computer, 886 F.2d at 1117 ("[the corporation]'s massive investment in [a new product] demonstrates this good faith" belief that it will succeed). The plaintiffs presented no admissible evidence to the contrary. In sum, their argument distills to a contention that WOW should have predicted the collapse in sales that occurred in late 1987, long after the Debenture Offering. The corporation had no duty to do so. See VeriFone, 11 F.3d at 869 ("These alleged nondisclosures are, in substance, failures to make a forecast of future events. Put another way, what the complaint states is that [the issuer] omitted to state the 'fact' that future prospects were not as bright as past performance. Absent allegations that [the issuer] withheld financial data or other existing facts from which forecasts are typically derived, the alleged omissions are not of material, actual facts. Therefore, the forecasts need not have been disclosed, and the failure to make the omitted forecasts did not render the other statements that were made misleading."). We affirm the district court on this point.

* * *

NOTE ON FORWARD LOOKING STATEMENTS: THE PRIVATE SECURITIES LITIGATION REFORM ACT

Though a majority of circuits adopted the "bespeaks caution" doctrine prior to the 1995 Private Securities Litigation Reform Act (PSLRA), that Act created legislative safe harbors for forward-looking statements through § 21E of the Securities Exchange Act and § 27A of the Securities Act. The logic for a statutory exemption for forward-looking statements is straightforward. Investors care more about the future than the past; in fact, they care about the past only insofar as it helps predict the future. Also, predictions are inherently riskier and more subject to hindsight bias than historical facts. The bias against forward-looking predictions fell especially on high-tech firms, which had higher variance in outcomes, and therefore faced greater litigation risk. The threat of suit was substantial, and raised the cost of capital for these startup firms in an important industry. As for the judicial safe harbors, these were vaguer and more tenuous than a statutory exemption, which brought additional certainty to the practice.

Sections 21E and 27A apply only to a forward-looking statement made by

(1) an issuer that, at the time that the statement is made, is subject to the reporting requirements of § 13(a) or § 15(d);

(2) a person acting on behalf of such issuer;

(3) an outside reviewer retained by such issuer making a statement on behalf of such issuer; or

(4) an underwriter, with respect to information provided by such issuer or information derived from information provided by the issuer.[48]

---

[48] Sec. Ex. Act § 21E(a).

There are three different safe harbors in Securities Act § 27A(c) and Securities Exchange Act § 21E(c):

(1) Securities Act § 27(c)(1)(A) and Securities Exchange Act § 21E(c)(1)(A) may immunize a false forward-looking statement if the court concludes it was accompanied "by meaningful cautionary statements."

(2) Securities Act § 27A(c)(1)(B) and Securities Exchange Act § 21E(c)(1)(B) provide defendants with a safe harbor if he or she cannot offer and prove sufficient meaningful cautionary statements because the plaintiff is still required to prove the higher culpability standard of "actual knowledge" rather than the lower recklessness or negligence standard available today under the Securities Exchange Act § 10(b) and Rule 14a–9.

(3) The sections also provide safe harbors for oral forward-looking statements when appropriate reference is made to a readily available written document.

The safe harbors are buttressed by provisions that allow the Commission to further exempt forward-looking statements,[49] and that require the court to stay discovery during any motion for summary judgment concerning a covered forward-looking statement.[50]

The Securities Act § 27A(i) and Securities Exchange Act § 21E(i) define the term "forward-looking statement" in a manner similar to Securities Act Rule 175 and Securities Exchange Act Rule 3b–6. The safe harbors in the 1934 Act § 21E(i)(1), however, add definitions[51]:

(E) any report issued by an outside reviewer retained by an issuer, to the extent that the report assesses a forward-looking statement made by the issuer; or

(F) a statement containing a projection or estimate of such other items as may be specified by rule or regulation of the Commission.

The Managers Statement accompanying the legislation emphasized the significance of the bespeaks caution cases when it stated: "As part of the analysis of what constitutes a meaningful cautionary statement, courts should consider the factors identified in the statements. 'Important' factors mean the stated factors identified in the cautionary statement must be relevant to the projection and must be of a nature that the factor or factors could actually affect whether the forward-looking statement is realized."[52]

---

[49] See Sec. Act § 27A(c)(4); Sec. Ex. Act § 21E(c)(4); see also Sec. Act §§ 27A(g)–(h); Sec. Ex. Act §§ 21E(g)–(h).

[50] Sec. Act § 27A(f); Sec. Ex. Act § 21E(f).

[51] Sec. Act §§ 27A(i)(E)–(F) and Sec. Ex. Act §§ 21E(i)(E)–(F).

[52] 1995–1996 Fed. Sec. L. Rep. (CCH) ¶ 85,710 at 87,209.

Consider this case applying the provisions.

Harris v. Ivax Corp.

United States Court of Appeals, Eleventh Circuit, 1999.
182 F.3d 799.

■ Before: Cox and Hull, Circuit Judges, and Cohill, Senior District Judge.

■ Cox, Circuit Judge:

This appeal invites application of the safe harbor for forward-looking statements added to the Securities Exchange Act of 1934 by the Private Securities Litigation Reform Act of 1995, Pub. L. 104–67, 109 Stat. 737 (1995) (PSLRA). We affirm the district court's dismissal of the complaint under Fed R. Civ. P. 12(b)(6).

I. Background

According to the complaint—our only source of the facts—the defendant Ivax Corporation is a manufacturer of generic drugs, a highly volatile business. Ivax was profitable in 1995, but lost money in the second quarter of 1996. On August 2, 1996 Ivax issued a press release that, while acknowledging business problems, also showed some optimism. Ivax stock rose. On September 30, the last day of the quarter, Ivax announced in another press release that it anticipated a $43 million loss. On November 11, Ivax announced a $179 million loss for the third quarter, $104 million of which was a reduction in the carrying value of the goodwill ascribed to certain of Ivax's businesses. Neither of the earlier press releases had mentioned the possibility of this goodwill writedown based on third-quarter results. The price of Ivax stock plummeted.

Investors hoping to represent a class of purchasers of Ivax Corporation stock between August 2, 1996 and November 11, 1996 sued Ivax, its chairman and chief executive officer, and its chief financial officer. They claimed that the defendants had committed fraud under the Securities Exchange Act § 10(b), 15 U.S.C. § 78j, and Securities and Exchange Commission Rule 10b–5, 17 C.F.R. § 210.10b–5, as well as common-law negligent misrepresentation. There are two theories of liability: first, that Ivax's economic projections were fraudulent, and second, that Ivax's disclosure of factors affecting its projections misled by omitting the possibility of a goodwill writedown. The defendants moved to dismiss based on the safe-harbor provision * * *.

In a thoughtful opinion, the district court dismissed the complaint under Fed. R. Civ. P. 12(b)(6).

* * *

II. Discussion

* * *

The district court concluded that all of the statements alleged in the complaint to be fraudulent were forward-looking, and that the statements' "cautionary language" was "meaningful." The court thus concluded that Ivax's statements were anchored within the statutory safe harbor, and that the cautionary language shielded Ivax from liability.

* * *

All of the statements that the plaintiffs claim to be false or misleading are forward-looking. They were accompanied, moreover, by "meaningful cautionary language."

* * *

1. *Improving reorders.*

The August 2, 1996 press release contained the following sentence: "Reorders are expected to improve as customer inventories are depleted." This statement falls squarely in the middle of one of the categories of "forward-looking statements," as Congress has defined them: it is "a statement of the assumptions underlying" "a statement of future economic performance." 15 U.S.C. § 78u–5(*i*)(1)(D), (C). The text that follows in the press release (which we discuss below) is a general outlook for the third quarter. The arrangement of the text makes clear that an expected increase in reorders was one of the bases of the optimism. This was therefore a forward-looking statement within the statutory safe harbor.

2. *The "unique challenges."*

The August 2, 1996 press release also announced optimistically that "the challenges unique to this period in our history are now behind us." Taken in context, this statement is forward-looking. The two paragraphs of the press release preceding this statement describe two problems that contributed to a loss in the second quarter: excessive customer inventories, which reduced new orders, and a technical default in a revolving credit facility. Both problems, the statement said, were being resolved; inventories were becoming depleted, and the bank syndicate was expected to waive the default. Thus, the chairman and CEO announced that things were looking up.

"Forward-looking statement[s]" include "statements of future economic performance." 15 U.S.C. § 78u–5(i)(1)(c). The chairman and CEO's hopeful conclusion that conditions are better because of two anticipated improvements in business conditions is a prediction of economic performance, however couched. The plaintiffs' purely grammatical argument to the contrary—that a present-tense statement cannot predict the future—is unpersuasive; a statement about the state of a company whose truth or falsity is discernible only after it is made necessarily refers only to future performance. Whether the worst of Ivax's challenges were behind it was a matter verifiable only after the chairman so declared. This statement was thus forward-looking and in the safe harbor.

3. *Intact strategies.*

The August 2, 1996 press release continued with another hopeful outlook from Ivax's chairman and CEO, Phillip Frost, that "[o]ur fundamental business and its underlying strategies remain intact.... Only a limited number of companies are positioned to meaningfully participate in this rapidly growing market and, among them, IVAX is certainly very well positioned." Like the previous statement, this one is a prediction "of future economic performance." 15 U.S.C. § 78u–5(i)(1)(c). While it is true that the *state* of Ivax's "fundamental business" and "underlying strategies" is a question of present condition, whether they are intact is a fact only verifiable by seeing how they hold up in the future. Likewise, whether Ivax is "well positioned" is a statement whose truth can only be known after seeing how Ivax's future plays out. That puts this statement in the safe harbor, as well.

4. *The laundry list.*

The September 30, 1996 press release, which predicted third quarter results, contained a list of factors "relating to [Ivax's] generic drug business [that] will influence [Ivax's] third quarter results." Those five factors included high customer inventory levels and low orders; declining prices; "shelf stock adjustments" for existing customers; higher reserves for returns; and the bankruptcy of a major customer who owed Ivax $16 million. The list is a mixed bag, with some sentences that are forward-looking and some that are not. The statement's choice of language suggests that three of the factors had already been observed: "customer re-orders remain depressed"; "prices have continued to decline"; and "a wholesaler customer who owed us approximately $16 million filed a Chapter 11 bankruptcy petition." Observed facts of this kind are not "assumptions," and they are not any kind of prediction, either, that would put them within the definition of a forward-looking statement. These sentences are not, therefore, forward-looking. Two other factors, however, are worded as assumptions about future events: "we expect reserves for returns and inventory writeoffs to be well above typical quarters" and "lower prices ... will increase shelf stock adjustments." As "assumptions underlying" the predictions elsewhere in the press release, these sentences are forward-looking. 15 U.S.C. § 78u–5(i)(1)(D).

The mixed nature of this statement raises the question whether the safe harbor benefits the entire statement or only parts of it. Of course, if any of the individual sentences describing known facts (such as the customer's bankruptcy) were allegedly false, we could easily conclude that that smaller, non-forward-looking statement falls outside the safe harbor. But the allegation here is that the list *as a whole* misleads anyone reading it for an explanation of Ivax's projections, because the list omits the expectation of a goodwill writedown. If the allegation is that the whole list is misleading, then it makes no sense to slice the list into separate sentences. Rather, the list becomes a "statement" in the statutory sense, and a basis of liability, as a unit. It must therefore be either forward-looking or not forward-looking in its entirety. The next issue is what the character of the list is as a whole—forward-looking or not.

We conclude that the entire list is due forward-looking treatment. To begin with, there is no question under the statute that a material and misleading omission can fall within the forward-looking safe harbor. See 15 U.S.C. § 78u–15(c)(1) ("[I]n any private action arising under this chapter that is based on an untrue statement of material fact or *omission of a material fact necessary to make the statement not misleading*, a person referred to in subsection (a) of this section shall not be liable. . . .") (emphasis added). And while the statute does not tell us exactly what to do with a mixed statement, extrinsic sources of congressional intent point strongly toward treating the entire list as forward-looking. Congress enacted the safe-harbor provision in order to loosen the "muzzling effect" of potential liability for forward-looking statements, which often kept investors in the dark about what management foresaw for the company. See H.R. Conf. Rep. 104–369, at 42 (1995), reprinted in 1995 U.S.C.C.A.N. 730, 741. Forward-looking conclusions often rest both on historical observations and assumptions about future events. Thus, were we to banish from the safe harbor lists that contain both factual and forward-looking factors, we would inhibit corporate officers from fully explaining their outlooks. Indeed, liability-conscious officers would be relegated to citing only the factors that could individually be called forward-looking. That would hamper the communication that Congress sought to foster.

Treating mixed lists as forward-looking may open a loophole for misleading omissions, but there are two circumstances that should put investors on guard, anyway. First, a list or explanation will only qualify for this treatment if it contains assumptions underlying a forward-looking statement. Investors should know, under the current statutory scheme, that relying on assumptions is dangerous; there will often be no legal recourse even if the assumption is false. Second, a defendant can fully benefit from the safe harbor's shelter only when it has disclosed risk factors in a warning accompanying the forward-looking statement. This disclosure as well should warn investors against blind reliance on mixed lists.

For these reasons, we hold that when the factors underlying a projection or economic forecast include both assumptions and statements of known fact, and a plaintiff alleges that a material factor is missing, the entire list of factors is treated as a forward-looking statement. This list is therefore in the safe harbor.

C. *Cautionary Language*

The district court was correct that adequate cautionary language accompanies the forward-looking statements here. The italicized warning that Ivax appended to both press releases is detailed and informative; it tells the reader in detail what kind of misfortunes could befall the company and what the effect could be. We can reject out of hand, therefore, the plaintiffs' arguments that the cautionary statements are "mere boilerplate." That leaves, however, another question: the plaintiffs here allege fraud by material omission. Neither of the statements mentions the possibility of a large goodwill writedown. To be "meaningful," 15 U.S.C. § 78u–5(c)(I)(A)(i), must the cautionary language explicitly mention *the* factor that ultimately belies a forward-looking statement?

We think not. The statute requires the warning only to mention "important factors that could cause actual results to differ materially from those in the forward-looking statement." 15 U.S.C. § 78u–5(c)(1)(A)(i). It does not require a listing of *all* factors. The conference report, moreover, that accompanied the PSLRA specified that "failure to include the particular factor that ultimately causes the forward-looking statement not to come true will not mean that the statement is not protected by the safe harbor." H.R. Conf. Rep. 104–369, at 44 (1995). In short, when an investor has been warned of risks of a significance similar to that actually realized, she is sufficiently on notice of the danger of the investment to make an intelligent decision about it according to her own preferences for risk and reward. This statement satisfies Ivax's burden to warn under the statute, and it excuses Ivax from liability.

* * *

For the foregoing reasons, we affirm the district court's dismissal of the complaint.

Affirmed.

(3) REASONS, OPINIONS, AND BELIEFS

Important components of Rule 10b–5 were set forth in the following case, which is really a Rule 14a–9 case.

Virginia Bankshares, Inc. v. Sandberg
Supreme Court of the United States, 1991.
501 U.S. 1083, 111 S.Ct. 2749, 115 L.Ed.2d 929.

■ JUSTICE SOUTER delivered the opinion of the Court.

* * *

I

In December 1986, First American Bankshares, Inc., (FABI), a bank holding company, began a "freeze-out" merger, in which the First American Bank of Virginia (Bank) eventually merged into Virginia Bankshares, Inc., (VBI), a wholly owned subsidiary of FABI. VBI owned 85% of the Bank's shares, the remaining 15% being in the hands of some

2,000 minority shareholders. FABI hired the investment banking firm of Keefe, Bruyette & Woods (KBW) to give an opinion on the appropriate price for shares of the minority holders, who would lose their interests in the Bank as a result of the merger. Based on market quotations and unverified information from FABI, KBW gave the Bank's executive committee an opinion that $42 a share would be a fair price for the minority stock. The executive committee approved the merger proposal at that price, and the full board followed suit.

Although Virginia law required only that such a merger proposal be submitted to a vote at a shareholders' meeting, and that the meeting be preceded by circulation of a statement of information to the shareholders, the directors nevertheless solicited proxies for voting on the proposal at the annual meeting set for April 21, 1987.[3] In their solicitation, the directors urged the proposal's adoption and stated they had approved the plan because of its opportunity for the minority shareholders to achieve a "high" value, which they elsewhere described as a "fair" price, for their stock.

* * *

The jury * * * [found] violations of Rule 14a–9 by all defendants and a breach of fiduciary duties by the Bank's directors. The jury awarded Sandberg $18 a share, having found that she would have received $60 if her stock had been valued adequately.

* * *

II
* * *

A

We consider first the actionability *per se* of statements of reasons, opinion or belief. Because such a statement by definition purports to express what is consciously on the speaker's mind, we interpret the jury verdict as finding that the directors' statements of belief and opinion were made with knowledge that the directors did not hold the beliefs or opinions expressed, and we confine our discussion to statements so made.[5] That such statements may be materially significant raises no serious question. The meaning of the materiality requirement for liability under § 14(a) was discussed at some length in TSC Industries, Inc. v. Northway, Inc., 426 U.S. 438 (1976), where we held a fact to be material "if there is a substantial likelihood that a reasonable shareholder would consider it important in deciding how to vote." We think there is no room to deny that a statement of belief by corporate directors about a

---

[3] Had the directors chosen to issue a statement instead of a proxy solicitation, they would have been subject to an SEC antifraud provision analogous to Rule 14a–9. See 17 CFR 240.14c–6 (1990). See also 15 U.S.C. § 78n(c).

[5] In TSC Industries, Inc. v. Northway, Inc., we reserved the question whether scienter was necessary for liability generally under § 14(a). We reserve it still.

recommended course of action, or an explanation of their reasons for recommending it, can take on just that importance. Shareholders know that directors usually have knowledge and expertness far exceeding the normal investor's resources, and the directors' perceived superiority is magnified even further by the common knowledge that state law customarily obliges them to exercise their judgment in the shareholders' interest. Naturally, then, the share owner faced with a proxy request will think it important to know the directors' beliefs about the course they recommend and their specific reasons for urging the stockholders to embrace it.

B

1

But, assuming materiality, the question remains whether statements of reasons, opinions, or beliefs are statements "with respect to . . . material fact[s]" so as to fall within the strictures of the Rule. Petitioners argue that we would invite wasteful litigation of amorphous issues outside the readily provable realm of fact if we were to recognize liability here on proof that the directors did not recommend the merger for the stated reason and they * * * [urge] us to recognize sound policy grounds for placing such statements outside the scope of the Rule.

* * *

Attacks on the truth of directors' statements of reasons or belief, however, need carry no such threats. * * * Reasons for directors' recommendations or statements of belief are, in contrast, characteristically matters of corporate record subject to documentation, to be supported or attacked by evidence of historical fact outside a plaintiff's control. Such evidence would include not only corporate minutes and other statements of the directors themselves, but circumstantial evidence bearing on the facts that would reasonably underlie the reasons claimed and the honesty of any statement that those reasons are the basis for a recommendation or other action, a point that becomes especially clear when the reasons or beliefs go to valuations in dollars and cents.

It is no answer to argue, as petitioners do, that the quoted statement on which liability was predicated did not express a reason in dollars and cents, but focused instead on the "indefinite and unverifiable" term, "high" value, much like the similar claim that the merger's terms were "fair" to shareholders. The objection ignores the fact that such conclusory terms in a commercial context are reasonably understood to rest on a factual basis that justifies them as accurate, the absence of which renders them misleading. * * * In this case, whether $42 was "high," and the proposal "fair" to the minority shareholders depended on whether provable facts about the Bank's assets, and about actual and potential levels of operation, substantiated a value that was above, below, or more or less at the $42 figure, when assessed in accordance with recognized methods of valuation.

Respondents adduced evidence for just such facts in proving that the statement was misleading about its subject matter and a false expression of the directors' reasons. Whereas the proxy statement described the $42 price as offering a premium above both book value and market price, the evidence indicated that a calculation of the book figure based on the appreciated value of the Bank's real estate holdings eliminated any such premium. The evidence on the significance of market price showed that KBW had conceded that the market was closed, thin, and dominated by FABI, facts omitted from the statement. There was, indeed, evidence of a "going concern" value for the Bank in excess of $60 per share of common stock, another fact never disclosed. However conclusory the directors' statement may have been, then, it was open to attack by garden-variety evidence, subject neither to a plaintiff's control nor ready manufacture, and there was no undue risk of open-ended liability or uncontrollable litigation in allowing respondents the opportunity for recovery on the allegation that it was misleading to call $42 "high."

* * *

2

Under § 14(a), then, a plaintiff is permitted to prove a specific statement of reason knowingly false or misleadingly incomplete, even when stated in conclusory terms. In reaching this conclusion we have considered statements of reasons of the sort exemplified here, which misstate the speaker's reasons and also mislead about the stated subject matter (e.g., the value of the shares). A statement of belief may be open to objection only in the former respect, however, solely as a misstatement of the psychological fact of the speaker's belief in what he says. In this case, for example, the Court of Appeals alluded to just such limited falsity in observing that "the jury was certainly justified in believing that the directors did not believe a merger at $42 per share was in the minority stockholders' interest but, rather, that they voted as they did for other reasons, e.g., retaining their seats on the board."

The question arises, then, whether disbelief, or undisclosed belief or motivation, standing alone, should be a sufficient basis to sustain an action under § 14(a), absent proof by the sort of objective evidence described above that the statement also expressly or impliedly asserted something false or misleading about its subject matter. We think that proof of mere disbelief or belief undisclosed should not suffice for liability under § 14(a), and if nothing more had been required or proven in this case we would reverse for that reason.

* * *

NOTES ON REASONS, OPINIONS, AND BELIEFS

1. *Omnicare and Opinions.* In Omnicare, Inc. v. Laborers District Council Construction Industry Pension Fund, which is covered in Chapter 11, the Supreme Court also addressed the issue presented in *Virginia Bankshares*, that of the actionability of statements couched in terms of beliefs. Although the cases come to opposite conclusions—beliefs were held nonactionable in *Virginia Bankshares* and actionable in *Omnicare*—the latter did not necessarily overrule the former. The *Omnicare* Court did not say it was overruling its prior opinion, and in the absence of a clear indication there is reason to believe it remains good law. Moreover, *Virginia Bankshares* involved liability under § 14 and Rule 14a–9 promulgated thereunder, while *Omnicare* involved § 11. This difference matters because unlike § 14, § 11 is a strict liability statute, and thus the Court construed its reach further in light of this fact. As the Sixth Circuit wrote in the lower-court opinion in *Omnicare* when distinguishing *Virginia Bankshares*, "it would be unwise for this Court to add an element to Section 11 claims based on little more than a tea-leaf reading in a Section 14(a) case." This difference points to an important element of securities law practice, if not legal practice more generally: the precise statute or rule at issue in a particular case matters a great deal. This is especially true in securities litigation, where there are multiple antifraud provisions that could arguably cover the same conduct, each of which has different elements, defenses, damages, and interpretations at the SEC and in the courts. That said, it seems likely that the reasoning in *Omnicare* may well bleed over into other securities causes of action.

2. *Puffing.* *Virginia Bankshares* also addressed "soft" or "puffing" statements, finding they lack materiality. Some cases following *Virginia Bankshares* take the position statements—such as one characterizing a marketplace for a particular group of products "with an expected annual growth rate of 10% to 30% over the next several years"—lack materiality "because the market price of a share is not inflated by vague statements predicting growth."[53] In San Leandro Emergency Medical Group Profit Sharing Plan v. Philip Morris Companies, Inc.,[54] the court concluded:

> In any event, even the most positive statements by Philip Morris representatives at that time consisted of relatively subdued general comments, such as the company "*should* deliver income growth consistent with its historically superior performance" (emphasis added) and "we are optimistic about 1993." These statements "lack the sort of definite positive projections that

---

[53] Raab v. General Physics Corp., 4 F.3d 286, 289 (4th Cir. 1993); Longman v. Food Lion, Inc., 197 F.3d 675, 685 (4th Cir. 1999) ("[T]hese statements are the kind of puffery and generalizations that reasonable investors could not have relied upon when deciding whether to buy stock"). See generally Jennifer O'Hare, The Resurrection of the Dodo: The Unfortunate Re-emergence of the Puffery Defense in Private Securities Fraud Actions, 59 Ohio St. L.J. 1697 (1998).

[54] 75 F.3d 801 (2d Cir. 1996).

might require later correction." Time Warner, 9 F.3d at 267. As noted above, such puffery is not actionable.[55]

Problem

PROBLEM 12-3

Tel-Cel is a corporation comprised of local telephone companies and cellular phone systems. The cellular phone business was hot, and the local telephone business cool. Tel-Cel's board believed that the combination was unlovely to investors and that the firm's assets would be worth more if the company was sold.

Rather than just seek out a possible purchaser and negotiate privately, Tel-Cel decided to organize an auction at which bidders could bid on the whole company or on parts of it as they wished. The auction was intimated in a public announcement by Tel-Cel on January 23 that it had hired two prominent investment banks to "explore strategic alternatives to maximize shareholder value, including the possible sale of the company." On the day of the announcement, the price of Tel-Cel's shares rose from $37 to almost $48.

On March 5, GTE, a potential bidder, announced that it would not participate in the auction. Although Tel-Cel responded by bravely claiming that "[w]e believe that this [GTE's statement] has no impact on our process [and w]e continue to move along," a week later it met with its investment bankers in private to consider the viability of a "survivor entity" consisting of those assets of Tel-Cel that would not fetch an attractive price at the auction. The conclusion (not publicly announced) of the participants at the meeting was that any such entity would "very clearly bear the taint of a nonsaleable Tel-Cel property which has been aggressively (and publicly) marketed to 'the world.'"

On March 25, Pacific Telesis, one of the Baby Bells and a potential bidder for Tel-Cel's Nevada properties, a major asset, announced that it also wouldn't bid for them after all. Tel-Cel reacted with a public statement that "the bidding process continues to go very smoothly." By this time, several other large potential purchasers had expressed a lack of interest as well. The price of Tel-Cel's stock drifted lower than its peak on January 23, but it was still above $40.

April 16 was the deadline for the submission of bids. On April 13, Tel-Cel's chief executive officer announced publicly that there was "widespread interest almost down to every [Tel-Cel telecommunications] exchange."

The auction was held on April 16 as scheduled, but it was a bust. Only seven bids were submitted, none for the whole company. Although Tel-Cel kept mum, it accepted none of the bids. Instead, it approached Sprint hat in hand and quickly negotiated a sale of the entire company to Sprint at a price equivalent to $33.50 a share, which was $9 below the then current market

---

[55] Id. at 811. Compare Lasker v. New York State Elec. & Gas Corp., 85 F.3d 55 (2d Cir. 1996).

price and roughly 10 percent below the market price before the auction was first intimated. As soon as the deal with Sprint was announced, on May 27, the value of Tel-Cel's shares plummeted, from $42.50 to $32.

1. Did Tel-Cel make a material misrepresentation or omission in violation of Rule 10b–5?

2. What effect on liability would there be if Tel-Cel had added to its January 23rd announcement: "Of course we cannot guarantee that any strategic alternative will succeed or will generate an offer in excess of current market price"?

C. THE "IN CONNECTION WITH" REQUIREMENT

Courts have generally construed the requirement that fraud be "in connection with the purchase or sale of any security" broadly to encompass activities not directly about the purchase or sale of a security. For instance, the misappropriation of private information for use in valuing securities has been held to be sufficiently connected to the purchase or sale of securities to constitute securities fraud. But, as seen in the Supreme Court's recent opinion in *Trioce*, the "in connection with" requirement was not satisfied when the alleged fraud involved the sale of something whose value was based in part on the value of underlying securities. The following cases explore the boundaries of the "in connection with" requirement.

Semerenko v. Cendant Corp.
United States Court of Appeals, Third Circuit, 2000.
223 F.3d 165.

■ Before: MANSMANN and GREENBERG, CIRCUIT JUDGES and ALARCON, SENIOR CIRCUIT JUDGE.*

■ ALARCON, SENIOR CIRCUIT JUDGE:

I

The P. Schoenfeld Asset Management LLC and the class of similarly situated investors (collectively, the "Class") appeal from the order of the district court dismissing their claims for securities fraud pursuant to Rule 12(b)(6) of the Federal Rules of Civil Procedure. The Class's complaint was filed under § 10(b) of the Securities Exchange Act of 1934 (the "Exchange Act") and Rule 10b–5. The complaint also alleged that the individual defendants were liable for the underlying violations of § 10(b) and Rule 10b–5 as control persons under § 20(a) of the Exchange Act.

* * *

---

* The Honorable Arthur L. Alarcon, Senior Judge of the United States Court of Appeals for the Ninth Circuit, sitting by designation.

II

The Class filed this action against the Cendant Corporation ("Cendant"), its former officers and directors Walter A. Forbes, E. Kirk Shelton, Christopher K. McLeod, and Cosmo Corigliano (the "individual defendants"), and its accountant Ernst & Young LLP ("Ernst & Young") (collectively, the "defendants"). The Class alleges that the defendants violated § 10(b) and Rule 10b–5 by making certain misrepresentations about Cendant during a tender offer for shares of American Bankers Insurance Group, Inc. ("ABI") common stock. The Class consists of persons who purchased shares of ABI common stock during the course of the tender offer. The class period runs from January 27, 1998 to October 13, 1998. The complaint does not allege that any member of the Class purchased securities issued by Cendant, or that any member of the Class tendered shares of ABI common stock to Cendant. Instead, it alleges that the defendants made certain misrepresentations about Cendant that artificially inflated the price at which the Class purchased their shares of ABI common stock, and that the Class suffered a corresponding loss when those misrepresentations were disclosed to the public and the merger agreement was terminated. In light of the procedural posture of this case, we must assume the truth of the facts alleged in the complaint.

* * *

IV

* * *

A.

We must first decide whether the Class's complaint pleads sufficient facts to satisfy the "in connection with" requirement of § 10(b) and Rule 10b–5. The parties have expressed much disagreement over the standard that this court applies in determining whether an alleged misrepresentation was made "in connection with" the purchase or the sale of a security. The defendants, in varying respects, contend that the alleged misrepresentations must speak directly to the investment value of the security that is bought or sold, and that they must have been made with the specific purpose or objective of influencing an investor's decision. In contrast, the Class and the SEC, as amicus curiae, argue that the "in connection with" requirement is satisfied whenever a misrepresentation is made in a manner that is reasonably calculated to influence the investment decisions of market participants. Recognizing that "the 'in connection with' phrase is not the least difficult aspect of the 10b–5 complex to tie down," we take this opportunity to clarify the standard that governs this matter. Chemical Bank v. Arthur Andersen & Co., 726 F.2d 930, 942 (2d Cir. 1984) (noting the difficulty in establishing a test for the "in connection with" requirement) (quotations and citations omitted).

In Ketchum v. Green, 557 F.2d 1022 (1977), this court considered the question whether certain misrepresentations arising out of an internal contest for the control of a closely held corporation were made "in connection with" the subsequent forced redemption of the losing parties' stock. There, a group of minority shareholders secretly conspired to remove the two majority shareholders from their respective positions as the chairman of the board of directors and as the president of the corporation. By misrepresenting their intentions concerning the election of corporate officers, the minority shareholders were able to persuade the majority shareholders to elect them to a majority of the seats on the board of directors. After gaining control of the board of directors, the minority shareholders immediately voted to remove the two majority shareholders from their officerships. To entrench themselves, they also passed resolutions terminating the majority shareholders' employment and authorizing the mandatory repurchase of the majority shareholders' stock pursuant to a stock retirement agreement. The majority shareholders brought an action pursuant to § 10(b) and Rule 10b–5 to enjoin their ouster from the corporation and to obtain damages. On review, this court held that the majority shareholders failed to establish that the complained of misrepresentations were made "in connection with" the purchase or the sale of a security. In addition to noting that the case fell within an "internal corporate mismanagement" exception to § 10(b) and Rule 10b–5, the court reasoned that the degree of proximity between the claimed fraud and the securities transaction was simply too attenuated for the case to fall within the scope of the federal securities laws.

This court again considered the contours of the "in connection with" requirement in Angelastro v. Prudential-Bache Sec., Inc., 764 F.2d 939 (3d Cir. 1985), when it addressed the question whether a brokerage firm could be held liable under § 10(b) and Rule 10b–5 for making misrepresentations concerning the terms of its margin accounts. In that case, a class of investors sued a national brokerage firm for misrepresenting both the specific interest rates that it would charge in connection with a margin purchase and the formula that it would apply in calculating those rates. The district court dismissed the investors' complaint on the basis that the alleged misrepresentations were not made "in connection with" the purchase or the sale of a security. This court reversed, holding that the investors could pursue their claims under § 10(b) and Rule 10b–5. The court reasoned that the requisite causal connection was satisfied by the brokerage firm's fraudulent course of dealing, notwithstanding the fact that the alleged misrepresentations did not relate to the merits of a security. In holding in favor of the class, the court specifically noted that "Rule 10b–5 also encompasses misrepresentations beyond those implicating the investment value of a particular security."

While the decisions in *Ketchum* and *Angelastro* are illustrative of the point that the "in connection with" language requires a causal connection between the claimed fraud and the purchase or the sale of a security, and that the misrepresentations need not refer to a particular security, they are not helpful in applying the standard to the facts of this case. This case does not present a claim based on allegations of internal corporate misconduct arising from a contest for the control of a closely held corporation. See Ketchum, 557 F.2d at 1028. Nor does it concern a fraudulent course of dealing by a brokerage firm. See Angelastro, 764 F.2d at 944. Rather, it involves the public dissemination of allegedly misleading information into an efficient securities market. In light of the law of this circuit that the scope of the "in connection with" requirement must be determined on a case-by-case basis, we are compelled to look elsewhere in deciding the standard that governs this matter. See Ketchum, 557 F.2d at 1027; Angelastro, 764 F.2d at 942–43, 945.

In resolving the issue before us, we are persuaded by recent decisions in the Second Circuit and the Ninth Circuit that have addressed the scope of the "in connection with" requirement when the alleged fraud involves the public dissemination of false and misleading information. Those courts have generally adopted the standard articulated in Securities & Exch. Comm'n v. Texas Gulf Sulphur Co., 401 F.2d 833, 862 (2d Cir. 1968) (en banc), and applied an objective analysis that considers the alleged misrepresentation in the context in which it was made. They have held that, where the fraud alleged involves the public dissemination of information in a medium upon which an investor would presumably rely, the "in connection with" element may be established by proof of the materiality of the misrepresentation and the means of its dissemination. Under that standard, it is irrelevant that the misrepresentations were not made for the purpose or the object of influencing the investment decisions of market participants.

We conclude that the materiality and public dissemination approach should apply in this case. The purpose underlying § 10(b) and Rule 10b–5 is to ensure that investors obtain fair and full disclosure of material facts in connection with their decisions to purchase or sell securities. That purpose is best satisfied by a rule that recognizes the realistic causal effect that material misrepresentations, which raise the public's interest in particular securities, tend to have on the investment decisions of market participants who trade in those securities. We therefore adopt the reasoning of the Second Circuit and the Ninth Circuit and hold that the Class may establish the "in connection with" element simply by showing that the misrepresentations in question were disseminated to the public in a medium upon which a reasonable investor would rely, and that they were material when disseminated. We also point out that, under the standard which we adopt, the Class is not required to establish that the defendants actually envisioned that members of the Class would rely upon the alleged misrepresentations when making their investment decisions. Rather, it must only show that the alleged misrepresentations were reckless. See In re Advanta Corp. Sec. Litig., 180 F.3d 525, 535 (3d

Cir. 1999) (reaffirming that § 10(b) and Rule 10b–5 cover reckless misrepresentations).

* * *

SEC v. Zandford
United States Supreme Court, 2002.
535 U.S. 813, 122 S.Ct. 1899, 153 L.Ed.2d 1.

■ STEVENS, J., delivered the opinion for a unanimous Court.

The Securities and Exchange Commission (SEC) filed a civil complaint alleging that a stockbroker violated both § 10(b) of the Securities Exchange Act of 1934, 48 Stat. 891, as amended, 15 U.S.C. § 78j(b), and the SEC's Rule 10b–5, by selling his customer's securities and using the proceeds for his own benefit without the customer's knowledge or consent. The question presented is whether the alleged fraudulent conduct was "in connection with the purchase or sale of any security" within the meaning of the statute and the Rule.

I

Between 1987 and 1991, respondent was employed as a securities broker in the Maryland branch of a New York brokerage firm. In 1987, he persuaded William Wood, an elderly man in poor health, to open a joint investment account for himself and his mentally retarded daughter. According to the SEC's complaint, the "stated investment objectives for the account were 'safety of principal and income.'" The Woods granted respondent discretion to manage their account and a general power of attorney to engage in securities transactions for their benefit without prior approval. Relying on respondent's promise to "conservatively invest" their money, the Woods entrusted him with $419,255. Before Mr. Wood's death in 1991, all of that money was gone.

In 1991, the National Association of Securities Dealers (NASD) conducted a routine examination of respondent's firm and discovered that on over 25 separate occasions, money had been transferred from the Woods' account to accounts controlled by respondent. In due course, respondent was indicted in the United States District Court for the District of Maryland on 13 counts of wire fraud in violation of 18 U.S.C. § 1343. The first count alleged that respondent sold securities in the Woods' account and then made personal use of the proceeds. Each of the other counts alleged that he made wire transfers between Maryland and New York that enabled him to withdraw specified sums from the Woods' accounts. Some of those transfers involved respondent writing checks to himself from a mutual fund account held by the Woods, which required liquidating securities in order to redeem the checks. Respondent was convicted on all counts, sentenced to prison for 52 months, and ordered to pay $10,800 in restitution.

After respondent was indicted, the SEC filed a civil complaint in the same District Court alleging that respondent violated § 10(b) and Rule 10b–5 by engaging in a scheme to defraud the Woods and by misappropriating approximately $343,000 of the Woods' securities without their knowledge or consent.

* * *

II.

* * *

In its role enforcing the Act, the SEC has consistently adopted a broad reading of the phrase "in connection with the purchase or sale of any security." It has maintained that a broker who accepts payment for securities that he never intends to deliver, or who sells customer securities with intent to misappropriate the proceeds, violates § 10(b) and Rule 10b–5. This interpretation of the ambiguous text of § 10(b), in the context of formal adjudication, is entitled to deference if it is reasonable, see United States v. Mead Corp., 533 U.S. 218, 229–230, and n.12 (2001). For the reasons set forth below, we think it is. While the statute must not be construed so broadly as to convert every common-law fraud that happens to involve securities into a violation of § 10(b), Marine Bank v. Weaver, 455 U.S. 551, 556 (1982) ("Congress, in enacting the securities laws, did not intend to provide a broad federal remedy for all fraud"), neither the SEC nor this Court has ever held that there must be a misrepresentation about the value of a particular security in order to run afoul of the Act.

The SEC claims respondent engaged in a fraudulent scheme in which he made sales of his customer's securities for his own benefit. Respondent submits that the sales themselves were perfectly lawful and that the subsequent misappropriation of the proceeds, though fraudulent, is not properly viewed as having the requisite connection with the sales; in his view, the alleged scheme is not materially different from a simple theft of cash or securities in an investment account. We disagree.

According to the complaint, respondent "engaged in a scheme to defraud" the Woods beginning in 1988, shortly after they opened their account, and that scheme continued throughout the 2-year period during which respondent made a series of transactions that enabled him to convert the proceeds of the sales of the Woods' securities to his own use. The securities sales and respondent's fraudulent practices were not independent events. This is not a case in which, after a lawful transaction had been consummated, a broker decided to steal the proceeds and did so. Nor is it a case in which a thief simply invested the proceeds of a routine conversion in the stock market. Rather, respondent's fraud coincided with the sales themselves.

Taking the allegations in the complaint as true, each sale was made to further respondent's fraudulent scheme; each was deceptive because it was neither authorized by, nor disclosed to, the Woods. With regard to the sales of shares in the Woods' mutual fund, respondent initiated these transactions by writing a check to himself from that account, knowing that redeeming the check would require the sale of securities. Indeed, each time respondent "exercised his power of disposition for his own benefit," that conduct, "without more," was a fraud. United States v. Dunn, 268 U.S. 121 (1925). In the aggregate, the sales are properly viewed as a "course of business" that operated as a fraud or deceit on a stockbroker's customer.

Insofar as the connection between respondent's deceptive practices and his sale of the Woods' securities is concerned, the case is remarkably similar to Superintendent of Ins. of N. Y. v. Bankers Life & Casualty Co., 404 U.S. 6 (1971). In that case the directors of Manhattan Casualty Company authorized the sale of the company's portfolio of treasury bonds because they had been "duped" into believing that the company would receive the proceeds of the sale. We held that "Manhattan was injured as an investor through a deceptive device which deprived it of any compensation for the sale of its valuable block of securities." In reaching this conclusion, we did not ask, as the Fourth Circuit did in this case, whether the directors were misled about the value of a security or whether the fraud involved "manipulation of a particular security." In fact, we rejected the Second Circuit's position in Superintendent of Ins. of N. Y. v. Bankers Life & Casualty Co., 430 F.2d 355, 361 (1970), that because the fraud against Manhattan did not take place within the context of a securities exchange it was not prohibited by § 10(b). 404 U.S., at 10. We refused to read the statute so narrowly, noting that it "must be read flexibly, not technically and restrictively." Although we recognized that the interest in " 'preserving the integrity of the securities markets' " was one of the purposes animating the statute, we rejected the notion that § 10(b) is limited to serving that objective alone. ("We agree that Congress by § 10(b) did not seek to regulate transactions which constitute no more than internal corporate mismanagement. But we read § 10(b) to mean that Congress meant to bar deceptive devices and contrivances in the purchase or sale of securities whether conducted in the organized markets or face to face").

Like the company directors in *Bankers Life*, the Woods were injured as investors through respondent's deceptions, which deprived them of any compensation for the sale of their valuable securities. They were duped into believing respondent would "conservatively invest" their assets in the stock market and that any transactions made on their behalf would be for their benefit for the " 'safety of principal and income.' " The fact that respondent misappropriated the proceeds of the sales provides persuasive evidence that he had violated § 10(b) when he made the sales, but misappropriation is not an essential element of the offense. Indeed, in *Bankers Life*, we flatly stated that it was "irrelevant" that "the proceeds of the sale that were due the seller were misappropriated." It is enough that the scheme to defraud and the sale of securities coincide.

* * *

More recently, in Wharf (Holdings) Ltd. v. United Int'l Holdings, Inc., 532 U.S. 588 (2001), our decision that the seller of a security had violated § 10(b) focused on the secret intent of the seller when the sale occurred. The purchaser claimed "that Wharf sold it a security (the option) while secretly intending from the very beginning not to honor the option." Although Wharf did not specifically argue that the breach of contract underlying the complaint lacked the requisite connection with a sale of securities, it did assert that the case was merely a dispute over ownership of the option, and that interpreting § 10(b) to include such a claim would convert every breach of contract that happened to involve a security into a violation of the federal securities laws. We rejected that argument because the purchaser's claim was not that the defendant failed to carry out a promise to sell securities; rather, the claim was that the defendant sold a security while never intending to honor its agreement in the first place. Similarly, in this case the SEC claims respondent sold the Woods' securities while secretly intending from the very beginning to keep the proceeds. In *Wharf*, the fraudulent intent deprived the purchaser of the benefit of the sale whereas here the fraudulent intent deprived the seller of that benefit, but the connection between the deception and the sale in each case is identical.

In United States v. O'Hagan, 521 U.S. 642 (1997), we held that the defendant had committed fraud "in connection with" a securities transaction when he used misappropriated confidential information for trading purposes. We reasoned that "the fiduciary's fraud is consummated, not when the fiduciary gains the confidential information, but when, without disclosure to his principal, he uses the information to purchase or sell securities. The securities transaction and the breach of duty thus coincide. This is so even though the person or entity defrauded is not the other party to the trade, but is, instead, the source of the nonpublic information." The Court of Appeals distinguished *O'Hagan* by reading it to require that the misappropriated information or assets not have independent value to the client outside the securities market. We do not read *O'Hagan* as so limited. In the chief passage cited by the Court of Appeals for this proposition, we discussed the Government's position that "[t]he misappropriation theory would not. . . . apply to a case in which a person defrauded a bank into giving him a loan or embezzled cash from another, and then used the proceeds of the misdeed to purchase securities," because in that situation "the proceeds would have value to the malefactor apart from their use in a securities transaction, and the fraud would be complete as soon as the money was obtained." if this passage could be read to introduce a new requirement into § 10(b), it would not affect our analysis of this case, because the Woods' securities did not have value for respondent apart from their use in a securities transaction and the fraud was not complete before the sale of securities occurred.

As in *Bankers Life*, *Wharf*, and *O'Hagan*, the SEC complaint describes a fraudulent scheme in which the securities transactions and breaches of fiduciary duty coincide. Those breaches were therefore "in connection with" securities sales within the meaning of § 10(b).[4] Accordingly, the judgment of the Court of Appeals is reversed, and the case is remanded for further proceedings consistent with this opinion.

It is so ordered.

NOTE ON THE "IN CONNECTION WITH" REQUIREMENT

The lower courts have generally construed the "in connection with" element as set forth in *Superintendent of Insurance*[56] to require "some nexus but not necessarily a direct and close relationship" between the fraud and the purchase or sale of a security.[57] In Chemical Bank v. Arthur Andersen & Co.,[58] Frigitemp had pledged 100 percent of the stock in its wholly owned subsidiary, Elsters, as security for bank loans. The banks alleged that auditor Arthur Andersen had made knowing misrepresentations concerning Frigitemp's financial condition, however, this was not enough to allege a misstatement in connection with the banks' purchase or Frigitemp's sale of Elsters' stock. Judge Friendly wrote:

> The purpose of § 10(b) and Rule 10b–5 is to protect persons who are deceived in securities transactions—to make sure that buyers of securities get what they think they are getting and that sellers of securities are not tricked into parting with something for a price known to the buyer to be inadequate or for a consideration to the buyer not to be what it purports to be. Andersen is not alleged to have deceived the Banks with respect to the pledge of the Elsters' stock; the Banks got exactly what they expected. Their showing is simply that but for Andersen's description of Frigitemp they would not have renewed the Frigitemp loans or made the Elsters' loan which Frigitemp guaranteed, and that if they had not done this, there would have been no pledge of Elsters' stock. Such "but-for" causation is not enough. The Act and Rule impose liability for a proscribed act in connection with the purchase or sale of a security; it is not

---

[4] Contrary to the Court of Appeals' prediction, our analysis does not transform every breach of fiduciary duty into a federal securities violation. If, for example, a broker embezzles cash from a client's account or takes advantage of the fiduciary relationship to induce his client into a fraudulent real estate transaction, then the fraud would not include the requisite connection to a purchase or sale of securities. Likewise if the broker told his client he was stealing the client's assets, that breach of fiduciary duty might be in connection with a sale of securities, but it would not involve a deceptive device or fraud.

[56] 404 U.S. 6 (1971).

[57] See, e.g., Abrams v. Oppenheimer Gov't Sec., Inc., 737 F.2d 582 (7th Cir. 1984).

[58] 726 F.2d 930, 943 (2d Cir. 1984).

sufficient to allege that a defendant has committed a proscribed act in a transaction of which the pledge of a security is a part.

The Second Circuit subsequently distinguished *Chemical Bank* in SEC v. Drysdale, where the court held misrepresentations of the company's financial condition that directly involved the consideration for a securities transaction were sufficiently "in connection with the purchase or sale of securities."[59] The court noted that the "securities were transferred as a direct result of a misrepresentation, whereas in *Chemical Bank* the direct result of the misrepresentations was a loan and not a securities transfer."[60]

D. CULPABILITY

Ernst & Ernst v. Hochfelder
Supreme Court of the United States, 1976.
425 U.S. 185, 96 S.Ct. 1375, 47 L.Ed.2d 668.

■ MR. JUSTICE POWELL delivered the opinion of the Court.

The issue in this case is whether an action for civil damages may lie under § 10(b) of the Securities Exchange Act of 1934 (1934 Act) and Securities and Exchange Commission Rule 10b–5, in the absence of an allegation of intent to deceive, manipulate, or defraud on the part of the defendant.

I

Petitioner, Ernst & Ernst, is an accounting firm. From 1946 through 1967 it was retained by First Securities Company of Chicago (First Securities), a small brokerage firm and member of the Midwest Stock Exchange and of the National Association of Securities Dealers, to perform periodic audits of the firm's books and records. In connection with these audits Ernst & Ernst prepared for filing with the Securities and Exchange Commission (Commission) the annual reports required of First Securities under § 17(a) of the 1934 Act. It also prepared for First

---

[59] SEC v. Drysdale Sec. Corp., 785 F.2d 38, 41–43 (2d Cir. 1986).

[60] Id. at 43. In Ames Dep't Stores Inc. Stock Litig., 991 F.2d 953, 963 (2d Cir. 1993), the Second Circuit reversed a district court dismissal for failure to state a claim, stating in part:

> [T]he district court evidently assumed that the only statements that are made in connection with the sale of stock are those made in the issuing documents. This reasoning would eliminate the vast majority of private Rule 10b–5 actions and subvert the 1934 Act's efforts to protect investors from deliberate fraud. The securities markets are highly sensitive to press releases and to information contained in all sorts of publicly released corporate documents, and the investor is foolish who would ignore such releases. In light of this, defendants have been held liable for misrepresentations in press releases, Basic Inc. v. Levinson, 485 U.S. 224 (1988), and for misrepresentations in corporate documents other than those issued to shareholders, Fischman v. Raytheon, 188 F.2d 783.

Similarly, in United States v. Russo, 74 F.3d 1383, 1391–92 (2d Cir. 1996), the court relied on Ames to conclude that fraudulent short sales made for the express purpose of financing a stock kiting scheme were sufficiently "in connection with" a manipulation to violate § 10(b) and Rule 10b–5.

Securities responses to the financial questionnaires of the Midwest Stock Exchange (Exchange).

Respondents were customers of First Securities who invested in a fraudulent securities scheme perpetrated by Leston B. Nay, president of the firm and owner of 92% of its stock. Nay induced the respondents to invest funds in "escrow" accounts that he represented would yield a high rate of return. Respondents did so from 1942 through 1966, with the majority of the transactions occurring in the 1950's. In fact, there were no escrow accounts as Nay converted respondents' funds to his own use immediately upon receipt. These transactions were not in the customary form of dealings between First Securities and its customers. The respondents drew their personal checks payable to Nay or a designated bank for his account. No such escrow accounts were reflected on the books and records of First Securities, and none was shown on its periodic accounting to respondents in connection with their other investments. Nor were they included in First Securities' filings with the Commission or the Exchange.

This fraud came to light in 1968 when Nay committed suicide, leaving a note that described First Securities as bankrupt and the escrow accounts as "spurious." Respondents subsequently filed this action for damages against Ernst & Ernst in the United States District Court for the Northern District of Illinois under § 10(b) of the 1934 Act. The complaint charged that Nay's escrow scheme violated § 10(b) and Commission Rule 10b–5, and that Ernst & Ernst had "aided and abetted" Nay's violations by its "failure" to conduct proper audits of First Securities. As revealed through discovery, respondents' cause of action rested on a theory of negligent nonfeasance. The premise was that Ernst & Ernst had failed to utilize "appropriate auditing procedures" in its audits of First Securities, thereby failing to discover internal practices of the firm said to prevent an effective audit. The practice principally relied on was Nay's rule that only he could open mail addressed to him at First Securities or addressed to First Securities to his attention, even if it arrived in his absence. Respondents contended that if Ernst & Ernst had conducted a proper audit, it would have discovered this "mail rule." The existence of the rule then would have been disclosed in reports to the Exchange and to the Commission by Ernst & Ernst as an irregular procedure that prevented an effective audit. This would have led to an investigation of Nay that would have revealed the fraudulent scheme. Respondents specifically disclaimed the existence of fraud or intentional misconduct on the part of Ernst & Ernst.

After extensive discovery the District Court granted Ernst & Ernst's motion for summary judgment and dismissed the action. The court rejected Ernst & Ernst's contention that a cause of action for aiding and abetting a securities fraud could not be maintained under § 10(b) and Rule 10b–5 merely on allegations of negligence. It concluded, however, that there was no genuine issue of material fact with respect to whether

Ernst & Ernst had conducted its audits in accordance with generally accepted auditing standards.

The Court of Appeals for the Seventh Circuit reversed and remanded, holding that one who breaches a duty of inquiry and disclosure owed another is liable in damages for aiding and abetting a third party's violation of Rule 10b–5 if the fraud would have been discovered or prevented but for the breach. * * *.

We granted *certiorari* to resolve the question whether a private cause of action for damages will lie under § 10(b) and Rule 10b–5 in the absence of any allegation of "scienter"—intent to deceive, manipulate, or defraud. We conclude that it will not and therefore we reverse.

II

* * *

Although § 10(b) does not by its terms create an express civil remedy for its violation, and there is no indication that Congress, or the Commission when adopting Rule 10b–5, contemplated such a remedy, the existence of a private cause of action for violations of the statute and the Rule is now well established. During the 30-year period since a private cause of action was first implied under § 10(b) and Rule 10b–5, a substantial body of case law and commentary has developed as to its elements. Courts and commentators long have differed with regard to whether scienter is a necessary element of such a cause of action, or whether negligent conduct alone is sufficient. In addressing this question, we turn first to the language of § 10(b), for "[t]he starting point in every case involving construction of a statute is the language itself." Blue Chip Stamps, (Powell, J., concurring); see FTC v. Bunte Brothers, Inc., 312 U.S. 349, 350 (1941).

A

Section 10(b) makes unlawful the use or employment of "any manipulative or deceptive device or contrivance" in contravention of Commission rules. The words "manipulative or deceptive" used in conjunction with "device or contrivance" strongly suggest that § 10(b) was intended to proscribe knowing or intentional misconduct. See SEC v. Texas Gulf Sulphur Co., 401 F.2d 833, 868 (C.A.2 1968) (Friendly, J., concurring), cert. denied sub nom.

In its *amicus curiae* brief, however, the Commission contends that nothing in the language "manipulative or deceptive device or contrivance" limits its operation to knowing or intentional practices. In support of its view, the Commission cites the overall congressional purpose in the 1933 and 1934 Acts to protect investors against false and deceptive practices that might injure them. The Commission then reasons that since the "effect" upon investors of given conduct is the same regardless of whether the conduct is negligent or intentional, Congress must have intended to bar all such practices and not just those done knowingly or intentionally. The logic of this effect-oriented approach would impose liability for wholly faultless conduct where such conduct results in harm to investors, a result the Commission would be unlikely to support. But apart from where its logic might lead, the Commission would add a gloss to the operative language of the statute quite different from its commonly accepted meaning. The argument simply ignores the use of the words "manipulative," "device," and "contrivance" terms that make unmistakable a congressional intent to proscribe a type of conduct quite different from negligence. Use of the word "manipulative" is especially significant. It is and was virtually a term of art when used in connection with securities markets. It connotes intentional or willful conduct designed to deceive or defraud investors by controlling or artificially affecting the price of securities.

In addition to relying upon the Commission's argument with respect to the operative language of the statute, respondents contend that since we are dealing with "remedial legislation," Tcherepnin v. Knight, 389 U.S. 332, 336 (1967), it must be construed "'not technically and restrictively, but flexibly to effectuate its remedial purposes.'" Affiliated Ute Citizens v. United States, supra, at 151, quoting SEC v. Capital Gains Research Bureau, supra, at 186. They argue that the "remedial purposes" of the Acts demand a construction of § 10(b) that embraces negligence as a standard of liability. But in seeking to accomplish its broad remedial goals, Congress did not adopt uniformly a negligence standard even as to express civil remedies. In some circumstances and with respect to certain classes of defendants, Congress did create express liability predicated upon a failure to exercise reasonable care. E.g., 1933 Act § 11(b)(3)(B) (liability of "experts," such as accountants, for misleading statements in portions of registration statements for which they are responsible). But in other situations good faith is an absolute defense. 1934 Act § 18 (misleading statements in any document filed pursuant to the 1934 Act). And in still other circumstances Congress created express liability regardless of the defendant's fault, 1933 Act § 11(a) (issuer liability for misleading statements in the registration statement).

It is thus evident that Congress fashioned standards of fault in the express civil remedies in the 1933 and 1934 Acts on a particularized basis. Ascertainment of congressional intent with respect to the standard of liability created by a particular section of the Acts must therefore rest primarily on the language of that section. Where, as here, we deal with a judicially implied liability, the statutory language certainly is no less important. In view of the language of § 10(b) which so clearly connotes intentional misconduct, and mindful that the language of a statute controls when sufficiently clear in its context, further inquiry may be unnecessary. We turn now, nevertheless, to the legislative history of the 1934 Act to ascertain whether there is support for the meaning attributed to § 10(b) by the Commission and respondents.

B

Although the extensive legislative history of the 1934 Act is bereft of any explicit explanation of Congress' intent, we think the relevant portions of that history support our conclusion that § 10(b) was addressed to practices that involve some element of scienter and cannot be read to impose liability for negligent conduct alone.

* * *

Neither the intended scope of § 10(b) nor the reasons for the changes in its operative language are revealed explicitly in the legislative history of the 1934 Act, which deals primarily with other aspects of the legislation. There is no indication, however, that § 10(b) was intended to proscribe conduct not involving scienter. The extensive hearings that preceded passage of the 1934 Act touched only briefly on § 10, and most of the discussion was devoted to the enumerated devices that the Commission is empowered to proscribe under § 10(a). The most relevant exposition of the provision that was to become § 10(b) was by Thomas G. Corcoran, a spokesman for the drafters. Corcoran indicated:

> "Subsection (c) [§ 9(c) of H.R. 7852—later § 10(b)] says, 'Thou shalt not devise any other cunning devices.'
>
> "Of course subsection (c) is a catch-all clause to prevent manipulative devices. I do not think there is any objection to that kind of clause. The Commission should have the authority to deal with new manipulative devices." Hearings on H.R. 7852 and H.R. 8720 before the House Comm. on Interstate and Foreign Commerce, 73d Cong., 2d Sess., 115 (1934).

This brief explanation of § 10(b) by a spokesman for its drafters is significant. The section was described rightly as a "catch-all" clause to enable the Commission "to deal with new manipulative [or cunning] devices." It is difficult to believe that any lawyer, legislative draftsman, or legislator would use these words if the intent was to create liability for merely negligent acts or omissions. Neither the legislative history nor the briefs supporting respondents identify any usage or authority for construing "manipulative [or cunning] devices" to include negligence.

* * *

C

* * *

The Commission argues that Congress has been explicit in requiring willful conduct when that was the standard of fault intended, citing § 9 of the 1934 Act, which generally proscribes manipulation of securities prices. Sections 9(a)(1) and (a)(2), for example, respectively prohibit manipulation of security prices "[f]or the purpose of creating a false or misleading appearance of active trading in any security . . . or . . . with respect to the market for any such security," and "for the purpose of inducing the purchase or sale of such security by others." See also

§ 9(a)(4). Section 9(e) then imposes upon "[a]ny person who willfully participates in any act or transaction in violation of" other provisions of § 9 civil liability to anyone who purchased or sold a security at a price affected by the manipulative activities. From this the Commission concludes that since § 10(b) is not by its terms explicitly restricted to willful, knowing, or purposeful conduct, it should not be construed in all cases to require more than negligent action or inaction as a precondition for civil liability.

The structure of the Acts does not support the Commission's argument. In each instance that Congress created express civil liability in favor of purchasers or sellers of securities it clearly specified whether recovery was to be premised on knowing or intentional conduct, negligence, or entirely innocent mistake. See 1933 Act, §§ 11, 12, 15; 1934 Act §§ 9, 18, 20. For example, § 11 of the 1933 Act unambiguously creates a private action for damages when a registration statement includes untrue statements of material facts or fails to state material facts necessary to make the statements therein not misleading. Within the limits specified by § 11(e), the issuer of the securities is held absolutely liable for any damages resulting from such misstatement or omission. But experts such as accountants who have prepared portions of the registration statement are accorded a "due diligence" defense. In effect, this is a negligence standard. An expert may avoid civil liability with respect to the portions of the registration statement for which he was responsible by showing that "after reasonable investigation" he had "reasonable ground[s] to believe" that the statements for which he was responsible were true and there was no omission of a material fact.[26] § 11(b)(3)(B)(i). See, e.g., Escott v. BarChris Construction Corp., 283 F.Supp. 643, 697–703 (S.D.N.Y.1968). The express recognition of a cause of action premised on negligent behavior in § 11 stands in sharp contrast to the language of § 10(b), and significantly undercuts the Commission's argument.

We also consider it significant that each of the express civil remedies in the 1933 Act allowing recovery for negligent conduct, see §§ 11, 12(2), 15, is subject to significant procedural restrictions not applicable under § 10(b).[28] Section 11(e) of the 1933 Act, for example, authorizes the court

---

[26] Other individuals who sign the registration statement, directors of the issuer, and the underwriter of the securities similarly are accorded a complete defense against civil liability based on the exercise of reasonable investigation and a reasonable belief that the registration statement was not misleading. §§ 11(b)(3)(A), (C), (D), (c). See, e.g., Feit v. Leasco Data Processing Equipment Corp., 332 F.Supp. 544, 575–583 (E.D.N.Y.1971) (underwriters, but not officer-directors, established their due diligence defense).

[28] Each of the provisions of the 1934 Act that expressly create civil liability, except those directed to specific classes of individuals such as directors, officers, or 10% beneficial holders of securities, see § 16(b), Foremost-McKesson, Inc. v. Provident Securities Co., supra; Kern County Land Co. v. Occidental Petroleum Corp., 411 U.S. 582 (1973), contains a state-of-mind condition requiring something more than negligence. Section 9(e) creates potential civil liability for any person who "willfully participates" in the manipulation of securities on a national exchange. § 9(e). Section 18 creates potential civil liability for misleading statements filed with the Commission, but provides the defendant with the defense that "he acted in good faith and had no knowledge that such statement was false or misleading." And § 20, which imposes liability

to require a plaintiff bringing a suit under § 11, § 12(2), or § 15 thereof to post a bond for costs, including attorneys' fees, and in specified circumstances to assess costs at the conclusion of the litigation. Section 13 specifies a statute of limitations of one year from the time the violation was or should have been discovered, in no event to exceed three years from the time of offer or sale, applicable to actions brought under § 11, § 12(2), or § 15. These restrictions, significantly, were imposed by amendments to the 1933 Act adopted as part of the 1934 Act. Prior to amendment § 11(e) contained no provision for payment of costs. The amendments also substantially shortened the statute of limitations provided by § 13. Compare Pub.L. No. 22, supra, § 13, 48 Stat. 84, with 15 U.S.C. § 77m. See 1934 Act, § 207, 48 Stat. 908. We think these procedural limitations indicate that the judicially created private damages remedy under § 10(b)—which has no comparable restrictions—cannot be extended, consistently with the intent of Congress, to actions premised on negligent wrongdoing. Such extension would allow causes of action covered by § 11, § 12(2), and § 15 to be brought instead under § 10(b) and thereby nullify the effectiveness of the carefully drawn procedural restrictions on these express actions. We would be unwilling to bring about this result absent substantial support in the legislative history, and there is none.[31]

D

We have addressed, to this point, primarily the language and history of § 10(b). The Commission contends, however, that subsections [(2)] and [(3)] of Rule 10b–5 are cast in language which—if standing alone—could encompass both intentional and negligent behavior. These subsections respectively provide that it is unlawful "[t]o make any untrue statement

---

upon "controlling persons" for violations of the Act by those they control, exculpates a defendant who "acted in good faith and did not ... induce the act ... constituting the violation...." Emphasizing the important difference between the operative language and purpose of § 14(a) of the 1934 Act as contrasted with § 10(b), however, some courts have concluded that proof of scienter is unnecessary in an action for damages by the shareholder recipients of a materially misleading proxy statement against the issuer corporation. Gerstle v. Gamble-Skogmo, Inc., 478 F.2d 1281, 1299 (C.A.2 1973).

[31] Section 18 of the 1934 Act creates a private cause of action against persons, such as accountants, who "make or cause to be made" materially misleading statements in reports or other documents filed with the Commission. We need not consider the question whether a cause of action may be maintained under § 10(b) on the basis of actions that would constitute a violation of § 18. Under § 18 liability extends to persons who, in reliance on such statements, purchased or sold a security whose price was affected by the statements. Liability is limited, however, in the important respect that the defendant is accorded the defense that he acted in "good faith and had no knowledge that such statement was false or misleading." Consistent with this language, the legislative history of the section suggests something more than negligence on the part of the defendant is required for recovery. The original version of § 18(a), § 17(a) of S. 2693, H.R. 7852 and H.R. 7855, provided that the defendant would not be liable if "he acted in good faith and in the exercise of reasonable care had no ground to believe that such statement was false or misleading." The accounting profession objected to this provision on the ground that liability would be created for honest errors in judgment. In subsequent drafts the current formulation was adopted. It is also significant that actions under § 18 are limited by a relatively short statute of limitations similar to that provided in § 13 of the 1933 Act, § 18(c). Moreover, as under § 11(e) of the 1933 Act a District Court is authorized to require the plaintiff to post a bond for costs, including attorney's fees, and to assess such costs at the conclusion of the litigation. § 18(a).

of a material fact or to omit to state a material fact necessary in order to make the statements made, in light of the circumstances under which they were made, not misleading . . ." and "[t]o engage in any act, practice, or course of business which operates or would operate as a fraud or deceit upon any person. . . ." Viewed in isolation the language of subsection [(2)], and arguably that of subsection [(3)], could be read as proscribing, respectively, any type of material misstatement or omission, and any course of conduct, that has the effect of defrauding investors, whether the wrongdoing was intentional or not.

We note first that such a reading cannot be harmonized with the administrative history of the Rule, a history making clear that when the Commission adopted the Rule it was intended to apply only to activities that involved scienter. More importantly, Rule 10b–5 was adopted pursuant to authority granted the Commission under § 10(b). The rulemaking power granted to an administrative agency charged with the administration of a federal statute is not the power to make law. Rather, it is " 'the power to adopt regulations to carry into effect the will of Congress as expressed by the statute.' " Dixon v. United States, 381 U.S. 68, 74 (1965), quoting Manhattan General Equipment Co. v. Commissioner, 297 U.S. 129, 134 (1936). Thus, despite the broad view of the Rule advanced by the Commission in this case, its scope cannot exceed the power granted the Commission by Congress under § 10(b). For the reasons stated above, we think the Commission's original interpretation of Rule 10b–5 was compelled by the language and history of § 10(b) and related sections of the Acts. When a statute speaks so specifically in terms of manipulation and deception, and of implementing devices and contrivances—the commonly understood terminology of intentional wrongdoing—and when its history reflects no more expansive intent, we are quite unwilling to extend the scope of the statute to negligent conduct.

III

Recognizing that § 10(b) and Rule 10b–5 might be held to require proof of more than negligent nonfeasance by Ernst & Ernst as a precondition to the imposition of civil liability, respondents further contend that the case should be remanded for trial under whatever standard is adopted. Throughout the lengthy history of this case respondents have proceeded on a theory of liability premised on negligence, specifically disclaiming that Ernst & Ernst had engaged in fraud or intentional misconduct. In these circumstances, we think it inappropriate to remand the action for further proceedings.

The judgment of the Court of Appeals is *Reversed*.

* * *

NOTES ON THE REQUIRED CULPABILITY OF THE DEFENDANT

1. *Is Recklessness Enough?* In footnote 7 of *Ernst & Ernst*, the Supreme Court reserved the question as to whether "reckless" behavior might be a sufficient basis for culpability in an action under Rule 10b–5, conceding only that a conscious "intent to deceive, manipulate, or defraud" was sufficient. The text of footnote 7 reads:

> In support of this holding, the Court of Appeals cited its decision in Hochfelder v. Midwest Stock Exchange, supra, where it detailed the elements necessary to establish a claim under Rule 10b–5 based on a defendant's aiding and abetting a securities fraud solely by inaction. In such a case the plaintiff must show "that the party charged with aiding and abetting had knowledge of or, but for the breach of a duty of inquiry, should have had knowledge of the fraud, and that possessing such knowledge the party failed to act due to an improper motive or breach of a duty of disclosure." The court explained in the instant case that these "elements constitute a flexible standard of liability which should be amplified according to the peculiarities of each case." In view of our holding that an intent to deceive, manipulate, or defraud is required for civil liability under § 10(b) and Rule 10b–5, we need not consider whether civil liability for aiding and abetting is appropriate under the section and the rule, nor the elements necessary to establish such a cause of action. See, e.g., Brennan v. Midwestern United Life Ins. Co., 259 F.Supp. 673 (1966), 286 F.Supp. 702 (N.D.Ind.1968), aff'd, 417 F.2d 147 (7th Cir. 1969), cert. denied, 397 U.S. 989 (1970) (defendant held liable for giving active and knowing assistance to a third party engaged in violations of the securities laws). See generally Ruder, Multiple Defendants in Securities Law Fraud Cases: Aiding and Abetting, Conspiracy, In Pari Delicto, Indemnification and Contribution, 120 U.Pa.L.Rev. 597, 620–645 (1972).

After *Ernst & Ernst*, lower courts adopted the view that "recklessness" is a sufficient basis for liability, answering the question left open by the Supreme Court in *Ernst & Ernst*'s soon famous footnote 7.[61] These courts generally followed the definition of "recklessness" first set out by the Seventh Circuit in Sundstrand Corp. v. Sun Chemical Corp.,[62] as follows:

> Reckless conduct may be defined as a highly unreasonable [conduct], involving not merely simple, or even inexcusable

---

[61] 1st Circuit: Cook v. Avien, Inc., 573 F.2d 685, 692 (1st Cir. 1978); Hoffman v. Estabrook & Co., Inc., 587 F.2d 509, 516 (1st Cir. 1978) (approving district court instruction defining recklessness as "carelessness approaching indifference"); Cleary v. Perfectune, Inc., 700 F.2d 774, 777 (1st Cir. 1983); SEC v. Lehman Bros., 157 F.3d 2, 7 (1st Cir. 1998) (scienter could be established when someone "deliberately averted his eyes from evident misconduct").

[62] 553 F.2d 1033 (7th Cir. 1977).

negligence, but an extreme departure from the standards of ordinary care, and which presents a danger of misleading buyers or sellers that is either known to the defendant or is so obvious that the actor must have been aware of it.[63]

Whether phrased as "a lesser form of intent," "an extreme departure from the standards of ordinary care," or "severe recklessness," all circuits have followed the Seventh Circuit standard.[64]

2. *Ignoring Ernst & Ernst.* As discussed in Chapter 9, the Commission long had the view that any action that distorted the market could violate Rule 10b–5, regardless of the defendant's mental state. After *Ernst & Ernst*, this position was increasingly untenable. But, despite the clear Supreme Court command that scienter was an essential element of a Rule 10b–5 action, lower courts and the Commission occasionally ignore this requirement. For instance, courts have held that charging differential commissions constitutes securities fraud, even in the absence of any allegation of scienter.

3. *Scienter and Forward-Looking Statements.* The Private Securities Litigation Reform Act of 1995 amended § 17A of the Securities Act and § 21E of the Securities Exchange Act to create a safe harbor when a plaintiff alleged a fraudulent forward-looking statement unless the statement was made with "actual knowledge." This standard means that plaintiffs now can rely on a defendant's recklessness only in alleging claims concerning historical facts. Indeed, since the 1995 Act, several courts have affirmed that the Act did not alter the prevailing recklessness standard for historical facts.[65]

---

[63] Id. at 1045.

[64] In re Genzyme Corp. Sec. Litig., 754 F.3d 31, 40 (1st Cir. 2014) ("Scienter may be pled by showing that defendants either consciously intended to defraud, or that they acted with a high degree of recklessness." (citations omitted)); In re Advanced Battery Technologies, Inc., 781 F.3d 638, 644 (2d Cir. 2015) ("[R]ecklessness must be conduct that is highly unreasonable, representing an extreme departure from the standards of ordinary care, not merely a heightened form of negligence." (citations omitted)); In re Ikon Office Solutions, Inc., 277 F.3d 658, 672 n.16 (3d Cir. 2002) (requiring "recklessness bordering on an intent to deceive"); Ottmann v. Hanger Orthopedic Grp., Inc., 353 F.3d 338, 344 (4th Cir. 2003) (requiring "severe recklessness [which] is, in essence, a slightly lesser species of intentional misconduct"); Masel v. Villareal, 924 F.3d 734, 747 (5th Cir. 2019) (requiring "severe recklessness"); PR Diamonds, Inc. v. Chandler, 364 F.3d 671, 681 (6th Cir. 2004) (defining recklessness as a mental state akin to "conscious disregard"); Searls v. Glasser, 64 F.3d 1061, 1066 (7th Cir. 1995) (requiring "recklessness so severe that it is the functional equivalent of intent"); Kushner v. Beverly Enters., Inc., 317 F.3d 820, 828 (8th Cir. 2003) (requiring "severe recklessness"); Reese v. Malone, 747 F.3d 557, 569 (9th Cir. 2014) (requiring "[d]eliberate recklessness," "mean[ing] that the reckless conduct 'reflects some degree of intentional or conscious misconduct.'" (citation omitted)); City of Phila. v. Fleming Cos., 264 F.3d 1245, 1258 (10th Cir. 2001) (defining recklessness as "conduct that is an extreme departure from the standards of ordinary care"); Ziemba v. Cascade Int'l, Inc., 256 F.3d 1194, 1202 (11th Cir. 2001) (requiring "severe recklessness"); Dolphin & Bradbury, Inc. v. SEC, 512 F.3d 634, 639 (D.C. Cir. 2008) (requiring "[e]xtreme recklessness," defined as "an extreme departure from the standards of ordinary care . . . which presents a danger of misleading buyers or sellers that is either known to the defendant or is so obvious that the actor must have been aware of it" (citations omitted)).

[65] See, e.g., Nathenson v. Zonagen Inc., 267 F.3d 400, 408 (5th Cir. 2001) ("It seems clear to us that the PSLRA has not generally altered the substantial scienter requirement for claims brought under section 10(b) and Rule 10b–5 . . ."), citing Greebel v. FTP Software, Inc., 194 F.3d 185, 198–201 (1st Cir. 1999); Advanta Corp. Sec. Litig., 180 F.3d 525, 534 (3d Cir. 1999);

4. *Who Is Culpable?* In the 2011 case, Janus Capital Group, Inc. v. First Derivative Traders,[66] the Supreme Court held that "the maker of a statement is the person or entity with ultimate authority over the statement, including its content and whether and how to communicate it," and emphasized that "[w]ithout control, a person or entity can merely suggest what to say, not 'make' a statement in its own right." Following *Janus*, there was confusion as to who was a "maker" of a misstatement.

The Supreme Court addressed this question in Lorenzo v. SEC.[67] The Court held persons who "disseminate[ ] false or misleading statements with the intent to defraud" can be liable under Rule 10b–5(a) and (c) "even if the disseminator did not 'make' the statements."[68] In its opinion the Court distinguished between the petitioner, who "sent false statements directly to investors, invited them to follow up with questions, and did so in his capacity as vice president of an investment banking company" and a "mailroom clerk," stating liability would typically be inappropriate for the latter.[69]

Problem

PROBLEM 12-4

(1) Rexford is the Chief Executive Officer of Hughes Gyros Inc. Bachman is the Chief Financial Officer. Earlier this year Rexford was criminally convicted for a scheme in which he secretly sold gyroscope parts from Hughes' inventory. The SEC has now commenced a civil action under Rule 10b–5 against Bachman.

Bachman argues that he did not act with the required culpability when he assisted Rexford and the others to purchase and resell inventory. He obtained cashier's checks with which to purchase the inventory but directed that his name not appear on these checks. The cashier's checks bore the names of a nominee account holder. Bachman transferred the proceeds of the sale among various noncorporate accounts held by Rexford, even though he concedes that these transactions had no apparent business purpose. Bachman has employed a Nuremberg defense by arguing that he simply did what he was told and was not in a position to question the orders given to him by his employer. What result?

(2) Hughes Gyros also published an earnings forecast in its latest Form 10-K annual report based on a linear extrapolation of prior year earnings, including those artificially inflated as a result of the secret inventory sales. What result if Bachman is sued and asserts § 21E of the Securities Exchange Act in defense?

Comshare Inc. Sec. Litig., 183 F.3d 542, 548–49 (6th Cir. 1999); Bryant v. Avado Brands, Inc., 187 F.3d 1271, 1283–84 (11th Cir. 1999); Novak v. Kasaks, 216 F.3d 300, 306 (2d Cir. 2000).

[66] 564 U.S. 135, 142 (2011).
[67] 139 S.Ct. 1094 (2019).
[68] Id. at 1100.
[69] Id. at 1101.

E. Reliance and Causation

(1) Reliance and the Fraud-on-the-Market Presumption

Basic Incorporated v. Levinson
Supreme Court of the United States, 1988.
485 U.S. 224, 108 S.Ct. 978, 99 L.Ed.2d 194.

■ BLACKMUN, J., delivered the opinion of the Court, in which BRENNAN, MARSHALL, and STEVENS, JJ., joined, and in Parts I, II, and III of which WHITE and O'CONNOR, JJ., joined. WHITE, J., filed an opinion concurring in part and dissenting in part, in which O'CONNOR, J., joined. REHNQUIST, C.J. and SCALIA and KENNEDY, JJ., took no part in the consideration or decision of the case.

■ JUSTICE BLACKMUN:

* * *

IV

A

We turn to the question of reliance and the fraud-on-the-market theory. Succinctly put:

> "The fraud on the market theory is based on the hypothesis that, in an open and developed securities market, the price of a company's stock is determined by the available material information regarding the company and its business.... Misleading statements will therefore defraud purchasers of stock even if the purchasers do not directly rely on the misstatements.... The causal connection between the defendants' fraud and the plaintiffs' purchase of stock in such a case is no less significant than in a case of direct reliance on misrepresentations." Peil v. Speiser, 806 F.2d 1154, 1160–1161 (C.A.3 1986).

Our task, of course, is not to assess the general validity of the theory, but to consider whether it was proper for the courts below to apply a rebuttable presumption of reliance, supported in part by the fraud-on-the-market theory.

This case required resolution of several common questions of law and fact concerning the falsity or misleading nature of the three public statements made by Basic, the presence or absence of scienter, and the materiality of the misrepresentations, if any. In their amended complaint, the named plaintiffs alleged that in reliance on Basic's statements they sold their shares of Basic stock in the depressed market created by petitioners. Requiring proof of individualized reliance from each member of the proposed plaintiff class effectively would have prevented respondents from proceeding with a class action, since individual issues then would have overwhelmed the common ones. The

District Court found that the presumption of reliance created by the fraud-on-the-market theory provided "a practical resolution to the problem of balancing the substantive requirement of proof of reliance in securities cases against the procedural requisites of [Fed. Rule Civ. Proc.] 23." The District Court thus concluded that with reference to each public statement and its impact upon the open market for Basic shares, common questions predominated over individual questions, as required by Fed. Rule Civ. Proc. 23(a)(2) and (b)(3).

Petitioners and their *amici* complain that the fraud-on-the-market theory effectively eliminates the requirement that a plaintiff asserting a claim under Rule 10b–5 prove reliance. They note that reliance is and long has been an element of common-law fraud, and argue that because the analogous express right of action includes a reliance requirement, see, e.g., § 18(a) of the 1934 Act, as amended, 15 U.S.C. § 78r(a), so too must an action implied under § 10(b).

We agree that reliance is an element of a Rule 10b–5 cause of action. See Ernst & Ernst v. Hochfelder, 425 U.S., at 206 (quoting Senate Report). Reliance provides the requisite causal connection between a defendant's misrepresentation and a plaintiff's injury. There is, however, more than one way to demonstrate the causal connection. Indeed, we previously have dispensed with a requirement of positive proof of reliance, where a duty to disclose material information had been breached, concluding that the necessary nexus between the plaintiffs' injury and the defendant's wrongful conduct had been established. See Affiliated Ute Citizens v. United States, 406 U.S., at 153–154. Similarly, we did not require proof that material omissions or misstatements in a proxy statement decisively affected voting, because the proxy solicitation itself, rather than the defect in the solicitation materials, served as an essential link in the transaction. See Mills v. Electric Auto-Lite Co., 396 U.S. 375, 384–385 (1970).

The modern securities markets, literally involving millions of shares changing hands daily, differ from the face-to-face transactions contemplated by early fraud cases, and our understanding of Rule 10b–5's reliance requirement must encompass these differences.

> "In face-to-face transactions, the inquiry into an investor's reliance upon information is into the subjective pricing of that information by that investor. With the presence of a market, the market is interposed between seller and buyer and, ideally, transmits information to the investor in the processed form of a market price. Thus the market is performing a substantial part of the valuation process performed by the investor in a face-to-face transaction. The market is acting as the unpaid agent of the investor, informing him that given all the information available to it, the value of the stock is worth the market price." In re LTV Securities Litigation, 88 F.R.D. 134, 143 (N.D.Tex.1980).

B

Presumptions typically serve to assist courts in managing circumstances in which direct proof, for one reason or another, is rendered difficult. The courts below accepted a presumption, created by the fraud-on-the-market theory and subject to rebuttal by petitioners, that persons who had traded Basic shares had done so in reliance on the integrity of the price set by the market, but because of petitioners' material misrepresentations that price had been fraudulently depressed. Requiring a plaintiff to show a speculative state of facts, i.e., how he would have acted if omitted material information had been disclosed, or if the misrepresentation had not been made, would place an unnecessarily unrealistic evidentiary burden on the Rule 10b–5 plaintiff who has traded on an impersonal market.

* * *

C

* * *

Any showing that severs the link between the alleged misrepresentation and either the price received (or paid) by the plaintiff, or his decision to trade at a fair market price, will be sufficient to rebut the presumption of reliance. For example, if petitioners could show that the "market makers" were privy to the truth about the merger discussions here with Combustion, and thus that the market price would not have been affected by their misrepresentations, the causal connection could be broken: the basis for finding that the fraud had been transmitted through market price would be gone.[28] Similarly, if, despite petitioners' allegedly fraudulent attempt to manipulate market price, news of the merger discussions credibly entered the market and dissipated the effects of the misstatements, those who traded Basic shares after the corrective statements would have no direct or indirect connection with the fraud.[29] Petitioners also could rebut the presumption of reliance as to plaintiffs who would have divested themselves of their Basic shares without relying on the integrity of the market. For example, a plaintiff who believed that Basic's statements were false and that Basic was indeed engaged in merger discussions, and who consequently believed that Basic stock was artificially underpriced, but sold his shares

---

[28] By accepting this rebuttable presumption, we do not intend conclusively to adopt any particular theory of how quickly and completely publicly available information is reflected in market price. Furthermore, our decision today is not to be interpreted as addressing the proper measure of damages in litigation of this kind.

[29] We note there may be a certain incongruity between the assumption that Basic shares are traded on a well-developed, efficient, and information-hungry market, and the allegation that such a market could remain misinformed, and its valuation of Basic shares depressed, for 14 months, on the basis of the three public statements. Proof of that sort is a matter for trial, throughout which the District Court retains the authority to amend the certification order as may be appropriate. See Fed. Rule Civ. Proc. 23(c)(1) and (c)(4). See 7B C. Wright, A. Miller & M. Kane, Federal Practice and Procedure 128–132 (1966). Thus, we see no need to engage in the kind of factual analysis the dissent suggests that manifests the "oddities" of applying a rebuttable presumption of reliance in this case.

nevertheless because of other unrelated concerns, e.g., potential antitrust problems, or political pressures to divest from shares of certain businesses, could not be said to have relied on the integrity of a price he knew had been manipulated.

* * *

■ THE CHIEF JUSTICE, JUSTICE SCALIA, and JUSTICE KENNEDY took no part in the consideration or decision of this case.

■ JUSTICE WHITE, with whom JUSTICE O'CONNOR joins, concurring in part and dissenting in part.

* * *

I

Even when compared to the relatively youthful private cause-of-action under § 10(b), see Kardon v. National Gypsum Co., 69 F.Supp. 512 (E.D. Pa. 1946), the fraud-on-the-market theory is a mere babe. Yet today, the Court embraces this theory with the sweeping confidence usually reserved for more mature legal doctrines. In so doing, I fear that the Court's decision may have many adverse, unintended effects as it is applied and interpreted in the years to come.

* * *

C

At the bottom of the Court's conclusion that the fraud-on-the-market theory sustains a presumption of reliance is the assumption that individuals rely "on the integrity of the market price" when buying or selling stock in "impersonal, well-developed market[s] for securities." Even if I was prepared to accept (as a matter of common sense or general understanding) the assumption that most persons buying or selling stock do so in response to the market price, the fraud-on-the-market theory goes further. For in adopting a "presumption of reliance," the Court *also* assumes that buyers and sellers rely—not just on the market price—but on the *"integrity"* of that price. It is this aspect of the fraud-on-the-market hypothesis which most mystifies me.

To define the term "integrity of the market price," the majority quotes approvingly from cases which suggest that investors are entitled to " 'rely on the price of a stock as a reflection of its value.' " But the meaning of this phrase eludes me, for it implicitly suggests that stocks have some "true value" that is measurable by a standard other than their market price. While the scholastics of medieval times professed a means to make such a valuation of a commodity's "worth," I doubt that the federal courts of our day are similarly equipped.

Even if securities had some "value"—knowable and distinct from the market price of a stock—investors do not always share the Court's presumption that a stock's price is a "reflection of [this] value." Indeed, "many investors purchase or sell stock because they believe the price *inaccurately* reflects the corporation's worth." See Black, Fraud on the Market: A Criticism of Dispensing with Reliance Requirements in Certain Open Market Transactions, 62 N.C. L.Rev. 435, 455 (1984) (emphasis added). If investors really believed that stock prices reflected a stock's "value," many sellers would never sell, and many buyers never buy (given the time and cost associated with executing a stock transaction). As we recognized just a few years ago: "[I]nvestors act on inevitably incomplete or inaccurate information, [consequently] there are always winners and losers; but those who have 'lost' have not necessarily been defrauded." Dirks v. SEC, 463 U.S. 646, 667, n.27 (1983). Yet today, the Court allows investors to recover who can show little more than that they sold stock at a lower price than what might have been.[7]

* * *

III

Finally, the particular facts of this case make it an exceedingly poor candidate for the Court's fraud-on-the-market theory, and illustrate the illogic achieved by that theory's application in many cases.

Respondents here are a class of sellers who sold Basic stock between October 1977 and December 1978, a fourteen-month period. At the time the class period began, Basic's stock was trading at $20 a share (at the time, an all-time high); the last members of the class to sell their Basic stock got a price of just over $30 a share. It is indisputable that virtually every member of the class made money from his or her sale of Basic stock.

The oddities of applying the fraud-on-the-market theory in this case are manifest. First, there are the facts that the plaintiffs are sellers and the class period is so lengthy—both are virtually without precedent in prior fraud-on-the-market cases.

* * *

Second, there is the fact that in this case, there is no evidence that petitioner Basic's officials made the troublesome misstatements for the purpose of manipulating stock prices, or with any intent to engage in underhanded trading of Basic stock. Indeed, during the class period, petitioners do not appear to have purchased or sold *any* Basic stock whatsoever. I agree with *amicus* who argues that "[i]mposition of damages liability under Rule 10b–5 makes little sense ... where a defendant is neither a purchaser nor a seller of securities." See Brief for

---

[7] This is what the Court's rule boils down to in practical terms. For while, in theory, the Court allows for rebuttal of its "presumption of reliance"—a proviso with which I agree,—in practice the Court must realize, as other courts applying the fraud-on-the-market theory have, that such rebuttal is virtually impossible in all but the most extraordinary case. See Blackie v. Barrack, 524 F.2d at 906–907, n.22; In re LTV Securities Litigation, 88 F.R.D. 134, 143, n.4 (N.D.Tex.1980).

Consequently, while the Court considers it significant that the fraud-on-the-market presumption it endorses is a rebuttable one, ante, at 17, 23, the majority's implicit rejection of the "pure causation" fraud-on-the-market theory rings hollow. In most cases, the Court's theory will operate just as the causation theory would, creating a non-rebuttable presumption of "reliance" in future 10b–5 actions.

American Corporate Counsel Association as Amicus Curiae 13. In fact, in previous cases, we had recognized that Rule 10b–5 is concerned primarily with cases where the fraud is committed by one trading the security at issue. See e.g., Blue Chip Stamps v. Manor Drug Stores, 421 U.S. 723, 736, n.8 (1975). And it is difficult to square liability in this case with § 10(b)'s express provision that it prohibits fraud *"in connection with the purchase or sale of any security."* See 15 U.S.C. § 78j(b) (emphasis added).

Third, there are the peculiarities of what kinds of investors will be able to recover in this case. As I read the District Court's class certification order, there are potentially many persons who did not purchase Basic stock until *after* the first false statement (October 1977), but who nonetheless *will* be able to recover under the Court's fraud-on-the-market theory. Thus, it is possible that a person who heard the first corporate misstatement and *disbelieved* it—i.e., someone who purchased Basic stock thinking that petitioners' statement was false—may still be included in the plaintiff-class on remand. How a person who undertook such a speculative stock-investing strategy—and made $10 a share doing so (if he bought on October 22, 1977, and sold on December 15, 1978)—can say that he was "defrauded" by virtue of his reliance on the "integrity" of the market price is beyond me. And such speculators may not be uncommon, at least in this case.

* * *

The question in the next case, commonly referred to as *Halliburton II*, was whether to overrule *Basic* and replace it with a different test for reliance and class certification, or, perhaps, end private securities class actions altogether. The Court chose to preserve *Basic*, but it added a new defense at the class-certification stage—defendants can now introduce evidence that there was no price impact from the alleged fraud.

Halliburton Co. v. Erica P. John Fund, Inc.
Supreme Court of the United States, 2014.
573 U.S. 258, 134 S.Ct. 2398, 189 L.Ed.2d 339.

* * *

II

Halliburton urges us to overrule *Basic*'s presumption of reliance and to instead require every securities fraud plaintiff to prove that he actually relied on the defendant's misrepresentation in deciding to buy or sell a company's stock. Before overturning a long-settled precedent, however, we require "special justification," not just an argument that the precedent was wrongly decided. *Dickerson v. United States,* 530 U.S. 428,

443, 120 S.Ct. 2326, 147 L.Ed.2d 405 (2000) (internal quotation marks omitted). Halliburton has failed to make that showing.

A

Section 10(b) of the Securities Exchange Act of 1934 and the Securities and Exchange Commission's Rule 10b–5 prohibit making any material misstatement or omission in connection with the purchase or sale of any security. Although section 10(b) does not create an express private cause of action, we have long recognized an implied private cause of action to enforce the provision and its implementing regulation. To recover damages for violations of section 10(b) and Rule 10b–5, a plaintiff must prove " '(1) a material misrepresentation or omission by the defendant; (2) scienter; (3) a connection between the misrepresentation or omission and the purchase or sale of a security; (4) reliance upon the misrepresentation or omission; (5) economic loss; and (6) loss causation.' " *Amgen Inc. v. Connecticut Retirement Plans and Trust Funds*, 568 U.S. 455, 460–61, 133 S.Ct. 1184, 1192, (quoting *Matrixx Initiatives, Inc. v. Siracusano,* 563 U.S. 27, 37–38, 131 S.Ct. 1309, 1317–1318).

The reliance element " 'ensures that there is a proper connection between a defendant's misrepresentation and a plaintiff's injury.' " 133 S.Ct., at 1192 (quoting *Halliburton I,* 131 S.Ct., at 2184–2185). "The traditional (and most direct) way a plaintiff can demonstrate reliance is by showing that he was aware of a company's statement and engaged in a relevant transaction—*e.g.,* purchasing common stock—based on that specific misrepresentation." *Id.,* at 1192.

In *Basic,* however, we recognized that requiring such direct proof of reliance "would place an unnecessarily unrealistic evidentiary burden on the Rule 10b–5 plaintiff who has traded on an impersonal market." 108 S.Ct. 978. That is because, even assuming an investor could prove that he was aware of the misrepresentation, he would still have to "show a speculative state of facts, *i.e.,* how he would have acted ... if the misrepresentation had not been made." *Ibid.*

We also noted that "[r]equiring proof of individualized reliance" from every securities fraud plaintiff "effectively would ... prevent [ ] [plaintiffs] from proceeding with a class action" in Rule 10b–5 suits. *Id.,* 978. If every plaintiff had to prove direct reliance on the defendant's misrepresentation, "individual issues then would ... overwhelm[ ] the common ones," making certification under Rule 23(b)(3) inappropriate. *Ibid.*

To address these concerns, *Basic* held that securities fraud plaintiffs can in certain circumstances satisfy the reliance element of a Rule 10b–5 action by invoking a rebuttable presumption of reliance, rather than proving direct reliance on a misrepresentation. The Court based that presumption on what is known as the "fraud-on-the-market" theory, which holds that "the market price of shares traded on well-developed markets reflects all publicly available information, and, hence, any material misrepresentations." *Id.,* 978. The Court also noted that, rather than scrutinize every piece of public information about a company for himself, the typical "investor who buys or sells stock at the price set by the market does so in reliance on the integrity of that price"—the belief that it reflects all public, material information. *Id.,* 978. As a result, whenever the investor buys or sells stock at the market price, his "reliance on any public material misrepresentations ... may be presumed for purposes of a Rule 10b–5 action." *Ibid.*

Based on this theory, a plaintiff must make the following showings to demonstrate that the presumption of reliance applies in a given case: (1) that the alleged misrepresentations were publicly known, (2) that they were material, (3) that the stock traded in an efficient market, and (4) that the plaintiff traded the stock between the time the misrepresentations were made and when the truth was revealed. See *id.,* 978; *Halliburton I,* 131 S.Ct., at 2185–2186.

At the same time, *Basic* emphasized that the presumption of reliance was rebuttable rather than conclusive. Specifically, "[a]ny showing that severs the link between the alleged misrepresentation and either the price received (or paid) by the plaintiff, or his decision to trade at a fair market price, will be sufficient to rebut the presumption of reliance." 108 S.Ct. 978. So for example, if a defendant could show that the alleged misrepresentation did not, for whatever reason, actually affect the market price, or that a plaintiff would have bought or sold the stock even had he been aware that the stock's price was tainted by fraud, then the presumption of reliance would not apply. In either of those cases, a plaintiff would have to prove that he directly relied on the defendant's misrepresentation in buying or selling the stock.

B

Halliburton contends that securities fraud plaintiffs should *always* have to prove direct reliance and that the *Basic* Court erred in allowing them to invoke a presumption of reliance instead. According to Halliburton, the *Basic* presumption contravenes congressional intent and has been undermined by subsequent developments in economic theory. Neither argument, however, so discredits *Basic* as to constitute "special justification" for overruling the decision.

1

Halliburton first argues that the *Basic* presumption is inconsistent with Congress's intent in passing the 1934 Exchange Act. Because "[t]he Section 10(b) action is a 'judicial construct that Congress did not enact,' " this Court, Halliburton insists, "must identify—and borrow from—the express provision that is 'most analogous to the private 10b–5 right of action.' " Brief for Petitioners 12 (quoting *Stoneridge Investment Partners, LLC v. Scientific-Atlanta, Inc.,* 552 U.S. 148, 164, 128 S.Ct. 761, 169 L.Ed.2d 627 (2008); *Musick, Peeler & Garrett v. Employers Ins. of Wausau,* 508 U.S. 286, 294, 113 S.Ct. 2085, 124 L.Ed.2d 194 (1993)).

According to Halliburton, the closest analogue to section 10(b) is section 18(a) of the Act, which creates an express private cause of action allowing investors to recover damages based on misrepresentations made in certain regulatory filings. 15 U.S.C. § 78r(a). That provision requires an investor to prove that he bought or sold stock "in reliance upon" the defendant's misrepresentation. *Ibid.* In ignoring this direct reliance requirement, the argument goes, the *Basic* Court relieved Rule 10b–5 plaintiffs of a burden that Congress would have imposed had it created the cause of action.

EPJ Fund contests both premises of Halliburton's argument, arguing that Congress has affirmed *Basic*'s construction of section 10(b) and that, in any event, the closest analogue to section 10(b) is not section 18(a) but section 9, 15 U.S.C. § 78i—a provision that does not require actual reliance.

We need not settle this dispute. In *Basic,* the dissenting Justices made the same argument based on section 18(a) that Halliburton presses here. See 108 S.Ct. 978 (White, J., concurring in part and dissenting in part). The *Basic* majority did not find that argument persuasive then, and Halliburton has given us no new reason to endorse it now.

2

Halliburton's primary argument for overruling *Basic* is that the decision rested on two premises that can no longer withstand scrutiny. The first premise concerns what is known as the "efficient capital markets hypothesis." *Basic* stated that "the market price of shares traded on well-developed markets reflects all publicly available information, and, hence, any material misrepresentations." *Id.,* 978. From that statement, Halliburton concludes that the *Basic* Court espoused "a robust view of market efficiency" that is no longer tenable, for " 'overwhelming empirical evidence' now 'suggests that capital markets are not fundamentally efficient.' " Brief for Petitioners 14–16 (quoting Lev & de Villiers, Stock Price Crashes and 10b–5 Damages: A Legal, Economic, and Policy Analysis, 47 Stan. L. Rev. 7, 20 (1994)). To support this contention, Halliburton cites studies purporting to show that "public information is often not incorporated immediately (much less rationally) into market prices." Brief for Petitioners 17; see *id.,* at 16–20. See also Brief for Law Professors as *Amici Curiae* 15–18.

Halliburton does not, of course, maintain that capital markets are *always* inefficient. Rather, in its view, *Basic*'s fundamental error was to ignore the fact that " 'efficiency is not a binary, yes or no question.' " Brief for Petitioners 20 (quoting Langevoort, *Basic* at Twenty: Rethinking Fraud on the Market, 2009 Wis. L.Rev. 151, 167). The markets for some securities are more efficient than the markets for others, and even a single market can process different kinds of information more or less efficiently, depending on how widely the information is disseminated and how easily it is understood. Yet *Basic,* Halliburton asserts, glossed over these nuances, assuming a false dichotomy that renders the presumption of reliance both underinclusive and overinclusive: A misrepresentation can distort a stock's market price even in a generally inefficient market, and a misrepresentation can leave a stock's market price unaffected even in a generally efficient one.

Halliburton's criticisms fail to take *Basic* on its own terms. Halliburton focuses on the debate among economists about the degree to which the market price of a company's stock reflects public information about the company—and thus the degree to which an investor can earn an abnormal, above-market return by trading on such information. See Brief for Financial Economists as *Amici Curiae* 4–10 (describing the debate). That debate is not new. Indeed, the *Basic* Court acknowledged it and declined to enter the fray, declaring that "[w]e need not determine by adjudication what economists and social scientists have debated through the use of sophisticated statistical analysis and the application of economic theory." 108 S.Ct. 978. To recognize the presumption of reliance, the Court explained, was not "conclusively to adopt any particular theory of how quickly and completely publicly available information is reflected in market price." *Id.*, 978, n. 28. The Court instead based the presumption on the fairly modest premise that "market professionals generally consider most publicly announced material statements about companies, thereby affecting stock market prices." *Id.*, 108 S.Ct. 978. *Basic*'s presumption of reliance thus does not rest on a "binary" view of market efficiency. Indeed, in making the presumption rebuttable, *Basic* recognized that market efficiency is a matter of degree and accordingly made it a matter of proof.

The academic debates discussed by Halliburton have not refuted the modest premise underlying the presumption of reliance. Even the foremost critics of the efficient-capital-markets hypothesis acknowledge that public information generally affects stock prices. Halliburton also conceded as much in its reply brief and at oral argument. Debates about the precise *degree* to which stock prices accurately reflect public information are thus largely beside the point. "That the . . . price [of a stock] may be inaccurate does not detract from the fact that false statements affect it, and cause loss," which is "all that *Basic* requires." *Schleicher v. Wendt*, 618 F.3d 679, 685 (C.A.7 2010) (Easterbrook, C.J.). Even though the efficient capital markets hypothesis may have "garnered substantial criticism since *Basic*," *post*, at 2420 (THOMAS, J., concurring in judgment), Halliburton has not identified the kind of fundamental shift in economic theory that could justify overruling a precedent on the ground that it misunderstood, or has since been overtaken by, economic realities.

Halliburton also contests a second premise underlying the *Basic* presumption: the notion that investors "invest 'in reliance on the integrity of [the market] price.'" Reply Brief 14 (quoting 485 U.S., at 247, 108 S.Ct. 978; alteration in original). Halliburton identifies a number of classes of investors for whom "price integrity" is supposedly "marginal or irrelevant." The primary example is the value investor, who believes that certain stocks are undervalued or overvalued and attempts to "beat the market" by buying the undervalued stocks and selling the overvalued ones. If many investors "are indifferent to prices," Halliburton contends, then courts should not presume that investors rely on the integrity of those prices and any misrepresentations incorporated into them.

But *Basic* never denied the existence of such investors. As we recently explained, *Basic* concluded only that "it is reasonable to presume that *most* investors—knowing that they have little hope of outperforming the market in the long run based solely on their analysis of publicly available information—will rely on the security's market price as an unbiased assessment of the security's value in light of all public information." *Amgen,* 568 U.S. at 462 (emphasis added).

In any event, there is no reason to suppose that even Halliburton's main counterexample—the value investor—is as indifferent to the integrity of market prices as Halliburton suggests. Such an investor implicitly relies on the fact that a stock's market price will eventually reflect material information—how else could the market correction on which his profit depends occur? To be sure, the value investor "does not believe that the market price accurately reflects public information *at the time he transacts.*" *Post,* at 2423. But to indirectly rely on a misstatement in the sense relevant for the *Basic* presumption, he need only trade stock based on the belief that the market price will incorporate public information within a reasonable period. The value investor also presumably tries to estimate *how* undervalued or overvalued a particular stock is, and such estimates can be skewed by a market price tainted by fraud.

C

The principle of *stare decisis* has " 'special force' " "in respect to statutory interpretation" because " 'Congress remains free to alter what we have done.' " *John R. Sand & Gravel Co. v. United States,* 552 U.S. 130, 139, 128 S.Ct. 750, 169 L.Ed.2d 591 (2008) (quoting *Patterson v. McLean Credit Union,* 491 U.S. 164, 172–173, 109 S.Ct. 2363, 105 L.Ed.2d 132 (1989)). So too with *Basic*'s presumption of reliance. Although the presumption is a judicially created doctrine designed to implement a judicially created cause of action, we have described the presumption as "a substantive doctrine of federal securities-fraud law." *Amgen, supra,* at 462. That is because it provides a way of satisfying the reliance element of the Rule 10b–5 cause of action. As with any other element of that cause of action, Congress may overturn or modify any aspect of our interpretations of the reliance requirement, including the *Basic* presumption itself. Given that possibility, we see no reason to exempt the *Basic* presumption from ordinary principles of *stare decisis.*

To buttress its case for overruling *Basic,* Halliburton contends that, in addition to being wrongly decided, the decision is inconsistent with our more recent decisions construing the Rule 10b–5 cause of action. As

Halliburton notes, we have held that "we must give 'narrow dimensions . . . to a right of action Congress did not authorize when it first enacted the statute and did not expand when it revisited the law.'" *Janus Capital Group, Inc. v. First Derivative Traders,* 131 S.Ct. 2296, 2302. Yet the *Basic* presumption, Halliburton asserts, does just the opposite, *expanding* the Rule 10b–5 cause of action.

Not so. In *Central Bank* and *Stoneridge,* we declined to extend Rule 10b–5 liability to entirely new categories of defendants who themselves had not made any material, public misrepresentation. Such an extension, we explained, would have eviscerated the requirement that a plaintiff prove that he relied on a misrepresentation made *by the defendant*. The *Basic* presumption does not eliminate that requirement but rather provides an alternative means of satisfying it. While the presumption makes it easier for plaintiffs to prove reliance, it does not alter the elements of the Rule 10b–5 cause of action and thus maintains the action's original legal scope.

Halliburton also argues that the *Basic* presumption cannot be reconciled with our recent decisions governing class action certification under Federal Rule of Civil Procedure 23. Those decisions have made clear that plaintiffs wishing to proceed through a class action must actually *prove*—not simply plead—that their proposed class satisfies each requirement of Rule 23, including (if applicable) the predominance requirement of Rule 23(b)(3). According to Halliburton, *Basic* relieves Rule 10b–5 plaintiffs of that burden, allowing courts to presume that common issues of reliance predominate over individual ones.

That is not the effect of the *Basic* presumption. In securities class action cases, the crucial requirement for class certification will usually be the predominance requirement of Rule 23(b)(3). The *Basic* presumption does not relieve plaintiffs of the burden of proving—before class certification—that this requirement is met. *Basic* instead establishes that a plaintiff satisfies that burden by proving the prerequisites for invoking the presumption—namely, publicity, materiality, market efficiency, and market timing. The burden of proving those prerequisites still rests with plaintiffs and (with the exception of materiality) must be satisfied before class certification. *Basic* does not, in other words, allow plaintiffs simply to plead that common questions of reliance predominate over individual ones, but rather sets forth what they must prove to demonstrate such predominance.

Basic does afford defendants an opportunity to rebut the presumption of reliance with respect to an individual plaintiff by showing that he did not rely on the integrity of the market price in trading stock. While this has the effect of "leav[ing] individualized questions of reliance in the case," *post,* at 2424, there is no reason to think that these questions will overwhelm common ones and render class certification inappropriate under Rule 23(b)(3). That the defendant might attempt to pick off the occasional class member here or there through individualized rebuttal does not cause individual questions to predominate.

Finally, Halliburton and its *amici* contend that, by facilitating securities class actions, the *Basic* presumption produces a number of serious and harmful consequences. Such class actions, they say, allow plaintiffs to extort large settlements from defendants for meritless claims; punish innocent shareholders, who end up having to pay settlements and judgments; impose excessive costs on businesses; and consume a disproportionately large share of judicial resources.

These concerns are more appropriately addressed to Congress, which has in fact responded, to some extent, to many of the issues raised by Halliburton and its *amici*. Congress has, for example, enacted the Private Securities Litigation Reform Act of 1995 (PSLRA), 109 Stat. 737, which sought to combat perceived abuses in securities litigation with heightened pleading requirements, limits on damages and attorney's fees, a "safe harbor" for certain kinds of statements, restrictions on the selection of lead plaintiffs in securities class actions, sanctions for frivolous litigation, and stays of discovery pending motions to dismiss. And to prevent plaintiffs from circumventing these restrictions by bringing securities class actions under state law in state court, Congress also enacted the Securities Litigation Uniform Standards Act of 1998, 112 Stat. 3227, which precludes many state law class actions alleging securities fraud. Such legislation demonstrates Congress's willingness to consider policy concerns of the sort that Halliburton says should lead us to overrule *Basic*.

III

Halliburton proposes two alternatives to overruling *Basic* that would alleviate what it regards as the decision's most serious flaws. The first alternative would require plaintiffs to prove that a defendant's misrepresentation actually affected the stock price—so-called "price impact"—in order to invoke the *Basic* presumption. It should not be enough, Halliburton contends, for plaintiffs to demonstrate the general efficiency of the market in which the stock traded. Halliburton's second proposed alternative would allow defendants to rebut the presumption of reliance with evidence of a *lack* of price impact, not only at the merits stage—which all agree defendants may already do—but also before class certification.

A

As noted, to invoke the *Basic* presumption, a plaintiff must prove that: (1) the alleged misrepresentations were publicly known, (2) they were material, (3) the stock traded in an efficient market, and (4) the plaintiff traded the stock between when the misrepresentations were made and when the truth was revealed. Each of these requirements follows from the fraud-on-the-market theory underlying the presumption. If the misrepresentation was not publicly known, then it could not have distorted the stock's market price. So too if the misrepresentation was immaterial—that is, if it would not have " 'been viewed by the reasonable investor as having significantly altered the "total mix" of information made available,' " *Basic, supra,* at 231–232, 108 S.Ct. 978 (quoting *TSC Industries, Inc. v. Northway, Inc.,* 426 U.S. 438, 449, 96 S.Ct. 2126, 48 L.Ed.2d 757 (1976))—or if the market in which the stock traded was inefficient. And if the plaintiff did not buy or sell the stock after the misrepresentation was made but before the truth was revealed, then he could not be said to have acted in reliance on a fraud-tainted price.

The first three prerequisites are directed at price impact—"whether the alleged misrepresentations affected the market price in the first place." *Halliburton I,* 131 S.Ct., at 2182. In the absence of price impact, *Basic's* fraud-on-the-market theory and presumption of reliance collapse. The "fundamental premise" underlying the presumption is "that an investor presumptively relies on a misrepresentation so long as it was reflected in the market price at the time of his transaction." 131 S.Ct., at 2186. If it was not, then there is "no grounding for any contention that [the] investor[ ] indirectly relied on th[at] misrepresentation[ ] through [his] reliance on the integrity of the market price." *Amgen, supra,* at 473.

Halliburton argues that since the *Basic* presumption hinges on price impact, plaintiffs should be required to prove it directly in order to invoke the presumption. Proving the presumption's prerequisites, which are at best an imperfect proxy for price impact, should not suffice.

Far from a modest refinement of the *Basic* presumption, this proposal would radically alter the required showing for the reliance element of the Rule 10b–5 cause of action. What is called the *Basic* presumption actually incorporates two constituent presumptions: First, if a plaintiff shows that the defendant's misrepresentation was public and material and that the stock traded in a generally efficient market, he is entitled to a presumption that the misrepresentation affected the stock price. Second, if the plaintiff also shows that he purchased the stock at the market price during the relevant period, he is entitled to a further presumption that he purchased the stock in reliance on the defendant's misrepresentation.

By requiring plaintiffs to prove price impact directly, Halliburton's proposal would take away the first constituent presumption. Halliburton's argument for doing so is the same as its primary argument for overruling the *Basic* presumption altogether: Because market efficiency is not a yes-or-no proposition, a public, material misrepresentation might not affect a stock's price even in a generally efficient market. But as explained, *Basic* never suggested otherwise; that is why it affords defendants an opportunity to rebut the presumption by showing, among other things, that the particular misrepresentation at issue did not affect the stock's market price. For the same reasons we declined to completely jettison the *Basic* presumption, we decline to effectively jettison half of it by revising the prerequisites for invoking it.

B

Even if plaintiffs need not directly prove price impact to invoke the *Basic* presumption, Halliburton contends that defendants should at least be allowed to defeat the presumption at the class certification stage through evidence that the misrepresentation did not in fact affect the stock price. We agree.

1

There is no dispute that defendants may introduce such evidence at the merits stage to rebut the *Basic* presumption. *Basic* itself "made clear that the presumption was just that, and could be rebutted by appropriate evidence," including evidence that the asserted misrepresentation (or its correction) did not affect the market price of the defendant's stock. *Halliburton I, supra,* at 2185.

Nor is there any dispute that defendants may introduce price impact evidence at the class certification stage, so long as it is for the purpose of countering a plaintiff's showing of market efficiency, rather than directly rebutting the presumption. As EPJ Fund acknowledges, "[o]f course . . . defendants can introduce evidence at class certification of lack of price impact as some evidence that the market is not efficient." Brief for Respondent 53.

After all, plaintiffs themselves can and do introduce evidence of the *existence* of price impact in connection with "event studies"—regression analyses that seek to show that the market price of the defendant's stock tends to respond to pertinent publicly reported events. In this case, for example, EPJ Fund submitted an event study of various episodes that might have been expected to affect the price of Halliburton's stock, in order to demonstrate that the market for that stock takes account of material, public information about the company. The episodes examined by EPJ Fund's event study included one of the alleged misrepresentations that form the basis of the Fund's suit.

Defendants—like plaintiffs—may accordingly submit price impact evidence prior to class certification. What defendants may not do, EPJ Fund insists and the Court of Appeals held, is rely on that same evidence prior to class certification for the particular purpose of rebutting the presumption altogether.

This restriction makes no sense, and can readily lead to bizarre results. Suppose a defendant at the certification stage submits an event study looking at the impact on the price of its stock from six discrete events, in an effort to refute the plaintiffs' claim of general market efficiency. All agree the defendant may do this. Suppose one of the six events is the specific misrepresentation asserted by the plaintiffs. All agree that this too is perfectly acceptable. Now suppose the district court determines that, despite the defendant's study, the plaintiff has carried its burden to prove market efficiency, but that the evidence shows no price impact with respect to the specific misrepresentation challenged in the suit. The evidence at the certification stage thus shows an efficient market, on which the alleged misrepresentation had no price impact. And yet under EPJ Fund's view, the plaintiffs' action should be certified and proceed as a class action (with all that entails), even though the fraud-on-the-market theory does not apply and common reliance thus cannot be presumed.

Such a result is inconsistent with *Basic*'s own logic. Under *Basic*'s fraud-on-the-market theory, market efficiency and the other prerequisites for invoking the presumption constitute an indirect way of showing price impact. As explained, it is appropriate to allow plaintiffs to rely on this indirect proxy for price impact, rather than requiring them to prove price impact directly, given *Basic*'s rationales for recognizing a presumption of reliance in the first place.

But an indirect proxy should not preclude direct evidence when such evidence is available. As we explained in *Basic*, "[a]ny showing that severs the link between the alleged misrepresentation and . . . the price received (or paid) by the plaintiff . . . will be sufficient to rebut the presumption of reliance" because "the basis for finding that the fraud had been transmitted through market price would be gone." 108 S.Ct. 978. And without the presumption of reliance, a Rule 10b–5 suit cannot proceed as a class action: Each plaintiff would have to prove reliance individually, so common issues would not "predominate" over individual ones, as required by Rule 23(b)(3). *Id.*, at 978. Price impact is thus an essential precondition for any Rule 10b–5 class action. While *Basic* allows plaintiffs to establish that precondition indirectly, it does not require courts to ignore a defendant's direct, more salient evidence showing that the alleged misrepresentation did not actually affect the stock's market price and, consequently, that the *Basic* presumption does not apply.

2

The Court of Appeals relied on our decision in *Amgen* in holding that Halliburton could not introduce evidence of lack of price impact at the class certification stage. The question in *Amgen* was whether plaintiffs could be required to prove (or defendants be permitted to disprove) materiality before class certification. Even though materiality is a prerequisite for invoking the *Basic* presumption, we held that it should be left to the merits stage, because it does not bear on the predominance requirement of Rule 23(b)(3). We reasoned that materiality is an objective issue susceptible to common, classwide proof. We also noted that a failure to prove materiality would necessarily defeat every plaintiff's claim on the merits; it would not simply preclude invocation of the presumption and thereby cause individual questions of reliance to predominate over common ones. In this latter respect, we explained, materiality differs from the publicity and market efficiency prerequisites, neither of which is necessary to prove a Rule 10b–5 claim on the merits.

EPJ Fund argues that much of the foregoing could be said of price impact as well. Fair enough. But price impact differs from materiality in a crucial respect. Given that the other *Basic* prerequisites must still be proved at the class certification stage, the common issue of materiality can be left to the merits stage without risking the certification of classes in which individual issues will end up overwhelming common ones. And because materiality is a discrete issue that can be resolved in isolation from the other prerequisites, it can be wholly confined to the merits stage.

Price impact is different. The fact that a misrepresentation "was reflected in the market price at the time of [the] transaction"—that it had price impact—is "*Basic*'s fundamental premise." *Halliburton I,* 131 S.Ct., at 2186. It thus has everything to do with the issue of predominance at the class certification stage. That is why, if reliance is to be shown through the *Basic* presumption, the publicity and market efficiency prerequisites must be proved before class certification. Without proof of those prerequisites, the fraud-on-the-market theory underlying the presumption completely collapses, rendering class certification inappropriate.

But as explained, publicity and market efficiency are nothing more than prerequisites for an indirect showing of price impact. There is no dispute that at least such indirect proof of price impact "is needed to ensure that the questions of law or fact common to the class will 'predominate.'" *Amgen,* 568 U.S. at 467 (emphasis deleted); That is so even though such proof is also highly relevant at the merits stage.

Our choice in this case, then, is not between allowing price impact evidence at the class certification stage or relegating it to the merits. Evidence of price impact will be before the court at the certification stage in any event. The choice, rather, is between limiting the price impact inquiry before class certification to indirect evidence, or allowing consideration of direct evidence as well. As explained, we see no reason to artificially limit the inquiry at the certification stage to indirect evidence of price impact. Defendants may seek to defeat the *Basic* presumption at that stage through direct as well as indirect price impact evidence.

* * *

More than 25 years ago, we held that plaintiffs could satisfy the reliance element of the Rule 10b–5 cause of action by invoking a presumption that a public, material misrepresentation will distort the price of stock traded in an efficient market, and that anyone who purchases the stock at the market price may be considered to have done so in reliance on the misrepresentation. We adhere to that decision and decline to modify the prerequisites for invoking the presumption of reliance. But to maintain the consistency of the presumption with the class certification requirements of Federal Rule of Civil Procedure 23, defendants must be afforded an opportunity before class certification to defeat the presumption through evidence that an alleged misrepresentation did not actually affect the market price of the stock.

Because the courts below denied Halliburton that opportunity, we vacate the judgment of the Court of Appeals for the Fifth Circuit and remand the case for further proceedings consistent with this opinion.

It is so ordered.

NOTES ON THE FRAUD ON THE MARKET THEORY

1. *Class Actions.* The fraud on the market doctrine is key to any Rule 10b–5 class action. As the *Halliburton II* Court reiterated, the *Basic* plurality opinion notes, without such a presumption, "it would be impractical to certify a class." The *Basic* Court also notes that "[r]equiring proof of individualized reliance from each member of the proposed plaintiff class effectively would have prevented respondents from proceeding with a class action, since individual issues then would have overwhelmed the common ones." Following *Halliburton II*, the Second Circuit clarified the fraud on the market theory of reliance at the class certification stage. The court addressed *Basic*'s presumption of reliance in Waggoner v. Barclays PLC,[70] affirming a decision certifying a class based on the price maintenance theory[71] and clarifying that defendants seeking to rebut the *Basic* presumption at the class certification stage must do so by a preponderance of the evidence.[72]

2. *"Efficient" Markets.* Courts examine the nature of the market for a firm's stock before allowing reliance through the presumption. In Freeman v. Laventhol & Horwath,[73] the court stated that among the factors to be considered in determining whether there is an "efficient market" for the fraud-on-the-market theory are: a large weekly trading volume, the existence of a significant number of reports by security analysts, the existence of market makers and arbitrageurs in the security, the company's eligibility to file an S-3 Registration Statement and a history of immediate movement of the stock price caused by unexpected corporate events or financial releases. These factors, then, become relevant at the rebuttal stage.

---

[70] 875 F.3d 79 (2d. Cir. 2017).

[71] Price maintenance theory recognizes "that statements that merely maintain inflation already extant in a company's stock price, but do not add to that inflation, nonetheless affect a company's stock price." Waggoner v. Barclays PLC, 875 F.3d 79, 104 (quoting In re Vivendi, 838 F.3d 223, 256 (2d. Cir. 2016)).

[72] Id. The burden of proof standard was reaffirmed in In Ark. Teachers Ret. Sys. v. Goldman Sachs Grp., Inc., clarifying that defendants did not need to "conclusively prove a complete absence of price impact." 879 F.3d 474 (2d. Cir. 2018). While declining to adopt a particular test for market efficiency, the Second Circuit held it was proper for the district court to decline to "view direct and indirect evidence as distinct requirements, opting instead for a holistic analysis based on the totality of the evidence presented." In re Petrobras Securities Litig., 862 F.3d 250, 277 (2d Cir. 2017).

[73] 915 F.2d 193 (6th Cir. 1990).

The lower courts have generally held that the over-the-counter securities markets, like the stock exchanges, can be efficient markets for the purposes of the fraud-on-the-market doctrine.[74] Nevertheless, the focus on market efficiency means cases against larger companies traded in more liquid markets are easier to bring than cases against smaller companies in less liquid markets. Yet, fraud is actually more likely in smaller companies with fewer analysts following them and less oversight by large auditing firms.

3. *New Issues of Securities.* Does the doctrine reach new securities issues sold before an established market for the trading of the securities exists? In Shores v. Sklar,[75] decided before *Basic*, the Fifth Circuit declined to hold that the fraud-on-the-market theory was applicable to a new issue of municipal bonds, but held that a plaintiff could recover if the bonds were "fraudulently" marketed. "The securities laws allow an investor to rely on the integrity of the market to the extent that the securities it offers to him for purchase are entitled to be in the market place."[76] On the other hand, a plaintiff could not recover in a new issue context if all that he or she could prove was "that the bonds would have been offered at a lower price or a higher rate, rather than that they would never have been issued or marketed * * *."[77] It is not clear why a plaintiff should be deprived of a remedy if the securities could only have been sold at a materially lower price.

Cases discussing the issue define "unmarketable" strictly. The Sixth Circuit breaks the term into two categories: (1) "economic unmarketability," which occurs when a security is patently worthless, and (2) "legal unmarketability," which occurs when a regulatory or municipal agency would have been required by law to prevent or forbid the issuance of the security.[78]

4. *Truth on the Market.* If the truth enters the market in some manner, the fraud-on-the market theory allows for rebuttal. In Kaplan v. Rose,[79] for example, the court reasoned: "If, however, the information that defendants are alleged to have withheld from or misrepresented to the market has entered the market through other channels, the market will not have been misled, and the stock price will reflect the full universe

---

[74] See, e.g., Cammer v. Bloom, 711 F.Supp. 1264 (D.N.J.1989); Hurley v. Federal Deposit Ins. Corp., 719 F.Supp. 27, 33–34 (D. Mass. 1989) (fraud-on-the-market theory applies equally to New York Stock Exchange, American Stock Exchange, and over-the counter trading); Rospatch Sec. Litig., 1991 Fed. Sec. L. Rep. (CCH) ¶ 96,160 at 90,873–90,874 (W.D.Mich.1991).

[75] 647 F.2d 462 (5th Cir. 1981).

[76] Id. at 471.

[77] Id. at 407.

[78] Ockerman v. May Zima & Co., 27 F.3d 1151, 1160 (6th Cir. 1994). Cf. Ross v. Bank South, 885 F.2d 723, 729 (11th Cir. 1989) (en banc) ("[T]he fraud must be so pervasive that it goes to the very existence of the bonds and the validity of their presence on the market.").

[79] 49 F.3d 1363, 1376 (9th Cir. 1994).

of information, despite the defendants' misrepresentations." This has been called the "truth on the market" defense.[80]

5. *No Effect on the Stock Price.* Securities fraud defendants also attempt to rebut the fraud-on-the-market presumption by presenting evidence that the alleged misstatements had no effect on the price of the issuer's stock. For example, in *In re Moody*'s, the defendants' expert conducted an "event study" to show that none of the alleged misstatements were associated with a statistically significant, positive change in Moody's stock price.[81] Additionally, the event study indicated that during the class period no disclosure correcting those misstatements was correlated with a statistically significant, negative change in the stock price. The court accordingly denied class certification. Nevertheless, this issue is subject to debate, because a lack of price movement can, in fact, be attributed to price maintenance, or, put differently, a fraud might be aimed at maintaining a stock price, not increasing it.[82]

6. *Measuring Price Impact.* Under *Halliburton II*, defendants have made various arguments and deployed economic analysis to argue the alleged misstatements did not affect the market price; plaintiffs have responded with their own economists who will testify that it did. Markets vary in the speed with which they incorporate information. Moreover, the significance of the information matters, so it can be a challenging task to establish whether a statement affected the market price. That challenge can be particularly daunting if a company releases multiple pieces of information at the same time. With the burden of proof on defendants, many trial judges—faced with conflicting economic evidence that they are scarcely equipped to evaluate—may opt to certify a class. Despite the limited prospects for success and the added litigation expense, it will be the rare defense lawyer that does not take advantage of the opportunity afforded by the *Halliburton II* decision; after all, they bill by the hour.

7. *Stare Decisis.* The *Halliburton II* Court made it clear that *stare decisis* played an important role in the outcome. Arguably, the Court also lacks the requisite institutional expertise for reform. The members of the Court are all former government officials, academics, and appellate advocates. They are all highly talented lawyers but, are not necessarily equipped to confront the highly technical field of securities law. It has been almost 30 years since the last justice with substantial experience as a corporate lawyer—Lewis F. Powell Jr.—retired from the Court. The Court has made it clear that it prefers to leave the field to Congress.

8. *Will Congress Act?* Is it realistic to expect reform to come from Congress? Not anytime soon. Although Congress's decision to enact legislation around the 10b–5 class action arguably indirectly addresses

---

[80] Schaffer v. Timberland Co., 924 F.Supp. 1298, 1308–09 (D.N.H. 1996).
[81] In re Moody's Corp. Sec. Litig., 274 F.R.D. 480 (S.D.N.Y. 2011).
[82] See e.g., Waggoner v. Barclays PLC, 875 F.3d 79 (2d. Cir. 2017).

the cause of action, as noted above, Congress did not directly address the question of the FOTM presumption when it adopted the PSLRA in 1995. Why? Political reality: two powerful constituencies were diametrically opposed. For the plaintiffs' bar, the FOTM presumption was the foundation of their livelihood. On the other side of the battle was corporate America, particularly the high-tech sector, wailing that lawsuits were chilling growth and destroying jobs. Neither side had the political clout to declare outright victory. Congress tightened the screws on securities class actions, but never seriously threatened to end FOTM suits.

(2) REASONABLE RELIANCE

Semerenko v. Cendant Corp.
United States Court of Appeals, Third Circuit, 2000.
223 F.3d 165.

■ Before: MANSMANN and GREENBERG, CIRCUIT JUDGES and ALARCON, SENIOR CIRCUIT JUDGE.

■ ALARCON, SENIOR CIRCUIT JUDGE:

[Eds. The beginning of this case appears earlier in the Chapter. Recall that the alleged misrepresentations were made by Cendant and others about Cendant during a tender offer for shares of American Bankers Insurance Group, Inc. The purchasers bought stock in ABI in reliance on the misrepresentations about Cendant, and argued they suffered a loss when the misrepresentations became public and the merger agreement was terminated.]

* * *

II

* * *

[Eds. On December 22, 1997, the American International Group, Inc. ("AIG") announced that it would acquire one hundred percent of the outstanding shares of ABI common stock for $47 per share. On January 27, 1998, Cendant made a competing tender offer at a price of $58 per share, or approximately $2.7 billion. Cendant also filed a Schedule 14D-1 that overstated its income for prior financial reporting periods.

On March 3, 1998, AIG matched Cendant's bid. Cendant eventually raised its bid to $67 per share, payable in cash and in shares of Cendant common stock. Cendant filed an amendment to its Schedule 14D-1 on March 23, 1998 with the terms of the merger agreement and, eight days later, filed a Form 10-K with 1997 financial results.

But, after the close of trading on April 15, 1998, Cendant announced potential accounting irregularities, and that its Audit Committee had engaged Willkie, Farr & Gallagher and Arthur Andersen LLP to do an independent investigation and Deloitte & Touche LLP to reaudit its financial statements. The announcement also reported that the irregularities occurred in a single business unit that "accounted for less than one third" of Cendant's net income, and that it would restate annual and quarterly earnings for the 1997 fiscal year by $0.11 to $0.13 per share. Immediately after Cendant disclosed the accounting irregularities, the price of ABI common stock dropped from $64–7/8 to $57–3/4, or an eleven percent decrease.

Cendant later made several public statements in reiterating commitment to completing the merger. On April 27, 1998, Walter A. Forbes, the chairman of the board of directors of Cendant, and Henry R. Silverman, the president and the chief executive officer of Cendant, issued a letter to Cendant shareholders, which was published in the financial press. That letter states:

> We are outraged that the apparent misdeeds of a small number of individuals within a limited part of our company has adversely affected the value of your investment—and ours—in Cendant. We are working together diligently to clear this matter up as soon as possible. We fully support the Audit Committee's investigation and continue to believe that the strategic rationale and industrial logic of the HFS/CUC merger that created Cendant is as compelling as ever.
>
> Cendant is strong, highly liquid, and extremely profitable. The vast majority of Cendant's operating businesses and earnings are unaffected and the prospects for the Company's future growth and success are excellent.
>
> We have reaffirmed our commitment to completing all pending acquisitions: American Bankers, National Parking Corporation and Providian Insurance.

Then, in May 5, 1998, Cendant stated that "over eighty percent of the Company's net income for the first quarter of 1998 came from Cendant business units not impacted by the potential accounting irregularities."

Later, on July 14, 1998, Cendant revealed that the April 15, 1998 announcement was inaccurate, that the reduction in income would be twice as large, that its investigation had uncovered accounting irregularities, affecting other business units and fiscal years. After the July 14, 1998 disclosure, the price of ABI common stock dropped until Cendant issued several public statements indicating that it intended to continue the tender offer and that it was "contractually committed" to completing the ABI merger.

On August 13, 1998, Cendant stated its investigation was complete and stated that it would restate earnings by $0.28 per share in 1997, by $0.19 per share in 1996, and by $0.14 per share in 1995. On August 27, 1998, Cendant issued a statement that the board of directors had adopted the audit report, which was publicly filed with the SEC on August 28,

1998 and a copy given to the United States Attorney for the District of New Jersey. The report found that "fraudulent financial reporting" and other "errors" inflated Cendant's pretax income by approximately $500 million from 1995 to 1997, and that Forbes and Shelton were "among those who must bear responsibility." The price of ABI common stock closed at $53–1/2 per share on August 28, 1998 and fell further to a closing price of $51–7/8 per share on August 31, 1998, the first day of trading following the disclosure.

On September 29, 1998, Cendant filed an amended Form 10-K for the 1997 fiscal year announcing that it had lost $217.2 million in 1997, not $55.5 million. ABI common stock to dropped further to $43 per share by the close of trading. On October 13, 1998, Cendant and ABI announced that they were terminating the merger agreement, and that Cendant would pay ABI a $400 million dollar break up fee. The termination agreement, provided that the termination of the merger would not result in liability on the part of Cendant or ABI, or on the part of any of their directors, officers, employees, agents, legal and financial advisors, or shareholders. In response to the disclosure, the price of ABI common stock dropped to $35–1/2 per share by the end of the day.

On October 14, 1998, the Class filed a complaint in the United States District Court for the District of New Jersey alleging that Cendant and the individual defendants violated § 10(b) and Rule 10b–5 by making fraudulent misrepresentations concerning Cendant's financial condition, its willingness to complete the tender offer, and its willingness to complete the proposed merger. The complaint also alleged that the individual defendants were liable for those violations as control persons under § 20(a). The Class subsequently amended its complaint to expand the class period and to name Ernst & Young as an additional defendant in its claims under § 10(b) and Rule 10b–5.]

* * *

IV.

* * *

B.

We next turn to the question whether the Class's complaint alleges sufficient facts to establish the element of reliance. It is axiomatic that a private action for securities fraud must be dismissed when a plaintiff fails to plead that he or she reasonably and justifiably relied on an alleged misrepresentation. See Weiner, 129 F.3d at 315 (setting forth reliance as an element of a private right of action under § 10(b) and Rule 10–5); In re Burlington Coat Factory Sec. Litig., 114 F.3d at 1417 (same). The defendants claim that the complaint fails to establish the element of reliance, because it alleges that the defendants' misrepresentations were made in the context of a tender offer and a proposed merger, that AIG made a competing tender offer to purchase shares of ABI common stock at $58 per share, and that Cendant issued a press release on April 15,

1998 warning investors not to rely on its prior representations concerning its financial condition.

Traditionally, purchasers and sellers of securities were required to establish that they were aware of, and directly misled by, an alleged misrepresentation to state a claim for securities fraud under § 10(b) and Rule 10b–5. See Peil v. Speiser, 806 F.2d 1154, 1160 (3d Cir. 1986) (discussing theories of reliance). Recognizing that the requirement of showing direct reliance presents an unreasonable evidentiary burden in a securities market where face-to-face transactions are rare and where lawsuits are brought by classes of investors, however, this court has adopted a rule that creates a presumption of reliance in certain cases. Under the fraud on the market theory, a plaintiff in a securities action is generally entitled to a rebuttable presumption of reliance if he or she purchased or sold securities in an efficient market. See In re Burlington Coat Factory Sec. Litig., 114 F.3d at 1419 n.8 (holding that a purchaser of securities in an open and developed market is entitled to a presumption of reliance).

The fraud on the market theory of reliance is, in essence, a theory of indirect actual reliance under which a plaintiff is entitled to three separate presumptions in attempting to establish the element of direct reliance. Under the fraud on the market theory of reliance, the court presumes (1) that the market price of the security actually incorporated the alleged misrepresentations, (2) that the plaintiff actually relied on the market price of the security as an indicator of its value, and (3) that the plaintiff acted reasonably in relying on the market price of the security. The fraud on the market theory of reliance, however, creates only a presumption, which a defendant may rebut by raising any defense to actual reliance. This court has pointed out that the presumption of reliance may be rebutted by showing that the market did not respond to the alleged misrepresentations, or that the plaintiff did not actually rely on the market price when making his or her investment decision. See Zlotnik, 836 F.2d at 822; Peil, 806 F.2d at 1161. This court has also held that a defendant may defeat the presumption of reliance by showing that the plaintiff's reliance on the market price was actually unreasonable. See Zlotnik, 836 F.2d at 822; Peil, 806 F.2d at 1161.

In the present case, we are persuaded that the Class has sufficiently pleaded the element of reliance to withstand a challenge under Rule 12(b)(6) with respect to at least some of the alleged misrepresentations. The complaint alleges that ABI common stock traded in an open and developed market throughout the class period, that the market price of ABI common stock incorporated the alleged misrepresentations, and that the Class members purchased shares of ABI common stock in reliance on that price. The complaint also states that the Class was directly misled by the alleged misrepresentations. Those allegations, if true, are sufficient to establish direct reliance and to create a presumption of indirect actual reliance so long as the Class's reliance on the purported misrepresentations or the market price of ABI common stock was not unreasonable as a matter of law.

We conclude that it was reasonable for the Class members who purchased shares prior to March 3, 1998 to rely on the alleged misrepresentations occurring prior to that date. The defendants have not provided us with a legitimate reason for us to conclude to the contrary. Their arguments concern only the reasonableness of the reliance of the Class members who purchased shares of ABI common stock after March 3, 1998. They have no bearing on the investment decisions of persons who purchased shares of ABI common stock prior to that date, because the reasonableness of reliance is determined at the time of the transaction in question. See Hayes v. Gross, 982 F.2d 104, 107 (3d Cir. 1992) (requiring an investor to rely on an alleged misrepresentation at the time of the purchase or the sale of securities); Zlotnik, 836 F.2d at 823 (same); Gannon v. Continental Ins. Co., 920 F.Supp. 566, 578 (D.N.J.1996) (holding that an investor cannot rely on statements that are made subsequent to the purchase of securities).

To the extent that the defendant's arguments suggest that it is unreasonable as a matter of law to rely on information concerning a tender offer or a merger before the transaction is finalized, we disagree. The Supreme Court has cautioned that "[n]o particular event or factor short of closing the transaction need be either necessary or sufficient by itself to render merger discussions material." Basic, Inc., 485 U.S. at 239. And, other courts have similarly held that information concerning a tender offer may be material while the transaction is still in the planning stage. Maio, 51 F.3d at 637; Mayhew, 916 F.Supp. at 131. If it may be reasonable for an investor to find information concerning a tentative tender offer or a merger important when making an investment decision, we see no reason why the conditional nature of those transactions should necessarily prevent the investor from reasonably relying on that information as well.

We are also persuaded that the Class members who purchased shares of ABI common stock between March 3, 1998 and April 15, 1998 alleged sufficient facts to satisfy the element of reliance. With respect to those purchasers, the defendants maintain that AIG's $58 tender offer provided an independent valuation of ABI common stock upon which the Class members directly or indirectly relied. In effect, the defendants suggest that the market did not incorporate the alleged misrepresentations into the price of ABI common stock during the competing tender offer, and that the Class members would have purchased shares of ABI common stock to tender to AIG even if they had known the truth about Cendant. See Basic, Inc., 485 U.S. at 249 (noting that the presumption of indirect actual reliance may be rebutted by showing that the plaintiff would have completed the transaction regardless of the alleged misrepresentations); Zlotnik, 836 F.2d at 822 (stating that the presumption of indirect actual reliance may be rebutted by showing that the market price was not affected by the alleged misrepresentations). While those arguments are facially appealing, we do not find them persuasive given the procedural posture of this case.

In reviewing a motion to dismiss under Rule 12(b)(6), we must accept the allegations of the complaint as true and draw all reasonable inferences in the light most favorable to the plaintiffs. In this case, the Class's complaint alleges that the market price of ABI common stock was inflated due to the alleged misrepresentations, and it states that the Class purchased "ABI shares believing they would receive $58 per share ... in a combination of cash and Cendant stock." Though we agree with the defendants that the market price of ABI common stock incorporated information concerning AIG's $58 tender offer, we may not assume for the present purposes that it did not also incorporate information concerning a potential acquisition by Cendant, or that Cendant's tender offer did not have an actual effect on the Class. Indeed, it is likely that the shares of ABI common stock traded at a relative premium during the competing tender offer based on the fact that two purportedly willing and able suitors sought to acquire the company. It is also possible that members of the Class would not have purchased shares of ABI common stock had they been unable to exchange them for shares of Cendant. Because we must assume the truth of the allegations of the complaint, and resolve all competing allegations and inferences in favor of the Class, we agree that the existence of a competing tender offer did not effect the Class's reliance on the defendants' alleged misrepresentations. See In re Burlington Coat Factory Sec. Litig., 114 F.3d at 1420 (stating that a court must credit the allegations of the complaint and not the defendant's responses when resolving conflicting allegations on a motion to dismiss). We also note that the effect of the $58 tender offer would have been limited to those members of the Class who purchased shares from March 3, 1998, when the tender offer was made, and March 17, 1998, when Cendant raised its bid price to $67 per share.

We agree that the Class has failed to demonstrate that it was reasonable for its members to rely on the defendants' *prior* financial statements and auditors' reports following the April 15, 1998 disclosure of the accounting irregularities. The complaint states that Cendant disclosed on April 15, 1998 that it had uncovered accounting irregularities, and that it warned investors not to rely on its prior financial statements and auditor's reports when making an investment decision. The complaint further alleges that the common stock of both Cendant and ABI traded in an efficient market, and that the market price of each stock instantly dropped after Cendant issued the warning. In light of the curative nature of the warning statement, and given the instantaneous decline in the market price of both companies' common stock, we conclude that the announcement immediately rendered the prior misrepresentations concerning Cendant's financial condition thereafter immaterial as a matter of law. See Weiner, 129 F.3d at 321 (holding that a public statement curing the misleading effect of a prior misrepresentation renders the prior misrepresentation immaterial); In re Burlington Coat Factory Sec. Litig., 114 F.3d at 1425 (stating that an efficient market immediately incorporates information into the price of a security); Teamsters Local 282 Pension Trust Fund v. Angelos, 762 F.2d 522, 530 (7th Cir. 1985) (dicta) (stating that an investor may not ask a court to focus on a misrepresentation and ignore information that has already been disseminated). Thus, neither the market nor the Class members could have reasonably relied upon Cendant's prior financial statements or its audit reports after April 15, 1998. Because it made no misrepresentations after the curative statement was issued, Ernst & Young may not be held liable to members of the Class who purchased shares of ABI common stock after April 15, 1998.

Nevertheless, we do not accept the defendants' contention that the Class could not have reasonably relied on the alleged misrepresentations that were *included* in the April 15, 1998 announcement. The Class claims that the April 15, 1998 announcement misrepresented Cendant's financial condition by stating that the company expected to restate its 1997 earnings by $0.11 to $0.13 per share and to reduce its net income prior to restructuring and unusual charges by approximately $100 to $115 million. The defendants claim that the Class was not entitled to rely on those statements or on any subsequent statements, because the announcement warned that the representations were subject to "known and unknown risks and uncertainties including, but not limited to, the outcome of the Audit Committee's investigation." Their argument is based upon both the bespeaks caution doctrine, which renders alleged misrepresentations immaterial, and the common sense principle that investors do not act reasonably in relying on statements that are accompanied by meaningful cautionary language.

The parties disagree as to whether the bespeaks caution doctrine applies to the statements made in the April 15, 1998 announcement that predicted the amount by which Cendant would restate its results for the 1997 year. The Class and the SEC maintain that the "bespeaks caution" doctrine is inapplicable, because the statements related to present and historical facts that were capable of verification and, as such, not forward-looking. See Grossman v. Novell, Inc., 120 F.3d 1112, 1123 (10th Cir. 1997) (holding that the bespeaks caution doctrine applies only to forward-looking information). The defendants, in contrast, characterize the statements concerning the restatement as forward-looking, and thus subject to the bespeaks caution doctrine, because Cendant had not completed a reaudit when it disclosed the amount of the anticipated restatement. See Harris v. Ivax Corp., 182 F.3d 799, 802–3 (11th Cir. 1999) (holding that statements made on the last day of a quarter concerning the results for the quarter are forward-looking).

We need not decide whether the alleged misrepresentations in the April 15, 1998 announcement were forward-looking statements, however, because we conclude that the accompanying warnings were not sufficiently cautionary to warn against the danger of relying on the specific numbers identified in the announcement. In In re Trump Casino Sec. Litig., 7 F.3d 357, 369 (3d Cir. 1993), this court instructed that cautionary language must be "extensive yet specific" to prevent a reasonable investor from relying on specific projections. There, the court explained:

> a vague or blanket (boilerplate) disclaimer which merely warns the reader that the investment has risks will ordinarily be inadequate to prevent misinformation. To suffice, the cautionary statements must be substantive and tailored to the specific future projections, estimates or opinions in the prospectus which the plaintiffs challenge.

In Kline v. First Western Gov't Sec., Inc., 24 F.3d 480, 489 (3d Cir. 1994), this court clarified that "*Trump* requires that the language bespeaking caution relate directly to that by which plaintiffs claim to have been misled."

In the present case, the cautionary language set forth in the April 15, 1998 announcement generally pertains only to the risk that the results of operations could vary in *future* fiscal years. In fact, the only risk factor that is apparently applicable to the restatement of Cendant's results for the 1997 fiscal year relates to the risk that the announcement's calculations might differ from those made by the Audit Committee. We are not persuaded that such a general statement of risk is sufficiently substantive and tailored to satisfy the requirements of the bespeaks caution doctrine. Nor are we persuaded that it is adequate to give investors reasonable notice that the projected restatement of Cendant's financial statements should not be trusted so as to make any reliance unreasonable as a matter of law. In our opinion, a reasonable investor may be willing to rely on the announcement's specific calculations concerning the restatement in the absence of a more detailed explanation of the reasons that the calculations might be incorrect and of the effect of any error. The announcement's blanket warning—that the amount of the restatement could later turn out to be wrong—was simply not sufficient to caution reasonable investors against relying on the defendants' representations. See Kline, 24 F.3d at 489–90 (holding that cautionary statements in an opinion letter were not sufficiently cautionary to preclude reliance where they suggested nothing more than the possibility that the speaker "might have gotten the law wrong or incorrectly assessed the risk that the IRS would deny deductions"); see, e.g., Harris, 182 F.3d at 810, 813–14 (setting forth meaningful and specific cautionary language as an appendix to the opinion). Because we conclude that the alleged misrepresentations concerning the restatement of Cendant's 1997 financial information did not include sufficient cautionary language, we agree that the Class could reasonably rely on the anticipated restatement in the April 15, 1998 announcement. For the same reason, we conclude that the Class members were not necessarily prevented from reasonably relying on the defendants' subsequent statements concerning Cendant's intent to merge with ABI.

The Class was not entitled, however, to rely indefinitely upon the April 15, 1998 misrepresentations. Cendant announced on July 14, 1998 that it had revised the restatement of its 1997 income, and it disseminated the formal results of the Audit Committee's investigation one month later. We think that it is possible that either, if not both, of those announcements might have cured the effect of the alleged misrepresentations in the April 15, 1998 announcement and rendered the disclosure thereafter unreliable. However, in light of our decision to remand this case, and given that the parties have not discussed the issue, we leave it for the district court to decide in the first instance the point at which the particular misrepresentations could no longer be trusted.

* * *

NOTES ON REASONABLE RELIANCE AND CAUSATION

1. *Transaction Causation, Loss Causation, and the "in Connection with" Requirement.* Semerenko is typical of recent cases in recognizing that in addition to the "in connection with" element a plaintiff may also have to prove transaction causation (often, as in *Semerenko*, called reliance) and loss causation (invariably meaning proximate causation).

2. *Reliance and Omissions.* Transaction causation or reliance is often presumed, either through the fraud-on-the-market doctrine or in cases like Affiliated Ute Citizens v. United States,[83] where the plaintiff's claim was based on a defendant's material omission.[84] The basis for a presumption with respect to a material omission was aptly articulated by a later Second Circuit decision: "Because, in such situations, the plaintiff is unaware of the omitted information, the record generally fails to provide a basis from which a finder of fact may evaluate how the plaintiff would have reacted if he or she had been aware of the withheld information. * * * To saddle a plaintiff with proving the 'generally indeterminable fact of what would have happened but for the omission [or the misrepresentations that skewed the market value of stock] would reduce the protection against fraud afforded by Section 10(b).' "[85]

3. *Justifiable Reliance and Oral Misstatements.* Several Rule 10b–5 decisions have also articulated a "justifiable reliance" requirement.[86] As described by the Fourth Circuit in Myers v. Finkle[87]:

---

[83] 406 U.S. 128, 153–54 (1972).
[84] Affiliated Ute referred to this requirement as "causation in fact."
[85] Litton Indus., Inc. v. Lehman Bros. Kuhn Loeb Inc., 967 F.2d 742, 748 (2d Cir. 1992).
[86] See, e.g., Kennedy v. Josephthal & Co., Inc., 814 F.2d 798, 804 (1st Cir. 1987) (citing factors used by courts in examining whether reliance on misrepresentations is justified).
[87] 950 F.2d 165, 167 (4th Cir. 1991).

A determination of whether an investor may be justified in relying on oral representations that conflict with contemporaneous written statements in the investor's possession requires a consideration of all relevant factors, including:

(1) [T]he sophistication and expertise of the plaintiff in financial and securities matters; (2) the existence of long standing business or personal relationships; (3) access to relevant information; (4) the existence of a fiduciary relationship; (5) concealment of the fraud; (6) the opportunity to detect the fraud; (7) whether the plaintiff initiated the stock transaction or sought to expedite the transaction; and (8) the generality or specificity of the misrepresentations.

Because no single factor is dispositive, consideration of all factors is necessary.

Justifiable reliance need not be proven when the plaintiff is entitled to the fraud-on-the-market presumption of reliance.

(3) Loss Causation

The loss causation, or proximate cause, element has created other complexities. The Supreme Court addressed loss causation in two recent opinions. The first addresses pleading, and the second addresses class certification.

Dura Pharmaceuticals, Inc. v. Michael Broudo
Supreme Court of the United States, 2005.
544 U.S. 336, 125 S.Ct. 1627, 161 L.Ed.2d 577.

■ JUSTICE BREYER delivered the opinion of the Court.

A private plaintiff who claims securities fraud must prove that the defendant's fraud caused an economic loss. 15 U.S.C. § 78u–4(b)(4). We consider a Ninth Circuit holding that a plaintiff can satisfy this requirement—a requirement that courts call "loss causation"—simply by alleging in the complaint and subsequently establishing that "the price" of the security *on the date of purchase* was inflated because of the misrepresentation." 339 F.3d 933, 938 (2003) (internal quotation marks omitted). In our view, the Ninth Circuit is wrong, both in respect to what a plaintiff must prove and in respect to what the plaintiffs' complaint here must allege.

I

Respondents are individuals who bought stock in Dura Pharmaceuticals, Inc., on the public securities market between April 15, 1997, and February 24, 1998. They have brought this securities fraud class action * * * against Dura and some of its managers and directors (hereinafter Dura) in federal court. In respect to the question before us, their detailed amended * * * complaint makes substantially the following allegations:

(1) Before and during the purchase period, Dura (or its officials) made false statements concerning both Dura's drug profits and future Food and Drug Administration (FDA) approval of a new asthmatic spray device.

(2) In respect to drug profits. Dura falsely claimed that it expected that its drug sales would prove profitable.

(3) In respect to the asthmatic spray device, Dura falsely claimed that it expected the FDA would soon grant its approval.

(4) On the last day of the purchase period, February 24, 1998, Dura announced that its earnings would be lower than expected, principally due to slow drug sales.

(5) The next day Dura's shares lost almost half their value (falling from about $39 per share to about $21).

(6) About eight months later (in November 1998), Dura announced that the FDA would not approve Dura's new asthmatic spray device.

(7) The next day Dura's share price temporarily fell but almost fully recovered within one week.

Most importantly, the complaint says the following (and nothing significantly more than the following) about economic losses attributable to the spray device misstatement: *"In reliance on the integrity of the market, [the plaintiffs] . . . paid artificially inflated prices for Dura securities"* and the plaintiffs suffered *"damage[s]"* thereby. (emphasis added).

The District Court dismissed the complaint. In respect to the plaintiffs' drug-profitability claim, it held that the complaint failed adequately to allege an appropriate state of mind, i.e., that defendants had acted knowingly, or the like. In respect to the plaintiffs' spray device claim, it held that the complaint failed adequately to allege "loss causation."

The Court of Appeals for the Ninth Circuit * * * held that the complaint adequately alleged "loss causation." The Circuit wrote that "plaintiffs establish loss causation if they have shown that the price *on the date of purchase* was inflated because of the misrepresentation." It added that "the injury occurs at the time of the transaction." Since the complaint pleaded "that the price at the time of purchase was overstated," and it sufficiently identified the cause, its allegations were legally sufficient.

* * *

II

* * *

A

We begin with the Ninth Circuit's basic reason for finding the complaint adequate, namely, that at the end of the day plaintiffs need only "establish," i.e., prove, that "the price *on the date of purchase* was inflated because of the misrepresentation." In our view, this statement of the law is wrong. Normally, in cases such as this one (i.e., fraud-on-the-market cases), an inflated purchase price will not itself constitute or proximately cause the relevant economic loss.

For one thing, as a matter of pure logic, at the moment the transaction takes place, the plaintiff has suffered no loss; the inflated purchase payment is offset by ownership of a share that *at that instant* possesses equivalent value. Moreover, the logical link between the inflated share purchase price and any later economic loss is not invariably strong. Shares are normally purchased with an eye toward a later sale. But if, say, the purchaser sells the shares quickly before the relevant truth begins to leak out, the misrepresentation will not have led to any loss. If the purchaser sells later after the truth makes its way into the market place, an initially inflated purchase price *might* mean a later loss. But that is far from inevitably so. When the purchaser subsequently resells such shares, even at a lower price, that lower price may reflect, not the earlier misrepresentation, but changed economic circumstances, changed investor expectations, new industry-specific or firm specific facts, conditions, or other events, which taken separately or together account for some or all of that lower price. (The same is true in respect to a claim that a share's higher price is lower than it would otherwise have been—a claim we do not consider here.) Other things being equal, the longer the time between purchase and sale, the more likely that this is so, i.e., the more likely that other factors caused the loss.

Given the tangle of factors affecting price, the most logic alone permits us to say is that the higher purchase price will *sometimes* play a role in bringing about a future loss. It may prove to be a necessary condition of any such loss, and in that sense one might say that the inflated purchase price suggests that the misrepresentation (using language the Ninth Circuit used) "touches upon" a later economic loss. But, even if that is so, it is insufficient. To "touch upon" a loss is not to cause a loss, and it is the latter that the law requires. 15 U.S.C. § 78u–4(b)(4).

For another thing, the Ninth Circuit's holding lacks support in precedent. Judicially implied private securities-fraud actions resemble in many (but not all) respects common-law deceit and misrepresentation actions. The common law of deceit subjects a person who "fraudulently" makes a "misrepresentation" to liability "for pecuniary loss caused" to one who justifiably relies upon that misrepresentation. Restatement

(Second) of Torts § 525, p. 55 (1976) (hereinafter Restatement of Torts); see also Southern Development Co. v. Silva, 125 U.S. 247, 250 (1888) (setting forth elements of fraudulent misrepresentation). And the common law has long insisted that a plaintiff in such a case show not only that had he known the truth he would not have acted but also that he suffered actual economic loss. See, e.g., Pasley v. Freeman, 3 id. T.R. 51,65. 100 Eng. Rep. 450, 457 (1789) (if "no injury is occasioned by the lie, it is not actionable: but if it be attended with a damage, it then becomes the subject of an action"); Freeman v. Venner, 120 Mass. 424, 426 (1876) (a mortgagee cannot bring a tort action for damages stemming from a fraudulent note that a misrepresentation led him to execute unless and until the note has to be paid); see also M. Bigelow, Law of Torts 101 (8th ed. 1907) (damage "must already have been suffered before the bringing of the suit"); 2 T. Cooley, Law of Torts 348, p. 551 (4th ed. 1932) (plaintiff must show that he "suffered damage" and that the "damage followed proximately the deception"); W. Keeton, D. Dobbs, R. Keeton, & D. Owen, Prosser and Keeton on Law of Torts § 110, p. 765 (5th ed. 1984) (hereinafter Prosser and Keeton) (plaintiff "must have suffered substantial damage," not simply nominal damages, before "the cause of action can arise").

Given the common-law roots of the securities fraud action (and the common-law requirement that a plaintiff show actual damages), it is not surprising that other Courts of Appeals have rejected the Ninth Circuit's "inflated purchase price" approach to proving causation and loss. See, e.g., Emergent Capital, 343 F.3d at 198 (inflation of purchase price alone cannot satisfy loss causation); Semerenko, 223 F.3d at 185 (same), Robbins, 116 F.3d at 1448 (same); cf., Bastian, 892 F.2d at 685. Indeed, the Restatement of Torts, in setting forth the judicial consensus, says that a person who "misrepresents the financial condition of a corporation in order to sell its stock" becomes liable to a relying purchaser "for the loss" the purchaser sustains "when the facts . . . become generally known" and "as a result" share value "depreciate[s]." § 548A, Comment b, at 107. Treatise writers, too, have emphasized the need to prove proximate causation. Prosser and Keeton § 110, at 767 (losses do "not afford any basis for recovery" if "brought about by business conditions or other factors").

We cannot reconcile the Ninth Circuit's "inflated purchase price" approach with these views of other courts. And the uniqueness of its perspective argues against the validity of its approach in a case like this one where we consider the contours of a judicially implied cause of action with roots in the common law.

Finally, the Ninth Circuit's approach overlooks an important securities law objective. The securities statutes seek to maintain public confidence in the marketplace. They do so by deterring fraud, in part, through the availability of private securities fraud actions. But the statutes make these latter actions available, not to provide investors with broad insurance against market losses, but to protect them against those economic losses that misrepresentations actually cause. Cf. Basic, 485 U.S., at 252 (White, J., joined by O'Connor, J., concurring in part and dissenting in part) ("[A]llowing recovery in the face of affirmative evidence of nonreliance—would effectively convert Rule 10b–5 into a scheme of investor's insurance. There is no support in the Securities Exchange Act, the Rule, or our cases for such a result.")

The statutory provision at issue here and the paragraphs that precede it emphasize this last mentioned objective. Private Securities Litigation Reform Act of 1995. The statute insists that securities fraud complaints "specify" each misleading statement; that they set forth the facts "on which [a] belief" that a statement is misleading was "formed"; and that they "state with particularity facts giving rise to a strong inference that the defendant acted with the required state of mind." 15 U.S.C. §§ 78u–4(b)(1), (2). And the statute expressly imposes on plaintiffs "the burden of proving" that the defendant's misrepresentations "caused the loss for which the plaintiff seeks to recover." § 78u–4(b)(4).

The statute thereby makes clear Congress' intent to permit private securities fraud actions for recovery where, but only where, plaintiffs adequately allege and prove the traditional elements of causation and loss. By way of contrast, the Ninth Circuit's approach would allow recovery where a misrepresentation leads to an inflated purchase price but nonetheless does not proximately cause any economic loss. That is to say, it would permit recovery where these two traditional elements in fact are missing.

In sum, we find the Ninth Circuit's approach inconsistent with the law's requirement that a plaintiff prove that the defendant's misrepresentation (or other fraudulent conduct) proximately caused the plaintiff's economic loss. We need not, and do not, consider other proximate cause or loss-related questions.

B

Our holding about plaintiffs' need to *prove* proximate causation and economic loss leads us also to conclude that the plaintiffs' complaint here failed adequately to *allege* these requirements. We concede that the Federal Rules of Civil Procedure require only "a short and plain statement of the claim showing that the pleader is entitled to relief." Fed. Rule Civ. Proc. 8(a)(2). And we assume, at least for argument's sake, that neither the Rules nor the securities statutes impose any special further requirement in respect to the pleading of proximate causation or economic loss. But, even so, the "short and plain statement" must provide the defendant with "fair notice of what the plaintiff's claim is and the grounds upon which it rests." Conley v. Gibson, 355 U.S. 41 (1957). The complaint before us fails this simple test.

As we have pointed out, the plaintiffs' lengthy complaint contains only one statement that we can fairly read as describing the loss caused by the defendants' "spray device" misrepresentations. That statement says that the plaintiffs "paid artificially inflated prices for Dura['s] securities" and suffered "damage[s]." The statement implies that the plaintiffs' loss consisted of the "artificially inflated" purchase "prices." The complaint's failure to claim that Dura's share price fell significantly after the truth became known suggests that the plaintiffs considered the allegation of purchase price inflation alone sufficient. The complaint contains nothing that suggests otherwise.

For reasons set forth in Part II-A supra, however, the "artificially inflated purchase price" is not itself a relevant economic loss. And the complaint nowhere else provides the defendants with notice of what the relevant economic loss might be or of what the causal connection might be between that loss and the misrepresentation concerning Dura's "spray device."

We concede that ordinary pleading rules are not meant to impose a great burden upon a plaintiff. But it should not prove burdensome for a plaintiff who has suffered an economic loss to provide a defendant with some indication of the loss and the causal connection that the plaintiff has in mind. At the same time, allowing a plaintiff to forgo giving any indication of the economic loss and proximate cause that the plaintiff has in mind would bring about harm of the very sort the statutes seek to avoid. Cf. H. R. Conf. Rep. No. 104–369, p. 31 (1995) (criticizing "abusive" practices including "the routine filing of lawsuits . . . with only [a] faint hope that the discovery process might lead eventually to some plausible cause of action"). It would permit a plaintiff "with a largely groundless claim to simply take up the time of a number of other people, with the right to do so representing an *in terrorem* increment of the settlement value, rather than a reasonably founded hope that the [discovery] process will reveal relevant evidence." Blue Chip Stamps, 421 U.S. at 741. Such a rule would tend to transform a private securities action into a partial downside insurance policy.

For these reasons, we find the plaintiffs' complaint legally insufficient. We reverse the judgment of the Ninth Circuit, and we remand the case for further proceedings consistent with this opinion.

It is so ordered.

Erica P. John Fund, Inc. v. Halliburton Co.

Supreme Court of the United States, 2011.
563 U.S. 804, 131 S.Ct. 2179, 180 L.Ed.2d 24.

■ CHIEF JUSTICE ROBERTS delivered the opinion of the Court.

To prevail on the merits in a private securities fraud action, investors must demonstrate that the defendant's deceptive conduct caused their claimed economic loss. This requirement is commonly referred to as "loss causation." The question presented in this case is whether securities fraud plaintiffs must also prove loss causation in order to obtain class certification. We hold that they need not.

I

Petitioner Erica P. John Fund, Inc. (EPJ Fund), is the lead plaintiff in a putative securities fraud class action filed against Halliburton Co. and one of its executives (collectively Halliburton). The suit was brought on behalf of all investors who purchased Halliburton common stock between June 3, 1999, and December 7, 2001.

EPJ Fund alleges that Halliburton made various misrepresentations designed to inflate its stock price, in violation of § 10(b) of the Securities Exchange Act of 1934 and Securities and Exchange Commission Rule 10b–5. The complaint asserts that Halliburton deliberately made false statements about (1) the scope of its potential liability in asbestos litigation, (2) its expected revenue from certain construction contracts, and (3) the benefits of its merger with another company. EPJ Fund contends that Halliburton later made a number of corrective disclosures that caused its stock price to drop and, consequently, investors to lose money.

After defeating a motion to dismiss, EPJ Fund sought to have its proposed class certified pursuant to Federal Rule of Civil Procedure 23. The parties agreed, and the District Court held, that EPJ Fund satisfied the general requirements for class actions set out in Rule 23(a): The class was sufficiently numerous, there were common questions of law or fact, the claims of the representative parties were typical, and the representative parties would fairly and adequately protect the interests of the class.

The District Court also found that the action could proceed as a class action under Rule 23(b)(3), but for one problem: Circuit precedent required securities fraud plaintiffs to prove "loss causation" in order to obtain class certification. As the District Court explained, loss causation is the " 'causal connection between the material misrepresentation and the [economic] loss' " suffered by investors. After reviewing the alleged misrepresentations and corrective disclosures, the District Court concluded that it could not certify the class in this case because EPJ Fund had "failed to establish loss causation with respect to any" of its claims. The court made clear, however, that absent "this stringent loss causation requirement," it would have granted the Fund's certification request.

The Court of Appeals affirmed the denial of class certification. It confirmed that, "[i]n order to obtain class certification on its claims, [EPJ Fund] was required to prove loss causation, i.e., that the corrected truth of the former falsehoods actually caused the stock price to fall and resulted in the losses." Like the District Court, the Court of Appeals concluded that EPJ Fund had failed to meet the "requirements for proving loss causation at the class certification stage."

We granted the Fund's petition for certiorari to resolve a conflict among the Circuits as to whether securities fraud plaintiffs must prove loss causation in order to obtain class certification. Compare 597 F.3d at 334 (case below), with In re Salomon Analyst Metromedia Litigation, 544 F.3d 474, 483 (2d Cir. 2008) (not requiring investors to prove loss causation at class certification stage); Schleicher v. Wendt, 618 F.3d 679, 687 (7th Cir. 2010) (same); In re DVI, Inc. Secs. Litig., 2011 WL 1125926, *7 (3d Cir., Mar. 29, 2011) (same; decided after certiorari was granted).

II

EPJ Fund contends that the Court of Appeals erred by requiring proof of loss causation for class certification. We agree.

A

As noted, the sole dispute here is whether EPJ Fund satisfied the prerequisites of Rule 23(b)(3). In order to certify a class under that Rule, a court must find "that the questions of law or fact common to class members predominate over any questions affecting only individual members, and that a class action is superior to other available methods for fairly and efficiently adjudicating the controversy." Fed. Rule Civ. Proc. 23(b)(3). Considering whether "questions of law or fact common to class members predominate" begins, of course, with the elements of the underlying cause of action. The elements of a private securities fraud claim based on violations of § 10(b) and Rule 10b–5 are: " '(1) a material misrepresentation or omission by the defendant; (2) scienter; (3) a connection between the misrepresentation or omission and the purchase or sale of a security; (4) reliance upon the misrepresentation or omission; (5) economic loss; and (6) loss causation.' " Matrixx Initiatives, Inc. v. Siracusano, 563 U.S. 27, 37–38 (2011) (quoting Stoneridge Investment Partners, LLC v. Scientific-Atlanta, Inc., 552 U.S. 148, 157 (2008)).

Whether common questions of law or fact predominate in a securities fraud action often turns on the element of reliance. The courts below determined that EPJ Fund had to prove the separate element of loss causation in order to establish that reliance was capable of resolution on a common, classwide basis.

"Reliance by the plaintiff upon the defendant's deceptive acts is an essential element of the § 10(b) private cause of action." Stoneridge at 159. This is because proof of reliance ensures that there is a proper "connection between a defendant's misrepresentation and a plaintiff's injury." Basic Inc. v. Levinson, 485 U.S. 224, 243 (1988). The traditional (and most direct) way a plaintiff can demonstrate reliance is by showing that he was aware of a company's statement and engaged in a relevant transaction—*e.g.*, purchasing common stock—based on that specific misrepresentation. In that situation, the plaintiff plainly would have relied on the company's deceptive conduct. A plaintiff unaware of the relevant statement, on the other hand, could not establish reliance on that basis.

We recognized in *Basic*, however, that limiting proof of reliance in such a way "would place an unnecessarily unrealistic evidentiary burden on the Rule 10b–5 plaintiff who has traded on an impersonal market." We also observed that "[r]equiring proof of individualized reliance from each member of the proposed plaintiff class effectively would" prevent such plaintiffs "from proceeding with a class action, since individual issues" would "overwhelm[ ] the common ones."

The Court in *Basic* sought to alleviate those related concerns by permitting plaintiffs to invoke a rebuttable presumption of reliance based on what is known as the "fraud-on-the-market" theory. According to that theory, "the market price of shares traded on well-developed markets reflects all publicly available information, and, hence, any material misrepresentations." Because the market "transmits information to the investor in the processed form of a market price," we can assume, the Court explained, that an investor relies on public misstatements whenever he "buys or sells stock at the price set by the market." The Court also made clear that the presumption was just that, and could be rebutted by appropriate evidence.

B

It is undisputed that securities fraud plaintiffs must prove certain things in order to invoke *Basic*'s rebuttable presumption of reliance. It is common ground, for example, that plaintiffs must demonstrate that the alleged misrepresentations were publicly known (else how would the market take them into account?), that the stock traded in an efficient market, and that the relevant transaction took place "between the time the misrepresentations were made and the time the truth was revealed."

According to the Court of Appeals, EPJ Fund also had to establish loss causation at the certification stage to "trigger the fraud-on-the-market presumption." (EPJ Fund must "establish a causal link between the alleged falsehoods and its losses in order to invoke the fraud-on-the-market presumption"). The court determined that, in order to invoke a rebuttable presumption of reliance, EPJ Fund needed to prove that the decline in Halliburton's stock was "because of the correction to a prior misleading statement" and "that the subsequent loss could not otherwise be explained by some additional factors revealed then to the market." This is the loss causation requirement as we have described it. See Dura Pharmaceuticals at 342; see also 15 U.S.C. § 78u–4(b)(4).

The Court of Appeals' requirement is not justified by Basic or its logic. To begin, we have never before mentioned loss causation as a precondition for invoking Basic's rebuttable presumption of reliance. The term "loss causation" does not even appear in our Basic opinion. And for good reason: Loss causation addresses a matter different from whether an investor relied on a misrepresentation, presumptively or otherwise, when buying or selling a stock.

We have referred to the element of reliance in a private Rule 10b–5 action as "transaction causation," not loss causation. *Dura Pharmaceuticals* at 341–342 (citing *Basic* at 248–249). Consistent with that description, when considering whether a plaintiff has relied on a misrepresentation, we have typically focused on facts surrounding the investor's decision to engage in the transaction. Under *Basic*'s fraud-on-the-market doctrine, an investor presumptively relies on a defendant's misrepresentation if that "information is reflected in [the] market price" of the stock at the time of the relevant transaction.

Loss causation, by contrast, requires a plaintiff to show that a misrepresentation that affected the integrity of the market price *also* caused a subsequent economic loss. As we made clear in *Dura Pharmaceuticals*, the fact that a stock's "price on the date of purchase was inflated because of [a] misrepresentation" does not necessarily mean that the misstatement is the cause of a later decline in value. We observed that the drop could instead be the result of other intervening causes, such as "changed economic circumstances, changed investor expectations, new industry-specific or firm-specific facts, conditions, or other events." If one of those factors were responsible for the loss or part of it, a plaintiff would not be able to prove loss causation to that extent. This is true even if the investor purchased the stock at a distorted price, and thereby presumptively relied on the misrepresentation reflected in that price.

According to the Court of Appeals, however, an inability to prove loss causation would prevent a plaintiff from invoking the rebuttable presumption of reliance. Such a rule contravenes *Basic's* fundamental premise—that an investor presumptively relies on a misrepresentation so long as it was reflected in the market price at the time of his transaction. The fact that a subsequent loss may have been caused by factors other than the revelation of a misrepresentation has nothing to do with whether an investor relied on the misrepresentation in the first place, either directly or presumptively through the fraud-on-the-market theory. Loss causation has no logical connection to the facts necessary to establish the efficient market predicate to the fraud-on-the-market theory.

The Court of Appeals erred by requiring EPJ Fund to show loss causation as a condition of obtaining class certification.

C

Halliburton concedes that securities fraud plaintiffs should not be required to prove loss causation in order to invoke *Basic*'s presumption of reliance or otherwise achieve class certification. Halliburton nonetheless defends the judgment below on the ground that the Court of Appeals did not actually require plaintiffs to prove "loss causation" as we have used that term. See id., at 27 ("it's not loss causation as this Court knows it in *Dura*"). According to Halliburton, "loss causation" was merely "shorthand" for a different analysis. The lower court's actual inquiry,

Halliburton insists, was whether EPJ Fund had demonstrated "price impact"—that is, whether the alleged misrepresentations affected the market price in the first place. See, e.g., id., at 16–19, 24–27, 50–51; see also Tr. of Oral Arg. 27 (stating that the Court of Appeals' "test is simply price impact" and that EPJ Fund's "only burden under the Fifth Circuit case law was to show price impact").

"Price impact" simply refers to the effect of a misrepresentation on a stock price. Halliburton's theory is that if a misrepresentation does not affect market price, an investor cannot be said to have relied on the misrepresentation merely because he purchased stock at that price. If the price is unaffected by the fraud, the price does not reflect the fraud.

We do not accept Halliburton's wishful interpretation of the Court of Appeals' opinion. As we have explained, loss causation is a familiar and distinct concept in securities law; it is not price impact. While the opinion below may include some language consistent with a "price impact" approach, we simply cannot ignore the Court of Appeals' repeated and explicit references to "loss causation," see id., at 334 (three times), 334 n. 2, 335, 335 n. 10 (twice), 335 n. 11, 336, 336 n. 19, 336 n. 20, 337, 338, 341 (twice), 341 n. 46, 342 n. 47, 343, 344 (three times).

Whatever Halliburton thinks the Court of Appeals meant to say, what it said was loss causation: "[EPJ Fund] was required to prove loss causation, i.e., that the corrected truth of the former falsehoods actually caused the stock price to fall and resulted in the losses." 597 F.3d at 334; see id., at 335 ("we require plaintiffs to establish loss causation in order to trigger the fraud-on-the-market presumption" (internal quotation marks omitted)). We take the Court of Appeals at its word. Based on those words, the decision below cannot stand.

* * *

Because we conclude the Court of Appeals erred by requiring EPJ Fund to prove loss causation at the certification stage, we need not, and do not, address any other question about *Basic*, its presumption, or how and when it may be rebutted. To the extent Halliburton has preserved any further arguments against class certification, they may be addressed in the first instance by the Court of Appeals on remand.

The judgment of the Court of Appeals is vacated, and the case is remanded for further proceedings consistent with this opinion.

It is so ordered.

NOTES ON LOSS CAUSATION

1. *Pleading Loss Causation.* In *Dura Pharmaceuticals* the Supreme Court held that a complaint adequately alleges loss causation if it "provides the defendants with notice of what the relevant economic loss might be or of what the causal connection might be between that loss

and the misrepresentation."[88] The Supreme Court stopped short, however, of dictating a specified standard to which plaintiffs' pleadings must adhere.

Since *Dura*, courts have treated *Dura* in various ways. The most stringent standard comes out of the Fourth Circuit. The Fourth Circuit requires that a plaintiff pleading loss causation must satisfy the heightened pleading standard of Rule 9(b).[89] The Seventh Circuit imposes a standard requiring that a complaint "specify . . . a causal connection between the material misrepresentation and the loss, not simply that the misrepresentation 'touches upon' a later economic loss."[90]

Other courts have imposed a lesser burden on plaintiffs' pleadings by subjecting loss causation to the ordinary pleading standards under Rule 8(a).[91] Applying Rule 8(a), the Fifth Circuit held that a complaint must allege only "a facially 'plausible' causal relationship between the fraudulent statements or omissions and plaintiff's economic loss."[92] The Second Circuit employs a unique approach. Applying an analysis similar to the tort-law concept of proximate cause, the Second Circuit requires a "causal connection" between the defendant's alleged misstatements and the plaintiff's purported loss in order to satisfy the pleading requirements.[93]

2. *Is a Misstatement That Does Not Itself Cause Price Inflation Actionable?* The Eleventh Circuit answered this question affirmatively in Findwhat Investor Group v. Findwhat.com.[94] In this case, plaintiffs sought recovery from an Internet commerce company that provided "pay-per-click" advertising services. The plaintiffs alleged that the defendants committed "click fraud," the practice of clicking on an Internet advertisement to force the advertising client to pay for the clicks. The plaintiffs alleged that the click fraud practice helped the company maintain its stock prices. The plaintiffs' expert opined that statements

---

[88] Dura Pharmaceuticals, Inc. v. Broudo, 544 U.S. 336, 347, 125 S.Ct. 1627 (2005).

[89] See Katyle v. Penn Nat'l Gaming, Inc., 637 F.3d 462, 466 (4th Cir. 2011) ("[P]leading practice requires that a plaintiff, as a precursor to proof, allege loss causation in the complaint with sufficient specificity to enable the court to evaluate whether the necessary causal link exists."); Teachers' Retirement System of Louisiana v. Hunter, 477 F.3d 162, 186 (4th Cir. 2007) ("[a] strong case can be made that because loss causation is among the 'circumstances constituting fraud for which Rule 9(b) demands particularity' ").

[90] Tricontinental Industries, Ltd. v. PricewaterhouseCoopers, 475 F.3d 824, 84 (7th Cir. 2007) ("complaint must specify each misleading statement, and that there must be a causal connection between the material misrepresentation and the loss, not simply that the misrepresentation 'touches upon' a later economic loss").

[91] See In re Gilead Scis. Sec. Litig., 536 F.3d 1049, 1057 (9th Cir. 2008) ("So long as the complaint alleges facts that, if taken as true, plausibly establish loss causation, a Rule 12(b)(6) dismissal is inappropriate. This is not 'a probability requirement . . . it simply calls for enough fact to raise a reasonable expectation that discovery will reveal evidence of loss causation." (citing Bell Atlantic v. Twombly, 127 S.Ct. at 1965)).

[92] Lormand v. US Unwired, Inc., 565 F.3d 228, 267 (5th Cir. 2009).

[93] Lentell v. Merrill Lynch & Co., 396 F.3d 161, 173 (2d Cir. 2005).

[94] 658 F.3d 1282 (11th Cir. 2011).

by the company's CEO, stating the company had eliminated click fraud, continued to prop up the already inflated stock price.

The district court dismissed the plaintiffs' allegations, finding that plaintiffs failed adequately to plead loss causation and damages. On appeal, the Eleventh Circuit disagreed, stating that "[t]he district court erroneously assumed that simply because confirmatory false statements have no immediate effect on an already inflated stock price in an efficient market, these statements cannot cause harm."[95] The Court opined that:

> [F]raudulent misstatements that prolong inflation can be just as harmful to subsequent investors as statements that create inflation in the first instance. Inflation creates an ongoing risk of harm. Every investor who purchases at an inflated price—whether at the beginning, middle, or end of the inflationary period—is at risk of losing the inflationary component of his investment when the truth underlying the misrepresentation comes to light. . . . When the truth underlying the falsehood is finally revealed, however, the market will digest the new information and cease attributing the artificial inflation to the price. At that time, investors who purchased at inflated prices (and who still hold their stock) will suffer economic loss, because they will no longer be able to recoup the inflationary component of their purchase price by reselling their stock in the newly calibrated marketplace.[96]

Not every circuit agrees with the Eleventh Circuit's view about maintenance of stock price inflation. The Fifth Circuit, for example, rejects this view.[97]

3. *Event Studies.* *Dura*'s requirement that plaintiffs prove that the defendant's misrepresentation proximately caused the loss has enhanced reliance on expert testimony in securities fraud cases. The use of an event study—a regression analysis of the effect of a particular event on the movement of a company's stock price—is the most common way a plaintiffs' expert will attempt to show a change in the value of their investment caused by the fraud. Many circuits sustain the use of event studies,[98] and a court will grant summary judgment in favor of the defendants if the plaintiffs fail to offer an adequate event study.[99]

4. *Query.* Basic, Inc. v. Levinson said that the fraud on the market presumption was rebuttable. But when can defendants seek to rebut the presumption? Under *Halliburton I*, the most likely answer is at the summary judgment stage, but the possibility remains open that rebuttal

---

[95] Id. at 1314.

[96] Id. at 1314–15.

[97] Greenberg v. Crossroads Sys., 364 F.3d 657, 666 (5th Cir. 2004) ("Because the presumption of reliance is based upon actual movement of the stock price, confirmatory information cannot be the basis for a fraud-on-the-market claim.").

[98] See Findwhat Investor Group v. Findwhat.com, 658 F.3d at 1313.

[99] In re Williams Secs. Litig.—WCG Subclass, 558 F.3d 1130 (10th Cir. 2009).

could occur earlier at the motion to dismiss stage if there were no factual issues.

Problem

PROBLEM 12-5

Larry Abel, the Chief Executive Officer of Kain, Inc., a closely held corporation, recently had dinner with his business school classmate, Margaret Jones, Chief Executive Officer of Franklin Press, a thinly traded over-the-counter corporation. At the conclusion of dinner, they agreed to merge Kain, Inc. and Franklin Press. Three days later, a formal merger agreement was signed, and a press conference to make the announcement public was scheduled one week later.

The day after the merger agreement was signed, Afterman, a shareholder in Franklin Press, telephoned Franklin's public relations officer, and asked about "rumors of an impending major event." The public relations officer emphatically denied the rumors. Afterman promptly sold her Franklin stock at $20. After the merger was announced, Franklin's stock rose to $30.

1. Can Afterman rely on the fraud-on-the-market presumption to prove reliance?

2. Could Afterman prove reliance if her stock sale order had been placed before the conversation with the public relations officer?

3. Would an earlier originated stock sale order be "in connection with" a stock sale that occurred after Franklin's public relations officer made a material misrepresentation about Franklin's future?

4. Suppose Afterman could satisfy the reliance and "in connection with" requirements. Could Afterman establish loss causation for the difference between her $20 sales price per Franklin share and the $30 price at which Franklin was quoted after the merger announcement if the relevant stock market index was up 25 percent?

5. Could Afterman establish loss causation if the Baucus Brothers decided the day after the merger agreement was signed to seek control of Franklin Press and their open market purchases pushed the trading price of Franklin to $25?

F. STANDING

Blue Chip Stamps v. Manor Drug Stores
Supreme Court of the United States, 1975.
421 U.S. 723, 95 S.Ct. 1917, 44 L.Ed.2d 539.

■ MR. JUSTICE REHNQUIST delivered the opinion of the Court.

This case requires us to consider whether the offerees of a stock offering, made pursuant to an antitrust consent decree and registered under the Securities Act of 1933, 15 U.S.C. § 77a et seq. ("1933 Act"), may maintain a private cause of action for money damages where they allege that the offeror has violated the provisions of Rule 10b–5 of the Securities and Exchange Commission, but where they have neither purchased nor sold any of the offered shares. See Birnbaum v. Newport Steel Corp., 193 F.2d 461 (CA2), cert. denied, 343 U.S. 956 (1952).

I

In 1963 the United States filed a civil antitrust action against Blue Chip Stamp Company (Old Blue Chip), a company in the business of providing trading stamps to retailers, and nine retailers who owned 90% of its shares. In 1967 the action was terminated by the entry of a consent decree. United States v. Blue Chip Stamp Co., 272 F.Supp. 432 (C.D.Cal.1967), aff'd sub nom. Thrifty Shoppers Scrip Co. v. United States, 389 U.S. 580 (1968). The decree contemplated a plan of reorganization whereby Old Blue Chip was to be merged into a newly formed corporation, Blue Chip Stamps (New Blue Chip). The holdings of the majority shareholders of Old Blue Chip were to be reduced, and New Blue Chip, one of the petitioners here, was required under the plan to offer a substantial number of its shares of common stock to retailers who had used the stamp service in the past but who were not shareholders in the old company. Under the terms of the plan, the offering to nonshareholder users was to be proportional to past stamp usage and the shares were to be offered in units consisting of common stock and debentures.

The reorganization plan was carried out, the offering was registered with the SEC as required by the 1933 Act, and a prospectus was distributed to all offerees as required by § 5 of that Act. Somewhat more than 50% of the offered units were actually purchased. In 1970, two years after the offering, respondent, a former user of the stamp service and therefore an offeree of the 1968 offering, filed this suit in the United States District Court for the Central District of California. Defendants below and petitioners here are Old and New Blue Chip, eight of the nine majority shareholders of Old Blue Chip, and the directors of New Blue Chip (collectively called Blue Chip).

Respondent's complaint alleged, *inter alia*, that the prospectus prepared and distributed by Blue Chip in connection with the offering was materially misleading in its overly pessimistic appraisal of Blue Chip's status and future prospects. It alleged that Blue Chip intentionally made the prospectus overly pessimistic in order to discourage respondent and other members of the allegedly large class whom it represents from accepting what was intended to be a bargain offer, so that the rejected shares might later be offered to the public at a higher price. The complaint alleged that class members because of and in reliance on the false and misleading prospectus failed to purchase the offered units. Respondent therefore sought on behalf of the alleged class some $21,400,000 in damages representing the lost opportunity to purchase the units; the right to purchase the previously rejected units at the 1968 price; and in addition, it sought some $25,000,000 in exemplary damages.

The only portion of the litigation thus initiated which is before us is whether respondent may base its action on Rule 10b–5 of the Securities and Exchange Commission without having either bought or sold the securities described in the allegedly misleading prospectus.

* * *

II.

* * *

Despite the contrast between the provisions of Rule 10b–5 and the numerous carefully drawn express civil remedies provided in the Acts of both 1933 and 1934, it was held in 1946 by the United States District Court for the Eastern District of Pennsylvania that there was an implied private right of action under the Rule. Kardon v. National Gypsum Co., 69 F.Supp. 512 (1946). This Court had no occasion to deal with the subject until 25 years later, and at that time we confirmed with virtually no discussion the overwhelming consensus of the District Courts and Courts of Appeals that such a cause of action did exist. Such a conclusion was, of course, entirely consistent with the Court's recognition in J.I. Case Co. v. Borak, 377 U.S. 426, 432 (1964), that private enforcement of Commission rules may "[provide] a necessary supplement to Commission action."

* * *

III

The panel which decided *Birnbaum* consisted of Chief Judge Swan and Judges Learned Hand and Augustus Hand: the opinion was written by the [latter]. Since both § 10(b) and Rule 10b–5 proscribed only fraud "in connection with the purchase or sale" of securities, and since the history of § 10(b) revealed no congressional intention to extend a private civil remedy for money damages to other than defrauded purchasers or sellers of securities, in contrast to the express civil remedy provided by § 16(b) of the 1934 Act, the court concluded that the plaintiff class in a Rule 10b–5 action was limited to actual purchasers and sellers.

* * *

In 1957 and again in 1959, the Securities and Exchange Commission sought from Congress amendment of § 10(b) to change its wording from "in connection with the purchase or sale of any security" to "in connection with the purchase or sale of, *or any attempt to purchase or sell,* any security." 103 Cong.Rec. 11636 (1957) (emphasis added); SEC Legislation, Hearings before Subcom. of Sen. Com. on Banking & Currency on S. 1178–1182, 86th Cong., 1st Sess., 367–368 (1959); S. 2545, 85th Cong., 1st Sess. (1957); S. 1179, 86th Cong., 1st Sess. (1959). In the words of a memorandum submitted by the Commission to a congressional committee, the purpose of the proposed change was "to make section 10(b) also applicable to manipulative activities in connection with any attempt to purchase or sell any security." Hearings on S. 1178–1182, supra, at 331. Opposition to the amendment was based on fears of the extension of civil liability under § 10(b) that it would cause. Id., at 368. Neither change was adopted by Congress.

The longstanding acceptance by the courts, coupled with Congress' failure to reject *Birnbaum*'s reasonable interpretation of the wording of § 10(b), wording which is directed towards injury suffered "in connection with the purchase or sale" of securities, argues significantly in favor of acceptance of the *Birnbaum* rule by this Court. Blau v. Lehman, 368 U.S. 403, 413 (1962).

Available [*extrinsic*] evidence from the texts of the 1933 and 1934 Acts as to the congressional scheme in this regard, though not conclusive, supports the result reached by the *Birnbaum* court. The wording of § 10(b) directed at fraud "in connection with the purchase or sale" of securities stands in contrast with the parallel antifraud provision of the 1933 Act, § 17(a)[6] reaching fraud "in the offer or sale" of securities. Cf. § 5 of the 1933 Act. When Congress wished to provide a remedy to those who neither purchase nor sell securities, it had little trouble in doing so expressly. Cf. § 16(b) of the 1934 Act, 15 U.S.C. § 78p.

Section 28(a) of the 1934 Act which limits recovery in any private damages action brought under the 1934 Act to "actual damages," likewise provides some support for the purchaser-seller rule. While the damages suffered by purchasers and sellers pursuing a § 10(b) cause of action may on occasion be difficult to ascertain, in the main such purchasers and sellers at least seek to base recovery on a demonstrable number of shares traded. In contrast, a putative plaintiff, who neither purchases nor sells securities, but sues instead for intangible economic injury such as loss of a noncontractual opportunity to buy or sell, is more likely to be seeking a largely conjectural and speculative recovery in which the number of shares involved will depend on the plaintiff's subjective hypothesis.

One of the justifications advanced for implication of a cause of action under § 10(b) lies in § 29(b) of the 1934 Act providing that a contract made in violation of any provision of the 1934 Act is voidable at the option of the deceived party. But that justification is absent when there is no actual purchase or sale of securities, or a contract to [do so], affected or tainted by a violation of § 10(b).

The principal express nonderivative private civil remedies, created by Congress contemporaneously with the passage of § 10(b), for

---

[6] * * * We express, of course, no opinion on whether § 17(a) in light of the express civil remedies of the 1933 Act gives rise to an implied cause of action. Compare Greater Iowa Corp. v. McLendon, 378 F.2d 783, 788, 791 (C.A.8 1967), with Fischman v. Raytheon Mfg. Corp., 188 F.2d 783, 787 (C.A.2 1951). See, e.g., SEC v. Texas Gulf Sulphur Co., 401 F.2d 833, 867 (C.A.2 1968) (Opinion of Friendly, J., concurring), cert. denied, 394 U.S. 976 (1969); 3 L. Loss, Securities Regulation 1785 (1961).

violations of various provisions of the 1933 and 1934 Acts are by their terms expressly limited to purchasers or sellers of securities. Thus § 11(a) of the 1933 Act confines the cause of action it grants to "any person acquiring such security" while the remedy granted by § 12 of that Act is limited to the "person purchasing such security." Section 9 of the 1934 Act, prohibiting a variety of fraudulent and manipulative devices, limits the express civil remedy provided for its violation to "any person who shall purchase or sell any security" in a transaction affected by a violation of the provision. Section 18 of the 1934 Act, prohibiting false or misleading statements in reports or other documents required to be filed by the 1934 Act, limits the express remedy provided for its violation to "any person . . . who . . . shall have purchased or sold a security at a price which was affected by such statement. . . ." It would indeed be anomalous to impute to Congress an intention to expand the plaintiff class for a judicially implied cause of action beyond the bounds it delineated for comparable express causes of action.

Having said all this, we would by no means be understood as suggesting that we are able to divine from the language of § 10(b) the express "intent of Congress" as to the contours of a private cause of action under Rule 10b–5. When we deal with private actions under Rule 10b–5, we deal with a judicial oak which has grown from little more than a legislative acorn. Such growth may be quite consistent with the congressional enactment and with the role of the federal judiciary in interpreting it, but it would be disingenuous to suggest that either Congress in 1934 or the Securities and Exchange Commission in 1942 foreordained the present state of the law with respect to Rule 10b–5. It is therefore proper that we consider, in addition to the factors already discussed, what may be described as policy considerations when we come to flesh out the portions of the law with respect to which neither the congressional enactment nor the administrative regulations offer conclusive guidance.

Three principal classes of potential plaintiffs are presently barred by the *Birnbaum* rule. First are potential purchasers of shares, either in a new offering or on the Nation's post-distribution trading markets, who allege that they decided not to purchase because of an unduly gloomy representation or the omission of favorable material which made the issuer appear to be a less favorable investment vehicle than it actually was. Second are actual shareholders in the issuer who allege that they decided not to sell their shares because of an unduly rosy representation or a failure to disclose unfavorable material. Third are shareholders, creditors, and perhaps others related to an issuer who suffered loss in the value of their investment due to corporate or insider activities in connection with the purchase or sale of securities which violate Rule 10b–5. It has been held that shareholder members of the second and third of these classes may frequently be able to circumvent the *Birnbaum* limitation through bringing a derivative action on behalf of the corporate issuer if the latter is itself a purchaser or seller of securities. But the first of these classes, of which respondent is a member, cannot claim the benefit of such a rule.

A great majority of the many commentators on the issue before us have taken the view that the *Birnbaum* limitation on the plaintiff class in a Rule 10b–5 action for damages is an arbitrary restriction which unreasonably prevents some deserving plaintiffs from recovering damages which have in fact been caused by violations of Rule 10b–5. See, e.g., Lowenfels, The Demise of the Birnbaum Doctrine: A New Era for Rule 10b–5, 54 Va. L. Rev. 268 (1968). The Securities and Exchange Commission has filed an *amicus* brief in this case espousing that same view. We have no doubt that this is indeed a disadvantage of the *Birnbaum* rule, and if it had no countervailing advantages it would be undesirable as a matter of policy, however much it might be supported by precedent and legislative history. But we are of the opinion that there are countervailing advantages to the *Birnbaum* rule, purely as a matter of policy, although those advantages are more difficult to articulate than is the disadvantage.

* * *

We believe that the concern expressed for the danger of vexatious litigation which could result from a widely expanded class of plaintiffs under Rule 10b–5 is founded in something more substantial than the common complaint of the many defendants who would prefer avoiding lawsuits entirely to either settling them or trying them. These concerns have two largely separate grounds.

The first of these concerns is that in the field of federal securities laws governing disclosure of information even a complaint which by objective standards may have very little chance of success at trial has a settlement value to the plaintiff out of any proportion to its prospect of success at trial so long as he may prevent the suit from being resolved against him by dismissal or summary judgment. The very pendency of the lawsuit may frustrate or delay normal business activity of the defendant which is totally unrelated to the lawsuit.

* * *

The second ground for fear of vexatious litigation is based on the concern that, given the generalized contours of liability, the abolition of the *Birnbaum* rule would throw open to the trier of fact many rather hazy issues of historical fact the proof of which depended almost entirely on oral testimony. We in no way disparage the worth and frequent high value of oral testimony when we say that dangers of its abuse appear to exist in this type of action to a peculiarly high degree.

* * *

But in the absence of the *Birnbaum* rule, it would be sufficient for a plaintiff to prove that he had failed to purchase or sell stock by reason of a defendant's violation of Rule 10b–5. The manner in which the defendant's violation caused the plaintiff to fail to act could be as a result of the reading of a prospectus, as respondent claims here, but it could just as easily come as a result of a claimed reading of information contained in the financial pages of a local newspaper. Plaintiff's proof would not be that he purchased or sold stock, a fact which would be capable of documentary verification in most situations, but instead that he decided *not* to purchase or sell stock. Plaintiff's entire testimony could be dependent upon uncorroborated oral evidence of many of the crucial elements of his claim, and still be sufficient to go to the jury. The jury would not even have the benefit of weighing the plaintiff's version against the defendant's version, since the elements to which the plaintiff would testify would be in many cases totally unknown and unknowable to the defendant. The very real risk in permitting those in respondent's position to sue under Rule 10b–5 is that the door will be open to recovery of substantial damages on the part of one who offers only his own testimony to prove that he ever consulted a prospectus of the issuer, that he paid any attention to it, or that the representations contained in it damaged him. The virtue of the *Birnbaum* rule, simply stated, in this situation, is that it limits the class of plaintiffs to those who have at least dealt in the security to which the prospectus, representation, or omission relates. And their dealing in the security, whether by way of purchase or sale, will generally be an objectively demonstrable fact in an area of the law otherwise very much dependent upon oral testimony. In the absence of the *Birnbaum* doctrine, bystanders to the securities marketing process could await developments on the sidelines without risk, claiming that inaccuracies in disclosure caused non-selling in a falling market and that unduly pessimistic predictions by the issuer followed by a rising market caused them to allow retrospectively golden opportunities to pass.

* * *

IV

The majority of the Court of Appeals in this case expressed no disagreement with the general proposition that one asserting a claim for damages based on the violation of Rule 10b–5 must be either a purchaser or seller of securities. However, it noted that prior cases have held that persons owning contractual rights to buy or sell securities are not excluded by the *Birnbaum* rule. Relying on these cases, it concluded that respondent's status as an offeree pursuant to the terms of the consent decree served the same function, for purposes of delimiting the class of plaintiffs, as is normally performed by the requirement of a contractual relationship.

* * *

Even if we were to accept the notion that the *Birnbaum* rule could be circumvented on a case-by-case basis through particularized judicial inquiry into the facts surrounding a complaint, this respondent and the members of its alleged class would be unlikely candidates for such a judicially created exception. While the *Birnbaum* rule has been flexibly interpreted by lower federal courts, we have been unable to locate a single decided case from any court in the 20-odd years of litigation since the *Birnbaum* decision which would support the right of persons who were in the position of respondent here to bring a private suit under Rule 10b–5. Respondent was not only not a buyer or seller of any security but it was not even a shareholder of the corporate petitioners.

* * *

NOTES ON STANDING: THE PURCHASER SELLER REQUIREMENT UNDER RULE 10b–5

As with causation, much of the complexity of defining Rule 10b–5's standing requirement is a consequence of the somewhat imprecise terms, "in connection with a purchase or sale" of securities. The courts have settled several applications of this concept.

1. *Purchases and Sales and Injunctions.* In 1984, the District of Columbia Circuit Court applied the rationale of *Blue Chip Stamps* to a case in which a plaintiff sought an injunction to prevent the company from making misrepresentations and omissions.[100] The court held that the standing requirement for equitable relief was the same as that for a damages-based action.

2. *Issuance of Its Own Securities.* In Hooper v. Mountain States Securities Corp.,[101] the Fifth Circuit decided a corporation's issuance of its own securities was a "sale" within the meaning of Rule 10b–5 (and, of course, a "purchase" by the other party to the transaction), and other courts have followed this holding.[102]

3. *Repurchase of Its Own Securities.* The repurchase by a corporation of its own outstanding securities involves a purchase and sale. Cochran v. Channing Corp.[103] held that a repurchase by a corporation of its own shares could be the basis of an action under Rule 10b–5. Many of the early nondisclosure cases involved a purchase of minority shares by the issuing corporation, rather than by the controlling shareholders, while there existed allegedly material, nondisclosed inside information.

---

[100] Cowin v. Bresler, 741 F.2d 410 (D.C. Cir. 1984).

[101] Hooper v. Mountain States Sec. Corp., 282 F.2d 195, 200–03 (5th Cir. 1960), cert. denied, 365 U.S. 814 (1961).

[102] See, e.g., Ruckle v. Roto Am. Corp., 339 F.2d 24, 27–28 (2d Cir. 1964); Dasho v. Susquehanna Corp., 380 F.2d 262, 270 (7th Cir. 1967), cert. denied sub nom. Bard v. Dasho, 389 U.S. 977 (1967); Schoenbaum v. Firstbrook, 405 F.2d 215, 219 (2d Cir. 1968), cert. denied sub nom. Manley v. Schoenbaum, 395 U.S. 906 (1969); Miller v. San Sebastian Gold Mines, Inc., 540 F.2d 807, 809 (5th Cir. 1976); Harris v. Union Elec. Co., 787 F.2d 355, 368 (8th Cir. 1986), cert. denied, 479 U.S. 823 (1986).

[103] 211 F.Supp. 239 (S.D.N.Y. 1962); see also Mutual Shares Corp. v. Genesco, Inc., 384 F.2d 540 (2d Cir. 1967) (the problem was that the plaintiffs had not been the ones who had sold).

4. *Employee Benefit Plans*. In International Brotherhood Teamsters v. Daniel,[104] the Supreme Court held that an interest in a "noncontributory, compulsory pension plan" is not a security because it fails the Howey test,[105] discussed in earlier chapters. This decision has been extended by lower courts to include stock option awards.[106] Individually negotiated compensation packages that include stock, however, may be considered securities. [107]

5. *Privity*. In its first case involving a private action under Rule 10b–5, the Supreme Court "read § 10(b) to mean that Congress meant to bar deceptive devices and contrivances in the purchase or sale of securities whether conducted in the organized markets or [as in that case] face-to-face."[108]

6. *Contemporaneous Traders*. In the 1988 Insider Trading and Securities Fraud Enforcement Act, Congress adopted § 20A of the Securities Exchange Act to provide standing for "contemporaneous traders." Section 20A(a) specifically provides a private right of action "to any person who, contemporaneously with the purchase or sale of securities that is the subject of [a violation of any provision of the 1934 Act or its rules by purchasing or selling a security while in possession of material nonpublic information], has purchased * * * or sold * * * securities *of the same class*." [Emphasis added.]

The Act did not define "contemporaneous traders," and the House Committee on Energy and Commerce explained that the term "has developed through case law."[109] The Committee cited Shapiro v. Merrill Lynch, Pierce, Fenner & Smith, Inc.,[110] which held defendants liable "not only to the purchasers of the actual shares sold by defendants (in the unlikely event they can be identified) but to all persons who during the same period purchased Douglas Stock in the open market without knowledge of the material inside information which was in the possession of defendants."[111] The Committee also cited Wilson v. Comtech

---

[104] 439 U.S. 551 (1979).

[105] Id. at 552 ("With respect to the investment-of-money element, in such a pension plan the purported investment is a relatively insignificant part of the total and indivisible compensation package of an employee, who, from the standpoint of the economic realities, is selling his labor to obtain a livelihood, not making an investment for the future. And with respect to the expectation-of-profits element, while the pension fund depends to some extent on earnings from its assets, the possibility of participating in asset earnings is too insubstantial to bring the entire transaction within the Securities Acts.")

[106] See, e.g., Fraser v. Fiduciary Trust Co. Int'l, 417 F.Supp.2d 310, 318 (S.D.N.Y. 2006) ("When an employee does not give anything of value for stock other than the continuation of employment nor independently bargains for ... stock, there is no 'purchase or sale' of securities.") (quoting In re Cendant Corp. Sec. Litig., 76 F.Supp.2d 539, 543–546 (D.N.J. 1999)).

[107] SEC v. Longfin Corp., 316 F.Supp.3d 743 (S.D.N.Y. 2018) ("A person who works for an issuer in exchange for stock compensation is a purchaser of securities.") (citing Yoder v. Orthomolecular Nutrition Institute, Inc., 751 F.2d 555 (2d Cir. 1985)).

[108] Superintendent of Ins. of State of N.Y. v. Bankers Life & Casualty Co., 404 U.S. 6, 12 (1971).

[109] H.R. Rep. No. 100–910, 100th Cong., 2d Sess. 27 n.22 (1988).

[110] 495 F.2d 228 (2d Cir. 1974).

[111] Id. at 237.

Telecommunications Corp.,[112] which observed of the "during the same period" concept in *Shapiro* that "the entire period * * * was only four days."[113] *Wilson* then added significantly:

> To extend the period of liability well beyond the time of the insider's trading simply because disclosure was never made could make the insider liable to all the world. Any duty of disclosure is owed only to those investors trading contemporaneously with the insider; non-contemporaneous traders do not require the protection of the "disclose or abstain" rule because they do not suffer the disadvantage of trading with someone who has superior access to information.[114]

7. *Private Plaintiffs.* As *Blue Chip Stamps* makes clear, a private plaintiff has to be an actual buyer or seller.[115] The *Birnbaum* case, cited in *Blue Chip Stamps*, was a so-called sale of control case. In such a case, the controlling shareholder may be held liable, either to the corporation or to the minority shareholders, for his or her sale of the control block to a third party. Because neither the corporation nor the other shareholders in the typical case have purchased or sold any securities, Rule 10b–5 is unavailable. A shareholder who does not tender in a tender offer also has no standing to sue the offeror or the target company under Rule 10b–5.[116] A shareholder who merely claims that the defendant's acts depreciated the value of her stock has no standing under Rule 10b–5 either individually[117] or derivatively unless the wrongful acts of the defendant involved some purchase or sale of securities by the corporation.

Who is a purchaser or seller for the purpose of applying this limitation? A trust beneficiary has standing to bring an action against the trustee alleging fraud in selling securities of the trust corpus because the beneficial interest of the beneficiary was sold and therefore he was a "seller."[118] A secured party was a seller in a case where the securities were sold on foreclosure,[119] and the pledgor is a seller when the pledgee sells the securities on foreclosure.[120] In both cases they have an interest in the proceeds of the sale (although the pledgor does only if a surplus over the amount of the debt is produced by the sale). The Supreme Court

---

[112] 648 F.2d 88 (2d Cir. 1981).

[113] Id. at 94.

[114] Id. at 94–95.

[115] In a criminal or Commission action, the "in connection with" requirement merely requires that someone buy or sell during the period of allegedly fraudulent activity. See, e.g., SEC v. National Sec., Inc., 393 U.S. 453 (1969), cited in Blue Chip Stamps, 421 U.S. at 751 n.14; United States v. Carpenter, 791 F.2d 1024, 1033 (2d Cir. 1986), aff'd 484 U.S. 19 (1987).

[116] See Petersen v. Federated Dev. Co., 387 F.Supp. 355 (S.D.N.Y. 1974).

[117] Sargent v. Genesco, Inc., 492 F.2d 750 (5th Cir. 1974).

[118] Norris v. Wirtz, 719 F.2d 256 (7th Cir. 1983); Kirshner v. United States, 603 F.2d 234 (2d Cir. 1978); James v. Gerber Products Co., 483 F.2d 944 (6th Cir. 1973).

[119] Falls v. Fickling, 621 F.2d 1362 (5th Cir. 1980); Bosse v. Crowell Collier and Macmillan, 565 F.2d 602 (9th Cir. 1977).

[120] Dopp v. Franklin National Bank, 374 F.Supp. 904 (S.D.N.Y. 1974).

held that a pledge of stock is itself a "sale" for the purposes of Rule 10b–5.[121]

In a stockholders' derivative action, it is the corporation, not the private plaintiff that must have bought or sold the relevant security.[122] In contrast, courts have held that the dissolution of a partnership involves a sale by a limited partner of its limited partnership interests.[123]

8. *The "Forced Seller."* In Vine v. Beneficial Finance Co., Inc.,[124] the Second Circuit held that a minority shareholder in a corporation who was "cashed out" by the effectuation of a short-form merger of his or her corporation with its corporate parent was a "forced seller" and entitled to sue under Rule 10b–5. This same rationale has been applied to a liquidation[125] and to an ordinary merger.[126] Judge Friendly reaffirmed the *Vine* case in Mayer v. Oil Field Systems Corp.[127] In *Mayer*, a limited partner was forced to accept stock in a corporation in exchange for his limited partnership interest in a transaction which had to be approved only by the general partner. The court said that the fact that the limited partner had no choice in the matter, as in the *Vine* case, did not prevent him from being a "seller" under the forced-seller doctrine. Presumably, he was also a "purchaser" of the stock of the corporation he received, but the court does not analyze that side of the transaction.

The doctrine is limited to instances where the plaintiff is forced to surrender a security for cash or a fundamentally different security. It does not reach, for example, a plaintiff who retains shares in a "going concern" but the issuance of new shares dilutes the value of the plaintiff's investment.[128] Similarly, the courts have treated an arm's length stock-for-assets exchange between two independent corporations as constituting a purchase or sale for the purposes of § 10(b).[129] But, a transfer of securities from a wholly owned subsidiary to its parent, or between two corporations wholly controlled by a third corporation, does

---

[121] Rubin v. United States, 449 U.S. 424 (1981).

[122] See, e.g., Blue Chip Stamps v. Manor Drug Stores, 421 U.S. 723, 738 (1975); Frankel v. Slotkin, 984 F.2d 1328, 1332–34 (2d Cir. 1993).

[123] 7547 Corp. v. Parker & Parsley Dev. Partners, L.P., 38 F.3d 211, 228–29 (5th Cir. 1994); Bolger v. Laventhol, Krekstein, Horwath & Horwath, 381 F.Supp. 260 (S.D.N.Y. 1974); Houlihan v. Anderson-Stokes, Inc., 434 F.Supp. 1330 (D.D.C. 1977).

[124] 374 F.2d 627 (2d Cir. 1967). Cf. Isquith v. Caremark Int'l, Inc., 136 F.3d 531 (7th Cir. 1998), where the court held that a spinoff was not a sale of securities since it did not effect a fundamental change in the plaintiff's holdings. Isquith criticized the "defunct forced seller doctrine" and characterized it as succeeded by a related "fundamental change" doctrine. Id. at 535–37.

[125] Coffee v. Permian Corp., 434 F.2d 383 (5th Cir. 1970); Dudley v. Southeastern Factor and Fin. Corp., 446 F.2d 303 (5th Cir. 1971); Alley v. Miramon, 614 F.2d 1372 (5th Cir. 1980).

[126] Mader v. Armel, 402 F.2d 158 (6th Cir. 1968).

[127] 721 F.2d 59 (2d Cir. 1983).

[128] See Sargent v. Genesco, Inc., 492 F.2d 750, 764–65 (5th Cir. 1974); Jeanes v. Henderson, 703 F.2d 855, 860 (5th Cir. 1983); Ray v. Karris, 780 F.2d 636, 640 n.1 (7th Cir. 1985); Mosher v. Kane, 784 F.2d 1385, 1389 (9th Cir. 1986), rev'd on other grounds sub nom. Washington Pub. Power Supply Sys. Sec. Litig., 823 F.2d 1349 (9th Cir. en banc 1987).

[129] See, e.g., Swanson v. American Consumer Indus. Inc., 415 F.2d 1326, 1330 (7th Cir. 1969).

not amount to a purchase or sale and is only "a mere transfer between corporate pockets."[130]

9. *Contracts to Buy or Sell Securities.* A contract to sell securities is itself a "sale" for the purposes of the rule in the *Blue Chip* case;[131] however, parties who negotiate for the purchase and sale of securities but never arrive at any enforceable contract cannot sue under Rule 10b–5.[132] An oral agreement to sell is not sufficient to satisfy the purchase or sale requirement of Rule 10b–5 if it is unenforceable under the statute of frauds.[133] In A.T. Brod & Co. v. Perlow,[134] the court held that a contract of purchase entered into without the intention of paying for the securities was a "sale" within the Rule. And, Commerce Reporting Co. v. Puretec, Inc.[135] held that a contract of sale entered into by the defendant without any intention of performing it, but merely for the purpose of getting a better offer from a third party, was a "purchase" by the other party within the Rule.

3. RULE 14a–9: PROXY FRAUD

Section 14(a) of the Securities Exchange Act authorizes the SEC to adopt rules for the solicitation of proxies. Rule 14a–9 prohibits material misrepresentations and omissions in proxy solicitations. The remedy it provides is broad, including antifraud remedies for false or misleading facts or omissions made in a proxy statement, form of proxy, notice of meeting, or other communication used in a proxy solicitation.[136] Litigation under the Rule has played a significant role in the development of implied causes of action under the federal securities laws and in the meaning of terms such as "materiality." In this section of the Chapter, we explore Rule 14a–9 and its elements.

Rule 14a–9(a) provides:

No solicitation subject to this regulation shall be made by means of any proxy statement, form of proxy, notice of meeting, or other communication, written or oral, containing any statement which, at the time and in the light of the circumstances under which it is made, is false or misleading with respect to any

---

[130] Blau v. Mission Corp., 212 F.2d 77, 80 (2d Cir. 1954); International Controls Corp. v. Vesco, 490 F.2d 1334, 1343 (2d Cir. 1974); Rathborne v. Rathborne, 683 F.2d 914, 918–19 (5th Cir. 1982); Gelles v. TDA Indus., Inc., 44 F.3d 102, 105 (2d Cir. 1994) ("Gelles held literally the exact same shares before and after the transaction").

[131] Mosher v. Kane, 784 F.2d 1385 (9th Cir. 1986), rev'd on other grounds sub nom. Washington Pub. Power Supply Sys. Sec. Litig., 823 F.2d 1349 (9th Cir. en banc 1987); Griggs v. Pace Am. Group, Inc., 170 F.3d 877, 880 (9th Cir. 1999).

[132] Reprosystem, B.V. v. SCM Corp., 727 F.2d 257 (2d Cir. 1984); Northland Capital Corp. v. Silver, 735 F.2d 1421 (D.C. Cir. 1984).

[133] Kagan v. Edison Bros. Stores, Inc., 907 F.2d 690 (7th Cir. 1990); Pelletier v. Stuart-James Co., Inc., 863 F.2d 1550 (11th Cir. 1989).

[134] 375 F.2d 393 (2d Cir. 1967).

[135] 290 F.Supp. 715 (S.D.N.Y. 1968).

[136] On the proxy solicitation process generally, including the other proxy rules such as Rule 14a–8, see 4 Louis Loss & Joel Seligman Ch. 6.C (3d ed. rev. 2000).

material fact, or which omits to state any material fact necessary in order to make the statements therein not false or misleading or necessary to correct any statement in any earlier communication with respect to the solicitation of a proxy for the same meeting or subject matter which has become false or misleading.[137]

A. IMPLIED CAUSE OF ACTION

The basis for private right of action under Rule 14a–9, as elsewhere, is confused. Since J.I. Case Co. v. Borak, 377 U.S. 426 (1964), courts have not questioned that a private right of action exists under Rule 14a–9 for a violation of the proxy rules. Nevertheless, the Supreme Court repudiated the *Borak* court's reliance upon § 27 of the 1934 Act as a basis for implying a private right of action under any section of the 1934 Act.[138] Specifically, § 27 confers upon the federal courts exclusive jurisdiction to entertain any suits "to enforce any liability or duty" created by that Act. But then in Franklin v. Gwinnett County Pub. Sch. (1992),[139] the Court cited *Borak* with approval for "the general rule that all appropriate relief is available in an action brought to vindicate a federal right when Congress has given no indication of its purpose with respect to remedies."[140]

B. MATERIALITY

Under the basic federal securities law antifraud provisions, the central questions are whether a particular statement or omission is false and misleading and whether the statement or omission is material. These two questions tend to merge here as they do in other fraud provisions both in securities law and at common law. But, importantly, proof of (1) a false and misleading statement or omission and (2) materiality are two separate elements.

A note to Rule 14a–9 gives some examples of what, depending upon particular facts and circumstances, may be misleading:

(a) Predictions as to specific future market values.[141]

---

[137] See generally 4 Louis Loss & Joel Seligman, Securities Regulation 2071–2105 (3d ed. rev. 2000).

[138] See Touche Ross & Co. v. Redington, 442 U.S. 560, 577 (1979).

[139] 503 U.S. 60, 68 (1992).

[140] See also Roosevelt v. E.I. Du Pont de Nemours & Co., 958 F.2d 416 (D.C. Cir. 1992) (Section 14(a) of the 1934 Act implies cause of action for Rule 14a–8 violations); United Paperworkers Int'l Union v. International Paper Co., 985 F.2d 1190, 1197–1198 (2d Cir. 1993) (either the proponent of a Rule 14a–8 proposal or another shareholder has standing to bring a Rule 14a–9 lawsuit); Koppel v. 4987 Corp., 167 F.3d 125 (2d Cir. 1999) (implied causes of action under Rules 14a–4(a)(3) and 14a–4(b)(1)).

[141] Until the 1979 adoption of Rule 3b–6, a "safe harbor" Rule for projections, Note (a) referred to "market value, earnings, or dividends." Regarding the revision of this Note, see Walker v. Action Indus., Inc., 802 F.2d 703, 707–710 (4th Cir. 1986), cert. denied, 479 U.S. 1065 (1987).

(b) Material which directly or indirectly impugns character, integrity or personal reputation, or directly or indirectly makes charges concerning improper, illegal or immoral conduct or associations, without factual foundation.

(c) Failure to so identify a proxy statement, form of proxy and other soliciting material as to clearly distinguish it from the soliciting material of any other person or persons soliciting for the same meeting or subject matter.

(d) Claims made prior to a meeting regarding the results of a solicitation.

In proxy fights, some flexibility is permitted. For example, in the analogous context of a contested tender offer Judge Friendly cautioned: "Courts should tread lightly in imposing a duty of self-flagellation on offerors with respect to matters that are known as well, or almost as well, to the target company; some issues concerning a contested tender offer can safely be left for the latter's riposte."[142] This sentiment was echoed in another case, which noted: " 'There is no requirement that a material fact be expressed in certain words or in a certain form of language.' Fair accuracy, not perfection, is the appropriate standard."[143]

NOTES ON MATERIALITY: WHAT FACTS ARE MATERIAL?

1. *The General Standard.* The standard of materiality is explored earlier in this Chapter with respect to Rule 10b–5. The same standard applies here. As described in *Virginia Bankshares*,[144] "[An omitted] fact [is] material 'if there is a substantial likelihood that a reasonable shareholder would consider it important in deciding how to vote.' " (quoting *TSC Industries Inc. v. Northway Inc.*, 426 U.S. 438, 449).[145] This definition of "materiality" has been applied, not only in actions under § 14(a) of the 1934 Act, but also in actions brought under Rule 10b–5,[146] § 11 of the 1933 Act,[147] § 12(a)(2) of the 1933 Act,[148] § 13(d) of the 1934 Act,[149] and §§ 14(d) and 14(e) of the 1934 Act.[150] Cases after *TSC Industries* have substantially amplified this general definition of materiality.

---

[142] Mo. Portland Cement Co. v. Cargill, Inc., 498 F.2d 851, 873 (2d Cir. 1974), cert. denied, 419 U.S. 883 (1974).

[143] See, e.g., Kennecott Copper Corp. v. Curtiss-Wright Corp., 584 F.2d 1195, 1200 (2d Cir. 1978).

[144] 501 U.S. 1083 (1991).

[145] Id. at 1090.

[146] Basic Inc. v. Levinson, 485 U.S. 224, 232 (1988).

[147] Kronfeld v. Trans World Airlines, Inc., 832 F.2d 726, 731 (2d Cir. 1987), cert. denied, 485 U.S. 1007 (1988).

[148] Simpson v. Southeastern Inv. Trust, 697 F.2d 1257, 1259 (5th Cir. 1983).

[149] SEC v. Savoy Indus., Inc., 587 F.2d 1149, 1166 (D.C. Cir. 1978), cert. denied, 440 U.S. 913 (1979).

[150] Seaboard World Airlines, Inc. v. Tiger Int'l, Inc., 600 F.2d 355, 360–361 (2d Cir. 1979); Macfadden Holdings, Inc. v. JB Acquisition Corp., 802 F.2d 62, 69 n. 3 (2d Cir. 1986).

2. *The "Total Mix."* In United Paperworkers International Union v. International Paper Co.,[151] the court addressed the concept of the "total mix":

> The mere fact that a company has filed with a regulatory agency documents containing factual information material to a proposal as to which proxies are sought plainly does not mean that the company has made adequate disclosure to shareholders under Rule 14a–9. Corporate documents that have not been distributed to the shareholders entitled to vote on the proposal should rarely be considered part of the total mix of information reasonably available to those shareholders.
>
> The "total mix" of information may also include "information already in the public domain and facts known or reasonably available to the shareholders." Thus, when the subject of a proxy solicitation has been widely reported in readily available media, shareholders may be deemed to have constructive notice of the facts reported, and the court may take this into consideration in determining whether representations in or omissions from the proxy statement are materially misleading. However, the mere presence in the media of sporadic news reports does not give shareholders sufficient notice that proxy solicitation statements sent directly to them by the company may be misleading, and such reports should not be considered to be part of the total mix of information that would clarify or place in proper context the company's representations in its proxy materials.
>
> In the present case, the district court properly rejected Paper Co.'s contention that public press reports and its 10-K Report should be viewed as part of the total mix of information reasonably available to shareholders. Though the Company argued that news articles should be considered, the articles were few in number, narrow in focus, and remote in time.

3. *Known Facts.* Information that is equally available to both parties, such as the effect of tight money on the mortgage market or current market quotations, need not be disclosed.[152] Simply put, an omitted fact will not be material if it is already well known to the securities market.[153]

---

[151] 985 F.2d 1190, 1199 (2d Cir. 1993).

[152] See, e.g., Seibert v. Sperry Rand Corp., 586 F.2d 949, 952 (2d Cir. 1978) (holding that where the registrant had long and highly publicized labor troubles, " 'there is no duty to disclose information to one who reasonably should already be aware of it,' " and a party's " 'reasonable belief that the other party already has access to the facts should excuse him from new disclosures which reasonably appear to be repetitive.' "); Apple Computer Sec. Litig., 886 F.2d 1109, 1115 (9th Cir. 1989) (holding that "the defendant's failure to disclose material information may be excused where that information has been made credibly available to the market by other sources").

[153] Longman v. Food Lion, Inc., 197 F.3d 675, 684 (4th Cir. 1999). But see Judge Murnaghan's dissent on the ground that the information did not reach the market from a credible source. Id. at 686–688.

4. *Buried Facts.* "Under the 'buried facts' doctrine, a disclosure is deemed inadequate if it is presented in a way that conceals or obscures the information sought to be disclosed. The doctrine applies when the fact in question is hidden in a voluminous document or is disclosed in a piecemeal fashion which prevents a reasonable shareholder from realizing the 'correlation and overall import of the various facts interspersed throughout' the document."[154]

5. *Undisclosed Conduct.* In *TSC Industries*, the Supreme Court was unwilling to require disclosure of information that might *suggest* the existence of market manipulation in the absence of some showing that there was in fact market manipulation.[155] Subsequently, in a criminal case, the Second Circuit held that uncharged criminal conduct need not be disclosed under Rule 14a–9 unless an express Commission rule requires it.[156] As one district court stated, " '[n]o case has * * * held that the proxy rules are violated because management has allegedly mismanaged the company, and the proxy statement does not say so.' "[157] Nor must the registrant characterize or state conclusions about disclosed facts.[158]

6. *Conflicts of Interest.* In *TSC Industries*, the Court held that two omitted facts relating to another company's (National's) potential influence or control over the management of TSC were not material as a matter of law: (1) the chairman of the TSC board, Stanley Yarmuth, was National's president and chief executive officer, and the chairman of the TSC executive committee was Charles Simonelli, National's executive vice president; and (2) neither TSC nor National indicated that National "may be deemed to be a 'parent' of TSC as that term is defined in [SEC] Rules and Regulations under the Securities Act of 1933."[159] In a footnote the Court, nonetheless, emphasized that, *as a matter of law*, the total omission of material information concerning a conflict of interest would have to be disclosed.[160]

---

[154] Werner v. Werner, 267 F.3d 288, 297 (3d Cir. 2001), citing Kas v. Financial Gen. Bankshares, Inc., 796 F.2d 508, 516 (D.C. Cir. 1986).

[155] 426 U.S. at 460–463.

[156] United States v. Matthews, 787 F.2d 38, 49 (2d Cir. 1986); but see Roeder v. Alpha Indus., Inc., 814 F.2d 22, 25–26 (1st Cir. 1987).

[157] Markewich v. Adikes, 422 F.Supp. 1144, 1147 (E.D.N.Y.1976); quoted in Goldberger v. Baker, 442 F.Supp. 659, 667 (S.D.N.Y.1977); Bank & Trust Co. of Old York Road v. Hankin, 552 F.Supp. 1330, 1335–1336 (E.D.Pa.1982). Cf. Gaines v. Haughton, 645 F.2d 761, 776–777 (9th Cir. 1981), cert. denied, 454 U.S. 1145 (1982).

[158] In re Gap Sec. Litig., 1989–1990 Fed. Sec. L. Rep. (CCH) ¶ 94,724 (N.D.Cal.1988) (defendants were not required to disclose the causes and trends ascribed to a buildup in inventory when they fully disclosed the dollar amounts by which the inventory had increased); In re New Am. High Income Fund Sec. Litig., 834 F.Supp. 501, 506 (D.Mass.1993), aff'd in relevant part, rev'd on other grounds sub nom. Lucia v. Prospect St. High Income Portfolio, Inc., 36 F.3d 170 (1st Cir. 1994) ("There is, however, no obligation to disclose all securities information simply because the market would be interested, as long as the data that is disclosed is accurate and complete.").

[159] 426 U.S. at 451–453.

[160] Id. at 453 n.15.

The lower federal courts have also often required disclosure of conflicts of interest.[161] In Kronfeld v. Trans World Airlines, Inc.[162] the court held that the fact that a parent corporation was considering the possibility of a spinoff of its operating airline subsidiary (although no final decision had been made) was material to the purchasers of preferred stock of the subsidiary being offered in a registered offering because it would cut the financial ties between the parent and the subsidiary, and therefore eliminate the possibility that the parent corporation would support the operations of the subsidiary even though it had no legal obligation to do so.

7. *Required Disclosures.* In Howing Company v. Nationwide Corporation,[163] the Sixth Circuit agreed with the District Judge that the *TSC Industries* test of materiality applied in connection with the alleged omission of certain information required by Rule 13e–3 in a going-private transaction, but it ruled that the fact that this information was required by Rule 13e–3 created a "presumption" of materiality. The court said: "Although we agree with the District Court that the general *TSC* standard of materiality is applicable to transactions governed by Rule 13e–3, the clear and specific language of the instructions to Item 8 creates in effect a presumption that a discussion of book, going concern and liquidation value in the proxy statement would be material to a reasonable shareholder. The presumed fact—that the investor would likely find disclosure of such information significant—follows from Item 8's insistence that the information be stated."[164]

8. *Quantitative Materiality.* As a practical matter, lawyers and accountants have long determined whether information is material by applying quantitative tests. In the lore of securities law, there is a presumption that information that accounts for more than a ten percent movement in stock price of an issuer or registrant's total assets, gross sales or net earnings is presumed to be material. Information that accounts for less than five percent is presumed not to be material, with a gray area between five and ten percent. These five and ten percent benchmarks are derived in part from SEC rules, such as Rule 14a–8(i)(5), which under certain circumstances does not require a registrant's

---

[161] See, e.g., Wilson v. Great Am. Indus., Inc., 855 F.2d 987, 993–994 (2d Cir. 1988) (focusing on failure to disclose that general counsel of corporation A personally represented senior executives of corporation B and he and his firm served as counsel to several entities controlled by these executives while effecting merger between corporations A and B); cf. Kas v. Financial Gen. Bankshares, Inc., 796 F.2d 508, 513 (D.C. Cir. 1986) ("The violation arising from the failure to disclose such a potential conflict of interest does not turn on the failure to disclose a director's true motivations but rather stems from the failure to disclose a fact that puts the shareholder on notice of a potential impairment of the director's judgment"); Cooperman v. Individual, Inc., 171 F.3d 43, 49 (1st Cir. 1999) (a board level conflict over the future direction of a company can be material). See also Kramer v. Time Warner Inc., 937 F.2d 767, 777 (2d Cir. 1991) ("That inside directors stand to gain from a recommended transaction is material information that must be disclosed to shareholders considering a tender offer.").

[162] 832 F.2d 726 (2d Cir. 1987).

[163] 927 F.2d 263 (6th Cir. 1991), judgment vacated, 502 U.S. 801 (1991).

[164] Id. at 265.

management to circulate a shareholder proposal relating to operations if it accounts for less than five percent of an issuer's total assets and is less than five percent of its net earnings and gross sales for its most recent fiscal year. Similarly, Instruction 2 to Regulation S–K Item 103 uses a ten percent threshold to determine when certain pending legal proceedings must be disclosed.

On occasion, numerical benchmarks have received the judiciary's imprimatur. For example, in equity transactions the courts have affirmed SEC rulings that markups of more than 10 percent are fraudulent.[165] But generally courts have been more skeptical of numerical benchmarks as materiality measures, and the SEC has declined to set a fixed or overall percentage for materiality.

C. Culpability

In Adams v. Standard Knitting Mills, Inc.,[166] the Sixth Circuit addressed the state of mind necessary for a § 14 claim:

> We turn to the question of the standard of liability under Rule 14a–9 pertaining to statements made in proxy solicitations. There has been relatively little case law on the standard of liability following the Supreme Court decision in J.I. Case Co. v. Borak, 377 U.S. 426 (1964), which established a private right of action under 14(a) and Rule 14a–9. Two circuits have examined the issue. Both have prescribed a negligence standard for the corporation issuing the proxy statement. One held that the negligence standard also applies to outside, nonmanagement directors, Gould v. American-Hawaiian Steamship Co., 535 F.2d 761, 777–78 (3d Cir. 1976); and the other intimated in dicta, without deciding the issue, that a *scienter* standard probably should apply to outside directors and accountants, Gerstle v. Gamble-Skogmo, Inc., 478 F.2d 1281, 1300–1301 (2d Cir. 1973).
>
> * * *
>
> It is not simply a question of statutory interpretation. Federal courts created the private right of action under section 14, and they have a special responsibility to consider the consequences of their rulings and to mold liability fairly to reflect the circumstances of the parties. Although we are not called on in this case to decide the standard of liability of the corporate issuer of proxy material, we are influenced by the fact that the accountant here, unlike the corporate issuer, does not directly benefit from the proxy vote and is not in privity with the

---

[165] See, e.g., Alstead, Dempsey & Co., Inc., 47 SEC 1034, 1035 (1984). Cf. Adams v. Standard Knitting Mills, Inc., 623 F.2d 422, 433 (6th Cir. 1980), cert. denied, 449 U.S. 1067 (1980), where the court characterized a four percent variance between an accountant's inventory count and that of the issuer as "insufficient to render the inventory figure a material misstatement of fact."

[166] 623 F.2d 422, cert denied, 449 U.S. 1067 (1980).

stockholder. Unlike the corporate issuer, the preparation of financial statements to be appended to proxies and other reports is the daily fare of accountants, and the accountant's potential liability for relatively minor mistakes would be enormous under a negligence standard. In contrast to section 12(2) of the 1933 Act which imposes liability for negligent misrepresentation in a prospectus, Rule 14a–9 does not require privity. In contrast to section 11 of the 1933 Act which imposes liability for negligent misrepresentation in registration statements, Rule 14a–9 does not require proof of actual investor reliance on the misrepresentation. Rule 14a–9, like 10b–5, substitutes the less exacting standard of materiality for reliance, TSC Ind., Inc. v. Northway, Inc., 426 U.S. 438 (1976), and in the instant case there was no proof of investor reliance on the notes to the financial statements which erroneously described the restriction on payment of dividends. We can see no reason for a different standard of liability for accountants under the proxy provisions than under 10(b).[6]

We may not end our consideration there, however. We must turn to the legislative history of the proxy provisions. Section 14(a) and Rule 14a–9 are silent regarding the proper standard of liability. The Senate Report to the 1934 Act, commonly known as the Fletcher Report, discussed the sort of proxy abuse that Congress was trying to stop, that of corporate officers using the proxy mechanism to ratify their own frauds upon the shareholders, or outsiders soliciting shareholders' approval to plunder a ripe company. The words "unscrupulous," "concealing," and "distorting" all imply knowledge or scienter; and we interpret "promiscuous" to mean reckless. In addition the characterization of irresponsible outsiders trying to "wrest control ... from *honest* ... corporate officials," implies dishonesty—and hence scienter—on the part of the outsiders. Consequently, the Report leads us to believe that its authors contemplated that 14(a) would be applied only against the knowing or reckless wrongdoing of outsiders.

---

[6] Indeed section 18 of the 1934 Act, dealing with misstatements in reports filed with the SEC, requires both scienter and reliance for civil liability. Section 14 is much more similar to section 18 than it is to section 11 of the 1933 Act. Under the current regulatory scheme, proxy materials must be filed in advance of the solicitation with the SEC, see 17 C.F.R. § 240.14a–6, and are therefore subject to the provisions of section 18. In contrast, proxy solicitations per se do not put the solicitor within the ambit of section 11. The District Court found that the plaintiffs could not recover under section 18 because they had not shown the reliance which is required by that section. This was, of course, true. At the same time, the defendants argue that the specific remedy provided by section 18 precludes implication of a cause of action under either section 10 or section 14, when the requirements of section 18 are not met. Only one circuit has directly discussed this question, finding that inability to satisfy the requirements of section 18 does not bar a less restrictive implied action brought under section 10, Ross v. A. H. Robins Co., Inc., 607 F.2d 545 (2d Cir. 1979). This question was not specifically addressed by the District Court and, because we find that in all events, the plaintiffs cannot recover under sections 10 or 14, we need not decide this question here.

* * *

We conclude that 14(a) and 14(e) should be governed by the same standard of liability insofar as accountants' liability is concerned, and that an action under 14(a) requires proof of scienter. Finding no evidence of scienter, we reverse the imposition of liability under 14(a) and Rule 14a–9.

* * *

NOTES ON CULPABILITY UNDER RULE 14a–9

1. *Issuer.* In a Judge Friendly opinion, Gerstle v. Gamble-Skogmo, Inc.,[167] the Second Circuit held that, with respect to the corporate issuer, simple negligence is a sufficient basis for liability under Rule 14a–9.[168] Judge Friendly noted the absence of any "evil-sounding language" in either § 14(a) or Rule 14a–9. What are the appropriate legal materials for courts to consider when making this determination?

2. *Collateral Participants.* The *Adams* case is not necessarily inconsistent with the *Gerstle* case. In *Gerstle*, Judge Friendly limited his holding to the liability of the corporate issuer of the proxy statement and did not rule on the culpability of a collateral participant, like the accountant in *Adams*. Is there a sound basis for this distinction?

3. *Directors and Officers.* In Wilson v. Great American Industries, Inc.,[169] the Second Circuit reaffirmed the *Gerstle* case and extended its holding to directors and officers of the issuer who drafted, or had knowledge of, the false or misleading statements in the proxy statement. The court stated that "the preparation of a proxy statement by corporate insiders containing materially false or misleading statements or omitting a material fact is sufficient to satisfy the *Gerstle* negligence standard."[170] The *Wilson* court found, however, that the corporate directors and officers *knew* that the statements in the proxy statement were false or misleading at the time the proxy statement was issued.

D. CAUSATION

In Mills v. Electric Auto-Lite Co.,[171] the Supreme Court held that proof that a misstatement or omission was material normally did not need to be supplemented "with a requirement of proof of whether the defect actually had a decisive effect on the voting."[172] Alternatively, the

---

[167] 478 F.2d 1281 (2d Cir. 1973).
[168] See also, Gould v. American-Hawaiian Steamship Co., 535 F.2d 761 (3d Cir. 1976); National Home Products, Inc. v. Gray, 416 F.Supp. 1293 (D. Del. 1976).
[169] 855 F.2d 987 (2d Cir. 1988).
[170] Id. at 995.
[171] 396 U.S. 375 (1970).
[172] Id. at 384–385.

Court held that once the plaintiffs establish materiality, causation is presumed.

In footnote 7, the Court allowed one possible exception:

> We need not decide in this case whether causation could be shown where the management controls a sufficient number of shares to approve the transaction without any votes from the minority. Even in that situation, if the management finds it necessary for legal or practical reasons to solicit proxies from minority shareholders, at least one court has held that the proxy solicitation might be sufficiently related to the merger to satisfy the causation requirement[.][173]

In 1991, a 5–4 majority of the Supreme Court returned to this unresolved question in Virginia Bankshares, Inc. v. Sandberg,[174] and reasoned that where management possessed sufficient votes to approve a merger and plaintiffs could identify *no* remedy that was lost because of the alleged material misrepresentations or omissions, the plaintiffs would fail to demonstrate causation.

The majority decision on causation in *Virginia Bankshares* is quite narrow. Justice Souter specifically found that there was *no* link between the alleged misrepresentations to the minority stockholder and any lost state remedy. This holding left for another day the question of whether minority shareholders could establish causation if they were induced "to forfeit a state-law right to an appraisal remedy by voting to approve a transaction," or "had been deterred from obtaining an order enjoining a damaging transaction by a proxy solicitation that misrepresent[ed] the facts on which an injunction could properly have been issued."[175]

In Howing Co. v. Nationwide Corp.,[176] the Sixth Circuit applied *Virginia Bankshares* to a claim under a different section of the Securities Exchange Act, and concluded that plaintiffs, there minority stockholders, could recover under a theory of loss of state law remedy.

4. SECTION 18

Section 18 imposes liability on any person who shall make or cause to be made any materially false or misleading statement in a filing required by the Securities Exchange Act of 1934. A private right of action was created for any person who, "in reliance upon such statement, shall have purchased or sold a security at a price which was affected by such statement, for damages caused by such reliance, unless the person sued

---

[173] Id. at 385 n.7.
[174] 501 U.S. 1083, 1099–1108 (1991).
[175] Id. at 1107.
[176] 972 F.2d 700, 709–710 (6th Cir. 1992), judgement vacated, 502 U.S. 801 (1991).

shall prove that he acted in good faith and had no knowledge that such statement was false or misleading."[177]

A plaintiff has very high hurdles under § 18.[178] First, that they actually relied on the particular misstatement[179] and second, that the misstatement affected the price at which a security was sold. In addition to these two issues, § 18 is not frequently used due to procedural rules, such as statute of limitations and imposition of attorney's fees, and a good faith defense. Nonetheless, plaintiffs, particularly financial institutions, have used § 18 to pursue claims that would qualify under the anti-fraud provision of Rule 10b–5, discussed earlier in this Chapter, to avoid the higher pleading standard.[180]

---

[177] 15 U.S.C. § 78r.

[178] Section 18 is not an exclusive remedy and its high hurdles can be avoided by allowing a suit under Rule 10b–5, which presumes reliance once materiality of the omission is established. Ross v. A.H. Robins Co., 607 F.2d 545, 552–553 (2d Cir. 1979).

[179] Actual reliance stands in contrast to the constructive reliance requirement under Section 11. See Heit v. Weitzen, 402 F. 2d 909, 916 (2d Cir. 1968). Courts have suggested that an "eyeball" test may be sufficient. See Gould v. Winstar Comm., Inc., 686 F.3d 108 (2d Cir. 2012).

[180] E.g. Wachovia Bank & Trust Co. v. National Student Marketing Corp., 650 F.2d 342 (D.C. Cir. 1980), cert. denied, 452 U.S. 954 (1981); Ross v. A.H. Robins Co., 607 F.2d 545 (2d Cir. 1979).

CHAPTER 13

INSIDER TRADING

Statutes and Regulations

Exchange Act, §§ 10, 20A, 21A, 13(d), 14(d), 14(e), 16.

Rules 10b–5, 10b5–1, 10b5–2, 14e–3, 16a, 16b.

Sarbanes-Oxley Act, Section 306.

Insider trading may well be the archetypal white collar crime. The public learns about it from frequent T.V. news stories in which professionals—investment bankers, attorneys, and corporate executives—are arrested or sentenced. During the first five years in office, the former U.S. Attorney for the Southern District of New York, Preet Bharara, brought nearly 100 insider trading prosecutions. Dozens of corporate officers (classic "insiders") as well as various investors (known as "tippees") are currently in federal prison for trading on nonpublic information about stock prices. As will be discussed later in this chapter, Matthew Martoma, a former employee at SAC Capital, was sentenced to nine years in jail for trading in advance of a drug company's public release of negative results about one of its drugs.

These prosecutions (and the nearly 100% conviction rate in jury trials that Mr. Bharara achieved) no doubt suggest that the public deeply disapproves of individuals trading with information that others do not have. But, as a matter of economic theory, no trading (or very little) would happen in a world of information parity. So some informational asymmetries must exist in order for markets to work, and for traders to invest in the production of information about companies—a public good. Thus, it makes sense to begin this chapter by considering what are the harms (and possible benefits) from insider trading. Students tend to assume that the chief harm is to the counterparty (the other trader who might have sold at a higher price or purchased at a lower price if the material, nonpublic information had been disclosed). That could be true, but it is equally possible that the same counterparty would have sold or purchased at the same inferior price if the insider had not traded. Hence, other harms may be at least as important, including:

1. *Harm to the Corporation.* When insiders use information given to them for a corporate purpose to trade for their own personal benefit, the result may often be that their corporation is injured. This could happen because the insider's trading produces market rumors, which affect the stock price. In the landmark case of *SEC v. Texas Gulf Sulphur Co.*,[1] heavy insider trading followed after the company made initial drillings that seemed to show a major ore strike in Ontario, Canada; this

---

[1] 401 F.2d 833 (2d Cir. 1968).

trading resulted in market-moving rumors that forced the premature disclosure of the discovery, which inhibited the corporation's ability to exploit its discovery by acquiring the surrounding land at a cheap price. The shareholders thus lost a valuable opportunity. Alternatively, consider the case of a corporation that is intending to make a tender offer for another company. If the insiders of either company begin to buy the target stock in advance of the tender offer's announcement, this may drive the target's stock price up (and also fuel rumors of an impending bid), thereby increasing the acquisition price to the acquiring company.

Another harm to the corporation may involve the internal dynamics within the firm. If significant gains are possible from insider trading, corporate employees (high and low) may spend less time on their assigned tasks and more at searching for undisclosed material information. Fearing premature disclosure of proprietary or confidential information, corporate superiors may respond by restricting access to corporate information in a manner that produces suboptimal information flow within the firm, depriving the firm of internal dialogue, criticism and advice.[2]

Still another possibility is reputational injury to the corporation that is the subject of heavy insider trading. Some evidence suggests that the stock market discounts the prices of stocks that are subject to such trading,[3] and this could increase the firm's cost of capital.[4]

2. *Harm to the Market.* Intermediaries (market makers and professional traders) make the market in stocks, buying and selling in large volume. If market makers perceive that others have an informational advantage over them, they will likely respond defensively by widening their spreads (that is, lowering the price at which they buy and raising the price at which they sell). This reaction will affect many stocks (not just the corporation whose stock is being traded by insiders), and it will imply that all investors trading in these stocks will receive inferior prices. Indeed, a narrow bid/asked spread is a test of an efficient market, and spreads should logically widen if some traders have inherent informational advantages over others.

On the other side of the debate, some argue that permitting insider trading increases market efficiency by increasing the flow of information to the market.[5] But this view that information will reach the market more quickly (and in a less biased fashion) has been challenged by others. These critics argue that insiders will rationally seek to delay the release of information in order to "bunch" it, because the release of aggregated

---

[2] For this view, see Robert Haft, The Effect of Insider Trading Rules on the Internal Efficiency of the Large Corporation, 80 Mich. L. Rev. 1051 (1982).

[3] See Harold Demsetz, Corporate Control, Insider Trading, and Rates of Return, 76 Am. Econ. Rev. 313 (1986).

[4] See Victor Brudney, Insiders, Outsiders, and Informational Advantages under the Federal Securities Laws, 93 Harv. L. Rev. 322, 356 (1979).

[5] Henry Manne, INSIDER TRADING AND THE STOCK MARKET (1966).

items of information (all positive or all negative) is more likely to move the market.[6] Thus, insiders might seek to separate positive and negative information, disclosing them separately to create a more volatile market in which they could reap greater profits. Other critics of the view that insider trading improves market efficiency argue that because there is market risk to insider trading, most such traders only buy or sell a few days (or hours) before a major announcement (such as a merger or major discovery). Hence, market efficiency is only enhanced for a relatively minor period that does not affect the company's long-term cost of capital.

The law of insider trading has never sought to examine these arguments in much depth. This is primarily because American law has always assumed that a company's confidential business information "qualifies as property to which the company has a right of exclusive use."[7] Thus, when an officer or employee deprives the corporation of exclusive use, such person is effectively stealing or embezzling the information, and this is sufficient to violate the federal securities laws as well.

Curiously, however, no federal statute specifically forbids trading by insiders based on information not known to those whom they trade against.[8] Instead, the legality of insider trades is based on a statute combined with rules and interpretations of the SEC, and a body of case law interpreting these. Section 10(b) of the Securities Exchange Act of 1934 is the wellspring of this body of law: "It shall be unlawful for any person . . . [t]o use or employ, in connection with the purchase or sale of any security . . . , any manipulative or deceptive device. . . ."[9] The statute does not state that trades based on asymmetric information on an anonymous exchange are "manipulative or deceptive." It only delegates to the SEC the authority to write rules to implement the language for "the public interest or for the protection of investors."[10]

The relevant SEC rule is not a model of clarity either. Rule 10b–5 makes it unlawful to use interstate commerce to, among other things, "employ any . . . scheme . . . to defraud . . . in connection with the purchase or sale of any security."[11] The result of executive agency ambiguity layered on top of congressional ambiguity is judicial power to decide what is and what is not illegal. The law of insider trading is

---

[6] See Roy Schotland, Unsafe at any Price: A Reply to Manne, 53 Va. L. Rev. 1925 (1967).

[7] See United States v. O'Hagan, 521 U.S. 642, at 654 (1997); Carpenter v. United States, 484 U.S. 19, 25–27 (1987). In *Carpenter*, a reporter for The Wall Street Journal who tipped a broker of his forthcoming stories in the Journal was convicted of wire fraud for depriving his employer of the exclusive possession of this confidential information, even though no competitive injury to his employer was alleged. Note that it is not necessary under this wire fraud theory that there even be a purchase or sale of a security.

[8] Legislation has, however, been recently drafted. In December 2019, the Insider Trading Prohibition Act passed the House of Representatives by the overwhelming vote of 410 to 13, clearly showing that Congress has no sympathy for insider trading.

[9] Section 10(b) of the Securities Exchange Act of 1934, 15 U.S.C. § 78j(b), and Rule 10b–5 promulgated thereunder, 17 C.F.R. § 240.10b–5.

[10] 15 U.S.C. § 78j.

[11] See Rule 10b–5, 17 C.F.R. § 240.10b–5.

effectively federal common law or, as Chief Justice Rehnquist wrote, "a judicial oak which has grown from little more than a legislative acorn."[12]

As the chief prosecutor of these cases, the SEC's point of view has considerable influence. The SEC has fairly consistently taken the view that insiders have a duty to disclose all material information available to them before trading—the so-called "disclose or abstain" rule.[13] The rule was first announced in *Cady, Roberts & Co.*, an administrative enforcement proceeding in 1961.[14] The SEC found liability in the case of an outside director who tipped his partner in a brokerage business about an upcoming dividend cut.[15] Relying on two separate theories—first, that the director expropriated corporate information for personal use; and second, that there is "inherent unfairness" in trading on information knowing it is not known by the other side—the SEC declared an insider in possession of material, nonpublic information (hereinafter "inside" information) must disclose such information before trading or abstain from trading.[16]

The Second Circuit endorsed this view several years later in SEC v. Texas Gulf Sulphur, holding that insiders of a mining company trading in advance of public disclosure of a favorable geology report violated Rule 10b–5.[17] The court specifically blessed the disclose-or-abstain rule the SEC announced in *Cady, Roberts*, noting this rule "is based in policy on the justifiable expectation of the securities marketplace that all investors trading on impersonal exchanges have relatively equal access to material information."[18]

---

[12] Blue Chip Stamps v. Manor Drug Stores, 421 U.S. 723 (1975).

[13] The SEC's position in litigation over the years has been that liability could arise from trades made by any person that has an informational advantage, no matter how that informational advantage arose. There is deep irony here. The expert agency tasked with writing and executing rules interpreting the securities statutes, takes a position—trading only based on equal access to information—that is fundamentally inconsistent with markets arising in the first place. A more generous reading of the SEC's position is that it understands the need for informational asymmetry, but given limited monitoring and enforcement resources has to lower the burden to make out any particular case in order to achieve the optimal deterrence of socially destructive trading by insiders. After all, people do not want to trade in markets that they perceive to be unfair. Whatever the rationale, the judiciary, especially the Supreme Court, has consistently rejected the SEC's attempts to broadly define insider trading when involving third parties like journalists, printers, and others unrelated or tangentially related to the inside information. The basic SEC approach regarding insiders is, however, long standing and largely undisturbed by courts.

[14] Cady, Roberts & Co., 40 S.E.C. 907 (1961),

[15] Id.

[16] Id.

[17] 401 F.2d 833 (2d Cir. 1968).

[18] Id. ("It was the intent of Congress that all members of the investing public should be subject to identical market risks . . . The investors were not trading on equal footing with outside investors")

1. "INSIDER" TRADING

The SEC in In re Cady, Roberts & Co.,[19] and the Second Circuit in SEC v. Texas Gulf Sulphur Co.,[20] popularized what came to be known as the "disclose or abstain" duty. As the court in *Texas Gulf Sulphur* phrased this duty:

> The essence of the Rule is that anyone who, trading for his own account in the securities of a corporation has "access, directly or indirectly, to information intended to be available only for a corporate purpose and not for the personal benefit of anyone" may not take "advantage of such information knowing it is unavailable to those with whom he is dealing," i.e., the investing public. Matter of Cady, Roberts & Co., 40 SEC 907, 912 (1961). Insiders, as directors or management officers are, of course, by this Rule, precluded from so unfairly dealing, but the Rule is also applicable to one possessing the information who may not be strictly termed an "insider" within the meaning of Sec. 16(b) of the Act. Cady, Roberts, supra. Thus, anyone in possession of material inside information must either disclose it to the investing public, or, if he is disabled from disclosing it in order to protect a corporate confidence, or he chooses not to do so, must abstain from trading in or recommending the securities concerned while such inside information remains undisclosed.[21]

The concept of a disclose-or-abstain duty has endured, but the *Texas Gulf Sulphur* intimation that the duty was universal has not. Three key Supreme Court decisions have sharpened the scope of who is subject to the disclose-or-abstain duty, dividing the duties into several categories.

A. CLASSICAL INSIDER TRADING

Chiarella v. United States
Supreme Court of the United States, 1980.
445 U.S. 222, 100 S.Ct. 1108, 63 L.Ed.2d 348.

■ JUSTICE POWELL delivered the opinion of the Court.

The question in this case is whether a person who learns from the confidential documents of one corporation that it is planning an attempt to secure control of a second corporation violates § 10(b) of the Securities Exchange Act of 1934 if he fails to disclose the impending takeover before trading in the target company's securities.

---

[19] 40 SEC 907 (1961).
[20] 401 F.2d 833 (2d Cir. 1968).
[21] Id. at 848.

I

Petitioner is a printer by trade. In 1975 and 1976, he worked as a "markup man" in the New York composing room of Pandick Press, a financial printer. Among documents that petitioner handled were five announcements of corporate takeover bids. When these documents were delivered to the printer, the identities of the acquiring and target corporations were concealed by blank spaces or false names. The true names were sent to the printer on the night of the final printing.

The petitioner, however, was able to deduce the names of the target companies before the final printing from other information contained in the documents. Without disclosing his knowledge, petitioner purchased stock in the target companies and sold the shares immediately after the takeover attempts were made public. By this method, petitioner realized a gain of slightly more than $30,000 in the course of 14 months. Subsequently, the Securities and Exchange Commission (Commission or SEC) began an investigation of his trading activities. In May 1977, petitioner entered into a consent decree with the Commission in which he agreed to return his profits to the sellers of the shares. On the same day, he was discharged by Pandick Press.

In January 1978, petitioner was indicted on 17 counts of violating § 10(b) of the Securities Exchange Act of 1934 (1934 Act) and SEC Rule 10b–5. After petitioner unsuccessfully moved to dismiss the indictment, he was brought to trial and convicted on all counts.

The Court of Appeals for the Second Circuit affirmed petitioner's conviction. 588 F.2d 1358 (1978). We granted certiorari, 441 U.S. 942 (1979), and we now reverse.

II

Section 10(b) of the 1934 Act prohibits the use "in connection with the purchase or sale of any security . . . [of] any manipulative or deceptive device or contrivance in contravention of such rules and regulations as the Commission may prescribe." Pursuant to this section, the SEC promulgated Rule 10b–5 * * *.

This case concerns the legal effect of the petitioner's silence. The District Court's charge permitted the jury to convict the petitioner if it found that he willfully failed to inform sellers of target company securities that he knew of a forthcoming takeover bid that would make their shares more valuable. In order to decide whether silence in such circumstances violates § 10(b), it is necessary to review the language and legislative history of that statute as well as its interpretation by the Commission and the federal courts.

Although the starting point of our inquiry is the language of the statute, Ernst & Ernst v. Hochfelder, 425 U.S. 185, 197 (1976), § 10(b) does not state whether silence may constitute a manipulative or deceptive device. Section 10(b) was designed as a catch-all clause to prevent fraudulent practices. Id., at 202, 206. But neither the legislative history nor the statute itself affords specific guidance for the resolution of this case. When Rule 10b–5 was promulgated in 1942, the SEC did not discuss the possibility that failure to provide information might run afoul of § 10(b).

* * *

The Federal courts have found violations of § 10(b) where corporate insiders used undisclosed information for their own benefit. E.g., SEC v. Texas Gulf Sulphur Co., 401 F.2d 833 (C.A.2 1968), cert. denied, 404 U.S. 1005 (1971). The cases also have emphasized, in accordance with the common-law rule, that "[t]he party charged with failing to disclose market information must be under a duty to disclose it." Frigitemp Corp. v. Financial Dynamics Fund, Inc., 524 F.2d 275, 282 (C.A.2 1975). Accordingly, a purchaser of stock who has no duty to a prospective seller because he is neither an insider nor a fiduciary has been held to have no obligation to reveal material facts.

* * *

Thus, administrative and judicial interpretations have established that silence in connection with the purchase or sale of securities may operate as a fraud actionable under § 10(b) despite the absence of statutory language or legislative history specifically addressing the legality of nondisclosure. But such liability is premised upon a duty to disclose arising from a relationship of trust and confidence between parties to a transaction. Application of a duty to disclose prior to trading guarantees that corporate insiders, who have an obligation to place the shareholder's welfare before their own, will not benefit personally through fraudulent use of material, nonpublic information.[12]

III

In this case, the petitioner was convicted of violating § 10(b) although he was not a corporate insider and he received no confidential information from the target company. Moreover, the "market information" upon which he relied did not concern the earning power or operations of the target company, but only the plans of the acquiring company. Petitioner's use of that information was not a fraud under § 10(b) unless he was subject to an affirmative duty to disclose it before trading. In this case, the jury instructions failed to specify any such duty. In effect, the trial court instructed the jury that petitioner owed a duty to everyone; to all sellers, indeed, to the market as a whole. The jury simply was told to decide whether petitioner used material, nonpublic

---

[12] "Tippees" of corporate insiders have been held liable under § 10(b) because they have a duty not to profit from the use of inside information that they know is confidential and know or should know came from a corporate insider, Shapiro v. Merrill Lynch, Pierce, Fenner & Smith, 495 F.2d 228, 237–238 (C.A.2 1974). The tippee's obligation has been viewed as arising from his role as a participant after the fact in the insider's breach of a fiduciary duty. Subcommittees of American Bar Association Section of Corporation, Banking, and Business Law, Comment Letter on Material, Non-Public Information (Oct. 15, 1973) reprinted in BNA, Securities Regulation & Law Report No. 233, at D-1, D-2 (Jan. 2, 1974).

information at a time when "he knew other people trading in the securities market did not have access to the same information."

The Court of Appeals affirmed the conviction by holding that "[a]nyone—corporate insider or not—who regularly receives material nonpublic information may not use that information to trade in securities without incurring an affirmative duty to disclose." Although the court said that its test would include only persons who regularly receive material nonpublic information, its rationale for that limitation is unrelated to the existence of a duty to disclose. The Court of Appeals, like the trial court, failed to identify a relationship between petitioner and the sellers that could give rise to a duty. Its decision thus rested solely upon its belief that the federal securities laws have "created a system providing equal access to information necessary for reasoned and intelligent investment decisions." The use by anyone of material information not generally available is fraudulent, this theory suggests, because such information gives certain buyers or sellers an unfair advantage over less informed buyers and sellers.

This reasoning suffers from two defects. First, not every instance of financial unfairness constitutes fraudulent activity under § 10(b). See Santa Fe Industries, Inc. v. Green, 430 U.S. 462, 474–477 (1977). Second, the element required to make silence fraudulent—a duty to disclose—is absent in this case. No duty could arise from petitioner's relationship with the sellers of the target company's securities, for petitioner had no prior dealings with them. He was not their agent, he was not a fiduciary, he was not a person in whom the sellers had placed their trust and confidence. He was, in fact, a complete stranger who dealt with the sellers only through impersonal market transactions.

We cannot affirm petitioner's conviction without recognizing a general duty between all participants in market transactions to forgo actions based on material, nonpublic information. Formulation of such a broad duty, which departs radically from the established doctrine that duty arises from a specific relationship between two parties, should not be undertaken absent some explicit evidence of congressional intent.

As we have seen, no such evidence emerges from the language or legislative history of § 10(b). Moreover, neither the Congress nor the Commission ever has adopted a parity-of-information rule. Instead the problems caused by misuse of market information have been addressed by detailed and sophisticated regulation that recognizes when use of market information may not harm operation of the securities markets. For example, the Williams Act limits but does not completely prohibit a tender offeror's purchases of target corporation stock before public announcement of the offer. Congress' careful action in this and other areas contrasts, and is in some tension, with the broad rule of liability we are asked to adopt in this case.

Indeed, the theory upon which the petitioner was convicted is at odds with the Commission's view of § 10(b) as applied to activity that has the same effect on sellers as the petitioner's purchases. "Warehousing" takes place when a corporation gives advance notice of its intention to launch a tender offer to institutional investors who then are able to purchase stock in the target company before the tender offer is made public and the price of shares rises. In this case, as in warehousing, a buyer of securities purchases stock in a target corporation on the basis of market information which is unknown to the seller. In both of these situations, the seller's behavior presumably would be altered if he had the nonpublic information. Significantly, however, the Commission has acted to bar warehousing under its authority to regulate tender offers after recognizing that action under § 10(b) would rest on a "somewhat different theory" than that previously used to regulate insider trading as fraudulent activity.

We see no basis for applying such a new and different theory of liability in this case. As we have emphasized before, the 1934 Act cannot be read "'more broadly than its language and the statutory scheme reasonably permit.'" Touche Ross & Co. v. Redington, 442 U.S. 560, 578 (1979), quoting SEC v. Sloan, 436 U.S. 103, 116 (1978). Section 10(b) is aptly described as a catch-all provision, but what it catches must be fraud. When an allegation of fraud is based upon nondisclosure, there can be no fraud absent a duty to speak. We hold that a duty to disclose under § 10(b) does not arise from the mere possession of nonpublic market information. The contrary result is without support in the legislative history of § 10(b) and would be inconsistent with the careful plan that Congress has enacted for regulation of the securities markets.

IV

In its brief to this Court the United States offers an alternative theory to support petitioner's conviction. It argues that petitioner breached a duty to the acquiring corporation when he acted upon information that he obtained by virtue of his position as an employee of a printer employed by the corporation. The breach of this duty is said to support a conviction under § 10(b) for fraud perpetrated upon both the acquiring corporation and the sellers.

We need not decide whether this theory has merit for it was not submitted to the jury. The jury was told, in the language of Rule 10b–5, that it could convict the petitioner if it concluded that he either (i) employed a device, scheme or artifice to defraud or (ii) engaged in an act, practice, or course of business which operated or would operate as a fraud or deceit upon any person. The trial judge stated that a "scheme to defraud" is a plan to obtain money by trick or deceit and that "a failure by Chiarella to disclose material, non-public information in connection with his purchase of stock would constitute deceit." Accordingly, the jury was instructed that the petitioner employed a scheme to defraud if he "did not disclose . . . material non-public information in connection with the purchases of the stock."

* * *

The judgment of the Court of Appeals is *Reversed*.

NOTE: From early on, it had long been clear that officers and directors[22] and majority or other controlling shareholders[23] were subject to the disclose-or-abstain rule.

B. TEMPORARY INSIDERS, TIPPERS, AND TIPPEES

Dirks v. SEC
Supreme Court of the United States, 1983.
463 U.S. 646, 103 S.Ct. 3255, 77 L.Ed.2d 911.

■ JUSTICE POWELL delivered the opinion of the Court.

Petitioner Raymond Dirks received material nonpublic information from "insiders" of a corporation with which he had no connection. He disclosed this information to investors who relied on it in trading in the shares of the corporation. The question is whether Dirks violated the antifraud provisions of the federal securities laws by this disclosure.

I

In 1973, Dirks was an officer of a New York broker-dealer firm who specialized in providing investment analysis of insurance company securities to institutional investors. On March 6, Dirks received information from Ronald Secrist, a former officer of Equity Funding of America. Secrist alleged that the assets of Equity Funding, a diversified corporation primarily engaged in selling life insurance and mutual funds, were vastly overstated as the result of fraudulent corporate practices. Secrist also stated that various regulatory agencies had failed to act on similar charges made by Equity Funding employees. He urged Dirks to verify the fraud and disclose it publicly.

Dirks decided to investigate the allegations. He visited Equity Funding's headquarters in Los Angeles and interviewed several officers and employees of the corporation. The senior management denied any wrongdoing, but certain corporation employees corroborated the charges of fraud. Neither Dirks nor his firm owned or traded any Equity Funding stock, but throughout his investigation he openly discussed the information he had obtained with a number of clients and investors. Some of these persons sold their holdings of Equity Funding securities, including five investment advisers who liquidated holdings of more than $16 million.

---

[22] See, e.g., List v. Fashion Park, Inc., 340 F.2d 457 (2d Cir. 1965); Kardon v. National Gypsum Co., 69 F.Supp. 512 (E.D.Pa. 1946), 73 F.Supp. 798 (E.D.Pa. 1947), 83 F.Supp. 613 (E.D.Pa. 1947); Northern Trust Co. v. Essaness Theatres Corp., 103 F.Supp. 954 (N.D.Ill. 1952).

[23] See, e.g., Speed v. Transamerica Corp., 99 F.Supp. 808 (D.Del. 1951), 135 F.Supp. 176 (D.Del. 1955), aff'd, 235 F.2d 369 (3d Cir. 1956).

* * *

During the two-week period in which Dirks pursued his investigation and spread word of Secrist's charges, the price of Equity Funding stock fell from $26 per share to less than $15 per share. This led the New York Stock Exchange to halt trading on March 27. Shortly thereafter California insurance authorities impounded Equity Funding's records and uncovered evidence of the fraud. Only then did the Securities and Exchange Commission (SEC) file a complaint against Equity Funding and only then, on April 2, did the Wall Street Journal publish a front-page story based largely on information assembled by Dirks. Equity Funding immediately went into receivership.

The SEC began an investigation into Dirks' role in the exposure of the fraud. After a hearing by an administrative law judge, the SEC found that Dirks had aided and abetted violations of § 17(a) of the Securities Act of 1933, § 10(b) of the Securities Exchange Act of 1934, and SEC Rule 10b–5, by repeating the allegations of fraud to members of the investment community who later sold their Equity Funding stock. The SEC concluded: "Where 'tippees'—regardless of their motivation or occupation—come into possession of material 'information that they know is confidential and know or should know came from a corporate insider,' they must either publicly disclose that information or refrain from trading." 21 S.E.C. Docket 1401, 1407 (1981) (footnote omitted) (quoting Chiarella v. United States, 445 U.S. 222, 230 n. 12 (1980)). Recognizing, however, that Dirks "played an important role in bringing [Equity Funding's] massive fraud to light," 21 S.E.C. Docket, at 1412, the SEC only censured him. [Dirks appealed to the D.C. Court of Appeals, which entered a judgment against him.]

* * *

In view of the importance to the SEC and to the securities industry of the question presented by this case, we granted a writ of certiorari. We now reverse.

II

In the seminal case of In re Cady, Roberts & Co., 40 S.E.C. 907 (1961), the SEC recognized that the common law in some jurisdictions imposes on "corporate 'insiders,' particularly officers, directors, or controlling stockholders" an "affirmative duty of disclosure . . . when dealing in securities."[10] The SEC found that not only did breach of this common-law duty also establish the elements of a Rule 10b–5 violation, but that individuals other than corporate insiders could be obligated

---

[10] The duty that insiders owe to the corporation's shareholders not to trade on inside information differs from the common-law duty that officers and directors also have to the corporation itself not to mismanage corporate assets, of which confidential information is one. In holding that breaches of this duty to shareholders violated the Securities Exchange Act, the Cady, Roberts Commission recognized, and we agree, that "[a] significant purpose of the Exchange Act was to eliminate the idea that use of inside information for personal advantage was a normal emolument of corporate office." See 40 S.E.C., at 912, n.15.

either to disclose material nonpublic information before trading or to abstain from trading altogether. In *Chiarella*, we accepted the two elements set out in *Cady, Roberts* for establishing a Rule 10b–5 violation: "(i) the existence of a relationship affording access to inside information intended to be available only for a corporate purpose, and (ii) the unfairness of allowing a corporate insider to take advantage of that information by trading without disclosure." In examining whether Chiarella had an obligation to disclose or abstain, the Court found that there is no general duty to disclose before trading on material nonpublic information, and held that "a duty to disclose under § 10(b) does not arise from the mere possession of nonpublic market information." Such a duty arises rather from the existence of a fiduciary relationship.

* * *

III

We were explicit in *Chiarella* in saying that there can be no duty to disclose where the person who has traded on inside information "was not [the corporation's] agent, . . . was not a fiduciary, [or] was not a person in whom the sellers [of the securities] had placed their trust and confidence." Not to require such a fiduciary relationship, we recognized, would "depar[t] radically from the established doctrine that duty arises from a specific relationship between two parties" and would amount to "recognizing a general duty between all participants in market transactions to forgo actions based on material, nonpublic information." This requirement of a specific relationship between the shareholders and the individual trading on inside information has created analytical difficulties for the SEC and courts in policing tippees who trade on inside information. Unlike insiders who have independent fiduciary duties to both the corporation and its shareholders, the typical tippee has no such relationships.[14] In view of this absence, it has been unclear how a tippee acquires the *Cady, Roberts* duty to refrain from trading on inside information.

A

The SEC's position, as stated in its opinion in this case, is that a tippee "inherits" the *Cady, Roberts* obligation to shareholders whenever he receives inside information from an insider * * *.

---

[14] Under certain circumstances, such as where corporate information is revealed legitimately to an underwriter, accountant, lawyer, or consultant working for the corporation, these outsiders may become fiduciaries of the shareholders. The basis for recognizing this fiduciary duty is not simply that such persons acquired nonpublic corporate information, but rather that they have entered into a special confidential relationship in the conduct of the business of the enterprise and are given access to information solely for corporate purposes. When such a person breaches his fiduciary relationship, he may be treated more properly as a tipper than a tippee. See Shapiro v. Merrill Lynch, Pierce, Fenner & Smith, Inc., 495 F.2d 228, 237 (C.A.2 1974) (investment banker had access to material information when working on a proposed public offering for the corporation). For such a duty to be imposed, however, the corporation must expect the outsider to keep the disclosed nonpublic information confidential, and the relationship at least must imply such a duty.

This view differs little from the view that we rejected as inconsistent with congressional intent in *Chiarella*. In that case, the Court of Appeals agreed with the SEC and affirmed Chiarella's conviction, holding that " '[a]*nyone*—corporate insider or not—who regularly receives material nonpublic information may not use that information to trade in securities without incurring an affirmative duty to disclose.' " Here, the SEC maintains that anyone who knowingly receives nonpublic material information from an insider has a fiduciary duty to disclose before trading.[15]

In effect, the SEC's theory of tippee liability in both cases appears rooted in the idea that the antifraud provisions require equal information among all traders. This conflicts with the principle set forth in *Chiarella* that only some persons, under some circumstances, will be barred from trading while in possession of material nonpublic information.[16] Judge Wright correctly read our opinion in *Chiarella* as repudiating any notion that all traders must enjoy equal information before trading: "[T]he 'information' theory is rejected. Because the disclose-or-refrain duty is extraordinary, it attaches only when a party has legal obligations other than a mere duty to comply with the general antifraud proscriptions in the federal securities laws." 220 U.S.App.D.C., at 322, 681 F.2d, at 837. See Chiarella, 445 U.S., at 235, n.20. We reaffirm today that "[a] duty [to disclose] arises from the relationship between parties . . . and not merely from one's ability to acquire information because of his position in the market." 445 U.S., at 231–232, n.14.

Imposing a duty to disclose or abstain solely because a person knowingly receives material nonpublic information from an insider and

---

[15] Apparently the SEC believes this case differs from Chiarella in that Dirks' receipt of inside information from Secrist, an insider, carried Secrist's duties with it, while Chiarella received the information without the direct involvement of an insider and thus inherited no duty to disclose or abstain. The SEC fails to explain, however, why the receipt of nonpublic information from an insider automatically carries with it the fiduciary duty of the insider. As we emphasized in Chiarella, mere possession of nonpublic information does not give rise to a duty to disclose or abstain; only a specific relationship does that. And we do not believe that the mere receipt of information from an insider creates such a special relationship between the tippee and the corporation's shareholders.

Apparently recognizing the weakness of its argument in light of Chiarella, the SEC attempts to distinguish that case factually as involving not "inside" information, but rather "market" information, i.e., "information originating outside the company and usually about the supply and demand for the company's securities." This Court drew no such distinction in Chiarella and, as The Chief Justice noted, "[i]t is clear that § 10(b) and Rule 10b–5 by their terms and by their history make no such distinction." 445 U.S., at 241, n. 1 (dissenting opinion). See ALI Fed.Sec.Code § 1603, Comment (2)(j) (Proposed Official Draft 1978).

[16] In Chiarella, we noted that formulation of an absolute equal information rule "should not be undertaken absent some explicit evidence of congressional intent." Rather than adopting such a radical view of securities trading, Congress has expressly exempted many market professionals from the general statutory prohibition set forth in § 11(a)(1) of the Securities Exchange Act, 15 U.S.C. § 78k(a)(1), against members of a national securities exchange trading for their own account. We observed in Chiarella that "[t]he exception is based upon Congress' recognition that [market professionals] contribute to a fair and orderly marketplace at the same time they exploit the informational advantage that comes from their possession of [nonpublic information]."

trades on it could have an inhibiting influence on the role of market analysts, which the SEC itself recognizes is necessary to the preservation of a healthy market.[17] It is commonplace for analysts to "ferret out and analyze information," 21 S.E.C., at 1406,[18] and this often is done by meeting with and questioning corporate officers and others who are insiders. And information that the analysts obtain normally may be the basis for judgments as to the market worth of a corporation's securities. The analyst's judgment in this respect is made available in market letters or otherwise to clients of the firm. It is the nature of this type of information, and indeed of the markets themselves, that such information cannot be made simultaneously available to all of the corporation's stockholders or the public generally.

B

The conclusion that recipients of inside information do not invariably acquire a duty to disclose or abstain does not mean that such tippees always are free to trade on the information. The need for a ban on some tippee trading is clear. Not only are insiders forbidden by their fiduciary relationship from personally using undisclosed corporate information to their advantage, but they may not give such information to an outsider for the same improper purpose of exploiting the information for their personal gain. See 15 U.S.C. § 78t(b) (making it unlawful to do indirectly "by means of any other person" any act made unlawful by the federal securities laws). Similarly, the transactions of those who knowingly participate with the fiduciary in such a breach are "as forbidden" as transactions "on behalf of the trustee himself." Mosser v. Darrow, 341 U.S. 267, 272 (1951). As the court explained in *Mosser*, a contrary rule "would open up opportunities for devious dealings in the name of the others that the trustee could not conduct in his own." Thus,

---

[17] The SEC expressly recognized that "[t]he value to the entire market of [analysts'] efforts cannot be gainsaid; market efficiency in pricing is significantly enhanced by [their] initiatives to ferret out and analyze information, and thus the analyst's work redounds to the benefit of all investors." 21 S.E.C., at 1406. The SEC asserts that analysts remain free to obtain from management corporate information for purposes of "filling in the 'interstices in analysis'...." Brief for Respondent 42 (quoting Investors Management Co., 44 S.E.C., at 646). But this rule is inherently imprecise, and imprecision prevents parties from ordering their actions in accord with legal requirements. Unless the parties have some guidance as to where the line is between permissible and impermissible disclosures and uses, neither corporate insiders nor analysts can be sure when the line is crossed. Cf. Adler v. Klawans, 267 F.2d 840, 845 (C.A.2 1959) (Burger, J., sitting by designation).

[18] On its facts, this case is the unusual one. Dirks is an analyst in a broker-dealer firm, and he did interview management in the course of his investigation. He uncovered, however, startling information that required no analysis or exercise of judgment as to its market relevance. Nonetheless, the principle at issue here extends beyond these facts. The SEC's rule—applicable without regard to any breach by an insider—could have serious ramifications on reporting by analysts of investment views.

Despite the unusualness of Dirks' "find," the central role that he played in uncovering the fraud at Equity Funding, and that analysts in general can play in revealing information that corporations may have reason to withhold from the public, is an important one. Dirks' careful investigation brought to light a massive fraud at the corporation. And until the Equity Funding fraud was exposed, the information in the trading market was grossly inaccurate. But for Dirks' efforts, the fraud might well have gone undetected longer.

the tippee's duty to disclose or abstain is derivative from that of the insider's duty. As we noted in *Chiarella*, "[t]he tippee's obligation has been viewed as arising from his role as a participant after the fact in the insider's breach of a fiduciary duty."

Thus, some tippees must assume an insider's duty to the shareholders not because they receive inside information, but rather because it has been made available to them *improperly*.[19] And for Rule 10b–5 purposes, the insider's disclosure is improper only where it would violate his *Cady, Roberts* duty. Thus, a tippee assumes a fiduciary duty to the shareholders of a corporation not to trade on material nonpublic information only when the insider has breached his fiduciary duty to the shareholders by disclosing the information to the tippee and the tippee knows or should know that there has been a breach.[20] As Commissioner Smith perceptively observed in *Investors Management Co.*: "[T]ippee responsibility must be related back to insider responsibility by a necessary finding that the tippee knew the information was given to him in breach of a duty by a person having a special relationship to the issuer not to disclose the information. . . ." 44 S.E.C., at 651 (concurring in the result). Tipping thus properly is viewed only as a means of indirectly violating the *Cady, Roberts* disclose-or-abstain rule.[21]

---

[19] The SEC itself has recognized that tippee liability properly is imposed only in circumstances where the tippee knows, or has reason to know, that the insider has disclosed improperly inside corporate information. In Investors Management Co., supra, the SEC stated that one element of tippee liability is that the tippee knew or had reason to know that the information "was non-public and had been obtained *improperly* by selective revelation or otherwise." 44 S.E.C., at 641 (emphasis added). Commissioner Smith read this test to mean that a tippee can be held liable only if he received information in breach of an insider's duty not to disclose it. Id., at 650 (concurring in the result).

[20] Professor Loss has linked tippee liability to the concept in the law of restitution that "'[w]here a fiduciary in violation of his duty to the beneficiary communicates confidential information to a third person, the third person, if he had notice of the violation of duty, holds upon a constructive trust for the beneficiary any profit which he makes through the use of such information.'" 3 L. Loss, Securities Regulation 1451 (2d ed. 1961) (quoting Restatement of Restitution § 201(2) (1937)). Other authorities likewise have expressed the view that tippee liability exists only where there has been a breach of trust by an insider of which the tippee had knowledge.

[21] We do not suggest that knowingly trading on inside information is ever "socially desirable or even that it is devoid of moral considerations." Dooley, Enforcement of Insider Trading Restrictions, 66 Va. L. Rev. 1, 55 (1980). Nor do we imply an absence of responsibility to disclose promptly indications of illegal actions by a corporation to the proper authorities—typically the SEC and exchange authorities in cases involving securities. Depending on the circumstances, and even where permitted by law, one's trading on material nonpublic information is behavior that may fall below ethical standards of conduct. But in a statutory area of the law such as securities regulation, where legal principles of general application must be applied, there may be "significant distinctions between actual legal obligations and ethical ideals." SEC, Report of the Special Study of Securities Markets, H.R.Doc. No. 95, 88th Cong., 1st Sess., pt. 1, pp. 237–238 (1963). The SEC recognizes this. At oral argument, the following exchange took place:

"QUESTION: So, it would not have satisfied his obligation under the law to go to the SEC first?

"[SEC's counsel]: That is correct. That an insider has to observe what has come to be known as the abstain or disclosure rule. Either the information has to be disclosed to the market if it is inside information . . . or the insider must abstain." Tr. of Oral Arg. 27.

C

In determining whether a tippee is under an obligation to disclose or abstain, it thus is necessary to determine whether the insider's "tip" constituted a breach of the insider's fiduciary duty. All disclosures of confidential corporate information are not inconsistent with the duty insiders owe to shareholders. In contrast to the extraordinary facts of this case, the more typical situation in which there will be a question whether disclosure violates the insider's *Cady, Roberts* duty is when insiders disclose information to analysts. In some situations, the insider will act consistently with his fiduciary duty to shareholders, and yet release of the information may affect the market. For example, it may not be clear—either to the corporate insider or to the recipient analyst—whether the information will be viewed as material nonpublic information. Corporate officials may mistakenly think the information already has been disclosed or that it is not material enough to affect the market. Whether disclosure is a breach of duty therefore depends in large part on the purpose of the disclosure. This standard was identified by the SEC itself in *Cady, Roberts*: a purpose of the securities laws was to eliminate "use of inside information for personal advantage." Thus, the test is whether the insider personally will benefit, directly or indirectly, from his disclosure. Absent some personal gain, there has been no breach of duty to stockholders. And absent a breach by the insider, there is no derivative breach. As Commissioner Smith stated in *Investors Management Co.*: "It is important in this type of case to focus on policing insiders and what they do . . . rather than on policing information *per se* and its possession. . . ." 44 S.E.C., at 648 (concurring in the result).

The SEC argues that, if inside-trading liability does not exist when the information is transmitted for a proper purpose but is used for trading, it would be a rare situation when the parties could not fabricate some ostensibly legitimate business justification for transmitting the information. We think the SEC is unduly concerned. In determining whether the insider's purpose in making a particular disclosure is fraudulent, the SEC and the courts are not required to read the parties' minds. Scienter in some cases is relevant in determining whether the tipper has violated his *Cady, Roberts* duty.[23] But to determine whether

---

Thus, it is clear that Rule 10b–5 does not impose any obligation simply to tell the SEC about the fraud before trading.

[23] Scienter—"a mental state embracing intent to deceive, manipulate, or defraud," Ernst & Ernst v. Hochfelder, 425 U.S. 185, 193, n. 12 (1976)—is an independent element of a Rule 10b–5 violation. See Aaron v. SEC, 446 U.S. 680, 695 (1980). Contrary to the dissent's suggestion, motivation is not irrelevant to the issue of scienter. It is not enough that an insider's conduct results in harm to investors; rather, a violation may be found only where there is "intentional or willful conduct designed to deceive or defraud investors by controlling or artificially affecting the price of securities." Ernst & Ernst v. Hochfelder, supra, 425 U.S., at 199. The issue in this case, however, is not whether Secrist or Dirks acted with scienter, but rather whether there was any deceptive or fraudulent conduct at all, i.e., whether Secrist's disclosure constituted a breach of his fiduciary duty and thereby caused injury to shareholders. Only if there was such a breach did Dirks, a tippee, acquire a fiduciary duty to disclose or abstain.

the disclosure itself "deceive[s], manipulate[s], or defraud[s]" shareholders, Aaron v. SEC, 446 U.S. 680, 686 (1980), the initial inquiry is whether there has been a breach of duty by the insider. This requires courts to focus on objective criteria, i.e., whether the insider receives a direct or indirect personal benefit from the disclosure, such as a pecuniary gain or a reputational benefit that will translate into future earnings. Cf. 40 S.E.C., at 912, n. 15; Brudney, Insiders, Outsiders, and Informational Advantages Under the Federal Securities Laws, 93 Harv.L.Rev. 324, 348 (1979) ("The theory . . . is that the insider, by giving the information out selectively, is in effect selling the information to its recipient for cash, reciprocal information, or other things of value for himself. . . ."). There are objective facts and circumstances that often justify such an inference. For example, there may be a relationship between the insider and the recipient that suggests a *quid pro quo* from the latter, or an intention to benefit the particular recipient. The elements of fiduciary duty and exploitation of nonpublic information also exist when an insider makes a gift of confidential information to a trading relative or friend. The tip and trade resemble trading by the insider himself followed by a gift of the profits to the recipient.

Determining whether an insider personally benefits from a particular disclosure, a question of fact, will not always be easy for courts. But it is essential, we think, to have a guiding principle for those whose daily activities must be limited and instructed by the SEC's inside-trading rules, and we believe that there must be a breach of the insider's fiduciary duty before the tippee inherits the duty to disclose or abstain. In contrast, the rule adopted by the SEC in this case would have no limiting principle.

IV

Under the inside-trading and tipping rules set forth above, we find that there was no actionable violation by Dirks. It is undisputed that Dirks himself was a stranger to Equity Funding, with no pre-existing fiduciary duty to its shareholders. He took no action, directly or indirectly, that induced the shareholders or officers of Equity Funding to repose trust or confidence in him. There was no expectation by Dirks' sources that he would keep their information in confidence. Nor did Dirks misappropriate or illegally obtain the information about Equity Funding. Unless the insiders breached their *Cady, Roberts* duty to shareholders in disclosing the nonpublic information to Dirks, he breached no duty when he passed it on to investors as well as to the Wall Street Journal.

It is clear that neither Secrist nor the other Equity Funding employees violated their *Cady, Roberts* duty to the corporation's shareholders by providing information to Dirks.[27] The tippers received

---

[27] In this Court, the SEC appears to contend that an insider invariably violates a fiduciary duty to the corporation's shareholders by transmitting nonpublic corporate information to an outsider when he has reason to believe that the outsider may use it to the disadvantage of the shareholders. "Thus, regardless of any ultimate motive to bring to public

no monetary or personal benefit for revealing Equity Funding's secrets, nor was their purpose to make a gift of valuable information to Dirks. As the facts of this case clearly indicate, the tippers were motivated by a desire to expose the fraud. In the absence of a breach of duty to shareholders by the insiders, there was no derivative breach by Dirks. See n. 20, supra. Dirks therefore could not have been "a participant after the fact in [an] insider's breach of a fiduciary duty." Chiarella, 445 U.S., at 230, n. 12.

V

We conclude that Dirks, in the circumstances of this case, had no duty to abstain from use of the inside information that he obtained. The judgment of the Court of Appeals therefore is

Reversed.

---

attention the derelictions at Equity Funding, Secrist breached his duty to Equity Funding shareholders." Brief for Respondent 31. This perceived "duty" differs markedly from the one that the SEC identified in *Cady, Roberts* and that has been the basis for federal tippee-trading rules to date. In fact, the SEC did not charge Secrist with any wrongdoing, and we do not understand the SEC to have relied on any theory of a breach of duty by Secrist in finding that Dirks breached his duty to Equity Funding's shareholders. See App. 250 (decision of administrative law judge) ("One who knows himself to be a beneficiary of non-public, selectively disclosed inside information must fully disclose or refrain from trading."); SEC's Reply to Notice of Supplemental Authority before the SEC 4 ("If Secrist was acting properly, Dirks inherited a duty to [Equity Funding]'s shareholders to refrain from improper private use of the information."); Brief on behalf of the SEC in the Court of Appeals, at 47–50; id., at 51 ("[K]nowing possession of inside information by any person imposes a duty to abstain or disclose."); id., at 52–54; id., at 55 ("[T]his obligation arises not from the manner in which such information is acquired. . . ."); 220 U.S. App. D.C., at 322–323, 681 F.2d, at 837–838 (Wright, J.).

The dissent argues that "Secrist violated his duty to Equity Funding shareholders by transmitting material nonpublic information to Dirks with the intention that Dirks would cause his clients to trade on that information." By perceiving a breach of fiduciary duty whenever inside information is intentionally disclosed to securities traders, the dissenting opinion effectively would achieve the same result as the SEC's theory below, i.e., mere possession of inside information while trading would be viewed as a Rule 10b–5 violation. But *Chiarella* made it explicitly clear there is no general duty to forgo market transactions "based on material, nonpublic information." Such a duty would "depar[t] radically from the established doctrine that duty arises from a specific relationship between two parties."

* * *

Moreover, to constitute a violation of Rule 10b–5, there must be fraud. See Ernst & Ernst v. Hochfelder, 425 U.S. 185, 199 (statutory words "manipulative," "device," and "contrivance . . . connot[e] intentional or willful conduct designed to *deceive or defraud* investors by controlling or artificially affecting the price of securities") (emphasis added). There is no evidence that Secrist's disclosure was intended to or did in fact "deceive or defraud" anyone. Secrist certainly intended to convey relevant information that management was unlawfully concealing, and—so far as the record shows—he believed that persuading Dirks to investigate was the best way to disclose the fraud. Other efforts had proved fruitless. Under any objective standard, Secrist received no direct or indirect personal benefit from the disclosure.

The dissenting opinion focuses on shareholder "losses," "injury," and "damages," but in many cases there may be no clear causal connection between inside trading and outsiders' losses. In one sense, as market values fluctuate and investors act on inevitably incomplete or incorrect information, there always are winners and losers; but those who have "lost" have not necessarily been defrauded. On the other hand, inside trading for personal gain is fraudulent, and is a violation of the federal securities laws. See Dooley, supra, at 39–41, 70. Thus, there is little legal significance to the dissent's argument that Secrist and Dirks created new "victims" by disclosing the information to persons who traded. In fact, they prevented the fraud from continuing and victimizing many more investors.

TIPPERS AND TIPPEES

1. *No Good Deed Goes Unpunished.* Think about the government's case here: Dirks played an important role in revealing a massive ongoing fraud, and the government's response was to try to send him to prison, among other things. Do you think this fact contributed to the Court's decision to reverse? Is this an example of Holmes's aphorism that "hard cases make bad law?"

2. *Constructive Insiders.* Footnote 14 in *Dirks* is significant because it transforms such "outsiders" as an underwriter, accountant, lawyer, or corporate consultant into constructive insiders ("fiduciaries of the shareholders") when they "[enter] into a special confidential relationship in the conduct of the business of the enterprise and are given access to information solely for corporate purposes."[24]

The Court underlined that "[f]or such a duty to be imposed * * * the corporation must expect the outsider to keep the disclosed nonpublic information confidential and the relationship at least must imply such a duty."[25] *Dirks* did not, however, define what it meant by a special confidential relationship.

The *Dirks* court added one more point concerning constructive insiders. "When such a person breaches his fiduciary relationship, he may be treated more properly as a tipper than a tippee."[26] This eliminates the need to prove (1) that the constructive insider received material nonpublic information in violation of a traditional insider's fiduciary duties—normally, of course, the constructive insider will receive the data without violating a traditional insider's duties—and (2) that the constructive insider knew or should have known that the data were given to him or her in violation of a traditional insider's duties. *Dirks* requires these proofs in a case against a tippee.

3. *Tippers and Tippees.* In a Second Circuit case preceding *Dirks*, the court had held that an insider can be held liable for conveying nonpublic material information to outsiders who trade, even when the insider does not trade.[27]

In *Dirks,* the Supreme Court similarly held: "Not only are insiders forbidden by their fiduciary relationship from personally using undisclosed corporate information to their advantage, but they also may not give such information to an outsider for the same improper purpose

---

[24] 463 U.S. at 655 n.14.
[25] Id.
[26] Id.
[27] Shapiro v. Merrill Lynch, Pierce, Fenner & Smith, Inc., 495 F.2d 228, 237–238 (2d Cir. 1974).

of exploiting the information for their personal gain."[28] That is to say, an insider may not use a tippee as a surrogate or agent for illegal trading. But this does not address information that is communicated consistently with fiduciary duties, for example, to secure a corporate loan or business relationship. Granted that the tipper no longer may be held liable for communicating this information, are all "tippees" then free to trade while in possession of appropriately communicated information?

In *Dirks*, the Court's response was equivocal. In certain circumstances these types of outsiders may become constructive insiders under the logic of footnote 14. But the general rule is that "[t]ippees must assume an insider's duty to the shareholders not because they receive inside information, but rather because it has been made available to them *improperly*."[29] [Emphasis in original.] The key to the test "is whether the insider personally will benefit, directly or indirectly, from his disclosure. Absent some personal gain, there has been no breach of duty to stockholders. And absent a breach by the insider, there is no derivative breach."[30]

Dirks also complicated proof of a Rule 10b–5 violation, as SEC v. Switzer[31] illustrates. In *Switzer*, a university football coach, while sitting in the stands at a track meet, overheard a business executive give his wife material nonpublic information concerning a firm in which the executive served as a director. To prove a violation of Rule 10b–5, a plaintiff must show that the tip was made with scienter. In *Switzer*, the Commission was unable to persuade the judge that the business executive had intentionally or recklessly tipped the coach, with the result that the coach and other more remote tippees were allowed to retain substantial profits.

In United States v. Chestman,[32] a tipper-tippee theory also proved unsuccessful when a corporate insider informed his sister about a pending tender offer for the presumably innocent purpose of helping her tender her shares. The sister informed her daughter who in turn told her husband who told his stockbroker, Chestman. In this context, the Second Circuit held that "marriage does not, without more, create a fiduciary relationship." Since the tips from the insider to his sister and her tip to her daughter and her daughter's tip to her husband could not establish the requisite fiduciary relationship, the *Dirks* tipper-tippee analysis did not result in liability. The SEC soon promulgated Rule 10b5–2 to clarify, for purposes of the misappropriation theory, when fiduciary duties arise in non-business relationships. Rule 10b5–2 effectively overruled

---

[28] 463 U.S. at 659.
[29] Id. at 660.
[30] Id. at 662.
[31] 590 F.Supp. 756 (W.D.Okla.1984).
[32] 947 F.2d 551 (2d Cir. en banc 1991).

Chestman. See notes following Securities and Exchange Commission v. Yun, 327 F.3d 1263 (11th Cir. 2003).

C. THE MISAPPROPRIATION THEORY

United States v. O'Hagan
Supreme Court of the United States, 1997.
521 U.S. 642, 117 S.Ct. 2199, 138 L.Ed.2d 724.

■ JUSTICE GINSBURG delivered the opinion of the Court.

This case concerns the interpretation and enforcement of § 10(b) and § 14(e) of the Securities Exchange Act of 1934, and rules made by the Securities and Exchange Commission pursuant to these provisions, Rule 10b–5 and Rule 14e–3(a). Two prime questions are presented. The first relates to the misappropriation of material, nonpublic information for securities trading; the second concerns fraudulent practices in the tender offer setting. In particular, we address and resolve these issues: (1) Is a person who trades in securities for personal profit, using confidential information misappropriated in breach of a fiduciary duty to the source of the information, guilty of violating § 10(b) and Rule 10b–5? (2) Did the Commission exceed its rulemaking authority by adopting Rule 14e–3(a), which proscribes trading on undisclosed information in the tender offer setting, even in the absence of a duty to disclose? Our answer to the first question is yes, and to the second question, viewed in the context of this case, no.

I

Respondent James Herman O'Hagan was a partner in the law firm of Dorsey & Whitney in Minneapolis, Minnesota. In July 1988, Grand Metropolitan PLC (Grand Met), a company based in London, England, retained Dorsey & Whitney as local counsel to represent Grand Met regarding a potential tender offer for the common stock of the Pillsbury Company, headquartered in Minneapolis. Both Grand Met and Dorsey & Whitney took precautions to protect the confidentiality of Grand Met's tender offer plans. O'Hagan did no work on the Grand Met representation. Dorsey & Whitney withdrew from representing Grand Met on September 9, 1988. Less than a month later, on October 4, 1988, Grand Met publicly announced its tender offer for Pillsbury stock.

On August 18, 1988, while Dorsey & Whitney was still representing Grand Met, O'Hagan began purchasing call options for Pillsbury stock. Each option gave him the right to purchase 100 shares of Pillsbury stock by a specified date in September 1988. Later in August and in September, O'Hagan made additional purchases of Pillsbury call options. By the end of September, he owned 2,500 unexpired Pillsbury options, apparently more than any other individual investor. O'Hagan also purchased, in September 1988, some 5,000 shares of Pillsbury common stock, at a price just under $39 per share. When Grand Met announced its tender offer in

October, the price of Pillsbury stock rose to nearly $60 per share. O'Hagan then sold his Pillsbury call options and common stock, making a profit of more than $4.3 million.

The Securities and Exchange Commission (SEC or Commission) initiated an investigation into O'Hagan's transactions, culminating in a 57-count indictment. The indictment alleged that O'Hagan defrauded his law firm and its client, Grand Met, by using for his own trading purposes material, nonpublic information regarding Grand Met's planned tender offer. According to the indictment, O'Hagan used the profits he gained through this trading to conceal his previous embezzlement and conversion of unrelated client trust funds. O'Hagan was charged with 20 counts of mail fraud, in violation of 18 U.S.C. § 1341; 17 counts of securities fraud, in violation of § 10(b) of the Securities Exchange Act of 1934 (Exchange Act), 48 Stat. 891, 15 U.S.C. § 78j(b), and SEC Rule 10b–5, 17 CFR § 240.10b–5 (1996); 17 counts of fraudulent trading in connection with a tender offer, in violation of § 14(e) of the Exchange Act, 15 U.S.C. § 78n(e), and SEC Rule 14e–3(a), 17 CFR § 240.14e–3(a) (1996); and 3 counts of violating federal money laundering statutes, 18 U.S.C. §§ 1956(a)(1)(B)(i), 1957. A jury convicted O'Hagan on all 57 counts, and he was sentenced to a 41-month term of imprisonment.

A divided panel of the Court of Appeals for the Eighth Circuit reversed all of O'Hagan's convictions. 92 F.3d 612 (1996). Liability under § 10(b) and Rule 10b–5, the Eighth Circuit held, may not be grounded on the "misappropriation theory" of securities fraud on which the prosecution relied. The Court of Appeals also held that Rule 14e–3(a)—which prohibits trading while in possession of material, nonpublic information relating to a tender offer—exceeds the SEC's § 14(e) rulemaking authority because the Rule contains no breach of fiduciary duty requirement. The Eighth Circuit further concluded that O'Hagan's mail fraud and money laundering convictions rested on violations of the securities laws, and therefore could not stand once the securities fraud convictions were reversed. Judge Fagg, dissenting, stated that he would recognize and enforce the misappropriation theory, and would hold that the SEC did not exceed its rulemaking authority when it adopted Rule 14e–3(a) without requiring proof of a breach of fiduciary duty.

Decisions of the Courts of Appeals are in conflict on the propriety of the misappropriation theory under § 10(b) and Rule 10b–5, and on the legitimacy of Rule 14e–3(a) under § 14(e). We granted certiorari, 519 U.S. 1087 (1997), and now reverse the Eighth Circuit's judgment.

II

We address first the Court of Appeals' reversal of O'Hagan's convictions under § 10(b) and Rule 10b–5. Following the Fourth Circuit's lead, see United States v. Bryan, 58 F.3d 933, 943–959 (1995), the Eighth Circuit rejected the misappropriation theory as a basis for § 10(b) liability. We hold, in accord with several other Courts of Appeals, that criminal liability under § 10(b) may be predicated on the misappropriation theory.[4]

A

* * *

Under the "traditional" or "classical theory" of insider trading liability, § 10(b) and Rule 10b–5 are violated when a corporate insider trades in the securities of his corporation on the basis of material, nonpublic information. Trading on such information qualifies as a "deceptive device" under § 10(b), we have affirmed, because "a relationship of trust and confidence [exists] between the shareholders of a corporation and those insiders who have obtained confidential information by reason of their position with that corporation." Chiarella v. United States, 445 U.S. 222, 228 (1980). That relationship, we recognized, "gives rise to a duty to disclose [or to abstain from trading] because of the 'necessity of preventing a corporate insider from . . . tak[ing] unfair advantage of . . . uninformed . . . stockholders.'" Id., at 228–229. The classical theory applies not only to officers, directors, and other permanent insiders of a corporation, but also to attorneys, accountants, consultants, and others who temporarily become fiduciaries of a corporation. See Dirks v. SEC, 463 U.S. 646, 655, n.14 (1983).

The "misappropriation theory" holds that a person commits fraud "in connection with" a securities transaction, and thereby violates § 10(b) and Rule 10b–5, when he misappropriates confidential information for securities trading purposes, in breach of a duty owed to the source of the information. Under this theory, a fiduciary's undisclosed, self-serving use of a principal's information to purchase or sell securities, in breach of a duty of loyalty and confidentiality, defrauds the principal of the exclusive use of that information. In lieu of premising liability on a fiduciary relationship between company insider and purchaser or seller of the company's stock, the misappropriation theory premises liability on a fiduciary-turned-trader's deception of those who entrusted him with access to confidential information.

The two theories are complementary, each addressing efforts to capitalize on nonpublic information through the purchase or sale of securities. The classical theory targets a corporate insider's breach of duty to shareholders with whom the insider transacts; the misappropriation theory outlaws trading on the basis of nonpublic

---

[4] Twice before we have been presented with the question whether criminal liability for violation of § 10(b) may be based on a misappropriation theory. In Chiarella v. United States, 445 U.S. 222, 235–237 (1980), the jury had received no misappropriation theory instructions, so we declined to address the question. In Carpenter v. United States, 484 U.S. 19, 24 (1987), the Court divided evenly on whether, under the circumstances of that case, convictions resting on the misappropriation theory should be affirmed. See Aldave, The Misappropriation Theory: Carpenter and Its Aftermath, 49 Ohio St. L.J. 373, 375 (1988) (observing that "Carpenter was, by any reckoning, an unusual case," for the information there misappropriated belonged not to a company preparing to engage in securities transactions, e.g., a bidder in a corporate acquisition, but to the Wall Street Journal).

information by a corporate "outsider" in breach of a duty owed not to a trading party, but to the source of the information. The misappropriation theory is thus designed to "protec[t] the integrity of the securities markets against abuses by 'outsiders' to a corporation who have access to confidential information that will affect th[e] corporation's security price when revealed, but who owe no fiduciary or other duty to that corporation's shareholders."

In this case, the indictment alleged that O'Hagan, in breach of a duty of trust and confidence he owed to his law firm, Dorsey & Whitney, and to its client, Grand Met, traded on the basis of nonpublic information regarding Grand Met's planned tender offer for Pillsbury common stock. This conduct, the Government charged, constituted a fraudulent device in connection with the purchase and sale of securities.[5]

B

We agree with the Government that misappropriation, as just defined, satisfies § 10(b)'s requirement that chargeable conduct involve a "deceptive device or contrivance" used "in connection with" the purchase or sale of securities. We observe, first, that misappropriators, as the Government describes them, deal in deception. A fiduciary who "[pretends] loyalty to the principal while secretly converting the principal's information for personal gain," Brief for United States 17, "dupes" or defrauds the principal. See Aldave, Misappropriation: A General Theory of Liability for Trading on Nonpublic Information, 13 Hofstra L. Rev. 101, 119 (1984).

We addressed fraud of the same species in Carpenter v. United States, 484 U.S. 19 (1987), which involved the mail fraud statute's proscription of "any scheme or artifice to defraud," 18 U.S.C. § 1341. Affirming convictions under that statute, we said in *Carpenter* that an employee's undertaking not to reveal his employer's confidential information "became a sham" when the employee provided the information to his co-conspirators in a scheme to obtain trading profits. A company's confidential information, we recognized in *Carpenter*, qualifies as property to which the company has a right of exclusive use. The undisclosed misappropriation of such information, in violation of a fiduciary duty, the Court said in *Carpenter*, constitutes fraud akin to embezzlement—" 'the fraudulent appropriation to one's own use of the money or goods entrusted to one's care by another.' " *Carpenter's* discussion of the fraudulent misuse of confidential information, the Government notes, "is a particularly apt source of guidance here, because

---

[5] The Government could not have prosecuted O'Hagan under the classical theory, for O'Hagan was not an "insider" of Pillsbury, the corporation in whose stock he traded. Although an "outsider" with respect to Pillsbury, O'Hagan had an intimate association with, and was found to have traded on confidential information from, Dorsey & Whitney, counsel to tender offeror Grand Met. Under the misappropriation theory, O'Hagan's securities trading does not escape Exchange Act sanction, as it would under Justice Thomas' dissenting view, simply because he was associated with, and gained nonpublic information from, the bidder, rather than the target.

[the mail fraud statute] (like Section 10(b)) has long been held to require deception, not merely the breach of a fiduciary duty."

Deception through nondisclosure is central to the theory of liability for which the Government seeks recognition. As counsel for the Government stated in explanation of the theory at oral argument: "To satisfy the common law rule that a trustee may not use the property that [has] been entrusted [to] him, there would have to be consent. To satisfy the requirement of the Securities Act that there be no deception, there would only have to be disclosure." Tr. of Oral Arg. 12; see generally Restatement (Second) of Agency §§ 390, 395 (1958) (agent's disclosure obligation regarding use of confidential information).[6]

The misappropriation theory advanced by the Government is consistent with Santa Fe Industries, Inc. v. Green, 430 U.S. 462 (1977), a decision underscoring that § 10(b) is not an all-purpose breach of fiduciary duty ban; rather, it trains on conduct involving manipulation or deception. In contrast to the Government's allegations in this case, in *Santa Fe Industries*, all pertinent facts were disclosed by the persons charged with violating § 10(b) and Rule 10b–5; therefore, there was no deception through nondisclosure to which liability under those provisions could attach. Similarly, full disclosure forecloses liability under the misappropriation theory: Because the deception essential to the misappropriation theory involves feigning fidelity to the source of information, if the fiduciary discloses to the source that he plans to trade on the nonpublic information, there is no "deceptive device" and thus no § 10(b) violation—although the fiduciary-turned-trader may remain liable under state law for breach of a duty of loyalty.

We turn next to the § 10(b) requirement that the misappropriator's deceptive use of information be "in connection with the purchase or sale of [a] security." This element is satisfied because the fiduciary's fraud is consummated, not when the fiduciary gains the confidential information, but when, without disclosure to his principal, he uses the information to purchase or sell securities. The securities transaction and the breach of duty thus coincide. This is so even though the person or entity defrauded is not the other party to the trade, but is, instead, the source of the nonpublic information. See Aldave, 13 Hofstra L. Rev., at 120 ("a fraud or deceit can be practiced on one person, with resultant harm to another person or group of persons"). A misappropriator who trades on the basis of material, nonpublic information, in short, gains his advantageous

---

[6] Under the misappropriation theory urged in this case, the disclosure obligation runs to the source of the information, here, Dorsey & Whitney and Grand Met. Chief Justice Burger, dissenting in *Chiarella*, advanced a broader reading of § 10(b) and Rule 10b–5; the disclosure obligation, as he envisioned it, ran to those with whom the misappropriator trades. 445 U.S., at 240 ("a person who has misappropriated nonpublic information has an absolute duty to disclose that information or to refrain from trading"). The Government does not propose that we adopt a misappropriation theory of that breadth.

market position through deception; he deceives the source of the information and simultaneously harms members of the investing public.

The misappropriation theory targets information of a sort that misappropriators ordinarily capitalize upon to gain no-risk profits through the purchase or sale of securities. Should a misappropriator put such information to other use, the statute's prohibition would not be implicated. The theory does not catch all conceivable forms of fraud involving confidential information; rather, it catches fraudulent means of capitalizing on such information through securities transactions.

* * *

The misappropriation theory comports with § 10(b)'s language, which requires deception "in connection with the purchase or sale of any security," not deception of an identifiable purchaser or seller. The theory is also well-tuned to an animating purpose of the Exchange Act: to insure honest securities markets and thereby promote investor confidence. See 45 Fed.Reg. 60412 (1980) (trading on misappropriated information "undermines the integrity of, and investor confidence in, the securities markets"). Although informational disparity is inevitable in the securities markets, investors likely would hesitate to venture their capital in a market where trading based on misappropriated nonpublic information is unchecked by law. An investor's informational disadvantage vis-a-vis a misappropriator with material, nonpublic information stems from contrivance, not luck; it is a disadvantage that cannot be overcome with research or skill.

* * *

In sum, considering the inhibiting impact on market participation of trading on misappropriated information, and the congressional purposes underlying § 10(b), it makes scant sense to hold a lawyer like O'Hagan a § 10(b) violator if he works for a law firm representing the target of a tender offer, but not if he works for a law firm representing the bidder. The text of the statute requires no such result.[9] The misappropriation at issue here was properly made the subject of a § 10(b) charge because it meets the statutory requirement that there be "deceptive" conduct "in connection with" securities transactions.

---

[9] As noted earlier, however, the textual requirement of deception precludes § 10(b) liability when a person trading on the basis of nonpublic information has disclosed his trading plans to, or obtained authorization from, the principal—even though such conduct may affect the securities markets in the same manner as the conduct reached by the misappropriation theory. Contrary to Justice Thomas' suggestion, the fact that § 10(b) is only a partial antidote to the problems it was designed to alleviate does not call into question its prohibition of conduct that falls within its textual proscription. Moreover, once a disloyal agent discloses his imminent breach of duty, his principal may seek appropriate equitable relief under state law. Furthermore, in the context of a tender offer, the principal who authorizes an agent's trading on confidential information may, in the Commission's view, incur liability for an Exchange Act violation under Rule 14e–3a.

C

* * *

Chiarella involved securities trades by a printer employed at a shop that printed documents announcing corporate takeover bids. Deducing the names of target companies from documents he handled, the printer bought shares of the targets before takeover bids were announced, expecting (correctly) that the share prices would rise upon announcement. In these transactions, the printer did not disclose to the sellers of the securities (the target companies' shareholders) the nonpublic information on which he traded. For that trading, the printer was convicted of violating § 10(b) and Rule 10b–5. We reversed the Court of Appeals judgment that had affirmed the conviction.

* * *

The Court did not hold in *Chiarella* that the *only* relationship prompting liability for trading on undisclosed information is the relationship between a corporation's insiders and shareholders. That is evident from our response to the Government's argument before this Court that the printer's misappropriation of information from his employer for purposes of securities trading—in violation of a duty of confidentiality owed to the acquiring companies—constituted fraud in connection with the purchase or sale of a security, and thereby satisfied the terms of § 10(b). The Court declined to reach that potential basis for the printer's liability, because the theory had not been submitted to the jury. But four Justices found merit in it. See id., at 239 (Brennan, J., concurring in judgment); id., at 240–243 (Burger, C. J., dissenting); id., at 245 (Blackmun, J., joined by Marshall, J., dissenting). And a fifth Justice stated that the Court "wisely le[ft] the resolution of this issue for another day." Id., at 238 (Stevens, J., concurring).

Chiarella thus expressly left open the misappropriation theory before us today. Certain statements in *Chiarella*, however, led the Eighth Circuit in the instant case to conclude that § 10(b) liability hinges exclusively on a breach of duty owed to a purchaser or seller of securities. The Court said in *Chiarella* that § 10(b) liability "is premised upon a duty to disclose arising from a relationship of trust and confidence *between parties to a transaction*," and observed that the printshop employee defendant in that case "was not a person in whom the sellers had placed their trust and confidence." These statements rejected the notion that § 10(b) stretches so far as to impose "a general duty between all participants in market transactions to forgo actions based on material, nonpublic information," and we confine them to that context. The statements highlighted by the Eighth Circuit, in short, appear in an opinion carefully leaving for future resolution the validity of the misappropriation theory, and therefore cannot be read to foreclose that theory.

Dirks, too, left room for application of the misappropriation theory in cases like the one we confront. *Dirks* involved an investment analyst who had received information from a former insider of a corporation with which the analyst had no connection. The information indicated that the corporation had engaged in a massive fraud. The analyst investigated the fraud, obtaining corroborating information from employees of the corporation. During his investigation, the analyst discussed his findings with clients and investors, some of whom sold their holdings in the company the analyst suspected of gross wrongdoing.

The SEC censured the analyst for, *inter alia*, aiding and abetting § 10(b) and Rule 10b–5 violations by clients and investors who sold their holdings based on the nonpublic information the analyst passed on. In the SEC's view, the analyst, as a "tippee" of corporation insiders, had a duty under § 10(b) and Rule 10b–5 to refrain from communicating the nonpublic information to persons likely to trade on the basis of it. This Court found no such obligation, and repeated the key point made in *Chiarella*: There is no " 'general duty between all participants in market transactions to forgo actions based on material, nonpublic information.' " 463 U.S. at 655 (quoting Chiarella, 445 U.S., at 233); see Aldave, 13 Hofstra L. Rev., at 122 (misappropriation theory bars only "trading on the basis of information that the wrongdoer converted to his own use in violation of some fiduciary, contractual, or similar obligation to the owner or rightful possessor of the information").

No showing had been made in *Dirks* that the "tippers" had violated any duty by disclosing to the analyst nonpublic information about their former employer. The insiders had acted not for personal profit, but to expose a massive fraud within the corporation. Absent any violation by the tippers, there could be no derivative liability for the tippee. Most important for purposes of the instant case, the Court observed in *Dirks*: "There was no expectation by [the analyst's] sources that he would keep their information in confidence. Nor did [the analyst] misappropriate or illegally obtain the information. . . ." *Dirks* thus presents no suggestion that a person who gains nonpublic information through misappropriation in breach of a fiduciary duty escapes § 10(b) liability when, without alerting the source, he trades on the information.

* * *

In sum, the misappropriation theory, as we have examined and explained it in this opinion, is both consistent with the statute and with our precedent.[11] Vital to our decision that criminal liability may be

---

[11] The United States additionally argues that Congress confirmed the validity of the misappropriation theory in the Insider Trading and Securities Fraud Enforcement Act of 1988 (ITSFEA), § 2(1), 102 Stat. 4677, note following 15 U.S.C. § 78u–1. See Brief for United States 32–35. ITSFEA declares that "the rules and regulations of the Securities and Exchange Commission under the Securities Exchange Act of 1934 . . . governing trading while in possession of material, nonpublic information are, as required by such Act, necessary and appropriate in the public interest and for the protection of investors." Note following 15 U.S.C. § 78u–1. ITSFEA also includes a new § 20A(a) of the Exchange Act expressly providing a private

sustained under the misappropriation theory, we emphasize, are two sturdy safeguards Congress has provided regarding scienter. To establish a criminal violation of Rule 10b–5, the Government must prove that a person "willfully" violated the provision. See 15 U.S.C. § 78ff(a). Furthermore, a defendant may not be imprisoned for violating Rule 10b–5 if he proves that he had no knowledge of the Rule. See ibid.[13] O'Hagan's charge that the misappropriation theory is too indefinite to permit the imposition of criminal liability, thus fails not only because the theory is limited to those who breach a recognized duty. In addition, the statute's "requirement of the presence of culpable intent as a necessary element of the offense does much to destroy any force in the argument that application of the [statute]" in circumstances such as O'Hagan's is unjust. Boyce Motor Lines, Inc. v. United States, 342 U.S. 337, 342 (1952).

The Eighth Circuit erred in holding that the misappropriation theory is inconsistent with § 10(b). The Court of Appeals may address on remand O'Hagan's other challenges to his convictions under § 10(b) and Rule 10b–5.

* * *

WHO HAS A DUTY TO DISCLOSE AND SEC REGULATIONS

1. *Generally.* *Chiarella*, *Dirks*, and *O'Hagan* make clear that only one with a duty to disclose is subject to the Rule 10b–5 disclose or abstain rule. *Chiarella* emphatically rejected the "egalitarian" or parity-of-information theory implicit in the Second Circuit's holding that "[a]nyone corporate insider or not who regularly receives material nonpublic information may not use that information to trade in securities without incurring an affirmative duty to disclose."[33]

2. *The Misappropriation Theory.* In *O'Hagan* the Court held that "a person commits fraud 'in connection with' a securities transaction, and thereby violates § 10(b) and Rule 10b–5, when he misappropriates confidential information for securities trading purposes, in breach of a duty to the source of the information. * * * In lieu of premising liability on a fiduciary relationship between company insider and purchaser or seller of the company's stock, the misappropriation theory premises

---

cause of action against persons who violate the Exchange Act "by purchasing or selling a security while in possession of material, nonpublic information;" such an action may be brought by "any person who, contemporaneously with the purchase or sale of securities that is the subject of such violation, has purchased ... or sold ... securities of the same class." 15 U.S.C. § 78t–1(a). Because we uphold the misappropriation theory on the basis of § 10(b) itself, we do not address ITSFEA's significance for cases of this genre.

[13] The statute provides no such defense to imposition of monetary fines. See ibid.

[33] United States v. Chiarella, 588 F.2d 1358, 1365 (2d Cir. 1978). Necessarily this also amounted to a rejection of the similar egalitarian theory articulated in SEC v. Texas Gulf Sulphur Co., 401 F.2d 833, 848 (2d Cir. 1968), cert. denied sub nom. Coates v. SEC, 394 U.S. 976 (1969).

liability on a fiduciary-turned-trader's deception of those who entrusted him with access to confidential information."[34]

O'Hagan suggests (but does not clearly conclude) that if the owner of the information authorizes the trader to use the information, there would be no misappropriation, and therefore no liability under Rule 10b–5. Thus, if the client gave the permission to trade, and the law firm authorized the lawyer to trade (or to tip), there would be no case. Does the fact that no law firms or any other firms with access to this kind of information has authorized this kind of trading (that we know of) suggest something about the appropriateness of insider-trading rules? Note also that if a CEO disclosed material nonpublic information to an investor and authorized the investor to trade on it, this would amount to selective disclosure and likely violate Regulation FD, which is discussed shortly. Also, such a disclosure might amount to a "gift" of information in violation of *Dirks*.

3. *Proving Misappropriation.* Proof of misappropriation requires proof of deception of the source of the information. Here O'Hagan deceived both his law firm and Grand Met, the firm that employed the law firm. The misappropriation theory does not create a duty that runs to those with whom the misappropriator traded. Although not directly addressed in *O'Hagan*, the Supreme Court's approach would seem capable of reaching "a judge's law clerk who trades on information in an unpublished opinion or a Government employee who trades on a secret report."[35] The misappropriation theory has also been applied in instances that did not involve a violation of a duty to an employer.[36]

Under the misappropriation theory the plaintiff's burden is simplified. Proving a tippee's scienter can be a major stumbling block. The tippee must know of a benefit to the tipper. The same tippee, however, can be held liable under the misappropriation theory if it can be shown that the misappropriator knew that he or she wrongly took another's information. The misappropriation scienter element seems far more appropriate for certain types of wrongdoing. For example, if a businessperson in Corporation *A* proposes a transaction to a second businessperson in Corporation *B* solely for the purpose of fraudulently securing Corporation *B*'s proprietary information, it would be highly difficult to establish tipping liability. Disclosure of this data by the Corporation *B* businessperson would appear to be consistent with his other underlying fiduciary duties. Under tipping analysis, since the Corporation *A* businessperson would know that the Corporation *B* businessperson had not violated a fiduciary duty, he or she would appear

---

[34] 521 U.S. 642, 652.

[35] These had been Burger's concerns in *Chiarella*. See 445 U.S. 222, 242 n.3.

[36] SEC v. Willis, 777 F.Supp. 1165 (S.D.N.Y. 1991) (holding liable a psychiatrist who traded on the basis of a patient's disclosures about her husband's inside information).

to be free to trade. The result is troubling, because the *A* businessperson had engaged in a fraud or deceit to secure the data.

Under misappropriation analysis, if the plaintiff can prove that a businessperson secretly traded on the basis of the confidential data, insider trading can be proved. This type of scienter analysis better aligns the proof of a fraud or deceit with the knowledge of a wrong than tippee liability under the *Dirks* paradigm, preventing a free ride for tippees who trade for personal benefit whenever the tipper has not also secured a personal benefit.

4. *Rule 10b5–1: The SEC Responds to the "Use or Possession" Debate.* An unsettled issue in insider trading law had surrounded the need, if any, to show a causal connection between the trader's possession of inside information and the trader's decision to trade. The SEC had argued that it need show only "knowing possession," but some cases have required a showing of "use," recognizing that possession may establish a strong inference of use.[37] To resolve this conflict, the SEC adopted Rule 10b5–1.

Rule 10b5–1 defines a trade or sale to have occurred "on the basis of" material nonpublic information at the time of the purchase or sale. However, the rule also created an important safe harbor from liability when the trade results from a preexisting plan, contract, or instruction made in good faith.

Specifically, Rule 10b5–1(c)(1)(i) creates an affirmative defense from the general rule of liability if the following factors can be established:

1. Before becoming aware of the information, the person entered into a binding contract to purchase or sell the security, provided instructions to another person to execute the trade for its account, or adopted a written plan for trading securities;

2. The contract, instruction or plan either expressly specified the amount, price, and date or provided a written formula or algorithm, and dates, or did not permit the person to exercise any subsequent influence.

3. No alteration or deviation from the prior contract, instruction, or plan occurred after the time that the person became aware of the material nonpublic information.

Thus, if (i) a corporate executive establishes a written plan with his broker instructing the broker to sell 10% of the executive's holdings in the company each year (or quarter), (ii) the broker was not itself aware of the material nonpublic information, and (iii) the executive did not modify the plan after becoming aware of material, nonpublic information or otherwise exercise influence over the broker's trading, the written plan or instruction enables the executive to buy or sell his company's stock

---

[37] See SEC v. Adler, 137 F.3d 1325, 1337 (11th Cir. 1998); United States v. Smith, 155 F.3d 1051, 1069 & n.27 (9th Cir. 1998) ("use" must be proven in a criminal case).

without fear of incurring insider trading liability. Rule 10b5–1 plans are becoming a standard part of corporate life. They enable executives to meet expected financial commitments through stock sales and simplify the need for pre-clearance by corporate counsel. In addition, they permit the executive to exercise stock options and immediately sell the underlying stock on a pre-arranged timetable. The corporation, itself, can also use such a plan to effect stock repurchases without having to halt them when it becomes aware of material information.

The cancellation of a 10b5–1 trading plan, while in possession of material nonpublic information, does not implicate § 10(b) or Rule 10b–5 liability. The SEC limits liability to transactions "in connection with" the *purchase* or *sale* of any security. A refusal to trade on material nonpublic information, standing alone, creates no insider trading liability. This interpretation of Rule 10b5–1 creates a valuable option for insiders at little or no cost. Consider an insider who is highly confident that in nine months the FDA will approve the firm's only drug. The insider nevertheless enters into a Rule 10b5–1 trading plan to sell a large block of stock a few weeks before the FDA's scheduled announcement. If as the announcement approaches the insider learns the drug will be approved as expected, the insider merely cancels the planned trades. But, if the insider learns the FDA is likely to rule the other way, the planned trades execute. In this case, the government's case against the insider will be much more difficult than had a plan not been used. Circumstantial evidence, especially coincidental timing, is a large part of the proof of these cases, and proving an insider had knowledge nine months earlier is more difficult than proving an insider had knowledge three weeks before announcement.

The cancellation of a Rule 10b5–1(c) plan may, however, call into doubt whether the plan was initially "entered into in good faith and not as a part of a plan or scheme to evade" insider trading rules. Canceling a Rule 10b5–1(c) plan may, additionally, limit the affirmative defense's future availability if the individual that cancelled the plan attempts to enter into another 10b–5(1)(c) plan at a later date. At that time, all of the surrounding facts and circumstances of the earlier plan, its cancellation, and the timing of the cancellation, are relevant in determining whether the person established the new plan "in good faith and not as part of a plan or scheme to evade."

The empirical evidence strongly suggests insiders are using Rule 10b5–1 to *increase* abnormal trading returns, which is contrary to the SEC's stated intent in adopting the Rule. Studies by Alan Jagolinzer, and Todd Henderson, and Karl Muller show that insiders trading in these plans systematically outperform what random trades would suggest, and that, counter-intuitively, insiders who disclose more details about their trading plans earn the greatest abnormal returns.[38] Why would that be?

5. *Rule 10b5–2.* Another unsettled issue in insider trading law involves the circumstances under which non-business relationships, such as family and personal relationships, give rise to the duty of trust or confidence required under misappropriation theory. In United States v. Chestman,[39] a wife passed information about an approaching merger and tender offer to her husband, who then tipped his broker who traded. Nonetheless, the Second Circuit found no liability under Rule 10b–5, because it said no fiduciary relationship existed between the husband and wife with respect to confidential business information. Rule 10b5–2 effectively overrules *Chestman* and curtails the need in many instances to inquire into the minute details of personal relationships. It specifies three non-exclusive situations in which a duty of trust or confidence arises for purposes of misappropriation theory and Rule 10b–5:

1. Whenever a person agrees to maintain information in trust or confidence;

2. When two people have a history, pattern or practice of sharing confidences such that the recipient of the information knows or reasonably should know that the person communicating the material nonpublic information expects that the recipient will maintain its confidentiality; and

3. When a person receives or obtains material nonpublic information from certain enumerated close family members: spouses, parents, children, and siblings. An affirmative defense is available if the defendant can show that no duty of trust or confidence existed in the actual family relationship.

Rule 10b5–2 effectively "federalizes" the state law of family relationships for purposes of Rule 10b–5. Long-time domestic partners who are unmarried are potentially subject to liability under clause 2 above, not the automatic language of clause 3.

---

[38] See Alan D. Jagolinzer, "SEC Rule 10b5–1 and Insiders' Strategic Trade," 55 *Mgmt. Science* 224 (2009); M. Todd Henderson, et al., "Offensive Disclosure: How Voluntary Disclosure Can Increase Returns from Insider Trading," 103 Geo. L. J. 1775 (2015).

[39] 947 F.2d 551 (2d Cir. 1991) (en banc).

D. The Second Circuit's Gift Theory

United States v. Martoma
United States Court of Appeals, Second Circuit, 2017 (Amended 2018).
894 F.3d 64.

■ Before: Katzmann, Chief Judge, Pooler and Chin Circuit Judges.

■ Katzmann, Chief Judge:

Defendant-appellant Mathew Martoma was convicted, following a four-week jury trial, of one count of conspiracy to commit securities fraud in violation of 18 U.S.C. § 371 and two counts of securities fraud in violation of 15 U.S.C. §§ 78j(b) & 78ff in connection with an insider trading scheme. On appeal, Martoma argues that the jury was improperly instructed and that there was insufficient evidence to sustain his conviction.

Martoma's contentions focus on the "personal benefit" element of insider trading law. In *Dirks v. S.E.C.*, the Supreme Court held that a "tippee"—someone who receives confidential information from a corporate insider, or "tipper," and then trades on the information—can be held liable under the insider trading laws "only when the insider has breached his fiduciary duty to the shareholders by disclosing the information to the tippee and the tippee knows or should know that there has been a breach." 463 U.S. 646, 660 (1983). "[T]he test" for whether there has been a breach of the tipper's duty "is whether the [tipper] personally will benefit, directly or indirectly, from his disclosure" to the tippee. *Id.* at 662. *Dirks* set forth several personal benefits that could prove the tipper's breach, including, for example, "a relationship" between the tipper and tippee "that suggests a *quid pro quo* from the latter," the tipper's "intention to benefit" the tippee, and "a gift of confidential information to a trading relative or friend" where "[t]he tip and trade resemble trading by the insider himself followed by a gift of the profits to the recipient." *Id.* at 664.

Martoma first argues that the jury in his case was not properly instructed in light of the Second Circuit's decision in *United States v. Newman*, 773 F.3d 438 (2d Cir. 2014). Martoma asserts that, under *Newman*, evidence that the tipper made a gift of inside information to a trading relative or friend establishes a "personal benefit" only if tipper and tippee share a "meaningfully close personal relationship." *See Newman*, 773 F.3d at 452. Martoma contends that the jury instructions were flawed because they did not qualify that evidence of a gift to a trading relative or friend establishes a personal benefit only where there is a "meaningfully close personal relationship." Second, Martoma argues that the evidence at trial was insufficient to sustain a conviction under any theory of personal benefit.

We agree that the jury instructions are inconsistent with *Newman*, though not for the reasons Martoma advances. *Newman* held that a personal benefit in the form of "a gift of confidential information to a trading relative or friend," *see Dirks*, 463 U.S. at 664, requires proof that the tipper and tippee shared what the decision called a "meaningfully close personal relationship," *see Newman*, 773 F.3d at 452. The Court explained that this standard "requires evidence of 'a relationship between the insider and the recipient that suggests a *quid pro quo* from the latter, or an intention to benefit the [latter].'" *Id.* (quoting *United States v. Jiau*, 734 F.3d 147, 153 (2d Cir. 2013) (quoting *Dirks*, 463 U.S. at 664)). Thus, Martoma's jury instructions were erroneous, not because they omitted the term "meaningfully close personal relationship," but because they allowed the jury to find a personal benefit in the form of a "gift of confidential information to a trading relative or friend" without requiring the jury to find either that tipper and tippee shared a relationship suggesting a *quid pro quo* or that the tipper gifted confidential information with the intention to benefit the tippee.

We nonetheless conclude that this instructional error did not affect Martoma's substantial rights. At trial, the government presented compelling evidence that at least one tipper received a different type of personal benefit from disclosing inside information: $70,000 in "consulting fees." This evidence establishes the existence of a relationship suggesting a *quid pro quo* between the tipper and tippee. For this reason, Martoma's challenge to the sufficiency of the personal benefit evidence fails. Moreover, the government presented sufficient evidence for a rational trier of fact to conclude that at least one tipper received a personal benefit by disclosing inside information with the intention to benefit Martoma. Accordingly, we AFFIRM the judgment of the district court.

BACKGROUND

Martoma's convictions stem from an insider trading scheme involving securities of two pharmaceutical companies, Elan Corporation, plc ("Elan") and Wyeth, that were jointly developing an experimental drug called bapineuzumab to treat Alzheimer's disease. Martoma worked as a portfolio manager at S.A.C. Capital Advisors ("SAC"), a hedge fund owned and managed by Steven A. Cohen. In that capacity, Martoma managed an investment portfolio with buying power of between $400 and $500 million that was focused on pharmaceutical and healthcare companies. He also recommended investments to Cohen, who managed SAC's largest portfolio. While at SAC, Martoma began to acquire shares in Elan and Wyeth in his portfolio and recommended that Cohen acquire shares in the companies as well.

In order to obtain information about bapineuzumab, Martoma contacted expert networking firms and arranged paid consultations with doctors knowledgeable about Alzheimer's disease, including two who were working on the bapineuzumab clinical trial. Dr. Sidney Gilman, chair of the safety monitoring committee for the bapineuzumab clinical trial, participated in approximately 43 consultations with Martoma at the rate of around $1,000 per hour.[1] As a member of the safety monitoring committee, Dr. Gilman had an obligation to keep the results of the clinical trial confidential. His consulting contract reiterated that he was not to disclose any confidential information in a consultation. He nevertheless provided Martoma, whom he knew to be an investment manager seeking information to help make securities trading decisions, with confidential updates on the drug's safety that he received during meetings of the safety monitoring committee. Dr. Gilman also shared with Martoma the dates of upcoming safety monitoring committee meetings, which allowed Martoma to schedule consultations with Dr. Gilman shortly after each one. Another consultant, Dr. Joel Ross, one of the principal investigators on the clinical trial, met with Martoma on many occasions between 2006 and July 2008 and charged approximately $1,500 per hour. Like Dr. Gilman, Dr. Ross had an obligation to maintain the confidentiality of information about the bapineuzumab clinical trial. Nevertheless, during their consultations, Dr. Ross provided Martoma with information about the clinical trial, including information about his patients' responses to the drug and the total number of participants in the study, that Dr. Ross recognized was not public. . . .

In mid-July of 2008, the sponsors of the bapineuzumab trial selected Dr. Gilman to present the results at the July 29 conference. It was only at this point that Dr. Gilman was unblinded as to the final efficacy results of the trial. Dr. Gilman was "initially euphoric" about the results, but identified "two major weaknesses in the data" that called into question the efficacy of the drug as compared to the placebo. Tr. 1419–20. On July 17, 2008, the day after being unblinded to the results, Dr. Gilman spoke with Martoma for about 90 minutes by telephone about what he had learned. That same day, Martoma purchased a plane ticket to see Dr. Gilman in person at his office in Ann Arbor, Michigan. That meeting occurred two days later, on July 19, 2008. At that meeting, Dr. Gilman showed Martoma a PowerPoint presentation containing the efficacy results and discussed the data with him in detail.

The next morning, Sunday, July 20, Martoma sent Cohen, the owner of SAC, an email with "It's important" in the subject line and asked to speak with him by telephone. The two had a telephone conversation lasting about twenty minutes, after which Martoma emailed Cohen a summary of SAC's Elan and Wyeth holdings. The day after Martoma spoke to Cohen, on July 21, 2008, SAC began to reduce its position in Elan and Wyeth securities and entered into short-sale and options trades that would be profitable if Elan's and Wyeth's stock fell.

---

[1] Martoma did not pay Dr. Gilman or any other consultant directly. Instead, SAC would pay the expert networking firm, and the expert networking firm would in turn pay Dr. Gilman and the other consultants.

Dr. Gilman publicly presented the final results from the bapineuzumab trial at the International Conference on Alzehimer's Disease in the afternoon of July 29, 2008. Elan's share price began to decline during Dr. Gilman's presentation and at the close of trading the next day, the share prices of Elan's and Wyeth had declined by about 42% and 12%, respectively. The trades that Martoma and Cohen made in advance of the announcement resulted in approximately $80.3 million in gains and $194.6 million in averted losses for SAC. Martoma personally received a $9 million bonus based in large part on his trading activity in Elan and Wyeth.

At Martoma's trial, the district court instructed the jury on the personal benefit element of insider trading law as follows:

> If you find that Dr. Gilman or Dr. Ross disclosed material, non-public information to Mr. Martoma, you must then determine whether the government proved beyond a reasonable doubt that Dr. Gilman and Dr. Ross received or anticipated receiving some personal benefit, direct or indirect, from disclosing the material, non-public information at issue.
>
> The benefit may, but need not be, financial or tangible in nature; it could include obtaining some future advantage, developing or maintaining a business contact or a friendship, or enhancing the tipper's reputation.
>
> A finding as to benefit should be based on all the objective facts and inferences presented in the case. You may find that Dr. Gilman or Dr. Ross received a direct or indirect personal benefit from providing inside information to Mr. Martoma if you find that Dr. Gilman or Dr. Ross gave the information to Mr. Martoma with the intention of benefiting themselves in some manner, or with the intention of conferring a benefit on Mr. Martoma, or as a gift with the goal of maintaining or developing a personal friendship or a useful networking contact.

Tr. 3191.

After Martoma was convicted and while his appeal was pending, this Court decided *United States v. Newman,* 773 F.3d 438 (2d Cir. 2014), an insider trading case that considered one of the personal benefits described in *Dirks* and mentioned in Martoma's jury instructions—making a "gift" of inside information to "a trading relative or friend."[2] This Court stated:

> To the extent *Dirks* suggests that a personal benefit may be inferred from a personal relationship between the tipper and tippee, where the tippee's trades 'resemble trading by the insider himself followed by a gift of the profits to the recipient,' see 463 U.S. at 664, we hold that such an inference is

---

[2] For convenience, we sometimes refer to this as the "gift theory" of personal benefit.

impermissible in the absence of proof of a meaningfully close personal relationship that generates an exchange that is objective, consequential, and represents at least a potential gain of a pecuniary or similarly valuable nature.

773 F.3d at 452. An initial round of briefing focused in large part on whether Martoma's conviction could stand in light of this passage from *Newman*.

Shortly thereafter, the Supreme Court decided *Salman v. United States,* 137 S.Ct. 420 (2016), another case involving the gift theory. The defendant, relying on *Newman*, urged the Supreme Court to hold that a " 'gift of confidential information to a trading relative or friend' " is insufficient to establish insider trading liability "unless the tipper's goal in disclosing inside information [wa]s to obtain money, property, or something of tangible value." *Id.* at 426 (quoting *Dirks,* 463 U.S. at 664). The Supreme Court rejected the defendant's argument and "adhere[d] to *Dirks,*" *id.* at 427, observing that "[t]o the extent the Second Circuit held that the tipper must also receive something of a 'pecuniary or similarly valuable nature' in exchange for a gift to family or friends, . . . this requirement is inconsistent with *Dirks,*" *id.* at 428 (quoting *Newman,* 773 F.3d at 452); *see also id.* ("Here, by disclosing confidential information as a gift to his brother with the expectation that he would trade on it, Maher breached his duty of trust and confidence to Citigroup and its clients. . . .").

The government now takes the position that *Salman* fully abrogated *Newman*'s interpretation of the personal benefit element, whereas Martoma argues that *Newman*'s "meaningfully close personal relationship" standard survived *Salman*. However, because there are many ways to establish a personal benefit, we conclude that we need not decide whether *Newman*'s gloss on the gift theory is inconsistent with *Salman*. At trial, the government presented compelling evidence that Dr. Gilman received a different type of personal benefit: $70,000 in consulting fees, which can be seen either as evidence of a *quid pro quo*-like relationship, or simply advance payments for the tips of inside information that Dr. Gilman went on to supply. The government also introduced sufficient evidence to prove Dr. Gilman received a personal benefit by disclosing inside information with the intention to benefit Martoma. We accordingly conclude that Martoma has provided no basis for his judgment of conviction to be vacated or reversed.

DISCUSSION

As noted above, Martoma challenges both the adequacy of the district court's jury instructions and the sufficiency of the evidence presented at trial . . .

* * *

I.

We first turn to Martoma's challenge to the district court's jury instructions, which focuses on *Dirks*' statement that the personal benefit necessary to establish insider trading liability in a tipping case can be inferred from a "gift of confidential information to a trading relative or friend." *Dirks*, 463 U.S. at 663–64; *see also Salman*, 137 S.Ct. at 428. Martoma argues that the district court's jury instructions ran afoul of this Court's decision in *Newman* by permitting the jury to conclude that a gift of confidential information given with the goal of "developing or maintaining . . . a friendship" qualifies as a personal benefit. According to Martoma, the jury should have been instructed that the tipper and tippee must share a "meaningfully close personal relationship" in order to find a personal benefit based on a gift of inside information to a friend.

A. The Personal Benefit Requirement

The Supreme Court long ago held that there is no "general duty between all participants in market transactions to forgo actions based on material, nonpublic information." *Chiarella v. United States*, 445 U.S. 222, 233 (1980). However, the "traditional" or "classical theory" of insider trading provides that a corporate insider violates § 10(b) of the Securities Exchange Act of 1934, 15 U.S.C. § 78j(b), and Rule 10b–5 when he "trades in the securities of his corporation on the basis of material, non-public information" because "a relationship of trust and confidence [exists] between the shareholders of a corporation and those insiders who have obtained confidential information by reason of their position with that corporation." *United States v. O'Hagan*, 521 U.S. 642, 651–52 (1997) (alteration in original) (quoting *Chiarella*, 445 U.S. at 228). Similarly, the "misappropriation theory" of insider trading provides "that a person . . . violates § 10(b) and Rule 10b–5 when he misappropriates confidential information for securities trading purposes, in breach of a duty owed to the source of the information." *Id.* at 652. It is thus the breach of a fiduciary duty or other "duty of loyalty and confidentiality" that is a necessary predicate to insider trading liability. *See id.*[5]

The personal benefit element has its origin in *Dirks*, where the Supreme Court examined how a recipient of inside information who was not himself a corporate insider—*i.e.*, a tippee—can acquire a duty to disclose or abstain from trading. The Supreme Court held that a tippee acquires the duty to disclose or abstain only if the insider disclosed the confidential information in breach of a fiduciary duty to the firm. *Dirks*, 463 U.S. at 660–61. "Whether disclosure is a breach of duty," the Supreme Court explained, "depends in large part on the purpose of the disclosure." *Id.* at 662. The personal benefit requirement is designed to

---

[5] Although many of the cases refer to "insiders" and "fiduciary" duties because those cases involve the "classical theory" of insider trading, the *Dirks* articulation of tipper and tippee liability also applies under the misappropriation theory, where the misappropriator violates some duty owed to the source of the information. *See S.E.C. v. Obus*, 693 F.3d 276, 286–88 (2d Cir. 2012); *see also Newman*, 773 F.3d at 445–46.

test the propriety of the tipper's purpose. *See id.* at 661–63. This logic is sound. A firm's confidential information belongs to the firm itself, and an insider entrusted with it has a fiduciary duty to use it only for firm purposes. The insider who personally benefits—*i.e.*, whose purpose is to help himself—from disclosing confidential information therefore breaches that duty; the insider who discloses for a legitimate corporate purpose does not. Identifying personal benefits is not, however, the central focus of insider trading law, but simply how courts and juries analyze breaches of fiduciary duty.

The Supreme Court defined personal benefit broadly. As noted above, the test for a personal benefit is whether objective evidence shows that "the insider personally will benefit, directly or indirectly, from his disclosure" of confidential information to the tippee. *Id.* at 662. *Dirks* set forth numerous examples of personal benefits that prove the tipper's breach: a "pecuniary gain," a "reputational benefit that will translate into future earning," a "relationship between the insider and the recipient that suggests a *quid pro quo* from the latter," the tipper's "intention to benefit the particular recipient," and a "gift of confidential information to a trading relative or friend" where "[t]he tip and trade resemble trading by the insider himself followed by a gift of the profits to the recipient." *Id.* at 663–64. The tipper's personal benefit need not be pecuniary in nature. *See Salman,* 137 S.Ct. at 428.

We have applied *Dirks* to uphold a wide variety of personal benefits. We held that a jury could infer a personal benefit from the fact that a tipper "hoped to curry favor with his boss," *Obus,* 693 F.3d at 292, and from the fact that another tipper and the tippee "were friends from college," *id.* at 291. We found evidence of a personal benefit sufficient where the tippee gave one tipper "an iPhone, live lobsters, a gift card, and a jar of honey," and where the tippee had another tipper admitted into an investment club where the tipper "had the opportunity to access information that could yield future pecuniary gain" (even though he never realized that opportunity). *Jiau,* 734 F.3d at 153. In another case, we held that the government "need not show that the tipper expected or received a specific or tangible benefit in exchange for the tip," and that the personal benefit element is satisfied where there is evidence that the tipper "intend[ed] to benefit the . . . recipient." *S.E.C. v. Warde,* 151 F.3d 42, 48 (2d Cir. 1998) (internal quotation marks omitted).

As we understand the dissent, our core disagreement is over whether intent to benefit is a standalone personal benefit under *Dirks*. The dissent argues that it is not, claiming instead that the correct formulation is a "relationship . . . that suggests . . . an intention to benefit" the tippee. *See* Dissent, op. at 53–54. The key sentence of *Dirks* is admittedly ambiguous, and we acknowledge that the dissent has offered a plausible reading. *See* 463 U.S. at 664 ("For example, there may be a relationship between the insider and the recipient that suggests a *quid pro quo* from the latter, or an intention to benefit the particular recipient."). But that is not the only reading. The comma separating the "intention to benefit" and "relationship . . . suggesting a *quid pro quo*" phrases can be read to sever any connection between them. The sentence, so understood, effectively reads, "there may be a relationship between the insider and the recipient that suggests a *quid pro quo* from the latter, or there may be an intention to benefit the particular recipient." And that is the reading this Court adopted in *Warde*, where we read the "intention to benefit" language independently of the language of relationships: "The 'benefit' element of § 10(b) is satisfied when the tipper 'intend[s] to benefit the . . . recipient' or 'makes a gift of confidential information to a trading relative or friend.'" *Warde*, 151 F.3d at 48 (quoting *Dirks*, 463 U.S. at 664). We adhere to *Warde*.

Our understanding is also more consonant with *Dirks* as a whole. Because the existence of a breach "depends in large part on the purpose of the disclosure," *Dirks*, 463 U.S. at 662, it makes perfect sense to permit the government to prove a personal benefit with objective evidence of the tipper's intent, without requiring in every case some additional evidence of the tipper-tippee relationship. *Cf. United States v. Falcone*, 257 F.3d 226, 230 (2d Cir. 2001) (Sotomayor, J.) (explaining that "the key factor" in proving a personal benefit is "the tipper's intent in providing the information"). For example, suppose a tipper discloses inside information to a perfect stranger and says, in effect, you can make a lot of money by trading on this. Under the dissent's approach, this plain evidence that the tipper intended to benefit the tippee would be insufficient to show a breach of the tipper's fiduciary duty to the firm due to the lack of a personal relationship. *Dirks* and *Warde* do not demand such a result. Rather, the statement "you can make a lot of money by trading on this," following the disclosure of material non-public information, suggests an intention to benefit the tippee in breach of the insider's fiduciary duty.

We are not persuaded by our dissenting colleague's arguments to the contrary. The dissent contends that proof that the tipper had an intent to benefit the *tippee* does not prove that the *tipper* truly "received" a personal benefit. *See* Dissent, op. at 84–85. The dissent would evidently have there be proof of something more concrete. However, as we have explained, it is settled law that personal benefits may be indirect and intangible and need not be pecuniary at all. The tipper's intention to benefit the tippee proves a breach of fiduciary duty because it demonstrates that the tipper improperly used inside information for personal ends and thus lacked a legitimate corporate purpose. That is precisely what, under *Dirks*, the personal benefit element is designed to test. *See* 463 U.S. at 662. Is evidence that an insider intended to benefit an outsider with valuable confidential information any less probative of the absence of a legitimate corporate purpose than evidence that the tippee gave the tipper trivialities like shellfish and a gift card? *See Jiau*, 734 F.3d at 153.

The dissent argues that its formulation is more faithful to the personal benefit standard because evidence of a relationship suggesting an intent to benefit the tippee "provides reason to believe that the tipper benefits by benefitting, since the tipper is understood as contributing to a relationship from which both tipper and tippee benefit," a rationale that does not apply where there has been no proof of a relationship. Dissent, op. at 86. We disagree. That rationale would justify a personal benefit in the form of a relationship suggesting an intention to benefit both tipper and tippee, from which it is straightforward to infer that the tipper personally benefited from the tip. But what *Dirks* in fact refers to is an intention to benefit the tippee alone. *See* 463 U.S. at 664. Whichever way *Dirks* is read, it recognizes that purposely benefitting the tippee with inside information proves that the tipper has received a personal benefit in breach of a fiduciary duty. The question is whether *Dirks* requires that to be proved with evidence of a relationship or not. We think it clear that the answer is no. And although few reported decisions have relied on the intent to benefit theory, its legitimacy has until today been uncontroversial. To take an example close to home, it featured in the jury instructions in this very case, *see* Tr. 3191, and no objection was raised, nor was any challenge to this language pressed on appeal.

Finally, we are warned that this approach creates a "subjective" test and allows for convictions based on sheer speculation into the tipper's motives. *See* Dissent, op. at 83–84, 88. These fears are unwarranted. Intent elements are everywhere in our law and are generally proved with circumstantial evidence. *See, e.g., United States v. Heras,* 609 F.3d 101, 106 (2d Cir. 2010) "The law has long recognized that criminal intent may be proved by circumstantial evidence alone."); *United States v. Salameh,* 152 F.3d 88, 143 (2d Cir. 1998) "[A]s a general rule most evidence of intent is circumstantial."). Insider trading is no different. A factfinder may infer the tipper intended to benefit the tippee from the sort of objective evidence that is commonly offered in insider trading cases. To return to the example above, the statement "you can make a lot of money by trading on this" is strong circumstantial evidence of the tipper's intention to benefit the tippee. And the requirement of proof beyond a reasonable doubt remains a formidable barrier to convictions resting on speculation. *See United States v. Torres,* 604 F.3d 58, 66 (2d Cir. 2010).

We are thus satisfied that the personal benefit element can be met by evidence that the tipper's disclosure of inside information was intended to benefit the tippee. And as is clear from the purpose of the personal benefit element, the "broad definition of personal benefit set forth in *Dirks*," and the variety of benefits we have upheld, the evidentiary "bar is not a high one." *Obus,* 693 F.3d at 292.

B. This Court's Decision in Newman

It is against that background that we must assess how *Newman* affected this Court's insider trading law. The central question in *Newman* was an issue of scienter on which our district courts had been split: whether a tippee must be aware, not only that the tipper breached a fiduciary duty in disclosing inside information, but also that the tipper received a personal benefit. *Newman*, 773 F.3d at 447–51. The Court persuasively explained that both were required. *Id.* at 449 ("[A] tippee's knowledge of the insider's breach necessarily requires knowledge that the insider disclosed confidential information in exchange for personal benefit."). This important teaching of *Newman* is not before us. We observe that, unlike the defendants in *Newman*, Martoma received confidential information directly from the tipper, and he does not claim that he was unaware of any personal benefit Dr. Gilman received. *Cf.* id. at 448 ("In *Jiau*, the defendant knew about the benefit because she provided it.").

Newman's second holding is the focus of this appeal. After resolving the scienter question, *Newman* considered the sufficiency of the personal benefit evidence for two tippers, where the government relied chiefly on evidence that they were friendly with their tippees. The first tipper and tippee were not "close" friends but "had known each other for years, having both attended business school and worked at Dell together," and the tippee had provided modest "career advice and assistance" to the tipper. *Id.* at 452. The second tipper and tippee were "family friends" that "had met through church and occasionally socialized together." *Id.* The government argued that these relationships were "sufficient to prove that the tippers derived some benefit from the tip." *Id.*

The *Newman* panel rejected the government's argument, holding that the personal benefit "standard, although permissive, does not suggest that the Government may prove the receipt of a personal benefit by the mere fact of a friendship, particularly of a casual or social nature." *Id.* As the *Newman* Court reasoned, if that were enough, then "practically anything would qualify," and "the personal benefit requirement would be a nullity." *Id.* And in the sentence that forms the basis of Martoma's argument on appeal, *Newman* stated as follows:

> To the extent *Dirks* suggests that a personal benefit may be inferred from a personal relationship between the tipper and tippee, where the tippee's trades 'resemble trading by the insider himself followed by a gift of the profits to the recipient,' we hold that such an inference is impermissible in the absence of proof of a meaningfully close personal relationship . . . .

Id. at 452 (citation omitted) (quoting *Dirks*, 463 U.S. at 664). On the facts before it, the *Newman* Court found that standard had not been satisfied. *Id.* at 452–53.

Martoma focuses on this single sentence of *Newman* to argue that a jury may not infer that a tipper received a personal benefit from gifting confidential information in the absence of a "meaningfully close personal relationship." The term "meaningfully close personal relationship" is new to our insider trading jurisprudence, and, viewed in isolation, it might admit multiple interpretations. But *Newman* provided substantial guidance. Immediately after introducing the "meaningfully close personal relationship" concept, *Newman* held that it "requires evidence of 'a relationship between the insider and the recipient that suggests a *quid pro quo* from the latter, or an intention to benefit the [latter].'" *Newman*, 773 F.3d at 452 (quoting *Jiau*, 734 F.3d at 153 (quoting *Dirks*, 463 U.S. at 664)). As explained above, each of these is an independently sufficient basis to infer a personal benefit under *Dirks* and its progeny. *See, e.g., Jiau*, 734 F.3d at 153 (*quid pro quo*-like relationship). In other words, *Newman* cabined the gift theory using two *other* freestanding personal benefits that have long been recognized by our case law. And although the dissent urges in strong terms that this reading is mistaken or even improper, its dispute is in truth with the plain language of *Dirks*, as construed by *Warde*. We do no more than read literally *Newman*'s own explanation of its novel standard in light of these decisions, thereby fulfilling our legitimate function to construe and give effect to prior panel decisions.

With that understanding of *Newman*, we conclude that the personal benefit jury instructions in Martoma's trial, issued prior to that decision, were erroneous. The instructions allowed the jury to find a personal benefit based solely on the conclusion that Dr. Gilman tipped Martoma in order to "develop[ ] or maintain[ ] . . . a friendship." Under *Newman*, this articulation of the gift theory is incomplete. A properly instructed jury would have been informed that it could find a personal benefit based on a "gift of confidential information to a trading relative or friend" only if it also found that Dr. Gilman and Martoma shared a relationship suggesting a *quid pro quo* or that Dr. Gilman intended to benefit Martoma with the inside information. But, of course, there was no error in the district court's instructions that the jury could also find a personal benefit based on either of those two factors alone, *i.e.*, if it concluded that Dr. Gilman disclosed confidential information "with the intention of conferring a benefit on Mr. Martoma," or "with the intention of benefiting [himself] in some manner." *See* Tr. 3191. Each of these personal benefits is unaffected by *Newman*'s interpretation of the gift theory, and neither requires proof that Dr. Gilman and Martoma share any type of "personal relationship."

Although the jury instructions were inaccurate, we conclude that the error did not affect Martoma's substantial rights. *See Nouri*, 711 F.3d at 139–40. The government produced compelling evidence that Dr. Gilman, the tipper, "entered into a relationship of *quid pro quo*" with Martoma. *See Jiau*, 734 F.3d at 153. Dr. Gilman, over the course of approximately 18 months and 43 paid consultation sessions for which he billed $1,000 an hour, regularly and intentionally provided Martoma with confidential information from the bapineuzumab clinical trial. Martoma kept coming back, specifically scheduling consultation sessions so that they would occur shortly after the safety monitoring committee meetings, when Dr. Gilman would have new information to pass along. Starting at least in

August 2007, Dr. Gilman would reschedule his conversations with Martoma if he had no new information to reveal at the time they were scheduled to meet. By that point, the consulting relationship between Dr. Gilman and Martoma involved no legitimate service, *see* Dissent, op. at 88; as Dr. Gilman testified at trial, "the purpose of those consultations was for [him] to disclose to [Martoma] confidential information about the results . . . of the last Safety Monitoring Committee [meeting]." Tr. 1274. And because Martoma continued to see Dr. Gilman to receive confidential information, Dr. Gilman continued to receive consulting fees. The fact that Dr. Gilman did not specifically bill for his July 17 and 19, 2008 conversations with Martoma in which Dr. Gilman divulged the final drug efficacy data is also of no moment because, as he admitted at trial, doing so "would [have been] tantamount to confessing that [he] was . . . giving [Martoma] inside information." Tr. 1918. In the context of their ongoing "relationship of *quid pro quo*," Dr. Gilman's disclosures of confidential information were designed to "make good on the substantial pecuniary benefit he had already earned," *Dirks*, 463 U.S. at 663, and as a result, "it is clear beyond a reasonable doubt that a rational jury would have found [Martoma] guilty absent [any] error." *Mahaffy*, 693 F.3d at 136 (internal quotation marks omitted).

The dissent argues that under our analysis, a fact-finder must always find that tipper and tippee had a *quid pro quo*-like relationship whenever a tip is exchanged within a paid consulting relationship. Dissent, op. at 88. Not so. We merely hold that on the compelling facts of this case, it is clear beyond a reasonable doubt that a properly instructed jury would have found Martoma guilty. Nor does our decision mean that a tipper who accidentally or unknowingly reveals inside information can be found guilty. *See id.* at 16. Such a tipper would be protected by the requirement that the tipper know (or is reckless in not knowing) that the information is material and non-public, *see Obus*, 693 F.3d at 286, or by the requirement that the tipper expect the tippee to trade, *see United States v. Gansman*, 657 F.3d 85, 92 (2d Cir. 2011).

II.

We next turn to Martoma's challenge to the sufficiency of the personal benefit evidence and whether, "evaluating . . . the evidence in the light most favorable to the government," a rational jury could have found Martoma guilty of insider trading. *See Coplan*, 703 F.3d at 62. As an initial matter, it follows from our conclusion that the faulty jury instructions were harmless because of the compelling evidence that Dr. Gilman and Martoma shared a relationship suggesting a *quid pro quo* that this evidence was also sufficient to support his conviction. In particular, the jury was free to place no weight on the fact that Dr. Gilman did not bill Martoma for the July 17 and 19, 2008 sessions. We reiterate, however, that while the government presented compelling evidence on this point, the evidentiary bar is "modest." *Jiau*, 734 F.3d at 153.

Moreover, even if a jury were inclined to accept Martoma's argument that there was no *quid pro quo*-like relationship because Dr. Gilman did not bill Martoma for two key sessions, a rational jury could nonetheless find that Dr. Gilman personally benefited by disclosing inside information with the "intention to benefit" Martoma. *See Dirks,* 463 U.S. at 664. We think a jury can often infer that a corporate insider receives a personal benefit (*i.e.*, breaches his fiduciary duty) from deliberately disclosing valuable, confidential information without a corporate purpose and with the expectation that the tippee will trade on it. *See id.* at 659 (explaining that "insiders [are] forbidden by their fiduciary relationship" from giving inside information "to an outsider for the . . . improper purpose of exploiting the information for their personal gain"); *cf. Salman,* 137 S.Ct. at 428 (recognizing that where a tipper discloses information with the "expectation that [the recipient will] trade on it," the information is "the equivalent of . . . cash"). Here, as previously noted, Dr. Gilman knew that Martoma was an investment manager who was seeking information on which to base securities trading decisions. And Dr. Gilman plainly understood the valuable nature of the information about the bapineuzumab clinical trial, as Martoma had previously paid him $1,000 per hour over the course of 43 consultations to convey his knowledge on the subject, and had visited Dr. Gilman in his Ann Arbor office to receive the key drug efficacy results firsthand. From these facts, a reasonable jury could infer that Dr. Gilman personally benefited by conveying inside information about the trial with the purpose of benefiting Martoma, even if it was not persuaded that the two had a relationship suggesting a *quid pro quo* (or a personal relationship, for that matter). *See Dirks,* 463 U.S. at 667. * * *

CONCLUSION

We have considered Martoma's remaining arguments and find them without merit. Accordingly, we **AFFIRM** the judgment of the district court.

---

1. *Martoma's Impact.* When remote tippees receive material, nonpublic information from an earlier tippee in the chain, it is often difficult for the prosecution to show that they knew of any personal benefit paid by the original tippee to the original tipper. After all, why would a tippee convey this information to a subsequent tippee? *Martoma* may have been a conscious attempt on the part of the court to simplify the proof that the prosecution must show. Instead of showing a benefit to the tipper, the prosecution under it need show only that the original tipper in the chain was seeking to benefit the original tippee. On the case's facts, Dr. Gilman did know defendant Martoma and may have wanted to benefit him (although he was even more likely motivated by the high consulting fees he was receiving indirectly from Martoma). Suppose the relationship between tipper and tippee is even more

attenuated. For example, a slightly tipsy investment banker on New Year's Eve tells everyone at the bar at his social club that they should buy XYZ Inc's stock because it has made a major medical discovery that will be announced soon (and some do buy). But the investment banker does not even know the names of his tippees. Do you believe that the *Dirks* court would have wanted there to be liability under its gift theory in such a case?

E. THE STOCK ACT

Until 2012, it was an open question whether members of Congress, or their employees, could violate the insider trader prohibition by trading on the basis of material, nonpublic information that they acquired in the performance of their official duties. This was because they were not subject to any clear-cut legal duty and were certainly not fiduciaries to the shareholders of the company in whose stock they traded. But, after a wave of unfavorable publicity, Congress passed the "Stop Trading on Congressional Knowledge Act of 2012" (or the STOCK Act), which was signed into law on April 4, 2012.[40] The STOCK Act specifically states that "Members of Congress and employees of Congress are not exempt from the insider trading prohibitions arising under the securities laws, including Section 10(b) of the Securities Exchange Act of 1934 and Rule 10b–5 thereunder."[41]

In addition, the Act amended Section 21A of the Securities Exchange Act to provide:

> "[E]ach Member of Congress or employee of Congress owes a duty arising from a relationship of trust and confidence to the Congress, the United States Government, and the citizens of the United States with respect to material, nonpublic information derived from such a person's position as a Member of Congress or employee of Congress or gained from the performance of such person's official responsibilities."[42]

Not content to restrict only itself, Congress also added Section 21A(h) to the Securities Exchange Act, which similarly covers each "executive branch employee," "judicial officer," and "judicial employee," providing that they also owe "a duty arising from a relationship of trust and confidence to the United States Government and the citizens of the United States." These terms are defined in Section 21A(h)(2).[43] On the other hand, late in the legislation process, the House stripped language from the STOCK Act that would have covered "political intelligence" firms and the exchange of such information.

---

[40] Pub. L. No. 112–105, 126 Stat. 291 (2012).
[41] Section 4(a) of the STOCK Act.
[42] See Section 21A(g) of the Securities Exchange Act of 1934.
[43] Prospective judicial law clerks should take note that they are covered by the STOCK Act and gossip by them might be viewed by the SEC as unlawful tipping if the information were material and the recipient (or others) traded upon it.

Interpretive problems are certain to arise under the STOCK Act. For example, although it is clear that a member of Congress who knows of a still nonpublic bill or appropriation that is likely to benefit a particular corporation cannot trade in its stock, can she tip the corporation's officers, agents or lobbyists that the appropriation is coming? If she does so (which is the usual practice in Washington), can these persons trade? Alternatively, suppose a CEO of a major corporation plays golf with that Congressmember and confides in her news about a major development affecting her firm that has not yet been announced publicly? Was this information "derived" because of the Congress person's "position" (as Section 21A(g) requires)? How would the prosecution prove this?

Probably the most dangerous scenario involves a Congressperson who alerts a "political intelligence" firm in Washington that a deal has been reached on major, market-moving legislation, and that firm's clients then trade minutes later on this still non-public information. *Query*: Would it make a difference if the member of Congress expected (or had received) a campaign contribution from the political intelligence firm?

A Constitutional issue also lurks here involving the scope of the Speech or Debate Clause of the U.S. Constitution, which provides that "for Speech or Debate in either House, [Members of Congress] shall not be questioned in any other place."[44] The Court has broadly construed this language to immunize "legislative acts,"[45] which includes many activities that are normally incident to the legislation process. For example, gossip among Congressional staffers who give and receive no benefit seems unlikely to fall within the STOCK Act, as construed in light of the Speech and Debate Clause. Some judicial balancing remains to be done here.

Problem

PROBLEM 13-1

Wyoming was employed as Director of Fiduciary Services by the St. Louis law firm of Larsen & Gould. She controlled the selection of stockbrokers for the placing of securities trades on behalf of the trust accounts managed by Larsen & Gould. Murtagh was employed as a stockbroker by Morgan Merrill. Wyoming directed a large share of Larsen & Gould's business to Murtagh. Murtagh and Wyoming also shared a personal and financial relationship.

From December 7, until December 12, Larsen & Gould represented the Bank of St. Louis in connection with a potential merger with MoBanks. This was a highly confidential transaction. Though few lawyers at Larsen & Gould were involved in the transactions, Wyoming had daily contact with at least one, John Green. Green visited Wyoming's office frequently to check

---

[44] U.S. Constitution, art. I, § 6, cl. 1.

[45] See, e.g., United States v. Helstoski, 442 U.S. 477, 481 (1979); Eastland v. U.S. Servicemen's Fund, 421 U.S. 491, 502 (1975). Clearly, the payment of a bribe to introduce legislation is not protected by this Clause. See United States v. Brewster, 408 U.S. 501 (1972).

stock prices and monitor his personal account. Computer records indicate that Wyoming opened Green's account summary on Wyoming's computer at 3:27 p.m. and 3:28 p.m. on December 12.

At 3:29 p.m., one minute after opening Green's account summary, Wyoming placed a call to Murtagh. The call lasted one minute and twelve seconds. Immediately after Wyoming's call, Murtagh called his trading assistant, Abby Lincoln, and entered orders to purchase approximately 11,000 shares of MoBanks stock, priced at $85 per share, for his own account, and those of other family members. Lincoln also purchased 400 shares of MoBanks stock for her own account. To her knowledge, Murtagh never had bought across all of his family accounts at once.

Lincoln on December 12th also telephoned her fiancée, Jim Washington, and said "buy MoBanks." Washington instantly bought 1000 shares.

After the market closed on December 12, Bank of St. Louis and MoBanks announced their merger. As a result of the merger, MoBanks stock price increased by $8 a share (or 28 percent) before the market opened on December 13.

Have (1) Wyoming, (2) Murtagh, (3) Lincoln, or (4) Washington violated Rule 10b–5? If so, why?

F. 18 U.S.C. § 1348

Section 1348 was enacted as part of the Sarbanes-Oxley Act in 2002.[46] Although it had been used with respect to frauds in the commodities markets, it had not been employed to prosecute insider trading in the securities markets until *Newman* seemed to make it harder to show the requisite "personal benefit."[47] As the *Blaszczak* decision shows, Section 1348 may offer prosecutors a much more friendly playing field:

---

[46] 18 U.S.C. § 1348 reads as follows:

"Whoever knowingly executes, or attempts to execute, a scheme or artifice–

(1) to defraud any person in connection with any commodity for future delivery, or any option on a commodity for future delivery, or any security of an issuer with a class of securities registered under section 12 of the Securities Exchange Act of 1934 (15 U.S.C. 78*l*) or that is required to file reports under section 15(d) of the Securities Exchange Act of 1934 (15 U.S.C. 78*o*(d)); or

(2) to obtain, by means of false or fraudulent pretenses, representations, or promise, any money or property in connection with the purchase or sale of any commodity for future delivery, or any security of an issuer with a class of securities registered under section 12 of the Securities Exchange Act of 1934 (15 U.S.C. 78*l*) or that is required to file reports under section 15(d) of the Securities Exchange Act of 1934 (15 U.S.C. 78*o*(d));

Shall be fined under this title, or imprisoned not more than 25 years, or both."

[47] United States v. Newman, 773 F.3d 438 (2d Cir. 2014).

United States v. Blaszczak
United States Court of Appeals, Second Circuit, 2019.
947 F.3d 19.

- Before: KEARSE, DRONEY and SULLIVAN, CIRCUIT JUDGES.
- SULLIVAN, CHIEF JUDGE:

These consolidated appeals require us to consider whether the federal wire fraud, securities fraud, and conversion statutes, codified at 18 U.S.C. §§ 1343, 1348, and 641, respectively, reach misappropriation of a government agency's confidential nonpublic information relating to its contemplated rules. Defendants David Blaszczak, Theodore Huber, Robert Olan, and Christopher Worrall were charged with violating these statutes—and with engaging in securities fraud in violation of Section 10(b) of the Securities and Exchange Act, 15 U.S.C. § 78j(b), and SEC Rule 10b–5 ("Title 15 securities fraud")—by misappropriating confidential nonpublic information from the Centers for Medicare & Medicaid Services ("CMS"). The indictment principally alleged that CMS employees, including Worrall, disclosed the agency's confidential information to Blaszczak, a "political intelligence" consultant for hedge funds, who in turn tipped the information to Huber and Olan, employees of the healthcare-focused hedge fund Deerfield Management Company, L.P. ("Deerfield"), which traded on it. After a one-month trial before the United States District Court for the Southern District of New York (Kaplan, J.), a jury found Defendants guilty of wire fraud, conversion, and, with the exception of Worrall, Title 18 securities fraud and conspiracy. The jury acquitted Defendants on all counts alleging Title 15 securities fraud.

Defendants now challenge their convictions on various grounds. For the reasons set forth below, we reject these challenges. In doing so, we hold, *inter alia*, that (1) confidential government information such as the CMS information at issue here may constitute "property" in the hands of the government for purposes of the wire fraud and Title 18 securities fraud statutes, and (2) the "personal-benefit" test established in *Dirks v. SEC*, 463 U.S. 646 (1983), does not apply to these Title 18 fraud statutes. Because we also discern no prejudicial error with respect to the remaining issues raised on appeal, we affirm the judgments of the district court.

I. BACKGROUND

A. Facts

The jury returned guilty verdicts on counts charging two insider-trading schemes: (1) a scheme relating to Deerfield that involved all defendants to varying degrees, and (2) a scheme relating to another hedge fund investment manager, Visium Asset Management, L.P. ("Visium"), that involved Blaszczak only. We recite the facts pertaining to each of these schemes in turn, construing the evidence at trial underlying the counts of conviction in the light most favorable to the prosecution. *See United States v. Kirk Tang Yuk,* 885 F.3d 57, 65 (2d Cir. 2018).

1. The Deerfield Scheme

At various times between 2009 and 2014, Olan, Huber, and fellow Deerfield partner Jordan Fogel—a cooperating witness who pleaded guilty and testified at trial—approached Blaszczak for the purpose of obtaining so-called "predecisional" information concerning CMS's contemplated rules and regulations. The three Deerfield partners knew that Blaszczak, who had worked at CMS before becoming a consultant for hedge funds, enjoyed unique access to the agency's predecisional information through his inside sources at the agency. Because other consultants did not have access to Blaszczak's sources, the Deerfield partners counted him as a particularly lucrative fount of illegal market "edge." App'x at 567, 606.

This illegal market edge first paid off for the three Deerfield partners in July 2009, after Blaszczak passed them nonpublic CMS information concerning both the timing and substance of an upcoming proposed CMS rule change that would reduce the reimbursement rate for certain radiation oncology treatments. The Deerfield partners sought to maximize this market edge by trading while "the information wasn't known to others, and . . . wasn't public." *Id.* at 593. In late June 2009, Olan, Huber, and Fogel directed Deerfield to enter orders shorting approximately $33 million worth of stock in radiation-device manufacturer Varian Medical Systems ("Varian"), a company that would be hurt by CMS's proposed rule. Blaszczak's information was consistent with the proposed rule that CMS ultimately announced on July 1, 2009, and as a result of the Varian trade, Deerfield made $2.76 million in profits.

Deerfield again traded on confidential CMS information obtained from Blaszczak in 2012. This time, Blaszczak obtained the predecisional information at issue from Worrall, a CMS employee who had previously worked with Blaszczak at the agency and remained friends with him after Blaszczak left CMS to become a hedge fund consultant. Blaszczak met Worrall at CMS's headquarters in Maryland on May 8, 2012; the following day, Blaszczak emailed Fogel to set up a phone call so that he could update him on one of Fogel's "favorite topics." *Id.* at 2439. On the call, Blaszczak provided Fogel with predecisional CMS information about additional radiation oncology reimbursement rate changes. Fogel, in turn, shared this information with Huber and Olan, and together the three of them relied on it—in combination with other confidential CMS information that Blaszczak passed them over the next few weeks—in recommending that Deerfield short millions of dollars in the shares of companies that would be hurt by the reimbursement changes. Deerfield earned profits of $2.73 million from trades relating to this radiation oncology rule, which was publicly announced on July 6, 2012.

In February 2013, shortly after Fogel moved to a different group within Deerfield, he reached out to Blaszczak in the hopes of "re-ignit[ing] the Blaszczak-Fogel money printing machine." Supp. App'x at 6. As Fogel testified at trial, the "Blaszczak-Fogel money printing machine" meant that "Blaszczak had a long history of providing [Fogel] and [his] teammates nonpublic information that [they] could trade on, and it was a great asset to get edge for investments." App'x at 581.

Fogel did not have to wait long for the machine to reignite. In June 2013, Blaszczak told Fogel that he expected CMS to propose cutting the reimbursement rate for end-stage renal disease ("ESRD") treatments by 12 percent. Although Blaszczak did not reveal the source of his information to Fogel, the prediction was so specific—and so different from the market consensus—that Fogel believed it came "from a credible source inside of CMS." *Id.* at 582. Still, Fogel remained anxious about the outlier status of Blaszczak's prediction and continued to check in with him about his level of certainty. On June 25, 2013, less than a week before CMS announced the ESRD rule, Blaszczak told Fogel that there was "[n]o change in [his] numbers" and that he was "pretty confident" in his information. *Id.* at 2024. Fogel again took this to mean that Blaszczak obtained the information from a reliable inside source, and further inferred that the public announcement of the proposed rate cut (the timing of which was also nonpublic) was around the corner and thus less likely to change. On the basis of this confidential nonpublic information, Fogel directed Deerfield to enter orders shorting stock in Fresenius Medical Care, a public company that would be hurt by the reimbursement rate cuts. CMS publicly announced the 12 percent rate cut on July 1, 2013, and Deerfield earned approximately $860,000 in profits from the trade.

Blaszczak continued to provide Fogel with predecisional CMS information in advance of CMS's announcement of the final ESRD rule on November 22, 2013. In particular, Blaszczak informed Fogel that the final ESRD rule would keep the 12 percent rate cut but would be phased in over three to four years. Based on that information, Fogel recommended that Deerfield enter orders to short stock in Fresenius and DaVita Healthcare Partners Inc. Deerfield did so, earning profits of approximately $791,000. Immediately after CMS announced the final ESRD rule, Fogel emailed his colleagues at Deerfield to praise Blaszczak for his ESRD reimbursement predictions: "I told u guys blazcack [sic] is the man. . . . [H]e has crushed it on these two rules both times round." Supp. App'x at 10. . . .

B. Procedural History

On March 5, 2018, the government filed an eighteen-count superseding indictment in the United States District Court for the Southern District of New York setting forth allegations relating to the Deerfield scheme (Counts One through Sixteen) and Visium scheme (Counts Seventeen and Eighteen). Counts One and Two charged

Defendants with participating in conspiracies centering on the misappropriation of confidential CMS information between 2009 and 2014. In Counts Three through Ten, the indictment charged Defendants with conversion of U.S. property (Count Three), Title 15 securities fraud (Counts Four through Eight), wire fraud (Count Nine), and Title 18 securities fraud (Count Ten), relating to the misappropriation of confidential CMS information that pertained to the July 2012 proposed radiation oncology rule. . . .

On April 2, 2018, the case proceeded to a jury trial before Judge Kaplan. The parties rested their cases three weeks later, on April 23, 2018, and after summations, the district court charged the jury. In particular, the district court instructed the jury pursuant to *Dirks* that, (1) in order to convict Worrall of Title 15 securities fraud, it needed to find that he tipped confidential CMS information in exchange for a "personal benefit;" (2) in order to convict Blaszczak of Title 15 securities fraud, it additionally needed to find that he knew that Worrall disclosed the information in exchange for a personal benefit; and (3) in order to convict Huber or Olan of Title 15 securities fraud, it needed to find that Huber or Olan knew that a CMS insider tipped the information in exchange for a personal benefit. App'x at 1042–43. The district court, however, refused to give *Dirks*-style instructions on the wire fraud and Title 18 securities fraud counts. The district court instead instructed the jury that wire fraud "includes the act of embezzlement, which is . . . the fraudulent appropriation to one's own use of the money or property entrusted to one's care by someone else." *Id.* at 1044–45; *see Carpenter v. United States,* 484 U.S. 19, 27 (1987). The district court similarly instructed the jury, for the Title 18 securities fraud counts, that it could find the existence of a scheme to defraud if a defendant "participated in a scheme to embezzle or convert confidential information from CMS by wrongfully taking that information and transferring it to his own use or the use of someone else." App'x at 1045. For both Title 18 fraud offenses, the district court further instructed the jury that it could only convict if it found that the defendant it was considering knowingly and willfully participated in the fraudulent scheme.

On May 3, 2018, after four days of deliberations, the jury returned a split verdict. The jury acquitted all defendants on the Title 15 securities fraud counts. . . . The jury nevertheless found all defendants guilty of the conversion and wire fraud offenses charged in Counts Three and Nine, respectively; all defendants but Worrall guilty of the conspiracy offenses charged in Counts One and Two as well as Title 18 securities fraud as charged in Count Ten; and Blaszczak alone guilty of the offenses charged in Counts Thirteen and Fifteen through Eighteen. . . .

III. DISCUSSION

Defendants challenge their convictions on several grounds. They argue that (1) the confidential CMS information at issue is not "property" in the hands of CMS for purposes of the wire fraud and Title 18 securities fraud statutes; (2) the district court erred by refusing to instruct the jury on the *Dirks* personal-benefit test as to the Title 18 fraud counts; (3) Defendants' convictions for converting U.S. property were infected by a series of legal and factual errors; (4) the evidence at trial was insufficient on all counts; (5) Counts Seventeen and Eighteen, charging Blaszczak alone in the Visium scheme, were misjoined with the other counts; and (6) the district court made a variety of evidentiary errors. We address each of these arguments in turn. . . .

B. Whether *Dirks v. SEC* applies to 18 U.S.C. §§ 1343 and 1348

Under *Dirks*, an insider may not be convicted of Title 15 securities fraud unless the government proves that he breached a duty of trust and confidence by disclosing material, nonpublic information in exchange for a "personal benefit." 463 U.S. at 663. Similarly, a tippee may not be convicted of such fraud unless he utilized the inside information knowing that it had been obtained in breach of the insider's duty. *See United States v. Newman*, 773 F.3d 438, 447–49 (2d Cir.2014), *abrogated on other grounds by Salman v. United States,* 137 S.Ct. 420 (2016). Here, Defendants claim that the district court erred by not instructing the jury that *Dirks*'s personal-benefit test also applied to the wire fraud and Title 18 securities fraud counts. In essence, Defendants argue that the term "defraud" should be construed to have the same meaning across the Title 18 fraud provisions and Rule 10b–5, so that the elements of insider-trading fraud are the same under each of these provisions. We disagree.

We begin by noting what the Title 18 fraud statutes and Title 15 fraud provisions have in common: their text does not mention a "personal benefit" test. Rather, these provisions prohibit, with certain variations, schemes to "defraud." 18 U.S.C. §§ 1343, 1348(1); 17 C.F.R. § 240.10b–5(a); *see* 18 U.S.C. § 1348(2) (prohibiting schemes to obtain certain property "by means of false or fraudulent pretenses"); 15 U.S.C. § 78j(b) (prohibiting the use of any "manipulative or deceptive device"). For each of these provisions, the term "defraud" encompasses the so-called "embezzlement" or "misappropriation" theory of fraud. *See United States v. O'Hagan,* 521 U.S. 642, 653–54 (1997) (Title 15 securities fraud); *Carpenter,* 484 U.S. at 27 (mail and wire fraud); *see also, e.g., United States v. Mahaffy,* 693 F.3d 113, 123 (2d Cir. 2012) (Title 18 securities fraud). According to this theory, "[t]he concept of 'fraud' includes the act of embezzlement, which is 'the fraudulent appropriation to one's own use of the money or goods entrusted to one's care by another.'" *Carpenter,* 484 U.S. at 27 (quoting *Grin v. Shine,* 187 U.S. 181, 189, 23 S.Ct. 98, 47 L.Ed. 130 (1902)). The undisclosed misappropriation of confidential information, in breach of a fiduciary or similar duty of trust and confidence, "constitutes fraud akin to embezzlement." *O'Hagan, 521 U.S. at 654; see also United States v. Chestman,* 947 F.2d 551, 566–67, 571 (2d Cir. 1991) (en banc).

While the Title 18 fraud statutes and Title 15 fraud provisions thus share similar text and proscribe similar theories of fraud, these common features have little to do with the personal-benefit test. Rather, the personal-benefit test is a judge-made doctrine premised on the Exchange Act's statutory purpose. As *Dirks* explained, in order to protect the free flow of information into the securities markets, Congress enacted the Title 15 fraud provisions with the limited "purpose of . . .eliminat[ing] [the] use of inside information for *personal advantage*." 463 U.S. at 662 (emphasis added) (internal quotation marks omitted). *Dirks* effectuated this purpose by holding that an insider could not breach his fiduciary duties by tipping confidential information unless he did so in exchange for a personal benefit. *Id.* at 662–64; *see also Chestman,* 947 F.2d at 581 (Winter, J., concurring in part and dissenting in part) (observing that whereas the theory of fraud recognized in *Carpenter* "is derived from the law of theft or embezzlement," the "*Dirks* rule is derived from securities law, and . . . [is] influenced by the need to allow persons to profit from generating information about firms so that the pricing of securities is efficient"); *United States v. Pinto-Thomaz,* 352 F.Supp.3d 287, 298 (S.D.N.Y. 2018) (Rakoff, J.) ("Although [the *Dirks* personal-benefit test] was novel law, the Court reasoned that this test was consistent with the 'purpose of the [Title 15] securities laws . . . to eliminate use of inside information for personal advantage.'" (quoting *Dirks,* 463 U.S. at 662)).

But once untethered from the statutory context in which it arose, the personal-benefit test finds no support in the embezzlement theory of fraud recognized in *Carpenter*. In the context of embezzlement, there is no additional requirement that an insider breach a duty to the owner of the property, since "it is impossible for a person to embezzle the money of another without committing a fraud upon him." *Grin,* 187 U.S. at 189. Because a breach of duty is thus inherent in *Carpenter*'s formulation of embezzlement, there is likewise no additional requirement that the government prove a breach of duty in a specific manner, let alone through evidence that an insider tipped confidential information in exchange for a personal benefit. . . . In short, because the personal-benefit test is not grounded in the embezzlement theory of fraud, but rather depends entirely on the purpose of the *Exchange Act,* we decline to extend *Dirks* beyond the context of that statute.

Our conclusion is the same for both the wire fraud and Title 18 securities fraud statutes. While it is true that Section 1348 of Title 18, unlike the wire fraud statute, concerns the general subject matter of securities law, Section 1348 and the Exchange Act do not share the same statutory purpose. . . .In particular, Congress intended for Section 1348 to "supplement the patchwork of existing technical securities law violations with a more general and less technical provision, with elements and intent requirements comparable to current bank fraud and health care fraud statutes." S. Rep. No. 107–146, at 14. Given that Section 1348 was intended to provide prosecutors with a different—and broader—enforcement mechanism to address securities fraud than what had been previously provided in the Title 15 fraud provisions, we decline to graft the *Dirks* personal-benefit test onto the elements of Title 18 securities fraud.

Finally, Defendants argue that we should extend *Dirks* beyond the Title 15 fraud provisions because otherwise the government may avoid the personal-benefit test altogether by prosecuting insider-trading fraud with less difficulty under the Title 18 fraud statutes—particularly the Title 18 securities fraud statute, which (unlike the wire fraud statute) does not require proof that wires were used to carry out the fraud. But whatever the force of this argument as a policy matter, we may not rest our interpretation of the Title 18 fraud provisions "on such enforcement policy considerations." *O'Hagan,* 521 U.S. at 678 n.25. "The Federal Criminal Code is replete with provisions that criminalize overlapping conduct," and so "[t]he mere fact that two federal criminal statutes criminalize similar conduct says little about the scope of either." *Pasquantino,* 544 U.S. at 358 n.4. Congress was certainly authorized to enact a broader securities fraud provision, and it is not the place of courts to check that decision on policy grounds.

Accordingly, we hold that the personal-benefit test does not apply to the wire fraud and Title 18 securities fraud statutes, and thus the district court did not err by refusing to instruct the jury on the personal benefit test for those offenses. . . .

IV. CONCLUSION

In upholding the jury's verdict, we pause to reject Defendants' thematic claim that the government's positions, if accepted, would herald an unprecedented expansion of federal criminal law. It is Defendants who ask us to break new ground by rejecting well-recognized theories of property rights and by adding, in effect, a "personal benefit" element to the Title 18 fraud statutes. We decline these requests, holding instead that (1) a government agency's confidential information relating to its contemplated rules may constitute "property" for purposes of the wire fraud and Title 18 securities fraud statutes, and (2) *Dirks*'s "personal-benefit" framework does not apply to these Title 18 fraud statutes. Our remaining holdings confirm that Defendants' misappropriation of CMS's predecisional information, as proven at trial, fall comfortably within the Title 18 securities fraud, wire fraud, conversion, and conspiracy statutes. To the extent that the government's decision to prosecute any or all of these crimes in this case raises broader enforcement policy concerns, that is a matter for Congress and the Executive, not the Judiciary. Our inquiry is a more limited one, and having now completed it, we AFFIRM the judgments of the district court.

---

1. *The Impact of* Blaszczak. As a practical matter, *Blaszczak* enables prosecutors to outflank the "personal benefit" rule of *Dirks* and subsequent cases. As *Blaszczak*, itself, shows, juries may acquit

defendants of insider trading under the *Dirks* standard and yet convict under wire fraud or § 1348.

Does this result in overcriminalization? It could, but that district court (Judge Lewis Kaplan) instructed the jury (and the Second Circuit approved and emphasized this charge in its opinion) that, to convict under § 1348, the jury had to find some misappropriation or embezzlement of the information. This protects defendants from being charged under § 1348 because they traded on material nonpublic information that they themselves developed. For example, a prospective bidder in a hostile tender offer who buys stock in the open market before announcing its tender offer may be trading on material, nonpublic information, but it has not misappropriated this information from anyone else.

How could the scope of *Blaszczak* extend beyond that of *Dirks*? Consider again the basic facts of *Dirks*. A whistleblower approached Ray Dirks, soliciting and obtaining his assistance in exposing a fraud. Although neither the whistleblower nor Dirks breached any duty owed to the shareholders of the corporation, Dirks did use information provided to him by the whistleblower for the benefit of his clients and himself. Did Dirks thereby misappropriate information from the whistleblower? Under the *Dirks* decision, we look only to see if the corporate official who tipped Dirks breached a duty to the shareholders. If he did not, others may use the information safely as they stand in the tipper's shoes. But under *Blaszczak*, we could look to whether Dirks misappropriated information from his whistleblower. This is not to conclude that courts under § 1348 would necessarily reach a different decision than under *Dirks*, but the full implications of *Blaszczak* have yet to be fully assessed.

2. *Future Directions*. In early 2020, the Bharara Task Force on Insider Trading issued its report, which called for federal legislation codifying the prohibition on insider trading and eliminating the "personal benefit" requirement.[48] Also, it endorsed an approach that went beyond the law of fraud and also covered material information that had been "wrongfully" obtained by any means, including computer hacking, extortion, misrepresentation, misappropriation, theft or a fiduciary breach.[49]

In December 2019, the House of Representatives passed the Insider Trading Prohibition Act by the overwhelming margin of 410 to 13. That bill, largely drafted and coordinated by Congressman Jim Himes (D-Conn.), had originally eliminated the "personal benefit" requirement, but on the eve of its passage by the House, this requirement was restored (at least in cases based on a fiduciary breach) in order to obtain Republican

---

[48] See Report of the Bharara Task Force on Insider trading (January, 2020). Professor Coffee was one of the eight members of this Task Force.

[49] The SEC has been able sometimes to prosecute insider trading when the information was obtained through computer hacking. See SEC v. Dorozhko, 574 F.3d 42, 48–50 (2d Cir. 2009). But it must show that deception was used in obtaining this information.

support. This legislation focuses on whether the material, nonpublic information was "wrongfully" obtained, and does not require prosecutors to show deception or manipulation (as § 10(b) requires). Although this legislation sailed through the House, the Senate never considered it and thus, with the Session ending, the legislation will have to start over with a new Congress in 2021. Its future seems highly uncertain.

For the future, it seems increasingly likely that prosecutors will plead multiple theories under both Section 10(b), the mail and wire fraud statutes, and Section 1348, thereby escaping the need to prove a "personal benefit" under the latter two theories. However, it must be remembered that the SEC cannot use § 1348 or the mail and wire fraud statutes, but only has standing to assert securities fraud theories under Title 15. Thus and curiously, theories of criminal liability will reach further (and be easier to satisfy) than theories of civil liability.

2. REGULATION FD

In August, 2000 the SEC adopted Regulation FD. The adoption Release explained:

> Regulation FD (Fair Disclosure) is a new issuer disclosure rule that addresses selective disclosure. The regulation provides that when an issuer, or person acting on its behalf, discloses material nonpublic information to certain enumerated persons (in general, securities market professionals and holders of the issuer's securities who may well trade on the basis of the information), it must make public disclosure of that information. The timing of the required public disclosure depends on whether the selective disclosure was intentional or non-intentional; for an intentional selective disclosure, the issuer must make public disclosure simultaneously; for a non-intentional disclosure, the issuer must make public disclosure promptly. Under the regulation, the required public disclosure may be made by filing or furnishing a Form 8-K, or by another method or combination of methods that is reasonably designed to effect broad, non-exclusionary distribution of the information to the public.[50]

The SEC's decision to adopt Regulation FD in the face of considerable opposition from securities analysts and investment banking firms (but much vocal support from individual investors) was based on several different considerations:

First, the SEC recognized that there was considerable legal doubt as to whether Rule 10b–5 could be stretched to reach corporate disclosures to securities analysts or institutional investors that were not accompanied by actual bribes or other tangible inducements.

---

[50] Sec. Ex. Act Rel. 43,154, 53 SEC Dock. 3, 1 (2000).

Second, in addition to giving unequal access to material information to privileged investors, selective disclosure involved an independent danger not generally associated with insider trading: it could be used to undermine the independence of securities analysts, upon whose efforts market efficiency might substantially depend. Evidence indicated that issuers could and did use information as a means of securing the acquiescence and support of securities analysts, by, for example, cutting off a critical analyst from the flow of future sensitive information.

Third, the SEC believed that selective disclosure was becoming pervasive and in the words of the adoption release that, "voluntary steps" to remedy the problem "have been far from fully effective."[51]

The Commission balanced concerns that a rule against selective disclosure might "chill" issuer communications and result in less information reaching the market. The result was a rule more narrow than originally proposed:

(1) As adopted, Regulation FD applies only to communications made to a limited number of persons (securities market professionals and holders of the issuer's securities under circumstances where it was reasonably foreseeable that the holder would trade on the basis of the information);

(2) The Rule applies only to certain issuer personnel (senior officials and lower-ranking persons regularly engaged in communications with securities market professionals or securities holders);

(3) Private liability cannot result from a Regulation FD violation;

(4) Statements made in connection with marketing securities offerings (such as at roadshows) are expressly excluded from The Rule's coverage.

As so narrowed, Rule 100 of Regulation FD applies, as explained in the adopting Release:

[W]henever:

(1) an issuer, or person acting on its behalf,

(2) discloses material nonpublic information,

(3) to certain enumerated persons (in general, securities market professionals or holders of the issuer's securities who may well trade on the basis of the information),

(4) the issuer must make public disclosure of that same information: (a) simultaneously (for intentional disclosures), or (b) promptly (for non-intentional disclosures).

---

[51] Id. at 4.

As a whole, the regulation requires that when an issuer makes an intentional disclosure of material nonpublic information to a person covered by the regulation, it must do so in a manner that provides general public disclosure, rather than through a selective disclosure. For a selective disclosure that is non-intentional, the issuer must publicly disclose the information promptly after it knows (or is reckless in not knowing) that the information selectively disclosed was both material and nonpublic.[52]

Regulation FD applies only to reporting companies. In addition, Rule 100(b)(2) of Regulation FD sets out three specific exclusions from coverage: (1) communications made to persons who owe the issuer a duty of trust or confidence (for example, lawyers or investment bankers working for the issuer); (2) communications to persons who expressly agree to maintain the information in confidence (for example, selective disclosure might be made to offerees in a private placement if they agree to maintain the information so disclosed in confidence); and (3) communications made in connection with securities offerings. Before Congress passed the Dodd-Frank Act, Regulation FD also excluded disclosures to nationally recognized statistical ratings organizations and credit ratings agencies. Section 939B of the Dodd-Frank Act mandated that the SEC remove this exclusion. The third exclusion for communications in connection with securities offerings raises special problems that the Commission will ultimately need to face. Why should selective disclosure be permitted at a roadshow, for example, where the audience consists of institutional investors and analysts who are likely to trade promptly in the secondary market upon learning of material information? Put differently—if selective disclosure is undesirable—why should Regulation FD exempt it in the public offering process?

Rule 101(e) defines the type of "public disclosure" that will satisfy the requirements of Regulation FD. As adopted, it says that issuers can make public disclosure for purposes of Regulation FD by filing or furnishing a Form 8-K, or by disseminating information "through another method (or by a combination of methods) of disclosure that is reasonably designed to provide broad, non-exclusionary distribution of the information to the public." In the adoption Release, the Commission recommended (but did not require) the following "model":

First, issue a press release, distributed through regular channels, containing the information;

Second, provide adequate notice, by a press release and/or website posting, of a scheduled conference call to discuss the announced results, giving investors both the time and date of the conference call, and instructions on how to access the call; and

---

[52] Id. at 6–7.

Third, hold the conference call in an open manner, permitting investors to listen in either by telephonic means or through Internet webcasting.

By following these steps, an issuer can use the press release to provide the initial broad distribution of the information, and then discuss its release with analysts in the subsequent conference call, without fear that if it should disclose additional material details related to the original disclosure it will be engaging in a selective disclosure of material information.[53]

3. SEC RULE 14e–3 AND TENDER OFFERS

In 1980, after the *Chiarella* decision, there was a gaping hole in insider trading regulation. Anyone without a fiduciary duty could obtain information and trade on it without any obvious legal remedy. In the classic 1980s hostile takeover scenario, fictionalized in Oliver Stone's movie "Wall Street," this would allow a banker working on the takeover of a target firm to use the information about the pending takeover to buy and sell shares in the target company with impunity. After all, the banker or lawyer working for the acquiring company owes no fiduciary duty to the target company or its shareholders.

To close this loophole, the SEC adopted Rule 14e–3, which is applicable when (1) any person has taken a substantial step or steps to commence, or has commenced, a tender offer *and* another person is in possession of material information relating to the tender offer; (2) the information that the other person knows or has reason to know is nonpublic; (3) that information has been acquired directly or indirectly from the offeror, from the issuer of the securities sought or to be sought by the tender offer (the target), or from any officer, director, partner, employee, or any other person acting on behalf of the offeror or the target; and (4) the other person purchases or sells or causes the purchase or sale of any security to be sought or in fact sought in the tender offer *or* any other security convertible into or exchangeable for that security *or* any option or right to obtain or to dispose of that security, unless (5) within a reasonable time before any purchase or sale the information *and* its source are publicly disclosed by a press release or otherwise.[54] The Supreme Court addressed this rule in the second half of the *O'Hagan* opinion.

---

[53] Securities Exchange Act Rel. 43,154 at 15–16.

[54] See generally 8 Louis Loss & Joel Seligman, Securities Regulation 3729–3739 (3d ed. 1991). The First Circuit has held that "there is simply no language in [Rule 14e–3] indicating that a defendant must know that the nonpublic information in his possession relates to a tender offer." SEC v. Sargent, 229 F.3d 68, 78 (1st Cir. 2000).

United States v. O'Hagan
Supreme Court of the United States, 1997.
521 U.S. 642, 117 S.Ct. 2199, 138 L.Ed.2d 724.

■ JUSTICE GINSBURG delivered the opinion of the Court.

* * *

III

We consider next the ground on which the Court of Appeals reversed O'Hagan's convictions for fraudulent trading in connection with a tender offer, in violation of § 14(e) of the Exchange Act and SEC Rule 14e–3(a). A sole question is before us as to these convictions: Did the Commission, as the Court of Appeals held, exceed its rulemaking authority under § 14(e) when it adopted Rule 14e–3(a) without requiring a showing that the trading at issue entailed a breach of fiduciary duty? We hold that the Commission, in this regard and to the extent relevant to this case, did not exceed its authority.

The governing statutory provision, § 14(e) of the Exchange Act, reads in relevant part:

> "It shall be unlawful for any person . . . to engage in any fraudulent, deceptive, or manipulative acts or practices, in connection with any tender offer. . . . The [SEC] shall, for the purposes of this subsection, by rules and regulations define, and prescribe means reasonably designed to prevent, such acts and practices as are fraudulent, deceptive, or manipulative." 15 U.S.C. § 78n(e).

* * *

Through § 14(e) and other provisions on disclosure in the Williams Act, Congress sought to ensure that shareholders "confronted by a cash tender offer for their stock [would] not be required to respond without adequate information." Rondeau v. Mosinee Paper Corp., 422 U.S. 49, 58 (1975); see Lewis v. McGraw, 619 F.2d 192, 195 (C.A.2 1980) (per curiam) ("very purpose" of Williams Act was "informed decisionmaking by shareholders"). As we recognized in Schreiber v. Burlington Northern, Inc., 472 U.S. 1 (1985), Congress designed the Williams Act to make "disclosure, rather than court-imposed principles of 'fairness' or 'artificiality,' . . . the preferred method of market regulation." Section 14(e), we explained, "supplements the more precise disclosure provisions found elsewhere in the Williams Act, while requiring disclosure more explicitly addressed to the tender offer context than that required by § 10(b)."

Relying on § 14(e)'s rulemaking authorization, the Commission, in 1980, promulgated Rule 14e–3(a). That measure provides:

> "(a) If any person has taken a substantial step or steps to commence, or has commenced, a tender offer (the 'offering

person'), it shall constitute a fraudulent, deceptive or manipulative act or practice within the meaning of section 14(e) of the [Exchange] Act for any other person who is in possession of material information relating to such tender offer which information he knows or has reason to know is nonpublic and which he knows or has reason to know has been acquired directly or indirectly from:

"(1) The offering person,

"(2) The issuer of the securities sought or to be sought by such tender offer, or

"(3) Any officer, director, partner or employee or any other person acting on behalf of the offering person or such issuer, to purchase or sell or cause to be purchased or sold any of such securities or any securities convertible into or exchangeable for any such securities or any option or right to obtain or to dispose of any of the foregoing securities, unless within a reasonable time prior to any purchase or sale such information and its source are publicly disclosed by press release or otherwise." 17 CFR § 240.14e–3(a) (1996).

As characterized by the Commission, Rule 14e–3(a) is a "disclose or abstain from trading" requirement. 45 Fed.Reg. 60410 (1980).[15] The Second Circuit concisely described the Rule's thrust:

"One violates Rule 14e–3(a) if he trades on the basis of material nonpublic information concerning a pending tender offer that he knows or has reason to know has been acquired 'directly or indirectly' from an insider of the offeror or issuer, or someone working on their behalf. Rule 14e–3(a) is a disclosure provision. It creates a duty in those traders who fall within its ambit to abstain or disclose, *without regard to whether the trader owes a pre-existing fiduciary duty* to respect the confidentiality of the information." United States v. Chestman, 947 F.2d 551, 557 (1991) (en banc) (emphasis added), cert. denied, 503 U.S. 1004 (1992).

* * *

In the Eighth Circuit's view, because Rule 14e–3(a) applies whether or not the trading in question breaches a fiduciary duty, the regulation exceeds the SEC's § 14(e) rulemaking authority. In support of its holding, the Eighth Circuit relied on the text of § 14(e) and our decisions in *Schreiber* and *Chiarella*.

* * *

---

[15] The Rule thus adopts for the tender offer context a requirement resembling the one Chief Justice Burger would have adopted in *Chiarella* for misappropriators under § 10(b).

The United States urges that the Eighth Circuit's reading of § 14(e) misapprehends both the Commission's authority to define fraudulent acts and the Commission's power to prevent them. "The 'defining' power," the United States submits, "would be a virtual nullity were the SEC not permitted to go beyond common law fraud (which is separately prohibited in the first [self-operative] sentence of Section 14(e))."

* * *

We need not resolve in this case whether the Commission's authority under § 14(e) to "define . . . such acts and practices as are fraudulent" is broader than the Commission's fraud-defining authority under § 10(b), for we agree with the United States that Rule 14e–3(a), as applied to cases of this genre, qualifies under § 14(e) as a "means reasonably designed to prevent" fraudulent trading on material, nonpublic information in the tender offer context.[17] A prophylactic measure, because its mission is to prevent, typically encompasses more than the core activity prohibited. As we noted in *Schreiber*, § 14(e)'s rulemaking authorization gives the Commission "latitude," even in the context of a term of art like "manipulative," "to regulate nondeceptive activities as a 'reasonably designed' means of preventing manipulative acts, without suggesting any change in the meaning of the term 'manipulative' itself." We hold, accordingly, that under § 14(e), the Commission may prohibit acts, not themselves fraudulent under the common law or § 10(b), if the prohibition is "reasonably designed to prevent . . . acts and practices [that] are fraudulent." 15 U.S.C. § 78n(e).[18]

Because Congress has authorized the Commission, in § 14(e), to prescribe legislative rules, we owe the Commission's judgment "more than mere deference or weight." Batterton v. Francis, 432 U.S. 416, 424–426 (1977). Therefore, in determining whether Rule 14e–3(a)'s "disclose or abstain from trading" requirement is reasonably designed to prevent fraudulent acts, we must accord the Commission's assessment "controlling weight unless [it is] arbitrary, capricious, or manifestly contrary to the statute." Chevron U.S.A. Inc. v. Natural Resources Defense Council, Inc., 467 U.S. 837, 844 (1984). In this case, we conclude, the Commission's assessment is none of these.

In adopting the "disclose or abstain" rule, the SEC explained:

---

[17] We leave for another day, when the issue requires decision, the legitimacy of Rule 14e–3(a) as applied to "warehousing," which the Government describes as "the practice by which bidders leak advance information of a tender offer to allies and encourage them to purchase the target company's stock before the bid is announced." As we observed in *Chiarella*, one of the Commission's purposes in proposing Rule 14e–3(a) was "to bar warehousing under its authority to regulate tender offers." 445 U.S., at 234. The Government acknowledges that trading authorized by a principal breaches no fiduciary duty. The instant case, however, does not involve trading authorized by a principal: therefore, we need not here decide whether the Commission's proscription of warehousing falls within its § 14(e) authority to define or prevent fraud.

[18] The Commission's power under § 10(b) is more limited. See supra, at 6 (Rule 10b–5 may proscribe only conduct that § 10(b) prohibits).

"The Commission has previously expressed and continues to have serious concerns about trading by persons in possession of material, nonpublic information relating to a tender offer. This practice results in unfair disparities in market information and market disruption. Security holders who purchase from or sell to such persons are effectively denied the benefits of disclosure and the substantive protections of the Williams Act. If furnished with the information, these security holders would be able to make an informed investment decision, which could involve deferring the purchase or sale of the securities until the material information had been disseminated or until the tender offer had been commenced or terminated." 45 Fed.Reg. 60412 (1980) (footnotes omitted).

The Commission thus justified Rule 14e–3(a) as a means necessary and proper to assure the efficacy of Williams Act protections.

The United States emphasizes that Rule 14e–3(a) reaches trading in which "a breach of duty is likely but difficult to prove." "Particularly in the context of a tender offer," as the Tenth Circuit recognized, "there is a fairly wide circle of people with confidential information," Peters, 978 F.2d, at 1167, notably, the attorneys, investment bankers, and accountants involved in structuring the transaction. The availability of that information may lead to abuse, for "even a hint of an upcoming tender offer may send the price of the target company's stock soaring." SEC v. Materia, 745 F.2d 197, 199 (C.A.2 1984). Individuals entrusted with nonpublic information, particularly if they have no long-term loyalty to the issuer, may find the temptation to trade on that information hard to resist in view of "the very large short-term profits potentially available [to them]." Peters, 978 F.2d, at 1167.

"[I]t may be possible to prove circumstantially that a person [traded on the basis of material, nonpublic information], but almost impossible to prove that the trader obtained such information in breach of a fiduciary duty owed either by the trader or by the ultimate insider source of the information." Ibid. The example of a "tippee" who trades on information received from an insider illustrates the problem. Under Rule 10b–5, "a tippee assumes a fiduciary duty to the shareholders of a corporation not to trade on material nonpublic information only when the insider has breached his fiduciary duty to the shareholders by disclosing the information to the tippee and the tippee knows or should know that there has been a breach." Dirks, 463 U.S., at 660. To show that a tippee who traded on nonpublic information about a tender offer had breached a fiduciary duty would require proof not only that the insider source breached a fiduciary duty, but that the tippee knew or should have known of that breach. "Yet, in most cases, the only parties to the [information transfer] will be the insider and the alleged tippee." Peters, 978 F.2d, at 1167.

In sum, it is a fair assumption that trading on the basis of material, nonpublic information will often involve a breach of a duty of confidentiality to the bidder or target company or their representatives. The SEC, cognizant of the proof problem that could enable sophisticated traders to escape responsibility, placed in Rule 14e–3(a) a "disclose or abstain from trading" command that does not require specific proof of a breach of fiduciary duty. That prescription, we are satisfied, applied to this case, is a "means reasonably designed to prevent" fraudulent trading on material, nonpublic information in the tender offer context. See Chestman, 947 F.2d, at 560 ("While dispensing with the subtle problems of proof associated with demonstrating fiduciary breach in the problematic area of tender offer insider trading, [Rule 14e–3(a)] retains a close nexus between the prohibited conduct and the statutory aims."); accord, Maio, 51 F.3d, at 635, and n. 14; Peters, 978 F.2d, at 1167.[21] Therefore, insofar as it serves to prevent the type of misappropriation charged against O'Hagan, Rule 14e–3(a) is a proper exercise of the Commission's prophylactic power under § 14(e).

RULE 14e–3 ISSUES

1. *Generally.* O'Hagan resolved that Rule 14e–3 was validly adopted. The Court did not address the meaning of such potentially ambiguous concepts as a "substantial step . . . to commence" a tender offer. The Rule 14e–3 adoption Release articulated the Commission's belief

> that a substantial step or steps to commence a tender offer include, but are not limited to, voting on a resolution by the offering person's board of directors relating to the tender offer; the formulation of a plan or proposal to make a tender offer by the offering person or the person(s) acting on behalf of the offering person; or activities which substantially facilitate the tender offer such as: arranging financing for a tender offer; preparing or directing or authorizing the preparation of tender offer materials; or authorizing negotiations, negotiating or entering into agreements with any person to act as a dealer manager, soliciting dealer, forwarding agent or depository in connection with the tender offer.[55]

2. *When Does Conduct Violate Rule 14e–3?* In O'Connor & Assoc. v. Dean Witter Reynolds, Inc.,[56] the court found that allegedly fraudulent

---

[21] Justice Thomas insists that even if the misappropriation of information from the bidder about a tender offer is fraud, the Commission has not explained why such fraud is "in connection with" a tender offer. What else, one can only wonder, might such fraud be "in connection with"?

[55] Sec. Ex. Act Rel. 17,120, 20 SEC Dock. 1350 n.33 (Sept. 4, 1980).

[56] 529 F.Supp. 1179 (S.D.N.Y. 1981).

conduct when the offer was still in a proposed state could violate Rule 14e–3, even if the offer never became effective because it was conditioned upon the target board's approval and the board rejected the proposal at the same time that it publicly announced it.[57] A substantial step to commence a tender offer can occur even absent an actual tender offer. For example, a court had no difficulty in concluding that a substantial step had been taken to accomplish a tender offer when the two firms had hired a consulting firm, signed confidentiality agreements, and held meetings between top officials.[58] Similarly, the Second Circuit held that when a potential bidder acquired a large portion in a target from which it could launch a tender offer, it constituted a substantial step even if no meetings between the bidder and the target had occurred.[59] Finally, in SEC v. Maio,[60] the court held that a meeting before the parties signed a confidentiality agreement was a substantial step toward commencing a tender offer, because one of the two corporations had earlier solicited a tender offer.

3. *Sections 13(d), 14(d), and 14(e) of the 1934 Act.* When litigation under the Williams Act came along, the initial Circuit Court decisions were in favor of the full implication of liability under § 14(e),[61] despite some initial misgivings expressed by a few district court judges.[62] The holding of these cases, that a defeated tender offeror had an implied cause of action to collect damages from the target company and its directors and officers and other persons, was, however, overruled by the Supreme Court decision in the *Piper* case.[63] The Supreme Court seemed to accept the idea, although it expressly did not rule on it since the issue was not before it, that a cause of action could be asserted under § 14(e) by the shareholders of the target company for whose "special benefit" the Williams Act was enacted. But it is difficult to see, however, how the shareholders of the target company could allege that they were injured in any way by having tendered as a result of false statements by the tender offeror, because the offer is usually at a substantial premium above market. As to those shareholders who fail to tender, this would hardly be the result of statements made by the tender offeror, which is attempting to induce them to accept, not reject, the offer. In any event, they are frequently cashed out at the same price as was paid in the tender offer.

---

[57] Id. at 1188–1193.
[58] SEC v. Mayhew, 121 F.3d 44, 52–53 (2d Cir. 1997).
[59] SEC v. Warde, 151 F.3d 42, 49 (2d Cir. 1998).
[60] 51 F.3d 623, 636 (7th Cir. 1995).
[61] See, e.g., H.K. Porter Co., Inc. v. Nicholson File Co., 482 F.2d 421 (1st Cir. 1973).
[62] See, e.g., Washburn v. Madison Square Garden Corp., 340 F.Supp. 504 (S.D.N.Y.1972).
[63] Piper v. Chris-Craft Indus., Inc., 430 U.S. 1 (1977).

In Kalmanovitz v. G. Heileman Brewing Co., Inc.,[64] the Third Circuit held that an unsuccessful tender offeror who was also a shareholder of the target company did not have standing under the *Piper* case to bring a suit for damages under § 14(e). The court stated that one who occupies those dual roles may be considered to be only an offeror for the purposes of judging his standing to bring claims under § 14(e). The court also said:

> In *Piper*, the Supreme Court left open the questions whether a private right of action exists under § 14(e) and, if so, whether a shareholder has standing to assert such a claim. * * * Although plaintiff's contention [that a private right of action exists in favor of a shareholder of the target company in view of the Supreme Court's explicit statement that the act was passed to protect such shareholders] arguably may be correct, our disposition of this case does not require us to decide that issue.[65]

With respect to false statements by management and its allies in connection with such a takeover battle, in Panter v. Marshall Field & Co.[66] the Seventh Circuit held that the shareholders of the target company could not establish any cause of action under § 14(e) in a case where the tender offer was withdrawn, since they had not "relied" on the allegedly false statements in not tendering—they had never been given an opportunity to tender. If the *Panter* case is correct, the holding seems to leave only a situation where the tender offer is not withdrawn but is defeated by allegedly false statements of the management, and the price of the stock later declines. In such a situation, the shareholders of the target company might be able to state a cause of action under § 14(e) by claiming that they had not tendered in reliance on the false statements of the management. This discussion, of course, relates to actions for damages and not for injunctive relief, which may be subject to different considerations.

The cases have generally held that an issuer has an implied private right of action under § 13(d) to seek injunctive relief, since Congress must have intended to confer a private remedy upon the issuer as the only party with the capability and the incentive to pursue violations of the reporting statute. In Gearhart Industries, Inc. v. Smith International, Inc.,[67] the court stated:

> [T]o conclude that such relief is available in no circumstances whatever—however flagrant—would be all but to license the filing of deliberately misleading 13(d) and 14(e) disclosure statements on pain of nothing more than a possible damage suit by sellers or intervention by the SEC—a body that assures us on amicus brief that its resources are inadequate to police the

---

[64] 769 F.2d 152 (3d Cir. 1985).
[65] Id. at 158–159.
[66] 646 F.2d 271 (7th Cir. 1981). See also Lewis v. McGraw, 619 F.2d 192 (2d Cir. 1980).
[67] 741 F.2d 707 (5th Cir. 1984).

myriad of 13(d) filings made each year so as to insure truthful disclosures.[68]

Reversing the district judge's holding, however, the court held that enjoining both the tender offer and the voting of the shares acquired was too "drastic" a remedy and that the injunction should hold up the tender offer only until corrective disclosures were filed.

Several circuits have now implied a private cause of action for target company stockholders under § 14(d)(7), the "Best Price" provision of the Williams Act.[69]

Problem

PROBLEM 13-2

Former business school classmates, Mike Jones and Sara Sanchez, share a one room business office in Silicon Valley. Each operates a separate financial consulting firm. Recently Jones overheard Sanchez discuss "the Incubator deal" with a client. Jones knows that Sanchez is on retainer to Incubator, Inc. Jones telephones his broker, Kelley Gunn, and asks for a research report on Incubator, a local biotech firm. Gunn telephones later that day with an upbeat report and Jones buys 1,000 shares of Incubator.

The next day Macrohard announced a friendly tender offer for Incubator at a 50 percent premium above the prior day's stock market.

Has Sara Sanchez or Mike Jones violated Rule 10b–5?

Has Mike Jones violated Rule 14e–3?

4. SECTION 16(b) LIABILITY FOR SHORT SWING PROFITS

A. INTRODUCTION

Section 16 was the original and only express "insider" trading provision in the 1934 Act. The 1934 report of the Senate Banking and Currency Committee explained:

> Among the most vicious practices unearthed at the hearings before the subcommittee was the flagrant betrayal of their fiduciary duties by directors and officers of corporations who

---

[68] 741 F.2d at 714–715. Accord: Dan River, Inc. v. Unitex Ltd., 624 F.2d 1216 (4th Cir. 1980); Chromalloy Am. Corp. v. Sun Chem. Corp., 611 F.2d 240 (8th Cir. 1979); Indiana Nat'l Corp. v. Rich, 712 F.2d 1180 (7th Cir. 1983); General Aircraft Corp. v. Lampert, 556 F.2d 90 (1st Cir. 1977). But see Liberty Nat'l Ins. Holding Co. v. Charter Co., 734 F.2d 545 (11th Cir. 1984) (no private cause of action for issuer under § 13(d) or § 14(d)); cf. Florida Commercial Banks v. Culverhouse, 772 F.2d 1513 (11th Cir. 1985) (interpreting Liberty National as limited to a right of divestiture of the shares acquired by a tender offeror).

[69] See, e.g., Field v. Trump, 850 F.2d 938, 946 (2d Cir. 1988); Polaroid Corp. v. Disney, 862 F.2d 987, 996 (3d Cir. 1988); Epstein v. MCA, Inc., 50 F.3d 644, 652 (9th Cir. 1995), reversed on other grounds, 516 U.S. 367, 370 n.1 (1996) (expressing no opinion whether an implied private cause of action exists under § 14(d)(6) or § 14(d)(7)).

used their positions of trust and the confidential information which came to them in such positions, to aid them in their market activities. Closely allied to this type of abuse was the unscrupulous employment of inside information by large stockholders who, while not directors and officers, exercised sufficient control over the destinies of their companies to enable them to acquire and profit by information not available to others.[70]

In one case described in the Committee's report on the bill, "the president of a corporation testified that he and his brothers controlled the company with a little over 10 percent of the shares; that shortly before the company passed a dividend, they disposed of their holdings for upward of $16 million and later repurchased them for about $7 million, showing a profit of approximately $9 million on the transaction."[71]

Section 16(a) provides that every officer or director of a company with an equity security registered under § 12, as well as every person "who is directly or indirectly the beneficial owner of more than 10 percent of any class of any equity security" so registered, shall file with the Commission, as well as any exchange on which the security is listed, an initial report of his or her holdings of *all* the issuer's equity securities, and a further report within two days after the close of each calendar month in which there has been any change in his or her holdings.[72] The factor that touches off the reporting requirement is the registration of an *equity* security. If a particular company has only its common stock registered, § 16 applies also to its preferred stock. But the Section does not apply to any of the securities—even equity securities—of a company that has only a nonconvertible bond issue registered. Similarly a 10+ percent owner of an *unregistered* equity security who is neither a director nor an officer is not subject to § 16 even with respect to equity securities that are registered. This is pure disclosure, except that § 16(a) serves the further function of facilitating the enforcement of § 16(b).[73]

Section 16(b) was designed to protect "outside" stockholders against short swing speculation by "insiders" with advance information. It was described by the Administration's spokesman in the 1934 hearings as a "crude rule of thumb."[74]

---

[70] S. Rep. No. 1455, 73d Cong., 2d Sess. 55 (1934).

[71] S. Rep. No. 792, 73d Cong., 2d Sess. 9 (1934).

[72] Section 403 of the Sarbanes-Oxley Act amended § 16(a) to require insider reports to be filed within ten days after a person becomes a beneficial owner, director, or officer and within two days after a change of ownership. Reports are electronically filed. Section 929R of the Dodd-Frank Act gave the SEC rulemaking power to shorten the ten-day reporting period.

[73] Because compliance with § 16(a) was a longstanding problem, the Commission in the 1991 rules revision adopted Item 405 of Regulation S–K, which requires the *registrant* to disclose, in its proxy and information statements and annual reports, the names of delinquents together with the number of transactions and number of delinquent filings for each such person.

[74] 15 Stock Exchange Practices, Hearings before Senate Comm. on Banking & Currency, 73d Cong., 2d Sess. 6557 (1934) (testimony of Thomas G. Corcoran).

Nonetheless, § 16(b) has proven to be quite controversial. Because § 16(b) imposes a form of strict liability on statutory insiders who buy and sell (or sell and buy) any equity security within any period of less than six months, the Section is vulnerable to criticism that it can impose liability upon entirely innocent persons.[75]

At the same time, the provision's simplicity (in the usual case) has undoubtedly had a substantial deterrent effect.[76] The elements of the action are simple, and the defendant is apt to find that he or she has no practical alternative but to pay up. Consequently, the number of reported decisions is probably no indicator of the total amount of short term profits recaptured or, once the Section became well known, simply foregone.[77] Conversely, although there have been quite a few reported cases, they all involved some legal question that counsel obviously thought was worth the expense of a defense.

B. Purchases and Sales

Kern County Land Co. v. Occidental Petroleum Corp.

Supreme Court of the United States, 1973.
411 U.S. 582, 93 S.Ct. 1736, 36 L.Ed.2d 503.

■ JUSTICE WHITE delivered the opinion of the Court.

Section 16(b) of the Securities Exchange Act of 1934 provides that officers, directors, and holders of more than 10% of the listed stock of any company shall be liable to the company for any profits realized from any purchase and sale or sale and purchase of such stock occurring within a period of six months. Unquestionably, one or more statutory purchases occur when one company, seeking to gain control of another, acquires more than 10% of the stock of the latter through a tender offer made to

---

[75] In Western Auto Supply Co. v. Gamble-Skogmo, Inc., 348 F.2d 736 (8th Cir. 1965), cert. denied, 382 U.S. 987 (1966), Gamble-Skogmo purchased 25,942 shares of the stock of its subsidiary, Western Auto Supply Company at $32.35 per share, and simultaneously contributed these shares to its profit-sharing trust for the benefit of its employees. Within less than six months it sold all of its previous holdings in Western Auto, over 1,200,000 shares, to Beneficial Finance Co. for $36.00 per share. Beneficial through its new subsidiary, Western Auto, recovered from Gamble-Skogmo over $94,000 representing the "profit" obtained by matching the purchase of the 25,942 shares with the sale of that number of shares to Beneficial. The court stated: "We * * * have noted the reference to the ethical position of Beneficial in seeking to recover, in effect, a part of the purchase price it willingly paid for the stock. The punctilios of the parties are not an issue here." Id. at 743 n.7.

The Western Auto Supply Company case is typical of many reported § 16(b) opinions. The courts themselves have employed such phrases as "draconian" and "purposeless harshness" in connection with § 16(b).

[76] See Whiting v. Dow Chem. Co., 523 F.2d 680, 689 (2d Cir. 1975). In 1987 an ABA Task Force endorsed retention of § 16(b) on deterrence grounds, but also suggested a few changes. Report of the Task Force on Regulation of Insider Trading Part II: Reform of Section 16, 42 Bus. Law. 1087 (1987).

[77] See Arrow Distrib. Corp. v. Baumgartner, 783 F.2d 1274, 1278 (5th Cir. 1986), amended per curiam on other grounds & reh'g denied, 783 F.2d 1274 (5th Cir. 1986).

its shareholders. But is it a § 16(b) "sale" when the target of the tender offer defends itself by merging into a third company and the tender offeror then exchanges his stock for the stock of the surviving company and also grants an option to purchase the latter stock that is not exercisable within the statutory six-month period? This is the question before us in this case.

I

On May 8, 1967, after unsuccessfully seeking to merge with Kern County Land Co. (Old Kern), Occidental Petroleum Corp. (Occidental) announced an offer, to expire on June 8, 1967, to purchase on a first-come, first-served basis 500,000 shares of Old Kern common stock at a price of $83.50 per share plus a brokerage commission of $1.50 per share. By May 10, 1967, 500,000 shares, more than 10% of the outstanding shares of Old Kern, had been tendered. On May 11, Occidental extended its offer to encompass an additional 500,000 shares. At the close of the tender offer, on June 8, 1967, Occidental owned 887,549 shares of Old Kern.

Immediately upon the announcement of Occidental's tender offer, the Old Kern management undertook to frustrate Occidental's takeover attempt. A management letter to all stockholders cautioned against tender and indicated that Occidental's offer might not be the best available, since the management was engaged in merger discussions with several companies. When Occidental extended its tender offer, the president of Old Kern sent a telegram to all stockholders again advising against tender. In addition, Old Kern undertook merger discussions with Tenneco, Inc. (Tenneco), and, on May 19, 1967, the Board of Directors of Old Kern announced that it had approved a merger proposal advanced by Tenneco. Under the terms of the merger, Tenneco would acquire the assets, property, and goodwill of Old Kern, subject to its liabilities, through "Kern County Land Company" (New Kern), a new corporation to be formed by Tenneco to receive the assets and carry on the business of Old Kern. The shareholders of Old Kern would receive a share of Tenneco cumulative convertible preference stock in exchange for each share of Old Kern common stock which they owned. On the same day, May 19, Occidental, in a quarterly report to stockholders, appraised the value of the new Tenneco stock at $105 per share.

Occidental, seeing its tender offer and takeover attempt being blocked by the Old Kern-Tenneco "defensive" merger, countered on May 25 and 31 with two mandamus actions in the California courts seeking to obtain extensive inspection of Old Kern books and records. Realizing that, if the Old Kern-Tenneco merger were approved and successfully closed, Occidental would have to exchange its Old Kern shares for Tenneco stock and would be locked into a minority position in Tenneco, Occidental took other steps to protect itself. Between May 30 and June 2, it negotiated an arrangement with Tenneco whereby Occidental granted Tenneco Corp., a subsidiary of Tenneco, an option to purchase at

$105 per share all of the Tenneco preference stock to which Occidental would be entitled in exchange for its Old Kern stock when and if the Old Kern-Tenneco merger was closed. The premium to secure the option, at $10 per share, totaled $8,866,230 and was to be paid immediately upon the signing of the option agreement. If the option were exercised, the premium was to be applied to the purchase price. By the terms of the option agreement, the option could not be exercised prior to December 9, 1967, a date six months and one day after expiration of Occidental's tender offer. On June 2, 1967, within six months of the acquisition by Occidental of more than 10% ownership of Old Kern, Occidental and Tenneco Corporation executed the option. Soon thereafter, Occidental announced that it would not oppose the Old Kern-Tenneco merger and dismissed its state court suits against Old Kern.

The Old Kern-Tenneco merger plan was presented to and approved by Old Kern shareholders at their meeting on July 17, 1967. Occidental refrained from voting its Old Kern shares, but in a letter read at the meeting Occidental stated that it had determined prior to June 2 not to oppose the merger and that it did not consider the plan unfair or inequitable. Indeed, Occidental indicated that had it been voting, it would have voted in favor of the merger.

* * *

The Old Kern-Tenneco merger transaction was closed on August 30. Old Kern shareholders thereupon became irrevocably entitled to receive Tenneco preference stock, share for share in exchange for their Old Kern stock. Old Kern was dissolved and all of its assets including "all claims, demands, rights and choses in action accrued or to accrue under and by virtue of the Securities Exchange Act of 1934 . . . ," were transferred to New Kern.

The option granted by Occidental on June 2, 1967, was exercised on December 11, 1967. Occidental, not having previously availed itself of its rights, exchanged certificates representing 887,549 shares of Old Kern stock for a certificate representing a like number of shares of Tenneco preference stock. The certificate was then endorsed over to the optionee-purchaser, and in return $84,229,185 was credited to Occidental's accounts at various banks. Adding to this amount the $8,886,230 premium paid in June, Occidental received $93,905,415 for its Old Kern stock (including the 1,900 shares acquired prior to issuance of its tender offer). In addition, Occidental received dividends totaling $1,793,439.22. Occidental's total profit was $19,506,419.22 on the shares obtained through its tender offer.

On October 17, 1967, New Kern instituted a suit under § 16(b) against Occidental to recover the profits which Occidental had realized as a result of its dealings in Old Kern stock. The complaint alleged that the execution of the Occidental-Tenneco option on June 2, 1967, and the exchange of Old Kern shares for shares of Tenneco to which Occidental became entitled pursuant to the merger closed on August 30, 1967, were both "sales" within the coverage of § 16(b). Since both acts took place within six months of the date on which Occidental became the owner of more than 10% of the stock of Old Kern, New Kern asserted that § 16(b) required surrender of the profits realized by Occidental.

* * *

II.

* * *

Although traditional cash-for-stock transactions that result in a purchase and sale or a sale and purchase within the six-month, statutory period are clearly encompassed within the purview of § 16(b), the courts have wrestled with the question of inclusion or exclusion of certain "unorthodox" transactions. The statutory definitions of "purchase" and "sale" are broad and, at least arguably, reach many transactions not ordinarily deemed a sale or purchase. In deciding whether borderline transactions are within the reach of the statute, the courts have come to inquire whether the transaction may serve as a vehicle for the evil which Congress sought to prevent—the realization of short-swing profits based upon access to inside information—thereby endeavoring to implement congressional objectives without extending the reach of the statute beyond its intended limits. The statute requires the inside, short-swing trader to disgorge all profits realized on all "purchases" and "sales" within the specified time period, without proof of actual abuse of insider information, and without proof of intent to profit on the basis of such information. Under these strict terms, the prevailing view is to apply the statute only when its application would serve its goals. "[W]here alternative constructions of the terms of § 16(b) are possible, those terms are to be given the construction that best serves the congressional purpose of curbing short-swing speculation by corporate insiders." Reliance Electric Co. v. Emerson Electric Co., supra, at 424. See Blau v. Lamb, 363 F.2d 507 (C.A.2 1966), cert. denied 385 U.S. 1002 (1967). Thus, "[i]n interpreting the terms 'purchase' and 'sale,' courts have properly asked whether the particular type of transaction involved is one that gives rise to speculative abuse." Reliance Electric Co. v. Emerson Electric Co., supra, at 424, n.4.

In the present case, it is undisputed that Occidental became a "beneficial owner" within the terms of § 16(b) when, pursuant to its tender offer, it "purchased" more than 10% of the outstanding shares of Old Kern. We must decide, however, whether a "sale" within the ambit of the statute took place either when Occidental became irrevocably bound to exchange its shares of Old Kern for shares of Tenneco pursuant to the terms of the merger agreement between Old Kern and Tenneco or when Occidental gave an option to Tenneco to purchase from Occidental the Tenneco shares so acquired.[28]

III

On August 30, 1967, the Old Kern-Tenneco merger agreement was signed, and Occidental became irrevocably entitled to exchange its shares of Old Kern stock for shares of Tenneco preference stock. Concededly, the transaction must be viewed as though Occidental had made the exchange on that day. But, even so, did the exchange involve a "sale" of Old Kern shares within the meaning of § 16(b)? We agree with the Court of Appeals that it did not, for we think it totally unrealistic to assume or infer from the facts before us that Occidental either had or was likely to have access to inside information, by reason of its ownership of more than 10% of the outstanding shares of Old Kern, so as to afford it an opportunity to reap speculative, short-swing profits from its disposition within six months of its tender offer purchases.

It cannot be contended that Occidental was an insider when, on May 8, 1967, it made an irrevocable offer to purchase 500,000 shares of Old Kern stock at a price substantially above market. At that time, it owned only 1,900 shares of Old Kern stock, far fewer than the 432,000 shares needed to constitute the 10% ownership required by the statute. There is no basis for finding that, at the time the tender offer was commenced, Occidental enjoyed an insider's opportunity to acquire information about Old Kern's affairs.

* * *

The possibility that Occidental had, or had the opportunity to have, any confidential information about Old Kern before or after May 11, 1967, seems extremely remote. Occidental was, after all, a tender offeror, threatening to seize control of Old Kern, displace its management, and use the company for its own ends. The Old Kern management vigorously and immediately opposed Occidental's efforts. Twice it communicated with its stockholders, advising against acceptance of Occidental's offer and indicating prior to May 11 and prior to Occidental's extension of its offer, that there was a possibility of an imminent merger and a more profitable exchange. Old Kern's management refused to discuss with Occidental officials the subject of an Old Kern-Occidental merger. Instead, it undertook negotiations with Tenneco and forthwith concluded an agreement, announcing the merger terms on May 19. Requests by Occidental for inspection of Old Kern records were sufficiently frustrated

---

[28] Both events occurred within six months of Occidental's first acquisition of Old Kern shares pursuant to its tender offer. Although Occidental did not exchange its Old Kern shares until December 11, 1967, it is not contended that that date, rather than the date on which Occidental became irrevocably bound to do so, should control. Similarly, although the option was not exercised until December 11, 1967, no liability is asserted with respect to that event, because it occurred more than six months after Occidental's last acquisition of Old Kern stock.

by Old Kern's management to force Occidental to litigate to secure the information it desired.

* * *

Once the merger and exchange were approved, Occidental was left with no real choice with respect to the future of its shares of Old Kern. Occidental was in no position to prevent the issuance of a ruling by the Internal Revenue Service that the exchange of Old Kern stock for Tenneco preferred would be tax-free; and, although various lawsuits were begun in state and federal courts seeking to postpone the merger closing beyond the statutory six-month period, those efforts were futile. The California Corporation Commissioner issued the necessary permits for the closing that took place on August 30, 1967.[a] The merger left no right in dissenters to secure appraisal of their stock. Occidental could, of course, have disposed of its shares of Old Kern for cash before the merger was closed. Such an act would have been a § 16(b) sale and would have left Occidental with a prima facie § 16(b) liability. It was not, therefore, a realistic alternative for Occidental as long as it felt that it could successfully defend a suit like the present one. We do not suggest that an exchange of stock pursuant to a merger may never result in § 16(b) liability. But the involuntary nature of Occidental's exchange, when coupled with the absence of the possibility of speculative abuse of inside information, convinces us that § 16(b) should not apply to transactions such as this one.

---

[a] [Eds.] This cryptic reference to "various lawsuits" and to the proceedings before the California Commissioner of Corporations conceals a monumental legal battle initiated when Occidental woke up after the shareholders' meeting to the fact that it had a § 16(b) problem if the sale of assets was consummated within six months of its purchases of stock of Old Kern, although it would seem that it would have been relatively easy for Occidental to have negotiated a postponement of the closing at the time it made its option deal with Tenneco if it had recognized the problem then. A flurry of lawsuits were filed all over the United States to enjoin the transaction until the six months had passed; an attempt was made to get the California Commissioner of Corporations to deny the permit necessary for the closing on the basis that the transaction was not "fair, just and equitable" to the shareholders of Old Kern, although Occidental had publicly read a letter to the shareholders' meeting stating that in its opinion the transaction was the "best deal" that those shareholders could get; and application was made to the Securities and Exchange Commission for a special exemptive rule to relieve Occidental of its potential Section 16(b) liability. In one county in Texas where an injunction action had been filed, Louis Nizer was flown in from New York City to represent Occidental and local counsel for Tenneco wrote a classic brief in which the country bumpkin lawyer took on the city slicker and illustrated each point of his argument with a quotation from one of Mr. Nizer's published literary efforts extolling his own exploits as an attorney. (Occidental and Mr. Nizer of course had the last laugh, when the Second Circuit reversed a $23,500,000 judgment against Occidental and the Supreme Court affirmed.) None of this effort succeeded and the transaction closed on schedule; and then the race by the 16(b) Bar to the courthouse began, initiating six years of litigation over the liability question. If the judgment against Occidental had been affirmed, the result would have been that the public shareholders of Occidental would have been forced to make a gift of $23,500,000 to the public shareholders of Tenneco. Total fees paid to lawyers throughout this fiasco are unknown, but undoubtedly ran into the millions. Cui bono?

IV

Petitioner also claims that the Occidental-Tenneco option agreement should itself be considered a sale, either because it was the kind of transaction the statute was designed to prevent or because the agreement was an option in form but a sale in fact. But the mere execution of an option to sell is not generally regarded as a "sale." See Booth v. Varian Associates, 334 F.2d 1 (C.A.1 1964), cert. denied 379 U.S. 961 (1965); Allis-Chalmers Mfg. Co. v. Gulf & Western Industries, 309 F.Supp. 75 (E.D. Wis. 1970); Marquette Cement Mfg. Co. v. Andreas, 239 F.Supp. 962 (S.D.N.Y. 1965). And we do not find in the execution of the Occidental-Tenneco option agreement a sufficient possibility for the speculative abuse of inside information with respect to Old Kern's affairs to warrant holding that the option agreement was itself a "sale" within the meaning of § 16(b). The mutual advantages of the arrangement appear quite clear. As the District Court found, Occidental wanted to avoid the position of a minority stockholder with a huge investment in a company over which it had no control and in which it had not chosen to invest. On the other hand, Tenneco did not want a potentially troublesome minority stockholder that had just been vanquished in a fight for the control of Old Kern. Motivations like these do not smack of insider trading; and it is not clear to us, as it was not to the Court of Appeals, how the negotiation and execution of the option agreement gave Occidental any possible opportunity to trade on inside information it might have obtained from its position as a major stockholder of Old Kern. Occidental wanted to get out, but only at a date more than six months thence. It was willing to get out at a price of $105 per share, a price at which it had publicly valued Tenneco preferred on May 19 when the Tenneco-Old Kern agreement was announced. In any event, Occidental was dealing with the putative new owners of Old Kern who undoubtedly knew more about Old Kern and Tenneco's affairs than did Occidental. If Occidental had leverage in dealing with Tenneco, it is incredible that its source was inside information rather than the fact of its large stock ownership itself.

Neither does it appear that the option agreement, as drafted and executed by the parties, offered measurable possibilities for speculative abuse. What Occidental granted was a "call" option. Tenneco had the right to buy after six months, but Occidental could not force Tenneco to buy. The price was fixed at $105 for each share of Tenneco preferred. Occidental could not share in a rising market for the Tenneco stock. See Silverman v. Landa, 306 F.2d 422 (C.A.2 1962). If the stock fell more than $10 per share, the option might not be exercised, and Occidental might suffer a loss if the market further deteriorated to a point where Occidental was forced to sell. Thus, the option, by its very form, left Occidental with no choice but to sell if Tenneco exercised the option, which it was almost sure to do if the value of Tenneco stock remained relatively steady. On the other hand, it is difficult to perceive any speculative value to Occidental if the stock declined and Tenneco chose not to exercise its option.

The option, therefore, does not appear to have been an instrument with potential for speculative abuse, whether or not Occidental possessed inside information about the affairs of Old Kern. In addition, the option covered Tenneco preference stock, a stock as yet unissued, unregistered, and untraded. It was the value of this stock that underlay the option and that determined whether the option would be exercised, whether Occidental would be able to profit from the exercise, and whether there was any real likelihood of the exploitation of inside information.

* * *

Nor can we agree that we must reverse the Court of Appeals on the ground that the option agreement was in fact a sale because the premium paid was so large as to make the exercise of the option almost inevitable, particularly when coupled with Tenneco's desire to rid itself of a potentially troublesome stockholder. The argument has force, but resolution of the question is very much a matter of judgment, economic and otherwise, and the Court of Appeals rejected the argument. That court emphasized that the premium paid was what experts had said the option was worth, the possibility that the market might drop sufficiently in the six months following execution of the option to make exercise unlikely, and the fact that here, unlike the situation in Bershad v. McDonough, 428 F.2d 693 (C.A.7 1970), the optionor did not surrender practically all emoluments of ownership by executing the option. Nor did any other special circumstances indicate that the parties understood and intended that the option was in fact a sale. We see no satisfactory basis or reason for disagreeing with the judgment of the Court of Appeals in this respect.

The judgment of the Court of Appeals is *affirmed*.

So ordered.

* * *

"PURCHASE" AND "SALE"

1. *Generally.* The unorthodox transaction analysis in *Kern* is limited to involuntary transactions. For example, in Colan v. Mesa Petroleum Co.,[78] where Mesa abandoned its tender offer for Unocal and participated in a recapitalization incident to Unocal's self-tender offer by exchanging Unocal stock that it had bought in the market three months earlier for Unocal bonds created in the recapitalization, the court distinguished *Kern* on the ground that Mesa's exchange was voluntary.

---

[78] 951 F.2d 1512 (9th Cir. 1991). See also C.R.A. Realty Corp. v. Fremont Gen. Corp., 5 F.3d 1341 (9th Cir. 1993).

The broader issue implicated by *Kern* is the meaning of "purchase" and "sale." A "purchase" or "sale" for the purposes of § 16(b) may occur even though there is not a cash transaction, but an exchange of stock for property or for other stock. The courts long struggled with discerning when convertible securities transactions would involve a "purchase" or "sale."[79] Similarly, with respect to the options, *Kern* rejected the acquisition of an option, in contrast to exercise of the option, as a purchase under § 16(b). This approach was subject to sharp criticism.[80]

2. *Derivative Securities.* In 1991 the Commission adopted Rule 16a–1(c), which generally defines the term "derivative securities" to mean "any option, warrant, convertible security, stock appreciation right, or similar right with an exercise or conversion privilege at a price related to an equity security."[81] Call options are options to purchase; put options are options to sell. Both under the 1991 rules and earlier, the purchase *and* sale of a derivative security can be actionable under § 16(b), whether derivative securities are purchased in the open market, from the issuer, or in any other way.[82] As *Kern* suggests, § 16(b) attaches also to any purchase or sale of stock through the exercise of a derivative security.[83]

The premise of Rule 16b–6 was that holding a derivative security is functionally equivalent, for § 16 purposes, to holding the underlying security:

> The former Commission Section 16 rules and case law, by failing to recognize the functional equivalence of derivative securities

---

[79] Cf. Park & Tilford v. Schulte, 160 F.2d 984, 987 (2d Cir. 1947) (conversion of senior security into common stock was a "purchase"); Ferraiolo v. Newman, 259 F.2d 342 (6th Cir. 1958) (conversion of preferred stock into common stock did not involve "purchase").

[80] See, e.g., Kern County Land Co. v. Occidental Petroleum Corp., 411 U.S. 582, 605 (1973) (Douglas, J., dissenting); Seinfeld v. Hospital Corp. of Amer., 685 F.Supp. 1057, 1065–1067 (N.D. Ill.1988).

[81] Sec. Ex. Act Rel. 28,869, 48 SEC Dock. 216 (1991). There are several exceptions.
A "blocker" provision limiting a shareholder's ability to convert shares into common stock to 4.99 percent prevented a defendant from being subject to § 16(b). Levy v. Marshall Capital Management, Inc., 2000–2001 Fed.Sec.L.Rep. (CCH) ¶ 91,230 (E.D.N.Y. 2000). See also Schaffer v. CC Inv., LDC, 115 F.Supp.2d 440 (S.D.N.Y. 2000) (similar conversion cap).

[82] See Rule 16a–4.
Several other items are defined in the 1991 rules. See Rules 16a–1(b) ("call equivalent position"); 16a–1(h) ("put equivalent position"); 16a–1(d) ("equity security of such issuer").
In Magma Power Co. v. Dow Chem. Co., 136 F.3d 316, 322–323 (2d Cir. 1998), the court concluded: "The establishment of a 'call equivalent position' constitutes a purchase of the underlying security for purposes of section 16(b)."

[83] See, e.g., Seinfeld v. Hospital Corp. of Am., 685 F.Supp. 1057, 1065 (N.D. Ill. 1988).
In Gwozdzinsky v. Zell/Chilmark Fund, L.P., 156 F.3d 305, 308–309 (2d Cir. 1998), the court concluded:
In the case of derivative securities, the SEC has defined the terms "purchase" and "sale" broadly. See, e.g., 17 C.F.R. § 16(b)–6(a). Thus, under Rule 16b–6(d), any insider who writes a put option on securities of the issuer is liable under § 16(b) to the extent of any premium received for writing the option if the option is either canceled or expires unexercised within six months of its writing, an event that is deemed a "sale" for purposes of § 16(b). This rule is designed to prevent a scheme whereby an insider with inside information favorable to the issuer writes a put option, and receives a premium for doing so, knowing, by virtue of his inside information, that the option will not be exercised within six months.

and the underlying equity securities, and by therefore focusing on the exercise, rather than the acquisition, of the derivative security, have left open a significant potential for short-swing abuse in trading derivative securities, while permitting recovery in situations that represent long-term investments.[84] For example, an insider with knowledge of a positive material development, to be announced shortly, determines that while he wants to retain his existing equity position, he wants to take advantage of the information, so he purchases issuer warrants. After the public announcement and rise in stock price the insider sells his common stock, obtaining a short-swing profit, knowing that he holds the warrants. Under the former rules, he could simply wait six months and a day to exercise the warrants so the profit would not be subject to Section 16(b) and not recoverable by the company. Ironically, however, an insider who purchased a warrant for investment purposes, exercised the warrant after a year and sold the underlying stock five months later—17 months after the purchase of the warrant, far beyond the six month period the statute defines as short-swing—would be subject to short-swing profit recovery.

Given the short-swing profit potential presented by transactions in derivative securities, the Commission has amended the rules to make it clear that ownership of derivative securities constitutes beneficial ownership of the underlying equity securities for purposes of Section 16. Therefore, transactions in options, convertible securities, warrants and similar derivative securities will be matchable with transactions in other derivative securities and in the underlying equity, and the profits recoverable by the corporation.[85]

3. *Mergers and Tender Offers.* The SEC has impliedly ruled that statutory mergers and consolidations are covered generally, because some transactions are exempt in Rule 16b–7. That rule provides that where one of the corporations involved in a merger or consolidation owns 85 percent or more of the stock of the other corporation before the merger, or had 85 percent or more of the combined assets of all corporations involved in the merger or consolidation, any acquisition or disposition of securities by its shareholders in connection with the merger or consolidation is not a purchase or sale under § 16(b). In other words, if there is a "downstairs" merger of a corporation into its own subsidiary, or a merger of a "giant" corporation into a "pygmy," and in either case the percentage test is met, the shareholders of the merging corporation have not made a sale of their stock in the merging corporation nor a purchase of the stock received by them in the continuing corporation, for the

---

[84] Nonetheless Kern County held that the mere grant of an option is not a sale, or, implicitly, a purchase. 411 U.S. 582, 601.

[85] Sec. Ex. Act Rel. 28,869, 48 SEC Dock. 216, 226, 229 (1991).

purpose of § 16(b). The rule does not apply if the person makes both a purchase of a security of a corporation involved in the merger and a sale of a security of any other corporation involved in the merger (other than the merger transaction itself) during a six-month period within which the merger occurs.

Where the merger or sale of assets falls outside the terms of this exemptive rule, the *Kern* case holds that it *may be* a sale of the stock of the acquired corporation (and presumably a purchase of stock of the acquiring corporation). Note that in the case of such an "unorthodox" transaction, it will not be a purchase or sale if there is no "possibility" that the transaction could "lend itself" to the abuses which § 16(b) was designed to prevent. In American Standard, Inc. v. Crane Co.,[86] the Second Circuit held that where an unsuccessful tender offeror was forced to exchange its holdings for those of another company with which the target company had arranged a "defensive merger," that exchange was not a sale of the securities purchased nor a purchase of the securities received in the merger which could be matched with its sale of those securities within six months. The court also held that the tender offeror's original purchases of stock of the target company which disappeared in the merger could not be matched with its sale of the securities received in the merger, although those also were within a period of six months, because they were securities of different issuers.

The cases have generally held that a transaction in which a hostile tender offeror tenders the shares acquired by him to a "white knight" or sells them back to the issuer in a "greenmail" transaction is not an "unorthodox transaction" within the meaning of the *Kern* case, since it is merely a voluntary sale for cash.[87] On the other hand, the Second Circuit held that a defeated tender offeror that was forced to accept securities of a rival bidder, when the target company was merged with a subsidiary of the white knight, was not liable under § 16(b) under the rationale of the *Kern* case. The exchange of securities was involuntary (the defendant voted against the merger) and there was no possibility of access to inside information in view of the relationship of the defendant to the issuer.[88]

In Gollust v. Mendell,[89] the Supreme Court held that where a merger of a subsidiary corporation into its parent was carried out after the institution of a suit under Section 16(b) by a shareholder of the subsidiary, and the plaintiff shareholder received stock of the parent corporation in the merger, the plaintiff shareholder was not divested of standing to pursue the litigation. The literal language of the statute requires only that the plaintiff be a shareholder of the "issuer" at the time the suit is "*instituted*." A cash-out merger divesting the plaintiff of any

---

[86] 510 F.2d 1043 (2d Cir. 1974), cert. denied, 421 U.S. 1000 (1975).

[87] Texas Int'l Airlines v. National Airlines, Inc., 714 F.2d 533 (5th Cir. 1983); Super Stores, Inc. v. Reiner, 737 F.2d 962 (11th Cir. 1984).

[88] Heublein, Inc. v. General Cinema Corp., 722 F.2d 29 (2d Cir. 1983).

[89] 501 U.S. 115 (1991).

interest in the parent corporation or the subsidiary, whether carried out before or after the institution of the action under § 16(b), would deprive the shareholder of any standing to bring that action. The Court said that the plaintiff must have a "continuing interest" in the litigation until judgment in order to avoid raising a serious question under the constitutional requirement in Article III of a "case or controversy."

"ANY PERIOD OF LESS THAN SIX MONTHS"

Any purchase or sale may be matched under § 16(b) with any sale or purchase within six months before or after its date, not merely three months before or after such date.[90] A "period of less than six months" means, since the law does not take account of fractions of days, a period commencing at 0001 hours on one day and ending at midnight on the day two days before the corresponding date in the sixth succeeding month; e.g., from January 15, through July 13, inclusive, in any year. On the other hand, a purchase at 8:00 a.m. on January 15 followed by a sale at 4:00 p.m. on July 14 would be in a period of exactly six months (since January 15 and July 14 are counted as full days), and not within a period of "less than" six months.[91]

"PROFIT REALIZED"

The 1943 Second Circuit opinion, Smolowe v. Delendo Corp.,[92] has long been the controlling precedent on how to calculate the "profit realized" when there is more than one pair of transactions within a six month period:

> We must suppose that the statute was intended to be thoroughgoing, to squeeze all possible profits out of stock transactions, and thus to establish a standard so high as to prevent any conflict between the selfish interest of a fiduciary officer, director, or stockholder and the faithful performance of his duty. The only rule whereby all possible profits can be surely

---

[90] Gratz v. Claughton, 187 F.2d 46 (2d Cir. 1951). To calculate "how long is six months when measured from the last day of a month with thirty one days to a month with no corresponding thirty first day," the court in Jammies Int'l, Inc. v. Nowinski, 700 F.Supp. 189 (S.D.N.Y. 1988), picked the last day of the sixth month rather than the first day of the seventh month. The "draconian penalties" of § 16(b) should not be applied when confusion exists regarding whether its terms have been violated. Id. at 192.

[91] Stella v. Graham-Paige Motors Corp., 132 F.Supp. 100, 103–104 (S.D.N.Y. 1955), rev'd on other grounds, 232 F.2d 299 (2d Cir. 1956); Colonial Realty Corp. v. MacWilliams, 381 F.Supp. 26 (S.D.N.Y.1974); Morales v. Reading & Bates Offshore Drilling Co., 392 F.Supp. 41 (N.D. Okla. 1975) (citing this casebook).

[92] 136 F.2d 231, 239 (2d Cir. 1943).

recovered is that of lowest price in, highest price out—within six months—as applied by the district court.

More specifically the calculation proceeds as follows:

Listed in one column are all the purchases made during the period for which recovery of profits is sought. In another column are listed all of the sales during that period. Then the shares purchased at the lowest price are matched against an equal number of the shares sold at the highest price within six months of such purchase, and the profit computed. After that the next lowest price is matched against the next highest price and that profit is computed. Then, the same process is repeated until all the shares in the purchase column which may be matched against shares sold for higher prices in the sale column have been matched off. Where necessary to accurate computation it would seem proper to split a larger denomination or lot of shares in order to match off part of the lot against an equal amount on the other side. The gross recovery is the sum of the profits thus determined.[93]

But "obviously no transaction can figure in more than one equation."[94] If there is a purchase of 100 shares on February 1 followed by a sale of 100 shares on March 1 and another purchase of 100 shares on April 1, the sale on March 1 can be matched against either purchase (the plaintiff, of course, will pick the one at the lower price) but not both. On the other hand, if the case were the same except that 200 shares were sold on March 1, presumably 100 of that figure could be match against the February 1 purchase and the other 100 against the April 1 purchase.

C. OFFICERS AND DIRECTORS

Feder v. Martin Marietta Corp.
United States Court of Appeals, Second Circuit, 1969.
406 F.2d 260.

- Before WATERMAN, SMITH and HAYS, CIRCUIT JUDGES.

- WATERMAN, CIRCUIT JUDGE:

Plaintiff-appellant, a stockholder of the Sperry Rand Corporation ("Sperry") after having made the requisite demand upon Sperry which was not complied with, commenced this action pursuant to § 16(b) of the Securities Exchange Act of 1934, 15 U.S.C. § 78p(b) (1964), to recover for Sperry "short-swing" profits realized upon Sperry stock purchases and sales by the Martin Marietta Corporation ("Martin"). Plaintiff alleged that George M. Bunker, the President and Chief Executive of Martin

---

[93] Robert S. Rubin & Myer Feldman, Statutory Inhibitions upon Unfair Use of Corporate Information by Insiders, 95 U. Pa. L. Rev. 468, 482–483 (1947).

[94] Gratz v. Claughton, 187 F.2d 46, 52 (2d Cir. 1951).

Marietta, was deputized by, or represented, Martin Marietta when he served as a member of the Sperry Rand Board of Directors and therefore during his membership Martin Marietta was a "director" of Sperry Rand within the meaning of Section 16(b). The United States District Court for the Southern District of New York, Cooper, J., sitting without a jury, finding no deputization, dismissed plaintiff's action. 286 F.Supp. 937 (S.D.N.Y. 1968). We hold to the contrary and reverse the judgment below.

The purpose of § 16(b) as succinctly expressed in the statute itself is to prevent "unfair use of information" by insiders and thereby to protect the public and outside stockholders. The only remedy which the framers of § 16(b) deemed effective to curb insider abuse of advance information was the imposition of a liability based upon an objective measure of proof, e.g., Smolowe v. Delendo Corp., 136 F.2d 231, 235 (2d Cir.), cert. denied 320 U.S. 751 (1943). Thus, application of the act is not conditional upon proof of an insider's intent to profit from unfair use of information, e.g., Blau v. Lamb, 363 F.2d 507, 515 (2 Cir. 1966), cert. denied 385 U.S. 1002 (1967), or upon proof that the insider was privy to any confidential information, e.g., Ferraiolo v. Newman, 259 F.2d 342, 344 (6th Cir. 1958), cert. denied, 359 U.S. 927 (1959). Rather, Section 16(b) liability is automatic, and liability attaches to any profit by an insider on any short-swing transaction embraced within the arbitrarily fixed time limits of the statute.

The judicial tendency, especially in this circuit, has been to interpret Section 16(b) in ways that are most consistent with the legislative purpose, even departing where necessary from the literal statutory language. See, e.g., cases cited in Blau v. Oppenheim, 250 F.Supp. 881, 884–885 (S.D.N.Y.1966) (Weinfeld, J.). But the policy underlying the enactment of § 16(b) does not permit an expansion of the statute's scope to persons other than directors, officers, and 10% shareholders. Blau v. Lehman, 368 U.S. 403, 410–411 (1962). Through the creation of a legal fiction, however, our courts have managed to remain within the limits of § 16(b)'s literal language and yet have expanded the Act's reach.

In Rattner v. Lehman, 193 F.2d 564 (2d Cir. 1952), Judge Learned Hand in his concurring opinion planted the seed for a utilization of the theory of deputization upon which plaintiff here proceeds. In discussing the question whether a partnership is subject to Section 16(b) liability whenever a partner is a director of a corporation whose stock the partnership traded, Judge Hand state[d]:

> I agree that § 16(b) does not go so far; but I wish to say nothing as to whether, if a firm deputed a partner to represent its interests as a director on the board, the other partners would not be liable. True, they would not even then be formally "directors"; but I am not prepared to say that they could not be so considered; for some purposes the common law does treat a firm as a jural person. 193 F.2d at 567.

The Supreme Court in Blau v. Lehman, 368 U.S. 403, 408–410 (1962), affirming 286 F.2d 786 (2d Cir. 1960), affirming 173 F.Supp. 590 (S.D.N.Y. 1959) more firmly established the possibility of an entity, such as a partnership or a corporation, incurring Section 16(b) liability as a "director" through the deputization theory. Though the Court refused to reverse the lower court decisions that had held no deputization, it stated:

> Although admittedly not "literally designated" as one, it is contended that Lehman is a director. No doubt Lehman Brothers, though a partnership, could for purposes of § 16 be a "director" of Tide Water and function through a deputy * * *. 368 U.S. at 409.

In Marquette Cement Mfg. Co. v. Andreas, 239 F.Supp. 962, 967 (S.D.N.Y. 1965), relying upon Blau v. Lehman, the availability of the deputization theory to impose § 16(b) liability was again recognized.

In light of the above authorities, the validity of the deputization theory, presumed to be valid here by the parties and by the district court, is unquestionable. Nevertheless, the situations encompassed by its application are not as clear. The Supreme Court in Blau v. Lehman intimated that the issue of deputization is a question of fact to be settled case by case and not a conclusion of law. Therefore, it is not enough for appellant to show us that inferences to support appellant's contentions should have been drawn from the evidence. Rather our review of the facts and inferences found by the court below is imprisoned by the "unless clearly erroneous" standard. Fed. R. Civ. P. 52(a). In the instant case, applying that standard, though there is some evidence in the record to support the trial court's finding of no deputization, we, upon considering the entire evidence, are left with the definite and firm conviction that a mistake was committed. Consequently, we reverse the result reached below.

Bunker served as a director of Sperry from April 29, 1963 to August 1, 1963, when he resigned. During the period December 14, 1962 through July 24, 1963, Martin Marietta accumulated 801,300 shares of Sperry stock of which 101,300 shares were purchased during Bunker's directorship. Between August 29, 1963 and September 6, 1963, Martin Marietta sold all of its Sperry stock. Plaintiff seeks to reach, on behalf of the Sperry Rand Corporation, the profits made by Martin Marietta from the 101,300 shares of stock acquired between April 29 and August 1, all of which, of course, were sold within six months after purchase.

The district court, in determining that Bunker was not a Martin deputy, made the following findings of fact to support its decision: (1) Sperry initially invited Bunker to join its Board two and a half months before Martin began its accumulation of Sperry stock; (2) Bunker turned down a second offer by Sperry at a time when Martin already held 400,000 shares of Sperry stock; (3) Sperry, not Martin, took the initiative to encourage Bunker to accept the directorship; (4) no other Martin man was ever mentioned for the position in the event Bunker absolutely declined; and (5) Bunker's fine reputation and engineering expertise was the prime motivation for Sperry's interest in him. In addition, the testimony of the only two witnesses who testified at trial, Mr. Bunker and a Mr. Norman Frost, a Sperry director and its chief counsel, were fully believed and accepted as truthful by the court. We assume all of the foregoing findings have a basis of fact in the evidence, but we find there was additional, more germane, uncontradicted evidence, overlooked or ignored by the district court, which we are firmly convinced require us to conclude that Martin Marietta was a "director" of Sperry Rand.

First and foremost is Bunker's testimony that as chief executive of Martin Marietta he was "ultimately responsible for the total operation of the corporation" including personal approval of all the firm's financial investments, and, in particular, all of Martin's purchases of Sperry stock. As the district court aptly recognized, Bunker's control over Martin Marietta's investments, coupled with his position on the Board of Directors of Sperry Rand, placed him in a position where he could acquire inside information concerning Sperry and could utilize such data for Martin Marietta's benefit without disclosing this information to any other Martin Marietta personnel. Thus, the district court's findings that Bunker "never disclosed inside information relevant to investment decisions" and that the "information that he obtained while a director 'simply wasn't germane to that question at all'" are not significant. Nor are these findings totally supported by the evidence. Bunker's testimony revealed that while he was a Sperry director three Sperry officials had furnished him with information relating to the "short-range outlook" at Sperry, and, in addition, Bunker admitted discussing Sperry's affairs with two officials at Martin Marietta and participating in sessions when Martin's investment in Sperry was reviewed. Moreover, an unsigned document concededly originating from the Martin Marietta files, entitled "Notes on Exploratory Investment in Sperry Rand Corporation," describing the Sperry management, evaluating their abilities, and analyzing the merit of Sperry's forecasts for the future, further indicates that Martin Marietta may have benefited, or intended to benefit, from Bunker's association with Sperry Rand.

In contrast, in Blau v. Lehman, where Lehman Brothers was the alleged "director," the Lehman partner exercised no power of approval concerning the partnership's investment; was not consulted for advice; had no advance knowledge of Lehman Brothers' intention to purchase the stock of the corporation of which he was a member of the board of directors; and never discussed the operating details of that corporation's affairs with any member of Lehman Brothers. Similarly, in Rattner v. Lehman, the court's decision was premised on the assumption that the defendant's purchases and sales were made without any advice or concurrence from the defendant's partner sitting on the Board of the company in whose stock the defendant traded.

It appears to us that a person in Bunker's unique position could act as a deputy for Martin Marietta even in the absence of factors indicating an intention or belief on the part of both companies that he was so acting. We do not hold that, without more, Bunker's control over Martin Marietta, or the possibility that inside information was obtained or disclosed, mandates that Bunker was Martin's deputy. However, additional evidence detailed hereafter which indicates that the managements of Sperry Rand and of Martin Marietta intended that Bunker should act as Martin's deputy on the Sperry Board, and believed he was so acting, lends valuable support to our factual conclusion.

First, in Bunker's letter of resignation to General MacArthur, the Chairman of the Board of Directors of Sperry Rand, he stated:

> When I became a member of the Board in April, it appeared to your associates that the Martin Marietta ownership of a substantial number of shares of Sperry Rand should have representation on your Board. This representation does not seem to me really necessary and I prefer not to be involved in the affairs of Sperry Rand when there are so many other demands on my time * * *.

Martin Marietta urges that we should not read this letter to mean what it so clearly says. They would have us believe that this letter was so phrased because Bunker intended "to write a gentle letter of resignation to a great (but elderly) man whom he admired, in terms that he would understand." No matter how advanced in years the Chairman of the Sperry Board may have been, we are puzzled by defendant's contention that he, and only he, of all those on the Sperry Board, considered Bunker to be representing Martin's interests. Furthermore, if, throughout Bunker's service, the Chairman of the Board misunderstood the purpose of Bunker's directorship, why Bunker upon resignation would want this misunderstanding perpetuated is even more perplexing. Certainly the more logical inference from the wording of Bunker's letter of resignation is the inference that Bunker served on the Sperry Board as a representative of Martin Marietta so as to protect Martin's investment in Sperry.

Second, the Board of Directors of Martin Marietta formally consented to and approved Bunker's directorship of Sperry prior to Bunker's acceptance of the position. While Martin's organizational policy required that Bunker secure that Board's approval of any corporate directorship he were [sic] offered, the approval was not obtained until, significantly, the Board had been informed by Bunker that Martin had a 10 million dollar investment in Sperry stock at the time. Bunker testified that he "thought the Board would draw the inference that his presence on Sperry's Board would be to Martin's interest." Indeed, as noted by the district court, "the logic behind such an inference is obvious when we stop to consider that a directorship, by its very nature, carries with it potential access to information unavailable to the ordinary investor." Surely such conduct by the Martin Board supports an inference that it deputized Bunker to represent its interests on Sperry's Board. The trial court's finding to the contrary leaves us with the definite and firm conviction that a mistake was indeed committed.

* * *

In summary, it is our firm conviction that the district court erred in apportioning the weight to be accorded the evidence before it. The control possessed by Bunker, his letter of resignation, the approval by the Martin Board of Bunker's directorship with Sperry, and the functional similarity between Bunker's acts as a Sperry director and the acts of Martin's representatives on other boards, as opposed to the factors relied upon by the trial court, are all definite and concrete indicatives that Bunker, in fact, was a Martin deputy, and we find that indeed he was.

The trial court's disposition of the case obviated the need for it to determine whether § 16(b) liability could attach to the corporate director's short-swing profits realized after the corporation's deputy had ceased to be a member of the board of directors of the corporation whose stock had been so profitably traded in. It was not until after Bunker's resignation from the Sperry Board had become effective that Martin Marietta sold any Sperry stock. The issue is novel and until this case no court has ever considered the question. We hold that the congressional purpose dictates that Martin must disgorge all short-swing profits made from Sperry stock purchased during its Sperry directorship and sold after the termination thereof if sold within six months of purchase.

* * *

OFFICER OR DIRECTOR

1. *Defined.* The term "officer" is defined by the SEC to mean "an issuer's president, principal financial officer, or principal accounting officer (or, if there is no such accounting officer, the controller), any vice-president of the issuer in charge of a principal business unit, division or function (such as sales, administration or finance), any other officer who performs a policy-making function, or any other person who performs similar policy-making functions for the issuer. Officers of the issuer's parent(s) or subsidiaries shall be deemed officers of the issuer if they perform such policy-making functions for the issuer."[95] An officer of a subsidiary of the issuer has been held not to be subject to § 16(b), unless he or she is in fact performing the functions of an officer of the parent corporation.[96]

---

[95] Rule 16a–1(f).

[96] Lee Nat'l Corp. v. Segur, 281 F.Supp. 851 (E.D. Pa. 1968). However, a person who was the "Executive Vice-President of International Operations" of a corporation and "one of the more active members of the executive committee" did not get anywhere with the argument that he

In Merrill Lynch, Pierce, Fenner & Smith, Inc. v. Livingston,[97] the Ninth Circuit held that a securities salesman with the "honorary" title of vice president was not an officer with access to inside information within the coverage of § 16(b).[98] The court held that it must look behind the title of the person to ascertain his real duties and that "a person who does not have the title of an officer, may, in fact, have a relationship to the company which gives him the very access to insider information that the statute was designed to reach."[99]

The SEC rules adopted in 1991 have embodied the approach of these cases in making the determination of whether an individual is an officer dependent upon function rather than title. In a note to Rule 16a–1(f), the Commission indicated that " '[p]olicy-making function' is not intended to include policy-making functions that are not significant."

2. *Timing of Liability*. Officers or directors may be liable for short-swing profits on stock which was registered at the time of the purchase or sale, although not at the time of the matching transaction less than six months earlier.[100] The *Feder* case reached the same result, where the defendant was only an officer or director at the time of the purchase and not at the time of the subsequent sale after he left office. Both the Second Circuit[101] and the Third Circuit[102] have held, however, that liability should not be imposed upon a director or officer where both ends of the transaction occurred after he left office, even though within six months thereafter.

The 1991 Section 16 Rules have overruled the first result of the cases mentioned above by exempting the front end of any transaction which occurs before a person becomes an officer or director, on the theory that the person could not normally have had any access to inside information before he became an insider; and if in fact he did, a remedy would exist under Rule 10b–5. Those rules, however, have adopted all of the other results of the cases cited above.

D. BENEFICIAL OWNERSHIP

In the past, if a statutory insider owned or controlled one or more companies that traded in the securities of the corporation in which the statutory insider held office, the courts had held that the benefit to the insider was too "indirect" (whether the insider was a director of the

---

was "merely a figurehead" and should not be liable under § 16(b). Selas Corp. of Am. v. Voogd, 365 F.Supp. 1268 (E.D. Pa. 1973).

[97] 566 F.2d 1119 (9th Cir. 1978).

[98] This holding was limited, however, in the subsequent Ninth Circuit case of National Medical Enterprises, Inc. v. Small, 680 F.2d 83, 84 (9th Cir. 1982), to a situation where the person's title "is essentially honorary or ceremonial."

[99] 566 F.2d at 1122.

[100] Arrow Distributing Corp. v. Baumgartner, 783 F.2d 1274 (5th Cir. 1986).

[101] Lewis v. Varnes, 505 F.2d 785 (2d Cir. 1974).

[102] Lewis v. Mellon Bank, 513 F.2d 921 (3d Cir. 1975).

corporation or a 10% holder) to hold this insider responsible for disgorgement of profits under § 16(b).[103] But the Second Circuit seemingly reversed this rule in Feder v. Frost.[104] There, the individual who was CEO and Chairman of the Board of IVAX Corporation also controlled another entity, FNLP, which in turn controlled still another entity, NAVI. During a six month period, NAVI sold IVAX stock and the CEO and FNLP purchased it, resulting in short-swing profits. The Second Circuit required both the CEO and his controlled entity (FNLP) to disgorge these profits, relying on revised SEC Rule 16–1(a)(2). That Rule specified that "the term beneficial owner shall mean any person who, directly or indirectly, . . . has or shares a direct or indirect pecuniary interest in the equity securities" and specifically included "a general partner's proportionate interest in the portfolio securities in the general or limited partnership." Is this a trap for the unwary? Or should the CEO have recognized that his controlled companies were doing what he could not do?

TEN PERCENT HOLDER

In 1976 the Supreme Court decided the case of Foremost-McKesson, Inc. v. Provident Securities Co.,[105] holding that the defendant had to be a 10% holder *before* the purchase in order to impose liability upon it under § 16(b). The Court stated:

> Our construction of § 16(b) also is supported by the distinction Congress recognized between short-term trading by mere stockholders and such trading by directors and officers. The legislative discourse revealed that Congress thought that all short-swing trading by directors and officers was vulnerable to abuse because of their intimate involvement in corporate affairs. But trading by mere stockholders was viewed as being subject to abuse only when the size of their holdings afforded the potential for access to corporate information. These different perceptions simply reflect the realities of corporate life.
>
> It would not be consistent with this perceived distinction to impose liability on the basis of a purchase made when the percentage of stock ownership requisite to insider status had not been acquired. To be sure, the possibility does exist that one who becomes a beneficial owner by a purchase will sell on the basis of information attained by virtue of his newly acquired holdings. But the purchase itself was not one posing dangers that Congress considered intolerable, since it was made when the purchaser owned no shares or less than the percentage deemed

---

[103] See Mayer v. Chesapeake Insurance Co., 877 F.2d 1154 (2d 1989).
[104] 220 F.3d 29 (2d Cir. 2000).
[105] 423 U.S. 232 (1976).

necessary to make one an insider. Such a stockholder is more analogous to the stockholder who never owns more than 10% and thereby is excluded entirely from the operation of § 16(b), than to a director or officer whose every purchase and sale is covered by the statute. While this reasoning might not compel our construction of the exemptive provision, it explains why Congress may have seen fit to draw the line it did. Cf. Adler v. Klawans, 267 F.2d 840, 845 (C.A.2 1959).[106]

In Reliance Electric Co. v. Emerson Electric Co.,[107] the Supreme Court held that where a 10% holder sold an amount of stock sufficient to bring him below the 10% level and then sold the remainder of his holdings, both sales being within six months of a purchase, only the first sale could be matched with the purchase to produce § 16(b) liability, even though the sales were arranged in this way for the express purpose of avoiding such liability with respect to the second sale. The Court said: "In this case, the respondent, the owner of 13.2% of a corporation's shares, disposed of its entire holdings in two sales, both of them within six months of purchase. The first sale reduced the respondent's holdings to 9.96% and the second disposed of the remainder. The question presented is whether the profits derived from the second sale are recoverable by the Corporation under § 16(b). We hold that they are not."

In Chemical Fund, Inc. v. Xerox Corp.,[108] a mutual fund purchased more than 10% of an outstanding issue of convertible debentures of Xerox Corp. The debentures were a registered security and an "equity security" as defined in the 1934 Act, but these debentures were convertible into only approximately 2.72% of the Xerox common stock. The fund purchased convertible debentures of Xerox and sold common stock of Xerox within a six month period. The Second Circuit held:

> Thus the question is: are the Debentures by themselves a "class of any equity security," or does the class consist of the common stock augmented, as to any beneficial holder in question, by the number of shares into which the Debentures it owns are convertible? We think that the Debentures are not a class by themselves; the total percentage of common stock which a holder would own following a hypothetical conversion of the Debentures it holds is the test of liability under section 16(b). The history of the legislation, the stated purpose of the Act, and the anomalous consequences of any other meaning all support this conclusion.[109]

---

[106] 423 U.S. at 253–254.
[107] 404 U.S. 418, 419–420 (1972).
[108] 377 F.2d 107 (2d Cir. 1967).
[109] 377 F.2d at 110. Compare with the Chemical Fund case, Ellerin v. Massachusetts Mut. Life Ins. Co., 270 F.2d 259 (2d Cir. 1959), in which the court held that two "series" of preferred stock, differing as to dividend rates, redemption prices and sinking fund provisions,

Problem

PROBLEM 13-3

(1) If a person acquires 120,000 shares of a registered security, of which there are 1,000,000 shares outstanding, on May 1; purchases an additional 50,000 shares on July 1; sells 70,001 shares on September 1; and sells all of his remaining 99,999 shares on September 5; for which, if any, shares would the person be liable under § 16(b)?

(2) Suppose that a corporation has a listed common stock outstanding and also a convertible preferred which is neither listed nor registered under § 12(g) (because not held by more than 500 persons). A owns 90% of the preferred issue, which is convertible into more than 10% of the common, assuming complete conversion. The owner purchases and sells preferred within a period of six months. Under the *Chemical Fund* rationale, is the owner subject to liability under § 16(b) as a 10% holder of a *registered* security?

E. RULE 16b–3 AND EMPLOYEE BENEFIT PLANS

There are several statutory and rule exemptions from §§ 16(a) and (b). The most frequently amended and litigated of these exemptive rules is Rule 16b–3 which exempts certain employee benefit plans from § 16(b).

In 1996, the SEC adopted a new version of Rule 16b–3. The adopting Release explained in part:

> New Rule 16b–3 exempts from short-swing profit recovery any acquisitions and dispositions of issuer equity securities (including those that occur upon the exercise or conversion of a derivative security, whether in-or out-of-the money) between an officer or director and the issuer, subject to simplified conditions. A transaction with an employee benefit plan sponsored by the issuer will be treated the same as a transaction with the issuer. However, unlike the current rule, a transaction need not be pursuant to an employee benefit plan or any compensatory program to be exempt, nor need it specifically have a compensatory element.
>
> A transaction will be exempt if it satisfies the appropriate conditions set forth among four alternative categories: Tax-Conditioned and Related Plans; Discretionary Transactions; Grants, Awards and Other Acquisitions from the Issuer; and Dispositions to the Issuer. New Rule 16b–3 eliminates many of the conditions of current Rule 16b–3, such as general written plan conditions, the prohibition against transfer of derivative securities, shareholder approval as a general condition for plan exemption, the six-month holding period as a general condition

---

nevertheless constituted a single "class" for the purpose of determining whether a person was a 10% holder under § 16(b).

for the exemption of grant and award transactions, the disinterested administration or formula plan requirements regarding grant transactions, and the window period requirement for fund-switching transactions and stock appreciation right exercises.[110]

Under the 1996 rules, derivative securities will get two bites at the apple. Under Note (1) to Rule 16b–3, if they do not satisfy that Rule they may be exempt if they satisfy Rule 16b–6(b). On the other hand, under the Note to Rule 16b–6(b), the exercise or conversion of a derivative security that does not satisfy Rule 16b–6(b) may be exempted under Rule 16b–3.

THE SARBANES-OXLEY ACT

Section 306 of the Sarbanes-Oxley Act prohibits director or executive officer trades during pension fund blackout periods.

Section 306(a)(4) defines a blackout period with respect to an issuer's equity securities:

(A) means any period of more than 3 consecutive business days during which the ability of not fewer than 50 percent of the participants or beneficiaries under all individual account plans maintained by the issuer to purchase, sell, or otherwise acquire or transfer an interest in any equity of such issuer held in such an individual account plan is temporarily suspended by the issuer or by a fiduciary of the plan; and

(B) does not include, under regulations which shall be prescribed by the Commission—

(i) a regularly scheduled period in which the participants and beneficiaries may not purchase, sell, or otherwise acquire or transfer an interest in any equity of such issuer, if such period is—

(I) incorporated into the individual account plan; and

(II) timely disclosed to employees before becoming participants under the individual account plan or as a subsequent amendment to the plan; or

(ii) any suspension described in subparagraph (A) that is imposed solely in connection with person becoming participants or beneficiaries, or ceasing to be participants or beneficiaries, in an individual account plan by reason of a corporate merger, acquisition, divestiture, or similar transaction involving the plan or plan sponsor.

---

[110] Sec. Ex. Act Rel. 37,260, 62 SEC Dock. 138, 143 (May 31, 1996).

5. DAMAGES FOR INSIDER TRADING

Elkind v. Liggett & Myers, Inc.
United States Court of Appeals, Second Circuit, 1980.
635 F.2d 156.

- Before: MANSFIELD and NEWMAN, CIRCUIT JUDGES.*

- MANSFIELD, CIRCUIT JUDGE:

This case presents a number of issues arising out of what has become a form of corporate brinkmanship—non-public disclosure of business-related information to financial analysts. The action is a class suit by Arnold B. Elkind on behalf of certain purchasers (more fully described below) of the stock of Liggett & Myers, Inc. (Liggett) against it. They seek damages for * * * the [officers' and directors'] alleged wrongful tipping of inside information to certain persons who then sold Liggett shares on the open market.

* * *

On July 17, preliminary earnings data for June and six-month totals became available to the Board of Directors. June earnings were $.20 per share (compared to $.44 in June 1971). The first half earnings for 1972 were approximately $1.46 per share, down from $1.82 the previous year. The Board decided to issue a press release the following day. That release, issued at about 2:15 P.M. on July 18, disclosed the preliminary earnings figures and attributed the decline to shortcomings in all of Liggett's product lines.

The district court found two "tips" of material inside information in the days before the July 18 press release. On July 10, analyst Peter Barry of Kuhn Loeb & Co. spoke by telephone with Daniel Provost, Liggett's Director of Corporate Communications. According to Barry's deposition testimony, apparently adopted by the court below, Provost confirmed Barry's suggestions that J & B sales were slowing due to earlier stockpiling and that a new competing dog food was affecting Alpo sales adversely. Barry asked if a projection of a 10% earnings decline would be realistic, and received what he characterized as a noncommittal response. Barry testified that Provost told him that a preliminary earnings statement would be coming out in a week or so. Since Barry knew of no prior instances in which Liggett had issued such a preliminary statement, he deduced that the figures would be lower than expected. Barry sent a wire * * * to Kuhn Loeb's offices. The information was conveyed to three clients. Two of them, holders of a total of over 600,000 shares, did not sell. A third client sold the 100 shares he owned. No other Kuhn Loeb customers sold between the time of the July 10 "tip"

---

* Pursuant to § 0.14 of the Rules of this Court, this appeal is being determined by Judges Mansfield and Newman, who are in agreement on this opinion.

and the release of preliminary earnings figures on July 18; Kuhn Loeb customers bought some 5,000 shares during this period.

The second "tip" occurred on July 17, one day before the preliminary earnings figures for the first half were released. Analyst Robert Cummins of Loeb Rhoades & Co. questioned Ralph Moore, Liggett's chief financial officer, about the recent decline in price of Liggett's common stock, as well as performance of the various subsidiaries. According to Cummins' deposition, he asked Moore whether there was a good possibility that earnings would be down, and received an affirmative ("grudging") response. Moore added that this information was confidential. Cummins sent a wire to his firm, and spoke with a stockholder who promptly sold 1,800 shares of Liggett stock on behalf of his customers.

The district court held that each of these disclosures was a tip of material information in violation of Rule 10b–5, rendering Liggett liable to all persons who bought the company's stock during the period from July 11 to July 18, 1972, inclusive, without knowledge of the tipped information. However, the court rejected plaintiff's claims that Liggett was under a legal obligation to correct the analysts' earlier erroneous predictions, relying on this court's decision in Electronic Specialty Co. v. International Controls Corp., 409 F.2d 937 (2d Cir. 1969). It also rejected plaintiff's claims that Liggett's earlier statements to analysts and stockholders were misrepresentations and that Liggett was under a duty to issue a preliminary earnings statement in June when it received its May figures.

* * *

DISCUSSION
* * *

4. Damages

This case presents a question of measurement of damages which we have previously deferred, believing that damages are best addressed in a concrete setting. See Shapiro v. Merrill Lynch, Pierce, Fenner & Smith, Inc., 495 F.2d at 241–42; Heit v. Weitzen, 402 F.2d 909, 917 & n.8 (2d Cir. 1968), cert. denied, 395 U.S. 903 (1969). We ruled in *Shapiro* that defendants selling on inside information would be liable to those who bought on the open market and sustained "substantial losses" during the period of insider trading.

The district court looked to the measure of damages used in cases where a buyer was induced to purchase a company's stock by materially misleading statements or omissions. In such cases of fraud by a fiduciary intended to induce others to buy or sell stock the accepted measure of damages is the "out-of-pocket" measure. This consists of the difference between the price paid and the "value" of the stock when brought (or when the buyer committed himself to buy, if earlier).[25] Except in rare face-to-face transactions, however, uninformed traders on an open, impersonal market are not induced by representations on the part of the tipper or tippee to buy or sell. Usually they are wholly unacquainted with and uninfluenced by the tippee's misconduct. They trade independently and voluntarily but without the benefit of information known to the trading tippee.

* * *

It is the combination of the tip and the tippee's trading that poses the evil against which the open market investor must be protected. The reason for the "disclose or abstain" rule is the unfairness in permitting an insider to trade for his own account on the basis of material inside information not available to others. The tipping of material information is a violation of the fiduciary's duty but no injury occurs until the information is used by the tippee. The entry into the market of a tippee with superior knowledge poses the threat that if he trades on the basis of the inside information he may profit at the expense of investors who are disadvantaged by lack of the inside information. For this both the tipper and the tippee are liable. If the insider chooses not to trade, on the other hand, no injury may be claimed by the outside investor, since the public has no right to the undisclosed information.

* * *

Within the flexible framework thus authorized for determining what amounts should be recoverable by the uninformed trader from the tipper and tippee trader, several measures are possible. First, there is the traditional out-of-pocket measure used by the district court in this case. For several reasons this measure appears to be inappropriate. In the first place, as we have noted, it is directed toward compensating a person for losses directly traceable to the defendant's fraud upon him. No such fraud or inducement may be attributed to a tipper or tippee-trading on an impersonal market. Aside from this the measure poses serious proof problems that may often be insurmountable in a tippee-trading case. The "value" of the stock traded during the period of nondisclosure of the tipped information (i.e., the price at which the market would have valued the stock if there had been a disclosure) is hypothetical. Expert testimony regarding that "value" may, as the district court found in the present

---

[25] Some cases have suggested the availability as an alternative measure of damages of a modified rescissionary measure, consisting of the difference between the price the defrauded party paid and the price at the time he learned or should have learned the true state of affairs. The theory of this measure is to restore the plaintiff to the position where he would have been had he not been fraudulently induced to trade. See, e.g., Mitchell v. Texas Gulf Sulphur Co., 446 F.2d 90, 104–06 (10th Cir.), cert. denied, 404 U.S. 1004 (1971). The soundness of this measure has been vigorously disputed in the case of open market trading. Green v. Occidental Petroleum Corp., 541 F.2d 1335, 1341–44 (9th Cir. 1976) (Sneed, J., concurring). While the district court cited to Mitchell, its opinion makes clear that it was applying the out-of-pocket measure of damages. Since the district court did not apply this modified rescissionary measure, we need not pass on it here.

case, be entirely speculative. This has led some courts to conclude that the drop in price of the stock after actual disclosure and after allowing a period of time to elapse for the market to absorb the news may sometimes approximate the drop which would have occurred earlier had the tip been disclosed. The court below adopted this approach of using post-public disclosure market price as *nunc pro tunc* evidence of the "value" of the stock during the period of non-disclosure.

Whatever may be the reasonableness of the *nunc pro tunc* "value" method of calculating damages in other contexts, it has serious vulnerabilities here. It rests on the fundamental assumptions (1) that the tipped information is substantially the same as that later disclosed publicly, and (2) that one can determine how the market would have reacted to the public release of the tipped information at an earlier time by its reaction to that information at a later, proximate time. This theory depends on the parity of the "tip" and the "disclosure." When they differ, the basis of the damage calculation evaporates. One could not reasonably estimate how the public would have reacted to the news that the Titanic was near an iceberg from how it reacted to news that the ship had struck an iceberg and sunk. In the present case, the July 10 tip that preliminary earnings would be released in a week is not comparable to the later release of the estimated earnings figures on July 18. Nor was the July 17 tipped information that there was a good possibility that earnings would be down comparable to the next day's release of the estimated earnings figures.

An equally compelling reason for rejecting the theory is its potential for imposition of Draconian, exorbitant damages, out of all proportion to the wrong committed, lining the pockets of all interim investors and their counsel at the expense of innocent corporate stockholders. Logic would compel application of the theory to a case where a tippee sells only 10 shares of a heavily traded stock (e.g., IBM), which then drops substantially when the tipped information is publicly disclosed. To hold the tipper and tippee liable for the losses suffered by every open market buyer of the stock as a result of the later decline in value of the stock after the news became public would be grossly unfair. While the securities laws do occasionally allow for potentially ruinous recovery, we will not readily adopt a measure mandating "large judgments, payable in the last instance by innocent investors [here, Liggett shareholders], for the benefit of speculators and their lawyers," SEC v. Texas Gulf Sulphur Co., 401 F.2d at 867 (Friendly, J., concurring); cf. Blue Chip Stamps v. Manor Drug Stores, 421 U.S. 723, 739–40 (1975), unless the statute so requires.

An alternative measure would be to permit recovery of damages caused by erosion of the market price of the security that is traceable to the tippee's wrongful trading, i.e., to compensate the uninformed investor for the loss in market value that he suffered as a direct result of the tippee's conduct. Under this measure an innocent trader who bought

Liggett shares at or after a tippee sold on the basis of inside information would recover any decline in value of his shares caused by the tippee's trading. Assuming the impact of the tippee's trading on the market is measurable, this approach has the advantage of limiting the plaintiffs to the amount of damage actually caused in fact by the defendant's wrongdoing and avoiding windfall recoveries by investors at the expense of stockholders other than the tippee trader, which could happen in the present action against Liggett. The rationale is that if the market price is not affected by the tippee's trading, the uninformed investor is in the same position as he would have been had the insider abstained from trading. In such event the equilibrium of the market has not been disturbed and the outside investor has not been harmed by the informational imbalance. Only where the market has been contaminated by the wrongful conduct would damages be recoverable.

* * *

A third alternative is (1) to allow any uninformed investor, where a reasonable investor would either have delayed his purchase or not purchased at all if he had had the benefit of the tipped information, to recover any post-purchase decline in market value of his shares up to a reasonable time after he learns of the tipped information or after there is a public disclosure of it but (2) limit his recovery to the amount gained by the tippee as a result of his selling at the earlier date rather than delaying his sale until the parties could trade on an equal informational basis. Under this measure if the tippee sold 5,000 shares at $50 per share on the basis of inside information and the stock thereafter declined to $40 per share within a reasonable time after public disclosure, an uninformed purchaser buying shares during the interim (e.g., at $45 per share) would recover the difference between his purchase price and the amount at which he could have sold the shares on an equal informational basis (i.e., the market price within a reasonable time after public disclosure of the tip), subject to a limit of $50,000, which is the amount gained by the tippee as a result of his trading on the inside information rather than on an equal basis. Should the intervening buyers, because of the volume and price of their purchases, claim more than the tippee's gain, their recovery (limited to that gain) would be shared *pro rata.*

This third alternative, which may be described as the disgorgement measure, has in substance been recommended by the American Law Institute in its 1978 Proposed Draft of a Federal Securities Code, §§ 1603, 1703(b), 1708(b), 1711(j). It offers several advantages. To the extent that it makes the tipper and tippees liable up to the amount gained by their misconduct, it should deter tipping of inside information and tippee-trading. On the other hand, by limiting the total recovery to the tippee's gain, the measure bars windfall recoveries of exorbitant amounts bearing no relation to the seriousness of the misconduct. It also avoids the extraordinary difficulties faced in trying to prove traditional out-of-pocket damages based on the true "value" of the shares purchased or damages claimed by reason of market erosion attributable to tippee trading. A plaintiff would simply be required to prove (1) the time, amount and price per share of his purchase, (2) that a reasonable investor would not have paid as high a price or made the purchase at all if he had had the information in the tippee's possession, and (3) the price to which the security had declined by the time he learned the tipped information or at a reasonable time after it became public, whichever event first occurred. He would then have a claim and, up to the limits of the tippee's gain, could recover the decline in market value of his shares before the information became public or known to him. In most cases the damages recoverable under the disgorgement measure would be roughly commensurate to the actual harm caused by the tippee's wrongful conduct. In a case where the tippee sold only a few shares, for instance, the likelihood of his conduct causing any substantial injury to intervening investors buying without benefit of his confidential information would be small. If, on the other hand, the tippee sold large amounts of stock, realizing substantial profits, the likelihood of injury to intervening uninformed purchasers would be greater and the amount of potential recovery thereby proportionately enlarged.

We recognize that there cannot be any perfect measure of damages caused by tippee-trading. The disgorgement measure, like others we have described, does have some disadvantages. It modifies the principle that ordinarily gain to the wrongdoer should not be a prerequisite to liability for violation of Rule 10b–5. It partially duplicates disgorgement remedies available in proceedings by the SEC or others. Under some market conditions such as where the market price is depressed by wholly unrelated causes, the tippee might be vulnerable to heavy damages, permitting some plaintiffs to recover undeserved windfalls. In some instances the total claims could exceed the wrongdoer's gain, limiting each claimant to a pro rata share of the gain. In other situations, after deducting the cost of recovery, including attorneys' fees, the remainder might be inadequate to make a class action worthwhile. However, as between the various alternatives we are persuaded, after weighing the pros and cons, that the disgorgement measure, despite some disadvantages, offers the most equitable resolution of the difficult problems created by conflicting interests.

In the present case the sole Rule 10b–5 violation was the tippee-trading of 1,800 Liggett shares on the afternoon of July 17, 1972. Since the actual preliminary Liggett earnings were released publicly at 2:15 P.M. on July 18 and were effectively disseminated in a Wall Street Journal article published on the morning of July 19, the only outside purchasers who might conceivably have been damaged by the insider-trading were those who bought Liggett shares between the afternoon of July 17 and the opening of the market on July 19. Thereafter all purchasers bought on an equal informational footing, and any outside purchaser who bought on July 17 and 18 was able to decide within a reasonable time after the July 18–19 publicity whether to hold or sell his shares in the light of the publicly-released news regarding Liggett's less favorable earnings.

The market price of Liggett stock opened on July 17, 1972, at $55–5/8, and remained at substantially the same price on that date, closing at $55–1/4. By the close of the market on July 18 the price declined to $52–1/2 per share. Applying the disgorgement measure, any member of the plaintiff class who bought Liggett shares during the period from the afternoon of July 17 to the close of the market on July 18 and met the reasonable investor requirement would be entitled to claim a *pro rata* portion of the tippee's gain, based on the difference between their purchase price and the price to which the market price declined within a reasonable time after the morning of July 19. By the close of the market on July 19 the market price had declined to $46–3/8 per share. The total recovery thus would be limited to the gain realized by the tippee from the inside information, i.e., 1,800 shares multiplied by approximately $9.35 per share.

The finding of liability based on the July 10, 1972, tip is reversed. The award of damages is also reversed and the case is remanded for a determination of damages recoverable for tippee-trading based on the July 17, 1972, tip, to be measured in accordance with the foregoing. Each party will bear [its] own costs.

STATUTORY DEVELOPMENTS

When Congress added § 20A to the 1934 Act in the Insider Trading and Securities Fraud Enforcement Act of 1988, creating an express cause of action in favor of contemporaneous market traders for violations of the insider trading rules, it adopted the decision of the *Elkind* case and applied it to both insiders and their tippees. Subsection (b)(1) provides that "[t]he total amount of damages imposed [in favor of such traders] * * * shall not exceed the profit gained or loss avoided [by the defendant] in the transaction or transactions that are the subject of the violation." It also provides that any amount that has been "disgorged" by the defendant as a result of action by the SEC should be deducted from the recovery.[111] Therefore, if the defendant has settled with the Commission by giving up all of his profit, the class action lawyers are out of luck.

Even before this private cause of action for insider trading was created in 1988, Congress gave the SEC authority to seek up to treble damages as a civil penalty against a person who trades unlawfully "while in possession of material, nonpublic information." Under the Insider Trading Sanctions Act of 1984, which added Section 21A(a)(2) to the Securities Exchange Act, the court in its discretion may award up to

---

[111] § 20A(b)(2).

three times the profit gained or loss avoided. Recently, courts have tended to award double the gain or loss. In addition, Section 21A(a)(3) of the Securities Exchange Act further authorizes the court "in light of the facts and circumstances" to award an additional penalty against a "controlling person" of up to the greater of $1 million or three times the amount of the profit gained or loss avoided as the result of such trading. Thus, if a broker working at brokerage firm engages in insider trading, not only does he face liability under Section 21A(a)(2), as described above, but so does the employee's employer if such employer is found to be a controlling person. Thus, even when the employer has received no benefit at all (because the broker traded for a personal account or for a client's account), the employer can be held liable. However, under Section 21A(b), the controlling person's liability is dependent upon the SEC showing that the controlling person "knew or recklessly disregarded the fact that such controlled person was likely to engage in the act or acts constituting the violation and failed to take appropriate steps" or "recklessly failed to establish, maintain, or enforce any policy or procedure required under section 15(f)" of the 1934 Act or Section 204A of the Investment Advisers Act.

CHAPTER 14

SEC ENFORCEMENT ACTIONS

Statutes and Regulations

Dodd-Frank Act, §§ 403, 407, 408, 922, 925, 929E, 929U, 953, 954, 955, 956.

Investment Advisers Act, § 203.

SEC Rules of Practice, 17 C.F.R. § 201.100 et seq.

Securities Act, §§ 8, 20.

Exchange Act, §§ 10A, 12(k), 13(b)(2), 15(b), 21, 21F.

Sarbanes-Oxley Act, §§ 201, 202, 206, 301, 302, 303, 304, 308, 602.

The Commission investigates and prosecutes civil violations of the securities laws. It has a distinctive pattern of procedures and a broad array of remedies available to it. Despite this power, the Commission depends on Congress for funding. The Dodd-Frank Wall Street Reform and Consumer Protection Act of 2010 ("Dodd-Frank Act") proposed to double the Commission's budget and create a $100 million Reserve Fund funded by the registration fees the Commission collects.[1] The SEC relies upon its budget to meet its mission to (1) protect investors, (2) maintain fair, orderly, and efficient markets, and (3) facilitate capital formation. Sufficient funding is necessary not only to carry out these various roles, but also to keep up with the growing complexity of the financial markets.[2]

This chapter begins with a discussion of how the SEC's enforcement process works procedurally. The next section examines both the SEC's remedies for enforcement actions and the situations in which these remedies are available.

The SEC can bring enforcement actions against broker-dealers, investment advisers, securities attorneys, accountants, corporate registrants, officers, and directors—employing causes of action unavailable to private litigants. Section 3 of this chapter considers the most significant of these actions.

The SEC, however, has no power to bring criminal actions for willful violation of the federal securities laws. The Commission's authority is limited to referring potential criminal actions to the Justice Department. Chapter 15 discusses criminal enforcement of the federal securities laws.

---

[1] Dodd-Frank Wall Street Reform and Consumer Protection Act, Pub. L. 111–203, § 991, 15 U.S.C. § 78m (2010).

[2] *What We Do*, Securities and Exchange Commission, https://www.sec.gov/Article/whatwedo.html.

Finally, both the SEC and the Justice Department face similar jurisdictional and choice of law problems when they seek to enforce the federal securities laws extraterritorially. Chapter 16 addresses these topics.

1. PROCEDURES

An SEC investigation into a possible violation of the federal securities laws is typically divided into two stages. The first stage is an informal SEC staff inquiry into allegations of misconduct. At this stage, the staff investigators may interview prospective witnesses, but they may not issue subpoenas, administer oaths, or otherwise compel testimony. The staff will seek the voluntary cooperation of the issuer and the other objects of its investigation. Defense counsel often face difficult tactical issues at this juncture, balancing their desire to cooperate in order to allay the staff's suspicions against the dangers of a wholesale disclosure of confidential corporate information.

Information about misconduct comes to the SEC staff through many different sources (e.g., suggestions from other SEC divisions, referrals from self-regulatory organizations (FINRA), complaints from market professionals of manipulation, newspaper reports, or anonymous informants). An increasingly important source of the SEC's information is likely to be through whistleblowers, employees who voluntarily provide the SEC with information of a possible violation of federal securities laws.

In a 2010 paper, Alexander Dyck, Adair Morse, and Luigi Zingales looked for the source of discovery for all cases of corporate fraud in large companies between 1996 and 2004. They found: "[o]nly 6% of the frauds are revealed by the SEC and 14% by the auditors. More important monitors are media (14%), industry regulators (16%), and employees (19%)."[3]

The Dodd-Frank Act provides substantial incentives for whistleblowers to come forward and aid in SEC investigations. Prior to the Dodd-Frank Act, the Commission could reward whistleblowers only in insider trading cases. The Dodd-Frank Act added § 21F to the Securities Act of 1934. This section entitles whistleblowers to a reward if they voluntarily provide the Commission with original information about a violation of the securities laws that leads to an enforcement action resulting in monetary sanctions exceeding $1 million. The whistleblowers are entitled to between 10% and 30% of any government recovery in excess of $1 million, which is to be paid out of the Investor Protection Fund.

---

[3] Alexander Dyck, et al., "Who Blows the Whistle on Corporate Fraud?" 65 J. FIN. 2213 (2010).

On May 25, 2011, the Commission adopted rules to implement the whistleblower program.[4] The Dodd-Frank Act defines a "whistleblower" as "any individual who provides. . .information relating to a violation of the securities laws to the Commission."[5] The rules require the Commission to consider a multitude of factors when determining the amount of an award including: the significance of the information, the success of any proceeding brought against wrongdoers, the extent of the assistance provided, and the culpability, if any, of the whistleblower.[6] The rules permit anonymous reporting. A whistleblower that chooses to report anonymously, however, must submit his or her information through an attorney in order to be considered for an award.[7]

The Dodd-Frank Act buttresses these whistleblower incentives with statutory protections for whistleblowers. For example, it expressly prohibits retaliation by employers against individuals who become whistleblowers, even if they do not ultimately recover a whistleblower award. In order to receive protection under the anti-retaliation provision, the individual must have reported the alleged misconduct to the SEC.[8] Section 922(a) provides whistleblowers with a private right of action against retaliating employers. As a result, they can bypass administrative remedies and pursue their claim directly in federal court. Successful employees may obtain: reinstatement without loss of seniority, double back-pay, and reasonable attorneys' fees and litigation costs. Employees also have up to six years after the violation occurred, or three years after they knew or reasonably should have known of facts material to the violation, to bring their claims, so long as the complaint is filed within ten years of the violation.

Query: given the fact that the literature documents overwhelmingly negative outcomes for whistleblowers in terms of career prospects and overall well-being, what kind of legal assurances would you require before you decided to blow the whistle on corporate fraud? If the answer is, "more than those described above," what legal changes would you recommend to encourage the optimal amount of whistleblowing? Or, should government and SRO investigators focus on alternative regulatory channels for uncovering corporate fraud?

NOTE ON PROCEDURES: FORMAL INVESTIGATIONS

In order to progress to the second or "formal" stage, the staff must present to the Commission a request for an order instituting a "formal investigation." This order of investigation authorizes the staff to issue subpoenas and to examine witnesses under oath, but it is not a formal adjudication or fact finding. Commission investigative subpoenas are not

---

[4] 17 C.F.R. §§ 240.21F–1 et seq.
[5] 15 U.S.C. § 78u–6(a)(6).
[6] 17 C.F.R. § 240.21F–6.
[7] 17 C.F.R. § 240.21F–7.
[8] Digital Realty Trust, Inc. v. Somers, 138 S.Ct. 767 (2018).

self-enforcing. Thus, if a witness refuses to comply, Commission staff must apply under § 21(c) of the 1934 Act to the federal district court "within the jurisdiction in which such investigation or proceeding is carried on, or where such person resides or carries on business" to enforce the subpoena. Staff need not demonstrate that probable cause exists to believe that the securities laws have been violated.[9] Few defendants, however, want to cross the staff. Although a respondent can challenge the subpoena on the ground that the investigation is not for a legitimate purpose or that the information is not relevant to the investigation (or is already known to the SEC),[10] such challenges are rarely successful. More importantly, the SEC need not notify the target of an investigation before it directs a subpoena to third parties.[11]

One of ongoing debates has been who can issue subpoenas. In 2009, one of newly-appointed SEC Chairman Mary Schapiro's first actions was to grant authority to issue formal orders of investigation directly to the SEC's enforcement division. This grant of power included the authority to issue subpoenas in connection with SEC investigations.[12] The purpose of this change was to expedite the investigative process and provide more authority to senior enforcement attorneys.[13] Prior to this grant, investigators had to come before the agency's commissioners to request permission to file subpoenas, a process some viewed as an impediment to conducting quick probes into financial wrongdoing. In 2017, the media reported that the acting head of the SEC, Chairman Piwowar, narrowed this delegation of power. Piwowar reportedly revoked the subpoena authority of approximately 20 senior enforcement attorneys. The head of the enforcement division still had subpoena power under Piwowar's plan.[14] Congress also increased the SEC's subpoena power with the passage of the Dodd-Frank Act. Until the passage of the Act, witnesses could be compelled to appear only if they resided within 100 miles of the courthouse. This provision restricted the Commission's ability to compel witnesses to travel long distances to testify at trials and often dictated where the Commission would file its actions. Section 929E of the Act permits the SEC to serve subpoenas nationwide. Now witnesses located anywhere in the United States may be required to appear at SEC civil injunctive actions. This change puts the Commission's subpoena power on par with most other federal agencies.

---

[9] See United States v. Morton Salt Co., 338 U.S. 632 (1950); SEC v. Brigadoon Scotch Distrib. Co., 480 F.2d 1047, 1052–53 (2d Cir. 1973).

[10] See United States v. Powell, 379 U.S. 48 (1964); SEC v. Arthur Young & Co., 584 F.2d 1018, 1020–31 (D.C. Cir. 1978).

[11] See SEC v. Jerry T. O'Brien, Inc., 467 U.S. 735 (1984).

[12] 17 CFR 200.30–4.

[13] See SEC Release No. 34–60448 (Aug. 5, 2009).

[14] Dave Michaels, *SEC Chief Scales Back Powers of Enforcement Staff*, Wall Street Journal (Feb. 15, 2017) https://www.wsj.com/articles/sec-chief-scales-back-powers-of-enforcement-staff-1487199642.

A. Special Issues: Proper Purpose

One issue that can arise at this stage is whether the Commission's investigation is the product of improper influence or political pressure. In SEC v. Wheeling-Pittsburgh Steel Corp.,[15] Wheeling-Pittsburgh sought to quash an SEC subpoena on the ground that the investigation into its proxy disclosures was the coerced result of pressure on the Commission from United States Senator Lowell Weicker, who was allied with one of Wheeling-Pittsburgh's principal competitors. The District Court found that the SEC had permitted the "abuse of its investigating function," but declined to find that the SEC was acting in bad faith.

On appeal, the Third Circuit focused on the issue of "bad faith," saying that judicial enforcement of an administrative subpoena "would constitute an abuse of the court's process" in such circumstances. In remanding the case to the district court for further findings, it framed the issue as follows:

> At bottom, this case raises the question whether, based on objective factors, the SEC's decision to investigate reflected its independent determination, or whether that decision was the product of external influences. * * * That the SEC commenced these proceedings as a result of the importunings of Senator Weicker * * * even with malice on [his] part, is not a sufficient basis to deny enforcement of the subpoena. But beginning an informal investigation by collecting facts at the request of a third party, even one harboring ulterior motives, is much different from entering an order directing a private formal investigation without an objective determination by the Commission and only because of political pressure. The respondents are not free from an informal investigation instigated by anyone, in or out of government. But they *are* entitled to a decision by the SEC, itself, free from third-party political pressure. The SEC order must be supported by an independent agency determination, not one dictated or pressured by external forces."[16]

B. Right to Counsel

A witness subpoenaed to testify at an SEC investigation has the right to be "accompanied, represented and advised by counsel."[17] Persons under investigation have no right to have counsel present during testimony from other witnesses.[18] Counsel may circumvent this rule by

---

[15] 648 F.2d 118 (3d Cir. 1981).
[16] Id. at 130.
[17] See 17 C.F.R. § 203.7(b).
[18] The Commission has a "sequestration" rule that denies both the witness, even if the witness is the target of the investigation, and its counsel the right to hear the testimony of other witnesses. See 17 C.F.R. § 203.7(b). This rule was upheld in SEC v. Meek, 1979–1980 Fed. Sec. L. Rep. (CCH) ¶ 97,323 (10th Cir. 1980).

seeking to represent multiple witnesses (for example, the corporation and each of its subpoenaed officers). The SEC has long sought to prevent such joint representation by taking the position that an attorney could not represent two or more witnesses, because this would give one defense attorney access to most of the evidence in an investigation. Courts refused to accept the SEC's attempt to extend legal ethics in this regard, and have held that the Commission may bar a counsel from representing multiple witnesses (or may sequester the attorney while any of the clients testify) only when it has "concrete evidence" that the attorney's presence would obstruct or impede the investigation.[19]

C. CONFIDENTIALITY

The Commission has always insisted upon the secrecy of its investigations, even after the formal order of investigation has been issued. Typically, the SEC attorney conducting the investigation will warn witnesses that they are not permitted to reveal to anyone the testimony they have given. Unlike grand jury proceedings, whose secrecy is mandated by law, there appears to be no statutory basis for the Commission's position.[20] The right of the Commission to refuse to release information acquired in the course of an investigation is, however, recognized by the Freedom of Information Act, subject to limited exceptions.[21]

D. WELLS SUBMISSIONS

After the staff completes its investigation, it must secure Commission approval to initiate any enforcement action. The Commission will make its decision at a nonpublic meeting, with no right on the target's part to appear or receive advance notice. The staff, as a matter of discretion, customarily informs the subjects of its recommendation and offers them an opportunity to file a written statement, known as a "Wells submission," with the Commission. The term comes from the recommendations of the SEC's Advisory Committee on Enforcement Policies (called the "Wells Committee" after its chair).[22] In theory, a Wells submission is supposed to address the legal and policy issues in the case, as opposed to factual issues, that should incline the Commission not to initiate an enforcement action. In practice, however, most attorneys address factual issues as well. Defense counsel must

---

[19] See SEC v. Higashi, 359 F.2d 550 (9th Cir. 1966); SEC v. Csapo, 533 F.2d 7 (D.C. Cir. 1976); SEC v. Whitman, 613 F.Supp. 48 (D.D.C. 1985).

[20] The secrecy of grand jury proceedings is established by Rule 6(e) of the Federal Rules of Criminal Procedure. See United States v. DiBona, 601 F.Supp. 1162, 1166 (E.D. Pa. 1984), aff'd on reconsideration, 610 F.Supp. 449 (E.D. Pa. 1985).

[21] See 5 U.S.C. § 552(b)(7).

[22] These recommendations were adopted in Sec. Act Rels. 5310 (1972); 5320 (1972). See generally 10 Louis Loss & Joel Seligman, Securities Regulation 4888–4891 (3d ed. rev. 1996); Kenneth B. Winer & Samuel J. Winer, Effective Representation in the SEC Wells Process, 34 Rev. Sec. & Commodities Reg. 59 (2001).

make the decision to file a Wells submission carefully, particularly when a criminal reference is possible. Statements in the submission may be taken as admissions, may be used for impeachment purposes, and may be discoverable in later civil litigation with private plaintiffs.

The Dodd-Frank Act imposes new time limitations on SEC inspections and enforcement actions. Specifically, § 929U of the Act requires that the SEC bring an action against a target, or issue a notice of intent not to do so, within 180 days of that target being provided a Wells notice. That section also limits the SEC to 180 days after it completes the fieldwork portion of an inspection to inform the target either that the inspection has concluded without findings or request that the target take corrective action.

E. RULES OF PRACTICE

The Commission has promulgated formal Rules of Practice to govern the conduct of administrative hearings.[23] An SEC hearing is initiated by the issuance of a Commission order, the Order of Proceedings, which is analogous to a complaint in a civil action. Once the Commission's order is served on the named respondents, they have 20 days to answer.[24] If the case is not resolved by settlement, an evidentiary hearing is typically held before an Administrative Law Judge (or "ALJ"). Prior to 2018 and the Lucia v. SEC opinion, the SEC staff members appointed ALJs.[25] In *Lucia*, the Supreme Court considered a challenge to the constitutionality of ALJs.[26] The Court held that ALJs are "Officers of the United States" and subject to the Appointments clause. Therefore, only the President, a court of law, or a head of a department can appoint ALJs.[27]

ALJ hearings are conducted much like a civil trial, with the Commission's staff and respondents each having the right to present evidence and testimony and cross-examine witnesses. At the conclusion of the hearing, the ALJ will file an "initial decision," including findings and conclusions and an appropriate order.[28] Once this decision is rendered, any party to the proceeding may file a petition for Commission review of the initial decision.[29] The Commission may also order a review on its own initiative.

The Commission's factual findings in its decision are conclusive if supported by substantial evidence.[30] A party aggrieved by a final order entered by the Commission may obtain judicial review in the United

---

[23] The current Rules of Practice were adopted in 2005. See 17 C.F.R. § 201.100 et seq.
[24] 17 C.F.R. § 201.220.
[25] See Lucia v. S.E.C., 138 S.Ct. 2044, 2052 (2018).
[26] See Lucia v. S.E.C., 138 S.Ct. 2044 (2018).
[27] Id. at 2055.
[28] 17 C.F.R. § 201.410.
[29] 17 C.F.R. § 201.411.
[30] See § 9(a) of the 1933 Act and § 25(a)(4) of the 1934 Act.

States Court of Appeals for the District of Columbia or in the circuit where the party resides or has its principal place of business.[31]

Because of the broad discretion given to the Commission and the severe penalties authorized by some provisions of the federal securities laws, a series of cases in the late 1970s held that the Commission could not impose certain severe sanctions, such as expulsion and suspension, except upon a showing of "clear and convincing evidence" of a securities violation.[32] This position eventually produced a split among the circuits that attracted the Supreme Court's attention. In 1981, the Supreme Court resolved the circuit split, holding that the preponderance standard was correct.[33] Notably, FINRA, which administers the licensing for broker-dealers, also can suspend or expel members of the industry, subject to review only by the Commission and the courts. FINRA does not have legal authority to compel payment of the fines it levies, and so it relies on the threat of licensure removal or denial to do so. Where these fail, FINRA would have to seek judicial enforcement, but that would involve effectively re-litigating the issues in district court. In practice, FINRA does not do this, but rather collects only the fines violators are willing to pay.

F. EXPANDED AUTHORITY IN ADMINISTRATIVE PROCEEDINGS

The Dodd-Frank Act expanded the Commission's authority to litigate in administrative proceedings. In general, the Commission would prefer to litigate all of its cases in administrative proceedings, as opposed to in federal court, because of the procedural advantages including: the absence of juries, the absence of meaningful pre-trial discovery and motion practice, the short deadlines imposed on completion, the more flexible rules of evidence, and the right of appeal from a decision of an ALJ to the SEC Commissioners rather than to a Court of Appeals.[34]

Prior to the passage of Dodd-Frank, the Commission was constrained by its inability to seek certain remedies in these administrative proceedings. Specifically, the Commission could not impose monetary penalties against people who were not associated with regulated entities (e.g., employees of public companies and accountants). Section 929P(a) of Dodd-Frank eliminated this limitation and permits the Commission to obtain monetary penalties against any person in administrative proceedings. As a result, the Commission may bring more enforcement actions as administrative proceedings.

---

[31] Id.
[32] See Collins Sec. Corp. v. SEC, 562 F.2d 820 (D.C. Cir. 1977).
[33] Steadman v. SEC, 450 U.S. 91 (1981).
[34] See generally § 201.100 et seq.

2. REMEDIES

Few areas of securities law have changed as dramatically in recent years as the remedies available to the SEC. Traditionally, the SEC relied heavily on two principal enforcement tools: civil injunctions and administrative proceedings. These two tools remain the backbone of the Commission's enforcement arsenal. In 2019, the SEC filed 862 enforcement actions.[35] This number has remained consistent over the past five years: there were, for instance, 807 in 2015 and 754 in 2017.

Both judicial and administrative proceedings are usually settled by a consent decree negotiated by the parties; they are routinely implemented through a court or SEC order. The incentives for such a negotiated resolution are strong on both sides. The defendants avoid the embarrassment of being found to have violated the securities law and, in cases of lesser gravity, typically consent to the entry of an injunction that only orders them not to commit future violations of the federal securities laws. More importantly, defendants avoid the collateral estoppel effect of an adverse judgment in the SEC's action, which plaintiffs could use offensively in an action for damages.[36] As a practical matter, the risk that an SEC victory in an injunctive action would entail high financial liability to plaintiffs in a securities class action often dissuades defendants from litigating with the SEC.

From the SEC's standpoint, the advantages of the consent decree procedure are primarily economic. Both in terms of financial cost and staff resources, the SEC could not realistically hope to litigate annually over 100 cases (many with multiple defendants) through trial. Instead, by settling for an order barring future violations of the securities laws (plus disgorgement of any profits from the violation) in most cases, and by seeking special ancillary relief in a limited number of significant cases, the SEC has sought to employ its enforcement resources efficiently to maximize their impact.

In 1990, the Securities Law Enforcement Remedies and Penny Stock Reform Act dramatically expanded the Commission's enforcement arsenal by adding three significant new tools: civil fines; cease and desist orders; and corporate bar orders. Increasingly these new tools have had effect. For example, in 2019, the SEC ordered monetary sanctions in excess of $4.3 billion.[37] The frequency of cease and desist orders and corporate bar orders have increased.[38]

---

[35] Division of Enforcement: Annual Report 2019, SEC (Nov. 6, 2019) https://www.sec.gov/files/enforcement-annual-report-2019.pdf.

[36] See Parklane Hosiery Co. v. Shore, 439 U.S. 322 (1979).

[37] Division of Enforcement: Annual Report 2019, SEC (Nov. 6, 2019) https://www.sec.gov/files/enforcement-annual-report-2019.pdf.

[38] See, e.g., 10 Louis Loss & Joel Seligman, Securities Regulation 4981–4995 (3d ed. rev. 1996).

A. INJUNCTIONS AND ANCILLARY RELIEF

The Commission can sue for an injunction under each federal securities statute.[39] In most Commission injunction actions, the practical problem often concerns whether a violation occurred recently enough to warrant the conclusion that there is a threat of recurrence.[40] Among the factors that courts have considered in assessing the likelihood of future violations are: (1) whether the defendant committed a past violation; (2) whether and to what degree scienter was present in the past violation; (3) whether the past violation can be properly characterized as an isolated occurrence; (4) whether the defendant has acknowledged the wrongfulness of the past conduct and given assurance that the violation will not be repeated; and (5) whether the defendant's occupation puts him or her in a position to commit further violations.[41]

The courts have added: "To obtain injunctive relief the Commission must offer positive proof of the likelihood that the wrongdoing will recur. The Commission needs to go beyond the mere fact of past violations."[42] It is not inevitable that the Commission can meet this threshold, as the following case illustrates.

SEC v. Unifund SAL
United States Court of Appeals, Second Circuit, 1990.
910 F.2d 1028.

■ Before: VAN GRAAFEILAND, NEWMAN and KEARSE, CIRCUIT JUDGES.

■ JON O. NEWMAN, CIRCUIT JUDGE:

This is an appeal by two securities purchasers from a preliminary injunction obtained by the Securities and Exchange Commission in a case of alleged insider trading. This case is unusual in that, as the Commission acknowledged at oral argument, it is the first insider trading case in which the Commission has sought relief against alleged tippees before identifying the alleged tipper. Unifund SAL ("Unifund") and Tamanaco Saudi & Gulf Investment Group ("Tamanaco") appeal, respectively, from *** orders of the District Court for the Southern District of New York (Shirley Wohl Kram, Judge) granting a preliminary injunction at the request of the Commission. The injunction (a) prohibits violation of section 10(b) of the Securities and Exchange Act, and rule 10b–5, (b) freezes appellants' accounts, subject to trading approved by

---

[39] See, e.g., Sec. Act § 20(b); Sec. Ex. Act § 21(d)(1).

[40] See, e.g., Rondeau v. Mosinee Paper Corp., 422 U.S. 49, 59 (1975), (characterizing "the usual basis for injunctive relief, 'that there exists some cognizable danger of recurrent violation'"); see also SEC v. Manor Nursing Centers, Inc., 458 F.2d 1082, 1100–1101 (2d Cir. 1972).

[41] Quoting 10 Louis Loss & Joel Seligman, Securities Regulation 4737 (3d ed. rev. 1996).

[42] SEC v. Caterinicchia, 613 F.2d 102, 105 (5th Cir. 1980). See generally Daniel J. Morrissey, SEC Injunctions, 68 Tenn. L. Rev. 427 (2001).

the Commission, and (c) bars disposal or alteration of appellants' books and records.

* * *

BACKGROUND

The case concerns trading in the stock and stock options of Rorer Group, Inc. ("Rorer"), a United States pharmaceutical company incorporated in Pennsylvania. Rorer common stock is listed on the New York Stock Exchange, and option contracts for its common stock are listed on the American Stock Exchange. In the summer of 1989, Rorer began confidential merger negotiations with Rhone-Poulenc, S.A. ("Rhone"), a French corporation. The discussions intensified in December and in early January 1990. In mid-January, prior to any public announcement of merger negotiations, massive trading occurred in Rorer stock and options.

* * *

The heavy trading volume prompted the Commission to investigate. It quickly identified unusually large Rorer stock and option transactions in brokerage accounts maintained by foreign investors, including appellants Unifund and Tamanaco. Unifund is an investment company based in Lebanon and incorporated under Lebanese law. Tamanaco is an investment company incorporated in Panama. On January 4 Unifund purchased 40,000 shares of Rorer for approximately $2 million through the Beirut office of Merrill Lynch, Pierce, Fenner & Smith, Inc. ("Merrill Lynch"). From January 4 through 12 it bought 810 Rorer call option contracts for approximately $300,000. After the merger announcement, Unifund liquidated its position, making $564,000 on the stock and $980,000 on the options. On January 10, Tamanaco purchased 500 Rorer call options for approximately $150,000 through Compagnie Financiere Esperito Santo ("Esperito Santo"), a Swiss bank in Lausanne. Two days later Tamanaco bought an additional 100 call options through the same bank. The purchases were made through Esperito Santo's account at the Lausanne branch of Dean Witter Reynolds Inc. ("Dean Witter"). Within one week the value of the options quadrupled, producing a profit of approximately $660,000.

On January 17, two days after the merger announcement, the Commission filed this lawsuit against Unifund and other purchasers of Rorer stock and obtained a temporary restraining order. Tamanaco had not yet been identified as the name of one of the purchasers. The TRO barred future violations of section 10(b) and rule 10b–5, required retention of unsold Rorer stock and options as well as the proceeds from those securities that had already been sold, and froze defendants' accounts. The TRO permitted trading in Rorer options and in the frozen accounts with the Commission's permission.

* * *

In an opinion dated March 2, Judge Kram detailed the basis for issuing [a preliminary] injunction.

* * *

On the merits, Judge Kram stated that the standard for a preliminary injunction requested by the Commission is a strong prima facie case of a violation of section 10(b) and a reasonable likelihood that the wrong will be repeated. She found this standard met by various items of circumstantial evidence. Initially, she relied on the unusual trading activity in Rorer securities by Tamanaco and Unifund. There was evidence that in the Espirito Santo account at Dean Witter in Lausanne, through which the Tamanaco's Rorer options had been purchased, no other options had been traded since August 1989. Unifund's January 4 purchase of 40,000 Rorer shares represented 13 percent of the total Rorer shares traded that day. Unifund's stock purchase was nearly twice the size of its next largest investment in any company, even when those investments were aggregated over time. Moreover, its prior equity positions had been partially hedged, but its position in Rorer was not.

To show that the purchases were based on inside information, Judge Kram relied on the following circumstances. On January 10, 1990, Espirito Santo, through which Tamanaco purchased its Rorer options, purchased 3,000 shares of Rorer through the Nyon, Switzerland office of Raymond Jones & Associates, Inc. ("Raymond Jones"), stockbrokers based in Tampa, Florida. Espirito Santo's broker at Raymond Jones, Candid Peyer, told Commission investigators in a telephone interview that in mid-December 1989 a close friend, identified only as an independent money manager in Geneva, had told him that "if you want a Christmas gift, buy February 60 calls in Rorer." Peyer said that in his opinion his friend had "inside information" concerning a takeover of Rorer. Peyer said his friend received the information from an unnamed stockbroker at a Canadian brokerage firm in Lausanne. After a pause in the interview, during which Peyer consulted with a Raymond Jones compliance officer, Peyer said he thought the recommendation was based on inside information because the price of Rorer stock continued to go up. In a subsequent interview after the lawsuit was filed, Peyer revealed that his friend had said that the information came from "the direction" of one of the entities mentioned in connection with the lawsuit.

Judge Kram found that the Peyer "admission" was pertinent not only to Tamanaco but also to Unifund. As the link to Unifund, she pointed to Bank Audi, a Lebanese bank. The connection Judge Kram relied upon was that Ralph Audi, the principal shareholder of Unifund, is related to individuals who run Bank Audi and its Swiss affiliate, Bank Audi Suisse, and that Bank Audi Suisse had purchased Rorer call options in the week prior to the merger announcement and had made the purchases through Raymond Jones, the brokerage firm that employed Candid Peyer. Ralph Audi's relatives, George W. Audi and Raymond W. Audi, are, respectively, chairman and director of Bank Audi; Raymond is also chairman of Bank Audi Suisse. Ralph Audi has borrowed funds from Bank Audi.

* * *

Judge Kram explicitly declined to credit Unifund's innocent explanation for its Rorer purchases. In an affidavit, Ralph Audi stated that Unifund frequently invests in possible takeover targets, that Rorer had been the subject of takeover speculation since August 1989, that his bank in Paris had informed him in the last week of December that additional collateral was needed to secure Unifund's line of credit, and that the "first stock that came to mind for me was Rorer," because of the prior takeover rumors. Judge Kram found this explanation unconvincing because Audi had not bought Rorer in August, when he claims to have first heard takeover rumors, but did so on January 4, 1990, just after Merrill Lynch had advised against a purchase in December.

Having found a "strong *prima facie*" case of rule 10b–5 violations by both Unifund and Tamanaco, Judge Kram also found a sufficient likelihood of future violations, a conclusion based primarily on the fact that both defendants regularly trade securities. She therefore issued the preliminary injunction.

* * *

IV. Sufficiency of the Evidence for
Preliminary Injunctive Relief.

The major issue on appeal is whether the evidence presented by the Commission sufficed to warrant a preliminary injunction. We begin our consideration of that issue with an examination of the pertinent statute and the standards that have evolved in applying it. Section 21(d) of the Exchange Act provides:

> Whenever it shall appear to the Commission that any person is engaged or is about to engage in acts or practices constituting a violation of any provision of this chapter, the rules or regulations thereunder, [or rules of exchanges and other designated entities], it may in its discretion bring an action in the proper district court . . . to enjoin such acts or practices, and upon a proper showing a permanent or temporary injunction or restraining order shall be granted without bond.

15 U.S.C. § 78u(d) (1988).

* * *

In our earliest encounters with injunction requests by the Commission, we relieved the Commission of the obligation, imposed on private litigants, to show risk of irreparable injury, SEC v. Torr, 87 F.2d 446, 450 (2d Cir. 1937), or the unavailability of remedies at law, SEC v. Jones, 85 F.2d 17 (2d Cir.), cert. denied, 299 U.S. 581 (1936). That rule remains the law of this Circuit. See SEC v. Management Dynamics, Inc., 515 F.2d 801, 808–09 (2d Cir. 1975).

Though the Commission faces a reduced burden in these respects, compared to private litigants, there is some uncertainty whether in other respects its burden in obtaining a preliminary injunction is the same as or greater than that of private litigants. The uncertainty concerns (1) whether the Commission's showing on the merits must be more than the "likelihood of success" standard required of private litigants, and (2) whether the alternative test for a preliminary injunction—irreparable harm plus an issue that is a fair ground for litigation and a balance of hardships that tips decidedly to the plaintiff, id.—is available to the Commission. The statutory standard set forth in section 21(d) of the Exchange Act—"a proper showing"—is singularly unenlightening in resolving these issues.

* * *

C. *Application of Preliminary Injunction Standards*

Since the test of sufficiency varies with the nature of the relief sought, we consider separately each of the two principal forms of relief that were ordered—the prohibition against future insider trading violations and the freeze order.

(i) *Prohibition Against Future Securities Law Violations.*

The prohibition against future securities law violations is among the sanctions that we have characterized as having grave consequences. Such an order subjects the defendant to contempt sanctions if its subsequent trading is deemed unlawful and also has serious collateral effects. Though the order is prohibitory in form, rather than mandatory, it accomplishes significantly more than preservation of the status quo. For this form of relief, the Commission has to make a substantial showing of likelihood of success as to both a current violation and the risk of repetition. An insider trading violation requires proof not only that the defendant traded on the basis of material nonpublic information but also that in doing so he knew or should have known that he was breaching a fiduciary duty.

In this case, the Commission has not identified the person or entity alleged to have conveyed inside information to either appellant. It is therefore more difficult than in the typical tipping case to determine whether, even if the appellants obtained inside information, they traded upon it in breach of a fiduciary duty that they knew or should have known existed. Though a "tippee's duty to disclose or abstain is derivative from that of the insider's duty," Dirks v. SEC, we do not know from whom such a duty might derive in this case.

The Commission attempts to bridge this fundamental gap in its evidence with speculation. Even if we assume that it has sufficiently shown an adequate probability that Candid Peyer, Espirito Santo's broker at Raymond Jones, had material nonpublic information from an insider, we are then asked to infer the requisite relationship to Unifund and Tamanaco from wholly inadequate circumstances. The evidence showed that Unifund's principal is related, familially and financially, to a bank that bought Rorer securities through Raymond Jones. The link to Unifund assumes that Peyer's information was conveyed to Raymond Jones, then to Bank Audi, and then to Unifund, under circumstances where Unifund knew or should have known of a nondisclosure obligation. These assumptions are unsupported on this record. Nor are they provided by the commonality of surnames between an officer of Bank Audi and a shareholder of Unifund (both named Karam), or between an executive of Rhone and an incorporator of Unifund (both named Khoury).

The linkage is no better with respect to Tamanaco. It assumes that Peyer's information was conveyed to Raymond Jones, then to Espirito Santo, and then to Tamanaco. These assumptions are also unsupported.

What the record discloses is unusual trading by both Unifund and Tamanaco on the eve of the merger announcement. They may well have had inside information, but possession of such information without more does not give rise to a duty to disclose or abstain from trading, Dirks v. SEC, at least where the recipient of the information is an ordinary investor. Whatever adverse inferences might be drawn from the recalcitrance to discovery that Judge Kram attributed to appellants are not sufficient to remedy the gap in the Commission's showing of a probable insider trading violation.

(ii) *Freeze Order.*

We reach a different conclusion with respect to the freeze order, though we modify the terms of the order. In seeking to freeze appellants' accounts, the Commission is requesting ancillary relief to facilitate enforcement of any disgorgement remedy that might be ordered in the event a violation is established at trial. Unlike the injunction against securities law violations, the freeze order does not place appellants at risk of contempt in all future securities transactions. It simply assures that any funds that may become due can be collected. The order functions like an attachment. That does not mean, however, that its issuance must be tested against state law standards, as would be the case if the relief were sought pursuant to rule 64 of the Federal Rules of Civil Procedure. Congress has authorized the Commission to obtain preliminary injunctive relief upon a "proper showing," and it is a matter of federal law whether the showing the Commission has made is sufficient to support an interlocutory freeze order. Cf. FTC v. H.N. Singer, Inc., 668 F.2d 1107, 1112 (9th Cir. 1982) (unavailability of attachment does not preclude other provisional remedies). Moreover, an ancillary remedy may be granted, even in circumstances where the elements required to support a traditional SEC injunction have not been established, see SEC v. Commonwealth Chemical Securities, Inc., 574 F.2d at 103 n.13 (approving disgorgement remedy despite failure to show likelihood of recurring violation), and such a remedy is especially warranted where it is sought for a limited duration, see SEC v. Levine, 881 F.2d 1165, 1177 (2d Cir. 1989).

Though the Commission has not presented at this stage sufficient evidence to warrant a preliminary injunction of traditional scope, its evidence suffices to warrant some form of freeze order. There is a basis to infer that the appellants traded on inside information, and while the Commission is endeavoring to prove at trial the requisite element of trading in breach of a fiduciary duty of which the defendants were or should have been aware, the Commission should be able to preserve its opportunity to collect funds that may yet be ordered disgorged.

Three aspects of the freeze order in this case require further consideration. First, the order freezes funds in an amount sufficient to cover not just the profits that might have to be disgorged but the civil penalty, equal to three times the profits, that the Commission may recover under section 21A of the Exchange Act upon proof of a violation. Appellants challenge this aspect of the order, relying on SEC v. Manor Nursing Centers, Inc., 458 F.2d 1082 (2d Cir. 1972), where we said that a freeze order could be imposed so long as it orders " 'remedial relief and is not a penalty assessment.' " That observation was made in setting aside that portion of an order requiring surrender of the income earned on proceeds required to be disgorged. Though recognizing that surrendering the earned income might add to the deterrent effect of securities law enforcement, we concluded that this incremental remedy would be arbitrary in the circumstances presented.

With the enactment of section 21A in 1988, Congress has made the judgment that a civil penalty equal to three times the profits of insider trading should be an available remedy for the Commission. Our reluctance in *Manor Nursing Centers* to permit a freeze order to reach funds not normally forfeitable is not authority for denying the Commission the opportunity to collect funds that Congress has expressly determined are appropriate for forfeiture.

Second, and more troublesome, is the fact that the freeze order obliges appellants not merely to maintain in their accounts funds sufficient to pay the amounts that might eventually be due but also to refrain from any trading in the accounts without the Commission's approval. The Commission understandably prefers such a remedy, which enables it to insist upon high-grade investments to maximize the prospect that sufficient funds will be available in the accounts to pay the civil penalties. But bearing in mind the basic principle that burdensome forms of interim relief require correspondingly substantial justification, we conclude that the Commission's showing in this case is inadequate to support the extensive trading restriction in the freeze order. The Commission has presented a thin case for any ancillary relief. At most, its meager showing entitles it to an order that provides reasonable security for collecting a judgment, with a trading restriction imposed only if that security becomes deficient. The freeze order should be modified to provide that the appellants shall maintain in their accounts funds and securities in an amount equal to three times the profits earned on the

Rorer trades, with the proviso that, should either appellant's account balance, at fair market values, decrease to a level at or below twice that appellant's Rorer profits, that appellant must restore the account to a level equal to three times its Rorer profits, failing which the Commission may reimpose its restriction on permissible trading. Though this modified remedy tolerates a risk that unsuccessful trading might erode some of the value of the accounts from which the Commission hopes to collect any penalties that may be assessed, it gives the Commission substantial security without unduly burdening the appellants by denying them the opportunity to invest as they see fit. Presumably, they are as anxious to see their account balances grow as is the Commission, though we acknowledge that the appellants will now have the opportunity to make their more risky investments from the accounts previously frozen so extensively. In any event, we are satisfied that this mild thaw in the freeze order appropriately adjusts it to the maximum interim relief to which the Commission is entitled in view of its minimal showing of a violation.

Third, though we are willing to approve a modified freeze order, we do not believe that the Commission is entitled to keep even the modified order in force for whatever period of time the Commission may take to prepare for trial. In view of the Commission's meager showing on the merits, it should not be entitled to interfere with the appellants' unrestricted use of their accounts for more than a brief interval. In view of the time that has already elapsed since the injunction issued, we will direct that the freeze order, as modified, shall terminate thirty days after the issuance of our mandate, unless within such time the Commission advises the District Court of its readiness for immediate trial.

The orders of the District Court are vacated in part and modified in part, and the cause is remanded for entry of orders revised in conformity with this opinion.

B. Disgorgement and Ancillary Relief

The following case illustrates the broad power of the SEC and the courts to fashion appropriate remedies, including disgorgement.

Liu v. SEC
Supreme Court of the United States, 2020.
591 U.S. ___, 140 S.Ct. 1936, 207 L.Ed.2d 401 (2020).

■ JUSTICE SOTOMAYOR delivered the opinion of the Court in an 8–1 decision. JUSTICE THOMAS' dissent is omitted.

In Kokesh v. SEC, this Court held that a disgorgement order in a Securities and Exchange Commission (SEC) enforcement action imposes a "penalty" for the purposes of 28 U. S. C. § 2462, the applicable statute of limitations. In so deciding, the Court reserved an antecedent question: whether, and to what extent, the SEC may seek "disgorgement" in the first instance through its power to award "equitable relief" under 15 U. S. C. § 78u(d)(5), a power that historically excludes punitive sanctions. The Court holds today that a disgorgement award that does not exceed a wrongdoer's net profits and is awarded for victims is equitable relief permissible under § 78u(d)(5). The judgment is vacated, and the case is remanded for the courts below to ensure the award was so limited.

I

A

Congress authorized the SEC to enforce the Securities Act of 1933, 48 Stat. 74, as amended, 15 U. S. C. § 77a *et seq.*, and the Securities Exchange Act of 1934, 48 Stat. 881, as amended, 15 U. S. C. § 78a *et seq.*, and to punish securities fraud through administrative and civil proceedings. In administrative proceedings, the SEC can seek limited civil penalties and "disgorgement." See § 77h–1(e) ("In any cease-and-desist proceeding under subsection (a), the Commission may enter an order requiring accounting and disgorgement"); see also § 77h–1(g) ("Authority to impose money penalties"). In civil actions, the SEC can seek civil penalties and "equitable relief." See, *e.g.*, § 78u(d)(5) ("In any action or proceeding brought or instituted by the Commission under any provision of the securities laws, . . . any Federal court may grant . . . any equitable relief that may be appropriate or necessary for the benefit of investors"); see also § 78u(d)(3) ("Money penalties in civil actions" (quotation modified)).

Congress did not define what falls under the umbrella of "equitable relief." Thus, courts have had to consider which remedies the SEC may impose as part of its § 78u(d)(5) powers.

Starting with SEC v. Texas Gulf Sulphur Co., 446 F. 2d 1301 (CA2 1971), courts determined that the SEC had authority to obtain what it called "restitution," and what in substance amounted to "profits" that "merely depriv[e]" a defendant of "the gains of . . . wrongful conduct." Id., at 1307–1308. Over the years, the SEC has continued to request this remedy, later referred to as "disgorgement," and courts have continued to award it.). * * *

In *Kokesh*, this Court determined that disgorgement constituted a "penalty" for the purposes of 28 U. S. C. § 2462, which establishes a 5-year statute of limitations for "an action, suit or proceeding for the enforcement of any civil fine, penalty, or forfeiture." The Court reached this conclusion based on several considerations, namely, that disgorgement is imposed as a consequence of violating public laws, it is assessed in part for punitive purposes, and in many cases, the award is not compensatory. * * * But the Court did not address whether a § 2462 penalty can nevertheless qualify as "equitable relief" under § 78u(d)(5), given that equity never "lends its aid to enforce a forfeiture or penalty." Marshall v. Vicksburg, 15 Wall. 146, 149 (1873). The Court cautioned, moreover, that its decision should not be interpreted "as an opinion on whether courts possess authority to order disgorgement in SEC enforcement proceedings." Kokesh, 581 U. S., at ___, n. 3. This question is now squarely before the Court.

B

The SEC action and disgorgement award at issue here arise from a scheme to defraud foreign nationals. Petitioners Charles Liu and his wife, Xin (Lisa) Wang, solicited nearly $27 million from foreign investors under the EB-5 Immigrant Investor Program (EB-5 Program). 754 Fed. Appx. 505, 506 (CA9 2018). The EB-5 Program, administered by the U. S. Citizenship and Immigration Services, permits noncitizens to apply for permanent residence in the United States by investing in approved commercial enterprises that are based on "proposals for promoting economic growth." See USCIS, EB-5 Immigrant Investor Program, https://www.uscis.gov/eb-5. Investments in EB-5 projects are subject to the federal securities laws.

Liu sent a private offering memorandum to prospective investors, pledging that the bulk of any contributions would go toward the construction costs of a cancer-treatment center. The memorandum specified that only amounts collected from a small administrative fee would fund " 'legal, accounting and administration expenses.' " 754 Fed. Appx., at 507. An SEC investigation revealed, however, that Liu spent nearly $20 million of investor money on ostensible marketing expenses and salaries, an amount far more than what the offering memorandum permitted and far in excess of the administrative fees collected. 262 F.Supp.3d 957, 960–964 (C.D. Cal. 2017). The investigation also revealed that Liu diverted a sizable portion of those funds to personal accounts and to a company under Wang's control. Id., at 961, 964. Only a fraction of the funds were put toward a lease, property improvements, and a proton-therapy machine for cancer treatment. Id., at 964–965.

The SEC brought a civil action against petitioners, alleging that they violated the terms of the offering documents by misappropriating millions of dollars. The District Court found for the SEC, granting an injunction barring petitioners from participating in the EB-5 Program and imposing a civil penalty at the highest tier authorized. Id., at 975, 976. It also ordered disgorgement equal to the full amount petitioners had raised from investors, less the $234,899 that remained in the corporate accounts for the project. Id., at 975–976.

Petitioners objected that the disgorgement award failed to account for their business expenses. The District Court disagreed, concluding that the sum was a "reasonable approximation of the profits causally connected to [their] violation." Ibid. The court ordered petitioners jointly and severally liable for the full amount that the SEC sought. App. to Pet. for Cert. 62a.

The Ninth Circuit affirmed. It acknowledged that *Kokesh* "expressly refused to reach" the issue whether the District Court had the authority to order disgorgement. 754 Fed. Appx., at 509. The court relied on Circuit precedent to conclude that the "proper amount of disgorgement in a scheme such as this one is the entire amount raised less the money paid back to the investors." Ibid.; see also SEC v. JT Wallenbrock & Assocs., 440 F. 3d 1109, 1113, 1114 (CA9 2006) (reasoning that it would be "unjust to permit the defendants to offset . . . the expenses of running the very business they created to defraud . . . investors").

We granted certiorari to determine whether § 78u(d)(5) authorizes the SEC to seek disgorgement beyond a defendant's net profits from wrongdoing. * * *

II

Our task is a familiar one. In interpreting statutes like § 78u(d)(5) that provide for "equitable relief," this Court analyzes whether a particular remedy falls into "those categories of relief that were *typically* available in equity." * * *

These works on equity jurisprudence reveal two principles. First, equity practice long authorized courts to strip wrongdoers of their ill-gotten gains, with scholars and courts using various labels for the remedy. Second, to avoid transforming an equitable remedy into a punitive sanction, courts restricted the remedy to an individual wrongdoer's net profits to be awarded for victims.

A

Equity courts have routinely deprived wrongdoers of their net profits from unlawful activity, even though that remedy may have gone by different names. * * *

No matter the label, this "profit-based measure of unjust enrichment," Restatement (Third) § 51, Comment *a*, at 204, reflected a foundational principle: "[I]t would be inequitable that [a wrongdoer] should make a profit out of his own wrong," Root v. Railway Co., 105 U. S. 189, 207 (1882). At the same time courts recognized that the wrongdoer should not profit "by his own wrong," they also recognized the countervailing equitable principle that the wrongdoer should not be punished by "pay[ing] more than a fair compensation to the person wronged." Tilghman v. Proctor, 125 U. S. 136, 145–146 (1888).

Decisions from this Court confirm that a remedy tethered to a wrongdoer's net unlawful profits, whatever the name, has been a mainstay of equity courts. In Porter v. Warner Holding Co., 328 U. S. 395 (1946), the Court interpreted a section of the Emergency Price Control Act of 1942 that encompassed a "comprehensiv[e]" grant of "equitable jurisdiction." Id., at 398. "[O]nce [a District Court's] equity jurisdiction has been invoked" under that provision, the Court concluded, "a decree compelling one to disgorge profits . . . may properly be entered." Id., at 398–399.

Subsequent cases confirm the "'protean character' of the profits-recovery remedy." Petrella v. Metro-GoldwynMayer, Inc., 572 U. S. 663, 668, n. 1 (2014). In Tull v. United States, 481 U. S. 412 (1987), the Court described "disgorgement of improper profits" as "traditionally considered an equitable remedy." Id., at 424. While the Court acknowledged that disgorgement was a "limited form of penalty" insofar as it takes money out of the wrongdoer's hands, it nevertheless compared disgorgement to restitution that simply "'restor[es] the status quo,'" thus situating the remedy squarely within the heartland of equity. Ibid. In Great-West, the Court noted that an "accounting for profits" was historically a "form of equitable restitution." 534 U. S., at 214, n. 2. And in Kansas v. Nebraska, 574 U. S. 445 (2015), a "'basically equitable'" original jurisdiction proceeding, the Court ordered disgorgement of Nebraska's gains from exceeding its allocation under an interstate water compact. Id., at 453, 475.

Most recently, in SCA Hygiene Products Aktiebolag v. First Quality Baby Products, LLC, 580 U. S. ___ (2017), the Court canvassed pre-1938 patent cases invoking equity jurisdiction. It noted that many cases sought an "accounting," which it described as an equitable remedy requiring disgorgement of ill-gotten profits. * * * This Court's "transsubstantive guidance on broad and fundamental" equitable principles, Romag Fasteners, Inc. v. Fossil Group, Inc., 590 U. S. ___, ___ (2020), thus reflects the teachings of equity treatises that identify a defendant's net profits as a remedy for wrongdoing.

Contrary to petitioners' argument, equity courts did not limit this remedy to cases involving a breach of trust or of fiduciary duty. As petitioners acknowledge, courts authorized profits-based relief in patent-infringement actions where no such trust or special relationship existed. Id., at 29; see also Root, 105 U. S., at 214 ("[I]t is nowhere said that the patentee's right to an account is based upon the idea that there is a fiduciary relation created between him and the wrong-doer by the fact of infringement").

* * *

B

While equity courts did not limit profits remedies to particular types of cases, they did circumscribe the award in multiple ways to avoid transforming it into a penalty outside their equitable powers. See *Marshall*, 15 Wall., at 149.

For one, the profits remedy often imposed a constructive trust on wrongful gains for wronged victims. The remedy itself thus converted the wrongdoer, who in many cases was an infringer, "into a trustee, as to those profits, for the owner of the patent which he infringes." Burdell v. Denig, 92 U. S. 716, 720 (1876). In "converting the infringer into a trustee for the patentee as regards the profits thus made," the chancellor "estimat[es] the compensation due from the infringer to the patentee."

Packet Co. v. Sickles, 19 Wall. 611, 617–618 (1874); see also Clews v. Jamieson, 182 U. S. 461, 480 (1901) (describing an accounting as involving a " 'distribution of the trust moneys among all the beneficiaries who are entitled to share therein' " in an action against the governing committee of a stock exchange).

Equity courts also generally awarded profits-based remedies against individuals or partners engaged in concerted wrongdoing, not against multiple wrongdoers under a joint-and-several liability theory. See Ambler v. Whipple, 20 Wall. 546, 559 (1874) (ordering an accounting against a partner who had "knowingly connected himself with and aided in . . . fraud"). In Elizabeth v. Pavement *Co.*, 97 U. S. 126 (1878), for example, a city engaged contractors to install pavement in a manner that infringed a third party's patent. The patent holder brought a suit in equity to recover profits from both the city and its contractors. The Court held that only the contractors (the only parties to make a profit) were responsible, even though the parties answered jointly. Id., at 140; see also ibid. (rejecting liability for an individual officer who merely acted as an agent of the defendant and received a salary for his work). The rule against joint-and-several liability for profits that have accrued to another appears throughout equity cases awarding profits. See, *e.g.*, Belknap v. Schild, 161 U. S. 10, 25–26 (1896) ("The defendants, in any such suit, are therefore liable to account for such profits only as have accrued to themselves from the use of the invention, and not for those which have accrued to another, and in which they have no participation"); Keystone Mfg. Co. v. Adams, 151 U. S. 139, 148 (1894) (reversing profits award that was based not on what defendant had made from infringement but on what third persons had made from the use of the invention); Jennings v. Carson, 4 Cranch 2, 21 (1807) (holding that an order requiring restitution could not apply to "those who were not in possession of the thing to be restored" and "had no power over it") (citing Penhallow v. Doane's Administrators, 3 Dall. 54 (1795) (reversing a restitution award in admiralty that ordered joint damages in excess of what each defendant received)).

Finally, courts limited awards to the net profits from wrongdoing, that is, "the gain made upon any business or investment, when both the receipts and payments are taken into the account." Rubber Co. v. Goodyear, 9 Wall. 788, 804 (1870); see also Livingston v. Woodworth, 15 How. 546, 559–560 (1854) (restricting an accounting remedy "to the actual gains and profits . . . during the time" the infringing machine "was in operation and during no other period" to avoid "convert[ing] a court of equity into an instrument for the punishment of simple torts"); Seymour v. McCormick, 16 How. 480, 490 (1854) (rejecting a blanket rule that infringing one component of a machine warranted a remedy measured by the full amounts of the profits earned from the machine); Mowry v. Whitney, 14 Wall. 620, 649 (1872) (vacating an accounting that exceeded the profits from infringement alone); Wooden-Ware Co. v. United States,

106 U. S. 432, 434–435 (1882) (explaining that an innocent trespasser is entitled to deduct labor costs from the gains obtained by wrongfully harvesting lumber).

The Court has carved out an exception when the "entire profit of a business or undertaking" results from the wrongful activity. Root, 105 U. S., at 203. In such cases, the Court has explained, the defendant "will not be allowed to diminish the show of profits by putting in unconscionable claims for personal services or other inequitable deductions." Ibid. In Goodyear, for example, the Court affirmed an accounting order that refused to deduct expenses under this rule. The Court there found that materials for which expenses were claimed were bought for the purposes of the infringement and "extraordinary salaries" appeared merely to be "dividends of profit under another name." 9 Wall., at 803; see also Callaghan v. Myers, 128 U. S. 617, 663–664 (1888) (declining to deduct a defendant's personal and living expenses from his profits from copyright violations, but distinguishing the expenses from salaries of officers in a corporation).

Setting aside that circumstance, however, courts consistently restricted awards to net profits from wrongdoing after deducting legitimate expenses. Such remedies, when assessed against only culpable actors and for victims, fall comfortably within "those categories of relief that were typically available in equity." *Mertens*, 508 U. S., at 256.

C

By incorporating these longstanding equitable principles into § 78u(d)(5), Congress prohibited the SEC from seeking an equitable remedy in excess of a defendant's net profits from wrongdoing. To be sure, the SEC originally endeavored to conform its disgorgement remedy to the common law limitations in § 78u(d)(5). Over the years, however, courts have occasionally awarded disgorgement in three main ways that test the bounds of equity practice: by ordering the proceeds of fraud to be deposited in Treasury funds instead of disbursing them to victims, imposing joint-and-several disgorgement liability, and declining to deduct even legitimate expenses from the receipts of fraud. The SEC's disgorgement remedy in such incarnations is in considerable tension with equity practices.

Petitioners go further. They claim that this Court effectively decided in *Kokesh* that disgorgement is necessarily a penalty, and thus not the kind of relief available at equity. Not so. *Kokesh* expressly declined to pass on the question. 581 U. S., at ___, n. 3. To be sure, the Kokesh Court evaluated a version of the SEC's disgorgement remedy that seemed to exceed the bounds of traditional equitable principles. But that decision has no bearing on the SEC's ability to conform future requests for a defendant's profits to the limits outlined in common-law cases awarding a wrongdoer's net gains.

The Government, for its part, contends that the SEC's interpretation of the equitable disgorgement remedy has Congress' tacit support, even if it exceeds the bounds of equity practice. It points to the fact that Congress has enacted a number of other statutes referring to "disgorgement."

That argument attaches undue significance to Congress' use of the term. It is true that Congress has authorized the SEC to seek "disgorgement" in administrative actions. 15 U. S. C. § 77h–1(e) ("In any cease-and-desist proceeding under subsection (a), the Commission may enter an order requiring accounting and disgorgement"). But it makes sense that Congress would expressly name the equitable powers it grants to an agency for use in administrative proceedings. After all, agencies are unlike federal courts where, "[u]nless otherwise provided by statute, all . . . inherent equitable powers . . . are available for the proper and complete exercise of that jurisdiction." Porter, 328 U. S., at 398.

Congress does not enlarge the breadth of an equitable, profit-based remedy simply by using the term "disgorgement" in various statutes. The Government argues that under the prior-construction principle, Congress should be presumed to have been aware of the scope of "disgorgement" as interpreted by lower courts and as having incorporated the (purportedly) prevailing meaning of the term into its subsequent enactments. But "that canon has no application" where, among other things, the scope of disgorgement was "far from 'settled.' " Armstrong v. Exceptional Child Center, Inc., 575 U. S. 320, 330 (2015).

At bottom, even if Congress employed "disgorgement" as a shorthand to cross-reference the relief permitted by § 78u(d)(5), it did not silently rewrite the scope of what the SEC could recover in a way that would contravene limitations embedded in the statute. After all, such "statutory reference[s]" to a remedy grounded in equity "must, absent other indication, be deemed to contain the limitations upon its availability that equity typically imposes." *Great-West*, 534 U. S., at 211, n. 1. Accordingly, Congress' own use of the term "disgorgement" in assorted statutes did not expand the contours of that term beyond a defendant's net profits—a limit established by longstanding principles of equity.

III

Applying the principles discussed above to the facts of this case, petitioners briefly argue that their disgorgement award is unlawful because it crosses the bounds of traditional equity practice in three ways: It fails to return funds to victims, it imposes joint-and-several liability, and it declines to deduct business expenses from the award. Because the parties focused on the broad question whether any form of disgorgement may be ordered and did not fully brief these narrower questions, we do not decide them here. We nevertheless discuss principles that may guide the lower courts' assessment of these arguments on remand.

A

Section 78u(d)(5) restricts equitable relief to that which "may be appropriate or necessary for the benefit of investors." The SEC, however, does not always return the entirety of disgorgement proceeds to investors, instead depositing a portion of its collections in a fund in the Treasury. See SEC, Division of Enforcement, 2019 Ann. Rep. 16–17. Congress established that fund in the Dodd-Frank Wall Street Reform and Consumer Protection Act for disgorgement awards that are not deposited in "disgorgement fund[s]" or otherwise "distributed to victims." 124 Stat. 1844. The statute provides that these sums may be used to pay whistleblowers reporting securities fraud and to fund the activities of the Inspector General. Ibid. Here, the SEC has not returned the bulk of funds to victims, largely, it contends, because the Government has been unable to collect them.

The statute provides limited guidance as to whether the practice of depositing a defendant's gains with the Treasury satisfies the statute's command that any remedy be "appropriate or necessary for the benefit of investors." The equitable nature of the profits remedy generally requires the SEC to return a defendant's gains to wronged investors for their benefit. After all, the Government has pointed to no analogous common-law remedy permitting a wrongdoer's profits to be withheld from a victim indefinitely without being disbursed to known victims. Cf. *Root*, 105 U. S., at 214–215 (comparing the accounting remedy to a breach-of-trust action, where a court would require the defendant to "refund the amount of profit which they have actually realized").

The Government maintains, however, that the primary function of depriving wrongdoers of profits is to deny them the fruits of their ill-gotten gains, not to return the funds to victims as a kind of restitution. See, *e.g.*, SEC, Report Pursuant to Section 308(C) of the Sarbanes Oxley Act of 2002, p. 3, n. 2 (2003) (taking the position that disgorgement is not intended to make investors whole, but rather to deprive wrongdoers of ill-gotten gains); see also 6 T. Hazen, Law of Securities Regulation § 16.18, p. 8 (rev. 7th ed. 2016) (concluding that the remedial nature of the disgorgement remedy does not mean that it is essentially compensatory and concluding that the "primary function of the remedy is to deny the wrongdoer the fruits of ill-gotten gains"). Under the Government's theory, the very fact that it conducted an enforcement action satisfies the requirement that it is "appropriate or necessary for the benefit of investors."

But the SEC's equitable, profits-based remedy must do more than simply benefit the public at large by virtue of depriving a wrongdoer of ill-gotten gains. To hold otherwise would render meaningless the latter part of § 78u(d)(5). Indeed, this Court concluded similarly in Mertens when analyzing statutory language accompanying the term "equitable remedy." 508 U. S., at 253 (interpreting the term "appropriate equitable relief"). There, the Court found that the additional statutory language must be given effect since the section "does not, after all, authorize . . . 'equitable relief' at large." Ibid. As in *Mertens*, the phrase "appropriate or necessary for the benefit of investors" must mean something more than depriving a wrongdoer of his net profits alone, else the Court would violate the "cardinal principle of interpretation that courts must give effect, if possible, to every clause and word of a statute." Parker Drilling Management Services, Ltd. v. Newton, 587 U. S. ___, ___ (2019).

The Government additionally suggests that the SEC's practice of depositing disgorgement funds with the Treasury may be justified where it is infeasible to distribute the collected funds to investors. Brief for Respondent 37. It is an open question whether, and to what extent, that practice nevertheless satisfies the SEC's obligation to award relief "for the benefit of investors" and is consistent with the limitations of § 78u(d)(5). The parties have not identified authorities revealing what traditional equitable principles govern when, for instance, the wrongdoer's profits cannot practically be disbursed to the victims. But we need not address the issue here. The parties do not identify a specific order in this case directing any proceeds to the Treasury. If one is entered on remand, the lower courts may evaluate in the first instance whether that order would indeed be for the benefit of investors as required by § 78u(d)(5) and consistent with equitable principles.

B

The SEC additionally has sought to impose disgorgement liability on a wrongdoer for benefits that accrue to his affiliates, sometimes through joint-and-several liability, in a manner sometimes seemingly at odds with the common-law rule requiring individual liability for wrongful profits. See, *e.g.*, SEC v. Contorinis, 743 F. 3d 296, 302 (CA2 2014) (holding that a defendant could be forced to disgorge not only what he "personally enjoyed from his exploitation of inside information, but also the profits of such exploitation that he channeled to friends, family, or clients"); SEC v. Clark, 915 F. 2d 439, 454 (CA9 1990) ("It is well settled that a tipper can be required to disgorge his tippee's profits"); SEC v. Whittemore, 659 F. 3d 1, 10 (CADC 2011) (approving joint-and-several disgorgement liability where there is a close relationship between the defendants and collaboration in executing the wrongdoing).

That practice could transform any equitable profits-focused remedy into a penalty. Cf. *Marshall*, 15 Wall., at 149. And it runs against the rule to not impose joint liability in favor of holding defendants "liable to account for such profits only as have accrued to themselves . . . and not for those which have accrued to another, and in which they have no participation." *Belknap*, 161 U. S., at 25–26; see also Elizabeth v. Pavement Co., 97 U. S. 126 (1878).

The common law did, however, permit liability for partners engaged in concerted wrongdoing. See, *e.g.*, *Ambler*, 20 Wall., at 559. The historic profits remedy thus allows some flexibility to impose collective liability. Given the wide spectrum of relationships between participants and beneficiaries of unlawful schemes—from equally culpable codefendants to more remote, unrelated tipper-tippee arrangements—the Court need not wade into all the circumstances where an equitable profits remedy might be punitive when applied to multiple individuals.

Here, petitioners were married. 754 Fed. Appx. 505; 262 F.Supp.3d, at 960–961. The Government introduced evidence that Liu formed business entities and solicited investments, which he misappropriated. Id., at 961. It also presented evidence that Wang held herself out as the president, and a member of the management team, of an entity to which Liu directed misappropriated funds. Id., at 964. Petitioners did not introduce evidence to suggest that one spouse was a mere passive recipient of profits. Nor did they suggest that their finances were not commingled, or that one spouse did not enjoy the fruits of the scheme, or that other circumstances would render a joint-and-several disgorgement order unjust. Cf. SEC v. Hughes Capital Corp., 124 F. 3d 449, 456 (CA3 1997) (finding that codefendant spouse was liable for unlawful proceeds where they funded her "lavish lifestyle"). We leave it to the Ninth Circuit on remand to determine whether the facts are such that petitioners can, consistent with equitable principles, be found liable for profits as partners in wrongdoing or whether individual liability is required.

C

Courts may not enter disgorgement awards that exceed the gains "made upon any business or investment, when both the receipts and payments are taken into the account." *Goodyear*, 9 Wall., at 804; see also Restatement (Third) § 51, Comment h, at 216 (reciting the general rule that a defendant is entitled to a deduction for all marginal costs incurred in producing the revenues that are subject to disgorgement). Accordingly, courts must deduct legitimate expenses before ordering disgorgement under § 78u(d)(5). A rule to the contrary that "make[s] no allowance for the cost and expense of conducting [a] business" would be "inconsistent with the ordinary principles and practice of courts of chancery." Tilghman, 125 U. S., at 145–146; cf. SEC v. Brown, 658 F. 3d 858, 861 (CA8 2011) (declining to deduct even legitimate expenses like payments to innocent third-party employees and vendors).

The District Court below declined to deduct expenses on the theory that they were incurred for the purposes of furthering an entirely fraudulent scheme. It is true that when the "entire profit of a business or undertaking" results from the wrongdoing, a defendant may be denied "inequitable deductions" such as for personal services. Root, 105 U. S., at 203. But that exception requires ascertaining whether expenses are legitimate or whether they are merely wrongful gains "under another name." *Goodyear*, 9 Wall., at 803. Doing so will ensure that any disgorgement award falls within the limits of equity practice while preventing defendants from profiting from their own wrong. *Root*, 105 U. S., at 207.

Although it is not necessary to set forth more guidance addressing the various circumstances where a defendant's expenses might be considered wholly fraudulent, it suffices to note that some expenses from petitioners' scheme went toward lease payments and cancer-treatment equipment. Such items arguably have value independent of fueling a fraudulent scheme. We leave it to the lower court to examine whether including those expenses in a profits-based remedy is consistent with the equitable principles underlying § 78u(d)(5).

* * *

For the foregoing reasons, we vacate the judgment below and remand the case to the Ninth Circuit for further proceedings consistent with this opinion.

It is so ordered.

NOTES ON DISGORGEMENT REMEDY

1. *The Authority of the SEC to Obtain Disgorgement.* The SEC has the power seek equitable remedies from violators of the securities laws. Prior to Liu v. SEC,[43] the court reserved as an open question in SEC v. Kokesh[44] whether the SEC had the authority to seek disgorgement as a form of equitable relief under 15 U.S.C. § 78u(d)(5). In *Liu,* the Court held that issuing a disgorgement order can be a form of equitable relief with some limitations. The Court highlighted three issues that impact whether a disgorgement order is a penalty and, therefore, not allowed: (1) whether the disgorgement funds are paid directly to injured investors; (2) whether the SEC seeks disgorgement from multiple parties on an individual liability basis or on a joint-and-several liability basis; and (3) whether the disgorgement award exceeds the wrongdoer's net gains.

2. *The Distribution of Disgorgement Funds.* The SEC has a practice in some cases of distributing disgorgement funds to a U.S. Treasury Fund established by Dodd-Frank—instead of directly to the injured investors. The SEC typically chooses to distribute funds to the U.S. Treasury when the costs of returning the funds to investors would be too high in light of the amount of money collected. The Court did not decide this issue, but it did caution that the disgorgement order would need to "do more than simply benefit the public at large" and "be for the benefit of investors."

3. *The Basis of Liability.* The Court also did not decide whether the SEC can seek disgorgement from multiple parties on a joint-and-several liability basis. The Court did, however, caution that seeking disgorgement from multiple parties on a joint-and-several liability basis conflicts with the common-law rule, which requires individual liability for recovery of wrongful profits. Nevertheless, the common law does allow

---

[43] 591 U.S. ___, 140 S.Ct. 1936 (2020).
[44] 581 U.S. ___, 137 S.Ct. 1635 (2017).

for collective liability in the case of partners engaged in "concerted wrongdoing."

4. *The Amount of the Disgorgement Award.* The Court held in *Liu* that disgorgement awards cannot exceed the wrongdoers' net gains. As a result, courts should deduct "legitimate expenses" from gross profits to determine the amount of the disgorgement award. The Court left it up to the lower courts to determine "legitimate expenses," noting that the courts must determine "whether expenses are legitimate or whether they are merely wrongful gains 'under another name.'" The definition of legitimate expenses will likely be the subject of future litigation.

NOTES ON INJUNCTIONS AND RECEIVERSHIPS

1. *The Power of SEC Injunctions from "Further Violations."* Several statutory provisions in both the federal and state securities laws disqualify a person who has been enjoined from violating the securities law from engaging in almost any aspect of the securities business, at least without the prior consent of the appropriate regulatory agency. For example, professionals, including attorneys, who "practice" before the Commission may be suspended from practice under Rule 102(e) if they have been permanently enjoined from violating the securities laws; brokers and dealers may be similarly disciplined under § 15(b)(4) of the 1934 Act.[45]

FINRA has similar powers. FINRA has authority to deny the membership of associated persons as set forth in § 15A(g)(2) of the Securities Exchange Act of 1934. Article III, § 3(d) of FINRA's By-Laws permits a disqualified person to request permission to return to the industry.

SEC injunctions are often accompanied by an asset freeze.[46] Sarbanes-Oxley amended § 21C(c)(3) of the 1934 Act to expand the SEC's power to obtain a court order to freeze assets. The SEC can now seek a temporary freeze order from a district court whenever it appears that a corporation may make "extraordinary payments" to a corporate officer, director, partner, control person, agent, or employee.

Private securities class actions sometimes follow SEC injunctions. If the injunction resulted from a litigated decision (and not a negotiated settlement), the defendant will be collaterally estopped from denying any facts determined by the court. Under Parklane Hosiery Co. v. Shore,[47] private plaintiffs can make offensive use of collateral estoppel even though they were not parties to the earlier proceeding.

---

[45] For a full discussion, see Thomas J. Andre, Jr., The Collateral Consequences of SEC Injunctive Relief: Mild Prophylactic or Perpetual Hazard?, 1981 U. Ill. L. Rev. 625.

[46] For a full discussion, see Thomas J. Andre, Jr., The Collateral Consequences of SEC Injunctive Relief: Mild Prophylactic or Perpetual Hazard?, 1981 U. Ill. L. Rev. 625.

[47] 439 U.S. 322 (1979).

2. *Receiverships.* In many of its civil injunctive actions, the Commission has sought and obtained a variety of other ancillary remedies designed to address consequences of past violations or to reduce the likelihood of future violations or both. Where a drastic remedy is necessary to protect the rights of investors, the Commission may seek the appointment of a receiver.[48] In SEC v. Wencke,[49] the Ninth Circuit held that the court could stay state court actions against a corporation, including a bankruptcy proceeding, even if the persons in the other proceeding are not part of the SEC action.

The most controversial of these ancillary relief measures have been those designed to give the Commission (or the court) control over the future conduct of the corporation and its business, short of imposing a receivership. Typical of these measures have been: (1) the appointment of "special counsel," as illustrated by the *First Jersey* case, who is required to be satisfactory to or approved by the Commission, to make an investigation of the past misdeeds of management and report, not only to the board of directors of the corporation, but also to the Commission (or the court);[50] (2) the required resignation of officers and directors;[51] and (3) the election to the board of directors of one or more "independent directors" who are not beholden to the existing management, to control the future conduct of the corporation in specific areas or generally. Such independent director or directors usually must be approved (i.e., in effect nominated) by the Commission. In SEC v. Mattel, Inc.,[52] the Commission negotiated a consent injunction under which for five years a majority of the directors on both the board of directors and the executive committee were to be chosen from a list selected by the Commission. In addition, a special counsel was to be selected to investigate and prosecute litigation against the old management for securities law violations.

Typically, the SEC imposes remedies with the consent of the defendant corporation either in a provision of a consent injunction or pursuant to an "undertaking" given by the corporation to the Commission. In SEC v. Falstaff Brewing Corp.,[53] the district court refused to order a restructuring of the corporation's board of directors, stating, "the court should not, without considerable justification, impose

---

[48] See, e.g., Los Angeles Trust Deed & Mortgage Exch. v. SEC, 285 F.2d 162 (9th Cir. 1960), cert. denied, 366 U.S. 919 (1961); SEC v. Manor Nursing Centers, Inc., 458 F.2d 1082 (2d Cir. 1972); SEC v. Bilzerian, 127 F.Supp.2d 232 (D.D.C. 2000).

[49] 622 F.2d 1363 (9th Cir. 1980).

[50] In SEC v. Materia, 745 F.2d 197 (2d Cir. 1984), the court held that once equity jurisdiction is properly invoked, "the court has power to order all equitable relief necessary under the circumstances." For cases in which such a special counsel has been appointed, see Handler v. SEC, 610 F.2d 656 (9th Cir. 1979); SEC v. Medic-Home Enter., Inc., 1979–1980 Fed. Sec. L. Rep. (CCH), ¶ 97,291 (S.D.N.Y. 1980).

[51] Such relief has usually been negotiated by a consent decree, but in one litigated case the court did conditionally bar the defendant from future service with the corporation. See SEC v. Techni-Culture, Inc., 1973–1974 Fed. Sec. L. Rep. (CCH) ¶ 94,501 (D.Ariz.1974); see also SEC v. Florafax Int'l, Inc., Litig. Rel. 10,617 (N.D. Okla.1984).

[52] 1974–1975 Fed. Sec. L. Rep. (CCH) ¶ 94,807 (D.D.C. 1974).

[53] Fed. Sec. L. Rep. (CCH) ¶ 96,583 (D.D.C. 1978), aff'd, 629 F.2d 62 (D.C. Cir. 1980).

a remedy which would in effect regulate areas traditionally left to internal corporate management." Some commentators have questioned whether ancillary remedies of that character intrude upon the rights of shareholders to elect their own directors and of the states to regulate corporate governance.[54]

Even consent judgments calling for only a monetary settlement are not always given a judicial rubber-stamp. The following much-noted 2010 decision by U.S. District Judge Jed Rakoff, which rejected the SEC's proposed settlement of its enforcement action against Bank of America, has triggered an important national debate over the effectiveness of SEC enforcement. And, as the discussion following the case points out, this is the first, but not the last word on this issue from Judge Rakoff.

Securities and Exchange Commission v. Bank of America Corporation

United States District Court, Southern District of New York, 2009.
653 F.Supp.2d 507.

■ RAKOFF, DISTRICT JUDGE:

In the Complaint in this case, filed August 3, 2009, the Securities and Exchange Commission ("SEC") alleges, in stark terms, that defendant Bank of America Corporation materially lied to its shareholders in the proxy statement of November 3, 2008 that solicited the shareholders' approval of the $50 billion acquisition of Merrill Lynch & Co. ("Merrill"). The essence of the lie, according to the Complaint, was that Bank of America "represented that Merrill had agreed not to pay year-end performance bonuses or other discretionary incentive compensation to its executives prior to the closing of the merger without Bank of America's consent [when] [i]n fact, contrary to the representation . . ., Bank of America had agreed that Merrill could pay up to $5.8 billion—nearly 12% of the total consideration to be exchanged in the merger—in discretionary year-end and other bonuses to Merrill executives for 2008." Along with the filing of these very serious allegations, however, the parties, on the very same day, jointly sought this Court's approval of a proposed final Consent Judgment by which Bank of America, without admitting or denying the accusations, would be enjoined from making future false statements in proxy solicitations and would pay to the SEC a fine of $33 million.

In other words, the parties were proposing that the management of Bank of America—having allegedly hidden from the Bank's shareholders that as much as $5.8 billion of their money would be given as bonuses to the executives of Merrill who had run that company nearly into

---

[54] See George W. Dent, Jr., Ancillary Relief in Federal Securities Law: A Study in Federal Remedies, 67 Minn. L. Rev. 865 (1983). But see James R. Farrand, Ancillary Remedies in SEC Enforcement Suits, 89 Harv. L. Rev. 1779 (1976).

bankruptcy—would now settle the legal consequences of their lying by paying the SEC $33 million more of their shareholders' money.

This proposal to have the victims of the violation pay an additional penalty for their own victimization was enough to give the Court pause. The Court therefore heard oral argument on August 10, 2009 and received extensive written submissions on August 24, 2009 and September 9, 2009. Having now carefully reviewed all these materials, the Court concludes that the proposed Consent Judgment must be denied.

In reaching this conclusion, the Court is very mindful of the considerable deference it must accord the parties' proposal, since it would seemingly result in the consensual resolution of the case. Society greatly benefits when lawsuits are amicably resolved, and, for that reason, an ordinary civil settlement that includes dismissal of the underlying action is close to unreviewable. When, however, as in the case of a typical consent judgment, a federal agency such as the SEC seeks to prospectively invoke the Court's own contempt power by having the Court impose injunctive prohibitions against the defendant, the resolution has aspects of a judicial decree and the Court is therefore obliged to review the proposal a little more closely, to ascertain whether it is within the bounds of fairness, reasonableness, and adequacy—and, in certain circumstances, whether it serves the public interest. But even then, the review is highly deferential.

Here, however, the Court, even upon applying the most deferential standard of review for which the parties argue, is forced to conclude that the proposed Consent Judgment is neither fair, nor reasonable, nor adequate.

It is not fair, first and foremost, because it does not comport with the most elementary notions of justice and morality, in that it proposes that the shareholders who were the victims of the Bank's alleged misconduct now pay the penalty for that misconduct. The SEC admits that the corporate penalties it here proposes will be "indirectly borne by [the] shareholders." But the SEC argues that this is justified because "[a] corporate penalty ... sends a strong signal to shareholders that unsatisfactory corporate conduct has occurred and allows shareholders to better assess the quality and performance of management." This hypothesis, however, makes no sense when applied to the facts here: for the notion that Bank of America shareholders, having been lied to blatantly in connection with the multi-billion-dollar purchase of a huge, nearly-bankrupt company, need to lose another $33 million of their money in order to "better assess the quality and performance of management" is absurd.

The SEC, while also conceding that its normal policy in such situations is to go after the company executives who were responsible for the lie, rather than innocent shareholders, says it cannot do so here because "[t]he uncontroverted evidence in the investigative record is that lawyers for Bank of America and Merrill drafted the documents at issue and made the relevant decisions concerning disclosure of the bonuses." But if that is the case, why are the penalties not then sought from the lawyers? And why, in any event, does that justify imposing penalties on the victims of the lie, the shareholders?

Bank of America, for its part, having originally agreed to remain silent in the face of these charges, now, at the Court's request that it provide the Court with the underlying facts, vigorously asserts that the proxy statement, when read carefully, is neither false nor misleading, or that, even if it is false or misleading, the misstatements were immaterial because "[it] was widely acknowledged in the period leading up to the shareholder vote that Merrill Lynch intended to pay year-end incentive compensation." The SEC responds, however, that these arguments are hollow. The Bank's argument that the proxy statement was not misleading rests in material part on reference to a schedule that was not even attached to the proxy statement, and "[s]hareholders are entitled to rely on the representations in the proxy itself, and are not required to puzzle out material information from a variety of external sources." As for the Bank's argument that the investors were not materially misled because the press was already reporting the imminent payment of Merrill bonuses, "investors were not required to ignore Bank of America's express statements in the proxy materials and rely instead on media speculation that may have suggested that these statements were misleading."

Moreover, it is noteworthy that, in all its voluminous papers protesting its innocence, Bank of America never actually provides the Court with the particularized facts that the Court requested, such as precisely how the proxy statement came to be prepared, exactly who made the relevant decisions as to what to include and not include so far as the Merrill bonuses were concerned, etc.

But all of this is beside the point because, if the Bank is innocent of lying to its shareholders, why is it prepared to pay $33 million of its shareholders' money as a penalty for lying to them? All the Bank offers in response to this obvious question is the statement in the last footnote of its Reply Memorandum that "Because of the SEC's decision to bring charges, Bank of America would have to spend corporate funds whether or not it settled,"—the implication being that the payment was simply an exercise of business judgment as to which alternative would cost more: litigating or settling. But, quite aside from the fact that it is difficult to believe that litigating this simple case would cost anything like $33 million, it does not appear, so far as one can tell from this single sentence in a footnote, that this decision was made by disinterested parties. It is one thing for management to exercise its business judgment to determine how much of its shareholders money should be used to settle a case brought by former shareholders or third parties. It is quite something else for the very management that is accused of having lied to its shareholders to determine how much of those victims' money should be used to make the case against the management go away.[1] And even if this decision is arguably within their purview, it calls for greater scrutiny by the Court than would otherwise be the case.

Overall, indeed, the parties' submissions, when carefully read, leave the distinct impression that the proposed Consent Judgment was a contrivance designed to provide the SEC with the facade of enforcement and the management of the Bank with a quick resolution of an embarrassing inquiry—all at the expense of the sole alleged victims, the shareholders. Even under the most deferential review, this proposed Consent Judgment cannot remotely be called fair.

Nor is the proposed Consent Judgment reasonable. Obviously, a proposal that asks the victims to pay a fine for their having been victimized is, for all the reasons already given, as unreasonable as it is unfair. But the proposed Consent Judgment is unreasonable in numerous other respects as well.

For example, the Consent Judgment would effectively close the case without the SEC adequately accounting for why, in contravention of its own policy, it did not pursue charges against either Bank management or the lawyers who allegedly were responsible for the false and misleading proxy statements. The SEC says this is because charges against individuals for making false proxy statements require, at a minimum, proof that they participated in the making of the false statements knowing the statements were false or recklessly disregarding the high probability the statements were false. But how can such knowledge be lacking when, as the Complaint in effect alleges, executives at the Bank expressly approved Merrill's making year-end bonuses before they issued the proxy statement denying such approval?[2] The SEC states, as noted, that culpable intent was nonetheless lacking because the lawyers made all the relevant decisions. But, if so, then how can the lawyers be said to lack intent? Under these circumstances, how can a

---

[1] Undoubtedly, the decision to spend this money was made even easier by the fact that the U.S. Government provided the Bank of America with a $40 billion or so "bail out," of which $20 billion came after the merger. Since $3.6 billion of that money had already been spent, indirectly, to compensate the Bank for the Merrill bonuses—not to mention the $20 billion in taxpayer funds that effectively compensated the Bank for the last-minute revelations that Merrill's loss for 2008 was $27 billion instead of $7 billion—what impediment could there be to paying a mere $33 million (—or more than most people will see in their lifetimes—) to get rid of a lawsuit saying that the bonuses had been concealed from the shareholders approving the merger? To say, as the Bank now does, that the $33 million does not come directly from U.S. funds is simply to ignore the overall economics of the Bank's situation.

[2] Lurking in the background is the suggestion, affirmed by the Bank's counsel at the August 10 hearing, that the highest executives of Bank of America, upon learning that Merrill's loss was $20 billion more than had been represented at the time the merger was negotiated, were prepared to walk away from the merger until "coerced" by the Government into going through with it, following which the Government provided the Bank with an additional $20 billion in bail-out funds. But, quite aside from the fact that none of this appears to have been revealed to the shareholders prior to the merger, neither party suggests that any such coercion played any role in the alleged decision not to reveal the Merrill bonuses. The huge increase in Merrill's losses, however, did arguably render the providing of the bonuses more material, as well as more inexplicable.

Court find reasonable a proposed Consent Judgment that otherwise violates SEC policy?[3]

To give a different example, the proposed Consent Judgment seeks injunctive relief forbidding the Bank, on pain of contempt of court, from issuing false or misleading statements in the future. On its face, the proposed injunction appears too nebulous to comply with Rule 65(d) of the Federal Rules of Civil Procedure, which requires, among other things, that an injunction "describe in reasonable detail . . . the act or acts restrained. . . ." Moreover, since the Bank contends that it never made any false or misleading statements in the past, the Court at this point lacks a factual predicate for imposing such relief.

To be sure, the Bank's initial position was that it neither admitted nor denied the allegations, and such a position, when coupled with proof by the SEC that the alleged violations have occurred, may often be sufficient to support certain forms of injunctive relief. But here the further submissions of the Bank make clear its position that the proxy statement in issue was totally in accordance with the law: meaning that, notwithstanding the injunctive relief here sought by the SEC, the Bank would feel free to issue exactly the same kind of proxy statement in the future. Under these circumstances, the broad but vague injunctive relief here sought would be a pointless exercise, since the sanction of contempt may only be imposed for violation of a particularized provision known and reasonably understood by the contemnor, all of which would be lacking here.

Without multiplying examples further, the point is that the Court finds the proposed Consent Judgment not only unfair but also unreasonable.

Finally, the proposed Consent Judgment is inadequate. The injunctive relief, as noted, is pointless. The fine, if looked at from the standpoint of the violation, is also inadequate, in that $33 million is a trivial penalty for a false statement that materially infected a multi-billion-dollar merger. But since the fine is imposed, not on the individuals putatively responsible, but on the shareholders, it is worse than pointless: it further victimizes the victims.

Oscar Wilde once famously said that a cynic is someone "who knows the price of everything and the value of nothing." Oscar Wilde, Lady Windermere's Fan (1892). The proposed Consent Judgment in this case

---

[3] The SEC also claims it was stymied in determining individual liability because the Bank's executives said the lawyers made all the decisions, but the Bank refused to waive attorney-client privilege. But it appears that the SEC never seriously pursued whether the this constituted a waiver of the privilege, let alone whether it fit within the crime/fraud exception to the privilege. And even on its face, such testimony would seem to invite investigating the lawyers. The Bank, for its part, claims that it has not relied on a defense of advice of counsel and so no waiver has occurred. But, as noted earlier, the Bank has failed to provide its own particularized version of how the proxies came to be and how the key decisions as to what to include or exclude were made, so its claim of not relying on an advice of counsel is simply an evasion.

suggests a rather cynical relationship between the parties: the SEC gets to claim that it is exposing wrongdoing on the part of the Bank of America in a high-profile merger; the Bank's management gets to claim that they have been coerced into an onerous settlement by overzealous regulators. And all this is done at the expense, not only of the shareholders, but also of the truth.

Yet the truth may still emerge. The Bank of America states unequivocally that if the Court disapproves the Consent Judgment, it is prepared to litigate the charges. The SEC, having brought the charges, presumably is not about to drop them. Accordingly, the Court, having hereby disapproved the Consent Judgment, directs the parties to file with the Court, no later than one week from today, a jointly proposed Case Management Plan that will have this case ready to be tried on February 1, 2010.

Seven months after Judge Rakoff rejected the $33 million dollar settlement in the above opinion he "reluctantly" approved a $150 million settlement between the parties.[55] The settlement required Bank of America not only to pay a $150 million penalty, but also to implement several corporate governance reforms including: retaining disclosure counsel, using an independent compensation consultant, and putting executive compensation to a non-binding shareholder vote.[56] In his approval of the settlement, Judge Rakoff opined that although the settlement was "half-baked justice at best," the law required him to give "substantial deference" to the SEC in approving it.[57]

Then, in November of 2011, Judge Rakoff again rejected a settlement agreement, this time between the SEC and Citigroup Global Markets Inc.[58] According to his opinion, the applicable standard of review is not just whether the agreement is fair, reasonable, and adequate, but also the "overall fairness to beneficiaries and consistency with the public interest."[59] The SEC pushed back on this aspect of the standard, but Judge Rakoff held firm. Indeed, he found that the proposed settlement met none of the standards, noting that the relief requested, wide-ranging injunctive remedies, enforceable by judicial contempt, requires that the parties provide the court, and the public, with some information about the underlying facts.[60] Of course, this revelation-of-facts standard is at odds with the longstanding approach of the SEC, and defendants, in settling cases without admissions.

---

[55] SEC v. Bank of America, 2010 U.S. Dist. LEXIS 15460 (S.D.N.Y. Feb. 22, 2010).
[56] Id.
[57] Id. at *19.
[58] U.S. S.E.C. v. Citigroup Global Markets Inc., 2011 WL 5903733 (S.D.N.Y. 2011).
[59] Id. at *3.
[60] Id. at *4.

Judge Rakoff also noted that the settlement was substantial, $160 million in profits, $30 million in interest, and $95 million in the form of a penalty, but, given the allegations, the court could not approve it without more information. Indeed, he stated that if the allegations were true, Citigroup was getting a "very good deal" and, if they were untrue, "it was a mild and modest cost of doing business."[61] In sum, the court rejected the settlement stating:

> It is not reasonable, because how can it ever be reasonable to impose substantial relief on the basis of mere allegations? It is not fair, because, despite Citigroup's nominal consent, the potential for abuse in imposing penalties on the basis of facts that are neither proven nor acknowledged is patent. It is not adequate, because, in the absence of any facts, the Court lacks a framework for determining adequacy. And, most obviously, the proposed Consent Judgment does not serve the public interest, because it asks the Court to employ its power and assert its authority when it does not know the facts.[62]

The ruling provoked a strong response from the SEC, in part because it "shook a central pillar of federal securities law, potentially upending a practice that allows the S.E.C. to settle hundreds of enforcement cases each year."[63] In addition, the SEC appealed the decision, arguing legal error, and requested a stay of Judge Rakoff's order denying the settlement. Judge Rakoff denied the stay, took issue with the appeal, which was interlocutory in nature, and issued an opinion noting that there was little legal basis for an appeal in this instance.[64]

While many laud Judge Rakoff's willingness to question settlement deals between the Commission and regulated entities, there is a paradox at the heart of his refusal to approve the initial settlement: there is nothing a judge can do to force a prosecutor or regulator to bring a particular case or to prosecute a case with full intensity. In other words, regulators dead set on treating regulated entities with kid gloves will continue to be able to do so, and there is not much judges can do about it. Even Congress may be unable to fully resolve this problem, since statutes compelling particular actions are difficult to design and enforce. For instance, in a study of district court compliance with a congressional mandate to make particular findings in every securities case, Professors Todd Henderson and William Hubbard found courts followed the law in less than 14% of cases.[65]

---

[61] Id. at *5.

[62] Id. at *6.

[63] Edward Wyatt, Citing "Legal Error," S.E.C. Says It Will Appeal Rejection of Citigroup Settlement, New York Times (Dec. 15, 2011).

[64] U.S. S.E.C. v. Citigroup Global Markets Inc., 2011 WL 6762964 (Dec. 27, 2011).

[65] See M. Todd Henderson & William H. J. Hubbard, "Judicial Noncompliance with Mandatory Procedural Rules Under the PSLRA," S87 J. LEGAL STUD. S91 (2015).

Problem

PROBLEM 14-1

Last year, Hottentot, a securities broker licensed by the National Association of Securities Dealers, was affiliated with two companies, FCN Financial Services and Burnett Grey & Co. These companies were approached by the principals of a company called EDP to help create a market for EDP stock. The stock was not registered with the SEC. At the time, Hottentot was President of Burnett Grey, a broker-dealer firm, and Secretary of FCN, a company that advised clients on taking private companies public, meeting regulatory and compliance requirements relating to such undertakings, and promoting such companies to brokerage firms. In these capacities, she became involved in marketing EDP stock. Last year, Burnett Grey and FCN made four trades of unregistered EDP stock, in blocks ranging from 75 to 4200 shares.

In marketing the stock, Hottentot did not ensure that EDP had registered its offering with the SEC. Hottentot relied on advice from Peterson, her personal attorney, who heard her oral description of EDP, then stated "this sounds like an exempt transaction to me." Neither Hottentot nor Petersen learned that EDP was apparently a "sham" corporation, which had overstated the value of its assets and which had no real headquarters or employees.

Can the SEC permanently enjoin Hottentot from future violations of the securities laws?

C. EX PARTE SANCTIONS

The Commission is authorized to employ one remedial sanction without notice or a hearing to the issuer affected thereby. Section 12(k) of the 1934 Act authorizes the Commission to "summarily to suspend trading in any security (other than an exempted security) for a period not exceeding 10 business days," or to suspend all trading on any national securities exchange for a period not to exceed 90 calendar days, although in the latter case only with the approval of the President. Until 1978, the Commission used this authority to affect a permanent suspension of trading (unless lifted by the Commission) in the stock of a particular company, by simply routinely renewing the suspension of trading for another ten days at the end of each ten-day period. In one case the suspension of trading continued in this fashion for thirteen years.[66]

In SEC v. Sloan,[67] the United States Supreme Court held that action was unauthorized and illegal where the subsequent suspensions of trading were not based on any new circumstances arising after the initial suspension. Justice Brennan's concurring opinion stated that:

---

[66] See the concurring opinion of Justice Brennan in SEC v. Sloan, 436 U.S. 103, 123 (1978).

[67] 436 U.S. 103 (1978).

[T]he SEC's procedural implementation of its § 12(k) power mocks any conclusion other than that the SEC simply could not care whether its § 12(k) orders are justified. So far as this record shows, the SEC never reveals the reasons for its suspension orders. To be sure, here respondent was able long after the fact to obtain some explanation through a Freedom of Information Act request, but even the information tendered was heavily excised and none of it even purports to state the reasoning of the Commissioners under whose authority § 12(k) orders issue. Nonetheless, when the SEC finally agreed to give respondent a hearing on the suspension of Canadian Javelin stock, it required respondent to state, in a verified petition (that is, under oath) why he thought the unrevealed conclusions of the SEC to be wrong. This is obscurantism run riot.[68]

In the wake of *Sloan*, the Commission still employs back-to-back suspension orders under § 12(k), but it is now "very careful to find a different ground for a second order."[69]

D. NEW STATUTORY REMEDIES

Today the SEC has a much larger range of administrative enforcement remedies than those originally contemplated at the time its creation. The Securities Enforcement Remedies and Penny Stock Reform Act of 1990 (the "Remedies Act") arms the SEC with three types of civil remedies: (a) civil fines; (b) cease and desist orders; and (c) corporate bar orders. The Sarbanes Oxley Act of 2002 ("Sarbanes-Oxley") and the 2010 Dodd-Frank Wall Street Reform and Consumer Protection Act expanded the available remedies even further.

(1) CIVIL FINES

The Remedies Act amended § 20 of the Securities Act, § 21 of the Exchange Act, § 42 of the Investment Company Act, and § 209 of the Investment Advisers Act, to allow the SEC to seek a monetary penalty in any civil injunctive action brought under these acts. In addition to disgorgement of profits, the SEC can now obtain the following civil penalties:[70]

1. up to $5,000 per violation for individuals and $50,000 per violation for a corporation;

2. up to $50,000 per violation for individuals and $250,000 for corporations for misconduct involving "fraud, deceit, manipulation, or deliberate or reckless disregard of a regulatory requirement"; or

---

[68] 436 U.S. at 124–125.
[69] See 4 Louis Loss & Joel Seligman. Securities Regulation 1912 (3d. rev. 2000).
[70] Pub. L. No. 101–429, 104 Stat. 931.

3. up to $100,000 per violation for individuals and $500,000 for corporations if, in addition to misconduct involving "fraud, deceit, manipulation, or deliberate or reckless disregard of a regulatory requirement," the "violation directly or indirectly resulted in substantial losses or created a significant risk of substantial losses to other persons."

These provisions extend the Commission's earlier authority to seek civil fines in the context of insider trading,[71] covering "such areas as the fraudulent sales techniques and price manipulation of the penny stock market, violations of beneficial ownership disclosure rules including 'parking,' and trading violations such as those that occurred during the market break of 1987."[72] Particular concern was expressed about the "disturbingly low level of compliance" with the insider reporting requirement in § 16(a) of the 1934 Act.[73]

Alternatively, in any proceeding against a registered broker-dealer or other regulated person subject to the Exchange Act's § 15(b)(4), § 15(b)(6), § 15B, § 15C, or § 17A, the Commission may impose a civil penalty if it finds that the broker-dealer has committed any of a series of acts of the general kind specified in § 15(b)(4).[74]

The Commission may consider six factors in determining whether a penalty is in the public interest, including whether: (1) the act or omission involves "fraud, deceit, manipulation, or deliberate or reckless disregard of a regulatory requirement"; (2) the resulting harm to other persons; (3) the extent of any person's unjust enrichment (any restitution being taken into account); (4) the degree of recidivism; (5) the need to "deter such person and other persons from committing such acts or omissions"; and (6) "such other matters as justice may require" (a factor borrowed from the Federal Trade Commission Act).[75]

Prior to the passage of Sarbanes-Oxley, the SEC typically distributed disgorgement penalties to investors while civil penalties were directed to the U.S. Treasury. With the passage of Sarbanes-Oxley Congress altered this scheme. Known as the "fair fund" provision, § 308 of Sarbanes-Oxley provides that specified civil penalties recovered by the SEC can be added to disgorgement funds for the benefit of investors. This "fair fund" provision attempts to make victims whole by allowing the SEC to impose a more severe penalty against offending officers and directors when the amount of disgorgement that would be otherwise obtainable

---

[71] This was initially adopted in the Insider Trading Sanctions Act of 1984 and reenacted in the Insider Trading and Securities Fraud Enforcement Act of 1988. See 8 Louis Loss & Joel Seligman, Securities Regulation 3746–3758 (3d ed. 1991).

[72] H.R. Rep. No. 101–616, 101st Cong., 2d Sess. 17 (1990).

[73] Id. at 23; S. Rep. No. 101–337, 101st Cong., 2d Sess. 17 (1990).

[74] Sec. Ex. Act § 21B; Inv. Co. Act § 9(d); Inv. Adv. Act § 203(i).

[75] Sec. Ex. Act § 21B(c); Inv. Co. Act § 9(d)(3); Inv. Adv. Act § 203(i)(3). Consideration of these factors is "permissive and not mandatory, because not all of the factors would apply in any given case." H.R. Rep. No. 101–616, 101st Cong. 2d Sess. 20 (1990).

may be insufficient. In recent years, the SEC "fair fund" provision enabled the Commission to distribute millions of dollars to injured investors. In 2019, 2018, and 2017, the SEC distributed $950 million, $491 million, and $1,056 million respectively.

FINRA also has the ability to levy fines. In 2019, FINRA brought 854 disciplinary actions compared to 921 disciplinary actions in 2018 and 1,369 disciplinary actions in 2017. FINRA has issued fines of approximately $39 million, $61 million, and $65 million in 2019, 2018, and 2017, respectively. FINRA also expelled 6 firms, suspended 21 firms, barred 348 individuals, and suspended 415 individuals in 2019.

But, because FINRA is not a government agency, its fines do not carry the force of law. In Fiero v. FINRA, the Second Circuit went further, holding that nothing in the securities laws authorizes FINRA to bring court actions to collect disciplinary fines.[76] Under *Fiero*, if FINRA wants to enforce a fine, it must prove the allegations in a judicial proceeding. In practice, this means if a registered representative or entity refuses to pay the fine, FINRA can only threaten to revoke the license to compel payment. Since many fines are levied in cases involving bars from the industry, this means most FINRA fines remain uncollected.

(2) CEASE AND DESIST ORDERS

The Remedies Act also amended § 8 of the 1933 Act, § 9 of the Investment Company Act, and § 203 of the Investment Advisers Act, and added a new § 21C to the 1934 Act, to provide the SEC with an administrative cease and desist authority. Now the Commission may proceed against any respondent the Commission suspects has violated or is about to violate the federal securities laws, and order the respondent to cease the violation, disgorge profits, and take affirmative steps to comply with the securities laws. The Commission also has the power to issue a temporary cease and desist order without notice to the respondent and *without* a hearing. This temporary order will remain in effect until the administrative proceeding for the permanent order is resolved, unless the respondent appeals the temporary order to the Commission and, in turn, to a federal district court.

A theoretical advantage of the administrative cease and desist procedure is that it does not require the Commission—as it must in an injunctive proceeding—to show a likelihood of future violation. Nonetheless, in 2001 the Commission concluded that there must be some likelihood of future violations when it issues a cease and desist order.[77]

---

[76] 660 F.3d 569 (2d Cir. 2011).

[77] KPMG Peat Marwick, LLP, AAER 1360, 74 SEC Dock. 357, 380 (2001). But the Commission concluded that this likelihood is less than necessary to issue an injunction:

> Though "some" risk is necessary, it need not be very great to warrant issuing a cease and desist order. Absent evidence to the contrary, a finding of violation raises a sufficient risk of future violation. To put it another way, evidence showing that a respondent violated the law probably also shows a risk of repetition that merits our ordering to cease and desist. Our conclusion is suggested, though not compelled, by the

Since enactment of the Remedies Act, the SEC has made frequent use of the cease and desist order.[78]

Valicenti Advisory Services, Inc. v. SEC

United States Court of Appeals for the Second Circuit, 1999.
198 F.3d 62, cert. denied, 530 U.S. 1276 (2000).

■ Before: FEINBERG, CALABRESI and SOTOMAYOR, CIRCUIT JUDGES.

■ PER CURIAM:

Petitioners Valicenti Advisory Services, Inc. ("VAS") and Vincent R. Valicenti appeal from an opinion and order of the Securities and Exchange Commission ("SEC" or "Commission") finding that VAS, aided and abetted by Valicenti, willfully violated various anti-fraud provisions of the Investment Advisers Act ("IAA"), and imposing various sanctions. For the reasons to be discussed, we affirm.

BACKGROUND

Valicenti is the president and sole owner of VAS, an advisory organization registered with the SEC. Throughout 1992, petitioners distributed a packet of marketing materials to prospective clients. That packet contained a chart developed by petitioners which purported to show VAS's rates of return on its "Total Portfolio" between 1987 and 1991 (the "Chart"). On the Chart, a footnote next to "Total Portfolio" indicated that the displayed figures represented a "composite of discretionary accounts with a balanced objective."

In December 1993, the SEC commenced an inspection of VAS, at which time the Commission became aware of the Chart. The SEC found the Chart to be materially misleading because: (1) a reasonable investor would have understood a "composite" to include *all* "discretionary accounts with a balanced objective"; (2) the Chart reflected the performance of only a selected portion of VAS's "balanced" accounts; and (3) the rate of return ("ROR") for 1991 indicated on the Chart was more than seven percentage points higher than it would have been had the Chart incorporated all of VAS's balanced accounts for that year.

The Commission also found that petitioners acted with a deliberate intent to defraud. In so finding the Commission relied upon the following facts:

---

statutory language. The statute specifies that we may impose a cease and desist order on a person who "has violated" the securities laws. This contrasts with our authority to seek injunctive relief in those instances when a person "is engaged or about to engage" in violative conduct.

Id. See also Andrew M. Smith, SEC Cease-and-Desist Orders, 51 Admin. L. Rev. 1197 (1999); Larry S. Gondelman & Thais R. Rencher, What the SEC Won't Tell You about Cease-and-Desist Orders, 28 Sec. Reg. L.J. 163 (2000); Stephen J. Crimmins & Mitchell E. Herr, SEC Resolves Long-Standing Questions About Its Cease-and-Desist Remedy, 33 Sec. Reg. & L. Rep. (BNA) 1084 (2001).

[78] See 10 Louis Loss & Joel Seligman, Securities Regulation 4987–4993 (3d ed. rev. 1996). See also S. Rep. No. 101–337, 101st Cong., 2d Sess. 20–21 (1990).

- Valicenti rejected recommendations by the VAS marketing manager that the Chart disclose more information, including, *inter alia,* methodology, the number of accounts reflected in the Chart, and the value of the largest and smallest accounts.
- Valicenti included in the Chart only a small and distorted subset of balanced accounts. Specifically:
  (1) Valicenti excluded from the Chart accounts valued under $100,000. The Chart did not mention this exclusion, even though 27% to 45% of VAS's balanced accounts between 1987 and 1991 were valued under $100,000.
  (2) After reviewing a preliminary calculation that reflected an overall performance of -0.84% for 1987, Valicenti directed the VAS marketing manager to exclude from the final calculation six accounts with negative RORs for that year and to add two other accounts that had performed positively that year. As a result of these changes, the total performance figure for 1987 went from -0.84% to $+2.60\%$.
- Valicenti included accounts that fell outside his definition of a "balanced" account, i.e., the equity portion of the account be no greater than 70% and no less than 30%.[2]
- Valicenti created and distributed in the marketing packet another document containing a bar graph that distorted VAS's performance relative to other investment advisers by using data that were not comparable.[3]

Accordingly, the SEC found that both petitioners had violated § 206(1), § 206(2), and § 206(4) of the IAA, 15 U.S.C. §§ 80b–6(1), 80b–6(2), 80(b)–6(4), as well as SEC Rule 206(4)–1(a)(5), 17 C.F.R. § 275.206(4)–1(a)(5). In light of these findings, the SEC sanctioned petitioners with a censure, a cease and desist order, and fines of $50,000 against VAS and $25,000 against Valicenti. The Commission also required petitioners to send copies of the Commission's opinion and order to all existing clients of VAS and, in the following year, to all prospective clients.

* * *

DISCUSSION

* * *

---

[2] In a letter to the Commission, Valicenti explicitly defined a "balanced" account as an account with an asset mix ranging from 70% equity and 30% fixed income to 30% equity and 70% income ("the 70/30 definition"). He later testified, however, that the 70/30 definition was a "guideline" and that a "balanced" account was defined in terms of its investment objectives instead of its asset mix.

[3] Valicenti does not appeal this particular finding.

IV. Sanctions

Petitioners challenge the SEC's imposition of monetary sanctions, the issuance of a cease and desist order, and the requirement that current and future clients be provided with a copy of the Commission's opinion and order ("the distribution requirement"). We review the Commission's imposition of sanctions for abuse of discretion.

We will find an abuse of discretion if the sanctions imposed are either unwarranted in law or without justification in fact. The sanctions imposed in this case are both within the SEC's statutory authority and justified under the circumstances. The Commission is empowered to assess monetary penalties of $50,000 against a natural person or $250,000 against a company for willful and fraudulent violations of the IAA. 15 U.S.C. § 80b–3(i)(2)(B) (1994). The Commission may also issue cease and desist orders that would "require [a violator] to comply, or take steps to effect compliance" with the provisions they violated. 15 U.S.C. § 80b–3(k)(1) (1994). Moreover, the Commission is empowered to "place limitations on the activities" of violators, suspend them for up to twelve months, or bar them entirely from the investment advising business. 15 U.S.C. § 80b–3(e), (f) (1994 & Supp. 1999). In determining whether to impose any or all of these statutorily authorized penalties, the Commission is to consider "whether the act or omission for which such penalty is assessed involved fraud, deceit, manipulation, or deliberate or reckless disregard of a regulatory requirement." 15 U.S.C. § 80b–3(i)(3)(A) (1994). Having upheld the SEC's finding that petitioners acted with an intent to defraud, we conclude that the monetary sanctions, the cease and desist order, and the distribution requirement were all justified under the circumstances.

Petitioners argue further that the Commission abused its discretion by imposing the distribution requirement because the imposition of such a sanction was "excessive" and "bore no rational relationship to the violations found." Although we recognize that the imposition of a sanction that is "palpably disproportionate to the violation" may be an abuse of discretion, see Reddy v. Commodity Futures Trading Comm'n, 191 F.3d 109, 124 (2d Cir. 1999), the distribution requirement here was rationally connected to the particular conduct at issue. As we observed above, the IAA authorizes the SEC to "place limitations on the activities" of violators of the statute. 15 U.S.C. § 80b–3(e), (f). We see no reason why the distribution requirement might not be an appropriate and reasonable "limitation" in certain circumstances. In this regard, we note that the IAA explicitly permits the imposition of sanctions that are plausibly *more severe* than the distribution requirement, including revocation of the petitioners' registration and suspension for up to 12 months, each of which would likely result in greater loss of income and stigmatization than having to furnish copies of the SEC's opinion and order to existing and prospective clients for one year.

Moreover, the SEC has provided at least two reasonable explanations justifying the imposition of the distribution requirement as a reasonable "limitation" on petitioners' investment adviser activities. First, the distribution requirement will apprise present and prospective clients of the Commission's findings so that these investors may be fully informed in deciding whether they wish to do business with petitioners. Second, the distribution requirement may discourage petitioners from committing further violations. Given the serious nature of the petitioners' violations, we cannot deny that the distribution requirement is a rational means to alert actual and prospective clients of petitioners' misconduct and to discourage any further such conduct. See Reddy, 191 F.3d at 124 ("[S]o long as an agency has articulate[d] a satisfactory explanation for its action including a rational connection between the facts found and the choice made, we will uphold its choice of sanctions.") (citations and internal quotation marks omitted); County Produce, Inc. v. United States Dep't of Agric., 103 F.3d 263, 266 (2d Cir. 1997) (noting the "fundamental principle that where Congress has entrusted an administrative agency with the responsibility of selecting the means of achieving the statutory policy[,] the relation of remedy to policy is peculiarly a matter for administrative competence") (citation and internal quotation marks omitted).

Finally, petitioners argue that the distribution requirement was an abuse of discretion because the Commission has never before imposed such a sanction against an investment adviser in a litigated case. The Commission, however, has previously imposed sanctions similar to the distribution requirement here in investment adviser advertising cases that have been settled. We find no indication that the SEC singled out petitioners for particularly severe punishment. Cf. Winkler v. SEC, 377 F.2d 517, 518 (2d Cir. 1967) (warning that the court must be "watchful" of whether sanctions have been applied in an "unduly harsh" or "discriminatory" manner). Moreover, petitioners have not identified any particular instances in which persons who intentionally misled their clients received more lenient treatment. Accordingly, we find that the sanctions imposed by the Commission do not constitute an abuse of discretion.

CONCLUSION

Having reviewed the record and examined petitioners' arguments and having found those arguments to be without merit, we affirm the opinion and order of the Securities and Exchange Commission.

WHX Corporation v. Securities and Exchange Commission

United States Court of Appeals, District of Columbia Circuit, 2004.
362 F.3d 854.

■ Before: EDWARDS and HENDERSON, CIRCUIT JUDGES, and WILLIAMS, SENIOR CIRCUIT JUDGE.

■ WILLIAMS, SENIOR CIRCUIT JUDGE:

The Securities and Exchange Commission found that WHX Corporation violated the All Holders Rule, SEC Rule 14d–10(a)(1), 17 C.F.R. § 240.14d–10(a)(1), and issued a cease-and-desist order prohibiting the company from committing or causing any future violations of that Rule. WHX petitioned for review. We find that the SEC's decision to issue a cease-and-desist order was arbitrary and capricious, and therefore vacate the order.

* * *

In March 1997 WHX decided to attempt a hostile takeover of Dynamics Corporation of America ("DCA"). But DCA's charter had a poison pill that allowed shareholders to purchase new shares at rock-bottom prices if any party acquired 20 percent of DCA's stock without the approval of DCA's board. Further, New York law (New York Business Corporation Law § 912(b)) forbids a New York corporation from entering into a "business combination" with any shareholder owning 20 percent of the corporation's stock until the shareholder has held the stock for at least five years, unless the shareholder first secures board approval.

To overcome the opposition of the incumbent board, WHX planned a two-stage takeover strategy. First, it would make a cash tender offer for 19.9 percent of DCA's common stock, offering $40 a share. Second, it would conduct a proxy contest seeking to oust the DCA board and replace it with a new one that would revoke the pill and approve a merger with WHX. Under the terms of this merger, WHX would purchase all remaining DCA shares for $40 cash.

The timing of WHX's planned tender offer posed an additional problem. The next annual DCA shareholder meeting was scheduled for May 2, 1997. But the record date for that meeting was March 14, 1997, which had already passed by the time WHX was ready to launch its offer. Because only holders of record (or holders of proxies from record holders) could vote at the shareholder meeting, an ordinary tender offer for common stock would yield WHX at least some (and possibly many) shares that couldn't vote at the May 2 meeting. As WHX's purpose was to maximize its voting power without running afoul of DCA's poison pill, it wanted to avoid buying shares that would be effectively useless.

WHX's solution triggered the SEC sanction at issue here. It proposed to include in its offer a condition under which the offer would extend only to those shareholders who were holders as of the March 14 record date, or who were able to obtain a valid proxy. WHX's attorney recognized that this condition might be thought to violate the so-called All Holders Rule, see Opinion at 4, which was promulgated under § 14(d) of the 1934 Securities Exchange Act, 15 U.S.C. 78n(d), and which provides:

(a) No bidder shall make a tender offer unless:

(1) The tender offer is open to all security holders of the class of securities subject to the tender offer.

17 C.F.R. § 240.14d–10(a)(1). The SEC adopted this rule in 1986 in response to concerns about "discriminatory tender offers" that would pressure "security holders who are excluded from the offer . . . to sell to those in the included class" in order to receive the premium price, but who "would not receive the information required by the Williams Act, would have their shares taken up on a first-come first-served basis and would have no withdrawal rights." Amendments to Tender Offer Rules: All-Holders and Best-Price, Exchange Act Release No. 34–23421 (July 17, 1986). Moreover, the SEC explained that, without this rule, the "equal treatment" provisions of the Exchange Act would easily be circumvented: an offeror could simply address an offer to "a privileged group of security holders who hold the desired number of shares" rather than purchasing the desired number of shares from all tenderers on a pro rata basis for the same consideration. In adopting the All Holders Rule, the SEC appears to have been reacting in part to the decision in Unocal Corp. v. Pickens, 608 F.Supp. 1081 (C.D. Cal. 1985), which upheld as lawful a defensive self-tender that offered a high premium but excluded the shareholder attempting the takeover.

Seeking guidance, WHX faxed the SEC's Office of Mergers and Acquisitions a letter on March 24, asking for either a no-action letter or an exemption from the rule. The letter suggested several reasons why WHX thought the All Holders Rule should not apply to its proposed condition. First, it contrasted the condition with the highly discriminatory offers which precipitated the rule, such as that involved in *Unocal*, where shares tendered by or on behalf of the would-be acquirer were deliberately excluded from what in essence would be a dividend to the eligible shareholders. Under WHX's offer, by contrast, even a shareholder who had bought after the record date had some possibility of securing a proxy, and in any event would receive "the same per share price . . . in the cash merger following successful completion of the tender offer."

Second, WHX argued that here the only "discrimination" reflected a virtually universal disenfranchisement of shareholders inherent in the practicalities of limiting voting to holders as of the record date. If it is legitimate to have a record date at all—which by its nature deprives late purchasers of the right to vote at the annual meeting—then why, WHX asked, should the All Holders Rule embrace all holders on the last day of the tender offer?

A staffer with the SEC's Office of Mergers and Acquisitions called WHX's lawyer back the same day to inform him that the Commission did not issue no-action letters on All Holders Rule issues and that WHX should withdraw its no-action letter request. WHX did so that afternoon. Although the staffer said only that the SEC didn't give no action letters on that subject, not that it refused to give such a letter on these facts, and although WHX's lawyer found the staffer not at all clear, he interpreted the statement as an indication that the Office of Mergers and Acquisition staff informally believed that the proposed condition would violate the All Holders Rule. Nonetheless, in light of counsel's belief that there were strong arguments why the condition did not violate the All Holders Rule, and the lack of contrary Commission precedents, WHX decided to proceed. It announced its hostile tender offer, including the record holder condition, on March 31, 1997. The tender offer letter noted that the SEC staff had "informally advised" WHX that the record holder condition might offend the All Holders Rule, but explained that WHX believed "special circumstances" justified the condition.

On April 4, 1997 staff of the Office of Mergers and Acquisitions contacted WHX to say that the staff believed that the condition violated the All Holders Rule and was prepared to recommend enforcement action to enjoin the tender offer unless WHX withdrew the condition. In response, WHX's counsel wrote to the SEC Commissioners "to explain the rationale for [the record holder provision] and to respectfully suggest that no remedial relief is necessary based on the unusual circumstances at hand." The letter went on to argue that the All Holders Rule was adopted to prevent tender offers that discriminated against particular identifiable shareholders, and that WHX's condition did no such thing. WHX reiterated its commitment to buy all outstanding shares at the tender offer price if its takeover bid should succeed.

After receiving its copy of WHX's letter, the SEC staff phoned WHX on April 7 to say that it would that day ask the Commission for authority to seek injunctive relief against the offer. WHX responded with an April 7 letter to the Commission, arguing that its record holder condition was "in fact no different from a standard condition in virtually *every single* contested tender offer: namely, that valid tenders will only be accepted from holders of rights issued under a target's poison pill plan."

WHX's pleas were unavailing. On April 8, the Commission authorized an enforcement action to enjoin the tender offer. WHX immediately withdrew the record holder condition. This withdrawal eliminated any occasion for injunctive action, and WHX proceeded with its takeover bid, which ultimately failed because of a competing bid by a "white knight."

On June 25, 1998, over a year later, the SEC started cease-and-desist proceedings against WHX under Section 21C of the Exchange Act, 15 U.S.C. 78u–3. An Administrative Law Judge found no violation of the All Holders Rule. Although finding that as a practical matter it would be very difficult for those who purchased shares between March 14 and March 31 to obtain voting rights, and that therefore it was "questionable" whether the offer was really open to these shareholders, the ALJ reasoned that the kinds of offers that had given rise to the rule had pressured ineligible shareholders to sell to eligible ones, and that no such pressure could arise here.

The ALJ also stressed WHX's good faith arguments for the innocence of its condition under the All Holders Rule, its reliance on counsel's prediction that its interpretation would be upheld, and its immediate removal of the condition after the SEC authorized an enforcement action. Moreover, the ALJ observed that "[n]o harm was done by the few days the offer was arguably out of compliance," and that a sanction would be "counterproductive" because "[t]o impose a sanction after WHX changed its offer to conform to the Commission's instructions is a disincentive for similarly situated parties to comply with the Commission's views in the future."

The SEC reversed the ALJ and imposed an order requiring WHX to "cease and desist from committing or causing any violations or future violations of Section 14(d)(4) of the Securities Exchange Act of 1934 or Rule 14d–10(a)(1) thereunder." The Commission first found that the record holder condition violated the All Holders Rule, rejecting WHX's arguments to the contrary. It found that a violation of the All Holders Rule required neither scienter or negligence, nor a finding of harm. Insofar as its opinion addressed WHX's arguments distinguishing its condition from the cases giving rise to the All Holders Rule, the SEC offered only a conclusory statement that the condition "unfairly disadvantaged shareholders who bought DCA stock between March 14 and March 31 because . . . [they] would not have been able to obtain proxies and could not participate in the tender offer."

Before us WHX argues that (1) the SEC lacked statutory authority to promulgate the All Holders Rule in the first place; (2) even if the All Holders Rule is lawful under the statute, the SEC's interpretation of that rule as covering these facts was arbitrary and capricious; (3) even if the SEC could lawfully find that WHX's record holder condition violated the All Holders Rule, the Commission failed to provide fair notice of its interpretation to WHX, and therefore cannot impose a sanction without offending the Due Process Clause, see General Electric Co. v. EPA, 53 F.3d 1324 (D.C. Cir. 1995); and (4) even if each of the first three defenses failed, the imposition of a cease-and-desist order was arbitrary and capricious given the circumstances of WHX's violation. Because we agree with WHX's last claim, we need not reach its other arguments.

We accord great deference to the SEC's decisions as to choice of sanction, inquiring only whether a sanction "was arbitrary, capricious, an abuse of discretion, or otherwise not in accordance with law." KPMG, LLP v. SEC, 289 F.3d 109, 121 (D.C. Cir. 2002). But review does include verifying whether the Commission complied with its own standard for issuing a cease-and-desist order. It is on that requirement that the Commission's action founders.

The Commission noted that there "must be a showing of 'some risk' of future violation," though not necessarily a very great risk. It believed the risk of future violation by WHX to be "much greater" than needed, and it went on to say that in exercising its discretion it applied a "range of traditional factors," including

> the seriousness of the violation, the isolated or recurrent nature of the violation, the respondent's state of mind, the sincerity of the respondent's assurances against future violations, the respondent's recognition of the wrongful nature of his or her conduct, and the respondent's opportunity to commit future violations. In addition, we consider whether the violation is recent, the degree of harm to investors or the marketplace resulting from the violation, and the remedial function to be served by the cease-and-desist order in the context of any other sanctions being sought in the same proceedings.

Opinion at 20, citing In re KPMG Peat Marwick, LLP, 2001 WL 47245 at *26 (Jan. 19, 2001). No one criterion, it said, was dispositive.

The Commission's discussion, however, failed to explain how any reasonable application of these factors could support the imposition of a cease-and-desist order. First, the Commission stressed that there was a sufficient risk of a future violation because "WHX has made a career of establishing and promoting public companies and will be presented with opportunities to violate the law in the future." Under this view, apparently, the "risk of future violation" element is satisfied if (1) a party has committed a violation of a rule, and (2) that party has not exited the market or in some other way disabled itself from recommission of the offense. Given that the first condition is satisfied in every case where the Commission seeks a cease-and-desist order on the basis of past conduct, and the second condition is satisfied in almost every such case, this can hardly be a significant factor in determining when a cease-and-desist order is warranted. The Commission itself has disclaimed any notion that a cease-and-desist order is "automatic" on the basis of such an almost inevitably inferred risk of future violation.

The Commission urges that the "seriousness of the violation" factor weighs heavily in favor of imposing a cease-and-desist order here. The Commission's assertion that WHX's violation was "serious" is premised on two claims: first, that the All Holders Rule is clear and unambiguous, so that WHX's violation indicates willful and deliberate disregard of the rule; and second, that WHX ignored SEC staff warnings that its conduct violated the rule, and so proceeded at its peril. Neither claim passes even a weak rationality standard.

We see no basis for the Commission's idea that the plain language of the All Holders Rule clearly and unambiguously applies to WHX's record holder condition. Nothing on the face of the regulation indicates its applicability to such a condition, and WHX made a number of reasonable, good faith arguments to the SEC as to why the rule was in fact inapplicable. The Commission thought otherwise, and its interpretation of an ambiguous regulation is generally entitled to substantial deference. But if the Commission had endorsed WHX's interpretation of the All Holders Rule, we could not have rejected that alternative interpretation as "plainly inconsistent" with the rule—an observation which suggests that WHX's position did not contravene the rule's unambiguous meaning. Although WHX received informal indications that its provision violated the staff's understanding of the rule (on which more below), there was no formal Commission precedent or official interpretive guideline on point. In sum, the Commission had no basis for treating WHX's violation as "serious" because of the alleged clarity of the All Holders Rule.

The Commission's second argument for the seriousness of the violation rests on the view that WHX "acted at its peril in following counsel's recommendation to refuse to remove the Record Holder Condition in the face of the staff's warning" that the condition violated the All Holders Rule. Presumably, the Commission was referring to the staff warnings on April 4 and April 7 that it would recommend enforcement action if WHX did not remove the record holder condition, since in the March 24 exchange the staff had merely said that the Commission "did not issue" no-action letters on All Holders Rule matters, a statement that on its face did not address the merits.

It is difficult to understand why WHX's persistence after the staff said it would recommend an enforcement action should establish that WHX's violation was "serious" or "willful." True, at that point WHX had a clear idea where the Office of Mergers and Acquisitions stood on the matter. But under SEC rules parties at risk of enforcement actions are entitled to make "Wells submissions" to the Commissioners, presenting arguments why the Commissioners should reject the staff's recommendation for enforcement, see 17 C.F.R. § 202.5(c), an entitlement obviously based on recognition that staff advice is not authoritative. That procedure appears to be precisely what WHX followed in this case. In fact, the SEC staffer who informed WHX's counsel that the staff would recommend enforcement not only acknowledged the propriety of WHX's making a Wells submission under 17 C.F.R. § 202.5(c), but actually told counsel "to go to the Commission if he wanted to put something in the nature of a Wells Submission, that he should feel free to do so." Finding a violation "serious" and "willful" simply because of a failure to comply immediately with the staff's interpretation effectively punishes parties who make Wells submissions that are ultimately unsuccessful. To do so is arbitrary and capricious, at least in the absence of a more compelling explanation than the SEC offered in its Opinion. We further note that SEC counsel at oral argument acknowledged that there was no other way for WHX to secure a Commission view in time for a real-world decision.

Thus the SEC's stated bases for the cease-and-desist order fall apart. The "risk of future violation" cannot be the sole basis for its imposition of the order, as the SEC's standard for finding such a risk is so weak that it would be met in (almost) every case; and the finding that the violation was serious depends on the mistakenly assumed clarity of the rule and on WHX's good faith use of procedures made available by the Commission expressly for parties in WHX's position.

There is no indication that the other factors the SEC says it evaluates when considering a cease-and-desist order would assist it in this case. Other than a brief and underdeveloped argument, the Commission fails to establish any serious harm to shareholders or the marketplace caused by the record holder condition. At no point does it consider the possibility that allowing conditions such as WHX's might actually have benefited all DCA shareholders, including those excluded by WHX's condition, by increasing the chances that a lucrative merger would succeed, or might benefit shareholders generally by increasing the capacity of the market for corporate control to discipline management. Moreover, though the Commission may be right in its view that harm is not an element of a violation of the All Holders Rule (a position we assume but do not decide), so that the ALJ's (unreversed) finding of no harm may not undermine the finding of a violation, it is clearly a factor the Commission claims to consider when deciding whether to impose a cease-and-desist order. Yet the section of its order on the appropriateness of the sanction omits any discussion of harm to shareholders—beyond bland assertions that the All Holders Rule is important.

WHX committed (at most) a single, isolated violation of the rule, it immediately withdrew the offending condition once the Commission had made its official position clear, and the Commission has offered no reason to doubt WHX's assurances that it will not violate the rule in the future. In light of these factors, none of which the Commission seems to have considered seriously, the imposition of the cease-and-desist order seems all the more gratuitous.

* * *

The Commission erred in imposing a cease-and-desist order without a rational explanation of why such a sanction was appropriate under the Commission's own standards. We vacate the Order Imposing Remedial Sanctions and the portion of the Opinion finding the cease-and-desist order justified.

So ordered.

(3) CORPORATE BAR ORDERS

The Remedies Act also amended § 20(e) of the 1933 Act and § 21(d)(1) of the 1934 Act to enable courts to bar an individual from serving as an officer or director of any publicly reporting corporation. The Senate Report explained, in part: "Although this remedy represents a potentially severe sanction for individual misconduct, persons who have demonstrated a blatant disregard for the requirements of the Federal securities laws should not be placed in a position of trust with a publicly held corporation."[79]

SEC v. Patel
United States Court of Appeals, Second Circuit, 1995.
61 F.3d 137.

- Before: MINER, ALTIMARI and CABRANES, CIRCUIT JUDGES.
- MINER, CIRCUIT JUDGE:

Defendant-appellant Ratilal K. Patel appeals from a judgment entered in the United States District Court for the Southern District of New York (Patterson, J.) in an action brought against him by plaintiff-appellee Securities and Exchange Commission ("SEC") for violations of federal securities laws. The judgment permanently enjoins Patel from future violations, orders him to disgorge $453,203 in illegal profits plus prejudgment interest and bars him from serving as an officer or director of any public company. On appeal, Patel contends that the district court erred in calculating the "avoided losses" that it ordered him to disgorge. He also contends that the district court considered improper factors in barring him permanently from serving as an officer or director of any public company.

BACKGROUND

The parties have no dispute regarding the factual background of this case. Patel was a founder, director and senior vice president for research and development of Par Pharmaceutical, Inc. ("Par"), a manufacturer of generic drugs. In November of 1987, Par submitted to the Food and Drug Administration ("FDA") an Abbreviated New Drug Application ("the Application") for a generic version of the drug known as Maxzide, which is used for the treatment of hypertension. The Application falsely represented that Par's generic Maxzide, of which sodium bicarbonate was an ingredient, had been tested in bioequivalency studies required by the FDA. This misrepresentation came in the form of a certificate of analysis for sodium bicarbonate. The certificate was backdated to conceal the fact that the bioequivalency studies were performed with a formulation of Maxzide that did not contain the sodium bicarbonate. Patel knew that the Application was false and, in February and March of 1988, sold 75,000 shares of common stock in Par. The average sale price was approximately $21.00 per share, and Patel realized a total of $1,576,358.

---

[79] S. Rep. No. 101–337, 101st Cong., 2d Sess. 21–22 (1990). Cf. SEC v. Posner, 16 F.3d 520 (2d Cir. 1994) (director and officer bar based on District Court's general equitable powers); SEC v. First Pac. Bancorp, 142 F.3d 1186, 1193–1194 (9th Cir. 1998).

It was not until July 24, 1989 that Par publicly disclosed that it was recalling its Maxzide tablets.

Par had experienced a number of adverse events before it revealed its problems with Maxzide. In July of 1988, a congressional subcommittee (the Dingell Subcommittee), which had begun an investigation into the generic pharmaceutical industry, focused on Par. A subcommittee subpoena for Par records was served on July 5, 1988, and the press later reported that Par was involved in the Dingell Subcommittee's inquiry into allegations of bribes and payoffs to FDA officials. It seems certain that this information had a negative impact on the price of Par's stock. Another, more serious, decline in the price of the stock occurred in October of 1988, following Par's announcement that it was a target of a grand jury investigation into various improprieties, including bribery, in the generic drug industry.

In April of 1989, the press reported that Ashok Patel, another Senior Vice President of Par, had resigned his position with Par and had agreed to plead guilty to unspecified charges. Later that month, the press reported the indictment of two FDA officials on bribery charges, in an article that referred to Par, Ashok Patel and Dilip Shah. Shah later resigned from the Board of Directors of a Par subsidiary known as Quad Pharmaceuticals, Inc. In May of 1989, the Dingell Subcommittee held public hearings in connection with its investigation into the generic drug approval process. The following month, there were negative press reports on the relationship between FDA officials and Ashok Patel and Dilip Shah. Thereafter, on July 11, it was reported that a third FDA employee had been criminally charged and, on July 17, it was reported that Par had agreed to plead guilty to a charge of providing an unlawful gratuity to an FDA employee. As was to be expected, all the negative news resulted in depressions in the price of Par stock.

When Par announced on July 24, 1989 that it was recalling its Maxzide product and suspending all shipments of the drug, it also announced that it had intentionally furnished a false report to the FDA during a recent inspection; that Ratilal Patel was taking a leave of absence from the company; that its vice president for regulatory affairs and its executive vice-president were taking leaves of absence from the Board of Directors; and that the company was postponing its annual shareholders' meeting in light of the ongoing investigation. Following that announcement, the price of Par stock closed on July 24 at $8.375 per share, down $1.625 from the $10 closing price on Friday, July 21, the previous trading day. On July 25, the next trading day, the stock closed at $7.125 per share. The total decline from the July 21 closing price was $2.875 or 28.75%. On July 26, 1989, the third day after the disclosure, Par stock rallied from $7.125 to close at $7.625.

On September 8, 1989, Patel resigned as a director and senior vice president of Par and as a director of its subsidiary, Quad Pharmaceuticals, Inc. In March of 1992, he settled a securities fraud class action claim with the payment of 500,000 shares of Par stock valued at approximately $3,000,000. In January of 1993, Patel pled guilty to conspiracy to defraud the FDA in connection with the generic Maxzide Application and thereafter was sentenced to a 27-month term of imprisonment, two years of supervised release and a $25,000 fine.

* * *

II. Injunction Against Service as Officer and Director

For violations of the antifraud provisions of the securities laws,

> the court may prohibit, conditionally or unconditionally, and permanently or for such period of time as it shall determine, any person who violated [the applicable provisions] from acting as an officer or director [of a public company] if the person's conduct demonstrates substantial unfitness to serve as an officer or director. . . .

15 U.S.C. §§ 77t(e) and 78u(d)(2) (enacted in 1990).

In permanently enjoining Patel from serving as an officer or director of any public company at the behest of the SEC, the district court necessarily determined that Patel was substantially unfit to hold such positions. The court identified six factors that it considered in resolving the issue of substantial unfitness: "(1) the 'egregiousness' of the underlying securities law violation; (2) the defendant's 'repeat offender' status; (3) the defendant's 'role' or position when he engaged in the fraud; (4) the defendant's degree of scienter; (5) the defendant's economic stake in the violation; and (6) the likelihood that misconduct will recur." These factors were suggested in a law review article by Jayne W. Barnard entitled When is a Corporate Executive "Substantially Unfit to Serve"?, 70 N. C. L. Rev. 1489, 1492–93 (1992).

* * *

The district court properly considered Patel's involvement in the "Maxzide affair" as part and parcel of his conduct in the securities law violations. His deception of the FDA, although perhaps not originally designed to obtain profits or avoid losses in the sale of his stock, set in motion the scheme that culminated in his breach of fiduciary duties and in the resultant detriment to investors. Also, the district court properly took into account the six factors that it identified in evaluating substantial unfitness. These factors are useful in making the unfitness assessment, although we do not mean to say that they are the only factors that may be taken into account or even that it is necessary to apply all these factors in every case. A district court should be afforded substantial discretion in deciding whether to impose a bar to employment in a public company.

We do find a problem in this case, however, with the district court's finding regarding the likelihood of future misconduct, which is always an important element in deciding whether the substantial unfitness found justifies the imposition of a lifetime ban. The only findings that the district court made in this regard were that "Patel was a founder of Par and used his position as an officer and director to engage in misconduct." This is merely a general statement of events and can in no way justify the prediction that future misconduct will occur.

Moreover, we think that it was error for the district court to say that the likelihood of future misconduct based on the foregoing statement "is sufficient to warrant the imposition of the injunctive relief requested." The loss of livelihood and the stigma attached to permanent exclusion from the corporate suite certainly requires more. In a case in which we approved lifetime banishment as a common law remedy, we noted that the defendants "had committed securities law violations with a 'high degree of scienter' and that their past securities law violations and lack of assurances against future violations demonstrated that such violations were likely to continue." Posner, 16 F.3d at 521–22. Although it is not essential for a lifetime ban that there be past violations, we think that it is essential, in the absence of such violations, that a district court articulate the factual basis for a finding of the likelihood of recurrence.

Finally, we take note of the fact that the governing statute provides that a bar on service as an officer or director that is based on substantial unfitness may be imposed "conditionally or unconditionally" and "permanently or for such period of time as [the court] shall determine." We take these provisions to suggest that, before imposing a permanent bar, the court should consider whether a conditional bar (e.g., a bar limited to a particular industry) and/or a bar limited in time (e.g., a bar of five years) might be sufficient, especially where there is no prior history of unfitness. In this connection, we do not think that it would be improper for the district court to take into account any prior punishment that may have been imposed in a criminal proceeding. If the district court decides that a conditional ban or a ban limited in time is not warranted, it should give reasons why a lifetime injunction is imposed.

CONCLUSION

We affirm the judgment to the extent that it enjoins future securities law violations and orders the disgorgement of avoided losses.

* * *

NOTE ON THE CORPORATE BAR ORDER: SARBANES-OXLEY

The passage of the Sarbanes-Oxley Act expanded the corporate bar order in two significant ways. First, Sarbanes-Oxley amended the securities laws to authorize the federal courts to issue a corporate bar order upon the SEC's showing of "unfitness to serve."[80] This showing is presumably less than the *Patel* "substantial unfitness" standard, but

---

[80] See § 20(e) of the Securities Act and § 21(d)(2) of the Exchange Act.

Courts appear to still focus on egregious and other significant behavior.[81] Sarbanes-Oxley also granted the SEC the authority to issue corporate bar orders (both temporary and permanent) in administrative proceedings.[82] Prior to Sarbanes-Oxley only the courts had the authority to impose this sanction.

(4) COLLATERAL BAR ORDERS

The ability to impose a collateral bar, a permanent bar from the securities industry, is a new tool in the SEC's enforcement arsenal. Prior to the passage of the Dodd-Frank Act, the SEC had only the authority to bar violators from association with regulated entities of the same type with which they were associated at the time the violation occurred.[83] Section 925 of the Dodd-Frank Act provides the SEC with authority to suspend or bar offenders of the securities laws from associating with *any* type of regulated entity, regardless of the conduct involved.

3. SEC ENFORCEMENT AND PROFESSIONALS

The prior section addressed the various remedies the SEC deploys in its enforcement actions. This section looks at enforcement actions against specific types of defendants. In some situations, the SEC uses a particular statute or provision when bringing an enforcement action. In others, the SEC might choose to pursue a defendant for aiding and abetting a securities violation. Note that the standard for aiding and abetting has varied over the years. Some of the cases in this section, for example, use "knowing" as the standard. Section 929O of the Dodd-Frank Act specifies that the standard is now mere recklessness. In addition, Dodd-Frank also clarifies that aiding and abetting is available for civil penalties under the Securities Act and the Investment Company Act of 1940. Private plaintiffs may not bring aiding and abetting claims. Chapter 12 addresses that issue.

A. SECURITIES ATTORNEYS AND ACCOUNTANTS

(1) INTRODUCTION TO RULE 102(e)

Rule 102(e) (until 1995 Rule 2(e)) of the Commission's Rules of Practice provides that the SEC may deny, temporarily or permanently, the privilege of appearing or practicing before it in any way. The bases specified in Rule 102(e)(1)(i)–(iii) for such a suspension or disbarment of an attorney or accountant from practice before the Commission are that the Commission finds the person:

---

[81] See SEC v. Bankosky, 716 F.3d 45 (2d Cir. 2013), which affirmed that the Patel factors are still relevant even though the "unfitness" standard is a lower hurdle than Patel's "substantial unfitness" standard.

[82] See § 8A(f) of the Securities Act and § 21C(f) of the Exchange Act.

[83] See Teicher v. SEC, 177 F.3d 1016 (D.C. Cir. 1999), which held that the imposition of collateral bars exceeded the Commission's authority under § 15(b)(6) of the Exchange Act.

(i) not to possess the requisite qualifications to represent others; or (ii) to be lacking in character or integrity or to have engaged in unethical or improper professional conduct; or (iii) to have willfully violated, or willfully aided and abetted the violation of any provision of the Federal securities laws, or the rules and regulations thereunder.

In addition, attorneys who have been suspended or disbarred, or other persons whose professional licenses have been revoked or suspended, or who have been convicted of a felony, or of a misdemeanor "involving moral turpitude" are automatically suspended.[84]

The basic provisions of Rule 102(e)(1)(i)–(iii) have been in effect since 1935. During the first 40 years of its existence, this Rule generated very little discussion or controversy. During the 1980s, however, it became a very serious bone of contention between the Securities and Exchange Commission and the accounting and legal professions. Originally, the Commission instituted such proceedings only where the respondent's conduct constituted a direct and egregious interference with the functioning of the Commission's process. In the late 1970s and early 1980s, the Commission sometimes used this Rule as a basis for asserting jurisdiction to regulate the practice by attorneys and accountants of their professions, even where there was no proceeding before the Commission, as long as the conduct of the respondent allegedly facilitated in some fashion a violation of the federal securities laws.

Although the Commission's initial authority to promulgate the rule was questioned, courts consistently upheld it as necessary to protect the integrity of the SEC's processes.[85] The use of Rule 102(e) proceedings remains controversial both within the bar and within the Commission. In the case of In the Matter of Keating, Muething & Klekamp,[86] then-Commissioner Roberta Karmel dissented from the imposition of sanctions under Rule 2(e) on a law firm (even though it had consented to the order), on the basis that the Commission had no statutory authorization to discipline attorneys who practice before it. She wrote:

> When Rule 2(e) is invoked to discipline attorneys for misconduct which does not directly obstruct the administrative process, in my opinion it is done so improperly as a matter of law and as a matter of policy. In the *Emanuel Fields* case[87] the Commission barred an attorney on the theory that the Commission can regulate the manner in which lawyers counsel clients and render opinions in securities transactions in order to protect investors. A primary rationale for so using Rule 2(e) had been

---

[84] Rule 102(e)(2).

[85] See Davy v. SEC, 792 F.2d 1418 (9th Cir. 1986); Touche Ross & Co. v. SEC, 609 F.2d 570 (2d Cir. 1979); Checkosky v. SEC, 23 F.3d 452, 455 (D.C. Cir. 1994); Sheldon v. SEC, 45 F.3d 1515, 1518 (11th Cir. 1995).

[86] 47 SEC 95 (1979).

[87] 45 SEC 262 (1973).

that "the task of enforcing the securities laws rests in overwhelming measure on the bar's shoulders" and that given "its small staff, limited resources, and onerous tasks, the Commission is peculiarly dependent on the probity and diligence of the professionals who practice before it." However, Congress did not authorize the Commission to conscript attorneys to enforce their clients' responsibilities under the federal securities laws. Furthermore, institutional limitations alone cannot justify the creation of a new remedy not contemplated by the Congress.

I am firmly convinced that such conscription, or the promulgation and enforcement of regulatory standards of conduct for securities lawyers by the Commission, is very bad policy. It undermines the willingness and ability of the bar to exercise professional responsibility and sows the seeds for government abuse of power.

Two years later, matters came to a head in the following case.

(2) RULE 102(e) AND ATTORNEYS

Carter & Johnson
47 SEC 471 (1981).

OPINION OF THE COMMISSION

William R. Carter and Charles J. Johnson, Jr., respondents, appeal from the initial decision of the Administrative Law Judge in this proceeding brought under Rule 2(e) of the Commission's Rules of Practice. In an opinion dated March 7, 1979, the Administrative Law Judge found that, in connection with their representation of National Telephone Company, Inc. during the period from May 1974 to May 1975, Carter and Johnson willfully violated and willfully aided and abetted violations of Sections 10(b) and 13(a) of the Securities Exchange Act of 1934 (the "Exchange Act") and Rules 10b–5, 12b–20 and 13a–11 thereunder and that they engaged in unethical and improper professional conduct. In light of these findings, the Administrative Law Judge concluded that Carter and Johnson should be suspended from appearing or practicing before the Commission for periods of one year and nine months, respectively.

For the reasons stated more fully below, we reverse the decision of the Administrative Law Judge with respect to both respondents. We have concluded that the record does not adequately support the Administrative Law Judge's findings of violative conduct by respondents. Moreover, we conclude that certain concepts of proper ethical and professional conduct were not sufficiently developed, at the time of the conduct here at issue, to permit a finding that either respondent breached applicable ethical or professional standards. In addition, we are today giving notice of an interpretation by the Commission of the term "unethical or improper professional conduct," as that term is used in Rule 2(e)(1)(ii). This interpretation will be applicable prospectively in cases of this kind.

* * *

III. RESPONDENTS' CONDUCT

* * * The conduct [at] issue in these proceedings occurred in connection with respondents' legal representation of National Telephone Company, Inc. ("National") during the period from mid-1974 through mid-1975. National, a Connecticut corporation with its principal offices located in East Hartford, Connecticut, was founded in 1971 to lease sophisticated telephone equipment systems to commercial customers pursuant to long-term (5- to 10-year) leases. National enjoyed an impressive growth rate in its first three years, increasing its total assets from $320,123 to $19,028,613 and its net income from $2,390 to $633,485 during this period. At the same time, the company's backlog grew from $66,000 to $2,610,000 and the value of equipment leases written by it increased from $255,422 to $13,292,549.

The architect of National's meteoric rise was Sheldon L. Hart, one of its founders and, at all times relevant to these proceedings, its controlling stockholder. From its incorporation until his resignation on May 24, 1975, Hart was National's chief executive officer, chairman of the board of directors, president and treasurer. National's chief in-house counsel was Mark I. Lurie who, assisted by Brian Kay, was one of respondents' principal contacts with the company.

In large measure, National was a prisoner of its own success. As is commonly the case with equipment leasing companies, the greater part of National's costs in connection with a new lease, including equipment, marketing and installation expenses, was incurred well before rental payments commenced. Since rental payments were National's only significant source of revenues, the company's cash flow situation worsened with each new lease, and continued growth and operations could only be sustained through external financing. Between 1971 and 1973, National managed to obtain needed capital from an initial public offering of stock under Regulation A, short-term loans from local banks, and an offering of convertible debentures in September of 1973.

National's last successful effort to secure significant outside financing resulted in the execution, in May and June of 1974, of a $15 million credit agreement (the "Credit Agreement") with a group of five banks. Although the Credit Agreement was not closed (in amended form) until December 1974, the banks were willing to advance substantial sums to National under a variety of demand arrangements prior to the closing. In fact, by the time of the closing on December 20, 1974, these advances totaled some $16.8 million. The Credit Agreement was amended to cover this amount, plus $2.2 million for general corporate purposes and an additional $2 million available only upon the implementation of a special business plan limiting National's business growth if other sources of money could not be located. Unfortunately, funds available under the Credit Agreement, as amended, were not sufficient to finance National's expansion and operations much beyond the closing, and the pressure on National's cash flow continued.

National finally ran out of time in July of 1975, after being unable to secure sufficient external financing after the closing of the Credit Agreement. On July 2, 1975, National was forced to file a petition for an arrangement under Chapter XI of the Bankruptcy Act, 11 U.S.C. 701, et seq.; in March of 1976 this proceeding was converted into a reorganization under Chapter X of the Bankruptcy Act, 11 U.S.C. 501, et seq.

* * *

Carter, an attorney admitted to practice in the State of New York, was born in 1917. He received his law degree from Harvard Law School and has been working for the law firm known as Brown, Wood, Ivey, Mitchell & Petty ("Brown, Wood") since 1945, having become a partner of the firm in 1954. Carter's principal areas of practice have been securities, general corporate and antitrust law. Johnson, also admitted to practice as an attorney in the State of New York, as well as in the State of Connecticut, was born in 1932. He received his legal education at Harvard Law School and joined Brown, Wood's predecessor firm in 1956, becoming a partner in 1967. Johnson's principal areas of practice have been corporate and securities law.

Kenneth M. Socha worked with Carter and Johnson on a variety of legal matters affecting National, including all of the matters which are the basis of these proceedings. Socha joined Brown, Wood as an associate in 1970 and continued in that capacity during all periods relevant to these proceedings.

* * *

During 1974 and 1975, Brown, Wood, principally through Carter, Johnson and Socha, provided a wide range of legal services to National, including the preparation of a Form S-8 registration statement, proxy materials and an annual report for the company's 1974 annual stockholders meeting, other Commission filings, press releases and communications to National's stockholders. Johnson was charged with the overall coordination of Brown, Wood's legal efforts on National's behalf and was generally kept aware of progress on all significant projects. In March of 1974, after another Brown, Wood partner left the firm, Johnson asked Carter to assist Socha in working on the Credit Agreement. Thereafter Carter assumed primary responsibility for that project.

* * *

In May and June of 1974, negotiations with a consortium of five banks, in which Carter, Johnson and Socha were all participants, culminated in the execution of the Credit Agreement, which was dated as of April 30, 1974. The Credit Agreement provided for an interim revolving loan of up to $15 million, evidenced by rolling 90-day notes, until November 29, 1974, at which time National had the option to convert the principal amount then outstanding into six-year term notes. As discussed below, the Credit Agreement (as amended) was not formally closed until December 20, 1974, in part because National was unable to satisfy the closing conditions relating to its liquidity and debt-to-net-worth ratios. Ultimately the banks agreed to waive these conditions.

Since the Credit Agreement contemplated that the loans thereunder would be secured by substantially all of National's assets, it was necessary for National to transfer these assets to Systems, a transfer which in turn required the approval of National's stockholders. In order to secure this approval, National called its annual stockholders meeting for June 27, 1974, and Brown, Wood was asked to prepare the proxy materials for this meeting. Carter and Johnson also participated in the preparation of National's 1974 Annual Report. These proxy materials, along with National's 1974 Annual Report, were sent to National's stockholders on June 17 and filed with the Commission on June 19.

In urging approval of the asset transfers necessitated by the Credit Agreement, National's proxy statement disclosed that

> [t]he future growth and operations of the Company are dependent upon its ability to obtain financing such as is supplied by the Credit Agreement.

National's 1974 Annual Report contained projections of future lease installations which showed, by each quarter, a doubling of annual installations from approximately $13.3 million in fiscal 1974 to approximately $27 million in fiscal 1975. In response to a specific request from Hart, Carter advised National orally and in writing that, in light of Securities Act Release No. 5362 (Feb. 2, 1973), a copy of which Carter sent to Hart, it was permissible to include projections in the Annual Report, but that the assumptions underlying the projections should also be disclosed. Hart ignored this advice and the Annual Report was distributed without assumptions. This incident is the first example in the record of Hart's uncooperative reaction to respondents' advice concerning the disclosure demands of the federal securities laws.

* * *

At the September 11 meeting with the banks, Hart indicated that the projected equity offering had been ruled out by National's investment bankers, due to deteriorating market conditions. He further reported that National's cash flow problems had caused the company voluntarily to institute a "wind-down" program, effective September 1. As he described it, this program, projected to last five months, was a severe retrenchment, designed to protect the banks' existing investment. Under it, National would limit its operations to the conversion of present inventory—approximately $5 million—into installed systems under new leases, phase out further marketing and installation efforts and reduce the company to a "pure maintenance organization." Hart requested an increase in the total amount of the banks' planned loan from $15 to $21 million in order to finance this wind-down program. The banks, however, hesitated, agreeing only that no decision would be made on lending National additional funds until the pending $15 million Credit Agreement was closed.

Hart, in fact, had lied to the banks. No wind-down program had been instituted or, as it turned out, would be until almost eight months later, in May of 1975. There is, however, no evidence in the record that respondents were, or ever became, aware of Hart's September 11, 1974 deception.

* * *

In light of his presence at the July 1, August 19 and October 15 board meetings, as well as the October 18 bank meeting, Johnson was well aware of National's cash crisis, its continuing failure to obtain needed financing and its purported "wind-down" program. This, in addition to the well-known depressed state of the credit markets and the fact that National had projected, confirmed and continued to report, without obviously relevant qualifications, rapidly growing sales and earnings, undoubtedly prompted Johnson to instruct Socha to draft a disclosure letter to National's stockholders approximately two days after the October 18 bank meeting.

The proposed stockholders letter, which was reviewed by both Carter and Johnson and sent to the company in early November, was a candid summary of National's financial predicament, noting that National would "in the near future" have to obtain significant financing in addition to the Credit Agreement. It concluded:

> The Company's efforts to obtain additional financing have been adversely affected by tight credit conditions, increased interest costs, a generally unfavorable equity market and certain factors that are peculiar to its business such as the negative cash flow described above. In view of these factors the Company has determined that it would be prudent to curtail its sales operations and, therefore, to emphasize the liquidity rather than growth until such time as additional debt or equity financing can be obtained.

Johnson subsequently told Lurie that this was the type of communication "that a company . . . interested in keeping its stockholders advised on a regular basis should be making." Despite this advice, National's management declined to issue the letter. Neither respondent elected to pursue the matter.

* * *

It is important to note, at this point, that both Carter and Johnson must have been aware that, if National were to implement the wind-down plan, the company would have no reasonable opportunity to meet the projections of $27 million in lease installations which were set forth in the 1974 Annual Report and indirectly reconfirmed in the company's September 12 letter to its stockholders. The wind-down plan, which Socha summarized in a December 2 memorandum to Johnson, provided that National would not be permitted to enter into any further leases. Obviously, under these circumstances, the company's sales and earnings growth would be halted—short of projected levels.

In early December, Socha received from National a draft of the company's quarterly report to its stockholders for the second fiscal quarter ended September 30, 1974. The report contained a series of graphs, illustrating the successful results of National's operations, but once again made no mention of the dire financial straits in which the company found itself in December. Such an omission was especially significant in light of the disclosure recommendations which Brown, Wood had by then made to National. When Socha inquired whether the use of the graphs had been cleared by Johnson, Lurie informed him that they had. This was not true, as Johnson noted on the copy of the draft report circulated to him by Socha. The quarterly report was mailed as proposed, and neither respondent ever spoke with the company's management about the disclosure problems it presented or about Lurie's misrepresentation to Socha.

* * *

In the final days leading to the closing, National's "wind-down" plan was renegotiated somewhat and finally emerged with a new name, the lease maintenance plan ("LMP"). All the witnesses speaking to the question agreed that the term "lease maintenance plan" had no generally accepted meaning in the industry and that they had never used or heard this term before. Moreover, the terms "wind-down plan," "contingency plan," and "lease maintenance plan," were all intended to refer to the same thing.

The need to revise the original wind-down plan emerged when the consulting firm hired by National to evaluate the plan reported to the banks that, in its original form, the plan was neither feasible nor in the best interests of the banks. Rather, the independent consultants advised that the best course would be to allow National limited continuing growth, financed with additional bank borrowings, and that a wind-down should be implemented only as a last resort and only if the company were unable to obtain additional outside financing.

At a meeting held on December 11, with Carter and representatives of National and the banks present, final details of the Amendment were negotiated. A draft of the Amendment dated December 13, 1974, which was prepared by White & Case, contemplated an arrangement under which the banks would permit Systems to borrow up to $19 million at any time on or before April 30, 1975. These borrowings were to be secured by the telephone leases and equipment transferred to Systems by National and guaranteed by National. If either (1) National and/or Systems attempted to borrow in excess of $19 million from the existing bank group or (2) National failed to meet a specified liquidity test, National and Systems were required to implement the LMP. Their failure to do so in accordance with the provisions of the LMP was an event of default under the Credit Agreement, as modified by the Amendment (the "Amended Credit Agreement"), and resulted in all outstanding indebtedness under that Agreement becoming due and payable upon demand.

The December 13 draft of the Amendment for the first time contained a reference to a "lease maintenance plan" and indicated that the LMP was to be attached as an exhibit to the Amendment. The effect of the implementation of the LMP on National's operations and growth would obviously be both dramatic and devastating. Indeed, as one expert called by respondents testified, the LMP was "a sort of a holding pattern short of bankruptcy or levy by the creditors." The LMP required National to terminate all sales activities, dismiss all sales personnel, and limit its operations to those necessary to service existing leases. In effect, the company would be transformed into a mere service agency, maintaining existing leases, but writing no new ones. Moreover, the final $2 million of the funds to be provided by the banks was only available until June 30, 1975 and could only be used to implement the LMP, principally by financing the installation of equipment already in inventory to complete existing orders.

* * *

On December 19, the day immediately preceding the closing under the Amended Credit Agreement, at a day-long pre-closing meeting, Hart told Carter that he did not want the terms of the LMP made public or filed with the Commission. Although Carter testified that he could not recall the reason for this request, he speculated that Hart sought not to publicize the LMP because he was concerned that the disclosure of the LMP's effects on the company's business would have a negative impact on the morale of National's sales personnel. After reading the LMP, Carter advised Hart that the LMP would have to be filed with the Commission if it were an exhibit to the Amendment, as originally had been contemplated. However, Carter added that the LMP need not be filed with the Commission or publicized if it were not an exhibit but rather merely referred to in the Amendment. Hart agreed, and the Amendment was modified to delete the LMP as an exhibit.

Also at the December 19 pre-closing conference, Carter reviewed and extensively revised a press release prepared by National announcing the closing of the Amended Credit Agreement. The revised press release was reviewed by all parties at the meeting, including the company's management. No one raised any objections to the revisions proposed by Carter.

On December 20, the Amended Credit Agreement was closed and National immediately borrowed $18 million from the banks. Of this amount, over $16.8 million was used to repay existing demand indebtedness based on advances the banks had made to National since the original Credit Agreement had been signed six months earlier.

* * *

Immediately after the closing, National issued the press release that Carter had redrafted the day before. The release stated, in its entirety:

<u>PRESS RELEASE—FOR IMMEDIATE RELEASE</u>
EAST HARTFORD, CONN., DECEMBER 20, 1974

National Telephone Company today announced the execution of a $6,000,000 extension of a $15,000,000 Credit Agreement with a group of banks headed by Bankers Trust Company of New York. Included in the $21 million is a contingency fund of $2 million which is available until June 30, 1975 and which may be utilized by the Company only for the purpose of funding a lease maintenance program in the event additional financing is not otherwise available.

Of the $21 million, the Company has borrowed $18 million pursuant to a seven-year term loan, of which approximately $16,500,000 was used to repay outstanding short-term loans. The balance will be used for general operating expenses. Participating in the loans are Bankers Trust Company of New York, Mellon Bank N.A. of Pittsburgh, Central National Bank of Cleveland, The Connecticut Bank and Trust Company and The Hartford National Bank and Trust Company of Hartford, Connecticut.

The press release did not discuss either of the following matters each of which was then within the knowledge of Carter and Johnson.

(1) The precise nature and effects on National's business of the LMP and the likelihood that National would be required to implement the LMP within a short period of time; and

(2) The substantial limitations placed on National's operations by the Amended Credit Agreement.

It is also apparent from the record that the press release's statement indicating that the balance of the financing remaining after the repayment of outstanding bank debt "will be used for general operating expenses" was misleading, in light of the substantial overdue obligations of National then existing.

The second major item of public disclosure concerning the closing was a stockholders' letter mailed, without respondents' knowledge, by National on or about December 23. This letter, which was issued in the face of Socha's advice to National that no further public statements should be issued concerning the Amended Credit Agreement unless such statements were cleared by Brown, Wood, contained numerous misstatements and omissions, including the following:

(1) The letter indicated that the company "was stronger now than ever before in its history" and that it had "a greater availability of capital, expanding productivity and growing earnings" and was "looking forward to an outstanding year in calendar 1975."

(2) The letter indicated that the entire additional $6 million loan to National could be used for future operating expenses.

(3) The letter made no reference to National's repayment of existing bank loans and other pre-existing debts with the proceeds of the financing, its continuing cash needs and shortages, or the LMP.

Respondents first learned of the letter on December 27, when Brian Kay, who was aware that National had ignored Socha's advice that all public disclosure should be reviewed by them, voluntarily telephoned Socha and dictated the letter to him. Socha thought that the letter's description of the Amended Credit Agreement was "seriously inadequate" and immediately gave a copy of it to Johnson. Carter, too, was consulted. While respondents felt that the letter did not make "adequate disclosure" with respect to the Amended Credit Agreement, they concluded that, when read together with the earlier December 20 press release which Carter had revised, it was not materially false or misleading, and that no corrective action by National was therefore required. Johnson later did, however, orally express his dissatisfaction with the letter to Lurie.

* * *

On January 9, 1975, National filed a current report on Form 8-K for the month of December 1974, reporting on the closing under the Amended Credit Agreement. This document was drafted by Carter, who accepted full responsibility for it.

The Amended Credit Agreement, which was attached to the Form 8-K as an exhibit, made frequent reference to the LMP. And the 8-K itself stated that $2 million of National's recent $21 million loan arrangement was "a contingency fund available until June 30, 1975 only for the purpose of financing a lease maintenance program in the event additional financing is not otherwise available." As previously requested by Hart, however, the LMP itself was not included as an exhibit to the Agreement or the filing; nor was the term "lease maintenance plan" specifically defined or the effects which it would have on the company discussed.

Between the January 9, 1975 filing of National's Form 8-K and mid-March, National's financial condition deteriorated even further, to a degree requiring the implementation of the LMP. In addition, the gap between National's public disclosure posture and its private financial condition continued to widen and National's board of directors was becoming increasingly uncomfortable with the situation. There is no indication in the record that either respondent directly or indirectly became aware of the growing seriousness of the situation until a March 17 telephone call from the banks' counsel, described below.

* * *

On March 17—nearly one month after the February 20 consultants report, and over six weeks after the LMP had in fact been triggered—Brown, Wood was informed for the first time, by the banks' lawyers, White & Case, that events requiring implementation of the LMP had occurred. The White & Case lawyers had received a telephone call from a vice president of one of the banks informing them of this fact and reporting that no public disclosure had been made by National. The bank vice president also sought White & Case's advice on how to respond to trade creditors of National who were making inquiries to the banks about the company.

During their March 17 conversation, the White & Case lawyers advised Carter that National and its counsel, Brown, Wood, had the responsibility to determine what disclosure, if any, would be appropriate under the circumstances, and they sought assurances that, if proper disclosure were deemed necessary, it would be forthcoming. Carter, who admittedly considered the triggering of the LMP clearly material, assured White & Case that, if what they said were true, Brown, Wood would contact National and "get a statement out." The White & Case lawyers then called the bank's vice president and relayed the content of their conversation with Carter.

On the following day, March 18, Carter telephoned Lurie and informed him of the call from the White & Case lawyers. Lurie neither confirmed nor denied that the LMP had been triggered. Rather, he dissembled, stating that the situation was "tight," but adding that, "if they were careful, they would be all right." Carter advised Lurie that, if the LMP had indeed been triggered, the fact should be disclosed publicly, although he did not press Lurie for a definite answer on whether the LMP had in fact been triggered, or on whether National's management was in fact implementing the LMP as required by the Amended Credit Agreement.

* * *

On April 23, 1975 both respondents met with Hart and advised him in no uncertain terms that immediate disclosure was required. In response to Hart's protestations that National would soon obtain additional financing, respondents advised him that these hopes, as well as any negotiations for a waiver of the LMP by the banks, did not serve to excuse National's legal obligation to make prompt disclosure.

Shortly before the April 23 meeting, the vice president of one of the lending banks had written to Hart requesting, among other things, a "written response from your counsel regarding [National's] obligation to make public disclosure regarding significant transactions which may have transpired during the last several months, particularly with regard to the implementing of the lease maintenance plan." Presumably as a result of this request, Hart telephoned Johnson on April 28—only five days after having received the unambiguous and forceful advice that disclosure was required—to request that Johnson issue a legal opinion for the banks to the effect that disclosure of the triggering of the LMP was *not* necessary. Johnson testified that he replied as follows:

> I'm incredulous. I just can't believe this. You sat in my office last week and I told you as clearly and positively and precisely as I could that my advice was that you should disclose that you had gone into the lease maintenance mode.

Ultimately, Hart responded to the bank's request for an opinion of counsel with a letter from National stating that no disclosure had been made because, "in the opinion of the company," none was required.

In late April, after the telephone encounter with Hart described above, Johnson instructed Socha to draft a disclosure document for National to issue, either in its next report to the Commission or in a special letter to the stockholders. In doing so, Johnson specified that the draft should be one that would be "acceptable to a person as emotionally involved as Hart." Both respondents reviewed and approved the draft prepared by Socha and it was forwarded to Hart on or about May 1, with the suggestion that Hart call Carter or Johnson about it.

* * * National did not issue this disclosure document in any form and the record does not indicate any response to Brown, Wood's disclosure advice. Neither respondent questioned anyone at the company about management's failure to make the suggested disclosure.

On May 9, Kay called Socha to seek his approval of a draft of the company's proposed current report on Form 8-K for the month of April. Socha reiterated Brown, Wood's earlier advice that disclosure should be made concerning National's present status under the Amended Credit Agreement and of the event of default that resulted from the company's failure to implement the LMP. Although Kay agreed to include the suggested disclosure, the report actually filed with the Commission did not contain any such disclosure, because Lurie would not permit it.

* * *

Later the same day, Socha called Kay and asked for a copy of the company's April Form 8-K. Kay replied that Lurie would not permit him to mail a copy to Brown, Wood or to the Commission. The April Form 8-K was eventually filed with the Commission on May 15, 1975. Socha testified that he was required to obtain a copy of it from the Commission.

* * *

The internal and external tensions which had been developing around National came to a head on Saturday afternoon, May 24, at the special meeting of the board of directors in Hartford, Connecticut. Johnson was there, acting as secretary, having been asked to attend by Hart. Also present at the meeting was independent counsel who had been consulted by the outside directors and asked to attend the meeting in the expectation that Johnson would not be there. It was at this meeting that the outside directors learned for the first time that, for over a month, Brown, Wood had been recommending disclosure and Johnson read a draft of the letter which Brown, Wood had sent to Hart on May 1, disclosing that the LMP had been triggered and its effect on the company. One of the nonmanagement directors testified that he had no prior indication that Brown, Wood had been recommending this disclosure to Hart and that when he heard the letter read by Johnson he "was shocked to the core."

At the May 24 meeting, Hart resigned each of his corporate offices, although he remained a director of the company, Johnson prepared a press release which was unanimously approved by the Board and it was decided that Brown, Wood would continue as company counsel. Johnson, however, resigned as secretary of the company.

* * *

IV. AIDING AND ABETTING

Rule 2(e)(1)(iii) provides that the Commission may deny, temporarily or permanently, the privilege of appearing or practicing before it to any person who is found by the Commission, after notice of and opportunity for hearing, to have willfully violated, or willfully aided and abetted the violation of, any provision of the federal securities laws or the rules and regulations thereunder.

A. *The Findings Below.*

The Administrative Law Judge summarized the bases for his findings that respondents had "willfully violated and aided and abetted violations" of Sections 10(b) and 13(a) of the Exchange Act and Rules 10b–5, 12b–20 and 13a–11 thereunder as follows:

(i) that the December 20, 1974 press release, revised by Carter, in describing the closing under the Amended Credit Agreement was materially false and misleading in its failure to disclose adequately the nature of the LMP and that Carter was responsible for preparing it;

(ii) that the December 23, 1974 letter which Hart sent to National's stockholders was materially false and misleading, and that neither respondent took action to correct it, or to see that adequate disclosure would be made to clear up the misperceptions created by it, after they learned of the letter on December 27;

(iii) that National's Form 8-K for December 1974 was materially false and misleading in its failure to describe adequately the nature of the LMP, and that Carter has accepted full responsibility for preparing it;

(iv) that respondents failed to communicate with the board of directors of National, or otherwise take steps to insure that adequate disclosures were made in filings with the Commission, in press releases, and in letters to stockholders, despite the optimistic information about the company which they knew had been disseminated to the marketplace; and

(v) that respondents (a) from May 1974 to May 1975, assisted National's management in its efforts to conceal material facts concerning the company's financial condition, and (b) at least from October 1974 to May 1975, failed to inform the company's board of directors concerning management's unwillingness to make required disclosures.

* * * [G]iven the circumstances of this case, we do not believe that respondents' involvement in the affairs or decision-making processes of the company was sufficient to justify a finding against them as direct, primary violators of Section 10(b) or Rule 10b–5 as a result of the antifraud violations growing out of National's statements. We therefore will consider respondents' conduct only as it may constitute willful aiding and abetting of a federal securities law violation by National.

B. *Securities Law Violations by National.*

We have no doubt that National's failure to disclose the nature of the LMP in the December 20 press release and the December Form 8-K constituted a violation of Sections 10(b) and 13(a) of the Exchange Act and Rules 10b–5, 12b–20 and 13a–11 thereunder. Respondents' position to the contrary rests on the purported knowledge of the marketplace that a leasing company must have new infusions of capital to grow, and that the press release and Form 8-K adequately disclosed that the closing of the Amended Credit Agreement in December made no substantial funds available to finance new leases.

Whatever our doubts about that proposition, it is clear that the LMP involved a great deal more than merely confirming the temporary absence of funds for new leases. It required, among other things, the cessation of all leasing activity and the termination of substantially all sales personnel.

* * *

These limiting provisions were highly unusual and their import is not conveyed by the mere repetition of the words "lease maintenance plan" in the press release and in the December Form 8-K. Nor do we find persuasive respondents' argument that the likelihood of the LMP being triggered was so remote that its provisions were not material.

* * *

Respondents assert that the disclosure system deals with facts, not contingencies. But the existence of this contingency—the uncertainty of additional financing and its relationship to the LMP—is itself a fact about which investors are entitled to make their own judgments.

* * *

C. *Aiding and Abetting.*

Our primary concern, however, is with the respondents' relationship to these violations of the securities laws. Although "[t]he elements of an aiding and abetting claim have not yet crystallized into a set pattern,"[56] we have examined the decisions of the various circuits and conclude that certain legal principles are common to all the decisions.

In the context of the federal securities laws, these principles hold generally that one may be found to have aided and abetted a violation when the following three elements are present:

1. there exists an independent securities law violation committed by some other party;
2. the aider and abettor knowingly and substantially assisted the conduct that constitutes the violation; and
3. the aider and abettor was aware or knew that his role was part of an activity that was improper or illegal.

As noted above, we have no difficulty in finding that National committed numerous substantial securities law violations. The second element—substantial assistance—is generally satisfied in the context of a securities lawyer performing professional duties, for he is inevitably deeply involved in his client's disclosure activities and often participates in the drafting of the documents, as was the case with Carter. And he does so knowing that he is participating in the preparation of disclosure documents—that is his job.

In this connection, we do not distinguish between the professional advice of a lawyer given orally or in writing and similar advice which is embodied in drafting documents to be filed with the Commission. Liability in these circumstances should not turn on such artificial distinctions, particularly in light of the almost limitless range of forms which legal advice may take. Moreover, the opposite approach, which would permit a lawyer to avoid or reduce his liability simply by avoiding participation in the drafting process, may well have the undesirable effect of reducing the quality of the disclosure by the many to protect against the defalcations of the few.

For these reasons, the crucial inquiry in a Rule 2(e) proceeding against a lawyer inevitably tends to focus on the awareness or the intent element of the offense of aiding and abetting. It is that element which

---

[56] Woodward v. Metro Bank of Dallas, 522 F.2d 84, 94 (C.A.5 1975).

has been the source of the most disagreement among commentators and the courts. We do not seek to resolve that disagreement today. We do hold, however, that a finding of willful aiding and abetting within the meaning of Rule 2(e)(2)(iii) requires a showing that respondents were aware or knew that their role was part of an activity that was improper or illegal.

* * *

If a securities lawyer is to bring his best independent judgment to bear on a disclosure problem, he must have the freedom to make innocent—or even, in certain cases, careless—mistakes without fear of legal liability or loss of the ability to practice before the Commission. Concern about his own liability may alter the balance of his judgment in one direction as surely as an unseemly obeisance to the wishes of his client can do so in the other. While one imbalance results in disclosure rather than concealment, neither is, in the end, truly in the public interest. Lawyers who are seen by their clients as being motivated by fears for their personal liability will not be consulted on difficult issues.

* * *

V. ETHICAL AND PROFESSIONAL RESPONSIBILITIES

A. *The Findings of the Administrative Law Judge.*

The Administrative Law Judge found that both respondents "failed to carry out their professional responsibilities with respect to appropriate disclosure to all concerned, including stockholders, directors and the investing public ... and thus knowingly engaged in unethical and improper professional conduct, as charged in the Order." In particular, he held that respondents' failure to advise National's board of directors of Hart's refusal to disclose adequately the company's perilous financial condition was itself a violation of ethical and professional standards referred to in Rule 2(e)(1)(ii).

Respondents argue that the Commission has never promulgated standards of professional conduct for lawyers and that the Commission's application in hindsight of new standards would be fundamentally unfair. Moreover, even if it is permissible for the Commission to apply—without specific adoption or notice—generally recognized professional standards, they argue that no such standards applicable to respondents' conduct existed in 1974–75, nor do they exist today.

We agree that, in general, elemental notions of fairness dictate that the Commission should not establish new rules of conduct and impose them retroactively upon professionals who acted at the time without reason to believe that their conduct was unethical or improper. At the same time, however, we perceive no unfairness whatsoever in holding those professionals who practice before us to generally recognized norms of professional conduct, whether or not such norms had previously been explicitly adopted or endorsed by the Commission. To do so upsets no justifiable expectations, since the professional is already subject to those norms.[64]

The ethical and professional responsibilities of lawyers who become aware that their client is engaging in violations of the securities laws have not been so firmly and unambiguously established that we believe all practicing lawyers can be held to an awareness of generally recognized norms.[65] We also recognize that the Commission has never articulated or endorsed any such standards. That being the case, we reverse the Administrative Law Judge's findings under subparagraph (ii) of Rule 2(e)(1) with respect to both respondents. Nevertheless, we believe that respondents' conduct raises serious questions about the obligations of securities lawyers, and the Commission is hereby giving notice of its interpretation of "unethical or improper professional conduct" as that term is used in Rule 2(e)(1)(ii). The Commission intends to issue a release soliciting comment from the public as to whether this interpretation should be expanded or modified.

B. *Interpretive Background.*

Our concern focuses on the professional obligations of the lawyer who gives essentially correct disclosure advice to a client that does not follow that advice and as a result violates the federal securities laws. The subject of our inquiry is not a new one by any means and has received extensive scholarly treatment[66] as well as consideration by a number of local bar ethics committees and disciplinary bodies. Similar issues are also presently under consideration by the ABA's Commission on Evaluation of Professional Standards in connection with the review and proposed revision of the ABA's Code of Professional Responsibility.

---

[64] For example, the universally recognized requirement that a lawyer refrain from acting in an area where he does not have an adequate level of preparation or care, e.g., ABA Code of Professional Responsibility, Disciplinary Rule ("ABA D.R.") 6–101.

[65] We are aware that ABA D.R. 1–102(A)(4) provides that "a lawyer shall not . . . engage in conduct involving dishonesty, fraud, deceit or misrepresentation" and that ABA D.R. 7–102(A)(7) provides that a lawyer may not, in the course of his representation, "counsel or assist his client in conduct that the lawyer knows to be illegal or fraudulent." Although we believe the prohibitions embodied in ABA D.R. 1–102(A)(4) and 7–102(A)(7) to be of such a fundamental nature that we would not hesitate to hold that their coverage plainly falls within the area of conduct prohibited by Rule 2(e)(1)(ii), two factors convince us not to apply them in this case. First, it is unclear whether the operative terms used in these Disciplinary Rules are coextensive with the use of such terms in the statutory prohibitions of Section 10(b) of the Exchange Act. Second, it is not apparent that the reach of ABA D.R. 1–102(A)(4) or 7–102(A)(7) is greater or any different from the reach of Rule 2(e)(1)(ii) in the case of a lawyer who willfully aids and abets a violation of Section 10(b). Accordingly, in this opinion, we have elected to analyze respondents' actions in the context of the provisions of subparagraph (iii), as discussed above, rather than under subparagraph (ii) of Rule 2(e)(1).

[66] E.g., Hoffman, On Learning of a Corporate Client's Crime or Fraud—The Lawyer's Dilemma, 33 Bus. Lawyer 1389 (1978); Association of the Bar of The City of New York, Report By Special Committee on The Lawyers' Role in Securities Transactions, 32 Bus. Lawyer 1879 (1977); Cooney, The Registration Process: The Role of the Lawyer in Disclosure, 33 Bus. Lawyer 1329 (1978); Cutler, The Role of the Private Law Firm, 33 Bus. Lawyer 1549 (1978); Sonde, The Responsibility of Professionals under the Federal Securities Laws—Some Observations, 68 Nw. U. L. Rev. 1 (1973); New York Law Journal, "Expanding Responsibilities under the Securities Laws" (1972), 29 (remarks of Manuel F. Cohen, Esq.).

While precise standards have not yet emerged, it is fair to say that there exists considerable acceptance of the proposition that a lawyer must, in order to discharge his professional responsibilities, make all efforts within reason to persuade his client to avoid or terminate proposed illegal action. Such efforts could include, where appropriate, notification to the board of directors of a corporate client. In this connection, it is noteworthy that a number of commentators responding to the Commission's request, in Securities Exchange Act Release No. 16045, for written comments on a rulemaking petition concerning the disclosure of relationships between registrants and their lawyers (the "Georgetown Petition"), volunteered their beliefs that such a professional obligation already exists. This informal expression of views is, of course, not conclusive, and there continues to be a lively debate surrounding the lawyer's proper reaction to his client's wrongdoings.

We are mindful that, when a lawyer represents a corporate client, the client—and the entity to which he owes his allegiance—is the corporation itself and not management or any other individual connected with the corporation. Moreover, the lawyer should try to "insure that decisions of his client are made only after the client has been informed of relevant considerations." These unexceptionable principles take on a special coloration when a lawyer becomes aware that one or more specific members of a corporate client's management is deciding not to follow his disclosure advice, especially if he knows that those in control, such as the board of directors, may not have participated in or been aware of that decision. Moreover, it is well established that no lawyer, even in the most zealous pursuit of his client's interests, is privileged to assist his client in conduct the lawyer knows to be illegal. The application of these recognized principles to the special role of the securities lawyer giving disclosure advice, however, is not a simple task.

The securities lawyer who is an active participant in a company's ongoing disclosure program will ordinarily draft and revise disclosure documents, comment on them and file them with the Commission. He is often involved on an intimate, day-to-day basis in the judgments that determine what will be disclosed and what will be withheld from the public markets. When a lawyer serving in such a capacity concludes that his client's disclosures are not adequate to comply with the law, and so advises his client, he is "aware," in a literal sense, of a continuing violation of the securities laws. On the other hand, the lawyer is only an adviser, and the final judgment—and, indeed, responsibility—as to what course of conduct is to be taken must lie with the client. Moreover, disclosure issues often present difficult choices between multiple shades of gray, and while a lawyer's judgment may be to draw the disclosure obligation more broadly than his client, both parties recognize the degree of uncertainty involved.

The problems of professional conduct that arise in this relationship are well-illustrated by the facts of this case. In rejecting Brown, Wood's advice to include the assumptions underlying its projections in its 1974 Annual Report, in declining to issue two draft stockholders letters offered by respondents and in ignoring the numerous more informal urgings by both respondents and Socha to make disclosure, Hart and Lurie indicated that they were inclined to resist any public pronouncements that were at odds with the rapid growth which had been projected and reported for the company.

If the record ended there, we would be hesitant to suggest that any unprofessional conduct might be involved. Hart and Lurie were, in effect, pressing the company's lawyers hard for the minimum disclosure required by law. That fact alone is not an appropriate basis for a finding that a lawyer must resign or take some extraordinary action. Such a finding would inevitably drive a wedge between reporting companies and their outside lawyers; the more sophisticated members of management would soon realize that there is nothing to gain in consulting outside lawyers.

However, much more was involved in this case. In sending out a patently misleading letter to stockholders on December 23 in contravention of Socha's plain and express advice to clear all such disclosure with Brown, Wood, in deceiving respondents about Johnson's approval of the company's quarterly report to its stockholders in early December and in dissembling in response to respondents' questions about the implementation of the LMP, the company's management erected a wall between National and its outside lawyers—a wall apparently designed to keep out good legal advice in conflict with management's improper disclosure plans.

Any ambiguity in the situation plainly evaporated in late April and early May of 1975 when Hart first asked Johnson for a legal opinion flatly contrary to the express disclosure advice Johnson had given Hart only five days earlier, and when Lurie soon thereafter prohibited Kay from delivering a copy of the company's April 1975 Form 8-K to Brown, Wood.

These actions reveal a conscious desire on the part of National's management no longer to look to Brown, Wood for independent disclosure advice, but rather to embrace the firm within Hart's fraud and use it as a shield to avoid the pressures exerted by the banks toward disclosure. Such a role is a perversion of the normal lawyer-client relationship, and no lawyer may claim that, in these circumstances, he need do no more than stubbornly continue to suggest disclosure when he knows his suggestions are falling on deaf ears.

C. *"Unethical or Improper Professional Conduct."*

The Commission is of the view that a lawyer engages in "unethical or improper professional conduct" under the following circumstances: When a lawyer with significant responsibilities in the effectuation of a company's compliance with the disclosure requirements of the federal securities laws becomes aware that his client is engaged in a substantial and continuing failure to satisfy those disclosure requirements, his continued participation violates professional standards unless he takes prompt steps to end the client's noncompliance. The Commission has determined that this interpretation will be applicable only to conduct occurring after the date of this opinion.

We do not imply that a lawyer is obliged, at the risk of being held to have violated Rule 2(e), to seek to correct every isolated disclosure action or inaction which he believes to be at variance with applicable disclosure standards, although there may be isolated disclosure failures that are so serious that their correction becomes a matter of primary professional concern. It is also clear, however, that a lawyer is not privileged to unthinkingly permit himself to be co-opted into an ongoing fraud and cast as a dupe or a shield for a wrong doing client.

Initially, counseling accurate disclosure is sufficient, even if his advice is not accepted. But there comes a point at which a reasonable lawyer must conclude that his advice is not being followed, or even sought in good faith, and that his client is involved in a continuing course of violating the securities laws. At this critical juncture, the lawyer must take further, more affirmative steps in order to avoid the inference that he has been co-opted, willingly or unwillingly, into the scheme of non-disclosure.

The lawyer is in the best position to choose his next step. Resignation is one option, although we recognize that other considerations, including the protection of the client against foreseeable prejudice, must be taken into account in the case of withdrawal. A direct approach to the board of directors or one or more individual directors or officers may be appropriate; or he may choose to try to enlist the aid of other members of the firm's management. What is required, in short, is some prompt action[77] that leads to the conclusion that the lawyer is engaged in efforts to correct the underlying problem, rather than having capitulated to the desires of a strong-willed, but misguided client.

Some have argued that resignation is the only permissible course when a client chooses not to comply with disclosure advice. We do not agree. Premature resignation serves neither the end of an effective lawyer-client relationship nor, in most cases, the effective administration of the securities laws. The lawyer's continued interaction with his client will ordinarily hold the greatest promise of corrective action. So long as a lawyer is acting in good faith and exerting reasonable efforts to prevent violations of the law by his client, his professional obligations have been met. In general, the best result is that which promotes the continued, strong-minded and independent participation by the lawyer.

---

[77] In those cases where resignation is not the only alternative, should a lawyer choose not to resign, we do not believe the action taken must be successful to avoid the inference that the lawyer had improperly participated in his client's fraud. Rather, the acceptability of the action must be considered in the light of all relevant surrounding circumstances. Similarly, what is "prompt" in any one case depends on the situation then facing the lawyer.

We recognize, however, that the "best result" is not always obtainable, and that there may occur situations where the lawyer must conclude that the misconduct is so extreme or irretrievable, or the involvement of his client's management and board of directors in the misconduct is so thoroughgoing and pervasive that any action short of resignation would be futile. We would anticipate that cases where a lawyer has no choice but to resign would be rare and of an egregious nature.[78]

D. *Conclusion.*

As noted above, because the Commission has never adopted or endorsed standards of professional conduct which would have applied to respondents' activities during the period here in question, and since generally accepted norms of professional conduct which existed outside the scope of Rule 2(e) did not, during the relevant time period, unambiguously cover the situation in which respondents found themselves in 1974–75, no finding of unethical or unprofessional conduct would be appropriate. That being the case, we reverse the findings of the Administrative Law Judge under Rule 2(e)(1)(ii). In future proceedings of this nature, however, the Commission will apply the interpretation of subparagraph (ii) of Rule 2(e)(1) set forth in this opinion.

An appropriate order will issue.

* * *

NOTES ON RULE 102(e): OVER TIME

1. *The SEC's Authority.* Although the *Carter & Johnson* case was expected to result in judicial review and clarification of the SEC's authority under what is now Rule 102(e), the Commission neatly sidestepped any judicial test of its power by declining to impose any sanction on the respondents (while threatening to do so in future cases). In 1982, the Commission's general counsel indicated that the Commission would normally limit its discipline of attorneys to instances where the conduct also violated established ethical rules of state bar organizations.[88] The Commission ratified this policy in 1988, stating:

> With respect to attorneys, the Commission generally has not sought to develop or apply independent standards of professional conduct. The great majority of Rule 2(e) proceedings against attorneys involve allegations of violations of the law (not of professional standards); thus, the Commission as a matter of policy, generally refrains from using its

---

[78] This case does not involve, nor do we here deal with, the additional question of when a lawyer, aware of his client's intention to commit fraud or an illegal act, has a professional duty to disclose that fact either publicly or to an affected third party. Our interpretation today does not require such action at any point, although other existing standards of professional conduct might be so interpreted. See, e.g., ABA D.R. 7–102(B).

[88] See Greene, Lawyer Disciplinary Proceedings Before the Securities and Exchange Commission, 14 Sec. Reg. L. Rep. (BNA) 168 (1982).

administrative forum to conduct *de novo* determinations of the professional obligations of attorneys.[89]

Since the Commission's 1981 proceeding in *Carter & Johnson* all, or virtually all, Rule 102(e) proceedings against lawyers have followed injunctions (or occasionally convictions) for securities law violations.[90]

2. *Rule 102(e)'s Required Mental State.* In Checkosky v. SEC,[91] ("*Checkosky I*") the D.C. Circuit Court remanded, *per curiam*, a Rule 2(e) proceeding so that the Commission could state unequivocally whether it regarded negligent acts, without more, as constituting a violation of Rule 2(e). Judge Silberman's opinion stated:

> If the Commission were to determine that an accountant's negligence is a per se violation of Rule 2(e), it would have to consider not only the administrative burden such a position would entail but also whether it would constitute a de facto substantive regulation of the profession and thus raise questions as to the legitimacy of Rule 2(e)(1)(ii)—or at least its scope.[92]

Judge Randolph conceded that the Commission did regard negligence as a sufficient basis for a Rule 2(e) violation but would have vacated and remanded the order to give the SEC the opportunity to justify this aspect of its order.[93]

Judge Reynolds believed that the SEC concluded that the defendants were "*at least* negligent,"[94] but would have affirmed. "The SEC did not have to find scienter to invoke Rule 2(e)(1)(ii) in this case."[95]

On remand in 1997 the Commission concluded:

> We believe that Rule 2(e)(1)(ii) does not mandate a particular mental state and that negligent actions by a professional may, under certain circumstances, constitute improper professional conduct. Unlike Rule 2(e)(1)(iii), Rule 2(e)(1)(ii) does not require that the conduct be "willful." Nor do we believe that Respondents are correct that the overall structure of the securities laws mandates that scienter is an element of Rule 2(e)(1)(ii). Respondents observe that Section 10(b) of the Exchange Act requires scienter. However, other provisions of the securities laws that can involve accountants do not. The

---

[89] Sec. Ex. Act Rel. 25,893, 41 SEC Dock. 388 (1988); see also Goelzer & Wyderko, Rule 2(e): Securities and Exchange Commission Discipline of Professionals, 85 Nw. U. L. Rev. 652 (1991).

[90] Robert W. Emerson, Rule 2(e) Revisited: SEC Disciplining of Attorneys Since In re Carter, 29 Am. Bus. L.J. 155, 213 (1991); Ann Maxey, SEC Enforcement Actions Against Securities Lawyers: New Remedies vs. Old Policies, 22 Del. J. Corp. L. 537 (1997).

[91] 23 F.3d 452 (D.C. Cir. 1994).

[92] Id. at 459.

[93] Id. at 467.

[94] Id. at 494.

[95] Id.

Office of the Chief Accountant directs our attention to Section 11 of the Securities Act of 1933, which imposes civil liability on auditors in the absence of scienter. Moreover, other provisions of the Exchange Act that may impose liability based on audited financial reports filed with us, such as Sections 15(c)(3) and 13(a) similarly do not contain a scienter requirement.[96]

Commissioner Johnson dissented: "I think that this Commission's processes can be protected sufficiently by disciplining professionals under Rule 2(e)(1)(ii) only when it is demonstrated that they acted with scienter."[97]

The following year, the District of Columbia Circuit returned to the fray. In Checkosky v. SEC ("*Checkosky II*"),[98] the Court of Appeals expressed displeasure at the Commission's 1997 Opinion, stating that it again "failed to adequately explain its interpretation of [Rule 102(e)],"[99] "voicing instead a multiplicity of inconsistent interpretations."[100] The court then took the rare step of remanding the case with instructions to dismiss the proceeding.

The court took particular exception to the standard in the Commission's 1997 Opinion:

> We believe that Rule 2(e)(1)(ii) does not mandate a particular mental state and that negligent actions by a professional may, *under certain circumstances*, constitute improper professional conduct."[101] As the court explained: "Elementary administrative law norms of fair notice and reasoned decision making demand that the Commission define those circumstances with some degree of specificity. It has not done so.[102]

In 1998, the Commission amended Rule 102(e), again over a lengthy dissent by Commissioner Johnson. As amended Rule 102(e) adds a new paragraph (iv):

> (iv) With respect to persons licensed to practice as accountants, "improper professional conduct" under § 201.102(e)(1)(ii) means:
>
> (A) Intentional or knowing conduct, including reckless conduct, that results in a violation of applicable professional standards; or
>
> (B) Either of the following two types of negligent conduct:

---

[96] David J. Checkosky, AAER 871, 63 SEC Dock. 1691, 1700–1701 (1997).
[97] Id. at 1704.
[98] 139 F.3d 221 (D.C. Cir. 1998).
[99] 139 F.3d at 222.
[100] Id.
[101] Id. at 224.
[102] Id.

(1) A single instance of highly unreasonable conduct that results in a violation of applicable professional standards in circumstances in which an accountant knows, or should know, that heightened scrutiny is warranted.

(2) Repeated instances of unreasonable conduct, each resulting in a violation of applicable professional standards, that indicate a lack of competence to practice before the Commission.[103]

The Commission majority viewed this standard as responding to the *Checkosky II* criticism that it had not clearly articulated when an accountant would have engaged in "improper professional conduct."[104] Commissioner Johnson urged in dissent his view that the Commission lacked authority to promulgate Rule 102(e) and that in any event it lacks the authority to adopt a negligence standard under Rule 102(e).[105]

In 2002, § 602 of the Sarbanes-Oxley Act codified Rule 102(e), thus removing any question as to the Commission's ability to adopt the Rule or its culpability standard.

3. *The National Student Marketing Case.* Do the professional responsibilities of lawyers to their clients, and to others, differ from those normally applicable because they are advising their clients with respect to compliance with the federal securities laws? The *National Student Marketing* case involved the acquisition by National Student Marketing Corporation (NSMC) of Interstate National Corporation (INC) for stock of NSMC. The accountants refused to give a "comfort letter" at the closing as required by the merger agreement. Instead, they provided a letter detailing material misstatements in the interim financial statements of NSMC that had been furnished to the shareholders of INC when they voted on the merger. White & Case represented NSMC. Lord, Bissell & Brooks (LBB), an equally prestigious Chicago law firm, represented INC. The INC representatives present at the closing agreed to waive the requirement of a clean comfort letter from the accountants. They constituted a majority of the Board of Directors of INC and themselves held a majority of its stock (and would receive more than half of the stock being issued by NSMC in the merger transaction).

The SEC asserted that the lawyers violated Rule 10b–5 by their failure to put a stop to the closing of the transaction after receipt of the "noncomfort" letter—by refusing to give the opinions required of them at the closing. According to the SEC, the lawyers should have insisted upon a resolicitation of the shareholders of INC with corrected financial information regarding NSMC.

---

[103] Sec. Act Rel. 7593, 68 SEC Dock. 489 (1998) (adoption). Cf. Russell Ponce, AAER 1297, 73 SEC Dock. 358 (2000) (auditor knew or was reckless in not knowing about false statements).
[104] Sec. Act Rel. 7593, 68 SEC Dock. at 491–492.
[105] Id. at 510–516.

In SEC v. National Student Marketing Corp.,[106] Judge Parker of the federal district court held that LBB and its partners (White & Case in the meantime had settled with the SEC out of court) had been guilty of aiding and abetting a violation of Rule 10b–5. Judge Parker said:

> Upon receipt of the unsigned comfort letter, it became clear that the merger had been approved by the Interstate shareholders on the basis of materially misleading information. In view of the obvious materiality of the information, especially to attorneys learned in securities law, the attorneys' responsibilities to their corporate client required them to take steps to ensure that the information would be disclosed to the shareholders. However, it is unnecessary to determine the precise extent of their obligations here, since it is undisputed that they took no steps whatsoever to delay the closing pending disclosure to and resolicitation of the Interstate shareholders. But, at the very least, they were required to speak out at the closing concerning the obvious materiality of the information and the concomitant requirement that the merger not be closed until the adjustments were disclosed and approval of the merger was again obtained from the Interstate shareholders. Their silence was not only a breach of this duty to speak, but in addition lent the appearance of legitimacy to the closing, see Kerbs v. Fall River Industries, Inc., supra. [502 F.2d 731 (10th Cir. 1974)]. The combination of these factors clearly provided substantial assistance to the closing of the merger.
>
> Contrary to the attorney defendants' contention, imposition of such a duty will not require lawyers to go beyond their accepted role in securities transactions, nor will it compel them to "err on the side of conservation, . . . thereby inhibiting clients' business judgments and candid attorney-client communications." Courts will not lightly overrule an attorney's determination of materiality and the need for disclosure. However, where, as here, the significance of the information clearly removes any doubt concerning the materiality of the information, attorneys cannot rest on asserted "business judgments" as justification for their failure to make a legal decision pursuant to their fiduciary responsibilities to client shareholders.[107]

The judge, however, refused to issue an injunction against the lawyers because the Commission failed to demonstrate a likelihood that the lawyers were going to repeat the type of conduct of which they had been found guilty.

In a related case against a different lawyer, the District Court denied summary judgment to a lawyer who rendered an opinion to National

---

[106] 457 F.Supp. 682 (D.D.C. 1978).
[107] Id. at 713–714.

Student Marketing that permitted its accountants to record a transfer of a subsidiary in a certain fashion. The court also denied the SEC's motion for summary judgment.[108] The lawyer's opinion that "all of the risks and benefits of ownership"[109] of the subsidiary had passed to the purchaser as of the end of the fiscal year, permitted the elimination of the subsidiary's losses on the consolidated statements of National Student Marketing. The attorney knew that the transaction had actually been carried out after the end of the fiscal year and antedated, and that the transaction had no economic substance because the purchaser assumed no obligation to pay the purchase price.

In Barker v. Henderson, Franklin, Starnes & Holt,[110] the Seventh Circuit addressed the plaintiff's assertion that a law firm representing a charitable foundation (and an accounting firm working for the foundation) should have "blown the whistle" on the activities of the client:

> The extent to which lawyers and accountants should reveal their clients' wrongdoing—and to whom they should reveal—is a question of great moment. There are proposals to change the rules of legal ethics and the SEC's regulations governing accountants. The professions and the regulatory agencies will debate questions raised by cases such as this one for years to come. We express no opinion on whether the firms did what they should, whether there was malpractice under state law, or whether the rules of ethics (or other fiduciary doctrines) ought to require lawyers and accountants to blow the whistle in equivalent circumstances. We are satisfied, however, that an award of damages under the securities laws is not the way to blaze the trail toward improved ethical standards in the legal and accounting professions. Liability depends on an *existing* duty to disclose. The securities law therefore must lag behind changes in ethical and fiduciary standards. The plaintiffs have not pointed to any rule imposing on either Firm a duty to blow the whistle.[111]

This line of cases was called into doubt by the Supreme Court's holding in Central Bank of Denver v. First Interstate Bank of Denver, which held lawyers cannot be held liable for aiding and abetting violations of Rule 10b–5 actions.[112] *Central Bank* was extended in Stoneridge Investment Partners v. Scientific-Atlanta, which held that secondary actors, like lawyers and accountants, are liable under Rule 10b–5 only if their conduct independently violates the securities laws.[113]

---

[108] SEC v. National Student Marketing Corp., 402 F.Supp. 641 (D.D.C. 1975).
[109] Id. at 645.
[110] 797 F.2d 490 (7th Cir. 1986).
[111] Id. at 497.
[112] 511 U.S. 164 (1994).
[113] 552 U.S. 148 (2008).

In response, Congress amended § 20 of the Securities Exchange Act to permit the Commission to bring enforcement actions against "any person that knowingly or recklessly provides substantial assistance to another person in violation of . . . any rule or regulation" of the securities laws. *Central Bank* and *Stoneridge* still foreclose private suits for aiding and abetting or scheme liability.

4. *Post Carter & Johnson 102(e) Proceedings.* After *Carter & Johnson,* the SEC refrained from bringing similar Rule 102(e) cases.[114] It pursues attorneys under other securities provisions.

In SEC v. Spectrum, Ltd.,[115] the Second Circuit held an attorney liable in an injunction action by the Commission for the negligent issuance of legal opinions permitting the distribution of unregistered securities in violation of the 1933 Act. The court said: "In assessing liability as an aider and abettor, however, the district judge formulated a requisite standard of culpability—actual knowledge of the improper scheme plus an intent to further that scheme—which we find to be a sharp and unjustified departure from the negligence standard which we have repeatedly held to be sufficient in the context of enforcement proceedings seeking equitable or prophylactic relief."[116] The Supreme Court in the *Aaron* case[117] apparently confirmed the actual results of these cases, although that decision will require the Commission to proceed under § 17(a) of the 1933 Act rather than Rule 10b–5.

In a 1981 Securities Exchange Act Release,[118] the Commission criticized an attorney for an underwriter in connection with an exempt offering of industrial revenue bonds for failing to make any investigation of the issuer or to protest the failure to include in the offering circular any financial statements regarding the past operations of the issuer. The attorney's opinion for the transaction went to the questions of exemptions from the 1933 Act and the Trust Indenture Act of 1939. The Commission stated, however, that "although the opinion letter states that the signator has not independently checked or verified most of the material statements in the offering circular, Mr. Gotten [the underwriter's counsel], who knew that the issuer was a going concern that had been in operation for a number of years, signed and issued the opinion letter

---

[114] SEC Rule 102(e) proceedings have recently experienced somewhat of a revival. See e.g., In the Matter of Steven Altman, Esq., SEC Release No. 34–63306 (Nov. 10, 2010) (permanent bar issued against attorney who proposed "quid pro quo"); In the Matter of Jay Lapine, Esq. Respondent., SEC Release No. 34–62238 (June 8, 2010) (after consenting to an injunction, attorney suspended (with option to seek reinstatement after five years) based on participation in fraudulent scheme); In the Matter of J. Bennett Grocock, Esq. Respondent, SEC Release No. 34–61511 (Feb. 8, 2010); In the Matter of Joseph I. Emas Respondent, SEC Release No. 34–61386 (Jan. 20, 2010); In the Matter of Rex R. Rogers, Respondent, Release No. 34–59297 (Jan. 26, 2009) (two-year suspension of former Enron associate general counsel); In re Bua, Release No. 34–58919 (Nov. 7, 2008).

[115] 489 F.2d 535 (2d Cir. 1973).

[116] Id. at 541.

[117] But see SEC v. Haswell, 654 F.2d 698 (10th Cir. 1981).

[118] Sec. Ex. Act Rel. 17,831, 22 SEC Dock. 1200 (1981).

without questioning the omission from the offering circular of financial statements concerning the issuer's prior operating history, reviewing any documents as to the financial status of the issuer, or making inquiry as to results of the operations of prior years. This inquiry was totally inadequate and facilitated the bond closing and the bond sales to the public."

The issuer's counsel functions as the "quarterback" in preparing the nonfinancial portions of a 1933 Act registration statement. For this reason, the Commission has repeatedly cautioned, "the task of enforcing the securities laws rests in overwhelming measure on the bar's shoulders."[119] If a Commissioner's statement in an address to a bar group that "a lawyer preparing a registration statement has an obligation to do more than simply act as the blind scrivener of the thoughts of his client" can be discounted as an able lawyer's rhetoric, it is not quite so easy to discount the further suggestion that "in securities matters (other than those where advocacy is clearly proper) the attorney will have to function in a manner more akin to that of the auditor than to that of the advocate."[120]

5. *The George C. Kern Case.* The question of how far this responsibility of a lawyer is "akin to an auditor" was again raised with considerable controversy in the *George C. Kern* case,[121] an administrative proceeding brought under § 15(c)(4) of the 1934 Act. Section 15(c)(4) was not in the original 1934 Act, but was added in 1964, chiefly to give the SEC an administrative remedy for late or tardy filings. Its scope was significantly expanded in 1984, and it currently reaches "any person subject to the provisions of Section 12, 13, or 14 or subsection (d) of Section 15" of the 1934 Act (which Sections cover the periodic reporting, proxy and tender offer rules) who "has failed to comply with any such provision, rule, or regulation in any material respect." The 1984 amendments also increased its importance by extending its reach to cover any person who "was a cause" of a violation of those Sections. As a result, it seemingly gives the SEC authority equivalent to an administrative injunction over not only the corporate issuer, but also its officers, directors, employees, and even its outside counsel, where such person "was a cause" of a violation.

In 1987, the Commission instituted a proceeding under § 15(c)(4) against George Kern, a director of Allied Stores Corporation and a prominent "mergers and acquisitions" attorney in New York City. Its

---

[119] Emanuel Fields, 45 SEC 262, 266 n.20 (1973).

[120] See generally Richard W. Painter & Jennifer E. Duggan, Lawyer Disclosure of Corporate Fraud: Establishing a Firm Foundation, 50 SMU L. Rev. 225 (1996); Donald C. Langevoort, The Epistemology of Corporate Securities Lawyering: Beliefs, Biases and Organizational Behavior, 63 Brook. L. Rev. 629 (1997); Edward Cohen, Lawyers Investing in Their Clients: The Rules of Professional Responsibility, 14 Insights No. 8 at 2 (2000); Michael S. Sackheim, Ethical Standards for New York Brokerage House Attorneys, 33 Rev. Sec. & Commodities Reg., 199 (2000).

[121] 50 SEC 596 (1991).

theory was that Kern caused Allied Stores to fail to comply with its reporting obligations under the Williams Act when it undertook defensive negotiations with a potential "white knight" in response to a hostile takeover bid from Campeau Corporation. Specifically, the SEC charged that Kern, as the lawyer principally responsible for Allied Stores' SEC filings, failed on repeated occasions, to amend its Schedule 14D-9 to reflect ongoing material negotiations by which Allied Stores was arranging to sell its real estate to a major developer in order to thwart Campeau.[122] In 1988, the Administrative Law Judge sustained the SEC's position on the merits,[123] but found that because Allied Stores no longer existed as a public company (Campeau had taken it over in a successful tender offer), there was no basis on which he could grant an order against Kern. In his view, it would be pointless to order Kern to cause future compliance by Allied Stores and no authority existed under § 15(c)(4) to grant generalized compliance orders with respect to Kern's conduct regarding other issuers. On its own motion, the Commission decided to review the *Kern* decision, but delayed three years until mid-1991 before releasing its decision. Essentially, the Commission (which had a very different composition in 1991 from the Commission that took the appeal in 1988) affirmed the ALJ's determination to discontinue the proceeding, and it vacated the opinion below, based on its decision that it lacked the power to issue general, forward looking compliance orders under § 15(c)(4).[124] This reversed prior Commission statements, but the Commission's retreat appeared to have been based on the new "cease and desist" powers that the Congress gave it in 1990 under the Remedies Act, which expressly authorized administrative orders against future violations of any provision, rule, or regulation.

6. *Sarbanes-Oxley § 307 and SEC Rule of Practice 205.* Section 307 of the Sarbanes-Oxley Act required that the SEC provide rules setting forth minimum standards of professional conduct for attorneys appearing and practicing before the Commission in any way in the representation of public companies.

SEC Rule of Practice 205 sets out various provisions designed to clarify that lawyers who represent issuers before the SEC are representing the entity and not individual officers or directors.[125] Under Rule 205.3(b)(1), lawyers have obligations to report material violations of

---

[122] Section 14(d)(4) of the 1934 Act requires that any solicitation or recommendation to holders of a security to accept or reject a tender offer be made in accordance with rules and regulations promulgated by the Commission. Rule 14d–9(b) requires the filing of a Schedule 14D-9 as soon as practicable after the solicitation or recommendation is sent or given to security holders. Rule 14d–9(c) then requires that an amendment be filed to the Schedule 14D-9 disclosing any material change "promptly." Thus, Kern was charged under § 15(c)(4) with failing to cause Allied Stores to file such a prompt amendment.

[123] See George C. Kern, Jr. (Allied Stores Corp.), 52 SEC Dock. 451 (Mar. 21, 1988) (Opinion by Chief Administrative Law Judge Blair), 1988–1989 Fed. Sec. L. Rep. (CCH) ¶ 84,342 (1988).

[124] George C. Kern, Jr., 50 SEC 596 (1991).

[125] Rule 205.3(a).

federal or state securities laws or breaches of fiduciary duties. They can report to the issuer's chief legal officer or to the chief legal officer and the chief executive officer. Once the matter is reported, the chief legal officer must investigate it. If she determines that a material violation occurred, she must ensure that the company responds appropriately. In addition, she must report back to the lawyer who raised the issue.[126] At this point in the process, the lawyer must determine whether the response was sufficient and reasonably timely. If it was not, the lawyer must report the matter to one of several bodies: the audit committee; another committee composed solely of independent directors; the full board; or, if the issuer has one, the "qualified legal compliance committee."[127] Qualified legal compliance committees were newly created entities and must have at least one audit committee member and at least two independent directors.[128]

In some circumstances, Rule 205.3(d) allows lawyers to report the matter, including confidential information, to the SEC, without issuer consent. First, the lawyer may disclose confidential information in order to "prevent the issuer from committing a material violation that is likely to cause substantial injury to the financial interest or property of the issuer or investors." Second, the lawyer may reveal the information to address the consequences of a previously occurring violation. Third, the lawyer may make such a disclosure to prevent issuer perjury in an SEC enforcement action or investigation or perpetuation of a fraud on the SEC.

SEC v. Fehn
United States Court of Appeals for the Ninth Circuit, 1996.
97 F.3d 1276, cert. denied, 522 U.S. 813 (1997).

■ Before: GOODWIN and HAWKINS, CIRCUIT JUDGES, and FITZGERALD, DISTRICT JUDGE.

■ MICHAEL DALY HAWKINS, CIRCUIT JUDGE:

* * *

California attorney H. Thomas Fehn appeals the district court's final judgment and permanent injunction order of April 1, 1994, which ordered Fehn to refrain from aiding and abetting violations of Section 10(b) and Section 15(d) of the Securities Exchange Act of 1934 and related regulations. Fehn advances three distinct challenges to the district court's injunction. He first contends that the Supreme Court's decision in Central Bank of Denver v. First Interstate Bank of Denver, 511 U.S. 164 (1994), which held that a private plaintiff may not maintain an action for aiding and abetting violations of Section 10(b) of the Securities Exchange

---

[126] Rule 205.3(b)(2).
[127] Rule 205.3(b)(3).
[128] Rule 205.3(c).

Act, should extend to SEC injunctive actions like the one that precipitated this case. Fehn argues, in the alternative, that even if *Central Bank* does not preclude the SEC's injunctive action against him, the district court erroneously concluded that he aided and abetted violations of Section 10(b) and Section 15(d) and related regulations. Finally, Fehn contends that the district court abused its discretion in entering a permanent injunction against him.

* * * We affirm the district court's permanent injunction order because we conclude that the court correctly found that Fehn had aided and abetted violations of Section 10(b) and Section 15(d) of the Securities Exchange Act and related regulations, and did not abuse its discretion in permanently enjoining him from future aiding and abetting violations.

FACTUAL AND PROCEDURAL BACKGROUND

I. The Initial Public Offering by CTI Technical, Inc.

CTI Technical, Inc. was incorporated in Nevada in January 1987 by its promoter, Las Vegas resident Edwin "Bud" Wheeler. Although Wheeler directed CTI's operations from the date of its incorporation, his status as company president and chief executive officer was not disclosed publicly until August 1988. In June 1987, seeking to raise capital to acquire other businesses, CTI conducted a $200,000 "blind pool" initial public offering of securities ("IPO").

The CTI offering was tainted by violations of state and federal securities laws. First, CTI violated state blue sky laws by failing to register its securities with the states in which those securities were sold. Second, although CTI filed a Form S-18 registration statement with the SEC, it violated the Securities Act of 1933 and SEC regulations by failing to disclose that Wheeler was the promoter of the company and controlled its nominal directors. Finally, Wheeler and Stoneridge Securities, Inc., underwriter for the IPO, attempted to defraud investors by manipulating the price of the securities in aftermarket trading.

II. The SEC Investigation of CTI's Initial Public Offering

In early 1988, the SEC launched a formal investigation of CTI's IPO. That investigation was to culminate in the SEC's September 1989 complaint against CTI and Wheeler. As a result of the SEC's action, the defendants consented to a permanent injunction against future securities laws violations, and Wheeler was convicted of securities fraud for misstatements and omissions in CTI's registration statement.

In connection with the SEC investigation, defendant-appellant Fehn was retained to represent CTI and Wheeler, as well as CTI's underwriter and various CTI officers and directors. Fehn is a California attorney who has specialized in securities law during nearly three decades of practice. He has represented clients in connection with the registration and offering of securities under the Securities Act of 1933, compliance with reporting and disclosure requirements under the Securities Exchange Act of 1934, and litigation of various securities matters. Prior to Fehn's retention in connection with the SEC investigation, Fehn's law firm had represented underwriter Stoneridge Securities during CTI's IPO.

During the SEC investigation of CTI and Wheeler, Fehn became aware that CTI was not in compliance with certain reporting requirements of the Securities Exchange Act of 1934. First, Fehn learned that after the IPO, CTI had failed to file Form 10-Q quarterly reports as required by Section 15(d) of the Securities Exchange Act and related regulations. Second, Wheeler's investigative testimony before the SEC revealed that the Food and Drug Administration had banned sales of a diet product known as "Accupatch," CTI's main product and the source of gross sales of $1 million a month, and had impounded CTI's existing inventory of the product. CTI's registration documents, however, failed to disclose these FDA actions.

Fehn advised Wheeler that CTI was required to file the quarterly Form 10-Q's, and that it must disclose, in particular, the FDA's restriction of its Accupatch product. He also discussed with Wheeler whether the Securities Exchange Act required disclosure, in the Form 10-Q's, of Wheeler's and CTI's apparent violations of the Securities Act of 1933 in connection with the IPO. Wheeler flatly refused to make such disclosures. Fehn later testified that he told Wheeler it was his professional opinion that such disclosures were unnecessary under the regulations, and furthermore could impair Wheeler's ability to assert his Fifth Amendment privilege against self-incrimination with respect to those earlier violations.

Because Wheeler wished to limit CTI's expenses, he had a non-lawyer employee of CTI—rather than Fehn—draft the Form 10-Q's. Fehn gave Wheeler a copy of Regulation S–K, which outlines disclosure requirements for Form 10-Q, an instruction booklet describing how to fill out a Form 10-Q, and a sample Form 10-Q. The employee prepared a draft of the Form 10-Q for the quarter ending March 31, 1988, which disclosed the FDA's ban on CTI's Accupatch product. However, the Form 10-Q mischaracterized Wheeler's true role in CTI, describing him as CTI's recently appointed CEO and president rather than the individual who in fact had promoted, incorporated, and controlled the company since its inception. The form also failed to disclose the potential civil liability stemming from Wheeler's and CTI's earlier violations of state and federal securities laws. Fehn reviewed and edited the draft of the Form 10-Q, incorporating financial statements he had obtained from CTI's accountant. Fehn maintains that he made no substantive changes to the document, and, in particular, did not delete from the report any information the SEC later contended was improperly omitted. Fehn's secretary mailed the final Form 10-Q to the SEC, where it was filed in August 1988.

Based on CTI's Form 10-Q for the quarter ending March 31, 1988, Fehn's law firm prepared and mailed two other Form 10-Q's, for the quarters ending December 31, 1987, and June 30, 1988, respectively.

These forms, too, mischaracterized Wheeler's relationship to CTI, and failed to mention contingent liabilities stemming from CTI's and Wheeler's earlier securities law violations. Fehn insists that his involvement in the preparation of these later Form 10-Q's was minimal, but the SEC points out that editing notations in Fehn's handwriting appeared on drafts of these Form 10-Q's. These Form 10-Q's were filed in November 1988.

III. The SEC Injunctive Action Against Fehn

In November 1992, the SEC filed a complaint against Fehn, alleging that in preparing and filing the three Form 10-Q's, Fehn had aided and abetted violations of Sections 10(b) and 15(d) of the Securities Exchange Act, 15 U.S.C. §§ 78j(b) and 78o(d), and violations of Rules 10b–5, 12b–20, and 15d–13, 17 C.F.R. §§ 240.10b–5, 240.12b–20, and 240.15d–13. Pursuant to Section 20(b) of the Securities Act of 1933, 15 U.S.C. § 77t(b), and Sections 21(d) and 21(e) of the Securities Exchange Act of 1934, 15 U.S.C. §§ 78u(d) and 78u(e), the SEC brought an action to permanently enjoin Fehn from future securities laws violations. The SEC alleged that CTI and Wheeler had violated Section 10(b) and Section 15(d) by preparing and filing Form 10-Q's that contained false accounts of Wheeler's role in the promotion, formation and management of CTI and his control over CTI stock and directors, and failed to disclose "material contingent liabilities" stemming from CTI's violations of state and federal securities laws in connection with its 1987 IPO. Additionally, the SEC alleged that Fehn had knowingly lent "substantial assist[ance]" to Wheeler and CTI in the preparation and filing of the faulty Form 10-Q's.

On April 1, 1994, following a bench trial, the district court entered final judgment against Fehn, based on its findings that Fehn had aided and abetted violations of Sections 10(b) and 15(d) of the Securities Exchange Act, the Act's antifraud and reporting provisions, respectively, along with Rules 10b–5, 12b–20, and 15d–13. Because it concluded that there was a reasonable likelihood of future violations on Fehn's part, the district court entered an order permanently enjoining Fehn from future aiding and abetting violations of the securities laws. Fehn timely appealed.

ANALYSIS

* * *

II. Whether the District Court Erred in Finding Fehn Liable for Aiding and Abetting Violations of Section 10(b) and Section 15(d) of the Securities Exchange Act and Related Regulations

* * *

A. The Elements of Aiding and Abetting Liability under Section 104 of the Private Securities Litigation Act of 1995

In authorizing the SEC to pursue injunctive actions for aiding and abetting violations of certain securities laws, Congress provided that

Section 104 governs the "[l]iability of controlling persons *and persons who aid and abet violations.*" Section 104 provides:

> (f) Prosecution of persons who aid and abet violations. For purposes of any action brought by the Commission under paragraph (1) or (3) of Section 78u(d) of this title, *any person that knowingly provides substantial assistance to another person in violation of a provision of this chapter, or of any rule or regulation issued under this chapter*, shall be deemed to be in violation of such provision to the same extent as the person to whom such assistance is provided. (emphasis added)

We note that Congress employed language identical to that used by lower federal courts in articulating the elements of aiding and abetting under Section 10(b) before *Central Bank* eliminated private causes of action for aiding and abetting. Before *Central Bank*, the elements of aiding and abetting under Section 10(b) were: (1) the existence of an independent primary violation; (2) actual knowledge by the alleged aider and abettor of the primary violation and of his or her own role in furthering it; and (3) "substantial assistance" by the defendant in the commission of the primary violation. Hauser, 14 F.3d at 1343. The new Section 104 defines aiding and abetting as follows: (1) the defendant acted "knowingly," (2) the defendant "provide[d] substantial assistance," and (3) that assistance was given "to another person in violation of a provision of this chapter, or of any rule or regulation issued under this chapter." The elements of the new Section 104 clearly mirror the elements this Court and others traditionally used to define aiding and abetting under Section 10(b). In our view, the symmetry between the elements of aiding and abetting *before Central Bank* and *after* Section 104 is a strong indication that Congress intended Section 104 to preserve the definition of aiding and abetting as it existed pre-*Central Bank*.

* * *

1. The Existence of a Primary Violation
a. Disclosure Requirements under Section 10(b) and Section 15(d)

* * *

Section 15(d) is a key reporting and disclosure provision of the Securities Exchange Act, 15 U.S.C. § 78*o*(d). It provides that issuers that have filed registration statements with the SEC shall

> file with the Commission, in accordance with such rules and regulations as the Commission may prescribe as necessary or appropriate in the public interest or for the protection of investors, *such supplementary and periodic information*, documents, and reports as may be required

by other provisions of the securities laws and SEC regulations. 15 U.S.C. § 78*o*(d) (emphasis added).

Rule 15d–13 implements Section 15(d)'s disclosure provision by requiring issuers to file quarterly 10-Q reports. Rule 12b–20 requires that, in addition to information explicitly required by other securities regulations,

> there shall be added such further material information, if any, as may be necessary to make the required statements, in the light of the circumstances under which they are made not misleading.

Rule 12b–20, 17 C.F.R. § 240.12b–20.

Fehn insists that the securities laws impose no duty to disclose, in a quarterly Form 10-Q, a failure to identify a company's promoter at the time of an initial public offering or the existence of prior securities law violations.

We disagree. Read against the backdrop of events in this case, these provisions required CTI and Wheeler to describe correctly Wheeler's role at CTI and to disclose the contingent liabilities stemming from earlier securities law violations.

* * *

2. Fehn's "Substantial Assistance" in the Primary Violation

The term "substantial assistance" has been interpreted to include "participation in the editing" of information for the purpose of marketing securities. Molecular Technology Corp. v. Valentine, 925 F.2d 910, 918 (6th Cir. 1991). Fehn admits that he reviewed the initial draft Form 10-Q prepared by Wheeler's non-lawyer employee, and admits that he personally altered that document. Although he claims to have had less involvement in the preparation of subsequent Form 10-Q's, these documents, too, reflect Fehn's editing notations, and were prepared by Fehn's law firm. Because Fehn had a hand in the editing the Form 10-Q's, and because he failed to properly advise Wheeler and CTI of the material omissions in the Form 10-Q's, instead submitting those forms to the SEC for filing, we conclude that Fehn lent the requisite "substantial assistance" to the primary violation of Section 10(b) and Section 15(d) of the Securities Exchange Act and related regulations.

Fehn urges us that he acted in good faith in rendering professional advice to CTI and Wheeler, and that this alleged good faith precludes a finding that he rendered "substantial assistance" in the primary violations of Sections 10(b) and 15(d). He relies on In re Carter and Johnson, 47 SEC 471 (Feb. 28, 1981), in which the SEC explained that "[s]o long as a lawyer is acting in good faith and exerting reasonable efforts to prevent violations of the law by his client, his professional obligations have been met." We reject Fehn's argument because we find that his efforts were not "reasonable" in light of the well-established disclosure requirements imposed by the aforementioned SEC regulations. Rules 10b–5 and 12b–20 clearly prohibited the misstatements and omissions contained in CTI's Form 10-Q's.

We observe, furthermore, that effective regulation of the issuance and trading of securities depends, fundamentally, on securities lawyers such as Fehn properly advising their clients of the disclosure requirements and other relevant provisions of the securities regulations. Securities regulation in this country is premised on open disclosure, and it is therefore incumbent upon practitioners like Fehn to be highly familiar with the disclosure requirements and to insist that their clients comply with them.

* * *

We express no opinion as to whether Fehn's representation of Wheeler and CTI in connection with the SEC investigation was "compatible" with counseling these same parties about compliance with SEC disclosure requirements. What *is* clear, however, is that the SEC disclosure requirements mandated disclosure of Wheeler's role as CTI's promoter and of the contingent liabilities stemming from CTI's and Wheeler's earlier securities law violations. In failing to make the Form 10-Q's comply with these disclosure requirements, Fehn "substantially assist[ed]" in the primary disclosure violations.

3. Fehn's Scienter in Aiding and Abetting the Primary Violation

The new Section 104, in authorizing SEC injunctive actions against aiders and abettors of the securities laws, makes clear that the requisite scienter for aiding and abetting liability is "knowingly." This requirement is in keeping with the traditional scienter necessary to give rise to aiding and abetting liability under Section 10(b). See Hauser, 14 F.3d at 1343 (requiring "actual knowledge" of the primary wrong and of the aider and abettor's "role in furthering [that violation]").

Fehn's knowledge of the primary violations was plainly established in this case. First, Fehn knew that the representations in CTI's registration statement with respect to Wheeler's role as promoter were inaccurate. In light of the information Fehn possessed when he undertook to review and edit the Form 10-Q's, Fehn must have known that the Form 10-Q's he helped to prepare perpetuated this inaccuracy and, furthermore, contained additional untrue statements about Wheeler's historical relationship with CTI. Second, Fehn knew there was material information about CTI that Wheeler did not wish to disclose in the quarterly Form 10-Q reports, since Wheeler informed Fehn in no uncertain terms of his refusal to disclose in the Form 10-Q's his potential liability for past securities law violations. The "knowledge" element was therefore clearly established in this case.

* * *

CONCLUSION

We affirm the district court's final judgment against Fehn and its order permanently enjoining Fehn from future aiding and abetting of violations of Sections 10(b) and 15(d) of the Securities Exchange Act of 1934 and related regulations.

Problem

PROBLEM 14-2

June Lui, an associate of the major Wall Street firm of Smith & Folk ["S & F"] has been asked by partner Richard B. Ito to research the proper response to a "client problem."

S & F's largest client, World Bank, has hired S & F to complete due diligence on a $1.2 billion debt underwriting to be filed on the SEC's abbreviated Form S-3.

Currently, interest rates are extremely favorable. World Bank would like Ito to complete his due diligence within three days.

Lui is concerned that World Bank has not produced Board of Directors Executive Committee Minutes for the previous year. She has repeatedly requested the Minutes and has repeatedly been informed, "They are in illegible handwritten form. There isn't time to type them up. There is nothing of significance in them."

Lui is aware of rumors that the Internal Revenue Service is conducting an investigation of World Bank, but has found no document to substantiate the rumors. World Bank's Chief Financial Officer has specifically denied such an IRS investigation.

(1) If Ito signs off on the World Bank underwriting without review of the Executive Committee Meeting Minutes, what risk is there of an S & F Rule 102(e) violation?

(2) Assuming that World Bank refuses to produce the Minutes, what can Ito do that would be consistent with both applicable ABA Model Rules of Professional Conduct and the federal securities laws?

(3) ACCOUNTANTS' INDEPENDENCE

a. SEC Actions

The SEC has long expressed strong views with respect to the independence of the outside certifying accountant.[129] To fortify the

---

[129] An accountant, as we have seen, can be liable under § 11 of the Securities Act of 1933; in an SEC aiding and abetting action; under Rule 102(e); or state common law. See generally 2 Louis Loss & Joel Seligman, Securities Regulation 751–766 (3d ed. rev. 1999), Douglas M. Schwab, George Greer & Scott Wiener, Claims between Auditors and Their Clients, in Accountants' Liability After Enron, 29 (PLI Corp. Law & Practice Course, Handbook Series no. 1309, 2002). Paul R. Brown, Jeanne A. Calderon & Baruch Lev, Administrative and Judicial Approaches to Auditor Independence, 30 Seton Hall L. Rev. 443 (2000); cf. Ross D. Fuerman, The Role of Auditor Culpability in Naming Auditor Defendants in United States Securities Class Actions, 10 Crit. Perspectives on Acct. 315 (1999) (nonculpable auditors were not routinely named defendants in securities class actions before the 1995 Act); Ross D. Fuerman, Auditors and the Post-Litigation Reform Act Environment, 14 Research Acct. Reg. 199 (2000) (auditors are named as defendants less frequently in federal securities class actions than in parallel proceedings).

independence of certified public accountants, the Commission in 1974 required that whenever the auditor for a registered company is dismissed or resigns, a report must be filed on Form 8-K of any "disagreements" between the auditor and the management of the company within the prior two years.[130]

In 1995, as part of the Private Securities Litigation Reform Act, § 10A was added to the Securities Exchange Act to authorize the Commission to modify or supplement generally accepted auditing standards to establish:

(1) procedures designed to provide reasonable assurance of detecting illegal acts that would have a direct and material effect on the determination of financial statement amounts;

(2) procedures designed to identify related party transactions that are material to the financial statements or otherwise require disclosure therein; and

(3) an evaluation of whether there is substantial doubt about the ability of the issuer to continue as a going concern during the ensuring fiscal year.[131]

If an independent public accountant detects or otherwise becomes aware of information indicating that an illegal act (whether or not material) has occurred or may occur, the accountant must inform the appropriate level of management of the issuer and assure that the audit committee or the board is adequately informed with respect to the illegal acts.[132] Failure by management to respond to a *material* illegal act will require the accountant to report its conclusions to the board,[133] or to resign or to furnish to the Commission a copy of its report.[134]

As adopted in 1997, Rule 10A–1(a) requires an issuer who receives a report requiring a notice to the Commission in accordance with § 10A(b)(3) to provide the notice to the Office of the Chief Accountant with the issuer having the option to provide either a summary of the report or a copy of the report itself. If a summary is provided, it must describe "the act that the independent accountant has identified as a likely illegal act and the possible effect of that act on all affected financial statements of the issuer or those related to the most current three-year period, whichever is shorter."[135] Separately, the independent accountant must provide the Office of the Chief Accountant with a copy of its report (or documentation of any oral report).[136]

---

[130] Sec. Act Rel. 5550, 5 SEC Dock. 799 (1974).
[131] Sec. Ex. Act § 10A(a).
[132] Sec. Ex. Act § 10A(b)(1).
[133] See Sec. Ex. Act § 10A(b)(2).
[134] Sec. Ex. Act § 10A(b)(3).
[135] Rule 10A–1(a)(2)(iii)(A).
[136] Rule 10A–1(b)(1). See also Edward Cohen, New Section 10A: Illegal Conduct Identified in an Audit, 14 Insights No. 3 at 2 (2000).

By the late 1990s, the extent to which management consulting and other services had become more significant to many outside auditor-corporate relationships, rather than auditing itself, emerged as the most significant SEC accounting issue.[137]

Estimated U.S. Revenues for Big 5/Big 6 Public Accounting Firms

	1999	1998	1997	1996	1995	1994	1993
Total	$30,616	$25,917	$20,492	$17,305	$15,051	$13,291	$12,162

Estimated Revenue Mix by Service Line

	1999	1998	1997	1996	1995	1994	1993
A&A	30%	30%	33%	36%	38%	44%	45%
Tax	19%	19%	20%	20%	20%	20%	22%
MCS	51%	51%	47%	44%	42%	36%	32%

In its 2000 proposed rule amendments concerning auditor independence, the Commission stated in part:

How Non-Audit Services Can Affect Auditor Independence.

The dramatic expansion of non-audit services may fundamentally alter the relationships between auditors and their audit clients in two principal ways. First, as auditing becomes an ever-smaller portion of a firm's business with its audit clients, auditors become increasingly vulnerable to economic pressures from audit clients. Second, certain non-audit services, by their very nature, raise independence issues. These concerns * * * have led us to consider whether our rules should limit—or even completely bar—an auditor's provision of non-audit services to audit clients.[138]

In November 2000, the Commission adopted a revision of Rule 2–01 of Regulation S–X, the auditor's independence requirements.[139] The Commission chose *not* to adopt a total ban on non-audit services and

---

[137] Cf. Address by Arthur Levitt, Reviewing the Covenant with Investors (N.Y.U. Center for Law and Bus. May 10, 2000):

In fact, today auditing no longer dominates the practices of the largest firms. It accounts for just 30 percent of total revenues—down from 70 percent in 1977. Consulting and other management advisory services now represent over half—up from 12 percent in 1977. Since 1993, auditing revenues have been growing by 9 percent per year on average—while consulting and similar services have been growing at a rate of 27 percent each year.

Id. at 3.

Later in 2000, the Commission proposed rule amendments concerning auditor independence. Sec. Ex. Act Rel. 42,994, 72 SEC Dock. 1901 (2000). Appendix B amplified the trend away from accounting and advisory services (A & A) towards management consulting and other services (MCS) for what are now the "Big 5" Public Accounting Firms.

[138] Sec. Ex. Act Rel. 42,994, 72 SEC. Dock. 1901, 1908 (2000).

[139] Sec. Ex. Act Rel. 43,602, 73 SEC Dock. 1885 (2000) (adoption).

instead identified certain non-audit services that render the auditor not independent of the client.[140]

A preliminary Note to Rule 2–01 of Regulation S–X explains:

Rule 2–01(b) sets forth the general standard of auditor independence. Paragraphs (c)(1) to (c)(5) reflect the application of the general standard to particular circumstances. The rule does not purport to, and the Commission could not, consider all circumstances that raise independence concerns, and these are subject to the general standard in paragraph 2–01(b). In considering this standard, the Commission looks in the first instance to whether a relationship or the provision of a service: (a) creates a mutual or conflicting interest between the accountant and the audit client; (b) places the accountant in the position of auditing his or her own work; (c) results in the accountant acting as management or an employee of the audit client; or (d) places the accountant in a position of being an advocate for the audit client.

The most significant addition was Rule 2–01(c)(4), which defines when an accountant will be independent with respect to non-audit services. Rule 2–01(c)(4) begins:

(4) Non-audit services. An accountant is not independent if, at any point during the audit and professional engagement period, the accountant provides the following non-audit services to an audit client.

The Rule then elaborates at length concerning (i) bookkeeping or other services relating to the audit client's accounting records or other financial statements; (ii) financial information systems design and implementation; (iii) appraisal or valuation services; (iv) actuarial services; (v) internal audit services; (vi) management functions; (vii) human resources; (viii) broker-dealer services; (ix) legal services; and (x) expert services unrelated to the audit.[141]

In the period following adoption of the revised Rule 2–01, the Commission brought high profile cases against Big Five accounting firms. For example, early in 2001 the Commission ruled in a Rule 102(e) proceeding that KPMG Peat Marwick could not be considered independent when it conducted an audit of a registrant while a loan from the accounting firm to an officer of the registrant was outstanding.[142] Then in Arthur Andersen LLP,[143] the Commission settled a Rule 102(e) action with a major accounting firm after the Commission found that the

---

[140] Id. at 1888–1889.

[141] Simultaneously, the Commission reinstated earlier proxy statement disclosure in Item 9(e) of Proxy Schedule 14A to require independent public accountants to disclose aggregate fees for audit and nonaudit services.

[142] KMPG Peat Marwick LLP, Sec. Ex. Act Release No. 43,862, 54 SEC 1135 (2001) (former Rule 2–01(b)).

[143] Sec. Ex. Act Release No. 43,862.

firm failed "to stand up to management in the face of improper accounting practices but instead issue[d] unqualified audit reports on financial statements that it [knew] or [was] reckless in not knowing [were] materially misstated."[144]

b. *The Sarbanes-Oxley Act*

In Congressional hearings preceding the Sarbanes-Oxley Act, particular attention was devoted to the wisdom of separating accounting firm audit services from consulting. One early result of Enron was an acceleration of this process by voluntary means in the Big Five accounting firms. Former SEC Chairman David Ruder thoughtfully explained:

> One of the substantial worries regarding the Andersen audit of Enron has been that Andersen not only audited Enron, but also was paid approximately the same amount for non-audit services. It has been reported that in the year 2000 Andersen was paid audit fees of approximately $25 million and non-audit fees of approximately $27 million. Comparisons of the amounts of audit fees to non-audit fees for a range of companies and auditors have revealed ratios of non-audit to audit fees ranging as high as nine to one. The expressed general concern is that an audit cannot be objective if the auditor is receiving substantial non-audit fees.
>
> The accounting profession seems to have recognized that management consulting services, which involve accounting firms in helping management make business decisions, should not be performed for an audit client. Three of the Big Five accounting firms (Andersen, Ernst & Young, and KPMG) have now separated their management consulting units from their audit units by contractual splits and spinoffs, and a fourth (PricewaterhouseCoopers) has announced its intention to split off its management consulting unit in a public offering. (Wall Street Journal, p3, January 31, 2002) The fifth firm should also do so, or at least refrain from offering management consulting services to audit clients.[145]

The Sarbanes-Oxley Act is quite prohibitive. Section 201 amends § 10A of the 1934 Act to provide:

> (g) *Prohibited Activities*. Except as provided in subsection (h), it shall be unlawful for a registered public accounting firm (and any associated person of that firm, to the extent determined appropriate by the Commission) that performs for any issuer

---

[144] Id. at 511.

[145] Senate Comm. On Banking, Housing & Urban Affairs, Hearing on "Accounting and Investor Protection Issues Raised in Enron and Other Public Companies," Feb. 12, 2002 (testimony of David S. Ruder), at 2, available at http://www.eastwestlaw.com/E_int/ShowArticle.asp?id=2.

any audit required by this title or the rules of the Commission under this title or, beginning 180 days after the date of commencement of the operations of the Public Company Accounting Oversight Board * * * to provide to that issuer, contemporaneously with the audit, any non-audit service, including—

> (1) bookkeeping or other services related to the accounting records or financial statements of the audit client;
>
> (2) financial information systems design and implementation;
>
> (3) appraisal or valuation services, fairness opinions, or contribution-in-kind reports;
>
> (4) actuarial services;
>
> (5) internal audit outsourcing services;
>
> (6) management functions or human resources;
>
> (7) broker or dealer, investment adviser, or investment banking services;
>
> (8) legal services and expert services unrelated to the audit; and
>
> (9) any other service that the Board determines, by regulation, is impermissible.
>
> (h) *Preapproval Required for Non-Audit Services.* A registered public accounting firm may engage in any non-audit service, including tax services, that is not described in any of paragraphs (1) through (9) of subsection (g) for an audit client, only if the activity is approved in advance by the audit committee of the issuer, in accordance with subsection (i) of this section.

Section 201(b) authorizes the Board to exempt any person, issuer, public accounting firm, or transaction from the prohibitions in § 10A(g) on a case by case basis.

Section 202 then adds a new § 10A(i) to create a preapproval requirement for audit committees both with respect to audit and non-audit services provided to the issuer by an auditor. Under the new § 10A(i)(B), preapproval is waived with respect to non-audit services that constitute not more than 5 percent of the total amount of revenues paid by the issuer to the auditor.

Section 206 further prohibits a public accounting firm from performing any audit service for an issuer if a senior officer of the issuer was employed by the auditor within the prior year.

The Sarbanes-Oxley Act does not prohibit auditors from providing non-audit services, but it limits such services to immaterial amounts.

Perhaps of greater significance is the fact that the Sarbanes-Oxley Act does not require the division of an accounting firm into an audit firm and a separate non-audit firm. It requires instead that for each audit client there is a prohibition of nine non-audit services and a preapproval requirement for other non-audit services. This means an audit firm can continue to provide non-audit services to other clients.

B. CORPORATE REGISTRANTS, OFFICERS, AND DIRECTORS

In recent years, the Commission has increasingly relied on the internal accounting controls required by § 13(b)(2) of the Securities Exchange Act and the corporate audit committee to ensure accurate corporate reporting.

In 1977, as part of the Foreign Corrupt Practices Act ("FCPA"), Congress enacted § 13(b)(2). That Section requires every corporation subject to § 12 or § 15(d) of the 1934 Act to:

(A) make and keep books, records, and accounts, which, in reasonable detail, accurately and fairly reflect the transactions and dispositions of the assets of the issuer;

(B) devise and maintain a system of internal accounting controls sufficient to provide reasonable assurances that

(i) transactions are executed in accordance with management's general or specific authorization;

(ii) transactions are recorded as necessary (I) to permit preparation of financial statements in conformity with generally accepted accounting principles or any other criteria applicable to such statements, and (II) to maintain accountability for assets;

(iii) access to assets is permitted only in accordance with management's general or specific authorization; and

(iv) the recorded accountability for assets is compared with the existing assets at reasonable intervals and appropriate action is taken with respect to any differences.

In 1988 Congress adopted the Foreign Corrupt Practices Act Amendments, which added §§ 13(b)(4)–(7).[146] These new sections limit criminal liability to persons who *knowingly* violate § 13(b)(2); discharge the liability of an issuer owning 50 percent or less of a subsidiary when the issuer makes a good faith effort to cause the subsidiary to comply with § 13(b)(2); and define the terms *reasonable assurances* and *reasonable detail* to mean "such level of detail and degree of assurance as would satisfy prudent officials in the conduct of their own affairs."[147]

---

[146] See H.R. Rep. No. 100–576, 100th Cong., 2d Sess. 916–917 (1988).

[147] See generally Symposium, A Review of the Foreign Corrupt Practices Act on Its Twentieth Anniversary: Its Application, Defense and International Aftermath, 18 Nw. J. Int'l L. & Bus. 269 (1998); Kathleen A. Lacey & Barbara Crutchfield George, Expansion of SEC Authority into Internal Corporate Governance: The Accounting Provisions of the Foreign Corrupt Practices Act (A Twentieth Anniversary Review), 7 J. Transnat'l L. & Pol'y 119 (1998);

The FCPA has become an increasingly powerful enforcement tool for both the SEC and the DOJ, and the penalties collected from violators are often substantial. The largest penalty collected to date under the FCPA was from Petroleo Brasileiro S.A. ("Petrobras"), Brazil's state energy company. The complaint against Petrobas alleged that Petrobas senior executives, many of whom served on the company's board, engaged in bid-rigging and bribery schemes. Specifically, they worked with the company's largest contractors and suppliers to inflate the cost of its infrastructure projects by billions of dollars resulting in an estimated $2.5 billion overstatement of assets. The companies receiving that money then paid billions in kickbacks to Petrobras executives, who in turn made corrupt payments to Brazilian politicians and political parties.[148]

SEC § 13(b)(2) proceedings are initiated against the corporate registrant or its officers and directors. In effect this creates a second set of individuals—in addition to the corporation's auditors—with responsibility for corporate books and records.

Consider the following case.

SEC v. World-Wide Coin Investments, Ltd.
United States District Court, N.D. Ga., 1983.
567 F.Supp. 724.

■ VINING, DISTRICT JUDGE:

This is a securities fraud action in which the Securities and Exchange Commission (SEC) seeks a permanent injunction against World-Wide Coin Investments, Ltd. (World-Wide) and the individual defendants as well as an order for a full accounting and disclosure of wrongfully received benefits. In an order entered March 29, 1983, this court directed the clerk to enter judgment for the SEC on all counts of the complaint and further directed defendants Hale and Seibert to (1) retain an independent auditor to perform a full accounting of World-Wide of all receipts and disbursements of cash and all purchases and sales and other acquisitions and dispositions of inventory and assets since July 1, 1979, and (2) return whatever shares of World-Wide stock they might hold to World-Wide. Finally, the court ordered World-Wide to make a full disclosure to its present shareholders with respect to all material information relating to its operations since July 1, 1979. The following memorandum opinion will constitute this court's findings of fact and conclusions of law as required by Fed. R. Civ. P. 52(a).

Kenneth B. Winer, Securities Firms and the Foreign Corrupt Practices Act, 33 Rev. Sec. & Commodities Reg. 61 (2000).

[148] Press Release, Petrobras Reaches Settlement with SEC for Misleading Investors, (Sept. 27, 2018), available at https://www.sec.gov/news/press-release/2018-215?utm_medium=email&utm_source=govdelivery.

Factual Background

World-Wide Coin Investments, Ltd., is a Delaware corporation with its principal offices in Atlanta, Georgia, and is engaged primarily in the wholesale and retail sale of rare coins, precious metals, gold and silver coins, bullion, and, until 1979, in the retail sale of camera equipment. Its operations also include the sale of Coca-Cola collector items and certain commemorative items. Its inventory of rare coins comes from its purchases of collections from estates and private individuals, purchases from dealers, purchases on domestic commodities exchanges, and purchases at coin shows. Sales are transacted at the Atlanta office and at many major coin shows held in the United States. For some time it published a trade journal, The Coin Wholesaler, which carried both news and feature stories of special interest to coin collectors and investors, who comprised the majority of subscribers. Until August 1979, through its subsidiary World-Wide Camera Fair, Inc., World-Wide operated retail stores in Augusta, Athens, Savannah, Columbus, Georgia, and Jacksonville, Florida, selling camera and photographic equipment. All five stores were sold during the first quarter of fiscal year 1980.

World-Wide's common stock is registered with the SEC pursuant to the Securities Exchange Act of 1934, 15 U.S.C. § 78l(b), and until late 1981 was listed on the Boston Stock Exchange. Prior to July 1979, the company's assets totaled over $2,000,000, and it had over 40 employees. In August 1981, the time of the filing of this lawsuit, the company's assets amounted to less than $500,000, and it had only three employees.

Defendant Joseph H. Hale took over the management and control of World-Wide on July 24, 1979, as the controlling shareholder, chairman of the board, chief executive officer, and president.

* * *

On November 5, 1979, Kanes, Benator, as World-Wide's independent auditor, warned Hale and World-Wide that a good and sound internal accounting control system was necessary to ensure the safeguarding of assets against losses from unauthorized use of dispositions and of financial records for preparing financial statements and maintaining accountability for assets. Although the company was notified of the importance of a good system of internal controls, this warning was ignored, and any control system that had existed at World-Wide ceased to exist. The problems that occurred at the company with respect to internal controls and accounting procedures can be divided into three areas: (1) inventory problems, (2) problems with separation of duties and the lack of documentation of transactions, and (3) problems with the books, records, and accounting procedures of the company.

(1) Inventory Problems

The safeguarding of World-Wide's physical inventory was one of its most severe problems; there was considerable testimony at trial to the effect that the company's vault, where most of the rare coins were kept, was unguarded and left open all day to all employees. Furthermore, no one employee was responsible for the issuance of coins from the vault, according to the accountants from May, Zima, who performed the 1980 audit. Scrap silver and bags of silver coins were left unattended in the hallways and in several cluttered, unlocked rooms at World-Wide's offices. During the trial, Hale admitted that he was worried about thefts due both to faulty record-keeping and the system of safeguarding the assets.

Hale also failed to initiate an adequate system of itemizing World-Wide's physical inventory. Rather than maintaining a perpetual inventory system, the company relied on a manual quarterly system, which, in light of the company's inadequate securities measures, was not effective in safeguarding the assets or in keeping an accurate account of the inventory. World-Wide's system made it relatively simple for an employee to improperly value and/or misappropriate large items of inventory undetected. Furthermore, employees were allowed to take large amounts of inventory off the premises of World-Wide for purposes of effecting a sale without giving a receipt.

An accurate valuation of World-Wide's inventory was never accomplished, and Clifford Haygood, the accountant from May, Zima who performed the field work for the 1980 audit, testified that a major reason for the disclaimed opinion in 1980 was the inability to determine the valuation of the cost inventory. Haygood also testified that he was unable to determine the cost of inventory, since World-Wide failed to have adequate purchase orders as documentation to determine the correct cost.[22]

Haygood, along with Robert Nofal, a coin expert hired by May, Zima to determine the value of World-Wide's coin inventory, inspected the offices of World-Wide for approximately 4-1/2 days beginning July 30, 1980. After Nofal's examination of the coins, Haygood concluded that the value of inventory by Hale required a substantial write-down of 10% of the value at which they were being carried on World-Wide's books. With respect to the $225,000 "appraisal" of the medallions involved in the 1979 stock swap, Haygood stated that no actual appraisal was ever done since the items were never actually physically inspected, which is necessary for an accurate appraisal.

Nofal testified that he could not determine how much was actually paid for the coins in World-Wide's inventory, since there were no backup documents and only a few coins were cost-coded.[23] Nofal further testified

---

[22] Under GAAP (generally accepted accounting principles), a company's inventory must be stated at the lower of cost price or market price. Since World-Wide had no records or purchase orders with respect to its inventory, Haygood was unable to determine the cost under either method.

[23] Cost-coding is a form of internal control device used in the coin business; coins are marked with a special code indicating their purchase price and date of purchase. Nofal testified that this type of device is an excellent control over theft problems, which are prevalent in a business with a large inventory such as coins.

that there was no organization of the inventory and that the vault was open without a guard when he came into the store.

(2) Separation of Duties

The lack of qualified personnel working in World-Wide's offices and the company's policy of allowing one individual to accomplish numerous transactions was another primary reason for May, Zima's disclaimed opinion, and was a major concern of Kanes, Benator in its letter of November 5, 1979. This court has previously noted the lack of supervision over the accounting department, managed by Patricia Allen, and her lack of expertise in the area. World-Wide maintains no separation of duties in the area of purchase and sales transactions, and valuation procedures for ending inventory. For instance, a single salesperson can do all the following tasks without supervision or review by another employer or officer: appraise a particular coin offered for purchase by a customer, purchase that coin with a check that the salesperson alone has drawn, count that same coin into inventory, value the coin for inventory purposes, and sell the coin to another purchaser.

Employees, none of whom was bonded, were also allowed to take large amounts of inventory off the company's premises for purposes of effecting a sale without giving a receipt, as well as being given cash to purchase the precious metals and coins at various locations, also without giving a receipt. Nor were employees required to write source documents relating to the purchase and sale of coins, bullion, and other inventory, making it impossible, as Haygood testified, to ascertain whether a particular inventory item had been sold at a profit or loss, or whether it had even been sold. Although pre-numbered invoices could have been used to help alleviate this problem, they were not; there was a complete lack of control over any retail countersales, and Haygood testified that he could not match cash coming in or out with the merchandise going out. The company apparently did have a daily report of cash coming in, but there was no record of items purchased or sold. Hale himself admitted that he told his employees to write down the sales of total bullion rather than writing receipts for individual coins.

Additionally, there were no procedures enforced with respect to writing checks; for instance, no system has been implemented to ensure that the purpose for which a check is written can be ascertained. Since employees have been allowed to write checks without noting the purpose of the transaction on the instrument or on any other document, source documents for most checks do not exist. All employees have had access to presigned checks, and there has been no dollar limit over which an employee cannot write a check. Furthermore, employees have not been required to get approval before writing a check. These policies have caused World-Wide to bounce over 100 checks since Hale took over the management of the company. Because of World-Wide's propensity for having their checks returned due to insufficient funds, the National Bank of Georgia, the company's transfer agent, requested World-Wide to close its account and take its business elsewhere.

Evidence introduced at trial further revealed that approximately $1.7 million worth of checks were written to Hale, his affiliates, or to cash, all without supporting documentation or any indication of the purpose of the checks. Hale testified that approximately $250,000 worth of these checks were repayments of loans he had personally made to the company, but he failed to introduce any executed promissory notes or any document to support that claim. The SEC also introduced various checks to and/or bills from local bars and restaurants written by Hale and reimbursed by either World-Wide or East Coast Coin. Numerous checks written to Hale on World-Wide's account were superimposed over purchase orders, supposedly as source documentation for the transactions.

(3) Books and Records

The lack of qualified accounting personnel not only created problems with World-Wide's inventory but also resulted in completely inaccurate and incomplete books and records. World-Wide, Hale, and Seibert have failed to make and keep books, records, and accounts which accurately and clearly reflect the transactions and dispositions of World-Wide's assets. As discussed previously, World-Wide employees have not been required to write purchase orders or any source document relating to the purchase and sale of coins and bullion, rendering it impossible to arrive at an accurate count or valuation of the inventory.

During his inspection of World-Wide's offices, Haygood stated that the records of operations for Hale's subsidiaries, such as World-Wide Camera Fair, were scattered throughout the office and were not in any order. Although Haygood was aware of the existence of World-Wide Camera Fair following a review of Kanes, Benator's work papers from 1979, he stated that he was unsure about the documentation and the sale of other companies such as World-Wide Rare Metals and Chattanooga Coin and Stamp. With respect to this latter subsidiary, Haygood was unable to identify it as a separate and existing corporation since it had been merged into World-Wide's balance sheet, making it impossible to differentiate between the good will of World-Wide and that of Chattanooga Coin and Stamp. Furthermore, this failure to consolidate the subsidiaries into the form and financial statements rendered the 10Q reports incorrect for fiscal year 1980.

Haygood also testified the company's books were chaotic with respect to the deferred revenue received from subscriptions to the company newspaper, The Coin Wholesaler. There were no accurate records setting out the dates of subscriptions; therefore, the amount of deferred revenue simply had to be estimated on the company's books.

During May, Zima's inspection at the premises, on July 31, 1980, Haygood and other representatives from May, Zima met with Jones and

Seibert to express their concern about the state of World-Wide's control procedures and accounting methods. Each item of concern was discussed in detail including questions from Seibert and Jones relative to the evaluation of the potential effects on the company and the continued trading of the common stock. May, Zima explained the position of Robert Nofal and offered to have a second opinion in order to confirm his initial evaluation that the grading policy and inventory values were significantly higher than was appropriate. Seibert and Jones acknowledged the problems noted and agreed that a totally separate inventory would be prepared by Nofal and later compared to the inventory prepared by the company's employee with appropriate reconciliation of differences in order to establish an acceptable, reasonable valuation of inventory. Robert Johnson, a partner at May, Zima, suggested that the company immediately obtain and consult with a securities attorney relative to the necessary action that should be taken as a result of the information May, Zima provided concerning its evaluation of the company's internal accounting control system and the effect on May, Zima's opinion. Johnson further indicated that there was a possible violation of the Foreign Corrupt Practices Act and that World-Wide should seek advice concerning that possibility. Johnson explained that the May, Zima would be willing to assist World-Wide through further discussions of these matters and/or offer suggestions to remedy the situations noted. Furthermore, Haygood offered to go to the Securities and Exchange Commission with the company to resolve their problems, but Seibert stated that he would rather take his chances and not contact the SEC in the hope that the SEC would not contact him.

World-Wide eventually agreed to retain the law firm of Jones, Bird & Howell and met with Frank Bird of that firm on August 18, 1980. At that meeting, there was a discussion of how World-Wide should communicate to the SEC. Bird agreed that the disclosure should be made immediately and that a Form 8K should be filed on the report received from the company's auditors advising it of a possible problem with the provisions of the Foreign Corrupt Practices Act, a possible disclaimer of opinion on the company's financial statements and the effects on the company's estimated net income resulting from the write-off of investments and subsidiaries. Seibert agreed to draft a Form 8K to disclose these items and to make a press release on the revised estimated income.

Following the initial meeting on July 31, 1980, May, Zima wrote a letter to World-Wide on August 21, 1980, detailing the weaknesses noted in its system of internal accounting controls. In this letter, May, Zima listed the following deficiencies: (1) a lack of supervision in the accounting department, (2) a lack of reliability in the bookkeeping department because of no supervision, (3) a lack of segregation of duties in the accounting department, emphasizing that the segregation of duties would allow for proper checks and balances in the company's accounting system, (4) a lack of control over retail counter sales in that there were no prenumbered invoices and the company could not match cash coming in with merchandise going out, (5) a lack of segregation of duties in the department of purchases and sales of coins, (6) the lack of determined value on some of the items of inventory such as the Coca-Cola memorabilia, (7) problems with "related-party" transactions (transactions between World-Wide and insiders or stockholders).

On October 22, 1980, May, Zima wrote a memorandum to the board of directors of World-Wide, setting forth certain recommendations of procedures which the accounting firm felt would improve and strengthen the company's present system. May, Zima suggested (1) a change in the company's system of cash received and disbursements, suggesting that a listing of mail receipts be prepared by the individual who opens the mail and compared to the bank deposit slip and amounts recorded in the cash receipts journal, (2) petty cash reimbursements should be drawn to the petty cash custodian and not to cash, (3) aging accounts receivable should be reviewed on a periodic basis by an appropriate official separate from the accounting department, (4) an improvement in the safeguarding of the assets of the company, and a provision for regular inspection of the assets, (5) routine procedures to be developed providing for prompt and adequate reporting to the accounting department of sales and/or disposals of property and equipment, (6) utilization of prenumbered inventory tags to facilitate accounting for, and control of, the inventory, (7) obtaining cancelled notes payable from creditors when paid, (8) the maintenance of personnel files for all employees and the rotation of the distribution of payroll checks among appropriate officials, (9) the bonding of employees who receive, disburse, or handle cash or who have access to assets and records, (10) full documentation of travel and entertainment expenses, and (11) a mathematical check for sales and vendor invoices.

Although notified of a possible violation of the Foreign Corrupt Practices Act and of severe problems in the company's internal controls system and accounting procedures, World-Wide did little, if anything, to change its methods of operation. Steve Watson, a staff accountant with the SEC, reviewed World-Wide's accounting records in September 1981 and concluded that there was still inadequate documentation to support purchases made and that the internal controls of the company were inadequate. Watson indicated at trial that the company currently issues receipts for cash sales and has started taking quarterly inventories but that the controls of the company are still inadequate since there are no controls over the inventory itself. He further stated that he was unable to determine the cost of inventory in accordance with generally accepted accounting principles.

* * *

APPLICATION OF LAW
I. FOREIGN CORRUPT PRACTICES ACT

The Foreign Corrupt Practices Act, 15 U.S.C. § 78m(b)(2) (Amend. 1977) ("FCPA") was enacted by Congress as an amendment to the 1934 Securities Exchange Act and was the legislative response to numerous questionable and illegal foreign payments by United States corporations in the 1970's. Although one of the major substantive provisions of the FCPA is to require corporate disclosure of assets as a deterrent to foreign bribes, the more significant addition of the FCPA is the accounting controls or "books and records" provision, which gives the SEC authority over the entire financial management and reporting requirements of publicly held United States corporations.

* * *

Section 13(b)(2) contains two separate requirements for issuers in complying with the FCPA's accounting provisions: (1) a company must keep accurate books and records reflecting the transactions and dispositions of the assets of the issuer, and (2) a company must maintain a reliable and adequate system of internal accounting controls. In applying these two separate requirements to the instant case, the court will examine the requirements of each provision and the problems inherent in their interpretation.

The "books and records" provision, contained in section 13(b)(2)(A) of the FCPA has three basic objectives: (1) books and records should reflect transactions in conformity with accepted methods of reporting economic events, (2) misrepresentation, concealment, falsification, circumvention, and other deliberate acts resulting in inaccurate financial books and records are unlawful, and (3) transactions should be properly reflected on books and records in such a manner as to permit the preparation of financial statements in conformity with GAAP and other criteria applicable to such statements.

Congress' use of the term "records" suggests that virtually any tangible embodiment of information made or kept by an issuer is within the scope of section 13(b)(2)(A) of the FCPA, such as tape recordings, computer print-outs, and similar representations. As indicated above, the purpose of this provision is to strengthen the accuracy of records and the reliability of audits.

* * * Congress did make it clear that:

> The term "accurately" in the bill does not mean exact precision as measured by some abstract principle. Rather, it means that an issuer's records should reflect transactions in conformity with accepted methods of recording economic events.

The only express congressional requirement for accuracy is the phrase "in reasonable detail." Although section 13(b)(2) expects management to see that the corporation's recordkeeping system is adequate and effectively implemented, how the issuer goes about this task is up to management; the FCPA provides no guidance, and this court cannot issue any kind of advisory opinion.

Just as the degree of error is not relevant to an issuer's responsibility for any inaccuracies, the motivations of those who erred are not relevant. * * * The concept that the books and records provision of the Act embodies a scienter requirement would be inconsistent with the language of section 13(b)(2)(A), which contains no words indicating that Congress intended to impose such a requirement. Furthermore, either inadvertent or intentional errors could cause the misapplication or unauthorized use of corporate assets that Congress seeks to prevent. Also, a scienter requirement is inappropriate because the difficulty of proving intent would render enforcement extremely difficult. As a practical matter, the standard of accuracy in records will vary with the nature of the transaction involved.

The second branch of the accounting provisions—the requirement that issuers maintain a system of internal accounting controls—appears in section 13(b)(2)(B). Like the recordkeeping provisions of the Act, the internal controls provision is not limited to material transactions or to those above a specific dollar amount.* * *

Internal accounting control is, generally speaking, only one aspect of a company's total control system; in order to maintain accountability for the disposition of its assets, a business must attempt to make it difficult for its assets to be misappropriated. The internal accounting controls element of a company's control system is that which is specifically designed to provide reasonable, cost-effective safeguards against the unauthorized use or disposition of company assets and reasonable assurances that financial records and accounts are sufficiently reliable for purposes of external reporting. "Internal accounting controls" must be distinguished from the accounting system typically found in a company. Accounting systems process transactions and recognize, calculate, classify, post, summarize, and report transactions. Internal controls safeguard assets and assure the reliability of financial records, one of their main jobs being to prevent and detect errors and irregularities that arise in the accounting systems of the company. Internal accounting controls are basic indicators of the reliability of the financial statements and the accounting system and records from which financial statements are prepared.

Among the factors that determine the internal accounting control environment of a company are its organizational structure, including the competence of personnel, the degree and manner of delegation and responsibility, the quality of internal budgets and financial reports, and the checks and balances that separate incompatible activities. The efficiency of the internal control system of a company cannot be evaluated without considering the company's organizational structure, the caliber of its employees, the strength of its audit committee, the effectiveness of its internal audit operation, and a host of other factors which, while not part of the internal control system itself, have an impact on the function of the system.

Although not specifically delineated in the Act itself, the following directives can be inferred from the internal controls provisions: (1) Every company should have reliable personnel, which may require that some be bonded, and all should be supervised. (2) Account functions should be segregated and procedures designed to prevent errors or irregularities. The major functions of recordkeeping, custodianship, authorization, and operation should be performed by different people to avoid the temptation for abuse of these incompatible functions. (3) Reasonable assurances should be maintained that transactions are executed as authorized. (4) Transactions should be properly recorded in the firm's accounting records to facilitate control, which would also require standardized procedures for making accounting entries. Exceptional entries should be investigated regularly. (5) Access to assets of the company should be limited to authorized personnel. (6) At reasonable intervals, there should be a comparison of the accounting records with the actual inventory of assets, which would usually involve the physical taking of inventory, the counting of cash, and the reconciliation of accounting records with the actual physical assets. Frequency of these comparisons will usually depend on the cost of the process and upon the materiality of the assets involved.

* * *

The definition of accounting controls does comprehend reasonable, but not absolute, assurances that the objectives expressed in it will be accomplished by the system. The concept of "reasonable assurances" contained in section 13(b)(2)(B) recognizes that the costs of internal controls should not exceed the benefits expected to be derived. It does not appear that either the SEC or Congress, which adopted the SEC's recommendations, intended that the statute should require that each affected issuer install a fail-safe accounting control system at all costs. It appears that Congress was fully cognizant of the cost-effective considerations which confront companies as they consider the institution of accounting controls and of the subjective elements which may lead reasonable individuals to arrive at different conclusions. Congress has demanded only that judgment be exercised in applying the standard of reasonableness. The size of the business, diversity of operations, degree of centralization of financial and operating management, amount of contact by top management with day-to-day operations, and numerous other circumstances are factors which management must consider in establishing and maintaining an internal accounting controls system. However, an issuer would probably not be successful in arguing a cost-benefit defense in circumstances where the management, despite warnings by its auditors or significant weaknesses of its accounting control system, had decided, after a cost benefit analysis, not to strengthen them, and then the internal accounting controls proved to be so inadequate that the company was virtually destroyed. It is also true that the internal accounting controls provisions contemplate the financial principle or proportionality—what is material to a small company is not necessarily material to a large company.

This court has already declined to adopt the defense offered by the defendants that the accounting controls provisions of the FCPA require a scienter requirement. The remainder of World-Wide's defense appears to be that such a small operation should not be required to maintain an elaborate and sophisticated internal control system, since the costs of implementing and maintaining it would financially destroy the company. It is true that a cost/benefit analysis is particularly relevant here, but it remains undisputed that it was the lack of any control over the inventory and inadequate accounting procedures that primarily contributed to World-Wide's demise. No organization, no matter how small, should ignore the provisions of the FCPA completely, as World-Wide did. Furthermore, common sense dictates the need for such internal controls and procedures in a business with an inventory as liquid as coins, medals, and bullion.

The evidence in this case reveals that World-Wide, aided and abetted by Hale and Seibert, violated the provisions of section 13(b)(2) of the FCPA. As set forth in the factual background portion of this order, the internal recordkeeping and accounting controls of World-Wide has been sheer chaos since Hale took over control of the company. For example, there has been no procedure implemented with respect to writing checks: employees have had access to presigned checks; source documents were not required to be prepared when a check was drawn; employees have not been required to obtain approval before writing a check; and, even when a check was drawn to "cash," supporting documentation was usually not prepared to explain the purpose for which the check was drawn. In addition to extremely lax security measures such as leaving the vault unguarded, there has been no separation of duties in the areas of purchase and sales transactions, and valuation procedures for ending inventory. Furthermore, no promissory notes or other supporting documentation has been prepared to evidence purported loans to World-Wide by Hale or by his affiliate companies.

Since Hale obtained control of World-Wide, employees have not been required to write source documents relating to the purchase and sale of coins, bullion, or other inventory. Because of this total lack of an audit trail with respect to these transactions and the disposition of World-Wide's assets, it has been virtually impossible to determine if an item has been sold at a profit or at a loss. Furthermore, there are more than $1,700,000 worth of checks drawn to Hale or to Hale's affiliates, or to cash, for which no adequate source documentation exists. Furthermore, Hale and Seibert knew that the medallions that were sold to World-Wide by Hale in 1979 were overvalued and unmarketable. Even so, they allowed the incorrect value of the medallions to be entered on the books of World-Wide. They also knew that the company's books and records were neither accurate nor complete. Pursuant to their directives, source documents were not prepared with respect to the transfer of funds; additionally, no audit trail was maintained for the acquisition and disposition of inventory. Furthermore, it appears that there were numerous false and misleading statements and omissions in the company's numerous reports to the SEC, many of which were filed late or not at all.

Individually, the acts of these defendants do not appear so egregious as to warrant the full panoply of relief requested by the SEC nor to impose complete liability under the FCPA. However, the court cannot ignore the all-pervasive effect of the combined failure to act, failure to keep accurate records, failure to maintain any type of inventory control, material omissions and misrepresentations, and other activities which caused World-Wide to decrease from a company of 40 employees and assets over $2,000,000 to a company of only three employees and assets of less than $500,000. It is evident that World-Wide, Hale, and Seibert violated all provisions contained in section 13(b)(2)(A) and (B) and the SEC's rules promulgated thereunder.

* * *

NOTES ON SARBANES-OXLEY AND DODD-FRANK

Much of the Sarbanes-Oxley Act addressed breakdowns in the system of corporate responsibility. As the fervor of Congress increased in late July 2002, the dimensions of the legislative response increased exponentially. Then, in the years prior to the passage of the Dodd Frank Act, the relationship (or lack thereof) between executive compensation and an issuer's financial performance attracted more attention. Title IX of the Dodd-Frank Act addresses these issues.

1. *Section 302.* Section 302 of the Sarbanes-Oxley Act requires each quarterly and annual report filed under § 13(a) or 15(d) of the 1934 Act to be certified by the principal executive officer or officers *and* the principal financial officer or officers. Each signing officer must certify that:

1. the signing officer has reviewed the report;
2. based on the officer's knowledge, the report does not contain any untrue statement of a material fact or omit to state a material fact necessary in order to make the statements made, in light of the circumstances under which such statements were made, not misleading;
3. based on such officer's knowledge, the financial statements, and other financial information included in the report, fairly present in all material respects the financial

condition and results of operations of the issuer as of, and for, the periods presented in the report;

4. the signing officers—
   A. are responsible for establishing and maintaining internal controls;
   B. have designed such internal controls to ensure that material information relating to the issuer and its consolidated subsidiaries is made known to such officers by others within those entities, particularly during the period in which the periodic reports are being prepared;
   C. have evaluated the effectiveness of the issuer's internal controls as of a date within 90 days prior to the report; and
   D. have presented in the report their conclusions about the effectiveness of their internal controls based on their evaluation as of that date;
5. the signing officers have disclosed to the issuer's auditors and the audit committee of the board of directors (or persons fulfilling the equivalent function)—
   A. all significant deficiencies in the design or operation of internal controls which could adversely affect the issuer's ability to record, process, summarize, and report financial data and have identified for the issuer's auditors any material weaknesses in internal controls; and
   B. any fraud, whether or not material, that involves management or other employees who have a significant role in the issuer's internal controls; and
6. the signing officers have indicated in the report whether or not there were significant changes in internal controls or in other factors that could significantly affect internal controls subsequent to the date of their evaluation, including any corrective actions with regard to significant deficiencies and material weaknesses.

2. *Section 303.* Section 303 created a new violation for any officer or director or any person acting under the direction of any officer or director who takes *any* action in contradiction of SEC rules "to fraudulently influence, coerce, manipulate, or mislead any independent public or certified accountant engaged in the performance of an audit of the financial statements of that issuer for the purpose of rendering such financial statements materially misleading." This is a far more defensible standard than § 302 because it directly precludes inappropriate behavior.

3. *Section 301.* In 1977, the Commission approved a rule change in the listing requirements of the New York Stock Exchange to require each domestic company with common stock listed on that exchange, "as a condition of initial and continued listing of its securities * * * to establish not later than June 30, 1978, and maintain thereafter, an audit committee composed solely of directors independent of management and free from any relationship that, in the opinion of the board of directors, would interfere with the exercise of independent judgment as a committee member."[149]

Section 301 of the Sarbanes-Oxley Act adds § 10A(m) of the 1934 Act and expressly directs that:

> The audit committee of each issuer, in its capacity as a committee of each issuer, in its capacity as a committee of the board of directors, shall be directly responsible for the appointment, compensation, and oversight of the work of any registered public accounting firm employed by that issuer (including resolution of disagreements between management and the auditor regarding financial reporting) for the purpose of preparing or issuing an audit report or related work, and each registered public accounting firm shall report directly to the audit committee.

The audit committee must be comprised entirely of independent directors and be authorized to engage independent counsel and other advisors.

The NYSE Corporate Accountability and Listing Standards Committee, "in the aftermath of the 'meltdown' of significant companies due to failures of diligence, ethics, and controls," recommended a broader set of corporate governance reforms to the NYSE Board of Directors which, in turn, adopted the recommendations, later adopted by the SEC.[150]

4. *Clawback of Executive Compensation.* One attempt by Congress to combat the disconnect between executive compensation and an issuer's financial performance has been to expand the power of the SEC to seek a "clawback" of executive compensation in the event of an earnings restatement.

Clawbacks were first authorized by § 304 of the Sarbanes-Oxley Act. This section requires that the chief executive and financial officers forfeit bonuses or other incentive-based compensation received during the 12 months following a financial disclosure that later requires an accounting restatement as a result of the issuer's misconduct.

Section 954 of the Dodd-Frank Act significantly expands this clawback authority. Section 954 directs national securities exchanges to

---

[149] Sec. Ex. Act Rel. 13,346, 11 SEC Dock. 1945 (1977).

[150] The NYSE Corporate Accountability and Listing Standards Committee (Aug. 1, 2002), available at https://www.iasplus.com/en/binary/resource/nysegovf.pdf.

prohibit the listing of any issuer that does not have adequate clawback policies. The issuer must have a policy providing for disclosure of incentive-based compensation and a policy for the recovery of incentive-based compensation from current or former executives in the event of accounting restatements caused by material problems with financial reporting.

Section 954 is independent from § 304 of Sarbanes-Oxley. Section 954, unlike § 304, affects all current and former executive officers of the issuer (rather than just an issuer's CEO or CFO) and applies to incentive-based compensation during the three years (rather than just the prior year) preceding the date on which the issuer is required to prepare an accounting restatement. Dodd-Frank also specifies that the compensation to be recovered is only that which would not have been earned had the financial statements been presented correctly. Finally, the standard under Dodd-Frank for recovery is "material noncompliance" of the issuer with any financial reporting requirements, as opposed to the "misconduct" standard in Sarbanes-Oxley.

These clawback provisions interact with another provision of Sarbanes-Oxley. Section 402 adds § 13(k) to the Exchange Act. It makes it unlawful for any issuer, "directly or indirectly . . . to extend or maintain credit . . . in the form of a personal loan to or for any director or executive officer . . . of that issuer." In effect, this provision bans deferred compensation to executives if it is delivered in the form of a loan. Loans could be a substitute for or complement to clawback provisions, since repayment can be made contingent on not violating the law or firm policies. For instance, a loan of $1 million could be forgiven after a period of time (say, five years after retirement) if there is no evidence that the borrower did anything wrong. This is just the flipside of paying the executive $1 million in cash, and then hoping to clawback the money in the event of wrongdoing. The effectiveness of calling loans (or canceling in-kind compensation, such as fringe benefits) versus clawing back compensation determines which is the more effective and efficient compensation strategy.[151]

5. *Additional Compensation Disclosure.* The Dodd-Frank Act also calls for the SEC to adopt rules requiring greater transparency on the part of issuers regarding executive compensation. Section 953 of the Act directs the SEC to adopt rules requiring additional disclosure about specific compensation matters, including the relationship between the compensation actually paid and the issuer's financial performance and the ratio between the CEO's annual compensation and the median annual compensation for all other company employees. Section 955 of the Act requires issuers to disclose whether directors and employees are

---

[151] For a discussion of these issues and a defense of corporate loans and in-kind compensation, see M. Todd Henderson & James C. Spindler, "Corporate Heroin: A Defense of Perks, Executive Loans, and Conspicuous Consumption," 93 GEORGETOWN L. JOURNAL 1885 (2005).

permitted to hedge any decrease in market value of the company's stock. On September 18, 2013, the Commission promulgated proposed rules to implement the pay ratio statutory requirement, over the dissent of two commissioners.[152] Although a pay ratio sounds relatively simple to produce and disclose, commenters argue that it is likely to be very costly for issuers, especially large issuers, to determine a ratio that is not misleading. Do you think shareholders care about pay ratios?

6. *Disclosure of Incentive-Based Compensation.* Section 956 of the Dodd-Frank Act requires a "covered financial institution" to disclose to its respective regulator the structure of the incentive-based compensation paid to executives to enable the regulator to prohibit excessive incentive-based compensation that could encourage inappropriate risk. The principal set of regulators (including the SEC) has proposed rules to implement this section.[153] The proposed rules would require financial institutions with $1 billion or more in assets to submit an annual report to their federal regulator describing the structure of their incentive compensation arrangements. In the case of larger financial institutions, generally those with $50 billion or more in assets, the rules require that they defer at least 50% of the incentive compensation of certain officers for at least three years and that the amounts ultimately paid reflect losses or other aspects of performance over time.

7. *Compensation Committee Independence.* Section 952 of the Dodd-Frank Act adds § 10C to the Exchange Act. Section 10C–1(b) requires that issuers ensure the independence of the members of their compensation committees as well as requires further disclosure about the role of, and potential conflicts involving, compensation consultants. Section 10C–1(a) requires that national securities exchanges must prohibit the "initial or continued listing of any equity security of an issuer" that is not in compliance with these independence requirements.[154]

C. BROKER-DEALERS

Broker-dealers play an important role in the securities industry. They help investors make significant financial decisions and act as intermediaries to connect investors to a range of investments. Sections 15(b)(4) and (6) of the Exchange Act give the SEC authority to impose sanctions against broker-dealers and their associated persons. The following case illustrates how, in addition to discipline for direct misconduct, a broker-dealer may also be subject to sanctions for failure

---

[152] Press Release, SEC Proposes Rules for Pay Ratio Disclosure (Sept. 18, 2013) http://www.sec.gov/News/PressRelease/Detail/PressRelease/1370539817895#.VLWBBSTY-6w.

[153] See Securities Exchange Act Release No. 34–641040 (Apr. 14, 2011).

[154] See §§ 240.10C–1(a)–(b).

to supervise their employees who commit violations of the securities laws.

In the Matter of John H. Gutfreund, et al.
51 SEC 93 (1992).

Order Instituting Proceedings Pursuant to Section 15(b) of the Securities Exchange Act of 1934, Making Findings, and Imposing Remedial Sanctions and Report of Investigation Pursuant to Section 21(a) of the Securities Exchange Act of 1934.

I.

The Commission deems it appropriate and in the public interest that public administrative proceedings be and they hereby are instituted against John H. Gutfreund, Thomas W. Strauss, and John W. Meriwether pursuant to Section 15(b) of the Securities Exchange Act of 1934 ("Exchange Act").

II.

In anticipation of the institution of these administrative proceedings, Gutfreund, Strauss, and Meriwether have each submitted Offers of Settlement which the Commission has determined to accept. Solely for the purposes of these proceedings and any other proceedings brought by or on behalf of the Commission or to which the Commission is a party, prior to a hearing pursuant to the Commission's Rules of Practice, and without admitting or denying the facts, findings, or conclusions herein, Gutfreund, Strauss, and Meriwether each consent to entry of the findings, and the imposition of the remedial sanctions, set forth below.

III.

The Commission also deems it appropriate and in the public interest that a report of investigation be issued pursuant to Section 21(a) of the Exchange Act with respect to the supervisory responsibilities of brokerage firm employees in certain circumstances. Donald M. Feuerstein consents to the issuance of this Report, without admitting or denying any of the statements contained herein.

IV.

On the basis of this Order and the Respondents' Offers of Settlement, the Commission finds the following:

A. FACTS

1. *Brokerage Firm Involved*

Salomon Brothers Inc. ("Salomon") is a Delaware corporation with its principal place of business in New York, New York. At all times relevant to this proceeding, Salomon was registered with the Commission as a broker-dealer pursuant to Section 15(b) of the Exchange Act.

Salomon has been a government-designated dealer in U.S. Treasury securities since 1939 and a primary dealer since 1961.

2. Respondents

John H. Gutfreund was the Chairman and Chief Executive Officer of Salomon from 1983 to August 18, 1991. He had worked at Salomon since 1953.

Thomas W. Strauss was the President of Salomon from 1986 to August 18, 1991. During that time period, Strauss reported to Gutfreund. He had worked at Salomon since 1963.

John W. Meriwether was a Vice Chairman of Salomon and in charge of all fixed income trading activities of the firm from 1988 to August 18, 1991. During that period, Meriwether reported to Strauss. During the same period, Paul W. Mozer, a managing director and the head of Salomon's Government Trading Desk, reported directly to Meriwether.

3. Other Individual

Donald M. Feuerstein was the chief legal officer of Salomon Inc. and the head of the Legal Department of Salomon until August 23, 1991. From 1987 until August 23, 1991, the head of Solomon's Compliance Department reported directly to Feuerstein.

4. Summary

In late April of 1991, three members of the senior management of Salomon—John Gutfreund, Thomas Strauss, and John Meriwether—were informed that Paul Mozer, the head of the firm's Government Trading Desk, had submitted a false bid in the amount of $3.15 billion in an auction of U.S. Treasury securities on February 21, 1991. The executives were also informed by Donald Feuerstein, the firm's chief legal officer, that the submission of the false bid appeared to be a criminal act and, although not legally required, should be reported to the government. Gutfreund and Strauss agreed to report the matter to the Federal Reserve Bank of New York. Mozer was told that his actions might threaten his future with the firm and would be reported to the government. However, for a period of months, none of the executives took action to investigate the matter or to discipline or impose limitations on Mozer. The information was also not reported to the government for a period of months. During that same period, Mozer committed additional violations of the federal securities laws in connection with two subsequent auctions of U.S. Treasury securities.

The Respondents in this proceeding are not being charged with any participation in the underlying violations. However, as set forth herein, the Commission believes that the Respondents' supervision was deficient and that this failure was compounded by the delay in reporting the matter to the government.

* * *

8. Mozer's Disclosure to John Meriwether of the Submission of One False Bid

[On April 24, 1991, Mozer] went to the office of John Meriwether, his immediate supervisor, * * * [and informed him of the first false bid in the name of Mercury Asset Management (Mercury)]. * * * After expressing shock at Mozer's conduct, Meriwether told him that his behavior was career-threatening, and he asked Mozer why he had submitted the bid. Mozer told Meriwether that the Government Trading Desk had needed a substantial amount of the notes, that there was also demand from the Government Arbitrage Desk for the notes, and that he had submitted the false bid to satisfy those demands.

Meriwether then asked Mozer if he had ever engaged in that type of conduct before or since. Mozer responded that he had not. Meriwether told Mozer that he would have to take the matter immediately to Thomas Strauss. Mozer then told Meriwether of his conversation with the Mercury Senior Director in which he had told that individual that the bid was an "error" and had asked him to keep the matter confidential. Meriwether listened to Mozer's description of the conversation, but did not respond.

* * *

9. Discussions Among Senior Management

Meriwether then called Thomas Strauss. Strauss was not in, but he returned Meriwether's call later that day. Meriwether told Strauss that Mozer had informed him that he had submitted an unauthorized customer bid in an auction of U.S. Treasury securities. Strauss indicated that they should meet to discuss the matter first thing the next morning.

Meriwether met with Strauss at 9:15 a.m. the following morning, April 25, in Strauss' office. Prior to the meeting, Strauss had arranged for Donald Feuerstein, the firm's chief legal officer, to attend, and Feuerstein was in Strauss' office when Meriwether arrived. Meriwether began the meeting by describing his conversation with Mozer the previous day. He told Strauss and Feuerstein that Mozer had come to him and had informed him that he had submitted an unauthorized customer bid in an auction of U.S. Treasury securities. He said that he had informed Mozer that his conduct was career-threatening and that Mozer had denied that he had ever before or since engaged in that type of conduct. He indicated that Mozer had received a letter from the Treasury Department inquiring about the bid and that Mozer had shown him a copy of that letter. Meriwether also reported that Mozer had said that he had submitted the bid to satisfy demand for the securities from the Government Trading Desk and from Salomon's Government Arbitrage Desk. Finally, he told Strauss and Feuerstein that Mozer had informed him that he had contacted an individual at Mercury Asset Management who had also received the letter from the Treasury Department. Meriwether indicated that Mozer had told that individual that the submission of the bid was an error, and had attempted to persuade him not to inform the government of that fact.

When Meriwether was finished, Feuerstein said that Mozer's conduct was a serious matter and should be reported to the government. Feuerstein asked to see a copy of the April 17 letter. Meriwether returned to the trading floor and retrieved the letter from Mozer. He then returned to Strauss' office and provided the letter to Feuerstein. After some discussion about the letter, Strauss said he wanted to discuss the matter with Gutfreund, who was then out of town, and the meeting ended.

A meeting was then held early the following week, on either Monday, April 29 or Tuesday, April 30, with Gutfreund. The meeting was attended by Meriwether, Feuerstein, Strauss and Gutfreund and was held in Strauss' office. Meriwether summarized his conversation with Mozer. Meriwether also indicated that he believed that the incident was an aberration and he expressed his hope that it would not end Mozer's career at Salomon.

After Meriwether's description, Feuerstein told the group that he believed that the submission of the false bid was a criminal act. He indicated that, while there probably was not a legal duty to report the false bid, he believed that they had no choice but to report the matter to the government. The group then discussed whether the bid should be reported to the Treasury Department or to the Federal Reserve Bank of New York. The hostile relationship that had developed between Mozer and the Treasury Department over the adoption of the 35% bidding limitation in the Summer of 1990 was noted, as was the role of the Federal Reserve Bank of New York as Salomon's regulator in the area of U.S. Treasury securities, and the group concluded that the preferable approach would be to report the matter to the Federal Reserve Bank of New York. The meeting then ended.

At the conclusion of the meeting, each of the four executives apparently believed that a decision had been made that Strauss or Gutfreund would report the false bid to the government, although each had a different understanding about how the report would be handled. Meriwether stated that he believed that Strauss would make an appointment to report the matter to Gerald Corrigan, the President of the Federal Reserve Bank of New York. Feuerstein stated that he believed that Gutfreund wanted to think further about how the bid should be reported. He then spoke with Gutfreund the next morning. Although the April 17 letter had been sent from the Treasury Department, Feuerstein told Gutfreund that he believed the report should be made to the Federal Reserve Bank of New York, which could then, if it wanted, pass the information on to the Treasury Department. Strauss stated that he believed that he and Gutfreund would report the matter in a personal visit with Corrigan, although he believed that Gutfreund wanted to think further about how the matter should be handled. Gutfreund stated that he believed that a decision had been made that he and Strauss, either separately or together, would speak to Corrigan about the matter.

Aside from the discussions referred to above regarding reporting the matter to the government, there was no discussion at either meeting in late April about investigating what Mozer had done, about disciplining him, or about placing limits on his activities. There was also no discussion about whether Mozer had acted alone or had been assisted by others on the Government Trading Desk, about whether false records had been created, about the involvement of the Government Arbitrage Desk, which Mozer had said had sought securities from the auction, or about what had happened with the securities obtained pursuant to the bid. Similarly, there was no discussion about whether Salomon had violated the 35% bidding limitation by also submitting a bid in its own name.

For almost three months, no action was taken to investigate Mozer's conduct in the February 21 auction. That conduct was investigated only after other events prompted an internal investigation by an outside law firm, as is discussed below. During the same period, no action was taken to discipline Mozer or to place appropriate limitations on his conduct. Mozer's employment by Salomon was terminated on August 9, 1991, after an internal investigation had discovered that he had been involved in additional improper conduct.

Each of the four executives who attended the meetings in late April placed the responsibility for investigating Mozer's conduct and placing limits on his activities on someone else. Meriwether stated that he believed that, once he had taken the matter of Mozer's conduct to Strauss and Strauss had brought Feuerstein and Gutfreund into the process, he had no further responsibility to take action with respect to the false bid unless instructed to do so by one of those individuals. Meriwether stated that he also believed that, though he had the authority to recommend that action be taken to discipline Mozer or limit his activities, he had no authority to take such action unilaterally. Strauss stated that he believed that Meriwether, who was Mozer's direct supervisor, and Feuerstein, who was responsible for the legal and compliance activities of the firm, would take whatever steps were necessary or required as a result of Mozer's disclosure. Feuerstein stated that he believed that, once a report to the government was made, the government would instruct Salomon about how to investigate the matter. Gutfreund stated that he believed that the other executives would take whatever steps were necessary to properly handle the matter. According to the executives, there was no discussion among them about any action that would be taken to investigate Mozer's conduct or to place limitations on his activities.

10. Violations After Disclosure by Mozer to Management

After Mozer's disclosure of one unauthorized bid on April 24, 1991, he submitted two subsequent unauthorized bids in auctions of U.S. Treasury securities.

* * *

12. The Internal Investigation

* * * [In July, 1991, Saloman received a call from its lawyers. The lawyers had been contacted about representing the government, but declined because of a prior relationship with Salomon. After the lawyers notified Salomon, Salomon retained them to do an internal investigation. The lawyers produced the results of their investigation to Feuerstein on August 6, 1991.]

* * *

On August 9, 1991, after consultation with and review by outside counsel, Salomon issued a press release stating that it had "uncovered irregularities and rule violations in connection with its submission of bids in certain auctions of Treasury securities." The release described several of the violations and stated that Salomon had suspended two managing directors on the Government Trading Desk and two other employees.

In telephone conversations on August 9, 1991 in which they reported on the results of the internal investigation, Gutfreund and Strauss disclosed to government officials for the first time that the firm had known of a false bid in a U.S. Treasury auction since late April of 1991. On August 14, 1991, Salomon issued a second press release which publicly disclosed for the first time that Gutfreund, Strauss and Meriwether had been "informed in late April by one of the suspended managing directors that a single unauthorized bid had been submitted in the February 1991 auction of five-year notes."

On Sunday, August 18, at a special meeting of the Board of Directors of Salomon Inc, Gutfreund and Strauss resigned their positions with Salomon and Salomon Inc, and Meriwether resigned his position with Salomon. On August 23, 1991, Feuerstein resigned his position as Chief Legal Officer of Salomon.

* * *

B. FINDINGS

1. Legal Principles

Section 15(b)(4)(E) of the Exchange Act authorizes the Commission to impose sanctions against a broker-dealer if the firm has:

> failed reasonably to supervise, with a view to preventing violations [of federal securities laws], another person who commits such a violation, if such person is subject to his supervision.

Section 15(b)(6) of the Exchange [Act] incorporates Section 15(b)(4)(E) by reference and authorizes the Commission to impose sanctions for deficient supervision on individuals associated with broker-dealers.

The principles which govern this proceeding are well-established by the Commission's cases involving failure to supervise. The Commission has long emphasized that the responsibility of broker-dealers to supervise their employees is a critical component of the federal regulatory scheme. As the Commission stated in *Wedbush Securities, Inc.*:

> In large organizations it is especially imperative that those in authority exercise particular vigilance when indications of irregularity reach their attention.

> The supervisory obligations imposed by the federal securities laws require a vigorous response even to indications of wrongdoing. Many of the Commission's cases involving a failure to supervise arise from situations where supervisors were aware only of "red flags" or "suggestions" of irregularity, rather than situations where, as here, supervisors were explicitly informed of an illegal act.

> Even where the knowledge of supervisors is limited to "red flags" or "suggestions" of irregularity, they cannot discharge their supervisory obligations simply by relying on the unverified representations of employees. Instead, as the Commission has repeatedly emphasized, "[t]here must be adequate follow-up and review when a firm's own procedures detect irregularities or unusual trading activity...." Moreover, if more than one supervisor is involved in considering the actions to be taken in response to possible misconduct, there must be a clear definition of the efforts to be taken and a clear assignment of those responsibilities to specific individuals within the firm.

2. The Failure to Supervise

As described above, in late April of 1991 three supervisors of Paul Mozer—John Meriwether, Thomas Strauss, and John Gutfreund—learned that Mozer had submitted a false bid in the amount of $3.15 billion in an auction of U.S. Treasury securities. Those supervisors learned that Mozer had said that the bid had been submitted to obtain additional securities for another trading area of the firm. They also learned that Mozer had contacted an employee of the customer whose name was used on the bid and falsely told that individual that the bid was an error. The supervisors also learned that the bid had been the subject of a letter from the Treasury Department to the customer and that Mozer had attempted to persuade the customer not to inform the Treasury Department that the bid had not been authorized. The supervisors were also informed by Salomon's chief legal officer that the submission of the false bid appeared to be a criminal act.

The information learned by the supervisors indicated that a high level employee of the firm with significant trading discretion had engaged in extremely serious misconduct. As the cases described above make clear, this information required, at a minimum, that the supervisors take action to investigate what had occurred and whether there had been other instances of unreported misconduct. While they could look to counsel for guidance, they had an affirmative obligation to undertake an appropriate inquiry. If they were unable to conduct the inquiry themselves or believed it was more appropriate that the inquiry be conducted by others, they were required to take prompt action to ensure that others in fact undertook those efforts. Such an inquiry could have been conducted by the legal or compliance departments of the firm, outside counsel, or others who had the ability to investigate the matter adequately. The supervisors were also required, pending the outcome of such an investigation, to increase supervision of Mozer and to place appropriate limitations on his activities.

The failure to recognize the need to take action to limit the activities of Mozer in light of his admitted misconduct is particularly troubling because Gutfreund and Strauss did place limitations on Mozer's conduct in connection with the June two-year U.S. Treasury note auction at a time when they thought the firm had not engaged in misconduct, but press reports had raised questions about the firm's activities. Although they had previously been informed that a serious violation had in fact been committed by Mozer, they failed for over three months to take any action to place limitations on his activities to deal with that misconduct.

The need to take prompt action was all the more critical in view of the fact that the potential unlawful conduct had taken place in the market for U.S. Treasury securities. The integrity of that market is of vital importance to the capital markets of the United States, as well as to capital markets worldwide, and Salomon occupied a privileged role as a government-designated primary dealer. The failure of the supervisors to take vigorous action to address known misconduct by the head of the firm's Government Trading Desk caused unnecessary risks to the integrity of this important market.

To discharge their obligations, the supervisors should at least have taken steps to ensure that someone within the firm questioned other employees on the Government Trading Desk, such as the desk's clerk or the other managing director on the Desk. Since the supervisors were informed that Mozer had said that he submitted the false bid to obtain additional securities for another trading desk of the firm, they should also have specifically investigated any involvement of that area of the firm in the matter. The supervisors should also have reviewed, or ensured that others reviewed, documentation concerning the February 21, 1991 auction. Such a review would have revealed, at a minimum, that a second false bid had been submitted in the auction and that false trade tickets and customer confirmations had been created in connection with both false bids. Those facts would have raised serious questions about the operations of the Government Trading Desk, and inquiries arising from those questions might well have led to discovery of the additional false bids described above. For instance, two of the other false bids, those submitted in the December 27, 1990 and February 7, 1991 auctions, involved the same pattern of fictitious sales to and from customer accounts and the suppression of customer confirmations used in connection with the February 21, 1991 auction. Inasmuch as Mozer had admitted to committing one apparently criminal act, the supervisors had reason to be skeptical of Mozer's assurances that he had not engaged in other misconduct.

Each of the three supervisors apparently believed that someone else would take the supervisory action necessary to respond to Mozer's misconduct. There was no discussion, however, among any of the supervisors about what action should be taken or about who would be responsible for taking action. Instead, each of the supervisors assumed that another would act. In situations where supervisors are aware of wrongdoing, it is imperative that they take prompt and unequivocal action to define the responsibilities of those who are to respond to the wrongdoing. The supervisors here failed to do that. As a result, although there may be varying degrees of responsibility, each of the supervisors bears some measure of responsibility for the collective failure of the group to take action.

After the disclosure of one unauthorized bid to Meriwether, Mozer committed additional violations in connection with the submission of two subsequent unauthorized customer bids. Had limits been placed on his activities after the one unauthorized bid was disclosed, these violations might have been prevented. While Mozer was told by Meriwether that his conduct was career-threatening and that it would be reported to senior management and to the government, these efforts were not a sufficient supervisory response under the circumstances. The supervisors were required to take action reasonably designed to prevent a repetition of the misconduct that had been disclosed to them. They could, for instance, have temporarily limited Mozer's activities so that he was not involved in the submission of customer bids pending an adequate review of what had occurred in the February 21, 1991 auction, or they could have instituted procedures to require verification of customer bids.

Under the circumstances of this case, the failure of the supervisors to take action to discipline Mozer or to limit his activities constituted a serious breach of their supervisory obligations. Gutfreund, Strauss and Meriwether thus each failed reasonably to supervise Mozer with a view to preventing violations of the federal securities laws.[20]

As Chairman and Chief Executive Officer of Salomon, Gutfreund bore ultimate responsibility for ensuring that a prompt and thorough inquiry was undertaken and that Mozer was appropriately disciplined. A chief executive officer has ultimate affirmative responsibility, upon learning of serious wrongdoing within the firm as to any segment of the securities market, to ensure that steps are taken to prevent further violations of the securities laws and to determine the scope of the

---

[20] Salomon did not have established procedures, or a system for applying those procedures, which together reasonably could have been expected to detect and prevent the violations. The affirmative defense provisions of Section 15(b)(4)(E) thus do not apply in this case.

wrongdoing. He failed to ensure that this was done. Gutfreund also undertook the responsibility to report the matter to the government, but failed to do so, although he was urged to make the report on several occasions by other senior executives of Salomon. The disclosure was made only after an internal investigation prompted by other events. Gutfreund's failure to report the matter earlier is of particular concern because of Salomon's role in the vitally-important U.S. Treasury securities market. The reporting of the matter to the government was also the only action under consideration within the firm to respond to Mozer's actions. The failure to make the report thus meant that the firm failed to take any action to respond to Mozer's misconduct.

Once improper conduct came to the attention of Gutfreund, he bore responsibility for ensuring that the firm responded in a way that recognized the seriousness and urgency of the situation. In our view, Gutfreund did not discharge that responsibility.

Strauss, as the President of Salomon, was the official within the firm to whom Meriwether first took the matter of Mozer's misconduct for appropriate action. As its president, moreover, Strauss was responsible for the operations of Salomon as a brokerage firm.[21] Though he arranged several meetings to discuss the matter, Strauss failed to direct that Meriwether, Feuerstein, or others within the firm take the steps necessary to respond to the matter. Even if Strauss assumed that Meriwether or Feuerstein had taken the responsibility to address the matter, he failed to follow-up and ascertain whether action had in fact been taken. Moreover, it subsequently became clear that no meaningful action was being taken to respond to Mozer's misconduct. Under these circumstances, Strauss retained his supervisory responsibilities as the president of the brokerage firm, and he failed to discharge those responsibilities.

Meriwether was Mozer's direct supervisor and the head of all fixed-income trading activities at Salomon. Meriwether had also been designated by the firm as the person responsible for supervising the firm's fixed-income trading activities, including the activities of the Government Trading Desk.

When he first learned of Mozer's misconduct, Meriwether promptly took the matter to senior executives within the firm. In so doing, he took appropriate and responsible action. However, Meriwether's responsibilities did not end with communication of the matter to more senior executives. He continued to bear direct supervisory responsibility for Mozer after he had reported the false bid to others within the firm. As

---

[21] As we noted in Universal Heritage Investments Corporation, 47 S.E.C. 839, 845 (1982):

The president of a corporate broker-dealer is responsible for compliance with all of the requirements imposed on his firm unless and until he reasonably delegates particular functions to another person in that firm, and neither knows nor has reason to know that such person's performance is deficient.

a result, until he was instructed not to carry out his responsibilities as Mozer's direct supervisor, Meriwether was required to take appropriate supervisory action. Meriwether's efforts in admonishing Mozer and telling him that his misconduct would be reported to the government were not sufficient under the circumstances to discharge his supervisory responsibilities.

C. DONALD M. FEUERSTEIN

Donald Feuerstein, Salomon's chief legal officer, was informed of the submission of the false bid by Paul Mozer in late April of 1991, at the same time other senior executives of Salomon learned of that act. Feuerstein was present at the meetings in late April at which the supervisors named as respondents in this proceeding discussed the matter. In his capacity as a legal adviser, Feuerstein did advise Strauss and Gutfreund that the submission of the bid was a criminal act and should be reported to the government, and he urged them on several occasions to proceed with disclosure when he learned that the report had not been made. However, Feuerstein did not direct that an inquiry be undertaken, and he did not recommend that appropriate procedures, reasonably designed to prevent and detect future misconduct, be instituted, or that other limitations be placed on Mozer's activities. Feuerstein also did not inform the Compliance Department, for which he was responsible as Salomon's chief legal officer, of the false bid.[22]

Unlike Gutfreund, Strauss and Meriwether, however, Feuerstein was not a direct supervisor of Mozer at the time he first learned of the false bid. Because we believe this is an appropriate opportunity to amplify our views on the supervisory responsibilities of legal and compliance officers in Feuerstein's position, we have not named him as a respondent in this proceeding.[23] Instead, we are issuing this report of investigation concerning the responsibilities imposed by Section 15(b)(4)(E) of the Exchange Act under the circumstances of this case.

Employees of brokerage firms who have legal or compliance responsibilities do not become "supervisors" for purposes of Sections 15(b)(4)(E) and 15(b)(6) solely because they occupy those positions. Rather, determining if a particular person is a "supervisor" depends on whether, under the facts and circumstances of a particular case, that person has a requisite degree of responsibility, ability or authority to affect the conduct of the employee whose behavior is at issue.[24] Thus,

---

[22] In late May or early June, Feuerstein did speak with the head of the Compliance Department about the need to develop compliance procedures with respect to the firm's activities in government securities.

[23] We note that Feuerstein has represented that he does not intend to be employed in the securities industry in the future.

[24] Although it did not represent an opinion of the Commission, the concurring opinion in Arthur James Huff, Exchange Act Release No. 29,017 (March 28, 1991), is consistent with this principle. The operative portion of that opinion, Part VI, explains that in each situation a person's actual responsibilities and authority, rather than, for example, his or her "line" or "non-line" status, will determine whether he or she is a "supervisor" for purposes of Sections 15(b)(4)(E) and (6).

persons occupying positions in the legal or compliance departments of broker-dealers have been found by the Commission to be "supervisors" for purposes of Sections 15(b)(4)(E) and 15(b)(6) under certain circumstances.

In this case, serious misconduct involving a senior official of a brokerage firm was brought to the attention of the firm's chief legal officer. That individual was informed of the misconduct by other members of senior management in order to obtain his advice and guidance, and to involve him as part of management's collective response to the problem. Moreover, in other instances of misconduct, that individual had directed the firm's response and had made recommendations concerning appropriate disciplinary action, and management had relied on him to perform those tasks.

Given the role and influence within the firm of a person in a position such as Feuerstein's and the factual circumstances of this case, such a person shares in the responsibility to take appropriate action to respond to the misconduct. Under those circumstances, we believe that such a person becomes a "supervisor" for purposes of Sections 15(b)(4)(E) and 15(b)(6). As a result, that person is responsible, along with the other supervisors, for taking reasonable and appropriate action. It is not sufficient for one in such a position to be a mere bystander to the events that occurred.

Once a person in Feuerstein's position becomes involved in formulating management's response to the problem, he or she is obligated to take affirmative steps to ensure that appropriate action is taken to address the misconduct. For example, such a person could direct or monitor an investigation of the conduct at issue, make appropriate recommendations for limiting the activities of the employee or for the institution of appropriate procedures, reasonably designed to prevent and detect future misconduct, and verify that his or her recommendations, or acceptable alternatives, are implemented. If such a person takes appropriate steps but management fails to act and that person knows or has reason to know of that failure, he or she should consider what additional steps are appropriate to address the matter. These steps may include disclosure of the matter to the entity's board of directors, resignation from the firm, or disclosure to regulatory authorities.[26]

These responsibilities cannot be avoided simply because the person did not previously have direct supervisory responsibility for any of the activities of the employee. Once such a person has supervisory obligations by virtue of the circumstances of a particular situation, he

---

[26] Of course, in the case of an attorney, the applicable Code of Professional Responsibility and the Canons of Ethics may bear upon what course of conduct that individual may properly pursue.

must either discharge those responsibilities or know that others are taking appropriate action.

V. ORDER

In view of the foregoing, the Commission deems it appropriate and in the public interest to impose the sanctions specified in the Offers of Settlement submitted by John H. Gutfreund, Thomas W. Strauss, and John W. Meriwether.

NOTES ON BROKER-DEALERS: DISCIPLINARY PROCEEDINGS

1. *Section 15(b)(4)*. Section 15(b)(4) of the 1934 Act empowers the SEC to censure, place limits on activities, functions, or operations, suspend for a period not exceeding 12 months, or revoke the registration on any of eight grounds. The grounds are: (A) misstatements in an application; (B) criminal convictions; (C) injunctions with respect to specified securities or commodities activities; (D) willful violations of the federal securities laws; (E) aiding and abetting or failure to supervise; (F) bars or suspension of an associated person; (G) violations of foreign financial regulations and statutes; and (H) bars or orders from state securities regulators. Section 15(b)(6) establishes a parallel enforcement mechanism allowing the SEC to directly discipline an associate of a broker-dealer firm.[155]

2. *Notable Cases*. The SEC has employed § 15(b)(4)(E) to inspire more rigorous compliance by broker-dealer firms.[156] The SEC, for example, employed § 15(b)(4)(E) against Prudential Securities for its failure to adequately supervise the sale of approximately $8 billion of limited partnership interests in more than 700 offerings between 1980 and 1990. The Commission alleged that Prudential "made material misstatements and omissions in the sale of limited partnership interests relating, among other things, to the nature, potential yields, safety, and purported liquidity of the investments."[157]

---

[155] See generally 6 Louis Loss & Joel Seligman, Securities Regulation 3028–3086 (3d ed. rev. 2002).

[156] See, e.g., Graham v. SEC, 222 F.3d 994 (D.C. Cir. 2000); Shearson Lehman Bros., Inc., 49 SEC 619 (1986) ("a system of supervisory procedures which rely solely on the branch manager is insufficient"); Dean Witter Reynolds, Inc., 49 SEC 956 (1988) ("a firm's failure to establish guidelines to ensure that its Compliance Department's directives are enforced is symptomatic of a failure to reasonably supervise").

[157] Prudential Sec. Inc., 51 SEC 726, 737 (1993); Litig. Rel. 13,840, 55 SEC Dock. 709 (1993). See also 55 SEC Dock. 624, 631 (1993).

Similar shortcomings were later found in PaineWebber's offer and sale of approximately $3 billion in limited partnership and direct investment interests between 1986 and 1992. PaineWebber Inc., Sec. Ex. Act Rel. 36,724, 61 SEC Dock. 121 (1996).

For another account of a breakdown in supervision, see Lynch, Report of Inquiry into False Trading Profits at Kidder Peabody & Co., Inc. 11 (Aug. 4, 1994) ("The principal shortcoming that contributed to the non-detection of Jett's false profits was the failure of Jett's immediate supervisors to understand the nature of his trading activity").

The most egregious failure-to-supervise cases have involved "rogue brokers." As the GAO reported: "Of the almost 470,000 active brokers listed in CRD as of November 30, 1993, about 10,000 had at least 1 formal disciplinary action against them for a variety of violations, including sales practice abuse violations and such criminal acts as driving while intoxicated, and 816 had 3 or more disciplinary actions."[158]

Other practices that have been the subject of recent SEC failure-to-supervise cases have been pre-announced, rather than surprise compliance examinations,[159] failure to adequately review new hires,[160] and failure to dismiss or institute heightened supervision of a registered representative when the supervisor learns that the representative has engaged in misconduct.[161]

3. *Supervisors.* In *Gutfreund*, the Commission emphasized the supervisor's responsibility. Often the supervisor will be a branch manager with responsibilities for several registered representatives in a specific office. The Commission has also focused on the quality of compliance procedures. If the Commission finds a violation, the broker-dealer may make restitution to the customer. The registered representative or supervisor may be subject to sanctions, including education, special supervision, censure, full disclosure to customers, or dismissal.

Problem

PROBLEM 14-3

Finance Franchises (FF) is a registered broker-dealer that has adopted a series of cutting-edge approaches to supervision. Virtually all of its registered representatives are independent contractors, rather than employees. Most operate in single person offices. Much supervision is done by computer programs that review daily trading records.

Pam Backman, Chief of Compliance, recently became concerned that John Caviness, an FF independent contractor, may have been excessively trading six specific accounts.

---

[158] GAO, Actions Needed to Better Protect Investors against Unscrupulous Brokers 3 (1994). See also Special Report, "Rogue Broker" Problem Raises Troubling Issues for Firms, Regulators, 26 Sec. Reg. & L. Rep. (BNA) 1207 (1994); Testimony of SEC Chairman Arthur Levitt Concerning the Large Firm Project, Subcomm. on Telecommunications & Fin., House Comm. on Energy & Commerce (Sept. 14, 1994), reprinted in 1994–1995 Fed. Sec. L. Rep. (CCH) ¶ 85,433 (1994). See also Joint Regulatory Sales Practice Sweep Report, 1995–1996 Fed. Sec. L. Rep. (CCH) ¶ 85,742 (1996); GAO, Responses to GAO and SEC Recommendations Related to Microcap Stock Fraud (GAO/GGD-98-204) (Sept. 1998).

Later, the Justice Department announced, in May 1997, that it had charged or convicted 17 rogue brokers in ten states. Justice Announces Prosecutions of 17 "Rogue" Brokers in 10 States, 29 Sec. Reg. & L. Rep. (BNA) 739 (1997).

[159] Royal Alliance Assoc., Inc., Sec. Ex. Act Rel. 38,174, 63 SEC Dock. 1606 (1997).
[160] Cf. Clarence Z. Wurts, Sec. Ex. Act Rel. 43,842, 74 SEC Dock. 281 (2001).
[161] Quest Capital Strategies, Inc., Sec. Ex. Act Rel. 44,935, 76 SEC Dock. 102 (2001).

Should she:

(1) Telephone Caviness and ask for an explanation?

(2) Plan an unscheduled examination of his office?

(3) Report the pattern of trading to Caviness's line supervisor?

(4) Report the trading pattern to Paul Gorgen, FF's chief executive officer?

(5) Review FF's compliance procedures?

(6) Seek to fire Caviness if he is found to have excessively traded?

NOTES ON BROKER-DEALERS: SRO REGULATION

The SEC and Self-Regulatory Organizations (SROs), mainly FINRA for registered broker-dealers that deal with the public, share responsibility for supervising the conduct of broker-dealers. Before a broker-dealer begins doing business, it must become a member of an SRO. SROs impose their own rules of conduct and disclosure obligations that broker-dealers must satisfy. There are generally three ways in which an SRO may adversely affect the interest of a particular person: imposing disciplinary sanctions on its members, or a person who is affiliated with a member; denying membership to an applicant; or requiring its members to cease doing business with a particular non-member or a particular security.

1. *Andrews v. Prudential Securities*.[162] The Andrews v. Prudential Securities case illustrates the importance of truthful disclosures when brokerage firms act in compliance with their obligations to SROs to ensure they do not become subject to potential defamation claims by former employees.

In *Andrews*, a brokerage firm amended the Form U-5, Uniform Termination Notice for Securities Industry Registration it had previously filed with the National Association of Securities Dealers (NASD, now FINRA) in response to customer complaints in connection with limited partnerships the brokers sold.[163] Under NASD bylaws, even though at the time of the filing the brokers were no longer working for the firm, the firm was required to file an amended Form U-5 if it believed that it had information that was required to be disclosed on the form.[164]

As a result of the amended Form U-5, the plaintiffs filed a complaint with the District Court alleging defamation because Prudential checked affirmatively section (2) of Item 13 on the amended Form U-5.[165] Item 13 of the Form U-5 requires a firm to make the following disclosure:

---

[162] Andrews v. Prudential Sec., 160 F.3d 304 (6th Cir. 1998).
[163] Id.
[164] Id. at 306.
[165] Id. at 308.

WHILE EMPLOYED BY OR ASSOCIATED WITH YOUR FIRM, WAS THE INDIVIDUAL:

. . . .

B. the subject of an investment-related, consumer-initiated complaint that:

(1) alleged compensatory damages of $10,000 or more, fraud, or wrongful taking of property?

(2) was settled or decided against the individual for $5,000 or more, or found fraud, or the wrongful taking of property?

The Sixth Circuit found that Prudential had been truthful in its disclosure on the U-5 form and held that the truth contained in the U-5 forms was a complete defense to the plaintiff's defamation claim.[166]

2. *Qualified Immunity.* Some have suggested that "rogue brokers" (really, registered representatives) are too easily employed by other broker-dealers because earlier broker-dealers are reluctant to candidly acknowledge the reason for a registered representative's departure in the joint SEC-State Form 4-5, Uniform Termination Notice for Securities Industry Registration.

In 1998 the NASD proposed qualified immunity in securities arbitration proceedings for statements made on Form U-5 and Form U-4, the Uniform Application for Securities Registration or Transfer.[167] The Commission did not adopt the proposal, in part, because of a belief that it was better addressed by the states. Others have proposed absolute immunity as an alternative approach.

Securities administrators or self-regulatory organizations generally are subject to absolute or qualified immunity for actions of their employees within the course of their official duties.[168]

No state has rejected immunity in this context by judicial decision, and a number of states have adopted qualified immunity by judicial decision.[169]

The Uniform Securities Act adopted a qualified immunity provision in the summer of 2002.[170] According to the National Conference of Commissioners on Uniform State Laws (NCCUSL), seventeen states and

---

[166] Id. at 309.

[167] Sec. Ex. Act Rel. 39,892, 66 SEC Dock. 2473 (1998).

[168] See 10 Louis Loss & Joel Seligman, Securities Regulation 4818–4821 (3d ed. rev. 1996).

[169] See, e.g., Eaton Vance Distrib., Inc. v. Ulrich, 692 So.2d 915 (Fla. Dist. Ct. App.1997); Baravati v. Josephthal, Lyon & Ross, Inc., 28 F.3d 704 (7th Cir. 1994) (Illinois); Andrews v. Prudential Sec., Inc., 160 F.3d 304 (6th Cir. 1998) (Michigan) (not addressing lower Court's holding that the statements were protected by qualified privilege); Prudential Sec., Inc. v. Dalton, 929 F.Supp. 1411 (N.D. Okla. 1996) (Oklahoma); Glennon v. Dean Witter Reynolds, Inc., 83 F.3d 132 (6th Cir. 1996) (Tennessee).

[170] Uniform Securities Act, § 507 (2002).

the U.S. Virgin Islands have adopted the Uniform Act in their securities statutes.[171]

An agent who has been the subject of a Form U-5, Uniform Termination Notice for Securities Industry Registration, may respond to specified adverse disclosures and have those responses included in the Form U-5.

D. INVESTMENT ADVISERS

As initially adopted, the Investment Advisers Act of 1940 was little more than a continuing census of the nation's investment advisers.[172] But it was substantially tightened by a series of amendments in 1960, 15 years after the Commission had first urged such action in a special report to Congress.[173] Congress again amended it in the Investment Company Amendments Act of 1970 and the Securities Acts Amendments of 1975.

The 1975 Amendments were designed to conform the registration and disciplinary procedures more closely to those concurrently prescribed for broker-dealers in the same legislation.

A more significant development occurred in 1996 when Title III of the National Securities Markets Improvement Act, separately titled The Investment Advisers Supervision Coordination Act, subjected with assets under management of $25 million or less (later raised to $30 million) to state regulation advisers.[174] Any adviser with assets under management of $30 million or more, or who is an investment adviser to an investment company registered under the Investment Company Act of 1940, will register solely under § 203 of the Investment Advisers Act and not state law. In essence, this new division of labor largely eliminated duplicative regulation of investment advisers.

The Investment Advisers Act is limited in two significant respects. First, unlike state securities statutes, only investment advisers, not investment adviser representatives, must register. Second, private rights of action are quite limited. In 1979 the Supreme Court held there could be no implied action for damages under § 206, the Investment Advisers Act's equivalent to Rule 10b–5.[175]

Each investment adviser who registers under the Investment Advisers Act after 2001 must electronically file Form ADV[176] through the

---

[171] Legislative Fact Sheet-Securities Act, available at http://www.nccusl.org/Legislative FactSheet.aspx?title=SecuritiesAct.

[172] See generally 7 Louis Loss & Joel Seligman, Securities Regulation ch. 8.C (3d ed. 1991).

[173] SEC, Protection of Clients' Securities and Funds in Custody of Investment Advisers (1945), summarized in Inv. Adv. Act Rel. 39 (1945).

[174] Rule 203A–1.

[175] Transamerica Mortgage Advisors, Inc. v. Lewis, 444 U.S. 11 (1979).

[176] See 7 Louis Loss & Joel Seligman, Securities Regulation 3332–3344 (3d ed. 1991).

Investment Adviser Registration Depository (IARD).[177] Under the Investment Adviser Act there are other substantive requirements addressing (1) recordkeeping;[178] (2) inspection;[179] (3) performance fees (i.e., a statutory prohibition on an investment adviser sharing capital gains);[180] (4) assignment of advisory compacts;[181] and (5) use of the title "investment counsel."[182]

This section examines the considerable litigation under the Act focused on the definition of investment adviser and on novel forms of advisory fraud. It concludes with a discussion of the significant changes in the Dodd-Frank Act, which impact the regulation of Investment Advisers.

(1) DEFINITION OF "INVESTMENT ADVISER"

Lowe v. SEC
Supreme Court of the United States, 1985.
472 U.S. 181, 105 S.Ct. 2557, 86 L.Ed.2d 130.

■ JUSTICE STEVENS delivered the opinion of the Court.

The question is whether petitioners may be permanently enjoined from publishing nonpersonalized investment advice and commentary in securities newsletters because they are not registered as investment advisers under § 203(c) of the Investment Advisers Act of 1940 (Act), 54 Stat. 850, 15 U.S.C. § 80b–3(c).

Christopher Lowe is the president and principal shareholder of Lowe Management Corporation. From 1974 until 1981, the corporation was registered as an investment adviser under the Act. During that period Lowe was convicted of misappropriating funds of an investment client, of engaging in business as an investment adviser without filing a registration application with New York's Department of Law, of tampering with evidence to cover up fraud of an investment client, and of stealing from a bank. Consequently, on May 11, 1981, the Securities and Exchange Commission (Commission), after a full hearing before an Administrative Law Judge, entered an order revoking the registration of the Lowe Management Corporation, and ordering Lowe not to associate thereafter with any investment adviser.

In fashioning its remedy, the Commission took into account the fact that petitioners "are now solely engaged in the business of publishing advisory publications." The Commission noted that unless the

---

[177] Inv. Adv. Act Rel. 1897, 73 SEC Dock. 595 (2000). Simultaneously IARD can be used to file Form ADV with appropriate states.

[178] See 7 Louis Loss & Joel Seligman, Securities Regulation 3376–3382 (3d ed. 1991).

[179] Id. at 3383–3384.

[180] Id. at 3385–3392. There are several exceptions that have been adopted, by rule or, in 1996, by statute.

[181] Id. at 3393–3395.

[182] Id. at 3396.

registration was revoked, petitioners would be "free to engage in all aspects of the advisory business" and that even their publishing activities afforded them "opportunities for dishonesty and self-dealing."

A little over a year later, the Commission commenced this action by filing a complaint in the United States District Court for the Eastern District of New York, alleging that Lowe, the Lowe Management Corporation, and two other corporations, were violating the Act, and that Lowe was violating the Commission's order. The principal charge in the complaint was that Lowe and the three corporations (petitioners) were publishing two investment newsletters and soliciting subscriptions for a stock-chart service. The complaint alleged that, through those publications, the petitioners were engaged in the business of advising others "as to the advisability of investing in, purchasing, or selling securities . . . and as a part of a regular business . . . issuing reports concerning securities." Because none of the petitioners was registered or exempt from registration under the Act, the use of the mails in connection with the advisory business allegedly violated § 203(a) of the Act. The Commission prayed for a permanent injunction restraining the further distribution of petitioners' investment advisory publications; for a permanent injunction enforcing compliance with the order of May 11, 1981; and for other relief.

Although three publications are involved in this litigation, only one need be described. A typical issue of the Lowe Investment and Financial Letter contained general commentary about the securities and bullion markets, reviews of market indicators and investment strategies, and specific recommendations for buying, selling, or holding stocks and bullion. The newsletter advertised a "telephone hotline" over which subscribers could call to get current information. The number of subscribers to the newsletter ranged from 3,000 to 19,000. It was advertised as a semimonthly publication, but only eight issues were published in the 15 months after the entry of the 1981 order.

Subscribers who testified at the trial criticized the lack of regularity of publication, but no adverse evidence concerning the quality of the publications was offered. There was no evidence that Lowe's criminal convictions were related to the publications; no evidence that Lowe had engaged in any trading activity in any securities that were the subject of advice or comment in the publications; and no contention that any of the information published in the advisory services had been false or materially misleading.

* * *

I

We granted certiorari to consider the important constitutional question whether an injunction against the publication and distribution of petitioners' newsletters is prohibited by the First Amendment. 469 U.S. 816 (1984). Petitioners contend that such an injunction strikes at the very foundation of the freedom of the press by subjecting it to license and censorship, see, e. g., Lovell v. City of Griffin, 303 U.S. 444, 451 (1938). In response the Commission argues that the history of abuses in the securities industry amply justified Congress' decision to require the registration of investment advisers, to regulate their professional activities, and, as an incident to such regulation, to prohibit unregistered and unqualified persons from engaging in that business. In reply, petitioners acknowledge that person-to-person communication in a commercial setting may be subjected to regulation that would be impermissible in a public forum, cf. Ohralik v. Ohio State Bar Assn., 436 U.S. 447, 455 (1978), but contend that the regulated class—investment advisers—may not be so broadly defined as to encompass the distribution of impersonal investment advice and commentary in a public market.

* * *

III

The basic definition of an "investment adviser" in the Act reads as follows:

> " 'Investment adviser' means any person who, for compensation, engages in the business of advising others, either directly or through publications or writings, as to the value of securities or as to the advisability of investing in, purchasing, or selling securities, or who, for compensation and as part of a regular business, issues or promulgates analyses or reports concerning securities. . . ."

Petitioners' newsletters are distributed "for compensation and as part of a regular business" and they contain "analyses or reports concerning securities." Thus, on its face, the basic definition applies to petitioners. The definition, however, is far from absolute. The Act excludes several categories of persons from its definition of an investment adviser, lists certain investment advisers who need not be registered, and also authorizes the Commission to exclude "such other person" as it may designate by rule or order.

One of the statutory exclusions is for "the publisher of any bona fide newspaper, news magazine or business or financial publication of general and regular circulation." Although neither the text of the Act nor its legislative history defines the precise scope of this exclusion, two points seem tolerably clear. Congress did not intend to exclude publications that are distributed by investment advisers as a normal part of the business of servicing their clients. The legislative history plainly demonstrates that Congress was primarily interested in regulating the business of rendering personalized investment advice, including publishing activities that are a normal incident thereto. On the other hand, Congress, plainly sensitive to First Amendment concerns, wanted to make clear that it did not seek to regulate the press through the licensing of nonpersonalized publishing activities.

Congress was undoubtedly aware of two major First Amendment cases that this Court decided before the enactment of the Act. The first, Near v. Minnesota ex rel. Olson, 283 U.S. 697 (1931), established that "liberty of the press, and of speech, is within the liberty safeguarded by the due process clause of the Fourteenth Amendment from invasion by state action." In *Near*, the Court emphatically stated that the "chief purpose" of the press guarantee was "to prevent previous restraints upon publication," and held that the Minnesota nuisance statute at issue in that case was unconstitutional because it authorized a prior restraint on publication.

Almost seven years later, the Court decided Lovell v. City of Griffin, 303 U.S. 444 (1938), a case that was expressly noted by the Commission during the Senate Subcommittee hearings. In striking down an ordinance prohibiting the distribution of literature within the city without a permit, the Court wrote:

> "We think that the ordinance is invalid on its face. Whatever the motive which induced its adoption, its character is such that it strikes at the very foundation of the freedom of the press by subjecting it to license and censorship. The struggle for the freedom of the press was primarily directed against the power of the licensor. It was against that power that John Milton directed his assault by his 'Appeal for the Liberty of Unlicensed Printing.' And the liberty of the press became initially a right to publish '*without* a license what formerly could be published only *with* one.' While this freedom from previous restraint upon publication cannot be regarded as exhausting the guaranty of liberty, the prevention of that restraint was a leading purpose in the adoption of the constitutional provision. . . .
>
> "The liberty of the press is not confined to newspapers and periodicals. It necessarily embraces pamphlets and leaflets. These indeed have been historic weapons in the defense of liberty, as the pamphlets of Thomas Paine and others in our own history abundantly attest. The press in its historic connotation comprehends every sort of publication which affords a vehicle of information and opinion. What we have had recent occasion to say with respect to the vital importance of protecting this essential liberty from every sort of infringement need not be repeated. Near v. Minnesota. . . ." Id., at 451–452 (emphasis in original) (footnote omitted).

The reasoning of *Lovell*, particularly since the case was cited in the legislative history, supports a broad reading of the exclusion for publishers.

The exclusion itself uses extremely broad language that encompasses any newspaper, business publication, or financial publication provided that two conditions are met. The publication must be "bona fide," and it must be "of regular and general circulation."

Neither of these conditions is defined, but the two qualifications precisely differentiate "hit and run tipsters" and "touts" from genuine publishers. Presumably a "bona fide" publication would be genuine in the sense that it would contain disinterested commentary and analysis as opposed to promotional material disseminated by a "tout." Moreover, publications with a "general and regular" circulation would not include "people who send out bulletins from time to time on the advisability of buying and selling stocks," see Hearings on H. R. 10065, at 87, or "hit and run tipsters." Ibid. Because the content of petitioners' newsletters was completely disinterested, and because they were offered to the general public on a regular schedule, they are described by the plain language of the exclusion.

* * *

The language of the exclusion, read literally, seems to describe petitioners' newsletters. Petitioners are "publishers of any bona fide newspaper, news magazine or business or financial publication." The only modifier that might arguably disqualify the newsletters are the words "bona fide." Notably, however, those words describe the publication rather than the character of the publisher; hence Lowe's unsavory history does not prevent his newsletters from being "bona fide." In light of the legislative history, this phrase translates best to "genuine"; petitioners' publications meet this definition: they are published by those engaged solely in the publishing business and are not personal communications masquerading in the clothing of newspapers, news magazines, or financial publications. Moreover, there is no suggestion that they contained any false or misleading information, or that they were designed to tout any security in which petitioners had an interest. Further, petitioners' publications are "of general and regular circulation." Although the publications have not been "regular" in the sense of consistent circulation, the publications have been "regular" in the sense important to the securities market: there is no indication that they have been timed to specific market activity, or to events affecting or having the ability to affect the securities industry.

The dangers of fraud, deception, or overreaching that motivated the enactment of the statute are present in personalized communications but are not replicated in publications that are advertised and sold in an open market. To the extent that the chart service contains factual information about past transactions and market trends, and the newsletters contain commentary on general market conditions, there can be no doubt about the protected character of the communications, a matter that concerned Congress when the exclusion was drafted. The content of the publications and the audience to which they are directed in this case reveal the specific limits of the exclusion. As long as the communications between petitioners and their subscribers remain entirely impersonal and do not develop into the kind of fiduciary, person-to-person relationships that were discussed at length in the legislative history of the Act and that are characteristic of investment adviser-client relationships, we believe the publications are, at least presumptively, within the exclusion and thus not subject to registration under the Act.

We therefore conclude that petitioners' publications fall within the statutory exclusion for bona fide publications and that none of the petitioners is an "investment adviser" as defined in the Act. It follows that neither their unregistered status, nor the Commission order barring Lowe from associating with an investment adviser, provides a justification for restraining the future publication of their newsletters. It also follows that we need not specifically address the constitutional question we granted certiorari to decide.

The judgment of the Court of Appeals is reversed.

It is so ordered.

NOTES ON WHO IS AN INVESTMENT ADVISER

The definition in § 202(a)(11) is broad enough to cover every person, who for compensation, gives advice with respect to securities. This reaches from the highest-grade investment counselor who renders personalized service to the publisher of the lowliest tipster sheet.[183]

A considerable gray area nevertheless survives the exclusions in § 202(a)(11) (A)–(F).

1. *Financial Planners.* In recent years both the SEC and state securities administrators have focused on financial planners. Financial planners provide advisory services as a component of other financially related services—for example, financial or pension consultants or sports or entertainment representatives, as distinct from the lawyers and brokers and others whose advisory services may also be incidental but are not specifically excluded by Clauses (B) and (C). The SEC staff wrote in a 1987 interpretative release:

> Financial planning typically involves providing a variety of services, principally advisory in nature, to individuals or families regarding the management of their financial resources based upon an analysis of individual client needs. Generally, financial planning services involve preparing a financial program for a client based on the client's financial circumstances and objectives. This information normally would cover present and anticipated assets and liabilities, including insurance, savings, investments, and anticipated retirement or other employee benefits. The program developed for the client usually includes general recommendations for a course of activity, or specific actions, to be taken by the client. For example, recommendations may be made that the client obtain

---

[183] See generally 7 Louis Loss & Joel Seligman, Securities Regulation 3344–3375 (3d ed. rev. 1991).

insurance or revise existing coverage, establish an individual retirement account, increase or decrease funds held in savings accounts, or invest funds in securities. A financial planner may develop tax or estate plans for clients or refer clients to an accountant or attorney for these services.

* * *

Whether a person providing financially related services of the type discussed in this release is an investment adviser within the meaning of the Advisers Act depends upon all the relevant facts and circumstances. As a general matter, if the activities of any person providing integrated advisory services satisfy the elements of the definition, the person would be an investment adviser within the meaning of the Advisers Act, unless entitled to rely on one of the exclusions from the definition of investment adviser in clauses (A) to (F) of Section 202(a)(11). A determination as to whether a person providing financial planning, pension consulting, or other integrated advisory services is an investment adviser will depend upon whether such person: (1) provides advice, or issues reports or analyses, regarding securities; (2) is in the business of providing such services; or (3) provides such services for compensation.[184]

2. *Brokers and Dealers.* Two related questions are presented under § 202(a)(11)(C): the meaning of "solely incidental" and what constitutes "special compensation."

The Commission views a broker or dealer whose business consists almost exclusively of managing discretionary accounts as an investment adviser.

With respect to the meaning of "special compensation," the Commission's General Counsel stated early:

> Clause (C) of Section 202(a)(11) amounts to a recognition that brokers and dealers commonly give a certain amount of advice to their customers in the course of their regular business, and that it would be inappropriate to bring them within the scope of the Investment Advisers Act merely because of this aspect of their business. On the other hand, that portion of clause (C) which refers to "special compensation" amounts to an equally clear recognition that a broker or dealer who is specially compensated for the rendition of advice should be considered an investment adviser and not be excluded from the purview of the Act merely because he is also engaged in effecting market transactions in securities. It is well known that many brokers and dealers have investment advisory departments which furnish investment advice for compensation in the same manner as does an investment adviser who operates solely in an

---

[184] Inv. Adv. Act Rel. 1092, 39 SEC Dock. 494, 495–496 (1987).

advisory capacity. The essential distinction to be borne in mind in considering borderline cases * * * is the distinction between compensation for advice itself and compensation for services of another character to which advice is merely incidental.[185]

This approach applies equally in principle to dealers as well as brokers. Because dealers, however, historically did not ordinarily disclose their profits or spreads, determining whether the profit or spread in a particular case was greater because of the amount of incidental investment advice rendered was difficult. Similar problems have resulted from the "unbundling" of rates and the discounting that followed the abolition of fixed stock exchange commissions in 1975. It would be fatal, not surprisingly, for a firm to make two general fee schedules available whose difference is attributable primarily to the presence or absence of investment advice. But the staff does not consider that there is "special compensation" merely because a "full service" firm, for example, charges higher rates than a "discount" firm, or a firm negotiates different fees with different clients for similar transactions.[186]

3. *Professional Persons.* A lawyer, accountant, engineer, or teacher of any kind can be an investment adviser if the advice rendered is not solely incidental to the practice of the profession.[187] Much of what will be said with reference to the exclusion of certain brokers and dealers by Clause (C) is equally applicable here. Arguably, however, it is not essential that every advisory client of the lawyer be a legal client if the lawyer does not hold himself or herself out to the public as an investment adviser and is first and foremost a lawyer whose advisory services are "solely incidental" to his or her law practice.

NOTES ON INVESTMENT ADVISERS: THE DODD-FRANK ACT

The Dodd-Frank Act makes significant changes to the registration, reporting, and recordkeeping requirements under the Investment Advisers Act of 1940. It may also signify an important change in the landscape of SEC regulation of broker-dealers and investment advisers.

1. *Advisers to Private Funds Lose Their Exemption.* Historically, advisers to private funds (hedge funds and private equity funds) were exempt from registration under § 203(b)(3) of the Investment Advisers Act. The Dodd-Frank Act removed this exemption and replaced it with several narrower exemptions for advisers that advise exclusively venture

---

[185] Inv. Adv. Act Rel. 2 (1940).

[186] Inv. Adv. Act Rel. 626, 14 SEC Dock. 946, 950–951 (1978).

[187] Section 202(a)(11)(B). "The term 'solely incidental' has been interpreted to mean that the exclusion will be lost if a professional holds itself out to the public as an adviser or financial planner; provides advisory services that are not reasonably related to other professional activities; or calculates advisory service charges differently from usual professional charges." SEC Staff Report on Financial Planners, Subcomm. On Telecommunications & Fin., House Comm. on Energy & Commerce, 101st Cong., 1st Sess. B-4 (1988).

capital firms, family offices, advisers managing less than $150 million of private funds, foreign private advisers, and advisers to licensed small business investment companies.[188] These exempt advisers will still be required to file, and periodically update, reports with the SEC that contain a more limited set of disclosures.[189]

2. *New Reporting Requirements.* To facilitate its increased responsibility for private fund advisers arising from the Dodd-Frank Act, the SEC amended the investment adviser registration form, Form ADV, to require additional disclosures.[190] These disclosures include an expansion of the data advisers provide about the private funds they advise, including identification of five categories of "gatekeepers" that perform critical roles for advisers and the private funds they manage (i.e., auditors, prime brokers, custodians, administrators, and marketers). In addition, the amendments require all registered advisers to provide data on their clients, their employees, and their advisory activities, as well as about their business practices that may present conflicts of interest. Finally, the amendments require additional information about advisers' non-advisory activities and their financial industry affiliations.

3. *Regulation of "Mid-Sized" Advisers.* The responsibility of regulating investment advisers is divided between the SEC and the states. Under existing law, advisers generally may not register with the SEC unless they manage at least $25 million for their clients.[191] The Dodd-Frank Act reallocates the responsibility for regulating advisers who manage between $25 million and $100 million in assets from the SEC to the states by creating a new category of advisers called "mid-sized advisers."[192] As a result of this amendment, the SEC estimates that about 3,200 of the current 11,500 registered advisers will switch from SEC to state registration.[193] These advisers will continue to be subject to the Advisers Act's general anti-fraud provisions.

4. *Systemic Risk Reporting.* Section 404 of the Dodd-Frank Act, which amends § 204(b) of the Investment Advisers Act, gives the SEC authority to impose reporting and recordkeeping requirements on investment advisers for the purpose of assessing systemic risk. Pursuant to this authority, the SEC, jointly with the Commodities Futures Trading Commission (CFTC), proposed rules that would require investment advisers registered with the SEC that advise one or more private funds to file new confidential reports to report systemic risk information.

---

[188] See §§ 403, 407 and 408 of The Dodd-Frank Act.

[189] See Rule 204–4 under the Investment Advisers Act of 1940.

[190] See Rules Implementing Amendments to the Investment Advisers Act of 1940, Release No. IA-3221, (June 22, 2011).

[191] See National Securities Markets Improvement Act of 1996, Pub. L No. 104–290, 110 Stat. 3416 § 306 (1996) (allocating to the states certain responsibility for small investment advisers with less than $25 million in management).

[192] See § 410 of Dodd-Frank, § 203A of the Investment Advisers Act.

[193] See Rules Implementing Amendments to the Investment Advisers Act of 1940, Release No. IA-3221, (June 22, 2011).

5. *Control Person Liability in SEC Enforcement Actions.* The Dodd-Frank Act clarifies that control person liability under § 20(a) of the 1934 Act is not limited to private actions. Prior to the passage of Dodd-Frank, a split of authority existed as to whether the SEC could maintain an enforcement action under § 20(a). Both the Second and Third Circuits had held that the SEC could maintain an enforcement action under § 20(a),[194] but the Sixth Circuit issued conflicting opinions on the issue.[195] Section 929P(c) of the Dodd-Frank Act resolves this conflict by providing the SEC with express authorization to pursue enforcement actions against controlling persons, unless they acted in "good faith" and did not "directly or indirectly induce" the alleged violation.

6. *Fiduciary Standard of Conduct for Investment Advisers and Broker-Dealers.* Section 913 of Dodd-Frank required the Commission to conduct a study to evaluate the effectiveness of the current standards regulating investment advisers and broker-dealers, and whether there are legal or regulatory gaps in the standards for the protection of retail customers that should be addressed. In 2019, the SEC addressed this issue with Regulation Best Interest, discussed in Chapter 9.

7. *Section 919B.* Section 919B of the Dodd-Frank Act directed the Commission to conduct a study of ways to improve the access of retail investors to registration information about investment advisers and broker-dealers and to identify additional information that should be made publicly available. On January 26, 2011, the SEC published a study pursuant to this mandate recommending a unified public disclosure database as the optimal means to achieve this goal. The SEC implemented this recommendation by expanding the Investment Adviser Search on the Investment Adviser Public Disclosure's ("IAPD") website to include results from FINRA's BrokerCheck website.

Problem

PROBLEM 14-4

The SEC has filed a four-count complaint against Defendants Yun Soo Oh Park, a.k.a. Tokyo Joe ("Park"), and Tokyo Joe's Societe Anonyme Corp. (collectively, the "Defendants"), as a result of Defendants' conduct on their web site, which allegedly violates various SEC regulations.

In year three, Park incorporated Tokyo Joe's Society Anonyme Corp. (hereinafter "Societe Anonyme"). Societe Anonyme was never registered under the Investment Advisers Act of 1940.

In year one, Park began posting messages on various public financial Internet bulletin boards, which allow people to electronically post and reply

---

[194] SEC v. First Jersey Secs., Inc., 101 F.3d 1450, 1472 (2d Cir. 1996); SEC v. J.W. Barclay & Co., Inc., 442 F.3d 834, 842 (3d Cir. 2006).

[195] Compare SEC v. Coffey, 493 F.2d 1304, 1318 (6th Cir. 1974) (holding that Section 20(a) may not be relied upon by the SEC in an injunctive enforcement action) with United States v. Smith, 208 Fed. Appx. 402 (6th Cir. 2006) (affirming summary judgment against the defendant under § 20(a)).

to messages regarding stocks, investing, and other financial subjects. During year two, Park posted thousands of messages under the names "Tokyo Joe" or "TokyoMex." Early year two, individuals from these bulletin boards began directly contacting Park, soliciting further information about stock picks and trading. As a result, in March of year two, Park created an e-mail list and sent individuals on the list his stock picks.

In July of year two, Park set up Tokyo Joe's Internet site, at tokyo-joe.com, which operated under Park's control. From July to December of year two, Tokyo Joe's consisted of two areas. One was a limited area of the web site accessible to the general public, and the other consisted of a more expanded area of the web site accessible only to fee-paying members. From about July to about November of year two, the fee was $299 per year to become a Societe Anonyme member. Members received, among other things, exclusive e-mails of Park's daily stock picks and unlimited access to the members only areas of Park's web site. On or about December of year two, Park added a "chat room" to the members-only area of the web site. The chat room served as a forum in which Park conducted two-way electronic dialogues with Societe Anonyme members about Park's stock picks and other investment advice. Between July of year two and May of year three, Societe Anonyme's membership increased from about 200 to 3,800 subscribers.

The SEC brought suit, for among other reasons, Park's failure to register under the Investment Advisers Act. Park moved to dismiss claiming that he is not subject to the Investment Advisers Act after *Lowe*.

What result should a court reach on Park's motion?

(2) SCALPING

SEC v. Capital Gains Research Bureau, Inc.
Supreme Court of the United States, 1963.
375 U.S. 180, 84 S.Ct. 275, 11 L.Ed.2d 237.

■ MR. JUSTICE GOLDBERG delivered the opinion of the Court.

We are called upon in this case to decide whether under the Investment Advisers Act of 1940 the Securities and Exchange Commission may obtain an injunction compelling a registered investment adviser to disclose to his clients a practice of purchasing shares of a security for his own account shortly before recommending that security for long-term investment and then immediately selling the shares at a profit upon the rise in the market price following the recommendation. The answer to this question turns on whether the practice—known in the trade as "scalping"—"operates as a fraud or deceit upon any client or prospective client" within the meaning of the Act. We hold that it does and that the Commission may "enforce compliance" with the Act by obtaining an injunction requiring the adviser to make full disclosure of the practice to his clients.

The Commission brought this action against respondents in the United States District Court for the Southern District of New York. At the hearing on the application for a preliminary injunction, the following facts were established. Respondents publish two investment advisory services, one of which—"a Capital Gains Report"—is the subject of this proceeding. The Report is mailed monthly to approximately 5,000 subscribers who each pay an annual subscription price of $18. It carries the following description:

> "An Investment Service devoted exclusively to (1) The protection of investment capital. (2) The realization of a steady and attractive income therefrom. (3) The accumulation of CAPITAL GAINS thru the timely purchase of corporate equities that are proved to be undervalued."

Between March 15, 1960, and November 7, 1960, respondents, on six different occasions, purchased shares of a particular security shortly before recommending it in the Report for long-term investment. On each occasion, there was an increase in the market price and the volume of trading of the recommended security within a few days after the distribution of the Report. Immediately thereafter, respondents sold their shares of these securities at a profit. They did not disclose any aspect of these transactions to their clients or prospective clients.

* * *

The decision in this case turns on whether Congress, in empowering the courts to enjoin any practice which operates "as a fraud or deceit upon any client or prospective client," intended to require the Commission to establish fraud and deceit "in their technical sense," including intent to injure and actual injury to clients, or whether Congress intended a broad remedial construction of the Act which would encompass nondisclosure of material facts. For resolution of this issue we consider the history and purpose of the Investment Advisers Act of 1940.

I.

The Investment Advisers Act of 1940 was the last in a series of Acts designed to eliminate certain abuses in the securities industry, abuses which were found to have contributed to the stock market crash of 1929 and the depression of the 1930's.

* * *

The Public Utility Holding Company Act of 1935 "authorized and directed" the Securities and Exchange Commission "to make a study of the functions and activities of investment trusts and investment companies * * *." Pursuant to this mandate, the Commission made an exhaustive study and report which included consideration of investment counsel and investment advisory services. This aspect of the study and report culminated in the Investment Advisers Act of 1940.

The report reflects the attitude—shared by investment advisers and the Commission—that investment advisers could not "completely perform their basic function—furnishing to clients on a personal basis competent, unbiased, and continuous advice regarding the sound management of their investments—unless all conflicts of interest between the investment counsel and the client were removed." The report stressed that affiliations by investment advisers with investment bankers, or corporations might be "an impediment to a disinterested, objective, or critical attitude toward an investment by clients * * *."

This concern was not limited to deliberate or conscious impediments to objectivity. Both the advisers and the Commission were well aware that whenever advice to a client might result in financial benefit to the adviser—other than the fee for his advice—"that advice to a client might in some way be tinged with that pecuniary interest [whether consciously or] subconsciously motivated * * *." The report quoted one leading investment adviser who said that he "would put the emphasis * * * on subconscious" motivation in such situations. It quoted a member of the Commission staff who suggested that a significant part of the problem was not the existence of a "deliberate intent" to obtain a financial advantage, but rather the existence "subconsciously [of] a prejudice" in favor of one's own financial interests. The report incorporated the Code of Ethics and Standards of Practice of one of the leading investment counsel associations, which contained the following canon:

> "[An investment adviser] should continuously occupy an impartial and disinterested position, as free as humanly possible from the *subtle* influence of prejudice, *conscious or unconscious*; he should scrupulously avoid any affiliation, or any act, which subjects his position to challenge in this respect." (Emphasis added.)

Other canons appended to the report announced the following guiding principles: that compensation for investment advice "should consist exclusively of direct charges to clients for services rendered"; that the adviser should devote his time "exclusively to the performance" of his advisory function; that he should not "share in profits" of his clients; and that he should not "directly or indirectly engage in any activity which may jeopardize [his] ability to render unbiased investment advice." These canons were adopted "to the end that the quality of services to be rendered by investment counselors may measure up to the high standards which the public has a right to expect and to demand."

One activity specifically mentioned and condemned by investment advisers who testified before the Commission was *"trading by investment counselors for their own account in securities in which their clients were interested * * *."*

This study and report—authorized and directed by statute—culminated in the preparation and introduction by Senator Wagner of the bill which, with some changes, became the Investment Advisers Act of 1940.

* * *

Although certain changes were made in the bill following the hearings, there is nothing to indicate an intent to alter the fundamental purposes of the legislation. The broad proscription against "any * * * practice * * * which operates * * * as a fraud or deceit upon any client or prospective client" remained in the bill from beginning to end. And the Committee Reports indicate a desire to preserve "the personalized character of the services of investment advisers," and to eliminate conflicts of interest between the investment adviser and the clients as safeguards both to "unsophisticated investors" and to "bona fide investment counsel." The Investment Advisers Act of 1940 thus reflects a congressional recognition "of the delicate fiduciary nature of an investment advisory relationship," as well as a congressional intent to eliminate, or at least to expose, all conflicts of interest which might incline [an] investment adviser—consciously or unconsciously—to render advice which was not disinterested. It would defeat the manifest purpose of the Investment Advisers Act of 1940 for us to hold, therefore, that Congress, in empowering the courts to enjoin any practice which operates "as a fraud or deceit," intended to require proof of intent to injure and actual injury to clients.

This conclusion moreover, is not in derogation of the common law of fraud, as the District Court and the majority of the Court of Appeals suggested. To the contrary, it finds support in the process by which the courts have adapted the common law of fraud to the commercial transactions of our society. It is true that at common law intent and injury have been deemed essential elements in a damage suit between parties to an arm's-length transaction. But this [is] not such an action. This is a suit for a preliminary injunction in which the relief sought is, as the dissenting judges below characterized it, the "mild prophylactic," of requiring a fiduciary to disclose to his clients, not all his security holdings, but only his dealings in recommended securities just before and after the issuance of his recommendations.

The content of common-law fraud has not remained static as the courts below seem to have assumed. It has varied, for example, with the nature of the relief sought, the relationship between the parties, and the merchandise in issue. It is not necessary in a suit for equitable or prophylactic relief to establish all the elements required in a suit for monetary damages.

* * *

Nor is it necessary in a suit against a fiduciary, which Congress recognized the investment adviser to be, to establish all the elements required in a suit against a party to an arm's-length transaction. Courts have imposed on a fiduciary an affirmative duty of "utmost good faith, and full and fair disclosure of all material facts," as well as an affirmative obligation "to employ reasonable care to avoid misleading" his clients. There has also been a growing recognition by common-law courts that the doctrines of fraud and deceit which developed around transactions involving land and other tangible items of wealth are ill-suited to the sale of such intangibles as advice and securities, and that, accordingly, the doctrines must be adapted to the merchandise in issue. The 1909 New York case of Ridgely v. Keene, 134 App. Div. 647, 119 N.Y. 451, illustrates this continuing development. An investment adviser who, like respondents, published an investment advisory service, agreed, for compensation, to influence his clients to buy shares in a certain security. He did not disclose the agreement to his client but sought "to excuse his conduct by asserting that * * * he honestly believed, that his subscribers would profit by his advice * * *." The court, holding that "his belief in the soundness of his advice is wholly immaterial," declared the act in question "a palpable fraud."

We cannot assume that Congress, in enacting legislation to prevent fraudulent practices by investment advisers, was unaware of these developments in the common law of fraud. Thus, even if we were to agree with the courts below that Congress had intended, in effect, to codify the common law of fraud in the Investment Advisers Act of 1940, it would be logical to conclude that Congress codified the common law "remedially" as the courts had adapted it to the prevention of fraudulent securities transactions by fiduciaries, not "technically" as it has traditionally been applied in damage suits between parties to arm's-length transactions involving land and ordinary chattels.

The foregoing analysis of the judicial treatment of common-law fraud reinforces our conclusion that Congress, in empowering the courts to enjoin any practice which operates "as a fraud or deceit" upon a client, did not intend to require proof of intent to injure and actual injury to the client. Congress intended the Investment Advisers Act of 1940 to be construed like other securities legislation "enacted for the purpose of avoiding frauds," not technically and restrictively, but flexibly to effectuate its remedial purposes.

II.

We turn now to a consideration of whether the specific conduct here in issue was the type which Congress intended to reach in the Investment Advisers Act of 1940. It is arguable—indeed it was argued by "some investment counsel representatives" who testified before the Commission—that any "trading by investment counselors for their own account in securities in which their clients were interested * * *" creates a potential conflict of interest which must be eliminated. We need not go that far in this case, since here the Commission seeks only disclosure of a conflict of interests with significantly greater potential for abuse than in the situation described above. An adviser who, like respondents, secretly trades on the market effect of his own recommendation may be motivated—consciously or unconsciously—to recommend a given security not because of its potential for long-run price increase (which would profit the client), but because of its potential for short-run price increase in response to anticipated activity from the recommendation (which would profit the adviser). An investor seeking the advice of a registered investment adviser must, if the legislative purpose is to be served, be permitted to evaluate such overlapping motivations, through appropriate disclosure, in deciding whether an adviser is serving "two masters" or only one, "especially * * * if one of the masters happens to be economic self-interest." United States v. Mississippi Valley Generating Co., 364 U.S. 520, 549. Accordingly, we hold that the Investment Advisers Act of 1940 empowers the courts, upon a showing such as that made here, to require an adviser to make full and frank disclosure of his practice of trading on the effect of his recommendations.

III.

Respondents offer three basic arguments against this conclusion. They argue first that Congress could have made, but did not make, failure to disclose material facts unlawful in the Investment Advisers Act of 1940, as it did in the Securities Act of 1933, and that absent specific language, it should not be assumed that Congress intended to include failure to disclose in its general proscription of any practice which operates as a fraud or deceit. But considering the history and chronology of the statutes, this omission does not seem significant. The Securities Act of 1933 was the first experiment in federal regulation of the securities industry. It was understandable, therefore, for Congress, in declaring certain practices unlawful, to include both a general proscription against fraudulent and deceptive practices and, out of an abundance of caution, a specific proscription against nondisclosure. It soon became clear, however, that the courts, aware of the previously outlined developments in the common law of fraud, were merging the proscription against nondisclosure into the general proscription against fraud, treating the former, in effect, as one variety of the latter. * * * In light of this, and in light of the evident purpose of the Investment Advisers Act of 1940 to substitute a philosophy of disclosure for the philosophy of *caveat emptor*, we cannot assume that the omission in the 1940 Act of a specific proscription against nondisclosure was intended to limit the application of the antifraud and antideceit provisions of the Act so as to render the Commission impotent to enjoin suppression of material facts. The more reasonable assumption, considering what had transpired between 1933 and 1940, is that Congress, in enacting the Investment Advisers Act of 1940 and proscribing any practice which operates "as a fraud or deceit," deemed a specific proscription against nondisclosure surplusage.

Respondents also argue that the 1960 amendment to the Investment Advisers Act of 1940 justifies a narrow interpretation of the original enactment. The amendment made two significant changes which are relevant here. "Manipulative" practices were added to the list of those specifically proscribed. There is nothing to suggest, however, that with respect to a requirement of disclosure, "manipulative" is any broader than fraudulent or deceptive. Nor is there any indication that by adding the new proscription Congress intended to narrow the scope of the original proscription. The new amendment also authorizes the Commission "by rules and regulations [to] define, and prescribe means reasonably designed to prevent, such acts, practices, and courses of business as are fraudulent, deceptive, or manipulative." The legislative history offers no indication, however, that Congress intended such rules to substitute for the "general and flexible" antifraud provisions which have long been considered necessary to control "the versatile inventions of fraud-doers." Moreover, the intent of Congress must be culled from the events surrounding the passage of the 1940 legislation. "[O]pinions attributed to a Congress twenty years after the event cannot be considered evidence of the intent of the Congress of 1940." Securities & Exchange Comm'n v. Capital Gains Research Bureau, Inc., 306 F.2d 606, 615 (dissenting opinion).

Respondents argue, finally, that their advice was "honest" in the sense that they believed it was sound and did not offer it for the purpose of furthering personal pecuniary objectives. This, of course, is but another way of putting the rejected argument that the elements of technical common-law fraud—particularly intent—must be established before an injunction requiring disclosure may be ordered. It is the practice itself, however, with its potential for abuse, which "operates as a fraud or deceit" within the meaning of the Act when relevant information is suppressed. The Investment Advisers Act of 1940 was "directed not only at dishonor, but also at conduct that tempts dishonor." United States v. Mississippi Valley Generating Co., 364 U.S. 520, 549. Failure to disclose material facts must be deemed fraud or deceit within its intended meaning, for, as the experience of the 1920's and 1930's amply reveals, the darkness and ignorance of commercial secrecy are the conditions upon which predatory practices best thrive. To impose upon the Securities and Exchange Commission the burden of showing deliberate dishonesty as a condition precedent to protecting investors through the prophylaxis of disclosure would effectively nullify the protective purposes of the statute. Reading the Act in light of its background we find no such requirement commanded. Neither the Commission nor the courts should be required "to separate the mental urges," Peterson v. Greenville, 373 U.S. 244, 248, of an investment adviser, for "[t]he motives of man are too complex * * * to separate * * *." Mosser v. Darrow, 341 U.S. 267, 271. The statute, in recognition of the adviser's fiduciary relationship to his clients, requires that his advice be disinterested. To insure this it empowers the courts to require disclosure of material facts. It misconceives the purpose of the statute to confine its application to "dishonest" as opposed to "honest" motives. As Dean Shulman said in discussing the nature of securities transactions, what is required is "a picture not simply of the show window, but of the entire store * * * not simply truth in the statements volunteered, but disclosure." The high standards of business morality exacted by our laws regulating the securities industry do not permit an investment adviser to trade on the market effect of his own recommendations without fully and fairly revealing his personal interests in these recommendations to his clients.

Experience has shown that disclosure in such situations, while not onerous to the adviser, is needed to preserve the climate of fair dealing which is so essential to maintain public confidence in the securities industry and to preserve the economic health of the country.

The judgment of the Court of Appeals is reversed and the case is remanded to the District Court for proceedings consistent with this opinion.

Reversed and remanded.

Problem

PROBLEM 14-5

A commentator on a financial news TV show made highly laudatory statements about Zweig, Inc., the day after purchasing 5000 shares of Zweig's stock. The next day the Zweig stock rose 15 percent. Has the commentator violated the Investment Advisers Act? Has the commentator violated Rule 10b–5 of the Securities Exchange Act? In either case, is it a defense that every statement made was believed to be true?

CHAPTER 15

CRIMINAL ENFORCEMENT OF THE FEDERAL SECURITIES LAWS

Statutes

Securities Act, § 24.

Exchange Act, § 32(a).

Federal Mail and Wire Fraud Statutes, 18 U.S.C. §§ 1341, 1343, 1346.

18 U.S.C. § 1348 ("Securities Fraud")

18 U.S.C. § 1350 ("Failure of Corporate Officers to Certify Financial Reports")

18 U.S.C. § 1513(e) (retaliation against whistle-blowers)

18 U.S.C. § 1519 ("Destruction, Alteration or Falsification of Records in Federal Investigations and Bankruptcy")

18 U.S.C. § 1520 ("Destruction of Corporate Audit Records")

RICO, 18 U.S.C. §§ 1961–1968.

Criminal prosecutions under the federal securities laws are increasingly common, most notably in response to corporate scandals including the insider trading scandals of the 1980s, the accounting scandals at Enron, WorldCom, and elsewhere in the early 2000s, and insider trading by hedge funds in the early 2010s. The criminal provisions of the federal securities laws do not focus on insider trading or even on fraud offenses. Both § 24 of the 1933 Act and § 32(a) of the 1934 Act are considerably broader in scope, each making it a felony for any person to "willfully" violate any statutory provision of either statute, or any rule or regulation promulgated thereunder. Any SEC rule or regulation, or any false filing with the SEC, can support a criminal prosecution. Section 24 provides for a sentence of up to five years and § 32(a) authorizes a sentence of up to 20 years.

Federal prosecutors are not limited to the use of the federal securities laws. Indeed, the federal mail and wire fraud statutes are popular weapons.[1] They provide a general catch-all backstop for cases

---

[1] 18 U.S.C. §§ 1341, 1343. After the Sarbanes-Oxley Act, these crimes now carry a maximum 20-year sentence. The mail and wire fraud statutes expanded rapidly in the 1980's to cover conduct involving a breach of fiduciary duty. See John C. Coffee, Jr., The Metastasis of Mail Fraud: The Continuing Story of the "Evolution" of a White Collar Crime, 21 Amer. Crim. L. Rev. 1 (1983); John C. Coffee, Jr. & Charles K. Whitehead, The Federalization of Fraud: Mail and Wire Fraud Statutes, in Otto G. Obermaier & Robert G. Morvillo, White Collar Crime:

where all of the elements of securities fraud cannot be proved, but prosecutors believe the defendants engaged in bad conduct. We have already seen this provision in action in the *O'Hagan* case. Prosecutors can also seek a harsher sentence, a special forfeiture sanction, and a pretrial freeze of the defendant's assets under the RICO statute.[2] In 1995, however, Congress ended an earlier express private cause of action for securities violations under RICO. More recently, 18 U.S.C. § 1348 ("Securities Fraud"), which was part of the Sarbanes-Oxley Act, has come into increasing use, especially in insider trading cases because (as later explained) it does not require the prosecution to prove all the elements that are required by Dirks v. SEC.[3]

1. PROCEDURAL ISSUES

United States Attorneys bring criminal prosecutions in the federal courts. The SEC has neither authority nor practical control over the decision of a U.S. Attorney to initiate a criminal prosecution. Section 21(d) of the 1934 Act does authorize the Commission to:

> transmit such evidence as may be available concerning such acts or practices as may constitute a violation of any provision of this [title] or the rules or regulations thereunder to the Attorney General, who may, in his discretion, institute the necessary criminal proceedings under this [title].

Typically, personnel within the SEC's Division of Enforcement perform the initial investigative work in a criminal prosecution.[4] At some point, personnel within the Division of Enforcement or a regional office may decide that the matter under investigation is sufficiently serious to warrant a criminal prosecution. They can then pursue one of two courses of action: a formal "criminal reference," or an informal reference. In order to make a "criminal reference," the Commission must vote to request that the Department of Justice commence an investigation and transmit any

---

Business and Regulatory Offenses (1990). However, this expansion came to a screeching halt in 2010 when the Supreme Court ruled in Skilling v. United States, 561 U.S. 358 (2010), that 18 U.S.C. § 1346 ("Definition of a 'scheme or artifice to defraud'") covered only schemes involving bribery or kickbacks. Even as so cut back, these statutes are satisfied by any loss of money or property, including through an embezzlement or misappropriation, which allows them to easily match the reach of Rule 10b–5.

For criminal law specialists, the observation of Judge Rakoff is particularly memorable: "To federal prosecutors of white collar crime, the mail fraud statute is our Stradivarius, our Colt 45, our Louisville Slugger, our Cuisinart—and our true love. We may flirt with RICO, show off with 10b–5, and call the conspiracy law darling, but we always come home to the virtues of 18 U.S.C. § 1341, with its simplicity, adaptability, and comfortable familiarity." Jed S. Rakoff, The Federal Mail Fraud Statute (Part I), 18 Duquesne L. Rev. 771, 771 (1980).

[2] 18 U.S.C. §§ 1961–1968.

[3] 463 U.S. 646 (1989) (requiring a showing of a breach of a fiduciary or similar duty to prove unlawful insider trading).

[4] Some criminal prosecutions for securities law violations can originate in a U.S. Attorney's office. These are often the result of plea bargain negotiations with defendants in other cases who have an incentive to cooperate by revealing other crimes, including those by third parties.

evidence pursuant to § 21(d). More often, Commission staff will make an informal reference, advising their counterparts in a U.S. Attorney's office (with whom they may have frequent contact on other pending matters) about a case and inviting them to request to see the Commission's file. The SEC will invariably comply with such a request.[5] Such informal references without a Commission vote have been held not to violate any rights of the accused.[6]

A criminal reference does not mean the Commission suspends its own enforcement activity. It may still pursue injunctive or administrative relief (such as disgorgement or civil penalties). From defense counsel's perspective, the most important consideration in any SEC investigation is often to protect the client from a criminal reference. In the past, defense counsel would bargain in its negotiations for an express promise by the SEC staff that it would not make a criminal reference in return for agreed-upon relief.

This practice changed, however, following the case of United States v. Fields.[7] There, enforcement staff gave defense counsel the impression that in return for a civil settlement, they would not make an informal criminal referral. In fact, they did recommend criminal prosecution, and the defendant was indicted. Although the Second Circuit found the implicit promise not binding on the U.S. Attorney (who had no notice of it), it condemned the SEC staff attorneys' conduct as unprofessional and indicated that under some circumstances such a promise could be binding.

In response, the SEC adopted a formal policy of refusing to comment on whether a criminal reference would be made.[8] This rule has greatly complicated life for defense counsel, who still naturally desire "global" settlements of all pending SEC and criminal charges (and who fear even making submissions to the SEC (pursuant to Wells Notices) if the material in them might be turned over to a U.S. Attorney). Sometimes, before settling potentially criminal charges with the SEC (such as insider trading charges), defense counsel will approach the U.S. Attorney's staff and ask it to sign off by indicating its lack of interest in criminal prosecution. The premise here is that the U.S. Attorney will read the SEC staff's silence as indicating its implied consent to a noncriminal

---

[5] The Commission's policy is that it does not have "the authority or responsibility for instituting, conducting, settling, or otherwise disposing of criminal proceedings. That authority and responsibility are vested in the Attorney General and representatives of the Department of Justice." See 17 C.F.R. § 202.5(f).

[6] See United States v. Bloom, 450 F.Supp. 323 (E.D.Pa.1978).

[7] 1977–1978 Fed.Sec.L.Rep. (CCH) ¶ 96,074 (S.D.N.Y.1977), aff'd in part, rev'd in part, 592 F.2d 638 (2d Cir. 1978).

[8] See 17 C.F.R. § 202.5(f): "[A]ny person involved in an enforcement matter before the Commission who consents, or agrees to consent, to any judgment or order does so solely for the purpose of resolving the claims against him in that investigative, civil, or administrative matter and not for the purpose of resolving any criminal charges that have been, or might be, brought against him."

resolution of the case (although, of course, the staff or the Commission could make a post-settlement request).

A different problem surfaces when parallel SEC and criminal investigations overlap. Discovery in the federal criminal process is limited and is essentially conducted through the mechanism of the grand jury. Before the grand jury, the defendant has a Fifth Amendment right to silence and non-cooperation. Yet, as discussed below, the Fifth Amendment supplies much less protection in a civil proceeding before the SEC (at which the defendant could be barred from the securities business for life or fined a substantial amount) because an adverse inference can be taken by the court or jury when the defendant takes the Fifth Amendment in a civil case. Also, it simply does not apply in FINRA investigations, which are increasingly connected to SEC investigations, in the same way that SEC investigations are connected to those of U.S. Attorneys. This relative difference in legal protections and the intensity of the legal inquiry creates an incentive to use civil discovery to supplement the criminal investigatory process.

SEC v. Dresser Industries, Inc.
United States Court of Appeals, District of Columbia Circuit, 1980.
628 F.2d 1368, cert. denied, 449 U.S. 993 (1980).

■ Before: WRIGHT, CHIEF JUDGE, and MCGOWAN, TAMM, ROBINSON, MACKINNON, ROBB, WILKEY, WALD, MIKVA, and EDWARDS, CIRCUIT JUDGES.

■ J. SKELLY WRIGHT, CHIEF JUDGE:

Dresser Industries, Inc. (Dresser) appeals from a decision of the District Court requiring obedience to a subpoena *duces tecum* issued by the Securities and Exchange Commission (SEC) on April 21, 1978, and denying Dresser's motion to quash the subpoena. The subpoena was issued in connection with an SEC investigation into Dresser's use of corporate funds to make what are euphemistically called "questionable foreign payments," and into the adequacy of Dresser's disclosures of such payments under the securities laws.

The principal issue facing this *en banc* court is whether Dresser is entitled to special protection against this SEC subpoena because of a parallel investigation into the same questionable foreign payments now being conducted by a federal grand jury under the guidance of the United States Department of Justice (Justice). Dresser argues principally that the SEC subpoena abuses the civil discovery process of the SEC for the purpose of criminal discovery and infringes the role of the grand jury in independently investigating allegations of criminal wrongdoing. On November 19, 1979 a panel of this court issued a decision affirming the District Court but, with Judge Robb dissenting, attaching a condition prohibiting the SEC from providing Justice with the information received from Dresser under this subpoena. Because of the importance of this issue to enforcement of the regulatory laws of the United States, this court voted to vacate the panel opinions and rehear the case en banc.

I. BACKGROUND

A. Origin of the Investigations

Illegal and questionable corporate payments surfaced as a major public problem in late 1973, when several major scandals implicated prominent American corporations in improper use of corporate funds to influence government officials in the United States and foreign countries. The exposure of these activities disrupted public faith in the integrity of our political system and eroded international trust in the legitimacy of American corporate operations abroad.[3] SEC investigation revealed that many corporate officials were falsifying financial records to shield questionable foreign and domestic payments from exposure to the public and even, in many cases, to corporate directors and accountants. Since the completeness and accuracy of corporate financial reporting is the cornerstone of federal regulation of the securities markets, such falsification became a matter of grave concern to the SEC.

Beginning in the spring of 1974 the SEC brought a series of injunctive actions against certain American corporations. It obtained consent decrees prohibiting future violations of the securities laws and establishing internal corporate procedures for investigation, disclosure, and prevention of illegal corporate payments. However, the problem of questionable foreign payments proved so widespread that the SEC devised a "Voluntary Disclosure Program" to encourage corporations to conduct investigations of their past conduct and make appropriate disclosures without direct SEC coercion. Participation in the Voluntary Disclosure Program would not insulate a corporation from an SEC enforcement action, but the Commission would be less likely to exercise its discretion to initiate enforcement actions against participants. The most important elements of the Voluntary Disclosure Program were (1) an independent committee of the corporation would conduct a thorough investigation into questionable foreign and domestic payments made by the corporation; (2) the committee would disclose the results of this investigation to the board of directors in full; (3) the corporation would disclose the substance of the report to the public and the SEC on Form 8-K; and (4) the corporation would issue a policy statement prohibiting future questionable and illegal payments and maintenance of false or incomplete records in connection with them. Except in "egregious cases"

---

[3] The Senate Committee on Banking, Housing, and Urban Affairs reported in May 1977:

Recent investigations by the SEC have revealed corrupt foreign payments by over 300 U.S. companies involving hundreds of millions of dollars. These revelations have had severe adverse effects. Foreign governments friendly to the United States in Japan, Italy, and the Netherlands have come under intense pressure from their own people. The image of American democracy abroad has been tarnished. Confidence in the financial integrity of our corporations has been impaired. The efficient functioning of our capital markets has been hampered.

S. Rep. No. 114, 95th Cong., 1st Sess. 3 (1977).

the SEC would not require that public disclosures include specific names, dates, and places. Rather, the disclosure might be "generic" in form. Thus companies participating in the Voluntary Disclosure Program would ordinarily be spared the consequences to their employees, property, and business that might result from public disclosure of specific instances of foreign bribery or kickbacks. However, companies participating in the Voluntary Disclosure Program had to agree to grant SEC requests for access to the final report and to the unexpurgated underlying documentations.

B. The Dresser Investigations

On January 27, 1976 an attorney and other representatives of Dresser met with members of the SEC staff to discuss a proposed filing. At the meeting Dresser agreed to conduct an internal inquiry into questionable foreign payments, in accordance with the terms of the Voluntary Disclosure Program. The next day Dresser submitted a Form 8-K describing, in generic terms, one questionable foreign payment. On November 11, 1976 Dresser filed a second Form 8-K reporting the results of the internal investigation. On February 10, 1977 the company supplemented this report with a third Form 8-K concerning a questionable payment not reported in the earlier reports. The reports concerned Dresser's foreign activities after November 1, 1973. All disclosures were in generic, not specific, terms.

As part of its general monitoring program the SEC staff requested access to the documents underlying Dresser's report. On July 15, 1977 Dresser refused to grant such access. The company argued that allowing the staff to make notes or copies might subject its documents to public disclosure through the Freedom of Information Act. Dresser stated that such disclosure could endanger certain of its employees working abroad. During the ensuing discussions with the staff Dresser attempted to impose conditions of confidentiality upon any SEC examination of its documents, but the staff did not agree. Instead, it issued a recommendation to the Commission for a formal order of investigation in the Dresser case.

* * *

Meanwhile, the Department of Justice had established a task force on transnational payments to investigate possible criminal violations arising from illegal foreign payments. Two SEC attorneys participated in the task force. In the summer of 1977 the Justice task force requested access to SEC files on the approximately 400 companies, including Dresser, that had participated in the Voluntary Disclosure Program. Pursuant to Commission authorization the SEC staff transmitted all such files to the Justice task force in August 1977. After its preliminary investigation of the Form 8-K's submitted by Dresser under the Voluntary Disclosure Program, Justice presented Dresser's case to a grand jury in the District of Columbia on January 25, 1978.

Before any summons or subpoena had issued in either the SEC or the grand jury investigation, Dresser filed suit in the Southern District of Texas against the SEC and Justice to enjoin any further investigation of it by either agency. While Dresser's suit was pending in the Southern District of Texas, the District of Columbia grand jury subpoenaed Dresser's documents on April 21, 1978. At roughly the same time the SEC issued a formal order of private investigation, authorizing the staff to subpoena the documents and to obtain other relevant evidence. Pursuant to that order the staff issued a subpoena *duces tecum*, returnable on May 4, 1978. This subpoena covered substantially the same documents and materials subpoenaed by the grand jury, and more. Dresser did not respond to the subpoena.

* * *

II. GENERAL PRINCIPLES

A. Parallel Investigations

The civil and regulatory laws of the United States frequently overlap with the criminal laws, creating the possibility of parallel civil and criminal proceedings, either successive or simultaneous. In the absence of substantial prejudice to the rights of the parties involved, such parallel proceedings are unobjectionable under our jurisprudence. As long ago as 1912 the Supreme Court recognized that under one statutory scheme—that of the Sherman Act—a transaction or course of conduct could give rise to both criminal proceedings and civil suits. Standard Sanitary Manufacturing Co. v. United States, 226 U.S. 20, 52 (1912). The Court held that the government could initiate such proceedings either "simultaneously or successively," with discretion in the courts to prevent injury in particular cases.

* * *

The Constitution, therefore, does not ordinarily require a stay of civil proceedings pending the outcome of criminal proceedings. See Baxter v. Palmigiano, 425 U.S. 308 (1976); DeVita v. Sills, 422 F.2d 1172, 1181 (3d Cir. 1970). Nevertheless, a court may decide in its discretion to stay civil proceedings, postpone civil discovery, or impose protective orders and conditions "when the interests of justice seem[ ] to require such action, sometimes at the request of the prosecution, * * * sometimes at the request of the defense[.]" United States v. Kordel, 397 U.S. at 12 n.27 (citations omitted); see Horne Brothers, Inc. v. Laird, 463 F.2d 1268, 1271–1272 (D.C.Cir. 1972). The court must make such determinations in the light of the particular circumstances of the case.

Other than where there is specific evidence of agency bad faith or malicious governmental tactics, the strongest case for deferring civil proceedings until after completion of criminal proceedings is where a party under indictment for a serious offense is required to defend a civil or administrative action involving the same matter. The noncriminal proceeding, if not deferred, might undermine the party's Fifth

Amendment privilege against self-incrimination, expand rights of criminal discovery beyond the limits of Federal Rule of Criminal Procedure 16(b), expose the basis of the defense to the prosecution in advance of criminal trial, or otherwise prejudice the case. If delay of the noncriminal proceeding would not seriously injure the public interest, a court may be justified in deferring it. See, e.g., United States v. Henry, 491 F.2d 702 (6th Cir. 1974); Texaco, Inc. v. Borda, 383 F.2d 607, 608–609 (3d Cir. 1967); Silver v. McCamey, 221 F.2d 873, 874–875 (D.C.Cir. 1955). * * * In some such cases, however, the courts may adequately protect the government and the private party by merely deferring civil discovery or entering an appropriate protective order. Gordon v. FDIC, 427 F.2d 578, 580–581 (D.C.Cir. 1970). The case at bar is a far weaker one for staying the administrative investigation. No indictment has been returned; no Fifth Amendment privilege is threatened; Rule 16(b) has not come into effect, and the SEC subpoena does not require Dresser to reveal the basis for its defense.

B. SEC Investigations

The case at bar concerns enforcement of the securities laws of the United States, especially the Securities Act of 1933 ('33 Act) and the Securities Exchange Act of 1934 ('34 Act). These statutes explicitly empower the SEC to investigate possible infractions of the securities laws with a view to both civil and criminal enforcement, and to transmit the fruits of its investigations to Justice in the event of potential criminal proceedings. The '34 Act provides in relevant part: "The Commission may, in its discretion, make such investigations as it deems necessary to determine whether any person has violated, is violating, or is about to violate any provision of this chapter[.]" Section 21(a) of the '34 Act (1976). This investigative authority includes the power to administer oaths and affirmations, subpoena witnesses, take evidence, and require production of any books, papers, correspondence, memoranda, or other records which the SEC deems relevant or material. Id., Section 21(b). If it determines that a person "is engaged or is about to engage in acts or practices constituting a violation" of the Act, the SEC may bring an action in federal district court to enjoin such acts or practices. Id., Section 21(d). Under the same subsection of the '34 Act the SEC may "transmit such evidence as may be available concerning such acts or practices * * * to the Attorney General, who may, in his discretion, institute the necessary criminal proceedings under this chapter." Id. The '33 Act is to similar effect. See Sections 19(b), 20(a), (b) of the '33 Act.

Effective enforcement of the securities laws requires that the SEC and Justice be able to investigate possible violations simultaneously. Dissemination of false or misleading information by companies to members of the investing public may distort the efficient workings of the securities markets and injure investors who rely on the accuracy and completeness of the company's public disclosures. If the SEC suspects that a company has violated the securities laws, it must be able to respond quickly: it must be able to obtain relevant information concerning the alleged violation and to seek prompt judicial redress if necessary. Similarly, Justice must act quickly if it suspects that the laws have been broken. Grand jury investigations take time, as do criminal prosecutions. If Justice moves too slowly the statute of limitations may run, witnesses may die or move away, memories may fade, or enforcement resources may be diverted. The SEC cannot always wait for Justice to complete the criminal proceedings if it is to obtain the necessary prompt civil remedy; neither can Justice always await the conclusion of the civil proceeding without endangering its criminal case. Thus we should not block parallel investigations by these agencies in the absence of "special circumstances" in which the nature of the proceedings demonstrably prejudices substantial rights of the investigated party or of the government. See United States v. Kordel, supra, 397 U.S. at 11–13.

* * *

In essence, Dresser has launched this attack on the parallel SEC and Justice proceedings in order to obtain protection against the bare SEC proceeding, which it fears will result in public disclosure of sensitive corporate documents. The prejudice Dresser claims it will suffer from the parallel nature of the proceedings is speculative and undefined if indeed Dresser would suffer any prejudice from it at all. Any entitlement to confidential treatment of its documents must arise under the laws pertaining to the SEC; the fortuity of a parallel grand jury investigation cannot expand Dresser's rights in this SEC enforcement action. Thus Dresser's invocation of *LaSalle* [United States v. LaSalle National Bank, 437 U.S. 298 (1978)] can avail the company nothing.

IV. COOPERATION BETWEEN SEC AND JUSTICE

In its initial decision in this case a panel of this court ruled that "the broad prophylactic rule enunciated in *LaSalle* is inappropriate where the SEC and the Justice Department are simultaneously pursuing civil and criminal investigations." The panel therefore affirmed the District Court and ordered enforcement of the SEC subpoena. Out of a concern that the SEC subpoena might somehow "subvert the limitations of criminal discovery," however, the panel, with one judge dissenting, modified the terms of the subpoena enforcement order. It required that "once the Justice Department initiates criminal proceedings by means of a grand jury, the SEC may not provide the Justice Department with the fruits of the Commission's civil discovery gathered after the decision to prosecute." We affirm the judgment of the District Court and reject the panel's modification.

First, we note that no party to this case had suggested or requested a modification such as that imposed by the panel majority, either in the District Court or in this court.

* * *

Second, we note that there is no support for the panel's modification in either the relevant statutes or legislative history. Both the '33 Act and the '34—Act and other statutes related to securities law enforcement as well—expressly authorize the SEC to "transmit such evidence as may be available * * * to the Attorney General, who may, in his discretion, institute the necessary criminal proceedings under this subchapter." Section 20(b) of the '33 Act; Section 21(d) of the '34 Act. The statutes impose no limitation on when this transmittal may occur. The parties have not cited any portions of the legislative histories of these Acts relevant to this question, nor have we found any. But the SEC and Justice find considerable support for their interpretation in the legislative history of the Foreign Corrupt Practices Act of 1977, 91 Stat. 1494, Title I, 15 U.S.C. §§ 78a, 78m, 78dd–1, 78dd–2, 78ff (Supp. I 1977).

* * *

Congress manifestly did not intend that the SEC be forbidden to share information with Justice at this stage of the investigation. Under the panel majority's theory of the case the SEC would be foreclosed from sharing the fruits of its investigation with Justice as soon as Justice begins its own investigation through a grand jury. Only by waiting until the close of the SEC proceeding before initiating its own grand jury investigation could Justice obtain access to the evidence procured by the SEC. In view of Congress' concern that the agencies share information "at the earliest stage of any investigation in order to insure that the evidence needed for a criminal prosecution does not become stale," S.Rep. No. 114, and that the agencies avoid "a costly duplication of effort," H.R.Rep. No. 640, it would be unreasonable to prevent a sharing of information at this point in the investigation.

Third, we note that there is little or no judicial precedent for the panel's modification.

* * *

Finally, we note that the panel's modification would serve no compelling purpose, and might interfere with enforcement of the securities laws by the SEC and Justice. As the Second Circuit has said, the procedure permitting the SEC to communicate with Justice during the preliminary stages of an investigation has "significant advantages." United States v. Fields, 592 F.2d at 646.

> Allowing early participation in the case by the United States Attorney minimizes statute of limitations problems. The more time a United States Attorney has, the easier it is for him to become familiar with the complex facts of a securities fraud case, to prepare the case, and to present it to a grand jury before expiration of the applicable statute of limitations. Earlier initiation of criminal proceedings moreover is consistent with a defendant's right to a speedy trial. * * *

Id. The panel's modification would "interfere with this commendable example of inter-agency cooperation," to the detriment of securities law enforcement and in contravention of the will of Congress. On the other side of the balance, the panel's concern for preserving the limitations on criminal discovery is largely irrelevant at this stage of the proceedings, as Dresser agrees. Thus this would be an inappropriate situation to impose a "prophylactic" rule against cooperation between the agencies. We believe the courts can prevent any injustice that may arise in the particular circumstances of parallel investigations in the future. We decline to adopt the position of the panel majority.

* * *

The judgments of the District Court are *Affirmed*.

■ Concurring Opinion of CIRCUIT JUDGE EDWARDS:

I concur in the opinion of the court in this case. I wish to point out, however, that I do not read the court's opinion as expressing any view as to the proper outcome in a case of this sort once an indictment has issued. * * * Once an indictment has issued, the policy interest expressed in United States v. LaSalle National Bank, concerning the impermissibility of broadening the scope of criminal discovery through the summons authority of an agency, may come into play. I express no opinion as to whether or not the summons authority of a government agency may continue once an indictment has been issued or, if it may, whether protective conditions need be placed on the exercise of that power. These issues raise questions which are not presented here. The resolution of these questions, therefore, must await another day.

A. PARALLEL PROCEEDINGS

1. *Defined.* In one sense, all SEC proceedings are potentially "parallel," because the U.S. Attorney can commence a criminal prosecution at any time within the statute of limitations, and the SEC will never agree to discuss the issue of a criminal reference with the target of its investigation. In the usual sense of the term, however, the phrase "parallel proceeding" refers to a situation where the SEC investigation is continuing at the same time that the Justice Department is conducting a grand jury investigation with respect to the same subject matter. In United States v. LaSalle National Bank,[9] the Supreme Court held unenforceable an Internal Revenue Service summons issued after it made a recommendation for prosecution by the Department of Justice: "Nothing in § 7602 [of the Internal Revenue Code] or its legislative history suggests that Congress intended the summons authority to broaden the Justice Department's right of criminal litigation discovery or to infringe on the role of the grand jury as the principal tool of criminal accusation."[10] Yet, in *Dresser Industries*, the D.C. Circuit distinguished

---

[9] 437 U.S. 298 (1978).
[10] Id. at 312.

LaSalle and earlier cases on the ground that different statutory provisions were involved. Is there a sound basis for distinguishing an SEC subpoena from an IRS summons once a criminal referral has been made? What if the SEC feared that investors would continue to be misled by fraudulent financial statements? Is *Dresser* such a case?

2. *Testimony.* A defendant who testifies at an SEC investigation effectively forfeits the privilege against self-incrimination because a transcript of the testimony will in all likelihood be made available to the prosecutor and the grand jury, and may be used for impeachment purposes at trial. If the defendant invokes the Fifth Amendment at a civil hearing or trial, the court or administrative law judge may permissibly draw an adverse inference,[11] and it is likely that the defendant will lose the case. In short, the defendant faces Hobson's choice when there are parallel proceedings.

3. *Stays.* A defendant faced with simultaneous civil litigation and a criminal investigation (or a pending trial) can seek to stay the civil proceedings (or at least any deposition or scheduled testimony of the defendant in the civil case) pending the resolution of the criminal case. Such stays are discretionary, but, in the securities law context, defendants have not been noticeably successful in obtaining stays.[12]

2. CRIMINAL PROSECUTIONS UNDER THE FEDERAL SECURITIES LAWS

Section 24 of the 1933 Act and § 32(a) of the 1934 Act each criminalize any "willful" violation of the statutory provisions in their respective statutes or any rule or regulation adopted thereunder. However, there is one significant difference between these two provisions: § 32 criminalizes a false filing only if it is made "willfully and knowingly." This phrasing raises an interpretive issue: What does "knowingly" add to "willfully?" Does it require some knowledge of guilt or at least bad faith? The final clause of § 32(a) compounds this problem by adding that, even if convicted, "no person shall be subject to imprisonment under this section for the violation of any rule or regulation if he proves that he had no knowledge of such rule or regulation." But how can one have "no knowledge" if one must act "knowingly" (in the case of a false filing) to be convicted in the first instance?

---

[11] See Baxter v. Palmigiano, 425 U.S. 308 (1976).

[12] See United States v. Kordel, 397 U.S. 1 (1970); SEC v. Drucker, 1979 Fed.Sec.L.Rep. (CCH) ¶ 96,821 (S.D.N.Y.1979); see generally Note, Unjust Justice in Parallel Proceedings: Preventing Circumvention of Criminal Discovery Rules, 27 Hofstra L. Rev. 109 (1998).

United States v. Dixon
United States Court of Appeals, Second Circuit, 1976.
536 F.2d 1388.

- Before: LUMBARD, FRIENDLY and MULLIGAN, CIRCUIT JUDGES.

- FRIENDLY, CIRCUIT JUDGE:

[Lloyd Dixon, Jr., the president of AVM Corporation, a "reporting" company under the 1934 Act, was convicted under § 32(a) based on the failure of AVM's proxy statement and Form 10-K to disclose that it had lent him amounts in excess of $65,000 during 1970. Under the then applicable requirements, disclosure was required on the proxy statement if the officer's indebtedness exceeded $10,000 and on the Form 10-K if it exceeded $20,000. Just before the close of its fiscal year, Dixon caused AVM to switch some of his indebtedness to his father's account and Dixon also temporarily paid down the loan from AVM by taking out a bank loan. Thus, on December 31, 1970, the loan balance to AVM was only $19,100. In February, 1971, Dixon took out a new loan with AVM and used it to repay the bank loan. AVM's general counsel, Entwisle, made AVM's filings and did not know of Dixon's indebtedness to AVM].

* * *

The evidence thus established that the proxy statement sent out March 19, 1971 and the 10-K report filed on March 25, 1971 did not contain the information on Dixon's indebtedness that was required. Dixon's principal defense was that he thought the "SEC rules" provided for a $20,000 exemption, determined on the basis of year-end indebtedness, rather than by the highest aggregate balance during the year. Since Dixon's year-end balance still exceeded the $10,000 exemption in the proxy rules, it seems, although the record and briefs are not altogether clear on this, that the defense encompassed an assertion that Dixon thought a $20,000 year-end balance was the test for exemption from both rules.

* * *

The most important exculpatory item was testimony by Lewis that Sam Hale, the Ernst & Ernst account executive, had said "sometime around 1967", probably in connection with the 10-K report, that Dixon's loans had to be reduced below $20,000 by year-end in order to avoid having to file a Schedule II. As against this Lewis testified that at some time Lyons, an AVM financial officer, had given him the correct information and that it was Lewis' practice to pass information regarding the accounts to Dixon.

* * *

The preparation of the proxy statement was primarily the work of Entwisle. He would prepare a draft based on such information as he had "and then submit it to Mr. Lewis with a copy to Mr. Dixon for input." The first draft would have, "many, many blanks" which would call for information including a paragraph on "Transactions" which was to disclose those transactions between the officers and employees of AVM and AVM itself; stock options and purchases, salaries and vested retirement benefits, were, for example, included by the AVM staff to be written up in the final copy by Entwisle. But Dixon did not inform Entwisle of the loans; the latter learned of them only in 1972 when a grand jury was investigating possible bribery of municipal officials and Entwisle examined the books. After this, AVM in October 1972 filed an 8-K report with the SEC stating that:

> Due to a misunderstanding of the rule, the Company has failed to report publicly outstanding loans to two of its executives.

* * *

We shall deal first with Dixon's convictions on the two counts, II and VI, of violating the Securities Exchange Act. The failure to include a statement of Dixon's indebtedness in the proxy statement and a Schedule II in the 10-K report were clear violations of "any provision of this chapter, or any rule or regulation thereunder the violation of which is made unlawful or the observance of which is required under the terms of this chapter," the language of the first clause of § 32(a). The principal questions before us are whether Dixon was shown to have had the state of mind required for a conviction and whether the jury was properly charged.

In United States v. Peltz, 433 F.2d 48, 54–55 (2d Cir. 1970), cert. denied, 401 U.S. 955 (1971), we pointed out that in regard to violations of the statute or applicable rules or regulations, § 32(a) requires only willfulness; that the "willfully and knowingly" language occurs only in the second clause of § 32(a) relating to false or misleading statements in various papers required to be filed; that the final proviso that "no person shall be subject to imprisonment under this section for the violation of any rule or regulation if he proves that he had no knowledge of such rule or regulation" shows that "A person can willfully violate an SEC rule even if he does not know of its existence"; and that whatever may be true in other contexts,[6] "willfully" thus has a more restricted meaning in § 32(a). However, since the term must have some meaning, we held, as the late Judge Herlands wrote in the very year the statute was passed and long before his appointment to the federal bench, the prosecution need only establish "a realization on the defendant's part that he was doing a wrongful act," Criminal Law Aspects of the Securities Exchange Act of 1934, 21 U. of Va.L.Rev. 139, 144–49 (1934); it is necessary, we added, only that the act be "wrongful under the securities laws and that the

---

[6] As the Supreme Court has pointed out, " '[W]illful' is a word 'of many meanings, its construction often being influenced by its context,' " Screws v. United States, 325 U.S. 91, 101 (1945), quoting Spies v. United States, 317 U.S. 492 (1943). The Model Penal Code would have requirements of "willfulness" satisfied by proof that the person had acted "knowingly." ALI Proposed Official Draft § 2.02 (1962).

knowingly wrongful act involve a significant risk of effecting the violation that has occurred."

While evidence was scarcely needed to show that the chief officer of a corporation required to file 10-K reports and issue proxy statements knew that the content of these was prescribed by statute or rule, the testimony of Lewis and Entwisle sufficed to meet any burden the Government had on that score. Indeed, Dixon does not deny his knowledge that there were SEC rules requiring the reporting of loans to officers, of which there clearly was sufficient evidence; his contention is that he was incorrectly informed of their content. As the sentencing minutes show, Chief Judge Curtin believed Dixon knew that the exemptive provisions of those rules were not satisfied by a sufficiently low balance at year-end, however high the figure had previously been. Dixon contends the evidence of the latter was not sufficient to convince a reasonable juror beyond a reasonable doubt, United States v. Taylor, 464 F.2d 240 (2 Cir. 1972). Both the factual issue and the question of the effect of a decision on it favorable to Dixon may be close ones, but we need not resolve them. We do not have here the case of a defendant manifesting an honest belief that he was complying with the law. Dixon did a "wrongful act," in the sense of our decision in *Peltz*, when he caused the corporate books to show, as of December 31, 1970, debts of his father and of Lewis which in fact were his own. True, Dixon may have thought his year-end thimblerig would provide escape from a rule different from the one that existed. But such acts are wrongful "under the Securities Acts" if they lead, as here, to the very violations that would have been prevented if the defendant had acted with the aim of scrupulously obeying the rules (which would have necessarily involved correctly ascertaining them) rather than of avoiding them. Such an intention to deceive is enough to meet the modest requirements of the first clause of § 32(a) when violations occur.

* * *

A. KNOWING VERSUS WILLFUL

1. *Convictions.* Dixon was convicted under the first clause of § 32(a), which applies to a failure to comply with an SEC rule or regulation (here, the failure to disclose the indebtedness). What if the prosecution had instead been for a false filing so that the "willfully and knowingly" language of the second clause of § 32(a) became applicable? Some commentators have said that the word "knowingly" in the second clause is redundant.[13] In *Dixon*, however, Judge Friendly notes "the difference seems to have been deliberate."[14] Assuming that the defendant requested a jury charge on the meaning of "knowingly," would it have been necessary for the prosecution to prove more than voluntary and

---

[13] 10 Louis Loss & Joel Seligman, Securities Regulation 4757–4759 (3d ed. rev. 1996).
[14] 536 F.2d at 1396.

intentional conduct? For example, that the defendant knew he was acting illegally?[15] A subsequent Second Circuit decision held that the terms "willfully" and "knowingly" do not require the government to prove the element of specific intent to defraud.[16] Other courts have held that a conviction under § 32(a) can be both "willful" and done knowingly when based upon "reckless, deliberate indifference to or disregard for truth and falsity"[17]—a standard similar to the culpability standard under § 10(b).

2. *Sentencing.* The final clause of § 32(a) of the Securities Exchange Act of 1934 provides: "[N]o person shall be subject to imprisonment under this section in violation of any rule or regulation if he proves that he had no knowledge of such rule or regulation." The "no knowledge" clause was interpreted in United States v. Lilley[18] to mean that:

> Congress intended to charge every man with knowledge of the standards prescribed in the securities acts themselves. It would frustrate the intent of Congress to permit a person whose conduct is expressly prohibited by statute to attempt to prove no knowledge of a parallel rule provision. Allowing these defendants to invoke the "no knowledge" clause would have precisely this effect. * * * It was not intended by the Congress that the "no knowledge" clause of the penalty statute should be available to persons who were charged with knowing their conduct to be in violation of law, but did not happen to know it was in violation of a particular rule or regulation of the SEC such as Rule 10b–5.
>
> * * *
>
> * * * Proof of no knowledge cannot mean proof that defendants did not know, for example, the precise number or common name of the rule, the book and page where it was to be found, or the date upon which it was promulgated. It does not even mean proof of a lack of knowledge that their conduct was proscribed by rule rather than by statute. Proof of "no knowledge" of the rule can only mean proof of an ignorance of the substance of the rule, proof that they did not know that their conduct was contrary to law.

The "no knowledge" clause is relevant only to whether a sentence of incarceration may be imposed. The person convicted has the burden of

---

[15] See United States v. Kaiser, 609 F.3d 556 (2d Cir. 2010) ("whatever "willful" might mean for purposes of other statutes, for the purposes of Section 32(a), it does not encompass the requirement that a defendant knew he was violating the law").

[16] United States v. Chiarella, 588 F.2d 1358, 1370–1371 (2d Cir. 1978), rev'd on other grounds, 445 U.S. 222 (1980). Cf. United States v. DeSantis, 134 F.3d 760, 764 (6th Cir. 1998) (a specific intent to defraud and recklessness are alternative standards).

[17] United States v. Weiner, 578 F.2d 757, 786–787 (9th Cir. 1978); United States v. Boyer, 694 F.2d 58 (3d Cir. 1982).

[18] 291 F.Supp. 989, 992–993 (S.D.Tex.1968).

persuasion to prove no knowledge at sentencing. This section has been held not to raise a constitutional problem because it does not impose a burden on the defendant to disprove the elements of a crime.[19]

B. RELIANCE ON THE ADVICE OF COUNSEL

In United States v. Crosby,[20] the Second Circuit reversed the convictions of four broker-dealers who sold unregistered stock of a control person, "which * * * made the broker defendants technically 'underwriters'."[21] The defendants had relied on their counsel's advice that the shares were exempt from registration under former Rule 133. Given this advice, the Second Circuit said that the "knowingly" requirement of § 32(a) had not been satisfied: "While such a theory is probably invalid * * *, we cannot say that on its face the legal opinions tendered were so patently erroneous as to permit the jury to speculate on the good faith of the defendants."[22]

In contrast, in United States v. Bilzerian,[23] the defendant sought to testify as to his own good faith, but the court ruled that, by doing so, he would become subject to cross-examination as to the basis of his understanding that his actions were legal. This placed in jeopardy the attorney/client privilege to the extent that the prosecution could ask him if he had discussed his conduct with counsel and what advice he had received. In short, by seeking to testify as to his good faith, Bilzerian put into issue whether he might have received contrary indications from his counsel. Although neither the trial court nor the Second Circuit held that he waived his attorney/client privilege, they both suggested that it was in some jeopardy.

3. STOCK PARKING AND "REGULATORY" VIOLATIONS

Few dispute the use of criminal sanctions to punish "true" fraud. But some forms of misconduct in the securities markets raise issues as to whether they are either too technical or too marginal to justify the use of criminal sanctions. Here, the leading example may be "stock parking." Stock parking schemes can vary considerably. In United States v. Regan,[24] the general partners of Princeton/Newport Partners, L.P., an investment firm, were convicted for stock parking. The scheme in *Regan* was entirely different from that in *Bilzerian*. In *Bilzerian*, the motive was to outflank the § 13(d) requirements of the Williams Act and to hide the identity of the silent partner financing Bilzerian. In *Regan*, the

---

[19] United States v. Mandel, 296 F.Supp. 1038, 1040 (S.D.N.Y.1969).
[20] 294 F.2d 928 (2d Cir. 1961).
[21] 294 F.2d at 939–40. See also United States v. Wolfson, 405 F.2d 779 (2d Cir. 1968) (affirming a criminal conviction for similar conduct).
[22] 294 F.2d at 942. But see United States v. Peterson, 101 F.3d 375, 381–83 (5th Cir. 1996): "A good faith reliance on the advice of counsel is not a defense to securities fraud."
[23] 926 F.2d 1185 (2d Cir. 1991).
[24] 937 F.2d 823 (2d Cir. 1991).

government alleged that Princeton/Newport Partners arranged to sell securities to Drexel Burnham Lambert, Inc., subject to secret repurchase agreements allowing it to buy back the securities without regard to their market value at the time of the repurchase. One alleged purpose of this scheme was to permit Princeton/Newport to retain effective economic ownership of the securities while appearing to sell them for tax purposes. Another alleged motive was to allow Drexel to hide its stock ownership in other companies, to permit Drexel to hold a larger ownership percentage than management of the company would have tolerated or to manipulate the company's stock price downward (allegedly so that Drexel could negotiate a better price on an underwriting of convertible bonds it was handling for the company).

"Stock parking" is not itself an independent criminal offense. Rather, it requires violations of specific 1934 Act rules. In the case of a broker-dealer, however, such proof is relatively simple. Rules 17a–3 and 17a–4 under the 1934 Act require a broker-dealer to keep accurate financial records—known as "blotters" and "ledger accounts"—showing all transactions in securities, including any repurchase agreements.

These cases raise an important policy question: should violations of such technical rules be prosecuted as federal felonies? Did Congress really intend that every SEC regulation, however technical or mundane, could be the subject of a federal criminal prosecution under which sentences of up to 10 years are authorized? In *Regan*, the principal stock parking transactions were designed to achieve a tax purpose (which was subject to independent criminal prosecution if unlawful) and did not seek to defraud investors. Although no one challenges that the SEC could and should be entitled to injunctive or administrative relief on detecting such a violation, a continuing debate surrounds the question of whether "overcriminalization" results from the use of criminal sanctions in such cases.[25] Defense counsel have repeatedly asserted that defendants were informed that they would not have been criminally prosecuted if they had cooperated in the government's investigation of other defendants in these cases. In this light, does attaching criminal sanctions to every SEC regulation give the prosecution too much leverage in plea bargaining? In a more recent stock parking case, the Ninth Circuit appeared to tighten the standard.[26]

---

[25] These issues are reconsidered in light of the 1980s insider trading scandals in John C. Coffee, Jr., *Hush! The Criminal Status of Confidential Business Information After McNally and Carpenter and the Enduring Problem of Overcriminalization*, 26 Am. Crim. L. Rev. 121 (1988).

[26] In Yoshikawa v. SEC, 192 F.3d 1209, 1214 (9th Cir. 1999), the court concluded:
Based on our review and analysis of the "parking" caselaw, we conclude that securities "parking" is, at a minimum, comprised of the following elements:
(1) a pre-arrangement to sell and then buy back securities (to conceal true ownership);
(2) on the same, or substantially the same, terms (thus keeping the market risk entirely on the seller);

The next case involves both stock parking and manipulation charges and may show some judicial resistance to the criminalization of "regulatory" offenses:

United States v. Mulheren
United States Court of Appeals, Second Circuit, 1991.
938 F.2d 364.

■ Before: VAN GRAAFEILAND, MESKILL and McLAUGHLIN, CIRCUIT JUDGES.

■ McLAUGHLIN, CIRCUIT JUDGE:

In the late 1980's a wide prosecutorial net was cast upon Wall Street. Along with the usual flotsam and jetsam, the government's catch included some of Wall Street's biggest, brightest, and now infamous—Ivan Boesky, Dennis Levine, Michael Milken, Robert Freeman, Martin Siegel, Boyd L. Jeffries, and Paul A. Bilzerian—each of whom either pleaded guilty to or was convicted of crimes involving illicit trading scandals. Also caught in the government's net was defendant-appellant John A. Mulheren, Jr., the chief trader at and general partner of Jamie Securities Co. ("Jamie"), a registered broker-dealer.

Mulheren was charged in a 42-count indictment handed-up on June 13, 1989. The indictment alleged that he conspired to and did manipulate the price on the New York Stock Exchange (the "NYSE") of the common stock of Gulf & Western Industries, Inc. ("G & W" or the "company") * * * by purchasing 75,000 shares of G & W common stock on October 17, 1985 for the purpose of raising the price thereof to $45 per share (Counts One through Four); that he engaged in "stock parking" transactions to assist the Seemala Corporation, a registered broker-dealer controlled by Boesky, in evading tax and other regulatory requirements * * *; that he committed mail fraud in connection with the stock parking transactions * * *; and that Mulheren caused Jamie to make and keep false books and records.

* * *

This appeal thus focuses solely on the convictions concerning Mulheren's alleged manipulation of G & W common stock. The government sought to prove that on October 17, 1985, Mulheren purchased 75,000 shares of G & W common stock with the purpose and intent of driving the price of that stock to $45 per share. This, the government claimed, was a favor to Boesky, who wanted to sell his enormous block of G & W common stock back to the company at that price. Mulheren assails the convictions on several grounds.

---

(3) for a bad-faith purpose, accomplished through a sham transaction in which nominal title is transferred to the purported buyer while the economic incidents of ownership are left with the purported seller.

First, Mulheren claims that the government failed to prove beyond a reasonable doubt that when he purchased the 75,000 shares of G & W common stock on October 17, 1985, he did it for the sole purpose of raising the price at which it traded on the NYSE, rather than for his own investment purposes. Second, Mulheren argues that even if his sole intent had been to raise the price of G & W stock, that would not have been a crime because, he claims, (1) he neither misrepresented any fact nor failed to disclose any fact that he was under a duty to disclose concerning his G & W purchases; (2) his subjective intent in purchasing G & W stock is not "material"; and (3) he did not act for the purpose of deceiving others. Finally, Mulheren cites various alleged evidentiary and sentencing errors that he believes entitle him to either a new trial or resentencing.

Although we harbor doubt about the government's theory of prosecution, we reverse on Mulheren's first stated ground because we are convinced that no rational trier of fact could have found the elements of the crimes charged here beyond a reasonable doubt.

BACKGROUND

Reviewing the evidence "in the light most favorable to the government, and construing all permissible inferences in its favor," the following facts were established at trial.

In 1985, at the suggestion of his long-time friend, Carl Icahn, a prominent arbitrageur and corporate raider, Ivan Boesky directed his companies to buy G & W stock, a security that both Icahn and Boesky believed to be "significantly undervalued." Between April and October 1985, Boesky's companies accumulated 3.4 million shares representing approximately 4.9 percent of the outstanding G & W shares. According to Boesky, Icahn also had a "position of magnitude."

On September 5, 1985, Boesky and Icahn met with Martin Davis, the chairman of G & W. At the meeting, Boesky expressed his interest in taking control of G & W through a leveraged buyout or, failing that, by increasing his position in G & W stock and securing seats on the G & W board of directors. Boesky told Davis that he held 4.9 percent of G & W's outstanding shares. Davis said he was not interested in Boesky's proposal, and he remained adamant in subsequent telephone calls and at a later meeting on October 1, 1985.

At the October 1, 1985 meeting, which Icahn also attended, Boesky added a new string to his bow: if Davis continued to reject Boesky's attempts at control, then G & W should buy-out his position at $45 per share. At that time, G & W was, indeed, reducing the number of its outstanding shares through a repurchase program, but, the stock was trading below $45 per share. Davis stated that, although he would consider buying Boesky's shares, he could not immediately agree to a price. Icahn, for his part, indicated that he was not yet sure whether he would sell his G & W stock.

During—and for some time before—these negotiations, Mulheren and Boesky also maintained a relationship of confidence and trust. The two had often shared market information and given each other trading tips. At some point during the April–October period when Boesky was acquiring G & W stock, Mulheren asked Boesky what he thought of G & W and whether Icahn held a position in the stock. Boesky responded that he "thought well" of G & W stock and that he thought Icahn did indeed own G & W stock. Although Boesky told Mulheren that G & W stock was "a good purchase and worth owning," Boesky never told Mulheren about his meetings or telephone conversations with Davis because he considered the matter "very confidential." Speculation in the press, however, was abound. Reports in the August 19, 1985 issue of Business Week and the September 27, 1985 issue of the Wall Street Journal indicated that Boesky and Icahn each owned close to five percent of G & W and discussed the likelihood of a take-over of the company. Mulheren, however, testifying in his own behalf, denied reading these reports and denied knowing whether Boesky and Icahn held positions in G & W.

On October 3, 1985, two days after his meeting with Boesky and Icahn, Davis met with Mulheren. Mulheren stated that he had a group of investors interested in knowing whether G & W would join them in acquiring CBS. According to Davis, Mulheren also volunteered that he could be "very helpful in monitoring the activities of Ivan Boesky [in G & W stock;] [Mulheren] knew that [Davis] considered Mr. Boesky adversarial;" and Mulheren agreed with Davis' unflattering assessment of Boesky. In a telephone conversation sometime between this October 3 meeting and a subsequent meeting between the two on October 9, 1985, Mulheren told Davis that he believed that Boesky did not own any G & W securities. Mulheren also said that he did not own any G & W stock either. When Davis and Mulheren met again on October 9, they spoke only about Mulheren's CBS proposal.

In the meantime, Boesky continued to press Davis to accept his proposals to secure control of G & W. When Boesky called Davis after their October 1, 1985 meeting, Davis "told [Boesky] as clearly as [he] could again that [G & W] had no interest whatsoever in doing anything with [Boesky]." Boesky then decided to contact his representative at Goldman, Sachs & Co. to arrange the sale of his massive block of stock to G & W. Boesky advised Goldman, Sachs that G & W common stock was not trading at $45 per share at the time, "but that should it become 45," he wanted to sell. A Goldman, Sachs representative met with Davis shortly thereafter regarding the company's repurchase of Boesky's G & W shares.

Sometime after the close of the market on October 16, 1985, Boesky called Davis, offering to sell his block of shares back to G & W at $45 per share. NYSE trading had closed that day at $44–3/4 per share, although at one point during that day it had reached $45. Davis told Boesky that the company would buy his shares back, but only at the "last sale"—the price at which the stock traded on the NYSE at the time of the sale—and that Boesky should have his Goldman, Sachs representative contact Kidder Peabody & Co. to arrange the transaction.[1]

After this conversation with Davis, but before 11:00 a.m. on October 17, 1985, Boesky called Mulheren. According to Boesky's testimony, the following, critical exchange took place:

> BOESKY: Mr. Mulheren asked me if I liked the stock on that particular day, and I said yes, I still liked it. At the time it was trading at 44–3/4. I said I liked it; however, I would not pay more than 45 for it and it would be great if it traded at 45. The design for the comment—
>
> DEFENSE COUNSEL MR. PUCCIO: Objection to the "design of the comment." I would ask only for the conversation.
>
> A.U.S.A. GILBERT: What if anything did he say to you?
>
> BOESKY: I understand.

Shortly after 11:00 a.m. on October 17, 1985, Jamie (Mulheren's company) placed an order with Oliver Ihasz, a floor broker, to purchase 50,000 shares of G & W at the market price. Trading in G & W had been sluggish that morning (only 32,200 shares had traded between 9:30 a.m. and 11:03 a.m.), and the market price was holding steady at $44–3/4, the price at which it had closed the day before. At 11:04 a.m., Ihasz purchased 16,100 shares at $44–3/4 per share. Unable to fill the entire 50,000 share order at $44–3/4, Ihasz purchased the remaining 33,900 shares between 11:05 a.m. and 11:08 a.m. at $44–7/8 per share.

At 11:09 a.m., Ihasz received another order from Jamie; this time, to purchase 25,000 shares of G & W for no more than $45 per share. After attempting to execute the trade at $44–7/8, Ihasz executed the additional 25,000 share purchase at $45 per share at 11:10 a.m. In sum, between 11:04 a.m. and 11:10 a.m., Jamie purchased a total of 75,000 shares of G & W common stock, causing the price at which it traded per share to rise from $44–3/4 to $45. At 11:17 a.m., Boesky and Icahn sold their G & W stock—6,715,700 shares between them—back to the company at $45 per share. Trading in G & W closed on the NYSE on October 17, 1985 at $43–5/8 per share. At the end of the day, Jamie's trading in G & W common stock at Mulheren's direction had caused it to lose $64,406.

DISCUSSION

A convicted defendant, of course, bears "a very heavy burden" to demonstrate that the evidence at trial was insufficient to prove his guilt

---

[1] Around the same time, Mulheren received a call from a broker at another firm who had failed to execute an order that day to buy 25,000 shares of G & W for an institutional customer. The broker asked Mulheren if Mulheren would sell him the 25,000 shares he needed. Mulheren, who, at the time, did not own any shares of G & W, checked the stock, noted "it was up a dollar that day" and agreed to "short" the broker—sell what he did not own—25,000 shares. Obviously, Mulheren would soon be obligated to cover his short position, i.e. buy 25,000 shares of G & W.

beyond a reasonable doubt. "A jury's verdict will be sustained if there is *substantial evidence*, taking the view most favorable to the government, to support it." (emphasis added). Where " '*any* rational trier of fact could have found the essential elements of the crime,' the conviction must stand." United States v. Badalamenti, 794 F.2d 821, 828 (2d Cir. 1986) (quoting Jackson v. Virginia, 443 U.S. 307, 319 (1979)) (emphasis in original).

On this appeal, however, we are reminded that "in America we still respect the dignity of the individual, and [a defendant] . . . is not to be imprisoned except on definite proof of a specific crime." United States v. Bufalino, 285 F.2d 408, 420 (2d Cir. 1960) (Clark, J., concurring). To that end, it is "imperative that we not rend the fabric of evidence and examine each shred in isolation; rather, the reviewing court 'must use its experience with people and events in weighing the chances that the evidence correctly points to guilt against the possibility of innocent or ambiguous inference.'" United States v. Redwine, 715 F.2d 315, 319 (7th Cir. 1983) (quoting United States v. Kwitek, 467 F.2d 1222, 1226 (7th Cir. 1972)).

The government's theory of prosecution in this case is straightforward. In its view, when an investor, who is neither a fiduciary nor an insider, engages in securities transactions in the open market with the sole intent to affect the price of the security, the transaction is manipulative and violates Rule 10b–5.[2] Unlawful manipulation occurs, the argument goes, even though the investor has not acted for the "purpose of inducing the purchase or sale of such security by others," an element the government would have had to prove had it chosen to proceed under the manipulation statute, § 9(a)(2). Mulheren was not charged with violating § 9(a)(2). When the transaction is effected for an investment purpose, the theory continues, there is no manipulation, even if an increase or diminution in price was a foreseeable consequence of the investment.

Although we have misgivings about the government's view of the law, we will assume, without deciding on this appeal, that an investor may lawfully be convicted under Rule 10b–5 where the purpose of his transaction is solely to affect the price of a security. The issue then becomes one of Mulheren's subjective intent. The government was obligated to prove beyond a reasonable doubt that when Mulheren purchased 75,000 shares of G & W common stock on October 17, 1985, he did it with the intent to raise its price, rather than with the intent to invest. We conclude that the government failed to carry this burden.

---

[2] The government also appears to argue in the alternative that the violation occurs not by simply engaging in a securities transaction with the intent to affect the price of a security, but rather by failing to disclose that subjective intent to the market. The government contends that all investors are under a "general duty" not to manipulate; thus, absent disclosure of an intent to manipulate, Rule 10b–5 is violated. We express no view on this theory.

In order to convict, the government had to demonstrate, in the first place, that Mulheren was aware that Boesky had a stake in G & W. In proof of knowledge, the government makes three arguments.

First, the government suggests that Boesky himself told Mulheren of his G & W positions. Boesky, however, never so testified; and the greatest puzzle in this record is why that critical question was never directly put to Boesky.[3]

Second, the government relies on the speculation reported in the media, specifically the Wall Street Journal and Business Week, and the rumors floating on Wall Street that Boesky and Icahn owned substantial positions in G & W. There was no evidence, however, that Mulheren read these articles or heard these rumors. On the contrary, Mulheren flatly denied knowing of their existence. Moreover, knowledge of a rumor, particularly one on Wall Street, can hardly substitute for knowledge of a fact.

Third, the government contends that Mulheren's knowledge of Boesky's position is evident in the October 3, 1985 meeting between Davis and Mulheren. In that meeting, Mulheren told Davis that he knew that Davis and Boesky had an "adversarial" relationship and Mulheren "understood" Davis' "position" and offered to help Davis "in any way he could" to "monitor" Boesky's G & W transactions. While this evidence, taken in isolation, might create an inference that Mulheren knew of Boesky's G & W holdings (as the source of the Boesky-Davis adversarial relationship), the rest of Davis' testimony casts a considerable shadow on the inference. Davis went on to testify that in a telephone conversation sometime between their October 3 and October 9 meetings Mulheren stated that he did not believe Boesky owned any G & W stock at all. By this time, of course, Boesky had already told Davis (at their September 5 meeting) that he owned 4.9 percent of G & W's outstanding shares. Given that Mulheren was at the time attempting to curry favor from Davis in connection with Mulheren's CBS proposal, it was hardly in Mulheren's best interest to lie to Davis by telling him that Boesky owned *no* shares, if in fact Mulheren knew that Boesky owned 3.4 million shares. In sum, the evidence of Mulheren's knowledge that Boesky had an interest in G & W rests on a very slender reed.

Even were we to conclude otherwise, however, the convictions still could not be sustained. Assuming that Mulheren knew that Boesky held a substantial position in G & W stock, the government nevertheless failed to prove that Mulheren agreed to and then purchased the 75,000 shares

---

[3] The closest Boesky came to testifying that he told Mulheren about his G & W holdings is the following exchange on direct examination concerning a telephone conversation between Mulheren and Boesky sometime in the period between April and the end of September 1985:

A.U.S.A. GILBERT: What in fact did you tell [Mulheren] about the stock?

BOESKY: As my position was being accumulated, I told him that's how I felt about it, that it was a good purchase and worth owning.

for the sole purpose of raising the price at which G & W common stock traded.

The strongest evidence supporting an inference that Mulheren harbored a manipulative intent, is the telephone conversation between Boesky and Mulheren that occurred either late in the day on October 16 or before 11:00 a.m. on October 17, 1985. In discussing the virtues of G & W stock, Boesky told Mulheren that he "would not pay more than 45 for it and it would be great if it traded at 45." To this Mulheren replied "I understand." The meaning of this cryptic conversation is, at best, ambiguous, and we reject the government's contention that this conversation "*clearly* conveyed Boesky's request that the price of the stock be pushed up to $45 . . . [and Mulheren's] agreement to help." Boesky never testified (again, he was not asked) what he meant by his words.[4]

We acknowledge that, construed as an innocent tip—*i.e.* G & W would be a "great" buy at a price of $45 or below—the conversation appears contradictory. It seems inconsistent for Boesky to advise, on one hand, that he would not pay more than $45, yet on the other to exclaim that it would be a bargain ("great") at $45. The conversation does not make any more sense, however, if construed as a request for illicit manipulation. That Boesky put a limit on the price he would pay for the stock ("I would not pay more than 45 for it") seems inconsistent with a request to drive up the price of the stock. If a conspiracy to manipulate for his own selfish benefit had been Boesky's intent, and if Davis were poised to repurchase the shares at the "last sale," Boesky would obviously have preferred to see Mulheren drive the trading in G & W stock to a price above $45. In this regard, it is noteworthy that there was *no* evidence whatever that Mulheren knew of Boesky's demand to get $45 per share from G & W. Moreover, during the four to six weeks preceding this conversation, Mulheren repeatedly asked Boesky what he thought of G & W—evincing Mulheren's predisposition (and Boesky's knowledge thereof) to invest in the company. In fact, Mulheren took a position in G & W when he shorted a broker 25,000 shares of G & W after the market closed on October 16.

Clearly, this case would be much less troubling had Boesky said "I want you to bring it up to 45" or, perhaps, even, "I'd like to see it trading at 45." But to hang a conviction on the threadbare phrase "it would be great if it traded at 45," particularly when the government does not suggest that the words were some sort of sinister code, defies reason and a sense of fair play. Any doubt about this is dispelled by the remaining evidence at trial.

First, and perhaps most telling, is that Jamie *lost* over $64,000 on Mulheren's October 17th transactions. This is hardly the result a market

---

[4] Defense counsel objected after Boesky testified "[t]he design of the comment. . . ." No ruling was made on the objection and the government—for reasons known only to itself—abandoned further inquiry into Boesky's state of mind.

manipulator seeks to achieve. One of the hallmarks of manipulation is some profit or personal gain inuring to the alleged manipulator.

Second, the unrebutted trial testimony of the G & W specialist demonstrated that if raising the price of G & W to $45 per share was Mulheren's sole intent, Mulheren purchased significantly more shares (and put Jamie in a position of greater risk) than necessary to achieve the result. The G & W specialist testified that at the time Jamie placed its second order, 5,000 shares would "definitely" have raised the trading price from $44 7/8 to $45 per share. Yet, Jamie bought 25,000 shares.

Although there was no evidence that Mulheren received a *quid pro quo* from Boesky for buying G & W stock, the government, nevertheless, claims that Mulheren had a "strong pecuniary interest" in accommodating Boesky in order to maintain the close and mutually profitable relationship they enjoyed. With this argument the government is hoist with its own petard. Precisely because of this past profitable relationship, the more reasonable conclusion is that Mulheren understood Boesky's comment as another tip—this time to buy G & W stock. Indeed, there was no evidence that Boesky had ever asked Mulheren to rig the price of a stock in the past.

None of the traditional badges of manipulation are present in this case. Mulheren conspicuously purchased the shares for Jamie's account in the open market. Compare United States v. Scop, 846 F.2d 135, 137 (matched orders through fictitious nominees), modified on other grounds, 856 F.2d 5 (2d Cir. 1988); United States v. Gilbert, 668 F.2d 94, 95 (2d Cir. 1981) (matched orders and wash sales),[5] cert. denied, 456 U.S. 946 (1982); United States v. Minuse, 114 F.2d 36, 38 (2d Cir. 1940) (fictitious accounts, matched orders, wash sales, dissemination of false literature). The government argues that Mulheren's deceptive intent can be inferred from the fact that (1) he purchased the G & W shares through Ihasz, a floor broker whom the government claims was used only infrequently by Jamie; and (2) Ihasz never informed anyone that the purchases were made for Jamie. These arguments are factually flawed.

There was no evidence that there was anything unusual about Ihasz's execution of the trades. Oliver Ihasz testified that Jamie was a customer of his company. There was no testimony that his company was used infrequently, or that Mulheren's request was in any way out of the ordinary. Nor is there anything peculiar about the fact that Ihasz disclosed only the name of the clearing broker and not Jamie, as the purchaser, when he executed the trade. As Ihasz testified, in an open market transaction, the only information the floor broker provides to the seller is the name of the clearing broker, not the ultimate buyer. Jamie

---

[5] In a wash sale transaction, beneficial ownership of the stock does not change. A matched order involves the prearranged purchase and sale, usually through different brokers, of the same amount of securities at substantially the same price and time. Both practices give the appearance of legitimate market activity.

was conspicuously identified as the ultimate buyer of the G & W securities on Ihasz's order tickets, where it is supposed to appear.

The government also argues that manipulative intent can be inferred from the fact that Mulheren's purchase on October 17, 1985 comprised 70 percent of the trading in G & W common stock during the period between the opening of the market and 11:10 a.m. Such market domination, the government contends, is indicative of manipulation. While we agree, as a general proposition, that market domination is a factor that supports a manipulation charge, the extent to which an investor controls or dominates the market at any given period of time cannot be viewed in a vacuum. For example, if only ten shares of a stock are bought or sold in a given hour and only by one investor, that investor has created 100 percent of the activity in that stock in that hour. This alone, however, does not make the investor a manipulator. The percent of domination must be viewed in light of the time period involved and other indicia of manipulation. Taken in this context, the cases upon which the government relies, United States v. Gilbert, 668 F.2d 94 (2d Cir. 1981); United States v. Stein, 456 F.2d 844 (2d Cir. 1972); In re Delafield & Delafield, [1967–69 Transfer Binder] Fed.Sec.L.Rep. (CCH) ¶ 77, 648 (SEC 1969), are readily distinguishable.

Gilbert, for example, involved the manipulation of the shares of Conrac Corporation where, over a one-year period, the defendant's trading constituted more than 50 percent of the overall trading. In *Stein*, the manipulator's transactions accounted for 28.8 percent of the daily exchange volume of transactions in Buckeye Corporation stock over a four month period. When domination is sustained over such an extended period of time, evidence of manipulation is strong. But, if the percentage of control be measured in terms of minutes or hours, anyone could find himself labeled as a manipulator.

In re Delafield & Delafield is the only case that gives us pause. There, the respondents entered into a consent decree with the Securities and Exchange Commission concerning allegations that they had manipulated the Class A common stock of the Mary Carter Paint Company by selling 17,600 shares of the stock between 2:00 p.m. and the close of the market on January 9, 1968. Respondents' transactions represented 83 percent of the transactions in the stock during that period. Significantly, however, the sales "were effected in the name of two foreign banks to conceal the identity" of the true seller. No such chicanery exists here. Thus, in the absence of other indicia of manipulation—and there are none—the fact that Mulheren dominated the market between 9:30 a.m. and 11:10 a.m. on October 17, 1985 (noting that Mulheren's purchases represented a small fraction of the total October 17th activity in G & W stock) carries little weight.

The government also urges that Mulheren's manipulative intent—as opposed to investment intent—can be inferred from certain of Mulheren's actions after his purchase of the G & W shares. For example,

Mulheren sold G & W call options in the afternoon of October 17, 1985 that were designed to create a hedge in the event of a drop in the price of stock. Had Mulheren known, however, that Boesky and Icahn were going to unload 6.7 million shares of G & W stock—which had the inevitable effect of driving the price down—surely Mulheren would have had the foresight to write the options before Boesky and Icahn had a chance to sell. That Mulheren wrote the options in the afternoon suggests only that he was attempting to mitigate his losses.

Finally, the government contends that the fact that Mulheren continued to do favors for Boesky after G & W repurchased Boesky and Icahn's shares is inconsistent with his claim that he was "duped" by Boesky into purchasing the 75,000 G & W shares. We disagree. First, the evidence of "favors" rests largely on the unproven "stock parking" charges. Second, Mulheren's conduct after his G & W purchases is equally consistent with that of a sophisticated businessman who turns the other cheek after being slapped by the hand that usually feeds him.

We acknowledge that this case treads dangerously close to the line between legitimate inference and impermissible speculation. We are persuaded, however, that to come to the conclusion it did, "the jury must have engaged in false surmise and rank speculation." United States v. Wiley, 846 F.2d 150, 155 (2d Cir. 1988) (citing United States v. Starr, 816 F.2d 94, 99 (2d Cir. 1987)). At best, Mulheren's convictions are based on evidence that is "at least as consistent with innocence as with guilt," United States v. Mankani, 738 F.2d 538, 547 (2d Cir. 1984), and "on inferences no more valid than others equally supported by reason and experience." United States v. Bufalino, 285 F.2d 408, 419 (2d Cir. 1960). Accordingly, the judgments of conviction are reversed and Counts One through Four of the indictment are dismissed.

---

1. *The Meaning of Manipulation.* Only weeks before the *Mulheren* decision, another Second Circuit panel upheld the conviction of Princeton/Newport Partners, the same defendants discussed above in the note on stock parking, for stock manipulation. According to the government's theory in *Regan*,[27] Drexel Burnham arranged with Princeton/Newport, an arbitrage and hedge trading firm, for the latter to sell short the stock of one of its clients, C.O.M.B., Inc., whose convertible bonds Drexel was about to underwrite. Drexel apparently feared that its client, C.O.M.B., Inc., was manipulating the price of its common stock upwards (in order to get a lower interest rate concession on its soon-to-be-issued bonds, because the more attractive the bonds' conversion price, the lower the interest rate necessary to attract purchasers). In response, Drexel sought to drive C.O.M.B.'s stock price downward on the eve of the underwriting. On appeal, the defendants claimed that because they owed no fiduciary duty to the parties they traded with in their sales of

---

[27] 937 F.2d 823 (2d Cir. 1991).

C.O.M.B. stock they had no duty to disclose the fact that the market had been manipulated. The Second Circuit panel in *Regan* rejected this theory, concluding:

> Failure to disclose that [the] market prices are being artificially depressed operates as a deceit on the market place and is an omission of a material fact * * * Appellants' argument that a fiduciary relationship must exist before liability can be found is without merit.[28]

Regan thus seemingly accepted the government's theory that there is a general obligation to disclose the fact that one has manipulated market prices. But this was precisely the theory as to which the *Mulheren* panel said "we harbor doubt about the government's theory of prosecution."[29] Interestingly, one judge sat on both panels. The issue seems to be whether courts view stock manipulation as a disclosure crime (in which case omissions are normally actionable only if there is a duty to speak) or as a crime of conduct (in which case purchases made with a "manipulative intent" to raise or depress the market price artificially are themselves unlawful without more).[30]

2. *Legislative Enhancements to Criminal Liability.* Congress continues to enhance prosecutors' criminal enforcement abilities under the Federal Securities Laws, both in the Sarbanes-Oxley Act of 2002, and to a lesser extent, in the Dodd-Frank Act of 2010.

Section 802 of Title VIII of Sarbanes-Oxley introduced §§ 1519 and 1520 to Title 18 of the United States Code. Section 1519 criminalizes the

---

[28] Id. at 829.

[29] United States v. Mulheren, 938 F.2d 364, 366 (2d Cir. 1991). Some commentators deny that there is any objective meaning to the term "manipulation" and recommend that the entire concept be abandoned as founded on "conceptual confusion." See Daniel R. Fischel & David J. Ross, Should The Law Prohibit "Manipulation" in Financial Markets?, 105 Harv. L. Rev. 503 (1991). Cf. Steve Thel, $850,000 in Six Minutes—The Mechanics of Securities Manipulation, 79 Cornell L. Rev. 219 (1994); Judith R. Starr & David Herman, The Same Old Wine in a Brand New Bottle: Applying Market Manipulation Principles to Internet Stock Scams, 29 Sec. Reg. L.J. 236 (2001).

[30] In SEC v. Kimmes, 799 F.Supp. 852, 859 (N.D.Ill.1992); the court generalized:

[A]ny activities that falsely persuade the public that activity in an over-the-counter security is "the reflection of a genuine demand instead of a mirage" are outlawed by 1933 Act § 17(a) and 1934 Act § 10(b) (SEC v. Resch-Cassin & Co., 362 F.Supp. 964, 975 (S.D.N.Y.1973)). Such activities may include (1) fraudulent promises of quick profits made by salesmen to friends and customers (United States v. Blitz, 533 F.2d 1329, 1338 (2d Cir. 1976)); (2) directed and controlled trading in a security (United States v. Cohen, 518 F.2d 727, 734 (2d Cir. 1975); United States v. Corr, 543 F.2d 1042, 1045–46 (2d Cir. 1976); (3) the use of wash sales and matched orders (Edward J. Mawod & Co. v. SEC, 591 F.2d 588, 595 (10th Cir. 1979)); (4) the use of undisclosed nominees (SEC v. Commonwealth Chemical Securities, Inc., 410 F.Supp. 1002, 1017–18 (S.D.N.Y.1976), aff'd in part and modified in part on other grounds, 574 F.2d 90 (2d Cir. 1978); and (5) the use of material misrepresentations in newsletters and otherwise (United States v. Mahler, 579 F.2d 730, 732 (2d Cir. 1978)).

In a manipulation case, individual purchases or sales are not the appropriate unit of prosecution; "these retail events were only a step in the advancement of the scheme as a whole. On the facts here, each count properly charged a manipulation of the securities of each of the three separate companies—each involving a discrete scheme." United States v. Haddy, 134 F.3d 542, 549 (3d Cir. 1998).

alteration or falsification of records in federal investigation and bankruptcy proceedings and allows a sentence of up to 20 years imprisonment. Section 1520 creates a criminal provision with up to ten years imprisonment for destruction of corporate audit records. The indictment and ensuing criminal trial of Arthur Andersen LLP inspired these sections. Arthur Andersen allegedly destroyed documents in anticipation of investigation, and the only criminal remedy available to prosecutors was 18 U.S.C. § 1512 for obstruction of justice. Arthur Anderson was convicted, but the Supreme Court later reversed the convictions.[31] (The reversal was cold comfort for the employees and owners of Arthur Anderson, which disbanded after its initial conviction, highlighting that in criminal cases against entities, the ultimate resolution of the case may be of less importance than the existence of a case in the first place.) Section 807 of Title VII also adds a provision that allows up to 25 years imprisonment for securities fraud.

Title IX (the "White Collar Crime Penalty Enforcement Act of 2002") also enhances several criminal penalties. Section 1350 establishes criminal penalties for chief executive officers and chief financial officers who falsely certify (or fail to certify) their companies' periodic financial reports. A willful violation of this Section can result in a fine of up to $5 million and 20 years imprisonment. Section 1106 amends § 32(a) of the 1934 Act to increase specified criminal penalties up to $5 (or $25 million in the case of corporations or other entities) and 20 years imprisonment. Section 1107 amends 18 U.S.C. § 1513(e) punishes retaliation against whistle-blowers with up to 10 years imprisonment. Section 1079A of the Dodd-Frank Act also extended the statute of limitations for securities offenses to 6 years after the offense from 5 years.

This increasing use of criminal penalties to enforce securities laws has come under some criticism. On the one hand, criminal sanctions can be highly effective at deterring wrongdoing, especially when it is difficult to detect and when potential defendants may be judgment proof. (If there is only a 10% chance of being caught stealing $1 million, damages must be set at $10 million to deter this crime, but defendants may not be able to bear those losses.) On the other hand, excessive use of criminal penalties may chill risk taking and otherwise socially productive behavior. As in other areas of law, if the legal system sorts perfectly the good and bad cases, and sets penalties accurately, then these risks are mitigated. But, if there are errors in sorting cases or penalties are not finely calibrated, productive activity can be deterred. Overdeterrence may be especially worrisome when using criminal sanctions, given the high cost of losing one's liberty and given the large reputational sanctions of criminal convictions, especially among white collar workers.

---

[31] Arthur Andersen LLP v. United States, 544 U.S. 696 (2005).

Problem

PROBLEM 15-1

You are assisting the general counsel of FINRA in formulating a policy regarding the sharing of the results of FINRA investigations with investigators from the SEC and with the FBI. Write down a list of pros and cons of a policy of open collaboration, in which FINRA's Department of Enforcement routinely shares data, testimony, and findings of FINRA investigations with government investigators.

4. CRIMINAL PROSECUTIONS UNDER TITLE 18

Traditionally, when federal prosecutors decided to prosecute a fraud (whether insider trading or a "pump and dump" scheme), they would use Rule 10b–5 (and the SEC could bring a parallel action also relying on Rule 10b–5). But this pattern appears to be changing. Federal prosecutors have long used the mail and wire fraud statutes to reach all varieties of frauds, and in Carpenter v. United States,[32] they successfully prosecuted insider trading on the theory that an employee who trades based on "confidential information" belonging to the employer has essentially embezzled property from the employer. More recently, in the Sarbanes-Oxley Act, Congress enacted 18 U.S.C. § 1348 ("Securities Fraud") for the express purpose of enabling prosecutors to overcome the "technical legal requirements" of Title 15 fraud provisions.[33] As *Dirks*'s standards for insider trading (which requires both some form of a fiduciary breach and receipt of a personal benefit paid to the tipper by the tippee) became more complicated to apply, prosecutors turned increasingly to section 1348. But this raises the question of whether section 1348 should be read *in pari materia* with Rule 10b–5, as both are specifically aimed at stock trading.

In United States v. Blaszczak,[34] the Second Circuit (with one dissent) ruled that the doctrine of *in pari materia* did not apply because § 1348 had a very different purpose than the Securities Exchange Act. There, the defendant had used material non-public information taken from a federal agency to sell stocks that would be adversely affected when a new governmental policy was announced. U.S. attorneys indicted the defendant under each of Rule 10b–5, wire fraud, § 1348, and 18 U.S.C. 641 (which prohibits conversion of governmental property). Interestingly, the jury acquitted the defendants on the Rule 10b–5 charge (where they were required to find a "personal benefit" paid by the tippee to the tipper), but convicted the defendant on all the other counts. On appeal, defendants argued that insider trading should not be differently defined in two related statutes that were both intended to address the

---

[32] 484 U.S. 19, 26 (1987). All that is necessary is that the defendants deprive their employer of "exclusive possession" of the confidential information.
[33] See U.S. v. Hoskins, 902 F.3d 69, 81 n. 5 (2d Cir. 2018).
[34] 947 F.3d 19 (2d Cir. 2019).

same topic—but lost.[35] This raises the question of whether *Dirks*'s other standards also carried over to § 1348. For example, Rule 10b–5 clearly requires that there must be a purchase or sale of securities before it applies.[36] But is a purchase or sale also necessary for §§ 1348 and 1349 (which criminalizes attempts or conspiracies to violate § 1348).[37]

Another consequence of this increased use of § 1348 and the mail and wire fraud statutes is that the SEC is left out. It has jurisdiction to sue under Title 15, but not under Title 18. Of course, it can still sue under Rule 10b–5 (but it now faces a greater burden than the criminal prosecutors because it must now prove the *Dirks* standard). At some point, this issue may again make its way to the Supreme Court.

---

[35] The district court in *Blaszczak* did, however, charge the jury that to convict under Section 1348, they had to find that information had been either misappropriated or embezzled.

[36] See Blue Chip Stamps v. Manor Drug Stores, 421 U.S. 723 (1975).

[37] Section 1348(1) does not refer to "in connection with a purchase or sale," but Section 1348(2) does. For a discussion of how little must be shown under Section 1348, see United States v. Mahaffy, 693 F.3d 113, 125–126 (2d Cir. 2012) (Section 1348 does not require proof of false representations or material omissions); United States v. Motz, 652 F.Supp.2d 284 (E.D.N.Y. 2009).

CHAPTER 16

INTERNATIONAL ENFORCEMENT

Statutes and Regulations

Dodd-Frank Act, §§ 929P(b), 929Y.

Securities Act, § 17(a).

Exchange Act, §§ 10(b), 27.

Rule 10b–5.

Securities markets are increasingly global. U.S. investors have expanded their holdings of foreign securities and foreign issuers have made greater use of the U.S. capital markets. In 2018, U.S. investors held $11.3 trillion in foreign securities.[1] Conversely, in 2019, foreign investors held $20.5 trillion, in U.S. securities.[2]

A variety of factors are driving this movement to a globalized securities market including:

- Capital market imbalances caused by differences in national savings rates and investment opportunities, resulting in some nations (i.e., the OPEC countries early in the 1980s, Japan later in the decade, and increasingly China in the 2000s) becoming capital suppliers;
- New technology developments, which facilitate international trading;
- Investors who desire to hold an internationally diversified portfolio of securities to reduce exposure to economic downturn in any one country;
- Issuers who tap international equity markets to reduce their cost of capital; and
- U.S. financial services industry fears that without accommodation of foreign issuers, U.S. dealers would be excluded from profitable business, and foreign securities markets would gradually surpass U.S. markets in depth and liquidity.

---

[1] DEP'T OF THE TREASURY, FED. RESERVE BANK OF N.Y., & BD. OF GOVERNORS OF THE FED. RESERVE SYS., U.S. PORTFOLIO HOLDINGS OF FOREIGN SECURITIES AS OF DECEMBER 31, 2018 5 (2019), http://www.treasury.gov/resource-center/data-chart-center/tic/Pages/fpis.aspx#usclaims.

[2] DEP'T OF THE TREASURY, FED. RESERVE BANK OF N.Y., & BD. OF GOVERNORS OF THE FED. RESERVE SYS., FOREIGN PORTFOLIO HOLDINGS OF U.S. SECURITIES AS OF JUNE 28, 2019 4 (2020), http://www.treasury.gov/resource-center/data-chart-center/tic/Pages/fpis.aspx#usclaims.

The internationalization of securities markets results in profound implications for the world's securities market regulators. Securities suits against foreign issuers have been a significant part of overall securities lawsuit filings in recent years. For example, from 1997 to 2019, the percentage of securities class action filings against foreign issuers rose from just 3% to 23%.[3] Yet, the extraterritorial reach of the United States securities laws remains uncertain.

1. THE JURISDICTION OF U.S. COURTS OVER CLAIMS BY PRIVATE PLAINTIFFS

For many years, case law developed around the question of whether and when private plaintiffs could sue over "foreign" securities transactions. The federal securities fraud laws are silent on the question of their extraterritorial reach. Courts had, however, construed them to cover certain foreign transactions.

Schoenbaum v. Firstbrook,[4] the first significant decision to consider the extraterritorial application of the federal securities laws, established the principle that the application of § 10(b) could be premised upon some effect on American securities markets or investors, regardless of the location of the transaction. Over the next forty years, courts continued to address the issue through jurisdictional principles, with a focus on the conduct surrounding the transaction and the location of the injuries where the effects were felt. As a result, the issue became one about the reach of the statute. The Supreme Court addressed this issue in Morrison v. National Australia Bank, Ltd. and significantly redefined the extraterritorial application of the federal securities laws.

The *Morrison* opinion did away with many years of jurisdictional jurisprudence. Instead, Justice Scalia relied on the presumption against extraterritorial application of U.S. law and limited the jurisdiction of § 10(b) to alleged frauds in connection with the "purchase or sale of a security listed on an American stock exchange, and the purchase or sale of any other security in the United States."[5]

Morrison addresses a so-called "f-cubed" securities case, involving foreign plaintiffs, suing foreign defendants, for a foreign securities transaction, that is, one that took place outside of the United States. As discussed in the notes following the *Morrison* case, however, the reach of the opinion is broader than just the f-cubed cases.

---

[3] Stanford Law School Securities Class Action Clearinghouse and Cornerstone Research, Securities Class Action Filings: 2016 A Year In Review 21 fig.18, http://securities.stanford.edu/research-reports/1996-2016/Cornerstone-Research-Securities-Class-Action-Filings-2016-YIR.pdf; Stanford Law School Securities Class Action Clearinghouse and Cornerstone Research, Securities Class Action Filings: 2019 A Year In Review 30 fig.29, https://www.cornerstone.com/Publications/Reports/Securities-Class-Action-Filings%E2%80%942019-Year-in-Revie.

[4] 405 F.2d 200 (2d Cir. 1968).

[5] Morrison v. National Austl. Bank Ltd., 561 U.S. 247, 130 S.Ct. 2869, 2888 (2010).

Morrison v. National Australia Bank, Ltd.
Supreme Court of the United States, 2010.
561 U.S. 247, 130 S.Ct. 2869, 177 L.Ed.2d 535.

■ JUSTICE SCALIA delivered the opinion of the Court.

We decide whether § 10(b) of the Securities Exchange Act of 1934 provides a cause of action to foreign plaintiffs suing foreign and American defendants for misconduct in connection with securities traded on foreign exchanges.

I

Respondent National Australia Bank Limited (National) was, during the relevant time, the largest bank in Australia. Its Ordinary Shares—what in America would be called "common stock"—are traded on the Australian Stock Exchange Limited and on other foreign securities exchanges, but not on any exchange in the United States. There are listed on the New York Stock Exchange, however, National's American Depositary Receipts (ADRs), which represent the right to receive a specified number of National's Ordinary Shares.

The complaint alleges the following facts, which we accept as true. In February 1998, National bought respondent HomeSide Lending, Inc., a mortgage servicing company headquartered in Florida. HomeSide's business was to receive fees for servicing mortgages (essentially the administrative tasks associated with collecting mortgage payments, see J. Rosenberg, Dictionary of Banking and Financial Services 600 (2d ed. 1985)). The rights to receive those fees, so-called mortgage-servicing rights, can provide a valuable income stream. How valuable each of the rights is depends, in part, on the likelihood that the mortgage to which it applies will be fully repaid before it is due, terminating the need for servicing. HomeSide calculated the present value of its mortgage-servicing rights by using valuation models designed to take this likelihood into account. It recorded the value of its assets, and the numbers appeared in National's financial statements.

From 1998 until 2001, National's annual reports and other public documents touted the success of HomeSide's business, and respondents Frank Cicutto (National's managing director and chief executive officer), Kevin Race (HomeSide's chief operating officer), and Hugh Harris (HomeSide's chief executive officer) did the same in public statements. But on July 5, 2001, National announced that it was writing down the value of HomeSide's assets by $450 million; and then again on September 3, by another $1.75 billion. The prices of both Ordinary Shares and ADRs slumped. After downplaying the July write-down, National explained the September write-down as the result of a failure to anticipate the lowering of prevailing interest rates (lower interest rates lead to more refinancings, i.e., more early repayments of mortgages), other mistaken assumptions in the financial models, and the loss of goodwill. According to the complaint, however, HomeSide, Race, Harris, and another

HomeSide senior executive who is also a respondent here had manipulated HomeSide's financial models to make the rates of early repayment unrealistically low in order to cause the mortgage-servicing rights to appear more valuable than they really were. The complaint also alleges that National and Cicutto were aware of this deception by July 2000, but did nothing about it.

As relevant here, petitioners Russell Leslie Owen and Brian and Geraldine Silverlock, all Australians, purchased National's Ordinary Shares in 2000 and 2001, before the write-downs.[1] They sued National, HomeSide, Cicutto, and the three HomeSide executives in the United States District Court for the Southern District of New York for alleged violations of §§ 10(b) and 20(a) of the Securities and Exchange Act of 1934, 48 Stat. 881, 15 U.S.C. §§ 78j(b) and 78t(a), and SEC Rule 10b–5, 17 CFR § 240.10b–5 (2009), promulgated pursuant to § 10(b). They sought to represent a class of foreign purchasers of National's Ordinary Shares during a specified period up to the September write-down.

Respondents moved to dismiss for lack of subject-matter jurisdiction under Federal Rule of Civil Procedure 12(b)(1) and for failure to state a claim under Rule 12(b)(6). The District Court granted the motion on the former ground, finding no jurisdiction because the acts in this country were, "at most, a link in the chain of an alleged overall securities fraud scheme that culminated abroad." The Court of Appeals for the Second Circuit affirmed on similar grounds. The acts performed in the United States did not "compris[e] the heart of the alleged fraud."

II

Before addressing the question presented, we must correct a threshold error in the Second Circuit's analysis. It considered the extraterritorial reach of § 10(b) to raise a question of subject-matter jurisdiction, wherefore it affirmed the District Court's dismissal under Rule 12(b)(1). In this regard it was following Circuit precedent, see Schoenbaum v. Firstbrook, 405 F.2d 200, 208, modified on other grounds en banc, 405 F.2d 215 (1968). The Second Circuit is hardly alone in taking this position.

But to ask what conduct § 10(b) reaches is to ask what conduct § 10(b) prohibits, which is a merits question. Subject-matter jurisdiction, by contrast, "refers to a tribunal's 'power to hear a case.' " It presents an issue quite separate from the question whether the allegations the plaintiff makes entitle him to relief. The District Court here had jurisdiction under 15 U.S.C. § 78aa to adjudicate the question whether § 10(b) applies to National's conduct.

---

[1] Robert Morrison, an American investor in National's ADRs, also brought suit, but his claims were dismissed by the District Court because he failed to allege damages. Petitioners did not appeal that decision, and it is not before us. Inexplicably, Morrison continued to be listed as a petitioner in the Court of Appeals and here.

In view of this error, which the parties do not dispute, petitioners ask us to remand. We think that unnecessary. Since nothing in the analysis of the courts below turned on the mistake, a remand would only require a new Rule 12(b)(6) label for the same Rule 12(b)(1) conclusion. As we have done before in situations like this, we proceed to address whether petitioners' allegations state a claim.

III

A

It is a "longstanding principle of American law 'that legislation of Congress, unless a contrary intent appears, is meant to apply only within the territorial jurisdiction of the United States.'" EEOC v. Arabian American Oil Co., 499 U.S. 244, 248 (1991) (*Aramco*). This principle represents a canon of construction, or a presumption about a statute's meaning, rather than a limit upon Congress's power to legislate. It rests on the perception that Congress ordinarily legislates with respect to domestic, not foreign matters. Thus, "unless there is the affirmative intention of the Congress clearly expressed" to give a statute extraterritorial effect, "we must presume it is primarily concerned with domestic conditions." The canon or presumption applies regardless of whether there is a risk of conflict between the American statute and a foreign law.

Despite this principle of interpretation, long and often recited in our opinions, the Second Circuit believed that, because the Exchange Act is silent as to the extraterritorial application of § 10(b), it was left to the court to "discern" whether Congress would have wanted the statute to apply. This disregard of the presumption against extraterritoriality did not originate with the Court of Appeals panel in this case. It has been repeated over many decades by various courts of appeals in determining the application of the Exchange Act, and § 10(b) in particular, to fraudulent schemes that involve conduct and effects abroad. That has produced a collection of tests for divining what Congress would have wanted, complex in formulation and unpredictable in application.

As of 1967, district courts at least in the Southern District of New York had consistently concluded that, by reason of the presumption against extraterritoriality, § 10(b) did not apply when the stock transactions underlying the violation occurred abroad. See Schoenbaum v. Firstbrook, 268 F.Supp. 385, 392 (1967). *Schoenbaum* involved the sale in Canada of the treasury shares of a Canadian corporation whose publicly traded shares (but not, of course, its treasury shares) were listed on both the American Stock Exchange and the Toronto Stock Exchange. Invoking the presumption against extraterritoriality, the court held that § 10(b) was inapplicable (though it incorrectly viewed the defect as jurisdictional). The decision in *Schoenbaum* was reversed, however, by a Second Circuit opinion which held that "neither the usual presumption against extraterritorial application of legislation nor the specific language of [§]30(b) show Congressional intent to preclude application of the Exchange Act to transactions regarding stocks traded in the United States which are effected outside the United States...." It sufficed to apply § 10(b) that, although the transactions in treasury shares took place in Canada, they affected the value of the common shares publicly traded in the United States. Application of § 10(b), the Second Circuit found, was "necessary to protect American investors."

The Second Circuit took another step with Leasco Data Processing Equip. Corp. v. Maxwell, which involved an American company that had been fraudulently induced to buy securities in England. There, unlike in *Schoenbaum*, some of the deceptive conduct had occurred in the United States but the corporation whose securities were traded (abroad) was not listed on any domestic exchange. *Leasco* said that the presumption against extraterritoriality applies only to matters over which the United States would not have prescriptive jurisdiction. Congress had prescriptive jurisdiction to regulate the deceptive conduct in this country, the language of the Act could be read to cover that conduct, and the court concluded that "if Congress had thought about the point," it would have wanted § 10(b) to apply.

With *Schoenbaum* and *Leasco* on the books, the Second Circuit had excised the presumption against extraterritoriality from the jurisprudence of § 10(b) and replaced it with the inquiry whether it would be reasonable (and hence what Congress would have wanted) to apply the statute to a given situation. As long as there was prescriptive jurisdiction to regulate, the Second Circuit explained, whether to apply § 10(b) even to "predominantly foreign" transactions became a matter of whether a court thought Congress "wished the precious resources of United States courts and law enforcement agencies to be devoted to them rather than leave the problem to foreign countries."

The Second Circuit had thus established that application of § 10(b) could be premised upon either some effect on American securities markets or investors (*Schoenbaum*) or significant conduct in the United States (*Leasco*). It later formalized these two applications into (1) an "effects test," "whether the wrongful conduct had a substantial effect in the United States or upon United States citizens," and (2) a "conduct test," "whether the wrongful conduct occurred in the United States." These became the north star of the Second Circuit's § 10(b) jurisprudence, pointing the way to what Congress would have wished. Indeed, the Second Circuit declined to keep its two tests distinct on the ground that "an admixture or combination of the two often gives a better picture of whether there is sufficient United States involvement to justify the exercise of jurisdiction by an American court." The Second Circuit never put forward a textual or even extratextual basis for these tests. As early as *Bersch*, it confessed that "if we were asked to point to language in the statutes, or even in the legislative history, that compelled these conclusions, we would be unable to respond."

As they developed, these tests were not easy to administer. The conduct test was held to apply differently depending on whether the harmed investors were Americans or foreigners: When the alleged damages consisted of losses to American investors abroad, it was enough that acts "of material importance" performed in the United States "significantly contributed" to that result; whereas those acts must have "directly caused" the result when losses to foreigners abroad were at issue. And "merely preparatory activities in the United States" did not suffice "to trigger application of the securities laws for injury to foreigners located abroad." This required the court to distinguish between mere preparation and using the United States as a "base" for fraudulent activities in other countries. But merely satisfying the conduct test was sometimes insufficient without " 'some additional factor tipping the scales' " in favor of the application of American law. District courts have noted the difficulty of applying such vague formulations. There is no more damning indictment of the "conduct" and "effects" tests than the Second Circuit's own declaration that "the presence or absence of any single factor which was considered significant in other cases . . . is not necessarily dispositive in future cases."

Other Circuits embraced the Second Circuit's approach, though not its precise application. Like the Second Circuit, they described their decisions regarding the extraterritorial application of § 10(b) as essentially resolving matters of policy. While applying the same fundamental methodology of balancing interests and arriving at what seemed the best policy, they produced a proliferation of vaguely related variations on the "conduct" and "effects" tests. As described in a leading Seventh Circuit opinion: "Although the circuits . . . seem to agree that there are some transnational situations to which the antifraud provisions of the securities laws are applicable, agreement appears to end at that point."

At least one Court of Appeals has criticized this line of cases and the interpretive assumption that underlies it. In Zoelsch v. Arthur Andersen & Co., the District of Columbia Circuit observed that rather than courts' "divining what 'Congress would have wished' if it had addressed the problem[, a] more natural inquiry might be what jurisdiction Congress in fact thought about and conferred." Although tempted to apply the presumption against extraterritoriality and be done with it, that court deferred to the Second Circuit because of its "preeminence in the field of securities law." See also Robinson v. TCI/US West Communications Inc., 117 F.3d 900, 906–907 (5th Cir. 1997) (expressing agreement with Zoelsch's criticism of the emphasis on policy considerations in some of the cases).

Commentators have criticized the unpredictable and inconsistent application of § 10(b) to transnational cases. Some have challenged the premise underlying the Courts of Appeals' approach, namely that Congress did not consider the extraterritorial application of § 10(b) (thereby leaving it open to the courts, supposedly, to determine what Congress would have wanted). Others, more fundamentally, have noted that using congressional silence as a justification for judge-made rules violates the traditional principle that silence means no extraterritorial application.

The criticisms seem to us justified. The results of judicial-speculation-made-law—divining what Congress would have wanted if it had thought of the situation before the court—demonstrate the wisdom of the presumption against extraterritoriality. Rather than guess anew in each case, we apply the presumption in all cases, preserving a stable background against which Congress can legislate with predictable effects.

B

Rule 10b–5, the regulation under which petitioners have brought suit, was promulgated under § 10(b), and "does not extend beyond conduct encompassed by § 10(b)'s prohibition." United States v. O'Hagan, 521 U.S. 642, 651 (1997). Therefore, if § 10(b) is not extraterritorial, neither is Rule 10b–5.

On its face, § 10(b) contains nothing to suggest it applies abroad:

"It shall be unlawful for any person, directly or indirectly, by the use of any means or instrumentality of interstate commerce or of the mails, or of any facility of any national securities exchange ... [t]o use or employ, in connection with the purchase or sale of any security registered on a national securities exchange or any security not so registered, ... any manipulative or deceptive device or contrivance in contravention of such rules and regulations as the [Securities and Exchange] Commission may prescribe...." 15 U.S.C. 78j(b).

Petitioners and the Solicitor General contend, however, that three things indicate that § 10(b) or the Exchange Act in general has at least some extraterritorial application.

First, they point to the definition of "interstate commerce," a term used in § 10(b), which includes "trade, commerce, transportation, or communication ... between any foreign country and any State." 15 U.S.C. § 78c(a)(17). But "we have repeatedly held that even statutes that contain broad language in their definitions of 'commerce' that expressly refer to '*foreign* commerce' do not apply abroad." The general reference to foreign commerce in the definition of "interstate commerce" does not defeat the presumption against extraterritoriality.

Petitioners and the Solicitor General next point out that Congress, in describing the purposes of the Exchange Act, observed that the "prices established and offered in such transactions are generally disseminated and quoted throughout the United States and foreign countries." 15 U.S.C. § 78b(2). The antecedent of "such transactions," however, is found in the first sentence of the section, which declares that "transactions in securities as commonly conducted upon securities exchanges and over-the-counter markets are affected with a national public interest." § 78b. Nothing suggests that this *national* public interest pertains to transactions conducted upon *foreign* exchanges and markets. The fleeting reference to the dissemination and quotation abroad of the prices of securities traded in domestic exchanges and markets cannot overcome the presumption against extraterritoriality.

Finally, there is § 30(b) of the Exchange Act, 15 U.S.C. § 78dd(b), which does mention the Act's extraterritorial application: "The provisions of [the Exchange Act] or of any rule or regulation thereunder shall not apply to any person insofar as he transacts a business in securities without the jurisdiction of the United States," unless he does so in violation of regulations promulgated by the Securities and Exchange Commission "to prevent . . . evasion of [the Act]." (The parties have pointed us to no regulation promulgated pursuant to § 30(b).) The Solicitor General argues that "[this] exemption would have no function if the Act did not apply in the first instance to securities transactions that occur abroad."

We are not convinced. In the first place, it would be odd for Congress to indicate the extraterritorial application of the whole Exchange Act by means of a provision imposing a condition precedent to its application abroad. And if the whole Act applied abroad, why would the Commission's enabling regulations be limited to those preventing "evasion" of the Act, rather than all those preventing "violation"? The provision seems to us directed at actions abroad that might conceal a domestic violation, or might cause what would otherwise be a domestic violation to escape on a technicality. At most, the Solicitor General's proposed inference is possible; but possible interpretations of statutory language do not override the presumption against extraterritoriality.

The Solicitor General also fails to account for § 30(a), which reads in relevant part as follows:

> "It shall be unlawful for any broker or dealer . . . to make use of the mails or of any means or instrumentality of interstate commerce for the purpose of effecting on an exchange not within or subject to the jurisdiction of the United States, any transaction in any security the issuer of which is a resident of, or is organized under the laws of, or has its principal place of business in, a place within or subject to the jurisdiction of the United States, in contravention of such rules and regulations as the Commission may prescribe. . . ." 15 U.S.C. § 78dd(a).

Subsection 30(a) contains what § 10(b) lacks: a clear statement of extraterritorial effect. Its explicit provision for a specific extraterritorial application would be quite superfluous if the rest of the Exchange Act already applied to transactions on foreign exchanges—and its limitation of that application to securities of domestic issuers would be inoperative.

Even if that were not true, when a statute provides for some extraterritorial application, the presumption against extraterritoriality operates to limit that provision to its terms. No one claims that § 30(a) applies here.

The concurrence claims we have impermissibly narrowed the inquiry in evaluating whether a statute applies abroad, citing for that point the dissent in *Aramco*. But we do not say, as the concurrence seems to think, that the presumption against extraterritoriality is a "clear statement rule," if by that is meant a requirement that a statute say "this law applies abroad." Assuredly context can be consulted as well. But whatever sources of statutory meaning one consults to give "the most faithful reading" of the text, there is no clear indication of extraterritoriality here. The concurrence does not even try to refute that conclusion, but merely puts forward the same (at best) uncertain indications relied upon by petitioners and the Solicitor General. As the opinion *for the Court* in *Aramco* (which we prefer to the dissent) shows, those uncertain indications do not suffice.

In short, there is no affirmative indication in the Exchange Act that § 10(b) applies extraterritorially, and we therefore conclude that it does not.

IV

A

Petitioners argue that the conclusion that § 10(b) does not apply extraterritorially does not resolve this case. They contend that they seek no more than domestic application anyway, since Florida is where HomeSide and its senior executives engaged in the deceptive conduct of manipulating HomeSide's financial models; their complaint also alleged that Race and Hughes made misleading public statements there. This is less an answer to the presumption against extraterritorial application than it is an assertion—a quite valid assertion—that that presumption here (as often) is not self-evidently dispositive, but its application requires further analysis. For it is a rare case of prohibited extraterritorial application that lacks *all* contact with the territory of the United States. But the presumption against extraterritorial application would be a craven watchdog indeed if it retreated to its kennel whenever *some* domestic activity is involved in the case. The concurrence seems to imagine just such a timid sentinel, but our cases are to the contrary. In *Aramco,* for example, the Title VII plaintiff had been hired in Houston, and was an American citizen. The Court concluded, however, that neither that territorial event nor that relationship was the "focus" of congressional concern, but rather domestic employment.

Applying the same mode of analysis here, we think that the focus of the Exchange Act is not upon the place where the deception originated, but upon purchases and sales of securities in the United States. Section 10(b) does not punish deceptive conduct, but only deceptive conduct "in connection with the purchase or sale of any security registered on a national securities exchange or any security not so registered." 15 U.S.C. § 78j(b). Those purchase-and-sale transactions are the objects of the statute's solicitude. It is those transactions that the statute seeks to "regulate," see Superintendent of Ins. of N.Y. v. Bankers Life & Casualty Co., 404 U.S. 6, 12 (1971); it is parties or prospective parties to those transactions that the statute seeks to "protec[t]." And it is in our view only transactions in securities listed on domestic exchanges, and domestic transactions in other securities, to which § 10(b) applies.

The primacy of the domestic exchange is suggested by the very prologue of the Exchange Act, which sets forth as its object "[t]o provide for the regulation of securities exchanges . . . operating in interstate and foreign commerce and through the mails, to prevent inequitable and unfair practices on such exchanges. . . ." 48 Stat. 881. We know of no one who thought that the Act was intended to "regulat[e]" *foreign* securities exchanges—or indeed who even believed that under established principles of international law Congress had the power to do so. The Act's registration requirements apply only to securities listed on national securities exchanges. 15 U.S.C. § 78*l*(a).

With regard to securities not registered on domestic exchanges, the exclusive focus on domestic purchases and sales[10] is strongly confirmed by § 30(a) and (b), discussed earlier. The former extends the normal scope of the Exchange Act's prohibitions to acts effecting, in violation of rules prescribed by the Commission, a "transaction" in a United States security "on an exchange not within or subject to the jurisdiction of the United States." § 78dd(a). And the latter specifies that the Act does not apply to "any person insofar as he transacts a business in securities without the jurisdiction of the United States," unless he does so in violation of regulations promulgated by the Commission "to prevent evasion [of the Act]." § 78dd(b). Under both provisions it is the foreign location of the transaction that establishes (or reflects the presumption of) the Act's inapplicability, absent regulations by the Commission.

The same focus on domestic transactions is evident in the Securities Act of 1933, enacted by the same Congress as the Exchange Act, and forming part of the same comprehensive regulation of securities trading. That legislation makes it unlawful to sell a security, through a prospectus or otherwise, making use of "any means or instruments of transportation or communication in interstate commerce or of the mails," unless a registration statement is in effect. 15 U.S.C. § 77e(a)(1). The

---

[10] That is in our view the meaning which the presumption against extraterritorial application requires for the words "purchase or sale, of . . . any security not so registered" in § 10(b)'s phrase "in connection with the purchase or sale of any security registered on a national securities exchange *or any security not so registered*" (emphasis added). Even without the presumption against extraterritorial application, the only alternative to that reading makes nonsense of the phrase, causing it to cover all purchases and sales of registered securities, and all purchases and sales of nonregistered securities—a thought which, if intended, would surely have been expressed by the simpler phrase "all purchases and sales of securities."

Commission has interpreted that requirement "not to include . . . sales that occur outside the United States." 17 CFR § 230.901 (2009).

Finally, we reject the notion that the Exchange Act reaches conduct in this country affecting exchanges or transactions abroad for the same reason that *Aramco* rejected overseas application of Title VII to all domestically concluded employment contracts or all employment contracts with American employers: The probability of incompatibility with the applicable laws of other countries is so obvious that if Congress intended such foreign application "it would have addressed the subject of conflicts with foreign laws and procedures." Like the United States, foreign countries regulate their domestic securities exchanges and securities transactions occurring within their territorial jurisdiction. And the regulation of other countries often differs from ours as to what constitutes fraud, what disclosures must be made, what damages are recoverable, what discovery is available in litigation, what individual actions may be joined in a single suit, what attorney's fees are recoverable, and many other matters. The Commonwealth of Australia, the United Kingdom of Great Britain and Northern Ireland, and the Republic of France have filed amicus briefs in this case. So have (separately or jointly) such international and foreign organizations as the International Chamber of Commerce, the Swiss Bankers Association, the Federation of German Industries, the French Business Confederation, the Institute of International Bankers, the European Banking Federation, the Australian Bankers' Association, and the Association Francaise des Entreprises Privees. They all complain of the interference with foreign securities regulation that application of § 10(b) abroad would produce, and urge the adoption of a clear test that will avoid that consequence. The transactional test we have adopted—whether the purchase or sale is made in the United States, or involves a security listed on a domestic exchange—meets that requirement.

B

The Solicitor General suggests a different test, which petitioners also endorse: "[A] transnational securities fraud violates [§]10(b) when the fraud involves significant conduct in the United States that is material to the fraud's success." Neither the Solicitor General nor petitioners provide any textual support for this test. The Solicitor General sets forth a number of purposes such a test would serve: achieving a high standard of business ethics in the securities industry, ensuring honest securities markets and thereby promoting investor confidence, and preventing the United States from becoming a "Barbary Coast" for malefactors perpetrating frauds in foreign markets. But it provides no textual support for the last of these purposes, or for the first two as applied to the foreign securities industry and securities markets abroad. It is our function to give the statute the effect its language suggests, however modest that may be; not to extend it to admirable purposes it might be used to achieve.

If, moreover, one is to be attracted by the desirable consequences of the "significant and material conduct" test, one should also be repulsed by its adverse consequences. While there is no reason to believe that the United States has become the Barbary Coast for those perpetrating frauds on foreign securities markets, some fear that it has become the Shangri-La of class-action litigation for lawyers representing those allegedly cheated in foreign securities markets.

As case support for the "significant and material conduct" test, the Solicitor General relies primarily on Pasquantino v. United States, 544 U.S. 349 (2005). In that case we concluded that the wire-fraud statute, 18 U.S.C. § 1343 (2009 ed., Supp. II), was violated by defendants who ordered liquor over the phone from a store in Maryland with the intent to smuggle it into Canada and deprive the Canadian Government of revenue. Section 1343 prohibits "any scheme or artifice to defraud,"—fraud *simpliciter*, without any requirement that it be "in connection with" any particular transaction or event. The *Pasquantino* Court said that the petitioners' "offense was complete the moment they executed the scheme inside the United States," and that it was "[t]his domestic element of petitioners' conduct [that] the Government is punishing." Section 10(b), by contrast, punishes not all acts of deception, but only such acts "in connection with the purchase or sale of any security registered on a national securities exchange or any security not so registered." Not deception alone, but deception with respect to certain purchases or sales is necessary for a violation of the statute.

The Solicitor General points out that the "significant and material conduct" test is in accord with prevailing notions of international comity. If so, that proves that if the United States asserted prescriptive jurisdiction pursuant to the "significant and material conduct" test it would not violate customary international law; but it in no way tends to prove that that is what Congress has done.

Finally, the Solicitor General argues that the Commission has adopted an interpretation similar to the "significant and material conduct" test, and that we should defer to that. In the two adjudications the Solicitor General cites, however, the Commission did not purport to be providing its own interpretation of the statute, but relied on decisions of federal courts—mainly Court of Appeals decisions that in turn relied on the *Schoenbaum* and *Leasco* decisions of the Second Circuit that we discussed earlier. We need "accept only those agency interpretations that are reasonable in light of the principles of construction courts normally employ." Since the Commission's interpretations relied on cases we disapprove, which ignored or discarded the presumption against extraterritoriality, we owe them no deference.

* * *

Section 10(b) reaches the use of a manipulative or deceptive device or contrivance only in connection with the purchase or sale of a security listed on an American stock exchange, and the purchase or sale of any other security in the United States. This case involves no securities listed on a domestic exchange, and all aspects of the purchases complained of by those petitioners who still have live claims occurred outside the United States. Petitioners have therefore failed to state a claim on which relief can be granted. We affirm the dismissal of petitioners' complaint on this ground.

It is so ordered.

■ JUSTICE SOTOMAYOR took no part in the consideration or decision of this case.

■ JUSTICE BREYER, concurring in part and concurring in the judgment.

Section 10(b) of the Securities Exchange Act of 1934 applies to fraud "in connection with" two categories of transactions: (1) "the purchase or sale of any security registered on a national securities exchange" or (2) "the purchase or sale of . . . any security not so registered." 15 U.S.C. § 78j(b). In this case, the purchased securities are listed only on a few foreign exchanges, none of which has registered with the Securities and Exchange Commission as a "national securities exchange." See § 78f. The first category therefore does not apply. Further, the relevant purchases of these unregistered securities took place entirely in Australia and involved only Australian investors. And in accordance with the presumption against extraterritoriality, I do not read the second category to include such transactions. Thus, while state law or other federal fraud statutes, see, e.g., 18 U.S.C. § 1341 (mail fraud), § 1343 (wire fraud), may apply to the fraudulent activity alleged here to have occurred in the United States, I believe that § 10(b) does not. This case does not require us to consider other circumstances.

To the extent the Court's opinion is consistent with these views, I join it.

■ JUSTICE STEVENS, with whom JUSTICE GINSBERG joins, concurring in the judgment.

While I agree that petitioners have failed to state a claim on which relief can be granted, my reasoning differs from the Court's. I would adhere to the general approach that has been the law in the Second Circuit, and most of the rest of the country, for nearly four decades.

I

Today the Court announces a new "transactional test," for defining the reach of § 10(b) of the Securities Exchange Act of 1934, and SEC Rule 10b–5: Henceforth, those provisions will extend only to "transactions in securities listed on domestic exchanges . . . and domestic transactions in other securities." If one confines one's gaze to the statutory text, the Court's conclusion is a plausible one. But the federal courts have been construing § 10(b) in a different manner for a long time, and the Court's textual analysis is not nearly so compelling, in my view, as to warrant the abandonment of their doctrine.

The text and history of § 10(b) are famously opaque on the question of when, exactly, transnational securities frauds fall within the statute's compass. As those types of frauds became more common in the latter half of the 20th century, the federal courts were increasingly called upon to wrestle with that question. The Court of Appeals for the Second Circuit, located in the Nation's financial center, led the effort. Beginning in earnest with Schoenbaum v. Firstbrook, that court strove, over an extended series of cases, to "discern" under what circumstances "Congress would have wished the precious resources of the United States courts and law enforcement agencies to be devoted to [transnational] transactions." Relying on opinions by Judge Henry Friendly,[1] the Second Circuit eventually settled on a conduct-and-effects test. This test asks "(1) whether the wrongful conduct occurred in the Unites States, and (2) whether the wrongful conduct had a substantial effect in the United States or upon United States citizens." Numerous cases flesh out the proper application of each prong.

The Second Circuit's test became the "north star" of § 10(b) jurisprudence, not just regionally but nationally as well. With minor variations, other courts converged on the same basic approach. See Brief for United States as Amicus Curiae 15 ("The courts have uniformly agreed that Section 10(b) can apply to a transnational securities fraud either when fraudulent conduct has effects in the United States or when sufficient conduct relevant to the fraud occurs in the United States"); see also 1 Restatement (Third) of Foreign Relations Law of the United States § 416 (1986) (setting forth conduct-and-effects test). Neither Congress nor the Securities Exchange Commission (Commission) acted to change the law. To the contrary, the Commission largely adopted the Second Circuit's position in its own adjudications.

In light of this history, the Court's critique of the decision below for applying "judge-made rules" is quite misplaced. This entire area of law is replete with judge-made rules, which give concrete meaning to Congress' general commands. "When we deal with private actions under Rule 10b–5," then-Justice Rehnquist wrote many years ago, "we deal with a judicial oak which has grown from little more than a legislative acorn." Blue Chip Stamps v. Manor Drug Stores, 421 U.S. 723, 737 (1975). The " 'Mother Court' " of securities law tended to that oak. Id., at 762 (Blackmun, J., dissenting) (describing the Second Circuit). One of our greatest jurists—the judge who, "without a doubt, did more to shape the law of securities regulation than any [other] in the country"—was its master arborist.

The development of § 10(b) law was hardly an instance of judicial usurpation. Congress invited an expansive role for judicial elaboration

---

[1] See, e.g., IIT, Int'l Inv. Trust v. Cornfeld, 619 F.2d 909 (2d Cir. 1980); IIT v. Vencap, Ltd., 519 F.2d 1001 (2d Cir. 1975); Bersch v. Drexel Firestone, Inc., 519 F.2d 974 (2d Cir. 1975); Leasco Data Processing Equip. Corp. v. Maxwell, 468 F.2d 1326 (2d Cir.1972).

when it crafted such an open-ended statute in 1934. And both Congress and the Commission subsequently affirmed that role when they left intact the relevant statutory and regulatory language, respectively, throughout all the years that followed. Unlike certain other domains of securities law, this is "a case in which Congress has enacted a regulatory statute and then has accepted, over a long period of time, broad judicial authority to define substantive standards of conduct and liability," and much else besides. Stoneridge Investment Partners, LLC v. Scientific-Atlanta, Inc., 552 U.S. 148, 163 (2008).

* * *

Thus, while the Court devotes a considerable amount of attention to the development of the case law, it draws the wrong conclusions. The Second Circuit refined its test over several decades and dozens of cases, with the tacit approval of Congress and the Commission and with the general assent of its sister Circuits. That history is a reason we should give additional weight to the Second Circuit's "judge-made" doctrine, not a reason to denigrate it. "The longstanding acceptance by the courts, coupled with Congress' failure to reject [its] reasonable interpretation of the wording of § 10(b), . . . argues significantly in favor of acceptance of the [Second Circuit] rule by this Court." Blue Chip, 421 U.S., at 733.

II

The Court's other main critique of the Second Circuit's approach—apart from what the Court views as its excessive reliance on functional considerations and reconstructed congressional intent—is that the Second Circuit has "disregard[ed]" the presumption against extraterritoriality. It is the Court, however, that misapplies the presumption, in two main respects.

First, the Court seeks to transform the presumption from a flexible rule of thumb into something more like a clear statement rule. We have been here before. In the case on which the Court primarily relies, EEOC v. Arabian American Oil Co., Chief Justice Rehnquist's majority opinion included a sentence that appeared to make the same move. See id., at 258 ("Congress' awareness of the need to make a clear statement that a statute applies overseas is amply demonstrated by the numerous occasions on which it has expressly legislated the extraterritorial application of a statute"). Justice Marshall, in dissent, vigorously objected. See id., at 261 ("[C]ontrary to what one would conclude from the majority's analysis, this canon is not a 'clear statement' rule, the application of which relieves a court of the duty to give effect to all available indicia of the legislative will").

Yet even *Aramco*—surely the most extreme application of the presumption against extraterritoriality in my time on the Court—contained numerous passages suggesting that the presumption may be overcome without a clear directive. See id., at 248–255 (majority opinion) (repeatedly identifying congressional "intent" as the touchstone of the presumption). And our cases both before and after *Aramco* make perfectly clear that the Court continues to give effect to "*all available evidence* about the meaning" of a provision when considering its extraterritorial application, lest we defy Congress' will. Contrary to Justice Scalia's personal view of statutory interpretation, that evidence legitimately encompasses more than the enacted text. Hence, while the Court's dictum that "[w]hen a statute gives no clear indication of an extraterritorial application, it has none," makes for a nice catchphrase, the point is overstated. The presumption against extraterritoriality can be useful as a theory of congressional purpose, a tool for managing international conflict, a background norm, a tiebreaker. It does not relieve courts of their duty to give statutes the most faithful reading possible.

Second, and more fundamentally, the Court errs in suggesting that the presumption against extraterritoriality is fatal to the Second Circuit's test. For even if the presumption really were a clear statement (or "clear indication,") rule, it would have only marginal relevance to this case.

It is true, of course, that "this Court ordinarily construes ambiguous statutes to avoid unreasonable interference with the sovereign authority of other nations," and that, absent contrary evidence, we presume "Congress is primarily concerned with domestic conditions." Accordingly, the presumption against extraterritoriality "provides a sound basis for concluding that Section 10(b) does not apply when a securities fraud with no effects in the United States is hatched and executed entirely outside this country." Brief for United States as Amicus Curiae 22. But that is just about all it provides a sound basis for concluding. And the conclusion is not very illuminating, because no party to the litigation disputes it. No one contends that § 10(b) applies to wholly foreign frauds.

Rather, the real question in this case is how much, and what kinds of, *domestic* contacts are sufficient to trigger application of § 10(b). In developing its conduct-and-effects test, the Second Circuit endeavored to derive a solution from the Exchange Act's text, structure, history, and purpose. Judge Friendly and his colleagues were well aware that United States courts "cannot and should not expend [their] resources resolving cases that do not affect Americans or involve fraud emanating from America."

* * *

This approach is consistent with the understanding shared by most scholars that Congress, in passing the Exchange Act, "expected U.S. securities laws to apply to certain international transactions or conduct." Buxbaum, Multinational Class Actions Under Federal Securities Law: Managing Jurisdictional Conflict, 46 Colum. J. Transnat'l L. 14, 19 (2007); see also Leasco Data Processing Equip. Corp. v. Maxwell, 468 F.2d 1326, 1336 (2d Cir. 1972) (Friendly, J.) (detailing evidence that

Congress "meant § 10(b) to protect against fraud in the sale or purchase of securities whether or not these were traded on organized United States markets"). It is also consistent with the traditional understanding, regnant in the 1930's as it is now, that the presumption against extraterritoriality does not apply "when the conduct [at issue] occurs within the United States," and has lesser force when "the failure to extend the scope of the statute to a foreign setting will result in adverse effects within the United States." And it strikes a reasonable balance between the goals of "preventing the export of fraud from America," protecting shareholders, enhancing investor confidence, and deterring corporate misconduct, on the one hand, and conserving United States resources and limiting conflict with foreign law, on the other.

Thus, while § 10(b) may not give any "clear indication" on its face as to how it should apply to transnational securities frauds, it does give strong clues that it should cover at least some of them. And in my view, the Second Circuit has done the best job of discerning what sorts of transnational frauds Congress meant in 1934—and still means today—to regulate. I do not take issue with the Court for beginning its inquiry with the statutory text, rather than the doctrine in the Courts of Appeals. I take issue with the Court for beginning *and ending* its inquiry with the statutory text, when the text does not speak with geographic precision, and for dismissing the long pedigree of, and the persuasive account of congressional intent embodied in, the Second Circuit's rule.

Repudiating the Second Circuit's approach in its entirety, the Court establishes a novel rule that will foreclose private parties from bringing § 10(b) actions whenever the relevant securities were purchased or sold abroad and are not listed on a domestic exchange.[12] The real motor of the Court's opinion, it seems, is not the presumption against extraterritoriality but rather the Court's belief that transactions on domestic exchanges are "the focus of the Exchange Act" and "the objects of [its] solicitude." In reality, however, it is the "public interest" and "the interests of investors" that are the objects of the statute's solicitude. And while the clarity and simplicity of the Court's test may have some salutary consequences, like all bright-line rules it also has drawbacks.

Imagine, for example, an American investor who buys shares in a company listed only on an overseas exchange. That company has a major American subsidiary with executives based in New York City; and it was in New York City that the executives masterminded and implemented a massive deception which artificially inflated the stock price—and which

---

[12] The Court's opinion does not, however, foreclose the Commission from bringing enforcement actions in additional circumstances, as no issue concerning the Commission's authority is presented by this case. The Commission's enforcement proceedings not only differ from private § 10(b) actions in numerous potentially relevant respects, but they also pose a lesser threat to international comity, id., at 26–27; cf. Empagran, 542 U.S., at 171 (" '[P]rivate plaintiffs often are unwilling to exercise the degree of self-restraint and consideration of foreign governmental sensibilities generally exercised by the U.S. Government' " (quoting Griffin, Extraterritoriality in U.S. and EU Antitrust Enforcement, 67 Antitrust L. J. 159, 194 (1999); alteration in original)).

will, upon its disclosure, cause the price to plummet. Or, imagine that those same executives go knocking on doors in Manhattan and convince an unsophisticated retiree, on the basis of material misrepresentations, to invest her life savings in the company's doomed securities. Both of these investors would, under the Court's new test, be barred from seeking relief under § 10(b).

The oddity of that result should give pause. For in walling off such individuals from § 10(b), the Court narrows the provision's reach to a degree that would surprise and alarm generations of American investors—and, I am convinced, the Congress that passed the Exchange Act. Indeed, the Court's rule turns § 10(b) jurisprudence (and the presumption against extraterritoriality) on its head, by withdrawing the statute's application from cases in which there is *both* substantial wrongful conduct that occurred in the United States *and* a substantial injurious effect on United States markets and citizens.

III

In my judgment, if petitioners' allegations of fraudulent misconduct that took place in Florida are true, then respondents may have violated § 10(b), and could potentially be held accountable in an enforcement proceeding brought by the Commission. But it does not follow that shareholders who have failed to allege that the bulk or the heart of the fraud occurred in the United States, or that the fraud had an adverse impact on American investors or markets, may maintain a private action to recover damages they suffered abroad. Some cases involving foreign securities transactions have extensive links to, and ramifications for, this country; this case has Australia written all over it. Accordingly, for essentially the reasons stated in the Court of Appeals' opinion, I would affirm its judgment.

The Court instead elects to upend a significant area of securities law based on a plausible, but hardly decisive, construction of the statutory text. In so doing, it pays short shrift to the United States' interest in remedying frauds that transpire on American soil or harm American citizens, as well as to the accumulated wisdom and experience of the lower courts. I happen to agree with the result the Court reaches in this case. But "I respectfully dissent," once again, "from the Court's continuing campaign to render the private cause of action under § 10(b) toothless." Stoneridge, 552 U.S., at 175 (Stevens, J., dissenting).

NOTES ON *MORRISON*

1. *10b–5 Private Rights of Action.* The *Morrison* opinion certainly eliminates private 10b–5 claims in, at least, f-cubed situations. In so doing, the Court rejected forty years of precedent. Do you think the majority is persuasive in light of this existing body of law? Or, should the lower-court precedent be irrelevant to the Supreme Court's analysis?

2. *The Single-Transaction Based Test.* After rejecting the conduct and effects test, the *Morrison* court adopted a test that focuses on fraud in connection with "transactions in securities listed on domestic exchanges and domestic transactions in other securities."[6] Courts have, however, interpreted *Morrison's* pronouncements on extraterritoriality very narrowly. *Morrison* has been invoked:

> To dismiss "foreign squared" claims—claims asserted by American investors who have purchased securities of foreign issuers on foreign exchanges;[7]

> To reject an argument that listing some shares on a U.S. exchange subjects all transactions in that company's shares to 10b–5, regardless of where the transactions take place;[8] and

> To dismiss a case against a fund manager because the transaction was not "completed in" the U.S., interpreting *Morrison* as suggesting "that inquiry into the location of solicitation [or to 'events preparatory to the transaction'] [are] irrelevant to the inquiry";[9]

3. *The Domestic Purchase and Sale Test.* In Absolute Activist Value Master Fund Ltd. v. Ficeto,[10] the Second Circuit defined what constituted a domestic purchase or sale under *Morrison*. It held that "to sufficiently allege the existence of a 'domestic transaction in other securities,' plaintiffs must allege facts indicating that irrevocable liability was incurred or that title was transferred within the United States."[11]

Plaintiffs, nine Cayman Island hedge funds that purchased shares of U.S. penny stock companies not traded on a domestic exchange, sued officers of Absolute Capital Management Holdings Ltd., an investment management company retained by the funds, and principals of a domestic broker-dealer. The plaintiffs filed a complaint alleging fraud under § 10(b), Rule 10b–5, and the common law.[12] They claimed losses of at least $195 million in connection with the sale to the hedge funds of shares at inflated prices in a "pump-and-dump" scheme.[13] The District Court dismissed for lack of subject matter jurisdiction pursuant to *Morrison*.[14]

The Court of Appeals noted that "[w]hile *Morrison* holds that § 10(b) can be applied to domestic purchases or sales, it provides little guidance

---

[6] Morrison v. National Austl. Bank Ltd., 561 U.S. 247 130 S.Ct. 2869, 2888 (2010).
[7] Cornwell v. Credit Suisse Group, 729 F.Supp.2d 620 (S.D.N.Y. 2010).
[8] In re Royal Bank of Scot. Group PLC Sec. Litig., 765 F.Supp.2d 327 (S.D.N.Y. 2011).
[9] Cascade Fund, LLLP v. Absolute Capital Mgmt. Holdings Ltd., 2011 U.S. Dist. LEXIS 34748 at *21 (D. Colo. 2011).
[10] 677 F.3d 60 (2d Cir. 2012).
[11] Id. at 62.
[12] Id. at 65.
[13] Id. at 63.
[14] Id. at 65.

as to what constitutes a domestic purchase or sale."[15] The Court then reasoned that since:

> the point at which the parties become irrevocably bound is used to determine the timing of a purchase and sale, we similarly hold that the point of irrevocable liability can be used to determine the locus of a securities purchase or sale. Thus, in order to adequately allege the existence of a domestic transaction, it is sufficient for a plaintiff to allege facts leading to the plausible inference that the parties incurred irrevocable liability within the United States: that is, that the purchaser incurred irrevocable liability within the United States to take and pay for a security, or that the seller incurred irrevocable liability within the United States to deliver a security.[16]

The Court stated that was not the only test, however, because "a sale of securities can be understood to take place at the location in which title is transferred," citing the Eleventh Circuit opinion in *Quail Cruises*.[17]

The Second Circuit held that the plaintiffs failed to sufficiently allege that irrevocable liability was incurred in the United States. It examined the complaint and identified only one "conclusory" allegation stating that the transaction occurred in the United States.[18] The Court remanded allowing the plaintiffs to replead, because their complaint was filed before the *Morrison* decision, and before the Second Circuit "provided guidance about how to adequately plead a domestic purchase or sale."[19]

The Second Circuit then applied *Absolute Activist*, to affirm the dismissal of a foreign-squared claim in City of Pontiac Policemen's and Firemen's Retirement System v. UBS AG.[20] Here, the Court considered "whether the mere placement of a buy order in the United States for the purchase of foreign securities on a foreign exchange is sufficient to allege that a purchaser incurred irrevocable liability in the United States."[21] Plaintiffs included a group of foreign and domestic institutional investors and alleged the defendants, directors and officers of UBS, made fraudulent statements in conjunction with the issuance of ordinary shares listed on foreign exchanges and the New York Stock Exchange, in violation of §§ 10(b) and 20(a) of the Exchange Act.[22] The Second Circuit, noted that *Absolute Activist* "made clear that 'a purchaser's citizenship

---

[15] Id. at 67.

[16] Id. at 68.

[17] Id. at 68 (citing Quail Cruises v. Agencia de Viagens, 645 F.3d 1307 (11th Cir. 2011) (holding that for the purposes of a motion to dismiss, allegations that a transaction closed in the United States were sufficient under *Morrison*)).

[18] Id. at 70.

[19] Id. at 71.

[20] 752 F.3d 173 (2d Cir. 2014).

[21] Id. at 181.

[22] Id. at 176–77.

or residency does not affect where a transaction occurs,'"[23] and held that a domestic plaintiff does not automatically incur irrevocable liability when that plaintiff places a "buy order in the United States that was then executed on a foreign exchange."[24]

More recently in Parkcentral Global Hub Ltd. v. Porsche Automobile Holdings SE,[25] the Second Circuit held that § 10(b) does not reach foreign squared transactions involving "securities-based swap agreements based on the price movements of foreign securities" where the claim is based on "largely foreign conduct" and the "foreign defendants [had] not alleged involvement in plaintiffs' transactions."[26] In this case, international hedge funds brought suit against Porsche and two of its officers alleging violations of U.S. securities laws. They claimed the defendants "made various fraudulent statements and took various manipulative actions to deny and conceal Porsche's intention to take over [Volkswagen AG]."[27] Plaintiffs subsequently relied on these statements when making their swap agreements and suffered large losses when Porsche's intentions became public and "the price of VW shares rose dramatically."[28] The court held that "while [*Morrison*] unmistakably made a domestic securities transaction (or transaction in a domestically listed security) necessary to a properly domestic invocation of § 10(b), such a transaction is not alone sufficient to state a properly domestic claim under the statute."[29] The court did not opine as to whether liability became irrevocable or title changed hands and instead, found the claims to be "so predominantly foreign as to be impermissibly extraterritorial."[30]

The Ninth Circuit, however, rejected *Parkcentral*'s necessary but not sufficient test in Stoyas v. Toshiba Corp.,[31] holding that "*Parkcentral*'s analysis relies heavily on the foreign location of the allegedly deceptive conduct, which *Morrison* held to be irrelevant to the Exchange Act's applicability, given Section 10(b)'s exclusive focus on transactions."[32] In *Stoyas*, the court determined that the presence of a domestic transaction is sufficient and whether liability applies should be decided under the "in connection with" requirement. On remand, the district court denied Toshiba's motion to dismiss finding sufficient allegations of irrevocable liability "to take and pay for" the ADRs occurred in the United States."[33]

---

[23] Id. at 181.
[24] Id.
[25] 763 F.3d 198 (2d Cir. 2014).
[26] Id. at 201. A securities-based swap agreement is "a private contract between two parties in which they 'agree to exchange cash flows that depend on the price of a reference security, here VW shares.'" Id. at 205 (citation omitted).
[27] Id. at 201.
[28] Id.
[29] Id. at 215.
[30] Id. at 216.
[31] 896 F.3d 933 (9th Cir. 2018).
[32] Id. at 950.
[33] Stoyas v. Toshiba Corporation, 424 F.Supp.3d 821, 826 (C.D. Ca. 2020).

4. *American Depository Receipts and the OTC Market.* The *Morrison* case did not address trading in ADRs because they were not at issue. ADRs are stocks trading in the U.S., but they represent shares of a foreign corporation. They are bought and sold on American markets and issued/sponsored by U.S. banks or brokerages. Post-*Morrison*, the fate of litigation over ADRs is unclear. In Stackhouse v. Toyota,[34] the court assumed that ADRs listed on a U.S. exchange were covered. But, in In re Societe Generale Sec. Litig.,[35] the court found that trading in ADRs in the U.S. is predominantly foreign. The approach of the Societe Generale court seems incorrect for two reasons. First, the ADRs were traded in the U.S., though over the counter, not on an exchange. Second, *Morrison* eschewed measures of predominance, decidedly preferring the bright line test focused on the transaction location.

The Second Circuit in *City of Pontiac* rejected the "listing theory," the idea that ADRs listed for trading on a U.S. stock exchange would survive the presumption against extraterritoriality under *Morrison*, as "irreconcilable with *Morrison* read as a whole."[36] The Court noted the Supreme Court's emphasis on " 'location of the securities transaction and not the location where the security may be dually listed' "[37] due to the Exchange Act's focus on "*purchases* and *sales* of securities in the United States."[38] In short, "*Morrison* does not support the application of § 10(b) of the Exchange Act to claims by a foreign purchaser of foreign-issued shares on a foreign exchange simply because those shares are also listed on a domestic exchange."[39]

The *Morrison* case also did not address trading on the U.S. over-the-counter (OTC) market. In United States v. Georgiou[40], the Third Circuit held "[g]iven that a "national securities exchange" is explicitly listed in Section 10(b)—to the exclusion of the OTC markets—and coupled with the absence of the Pink Sheets and the OTCBB on the list of registered national security exchanges on the SEC Webpage on Exchanges, we are persuaded that those exchanges are not national securities exchanges within the scope of *Morrison*."[41] Although *Morrison's* first prong was not satisfied in this case, the court found the "evidence [was] sufficient to demonstrate . . . the second prong of *Morrison*" under the irrevocable liability theory set forth in *Absolute Activist*.[42]

---

[34] 2010 U.S. Dist. LEXIS 79837 (C.D. Cal. 2010).
[35] 2010 U.S. Dist. LEXIS 107719 (S.D.N.Y. 2010).
[36] 752 F.3d 173, 180 (2d 2014).
[37] Id. (quoting In re UBS Sec. Litig., 2011 WL 4059356, *5 (S.D.N.Y.)).
[38] Id. (quoting Morrison, 561 U.S. at 266).
[39] Id. at 181.
[40] 777 F.3d 125 (3d. Cir. 2015).
[41] Id. at 135.
[42] Id. at 137. See also Stoyas v. Toshiba Corporation, 896 F.3d 933, 947 (9th Cir. 2018) (finding OTC Link is not an "exchange" under the Exchange Act). Not all courts, however, agree. See United States v. Isaacson, 752 F.3d 1291, 1299 (11th Cir. 2014) (holding expert testimony stating that Over-the-Counter Bulletin Board or Pink Sheets are "similar to" the NYSE and

5. *Non 10b–5 Claims*. The issues arising in these cases are quite difficult. Consider a situation involving solicitations to U.S. investors, for a transaction that actually closes offshore. The language of *Morrison* refers only to purchases and sales, and not to offers, thus, one might argue that the other provisions of the statutes should not be similarly limited. At least two opinions have differed. For example, in In re Royal Bank of Scotland,[43] the court dismissed §§ 11 and 12 claims based on a transaction that took place mainly abroad. But, in SEC v. Goldman Sachs,[44] the court applied *Morrison* to find that claims under § 17(a), which bars fraudulent offers, not just purchases and sales, could be interpreted more broadly.[45]

6. *State Court Alternative*. In July 2011, the Southern District of New York dismissed a lawsuit filed by Basis Yield Alpha Fund, an Australian hedge fund, against Goldman Sachs relating to misrepresentations in a 2007 sale of collateralized-debt obligations ("CDO").[46] The Court dismissed the case on the basis of *Morrison's* requirement of a domestic transaction, because the CDO was not listed on a U.S. exchange and the swap agreements were executed overseas. The case was dismissed without prejudice with 30 days to refile. Instead of refiling in federal court, Basis chose to bring a case in New York State Court seeking damages under state and common law causes of action including fraud, breach of contract, and negligent misrepresentation.[47] *Basis Yield Alpha Fund* is not the first instance of a foreign plaintiff refiling in state court after having its federal claims dismissed under *Morrison*.[48]

7. *Study on a Private Right of Action*. Section 929Y the Dodd-Frank Act is also a response to the *Morrison* decision. Section 929Y directs the SEC to conduct a study to determine the extent to which a private right of action under the securities laws should extend extraterritorially, and to report back to Congress by January 21, 2012. The SEC published its 929Y report in April 2012. The study set forth four possible ways to clarify the transaction test:

NASDAQ in conjunction with evidence that the fund was run out of the U.S. was sufficient to satisfy *Morrison*).

[43] 765 F.Supp.2d 327 (S.D.N.Y. 2011). See also In re Vivendi Universal, S.A., Sec. Litig., 842 F.Supp.2d 522, 529 (S.D.N.Y. 2012) (applying *Morrison* to §§ 11, 12(a)(2), and 15 of the Securities Act).

[44] 790 F.Supp.2d 147 (S.D.N.Y. 2011).

[45] Id. (denying Goldman's motion to dismiss the SEC's § 17(a) claims to the extent it alleged offers and not sales outside the United States).

[46] Basis Yield Alpha Fund v. Goldman Sachs Group, Inc., 798 F.Supp.2d 533 (S.D.N.Y. 2011).

[47] Summons, Basis Yield Alpha Fund v. Goldman Sachs Group, Inc., 2011 WL 5119725 (N.Y. Sup. 2011).

[48] See Heungkuk Life Insurance Co. v. The Goldman Sachs Group, Inc., 2011 WL 1398953 (N.Y. Sup. 2011); Norex Petroleum Ltd. v. Blavatnik, New York State Supreme Court, New York County, 650591 (2011).

— Permit investors to pursue a section 10(b) private action for the purchase or sale of any security that is of the same class of securities registered in the United States, irrespective of the actual location of the transaction;

— Authorize section 10(b) private actions against securities intermediaries that engage in securities fraud while purchasing or selling securities overseas for U.S. investors;

— Permit investors to pursue a section 10(b) private action if they can demonstrate that they were induced while in the United States to engage in the transaction, irrespective of where the actual transaction occurred; and

— Clarify that an off-exchange transaction takes place in the United States if either party made the offer to sell or purchase, or accepted the offer to sell or purchase, while in the United States.

The SEC did not endorse any of these proposals, but merely set for the policy considerations for Congress to consider if it wanted to clarify the transaction test.

8. *Class Actions.* In *In re Petrobras Securities Litig.*,[49] the Second Circuit held that, in a securities class action arising out of the over-the-counter sale of securities, a district court considering class certification must determine whether each individual purchase was made in the United States, a determination that is difficult to make on a class-wide basis. In other words, purported class members had to show, on an individualized basis, that they purchased their securities in "domestic transactions" in order to satisfy *Morrison*.

Petrobras is a Brazilian oil company. Unlike Petrobras's common stock, which traded on the New York Stock Exchange (and thus was within the scope of *Morrison*), the bonds could have traded outside the United States (such as in Brazil), even though the bonds had to clear through The Depository Trust Company in New York in order to qualify for the settlement. The possibility that the bonds had traded outside the United States implicated *Morrison*, and, more to the point, raised an "individual" issue as to the location of each bond's sale. Under Rule 23(b)(3) of the Federal Rules of Civil Procedure, applicable to class actions, a class action seeking monetary damages can be certified only if the common issues of law and fact "predominate" over the individual issues. The location of each trade (i.e., whether it was domestic or foreign, referred to as their "domesticity") was an individual issue, thus precluding certification, unless common evidence could establish the location of all trades by class members. The Second Circuit reversed Judge Rakoff's certification order and remanded the case to the district court for further proceeding to see if other evidence as to the bonds' domesticity could be obtained. This ruling seemed to imply that the

---

[49] 862 F.3d 250 (2d Cir. 2017).

Petrobras bonds (unlike the Petrobras common stock) could not be included in the class. *Petrobras*, according to some commentators, was the death knell for class action certification involving OTC securities sales.

On remand, the case took an unusual turn. In In re Petrobras Securities Litig.,[50] U.S. District Judge Jed Rakoff approved a $3 billion settlement against Petrobras, with the disputed bonds included in the settlement. Did this defy the appellate court's ruling? Judge Rakoff held that it did not, finding that the issue of "domesticity" did not relate to subject matter jurisdiction, but only to the merits. Defendants, he said, could waive any issue as to the merits, but not issues as to subject matter jurisdiction. Here, the district court was simply repeating a point that *Morrison*, itself, had stressed: extraterritoriality went to the merits, not the court's subject matter jurisdiction. Earlier Second Circuit decisions also made this same point in allowing the defendant to waive defenses and achieve certification. Thus, Judge Rakoff upheld and approved as a settlement class an action he could not have heard as a litigation class (if the defendant objected).

The bottom line is that, in these kinds of cases, defendants appear to have great discretion over whether cases that cannot be certified as litigation classes can instead be certified as settlement classes. If defendants have broad discretion in this regard, they may use that power to agree to a settlement class chiefly when the settlement terms favor it and undercompensate the class. Plaintiffs' counsel, having no ability to get to trial and thus being "disarmed," may agree to such a settlement either because (a) it is the best the class can get or (b) the fees the plaintiffs' attorneys will receive if the settlement is approved more than adequately compensate them (although not necessarily the class).

2. GOVERNMENT EXTRATERRITORIAL ENFORCEMENT OF THE SECURITIES LAWS

One of the key questions after *Morrison* was the case's impact on the SEC and DOJ. Once the Court interpreted the issue as being about the location of the purchases and sales, the jurisdictional cases that had been applied to the civil and criminal enforcement actions were no longer valid.

Shortly after the Court issued its opinion, however, Congress passed the Dodd-Frank Act and addressed the issue. Section 929P(b) of the Dodd-Frank Act adds a phrase to § 22 of the 1933 Act and § 27 of 1934 Act that grants the district courts of the United States jurisdiction over SEC or DOJ actions when "conduct within the United States ... constitutes significant steps in furtherance of the violation" (even if the securities are not traded in the United States)—exactly the result *Morrison* rejected for private litigants. The legislative history makes it

---

[50] 317 F.Supp.3d 858 (S.D.N.Y. 2018).

clear that Congress intended that § 929P(b) of the Dodd-Frank Act would rebut the presumption against extraterritoriality and reinstate the "conduct" and "effects" test to SEC and DOJ enforcement actions.[51]

Justice Scalia stated the Second Circuit's conduct and effects test in *Morrison*:

> The Second Circuit . . . established that application of § 10(b) could be premised upon either some effect on American securities markets or investors (*Schoenbaum*) or significant conduct in the United States (*Leasco*). It later formalized these two applications into (1) an "effects test," "whether the wrongful conduct had a substantial effect in the United States or upon United States citizens," and (2) a "conduct test," "whether the wrongful conduct occurred in the United States." These became the north star of the Second Circuit's § 10(b) jurisprudence, pointing the way to what Congress would have wished. Indeed, the Second Circuit declined to keep its two tests distinct on the ground that "an admixture or combination of the two often gives a better picture of whether there is sufficient United States involvement to justify the exercise of jurisdiction by an American court."[52]

A. SECTION 929P(b) OF DODD-FRANK ACT

Justice Scalia stated that the controlling issue in *Morrison* was not jurisdiction, but the fact that § 10(b) does not provide for relief of extraterritorial claims—a question of the merits. According to Scalia, the federal courts have jurisdiction over cases brought under § 10(b), but § 10(b) did not provide a cause of action for the f-cubed situation alleged in the case.[53]

The Dodd-Frank Act provisions on extraterritoriality speak only to jurisdiction and not the merits of an SEC or DOJ claim under § 10(b). The Dodd-Frank Act provisions on extraterritoriality were proposed before the *Morrison* decision anticipating that the court in *Morrison* would bar f-cubed claims. Thus, the provisions focused on subject matter jurisdiction. Accordingly, the Dodd-Frank Act expressly restored the federal courts jurisdiction over SEC and DOJ suits concerning securities transactions outside the United States.[54] It did not address the substantive reach of § 10(b).

---

[51] See Study on Extraterritorial Private Rights of Action, SEC Release No. 34–63174 (October 25, 2010), *available at* www.sec.gov/rules/other/2010/34-63174.pdf.
[52] Morrison v. Nat'l Austl. Bank Ltd., 561 U.S. 247, 257–58 (2010).
[53] See Id.
[54] The language ultimately adopted in Dodd-Frank § 929P is under the heading "Extraterritorial Jurisdiction of the Antifraud Provisions of the Federal Securities Laws," and reads:
> Section 27 of the Securities Exchange Act of 1934 (15 U.S.C. 78aa) is amended . . . by adding at the end the following new subsection:

New York lawyer George Conway III, who successfully argued the *Morrison* case before the Court, has argued that because the Dodd-Frank provision addresses only jurisdiction, it does not effectively reverse *Morrison* for SEC and DOJ actions.[55] Some legal scholars have similarly recognized that the literal language of the statute may frustrate Congressional intent in this regard and have concluded that Congress should revise the statutory language.[56] Other scholars point out that *Morrison* said that the presumption against extraterritorial jurisdiction did not have to be expressly cancelled, rather, it acknowledged that "context be consulted as well."[57] If one considers the context in which the Dodd-Frank provision was enacted, it seems to show that Congress was trying to re-arm the SEC with the ability to challenge extraterritorial transactions so long as either of the traditional tests, conduct or effects, were met.[58]

Will future courts look to Congressional intent or the language of the statute to determine whether the SEC or DOJ can enforce the securities laws extraterritorially? How should courts take account of the many congresses problem when considering such statutes?

In SEC v. Goldman Sachs,[59] the S.D.N.Y. adopted *Morrison* against the SEC. The SEC alleged that, in 2007, Goldman structured and marketed a synthetic collateralized debt obligation ("CDO") called Abacus 2007-AC1 ("Abacus"), which was based on the performance of subprime residential mortgage-backed securities ("RMBS"). The SEC further alleged that Goldman marketed the CDOs without disclosing that the Paulson & Co hedge fund, which had assisted Goldman in selecting the RMBSs underlying Abacus, had bet against the RMBSs. Fabrice Tourre was allegedly the Goldman employee primarily responsible for the Abacus transaction.

"(b) *Extraterritorial Jurisdiction.* The district courts of the United States and the United States courts of any Territory shall have jurisdiction of an action or proceeding brought or instituted by the Commission or the United States alleging a violation of the antifraud provisions of this title involving—

"(1) conduct within the United States that constitutes significant steps in furtherance of the violation, even if the securities transaction occurs outside the United States and involves only foreign investors; or

"(2) conduct occurring outside the United States that has a foreseeable substantial effect within the United States."

The Dodd-Frank Act contains similar provisions with respect to § 17A of the 1933 Act and § 214 of the Investment Advisors Act of 1940.

[55] See George T. Conway III, Extraterritoriality After Dodd-Frank (Aug. 5, 2010), http://blogs.law.harvard.edu/corpgov/2010/08/05/extraterritoriality-after-dodd-frank.

[56] See Richard Painter, Douglas Dunham & Ellen Quackenbos, When Courts and Congress Don't Say What They Mean: Initial Reactions to Morrison v. National Australia Bank and to the Extraterritorial Jurisdiction Provisions of the Dodd-Frank Act, 20 Minn. J. Int'l L. 1, 25 (2011).

[57] Morrison v. National Austl. Bank Ltd., 561 U.S. 247, 265, 130 S.Ct. 2869, 2883 (2010).

[58] John C. Coffee, Jr., The Gray Edges of 'Morrison', Corporate Update New York Law Journal (Online), May 19, 2011.

[59] 790 F.Supp.2d 147 (S.D.N.Y. 2011).

The closing of the transaction occurred in New York City. Goldman delivered the notes through the book entry facilities of Depository Trust Company in New York City, however, Goldman Sachs International, located in London, was listed as the seller of the Abacus securities. The securities were not listed on any exchange, and their sole investor was IKB, a German commercial bank.

The SEC brought claims against Tourre pursuant to § 17 of the Securities Act and § 10(b) of the Exchange Act. Tourre moved to dismiss arguing that the SEC could not meet its burden under *Morrison* to demonstrate that the securities transactions took place in the United States.

With respect to the Exchange Act claims the court held that the SEC could not maintain a fraud claim related to the IKB purchases. The court determined that the purchase (or sale) of a security under the Exchange Act does not occur until the buyer has "incurred an *irrevocable* liability to take and pay for the stock"[60] and held that the SEC provided no facts to support the reasonable inference that any party to the Abacus transaction incurred irrevocable liability in the United States.

The court rejected the SEC's argument that the structuring and marketing of the Abacus securities (which occurred in New York) was sufficient to support the charges, stating "[t]he shortcoming of all of this U.S.-based conduct is precisely that—it is just conduct." The court also rejected the SEC's argument that courts must look to the "entire selling process" to determine whether a securities transaction is foreign or domestic.

The court then considered whether *Morrison* applied to the SEC's claims under § 17(a) of the Securities Act. The court found that in some circumstances *Morrison* applied to § 17(a), because "*Morrison* itself expressly state[d] that the Exchange Act and the Securities Act share '[t]he same focus on domestic transactions.' " The court noted, however, that § 17(a), unlike § 10(b) applies to both "offers" and "sales" and found that the SEC's allegations of Tourre's marketing and solicitation of the Abacus securities in New York City constituted domestic offers of securities or swaps. Thus, the § 17(a) claim survived, to the extent that it alleged offers as opposed to sales. The court then granted the SEC's later motion for summary judgment with respect to the domestic element of § 17(a) stating "[i]t defies reason to adopt a construction of Section 17(a) that could permit the SEC to prove that each and every element of its claim occurred—and occurred in the United States—only to require dismissal because a separate "sale" took place abroad."[61]

The *Goldman Sachs* case was brought before Congress passed the Dodd-Frank Act. Since then, there has been a debate as to whether

---

[60] Id. at 158 (citing Plumbers' Union Local No. 12 Pension Fund v. Swiss Reinsurance Company, 753 F.Supp.2d 166, 177 (S.D.N.Y. 2010)).

[61] SEC v. Tourre, 2013 U.S. Dist. LEXIS 78297, at *27 (S.D.N.Y. 2013).

Section 929P(b) is to have any practical effect, as the wording merely amends the subject-matter jurisdiction provisions rather than expanding the territorial scope of any substantive regulatory provision under the Securities Act, the Exchange Act, and the Investment Advisers Act.[62] Since the provisions' passing, some courts have held that although "the plain language of Section 929P(b) did not explicitly overturn the core holdings of *Morrison*"[63] the "context and historical background" of Section 929P(b), in addition to its section title of "Strengthening Enforcement by the Commission", make clear that "Congress undoubtedly intended that the substantive antifraud provisions should apply extraterritorially when the statutory conduct-and-effects test is satisfied."[64]

B. CRIMINAL ENFORCEMENT OF THE SECURITIES LAWS

Although *Morrison* did not answer the question of criminal liability under § 10(b) and Rule 10b–5, the Second Circuit in United States v. Vilar[65] extended *Morrison* to criminal prosecution.[66] The court held:

> Section 10(b) and its implementing regulation, Rule 10b–5, do not apply to extraterritorial conduct, regardless of whether liability is sought criminally or civilly. Accordingly, a defendant may be convicted of securities fraud under Section 10(b) and Rule 10b–5 only if he has engaged in fraud in connection with (1) a security listed on a U.S. exchange, or (2) a security purchased or sold in the United States.[67]

In *Vilar*, the securities in question were not listed on an American exchange. The court found that the plaintiffs satisfied the second prong of *Morrison* and that the defendants "engaged in fraud in connection with a *domestic* purchase or sale of securities" pursuant to the irrevocable liability test set forth in *Absolute Activist* as victims "entered into and renewed their agreements" in the United States.[68]

The significance of *Vilar*, however, would be severely limited if § 929P(b) succeeded in overruling *Morrison* by broadly defining the

---

[62] Id.

[63] SEC v. Traffic Monsoon, LLC, 245 F.Supp.3d 1275, 1288–1294 (D. Utah 2017) ("the legal context in which th[e] amendment was drafted, [the] legislative history, and the expressed purpose of the amendment all point to a congressional intent that, in actions brought by the SEC, Sections 10(b) and 17(a) should be applied to extraterritorial transactions to the extent that the conduct and effects test can be satisfied").

[64] SEC v. Scoville, 913 F.3d 1204, 1218 (10th Cir. 2019).

[65] 729 F.3d 62 (2d Cir. 2013), cert denied, 134 S.Ct. 2684 (2014).

[66] The counts included conspiracy to commit fraud, securities fraud, investment adviser fraud, mail fraud, wire fraud, money laundering, and making false statements to the SEC. Id. at 69. The Eleventh Circuit, however, has declined to follow *Vilar* and has not extended *Morrison* to limit "the scope of criminal liability . . . to the same extent it limits the scope of civil liability." United States v. Isaacson, 752 F.3d 1291 (11th Cir. 2014).

[67] *Vilar*, 729 F.3d at 67.

[68] Id. at 76–77.

substantive reach of § 10(b) with respect to actions brought by the SEC or DOJ, rather than simply conferring jurisdiction.

Problem

PROBLEM 16-1

The sole business of Southeast Asian and European Overseas Traders (SAED), a Panamanian Corporation, is to invest in securities. It is wholly owned by Allen Truck, a citizen of Canada. While vacationing in Florida, Truck made offers by telephone and e-mail, and closed a transaction with a French bank, located in Paris, to sell SAED securities.

(1) Would such conduct be sufficient to establish jurisdiction in a private action under the Securities Exchange Act?

(2) Assuming all facts are the same, but the SEC decided to bring an enforcement action, would they be able to establish jurisdiction?

C. THE CHALLENGES TO GOVERNMENTAL ENFORCEMENT EFFORTS

It is a challenge for the SEC and DOJ to get collect information when trading takes place through financial institutions outside of the U.S. that are protected by secrecy or blocking laws of their home countries. One way the SEC overcomes this obstacle is to employ the discovery process provided by Rule 37 of the Fed. R. Civ. P., which permits court-ordered sanctions against U.S. subsidiaries of foreign financial institutions. Another way is collaboration with other countries.

Collaboration is a necessary element to the SEC's international enforcement of securities. In 2016, there were 1,027 SEC requests to foreign authorities for enforcement assistance, and 636 requests from foreign authorities for enforcement assistance.[69] The SEC's cooperation with other countries is also accomplished through bilateral and multilateral agreements with foreign regulators.[70]

In 1990, in an effort to increase bilateral cooperation, Congress enacted the International Securities Enforcement Cooperation Act, which amended § 24 of the Securities Exchange Act. In § 24(d) the SEC can withhold disclosure under the Freedom of Information Act of records obtained from a foreign securities authority.

---

[69] SEC, Agency Financial Report: Fiscal Year 2016 27 (2016).

[70] See 10 Louis Loss & Joel Seligman, Securities Regulation 5122–5123 (3d ed. rev. 1996); Michael D. Mann, Paul A. Leder & Elizabeth Jacobs, The Establishment of International Mechanisms for Enforcing Provisional Orders and Final Judgments Arising from Securities Law Violations, 55 Law & Contemp. Probs. 303 (Autumn 1992); Michael D. Mann, Joseph G. Mari & George Lavdas, International Agreements and Understandings for the Production of Information and Other Mutual Assistance, 29 Int'l L. 780 (1995); Hendrik F. Jordaan, "Has IOSCO Advanced International Securities Law Enforcement?": An Analysis in Light of SEC MOUs with Emerging Markets, 26 Sec. Reg. L. J. 269 (1998).

There are also a limited number of treaties for mutual assistance in criminal matters.[71] The first treaty, the 1977 Treaty on Mutual Assistance on Criminal Matters between the Swiss Confederation and the United States, "provides for broad assistance in criminal matters, including assistance in locating witnesses, production and authentication of business records, and service of judicial and administrative documents." It does not, however, provide for extradition, which has been enforced with quite limited success, after agonizing delays.[72]

In 1982 the United States entered into an MOU with the Swiss Government for improving international law enforcement cooperation in the field of insider trading. Attached to the memorandum was an agreement with the Swiss Bankers' Association with respect to requests for information from the SEC on the misuse of inside information.[73] In December 1987 the Swiss Federal Assembly adopted a new 1–1/2 page Article 161 of the Penal Code with respect to insider trading. This treaty went into effect in December 1988.[74]

The International Organization of Securities Commissions (IOSCO) is an association of international securities regulators formed to promote high standards of regulation and cooperation between the countries. In 2002, the IOSCO created a Multilateral Memorandum of Understanding (MMoU), a global multilateral information-sharing arrangement among securities regulators. As of May 2020, 124 foreign regulators had become signatories to the MMoU.[75] The MMoU provide for information and documents sharing between regulators; obtaining information and documents regarding financial transactions; and taking or compelling a person's statement or, where permissible, a person's testimony.[76]

An Enhanced MMoU (EMMoU) was promulgated in 2016 with the goal of further facilitating international cooperation. The EMMoU

---

[71] See SEC, Staff Report on Internationalization of the Securities Markets VII-49 to VII-60 (1987) (describing four treaties for mutual assistance in criminal matters with Italy, the Netherlands, Switzerland, and Turkey).

[72] Id. at VII-50; see, e.g., SEC v. Certain Unknown Purchasers, 1984–1985 Fed. Sec. L. Rep. (CCH) ¶ 91,951 (S.D.N.Y. 1985); cf. SEC v. Banca Della Svizzera Italiana, 92 F.R.D. 111 (S.D.N.Y. 1981).

The Swiss Federal Office for Police Matters has taken the position that the rule of specialty implicit in Article IX of the Treaty for the Extradition of Criminals between the United States and Switzerland, 31 Stat. 1928 (May 14, 1900), will not block a civil enforcement action filed by the SEC. SEC v. Eurobond Exch., Ltd., 13 F.3d 1334, 1336, 1337 (9th Cir. 1994).

Cf. Colello v. SEC, 908 F.Supp. 738 (C.D.Cal.1995) (holding it is a violation of the Fifth Amendment to freeze assets under the Mutual Assistance in Criminal Matters treaty without affording defendants a notice of an asset freeze or a hearing and that the Swiss asset freeze constituted an unreasonable search under the Fourth Amendment).

[73] Int'l Sec. Rel. 2, 43, SEC Dock. 123 (1989).

[74] Lionel Frei & Stefan Treschsel, Origins and Applications of the United States-Switzerland Treaty on Mutual Assistance in Criminal Matters, 31 Harv. Int'l L. J. 77 (1990).

[75] Int'l Org. of Sec. Comm'n, Signatories to Appendix A and Appendix B List, https://www.iosco.org/about/?subSection=mmou&subSection1=signatories.

[76] See SEC, Cooperative Arrangement Fact Sheet, http://www.sec.gov/about/offices/oia/oia_coopfactsheet.htm.

signatories "agree to new forms of assistance critical to effective enforcement, such as obtaining compelled testimony and obtaining asset freezes to protect custom funds, among other powers."[77] In May of 2019, the SEC and the CFTC became two of eleven regulatory bodies to sign the EMMoU. In light of the MMoU, "SEC staff now strongly recommends the negotiation of bilateral MOUs only if a foreign securities authority is empowered to provide assistance beyond that required by the ISOCO MMoU."[78]

---

[77] Press Release, SEC, SEC and CFTC Participate in the Signing Ceremony for the IOSCO Enhanced Multilateral Memorandum of Understanding Concerning Cross-Border Enforcement (May 20, 2019), https://www.sec.gov/news/press-release/2019-71. Other forms of assistance include obtaining and sharing Audit papers, internet service provider records, and telephone records. Int'l Org. of Sec. Comm'n, Enhanced Multilateral Memorandum of Understanding Concerning Consultation and Cooperation and the Exchange of Information, https://www.iosco.org/about/?subsection=emmou.

[78] SEC, Cooperative Arrangement Fact Sheet, https://www.sec.gov/about/offices/oia/oia_coopfactsheet.htm.

INDEX

References are to Pages

ACCOUNTANTS
Securities accountants. SEC Enforcement Actions, this index

ADMINISTRATIVE PROCEDURE ACT
Generally, 58–60

AFFILIATES
Offerings by Underwriters, Affiliates, and Dealers, this index

ALTERNATIVE TRADING SYSTEMS
Generally, 30, 31
Securities Markets, this index

ANALYSTS
Role of securities analysts, 87–92

ANNUITIES
Variable annuities, exempted securities, 371, 372

ARBITRATION
Brokerage agreements, 765

ATTORNEYS
SEC enforcement actions, right to counsel, 1293, 1294
Securities attorneys. SEC Enforcement Actions, this index

BANKS
Exempted securities, bank issued or guaranteed, 368–370

BAR ORDERS
SEC Enforcement Actions, this index

BEST INTEREST
Regulation Best Interest. Broker-Dealers, this index

BLANK CHECK OFFERINGS
Registration process, 270–272

BLUE SKY REGULATION
Generally, 64–66
Uniform Limited Offering Exemption, 435, 436

BROKER-DEALERS
Generally, 727–789
Activities during registration, 108–110
Arbitration provisions in brokerage agreements, 765
Avoiding broker characterization, 733, 734
Best execution, duty of, 772, 773
Best interest. Regulation Best Interest, below
Broker/investment adviser turf war, 788, 789
Churning
    Generally, 775–785
    Damages, 783, 784
    Excessive trading, 782, 783
    Litigation, 781, 782
    Unauthorized transactions, churning, and "in connection with" requirement, 784, 785
Common law duties, 736–738
Credit regulation, 762–765
Criminal liability, 738
Customers, duties to
    Generally, 766–789
    Best execution, duty of, 772, 773
    Churning, above
    Financial services middle market, 788, 789
    Limit orders, duty to protect, 773–775
    Penny Stock Reform Act of 1990, below
    Regulation Best Interest, below
Defined, 733, 734
Dodd-Frank, impact of, 739, 740
Duties
    Common law duties, 736–738
    Customers, duties to, above
Enforcement actions. SEC Enforcement Actions, this index
Entry into profession, SEC requirements, 733
Exemptions from registration requirements, 735
Fiduciary duty standard, 738–740
Financial services middle market, 788, 789
Financial soundness requirements, 733
FINRA
    Disciplinary process, 731
    Powers, 730, 731
    Suitability doctrine, 738, 739, 770
Fraud and manipulation
    Generally, 741–758
    Anti-fraud rules, generally, 733
    General fraud sections as applied to broker-dealers, 756, 757
    Hot issues, free-riding and withholding, SEC and NASD interpretations, 750 et seq.
    IPO allocation process, 752–755
    Laddering, 747, 748
    Manipulation, general issues, 755, 756
    Regulation M, below
    Scienter requirements, 750
    Shelf registration and trading practices, 749, 980
    Shingle theory, 740, 757, 758
    Short sales, below

Spinning, 752–755
Stabilizing activities, 748, 749
Free-riding and withholding, SEC and NASD interpretations, 750–752
High risk and insolvency, regulation aimed at protection from
    Generally, 758–765
    Arbitration provisions in brokerage agreements, 765
    Credit regulation, 762–765
    Margin requirements, 762–765
    Net capital rules, 760, 761
    Recordkeeping by broker-dealers, 759
    Securities Investor Protection Corporation (SIPC), 761, 762
Hot issues, SEC and NASD interpretations, 750–752
Internalization, 31, 32
IPO allocation process, 752–755
Laddering, 747, 748
Limit orders, duty to protect, 773–775
Manipulation. Fraud and manipulation, above
Margin requirements, 762–765
Net capital rules, 760, 761
Offerings by Underwriters, Affiliates, and Dealers, this index
OTC trading by dealers, 32
Penny Stock Reform Act of 1990
    Generally, 785–788
    Revised SEC rules, 785, 786
    Rule 15c2–11, 786–788
Recordkeeping requirements, 759
Registration, activities during, 108–110
Regulation Best Interest
    Generally, 728, 729, 767–772
    Care obligation, 767
    Compliance obligation, 768
    Conflict of interest obligation, 767, 768
    Disclosure obligation, 767
    Form CRS, 770
    Gray areas, 769
    Institutional investors, 770–772
    Likely impacts, 768
    Litigation, 770
    Non-covered matters, 768
    Preemption, 768, 769
    Suitability obligations, 770
Regulation M, manipulation during distribution
    Generally, 745–747
    Chinese walls, 747
    Exceptions, 746, 747
    Intrastate offerings, 746
    Restricted periods, 746
Rogue brokers, 789
Scienter, violation of trading practices rules, 750
SEC authority
    Generally, 725, 731–735
    Entry into profession, 733
    Financial soundness, 733
    Fraud and manipulation, above
SEC Enforcement Actions, this index

Securities Investor Protection Corporation (SIPC), 761, 762
Self-Regulation, this index
Shelf registration and trading practices, 749, 980
Shingle theory, 740, 757, 758
Short sales, regulation of
    Generally, 741–745
    Naked short selling, 743, 744
    Public offering, short selling in anticipation of, 744, 745
    Regulation SHO, 743, 744
    Tick test, 742, 743
Spinning, 752–755
Stabilizing activities, 748, 749
State authority, 735, 736
Suitability doctrine, 738, 739, 770
Unauthorized transactions, churning, and "in connection with" requirement, 784, 785
Waiting period, broker's card, 121, 122

BUYOUTS
Tender Offers, Management Buyouts, and Takeover Contests, this index

CAPITAL MARKETS OVERVIEW
Institutional and Regulatory Framework, this index

CAUSATION
Civil liability under Securities Act of 1933, 971–975
Proxy Fraud (Rule 14a–9), 1184, 1185
Rule 10b–5 Enforcement Actions, this index

CEASE AND DESIST ORDERS
SEC enforcement actions, 1329–1340

CERTIFICATES OF DEPOSIT
Security, defined, 345–347

CHARITABLE ORGANIZATIONS
Exempted securities, 371

CHURNING
Broker-Dealers, this index

CIVIL LIABILITY UNDER SECURITIES ACT OF 1933
Generally, 919–1030
Causation, 971–975
Concurrent jurisdiction, state and federal courts, 994, 995
Damages
    Generally, 971–976
    Amount recoverable, 975, 976
Defendants under § 11, 962, 963
Documents other than registration statement, 980
Due diligence defense
    Generally, 922–971
    Back door due diligence requirement, 992, 993
    Expert liability, 967–969
    How much diligence is due, 970

Inside directors and officers, 964–966
Outside directors, 964–966
Reasonable care defense compared, 1025–1027
Securities offering reform, 969, 970
Underwriters, 966, 967
Who are § 11 defendants, 962, 963
Expert liability, 967–969
Free writing prospectus liability, 1023
Inside directors and officers, 964–966
Material misrepresentations or omissions.
Section 12 liability, below
Oral presentations, 980
Outside directors, 964–966
Plaintiffs under § 11
Generally, 976–982
Purchaser requirement, 980, 981
Tracing, 981
Section 11 liability
Generally, 919–921
Defendants, 962, 963
Due diligence defense, above
Introductory note, 919–921
Misstatements, what counts as, 982–993
Plaintiffs, above
Section 12 liability
Generally, 995–1028
Due diligence and reasonable care defenses compared, 1025–1027
Free writing prospectus liability, 1023
Material misrepresentations or omissions, 1005–1028
Reasonable care defense, 1005, 1024, 1025
Rule 159, 1023
Seller liability, 995–1005
Standing, 1023
Section 17(a), 1028–1030
Securities offering reform, 969, 970
Seller liability, 995–1005
Statute of limitations, 993, 994
Tracing by open market purchaser, 981
Underwriters, 966, 967

CLASS ACTIONS
Generally, 910–917
Certification of class
Evolving law, 915–917
Rule 10b–5 materiality, 1079, 1080
Fraud-on-the-market theory, 1140
International enforcement, 1497, 1498
Lead plaintiff and counsel, 913, 914
Notice to class members, 914
Private Securities Litigation Reform Act of 1995, 912–915
SEC injunctions and subsequent class actions, 1317
Securities litigation, provisions unique to, 910–917
Stay of discovery, 915

COMMERCIAL PAPER
Security and exempted securities, defined, 344, 345, 370, 371

COMMODITIES FUTURES TRADING COMMISSION
Generally, 51, 52

COMPENSATION
Executive compensation
Clawback, 1402, 1403
Dodd-Frank provisions, 203, 204, 1402–1404
Registration disclosures, 203, 204
Underwriters, FINRA review, 262, 263

CONCURRENT JURISDICTION
State and federal courts, 994, 995

CONDOMINIUMS
Security, defined, 312–316

CONFIDENTIALITY
SEC enforcement actions, 1294

CONFLICTS OF INTEREST
Broker-dealers, conflict of interest obligation, 767, 768
Proxy fraud, materiality, 1180, 1181

CONTROLLING PERSONS
Offerings by Underwriters, Affiliates, and Dealers, this index

CORPORATE REGISTRANTS, OFFICERS, AND DIRECTORS
SEC Enforcement Actions, this index

COST-BENEFIT ANALYSIS
Regulatory process, 60, 61

CREDIT RATINGS
Nationally recognized statistical rating organizations, 57

CRIMINAL ENFORCEMENT
Generally, 1441–1472
Advice of counsel, reliance on, 1457
Extraterritorial enforcement, 1502, 1503
Federal securities laws, prosecutions under
Generally, 1452–1457
Advice of counsel, reliance on, 1457
Knowing vs. willful, 1455–1457
Sentencing, 1456, 1457
Legislative enhancements to criminal liability, 1469, 1470
Parallel proceedings, 1451, 1452
Privilege against self-incrimination, 1452
Procedural issues, 1442–1452
Reference to DOJ, 1442, 1443
Stay of parallel civil proceedings, 1452
Stock parking and regulatory violations
Generally, 1457–1471
Legislative enhancements to criminal liability, 1469, 1470
Manipulation, meaning of, 1468, 1469

Title 18 prosecutions, 1471, 1472

CROWDFUNDING
Limited and Other Offering Exemptions, this index

CULPABILITY
Proxy Fraud (Rule 14a–9), this index
Rule 10b–5 Enforcement Actions, this index

DAMAGES
Churning, 783, 784
Civil Liability under Securities Act of 1933, this index
Insider trading, 1286, 1287

DEFINITIONS OF SECURITY
Generally, 273–366
Certificates of deposit, 345–347
Commercial paper, 344, 345
Condominiums, 312–316
Digital assets, 356–366
Economic realities test
    Generally, 301–326
    Condominiums and real estate developments, 312–316
    Investment vs. consumption, 306, 307
    Investment vs. entertainment, 307
    Partnerships, limited partnerships and LLCs, above in this group
Exempted Securities, this index
Fixed returns, 300
Howey test, 287, 356
Internet, commonality and, 296
Investment contracts, 273–301
Loan participations, 350–353
Managerial efforts, 287, 288
Notes, 332–343
Partnerships, limited partnerships and LLCs
    Generally, 316–326
    Control in limited partnership, 316–322
    Limited partnerships, 325
    Partnerships, 324, 325
    Special case of LLCs, 322–324
Real estate development, 312–316
Risk reduction, 347–349
Special debt obligations, 343–356
Statutory interpretation, study in, 273–275
Stock, return of formalism, 326–332
Swaps, 353–356
Tokens and other digital assets, 356–366
Unique investments, 279
Vertical vs. horizontal commonality, 293–296, 315

DERIVATIVES MARKETS
Institutional and Regulatory Framework, this index

DIGITAL ASSETS
Security, defined, 356–366

DISCLOSURE
Broker-dealers, disclosure obligation, 767
Crowdfunding, 503, 504
Executive compensation, 203, 204
Insider trading, who has duty to disclose and SEC regulations, 1215–1219
Integrated disclosure system. Registration Process, this index
JOBS Act, required disclosures, 142, 143
Litigation and enforcement, role of disclosure, 909, 910
Omissions, actionable, and duty to disclose, 1050
Proxy fraud, required disclosures and materiality, 1181
Registration Process, this index
Standardizing disclosure, 6, 7
Williams Act requirements, 799–803

DISGORGEMENT
SEC Enforcement Actions, this index
Tender offers, disgorgement remedy, 836

DISTRIBUTION OF SECURITIES
Underwriters and Underwriting, this index

DUE DILIGENCE
Civil Liability under Securities Act of 1933, this index
Rule 10b–5 enforcement actions, 1046
Shelf registration, 166–169

ELECTRONIC/GRAPHIC COMMUNICATIONS
Waiting Period, this index

EMERGING GROWTH COMPANIES
JOBS Act, this index

EMPLOYEE BENEFIT PLANS
Insider trading, employee benefit plans and Rule 16b–3, 1278, 1279

ENFORCEMENT
Criminal Enforcement, this index
International Enforcement, this index
Rule 10b–5 Enforcement Actions, this index
SEC Enforcement Actions, this index

ENVIRONMENTAL LIABILITIES
Registration process, 204–206

EQUITY AND NON-EQUITY MARKETS
Institutional and Regulatory Framework, this index

EXCHANGES
Securities Markets, this index

EXCHANGES AND REORGANIZATIONS
Limited and Other Offering Exemptions, this index

EXECUTIVE COMPENSATION
Compensation, this index

EXEMPTED SECURITIES
Generally, 366–372
Bank, securities issued or guaranteed by, 368–370
Charitable organizations, 371
Commercial paper, 370, 371
IRAs, 370
Keogh plans, 370
Municipal securities, 367, 368
Section 3(a)(2), 366–370
Section 3(a)(3), 370, 371
Sections 3(a)(4) to 3(a)(8), 371, 372
Variable annuities, 371, 372

EXPERTS
Civil liability under Securities Act of 1933, 967–969

FAST ACT
Generally, 146

FIDUCIARY DUTY
Broker-dealers, 738–740
Investment advisers, 1431
State law fiduciary breaches, 1043, 1044

FINANCIAL STABILITY OVERSIGHT COUNCIL
Generally, 55

FINES
SEC enforcement actions, civil fines, 1327–1329

FINRA
Disciplinary process, 731
Fines, ability to levy, 1329
IPO allocation process, 752–755
Membership of associated persons, authority to deny, 1317
Powers, 730, 731
Research rules, 110–112
Suitability doctrine, 738, 739, 770
Underwriter's compensation, FINRA review, 262, 263

FRAUD
Broker-Dealers, this index
Crowdfunding, use of intermediaries to reduce fraud risk, 504, 505
Fraud-on-the-market doctrine
    Class actions, 1140
    Market efficiency, 257, 258
Materially false or misleading statement, § 18 liability, 1185, 1186
Proxy Fraud (Rule 14a–9), this index
Rule 10b–5 Enforcement Actions, this index

FREE WRITING
Prospectus, this index

GUN-JUMPING
Pre-Filing Period, this index
Tender offer process, reforming, 870, 871

HEDGE FUNDS
Securities markets, forces reshaping, 37, 38
Tender offers, impact of hedge fund activism, 903

IDENTIFYING STATEMENT
Waiting period, 118–120

INITIAL PUBLIC OFFERINGS
Generally, 80–86
Costs of IPOs, 149, 150, 176, 177
Decline in IPOs, 48–50
Direct listings, 147–149
Disadvantages of going public, 175, 176
Motivations for going public, 175
Mutual fund investors, 150
New issues market, 80–86
Pricing ratchet, 150
Registration Process, this index
Underpricing, 82–86
Underwriters and Underwriting, this index
Venture capital market, 23, 24

INJUNCTIONS
SEC Enforcement Actions, this index

INSIDER TRADING
Generally, 1187–1287
Beneficial ownership. Short swing profits, § 16(b) liability, below
Classical insider trading, 1191–1196
Constructive insiders, 1205
Corporation, harm to, 1187, 1188
Damages
    Generally, 1280–1286
    Statutory developments, 1286, 1287
Disclose or abstain duty, 1191
Employee benefit plans and Rule 16b–3, 1278, 1279
Gift theory (Second Circuit), 1220–1233
Market, harm to, 1188–1190
Misappropriation theory
    Generally, 1207–1219
    Proving misappropriation, 1216, 1217
    Rule 10b5–1, SEC responds to "use or possession" debate, 1217–1219
    Rule 10b5–2, non-business relationships, 1219
    Who has duty to disclose and SEC regulations, 1215–1219
Officers and directors. Short swing profits, § 16(b) liability, below
Purchases and sales. Short swing profits, § 16(b) liability, below
Regulation FD, 1244–1247
Section 1348 and personal benefit rule, 1235–1244
Short swing profits, § 16(b) liability
    Generally, 1255–1280
    Any period of less than six months, 1268
    Beneficial ownership
        Generally, 1275–1278
        Ten percent holder, 1276, 1277

Derivative securities, defined, 1265, 1266
Deterrent effect, 1257
Employee benefit plans and Rule 16b–3, 1278, 1279
Mergers and tender offers, 1266–1268
Officers and directors
    Generally, 1269–1275
    Defined, 1274
    Timing of liability, 1275
Purchases and sales
    Generally, 1257–1269
    Any period of less than six months, 1268
    Derivative securities, 1265, 1266
    Mergers and tender offers, 1266–1268
    Profit realized, 1268, 1269
    Terms defined, 1264–1268
Strict liability, 1257
STOCK Act, 1233–1235
Temporary insiders, tippers, and tippees, 1196–1207
Tender offers and SEC Rule 14e–3
    Generally, 1247–1255
    Applicability of Rule 14e–3, 1247
    When does conduct violate Rule 14e–3, 1252, 1253
    Williams Act, 1253–1255

INSTITUTIONAL AND REGULATORY FRAMEWORK
Generally, 3–66
Administrative Procedure Act, 58–60
Alternative trading systems, 30, 31
Blue sky regulation, 64–66
Broker-dealer internalization, 31, 32
Commodities Futures Trading Commission, 51, 52
Cost-benefit analysis, 60, 61
Dark pools, 31
Derivatives market
    Generally, 19–22
    Futures, 20, 21
    Swaps, 21, 22
    Traded options, 20
Electronic communications networks, 30, 31
Equity market (public)
    Generally, 22–32
    Alternative trading systems, 30, 31
    Broker-dealer internalization, 31, 32
    Dark pools, 31
    Electronic communications networks, 30, 31
    Exchanges, redefining role, 24–32
    OTC trading by dealers, 32
    Venture capital market, 23, 24
Exchanges, redefining role, 24–32
Financial markets overview
    Generally, 11–32
    Derivatives market, above
    Equity market, above
    Non-equity markets, below
Goals of securities regulation
    Generally, 3–11
    Allocative efficiency, 7–9
    Consumer protection, 4–6
    Corporate governance and agency costs, 9
    Economic growth, innovation, and access to capital, 9, 10
    Inadequate incentives to disclose, 7
    Reducing cost of capital and tradeoffs, 10, 11
    Standardizing disclosure, 6, 7
    Systemic risk and financial stability, 6
Non-equity markets
    Generally, 13–22
    Corporate debt market, 17, 18
    Derivatives market, above
    Government securities market, 15, 16
    Money market, 14, 15
    Municipal securities market, 16, 17
    Securitizations, 18, 19
Regulatory framework
    Generally, 50–58
    Blue sky regulation, 64–66
    Commodities Futures Trading Commission, 51, 52
    Securities and Exchange Commission, below
    Summaries of securities statutes, 53–58
Regulatory process
    Generally, 58–64
    Administrative Procedure Act, 58–60
    Cost-benefit analysis, 60, 61
    Self-regulatory organizations, 61–64
Securities and Exchange Commission
    Generally, 51
    Administration of securities statutes, 53
    Organization, 52, 53
Securities markets, forces reshaping. Securities Markets, this index
Self-regulatory organizations, 61–64
Summaries of securities statutes, 53–58
Venture capital market, 23, 24

INTEGRATION OF EXEMPTIONS
Limited and Other Offering Exemptions, this index

INTERNATIONAL ENFORCEMENT
Generally, 1473–1505
Government extraterritorial enforcement
    Generally, 1498–1505
    Challenges to governmental enforcement efforts, 1503–1505
    Criminal enforcement, 1502, 1503
    Dodd-Frank § 929P(b), 1499–1502
Jurisdiction of U.S. courts over claims by private plaintiffs
    Generally, 1474–1498
    ADRs and OTC market, 1495

Class actions, 1497, 1498
Domestic purchase and sale test, 1492–1494
Non-10b–5 claims, 1496
Private rights of action under 10b–5, 1491
Single-transaction based test, 1492
State court alternative, 1496
Study on private right of action, 1496, 1497

INTRASTATE OFFERINGS
Limited and Other Offering Exemptions, this index

INVESTMENT ADVISERS
See also SEC Enforcement Actions, this index
Advisers Act, 58
Broker/investment adviser turf war, 788, 789
Defined, 1422–1432
Dodd-Frank, 1429–1431
Fiduciary standard of conduct, 1431
Mid-sized advisers, regulation of, 1430
Private funds, advisers to, 1429, 1430
Reporting requirements, 1430
Retail investors, access to registration information, 1431
Scalping, 1432–1439
Systemic risk reporting, 1430

INVESTMENT COMPANY ACT
Generally, 58

INVESTMENT CONTRACTS
Security, defined, 273–301

JOBS ACT
Generally, 141–147
Accounting standards, 143
Benefits, 141–144
Corporate governance rules, 143
Crowdfunding, 501 et seq.
Disclosures, required, 142, 143
Registration statement, confidential review, 141, 142
Research reports, 144
Test-the-waters communications, 142

JURISDICTION
Concurrent jurisdiction, state and federal courts, 994, 995
International Enforcement, this index
Self-regulation, SEC jurisdiction, 725

LIMITED AND OTHER OFFERING EXEMPTIONS
Generally, 401–521
Crowdfunding
  Generally, 501–507
  Disclosure requirements, 503, 504
  Fraud risk, use of intermediaries to reduce, 504, 505
  Investor limits, 502, 503
  Issuer eligibility, 502
  Material misstatements or omissions, liability for, 506

  State regulation, 503
Exchanges and reorganizations, exempted
  Generally, 475–501
  Amendments of articles or indentures, exchanges and, 479
  Bankruptcy Code provisions
    Generally, 494–497
    Benefits of § 1145, 498–500
    Trustee's issuance of securities in ordinary course of business, 501, 502
  Free stock, 477, 478
  Pledge of securities, 478
  Section 2(a)(3) and theory of sale
    Generally, 475–479
    Free stock, 477, 478
    Pledge of securities, 477
    Stock dividends, 477
    Warrants, options, and conversion rights, 475, 476
  Section 3(a)(9) exchanges
    Generally, 480–490
    Convertible securities, 488, 489
    Existing security holder requirement, 480, 481
    Integration of transactions, 481, 482
    Issuer identity, 480, 481
    No additional consideration requirement, 480, 481
    Remuneration for solicitation, 481, 483
    Securities Act Release No. 646, 484–486
    Securities Act Release No. 2029, 486–488
    Subsequent resales, 489, 490
  Section 3(a)(10) exchanges
    Generally, 490–497
    Advantages to issuer, 494, 495
    Conditions to be satisfied, 490–493
    Financially-distressed entities, reorganization of, 495
    Resales, 496, 497
    Securities Act Release No. 312, 493, 494
    Settlement of litigation, 495, 496
  Stock dividends, 477
  Warrants, options, and conversion rights, 475, 476
Integration of exemptions
  Generally, 507–521
  Foreign offerings, 514
  Genesis of doctrine, 508–511
  Rules 152 and 155, 511–513
  Uncertainty, 514
Intrastate offerings
  Generally, 444–469
  Out-of-state residents, offers to, 445

Principal place of business, 445
Rules 147 and 147A
    Generally, 457–468
    Doing business within requirement, 468
    Secondary transactions, 468
    Securities Act Release No. 5450, 457–467
    State regulation and National Securities Market Improvement Act, 467, 468
Section 3(a)(11)
    Generally, 446–456
    Leading cases, 454–456
    Recurring issues, 454
    Securities Act Release No. 4434, 446–451
Regulation A offerings
    Generally, 403, 404, 436–444
    Abandoned offerings, 443, 444
    Eligible securities, 437
    Integration rule, 442, 443
    Non-public review of offering statement, 440
    Offering process, 438, 439
    Prior offerings, 443
    Regulation D compared, 439–441, 440
    Testing the waters procedure, 441, 442
    Tiers 1 and 2, 403, 404, 437
Regulation CE, 473–475
Regulation D safe harbor
    Generally, 405–436
    Accredited investor status, reasonable steps to verify, 427–431
    Bad actor disqualification, 432, 433
    Blue sky exemptions and Uniform Limited Offering Exemption, 435, 436
    Fraud and Rule 504, 434, 435
    General solicitation or general advertising, 424–431
    Historical background, 401, 402
    Inflation adjusted definition of "accredited investor," 431, 432
    Reasons for popularity, 403
    Rule 135c, 435
    Rule 144, 431
    Rule 503, 433
    Rule 508, 433, 434
    Securities Act Release No. 6389, 405–415
    Securities Act Release No. 6455, 416–424
Reorganizations. Exchanges and reorganizations, exempted, above
Rule 701 and non-reporting issuers
    Generally, 469–473
    Consultants or advisers, offers to, 471, 472
    Disclosure requirements, 471
    Limits on amount of securities sold, 470
    Options, special rules, 470, 472

LIMITED LIABILITY COMPANIES
Security, defined, 322–324

LIMITED PARTNERSHIPS
Security, defined, 316–322, 325

LOAN PARTICIPATIONS
Security, defined, 350–353

MANAGEMENT BUYOUTS
Tender Offers, Management Buyouts, and Takeover Contests, this index

MARKETS
Equity and non-equity markets. Institutional and Regulatory Framework, this index
Market efficiency. Registration Process, this index
Overview of financial markets. Institutional and Regulatory Framework, this index
Securities Markets, this index

MATERIALITY
Litigation and enforcement, role of materiality, 909, 910
Proxy Fraud (Rule 14a–9), this index
Rule 10b–5 Enforcement Actions, this index
Tender offers, materiality of financial information about bidder, 866

MISAPPROPRIATION
Insider Trading, this index

MUNICIPAL SECURITIES
Exempted securities, defined, 367, 368

MUTUAL FUNDS
Forces reshaping securities markets, 35, 36
Initial public offerings, mutual fund investors, 150

NOTES
Security, defined, 332–343

OFFERING EXEMPTIONS
Limited and Other Offering Exemptions, this index
Private Offering Exemptions, this index

OFFERINGS BY UNDERWRITERS, AFFILIATES, AND DEALERS
Generally, 523–651
Broker's exemption, 571–573
Changing circumstances doctrine, 580, 581
Concept of underwriter, 523 et seq.
Control shares and restricted securities, restrictions on resale under Rule 144
    Generally, 584–600
    Amount sold, limitation on, 590–592
    Applicability and availability of Rule 144, 584–586
    Brokers' transactions, 592, 593

Current public information
requirement, 586, 587
Exclusivity and operation of Rule
144, 593
Fully paid requirement, 587, 588
Fungibility, 588
Holding period, 587–590, 593
Issuers with no or only nominal
operations, 593
Manner of sale, 592, 593
Market makers, 592
Rule 145 transactions, 594–596
Tacking holding period, 589, 590
Controlling persons or affiliates, statutory
restrictions on distributions by
Generally, 557–583
Broker's exemption, 571–573
Changing circumstances doctrine,
580, 581
Dealer's exemption, 570, 571
Defining control, 576
Fungibility concept, 581, 582
Investment intent and resales of
securities purchased in
private offerings, 579, 580
Sales by controlling persons, 577,
578
Shelf registration, 576, 577
Who is controlling person, 564–569
Dealer's exemption, 570, 571
Fungibility concept, 581, 582
Going public by back door
Generally, 537–546
Continuing use of back door, 545,
546
Restricted securities, 544
Restricting back door entry, 541–
544
Rule 15c2–11, 544, 545
Spin-offs, reverse mergers, and shell
game, 541–546
Investment intent and resales of
securities purchased in private
offerings, 579, 580
Offshore offers and sales. Regulation S
exemption for offerings outside U.S.,
below
Participation standard, 535, 536
Presumptive underwriters, 525–527, 595,
596
Private resale market and Rule 144A
Generally, 600–608
Documentation and form, 606
Fungibility exclusion, 606, 607
General solicitation, 605
Information requirement, 606
PORTAL, 605, 606
Restricted securities, resale of, 602–
605
Rules 138 and 139, 607
Promoters, 530
Regulation S exemption for offerings
outside U.S.
Generally, 610–636
Abuse of Regulation S, 630, 631

Business implications of Regulation
S, 632, 633
Categories of issuers, 611, 612
Morrison, impact of, 635, 636
Offshore offers and sales, 612 et seq.
Reforms (1988), 631
Relationship with Rule 144A, 633
Resales in U.S., 634, 635
Resales outside U.S., 633, 634
Rule 901, 631, 632
Structure of Regulation S, 630
TEFRA D, 632
Rule 144. Controlling persons or affiliates,
statutory restrictions on
distributions by, above
Sales by controlling persons, 577, 578
Section 4(1½) exemption
Generally, 546–557
Future of exemption, 556, 557
General solicitations, 556
Private resales of restricted
securities, 547–555
Purchaser sophistication, 555, 556
Section 4(a)(7), private resale of securities
acquired in unregistered offerings,
608, 609
Spin-offs, reverse mergers, and shell
game, 541–546
Statutory underwriters, 523–525

OFFSHORE OFFERS AND SALES
Regulation S exemption. Offerings by
Underwriters, Affiliates, and
Dealers, this index

ONLINE OFFERINGS
Post-effective period, 139

OVER-THE-COUNTER MARKET
Generally, 709–716
Dealers, OTC trading, 32
Mark-up policy, 713–716

PARTNERSHIPS
Security, defined, 324, 325

**PENNY STOCK REFORM ACT OF
1990**
Broker-Dealers, this index
Registration process, 270–272

**PENSIONS AND RETIREMENT
PLANS**
Exempted securities, IRAs and Keogh
plans, 370
Securities markets, forces reshaping, 36,
37

POST-EFFECTIVE PERIOD
Generally, 133–140
Online offerings, 139
Procedure surrounding effectiveness
(Rules 430A and 430B), 133, 134
Prospectus requirements. Prospectus, this
index
Shelf registration, 171–174

POST-FILING REVIEW AND RESTRICTIONS
Registration Process, this index

PRE-FILING PERIOD
  Generally, 96–115
Biased research, 110–112
Broker-dealer activities during registration, 108–110
Guidelines for release of information, issuers whose securities are in registration, 103–105
Initial steps, 97–99
Preliminary negotiations between issuer and underwriter
  Generally, 96–99
  Initial steps, 97–99
Quiet period, SEC's revised rules, 105–108
Research, biased, 110–112
Sales publicity and timely disclosures of corporate information, traditional dividing line, 100–105
SEC staff availability, 183

PRIVATE OFFERING EXEMPTIONS
  Generally, 373–400
ABA's position, 398
Access and furnishing information, 397, 398
Administrative interpretations, 377, 378
Dual standard, 383–386
Information, availability and access to, 377
Issuer, definition and scope, 373–375
Limitation on resales, 378
Manner of offering, 378
Offerees, number and nature, 377, 378
Pre-screening procedures, 395, 396
Regulation D safe harbor
  Generally, 379, 380
  See also Limited and Other Offering Exemptions, this index
Rules vs. standards, 398, 399
Sophisticated investors, 394, 396, 397
Statutory standard, 377
Types of exempt transactions, 375–377

PRIVATE RESALE MARKET
Offerings by Underwriters, Affiliates, and Dealers, this index

PRIVATE SECURITIES LITIGATION REFORM ACT OF 1995
Generally, 912–915

PROSPECTUS
Delivery during waiting period, 129–133
Free writing prospectus
  Generally, 122–125
  Civil liability, 1023
  Conditions for use of, 123
  Filing with SEC, 124
  Legend, 123
  Media interviews, 124
  Post-effective period, 136, 137

Post-effective period, prospectus requirements
  Generally, 134–139
  Delivery rules, 134–136
  Duration of delivery obligation, 137–139
  Free writing, 136, 137
Preliminary or red herring prospectus
  Generally, 116–118
  Prior delivery of preliminary prospectus, 129, 130
Summary prospectus, 118

PROXY FRAUD (RULE 14a–9)
  Generally, 1176–1185
Causation, 1184, 1185
Culpability
  Generally, 1182–1184
  Collateral participants, 1184
  Directors and officers, 1184
  Issuer, 1184
Implied private cause of action, 1177
Materiality
  Generally, 1177–1182
  Buried facts, 1180
  Conflicts of interest, 1180, 1181
  Disclosures, required, 1181
  Known facts, 1179
  Quantitative materiality, 1181, 1182
  Total mix of information, 1179
  Undisclosed conduct, 1180
  What facts are material, 1178–1182

PUBLIC UTILITIES HOLDING COMPANY ACT
Generally, 57

QUIET PERIOD
SEC's revised rules, 105–108

REAL ESTATE DEVELOPMENTS
Security, defined, 312–316

RECEIVERSHIPS
SEC injunctive actions, 1318

REGISTRATION OF RESALES
Offerings by Underwriters, Affiliates, and Dealers, this index

REGISTRATION PROCESS
  Generally, 153–272
Acceleration, 187, 260
Antisocial conduct not involving violations of law, 202, 203
Basic information package, 155–157
Blank check offerings, 270–272
Code of ethics, 225
Comment letter and issuer's response, 184–186
Delaying amendments, 258, 259
Disclosure
  Integrated disclosure system, below
  Management discussion and analysis, 208–216
  Mandatory disclosure system, case for, 248–258

Market efficiency, disclosure policy and, below
New approaches, 206 et seq.
Plain English disclosure, 217–220
Principles-based approach to disclosure, 214
Qualitative disclosure, below
Sarbanes-Oxley and post-Enron disclosure, below
SEC enforcement, 215, 216
Soft information, 206 et seq.
Division of Corporation Finance, 178–180
Efficient Capital Market Hypothesis (ECMH)
    Generally, 225 et seq.
    Behavioral theories, 244, 245
    Noise trading critique, 233–244, 246
Environmental liabilities, 204–206
Executive certifications, 221
Executive compensation, 203, 204
Fraud-on-market doctrine and market efficiency, 257, 258
Going effective, 187, 188
Informal appeal process, 188, 189
Integrated disclosure system
    Generally, 153–161
    EDGAR, 160, 161
    Efficient market theory, 158, 159
    Management's discussion and analysis, 160
    Smaller reporting companies, 159, 160
Integrity disclosures, 196–199
Internal control report, 224
Law violations not involving senior management, 201, 202
Management discussion and analysis disclosure, 208–216
Market efficiency, disclosure policy and
    Generally, 225–258
    Behavioral economics, recurring heuristics, 246–248
    Efficient Capital Market Hypothesis (ECMH), above
    Fraud-on-market doctrine, 257, 258
    Mandatory disclosure system, case for, 248–258
    Policy implications, 248–258
    Underwriters, role of, 229–232
Off-balance sheet items and pro forma figures, 222–224
Penny stocks, 270–272
Plain English disclosure, 217–220
Post-filing review and restrictions
    Generally, 258–261
    Acceleration, 260
    Delaying amendments, 258, 259
    Exchange Act, entry into, 259
    Proceeds, use of, 260
    Processing, post-filing, 258–261
    Refusal of registration statement and stop orders, 260, 261
    Withdrawal of registration statement, 261
Pre-Filing Period, this index

Preparation of registration statement, 174–190
Presentation of registration statement, 182, 183
Principles-based approach to disclosure, 214
Private litigation, 201, 214, 215
Proceeds, use of, 260
Public companies, SEC review of disclosures, 225
Qualitative disclosure
    Generally, 190–206
    Antisocial conduct not involving violations of law, 202, 203
    Case law, 199, 200
    Environmental liabilities, 204–206
    Executive compensation, 203, 204
    Integrity disclosures, 196–199
    Law violations not involving senior management, 201, 202
    Private litigation, 201
    Unadjudicated charges, 200, 201
Real time issuer disclosures, 221, 222
Refusal of registration statement and stop orders, 260, 261
Registration statement
    Preparation, 174–190
    Presentation, 182, 183
    Refusal and stop orders, 260, 261
    Withdrawal, 261
Sarbanes-Oxley and post-Enron disclosure
    Generally, 220 et seq.
    Code of ethics, 225
    Executive certifications, 221
    Internal control report, 224
    Off-balance sheet items and pro forma figures, 222–224
    Public companies, SEC review of disclosures, 225
    Real time issuer disclosures, 221, 222
SEC enforcement, MD&A requirement, 215, 216
Selective review process, 180–182
Shelf registration
    Generally, 161–174
    Automatic shelf registration
        Generally, 169–174
        Classes of issuers, 170, 171
        Post-effective procedure, 171–174
        Well-known seasoned issuer, 169, 170
    Civil liability under Securities Act of 1933, 980
    Controlling persons or affiliates, distribution by, 576, 577
    Debate over Rule 415, 161–164
    Due diligence, 166–169
    Equity offerings, 165, 166
    Rule 415, 161 et seq.
    Trading practices, 749
    Underwriting fees, 164, 165
Statement. Registration statement, above
Unadjudicated charges, 200, 201

Underwriters and Underwriting, this index
Withdrawal of registration statement, 261

REGULATION A
Limited and Other Offering Exemptions, this index

REGULATION BEST INTEREST
Broker-Dealers, this index

REGULATION D
Limited and Other Offering Exemptions, this index

REGULATION NMS
Securities Markets, this index

REGULATORY FRAMEWORK
Institutional and Regulatory Framework, this index

RESALES
Offerings by Underwriters, Affiliates, and Dealers, this index

RESEARCH
Analysts, role of, 87–92
JOBS Act, research reports, 144
Pre-filing period, biased research, 110–112

ROAD SHOWS
Waiting period, 75, 125–128

RULE 10b–5 ENFORCEMENT ACTIONS
Generally, 1031–1176
Causation
    Loss causation, below
    Reasonable reliance and causation, 1151, 1152
    Transaction causation, loss causation, and "in connection with" requirement, 1151
Cause of action, notes on, 1032–1037
Culpability of defendant
    Generally, 1112–1122
    Ignoring *Ernst & Ernst*, 1121
    Recklessness, 1120, 1121
    Scienter and forward looking statements, 1121
    Who is culpable, 1122
Due diligence, plaintiff's, 1046
Duty to disclose, when omissions actionable, 1050
Duty to update and duty to correct
    Generally, 1047–1061
    Duty to disclose, 1050
    Third-party statements, 1050, 1051
FINRA rules, violations of, 1035–1037
Forward looking statements. Materiality, below
Fraud in connection with purchase or sale of security
    Generally, 1037 et seq.
    Culpability of defendant, above
    Duty to update and duty to correct, above
    Fraud requirement, 1037–1061
    In connection with requirement, 1103–1112
    Materiality, below
    Misstatements and omissions, below
    Reliance, below
    Standing, below
Half-truths and materiality, 1080
Implied private cause of action, 1032, 1033
In connection with requirement, 1103–1112
Justifiable reliance and oral misstatements, 1151, 1152
Loss causation
    Generally, 1152–1165
    Event studies, 1164
    Misstatement not itself causing price inflation, 1163, 1164
    Pleading, 1162, 1163
Materiality
    Generally, 1061–1103
    Class certification, 1079, 1080
    Forward looking statements
        Generally, 1081–1097
        Private Securities Litigation Reform Act, 1091–1093
        Scienter, 1121
    Half-truths, 1080
    Puffing, 1101, 1102
    Reasons, opinions, and beliefs, 1097–1103
Mismanagement, Rule 10b–5 as remedy for, 1043–1047
Misstatements and omissions
    Generally, 1037–1043
    Due diligence, plaintiff's, 1046
    Oral misstatements, below
Nonreliance/integration clauses, 1046, 1047
Omissions, reliance and, 1151
Oral misstatements
    Generally, 1044–1046
    Justifiable reliance, 1051, 1052
Overlapping causes of action, 1033–1035
Person, defined, 1033–1035
Private Securities Litigation Reform Act and materiality, 1091–1093
Puffing and materiality, 1101, 1102
Reliance and fraud-on-the-market presumption
    Generally, 1123–1143
    Class actions, 1140
    Efficient markets, 1140, 1141
    New issues of securities, 1141
    Price impact, measuring, 1142
    Stare decisis and *Halliburton II*, 1142
    Stock price, no effect on, 1142
    Truth on the market, 1141, 1142
Reliance, reasonable
    Generally, 1143–1152
    Causation and reasonable reliance, 1151, 1152
    Justifiable reliance and oral misstatements, 1151, 1152

Omissions, reliance and, 1151
Standing
    Generally, 1165–1176
    Contemporaneous traders, 1173, 1174
    Contracts to buy or sell, 1176
    Employee benefit plans, 1173
    Equitable relief, 1172
    Forced seller, 1175
    Issuance of own securities, 1172
    Private plaintiffs, 1174, 1175
    Privity, 1173
    Purchaser seller requirement, 1172–1176
    Repurchase of own securities, 1172
State law fiduciary breaches, 1043, 1044
Stock exchange rules, violations of, 1035–1037
Types of fraud covered, 1031

RULE 701 AND NON-REPORTING ISSUERS
Limited and Other Offering Exemptions, this index

SANCTIONS
SEC enforcement actions, ex parte sanctions, 1326, 1327

SEC ENFORCEMENT ACTIONS
Generally, 1289 et seq.
Accountants. Securities attorneys and accountants, below
ALJ hearings, 1295
Ancillary relief
    Disgorgement and ancillary relief, below
    Injunctions and ancillary relief, below
Asset freezes, 1317
Attorneys. Securities attorneys and accountants, below
Broker-dealers
    Generally, 1404–1421
    Disciplinary proceedings, 1417, 1418
    Fiduciary standard of conduct, 1431
    Investment advisers, defined, 1428, 1429
    SRO regulation, 1419–1421
    Supervisor's responsibility, 1418
Cease and desist orders, 1329–1340
Civil fines, 1327–1329
Collateral bar orders, 1345
Confidentiality, 1294
Consent decrees, 1297
Corporate bar orders
    Generally, 1340–1345
    Sarbanes-Oxley, 1344, 1345
Corporate registrants, officers, and directors
    Generally, 1388–1404
    Audit committees, 1402
    Certification of quarterly and annual reports, 1400, 1401
    Clawback of executive compensation, 1402, 1403
    Compensation committee independence, 1404
    Compensation disclosure requirements, 1403, 1404
    Foreign Corrupt Practices Act, 1388 et seq.
    Incentive-based compensation, disclosure of, 1404
    Misleading financial statements, 1401
    Sarbanes-Oxley and Dodd-Frank, 1400–1404
Counsel, right to, 1293, 1294
Disgorgement and ancillary relief
    Generally, 1305–1326
    Amount of award, 1317
    Ancillary relief, 1318, 1319
    Basis of liability, 1316, 1317
    Distribution of funds, 1316
    SEC authority to obtain, 1316
Ex parte sanctions, 1326, 1327
Expanded authority in administrative proceedings, 1296
Financial planners as investment advisers, 1427, 1428
Formal investigations, 1291, 1292
Informal staff inquiry, 1200
Injunctions and ancillary relief
    Generally, 1298–1305
    Asset freezes, 1317
    Class actions and collateral estoppel, 1317
    Further violations, enjoining, 1317
    Receiverships, 1318
Investment advisers
    Generally, 1421–1439
    Brokers and dealers, 1428, 1429
    Control person liability, 1431
    Defined, 1422–1432
    Dodd-Frank, 1429–1431
    Fiduciary standard of conduct, 1431
    Financial planners, 1427, 1428
    Mid-sized advisers, regulation of, 1430
    Private funds, advisers to, 1429, 1430
    Professional persons, 1429
    Reporting requirements, 1430
    Retail investors, access to registration information, 1431
    Scalping, 1432–1439
    Systemic risk reporting, 1430
Judicial review, standard of, 1296
Management discussion and analysis requirement, 215, 216
Procedures, generally, 1290 et seq.
Proper purpose, 1293
Receiverships, 1318
Remedies, 1297 et seq.
Remedies Act, 1327 et seq.
Rules of Practice
    Generally, 1295, 1296
    Sarbanes-Oxley § 307 and Rule of Practice 205, 1374, 1375
Sanctions, ex parte, 1326, 1327

Securities attorneys and accountants (Rule 102(e))
    Generally, 1345–1388
    Aiding and abetting liability under Rule 10b–5, 1371, 1372
    Attorneys and Rule 102(e), 1347–1382
    Authority of SEC, 1366, 1367
    Independence of accountants
        Sarbanes-Oxley Act, 1386–1388
        SEC actions, 1382–1386
    Mental state required by Rule 102(e), 1367–1369
    Negligent acts, 1367–1369
Standard of judicial review, 1296
Subpoenas, 1291, 1292
Time limitations, 1295
Wells submissions, 1294, 1295
Whistleblower incentives and protections, 1290, 1291

SECURITIES ACT OF 1933
Generally, 54, 93 et seq.
Civil Liability, this index
Exempted Securities, this index
Gun-jumping. Pre-Filing Period, this index
JOBS Act, this index
Limited and Other Offering Exemptions, this index
Post-Effective Period, this index
Pre-Filing Period, this index
Private Offering Exemptions, this index
Prospectus, this index
Registration Process, this index
Statutory framework, 93–96
Underwriters and Underwriting, this index
Waiting Period, this index

SECURITIES MARKETS
Generally, 653–726
Alternative trading systems
    Generally, 690 et seq.
    Crossing systems, 690
    Market access, transparency, and surveillance issues, 694, 695
    Matching systems, 690
    Regulation ATS, 696, 697
    Regulation of exchanges, Release No. 38672, 691–693
    SEC's concerns, 693–697
    Single-price auction systems, 690, 691
Amendments to Securities Exchange Act (1975), 657, 658
Change in markets, 653 et seq.
Critiques of contemporary markets, 667–671
Dark pools, 31, 664, 668–670
Electronic Communications Network (ECN), 30, 659–661, 680, 681
Exchanges
    Generally, 683–697
    Alternative trading systems, above
    Defined, 683–686
    NASDAQ, 28, 29
    NYSE, 28
    OTC Markets Group, 29
    Redefining role, 24–32
    Regulation of exchanges, Release No. 38672, 691–693
    Survey from 1934 Act to Regulation ATS, 683–697
Exotic orders, 670, 671
Forces reshaping
    Generally, 32–50
    Deregulation and reconsideration, 41, 42
    Financial services industry, restructuring, 41, 42
    Gatekeepers, role of, 45–48
    Globalization, causes and consequences, 38–41
    Hedge funds, 37, 38
    Institutional investors, rise of, 33–38
    IPOs, decline in, 48–50
    Mutual funds, 35, 36
    Pension funds, 36, 37
    Systemic risk, problem of, 42–45
Gatekeepers, role of, 45–48
Globalization, 38–41, 653
High frequency traders, 655, 656, 667 et seq.
Institutional investors, rise of, 33–38
Internal structure of markets, 663
Latency arbitrage, 667, 668
Market data and data fees, 716–719
Market structure, impact of regulation
    Generally, 657–667
    Amendments to Securities Exchange Act (1975), 657, 658
    Dark pools, 31, 664, 668–670
    Electronic Communications Network (ECN), 30, 659–661, 680, 681
    Internal structure of markets, 663
    NASDAQ collusion scandal and SEC's response, 659–662
    Regulation NMS, 662–667
NASDAQ collusion scandal and SEC's response, 659–662
National market system
    Generally, 671–683
    Fostering competition vs. fear of market fragmentation, 672
    Regulation NMS, below
Over-the-counter market
    Generally, 709–716
    Mark-up policy, 713–716
Pinging and spoofing, 670
Primary jurisdiction and struggle for competitive rates
    Generally, 697–709
    Agency referrals, 705
    Soft dollars and § 28(e), 706–709
Regulation ATS, 696, 697
Regulation NMS
    Generally, 662–667, 672–683
    Access rule, 676

Decimalization, 682
ECNs, rise and fall, 680, 681
Evolution of NMS, 678–682
Firm quotations, 680
Internalization, 682
Market data rules, 677
Off-board trading restrictions, 680
Sub-penny rule, 676
Trade-through rule, 675 et seq.
Transaction and quotation information, 678–680
Regulation SCI, 720–722
Regulatory change in markets, 653 et seq.
Securities information processors (SIPs), 716 et seq.
Self-Regulation, this index
Systemic risk, problem of, 42–45
Technology and infrastructure, 720–722
Volker Rule, 44, 45

SELF-REGULATION
Generally, 61–64, 722–726
Cartelization problem, 731
Enforcement, 724
FINRA, 730, 731
Governance, 723, 724
Immunity, 724, 725
Origins, 729, 730
Pros and cons, 725, 726
Rule-making, 724
SEC jurisdiction, 725

SHELF REGISTRATION
Registration Process, this index

SHORT SALES
Broker-Dealers, this index
Underwriters, short selling around public offerings, 269, 270

SHORT SWING PROFITS
Insider Trading, this index

SPECIAL DEBT OBLIGATIONS
Security, defined, 343–356

STANDING
Rule 10b–5 Enforcement Actions, this index
SEC Enforcement Actions, this index

STATE ANTI-TAKEOVER LEGISLATION
Tender Offers, Management Buyouts, and Takeover Contests, this index

STATUTE OF LIMITATIONS
Civil liability under Securities Act of 1933, 993, 994

STOCK PARKING
Generally, 836
Criminal Enforcement, this index

SUBPOENAS
SEC enforcement actions, 1291, 1292

SWAPS
Generally, 21, 22
Security, defined, 353–356

TAKEOVER CONTESTS
Tender Offers, Management Buyouts, and Takeover Contests, this index

TENDER OFFERS, MANAGEMENT BUYOUTS, AND TAKEOVER CONTESTS
Generally, 791–908
Commencement of offer, 815, 871, 872
Cross-border tender offers, 903–906
Debt tender offers, 906, 907
Defensive tactics
    Generally, 873–880
    Federal securities law implications, 875–880
    Greenmail, 878–880
    Issuer repurchases, 876–878
    NYSE's 20% rule, 880
    Supervoting stock and one share/one vote controversy, 875, 876
    Williams Act, application to target, 873, 874
Definitional issues ("bidders")
    Generally, 858–866
    Materiality of financial information about bidder, 866
Definitional issues ("group")
    Generally, 817–837
    Investment purpose, 828, 829
    Swaps conferring beneficial ownership, 829 et seq.
    What makes a group, 827, 828
    Who can form, 826, 827
Definitional issues ("tender offer")
    Generally, 837–858
    Street sweeps, 857
    Unconventional offers, 856, 857
Disgorgement remedy, 836
Friendly tender offer, 902, 903
Greenmail, 878–880
Hedge fund activism, impact of, 903
Historical review, 791 et seq.
Issuer repurchases, 876–878
Materiality of financial information about bidder, 866
Mini-tenders, 907, 908
NYSE's 20% rule, 880
Overinclusion and employment agreements, 814, 815
Private remedies, 836, 837
Proxy rule reform, 871
Publicity and gun-jumping, 870, 871
Reforming tender offer process
    Generally, 867–873
    Commencement of offer, 815, 871, 872
    Disclosure forms, 872
    Impact, 872, 873
    Proxy rule reform, 871
    Publicity and gun-jumping, 870, 871

Rule 14e–5, 872
Securities Act Release No. 7760, 867–869
Subsequent offering period, 872
Transaction parity, goal of, 870
SEC Rule 14e–3 and tender offers. Insider Trading, this index
State anti-takeover legislation
    Generally, 880–902
    Case law, 881–900
    Constituency and disgorgement statutes, 900–902
    Moratorium or business combination statutes, 890 et seq.
Stock parking
    Generally, 836
    Criminal Enforcement, this index
Street sweeps, 857
Supervoting stock and one share/one vote controversy, 875, 876
Swaps conferring beneficial ownership, 829 et seq.
Transaction parity, goal of reforms, 870
Unconventional offers, 856, 857
Williams Act
    Generally, 797–817
    Anti-discrimination rules, 806 et seq.
    Commencement of offer, 815
    Disclosure requirements, 799–803
    Historical background, 791 et seq.
    Legislative history, 795
    Litigation issues, 816, 817
    MCA distinguished, 812–814
    Overinclusion and employment agreements, 814, 815
    Substantive rules, 803–815
    Target, application to, 873, 874
    Timing and duration rules, 804, 805
    Trip wire (§ 13(d)), 797–799
    Withdrawal and proration, 805, 806

TOKENS AND OTHER DIGITAL ASSETS
Security, defined, 356–366

TOMBSTONE AD
Generally, 118, 121

TRADING IN SECURITIES
Broker-Dealers, this index
Securities Markets, this index
Tender Offers, Management Buyouts, and Takeover Contests, this index

TRUST INDENTURE ACT
Generally, 58

UNDERWRITERS AND UNDERWRITING
Generally, 67–92
All or none offerings, 70
Analysts, role of, 87–92
Compensation, FINRA review, 262, 263
Direct listings, 71, 72, 147–149
Direct offerings, 69–71
Due diligence defense, 966, 967
Dutch auction, 69, 70
Fixed price offering and resale price maintenance, 86, 87
Hot issues, 263–266
IPO fees, 149
JOBS Act, this index
Letter of intent, 74
Market efficiency, role of underwriters, 229–232
New issues market, 80–86
Non-GAAP financial metrics, increased use of, 150, 151
Offerings by Underwriters, Affiliates, and Dealers, this index
Oversubscription, free riding and problem of asymmetric information, 263–266
Post-Effective Period, this index
Pre-Filing Period, this index
Presumptive underwriters, 523–525, 595, 596
Private placements, 70, 71
Regulation of underwriters and distribution process, 262–270
Rights offerings, 69
Road shows, 75, 125–128
SEC's trading rules, 266–268
Securities Act of 1933, underwriting process under, 67–92
Shelf registration, underwriting fees, 164, 165
Short selling around public offerings, 269, 270
Stabilization, 268, 269
Statutory underwriters, 523–525
Syndicates, 73, 74, 76–80
Terms defined, 72
Types of underwritings, 72 et seq.
Underpricing, 75, 76, 82–86
Waiting Period, this index

VOLKER RULE
Generally, 44, 45

WAITING PERIOD
    Generally, 115–133
Broker's card, 121, 122
Delivery of prospectus during waiting period, 129–133
Electronic/graphic communications
    Generally, 125–128
    Hyperlinks, 128
Identifying statement, 118–120
Offering documents, traditional, 116–122
Prospectus, this index
Road shows, 125–128
Tombstone ad, 118, 121

WHISTLEBLOWERS
SEC enforcement actions, 1290, 1291

WILLIAMS ACT
Tender Offers, Management Buyouts, and Takeover Contests, this index